The Oxford Companion to English Literature

THE OXFORD COMPANION TO

English Literature

SEVENTH EDITION

EDITED BY

DINAH BIRCH

Fifth and Sixth editions edited by

MARGARET DRABBLE

OXFORD
UNIVERSITY PRESS

OXFORD
UNIVERSITY PRESS

Great Clarendon Street, Oxford OX2 6DP

Oxford University Press is a department of the University of Oxford.
It furthers the University's objective of excellence in research, scholarship,
and education by publishing worldwide in

Oxford New York

Auckland Cape Town Dar es Salaam Hong Kong Karachi
Kuala Lumpur Madrid Melbourne Mexico City Nairobi
New Delhi Shanghai Taipei Toronto

With offices in

Argentina Austria Brazil Chile Czech Republic France Greece
Guatemala Hungary Italy Japan Poland Portugal Singapore
South Korea Switzerland Thailand Turkey Ukraine Vietnam

Oxford is a registered trade mark of Oxford University Press
in the UK and in certain other countries

Published in the United States
by Oxford University Press Inc., New York

First edition 1932
Second edition 1937
Third edition 1946
Fourth edition 1967
Fifth edition 1985
Sixth edition 2000
Seventh edition 2009

British Library Cataloguing in Publication Data

Data available

Library of Congress Cataloging in Publication Data

Data available

Typeset by SPI Publisher Services, Pondicherry, India
Printed in Italy by
Rotolito Lombarda S.p.A.

ISBN 978–0–19–280687–1

1 3 5 7 9 10 8 6 4 2

Associate Editors

Contents

Preface

In her introduction to the Sixth Edition of *The Oxford Companion to English Literature,* published in 2000, Dame Margaret Drabble remarked that 'the role of the work of reference is changing rapidly'. Her observation still holds true, and this edition represents a thorough revision of the *Companion* in the light of the evolving needs of its readers. Most entries have been updated, many have been completely rewritten, and a good deal of material has been added. Throughout this remodelling, I have kept sight of the purpose that has always shaped the *Companion*: to provide a lively and authoritative source of reference for general readers, scholars, students, and journalists looking for a guide to English literature in its broadest context. Contemporary writers have been included alongside explorations of the ideas that have influenced their work, while entries on authors, institutions, texts, and movements from earlier periods have been amended to reflect recent developments in literary research. Areas of literature whose richness and variety are now attracting increasing levels of interest, including children's literature, black British writing, postcolonial literature, science fiction, travel writing, and fantasy, have received generously enhanced coverage in this edition, as has the relation between literature, film, and television. The *Companion* has always been distinguished by its informative treatment of authors and works from literary cultures other than those of Great Britain, including American, European, and Asian writing. This aspect of the *Companion* has also been updated and revised, with the aim of making the impact of these traditions on English literature clearer. The result is a volume offering much that is fresh, while retaining the lucid and wide-ranging coverage that has earned the *Companion* the grateful affection of generations of readers.

This rebalancing has called for careful principles of selection. Entries on cultural figures or issues without literary associations have been removed. The recent proliferation of detailed reference works devoted to individual authors or major texts has made separate character entries less useful, and many have disappeared, though characters with a persistent life of their own (Shylock, for instance) are still represented. The selection of writers with newly established reputations has inevitably been challenging. Here the *Companion* can make no claim to comprehensive coverage, though I hope that the new authors included in this volume will give a representative picture of the range of excellent writing that has emerged since the millennium. To help create the space needed to accommodate expanding areas of interest, plot summaries have sometimes been abbreviated, though I have not wished to lose this useful and entertaining feature of the work. Cross-referencing within the entries has been extended, to make it easier for readers to identify related subjects.

Literary culture is increasingly diverse, and the growth of festivals, reading groups, book clubs, and prizes has created a keen appetite for knowledge among those who are not reading for professional or academic reasons. Such readers will not find themselves excluded from the resources of the *Companion*. Throughout the work, specialized vocabulary, where it occurs, has been explained, and information needed to identify people, or make sense of ideas, is included. Suggestions for further reading have been added as appropriate, but the entries are intended to be broadly self-contained, each providing the reader with a concise, clear and interesting account of a matter of literary consequence. The volume includes four substantial essays on areas of particular interest—cultures of reading, children's literature, literary culture and the novel in the new millennium, and black British writing—to stimulate and challenge the reader's thinking on these topics.

The work of revising and updating the volume would have been impossible without the small army of Associate Editors, contributors, and friends who have been so generous with their time and expertise. It is a pleasure to have the opportunity to thank them here. The unique worth of this new edition of the *Companion* rests on their committed work. I have been particularly fortunate in securing the services of scholars of the highest distinction in their fields, whose contributions have combined meticulous scholarship with style and flair. This volume continues the tradition of unsigned entries, but a list of new and heavily revised contributions will be found in an appendix at the end of the volume, together with the initials of the Associate Editors and contributors who were responsible for the work. My debt of gratitude, as General Editor, does not end with that list. Almost every entry has been scrutinized and amended, and though the changes have sometimes been too small to record separately, their cumulative effect on the *Companion* has been huge, and I am extremely grateful to all those who have taken such trouble over this essential work. Others have offered invaluable advice, encouragement, and help of many kinds, including Rosinka Chaudhuri, Philip Davis, Matthew O. Grenby, Nigel Griffin, Daniel Hahn, Andrew Hamer, Faye Hammill, Alexandra Harris, Philip Hensher, Rose Hepworth, Hermione Lee, Gordon McMullan, Robyn Marsack, Helen Moore, Dominic Moran, Peter Morey, Bernard O'Donoghue, Philip Pullman, Norman Vance, and Greg Woods. Special thanks are due to Paul Baines and Henry Woudhuysen, who have not faltered in the face of my frequent calls for help. Pamela Coote, formerly of Oxford University Press, who started the ball rolling, gave invaluable guidance in the early stages of the project, and Joanna Harris has proved a worthy successor in the role. Thanks are also due to their colleague Jo Spillane, whose administrative help has been unfailing. My family's patience and cheerful encouragement have been essential to the completion of this volume. My husband Sid, my daughter Rowena, and my son Joe have never complained about the looming presence of the *Companion* in the house, and I have often depended on their good advice. I'm very grateful.

My major debt is to Katy Hooper, my indefatigable, knowledgeable, and skilful editorial assistant, who has been my co-worker throughout the years in which this edition has been in preparation. Without her tactful encouragement and practical support, this volume would never have been completed.

Dinah Birch

Liverpool
January 2009

Editors and Contributors, Seventh Edition

GENERAL EDITOR

Dinah Birch is Professor of English Literature, University of Liverpool. She has published widely on nineteenth-century literature, and has edited novels by Anthony Trollope and George Eliot. Her books include *Ruskin's Myths* (1988), *Ruskin on Turner* (1990), and *Our Victorian Education* (2007). (DLB) **Victorian fiction**

ADVISER

Margaret Drabble is a distinguished novelist and biographer. Her many novels include *Jerusalem the Golden*, *The Needle's Eye*, *The Seven Sisters*, and *The Red Queen*. She has also written biographies of Arnold Bennett and Angus Wilson. She was the editor of the fifth and sixth editions of the *Companion*.

ASSOCIATE EDITORS

Linda Anderson is Professor of Modern English and American Literature at Newcastle University. Her research interests lie in autobiographical writing and twentieth-century women's poetry, and her publications include *Autobiography* (2000) and *Elizabeth Bishop: Poet of the Periphery* (2002). (LRA) **Life writing**

Paul Baines is Professor in the School of English, University of Liverpool. His recent books include *The Long Eighteenth Century* (2004) and *Edmund Curll, Bookseller* (2007, with Pat Rogers). He also works on crime and punishment in eighteenth-century satire. (PTB) **18th-century literature; Music**

Chris Baldick is Professor of English at Goldsmiths, University of London. His publications include the *Oxford Dictionary of Literary Terms* (2008), *The Modern Movement* (Oxford English Literary History, Vol. 10) (2004), and the *Oxford Book of Gothic Tales* (editor, 1990). (CGB) **Literary theory and terms**

Elleke Boehmer is Professor of World Literature in English, Faculty of English, University of Oxford; governing body Fellow, Wolfson College, Oxford. (EB) **Postcolonial literature**

Mishtooni Bose is Christopher Tower Student and Tutor in medieval poetry in English at Christ Church, Oxford, and CUF Lecturer in the Faculty of English, University of Oxford. (MCAB) **Old English and Medieval literature**

David Bradshaw is Reader in English Literature, University of Oxford, and a Fellow of Worcester College. Among the many volumes he has edited are *The Hidden Huxley* (2002), *To the Lighthouse* (2007), *A Concise Companion to Modernism* (2002), and *The Cambridge Companion to E. M. Forster* (2007). (DB) **Modernism**

John Bull is Professor of Film and Theatre, University of Reading. His publications include *New British Political Dramatists* (1984) and *Stage Right: Crisis and Recovery in Contemporary British Theatre* (1994). He has directed many plays from the modern and contemporary repertoire, as well as two of his own. (JB) **Contemporary drama**

J. B. Bullen is Professor Emeritus, University of Reading. (JBB) **Art**

John Carey is Emeritus Merton Professor of English Literature, University of Oxford. (JC) **17th-century literature**

Ian Christie is the author and editor of books on British, American, and Russian cinema, and Professor of Film and Media History at Birkbeck, University of London. He is a Fellow of the British Academy and was Slade Professor of Fine Art, University of Cambridge, in 2006. (IC) **Film**

Neil Corcoran is King Alfred Professor of English Literature in the University of Liverpool and previously taught at the universities of Sheffield, Swansea, and St Andrews. His books include *The Poetry of Seamus Heaney* (1998), *English Poetry since 1940* (1993), and *Elizabeth Bowen: The Enforced Return* (2004). (NC) **Contemporary poetry**

Anthony Cross is Professor Emeritus of Slavonic Studies, University of Cambridge. He has written widely on Russian culture, with particular emphasis on Anglo-Russian contacts and comparisons. (AGC) **Russian literature**

Patrick Crotty is Professor of Irish and Scottish Literature and Director of the Research Institute of Irish and Scottish Studies, University of Aberdeen. (PC) **Irish, Scottish, and Welsh literature**

Jane E. Everson is Professor of Italian Literature, School of Modern Languages, Literatures and Cultures, Royal Holloway, University of London. (JEE) **Italian literature**

Russell Goulbourne is Professor of Early Modern French Literature at the University of Leeds. He has published widely on seventeenth- and eighteenth-century French literature and has contributed to the new critical edition of Voltaire's works. (RG) **French literature**

Clive Griffin, Fellow and Tutor in Spanish, Trinity College, Oxford, teaches and researches principally in two areas: the history of the book in the sixteenth-century Iberian world, and modern Spanish American literature. (CHG) **Latin-American and Spanish literature**

Peter Kemp is fiction editor and chief fiction reviewer of the *Sunday Times*, and Visiting Fellow, Kellogg College, Oxford. He is the author of *Muriel Spark* (1974) and *H. G. Wells and the Culminating Ape* (1982; rev. 1996), and edited *The Oxford Dictionary of Literary Quotations* (1997; rev. 2003). He broadcasts frequently on *Front Row, Saturday Review, Open Book*, and *Nightwaves*, and was a Booker Prize judge in 1995. (PK) **Contemporary fiction**

Francis O'Gorman is Professor of Victorian Literature at the University of Leeds. His most recent book is *Victorian Literature and Finance* (2007). (FJO'G) **Victorian poetry**

Kimberley Reynolds is Professor of Children's Literature in Newcastle University's School of English. Founder of the National Centre for Research in Children's Literature, she helped develop Seven Stories: The Centre for Children's Books, and is Past President of the International Research Society for Children's Literature. (KGR) **Children's literature**

Isabel Rivers is a Research Professor in the Department of English, Queen Mary, University of London, and Co-Director of the Dr Williams's Centre for Dissenting Studies. Her books include *Reason, Grace, and Sentiment*, 2 vols (1991–2000). (IR) **Classical and biblical background**

David Seed is Professor of American Literature in the School of English at the University of Liverpool. He has published books on Thomas Pynchon, Joseph Heller, and brainwashing. His current research interests include the Cold War, science fiction, and the relation of fiction to film. (DS) **American literature, including African-American literature; science fiction; fantasy fiction**

James Simpson was until 2009 Senior Lecturer in German at the University of Liverpool, Director of the Combined Arts programme, and formerly lectured in Comparative Literature at the University of East Anglia. He has published on Goethe, Freud, Hoffmann, and Anglo-German literary relations. (JS) **German literature**

Angela Smith is Emeritus Professor, Department of English Studies, University of Stirling. (AMS) **African literature**

John Strachan is Professor of Romantic Literature at the University of Sunderland. He is the author and editor of over twenty books, including *Advertising and Satirical Culture in the Romantic Period* (2007). (JRS) **Romantic literature**

Stanley Wells is Chairman, The Shakespeare Birthplace Trust. He is General Editor of the Oxford and Penguin editions of Shakespeare and Co-General Editor of *Oxford Shakespeare Topics, The Oxford Companion to Shakespeare* (2001), and *Shakespeare: An Oxford Guide* (2003). His books also include *Re-Editing Shakespeare for the Modern Reader* (1984), *Shakespeare in the Theatre: An Anthology of Criticism* (1997), and (with Paul Edmondson) *Shakespeare's Sonnets* (2004). (SW) **Shakespeare and Renaissance drama**

Henry Woudhuysen is Professor of English at University College London. He contributed to the fifth and sixth editions of the *Oxford Companion to English Literature* (1985, 2000) and is co-General Editor (with M. F. Suarez, SJ) of the *Oxford Companion to the Book* (2010). (HRW) **16th-century literature (excluding Shakespeare and Renaissance drama); Book history**

Tim Youngs is Professor of English at Nottingham Trent University. He is founding editor of the scholarly journal *Studies in Travel Writing*. His book publications include *The Cambridge Companion to Travel Writing* (2002), edited with Peter Hulme. (TDY) **Travel writing**

ESSAYISTS

Kelvin Everest is Bradley Professor of Modern Literature at the University of Liverpool. He has edited Shelley's *Complete Poems* for the Longman Annotated English Poets series (2010), and has published widely on the English Romantic Poets, and on various topics in the theory of editing.

Bénédicte Ledent is a Professor at the University of Liège, where she teaches English language and postcolonial literature, mostly Caribbean and black British.

Hermione Lee, President, Wolfson College, Oxford, is a teacher, biographer, critic, and broadcaster. She taught at the University of York from 1977 to 1998 and then became Goldsmiths' Professor of English Literature at New College, Oxford, until 2008. Her books include major biographies of Virginia Woolf and Edith Wharton; from 1982 to 1986 she presented Channel Four TV's first books programme, *Book Four*.

Michael Rosen was born in 1946 and has been publishing children's books since 1978. He has a Ph.D. in children's literature and teaches at Birkbeck, University of London, where he is Visiting Professor. He was children's laureate 2007–9.

ADDITIONAL CONTRIBUTORS

Kirstie Blair is a Lecturer at the Department of English Literature, University of Glasgow. She is the author of *Victorian Poetry and the Culture of the Heart* (2006) and of numerous articles and chapters on Victorian poetry and poetics. Her current project is entitled *Form and Faith in Victorian Poetry and Religion*. (KB)

Roy Bridges is Emeritus Professor of History at the University of Aberdeen and President of the Hakluyt Society. He has written extensively on exploration and its literature, especially in relation to nineteenth-century Africa and its peoples. (RB)

Guy Cuthbertson is a lecturer at Merton College, Oxford. His research is mostly concerned with literature of the early twentieth century, especially Edward Thomas. He has also been a lecturer at St Edmund Hall, Oxford, and at Swansea University. (GC)

Leigh Dale teaches Australian and postcolonial literatures at the University of Queensland in Brisbane, and is editor of the journal *Australian Literary Studies*. (LD)

Tom Earle is King John II Professor of Portuguese Studies, University of Oxford, and Fellow of St Peter's College, with a special interest in Portuguese literature of the Renaissance period. (TFE)

Jasper Griffin was a Fellow of Balliol College, Oxford, for forty years, and Professor of Classical Literature at the University of Oxford until his retirement in 2004. He is the author of numerous works on Greek and Latin poetry, including *Homer: The Odyssey* (1987) and *Homer on Life and Death* (1980). (JG)

Alexandra Harris is a lecturer in English at the University of Liverpool. She works on twentieth-century British literature and painting. (AH)

Katharine Hodgson is Senior Lecturer in Russian at the University of Exeter. She is the author of two books on twentieth-century Russian poetry: *Written with the Bayonet: Soviet Russian Poetry of World War Two* (1996) and *Voicing the Soviet Experience: The Poetry of Ol'ga Berggol'ts* (2003). (KMH)

Peter Hunt is Professor Emeritus in English and Children's Literature, Cardiff University. He was the first specialist in children's literature to be appointed full Professor of English in a British University. He has written or edited 23 books, and written over 150 articles on the subject. (PLH)

Alan Jones taught Arabic, Turkish, and Islamic Studies at the University of Oxford from 1957 to 2000, when he retired from his post as Professor of Classical Arabic. He has wide interests in Arabic, Persian, and Turkish literature. His translation of the *Qur'ān* was published in 2007. (AJ)

W. Gareth Jones is Professor Emeritus of Russian at Bangor University. Author of *Nikolay Novikov: Enlightener of Russia* (1984), he has published extensively on aspects of the Russian eighteenth-century enlightenment, and nineteenth- and twentieth-century Russian literature. (WGJ)

N. H. Keeble is a Professor of English Studies and Senior Deputy Principal at the University of Stirling, Scotland. His research interests lie in English cultural history (and especially literary and religious history) of the early modern period. (NHK)

Jane Moore is a Reader in English Literature at Cardiff University. (JVM)

David Norton is Professor of English at Victoria University of Wellington, New Zealand. He has edited the King James Bible (*The New Cambridge Paragraph Bible*) (2005), and published books on its literary and textual history. (DWN)

Peter Parker is a writer, editor, and critic. He is author of *The Old Lie* (1987) and biographies of J. R. Ackerley (1989) and Christopher Isherwood (2004), associate editor for the *Oxford Dictionary of National Biography* (2004), and remains an advisory editor. (PP)

Alasdair Pettinger is an independent scholar and the editor of *Always Elsewhere: Travels of the Black Atlantic* (1998). (AP)

Deryn Rees-Jones is a poet and critic. Her books include *Quiver* (2004), *Consorting with Angels* (2005), and, as editor, *Modern Women Poets* (2005). She teaches literature in the School of English, University of Liverpool. (DR-J)

Nick Rennison is a writer and editor. He is author of *Contemporary British Novelists* (2005) and *The Good Reading Guide* (2006). (NR)

Christopher Rowe was until recently Professor of Greek at Durham University. His most recent publications are *Plato's Lysis* (with Terry Penner) (2005) and *Plato and the Art of Philosophical Writing* (2007). (CJR)

Andy Sawyer is Science Fiction Foundation Collection Librarian and Director of MA in Science Fiction Studies, University of Liverpool. He is Reviews Editor of *Foundation* and is the 2008 recipient of the Clareson Award for services to science fiction. (APS)

John Sloan, Fellow and Tutor in English, Harris Manchester College, Oxford, is a specialist in the literature of the late nineteenth and early twentieth centuries. His books include *George Gissing: The Cultural Challenge* (1989), *John Davidson: First of the Moderns* (1995), and *Oscar Wilde* ('Authors in Context' series) (2003). (JSl)

Eric Southworth is Fellow and Tutor in Spanish, St Peter's College, Oxford. (EAS)

Carl Thompson is Senior Lecturer in English, and a member of the Centre for Travel Writing Studies, at Nottingham Trent University. His publications include *The Suffering Traveller and the Romantic Imagination* (2007) and *Romantic-Era Shipwreck Narratives* (2007). (CET)

Sam Trainor is Attaché temporaire d'enseignement et de recherche, Charles-de-Gaulle University, Lille. He is a member of the CECILLE research centre (Centre d'Études 'Civilisations, Langues et Lettres Étrangères'). He was born in Birmingham in 1972. He studied and later taught at the University of Glasgow before moving to France. Examples of his writing can be found at www.samtrainor.com. (ST)

Norman Vance is Professor of English, University of Sussex. His book include *The Victorians and Ancient Rome* (1997) and *Irish Literature since 1800* (2002). (NV)

Edward Welch is Senior Lecturer in French at the University of Durham. He specializes in contemporary French visual and textual culture, with a particular interest in the radical socio-cultural changes affecting post-war France. He published *François Mauriac: The Making of an Intellectual* (2006). (EJW)

Richard White is Senior Lecturer, Department of History, University of Sydney. He teaches Australian history and the history of travel and tourism. (RW)

Anne Whitehead is Senior Lecturer in English Literature at Newcastle University. She is the author of *Trauma Fiction* (2004) and has co-edited *Theories of Memory: A Reader* (2007) and *W. G. Sebald: A Critical Companion* (2004). (AW)

Michael H. Whitworth, Tutorial Fellow, Merton College, Oxford, is author of *Einstein's Wake: Relativity, Metaphor and Modernist Literature* (2001) and *Virginia Woolf* (2005), and other articles and chapters on literature and science, modernism, and publishing history. (MHW)

Jane Wright is a Lecturer in English Literature at the University of Bristol. (JW)

Key to Contributor Initials

AGC	Anthony Cross
AH	Alexandra Harris
AJ	Alan Jones
AMS	Angela Smith
AP	Alasdair Pettinger
APS	Andy Sawyer
AW	Anne Whitehead
CET	Carl Thompson
CGB	Chris Baldick
CHG	Clive Griffin
CJR	Christopher Rowe
DB	David Bradshaw
DLB	Dinah Birch
DR-J	Deryn Rees-Jones
DS	David Seed
DWN	David Norton
EAS	Eric Southworth
EB	Elleke Boehmer
EJW	Edward Welch
FJO'G	Francis O'Gorman
GC	Guy Cuthbertson
HRW	Henry Woudhuysen
IC	Ian Christie
IR	Isabel Rivers
JB	John Bull
JBB	J. B. Bullen
JC	John Carey
JEE	Jane E. Everson
JG	Jasper Griffin
JRS	John Strachan
JS	James Simpson
JSl	John Sloan
JVM	Jane Moore
JW	Jane Wright
KB	Kirstie Blair
KGR	Kimberley Reynolds
KMH	Katharine Hodgson
LD	Leigh Dale
LRA	Linda Anderson
MCAB	Mishtooni Bose
MHW	Michael H. Whitworth
NC	Neil Corcoran
NHK	N. H. Keeble
NR	Nick Rennison
NV	Norman Vance
PC	Patrick Crotty
PK	Peter Kemp
PLH	Peter Hunt
PP	Peter Parker
PTB	Paul Baines
RB	Roy Bridges
RG	Russell Goulbourne
RW	Richard White
ST	Sam Trainor
SW	Stanley Wells
TDY	Tim Youngs
TFE	Tom Earle
WGJ	W. Gareth Jones

Contributors to Sixth Edition

GENERAL EDITOR

Margaret Drabble

CONTRIBUTORS

Dawn Ades
Brian Aldiss
Carole Angier
Lisa Appignanesi
Gillian Avery
Christopher Baldick
Robert Barnard
Jonathan Barnes
John Batchelor
D. Berman
Michael Billington
Paul Binding
J. W. Binns
V. Blain
A. Bold
C. Bryce
F. Burns
Ian Buruma
Marilyn Butler
Gordon Campbell
H. Carpenter
Helen Carr
Vincent Carretta
Ciaran Carson
Glen Cavaliero
Graham Caveney
Kate Clanchy
Susannah Clapp
Jeanne Clegg
Jonathan Coe
Michael Coveney
Michael Cox
Patricia Craig
Ursula Creagh
David Dabydeen
Stevie Davies
Hilary Dickinson
Charles Drazin
Dorothy Driver
Tony Durham
P. Edwards
A. C. Elias
G. Engle
Michael Erben
Lukas Erne
Magdalen Fergusson
Penelope Fitzgerald
Kate Flint
R. A. Foakes
Mark Ford
Margaret Forster
Ian Gibson
Stuart Gillespie
Nicholas Gleghorn
Gill Gregory
John Gribbin
V. Grosvenor Myer
P. S. Guptara
Daniel Hahn
Alethea Hayter
Andrew Hedgecock
L. Heyworth
Lesley Higgins
Michael Hofmann
R. V. Holdsworth
P. Holland
Richard Holmes
Michael Holroyd
Ted Honderich
Michael Horovitz
J. D. Hunt
F. L. Huntley
Simon James
Jeri Johnson
Hester Jones
P. Jones
Daniel Karlin
J. P. Kenyon
Paulina Kewes
Tom Keymer
Lynn Knight
Mary Lago
Sarah Lawson
John Levitt
Paul Levy
Ceridwen Lloyd-Morgan
Andrew McAllister
Peter McDonald
Helen McNeil
P. Merchant
J. Milton
Julian Mitchell
R. T. Mole
J. Moore
Sheridan Morley
Brian Morris
R. Musgrave
W. Myers
Ira Nadel
Benedict Nightingale
Sean O'Brien
Bernard O'Donoghue
Leonard Orr
Fintan O'Toole
Judith Palmer
Catherine Peters
Ralph Pite
Kate Pool
Roy Porter
Lois Potter
Jocelyn Powell
Richard Price
Tore Rem
Matthew Reynolds
R. Robbins
David Rodgers
Nicholas Royle
Salman Rushdie
M. Secrest
Roger Sharrock
Ned Sherrin
Jan Lo Shinebourne
Tom Shippey
Melanie Silgardo
Helen Small
R. D. Smith
Colin Smythe
Jane Spencer
Hilary Spurling
David Stafford
Meic Stephens
Anthony Storr
Michael F. Suarez, SJ
Matthew Sweet
Adam Swift
Clive Swift
Rebecca Swift
Helen Thomson
Anthony Thwaite
Antonia Till
E. M. Trahern
Jeremy Treglown
Jenny Turner
John Tydeman
Sue Vice
Brian Vickers
Stephen Wall
C. Webster
Duncan Webster
Stanley Wells
John Wilders
Jason Wilson
David Womersley
P. Wood
Gregory Woods

Abbreviations

anon.	anonymous
ASPR	Anglo-Saxon Poetic Records
b.	born
BCP	*Book of Common Prayer*
Bk	Book
c.	*circa*, about
CB	Companion of the Bath
CBE	Companion of the British Empire
cf.	*confer*, compare
CH	Companion of Honour
ch.	chapter
CIA	Central Intelligence Agency
CT	*The Canterbury Tales*
d.	died
DBE	Dame Commander of the British Empire
DCL	Doctor of Civil Law
DSO	Distinguished Service Order
ed., eds	editor, or edited by, editors
edn	edition
EETS	Early English Text Society
OS	Original Series
ES	Extra Series
SS	Supplementary Series
	If no series is specified, the volume referred to is in the Original Series
enl.	enlarged
est.	established
FBI	Federal Bureau of Investigation
ff.	and following
fl.	*floruit*, flourished
FRS	Fellow of the Royal Society
FRSL	Fellow of the Royal Society of Literature
introd.	introduction, or introduced by
KJB	King James Bible
l., ll.	line, lines
MA	Master of Arts
MBE	Member of the Order of the British Empire
MC	Military Cross
MD	doctor of medicine
ME	Middle English
MP	Member of Parliament
NT	New Testament
OBE	Officer of the Order of the British Empire
OE	Old English (Anglo-Saxon)
OED	*Oxford English Dictionary*
OM	Order of Merit
OS	Old Style dating, or calendar
OT	Old Testament
p., pp.	page, pages
perf.	performed
pron.	pronounced
Pt	Part
pub.	published
RA	Royal Academy of Arts
RADA	Royal Academy of Dramatic Art
repr.	reprinted
rev.	revised
Revd	Reverend
STS	Scottish Text Society
TLS	*Times Literary Supplement*
trans.	translation, or translated by
vol., vols	volume, volumes

Note to the Reader

The family names of real people are given in bold capital letters; the headwords of all other entries are in bold upper and lower case: italics for the titles of novels, plays, and other full-length works; roman in quotation marks for individual short stories, poems, essays; ordinary roman type for fictional characters, terms, places, and so on. Entries are in simple letter-by-letter alphabetical order, with spaces, hyphens, and the definite or indefinite article ignored. But where a work written in English has a title in a foreign language, the article conditions its alphabetical ordering: so 'L'Allegro' and 'La Belle Dame Sans Merci' are both listed under L. Names beginning with Mc or M' are ordered as though they were spelled Mac, St as though it were Saint, Dr as Doctor; but Mr and Mrs are ordered as they are spelled. An asterisk before a name, term, or title indicates that there is a separate entry for that subject. Modernized spelling has been preferred, for both titles of works and quotations.

LITERARY CULTURE AND THE NOVEL IN THE NEW MILLENNIUM

Hermione Lee

In 2007, three legendary English-language novelists lamented the current state of Western literary culture. Doris *Lessing, accepting the *Nobel Prize for Literature in December, scathingly compared the lack of educational resources in Africa to the privileged philistinism of our 'fragmenting culture', 'where it is common for young men and women who have had years of education, to know nothing about the world', to know only about 'computers' and 'the internet'. V. S. *Naipaul was scornful (not for the first time) about contemporary fiction: 'I find in myself an unwillingness to pick up a modern novel. What is against the form is that everybody can do it and everybody does it, and I think that this has debased it' (interview with James Campbell, *Guardian*, 12 Dec. 2007). Philip *Roth's fictional character Amy Bellette, in *Exit Ghost*, excoriated the superficiality of American literary journalism: 'There was a time when intelligent people used literature to think. That time is coming to an end…Now, in America, it is literature that has been expelled as a serious influence on how life is perceived… Cultural journalism—the more of it there is, the worse it gets…Who is the celebrity, what is the price, what is the scandal? If I had something like Stalin's power…I'd outlaw reading groups and Internet book chatter…'

These distinguished complaints were part of a general argument over whether print culture and literary traditions were being swallowed up by visual and popular media and a language of instant communication. The debasement of culture is not a new topic, of course. It has been a subject of debate since the invention of printing, and always surfaces at times of great technological change. Does mass journalism destroy the elite arts, or film destroy theatre, or television destroy reading? In the new millennium the debate was linked to 'the increasing commodification of the literary market-place'.

This 'commodification' involves a number of connected entities—writers, agents, publishers, bookshops, the media, and the reader. The process is well described by Claire Squires in *Marketing Literature: The Making of Contemporary Writing in Britain* (2007), from whom I take the phrase. Within the industry, there has been a large-scale process of the conglomeration and globalization of publishing companies, and some literary agencies. The demise of the net book agreement and the deregulation of book prices have led to the discounting of books in big bookstores and supermarkets, pushing many small booksellers out of business. The big bookstore chains put pressure on publishers to pay for displaying selected titles. There is a dwindling presence of minority titles, such as poetry books—which in general sell less and less—or specialist subjects. Bookshops organize their stock by genre—biography, travel, gardening—and publishers package fiction as brands (*horror, chick lit, *science fiction), like types of cereals or hand-creams. Fiction reviewers, literary editors, and prize judges have to get used to proof-copies flaunting the 'X meets Y' genre-indicator formula, as in 'Ian *McEwan meets John *Le Carré', or 'Roddy *Doyle meets Angela *Carter'. Online booksellers, like Amazon, with their lists of what 'readers who bought this book also bought', encourage categorizations. So writers find themselves 'niched' inside marketable genres. The process is particularly noticeable where nationality, race, or sexuality is involved. Indian novelists writing in English are marketed (in the critic Graham Huggan's phrase) as the 'postcolonial exotic'. Gay and lesbian novelists can find themselves typecast. Reading habits are directed, also, through a media fondness for competitive lists—best hundred books, best novels of the year—and through the powerful influence of media presenters' book selections and literary prizes.

Evidence of 'dumbing down', one of the new millennium's favourite phrases, is provided by the publishing of cheap, potted short classics, or popular television adaptations of great novels by Jane *Austen, Charles *Dickens, or Elizabeth *Gaskell. The celebrity cult of writers involves media coverage for authors on the basis of looks, youth, and notoriety as well as, or instead of, their writing. In order to attract attention in a highly competitive commercial environment, publishers must market their authors and their books as products. Proof-copies promise 'page-turning, unputdownable prose', 'gorgeous package', 'blanket lead review and feature coverage', '£100,000 marketing campaign including Central London bus sides', 'samplers to be handed out on the streets', or 'plasma screens at key commuter stations' as indicators that the object in hand is a novel worth reading. Literary reviewing in the major newspapers and on the radio is often confined to books by well-known writers or writers who are already attracting 'hype'. There is a dearth of literary programmes on television, which subsumes literature into cultural magazines or general arts programmes. State support for literature is limited by, for example, the underfunding of public libraries, or the Arts Council's recent preference for community-oriented projects rather than individual artwork. The provision of literature in schools is circumscribed by narrow choices on the national curricula and the deadening effect of too much testing. British writing is no longer as well transmitted abroad as it used to be by the British Council, which has been closing down its libraries of printed books all over Europe.

In the introduction to her book, Squires contrasts opposing views of our literary culture. Negative commentators (summed up as the 'lament school') 'cite what they see as falling standards of production, the globalising monopolies of a handful of companies, and a perceived impoverishment of an industry that forgoes diversity and quality in the pursuit of profit. The more positive accounts see a renewed vigour in the marketplace, particularly in the arena of literary fiction, and refer to the numerous new book retailing outlets, with their emphasis on accessibility and consumer choice, and the central place and impact of books in the media.'

There are, certainly, two sides to the story. Whatever Naipaul's views, the contemporary novel in English at the start of the new millennium is unstoppably adventurous, vigorous, and various. Media focus on individuals leads to enormous coverage (and sales) for, say, a new novel by Ian McEwan. Book purchasing on the web is easy for customers who have online facilities, and sites such as Amazon provide copious guidance for purchasers. The big bookshops' '3 for 1' paperback offers, especially at Christmas and holiday time, and their regular staging of 'meet-the-author' events, help to keep fiction sales healthy—of some titles, at least. There is considerable radio and print media coverage for new fiction, and online blogging has created an instantaneous, DIY reviewing culture. Regular newspaper features analysing major novels point to a readership interested in formal matters of narrative and style. An active and conscientious poet laureate, Andrew *Motion, brought poetry more vigorously into schools and onto the air. The Arts Council-funded organization Book Trust runs prizes and programmes to encourage readers of all ages, such as 'BookStart' and the 'Baby Book Award'. TV adaptations turn old classics—such as Elizabeth Gaskell's *Cranford*—into best-sellers. Readers' groups have become enough of a national fixture to be made into the subject of a television comedy series. The growth industry of literary festivals, at which readers can listen to, question, and have their books signed by authors, ranges from the massive international operation at Hay-on-Wye, where readers flock from tent to tent to hear celebrities, like passengers at an airport terminal, to smaller, more friendly and informal venues in Keswick, Ilkley, or Rye.

Though a great deal of literary activity has moved online, the much-anticipated death of the print-book and its replacement by e-books—in the shape, for example, of Sony's 'e-book' in 2005 or Amazon's 'Kindle' in 2007—has yet to be confirmed. The critic John Sutherland, a prolific commentator on contemporary literary culture, cited evidence in his brief guide to best-sellers (2007) that groups such as science-fiction readers and women readers of romance fiction were downloading increasing numbers of e-books. Squires, however, observed drily in 2007 that: 'Electronic delivery of novels has yet to make any major impact on the market.'

Sutherland notes that best-selling fiction has ranged from *Lolita*, *August 1914*, and *Doctor Zhivago* to *Love Story* and *The Carpetbaggers*: 'One could put together a very respectable educational curriculum from the bestseller lists. Or, alternatively, a scathing indictment of the utterly degraded British and American popular taste, as Q. D. *Leavis did in 1932.' Literary prizes, which sometimes create best-sellers, can similarly be thought of in terms of lament or celebration, as symptoms of a degraded, or an energetic, culture. They can be cynically regarded just as profit-making operations for publishers and the businesses that run the prizes. But they clearly, also, have some cultural value. The big prizes matter to the reading public. Heated public discussions surround, for instance, the overlooking of a favourite in a shortlist, the award of a prize to an unknown, or the appointment as literary judges of people who are not known primarily for their interest in books—such as the singer Lily Allen or the ex-politician Michael Portillo. The literary prize is a significant cultural pointer. Why?

Two historical reminders. When the Nobel Prize for Literature was started in 1901, the first ten recipients, who included Sully Prudhomme (1839–1907), Rudyard *Kipling, and Henryk Sienkiewicz (1846–1916), the author of **Quo Vadis*, notably did not include *Tolstoy, *Zola, or *Ibsen. Tolstoy did not win it because in *War and Peace* he had implied that human destiny was decided by blind chance, not by God. At least in its first ten years, the prize (as a 1991 survey by Kjell Espmark noted) was supposed to go to a work of 'lofty and sound idealism exhibiting a true nobility' and 'a contribution to humanity's struggle towards the ideal'. Zola was too sordid; Ibsen, a candidate in 1903, was too shocking.

The American *Pulitzer Prize was founded by Joseph Pulitzer and given by New York's Columbia University. In his will, Pulitzer required the novel prize to go to the book which should best give 'the whole atmosphere of American life'. But in 1917 the president of Columbia University changed the wording from 'whole' to 'wholesome'. So, in 1921, Edith *Wharton, frequently criticized at the time for the harsh realism of her subject matter, found to her ironical amusement that *The Age of Innocence*, a lacerating exposé of American sexual hypocrisy, had narrowly beaten Sinclair *Lewis's *Main Street* for the Pulitzer because it was deemed to be more 'wholesome'.

We smile at these examples, because the ideal that a good book should do you good is no longer a cultural assumption. It has become an arguable concept, the subject of provocative musings such as John Carey's *What Good Are the Arts* (2005). American and European literary prizes have left behind that yoking together of ethics and aesthetics—partly because the linking of moral virtue and the arts was discredited by its operations within Socialist Realism and Fascist art. Yet there is still a political, or social, or extra-aesthetic ingredient to some literary prizes. The Orange Prize for the best novel by a woman writer emerged in 1996 in ideological opposition to the perceived dominance of male writers on the *Booker Prize lists. The Nobel Prize, though its decision-making processes are shrouded in mystery, seems to have a political as well as an aesthetic ingredient. It is publicly maintained that the prize has no agenda of any kind except aesthetic excellence—no rotation among nations, for example, and no prejudice against American writers. But this is not widely believed. It strikes many observers as bizarre, for instance, that the greatest living American writer, Philip Roth, has (at the time of writing) been overlooked.

The history of the Man Booker Prize, like that of the Nobel, is not unpolitical. It emerged from the postcolonial history of the British Empire. In the 1940s and 1950s, the managing director of the Booker company, Jock Campbell, turned it from an expatriate colonial business with interests mainly in Guyana, into a UK-based company dealing in food distribution, engineering, shipping, and rum marketing. Campbell had literary interests and a friendship with Ian *Fleming, and he created an Authors Division of Booker, which purchased the copyrights of successful authors like Fleming, Agatha *Christie, and Georgette Heyer, to create tax loopholes for them and a profit for the company. In 1969, the publisher Tom Maschler persuaded Booker to set up a big literary prize like the Prix Goncourt. Commonwealth authors were included, reflecting Booker's history in Guyana. When John *Berger won in 1972 and announced he was going to give half his prize money to the Black Panthers in protest against Booker's colonialist policies in the West Indies, he may not have known that Booker gave regular financial assistance to Guyanese artists and writers.

The inclusion of Commonwealth writers (and the exclusion of American novelists, on the reasonable grounds that this would make the judges' task impossibly large) has always given rise to controversy. The awarding of the prize to novelists such as Thomas *Keneally, J. M. *Coetzee, Keri Hulme (1947–), Ben *Okri, Salman *Rushdie, Arundhati *Roy, Kiran *Desai, and Aravind Adiga (1974–) has provoked some Little Englander journalists to complain that the prize is for 'overseas writers with unpronounceable names'. In fact, one of the interests of the prize has always been its global reach. Since 2002, this has been developed by the addition of a Russian Man Booker Prize, the Caine Prize for African Writing, and the International Man Booker Prize.

My own experience of the Man Booker Prize spans a quarter of a century. When I first judged it in 1981 (with Malcolm *Bradbury as chair, Samuel Hynes, Brian *Aldiss, and Joan Bakewell) there was great excitement for us in awarding the prize to a dazzling, little-known young writer, Salman Rushdie, for *Midnight's Children* (which was later crowned the 'Booker of Bookers'). It was equally satisfying to revive the fortunes of the Anglo-Irish novelist Molly *Keane, who was then 77 and had not published for twenty years, and who leaped back into public view with our shortlisting of *Good Behaviour.* When I was co-presenting the television coverage of the prize in the 1980s, I was struck by the diversity of the winners, from the unknown New Zealander Keri Hulme, or the elegant dark horse Anita *Brookner, to the then still-admired old devil Kingsley *Amis.

By 2006, when I chaired the judging panel (made up of the poet Simon *Armitage, the actor Fiona Shaw, the film critic Anthony Quinn, and the novelist Candia McWilliam), it had become harder for our shortlisted or winning novels to make such a big impact. The effect of the prize on sales has become more variable and unpredictable. There are more novels to read now (I read 73 in 1981 and 112 in 2006). There are many more prizes in existence in Britain than in 1981, including the genre-crossing Whitbread, now the Costa Book Awards, the Orange Prize, the Samuel Johnson non-fiction prize, and the Commonwealth Writers' Prize. Though some good literary prizes, like the W. H. Smith, have vanished, there are numerous small-scale awards competing for attention, like the Duff Cooper or the James Tait Black, the Independent Foreign Fiction Prize and the Guardian First Book Prize, the Nestlé Smarties Book Prize for writing for children, the John Llewellyn Rhys Prize for a writer under 35, the Geoffrey Faber Prize, the Cheltenham Literature Festival Prize, the Betty Trask Prize for fiction with a romantic theme, and the David Cohen Prize for a writer's lifetime achievement. The field is crowded. Michael *Holroyd talked ruefully about the 'book-Prize circus' in *The Times* in August 2006: 'At literary festivals these days the epithet "prize-winning" is randomly used to describe all authors. The job of judging has grown so time-consuming and controversial that writers list the Prizes they have judged above those they have won in reference works.'

Yet, in spite of the saturation and the silliness, the frequent mistakes in judgement, and the pain and humiliation they can cause to writers, literary Prizes have a value that is not exclusively commercial. Nationally, they involve an energetic and engaged circle of library groups, reading groups, and highly opinionated bloggers. Internationally, they create links between the writers and readers of different countries. The Man Booker Prize, like the Nobel, can alter a writer's worldwide profile, either by confirming a towering reputation, or by promoting a relatively unknown novelist—as we did in 2006, when the 25-year-old Kiran Desai won for her second novel, *The Inheritance of Loss*. It can direct, and enlarge, people's reading, and encourage a vigorous public conversation about literature.

Our judging discussions in 2006 kept returning to well-trodden debates about the novel, with praise for moral seriousness and social responsibility jostling against an aesthetic pleasure in high style and a well-played game, pleasure in excess and outrageousness doing battle with a taste for fine-tuned poise and control. We travelled all over the world, and into other worlds, in our reading, and listened to an extraordinary array of voices, many of them at the far extreme of what written language can do. We read e-mail and chat-room novels, futuristic comedy written in invented dialect, realistic novels in raw street-speech, historical pastiche and poetic lyrics. We became acutely aware of the fears and preoccupations of the new millennium. There were many novels about children's vulnerability, women in repressive communities, old age, and institutions. There were plenty of male mid-life crises. We often came across characters looking for a secret past, searching for a lost parent, or uncovering a hidden trauma, characters questing for their true self. There was a great deal of anti-American feeling and many allusions to war and terrorism. Exile, displacement, and alienation were powerful themes.

At the end of the process, I asked my fellow judges what they had gained from their experience, and they gave me serious, even moral, answers: that it had been a privilege and a form of 'replenishment'; that in a time of anathema, novels are a free zone, a space where you can cross boundaries, and can imagine lives outside of and alien to your own. In spite of the swirl of biased, gossipy, and superficial commentary that always surrounds the Prize, judging it felt—most of the time—like a serious enterprise, having to do with things of value: the power of storytelling, the adventure of language, the future of reading.

The attention paid to literary Prizes is one indicator that the reading community in Britain is not confined to a small elite, as it is increasingly felt to be in North America. This community is catered for by a wide range of publications, from pulp fiction to 'writers' writers', like our 2006 Man Booker Prize runner-up, Edward *St Aubyn. Critical commentary on the novel at the start of the 21st century also spans a wide range. Between 2006 and 2008, a number of books on the novel were published in America and Britain, as various as the genre they described. A trawl of these early 21st-century critiques shows up an inexhaustible interest in analysing the genre, a belief in its political, intellectual, and ethical importance, and an awareness of different readerships wanting to be informed about the novel in a range of tones and approaches. These books were aimed, variously, at reading groups, students, scholars, browsers, theorists, anti-theorists, would-be novelists, and at Virginia *Woolf's ideal audience for fiction, 'the common reader'. They spoke different critical languages. But they could all be summed up by a phrase of Virginia Woolf's, used in the title of one of these books: 'A thing there was that mattered.'

The Czech novelist Milan *Kundera brought his own experience to bear in a Flaubertian meditation on European fiction, *The Curtain* (2007), which celebrates the 'everydayness' of the novel and praises the form's essential self-sufficiency: 'It refuses to exist as illustration of an historical era, as description of a society, as defence of an ideology, and instead puts itself exclusively at the service of "what only the novel can say".' Jane *Smiley gave a more personal, less rigorous American novelist's view in *13 Ways of Looking at the Novel* (2006). There are tips for aspiring novelists, emotional accounts of how fiction gets written, and brief, plain-spoken accounts of 101 selected novels, with simple, enthusiastic recommendations. Smiley places her emphasis on the reader's freedom to choose what she likes. She has no time for 'academic' theorizing about the novel, because 'novels were invented to be accessible'. Her central image, of 'Earth's big bookstore', implies that there is plenty for everyone. Novels, in her view, make an argument for democracy.

The American academic and Auden scholar Edward Mendelsohn, in *The Things That Matter: What Seven Classic Novels Have to Say about the Stages of Life* (2006), is more interested in the ethical than the political meanings of the novel. He makes an impassioned, didactic, and illuminating diagnosis of seven novels by women writers (Mary *Shelley, Charlotte and Emily *Brontë, George *Eliot, and Virginia Woolf) as humane lessons in how (or how not) to live a moral life. *Jane Eyre*, for instance, is read as a story about moral education. 'Everyone tells her to believe in different things in a different way—but she must find her beliefs by herself. In *Jane Eyre* as in life, the right choices are rarely new or surprising, but everyone has to discover anew the ways in which to learn to make those choices…[and] how to act on the truths you have chosen.'

In *How Novels Work* (2006), the British scholar and journalist John Mullan collected his weekly pieces for the *Guardian*, aimed at readers' groups and non-academics, on the mechanics and tactics of novel writing, into a useful and sensible diagnosis of novelistic strategies—beginnings and endings, paratexts and intertexts, first- and third-person narratives, present and past tenses, inadequate and multiple narrators. John Sutherland took the 'common reader' on a brisk, savvy trot through the jungle of the literary market-place in *How to Read a Novel: A User's Guide* (2006).

At the opposite end of the critical spectrum is the Stanford professor of comparative literature, Franco Moretti, editor of a two-volume, multi-authored encyclopedia, *The Novel* (2006). The first volume of this epic scholarly project, 'History, Geography and Culture', covers the centuries-long evolution of the genre and its worldwide crossing of borders and cross-fertilizations. The second volume, 'Forms and Themes', examines 'a morphology that ranges euphorically from war stories, pornography and melodrama, to syntactical labyrinths, metaphoric prose, and broken plot lines'. There are further divisions and subdivisions into large themes ('Space and Story', 'The European Acceleration'), narrower themes ('Inconceivable History: Storytelling as Hyperphasia and Disavowal'), individual case studies, and 'critical apparatus' ('The Semantic Field of Narrative'.) It is a solemn, ambitious, schematic enterprise.

The critic Jonathan Zwicker writes, in Moretti's collection, of a marginal note left by an anonymous Japanese reader in a 1908 library copy of Tolstoy's newly translated *Kreutzer Sonata*, whose title in translation was 'Chôkon', meaning 'long resentment'. 'A boring book. Where is the long resentment? The resentment is in having read the book. There is no value in its being translated.' That early 20th-century Japanese reader of Tolstoy, just like any judging panel or reading group today, shows that coming to conclusions about the novel is as personal, opinionated, and impure a process as writing one.

It is one of the few aspects of the novel generally agreed on in all these books that the novel's impurity makes classification difficult. Yet this is one of the favourite activities surrounding the genre, from publishers' and bookstores' 'genre-niching' activities, to scholarly systems of Nabokovian obsessiveness. The most awe-inspiring example of this in Moretti's volumes is the Society for the Analysis of Novelistic Topoi, a worldwide group of scholars 'engaged in systematic research to recover the topoi of French novels from the Middle Ages through the revolution and of generating an inventory in the form of a computerized database based on that research'. Nathalie Ferrand, who calls this 'a magnificent, but we might note, rather mad idea', gives various examples of such topoi—'Beauty held captive in a harem', 'Retreat to a convent occasioned by despondent love', 'Overheard conversations'—within which you can refine your web search to 'Someone overhears a conversation in a garden'. It could become a party game, with a Prize for the most examples of the following topoi in novels written in the 20th and 21st centuries: Estate agent has mid-life crisis; Teacher expelled from academic community charged with racial or sexual misdemeanour; Child grows up with telepathic powers transmitted through nose.

The classification of the novel into romance, epic, postcolonial, realist, socially committed, picaresque, idealist, bourgeois, fantastical, and so on, can be helpful, but needs to come with this warning, from Moretti's second volume (p. 195): 'All genres are hybrid, but some are more hybrid than others.' The critic James Wood, in his short book, part close reading, part philosophizing, on *How Fiction Works* (2008), dealing with traditional topics like narrating, detail, character, and dialogue, insists that 'The novel is the great virtuoso of exceptionalism: it always wriggles out of the rules thrown around it.'

Yet categories can be interestingly pursued when they are seen crossing cultural borders, as in an account by Jongyon Hwang (in Moretti), of how Korean fiction in the early 20th century began to adopt the genre of the **Bildungsroman* in order to move away from the previous generation's authoritarian culture (collapsed under Japanese colonialism), towards more Western desires for 'self-expression and social advancement'. Classification can be illuminating, too, when the category is seen as a shape-shifter, as in Bruce Robbins's essay, also in Moretti, on how the 'upward mobility story' in fiction shifted from social climbing to the making of a writer.

Almost all critics of the novel agree that one of its main functions is to tell the story of vulnerable, ordinary, eccentric, or obscure individuals so that we will better understand them. George Eliot is cited as the pre-eminent example of the novelist who widens and deepens her readers' sense of other people and makes us think harder about how we deal with the world. Her belief that 'the greatest benefit we owe to the artist...is the extension of our sympathies' is often cited, as by James Wood in a chapter called 'Sympathy and Complexity'. It follows from this belief in the value of the individual that the novel must draw us in, as individual readers. As Mendelsohn puts it, 'a reader who identifies with the characters in a novel is not reacting in a naive way that ought to be outgrown or transcended, but is performing one of the central acts of literary understanding'.

Simple processes of identification in novel reading are complicated by the duplicity of fiction, its acts of disguise, contradiction, and suppression. This is a frequent theme in these critical readings. The idea of the novel as the secret agent of literature, double-dealing, withholding information, is matched in these commentaries by an equally strong idea of the novel as polymorphous, expansive, and abundant. Even the most formal and aesthetically stringent of novelists can also have an appetite for excess. The inclusive, exhaustive tradition of *Balzac, or James Joyce's **Ulysses*, persists in contemporary fiction. In the course of their generalizations about the novel, these critics repeatedly seize on the stuff, the clutter, the prosaic detail, the 'thinginess' of fiction.

In reading about fiction, or in reading novels, past and present, one often comes on the idea of a journey: a worn path, a day's walking through a city, a quest, a progress, a journey through time or towards death. It is permissible to think about characters in novels as people, and it is not necessarily sentimental or naive to think about what might happen to them after we stop reading. The novels which haunt me most are those which give the effect of a journey continuing beyond the end of the book: Isabel Archer going back to her prison at the end of Henry James's *The *Portrait of a Lady*; the lovers walking away into the crowd in Charles Dickens's **Little Dorrit* and disappearing into everyday humanity; Newland Archer turning away from the windows of a house in Paris in Wharton's *The Age of Innocence*; Portia, the runaway girl about to return to the home she has to live in, in Elizabeth *Bowen's *The Death of the Heart*; the unknowable future for the married couple at the end of *Between the Acts*, set just before the outbreak of war and finished just before Woolf's suicide; the lonely narrator, all storytelling spent, looking out at the burning stars at the end of Roth's *I Married a Communist*; the reunion of the son and the father, coming through the utmost humiliation and impoverishment, on the last page of Kiran Desai's *The Inheritance of Loss*. As in all these examples, the journey of the literary novel (and its cultural context) does not end. This essay, and this *Companion*, mark a stage in a continuing process.

CULTURES OF READING

Kelvin Everest

It's temptingly easy to assume that people read less, less intelligently, more narrowly, somehow less seriously, than they used to. As Gore *Vidal has said, there are no famous novelists now. Literature is not at the heart of the general culture, but takes its place alongside the attractions and distractions of the internet, television, celebrity. Books get hyped nowadays like everything else. Authors and titles are marketed as celebrities, promoted, targeted on 'niche' categories of theme, setting, and style. It can seem diminishing; too commercialized, too fast-moving, a dumbed-down unserious consumerism of literature. A handful of novelists enjoy sales on a vast scale, while the range of good successful contemporary writers seems to narrow constantly. Bookselling has concentrated into a handful of chain stores. The publishing industry has become global big business. The best-seller lists are dominated by 'brand' writers, formulaic blockbusters, novels written to be bought in airports. If there is still something we could call a literary culture, the soul seems to have gone out of it. A few serious writers still find sustained success—John *Le Carré, Ian *McEwan—and some good writers—J. K. *Rowling—have had astonishing success. But most of the big sellers are unlikely to stand the test of time. Hardly anyone reads poetry, or indeed even publishes it. Literature is there to make money. Those who believed all along with Kingsley *Amis that the advent of mass higher education would bring an ugly dilution of our cultural experience have something to get their teeth into. The prediction that 'More means worse' encapsulates the fear underlying the conservative elitism of *modernism, so influentially articulated in the cultural pessimism of *The *Waste Land*. The culture of Europe after the First World War was in ruins, 'a heap of broken images'. T. S. *Eliot's poem brilliantly trades on a deliberately inaccessible allusiveness that anticipates the under-educated and ill-informed hordes that now dictate fashions in literature.

But what's wrong with a mass culture? We all live now in a cultural arena that is much bigger, more diverse, more inclusive. There is plenty of space and appetite for serious reading. There is room too for variety in what we read. Serious writing is permanently important, a form of high art which requires commitment and sometimes discipline, and which stimulates hard thought and passionate engagement. Its enjoyment does not necessarily come easily or quickly, and for many there are great benefits in the help of a teacher, the more readily to appreciate the depth, complexity, and power of a great book. But there are many kinds of pleasure in reading, some less enduring in their reward, but also less demanding and more directly accessible. The novels of Danielle Steele have sold hundreds of millions of copies, and obviously provide a valued entertainment. All readers enjoy different kinds of reading experience, be it *science fiction, thrillers, *detective novels, *fantasy, *life writing, or any one of numerous genres. Our contemporary culture can easily accommodate an intelligent and attentive readership for challenging and important literature, as one of many kinds and levels of reading for pleasure. And this variety is also normal and natural in the individual reader.

Reading remains one of the most important things we do. For many, it is the most important, a means to a wider, richer, and more various mental life than can easily be supported by the simple realities of our experience. Books take us into the lives and worlds of other people, who may be historically or culturally remote, utterly different in background, outlook, and prospect, and yet recognizable, sufficient in shared humanity to enable a sense of empathy, even identification. This familiar truth is no less potent for being obvious. Present-day reading tastes and fashions have recently placed an emphasis on certain recurring differences of time and place, colour, creed, and class: postcolonial countries, theatres of contemporary war, disadvantaged and dispossessed people. But the power of books to reach across divides of experience, to bring home to the imagination the reality of other lives, is a constant. For some this power in literature has assumed a quasi-religious significance. P. B. *Shelley believed that great literature acts like Love in enabling 'a going out of our own nature, and an identification of ourselves with the beautiful which exists in thought, action, or person, not our own…Poetry strengthens that faculty [imagination] which is the organ of the moral nature of man, in the same manner as exercise strengthens a limb.' For the Victorian Matthew *Arnold the European literary tradition had the capacity to take over the functions of religion itself. In our contemporary world, for many it is enough to acknowledge that books bring us into contact and relationship with a company far greater than can ever be encompassed in the ordinary goings-on of social life. They enable even the most solitary to feel the reality of their common humanity.

At times we all have leisure to read, on holiday, in retirement, as a programme of study, or on long journeys. But reading happens constantly, all around the ordinary commitments of time and space; travelling to work, in a lunch break, in the armchair, in the garden, or in bed. There is a complicated and elusive interconnectedness of social groups, institutions, and traditions that knits this personal activity into something much bigger, and which is inclusive of many kinds of reader. There is a kind of community and commonality of experience in this participation in a readership, which takes diverse forms. A professional metropolitan literary culture flourishes, in close relationship with the national press, and with the universities. This is a small and relatively enclosed group, but there is a broad regular audience for its commentary on current books and writers that makes its influence, through reviews and discursive journalism, real and considerable. We have strong and serious literary journalism, working through the major newspapers but also in a variety of journals: the *TLS*, the *LRB*, the *Literary Review*, the *New Statesman*. This broad audience merges with a much wider network of readers which has grown with the huge increase in people participating in higher education over the past 25 years. More has meant, not a worse, but a bigger and more various readership. The proportion of the population as a whole with some experience of higher education is now hugely greater than has ever before been the case, and there are hundreds of thousands who have studied the literature of the past. This makes a difference, both in sustaining the public appetite for new writing, but also in maintaining a level of literary awareness and sensitivity which ensures the continuing historical transmission of our literary heritage. There may be a far greater diversity in kinds and levels of reading taste, but this diversity encompasses a sheer scale of participation which is intrinsically robust. This participation is supplemented by popular television adaptations of classic English fiction, a vibrantly successful modern cultural form which constantly wins new readers and nurtures fresh interest. It is true that these adaptations of course edit drastically, and inevitably privilege narrative urgency and emotional extremity, but they reinforce the attractive power of their originals.

Beyond the specialized communities of writing, publishing, journalism, and the universities, and larger far than the audience they directly engage, is a general community of contemporary readers. These are the buyers of best-sellers and classics, people who meet in informal reading groups, borrow from libraries, give and receive books as gifts. When we read a book we participate in this national community, share, with or without explicit dialogue, in the common experience of our fellow contemporary readers, and become both a part and an agent of contemporary literary culture.

This quality in reading—a private experience of great intensity which is simultaneously shared with other readers—is repeated in a different way whenever we read a great work of literature which has survived through time. Take, for example, **Jane Eyre*. Since its first publication in 1847 Charlotte *Brontë's masterpiece has attracted probably millions of readers. It was admired from the first, W. M. *Thackeray describing it as 'the masterwork of a great genius'. Elizabeth *Gaskell in her biography of Brontë published in 1850 famously compared her work, favourably, with Jane *Austen's delineation of 'the surface of the lives of genteel English people'. In contrast with Austen ('only shrewd and observant', as Brontë herself described her work), Brontë offered 'what throbs fast and full, what the blood rushes through, what is the unseen seat of life and the sentient target of death'. This of course strikingly understates Austen's controlled passion and narrative drive. But it strikes a chord with all readers of *Jane Eyre*, because that novel has for generations articulated with a raw power the experience of thwarting social and personal circumstance, the inner life in painful struggle with constraining circumstances, the imperatives of self-fulfilment and the wish for a recognized presence in the world. The novel's first readers encountered these things, and each successive generation, in its shifting combination of forces and conditions, has encountered it anew. When we read *Jane Eyre* today we are drawn into a personal life in a social world that is both like and unlike our own, and there is a personal investment on our part in the experience and fate of the heroine. But we also share the like and unlike reading experience of the first readers, and of each generation, in our own and other places, and this connects us with a diverse array of other people, drawing our intellectual and emotional life back from the present into the layered past.

The ghostly company of earlier readers in our own experience of a book can even have an affinity with the physical presence of what we are reading, the material object of the book itself. When we read a work of literature in an old edition the imprint of previous owners and readers can be palpable, as in bookplates or annotation, or more subtly implicit in the evidence of previously turned pages, relaxed or broken bindings, down-turned corners, and the like. The book as an object is beautifully characterized in Craig *Raine's poem 'A Martian Sends a Postcard Home', where the alien's estranging gaze produces an insightfully distortive perspective:

Caxtons are mechanical birds with many wings
And some are treasured for their markings—

They cause the eyes to melt
Or the body to shriek without pain.

I have never seen one fly,
But sometimes they perch on the hand.

Books move us, make us think, and can be as directly affective as anything that we might experience. They are also portable, need no external power, and can be very durable; and this too bears on the meanings that they carry. There is a passage in James *Joyce's **Ulysses* when Stephen Dedalus pauses by a 'slanted bookcart' to browse second-hand books. He picks one up and muses as he flicks through the pages, 'Thumbed pages…read and read…Who has passed here before me?' This touches deftly on a major and pervasive theme in Joyce's great novel, the continuity, or contrast, between contemporary experience and that of the countless generations that precede it. *Ulysses* is a comedy, and wonderfully affirms the heroic grandeur of ordinary lives. All the mythic characters and legends that a culture inherits are archetypes abstracted from the detailed reality of uncountable lives, and the archetypes wake again from generation to generation, not least in the people of Dublin on 16 June 1904. The novel addresses what Leopold Bloom's wife Molly terms 'met-him-pike-hoses', *metempsychosis*, the transmigration of souls. There is a kind of temporary immortality that we can inhabit as readers of literature. The intellectual and emotional engagement with recognizable experiences in the past affirms something defining and constant of which we are ourselves the living agents.

Jane Eyre also vividly exemplifies another aspect of this doubleness in being a reader, the co-presence of a solitary and private activity with the sense of an experience shared with our own generation of readers, and also with all of the previous generations. Brontë's novel indeed itself evokes repeatedly a constant traffic between private subjectivity, and the objective presence of social conditions and other people. At one level the narrative portrays Jane growing up in a real social world, with an identifiable historical setting, England in the early 19th century. The story turns on recognizable institutions, social roles, and historical circumstances: the country house, schools, governesses, plantations in the West Indies, the legal system, and the place of women. But these materials are filtered through Jane's consciousness in a manner which imparts to the narrative a dreamlike subjectivity, as if external reality repeatedly shapes itself to the impulses and emerging desires of the heroine's personality. The novel moves through settings which embody newly emergent states of mind in Jane. The characters associated with each of these settings—Helen Burns, Miss Temple, Rochester—have an odd correspondence with recently quickening desires, new senses of self, in the heroine. Even the very names of the characters have obliquely symbolic connotations (as for instance in the various elemental associations of Rivers, Poole, Burns, Eyre, and so on). The action blends realism with a symbolism of inner development, so that the climactic fire which injures Rochester is the culminating instance of an elaborate patterning of fires and burning. The final impossible act of communication from Jane to Rochester, when their far distant cries to each other are apparently at some level actually heard, underpins the novel's merging of observed reality with the inner drama of developing subjective consciousness. Reading fiction always has this dimension: the novel is a determinate shareable thing, held in common by all of its readers and making reference to a common reality; but its precise force and meaning for the individual reader is always shaped by their unique circumstances, background, and time of life.

There are other ways in which reading can disturb our sense of the distinction between self and world, subjective consciousness and external reality. The potency with which literature presents to our waking intelligence the affective reality of imaginary representations of things, places, and people in the past can play strangely with our experience of time itself. Fiction and poetry both must comprise some representation of time. In poetry, this can be an elusive and puzzling thing, because except in certain cases where a specific historical reference is part of the meaning, verb tenses in poems do not work as they do in everyday speech. John *Keats's 'Ode to a Nightingale' begins in the present tense: 'My heart aches, and a drowsy numbness pains my sense'. This is obviously not a statement about a specific moment in historical time. The lines do not refer to a particular instant on Hampstead Heath in May 1819, but are permanently in the present tense for all subsequent readers. Present tenses in poems tend not to recede in time and become historically remote, as they do for example when they occur in documents of historical record. What happens in lyric poetry is always happening, and happens afresh with each reading. Here again is a kind of fleeting immortality that we are in touch with when we read, as we become the ephemeral agents of a poetic work of art that is not going to die. It is the effect in poetry that W. B. *Yeats had in mind in 'Among School Children': 'How can we know the dancer from the dance?' A dance, like a poem, is a permanent form, but to become real in time it needs the performance of real people, who, while they dance, partake of the immortality of the form to which they give temporary life.

Time in the novel bears somewhat differently on our experience as readers. Most kinds of fictional narrative make decisions about the representation of time, and many exercise a high degree of control and rigour. Often this can be a matter of explicit concern, as in Martin *Amis's *Time's Arrow*, and Ian McEwan's *The Child in Time* and *On Chesil Beach*, or of overt formal complexity and experimentation, for example in Ford Madox *Ford's *The Good Soldier* or Virginia *Woolf's *Mrs Dalloway*. **Wuthering Heights* begins with a date, which immediately alerts the reader to that novel's carefully unostentatious temporal complexity, moving backwards and forwards in a manner which complements the taxing similarity of character names in different generations. But most major works of fiction take great care with the coherence of their setting in time, and with the representation of the time that passes in the narrative. Jane Austen is at her most commandingly elegant in this respect. **Mansfield Park* for instance is plotted in time with subtle precision. It was published in 1811, and opens with the words 'About thirty years ago…', which takes us back to 1781, when Fanny Price's Aunt Maria married Sir Thomas Bertram. Fanny arrives at Mansfield Park around 1800, when she is 10, and is 'just eighteen' in 1808 when the main action of the novel takes place, covering a period of less than a year from July 1808, when the Crawfords arrive at the Parsonage, to the spring of 1809 when the novel ends with Fanny's return from Portsmouth. Only one actual date is specified through the whole course of the novel: Sir Thomas's ball for Fanny takes place on Thursday 22 December, which confirms a setting in 1808 and which indeed suggests that Austen probably used an almanac for that year in working out her plot. There is nothing remotely ostentatious about the controlled exactitude with which Austen organizes time in *Mansfield Park*. On the contrary it is never explicit, but enables a beautifully understated metaphor of the onset of winter, quietly delineated through numerous light touches of detail, which shadows Fanny's emotional descent following the theatricals (which take us into October) and through her deepening confusion about her feelings for Henry Crawford (he proposes to her in early January). The difficult period with her family in Portsmouth comes to a close with the accelerating denouements of the plot, which gather to a climax as the year moves in May from springtime into summer.

The span of time which is thus represented to pass in the course of the novel's action forms part of our experience as readers. Personal time is measured out against steady counters: the rhythm of night and day, of morning, afternoon, and evening, against the bigger but still steady and rhythmical background of the seasons and the climate. Within these rhythms our time is regulated by our time of life and circumstances, studying, working, travelling, retired. It is within these rhythms that reading takes place, but reading brings us into relationship with different orders of time. An hour or two of reading can encompass a fictional span of moments or years. There are novellas, such as Joseph *Conrad's 'Heart of Darkness', or Henry *James's *Turn of the Screw*, which can be read at a single sitting and whose formal brilliance offers an extraordinary narrative drive. Here the sense of time passing is accelerated as an effect of the tightening urgency of the action and the deepening intensity of the narrative voice. At a different extreme are the long and populous novels of 19th-century realism, which give a span of historical time and a sweep of social range and character. **Middlemarch*, or **Little Dorrit*, or **Vanity Fair*, can be read quickly but they need a basic investment of time, and for many people the demands of everyday life limit sustained periods of reading, such that the experience of these novels can extend for many days or weeks. They become a part of the texture of living, constantly paralleling, contrasting, supplementing our routine range of perception and interest.

These experiences stay with us. But unlike other kinds of powerful experience which change and mark our view of the world and our self-understanding, reading experiences can be revisited, and we do revisit them. **Persuasion*, or **Great Expectations*, or **Jude the Obscure*, are very different novels read at 18 and 58. It is not just that as readers of books that endure through time we participate in, or enjoy, a transient unity with a trans-historical community of other readers; we also reread ourselves, measure change, and weigh the import of shifted perspectives and changed horizons.

This aspect of our enjoyment of literature is perhaps at its most concentrated and profound in relation to drama. Relatively few people, other than specialists, spend much time reading non-poetic drama. But many go to the theatre, or watch productions of serious drama on television or in the cinema. When we see a production of a *Shakespeare play we of course have the specifics of the performance to consider and enjoy, and we are engaged by the subject matter, the characters, and the language. **Twelfth Night* is about love and the dubieties of sexual attraction, and the comical and not-so-comical possibilities of misunderstanding, self-delusion, and manipulation that come with this territory. It is shadowed by darker themes hinting at the cruelty in comedy, and the narrowness with which real tragedy is averted. Malvolio is not reconciled; affectations of strong feeling, or the need for its concealment, threaten the possibility of consummation. It is like **Romeo and Juliet* in a different mood. These themes are worked out in the drama across a range of characters who encompass different types and condition of lover. Orsino and Olivia start in poses of strong feeling which are sorely tested by circumstance. Viola must disguise her true feelings. Sir Toby, Aguecheek, and Maria are less illusioned but differently ill-judging and complacent; they are young lovers grown older, more worldly-wise and indulgent but shorn of idealism. Their ability to heighten the comedy in Malvolio's ridiculous gullibility is persisted in to the point of gratuitous cruelty, but between themselves they still display the capacity for mutual attraction and a sense of the pleasure in life, however self-deceiving. In short when we watch the play we follow a plot that involves a spectrum of human possibilities and conditions, and will find ourselves in correspondence, to a greater or lesser degree, with one of them. But we also find, as we see the play at intervals through the years, that we recognize ourselves differently. Orsino becomes Sir Toby; or even Andrew Aguecheek, with his oddly touching 'I was adored once'. This effect, of finding that a work of literature changes its meaning for us as we return to it again and again, is heightened in drama by the presence in live theatre of actors. Actors are real people who grow and age like the rest of us; sometimes we may ourselves be the actors. In a long career they will play the range of roles, from junior lead to ageing character part. An audience that has been moved and thrilled in the 1960s by the young David Warner's magnificent Hamlet, can have its enjoyment of his brilliant Falstaff in 2007 subtly intensified by the recollection of the earlier performance. The plays remain the same, but their human agents, the actors, flicker through the phases of life as a career passes. In this way great drama, which remains current in the canon of current performance, is guaranteed in its persisting truth of representation by this successive coming-to-life through constantly changing casts. The effect works powerfully in any drama where the performance is repeated in an extensive way. At the opposite end of the spectrum from Shakespeare's inclusive breadth lies Samuel *Beckett. His work plays self-consciously with the idea of theatre as an image of the human condition, continually re-enacting archetypes of experience through changing people, styles, and circumstances. The characters in **Waiting for Godot* are absolutely constrained by the literal conditions of their existence as characters in a play. It is a two-act play where the second act closely repeats numerous features of the first. Characters in the first act appear to be recalling things that happen in the second act, and that is possible because the second act precedes the first in the sense that the previous performance of the play involved the same characters; they have repeatedly moved through their lines and positions. They consequently know the limits of what can and will happen, and what has already happened. Beckett teases out with inexhaustible comic inventiveness the possibilities of play-in-performance as a metaphor for the human condition, and not just in his masterpiece *Godot*. *Endgame* ends with its dramatis personae frozen on stage in positions closely approximating to those they will be in when the next performance starts, and each performance starts with those characters under dustsheets, as if having been preserved from decay in their immoveable positions since the conclusion of the previous performance. Winnie in *Happy Days*, up to her waist in a mound of refuse in the first act, up to her neck in the second, keeps her determinedly cheerful banter going even when it gets so hot that the parasol she opens to protect herself catches fire, being dangerously close to the stage lighting. It's for a similar reason that Clov in *Endgame* is confident that it won't rain (the theatre being roofed), and it is also part of the joke when he turns his telescope on 'the without', and reports that through it he can see 'A multitude…in transports…of joy. (Pause.) That's what I call a magnifier.' He is of course looking out at the passively watching darkened audience.

Reading today remains central to our cultural life. There are those who argue or fear that the ubiquity of the internet poses a threat to literature. This seems unwarrantedly pessimistic. The internet certainly brings new kinds of problem and challenge. Copyright is a serious issue. The net brings bigger sales of books, with limitless choice at cheaper prices. But you tend to need to know what you are looking for in buying a book online; the bookshop pleasures of browsing, conversation, and accidental discovery are harder to replace. Reading itself however is not endangered. In practical terms it is not comfortable or easy to read extended prose fiction on a screen; and full-length novels, unlike music, are not usefully downloadable. Lyrical poetry is more accessible, and already exists on the web in a mode adapted to the special possibilities of typographical mutation, time-control, and hyperlink. But a poetry which is consciously intruded upon by the protean possibilities of electronic communication can also appear diminished and coercive. Poems, like novels, still work best when experienced in book form, where the medium itself has physically determinate boundaries and a stable form which can themselves be a part of the pleasure of reading. Hyperlinks are in their nature boundless and constitute an infinitely extendable distraction from the controlled wholeness of a work of literature.

Language is the principal medium of the internet, and while the world wide web is open to abuse like other human inventions, its speed and power of communication is a strength for the future of literature. We buy and sell books on the net, gather information, make and maintain connectivity with people, institutions, writers, and writing. It is the logical final form for the transmission of a mass and democratic literary culture, big enough to have room for every level, taste, and fashion, and certainly big enough to support a readership for serious literature which is these days far, far bigger than ever before in history.

BLACK BRITISH LITERATURE

BÉNÉDICTE LEDENT

In 1983, Salman *Rushdie observed (in an essay on 'Commonwealth Literature') that black British literature does not exist, that 'the category is a chimera' comprising different traditions united only by their proponents' pigmentation alongside their British citizenship or residence. The label 'black British' has often been seen as reductive and divisive, notably by literary practitioners; yet it has had wide currency since the 1980s. Writers cast as 'black British' frequently object that, despite the challenge implied in combining these two adjectives, the phrase suggests a marginalization in its relation to what might be called 'white British literature'—a much less common tag. Some resent being seen as an appendage to mainstream literature, or complain, like Fred *D'Aguiar in a 1986 piece entitled 'Against Black British Literature', that the assumptions of authenticity underlying the label confine their creative imagination which should '[know] no boundaries'. These questions are far-reaching. Other European nations, with imperial histories of their own, are confronted with comparable issues. But the complexities of colonial and postcolonial history have given them particular resonance in relation to our understanding of British literature.

When the term 'black British literature' became current in the 1970s, it was designed to describe writing by authors based in Britain but with origins in former British colonies in Asia, Africa, and the Caribbean. It was at that time a political rather than a purely racial label, pointing to a common experience of postcolonial migration, alienation, and discrimination, combined with an oblique yet potentially subversive assertion of attachment to Britain. This explains why writers of Asian origin such as Rushdie and Hanif *Kureishi, both of Indian heritage, or even Kazuo *Ishiguro with roots in Japan, were in the 1980s and 1990s unproblematically included in a wide-ranging category which also involved artists more obviously 'black' like Ben *Okri, born in Nigeria, or Linton Kwesi *Johnson, born in Jamaica. However, the term has lost some of its early scope, and now conventionally refers to authors of African and Caribbean descent. Writers with Asian roots are today often subsumed under the 'British Asian' or 'Asian British' banner, which is the case for a younger writer like Monica *Ali, whose best-selling debut novel *Brick Lane* (2003) is set in London's Bangladeshi community. This does not mean that the ethnic delineations of 'black British' writing have become neater—as illustrated, for example, by the presence in the 'black British' category of an author like Guyana-born Pauline Melville, who is of Caribbean heritage but ethnically white, or of David *Dabydeen, also born in Guyana but of East Indian descent. The shift in the limits of the term suggests changing relationships between so-called ethnic minorities in Britain and a growing gap between communities once bound by a shared status as racial and cultural outsiders, yet now increasingly divided, often along religious lines—in particular after 9/11 and 7/7.

While the term 'black' can lead to diverging though sometimes overlapping interpretations, 'British' might seem less problematic, referring as it does to either citizenship or residence, two criteria possibly less elusive than race or culture. The Britishness of some 'black British' writers has nonetheless been questioned on the ground that they display a plural sense of belonging. This has for example been the case of Chris Abani, a poet and novelist born in Nigeria but who spent several years in Britain before moving to the United States. Another notable instance of multiple cultural allegiances is Caryl *Phillips, a British writer born in St Kitts who lives in the United States. He has claimed a multi-faceted, Atlantic identity which he describes in *A New World Order* (2001) as encompassing the Africa of his ancestors, the Caribbean of his birth, and Britain where he was brought up and educated and which had a crucially formative effect on his world-view. It is not surprising that his writing provides an extensive reflection on the meaning of Britishness, even more than blackness, and explores various ways in which Britain has been shaped as a consequence of the arrival of migrants on its territories. While Abani's and Phillips's examples, which are not unique, testify to the inability of national labels to fully capture the complexities of literature in a global age, they also confirm the need to redefine existing tags, and even more importantly to see what each individual writer has to say and how she or he does it.

It is often assumed that 'black British literature' refers to a literary tradition which developed only after the Second World War, in the wake of the arrival of the *Empire Windrush*, the ship that in 1948 brought Jamaican immigrants to London and was therefore assumed to be the starting point of the black presence in Britain. It may be convenient to give a literary tradition such a precise starting point, but it should not be forgotten that there had been a sizeable body of texts pre-dating the work of pioneer figures like Samuel *Selvon or George *Lamming, two writers from the Caribbean who started to publish after their arrival in London in 1950, and had a major impact on the subsequent generations of writers coming from the former empire. An exclusive focus on this post-war period obliterates black contributions to British literature from earlier generations—such as Olaudah *Equiano's *Interesting Narrative* (1789), or Mary *Seacole's *Wonderful Adventures of Mrs. Seacole in Many Lands* (1857).

Similarly, the role played in the 1930s by literary figures like C. L. R. *James from Trinidad or Una Marson from Jamaica, who both spent a part of their lives in England and actively participated in intellectual debates in English radical circles, should not be underestimated. 'Black British literature' viewed as a time-limited phenomenon attached to post-war migration to England is likely to become irrelevant to a younger generation of writers born in England, some of whom are of mixed parentage, like Anglo-Jamaican Zadie *Smith or Anglo-Nigerian Diana Evans, and whose allegiance might for these reasons be more domestic than was the case for their predecessors. It will become difficult to view 'black British' literature as marked only by displacement and migration, as its representatives are increasingly born and bred Britons, more interested in the here and now than in their ancestral culture.

Generational expectations are, however, not the only ones to plague 'black British' writing. It also suffers from generic preconceptions. It is often thought to locate itself exclusively in fiction, the most popular and the most publicized contemporary genre, or in poetry, especially when it is performative, for this form is usually associated with artists coming from cultures with a strong oral tradition, like many African societies, and those of the Caribbean. It is true that most of the best performance poets in Britain today are from the black community. Famous names include John *Agard, Patience *Agbabi, Lemn *Sissay, Benjamin *Zephaniah, and particularly Linton Kwesi Johnson, who reads his politically committed poems to a reggae rhythm and is the second living poet, after Polish Czesław *Miłosz, to have his work published in the famous Penguin Classics series. Yet performance poetry is by no means the only field in which 'black British' poets excel. Though the difference between oral and written verse is not at all clear-cut, many of them have also written pieces intended to be read on the page, like David Dabydeen's *Turner* (1994), a long lyrical poem inspired by J. M. W. Turner's painting *The Slave Ship*, or Fred D'Aguiar's *Bill of Rights* (1998), a narrative poem about the 1978 Jonestown massacre in Guyana. In the field of drama too, 'black British' writing has had several outstanding ambassadors, like Michael Abbensetts (1938–), Mustapha Matura (1939–), or Winsome Pinnock (1961–), though their plays have been performed in fringe theatres, and have therefore not been very visible. Only recently, with a new generation of playwrights, has 'black British' theatrical production been given the recognition it deserves, particularly through the work of young dramatists like Roy Williams, Courttia Newland, or Kwame Kwei Armah (1967–), whose best-known play, *Elmina's Kitchen* (2003), was staged in the West End in 2004. Interestingly, 'black British' writing is rarely associated by the general reader with non-fiction, especially essay writing. However, many 'black British' writers, most of whom are university graduates, have used non-fictional forms to explore their ambiguous sense of belonging to Britain. Examples include George Lamming's *The Pleasures of Exile* (1960), Caryl Phillips's *The European Tribe* (1987), Mike *Phillips's *London Crossings: A Biography of Black Britain* (2001), and more recently Ekow Eshun's *Black Gold of the Sun: Searching for Home in England and Africa* (2005). 'Black British' writers have also produced challenging journalism, notably around issues of identity but also on more general political or cultural questions. Yasmin Alibhai-Brown, who has written for the major British dailies and is also the author of an autobiography called *No Place Like Home* (1995), is one of the most prominent instances of the 'black British' contribution to the debates that have interested the nation in recent times. So are Maya Jaggi and Gary Younge, both writing for the *Guardian*.

'Black British' literature is still associated with generational and generic preconceptions, but these may recede as the originality and vigour of the writing continues to promote its popularity. A measure of its growing reputation is the number of literary prizes awarded in the last ten years or so to British writers with roots in the Caribbean and Africa, whether it is the *Nobel Prize to V. S. *Naipaul in 2001, the Commonwealth Writers' Prize to Caryl Phillips's *A Distant Shore* in 2004, or the numerous awards garnered by Zadie Smith's *White Teeth* (2000) or by Andrea *Levy's *Small Island* (2004), two novels which concentrate on how British society has been changed by the immigration of Jamaicans and other citizens from the former empire. Also significant is the recognition that 'black British' writing has earned in academic circles, both in Britain and abroad, demonstrated by several significant publications on the topic in the last few years, such as Lyn Innes's *A History of Black and Asian Writing in Britain, 1700–2000* (2002), Mark Stein's *Black British Literature: Novels of Transformation* (2004), *A Black British Canon?*, a collection of critical essays edited by Gail Low and Marion Wynne-Davies (2006), and *'Black' British Aesthetics Today*, another collection edited by R. Victoria Arana (2007).

The current visibility of 'black British' literature owes much to the dynamism of cultural facilitators who have devoted their energy to promoting writing by black Britons and whose activism has, to some extent, compensated for the under-representation of 'black British' interests in the mainstream publishing industry. The cultural theorist Stuart Hall produced a major body of theoretical work at the University of Birmingham's Centre for Contemporary Cultural Studies, and at the Open University, and he was widely influential in establishing the parameters of the debate. Paul *Gilroy, who began his career as Hall's doctoral student at

Birmingham, has also had an impact, and his works, including *Ain't No Black in the Union Jack* (1987), *Small Acts* (1993), *The Black Atlantic* (1993), *Between Camps* (2000), and *After Empire: Multiculture or Postcolonial Melancholia* (2004), have been pivotal as reference points in these debates.

John La Rose, a poet and essayist from Trinidad who died in 2006, was also an active presence. He is celebrated for founding New Beacon Books in 1966, one of the first black publishing houses and bookshops in Britain, and for organizing the International Book Fair of Radical Black and Third World Books, held in London from 1982 to 1995. La Rose made an important contribution to the circulation of black writing in Britain and abroad. So did other well-known public figures like Margaret Busby, the co-founder of the publishing house Allison & Busby in 1967, and Kadija Sesay, the editor of several anthologies and of the literary magazine *Sable*. But it is probably Susheila Nasta, academic and editor, who has been most instrumental in advancing black letters in recent years. In 1984 she founded *Wasafiri*, a journal that is internationally known for its balanced mix of high-quality creative writing and literary criticism and is determined, to use its founder's own words, to open up 'previously marginalised spaces for artists and writers to be properly represented in Britain' and to work 'at the cutting edge of contemporary debates concerning the composite and diverse character of [today's] Britain'. Journals like *Wasafiri* have made 'black British' writing accessible to an international and not exclusively black readership, demonstrating by their judicious editorial choices that this literature should not be seen as sociological documentation to teach or convert the reader, but as art, conveying a unique message, and with its own distinctive language and form.

'Black British' writing is characterized by its variety and originality, qualities which have contributed to the invigorating effect it has had on English literature. It has played a decisive role in the thematic and formal renewal of a variety of literary traditions. It would be impossible to pin down a typical 'black British' fiction, a genre which displays notable versatility. It includes crime fiction (like Mike Phillips's *The Late Candidate*, 1990), children's fiction (Benjamin Zephaniah's *Refugee Boy*, 2001), fantasy fiction (Ben Okri's *The Famished Road*, 1991), or horror fiction (Courttia Newland, *Music for the Off-Key: Twelve Macabre Short Stories*, 2006). However, there are clearly recurrent preoccupations in 'black British' fictional writing which are part of its specificity—such as a keen interest in history, often combined with a special concern for 'otherness', not only racial, but also sexual and sometimes religious. These themes obviously have their origin in the writers' attempts to come to terms with their own complex cultural background and with their identity as individuals who do belong to Britain yet have been made to feel that they are not fully part of it. With a limited number of exceptions—for example Joan *Riley's London-based novels written in the 1980s—this sense of exclusion has not given rise to a literature of victimization or retaliation, simply reproducing the binaries of the colonial past and viewing the world as rigidly divided between black and white. Rather it has led to a tradition of writing that promotes complexity and heterogeneity, while remaining alert to the politics of culture, race, and gender.

This is illustrated by several novels dealing with transatlantic slavery published in the 1990s by British writers of Caribbean descent. Fred D'Aguiar's *The Longest Memory* (1994) and *Feeding the Ghosts* (1997), David Dabydeen's *Harlot's Progress* (1999), and Caryl Phillips's *Cambridge* (1991) and *Crossing the River* (1993), all revisit the history of slavery through the complex fate of several individuals, both black and white, many of whom are cultural hybrids needing to negotiate an identity marked by multiple allegiances. These novels are timely reminders of a painful episode in history which was long left uncharted, not to say obliterated, though it was the source of much of Britain's wealth and could to some extent be seen as establishing the black presence on British territory. They also establish a link between the exploitation of the past and continuing discrimination, racial or economic, in the present. As D'Aguiar puts it at the very beginning of *The Longest Memory*, 'the future is just more of the past waiting to happen'. In spite of this apparent fatalism, however, these texts are hopeful, for they also concentrate on the often ambiguous interactions between blacks and whites, slaves and masters, suggesting that they might share more than meets the eye, starting with their humanity. In that sense they encourage empathy, without offering easy remedies for suffering rooted in what happened centuries ago. To quote *The Longest Memory* again, 'Too much has happened to put right. I would need another life. No, several lives. Another hundred years. No, more, to unravel this knotted mess.... Maybe what's done is done. It cannot now be undone, only understood.'

These slavery novels are by no means the only ones that tackle the importance of history, both for the individual and the community. The epigraph from *The *Tempest* which opens Zadie Smith's *White Teeth* (2000)—'What's past is prologue'—could well be used for many other recent 'black British' fictions which address the past in different ways. Leone Ross's *Orange Laughter* (1999) does so through a haunting story set in the United States and touching upon the mental problems caused by the suppression of traumatic memories. Other novels explore former times by establishing a link between Britain and the ancestral homeland, in many cases Africa. Helen *Oyeyemi's *The Opposite House* (2007), for example, revisits Yoruba mythology through Cuba, the place of origin of the parents of the London-based protagonist, while Biyi *Bandele's *Burma Boy* (2007) focuses on a young Nigerian soldier who, like many other West Africans, fought on the British side in Burma during the Second World War. Bandele's dark humour is definitely his own, but he shares with many other 'black British' writers the impulse to give a voice to those who have been left out of history books and have for this reason remained unheard, be it a child soldier in this novel, a transvestite jazz trumpeter in Jackie *Kay's *Trumpet* (1998), or an asylum seeker from Zanzibar in Abdulrazak *Gurnah's *By the Sea* (2001). Complex ideas of otherness have been explored in recent novels such as Diana Evans's *26a* (2005) and Helen Oyeyemi's *The Icarus Girl* (2005) through their use of mixed-race twin characters, symbols of the ambiguity and inbetweenness that is part and parcel of 'black British' identity. This focus on the other as a means of identifying oneself also finds expression in intertextuality. This is sometimes viewed as a means of disrupting the English canon, but is often also a way for the writer to express multiple cultural affiliations, as in David Dabydeen's *The Intended* (1991), which echoes Joseph *Conrad's 'Heart of Darkness' (1902), or Zadie Smith's *On Beauty* (2005), which can be read as a transposition of E. M. *Forster's *Howards End* (1910).

The novelty of 'black British' fiction is not just thematic. It is also formal, marked by linguistic and structural inventiveness that is sometimes radical. In 1956, Samuel Selvon published *The Lonely Londoners*, an episodic novel that traces the lives of black immigrants in London and has now become a classic of the genre. Apart from a sensitive and humorous take on the hardships of displacement, this novel stands out for being written, both in its dialogue and its narration, in an artistic re-creation of Trinidadian English, a mongrel speech which was for Selvon a means of breaking the representational mould that had till then captured the 'black British' experience. Selvon's daring use of non-standard English has had a direct influence on the contemporary generation—on Diran *Adebayo and Courttia Newland, among others—but it might also have had a more general effect on these younger writers, in helping to liberate their style from the notion of a norm, leading to a type of linguistic transgression which, as John Agard humorously suggests in his well-known poem 'Listen Mr Oxford Don', has become synonymous with empowerment rather than inferiority. It is not surprising that 'black British' writing has become a field of linguistic ingenuity, as shown for example by Salman Rushdie's and Zadie Smith's often playfully inventive prose.

The formal disruption typical of 'black British' fiction goes well beyond vocabulary and grammar. It concerns the shape of the narrative itself, as well as the way the text often fundamentally transgresses generic or other conventions. 'Black British' fictions tend to display a fragmented narrative, developing the innovative models of modernism in order to express the discontinuity and the ambiguity at the heart of the 'black British' condition, but also reflecting the post-imperial nation. Significantly, some of these novels travel in time and space and are almost epic in scope, like Salman Rushdie's *Midnight's Children* (1981), which sweeps over the history of India, or Caryl Phillips's *The Nature of Blood* (1997), which brings together the Holocaust and the predicament of black people in the West. This tendency to cross narrative and other boundaries sometimes accompanies a fundamental questioning of the novel as a genre. Bernardine *Evaristo's books offer a striking illustration of this. Her first novels, *Lara* (1997) and *The Emperor's Babe* (2001), are both written in verse, a hybrid form which matches the identity of her protagonists, Lara, of mixed Nigerian and British descent, and Zuleika, a girl of Sudanese origin living in Roman London. Evaristo's more recent book, *Soul Tourists* (2005), is again stylistically bold. Comprising verse sections as well as many passages in prose (including letters, lists, and other types of documents), this unclassifiable book follows the European tour of two protagonists who come across the ghosts of significant African figures in European history, such as Shakespeare's 'Dark Lady' or the Chevalier de Saint Georges.

This reconciliatory and creative pattern is also apparent in other genres, and is especially visible among writers of the new generation. But it has a noteworthy precursor in Wilson *Harris, a writer of Guyanese origin settled in England for almost 50 years, who, from his first novel *Palace of the Peacock* (1960), has relentlessly worked at an alternative world vision which he calls 'cross-cultural'. In his 24 visionary novels to date, and also in his essays, he has developed a highly metaphorical style to further a renewal of the imagination, which he regards as a saving virtue that can redeem the modern world.

One of the writers whose work best exemplifies the major thematic and formal characteristics of 'black British' writing, and has also repeatedly addressed the changing meaning of Britishness, is Caryl Phillips, at once playwright, novelist, and essayist. His *Foreigners: Three English Lives* (2007) seems to crystallize the concern for the past and the 'other', as well as the formal innovativeness that has characterized the 'black British' tradition, while also providing subtle thoughts on identity. Each of the book's three sections focuses on a black man who lived in England and led an English life, yet was made to feel a foreigner, a disturbing paradox encapsulated in the title. The first part, 'Dr Johnson's Watch', is devoted to Samuel *Johnson's black servant, Francis Barber, of Jamaican origin, who retired to the countryside after his master's death in 1784 and died a pauper in spite of a generous bequest from his benefactor. The second, 'Made in Wales', concentrates on Randolph Turpin, a British-born mixed-race boxer, who in 1951 became Britain's first black world champion and eventually committed suicide. 'Northern Lights', the third part, is devoted to David Oluwale, a Nigerian who arrived as an illegal immigrant in England in 1949 and died at the hands of Leeds policemen twenty years later. By telling the lives of these three men, and chronicling their successes and ensuing downfalls, Phillips in a sense allegorizes several of the issues that are likely to affect 'black British' writers, who are sometimes also viewed as literary foreigners. The book notably touches upon the question of categorization (who belongs, and who does not?), the status of the outsider, especially when he or she is a public figure, the potential danger of fame and of being co-opted into the mainstream, as well as the expectation to conform that comes with otherness, racial or otherwise. Significantly, this hymn to difference is written in a composite, unpredictable form that combines true facts about these actual historical figures with a fictional exploration of their aspirations and flaws. It is a book at the interface between non-fiction and fiction, hard to pigeonhole. The three men are not allowed to speak for themselves, with the brief exception of Barber in the first piece. Yet each story is told in a distinctive way, using a specific language and a special narrative perspective that ranges from the distant (for Turpin) to the intimate (for Oluwale). One of the messages behind this unusual literary shape is that singularity should be recognized, giving each individual a chance to be understood and recover some lost dignity.

The tripartite structure of *Foreigners* is a reminder that, for all the undoubted changes that have transformed the opportunities available to blacks in contemporary Britain, they can still be seen as outsiders, with all the psychological consequences that can be imagined. At the same time, however, by enabling us to enter these three men's lives, the book suggests the capacity of the literary imagination to make us view the world from a different angle, or, as Phillips himself said in a recent lecture, 'to wrench us out of our ideological burrows and force us to engage with a world that is clumsily transforming itself, a world that is peopled with individuals we might otherwise never meet in our daily lives'.

CHILDREN'S LITERATURE

MICHAEL ROSEN

CHILDREN's literature is of course literature written for children. However, this poses certain problems: what should we say of the works which weren't written specifically for children but have ended up being read by many of them, or have been repeatedly adapted for a children's audience? It has been generally accepted by publishers and readers that these two kinds of literature (like folk tales and adaptations of such works as **Robinson Crusoe*) are both part of the world of children's literature. Meanwhile, both the notions of childhood and its lived reality have changed radically in the time that a specifically juvenile literature has been produced. At the age of 12 Charles *Dickens, like hundreds of thousands of others of the same age or less, was working a ten-hour day. He would have been a daily witness to children struggling to survive from begging, hard labour, and prostitution. This was the world that he reflected in **Oliver Twist*, which itself has often been adapted for a child audience. In the 21st century, no 12-year-old in the Western world is legally trying to eke out a living—though he or she may well be enjoying objects made in part by a 12-year-old from somewhere else in the world. However, there is a literature directed specifically at children which does show ways in which children suffer the privations of the modern world, through war, poverty, discrimination, or abuse. Leaving this to one side, our idea of children's literature also has to encompass the fact that many of the works we regard as being for children have always been understood by writers, illustrators, publishers, and audiences to be read by adults and children alongside each other—the books for the youngest children are a clear example of this.

Sociological, literary, and historical approaches can all enrich our understanding of children's literature. Three key institutions have had a vital part to play: the publishing industry, education, and, something more diffuse, the processes of child nurture. Adults create a set of activities around children, though it should be quickly added here that there is no uniform child reader across the ages or across any given society. Children have never been treated in the same way from one period to another nor from one child to another. While it has usually been the task of adults to protect and nourish children, there has also been infanticide, abandonment, and exploitation. Some children have been carefully educated to take the place of the adults, but there has also been widespread illiteracy and, until the 1960s, the production and distribution of printed material for children has been markedly differentiated from one kind of child to another. So, for example, a genre we might think of as one specific form, like the large full-colour picture book, has moved, thanks to publicly owned pre-school institutions, schools, and libraries, from being a luxury commodity consumed only by the well-off to something freely available to all. From the sociological standpoint, what distinguishes children's literature from other literatures is its unique position in relation to the three institutions of publishing, education, and nurture. The publishing industry customarily marks its productions as being child specific, age specific—and on occasions sex specific. Education makes selections of appropriate children's literature and controls much of children's critical reading of books, though both the selection and the critical approaches may be laid down in guidelines and contested by teachers. The present discourse around child nurture (carried out most influentially by the mass media, including television, women's magazines, and national newspapers) creates an environment where certain kinds of books and ways of reading are thought to be suitable for different kinds of child or home.

From a literary standpoint, it is possible to say that the literature itself has some common characteristics. There has long been an understanding that the spoken language of children develops in complexity with age, so one of the key markers of children's literature has been the modified linguistic registers of its texts—sometimes expressed as 'the use of simplified language'. Thematically, certain topics have, in different times, been thought to be more or less appropriate. Where once the subject of death was a central preoccupation of the stories and poems for children (especially in late 17th-century England), there have been whole periods when it was thought to be unsuitable. In the 19th century, the political aspirations of empire were made quite explicit in juvenile literature (especially in boys' magazines), while the mid-20th century marked a time when explicit political interventions were mostly, but not entirely, avoided. Throughout most of the history of children's literature, two important social taboos of the modern era, public talk in popular language about sex and bodily excretions, meant that these topics were off-limits. However, since the 1970s, there have been mass-produced books, freely available to all children, which do not regard such subjects as out of bounds. Structurally speaking, one generalization often thought to apply to children's literature is that the resolution of stories should involve some kind of redemption, reconciliation, hope, or sense of homecoming. Whether in jest or seriousness, more and more books for a young audience have broken with this constraint too. Underlying children's literature has also been the notion that the books should improve the child, or at the very least, not encourage behaviour that adults would regard as antisocial. Sometimes this idea of improvement has been explicit and didactic, whilst at other times, the improvement has been thought to derive indirectly through the process of responding to fiction's call for empathy with others, or even from the very fact that the child is exposed in an accessible way to the complexities of written language. It should be said, though, that there has also been a powerful strain in children's literature that has mocked improvement, starting perhaps with Heinrich Hoffmann's satire of moralistic teaching *Struwwelpeter* (Germany 1845; England 1848) and taken up in a different way (celebration of mischief, mostly) by comics such as *The Beano*, established in 1938. One strong current within the aspiration to improvement that we find throughout children's literature since the *Romantic period has been the idea that children's literature can develop or support the 'imagination' and that this has a key role to play in the development of personality.

Like its adult equivalent, children's literature has its novels, short stories, plays, and poetry, but it also has forms which are more widely read than their equivalents in adult literature: *picturebooks, pop-ups, and *'movables', comics, magazines made up of comic strips and stories, annuals, and illustrated story-book anthologies or miscellanies. In response to the demands of education, there has also been a specialist educational literature: many kinds of primers, 'readers', story-books and collections aimed specifically at helping children learn how to read. The selection and editing of the written folk or *fairy story has played a crucial part in many of these areas, and their place in publishing and education has helped shape the tales themselves. Meanwhile, all these forms and the reading habits of children have been affected by changing technology. In the present time, it's quite possible for a child to relate to a book through any or all of the following: a film, a TV programme, a computer game, a website, a radio programme, a music CD or download, a magazine article, toy, duvet cover, or any other piece of merchandising, along with some of the more traditional ways of mediating a book such as the classroom, library presentation, or cultural club, as with *The *Jungle Book* (Rudyard Kipling, 1894) and the 'Cubs'. Characters, such as *Winnie-the-Pooh (A. A. *Milne, 1926 and 1928) which once existed only in specific, authored books, may now live in several different formats and the original text may or may not be known to the child watching the TV programme or playing with the toy.

Children also create literature in their own right. The largely oral culture of their play produces jokes, stories, role play, verbal games, rhymes, and songs every day, and at various times this has been recorded (as for instance by Peter and Iona *Opie), anthologized, or embedded in written poetry (as in *The Poets' Tongue* (1935), an anthology chosen by W. H. *Auden and John Garrett). Works that children have composed, often while they are at school, and mostly as poems, have also been published and are now appearing more and more frequently on the internet.

The beginnings of this complex world of literature are mysterious. We will never know exactly what kinds of stories, jokes, and songs were made up specifically for or by children in the non-literate societies preceding our own. We can guess that adults sang lullabies and soothing rhythmic pieces to children, and it seems likely that they were included in storytelling and singing sessions. Once writing developed, some young children (usually the boys of the elite class) were taught to write and read, but clear examples of age-specific literature do not survive from the earliest literate societies. The first written forms aimed specifically at children are what we would now call lessons. For example, the 'Colloquy' of *Ælfric is a lively conversation in Latin between the teacher and his pupils designed as an aid to teach boys Latin. Geoffrey *Chaucer produced 'A Treatise on the Astrolabe' addressed to one 'Lyte Lowys' (Little Lewis), probably the poet's son. In the medieval period, there were also texts we can presume were for children such as alphabet poems and etiquette poems addressed to children on, say, how to behave at table. Manuscripts of *fables, exemplar tales (secular parables), legendary or miracle tales, and *bestiaries which circulated all over medieval Europe were read by or to some children, but were not specifically for them.

A key moment came with the production in 1658 of *Orbis Sensualum Pictus* (*The Visible World in Pictures*) by the Protestant Czech educator Jan Komenský or *Comenius. Each of its 151 little chapters (such as 'Aqua', 'Homo', or 'Mahometismus') is headed by a woodcut whilst underneath a set of words in Latin and German name parts of the picture and relate what Comenius regards as the facts. Though *Orbis Pictus* marks some kind of beginning, for some 100 years prior to this a popular literature of scurrilous and miraculous tales, crimes, ancient tales, rhymes, legends, and jokes circulated in the form of cheap sheets and booklets, known variously over the next 200 years as blackletter *ballads, broadsheet ballads, *broadsides, street ballads, and *chapbooks. Autolycus in *The *Winter's Tale* (1610) is a singer and pedlar who not only sells fabric, gloves, bracelets, perfume, and such like but also 'ballads'. If John *Bunyan's account is to be believed, he read this kind of popular literature when he was a child. Once again, this is not an age-specific literature but it could not have escaped the pedlars' notice that children were an audience for much of this literature. Interestingly, it was figures like Bunyan who in the 17th century produced didactic tales and poems for children as part of the *Puritan tradition, in part as a reaction against the frivolities of the cheap ballads which were seen as devil's work. A particular focus of these Christian works was the notion of original sin, interpreted by Puritans as the fallen condition of every newborn baby. Baptism would save the child from hell, so there developed a graphic, or, as some might say today, horrific children's literature relating the fate of those who missed baptism. Others wrote verses (like Bunyan's *A Book for Boys & Girls, or Country Rhymes for Children*, 1686) that told children how to observe, interpret, and love the world as God's creation, and how to perform the deeds of a good Christian. As the middle class grew during the 16th and 17th centuries, it found that it had sufficient wealth to produce many-roomed houses to live in (including rooms for children) and to endow schools and colleges to advance and perpetuate its status through the education of the younger generation. It also produced theories of how its children should be nursed and trained, and out of what we would now regard as the more liberal of these there appeared the first literature for children that looked to entertain the child. In 1744, in London, the printer Mary *Cooper published **Tommy Thumb's Pretty Song Book* in two volumes, of which only volume two survives. It is the earliest surviving example of a collection of *nursery rhymes, that is to say a set of verses mostly without known authors, made up of snatches from longer songs and ballads and songs culled from children's own singing. Over the years this body of popular verse has narrowed into a nursery rhyme canon. Crucially, 'Tommy Thumb' is a children's book that has no didactic, instructional, or religious intent. It includes versions of rhymes that have survived to this day ('London Bridge is falling down', 'Baa baa black sheep', 'Sing a song of sixpence') along with rhymes that would in the 19th and in most of the 20th century have been regarded as unsuitably bawdy or scatological for children ('Piss a Bed, | Piss a Bed, | Barley Butt, | Your Bum is so heavy, | You can't get up'). In the same year, the publisher John *Newbery, influenced by John *Locke's thoughts on education, produced *A Little Pretty Pocket-Book, Intended for the Amusement of Little Master Tommy and Pretty Miss Polly with Two Letters from Jack the Giant Killer*. Each letter of the alphabet has a rhyme and a moral and the book came with either a ball (for the boys) or a pincushion (for the girls). Meanwhile, the popular street literature of ballads, tales, legends, wonder-tales, and jokes with a mostly working-class readership continued to flourish. In the same decade, Sarah *Fielding produced what is thought of as the first full-length novel for children, *The Governess, or The Little Female Academy* (1749).

Over the following 100 years, the texts intended for children multiply and diversify. Each of the strands that were present by 1750 developed, often in reaction to each other. So, for example, in the hands of the *Religious Tract Society (founded in 1799), the didactic strain of Christian children's literature imitated the form and shape of street literature to produce illustrated moral tales for the same price. Authored poetry for children continued to focus on morally uplifting themes, but also incorporated fantasy and nonsense, in part borrowed from the folk nursery rhyme tradition (see in particular William *Roscoe's *The Butterfly's Ball and the Grasshopper's Feast*, 1806). It is in this period that the traditions of oral storytelling and French aristocratic fairy-story writing combine to produce the child-specific, illustrated versions taken from such original collections as Charles *Perrault's *Les Contes de ma mère l'oye* (1697; see *Mother Goose), Antoine *Galland's version of *Les Mille et une nuits* of 1704–17 (see *Arabian Nights Entertainments*), the *Grimms' *Kinder und Hausmärchen* (translated into English by Edgar Taylor with illustrations by George *Cruikshank in 1823 as *German Popular Stories*, 1812–15), and the more authored tales of E. T. A. *Hoffmann (1816) and Hans Christian *Andersen (1835). None of the tales in these original collections is a purely oral example of rural peoples' pre-literate culture. Both the original editions and the later child-friendly versions of these texts are complex hybrids of the oral and the written, marked with the social and political ideas of their day. For example, the Grimm brothers edited, altered, and rewrote the tales they had heard from their mostly middle-class female friends in order to fashion something that would help the much-divided German-speaking world of that time find itself culturally and would, they hoped, contribute to the creation of a modern, democratic state.

Much children's literature of the past 200 years has been made up of retellings of these tales. As a result, their many versions have been examined in detail with a view to discerning the psychological make-up or needs of children, the political and social intent of the adults presenting the stories, and the prevailing moral values of countries that have promoted or altered them. It is interesting to note that there are motifs in these tales (including attempted infanticide by parents, unpunished robbery, cannibalism, violence, rape, deception, and bargaining around sexual favours) that writers of new children's literature throughout this period are told by their publishers to avoid. The distancing created by the convention of anonymously saying 'Once upon a time...' (and all the other non-real techniques of such tales) has allowed these usually impermissible themes and images to circulate.

Children's literature in Britain and North America has now become a diverse industry, flanked on one side by largely publicly funded education and on the other by the massive multinational publishing, distribution, film, TV, and merchandising companies. In the midst of it all sits the parent or prime carer who inevitably plays a key role in the selection and availability of books in the home. This produces two opposite pulls: the one towards mass production of best-sellers and the other towards more locally or culturally specific books and readers. The child who is reading and consuming the Harry *Potter or *Disney products may well also be the child who is looking at a book with total sales of only a few thousand that ended up in her hands thanks to, say, the efforts of a small publisher, a book club, a librarian, or teacher. In some circumstances, parents can and do play this role, but for the mass of children, the route to the kind of book that may well cater for their more specific needs can only come through the central role of school or library.

In terms of theoretical availability, however, we are at a point where there has never been a greater diversity of books on offer. One reason for this is the internet. A great number of the children's books produced before 1900 are now available as downloads, while the internet book market of new and second-hand books has put small-scale productions of culturally specific books within the reach of millions (as well as millions of out-of-print books). Another is the nature of business itself. For some twenty years or so, the mass marketing of children's books has deemed it more profitable to produce more titles with a shorter 'shelf-life' in the book warehouses, than fewer titles with a long shelf-life. Meanwhile, the technology of book production has meant that it has become very easy to produce copies of non-illustrated books on demand.

Is it possible to discern any patterns or tendencies in all this? Clearly, the multi-media blockbusters of recent years, J. K. *Rowling's seven-volume Harry Potter sequence (1997–2007), Philip *Pullman's trilogy (1995–2000), the revival of C. S. *Lewis's seven-volume Narnia (1950–6) series and the work of J. R. R. *Tolkien (1937–55), has tilted the reading habits of children (aged roughly between 8 and 14) towards *fantasy fiction. Fantasy in the form of newly produced, child-specific novels starts in the 19th century. John *Ruskin's *King of the Golden River* (1851) can be credited with one of the first self-conscious fantasies intended for child readers, and this is followed by Charles *Kingsley's *The Water-Babies* (1863), Lewis *Carroll's

Alice's Adventures in Wonderland (1865), and George *MacDonald's *The Princess and the Goblin* (1872).

There are many ways of making cross-sections of the field of children's literature, each offering a different perspective. Issues of gender, class, and race have been much discussed since the early 1970s, with predictably divided responses. To take these in turn, it has been pointed out that apart from some notable classics (including those by Louisa May *Alcott and Laura Ingalls *Wilder, and some works by Frances Hodgson *Burnett, Edith *Nesbit, or Astrid Lindgren (1907–2002)), the role of girls and women in children's books of most kinds used to be largely domestic, and secondary to males. Meanwhile, others claimed that children's books helped to construct masculinity by repeatedly casting boys as adventurers. Scrutiny of the literature also showed a middle-class bias in children's literature, expressed in the kinds of schools, homes, and spending habits of its protagonists. The corollary to this, it was claimed, was that working-class characters were again and again cast as a mix of fools, victims, servants, or criminals. On the race front, there was an outpouring of books, comics, and boys' magazines between 1880 and 1914 which represented almost anyone in the human race other than people of northern European origin in the same way as working-class people, but also as childlike, cruel, and in need of chastisement or even, on occasions, summary execution. European white people were given implicitly or explicitly a mastering role at home and abroad.

The world of children's books has tried to change and a variety of books repositioning these roles have appeared. Sometimes this has been done through historical novels (like Mildred D. Taylor's *Roll of Thunder, Hear my Cry*, 1976); sometimes through modern realism (as in the work of Jacqueline *Wilson or Benjamin *Zephaniah); sometimes with picture books, like Mary Hoffmann's *Amazing Grace* (1991), or Allan *Ahlberg's *Peepo* (1981). Meanwhile, attention has been increasingly focused on such matters as whether young people are becoming less exposed to mild but necessary risk, or are unduly exposed to danger from adults through abuse, motor vehicles, and war, or through forms of cynical irony, explicit sex, and violence. Should children's books try to address these problems, or turn away, producing what is in effect an imaginative haven? In fact both kinds of books are being produced. Libby Hathorne's *Way Home* (1994) is a stark, gritty large-format picture book about urban homelessness, whilst Nick Butterworth's Percy the Park Keeper stories, which began to appear in 1989, are Edenic adventures with talking animals, a paternal Percy, and happy endings.

Another way of looking at this problem has been to focus on how books position readers through narrative technique. It has been claimed, for example, that some books over-explain and so patronize the child reader (a criticism levelled at Enid *Blyton, for example) whilst others offer complex narrative techniques (unreliable, 'self-conscious', or multiple narrators, flashbacks and flashforwards, deliberate gaps in narrative, inconclusive endings, and so on). Most notable of such authors for older readers have been Robert *Cormier and Aidan *Chambers, and for younger readers in a comic style, Janet and Allan Ahlberg and Jon Scieszka (1954–).

The age-ranking of children's books has been identified as a feature specific to children's literature, raising the question of whether children's books reinforce the tendency of modern culture to hold children in a false sequence of development. At either end of this sequence there are books which are marketed, distributed, and consumed as Baby Books and books for Young Adults or Teens. At one end you can find books you can play with or chew and at the other end, fiction which is largely adult in style but happens to focus on the lives of young people and children—rather in the way that J. D. *Salinger's *Catcher in the Rye* (1951), William

*Golding's *Lord of the Flies* (1954), or Harper *Lee's *To Kill a Mocking-Bird* (1960) have done. Incidentally, Judy *Blume can be credited with having written the first novel produced by a children's publisher which had a girl and boy talking about their genitals and having sex (see *Forever* 1975).

There is reason to think of the *picturebook as one of children's literature's greatest inventions. Originating in cave paintings, two-dimensional storytelling was taken up in church murals, which give accounts of biblical scenes, and medieval illuminated manuscripts of tales. Ballads and tales sold in the streets from the mid-16th century onwards were nearly always accompanied by illustration. *Orbis Sensualum Pictus* and the works of John *Bunyan followed the pattern. A splendid variety of illustrated books, often tinted by forced child labour, appeared in the 19th century. What has developed since is an art form, capable of telling stories with economy and complexity. It is a multiple approach, offering meanings through a variety of channels and in a variety of ways: print, sound (when read aloud), image, and, on occasions, touch. So, it is not simply a matter of a story with pictures. Several stories are told in a picturebook, with all kinds of features being present in one thread but not in the other. However, this is not simply a matter of objects or characters; it also involves the sensual effects of the images working in conjunction with, or even in ironic contrast to, aspects of the words. The words often have a percussive or musical quality themselves, through alliteration, rhythm, or rhyme. The images may well vary in size, intensity, focal spot, distance, so that neither eye nor ear will rest as the pages turn. The books of Beatrix *Potter opened the door for a long line of anthropomorphic, domestic, and pastoral picture books and her artwork in itself arises from the achievements of English, Victorian watercolourists. Far from being simple, easy-going tales, Potter's books are full of uneasy undercurrents of selfishness and danger. Mass production of cheap coloured children's books was pioneered in the Soviet Union in the 1930s and was taken up by publishers like Pere Castor in France, Little Golden Books in the USA, and Puffin Books in England, who delivered brightly coloured books for the very young into anyone's home and school. Maurice *Sendak single-handedly brought modern psychology into the picturebook with *Where the Wild Things Are* (1969) where a naughty boy quite literally deals with his demons. The modern picture book now tackles such subjects as the Holocaust, sex, or death alongside the happiest and lightest of themes.

Poetry for children has its own history, combining elements of the nursery rhyme, verse composed for children, poems not originally composed solely for children but later adopted by publishers and educationists in their anthologies, and children's own oral poetry. In this way, children have been exposed to a huge variety of poetry, from tiny, musical rhymes to complex First World War poetry by Wilfred *Owen. The nursery rhyme canon offers an abrupt, bold poetry: often surreal, violent, and mocking, full of characters who don't follow traditional etiquette or behaviour, though sometimes traditional role models are reinforced. 'Sing a Song of Sixpence' describes a king counting money in 'his' counting-house, while the queen eats bread and honey in 'the' parlour. Most of the canon is anonymous but several rhymes embedded in the English-speaking world's culture to this day are authored: 'Twinkle, twinkle little star' was written by Jane and Ann *Taylor (1806), 'Wee Willie Winkie' by William Miller (1841), 'Mary had a little lamb' by Sarah Josepha Hale (1830), and 'Old Mother Hubbard', which is based on an older rhyme, by Sarah Catherine Martin (1768–1826).

Etiquette, moral, and religious poetry for children in English emerged in the medieval period and continues in many different forms to the present day. The chapbook tradition produced many rhyming sheets based on such characters as *Tom Thumb or told short traditional tales in verse form. In the late 18th century, perhaps inspired in part by Bunyan, nursery rhymes, and chapbooks, a poetry for children emerges that takes pleasure in the observed world or creates absurd scenes, like 'Twinkle twinkle little star'. A major shift occurred with Edward *Lear, who applied all the skill of a great lyricist to create absurd, melancholic stories of loneliness and travel, or a gallery of oddballs in his *limericks. Lewis Carroll was a highly accomplished writer of narrative verse and parodies, mocking, in particular, the kinds of verses being given to children in Sunday Schools. The four best-known British writers of children's poetry prior to 1950 are Robert Louis *Stevenson, Hilaire *Belloc, A. A. Milne, and Walter *de la Mare, each contributing something very different. Stevenson is the first poet to celebrate his own childhood in poems intended for children. Hilaire Belloc built on the *Struwwelpeter* tradition with his 'Cautionary Tales', parodying moral verse. A. A. Milne took some of the themes from the poetry of adult humorous magazines and carried it over into children's books, while de la Mare created a dreamlike, mysterious, supernatural world. For older children in Britain from the late 19th century onwards there was a strand of patriotic and imperial poetry which celebrated Britain's role in battles defeating foreigners, most famously by Sir Henry *Newbolt.

Just as complex in its production and mediation is the history of drama for children. The pantomimes of the early 19th century were seen by whole families, and a work often seen as the first children's play, J. M. *Barrie's *Peter Pan* (1904), was also a family entertainment. Punch and Judy was always directed more specifically at children, while cut-out, paper, and cardboard theatres come with plays attached, such as dramatizations of 'Jack the Giant-Killer'. There are three strands to the modern world of theatre for children: the school- and museum-based touring companies; children's theatres; and Christmas shows for children, pantomimes along with such modern classics as dramatizations of Raymond *Briggs's *Snowman*. School-based touring companies started to develop in the 1960s and adopted the radical techniques (and in some cases the politics) of agitprop and Brechtian theatre. In the present time, these educational companies tend to produce plays on such matters as dental hygiene or road safety. Children's theatres usually offer a mix of adaptations of old and new fiction, plays with totally new stories along with the occasional 'old' play such as Maurice *Maeterlinck's *Blue Bird* (1908). Children themselves are involved in thousands of school- or club-based theatrical events, often writing them themselves. This too is a form of children's literature.

Clearly, the internet and the arrival of the electronic book have produced some major changes to what and how children will read in the future. Writers have become increasingly accessible to their readers through websites and chatrooms, and children themselves can publish what they write from the moment they can use a keyboard. However, the physical object of the book fits into another strand of children's activity—playing with toys. The tactile holding of a small object that releases possibilities, fantasies, fun, and speculation is perhaps not different in kind from a pile of building bricks. That said, the huge creative possibilities of texts and sounds delivered from hand-held screens have yet to be realized. New hybrids made up of moving photographic image, drawn image, computer-generated image, interactive game, linear text, music, sound effects, and *performance poetry or *rap are likely to emerge over the next few years. Indications of this can be found anywhere from modern art installations to the children's pages of the BBC website. What follows from this is that the production of literature for children will be subject to two forces: one global, delivering mass-produced entertainment into every child's hand; the other self-made and local. This is analogous to the production of the visual image for adults, where film is now widely available both as a mass-produced commodity and as part of a home-made process. Key to the creative power in this new era will be the role of education. Will those who control school curricula leave enough space and time for teachers and school students of all ages to make their own literatures? To do so will benefit the development of new artists of all kinds, but will also help develop a critical readership amongst young people.

Abbey Theatre, Dublin Opened on 27 December 1904 with a double bill of one-act plays, W. B. *Yeats's *On Baile's Strand* and *Spreading the News* by Lady *Gregory. The theatre rapidly became a focus of the *Irish Revival. In 1903 Annie *Horniman, a friend of Yeats from his London days, had been introduced by him to the Irish National Theatre Society, an amateur company led by F. J. and W. G. Fay, which had already produced several plays by contemporary Irish writers, including Yeats's *The Countess Cathleen* and George *Russell's (Æ's) *Deirdre*. She decided to provide a permanent Dublin home for the Society (which had Yeats for its president) and took over the disused theatre of the Mechanics' Institute in Abbey Street (built on the site of a previous Theatre Royal), together with the old city morgue next door, and converted them into the Abbey Theatre, with Lady Gregory as holder of the patent. The company, led by the Fays, with Sarah Allgood as principal actress, turned professional in 1906, with Yeats, Lady Gregory, and J. M. *Synge as directors, and in 1907 survived the riots provoked by Synge's *The *Playboy of the Western World*. The Fays left the following year, after a series of disagreements with Horniman, Yeats, and the leading players. In 1909 the company withstood strong pre-production pressure from the lord lieutenant to withdraw *The Shewing-up of Blanco Posnet*, by G. B. *Shaw, and staged the play almost uncut. It was a great success and there were no further threats to the theatre's patent. Meanwhile Horniman had become disenchanted with the company, and in 1910 refused to renew her subsidy; she offered the purchase of the theatre on generous terms, however, and Yeats and Lady Gregory became principal shareholders and managers. Over the years the early poetic dramas had been gradually replaced by more naturalistic works, by Padraic *Colum, St John *Ervine, Lennox Robinson (1886–1958), Sean *O'Casey, and others. Robinson took over the management from Yeats in 1910 and became director in 1923. There were successful, if contentious, tours of Ireland, Britain, and the USA. After the First World War the Abbey's finances became perilous, although O'Casey's *The Shadow of a Gunman* (1923), *Juno and the Paycock* (1924), and *The Plough and the Stars* (1926) brought some respite. In 1925 the Abbey received a grant from the government of the new Irish Free State, thus becoming the first state-subsidized theatre in the English-speaking world. From the late 1930s more plays were performed in Irish, and actors were required to be bilingual. In 1951 the theatre was burned down, and the company played in the Queen's Theatre until the new Abbey opened in 1966, where the tradition of new writing by Brian *Friel, Tom *Murphy, and others continues to flourish.

ABBO OF FLEURY (?945–1004) A French theologian, author of the *Epitome de Vitis Romanorum Pontificum* and of lives of the saints. He was invited to England by *Oswald (bishop of Worcester and archbishop of York) to teach in his monastery of Ramsey; it was at the request of the monks of Ramsey, he tells us, that Abbo wrote his 'Life of St Edmund' which was the source for *Ælfric's famous sermon. Abbo became abbot of Fleury, where he died; during his abbacy *Aristotle's *Categories* was commented on and his *Analytics* copied in Fleury.

Abbot, The A novel by Sir Walter *Scott, published 1820, a sequel to *The *Monastery*. This novel, set around the escape of *Mary Queen of Scots from Loch Leven, largely redeemed the relative failure of its predecessor. It is principally remembered today for the portrait of Mary herself, for attracting tourist trade to Loch Leven, and for being the first sequel novel in English, thus influencing the work of *Balzac, *Trollope, and many other 19th-century novelists.

Abbotsford The name of Sir Walter *Scott's property near Melrose on the Tweed, purchased 1811. It gave its name to the Abbotsford Club, founded in 1834 in Scott's memory for the purpose of publishing materials pertaining to the history or literature of any country dealt with in his writings. It ceased its publications in 1865.

ABBOTT, Edwin Abbott (1839–1926) Born in London; clergyman and author best known for *Flatland: A Romance of Many Dimensions* (1884). A mathematical fantasy satirizing the Victorian class system, *Flatland* describes a two-dimensional world, and speculates about 'lower' and 'higher' realms.

À BECKETT, Gilbert Abbott (1811–56) Born in London, educated at Westminster School, and called to the bar at Gray's Inn. He was the editor of *Figaro in London* and on the original staff of **Punch*. He was for many years a leader writer on *The *Times* and the *Morning Herald*, and was appointed a Metropolitan police magistrate in 1849. He wrote many plays and humorous works, including a *Comic History of England* (1847–8), a *Comic History of Rome* (1852), and a *Comic Blackstone* (1846).

À BECKETT, Gilbert Arthur (1837–91) Son of Gilbert Abbott *à Beckett, born in London and educated at

Westminster School and Christ Church, Oxford. He was, from 1879, like his father, a regular member of the staff of *Punch*. He wrote, in collaboration with W. S. *Gilbert, the successful comedy *The Happy Land* (1873).

ABELARD, Peter (1079–1142/4) A native of Brittany, a brilliant disputant and lecturer at the schools of Ste Geneviève and Notre-Dame in Paris, where *John of Salisbury was among his pupils. He was an advocate of rational theological enquiry, and his *Sic et Non* could be regarded as the first text in scholastic theology (*see* SCHOLASTICISM). He was primarily a dialectician rather than a theologian, though his theological views were condemned at Soissons (1121) and at Sens (1140), where he was vigorously opposed by St *Bernard. He was a student of Roscelin, who is regarded as the founder of the Nominalist school of thought, and against whose views Abelard reacted. The pre-eminence of the University of Paris in the 12th century owes much to Abelard's popularity as a teacher. He became the tutor and then the lover of Héloïse, the niece of Fulbert, a canon of Notre-Dame in whose house he lodged. Their love ended in a tragic separation and a famous correspondence in the 1130s. Héloïse died in 1163 and was buried in Abelard's tomb. Pope's poem *'Eloisa to Abelard' was published in 1717. See M. T. Clanchy, *Abelard: A Medieval Life* (1997).

ABERCROMBIE, Lascelles (1881–1938) Poet and critic, born in Cheshire. *Interludes and Poems* (1908) was followed by several further volumes of verse, including a collected edition in 1930 and *The Sale of St Thomas* (1931). Abercrombie contributed to *Georgian Poetry*, and to the four issues of *New Numbers* (1914), a journal he produced with his fellow 'Dymock Poets', Rupert *Brooke, John *Drinkwater, and W. W. *Gibson, who lived near the Gloucestershire village of Dymock. After the First World War, he taught at the universities of Liverpool, Leeds, London, and Oxford.

Abigail In 1 Samuel 25, the wife of Nabal and subsequently of David. The name came to signify a waiting-woman, from the name of the 'waiting-gentlewoman' in *The Scornful Lady* by *Beaumont and Fletcher, perhaps in allusion to the expression 'thine handmaid', frequently applied to herself by the biblical Abigail.

ABISH, Walter (1931–) Novelist, poet, and university teacher, born in Vienna. His family fled the Nazis and Abish moved to the USA in 1957, taking American citizenship in 1960. Although his first publication, *Duel Site* (1970), was a collection of poetry, Abish is best known for his experimental fiction which applies the arbitrary verbal and representational strategies characteristic of *postmodernism. His first novel, *Alphabetical Africa* (1971), contains alphabetically incremental words, and *How German Is It* (1980) presents a montage of images of Germany. His more recent publications include *Double Vision* (2004), an enquiry into his own past.

ABOULELA, Leila (1964–) Novelist who grew up in Khartoum and has lived in Egypt, Jakarta, Dubai, London, and Aberdeen. She focuses on religious identity in her two novels *The Translator* (1999) and *Minaret* (2005). Her story 'The Museum', from the collection *Coloured Lights* (2001), won the Caine Prize for African writing.

Absalom and Achitophel An allegorical poem by John *Dryden, published 1681. A *mock-biblical satire based on 2 Samuel 13–19, portraying the intrigues of the earl of *Shaftesbury and the ambition of the duke of Monmouth (1649–85) to replace James, duke of York (1633–1701; later James II) as Charles II's heir. Among public figures given biblical identities are Monmouth (Absalom), Shaftesbury (Achitophel), the duke of *Buckingham (Zimri), Charles II (David), Titus Oates (Corah), and Slingsby Bethel, sheriff of London (Shimei). David concludes the poem with a speech affirming Royalist principles, and asserting his determination to govern ruthlessly if he cannot do so mercifully. In 1682 a second part appeared, mainly written by Nahum *Tate, but with 200 lines by Dryden attacking two literary and political enemies, Thomas *Shadwell as Og and Elkanah *Settle as Doeg.

ABSE, Dannie (Daniel) (1923–) Poet, novelist, playwright, and memoirist, born in Cardiff and educated at University College, Cardiff, and King's College London. His first volume of poetry, *After Every Green Thing* (1948), was followed by more than a dozen others, including *Poems, Golders Green* (1968) and *Running Late* (2006). *New and Collected Poems* appeared in 2003. The title of *White Coat, Purple Coat*, a retrospective compilation from 1983, refers to Abse's dual career as physician (he worked as a chest specialist in London from 1954 to 1989) and poet. The most persistent dualism informing his precise, compassionate, and at times rueful verse concerns the relationship between his Welshness and his Jewishness ('I have two roots, that of Dafydd as well as David'). Abse's novels include *Ash on a Young Man's Sleeve* (1954) and *The Strange Case of Dr Simmonds and Dr Glas* (2002). *Goodbye, Twentieth Century* (2001) is the latest version of his autobiography. *The Presence*, a journal-memoir of his wife Joan, appeared in 2007.

Absentee, The A novel by Maria *Edgeworth, first published 1812 in *Tales of Fashionable Life*. This novel of (largely) Irish life was first written as a play, refused by Richard Brinsley *Sheridan, then turned into a novel. A swift, vivacious story, the greater part of which is in conversation, it begins with the extravagant London life of the absentee Irish landlord Lord Clonbrony and his ambitious, worldly wife. Their son Lord Colambre refuses to marry the heiress provided for him. A sensible young man, he gradually finds himself falling in love with his cousin Grace. Incognito, he visits the first of his father's estates, where he witnesses the dismissal, through a letter from Clonbrony, of the humane and honest agent Burke for not extorting sufficient income from the tenants. The next estate is managed by the brothers Garraghty. Here the castle is half ruined, the land is ill farmed, and the tenants are treated with callous indifference; but Clonbrony is satisfied because despite the Garraghtys' embezzlement money is forthcoming. Colambre returns to London and tells his father that he will himself pay off the debts, on condition that the Garraghtys are dismissed and the Clonbrony family returns to live on its Irish estates. After the sorting out of various troubles, he and Grace become engaged, his mother resigns herself to her return, and the family leave London to live in Ireland.

Absurd, Theatre of the A term coined by the theatre critic Martin Esslin to characterize the work of a number of European and American dramatists of the 1950s and early 1960s. As the name suggests, the function of such theatre is to give dramatic expression to the philosophical notion of the 'absurd', a notion that had received widespread diffusion following the publication of Albert *Camus's essay *Le Mythe de Sisyphe* in 1942. To define the world as absurd is to recognize its fundamentally mysterious nature, and this recognition is frequently associated with feelings of loss, purposelessness, and bewilderment. To such feelings, the Theatre of the Absurd gives ample expression, often leaving the observer baffled in the face of disjointed, meaningless, or repetitious dialogues, incomprehensible behaviour, and plots which deny all notion of logical or 'realistic' development. But the recognition of the absurdity of human existence also provided dramatists with a rich source of comedy, well illustrated in two early absurd plays, Eugène Ionesco's *La Cantatrice chauve*, written in 1948 (*The Bald Prima Donna*, 1958), and Samuel *Beckett's *En attendant Godot* (1952; trans. by the author, **Waiting for Godot*, 1954, subtitled 'A Tragicomedy in Two Acts'). The Theatre of the Absurd drew significantly on popular traditions of entertainment, on mime, acrobatics, and circus clowning, and, by seeking to redefine the legitimate concerns of 'serious' theatre, played an important role in extending the range of post-war drama. Amongst the dramatists associated with the Theatre of the Absurd are Arthur Adamov (1908–70), Edward *Albee, Beckett, Camus, Jean *Genet, Ionesco (1912–94), Alfred Jarry (1873–1907), Harold *Pinter, and Boris Vian (1920–59). See M. Esslin, *The Theatre of the Absurd* (1962).
See also Cruelty, Theatre of

Académie Française A prestigious French academy, established by *Richelieu in 1634 to set and maintain linguistic and literary standards in France. Its principal task since its creation has been the publication of a French dictionary: the first edition appeared in 1694, since when there have been seven more; the ninth is currently appearing in parts. Made up of 40 elected members, the Académie Française continues to exert a considerable influence on French cultural life.

Academies Associations first founded in Italy in the 15th century to promote intellectual and cultural debate on a wide range of topics. The earliest, like that of Ficino in Florence, were informal groups of humanist scholars who aimed to revive the ancient Platonic academy and its traditions of dialogue and debate. In the 16th century these informal groupings gave way to more formally constituted bodies, often characterized by punning titles, nicknames for members, witty emblems, and mottoes. Among the best known of this period are the Intronati (Siena), the *Della Crusca (Florence), and the Lincei (Rome), of which Galileo was a member. From an early date the Academies developed international links; the *Royal Society was modelled on, and had close connections with, several of the Academies in Italy. Among those surviving today are the Crusca, the Lincei, and the Arcadia.

Academy A periodical founded in 1869 as an Arnoldian platform for intellectual and cultural debate by a young Oxford don, Charles Appleton (1841–79), who edited it until his death, converting it in 1871 into a fortnightly and in 1874 into a weekly review. It included Matthew *Arnold, T. H. *Huxley, and Mark *Pattison among its early contributors. After Appleton's death in 1879 it grew less austere, and in 1896, under the control of John Morgan Richards, it became a lively literary journal, publishing work by Joseph *Conrad and Francis *Thompson. It ceased publication in 1916.

ACHEBE, Chinua (1930–) Writer, novelist, and poet, born and educated in Nigeria, graduating from University College, Ibadan, in 1953. At university he was invited to recognize his own people in such novels in English as Conrad's portrayal of the barbaric Africans in *'Heart of Darkness'. This led to Achebe's lifelong conviction that cultures must tell their own stories if they are to survive; in the words of the elder in *Anthills of the Savannah*, '"The story is our escort; without it, we are blind...it is the story that owns us and directs us."' Achebe published his first novel, *Things Fall Apart*, in 1958. He became the founding editor of the Heinemann African Writers Series in 1962 and of *Okike: An African Journal of New Writing*, in 1971. He was actively involved in politics during the Nigerian Civil War (Biafran War) of 1967–70; is a poet, short story writer, and emeritus professor at the University of Nigeria, Nsukka; has held academic posts in the USA; and has published widely on cultural, political, and social issues: *Morning Yet on Creation Day* (1975); *The Trouble with Nigeria* (1984); *Hopes and Impediments* (1988); *Home and Exile* (2000). Two of the titles of Achebe's novels, *Things Fall Apart* and *No Longer at Ease*, are quotations, from poems by W. B. *Yeats and T. S. *Eliot, signalling his dialogic engagement with canonical writers he studied at university. *Things Fall Apart* and *Arrow of God* (1964) imagine a precolonial Igboland which is evolving at its own pace, no Eden but a complex society with legal, religious, and social structures which are unrecognized by the newly arrived colonial powers. Proverbial language is woven into the books, providing the modern reader with a dynamic rather than archaic insight into traditional life: '"The world is like a Mask dancing."' *No Longer at Ease* (1960) engages with Nigeria's post-independence modernity, as does the coruscating satire of *A Man of the People*. *Anthills of the Savannah*, told in several narrative voices, pursues Achebe's bold, radical, and sardonic analysis of West African politics and corruption but concludes with a scene of female empowerment. See Ezenwa-Ohaeto, *Chinua Achebe* (1997).

ACKER, Kathy (1947–97) Novelist, poet, and performance artist, born in New York. On leaving university she worked as a stripper and pornographic film actor, these experiences providing material for her first self-published short stories. Her style and subject matter were established in early novels like *The Childlike Life of the Black Tarantula* (1975). Influenced by William *Burroughs, the poetry of the *Black Mountain School, and the erotic writings of Georges *Bataille, she rejected plot and character in favour of fragments of autobiography, plagiarized material, and disconnected dream-like sequences of explicit sexuality and violence. In the mid-1980s she settled in London, where the UK publication of *Blood and Guts in High School* (1984) brought her a wide audience, and was followed by *Don Quixote* (1986), *Empire of the Senseless* (1988), and *In Memoriam to Identity* (1990). She returned to the USA to make performance tours of her work. Books from this period include *My Mother: Demonology* (1995), *Pussy, King of the Pirates* (1995; also recorded as a CD with punk band the Mekons), *Bodies of Work* (1997, essays on art, culture, and sexuality), and *Eurydice in the Underworld* (1997).

ACKERLEY, J. R. (Joe Randolph) (1896–1967) Gay writer, educated at Rossall School, Lancashire, and Magdalene College, Cambridge. His play *The Prisoners of War* (1925) was based on his own experience as a prisoner of war. He was literary editor of the *Listener* (1935–59), where he encouraged W. H. *Auden and Stephen *Spender. *Hindoo Holiday* (1932) is based on his experiences as private secretary to the maharaja of Chhatarpurr; *My Dog Tulip* (1956) and his novel *We Think the World of You* (1960) describe his intense relationship with his Alsatian dog. *My Father and Myself* (1968) is an account of his discovery of his father's second family, also described by Ackerley's half-sister Diana Petre in *The Secret Garden of Roger Ackerley* (1975); see also *My Sister and Myself: The Diaries of J. R. Ackerley*, ed. Francis *King (1982). The Ackerley prize for autobiography, established in 1982, has been won, amongst others, by Edward Blishen (1920–96) and Alan *Bennett.

ACKERMANN, Rudolph (1764–1834) German lithographer who settled in London and opened a print shop in the Strand in 1795. He played a major role in establishing lithography as a fine art, and published handsome coloured-plate books with lithographs and hand-coloured aquatints in association with Samuel Prout (1783–1852), A. C. Pugin (1768/9–1832; father of A. W. N. *Pugin), Thomas *Rowlandson, and other artists. His publications include the *Repository of Arts, Literature, Fashions, etc.* (1809–28) and *The Microcosm of London* (3 vols, 1808–11), an antiquarian and topographical work by William *Combe.

ACKLAND, Rodney (1908–91) Playwright, born Nathan Ackland Bernstein and educated at Balham Grammar School; his work was greatly admired but considered insufficiently frivolous by West End managements. The only dramatist of his generation to see how Chekhov's revolutionary dramatic technique might be joined to the robust native tradition of mixing tragedy with comedy, his best early plays—*Strange Orchestra* (performed 1931; pub. 1932), *After October* (1936)—inhabit a world which recalls the seedy bohemian gentility of the novels of Jean *Rhys. *Birthday* (1934) is a study of hypocrisy and repression, while *The Dark River* (pub. 1937; performed 1943) is a more sombre and unsettling portrait of England in the shadow of the Second World War. His masterpiece, *The Pink Room* (1952), a tragicomedy set in a seedy London club in 1945, was reviewed savagely on its opening but triumphantly revived at the *National Theatre in 1995 under the title *Absolute Hell* (performed 1987; pub. 1990). See Charles Duff, *The Lost Summer* (1995).

ACKROYD, Peter (1949–) Novelist, biographer, poet, and reviewer. He was brought up in west London and educated at St Benedict's School, Ealing, Clare College, Cambridge, and Yale University. He worked for the **Spectator*, 1973–82, then joined *The *Times* as reviewer in 1986. Starting out as a poet (*London Lickpenny*, 1973), he also published two pieces of cultural criticism in the 1970s, *Notes for a New Culture* (1976) and *Dressing Up* (1979), a study of transvestism and drag. However he is best known as a biographer and novelist whose work explores the continuities between those two genres. His lives of Ezra *Pound (1980), T. S. *Eliot (1984), Charles *Dickens (1990), William *Blake (1995), and Sir Thomas *More (1998) have been widely praised. He has also been unafraid of experimenting with the form, as he does, most dramatically, perhaps, in *The Last Testament of Oscar Wilde* (1983) in which he has *Wilde himself looking back on his life from his last years in Paris. In his novels he has explored similar territory, questioning the nature of time and narrative as well as the distinction between invention and authenticity. His first novel, *The Great Fire of London* (1982), is based on Dickens's **Little Dorrit* and in this, and later novels, including *Hawksmoor* (1985) and *The House of Doctor Dee* (1993), he mixes historical retelling with present-day narratives. In *Chatterton* (1987), in which the poet's life provides the cue, his preoccupation with impersonation and history are at their subtlest. London has continued to loom large in Ackroyd's fiction, both as a physical location (especially its more sinister side) and as a metaphor. *Dan Leno and the Limehouse Golem* (1994) is set in 1880 and centres on a series of grisly murders in the East End of London. London itself has since become the focus or protagonist of such works as *London: The Biography* (2000) and *Thames: Sacred City* (2007). Ackroyd is a prolific writer who refuses to be contained by either history or fiction, as, for instance, in *Milton in America* (1996), where he transports *Milton to the New World. See Susanna Onega, *Peter Ackroyd* (1998).

Acmeism A school of Russian poetry, led by Nikolai *Gumilev and Sergei Gorodetsky (1884–1967), and including among its members Anna *Akhmatova and Osip *Mandelshtam. The Acmeist school originated in a group called the Guild of Poets, organized by Gumilev in November 1911. Their manifesto of 1913 rejected *symbolist mysticism and vagueness in favour of the depiction of the concrete world of everyday reality with brevity and clarity, and the precise and logical use of the poetic word. They announced their forerunners as *Shakespeare, *Villon, *Rabelais, and *Gautier. See Justin Doherty, *The Acmeist Movement in Russian Poetry* (1995).

Acrasia In Edmund *Spenser's **Faerie Queene*, II. xii, typifies Intemperance. She is captured and bound by Sir *Guyon, and her Bower of Bliss destroyed.

Actaeon In Greek myth a hunter who inadvertently saw the goddess Artemis (Roman Diana) bathing; to punish him she turned him into a stag, and his own hounds destroyed him. *Ovid tells the story in *Metamorphoses* Book 3. *Shakespeare's Orsino in **Twelfth Night* I. i figures himself as Actaeon, pursued by his desires 'like fell and cruel hounds'.

Action Française An extreme right-wing, monarchist, nationalistic, and anti-Semitic political group, founded in France in 1899, which flourished until the 1940s. In 1908 the newspaper *L'Action française* was founded, edited by Léon Daudet (1867–1942), a son of Alphonse *Daudet.

ACTON, Sir Harold Mario Mitchell (1904–94) Writer and aesthete, born at La Pietra near Florence and educated at Christ Church, Oxford, where his manner and antics inspired the character of Anthony Blanche in Evelyn *Waugh's *Brideshead Revisited* (1945). He spent much of the 1930s in Peking (Beijing), teaching English at the university and translating Chinese poetry and plays. After war service in RAF intelligence, he settled at La Pietra. Amongst his books are several volumes of modernist poetry, including *Aquarium* (1923) and *This Chaos* (1930); a mildly satirical novel set in Peking, *Peonies and Ponies* (1941); *The Soul's Gymnasium and Other Stories* (1982); and lively historical studies such as *The Last Medici* (1932) and *The Bourbons of Naples* (1956). He also wrote a memoir of Nancy *Mitford (1970) and two witty but discreet volumes of autobiography, *Memoirs of an Aesthete* (1948) and *More Memoirs of an Aesthete* (1970).

ACTON, Sir John Emerich Edward Dalberg, first Baron Acton (1834–1902) Customarily known as Lord Acton, historian, moralist, and critic, born at Naples, the son of a Roman Catholic English father and a German aristocrat mother. Brought up in a well-connected cosmopolitan world, he was educated at Paris, Oscott, Edinburgh, and Munich, where he studied under the distinguished German church historian Döllinger. In the *Rambler* (converted under his direction to the *Home and Foreign Review*) he advocated Döllinger's proposed reunion of Christendom, but stopped the *Review* on the threat of a papal veto. He opposed the definition by the Catholic Church of the dogma of papal infallibility, publishing his views in his *Letters from Rome on the Council* (1870). His copious literary activity was consistently formed by his rigorous morality and liberal Catholicism, taking the form of contributions to the *North British Review*, the **Quarterly Review*, and the *English Historical Review* (which he helped to found), besides lectures and addresses. Lord Acton was appointed Regius professor of modern history at Cambridge in 1895. One of his principal works was the planning of the *Cambridge Modern History* (1899–1912) for the *Cambridge University Press.

Acts and Monuments of these Latter and Perilous Days, Touching Matters of the Church Popularly known as the *Book of Martyrs*, by John *Foxe. It was first published in Latin at Basle 1559, printed in English in 1563, with woodcut illustrations, and in a revised and expanded form in 1570. This enormous work is a history of the Christian church from the earliest times, with special reference to the sufferings of the Christian martyrs of all ages, but more particularly of the Protestant martyrs of Mary's reign. The book is, in fact, a violent indictment of 'the persecutors of God's truth, commonly called papists'. The author is credulous in his acceptance of stories of martyrdom and partisan in their selection. The work, based on numerous histories and documents as well as oral testimony, is written in a simple, colloquial style and enlivened by vivid dialogues between the persecutors and their victims.

Acts of the Apostles *See* APOSTLES.

Adam *See* EDEN, GARDEN OF.

Adam The name given to a 12th-century Anglo-Norman play (also called the *Jeu d'Adam* and the *Mystère d'Adam*) in *octosyllabics, surviving in one 13th-century manuscript from Tours. There are three scenes: the Fall and expulsion of Adam and Eve from paradise; Cain and Abel; and a Prophets' Play (*Ordo Prophetarum*). It is generally thought that it was written in England *c*.1140, though the French scholar Joseph Bédier (1864–1938) doubted it, and it is regarded as important for the evolution of the medieval *mystery plays in England. Although it contains Latin as well as the vernacular, and is enacted with rudimentary staging at the church door, the play is not good evidence for the evolution from liturgical to secular staging, displaying as it does a theatrical sophistication far beyond most of the later mystery plays. There is an English edition, ed. Paul Studer (1918); see also M. D. Legge, *Anglo-Norman Literature and its Background* (1963).

Adam Bede A novel by George *Eliot, published 1859. The plot was suggested by a story told to George Eliot by her Methodist aunt Elizabeth Evans of a confession of child-murder made to her by a girl in prison. The action takes place at the close of the 18th century. Hetty Sorrel, pretty, vain, and self-centred, is the niece of the genial farmer Martin Poyser of Hall Farm. She is loved by Adam Bede, the village carpenter, a young man of dignity and character, but is deluded by the attentions of the thoughtless young squire, Arthur Donnithorne, and is seduced by him, in spite of Adam's efforts to save her. Arthur breaks off relations with her, and Hetty, broken-hearted, agrees to marry Adam. But before the marriage she discovers she is pregnant, flies from home to seek Arthur, fails to find him, and is arrested and convicted of infanticide. She is saved from the gallows at the last moment, her sentence commuted to transportation through Arthur's intervention. In prison she is comforted by her cousin Dinah Morris, a Methodist preacher, whose strong, serious, and calm nature is contrasted with Hetty's throughout the novel. In the last chapters, Adam discovers that Dinah loves him; his brother Seth, who had long and hopelessly loved Dinah, resigns her with a fine unselfishness.

The novel was immediately acclaimed for its realism, for which Eliot provides something close to a manifesto (chapter 17), for its picturesque portrayal of rural life, and for its humour; Mrs Poyser was greeted as a comic creation on the level of Charles *Dickens's Sam Weller and Mrs Gamp. Some critics objected to its insistence on the 'startling horrors of rustic reality' (*Saturday Review*) and its 'obstetric' details. Henry *James in 1866 found Hetty Sorrel 'the most successful' of George Eliot's female figures.

ADAMOV, Arthur *See* ABSURD, THEATRE OF THE.

ADAMS, Douglas (1952–2001) Scriptwriter and novelist born in Cambridge, whose *The Hitchhiker's Guide to the Galaxy* (1978) comedy radio series followed work on **Doctor Who*. Its success, charting the bemused Englishman Arthur Dent's adventures after the earth's demolition, resulted in a second series (1980), stage adaptations, records, computer games, five novels, and a film (2005). Adams's satire on bureaucracy and gift for character made him immensely popular, although the 'Dirk Gently' books (1987, 1988) did not achieve the stature of 'Hitchhiker's'. The unfinished *The Salmon of Doubt* was published in 2002. See M. J. Simpson's biography, *Hitchhiker* (2003).

ADAMS, Francis (1862–93) Novelist, poet, and journalist, born in Malta, and educated at Shrewsbury School and in Paris. He travelled to Australia in 1884 for health reasons (he was tubercular) and worked there successfully as a journalist, while publishing a collection of poems, *Songs of the Army of the Night* (1888). *The Melbournians* (1892) is a novella describing social and political life in Australia and the emerging sense of national identity; *The Australians* (1893) collects articles and essays on similar themes. Adams returned to England in 1890, where he was to commit suicide. His novel, *A Child of the Age*, was published posthumously in 1894 by John *Lane in the Keynotes Series. It vividly describes the schooldays (at 'Glastonbury') and poverty-stricken struggles of would-be poet and scholar, young orphan Bertram Leicester, and is understandably suffused with a *fin-de-siècle* melancholy.

ADAMS, Henry Brooks (1838–1918) American man of letters, and grandson and great-grandson of presidents of the United States. He was born and brought up in Boston and educated at Harvard University, and during the Civil War was in England, where his father Charles Francis Adams (1807–86) was a minister. On his return he taught history at Harvard, edited the *North American Review*, and, after moving to Washington, published two novels, *Democracy* (1880, anonymously) and *Esther* (1884, as 'Frances Snow Compton'). His ambitious *History of the United States during the Administrations of Thomas Jefferson and James Madison* appeared in nine volumes, 1889–91. He subsequently travelled widely in Europe; his *Mont-Saint-Michel and Chartres* (1904) is an interpretation of the spiritual unity of the 13th-century mind, which led to his autobiography, *The Education of Henry Adams* (1907), which describes the multiplicity of the 20th-century mind. In his preface, he invokes the names of *Rousseau and Benjamin *Franklin as predecessors in the field of autobiography, and proceeds (speaking of himself in the third person) to analyse the failures of his formal education (which he describes as not only useless but harmful), the complexity of the 'multiverse' we now inhabit, and the predicament of modern man in an increasingly technological world. In chapter XXV, 'The Dynamo and the Virgin', he contrasts the spiritual force that built Chartres with the dynamo—'He began to feel the forty-foot dynamos as a moral force, much as the early Christians had felt the Cross…'—and proceeds, in the final chapters, to define his own 'Dynamic Theory of History' and the acceleration of scientific progress. There are also interesting accounts of his residence in England, and of his 'diplomatic education' in the circle of Lord Palmerston (1784–1865), Lord John Russell (1792–1878), and *Gladstone; and a lively description of an encounter (through his friend Monckton *Milnes) with A. C. *Swinburne, whom he likened to 'a tropical bird, high-crested, long-beaked, quick-moving…a crimson macaw among owls'.

ADAMS, Richard (1920–) Children's writer and novelist, born in Newbury, Berkshire. He is best known for his highly successful fantasy *Watership Down* (1972), an anthropomorphic account of rabbit society. Other works include *Shardik* (1974) and *The Plague Dogs* (1977).

ADAMS, Sarah Flower (1805–48) Poet, born in Essex, the daughter of a radical journalist, Benjamin Flower (1755–1829), and brought up a *Unitarian: after her father's death she lived for some years in the family circle of W. J. *Fox, to whose *Monthly Repository* she contributed. She wrote a historical verse drama about martyrdom, *Vivia Perpetua* (1841), and was a writer of *hymns, which include 'Nearer, my God, to thee' (*c.*1834).

adaptation Meaning the transfer of any work from one medium to another, became a major commercial activity during the 19th century, with popular novels regularly adapted for the stage as plays and operas. Walter *Scott's romances were dramatized from as early as 1816, when **Guy Mannering* made its debut at Covent Garden, while the novels of Edward *Bulwer-Lytton, *Dickens, and R. L. *Stevenson also enjoyed wide stage success, with the latter's **Dr Jekyll and Mr Hyde* playing on both sides of the Atlantic within months of its publication. These traditional translations have continued, alongside adaptation for moving pictures, later for radio and television, and most recently for interactive computer games.

Early screen adaptations of popular works often drew on the stage versions, such as R. W. Paul's pioneering *Scrooge, or Marley's Ghost* (1901), and although highly condensed could assume the audience's familiarity with the story. On this basis, Dickens and Shakespeare were among the most popular early film subjects, while many popular Victorian melodramas enjoyed a new lease of life, such as Ellen Wood's **East Lynne*, filmed at least eight times before Theda Bara starred in a Fox version of 1916. Even a work considered the cornerstone of a new language of cinema, D. W. Griffith's controversial epic *The Birth of a Nation* (1915), was adapted from *The Clansman* (1905), a stage play based on a novel by Thomas *Dixon. Both Griffith and later Sergei Eisenstein would credit Dickens as the inspiration for such filmic techniques as the close-up and the flashback.

Most films, however, drew on less exalted models, as selling film rights became an important source of writers' income. In the 1920s Oswald Stoll's 'Eminent British Authors' series of adaptations of best-sellers by the likes of Jeffery Farnoll, A. E. W. Mason, Ethel Dell, and Baroness *Orczy became the mainstay of British cinema. Paradoxically, synchronized sound after 1929 meant that, while dialogue could be accurately reproduced, films were not necessarily more faithful to their sources. One outstanding British film-maker, Alfred *Hitchcock, understood the need to reinvent works for a different medium, claiming, 'I read a story once and, if I like the basic idea, I just forget all about the book and start to create cinema'. When William Wyler's **Wuthering Heights* (1939) was attacked for omitting half of the original, the critic Dilys Powell regretted a cinema 'still beset by people who bring the book with them'.

Radio, and later television, would offer new scope for much longer adaptations in their serial forms and 'classic serials' have been a staple of both media for over 50 years, with two landmark productions standing out from the generally high standard. In 1967, the BBC broadcast Galsworthy's *The *Forsyte Saga* as an unprecedented 26-part series, attracting a national and eventually international following. Fifteen years later, Granada produced an opulent eleven-part adaptation of Evelyn *Waugh's *Brideshead Revisited*, which became a new benchmark for scrupulous and evocative adaptation. Meanwhile, films are regularly 'novelized', adapted for the stage, and re-filmed; while films are now routinely accompanied by computer-game versions. 'Remediation' has been suggested by Jay Boulter and Richard Grusin in their book of the same title (2000) as an essential feature of how new media establish themselves.

ADCOCK, Fleur (1934–) Poet and translator, born in New Zealand, and educated partly in England. She read Classics at Victoria University, Wellington, and settled in England in 1963. Her volumes of poetry include *The Eye of the Hurricane* (1964), *High Tide in the Garden* (1971), a translated selection of medieval Latin poems, *The Virgin and the Nightingale* (1983), *Time-Zones* (1991), and *Looking Back* (1997). *Poems 1960–2000* appeared in 2000. She was awarded the Queen's Gold Medal for Poetry in 2006. Predominantly ironic and domestic in tone, her work suggests wider horizons through her evocations of travel and of varied landscapes, and in recent years she has written about public events (e.g. the fall of communism in Romania) and environmental issues. She edited the *Oxford Book of Contemporary New Zealand Poetry* (1983) and the *Faber Book of 20th Century Women's Poetry* in 1987. See Janet Wilson, *Fleur Adcock* (2006).

ADDISON, Joseph (1672–1719) Essayist, educated at Charterhouse with Richard *Steele and at the Queen's College, Oxford, and Magdalen, of which he became a fellow. In late 1704 he published *The Campaign*, a poem celebrating the victory at the battle of Blenheim. He was appointed under-secretary of state in 1705, and was elected to Parliament in 1708. In 1709 he went to Ireland as chief secretary to Lord Wharton, the lord lieutenant, losing office when the Whigs fell in 1710. He was a prominent member of the *Kit-Cat Club. From 1709 he contributed to Steele's **Tatler* and joined him in the production of the **Spectator*. For this he wrote several important literary essays: on **Paradise Lost* (5 January to 3 May 1712), on Imagination (21 June to 3 July 1712) and on traditional ballads. In the tenth issue Addison declared, 'I shall be ambitious to have it said of me, that I have brought philosophy out of closets and libraries, schools and colleges, to dwell in clubs and assemblies, at tea-tables and coffee-houses.' He popularized the ideas of John *Locke, and introduced a polite decorum to essays of social comment. His *neo-classical tragedy **Cato* (1713) was a hit, but his opera *Rosamund* (1707) failed and his comedy *The Drummer* (1715) met with only modest success. He resumed political office in 1714, but retired in 1718. Addison was buried in Westminster Abbey; his works were edited by Thomas *Tickell (1721). See Peter Smithers, *The Life of Joseph Addison* (1968); *The Letters of Joseph Addison*, ed. W. Graham (1941).

ADEBAYO, Diran (1968–) Reporter and journalist, born in London to Nigerian parents, and educated at Oxford; he has scripted documentaries for television. His prize-winning first novel *Some Kind of Black* (1996) interrogates the fashionable use of blackness, revealing the family and political anxieties under the protagonist's streetwise persona. *My Once upon a Time* (2000) is an inventive thriller set in London in the near future, fusing myth with metropolitan life and expanding the boundaries of the genre.

Adeline Mowbray A cautionary satire by Amelia *Opie, published 1804, based on the unconventional life of Mary *Wollstonecraft, with whom the author was acquainted. Raised by an intellectual mother to think independently, Adeline refuses marriage to Glenmurray (modelled on William *Godwin), living with him as his sexual equal. In consequence, she loses her respectable friends, her stepfather attempts to seduce her, and her formerly enlightened mother disowns her. On her premature deathbed, Adeline is reunited with her mother, repenting her conduct and wishing she had been taught more by experience than theory.

Adelphi Started in 1923 as a monthly journal under the editorship of John Middleton *Murry. Early issues published many posthumous works by Katherine *Mansfield. On the verge of folding in 1927, it was resumed (with financial aid from readers) as the *New Adelphi*, but as a quarterly. It was transformed into the *Adelphi* again in 1930, and ran until 1955. Though Murry formally ceased to be the editor in 1930, when the role was handed to Richard Rees and Max Plowman, he remained actively involved, and the exposition of his personal quest remained a dominant theme. Contributors to the three series include D. H. *Lawrence, T. S. *Eliot, Arnold *Bennett, H. G. *Wells, Cecil *Day-Lewis, George *Orwell, and W. H. *Auden.

ADICHIE, Chimamanda Ngozi (1977–) Novelist. She grew up in Nsukka, Nigeria, and is a graduate of two American universities. Her first novel, *Purple Hibiscus* (2003), is an exploration of a Nigerian family's tense but loving relationship. *Half of a Yellow Sun* (2006), set during the Nigerian Civil War (Biafran War), won the Orange Prize.

ADOMNAN, St (*c.*627–704) Abbot of Iona from 679, who, as *Bede says, was the author of a work on 'The Holy Places' (*Ecclesiastical History*, V. 15, 21), and who also wrote an extant life of St *Columba.

Adonais An elegy on the death of John *Keats, by P. B. *Shelley, written at Pisa and published 1821. Composed in 55 Spenserian stanzas, the poem was inspired partly by the Greek elegies of *Bion and *Moschus (both of which Shelley had translated) and partly by Milton's **Lycidas*. Keats is lamented under the name of Adonais, the Greek god of beauty and fertility, together with other poets who had died young, such as Thomas *Chatterton, Philip *Sidney, and *Lucan. His deathbed is attended by various figures, both allegorical and contemporary, including Lord *Byron, 'the Pilgrim of Eternity'. Shelley, the atheist, accepts the physical facts of death, but insists on some form of *Neoplatonic resurrection in the eternal Beauty of the universe, 'a portion of the loveliness | Which once he made more lovely'. The style is deliberately grand—'a highly wrought *piece of art*'—and lacks intimacy. Yet Shelley strongly identified himself with Keats's sufferings, and in his preface he attacks the Tory reviewers with a pen 'dipped in consuming fire'. The poem ends with astonishing clairvoyance: 'my spirit's bark is driven | Far from the shore...'

ADONIS (1930–) Pen-name of Ali Ahmad Said, poet and scholar, born in Syria, and educated at Damascus University; in 1956 he settled in Lebanon, where in 1968 he founded the influential magazine *Mawaqif*. Many of his poems, which explore classical themes as well as the tragedy of Beirut in the 1980s, have been translated into English, and he has himself translated into Arabic works by *Racine and *Saint-John Perse. His *Sufism and Surrealism* (trans. Judith Cumberbatch) was published in 2005.

Adonis *See* VENUS.

ADORNO, Theodor (1903–69) German social philosopher, musicologist, and cultural theorist, born in Frankfurt am Main, where he also completed his studies, subsequently teaching at the university. Because of his part-Jewish descent he was dismissed and eventually obliged to leave Germany, settling in America before returning to a position at the Frankfurt Institute of Social Research in 1950. With Max Horkheimer (1895–1973) he published *Dialektik der Aufklärung* (1947: *Dialectic of Enlightenment*). His application of Marxist insights to music, literature, film, and popular culture has been highly influential in Germany, Britain, and America, and the collection of aphorisms *Minima Moralia* (1951) is regarded as a seminal text for Critical Theory.

Advancement of Learning, The A treatise by Francis *Bacon, published 1605, in which he sets out his ideas for the reform of knowledge. He denounces medieval scholasticism and Ciceronian rhetoric, arguing that by pursuing tenuous theological subtleties and mere verbosity they have deflected knowledge from 'the benefit and use of man'.

Adventures of Master F.J., The *See* F.J.

***Adventures of Philip** on his Way through the World, Showing Who Robbed Him, Who Helped Him, and Who Passed Him by, The* The last complete novel of William Makepeace *Thackeray, serialized in the **Cornhill Magazine* January 1861–August 1862, with illustrations by the author and Fred Walker. The story is told by Arthur Pendennis, now a middle-aged married man. His young friend Philip is the son of a fashionable doctor, George Firmin, who, as 'George Brandon', had appeared as the seducer of Caroline Gann in 'A Shabby Genteel Story', an unfinished tale published in 1840 in **Fraser's Magazine*. Firmin had abandoned Caroline, having tricked her into a false marriage, and then run away with an heiress, Philip's mother, now dead. Firmin is being blackmailed by the disreputable parson Tufton Hunt, who performed the mock marriage ceremony with Caroline Gann and threatens to prove that the marriage was in fact valid. Caroline, calling herself Mrs Brandon, and known affectionately as 'the little Sister', is a nurse who has tended Philip through an attack of fever, and now looks on him as her own son. She refuses to give the evidence that will disinherit him. However, Dr Firmin, having lost his own money and Philip's fortune, absconds to America, and Philip's cousin Agnes, daughter of a pretentious toady, Talbot Twysden, breaks off her engagement to Philip. While visiting Pendennis and his family in Boulogne, Philip comes across

General Baynes, co-trustee with Dr Firmin of Philip's inheritance. Knowing that Baynes will be ruined by any financial claim on him, Philip does not pursue his legal rights. He falls in love with Baynes's daughter Charlotte, and marries her in spite of her mother's fierce opposition, Thackeray's prejudices against mothers-in-law being here prominently displayed. Philip is struggling to make a living as a journalist, in a manner that recalls Thackeray's own early career. A happy ending is achieved through the device of the suddenly rediscovered will of Lord Ringwood, Philip's great-uncle. Philip, the only one of the old man's haughty and capricious relatives never to flatter him, has been left a large legacy.

Æ Pseudonym of George William *Russell.

ÆLFRIC (*c.*950–*c.*1010) Benedictine monk, educated at Winchester (where he was a pupil of *Æthelwold), Cerne Abbas, and Eynsham near Oxford, where he became the first abbot. His chief works are the *Catholic Homilies* (990–5), largely drawn from the church *Fathers, which circulated widely, and the *Lives of the Saints*, also mostly translated from Latin, employing skilfully the alliteration and metrical organization associated with vernacular poetry whilst adopting a distinct and more direct idiom. Several other English works of his survive, including his Latin *Grammar* (his most popular work in the Middle Ages, judging by the number of manuscripts and by his being known as 'Grammaticus' in the 17th and 18th centuries); his *Colloquy* between a teacher and pupil on one side and representatives of various walks of life on the other; and a series of translations and adaptations of the Old Testament. Many of his English writings were produced specifically with the aim of disseminating orthodox doctrines among the laity. The greatest prose writer of his time, Aelfric is celebrated not only for his stylistic resourcefulness and varied subject matter, but also for his educational principles and the breadth of his learning as a product of the 10th-century Benedictine Revival in England. See *Catholic Homilies, First Series (Text)*, ed. P. Clemoes (EETS SS 17, 1995); *Homilies of Ælfric: A Supplementary Collection*, ed. J. C. Pope (EETS OS 259 and 260, 1967 and 1968); *Ælfric's Catholic Homilies, Series 2. Text*, ed. M. Godden (EETS SS 5, 1979).

Aeneid (written 29–19 BC) Epic in twelve books by *Virgil, reckoned the greatest poem in Latin literature. Unlike the **Iliad* and **Odyssey* it was not created from oral and pre-literate material, but was a sophisticated and intensely crafted composition, drawing on varied learning, in both Greek and Latin. While creating the national epic of Rome, Virgil deliberately recalls and challenges his predecessors. In addition to Homeric allusions and motifs, Virgil includes episodes and language evoking Greek tragedy and pastoral, and earlier Latin poetry and religion. The poem is composed in Homeric hexameters and features gods, heroes, battles, and tragic love in the grand epic style; but Virgil shows a new kind of sympathy for the characters. Aeneas, a survivor of the sack of Troy, is the son of Venus. He carries his old father, Anchises, out of burning Troy, sails west, and, after many adventures, founds Alba Longa, mother city of Rome. Famous for his *pietas* (religious and filial duty), he is the ancestor, through his son Iulus or Ascanius, of the emperor Augustus, Virgil's own patron. Key episodes include Aeneas's account to Dido, queen of Carthage, of the fall of Troy, their love affair, his departure, driven by Jupiter, for Italy and destiny, and her suicide (Books 2–4); and his descent at Cumae, led by the Sybil, to the world of the dead and the unborn, where his dead father Anchises prophesies the future greatness of his descendants, and where he encounters the unforgiving Dido (Book 6). Left unfinished, the *Aeneid* was immediately recognized as a masterpiece. It powerfully influenced subsequent poetry in Latin and later European literature, music, and painting. *Chaucer retold stories from the *Aeneid* in *The *House of Fame*; and the poem underlies the epic aspirations of Milton's **Paradise Lost* and the *mock-epic grandeur of Pope's **Dunciad*. Henry *Purcell in *Dido and Aeneas* and Hector *Berlioz in *Les Troyens* created magnificent operas from the early books of the poem. Notable English translations include those by Gawin *Douglas, *Dryden, William *Morris, Cecil *Day-Lewis, C. H. *Sisson, and Robert Fagles (1933–). See Jasper Griffin, *Virgil* (1986); Charles Martindale (ed.), *The Cambridge Companion to Virgil* (1997).

AESCHYLUS (?525/4–456/5 BC) Greek tragedian. He has some claim to be regarded as an inventor of the genre, since, where there had previously been the chorus and only one actor, he introduced a second actor and subordinated choral song to the dialogue. Only seven of between 70 and 90 plays have survived: the early plays, *The Persians*, *Seven against Thebes*, and *The Suppliants*; the trilogy forming the **Oresteia* (*Agamemnon, Choephoroe, Eumenides*), which introduces a third actor and is very different in terms of its dramatic structure; and *Prometheus Bound* (which may not be his). Aeschylus was hardly known in England before Thomas *Stanley's edition of the plays in 1663. His true popularity dates from the 19th century, centring initially on *Prometheus Bound*: Lord *Byron's 'Prometheus' (1816) was followed by P. B. *Shelley's **Prometheus Unbound* (1820), S. T. *Coleridge's essay *On the Prometheus of Aeschylus* (1825), and a translation of the play (1833) by Elizabeth Barrett *Browning. Several poets have translated the *Oresteia* in whole or in part, including Robert *Browning (*Agamemnon*, 1877), Louis *MacNeice (*Agamemnon*, 1936), Tony *Harrison (*Oresteia*, performed at the *National Theatre, 1981), and Ted *Hughes (*Oresteia*, also performed at the National, 1999). See P. E. Easterling (ed.), *The Cambridge Companion to Greek Tragedy* (1997); Archive of Performances of Greek and Roman Drama. *See* EURIPIDES; POETICS, THE; PROMETHEUS; SOPHOCLES.

AESOP (6th century BC) Said to have been a Phrygian slave, traditionally the author of the collection of Greek fables which comes down to us in several late versions. Aesop's fables often concern animals, who can sometimes talk, for example the Grasshopper and the Ant, and the Hare and the Tortoise. The fable of the Town Mouse and the Country Mouse was retold by *Horace, Robert *Henryson, Jonathan *Swift, and Beatrix

*Potter. Collections of *Erasmus' Latin edition were widely used in schools in the Renaissance. The fables have been frequently edited and adapted in English, for example by Roger *L'Estrange and Samuel *Richardson, and illustrated by artists such as Thomas *Bewick and Elisabeth Frink (1930–93). See B. E. Perry, *Aesopica* (1952); F. R. Adrados, *History of the Greco-Latin Fable*, 3 vols (1999–2003).

Aesthetic movement A cult of sensibility developed in the 1870s and 1880s, and influenced by the *Pre-Raphaelites, John *Ruskin, and Walter *Pater, in which art was separated from morality, and where form took precedence over content. Its female adherents often adopted anti-fashionable artistic dress. It was closely associated with Oscar *Wilde and was ridiculed by George *du Maurier in **Punch* and in Gilbert and Sullivan's **Patience* (1881), etc.
See also ART FOR ART'S SAKE; GROSVENOR GALLERY.

ÆTHELWOLD, St (b. between 904 and 909, d. 984) Born at Winchester. He entered the monastery of Glastonbury, of which *Dunstan was abbot, and became dean there. He subsequently re-established a monastic house at Abingdon, introducing the strict Benedictine Rule from Fleury, and he was appointed bishop of Winchester (963) after Edgar became king of England and Dunstan archbishop of Canterbury (960). He cooperated with Dunstan and *Oswald in the Benedictine Reforms of his century, expelling the secular clergy from Winchester, Chertsey, Milton, and Ely, and replacing them with monks. He rebuilt the church at Peterborough and built a new cathedral at Winchester. He was an important figure too in the revival of learning, as his pupil *Ælfric testifies; most significantly, he translated the *Rule* of St Benedict (*c.*960), and wrote the *Regularis Concordia*, the code of the new English rule in the 10th-century revival.

Aethiopica A Greek romance by the 3rd-century AD Syrian Heliodorus of Emesa, displays the common characteristics of the genre: the lovers Theagenes and Charicleia are parted, and there is the usual emphasis on travel through strange lands as they seek each other and on the maintenance of chastity in the face of temptations and dangers. As often happens, the intercalated stories have a 'realistic' character depicting Greek middle-class life, in sharp contrast to the romantic adventures that dominate the main narrative. The *Aethiopica* was first printed in 1534 and became widely known through Jacques *Amyot's French translation (1547) and Thomas *Underdowne's English version (*c.*1569). Its influence on later romances was considerable: *Tasso's **Jerusalem Delivered*, Sir Philip *Sidney's **Arcadia*, John *Barclay's *Argenis*, and Honoré D'Urfé's *L'Astrée* are all indebted to it.

Affectionate Shepherd, The *See* BARNFIELD, RICHARD.

African American literature The body of writing or performed art produced by African slaves and their descendants in America. One of its earliest forms was the slave narrative where the author describes the gradual achievement of freedom against extraordinary odds, including draconian laws against slave literacy in some states. Famous examples of this genre were produced by Olaudah *Equiano, William Wells *Brown, and Frederick *Douglass (*see* SLAVERY, LITERATURE OF). The publication in London of Phillis *Wheatley's *Poems on Various Subjects* in 1773 was a pivotal event, refuting the widely held belief that African Americans could not produce their own literature. From this period to the present African American literature has engaged in a running debate on the nature of American freedom and the impact of racism. At the turn of the 20th century authors like W. E. B. *Du Bois and Booker T. *Washington examined in their prose the nature of race relations in the USA. From around 1920 till the Second World War there was a great flourishing of cultural production in the *Harlem Renaissance, including a wide range of poetry and fiction from writers like Langston *Hughes and Zora Neale *Hurston, which drew on the vernacular tradition of spirituals, blues, and later jazz for their inspiration. This material formed a bedrock on which later writers like Richard *Wright and Ralph *Ellison depended for their depictions of the violence in American life. The civil rights movement occasioned a fresh burst of productivity, leading to the formation in the mid-1960s of the *Black Arts Movement, a loose coalition of groups collectively promoting a more political role for African American literature. Key figures here were Amiri *Baraka, Nikki *Giovanni, and the novelist Ishmael *Reed, although the latter was rather on the edge of the movement. Since the 1970s there has been a flourishing of African American writing in literature, criticism, and in rediscovering and republishing earlier works. The careers of figures like Alice *Walker and Toni *Morrison began in this period, the latter winning the *Nobel Prize for Literature in 1993. Among the critics, Henry Louis Gates Jr, has played a key role in formulating an autonomous tradition of signifying in African American literature with its roots in African folk tales, which argues for the continuing centrality of the vernacular in this material, while Maya *Angelou has provided the most famous continuation of the tradition of autobiographical memoir. African Americans have become important presences in science fiction (Samuel *Delany, Octavia *Butler), crime fiction (Walter *Mosley), and historical fiction (Edward P. Jones (1951–)), among other genres. See Henry Louis Gates, Jr, and Nellie Y. McKay (eds), *The Norton Anthology of African American Literature* (1997); William L. Andrews *et al.* (eds), *The Oxford Companion to African American Literature* (1997).

Agamemnon of Aeschylus, The A translation by Robert *Browning, published 1877. It sparked debate because of its literalness, which Browning defended in his preface, including his spelling of Greek names ('Olumpos' for 'Olympus', etc.). The translation (or 'transcription', as Browning termed it) diverted from Matthew *Arnold's Hellenism by insisting on the alien nature of the ancient Greek original. Violent murder and supernatural interventions in human life were persistent themes for Browning, finding new expression here.

AGARD, John (1949–) Born in Guyana and now living in Britain: 'I didn't graduate | I immigrate'. A dynamic performance poet, he writes witty plays, poetry, and short stories for children and adults, widening access to Caribbean culture. *Weblines* (2000) includes poems about Ananse, the trickster spider of creation myths.

Aga saga A journalistic term that was coined by Terence Blacker in 1992 in *Publishing News* to describe a kind of largely cosy fiction which dwells on middle-class life in English country towns and villages: the Aga (a stove of Swedish provenance) indicating traditional British rural values. The name of Joanna Trollope (1943–) is most often associated with the genre, though by no means all her work is as comforting and as comfortable as the label suggests, and she herself has often expressed annoyance that it is categorized in such an 'inaccurate and patronising' way.
See also ROMANTIC FICTION.

AGBABI, Patience (1965–) Performance poet, born to Nigerian parents in Britain. *Transformatrix* (2000) exemplifies her verbal and formal dexterity and dynamism. She writes, 'The written must be spoken. The chasm between page and stage must be healed.' Later books include *Bloodshot Monochrome* (2008).

AGEE, James (1909–55) American novelist, poet, film critic, and screenwriter, whose semi-autobiographical novel *A Death in the Family* (1957), about a Tennessee family shattered by the father's death, appeared posthumously. Two scripts produced classic films: *The African Queen* (John Huston, 1951) and Charles Laughton's only film as a director, *Night of the Hunter* (1955), while his collaborations with the photographers Walker Evans, in the book *Let Us Now Praise Famous Men* (1941), revealing the life of poor Alabama sharecroppers, and Helen Levitt (*In the Street*, 1945) remain influential.

Agenda A periodical of poetry, criticism, and translation, founded in 1959 and edited by William Cookson (1939–2003) and subsequently by Patricia McCarthy. It has had a bias towards poetry in the 'Poundian' and more generally *modernist line, and has published work by Ezra *Pound himself, David *Jones, Hugh *MacDiarmid, and Wyndham *Lewis. Renowned for its special issues devoted to individual writers, other contributors have included Charles *Tomlinson, C. H. *Sisson, Basil *Bunting, and Seamus *Heaney.

agents, literary The role of literary agent—that is, of middleman between author and publisher—began to develop towards the end of the 19th century, A. P. (Alexander Pollock) Watt (1834–1914) being frequently cited as the founder of the profession. Newspaper agencies and dramatic and lecture agents had existed earlier in the 19th century, and the *Society of Authors had recently been created to protect the rights of authors, but Watt appears to have been the first reputable literary agent, and his clients included Thomas *Hardy, Rudyard *Kipling, and Rider *Haggard. The firm he founded in 1875 still exists. Two other major figures in the early years were both Americans living in Britain—James Brand Pinker (1863–1922), who represented Joseph *Conrad and Arnold *Bennett and encouraged new authors, and Curtis Brown (1866–1945), who founded the firm that continues to bear his name in 1899. The influence of the agent was not universally acceptable; the Society of Authors was at first sceptical, as were some authors (including G. B. *Shaw) and many publishers, notably William Heinemann (1863–1920), who argued that an agent interfered with the natural relationship between author and publisher. By the end of the 1930s animosity had largely evaporated, all parties agreeing that agents could provide an indispensable service in terms of placing work, agreeing on contracts, intervening in disputes, etc. By the 1960s and 1970s most major writers had their own agents and publishers dealt increasingly with these agents rather than directly with the authors themselves. In recent decades, the power of literary agents such as Ed Victor and Andrew Wylie has continued to grow, as publishing has become more commercial and more competitive: agents have found themselves able to command very high advances for their more valuable (and not always their more literary) clients. Few agents have appeared in works of fiction and drama: an exception is the theatrical agent Peggy Ramsay (1908–91), who was portrayed on film by Vanessa Redgrave in *Prick up your Ears* (1987, from the life of Joe *Orton by John Lahr) and on stage in Alan Plater's *Peggy for You* (1999).

Age of Innocence, The *See* WHARTON, EDITH.

Age of Reason, The By Thomas *Paine, published as a whole 1795; the first part appeared in 1793, but no copies are extant. The work was written in Paris at the height of the Terror, the second part during Paine's imprisonment when his own life was at risk. In it he states, 'I believe in one God, and no more', and proceeds to attack Christianity and the Bible: the Old Testament consists of 'obscene stories and voluptuous debaucheries', whereas the New is inconsistent, and the account of the Virgin Birth, for example (a passage that was found particularly shocking), merely 'hearsay upon hearsay'. He concludes with a plea for religious tolerance. The work was widely attacked as blasphemous and scurrilous, occasionally praised as blunt and plain; its apparent flippancy was certainly intended to be provocative, and long remained so.

Agnes Grey A one-volume novel by Anne *Brontë, published 1847. It is the story of a rector's daughter, the narrator, who takes service as a governess, first with the Bloomfield family, whose undisciplined children are described as 'tigers' cubs', and then with the Murrays, where the conduct of her eldest charge, Rosalie, a heartless coquette, is contrasted with her own dignified, stoical, and gentle behaviour. Rosalie marries ambitiously and unhappily, but Agnes is happily united with Mr Weston, the curate, the only one to have shown kindness in her days of servitude. The novel, which reflects Anne Brontë's Christianity and her views on education, is lightened by passages showing Agnes's warm response to the natural world and in particular her feeling for the sea, which forms the background for her final reunion with Mr Weston.

Agrarians The name given to a group of writers from the Southern US states which included John Crowe *Ransom, Allen *Tate, and Robert Penn *Warren. They expressed their resistance to urbanization and the loss of tradition in their manifesto, the 1930 collection of essays *I'll Take my Stand*. Several of these writers subsequently retreated from their 1930 position.

Agravain, Sir In the Arthurian legends the second son of King Lot of Orkney and Arthur's sister Morgawse, the brother of *Gawain, *Gareth, and Gaheris. He conspires against Launcelot and discloses to Arthur Launcelot's love for Guinevere, and Launcelot kills him for this at Guinevere's door. He is called 'Agravayn a la Dure Mayn' (of the hard hand) in Sir **Gawain and the Green Knight* (l. 110), *Chrétien's *Perceval* (ll. 8139–40), and in the German **Parzifal* (dating from *c.*1205).

AGRIPPA, Henricus Cornelius, of Nettesheim (1486–1535) Scholar and writer on the occult sciences. He wrote *De Occulta Philosophia Libri Tres* (1533) and *De Incertitudine & Vanitate Scientiarum* (1527), and argued against the persecution of witches and veneration of relics. He spent a brief period in London in 1510. Jack Wilton and the earl of Surrey, characters in Thomas Nashe's picaresque *The *Unfortunate Traveller*, met him in the course of their travels. Agrippa is said to be the astrologer Herr Trippa of *Rabelais's Third Book. He is mentioned in Mary *Shelley's **Frankenstein* and, briefly, in the first Harry *Potter book.

AHLBERG, Allan (1938–) (born Croydon, Surrey) and **Janet** (1944–94) (born Huddersfield, Yorkshire) Admired husband-and-wife partnership who created many witty and inventive *picturebooks and series and pioneered highly allusive picturebooks, demonstrating that even very young children can read intertextually. These culminated in *The Jolly Postman* (1986), an international best-seller which incorporated removable letters, postcards, and, later in the series, other books and objects. Janet Ahlberg's detailed illustrations are particularly effective in books steeped in nostalgic period images (*Peepo!*, 1981) and in portraits of contemporary society (*Starting School*, 1988); they complement the restless ingenuity of Allan Ahlberg's verbal texts.

AICKMAN, Robert *See* GHOST STORIES.

AIDOO, Ama Ata (1942–) Ghanaian dramatist, poet, novelist, and short story writer, one of the most influential African authors of her generation. Her novel *Our Sister Killjoy* (1979) charts Sissie's journey on a scholarship to Europe, ironically described as 'a dress rehearsal for a journey to paradise'. An experimental fusion of prose and poetry in the narrative represents the protagonist's sceptical but compassionate recognition of her identity as an African. The oral tradition meets technological sophistication in her second novel, *Changes* (1991), which focuses on the complex cultural and political issues encountered by an independent career woman.

Aids to Reflection A religious and philosophical treatise by Samuel Taylor *Coleridge, published 1825. As a result of his 'Thursday classes' at Highgate, Coleridge compiled this unsystematic collection of commentaries and aphorisms on selected passages from the 17th-century Anglican Archbishop Leighton. Intended primarily as a religious guide to young men and a work of biblical scholarship, it stresses the importance of Christianity as a 'personal revelation'. Another 'main object' was to develop further his famous distinction between Reason and Understanding, originally drawn from *Kant, as the source respectively of 'Moral' and 'Prudential' action. The massive and frequently chaotic footnotes contain much fascinating literary material, such as discussions of symbolism and metaphor.

AIKEN, Conrad Potter (1889–1973) American author born in Georgia, brought up in Massachusetts, and educated at Harvard University, where he was in the class of 1911 with T. S. *Eliot. He made the first of many journeys to Europe in 1911, and lived in England for extended periods in the early 1920s and mid-1930s, writing at one time as London correspondent for the **New Yorker* as 'Samuel Jeake, Jr'. His first volume of poetry, *Earth Triumphant* (1914), was followed by many others, including *The Jig of Forslin* (1916); *Senlin: A Biography* (1918); *John Deth* (1930); and *Preludes for Memnon* (1931). His long poems, which he described as 'symphonies', show the somewhat diffused and diffuse influence of his *modernist contemporaries and friends. He also published several novels, which show a debt to James *Joyce and Sigmund *Freud, and his own desire to explore 'the fragmented ego'; these include *Blue Voyage* (1927) and *A Heart for the Gods of Mexico* (1939), both concerned with actual and metaphorical journeys. *Ushant* (1952) is a psychological autobiography, with portraits of Malcolm *Lowry and of Eliot, who appears as 'Tsetse', an illustration of Aiken's fondness for pun and verbal invention. His short stories were collected in 1960, and his criticism, *A Reviewer's ABC*, in 1958. His *Selected Letters* were published in 1978. He is the father of Joan *Aiken.

AIKEN, Joan (1924–2004) Novelist and writer of children's books, born Rye, Sussex, the daughter of Pulitzer Prize-winning author Conrad *Aiken. She wrote 92 novels, including 27 for adults, many in *Gothic and fantastic modes. Her major series, beginning with *The Wolves of Willoughby Chase* (1962), is set in an imagined 19th century in which the Stuart kings are on the throne, and the Hanoverians are pretenders—and wolves have come through the channel tunnel. Aiken's vivacious heroine, Dido Twite, first appears in

Black Hearts in Battersea (1964). She also had success with the 'Arabel and Mortimer' picture books (from 1972), illustrated by Quentin *Blake.

AIKIN, Anna Laetitia *See* BARBAULD, ANNA.

AIKIN, John (1747–1822) Physician, author, and Dissenter, and younger brother of Anna Laetitia *Barbauld, with whom he wrote the highly successful *Evenings at Home, or The Juvenile Budget Opened*, 6 vols (1792–6), for children. He was until 1806 literary editor of the **Monthly Magazine*. In 1811 Aitkin became editor of the **Annual Register*. He was a member of the coterie surrounding the radical bookseller Joseph *Johnson, the publisher of some of his works. The last decades of his life were spent in the radical and Dissenting stronghold of Stoke Newington, the home of his sister.

AINSWORTH, William Harrison (1805–82) Novelist. Born in Manchester, and educated at Manchester Free Grammar School, Ainsworth trained as a lawyer, but disliked the work. Having attempted a publishing career in London, he published his first novel, *Sir John Chiverton*, written with John Partington Aston (1805–82), anonymously in 1826: this was followed by his first success, *Rookwood* (1834, also anon.), romanticizing the career of Dick Turpin, and *Jack Sheppard* (1839), exalting the life of another highwayman. These 'Newgate' novels were satirized by W. M. *Thackeray in **Catherine* (1839–40). Meanwhile in 1837 Ainsworth had published *Crichton*, the story of a swashbuckling Scot in France. From 1840 to 1842 he edited **Bentley's Miscellany*, then from 1842 to 1853 *Ainsworth's Magazine*, and finally the **New Monthly Magazine*. He wrote 39 novels, chiefly historical; the Lancashire group, beginning with *The Lancashire Witches* (1848) and ending with *Mervyn Clitheroe* (1857), cover 400 years of northern history. Among the best known of the novels are *Jack Sheppard*, *Guy Fawkes* (1841), and *Old St Paul's* (1841). His interest in the supernatural is reflected in *Windsor Castle* (1843), which explores the legend of Herne the Hunter, and *The Lancashire Witches*. His vigorous narrative and vivid scene setting made him extremely popular, with enormous sales in the mid-century, but his popularity declined in his later years, and he is now little read.

aisling [lit. 'vision'; pronounced 'ashling'] A mode of lyrical poetry in late 17th- and 18th-century Irish in which the speaker encounters a *spéir-bhean* ('sky-woman'), a beautiful maiden representing Ireland, often suffering the advances of a lout understood to represent the Protestant English monarch. Her overseas betrothed, the Stuart Pretender, cannot defend her. Drawing on the medieval trope of the Sovereignty Goddess, the poems dramatize the collapse of the Gaelic world under the Williamite dispensation. Aisling is recalled in 19th-century popular songs like 'The Colleen Rue', in W. B. *Yeats's 'Red Hanrahan's Song about Ireland', and in poems by Ciaran *Carson and Paul *Muldoon.

AKENSIDE, Mark (1721–70) Poet, son of a Nonconformist butcher of Newcastle-upon-Tyne. He studied medicine at Edinburgh and Leiden and supported himself by literary work, the patronage of Jeremiah Dyson, and an increasingly prestigious medical practice. His influential didactic poem *The *Pleasures of Imagination* (1744) was published by Robert *Dodsley on *Pope's advice; Akenside began but did not finish a complete rewriting of the poem, from 1757. His *Odes on Several Subjects* (1745) marked an important shift in literary taste. His 'Hymn to the Naiads' (written 1746) displays much classical erudition; other poems explore the scientific theories of the *Enlightenment. Akenside also wrote notable political satire in verse. See *The Poetical Works of Mark Akenside*, ed. R. Dix (1996).

AKHMATOVA, Anna (1889–1966) Pseudonym of Anna Andreevna Gorenko, Russian poet. She was born near Odessa, but brought up in Tsarskoe Selo, outside St Petersburg. In 1903 she met the poet Nikolai *Gumilev, whom she married in 1910 and with whom she visited Paris, where she was drawn by the Italian artist Amedeo Modigliani (1884–1920). Her first poem appeared in 1907, and in 1911 she joined the Guild of Poets, the founders of Russian *Acmeism, along with Gumilev and Osip *Mandelshtam. She was divorced from Gumilev in 1918. Her collections of poetry, *Evening* (1912), *Rosary* (1914), *White Flock* (1917), *Plantain* (1921), *Anno Domini MCMXXI* (1922), won her enormous renown, but her focus on personal feelings was thought 'bourgeois' and irrelevant by the Soviet authorities. Her first volume of poetry since 1922, *From Six Books*, appeared in 1940. Her devastating cycle bearing witness to the Stalinist terror, *Requiem*, written secretly between 1935 and 1940, was published in Munich in 1963. During the war Akhmatova was able to publish her work and take part in poetry readings to great acclaim. Plans for the publication of a volume of her poetry were under way in 1946 when, in August, along with the prose writer Mikhail Zoshchenko (1895–1958), she was attacked by the Party during the post-war cultural freeze. Stalin's cultural henchman Andrei Zhdanov (1896–1948) notoriously called her poetic persona 'half-nun, half-whore', and she was expelled from the Union of Writers. From 1940 until 1965 she worked on *Poem without a Hero*, a complex analysis of her age and her relationship with it, including her significant meeting with Isaiah Berlin (1909–97) in 1945. The literary rehabilitation of Akhmatova began after the Soviet leader Khrushchev's 'secret speech' of February 1956. In 1962 she had a meeting in Leningrad with Robert *Frost, and in 1965 she visited Oxford to be awarded an honorary D.Litt. Major translations of Akhmatova's work include *Poems of Akhmatova* (trans. Stanley Kunitz and Max Hayward, 1973) and *Selected Poems* (trans. D. M. *Thomas, 2006). *The Complete Poems of Anna Akhmatova*, trans. J. Hemschemeyer and ed. R. Reeder, appeared in 1992. See Elaine *Feinstein, *Anna of All the Russias* (2005).

ALABASTER, William (1568–1640) Elizabethan theologian and Latin poet, educated at Westminster School and

Trinity College, Cambridge. Between 1588 and 1592 he produced an unfinished Latin *epic on Elizabeth I and a Latin tragedy *Roxana*. As chaplain to Robert Devereux, earl of *Essex, he took part in the Cadiz expedition, and in 1597 he became a Roman Catholic. His sonnets (first published in 1959) are among the earliest *metaphysical poems of devotion. His first major essay in mystical theology, *Apparatus in Revelationem Iesu Christi*, written in exile in the Low Countries, was declared heretical by the Catholic authorities. By 1613–14 he was again a Protestant, later becoming a doctor of divinity at Cambridge and chaplain to the king. In 1618 he married Katherine Fludd, a widow, so linking himself by marriage to the alchemist Robert *Fludd. He devoted his later years to theological studies.

ALAIN-FOURNIER (1886–1914) French novelist; born Henri Alban Fournier, he first published under the pseudonym 'Alain-Fournier' when he discovered that he shared his name with a prominent admiral and a celebrated racing driver. He was an ardent admirer of the works of Thomas *Hardy, which had a powerful influence upon him. He wrote *Le Grand Meaulnes* (1913; *The Wanderer*, 1928; *The Lost Domain*, 1959), a semi-autobiographical story of a schoolmaster's teenage son and his memories of an idealized friendship with the charismatic but irresponsible Augustin Meaulnes, who opens up his world to new possibilities and introduces him to the beautiful but elusive Yvonne de Galais. Although he had begun *Le Grand Meaulnes* as early as 1905, soon after meeting Yvonne de Quiévrecourt (with whom he fell in love, and who became the Yvonne of the novel), it was not completed until 1913, when he was back in Paris having completed his National Service. After five years of civilian life, during which he worked as a literary columnist and gave private French lessons (to a young T. S. *Eliot, among others), he was called up to fight in the First World War. He was killed in action on the Meuse in 1914. *Les Miracles*, a collection of stories and poems, was published in 1924.

À la recherche du temps perdu (*In Search of Lost Time*) A novel by Marcel *Proust, published in seven volumes between 1913 and 1927: *Du côté de chez Swann* (1913: *Swann's Way*), *À l'ombre des jeunes filles en fleurs* (1919: *Within a Budding Grove*), *Le Côté de Guermantes* (1920–1: *The Guermantes Way*), *Sodome et Gomorrhe* (1921–2: *Cities of the Plain*), *La Prisonnière* (1923: *The Captive*), *Albertine disparue* (1925: *The Sweet Cheat Gone*), and *Le Temps retrouvé* (1927: *Time Regained*). The novel's plot is circular: the narrator Marcel tells the story of his own life, which culminates in his discovering his artistic vocation, which leads him to write about his life in the very book the reader has just been reading. The dominant tone of the work is one of despair at the apparent irrecoverability of past experience and regret at the vanity of all human endeavour seen in the perspective of the destructive power of time. The search proclaimed in the novel's title is, however, vindicated by the narrator's discovery that the past is, in fact, eternally alive in the unconscious, and that it may be rescued from oblivion, either through the chance operation of sensory perception (the power of 'involuntary' memory) or through the agency of the work of art. But if the novel is fundamentally an account of an artistic vocation, it also offers a sustained analysis of a wide range of other subjects: the psychology of family relationships and of sexual relations, both homosexual and heterosexual; the fluidity that characterizes contemporary French society; and the aesthetics of the novel, music, and painting (Virigina *Woolf famously observed that if major Impressionist paintings were destroyed, they could be reconstructed from the descriptions in *À la recherche*). A definitive scholarly edition of the French text was published in the Pléiade series in 1987–9, ed. Jean-Yves Tadié. *Remembrance of Things Past* (1922–30), C. K. Scott Moncrieff's English translation of the first six volumes of Proust's novel was supplemented in 1970 by Andreas Mayor's translation of the final volume (*Time Regained*), and has since been revised by Terence Kilmartin (1981) and D. J. *Enright (1992). A new translation was published in 2003, edited by Christopher Prendergast.

Alastor A visionary poem by P. B. *Shelley, largely written in Windsor Great Park in the late summer of 1815, published 1816. 'Alastor' is a transliteration from the Greek, meaning the 'evil spirit or demon of solitude', who pursues the Poet to his death because he will not be satisfied by domestic affections and 'human sympathy'. Composed in Miltonic blank verse, laboured but sometimes translucently descriptive, the poem reflects Shelley's early wanderings: it tells how the Poet left his 'alienated home', abandoned an 'Arab maiden', and vainly pursued his vision of ideal love 'through Arabie | And Persia, and the wild Carmanian waste' until he reached a remote river in the Indian Caucasus, where he died alone, exhausted, and unfulfilled. This *rite de passage* includes the dream of a 'veilèd maid' who dances with shimmering erotic intensity (ll. 129–222). The work is closely associated with Shelley's prose essays 'On Love' and 'On Life'.

Albany (Albainn, Albin, Albania) Ancient poetic name of Gaelic origin for the northern part of Britain.

ALBEE, Edward Franklin (1928–) American playwright, associated with the Theatre of the *Absurd, whose later explorations of sexual fantasy, frustration, and domestic anguish also recall the plays of Tennessee *Williams. His works include the macabre one-act satiric comedy *The American Dream* (1961); the more naturalistic marital tragicomedy of academe *Who's Afraid of Virginia Woolf?* (1962); *Tiny Alice* (1965), a fantasy of wealth and corruption; and *A Delicate Balance* (1966), a tragicomedy set in a hard-drinking domestic environment. Later plays include *All Over* (1971), *Seascape* (1975), *The Lady from Dubuque* (1980), *The Man Who Had Three Arms* (1982), *Marriage Play* (1986), and *Three Tall Women* (perf. Vienna 1992, New York 1994), the leading character of which was based on Albee's adoptive mother. Albee is president of the Edward F. Albee Foundation, which maintains a writers' and artists' colony in New York State. Later works such as *The Goat* (2002) have included language games and word-play.

Albion An ancient name for Britain, perhaps derived from its white (Latin *albus*) cliffs. The author of *De Origine Gigantum* (1330s) claims that Albina, a Greek princess, populated the island with giant descendants (mentioned by *Geoffrey of Monmouth in *Historia Regum Britanniae*, I. 16) before Brutus renamed it. William *Blake uses Albion as a personification of England in such works as *Visions of the Daughters of Albion* (1793) and **Jerusalem*, adapting the presentation of England as a giant to his mythological purposes.

Albions England *See* WARNER, WILLIAM.

Album Amicorum An 'album of friends', the predecessor of the modern autograph album, popular from the 16th century with travelling students and scholars. Typically an entry would contain a biblical or classical motto, a personal device or coat of arms, a dedication, and an autograph. There are many examples in the British Library.

alcaics A verse form employing *quatrains with lines of 11, 11, 9, and 10 syllables. Named after the ancient Greek poet Alcaeus, the form was favoured by *Horace, and imitated in English by A. H. *Clough, A. C. *Swinburne, Alfred *Tennyson ('Milton: Experiments in Quantity'), W. H. *Auden, and Peter *Reading.

Alchemist, The A comedy by Ben *Jonson, performed by the King's Men 1610, printed 1612. Lovewit, during an epidemic of the plague, leaves his house in Blackfriars in London in charge of his servant Face, who sets up in business with Subtle, a fake alchemist, and Dol Common, a prostitute. They lure and fleece a variety of victims, including Sir Epicure Mammon, a voluptuous knight, Ananias and Tribulation Wholesome, fanatical Puritans, Dapper, a lawyer's clerk, Drugger, a tobacconist, and Kastril, a country bumpkin.

ALCOTT, Louisa May (1832–88) American author, born in Pennsylvania, the daughter of educationalist and Transcendentalist Amos Bronson Alcott (1799–1888). From an early age she published sketches, stories, etc., to help support her impractical father and family, achieving fame and financial security with **Little Women* (1868–9), based in part on childhood experiences, and its three sequels featuring Jo March. She wrote five other well-received children's books, sensational novels, melodramas, and straight adult novels, and was involved in various reform movements. There are several lives and studies including by Cheney (1889), Showalter (1988), Meigs (1993), and Keyser (1999).

ALCUIN (Albinus: English name Ealhwine) (*c.*735–804) Theologian, prolific man of letters, and the principal figure in the literary and educational programme of *Charlemagne in the 'Carolingian Renaissance'. He was born at York and educated in the cloister school there under Archbishop Egbert. At Parma in 781 he met Charlemagne, and became a member of the Frankish court. He became abbot of Tours in 796. As well as producing works of instruction in such fundamental disciplines as grammar, *rhetoric, and dialectic, he wrote liturgical, exegetical, hagiographical, philosophical, and polemical works, as well as numerous letters and poems in Latin, including an elegy on the destruction of Lindisfarne by the Danes. Although an educationalist rather than an original thinker, he was a committed opponent of heresy and influenced some continental liturgical practices. He adapted Tertullian's (b. *c.*150) words, 'What has Athens to do with Jerusalem?' in his famous question concerning heroic writing in monasteries: 'Quid Hinieldus cum Christo?' (Ingeld being a character in **Beowulf*). But his enduring legacy was the Carolingian educational curriculum and the Carolingian minuscule script developed in his writing school. See L. Wallach, *Alcuin and Charlemagne* (1959); J. Marenbon, *From the Circle of Alcuin to the School of Auxerre* (1981).

Alcyon In Edmund *Spenser's **Daphnaïda* and **Colin Clouts Come Home Againe*, is Sir Arthur *Gorges; *Daphnaïda* is an elegy on his wife's death.

ALDHELM, St (*c.*640–*c.*709) The first bishop of Sherborne (706). He was educated under *Theodore at Canterbury (*c.*671) and was a major figure in the intellectual movement led by him. He was the author of a number of Latin works which reveal a wide knowledge of classical and Christian authors. His ornate and difficult vocabulary—his *verborum garrulitas*—shows the influence of Irish models. He was abbot of Malmesbury and built churches at Sherborne (according to *William of Malmesbury), Wareham, and Bradford-on-Avon (Wiltshire). His most important work is *De Septenario, the Letter to Acircius* (i.e. Aldfrith, king of Northumbria) which contains his own Latin riddles, the *Aenigmata*. *Alfred says he was a popular vernacular poet but, as far as we know, none of this work survives. See *Aldhelmi Opera*, ed. R. Ehwald (1919).

ALDINGTON, Richard (1892–1962) Poet, novelist, and biographer, educated at Dover College and University College London, which he left without taking a degree. Early in his career he met Ezra *Pound, who introduced him to Hilda *Doolittle (known as H.D.), whom he married in 1913 (separated 1919, dissolved 1938), and Ford Madox *Ford. Aldington and H.D. worked as editors on the *imagist periodical the **Egoist* and in 1915 his first volume of poetry, *Images 1910–1915*, was published. Later volumes include *Images of War* (1919) and *A Fool i' the Forest* (1925), which shows an excessive debt to *The *Waste Land*. His *Collected Poems* were published in 1928. Aldington achieved popular success with his first novel, *Death of a Hero* (1929, abridged; Paris, 1930, unexpurgated), based on his own war experiences (he joined up in 1916). It relates the life and death, in 1918, of George Winterbourne.

The first two parts dwell on his youth and 'advanced' marriage, satirizing the complacency and frivolity of pre-war middle-class and bohemian England, and Part III is a horrifying description of life at the front in France. His subsequent novels (e.g. *The Colonel's Daughter*, 1931; *Soft Answers*, 1932; *All Men Are Enemies*, 1933) had less impact. From 1928 Aldington lived mainly abroad, in France and the United States. Of his later works the best known are his biographies, which include *Portrait of a Genius, but...*(1950), a controversial life of D. H. *Lawrence, and his even more controversial biography of T. E. *Lawrence, *Lawrence of Arabia: A Biographical Enquiry* (1955), which caused a furore through its debunking of Lawrence as an 'impudent mythomaniac'. Aldington's other works include many translations, an autobiography (*Life for Life's Sake*, 1941), and critical essays. See C. Doyle, *Richard Aldington* (1989); N. Gates, *Richard Aldington* (1992).

ALDISS, Brian W. (1925–) Novelist, poet, short story writer, and critic, born East Dereham, Norfolk. He has long championed *science fiction as a literary genre, editing many collections and anthologies and a history of the subject, *Billion Year Spree* (1973, revised, with David Wingrove, as *Trillion Year Spree*, 1986). His many works employing classic science fiction devices include *Non-Stop* (1958), *Hothouse*, (1962), and *Greybeard* (1964), but his association with the *New Wave of science fiction in the late 1960s resulted in intensification of his imaginative talents and satirical humour and a refusal to accept genre limitations. *Report on Probability A* (1968), *Barefoot in the Head* (1969), and *The Malacia Tapestry* (1976) are among the results. *Frankenstein Unbound* (1973) pays tribute to his view of Mary *Shelley's work as 'the first novel of the Scientific Revolution'. The best-selling non-science fiction *The Hand-Reared Boy* (1970) and sequels drew upon the author's military experience in India and Burma in the 1940s. The epic 'Helliconia' trilogy (1982–5) describes a planetary system in which seasons last for centuries, while *White Mars* (1999), written jointly with the mathematician Roger Penrose, explores utopian ideas. *Life in the West* (1980) and *Super-State* (2002) consider contemporary and near-future Europe. *Harm* (2007) engages with post-9/11 fears of terrorism. His short story 'Supertoys Last all Summer Long' was adapted by Stanley Kubrick for the film *A.I.: Artificial Intelligence* (2001), completed by Steven Spielberg. Collections include *Best Science Fiction Stories of Brian W. Aldiss* (1988) and *A Romance of the Equator: Best Fantasy Stories of Brian W. Aldiss* (1989). *The Twinkling of an Eye* (1998) is an autobiography; *When the Feast is Finished* (1999) is a moving reminiscence of his late wife Margaret. Collections of poetry include *At the Caligula Hotel* (1995). He received the OBE for services to literature in 2005.

ALDUS MANUTIUS (1449–1515) Scholar, printer, and publisher, born near Rome. He moved to Venice in 1490 and, after publishing his own Latin grammar (1493), in 1495 he opened his own press, which initially specialized in Greek texts, including a monumental edition of *Aristotle in five volumes. His roman and italic type, which was cut by Francesco da Bologna, and his Greek types greatly influenced the design of printers' letters. He introduced the publication of texts in octavo formats, including the works of Dante and Petrarch, and these small, inexpensive alternatives to large scholarly folios were sold in large numbers. His edition of *Erasmus' *Adages* in 1508 became a best-seller all over Europe. See M. Lowry, *The World of Aldus Manutius: Business and Scholarship in Renaissance Venice* (1979); M. Davies, *Aldus Manutius: Printer and Publisher of Renaissance Venice* (1995). *See also* Hypnerotomachia Poliphili.

ALEMBERT, Jean le Rond d' *See* Philosophes; Encyclopédie.

ALEXANDER VI *See* Borgia, Roderigo.

ALEXANDER OF HALES (*c.*1185–1245) Theologian, born in Hales (now Halesowen); he studied at Paris and taught theology there. For a short time he held various ecclesiastical appointments in England and became archdeacon of Coventry. Returning to Paris, he entered the Franciscan order and continued to teach theology, becoming the first member of this new order to hold the chair of theology there. He introduced the commentary on the *Sententiae* of *Peter Lombard to the syllabus. He began the *Summa Theologica* attributed to him, but it was completed by other Franciscans, who drew on his teachings. The work influenced the Italian-born theologian Bonaventura (1217–74). An Aristotelian, Alexander is important as evidencing a distinct Augustinian–Franciscan philosophical tradition in the first half of the 13th century. In the later Middle Ages he was called 'Doctor Irrefragabilis' (i.e. 'The Unanswerable Doctor').

ALEXANDER THE GREAT (356–323 BC) The most famous general in the classical world. Son of Philip II of Macedon and Olympias, and educated by *Aristotle, he became king of Macedon in 336 BC on the murder of his father, and in 334 he crossed the Hellespont with his army to conduct his father's planned war against Persia. Within a few years he conquered Phoenicia, Palestine, Egypt (where he founded Alexandria), and Persia, and he invaded India, where his famous horse Bucephalus died. He destroyed the Persian capital Persepolis, apparently at the instance of the courtesan Thaïs; his wives Roxana and Barsine were both Persian. He died of fever at Babylon when only 32 years old. Alexander was made the centre of a cluster of medieval legends, comparable to the cycles concerning *Charlemagne and King *Arthur. The chief romances concerning him are the great French *Roman d'Alexandre* of the 12th century and the English **King Alisaunder* of the early 14th century. The story of the rivalry of his two wives forms the subject of Nathaniel *Lee's tragedy *The *Rival Queens*.

ALEXANDER, C. F. (Cecil Frances) (1818–95) Irish hymn-writer and poet; her best-selling *Hymns for Little*

Children (1848) included 'There is a green hill far away', 'Once in royal David's city', and 'All things bright and beautiful'.

ALEXANDER, Sir William, earl of Stirling (?1567–1640) Scottish poet, courtier, and friend of *Drummond of Hawthornden, secretary of state for Scotland from 1626 until his death. His chief poetical works are a collection of songs and sonnets, *Aurora* (1604), a long poem on *Doomsday* (1614) in eight-line stanzas, and four tragedies on Darius, Croesus, Alexander, and Caesar, which are the source of some of the most striking lines in John *Webster's *The *White Devil* and *The *Duchess of Malfi*.

alexandrine A verse line of twelve syllables, which in English takes the form of an iambic *hexameter, most commonly found as the last line of the Spenserian *stanza, sometimes too as a variant line among *pentameters, and more rarely as the *metre of a whole *sonnet, as in the opening sonnet of Philip *Sidney's *Astrophel and Stella*. The line was the dominant metre of French verse from the 16th century to the 19th, taking its name from medieval French poems about Alexander the Great.

ALFIERI, Vittorio (1749–1803) Italian tragedian and poet. He gave up his own estates and, in his treatise *Della tirannide* (1777, rev. 1789: *On Tyranny*), advocated the revolutionary overthrow of all tyrannies. In another, *Del principe e delle lettere* (1778–86, rev. 1789: *On the Prince and on Letters*), he argued for the independence of writers from court patronage. Between 1775 and 1789 he wrote nineteen austerely concise tragedies on historical themes, of which the finest, *Saul* (1782), turns the king into a figure that may be compared with *Sturm und Drang* heroes. He hailed the French Revolution in the ode 'Parigi sbastigliata' (1789: 'Paris Unbastilled'), but satirized its excesses in *Il misogallo* (1793–9: *The Anti-Gaul*). His autobiography (*Vita*, 1803) is pre-Romantic both in its melancholy and in its strong-willed hatred of oppression. He was the devoted lover of the countess of Albany, wife of Charles Edward Stuart, the exiled claimant to the thrones of England, Scotland, and Ireland (the Young Pretender, or Bonnie Prince Charlie).

ALFRED (the Great) (848/9–99) King of the West Saxons from 871 to his death, important in the history of literature for the revival of letters that he effected in his southern kingdom and as the instigator of a tradition of English prose translation (though there were some Northumbrian translations of Latin before him). The systematic compilation of the *Anglo-Saxon Chronicles* began in the early 890s at Alfred's court. However, whether he actually wrote or simply authorized the English works traditionally ascribed to him is now acknowledged to be a complex and unresolved issue. A code of laws, drawing on the Mosaic and earlier English codes, was ascribed to him, as was the English translation of the *Cura Pastoralis* by *Gregory (*c.*890–6), which addresses the education of the clergy, states that there was decay of learning in England, and indicates Alfred's resolve to restore it. The translation of the *Historia Adversus Paganos* of *Orosius (*c.*890–1) also includes accounts of the celebrated voyage of the Norwegian Ohthere to the White Sea and that of the Anglian (or Danish) Wulfstan in the Baltic. The translation of *Bede's *Ecclesiastical History* includes a West Saxon version of the Hymn of *Cædmon. There is no evidence that the free translation of the *De Consolatione Philosophiae* of *Boethius, with some additions drawn from exegetes such as Remigius of Auxerre, was composed in Alfred's lifetime. The only claim that he translated the loose West Saxon version of *Augustine's *Soliloquia* appears in a 12th-century manuscript. Nevertheless, while the existence of some or all of these works may owe less to Alfred's authorship than to his regal authority, important for a pioneering and not uncontroversial vernacular translation project, they constitute a remarkable corpus of English writings that appropriate the original materials in ways that illuminate the priorities of their intended English readerships. See *Alfred the Great*, ed. S. Keynes and M. Lapidge (1983).

ALGER, Horatio, Jr (1832–99) American novelist, whose improving tales targeted the hopes of young male readers. Born in Chelsea (now Revere), Massachusetts, and educated in the Gates Academy in Marlborough, Massachusetts, and Harvard University, Alger was the son of a minister and had a religious upbringing before he moved to New York and turned his attention to the city poor. He published over 100 novels with titles like *Ragged Dick* (1868) and *From Canal Boy to President* (1881), many of which became best-sellers. His fiction promoted the belief that success can be attained with courage and determination. The 1928 biography by Herbert R. Mayes is largely fictional, based on bogus material.

ALGREN, Nelson (1909–61) American novelist, writer of short stories, and journalist, best known for his descriptions of the dispossessed of Chicago. Algren's first novel, *Somebody in Boots* (1935), describes the homeless of the Depression and in that same period he participated in the WPA (Works Progress Administration). *Never Come Morning* (1942) grew out of Algren's reportage on boxing, but he achieved real fame with his account of the Chicago drugs sub-culture, *The Man with the Golden Arm* (1949). Algren constantly questioned American notions of prosperity and success, focusing in his fiction on the underdogs of the cities. Thus *A Walk on the Wild Side* (1956) takes place largely in a New Orleans brothel. In *Chicago: City on the Make* (1951) he attacked corruption, and he sub-titled *Who Lost an American?* (1963), a collection of travel essays, as *Being a Guide to the Seamier Sides of New York City, Inner London, Paris, Dublin, Barcelona, Seville, Almeria, Istanbul, Crete and Chicago, Illinois*.

ALI, Monica (1967–) Novelist, born in Bangladesh and raised in Bolton, Greater Manchester; she read PPE (philosophy, politics, and economics) at Wadham College, Oxford. Her debut novel, *Brick Lane* (2003), documents the experiences of a young woman from Bangladesh who moves, after an arranged marriage to an older man, to the Bangladeshi community of London's Tower Hamlets (members of which community denounced the novel and strongly opposed the filming of it). *Alentejo Blue* (2006), less a novel than a collection of loosely linked short stories, is set in a village in southern Portugal.

Alice's Adventures in Wonderland (1865) By 'Lewis Carroll' (*see* DODGSON, CHARLES). Possibly the most famous and most-analysed children's book, it was first written as a present for the young Alice Liddell in 1864 (facsimile, *Alice's Adventures Underground*, 1886) and expanded, with illustrations by *Tenniel. Alice's episodic journey through Wonderland involves characters who have become deeply embedded in English culture, notably the White Rabbit, the Cheshire Cat, the Mad Hatter, and the Mock Turtle, and contains parodies of the verse of Isaac *Watts, Jane *Taylor, Robert *Southey, and others. Commonly seen as a landmark *'nonsense' text, liberating children from didactic fiction, it has been interpreted as a complex political satire, a commentary on Victorian girlhood, and an exploration of death, sexuality, drugs, and nihilism. Carroll wrote an equally complex sequel, **Through the Looking-Glass and What Alice Found There* (1871), in which the dreaming Alice walks through the looking-glass where she finds that the pieces from her chess set are alive and inhabit a landscape modelled on a chess board. Many famous characters, passages, and incidents associated with Alice are found in *Looking-Glass* including Tweedledum and Tweedledee, Humpty Dumpty, the Walrus and the Carpenter, and 'Jabberwocky'. In performance the two books are often combined. In 1890 Carroll produced the shorter, sentimentalized *The Nursery 'Alice'* for younger readers. See Martin Gardner's *The Annotated Alice* (2000).

alienation effect A term (from the German *Verfremdungseffekt*) used to describe attempts by author or director to prevent the reader or audience from identifying with, trusting, or taking for granted what is happening in the text or on stage: such devices can include narrative interventions, disruptions of mood and sequence, and introduction of non-realistic effects. Bertolt *Brecht was the most celebrated exponent of the technique, and first treats of it in detail in his essay 'Alienation Effects in Chinese Acting' (1936), but it has been very widely adopted.

ALISON, Archibald (1757–1839) Scottish episcopalian clergyman and aesthetician, born in Edinburgh and educated at Glasgow University and Balliol College, Oxford. He was the father of the historian and legal writer Sir Archibald Alison (1792–1867). In *Essays on the Nature and Principles of Taste* (1790; enl. 1811), a study of the role of the imagination and of the association of ideas in aesthetic perception, Alison claimed that poetry and drama are distinguished by their capacity to present a 'unity of character or expression', and condemned the appeal to mixed emotions in tragicomedy. He thus thought *Corneille a sounder dramatist than Shakespeare. *Essays* impressed Robert *Burns, and influenced Francis *Jeffrey and Walter *Scott.

allegory A kind of narrative or description that carries partially veiled meanings behind its actions and cast of characters, as for example when a dialogue between animals covertly echoes contemporary political conflicts, George Orwell's fable **Animal Farm* offering a well-known modern case. Allegorical works can be understood as systematically extended *metaphors, typically employing *personification of abstract qualities to establish legible correspondences between the overt action and the covert set of parallel meanings. Allegorical writing flourished especially in the later Middle Ages, in such works as **Piers Plowman* and the morality play **Everyman*, but is often found thereafter, notably in Edmund Spenser's *The *Faerie Queene*, in John Bunyan's *The *Pilgrim's Progress*, and in John Dryden's political allegory **Absalom and Achitophel*. Enigmatic suggestions of allegorical meaning are exploited teasingly in the novels and tales of Nathaniel *Hawthorne and Herman *Melville, as they are in the 20th century in the fiction of T. F. *Powys and of Muriel *Spark, among others.

ALLEN, Grant (Charles Grant Blairfindie) (1848–99) Science writer and novelist, born in Canada, educated in America, France, and at Merton College, Oxford. In 1873 he went to Queen's College, Jamaica, as professor of mental and moral philosophy, where his agnosticism and socialism led to the formulation of an evolutionary system of philosophy based on the works of Herbert *Spencer and Charles *Darwin. On his return to England in 1876 he published *Physiological Aesthetics* (1877), which introduced his name to the leaders of thought in London, and he was soon contributing articles on popular scientific and other subjects to the **Cornhill Magazine* and other journals. Next came *The Colour-Sense* (1879), which won praise from Alfred Russel *Wallace, Darwin, and Thomas Henry *Huxley. He began writing fiction, at first with stories for **Belgravia*, later collected as *Strange Stories* (1884). His first novel, *Philista* (1884), was followed by nearly 30 works of fiction including his best-selling *The Woman Who Did* (1895), intended as a protest against the subjection of women. It is the tale of a woman of advanced views who believes that marriage is a barbarous institution, incompatible with the emancipation of women; she lives with the man she loves, bears his child, but is left alone, when he inconveniently dies, to endure the consequent social ostracism. The novel attracted the criticism of both progressive and conservative circles. Millicent Garrett Fawcett and other feminists condemned its author as 'not a friend but an enemy' of the movement, and Victoria Crosse published *The Woman Who Didn't* (1895) in response. Allen was also a pioneer in *science fiction, notably in his novel on time travel, *The British Barbarians* (1895), and in crime writing, creating an engaging anti-hero in his conman and master of disguise Colonel Clay (*An African Millionaire*, 1897).

ALLEN, Ralph (1693–1764) Self-made businessman whose fortune was made in the postal service and other enterprises such as the supply of building stone for Bath and London. He was a friend of *Pope, who advised him on gardening and praised his covert philanthropy in the *Epilogue to the Satires*. Pope's friend William *Warburton married Allen's niece. Allen assisted Henry *Fielding, who portrayed him as Squire Allworthy in *Tom Jones* and dedicated *Amelia* to him. Allen provided for the education of Fielding's children. Samuel *Richardson, William Pitt the elder (1708–78), and Mary *Delany were among his friends. See B. Boyce, *The Benevolent Man* (1967).

ALLEN, Cardinal William (1532–94) Educated at Oriel College, he left Oxford in 1561 and was instrumental in the founding of seminaries for the training of Roman Catholic missionaries at Douai and Rome (where life at the English College is vividly described by Anthony *Munday in *The English Roman Life*, 1582), and Valladolid. As well as his own controversial writings he inspired and was involved in the translation of the Douai–Rheims Bible (1582–1609/10), for long the traditional Roman Catholic version of the Scriptures in the vernacular.

ALLENDE, Isabel (1942–) Best-selling Chilean writer born in Lima (Peru). Initially a journalist, she maintains that Pablo *Neruda encouraged her to write fiction. After Pinochet's 1973 military coup, she fled to Venezuela where she wrote her first and most famous novel, *La casa de los espíritus* (1982: *The House of the Spirits*), a family saga that explores four generations of women in a style that develops from *magical to brutal realism and incorporates her interests in Chilean politics and history from a feminist viewpoint. In the same vein she wrote *De amor y de sombra* (1984: *Of Love and Shadows*) and *Eva Luna* (1987). *El plan infinito* (1991: *The Infinite Plan*) is a New Age novel set in California, where she now lives (American citizenship 2003). Allende wrote movingly about the death of her daughter (*Paula*, 1994). Her prolific output includes historical romances, a memoir, and a trilogy for children. Her energetic, humane, and often humorous works combine popular appeal with a reflection upon writing. Her *Mi país inventado* (2003: *My Invented Country*) provides a good introduction to her work.

ALLESTREE, Richard (*fl.* 1617–43) *See* ALMANACS.

ALLESTREE, Richard (1619–81) *See* WHOLE DUTY OF MAN, THE.

ALLEYN, Edward (1566–1626) Actor (Richard *Burbage's chief rival) and partner of Philip *Henslowe, with whom he built the Fortune Theatre, Cripplegate. There he acted at the head of the Lord Admiral's Company, playing among other parts the leading roles in Christopher *Marlowe's *Tamburlaine*, *The *Jew of Malta*, and **Dr Faustus*. He acquired great wealth, bought the manor of Dulwich, and built and endowed Dulwich College. His first wife was Henslowe's stepdaughter, his second the daughter of John *Donne. He was a patron of Thomas *Dekker, John *Taylor (the 'water poet'), and other writers.

All for Love, *or The World Well Lost* A tragedy by John *Dryden produced and published 1678. Written in blank verse in acknowledged imitation of *Shakespeare's **Antony and Cleopatra*, it is Dryden's most performed and his best-known play. It concentrates on the last hours in the lives of its hero and heroine. In contrast to Shakespeare's play, it is an exemplary *neo-classical tragedy, notable for its elaborately formal presentation of character, action, and theme.

ALLIBONE, S. A. *See* CRITICAL DICTIONARY OF ENGLISH LITERATURE.

ALLINGHAM, Margery (1904–66) Short story writer, journalist, and novelist, born in London and educated at Endsleigh House School, Colchester, the Perse School, Cambridge, and the Regent Street Polytechnic, London. She introduced her aristocratic and deceptively vacuous detective hero Albert Campion in *The Crime at Black Dudley* (1929). Campion, along with his manservant Lugg and Charlie Luke of Scotland Yard, reappeared in many of her best-known works including *Flowers for the Judge* (1936), *More Work for the Undertaker* (1949), *The Tiger in the Smoke* (1952), and *The Beckoning Lady* (1955). Atmospheric, intelligent, and observant, her works have maintained their popularity despite their strong period flavour. See J. Thorogood, *Margery Allingham: A Biography* (1991). *See also* DETECTIVE FICTION.

ALLINGHAM, William (1824–89) Poet, diarist, and anthologist, born in Co. Donegal. He worked as a customs officer, first in Ireland, then in England, where he settled in 1863. His friends in the literary world included Coventry *Patmore, Thomas *Carlyle, D. G. *Rossetti, and Alfred *Tennyson. Allingham's diary, published in 1907, covers four decades and includes many accounts of Victorian literary culture. His first volume, *Poems* (1850), contains his best-known work 'The Fairies' ('Up the airy mountain'); it was followed by several others, including the long poem *Laurence Bloomfield in Ireland* (1864) and various collections and anthologies of verse for children, some with illustrations by Rossetti, John Everett *Millais, Kate *Greenaway, and his wife Helen (née Paterson; 1848–1926), who was a distinguished watercolourist.

All is True *See* HENRY VIII.

alliteration The repetition within the same phrase or line of similar consonantal sounds, most commonly at initial positions within neighbouring words or stressed syllables in poetry:

> Landscape-lover, lord of language.
> (Alfred *Tennyson)

Such effects were essential to the Old English and Middle English verse traditions that we refer to as *alliterative verse, in which vowel sounds could also be deemed to alliterate; but they subsequently became incidental or decorative devices. Alliteration may also be found in prose writing, especially in elaborately heightened styles such as that of John *Lyly.

alliterative prose A tradition of Old and Middle English prose elevated in style by the employment of some of the techniques of *alliterative verse. Its most distinguished exponents are *Ælfric and *Wulfstan in Old English, and the writers of the *Katherine Group in Middle English. R. W. *Chambers, in his essay 'On the Continuity of English Prose from Alfred to More' (1932), saw this alliterative thread as a common factor in English writing from Old English to the Renaissance.

Alliterative Revival A collective term for the group of alliterative poems written in the second half of the 14th century in which *alliteration, which had been the formal basis of Old English poetry, was again used in poetry of the first importance (such as *Piers Plowman* and *Sir *Gawain and the Green Knight*) as a serious alternative to the continental form, syllabic rhyming verse. Three views have been advanced to account for its emergence: (1) that it was a conscious return to traditional forms as politics became again more English than French, a nationalist movement like the attempted modern linguistic revivals in Wales or Ireland; (2) that it was merely a resurfacing of literature which had continued throughout the period since the Conquest but had not been officially published; (3) that it was a straightforward development of the loose alliterative poetry of the previous century which the new movement only enhanced. The last view, argued by Thorlac Turville Petre (*The Alliterative Revival*, 1977), is now thought the most persuasive. As well as their common formal elements, many of the poems are linked by a serious interest in contemporary politics and ethics (**Wynnere and Wastour, Death and Liffe, The Parlement of the Three Ages, Piers Plowman*).

alliterative verse The native Germanic tradition of English poetry and the standard form in Old English up to the 11th century, recurring in Middle English as a formal alternative to the syllable-counting, rhymed verse borrowed from French (*see* ALLITERATIVE REVIVAL). The Old English line was (normally) unrhymed, and made up of two distinct half-lines each of which contained two stressed syllables. The *alliteration was always on the first stress of the second half-line, which alliterated with either, or both, of the stresses in the first half-line; e.g.

x x x
Nāp nihtscūa, norþan snīwde

(**The Seafarer*, 31: The shade of night grew dark, it snowed from the north.)

In Middle English, even among the poets of the Revival, the alliterative rules were much less strict, although the alliteration was often very dense: 'I have lyved in londe', quod I, 'My name is Longe Wille'. (**Piers Plowman* B XV. 152) Nothing after Middle English could categorically be said to be 'alliterative verse', despite its recurrent use as a device throughout English poetry, except perhaps for the rather self-conscious revival of the form in the 20th century by such poets as W. H. *Auden and Cecil *Day-Lewis.

ALLNUTT, Gillian (1949–) British poet. Allnutt was born in London, educated at Cambridge and Sussex universities, but spent much of her childhood in the north-east of England, where she returned to live in the late 1980s. During her time in London she was a member of the collective Sheba Feminist Publishers, and the poetry editor of *City Limits*. Allnutt was initially best known as a feminist poet. While her interest in women's issues and gender has continued, her preoccupations, though always philosophical, have become increasingly spiritual. The dramatized voices and accumulating imagery of Allnutt's later work constitute a refashioning of biblical language, reminiscent in their intensity not only of Christopher *Smart but of her contemporary Selima *Hill. Her collections include *Spitting the Pips Out* (1981); *Beginning the Avocado* (1987); *Blackthorn* (1994); *Nantucket and the Angel* (1997); *Lintel* (2001); *Sojourner* (2004); and *How the Bicycle Shone: New and Selected Poems* (2007).

All Quiet on the Western Front *See* REMARQUE, ERICH.

All's Lost by Lust A tragedy by William *Rowley, acted by the Prince's Men *c.*1619, printed 1633. The story, taken from a legendary episode in Spanish history, concerns Roderick, king of Spain, his general Julianus, and Julianus' daughter Jacinta, who is raped by Roderick and later mutilated and murdered, along with her father, by Roderick's Moorish successor. The play remained popular throughout the 17th century, and was twice adapted during the Restoration. The story is also the subject of W. S. *Landor's *Count Julian* (1812) and Robert *Southey's *Roderick* (1814).

All's Well That Ends Well A comedy by *Shakespeare, first printed in the first *folio of 1623. It used to be thought to be the play referred to by Francis *Meres as *Love's Labour's Won*, which would mean that it was written before 1598; but it is now more usually dated 1606–7. Like **Measure for Measure* it is often classified as a 'tragicomedy' or 'problem comedy'.

Its chief source is Boccaccio's **Decameron* (Day 3, Tale 9), which Shakespeare may have read either in the translation by William *Painter, or in the French version by Antoine le Maçon. Bertram, the young count of Roussillon, on the death of his father is summoned to the court of the king of France, leaving his mother and with her Helena, daughter of the famous physician Gerard de Narbonne. The king is sick of a disease said to be incurable. Helena, who loves Bertram, goes to Paris and effects his cure by means of a prescription left by her father. As a reward she is allowed to choose her husband and names Bertram, who unwillingly obeys the king's order to wed her. But under the influence of the braggart Paroles, he at once takes service with the duke of Florence, writing to Helena that until she can get the ring from his finger 'which never shall come off', and is with child by him, she may not call him husband. Helena, passing through Florence on a pilgrimage, finds Bertram courting Diana, the daughter of her hostess there. Disclosing herself as his wife to them, she obtains permission to replace Diana at a midnight assignation with Bertram, having that day caused him to be informed that Helena is dead. Thereby she obtains from Bertram his ring, and gives him one that the king had given her. Bertram returns to his mother's house, where the king is on a visit. The latter sees on Bertram's finger the ring that he had given Helena, suspects Bertram of having destroyed her, and demands an explanation on pain of death. Helena appears, explains what has happened, and claims that the conditions named in Bertram's letter have been fulfilled. Bertram, filled with remorse, accepts her as his wife. Often heavily adapted in earlier times, the play has risen in esteem since the middle of the 20th century, largely as the result of some notable productions.

All the Year Round *See* HOUSEHOLD WORDS.

almanacs were, technically, tables of astronomical and astrological events of the coming year, and as such had existed since antiquity; with the advent of printing they proliferated, and by the 17th century in England were the most popular literary form, containing a wide range of material, from feast days, farming notes, tables of interest, to scurrilous verses and wild and colourful prophecies. They flourished particularly strongly from 1640 to 1700, when they engaged in political, social, and religious controversy, playing an active part in the ferment of the times. Well-known publishers and compilers of almanacs included Richard Allestree (active between 1617 and 1643, Derby and Coventry); the most famous of all, William *Lilly; John Gadbury (1627–1704), astrologer and physician; John Partridge (1644–1715), who published almanacs from 1678; and Francis Moore (1657–1714?), the original *Old Moore. In the 18th century growing scepticism and a declining interest in astrology led to a loss of vitality in the form, although Old Moore continued to be bought by the less educated classes in vast quantities, and still sells well today, as does the more prosaic reference book *Whitaker's Almanack* (*see* WHITAKER, JOSEPH). See Bernard Capp, *Astrology and the Popular Press: English Almanacs 1500–1800* (1979); Keith Thomas, *Religion and the Decline of Magic* (1971).

ALMOND, David (1951–) Born in Newcastle-upon-Tyne, educated at the University of East Anglia and Newcastle Polytechnic, best known for his children's books. These are set in the north-east of England, indebted to William *Blake, and incorporate *magic realist elements. Skellig (*Skellig*, 1998) is part tramp, part angel; in *Kit's Wilderness* (1999), the stories Kit writes inexplicably connect him to the past of the village to which he has moved; *The Fire-Eaters* (2003), set during the Cuban Missile Crisis, features a strange fire-eating performer, while *Clay* (2005) concerns a golem, a creature made from clay, and explores Almond's Catholic boyhood. *My Dad's a Birdman* (2007), a book for younger readers, treats mental disorder and its consequences with a life-affirming playfulness, while *The Savage* (2008) is a dark exploration of death and renewal.

A.L.O.E. (A Lady of England) Pen-name of Charlotte Maria Tucker (1821–93), writer and Indian missionary, born in Barnet, Middlesex, educated at home. Tucker's many novels were evangelical and didactic but entertaining, and popular in her day. *Rambles of a Rat* (1857) is typical: it sympathetically portrays the adventures of two likeable rats. Her writing encompassed anthropomorphic *allegories, *fables, and traditional Indian stories retold for British children and translated into Indian dialects. There is a life by Agnes Giberne (1895).

alternate history A sub-genre of *science fiction which developed partly under the influence of historical 'counterfactuals' such as those collected by J. C. Squire in *If It had Happened Otherwise* (1931), partly through the 'many worlds' theory devised by the physicist Hugh Everett in 1957 (although many stories, such as Murray Leinster's 'Sidewise in Time' (1934) pre-date this). Alternate histories often spring from a point of departure—the 'Jonbar point' after a world so named in Jack *Williamson's *The Legion of Time* (1938) to (for example) reverse the outcomes of the American Civil War (Ward *Moore) or the Second World War (Philip K. *Dick). The latter outcome is common in non-science fiction examples such as those by Len *Deighton or Robert *Harris. Alternates also arise through technological development, as in *The Difference Engine* by William *Gibson and Bruce *Sterling where the form's playful aspect is shown by the different roles played by characters like Benjamin *Disraeli. Kim Stanley *Robinson's *The Years of Rice and Salt* removes Europe from world history while Christopher *Priest's *The Separation* blends historical and personal branching of time-tracks. Philip *Roth's *The Plot against America* (2004) imagines an alternate history in a 1940s USA shadowed by anti-Semitism. Fantasies, like those by Diana Wynne *Jones, Philip *Pullman, and Susanna *Clarke, often present worlds that are alternate or parallel to our own.

ALTHER, Lisa (1944–) American novelist, short story writer, and magazine journalist, born in Tennessee. Her first novel *Kinflicks* (1976) humorously describes the escapades of a young woman negotiating the gender stereotypes of her time and was enthusiastically endorsed by Doris *Lessing. Although she moved away from the South, Alther has explained that the anecdotal style of conversation in the region helped form her style. Like her first novel, *Other Women* (1984), *Bedrock* (1990), and *Five Minutes to Heaven* (1995) trace out the experiences and mishaps of their female protagonists, all informed by Alther's wry humour. *Kinfolks* (2007) is an attempt by Alther to explore her family ancestry.

Alton Locke, Tailor and Poet: *An Autobiography* A novel by Charles *Kingsley, published 1850. Alton Locke, son of a small London tradesman and educated by a widowed

Baptist mother, is apprenticed to a tailor in whose sweatshop he experiences at first hand the miseries of the working classes and becomes imbued with the ideas of *Chartism. The material used in this section was first used by Kingsley in his polemical pamphlet *Cheap Clothes and Nasty*, on abuses within the clothing industry, published earlier the same year. Locke's gift for poetry gains him the friendship first of an old Scottish bookseller, Sandy Mackaye (partly modelled on Thomas *Carlyle), and then of a benevolent dean, his daughter Lillian (with whom he falls in love), and her cousin Eleanor. Under their influence he consents to the emasculation of his revolutionary poems before publication, a weakness he bitterly regrets. Roused by the taunts of his Chartist comrades, he undertakes a mission that involves him in a riot and is jailed for three years. On emerging, he learns that Lillian is engaged to his prosperous time-serving cousin. He falls ill (and during his fever undergoes an interesting evolutionary dream, seeing himself transformed from a group of polyps through higher forms of life to man) and is nursed by Eleanor, who converts him from Chartism to Christian Socialism. He emigrates to America and dies on the voyage. Despite its propagandist stridency, *Alton Locke* is a powerful social document, and had an impact similar to that of Benjamin *Disraeli's **Sybil* and Elizabeth *Gaskell's **Mary Barton*, the latter of which Kingsley much admired.

ALVAREZ, A. (Alfred) (1929–) Poet and critic, born in London, and educated at Oundle and Oxford. His works include *The Shaping Spirit* (1958), a study of modern poetry, and *The Savage God: A Study of Suicide* (1971), which contains an account of the death of Sylvia *Plath, whose work he published as poetry editor of the **Observer*. He edited an anthology of verse, *The New Poetry* (1962, featuring work by John *Berryman, Robert *Lowell, and Ted *Hughes), which included an influential introductory essay, 'Beyond the Gentility Principle'. He has also written on subjects as diverse as poker playing, mountain climbing, the oil industry, and divorce. His autobiography, *Where Did It All Go Right?*, appeared in 1999 and *New and Selected Poems* in 2002.

Amadis of Gaul (*Amadís de Gaula*) A Spanish or Portuguese romance, written in the form in which we have it by Garci Rodríguez de Montalvo in the second half of the 15th and printed early in the 16th century, but taken from 'ancient originals' now lost, perhaps by João de Lobeira (1261–1325) or by Vasco de Lobeira (d. 1403), the materials of the story being of French origin. Many continuations were written relating to the son and nephew of Amadis, Esplandian and Florisando. Perion, king of Gaul, falls in love with Elisena, daughter of Garinter, king of Lesser Britain; their child Amadis is cast away in a box on a river, and later washed ashore and reared by Gandales of Scotland. Until his identity is revealed he is known as 'The Child of the Sea'. He becomes the flower of chivalry, achieves wonderful feats of arms, and is often aided by the enchantress Urganda. He loves Oriana, daughter of Lisuarte, king of Great Britain, who is sought in marriage by the emperor of Rome and granted to him by her father, but rescued by Amadis. This provokes the emperor to attack with his fleet, but he is defeated and killed. Amadis then comes to the succour of Lisuarte, reconciliation follows, and all ends happily. The romance was translated into French by Herberay des Essarts in 1540, into English by Anthony *Munday (*c.*1590–1619), and an abridged version by Robert *Southey appeared in 1803. Translations of the romance's continuations appeared in the intervening years, and it remained a popular reference point in English poetry, prose, and drama into the 19th century. *Amadis of Gaul* and **Palmerin of England* were two of the works excepted from the holocaust of romances of chivalry in **Don Quixote* (I. 6). See John J. O'Connor, *Amadis de Gaule and its Influence on Elizabethan Literature* (1970); *Amadis de Gaule*, trans. Anthony Munday, ed. Helen Moore (2004).

Amadis of Greece A Spanish continuation of the seventh book of **Amadis of Gaul*, of which Lisuarte of Greece, the grandson of Amadis, is the hero. The work is by Feliciano de *Silva.

Amaryllis The name given to a shepherdess by *Theocritus, *Virgil, and *Ovid. Edmund *Spenser, in **Colin Clouts Come Home Againe*, uses the name to signify Alice (1559–1637), one of the daughters of Sir John Spencer of Althorp. She became the countess of Derby, for whom John *Milton wrote **Arcades*.

Amaurote or 'shadow city'. The capital of Sir Thomas *More's **Utopia*. *Rabelais (*La vie de Gargantua et de Pantagruel* II. xxiii) uses the name 'Amaurotes' for an imaginary people invaded by the Dipsodes.

Amazing Marriage, The A novel by George *Meredith, published 1895. Written in Meredith's opaque late manner, it is a vigorous exploration of the battle between the sexes, conducted on a very public stage amidst much gossip (Dame Gossip being one of the narrators). The marriage in question is that of the wild, courageous, and headstrong Carinthia, brought up in the Austrian mountains and left almost destitute on the death of her legendary father, the 'Old Buccaneer'. She marries Lord Fleetwood, wealthy and arrogant, who proposes to her impulsively at a dance and is held to his promise. He dramatically abandons her on the wedding night, and the novel describes their struggle for dominion within the marriage and her eventual triumph. Gower Woodseer, who is a friend to both parties and serves as go-between, is based on Robert Louis *Stevenson.

Amazing Stories (1926–94; 2004–6) Was the first *science fiction magazine. Created by Hugo *Gernsback, who lost control of it in 1929, *Amazing* popularized 'scientifiction' as inspirational and educational, emphasizing reprints by Jules *Verne and H. G. *Wells. With a stable of newer writers, *Amazing* developed an audience among fans of action-adventure space opera. During its long life its quality varied. Although adventurous material was published in the 1960s by Ursula K. *Le Guin and others, its last two decades saw erratic publication and a declining audience.

Ambassadors, The A novel by Henry *James, published 1903. This is one of the novels in which, with humour and delicacy of perception, James depicts the reaction of different American types to the European environment. Chadwick Newsome, the son of an overpowering Massachusetts widow, has been living in Paris and is reported to have entangled himself with a wicked woman. Mrs Newsome has decided to send out an ambassador to rescue Chad in the person of the elderly, amiable, guileless Lambert Strether. The story describes Strether's evolution in the congenial atmosphere of Paris, his desertion to the side of Chad and the bewitching comtesse de Vionnet, and his own mild flirtation with the pleasant cosmopolitan Maria Gostrey. An accident throws Strether unexpectedly into the company of Chad and Madame de Vionnet in circumstances which leave no doubt as to the nature of their real relations. Sadly disillusioned, but still insisting on the necessity of Chad's loyalty to Madame de Vionnet, Strether from a sense of duty turns his back on Paris.

Ambit A literary quarterly founded in 1959 by Martin Bax. Other editors have included J. G. *Ballard and Carol Ann *Duffy. It has published, among others, Peter *Porter, Edwin *Morgan, Fleur *Adcock, Gavin *Ewart, and Ruth *Fainlight. It is well known for its live readings in pubs and bookshops.

AMBLER, Eric (1909–98) Writer of thrillers, *spy fiction, and screenplays. His many works of fiction include *The Dark Frontier* (1936), *Uncommon Danger* (1937), *Epitaph for a Spy* (1938), *Cause for Alarm* (1938), *The Mask of Dimitrios* (1939), *Journey into Fear* (1940), *The October Man* (1948), *Judgement on Deltcher* (1951), *The Schirmer Inheritance* (1953), *Passage of Arms* (1959), *Dr Frigo* (1974), *Send No More Roses* (1977), and *The Care of Time* (1981). An edited volume, *To Catch a Spy: An Anthology of Favourite Spy Stories*, was published in 1964. *Here Lies: An Autobiography* appeared in 1985. *The Story So Far*, a collection of stories previously unpublished in book form together with reminiscences, was published in 1993.

Ambrose's Tavern The scene of the **Noctes Ambrosianae* published in **Blackwood's Magazine* from 1822 to 1835, is loosely based on a real Edinburgh tavern of the same name, first described by John *Lockhart in *Peter's Letters to his Kinsfolk* (1819).

Amelia A novel by Henry *Fielding, published 1752 (for 1751). **Joseph Andrews* and **Tom Jones* end with the title characters about to embark on married life; in *Amelia* Captain and Mrs Booth have already enjoyed some years together, and the book is much concerned with tenderness and family happiness. Amelia, loving, forgiving, yet strong and spirited, is a portrait of Fielding's wife Charlotte, who died in 1744, and Billy Booth has something of Fielding's own character, although Booth lacks Fielding's industry. Set in a London of pervasive squalor and violence, it opens in the court of Justice Thrasher, who throws the innocent Booth into Newgate because he cannot bribe his way out of trouble. In the filthy and corrupt prison Booth meets an old acquaintance, Miss Matthews, a courtesan who has the means to buy a clean cell which Booth guiltily shares with her. Colonel James, a distant connection, bails out Booth, and takes Miss Matthews as his mistress. Booth solicits an army commission, meanwhile wasting his half-pay on gambling: but even when Booth fails to return for her frugal but lovingly prepared meal of hashed mutton, Amelia does not upbraid him. Matters take a more sinister turn when 'My Lord', a flamboyant and menacing character who is never named, plots, with James, to ensnare Amelia. The Booths' landlady (secretly My Lord's procuress) arranges for Amelia to be attended at an oratorio by My Lord in disguise. My Lord affably offers to acquire a command for Booth, and showers presents on Amelia's adored children. Amelia is invited to a masquerade, but is warned off by a fellow lodger, the learned widow Mrs Bennet, whom My Lord once seduced by similar means. After more dangers and complications, their protector, the good clergyman Dr Harrison, pays off Booth's debts. Amelia discovers that she is heiress to her mother's fortune, and the Booths retire to a prosperous country life. The book sold well, and Samuel *Johnson read it through at an overnight sitting. Samuel *Richardson and Tobias *Smollett attacked it, but Fielding defended it in his *Covent-Garden Journal* (25 and 28 January 1752); it was his own favourite work.

American Democrat, The, *or Hints on the Social and Civic Relation of the United States of America* By James Fenimore *Cooper, published 1838. In this vigorous work, Cooper examined and set forth, to the offence of his countrymen, the defects and dangers of democracy as it flourished in America.

American dream A phrase popularized by James Truslow Adams (1878–1949) in his 1931 study *The Epic of America*, which expressed the conviction that in America every individual had the opportunity for self-fulfilment regardless of their birth or position. The phrase is used ironically in Edward *Albee's *The American Dream* (1961) and Norman *Mailer's *An American Dream* (1965).

American Senator, The A novel by Anthony *Trollope, published 1877. Elias Gotobed, senator for the fictional state of Mickewa, comes to England on a fact-finding tour, and finds 'irrational and salutary' English manners and customs more than he can understand. In this quiet exposition of country life in and around the town of Dillsborough, two stories of courtship are highlighted. The first is a conventional Trollopean love-triangle, in which Mary Masters prefers her childhood sweetheart Reginald Morton to a neighbouring gentleman-farmer, Larry Twentyman. The second deals with Arabella Trefoil's cynical pursuit of Lord Rufford, despite a prior engagement to Reginald's cousin John. Arabella's story highlights Trollope's dislike of the Victorian marriage market, and she emerges as both pitiable and grotesque in her hunt for a wealthy husband.

AMIEL, Henri-Frédéric (1821–81) Swiss poet and critic, author of a remarkable diary, *Journal intime*, extracts from which were first published in 1883 and translated by Mary Augusta *Ward in 1885. A complete critical edition in twelve volumes has been published (1976–94).

Aminta *See* TASSO, TORQUATO.

AMIS, Sir Kingsley (1922–95) Novelist and poet, born in south London, educated at the City of London School and St John's College, Oxford; he lectured in Swansea, then at Cambridge (1949–63). Beginning his literary career with two volumes of poetry, *Bright November* (1947) and *A Frame of Mind* (1953), he achieved popular success with his first novel, *Lucky Jim* (1954), whose hero, lower-middle-class lecturer Jim Dixon, with his subversive attitudes (anti-establishment, anti-pretension, anti-arts-and-crafts), was hailed as an *'Angry Young Man'. Its setting in a provincial university was also indicative of a new development in fiction (see William *Cooper, Philip *Larkin, John *Braine), something Amis confirmed with *That Uncertain Feeling* (1955) and *Take a Girl Like You* (1960). *I Like It Here* (1958), a slight, xenophobic novel set in Portugal, displays his deliberate cultivation, for comic effect, of a prejudiced and philistine pose which was to harden into an increasingly conservative and hostile view of contemporary life and manners. His subsequent work shows considerable versatility; although best known for satiric comedy (*One Fat Englishman*, 1963, set in America; *Ending up*, 1974, a savage study of old age; *Jake's Thing*, 1978, a dissertation on middle-aged impotence), he successfully attempted many other genres. *The Green Man* (1969) is a novel of the supernatural, *The Riverside Villas Murder* (1973) an imitation of a classic detective story, *The Alteration* (1976) an exercise in *alternate history. Amis's enthusiasm for Ian *Fleming's work expressed itself in *The James Bond Dossier* (1965) and *Colonel Sun* (1968), published under the pseudonym of Robert Markham. *Russian Hide-and-Seek* (1980) is set in the 21st century when England is being ruled by the Russians. *The Old Devils* (1986), which won the *Booker Prize, tells the story of a group of retired, heavy-drinking friends in Wales, whose lives are disrupted by the return of an obnoxious figure from their past. In *Difficulties with Girls* (1988), Patrick Standish and Jenny Bunn, from *Take a Girl Like You*, reappear as a married couple. *You Can't Do Both* (1994) is a semi-autobiographical story about a man's progress from south London suburbia, through Oxford, and on to a lectureship in a provincial university. *The Amis Collection: Selected Non-fiction 1954–1990* (1990) was followed by the publication of Amis's *Memoirs* (1991). A collection of short stories, *Mr Barrett's Secret*, appeared in 1993. His *Collected Poems 1944–1979* appeared in 1979. (*See* MOVEMENT.) A biography, *The Life of Kingsley Amis*, was published in 2006 by Zachary Leader, who also edited *The Letters of Kingsley Amis* (2000).

AMIS, Martin (1949–) Novelist and journalist, educated at Exeter College, Oxford, editorial assistant on *The *Times Literary Supplement*, literary editor of the *New Statesman* 1977–9. His early novels—*The Rachel Papers* (1973), *Dead Babies* (1975), and *Success* (1978)—are knowing semi-satires of affluent young metropolitans awash in sexual cynicism, drink, drugs, snobbery, and greed. *Other People* (1981), whose central character is an amnesiac, showed a taste for technical experimentation which is also on view in *Time's Arrow* (1991), the story of a Nazi war criminal in which events are recounted backwards, and *Night Train* (1997), a pastiche version of American noir *detective fiction. *Money* (1984), in which Amis's stylistic verve is used to most telling effect, is a scathing, scabrous comic novel that silhouettes rapacious monsters (especially its narrator, John Self) against a backdrop of 1980s New York and London, seen as hells of voracity and violence. His short story collection, *Einstein's Monsters* (1987), shows his fascination with menace and the toxic shifting to the subject of nuclear threat, as does his apocalyptic horror-comedy, *London Fields* (1989). Further broaching large and disturbing issues, later novels such as *The Information* (1995), *Yellow Dog* (2003), and *The House of Meetings* (2006) have divided opinion among readers and critics. His book about Stalin, *Koba the Dread* (2002), and his collection of stories and essays responding to the 9/11 attack on the World Trade Center, *The Second Plane* (2008), have also generated controversy. He has published volumes of essays and journalism such as *The Moronic Inferno and Other Visits to America* (1986), *Visiting Mrs Nabokov and Other Excursions* (1993), and *The War against Cliché* (2001), which, along with his novels, make clear his admiration for and indebtedness to Vladimir *Nabokov and Saul *Bellow. His autobiography, *Experience* (2000), is of especial interest, not least because of its account of his relationship with his father, Sir Kingsley *Amis.

Amis and Amiloun A late 13th-century romance of 2,508 lines, adapted from an Anglo-Norman *lay, about the virtue of friendship. Amis and Amiloun are two noble foster-brothers, bound in friendship. Amiloun takes the place of Amis in a trial by combat and is punished for this deception with leprosy. Amis is told by an angel that only a bath made from the blood of his two children will cure the leprosy, and he provides this for his friend. At the end the children are brought back to life. William *Morris and Walter *Pater (in *Studies in the History of the Renaissance*) tell the story as *Amis and Amile*. Criticism in the 1960s and 1970s argued the literary virtues of this popular romance, and its liveliness and complexity are now generally recognized. The standard edition is by MacEdward Leach (EETS OS 203, 1937).

AMMONS, Archie Randolph (1926–2001) American poet, born in North Carolina, whose work was informed by a close examination of nature, with an open, accessible style. His university degree in science shaped this scrutiny and in the 1990s Ammons held a professorship of poetry at Cornell University. *Garbage* (1993), a meditation on a smouldering heap of trash, won the National Book Award.

Amoret In Edmund *Spenser's *Faerie Queene*, III. vi, xii and IV. vii, daughter of the nymph Chrysogone and twin sister of *Belphoebe. She is 'Of grace and beautie noble Paragone', and has been married to Sir Scudamore, but carried off immediately after by the enchanter *Busirane and imprisoned by him until released by *Britomart. *Timias loves her, but being reproved by Belphoebe leaves her. This incident refers to *Elizabeth I's displeasure at the relations of Walter *Ralegh with Elizabeth Throckmorton.

Amoretti A series of 89 sonnets (sonnets 35 and 83 are identical) by Edmund *Spenser, which have been thought to illustrate the course of his courtship of Elizabeth Boyle. His marriage to her was celebrated in **Epithalamion*, which was printed following the *Amoretti* in 1595.

AMORY, Thomas (?1691–1788) Novelist, whose early life was spent in Ireland. His *Memoirs of Several Ladies of Great Britain* (1755), the only volume of a projected series to be published, was a rambling miscellany on Unitarian beliefs, antiquities, and medicine. It is set in the Hebrides and on Green Island, to the west of St Kilda, a luxuriant utopia inhabited by learned ladies. In 1756 and 1766 Amory published a fantasy autobiography, *The Life and Opinions of *John Buncle, Esq.*, which further expounds *Unitarianism and belief in the education of women. Amory was praised by William *Hazlitt and Leigh *Hunt.

Amos Barton, *The Sad Fortunes of the Rev* *See* SCENES OF CLERICAL LIFE.

amphibrach In English verse, a trisyllabic metrical *foot in which the second syllable is stressed.
See METRE.

Amphitryon A comedy by John *Dryden, produced and published 1690. Adapted from the comedies of *Plautus and *Molière on the same subject, it represents the story of *Jupiter's seduction of Alcmena in the guise of her husband Amphitryon. In this he is aided by *Mercury, who is disguised as Amphitryon's slave Sosia. The cruel abuse of mortal love by the gods is in striking contrast to the play's uninhibited eroticism. The same story was adapted by Jean *Giraudoux in his *Amphitryon 38* (1929).

AMYOT, Jacques (1513–93) French translator of, amongst other works, Plutarch's *Parallel Lives*. His translation was published in 1559 and translated into English by Sir Thomas *North in 1579.

anachrony The narration of events outside their logical sequence, normally in retrospective 'flashback' (analepsis), less commonly by anticipatory 'flashforward' (*prolepsis).

anacoluthon A Greek term for a change of grammatical construction in mid-sentence, of a kind that leaves the initial construction unfinished, as with the Gentleman's announcement of Goneril's suicide in **King Lear* (V. iii. 199):

> It came even from the heart of—O, she's dead!

ANACREON (6th century BC) A Greek lyric poet who is supposed to have written extensively on love and wine. Only a handful of complete poems survive, together with a number of fragments. A collection of *Hellenistic poems, the *Anacreonta*, were wrongly thought to be by him, and were translated into English several times and much imitated from the 17th to the 19th centuries, for example by Ben *Jonson, Robert *Herrick, Richard *Lovelace, Abraham *Cowley, and Thomas *Moore. 'Anacreontics' are verses that imitate both the themes and metres of Anacreon.

Analytical Review (1788–99) An important literary and radical periodical, published by Joseph *Johnson, which was an early influence in encouraging the growth of *Romanticism. William *Gilpin's theories on the *picturesque, and some of *Wordsworth's early poems were given sympathetic attention; the work of William *Bowles, Robert *Southey, Charles *Lamb, and other young writers was published. The *Review* attempted to comment, often fully, on every book published.

ANAND, Mulk Raj (1905–2004) Indian novelist in English, born in Peshawar, educated at the universities of Punjab and London. A student of the poet Muhammad Iqbal (1875–1938), Anand is recognized as one of the founders of the Indian novel in English, and among the most transnational, widely networked anglophone writers of the 20th century. After a peripatetic period between the two world wars during which he lived in London, interacted with the *Bloomsbury Group, and reported for the BBC, he settled in Bombay (Mumbai), having published early work in **Criterion*, *New Writing*, and other English periodicals. Anand made his name with the designedly proletarian novel *Untouchable* (1935), promoted by E. M. *Forster, which recounts a day in the life of street sweeper Bakha, roused to hopes of a casteless society by M. K. (Mahatma) Gandhi (who allegedly advised Anand on the manuscript). This was followed by other, more explicitly political novels describing the dispossessed, including *Coolie* (1936) and a trilogy (*The Village*, 1939; *Across the Black Waters*, 1940; *The Sword and the Sickle*, 1942) which recounts the life of a rebellious young Sikh peasant from the Punjab who fights for the British in the First World War. The Indian colonial government proscribed his first three novels. The best known of Anand's later works is *Private Life of an Indian Prince* (1953). In the 1930s Anand helped establish the Indian Progressive Writers' Association.

anapaest A trisyllabic metrical unit (*foot) in which the first two syllables are unstressed and the last is stressed; or in

Greek and Latin, where the first two are short and the last long. Anapaestic verse is rare in English, although it appears in modified form in the *limerick and in some jaunty songs ('With a hey, and a ho, and a hey-nonny-no'). Robert *Browning memorably exhibited its rhythmic effects in 'How they Brought the Good News from Ghent to Aix' (1845).

anaphora [Greek, 'carrying back'] The repetition of the same word or phrase in several successive clauses; for instance, 'Awake up, my glory; awake, lute and harp; I myself will awake right early' (Psalms 57: 9).

Anarchy, The Mask of *See* MASK OF ANARCHY.

Anatomy of Abuses, The *See* STUBBES, PHILIP

Anatomy of Melancholy, The By Robert *Burton, first published 1621, enlarged in successive editions between then and 1651. Ostensibly a treatise on abnormal psychology and its treatment, the *Anatomy* is written under the pseudonym of 'Democritus Junior' (*Democritus was 'the laughing philosopher') and its tone is, by turns, splenetic, satirical, mocking, self-mocking, confidential, scabrous, pessimistic, misanthropic, and tenderly humane. 'Melancholy', in Burton's usage, covers a vast range of obsessions, delusions, and mental malfunctions, including what is now called clinical depression. He concludes that the whole world is mad, including his readers and himself. Although it offers a copious array of cures and treatments, the *Anatomy* also warns that they are all useless. Self-contradiction is endemic. Colossally erudite, Burton quotes from and paraphrases a prodigious number of authors, covering every field of learning, and ranging from classical times to his own contemporaries, but he also says that erudition is a waste of time, and it is better to be ignorant. The book is made up of a lengthy introduction and three 'partitions', the first on the nature, causes, and symptoms of melancholy, the second on its cure, and the third on two special forms—love melancholy and religious melancholy. It made its author's reputation in his own lifetime, was admired by Samuel *Johnson, and Charles *Lamb, and gave John *Keats the story for *'Lamia'. The standard modern edition is the Clarendon Edition (1989–2001), which has three volumes of text, edited by Thomas C. Faulkner, Nicholas K. Kiessling, and Rhonda L. Blair, and three of commentary, edited by J. B. Bamborough and Martin Dodsworth.

Anchises *See* AENEID.

Ancient Mariner, The Rime of the A poem by Samuel Taylor *Coleridge, published 1798 in **Lyrical Ballads*. A revised version with marginal glosses was published in *Sibylline Leaves* (1817). An ancient mariner meets three gallants on their way to a marriage feast, and stops one of them in order to tell his story. His ship was drawn towards the South Pole by a storm. When the ship is surrounded by ice an albatross flies through the fog and is received with joy by the crew. The ice splits and the bird moves on with the ship; then, inexplicably, the mariner shoots it. After this act of cruelty a curse falls on the ship. She is driven north to the equator and is becalmed under burning sun in a rotting sea. The albatross is hung round the neck of the hated mariner. A skeleton ship approaches, on which Death and Life-in-Death are playing dice, and when it vanishes all the crew die except the mariner. Suddenly, watching the beauty of the watersnakes in the moonlight, he blesses them—and the albatross falls from his neck. The ship sails home and the mariner is saved, but for a penance he is condemned to travel from land to land and to teach by his example love and reverence for all God's creatures. The poem was derided when it first appeared, but has since come to be regarded as one of the great poems of *Romanticism. Its vivid imagery has prompted varied critical and symbolic interpretations: as a meditation on original sin, a re-enactment of the fall of man or the Crucifixion, a portrayal of a dark and unyielding form of medieval Catholicism, and—perhaps most commonly—as an allegory of what Coleridge's poem 'The Eolian Harp' calls the 'One life within us and abroad'. J. L. Lowes, in *The Road to Xanadu* (1927), traces the sources of Coleridge's story and imagery.

Ancrene Wisse A book of devotional and pastoral advice produced in the west Midlands (Herefordshire / Shropshire) and addressed to an initial audience of three anchoresses. It is possible that the author was a Dominican. The work draws on the intellectual currents of continental religious reform in the 12th and 13th centuries. Its emphasis on confession indicates that it was written after the Fourth Lateran Council in 1215: probably the 1220s, with later additions. The book is divided into eight sections, each dealing accessibly with one division of the religious rule, using memorable figurative language. Seventeen manuscripts, whole or partial, survive: nine in English (the language of the original), four in Latin, and four in French. It is admired as a work of great rhetorical resourcefulness and regarded as the greatest prose work of the Early Middle English period. It has important linguistic and thematic connections with the group of texts known (from the subject of one of them) as the *Katherine Group. *See Ancrene Wisse: A Corrected Edition of Cambridge, Corpus Christi College, MS 402*, ed. Bella Millett (EETS 325–6, 2005–6); selections (Parts VI and VII: on Penance, and on Love) ed. G. Shepherd (1959); trans. M. B. Salu (1956).

ANDERSEN, Hans Christian (1805–75) Danish writer, born in Odense, the son of a cobbler and a washerwoman. Andersen's earliest ambitions were theatrical; he trained as a singer and actor before achieving success as a playwright and novelist. From 1831 onwards he travelled widely in Europe, making his first visit to England in 1847. By this time he had already gained an international reputation for his *fairy stories, which first appeared in Danish from 1835 onwards, and in English in 1846 in three separate translations, by Charles Boner, Mary Howitt, and Caroline Peachey. These stories, in four collections, include such haunting tales as 'The Little Mermaid', 'The Snow Queen', 'The Ugly Duckling', 'The Red Shoes', and 'The Emperor's New Clothes'. They are deeply rooted in Danish folklore, but also shaped by Andersen's own psychological experiences and his at times morbidly acute sensitivity. Many of his narratives are wholly original, not least in their colloquial address and everyday settings; they shaped the modern literary fairy-tale. They were much admired by *Dickens, to whom Andersen dedicated *A Poet's Day Dreams* (1853) and with whom he stayed at Gad's Hill in 1857. Andersen's other works were also read and admired in England and internationally: his birthday, 2 April, is celebrated as International Children's Book Day. Recent studies include J. Wullschlager (2000), J. Zipes (2005).

ANDERSON, Poul (1926–2001) American author, born Bristol, Pennsylvania, of Scandinavian descent. His fiction, often set in a future dominated by interstellar trading and diplomacy, takes a libertarian stance. The 'Time Patrol' in *Guardians of Time* (1960) and other volumes protects history. The fantasy *The Broken Sword* (1954) is a remarkable reworking of the spirit of Norse saga, and *The Boat of a Million Years* (1989) follows the lives of a group of immortals through history.

ANDERSON, Sherwood (1876–1941) American writer, born in Ohio, who made his name as a leading naturalistic writer with his third book, *Winesburg, Ohio* (1919), a collection of short stories illustrating life in a small town. He published other collections, including *The Triumph of the Egg* (1921) and *Death in the Woods* (1933), in which he continued to illustrate the frustrations of contemporary life, a theme also explored in his novels, which include *Poor White* (1920), *Dark Laughter* (1925), and the semi-autobiographical *Tar: A Midwest Childhood* (1926). His *Memoirs* (1942) and *Letters* (1953) were posthumously published.

ANDRÉ, Bernard (*c.*1450–1522) French poet at the court of Henry VII. An Augustinian friar, he served as tutor to Henry's son, Prince Arthur. Although blind, he wrote poetry in Latin and French on public events, and in a variety of genres that included *panegyric and encomium (poetry devoted to praise). He continued writing into the reign of Henry VIII: the *Hymni Christiani* (1517) is a collection of just under 200 liturgical verses in various metres. André was an important link between the English court and continental exponents of humanism such as *Erasmus. See *Historia Regis Henrici Septimi*, ed. J. Gairdner, Rolls Series, 10 (1858).

Andreas An Old English poem of 1,722 lines divided into fifteen fits, or divisions, in the *Vercelli Book, based on a Latin version of the Greek Apocryphal *Acts of Andrew and Matthew amongst the Anthropophagi*. It was previously believed to be by *Cynewulf or by one of his followers influenced by **Beowulf*, but it is now thought probable that *Andreas* is later than Cynewulf, towards the end of the 9th century. See *Andreas and the Fates of the Apostles*, ed. K. R. Brooks (1961).

ANDREAS CAPELLANUS (*fl.* 1180s) Is usually believed to have been a chaplain to *Marie de Champagne, though the historical evidence for this is slim. His book *De Arte Honeste Amandi* (also entitled *De Amore*) is a handbook of procedure in love in three sections: Book I, concerned with the nature of love; Book II, on how love can be retained; and Book III, on the rejection of love. Andreas's work often draws explicitly on the writings of *Ovid; especially influential are the *Ars Amatoria* and the *Remedia Amoris*. The work's sceptical, Ovidian tone has made critics unsure of its sincerity, but it has been very authoritative in the definitions of *courtly love from Gaston Paris to the present day. Its excessive authority in English discussion is attributable principally to the prominence given to it by C. S. *Lewis in *The Allegory of Love* (1936). It has been edited (in the original Latin) by P. G. Walsh (1982) and translated by J. J. Parry as *The Art of Courtly Love* (1941).

ANDREEV, Leonid Nikolaevich (1871–1919) Russian prose writer and dramatist, born in Orel; he studied law first at St Petersburg University and then at Moscow University. His stories and articles in newspapers attracted the attention and encouragement of Maxim *Gorky, to whom Andreev dedicated his first collection of stories, published in 1901 to enormous popular and critical acclaim. Among his most important stories are 'The Abyss' and 'In the Fog' (1902), which treat sexual themes with a new frankness, 'The Red Laugh' (1904), a response to the 'madness' of the Russo-Japanese War, and 'The Story of the Seven Who Were Hanged' (1908), which examines political terrorism. He wrote more than twenty plays, including *The Life of a Man* (1906; translated by Maurice *Baring, 1908) and *He Who Gets Slapped* (1915), which brought him international fame. Translations of his major stories and plays began to appear from 1906 in England and in America, where his plays were much in vogue in the 1920s. Andreev supported the 1905 revolution but opposed the October Revolution and died in exile in Finland. A talented artist, he was also fascinated by photography. See Richard Davies (ed.), *Photographs by a Russian Writer* (1989).

ANDREWES, Lancelot (1555–1626) Theologian and preacher. Educated at Merchant Taylors' School, under Richard Mulcaster (1531/2–1611), and at Pembroke Hall, Cambridge, he took orders in 1581 and became chaplain to Henry Hastings, third earl of Huntingdon (1536?–95), and then, in 1588, vicar of St Giles's, Cripplegate. His fame as a preacher quickly spread, and he was appointed chaplain to Archbishop Whitgift (1530/1–1604) and to *Elizabeth I. His career prospered under *James I, who admired his preaching and his scholarship, and appointed him successively to the bishoprics of Chichester, Ely, and Winchester. He headed the list of divines chosen to translate the Authorized Version of the *Bible, and acted as general overseer of the project as well as leading the group responsible for Genesis to 2 Kings. He was a major influence in forming a distinctively Anglican theology, pitched between the extremes of *Puritanism and *Roman

Catholicism. His friends and associates included Walter *Ralegh, Sir Philip *Sidney, William *Camden, John *Selden, George *Herbert, and Isaac *Casaubon. In a sermon preached before James after the discovery of the Gunpowder Plot, he recommended the annual celebration of the king's and the nation's deliverance, a custom still observed. His sermons, in T. S. *Eliot's view, 'rank with the finest English prose of their time' (*For Lancelot Andrewes*, 1928). The opening of Eliot's 'Journey of the Magi' ('A cold coming we had of it') is drawn from Andrewes's *Sermon 15: Of the Nativitie*. He preached in the *metaphysical style that preceded the plainer preaching of the Puritans and John *Tillotson; and incorporates minute textual analysis, classical quotations, etymological analysis, and verbal play. His *Works* (11 vols, ed. J. P. Wilson and James Bliss) appeared 1841–54. See Peter McCullough, *Sermons at Court* (1998); *Lancelot Andrewes, Selected Sermons and Lectures*, ed. Peter McCullough (2005).

Anelida and Arcite An incomplete poem by *Chaucer in 357 lines. It is set, like 'The Knight's Tale' (*Canterbury Tales*, 1), in Theseus' Thebes and draws more on *Boccaccio's *Teseida* than on the sources it acknowledges, *Statius and Corinna. The simple story tells of the faithlessness of Arcite to Queen Anelida in 210 lines of *rhyme royal, as a preface to the elaborate *Compleynt* of Anelida in 140 lines of varying and accomplished metrical patterns.

Angel in the House, The A sequence of poems by Coventry *Patmore. The first and second parts, *The Betrothal* and *The Espousals*, in *octosyllabic quatrains, were published 1854 and 1856 respectively; the third and fourth parts, *Faithful for Ever* (1860) and *The Victories of Love* (1861), in octosyllabic couplets, were published as *The Victories of Love* in 1863.

The work is a celebration of married love, with lyrical and reflective passages linked by a narrative in which Felix courts and weds Honoria, a dean's daughter; in the last two parts Frederick, a rival for Honoria's hand, marries Jane and learns to love her before her early death. It was popular with its original readership, though its unironized sentiment and interest in material details of middle-class life made A. C. *Swinburne and Edmund *Gosse, among others, impatient. The title, largely thanks to Virginia *Woolf's 'Professions for Women' (1931), which spoke of the need for women writers to 'kill the Angel in the House', quickly established itself as shorthand, now much challenged, for a stereotype of Victorian womanhood. Patmore's enquiry into the nature of married love might be compared to those of Charles *Kingsley and Robert *Browning.

ANGELOU, Maya (1928–) African American autobiographer and poet, born in St Louis, Missouri. Rooted in a rich folk tradition of rural black culture, *I Know Why the Caged Bird Sings* (1970), the most famous of her five volumes of autobiography, charts her harrowing childhood in Arkansas, her segregated education in Southern schools, and the beginning of her enduring relationship with literature. The other volumes, *Gather Together in my Name* (1974), *Singin' and Swingin' and Gettin' Merry like Christmas* (1976), *The Heart of a Woman* (1981), and *All God's Children Need Traveling Shoes* (1986), record her flamboyant career as a singer and dancer, her years in the Harlem Writers' Guild, and her role within the civil rights movement. *A Song Flung up to Heaven* (2004) continues this emphasis in engaging with the assassinations of *Malcolm X and Martin Luther King (1929–68). An exuberant and technically assured poet with a commitment to the politics of race and gender, Angelou's works of poetry include *Just Give Me a Cool Drink of Water 'fore I Diiie* (1971), *And Still I Rise* (1978), and *I Shall Not Be Moved* (1990). In addition she has published a number of personal essay volumes including *Wouldn't Take Nothing for my Journey Now* (1993).

Anglo-Indian literature Also referred to as Indian literature in English, produced both in India and across the vast Indian diaspora, Anglo-Indian literature represents one of the most innovative and dynamic fields of world writing in English today. Indian writing in English has its roots in the 19th century, in the derivative if also startlingly precocious work of poets such as Henry Derozio (1809–31), Toru Dutt (1856–77), Manmohan Ghose (1869–1924), and Sarojini Naidu (1879–1949). The nationalist writer Bankimchandra Chatterjee (1838–94) wrote the first Indian novel in English, *Rajmohan's Wife* (1864), thereafter reverting to Bengali and achieving renown as a writer in that language, as did the poet Rabindranath *Tagore, India's only *Nobel Prize-winner for Literature to date (1913). In the late 20th century the reputation of the Indian novel in English came controversially to overshadow that of the equally vibrant vernacular literatures of the sub-continent, written in such languages as Malayalam and Hindi. For some Indian critics, this represents a loss, and English-language Indian writing an inauthentic colonial throwback. The vernacular languages nonetheless impress themselves upon the mainstream novelists' Indian English, as may be heard in the rhythms and diction of their reported speech, what the British Indian writer Salman *Rushdie calls 'chutnified' English.

Various reasons have been suggested to explain the vast critical and market success of Anglo-Indian literature both on the sub-continent and worldwide. These include imperial nostalgia, the promotion of Indian writing as exotic, the impetus of globalization, and the ways in which the English language was used to manage the empire, leading to high-quality middle-class education in English in the area since the early 1800s. Following independence in 1947, and despite moves to promote Hindi as the national language, English has been increasingly institutionalized as a unifying medium for the populous, many-tongued nation. Moreover, as in the autobiographical writing of first prime minister Jawaharlal Nehru, narrative in English was established as a mode of shaping Indian national identity. Several Indian writers including Rushdie, Mukul Kesavan, and Vikram *Seth imaginatively reflect upon this mode of national self-construction in their work. Critics are now perhaps more ready to acknowledge than they were at the time of the path-breaking success of

Rushdie's *Midnight's Children* (1981) that English is unquestionably a naturalized language and key literary medium, characterized by its own distinctive manner (as, too, is English in Nigeria or the Caribbean).

The two pioneers of the Indian novel in English are recognized to be the social realist Mulk Raj *Anand and the spiritual Raja *Rao. Anand was influenced by James *Joyce and *Marx, the *Bloomsbury Group, and the teachings of Gandhi. Raja Rao, a scholarly Sanskritist, wrote determinedly of the need to make an Indian English for himself; his choric Gandhian novel *Kanthapura* (1938) was much imitated. The comic social observationist R. K. *Narayan, his career straddling the second half of the 20th century, is the third important writer of this period, with his long line of short novels set in the south Indian town of Malgudi. In this same period the centenarian autobiographer Nirad *Chaudhuri was an influential if controversial presence, his *The Autobiography of an Unknown Indian* (1951) a study in cultural displacement. G. V. *Desani's *All About H. Hatterr* (1948) is a linguistically pyrotechnic novel, a precursor to Rushdie's *magical realism.

The fashioners of the influential late 20th-century Indian novel in English include several writers of the independence generation. Among them are Nehru's niece Nayantara Sahgal (1927–) with her early memoir of the heady days of the Independence struggle, *Prison and Chocolate Cake* (1954); the autobiographer Ved *Mehta; Ruth Prawer *Jhabvala; and Anita *Desai. Trinidad-born V. S. *Naipaul, like other diasporic South Asian writers, approaches the sub-continent as both outsider and insider. Naipaul's engagement with India, especially in his three non-fiction books, *An Area of Darkness* (1964), *A Wounded Civilization* (1977), and *India: A Million Mutinies Now* (1990), has been intense and controversial.

From the 1980s, a second literary generation established itself, with Rushdie its most influential member. Technically Pakistani, *Ice-Candy-Man* (1989), by the novelist Bapsi Sidhwa (1938–), is an outstanding response to Partition. The work of the US-based Gita Mehta (1943–) along with Githa Hariharan (1954–), Sara Suleri, and others confirms the quality of contemporary writing by Indian women.

A number of different modes in the writing are evolving, including the stark realism of Rohinton *Mistry, the light, Austen-esque prose of Seth, the mordant social observation of Upamanyu *Chatterjee, the flamboyance of Vikram Chandra (1961–) (*Love and Longing in Bombay*, 1997), the multi-layered historical studies of Amitav *Ghosh (*In an Antique Land*, 1992); and the elliptical understatement of Amit *Chaudhuri.

A third generation is now becoming prominent, including Kiran *Desai, Manju *Kapur, and the Keralan Arundhati *Roy with her ambitious, highly praised novel *The God of Small Things* (1997). Some writers of Indian descent, including Naipaul and Bharati *Mukherjee, now reject the ethnicizing label of 'Indian writer'.

Anglo-Norman The name given to the dialect of Medieval French introduced into Britain following the Norman Conquest and spoken and written there, albeit by an educated minority, until the end of the 14th century. It has had a marked influence on the vocabulary of modern English, and in particular legal vocabulary. Anglo-Norman writing occupies a significant place in the evolution of both Medieval French and Middle English literature. Perhaps the best-known work is a romance: the version of the Tristan legend by Thomas, dated to the 1170s, which survives only in fragments. One of the most prolific of Anglo-Norman writers was the Franciscan Nicole Bozon (*c*.1280–1330), whose output included saints' lives, satires, and *Contes moralisés* (*see* FABLE). *Macaronic verse, both religious and secular, is another characteristic of Anglo-Norman writing. There is some dispute over whether or not the *Mystère d'Adam* (*see* ADAM), the first French dramatic work wholly in the vernacular, can be included within the Anglo-Norman canon. The French of John *Gower in his *Cinkante Balades* is more continental than insular. See M. D. Legge, *Anglo-Norman Literature and its Background* (1963).

Anglo-Saxon The Latin form of the word (*Anglo-Saxonicus*) applies originally to the people and language of the Saxon race who colonized the southern parts of Britain (as distinct from the northern parts colonized by the Angles), to distinguish them from continental Saxons; hence, the 'Anglo' element is adverbial and the word does not mean, as was erroneously supposed, the combination of Angles and Saxons: i.e. the people and language of the whole of England. For the latter the term 'Old English' is more correct. The word became applied in the erroneous way very early; *Ælfric (*c*.1000) refers to the West Saxon he spoke as 'English'. So the 'correct' distinction, made by the *OED* and enforced by modern scholars (especially at Oxford), between 'Old English' and 'Anglo-Saxon' is a somewhat pedantic one (the term 'Anglo-Saxon' is still used at Cambridge, as in the 1941 book by the Chadwicks, *The Study of Anglo-Saxon*); since the revival of such studies in the 16th century, 'Anglo-Saxon' has been used as the general term, without a sense of geographical distinction.

Anglo-Saxon Chronicles, The Early records in English of events in England from the beginning of the Christian era to 1154, surviving in seven manuscripts which Plummer (see below) arranged in four groups: the Parker Chronicle, named from Matthew *Parker; the Abingdon Chronicles; the Worcester Chronicle; and the Laud Chronicle, named from William *Laud, of which the most famous version is the **Peterborough Chronicle*. The most important and fullest are the Parker and Laud chronicles. The Chronicles are believed to have developed from the brief annalistic entries in Easter tables, and the entries up to 449 are as brief as the single-sentence Latin annals in those tables. The entries after 449 are sporadically more lengthy, and the most celebrated are those for 449 itself (the arrival of *Hengist and Horsa), for 755 (the notably taut narrative of *Cynewulf and Cyneheard), for 893 to 897 (Alfred's last series of Danish wars), and for the disastrous years of Stephen's reign at the end of the Peterborough Chronicle. A famous, distinctive feature is the occurrence of the poem on the battle of *Brunanburh (937); other lyrical passages of poetry, semi-poetry, or memorable prose occur in the entries for 942, 959, 973 (in praise of King Edgar, ending in verse with his death in 975), 1011 (the martyrdom of Archbishop Ælfheah), and 1040 (the death of Prince Alfred). The organization of the Chronicles' records in a more orderly way has been attributed to *Alfred in the course of his literary ventures in the 890s. The Chronicles are of enormous importance in historical, linguistic, and literary terms. C. Plummer, *Two of the Saxon Chronicles Parallel* (2 vols, 1892); D. Whitelock, D. C. Douglas, and S. I. Tucker (trans., 1961); D. N. Dumville and S. Keynes, *The Anglo-Saxon Chronicle: A Collaborative Edition* (1983–).

Angria and **Gondal** Imaginary kingdoms invented by the *Brontë children, as a further development of games and stories inspired by a box of wooden soldiers brought home by their father in 1826. Early games created the Glass Town Confederacy on the west coast of Africa; the capital city, Glass Town or Verdopolis, owed much in its architecture to the engravings of John *Martin. Later Emily and Anne broke away and invented the kingdom of Gondal, which was to provide the setting for many of Emily's poems, including some of her finest; the initials and names attached to them (A.G.A., J. Brenzaida, R. Alcona, etc.) represent characters in the Gondal epic, of which no prose fragments remain. In 1834, Charlotte and Branwell jointly created the kingdom of Angria, of which the principal characters were Alexander Percy, the earl of Northangerland, and Arthur Wellesley, marquis of Douro, later known as duke of Zamorna. Charlotte wrote many Angrian tales, most of them tragic and Byronic tales of passion. The tales of 1837–9 ('Julia', 'Mina Laury', 'Caroline Vernon', and 'Henry Hastings') foreshadow many of the themes of her mature novels. See Frances Ratchford, *The Brontës' Web of Childhood* (1941); Juliet Barker, *The Brontës* (1994).

Angry Young Men A journalistic catchphrase loosely applied to a number of British playwrights and novelists from the mid-1950s, including Kingsley *Amis, John *Osborne, Alan *Sillitoe, and Colin *Wilson, whose political views were radical or anarchic, and who described various forms of social alienation. It is sometimes said to derive from the title of a work by the Irish writer Leslie Paul, *Angry Young Man* (1951).

Animal Farm By George *Orwell, published 1945; a satire in beast fable form on revolutionary and post-revolutionary Russia (and, by extension, on all revolutions). The animals of Mr Jones's farm revolt against their human masters and expel them, the pigs becoming their egalitarian leaders. However, dominated by Napoleon, their chief, the pigs become corrupted by power and a new tyranny replaces the old. The ultimate commandment runs 'ALL ANIMALS ARE EQUAL BUT SOME ANIMALS ARE MORE EQUAL THAN OTHERS'. Napoleon, ruthless and cynical, represents Stalin, and Snowball, the idealist whom he drives away, Trotsky. Boxer, the noble carthorse, stands for the strength, simplicity, and good nature of the common man, but he ends up in the knacker's yard.

animal stories (for children), originating from fables and folklore, have been predominantly didactic from Dorothy Kilner's *The Life and Perambulations of a Mouse* (1783) to **Black Beauty* and Marshall Saunders's *Beautiful Joe* (1894). They can be naturalistic, as in Ernest Thompson Seton's *Wild Animals I Have Known* (1898) and Jack *London's *White Fang* (1906); political and symbolic (*The *Jungle Book*), or concerned with humans in disguise (*The *Wind in the Willows* and much of Beatrix *Potter's work). Modern examples include Richard *Adams's *Watership Down*, books by E. B. *White and Dick *King-Smith, pony books, and many commercial *series books.

animation Early film animation developed in both drawn and puppet forms, with the former initially making use of existing *comic-strip characters, before launching its own range of animal characters, ranging from Felix the Cat to Walt *Disney's Mickey Mouse (1928). Puppet animation developed strongly in Russia and Eastern Europe, with Wladyslaw Starewicz (1892–1965) an innovative creator of sophisticated *fables, and the Czech *Surrealist Jan Svankmajer (1934–), widely admired today for his savage parables and such subversive literary *adaptations as *Alice* (1988) and *Faust* (1994). The animated versions of much juvenile literature produced by Disney, ranging from the *fairy story *Snow White* and such novels as *Pinocchio* and *Bambi*, to Rudyard *Kipling's *Jungle Book* and *101 Dalmations* by Dodie *Smith, may have all but eclipsed their originals. Yet animation remains a potent ideological medium. Halas and Batchelor's animated **Animal Farm* (1954) modified Orwell's politics, with CIA encouragement; while today Aardman's Wallace and Gromit have become wry emblems of English nostalgia.

'Annabel Lee' A poem by Edgar Allen *Poe.

Annales Cambriae A series of Latin chronicles of Irish, northern British, and Welsh history, compiled in Wales in the 10th century. Points of interest include information about *Gildas, and such aspects of the *Arthur story as the battle of Badon, which they place in 518, and the battle of Camlan in 539 in which, they say, Arthur and Mordred fell.

Annals of the Four Masters Chronicle of Irish history from the Deluge to AD 1616, compiled mainly from Gaelic manuscript sources in the Franciscan monastery in Donegal by the friar Mícheál Ó Cléirigh (*c.*1590–1643) with the assistance of Peregrine O'Clery, Fergus O'Mulconry, Peregrine O'Duignan, and others. The four-year labour of transcription and composition was completed in 1636. A full English translation by the scholar John O'Donovan (1806–61) appeared in six volumes from 1846 to 1851.

Annals of the Parish A novel by John *Galt, published 1821. The Revd Micah Balwhidder, a self-important minister, solemnly chronicles the events that impinge upon the lives of the parishioners of Dalmailing, Ayrshire, during the period 1760–1810. Juxtaposing the political (national and international) and the domestic to sometimes ludicrous effect, the book subtly charts the changes undergone by the parish, and is the source of the term 'utilitarian' adopted by John Stuart *Mill.

Anne of Geierstein, *or The Maiden of the Mist* A novel by Walter *Scott, published 1829. It is set in 15th-century Switzerland. For his material on the Vehmgericht, a secret criminal tribunal with its origins in Westphalia, Scott returned to an early favourite, *Goethe's *Götz von Berlichingen*, which he had translated in 1799. Written in the aftermath of Scott's bankruptcy, he found it a laborious task. To his surprise, it enjoyed considerable success.

Anne of Green Gables First of nine books (1908–37) by L. M. *Montgomery featuring the enduringly popular red-headed orphan Anne Shirley, who is mistakenly sent to work for ageing brother and sister Matthew and Marilla Cuthbert (they want a boy to help on their farm). Despite many mishaps arising from her highly developed imagination fed by a taste for romantic literature, she wins their love. In later books Anne becomes a teacher and marries her childhood tormentor, Gilbert Blythe.

Annual Register, The An annual review of the 'History, Politicks, and Literature' of the past year, founded by Robert *Dodsley and Edmund *Burke; the first volume, covering 1758, appeared on 15 May 1759. Burke's biographer Sir James Prior described it as 'the best and most comprehensive of all the periodical works'; it is still current.

Annus Mirabilis (*Year of Miracles*) A poem by John *Dryden, published 1667. The year he celebrates is 1666, and the 'miracles' are Britain's victory in the Second Dutch War, culminating in the St James's Day battle, and the fire of London, miraculous because it was stopped before it destroyed the city.

ANOUILH, Jean (1910–87) French dramatist, many of whose plays enjoyed success on the English stage in the 1950s and 1960s in translations by Christopher *Fry and Lucienne Hill, amongst others. His main works are *Le Bal des voleurs* (1938: *Thieves' Carnival*, 1952), *Antigone* (1944: 1946), *L'Invitation au château* (1947: *Ring round the Moon*, 1950), *La Valse des toréadors* (1952: *The Waltz of the Toreadors*, 1956), and a number of plays dealing with historical figures, including *L'Alouette* (1953: *The Lark*, 1955) on *Joan of Arc, *Pauvre Bitos* (1956: *Poor Bitos*, 1964) on Robespierre, and *Becket ou l'honneur de Dieu* (1959: *Becket, or The Honour of God*, 1960) on St Thomas *Becket. He also translated and adapted works from *Shakespeare, Oscar *Wilde, and Graham *Greene. See C. N. Smith, *Jean Anouilh* (1985).

ANSELM, St (*c.*1033–1109) Born in Aosta, northern Italy, and a pupil of *Lanfranc at the abbey of Bec in Normandy. He succeeded Lanfranc as prior of Bec, and as archbishop of Canterbury in 1093. His most original works are the *Monologion*, its sequel the *Proslogion*, and *Cur Deus Homo*, a justification of Christ's incarnation influenced by time spent with Gilbert Crispin, abbot of Westminster, who had discussed this element of Christian doctrine with Jews. The original title of the *Proslogion—Fides Quaerens Intellectum* ('faith seeking understanding')—encapsulates an intellectual method in which faith is subjected to meditative and logical examination. In this book is propounded the famous 'Ontological Argument': if God is defined as a Being than which no greater can be conceived, and such a Being can exist in the mind, then he must exist in reality, since what exists in the mind can be thought to exist in reality, which is greater than the mind. This argument was variously addressed by *Aquinas, *Descartes, *Kant, and Bertrand *Russell. *Anselm of Canterbury: The Major Works*, ed. with an introduction by Brian Davies and G. R. Evans (1998); R. W. Southern, *Saint Anselm: A Portrait in a Landscape* (1990).

ANSON, George, Baron Anson (1697–1762) Naval officer, administrator, and politician, who made his name circumnavigating the world in 1740–4. *A Voyage round the World by George Anson*, compiled by his chaplain Richard Walter, appeared in 1748. It was the source of William *Cowper's poem 'The *Castaway'.

ANSTEY, Christopher (1724–1805) Poet, educated at Cambridge University; author of the *New Bath Guide* (1766), a series of letters in colloquial verse, retailing the adventures of Squire Blunderhead and his family amid the fashionable entertainments of Bath. It greatly entertained Horace *Walpole and Thomas *Gray; later editions were illustrated by Thomas *Rowlandson and George *Cruikshank.

ANSTEY, F. (1856–1934) The pseudonym of Thomas Anstey Guthrie, born in London and educated in London and at Trinity Hall, Cambridge; author of many novels of fantasy and humour and of innumerable comic sketches and stories. The great success of *Vice Versa* (1882), in which Mr Bultitude is magically transformed into his schoolboy son, and vice versa, enabled Anstey to leave the bar in order to write. His long association with *Punch*, beginning in 1886, encouraged his skill in parody and burlesque; his series of *Voces Populi*, *Mr Punch's Pocket Ibsen*, and many others became very popular. His many novels of magic, besides *Vice Versa*, include *Tourmalin's Time Cheques* (1891), *The Brass Bottle* (1900), and *In Brief Authority* (1915).

anthem A form of Anglican church music sung antiphonally, i.e by two voices or choirs, and set to words from the *Bible; more generally, a song or hymn.

Anthology, The Greek (i.e. flower collection), a large number of epigrams (mostly short poems in elegiac couplets) by more than 300 Greek writers from the 4th century BC onwards, arranged in subjects in sixteen books; the subjects include Christian poems, sculpture, morality, homosexual love, and riddles. The anthology was put together in 10th-century Byzantium from several earlier collections. The manuscript of the Palatine anthology containing fifteen books was first discovered by *Salmasius in the Palatine Library at Heidelberg in 1606 but not published till the late 18th century; there were several 19th-century translations, e.g. by J. W. Mackail. A sixteenth book was assembled by the Byzantine monk Planudes *c.*1300; the Planudean anthology was published in 1494 and was widely read and imitated during the Renaissance. See Peter Jay (ed.), *The Greek Anthology* (1981).

Antichrist The name given in the Epistles of John to the enemies of Christ. This figure came to be associated with prophecies in the Books of Daniel and Revelation of an evil power who would reign before Christ's Second Coming. After the *Reformation, Protestants identified the pope with Antichrist.
See BIBLE.

anti-hero (or anti-heroine) An unheroic or inadequate *protagonist of a story or drama. Not to be confused with the villain or antagonist, the anti-heroic figure is an important type in the novel since *Cervantes and in some kinds of comic drama.

Anti-Jacobin, The, *or Weekly Examiner* (1797–8) A short-lived but remarkable journal founded by George *Canning and a group of brilliant, high-spirited friends, including George *Ellis and John *Frere, to combat the radical views supported by the **Monthly Magazine*, Coleridge's **Watchman*, and other *Jacobin influences, and to deride their supporters. Edited by William *Gifford, it was a political miscellany of strongly Tory outlook, which included much brilliant parody and satire: 'The Needy Knife-Grinder', a parody of Robert *Southey; 'The Loves of the Triangles', a parody of Erasmus *Darwin's 'The Loves of the Plants', 'The Rovers', a burlesque on the romantic solemnities of German drama; and 'New Morality', directed against French propaganda, are well-known examples. *The Anti-Jacobin* came to an end in 1798. Many of its chief contributors moved on in due course to the Tory **Quarterly Review*, but its crusade was continued briefly in enfeebled form by the *Anti-Jacobin Review and Magazine*. The journal's comic writing is included in G. Stones and J. Strachan (eds), *Parodies of the Romantic Age*, 5 vols (1999).

ANTIN, Mary (1881–1949) Jewish immigrant to America, whose memoir *Promised Land* (1912), describing childhood experiences in Russia (her birthplace), has become a classic of immigration literature. In 1914 she followed this with *They Who Knock at our Gates: A Complete Gospel of Immigration*.

antinomian One who maintains, through a misreading of arguments in *Paul's Epistles, that the moral law is not binding upon Christians under the law of grace. The term was coined by *Luther to attack Agricola (see Robert *Browning's 'Johannes Agricola in Meditation'), and it was often used against radical Protestants.
See HUTCHINSONIANS.

Antiquary, The A novel by Walter *Scott, published 1816. A gallant young officer, known as Major Neville, believed to be illegitimate, falls in love with Isabella Wardour who, deferring to the prejudices of her father Sir Arthur, rejects him. Assuming the name of Lovel, he follows her to Scotland, meeting on the way Jonathan Oldbuck, laird of Monkbarns, a learned and garrulous antiquary. Lovel saves the lives of Sir Arthur and his daughter at the peril of his own and rescues the former from the financial ruin that the deceptions of the German charlatan Dousterswivel have brought on him. In the end he is revealed as the son and heir of the earl of Glenallan and marries Isabella. The charm of the book, Scott's 'chief favourite among all his novels', lies in the character of Oldbuck, based, according to the author, on a friend of his boyhood, George Constable, but a recognizable portrait of Scott himself, and in the minor characters: the Mucklebackit family, the gossips in the village post office, and the shrewd and kindly Edie Ochiltree.

Antonio and Mellida A two-part play by John *Marston, printed 1602, probably acted two years earlier; it provided *Jonson with materials for his ridicule of Marston in *The *Poetaster*. In Part I, Antonio, son of Andrugio, duke of Genoa, is in love with Mellida, daughter of Piero, duke of Venice. The two states are at war and Genoa has been defeated, and a price set in Venice on the heads of Antonio and Andrugio. Antonio, disguised as an Amazon, comes to Piero's court to see Mellida. Mellida flees with Antonio but is captured. Andrugio offers himself as a victim to Piero, who appears to relent and assents to the marriage of Antonio and Mellida, and the first part closes joyfully.

In Part II Piero reveals his true character. He kills Andrugio, contrives the dishonour of Mellida in order to prevent the match, plots the death of Antonio, and gains the hand of Andrugio's widow. Mellida dies broken-hearted. Antonio, urged by the ghost of his father, assumes the disguise of a fool and kills Piero.

Antony and Cleopatra A tragedy by *Shakespeare probably written 1606, not printed until the first *folio of 1623. Its chief source is the *Life of Antony* by *Plutarch, as translated by Sir Thomas *North which Shakespeare followed extremely closely in places, as in Enobarbus' speech beginning: 'The barge she sat in, like a burnished throne | Burned on the water' (II. ii. 198–9). Minor sources include plays by the countess of *Pembroke and Samuel *Daniel.

The play presents Mark Antony, the great soldier and noble prince, at Alexandria, enthralled by the beauty of the Egyptian queen *Cleopatra. Recalled to Rome by the death of his wife

Fulvia and political developments, he tears himself from Cleopatra. His estrangement from Octavius Caesar is ended by his marriage to Octavia, Caesar's sister, provoking the intense jealousy of Cleopatra. But the reconciliation is short-lived, and Antony leaves Octavia and returns to Egypt. At the battle of Actium, the flight of the Egyptian squadron is followed by the retreat of Antony, pursued to Alexandria by Caesar. There, after a brief success, Antony is finally defeated. On the false report of Cleopatra's death, he falls upon his sword. He is carried to the monument where Cleopatra has taken refuge and dies in her arms. Cleopatra, fallen into Caesar's power but determined not to grace his triumph, takes her own life by the bite of an asp.
See also ALL FOR LOVE.

aphorism A short pithy statement into which much thought or observation is compressed, e.g. 'he who praises everybody praises nobody' (Samuel *Johnson). Notable aphorists in English include Johnson, William *Blake (in *The *Marriage of Heaven and Hell*), and Oscar *Wilde. See John Gross (ed.), *The Oxford Book of Aphorisms* (1983).

Apocalypse [from a Greek verb meaning 'to disclose'] A 'revelation' or an 'unveiling', and the title given to the book of Revelation in the New Testament. The term 'apocalyptic literature' is used in a broader sense to describe prophetic writings generally, and especially those presenting visions of the end of the world: the category includes many of the works of William *Blake, of W. B. *Yeats (e.g. 'The Second Coming'), and the 'disaster' novels of J. G. *Ballard and other *science fiction writers. Frank *Kermode's *The Sense of an Ending* (1967) discusses apocalyptic narrative in terms of the Judaeo-Christian view of history as linear, i.e. as possessing a beginning, a middle in which narrator and reader exist, and a necessarily different ending.
See NEW APOCALYPSE.

Apocrypha Books of Jewish origin in the Septuagint (Greek) version of the Old Testament which the Jews did not accept as part of the Hebrew canon of Scripture. *Jerome included them in the *Vulgate, with the name 'apocrypha' (i.e. non-canonical). At the *Reformation Protestants, unlike Catholics, excluded the Apocrypha from the canon. It forms a separate part of the Authorized Version (1611), in the order 1 and 2 Esdras, Tobit, Judith, the Rest of Esther, the Wisdom of Solomon, Ecclesiasticus, Baruch (with the Epistle of Jeremiah), the Song of the Three Holy Children, the History of Susanna, Bel and the Dragon, the Prayer of Manasses, and 1 and 2 Maccabees. Generally, 'apocrypha' and 'apocryphal' refer to non-canonical or inauthentic works or sayings.

APOLLINAIRE, Guillaume (1880–1918) French poet, prose writer, and art critic. He was a prominent figure in the avant-garde in Paris in the years before the First World War, and an ardent supporter of contemporary developments in poetry and painting (*Méditations esthétiques: les peintres cubistes*, 1913; English trans. 1944). His principal volumes of poetry are *Alcools* (1913; 1965) and *Calligrammes* (1918; 1980), both translated into English by Ann Hyde Greet. See F. Steegmuller, *Apollinaire* (1965).

Apollo (Phoebus) In classical mythology the most beautiful of the Olympian gods, son of Zeus (Roman *Jupiter) and Leto, and brother of Artemis (Roman Diana). He is identified by his bow and lyre: he is associated with the sun, archery, prophecy, music, and especially poetry, and hence is the leader of the *Muses and father of *Orpheus. He is prominent as Hector's supporter in the **Iliad* and is the subject of the Homeric *Hymn to Apollo*. In *Ovid's *Metamorphoses* he pursues the nymph Daphne and accidentally kills the boy he loves, Hyacinthus. In Milton's **Lycidas* and Keats's **Hyperion* he represents the poet's own artistic dedication. In *The Birth of Tragedy* (1872) the German philosopher Friedrich *Nietzsche contrasts Apollo with Dionysus as representatives of opposing principles within Greek culture.
See DELPHIC ORACLE; NIOBE.

APOLLONIUS OF RHODES (*fl.* 3rd century BC) Major Alexandrian Greek poet. He chose a conventionally heroic legend for his four-book epic *Argonautica*, the voyage of Jason and the Argonauts to recover the Golden Fleece, achieved with the help of the witch Medea, but he treated his subject with psychological insight, emphasized its romantic features, and left his readers keenly aware of his own presence as authoritative narrator. In short, he introduced into the genre many elements that were not found in *Homer. Apollonius had an important disciple in *Virgil. There are echoes of his verse in **Paradise Lost*, and he was William *Morris's main source for *The Life and Death of Jason*. See the translation by Richard Hunter, *Jason and the Golden Fleece* (1993).

Apology for Poetry, An *See* DEFENCE OF POETRY, A.

Apology for Smectymnuus *See* SMECTYMNUUS.

aporia A rhetorical figure in which the speaker appears perplexed by indecision over some question or choice. *Hamlet's soliloquy 'To be or not to be…' is the best-known extended example. In the terminology of *deconstruction, it is favoured as a term for an insoluble contradiction between two possible meanings of a given text or passage.

aposiopesis A rhetorical device in which the speaker suddenly comes to a halt in mid-sentence, usually as if dumbstruck by powerful emotion.

apostles [meaning 'messengers'] Who spread the gospel in the New Testament. The term refers both to the disciples, the twelve followers of Jesus, notably Peter, and to later apostles, notably *Paul, who is often simply called the

Apostle. The Acts of the Apostles narrates the early expansion of the church from Jerusalem to Rome.
See BIBLE.

Apostles an intellectual society ('Cambridge Conversazione Society') formed in Cambridge University in 1820 for the purpose of friendship and formal discussion. During the 19th century members included Arthur Henry *Hallam, Alfred *Tennyson, Monckton *Milnes, and Richard Trevenix *Trench. In the early 20th century, the philosopher G. E. Moore (1873–1958), the economist Maynard Keynes (1883–1946), Lytton *Strachey, Bertrand *Russell, Leonard *Woolf, and E. M. *Forster were among its members. Arthur *Clough's *The Bothie* mulled over the society's faith in reasoned discussion. See P. Levy, *G. E. Moore and the Cambridge Apostles* (1979); W. C. Lubenow, *The Cambridge Apostles* (1999).

apostrophe [Greek, 'to turn away'] A figure of speech in which the writer rhetorically addresses a dead or absent person or abstraction, e.g. 'Milton! thou shouldst be living at this hour' (William *Wordsworth, 'London, 1802').

APPERLEY, Charles James ('Nimrod') (1778–1843) Sporting writer and novelist. Educated at Rugby, Apperley was a professional soldier and amateur huntsman before money problems prompted him, from 1821 onwards, to write about field sports in the *Sporting Magazine* and the **Quarterly Review*. His essays in the latter were collected in *The Chace, the Turf, and the Road* (1837). He wrote a novel, *The Life of a Sportsman* (1842), and the first major sporting biography, *Memoirs of the Late John Mytton, Esquire* (1837), the story of the Shropshire squire, spendthrift, and sportsman, born into an inheritance of £500,000, who drank himself to death in debtors' prison at the age of 38.

Appius and Virginia (1) a tragedy printed in 1654 with a title-page ascription to John *Webster. It is now believed to be Webster's last play, dating from around 1627, and to have been written in collaboration with Thomas *Heywood, with Webster as the dominant partner. The plot is taken from the classical legend which forms one of the stories in William Painter's **Palace of Pleasure*. See *The Works of John Webster*, ed. David Gunby *et al.*, vol. ii (2003). (2) a tragedy by John *Dennis.

APPLETON, Victor House pseudonym for the ghost-written Tom *Swift series of adventure novels for children, published by the Stratemeyer Syndicate, which also produced the Nancy Drew and Bobbsey Twins series.

APULEIUS (*c.* AD 125–after 170) North African Roman poet, philosopher, and rhetorician, whose best-known work, the comic novel *Metamorphoses* or *The Golden Ass*, is the only complete work of Latin prose fiction to survive. Its interwoven stories became a quarry and model for the Italian and French novella: *Boccaccio borrowed three, and others appeared in the 15th-century **Cent nouvelles nouvelles*. The much-reprinted complete translation of 1566 by William Adlington, *The Golden Asse*, was known to William *Shakespeare. **Cupid and Psyche* is the most frequently retold of Apuleius' stories. See Robert H. F. Carver, *The Protean Ass: The 'Metamorphoses' of Apuleius from Antiquity to the Renaissance* (2007).

AQUINAS, St Thomas (*c.*1224–1274) Philosopher and Dominican friar from Aquino in southern Italy, now the most famous of the medieval *scholastic theologians, although in the Middle Ages he was a controversial figure whose authority took time to become widely established. His *Summa Theologica* represents the reconciliation of Christian theology with Aristotelian philosophy. Unfinished, it is a synthesis of the moral and political sciences within a theological and metaphysical framework. His other major works are the *Summa Contra Gentiles* and a series of commentaries on *Aristotle, whose works were translated from Greek into Latin under his aegis. He was later called 'Doctor Angelicus'. His followers (Thomists) have been an active school in contemporary philosophy, particularly in France. He is a fundamental influence on Dante's **Divina commedia* (see *Paradiso*, X–XIII). See B. Davies, *Aquinas* (2002); *Summa*, trans. in 20 vols (1911–25), by Fathers of the Dominican Province.

Arabia Deserta *See* DOUGHTY, CHARLES.

Arabian Nights Entertainments (*or A Thousand and One Nights*) A collection of Arabic stories, introduced in Europe through the French translation (from a Syrian manuscript and from oral sources) of Antoine *Galland, whose version appeared between 1704 and 1717. An anonymous *'Grub Street' version appeared in English *c.*1708, and E. W. *Lane's bowdlerized version appeared in 1838–40. A more complete English translation was by John Payne (1842–1916); it appeared in a limited edition, published by the Villon Society 1882–4. This was followed by Sir Richard *Burton's eccentric and prurient version (1885–8), also published through a subscription society to avoid prosecution for obscenity. The first version for children was published by Elizabeth Newbery (d. 1821) *c.*1791 as *The Oriental Moralist or Beauties of the Arabian Nights Entertainments*; other juvenile editions include *Dalziel's Illustrated Arabian Nights Entertainment* (1863–5), with illustrations by John *Tenniel, John Everett *Millais, and others, and one by Andrew *Lang (1898). The best modern translation (only partial) is by Husain Haddawy (2 vols, 1990, 1995).

The *Nights* evolved slowly through oral transmission, but with a certain amount of written backing. A Persian collection called *Hazar Afsaneh* (*A Thousand Tales*) translated into Arabic *c.* AD 850 probably provided a nucleus and possibly even the frame story of Shahriyar and Sheherazade. The tales, which vary in kind, from heroic epics, fables, and pornographic stories to magic-adventure tales such as those about Sinbad and Aladdin, derive mainly from Persian, Arabic, and Indian sources, with Sumerian, Akkadian, ancient Egyptian, Greek, and Turkish stories occasionally surfacing. The collection continued to change, sometimes, quite radically, as when large amounts of verse were added in medieval times, until the 19th century, when printed texts provided some stabilization.

There are many other large Arabic oral story collections, but the *Nights* has unequalled variety and verve. It captivated the European imagination, and contributed greatly to the vogue for *oriental tales in the 18th and early 19th centuries. Their influence continued through the 20th, and may be seen in the work of writers as diverse as John *Barth, Jorge *Borges, A. S. *Byatt, Angela *Carter, Pier Paolo *Pasolini, and Salman *Rushdie, and in numerous films. See *The Arabian Nights: A Companion* by R. Irwin (1994).

ARAGON, Louis (1897–1982) French poet, novelist, and political activist. He began his career under the influence of Dada. In 1919, with André *Breton and Philippe Soupault (1897–1990), he founded the review *Littérature*, which became the flagship of the French avant-garde. In 1924 he became one of the founding members of *Surrealism. His first collections of poetry were *Feu de joie* (1921) and *Le Mouvement perpétuel* (1926). In 1927 he joined the French Communist Party, before finally breaking with the Surrealist movement in 1932. During the Second World War he became one of the most popular of French Resistance poets, with *Les Yeux d'Elsa* (1942) and *La Diane française* (1945). His novels include the Surrealist *Le Paysan de Paris* (1926), the *Monde réel* trilogy—*Les Cloches de Bâle* (1934: *The Bells of Basel*), *Les Beaux Quartiers* (1936: *Residential Quarter*), and *Les Voyageurs de l'Impériale* (1942)—and *La Semaine sainte* (1958: *Holy Week*). See L. F. Becker, *Louis Aragon* (1971).

ARBER, Edward (1836–1912) He began his career as an admiralty clerk, 1854–78, but studied English literature at King's College London, and in 1881 became professor of English at Mason College, Birmingham. He produced *English Reprints* (1868–71), *A Transcript of the Registers of the Company of Stationers of London, 1554–1640* (1875–94), and *Term Catalogues, 1668–1709* (1903–6).

ARBUCKLE, James (d. 1742) Irish poet, educated at Glasgow, where he clashed with the Calvinist authorities for his active part in politics and student dramatics. He espoused the philosophy of the third earl of *Shaftesbury. In association with Francis *Hutcheson he wrote moral and aesthetic essays which were serialized in the *Dublin Weekly Journal* (1725–7) and later reissued as *Hibernicus's Letters* (1729), and he attempted a short-lived Dublin periodical, *The Tribune*, in 1729. His student poetry was published in broadsheets or in *The Edinburgh Miscellany* (1720). He was at one time befriended by Jonathan *Swift and in 1730 published the parody 'A Panegyric on the Reverend D—n S—t' formerly ascribed to Swift himself. Some classical translations and other manuscript poetry are now in the National Library of Wales.

ARBUTHNOT, John (1667–1735) MD of St Andrews, FRS, and from 1705 to 1714 physician to Queen Anne. The *Scriblerus Club met in his rooms. Arbuthnot's *History of *John Bull* and his pamphlet *The Art of Political Lying* (both 1712) were high Tory satires. He and *Pope assisted John *Gay in *Three Hours after Marriage* (1717) and he part-authored several other satires, often with scientific aspects. He wrote substantial works on probability, mathematics, ancient units of measurement, coins, geology, and medicine. His *Essay Concerning the Nature of Aliments* (1731), an account of the importance of diet, was followed by an *Essay Concerning the Effects of Air on Human Bodies* 1733). A serious poem, ΓΝΩΘΙ ΣΕΑΥΤΟΝ (*Know Thyself*) appeared in 1734; later that year Pope hastily assembled his *Epistle to Dr Arbuthnot*, turning a defence of satire into a tribute to his dying friend. Arbuthnot was a main author of the *Memoirs of *Martinus Scriblerus* (pub. 1741).

Arcades A *pastoral entertainment by John *Milton, written ?1634, in honour of Alice, dowager countess of Derby, for performance by members of the Bridgewater family for whom he wrote **Comus*. See Cedric C. Brown, *Milton's Aristocratic Entertainments* (1985).

Arcadia A district in the central Peloponnese which, through *Virgil's *Eclogues*, became the traditional location of the idealized world of *pastoral. Virgil himself was aware of the clash between the genre's realistic and idealizing purposes. Renaissance writers knew nothing about the real Arcadia and idealized landscape dominates their work.

Arcadia A series of verse eclogues connected by prose narrative, published 1504 by *Sannazar, occupied with the loves, laments, and other doings of various shepherds in Arcadia. The work, which was immensely popular, was a link between the *pastorals of *Theocritus and *Virgil and those of Jorge de *Montemayor, Philip *Sidney, Edmund *Spenser, and later writers.

Arcadia, The A prose romance by Philip *Sidney, including poems and pastoral eclogues in a wide variety of verse forms. It exists in two versions: the first, completed by 1581, and much of it written at *Wilton House, is known as the *Old Arcadia*. Its survival as an independent work that circulated in manuscript was discovered by Bertram Dobell in 1906–7; an edition was first printed in 1926. The second version, now known as the *New Arcadia*, was Sidney's radical revision, made about 1583–4 but never completed. It breaks down in the third book, having already run to twice the length of the original. This revised version was first printed, on its own, in 1590, with chapter divisions and summaries 'not of Sir *Philip Sidneis* dooing'. In 1593, and thereafter, books III–V of the *Old Arcadia* were added to the *New Arcadia* to make a complete-seeming but hybrid work. Until the 20th century, only the hybrid *Arcadia* was available to readers.

The *Old Arcadia* is in five 'Books or Acts', sometimes quasi-dramatic in use of dialogue, interspersed with a large number of poems and songs. The first four books are followed by pastoral eclogues on themes linked to or contrasted with the main narrative. The story is of the attempts of Arcadia's ruler, the foolish old duke Basilius, to prevent the fulfilment of an oracle by withdrawing to two rustic 'lodges' with his wife Gynecia and their daughters Pamela and Philoclea. Two young princes, the cousins Musidorus and Pyrocles, gain access to the retired court by disguising themselves as, respectively, a shepherd and an Amazon. A complicated series of intrigues ensues, with Basilius and Gynecia both falling in love with the disguised Pyrocles; Musidorus meanwhile becomes enmeshed with the family of Dametas, an ill-bred herdsman who has been made Pamela's guardian, his shrewish wife Miso, and their foolish daughter Mopsa. Pyrocles succeeds in seducing Philoclea, and Musidorus attempts to elope with Pamela and comes close to raping her, but their schemes go awry when Basilius appears to die of a potion believed by his wife to be an aphrodisiac, and Pyrocles and Philoclea are discovered in bed by Dametas. The climax of the narrative is a trial presided over by Euarchus, the just ruler of Macedon, who sentences Gynecia to be buried alive and Pyrocles and Musidorus to be executed. Euarchus does not recognize the young men as his own son and nephew, but even when their identities are revealed he asserts that 'If rightly I have judged, then rightly have I judged mine own children.' The day is saved, and all appears to end happily, by Basilius' awakening from what was only a sleeping potion. Among the minor characters Philisides, a melancholy gentleman-poet, is a version of Sidney himself. Strephon and Klaius, two shepherds in love with the mysterious Urania, recite two of the most elaborate love-complaints in the romance, the first being the double sestina 'Ye goat-herd gods, that love the grassy mountains'. Other memorable poems include the anatomical praise of Philoclea's beauties 'What tongue can her perfections tell', the echo poem in *hexameters 'Fair rocks, goodly rivers, sweet woods, when shall I see peace?', the asclepiadics (i.e. a lyric metre, consisting of a *spondee, two (or three) *choriambi, and an iambus) 'O sweet woods, the delight of solitariness', the beast fable on tyranny 'As I my little flock on Ister bank', and the sonnet 'My true love hath my heart, and I have his'.

No new poems were added in the *New Arcadia*, but the method of narration was made far more complex, both stylistically and thematically: the apparent pastoral comedy of the *Old Arcadia* gives way to heroic or epic and tragic writing. Major new characters include Basilius' wicked sister-in-law Cecropia and her well-meaning but unfortunate, melancholy son Amphialus, who is in love with Philoclea and beloved by Queen Helen of Corinth. The first two books are enlarged by the addition of tournaments and courtly spectacles and by detailed accounts of the exploits of Pyrocles and Musidorus before they reached Arcadia, including much about different forms of love and of government. In the third revised book mock battles give way to real ones, after the two Arcadian princesses and the disguised Pyrocles have been taken captive by Cecropia; their sufferings in prison are powerfully described, in particular those of the patient and dignified Pamela. Her prayer in prison was later alleged to have been used by Charles I, and in *Eikonoklastes* John *Milton attacked the monarch for his drawing on a prayer from a 'vain amatorious Poem'. The *New Arcadia* breaks off in mid-sentence just after Amphialus has appeared to kill himself and as rescue seems to be at hand for the imprisoned and besieged princesses.

The composite *Arcadia*, as printed from 1593 onwards, was attacked by William *Hazlitt as 'one of the greatest monuments of the abuse of intellectual power upon record', mainly because of its prose style. T. S. *Eliot, more damningly still, called it 'a monument of dulness'. It was, however, a highly popular book throughout the 17th century, and its plot material was frequently plundered by dramatists. *Shakespeare based the Gloucester plot of *King Lear* on Sidney's story of 'the *Paphlagonian* unkinde king', and Samuel *Richardson, who printed the last folio edition of the work in 1724, took the name of his first heroine, Pamela, from Sidney's romance. Like Charles *Lamb, Virginia *Woolf was an influential admirer of it, and the later 20th century showed signs that it was beginning to be appreciated again. C. S. *Lewis said that 'What a man thinks of it, far more than what he thinks of Shakespeare or Spenser or Donne, tests the depth of his sympathy with the sixteenth century.' Jean Robertson edited the *Old Arcadia* in 1973. *The New Arcadia*, ed. Victor Skretkowicz, was published in 1987.

ARCHER, William (1856–1924) Drama critic and translator, born in Perth, Scotland, and educated at Edinburgh University. He spent periods of his boyhood with his grandparents in Norway, where he learned the language; when he later became an influential drama critic in London (*see* THEATRE CRITICISM), he did much to popularize Henrik *Ibsen in England. His translation of Ibsen's *Pillars of Society* became in 1880 the first Ibsen play to be produced in London, although it attracted little notice. In 1889 the production of his translation of *A Doll's House* caused moral controversy, which increased with the production of *Ghosts* and *Hedda Gabler* in 1891, with Elizabeth Robins (1862–1952) in the role of Hedda. In 1890–1, Archer published his five-volume edition of Ibsen's prose dramas in translation (some with collaboration), and in 1892 he and his brother produced a translation of *Peer Gynt*. The collected works of Ibsen appeared in 1906–7. Archer campaigned extensively throughout his career to reform and modernize the English theatre. His books included: *English Dramatists of Today* (1882), *About the Theatre* (1886), *Masks and Faces?* (1888), and studies of the actors Henry *Irving (1883) and William *Macready (1890). His annual volumes of collected theatre criticism, *The Theatrical 'World'*, appeared between 1894 and 1898. In 1907, with Harley *Granville-Barker, he issued detailed proposals for a *National Theatre, and in 1919 he assisted with the establishment of the New Shakespeare Company at Stratford-upon-Avon. In *The Drama Old and New* (1923), he promoted the work of George Bernard *Shaw, whose career as a playwright he helped launch, and John *Galsworthy among others; in the same year his own play, *The Green Goddess*, was produced with great success in London after a successful run two years earlier in America. See the biography by P. Whitebrook (1993).

archetype A primary symbol, action, setting, or character-type that is found repeatedly in myth, folklore, and literature. Religious mystics have at various times proposed that there is a universal symbolic language of dreams and visions; and in the 20th century this notion was encouraged by the speculative anthropology of J. G. *Frazer and the psychology of *Jung, who claimed that human beings shared a 'collective unconscious' for which archetypal images, whether in dreams or in imaginative literature, provided evidence. Archetypal criticism (*see also* MYTH CRITICISM) under Jung's influence has sought to trace the recurrence of such symbols and types as the Earth Mother, the Quest, the Paradisal Garden, and the Trickster. Maud Bodkin's *Archetypal Patterns in Poetry* (1934) was an early example. The wider significance of archetypes in literature was explored by Northrop *Frye.

Archimago (Archimage) In Edmund *Spenser's **Faerie Queene*, is the great enchanter, symbolizing Hypocrisy, who deceives *Una by assuming the appearance of the *Redcrosse Knight (I. i). His deceits are exposed and Archimago is 'layd full low in dungeon deepe' (I. xii. 36). From this he emerges in Book II to seek vengeance on Sir *Guyon for what he has suffered at the hands of the Redcrosse Knight, and employs *Braggadochio for the purpose.

Arden (1) a large Warwickshire forest often figuring in romance literature. In Drayton's **Poly-olbion* it extends from the Severn to the Trent (XIII. 16); (2) the forest in Shakespeare's **As You Like It* (Ardenne in the Oxford edition), often assumed to be identical with (1) but also suggesting the forest north-east of Bordeaux and the forest of Ardennes in present Belgium; (3) the surname of Shakespeare's mother Mary; (4) the distinguishing name of a series of scholarly editions of Shakespeare's plays initiated by W. J. Craig and R. H. Case in 1899, and revised under the general editorship of Una Ellis-Fermor, H. F. Brooks, Harold Jenkins, and Brian Morris (1946–82); a third series under the general editorship of Richard Proudfoot, Ann Thompson, and David Scott Kastan was begun in 1995, since when Henry Woudhuysen has joined the editorial board.

ARDEN, John (1930–) Playwright, born in Barnsley, Yorkshire, and educated at the universities of Cambridge and Edinburgh, where he studied architecture. In 1957, the year in which he married Margaretta D'Arcy, with whom he collaborated as early as 1960 (*The Happy Haven*), he had his first professional production, at the *Royal Court, of *The Waters of Babylon*, a grotesque, satirical, sprawling play about a corrupt municipal lottery organized by a slum landlord. This was followed by *Live Like Pigs* (1958), dealing with social conflict and violence on a housing estate. *Serjeant Musgrave's Dance* (1959), set in a colliery town in the north of England in 1860–80, shows Musgrave, a deserter from the British army, attempting to exact revenge for the death of a colleague, but finding that violence breeds violence. Arden here mixes a rich, idiosyncratic, semi-historical prose with ballad and verse, as he does in *Armstrong's Last Goodnight* (1964), another fable about violence, set in the Border country in the 1530s. In a preface to *The Workhouse Donkey* (1963), a play about municipal corruption, Arden claims that 'the theatre must be catholic' and celebrate the Dionysian attributes of 'noise, disorder, drunkenness, lasciviousness, nudity, generosity, corruption, fertility and ease'. He was widely praised as one of the most innovatory dramatists of the 1960s, but fell out with the Royal Shakespeare Company, and the theatrical establishment over changes to the script of his *The Island of the Mighty* (1972), and it was the last of his plays to be performed by the British professional theatre. He and D'Arcy were already working with John *McGrath's 7:84 company and thereafter, from *The Ballygombeen Bequest* (1972) and *The Non-Stop Connolly Show* (1976) on, their work became more directly socialist and concerned with the politics of Ireland where they were staged. He has also had important works produced on BBC Radio, notably *Pearl* (1979) and *What is the Kingdom?* (1988). His fiction includes *Silence among the Weapons* (1982), and *The Stealing Steps*, a collection of short stories published in 2003.

Arden of Faversham: *The Lamentable and True Tragedy of Master Arden of Faversham in Kent, who was most wickedly murdered by the means of his disloyal and wanton wife* A play published anonymously in 1592 in a text that appears to be a memorial reconstruction. Ascribed to Shakespeare in a 1770 edition, it was included in Tucker Brooke's *The Shakespeare Apocrypha* (1908). Since then it has hovered on the fringes of the Shakespeare canon; the Revels editor, M. L. Wine (1973), considered it likely Shakespeare was the author, and the theory that Shakespeare wrote at least part of it has been revived more recently. The play deals with the persistent and eventually successful attempts of Mistress Arden and her lover Mosby to murder Arden: they hire two murderers, Black Will and Shakebag. The crime is discovered, and Mosby and Mrs Arden executed. The play derives from *Holinshed's account of an actual murder committed in February 1551. Modern revivals include performances by the Royal Shakespeare Company in 1970 and 1982. George *Lillo wrote a play on the same subject.

ARDIZZONE, Edward (1900–79) Painter, watercolourist, and printmaker, and one of the best known of 20th-century illustrators, of both adult and children's books.

ARENDT, Hannah (1906–75) Historian, philosopher, and social scientist, born in Hanover, educated at the universities of Marburg, Freiburg, and Heidelberg, where she studied under Karl Jaspers. She left Germany for France in 1933, and after the German invasion in 1940 fled to the United States where she later became a citizen. Her works include *On Revolution* (1963) and an influential analysis of the trial in 1961 of the Nazi leader Adolf Eichmann, *Eichmann in Jerusalem: A Report on the Banality of Evil* (1963, and subsequently revised), which proved an important contribution to the literature of the *Holocaust. *Men in Dark Times* (1970) contains among other writings valuable essays on Bertolt *Brecht, Walter *Benjamin, Hermann *Broch, and Gotthold *Lessing. She was a friend of Mary *McCarthy, and their correspondence was published as *Between Friends*, ed. C. Brightman (1995).

Areopagitica A tract championing freedom of the press by John *Milton, published in 1644. The title imitates the *Areopagiticus* of the Greek orator Isocrates (436–338 BC). Attempting (unsuccessfully) to persuade Parliament to repeal its licensing order of 14 June 1643, which effectively reinstated Stuart press censorship, Milton argues that readers should be free to choose between good and bad books, since good and evil are inseparable in the fallen world, and virtue lies in resisting evil, not being shielded from it. Truth is scattered, and can be recovered only by active search. However, he excludes *Roman Catholics from freedom to publish, regarding them as enemies of freedom themselves.

ARETINO, Pietro (the Aretine) (1492–1556) Italian dramatist, poet, and satirist, born at Arezzo, whence his name. He was the author of five comedies and a tragedy, and also of satires, pasquinades (*see* PASQUIL), and other works of a scandalous or licentious character. He is frequently mentioned in English works of the Elizabethan and later periods and differently appreciated, in comments ranging from 'It was one of the wittiest knaves that ever God made' of Thomas *Nashe (*The *Unfortunate Traveller*) to 'that notorious ribald of Arezzo' of John *Milton (**Areopagitica*). See C. Cairns, *Pietro Aretino and the Republic of Venice* (1985).

Argosy (1) *A Magazine of Tales, Travels, Essays and Poems*, a periodical owned and edited 1865–87 by Ellen *Wood (Mrs Henry Wood), who was herself a major contributor: it published work by many leading writers, including Anthony *Trollope, Charles *Kingsley, and Charles *Reade, and it survived until 1901; (2) *The World's Best Stories* (1926–40; as *The Argosy of Complete Stories*, 1940–74) consisted largely of reprints of work by established writers, including Joseph *Conrad, H. E. *Bates, Somerset *Maugham, William *Sansom, and many others.

Arianism A Christian heresy named after the 4th-century Alexandrian priest Arius, who taught that the Son of God was not co-eternal with the Father but created by him and endowed with divine status. Arius' principal opponent was Athanasius. Arianism spread widely in the Roman Empire in the 4th century but died out by the end of the 5th. It revived among English radicals in the 16th century, and was held both secretly and publicly by a number of important writers and thinkers in the 17th and 18th centuries, including John *Milton, John *Locke, Isaac *Newton, Samuel *Clarke, and Richard *Price.
See UNITARIANISM.

Ariel (1) an airy spirit in William *Shakespeare's *The *Tempest*. After Prospero releases him from imprisonment by the 'damned witch Sycorax', Ariel aids his magical schemes; (2) a rebel angel in Milton's **Paradise Lost* (VI. 371); (3) in Pope's **Rape of the Lock* (II. 53ff.) the chief of the sylphs whose 'humbler Province is to tend the Fair'.

Shakespeare's character (1) has inspired many later writers to identify the name 'Ariel' with poetic imagination. T. S. *Eliot called five Christmas poems (1927–54) 'Ariel poems', for instance, the first *Penguin paperback was *Maurois's life of P. B. *Shelley called *Ariel* (1935), and there have been several literary journals with 'Ariel' as title.
See also PLATH.

ARIOSTO, Ludovico (1474–1533) Italian poet and playwright, born at Reggio. He spent the greater part of his life at Ferrara and for many years was in the service, first of Cardinal Ippolito, and then of Duke Alfonso I, of *Este. He praised this family in his poem **Orlando furioso*, published in its final form in 1532, the greatest of Italian *chivalric or romance epics. He also wrote Italian and Latin lyrics, satires in imitation of *Horace (known to Sir Thomas *Wyatt), and four comedies, modelled on ancient Roman comedy but set in the contemporary world, of which one, *I suppositi* (1509), came through to *Shakespeare's *The *Taming of the Shrew* via George Gascoigne's **Supposes*. See C. P. Brand, *Ludovico Ariosto: A Preface to the 'Orlando furioso'* (1974).

ARISTOPHANES (*c*.450/460–386 BC) Athenian comic playwright. His eleven surviving comedies are *The Acharnians*; *The Knights*; *The Clouds*; *The Peace*; *The Wasps*; *The Birds*; *The Frogs*; *Plutus*; *Lysistrata*; *Ecclesiazusae*; and *Thesmophoriazusae*. They represent the rumbustious Old Comedy, combining personal attacks, obscenities, parodies, songs, and hymns with ideas on poetry, politics, religion, the sexes. *Socrates is ridiculed in *Clouds*; *Euripides in *Thesmophoriazusae*. In *Frogs*, Euripides and *Aeschylus compete in the underworld to determine which poet can save Athens. Aristophanes' earlier plays, *Acharnians* and *Knights*, are savage attacks on Athenian warmongering; *Wasps* attacks the democracy's jury system. *Birds* is a fantasy of escape from war. *Lysistrata* and *Ecclesiazusae* ridicule notions about the equality of the sexes. In *Plato's *Symposium*, Aristophanes makes a lively and engaging speech on love. Aristophanes' influence on English drama can be seen in Ben *Jonson, Thomas *Middleton, and especially Henry *Fielding. Robert *Browning's poem **Aristophanes' Apology* has the dramatist defend the naturalness of comedy. See M. S. Silk, *Aristophanes and the Definition of Comedy* (2002).

Aristophanes' Apology, *Including a Transcript from Euripides: Being the Last Adventure of Balaustion* A long poem in blank verse by Robert *Browning, published 1875 as a sequel to **Balaustion's Adventure* (1871). The core of the poem is a protracted argument between Balaustion and *Aristophanes as to the moral, social, and metaphysical value of the different aesthetics they espouse, Balaustion defending the visionary humanism of *Euripides, Aristophanes his own coarse realism. Part of Balaustion's argument consists in reading Euripides' play *Herakles* (whose plot, the madness of Herakles and his destruction of his family, constitutes the poem's thematic focus). The poem is not the straightforward defence of Euripides by Browning that it has been taken to be: Balaustion, not Browning, is the speaker. The structure—a monologue containing the narrative of a dialogue and the reading of a play—is arguably Browning's profoundest exploration of the relation of poetic discourse to absolute values such as 'truth' or 'reality'. The poem also contains the remarkable fragment 'Thamuris marching', which reworks some of the material of *' "Childe Roland to the Dark Tower Came" '.

ARISTOTLE (384–322 BC) Philosopher, born at Stagira (hence his name 'the Stagirite') in Macedon, where his father was physician to King Amyntas II. Sent to Athens in 367, he studied under *Plato for twenty years. After a period of travel, in 342 he was appointed by Philip II of Macedon as tutor to the future *Alexander the Great. Seven years later he returned to Athens, where he opened a school in the Lyceum, a grove outside the city; from its colonnades ('peripatoi'), where teaching took place, his school and its philosophical tradition later became known as the Peripatetic. His published works, including dialogues known to *Cicero, are lost; his extant works were probably written lectures. They cover logic, metaphysics, physics, zoology, psychology, ethics, politics, rhetoric, and poetics and demonstrate a strong commitment to the classification of empirical observations and the systematization of knowledge generally. Transmitted through translations, they shaped the development of medieval thought first in the Arab world, then in the Latin West, where Aristotle came to be regarded as the source of all knowledge. His logical treatises won a central place in the curriculum during the 12th century. After a brief struggle his ethical, metaphysical, and scientific works were harmonized with Christianity—to *Aquinas he was 'The Philosopher' and to *Dante he was 'the master of those who know'—and constituted the subject matter of higher education from the 13th to the 17th centuries. They shaped the thinking of Englishmen writing in Latin from *Grosseteste to *Herbert of Cherbury, but the 17th-century promoters of the new science saw Francis *Bacon as having overthrown Aristotle by his superior grasp of experimental observation and his method of induction. The humanists favoured the *Nicomachean Ethics* (identified by Edmund *Spenser as the source of the virtues in *The *Faerie Queene*), *Politics*, and *Poetics*. This last treatise, virtually unknown during the Middle Ages, came into prominence in the middle of the 16th century and contributed to the rise of *neo-classicism. See Jonathan Barnes (ed.), *The Cambridge Companion to Aristotle* (1995). *See* SCHOLASTICISM.

ARLEN, Michael (1895–1956) Novelist, born Dikran Kouyoumdjian in Bulgaria of Armenian descent; educated at Malvern College and, briefly, at Edinburgh University. Naturalized in 1922, he wrote a number of ornate and mannered novels of fashionable London life under the name he had acquired by deed poll, but is chiefly remembered for his best-seller *The Green Hat* (1924), which narrates the short life and violent death of *femme fatale* and dashing widow Iris Storm. Among further novels are *Men Dislike Women* (1931) and *Hell! Said the Duchess* (1934). In 1928 Arlen married and settled in the south of France, returning to London to offer his services during the war. He eventually moved to and died in New York.

Armadale A novel by Wilkie *Collins, published in 1866. This intricately plotted *sensation novel, Collins's longest, has two heroes, one fair, prosperous, and cheerful, the other penniless, dark, and disturbed. Both are named Allan Armadale, and both are infatuated with a compelling red-haired villainess, Lydia Gwilt. The complications stem from the previous generation, when the father of the dark Armadale murdered the father of the other. The dark Armadale, after a miserable childhood, adopts the name Ozias Midwinter, and meets the fair Armadale by chance. They become friends, but Armadale has a prophetic dream which convinces Midwinter that he is doomed to harm his friend. Lydia Gwilt, privy to the mystery surrounding them, marries Midwinter under his real name, becoming Mrs Armadale; her plan to murder Armadale and produce the marriage certificate in order to inherit his money is frustrated by Midwinter, and Lydia dies. The novel reflects Collins's characteristic interests in murder and detection, doubled identities, and the supernatural.

ARMAH, Ayi Kwei (1939–) Author, born in Ghana and educated at Achimota and Groton, before going to Harvard in 1960 and deciding that writing was 'the least parasitic option open to me'. He worked for a year in Paris on a journal, *Jeune Afrique*; his short stories and essays appeared in such journals as *Présence africaine* and *Harper's Magazine*. Since 1970 he has taught at universities in Tanzania (where he learnt Swahili), Lesotho, and the USA, and now lives in Senegal. His first novel, *The Beautyful Ones Are Not Yet Born* (1968), disconcerted readers by its savagely brilliant and witty attack on the corruption of independent Ghana. The opening scene shows a bus conductor savouring the pleasurably rotten stench of a banknote. Putrefaction pervades the dysfunctional world of the novel. Baako in *Fragments* (1970) is a Been-to; he has been educated in Britain and is expected to return with material prosperity for his family. His blind grandmother, Naana, sees the fragmentation of her society more clearly than anyone; it is epitomized for the reader by the death of Baako's baby nephew, killed by the icy blast of an electric fan. *Why Are We So Blest* (1972) asserts with vitriolic pessimism, from three different perspectives, that Africans 'have swallowed the wish for our destruction'. *Two Thousand Seasons* (1973), *The Healers* (1978), and *Osiris Rising* (1995) present an alternative position, focusing on healing through traditional storytelling and a revision of history.

Arminianism The doctrines of Jacobus Arminius (1560–1609), a Dutch Protestant theologian. In opposition to *Calvin's views, Arminius taught that Christ died for all, not only the elect, and that humans could choose whether or not to cooperate with divine grace. Though his doctrines were condemned by the synod of Dort (1618–19), they spread rapidly; in England they were on the whole detested by Puritans but were embraced by both bishops and theological radicals, including John *Milton. By the end of the 17th century the position of the Church of England had become largely if unofficially Arminian.

ARMITAGE, Simon (1963–) Poet, born in Huddersfield and educated at Portsmouth Polytechnic, where he studied Geography. He worked for some years as a probation officer. His first collection, *Zoom!* (1989), drew on that experience, and on the rhythms of Yorkshire vernacular, as well as on Frank *O'Hara and Paul *Muldoon. Its immediacy, wit, and originality brought him great critical and popular acclaim. *Book of Matches* (1993) was more introspective in nature, an element developed in *Dead Sea Poems* (1995), and coming to dominate in *CloudCuckooLand* (1997), which has a cosmic, or millenarian, intensity. He published a *Selected Poems* in 2001, and *Tyrannosaurus Rex versus the Cowboy Kid* in 2006. Armitage has also published novels, including *The White Stuff* (2004). He has made versions of *Euripides, the *Odyssey*, and the medieval English poem *Sir *Gawain and the Green Knight* (2007), which employs a distinctively northern and contemporary demotic while scrupulously recreating the alliterative metres of the original. *Moon Country* (1996), a collaboration with Glyn *Maxwell, retraces the journey to Iceland made by W. H. *Auden and Louis *MacNeice in 1936. Armitage has worked extensively as a poet in the media of radio, television, and film; and his public readings are immensely popular.

ARMSTRONG, John (1709–79) London-based Scottish poet and physician, and friend of James *Thomson (who portrayed him in *The *Castle of Indolence*), Tobias *Smollett, and Henry *Fuseli, with whom he made a continental tour in 1771. He is principally remembered for his four-volume didactic poem *The Art of Preserving Health* (1744) and for his satirical verse epistle, *Taste* (1753). He quarrelled with John *Wilkes over the latter's attacks on the Scots in the **North Briton*.

ARMSTRONG, William (Kinmont Willie) (*fl.* 1596) A Border moss-trooper (or outlaw), whose nickname is taken from his castle of Kinmont in Canonbie, Dumfriesshire. He was captured in 1587 but escaped; he was imprisoned in 1596 at Carlisle, but was rescued by the Scottish warden. His fate is unknown. He is the hero of the ballad 'Kinmont Willie', included in Walter *Scott's **Minstrelsy of the Scottish Border*.

ARNE, Thomas (1710–78) Theatre composer. He produced operas, including a setting of Joseph *Addison's *Rosamond* (1733), *masques, including an adaptation of *Milton's *Comus* (1738), and much incidental music for plays. His opera *Artaxerxes* (1762) held the stage into the 19th century; his setting of David *Mallet and James *Thomson's masque *Alfred* (1740) added 'Rule Britannia' to the canon of English song. His many *Shakespeare settings include 'Where the bee sucks' and 'Fear no more the heat of the sun'. He collaborated with David *Garrick for the Shakespeare Jubilee in an 'Ode upon Dedicating a Building to Shakespeare' (1769).

ARNOLD, Sir Edwin (1832–1904) Poet and journalist. Born in Gravesend, Kent, he won the *Newdigate Prize at Oxford in 1852, and was principal of the Deccan Sanskrit College at Poona, India, 1856–61. He then joined the staff of the **Daily Telegraph*, and became editor in 1873. He published several volumes of poems and translations, some from the Sanskrit, and is remembered for his *The Light of Asia, or The Great Renunciation* (1879), a poem of eight books in blank verse, in which he attempted 'by the medium of an imaginary Buddhist votary to depict the life and character and indicate the philosophy of that noble hero and reformer, Prince Gautama of India, founder of Buddhism'.

ARNOLD, Matthew (1822–88) Poet and critic, eldest son of Thomas *Arnold, born at Laleham-on-Thames, Middlesex, and educated at Rugby School, Winchester College, and at Balliol College, Oxford, where he formed a close friendship with A. H. *Clough, and won the *Newdigate Prize with a poem on Cromwell. He became a fellow of Oriel College, Oxford, then in 1847 secretary to Lord Lansdowne. In 1851 he became an inspector of schools, in which capacity he served for 35 years, travelling throughout England and observing at first hand the social conditions that prompted much of his later critical work. His first volume of poems, *The Strayed Reveller, and Other Poems* (by 'A', 1849), contains 'The Forsaken Merman', 'The Sick King in Bokhara', and sonnets written at Balliol, including 'Shakespeare'. In 1851 he married Fanny Lucy Wightman, who was to bear six children, three of whom predeceased him. Part of 'Dover Beach' (1867) may date from his honeymoon, which continued on the Continent, and also inspired his 'Stanzas from the Grande Chartreuse' (1855). **Empedocles on Etna, and Other Poems* appeared, anonymously, in 1852; it contained *'Tristram and Iseult' and some of the 'Marguerite' poems, including 'Yes! in the sea of life enisled', now thought to have been addressed to Mary Claude of Ambleside, whom he had met while staying at the Arnold holiday home at Fox How. In 1853 appeared a volume of poems containing extracts from the earlier books, and *'Sohrab and Rustum', 'The *Scholar-Gipsy', 'Memorial Verses to Wordsworth' (who had been a friend of the Arnolds), and 'Stanzas in Memory of the Author of "Obermann"', which show how Arnold had been affected by *Senancour's novel and by the *mal du siècle* of other European writers. Arnold's preface discusses the problems of writing poetry in an 'age wanting in moral grandeur' and his reason for repudiating *Empedocles on Etna* as insufficiently ennobling. *Poems, Second Series*, including **Balder Dead*, appeared in 1855; *Merope, a Tragedy* in 1858; and *New Poems*, including *'Thyrsis', 'Rugby Chapel', and 'Heine's Grave', in 1867.

In his maturity Arnold turned increasingly to prose, writing essays on literary, educational, and social topics that established him as the leading critic of the day and which greatly influenced writers as diverse as Max Weber, T. S. *Eliot, F. R. *Leavis, and Raymond *Williams. His lectures on translating

*Homer, with his definition of 'the grand style' (delivered in 1860, while he was professor of poetry at Oxford), were published in 1861 (*see* TRANSLATION); *Essays in Criticism (First Series)* in 1865 (*Second Series*, 1888); *On the Study of Celtic Literature* (which helped prompt Oxford to establish a chair of Celtic studies) in 1867; **Culture and Anarchy* in 1869; *Friendship's Garland* in 1871; *Literature and Dogma*, a study of the interpretation of the Bible, in 1873. In these and other works, Arnold sharply criticized the provincialism, *Philistinism, sectarianism, and *utilitarian materialism of English life and culture, and argued that England needed more intellectual curiosity, more ideas, and a more comparative, European outlook. The critic, he said, should be flexible, tactful, free of prejudice; his endeavour should be 'to see the object as in itself it really is'. Arnold's fame as a critic grew steadily, and in 1883 he delivered a series of lectures in America (undertaken partly to finance his feckless son Richard, who had inherited some of his father's early extravagances). He worked tirelessly to improve English education, visiting the Continent to study educational systems and producing reports (*The Popular Education of France*, 1861; *A French Eton*, 1864; *Schools and Universities on the Continent*, 1868) which argued that England badly needed more educational organization and could learn much from European models. He died in Liverpool, where he was awaiting the arrival of his daughter Lucy, who had married an American. See *Poems*, ed. and annotated Kenneth Allott and Miriam Allott (1979); *The Complete Prose Works of Matthew Arnold*, ed. R. H. Super, 11 vols (1960–77); Park Honan, *Matthew Arnold* (1981).

ARNOLD, Thomas (1795–1842) Educated at Winchester College and Corpus Christi College, Oxford, remembered principally as the headmaster (1828–42) of Rugby School, which, through various reforms, he raised from a state of decline to the rank of a great public school. His belief in the formation of the character of the Christian gentleman as the primary role of the public school had a profound and lasting influence, and he was held in great personal veneration by his pupils, who included his son Matthew *Arnold, Arthur Hugh *Clough, Arthur Penrhyn *Stanley, and Thomas *Hughes, author of *Tom Brown's Schooldays* (1857). A Broad Churchman, he wrote in favour of church reform and Catholic emancipation, and attacked the Tractarians of the *Oxford Movement. He was the author of several works on Roman history, influenced by *Niebuhr, and was appointed Regius professor of modern history in Oxford in 1841. The standard life is by A. P. *Stanley (1844).

Arraignment of Paris, The A pastoral play in verse by George *Peele, published 1584. It was written for and played before *Elizabeth I, whose beauty and virtue are duly celebrated. Paris is tending his flocks on Ida, with Oenone his wife, when he is called on to decide to which of the three goddesses, *Juno, Pallas, or Venus, the golden apple shall be awarded. He decides in favour of Venus, who carries away Paris, leaving Oenone disconsolate. Juno and Pallas formally accuse Paris of bias in his judgement. The case is referred to Diana. She evades the delicate choice by awarding the apple to the nymph Eliza, 'our Zabeta fair', i.e. Elizabeth I.

ARTAUD, Antonin (1896–1948) French actor, director, and dramatic theorist. In a series of manifestos, collected in *Le Théâtre et son double* (1938: *The Theatre and its Double*, 1958), he called for a return to the primitive and the ritualistic in drama (enshrined in the notion of a *'Theatre of Cruelty'), in opposition to the realistic theatre of a dominant rationalist culture. See M. Esslin, *Antonin Artaud* (1976).

Artegal (Archgallo in Geoffrey) Legendary king of Britain, son of the savage Morvidus and brother of Gorbonian whom he succeeds (described in *Geoffrey of Monmouth's *Historia Regum Britanniae*, III. 17). He was deposed for his crimes and replaced by his brother Elidurus the Dutiful; when he returned from exile Elidurus restored him to the throne. The story is the subject of William *Wordsworth's poem 'Artegal and Elidure'.

Artegall, Sir In Edmund *Spenser's **Faerie Queene*, V, the champion of Justice. *Britomart, to whom his image has been revealed by a magic mirror, is in love with him, and her quest for him ends in their union. Representing Lord Grey de Wilton, he undertakes the rescue of Irena (Ireland) from the tyrant Grantorto. Jointly with Prince *Arthur he slays the *soldan (Philip II of Spain). His name perhaps signifies 'equal to Arthur'.

art for art's sake A phrase associated with the aesthetic doctrine that art is self-sufficient and need serve no moral or political purpose. The phrase *l'art pour l'art* became current in France in the first half of the 19th century and Théophile *Gautier's formulation in his preface to *Mademoiselle de Maupin* (1835), which denied that art could or should be in any way useful, was admired by Walter *Pater, one of the leading influences on the English *'Aesthetic' movement of the 1880s. (*See* WILDE, OSCAR; DOWSON, ERNEST; JOHNSON, LIONEL; SYMONS, ARTHUR) A. C. *Swinburne in his study *William Blake* (written between 1862 and 1867) championed the morality of 'art for art's sake' and Pater in his conclusion to *The Renaissance* (1873) spoke of 'the desire of beauty, the love of art for art's sake'.

Arthour and of Merlin, Of A later 13th-century non-alliterative romance in 9,938 lines of short rhyming couplets, preserved in the *Auchinleck Manuscript (four other manuscripts contain a lesser, variant version). It seems to derive from a French source related to the Vulgate *Merlin* and is a leisurely narrative of the life of Merlin, the upbringing and crowning of Arthur and his many battles. It has been edited by O. D. Macrae-Gibson, *Of Arthour and of Merlin* (EETS OS 268, 1973).

Arthur, King The figure of King Arthur has probably some historical basis, and there is reason to think that, as *Nennius states, he was a chieftain or general (*dux bellorum*) in the 5th or 6th century. The **Annales Cambriae* place the battle of Mount Badon, 'in which Arthur carried the cross of our Lord Jesus Christ on his shoulders', in 518, and the 'battle of Camlan, in which Arthur and Medraut fell' in 539. The contemporary chronicler *Gildas makes no mention of Arthur (though he refers to the battle of Badon), nor do some of the principal Welsh bards of the 6th and 7th centuries. But there is mention of him in certain ancient poems contained in the **Black Book of Carmarthen* and more especially in the ancient Welsh romance *Culhwch and Olwen*, where he figures with Kay, Bedevere, and *Gawain (Gwalchmei). According to the *Arthur* of the marquis of Bath's manuscript (1428: ed. F. J. Furnivall, EETS os 2, 1864), he died in 542 after a reign of 22 years. He was said to be the father of *Mordred by his half-sister Morgawse; his sister was Anna. Guinevere was the daughter of Arthur's ally Leodegan. According to *Malory, the Grail was accomplished 454 years after the passing of Christ (i.e. in 487). The legend of the return of Arthur to rule Britain again is told by Malory and in the stanzaic *Le *Morte Arthur*. According to the alliterative **Morte Arthure*, he definitely died.

The Arthur of the cycle of legends first appears at length in the *Historia Regum Britanniae* of *Geoffrey of Monmouth. According to this, Arthur is the son of *Uther Pendragon and Ygaerne (*Igraine), wife of Gorlois of Cornwall, whom Uther wins through Merlin's magic. At the age of 15 he becomes king and, with his sword Caliburn (Excalibur), slays Childric, defeats the heathen, and conquers Scotland, Ireland, Iceland, and Orkney. He marries Guanhamara, a Roman lady, and holds his court at Caerleon on the Usk. He is summoned to pay tribute to the emperor Lucius of Rome, resists, and declares war. Guanhamara and the kingdom are left in the charge of Modred, his nephew. Arthur slays the giant of St Michael's Mount. When about to enter Rome, he is warned that Modred has seized Guanhamara and the kingdom. He returns with Walwain, who is slain on landing; Modred retreats to Cornwall where, with all his knights, he is slain in a final battle. Arthur is mortally wounded and is borne to the island of *Avalon for the healing of his wounds, and Guanhamara becomes a nun. This version was developed by the 12th-century Norman writer *Wace; the Round Table is first mentioned by him as a device for the settlement of disputes over precedence; and Wace says that the wounded king is expected to return to rule the Britons again. Wace was the principal source of *Laȝamon's *Brut*, the first English version of the story which adds to both the magical and martial aspects: Arthur is borne off after the last battle at Camelford to Argante (Morgan le Fay) in Avalon in a magic boat. The story was very significantly developed in the French *'matter of Britain', by such writers as *Marie de France, *Chrétien de Troyes, and the authors of the 13th-century Vulgate prose cycles, and it became the centre of a mass of legends in several languages, most importantly German. Other characters—*Merlin, *Gawain, *Launcelot, and *Tristram—gradually became associated with Arthur, and he himself is the central character only in the narratives describing his early years and his final battle and death; in the intervening tales his court is merely the starting point for the adventures of various knights. The story of Arthur as given here is the basis of Malory's *Le *Morte Darthur* which was the most authoritative version of the legend in the English tradition. Malory's version gives great prominence to the exploits of the knights of the Round Table, the quest of the Holy Grail, the love of Launcelot and Guinevere, and the love of Tristram and Isoud. For other Arthurian writings, *see* TENNYSON, ALFRED; WILLIAM OF MALMESBURY; GLASTONBURY. See J. D. Bruce, *The Evolution of Arthurian Romance from the Beginnings down to the Year 1300* (2 vols, 1923); R. S. Loomis (ed.), *Arthurian Literature in the Middle Ages* (1959); R. Barber, *King Arthur in Legend and History* (1973); N. J. Lacy and G. Ashe (ed.), *The New Arthurian Encyclopedia* (1996); A. Lupack, *The Oxford Guide to Arthurian Literature and Legend* (2005).

Arthur, Prince In Edmund *Spenser's **Faerie Queene* he symbolizes 'Magnificence', or Magnanimity, in the Aristotelian sense of the perfection of all the virtues. He enters into the adventures of the several knights and brings them to a fortunate conclusion. His chief deeds are the slaying of the three-bodied monster Geryoneo and the rescue from him of Belge (The Netherlands) (V. x, xi); and, jointly with *Artegall, the slaying of the *soldan (Philip II) in his 'charret hye' (the Armada) (V. viii).

art nouveau A decorative style that flourished throughout Europe and America from the 1880s to *c*.1914, characterized by asymmetry, sinuous lines, and a flame-like patterning of the surface with such motifs as the willowy, elongated, female figure with flowing hair and the fantastic curves of stylized flowers. English art nouveau tends to be sparser and more geometric than the continental version. The first British works are A. H. Mackmurdo's (1851–1942) chair of 1881, and a title page to *Wren's City Churches* (1883). Art-oriented literary periodicals played an important role; Mackmurdo's *Century Guild Hobby Horse* (1884) was followed by the **Dial* (1889–97), the **Yellow Book* (1894–7), and the **Savoy* (1896–8). The most distinguished illustrators were Aubrey *Beardsley, Charles *Ricketts, Laurence *Housman, Charles Conder (1868–1909), and Thomas Sturge *Moore. In the 1900s the severer style of the Glasgow school—of which Jessie M. King (1876–1949) was the most brilliant illustrator—dominated.

Art of English Poesie, The *See* PUTTENHAM, GEORGE.

Art of English Poesy, Observations in the An attack on the use of rhyme in English poetry by Thomas *Campion, published in 1602, to which Samuel *Daniel replied in his *Defence of Rhyme*.

Art of Rhetoric, The *See* WILSON, THOMAS.

Arts Council of Great Britain, the Incorporated by royal charter in 1946 for the purpose of developing greater knowledge, understanding, and practice of the fine arts and to increase their accessibility to the public. It grew out of the wartime Council for the Encouragement of Music and the Arts, which began in 1940 with a grant of £25,000 from the Pilgrim Trust. The first chairman was Lord Macmillan; the vice-chairman and prime mover Dr Thomas Jones, CH. John Maynard Keynes (1883–1946) was chairman from 1942 to 1945. In 1994, it was replaced by the Arts Council of England (since 2003, Arts Council England), the Arts Council of Wales, and the Scottish Arts Council, and in November of that year it began to receive funding from the National Lottery.
See also PATRONAGE.

Ascent of F6, The A play by W. H. *Auden and Christopher *Isherwood published 1936, first performed 1937. The central character, Michael Ransom, 'scholar and man of action', succumbs to his mother's persuasions and leads a mountaineering expedition up F6, a mysterious and haunted peak on the borders of disputed colonial territory; all his men die en route and he himself dies as he achieves his mission, destroyed by his own self-knowledge, having rejected the possibility of evasion and the contemplative life. The Establishment figures are presented satirically, the figures of the mother and the comrades with more ambiguity; Ransom himself was in part modelled on T. E. *Lawrence, the Truly Strong Weak Man. The play is a parable about the nature of power, will, and leadership, with both political and Freudian implications, and may be seen to reflect the apprehension of and attraction towards the 'strong man' in the 1930s.

ASCHAM, Roger (1514/15–68) Scholar, educated at St John's College, Cambridge, where he distinguished himself in Greek. In 1545 he published *Toxophilus*, a treatise on archery. Taking the form of a Ciceronian dialogue between Toxophilus (lover of shooting) and Philologus (lover of learning), the book was immediately popular. Dedicated to *Henry VIII, it gained Ascham a royal pension of £10 a year. He succeeded William Grindal as tutor to Princess Elizabeth, Prince Edward, and perhaps Lady Jane Grey in 1548, holding this post for under two years. In 1550–3 he travelled as secretary to Sir Richard Morison, English ambassador to the emperor Charles V, and on his return wrote his *Report of Germany*, which displays his knowledge of *Machiavelli's writing. In 1554 he became Latin secretary to Queen Mary, being tacitly permitted to continue in his *Protestantism, and he was renewed in this office under *Elizabeth I. He was afflicted by poverty in the last decade of his life; this was probably not caused, as William *Camden claimed, by his addiction to dicing and cock-fighting, but by his responsibility for a large family which included his mother-in-law and her younger children. His best-known work, *The Schoolmaster*, was published posthumously by his widow in 1570. Its three most distinctive features are: Ascham's dislike of corporal punishment; the Ciceronian technique of double translation, from Latin into English and back again; and his attitude to Italy. Although he valued Italian language and culture highly, Ascham felt that it was a dangerously corrupting country for English travellers. *The Schoolmaster* was an influence on Philip *Sidney's **Defence of Poetry*, as well as an important landmark in Renaissance educational theory. Ascham's English works are notable for their colloquial, personal style and for considerable economy of expression: they form an important bridge between the early Tudor writers and the Elizabethans. Samuel *Johnson wrote a *Life of Ascham* to accompany James Bennet's edition of 1761. There has been no complete edition of Ascham's *Works* since J. A. Giles's in 1864–5, but Lawrence V. Ryan has edited *The Schoolmaster* (1967) and has written a biography (1963).

ASHBERY, John (1927–) American poet, born in New York. He graduated from Harvard in 1949, by which time he had already composed the title poem of his first volume, *Song Trees*, which was published in the Yale Younger Poets series edited by W. H. *Auden in 1956. Ashbery spent most of the following decade in Paris, where his work grew more experimental and disjunctive. His second collection, *The Tennis Court Oath* (1962), is his most radical, and has proved an important influence on the development of the American school of the 1970s which became known as 'The *Language Poets'. Ashbery did not achieve canonical status until the publication of his sixth volume, *Self-Portrait in a Convex Mirror* (1975). He was the first of the so-called *'New York Poets'—normally seen as comprising Frank *O'Hara, Kenneth *Koch, and James *Schuyler—to achieve wide recognition. His poetry is characterized by its openness to the vagaries of consciousness, its wry, beguiling lyricism, and its innovative use of forms such as the pantoum (composed of four-line stanzas in which the second and fourth lines of each stanza serve as the first and third lines of the next) and the *sestina. Ashbery's art criticism is collected in *Reported Sightings* (1989). Ashbery's most vociferous advocate has been Harold *Bloom, who has frequently declared him the most significant poet since Wallace *Stevens.

ASHFORD, Daisy (1881–1972) Born in Petersham, child-author of *The Young Visiters*, published in 1919 with an introduction by J. M *Barrie, who verified that she was genuine. An unwitting parody of *romantic fiction, it tells the adventures of Ethel Monticue and her admirer Mr Salteena. The BBC filmed it in 2003.

ASHMOLE, Elias (1617–92) Antiquary and astrologer. He studied at Brasenose College, Oxford, and, as a Royalist, held several government appointments. His chief work was *The Institution, Laws and Ceremonies of the Order of the Garter* (1672), but he also edited work by Dr John *Dee and was associated with William *Lilly, whose autobiography appeared with Ashmole's *Memoirs* in the 1774 edition. In 1682 he presented his collection of curiosities, bequeathed to him by John *Tradescant, to Oxford University, thus founding the Ashmolean Museum. A five-volume edition of his autobiographical and historical notes, correspondence, and so on, edited by C. H. Josten, appeared in 1966.

ASIMOV, Isaac (1920–92) Born in Petrovitchi, Russia; educated in New York City public schools and Columbia University; American author credited with coining the term 'robotics' in a series of stories mostly published in **Astounding Science-Fiction* in the 1940s. Encouraged by the editor John W. *Campbell, Asimov developed the sequence, collected as *I, Robot* (1950), as a series of moral puzzles with the 'three laws of robotics' offering enough ambiguity to suggest ethical dilemmas. Further collections followed. In 1942, Asimov began an equally celebrated future history, collected as *Foundation* (1951), *Foundation and Empire* (1952), and *Second Foundation* (1953). A prolific writer of fiction and non-fiction, Asimov edited numerous anthologies and in 1977 'lent' his name to a science fiction magazine still (as *Asi*[illegible]*ence Fiction*) published to[illegible]egarded novels of the 1950s, including *Pebble in the Sky* (1950), *The Caves of Steel* (1954), and *The End of Eternity* (1955), were followed by a hiatus when he concentrated upon science writing, though *The Gods Themselves* (1972) won both *Hugo and Nebula awards in 1973. Later a series of novels attempted to link both major series; critical reaction was mixed, but *Foundation's Edge* (1982) won a Hugo. Asimov's popular and distinctively humanistic stories made him, according to critic John *Clute, the default voice of 20th-century science fiction.

ASLAM, Nadeem (1966–) Prize-winning novelist, born in Pakistan and now living in London. His painstakingly produced novels are *Season of the Rainbirds* (1993), *Maps for Lost Lovers* (2004), in which Aslam wanted each chapter to be like a Persian miniature, and *The Wasted Vigil* (2008).

Asloan Manuscript Compiled by John Asloan, a scribe and notary public from Edinburgh (*c*.1470–*c*.1530). It originally contained 71 items, of which 34 are now lost. Among its original contents were a still-extant treatise by John *Ireland and several works by Robert *Henryson. Ed. W. A. Craigie, 2 vols, STS (1923–5).

Asolando The last volume of poems by Robert *Browning, published 1889. The title derives from a fanciful verb 'asolare', 'to disport in the open air, to amuse oneself at random', attributed to *Bembo at the time of his residence in Asolo, in northern Italy (accent on first syllable). Asolo had played an important part in Browning's life and work (*see* PIPPA PASSES).

The poems fall into three main groups: an opening series of love lyrics; a group of narrative poems; and a concluding group of meditative or reminiscent dramatic monologues. The 'Epilogue', containing the self-description 'One who never turned his back but marched breast forward', is a high-water mark of Browning's optimism; 'Beatrice Signorini', returning to the subject of Italian painting, and 'Inapprehensiveness', on the decorum of affection, reveal that Browning's sensitivity to the unspoken was undiminished. Other poems meditate on moral conundrums and ambiguous human actions.

The Aspern Papers Novella written by Henry *James and published in 1888. The story, set in Venice, explores the obsession of an editor, the nameless narrator, who sets out to find Juliana Bordereau, now an old woman, who has once been the lover of a famous and now deceased early 19th-century American poet, Jeffrey Aspern, with a view to obtaining letters and papers which she has in her possession. The narrator befriends and courts her niece Miss Tita in order to further his ends. He is caught rifling Juliana's desk; after Juliana's death days later, Miss Tita proposes marriage as her price for th[illegible]. At first refusing, the narrat[illegible] and Miss Tita, showing maturity and dignity, reveals she has burned the letters.

ASSER (d. 909) Monk of St David's, Pembrokeshire, who, according to the Latin *Life* of King *Alfred (893) attributed to him, entered the household of the king (*c*.885) and studied with him for six months of each year. He received the monasteries of Amesbury and Banwell, and later a grant of Exeter and its district; he was bishop of Sherborne (892–910). The *Life* is written in an elaborate idiom and also draws heavily on the **Anglo-Saxon Chronicles* for 851–87. Its authenticity has been questioned, some scholars believing the work to be an 11th-century forgery. But there is no conclusive evidence that it does not belong to the 890s. See W. H. Stevenson (ed.), *Asser's Life of King Alfred: Together with the 'Annals of Saint Neots' Erroneously Ascribed to Asser* (1904).

assonance The repetition of similar vowel sounds in the stressed syllables (and sometimes too in those that follow) of neighbouring words:

> And round about the keel with faces pale
> (Alfred *Tennyson)

It is distinct from full *rhyme in that while the vowel sounds correspond, the consonants do not.

ASTELL, Mary (1666–1731) Daughter of a prosperous Newcastle coal merchant, educated by her clergyman uncle. *Letters Concerning the Love of God* (1695) was based on her correspondence with John *Norris. *A Serious Proposal to the Ladies for the Advancement of their True and Greatest Interest* (1694; part 2, 1697) sought to enhance women's situation and self-esteem through self-education. She proposed the establishment of a secular seminary for women who preferred intellectual pursuits to marriage. In *Some Reflections on Marriage* (1700) Astell argued that women who were not prepared to take the binding vows of obedience and subservience that marriage required of them should not marry (she herself remained unmarried). Astell's ideas on female education were publicized by Daniel *Defoe (*Essay upon Projects*, 1697) and absorbed into George *Berkeley's *Ladies Library* (1714). She was lampooned in the *Tatler* (nos. 32 and 63), but her influence on women writers was widespread.

Astounding Science-Fiction (now *Analog*) was established in 1930 (entitled *Astounding Stories of Super-Science*). From 1933 it featured some of the leading authors in science fiction. Following the appointment of John W. *Campbell as editor in 1937, it dominated the field, publishing debut stories from A. E. *Van Vogt, Robert A. *Heinlein, and others. From 1961, the *Analog* name suggested the connections between science and *hard science fiction which the magazine (now edited by Stanley Schmidt) has come to embody.

Astraea Redux *See* Dryden, John.

'Astrophel' A pastoral elegy, written by Edmund *Spenser *c.*1591–5 on the death of Philip *Sidney, and published in 1595 with *Colin Clouts Come Home Againe*. Spenser had previously lamented Sidney in 'The *Ruines of Time'. A. C. *Swinburne used the title for a volume of his poems in 1894.

Astrophel and Stella A sequence of 108 sonnets and 11 songs by Philip *Sidney, written *c.*1582. They plot the unhappy love of Astrophel ('star-lover') for Stella ('star'). As several sonnets make clear, e.g. 37, referring to one that 'Hath no misfortune, but that Rich she is', Stella is to be identified with Penelope *Rich; but the exact nature of Sidney's real, rather than poetic, relationship with her cannot be known. Apart from snatching a kiss while she is asleep, Astrophel achieves nothing in the sequence, and the story breaks off—'That therewith my song is broken'—rather than being resolved. Poetically, however, the sonnets are an outstanding achievement, being written throughout in versions of the exacting Italian sonnet form, and displaying a striking range of tone, imagery, and metaphor. Among the best known is 31, 'With how sad steps, ô Moone, thou climb'st the skies' (Philip *Larkin's 'Sad Steps', published in his 1974 collection, *High Windows*, takes its title from the sonnet). There were two editions of *Astrophel and Stella* in 1591 which began a craze for sonnet sequences; from 1598 it was included in editions of *The* **Arcadia*.

asyndeton The omission of conjunctions for rhetorical effect, either between clauses, as in 'I came, I saw, I conquered', or between nouns: 'The courtier's, soldier's, scholar's eye, tongue, sword' (**Hamlet*, III. i. 60); this second type is sometimes called brachylogia.

As You Like It A comedy by *Shakespeare, registered for publication 4 August 1600; probably written shortly before. It was first printed in the first *folio of 1623. Shakespeare's chief source was Thomas Lodge's **Rosalynde*, but some notable characters, such as Jaques and the clown Touchstone, have no original there, and unlike Lodge Shakespeare resolves the action with the appearance of Hymen (V. iv), the first of Shakespeare's scenes to include a god, anticipating the late romances.

Frederick has usurped his brother the duke, who is living with his faithful followers in the forest of Ardenne (*see* Arden). Celia, Frederick's daughter, and Rosalind, the duke's daughter, living at Frederick's court, watch a wrestling match in which Orlando, son of Sir Rowland de Bois, defeats a powerful adversary. Rosalind and Orlando fall in love. Orlando has been driven from home by the cruelty of his elder brother Oliver, who became his guardian on his father's death. Frederick, learning that Orlando is the son of Sir Rowland, a friend of the exiled duke, banishes Rosalind from his court. Celia accompanies her. Rosalind assumes a countryman's dress and calls herself Ganymede; Celia passes as Aliena, his sister. They live in the forest of Ardenne, and fall in with Orlando, who has joined the banished duke. Ganymede encourages Orlando to pay suit to her as though she were his Rosalind. Oliver comes to the forest to kill Orlando, but is saved by him from a lioness, and is filled with remorse. He falls in love with Aliena, and their wedding is arranged for the next day. Ganymede undertakes to Orlando that she will by magic produce Rosalind at the same time to be married to him. When all are gathered to celebrate the double wedding, Celia and Rosalind shed their disguise and appear in their own characters. News is brought that Frederick, setting out to destroy his brother and his followers, has been converted by 'an old religious man' and has restored the dukedom.

Conversation rather than plot dominates this play, much of it provided by the reflections of Jaques and Touchstone, and by the large number of songs, more than in any of Shakespeare's other plays, including 'Under the greenwood tree' (which Thomas *Hardy used as the title for a novel) and 'Blow, blow, thou winter wind' (in II. v and II. vii respectively).

Atalanta in Calydon A poetic drama by A. C. *Swinburne, published 1865. It tells the story of the hunting of the wild boar sent by Artemis to ravage Calydon in revenge for its neglect of her: Meleager slays the boar, presents the spoils to the virgin athlete and huntress Atalanta, and then himself dies through the intervention of his mother Althaea. The work brought Swinburne fame and was highly praised for its successful imitation of Greek models (though the subject had not been treated by any Greek dramatist); some critics pointed out its 'anti-theism', and W. M. *Rossetti compared it to P. B. *Shelley's **Prometheus Unbound*.

'Atheism, The Necessity of' A prose pamphlet by P. B. *Shelley and his friend Thomas Jefferson *Hogg, published anonymously at Oxford, 1811. Using the sceptical arguments of David *Hume and John *Locke, the authors—then both undergraduates—smartly demolish the grounds for a rational belief in the Deity. Shelley and Hogg were both expelled from the university for circulating the work to heads of colleges and to bishops, and for 'contumacy' (obstinate disobedience) in refusing to answer questions about it.

***Atheist's Tragedy,* The** A tragedy by Cyril *Tourneur, printed 1611. D'Amville, the 'atheist', plans to marry his son to Castabella and, to effect this, he sends her betrothed Charlemont abroad on active service. Charlemont is supposed dead, but returns, and is advised by the ghost of his father (whom D'Amville has meanwhile murdered) to forgo revenge. In the end D'Amville accidentally dashes out his own brains when raising an axe to execute Charlemont, and Charlemont and Castabella are united.
See REVENGE TRAGEDY.

Athelston A verse romance from the late 14th century, in 812 lines, whose historical resonances and literary affiliations have caused much critical speculation. It tells of the chance meeting in a forest of four messengers, one of whom, Athelston, becomes king of England, although this character shares nothing with the historical Athelstan except a successor named Edmund. Of the other three messengers, one becomes archbishop of Canterbury; another becomes earl of Dover, plots against the king, and is executed; and the fourth becomes earl of Stone and the father of Athelston's successor. Concern with relations between ecclesiastical and secular power is dramatized through the struggle between king and archbishop. See edition by A. M. Trounce (EETS 224, 1933; rev. 1951).

Athenaeum (1828–1921) James Silk *Buckingham's literary review, followed a general monthly magazine of this name (1807–9). The founder wished the journal to become a true 'Athenaeum', the resort of thinkers, poets, orators, and other writers, and he attacked the **Quarterly Review* for the political bias of its literary criticism. Co-proprietors included at various times John Hamilton *Reynolds, Thomas *Hood, and Allan *Cunningham. Charles Wentworth Dilke (1789–1864) was editor 1830–46, and the list of contributors in the 19th century included Charles *Lamb, George *Darley, James *Hogg, Hood, Walter Savage *Landor, Thomas *Carlyle, Robert *Browning, Andrew *Lang, and Walter *Pater. The scope of the review was enlarged in the 20th century, but its contributors were no less eminent; they included Thomas *Hardy, Katherine *Mansfield, T. S. *Eliot, Robert *Graves, Edmund *Blunden, Virginia *Woolf, and John Middleton *Murry, who became editor in 1919. Its reputation and authority altered little during its long history. In 1921 it merged with *Nation*, ran for ten years as *Nation and Athenaeum*, and in 1931 was purchased by the *New Statesman*. See L. A. Marchand, *The Athenaeum* (1941).

Athenian Gazette Later the *Athenian Mercury*, a periodical published by John *Dunton, a question-and-answer paper designed to resolve 'the nice and curious questions proposed by the Ingenious', and thus a precursor of **Notes and Queries*. It first appeared in March 1691, and flourished until 1697, with Samuel Wesley (1662–1735), father of John *Wesley, as partner. The queries ranged over a vast area, from the theological to the matrimonial, from the scientific to the literary, and it was praised and read by authors as diverse as the earl of *Halifax, Jonathan *Swift, Daniel *Defoe, and Sir William *Temple.

ATHERTON, Gertrude Franklin Horn (1857–1948) American novelist born in California who examined the history of her home state in novels like *Before the Gringo Came* (1894) and *The Californians* (1898). She used her fiction as a forum to campaign against the traces of Victorian prudery in America and in 1902 published *The Conqueror*, a novel based on her research into the life of Alexander Hamilton (1755–1804), one of the Founding Fathers of America. In 1895 she took up residence in England, then Germany, and soon after her return to America she published her autobiography *The Adventures of a Novelist* (1932). *Black Oxen* (1923), a novel which describes a glandular rejuvenation treatment she had in Europe, is also well known.

ATKINSON, Kate (1951–) Novelist and short story writer, born in York and educated at Dundee University. Her first novel, *Behind the Scenes at the Museum* (1995), a comedy of sibling rivalry and suppressed memory, is set largely in York during the 1950s but steps backwards in time to follow its central character's family history. *Human Croquet* (1997) and *Emotionally Weird* (2000) explore themes of identity and inheritance. She has also written idiosyncratic crime novels set mostly in Edinburgh such as *When Will There Be Good News?* (2008).

Atlantic Monthly Magazine founded in Boston in 1857 under the initial editorship of James Russell *Lowell. Subsequent editors included William Dean *Howells (1871–81). It was an important publishing forum for works by Henry *James, Charles *Chesnutt, Mark *Twain, and many others.

ATTERBURY, Francis (1662–1732) Clergyman, educated at Westminster School and Christ Church, Oxford. He engaged in the *Phalaris controversy and many theological and political disputes. A notable preacher, he held many important preferments, and became bishop of Rochester and dean of Westminster in 1713. He was arrested in 1722 and banished in 1723 for complicity in a *Jacobite plot. He was a close friend of Alexander *Pope, who gave evidence at his trial, and Jonathan *Swift.

ATWOOD, Margaret (1939–) Canadian poet and novelist, who spent much of her early life in the northern Ontario and Quebec bush country. Educated at the University of Toronto, Radcliffe College, and Harvard University, she taught for short spells in Canadian and American universities, and has maintained close connections with the academic community. Her first volume of poetry, *The Circle Game*, appeared in 1966, and she has since published poems prolifically, in magazines and regular collections. Her first novel, *The Edible Woman* (1969), was a biting account of a woman's escape from the stifling restrictions of a conventional life. It was followed by *Surfacing* (1972), *Lady Oracle* (1976), *Life before Man* (1979), and *Bodily Harm* (1981), all novels with political and feminist themes, and a controversial study of Canadian literature, *Survival* (1972). She also compiled *The New Oxford Book of Canadian Verse in English* (1983). She has published books for children, including *Up in the Tree* (1978), and *Princess Prunella and the Purple Peanut* (1995), and several collections of shorter fiction: *Dancing Girls* (1977), *Murder in the Dark* (1983), *Bluebeard's Egg and Other Stories* (1983), *Unearthing Suite* (1983), *Wilderness Tips* (1991), and *Good Bones* (1992). *The Handmaid's Tale* (1985) is a *dystopia set in the imaginary Republic of Gilead, where failing fertility results in the sexual enslavement of women for breeding purposes. *Cat's Eye* (1998) follows the thoughts of a painter as she comes to terms with memories of her childhood tormentors. *The Robber Bride* (1994) tells the story of three friends confronted by a disruptive *femme fatale* who they thought was dead. *Alias Grace* (1996) revisits the ambiguous history of a 16-year-old Canadian housemaid, convicted of the murder of her employer and his housekeeper in 1843. *The Blind Assassin* (2000; *Booker Prize) is the story of two sisters, whose relationship is revealed within complex layers of parallel narratives. *Oryx and Crake* (2003) contemplates a desolate future in a world ruined by misguided genetic manipulation, and reflects Atwood's long-standing interest in science and environmentalism. *The Penelopiad* (2005) is a novella in which Penelope remembers the events of Homer's **Odyssey*; it was dramatized by the Canadian National Arts Centre and the Royal Shakespeare Company (2007). Atwood's own views on the writer's craft are represented in her *Negotiating with the Dead: A Writer on Writing* (2002); see also Carol Beran, *Living over the Abyss: Margaret Atwood's Life before Man* (1994).

aubade A song or lyric poem in any verse form or *metre in which the coming of dawn is lamented because it brings the pains of separation to a pair of lovers. The classic English example is John *Donne's 'The Sunne Rising'. Shakespeare's **Romeo and Juliet* III. v is an extended dramatic adaptation of the aubade convention.

AUBIGNÉ, Théodore-Agrippa d' (1552–1630) French Huguenot leader and writer. After participating in the wars of religion and witnessing the accession of Henry IV, he withdrew to his Poitou domains in 1593 and, in order to escape further persecution, to Geneva in 1620. Soldier, architect, administrator, scholar, and poet, he was one of the complete men of his age. His literary output is as varied as it is innovatory. His early love lyrics, *Printemps* (first pub. 1874: *Spring*), are passionate and 'metaphysical'; his epic poem *Les Tragiques* (1616) is a violent and visionary representation of the fate of the Huguenots in 16th-century France; his *Histoire universelle* (1616–20) is a personal and historical narrative of religious and political events in France between 1550 and 1601; his burlesque novels, *Adventures du baron de Faeneste* (1617) and *Confession de Sancy* (pub. 1660), satirize religious absurdity and vice; and his autobiography, *Sa Vie à ses enfants* (*His Life to his Children*), justifies the course of a tumultuous life.

AUBIN, Penelope (?1679–?1731) Novelist, probably of French ancestry. She wrote three patriotic poems (1707–8). Her seven popular novels, from *The Strange Adventures of the Count de Vinevil* (1721) to *The Life and Adventures of the Young Count Albertus* (1728), portrayed virtue under pressure from seduction and other threats in attractively exotic settings. She produced four translations from French and edited a translation of an ethical work by Marin Le Roy, sieur de Gomberville. Aubin lectured on religious topics at York Buildings, Charing Cross, in 1729; her play *The Merry Masqueraders* had a brief run in 1730.

AUBREY, John (1626–97) Antiquary and biographer, born near Malmesbury, Wiltshire, the eldest surviving son of a well-to-do Herefordshire family. A lonely early childhood gave him delight in society, and he became familiar with many of the distinguished men of his time, including Thomas *Hobbes, whom he first met while still a boy, in 1634. His education at Trinity College, Oxford, was interrupted by the Civil War. In 1648 he was the first to discover the ruins of Avebury, and devoted much time to archaeological research, keenly deploring the neglect of antiquities; in 1662 he was nominated one of the original fellows of the *Royal Society. His *Miscellanies* (1696), a book of stories and folklore, was the only work completed and published in his lifetime. His 'Perambulation of Surrey', based on a tour in 1673, was included in Richard Rawlinson's *Natural History and Antiquities of Surrey* (1719), and his *Natural History of Wiltshire* appeared (ed. J. Britton) in 1847, but he is chiefly remembered for his *Lives* of eminent people, much used (and in his view somewhat abused) by Anthony *Wood. He collected these over a period of years, constantly adding to his notes, deploring his own lack of method ('I now set things down tumultuarily, as if tumbled out of a Sack'), and depositing his manuscripts in the Ashmolean Museum in 1693. Early editions (1813, 1898) were edited to erase bawdy references. The *Lives* are a lively and heterogeneous mixture of anecdote, first-hand observation, folklore, and erudition, a valuable, open-minded, entertaining (if at times inaccurate) portrait of an age. See Michael Hunter, *John Aubrey and the Realm of Learning* (1975).

Aucassin and Nicolette An early 13th-century courtly story in northern French, composed in alternating prose and heptasyllabic (seven-syllabled) verse, about the forbidden love of Aucassin, son of the Christian Count Garins of Beaucaire, for Nicolette, a Saracen captive, their various adventures, and their eventual marriage. The anonymous author deals playfully with the conventions of courtly love romances, such as in his treatment of the lovers' comic attempts to converse with shepherds. First translated into English in 1786, by the end of the 19th century *Aucassin and Nicolette* had aroused enormous interest, with Walter *Pater's essay on the story in *Studies in the History of the Renaissance* (1873) and two particularly successful translations published in 1887 by F. W. Bourdillon and Andrew *Lang. The most recent translation is that by Glyn

S. Burgess (1988). Charles *Causley's *The Ballad of Aucassin and Nicolette* is a play adaptation (performed 1978; pub. 1981).

Auchinleck Manuscript A major early miscellany of English poetry produced by a group of scribes in London, *c.*1330–40, and now in the National Library of Scotland. It includes many romances, and also saints' legends, religious debates, and satires. There is a facsimile edition, with an introduction by Derek Pearsall and I. C. Cunningham (1977).

AUCHINLOSS, Louis (1917–) American novelist, historian, and essayist. Trained originally as a lawyer, he then turned to the literature associated with his home city, New York. He is widely regarded as the heir to Edith *Wharton, about whom he published a critical study in 1972. Auchinloss's chosen subject is the New York aristocracy, which he has depicted in novels like *Pursuit of the Prodigal* (1959) and *Portrait in Brownstone* (1962).

AUDELAY, John (*fl.* 1417–26) Augustinian friar and author of most of the poems preserved in Oxford, Bodleian Library, MS Douce 302 (the attribution of some is disputed). Chantry priest (that is, a priest with the duty of celebrating masses for the dead in an endowed chantry chapel) to Richard Lestrange (d. 1449), lord of Knockin, at Haughmond Abbey, Shropshire, he describes himself in the poetry as blind and infirm. The poems in Douce 302 illustrate a range of contemporary concerns, and include didactic, devotional, and penitential lyrics, a life of St Bridget of Sweden, and an alliterative poem that recalls the idiom and subject matter of **Piers Plowman*. See *The Poems of John Audelay*, ed. Ella Keats Whiting, EETS os 184 (1931).

AUDEN, W. H. (Wystan Hugh) (1907–73) Poet. The youngest son of a doctor, he was born in York, brought up in Birmingham, and educated at Gresham's School, Holt. He began to be taken seriously as a poet while still at Christ Church, Oxford (1925–8), where he was much influenced by Anglo-Saxon and Middle English poetry, but also began to explore the means of preserving 'private spheres' (through poetry) in 'public chaos' which would become a hallmark of his work. Among his contemporaries were Louis *MacNeice, Cecil *Day-Lewis, and Stephen *Spender. After Oxford, Auden lived for a time in Berlin before returning to England in 1929 to work as a schoolteacher. However, he continued to visit Germany regularly, staying with his friend and future collaborator Christopher *Isherwood, with whom he had enjoyed a close relationship, intellectually and emotionally, since 1925. His *Poems* appeared in 1930. It was well received and established him as the most talented voice of his generation. *The Orators* followed in 1932 and *Look Stranger!* in 1936. In 1932 he became associated with the Group Theatre of the dancer and theatre director Rupert Doone (1903–66), which produced several of his plays (*The Dance of Death*, pub. 1933, performed 1934; and, with Isherwood, *The Dog beneath the Skin*, pub. 1935, performed 1936, *The *Ascent of F6*, pub. and performed in 1936, and *On the Frontier*, pub. and performed in 1938). All four owe something to the early plays of Bertolt *Brecht. Working from 1935 with the General Post Office film unit he became friendly with Benjamin *Britten, who set many of his poems to music and later used Auden's text for his opera *Paul Bunyan* (performed 1941). In 1935 the homosexual Auden married Erika Mann to provide her with a British passport and a means of escape from Nazi Germany; they never divorced. A visit to Iceland with MacNeice in 1936 produced their joint *Letters from Iceland* (1937); *Journey to a War* (1939, with Isherwood) records a journey to China. In 1937 he visited Spain for two months, to support the Republicans, but his resulting poem 'Spain' (1937) is less partisan and more detached in tone than might have been expected, and in January 1939 he and Isherwood left Europe for America (Auden became a US citizen in 1946) where he met Chester Kallman (1921–75), with whom he fell in love and who became his lifelong, if not always constant, companion. *Another Time* (1940), containing many of his most famous poems (including 'September 1939' and 'Lullaby'), was followed in 1941 by *The Double Man* (1941, published in London as *New Year Letter*), a long transitional verse epistle describing the 'baffling crime' of 'two decades of hypocrisy', rejecting political simplifications, accepting man's essential solitude, and ending with a prayer for refuge and illumination for the 'muddled heart'. From this time Auden's poetry became increasingly Christian in tone (to such an extent that he even altered some of his earlier work and disowned some of his political pieces), a transformation perhaps not unconnected with the death in 1941 of his devout Anglo-Catholic mother, to whom he dedicated *For the Time Being: A Christmas Oratorio* (1944). This was published with *The Sea and the Mirror*, a series of dramatic monologues inspired by *The *Tempest*. *The Age of Anxiety: A Baroque Eclogue* (1948) is a long dramatic poem, reflecting man's isolation. It opens in a New York bar at night and ends at dawn on the streets.

Auden's absence during the war led to a poor reception of his works in England, but his move to America rekindled his imaginative energies, and the high quality of his work from this period onwards soon saw him reinstated as a major poet. He was professor of poetry at Oxford from 1956 to 1961, and in 1962 he became a student (i.e. fellow) of Christ Church. His major later collections include *Nones* (1951, New York; 1952, London), *The Shield of Achilles* (1955), which includes 'Horae Canonicae' and 'Bucolics', and is considered by many his best single volume; and *Homage to Clio* (1960), which includes a high proportion of light verse. Auden had edited *The Oxford Book of Light Verse* in 1938, and subsequently many other anthologies and collections; his own prose criticism includes *The Enchafèd Flood* (1950, New York; 1951, London), *The Dyer's Hand* (1962, New York; 1963, London), and *Secondary Worlds* (1968, T. S. *Eliot Memorial Lectures). He also wrote several libretti, notably for Igor *Stravinsky's *The Rake's Progress* (1951, with Kallman). *About the House* (1965, New York; 1966, London) contains a tender evocation of his life with Kallman at their summer home in Austria. Auden spent his final year in Oxford and died suddenly in Vienna on his way back to England after his summer vacation. A posthumous volume,

Thank you, Fog (1974), appeared and his *Collected Poems*, edited by Edward Mendelson, came out in 1991.

Auden's influence on succeeding poets is incalculable, comparable in his era only with that of W. B. *Yeats (to whom Auden himself pays homage in 'In Memory of W. B. Yeats', 1939) and T. S. Eliot. His progress from the engaged, didactic, satiric poems of his youth to the complexity of his later work offered a wide variety of models—the urbane, the pastoral, the lyrical, the erudite, the public, and the introspective mingle with great fluency. He was a master of verse form and accommodated traditional patterns to a fresh, easy, and contemporary language. See Humphrey Carpenter, *W. H. Auden: A Biography* (1981); Edward Mendelson, *Early Auden* (1981); Edward Mendelson, *Later Auden* (1999).

AUDUBON, John James (1785–1851) American ornithologist of French descent, noted for his remarkable pictures of birds. The colour prints of his *The Birds of America* were issued serially in London in 1827–38, and the accompanying text, 'Ornithological Biography', in which he was assisted, in 1831–9. He also published, again with assistance, *Viviparous Quadrupeds of North America* (plates 1842–5; text 1846–54). His important *Journal* appeared in 1929.

Augustan age A term derived from the period of literary eminence under the Roman emperor Augustus (27 BC–AD 14), during which *Virgil, *Horace, and *Ovid flourished. In English literature it is generally taken to refer to the early and mid-18th century, though the earliest usages date back to the reign of Charles II. Augustan writers (such as Alexander *Pope, Joseph *Addison, Jonathan *Swift, and Richard *Steele) greatly admired their Roman counterparts, imitated their works, and themselves frequently drew parallels between the two ages. Oliver *Goldsmith, in *The Bee*, in an 'Account of the Augustan Age of England' (1759), identifies it with the reign of Queen Anne, and the era of William *Congreve, Matthew *Prior, and *Bolingbroke. See Howard Weinbrot, *Augustus Caesar in 'Augustan' England* (1978).
See also NEO-CLASSICISM.

AUGUSTINE, St (d. 26 May, between 604 and 609) First archbishop of Canterbury. He was prior of Pope Gregory's monastery of St Andrew in Rome and in 596 was sent by that pope with some 40 monks to preach the gospel in England, arriving there in 597. He was favourably received by King Æthelbert of Kent, who was afterwards converted to Christianity and gave Augustine a see (i.e. official seat as bishop) at Canterbury. Augustine was consecrated 'Bishop of the English' at Arles. He founded the monastery of Christ Church at Canterbury, and a number of other churches, none of which still survives. See M. Deanesly, *Augustine of Canterbury* (1964); H. Mayr-Harting, *The Coming of Christianity to Anglo-Saxon England* (rev. edn 1991).

AUGUSTINE, St, of Hippo (354–430) Born at Tagaste in North Africa; his mother Monica was a devout Christian. He was trained as a rhetorician and abandoned the Christianity in which he had been brought up (though not baptized). He had an illegitimate son, Adeodatus. He was a *Manichaean for some time, but was converted (387) after hearing the sermons of Ambrose, bishop of Milan, where Augustine taught rhetoric. The scene of his conversion is vividly described in his *Confessions* (*c.*400), which contains a celebrated account of his early life. He became bishop of Hippo (395) and was engaged in constant theological controversy, combating Manichaeans, Donatists, and *Pelagians. The most important of his numerous works is *De Civitate Dei* (416–22, *The City of God*), a treatise in vindication of Christianity. His principal tenet was the immediate efficacy of grace, and his theology remained an influence of profound importance on Franciscans, Cistercians, and others in the Middle Ages, when it was often characterized as being an alternative orthodoxy to the Dominican system of *Aquinas, and on 16th-century Protestant Reformers. His views on literature became standard in the Middle Ages, particularly as expressed in *De Doctrina Christiana* (*On Christian Doctrine*), and they have often been cited as an authority by 20th-century 'exegetical' critics of medieval literature, such as D. W. Robertson, who are sometimes called 'Augustinian critics'. See *On Christian Doctrine*, trans. D. W. Robertson (1958); *Confessions*, trans. Henry Chadwick (1991); *The City of God*, trans. Henry Bettenson (2003); Peter R. L. Brown, *Augustine of Hippo: A Biography* (2000).

'Auld Lang Syne' A song whose words were contributed by Robert *Burns to the fifth volume of James Johnson's **Scots Musical Museum* (1787–1803). Based on what he called a 'glorious fragment', Burns's lyric reworks lines and phrases that have been traced to sources including Allan *Ramsay's *Scots Songs* (1720) and the *Bannatyne Manuscript (1568). 'Auld Lang Syne' was matched to its now famous air by George Thomson (1757–1851) in the 1799 half-volume of his *Select Collection of Original Scottish Airs*.

AULNOY, Marie-Catherine Le Jumel de Barneville, comtesse d' (*c.*1650–1705) French writer of historical fiction, notably *Hypolite, comte de Duglas* (1691), set in the England of Henry VIII, and *Contes des fées* (1697: *Fairy Tales*) which enjoyed considerable popularity in England: of the 62 French fairy-tales that appeared in English between 1691 and 1729, eighteen were by Aulnoy.

Aureng-Zebe A tragedy by John *Dryden, produced 1675, published 1676. The plot is remotely based on the contemporary events by which the Mogul Aureng-Zebe wrested the empire of India from his father and his brothers. The hero is a figure of exemplary rationality, virtue, and patience, whose stepmother lusts after him and whose father pursues the woman with whom Aureng-Zebe is himself in love. Apparently highly schematic in its organization, this last of Dryden's rhymed heroic plays evinces a deeply disturbing awareness of the anarchy and impotence which threaten every aspect of human life, emotional, moral, and political.

Aurora Leigh A poem by Elizabeth Barrett *Browning, tells the life story of its eponymous heroine. Prior to publication in 1856 (dated 1857), its author explained that she wanted 'to write a poem of a new class', and later described *Aurora Leigh* (which is over 11,000 lines long) as a 'novel in verse'. Orphaned as a girl, Aurora grows to be an independent woman and poet who believes artists have a responsibility to highlight and assess concerns of the present day. The poem explores social accountability in connection with religion, art, and class, and relationships between the sexes. Aurora rejects a clumsy proposal from her philanthropic cousin Romney, but later accepts him after he has learned to appreciate her social and artistic perspectives. In a melodramatic sub-plot, Marian Erle (a seamstress) is raped and moves to Paris, where Aurora follows, and helps raise her child. Thought scandalous by a few, the poem was a great success with contemporary readers.

AUSTEN, Jane (1775–1817) Novelist, born in the rectory at Steventon, Hampshire, the sixth child in a family of seven. Her father, the Revd George Austen, was a cultivated man, comfortably prosperous, who taught Jane and encouraged her both in her reading and her writing. She was briefly tutored by a relative in Oxford, then in Southampton, and attended the Abbey House School, Reading (1785–6). As a child and young woman she read widely, including, among novelists, Henry *Fielding, Lawrence *Sterne, Samuel *Richardson, and Fanny *Burney; and among poets, Sir Walter *Scott, William *Cowper, and, her particular favourite, George *Crabbe. Her life is notable for its lack of events; she did not marry, although she had several suitors, one of whom she accepted one evening, only to withdraw her approval the following morning. She lived in the midst of a lively and affectionate family, with occasional visits to Bath, London, Lyme, and her brothers' houses. Any references there may have been to private intimacies or griefs were excised from Jane's letters by her sister Cassandra after the author's death, but the correspondence retains flashes of sharp wit and occasional coarseness that have startled some of her admirers. The letters cover the period 1796–1817, and her correspondents include Cassandra, her friend Martha Lloyd, and her nieces and nephews, to whom she confided her views on the novel (to Anna Austen, 9 September 1814: '3 or 4 families in a Country Village is the very thing to work on'; to J. Edward Austen, 16 December 1816: 'the little bit (two Inches wide) of Ivory on which I work with so fine a brush, as produces little effect after much labour'). In 1801, the family moved to Bath; in 1806, after Mr Austen's death, to Southampton; and in 1809 to Chawton, again in Hampshire; for a few weeks before her death Jane lodged in Winchester, where she died of Addison's disease. The novels were written between the activities of family life, and the last three (**Mansfield Park*, **Emma*, and **Persuasion*) are known to have been written in the busy family parlour at Chawton.

Her juvenilia, written in her early and mid-teens, are already incisive and elegantly expressed; *Love and Freindship (sic)* was written when she was 14, *A History of England* ('by a partial, ignorant and prejudiced historian') at 15; at 16 *A Collection of Letters*; and sometime during those same years, *Lesley Castle*. **Lady Susan* is also an early work, written probably in 1793–4. Of the major novels, **Sense and Sensibility* was published in 1811, **Pride and Prejudice* in 1813, *Mansfield Park* in 1814, *Emma* in 1816, **Northanger Abbey* and *Persuasion* posthumously in 1818. They were, however, begun or completed in a different order. The youthful sketch *Elinor and Marianne* (1795–6) was followed in 1797 by *First Impressions*, which was refused without reading by the publisher Cadell; the former was rewritten in 1797–8 as *Sense and Sensibility*. *Northanger Abbey* followed in 1798–9 and was, in 1803, sold to the publishers Crosby and Sons who paid the author £10 but did not publish. In 1809 *Sense and Sensibility* was again revised for publication, and *First Impressions* was recreated and renamed *Pride and Prejudice*.

Between the writing of *Northanger Abbey* and the revision of *Sense and Sensibility* she wrote an unfinished novel, *The *Watsons*, probably begun in 1804 and abandoned in 1805 on her father's death—an event which may account for her comparatively long silence at this period. *Mansfield Park* was begun at Chawton in 1811, *Emma* in 1814, *Persuasion* in 1815; and in 1817, the year of her death, the unfinished **Sanditon*. It is likely that although *Northanger Abbey* was, together with *Persuasion*, the last of the novels to be published, it was the earliest of the completed works as we now have them.

The novels were generally well received from publication onwards; the prince regent (whose librarian urged Austen to write 'an historical romance, illustrative of the history of the august house of Coburg') kept a set of novels in each of his residences, and Scott praised her work in the **Quarterly Review* in 1815; he later wrote of 'that exquisite touch which renders ordinary commonplace things and characters interesting'. There were, however, dissentient voices; Charlotte *Brontë and Elizabeth Barrett *Browning found her limited. Nonetheless, after the publication of J. E. Austen Leigh's *Memoir* in 1870 a Jane Austen cult began to develop. Since then her reputation has remained consistently high, though with interesting shifts of emphasis. D. W. Harding's 'Regulated Hatred: An Aspect of the Work of Jane Austen' (**Scrutiny*, 1940) presents her as a satirist more astringent than delicate and Marilyn Butler's *Jane Austen and the War of Ideas* (1975) situates the writer's work, so often seen as literary escapism, in its social and political context. See B. C. Southam (ed.), *Jane Austen: The Critical Heritage* (1968). The standard text of the novels, 6 vols (1923–54), is by R. W. Chapman, who also edited the letters (new edn 1995 by D. Le Faye). There are biographies by Claire *Tomalin and David Nokes, both 1997.

AUSTER, Paul (1947–) American novelist, poet, playwright, and film-maker, born in Newark, New Jersey, and educated at Columbia University. He began to write while earning his living as a translator, caretaker, switchboard operator, editor, and cook on an oil tanker. His earliest one-act plays were influenced by Harold *Pinter and Samuel *Beckett, and his first novel, *Squeeze Play*, was a *Chandleresque thriller published under the pseudonym 'Paul Benjamin'. He gained critical recognition with his *New York Trilogy* (*City of Glass*, 1985; *Ghosts*, 1986; and *The Locked Room*, 1987), which uses the conventions of the detective novel to investigate urban isolation, identity, and the link between language and meaning. Further examination of fictional genres followed with the dystopian fable *In the Country of Last Things* (1987), and *Moon Palace* (1989), which links a *picaresque plot to developments in American history. *The Music of Chance* (1991), an allegory of two men forced to build a wall, was filmed in 1993 by Philip Haas. In the early 1990s Auster worked on an adaptation of his own short tale, *Auggie Wren's Christmas Story*, with the director Wayne Wang. This collaboration produced first *Smoke* (with a script by Auster) and *Blue in the Face* (directed by Wang and Auster, both 1995), uncharacteristically optimistic stories of urban life. Subsequently, Wang directed *The Centre of the World* (2001), from Auster's story about a couple in Las Vegas; while Auster has written and directed *The Inner Life of Martin Frost* (2007), about a fictitious writer, with his daughter Sophie playing a leading part.

AUSTIN, Alfred (1835–1913) Poet, born at Headingley, near Leeds, of a Roman Catholic family, educated at Stonyhurst and Oscott College; his Catholicism is not evident in his writing. Inheriting a fortune from his uncle, he gave up a career as a barrister for literature. An ardent imperialist and follower of *Disraeli, he became in 1883 joint editor with the poet and scholar W. J. Courthope (1842–1917) of the newly founded *National Review*, and was its sole editor for eight years from 1887. Between 1871 and 1908 he published twenty volumes of verse. A prose work, *The Garden that I Love* (1894), proved popular, and in 1896 Austin was made *poet laureate, shortly afterwards publishing in *The* *Times an unfortunate ode celebrating the Jameson Raid. A waspish critic of his contemporaries, he was himself much derided and parodied as a poet. His *Autobiography* appeared in 1911. See N. B. Crowell, *Alfred Austin, Victorian* (1953).

autobiography has been recognized since the late 18th century as a distinct literary genre, with the first recorded uses of the term occurring around this time. However its definition was, even then, a matter of controversy and the history of the term has been bound up with ideological struggles about the status of the subject and the nature of authorship. The French critic Philippe Lejeune gives a widely quoted modern definition of autobiography as 'a retrospective prose narrative produced by a real person concerning his own existence, focusing on his individual life, in particular on the development of his personality'. Behind this definition lies the assumption that the author's intention to be truthful determines the truthfulness of a text. Paul *de Man's famous post-structuralist challenge to this is that there is no way of deciding what is truth and what fiction and that therefore autobiography, as distinct from fiction, does not really exist. The modern canon of autobiography looks back to the deeply reflective self-analysis of St *Augustine (354–430) in his *Confessions*. The earliest known autobiography in English, *The Boke of Margery Kempe* (*c*.1420), recounts the visions of a mystic; John *Bunyan made an impassioned record of his spiritual awakening; and the relationship between autobiography and religion would remain firm well into the 19th century, particularly among Nonconformists. The form's rise to popularity in the 18th century was also closely linked with the rise of the novel; indeed many early novels, including **Robinson Crusoe* (1719) and **Tristram Shandy* (1759–67), declared themselves to be autobiographies. Where the literary conceit of Defoe and Sterne was to publish anonymously and let their characters take the credit, Romantic writers turned attention to the figure of the author. In the greatest verse autobiography, *The *Prelude* (published 1850), William *Wordsworth traces the growth of his poetic imagination and accords this subject the status of epic. In the 20th century Virginia *Woolf turned to different autobiographical forms—diary and memoir—and experimented with ways of suggesting alternative feminine versions of selfhood which were fragmented or inchoate. Her draft memoir, published as 'Sketch of the Past', was one of many wartime autobiographies, including Henry *Green's *Pack my Bag* (1940) and Osbert *Sitwell's vast *Left Hand, Right Hand!* (1945–50), which sought to record personal visions of a lost pre-war world. *Roland Barthes by Roland Barthes* (1975) drew out the implications for autobiography of post-structuralism and 'the death of the author' by eschewing chronology and development and encouraging readers to view it 'as if spoken by a character in a novel'. Carolyn Steedman's *Landscape for a Good Woman* (1986) took issue with the inability of the genre to represent working-class experience, but modern approaches have emphasized the usefulness of autobiography for understanding different lives. Autobiographies can be forms of testimonial writing, bearing witness to overlooked or traumatic histories. Eva *Hoffman's *Lost in Translation* (1989), for instance, provided an account of exile and the experience of being a second-generation Holocaust survivor. Recent autobiographies have documented the experience of terminal illness, making public what has usually remained intensely private. Both John Diamond's *Because Cowards Have Cancer* (1998) and Ruth Picardie's *Before I Say Goodbye* (1998) were newspaper columns before being published as books. Other writers, like Blake *Morrison in *When Did You Last See your Father?* (1993) or Lorna Sage in *Bad Blood* (2000), have focused on the death of parents or difficult family circumstances. Today, autobiography is one of the best-selling genres, covering as it does a spectrum from the hugely popular and much-denigrated 'misery memoir', through such publishing phenomena as Frank McCourt's *Angela's Ashes* (1996), to experimental and challenging work which continues to push at the bounds of this most hybrid form.

Avalon In Arthurian legends, one of the Celtic 'Isles of the Blest' to which Arthur is carried after his death. The name is variously explained as the island of apples (by *Geoffrey of Monmouth, among others) and as the island of Avalloc, who ruled it with his daughters, including *Morgan. *Glastonbury has also been identified as the burial-place of Arthur and hence with Avalon. For discussion, see R. S. Loomis (ed.), *Arthurian Literature in the Middle Ages* (1959), 65–8.

AVELLANEDA, Alonso Fernández de *See* FERNÁNDEZ DE AVELLANEDA, ALONSO.

Averroës (Abū a'l-Walīd Muhammad bin Ahmad bin Rushd) (1126–98) A Muslim physician born at Córdoba in Spain (*Chaucer's Physician knows of him: **Canterbury Tales*, General Prologue, 433), and a philosopher, the author of a famous commentary on *Aristotle. He is placed in the limbo of the philosophers with *Avicenna by *Dante (*Inferno*, IV. 144). He is the inspiration for 'Latin Averroism' (1230 and afterwards), which regarded Aristotle as absolute in philosophy even when his view was not reconcilable with the absolute truth of Faith, an approach repeatedly opposed (as by *Aquinas) and condemned (as by Tempier, 1277) until *Ockham in the 14th century. Known among scholastic theologians as 'the Commentator', he is of immense and lasting importance as the conveyor of Aristotle back into the Western tradition. His controversial view that the active intellect was separable and distinct from the passive was opposed by Aquinas in *De Unitate Intellectus*.

Avicenna (Abū-a 'Ali al-Husayn bin Sīna) (980–1037) A Persian physician (a capacity in which he was known to *Chaucer's Physician—**Canterbury Tales*, General Prologue, 432—and Pardoner—VI. 889) and philosopher, who made commentaries on *Aristotle and *Galen. His views of love have been said to be influential on the ideas of *courtly love, by A. J. Denomy in *The Heresy of Courtly Love* (1947), and he was a major influence on the development of 13th-century *scholasticism in his reordering of *Neoplatonism on an Aristotelian basis. *Dante places him with *Averroës in the limbo of the philosophers (*Inferno*, IV. 143).

AWDRY, Revd W. (Wilbert) (1911–97). The 26 books about the railway on the island of Sodor, beginning with *The Three Railway Engines* (1945) and *Thomas the Tank Engine* (1946), supplemented by a further fourteen (1989–96) by Christopher Awdry, have been exhaustively marketed worldwide. The stories of Thomas, Gordon the express engine, the Fat Controller, and their companions evoke an idyllic England, but have class and gender overtones in the (female) carriages, the villainous diesels, and the (working-class) trucks.

Awkward Age, The A novel by Henry *James.

Awntyrs of Arthure at the Terne Wathelyne, The (*The Adventures of Arthur at the Tarn Wadling*, in Cumberland) A compelling alliterative poem in 715 lines, surviving in five 15th-century manuscripts. While hunting, *Gawain and Gaynor (*Guinevere) see the apparition of Gaynor's mother rise from the lake and ask that 30 trentals (sequences of 30 masses) be said for the relief of her suffering soul (a motif derived from the legend of the trental of St *Gregory). She attacks the vices of Gawain, Arthur, and the court, criticisms echoed in the second part of the poem, in which Sir Galeron of Galway (Galloway), demands the return of lands which Arthur had confiscated and given to Gawain. The lands are returned, and Gaynor has the masses said for her mother. The poem (in complex thirteen-line stanzas) is notable for its confident compression of many of the key elements of Arthurian romance, and displays a thoughtful ambivalence towards the materialism of Arthurian culture that is similar to the detachment of *Sir *Gawain and the Green Knight*. See the edition by R. Hanna (1974).

Ayala's Angel A novel by Anthony *Trollope, published 1881. Egbert Dormer fails to provide for his daughters, and on his death Lucy and Ayala are farmed out to relations. The romantic Ayala has a high ideal of the man she wishes to marry, but must choose from the vulgar Captain Batsby, her callow cousin Tom Tringle, and ugly Jonathan Stubbs. Stubbs's persistence and good sense overcome all Ayala's objections, and he ends the novel transfigured into her 'Angel of Light'. Meanwhile the practical Lucy has attached herself to a penniless but deserving sculptor. Incidental interest derives from the matrimonial tribulations of the daughters of the wealthy Sir Thomas Tringle. The novel reflects Trollope's characteristic interest in the moral choices imposed by courtship and marriage.

AYCKBOURN, Sir Alan (1939–) Playwright, born in London, whose first plays were produced at Scarborough, where he has since 1971 been artistic director of the Theatre-in-the-Round. His first London success, *Relatively Speaking* (1967), was followed by many others, including *Absurd Person Singular* (1973); *The Norman Conquests* (1974), a trilogy with elaborately overlapping action covering the same period of time and the same events from different points of view; *Absent Friends* (1975); and *Joking Apart* (1979). The plays are comedies of suburban and middle-class life, showing a keen sense of social nuance and of domestic misery and insensitivity, and displaying the virtuosity of Ayckbourn's stagecraft; Benedict Nightingale (*An Introduction to Fifty Modern British Plays*, 1982) comments that they succeed as comedies despite 'an intricacy of plot better fitted to farce, and themes sometimes more suited to tragedy', and detects, in common with other critics, an increasingly sombre note in his work. Later plays include *Sisterly Feelings* (1980), *A Chorus of Disapproval* (1986), and *Women in Mind* (1986), where his instinctive sympathy for the women as victims in his plays was most evident. In *Way Upstream* (1981) and *A Small Family Business* (1987) he addressed the politics of the Thatcher era from a social democratic perspective. He continues to produce work, though at a steadier pace, and is, after Shakespeare, the second most produced playwright in British theatrical history. See P. Allen, *Alan Ayckbourn: Grinning at the Edge* (2001).

Ayenbite of Inwit (*Prick of Conscience*) A devotional manual translated in 1340 by Dan Michel of Northgate, Canterbury, into English prose. Its source was the influential moral treatise *Le Somme des vices et des vertues*, also known as *Le Somme le roi* because it was composed for Philip III of France in 1279 by the Dominican Frère Loren of Orléans. Written in the Kentish dialect of the 14th century and often using allegorical imagery, the work covers the catechetical syllabus, including the Ten Commandments, the seven deadly sins and seven cardinal virtues, the seven gifts of the Holy Spirit, and the sacrament of confession. See the edition by R. Morris (EETS os 23, 1866), rev. P. O. E. Gradon (1965).

Ayesha (1) a novel by James Justinian *Morier; (2) a novel by Sir Henry Rider *Haggard.

Aymon, The Four Sons of A medieval French romance telling of *Charlemagne's struggle with these four noblemen, the eldest and most important of whom was Rinaldo. The English prose version of the romance is founded on William *Caxton's printed version (1489–91), there being no surviving manuscript. It has been edited by O. Richardson (1884; repr. 1973).

Ayrshire Legatees, The An *epistolary novel by John *Galt, serialized in *Blackwood's Magazine* and published 1821, recording the impressions of the family of a Scottish minister, Dr Zachariah Pringle, on a visit to London to take possession of a legacy. Rich in social detail, their alternately naive and shrewd comments on travellers, the sophistications of the English capital, and the 'douce folk' back home gently satirize Regency manners and values.

AYRTON, Michael (1921–75) Artist and writer, whose varied output of sculptures, illustrations, poems, and stories reveals an obsession with flight, myths, mirrors, and mazes. As a young man he worked for a while with Wyndham *Lewis, and an exhibition, *Word and Image* (National Book League, 1971), explored their literary and artistic connections. His writings include *The Testament of Daedalus* (1962, poetry), *Fabrications* (1972, short stories), and *The Maze Maker* (1967) and *The Midas Consequence* (1974), both novels.

AYTOUN, William Edmonstoune (1813–65) Poet and lawyer, born in Edinburgh, descendant of the poet Sir Robert Aytoun (1570–1638), who supposedly wrote the lines Robert *Burns turned into *'Auld Lang Syne'. Educated at Edinburgh University, he divided his life between law and literature, becoming professor of belles-lettres at Edinburgh in 1845, and sheriff of Orkney in 1852. He played an important role in the parodic *'Bon Gaultier' Ballads (1845), and was known also for his *Lays of the Scottish Cavaliers*. The first of the lays appeared in **Blackwood's Magazine* in April 1843, and the volume was published in 1849. These patriotic ballad-romances, based on stories of *Montrose, Dundee, and other Scottish heroes, were extremely popular. Aytoun also wrote *Firmilian, or The Student of Badajoz* (1854), a well-received mock-tragedy in which he parodied the poems of the *Spasmodic school. His novel *Norman Sinclair* (1861), set in early 19th-century Scotland, drew on his own memories.

B

Baal A Canaanite god, strongly opposed by the prophets of Israel in the Old Testament (e.g. Elijah in 1 Kings 18).

Bab Ballads A collection of humorous ballads by W. S. *Gilbert (who was called 'Bab' as a child by his parents), first published in *Fun*, 1866–71. They appeared in volume form as *Bab Ballads* (1869); *More Bab Ballads* (1873); *Fifty Bab Ballads* (1877).

Babbitt A 1922 novel by Sinclair *Lewis. 'Babbittry' became a term denoting middle-class conventionalism.

BABEL, Isaak Emmanuilovich (1894–1940) Russian writer born in Odessa into an Orthodox Jewish family. After graduating from the Kiev Institute of Financial and Business Studies in 1915, he went to Petrograd in search of a literary career. There Maxim *Gorky became his mentor, publishing Babel's first story in 1916. Guided by Gorky's advice to seek experience of life 'among the people', Babel served as soldier and war correspondent from 1917, and in 1920 published a short story cycle *On the Field of Honour*, based on the German front in the First World War. In the same year he took part in the First Cavalry's campaign to drive the Poles from Ukraine. From this came his masterpiece, the short story cycle *Red Cavalry* (1926) that examines Liutov, the intellectual, middle-class Jewish narrator, testing his values against the brutal machismo of the Cossack peasant soldiers. Many of Babel's other stories are loosely autobiographical such as 'The Story of My Dovecot' and 'First Love'. His four *Tales of Odessa* (1931)—'The King', 'How It Was Done in Odessa', 'The Father', and 'Liubka the Cossack'—written in 1921–4, hark back to his Jewish roots and are an entertaining caricature in hyperbole of life in Odessa's Jewish ghetto, dominated by the clownish gangster Benia Krik. With the 1930s Babel's exuberant, ornamental style, his sympathy for the underdog, and his Jewishness were reasons for increasing ostracism from the authorities. His anguish was expressed in his sardonic speech to the First Congress of the Writers' Union, chaired by Gorky in 1934. He was arrested in May 1939 and executed in January 1940. In 1954 he received a posthumous pardon. For translations see *Collected Stories*, ed. Walter Morison (1974); *Complete Works*, ed. Peter Constantine (2002); see also Milton Ehre, *Isaac Babel* (1986).

Babylon Middle Eastern empire to which the Jews were forcibly exiled, as described by the prophet Jeremiah. The Babylonian captivity is lamented in Psalm 137, 'By the rivers of Babylon'. In the Book of Revelation and St *Augustine's *City of God* the earthly Babylon is the symbolic opposite of the heavenly *Jerusalem. Protestant writers often identified Catholic Rome with Babylon.
See BIBLE.

BACH German family of musicians, of which Johann Sebastian (1685–1750) has become a central figure in music history since a revival of interest in the 19th century led by Samuel Wesley (1766–1837, son of Charles *Wesley) and Felix *Mendelssohn. His youngest son, Johann Christian (1735–82), settled in London in 1762 and became known as the 'English Bach': he became music-master to the family of George III and promoted a successful concert series. His operas were mainly in the prevailing Italian fashion, but he also wrote some arias in English and set folk songs. He was painted by Gainsborough and is buried in St Pancras churchyard.

BACON, Francis, First Baron Verulam and Viscount St Albans (1561–1626) Lord chancellor, politician, and philosopher, the fifth son of Sir Nicholas Bacon, lord keeper to *Elizabeth I 1558–79, by his second marriage, to Lady Anne Cooke (*c.*1528–1610), who was an exceptionally gifted scholar and translator in her own right. Born at York House in the Strand, Bacon was unusually precocious and at the age of 12 went up to Trinity College, Cambridge, with his brother Antony, where they were tutored by the master, John Whitgift (1530–1604), subsequently archbishop of Canterbury. As part of his grooming for high public office he spent from 1576 to 1579 with the queen's ambassador to France, Sir Amias Paulet (*c.*1532–88). His father died suddenly, in February 1579, leaving his estate unsettled. Deprived of an inheritance, Bacon returned to England to become a lawyer, entering Gray's Inn in 1579. His abilities were soon recognized, and he was appointed a lecturer in law and invited to sit on government legal committees while still in his twenties. In 1581 he became an MP (for Bossiney, Cornwall) and served in every Parliament until 1621. He achieved recognition as a parliamentary speaker, but his boldness in the 1593 session in opposing the unusually heavy taxes that the queen wanted led to his being expelled from royal favour, promotion to higher legal office going to his rival, Sir Edward *Coke. His finances were precarious and he was arrested for debt in 1598. The queen continued to employ him in various legal offices, severely testing his loyalty by appointing him one of the prosecutors of his former friend and patron the earl of *Essex, who was executed in 1601. In 1606 Bacon married Alice Barnham (1592–1650), the 14-year-old daughter of a London alderman and MP. Little is known of their marriage and he disinherited her in his will. With the accession of James I, Bacon's fortunes took an upward turn. He was a strong supporter of the royal prerogative, and rapidly achieved public office. Knighted in 1603, he became king's counsel in 1604, solicitor-general in 1607, attorney-general in 1613, a privy counsellor in 1616, lord keeper in 1617, and lord chancellor in 1618. He was elevated to the House of Lords as Baron Verulam in 1618, and created Viscount St Albans in 1621. But the higher reaches of state office carried their own dangers, and Bacon increasingly found that his carefully worked-out advice and counsel were ignored both by James and by the court favourite, the second duke of *Buckingham, George Villiers. In the absence of a proper salary structure, government officials under James depended for their livelihood on gifts from suitors and on selling their office, leading to a high degree of corruption. In 1621 a parliamentary group bent on reform, led by Coke and Sir Lionel Cranfield (1575–1645), attacked the system of monopolies, where lucrative patents were allocated and enforced by illegal means. Bacon, who as head of the Court of Chancery had issued licences to patentees at the king's request, was impeached on 23 charges of corruption. He did not attempt to defend himself, and both James and Buckingham abandoned him as scapegoat for their own unpopular policies. His career was ruined: he was fined £40,000, imprisoned in the Tower, and debarred from future office. But the fine was remitted; the imprisonment lasted three days, the whole affair being cynically intended to placate the reform party. Deprived of power, Bacon was vulnerable to Buckingham's greed, and was made to sell York House. Out of office, he devoted himself fully to writing, producing in quick succession *A History of the Life and Reign of King *Henry VII* (1622), the *De Dignitate & Augmentis Scientiarum* (1623, a Latin expansion of *The *Advancement of Learning*), the **Essays* (1625), and the posthumously published **New Atlantis* (1627). Until his downfall, Bacon's writings were the product of the vacations or other leisure time in a busy public career. Simultaneously a Protestant, humanist, or moderate Calvinist, as his posthumously published *Confession of Faith* (1641) shows, Bacon directed all his intellectual activities towards practical ends from which the whole of society would benefit. He outlined many schemes for reforming the laws, making them easier to understand and more coherent; he wanted the universities to widen their curriculum from the three traditional professions (theology, law, medicine) to take in the 'arts and sciences at large'; and he was ahead of his time in realizing that a continuous growth of knowledge was possible. Bacon's plan to reform the whole of natural philosophy (or science), outlined in the fragmentary *Instauratio Magna* (1620), of which the **Novum Organum* was the only more or less complete part, aimed to effect a new union between 'the mind and the universe', from which would spring a range of inventions to 'overcome the necessities and miseries of humanity'. Though he was not a scientist in the modern sense, he was regarded by succeeding generations as the instigator of the scientific revolution and the inventor of scientific method. He taught that men could 'arrive at the knowledge of the laws that govern the material world' by a process of induction—that is, by observation, experiment, and the testing of hypotheses, rather than by deduction from supposed first principles. He excluded religion from intellectual enquiry altogether, since that is a matter of faith whereas science is a matter of reason.

Bacon's writings inspired the founding of the *Royal Society in 1662, and had a considerable influence on Thomas *Hobbes, Robert *Boyle, John *Locke, Daniel *Defoe, and many others. The fullest edition of his works was prepared by James Spedding (14 vols, 1857–74); see also Lisa Jardine, *Francis Bacon: Discovery and the Art of Discourse* (1974); Julian Martin, *Francis Bacon, the State, and the Reform of Natural Philosophy* (1992); and SHAKESPEARE: AUTHORSHIP OF THE WORKS.

BACON, Roger (*c.*1214–*c.*1292) The 'Doctor Mirabilis', a philosopher who studied at Oxford and then Paris, where he probably became doctor before returning to England *c.*1247, after which time he was influenced by the Franciscan Robert *Grosseteste. It is thought that he joined the Franciscan order in *c.*1257. He incurred the suspicions of the Franciscans and was sent under surveillance to Paris, where he remained in confinement for ten years. He produced at the request of Pope Clement IV (1265–8) Latin treatises on the sciences (including grammar, logic, mathematics, physics, optics, and moral philosophy). His great work is the *Opus Maius*, and he also completed an *Opus Minus* and an *Opus Tertium*. He was again in confinement for his heretical propositions, *c.*1278–92, and is said to have died and been buried at Oxford. He advocated support for theology from an appeal to experience rather than from the *Scholastic method of argument. He states the causes of error to be ignorance of languages, especially Greek, bad Latin translations, and lack of knowledge of the natural sciences, especially mathematics. At the same time, his outlook remained partly mystical. His attack on the Scholastic method was taken up again and developed by William of *Ockham in the next century. Always a controversial, independent, and in some ways isolated thinker impatient with what he regarded as the conventional ideas and pedagogy of his time, he was also a man of immense learning, with a wide knowledge of the sciences and of languages, including Greek, Hebrew, and Aramaic. He was also a practical scientist; he invented spectacles and indicated the method by which a telescope might be constructed.

Badman, The Life and Death of Mr An allegory by John *Bunyan, published 1680. The allegory takes the form of a dialogue, in which Mr Wiseman relates the life of Mr Badman, recently deceased, and Mr Attentive comments on it. The youthful Badman shows early signs of his vicious disposition. He beguiles a rich damsel into marriage and ruins her; sets up in trade and swindles his creditors by fraudulent bankruptcies and his customers by false weights; breaks his leg when coming home drunk; and displays a short-lived sickbed repentance. His wife dies of despair and Badman marries again, but his second wife is as wicked as he is and they part 'as poor as Howlets'. Finally Badman dies of a complication of diseases. The story is entertaining as well as edifying and has a place in the evolution of the English novel.

BAEDEKER, Karl (1801–59) Editor and publisher, of Essen, Germany. He began the famous series of *guidebooks when his Koblenz publishing firm bought the rights to a guide to the Rhine. He developed a reputation for reliability and introduced the star rating system for cultural sites, hotels, and restaurants. His son Fritz transferred the business to Leipzig and expanded internationally, producing simultaneous English and French editions and eclipsing the guides of John *Murray. Baedeker became synonymous with the flourishing tourist industry and shaped the experience of generations of tourists. Deliberate bombing assaults on British cultural sites in the Second World War were termed 'Baedeker raids'.

BAGE, Robert (1728/30–1801) Novelist, who ran his family's paper-making business while pursuing his own course of study. A radical by conviction, he was much influenced by *Rousseau, and later friendly with William *Godwin. He lost money through a partnership in an ironworks with Erasmus *Darwin, and turned for solace to the writing of novels: *Mount Henneth* (1782); *Barham Downs* (1784); *The Fair Syrian* (1787); *James Wallace* (1788); *Man as He Is* (1792); and **Hermsprong, or Man as He Is Not* (1796), the best known. The novels, comic and satiric in tone, set fresh ideals of youth against the fossilized institutions of church and state; they were popular in spite of their *Jacobin leanings and were included in Anna Laetitia *Barbauld's 'British Novelists' and Walter *Scott's 'Ballantyne's Novelist's Library' series.

BAGEHOT, Walter (1826–77) Journalist, businessman, and essayist, born in Langport, Somerset, educated at Bristol and University College London. He was called to the bar and then joined the shipping and banking business of his father. He contributed articles on economic, political, historical, and literary subjects to various periodicals, became joint editor with R. H. *Hutton of the *National Review* from 1855, and editor of *The Economist* from 1860 until his death. He was author of *The English Constitution* (1867), which takes the form of a philosophical discussion appraising the constitution and remains a classic introduction to the study of English politics, in spite of historical change. His *Physics and Politics* (1872) was 'an attempt to apply the principles of natural selection and inheritance to political society'. *Lombard Street* (1873) is an analysis of the money market of his day. Among his other works are *Biographical Studies* (1881) and *Literary Studies* (1879–95), which includes critical essays on William *Shakespeare, Laurence *Sterne, and the notable 'Wordsworth, Tennyson, and Browning, or Pure, Ornate, and Grotesque Art in English Poetry'. See *Collected Works*, ed. N. A. F. St John-Stevas, 8 vols (1965–74); and *Life* by N. A. F. St John-Stevas (1959).

Bagford Ballads, The Illustrating the last years of the Stuarts' rule and the last years of the 17th century. They were published by the Ballad Society in 1878. The ballads were assembled by John Bagford (1651–1716), originally a shoemaker, a book-collector who made for Robert *Harley, first earl of Oxford, the collection that was subsequently acquired by the duke of *Roxburghe, and at the same time made a private collection for himself.

BAGNOLD, Enid Algerine, Lady Jones (1889–1981) Novelist and playwright, who spent much of her early childhood in the West Indies, returning to England to Prior's Field, an intellectually progressive school run by the mother of Aldous *Huxley. She worked as nurse and ambulance driver during the First World War (see her *Diary without Dates*, 1917) and married in 1920, but continued to write and move in artistic and bohemian circles, writing several novels, of which the best known and commercially most successful was *National Velvet* (1935, filmed 1944 with Elizabeth Taylor as the girl who wins the Grand National). Of her plays, the most successful was *The Chalk Garden* (1955). Her *Autobiography* was published in 1969.

BAILEY, Nathan (d. 1742) Teacher and author of the *Universal Etymological English Dictionary* (1721, second volume 1727), a popular forerunner of Samuel *Johnson's *Dictionary*. Johnson used Bailey's illustrated *Dictionarium Britannicum* (1730), while compiling his work.

BAILEY, Paul (1937–) London-born actor turned writer, the son of a road-sweeper, educated at Walter St John Grammar School, Battersea, and the Central School of Speech and Drama. His first book, *At the Jerusalem* (1967), won an Arts Council award for the best novel published between 1963 and 1967. Other novels include *Peter Smart's Confessions* (1977), which draws on Bailey's experiences in the theatre, and *Old Soldiers* (1980), one of several books showing an abiding fascination with London and the elderly. Characteristically mixing tragedy with the comic-grotesque, *Gabriel's Lament* (1986) details the relationship between a sensitive young man and his repulsive and reactionary old father who brought him up after the disappearance of his mother. *Kitty and Virgil* (1998) and *Uncle Rudolf* (2002) reflect a latter-day interest in Romania. Bailey has held several teaching posts and been a regular journalist and broadcaster. His non-fiction includes *An English Madam* (1982), a biography of Cynthia Payne; *An Immaculate Mistake: Scenes from Childhood and Beyond* (1990); and the biographical triptych *Three Queer Lives* (2001).

BAILEY, Philip James (1816–1902) Poet, born in Nottingham. After embarking on a career as a barrister, he retired in 1836 to his father's house at Old Basford, near Nottingham, where he wrote *Festus* (1839). A second edition appeared in 1845, and the final edition of 1889, which exceeded 40,000 lines, incorporated the greater part of three volumes of poetry that had appeared in the interval (*The Angel World*, 1850; *The Mystic*, 1855; *Universal Hymn*, 1867). *Festus* is Bailey's version of the *Faust story; it was strongly influenced by *Goethe and John

*Milton's *Paradise Lost*. Admired for its 'fire of imagination' (E. B. *Browning), it was a prominent representative of the so-called *Spasmodic school.

BAILLIE, Joanna (1762–1851) Scottish dramatist and poet. Born in Bothwell, Lanarkshire, and educated in Miss McDonald's boarding-school at Glasgow, she later settled in London. She published a book of verse (*Poems; Wherein It Is Attempted to Describe Certain Views of Nature and of Rustic Manners*) in 1790, but achieved success in 1798 with her first volume of *Plays on the Passions*, in which each verse drama displays the effect of one particular passion. *Basil*, on the subject of love, and *De Montfort*, on hatred, were the most successful; *De Montfort* was produced by Charles *Kemble and Sarah *Siddons in 1800. The volume brought her the friendship of Sir Walter *Scott, who called her 'the immortal Joanna', but her dramas were strongly criticized by Francis *Jeffrey in the **Edinburgh Review*. A second volume of the *Passions* appeared in 1802, *Miscellaneous Plays* in 1804, and a third *Passions* volume in 1812. Her tragedy *Constantine Paleologus, or The Last of the Caesars* (1804) was considered by John Stuart *Mill to be 'one of the best dramas of the last two centuries'. Her most successful play, *The Family Legend*, based on a bitter Scottish feud, was produced in 1810 with a prologue by Scott and an epilogue by Henry *Mackenzie. Scott described it as a 'complete and decided triumph' and it established Baillie as a literary and social success. Her house in Hampstead became a meeting place for many of the literary figures of her time. See *Joanna Baillie: A Selection of Poems and Plays*, ed. A. Gilroy and K. Hanley (1997).

BAILLIE, Robert (1599–1662) Scottish Presbyterian theologian, who was with the *Covenanters' army in 1639 and in 1640 went to London to draw up accusations against William *Laud. An opponent of religious toleration, he attacked the independents in *Anabaptism* (1647) as anarchists and sexual deviants. His *Letters and Journals*, ed. D. Laing (1842), are valuable records of the Civil War.

Bailly, Harry In Chaucer's **Canterbury Tales* the host of the Tabard Inn where the pilgrims meet in the General Prologue. We learn his name from the Cook's Prologue (l. 4358). He has been tentatively identified with an ostler of that name in the Subsidy Rolls for Southwark 1380/1 and perhaps with the member of Parliament for Southwark 1376/7 and 1378/9. He initiates the pilgrims' storytelling competition and serves as their goad and impromptu critic.

BAINBRIDGE, Dame Beryl (1934–) Novelist, born in Liverpool, educated at Merchant Taylor's School, Crosby, and the Cone-Ripman Ballet School in Tring, Hertfordshire. She began her career as an actress at the Liverpool Playhouse. Her first novels, *A Weekend with Claude* (1967) and *Another Part of the Wood* (1968), were little noticed, but in the 1970s a series of original and idiosyncratic works established her reputation. These include *Harriet Said* (1972), *The Bottle Factory Outing* (1974), and *Young Adolf* (1978). Short, laconic, and rich in black comedy, they deal with the lives of characters at once deeply ordinary and highly eccentric, in a world where violence and the absurd lurk beneath the daily routine of urban domesticity. In *Injury Time* (1977), a supposedly discreet dinner party becomes headline news when invaded by a gang of criminals who take its guests hostage. The juxtaposition of the banal and the bizarre is also a feature of the dialogue, which shows a fine ear for the oddities of contemporary speech. Other novels include *Winter Garden* (1980), *Filthy Lucre* (1986), and *An Awfully Big Adventure* (1989). Her *Collected Stories* were published in 1994. More recent novels have been set in the past, often drawing on real people or events: *Watson's Apology* (1984) reconstructs a Victorian murder; *The Birthday Boys* (1991) follows Robert Falcon *Scott to the Antarctic; *Every Man for Himself* (1996) takes place on board the *Titanic*; *Master Georgie* (1998) is set during the Crimean War; and *According to Queeney* (2001) is a child's-eye view of Samuel *Johnson. Her books have won numerous prizes and she was made DBE in 2000.

BAKER, Sir Samuel White (1821–93) Traveller and big-game hunter. As a young man he shot elephants and established a plantation in Sri Lanka. After his wife died he bought a Hungarian slave of the Turks, who accompanied him on expeditions to Africa and became his second wife. In 1864 he discovered Lake Albert Nyanza, so complementing John *Speke's Lake Victoria in the Nile system, and was later, for a very large salary, hired by the Khedive of Egypt to establish 'Equatoria' as a province at the head of the Nile. Baker exaggerated the size of his lake and the extent of his success in Equatoria. His brusque intolerance alienated Africans, especially the Banyoro of present-day Uganda, and the slave trade continued to flourish. *The Albert Nyanza* (1866) and *Ismailia* (1874) were the most important of the nine volumes and many articles he produced, including some adventure stories.

BAKHTIN, Mikhail Mikhailovich (1895–1975) Russian literary and cultural theorist, born in Orel, who studied classics and philology at Petrograd University. He developed his original theoretical approach in the 1920s and 1930s with a circle of collaborators including the Marxist scholars Valentin Voloshinov (1895–1936) and Pavel Medvedev (1892–1938). Between 1930 and 1960 he suffered periods of unemployment and internal exile, eventually securing a teaching position in Saransk. He returned to Moscow in 1969, where he enjoyed belated recognition and was finally able to see several works published. These included an extended version of *Problems of Dostoevsky's Poetics* (1963; trans. Caryl Emerson, 1984), originally published in 1929 just before his exile to Kazakhstan, *Rabelais and his World* (1965; trans. Helene Iswolsky, 1968), as well as a number of earlier essays, some of which were translated as *The Dialogic Imagination* (1981). Confusingly, works by Voloshinov and Medvedev also came to be attributed to Bakhtin. Bakhtin's influence has been widespread in Western academic criticism since the late 1970s, partly because of his attractive notion of the *carnivalesque in his study of *Rabelais, but more for his concept of 'dialogism', in which language (and truth) are viewed as an open field of interactive utterances, and literature—especially the novel—is valued for keeping in play a variety of voices and languages. See Caryl Emerson, *The First Hundred Years of Mikhail Bakhtin* (1997); Michael Holquist, *Dialogism: Bakhtin and his World* (1990); Sue Vice, *Introducing Bakhtin* (1997).

BALAKIREV, Mily Alexeyevich (1837–1910) Russian composer, conductor, and pianist. In 1859 he composed an overture to *King Lear*, performed the same year; further incidental music to the play, in part based on English song, was written in 1861, and revised in 1902–5. Balakirev was a crucially influential figure among the Russian nationalist school of composers, resistant to German orthodoxy. An uncompromising and sometimes intimidating character, it was he who pressed upon *Tchaikovsky the plan for a symphonic work based on *Romeo and Juliet*, and who similarly propelled the composer into writing the *Manfred* symphony.

Balaustion's Adventure: *Including a Transcript from Euripides* By Robert *Browning, published 1871. The story, suggested by a passage in *Plutarch's *Life of Nicias*, is set just after the defeat of the Athenian expedition against Sicily in 413 BC. A group of pro-Athenians from Rhodes, inspired by the young girl Balaustion, is intercepted on its voyage to Athens by a pirate ship and is forced to seek shelter in the harbour of Syracuse, where it is refused entry until it is discovered that Balaustion can recite a play by *Euripides, who was greatly admired in Sicily although neglected in his native Athens. The play is *Alcestis*, a performance of which Balaustion narrates, mingling with the text her own comments and descriptions. Browning is thus able to represent Euripides' play in his own interpretation, within the framework of another speaker's consciousness, a marriage of conventional drama with dramatic monologue which continues the experiment with form begun with *The *Ring and the Book*. The plot of the *Alcestis*, with its concentration on a woman's love for her husband and her rescue from Death by a heroic figure, also links the poem to *The Ring and the Book*, and the character of Balaustion has, like that of Pompilia, been thought to be modelled on Elizabeth Barrett (to whom there is a direct allusion at ll. 2668–71; *see* BROWNING, ELIZABETH BARRETT). Balaustion reappears in **Aristophanes' Apology*.

BALBOA, Vasco Núñez de *See* NÚÑEZ DE BALBOA, VASCO.

Balder Dead Long blank verse poem by Matthew *Arnold, published in 1855. It develops, like *'Sohrab and Rustum', from Arnold's argument in the 'Preface' to his *Poems* (1853) that action of permanent human interest should be at the centre of poetry. Here, Arnold retells the northern myth of the god Balder, maliciously slain and then confined to the underworld. Attempts to restore him to life fail and he remains in the murky realm of ghosts until the apocalypse. The narrative, an important instance of the northern Prose *Edda's reception among Victorian poets, was suffused with nervousness about Christian doctrine.

BALDWIN, James (1924–87) African American novelist, short story writer, playwright, poet, and essayist, born in Harlem, the stepson of a preacher. He was helped by Richard *Wright. His first novel, *Go Tell It on the Mountain* (1953), set in Harlem, was followed by several on a more international scale, dealing with both homosexuality and the situation of African Americans; they include *Giovanni's Room* (1956), *Another Country* (1962), and *Just above my Head* (1979). He also wrote short stories, political and autobiographical essays, and plays, including *Blues for Mister Charley* (1964). He campaigned through works like *The Fire Next Time* (1963) in the American civil rights movement.

BALDWIN, William (d. in or before 1563) Printer and author. He worked for Edward Whitchurch who printed his popular *Treatise of Moral Philosophy* (1547). By 1552 he had written a carnivalesque satirical work *Beware the Cat* (pub. 1570), and *c.*1554 he initiated *A *Mirror for Magistrates*.

BALE, John (1495–1563) Bishop of Ossory (in Ireland), author of religious plays, a catalogue of English writers, and numerous polemical and apocalyptic works promoting the Reformation. Of his 24 plays only five survive, the most notable being *King John*, performed in 1538, the first English historical play, forming a bridge between the *morality and the historical play proper.

'Balin and Balan' One of Tennyson's **Idylls of the King*, first published 1885. It is the story of two brothers who kill each other unwittingly, Balan mistaking for a demon the impassioned Balin, who is driven to frenzy by a conviction of Guinevere's adultery.

BALL, John Priest and leader of the *Peasants' Revolt of 1381. Chronicles associate him with seditious letters invoking *Piers Plowman.

ballad A traditional song in which some popular story is graphically narrated in short stanzas, commonly in *quatrains of alternate four- and three-stress lines with the shorter lines only rhymed, as in *'Sir Patrick Spens'; or a narrative poem written imitatively in this popular style. In the great collection of F. J. Child (1825–96), *English and Scottish Popular Ballads* (5 vols, 1882–98), the oldest of the 300 examples exhibited is 'Judas' (*c.*1300), with an uncharacteristically religious theme; ballads more traditionally deal with the pagan supernatural (e.g. 'Tam Lin'), with tragic love (e.g.*'Barbara Allan'), or with historical or legendary events, e.g. the Border ballads, or the *Robin Hood ballads. Most examples appear to date from the 15th and 16th centuries, at least in their surviving form, but arguments have been advanced for an oral tradition of greater antiquity. There was a notable awakening of interest in the form in Britain in the 18th century, which led to the researches and collections of Thomas *Percy (*Reliques*, 1765) and Joseph *Ritson, to the forgeries of Thomas *Chatterton and the adaptations of Robert *Burns, and to the deliberate antiquarian imitations of Thomas *Tickell ('Lucy and Colin'), Percy himself ('The Hermit of Warkworth'), David *Mallet ('William and Margaret'), Oliver *Goldsmith ('The Hermit'), and others. Walter *Scott's *Minstrelsy of the Scottish Border* is a mixture of traditional ballads, adaptations, and imitations, whereas the *Lyrical Ballads* of William *Wordsworth and S. T. *Coleridge manifests, in poems like 'The Idiot Boy' and the *Rime of the *Ancient Mariner*, their own interpretation and development of balladry. The form has continued to inspire poets, from John *Keats (*'La Belle Dame sans Merci') to William *Morris, Oscar *Wilde, Thomas *Hardy, W. B. *Yeats, and Charles *Causley, and flourishes in a popular folk form as well as in a more literary guise. The ingredients of ballads, both ancient and modern, vary, but frequently include the use of a refrain (sometimes altered slightly at the end of each stanza, to advance the story), stock descriptive phrases, and simple, terse dialogue. See M. J. C. Hodgart, *The Ballads* (2nd edn 1962).

ballade A French lyric verse-form that flourished in the hands of François *Villon, having already been adapted into English by Geoffrey *Chaucer (e.g. in 'To Rosemounde'). In its standard form, it consists of three eight-line stanzas rhyming *ababbcbc*, each ending with the same line as refrain, and usually followed by a four-line *envoy addressed to a prince. There are variant forms employing seven- or ten-line stanzas, and double ballades with six stanzas. A. C. *Swinburne and others revived the English ballade in the late 19th century.

ballad opera An English theatrical and musical form, in which the action of the play (usually comic) is carried in spoken prose, punctuated by songs set to traditional or fashionable melodies, sung by the actors in character. The first ballad opera, *The *Beggar's Opera* (1728) by Gay, with music for the 69 songs arranged by J. C. Pepusch, was enormously successful, touching off a burst of imitations, and the ballad opera became the chief mode of opposition to the Italian opera imported by *Handel and others; exotic kings and huge arias were exchanged for ordinary life and well-known tunes. Henry *Fielding made successful use of the form's satiric possibilities. But its vogue was short-lived and began to decline about 1735. English comic operas of the later 18th century, such as *Arne and *Bickerstaff's *Love in a Village* (1762) or *The Duenna* (1775), with music by Thomas Linley the elder (1733–95) and his son the younger Thomas Linley (1756–78), and libretto by Richard *Sheridan, bear some resemblance to the ballad opera.

BALLANTYNE, James (1772–1833) and **John** (1774–1821) Respectively a printer and publisher, who set up the unsuccessful publishing and bookselling business of John Ballantyne and Co. with Walter *Scott in 1809. James had printed *Minstrelsy of the Scottish Border* in 1802, and continued to issue Scott's works, but was bankrupted by the crash of Constable and Co. in 1826 (see CONSTABLE, A.). Scott planned Ballantyne's Novelist's Library (1821–4) solely for John's financial benefit, but only one volume was published before the latter's death.

BALLANTYNE, R. M. (Robert Michael) (1825–94) Prolific Scottish writer of boys' adventure stories, remembered for *The *Coral Island* (1858), a *Robinsonnade which influenced Robert Louis Stevenson's *Treasure Island* and William Golding's *Lord of the Flies* (1954). Born in Edinburgh, he left school to take up an apprenticeship with the Hudson's Bay Company in Canada, where he wrote *Snowflakes and Sunbeams*, retitled *The Young Fur Traders* (1856), based on his experiences there. Following its success he became a lecturer, writer, printer, and painter, creating picture books and novels. The books were often set in exotic locations including Africa (*Black Ivory*, 1873) and South America (*Martin Rattler*, 1858). He also wrote about adventurous careers, among them those of firefighters, miners, and fishermen. Ballantyne's books are didactic, designed to teach readers about geography, natural history, religion, morality, and the responsibilities of empire. His heroes are plucky, courageous, morally sound British boys.

BALLARD, J. G. (James Graham) (1930–2009) English novelist and short story writer, born in Shanghai and educated at Cambridge. He became known in the 1960s as the most prominent of the *'New Wave' science fiction writers. His first short story was published in 1956 in *New Worlds*, to which he continued to contribute during the influential editorship of Michael *Moorcock. His first novel, *The Drowned World* (1962), a 'catastrophe' novel in which the world turns into a vast swamp, was followed by *The Drought* (1965), in which he imagined post-apocalyptic landscapes and populated them with realistically observed, ultra-obsessive characters. *Crash* (1973) was an outstanding, outrageous work, years ahead of its time, if there could ever be a time when the eroticism of car accidents would be an acceptable subject for a novel. His collections of short stories include *The Terminal Beach* (1964) and *Vermilion Sands* (1971): a *Complete Stories* was issued in 2001. In *Empire of the Sun* (1984, filmed 1988) he turned away from science fiction to draw on his own wartime experiences in a Japanese prison camp in China. Other novels include *The Venus Hunters* (1986), *The Day of Creation* (1987), *Running Wild* (1988), *The Kindness of Women* (1991), and *Rushing to Paradise* (1994), a disturbing contemporary fable about eco-fanaticism. *Cocaine Nights* (1996), set in a high-security leisure-oriented Mediterranean resort complex, represents a new peak of Ballard's storytelling powers. Succeeding novels such as *Kingdom Come* (2006) explore the gated communities and designed Metro Centres of the coming century. Ballard is increasingly viewed as an important figure in the literary mainstream. See Roger Luckhurst, *The Angle between Two Walls* (1997).

Balor The chief of the *Fomorians of Gaelic mythology. One of his eyes had the power of destroying whatever it looked on. The eye was put out and Balor himself slain by Lugh, the sun god, at the great battle of Moytura.

BALZAC, Honoré de (1799–1850) French novelist, author of the great series of 89 separately titled but interlocking stories and novels known collectively as *La Comédie humaine* (*The Human Comedy*), published in seventeen volumes between 1842 and 1847. In his 1845 prospectus for the still incomplete collection, Balzac presents *La Comédie humaine* as having the form of a pyramid: at the base are *Études de mœurs* (*Studies of Mores*), fictions describing contemporary society, subdivided into those dealing with private, provincial, and country life, Paris, military matters, and politics; above these are *Études philosophiques* (*Philosophical Studies*), fictions considering the causes of social phenomena; and at the top are *Études analytiques* (*Analytical Studies*), fictions offering an analysis of the principles of life in society. The cast of *La Comédie humaine* comprises more than 2,000 characters, some of them, like the master criminal Vautrin or the moneylender Gobseck, appearing at different stages of their careers in several novels. Balzac is fascinated by the supernatural and the mysterious (especially in the *Études philosophiques*), the operation of the passions, the role of money in shaping personal and social relations, the determining effect of environment on the individual, and, conversely, by the various courses taken by energy and ambition in pursuit of social fulfilment. The best-known works in *La Comédie humaine* are *La Peau de chagrin* (1831: *The Wild Ass's Skin*), *Illusions perdues* (1837–43: *Lost Illusions*), *Le Médecin de campagne* (1833: *The Country Doctor*), *La Rabouilleuse* (1840: *The Black Sheep*), *La Cousine Bette* (1846: *Cousin Bette*), and *Le Cousin Pons* (1847: *Cousin Pons*). Balzac has long appealed to English readers: though Wilkie *Collins could lament in 1859 that 'he is little known because he is little translated', by the end of the 19th century there had appeared three different translations of his works in English, one of them, published in 40 volumes, masterminded by George Saintsbury; and in the 20th century, individual works have been translated by, amongst others, the poet Kathleen *Raine (*Cousin Bette*, 1948; *Lost Illusions*, 1951). Balzac's influence has been immense, and his work is an essential reference point in the history of the European novel. See G. Robb, *Balzac* (1994).

BAMBARA, Toni Cade (1939–95) African American novelist, short story writer, and documentary film-maker. She was active in the *Black Arts Movement and her short story collections, like *Gorilla, my Love* (1972), explore the importance of oral tradition. Her first novel, *The Salt Eaters* (1980), examines the role of activists within the community. In the 1980s, convinced that the film industry had 'colonized' African American subjects, she turned her attention to making documentaries, her first being *The Bombing of Osage Avenue* (1986). Her interest shifted next to a documentary about the life of W. E. B. *Du Bois, released in 1995. An important collection of essays and interviews, *Deep Sightings and Rescue Missions*, was published in 1995.

BAMFORD, Samuel (1788–1872) Weaver and poet, born in Middleton, Lancashire, and educated at Manchester Grammar School. He became a *Chartist activist, and in his *Passages in the Life of a Radical* (1840–4) gives a vivid first-hand description of the Peterloo massacre (1819) which both he and his wife witnessed: he was subsequently arrested and imprisoned for a year. He wrote a quantity of popular verse: his *Homely Rhymes, Poems and Reminiscences* (1839–41) collects some political poems, some pastoral, and a few written in dialect, many of them displaying considerable verve and energy. *Early Days*, an account of his childhood and of old Lancashire customs, was published 1848–9.

BANDELE, Biyi (1967–) Born in Nigeria and now living in London. He has written plays, several novels including *Burma Boy* (2007), adaptations of novels for the stage, and scripts for radio and television. He has worked with the *Royal Court Theatre and the Royal Shakespeare Company.

BANDELLO, Matteo (1485–1561) A Dominican friar, poet, and courtier who moved with his patron's widow to France in 1541 and was made bishop of Agen by Francis I; he was the best writer of Italian short stories in the 16th century. Many of his tales were translated by Belleforest into French (1564–82) and thirteen of these French versions were rendered into English by Geoffrey Fenton in his *Certaine Tragicall Discourses* (1567). Painter's **Palace of Pleasure* includes 25 of Bandello's tales, nine translated from the Italian and sixteen from Belleforest. Bandello is the source of plots for many English plays, including **Romeo and Juliet*, **Much Ado About Nothing*, **Twelfth Night*, and *The *Duchess of Malfi*.

BANIM, John (1798–1842) Irish Catholic novelist, dramatist, and poet, born in Kilkenny and educated at the Protestant Kilkenny Grammar School and at the Academy of the Royal Dublin Society. He is chiefly remembered for his depiction of rural Irish society in the highly successful *Tales by the O'Hara Family*, partly written with his brother Michael in self-conscious imitation of Walter *Scott and published in 1825, 1826, and 1827. Several novels later published separately first appeared in the *Tales*. Works mainly composed by John include *The Nowlans* (1833), a portrait of contemporary cabin life, and the historical novel *The Boyne Water* (1836). Michael Banim (1796–1874) claimed after his brother's death that he was himself responsible for thirteen of their 24 joint works; according to his claim, his own books include *The Croppy* (1828), a sombre, if somewhat obsequious tale of the 1798 uprising, and *The Mayor of Windgap* (1835).

BANKS, Iain Menzies (1954–) Scottish novelist, born in Dunfermline, educated at Stirling University. He came to controversial prominence with his first novel, *The Wasp Factory* (1984), a macabre tale of teenage fantasies of death and destruction, narrated by 16-year-old Frank Cauldhame, who lives with his 'scientist' father on the east coast of

Scotland: it was condemned by some for its graphic violence but praised by others for its targeting of macho values. Succeeding novels, such as *Walking on Glass* (1985), *The Bridge* (1986), *Espedair Street* (1987), *Complicity* (1993), *A Song of Stone* (1997, a post-apocalyptic story set around an ancestral castle in the aftermath of a civil war), *Dead Air* (2002), and *The Steep Approach to Garbadale* (2007), fulfilled his promise as an inventive and often fiercely comic moralist. As Iain M. Banks he has also written equally effective *science fiction novels, many set in a hard-edged utopian civilization known as the Culture, including *Consider Phlebas* (1987), *The Player of Games* (1988), *Feersum Endjinn* (1993), *Excession* (1996), *Look to Windward* (2000), and *The Algebraist* (2004). *The State of the Art* is a collection of short fiction, both science fiction and less classifiable, also published as by Iain M. Banks.

BANKS, Sir Joseph (1743–1820) Naturalist, born into a wealthy landed Lincolnshire family and educated at Harrow School, Eton College, and Christ Church, Oxford. A passion for botany took him to Newfoundland in 1766, and in 1768 he joined James *Cook's expedition to the Pacific. He returned famous, an authority on the South Seas and their peoples. When the Admiralty refused to accommodate his elaborate entourage on Cook's second voyage, he botanized in Iceland. He then enjoyed intellectual life in London, joining Samuel Johnson's *Club, and becoming president of the *Royal Society from 1778 until his death. He used his wealth and prestige to advance science, particularly botany, which was professionalized over his lifetime. He recommended Botany Bay (a name he had suggested) as a site for a convict settlement and took an active interest in the affairs of both Australia and Iceland. See Harold Carter, *Sir Joseph Banks* (1988).

BANKS, Lynne Reid (1929–) London-born novelist and children's writer, educated at the Royal Academy of Dramatic Art, whose first novel, *The L-Shaped Room* (1960), about Jane, a young girl, pregnant with an illegitimate child and living in a London bedsit, was a great success (film, 1962). This was followed by a number of other novels for adults, including *An End to Running* (1962), *Children at the Gate* (1968), *The Backward Shadow* (1970), and *Two is Lonely* (1974). From the 1970s she became better known as a writer for children and adolescents, notably for her series about miniature toys that come alive, beginning with *The Indian in the Cupboard* (1981–98; the first book was filmed in 1995), and *One More River* (1973) and its sequel *Broken Bridge* (1994), set during the Six Day War of 1967 and reflecting her interest in Israel, where she lived for a time.

Bannatyne Club Founded in 1823, with Walter *Scott as president, for the publication of old Scottish documents (see J. G. *Lockhart's *Scott*, lviii). The club was dissolved in 1861. George Bannatyne (1545–1608), in whose honour it was named, was the compiler in 1568 of a large collection of Scottish poems.

Bannatyne Manuscript A major manuscript of Scottish poetry compiled by George Bannatyne (completed 1568). Rediscovered in the 18th century, it is now in the National Library of Scotland. It includes 45 poems attributed to William *Dunbar, and works by Gawin *Douglas and Robert *Henryson. Ed. W. Tod Richie, 4 vols, STS (1928–34).
See BANNATYNE CLUB.

BANNERMAN, Helen *See* LITTLE BLACK SAMBO.

BANVILLE, John (1945–) Novelist, born in Wexford, where he received his secondary education at St Peter's College. He worked successively as a clerk and journalist before becoming literary editor of the *Irish Times* (1988–99). His fiction is characterized by an allusive, ironic style and a preoccupation with its own processes. *Long Lankin*, a collection of stories, appeared in 1970. Its concluding novella, 'The Possessed', was drawn on in Banville's first novel, *Nightspawn* (1971), whose narrator becomes a character in his own plot. The *'big house' novel *Birchwood* (1973) was followed by a trilogy of fictional portraits of famous scientists—*Doctor Copernicus* (1976), *Kepler* (1981), and *The Newton Letter* (1982)—in which the search for scientific certainty mirrors the quest for a persuasive artistic rendering of experience. *Mefisto*, the most explicitly Faustian of Banville's novels, appeared in 1986. *The Book of Evidence* (1989) introduced a second trilogy, completed by *Ghosts* (1993) and *Athena* (1994). Freddie Montgomery, the protagonist of all three works, is an aesthete and convicted murderer, obsessed with the issue of authenticity in the visual arts. The art curator at the centre of *The Untouchable* (1997), a deft transmutation of the *spy novel, can be recognized as a version of the 'Cambridge spy' Anthony Blunt. *The Sea* (2005), a meditative novel about a man who returns to the marine setting of a childhood trauma after the death of his wife, won the *Man Booker Prize. Banville publishes *detective fiction under the name Benjamin Black.

Baptists The title that in the 17th century superseded *Anabaptists* to designate those separatist Protestants who rejected infant baptism (*paedobaptism*) in favour of the baptism of adult believers (whence *anabaptists, rebaptizers*). General Baptists were Arminian in theology, Particular Baptists Calvinist. In England, the tradition derives from the Amsterdam congregation of John Smyth (?1570–1612), who in 1609 baptized himself (hence the sobriquet 'Se-Baptist') and then his church members, a number of whom in 1612 returned to England under Thomas Helwys (*c.*1550–*c.*1616) to establish the first English Baptist church. The Baptists' most notable literary figure is John *Bunyan.

BARAKA, Amiri (1934–) African American playwright, poet, and activist born in Newark, New Jersey, as Everett LeRoi Jones. Throughout his career he has used his writing as an extended polemic against American racism. He was instrumental in setting up organizations like the Black Arts Repertory Theatre and in founding the *Black Arts Movement in the 1960s.

In that same decade he converted to Islam and changed his name. Like Ralph *Ellison, Baraka's work has been influenced by jazz musicians, hence his assertion that 'poetry is music', and he has published a number of books on African American music. Indeed, although he has written novels (*The System of Dante's Hell*, 1965) and short stories, his main emphasis has fallen on the theatre and poetry in performance. His best-known play is *Dutchman* (1964), about a confrontation between a naive black man and a calculating white woman. Baraka has constantly raised controversies, most famously in 2002 with his poem about the bombings of the New York Trade Centre the previous year: 'Somebody Blew Up America', where he raised questions about US government complicity.

'Barbara Allan' A Scottish *ballad included in Percy's **Reliques*, on the subject of the death of Sir John Grehme for unrequited love of Barbara Allan, and her subsequent remorse. *Barbara Allen's Cruelty*, another ballad on the same theme, is also in the *Reliques*.

BARBAULD, Anna Laetitia (1743–1825) Née Aikin, poet and editor. Born in Kibworth Harcourt, Leicestershire, she was educated by her mother. Her father, a Nonconformist minister, taught at the Dissenting college at Warrington where he was a colleague of Joseph *Priestley, and the latter is supposed to have inspired her to compose verse. Her *Poems* appeared in 1773 and went though five editions by 1777. The volume's most notable poem is 'A Summer Evening's Meditation', a blank verse contemplation upon nature and the sublime. She published several popular volumes of prose for children with her brother John *Aikin, most notably the highly successful *Evenings at Home, or The Juvenile Budget Opened*, 6 vols (1792–6), and edited William *Collins (1794), Mark *Akenside (1794), and Samuel *Richardson's correspondence, 6 vols (1804). After the suicide in 1808 of her mentally unstable husband, the Revd Rochemont Barbauld, she threw herself into increased literary activity, editing *The British Novelists* in 50 volumes (1810). She was a friend of Hannah *More, Elizabeth *Montagu, and a circle of Dissenting radical intellectuals, and supported radical and philanthropic causes, notably Nonconformist liberties ('To Dr Priestley', 1792), and the abolition of the slave trade ('Epistle to William Wilberforce', 1791). She contributed to the **Monthly Magazine*. Her poem beginning 'Life, I know not what thou art' was much admired by *Wordsworth who sent her a copy of the 1800 version of the **Lyrical Ballads*. Her stately *Juvenalian satire in heroic couplets, *Eighteen Hundred and Eleven* (1811), condemns the ongoing war with France and foretells the decline of Britain's 'Midas dream' of wealth and the rise of prosperity and culture in America, whose tourists will come to visit with nostalgia 'the gray ruin and the mouldering stone' of England. Distressed by the poem's reception, especially the venomous politically motivated review of John *Croker in the Tory **Quarterly Review*, Barbauld resolved not to publish any more poetry, for fear of exposing herself—to quote her niece Lucy's memoir—'to the scorns of the unmanly, the malignant, and the base'. See *Anna Letitia Barbauld: Selected Poetry and Prose*, ed. W. McCarthy and E. Kraft (2003); W. McCarthy, *Anna Letitia Barbauld: Voice of the Enlightenment* (2008).

BARBELLION, W. N. P. Pseudonym of B. F. *Cummings.

BARBER, Mary (*c*.1685–1755) Poet, married to a Dublin woollen-draper. In the 1720s she attracted the attention of Lord Carteret (1690–1763) and Thomas *Tickell with her verse on public themes. Through such contacts she met Mary *Delany and Jonathan *Swift, who used (according to Laetitia *Pilkington) to preside over the 'correction' of her verse. He promoted a subscription edition of her poems vigorously, though she annoyed Alexander *Pope with her requests for assistance. In the preface to her *Poems* (1734) she adopted a self-deprecatory pose as a woman writer; the poems themselves comment amusingly and poignantly on a wide range of social customs.

BARBEY-D'AUREVILLY, Jules-Amédée (1808–89) French novelist and critic. He earned his living by literary journalism, and his collected articles—at once brilliant, prejudiced, and prophetic—fill several volumes. His major novels, *L'Ensorcelée* (1854: *The Bewitched*) and *Le Chevalier des Touches* (1864), and his short stories, *Les Diaboliques* (1874: *The She-Devils*), excel in their evocation of the desolate landscapes he had known as a child in the Cherbourg peninsula of Normandy, with their ancient Catholic and royalist traditions; and in their creation of proud, flamboyant, and tormented characters often susceptible to supernatural powers. His style combines spontaneity and elegance.

BARBOUR, John (*c*.1330–1395) Scottish poet, archdeacon of Aberdeen in 1356 and later one of the auditors of the Exchequer on several occasions. He probably studied at Oxford and Paris. The only poem ascribed to him with certainty is *The Bruce*, written in over 13,000 lines of *octosyllabic couplets, which dates from 1375; even if it is his, it has been argued that the poem was tampered with by John Ramsay, the writer of both the manuscripts in which the poem survives (from 1487 and 1489). The poem, in which Barbour also displays familiarity with the English *Alliterative Revival, is a chivalric romance version of the deeds of King Robert the Bruce and his follower James Douglas, and it contains a celebrated, graphic account of the battle of Bannockburn. Three other works were once attributed to him, but ultimately unconvincingly: *The Troy Book*, denied him on linguistic grounds; *The Lives of the Saints* (50 legends, certainly from Barbour's period and area of origin); and *The Buik of Alexander*, a translation of two French romances. See *The Bruce*, ed. W. W. Skeat in 4 vols (EETS ES 11, 21, 29, 55, 1870–89); *The Bruce*, ed. A. A. M. Duncan (1997).

Barchester Towers A novel by Anthony *Trollope, published 1857, the second in the *'Barsetshire' series. Archdeacon Grantly's hopes of succeeding his father as bishop of Barchester are dashed when an ineffectual evangelical, Dr Proudie, is set over him by a new Whig government. The novel is a record of the struggle for control of the diocese. Mrs Proudie, the bishop's overbearing wife, shows her strength when she selects Mr Quiverful as the future warden of Hiram's Hospital. Despite the efforts of Mr Slope, the bishop's oily chaplain, and Grantly to push the claims of Mr Harding (hero of *The *Warden*), Quiverful gains the appointment. When the old dean dies, Slope, anxious to take his place, persuades a national newspaper to advertise his own merits, and the conflict with Mrs Proudie intensifies. Slope's marital ambitions, however, start to get in his way. His designs on the fortune of Eleanor Bold, Harding's widowed daughter, are handicapped by his flirtation with the fascinating but penniless Signora Vesey-Neroni, and the scandal is his undoing. The Puseyite Dr Arabin succeeds to the deanery and marries Eleanor, while Mrs Proudie sees to it that Slope is dismissed from his chaplaincy.

BARCLAY, Alexander (*c*.1484–1552) Poet, scholar, and preacher, possibly of Scottish birth. He was successively a chaplain at the college of Ottery St Mary, Devon, a Benedictine monk at Ely, a Franciscan at Canterbury, and rector of All Hallows, Lombard Street, London. He translated Brant's *Narrenschiff* into English verse as *The *Ship of Fools* (1509) and wrote his **Eclogues* at Ely (*c*.1513–14). He also translated a life of St George from *Mantuan (*c*.1515) and *Sallust's *Bellum Jugurthinum* (*c*.1520).

BARCLAY, John (1582–1621) A Scot born at Pont-à-Mousson in France, author of the extremely popular Latin romance *Argenis* (1621), which refers to real historical events and personages under a veil of allegory. He also wrote *Euphormionis Satyricon* (?1603–7), a satire on the Jesuits in the form of a *picaresque novel, also in Latin.

BARCLAY, Robert (1648–90) Scottish Quaker whose *Apology for the True Christian Divinity* (1678) is a reasoned defence of Quakerism. His collected works, *Truth Triumphant*, with a preface by William *Penn, were published in 1692.

Bard, The A Pindaric *ode by Thomas *Gray, printed at Horace *Walpole's press in 1757. It is based on a tradition that Edward I suppressed the Welsh bards. From a crag the surviving bard curses the returning conqueror; the ghosts of dead comrades prophesy the fate of the Plantagenets, and the bard commits triumphant suicide. Though scorned by Samuel *Johnson, its portentous *sublime exerted a strong influence on poets and painters such as William *Blake and John *Martin.

bardic poetry A term of convenience to describe the corpus of verse in standardized literary language, and committed to quatrains in a variety of strict syllabic metres, that dominated poetic production in Ireland and Gaelic Scotland from 1250 to 1650, though examples of the mode can be found both before and after these dates. The authors were members of poetic families and underwent rigorous training in the poetic schools that owed something both to the medieval monastic model and to the pre-Christian academies of the druids. In ancient Ireland *bard* was used to designate a lesser order of versifier than the true poet or seer, the *fili*. In Wales *bardd* came to mean 'poet'. The Romantic conception of the Celtic bard popularized by James *Macpherson and Thomas *Gray has little historical authority. See Eleanor Knott, *Irish Classical Poetry* (1960).

BARETTI, Giuseppe Marc'Antonio (1719–89) Italian writer and literary critic, born at Turin. He came to London in 1751 and, among other pursuits, taught Italian. One of his pupils was Charlotte *Lennox, who introduced him to Samuel *Johnson. Baretti's standard work, *A Dictionary of the English and Italian Languages* (1760), was clearly influenced by Johnson's dictionary. Among his many eminent friends he numbered Joshua *Reynolds, Edmund *Burke, and David *Garrick. In 1768 he published *An Account of the Manners and Customs of Italy*, a riposte to the *Letters from Italy*, by Samuel Sharp, which he considered a grossly unfair portrayal of his native land. His *A Journey from London to Genoa* was published in 1770. In these and other works he stimulated interest in and understanding of Italian literature and culture. His *Easy Phraseology for the Use of Young Ladies* (1775) sprang from lessons in conversation with one of the daughters of Hester *Thrale, and was published with a preface by Johnson.

BARHAM, Richard Harris (1788–1845) Churchman and poet. Born in Canterbury, he held various preferments, including that of a minor canon of St Paul's. His *The Ingoldsby Legends; or Mirth and Marvels, by Thomas Ingoldsby Esquire* were first published from 1837 in **Bentley's Miscellany* and the **New Monthly Magazine*, and first collected in 1840. Their lively rhythms and inventive rhymes, comic and grotesque treatment of medieval legend, and quaint narratives made them immensely popular. One of the best known is the story of the Jackdaw of Rheims, who stole the archbishop's ring, was cursed, fell ill, but recovered when the curse was lifted, and became devout.

BARING, Maurice (1874–1945) Writer, educated at Eton College and Trinity College, Cambridge. Versatile, prolific, and successful, he produced articles, plays, biography, criticism, poetry, translations, stories and novels, and works on painting and music, amounting to some 50 volumes. A gift for languages led him to the Foreign Office, and later as a reporter to the Russo-Japanese War. He is credited with having discovered Anton *Chekhov's work in Moscow and helping to introduce it to the West. His *Landmarks in Russian Literature* appeared in 1910, *An Outline of Russian Literature* in 1914, and *The Oxford Book of Russian Verse* in 1924. Of his various novels *C* (1924), *Cat's Cradle* (1925), *Daphne Adeane* (1926), and *The Coat without Seam* (1929), all set in his own high social world, were very successful, and are still admired for their acute, intimate portrait of the period. Baring's conversion to the Roman Catholic faith is reflected in two historical novels of Tudor times, *Robert Peckham* (1930) and *In my End Is my Beginning* (1931). His novella *The Lonely Lady of Dulwich* (1934) is often held to be the best of his works.

BARING-GOULD, Sabine (1834–1924) Devout clergyman, folk-song collector, and writer. Baring-Gould travelled much on the Continent with his parents during his boyhood, then was educated at Clare College, Cambridge. In 1867 he defied family opposition to marry Grace Taylor, a mill girl, an experience described in his first novel *Through Fire and Flame* (1868): the marriage was lastingly happy, and they produced a family of fourteen children. From 1881 until his death he was both squire and rector of Lew Trenchard in Devon. An extremely prolific writer and an enthusiastic antiquary, he wrote dozens of works on travel, religion, folklore, local legend, and folk song, composed various hymns (including 'Onward Christian soldiers', 'Through the night of doubt and sorrow', and 'Now the day is over'), and wrote more than 40 novels, of which the most powerful, *Mehalah* (1880), was compared by A. C. *Swinburne to **Wuthering Heights*. He considered his collections of folk songs to have been his most significant achievement. He also wrote a life of Robert Stephen *Hawker, *The Vicar of Morwenstow* (1876).

BARKER, Clive (1952–) Born in Liverpool; writer, film-maker, and artist largely of *horror and *fantasy, resident in the USA. From the stories in the *Books of Blood* (1984–5), several of which have been adapted as films or graphic novels, he has explored fantasy's veins of visionary grotesque, often, as in *Weaveworld* (1987), *The Great and Secret Show* (1989), imagining dark otherworlds parallel to ours. The 'Abarat' series (2002–8) is for children. *Hellraiser* (1987), based upon his novella 'The Hellbound Heart', is perhaps the most successful film adaptation of his works. See Douglas E. Winter, *Clive Barker: The Dark Fantastic* (2001).

BARKER, George (1913–91) Poet, born in Essex of an English father and Irish mother, and educated (briefly) at the Regent Street Polytechnic. His first publication was *Thirty Preliminary Poems* (1933), which was followed by *Poems* (1935), *Calamiterror* (1937, a semi-political poem inspired by the Spanish Civil War), and *Lament and Triumph* (1940). In 1939 he taught in a Japanese university, then lived in America and Canada from 1940 and 1943; he then returned to England, though living for further periods in America and Italy. His relationship with Elizabeth *Smart at this period is recorded in her prose poem *By Grand Central Station I Sat Down and Wept* (1945). His subsequent volumes include *Eros in Dogma* (1944) and *The True Confession of George Barker* (1950; augmented 1965). Barker's earlier work is characteristically rhetorical, unruly, and surreal, though some critics have suggested that he achieves disorder more by accident than intent; a *Neo-Romantic and a self-styled 'Augustinian anarchist', he has a marked penchant for puns, distortion, and abrupt changes of tone. His *True Confession*, written as he reached the age of 35, presents the poet as irreverent, defiant, offhand, Rabelaisian, and guilt-ridden at once ('this rather dreary | Joke of an autobiography'); its later stanzas, and works such as *Villa Stellar* (1978) and the long title poem of *Anno Domini* (1983), have a more sombre and questioning tone, although they too have moments of exuberance. A huge *Collected Poems* was published in 1987. See Robert Fraser, *The Chameleon Poet: A Life of George Barker* (2002).

BARKER, Harley Granville- *See* GRANVILLE-BARKER, HARLEY.

BARKER, Howard (1946–) Playwright, born in London and educated at Sussex University. He came to prominence with a series of scathing dramas about the injustices of society: these included *Stripwell* (1975), and two plays set in a nightmarish Britain of the future, *That Good between Us* (1977) and *The Hang of the Gaol* (1978). From *Victory* (1983), a wonderfully grotesque epic about the birth of capitalism in 17th-century England, his work, never wholly realistic, gradually became more darkly comic in tone, more exotic in language and form, and less direct in its attack on Establishment targets: as witness *The Castle* (1985), *Seven Lears* (1989), and *Ten Dilemmas* (1992). He attacks the idea of a didactic theatre ('In theatre we imagine the world, we do not record it, we are not documentary makers. I hold all social realism and journalistic theatre in contempt') and insists that his audiences find their own meaning from what he has termed his 'Theatre of Catastrophe'. Despite its complexities, Barker's work has acquired a cult following, reflected in the formation in 1989 of the Wrestling School, a theatre company specializing in the production of his plays that was active until 2007.

BARKER, Jane (1652–1732) Poet and novelist. She converted to Catholicism and maintained strong *Jacobite links, living for long periods near the exiled court at Saint-Germain, and dying there. Some early poems appeared, without authority, as *Poetical Recreations* (1688); subsequent verse, unpublishable because of its political content, was held in manuscript. Her fiction includes a heroic romance on Jacobite themes, *Exilius, or The Banished Roman* (1715), and a semi-autobiographical trilogy: *The Amours of Bosvil and Galesia* (1713), the innovative story of a spinster and author; *A Patch-Work Screen for the Ladies* (1723); and *The Lining of the Patch-Work Screen* (1726).

BARKER, Nicola (1966–) Novelist and writer of short stories, born in Ely, Cambridgeshire, and educated at King's College, Cambridge. Her fiction, comic and surreal, explores the lives of wounded or hostile people, often in desolate settings. *Clear* (2004) is set in London at the time of David Blaine's four-day suspension over the capital in a transparent plastic box; *Darkmans* (2007), which won the Hawthornden Prize (2008), weaves together the lives of Edward IV's court jester and his biographer.

BARKER, Pat (1943–) Novelist, born in Thornaby-on-Tees, north Yorkshire, who read history at the London School of Economics, and, after a brief teaching career, made her fictional debut with *Union Street* (1982), an episodic account of women in an impoverished northern community. It was followed by *Blow your House Down* (1984), a novel about prostitutes terrorized by a serial killer, and *Liza's England* (originally published as *The Century's Daughter*, 1986), in which a working-class woman the same age as the century relates her harsh life story to a sympathetic social worker. After *The Man Who Wasn't There* (1989), which depicts the predicament of a fatherless boy, Barker achieved a breakthrough into wider recognition with *Regeneration* (1991). Based on an encounter at Craiglockhart War Hospital in 1917 between Siegfried *Sassoon and the psychologist and anthropologist William Rivers (1864–1922), it was followed by *The Eye in the Door* (1993) and *The Ghost Road* (1995, winner of the *Booker Prize). The acclaimed First World War trilogy these novels comprise is distinguished by vivid and knowledgeable evocation of the period both in Britain and on the Western Front, unflinching unsentimentality, a concern with characters under stress, and dialogue that brilliantly conveys a sense of intellectual and emotional alertness. *Another World* (1998), set in 1990s Newcastle, is much energized by the figure of a centenarian war veteran, Geordie. *Border Crossing* (2001) and *Double Vision* (2003), which focuses on a war photographer and a journalist who has witnessed atrocities in Sarajevo and Afghanistan, have contemporary settings. With *Life Class* (2007), a fictional portrayal of students and teachers from the Slade School of Art confronted by the ethical and aesthetic challenges presented by the First World War, Barker initiated a new sequence of novels dealing with the subject that so powerfully stirs her imagination.

Barkis In Charles *Dickens's **David Copperfield*, the carrier, who sent a message by David to Clara Peggotty that 'Barkis is willin''. The phrase has passed into the language.

Barlaam and Josaphat A medieval romance included in William *Caxton's **Golden Legend*, is a Christianized version of the legend of Buddha. Josaphat, the son of the Indian king, Abenner, is converted by the Christian hermit Barlaam. After Abenner's conversion and death, Josaphat abdicates to become a hermit. Edition by J. C. Hirsh (EETS os 290, 1986).

BARLOW, Joel (1754–1812) American poet and diplomat, born in Connecticut, who is remembered as the author of *The Columbiad* (1787, originally published as *The Vision of Columbus* and revised and renamed in 1807), a lengthy patriotic epic in heroic couplets, and of the more enjoyable *mock epic *The Hasty-Pudding* (1796). Barlow was one of the 'Hartford Wits', and was, like most of them, a graduate of Yale.

Barnaby Rudge A novel by Charles *Dickens published in 1841 as part of **Master Humphrey's Clock*. The earlier of Dickens's two historical novels, it is set at the period of the Gordon anti-popery riots of 1780, and Lord George Gordon himself appears as a character. Like the later *A *Tale of Two Cities*, it contains powerful evocations of mob violence, culminating in the sack of Newgate. Dickens wrote, 'my object has been to convey an idea of multitudes, violence and fury; and even to lose my own dramatis personae in the throng'. Reuben Haredale, a country gentleman, has been murdered, and the murderer never discovered. His brother Geoffrey Haredale, a Roman Catholic, and the smooth villain Sir John Chester (who models himself on Lord *Chesterfield) are enemies; Chester's son Edward is in love with Haredale's niece Emma, and the elders combine, despite their hatred, to thwart the match. The Gordon riots, secretly fomented by Chester, supervene. Haredale's house is burned and Emma carried off. Edward saves the lives of Haredale and Emma and wins Haredale's consent to his marriage with the latter. Haredale discovers the murderer of his brother, the steward Rudge, father of the half-witted Barnaby and the blackmailer of Barnaby's devoted mother Mrs Rudge. Rudge is hanged, Barnaby (who had been swept along as unwitting participant in the riots) is reprieved from the gallows at the last moment, and Chester is killed by Haredale in a duel.

The vivid description of the riots forms a principal interest of the book, which also displays Dickens's concern with the demoralizing effect of capital punishment in the characters of Dennis the Hangman and Hugh, the savage ostler who turns out to be Chester's son. Other characters involved in the plot include the upright locksmith Gabriel Varden, with his peevish wife and their coquettish daughter Dolly; Simon Tappertit, his aspiring and anarchic apprentice, and Miggs, his mean and treacherous servant; John Willett, host of the Maypole Inn, and Joe, his gallant son, who finally wins Dolly; and Grip, Barnaby's raven. Dolly Varden's appeal extended beyond the novel: she inspired songs, paintings, bonnets, and the 'Dolly Varden look' in ladies' clothes, fashionable for a while in the 1870s.

BARNARD, Lady Anne (1750–1825) Née Lindsay, Scottish writer, born at Balcarres in Fife, who in 1771 wrote 'Auld Robin Gray', a sentimental ballad of unsuitable marriage stoically endured. Published by David *Herd in 1776, the ballad became immensely popular and Lady Anne kept its authorship secret until she wrote to Walter *Scott in 1823 after he had quoted it in *The *Pirate*. Her journals and letters from the Cape of Good Hope, where her husband was colonial secretary from 1797 to 1801, are an important source of imperial history.

Barnavelt *See* OLDENBARNAVELT, SIR JOHN VAN.

BARNES, Barnabe (1568/9–1609) Poet and playwright, son of the bishop of Durham. He went up to Brasenose College, Oxford, in 1586, where his servitor was John *Florio. In 1591 he went to France with the earl of *Essex. His sonnet sequence **Parthenophil and Parthenophe* was published in 1593, and *A Divine Centurie of Spirituall Sonnets* in 1595. In 1598 he was arraigned for attempting to poison the recorder of Berwick, but managed to escape sentence. He published *Foure Bookes of Offices* in 1606, and in 1607 a Machiavellian drama, *The Divils Charter: A Tragaedie Conteining the Life and Death of Pope Alexander the Sixt*, said to have been performed before the king. It includes such melodramatic scenes as the murder of Lucrezia *Borgia with poisoned face wash. Another play, *The Battle of Evesham*, is lost. See *Parthenophil and Parthenophe*, ed. V. A. Doyno (1971).

BARNES, Djuna Chappell (1892–1982) American novelist, illustrator, journalist, short story writer, and playwright, born in Cornwall-on-Hudson; she studied art in New York, leading a bohemian life in Greenwich Village, then moved to Paris. Her publications include *A Book* (1923), a volume of plays, poems, and stories; *Ryder* (1928), a novel dealing with a man, his mother, and his mistress; *Ladies Almanack* (1928, privately printed in Paris), an erotic *pastiche of lesbian life; *The Antiphon* (1958), a verse drama. She is best remembered for *Nightwood* (1936, original text restored 1995), a novel originally published with a preface by T. S. *Eliot. It evokes, in highly wrought, high-coloured prose, a nightmare cosmopolitan world (chiefly located in Paris and New York) peopled by tormented and mutually tormenting characters, linked by the enigmatic doctor, priest of the secret brotherhood of the City of Darkness; it mingles elements of *fin-de-siècle* decadence with premonitions of the neo-Gothic. Her *Selected Works* appeared in 1962.

BARNES, John (1957–) American author, born in Indiana; his *science fiction has engaged with politics and globalization, most particularly in the 'Thousand Cultures' series from *A Million Open Doors* (1992) to *The Armies of Memory* (2006). *Mother of Storms* (1994) combines meteorological and social chaos to describe a crumbling near future.

BARNES, Julian (1946–) Novelist and essayist, born in Leicester, educated at the City of London School and Magdalen College, Oxford. He worked as a lexicographer on the *OED* supplement (1962–72), then as a book and television reviewer. His first, semi-autobiographical novel, *Metroland* (1980), follows a London schoolboy from suburbia to student Paris in 1968, and back to marriage and domesticity in 1977. *Before She Met Me* (1982) deals with sexual jealousy, a recurrent theme in Barnes's fiction, which resurfaces prominently in his two dialogue novels, *Talking It Over* (1991) and its sequel, *Love, Etc.* (2000). *Flaubert's Parrot* (1984), which mixes fiction, biographical detection, and literary commentary, exemplifies the elegant eclecticism typifying much of his work, and his fascination with French literature and life (*Cross Channel*, 1996, is a volume of stories about Anglo-French relationships). His most virtuoso work of fiction, *A History of the World in 10½ Chapters* (1989), inventively links a wide diversity of stories and essays by shared themes of shipwreck and survival. He has also written a part-fantastic novel about a female aviator, *Staring at the Sun* (1986), which explores ageing (as do the stories in *The Lemon Table*, 2004); a satiric fable about Eastern Europe, *The Porcupine* (1992); a caustic *dystopia, *England, England* (1998); and a novel which fictionalizes Arthur Conan *Doyle's real-life investigation of criminal activities in a late 19th-century Staffordshire village, *Arthur & George* (2005). There are two collections of stylish, ironic journalism, *Letters from London 1990–1995* (1995) and *Something to Declare* (2002), and a collection of pieces about food, *The Pedant in the Kitchen* (2003). His translation of the notebook Alphonse Daudet kept while dying from syphilis, *In the Land of Pain*, appeared in 2002. *Nothing to be Frightened Of* (2008) is a family memoir and meditation on mortality. He is also the author of four crime novels under the pseudonym Dan Kavanagh, the name a homage to his wife Pat Kavanagh (1940–2008), a celebrated literary agent. He became a Commandeur de l'Ordre des Arts et des Lettres in 2004.

BARNES, Peter (1931–2004) Playwright, born in east London, educated at Stroud Grammar School. His first real success came with *The Ruling Class* (1969), a bizarre farce exploring the mechanics of power, but despite his prolific output he did not sustain this success. The follow-up, *Leonardo's Last Supper* (1969), weighs up the economic advantages of a dead *Leonardo da Vinci over a live one. His plays espouse an extreme black comedy, fitting for a writer who so venerated Ben *Jonson. His use of humour to question and unsettle characterizes *Bewitched* (1974), like much of his work set in the past, a play that gleefully demonstrates his anarchic problematization of all religious and political creeds. However, it was *Laughter!* (1978) that was most controversial, with a first half set in 16th-century tsarist Russia, and the second culminating in a sudden and terrifying shift into Auschwitz concentration camp. His use of black humour was best seen in what was to be his last London production, *Red Noses* (1985), another disturbing 'misuse' of history.

BARNES, William (1801–86) Poet, born near Sturminster Newton, Dorset, of a farming family. He began work for a solicitor at the age of 14, then moved to Dorchester where he contributed poems to the local paper. He learned Greek, Latin, and music, taught himself wood engraving, and in 1823 became a schoolmaster at Mere. He married in 1827 and in 1835 moved his flourishing school to Dorchester. He was deeply interested in grammar and language, studied French, Italian, Welsh, Hebrew, Hindustani, and other languages, and waged a lifelong campaign to rid English of classical and foreign influences, suggesting many 'Saxonized' alternatives, such as 'sun-print' for photograph and 'fall-time' for autumn. He registered for a part-time degree requiring ten years' enrolment at St John's, Cambridge, in 1838, which he acquired in 1851. He was ordained in 1848, and took up the living of Whitcombe, moving to Cambe in 1862. *Orra: A Lapland Tale* appeared in 1822 and his *Poems of Rural Life in the Dorset Dialect* in 1844; *Hwomely Rhymes* followed in 1859 and *Poems of Rural Life*, written in standard English, in 1868. His collected dialect poems appeared as *Poems of Rural Life in the Dorset Dialect* in 1879.

As well as his volumes of poetry, Barnes contributed articles on archaeology and a range of subjects to the *Gentleman's Magazine* and, from 1852, to the **Retrospective Review*. He wrote textbooks, a primer of Old English (*Se Gefylsta*, 1849), *Philological Grammar* (1854), a *Grammar... of the Dorset Dialect* (1863), and other works reflecting his interest in philology and local history. He was one of the founders of the Dorchester Museum and as an old man became famed as a repository of old sentiments, customs, and manners.

According to his many admirers, who included Alfred *Tennyson, G. M. *Hopkins ('almost an admirer'), Thomas *Hardy, and Edmund *Gosse, Barnes was a lyric poet of the first rank and a vibrant force in regenerating poetic language through dialect. His poems evoke the Dorset landscape, country customs (as in 'Harvest Hwome' and 'Woodcom' Feast'), and happy childhood, although his few poems of grief, such as 'Woak Hill' and 'The Wind at the Door', written after the death of his wife, are among his most celebrated. He was interested in versification, prosody, and the techniques of verse (particularly in *alliteration), and the wide variety of his forms intrigued Hardy; his noun combinations ('heart-heaven', 'sun-sweep', and 'mind-sight') seem to foreshadow Hopkins. The dialect poems were written largely between 1834 and 1867; his standard English poems on either side of those dates. Hardy wrote an affectionate portrait in the **Athenaeum* on his death, and a poem, 'The Last Signal'.

BARNFIELD, Richard (1574–1620) Poet, educated at Brasenose College, Oxford. He published *The Affectionate Shepherd* in 1594, *Cynthia: With Certain Sonnets* in 1595, and *The Encomion of Lady Pecunia* (the praise of money) in 1598. Two of his *Poems, in Divers Humours* (1598) appeared also in *The *Passionate Pilgrim* (1599) and were long attributed to William *Shakespeare, the better known being the ode 'As it fell upon a day | In the merry month of May'. *The Affectionate Shepheard* is a pastoral (based on *Virgil's second eclogue) describing the homoerotic love of Daphnis for Ganymede, and includes a rather surprising digression on the 'indecencie of mens long haire'. The twenty sonnets in *Cynthia* are also addressed to Ganymede. Barnfield has the distinction of being the only Elizabethan poet other than Shakespeare known to have addressed love sonnets to a man.

baroque [from Portuguese *barroco*, Spanish *barrueco*, a rough or imperfect pearl] Originally a term of abuse applied to 17th-century Italian art and that of other countries, especially Germany, influenced by Italy. It is characterized by the unclassical use of classical forms, and by the interpenetration of architecture, sculpture, and painting to produce grandiose and emotional effects. In a literary context the word baroque is loosely used to describe highly ornamented verse or prose, abounding in extravagant conceits; it is rarely used of English writers (with the exception of the Italianate Richard *Crashaw), but frequently applied to Giambattista *Marino, whose name became synonymous with Marinism, and to Góngora, whose name supplied the term *Gongorism.

BARRÈS, Maurice (1862–1923) French novelist and essayist, deputy for Nancy (1889–93) and Paris (1906–23). Active in politics, Barrès was a committed nationalist-Boulangiste, anti-Dreyfusard, and militant of the Ligue de la Patrie Française. His reputation as a novelist rests largely upon his attempt to chronicle his times in three didactic trilogies. *Le Culte du moi* (*The Cult of the Self—Sous l'œil des barbares*, 1888: *Watched by the Barbarians*; *Un homme libre*, 1889: *A Free Man*; *Le Jardin de Bérénice*, 1891: *Berenice's Garden*) locates a source of moral energy in a sense of self that is at once disciplined and liberated. The spiritual benefits of a living relationship with family, local environment, and inherited tradition become the focus of attention in *Le Roman de l'énergie nationale* (*The Novel of National Energy—Les Déracinés*, 1897: *The Uprooted*; *L'Appel au soldat*, 1900: *The Appeal to the Soldier*; *Leurs Figures*, 1902: *Their Faces*), which follows the fortunes of seven young men who leave Lorraine, Barrès's own province, to pursue their careers in Paris. *Les Bastions de l'Est* (*The Bastions in the East—Au service de l'Allemagne*, 1905: *In the Service of Germany*; *Colette Baudoche*, 1909; *Le Génie du Rhin*, 1921: *The Genius of the Rhine*) explores the meeting of the French and German national characters in the eastern provinces of Alsace and Lorraine. *La Colline inspirée* (1913: *The Inspired Hill*) presents the conflict between the Roman Catholic Church and a religious community rooted in regional consciousness.

BARRETT, Elizabeth *See* BROWNING, ELIZABETH BARRETT.

BARRIE, Sir J. M. (James Matthew) (1860–1937) Baronet, OM, born in Kirriemuir, Scotland, son of a handloom weaver; educated at Glasgow Academy, Dumfries Academy, and Edinburgh University. He began work with the *Nottinghamshire Journal*, an experience described in *When a Man's Single*, published in 1888, the year he began his *'Kailyard school' stories and novels. These drew on his mother's memories and were set in Kirriemuir (as 'Thrums'); they included *Auld Licht Idylls* (1888), *A Window in Thrums* (1889), and the highly successful *The Little Minister* (1891). His first play, *Richard Savage* (with H. B. Marriot-Watson), was performed in London in 1891. In 1894 he married the actress Mary Ansell, but the marriage was unsuccessful and childless; they divorced in 1909. *Margaret Ogilvy*, an affectionate portrait of his mother, appeared in 1896, as did two self-revelatory books, *Sentimental Tommy* and *Tommy and Grizel*, which contain hints of **Peter Pan*. His theatrical successes included *Quality Street* (1901; filmed 1927, 1937), *The Admirable Crichton* (filmed 1957; *see* CRICHTON, JAMES), *What Every Woman Knows* (1906; filmed 1915, 1921, 1924), and *Dear Brutus* (1917).

Barrie's perceived whimsicality told against him in his later career, but his creation 'Peter Pan' has become a literary immortal. The story sprang from Barrie's relationship with the sons of Arthur and Sylvia Llewellyn Davies, and appears in several forms. The idea of Peter Pan first emerged in the novel *The Little White Bird* (1902), the Peter Pan episodes being reprinted as *Peter Pan in Kensington Gardens* in 1906. The play was first produced, with spectacular special effects, in

December 1904, and adapted as a novel, *Peter and Wendy*, in 1911. Barrie, and his complex relationship with the Llewellyn Davies family, has been explored by Andrew Birkin in BBC TV's *The Lost Boys* (1978) and his biography, *J. M. Barrie and the Lost Boys* (1979); by Alan Knee in the play *The Man Who was Peter Pan* (1998), and in the film *Finding Neverland* (Marc Forster, 2004). *Peter Pan* has been extensively analysed, notably by Jacqueline Rose in *The Case of Peter Pan* (1984).

BARRY, Elizabeth (1658–1713) A celebrated actress who owed her entrance to the stage to the patronage of the earl of *Rochester. She created more than 100 roles, including Monimia in Thomas *Otway's *The *Orphan*, Belvidera in **Venice Preserved*, and Zara in *The *Mourning Bride*. Otway was passionately devoted to her, but she did not return his affection.

BARRY, Sebastian (1955–) Playwright, poet, and novelist, born in Dublin and educated at Trinity College there. Barry's plays use lyrical, introspective language in place of overt dramatic conflict, and typically focus on the plight of people excluded from received narratives of Irishness. The protagonists of *Boss Grady's Boys* (1988) are rural bachelors, those of *Prayers of Sherkin* (1990) millenarians awaiting apocalypse on a remote island. *The Steward of Christendom* (1995) dramatizes the King Lear-like madness of a former officer of the pre-independence Dublin Metropolitan Police, while *Our Lady of Sligo* (1998) presents the last days of a middle-class woman dying of alcohol-induced cancer. Concerned respectively with a policeman driven from Ireland during the War of Independence, a group of Royal Dublin Fusiliers in Flanders, and a contemporary centenarian who has spent her life in a soon to be shut mental institution, the novels *The Whereabouts of Eneas McNulty* (1998), *A Long Long Way* (2005), and *The Secret Scripture* (2008) extend and enrich Barry's challenge to historical myths.

Barry Lyndon See LUCK OF BARRY LYNDON, THE.

Barsetshire Novels By Anthony *Trollope. They include the following: *The *Warden*, **Barchester Towers*, **Doctor Thorne*, **Framley Parsonage*, *The *Small House at Allington*, and *The *Last Chronicle of Barset*. They depict middle-class domestic and ecclesiastical life in the fictional English county of Barsetshire.

BARSTOW, Stan (1928–) Novelist, born in Yorkshire, the son of a miner, and educated at Ossett Grammar School. His first novel, *A Kind of Loving* (1960), is the first-person, present-tense narration of office-worker Vic Brown, trapped into marriage by his infatuation for small-minded Ingrid and harassed by his mother-in-law. It was followed by other vivid portrayals of Yorkshire life, including *Ask Me Tomorrow* (1962) and *Joby* (1964), which contributed to the development of the *regional novel associated with Alan *Sillitoe, Keith *Waterhouse (who adapted *A Kind of Loving* for the screen), John *Braine, and others. Later novels include *Just You Wait and See* (1986), *Give Us This Day* (1989), and *Next of Kin* (1991).

BARTH, Heinrich (1821–65) German scholar and explorer, educated at the University of Berlin, and employed by the British. Recommended by Carl Ritter, he was appointed to the Central African expedition to the Western Sudan of 1849–55. His companions died but Barth covered 10,000 miles, settled the question of the drainage of the Lake Chad area, and went on to Timbuktu. He recorded an immense amount of scientific, ethnographic, linguistic, and historical information, revealing the region to have literate and sophisticated societies. The results were published simultaneously in German and English as *Travels and Discoveries in North and Central Africa* (1857–8). Five volumes and 3,000 pages earned the enormous respect of scholars and a *Royal Geographical Society medal, and Barth was made a Companion of the Order of the Bath. But he did not gain the popularity of other African travellers. Somewhat disillusioned, Barth returned to academic life in Berlin and some further travels but died suddenly in 1865.

BARTH, John Simmons (1930–) American novelist, essayist, and short story writer, born in Maryland. He has combined writing with teaching English in universities. His 1967 essay 'The Literature of Exhaustion' argued that fiction was unable to keep up with the rapidly changing face of the post-war world, a position he modified in 1979 with 'The Literature of Replenishment'. His own work has tended towards *metafiction (*Giles Goat-Boy*, 1966), historical *pastiche (*The Sot-Weed Factor*, 1960), and academic parody (*Sabbatical*, 1992). *LETTERS* (1980) is a novel where both Barth and his own earlier characters appear. Barth has been drawn constantly to non-European story cycles, which have informed works like *The Tidewater Tales* (1987). His playful brand of *postmodernism—intrusive narrators, self-reflexive stories—suggests a body of work where means of representation form a major part of the subject. Two important essay collections are *The Friday Book* (1984) and *Further Fridays* (1995).

BARTHELME, Donald (1931–89) American novelist and short story writer. In 1961 he became the director of the Contemporary Arts Museum in Houston, the same year that he published his first story. His 1980 collection *Presents* consists of a series of collages. He consistently avoided mimetic realism in favour of short stories which assemble apparently unrelated details but which prove to be philosophically informed. His best-known story collection is *City Life* (1970) and his short novels include *Snow White* (1967) and *The Dead Father* (1975).

BARTHES, Roland (1915–80) French literary critic, essayist, and cultural theorist. After many years of research, writing, and journalism, in 1960 he became a director of studies at the École Pratique des Hautes Études in Paris; and in 1976 he was elected to a chair of literary semiology at the Collège de France. His first book, *Le Degré zéro de l'écriture*

(1953: *Writing Degree Zero*), is a response to Jean-Paul *Sartre on questions of literary style and political commitment. His witty articles on the workings of modern bourgeois ideology in all kinds of cultural product, from wrestling to popular magazines, were collected in *Mythologies* (1957), together with a more theoretical essay on the analysis of myths that is derived from Ferdinand de *Saussure. His commitment to *structuralism continued in *Éléments de sémiologie* (1965: *Elements of Semiology*), in his analysis of the codes of fashion writing in *Système de la mode* (1967: *The Fashion System*), and in essays proclaiming the 'death of the author'. As the scientific pretensions of structuralism came under assault from Jacques *Derrida and others, Barthes moved into a new phase of more personal and essayistic reflection in his book on Japan, *L'Empire des signes* (1970: *The Empire of Signs*), and in *S/Z* (1970), his influential study of *Balzac's *Sarrasine*, translated into English by Richard Miller in 1974. In these and later works of his 'post-structuralist' period, he emphasizes the multiple, open meanings of texts, and the *jouissance* (sexual bliss) of reading, notably in *Le Plaisir du texte* (1973: *The Pleasure of the Text*). The wistful and fragmentary late works *Roland Barthes par Roland Barthes* (1975), *Fragments d'un discours amoureux* (1977: *Fragments of a Lover's Discourse*), and *La Chambre claire* (1980: *Camera Lucida*) mix autobiography and aphorism in a manner remote from the certainties of the 1960s. His influence has been extensive, especially in his defence, partly inspired by Bertolt *Brecht, of *modernist experiment against the traditions of *realism. See L.-J. Calvet, *Roland Barthes* (1994).

BARTHOLOMAEUS ANGLICUS (before 1203–1272) A Franciscan, master of theology at Paris, and author of *De Proprietatibus Rerum* ('On the properties of things'), an encyclopedia of learning in nineteen books. A 14th-century English version was produced by John of *Trevisa.

Bartholomew, massacre of St The massacre of Huguenots throughout France ordered by Charles IX at the instigation of his mother Cathérine de Médicis (*see* MEDICI), and begun on the morning of the festival, 24 August 1572.

Bartholomew Fair A comedy by Ben *Jonson, performed by the Lady Elizabeth's Men 1614, printed 1631.

The play is set at the fair which took place at Smithfield on 24 August, St Bartholomew's day, and follows the fortunes of its various visitors: Littlewit, a proctor, his wife Win-the-fight, his mother-in-law Dame Purecraft, and her mentor, the ranting Puritan Zeal-of-the-land Busy, who come to eat roast pig; the rich fool Bartholomew Cokes, Wasp, his angry servant, and Grace Wellborn, who is unwillingly engaged to Cokes; Justice Adam Overdo, who attends the fair in disguise in order to discover its 'enormities'; and two gallants, Quarlous and Winwife, who intend to jeer at the fair people. Many mishaps and misunderstandings ensue, which result in Busy, Wasp, and Overdo being placed in the stocks, Cokes being robbed of all his possessions, including his future wife, who is won by Winwife, and Quarlous marrying Dame Purecraft. The play ends with the performance of a puppet play written by Littlewit, in imitation of Marlowe's **Hero and Leander*. Zeal-of-the-land Busy is defeated in a debate with a puppet about the morality of play-acting, and Overdo, reminded that he is 'but Adam, flesh and blood', agrees to give up his censoriousness and invites everyone home to supper. There are numerous editions, including E. A. Horsman's (1960) for the Revels plays.

'Bartleby the Scrivener' (1856) A short story by Herman *Melville. When the narrator, a New York lawyer, asks his scrivener (copier of legal documents) to help him, Bartleby replies, 'I would prefer not to', and with Bartleby's reiterated declaration what began as a humorous anecdote turns into a fable of existential refusal unto death.

BARTLETT, Elizabeth (1924–2008) British poet, born in Deal and raised in Kent. She left school at 15, and worked in a factory making hypodermic needles shortly before the outbreak of the Second World War. Her first collection, *A Lifetime of Dying*, was not published until 1979 and included poems written twenty years previously. Her hard-hitting depictions of the lonely, ill, and dispossessed offer a stark portrait of post-war Britain. Other titles include *Strange Territory* (1983); *The Czar is Dead* (1986); *Look No Face* (1991); *Two Women Dancing: New and Selected Poems* (1995); and more recently *Mrs Perkins and Oedipus* (2004).

BARTRAM, William (1739–1823) American Quaker naturalist and traveller, author of *Travels through North and South Carolina, Georgia, East and West Florida, the Cherokee Country, the Extensive Territories of the Moscogulges, or the Creek Confederacy, and the Country of the Chactaws* (1791), a travel book much admired by S. T. *Coleridge and William *Wordsworth, who both drew on its descriptions of the natural wonders of the new world.

BASHKIRTSEFF, Marie (Mariia Konstantinovna Bashkirtseva) (1858–84) Russian artist and diarist, born near Poltava in Ukraine. She studied painting in Paris, where she died of tuberculosis. Her *Journal de Marie Bashkirtseff*, abridged and censored by her family, first appeared posthumously in 1887 (English translation by Mathilde *Blind, 1890). A new sixteen-volume edition, from the original manuscript, was published in Paris (1995–2005).

Basil (1852) The second novel of Wilkie *Collins, and an early example of the *sensation genre: a sombre exploration of sexual obsession. Basil, a serious young man of good family, becomes infatuated with a veiled woman he sees on an omnibus, Margaret Sherwin, the young daughter of a linen draper. They marry, but the marriage is kept secret and unconsummated for a year. When Margaret goes to a party with Robert Mannion, her father's confidential clerk, who has a sinister power over her, Basil follows. He sees them leave together and go to a dubious hotel. Listening through a partition wall, he realizes they are lovers. When Mannion leaves, Basil attacks him, leaving him horribly disfigured and blinded in one eye. Basil collapses in delirium, but later recovers. Mannion reveals that his father was hanged for forgery, and that Basil's father refused to help him. Margaret, visiting Mannion in hospital, contracts typhus and dies. Basil flees London; Mannion pursues him to Cornwall. In a clifftop confrontation Mannion falls to his death. The novel is remarkable for its violent and explicit representations of madness, jealousy, and sexuality.

BASILE, Giambattista (1566?–1632) Neapolitan courtier, poet, and writer of novelle; he is best known for *Lo cunto de li cunti* or *Pentamerone* (1634/6), a collection of tales in Neapolitan dialect structured on the model of the **Decameron*. The work mixes folk tales, fables, and classical myths. Originally addressed to an elite, courtly audience, it later came to be viewed erroneously as a work of popular and children's literature. Individual tales provide the European source of many fairy stories including Cinderella, Puss-in-Boots, and Beauty and the Beast. *Perrault and the brothers *Grimm both drew on it. See N. M. Penzer (trans.), *The Pentamerone of Giambattista Basile* (1932; repr. 1975).

Basilikon Doron *See* JAMES I AND VI.

BASKERVILLE, John (1706–75) English typefounder and printer, first a writing-master. By 1754 he had established a printing office and type foundry in Birmingham. His books are notable for the quality of presswork, type, and paper. His first book was a Latin *Virgil, 1757, followed by a *Milton in 1758. He was the first to use 'wove' (smooth, unwatermarked) paper, and gave his pages a gloss by hot-pressing them after printing. In order to print the *Book of *Common Prayer* (3 editions, 1760–2) and the Bible (1763), Baskerville bought a nomination as supernumerary printer to the University of Cambridge. His books are among the masterpieces of English printing; but they did not sell, and after his death his types were sold to *Beaumarchais for his great edition of *Voltaire (1784–9): they are still in existence, and some are owned by *Cambridge University Press (see J. G. Dreyfus, *The Survival of Baskerville's Punches*, 1949). Baskerville gave his name to the roman typefaces based on his designs in current usage.

BASKETT, John (1664/5–1742) Stationer and printer. From 1710 he was Queen's printer and from 1713 printer to the University of Oxford. He produced editions of the *Book of *Common Prayer*, and the 'Vinegar' Bible in two volumes (1716–17), which was said to contain 'a basketful of errors'.
See BIBLE, THE ENGLISH.

BASSANI, Giorgio (1916–2000) Italian novelist, poet, short story writer, and editor. Born into an assimilated Jewish family in Ferrara, the main theme of his writings concerns the varied experiences of Jews in Fascist Italy and the impact of the racial laws of 1938. His best-known works are *Il romanzo di Ferrara*, a compendium of six works written between 1956 and 1972, including *Cinque storie ferraresi* (1956; rev. 1974: *Five Stories of Ferrara*, 1971), and *Il giardino dei Finzi Contini* (1962: *The Garden of the Finzi-Contini*), turned into a film by Vittorio De Sica (1970). Bassani was principally responsible for ensuring the publication of *Lampedusa's novel *Il gattopardo*.

BATAILLE, Georges (1897–1962) French writer and intellectual. His examination of the extremes of human existence and the margins of socially acceptable behaviour, and his radical analysis of the relationship between sex and death, made him an important touchstone for later thinkers such as Jacques *Derrida, Michel *Foucault, and Jacques *Lacan. He developed his ideas both in philosophical texts, including *La Part maudite* (3 vols, 1949; *The Accursed Share*, trans. Robert Hurley, 1991 and 1993), and in fictional works such as *Histoire de l'œil* (1928; *Story of the Eye*, trans. Joachim Neugroschel, 1977). See M. Surya, *Georges Bataille* (2002).

BATES, H. E. (Herbert Ernest) (1905–74) Novelist and short story writer, born in Northamptonshire and educated at Kettering Grammar School. With the encouragement of Eve *Garnett (of whom he wrote a brief study, 1950) he published his first novel, *The Two Sisters* (1926), which launched him on his writing career. Other novels and collections of short stories, usually with a rural setting, followed throughout the 1930s, including *The Fallow Land* (1932), *The Poacher* (1935), *A House of Women* (1936), and *My Uncle Silas* (1939). Wartime service with the RAF inspired several volumes of short stories published under the pseudonym 'Flying Officer X'. The Second World War also provided the backdrop for one of the best-known novels published under his own name, *Fair Stood the Wind for France* (1944), the story of a British bomber crew shot down in Occupied France. After the war, Bates continued to be a prolific novelist and short story writer. *The Purple Plain* (1947), *The Jacaranda Tree* (1949), and *The Scarlet Sword* (1950) all reflected his wartime experiences in India and Burma. Several novels (*The Darling Buds of May*, 1958; *A Breath of French Air*, 1959; *When the Green Woods Laugh*, 1960) featured the irrepressibly cheerful and life-embracing family, the Larkins. Many of Bates's novels have been successfully televised, most notably the Larkin books which were produced for TV by his son Richard. He also published three volumes of autobiography, *The Vanished World* (1969), *The Blossoming World* (1971), and *The World in Ripeness* (1972).

BATES, Henry Walter (1825–92) Self-taught naturalist, who visited Pará (at the mouth of the Amazon River) with Alfred Russel *Wallace in 1848 and the Amazon in 1851–9. He discovered 8,000 species new to science and his observation of butterflies led him to the theory of 'Batesian mimicry', by which a palatable and unprotected species imitated the appearance of an unpalatable or protected species. His findings lent support to the theory of evolution by natural selection.

Bates's *The Naturalist on the River Amazons* was published by John Murray in 1863.

Bath, Wife of *See* CANTERBURY TALES, 6.

bathos [Greek, 'depth'] A descent from the sublime to the ridiculous in literary style or subject. The term originates from Alexander *Pope's satire *Peri Bathous, or The Art of Sinking in Poetry* (1727).

Batrachomyomachia, *or The Battle of the Frogs and Mice* A burlesque Greek epic (*c.*5th century BC), formerly attributed to *Homer. It describes in *mock-epic Homeric style a battle between mice and frogs in which Zeus and Athena join. Thomas *Parnell's version of the *Batrachomyomachia* attacking John *Dennis and Lewis *Theobald appeared in 1717, relatively late in the history of the genre.

Battle of Alcazar, The A verse play by George *Peele, written *c.*1588/9, published 1594. It dramatizes the battle in 1578 between Sebastian, king of Portugal, and Abdelmelec, king of Morocco. Abdelmelec had recovered his kingdom from a usurper, Muly Mahamet, who invokes the assistance of Sebastian, offering to give up the kingdom of Morocco to him and to become his tributary. Sebastian sails with his fleet to Morocco and at the battle of Alcazar is killed, as is Abdelmelec. Muly Mahamet is drowned while fleeing the field. Sebastian is assisted by the adventurer Stukeley (Thomas Stucley, *c.*1520–1578), who is also killed in the battle. An interesting contemporary 'plot', or playhouse summary, survives, edited by W. W. *Greg. See David Bradley, *From Text to Performance in the Elizabethan Theatre* (1992) for a different interpretation; see also Charles Edelman's edition in *The Stukeley Plays* (2005).

Battle of the Books, The (*A Full and True Account of the Battel Fought Last Friday, between the Antient and the Modern Books in St James's Library*) A prose satire by Jonathan *Swift, written 1697, when Swift was residing with Sir William *Temple, published 1704. Temple had written an essay on the comparative merits of 'Ancient and Modern Learning' (the subject at that time of an animated controversy in Paris), which contained uncritical praise of the spurious **Epistles of Phalaris*; this drew the censure of William Wotton and Richard *Bentley. In Swift's treatment, the 'Battle' originates from a request by the moderns that the ancients shall evacuate the higher of the two peaks of Parnassus which they have hitherto occupied. The ancients, under the patronage of Pallas (Athena), are led by *Homer, *Pindar, Euclid, *Aristotle, and *Plato, with Temple commanding the allies; the moderns by John *Milton, John *Dryden, *Descartes, and Thomas *Hobbes, with the support of the malignant deity Criticism. Aristotle aims an arrow at Francis *Bacon but hits Descartes. Homer overthrows **Gondibert*. *Virgil encounters his translator Dryden, in a helmet nine times too big. In general the ancients have the advantage, but a parley ensues and the tale leaves the issue undecided.

BAUDELAIRE, Charles (1821–67) French poet, critic, translator, and essayist. His *Les Fleurs du mal* (1857: *The Flowers of Evil*) is one of the great collections of French verse. It represents a determined attempt to create order and beauty, notably by the discovery of hidden relations or 'correspondences', in a world which is largely perceived as ugly and oppressive. In musical language and evocative images, the poet explores his own sense of isolation, exile, and sin, his boredom and melancholy, the transporting power of love, and the attractions of evil and vice. When *Les Fleurs du mal* was first published, Baudelaire was fined and six of the poems were banned from subsequent editions as offensive to public morals; these were accordingly omitted from the second (1861) and the third, posthumous, edition (1868), by which time some 50 new poems had been added (the ban was only lifted in 1949). Baudelaire also wrote prose poems, published posthumously as *Le Spleen de Paris* (1869), and translations of Edgar Allan *Poe's tales: *Histoires extraordinaires* (1856) and *Nouvelles Histoires extraordinaires* (1857). He gave a detailed account of the effects of opium and hashish in *Les Paradis artificiels* (1860), which contains a commentary on the translated extracts from Thomas De Quincey's **Confessions of an English Opium Eater*. Most of his critical writings, including essays on the Paris salons of 1845, 1846, and 1859, Delacroix, *Gautier, *Flaubert, and *Wagner, were collected in the posthumous volumes *Curiosités esthétiques* and *L'Art romantique* (1868). His *Journaux intimes* were published in 1887. Baudelaire the poet has had a decisive influence on English verse: since 1890 there has been no decade without a major English translation, including versions by Edna St Vincent *Millay, Roy *Campbell, and Michael *Hamburger. The title story of Angela Carter's collection *Black Venus* (1985) describes Baudelaire from the point of view of his mistress, Jeanne Duval. See C. Pichois, *Baudelaire* (1989).

BAUDRILLARD, Jean (1929–2007) French philosopher, one of the principal theorists of *postmodernism. His pioneering work of the 1960s considers what he terms 'consumer society', exploring how human identity and relationships are mediated by a proliferating number of objects in the world. Later work dwells on the signs and meanings these objects produce, arguing that the contemporary world is saturated by 'simulacra', whose 'hyper-reality' appears to offer an escape from the banality of everyday life, but which in fact confront us with significant moral and ethical problems.

BAUM, L. (Lyman) **Frank** (1856–1919) Born Chittenago, New York. Baum worked as a salesman, reporter, actor, and director of opera houses before collaborating with the illustrator William Wallace Denslow on *Father Goose, his Book* (1899), and *The Wonderful *Wizard of Oz* (1900), which he adapted as a long-running musical.

BAWDEN, Nina (1925–) Née Mabey, CBE, novelist and children's writer, born in London, educated at Somerville College, Oxford. Her many well-crafted and closely observed novels are almost equally divided between those for adults and those for children. Several, notably *Family Money* (1991), have been televised. Her highly regarded children's books include *The Peppermint Pig* (1976) and *Carrie's War* (1973, BBC 1974; 2003), based on her experiences of wartime evacuation. Non-fiction includes a memoir, *In my Own Time* (1994), and *Dear Austen* (2005), addressed to her husband Austen Kark, who died in the Potter's Bar rail crash (2002).

BAX, Sir Arnold (1883–1953) English composer and writer. An early encounter with *Yeats's *Wanderings of Oisin* brought out a strong Celtic strain in Bax, and he spent much time in Ireland. As 'Dermot O'Byrne' he published plays, stories, and poetry, some of it influenced by the Easter Rising of 1916. As a composer he was prolific in all forms, from the early *Celtic Song Cycle* (1904, words by 'Fiona Macleod', i.e. William *Sharp) to the film score for *Oliver Twist* (1948). On the strength of his tone poem *Tintagel* (1917–19) and seven symphonies, he was for a while considered Britain's leading symphonist. He set many texts from all periods, from medieval poetry to Thomas *Hardy, A. E. *Housman, and Padraic *Colum. He was knighted in 1937 and made master of the king's music in 1942; his autobiographical sketch *Farewell my Youth* was published in 1943.

BAXTER, James Keir (1926–72) New Zealand poet, educated episodically at the University of Otago, and in Christchurch and Wellington. He wrote prolifically, producing plays as well as poetry, survived a period of alcoholism, and in 1961 became a Roman Catholic, devoting his last years to Franciscan austerity, investigations of Maori culture, and social work with the drunks, homeless, and drug addicts of Wellington and Auckland. His early volumes (*Beyond the Palisade*, 1944; *Blow, Wind of Fruitfulness*, 1948; *The Fallen House*, 1953) dealt with themes of nature, place, colonial alienation, and guilt, sometimes using the ballad form to satiric effect. In later work he expressed himself in a colloquial, hybridized, yet spiritual and questioning style, describing his own mission amongst the poor, and drawing on Christian imagery, small daily events, and the Maori language to create an intensely personal voice. Volumes include *Pig Island Letters* (1966), *Jerusalem Sonnets* (1970), and *Autumn Testament* (1972).

BAXTER, Richard (1615–91) A Presbyterian theologian who sided with Parliament and was a military chaplain during the Civil War. He was author of *The Saint's Everlasting Rest* (1650; the book that Mrs Glegg in George *Eliot's *The *Mill on the Floss* used to favour in a domestic crisis) and of *Call to the Unconverted* (1657), both of which played an important part in the evangelical tradition in England and America. Fined, imprisoned, and persecuted after the Act of Uniformity under both Charles II and James II for his Nonconformist preaching, he shared his sufferings with his young wife 'who cheerfully went with me into prison'. In her memory he wrote his moving *Breviate of the Life of Margaret Charlton* (1681). He was fined by the notoriously punitive Judge Jeffreys (1645–89) on the charge of libelling the Church in his *Paraphrase of the New Testament* (1685). His numerous writings include a lengthy autobiography, *Reliquiae Baxterianae* (1696), which gives a vivid portrait of the strife of the Interregnum and the Restoration, and several well-known hymns (e.g. 'Ye holy angels bright'). See N. H. Keeble, *Richard Baxter: Puritan Man of Letters* (1982).

BAXTER, Stephen (1957–) Liverpool-born writer of epic *science fiction. From *Raft* (1991), he has published numerous novels and short stories, including *The Time Ships* (1995), a sequel to H. G. *Wells's *The Time Machine*, the 'Manifold' sequence (1999–2002), and the 'Destiny's Children' sequence (2003–6). Novels written in collaboration with Arthur C. *Clarke include *The Light of Other Days* (2000). Baxter's command of the tradition of visionary speculation running from Wells through Olaf *Stapledon and Clarke makes him one of the field's most assured writers upon cosmological and evolutionary perspectives.

BAYAZET (or Bayayet; Turkish Bayezit) Ottoman sultan 1389–1402. After conquests in the Balkans and Anatolia, he turned his attentions to taking Constantinople. He was interrupted by the approach of Timur (Tamberlane). After a pitched battle near Ankara in July 1402, he was taken prisoner and died in captivity in March 1403. He figures in Christopher Marlowe's **Tamburlaine the Great* and Nicholas Rowe's **Tamerlane*.

BAYLE, Pierre (1647–1706) French Protestant scholar and philosopher, who lived in Rotterdam from 1681, where his major work, the *Dictionnaire historique et critique*, was published (2 vols, 1695, 1697; 2nd edn, rev. and enl., 1702). Most of the entries in the *Dictionnaire* were biographical articles on important figures from biblical, classical, and modern history, in the course of which, especially in the discursive footnotes, many theological and philosophical questions, some of them controversial, were subjected to rigorous critical analysis. Bayle's method rested on the systematic comparison of sources and scientific consideration of evidence. He deployed the learning that made his work a source-book of historical and religious criticism in a humane and enquiring spirit, impatient of superstition and intolerance. There were English translations of the *Dictionnaire* in 1710, 1734–8 (rev.), and 1734–41 (much enlarged, as *A General Dictionary, Historical and Critical*). See E. Labrousse, *Pierre Bayle*, trans. D. C. Potts (1983).

BAYLEY, Barrington J. (1937–2008) English author, born in Birmingham; he has published *science fiction since the 1950s. Time and awareness are features of novels published through the 1970s and 1980s, such as *The Fall of Chronopolis* (1974) and *Chronopolis* (1979). *Knights of the Limits* (1978;

reissued 2001) collects his Borgesian short stories, many published in *New Worlds.

BAYLEY, John (1925–) Critic and memoirist, born in Lahore; from 1975 to 1992 he was Warton professor of English literature at Oxford. He married Iris *Murdoch in 1956, and after her diagnosis of Alzheimer's disease, wrote a book about her decline (*Iris: A Memoir for Iris Murdoch*, 1998). After her death in 1999 he wrote further memoirs based on their life together.

BAYLY, Nathaniel Thomas Haynes (1797–1839) The author of many verses, including 'I'd be a butterfly' and 'She wore a wreath of roses' which have been the subject of some ridicule. He also wrote at great speed many pieces for the stage, including *Perfection* (1836), a successful farce.

Bay Psalm Book (1640) The first book printed in the American colonies. This metrical version of the *Psalms for the churches in Massachusetts was designed to replace that of *Sternhold and Hopkins. It was often reprinted and remained popular for over a hundred years.

BBC (British Broadcasting Corporation; initially, from 1922, the British Broadcasting Company Ltd), was established by royal charter as a publicly owned corporation supported by licence fee in 1927. Its first, highly influential manager, John, later Lord, Reith (1889–1971) established the remit of informing, educating, and entertaining. Adding *television to its *radio output in 1936 (interrupted during the war), it has continued to innovate, while its role as a national institution, popularly known as 'Auntie' and 'the Beeb', has also led to recurrent controversies. These have ranged from challenges over impartiality in reporting the General Strike (1926), the Suez Crisis (1956), and the Falklands War (1982) to political scandals resulting from programmes about Labour politicians (*Yesterday's Men*, 1971) and about intelligence justification for the Iraq War in 2003. Issues of taste have also been endemic, from Dorothy *Sayers's radio series on the life of Christ, *The Man Born to be King* (1941–2), to Dennis *Potter's earthy treatment of the same subject in his television play *Son of Man* (1969); and incidents such as Kenneth *Tynan uttering the word 'fuck' for the first time on BBC television in 1965, and obscene phone messages broadcast on a popular music programme in 2008, have provoked national debate about changing values.

The BBC remains the world's largest commissioner and producer of creative work in serious and popular music, drama, short stories, and documentary programmes, with much of its output re-transmitted by other broadcasters around the world. From the 1940s onwards, many writers also worked as BBC producers and regular contributors, including George *Orwell, Louis *MacNeice, P. H. *Newby, Terence Tiller (1916–87), George *MacBeth, Anthony *Thwaite, Roy *Campbell, Derek *Mahon, Patric Dickinson (1914–94), Paul *Muldoon, and Nigel Williams (1948–). BBC producers such as Douglas Cleverdon, Martin Esslin, Donald McWhinnie, Barbara Bray, Michael Bakewell, Richard Imison, and John Tydeman were instrumental in commissioning new, often first plays from Samuel *Beckett, Caryl *Churchill, Joe *Orton, Harold *Pinter, John *Mortimer, Robert *Bolt, Giles Cooper (1918–66), Tom *Stoppard, Bill Naughton (1910–92), John *Arden, David *Rudkin, Alun *Owen, James Saunders (1925–2004), and Alan *Plater. The tradition has continued with a new generation of dramatists, including Anthony Minghella (1954–2008), Martin *Crimp, Hanif *Kureishi, and Howard *Barker.

Apart from noted radio plays, original 'light entertainment' created for BBC radio includes *The Goon Show* (1951–60), Douglas *Adams's *The Hitchhiker's Guide to the Galaxy* (1978), and Sue *Townsend's *The Secret Diary of Adrian Mole* (1982), all of which have generated lasting devotion and *adaptations in many media. BBC television comedy has a distinguished tradition that includes series built around comedians such as Tony Hancock (*Hancock's Half Hour*, 1956–9, originally on radio), Ronnie Barker (*Porridge*, 1973–9), John Cleese (*Fawlty Towers*, 1975, 1979), and revue-style shows ranging from the satirical *That Was the Week That Was* (1962–3) to *Monty Python's Flying Circus* (1969–74). Radio comedy continues to launch new performers and formats which often migrate to television.

In 2009, the BBC operated four national television channels, with regional centres in Scotland, Wales, and Northern Ireland, a total of seven national radio networks, supplemented by a network of local radio stations, a widely admired and influential radio World Service and television News 24, which are transmitted internationally, and an ever-growing portfolio of digital services, made available through its extensive website at www.bbc.co.uk. It continues to be funded through a licence fee, supplemented by earnings from its trading activities.

See also ADAPTATION; RADIO; TELEVISION.

BEACH, Sylvia (1887–1962) Bookshop owner and publisher, born in Baltimore, Maryland; owner from 1919 of the Shakespeare and Company bookshop and lending library on the Left Bank in Paris, meeting place for writers as diverse as James *Joyce, Ernest *Hemingway, André *Gide, and Sherwood *Anderson. When Joyce could find no publisher for **Ulysses* after instalments of its serialization in the **Little Review* had been found obscene, she published it under the Shakespeare and Co. imprint in 1922, funding the enterprise through subscription. See Beach, *Shakespeare and Company* (1959); Noel Riley Fitch, *Sylvia Beach and the Lost Generation: A History of Literary Paris in the Twenties and Thirties* (1983).

Beach, The First novel of Alex Garland (b. London, 1970), published 1996 and filmed in 2000. A 'cult classic' provoking comparisons to William *Golding and Graham *Greene, it satirizes young international backpackers seeking authenticity in Thailand. They discover a paradisiacal beach untouched by mass tourism, but their community self-destructs.

'Beachcomber' The pseudonym attached to a column of fantastic and surreal humour published in the *Daily Express*: it was coined in 1919 by journalist and author Bevan Lewis (1891–1969), who bequeathed it to his friend John Cameron Morton (1893–1975). Morton wrote under this name from 1924 to 1975, at first daily, later weekly, and many of his articles have been published with illustrations by Nicolas Bentley in various collections.

'Beachy Head' An unfinished poem in blank verse by Charlotte *Smith, published posthumously in *Beachy Head, and Other Poems* (1807), which combines sublime imagery and natural description with historical narratives of war and nationhood, alongside mournful meditation on the poet's personal unhappiness, especially when compared to her youthful experience as 'An early worshipper at Nature's shrine'.

BEAGLE, Peter S. (1939–) American author, born in New York; known for the *fantasy *The Last Unicorn* (1968: filmed 1982). *A Fine and Private Place* (1960), *The Folk of the Air* (1986), *The Innkeeper's Song* (1993), and the collection *Giant Bones* (1997) play lyrically with fantasy motifs.

BEAR, Greg (1951–) American author, born in San Diego; his *science fiction and *fantasy novels frequently deal with biological or evolutionary themes. *Blood Music* (1985) is a visionary novel of post-human evolution—a theme continued in *Darwin's Radio* (1999) and *Darwin's Children* (2003).

BEARDSLEY, Aubrey (1872–98) Illustrator and writer, notorious in the 1890s as the outstanding artist of *fin-de-siècle* decadence. His disturbingly erotic drawings develop rapidly from the murky sensuality of *Pre-Raphaelite medievalism to rococo wit and grace. Beardsley's most important illustrations are for Oscar *Wilde's *Salome* (1894), Alexander *Pope's *The Rape of the Lock* (1896), the *Lysistrata* of *Aristophanes (1896), and Ben *Jonson's *Volpone* (1898). He was art editor of the **Yellow Book* in 1894; the Wilde scandal led to his dismissal in 1895; he then became art editor to the **Savoy*. Beardsley's most significant achievement as a writer is *The Story of Venus and Tannhauser*, a charmingly rococo and highly cultivated erotic romance. An expurgated version entitled *Under the Hill* was published in the *Savoy*; an unexpurgated edition was privately printed in 1907; it contains a cruel caricature of Wilde as 'Priapusa, the fat manicure and fardeuse'. In 1897 Beardsley, encouraged by John *Gray and his friend Marc-André Raffalovich (1864–1934), converted to Catholicism. He died of consumption. In 1916 his sister Mabel died of cancer; W. B. *Yeats, who had known them both, wrote a sequence of poems, 'Upon a Dying Lady', inspired by her. See Linda Zatlin, *Aubrey Beardsley* (1990).

Beat and Beat Generation 'Beat' was a term first used by the notorious hustler and drug addict Herbert Huncke (1916–96) to describe his own state of lawless drifting and social alienation. 'Beat' was quickly picked up by Jack *Kerouac as a triple entendre—an epithet that brought together a sense of being 'beaten' with the state of being 'beatific', as well as suggesting the pulse and 'beat' of music. The pioneers of the movement were Allen *Ginsberg, whose book *Howl* (1956) protested that America had seen 'the best minds of my generation destroyed by madness', and Kerouac, whose *On the Road* (1957) reinvented a mythic landscape of highways, bars, and male bonding. With other writers such as Gregory Corso (1930–2001) and William *Burroughs, the Beats developed an aesthetic based on the spontaneity of jazz, Buddhist mysticism, and the raw urgency of sex, in reaction against the perceived sterile conformity of post-war America. *Minor Characters* (1983) by Joyce Johnson (1935–) records the part played in the movement by women. See Ann Charters' *Portable Beat Reader* (1992).

Beatles, the A group of young musicians from Liverpool (George Harrison, John Lennon, Paul McCartney, and 'Ringo' Starr), whose songs and lifestyle, from 1962 until their break-up in 1970, attracted a vast following. Many of their lyrics (e.g. 'Penny Lane', 'Eleanor Rigby', 'She's Leaving Home') have been highly praised, and they had a considerable influence on the success of the *Liverpool poets and the underground poetry movement. Philip *Larkin described their work as 'an enchanting and intoxicating hybrid of Negro rock-and-roll with their own adolescent romanticism', and 'the first advance in popular music since the War'. John Lennon was murdered in New York in 1980, and George Harrison died in 2001.

BEATRICE (?1266–1290) Identified by *Boccaccio as Bice, daughter of Folco Portinari of Florence, and wife of Simone de' Bardi. The principal subject of *Dante's **Vita nuova*, in which he claims to have fallen in love with her when she was 9. After her death Dante comes to a new understanding of her role in his life. Beatrice acts as Dante's guide in the **Divina Commedia*, from *Purgatorio* XXX to *Paradiso* XXX.

BEATTIE, James (1735–1803) Scottish poet and philosopher, born near Laurencekirk, Kincardineshire, and educated at Marischal College, Aberdeen, where he was appointed professor of moral philosophy in 1760. His *Essay on the Nature and Immutability of Truth* (1770) was an attempt to refute David *Hume and George *Berkeley. As a poet he is remembered for *The Minstrel*, a poem in *Spenserian stanzas tracing 'the progress of a poetical Genius, born in a rude age, from the first dawning of fancy and reason'; Edwin, the son of a shepherd, a solitary and sensitive boy, finds his education in nature, in a manner that foreshadows Wordsworth's **Prelude*. Book I appeared in 1771, Book II in 1774, and they were many times reprinted, though the work remained unfinished.

Beauchamp's Career A novel by George *Meredith, published 1876. In this political novel, much concerned with the contemporary state of Britain, Nevil Beauchamp begins his career as an idealistic young naval officer. In spite of his mildly subversive views on social questions, he earns the approval of his wealthy aristocratic uncle Everard Romfrey, a traditionalist who detests radicals and their like. After the Crimean War, Nevil plunges into politics, stands unsuccessfully as a Radical candidate for Parliament, and becomes the friend of Dr Shrapnel, humanitarian, republican, and freethinker, detestable to Mr Romfrey and his friends. In his rage at various rumours and misrepresentations, Romfrey horsewhips Shrapnel, incurring the fury of his nephew, who demands that his uncle apologize to his friend. This hopeless enterprise becomes an obsession with Nevil, who is also distracted by his own inconclusive love affairs, torn between his early passion for Renée de Croisnel, a spirited and intelligent young woman (now the unhappy wife of an elderly Frenchman), and his love for a soft and decorous English girl, Cecilia Halkett. Gallantry and indecision lose him Renée, who has fled from her husband; and he also loses Cecilia, who is married by her father to Nevil's dull second cousin. Harassed and unhappy, Nevil falls desperately ill, near to death. His danger moves his proud uncle to present himself at Shrapnel's cottage, where Nevil lies, and to offer his apology at last. Nevil recovers and marries Shrapnel's ward Jenny Denham, a genial and sympathetic girl. But after a few months of happiness he is drowned trying to rescue an unknown child from the sea. The brilliant Renée was Meredith's favourite among all his women characters, representing the force of passion in a novel which examines the limitations which Beauchamp's impulsive and romantic nature places on his reasoned political idealism.

BEAUMARCHAIS, Pierre-Augustin Caron de (1732–99) French dramatist, author of farces and sentimental dramas, amongst the latter *Eugénie* (1767), successfully adapted, at the invitation of David *Garrick, by the playwright Elizabeth *Griffith as *The School for Rakes* (1769). But he is best known for his comedies about the resourceful valet Figaro: *Le Barbier de Séville* (1775: *The Barber of Seville*), and *Le Mariage de Figaro* (1784: *The Marriage of Figaro*). Both were quickly translated into English, the former again by Griffith in 1776, the latter by Thomas *Holcroft (*The Follies of a Day*, 1785), who learnt the play from performances in Paris. The Figaro plays also inspired operas by *Rossini (1816) and *Mozart (1786) respectively. See W. D. Howarth, *Beaumarchais and the Theatre* (1995).

BEAUMONT, Francis (15845–1616) Dramatist, born at Grace Dieu, Leicestershire, of an ancient family. He was admitted to Broadgates Hall (now Pembroke College), Oxford, at the age of 12, and entered the Inner Temple in 1600. His poem *Salmacis and Hermaphroditus* appeared anonymously in 1602. His most famous poem, on the Mermaid Tavern, is addressed to Ben *Jonson. The only play Beaumont is known to have written on his own, *The *Knight of the Burning Pestle* (1606/7), failed on its first appearance. Soon afterwards he began his celebrated collaboration with John *Fletcher. Initially they wrote five plays for boys' companies; the most popular was *The Scornful Lady*, which went into ten editions during the seventeenth century. According to John *Aubrey they lived together 'on the Bankside, not far from the [Globe] play-house, both bachelors; lay together; had one wench in the house between them...the same clothes and cloak, etc....'. The chronology of their work is uncertain, but at some point from 1608 to 1610 they began to write their four plays for the King's Men, including their greatest successes, **Philaster*, *A *King and No King*, and *The *Maid's Tragedy*. *Comedies and Tragedies written by Francis Beaumont and John Fletcher, Gentlemen* was published in 1647, but only about nine of the 34 plays and one *masque (by Beaumont) in this volume are now believed to have resulted from their collaboration. Philip *Massinger is the other major contributor. Beaumont's last work was the politically significant masque written for the Inner Temple and Gray's Inn to celebrate the marriage of Princess Elizabeth to Frederick V, elector palatine, in February 1613. In that year he married an heiress, Ursula Isley, by whom he had two daughters; he also suffered a stroke in 1613, and subsequently abandoned writing. He died in 1616 and was buried in Westminster Abbey. There is a major edition of the plays by Fredson Bowers (10 vols, 1966–96).

BEAUMONT, Sir George Howland (1753–1827) Artist, patron of art, and friend and benefactor of *Wordsworth, who frequently visited him at Coleorton Hall; in his dedication to Sir George of his 1815 volume, Wordsworth wrote, 'some of the best pieces were composed under the shade of your own groves, upon the classic ground of Coleorton'. Inspired by one of Beaumont's most notable landscapes, Wordsworth composed his 'Elegiac Stanzas Suggested by a Picture of Peele Castle in a Storm, Painted by Sir George Beaumont in 1806 in memory of his brother Captain John Wordsworth'. Walter *Scott described Beaumont as 'the man in the world most void of affectation', adding that he 'understood Wordsworth's poetry, which is a rare thing'. Beaumont also encouraged and supported *Coleridge and helped to procure his pension.

BEAUMONT, Jeanne-Marie Leprince de *See* LEPRINCE DE BEAUMONT JENNE-MARIE.

BEAUVOIR, Simone de (1908–86) French writer, philosopher, feminist, and political activist. A lifelong companion of Jean-Paul *Sartre, her early novels, which were quickly translated into English, reflect the major preoccupations of *existentialism: *L'Invitée* (1943: *She Came to Stay*), *Le Sang des autres* (1945: *The Blood of Others*), and *Les Mandarins* (1954), the novel for which she was awarded the Prix Goncourt. Her highly influential analysis of women's oppression, *Le Deuxième Sexe*, appeared in 1949 (*The Second Sex*, translated into English by H. M. Parshley in 1953) and paved the way for much modern *feminist criticism. She went on to publish four volumes of autobiography, including *Mémoires d'une jeune fille rangée* (1958: *Memoirs of a Dutiful Daughter*) and *La Force de l'âge* (1960: *The Prime of Life*), the former translated into

English by James *Kirkup in 1959. *Beloved Chicago Man: Letters to Nelson Algren 1947–64* (1997) collects her correspondence with her American lover, the writer Nelson *Algren. See D. Bair, *Simone de Beauvoir* (1990).
See also KRISTEVA.

Beaux' Stratagem, The George *Farquhar's final comedy, produced with great success in 1707. Aimwell and Archer, two spendthrifts, arrive at an inn at Lichfield, in search of adventure and money. To economize, Archer pretends to be Aimwell's servant, causing much speculation as to their identity. Dorinda, daughter of the wealthy Lady Bountiful, falls in love with Aimwell, who, thinking her a suitable prey, gets admission to her house by passing himself off as his elder brother Lord Aimwell. He is accompanied by Archer, who has formed a liaison with Mrs Sullen, the unhappy wife of Lady Bountiful's alcoholic son. The two men protect the women during an attack on the house. Overpowered by the trustfulness of Dorinda, Aimwell confesses the fraud. Mrs Sullen's brother brings news of Lord Aimwell's death and of Aimwell's accession to the title; Sullen agrees to the dissolution of his marriage, and Mrs Sullen is free to marry Archer.

BECCARIA, Cesare (1738–94) Italian aristocrat and jurist, whose essay *Dei delitti e delle pene* (1764: *Of Crimes and Punishments*), a masterpiece of the Italian Enlightenment, inspired European schemes to improve prison systems, followed in England by Jeremy *Bentham.

BECKET, St Thomas (*c.*1120–1170) Son of Gilbert Becket, educated in London and Paris; he subsequently studied canon law at Bologna and Auxerre. Henry II appointed him chancellor and made him his intimate friend and companion. In 1162 Thomas became archbishop of Canterbury, which required him to become the champion of ecclesiastical rights that Henry was attempting to curtail. In particular he opposed the Constitutions of Clarendon (1164). One measure in particular, that no clerical appeal to Rome could be made without the authority of the king, was contentious. Becket was exiled on the Continent for seven years; he returned to England in 1170 after a brief reconciliation with Henry was effected, but when the old arguments were revived he was assassinated on the king's orders in the cathedral at Canterbury on 29 December 1170. There was popular outrage. The king, officially at least, claimed that his orders had been misinterpreted, and harmony with the pope was only restored by his humiliation and flagellation at Avranches. Becket's shrine at Canterbury became the most famous in Christendom as a place where miracles were performed, and it was the objective of *Chaucer's pilgrims 200 years later. The story of Becket has been the subject of plays by *Tennyson, T. S. *Eliot (*Murder in the Cathedral*), and Christopher *Fry; and by Jean *Anouilh in French.

BECKETT, Samuel (1906–89) Author, born at Foxrock, Dublin, the second son of a quantity surveyor, and greatly affected in childhood by the evangelical Protestantism of his mother. He was educated at Portora Royal School, Enniskillen, and at Trinity College, Dublin, where he read English, French, and Italian. He taught briefly in Belfast before going to Paris as *lecteur d'anglais* at the École Normale Supérieure; there in 1928 he met James *Joyce, with whom he formed a lasting friendship. His first published work was an essay on Joyce (1929) and he assisted with the translation into French of the 'Anna Livia Plurabelle' section of **Finnegans Wake*. His first story, 'Assumption', appeared in **transition* (1929), and in 1930 he returned as lecturer to Trinity College, resigning after four terms to embark on five unsettled, solitary years in Germany, France, Ireland, and London, before settling permanently in France. During this period he reviewed, translated, published poems in various periodicals, and wrote a study of *Proust (1931). *More Pricks than Kicks* (1934, stories) was followed by several full-length novels, including *Murphy* (1938), a mordant evocation of London Irish life. Beckett emerged from his experience in the French Resistance during the Second World War as a francophone writer who had shed the slightly swaggering cleverness of his early work. His trilogy *Molloy* (1951); *Malone Meurt* (1951; Beckett's own English version, *Malone Dies*, 1958); and *L'Innommable* (1953; *The Unnamable*, 1960) was originally written in French, and all three of its constituent novels are interior monologues, desolate, terminal, obsessional, irradiated with flashes of black humour: *Malone Dies* opens with the characteristic sentence 'I shall soon be quite dead at last in spite of all', and the last volume trails away with '…where I am, I don't know, I'll never know, in the silence you don't know, you must go on, I can't go on, I'll go on'. Beckett's highly distinctive, despairing, yet curiously exhilarating voice reached a large audience with the Paris performance in 1953 of *En attendant Godot* (pub. 1952); the English version, **Waiting for Godot* (1955), also made a great impact, and Beckett became widely known as a playwright associated with the Theatre of the *Absurd, whose use of the stage and of dramatic narrative and symbolism revolutionized drama in England and influenced later playwrights, including Harold *Pinter, Athol *Fugard, and Tom *Stoppard. Subsequent stage plays include *Fin de partie* (first performed in French at the Royal Court, 1957; English version, *Endgame*, pub. 1958), a one-act drama of frustration, irascibility, and senility, featuring blind Hamm, his attendant Clov, and Hamm's parents, 'accursed progenitors' who spend the action in dustbins; *Krapp's Last Tape* (1958; pub. 1959), written for the Irish actor Patrick Magee, a monologue in which the shabby Krapp attempts to recapture the intensity of earlier days by listening to recordings of his own younger self; *Happy Days* (1961, pub. 1961), which portrays Winnie buried to her waist in a mound, but still attached to the carefully itemized contents of her handbag; *Come and Go* (1966; pub. 1967), a stark 'dramaticule' with three female characters and a text of 121 words; the even more minimal *Breath* (1969), a 30-second play consisting only of a pile of rubbish, a breath, and a cry; and *Not I* (1973; pub. 1973), a fragmented, disembodied monologue delivered by an actor of indeterminate sex of whom only the 'Mouth' is illuminated. Beckett has also written for television (*Eh Joe*, 1966) and, more frequently, for radio. His late prose fragments have excited considerable attention. He was awarded the *Nobel Prize in 1969. See James Knowlson, *Damned to Fame: The Life of Samuel Beckett* (1996).

BECKFORD, William (1760–1844) Author, born in London, educated privately. Indulging his passions for art, architecture, and music, he lavished his considerable fortune on the extravagant Fonthill Abbey and on continental travels, partly necessitated by homosexual scandal. He published **Vathek*, and books of travels, including *Dreams, Waking Thoughts and Incidents* (1783) and *Italy* (1834).

BEDDOES, Thomas Lovell (1803–49) Dramatist and poet, born in Clifton, Somerset, and educated at Charterhouse and Pembroke College, Oxford, the son of the physician, radical, and writer Dr Thomas Beddoes (1760–1808), who had been friend and doctor of *Coleridge, *Wordsworth, and *Southey. Thomas also studied medicine and in 1835 settled at Zurich, living thereafter mostly abroad. He published in 1821 *The Improvisatore* and in 1822 *The Brides' Tragedy.* His most important work, *Death's Jest-Book, or the Fool's Tragedy,* was begun in 1825 and repeatedly altered at various times, not being published until 1850, after his death by suicide at Basle. It is in blank verse, heavily influenced by Elizabethan and Jacobean tragedy, and shows Beddoes's obsession with the macabre, the supernatural, and bodily decay; these interests were to appeal strongly to *fin-de-siècle* poets such as A. W. *Symons, who compared Beddoes to *Baudelaire and *Poe, and wrote in praise, 'there is not a page without its sad, grotesque, gay or abhorrent imagery of the tomb'. He is now best known for his shorter pieces, such as 'Dream Pedlary' ('If there were dreams to sell, | What would you buy?') and the lyrics which appear in *Death's Jest-Book* ('If thou wilt ease thine heart | Of love and all its smart'), although some of his blank verse has undeniable power and originality. His poetical works were edited by Edmund *Gosse in 1890 and 1928, and H. W. Donner's edition, *Plays and Poems* (1950), has a biographical introduction.

BEDE (Baeda, or 'The Venerable Bede') (*c.*673–735) A distinguished, influential scholar and prolific writer, was placed when young in the charge of *Benedict Biscop, the abbot of Wearmouth. From there he went in 682 to Jarrow in the care of its first abbot, Ceolfrid, and there he spent most of his life. He was a diligent teacher and scholar of Latin and Greek, and he had many pupils among the monks of Wearmouth and Jarrow. He was buried at Jarrow, but his remains were moved to Durham during the first half of the 11th century. He was first called 'Venerabilis' during the 9th century. His *Historia Ecclesiastica Gentis Anglorum* (**Ecclesiastical History of the English People*) was finished in 731, by which time he had written nearly 40 works, including treatises, biblical commentaries, and homilies. His early treatise *De Natura Rerum* was modelled on the *Origines* of *Isidore of Seville and contains rudimentary natural science, referring phenomena to natural causes. His other influential work of history is the *Lives of the Abbots*, which gives an account of the earlier abbots in the Northumbrian Revival. There is a famous description of his death in a letter of his pupil Cuthbert. See B. Ward, *The Venerable Bede* (1990).

BEDE, Cuthbert Pseudonym of Edward *Bradley.

BEDFORD, Sybille (1911–2006) Author, born in Charlottenburg, Berlin, and initially brought up in a castle, though in reduced circumstances, by her aristocratic German father after he had been deserted by his part-English, part-Jewish, and wholly unreliable wife. When her father died, Bedford received a nominal education in England, Italy, and France while trailing in the wake of her increasingly erratic and morphine-addicted mother. They joined an expatriate bohemian community in Sanary-sur-Mer, where Bedford was encouraged to write by Aldous *Huxley, whose biography she would complete in two volumes (1973, 1974). *The Sudden View* (1953; reissued as *A Visit to Don Otavio*, 1960), describing travels in Mexico, was followed by a 'biographical novel', *A Legacy* (1956). Set largely in the years immediately preceding the First World War, this is a witty, sophisticated tragicomedy whose vivid portrait of two ill-matched families—one from the Roman Catholic aristocracy, the other from the Jewish *haute bourgeoisie*—drew upon Bedford's own background. *A Favourite of the Gods* (1962) and the boldly lesbian *A Compass Error* (1968) were semi-autobiographical novels with echoes of Henry *James, while *Jigsaw* (1989) is based closely on her travels round the south of France with her mother. Bedford worked as a reporter on notable criminal trials, producing two related books: *The Best We Can Do* (1958) and *The Faces of Justice* (1961). *As It Was* (1990) was chiefly made up of travel pieces, while *Quicksands* (2005) is an evocative, seemingly frank, but elusive memoir.

Bedlam A corruption of Bethlehem, applied to the Hospital of St Mary of Bethlehem, just outside Bishopsgate, London. It was founded as a priory in 1247, with the special duty of receiving and entertaining the clergy of St Mary of Bethlehem, the mother church. In 1329 it is mentioned as 'an hospital', and in 1402 as a hospital for lunatics. In 1346 it received the protection of the City of London, and on the dissolution of the monasteries it was granted to the mayor and citizens. In 1547 it was incorporated as a royal foundation for lunatics. From Bedlam are derived the expressions *Tom o' Bedlam and Bess o' Bedlam for wandering lunatics, or beggars posing as lunatics, and the hospital is referred to in plays by Thomas *Dekker, John *Ford, and Ben *Jonson.

Beelzebub The name of a demon or devil, derived from different biblical names. In the Old Testament, Baal-zebub is a false god (2 Kgs 1: 2–3), meaning in Hebrew 'lord of flies': in the New Testament, Beelzebub is 'prince of the devils' (Matt. 12: 24, Mark 3: 22) and associated with *Satan. He was seen in medieval and Renaissance times as Satan's second in command, a lurid figure in popular mythology and morality plays.

He accompanies Lucifer in Marlowe's *Dr Faustus*; Milton gives the name to one of the fallen angels, next to Satan in power (**Paradise Lost*, I. 79) and William *Golding adopted one version of it for the title of his novel **Lord of the Flies*.

BEER, Patricia (1919–99) Poet and critic. She was born in Devon, the daughter of a railway clerk and a mother who was a member of the Plymouth Brethren; she described her background vividly in her autobiographical *Mrs Beer's House* (1968). The legends and landscapes of the West Country also form the background for many of her poems (collections include *The Loss of the Magyar*, 1959; *The Estuary*, 1971; *Driving West*, 1975; *Selected Poems*, 1980; *The Lie of the Land*, 1983), and her historical novel *Moon's Ottery* (1978) is set in Elizabethan Devon. Her *Reader, I Married Him* (1974), a study of women characters in 19th-century fiction, was an early and influential example of the impact of feminism on academic criticism.

BEERBOHM, Sir Max (Henry Maximilian) (1872–1956) Drama critic, essayist, parodist, and caricaturist, born in London and educated at Charterhouse and Merton College, Oxford. He did not complete his classics course but drew on Oxford for his one completed novel, **Zuleika Dobson* (1911), a fantasized distillation of the Oxford atmosphere of the 1890s. His writing, like his personality, was characterized by elegance and a light but incisive touch in applying irony and wit to society's foibles and to the idiosyncrasies of writers, artists, and politicians. His first published book in this vein was somewhat audaciously entitled *The Works of Max Beerbohm* (1896), followed by *More* (1899), *Yet Again* (1909), *And Even Now* (1920). *A Christmas Garland* (1912) expertly parodied the literary styles of Henry *James, H. G. *Wells, Rudyard *Kipling, and other contemporary writers. His best short stories were collected in *Seven Men* (1919). As an associate in the 1890s of Oscar *Wilde and Aubrey *Beardsley, the *Rhymers Club circle and members of the New English Art Club, Beerbohm was well placed to observe and comment upon avant-garde tendencies. As half-brother of the actor-manager Beerbohm Tree (1852–1917), Max had entrée into theatrical circles and was brilliant, if not always happy, as a dramatic critic of the **Saturday Review* from 1898 to 1910; he succeeded George Bernard *Shaw, whose valedictory essay in that journal dubbed him 'the incomparable Max'. His dramatic criticism is collected in *Around Theatres* (1953) and *More Theatres* (1968). His caricatures, as elegant and as individual as his literary works, complement them with delicacy of line, witty captions, and unerring selection of salient characteristics. Among the best-known collections of these are *Caricatures of Twenty-Five Gentlemen* (1896), *The Poets' Corner* (1904), and *Rossetti and his Circle* (1922). In 1910 Max married the actress Florence Kahn and settled in Italy, his permanent home for the remainder of his life except for the periods of the two world wars. During visits to England in the 1930s he began a new career as broadcaster; his commentaries on England then and now are collected in *Mainly on the Air* (1957). See N. J. Hall, *Max Beerbohm: A Kind of Life* (2002).

BEETHOVEN, Ludwig van (1770–1827) German composer, whose immense reputation was established during his lifetime and spread relatively early to Britain: he dealt directly with the publishing firm of Clementi in London from 1807. In 1803 the Edinburgh publisher George Thomson asked him to write six sonatas based on Scottish folk tunes, and although this came to nothing, from 1809 onwards Beethoven made for Thomson arrangements with accompaniment for piano trio of some 140 Scottish, Irish, Welsh, and English folk songs, together with some variations for flute and piano on Scottish melodies. Beethoven made use of 'God Save the King' and *'Rule Britannia' in sets of piano variations (1802–3) and in the so-called 'Battle' Symphony (1813) written to celebrate *Wellington's victory at Vittoria. He knew the plays of *Shakespeare well, and is said to have linked the adagio of the String Quartet Op. 18 no. 2 with the tomb scene from **Romeo and Juliet*, and two piano sonatas, Op. 31 no. 2 (1802) and Op. 57 (1804–5), with *The *Tempest*. His opera *Fidelio* (1805) perhaps owes its name to Imogen's disguise in **Cymbeline*. His *Coriolan* overture (1807) was written for a play on the theme of Coriolanus by H. J. von Collin, who also began to write a libretto for **Macbeth* for which Beethoven sketched some never completed music. The Ninth Symphony (1824) was written for the Philharmonic Society of London, whose directors sent £100 for Beethoven's relief during the last months of his life.

Beggar's Bush, The A drama by John *Fletcher and Philip *Massinger, possibly with Francis *Beaumont; it was probably performed 1622, published 1647.

Florez, true heir of the earldom of Flanders, but ignorant of his rights and living as a rich merchant at Bruges, loves Bertha, who is heiress of Brabant, but has been stolen away and placed with the burgomaster of Bruges and is equally ignorant of her rights. Gerrard, father of Florez, who has been driven from Flanders, has concealed himself among the beggars near Bruges, is their king, and watches over the interests of Florez. Wolfort, the usurper, proposes to claim Brabant by marrying Bertha and restoring her inheritance. He sends Hubert, one of his nobles, who is in love with Jacqueline, Gerrard's daughter, to carry out his plans. Hubert, however, joins Jacqueline among the beggars, and successfully plots with Gerrard to get Wolfort into their power. The identity of Florez and Bertha is revealed and they are married.

The play has been admired for its intricate plot, and for the realistic portrayal of its 'ragged regiment' of beggars, whose dialogue is enlivened by thieves' cant. *Coleridge, in his *Table Talk* (17 Feb. 1833), declared, 'I could read the *Beggar's Bush* from morning to night. How sylvan and sunshiny it is!' *Pepys said it was the first play in which he saw women act.

'Beggar's Daughter of Bednall-Green, The' A ballad written in the reign of *Elizabeth I and included in Thomas *Percy's **Reliques*. Bessy, the fair daughter of a blind beggar, works at the inn at Romford and is courted by four suitors, a knight, a gentleman of good birth, a merchant of

London, and the innkeeper's son. They all withdraw their suit on being referred by her to her father, except the knight. The old beggar gives her £3,000 as dowry, two pounds for every one the knight puts down. It emerges that the beggar is Henry, son of Simon de Montfort, who has assumed the disguise of a beggar for safety. The story forms the basis of Henry *Chettle and John *Day's *The Blind-Beggar of Bednal-Green* (*c.*1600; printed 1659). Robert *Dodsley wrote a ballad opera, *The Blind Beggar of Bethnal Green*, and J. S. *Knowles also wrote a comedy on the subject.

Beggar's Opera, The A *ballad opera by *John Gay, produced with enormous success in 1728. The play arose out of Jonathan *Swift's suggestion for 'a Newgate pastoral, among the whores and thieves there'. The plot is founded in part on the career of the thief-taker Jonathan Wild (bap. 1683, d. 1725), represented by the businessman Peachum, whose daughter Polly marries a gallant but promiscuous highwayman, Macheath; Peachum has him imprisoned in Newgate in order to claim reward money. Newgate is run by Peachum's partner in crime Lockit; Macheath persuades Lockit's daughter Lucy, another 'wife', to help him escape. Lucy attempts to poison Polly, but the squabble (alluding to a feud between operatic sopranos) ends when Macheath is recaptured. In the condemned hold, he drinks and sings to bolster his courage, but announces himself ready for execution when several more 'wives' turn up. He is saved by a comically arbitrary reprieve. The humour of the play consists in giving recognizably 'low' characters from the criminal world the 'high' language and self-regard of Italian opera and fashionable society; this functions satirically to suggest that politicians like Sir Robert Walpole (1676–1745) resemble criminal gangs. Bertolt *Brecht and Kurt *Weill's *The Threepenny Opera* (1928) is a reworking of Gay's play.

BEHAN, Brendan (1923–64) Irish playwright, poet, songwriter, and memoirist, born into a working-class Republican family in Dublin. He was arrested in Liverpool in 1939 for IRA activities, and his subsequent period of incarceration is described in *Borstal Boy* (1958). His best-known plays are the anti-capital punishment *The Quare Fellow* (1954), and *The Hostage* (1958), a sprawling tragicomedy about a British soldier kidnapped and held hostage in a Dublin brothel, which Behan spun with the help of Joan *Littlewood out of his sparer original play in Irish, *An Giall*.

BEHN, Aphra (1640–89) Playwright and novelist, probably the daughter of a barber in Wye, near Canterbury. Her mother was nurse to the wealthy Culpeper family who may have brought up Aphra as a foster-child. In 1663 she visited a British sugar plantation in Surinam with members of her family. On her return to England the following year she married Johan Behn, a city merchant probably of Dutch descent, but the marriage was short-lived. She was employed in 1666 by Charles II as a spy in Antwerp in the Dutch war, but payment was not forthcoming and she was imprisoned for debt. On her release she began to write for her living. Her first play, *The Forced Marriage* (1670), was followed by some fourteen others, including her most popular, *The Rover* (in two parts, 1677–81), dealing with the adventures in Naples and Madrid of a band of English Cavaliers during the exile of Charles II; its hero, the libertine Willmore, was said to be based on *Rochester, though another model may have been her lover John Hoyle, lawyer and son of the regicide Thomas Hoyle. *The City Heiress* (1682) is a characteristic satiric comedy of London life and, like Thomas *Otway's **Venice Preserved*, contains a caricature of the first earl of *Shaftesbury. *The Lucky Chance* (1686) explores one of her favourite themes, the ill consequences of arranged marriage. Her friends included the second duke of *Buckingham, George *Etherege, John *Dryden, and Thomas Otway, and she was a staunch defender of the Stuart cause. She also wrote poems and novels and edited a *Miscellany* (1685). Her best-remembered work is **Oroonoko, or The History of the Royal Slave* (*c.*1688), based on her visit to Surinam. Perhaps the earliest English philosophical novel, it deplores the slave trade and Christian hypocrisy, holding up for admiration the nobility and honour of its African hero. Despite her success she had to contend with accusations of plagiarism and lewdness, attracted in her view by her sex. But Virginia Woolf in *A *Room of one's Own* (1928) acclaimed her as the first English woman to earn her living by writing, 'with all the plebeian virtues of humour, vitality and courage'. With the rise of women's studies her reputation has reached unprecedented heights. She was buried, 'scandalously but rather appropriately' in Woolf's view, in Westminster Abbey. See M. *Duffy, *The Passionate Shepherdess* (1977); Janet Todd, *The Secret Life of Aphra Behn* (1997).

Belgravia An illustrated monthly edited by Mary Elizabeth *Braddon, which ran from 1866 to 1899, and published work by many well-known writers, including Thomas *Hardy, Wilkie *Collins, Bret *Harte, and *Ouida.
See GHOST STORIES.

Belial Adapted from a Hebrew word probably meaning 'wickedness', but in the Authorized Version of the *Bible it is retained untranslated, as a proper name (e. g. Deut. 13: 13, 1 Sam. 2: 12, 2 Cor. 6: 15), often in the phrase 'sons (or children) of Belial'. It has thus come to mean the spirit of evil personified, and is used from early times as a name for *Satan or one of the fiends, and by Milton (**Paradise Lost*, I. 490) as the name of one of the fallen angels. The phrase 'sons of Belial' was a republican term of odium for *Cavaliers in the English Revolution: Milton evokes them in the same passage (I. 501–2).

Believe as You List A tragedy by Philip *Massinger, acted 1631, not published until 1849. The original play was banned because it dealt with recent Spanish and Portuguese history. Massinger ingeniously transferred the story back to the safer days of the Roman Empire.

Antiochus, king of lower Asia, returns years after his defeat and supposed death at the hands of the Romans. In his fight for recognition he is constantly opposed by the ruthless and indefatigable Roman envoy Flaminius. The Carthaginian Senate is afraid to back him, and Prusias, king of Bithynia, who at first shelters and encourages him, is intimidated into changing his mind. Antiochus, imprisoned and humiliated, refuses to deny his own identity, and is executed. The play is a fine study of the recurring conflict between nationalism and imperialism.

A manuscript of the play in Massinger's own hand survives, extensively worked over by the book-keeper of the King's Men to prepare it for performance. The play was acted by the Royal Shakespeare Company in 2005 as *Believe What You Will*.

BELL, Clive (1881–1964) Art critic, educated at Cambridge where he came under the influence of the philosopher G. E. Moore (1873–1958) and met members of what was to be the *Bloomsbury Group. In 1907 he married Vanessa Stephen (*see* BELL, VANESSA). In 1910 he met Roger *Fry, whose views contributed to his own theory of 'Significant Form', outlined in *Art* (1914), which held that form, independent of content, was the most important element in a work of art. With Fry, he was a champion of the *Post-Impressionists. In *Civilization* (1928) he argued (with provocative and ironical undertones) that civilization, in itself artificial and characterized by tolerance, discrimination, reason, and humour, depended on the existence of a (not necessarily hereditary) leisured elite. His other works include *Old Friends: Personal Recollections* (1956). See Richard Shone, *Bloomsbury Portraits* (1993).

BELL, Currer, Ellis, and **Acton** Pseudonyms of Charlotte, Emily, and Anne *Brontë.

BELL, Gertrude (1868–1926) Travel writer, born in County Durham, and educated at Lady Margaret Hall, Oxford. After a period spent travelling and mountaineering, in which she made several first ascents in the Alps, she conducted archaeological research in the Middle East between 1905 and 1914. From 1915 she worked for British military intelligence in the region. Appointed oriental secretary to the British high commissioner in Iraq in 1917, she played an important role in the creation of an independent Iraqi state. The author of numerous archaeological studies and political reports, she enjoyed popular success with works such as *Safar Nameh: Persian Pictures* (1894), *The Desert and the Sown* (1907), and *Amurath to Amurath* (1911). In these, and in her *Letters* (1927) and diaries—largely quoted in *Gertrude Bell: From her Personal Papers*, ed. Elizabeth Burgoyne (1958 and 1961)—she vividly conveyed Middle Eastern landscapes and personalities. An accomplished linguist in Arabic and Persian, she also published a translation of *Hāfiz. See H. V. F. Winstone, *Gertrude Bell* (1978; rev. edn 1993).

BELL, Quentin (1910–96) Artist, art historian and biographer, son of Clive and Vanessa *Bell and nephew of Virginia *Woolf. He wrote a highly praised biography of Virginia Woolf (2 vols, 1972). He also wrote a memoir, *Bloomsbury Recalled* (1996), which was less about himself than his parents and friends.

BELL, Vanessa (1879–1961) Née Stephen, painter, and elder sister of Virginia *Woolf. She married Clive *Bell in 1907 with whom she had two sons, Julian and Quentin. She had an open marriage and a number of affairs including one with Roger *Fry and another with the painter Duncan Grant (1885–1978) by whom she had a daughter, Angelica. From 1914, she, Grant, and Grant's homosexual lover David *Garnett shared a farmhouse, Charleston, near Firle, Sussex. As a central figure in the *Bloomsbury Group, she painted portraits of a number of the members including Virginia Woolf and designed dust-jackets for the Hogarth Press editions of Woolf's novels. Several of Woolf's female fictional characters show the influence of Bell, notably Katharine Hilbery in *Night and Day* (1919) and Lily Briscoe in *To the Lighthouse* (1927).

Bellamira A comedy by Sir Charles *Sedley, produced 1687. Founded on *Terence's *Eunuchus*, it is rough but lively. Dangerfield, a braggart and a bully, whose cowardice is exposed in an adventure similar to that of *Falstaff at Gadshill, is an amusing character.

BELLAMY, Edward (1850–98) American novelist and political theorist, born in Massachusetts, whose fame rests upon his popular *utopian novel *Looking Backward: 2000–1887* (1888). Its hero, Julian West, a young Bostonian, falls into a hypnotic sleep in 1887 and wakes in the year 2000 to find great social changes. Squalor and injustice have disappeared, private capitalism has been replaced by public, and everyone works for and is a member of the state. The moral, social, and cultural benefits of the new system are everywhere apparent. This work had an immense vogue; a Nationalist Party was formed to advocate its principles, and Bellamy lectured widely and wrote other works to further his views like *Equality* (1897). He was widely read in Europe, and imitated by, among others, H. G. *Wells.

'Belle Dame sans Merci, La' *See* 'LA BELLE DAME SANS MERCI'.

BELLENDEN, John (John Ballantyne) (*fl.* 1533–48) Scottish clergyman and poet, educated at the universities of St Andrews and Paris, who translated *Boece's *Historia Gentis Scotorum* and the first five books of *Livy's *History of Rome* into Scots prose.

Bellerophon In Greek myth the heroic tamer of the winged horse Pegasus. His feats included killing the monster Chimera. He was thrown down from his mount because of his attempt to reach Olympus and became a blind wanderer on earth. Both Bellerophon and Pegasus, whose hoof struck the fount of Hippocrene from Mount Helicon, sacred to the *Muses, became associated with poetic ambition. John

*Milton as narrator of *Paradise Lost* contrasts himself with Bellerophon (VII. 1–20).

Belle's Stratagem, The Comedy by Hannah *Cowley, produced in 1780. Doricourt returns from travelling to marry Letitia Hardy, in accordance with a childhood betrothal arranged by their parents, but finds her lacking in animation. She falls in love with him at once, and wins him by first assuming the manners of a country hoyden, and then dazzling him with her sprightliness at a masquerade, successfully proving that she '*can* be anything' to please him.

BELLI, Giuseppe Gioachino (1791–1863) Italian poet, whose vernacular Roman sonnets (*I sonetti*, ed. G. Vigolo, 1952) represent the outlook and customs of the Roman people. They were written between 1827 and 1849, but because of their blasphemous and erotic satire he kept them secret and seems to have tried to suppress them after the revolutionary threat of 1848–9. His dramatic use of sonnet form allows him to attribute forbidden thoughts to his speakers. In more than 2,000 sonnets he presents a *comédie humaine* that embraces the Bible, Roman history, ancient and modern, and the daily lives of characters ranging from popes to prostitutes and ghetto Jews. For the sounds of 'Romanesque' he devised his own spelling, yet he is not a 'dialect' poet: his idiom is his own, using all the resources of literary Italian, as well as popular speech, to explore an extreme range of poetic registers. He also wrote some 45,000 verses in academic Italian, of little poetic value. First described in English by Frances *Trollope, various of his works have been translated by Robert *Garioch, by Harold Norse, and by Anthony *Burgess.

Bell Jar, The A novel by Sylvia *Plath, published 1963 under the pseudonym of Victoria Lucas, and under her own name in 1966. Partly autobiographical, it describes how the narrator, Esther Greenwood, suffers a breakdown, undergoes electroconvulsive therapy, attempts suicide, and finally emerges from her therapy. The novel is written in a taut, controlled, colloquial yet poetic prose, and takes an ironic view of social norms of success.

BELLOC, Hilaire (1870–1953) Poet, critic, historian, novelist, travel writer, and Catholic apologist, born in France but educated at J. H. *Newman's Oratory School in Birmingham and at Balliol College, Oxford. His mother was Elizabeth Rayner ('Bessie') Parkes (1829–1925), feminist author and activist. For much of his life, Belloc lived in Sussex. From 1906 to 1909, and again in 1910, he was Liberal MP for South Salford. His first publications were, in 1896, *The Bad Child's Book of Beasts* and *Verses and Sonnets*; other books of verse included *Cautionary Tales* (1907) and *Sonnets and Verse* (1923). His witty and irreverent verses for children are fondly remembered, but poems such as 'Ha'nacker Mill', 'The South Country', and 'Tarantella' are also well known. A prolific and versatile writer, he was literary editor of the *Morning Post* from 1906 to 1910, and founded *The Eye-Witness*, which became *The New Witness*. His books attacking and satirizing Edwardian society (some with G. K. *Chesterton) include *Pongo and the Bull* (1910) and *The Servile State* (1912). His many works propounding Catholicism include *Europe and the Faith* (1920). He also wrote biographies such as *Danton* (1899), *Marie Antoinette* (1909), and *Charles II* (1939), and history books, including *The French Revolution* (1911) and a substantial *A History of England*, which appeared in the same year as *The Cruise of the 'Nona'* (1925), probably the most intimate of his books. His most successful book of travel, *The Path to Rome* (1902), which was published with his own sketches and illustrations, is an account of a journey which he undertook, largely on foot, from the valley of the Moselle to Rome, and it is interspersed with anecdotes, reflections, and dialogues between 'Lector' and 'Auctor'. *The Four Men: A Farrago* (1912), set in his beloved Sussex, also describes a walk. Of the novels, *Mr Clutterbuck's Election* (1908), *The Green Overcoat* (1912), and *Belinda* (1928) are among the more highly regarded. *Belinda*, the author's favourite, is a brief and highly individual love story, related with romantic feeling but much irony as well. See A. N. *Wilson, *Hilaire Belloc* (1984); Joseph Pearce, *Old Thunder* (2002).

BELLOW, Saul (1915–2005) American novelist, born in Canada of Russian-Jewish parents, who moved to Chicago, where he attended the University of Chicago (he later transferred to Northwestern University). Chicago is evoked in many of his works, including his first short novel *Dangling Man* (1944). *The Adventures of Augie March* (1953) also opens in Chicago and provides a lengthy, episodic, first-person account of Augie's progress from boyhood, moving to Mexico, then Paris. *Henderson the Rain King* (1959), designed on a grand and mythic scale, records American millionaire Gene Henderson's quest for revelation and spiritual power in Africa, where he becomes rainmaker and heir to a kingdom. *Herzog* (1964) reveals the inner life of a Jewish intellectual, Moses Herzog, driven to the verge of breakdown by his second wife's adultery with his close friend; he writes unsent letters about himself and civilization to the living and the dead. *The Dean's December* (1982) is a 'tale of two cities', Chicago and Bucharest. Bellow's last novel *Ravelstein* (2000) draws on his friendship with Allan Bloom (1930–92), portraying a professor of philosophy dying of Aids. Bellow's fiction constantly explores identity crises through reflective protagonists who meditate on the shortcomings of contemporary America. He also published a number of short story collections like *Him with his Foot in his Mouth* (1984) and *More Die of Heartbreak* (1987). *To Jerusalem and Back* (1976) is a memoir of a visit to Israel and *It All Adds up* (1994) is a collection of non-fiction pieces. Bellow also wrote a play (*The Last Analysis*, 1964), and lectured in many universities. He was awarded the *Nobel Prize for Literature in 1976. See James Atlas, *Bellow: A Biography* (2000).

Bells, The (1871) A dramatic adaptation by Leopold Lewis (1828–90) of *Le Juif polonais* by Erckmann-Chatrian (Émile Erckmann, 1822–99 and Alexandre Chatrian, 1826–90), the story of a burgomaster haunted by the consciousness of an undiscovered murder that he has committed. It provided Henry *Irving with one of his most successful parts.

Bells and Pomegranates The covering title of a series of plays and collections of shorter dramatic poems by Robert *Browning, published 1841–6, comprising *Pippa Passes* (1841), *King Victor and King Charles* (1842), *Dramatic Lyrics* (1842), *The Return of the Druses* (1843), *A *Blot in the 'Scutcheon* (1843), *Colombe's Birthday* (1844), **Dramatic Romances and Lyrics* (1845), and **Luria and A Soul's Tragedy* (1846). The title indicated 'an alternation, or mixture, of music with discoursing, sound with sense, poetry with thought; which looks too ambitious, thus expressed, so the symbol was preferred'. The 'symbol' derives from the Bible (Exod. 28: 33–4, where it relates to the ornamentation and embroidery of the high priest's robe). The separate numbers were bound together and sold as a single volume after 1846.

Beloved A novel by Toni *Morrison (1987), set in 1873 in America. The narrative technique is deliberately non-linear and complex, the language richly poetic and suffused with biblical references. Sethe, a former slave, lives with her daughter Denver and the ghost of her dead baby girl. The book opens with the unexpected arrival of Paul D., one of the five men with whom Sethe had formerly been enslaved at Sweet Home, a Kentucky farm. An uncanny girl called Beloved comes to live with them who proves to be an incarnation of the daughter Sethe had murdered, in desperation, in order to prevent her being enslaved. The title word transcends its character, and becomes a symbol for all dead and suffering slaves. The book is dedicated to 'Sixty Million and more'. *See* SLAVERY.

Belphoebe In Edmund *Spenser's **Faerie Queene*, the chaste huntress, daughter of the nymph Chrysogone and twin sister of *Amoret; she partly symbolizes *Elizabeth I. Belphoebe puts *Braggadochio to flight (II. iii), finds herbs to heal the wounded *Timias (III. v), and rescues Amoret from Corflambo (IV. vii).

Belshazzar's feast The feast made by Belshazzar, the son of Nebuchadnezzar and the last king of *Babylon, at which his doom was foretold by a hand writing on the wall, as described in the Old Testament Book of *Daniel (ch. 5). Babylon fell to the Persians in 539 BC. Belshazzar is the subject of a drama by Henry Hart *Milman, Robert *Landor's *The Impious Feast*, a poem by Lord *Byron, and oratorios by *Handel and William *Walton.

Belton Estate, The A novel by Anthony *Trollope, published 1866. Will Belton unexpectedly becomes the heir to an entailed estate in Somerset. On his first visit to Belton Castle he falls in love with the squire's daughter, Clara Amedroz, only to find that Clara has already promised herself to a lukewarm cousin, Captain Aylmer MP. When her father dies Clara, feeling bound by her engagement, goes to live for a trial period at Aylmer Park. But the family—particularly the ferociously condescending Lady Aylmer—find neither Clara's independence of mind nor her want of fortune to their liking. This inevitably leads to a quarrel with Captain Aylmer and, when Will Belton renews his suit, Clara is only too happy to accept the man to whom she has, all along, been attracted. The novel is characteristic of Trollope's many studies of courtship, with its emphasis on inheritance, divided loyalties, and restrictive social expectations.

BELY, Andrei (Boris Nikolaevich Bugaev) (1880–1934) Russian novelist, poet, and literary theorist, born in Moscow, who became a key figure in the Russian *symbolist movement. In 1904 he met Aleksandr *Blok, with whom he was to have a long 'inimical friendship', and for whose wife he conceived a complex passion. His reputation was established with three books of poetry, *Gold in Azure* (1904), *Ashes* (1909), and *The Urn* (1909), the last of which was inspired by his love for Liubov Blok. In 1912 he met Rudolf Steiner (1861–1925) and became a lifelong convert to anthroposophy, Steiner's individualistic and spiritualistic philosophy. After the revolution he engaged in teaching both literature and anthroposophy. During this period Bely wrote *Kotik Letaev* (serialized 1917–18; trans. Gerald Janecek, 1971), a fictionalized account of his consciousness as a young child, memorably described by Evgenii *Zamiatin as the only anthroposophical novel in existence. Bely's most important novel is *Petersburg* (1913–16), written in a rhythmical prose that at times approximates the rhythms of poetry. In the hallucinatory setting of St Petersburg during the 1905 Revolution a group of radicals attempt the assassination of a senator. *Petersburg* is overwhelmingly concerned with questions of identity and consciousness. The appearance of its definitive version the same year as Joyce's **Ulysses* is a remarkable coincidence, and their shared interest in neologism, leitmotif, mythology, parody, and experiment has been much noted. Its reputation as an inaccessible masterpiece was eventually modified by the appearance of an excellent translation (by Robert Maguire and John Malmstad, 1978). Bely's four-part memoirs, *Diary of an Eccentric* (1922), *Reminiscences of Blok* (1923), *On the Border of Two Centuries* (1930), and *Between Two Revolutions* (1934), are widely regarded as Russia's finest autobiography. See Konstantin Mochulsky, *Andrei Bely: His Life and Works* (1977).

BEMBO, Pietro (1470–1547) Italian humanist, poet, linguistic theorist, and historiographer of Venice, who became a cardinal (1539), bishop of Gubbio (1541) and Bergamo (1544). He wrote prose and verse in Latin and Italian, his Italian being studiously modelled on Petrarchan Tuscan, as his Latin was on the Ciceronian. He was a devoted admirer of Lucrezia *Borgia, to whom he dedicated his dialogue on love, *Gli Asolani* (1505); this work provided the title of Robert *Browning's last volume of poems, **Asolando* (Asolo is a small town north of Venice). *Gli Asolani*, modelled on *Plato's *Symposium*, also provided *Castiglione with the philosophical basis for his *Courtier* (in Bk IV of which Bembo himself figures prominently), and was useful to Edmund *Spenser in composing his *Fowre Hymnes*.

BENEDICT BISCOP, St (*c*.628–689) A thegn (a tenant by military service) of Oswiu, king of Northumbria, who after making two pilgrimages to Rome retired to the Isle of Lérins, where he adopted the monastic life. After two years he again went to Rome and was directed by the pope, Vitalian, to accompany Theodore of Tarsus from Rome to Canterbury. He was then appointed abbot of St Peter's, Canterbury (669), resigning the dignity two years later to visit Rome once more. During this journey he collected and brought back many volumes and relics. On his return he founded (674) the monastery of St Peter at the mouth of the river Wear, importing workmen to build a church of stone and to glaze the windows. After revisiting Rome, he founded the sister monastery of St Paul at Jarrow. He was buried at Wearmouth, having left directions for the careful preservation of his library. He is regarded as one of the originators of the artistic and literary development of Northumbria in the next century, celebrated by *Bede in his *Lives of the Abbots*.

BENET, Stephen Vincent (1898–1943) American poet, born in Pennsylvania and educated at Yale University. He is best known for his narrative poem of the Civil War, *John Brown's Body* (1928), and for some of the poems in *Ballads and Poems* (1931), including the popular 'American Names', with its resounding last line, 'Bury my heart at Wounded Knee'. He also wrote what he called 'bread-and-butter' novels and short stories, and worked as a screenwriter in Hollywood for some time. His folk opera *The Devil and Daniel Webster*, performed in 1939, for which he wrote the libretto, was based on his own short story (1937), and presents the successful appeal of the legendary *Webster against the devil's claim to the soul of New Hampshire farmer Jabez Stone.

BENFORD, Gregory (1941–) Born in Mobile, Alabama; author and physics professor whose profession illuminates his writing. The 'Galactic Centre' series (1977–95) ends in a distant future. In contrast *Timescape* (1980) and *Cosm* (1998) combine *Stapledon-like vision with perceptive descriptions of working scientists.

Ben-Hur: A Tale of the Christ A historical novel, published 1880, about the early days of Christianity by Lew (Lewis) Wallace (1827–1905), previously a general in the American Civil War. Already a successful stage *adaptation by 1900, it was first filmed in 1907, then as a major spectacle by MGM in 1925, opulently remade in 1959.

'Benito Cereno' (1856) A short story by Herman *Melville. A Gothic tale of white masters and implacable black revenge, it is set off the coast of Peru in 1799, where the amiable, condescendingly racist Yankee Captain Delano goes to the aid of a drifting slave ship. Delano suspects piracy and in fact the slaves have rebelled, enslaving the Spanish captain Don Benito Cereno and slaughtering their master Don Aranda, whose skeleton has been turned into a ghoulish figurehead with the slogan 'Follow Your Leader'. Cereno escapes with Delano, only to die later, and the recaptured slaves are executed, unrepentant. 'Benito Cereno' was dramatized by Robert *Lowell in 1967.

BENJAMIN, Walter (1892–1940) German critic and essayist, born in Berlin of a Jewish family, and educated in Berlin, Freiburg, Munich, and Bern. After failing to gain academic employment, he worked as a literary journalist, translator, and radio scriptwriter. Influenced by Marxist ideas, he became a friend of Bertolt *Brecht, whose dramatic methods he defended. Upon Hitler's seizure of power in 1933 he went into exile in Paris, where he undertook a study of Charles *Baudelaire and the urban experience. The invasion of France in 1940 led him to seek refuge in the USA, but on attempting to enter neutral Spain he was stopped at the Spanish border, where he took his own life. Despite unusual elements of Jewish mysticism, his posthumously published essays on literature, criticism, modern culture, and the philosophy of history, in part edited by Theodor *Adorno, have exercised extensive influence on *Marxist cultural and literary theory in the English- as well as German-speaking world. The essay on 'The Work of Art in the Age of Mechanical Reproduction', along with others in the collection *Illuminationen* (1955: *Illuminations*, 1968, ed. Hannah *Arendt), and *Versuche über Brecht* (1966: *Understanding Brecht*, 1973), have been widely discussed. Portions of his unfinished Paris project have been translated as *Charles Baudelaire: A Lyric Poet in the Era of High Capitalism* (1973).

BENLOWES, Edward (?1602–76) Poet, heir to a wealthy Catholic family, though he became a Protestant. He was a friend of Francis *Quarles and Phineas *Fletcher in Oxford. His principal work was *Theophila, or Love's Sacrifice* (1652), in thirteen cantos, celebrating the epic progress of the soul in learned, obscure, and occasionally grotesque conceits and language; it was praised by Sir William *D'Avenant but ridiculed by the poet Samuel *Butler ('Hudibras', 1613–80), Alexander *Pope, and William *Warburton. A critical biography by H. Jenkins appeared in 1952.

BENNETT, Alan (1934–) Dramatist and actor, born in Yorkshire and educated at Leeds Modern School and Exeter College, Oxford. He made his name with the satirical review *Beyond the Fringe* (1960; pub. 1963, with Jonathan Miller and others), and his other works, most of which are satirical comedies, include *Forty Years On* (1968), set in a public school, which has much fun at the expense of the *Bloomsbury Group, T. E. *Lawrence, and other fashionable cultural figures; *Getting on* (1971); and *Habeas Corpus* (1973). A more sombre work, *The Old Country* (1977), deals with the theme of exile through the life of an English spy in the Soviet Union; one of his many television plays, *An Englishman Abroad* (1983), deals with the same subject through a poignant evocation of Guy Burgess's real-life encounter in Moscow with the actress Coral Browne. Other works include *The Insurance Man* (1986); *Single Spies* (1988); *A Question of Attribution* (staged 1988, televised 1991), a brilliant treatment of the treachery of the spy and art historian Sir Anthony Blunt; *The Madness of George III* (1991); and *Talking Heads*, a series of six monologues originally written for television (1987). *Writing Home* (1994) is a collection of journal entries, reminiscences, and reviews, including his celebrated piece 'The Lady in the Van', on a female tramp who camped out in his garden. In 2004, he produced his most successful play, *The History Boys* (like *The Madness of George III* later made into a film) for the *National Theatre, a work that looks more seriously, though even more comically, at questions of historical veracity and education in a conscious recall of his first play, *Forty Years On*. *Untold Stories* (2005) is an autobiographical volume written after his diagnosis with cancer.

BENNETT, Arnold (1867–1931) Novelist, born in Burslem, Staffordshire, the son of a self-educated solicitor. He was destined to follow in his father's footsteps, but at the age of 21 he went to London where he worked as a legal clerk before establishing himself as a writer. His first stories were published in the popular weekly magazine *Tit Bits* (1890) and the **Yellow Book* (1895), and the first of his many novels, *A Man from the North*, appeared in 1898. In 1893 he became assistant editor and subsequently editor of the periodical *Woman*, launching himself on a career of remarkable versatility. In 1902 he moved to France, returning to England to settle permanently in 1912 with his French wife Marguerite Soulie, from whom he separated in 1921. In 1926, at the suggestion of his friend Max Beaverbrook (1879–1964), he began an influential and highly paid weekly article on books for the *Evening Standard* which continued until his death from typhoid. He had a lifelong passion for the theatre and wrote several successful plays, notably *Milestones* (1912, with the dramatist and novelist Edward Knoblock (1874–1945)), but his fame rests chiefly on his novels and short stories, the best known of which were set in the Potteries of his youth, a region he recreated as the 'Five Towns'. *Anna of the Five Towns* (1902), the story of a miser's daughter, shows clearly the influence of the French realists whom he much admired. *The Old Wives' Tale* (1908) was followed by the Clayhanger series (*Clayhanger*, 1910; *Hilda Lessways*, 1911; *These Twain*, 1916; *The Roll Call*, 1918). The novels portray the Five Towns with an ironic but affectionate detachment, describing provincial life and culture in documentary detail, and creating many memorable characters—Darius Clayhanger, the dictatorial printer who started work aged 7 in a pot-bank, the monstrous but good-hearted Auntie Hamps, Edwin Clayhanger, frustrated architect, and Hilda Lessways, the independent and strong-willed young woman who marries Edwin. Two volumes of short stories, *The Grim Smile of the Five Towns* (1907) and *The Matador of the Five Towns* (1912), are set in the same region, as are several minor novels. Bennett shows a concern for obscure and ordinary lives which also manifests itself in the best novel of his later period, *Riceyman Steps* (1923), the story of a miserly second-hand bookseller. But he also wrote many entertaining lighter works, displaying a love of luxury and fantasy, among them *The Grand Babylon Hotel* (1902), *The Card* (1911), and *Mr Prohack* (1922). His *Journal*, begun in 1896, modelled partly on that of the *Goncourt brothers, was published in 1932–3, and offers a striking portrait both of the period and of his own highly disciplined working life. Bennett's letters, ed. James Hepburn, were published in four volumes (1966–86). See Margaret *Drabble, *Arnold Bennett: A Biography* (1974).

BENOÎT DE SAINTE-MAURE A 12th-century trouvère, born probably at Sainte-Maure in Touraine and patronized by Henry II of England, for whom he composed a verse history of the dukes of Normandy. His best-known work is the *Roman de Troie*, based on the writings of *Dares Phrygius and *Dictys Cretensis. The *Roman* was translated into Latin prose by *Guido delle Colonne, and thus served as a source on which many subsequent writers drew, including *Boccaccio, followed by *Chaucer, who is believed to have made considerable direct use of Benoît. His works have been edited by L. Constance (6 vols, 1904–12).

BENSON, A. C. (Arthur Christopher) (1862–1925) author, eldest surviving son of E. W. Benson (1829–96), archbishop of Canterbury, and brother of R. H. and E. F. *Benson. He was educated at Eton College and King's College, Cambridge, and was from 1915 master of Magdalene College, Cambridge. He published many volumes of biography, family reminiscences, reflection, criticism, including *The House of Quiet: An Autobiography* (1904) and had a facility for writing public odes, typified by his 'Land of hope and glory'. From 1897 until 1925 he kept a diary, amounting to five million words; extracts were published by Percy *Lubbock in 1926, but the papers were locked away for 50 years. David Newsome makes use of them in his biography *On the Edge of Paradise: A. C. Benson, the Diarist* (1980), a work which reveals Benson's deeply depressive tendencies, and edited *Edwardian Excursions* (1981), selections from the manuscript covering 1898–1904.

BENSON, E. F. (Edward Frederic) (1867–1940) Prolific and popular novelist, brother of R. H. and A. C.*Benson. After studying at Cambridge University, he lived in Athens and London and then, from 1918, at Lamb House, Rye, once the home of Henry *James. His works include *Dodo* (1893, followed by other 'Dodo' novels) and *Queen Lucia* (1920, the first of the irresistibly catty 'Mapp and Lucia' novels), and various volumes of reminiscences, such as *As We Were* (1930) and *As We Are* (1932), which are a rich source of anecdote.

BENSON, Stella (1892–1933) Author, born in Shropshire, educated mainly at home due to ill health, with brief spells in Europe. Before and during the First World War, Benson worked for suffragist organizations and for the Charity Organization Society in London's East End. In 1918 she travelled to the United States and worked in California before leaving for

China, where in 1920 she met customs commissioner James O'Gorman Anderson, whom she married in London the following year, and with whom she was later to return to China. Their honeymoon journey by Ford across the United States is described in a book of travel pieces, *The Little World* (1925). Benson's numerous and critically neglected writings include eight novels, notably *The Far-Away Bride* (1930, published in Britain in 1931 as *Tobit Transplanted*); poetry; and the collections of short stories, *Hope against Hope* (1931) and *Christmas Formula* (1932). She published a second collection of travel essays, *Worlds within Worlds*, in 1928. Her 42 volumes of diaries were edited by Marlene B. Davis for microfilm publication by Adam Matthew in 2005.

BENTHAM, Jeremy (1748–1832) Social philosopher, educated at Westminster School and the Queen's College, Oxford. Called to the bar at Lincoln's Inn, he set himself to produce a simple, complete, and equitable legal system, rather than practise as a barrister. His ethical theory of Utility was propounded in *A Fragment on Government* (1776) and *An Introduction to the Principles of Morals and Legislation* (1789). 'It is the greatest happiness of the greatest number that is the measure of right and wrong.' When the pleasures and pains resulting from any act to all the members of the community affected have been measured, the moral quality of an act can be determined. Bentham believed it possible that the value of pains and pleasures as motives of action could be minutely calculated, giving scientific accuracy to legislation. Law and education must, by appropriate rewards and sanctions, induce the naturally self-interested individual to subordinate his own happiness to that of the community.

Chrestomathia, a series of papers on 'useful education', appeared in 1816. In 1823, with the assistance of James *Mill, Bentham founded the **Westminster Review*, the organ of the philosophical radicals, which lasted until 1914. John Stuart *Mill, in his essay 'Bentham' in this same review (1838), gives an interesting summary of Bentham's notorious hostility to imaginative literature, especially poetry. Bentham's democratic views are expressed in his extensive *Constitutional Code* (1830). He left his body to be dissected and his 'auto-icon', consisting of his skeleton dressed in his clothes, is on display at University College London.

BENTLEY, E. C. (Edmund Clerihew) (1875–1956) Son of a civil servant, born in Shepherd's Bush, London and educated at St Paul's (where began his lasting friendship with G. K. *Chesterton) and Merton College, Oxford. He studied law but made his living as a columnist on the **Daily News* and **Daily Telegraph*. As a schoolboy he invented the comical verse form named after him as the *clerihew, later exhibiting examples in *Biography for Beginners* (1905, illustrated by Chesterton), *More Biography* (1929), and *Baseless Biography* (1939), collected in *Clerihews Complete* (1951). His celebrated *detective novel *Trent's Last Case* (1913), intended as a spoof, heralded with its sprightly ingenuity the 'Golden Age' of that genre. His son Nicolas became a noted illustrator of books. See his memoir *Those Days* (1940).

BENTLEY, Phyllis *See* REGIONAL NOVEL.

BENTLEY, Richard (1662–1742) Classical scholar, born at Oulton in Yorkshire, educated at St John's College, Cambridge, and appointed by Edward Stillingfleet (1635–99) as tutor to his son, 1683–9. He made his reputation with his *Letter to Mill* (1691), a critical letter in Latin on the Greek dramatists, and the following year delivered the first *Boyle Lectures on *The Folly and Unreasonableness of Atheism*, checking his science with Isaac *Newton. As keeper of the king's libraries, he engaged during 1697–9 in a famous controversy, during which he proved the **Epistles of Phalaris* to be spurious and queried the antiquity of *Aesop's fables. In 1699 he was appointed master of Trinity College, Cambridge, but his mastership was a succession of quarrels, scandals, and litigation. His most controversial editorial work was a bold revision of the text of *Horace (1711); he proposed but did not complete editions of the New Testament and *Homer. Bentley's arbitrary revision of **Paradise Lost*, published in 1732 with over 800 suggested emendations, was based on the unlikely premiss that Milton had been ill served by an incompetent or malign amanuensis. He was caricatured in *The *Dunciad* (IV. 201 ff.) and elsewhere. See J. H. Monk, *The Life of Richard Bentley, D.D.* (1833).

BENTLEY, Richard (1794–1871) Publisher. He learned the printing and publishing trades with his uncle John *Nichols, and began in business on his own in 1819. He included Thomas *Moore, both *Disraelis, and *Dickens among his authors. In 1830 he joined with Henry *Colburn to found the firm of Colburn and Bentley, which in 1837 established **Bentley's Miscellany*, a magazine, first edited by Dickens, which was immensely popular. A cheap series of 'Standard Novels' in 127 volumes was also very successful. Bentley was succeeded in the business by his son George Bentley (1825–95), who introduced many novelists to the public, including Wilkie *Collins and Mrs Henry (Ellen) *Wood.

Bentley's Miscellany (1837–69) A very successful periodical consisting of essays, stories, and poems, but mainly of fiction, begun by Richard *Bentley. Charles *Dickens was the first editor, and **Oliver Twist* appeared in its pages in 1837–8. John Hamilton *Reynolds, Theodore *Hook, William *Maginn, Harrison *Ainsworth, and later W. M. *Thackeray and Henry Wadsworth *Longfellow were among its contributors. George *Cruikshank and John *Leech provided lively illustrations. In its early heyday the *Miscellany* covered, with biography or critical articles, all the important writers of the early 19th century.

Beowulf An Old English poem of 3,182 lines, surviving in a 10th-century manuscript. The poem's date is unknown. The young Beowulf, a Geatish hero, fights and kills Grendel, a monster who has attacked Heorot, the hall of the Danish king, Hrothgar. He then kills Grendel's mother, who has come to avenge her son. Fifty years later, when Beowulf has for a long time been king of the Geats, he fights a dragon which has attacked his people. He and the dragon are mortally wounded. The historical period of the poem's events can be dated in the 6th century, but much of the material of the poem is legendary and paralleled in Norse, Old English, and German literatures. A thread of tactful Christian commentary runs through the poem, distancing its readership from the heroic deeds and cultural assumptions of its characters even as it celebrates them. W. P. Ker (1855–1923) (in *Epic and Romance*, 1896) regarded the historical allusions as weighty and important. This view was most famously opposed by J. R. R. *Tolkien in 'The Monsters and the Critics' (1936), where he argued that it was the superhuman opposition of the heathen monsters that elevated the poem to heroic stature, and that all other allusions were related directly to the transient grandeur of Beowulf's life and battles. Both critical approaches are important, the monster plots showing the poet's control of pace and perspective, the skilful synthesis of Germanic myth and history marked by his keen awareness of its connections with Anglo-Saxon culture. The poem is also remarkable for its resourceful diction. *Beowulf* is the most important poem in Old English and it is the first major poem in a European vernacular. See the editions by F. Klaeber (1922, etc.) and George Jack (1994). Seamus *Heaney published a new translation in 1999. An animated film, *Beowulf*, loosely based on the poem, appeared in 2007.

Beppo: A Venetian Story A poem in **ottava rima* by Lord *Byron, published in 1818, in which the poet began to find the voice and style of **Don Juan*, a turning point in his career. Digressive, witty, and informal, it tells with great zest and style the story of a Venetian carnival, at which a lady's husband, Beppo, who has been absent for many years, returns in Turkish garb, and confronts her and her lover. Full reconciliation follows, in what the narrator implies is the civilized Venetian manner. Byron's praise of Italy's climate and women is offset by his lengthy satirical asides about English rain and English misses.

BÉRANGER, Pierre-Jean de (1780–1857) French poet and songwriter. He published a series of *Chansons* between 1815 and 1833, and from the 1830s to the end of the century his poetry was widely translated both in Britain and the USA. Many of his popular songs in the post-Napoleonic period display his sympathy for the oppressed and his hostility to the restored Bourbon monarchy. W. M. *Thackeray wrote four 'Imitations of Béranger', including a version of the anti-Napoleonic 'Le Roi d'Yvetot', and Robert Louis *Stevenson devoted a sympathetic entry to him in the **Encyclopaedia Britannica*.

BERENSON, Bernard (1865–1959) Art historian, connoisseur, and philosopher, born in Lithuania and educated in America. In 1887 he settled in Europe. In 1894 he published *The Venetian Painters of the Renaissance with an Index to their Works* followed by *The Central Italian Painters of the Renaissance* (1897), though it is *The Drawings of the Florentine Painters* (1903) that is considered his most thoroughly researched work. In *Italian Painters of the Renaissance* (first published as separate essays, 1894–1907) he developed the theory that the 'tactile values' of a work of art, that is, its ability to communicate a sense of form, stimulated in the spectator a state of increased awareness of 'life enhancement'. His ideas influenced Roger *Fry's theories about the primacy of form, which, in turn, stimulated the development of literary formalism in Britain. He built up a distinguished art collection and library at I Tatti, a large house outside Florence which was much admired by his close friend Edith *Wharton. Berenson also wrote on history, aesthetics, and politics.

BERESFORD, J. D. (1873–1947) English writer, born near Peterborough, son of a clergyman. His *scientific romances are reminiscent of H. G. *Wells, of whom he wrote an early study (1915), as speculations on social and evolutionary change. *The Hampdenshire Wonder* (1911) tells of a mutant 'superman'.

BERGER, John (1926–) Novelist and art critic, born in London and educated at the Chelsea College of Art and Central School of Art. He became well known as a broadcaster and journalist holding Marxist views, and also published several novels: *A Painter of our Time* (1958), *The Foot of Clive* (1962), *Corker's Freedom* (1964), *G* (*Booker Prize, 1972), and *To the Wedding* (1995). Works of non-fiction include *A Fortunate Man* (1967), the story of a country doctor. *Pig Earth* (1979), *Once in Europa* (stories, 1989), and *Lilac and Flag* (1991) form a trilogy. Other works include *Keeping a Rendezvous* (1992), a collection of essays and poems. One of his most influential texts has been *Ways of Seeing* (1972), which explores painting and commercial imagery in a context of cultural capitalism: it helped to popularize the concepts of Walter *Benjamin. See *Ways of Telling* (1986), a commentary by Geoff *Dyer.

BERGERAC, Cyrano *See* CYRANO DE BERGERAC.

BERGSON, Henri (1859–1941) French philosopher, professor at the Collège de France from 1900 to 1921, awarded the *Nobel Prize for Literature in 1927. His major works, vividly written and accessible to the non-specialist reader, are *Essai sur les données immédiates de la conscience* (1889: *Essay on the Immediate Data of Consciousness*), *Matière et mémoire* (1896: *Matter and Memory*), *L'Évolution créatrice* (1907: *Creative Evolution*), and *Les Deux Sources de la morale et de la religion* (1932: *The Two Sources of Morality and Religion*). In these studies Bergson defined his broad opposition to scientific materialism and positivism. Centring his enquiry on the self and its direct intuitions, he argued for the importance to a true understanding of experience of 'real duration', rather than to measured time, as a given fact of consciousness which is intuitively perceived. Consciousness is primarily the operation of memory, not mere habitual recollection but that pure memory which retains the totality of our conscious states, to be selected by the brain when necessary in order to guide spontaneous reaction in relation to events. This conviction of the primacy of inner experience was extended to the cosmic plane in the notion of the *élan vital*, or vital impulse, which Bergson conceived as directing the evolution of new forms and increasingly complex states of organization. Hence the pre-eminent value in morals and religion of what is spiritual, creative, 'open', over what is formal, fixed, 'closed'. Bergson explored the aesthetics of comedy in *Le Rire: essai sur la signification du comique* (1900: *Laughter: An Essay on the Meaning of the Comic*), where the comic is found to arise from the perception of those automatic, repetitive, or disjointed qualities that make against the spontaneity of life. Laughter is society's defence against such failure of adaptive power.

BERKELEY, George (1685–1753) Philosopher, born in Co. Kilkenny, and educated, like Jonathan *Swift, at Kilkenny school and Trinity College, Dublin. In 1712 he published controversial sermons on 'passive obedience' and a year later visited England, associating with Richard *Steele, Joseph *Addison, Alexander *Pope, John *Arbuthnot, and Swift, and contributed essays against freethinkers to the **Guardian*. His three-volume anthology *The Ladies Library* appeared in 1713 with a preface by Steele and was much reprinted. He travelled abroad for the next seven years, arriving back in the wake of the South Sea Bubble, about which he wrote a pamphlet, *An Essay towards Preventing the Ruin of Great Britain* (1721). He was appointed dean of Derry in 1724 and in 1728 went to America in connection with an abortive scheme for a missionary college in Bermuda. He was installed as bishop of Cloyne in 1734; in 1752 he retired to Oxford, where he died. His chief philosophical works are *An Essay towards a New Theory of Vision* (1709, 1710, 1732), *A Treatise Concerning the Principles of Human Knowledge* (1710, 1734), and *Three Dialogues between Hylas and Philonous* (1713, 1725, 1734). He defended his own philosophy in his dialogue *Alciphron* (1732, 1752) and *The Theory of Vision Vindicated and Explained* (1733). In 1734 he published *The Analyst*, criticizing Isaac *Newton's theory of fluxions; and in 1735–7 *The Querist*, dealing with questions of economic and social reform in Ireland. *Siris*, on the medical virtues of tar-water, appeared in 1744.

In his works on vision, Berkeley seeks to show the mind-dependence of the ideas derived from sight, and explains their 'arbitrary' though constant connection with the more primary ideas of touch by analogy with the way in which written words 'signify' speech. His philosophy is partly inspired by, and partly a reaction to, John *Locke's **Essay Concerning Human Understanding*. Only particular things exist, and since these are only a complex of sensations, if we abstract from them that of which we have perception, nothing remains. The 'support' of ideas or sensations is percipient mind. Locke's distinction between the primary and secondary qualities of bodies therefore has no validity; both are mind dependent. Samuel *Johnson famously claimed to have refuted Berkeley's idealism by kicking a large stone very hard, but Berkeley does not dispute the existence of matter so much as its status; its reality depends on perception, for the *esse* (being) of material things is *percipi* (to be perceived). We are directly aware of the existence of our own percipient minds, and the existence of other finite spirits is inferred by analogy from their effects. We believe in the existence of God because he speaks to us in the whole system of nature, through the sense-experiences produced in our minds in a regular and uniform manner. In *Alciphron*, Berkeley sees experience as functioning in the manner of a language, which to him implies a prior intelligence or design. See A. A. Luce, *The Life of George Berkeley* (1949); *The Works of George Berkeley*, ed. A. A. Luce and T. E. Jessup, 9 vols (1948–57).

BERKELEY, Sir Lennox (1903–89) English composer. Of aristocratic and partly French descent, he studied with Nadia Boulanger in Paris and worked in European modes of neo-classicism. Later he had a close association with Benjamin *Britten. His settings of English words include two groups by Walter *de la Mare, *5 Songs* and *Songs of the Half-Light* (1964); *5 Poems of W. H. Auden* (1958); *Herrick Songs* with accompaniment for harp (1974); and intense choral settings of *Crashaw, *Donne, George *Herbert, *Herrick, Robert *Bridges, G. M. *Hopkins, and many other English writers. With Cecil *Day-Lewis he wrote a *Hymn for Shakespeare's Birthday* (1972). He wrote incidental music for *The *Tempest* (1946) and *The *Winter's Tale* (1960) and four operas: *Nelson* (1954), with a libretto by Alan Pryce-Jones; *Ruth* (1956) to a text by Eric Crozier; and two one-act operas, *A Dinner Engagement* (1954) and *Castaway* (1967), both with words by Paul Dehn. He was knighted in 1974.

BERKENHEAD (Birkenhead), **Sir John** (1617–79) The principal editor and writer of the influential Royalist Oxford-based newsbook *Mercurius Aulicus* (1643–5), which was renowned for its cavalier insouciance and wit and condemned by its opponents as a 'Court Buffon', putting off everything with 'a jest and a jeer'. Berkenhead also wrote many pamphlets and much polite and satiric verse, including a mock-heroic piece called 'A Jolt', based on an incident when Oliver *Cromwell was thrown from his coach in Hyde Park. He is notable as one of the first writers to make a career in journalism, but he also maintained contact with the more fashionable world of letters, including among his friends Katherine *Philips and William *Cartwright. A life by P. W. Thomas appeared in 1969, which describes him as 'a caricaturist of invention and exceptional acuteness' and credits him with raising journalistic standards.
See also Newspapers.

BERKOFF, Steven (1937–) Actor, director, playwright, born of immigrant Russian Jewish parentage in the East End of London. After schooling in Hackney—like Harold *Pinter and Arnold *Wesker—he worked as a waiter and a salesman. He trained as an actor in London and with the mime artist Jacques le Coq in Paris. He formed the London Theatre Group in 1968 and caused a sensation with his adaptation of Franz *Kafka's *The Trial* (1969). He remained a vigorous maverick in the fringe theatre movement of the subsequent two decades, playing the leading role in his own productions of his own demotic verse plays *East* (1975), *Greek* (1979), *Decadence* (1981), and *West* (1983). His domestic fantasy *Kvetch* won the Best Comedy in the Evening Standard Awards in 1991. Success as a screen villain in Hollywood subsidizes his single-minded stage career, and a prolific writing output includes two essential volumes: *I Am Hamlet* (1989) and his memoirs *Free Association* (1996). More recent work includes *Shopping in the Santa Monica Mall* (2000), *The Secret Love Life of Ophelia* (2001), and *Requiem for Ground Zero* (2002).

BERLIOZ, Hector (1803–69) French composer who drew inspiration from English and European literature throughout his career. The overtures *Waverley* (1828) and *Rob Roy* (1831) signal allegiance to Walter *Scott. *Le Corsaire*, which seems to suggest *Byron in its final version (1852), was originally *La Tour de Nice* and later became *Le Corsaire rouge* (after James Fenimore *Cooper's *The Red Rover*). More specifically Byronic is the symphony with viola solo *Harold en Italie* (1834), written for Paganini. The *Neuf Mélodies irlandaises* (1830; later renamed *Irlande*) are settings of poems by Thomas *Moore, and include a powerful version of the *Elegy on the Death of Robert Emmet*. The overwhelming impact of Berlioz's passion for Harriet Smithson, the Irish actress whom he had first seen as Ophelia in September 1827, lies behind the Moore settings as well as his *Symphonie fantastique* (1830). Berlioz saw Smithson as the embodiment of the *Shakespeare heroine, an idealism which gradually poisoned their marriage (1833). Shakespeare continued to represent for Berlioz 'a voice of the burning bush, amid the storm clouds, the thunder and the lightning of a poetry that was new to me'. The *Fantaisie sur la Tempête* (1830) preceded the *Roi Lear* overture by a year: it was later incorporated in the lyric monodrama *Le Retour à la vie* (1832, later renamed *Lélio*) in which the composer's Shakespearian obsession is worked out in a mixture of music and spoken monologue. The huge dramatic symphony *Roméo et Juliette* was completed in 1839. Works on the theme of **Hamlet* include the 'Marche funèbre' (1848) and 'La Mort d'Ophélie' (1842). His last composition, the witty opera *Béatrice et Bénédict* (1862), was based on **Much Ado About Nothing*. Even *Les Troyens*, his vast Virgilian opera (1858), has its Shakespearian moment: the words for the love duet in Act IV are drawn from the last act of *The *Merchant of Venice*. 'It is Shakespeare who is the real author of both words and music,' wrote the composer. 'Strange that he, the poet of the North, should have intervened in the masterpiece of the poet of Rome… What singers, these two!' Berlioz wrote much music journalism; his revealing *Mémoires* were completed in 1865 but only published posthumously.

BERNANOS, Georges (1888–1948) French Catholic novelist and polemicist. A young member of *Action Française, his best-known novels, notably *Sous le soleil de Satan* (1926: *Under Satan's Sun*) and *Journal d'un curé de campagne* (1936: *The Diary of a Country Priest*), both of which were translated into English within a year of their publication, dramatize through the tormented lives of priests an intensely religious vision of the world. He moved to Majorca in 1936, where he denounced the Spanish fascists and became an ardent Republican. He emigrated to Brazil in 1938, and he spent his last years after the war in North Africa. See R. Speaight, *Georges Bernanos* (1973).

BERNARD, St (1090–1153) Abbot of the Cistercian foundation of Clairvaux at the age of 24 and developer of the Augustinian contemplative theological tradition with its emphasis on Faith rather than Reason. He was one of the foremost figures of the 12th-century monastic Reformation. He preached the Second Crusade, and opposed the dialectical theological method of *Abelard, which he had condemned at Soissons and Sens. The characteristic quality of his thought was a lively and personal mysticism; he developed and preached 'the Cistercian Programme', a progression from carnal to spiritual love which, in its literary application, became one of the most important elements of medieval poetry from the *troubadours to *Dante. In his mysticism the stress is on God's grace, according to the Augustinian school, rather than on the deliberate achievement of man's contemplative efforts, which was the aspect emphasized by the *Neoplatonists and their followers in the prose mysticism of the 14th century. See B. S. James, *St Bernard of Clairvaux* (1959).

BERNARDIN DE SAINT-PIERRE, Jacques-Henri (1737–1814) French novelist and natural philosopher, a friend and follower of Jean-Jacques *Rousseau. His *Études de la nature* (1784: *Studies of Nature*), a series of essays on natural history and philosophy, proved a popular success; in the third edition (1788), he included the work of fiction now regarded as his masterpiece and which was to achieve phenomenal popularity, *Paul et Virginie*. It tells the story of the idyllic childhood of two children of French parentage, Paul and Virginie, who are brought up as brother and sister by their mothers on the tropical island of Mauritius. The two mothers, refugees from social disgrace in France, determine that their children shall be reared in conformity with Nature's laws, and accordingly accustom them to a simple, frugal, and hard-working existence free from social prejudice, religious superstition, or fear of authority. In these conditions Paul and Virginie grow to adolescence, healthy, humane, pious, and benevolent, actively supporting their less fortunate neighbours. But at puberty Virginie is sent to Paris to join her great-aunt, who desires to educate her to receive her fortune. On her return, her ship is caught in a hurricane and thrown onto the reefs within sight of shore; a sailor offers to carry her to the shore if she undresses, but out of modesty she refuses, and is drowned. Paul and the two mothers die soon after of shock and grief. Helen Maria *Williams, a friend of Bernardin's, translated the novel in 1796. See M. Cook, *Bernardin de Saint-Pierre* (2006).

BERNERS, John Bourchier, second Baron (*c*.1467–1533) Soldier, statesman, and translator. He was made deputy of Calais in 1520, becoming chancellor of the Exchequer in 1524. He translated *Huon of Bordeaux (probably printed *c.*1515), Jean *Froissart's *Chronicles* (1523–5); a Spanish work, *The Castle of Love*, dating from after 1526 and printed *c.*1548; and Guevara's *The Golden Book of Marcus Aurelius* (1535).

BERNERS (Barnes), **Juliana** (*fl.* 1460) Once thought to have been prioress of a nunnery at Sopwell, near St Albans. She is also the alleged author of a treatise in verse on hunting contained in the *Book of St. Albans*, which was printed there in 1486. The treatise ends: 'Explicit Dame Julyans | Barnes in her boke of huntyng', but despite attestations to her existence by John Bale and others, Juliana Berners has yet to be satisfactorily identified.

BERNHARDT, Sarah (1844–1923) French actress. In a career that spanned 60 years and took her to many parts of the world, including numerous appearances in London and New York, she attained great celebrity in both tragedy and comedy. Among her famous roles were Doña Sol in Victor *Hugo's *Hernani*, Adrienne Lecouvreur in the play of the same name by Scribe and Legouvé, Phèdre in *Racine's tragedy, Marguerite in the younger Alexandre *Dumas's *La Dame aux camélias*, several parts in plays by Victorien Sardou, and Napoleon's son in Edmond *Rostand's *L'Aiglon*. From 1899 she managed her own Théâtre Sarah Bernhardt, taking the role of Hamlet there. Her memoirs, *Ma Double Vie* (*My Double Life*), were published in 1907.

BERNI, Francesco (1496/7–1535) A Tuscan poet, author of facetious, satirical, and burlesque compositions, whose style was imitated by Lord *Byron in his **Don Juan* and **Beppo*. Berni also wrote a Tuscan version of Boiardo's **Orlando innamorato*, published in 1542, which for a long time was better known than the original.

BERQUIN, Arnaud (1741–91) French writer of children's literature, best known for his collection of tales and dialogues *L'Ami des enfants* (1782–3: *The Children's Friend*), which was successfully adapted by Richard *Johnson as *The Looking-Glass for the Mind* (1787).

BERRIGAN, Ted (1934–83) American poet who was born in Providence, Rhode Island. He was active among the *New York School and his 1964 collection *The Sonnets* drew particular praise from Frank *O'Hara. Berrigan's *Collected Poems* was published in 2005.

BERRY, James (1924–) Born and educated in Jamaica; poet who came to London in 1948 and worked until 1977 as an overseas telegraphist. Since then he has done much work in the field of multicultural education, and edited various anthologies, including *Bluefoot Traveller: An Anthology of Westindian Poets in Britain* (1976), *Dance to a Different Drum* (1983, a Brixton Festival anthology), and *News for Babylon* (1984). His own collections include *Fractured Circles* (1979), *Lucy's Letter and Loving* (1982), *Chain of Days* (1985), *Hot Earth Cold Earth* (1995), and *Rough Sketch Beginning* (1996). *When I Dance* (1988) is a volume of poems, songs, and 'work-sing' for children, mixing inner-city subject matter with rural Caribbean motifs. *A Thief in the Village* (1987), *Anancy Spiderman* (1988), *The Future-Telling Lady* (1991), and *A Nest Full of Stars* (2002) are some of his collections of stories for children.
See JAZZ POETRY.

BERRYMAN, John (1914–72) American poet. Born John Smith in Oklahoma, he took his stepfather's name after his father's suicide. He was educated at Columbia University. Much of his poetry is anguished and confessional, exploring personal guilts and religious doubts, but it is also learned and often witty, and technically highly organized if idiosyncratic. His work includes *Poems* (1942), *The Dispossessed* (1948), and *Homage to Mistress Bradstreet* (1956), the last a complex biographical ode inspired by the first New England poet Anne *Bradstreet. *77 Dream Songs* (1964), with their imaginary and protean protagonist Henry, were completed by *His Toy, his Dream, his Rest* (1968), and together form his major work. He committed suicide in Minneapolis.

Bertram, *The Castle of St Aldobrand* A tragedy by Charles *Maturin, produced with great success by Edmund *Kean, 1816. An entertaining if overwrought drama, centred on a *Byronic hero, of love, madness, and suicide, it was the object of hostile criticism by S. T. *Coleridge in the **Biographia Literaria*.

BERTRAM, Charles (1723–65) English teacher at Copenhagen who between 1747 and 1757 sent to William *Stukeley a transcript of a manuscript itinerary and map of Roman Britain, allegedly by Richard of Cirencester. It was generally accepted as genuine until B. B. Woodward showed in the **Gentleman's Magazine* (1866) that the Latin was inauthentic.

BESANT, Sir Walter (1836–1901) Author, educated at King's College London, and Christ's College, Cambridge. He published *Early French Poetry* (1868) and *The French Humourists* (1873). He was secretary to the Palestine Exploration Fund (1868–86) and with W. H. Palmer wrote *Jerusalem* (1871). From 1871 to 1882 Besant collaborated with James *Rice and together they produced several best-selling novels, including *Ready-Money Mortiboy* (1872), *The Golden Butterfly* (1876), and *The Chaplain of the Fleet* (1881). He was deeply interested in the life of the poor, especially in the East End of London, and the grim social conditions of industrial workers, and draws attention to these in *All Sorts and Conditions of Men* (1882) and *Children of Gibeon* (1886); he stimulated the foundation of the People's Palace, Mile End (1887), for intellectual improvement and rational amusement. In 1884 he founded the *Society of Authors, and became editor of the *Author* in 1890; he defined the financial position of authors in *The Pen and the Book* (1899). His other books include the historical works *Rabelais* (1879) and *Captain Cook* (1890) and several histories of different parts of London. *A Survey of London* (1902–12) and his autobiography (1902) appeared posthumously.

BESTALL, Alfred *See* RUPERT BEAR

BESTER, Alfred (1913–87) American author and scriptwriter, born in New York; after publishing *science fiction stories in the early 1940s he spent several years writing comic book, radio, and television scripts before returning to science fiction with a baroque, fast-paced, cynical vision which made him one of the precursors of *cyberpunk. *The Demolished Man* (1953), winner of the first *Hugo award for best science fiction novel, considers how murder might be committed where telepaths could uncover the thought before the deed. *Tiger! Tiger!* (1956) is the revenge of an outsider in a decadent world. *Golem*^{100} (1980) is perhaps the best of his later novels.

bestiaries Medieval treatises derived from the Greek *Physiologus*, which was a collection of about 50 fabulous anecdotes from natural (mostly animal) history, followed by a 'moralization' of the anecdotes for a Christian purpose. The Greek original dates from some time between the 2nd and 4th centuries, and it was translated into many languages, most influentially Latin. In the 12th century additions began to be made to the Latin version from the popular encyclopedia of the Middle Ages, the *Etymologiae* of *Isidore of Seville. Those written in England in the 12th and 13th centuries were often richly illustrated with miniatures. The Old English poems 'The Panther' and 'The Whale' are isolated examples of the kind; the Middle English Bestiary, coming from the north-east Midlands in the second half of the 13th century, has 802 lines in various metres. Their method of moralization was influential on the relations between story and moral in many medieval texts, as well as being a popular source for such works as Sir Thomas *Browne's **Pseudodoxia Epidemica*.

See F. McCulloch, *Medieval Latin and French Bestiaries* (1960); T. H. *White, *The Book of Beasts* (1954: a translation of a 12th-century Latin bestiary); Middle English version ed. R. Morris in *An Old English Miscellany* (EETS os 49, 1872; repr. 1927, 1–25).

Bethgelert (Beddgelert) A village at the foot of Snowdon, where Llewelyn the Great lived. Gelert was a hound given by King John to Llewelyn. Returning from hunting, Llewelyn found the hound smeared with blood, his child's bed in disorder, and the child not to be seen. Thinking that the hound had devoured the child, the father killed Gelert with his sword. The child, awakened by the hound's dying yell, cried out from under a heap of coverings, and beneath the bed was found a great wolf which the hound had slain. The earliest published version of this story is in *Musical and Poetical Relicks of the Welsh Bards* (1784), by Edward Jones. It is also the subject of a ballad by William Robert Spencer (1769–1834, one of the many translators of Bürger's *'Lenore'), entitled 'Beth Gelert, or The Grave of the Greyhound', published in his *Poems* (1811).

BETJEMAN, Sir John (1906–84) Poet, born in Highgate; the name is of Dutch origin. He was educated at Marlborough College, and at Magdalen College, Oxford, where he became friendly with W. H. *Auden and Louis *MacNeice, and was encouraged by Maurice Bowra (1898–1971). Leaving without a degree, he worked briefly as a schoolmaster, then began to write, in 1931, for the *Architectural Review*; his first collection of verse, *Mount Zion*, appeared in that year. This was followed by many other collections, including *Continual Dew: A Little Book of Bourgeois Verse* (1937), *New Bats in Old Belfries* (1945), *A Few Late Chrysanthemums* (1954), and his extremely successful *Collected Poems* (1958; expanded 1962). His blank-verse autobiography, *Summoned by Bells* (1960), which covers his boyhood and life at Oxford, was followed by two more collections, *A Nip in the Air* (1972) and *High and Low* (1976). He was appointed *poet laureate in 1972. His poetry, which has reached an unusually wide audience (while numbering Auden and Philip *Larkin amongst its advocates), is predominantly witty, urbane, and satiric, a comedy of manners, place-names, and contemporary references. Many have commented, however, on the underlying melancholy, the chill of fear, the religion which dwells more on hope than faith; Larkin notes his 'heterogeneous world of farce and fury, where sports girls and old nuns jostle with town clerks and impoverished Irish peers'. In the preface to *Old Lights for New Chancels* (1940) Betjeman writes of his own 'topographical predilection' for 'suburbs and gaslights and Pont Street and Gothic Revival churches and mineral railways, provincial towns and garden cities', a predilection also displayed in his editing and writing of Shell Guides, some illustrated by his friend John Piper (1903–92), and various works on architecture, beginning with *Ghastly Good Taste* (1933). Betjeman's popularity as a public personality (notably in television appearances) and the apparent facility of his verse have contributed to the relative neglect of his poetry among academic critics, but it has always found admirers among poets themselves: Hugo *Williams edited a selection in 2006. *Letters 1926–1951*, edited by his daughter, was published in 1994. See Bevis Hillier, *Betjeman: The Biography* (2002).

Betrothed, The A novel by Walter *Scott, published 1825. This, the first of Scott's two *Tales of the Crusaders*, was so much disliked by James *Ballantyne and Archibald *Constable that publication was suspended while he embarked on *The *Talisman*. Eventually the two were published as a package, the success of *The Talisman* redeeming what Scott himself perceived as the failure of *The Betrothed*. The Crusades feature in the story only to explain the absence of Hugo de Lacy, to whom the heroine is betrothed, the action, which includes some fine battle descriptions, taking place entirely on the Welsh Marches.

BETTERTON, Mary (*c.*1637–1712) The wife of Thomas *Betterton, at first known on the stage by her maiden name Saunderson, the first notable actress on the English stage (until 1660 female parts were taken by men or boys). Mary

Betterton was the first woman to act William *Shakespeare's great female characters, such as Lady Macbeth, Ophelia, and Juliet. Samuel *Pepys called her 'Ianthe' after her part in Sir William *D'Avenant's *Siege of Rhodes*. With her husband she trained young performers. Anne *Bracegirdle was a pupil.

BETTERTON, Thomas (1635–1710) The greatest actor in the *Restoration. He joined Sir William *D'Avenant's company at Lincoln's Inn Fields, and was associated in the management of the Dorset Gardens Theatre from 1671. With most of his fellow actors he revolted against the harsh management of Christopher Rich (bap. 1647, d. 1714; father of John Rich (?1692–1761)) and established a rival company at Lincoln's Inn Fields in 1695, opening with William *Congreve's **Love for Love*. In 1705 his company moved into the theatre erected by Sir John *Vanbrugh in the Haymarket. His 180 roles included Hamlet, Mercutio, Sir Toby Belch, Macbeth, Bosola (in *The *Duchess of Malfi*), and Heartwell (in Congreve's *The *Old Bachelor*). His dramas include *The Roman Virgin*, acted 1669, adapted from John *Webster's *Appius and Virginia*; *The Prophetess* (1690), an opera from *The Prophetess* of Francis *Beaumont and John *Fletcher; *King Henry IV* (1700, in which he played *Falstaff) from William *Shakespeare; *The Amorous Widow* (1670), from *Molière's *George Dandin*.

BETTI, Ugo (1892–1953) Italian dramatist, poet, and short story writer, who pursued a legal career, rising to become a supreme court judge under the Fascist regime. After *Pirandello, he is the most significant Italian dramatist of the 20th century. Many of his 25 plays are concerned with aspects of justice—social, legal, moral, and existential—and with the dilemmas these provoke in human beings. The best known are *Frana allo Scalo nord* (1932/5), *Corruzione al palazzo di giustizia* (1944), *La regina e gli insorti* (1949), and *L'aiuola bruciata* (1952). See H. Reed (trans.), *Three Plays: The Queen and the Rebels, The Burnt Flowerbed, Summertime* (1956); G. H. McWilliam (trans.), *Three Plays on Justice: Landslide, Struggle till Dawn, The Fugitive* (1964).

BETTY, William Henry West (1791–1874) A phenomenally successful boy actor, known as 'the Young Roscius', in reference to the famous Roman actor. He made his debut in Belfast at the age of 12 playing four roles in four nights, one being that of Romeo. Proceeding to Dublin, he added Hamlet, Prince Arthur, and other parts to his repertoire. He continued his success in Scotland, and arrived in London in 1804, aged 13. At Covent Garden he played many major roles, including Richard III and Macbeth; there were riots for admission, he was presented to the royal family, and the House of Commons suspended a sitting to enable MPs to see his Hamlet. His final appearance as a boy actor was in 1808. He then went to Cambridge to study, returning to the stage in 1812. But his career as an adult actor was not a success, and he finally retired, a rich man, in 1824.

Beulah, Land of See Isaiah 62: 4. Derived from the Hebrew word for 'married', Beulah was traditionally equated with the erotic garden-paradise of the biblical Song of Solomon allegorized by Christians as the marriage of Christ and his church. In John *Bunyan's **Pilgrim's Progress* Beulah is a pastoral paradise of birdsong and eternal flowers. Hearing the 'voice of the turtle in the land' the pilgrims learn that 'the contract between the bride and the bridegroom' is renewed, and view the New *Jerusalem from its borders. William *Blake asssociated Beulah with the third state of vision and sexual love. In **Milton* and **Jerusalem* Beulah is a shadowy, moony place of rest between Eternity and Ulro; the daughters of Beulah are the poet's muses.
See BIBLE.

BEVINGTON, Louisa S. (1845–95) Poet and progressive thinker, born in London. She published several volumes of poetry, including *Key-Notes* (1876) and *Poems, Lyrics and Sonnets* (1882), which explore the nature of evolution, at times with a spare questioning lyricism. She also wrote and lectured on rationalism, religion, property, and evolutionary theory. Her last collection of poems, *Liberty Lyrics*, was published by James Tochatti's Liberty Press in 1895, and expressed her radical political sympathies. Bevington married a German artist, Ignatz Guggenberger, in 1883.

***Bevis:** The Story of a Boy* A novel by Richard *Jefferies, published 1882. In this intense evocation of a country childhood, revealing the secret world of two imaginative and adventurous boys, Bevis and Mark, Jefferies draws on his own rural boyhood in Wiltshire. The farm, the woods, the lake, become the Roman world (or any other world), the Unknown Island becomes the Hesperides, and the solemn games, adventures, and incidental terrors are played out in storm and sun, by day and under the stars, almost always out of doors.

Bevis of Hampton A popular verse romance from *c.*1324, exists in several versions ultimately derived from *Boeuve de Haumtone*, a 12th-century Anglo-Norman **chanson de geste*. The story was popular throughout Europe, from Ireland to Russia. Bevis's mother, the wife of Guy, earl of Hampton (possibly Littlehampton), has her husband murdered, marries the murderer, and sells Bevis into slavery in the East. The rest of the story narrates Bevis's conversion of and marriage to Josian, daughter of the king of Arabia, and their adventures in Europe, England (where he kills his father's murderer), and the East. Ed. E. Kölbing (EETS ES 46, 48, 65, 1885–94; repr. 1 vol., 1973); discussion in Jennifer Fellows and Ivana Djordjevic (eds), *Sir Bevis of Hampton in Literary Tradition* (2008).

BEWICK, Thomas (1753–1828) Wood-engraver, son of a Northumbrian farmer. He was apprenticed to, and subsequently partner of, Ralph Beilby (1744–1817), a metal-engraver in Newcastle. He engraved blocks for John *Gay's *Fables* (1779), *Select Fables* (1784), *A General History of Quadrupeds*

(1790), *Fables of Aesop* (1818), the poems of Oliver *Goldsmith and Thomas *Parnell (1795), and other books; his most celebrated and successful work was *A History of British Birds* (1797, 1804). John *Ruskin praised his 'flawless virtue', and his vignettes of country life were much admired by William *Wordsworth, Charlotte *Brontë, Thomas *Carlyle, and John James *Audubon, who visited him in his workshop in 1827. His *Memoir* (1862) is a vivid record of a north-country childhood and a craftsman's life.

Bhagavad-gitā A section of the **Mahābhārata*, in dialogue form, in which Krishna, an incarnation of the deity, instructs and exhorts his pupil and favourite, Arjuna, one of the five sons of the Pandavas, as they stand poised for battle. It was the first section to be translated into English by Charles Wilkins (1750–1836), a senior merchant in the East India Company, as *The Bhagvat-Geeta, or, Dialogues of Kreeshna and Arjoon* (1785), and has since been easily as influential in English translation as in its original Sanskrit, inspiring M. K. (Mahatma) Gandhi, the Theosophical movement (*see* BLAVATSKY, ELENA), and the Bengal nationalist movement, amongst others. In an advertisement prefacing the translation, Wilkins noted that he had been authorized by the Company's court of directors, at the particular desire of Warren Hastings (1732–1818). Hastings responded: 'I should not fear to place, in opposition to the best French versions of the most admired pages of the *Iliad* or the *Odyssey*, or the 1st or 6th books of our own Milton, highly as I venerate the latter, the English translation of the Mahabarat.'

BHATT, Sujata (1956–) Indian diaspora poet, born in Ahmadabad, now resident in Bremen, Germany; she has lived, studied, and worked in the USA and graduated from the Writers' Workshop at the University of Iowa. Her first collection *Brunizem* (1988) won the Commonwealth Poetry Prize, and attracted attention for its juxtaposition of bilingual Gujarati and English texts within the construct of the poems, a device used to invoke the alienation of the poet from the reader. She has published six collections of poems, all with Carcanet Press, including *Monkey Shadows* (1991), *The Stinking Rose* (1994), and *A Colour for Solitude* (2002), an exploration of the life of the German painter Paula Modersohn-Becker (1876–1907).

Biathanatos *See* DONNE, JOHN.

Bible, the Collected holy texts of Judaism (the Old Testament, OT), and (with the New Testament, NT) of Christianity. The OT, written almost entirely in Hebrew, begins with the heart of the Hebrew Bible, the Torah or Law, the five books of *Moses (Genesis, Exodus, Leviticus, Numbers, Deuteronomy). Genesis tells of the seven days of God's creation, and the fall of Adam and Eve, tempted by a serpent in the garden of Eden. Cain kills his brother Abel, the first murder. Seeing the later wickedness of man, God sends a flood, but saves Noah and his family and pairs or sevens of all animals. The subsequent rainbow symbolizes God's promise that there will be no more such destruction. These early myths are followed with stories of the ancestral figures of the Israelites, including Abraham, Isaac, Jacob (and Esau), and Joseph and his eleven brothers. After the exodus from Egypt led by Moses, and the giving of the Law (Exodus to Deuteronomy), comes the conquest of the promised land, Canaan (Joshua). For a period the twelve tribes of Israel are ruled by judges, including Samson, whose secret, that he will lose his strength if his hair is cut, is wheedled out of him by Delilah (Judges). In the time of the prophet Samuel, the people demand a king, and are ruled first by Saul, a tragic figure who loses God's favour, then *David, then his son, Solomon, famed for his wisdom and builder of the Temple in *Jerusalem. The kingdom becomes divided, a northern kingdom, Israel, whose kings invariably fail to do what is right in the eyes of God, and a southern kingdom, Judah, which includes Jerusalem, and has some righteous kings (1, 2 Samuel, 1, 2 Kings). Jerusalem is destroyed by the Babylonians and the people are exiled. The historical books end with the return to Jerusalem and the rebuilding of the Temple under Ezra and Nehemiah. The stories of faithful Ruth and of Queen Esther saving the people also come in this part of the OT.

The fall of Jerusalem and the exile are pivotal to the prophetic books, Isaiah to Malachi. As guardians of religious consciousness, the prophets observed the collective failure of the people and the two kingdoms to follow God and the Mosaic law, a failure often pictured in terms of sexual infidelity. They reported God's judgement on this failure or backsliding: the people and the nation would be destroyed. When that judgement was fulfilled, they began to offer consolation to the penitent people, envisioning spiritual redemption and leadership, and the coming of a Messiah or Saviour. With some uncertainties about the chronology, they divide into three groups. Amos, Hosea, first Isaiah (i.e. Isaiah 1–39), Micah, Habakkuk, Zephaniah, and Nahum are pre-exilic and emphasize sin and punishment. From the time of the exile come Jeremiah, Obadiah, Isaiah 40–55, Ezekiel, and, probably, Isaiah 56–66; they mix lament with promises of forgiveness. After the exile come several short books mixing hope and warning, Haggai, Zechariah 1–8, Malachi, Joel, and Zechariah 9–14. Jonah stands apart as a famous story about the duty of a prophet, and Daniel as the latest book of the OT, a combination of stories about the wisdom of Daniel and visions that reflect the situation of Israel prior to the 2nd-century BC restoration of the kingdom under the Maccabees.

In the Christian canon, which differs from the Jewish, books of wisdom (Job, Ecclesiastes, Proverbs) and poetry (Psalms and the Song of Solomon) come between the historical and the prophetic books. In Job poetic dialogues explore the problem of divine justice and human suffering, vividly expressed by the afflicted Job. Ecclesiastes is famous for its world-weary cynicism, 'vanity of vanities, all is vanity' (1: 2). The 150 psalms express faith and suffering in ways that have made them a perennial source of comfort. The poetic fragments of the Song of Solomon celebrate human love and, contrasting with the frequent use of images of infidelity in the prophets, are frequently read allegorically as expressing, for instance, Christ's love for the church (so interpreted in the King James Bible).

The *Apocrypha follows the OT in the Protestant canon, but is now omitted from most Bibles because of the secondary status of its contents as uninspired writings. It includes alternative versions of OT books (e.g. 1, 2 Esdras), some fine stories such as Tobit, wisdom writings, notably the Wisdom of Solomon, and two histories of the Maccabean revolt against Syrian oppression.

Four Gospels begin the NT: Matthew, Mark, and Luke, known as the Synoptic Gospels because of the similarity of their viewpoint, and John. Each gives a version of Jesus' life replete with famous stories from the coming of the three wise men through healing miracles to the events which define his significance as the Christian Messiah: his triumphal entry into Jerusalem, the last supper, his trial, crucifixion, and resurrection. Jesus' teaching stresses God's love and forgiveness, and the need for the sinful individual to 'love the Lord thy God with all thy heart', and to 'love thy neighbour as thyself' (Matt. 22: 37, 39). Much of the teaching uses parables which range from brief similes for the kingdom of God to extended homely tales such as the Good Samaritan and the Prodigal Son (Luke 10, 15).

Acts relates the early spread of Christianity from the coming of the Holy Ghost to Jesus' followers shortly after the resurrection to just before the death of Paul. Then comes the second heart of the NT, the Pauline epistles (*see* PAUL, ST), together with shorter epistles by or attributed to other apostles; most of these latter are concerned with false teaching and belief and were for general circulation (hence James to Jude are known as the Catholic Epistles).

The final book, Revelation or Apocalypse, is a fantastic series of visions of the end time, concluding with the coming of the holy city of God, new Jerusalem. Its prophetic-apocalyptic mode goes back to Ezekiel and Daniel.

The OT Hebrew texts were early translated into other languages. Most important was the Greek Septuagint, so called because of the legend that it was made in 70 days by 70 inspired Jewish scholars. Begun some time in the 3rd century BC, it was the Bible of Greek-speaking Judaism and early Christianity; it remains the OT for the Orthodox Church. Because it is older than any surviving Hebrew manuscripts, it sometimes preserves older readings; it also has a more extensive canon, and is the prime source for the Apocrypha. When Latin became the dominant language, early Christians made Latin versions of both Testaments. These were superseded by *Jerome's Vulgate, which became the standard Bible of Christendom until the *Reformation, and remained standard for Roman Catholics. Protestants fought to give the people Bibles in their own vernacular, and they usually insisted on translating from the Hebrew and Greek texts rather than the Vulgate. Some translations became classics, and also strong influences on their own language, notably *Luther's German (NT 1522, completed 1534), and *Tyndale and *Coverdale's English, in the form of the King James Bible (*see* BIBLE, THE ENGLISH). See *The Cambridge History of the Bible* (1963–70); *The Oxford Companion to the Bible* (1993).

Bible, the English The principal *Bible of English religion and culture since the 17th century is the King James Bible (KJB) or Authorized Version (1611). Its language became not just the model for religious expression, but also an inescapable example of a predominantly Anglo-Saxon, simply constructed way of writing. Some of its sayings became so familiar that they are commonly used to enhance a piece of writing; some such as 'fall by the wayside' have become clichés. Writers have depended upon the familiarity of the KJB's language and the entire contents of the Bible as their most widely used source of allusion, story, and teaching.

Before the *Reformation, English writers and readers knew the Bible from the *Vulgate, a few paraphrases and translations such as those of *Cædmon, *Bede, and *Ælfric, and from adaptations such as the **Cursor Mundi* and *mystery plays. The earliest complete English translation was the *Lollard or *Wyclif Bible. Its earlier form (*c.*1382), a highly literal rendering of the Vulgate, was revised into somewhat more natural English (*c.*1388); these versions were widely circulated in manuscript but had little influence on the later translations.

What became the KJB began while vernacular Bible translation was forbidden. William *Tyndale, working directly from the original Greek and Hebrew, completed the New Testament (NT; 1526, rev. 1535), the Pentateuch (1530), and Joshua to 2 Chronicles (published posthumously in the Matthew Bible, 1537). His combination of everyday English and a nearly literal fidelity to the originals created English biblical style. Relying heavily on *Luther and Latin versions, Miles *Coverdale revised and completed Tyndale's work, producing the first complete printed English Bible in 1535. This became the basis of the English church's first official Bible, the Great Bible (1539–40), later revised as the Bishops' Bible (1568).

Contemporary with Tyndale and Coverdale, other translators including George Joye (parts of the Old Testament, 1530–5) and Richard Taverner (1539) made translations that had little influence on later versions. In Mary's reign exiled Protestants in Geneva produced what became the most popular English Bible for a century, the Geneva (or Breeches) Bible (1560). Usually better printed and cheaper than the official Bibles, it also appealed through its extensive annotations. In *Elizabeth I's reign Roman Catholics, now exiled in their turn, produced the Rheims–Douai Bible (NT 1582, Old Testament (OT) 1609–10).

At a conference in 1604 called by *James I to try to create religious uniformity, the Puritans complained of mistranslations in the Great Bible and suggested there should be a new translation. Probably, they hoped the Geneva Bible would be adopted, but James vehemently disliked the Geneva annotations. He ordered that a new revision, free of notes, should be made, based on the Bishops' Bible, but using Tyndale, Coverdale, the Matthew Bible, the Great Bible, and Geneva where they were truer to the original languages. Six companies of translators, two each at Oxford, Cambridge, and Westminster, revised their predecessors' work, intending not 'to make a new translation...but to make a good one better, or out of many good ones one principal good one' (Preface). Some of the work was done by making interlinear revisions in the

Bishops' Bible. The Bodleian Library has a Bishops' Bible that contains the translators' early revisions to some parts of the NT, and their nearly final revisions to all of the OT except sections of Isaiah, Jeremiah, and Ezekiel. The result was a judicious combination of old work and new touches. Fidelity to the Hebrew and Greek originals was the chief aim.

Though quickly accepted by the learned as the most accurate translation into English, the KJB took 30 years to dominate the bible market, and longer to monopolize the English consciousness. After the 1760s it was generally acclaimed as fine, and, by many, as the greatest English literature. Popular affection and literary veneration grew as its scholarly reputation declined, eventually leading to the Revised Version (NT 1870, OT 1885), deliberately modelled on its style. This was never a literary success, but marked the start of increasingly frequent modern efforts either to improve the KJB while preserving a semblance of its style or to produce versions in contemporary language, such as the New English Bible (NT 1961, OT 1970). Many of these latter used literary advisers in a generally fruitless attempt to rival the literary success of the KJB. See Robert Alter and Frank Kermode (eds), *The Literary Guide to the Bible* (1987); David Norton, *A History of the English Bible as Literature* (2000).

biblical commentaries Works commenting on and interpreting the books of the *Bible have a long history and have had a powerful influence on literature and literary theory. *Paul in his epistles began the key process of interpreting events, persons, or things in the Old Testament as prefigurations or 'types' of corresponding events, persons, or things in the New Testament, a way of reading known as 'typology'. In the early Christian church, *Origen in his commentaries emphasized *allegory as the key to interpretation, and developed a threefold meaning of Scripture, literal, moral, and allegorical. Later a fourfold meaning was developed—literal, allegorical, tropological (moral), and anagogical (concerned with eternity)—which was influential until the *Reformation. Important early commentators in Latin include *Jerome, *Augustine, and *Bede. In the 18th and 19th centuries accessible commentaries in English, for example by Matthew Henry, Philip *Doddridge, and Thomas *Scott, were much reprinted and widely read in families.

Bibliographical Society Founded in 1892. Its *Transactions* were first published in 1893 and were merged with *The *Library* in 1920. The Society also published numerous separate monographs, including many dealing with the history of books in England, Scotland, and Ireland, such as dictionaries of printers and booksellers 1557–1775 (1907–32), accounts of printers' and publishers' devices (1913) and of title-page borders to 1640 (1932), engraved and etched title pages to 1691 (1934), the earliest English woodcuts (1935), and W. W. *Greg's *Bibliography of English Printed Drama to the Restoration* (1939–59). In 1926 it published A. W. *Pollard and G. R. Redgrave's *Short-Title Catalogue of English Books, 1475–1640*, and between 1976 and 1991 a completely revised second edition in three volumes. Among the Society's past presidents are R. *Garnett, T. J. *Wise, Greg, M. *Sadleir, and F. P. *Wilson.

BICKERSTAFF, Isaac (1733–?1808) Irish playwright. His two-act 'musical entertainment', *Thomas and Sally* (1760), with music by Thomas *Arne, prefigured the successful 'comic opera' *Love in a Village* (1762), another collaboration with Arne. *The Maid of the Mill* (1765), with music by Samuel Arnold, was based on Samuel *Richardson's **Pamela*. *Lionel and Clarissa* (1768) had music by Charles *Dibdin, who appeared blacked up in the role of Mungo in Bickerstaff's *The Padlock*, at David *Garrick's Drury Lane theatre; a comic success, the character was increasingly a focus for discontent about racial inequality (Bickerstaff wrote a lost version of the *Inkle and Yarico* story, based on **Spectator*, 11). *The Hypocrite* (1769) was adapted from *Molière's *Tartuffe* via Colley *Cibber's *The Non-juror*. In 1772 Bickerstaff fled to France, accused of a homosexual offence. Garrick, to whose Shakespeare Jubilee (1769) Bickerstaff had also contributed, was implicated in the scandal in the dramatist William Kenrick's *Love in the Suds*, subtitled 'the lamentations of Roscius for the loss of his Nyky'; Kenrick later suppressed this. Bickerstaff died, after 1808, in obscurity. See Peter Tasch, *The Dramatic Cobbler* (1971).

Bidpai* (*Pilpay*), *The Fables of (*Kalilah and Dimnah*) The title taken from the Arabic version of a lost original of the *Panchatantra*, a celebrated third-century Sanskrit collection of animal and human fables, the source of much European folklore. 'Bidpai' is a corruption of 'bidbah', the title of the chief scholar at the court of an Indian prince. The fables were translated into many European languages, the first English version coming via the Italian in a version by Sir Thomas *North as *The Morall Philosophie of Doni* (1570). See N. Penzer, *The Ocean of Story* (1928); R. Ballaster, *Fabulous Orients* (2005).

BIERCE, Ambrose (1842–?1914) American writer, born in Ohio. He served in the Civil War, 1861–5, and afterwards became a prominent journalist, living and working for a time in England (1872–6). He returned to San Francisco, and later worked as a correspondent in Washington. He published prolifically, and collected his writings in twelve volumes (1909–12), but is best known for his short stories, realistic, sardonic, and strongly influenced by Edgar Allan *Poe. They were published in *Tales of Soldiers and Civilians* (1891), a title which was changed to *In the Midst of Life* (1892; rev. edn 1898). Tired of life and America, he travelled to Mexico in 1913 and mysteriously disappeared, it is thought in the fighting of the Mexican Civil War.

Big Brother The head of the Party in George *Orwell's **Nineteen Eighty-Four* who never appears in person, but whose portrait, with the caption 'Big Brother is watching you', dominates every public space. The reality television programme *Big Brother* owes its name to Orwell's novel.

Biggles W. E. *Johns's national icon, Major James Bigglesworth, developed through 96 books for boys (from *The Camels are Coming*, 1932 to *Biggles Sees Too Much*, 1970) from sensitive First World War pioneer fighter pilot, into Second World War hero, finally becoming a post-war 'international air detective'. *See* WAR STORIES FOR CHILDREN.

'big house' fiction A genre of Irish fiction which centres on the decline of a country house of the Anglo-Irish ascendancy. A comparative term drawn from the speech of landless Catholics, 'big' is inflected with hostility and irony (as Elizabeth *Bowen suggested in her 1940 essay 'The Big House'). Maria *Edgeworth's **Castle Rackrent* introduced such staples of the mode as the improvidence of the gentry and the avarice of the middle classes. Later novels took on a political and historical dimension and paid more explicit attention to sectarian difference, incorporating responses to the Great Famine, the Land War, the Anglo-Irish War, and other disruptions. They include William *Carleton's *The Squanders of Castle Squander* (1852); Charles *Lever's *The Martins of Cro' Martin* (1856); *Somerville and Ross's *The Big House at Inver* (1925); Bowen's *The Last September* (1929); J. G. *Farrell's *Troubles* (1970); John *Banville's *Birchwood* (1973); Molly *Keane's *Good Behaviour* (1981); William *Trevor's *Fools of Fortune* (1983); and *The Captains and the Kings* (1972), *The Gates* (1973), *The Old Jest* (1979), and other works by Jennifer *Johnston. In George *Moore's *A Drama in Muslin* (1886) and Aidan *Higgins's *Langrishe, Go Down* (1966), the declining family is Catholic rather than Protestant. 'Big house' fiction embraces *tragedy, historical meditation, social comedy, and *Gothic, sometimes fusing elements of all four. Many short stories, from Bowen's 'The Happy Autumn Fields' (1945) to John *McGahern's 'Old-fashioned' and 'The Conversion of William Kirkwood' (both 1985), extend the tradition. Bowen's *Bowen's Court* (1942) and David Thomson's *Woodbrook* (1974) are 'big house' memoirs, the latter dealing with the family and demesne drawn upon for McGahern's Anglo-Irish stories. The motif also features in drama (Lennox Robinson's *The Big House*, 1926; W. B. *Yeats's *Purgatory*, 1939; Sean *O'Casey's *Purple Dust*, 1940; and Brian *Friel's *Aristocrats*, 1980) and poetry (Yeats's Coole Park poems; Richard *Murphy's 'The Woman of the House', 1959; John *Montague's 'Woodtown Manor', 1961; Louis *MacNeice's 'Soap Suds', 1963; Derek *Mahon's 'A Disused Shed in County Wexford', 1975; Paul *Muldoon's 'The Big House', 1977; Thomas *Kinsella's 'Tao and Unfitness at Inistiogue on the River Nore', 1978; and Seamus *Heaney's 'A Peacock's Feather', 1972/1987). See Vera Kreilcamp, *The Anglo-Irish Novel and the Big House* (1998).

Bildungsroman The German term for an 'education-novel' (education being understood in a broad sense that includes self-formation or personal development); thus a significant sub-genre of novel which relates the experiences of a youthful protagonist in meeting the challenges of adolescence and early adulthood. Such works, sometimes referred to in English as 'coming-of-age' novels, typically develop themes of innocence, self-knowledge, sexual awakening, and vocation. Although not the first example of the sub-genre, the most widely influential was *Goethe's *Wilhelm Meisters Lehrjahre* (1795–6), known in England through Thomas *Carlyle's translation (*Wilhelm Meister's Apprenticeship*, 1824). As a recognized generic description, the term *Bildungsroman* (plural *-romane*) was not widely adopted in English criticism until the early 20th century, but in the meantime many English novels of this type had appeared, for example **Great Expectations*; and the 20th century proved fertile for this tradition, as in D. H. *Lawrence's **Sons and Lovers* (1913) or Rosamond *Lehmann's *Dusty Answer* (1927). See Franco Moretti, *The Way of the World* (1987).

Billy Budd, Foretopman (written 1891; pub. 1924) A novella by Herman *Melville, a symbolic tale built out of Melville's egalitarian meditations on the mutiny at Spithead in 1797 and a family story of how Melville's elder brother presided over the court martial and execution of an insubordinate sailor. Billy, 'the handsome sailor', wrongly accused by the satanic master-at-arms Claggart and unable to defend himself verbally because of a stammer, strikes Claggart dead. After being tried by the liberal Captain Vere, Billy is hanged, his last words being 'God bless Captain Vere!' and he undergoes an apparently Christ-like apotheosis. Benjamin *Britten's setting of *Billy Budd* (1951) has become one of the most admired operas in the modern repertoire.

BINYON, Laurence (1869–1943) Author, educated at St Paul's School and Trinity College, Oxford; he entered the British Museum, where, in 1909, he became assistant keeper in the department of prints and drawings. He produced many works on art, chiefly English and oriental, including *Painting in the Far East* (1908), *English Water-Colours* (1933), and a study of oriental aesthetics, *The Flight of the Dragon* (1911). His plays include *Attila* (1907) and *Arthur* (1923), the latter with music by *Elgar. His much-anthologized poem 'For the Fallen' ('They shall grow not old, as we that are left grow old') was set to music by Elgar in 1916. Binyon later wrote two long odes, *The Sirens* (1924–5) and *The Idols* (1928). *Collected Poems* appeared in 1931. *The Burning of the Leaves* was published posthumously in 1944, and *The Madness of Merlin*, an unfinished verse drama, in 1947. See John Hatcher, *Laurence Binyon* (1995).

Biographia Britannica Edited by William Oldys (1696–1761) and others and published in seven folio volumes (1747–66), was a collection of lives of the most eminent people in Great Britain and Ireland from the earliest times to the mid-18th century. It was indebted to the method of Pierre *Bayle's *Dictionary* and Thomas *Birch's *General Dictionary*, and together with the unfinished second edition by Andrew Kippis (1725–95) in six volumes (1778–95) is the ancestor of the **Dictionary of National Biography*. See Isabel Rivers, *Books and their Readers in Eighteenth-Century England: New Essays* (2001).

Biographia Literaria A work of philosophical autobiography and Romantic literary criticism, by S. T. *Coleridge, published 1817. Originally conceived in 1814 as a short explanatory preface to the **Sibylline Leaves*, it rapidly expanded into a two-volume apologia for his 'literary life and opinions'. Part I is broadly autobiographical, describing Coleridge's friendship with Robert *Southey and with the *Wordsworths at Stowey, and going on to trace his struggle with the 'dynamic philosophy' of *Kant, *Fichte, and *Schelling in Germany. The narrative is gradually overwhelmed by Romantic metaphysics; ch. XIII contains his famous distinction between Fancy and Imagination. Part II is almost entirely critical, attacking Wordsworth's preface to the **Lyrical Ballads* and then marvellously vindicating the poetry itself. Coleridge concentrates on the psychology of the creative process, and propounds new theories of the origins of poetic language, metre, and form, as the interpenetration of 'passion and will' (chs XV–XVIII). Other chapters discuss the poetry of *Shakespeare, *Milton, Samuel *Daniel, George *Herbert, and others, as exemplary of true 'Imagination' and the 'language of real life'. Though maddeningly unsystematic in structure, the book is a touchstone of Romantic criticism; it also gives some impression of Coleridge in full conversational flight.

biography has flourished in recent decades, with some 3,500 examples appearing each year, a range of experimental new methods, and lively debate about the nature of life-writing. Biography in its current form is comparatively recent, but it has deep roots in older traditions. The earliest biographies in England were written in Latin in the Middle Ages, largely to glorify saints (*see* HAGIOGRAPHY) or to commemorate and justify secular rulers. The Renaissance emphasis on man as an individual prompted a new approach and the first biography in English, Thomas *More's life of Richard III (*c.*1513), was no saint's life but a coruscating portrait built up with human details and first-hand observations. Thomas North's 1579 translation of *Plutarch's paired character studies *Parallel Lives* had a considerable influence on English biography and particularly on Izaak *Walton, who wrote pious, affectionate, and artfully constructed lives of the poets John *Donne (1640) and George *Herbert (1670). The eccentric antiquary John *Aubrey gathered a splendid collection of donnish scurrilities and courtly tattle in his *Brief Lives* (manuscript 1693), though these were not published until 1813.

But it was in the 18th century that biography really became popular, with numerous biographical collections such as the lives of criminals in the **Newgate Calendar* (gathered in five volumes, 1773) and Samuel *Johnson's *The *Lives of the English Poets* (1779–81). The rich human appeal that Johnson saw in the new form was set out in his seminal essay 'On the Genius of Biography': 'No species of writing...can more certainly enchain the heart by irresistible interest, or more widely diffuse instruction to every diversity of condition...We are all prompted by the same motives, all deceived by the same fallacies, all animated by hope, obstructed by danger, entangled by desire, and seduced by pleasure.' But it was James *Boswell, in his celebrated *The Life of Samuel Johnson* (1791), who created the first distinctive masterpiece of English biography, using vividly dramatized scenes (worked up from his *Journals*) within a meticulous chronological narrative. Boswell gives Johnson both a sombre inner life and a robust social existence in tavern and drawing room, drawn with penetrating humour. The imaginative tension between private and public lives would become a hallmark of modern life-writing. Boswell's work clearly reflects the ethos of the European *Enlightenment (he knew David *Hume, *Voltaire, and Jean-Jacques *Rousseau): fearless and rational enquiry into the human condition, bringing better understanding of ourselves, and greater toleration of other natures and beliefs. The 19th century saw the flowering of biography and much debate about the role of biographers. Many saw themselves as dutiful celebrants paying homage to great lives, particularly where they were writing about a parent or friend. This was the case for Hallam Tennyson writing on his father in *Alfred Lord Tennyson: A Memoir* (1897), John *Lockhart on his father-in-law Walter *Scott (1837–8), John *Forster on his friend Charles *Dickens (1872–4), and Anne Thackeray Ritchie on her father, the novelist W. M. *Thackeray, in *Chapters from Some Memoirs* (1894). These were monuments to virtue and were welcomed as such, as were the didactic portraits in Samuel Smiles's *Self-Help* (1859) which proved extremely popular. The demand for flawless heroes affected even such a sympathetic study as Elizabeth *Gaskell's *Life of Charlotte Brontë* (1857), which aimed at new levels of openness. J. A. *Froude caused a protracted scandal by exposing aspects of Thomas *Carlyle's domestic life. Froude edged towards the objective, sometimes iconoclastic biographical stance that would be adopted uncompromisingly by Lytton *Strachey. His four elegant and mocking studies (with a satiric preface) in *Eminent Victorians* (1918)—of Cardinal *Manning, Florence *Nightingale, Dr Thomas *Arnold of Rugby, and General Gordon—liberated the artistic form of English biography once more. His work encouraged valuable experiments in the structure of biographical narrative, and a much more sophisticated approach to the contradictions of human character.

These experiments have become an influential part of the modern English tradition, already pioneered by Edmund *Gosse, who followed a standard Victorian life of his father, the naturalist and Christian fundamentalist Philip Henry Gosse (1890), with a devastating reappraisal in *Father and Son* (1907). Other influential experiments include Virginia *Woolf's *Orlando* (1928), a disguised life of Vita *Sackville-West through four centuries and a sex change, and *Flush* (1933), her life of Elizabeth Barrett Browning's dog. A. J. A. *Symons explored biography as an ornate and labyrinthine detective story in *The Quest for Corvo* (1934). An actual legal case, an embargo on biographical research brought by a living subject, turned Ian *Hamilton's *In Search of J. D. Salinger* (1988) into a mordant study of the ethics and psychology of life-writing itself. Julian *Barnes's *Flaubert's Parrot* (1984) was a brilliant postmodern parody of the art of biographical misinterpretation, interweaving the figure of a pedantic, fictional biographer with genuinely illuminating scholarship. Peter *Ackroyd's *Dickens* (1990), which included fictional interludes, prompted the question of how far a biographer is necessarily a creative writer. Far from undermining mainstream biography, these experiments have encouraged ever more detailed research, with finer and more stylish narrative techniques. This is especially true in literary biography, which has returned with great confidence to the large, comprehensive form of 'Life and Work' considered as a single dramatic and psychological unity. Outstanding among these are Richard *Ellmann's scholarly Irish trilogy, lives of W. B. *Yeats (1948), James *Joyce (1959), and Oscar *Wilde (1987), and Michael *Holroyd's flamboyant and socially expansive portraits of Lytton Strachey (1967–8), Augustus *John (1974–5), and George Bernard *Shaw (1988–92). Roy Foster's masterful biography of W. B. Yeats held to a chronological course on the basis that 'we do not, alas, live our lives in themes, but day by day', while Hermione *Lee's fine lives of Virginia Woolf (1996) and Edith *Wharton (2007) demonstrated the rich possibilities of a thematic approach. Notable work has also been done by Richard *Holmes on P. B. *Shelley and S. T. *Coleridge, Hilary *Spurling on Ivy *Compton-Burnett (1974, 1984), Victoria *Glendinning on the adventures of Vita Sackville-West (1983), and Claire *Tomalin on Mary *Wollstonecraft (1974) and the 19th-century actress Dorothy *Jordan (1994). Important work on non-literary subjects includes Martin Gilbert on *Churchill, John Sugden on Horatio Nelson, Jenny *Uglow's life of *Hogarth, and her 'group biography' *The Lunar Men* (2002). Recent biographies have also uncovered the lives of less eminent figures, answering Woolf's call for 'lives of the obscure'. Biographies of women have been particularly prolific, and women are now far better represented in the magisterial *Oxford Dictionary of National Biography*, founded by Colin Matthew in 1992 and continuing the work of Leslie *Stephen, who launched the **Dictionary of National Biography* in 26 volumes between 1885 and 1890.

Contemporary biographers are self-conscious about their art, questioning the boundaries between history and fiction, grappling with gaps in knowledge or different versions of events, and acknowledging that while they can offer *a* life of their subject, they cannot offer *the* life. There is now a considerable body of theoretical and discursive work on biography as an artistic form. Early explorations were Woolf's lively essays on 'The New Biography' (1927) and 'The Art of Biography' (1939). Robert *Gittings, biographer of Keats and Hardy, defended the form in his short but panoramic overview *The Nature of Biography* (1978); Richard Ellmann with mischievous wit in *Golden Codgers* (1976), which popularized Joyce's term 'biografiend'; and Leon *Edel (biographer of Henry *James) in his striking meditations *Writing Lives: Principia Biographica* (1984). Richard Holmes's seminal *Footsteps: Adventures of a Romantic Biographer* (1985) explored the overlap between biography and autobiography, and the emotive 'quest' for the subject. Helpful recent discussions of the genre include David Ellis's *Literary Lives* (2000) and Hermione Lee's *Biography: A Very Short Introduction* (2009). All these studies try to deal with a number of recurrent issues: the ethics of 'invading' privacy; the ambiguity of the links between art and life; the questionable objectivity of such sources as letters and diaries; the distortions involved in 'plotting' a life as a continuous narrative; the role of empathy and psychological 'transference' between author and subject; and the vexed question of the 'celebrity' life, which produces endless new and competing versions. These competing versions often become themselves part of the story the biographer tells. Many recent lives do not end with the death of the subject but go on to trace their various 'afterlives': the changes in reputation, the myths and apocrypha that grow up around a celebrated figure, and—importantly—the ways in which their life has been written.

BION (*fl. c.*100 BC) A Greek pastoral poet, said to have been born in Smyrna and to have died prematurely in Sicily. In literary history he is linked with *Theocritus and *Moschus. Little of his work survives. His best-known and only complete poem is his *Lament for Adonis*, which was imitated by *Ronsard and of which echoes can be found in Edmund *Spenser's *Astrophell* and William *Shakespeare's **Venus and Adonis*. John *Milton's **Lycidas* and P. B. *Shelley's **Adonais* draw directly from Bion's *Lament*.

BIRCH, Thomas (1705–66) Biographer, historian, secretary to the *Royal Society, and Anglican clergyman, born in Clerkenwell, London. He was the principal editor and author of *A General Dictionary, Historical and Critical*, 10 vols (1734–41); this is an expansion of Pierre *Bayle's *Dictionary*, and a major source of new information about English figures, including poets, politicians, scientists, and theologians. His many publications include lives and editions of Robert *Boyle, Catharine *Cockburn, John *Milton, and John *Tillotson. He was a keen collector of manuscripts, which he left to the *British Museum.

BIRD, Isabella (1831–1904) Travel writer, who also published as Isabella Bishop after her marriage in 1880. Born in Yorkshire, she spent much of her life when in Britain in Edinburgh and on the Isle of Mull. Advised to recuperate abroad after a spinal operation in 1850, she embarked on a life of travel that took her all around the world. Her vivid accounts of her journeys—among them *A Lady's Life in the Rocky Mountains* (1879), *Unbeaten Tracks in Japan* (1880), *The Golden Chersonese* (1883), and *Travels in Persia and Kurdistan* (1891)—achieved both popular and critical success, and in 1892 she became the first female Fellow of the *Royal Geographical Society. She appears as a character and as a type of the intrepid Victorian woman in Caryl Churchill's **Top Girls*.

BIRRELL, Augustine (1850–1933) Liberal chief secretary for Ireland, 1907–16, and literary critic, born in Wavertree, near Liverpool. He studied law at Trinity Hall, Cambridge. He made his name as an author with a volume of lightweight but witty essays, *Obiter Dicta* (1884), and then a second volume in 1887. He later wrote *More Obiter Dicta* (1924) and books on *Hazlitt (1902) and *Marvell (1905). His son Francis Birrell (1889–1935), journalist and dramatic critic, was associated with the *Bloomsbury Group.

BIRTWISTLE, Sir Harrison (1934–) Composer, born in Accrington, Lancashire, and educated at the Royal Manchester College of Music and the Royal Academy of Music. His work combines the violence of classical and pagan mythology and folk narratives with a modernist idiom and highly structured, cyclical forms. His first opera, *Punch and Judy* (1968), reworked the traditional story in a structured series of small-scale numbers. Birtwistle worked with Tony *Harrison on *Bow Down* (1977), based in part on Japanese *Nōh models, and produced the music for Peter *Hall's 1981 production of Aeschylus' **Oresteia*. His theatre music includes scores for several *Shakespeare productions from **Hamlet* (1975) onwards. His opera *Yan Tan Tethera* (1984) takes its cue from a pastoral myth, while *The Mask of Orpheus* (1986) presents an intricate mosaic of perspectives on the Greek story. *Gawain* (1991), to a libretto by David *Harsent, is based on the medieval alliterative poem *Sir *Gawain and the Green Knight*. Significant instrumental works include *Panic* (1995), on the nature god Pan. Birtwistle was knighted in 1988.

BISHOP, Elizabeth (1911–79) American poet, born in Massachusetts, and brought up by her maternal grandparents in Nova Scotia after the death of her father and mental collapse of her mother. She was educated at Vassar College, where in 1934 she met Marianne *Moore, with whose work her own has much affinity. She later travelled widely, finally settling in Brazil; the titles of some of her volumes (*North and South*, 1946; *Questions of Travel*, 1965; *Geography III*, 1976) reflect her preoccupation with place and movement, and her verse is reticent, objective, spare yet colloquial. Her *Complete Poems 1927–1979* appeared in 1983. Robert Giroux edited her *Collected Prose* (1984) and *One Art: The Selected Letters* (1994); see also Robert Giroux and Lloyd Schwartz (eds), *Elizabeth Bishop: Poems, Prose and Letters* (2008).

BISHOP, Sir Henry Rowley (1786–1855) Prolific composer of operas based on *Shakespeare and Walter *Scott among others; remembered now for the song 'Home, Sweet Home', which appeared as a 'Sicilian Air' in a volume of *National Airs* edited by Bishop in 1821, and was reused in the opera *Clari* (1823).

BISHOP, John Peale (1892–1944) American poet and story writer, educated at Princeton University with Edmund *Wilson and F. Scott *Fitzgerald. His *Collected Essays* and *Collected Poems* were published in 1948.

BISHOP, Michael (1945–) American author, born in Lincoln, Nebraska. *A Funeral for the Eyes of Fire* (1975) contains anthropological explorations of human–alien contact. *No Enemy But Time* (1982) and *Ancient of Days* (1985) similarly use humanity's distant past. *Brittle Innings* (1994) is an emotionally powerful updating of the *'*Frankenstein*' myth.

BLACK, William (1841–98) Scottish journalist and novelist, who gave up his post as assistant editor of the **Daily News* in 1875, following the international success of his moralizing romances *A Daughter of Heth* (1871), *The Strange Adventures of a Phaeton* (1872), and *A Princess of Thule* (1873). Later novels include *Macleod of Dare* (1878), *Shandon Bells* (1883), and *Judith Shakespeare* (1884).

Black Arts Movement Founded in Harlem in the mid-1960s by Amiri *Baraka and promoted by Larry Neal (1937–81), the movement supported cultural separatism and the Black Power movement, and sought to devise a distinctive African American aesthetic. Drawing on African art forms, it aimed at a total cultural revolution. Under its auspices a number of theatre venues were established. Other participants included Nikki Giovanni (1943–) and Sonia Sanchez (1934–). The movement was active until the mid-1970s.

Black Beauty, *his Grooms and Companions: The Autobiography of a Horse. Translated from the Original Equine* (1877) By Anna Sewell (1820–78), born in Yarmouth of a Quaker family. It is a *'crossover' book, written 'to induce kindness, sympathy, and an understanding treatment of horses'. Its particular target was the fashionable 'bearing rein', but its vividly dramatic episodes portray a wide spectrum of English life, from high society to the lowest slums. The 'innocent' eye of Black Beauty provides trenchant social comment made more powerful by the moving characterization of Beauty and his horse companions. Of these, Ginger's sad life featuring brutal treatment, hard and demeaning work, and ending in a cart on the way to the knacker's yard in particular has moved generations of readers. Sewell sold the copyright to Jarrold and Sons for £40; the book sold over 12,000 copies in its first year. It was promoted by the RSPCA, and pirated in the USA by George Angell, founder of the American Humane Education Society, which gave away over two million copies between 1890 and 1910. It has been highly influential in the genre of *animal stories, and has been filmed at least eleven times. There is a life, *Dark Horse*, by A. E. Gavin (2004).

Black Book of Carmarthen, The A Welsh manuscript of the 13th century, probably compiled by a scribe at the Priory of St John and St Teulyddog at Carmarthen. Its 108 pages contain medieval Welsh poems in a variety of modes, including eight on legendary and *Arthurian themes, and a group of prophecies relating to *Merlin.

black British literature *See introductory essay* pp. 16–22.

Black Dwarf, The A novel by Walter *Scott, published 1816. The first of the **Tales of my Landlord* and published anonymously, the novel's most interesting feature today is Scott's treatment of deformity. At the time of writing, he was preoccupied by the possible influence of Lord *Byron's lameness (which Scott himself shared) on his character. There are other correspondences between Scott's personal history and the situation of the Dwarf, who was superficially based on an actual dwarf, David Ritchie.

Blackfriars Theatre was built in the City of London within the boundaries of the old Dominican monastery lying between Ludgate Hill and the river. The first theatre on the site was adapted for performances by Richard Farrant, master of the Children of Windsor Chapel, in 1576; the second, in a different part of the old building, was bought and adapted by James *Burbage in 1596, but was handed over to the Children of the Chapel because of local opposition. It reverted to James's son Richard *Burbage in 1608. William *Shakespeare had a share in the new company that performed there. The building was demolished in 1655.

black humour A kind of humour which flourished from the late 1950s through to the 1970s in America, characterized by morbid or provocative treatment of subjects like death and disease. The typical unit of black humour narratives is the episode, and two of the best exemplars of this mode are Joseph *Heller's *Catch-22* (1961) and Stanley Kubrick's 1964 film *Dr Strangelove, or How I Learned to Stop Worrying and Love the Bomb*. The latter dramatizes a pathological sexual obsession with weaponry dominating the US military. Other practitioners include Terry *Southern, Kurt *Vonnegut, and Bruce Jay Friedman (1930–), who edited the anthology *Black Humour* in 1965.

BLACKLOCK, Thomas (1721–91) Scottish poet and essayist, born near Annan, Dumfriesshire, the son of an English bricklayer; he lost his sight to smallpox when six months old. He was befriended by both David *Hume and James *Beattie, and received a DD from Marischal College, Aberdeen, in 1767. There is an account of his meeting with Samuel *Johnson in James *Boswell's *Journal of a Tour to the Hebrides*. His collected poems, with a life by Henry *Mackenzie, appeared in 1793. His letter of praise for *Poems, Chiefly in the Scottish Dialect* is said to have dissuaded Robert *Burns from emigrating to Jamaica.

BLACKMAN, Malorie (1962–) Writer of short stories, picture books, and *young adult fiction. She was born in London, and educated at Thames Polytechnic and the National Film and Television School. Although her characters are often black, she rarely writes explicitly about race. *Hacker* (1992) is a thriller about IT; *Pig-Heart Boy* (1997, televised in 1999) deals with organ transplantation. *Noughts and Crosses* (2001) and its sequels *Knife Edge* (2004), *Checkmate* (2005), and *Double Cross* (2008) are set in an alternative world where race relations are reversed.

BLACKMORE, R. D. (Richard Doddridge) (1825–1900) Writer and fruit-farmer; the son of a clergyman, Blackmore was educated at Blundell's School, Tiverton, and at Exeter College, Oxford. He was called to the bar, but his epilepsy forced him to take up a country life, first as a schoolmaster, then as a fruit-grower at Teddington, where he lived till his death. He was happily married to an Irishwoman, Lucy Maguire, whose mother was a laundress. The wedding did not have the approval of Blackmore's family, and barriers of religion and social class thwarting the union of lovers frequently figure in his fiction. He published several volumes of poems and translations from *Theocritus and *Virgil, but his fame rests almost entirely on one of his novels, *Lorna Doone* (1869). He wrote thirteen other novels, including *Cradock Nowell* (1866), *The Maid of Sker* (1872), *Alice Lorraine* (1875), and *Springhaven* (1887). These pastoral tales, stirring in incident and with a slightly grotesque humour, are often ill constructed, and sometimes over-lush in style, but their descriptions of lovingly observed climate, wildlife, and vegetation are engaging. Blackmore was a kindly but reserved and eccentric man, absorbed in his experimental fruit-farming. See Waldo H. Dunn, *R. D. Blackmore, the Author of 'Lorna Doone'* (1956); M. K. Sutton, *R. D. Blackmore* (1979).

BLACKMORE, Sir Richard (1654–1729) Poet and doctor, educated at St Edmund Hall, Oxford. In 1695 he inaugurated his series of grand verse epics with *Prince Arthur*, a transparent panegyric on William III, who knighted him in 1697. He was physician to William and to Queen Anne, whom he celebrated in *Eliza* (1705). His orthodox *Creation: A Philosophical Poem* (1712) was added to **Lives of the English Poets* by Samuel *Johnson's own choice. Blackmore's humourless morality and prolixity were mocked by the wits, from Samuel *Garth onwards; Alexander *Pope catalogued his bombast in **Peri Bathous*, and in *The *Dunciad* mocked his 'sonorous strain'.

Black Mountain poets A group of American poets associated with Black Mountain College, an experimental liberal arts college founded in 1933 near Asheville, North Carolina, which became in the early 1950s a centre of anti-academic poetic revolt. A leading figure was Charles *Olson, rector of the college from 1951 to 1956, whose *Projective Verse* (1950) was a form of manifesto, laying much emphasis on the dynamic energy of the spoken word and phrase and attacking the domination of syntax, rhyme, and metre. His students and followers included Robert *Creeley, Robert Duncan (1919–88), and Denise *Levertov. The *Black Mountain Review* (1954–7; edited by Creeley) also published work by Allen *Ginsberg and Jack *Kerouac, thus heralding the *Beat Generation.

BLACKMUR, R. P. (Richard Palmer) (1904–65) American poet and critic, associated for many years with Princeton University, where he was professor from 1948 to 1965. His critical works, which include *The Expense of Greatness* (1940), *Language as Gesture* (1952), and *The Lion and the Honeycomb* (1955), link him with the *New Criticism; he was one of the early champions of the art of Wallace *Stevens.

BLACKSTONE, Sir William (1723–80) First Vinerian professor of common law at Oxford; his *Commentaries on the Laws of England* (4 vols, 1765–9) was a classic historical account of English law. It was criticized by Jeremy *Bentham in *A Fragment on Government* for accepting the existing legal system.

BLACKWOOD, Algernon (1869–1951) Journalist, short story writer, and novelist, born in Shooters Hill, Kent, now part of London. He led an adventurous early life in Canada and New York, where when almost starving he found work in journalism—described in *Episodes before Thirty* (1923). His work included travel, adventure, humour, and pantheistic fantasies, but the stories for which he is chiefly remembered deal in the psychic and macabre. His second collection, *The Listener and Other Stories* (1907), contains 'The Willows', highly regarded by H. P. *Lovecraft for its cosmic awe. More than 30 books followed, including *Tales of the Uncanny and Supernatural* (1949). See Mike Ashley, *Starlight Man: The Extraordinary Life of Algernon Blackwood* (2001).

BLACKWOOD, William (1776–1834) Scots publisher, founder of the firm of William Blackwood and Son, and of the highly successful **Blackwood's (Edinburgh) Magazine* in the conduct of which he took a decided interest. He early recognized the talent of John *Galt, whose *The *Ayrshire Legatees* he published, and of Susan *Ferrier. In 1810 he bought the *Edinburgh Encyclopaedia*, which he saw finally completed in 1830. His sons, in turn, became editors of *Blackwood's*; his son John (1818–79) was an admirer of George *Eliot, published much of her work, and became a friend.

Blackwood's Magazine (1817–1980) or 'the Maga', was an innovating monthly periodical founded by William *Blackwood as a Tory rival to the Whiggish **Edinburgh Review*. Beginning in April 1817 as the *Edinburgh Monthly Magazine*, it continued from October of that year until December 1905 as *Blackwood's Edinburgh Magazine*; in January 1906 it became *Blackwood's Magazine*. Although similar in politics to the **Quarterly Review*, it was intended to be sharper, brighter, and less ponderous. The first editors were soon replaced by John Gibson *Lockhart, John *Wilson, and James *Hogg, who gave the 'Maga' its forceful partisan tone. Its notoriety was early established with the publication in 1817 of the so-called *'Chaldee MS', in which many leading Edinburgh figures were pilloried; and, beginning in the same year, with the long series of attacks on the *'Cockney School' of poetry, directed chiefly against Leigh *Hunt, John *Keats, and William *Hazlitt. Blackwood had sometimes to pay damages, notably to Hazlitt, for the venom of his writers' pens. *Blackwood's* did however give considerable support to William *Wordsworth, P. B. *Shelley, Thomas *De Quincey, Henry *Mackenzie, John *Galt, Walter *Scott, and others, and did much to foster an interest in German literature. Unlike the *Edinburgh* and the *Quarterly* it published short stories and serialized novels. The carnivalesque series of sketches **Noctes Ambrosianae* was highly popular. Soon after 1830 the magazine became a purely literary review, and continued through the 19th century as a prosperous and respected literary miscellany, publishing Joseph *Conrad, Alfred *Noyes, Andrew *Lang, and many others. It continued, in a diminished form, until 1980.

BLAIR, Eric *See* Orwell, George.

BLAIR, Hugh (1718–1800) Scottish preacher and first Regius professor of rhetoric and belles lettres at Edinburgh University. He is remembered for his sermons (5 vols, 1777–1801) and for his influential and often reprinted *Lectures on Rhetoric and Belles Lettres* (2 vols, 1784). He belonged to a distinguished literary circle which included David *Hume, Alexander *Carlyle, Adam *Smith, and (briefly) Robert *Burns. He incurred Samuel *Johnson's wrath for his defence of James *Macpherson, his *A Critical Dissertation on the Poems of Ossian* (1763) finding that **Fingal* possessed 'all the essential requisites of a true and regular epic'.

BLAIR, Robert (1699–1746) Poet and Church of Scotland clergyman, educated at Edinburgh and in the Netherlands, and appointed minister of Athelstaneford, East Lothian, in 1731. His fame rests on *The Grave* (1743), a didactic poem of the *Graveyard School, consisting of 767 lines of *blank verse. It celebrates the horrors of death, the solitude of the tomb, the pains of bereavement, and the madness of suicide, and concludes on an orthodox Christian note some readers have found perfunctory. It has passages of considerable power and, like Edward *Young's **Night Thoughts*, was illustrated by William *Blake.

BLAKE, Quentin (1932–) MBE, Chevalier des Arts et des Lettres. This prolific artist has produced many distinguished *picturebooks and pioneering *'crossover' books, such as *The Green Ship* (1997). His work is lively and often anarchic. Blake illustrated Roald *Dahl's children's books, and was the first children's laureate (1999–2001).

BLAKE, William (1757–1827) Engraver and visionary poet, the third son of a London hosier. He did not go to school, but was apprenticed to James Basire, engraver to the Society of Antiquaries, and then became a student at the Royal Academy. From 1779 he was employed as an engraver by the bookseller Joseph *Johnson, and in 1780 met Henry *Fuseli and John *Flaxman, the latter a follower of Emanuel *Swedenborg, whose mysticism deeply influenced Blake. In 1782 he married Catherine Boucher, the daughter of a market-gardener; their childless marriage was a lasting communion. Flaxman at this period introduced him to the progressive intellectual circle of the Revd A. S. Mathew and his wife (which included Anna Laetitia *Barbauld, Hannah *More, and Elizabeth *Montagu), and Mathew and Flaxman financed the publication of Blake's first volume, *Poetical Sketches* (1783). In 1784, with help from Mrs Mathew, he set up a print shop at 27 Broad Street, and at about the same period (although not for publication) wrote the satirical *An *Island in the Moon*. He engraved and published his **Songs of Innocence* in 1789, and also *The Book of *Thel*, both works which manifest the early phases of his highly distinctive mystic vision, and in which he embarks on the evolution of his personal mythology; years later (in **Jerusalem*) he was to state, through the character Los, 'I must Create a System, or be enslav'd by another Man's', words which have been taken by some to apply to his own need to escape from the fetters of 18th-century versification, as well as from the materialist philosophy (as he conceived it) of the *Enlightenment, and a Puritanical or repressive interpretation of Christianity. *The Book of Thel* presents the maiden Thel lamenting transience and mutability by the banks of the river of Adona; she is answered by the lily, the cloud, the worm, and the clod who assure her that 'He, who loves the lowly' cherishes even the meanest; but this relatively conventional wisdom is challenged by a final section in which Thel visits the house of Clay, sees the couches of the dead, and hears 'a voice of sorrow' breathe a characteristically Blakean protest against hypocrisy and restraint—'Why a tender curb upon the youthful, burning boy? Why a tender little curtain of flesh upon the bed of our desire?'—a message which sends Thel back 'with a shriek' to the vales of Har. The ambiguity of this much-interpreted poem heralds the increasing complexity of his other works which include *Tiriel* (written 1789; pub. 1874), introducing the theme of the blind tyrannical father, 'the king of rotten wood, and of the bones of death', which reappears in different forms in many poems; *The *Marriage of Heaven and Hell* (engraved *c.*1790–3), his principal prose work, a book of paradoxical aphorisms; and the revolutionary works *The French Revolution* (1791); *America: A Prophecy* (1793); and *Visions of the Daughters of Albion* (also 1793), in which he develops his attitude of revolt against authority, combining political fervour (he had met Thomas *Paine at Joseph Johnson's) and visionary ecstasy; Urizen, the deviser of moral codes (described as 'the stony law' of the Decalogue) and Orc, the Promethean arch-rebel, emerge as principal characters in a cosmology that some scholars have related to that of *Gnosticism. By this time Blake had already established his poetic range; the long, flowing lines and violent energy of the verse combine with phrases of terse and aphoristic clarity and moments of great lyric tenderness, and he was once more to demonstrate his command of the lyric in **Songs of Experience* (1794), which includes 'Tyger! Tyger! burning bright', 'O Rose thou art sick', and other of his more accessible pieces.

Meanwhile the Blakes had moved to Lambeth in 1790; there he continued to work for the booksellers, and also to engrave his own works and to write, evolving his mythology further in *The Book of *Urizen* (1794); **Europe, a Prophecy* (1794); *The Song of Los* (1795); *The Book of Ahania* (1795); *The Book of Los* (1795); and *The *Four Zoas* (originally entitled *Vala*, written and revised 1797–1804). In 1800 he moved to Felpham, Sussex, where he lived for three years, working for his friend and patron William *Hayley, and working on **Milton* (1804–8); in 1803 he was charged at Chichester with high treason for having 'uttered seditious and treasonable expressions, such as "'D——n the King, d——n all his subjects..."', but was acquitted. In the same year he returned to London, to work on *Milton* and **Jerusalem: The Emanation of the Giant Albion* (written and etched, 1804–20). In 1805 he was commissioned by Robert *Cromek to produce a set of drawings for Robert *Blair's poem *The Grave*, but Cromek defaulted on the contract, and Blake earned neither the money nor the public esteem he had hoped for, and found his designs engraved and weakened by another hand. This was symptomatic of the disappointment of his later years, when he appears to have relinquished expectations of being widely understood, and quarrelled even with some of the circle of friends who supported him. Both his poetry and his art had failed to find a sympathetic audience, and a lifetime of hard work had brought him neither riches nor comfort. His last years were passed in obscurity, although he eventually began to attract the interest and admiration of younger artists. A commission in 1821 from the painter John Linnell produced his well-known illustrations for the Book of Job, published in 1826 (it was Linnell who introduced Blake to Samuel *Palmer in 1824.) A late poem, 'The Everlasting Gospel', written about 1818, shows undiminished power and attack; it presents Blake's own version of Jesus, in a manner that recalls the paradoxes of *The Marriage of Heaven and Hell*, attacking the conventional 'Creeping Jesus', gentle, humble, and chaste, and stressing his rebellious nature, his forgiveness of the woman taken in adultery, his reversing of the stony law of Moses, praising 'the Naked Human form divine', and sexuality as the means whereby 'the Soul Expands its wing', and elevating forgiveness above the 'Moral Virtues'.

At Blake's death, general opinion held that he had been, if gifted, insane; *Wordsworth's verdict, according to Henry Crabb *Robinson, was that 'There was no doubt that this poor man was mad, but there is something in the madness of this man which interests me more than the sanity of Lord Byron and Walter Scott', a view in some measure echoed by *Ruskin, who found his manner 'diseased and wild' but his mind 'great and wise'. It was not until Alexander Gilchrist's biography of 1863 (completed after his death by his wife Anne *Gilchrist), which significantly described Blake as 'Pictor Ignotus', that interest began to grow. This was followed by an appreciation by *Swinburne (1868) and by William Michael *Rossetti's edition of 1874, which added new poems to the canon and established his reputation, at least as a lyric poet; his rediscovered engravings considerably influenced the development of *art nouveau. In 1893 *Yeats, a devoted admirer, produced with E. J. Ellis a three-volume edition, with a memoir and an interpretation of the mythology, and the 20th century saw an enormous increase in interest. The bibliographical studies and editions of Geoffrey Keynes, culminating in *The Complete Writings of William Blake* (1966, 2nd edn), have added greatly to knowledge both of the man and his works, revealing him not only as an apocalyptic visionary but also as a writer of ribald and witty epigrams, a critic of spirit and originality, and an independent thinker who found his own way of resisting the orthodoxies of his age, and whose hostile response to the narrow vision and materialism (as he conceived it) of his *bêtes noires* Joshua *Reynolds, John *Locke, and Isaac *Newton was far from demented, but in part a prophetic warning of the dangers of a world perceived as mechanism, with man as a mere cog in an industrial revolution. There have been many interpretative studies, relating his work to traditional Christianity, to the *Neoplatonic and Swedenborgian traditions, to Jungian *archetypes, and to *Freudian and *Marxist theory; the Prophetic Books, once dismissed as incoherent, are now claimed by many as works of integrity as well as profundity. Blake had a marked influence on the *Beat Generation and the English poets of the underground movement, hailed by both as liberator; W. H. *Auden earlier acclaimed him (in the 'New Year Letter', 1941) as 'Self-educated Blake…' who 'Spoke to Isaiah in the Strand | And heard inside each mortal thing | Its holy emanation sing'.

See *Blake Books* (1977) by G. E. Bentley, Jr, including annotated catalogues of his writings and scholarly works about him; *The Complete Poetry and Prose of William Blake*, ed. D. V. Erdman (1965, 1988); *Blake's Illuminated Books*, 6 vols (1991–5), gen. ed. D. Bindman; J. Viscomi, *Blake and the Idea of the Book* (1993), an authoritative account of Blake's graphic process; and Erdman's *Blake: Prophet against Empire* (1954; 1977), a study of the poet's politics. There are modern biographies by M. Wilson, rev. G. Keynes (1971) and Peter *Ackroyd (1995). See also The William Blake Archive: www.blakearchive.org/blake (ed. M. Eaves, R. Essick, and J. Viscomi).

BLAMIRE, Susanna (1747–94) Poet, daughter of a Cumberland farmer, whose verse was circulated among friends or pinned to trees, and sometimes published, in single sheets, anthologies, or magazines. *The Poetical Works of Miss Susanna Blamire, 'The Muse of Cumberland'* (1842) was compiled by Patrick Maxwell of Edinburgh and Henry Lonsdale of Carlisle. The poems range from Scots or Cumberland dialect songs, such as 'The Siller Croun' and 'Wey, Ned, man!', to personal lyrics, chatty epistles to friends, and the heroic couplets of 'Stoklewath, or The Cumbrian Village', a complex picture of rural life and her most substantial poem.

BLANCH, Lesley (1904–2007) Romantic biographer, orientalist, and travel writer, best known for her memorably entitled group biography *The Wilder Shores of Love* (1954), dedicated to her then husband, novelist Romain Gary (1914–80). It tells the lives of four women 'enthralled by the Oriental legend': these include Isabel Burton, née Arundell (1831–96), wife of Sir Richard *Burton, and Frenchwoman Isabelle Eberhardt (1877–1904). *Pavilions of the Heart* (1974) is an anthology of various historic erotic venues. Blanch also edited the memoirs of Harriette *Wilson as *The Game of Hearts* (1957).

blank verse Verse written in unrhymed lines of iambic *pentameter. It was first used by *Surrey *c.*1540, subsequently adopted for dramatic verse by Thomas *Sackville and Thomas Norton (1530/2–84) in **Gorboduc* (1561), and most powerfully developed by Christopher *Marlowe and William *Shakespeare. It remained a standard form in non-dramatic verse, notably in the hands of John *Milton, William *Wordsworth, and Alfred *Tennyson.

Blast A periodical of literature and art edited by Wyndham *Lewis, subtitled 'Review of the Great English Vortex' (*see* Vorticism). Only two issues appeared, the first in June 1914, and the second, the 'War Number', in July 1915. The puce cover of the first issue and its striking typography made *Blast* one of the most self-consciously avant-garde of the British modernist periodicals. The first issue established its bearings in the opening pages by 'blasting' and 'blessing' British writers and institutions. Its contributors included Ezra *Pound, Ford Madox *Ford, T. S. *Eliot, Rebecca *West, Jessica Dismorr (1885–1939), and Helen Saunders (1885–1963).

Blatant Beast In Edmund *Spenser's **Faerie Queene*, Book VI, a monster, the personification of the calumnious voice of the world, begotten of Envy and Detraction. Sir *Calidore pursues it, finds it despoiling monasteries and defiling the church, overcomes it, and chains it up. But finally it breaks the chain, 'So now he raungeth through the world againe.'

BLAVATSKY, Madame Elena Petrovna (1831–91) Russian spiritualist, was born in Ekaterinoslav, Ukraine, but from 1848 travelled extensively throughout the world. In 1873 she emigrated to the United States, where she gained a reputation as a medium and in 1875 she founded, with Colonel Henry Steel Olcott (1832–1907) and William Quan Judge (1851–96), the Theosophical Society. Its aims to promote universal brotherhood, the study of Eastern literature and religion, and research into the laws of nature and the latent faculties of man were developed in her book *Isis Unveiled* (1877). In certain respects the Society's beliefs anticipate the 20th-century *New Age movement. By 1882 the Society's headquarters were located in India, near Madras, but Blavatsky finally moved to England, where her 'Inner Circle' of twelve disciples included Mrs Annie Besant (1847–1933). See Sylvia Cranston, *H.P.B.: The Extraordinary Life and Influence of Helena Blavatsky* (1993).

BLAYLOCK, James P. (1950–) American author, born in Long Beach, California. He turned from fantasies to 'steampunk' *science fiction in *The Digging Leviathan* (1984) and *Lord Kelvin's Machine* (1992). Like Tim *Powers, with whom he has collaborated in short stories, he explores and manipulates generic images and patterns.

blazon A heraldic term used to describe a catalogue of the different physical elements of a woman's beauty. The term is usually associated with poetry, as in Philip *Sidney's *Old Arcadia* poem 'What toong can her perfections tell' or William *Shakespeare's Sonnet 106, 'in the blazon of sweet beauty's best'.

Bleak House A novel by Charles *Dickens, published in monthly parts 1852–3. This dark and complex book combines a vigorous attack on the abuses of the old court of Chancery, the delays and costs of which brought misery and ruin on its suitors, with bitter satire on the callous neglect of the poor by the rich and powerful, and an intricate exploration of themes of hidden transgression, obsession, violence, and exposure. The complex plot centres on the fortunes of Richard Carstone, an irresolute youth, and his gentle cousin Ada Clare. They are wards of the court in the case of Jarndyce and Jarndyce, concerned with the distribution of an estate, which has gone on so long as to become a subject of heartless joking as well as a source of great profit to those professionally engaged in it. The wards are taken to live with their kind elderly relative John Jarndyce. They fall in love and secretly marry. Richard, incapable of sticking to any profession and lured by the will-o'-the-wisp of the fortune that is to be his when the case is settled, sinks gradually to ruin and death, and the case of Jarndyce and Jarndyce comes suddenly to an end on the discovery that the costs have absorbed the whole estate in dispute.

When Ada goes to live with John Jarndyce she is accompanied by Esther Summerson, a supposed orphan, self-effacing and loyal, and the narrative is partly supposed to be from her pen. Sir Leicester Dedlock, a pompous old baronet, is devotedly attached to his beautiful wife, Lady Dedlock, who hides a dreadful secret under her haughty exterior. Before her marriage she has loved a certain Captain Hawdon and has become the mother of a daughter, whom she believes dead. Hawdon is thought to have perished at sea. In fact the daughter lives in the person of Esther Summerson, and Hawdon in that of a penniless scrivener, or professional copyist. The accidental sight of his handwriting in a legal document reveals to Lady Dedlock the fact of his existence, and its effect on her alerts the cunning old lawyer Tulkinghorn to the existence of a mystery. Lady Dedlock's enquiries bring her, through the medium of the crossing-sweeper, Jo, a poverty-bitten and illiterate child, to the burial ground where her former lover's miserable career has just ended. Jo's unguarded revelation of his singular experience with this veiled lady sets Tulkinghorn on the track, until he possesses all the facts and tells Lady Dedlock that he is going to expose her next day to her husband. That night Tulkinghorn is murdered. Bucket, the detective who unfolds the mysteries at the heart of the novel, presently reveals to the baronet what Tulkinghorn had discovered, and arrests a former French maid of Lady Dedlock, a violent woman, who has committed the murder. Lady Dedlock, learning that her husband knows her secret, flies from the house in despair, and is found dead near the grave of her lover, in spite of the efforts of her husband and Esther to save her.

Much of the story is occupied with Esther's devotion to John Jarndyce; her acceptance of his offer of marriage from a sense of duty and gratitude, though she loves a young doctor, Woodcourt; Jarndyce's discovery of the state of her heart; and his surrender of her to Woodcourt.

There are a host of animated minor characters, including Harold Skimpole (drawn 'in the light externals of character' from Leigh *Hunt), who disguises his utter selfishness under an assumption of childish irresponsibility; Mrs Jellyby, who sacrifices her family to her selfish addiction to professional philanthropy; Jo, the crossing-sweeper, who is chivvied by the police to his death; Chadband, the pious, eloquent humbug; Turveydrop, the model of deportment; Krook, the 'chancellor' of the rag and bone department, who dies of spontaneous combustion; Guppy, the lawyer's clerk; Guster, the poor slavey; the law-stationer Snagsby; Miss Flite, the little lunatic lady who haunts the Chancery courts; and Jarndyce's friend, the irascible and generous Boythorn (drawn from Walter Savage *Landor).

For many of Dickens's contemporaries, this novel marked a decline in his reputation; individual characters (notably Jo and Bucket) were praised, but it was charged with verbosity and 'absolute want of construction'. Later readers, including George Bernard *Shaw, G. K. *Chesterton, Joseph *Conrad, and Lionel *Trilling, saw it as one of the high points of his achievement, and the herald of his last great phase. Its critical reputation remains high, and it is among the most intensively examined novels of the Victorian period. See Elliot Gilbert (ed.), *Critical Essays on Charles Dickens's Bleak House* (1989).

BLEASDALE, Alan (1946–) Playwright, born and educated in Liverpool. He is the author of several stage plays, including *Having a Ball* (1981), a comedy set in a vasectomy clinic, *Are You Lonesome Tonight?* (1985), about the singer Elvis Presley, and *On the Ledge* (*National Theatre, 1993), which is dramatically staged in a tower block with rioters below. He is perhaps best known for his TV work, which includes *Boys from the Blackstuff* (1982), about a group of unemployed men in Liverpool, and *G.B.H.* (1991), a seven-part serial about corrupt left-wing local politics. His streetwise Liverpool lad Scully first emerged on *BBC Radio 4, then on TV in 1984.

'Blessed Damozel, The' A poem by D. G. *Rossetti, of which the first version appeared in the *Germ* (1850); revised versions appeared subsequently. In this poem, inspired by *Dante, Rossetti described the blessed damozel leaning out from the ramparts of heaven, watching the worlds below and the souls mounting to God, and praying for union with her earthly lover in the shadow of the 'living mystic tree'. One of his earliest and most influential poems, it exemplified a *Pre-Raphaelite interest in medieval sacramental symbolism (she has three lilies in her hand, seven stars in her hair, a white rose in her robe) and was a powerful instance of Rossetti's representation—here in words—of variously eroticized women. He later painted the same subject.

BLESSINGTON, Marguerite, countess of (1789–1849) Author, born in Ireland. She travelled on the Continent with her second husband and with Count d'*Orsay, with whom she ultimately lived. She held court to several leading literary figures. Her publications include *Journal of a Tour through the Netherlands to Paris in 1821* (1822), *The Idler in Italy* (1839–40), and *The Idler in France* (1841), as well as a number of silver-fork novels (*see* FASHIONABLE NOVEL). Her best-known work is *Conversations of Lord Byron with the Countess of Blessington* (1834), which records her encounters with Lord *Byron in Italy, and is important to any consideration of Byron's life abroad.

BLIND, Mathilde (1841–96) Poet, born Mathilde Cohen in Mannheim, Germany; she took the name of her stepfather Karl Blind (1826–1907), who came to England in 1852 as a political refugee. Her brother Ferdinand committed suicide at the age of 17 after a failed assassination attempt upon Bismarck. Her unorthodox and eventful upbringing led her to challenge religious and social orthodoxies: she translated D. F. *Strauss's *The Old Faith and the New* (1873), became involved in the women's movement, and translated the journals of Marie *Bashkirtseff from the French (1890). Her first volume of poetry was published pseudonymously in 1867. This was followed by several others, all of which show a keen sense of social concern and a positivist outlook. They include *The Heather on Fire: A Tale of the Highland Clearances* (1886), and the intellectually ambitious and challenging *The Ascent of Man* (1889), a poem in three parts and varied verse forms, which gives a vivid account of Darwinian evolution from chaos, through the 'cruel strife', 'eternal hunger', and indifference of nature, to Man—'from Man's martyrdom in slow convulsion | Will be born the infinite goodness—God'. She wrote a life of George *Eliot (1884).

Blind Beggar of Bethnal Green, The *See* 'BEGGAR'S DAUGHTER OF BEDNALL-GREEN'.

Blind Harry *See* HARY'S WALLACE.

BLISH, James (1921–75) American author, born in New Jersey, later resident in the UK. Stories and novels published from 1950 and collected (1970) as the 'Cities in Flight' sequence explore the theories of cyclic history of the historian and philosopher Oswald Spengler (1880–1936). *A Case of Conscience* (1958) considers the implications for religious belief of the discovery of apparently sinless aliens. *Doctor Mirabilis* (1964) is a historical novel featuring the 13th-century theologian/scientist Roger *Bacon. Blish's *fanzine columns as 'William Atheling, Jr.' encouraged rigorous standards for the criticism of science fiction.

BLISS, Sir Arthur (1891–1975) Composer. His early works, such as *Madam Noy* (1918), with words by E. H. W. Meyerstein, and *Rout* (1920), which uses nonsense syllables in the vocal part, established him as a modernist. Subsequently he reverted to a more romantic idiom in the tradition of Edward *Elgar, who promoted his work through the Three Choirs Festival. His *Pastoral: Lie Strewn the White Flocks* (1928), for amateur chorus, brings together poems by Ben *Jonson, John *Fletcher, Wilfred *Owen, Robert *Nichols, and *Theocritus. The choral symphony *Morning Heroes* (1930), with words by *Homer, Walt *Whitman, and others, paid tribute to the dead of the First World War, in which he had served. He also wrote settings for G. M. *Hopkins, Cecil *Day-Lewis, Alexander *Pope, and T. S. *Eliot. In 1934–5 Bliss collaborated with H. G. *Wells on music for the film *Things to Come*. Works for the stage include several ballets, incidental music for *The *Tempest* (1921), and a full-scale opera, *The Olympians* (1949), with a libretto by J. B. *Priestley. He was knighted in 1950 and became master of the queen's music in 1953.

Blithedale Romance, The A novel by Nathaniel *Hawthorne, published 1852, and based on Hawthorne's own residence in 1841 at the *Transcendental utopian community at Brook Farm, near Boston. It is narrated by a poet, Miles Coverdale (named after the 16th-century reformer and translator of the Bible Miles *Coverdale), who visits Blithedale Farm, where he meets the exotic, wealthy, and queenly Zenobia (said to be based on Margaret *Fuller), the social reformer Hollingsworth, and the gentle, delicate girl Priscilla. Coverdale broods on the work of Charles *Fourier, Thomas *Carlyle, and Ralph Waldo *Emerson, while both the women fall in love with Hollingsworth; Zenobia is rejected and drowns herself, Hollingsworth marries Priscilla, and Coverdale remains a sceptical, solitary observer of mankind's aspirations and disappointments.

BLIXEN, Karen *See* DINESEN, ISAK.

BLOCH, Robert (1917–94) Chicago-born author of *fantasy and *horror stories who, like his mentor H. P. *Lovecraft, published widely in **Weird Tales*. Other influences included Edgar Allan *Poe, for his use of the grotesque, and 'Jack the Ripper' whom he returned to several times. His treatment of the macabre, though, could be wry and humorous. *Psycho* (1959) was filmed successfully by Alfred *Hitchcock (1960). Bloch's later career in television and screen-writing included three episodes for the original (1960s) series of **Star Trek*.

BLOK, Aleksandr Aleksandrovich (1880–1921) Russian *symbolist poet, playwright, and critic, born into an academic St Petersburg family. His early poetry was shaped by the ideas of the philosopher Vladimir Solovev (1853–1900) about Sophia, the feminine personification of Divine Wisdom ('Verses about the Beautiful Lady', 1904). In 1903 he married Liubov Dmitrievna Mendeleeva, whom he regarded, in part, as Solovev's Sophia incarnate, and in 1904 he met Andrei *Bely. Loss of faith in his ideal, the experience of urban life, and the disillusionment following the débâcle of the Russo-Japanese War and the failure of the 1905 Revolution are reflected in the gloom and pessimism of his second period (1904–8). Major works of these years are the narrative poem *The Night Violet* (1906), the cycles *The City* (1904–8), *The Snow Mask* (1907), and *Faina* (1906–8), and a bitter play satirizing his former ideals, *The Puppet Show* (1906). Some of Blok's most powerful work is contained in the cycles of his third period (1907–21), the urban poetry of *The Terrible World* (1907–16), *Italian Verses* (1909), *Carmen* (1914), resulting from his affair with the opera singer Liubov Delmas, and *Native Land* (1907–16), including his late poems on the theme of Russia. Blok responded to the Russian Revolution with his famous poem of January 1918, 'The Twelve', portraying it as an outbreak of elemental chaos. The poem ends with the ambiguous image of Christ leading a band of Red Guards. After the revolution he undertook various state literary activities, but ceased to write poetry. His *Selected Poems* (trans. Jon *Stallworthy and Peter France) appeared in 2000. See Avril Pyman, *The Life of Aleksandr Blok*, 2 vols (1979–80).

BLONDEL DE NESLE A French *trouvère who wrote in Picardy in the late 12th century and whose poems keep very close to the terminology and spirit of the troubadours. A famous legend makes him a friend of *Richard Cœur de Lion: Richard, on his return from the Holy Land in 1192, was imprisoned in Austria. Blondel set out to find him and, when he sat under a window of the castle where Richard was imprisoned, he sang a song in French that he and the king had composed together; halfway through he paused, and Richard took up the song and completed it. Blondel returned to England and told of the king's whereabouts.

Bloodaxe Books Independent poetry press, founded by Neil Astley in Newcastle-upon-Tyne in 1978, and based in Northumberland from 1997. Since its foundation, Bloodaxe has become a major force in poetry publishing in Britain. It has built up a large and diverse list of new and established English-language poets as well as European and international poetry in translation, which might otherwise fail to find a publisher in the United Kingdom. It has helped to establish the reputation of many interesting poets, including Simon *Armitage, Helen *Dunmore, Susan *Wicks, and Glyn *Maxwell. More established figures on its lists include Miroslav *Holub, Tony *Harrison, and Nobel laureates Rabindranath *Tagore, Eugenio *Montale, and Odysseus *Elytis. It has published a notably large number of modern women poets.

Bloody Brother, The, *or Rollo, Duke of Normandy* A play by John *Fletcher, Ben *Jonson, George *Chapman, and Philip *Massinger, performed *c.*1616, published 1639. It was very popular in the 17th century. An edition by J. D. Jump, published 1948, was reissued 1969.

The Duke of Normandy has bequeathed his dukedom to his two sons Rollo and Otto. Rollo, the elder, a resolute and violent man, in order to secure the whole heritage, kills his brother and orders the immediate execution of all who refuse to support him, including his old tutor Baldwin. Baldwin's daughter Edith pleads for his life, and her beauty captivates Rollo, but his reprieve comes too late. Edith resolves to avenge her father's death, intending to kill Rollo when he comes to woo her. His apparent repentance shakes her determination. While she hesitates, the brother of another of Rollo's victims enters and kills the tyrant. The scene between Latorch, Rollo's favourite, and the Astrologers was probably written by Jonson, as also part of Act IV, sc. i. It contains the lyric 'Take, O, take those lips away', which occurs with certain differences in *Measure for Measure*.

BLOOM, Harold (1930–) American critic, born in New York and educated at Cornell and Yale universities. He has spent his working life as a Yale professor, specializing in the Romantic literary tradition, as in *The Visionary Company* (1961), in opposition to T. S. *Eliot's classical critical orthodoxy. His works on individual poets include *Shelley's Myth-Making* (1959), *Yeats* (1970), and *Wallace Stevens* (1977); but he is better known for his ambitious reconsideration of poetic tradition in *The Anxiety of Influence* (1973) and *A Map of Misreading* (1975), which propose that major poets struggle against the suffocating weight of their predecessors, creating new poems by 'misreading' older ones through a complex series of rhetorical defence mechanisms. Several later works develop this thesis in more detail. A more popular work is *The Western Canon* (1994), which defends the 'great' writers against egalitarian critical trends.

BLOOM, Valerie (1956–) A Jamaican who came to Britain in 1979, and graduated from the University of Kent. A celebrated performance poet, she often writes in Jamaican patois. *Surprising Joy*, a novel for children, was followed by *The Tribe*, a coming-of-age novel concerning the Spanish conquest of the Caribbean.

BLOOMFIELD, Robert (1766–1823) Poet, born in Suffolk. He worked as a farm labourer and then as a shoemaker in London, enduring extreme poverty and often unable to afford paper to write on. He is remembered chiefly as author of *The Farmer's Boy* (1800, ed. Capel *Lofft, who portrayed the poet as a peasant prodigy in the manner of Robert *Burns), which was illustrated with engravings by Thomas *Bewick and which related the life of Giles, an orphan farm labourer, throughout the seasons. A vogue for tales of rustic life led to the immense sale of 26,000 copies in under three years, and translations into Italian and French. His other principal volumes are *Rural Tales* (1802), *Good Tidings, or News from the Farm* (1804), *Wild Flowers* (1806), and *The Banks of the Wye* (1811). These did not achieve the success of his first book and he died in penury. See S. White, *Robert Bloomfield, Romanticism and the Poetry of Community* (2007).

Bloomsbury Group The name given to a relatively loose association of like-minded people rather than an organized body of opinion, it has possibly acquired more significance and solidity than it warrants. Centred at first on 46 Gordon Square, Bloomsbury, which became the home of the artist Vanessa *Bell and her sister Virginia *Woolf (both then unmarried) in 1904, the Group was to include, among others, Geoffrey Keynes (1887–1982), Leonard *Woolf, Lytton *Strachey, David *Garnett, Duncan Grant (1885–1978), E. M. *Forster, Clive *Bell, and Roger *Fry. Based on friendship, an acerbic anti-Victorianism, and a deep interest in the arts, it derived many of its attitudes from G. E. Moore's *Principia*

Ethica (1903). Since the 1960s there have been many critical and biographical studies seeking to reassess the Group's influence and connectivity. See, for example, S. P. Rosenbaum, *The Bloomsbury Group* (1975) and *Aspects of the Bloomsbury Group* (1998); Regina Marler, *Bloomsbury Pie* (1997).

Blot in the 'Scutcheon, A A tragedy in blank verse by Robert *Browning, published in 1843 as no. V of **Bells and Pomegranates*. It was produced at Drury Lane in 1843, ran for three nights, and caused a final rift between Browning and William *Macready, who had rejected Browning's two previous plays and expressed doubts about the success of this one. Browning's friends accused Macready of sabotaging the production, and the quarrel was instrumental in Browning's decision to write no more stage plays. Set in an aristocratic household of the 18th century, the play concerns the tragic outcome of an illicit love affair between Mildred Tresham and Lord Henry Mertoun, although the central role is that of Mildred's brother and guardian, Lord Tresham.

BLOW, Dr John (1649–1708) Composer and organist, who became organist at Westminster Abbey at the age of 19, and from 1674 was master of the Children of the Chapel Royal. He was a friend and mentor of Henry *Purcell. Blow was a prolific composer of church anthems. His many court odes and secular songs include settings of Thomas *D'Urfey, Nahum *Tate, Abraham *Cowley, and John *Dryden. He composed what is usually considered the first true English opera, though it was described as a court masque at the time: the three-act *Venus and Adonis* (*c.*1683) antedates by about five years Purcell's *Dido and Aeneas*, for which it was an important model in its structure, plot, musical design, and sung dialogue.

Blue Bird, The *See* MAETERLINCK, MAURICE.

Blue Stockings An informal group of intelligent and sociable women, which flourished in London in the later 18th century, probably named after the worsted stockings worn to evening receptions by the impoverished Benjamin Stillingfleet (1702–71). Elizabeth Vesey began holding receptions for men and women of the fashionable and literary worlds in the 1750s; the other main hostesses were Elizabeth *Montagu, Elizabeth *Carter, Hester *Chapone, Mary *Delany, and Hannah *More. There were no cards, and no refreshment other than tea, coffee, or lemonade. Learned conversation was not be disfigured by pedantry; politics, scandal, and swearing were not allowed. Meetings were also held in the houses of Sir Joshua *Reynolds, Hester *Thrale, and many others; the most famous literary men in regular attendance were David *Garrick, Horace *Walpole, James *Boswell, and Samuel *Johnson, who according to Boswell found himself swamped with aristocratic company. More's poem *Bas Bleu* (1786) celebrates the pleasures of the society.

BLUME, Judy (1938–) Popular American writer who helped establish the dominant fashion for demotic, first-person 'problem novels' for children and *young adults with, for example, *Are You There, God? It's Me, Margaret* (1970). *Forever* (1975) is still one of the most-banned books in the USA, for its unjudgemental and explicit depiction of teenage sexuality. Blume has been active in combating literary censorship, and has written three adult novels, including *Wifey* (1978).

BLUNDEN, Edmund (1896–1974) Poet, born in London; educated at *Christ's Hospital and the Queen's College, Oxford. The longest-serving poet of the First World War, he wrote the experience of the trenches into such poems as 'Third Ypres' and 'Report on Experience'; guilt at his own survival became an important theme in his later writing. In 1920 he published an edition of the poems of John *Clare, whose work he rescued from obscurity. His prose account of the war, *Undertones of War*, which describes the double destruction of man and nature in Flanders, appeared in 1928, and his first *Collected Poems* followed in 1930. In 1931 he produced a collected edition of the work of Wilfred *Owen. Further volumes of his own poems were collected as *Poems 1930–1940*. In 1954 he published an edition of the poems of the almost unknown Ivor *Gurney. He was appointed professor of poetry at Oxford in 1966.

BLUNT, Wilfrid Scawen (1840–1922) Born in Petworth House, Sussex; poet, diplomat, traveller, anti-imperialist, and Arabist, who married in 1869 Annabella King-Noel, Lord *Byron's granddaughter. His own career as amorist appears to have been modelled on that of Byron, and his first volume of poetry, *Sonnets and Songs by Proteus* (1875, subsequently revised), passionately addresses various women. It was followed by several other volumes which include love lyrics, evocations of the Sussex countryside, and adaptations from the Arabic. He also wrote and agitated in support of Egyptian, Indian, and Irish independence, earning the support of G. B. *Shaw (see the preface to **John Bull's Other Island*) and a brief spell in an Irish prison. This inspired his sonnet sequence *In Vinculis* (1889). Blunt's many friends in the literary and political world included Lord *Lytton, Robert *Curzon (fourteenth Baron Zouche), William *Morris, Lady *Gregory, Alice *Meynell, and Oscar *Wilde. W. B. *Yeats and Ezra *Pound were later admirers. *My Diaries* appeared in two volumes, 1919–20. See Elizabeth Longford, *A Passionate Pilgrimage* (1979).

BLY, Robert (1926–) American poet, essayist, and translator. Bly's family was of Norwegian extraction and he has published translations from that and other languages. He has argued vigorously against the prominence given to American *modernist poets, finding stronger influences from writers like Rainer Maria *Rilke. In 1966 he co-founded American Writers Against the Vietnam War. In addition to numerous volumes of poetry, in 1990 he published *Iron John*, an analysis of one of the *Grimm brothers' folk tales, and this work has been credited with helping start the Mythopoetic Men's Movement in America.

BLYTHE, Ronald George (1922–) Author, born in Suffolk, educated at St Peter's and St Gregory's School, Sudbury. Blythe is best known for *Akenfield: Portrait of an English Village* (1969), a study of an East Anglian village, evoked through a series of tape recordings of conversations with its inhabitants, linked by the author's own descriptions and interpretations. Blythe was also involved in *Akenfield*, a film directed by Sir Peter *Hall in 1974, and *Akenfield Revisited*, a BBC documentary first screened in 2004, and he was interviewed by Craig Taylor in *Return to Akenfield* (2006). Other works include *The View in Winter: Reflections on Old Age* (1979), again based on tape-recorded interviews; and various critical and topographical studies. A long-term president of the John *Clare Society, Blythe's *Talking about John Clare* appeared in 1999. Further reflections on Clare, and on other writers, were collected in *A Writer's Day-Book* (2006).

BLYTON, Enid (1897–1968) London-born children's writer who trained to be a teacher at Ipswich High School. According to UNESCO, Blyton is the fourth most translated author in the world (after Agatha *Christie, Jules *Verne, and Lenin), with sales exceeding six million copies annually. She wrote around 650 titles, her most successful series being 'The Famous Five' (21 volumes) and 'Noddy' (at least 23 volumes). David Rudd's *Enid Blyton and the Mystery of Children's Literature* (2000) provides a detailed critical evaluation.

Boadicea (Bonduca) Corruptions of the name Boudicca, queen of the Iceni in the east of Britain. As described in *Tacitus' *Annals*, she led a revolt against the Romans but was defeated by Suetonius Paulinus in AD 61 and killed herself. She is the subject of a play by John *Fletcher and an ode by William *Cowper.

Boar's Head Inn An inn in Eastcheap, London, converted into a playhouse in 1599 and then used for several years by Worcester's and Queen Anne's Men. It is traditionally identified as *Falstaff's favourite tavern, though not actually named as such by *Shakespeare. It is the subject of a paper in Washington *Irving's *Sketch Book*, and provides the theme of one of Oliver *Goldsmith's essays, 'A Reverie at the Boar's-head-tavern in Eastcheap' originally published in 1760 in the *British Magazine*, where the author imagines himself dozing by the fire and transported back in time to the days of Mistress Quickly and her guests.

bob and wheel A metrical pattern used, for example, in *Sir *Gawain and the Green Knight*, at the end of the unrhymed strophes of the main narrative. The 'bob' is a short tag with one stress and the following 'wheel' is a *quatrain of three-stressed lines rhyming *abab*:

And al waz holȝ in with, nobot an olde cave
Or a crevisse of an olde cragge, he couþe hit noȝt deme
wiþ spelle.
'We! Lorde,' quoþ þe gentyle knyȝt,
'Wheþer þis be þe grene chapelle?
Here myȝt aboute mydnyȝt
Þe dele his matynnes tell!'
(*Sir Gawain*, ll. 2182–8)

Here the words 'with spelle' form the 'bob', leading into the 'wheel' of the quatrain.

BOCCACCIO, Giovanni (1313–75) Italian writer and humanist, born at or near Florence, the son of a Florentine merchant. His formative years, from about 1325 until 1340, were spent in Naples, where he began his literary studies and wrote his first works. His outlook was greatly conditioned by the aristocratic society in which he moved and especially by his contacts with the Angevin court, but the tradition that he fell in love with Maria d'Aquino, illegitimate daughter of King Robert of Naples, is now discredited. He returned to Florence in 1340, and witnessed the ravages of the Black Death in 1348, described in the introduction to the first day of *The *Decameron*. From 1350 onwards the municipality of Florence employed him on various diplomatic missions. His friendship with *Petrarch—whom he first met in 1350—gave a powerful impetus to his classical studies, and his house became an important centre of humanist activity. He wrote a life of *Dante and was the first to deliver a course of public lectures on the text of the **Divina commedia* (1373–4), on which he also wrote a commentary. Boccaccio's chief works, apart from *The Decameron*, were: *Filocolo*, a prose romance embodying the story of *Floris and Blancheflour; **Filostrato*, a poem on the story of Troilus and Cressida; *Teseida*, a poem on the story of Theseus, Palamon, and Arcite, which was translated by *Chaucer in the 'Knight's Tale'; *Ameto*, a combination of allegory and pastoral romance; the *Amorosa visione*, an uncompleted allegorical poem; *Fiammetta*, a psychological romance in prose, in which the woman herself recounts the various phases of her unhappy love; and the *Ninfale fiesolano*, an idyll translated into English (from a French version) by an Elizabethan, John Golburne. He also wrote a number of encyclopedic works in Latin which were widely read in England: the *De Genealogia Deorum*; the *De Claris Mulieribus*; and *De Casibus Virorum Illustrium*, the original source text of John *Lydgate's *The Fall of Princes*, which was also drawn upon by Chaucer, and for stories in *A *Mirror for Magistrates*. (See Willard Farnham, *The Medieval Heritage of Elizabethan Tragedy*, 1956.)

Boccaccio is an important figure in the history of literature, particularly of narrative fiction, and one of the earliest users, if not the inventor, of **ottava rima*. Among the poets who found inspiration in his works were Chaucer, *Shakespeare, John *Dryden, John *Keats, Henry Wadsworth *Longfellow, and *Tennyson. See V. Branca, *Boccaccio: The Man and his Works* (1976).

BODLEY, Sir Thomas (1545–1613) Educated at Geneva, where his parents had fled during the Marian persecution, and subsequently at Magdalen College, Oxford. From 1588 to 1596 he was English diplomatic representative at The Hague. He devoted the rest of his life to founding at Oxford the great Bodleian Library, opened in 1602. In 1609 Bodley endowed it with land in Berkshire and houses in London.

BOECE (Boëthius), **HECTOR** (?1465–1536) Historian, a native of Dundee and a student in the University of Paris, where in the College of Montaigu with *Erasmus he became a professor. In 1498 he was appointed first principal of the newly founded King's College in the University of Aberdeen. He published Latin lives of the bishops of Mortlach and Aberdeen (1522), and a Latin history of Scotland to the accession of James III (1526), the latter including many fabulous narratives, among others that of Macbeth and Duncan, which passed into *Holinshed's chronicles and thence to Shakespeare.

BOEHME, Jacob (1575–1624) Born of peasant stock near Görlitz in Germany, writer of a number of works setting out his unorthodox mystical and visionary theosophy. Largely suppressed during his lifetime, his posthumously published writings became known in England through translations by various hands which appeared in 1645–62. Boehme's ideas strongly influenced William *Law and early *Quaker religious thought. *The Works of Jacob Behmen the Teutonic Theosopher* published in London between 1764 and 1781 were admired by William *Blake.

BOETHIUS, Anicius Manlius Severinus (*c.*480–524) philosopher, born at Rome and consul in 510, in favour with Theodoric the Great, Ostrogothic king of Italy, but later suspected of treason, imprisoned, and finally cruelly executed. In prison he wrote *De Consolatione Philosophiae* (*On the Consolation of Philosophy*), a dialogue between himself and Philosophy. This is his most celebrated work and one of the most translated works in history; there are notable English translations by *Alfred, *Chaucer (as *Boece*), and *Elizabeth I. It was translated into French by Jean de Meun, and was one of the most influential books of the Middle Ages. It is now generally believed that he was a Christian, though this is rarely explicit in the *Consolation*, whose philosophy is broadly *Neoplatonic. Its form is *'Menippean Satire', i.e. alternating prose and verse. The verse often incorporates a story told by *Ovid or *Horace, used to illustrate the philosophy being expounded—a relationship that itself influenced medieval moral narrative. Before the Middle Ages, Boethius was of most importance for his translations of and commentaries on *Aristotle, which provided the main part of what was known of Aristotle before the recovery of most of his writings from Arabic scholars in the 12th century. See C. S. *Lewis, *The Discarded Image* (1964); Henry Chadwick, *Boethius: The Consolations of Music, Logic, Theology and Philosophy* (1981); Margaret Gibson (ed.), *Boethius: His Life, Thought and Influence* (1981).

BOGAN, Louise (1897–1970) American poet. Born in Maine, she married the poet and novelist Raymond Holden and began publishing poetry at this time. Most of her output pre-dated the Second World War. She has described her female speakers as the 'locus of intemperate, dangerous, antisocial desires'. She was closely associated with the poet Theodore *Roethke and served as poetry reviewer for the **New Yorker* from 1931 to 1969.

BOHN, Henry George (1796–1884) Publisher and translator, who amassed a valuable collection of rare books, publishing in 1841 his *Guinea Catalogue*, which became a standard reference work. In 1846 he started his popular Standard Library (followed by the Scientific Library, Antiquarian Library, Classical Library, etc.), the whole series numbering over 600 volumes. He was an accomplished scholar and translated several volumes for his 'Foreign Classics' series, and compiled a *Dictionary of Quotations* (1867).

BOIARDO, Matteo Maria (1441–94) Poet and courtier at the *Este court in Ferrara. He was one of the finest lyric poets of the Quattrocento, but his reputation rests centrally on his *chivalric epic, the unfinished **Orlando innamorato*. This was subsequently continued by Niccolò degli Agostini and more significantly by *Ariosto. It was revised in the 16th century by both Francesco *Berni and Ludovico Dolci (1508–68) and was widely read for centuries in Berni's version in standardized Tuscan Italian.

BOILEAU-DESPRÉAUX, Nicolas (1636–1711) French poet, satirist, and critic. A friend of *Molière, *La Fontaine, and *Racine, legislator and model for French *neo-classicism at its apogee, he achieved legendary status in his lifetime. His *Satires* (1660–1708), his *Épîtres* (1668–96: *Epistles*), and his *Art poétique* (1674: *Art of Poetry*), a four-canto poem in which he establishes canons of taste and defines principles of composition and criticism, achieved international currency. His *mock epic *Le Lutrin* (1674–83: *The Lectern*) was widely influential in England (see *The *Rape of the Lock*). John *Dryden, Alexander *Pope, and John *Oldham found in him a lesson in how to rework the Latin poets.

BOITO, Arrigo (1842–1918) Italian composer, poet, and librettist, whose chief importance in musical history is as a producer of libretti for other composers. His first attempt, a version of **Hamlet* (1865), showed exceptional sensitivity and ingenuity, and his two Shakespearian texts for *Verdi are among the best examples of the form ever produced. *Otello* (1887) makes some concessions to the operatic convention, particularly in the treatment of Iago, but the courageous decision to cut the first act cleverly tightens the dramatic structure and provides a superb operatic opening, as well as reflecting Samuel *Johnson's criticism of the original play. *Falstaff* (1893), based on *The *Merry Wives of Windsor*, is a still more remarkable achievement: Boito was ruthless in pruning the incoherent plot, and in his determination to 'squeeze all the juice out of that enormous Shakespearian orange without letting useless pips slip through into the glass' he reduced Shakespeare's scenes from 23 to 6, while filling out the figure of *Falstaff with passages lifted wholesale from both parts of *Henry IV.*

BOLAND, Eavan (1944–) Irish poet born in Dublin, daughter of a diplomat father and painter mother. She spent some of her childhood from the age of 15 in London, an experience evoked in several of her poems. She was educated at Trinity College, Dublin, where she read Latin and English and associated with fellow undergraduate poets Michael *Longley and Derek *Mahon. Her first collection, *New Territory* (1967), was followed by *The War Horse* (1975). Her work took a strongly feminist turn in *In her Own Image* (1980) and *Night Feed* (1982), a trend continued in such later volumes as *The Journey* (1987) and *Against Love Poetry* (2001). *Object Lessons* (1995) is a prose work reflecting on women, poetry, and the Irish literary tradition. Boland's verse draws on classical and Irish myth, on domestic life and maternal experience, and is informed by a strong visual sense. She writes evocatively of flowers and fabrics, of colours and cosmetics, of the 'sexuality, ritual and history' of female lives. Her verse is characteristically spare and condensed, if increasingly discursive. Boland has worked in Ireland and England and has been since 1995 a professor of English at Stanford University, California, and more recently director of the Creative Writing Program there.

BOLINGBROKE, Henry St John, first Viscount (1678–1751) Politician. There is no documentary record of his education, though Eton College, Christ Church, Oxford, and the dissenting Sheriffhales Academy are the usual candidates. He was elected to the House of Commons in 1701 for the family's seat, the riding of Wootton Basset, Wiltshire. He soon became a leading figure in the Tory party, defending the interests of country gentlemen in opposition to the financial interests associated with the Whigs. He was appointed secretary of war in 1704 and secretary of state in 1710; his efforts as minister were supported by his friend Jonathan *Swift in *The Conduct of the Allies* (1711) and other works. St John was made Viscount Bolingbroke in 1712 and took part in negotiating the Treaty of Utrecht in 1713. After the death of Queen Anne, Bolingbroke fled to France and declared his allegiance to the Pretender, James Stuart; convicted of high treason, his peerage was withdrawn. He wrote *A Letter to Sir William Wyndham* in 1717 to justify his conduct; it was widely circulated, but not published until 1753. In 1723 Bolingbroke received a qualified pardon, returning to England in 1725 to a life of political journalism in the company of Alexander *Pope, Swift, John *Gay, and George *Lyttelton. In the **Craftsman* Bolingbroke attacked the policies and practices of the Walpole administration, in particular, the 'corruption' which allowed the administration to maintain power in Parliament by awarding offices, honours, and salaries to supporters. These articles were later collected as *A Dissertation upon Parties* (1735) and *Remarks on the History of England* (1743). Bolingbroke's heavy influence on Pope, in such works as the **Essay on Man*, was as much personal and political as philosophical; the poet idolized him. He returned to France in 1735, but continued to produce works on the need for an active and united opposition to corruption (*A Letter on the Spirit of Patriotism*, written in 1736) and on the role of a monarch in a free government (*The Idea of a Patriot King*, written in 1738). This classical republican or civic humanist perspective also appears in *Letters on the Study and Use of History* (written 1736–8, published 1752); here he exhorted readers to find in history illustrations and examples which would inspire men to higher standards of public and private virtue. These writings were circulated among his friends on the understanding they would not be published. He returned to England in 1743, and after Pope's death he found Pope had printed an edition of *The Idea of a Patriot King*; in 1749 he brought out an official edition, with an 'advertisement' denouncing Pope's perfidious conduct. William *Warburton's response prompted Bolingbroke's *Familiar Epistle to the Most Impudent Man Living* (1749). His works were collected by David *Mallet (1754); his many posthumous publications excited intense hostility (from Warburton and Samuel *Johnson, among others) because of their scepticism towards revealed religion. The political essays had a lasting influence on movements for reform in England and America. See H. T. Dickinson, *Bolingbroke* (1970).

BÖLL, Heinrich (1917–85) German author of novels, short stories, and radio plays, mostly on the subject of wartime and post-war Germany. He has been highly acclaimed for his realistic portrayal of the problems of a society coming to terms with guilt and defeat, for example in *Und sagte kein einziges Wort* (1953: *And Never Said a Word*) and *Billard um halb zehn* (1959: *Billiards at Half-Past Nine*). He became a frequent visitor to Ireland and published his *Irisches Tagebuch* (1957: *Irish Journal*). Later works, such as *Ansichten eines Clowns* (1963: *The Clown*), *Gruppenbild mit Dame* (1971: *Group Portrait with Lady*), *Die verlorene Ehre der Katharina Blum* (1974: *The Lost Honour of Katharine Blum*), and *Fürsorgliche Belagerung* (1979: *The Safety Net*), voice an increasingly sharp criticism of state and society in the Federal Republic. On the basis of the novella *Katharina Blum*, which was made into a successful film, he was attacked for supposed sympathy with left-wing terrorism. Böll received the *Nobel Prize for Literature in 1972.

BOLT, Robert Oxton (1924–95) Dramatist and screenwriter, born and educated in Manchester. He worked in an insurance office and in the RAF before attending Exeter University: he then became a schoolmaster, writing many radio plays, until his first West End success in 1957 with *Flowering Cherry* (pub. 1958), a Chekhovian domestic drama about an insurance salesman incapable of fulfilling his own dreams of a better life. This was followed by *The Tiger and the Horse* (1960; pub. 1961), reflecting Bolt's own involvement with the campaign for nuclear disarmament, and *A Man for All Seasons* (1960; pub. 1960), his best-known work, based on the life of Sir Thomas *More, which was filmed effectively by Fred

Zinnemann in 1966. *Vivat, Vivat Regina* (1970) was based on the conflict between *Elizabeth I and *Mary Queen of Scots. Bolt became increasingly involved in cinema after writing a boldly iconoclastic script for David Lean's *Lawrence of Arabia* (1962), based on the exploits of T. E. *Lawrence, and also scripting *Dr Zhivago* (1965) and *Ryan's Daughter* (1970) for Lean. In 1972 he directed his wife Sarah Miles in an underrated film about Lord *Byron's circle, *Lady Caroline Lamb*. He continued to write for the screen and television until 1991.

BOND, Edward (1934–) Playwright, born in north London, and educated at Crouch End secondary modern school, where his interest in the theatre was aroused by a performance of **Macbeth*; after leaving school early and working at a series of dead-end jobs, he began to write for the theatre. *The Pope's Wedding* was given a Sunday night performance at the *Royal Court in 1962, and in 1965 his grim portrait of urban violence, **Saved*, aroused much admiration as well as a ban from the Lord Chamberlain (*see* CENSORSHIP). Other provocative works followed, including *Early Morning* (1969); *Lear* (1971), a savage reworking of Shakespeare; *The Sea* (1973), a black country-house comedy; *The Fool* (1975), based on the life of John *Clare; *Restoration* (1981), a *Brechtian revolutionary historical drama with songs; and *Summer* (1982). Bond's theatre is an outspoken indictment of capitalist society; his belief that violence occurs in 'situations of injustice' and that it therefore flourishes as 'a cheap consumer commodity' under capitalism, continues to arouse extreme responses from critics and audiences. At the *National Theatre in 1978, he had directed his own play *The Woman*, an excitingly innovative reworking of classical myth, and he was scheduled to co-direct his trilogy *The War Plays* for the Royal Shakespeare Company in 1985. He withdrew from the project, protesting at its treatment, and has never again allowed his work to be produced on the stages of the major subsidized theatres. However, there has been a regular stream of new plays, including *Jackets* (1989), *The Crime of the Twenty-First Century* (1999), and *Coffee* (2000). This major playwright continues to be produced on the Continent, but has largely turned his attention in England to producing work for young people with the Birmingham Theatre-in-Education group, Big Brum.

Bond, James Originally the suave and ruthless hero of thrillers by Ian *Fleming, reborn as a screen icon in a series of increasingly spectacular, and sardonic, films that followed the success of *Dr No* in 1962, starring Sean Connery. Later incarnations of '007, licensed to kill' have included Roger Moore, Timothy Dalton, Pierce Brosnan, and, since *Casino Royale* (2006), Daniel Craig.

Bondman, The A tragicomedy by Philip *Massinger with political implications, performed by the Lady Elizabeth's Men at the Cockpit and before Prince Charles at Whitehall in 1623, published 1624. A decadent aristocracy in Sicily has to import Timoleon to lead them into battle against the Carthaginians. Cleora, who despises the corruption of her society, is loved by Leosthenes, whose jealousy as he goes off to the wars makes her bind her eyes and swear she will not look at anyone until he returns. In the absence of the army, the oppressed slaves stage a rising under the leadership of the demagogue Marullo, but during the rising Marullo protects Cleora. When the army returns and eventually subdues the rebel slaves, Cleora rejects the overbearing Leosthenes and to everyone's horror throws in her lot with the imprisoned leader of the slaves. Fortunately he turns out to be her former suitor Pisander.

This is one of the best of Massinger's tragicomedies, with well-developed characters and fine satirical scenes. It is informed by his contempt for the arrogance of an effete aristocracy, perhaps reflecting Massinger's opinion of the Jacobean court.

Bonduca A tragedy by John *Fletcher, 1611–14, published 1647. The tragedy is based on the story of *Boadicea (Boudicca), as given by *Holinshed, but the principal character is her cousin, the wise and battle-hardened Caratach (*Caractacus), whose counsel to the impetuous Bonduca is disastrously ignored. After the defeat of the Britons in battle, Bonduca and her daughters defiantly commit suicide; the last act is devoted to the flight of Caratach and his young nephew Hengo, 'a brave boy', who is killed in a scene of carefully contrived pathos (greatly admired by *Swinburne). Caratach survives, yielding to the 'brave courtesies' of the Romans, to be led off to Rome as a prisoner.

Bon Gaultier The pseudonym (taken from *Rabelais) under which W. E. *Aytoun and Theodore *Martin published *A Book of Ballads* (1845), a collection of parodies and light poems. Among the authors parodied are Alfred *Tennyson (notably 'Locksley Hall', in 'The Lay of the Lovelorn') and, loosely, E. B. *Browning (in 'The Rhyme of Sir Lancelot Bogle'). Martin also used the pseudonym in his contributions to *Tait's Magazine* and **Fraser's Magazine*.

BONIFACE, St (?672/5–754) Missionary and martyr, whose original name was Wynfreth. He was born in Devon and educated at a monastery in Exeter and at Nursling near Winchester. He went to Rome in 718 and thence to Germany, where he preached, established monasteries, and organized the church. He was killed with his followers at Dokkum in Frisia. See T. Reuter (ed.), *The Greatest Englishman: Essays on St. Boniface and the Church at Crediton* (Exeter: Paternoster Press, 1980).

BONNEFOY, Yves (1923–) French poet and critic. He moved from his native Tours to Paris in 1944, where he met André *Breton and became involved with *Surrealism. His poetry engages with the here and now of lived experience. His first major collection, *Du mouvement et de l'immobilité de Douve* (1953: *Of the Movement and Immobility of Douve*), won him critical acclaim, and has been followed by other works which explore further the purposes and ethics of poetry, including *Hier régnant désert* (1958: *Yesterday's Wilderness*), *Dans le leurre du seuil* (1975: *In the Lure of the Threshold*), and *Début et fin de la neige* (1991: *Beginning and End of the Snow*). In 1981 he was awarded the *Académie Française's Grand Prix for poetry. He has also translated into French the poetry of W. B. *Yeats and many of the works of *Shakespeare. See M. A. Caws, *Yves Bonnefoy* (1984).

Booker Prize for Fiction *See* MAN BOOKER PRIZE FOR FICTION, and Appendix 4.

book history (the history of the book) A rather imprecise label used to identify an interdisciplinary field of historical study, whose origins can conveniently be traced to the publication in France of Lucien Febvre and Henri Jean Martin's *L'Apparition du livre* (1958). The field gained wider recognition, however, with the appearance in 1979 of works by two American scholars: Elizabeth Eisenstein's *The Printing Press as an Agent of Change* and Robert Darnton's *The Business of Enlightenment: A Publishing History of the Encylopédie*. During the 1980s the monumental *Histoire de l'édition française*, edited by Martin and Roger Chartier, initiated a series of national histories of the book. Book history has from the start traversed many disciplinary and national boundaries, involving an international network of sociologists, anthropologists, economists, art historians, librarians, and bibliographers as well as literary critics and theorists. The influence of the historically rigorous British bibliographical tradition exemplified by such scholars as R. B. *McKerrow and Philip Gaskell (1926–2001) is particularly noteworthy. Again, though the field is commonly identified with the study of the book, its object is the history of written communication encompassing the production, publication, distribution, control, collection, conservation, reading, and uses of script and print in all media, including manuscripts, pamphlets, periodicals, newspapers, books, and electronic forms. Building on such established areas of enquiry as author–publisher relations, the history of copyright legislation and censorship, libraries and collectors, bibliography, typography and book design, and the sociology of reading and reader response, book history has tried to open up new intellectual territories in a wide range of traditional disciplines, asking new questions, developing new methodologies, and identifying new sources. It has led to a reassessment of the significance of historical documents conceived not simply as sources of evidence but as themselves agents of historical change. In literary studies, it has insisted on the importance of material considerations in textual interpretation. Here book historians share some preoccupations with British Cultural Materialists like Raymond *Williams and American *New Historicists like Stephen Greenblatt, but their closest allies are the revisionist bibliographers and textual critics of the 1980s, notably Jerome McGann and D. F. McKenzie. Indeed, McKenzie's 'sociology of the text', first announced in the title of his Panizzi lectures in 1985 and intended there to point towards a radical transformation of Anglo-American bibliography, is often treated as a synonym for 'book history'. These various cross-disciplinary movements shaped the emergent field, and in the process initiated a significant reappraisal of such fundamental concepts as 'author', 'reader', and 'text'. Book historians insist, for example, on the historical importance of authors and readers, while recognizing that cultural intermediaries (printers, binders, publishers, booksellers, reviewers, etc.) have a significant role to play in the overall process of text production, transmission, and the formation of meaning. It follows from this that, for them, the history of successive versions of texts, where old works are put to new uses in new forms, offers primary evidence of cultural change. Starting from the premiss that the book, like any mode of inscription, is a complex system of signs—encompassing the publisher's imprint, typographical layout and design, paper, binding, illustrations, and the text itself—book historians have sought to rethink and rewrite social, political, and cultural history.

Book of Martyrs, The *See* ACTS AND MONUMENTS.

Book of the Duchess, The A dream-poem in 1,334 lines by *Chaucer, written *c.*1369–72, in octosyllabic couplets. It is believed, in accordance with a long-standing tradition (which was questioned in the 1950s), to be an allegorical lament on the death of Blanche of Lancaster, the first wife of *John of Gaunt, who died in September 1368. The love-lorn poet falls asleep reading the story of Ceix (Seys) and Alcyone and follows a hunting party. He meets a knight in black who laments the loss of his lady. The knight tells of her virtue and beauty and of their courtship, and in answer to the dreamer's question declares her dead. The hunting party reappears and a bell strikes twelve, awakening the poet, who finds his book still in his hand. The poem is one of Chaucer's earliest works, but it has great charm and accomplishment. It is founded on the French tradition of the dream as a vehicle for love poetry. 'A Complaynt of a Loveres Lyfe' by *Lydgate is based on it. For an account of the poem, see A. C. Spearing, *Medieval Dream-Poetry* (1976); B. A. Windeatt, *Chaucer's Dream-Poetry: Sources and Analogues* (1982).

Bookseller, The *See* WHITAKER, JOSEPH.

Book Trust An independent charitable organization founded in 1925 as the National Book Council; its function is to promote books and reading by working with all branches of the book world (booksellers, publishers, authors, printers, librarians, teachers, etc.). The Council was renamed the National Book League in 1945, and moved in 1980 from its central London premises at 7 Albemarle Street to Book House, Wandsworth. It took the name of Book Trust in 1986. Its services include the provision of a wide range of information to the public about books and the book trade, and the administration of literary prizes, including the John Llewellyn *Rhys Prize for a writer under 35, and the Orange Prize for fiction, awarded for the best novel written in English by a woman of any nationality. It also administers the children's laureate award and coordinates the annual Children's Book Week each October.

Boom, the A term used loosely to refer to a group of Latin American authors who, in the late 1950s and 1960s, put fiction from the sub-continent on the international map. The principal writers are Julio *Cortázar (Argentina), the Mexican Carlos Fuentes (1928–), Gabriel *García Márquez (Colombia), and Mario *Vargas Llosa (Peru). The Cuban Revolution of 1959 drew attention to Latin America and fostered a sense of a shared Latin American identity among left-leaning writers, while the promotion of the Boom by publishers, particularly in Spain and by the Paris-based magazine *Mundo nuevo*, ensured media attention. An earlier generation of Latin American writers had already drawn inspiration from European and North American *modernist authors like William *Faulkner, James *Joyce, and Virginia *Woolf, adapting them creatively to their own context, but the Boom authors did so in a way that caught the imagination of a wide readership. Fuentes's novel *La muerte de Artemio Cruz* (1962: *The Death of Artemio Cruz*) and Vargas Llosa's *La ciudad y los perros* (1963: *The Time of the Hero*) and *La casa verde* (1966: *The Green House*) were experimentally realist works which drew upon Faulkner's narrative and structural techniques to depict the complexity and violence of, respectively, Mexico and Peru. Cortázar and García Márquez, while sometimes writing in a realist mode, incorporated fantasy (notably the *magical realism of García Márquez's *Cien años de soledad* (1967: *One Hundred Years of Solitude*)) to create works that were at the same time ironic meditations on fiction. The Boom writers married experiment, which could make considerable demands upon their readers, with gripping storytelling, humour, and a political edge, rendering their works commercially successful. Although the Boom can be said to have ended by at least the 1980s, Latin American literature by then having consolidated an international public with a younger generation of writers having come to the fore, some of the original Boom authors continue to produce distinguished work into the 21st century.

Border Minstrelsy *See* MINSTRELSY OF THE SCOTTISH BORDER.

BOREMAN, Thomas (*fl.* 1715–43) Early and influential London bookseller and publisher specializing in—perhaps also conceiving and writing—generously (if unreliably) illustrated, attractively bound, informative books for children from *A Description of Three Hundred Animals* (1730) to ten miniature volumes of *Gigantick Histories* (1740–3), all sold through subscriptions.

BORGES, Jorge Luis (1899–1986) Argentine writer, born in Buenos Aires; he attended secondary school in Geneva (1914–18), but gained no educational qualifications. One of his grandmothers was English and from an early age he read literature in English (notably the works of Charles *Dodgson (Lewis Carroll), G. K. *Chesterton, Thomas *De Quincey, Rudyard *Kipling, Edgar Allan *Poe, Robert Louis *Stevenson, H. G. *Wells, and Oscar *Wilde), going on to gain an encyclopedic knowledge of world literature: he claimed to be a reader first, and only second a writer. In Spain after the First World War, he was associated with the literary movement *ultraísmo* (a form of Spanish *Expressionism). He returned in 1921 to Argentina, where for a time he championed the ultraist cause, partly through the periodical *Proa*. His first collection of poetry, *Fervor de Buenos Aires* (1923: *Fervour for Buenos Aires*), was followed by many other volumes of verse and engagingly eccentric essays, but he is best known for his short stories, of which the first volume, *Historia universal de la infamia* (1935: *A Universal History of Infamy*), has been acclaimed as a landmark in Latin American literature. Originally published in an Argentine newspaper, the vignettes which compose this collection are largely the fictionalized biographies of adventurers and criminals, and are an early illustration of Borges's enduring preoccupation with the relationship of fiction, truth, and identity; with violence; and with the puzzles of *detective fiction. In collaboration with his friend Adolfo Bioy Casares (1914–99) he wrote several tales of crime and detection. His two collections of short stories *Ficciones* (1944: *Fictions*) and *El aleph* (1949: *The Aleph*) are his most famous works, the publication of a selection entitled *Labyrinths* in Paris in 1953 establishing an international reputation which was consolidated by his sharing the Prix Formentor with Samuel *Beckett in 1961. Many of his best-known stories deal with the cyclical nature of time; they are themselves labyrinthine in form, and often dreamlike in their endlessly reflected facets of reality. Much of his fiction is humorous, drawing on an interest in philosophy and arcane knowledge, while parodying scholarly pedantry. Its metafictional nature and emphasis on the reader's role in forging meaning have made it attractive to many modern writers. Borges worked as a librarian in a Buenos Aires municipal library (1938–46) and some of his stories (e.g. 'La biblioteca de Babel': 'The Library of Babel') take on the quality of a bibliographer's nightmare. He was relieved of this post for political reasons, but with the overthrow of the Peronist regime he was appointed director of the National Library of Argentina in 1955 (he resigned in 1973). By the 1950s, however, his eyesight was failing, and he became almost totally blind. In later years he wrote more poetry than prose; among his later collections of stories are *El informe de Brodie* (1970: *Doctor Brodie's Report*), *El libro de arena* (1975: *The Book of Sand*), and *Veinticinco agosto 1983 y otros cuentos* (1983: *25 August 1983 and Other Stories*). See Gene H. Bell-Villada, *Borges and his Fiction* (2000).

BORGIA family Noble Catalan family who first came to prominence with the election of **Alonso Borgia** as Pope Calixtus III (1455). The most notorious members of the family were **Rodrigo** (Pope Alexander VI 1492–1503), his son **Cesare** (1475–1507), and his daughter **Lucrezia** (1480–1519). As Pope, Alexander's ambitions were directed towards the unscrupulous promotion of his family through dynastic marriages and the establishment of a fiefdom in central Italy for Cesare.

Alexander's generous patronage of the arts was continued by Lucrezia after her marriage to Alfonso d'Este (1502). She is celebrated in the works of *Ariosto, *Bembo, Titian, and *Aldus Manutius. Cesare, a ruthless and successful general, was the principal inspiration for *Machiavelli's *The Prince*. There is no evidence that the Borgia regularly poisoned their opponents, but anti-papal propaganda and the link to Machiavelli combined in Elizabethan England to blacken the family name. *The Divils Charter* (1607) by Barnabe *Barnes is one such account of the family.

BORON, Robert de A 12th- to 13th-century French poet who composed *c.*1202 a trilogy (*Joseph d'Arimathie* in 3,514 lines; *Merlin*, a fragment of 502 lines; and *Perceval*) in which he developed the early history of the Holy *Grail in Britain, linking it with the *Arthurian tradition.

Borough, The A poem by George *Crabbe published 1810, in twenty-four 'letters', describing, with much penetration and detail, the life and characters of the church, the school, the professions, the surroundings, the workhouse, the prisons, the sea, and other aspects of the town of Aldeburgh, Suffolk. The work, defining a distinctive form of poetic realism, took eight years to complete. Two of the best-known tales, concerning Peter *Grimes and Ellen *Orford, were combined in *Britten's opera *Peter Grimes* (1945).

BORROW, George (1803–81) Travel writer, educated at Edinburgh High School and at Norwich Grammar School. He was articled to a solicitor but after editing *Celebrated Trials, and Remarkable Cases of Criminal Jurisprudence* (1825) spent several years travelling through Europe and learning languages (though there is some suggestion that he exaggerated his linguistic achievements and his travels). Between 1833 and 1840 Borrow acted as agent for the British and Foreign Bible Society, visiting Russia, the Iberian Peninsula, and North Africa. He married in 1840 and settled in East Anglia. In 1844 he journeyed again to Europe and Asia. *Wild Wales* (1862) is the most famous result of his later British walking tours. His books, often characterized by a mixture of fact and fiction and by a fascination with outsiders and their language, also include: *The Zincali, or An Account of the Gypsies in Spain* (1841), *The Bible in Spain* (1843), **Lavengro* (1851), and *The *Romany Rye* (1857).

Borrowers, The (1952) A children's novel by Mary *Norton, awarded the Carnegie Medal; it has four sequels, to *The Borrowers Avenged* (1982). The Borrowers are small people who live under floors and 'borrow' items from the 'human beans' to survive; even their names—Pod, Homily, Arrietty—are 'borrowed'. The series epitomizes the conflict between the rural past and the uncertain future characteristic of post-war British children's books, and is notable for the complex multiple frames of the narratives. BBC television produced two series with Ian Boron (1992–3), and it was filmed with Jim Broadbent (1997, Peter Hewitt).

BOSCÁN DE ALMOGÁVER, Juan (*c.*1487–1542) A Spanish poet born in Barcelona, who did much to introduce Italian verse forms into the poetry of his country. He was a close friend of the innovative Spanish poet, *Garcilaso de la Vega, and the two are mentioned together by Lord *Byron in **Don Juan* (I. 95).

BOSSUET, Jacques Bénigne (1627–1704) French preacher. His reputation as the greatest French orator rests on his sermons, delivered chiefly in the course of his duties as bishop of Condom and bishop of Meaux, and especially on his funeral orations, celebrating many of the greatest figures at the court of Louis XIV, including Henrietta Maria, wife of Charles I, Marie Thérèse, wife of Louis XIV, and the Grand Condé. His style was usually simple, direct, and dignified, but capable of rising to grandeur when dealing with the mysteries of mortality and faith. A dogmatist on principle (he defined a heretic as 'he who has an opinion'), he was involved in a number of notorious disputes with Protestants. These had some effect on English religious controversies of the time.

BOSTON, Lucy M. (Maria) (1892–1990) Lancashire-born author of six distinguished fantasy-realism novels for children, beginning with *The Children of Green Knowe* (1954). All are set in Boston's house, the ancient Manor at Hemingford Grey, Cambridgeshire, and illustrated by her son. Boston's books for adults include *The Guardians of the House* (1974).

Bostonians, The A novel by Henry *James, published 1886. Basil Ransom, a young lawyer, comes north from Mississippi and the humiliations of the Civil War to Boston, where he calls on his cousin Olive Chancellor and her widowed sister, the girlishly arch Mrs Luna. Olive, a wealthy chill feminist, introduces him to a reformist group (acidly portrayed by James). Selah Tarrant, a charlatan faith healer and showman, is presenting his daughter Verena as an 'inspirational' speaker. There follows a struggle for Verena between Ransom and Olive, who has schooled her as a suffragette, which Ransom ultimately wins.

BOSWELL, James (1740–95) Lawyer, diarist, and biographer, the eldest son of Alexander Boswell, Lord Auchinleck (pron. Affleck), a Scottish judge who took his title from the family estate in Ayrshire. He reluctantly studied law at Edinburgh, Glasgow, and Utrecht universities, despite the literary and political ambitions demonstrated by numerous pamphlets and verses which he published anonymously from 1760 onwards, many of them also expressing his love of the theatre. He met Samuel *Johnson on 16 May 1763 in London; he then went to Holland (where he met and courted Isabelle de *Charrière) and on through Europe to Italy. His extraordinary persistence meant he met with *Rousseau and *Voltaire; Rousseau inspired him with zeal for the cause of Corsican liberty, and he visited Corsica in 1765, establishing a lifelong friendship with General Paoli. On his return to Scotland he 'passed advocate' and was to practise there and in England for the rest of his life. His first substantial work, *An Account of Corsica* (1768), was followed in December of the same year by a book of edited essays 'in favour of the brave Corsicans'; he was to remain loyal to this cause, creating a sensation by his appearance at the Shakespeare Jubilee in 1769 in Corsican dress. In this year he married his cousin Margaret Montgomerie, after many attempted courtships with others; she bore him seven children. Although his family remained in Scotland, Boswell visited London as frequently as possible, spending much time with Johnson, whose biography he already planned. They made their celebrated tour of Scotland and the Hebrides in 1773, in which year Boswell was elected a member of the *Club. From 1777 to 1783 he contributed a series of essays, as 'The Hypochondriack', to the **London Magazine*, on such subjects as drinking (a constant preoccupation), diaries, memory, and hypochondria. In 1782 his father (with whom his relationship had been complex and at times unhappy) died, and Boswell inherited the estate. His last meeting with Johnson was in 1784; his *Journal of a Tour of the Hebrides* appeared in 1785 after Johnson's death. The rest of Boswell's life was devoted to an unsuccessful pursuit of a political career (he was recorder of Carlisle, 1788–90) and to the immense task of assembling materials for his life of Johnson, a labour in which he was encouraged by Edmond *Malone. *The Life of Samuel *Johnson LLD* appeared in 1791. Boswell's volatility, promiscuity, fits of depression, ambitions, and emotional involvement in the affairs of his clients are revealed in his letters (notably to his two old university friends, William Johnson Temple and John Johnston) and in private papers and journals, many of which were discovered at Malahide Castle and Fettercairn House after his death; they cover his continental tour as well as his London visits, and have been edited from 1928 in various volumes, principally by F. A. Pottle, who also, with Frank Brady, wrote his biography. See also Peter Martin, *A Life of James Boswell* (1999); Adam Sisman, *Boswell's Presumptuous Task* (2000).

Bothie of Tober-na-Vuolich, The See CLOUGH, ARTHUR.

Botteghe oscure (literally 'dark shops') A review edited in Rome by Marguerite Caetani (1949–60), which established itself as a leading international periodical. The contributors, who included Dylan *Thomas, W. H. *Auden, Saul *Bellow, Günter *Grass, Albert *Camus, Eugenio *Montale, etc., were published in their own language.

BOTTICELLI, Sandro (*c.*1445–1510) Florentine painter, whose most famous paintings, *La Primavera* (*c.*1477–8) and *The Birth of Venus* (1485–90), are complex allegories that reflect the humanist and classical interests of the time. He also painted many altarpieces and portraits. His later works, perhaps in response to the teachings of *Savonarola, are wilder and more dramatic. At the time of his death Botticelli's decorative style had become old-fashioned, and he is only rarely mentioned again before the 19th century when his popularity soared. Walter *Pater's essay 'Sandro Botticelli' (1870), in which he describes Botticelli's work as refusing to conform to the current moral or religious orthodoxies, led to Botticelli being adopted by the cult of *Aestheticism. His influence can be seen in the work of Edward *Burne-Jones, Simeon Solomon (1840–1905), and other late 19th-century painters.

Bottom, Nick The weaver in Shakespeare's *A *Midsummer Night's Dream*. Whatever other associations it may have had, the name referred to the ball on which thread was wound. A *'droll' adapted from Shakespeare's play, *The Merry Conceited Humours of Bottom the Weaver*, was printed in 1661. Offered for both amateur and professional performance, it suggests that Oberon and Titania may double Theseus and Hippolyta, and that Pyramus, Thisbe, and Wall may also play fairies.

BOUCICAULT, Dion (originally Dion Boursiquot) (1820–90) Playwright, born in Dublin and educated at University College School, London. He began his career as an actor and achieved great success with his comedy *London Assurance* (1841), written under the pseudonym of Lee Morton. He subsequently wrote and adapted some 200 plays, including *The Corsican Brothers* (1852, from the French), *The Poor of New York* (1857), *The *Colleen Bawn, or The Brides of Garryowen* (1860), *Arra-na-Pogue, or The Wicklow Wedding* (1864), and *The Shaughraun* (1874). One of the dominant figures of 19th-century theatre, his career was marked by spectacular successes and reverses. He was responsible for important innovations, such as the introduction of a royalty from plays and copyright for dramatists in America. With the rise of realism and the emergence of Henrik *Ibsen and George Bernard *Shaw, his work fell out of fashion, but it influenced Sean *O'Casey, who praised his 'colour and stir', and some of his plays have been successfully revived. There is a life by Richard Fawkes, 1979.

Boudicca See BOADICEA.

BOUILLON, Godefroi de (Godfrey of Bouillon) (d. 1100) Duke of Lower Lorraine, leader of the First Crusade and proclaimed 'Protector of the Holy Sepulchre' in 1099. He appears in Tasso's **Jerusalem Delivered* and in Walter Scott's **Count Robert of Paris*.

BOULLE, Pierre (1912–94) French author (born Avignon) who drew upon his wartime experiences for *The Bridge over the River Kwai* (1952). His wry and philosophical *Monkey Planet* (1963) was adapted for the 1968 film *Planet of the Apes*, which saw several sequels and other adaptations.

Bounty, The Mutiny and Piratical Seizure of H.M.S., By Sir John Barrow (1764–1848), published 1831. HMS *Bounty*, which had been sent to the South Sea Islands to collect breadfruit plants, left Tahiti on 4 April 1789 for the Cape of Good Hope and the West Indies. It was hoped that the plants could be grown in the West Indies as a cheap source of food for slaves. On 28 April Fletcher Christian and others seized Lieutenant Bligh, the commander, and placed him with eighteen loyal members of the crew in an open boat, which they cast adrift. The boat eventually reached Timor and Bligh returned to Britain. Meanwhile the *Bounty* sailed east with 25 of the crew to Tahiti, where sixteen were put ashore. These men were later arrested and many of them were drowned when HMS *Pandora*, the ship that had sailed in November 1790 to search for the mutineers, sank in August 1791. Fletcher Christian and eight of his companions, together with some Tahitians, went on and settled on Pitcairn Island. There they founded a colony, of which Alexander Smith (now calling himself John Adams) became the leader, and which was eventually taken under the protection of the British government. These events form part of Lord *Byron's poem 'The *Island' (1823), and have been the subject of many books and films.

BOURDIEU, Pierre (1930–2002) French sociologist. His work investigates the mechanisms whereby social groups and classes vie for power at all levels of social activity, and highlights the role played by education and culture in this struggle. *Les Règles de l'art* (1992; *The Rules of Art*, trans. Susan Emanuel, 1996) considers the processes by which literary value and merit are established and challenged. While most of his research focuses on France, Bourdieu's theoretical framework can be effectively deployed to examine the pressures shaping cultural production in other societies.

bouts-rimés A poem composed to rhymes set in advance, popular as a game in 17th-century salons. Joseph *Addison discusses the bouts-rimés in the **Spectator*, 60.

BOUVIER, Nicolas (1929–98) Swiss travel writer, born in Grand-Lancy, near Geneva, and educated at the University of Geneva. In 1953–4 he travelled to Afghanistan in a Fiat Topolino with his friend Thierry Vernet, an experience vividly described in *L'Usage du monde* (1963; *The Way of the World*, trans. Robyn Marsack, 1992), widely regarded, after more than a decade of neglect, as a classic of post-war French travel literature. Bouvier continued his journey alone to Ceylon, where he spent seven months and experienced some form of breakdown, poignantly evoked in *Poisson-Scorpion* (1981; *Scorpion-Fish*, trans. Robyn Marsack, 1987). He went on to Japan, returning to Europe the following year. Bouvier revisited Japan several times and his writings on the country—historical essays interspersed with personal observations—are collected in *Chronique japonaise* (1989; *Japanese Chronicles*, trans. Anne Dickerson, 1992). *Journal d'Aran et d'autres lieux* (1990) includes accounts of travels to Ireland, South Korea, and China.

BOWDLER, Thomas (1754–1825) An Edinburgh doctor; his *Family Shakespeare*, published 1818, is dedicated to the memory of Mrs Elizabeth *Montagu; she had published a much-respected *Essay on the Writings and Genius of Shakespeare* in 1769. He may have been helped by his sister Henrietta Maria Bowdler (1754–1830), who also published poems and sermons. It has been argued that she was the prime mover, but the extent of her contribution has not been firmly established. The Bowdlers' love and admiration of Shakespeare, demonstrated in the prefaces, were profound; but they believed that nothing 'can afford an excuse for profaneness or obscenity; and if these could be obliterated, the transcendent genius of the poet would undoubtedly shine with more unclouded lustre'. Profanity they found only a small problem; 'God' as an expletive is always replaced by 'Heaven', and other brief passages and exclamations cut. But they confessed to enormous trouble with the indecency scattered throughout the plays. Their method was to cut, not to substitute; they in fact added almost nothing except prepositions and conjunctions. But the cutting is severe; for instance, Juliet's speech of longing for Romeo, 'Gallop apace...', is cut from 30 lines to 15, and many of her Nurse's comments have gone; in Lear's speech of madness, 'Ay, every inch a king...', 22 lines of verse are cut to seven. Bowdler found *1 and 2 *Henry IV* 'the most difficult of all the histories for family reading'. Doll Tearsheet is entirely removed, but Bowdler apologizes that even with the omission of many obscenities 'perfect delicacy of sentiment' could not be achieved. **Measure for Measure* was found to contain so many indecent expressions interwoven with the text that they could do nothing better than to print, with a warning, John Philip *Kemble's version for the stage. Failure is admitted with **Othello* ('unfortunately little suited to family reading'), and it is recommended that it be transferred 'from the parlour to the cabinet'.

The work was extremely successful, and went through many editions in both England and America. Similar excisions were inflicted on Gibbon's **Decline and Fall*. With the verb 'to bowdlerize', or expurgate, 'Dr Bowdler' joins the small band of those who have given their names to the language.

BOWEN, Elizabeth (1899–1973) Novelist and short story writer. Born in Dublin, where her father was a barrister, she spent much of her childhood at the family home in Co. Cork, the Anglo-Irish *'big house' she inherited in 1930 and described in *Bowen's Court* (1942). In 1923 she published her first collection of short stories, *Encounters*, and married Alan Cameron. They lived for ten years in London, a city vividly evoked in many of her works; her skill in describing urban and rural landscapes and her sensitivity to changes of light and season—changes characteristically made emblematic of psychological and social fluidities—are distinguishing features of her prose. Her novels include *The Hotel* (1927), *The Last September* (1929), *The House in Paris* (1935), and *Eva Trout* (1969). The best known are probably *The Death of the Heart* (1938) and *The Heat of the Day* (1949). The former focuses on the threat posed by the innocence of Portia, a 16-year-old orphan, to the precarious, sophisticated London lives of her half-brother and his wife; the latter centres on the tragic wartime love affair of Stella Rodney and Robert Kelway, and their reactions to the revelation that the latter is a spy. Bowen herself had some experience of the surreptitious, reporting to the Ministry of Information on her frequent wartime trips to neutral Ireland. The war inspired many of Bowen's best short stories, including 'Mysterious Kôr' (1944); other stories subtly invoke the supernatural. Wartime and otherworldly themes come together in the title story of *The Demon Lover* (1945). Bowen writes mainly of the upper middle classes, but within her narrow social range her perceptions are acute; her works convey a powerful sense of period through their re-creations of detail and atmosphere. Recent commentary has focused on the persistent, subversive presence of Ireland in her fiction. See Victoria *Glendinning, *Elizabeth Bowen: Portrait of a Writer* (1977); Neil Corcoran, *Elizabeth Bowen: The Enforced Return* (2004).

Bowge of Courte, The An allegorical poem in seven-line stanzas by John *Skelton, satirizing court life (1480/1498). The word 'bowge' is a corrupt form of 'bouche', meaning court rations, from the French 'avoir bouche à cour', to have free board at the king's table.

BOWLES, Caroline Anne (1786–1854) Poet and prose writer, born near Lymington, Hampshire, the only child of Captain Charles Bowles (East Indian Company, retired) and his wife Anne. Educated at home, Caroline grew up among adults in a largely female household where her writing and drawing accomplishments were encouraged from an early age. Left alone and impoverished at the age of 30, she sought advice about publication from Robert *Southey, thus beginning a correspondence (pub. 1880) and friendship lasting twenty years until their marriage in 1839 after the death of his first wife. Before this she published five volumes of verse, two of prose sketches (*Chapters on Churchyards*, 1829), and one of mixed genre (*Solitary Hours*, 1826). Her blank verse autobiography, *The Birth-Day* (1836), was much admired by the *Wordsworth household, but her work also encompassed comedy, satire, and social protest. Southey acknowledged her superior poetic gift, but owing to her choice of anonymous publication her reputation was never consolidated in her lifetime. Her *Poetical Works* appeared posthumously in 1867.

BOWLES, Jane (1917–73) Née Auer, American writer, wife of Paul *Bowles, chiefly remembered for her short novel *Two Serious Ladies* (1943), an exotic, disjointed, staccato work about two contrasted lives. Her play *In the Summer House* (perf. 1953) was praised by Tennessee *Williams as 'elusive and gripping'. Her *Collected Works* were published in 1984: *Everything is Nice* (1989) adds some previously uncollected short fiction. The story of her obsessional and self-destructive life is told in *A Little Original Sin* (1981) by Millicent Dillon.

BOWLES, Paul (1910–99) American novelist, poet, composer, translator, and short story writer, born in New York, educated at the University of Virginia, who married Jane Auer (*see* BOWLES, J.) in 1938. In 1948 they went to Tangier, where they lived intermittently for the rest of their lives, and where they became familiar landmarks in the expatriate gay community, and points of call for many literary visitors in search of the exotic. His works, most of which are set in Morocco, include *The Sheltering Sky* (1949), 'an adventure story in which the adventures take place on two planes simultaneously: in the actual desert and in the inner desert of the spirit'. *Let it Come Down* (1952) describes the disintegration of bank clerk Nelson Dyer in Tangier. *The Spider's House* (1955) is set in Fez and *Up above the World* (1966) follows a doomed American couple in Central America. Bowles produced a number of translations of Moroccan works. *Without Stopping* (1972) is an autobiography.

BOWLES, William Lisle (1762–1850) Educated at Winchester College and Trinity College, Oxford, vicar of Bremhill, chaplain to the prince regent, and canon of Salisbury. His *Fourteen Sonnets Written Chiefly on Picturesque Spots during a Journey* (1789) was admired by Charles *Lamb, Robert *Southey, and S. T. *Coleridge, whose early sonnets were professedly in Bowles's manner. Lord *Byron, however, described him as 'the maudlin prince of mournful sonneteers', and was roused to further anger by Bowles's hostile edition of Pope (1806).

Box and Cox A *farce by John Maddison *Morton, adapted from two French vaudevilles, published 1847. Box is a journeyman printer, Cox a journeyman hatter. Mrs Bouncer, a lodging-house keeper, has let the same room to both, taking advantage of the fact that Box is out all night and Cox out all day to conceal from each the existence of the other. Discovery comes when Cox unexpectedly gets a holiday. Indignation follows, and complications connected with a widow to whom both have proposed marriage; and finally a general reconciliation. It was adapted into an operetta, *Cox and Box*, by Sir Francis Cowley *Burnand.

BOYD, William (1952–) Novelist, born in Accra, Ghana, and educated at Gordonstoun, and at the universities of Nice, Glasgow, and Oxford. *A Good Man in Africa* (1981) is a comic tale of diplomatic life in a minor West African posting. A collection of stories, *On the Yankee Station*, appeared in 1981 and was followed by *An Ice-Cream War* (1982), a serio-comic tale set in East Africa during the First World War. *Stars and Bars* (1984) and *The New Confessions* (1987), the sadly comic autobiography of a self-styled genius, consolidated Boyd's reputation as an accomplished storyteller with an instinct for inventive comedy. *Brazzaville Beach* (1990), set in Africa, explores the theme of the origins of human and animal violence. *The Blue Afternoon* (1993), set in 1936, tells of a young female architect who meets an enigmatic stranger claiming to be her father. *Armadillo* (1998) recounts the amorous and financial adventures in late 20th-century London of a Romany-born loss adjuster with sleeping difficulties. *Any*

Human Heart (2002) provides a history of the 20th century through the journals of Logan Mountstuart while the complex and fast-moving plot of *Restless* (2006) focuses, through the narratives of a mother and daughter, on the role of spies and betrayal in the Second World War. Boyd has written television screenplays, two of which, *Good and Bad at Games* and *Dutch Girls*, were published together as *School Ties* (1985). *The Destiny of Nathalie 'X'* (1995) and *Fascination* (2004) are further collections of stories.

BOYDELL, John (1719–1804) Engraver and publisher, who with his nephew Josiah Boydell opened their Shakespeare Gallery in Pall Mall in 1789. Originally it contained 34 paintings of subjects from Shakespeare, by many of the most famous artists of the day, including Joseph *Wright of Derby (Prospero's Cell); Henry *Fuseli (scenes from *A *Midsummer Night's Dream*, **Macbeth*, and **Hamlet*); and Joshua *Reynolds (Henry VI at the deathbed of Beaufort). The collection was later expanded, and many engravings of the works were sold.

BOYER, Abel (1667–1729) French Huguenot publisher and translator, who settled in England in 1689. He published a yearly register of political and other occurrences, and a periodical, *The Political State of Great Britain* (1711–29). He also brought out an English–French and a French–English dictionary, a *History of William III* (3 vols, 1702–3) and a *History of the Life and Reign of Queen Ann* (1722). He translated into English the memoirs of Gramont (1714) and *Racine's *Iphigénie*.
See also HAMILTON, ANTHONY.

BOYLE, John, fifth earl of Orrery (1707–62) Biographer and writer of letters, a friend from the early 1730s of Jonathan *Swift and Alexander *Pope. His controversial *Remarks on the Life and Writings of Dr Jonathan Swift* (1751) gave a critical account of Swift's character, life, relations with Stella and Vanessa, and friendships with Pope, John *Gay, Patrick *Delany, and Edward *Young. In discussing Swift's work, Orrery deplored the misanthropy 'which induced him peevishly to debase mankind' (Letter VI); but he says that the character which Swift deserved was that of 'an enemy to tyranny and oppression in any shape whatever' (Letter XVII).

BOYLE, Kay (1902–92) American novelist, poet, short story writer, and political activist. She began her career within the American expatriate community in Paris between the wars. Returning to Paris in 1943, she was blacklisted during the McCarthy era and her writing became more overtly political. She was active in the anti-Vietnam War movement and was imprisoned a number of times. Her novels include *Plagued by the Nightingale* (1931), and one of her most substantial collections is *Fifty Stories* (1980). *Words That Must Somehow Be Said* (1985) gathers a selection of her essays and gives an indication of the range of her interests.

BOYLE, Robert (1627–91) Scientist, youngest son of Richard Boyle, first earl of Cork. After two years at Eton College he travelled abroad and was influenced, in Geneva, by the Huguenot Isaac Marcombes. Settling in Stalbridge, Dorset, he determined to devote his life to science and good works, and became the dominant figure in English science between Francis *Bacon and Isaac *Newton. Robert Hooke (1635–1703) was his technical assistant in experiments on air which led to the formulation of 'Boyle's Law', which describes the inversely proportional relation between the absolute pressure and volume of a gas, if the temperature is constant within a closed system. Boyle's 'corpuscularianism', a rendering of the mechanical philosophy, exercised great influence throughout Europe. He was one of the group of thinkers who met in Gresham College, London, and in Oxford and became the *Royal Society, of which he was a founder member. He published prolifically on scientific, philosophical and religious subjects. Best known among his scientific writings is *The Sceptical Chymist* (1661). *The Origin of Forms and Qualities* (1666) anticipates much of the philosophy of John *Locke. Among his early works were the romances *Seraphic Love* and *The Martyrdom of Theodora*, the latter being turned into an opera libretto for *Handel. Samuel *Butler ('Hudibras') and Jonathan *Swift wrote parodies of his *Occasional Reflections* (1665), a work which also supplied Swift with one of the central storylines in **Gulliver's Travels*. Boyle paid for the translation of the New Testament into Irish and other languages, and as a director of the East India Company promoted the spread of Christianity in the East. In his will he funded annual Boyle Lectures in defence of natural and revealed religion. The first series was delivered by Richard *Bentley in 1692. A complete new edition of his Works was edited by Michael Hunter and Edward B. Davis in 14 volumes (1999–2000) and of his Correspondence by Michael Hunter, Antonio Clericuzio, and Lawrence M. Principe (2001). The website of the Robert Boyle Project based at Birkbeck College, London, gives up-to-date news of Boyle studies.

BOYLE, Roger, first earl of Orrery (1621–79) Soldier and playwright, son of the first earl of Cork. Educated at Trinity College, Dublin, he had a distinguished military career against the Irish rebels in 1641, on the parliamentary side in the English Civil War, and during Oliver *Cromwell's conquest of Ireland. His works include *Parthenissa* (1654–65), the first English romance in the style of *La Calprenède and Madeleine de *Scudéry; *English-Adventures by a Person of Honour* (1676), a source for Thomas *Otway's *The Orphan*; a *Treatise on the Art of War* (1677), two comedies, and some rhymed tragedies, among them *Mustapha* (1665), based on de Scudéry's *Ibrahim* and the history of Richard *Knolles. His plays were edited in two volumes by W. S. Clark, 1937. See K. M. Lynch, *Roger Boyle* (1965).

Boz The pseudonym used by Charles *Dickens in his contributions to the **Morning Chronicle* and in the **Pickwick Papers*, 'was the nickname of a pet child, a younger brother, whom I had dubbed Moses, in honour of the Vicar of Wakefield; which being facetiously pronounced...became Boz' (Dickens, preface to *Pickwick Papers*, 1847 edn).

BRACEGIRDLE, Anne (?1673/4–1748) A leading *Restoration actress. William *Congreve, who was perhaps her lover, wrote Angelica in *Love for Love* and Millamant in *The Way of the World* for her. She also created Belinda in Sir John *Vanbrugh's *The *Provoked Wife*, and played Portia, Desdemona, Ophelia, Cordelia, and Mrs Ford. She had great success in breeches roles, and Colley *Cibber recorded that 'on the stage few spectators that were not past it could behold her without desire'. She was finally eclipsed by Anne Oldfield (1683–1730) in 1707 and retired from the stage. See Elizabeth Howe, *The First English Actresses* (1992).

BRACKENBRIDGE, Hugh Henry (1748–1816) American novelist, poet, and lawyer, born in Scotland and educated at the College of New Jersey (later Princeton). His satirical novel *Modern Chivalry*, published in instalments from 1792 to 1815, gives a good description of men and manners during the early days of the American republic, and manifests Brackenbridge's allegiance to the robust tradition of the English novel in Tobias *Smollett and Henry *Fielding.

BRACKETT, Leigh (1915–78) Screenwriter and novelist, born in Los Angeles, known for her adaptation of Raymond *Chandler's *The Big Sleep* (1946) and initial work on **Star Wars: The Empire Strikes Back* (1980), which drew upon her colourful *science fiction novels, such as *The Sword of Rhiannon* (1949).

BRADBURY, Sir Malcolm (1932–2000) Critic and novelist, born in Sheffield, and educated at the universities of Leicester, London, and Manchester; he held several academic appointments, and in 1970 became professor of American studies at the University of East Anglia, where he was instrumental in setting up an influential creative writing course. His critical works include *Possibilities: Essays on the State of the Novel* (1973), *The Modern American Novel* (1983), *No, Not Bloomsbury* (essays, 1987), *Ten Great Writers* (1989), *The Novel Today* (revised edn, 1990), *From Puritanism to Postmodernism* (1991), and studies of Evelyn *Waugh (1962) and Saul *Bellow (1982); his approach combines respect for pluralism with admiration for the experiments and fictive devices of the American novel and of British writers such as John *Fowles. His first three novels are satirical *campus novels, with widely differing backgrounds; *Eating People is Wrong* (1959) relates the amorous and pedagogic tribulations of an ageing liberal humanist professor in a redbrick university; *Stepping Westward* (1965) is set in the Midwest of America; and *The History Man* (1975) in the new plate-glass university of Watermouth. *Rates of Exchange* (1983), which sends an academic linguist on a lecture tour of a fictitious Eastern European country, satirizes cultural exchange, and *Cuts: A Very Short Novel* (1987) satirizes Thatcherite Britain. *Doctor Criminale* (1992) recounts the search for a great 20th-century thinker, the mysterious Dr Bazlo Criminale. In *To the Hermitage* (2000), the visit of the 18th-century philosopher Denis *Diderot to the court of *Catherine the Great is juxtaposed with a Bradbury-like novelist's comic misadventures in 20th-century St Petersburg.

BRADBURY, Ray (1920–) American *science fiction and *fantasy writer, playwright, and poet, born in Waukegan, Illinois, and living from 1934 in Los Angeles, where he educated himself in the public library and began to write stories. Perhaps his best-known single work is *Fahrenheit 451* (1953), set in an authoritarian future state where reading is banned: fireman Montag is employed to burn books but rebels and makes a bid for freedom. It was filmed by François Truffaut (1966). The stories published as *The Martian Chronicles* (1950) include some of his most poetic work, suffused with ambiguity and nostalgia. A Gothic sense of the macabre is added to the stories in *The Illustrated Man* (1951) and *Dandelion Wine* (1957)—to which *Farewell Summer* (2006) is a sequel—and the novel *Something Wicked This Way Comes* (1962). His scripting of John Huston's film of **Moby Dick* (1956) inspired stories collected as *Green Shadows, White Whale* (1992), and his career as a pulp writer is behind *Death is a Lonely Business* (1985). He has received many awards including the National Medal of Arts (2004). See Jonathan R. Eller and William F. Touponce, *Ray Bradbury* (2004); Sam Weller, *The Bradbury Chronicles* (2005).

BRADDON, Mary Elizabeth (1837–1915) Novelist and editor, privately educated. She was an actress for three years in order to support herself and her mother. She met John Maxwell, a publisher of periodicals, in 1860, and acted as stepmother to his five children before marrying him in 1874 upon the death of his insane wife; she had six children by him. She published several works, including *Garibaldi and Other Poems* (1861), before the appearance of the sensational **Lady Audley's Secret* (1862, first serialized in *Robin Goodfellow* and *The Sixpenny Magazine*), which won her fame and fortune. The bigamous pretty blonde heroine, who deserts her child, attempts to murder her husband, and contemplates poisoning her second husband, shocked Margaret *Oliphant who credited Miss Braddon as 'the inventor of the fair-haired demon of modern fiction'. The novel has been dramatized, filmed, and translated and remained in print throughout the author's life. She published a further 74 inventive, vivid novels including the successful *Aurora Floyd* (1863), *The Doctor's Wife* (1864; loosely based on Gustave *Flaubert's *Madame Bovary*), *Henry Dunbar* (1864), and *Ishmael* (1884) and edited several magazines including **Belgravia* and *Temple Bar*. She was often attacked for corrupting young minds by making crime and violence attractive, but she won some notable admirers including Edward *Bulwer-Lytton, Thomas *Hardy, Robert Louis *Stevenson, and W. M. *Thackeray. *See* SENSATION, NOVEL OF; GHOST STORIES. There is a life by Jennifer Carnell (2000).

BRADLAUGH, Charles (1833–91) Social reformer, atheist, and advocate of free thought, who, after being employed in various occupations, became a lecturer and pamphleteer on many popular causes, under the name 'Iconoclast'. His voice was to be heard on platforms throughout the country and in the *National Reformer* (of which he became proprietor) which was a chief outlet for his friend James *Thomson's poems. Elected MP for Northampton in 1880, he was unseated after having been refused the right to make affirmation of allegiance instead of taking the parliamentary oath. He was re-elected but it was not until 1886 that he took his seat, having agreed finally to take the oath. Bradlaugh became a popular debater in the House. He was engaged in several lawsuits to maintain freedom of the press. In association with Annie Besant (1847–1933), he republished a pamphlet, *The Fruits of Philosophy*, advocating birth control, which led to a six-month prison sentence and a £200 fine; the conviction was quashed on appeal.

BRADLEY, A. C. (Andrew Cecil) (1851–1935) Brother of the philosopher F. H. Bradley (1846–1924), professor of literature at Liverpool, then Glasgow, and from 1901 to 1906 professor of poetry at Oxford. He is particularly remembered for his contributions to Shakespearian scholarship; his best-known works are *Shakespearean Tragedy* (1904) and *Oxford Lectures on Poetry* (1909). L. C. Knights in his essay 'How many children had Lady Macbeth?' (1933) represented a new generation of critics in his mockery of Bradley's 'detective interest' in plot and emphasis on 'character' as a detachable object of study, but Knights's approach too has now dated, and Bradley's works remain classics of criticism.

BRADLEY, Edward (1827–89) Novelist, educated at University College, Durham (which suggested his pseudonym, 'Cuthbert Bede'), and rector of various country livings, remembered as the author of *The Adventures of Mr Verdant Green* (1853–7), a comic novel which traces the Oxford career of a gullible young undergraduate, fresh from Warwickshire, from his freshman days to graduation and marriage. It was reprinted in 1982 with an introduction by Anthony *Powell. Bradley also contributed extensively to periodicals, illustrated his own works, and drew for **Punch*.

BRADLEY, Marion Zimmer (1930–99) American author, born Albany, New York; best known for her 'Darkover' *science fiction series in which a lost colony develops psychic powers indistinguishable from magic. Later episodes such as *The Heritage of Hastur* (1975) are much nearer to *fantasy, while Bradley's closer attention to feminism and gender politics becomes evident, especially in the *The Mists of Avalon* (1982) which retells the Arthurian legends from the viewpoint of *Morgan le Fay (here Morgaine).

BRADSHAW, Henry (1831–86) Bibliographer, scholar, antiquary, and librarian of the University of Cambridge (1867–86), where he reorganized the early printed books and manuscripts. He established the method of studying *incunabula through an examination of their types and of ordering them by country, town, and press.

BRADSTREET, Anne (*c.*1612–1672) American poet. She was born in England and emigrated with her father Thomas Dudley and husband Simon Bradstreet in 1630, settling first at Ipswich, then in North Andover, Massachusetts. She had eight children. Her poems were published in London without her knowledge in 1650, under the title *The Tenth Muse Lately Sprung up in America*, and a posthumous second edition with her own corrections and additions was published in Boston (1678). She admired and was influenced by Francis *Quarles and Josuah Sylvester's translation of *Du Bartas, and her work was highly praised in her own time. Her later and shorter poems are now more highly regarded than her longer philosophical and historical discourses, and she has received much attention both as a woman writer and as the first poet of the New World. John *Berryman pays tribute to her in his *Homage to Mistress Bradstreet* (1956).

BRADWARDINE, Thomas (*c.*1300–1349) Oxford theologian appointed archbishop of Canterbury immediately before his death from plague in August 1349. His *De Causa Dei* reasserted the primacy of faith and divine grace in opposition to the rationalist sceptics (whom he characterized as New Pelagians) of the tradition of William of *Ockham and Robert *Holcot. Like his direct contemporary Richard *Fitzralph he was a member of the circle of Richard de *Bury. He has been called a determinist and a preacher of predestination because of his insistence on the involvement of God's will as a primary cause in every action of the human will, the independence of which is thus reduced. The effect of this, as of the arguments of his opponents, was to destroy the 13th-century synthesis of Faith and Reason, but in this case giving the primacy unconditionally to Faith/Theology over Reason/Philosophy. See G. Leff, *Bradwardine and the Pelagians* (1957).

BRAGG, Melvyn (1939–) Novelist, broadcaster, and public figure, born in Cumberland, where some of his works are set, educated at Oxford University, and appointed a Labour life peer in 1998. His twenty novels include *Without a City Wall* (1968), *The Silken Net* (1971), *The Maid of Buttermere* (1978), *A Time to Dance* (1990), and the powerful fictional sequence that began with *The Soldier's Return* (1999). He has also written popular histories. Best known as a media personality, he was producer-presenter of the television arts programme the *South Bank Show* (1978–2010), and presented influential *radio discussion programmes, including *The Routes of English* and *In our Time*.

Braggadochio In Edmund *Spenser's **Faerie Queene*, the typical braggart. His adventures and final exposure and humiliation occur in II. iii; III. viii, x; IV. iv, v, ix; V. iii.

BRAINE, John (1922–86) Novelist, born and educated in Bradford, who was for many years a librarian in the north of England. His first novel, *Room at the Top* (1957), set in a small Yorkshire town, was an instant success, and its hero, Joe Lampton, was hailed as a provincial *'Angry Young Man' of the 1950s. Lampton, a ruthless opportunist working at the town hall, seduces and marries the wealthy young Susan Browne, despite his love for an unhappily married older woman. *Life at the Top* (1962) continues the story of his success and disillusion. Braine's later novels express his increasing hostility to the radical views with which he was once identified. They include *The Crying Game* (1964), *Stay with Me till Morning* (1968), *The Queen of a Distant Country* (1972), *The Pious Agent* (1975), *Finger of Fire* (1977), *One and Last Love* (1981), and *The Two of Us* (1984).

BRANTÔME, Pierre de Bourdeilles, seigneur de (*c.*1540–1614) French memorialist. His career as an officer and courtier gave him the opportunity to observe the private conduct of the great figures of the day. His posthumously published memoirs (1665–6) include the notorious *Vie des dames galantes* (*Lives of Gallant Ladies*), which repeat the scandals of court intrigues in a lively and sympathetic style.

Branwen *See* MABINOGION.

BRATHWAITE, Kamau (1930–) A poet and academic, born in Barbados, educated there and at Cambridge and Sussex universities. He has written works on West Indian history and culture; his volumes of poetry include *The Arrivants: A New World Trilogy* (1973), which consists of *Rights of Passage* (1967), *Masks* (1968), and *Islands* (1969). The poem explores the complex Caribbean heritage and search for identity, using (but not exclusively) vernacular rhythms and diction, what he calls 'nation language'; its references range from Afro-Caribbean religious beliefs to cricket matches at the Oval. *Mother Poem* (1977), *Sun Poem* (1982), and *X-Self* (1987) form a trilogy about Barbados, 'most English of West Indian islands'. *Born to Slow Horses* (2005) meditates on exile.

Brat Pack A phrase coined by the media to describe a group of young novelists from New York which emerged in the mid- to late 1980s. Also known as 'The Blank Generation', they write fiction inhabiting a youth culture of fast-lane living—cocaine, nightclubs, Music Television (MTV), and hedonistic abandon. Bret Easton Ellis (1964–), in *Less than Zero* (1984), and Jay McInerney (1955–), in *Bright Lights, Big City* (1984), heralded this new mood of fashionable disaffection. Written in hypnotically deadpan voices, they described lives that consisted of a cool surface bereft of substance. Tama *Janowitz's collection of short stories *Slaves of New York* (1987) was a notable addition, and critics often tended (wrongly) to equate the writers with their characters. Their obsession with celebrity and vacuity reached apocalyptic proportions with Ellis's *American Psycho* (1991), a novel in which the narrator, Patrick Bateman, blends into the persona of a serial killer.

BRAUTIGAN, Richard (1935–84) American novelist and short story writer associated particularly with the San Francisco counter-culture of the 1960s. His 1967 novel *Trout Fishing in America* established him and set a keynote for his writing in using a faux-naïf style. His works also show some influence from Zen Buddhism and in the late 1960s he made an abortive attempt to collaborate with the *Beatles on a recording project. Ianthe Elizabeth Brautigan has recorded her memories of her father in *You Can't Catch Death* (2000).

Brave New World A novel by Aldous *Huxley, published 1932; a dystopian fable about a world state in the 7th century AF (after Ford), where social stability is based on a scientific caste system. Human beings, graded from highest intellectuals to lowest manual workers, hatched from incubators and brought up in communal nurseries, learn by methodical conditioning to accept their social destiny. The action of the story develops round Bernard Marx, an unorthodox and therefore unhappy Alpha-Plus (something had presumably gone wrong with his antenatal treatment), who visits a New Mexican Reservation and brings a Savage back to London. The Savage is at first fascinated by the new world, but finally revolted, and his argument with Mustapha Mond, World Controller, demonstrates the incompatibility of individual freedom and a scientifically trouble-free society. In *Brave New World Revisited* (1958) Huxley reconsiders his prophecies, fearing that some of them were coming true sooner than he thought.

BRAWNE, Fanny (1800–65) The young woman with whom John *Keats fell in love in 1818. To what extent she returned or understood his passion for her (expressed in many of his letters and several poems) is not clear, but some kind of engagement took place, and after his death she wore mourning for him for several years. She married in 1833. His letters to her were published in 1878 and in the collected edition of 1937; hers to his sister, also called Fanny, were published in 1937.

BRAZIL, Angela (1868–1947) Born in Preston, Lancashire, a formative influence on the development of modern girls' *school stories. She wrote 53 books from *The Fortunes of Philippa* (1906) to *The School on the Loch* (1946), and many short stories for annuals. Unlike most of her contemporaries, she did not write *series. Brazil favoured unidealized heroines and her books were criticized for their use of slang. There is a critical study by Gillian Freeman, *The Schoolgirl Ethic* (1976).

BRECHT, Bertolt (1898–1956) German dramatist and poet. His life and work, shaped by the great historical events of his times, can be considered in three distinct phases. Of the first of these, the years of the Weimar Republic, his best-known work for the stage is the satirical *Die Dreigroschenoper* (1928: *The Threepenny Opera*) with music by Kurt *Weill, an adaptation of

*The *Beggar's Opera*. As a result of the economic crisis which followed the First World War he began a study of *Marxism and, though never formally a member of the party, remained thereafter closely associated with the Communist cause. The second phase began with Hitler's seizure of power in 1933. He went into exile, settling first in Denmark, then Sweden and Finland. Finally he fled to the USA in 1941, where he looked to the film industry to earn a living. All the plays for which he is best known in the English-speaking world were written during the years of exile. Abandoning experiments with didactic agit-prop, he wrote *Leben des Galilei* (*Life of Galileo*) and *Mutter Courage und ihre Kinder* (*Mother Courage and her Children*), set in the Thirty Years War (1618–48) in 1938–9. These plays inaugurated the mature form of what he termed Epic Theatre; this was marked by a rejection of empathetic identification with the characters and any theatrical illusion of reality, extensive use of music, song, and verse, construction by 'loosely' connected scenes, and the *alienation effect. *Der gute Mensch von Sezuan* (1941–3: *The Good Woman of Setzuan*) and *Der kaukasische Kreidekreis* (1944: *The Caucasian Chalk Circle*) were both written in America where he collaborated with the actor Charles Laughton on an English version of *Life of Galileo* in 1946–7. After Hitler's defeat he was able to return to Europe, and in 1948 he settled in East Berlin where he led the Berliner Ensemble until his death. This third phase saw few original new works for the theatre, a fact due less to waning inspiration than to the practical demands of running a theatre company and the need to create a repertoire of adaptations, including one of George *Farquhar's *The Recruiting Officer* (*Pauken und Trompeten*, 1954). However, he was at last able to see his own works published in their final revised versions and staged in accordance with his theory, concisely formulated in *Kleines Organon für das Theater* (1949: *Short Organon for the Theatre*). His engagement with English literature, which he greatly admired, was both extensive and profound. In particular he studied the theatre of *Shakespeare and contemporaries such as Christopher *Marlowe, John *Heywood, John *Webster, and John *Ford: there were adaptations of **Edward II* in 1924, an unhappy collaboration with W. H. *Auden in 1944–6 on *The *Duchess of Malfi*, and a version of **Coriolanus* (1951–2; pub. 1959) for the Berliner Ensemble. In America he had attempted to interest both Christopher *Isherwood and Auden in translating his plays. Isherwood had already translated the verses from the novel *Dreigroschenroman* (1937: *A Penny for the Poor*) and Auden did produce versions of songs and poetry from *Mother Courage* and *Caucasian Chalk Circle*. He imitated the style of Rudyard *Kipling's ballads, venerated Jonathan *Swift, and felt a special kinship with P. B. *Shelley whom he called 'my brother'. The visit of the Berliner Ensemble to London in 1956 was warmly received by the critic Kenneth *Tynan, and Brecht's theatre had a notable impact on several British playwrights of the second half of the 20th century including Edward *Bond, John *Arden, Howard *Brenton, and David *Hare. Beyond the verse and songs contained in the plays, Brecht left a substantial and important body of lyric poetry and also some interesting prose narratives including one on Francis *Bacon. See K. Dickson, *Towards Utopia: A Study of Brecht* (1978); Ronald Hayman, *Bertolt Brecht: A Biography* (1983).

Breck, Alan A dashing character in Robert Louis *Stevenson's **Kidnapped and Catriona*. Based on Allan Breck Stewart, whose involvement in the notorious Appin murder case in 1752 also figures in Walter *Scott's fiction.

BREEZE, Jean Binta (1957–) Born in Jamaica. She studied at the School of Drama. She now lives in London, where she is a lecturer, performance poet, and joint editor of the **Critical Quarterly*. The first female *dub poet, she focuses on black women's experience in Kingston, Jamaica, and London.

BRENAN, Gerald (Edward Fitz-Gerald) (1894–1987) Author, born in Malta, who lived in Spain from 1920. He knew members of the *Bloomsbury Group, as recorded in his autobiography *A Life of one's Own* (1962), where he also describes his experiences in the First World War. *Personal Record 1920–1972* was published in 1974. See Jonathan Gathorne-Hardy, *The Interior Castle* (1992).

BRENDAN, St (*c*.484–578) or Brendan the Navigator. Irish monk said to have been born in West Kerry who founded the monastery of Clonfert, County Galway, and about whom there grew up a tradition of legendary voyages as a Christianized version of the Old Irish *immram* genre. Other examples include 'The Voyage of Bran' and 'The Voyage of Maeldune' The Latin allegory *Navigatio Sancti Brandani* has been dated to as early as the eighth century. The legends of Brendan have been periodically revived, for example by Matthew *Arnold. They include the story of his encountering Judas exercising his annual privilege of cooling himself on a rock on Christmas night; and of his landing on a whale, mistaking it for an island, and lighting a fire on its back. Folk tradition credits Brendan with reaching America nearly a thousand years before Columbus. Brendan is cited in the poetry of both Louis *MacNeice and Seamus *Heaney.

BRENNAN, Christopher (1870–1932) Australian poet and scholar, educated at the universities of Sydney and Berlin. A learned and rebellious figure influenced by Catholicism, Victorian poetry, German philosophy, and French literature (notably the *symbolists), whose poetry and criticism were neglected until the 1950s. Now known chiefly for his *Poems* (1914; often called *Poems [1913]*) which reflect what biographer Axel Clark argues, in *Christopher Brennan* (1980), was a lifelong search for 'wholeness', the 'Eden' of Stéphane *Mallarmé.

BRENT-DYER, Elinor M. (May) (1894–1969) Born in South Shields, Tyneside; she wrote over 100 books for girls. These included the 60 books in the popular 'Chalet School' series, from *The School at the Chalet* (1925) to *Prefects at the Chalet School* (1970), and the 'La Rochelle' series (1922–53). The exotic locations of the Chalet School, which moves from the Tyrol to the Channel Islands, to Wales, and to the Oberland, are matched by an acute understanding of girls' interests.

BRENTON, Howard (1942–) Playwright born in Portsmouth, educated at Cambridge University. His father was a policeman who later became a Methodist minister in Yorkshire. Police and clergy feature heavily in many of the short Brenton plays which powered the London fringe in the early 1970s. An avowed socialist, Brenton has a unique and powerful voice that combines jagged writing with raw, *Jacobean theatricality. His first full-scale *Royal Court play *Magnificence* (1973) was followed by a collaboration with David *Hare, *Brassneck* (1973), *The Churchill Play* (1974), and four highly successful productions at the *National Theatre: *Weapons of Happiness* (1976); a new version of Bertolt *Brecht's *Galileo*; *The Romans in Britain* (1980), an allegory of the British army presence in Northern Ireland, which attracted an ill-fated private prosecution by Mrs Mary Whitehouse; and, again with Hare, *Pravda* (1985), a savage attack on the power politics of the tabloid press. He has written a number of issue-based pieces with Tariq Ali, including *Moscow Gold* (1990). This and *Berlin Bertie* (1992) moved Brenton's work away from Britain and into the new Europe. He has written thirteen characteristically Gothic episodes for the popular television series *Spooks*. *Paul* (2005), with its denial of Jesus' resurrection, again aroused the controversy that has never been far away from Brenton; and *In Extremis* (2006) used the story of Eloise and *Abelard to consider the historical significance of the struggle between faith and reason. *Diving for Pearls* (1989) is a vivid novel, and *Hot Irons* (1995) a collection of occasional pieces and production diaries.

BRERETON, Jane (1685–1740) Poet. Separated from her husband, she lived at Wrexham and wrote verse to a circle of women friends, collected posthumously as *Poems on Several Occasions* (1744). During her lifetime she published an imitation of *Horace (1716), verse in the *Gentleman's Magazine*, and *Merlin: A Poem* (1735).

BRETON, André (1896–1966) French poet, essayist, and critic, one of the founders of *Surrealism. He collaborated with Philippe Soupault on *Les Champs magnétiques* (1920: *Magnetic Fields*), an early experiment in automatic writing, and he wrote his first *Manifeste du surréalisme* (*Manifesto of Surrealism*) in 1924, followed by a second in 1930. He published a number of volumes of poetry, including *Clair de terre* (1923: *Earthlight*), *Le Revolver à cheveux blancs* (1932: *The White-Haired Revolver*), and *L'Air de l'eau* (1934: *The Air of the Water*), as well as a series of prose narratives: *Nadja* (1928), *Les Vases communicants* (1932: *The Communicating Vessels*), *L'Amour fou* (1937: *Mad Love*), and *Arcane 17* (1944). His ongoing interest in art led to successive editions of *Le Surréalisme et la peinture* (1928, 1945, 1965: *Surrealism and Painting*). His essays and articles were collected in *Les Pas perdus* (1924: *Lost Footsteps*), *Point du jour* (1934: *Daybreak*), and *La Clé des champs* (1953: *The Key to the Fields*). See M. A. Caws, *André Breton* (1996).

BRETON, Nicholas (1554/5–*c.*1626) Educated at Oxford University, the author of miscellaneous satirical, religious, romantic, and political writings in verse and prose. His stepfather was George *Gascoigne. From *c.*1576 he seems to have settled in London, and between 1575 and 1622 he published well over 50 books including: *The Will of Wit, Wit's Will, or Will's Wit* (*c.*1582); *The Pilgrimage to Paradise, Joined with the Countess of Pembroke's Love* (1592); *Wit's Trenchmore* (a partly autobiographical dialogue on angling, 1597); *The Figure of Four, or A Handful of Sweet Flowers* (*c.*1597); *Pasquil's Mad-Cap* (1600); *The Soul's Heavenly Exercise* (1601); *Old Mad-Cap's New Gallimaufry* (1602); *Fantastics: Serving for a Perpetual Prognostication* (a collection of observations on men and nature arranged calendar-wise, *c.*1604); *The Honour of Valour* (1605); *The Good and the Bad, or Descriptions of the Worthies and Unworthies of this Age* (1616); *Conceited Letters, Newly Laid Open* (1618). His best poetry is to be found among his short lyrics in **Englands Helicon* (1600) and in his volume of pastoral poetry *The Passionate Shepherd* (1604). His works were edited by Alexander *Grosart in 1879, and poems not included by Grosart were edited, with much information about his works, by Jean Robertson in 1952.

Breton lays In medieval English literature, are short stories in rhyme like those of *Marie de France. Despite having analogues in several European languages, the English examples often owe their identification simply to the fact that they say they are Breton lays, or that the same story has been told by Marie in French. *See* Emaré; Orfeo, Sir; Degaré, Sir; the other English instances are *Sir Launfal*, *Lai le Freine*, *The Erle of Tolous*, *Sir Gowther*, Chaucer's 'The Franklin's Tale' (*see* Canterbury Tales, 12) and John *Gower's 'Tale of Rosiphelee' (*Confessio Amantis*, Bk IV). See T. C. Rumble (ed.), *The Breton Lays in Middle English* (1965).

Brewer's Dictionary of Phrase and Fable By the Revd Ebenezer Cobham Brewer (1810–97), first published 1870, regularly revised. It provides explanations and origins of the familiar and unfamiliar in English phrase and fable, including colloquial and proverbial phrases, embracing archaeology, history, religion, the arts, science, mythology, fictitious characters and titles.

BREYTENBACH, Breyten (1939–) South African poet, autobiographer, and essayist who writes in English and Afrikaans. In *True Confessions of an Albino Terrorist* (1984) he gives an account of his seven-year incarceration in maximum security prisons for political activism. His playful, angry, surreal prose eludes conventional categories.

Bride of Abydos, The A poem in irregular stanzas by Lord *Byron, one of his 'Turkish tales', published in December 1813: it sold 6,000 copies within a month. The beautiful Zuleika, daughter of the Pacha Giaffir, is destined to marry the rich, elderly Bey of Carasman, whom she has never seen. She confesses her grief to her beloved brother Selim, who takes her to his grotto, where he reveals himself in magnificent pirate garb and declares he is not her brother but her cousin. He begs her to share his future, but Giaffir and his soldiers arrive and Selim is killed. Zuleika dies of grief. In the first draft Zuleika and Selim were not cousins but half-brother and sister: a variation of the incest theme to which Byron was frequently drawn.

Bride of Lammermoor, The A novel by Walter *Scott, published 1819 in **Tales of my Landlord*, 3rd series. The darkness and fatalism of this novel have traditionally been ascribed to Scott's almost mortal illness while he was writing it, as have minor confusions in the plot; but recent research shows that most of it was written earlier. The pessimistic tone of what has been described as the most pure and powerful of his tragedies remains unexplained. The dramatic possibilities of the story of Lucy Ashton's frustrated love for the Byronic Master of Ravenswood, her stabbing of the alternative bridegroom forced upon her on the wedding night, and her own insanity and death, were to be seized on by *Donizetti for his opera *Lucia di Lammermoor*. The comic interest in the novel is provided by Ravenswood's henchman Caleb Balderstone, though Scott admitted that, in his creation, 'he had sprinkled too much parsley over his chicken'.

'Bridge of Sighs, The' A poem by Thomas *Hood, published 1843, one of the most popular of his serious works. It is a compassionate elegy on the suicide by drowning of a 'fallen woman', which dwells in some detail on her youth and beauty, her penitence for her 'evil behaviour', and the 'cold inhumanity' of the world which cast her out.

BRIDGES, Robert (1844–1930) Poet, born in Kent and educated at Eton College and Corpus Christi College, Oxford. He studied medicine at St Bartholomew's Hospital, London, and worked in various hospitals until 1881. At Oxford he met G. M. *Hopkins, and became his friend, adviser, and influential advocate of his poetry, later editing *The Poems of Gerard Manley Hopkins* (1918). Bridges's first book, *Poems*, was published in 1873. *The Growth of Love*, a sonnet sequence, appeared in 1876 with some success, and in an enlarged form in 1890. Two long poems followed, *Prometheus the Firegiver* (1883) and *Eros and Psyche* (1885). Between 1885 and 1894 he wrote eight plays. He also wrote *Milton's Prosody* (1893) and *John Keats* (1895), and between 1895 and 1908 wrote the words for four works by the composer Hubert *Parry. He was greatly interested in musical settings, and edited the *Yattendon Hymnal*. He had moved to Yattendon in Berkshire in 1882, and later moved to a house called Chilswell at Boars Hill, Oxford (he edited *The Chilswell Book of English Poetry* in 1924). His *Poetical Works* appeared in six volumes (1898–1905), and then in one volume in 1912, and received great critical and popular acclaim. The following year, he was appointed *poet laureate. In 1916, he produced a highly successful anthology, *The Spirit of Man*, which included six poems by Hopkins, whose work was mostly still unpublished. *October and Other Poems* (1920) and *New Verse* (1925) were followed by *The Testament of Beauty* (1929), a long poem, in four books, on his spiritual philosophy, which he saw as the culmination of his work as a poet, and which sold extremely well. His lyric verse was much anthologized, and some of it became widely known, but Bridges's poetry is no longer popular. His collected essays and papers were published between 1927 and 1936. One of the founders of the Society for Pure English, several of whose tracts he wrote or edited, he collaborated on tracts with his wife Monica as 'Matthew Barnes'. See Catherine Phillips, *Robert Bridges* (1992).

BRIDIE, James (1888–1951) Pseudonym of Osborne Henry Mavor, Scottish dramatist, born in Glasgow and educated at the University of Glasgow, where he studied medicine. He served in the Royal Army Medical Corps in both world wars, spending most of the intervening years in general practice until becoming a full-time writer in 1938. Though he helped found the Glasgow Citizens' Theatre in 1943, Bridie wrote mainly for the London stage. His plays, which delight in debate and the clash of ideas, and exhibit a wide variety of settings and styles, have sometimes been said to lack structure. They include *The Anatomist* (1930), *A Sleeping Clergyman* (1933), *Mr Bolfry* (1943), and *The Queen's Comedy* (1950).

BRIEUX, Eugène (1858–1932) French dramatist of contemporary morals, championed as 'the greatest writer France has produced since Molière' by George Bernard *Shaw, whose wife Charlotte (née Payne-Townshend, 1859–1943) translated his *Maternité* in *Three Plays by Brieux* (1913, with an introduction by Shaw). A second volume, *Woman on her Own, False Gods and The Red Robe: Three Plays by Brieux* (1916), has translations by Charlotte Shaw, J. B. Fagan, and A. B. Miall and an introduction by Brieux.

BRIGGS, Raymond (1934–) London-born author-illustrator of children's books, educated at Wimbledon School of Art and the Slade School of Fine Art; best known for his comic-strip style employed in long-standing favourites *Father Christmas* (1973), *Fungus the Bogeyman* (1977), and *The Snowman* (1979). *When the Wind Blows* (1982) is a remarkable portrayal of the reality of nuclear war for an ordinary couple, Jim and Hilda, as they take refuge in their hopelessly inadequate home-made fallout shelter. *Ethel and Ernest* (1998) is a memoir of his parents in comic-strip form. Notable *picturebook illustrations include those for Elfrida Vipont's *The Elephant and the Bad Baby* (1969). See Nicolette Jones, *Blooming Books* (2003).

BRIN, David (1950–) Born Glendale, California; novelist with a Ph.D. in space science, active in promoting *science fiction for its engagement with the future. His second novel, *Startide Rising* (1983) won the *Hugo award. *Earth* (1990) explores social and environmental issues over the next fifty years.

BRINK, André Philippus (1935–) South African playwright, novelist, short story writer, and critic educated at Potchefstroom University, the Sorbonne, and Rhodes

University. He is emeritus professor of English literature at the University of Cape Town. He writes most of his novels in both English and Afrikaans and was snubbed during the era of apartheid by the Afrikaans literary community for his dissidence. His *Kennis van die aand* (1973), translated into English as *Looking on Darkness* (1974), was banned by the South African government; it tells the story of a coloured actor who works against apartheid by cultural means. After a passionate affair with a white woman, he is executed by the Security Police. Brink's novels include *An Instant in the Wind* (1976), set in the interior; *Rumours of Rain* (1978) and *A Dry White Season* (1979, filmed 1989), both of which explore the moral ambiguities of Afrikaner nationalism; *A Chain of Voices* (1982), about a group of slaves accused of killing an Afrikaner farmer during the early 19th century; *The Wall of the Plague* (1984) where the Black Death is presented as a metaphor of apartheid; *States of Emergency* (1988), a love story set within the context of national violence; *An Act of Terror* (1991), a political thriller turning on a plot to assassinate the South African president; *On the Contrary* (1993), a *picaresque biography of an 18th-century adventurer, Estienne Barbier; and *Cape of Storms* (1993), an interracial 15th-century love story. After apartheid Brink has published seven novels all of which involve encounters between opposites: *Imaginings of Sand* (1996), a centenarian's tales told to her granddaughter; *Devil's Valley* (1998), in which a journalist hears conflicting stories in isolated mountains; *The Rights of Desire* (2000), about an ageing librarian who is disturbingly made to live in the present; *The Other Side of Silence* (2002), set at about 1905 and challenging gender stereotypes; *Before I Forget* (2004), in which an old writer is rejuvenated by a young sculptress; *Praying Mantis* (2005), the story of Cupido Cockroach, a 17th-century Khoi missionary; *The Blue Door* (2007), based on what-if? choices.

BRISCOE, Sophia (*fl.* 1771–8) Novelist, author of two epistolary novels: *Miss Melmoth, or The New Clarissa* (1771), and *The Fine Lady* (1772); for the latter she was paid 20 guineas. Lowndes, the publisher, also apparently paid her 12 guineas for *The Sylph* (1778), sometimes attributed to Georgiana, duchess of Devonshire.

BRISLEY, Joyce Lankester (1896–1978) Born in Bexhill, Sussex; writer-illustrator best known for her stories about Milly-Molly-Mandy (1928–67), first published in the *Christian Science Monitor* (1925). The stories describe the kindly Milly-Molly-Mandy's life in an idyllic village. The author's sister was Nina K. Brisley, designer of the first covers for *Brent-Dyer's Chalet School books.

Britannia or, according to its subtitle, *A Chorographical Description of the Most Flourishing Kingdoms of England, Scotland, and Ireland, and the Islands Adjoining, out of the Depth of Antiquity*, by William *Camden, first published in Latin (1586), the sixth (much-enlarged) edition appearing in 1607. It was translated in 1610 by Philemon *Holland; reprints continued in the 18th and 19th centuries. It is in effect a guidebook of the country, county by county, replete with archaeological, historical, physical, and other information.

Britannia's Pastorals *See* BROWNE, WILLIAM.

British Library London: the national library for the United Kingdom. It was established in 1973 under Act of Parliament by the amalgamation of the library departments of the *British Museum and other organizations, as the national centre for reference, lending, bibliographical, and other information services based on its vast collections of books, manuscripts, maps, music, periodicals, and other material. It moved from Bloomsbury to St Pancras in 1998. It is one of the six *legal deposit libraries, or copyright libraries, which are entitled to receive, free of charge, a copy of every work published in the United Kingdom and the Republic of Ireland. The other legal deposit libraries are the Bodleian Library, Oxford; the University Library, Cambridge; the National Library of Scotland, Edinburgh; the library of Trinity College Dublin; and the National Library of Wales, Aberystwyth.

British Museum Bloomsbury, occupying the site of Montagu House, acquired in 1753 to house the collections of Sir Hans Sloane (1660–1753). These were soon enormously increased by the purchase of the *Harleian Manuscripts, the gift by George IV of the royal library, the Elgin Marbles, and the acquisition of Egyptian antiquities (including the Rosetta Stone), and of the Layard Assyrian collections. New buildings, designed by Sir Robert Smirke, were erected in 1823–47. The great Reading Room, designed by Antonio *Panizzi, was opened in 1857; it closed in 1998, when the new British Library at St Pancras opened to the public.

Britomart The heroine of Book III of Edmund *Spenser's **Faerie Queene*, the daughter of King Ryence of Britain, and the female knight of chastity. She has fallen in love with Sir *Artegall, whose image she has seen in a magic mirror: her adventures in her quest for him are recounted in Books III and IV. She is the most powerful of several types of *Elizabeth I in the poem.

BRITTAIN, Vera (1893–1970) Writer, pacifist, and feminist. The daughter of a manufacturer, she was born in Newcastle-under-Lyme and educated at St Monica's School and Somerville College, Oxford. Her university education, opposed by her parents, was interrupted by the First World War, during which she served as a VAD (Voluntary Aid Detachment) nurse in France and Malta. Her *autobiographical *Testament of Youth* (1933) is a moving account of her early struggles, her war experiences, and her grief at the loss of both her fiancé, Roland Leighton, and brother Edward during the war. She returned to Oxford after the war, where she formed a close friendship with Winifred *Holtby, recorded in *Testament* *of Friendship* (1940). *Testament of Experience* (1957) continues her autobiography whilst her diaries, *Chronicles of Youth* (1981), which she drew on in *Testament of Youth*, were published posthumously. She was the mother of the politician Shirley Williams (1930–), who was among the founders of the Social Democratic Party in 1981. See Paul Berry and Mark Bostridge, *Vera Brittain: A Life* (1996).

BRITTEN, Benjamin (1913–76) English composer, born in Lowestoft and educated there, at Gresham's School, Holt, and at the Royal College of Music. Through writing music for documentaries he met W. H. *Auden, with whom he collaborated on *Our Hunting Fathers* (1936), an orchestral song cycle written in reaction to the Spanish Civil War. In 1939 Britten emigrated with the tenor Peter Pears (1910–86), who became his partner and for whom much of his vocal writing was designed, to America, where his first opera, *Paul Bunyan* (1941), to a libretto by Auden, was completed. Britten and Pears returned to England in 1942 and registered as conscientious objectors. Pacifism underlies *The War Requiem* (1962), written for the dedication of the new cathedral at Coventry: the Latin Mass for the Dead is punctuated by emotionally expressive settings for solo voice of poems by Wilfred *Owen. Britten's *Owen Wingrave* (1971), an opera for television based on Henry *James's story, is also on the theme of resistance to war.

In the *Serenade for Tenor, Horn and Strings* (1943), and the *Spring Symphony* (1949) Britten sets poems ranging from a medieval dirge through *Spenser, *Jonson, and *Herrick, to *Blake and *Tennyson. The darkly audacious opera *Peter Grimes* (1945), based on poems from George *Crabbe's *The Borough*, centres on an outsider figure; further operas, such as *The Rape of Lucretia* (1946), deal with themes of innocence destroyed or misunderstood. *Billy Budd* (1951) is based on Herman *Melville's novella via E. M. *Forster's libretto. *The *Turn of the Screw* (1954), derived from Henry James's story, is the first in a series of 'chamber operas', a move towards simplification paralleled in the three *Parables for Church Performance* (1964–68), stylized pieces on the model of the *Nōh play, and inflected by non-European harmonic patterns, all with libretti by William *Plomer, who provided the text for the poorly received 'coronation' opera, *Gloriana* (1953). More traditional operas include *A *Midsummer Night's Dream* (1960), and *Death in Venice* (1973), after Thomas *Mann. Britten founded the Aldeburgh Festival in 1976 and was created Baron Britten of Aldeburgh in 1976. See H. Carpenter, *Benjamin Britten: A Biography* (1992).

Broad Church A popular term especially current in the latter half of the 19th century for those in the Church of England who sought to interpret the creeds in a broad and liberal manner, and whose theological beliefs lay between Low and High Churchmen. The expression was used by Arthur Penrhyn *Stanley in one of his sermons, about 1847, though the term appears to have originally been proposed by Arthur Hugh *Clough. The existence of the Broad Church school owes much to the influence of Thomas *Arnold and to Romantic philosophy as interpreted by S. T. *Coleridge, who earned the title of 'Father of the Broad Church Movement'. Other characteristic representatives of the school were Thomas *Hughes, Benjamin *Jowett, Mark *Pattison, and most of the other writers for **Essays and Reviews*. The term is now often used to describe institutions tolerant of different ideas and beliefs.

broadside A sheet of paper printed on one side only, forming one large page; a term generally used of *ballads etc. so printed.

Broceliande A legendary region adjoining Brittany, in the Arthurian legends, home of *Merlin. *Wace in his *Roman de Rou* says that he made a disappointing visit there (i.e. to Brecheliant in Brittany) and found nothing (ii. 6395 ff.); there is a legendary Tomb of Merlin there still. Broceliande is made the magical forest of Calogrenant's story in *Chrétien de Troyes's *Yvain*.

BROCH, Hermann (1886–1951) Austrian writer, born in Vienna to Jewish parents. After publishing his vast pessimistic trilogy *Die Schlafwandler* (1930–2: *The Sleepwalkers*) he was imprisoned by the Nazis until his emigration to America was secured by influential friends including James *Joyce. There he wrote his best-known work, *Der Tod des Vergil* (1945: *The Death of Virgil*), which imagines the interior monologue of the dying poet as he reflects on the artistic value of the **Aeneid*. His correspondence with his publisher Daniel Brody, published in 1971, is of great interest to historians of book production.

BRODBER, Erna (1940–) Educated at the University of the West Indies; she is concerned as an academic and as a novelist with the untold stories of her native Jamaica. Her fiction, *Jane and Louisa Will Soon Come Home* (1980), *Myal* (1988), and *Louisiana* (1994), focuses on the spiritual power of the community, and particularly of women, to heal those isolated by the disruption caused by colonialism, slavery, gossip, and sectarianism. The characters' voices cover a range of vernaculars.

BRODERICK, Damien (1944–) Born Melbourne, Australia; writer, editor, and critic of *science fiction who may have first used the term 'virtual reality' in *The Judas Mandela* (1982). Later novels such as *Transcension* (2002) and *Godplayers* (2005) explore concepts like nanotechnology or alternative worlds.

BRODSKY, Joseph (1940–96) Russian poet, born in Leningrad. His early poetic talent was recognized by Anna *Akhmatova. In 1964 he was tried for 'parasitism', and spent eighteen months in exile in northern Russia. He was exiled from the Soviet Union in 1972, and settled in the United States, where he held a number of university posts. His first volume of poetry in English, *Joseph Brodsky: Selected Poems* (1973), shows that although his strength was a distinctive kind of dry, meditative soliloquy, he was immensely versatile and technically accomplished in a number of forms. In *A Part of Speech* (1980) he collaborated with a range of distinguished translators including Derek *Walcott, Richard *Wilbur, and David McDuff (1945–). The award of the *Nobel Prize in 1987 coincided with the first legal publication of his poetry in Russia. The following year saw the publication of *To Urania: Selected Poems 1965–1985*, which brings together translations of his earlier work with poems composed in English during his years of exile. In many of these poems he reflects on his exile, on memory and memories, and the passage of time. *Collected Poems in English* (2000) is the most extensive single volume of Brodsky's poetry in translation. He published two collections of essays in English, *Less than One* (1986) and *On Grief and Reason* (1995); these are made up of critical studies (Osip *Mandelshtam, W. H. *Auden, Thomas *Hardy, Rainer Maria *Rilke, Robert *Frost), autobiographical sketches, and portraits of a number of his contemporaries, including Anna Akhmatova, Nadezhda *Mandelshtam, Auden, and *Spender. His other prose writing includes *Watermark* (1992), an episodic account of his fascination with the character and history of Venice. He died in New York. See Liudmila Shtern, *Brodsky: A Personal Memoir* (2004).

Broken Heart, The A tragedy by John *Ford, written 1625/33, printed 1633. The scene is Sparta. Penthea, who was betrothed to Orgilus whom she loved, has been forced by her brother Ithocles to marry the jealous and contemptible Bassanes, who makes her life so miserable that she goes mad and dies. Ithocles falls in love with Calantha, the king's daughter, and she with him; the king sanctions their marriage. Orgilus, to avenge the fate of Penthea, entraps Ithocles and kills him. During a feast, Calantha hears, in close succession, of the deaths of Penthea, of her father, and of Ithocles. She dances on, apparently unmoved. When the feast is done, she sentences Orgilus to death, revealing that Ithocles' death has broken her heart just before she herself dies.

Spartan values of courage and self-control dominate the action. The stately language and emblematic imagery make this one of the greatest of Caroline tragedies. It has had successful modern revivals.

BROME, Alexander (1620–66) A Royalist poet and friend of Izaak *Walton and Charles *Cotton, both of whom addressed verses to him. He wrote many attacks on the Rump Parliament, including a ballad entitled *Bum-Fodder: or Waste-Paper Proper to Wipe the Nation's Rump with* (?1660). He also translated *Horace, wrote songs, and was the author of one comedy, *The Cunning Lovers* (1654).

BROME, Richard (*c.*1590–1652/3) Servant or perhaps secretary to Ben *Jonson, whose friendship he afterwards enjoyed and whose influence is clear in his works, as is that of Thomas *Dekker. *The *Northern Lass*, his first extant play, was printed in 1632. *The Sparagus Garden* (a place to which more or less reputable persons resorted to eat asparagus and otherwise amuse themselves), a comedy of manners, was acted in 1635. *The *City Wit* was printed in 1653. *A *Jovial Crew*, his best and latest play, was acted in 1641, often revived, and later turned into an operetta. Fifteen in all of his plays survive, including romantic dramas in the manner of John *Fletcher and Thomas *Middleton.

BRONTË, Anne (1820–49) Novelist and poet, sister of Charlotte and Emily *Brontë. She was educated largely at home, where, as the youngest of the motherless family, she may have fallen under the Wesleyan influence of her Aunt Branwell, who is thought to have encouraged her tendency to religious introspection. As a child she was particularly close to Emily; together they invented the imaginary world of Gondal, the setting of many of their poems. Anne accompanied Charlotte to Roe Head in 1836–7, and became governess to the Ingham family at Blake Hall in 1839; from 1840 to 1845 she was governess to the Robinson family at Thorp Green Hall, near York. Her brother Branwell joined her there as tutor in 1843, and became disastrously involved with Mrs Robinson. Anne's recollections of her experiences with the over-indulged young children and the worldly older children of these two households are vividly portrayed in **Agnes Grey* (1847). The novel appeared under the pseudonym Acton Bell, as did a selection of her poems, published with those of her sisters, in 1846. Her poems, which show the influence of William *Cowper and John *Wesley, explore religious doubt and confront Calvinist despair: among the most moving are 'To Cowper', 'My God (oh let me call thee mine)', and a Gondal lyric, 'Song: We know where deepest lies the snow'. Her second novel, *The *Tenant of Wildfell Hall* (1848), portrays in Arthur Huntingdon a violent, infantile, but sexually attractive drunkard clearly to some extent drawn from Branwell. Helen Huntingdon, Arthur's wife, takes her young son and establishes independence as a painter; in 1913 May *Sinclair remarked that 'the slamming of Helen Huntingdon's bedroom door against her husband reverberated throughout Victorian England'. Charlotte, in her 'Biographical Notice' (1850), felt obliged to comment that 'the choice of subject was an entire mistake', and insists that her sister's nature was 'naturally sensitive, reserved and dejected'. The novel may be read as a scathing indictment of sexual double standards enshrined in marriage law and the educational system. Anne died of tuberculosis at Scarborough, where she was buried. See *The Poems of Anne Brontë*, ed. E. Chitham (1979); E. Langland, *Anne Bronte* (1989); E. Chitham, *A Life of Anne Brontë* (1991).

BRONTË, Branwell (1817–48) Artist and writer, the brother of Charlotte, Emily, and Anne *Brontë. He was given a largely classical education at home by his father. As a boy, he was much involved with his sisters' literary efforts, and collaborated with Charlotte in creating the imaginary world of *Angria. His ambitions as a painter and writer were frustrated; he took to drink and opium, and after a brief spell as a tutor became assistant clerk to a railway company, but was dismissed in 1842 for culpable negligence. In 1843 he joined Anne at Thorp Green Hall as tutor, but became emotionally involved with his employer's wife, Mrs Robinson. The affair ended disastrously, and he returned to Haworth in 1845, where his rapid decline and death caused much suffering to his family. See *The Poems of Patrick Branwell Brontë*, ed. T. Winnifrith (1983).

BRONTË, Charlotte (1816–55) Novelist and poet, daughter of Patrick Brontë, an Irishman, perpetual curate of Haworth, Yorkshire, from 1820 until his death in 1861. Charlotte's mother died in 1821, leaving five daughters and a son to the care of their aunt, Elizabeth Branwell. Four of the daughters were sent to a Clergy Daughters' School at Cowan Bridge (which Charlotte portrayed as Lowood in **Jane Eyre*), an unfortunate step which Charlotte believed to have hastened the death in 1825 of her two elder sisters and to have permanently impaired her own health. The surviving children pursued their education at home; they read widely, and became involved in a rich fantasy life that owes much to their admiration of Lord *Byron, Walter *Scott, *The *Arabian Nights*, the *Tales of the Genii*, and the engravings of John *Martin. They began to write stories, to produce microscopic magazines in imitation of their favourite **Blackwood's Magazine*, and Charlotte and Branwell collaborated in the increasingly elaborate invention of the imaginary kingdom of *Angria, Emily and Anne in the invention of Gondal (for a discussion of the juvenilia, see F. E. Ratchford, *The Brontës' Web of Childhood*, 1941). In 1831–2 Charlotte was at Miss Wooler's school at Roe Head, returning as a teacher in 1835–8, where she met her two close friends, Ellen Nussey and Mary Taylor. In 1839 she was a governess with the Sidgwick family, near Skipton, and in 1841 with the White family at Rawdon. In 1842 she went with Emily to study languages at the Pensionnat Heger in Brussels; they were recalled at the end of the year by their aunt's death, and in 1843 Charlotte, whose thirst for wider experience was much greater than her sister's, returned alone for a further year. She fell deeply in love with M. Constantin Heger, who failed to respond to the letters she wrote to him after her return to Haworth; a project to establish her own school, with her sisters, also failed. In 1845 she 'discovered' (or so she alleged) the poems of Emily, and, convinced of their quality, projected a joint publication; a volume of verse entitled *Poems by Currer, Ellis, and Acton Bell* (the pseudonyms of Charlotte, Emily, and Anne) appeared in 1846, but did not sell and received little attention. By this time each had finished a novel; Charlotte's first, *The *Professor*, never found a publisher in her lifetime, but Emily's **Wuthering Heights* and Anne's **Agnes Grey* were accepted by Thomas Newby in 1847 and published in 1848. Undeterred by her own rejections, Charlotte immediately began **Jane Eyre* (in Manchester, where her father was undergoing an operation for cataract); it was published in 1847 by Smith, Elder and achieved immediate success, arousing much speculation about its authorship. To quell the suspicion (encouraged by the unscrupulous Newby) that the Bell pseudonyms concealed but one author, Charlotte and Anne visited Smith, Elder in July 1848 and made themselves known.

She was not able to enjoy her success and the many invitations now extended to her; Branwell, whose wildness and intemperance had caused the sisters much distress, died in September 1848, Emily in December of the same year, and Anne the following summer. Through this tragic period she persevered with the composition of **Shirley*, which appeared in 1849. The loneliness of her later years was alleviated by friendship with Elizabeth *Gaskell, whom she met in 1850 and who was to write her biography. In the same year she prepared and published a memorial edition of *Wuthering Heights* and *Agnes Grey*, with a preface to the former, a 'Biographical Notice of Ellis and Acton Bell', and a further selection of hitherto unpublished poems. **Villette*, founded on her memories of Brussels, appeared in 1853. Although her identity was by this time well known in the literary world, she continued to publish as Currer Bell. In 1854, after much persistence on his part and hesitation on hers, she married her father's curate, Arthur Bell Nicholls, but died a few months later of an illness probably associated with pregnancy. 'Emma', a fragment, was published in 1860 in the **Cornhill Magazine* with an introduction by W. M. *Thackeray, and many of her juvenile works have subsequently been published, adding to our knowledge of the intense creativity of her early years. In her lifetime, Charlotte was the most admired of the Brontë sisters, although she came in for some criticism (which deeply wounded her) on the grounds of alleged 'grossness' and emotionalism, considered particularly unbecoming in a clergyman's daughter. Matthew *Arnold wrote in a letter (1853) that her mind contained 'nothing but hunger, rebellion and rage', and Harriet *Martineau offended her by claiming that *Villette* dealt excessively with 'the need of being loved', and was passionately anti-Catholic. More widespread, however, was praise for her depth of feeling and her courageous realism, and her works continue to hold high popular and critical esteem. Biographies include Elizabeth Gaskell, *The Life of Charlotte Brontë* (1857), and W. Gérin, *Charlotte Brontë: The Evolution of Genius* (1967); see also Juliet Barker, *The Brontës* (1994); T. J. Wise and J. A. Symington (eds), *The Brontës: Their Lives, Friendships and Correspondence* (1932); *The Letters of Charlotte Brontë*, ed. M. Smith, 3 vols (1995–2004); M. Smith and C. Alexander, *The Oxford Companion to the Brontes* (2003).

BRONTË, Emily (1818–48) Novelist and poet, sister of Charlotte and Anne *Brontë. She briefly attended the school at Cowan Bridge with Charlotte in 1824–5, and was then educated largely at home, where she was particularly close to Anne, with whom she created the imaginary world of Gondal, the setting for many of her finest narrative and lyric poems. She was at Roe Head in 1835, but suffered from homesickness and returned after a few months to Haworth; she was even more intensely attached than her sisters to the moorland scenery her work evokes so vividly. She was for a time, probably in 1838, governess at Law Hill, near Halifax, and in 1842 spent nine months in Brussels with Charlotte, studying French, German, and music: her French 'Devoirs' from this period survive, as does M. Constantin Heger's praise of her abilities in music and logic. She returned on her aunt's death at the end of the year to Haworth, where she spent the rest of her life, and continued to pursue her studies of German and music. In 1845 Charlotte 'discovered' Emily's poems, and projected a joint publication, *Poems, by Currer, Ellis and Acton Bell*, which appeared in 1846. **Wuthering Heights* was written between October 1845 and June 1846, and published by T. C. Newby after some delay in December 1847. Unlike Charlotte's **Jane Eyre*, it met with more incomprehension than recognition, and it was only after Emily's death (of tuberculosis) that it became widely acknowledged as a masterpiece; in her posthumous 'Biographical Notice' (1850) Charlotte felt obliged to comment on the 'horror of great darkness' that seemed to her to brood over the work. Emily's response to her apparent lack of success, like so much in her character, remains enigmatic. Unlike Charlotte, she had no close friends, wrote few letters, and had few but strong loyalties; the veins of violence (exemplified in the story of her subduing the dog Keeper with her bare hands), of stoicism, and of mysticism in her personality have given rise to many legends but few certainties. She is now established as one of the most original poets of the century, remembered for her lyrics (e.g. 'The night is darkening round me'), for her passionate invocations from the world of Gondal ('Remembrance', 'The Prisoner'), and her apparently more personal visionary moments ('No coward soul is mine'). *Wuthering Heights*, which was at first regarded by many as excessively morbid and violent, was gradually reassessed, and by 1899 Mary Augusta *Ward was praising Emily's masterly fusion of romance and realism at the expense of Charlotte's didacticism.The 20th century produced a great deal of critical and biographical commentary. C. P. Sanger analysed her careful plotting in *The Structure of 'Wuthering Heights'* (1926), Frank *Kermode proposed a variety of readings in *The Classic* (1975), Terry *Eagleton proposed a Marxist reading in *Myths of Power* (1975), and J. Hillis Miller explored the complex narrative structure in *Fiction and Repetition* (1982). See E. Chitham, *A Life* (1987); Stevie Davies, *Emily Brontë: Heretic* (1994); Juliet Barker, *The Brontës* (1994); *The Belgian Essays*, ed. S. Lonoff (1996); *Poems*, ed. D. Roper and E. Chitham (1994).

BROOK, Peter (1925–) Theatre director, educated at Westminster School, Gresham School, Holt, and Magdalen College, Oxford. The most innovative director of post-war Britain and Europe, he has worked with the Royal Shakespeare Company and the *National Theatre, directing classics (memorably, *King Lear*, 1962, and *A Midsummer Night's Dream*, 1970) and modern plays, but is most celebrated internationally for his experimental work. Landmark productions include Peter *Weiss's *Marat/Sade* (1964), *The Ik* (1975, a multicultural drama of African famine based on an anthropological premiss), the **Mahābhārata* (1985; UK 1988), and *L'Homme qui* (1993), based on a work by Oliver *Sacks. Working with an international Paris-based company, the International Centre for Theatre Creation, travelling widely, and transcending conventional notions of text and theatrical space, he has been a powerful influence on 20th-century theatre, drawing inspiration from many sources. His travels to Iran in 1971 with Ted *Hughes resulted in Hughes's play in an invented language, *Orghast*. His *The Empty Space* (1968) is a highly influential work, and in 1998 he published a memoir, *Threads of Time*. In 2005, he directed *Tierno Bokar*, based on the life of an African mystic, adapted by Marie-Hélène Estienne from the West African writer Amadou Hampaté Bâ's *The Life and Teaching of Tierno Bokar: The Sage of Bandiagara* (1957; rev. 1980). *See also* CRUELTY, THEATRE OF. See Andrew Todd and Jean-Guy Lecat, *The Open Circle: Peter Brook's Theatre Environments* (2003).

BROOKE, Charlotte (1740–93) Irish translator, daughter of Henry *Brooke. Her dual language *Reliques of Irish Poetry* (1789) renders an annotated selection of Gaelic poems into polite English verse, providing the most remarkable Irish contribution to the vogue for literary antiquarianism associated with Thomas *Percy in England and Allan *Ramsay in Scotland, while prefiguring the 19th-century rapprochement between Gaelic and Anglo-Ireland.

BROOKE, Emma Frances (1844–1926) Radical novelist, journalist, and poet. Born in Macclesfield and educated at Newnham College, Cambridge, and the London School of Economics, she published *Millicent: A Poem* (1881) as 'E. Fairfax Byrrne', writing as Brooke after 1887. Her polemical *New Woman novels include *A Superfluous Woman* (1894), which deals with the plight of young women who unknowingly marry men with venereal disease, and *Life the Accuser* (1896), comparing the destinies of conventional and emancipated women. She contributed widely to periodicals and newspapers, was secretary to the Karl Marx Club, and joined the Fellowship of the New Life commune, before moving in the 1880s to a radical community in Kent. An early member of the Fabian Society, her socialist commitments informed her *Tabulation of the Factory Laws of European Countries* (1898). Critical and popular interest in her novels has recently revived; see A. Richardson and C. Willis (eds), *The New Woman in Fiction and in Fact* (2000).

BROOKE, Frances (1724–89) Novelist and dramatist, born in Claypole, Lincolnshire, largely educated by her mother. She conducted the periodical *The Old Maid* in 1755–6, then in 1760 published *Letters from Juliet Lady Catesby*, translated from Riccoboni. The pessimistic but highly successful epistolary novel *History of Lady Julia Mandeville* (1763) related the tragic story of the artless Harry and Lady Julia. Brooke lived with her clergyman husband in Quebec from 1763–7, hence the frozen Canadian setting of *The History of Emily Montague* (1769), which relates the love story of Emily with Edward Rivers. In 1777 came *The Excursion*, which exposes the superficial nature of 'good breeding'; Lord Melvile's education in correct behaviour is confusingly at odds with the generous impulses of his heart. The novel originally contained an attack on David *Garrick, motivated by his rejection of her tragedy *Virginia* (1756). *The Siege of Sinope* (1781) was more successful, as were two musical plays, *Rosina* (1783) and *Marian* (1788).

BROOKE, Henry (1703–83) Writer and playwright, educated in Dublin. He read law at the Temple in London, and returned in 1740 to Dublin, where he then chiefly lived. While in London he became a friend of Alexander *Pope and other literary men. In 1735 he published *Universal Beauty*, a poem which was thought to have greatly influenced Erasmus *Darwin's *The Botanic Garden*. Encouraged by David *Garrick, he wrote several plays, but his tragedy *Gustavus Vasa* (1739) was prohibited on the grounds that the villain resembled Sir Robert *Walpole. In 1765–70 he published his highly successful *The *Fool of Quality*, and in 1774 another novel, *Juliet Grenville*, both of which are notable for their looseness of structure and for a sustained tone of high sensibility. Brooke wrote much on Irish subjects, and advocated a relaxation of the anti-Catholic laws. He was the father of Charlotte *Brooke.

BROOKE, Jocelyn (1908–66) Novelist, educated at Bedales and Worcester College, Oxford, who spent some time as a regular soldier after serving during the war with the Royal Army Medical Corps, experience reflected in his semi-autobiographical trilogy *The Military Orchid* (1948), *A Mine of Serpents* (1949), and *The Goose Cathedral* (1950). Other works include two volumes of poems, *December Spring* (1946) and *The Elements of Death* (1952), and the novel *The Image of a Drawn Sword* (1950).

BROOKE, Rupert (1887–1915) Poet, born in Rugby and educated at Rugby School, where his father was a master, and then at King's College, Cambridge. *Poems* (1911) was followed by contributions to the first two volumes of **Georgian Poetry*, which he had helped to conceive. In 1913, having written a stark one-act play, *Lithuania* (1912), and a dissertation on John *Webster, he won a fellowship at King's, and suffered a serious breakdown, which led him in 1913 to travel in the USA, Canada, and the Pacific. In Tahiti, he had an affair with a local woman, and wrote 'Tiara Tahiti' and other poems, often thought to be among his best. In 1914 he was given a commission in the Royal Naval division and served as an officer on the Antwerp expedition. His five 'War Sonnets', including 'The Soldier', appeared in *New Numbers* in 1914 and then posthumously in *1914 and Other Poems* (1915). Brooke was dispatched to the Dardanelles, but he died of blood poisoning on the way and was buried on Skyros in April 1915. His war sonnets, 'The Soldier' especially, earned him a dazzling reputation which survived for many years. Other poems are also still read and studied, including the Tahiti poems, 'The Old Vicarage, Grantchester' (he had moved to Grantchester in 1909), 'The Great Lover', and 'I strayed about the deck'. A man of beauty and charm, Brooke had many friends, including Frances *Cornford, Henry *James, and Virginia *Woolf. James wrote the preface to Brooke's *Letters from America* (1916). *The Letters of Rupert Brooke* appeared in 1968, edited by Geoffrey Keynes, who also edited *The Poetical Works* (1946). *The Collected Poems*, with a memoir by his friend Edward *Marsh, had appeared in 1918. See Christopher Hassall, *Rupert Brooke* (1964).

BROOKE-ROSE, Christine (1926–) Novelist and critic, born in Geneva, brought up bilingually in Brussels, London, and Liverpool, and educated at Somerville College, Oxford, and University College London. She was professor of English language and literature at the University of Paris from 1975 to her retirement in 1988. Her first novel, *The Languages of Love* (1957), is a cosmopolitan Bloomsbury romance, much of it centred on the Reading Room of the *British Museum. She is best known for her experimental novels, marked by bilingual neologisms, which have some affinity with the **nouveau roman*; these include *Out* (1964), *Such* (1966), *Between* (1968), and *Thru* (1975). *Amalgamemnon* (1984), about a university teacher who is made redundant, was followed by *Xorandor* (1986), which concerns twins who make contact with a 4,000-year-old being through computer technology, *Verbivore* (1990), and *textermination* (1991). Her critical works include *A Rhetoric of the Unreal* (1981). *Remake* (1996), in which she refers to herself for much of the text as 'the old lady', gives a vivid, non-chronological account of her experiences as a young WAAF officer at Bletchley Park during the war, of her second marriage to a Polish poet, Janek (the novelist Jerzy Pieterkiewicz), and of her retirement in Provence. Her autobiography, *Life, End of*, appeared in 2006.

BROOKNER, Anita (1928–) Novelist and art historian, who was a reader at the Courtauld Institute of Art and the first woman to occupy the Slade chair of art at Cambridge (1967–8). She has published studies of the French painters Jean-Antoine *Watteau, Jean-Baptiste Greuze (1725–1805), and Jacques-Louis David (1748–1825). Her first work of fiction, *A Start in Life* (1981), tells the story of an authority on Honoré de *Balzac, whose life has been shaped by literature, and introduces a principal theme of her work: that of women whose lives, through circumstances or cultural conditioning, have become something to be endured rather than enjoyed. The finely delineated melancholy of Brookner's fictional world was leavened by wit in early novels such as *Providence* (1982), in which an academic working on the Romantic tradition becomes infatuated with a professor of medieval history. Her later novels chart the unlived lives of women of a certain age with rather less flamboyance. *Hotel du Lac* (1984), featuring a romantic novelist ironically named Edith Hope, won the *Booker Prize and was adapted for television by Christopher *Hampton in 1986. *Family and Friends* (1985), a compact family saga, drawing on Brookner's own background, marked a momentary change of direction, while *Lewis Percy* (1989) was the first of several novels featuring a male protagonist. For the most part, though, producing on average a novel every year, Brookner has confined herself to a distinctive type of heroine and a small but elegantly realized and instantly recognizable fictional milieu.

BROOKS, Cleanth (1906–94) American critic, born in Kentucky, and educated at Vanderbilt and Tulane universities, then at Oxford, before becoming a teacher at Louisiana State University and from 1947 at Yale. His college textbook

Understanding Poetry (with R. P. *Warren, 1938) helped to establish the methods of the *New Criticism in classrooms. His major works of poetic criticism, *Modern Poetry and the Tradition* (1939) and *The Well Wrought Urn* (1947), both regard irony and paradox as the typical virtues of poetry, in lucid developments from T. S. *Eliot's critical arguments. He collaborated with W. K. Wimsatt (1907–75) in *Literary Criticism: A Short History* (1957), and wrote two books on William *Faulkner. His later essays appeared in *The Hidden God* (1963) and *A Shaping Joy* (1971).

BROOKS, Gwendolyn (1917–2000) African American poet who was born in Kansas but spent most of her life in Chicago. She began publishing poems in her teens and taught creative writing at a number of universities including Columbia and Wisconsin. At a writers' conference in 1967 she announced her rediscovery of her blackness and the first major work to demonstrate this change was *In the Mecca* (1968), which uses free verse and reflects continuing influence from blues music. She published one novel, *Maud Martha*, in 1953. See George A. Kent, *A Life of Gwendolyn Brooks* (1990).

BROPHY, Brigid (1929–95) Writer and campaigner, born in London and educated at St Hugh's, Oxford; daughter of the author John Brophy (1899–1965), and married to the art historian Michael Levey. Her first novel, *Hackenfeller's Ape* (1953), concerned the attempt by a zoologist to prevent an ape being sent into space and marked an early interest in both animal rights and Mozart. These themes, along with those of the baroque, homosexuality, Freud, and 1890s aestheticism, would frequently recur in her work. Other novels include *Flesh* (1962), in which a young man transforms himself by a 'process of empathy' into 'a Rubens woman'; *The Finishing Touch* (1963), a pastiche of Ronald *Firbank set in a girls' school; *The Snow Ball* (1964), a comedy of manners influenced by the operas of Mozart and 'constructed as a baroque monumental tomb'; *In Transit* (1969), an experimental neo-Joycean 'trans-sexual comedy'; and the subversively satirical *Palace without Chairs* (1978). Among her works of non-fiction are *Black Ship to Hell* (1962), a Freudian investigation of the destructive impulse; *Mozart the Dramatist* (1964); two studies of Aubrey *Beardsley; and the magisterial *Prancing Novelist* (1973), 'a defence of fiction in the form of a critical biography in praise of Ronald Firbank'. She published three collections of her polemical essays and journalism, wrote an unconventional farce, *The Burglar* (1968), which failed in the West End, and an early volume of stories, which she subsequently disowned. Like her father, she was a leading campaigner for *Public Lending Right and to this end founded the Writers' Action Group with Maureen *Duffy.

BROUGHAM, Henry Peter, Baron Brougham and Vaux (1778–1868) Statesman, lawyer, and author. He was educated at Edinburgh High School and University, and rose to be lord chancellor. Brougham was a man of tremendous activity. His legal career was of great distinction, and included the defence of Queen Caroline in 1820, but he also took an important part in the founding of London University, and vigorously promoted the Mechanics' Institute and the Society for the Diffusion of Useful Knowledge. In literary history he is principally remembered as one of the founders, with Francis *Jeffrey and Sydney *Smith, of the **Edinburgh Review* in 1802. He also wrote *Observations on the Education of the People* (1825); *Historical Sketches of Statesmen in the Time of George III* (1839–43); *Demosthenes upon the Crown, Translated* (1840); and *The Life and Times of Lord Brougham*, published posthumously in 1871. He is said to have been the author of the disparaging article on **Hours of Idleness* in the *Edinburgh Review* of January 1808, an article which provoked Lord *Byron into writing **English Bards and Scotch Reviewers*. Of the many squibs written on Brougham's character and activities, the most famous is the lampoon in Thomas Love *Peacock's **Crotchet Castle*, where Brougham appears as the 'learned friend' who 'is for doing all the world's business as well as his own'. The brougham, a one-horse closed carriage, with two or four wheels, is named after him.

BROUGHTON, Rhoda (1840–1920) Novelist, born near Denbigh in north Wales, the daughter of a clergyman. She was largely taught at home by her father, and spent many years in Oxford with her widowed sister. Her many light, witty novels of country-house and town life, with their lively and articulate heroines, gained her a reputation for audacity of which a younger and more outspoken generation deprived her—to her own private amusement. 'I began by being the *Zola and I have now become the Charlotte *Yonge of English fiction,' she remarked towards the end of her life. She began her career with the three- and two-decker novels that were still popular (*Not Wisely, but Too Well*, 1867; *Cometh up as a Flower*, 1867; *Nancy*, 1873), but was possibly more at home with the form of her later short, sharp, observant one-volume novels, which include *Mrs Bligh* (1892), *Dear Faustina* (1897), *Lavinia* (1902, which boldly presents an anti-Boer War hero, fond of old lace), and *A Waif's Progress* (1905). Her early work is often forthright on the difficulties confronted by independently minded young women; despite the more conservative tone of her later fiction, she never lost her sense of the ridiculous, nor her compassion for women who find themselves helplessly hemmed in by social circumstances beyond their control.

BROWN, Charles Brockden (1771–1810) American novelist and editor, born in Philadelphia, who worked briefly as a lawyer before writing the four *Gothic novels for which he is remembered, *Wieland* (1798), *Arthur Mervyn* (1799), *Ormond* (1799), and *Edgar Huntly* (1799). Although obviously indebted to William *Godwin and Mary *Wollstonecraft, these were pioneer works which gave Gothic romance an American setting and combined fiction with historical fact. Brown's psychological interest in obsession, seduction, madness, and cruelty made him a precursor of Edgar Allan *Poe. He was admired in England, notably by Walter *Scott, John *Keats, and the *Shelleys. Brown's work fell into neglect until

Leslie *Fiedler reinstated him as formative figure in American literary history.

BROWN, Curtis *See* AGENTS, LITERARY.

BROWN, Eric (1960–) Born in Haworth, Yorkshire; novelist and short story writer. Many of his stories consider new art forms in the exotic universe loosely constructed in *Engineman* (1994). Virtual reality appears in near-future novels like *New York Nights* (2000) and its sequels.

BROWN, Fredric (1906–72) American author, born Cincinnati; prolific writer of humorous stories with a macabre twist for American magazines and paperbacks in the 1940s and 1950s. *The Fabulous Clipjoint* (1947) begins a detective sequence. *Martians Go Home* (1955) and *What Mad Universe* (1949) are *science fiction.

BROWN, George Douglas (1869–1902) Scottish novelist, born to unmarried parents in Ochiltree, Ayrshire, and educated at the University of Glasgow and Balliol College, Oxford, whose *The House with the Green Shutters* (1901) bitterly repudiated the *'Kailyard' idyll of Scottish village life. The novel allies a realist narrative style to a self-consciously tragic structure in its portrayal of John Gourlay, a tyrannical businessman whose power over the inhabitants of Barbie comes to a catastrophic end as a result of his inability to adapt to change. Brown published *Love and a Sword*, a boys' adventure novel, under the pseudonym Kennedy King in 1899.

BROWN, George Mackay (1921–96) Scottish poet, novelist, playwright, and short story writer, born and brought up in Stromness, Orkney, where he remained almost the whole of his life, only once visiting England. Educated at Newbattle Abbey College, under Edwin *Muir, and at the University of Edinburgh. Although versatile in the variety of its literary forms, all his work springs from a deep local source and is rooted in Norse saga, island folklore, the cycles of rural life, and a deep Christian faith (he converted to Roman Catholicism in 1961). His volumes of poetry include *Loaves and Fishes* (1959), *The Year of the Whale* (1969), and *Following a Lark* (1996). He also published several collections of short stories, including *A Calendar of Love* (1967) and *Winter Tales* (1995). His first novel, *Greenvoe* (1972), was set on an imaginary northern island, Hellya, which becomes the site for a military project called Operation Black Star. The story describes the resulting destruction of the village of Greenvoe against the unchanging and self-renewing backdrop of nature. This was followed by *Magnus* (1973) and in 1994 he published *Beside the Ocean of Time*, set on another fictitious Orcadian island, Norday, which evocatively describes the imaginings of Ragnarson, a crofter's son. Other works include *An Orkney Tapestry* (1969), a medley of prose and verse, and a posthumously published autobiography, *For the Islands I Sing* (1997).

BROWN, John (1800–59) American abolitionist, commemorated in the well-known marching song 'John Brown's Body' and in J. G. *Whittier's poem 'John Brown of Osawatomie'. He migrated in 1855 from Ohio to Kansas, where he became a leader of the anti-slavery movement. On the night of 16 October 1859, at the head of a small party of his followers, he seized the arsenal of Harper's Ferry, Virginia, intending to arm the slaves and start an uprising. He was quickly captured, tried by the Virginia authorities, and hanged at Charlestown. Set to an old Methodist hymn tune, 'John Brown's Body' became the most popular marching song of the Union forces.

BROWN, Dr John (1810–82) Scottish physician and essayist, born in Biggar, Lanarkshire, and educated at Edinburgh University, most of whose writings are contained in his three volumes of *Horae Subsecivae* (1858–82), including *Marjorie Fleming* and the memorable dog story *Rab and his Friends*.

BROWN, T. E. (Thomas Edward) (1830–97) Poet, born in the Isle of Man and educated there and at Oxford; ordained in 1855, he was second master at Clifton School 1864–93. He published *Betsy Lee: A Foc's'le Yarn* (1873), *Foc's'le Yarns* (1881), and other books of verse, most of it in the Manx dialect, and dealing with Manx life. Many of his non-dialect poems concerned West Country landscape; his narrative verses stirred some controversy with their swearing and unblushing accounts of prostitutes. His collected poems were issued in 1900 and reprinted in 1952 (2 vols) with a memoir by Arthur *Quiller-Couch, originally published in 1930.

BROWN, Thomas (1663–1704) Satirist, educated at Christ Church, Oxford, where he wrote 'I do not love you, Dr Fell' (*see* FELL, DR JOHN). He later settled in London as Tory pamphleteer, translator, and hack-writer. See B. Boyce, *Tom Brown of Facetious Memory* (1939).

BROWN, William Wells (1814–84) African American writer and abolitionist, born a slave in Kentucky. In 1834 he escaped north where he worked on Lake Erie steamboats and helped other fugitives reach Canada. He became an abolitionist lecturer, and moved to Boston, where he published *Narrative of William Wells Brown, a Fugitive Slave* (1847). Two years later he travelled to Britain and France and his account of his experiences, *Three Years in Europe* (1852), has been described as the first travel book written by an African American. Brown is also credited as the author of the first novel by an African American: *Clotel* (1853), which draws on the rumours that Thomas Jefferson was the father of some of his slaves; as well as the first play: *The Escape* (1858). His other works include *The Black Man: His Antecedents, his Genius, and his Achievements* (1863), and another volume of autobiography, *My Southern Home* (1880).

BROWNE, Charles Farrar *See* WARD, ARTEMUS.

BROWNE, Hablot Knight (1815–82) Under the pseudonym 'Phiz', he illustrated some of the works of Charles *Dickens, R. S. *Surtees, and F. E. *Smedley.

BROWNE, Sir Thomas (1605–82) Doctor and writer, born in London and educated at Winchester College, and Pembroke College, Oxford. He toured Ireland before studying medicine at Montpellier and Padua, and received a doctorate from Leiden. **Religio Medici*—first published without his consent in 1642—is one of the greatest works of English prose. Written in Browne's majestic, resonant style it strives to reconcile science and religion, and is reminiscent of *Montaigne's *Essays* (which, however, Browne said he had not read). An authorized edition was published in 1643. Its religious speculations displeased some and it was placed on the papal index of prohibited books in 1645. Browne settled in Norwich in about 1637 to practise medicine. In 1646 appeared his most learned and ambitious work, **Pseudodoxia Epidemica*, commonly known as *Vulgar Errors*, a compendium of esoteric learning, in which the spirit of Baconian enquiry battles, not always successfully, with superstition. In the 1650s he wrote for friends the shorter tracts **Hydriotaphia, Urn Burial*, a magnificent meditation on death arising from some Bronze Age burial urns dug up in Norfolk, *The *Garden of Cyrus*, in which the pattern of the quincunx is traced through the whole of nature from Roman fruit-tree plantations to the 'mystical mathematics of the kingdom of heaven', and *A Letter to a Friend* (published 1690), the latter overlapping in content with *Christian Morals*, a sententious piece said by his daughter Elizabeth to be a continuation of *Religio Medici*. *Certain Miscellany Tracts*, on a wide range of topics in human and natural history, were also published posthumously. Browne's admirers have included Thomas *De Quincey, S. T. *Coleridge, and Charles *Lamb, and, more recently, Herman *Melville (who was influenced by his style, and called him 'a cracked archangel'), W. G. *Sebald, and Jorge Luis *Borges. See *Pseudodoxia Epidemica*, ed. Robin Robbins (1981); Daniela Havenstein, *Democratizing Sir Thomas Browne* (1999); Claire Preston, *Sir Thomas Browne and the Writing of Early Modern Science* (2005). He is buried in St Peter Mancroft, Norwich, where a replica of his skull and other relics may be seen, on application.

BROWNE, William (?1590–1645) Poet, born in Tavistock, Devon, and educated at Exeter College, Oxford, and the Inner Temple. He published *Britannia's Pastorals* (Bks I and II, 1613, 1616), a narrative poem in couplets interspersed with lyrics; Book III, unfinished, remained in manuscript until 1852. He also contributed to *The Shepheard's Pipe* (1614) with George *Wither and others. Among various epitaphs he wrote the well-known lines on the dowager countess of *Pembroke, 'Underneath this sable hearse | Lies the subject of all verse'. His poetry has been praised for its sensuous richness and accurate observation of nature, and these qualities influenced John *Milton, who echoes him in *'L'Allegro' and **Lycidas*, and John *Keats. More recently Browne, with other Jacobean Spenserian poets, notably Wither and Christopher Brooke (*c.*1570–1638), have been viewed in the context of early Stuart political culture and seen as constituting a distinctive oppositional faction. See Michelle O'Callaghan, *The Shepheard's Nation* (2000).

BROWNING, Elizabeth Barrett (1806–61) Poet, born in County Durham, the eldest of twelve children of Edward Barrett Moulton Barrett, plantation owner, and his wife Mary. She spent her childhood at Hope End in Herefordshire, and was educated at home. Her early works were extensive, and *The Battle of Marathon* (1820) and *An Essay on Mind* (1826) were privately printed at her father's expense. Her individual voice began to develop during the 1830s in ballads including 'The Poet's Vow' and 'The Romaunt of the Page'. She learnt much from correspondence with Uvedale Price (1747–1829) and the blind scholar Hugh Stuart Boyd (1781–1848), both neighbours. She became versed in the classics and in prosodic theory, and later published translations from ancient and Byzantine Greek poetry. Her *Prometheus Bound, Translated from the Greek of Aeschylus, and Miscellaneous Poems* (1833)—as the production of a self-educated young woman—prompted critical praise. Mary Russell *Mitford, whom Elizabeth first met in 1836, became an encouraging friend. In 1832 the Barrett family moved to Sidmouth, and in 1835 to London; but by 1838, seriously ill, she was sent to Torquay where, two years later, her eldest brother Edward (known as 'Bro') was drowned, to her lifelong grief. The poems 'De Profundis' and 'Grief' record the pain of this period. She returned to London, still unwell, in 1841.

During the early 1840s, her health improved, and she continued to write. Following the royal commission for the investigation of child employment, 'The Cry of the Children' appeared in **Blackwood's* in 1843. The prolific creativity of 1841–4 culminated in *Poems* (1844), which confirmed her place as a significant poet. She was Alfred *Tennyson's rival for the laureateship of 1850. It was also this publication that prompted Robert *Browning to write to her for the first time in 1845. The two met in May that year and their courtship, from this time until their marriage in September 1846, is recorded in their collected correspondence. The marriage was necessarily secret since Elizabeth's strong-minded father forbade his adult children to marry (on his discovery of the union he disinherited her). The Brownings left England for Italy. Casa Guidi in Florence became their base, though they paid long visits to Rome, Siena, Bagni di Lucca, Paris, and London. Their only child, Robert Wiedemann (known as Penini, or Pen), was born in the Casa Guidi apartment in 1849. The **Sonnets from the Portuguese* (1850) bear eloquent witness to the conflicts and strength of her love for Browning, and were followed by *Casa Guidi Windows* (1851), on the theme of Italian liberation. Her principal work, **Aurora Leigh*, appeared in 1856.

Throughout her married life Elizabeth Barrett Browning's poetic reputation stood higher than Browning's in public opinion, though her progressive social ideas and audacious prosodic experiments were alarming for some. She was interested in Italian and French politics and an ardent partisan of Italian unity. She also became fascinated by spiritualism, though this—unlike her political views—played little part in her poetry. The highly political *Poems before Congress* (1860), which concluded with 'A Curse for a Nation', diminished her popularity; but *Last Poems*, issued posthumously in 1862, contained some of her best-known lyrics. The Brownings were friends with, among others, John *Ruskin, Thomas *Carlyle, Alfred Tennyson, W. M. *Thackeray, and D. G. *Rossetti, on all of whom Elizabeth's vivid intelligence made a lifelong impression. There are biographies by Dorothy Hewlett (1953), G. B. Taplin (1957), and Margaret *Forster (1988).

BROWNING, Robert (1812–89) Poet, the son of Robert Browning (d. 1866), a clerk in the Bank of England, and Sarah Anna Wiedemann (d. 1849), of German-Scottish descent. He was brought up with his only sister Sarianna in Camberwell in south-east London, receiving his education mainly in his father's large (6,000 vols) and eclectic library. The contrasting influences of his boyhood were those of his reading (particularly of P. B. *Shelley, Lord *Byron, and John *Keats) and an atmosphere of Nonconformist piety. He wrote a volume of lyric poems, *Incondita*, at the age of 12, but subsequently destroyed them: two survive. In 1828 he enrolled at the newly founded London University, but dropped out in his second term. His first published poem, *Pauline*, appeared anonymously in 1833 and attracted little notice. Browning travelled to Russia in 1834 and made his first trip to Italy in 1838. *Paracelsus* (1835) was a critical success, as a result of which Browning formed several important friendships, notably with John *Forster and William *Macready, who persuaded him to write for the stage; he also met Thomas *Carlyle, Charles *Dickens, and Alfred *Tennyson. In 1837 his play *Strafford* was produced at Covent Garden. The obscurity of his next published poem, *Sordello* (1840), led to a hostile reception which eclipsed his reputation for over twenty years. *Bells and Pomegranates* was completed by 1846. He began corresponding with Elizabeth Barrett (*see* BROWNING, E. B.) in January 1845 when, after returning from his second trip to Italy, he read and admired her 1844 *Poems*. He met her first in 1845; their relationship had to be kept a secret from her father, and they finally married and eloped to Italy in September 1846. They lived mainly in Italy (first in Pisa and then in Florence) until Elizabeth's death in 1861.They had one child, Robert Wiedemann Barrett Browning ('Pen', 1849–1913). In 1850 Browning published *Christmas-Eve and Easter-Day* and in 1855 the central work of his middle period, *Men and Women*, which, together with *Dramatis Personae* (1864), began to revive his reputation; the revival was completed by the success of *The *Ring and the Book* (1868–9), though Browning was never to achieve the commercial success of Tennyson. Meanwhile he had returned to England after the death of Elizabeth; from 1866, after his father died, he lived with his sister, generally spending the season in London, and the rest of the year in the country or abroad. He formed a wide circle of acquaintances in London society, and was awarded an honorary degree by Oxford University, and an honorary fellowship by Balliol College, Oxford, whose master Benjamin *Jowett was a close friend. The Browning Society was founded in 1881. Browning's publications after *The Ring and the Book* were: **Balaustion's Adventure* (1871), *Prince Hohenstiel-Schwangau* (1871), **Fifine at the Fair* (1872), **Red Cotton Night-Cap Country* (1873), **Aristophanes' Apology* (1875), *The *Inn Album* (1875), **Pacchiarotto... With Other Poems* (1876), *The *Agamemnon of Aeschylus* (1877), **La Saisiaz* and *The Two Poets of Croisic* (1878), **Dramatic Idyls* (1879), **Dramatic Idyls, Second Series* (1880), **Jocoseria* (1883), *Ferishtah's Fancies* (1884), **Parleying with Certain People of Importance in their Day* (1887), and **Asolando* (1889). Browning issued collections of his work in 1849, 1863, 1868, and 1888–9. Three complete scholarly editions are currently under way: the Longman, Ohio/Baylor, and Oxford editions. Browning's only prose works of importance are two essays on Thomas *Chatterton (1842) and Shelley (1852), the first in the form of a review (of a book on another subject) and the second as the introduction to a collection of letters of Shelley (which turned out to be forgeries). His correspondence with Elizabeth Barrett has been published, along with other separate volumes of letters; a collected edition is in progress. Browning died in Venice and is buried in Westminster Abbey.

BROWNJOHN, Alan (1931–) Poet, born in London and educated at Merton College, Oxford; taught in schools and other institutions 1953–79 before becoming a full-time writer. He was a member of Philip Hobsbaum's *Group, although he had then, and continues to have, affiliations with the *Movement poets. An early booklet of poems, *Travellers Alone* (1954), and his first volume, *The Railings* (1961), were followed by several other volumes. *The Observation Car* was published in 1990, *The Men around her Bed* in 2004, and a *Collected Poems* in 2006. Brownjohn's poetry is characteristically good-humoured, ironic, and urbane. In Peter *Porter's phrase, it unites 'wit and civic responsibility' in a survey of contemporary social, domestic, and literary life, reflecting both the attachments and the exacerbations of the contemporary liberal conscience. He has also written novels, children's books, and a study of Philip *Larkin.

BRUCE, Dorita Fairlie (1885–1970) Born Palos, Spain, educated at Clarence House, London. Bruce wrote popular girls' *school stories, notably nine 'Dimsie' books, from *The Senior Prefect* (1920; as *Dimsie Goes to School*, 1925) to *Dimsie Carries On* (1941). There is a study by E. M. Löfgren (1993).

BRUCE, James (1730–1794) Traveller and explorer. Born at Kinnaird, Stirlingshire, and educated at Harrow School, 'Abyssinian' Bruce was one of the most colourful characters in British exploration. His gargantuan, five-volume *Travels to Discover the Source of the Nile* (1790) recounts an epic journey into Abyssinia (modern-day Ethiopia), undertaken between 1768 and 1772 with an Italian draughtsman named Luigi Balugani (who died during the expedition). On Bruce's return to Britain in 1774, his lurid and often self-glorifying reports of Abyssinian life were met with disbelief and ridicule; it was also pointed out, by Samuel *Johnson among others, that the source of the Blue Nile had in fact been discovered already, by Jesuit missionaries in the 17th century. *Travels*, intended to rebut these charges, only renewed the controversy surrounding Bruce, but many of his claims and scientific findings were subsequently corroborated in a posthumous second edition, edited by Alexander Murray.

Bruce, The *See* BARBOUR, JOHN.

BRUEGEL, Pieter (*c.*1525/30–1569) Netherlandish genre, landscape, and religious painter, and a brilliant draughtsman. He first became known for his allegorical and satirical prints and his paintings crowded with little figures that look back to the demonic imagery of Hieronymus Bosch (*c.*1450–1516). Much of his imagery is drawn from proverb and folklore. In 1565 he painted his most famous works, great cosmic landscapes representing *The Months*, and in 1566–8 his celebrated scenes of rustic genre, *The Peasant Wedding Feast*. His latest works, such as *The Blind Leading the Blind*, are tragic indictments of the human condition. He has been the subject of considerable scholarly literature and virulent controversy, and his paintings have inspired writers, including William Carlos *Williams and, notably, W. H. *Auden, in his 'Musée des Beaux Arts', on the *Fall of Icarus*.

Brunanburh A poem in Old English (West Saxon dialect), included in four manuscripts of the **Anglo-Saxon Chronicles* under the year 937, dealing with the battle fought between the English (under Athelstan, the grandson of Alfred) and the Danes (under Olaf III Guthfrithson from Dublin, supported by Olaf's father-in-law, the Scots king Constantine II, and some Welsh). The site of the battle is currently unknown, but is thought to be somewhere on the west coast of England, between Chester and Dumfries. The poem is a triumphant celebration of the deeds of Athelstan and his brother and successor Edmund, in their defeat of the invaders. Alfred *Tennyson wrote a verse translation (*Ballads and Other Poems*, 1880). There is an edition by A. Campbell (1938).

BRUNNER, John (1934–1995) Born in Oxfordshire; British author of *science fiction, and thrillers such as *A Plague on Both your Causes* (1969). He was active in the early days of anti-nuclear protest, and his song 'The H-Bomb's Thunder' became the movement's theme. His political commitment influenced *dystopian novels such as *Stand on Zanzibar* (1968), on the pressures of overpopulation, and *The Sheep Look Up* (1972), where our world is destroyed by pollution. See Joseph De Bolt (ed.), *The Happening Worlds of John Brunner* (1975).

BRUNO, Giordano (1548–1600) Italian philosopher, born near Nola, who saw God as the unity reconciling spirit and matter. He was in early life a Dominican friar, but broke from his order and left Italy to avoid prosecution for heresy. He converted to Calvinism in Geneva, but was later excommunicated. He moved to France and then, in 1583, to England, where his scornful view of Oxford philosophy prompted him to embody his own views in a series of Italian dialogues, three on cosmology, including *La cena de le ceneri* (1584: *The Ash Wednesday Supper*) and three on moral topics, including *De gli heroici furori* (1585: *The Heroic Frenzies*). In 1585 he left for France and then Germany, where he was excommunicated by the Lutheran Church, and in 1591 returned to Italy in the mistaken belief that it would be safe to do so. He was accused of heresy, imprisoned for seven years, and finally burnt at the stake in Rome. He wrote a fine comedy, *Il candelaio* (1582: *The Candlemaker*). Some of his dialogues are dedicated to Philip *Sidney, under whose auspices he visited Oxford. His writings were much admired by James *Joyce, who mystified his friends by enigmatic references to 'the Nolan'. See Frances *Yates, *Giordano Bruno and the Hermetic Tradition* (1964).

Brut (Brutus) Legendary founder of the British race. *Geoffrey of Monmouth claims that Walter, archdeacon of Oxford, gave him an ancient book in the British language containing an account of the kings of Britain from Brutus to Cadwallader. Brutus was son of Sylvius, grandson of Ascanius, and great-grandson of Aeneas. Having killed his father, he brought a remnant of the Trojan race to England (uninhabited at the time 'except by a few giants'), landing at Totnes. He founded Troynovant or New Troy (later known as London) and was the progenitor of a line of British kings including Bladud, *Gorboduc, Ferrex and Porrex, *Lud, *Cymbeline, Coel, *Vortigern, and *Arthur. The name 'Troynovant' is a back-formation from 'Trinovantes', the name of the powerful British tribe that lived north and east of London. 'Brut' came to be used to mean 'chronicle of the Britons' in writings by Geoffrey of Monmouth's followers, such as the Norman poet *Wace, in his *Roman de Brut*, and the English *Laȝamon in the alliterative poem *Brut*. No doubt the phonetic echo (*cf.* Romulus/Rome) led to the adoption of this eponymous progenitor for the Britons.

Brut, The Prose The title given to a long English version, translated in the late 14th century, of the Anglo-Norman prose *Brut* which extends up to 1333. Over 180 copies are extant and this fluid narrative was extended several times to take account of events between 1377 and 1461. See the discussion in Lister M. Matheson, *The Prose* Brut: *The Development of a Middle English Chronicle* (1998).

BRUTUS, Dennis (1924–) Poet. He graduated from Fort Hare University, South Africa. In radical opposition to apartheid he became president of the South African Non-Racial Olympic Committee which resulted in the exclusion of South Africa from international sport and his own imprisonment on Robben Island. He now lives in the USA. His prison poems 'Letters to Martha' describe the self as its own labyrinth. His poetry records dogged resistance: *A Simple Lust* (1973), *Stubborn Hope* (1978), and most recently *Leafdrift* (2005).

BRUTUS, Marcus Junius (*c.*85–42 BC) Roman republican, leader of the conspiracy to assassinate Julius *Caesar, and enemy of Marcus Antonius; after defeat at the battle of Philippi he committed suicide. He is included in *Plutarch's lives, and is the principal character in *Shakespeare's **Julius Caesar*. In *Dante's *Inferno* he is a monster of ingratitude.

BRYAN, Sir Francis (d. 1550) Poet and courtier, nephew of Lord *Berners. A favourite of *Henry VIII's, he held various posts and took part in entertainments at court, and was sent on diplomatic missions. His reputation was for telling the king the truth; distancing himself from his cousin Anne Boleyn, he earned the nickname 'the vicar of hell' from Thomas Cromwell. Milton presumably refers to him in **Areopagitica* when he writes, 'I name not him for posterities sake, whom *Harry* the 8. nam'd in merriment his Vicar of hell.' Bryan, a friend of Thomas *Wyatt, who addressed his third satire to him, contributed to Richard *Tottel's *Miscellany* and his poetry was highly valued in his day, but is now, with the exception of a translation of Antonio de Guevara's *A Dispraise of the Life of a Courtier* (1548), almost entirely undiscoverable.

BRYANT, William Cullen (1794–1878) American poet and journalist, born in Massachusetts. He first practised law, but was for fifty years editor of the New York *Evening Post*. He began to make a name as a poet as early as 1817, when his Wordsworthian blank verse meditation 'Thanatopsis' was published in the **North American Review*, and confirmed his reputation with *Poems* (1821), which contains his well-known 'To a Waterfowl', 'The Yellow Violet', and 'Green River'. His subjects were taken from Nature, often informed by his Protestant beliefs.

BRYDGES, Sir Samuel Egerton (1762–1837) He devoted his life to antiquarian and literary work, considering himself to be a great writer, but he was successful only as a bibliographer. He published his valuable *Censura Literaria* (1805–9, 1815), *The British Bibliographer* (1810–14), and *Restituta, or Titles, Extracts, and Characters of Old Books in English Literature Revived* (1814–16). Of his novel *Arthur Fitz-Albini* (1798) Jane *Austen mildly observed, 'There is a very little story'. His enthusiasm for collecting and reprinting old books led him to establish a private press at Lee Priory, Kent.

BRYHER (1894–1983) The pseudonym of Winifred Ellerman, novelist, poet, and patron of the arts. The daughter of a wealthy shipping magnate, Bryher was born in Margate and educated privately and at Queenwood School, Eastbourne. She married twice, in 1921 and 1927, but by far her deepest relationship was with the poet Hilda *Doolittle (H.D.), whom she met in 1918 and to whom she remained devoted until H. D.'s death in 1961. Bryher published three autobiographical fictions, *Development* (1920), *Two Selves* (1923), and *West* (1925) at the beginning of her career and a further twelve books between 1948 and 1972.

BRYSON, Bill (1951–) American travel writer, born in Des Moines, Iowa, and educated at Drake University. He moved to England in 1977 and is best known for his humorous, ambling narratives and irreverent social commentary, starting with *The Lost Continent: Travels in Small Town America* (1989). *Neither Here Nor There* (1991) retraces a backpacking tour of Europe he made in his youth, and the hugely successful *Notes from a Small Island* (1995) recalls a valedictory trip around Britain before he returned to the United States. An Appalachian trek is the subject of *A Walk in the Woods* (1997) while *Notes from a Big Country* (1998) offers reflections on his homeland after twenty years abroad. Subsequent books include *Down Under* (2000), *Bill Bryson's African Diary* (2002), and a memoir, *The Life and Times of the Thunderbolt Kid* (2006). His books on the English language (*Mother Tongue*, 1990; *Made in America*, 1994) and science (*A Short History of Almost Everything*, 2004) have also proved popular.

BUCHAN John, Baron Tweedsmuir (1875–1940) Author and publisher. Born in Perth, Buchan was educated at Hutcheson's Grammar School, Glasgow, Glasgow University, and Brasenose College, Oxford. While still at Oxford he published a novel (*Sir Quixote of the Moors*, 1895) and a volume of essays (*Scholar Gipsies*, 1896). From the beginning he combined a literary career with a career in public life, culminating with the post of governor general of Canada, 1935–40. He wrote many non-fiction works, but is remembered for his adventure stories, the first of which was *Prester John* (1910), set in Africa, in which a young Scot becomes embroiled in a plot involving a legendary necklace of rubies, a villainous Portuguese, and a doomed African visionary with a mission to restore 'Africa to the Africans'. Many of his other tales feature a recurring group of heroes (Richard Hannay, Sandy Arbuthnot, Peter Pienaar, Edward Leithen, etc.). Favoured settings include Scotland, the Cotswolds, and South Africa, although his last novel, *Sick Heart River* (1941), prefiguring his own death, is set in the icy wastes of Canada. The novels are packed with action, often involving elaborate cross-country chases; the characterization is simple, the landscapes are lovingly evoked. The most popular include *The Thirty-Nine Steps* (1915; filmed by Alfred *Hitchcock, 1935), *Greenmantle* (1916), and *Mr Standfast* (1919). See Andrew Lownie, *John Buchan: The Presbyterian Cavalier* (1995).

BUCHANAN, George (1506–82) Poet, humanist scholar, and historian, born near Killearn in Stirlingshire; he studied at St Andrews and Paris, and became tutor to a natural son of James V. He satirized the Franciscans in several Latin poems, was condemned for heresy and imprisoned at St Andrews. Escaping to the Continent, he became a professor at Bordeaux, where he wrote four Latin plays (*Baptistes*, *Medea*, *Jephthes*, and *Alcestis*) and taught *Montaigne. In 1547 he went to teach in the University of Coimbra, but was confined by the Inquisition, put on trial for heresy, and sent to a monastery for instruction. During this period he produced a celebrated Latin version of the Psalms. Released in 1552, he went to Paris, later returning to Scotland and professing himself a Protestant. He became a bitter enemy of *Mary Queen of Scots after the murder of Darnley, writing his *Detectio Maria Scotorum Regina* in 1571. While continuing his deep involvement in public affairs, he was tutor to *James VI and I during 1570–8. In addition to writing Latin poems in a variety of metres, Buchanan produced *Sphaera*, an exposition of the Ptolemaic system against that of *Copernicus; an important political treatise, *De Iure Regni apud Scotos* (1579); and the *Rerum Scoticarum Historia* (1582), which was long regarded as a standard authority. In the 1570s, he produced two vernacular works: *Ane Admonition*, and the *Chamaeleon*, a satire against the courtier William Maitland of Lethington (1525/30–1573). See I. D. McFarlane, *Buchanan* (1981).

BUCHANAN, Robert Williams (1841–1901) Poet, essayist, novelist, and playwright, the son of a secularist tailor who owned several socialist journals in Glasgow. Buchanan came to London in 1860 and made a name for himself as a man of letters with many novels, poems, and plays. He is remembered now for his assaults on A. C. *Swinburne (whom he called unclean, morbid, and sensual, and satirized in a poem 'The Session of the Poets' in the **Spectator* 1866) and on the *Pre-Raphaelites, chiefly D. G. *Rossetti, whom he attacked in 'The Fleshly School of Poetry' in the *Contemporary Review* (1871) under the pseudonym 'Thomas Maitland'. The effect on Rossetti was serious. After Rossetti's death, Buchanan altered his argument in an essay in *A Look Round Literature* (1887), in which he declared that Rossetti 'uses amatory forms and carnal images to express ideas which are purely and remotely spiritual'.

BÜCHNER, Georg (1813–37) German dramatist, born near Darmstadt. He remained largely unknown in his own century, but has since received wide acclaim. *Dantons Tod* (*The Death of Danton*), set in 1794 at the height of the Terror, was the only drama to be published in his lifetime (1835). It expresses some of the radical ideas for which Büchner was forced to flee Germany after the distribution of his pamphlet (*Der hessische Landbote*, 1834) calling on the peasantry of Hesse to revolt. The play's questioning approach to revolutionary politics has had great influence. Stephen *Spender collaborated on a version for the Group Theatre in 1937, and a version by Howard *Brenton was performed at the National Theatre in 1982. *Woyzeck* (pub. 1879), whose eponymous hero, a mentally unstable soldier, murders his common-law wife out of jealousy, was left unfinished at his death from typhus in Zurich. All versions of the work, whose innovative style anticipates features of both *naturalism and *Expressionism, involve a high degree of editorial reconstruction and leave broad scope for conflicting interpretation. Frequently performed, it was also the basis of an opera by Alban Berg (*Wozzeck*, 1925).

BUCK, Pearl Sydenstricker (1892–1973) American novelist, playwright, and political commentator, who was educated and spent much of her early life in China, later attending Randolph-Macon Women's College and Cornell University. From her extensive output she is best known for her novel *The Good Earth* (1931), which describes the laborious rise to prosperity of a Chinese farmer. Buck championed the cause of cross-race adoptions and fervently opposed the Communist regime in China. She was awarded the Nobel Prize in 1938. Peter J. Conn's *Pearl S. Buck: A Cultural Biography* (1996) sheds much new light on her career, including her surveillance by the FBI.

BUCKERIDGE, Anthony (1912–2004) Educated at Seaford College and University College London, a London-born teacher who also wrote for magazines and radio, remembered for his many humorous *school stories about the well-intentioned schoolboy Jennings and his friend Darbishire. Beginning in 1948 with *Jennings Learns the Ropes*, a radio play for the BBC's *Children's Hour*; numerous episodes followed until 1962. *Jennings goes to School* (1950) was the first of twenty-two Jennings books, all based on Buckeridge's observations of his pupils.

BUCKHURST, Lord *See* SACKVILLE, THOMAS; SACKVILLE, CHARLES.

Buckingham, duke of In Shakespeare's **Richard III*; he acts as Richard's ally in murdering Lord Hastings and winning the throne, but defects to Richmond after his master fails to reward him. The line 'Off with his head! So much for Buckingham' occurs in Colley *Cibber's adaptation (1700), which was the stage version generally used until Henry *Irving's production in 1877.

BUCKINGHAM, George Villiers, second duke of (1628–87) A prominent figure in the reign of Charles II and an influential member of the cabal formed by his ministers Clifford, Arlington, Buckingham, Ashley (*see* SHAFTESBURY, FIRST EARL OF), and Lauderdale, and the Zimri of John *Dryden's **Absalom and Achitophel*. He was the author of verses, satires, and the burlesque *The *Rehearsal*, which was much performed in the 18th century with topical additions and substitutions. Famed for his debauchery and amorous adventures, as well as for the vicissitudes of his public life, he died miserably at Kirby Moorside; the death of 'this lord of useless thousands' in 'the worst inn's worst room' is described by Alexander *Pope in a famous passage in his *Epistle III* (**Epistles to Several Persons*). He also figures in Walter *Scott's **Peveril of the Peak*.

BUCKINGHAM, James Silk (1786–1855) Author, traveller, and social reformer. Buckingham was born near Falmouth, Cornwall, and spent his youth at sea. He founded the *Calcutta Journal* in 1818 and the **Athenaeum* in 1828. He served as MP for Sheffield 1832–7. He published many travel books on the Middle East, North America, and Europe, and, in 1855, two autobiographical volumes.

BUCKLE, Henry Thomas (1821–62) Historian. He received no formal training, but money inherited from his father allowed him to travel on the Continent. The first two volumes of his *History of Civilization in England* (1857, 1861) were to be part of a far larger work, which his death left incomplete. Buckle approached history as a science and attempted through it to understand the laws of nations. Charles *Darwin was among his admirers.

BUCKLEY, William F., Jr (1925–2008) American politician, novelist, and journalist. A conservative politician who supported Senator Joe McCarthy, Buckley founded the *National Review* in 1955. He had a running feud with Gore *Vidal in the late 1960s and 1970s, and in 1976 published his first Blackford Oakes espionage novel, the series being loosely based on James *Bond.

BUDÉ, Guillaume (1467–1540) French humanist. He did important work in Roman law and in numismatics, but was primarily celebrated for his contribution to Greek scholarship, notably the *Commentarii linguae graecae* (1529). He did much to encourage the revival of classical learning in France, was instrumental in the founding of what was to become the Collège de France, and, as royal librarian under Francis I, laid the basis for the future Bibliothèque Nationale.

BUFFON, Georges-Louis Leclerc, comte de (1707–88) French naturalist, curator of the Jardin du Roi and author of the monumental *Histoire naturelle* in 36 volumes (1749–88: *Natural History*), for which he enjoyed immense public esteem during his lifetime. Completed after Buffon's death in eight additional volumes (1788–1804) by E. de Lacépède, the *Histoire naturelle* aimed at a comprehensive view of living creatures in their environment and included (in *Théorie de la terre*, 1749 (*Theory of the Earth*), and *Époques de la nature*, 1778 (*Epochs of Nature*)) reconstructions of the geological periods of the earth. Buffon's method combines detailed observation with bold generalization and poetic vision: both his descriptions of animals and his hypothetical accounts of geological epochs are vividly rendered. He refused to enter into the controversy aroused by his conception of the earth's history, maintaining deistic views and the unity of all creation with man as its centre and crown. Buffon was a notable stylist. His ideals of order, harmony, and decorum are set out in his *Discours sur le style* (1753: *Discourse on Style*), originally his address on being received into the *Académie Française, later published as a supplement to the *Histoire naturelle*; it contains the celebrated dictum 'le style est l'homme même'.

BUJOLD, Lois McMaster (1949–) American *science fiction and *fantasy author, born Columbus, Ohio. In her 'Miles Vorkosigan' series, including the *Hugo award-winning *The Vor Game* (1990) and *Barrayar* (1991), she playfully combines generic modes from romantic comedy to dark psychological thriller.

BUKOWSKI, Charles (1920–94) American poet, novelist, and screenwriter. He was born in Germany but lived most of his life in Los Angeles. He started writing poetry in the 1950s and then produced a series of novels which included *Post Office* (1971) and *Women* (1978), all revolving around the semi-autobiographical persona of an uninhibited antisocial bachelor. Bukowski's writing, which tends to blur the boundary between poetry and prose, became popular in Europe before catching on in the USA. In his writing and his lifestyle he has been associated with the *Beat Generation. See Barry Miles, *Charles Bukowski* (2005).

BULGAKOV, Mikhail Afanasevich (1891–1940) Russian prose writer and dramatist, born in Kiev, the son of a professor of theology. He studied medicine and began his literary career by writing stories drawn from his experience as a doctor. After the revolution he worked in Moscow as a journalist and wrote satirical and humorous stories and plays. By the late 1920s his plays were banned from the repertoire and his prose could not be published. He wrote a letter to Stalin on 28 March 1930 asking permission to emigrate. Stalin replied with the offer of a post at the *Moscow Arts Theatre, and in 1932 intervened again by ordering a revival of Bulgakov's play *The Days of the Turbins*. Thereafter the relationship between the writer and the state became a central theme in Bulgakov's writing. His major works include stories: 'The Fatal Eggs' (1924), 'The Heart of a Dog' (1925); novels: *The White Guard* (1924, a sympathetic portrait of a White Russian family in Kiev after the Revolution), *A Theatrical Novel* (*Black Snow*) (1936–7); and plays: *The Days of the Turbins* (1925–6), an adaptation of *The White Guard, Flight* (1926–8), *A Cabal of Hypocrites* (a play about *Molière) (1930–6). His masterpiece, *The Master and Margarita* (1928–40; pub. 1966–7; trans. Michael Glenny, 1992), is a Faustian tale of the devil's appearance in contemporary Moscow and his relationship with a writer and his beloved, coupled with a narrative set in ancient Jerusalem in which Pilate condemns an innocent man to be crucified.

BULL, John (?1562–1628) English composer, court musician, and keyboard player. His compositions, some of which appeared with those of William *Byrd and Orlando *Gibbons in *Parthenia, or The Maydenhead* (1613), include the moody 'Doctor Bulls my Self' and the basic pattern of the tune 'God save the king'. Bull fled abroad in 1613 to escape prosecution for adultery and fornication, and never returned.

Bulletin, The (1880–) Weekly magazine founded in Sydney; important publishing venue for Australian and New Zealand writing, especially when the astute and forthright Alfred Stephens (1865–1933) was literary editor (1896–1906). The 'Red Page' (inside the pink front cover) under Stephens became a significant site of discussion of local writing: it was Stephens who declared *My Brilliant Career* (1901), by Miles Franklin (1879–1954) the first Australian novel. Among notable contributors in this period, particularly of their earliest writing, are Barbara Baynton (1857–1929), Victor Daley (1858–1905), Henry Lawson (1867–1922), Jack Lindsay (1900–90), Banjo Paterson (1864–1941), Brian Penton (1904–1951), Katharine Susannah Prichard (1883–1969), Kenneth *Slessor, and Kylie Tennant (1912–88). The magazine itself published books, major works including *On our Selection* (1899) by 'Steele Rudd' (1868–1935), the landmark novel *Such is Life* (1903) by Joseph Furphy (1843–1912), and *Jungfrau* (1936) by Dymphna Cusack (1902–81). Under the literary editorship of the poet Douglas Stewart (1913–85), who served from 1940 to 1961, work by notable authors, including Judith *Wright, Rosemary Dobson (1920–), Francis Webb (1925–73), and Hal Porter (1911–84), was published regularly.

BULLOUGH, Geoffrey (1901–82) Scholar and head of the department of English at King's College London (1946–68). His principal works were an edition of Fulke *Greville's poems and plays (1939) and his magisterial account and edition of the *Narrative and Dramatic Sources of Shakespeare* (8 vols, 1957–75).

BULMER, Kenneth (1921–2005) Born in London; active in the 1950s British *science fiction magazines, and later the author of pseudonymous historical and adventure novels as well as science fiction and *fantasy. He edited *New Writings in SF* from 1973 and was a Council member of the *Science Fiction Foundation.

BULWER-LYTTON, Edward George Earle Lytton, first Baron Lytton (1803–73) Novelist, playwright, poet, and editor, son of General Bulwer, who added his mother's surname to his own when he inherited Knebworth in 1843. Educated at Trinity Hall, Cambridge, he embarked on a career in politics as a keen Reform MP for St Ives in 1831; he was subsequently MP for Lincoln and in 1858–9 secretary for the colonies. He financed his extravagant life as a man of fashion by a versatile and prolific literary output, publishing either anonymously or under the name of Bulwer Lytton. His first success, **Pelham, or The Adventures of a Gentleman* (1828), was of the *fashionable school, a lively novel set in an aristocratic social and political world, bearing some resemblance to Disraeli's recent **Vivian Grey*; it brought him considerable acclaim and established his reputation as a wit and dandy. Walter *Scott found it 'easy and gentleman-like' but complained of 'a slang tone of morality which is immoral'. His *'Newgate' novels were more in the 'reforming' manner of William *Godwin, e.g. *Paul Clifford* (1830), about a philanthropic highwayman, and *Eugene Aram* (1832), about a repentant murderer. He also wrote novels of domestic life, such as *The Caxtons: A Family Picture* (1849); many popular *historical novels, including *The Last Days of Pompeii* (1834), in which the panoramic splendours show his admiration for John *Martin, *Rienzi, the Last of the Roman Tribunes* (1835), and *The Last of the Barons* (1843); tales of the occult, including *Zanoni* (1842) and *A Strange Story* (1862); and a *science fiction fantasy, *The *Coming Race* (1871)—an early example of its genre. Other novels include *Falkland* (1827), *The Disowned* and *Devereux* (1829), *Godolphin* (1833), *Ernest Maltravers* (1837), *Harold, the Last of the Saxons* (1848), *My Novel, or Varieties in English Life* (1853), *What Will He Do with It?* (1858), *Kenelm Chillingly* (1873), and *The Parisians* (1873, unfinished). He was also editor of the **New Monthly Magazine*, 1831–3, and the author of three plays, *The Lady of Lyons, or Love and Pride*, a romantic comedy first performed in 1838; *Richelieu, or the Conspiracy*, a historical play in blank verse performed in 1839; and **Money*, a comedy performed in 1840, all of which have been successfully revived. He published several volumes of verse, including his earliest *Byronic tale, *Ismael* (1820); *The New Timon* (1846), an anonymous satirical poem in which he attacked Alfred *Tennyson as 'School-Miss Alfred', thus aggravating previous criticisms and stinging Tennyson into a bitter response in verse, mocking Lytton as a rouged and padded fop; and an epic, *King Arthur* (1848–9). Bulwer-Lytton made many enemies in his turbulent career, which was not helped by his disastrous marriage and separation from his wife Rosina in 1836 (see below); he was the frequent butt of **Fraser's Magazine*, of John *Lockhart, and of W. M. *Thackeray. Nevertheless he had powerful friends and admirers, including Benjamin *Disraeli and Charles *Dickens. His vigorous works span many of the changes in 19th-century fiction and retain considerable literary interest. See L. G Mitchell, *Bulwer Lytton: The Rise and Fall of a Victorian Man of Letters* (2003).

BULWER LYTTON, Rosina, Lady (1802–82) Novelist, born in Ireland, the daughter of Francis and Anna Wheeler. Her mother was a radical feminist, her father an alcoholic: they separated when Rosina was 10 and she was brought up by relatives. Moving to London in her early twenties, she made friends with Letitia *Landon and Lady Caroline *Lamb, and in 1827 married Edward Bulwer, later *Bulwer-Lytton. Their stormy separation in 1836, after the birth of two children and his increasing unfaithfulness, permanently embittered her. Feeling acutely the powerlessness of a woman in her situation she turned to near-libellous publication, producing *Cheveley, or The Man of Honour* (1839), satirizing her husband's hypocrisy, followed by a string of equally spirited but less successful novels, as well as various public petitions and pamphlets. He retaliated by intimidating her publishers, withholding her allowance, denying her access to the children, and finally, in 1858, by having her forcibly committed to an asylum from which she was released only by public outcry. She published a memoir, *A Blighted Life*, in 1880. Her life was published in 1887 by Louisa Devey, incorporating material from *Letters of the Late Edward Bulwer, Lord Lytton, to his Wife*, ed. Louisa Devey (1884); see also *The Collected Letters of Rosina Bulwer Lytton*, ed. Marie Mulvey-Roberts and Steve Carpenter (2008).

Bumby, Mother A fortune-teller frequently alluded to by Elizabethan dramatists. John *Lyly wrote an Italianate, highly patterned comedy, *Mother Bombie* (1587–90, printed 1594), which is, says *Hazlitt, 'little else than a tissue of absurd mistakes, arising from the confusion of the different characters one with another, like another *Comedy of Errors*, and ends in their being (most of them), married…to the persons they particularly dislike'.

BUNIN, Ivan Alekseevich (1870–1953) Russian prose writer and poet. Born in Voronezh, central Russia, the son of impoverished gentry, he began his career as assistant editor of a provincial newspaper. Life in rural Russia is a prominent theme in his work. He began publishing poetry in the late 1880s and prose in the 1890s. In the early years of the 20th century he attained great popularity. Among his best works of the period are *The Village* (1910), *Sukhodol* (1912), and *The Gentleman from San Francisco* (1916). In these years he travelled widely in Europe, Asia, and Africa. Totally opposed to the October Revolution of 1917, he left Russia in 1918, eventually settling permanently in France. *The Accursed Days* (1935) is a diary of the post-revolutionary period, *The Life of Arsenev* (1930–9), an autobiographical novel based on the experiences of his youth. In 1933 Bunin became the first Russian to win the *Nobel Prize for Literature. His final volume of stories, *Dark Avenues*, appeared in 1943. Bunin is recognized as the finest writer of the first generation of Russian émigrés. He was a consistent opponent of *modernism, but remained aloof from other literary schools. He is the Russian translator of Lord *Byron's **Cain*, **Manfred*, and **Heaven and Earth*, Henry Wadsworth *Longfellow's *The Song of *Hiawatha*, and Alfred *Tennyson's *Lady Godiva*. There have been a number of translations of Bunin's work into English since the first, *The Gentleman from San Francisco and Other Stories*, translated by D. H. *Lawrence, S. S. Koteliansky, and Leonard *Woolf (1922).

BUNTING, Basil (1900–85) Poet, born in Scotswood-on-Tyne, near Newcastle, and educated at Quaker schools (Ackworth and Leighton Park). Having worked in Paris as a sub-editor on the *Transatlantic Review* 1923–4, in the 1930s he followed Ezra *Pound to Italy, where he met W. B. *Yeats and the American poet Louis *Zukofsky. From 1947 to 1952 he worked in Persia, where he married Sima Alladadian, a Kurdo-Armenian. He returned in 1952 to Newcastle to work on a local paper. Although he had been published abroad (*Redimiculum Matellarum*, Milan, 1930; *Poems*, Texas, 1950; *The Spoils*, 1951, *Poetry Chicago*) and had a considerable reputation among younger American poets as an important figure in the *modernist movement, he was virtually unknown in his own country until the appearance of his long, semi-autobiographical, and deeply Northumbrian poem *Briggflatts* (1966), which firmly established his presence. The poem was named after the Quaker hamlet of Briggflatts, now in Cumbria. His reappearance as a poet was largely due to the friendship and intervention of poet Tom *Pickard, who met him in 1964 and for whom he read *Briggflatts* in 1965 at the Newcastle poets' meeting place, Mordern Tower. His *Collected Poems* (1978) includes translations ('Overdrafts') from Latin and Persian. *The Complete Poems*, edited by Richard Caddel, was published in 1994.

BUNYAN, John (1628–88) Preacher and writer of religious works, born at Elstow, near Bedford, the son of a brazier. He learned to read and write at the village school and was early set to his father's trade. He was drafted into the Parliamentary army and was stationed at Newport Pagnell, 1644–6, an experience perhaps reflected in *The Holy War*. In 1649 he married his first wife, who introduced him to two religious works, Dent's *Plain Man's Pathway to Heaven* and Bayly's *Practice of Piety*; these, the *Bible, the Prayer Book, and John *Foxe's **Acts and Monuments* were his principal reading matter. In 1653 he joined a Nonconformist church in Bedford, preached there, and came into conflict with the Quakers (*see* FRIENDS, SOCIETY OF), against whom he published his first writings, *Some Gospel Truths Opened* (1656) and *A Vindication* (1657). He married his second wife Elizabeth *c.*1659, his first having died *c.*1656 leaving four children. As an itinerant tinker who presented his Puritan mission as apostolic and placed the poor and simple above the mighty and learned, Bunyan was viewed by the Restoration authorities as a militant subversive. Arrested in November 1660 for preaching without a licence, he was derided at his trial as 'a pestilent fellow', to which his wife riposted, 'Because he is a tinker, and a poor man, therefore he is despised and cannot have justice.' Bunyan spent most of the next twelve years in Bedford Jail. During the first half of this period he wrote nine books, including his spiritual autobiography, **Grace Abounding to the Chief of Sinners* (1666). In 1665 appeared *The Holy City, or The New Jerusalem*, inspired by a passage in the Book of Revelation. In 1672 he published *A Confession of my Faith, and a Reason of my Practice*. After his release in 1672 he was appointed pastor at the same church, but was imprisoned again for a short period in 1677 during which he probably finished the first part of *The *Pilgrim's Progress*, which had partly been written during the latter years of the first imprisonment. The first part was published in 1678, and the second, together with the whole work, in 1684. His other principal works are *The Life and Death of Mr *Badman* (1680) and *The Holy War* (1682). Bunyan preached in many places, his down-to-earth, humorous, and impassioned style drawing crowds of hundreds, but was not further molested. There are editions of his more important works by Roger Sharrock, who also wrote *John Bunyan* (1954), a biography. See also Christopher *Hill, *A Turbulent, Seditious and Factious People: John Bunyan and his Church* (1988).

BURBAGE, James (*c.*1531–1597) Actor, pioneer of the English stage, father of Richard *Burbage. Apprenticed as a joiner, he was leader of the Earl of Leicester's Players by 1572. He leased land in Shoreditch (1576), on which he erected The Theatre, England's first major building specially intended for plays. The fabric was removed in December 1598 to the Bankside and set up as the *Globe Theatre. In 1596 he converted the *Blackfriars with the aim of providing an indoor home for the Lord Chamberlain's Men but they were not able to occupy it until 1608.

BURBAGE, Richard (?1567–1619) Actor, son of James *Burbage, from whom he inherited a share in the *Blackfriars

Theatre and an interest in the *Globe Theatre. He acted as a boy at The Theatre in Shoreditch and rose to be an actor of chief parts, 1595–1618, in plays by William *Shakespeare, Ben *Jonson, and Francis *Beaumont and John *Fletcher. He excelled in tragedy. Burbage lived in Halliwell Street, Shoreditch, 1603–19. He is known also as a painter in oil colours and is known to have collaborated with Shakespeare on an 'impresa', a tilting shield for the earl of Rutland, in 1613.

BURCKHARDT, Jacob (1818–97) Swiss historian born in Basle. He is principally known for his great work *Die Kultur der Renaissance in Italien* (1860; trans. as *The Civilization of the Renaissance in Italy*, 1945), a discussion of the arts, politics, philosophy, culture, and society of the period which celebrates the concept of the many-sided *Renaissance man and propounds the view that it was at this time that man, previously conscious of himself 'only as a member of a race, people, party, family or corporation', became aware of himself as 'a spiritual *individual*'. Though often criticized subsequently, this concept of the Italian Renaissance has been highly influential for English understanding of Renaissance culture.

BURCKHARDT, Johann Ludwig (1784–1817) Traveller and scholar. He was born in Lausanne, educated in Leipzig and came to England in 1806. Engaged by Joseph *Banks to travel to Timbuktu and the Niger for the African Association, he studied Arabic at Cambridge and then Aleppo where he passed as an Arab. He met Lady Hester *Stanhope and was the first modern European to see Petra. Later, he travelled up the Nile and through Nubia before making a pilgrimage to Mecca of which he provided an earlier and better account than Richard *Burton. He died in Cairo before he could join a caravan for the Niger. Subsequently, the African Association published three major accounts of his travels and two other works on the Arabs. Burckhardt's influence fostered scholarly oriental studies while his love of the English and the Arabs helped to create the alleged bond between the two peoples built on 'gentlemanliness'.

BURDEKIN, Katherine (1896–1963) Novelist, born in Derbyshire. *Swastika Night* (1937), published under the pseudonym Murray Constantine, describes a future dominated by a victorious Nazi regime where the deification of Hitler and the brutal subjugation of women is slowly questioned when a young Englishman is given a book that reveals some of the truth. The influence on George *Orwell is clear. Other novels include *The Burning Ring* (1927) and the posthumously published *The End of This Day's Business* (1990).

burden The refrain or chorus of a song, a set of words recurring at the end of each verse, or the dominant theme of a song or poem.

BÜRGER, Gottfried August *See* 'LENORE'; WILD HUNTSMAN.

BURGESS, Anthony (John Anthony Burgess Wilson) (1917–93) Novelist, born in Manchester, of a Catholic family, and educated at the University of Manchester. His early career included years (1954–60) as an education officer in the colonial service in Malaya and Borneo, during which period he wrote his first three novels, *Time for a Tiger* (1956), *The Enemy in the Blanket* (1958), and *Beds in the East* (1959), published together as *The Malayan Trilogy* in 1972. *A Clockwork Orange* (1962), his dystopian vision of 'ultra violence', high technology, and authoritarianism, appeared in a film version by Stanley Kubrick in 1971. Numerous other works include a Rabelaisian sequence, brimming with pastiche, social satire, and linguistic panache, about a gross, fitfully inspired poet (*Inside Mr Enderby*, 1963, under the pseudonym 'Joseph Kell'; *Enderby Outside*, 1968; *The Clockwork Testament*, 1974; and *Enderby's Dark Lady*, 1984). *Earthly Powers* (1980), a long, ambitious novel narrated by an octogenarian writer, combines real and fictitious characters to produce a panorama of the 20th century. Among many other novels exhibiting Burgess's characteristic mix of the earthy and abstruse, bodily gusto, and relish for the recondite are *The Kingdom of the Wicked* (1985), about early Christianity, and *Any Old Iron* (1989), a debunking of myths about military glory and racial purity. He published novels about *Shakespeare (*Nothing Like the Sun*, 1964) and Christopher *Marlowe (*A Dead Man in Deptford*, 1993); two volumes of 'Confessions', *Little Wilson and Big God* (1987) and *You've Had your Time* (1990); biographies of Shakespeare (1970), Ernest *Hemingway (1978), and D. H. *Lawrence (1985); an abundance of critical works (notably on James *Joyce), translations, books on language, screenplays, television scripts, and a torrent of reviews (see *Urgent Copy*, 1968, and *Homage to* QWERTYUIOP, 1987). An accomplished composer (his original ambitions were musical), he also wrote symphonies, sonatas, concertos, a Shakespearian ballet suite, and a musical based on Joyce's **Ulysses*. Posthumously published, his last novel, *Byrne* (1995), deploys the **ottava rima* form of *Byron's *Don Juan* to recount the life of a philandering and pugnacious artist from a Lancashire Catholic working-class background strongly resembling Burgess's own.

BURGESS, Melvin (1954–) Born in Twickenham, Middlesex. He left school after A-levels. Controversial writer for children and young adults known for tackling topical issues, from animal rights to plastic surgery; best known for *Junk* (1996), about teenage runaways who become addicted to heroin and engage in stealing and prostitution, and two books about adolescent sexuality that became notorious, *Lady: My Life as a Bitch* (2001) and *Doing It* (2003, screened on US television as *Life as We Know It*, 2004–5). Burgess also writes film scripts and has retold the Icelandic *Volsund* saga in *Bloodtide* (1999) and *Bloodsong* (2005).

BURGHLEY, William Cecil, Lord (1520/21–98) Lord treasurer under *Elizabeth I, and her chief minister. Educated at St John's College, Cambridge, he was secretary to Lord Protector Somerset, secretary of state, 1550–3, and employed in negotiations by Queen Mary. He is introduced in Richard *Sheridan's *The *Critic* (1779), where, in Puff's tragedy, he comes on stage and shakes his head, being too much occupied with cares of state to talk, whence the expression, 'Burghley's nod'. See S. Alford, *Burghley* (2008).

BURGON, John William (1813–88) Clergyman and poet, appointed dean of Chichester in 1876. He published sermons and theological works and the poem 'Petra' (1845), containing the well-known line 'A rose-red city—"half as old as time"'.

'Burial of Sir John Moore, The' *See* WOLFE, CHARLES.

BURKE, Edmund (1729–97) Son of an Irish Protestant attorney and a Catholic mother, educated at Trinity College, Dublin. He came to London in 1750, and entered the Middle Temple. He made many lasting friendships with literary and artistic figures, including Samuel *Johnson (of whose *Club he was a founding member), Oliver *Goldsmith, Joshua *Reynolds, David *Garrick, and the *Blue Stockings; he championed emerging writers such as Fanny *Burney and George *Crabbe. In 1756 he published *A Vindication of a Natural Society*, in answer to the deism of *Bolingbroke, and in 1757 *A Philosophical Enquiry into…the *Sublime and Beautiful*. In 1759 he started the **Annual Register*, to which he contributed until 1788. In 1765 he was elected MP for Wendover. He published his *Thoughts on the Cause of the Present Discontents*, partly in relation to the *Wilkes crisis, in 1770. In 1773 he visited France, where he saw Marie Antoinette, a vision that inspired some passages of **Reflections on the Revolution in France* (1790). In 1774 he became MP for Bristol, making speeches *On American Taxation* (1774) and *On Conciliation with America* (1775); he was moved to the Malton seat in 1781. Burke's attacks on the conduct of the American war contributed to North's resignation in 1783. He was active in the investigation of the East India Company, delivering speeches on the East India Bill (1783) and *On the Nabob of Arcot's Private Debts* (1785), and he opened the case for the impeachment of Warren Hastings (1788). He supported William *Wilberforce in advocating abolition of the slave trade. The French Revolution prompted his *Reflections* and *An Appeal from the New to the Old Whigs* (1791), a defence against the charge of political inconsistency. *Two Letters on a Regicide Peace* (1796) appeared after his retirement in 1794; his *Letter to a Noble Lord* (1796) defends the pension he received. Burke's political life was devoted to several causes: the emancipation of the House of Commons from the control of George III and the 'King's friends'; the emancipation of the American colonies; the emancipation of Irish Catholics; the emancipation of India from the East India Company; and opposition to the Jacobinism of the French Revolution. For this last he was attacked by radicals, such as Thomas *Paine and William *Godwin, who considered he had betrayed his faith in political liberty. Goldsmith had described him in 1774 in a mock epitaph as one who 'born for the universe, narrowed his mind, | And to party gave up what was meant for mankind' (**Retaliation*). But *Wordsworth in *The *Prelude* saluted him as one who 'declares the vital power of social ties | Endeared by custom'. His prose was enormously admired by William *Hazlitt. Matthew *Arnold declared that 'almost alone in England, he brings thought to bear upon politics, he saturates politics with thought' (1864). See *The Writings and Speeches of Edmund Burke*, ed. P. Langford, 9 vols (1981–96); *The Correspondence of Edmund Burke*, general ed. R. P. Mcdowell, 10 vols (1958–78); F. P. Lock, *Edmund Burke*, 2 vols (1999–2006).

BURKE, Gregory (1968–) Playwright born in Dunfermline, Scotland, who shot to prominence with *Gagarin Way* (2001), a wildly comic play about the rise and fall of the Soviet Empire, named after a road in west Fife dedicated to the memory of the first Russian astronaut. His *Black Watch*, a very individual take on the history of the famous regiment, culminating in its deployment in Iraq, was the hit of the 2006 Edinburgh Festival.

BURKE, Kenneth (1897–1986) American literary theorist. He was born in Pittsburgh, and studied at Ohio State University and at Columbia University. He lived among artists in Greenwich Village, and acted as compositor for the first American printing of T. S. *Eliot's *The *Waste Land*. He worked as a music critic for New York magazines, and as a market gardener. His early writings include a novel, a book of short stories, a literary essay, *Counter-Statement* (1931), and a theoretical work on systems of interpretation, *Permanence and Change* (1935). *The Philosophy of Literary Form* (1941) collects his critical essays of the 1930s. His mature work on rhetoric and the psychology of human 'motives' embodied in language appears in *A Grammar of Motives* (1945), *A Rhetoric of Motives* (1950), and the essays collected in *Language as Symbolic Action* (1966). Written while Burke taught part-time at Bennington College, Vermont, these are complex investigations into the workings of metaphor and other 'master-tropes', and propose a scheme of analysis by which formal features of texts can be understood in larger political and psychological terms. Although sometimes grouped with the *New Critics, he worked to a much broader agenda that included constructive engagements with *psychoanalytic and *Marxist criticism.

burlesque [from the Italian *burla*, ridicule, mockery] A literary composition or dramatic representation which aims at exciting laughter by the comical treatment of a serious subject or the caricature of the spirit of a serious work. Notable examples include Samuel Butler's **Hudibras* and James Joyce's **Ulysses*.

BURNAND, Sir Francis Cowley (1836–1917) A regular contributor to **Punch* from 1863; his series 'Happy Thoughts' (1866) was very popular. He was editor of *Punch*, 1880–1906. He wrote many *burlesques and adaptations of French *farces, and his operetta *Cox and Box*, with music by

Arthur *Sullivan, adapted from J. M. Morton's **Box and Cox*, was performed in 1867.

BURNE-JONES, Sir Edward Coley (1833–98) Painter and designer, born in Birmingham, and educated at Oxford. There he came under the influence of William *Morris and the two young men abandoned prospective careers in the Church. In 1856 he met D. G. *Rossetti, under whom he studied painting. At first he was impressed by the medieval worlds of *Malory and of K. H. *Digby's *The Broad Stone of Honour* (1822), and by the Italian Primitive painters; later his painting took its inspiration from early Renaissance work, especially *Botticelli. In the 1870s his work was a strong influence on the *Aesthetic movement. Such pictures as the *Chant d'Amour* and *Laus Veneris* (inspired by his friend A. C. *Swinburne's famous poem) divided critical opinion when they were exhibited at the *Grosvenor Gallery in 1877; some deplored their 'unhealthy' sexual ambiguity. He was profoundly hostile to the materialism and mechanism of the 19th century. His best-known works (e.g. *The Golden Stairs* and *King Cophetua and the Beggar Maid*, 1884) are often set in dreamlike worlds far removed from the present, and many (e.g. *Pygmalion and the Image* and *The Briar Rose*) have literary subjects. He designed tapestry and stained glass for Morris and Co., and illustrations for the Kelmscott Press. Towards the end of the century he became a pillar of the artistic establishment and was offered a baronetcy in 1894.

Burnell the Ass Hero of the *Speculum Stultorum* by Nigel *Wireker. Burnell, who represents the monk who is dissatisfied with his lot, is an ass who wants a longer tail. He goes to Salerno and Paris to study, and finally loses his tail altogether. In the course of his travels he hears the tale that Chaucer alludes to in 'The Nun's Priest's Tale' (*CT* VII. 3312–16; *see* CANTERBURY TALES, 20): the priest's son Gandulf breaks a cock's leg by throwing a stone at it. Later, on the morning when he is to be ordained, the cock fails to crow in time to rouse him and he loses his benefice.

BURNET, Gilbert (1643–1715) A popular preacher, educated at Marischal College, Aberdeen, influenced by the *Cambridge Platonists, and a Whig. He refused four bishoprics before he was 29, and in 1674 was dismissed from the post of king's chaplain for his outspoken criticisms of Charles II. He went to the Continent, and in 1686 to The Hague, where he became an adviser of William of Orange. He became bishop of Salisbury in 1689. His account of the deathbed repentance of *Rochester, *Some Passages in the Life and Death of the Right Honourable John Wilmot Earl of Rochester*, appeared in 1680 and his *History of the Reformation in England* in three volumes, 1679, 1681, 1715. His best-known work, *The History of my Own Times*, is a mixture of history, autobiography, and anecdote, and was published posthumously (2 vols, 1724, 1734). Other works include *Memoirs of the... Dukes of Hamilton* (1677) and *Life of Sir Matthew Hale* (1682). The standard biography is by T. E. S. Clarke and H. C. Foxcroft (1907).

BURNET, Thomas (?1635–1715) Royal chaplain to William III and master of Charterhouse. He was the author of *The Sacred Theory of the Earth* (1681), English translation by Burnet himself from the Latin original, 2 vols, (1684–90). It argues that the earth is hollow, containing huge deposits of water, equivalent to nine oceans. These caused Noah's flood, which was a natural occurrence, and which left the surface of the globe, previously smooth and round, defaced by mountains and other geological features, resulting from the collapse of the earth's crust into subterranean cavities. It was probably the most widely read geological work in Europe in the 17th century and was translated into many languages. Burnet's *Archaeologiae Philosophicae* (1692) argued for an allegorical interpretation of the Creation account and fall of man in *Genesis, and caused consternation in ecclesiastical circles. See Stephen Jay Gould, *Ever since Darwin* (1977).

BURNETT, Frances Hodgson (1849–1924) Born in Manchester, a consummate writer of romances with fairy-tale roots. She moved to the USA, where she produced hack-work to support her family until becoming internationally successful with *That Lass o' Lowrie's* (1877) and *Little Lord Fauntleroy* (1886), in which a small, pure-hearted American boy overcomes the prejudices of his embittered noble English uncle. This book set a fashion for boys to be dressed in velvet suits with lace collars and long hair, endured by Compton *MacKenzie and A. A. *Milne, among others. Some indication of the book's popular appeal is that it has been filmed four times, in 1914, 1921, 1936, and 1980. Other lasting successes were *A Little Princess* (1905), developed from the novella *Sara Crewe* (1887), filmed in 1917, 1939, and 1995, and *The Secret Garden* (1911), adapted by the BBC in 1975. There is a memoir of her childhood (*The One I Knew Best of All*, 1893) and a life by Ann Thwaite (*Waiting for the Party*, 1974).

BURNEY, Dr Charles (1726–1814) Music historian, and father of Fanny *Burney. He worked for Thomas *Arne and was later the friend of David *Garrick, Joshua *Reynolds, Samuel *Johnson, and Joseph *Haydn. He toured France, Italy, the Low Countries and Germany, publishing accounts of his travels in 1771 and 1773 and a four-volume *History of Music*, based on this European research, in 1776–89. Virginia *Woolf describes his salon in 'Dr Burney's Evening Party' in *The Second Common Reader*.

BURNEY, Fanny (Frances, Mme d'Arblay) (1752–1840) Novelist, daughter of Charles *Burney, educated at home. She grew up in the midst of a London society which included Samuel *Johnson, Edmund *Burke, Sir Joshua *Reynolds, the *Thrales, the *Blue Stockings, and many members of the aristocracy. In 1778 she published **Evelina*, and the revelation of its authorship brought her immediate fame. She wrote, but suppressed, a satirical play, *The Witlings*; of her many other dramas, only one (the tragedy *Edwy and Elgiva*) was performed in her lifetime. She published **Cecilia* in 1782, and in 1786 was appointed second keeper of the robes to Queen Charlotte, an office she gladly relinquished on health grounds in 1791. In 1793 she married Alexandre-Jean-Baptiste d'Arblay, a French officer in exile from the French Revolution. In 1796 she published *Camilla. She and her husband were trapped in France by the Napoleonic Wars and lived near Paris from 1802 to 1812. In September 1811 she survived a mastectomy; her description of this trauma was used by Penelope *Fitzgerald in *The Blue Flower.* Her first three novels, which influenced Jane *Austen, depicted the entry into the social world of a young girl of beauty and understanding but no experience; the novels exposed their heroines to circumstances and events that developed and rewarded their character. Burney's last novel, *The *Wanderer* (1814), which reflected many darker kinds of 'female difficulties', was eagerly anticipated but not a success. In 1832 she edited the *Memoirs* of her father. Burney was herself a prodigious writer of lively letters and journals. Her *Diary and Letters...1778–1840*, including a vivid account of her life at court, was published in 1842–6, eliciting an appreciative essay by Thomas *Macaulay; her *Early Diary 1768–1778*, which includes attractive sketches of Johnson, David *Garrick, and many others, was published in 1889, with a modern edition by L. E. Troide appearing in 1988–94. An edition of her letters and journals (12 vols, 1972–84) appeared under the general editorship of J. Hemlow, who also wrote a life, *The History of Fanny Burney* (1958); see also C. Harman, *Fanny Burney: A Biography* (2000).

'Burning Babe, The' *See* SOUTHWELL, ST ROBERT.

BURNS, Robert (1759–96) Scottish poet, one of seven children born to a cotter near Alloway in Ayrshire. His father moved his family from one unprofitable farm to another, but was determined that his sons should be well educated. Though his formal schooling was intermittent, Robert received a good grounding in classic English authors from Shakespeare onwards, along with a reading knowledge of French and at least an elementary grasp of Latin and mathematics. He read voraciously, and began to write verses while still in his teens. Most of his time was taken up on the ailing farm as labourer and ploughman. His experience of poverty and injustice fuelled his egalitarian beliefs, and led to his involvement with the progressive New Light wing of the Church of Scotland and his enthusiasm for the French Revolution. After his father's death in 1784 he and his brother Gilbert continued to farm, now at Mossgiel in the parish of Mauchline, which is often mentioned in the poems he was beginning to write in some quantity. 'The *Cotter's Saturday Night', 'To a *Mouse', 'The Twa Dogs', *'Holy Willie's Prayer', the Epistles to Lapraik, 'The *Holy Fair', and many other of his best-known poems belong to this period. He was much influenced by Henry *Mackenzie's novel *The *Man of Feeling*, a book he loved 'next to the Bible'. In 1785 he met Jean Armour, who was eventually to become his wife, but continued his long series of entanglements with women, many of whom are mentioned in his poems (for instance, Mary Campbell in 'To Mary in Heaven'), and with some of whom he fathered children.

In this and the following year he wrote prolifically, but his problems, both financial and personal, became so acute that he made plans to emigrate to Jamaica. When *Poems, Chiefly in the Scottish Dialect* was printed by John Wilson in Kilmarnock in 1786, however, Burns became an overnight celebrity and set off instead for Edinburgh. He found himself fêted by the literary and polite society of the capital as, in Mackenzie's words, 'a Heaven-taught ploughman'. His attractive appearance and gregarious temperament led him into a life of dissipation and amorous complexity. In 1787 he met Mrs Agnes Maclehose, with whom he corresponded at length in high-flown terms, addressing her as 'Clarinda', signing himself 'Sylvander'. He was encouraged to write in the neoclassical and sentimental fashion of the day, and his poetry underwent a dramatic dip in quality that was not reversed until the composition of his masterpiece 'Tam o' Shanter' in 1790. Burns had, however, begun to transfer his creative energies from poetry to song writing (a 'home fiddler', he always mastered the tune before composing the words), and from 1786 until his death he collected, amended, and otherwise created more than 200 songs remarkable alike for their subtlety and their variety of tone and feeling. Many of his best-known lyrics, such as 'A red, red rose', 'Ae fond kiss', *'Auld Lang Syne', 'It was a' for our richtfu' king', and *'Scots wha hae', were songs contributed gratis out of a sense of patriotic obligation to James Johnson's **Scots Musical Museum* and George Thomson's *Select Collection of Original Scottish Airs*, multi-volume projects which would not fully see the light of day until long after the poet's death.

In 1788 Burns finally married Jean Armour, and settled on a poor farm at Ellisland, near Dumfries. A year later he secured a post as an excise officer, and in 1791 relinquished his farming life with relief and moved to Dumfries. Farming had always been a source of strain and anxiety to him, so it is doubtful that he ever, in the words of William *Wordsworth (whom he greatly influenced), 'walked in glory and in joy | Following his plough along the mountainside'. There is evidence that he experienced considerable difficulty in reconciling his political inclinations with his duties as a government employee, however, and his song for the Dumfries Volunteers, with whom he enlisted in 1795, has been interpreted variously as a repudiation of his earlier revolutionary ardour and as a radical's desperate dive for cover in the increasingly oppressive climate of the 1790s. In 1791 Burns published his last major poem, 'Tam o' Shanter'. He died of rheumatic heart disease in July 1796. 'Oh wert thou in the cauld blast', an exquisite song of protective male love, is said to have been written on his deathbed to Jessie Lewars, a local girl who assisted the family during Burns's illness.

Burns is a key figure where both the growth of British Romanticism and the development of the Scottish poetic tradition are concerned. Drawing on folk song and on the achievement of earlier *Scots-language poets, notably though not exclusively Allan *Ramsay and Robert *Fergusson, his work marries a stubborn local piety to the democratic values of the later Enlightenment. He was much admired by his contemporaries and immediate successors, not only in Scotland and England but also in Ireland, Europe, and America: Charles *Lamb spoke for many of his generation when he declared that in his youth 'Burns was the god of my idolatry'. The fierce political alertness of Burns's satires and songs is belied by the sentimentality of the Burns cult, and by the annual celebration of 'the Bard's' birthday in a tide of alcohol on 'Burns Night', 25 January. Burns's *Poems and Songs* (with music) were edited in three volumes by James Kinsley (1968); see also *The Letters of Robert Burns*, ed. J. Delancey Fergusson and G. Ross Roy (1985).

BURNSIDE, John (1955–) Scottish poet and novelist, born in Dunfermline, and educated at the Cambridge College of Art and Technology. Such early collections of poetry as *The Hoop* (1988) and *Feast Days* (1992) fuse autobiography with an interest in landscape, and communicate a sense of the ambiguous blessings of embodiment. A preoccupation with identity, memory, and the supernatural informs *The Myth of the Twin* (1994), in which the 'anima' is represented as inhabiting a parallel dimension to the self. Later volumes from *Light Trap* (2001) to *Gift Songs* (2007) are increasingly philosophical in manner. Darker and more violent than his poetry, Burnside's fiction includes six novels, from *The Dumb House* (1997) to *The Glister* (2008), along with a collection of short stories, *Burning Elvis* (2000). *A Lie about my Father*, a sometimes harrowing memoir, appeared in 2006.

BURRAGE, A. M. *See* GHOST STORIES.

BURROUGHS, Edgar Rice (1875–1950) Born in Chicago; creator of adventure stories about John Clayton, Lord Greystoke, known as 'Tarzan', reared by great apes in the African jungle after his parents' death. *Tarzan of the Apes* was published in *All-Story* magazine (1912) and issued as a novel in 1914. The character rapidly entered popular mythology as the hero of many sequels, films, radio programmes, and comic strips, and is one of the iconic figures of 20th-century literature. Other series include the John Carter adventures beginning with *A Princess of Mars* (1917), also first published in *All-Story*. Drawing upon Henry Rider *Haggard's lost-race romances, Burroughs invigorated popular *science fiction and *sword and sorcery.

BURROUGHS, John (1837–1921) American naturalist and essayist. Like Henry *Thoreau, his characteristic medium was the nature essay and Walt *Whitman encouraged him to get these into print. Apart from essay collections, Burroughs published *Whitman: A Study* (1896) and *John James Audubon* (1902), a biography.

BURROUGHS, William S. (Seward) (1914–97) American novelist, probably more famous for his life than his literature. His first novel, *Junkie* (1953), gave a semi-autobiographical account of his time as a drug addict. *The Naked Lunch* (1959) made him a *cause célèbre* through its graphic descriptions of sexual sadism, heroin abuse, and darkly satirical imaginings of a totalitarian state. Subsequent novels pursued these themes, with books like *The Soft Machine* (1961), *The Wild Boys* (1971), and *Cities of the Red Night* (1981) focusing on the nature of power and the dynamics of control. His belief that 'Language is a virus' led him, in collaboration with Brion Gysin, to employ the 'cut-up' technique—a process whereby words or sentences would be taken from any source and reassembled in a way that would *defamiliarize them. A similar philosophy underpinned his approach to painting, in 'shot-gun art', in which a can of paint would be placed in front of a canvas, and exploded by being shot at. The random and anarchic were seen as modes of opposition to a predetermined universe. Although a homosexual, he married twice and accidentally shot his second wife Joan during the staging of a William Tell act. His enthusiasm for firearms was unaffected by this event, and his unrepentant drug identity gave him an iconic status that would be used in such films as *Drugstore Cowboy* (1991) and by rock bands such as Nirvana and REM. Burroughs constantly experimented with different kinds of textual construction and frequently used 'routines' (a term taken from stand-up comedians) in his works, i.e. short, usually grotesque episodes.
See BEAT AND BEAT GENERATION.

BURTON, Sir Richard Francis (1821–90) Prolific travel writer (and sometimes primary explorer), ethnographer, co-founder of the racist Anthropological Society, formidable linguist, speaking 40 languages or dialects, and translator; but he was also a 'perpetual outsider'. Born in Torquay, Devon, he was expelled from Oxford, and joined the Indian army. Two books on Sind testify to his understanding of non-European cultures and—a constant interest—different sexual mores. He left India and sensationally made the *hajj* to Mecca in disguise. Then came several expeditions to Africa, most importantly that with John *Speke which discovered Lake Tanganyika in 1858 but led to controversies over the Nile source and bitter personal hostilities. Other travels followed and a series of unsatisfactory consular appointments to Fernando Po, Brazil, Damascus, and Trieste, where he died. In addition to more than 40 volumes of travel, he produced books and articles on folklore, poetry, and translations from Arabic, Latin, and Portuguese. Burton is best remembered for his unexpurgated versions of the **Arabian Nights* (1885–8), *The Kama Sutra* (1883), *The Perfumed Garden* (1886, from the French), and other works of Arabian erotology. His interest in sexual behaviour and deviance (shared with his friends Richard *Milnes and *Swinburne) and his frank ethnographical notes led him to risk prosecution for obscenity, and his more erotic works were published secretly or privately. On his death, his wife Isabel destroyed his papers and diaries, including his translation from the original Arabic of *The Perfumed Garden*, on which he had been working for fourteen years.

BURTON, Robert (1577–1640) Educated at Nuneaton and Sutton Coldfield schools and Brasenose College and

Christ Church, Oxford; rector of Segrave, Leicestershire. He was the author of *The *Anatomy of Melancholy.*

BURY, Richard de (1287–1345) Patron of learning and book-collector; named from his birthplace, Bury St Edmunds. He was tutor to Edward III when the latter was prince of Wales and became bishop of Durham. Possibly with the Dominican Robert *Holcot, he wrote *Philobiblon* in the form of an episcopal letter chastising different groups for their neglect of learning. A text and English translation by E. C. Thomas were edited by Michael MacLagan (1970).

Bush Theatre Founded in 1972 by Brian McDermott above a small public house in Shepherds Bush in west London. It rapidly became famous for its passionate commitment to new writing, and the skill with which actors, writers, and directors were matched, from Richard Wilson directing Alan Rickman in Dusty Hughes's *Commitments* (1980) to Conor *McPherson directing his own play *St Nicholas* with actor Brian Cox (1996). Many plays, including Liverpool-born playwright Jonathan Harvey's *Beautiful Thing* (1993), transferred to larger theatres, but the Bush's intimacy, with the audience perched on an L-shaped bank of seating, makes it a challenge in its own right, and it continues to serve as an important venue for new plays.

Busie Body, The Comedy by Susannah *Centlivre, produced 1709. Sir George Airy and Miranda love one another, but her guardian, Sir Francis Gripe, intends to marry her himself. Airy and Miranda are eventually united, and Gripe's son Charles wins Isabinda, whom her father, Sir Jealous Traffic, intends to marry off to a Spanish merchant. The devices through which this end is accomplished are constantly interrupted by the well-meant but misdirected energies of Marplot, the 'busybody'.

Busirane In Edmund *Spenser's **Faerie Queene* (III. xi and xii) the 'vile Enchaunter' symbolizing unlawful love. He is struck down by *Britomart in his castle and forced to release *Amoret. On the door of one of the castle's rooms was written: *'Be bold, be bold,* and every where *Be bold'*; but on another iron door, *'Be not too bold.'*

BUSSY, Dorothy (1865–1960) Née Strachey, novelist, daughter of Richard and Jane Strachey and sister of the writer Lytton *Strachey and James Strachey (1887–1967), Sigmund *Freud's first English translator. Her only novel, *Olivia* (1949), draws on her experience as pupil and teacher at the Marie Souvestre school for girls. A friend of André *Gide, she translated all his work into English.

Bussy D'Ambois A tragedy by George *Chapman, written for a boys' company, 1600–04, and later played by adults, published 1607. It was adapted by Thomas *D'Urfey in 1693, and directed by Jonathan Miller at the Old Vic, London, in 1988. Chapman's most famous play, it was very popular in its day, and was revived at the Restoration, when *Dryden attacked it in terms that nevertheless suggest its dramatic power: 'when I had taken up what I supposed a fallen star, I found I had been cozened with a jelly; nothing but a cold, dull mass, which glittered no longer than was shooting; a dwarfish thought, dressed up in gigantic words…' (1681).

Bussy D'Ambois (in real life, Louis de Bussy-d'Ambois), insolent and courageous, is raised from poverty and introduced to the court of Henri III of France by the king's brother Monsieur, his protector. He quarrels with the king's courtiers, killing three, and even with the duc de Guise. He embarks on an affair with Tamyra, wife of Montsurry (Montsoreau). Monsieur, who also desires Tamyra, betrays Bussy to Montsurry, who forces Tamyra to lure Bussy into a trap. Overpowered, he dies defiantly on his feet. ('Here like a Roman statue I will stand | Till death hath made me marble.') Chapman's sequel is *The *Revenge of Bussy D'Ambois.*

The story is also told by *Dumas *père* in *La Dame de Monsoreau* (1846).

BUTLER, Joseph (1692–1752) Moral philosopher, born in Wantage, Oxfordshire. Brought up as a Presbyterian, he was educated at a Dissenting academy and, after conforming to the Church of England, at Oriel College, Oxford. A youthful correspondence with Samuel *Clarke on natural theology was published in 1716. He was ordained in 1718, and in 1719 appointed preacher to the Rolls Chapel. Queen Caroline made him her clerk of the closet in 1736, and in 1738 he was appointed bishop of Bristol, from which he was translated to Durham in 1750. His reputation stemmed from *Fifteen Sermons* (1726), first preached at the Rolls Chapel, in which he defines his moral philosophy, affirming an intuitional theory of virtue against the arguments of Thomas *Hobbes and Bernard de *Mandeville. While recognizing benevolence and a due degree of self-love as elements in virtuous conduct, he regards conscience as governing and limiting them by considerations, not of happiness or misery, but of right and wrong. In 1736 appeared his *Analogy of Religion*, an enormously influential defence of Christianity against *Deism, in which Butler argues that belief in immortality, revelation, and miracles is as reasonable as the beliefs upon which natural religion is founded. He had a strong impact in very different ways on David *Hume, J. H. *Newman, Matthew *Arnold, and W. E. *Gladstone, who edited his *Works*. See Christopher Cunliffe (ed.), *Joseph Butler's Moral and Religious Thought* (1992).

BUTLER, Octavia (1947–2006) African American author born Pasadena, California, whose novels, such as the 'Xenogenesis' series (1987–89), frequently use concepts like genetic manipulation to explore race and gender issues. *Parable of the Talents* (1999) won a Nebula award as best *science fiction novel. Her short fiction collected in *Bloodchild and Other Stories* (1996) was also well received. Her most popular novel remains *Kindred* (1979) in which an African American woman time-travels back to the days of slavery.

BUTLER, Samuel ('Hudibras') (1613–80) Poet, born at Strensham, a hamlet south of Worcester, the son of a farmer, and educated at the King's School, Worcester. He is said to have served as a clerk to a local justice of the peace and later to have become secretary to the countess of Kent. By 1661 he was steward at Ludlow Castle to Richard Vaughan, earl of Carbery (1600?–86). The most significant event in an otherwise obscure life was the publication in 1663 of his **Hudibras*, which instantly became the most popular poem of its time. It was probably as a result of its success that he became secretary to the second duke of *Buckingham. In 1677 he was awarded an annual pension of £100 by Charles II, but by then he himself appears to have given currency to the complaint that, though a loyal satirist, he had been left to endure his old age in poverty. He wrote a number of shorter satirical poems, including 'The Elephant in the Moon', an attack on the *Royal Society, and a great many prose 'Characters'. See *Hudibras*, ed. John Wilders (1967); *Characters*, ed. C. W. Daves (1970); *Prose Observations*, ed. Hugh de Quehen (1980); *Hudibras Parts I and II and Selected Other Writings*, ed. Wilders and de Quehen (1973).

BUTLER, Samuel (1835–1902) The son of a clergyman and grandson of a bishop, educated at Shrewsbury School and St John's College, Cambridge. Religious doubts prevented his ordination and in 1859 he went to New Zealand, where he achieved success as a sheep-farmer. *A First Year in Canterbury Settlement* (1863), compiled by his father from Samuel's letters, was published in 1863 in a New Zealand journal and became the core of **Erewhon*. He returned to England in 1864 and settled in Clifford's Inn, where he began to study painting (at which he worked for ten years) and exhibited occasionally at the Royal Academy. In 1872 he published *Erewhon*, anonymously, which enjoyed a brilliant but brief success. In 1873 appeared *The Fair Haven*, an elaborate and ironic attack on the Resurrection, which brought him encouragement from Charles *Darwin and Leslie *Stephen. A journey to Canada in 1874–5 inspired his well-known poem 'A Psalm of Montreal' first printed in the **Spectator* in May 1878. Between 1877 and 1890 Butler produced a series of works of scientific controversy, many of them directed against certain aspects of Darwinism, in particular Darwin's theory of natural selection: they include *Evolution, Old and New* (1879), *Unconscious Memory* (1880), and three articles on 'The Deadlock in Darwinism' (*Universal Review*, 1890). Butler's espousal of the cause of *Lamarck and creative evolution won him the praise of George Bernard *Shaw in his preface to *Back to Methuselah* (1921); Shaw also praised Butler's outspoken views on religion and the 'importance of money' in his preface to **Major Barbara* (1907). In 1881 Butler published *Alps and Sanctuaries of Piedmont and the Canton Ticino*, the first of several works on art and travel. He experimented with musical composition, including a comic pastoral oratorio, *Narcissus* (1888), written in collaboration with his great friend Festing Jones. In 1896 appeared his *The Life and Letters of Dr Samuel Butler*, his revered grandfather, who had been headmaster, bishop, and geographer. A long interest in *Homer led to his theory of the feminine authorship of the *Odyssey* and its origin at Trapani in Sicily. *The Authoress of the 'Odyssey'* appeared in 1897, and translations of the **Iliad* and the **Odyssey* into vigorous colloquial prose in 1898 and 1900. A quirky study, *Shakespeare's Sonnets Reconsidered*, appeared in 1899, and **Erewhon Revisited* in 1901. Butler's most revealing work, on which he had been labouring for many years, was his semi-autobiographical novel *The *Way of All Flesh*, published posthumously in 1903. He left six large Notebooks, full of incident, self-revelation, and ideas; selections of these were published by Festing Jones in 1912. See Peter Raby, *Samuel Butler: A Biography* (1991).

BUTOR, Michel (1926–) French writer. Butor's novels of the 1950s, including *L'Emploi du temps* (1956; *Passing Time*, trans. Jean Stewart, 1960) and *La Modification* (1957; *Second Thoughts*, trans. Jean Stewart, 1958), aligned him with the **nouveau roman*, thanks to their interrogation of traditional narrative modes: *La Modification* is narrated entirely in the second person. *L'Emploi du temps* is also notable for its evocation of Manchester. Later work experiments constantly with representational techniques, *Mobile* (1962; trans. Richard Howard, 1963) deploying a montage of quotations in its depiction of the United States.

BUTTERWORTH, George (1885–1916) Composer of a small body of work in folk-song and pastoral vein, such as the orchestral idyll *The Banks of Green Willow* (1913). He set songs from A. E. *Housman's *A Shropshire Lad*, later developing the music into an orchestral rhapsody (1913), and produced settings of Oscar *Wilde, Robert Louis *Stevenson, and P. B. *Shelley. He was killed at the Somme.

BUTTS, Mary (1890–1937) Novelist and writer, born at Parkstone, Dorset, and educated locally; at St Leonard's School for Girls, St Andrews, Scotland; at Westfield College, London University; and at the London School of Economics. She contributed to the **Little Review* alongside T. S. *Eliot, Hilda *Doolittle (H.D.) and *Bryher (Winifred Ellerman), and in 1918 she married John *Rodker (they divorced in 1926). She brought out *Speed the Plough*, a volume of short stories, in 1923 and her first novel, *Ashe of Rings*, appeared in 1925; her second, *Armed with Madness*, followed in 1928, the same year as her *Imaginary Letters*, illustrated by Jean *Cocteau. In 1932 she made her home in Sennen Cove, Cornwall, and in 1934 she converted to Anglo-Catholicism. The 1930s saw her publish many books, including her third novel, *Death of Felicity Taverner* (1932), two volumes of short stories, *Several Occasions* (1932) and the posthumous *Last Stories* (1938), as well as a great many poems and articles and her autobiography, *The Crystal Cabinet: My Childhood at Salterns* (1937; repr. 1988). Her books were neglected after her death, but they began to be republished in the 1980s and her reputation continues to revive slowly but steadily. See Nathalie Blondel, *Mary Butts: Scenes from the Life* (1998); *The Journals of Mary Butts*, ed. N. Blondel (2002); Jane Garrity, *Step-Daughters of England: British Women Modernists and the National Imaginary* (2003).

BYATT, A. S. (Dame Antonia Susan) (1936–) Novelist and critic, born in Sheffield, and educated at the Mount School, York, and Newnham College, Cambridge. Her first novel, *Shadow of a Sun* (1964), describes a woman attempting to escape the shadow of her novelist father. *The Game* (1967) also explores the influence of art on life through the relationship of two sisters, one an Oxford don, the other a popular novelist. *The Virgin in the Garden* (1978), set largely in the coronation year of 1953, sees the second Elizabethan Age being celebrated by a performance at a Yorkshire country house of a new verse drama, in which schoolgirl Frederica Potter plays the role of the Virgin Queen. Rich in allegorical allusions to (among others) Edmund *Spenser, Walter *Ralegh, and *Shakespeare, the novel also provides a realistic and vivid portrait of provincial life in the 1950s. Frederica's story is continued in *Still Life* (1985), *Babel Tower* (1996), and *A Whistling Woman* (2002). Byatt's best-known novel is *Possession* (1990), which won the *Booker, Irish Times, and Commonwealth Writers' Prizes. It concerns a group of 20th-century academics who reconstruct the relationship between two fictitious Victorian poets, and is notable for its pastiches of 19th-century literary style. *Angels and Insects* (1992), comprising two novellas, *Morpho Eugenia* and *The Conjugal Angel*, is again set in the mid-19th century, while *The Matisse Stories* (1993) is a sequence of three stories loosely linked to paintings by Henri Matisse (1869–1954). *The Djinn in the Nightingale's Eye* (1994) is a collection of original *fairy stories, including two previously published in *Possession*. Other works include *Little Black Book of Stories* (2003); *The Children's Book* (2009); two critical studies of Iris *Murdoch; a volume of essays, *On Histories and Stories* (2000); and *Portraits in Fiction* (2001) about paintings in novels. Margaret *Drabble is her sister.

BYRD, William (?1540–1623) English composer. Byrd was a pupil and colleague of Thomas *Tallis and in his turn an influential teacher. He was organist at Lincoln Cathedral, 1563, and gentleman of the Chapel Royal from 1572. In London he gained the patronage of several Catholic nobles, and of *Elizabeth I, which shielded him from prosecution as a recusant, though his music for the Catholic rite (such as the masses for three, four, and five voices, completed in the early 1590s) was tinged with covert propaganda. Elizabeth required Byrd to compose a consort song to her own text, *Look and Bow Down*, on the defeat of the Spanish Armada, and he wrote other works in her praise, including the *madrigal *This Sweet and Merry Month of May* (1590). He produced a *Great Service* for the Anglican rite, but returned to Catholic format in the two volumes of *Gradualia* (1605 and 1607). He held a patent for music publishing, and produced with Tallis a volume of *Cantiones* in 1575. Independently he published two volumes of *Cantiones Sacrae* (1589 and 1591). The secular *Psalmes, Sonets and Songs* (1588) was one of the earliest books of English song; here and in *Songs of Sundrie Natures* (1589) and *Psalmes, Songs, and Sonnets* (1611) Byrd dealt circumspectly with the new Italianate form of the madrigal, a term he did not employ. Among the authors he set were Philip *Sidney, Walter *Ralegh, Edward *Dyer, and Thomas *Churchyard. Byrd also composed consort music and collected his keyboard pieces, which sometimes incorporate snatches of popular song, in a manuscript, *My Lady Nevilles Book*, dated 1591.

BYROM, John (1692–1763) Poet, born near Manchester, educated at Trinity College, Cambridge, under Richard *Bentley, in whose defence he wrote, and to whose daughter he may have addressed *A Pastoral*, published in the **Spectator*, 1714. He invented a popular system of shorthand or 'tychygraphy', and was elected a fellow of the *Royal Society in 1724. His *Private Journals and Literary Remains* (pub. 1854–7) include accounts of his friendship with William *Law. Byrom wrote the ambiguous toast beginning 'God bless the King! I mean the Faith's Defender'. His *Miscellaneous Poems* (1773) includes the hymn 'Christians, awake! Salute the happy morn'.

BYRON, George Gordon, sixth Baron (1788–1824) Poet, son of Captain John Byron, 'Mad Jack', who eloped with and married Lady Carmarthen, and had by her a daughter, Augusta, who was to be of great importance in Byron's life. As his second wife Captain Byron married Catherine Gordon of Gight, an impetuous Scot, who became Byron's mother. The boy was born in London, with a club-foot which (it is generally supposed) had a profound effect on his future temperament. Mary *Shelley was to write, 'No action of Lord Byron's life—scarce a line he has written—but was influenced by his personal defect.' Pursued by creditors, the family moved in 1789 to Aberdeen, where Byron was educated until he was 10. His father died in 1791, and the fifth baron's grandson was killed in 1794; so when the baron himself died in 1798, Byron inherited the title. He and his mother moved south, visited his future inheritance, the dilapidated Gothic Newstead Abbey, and Byron was eventually sent to Harrow School. Staying at Newstead in 1802 he probably first met his half-sister, Augusta. In 1805, an extremely handsome young man, he went up to Cambridge, where he attended intermittently to his studies between extravagant debauches there and in London. His first published collection of poems, **Hours of Idleness*, appeared in 1807, and was bitterly attacked, probably by Henry *Brougham, in the **Edinburgh Review*. Byron avenged himself in 1809 with his satire **English Bards and Scotch Reviewers*. In 1808 he returned to Newstead, in 1809 took his seat in the House of Lords, then left for the first of his prolonged travels abroad. Between 1809 and 1811 he visited Portugal, Spain, Malta, Greece, and the Levant. In 1809 he began the poem that was to become **Childe Harold* and completed two cantos; he swam the Hellespont; and he became fired with the wish, which was to lead to his return and death, that Greece should be freed from the Turks.

Back in England in 1811 he met Augusta again. In that year, and in 1813, he spoke effectively on liberal themes in the House of Lords. His first great literary triumph came with the publication of the first two cantos of *Childe Harold's Pilgrimage* in March 1812 (Byron wrote that 'I awoke... and found myself famous'). He was lionized by aristocratic and literary London, survived a hectic love affair with Lady Caroline *Lamb, and became the constant companion of Augusta. In 1813 he wrote

The *Bride of Abydos* in a week, and *The* *Corsair* in ten days: *The* *Giaour* appeared in the same year. In 1814 Augusta gave birth to a daughter, who was generally supposed to be Byron's and was almost certainly so. In the same year he wrote *Lara*. After a long and hesitant courtship he married in 1815 Lady Melbourne's niece Annabella Milbanke. In the same year their daughter Ada was born, and Byron published *Hebrew Melodies*. But his debts were accumulating, doubts were cast upon his sanity, and public horror at the rumours of his incest was rising. Annabella left him to live with her parents, and a legal separation was eventually arranged.

Ostracized and deeply embittered, Byron left England in 1816, never to return, and travelled to Geneva, where the *Shelleys and Claire *Clairmont had rented a villa. Here Byron wrote *The* *Prisoner of Chillon*; Claire was by now his mistress. He wrote two acts of *Manfred*, Canto III of *Childe Harold*, and several shorter poems, but after four months left for Italy. His daughter by Claire, Allegra, was born in January 1817 in England. Living a riotous life in Venice in the same year, he devised and published an Armenian dictionary and wrote the third act of *Manfred*. While travelling to Rome he began the fourth and last canto of *Childe Harold*. He returned to Venice and there wrote *Beppo*, his first work in the ironic, colloquial style which was to lead him to *Don Juan*. Newstead Abbey was at last sold, and Byron was free of financial worries. In 1818 he wrote *Mazeppa*, and began *Don Juan*, the first two cantos of which were published in 1819 by John *Murray, reluctantly and anonymously, and which were denounced in *Blackwood's* as 'a filthy and impious poem'. However, it was much admired by *Goethe, a fact which Byron found greatly encouraging. In this year he met Teresa, Countess Guiccioli, to whom he became deeply attached. They lived first in Venice, then he followed her and her household to Ravenna, where he wrote *The Prophecy of Dante*. In 1820 he continued with Cantos III and IV of *Don Juan*, wrote *Marino Faliero*, and became deeply involved with the cause of the Italian patriots. Teresa left her husband for Byron in 1821, and Shelley rented houses in Pisa both for Byron and for the Gambas, Teresa's family. In Ravenna and Pisa that year Byron became intensely interested in drama, and wrote *The* *Two Foscari*, *Sardanapalus*, *Cain*, the unfinished *Heaven and Earth*, and the unfinished *The* *Deformed Transformed*. He thought well of his dramatic works and regretted they were not better received. In the same productive year he also wrote his brilliant parody of *Southey, *The* *Vision of Judgment*, and continued with *Don Juan*. The death in 1822 of his daughter Allegra, whom he had continually failed to visit, was a great grief to him. With the Gambas he left Pisa for Livorno, where Leigh *Hunt joined them. Hunt and Byron cooperated in the production of the *Liberal* magazine, the three issues of which contained successively *The Vision of Judgment*, *Heaven and Earth*, and a translation from Luigi *Pulci. Now in Genoa, Byron wrote *Werner*, a verse drama based on a tale by Harriet and Sophia *Lee, and was much preoccupied with *Don Juan* and with thoughts of Greece. In 1823 he wrote *The Age of Bronze*, a satirical poem on the Congress of Verona, and *The* *Island*, but he had come to feel that action was more important than poetry, and he told Lady *Blessington, 'I have a presentiment I shall die in Greece.' By July he was ready to sail, and Goethe sent him good wishes in verse. In January 1824 after various mishaps and escapes, he arrived at Missolonghi. He formed the 'Byron Brigade' and gave large sums of money, and great inspiration, to the insurgent Greeks, but he was dismayed by their disarray. Before he saw any serious military action he died of fever in April. Memorial services were held all over Greece, but his body was refused by the deans of both Westminster and St Paul's. After his old friend John *Hobhouse had arranged for the coffin to lie in state for a few days in London, it was interred in the family vault at Hucknall Torkard, near Newstead.

Byron's poetry, although widely condemned on moral grounds, and frequently attacked by critics, was immensely popular in England and even more so abroad. He noted in his Journal in 1822 that his sales were better in Germany, France, and America than at home. Much of his poetry and drama exerted great influence on *Romanticism, and his legacy of inspiration in European poetry, music, the novel, opera, and painting has been immense. Bertrand *Russell wrote that 'As a myth his importance, especially on the continent, was enormous.' His *Byronic heroes, rejecting conventional morality, rebellious, proud, but often self-loathing, were influential in 19th-century English fiction, notably in Emily *Brontë's characterization of Heathcliff. Byron was also the leading figure, alongside William *Gifford and Thomas *Moore, in the flourishing satirical tradition of the late Georgian age.

He was an indefatigable writer of letters and journals, many of which (Moore asserted) were written with an eye to publication. They provide a brilliantly vivid commentary both on his own life and on the times in which he lived. Moore's life appeared in 1830 (*Letters and Journals of Lord Byron, with Notices of his Life*, 2 vols) and a three-volume biography by L. A. Marchand was published in 1958. Marchand also edited the letters, 12 vols (1973–82), and the *Complete Poetical Works*, 3 vols (1980–93), are edited by J. J. McGann and B. Weller.

BYRON, John (1723–86) As a midshipman on the *Wager*, one of the ships of George *Anson's squadron in his famous voyage, he was wrecked on an island off the coast of Chile in 1741. His 'Narrative' of the shipwreck, published in 1768, provided details for his grandson Lord *Byron's description of a wreck in *Don Juan*. Byron later led a circumnavigation of the globe, from 1764 to 1766, making no significant discoveries in the Pacific but causing a sensation with his reports of Patagonian giants. An account of the voyage was written by John *Hawkesworth and published in 1773.

BYRON, Robert (1905–41) Travel writer, Byzantinist, and aesthete, educated at Eton College and Merton College, Oxford. His works include *The Station* (1928), an account of a visit to Mount Athos; *The Byzantine Achievement* (1929); and *The Appreciation of Architecture* (1932). He is chiefly remembered for his classic study *The Road to Oxiana* (1937), a record in the form of diary jottings of a journey from Venice through the Middle

East and Afghanistan to India in search of the origins of Islamic architecture and culture. Its admirers include Bruce *Chatwin and William *Dalrymple. Byron died when the ship on which he was travelling as a war correspondent was hit by a torpedo.

Byron, *The Conspiracy and Tragedy of Charles, Duke of* A two-part play by George *Chapman, written for the Boys of St Paul's, published in 1608. Its portrayal of the French provoked a protest from the French ambassador with a request that Chapman be imprisoned. The plays deals with the intrigues of Charles Gontaut, duc de Biron, a brave soldier who had fought successfully and been nobly rewarded by Henri IV of France, but whose ambition made him disloyal to the king. His plots are discovered, he asks forgiveness, and is pardoned. But his restless aspirations lead to a new conspiracy, which is revealed to the king. He is arrested and condemned to death. He professes his innocence and is reduced to frenzy and despair when he realizes that he is to die.

Byronic Characteristic of or resembling Lord *Byron or his poetry; that is, contemptuous of and rebelling against conventional morality, or defying fate, or possessing the characteristics of Byron's romantic heroes, or imitating his dress and appearance; in the words of Thomas *Macaulay, 'a man proud, moody, cynical, with defiance on his brow, and misery in his heart, a scorner of his kind, implacable in revenge, yet capable of deep and strong affection'.

Byzantine The word used to designate the art, and especially the architecture, developed in the eastern division of the Roman Empire. This eastern division endured from the partition of the empire between the two sons of Theodosius in AD 395 to the capture of Constantinople, its capital, formerly known as Byzantium, by the Turks in 1453. Byzantine architecture is distinguished by its use of the round arch, cross, circle, dome, and rich mosaic ornament. Largely despised in the 18th century (by Edward *Gibbon and others), Byzantine art and architecture underwent a revival in the 19th, stimulated by John *Ruskin. His account of St Mark's in *The Stones of Venice* (1851–3) opened the eyes of a generation of readers to this neglected period and stimulated the interest of William *Morris and other Arts and Crafts writers towards the end of the century. W. B. *Yeats's poems 'Sailing to Byzantium' (written 1926) and 'Byzantium' (written 1930) represent the culmination of a romantic tradition where Byzantium is the symbol of the undying world of art, contrasted with the 'fury and the mire of human veins'. The word 'byzantine' is also sometimes used (with reference to history rather than art) to convey the suggestion of bureaucratic obstructionism or sinister *oriental intrigue.

C

CABELL, James Branch (1879–1958) American novelist who lived most of his life in Virginia. Although he started his writing career as a journalist, Cabell is best remembered for his novel *Jurgen: A Comedy of Justice* (1919), briefly banned for obscenity, which describes the sexual adventures of its protagonist. This novel formed part of the series *The Biography of Manuel*, which ran to eighteen volumes and which was mostly set in the pastiche French-medieval realm of Poictesme. Cabell's combination of erotic fantasy and word-play earned him the respect of contemporaries like H. L. *Mencken and subsequently influenced a number of post-war writers including Robert A. *Heinlein.

CABLE, George Washington (1844–1925) American novelist and short story writer, who lived in New Orleans and in 1885 moved to Massachusetts. His earliest writing was as a newspaper columnist; then he began his portraits of Louisiana Creole life for which he is best remembered. The latter include his short story collection *Old Creole Days* (1879) and his novel *The Grandissimes* (1880). Cable wrote a number of works attacking Southern racism and became a close friend of Mark *Twain, with whom he went on a reading tour around the USA. Cable was a pioneer of Southern Local Colour writing.

CADE, Jack, Rebellion of A revolt by men of Kent, Surrey, Sussex, Middlesex, and Essex in June and July 1450, against the administration of Henry VI and the circle of William de la Pole, duke of Suffolk. Its leader, Cade, marched into London, but after a fight on London Bridge, the rebellion met with decisive resistance by Londoners. A large number of the rebels received pardons, but Cade was killed in Sussex. He is portrayed in Shakespeare's 2 **Henry VI*.

Cadenus and Vanessa Jonathan *Swift's longest poem, written probably around 1713 for Esther Vanhomrigh ('Vanessa'). Vanessa, Venus' favourite child, beautiful, rich, and intelligent, is immune to conventional social follies but falls in love with 'Cadenus', an anagram of 'Decanus', or dean (Swift). The poem delicately and wittily narrates in Swift's habitual octosyllabic couplets the inconclusive exchanges and emotional manoeuvrings of their unusual pupil–teacher romance. It appeared in 1726, three years after Vanhomrigh's death.

CADIGAN, Pat (1953–) American author, born in Schenectady, New York, but resident in the UK since 1996. After editing the small-press magazine *Shayol* she published her first novel, *Mindplayers*, in 1987. Her stories and novels build upon the tarnished glamour of *cyberpunk to foreshadow obsession with celebrity and the use of information technology for entertainment purposes. *Synners* (1991) and *Fools* (1992) each won the Arthur C. Clarke Award for best *science fiction novel of the year.

Cadmus In Greek myth, warriors sprang up and fought each other when Cadmus sowed the dragon's teeth; the survivors supposedly founded Thebes (see *Ovid, *Metamorphoses*, Bk 3). Cadmus is also associated with the introduction of the alphabet. John *Milton in **Areopagitica* compares books to the dragon's teeth, springing up as armed men.

CADWALLADER The son of Cadwallon, died in 689 according to *Geoffrey of Monmouth. He is the last of the British kings of England, according to the various *Brut chronicles which conclude with him. After his day, which was characterized by plague and desolation, the British would be called Welsh (foreign) and the Saxons rule instead in England, until the time prophesied by *Merlin for the return of a British king. He joined Penda (according to Geoffrey, Cadwallader's maternal uncle) against Eadwine, the Anglian king of Northumbria.

CÆDMON (*fl.*670) Entered the monastery of Streaneshalch (Whitby) between 658 and 680, when already an elderly man. He is said by *Bede in his **Ecclesiastical History of the English People* to have been a herdsman who received the power of song in a vision and later put into English verse scriptural passages translated to him. The only work which can be attributed to him is the hymn which survives in several manuscripts of the *History* in various dialects.

CAESAR, Gaius Julius (100–44 BC) Roman politician who in his middle forties surfaced as a general of genius. Victor in the factional struggles that destroyed the republic, and eventually dictator, he prepared the ground for six centuries of imperial rule: Octavian, later the emperor Augustus, was his heir. He wrote a lucid third-person account of his campaigns in his *Commentaries: On the Gallic War*, which includes his invasions of Britain, and *On the Civil War*, which

opens with Caesar crossing the Rubicon with his army to invade Italy. During his Alexandrian campaign he began a love affair with *Cleopatra. He was assassinated on the Ides of March by a group of republican conspirators led by *Brutus. *Cicero is the principal contemporary source for the events of his lifetime; biographies were written later by *Plutarch and *Suetonius. Shakespeare's **Julius Caesar* and G. B. *Shaw's *Caesar and Cleopatra* are the most influential English retellings of his story. *On the Gallic War* was first translated into English by Arthur *Golding (1565), but for centuries the original Latin formed the basis of a classical education. Rex *Warner translated both sets of *Commentaries* and also wrote two novels about Caesar.
See CATO; LUCAN.

Caesar and Pompey A politically astute Roman tragedy by George *Chapman, written 1604, published 1631. It deals with the conflict between Caesar and Pompey, the events leading to the battle of Pharsalus (48 BC), the murder of Pompey, and the suicide of *Cato of Utica. Cato is the real hero of the play, of which the motto is 'Only a just man is a free man'.

caesura A pause within a line of verse, usually coinciding with a punctuated break between clauses or sentences. *Alliterative verse required a caesura at the middle of the line. The English *pentameter commonly displaces it to a position after the fourth or sixth syllable, but several other positions are permissible, and the caesura may not be employed at all.

CAHAN, Abraham (1860–1951) Lithuanian-born American novelist, short story writer, and journalist. Cahan produced a number of portraits of Jewish immigrant life in America, most notably *Yekl: A Tale of the New York Ghetto* (1896) and *The Rise of David Levinsky* (1917). He also served as editor and reporter for the *Yiddish press of New York.

CAIN, James Mallahan (1892–1977) American novelist, journalist, and screenwriter. One of the formative figures in the tradition of *hardboiled crime fiction, Cain is best remembered for his laconic first-person narratives like *The Postman Always Rings Twice* (1934), which was adapted for the cinema in 1946, directed by Carey Wilson. Cain insisted that his crime narratives were always motivated by a love story. In the 1930s and 1940s he worked as a screenwriter in Hollywood.

Cain: A Mystery A verse drama in three acts by Lord *Byron, published 1821. Cain, bewildered by the toil imposed on him by another's fault, and by the mystery of the 'evil' consequences of 'good' knowledge, is confronted by Lucifer, who teaches him to question the ways of God, the 'Omnipotent tyrant'. Cain expresses his doubts and fears to his sister-bride Adah and is reluctant to share his favoured brother Abel's sacrifice to Jehovah. In a fit of passion, revolted by the blood sacrifice and a God who could delight in such offerings, Cain strikes Abel and kills him, thus bringing into the world Death. Cursed by Eve, rejected by Adam, and marked on the brow by an angel of the Lord, Cain sets forth into exile with his wife and children, knowing that they will further the doom of mankind. This powerful enquiry into original sin, heredity, free will, and predestination caused intense indignation, and the publisher, John *Murray, was threatened with prosecution. Byron diplomatically denied that the views represented were his own.

CAINE, Hall (Sir Thomas Henry Hall) (1853–1931) novelist, who grew up in Liverpool, and worked as an architect's assistant, teacher, and journalist in his early years. In 1879 he delivered a lecture in Liverpool on D. G. *Rossetti, which brought him into correspondence with the poet. Caine spent the last few months of Rossetti's life as his housemate: see Caine's *Recollections of Dante Gabriel Rossetti* (1882). He edited an anthology, *Sonnets of Three Centuries* (1882), in which all three *Rossettis, and William Bell *Scott were represented. He then turned to fiction, and achieved spectacular success with a series of best-sellers, many set in the Isle of Man, where his father had originated and where he himself eventually settled. Titles included *The Deemster* (1887), *The Bondsman* (1890), *The Manxman* (1894), *The Christian* (1897), *The Eternal City* (1901), *The Prodigal Son* (1904), and a pro-woman's rights novel, *The Woman Thou Gavest Me* (1913). *The Woman of Knockaloe*, his last novel, appeared in 1923. See Vivian Allen's biography (1997).

CAIRD, Mona (1854–1932). One of the most militant of New Women writers who combined non-fictional feminist tracts that argued for equality in marriage (essays collected as *The Morality of Marriage*, 1897) with *New Woman fiction in which she interrogates the stifling effects of conventionality on women's lives. In *The Daughters of Danaus* (1894), the heroine leaves husband and family to study music. Other novels included *The Wing of Azrael* (1889), *A Romance of the Moors* (1891), and *The Stones of Sacrifice* (1915). Caird also campaigned extensively against vivisection: see *A Sentimental View of Vivisection* (1894), and *Beyond the Pale* (1896).

CALAMY, Edmund (1671–1732) Presbyterian minister and historian, born in London. He is best known for his carefully researched short lives of Nonconformist ministers ejected from the *Church of England in 1662, published between 1702 and 1727, which developed material in Richard *Baxter's *Reliquiae Baxterianae*. His very informative autobiography was first published in 1830.

CALDECOTT, Randolph (1846–86) RA, author/illustrator, and painter, born in Chester, educated at the Slade School, London. In 1878 the printer Edmund Evans commissioned *The House that Jack Built*, the first of sixteen *'toy books'. Caldecott is thought to be the first author/illustrator to negotiate royalty payments.

CALDERÓN DE LA BARCA, Pedro (1600–81) The great Spanish dramatist and successor of Lope de *Vega Carpio, born in Madrid where he was educated by the Jesuits. He later studied at Alcalá de Henares and Salamanca. After a turbulent early life he was ordained priest in 1651; he enjoyed royal favour, and in 1663 became chaplain to the king. He wrote some 120 plays—tragedies, comedies of manners, histories, philosophical dramas—and, in later life, more than 70 highly regarded *autos sacramentales*, allegorical religious plays with subjects from mythology and the Old and New Testaments, dramatizing aspects of faith. Of his secular plays, one of the best known is *El alcalde de Zalamea* (revised version published 1636?: *The Mayor of Zalamea*), in which the peasant-mayor takes revenge on the captain who has raped his daughter and is rewarded by Philip II by being made mayor for life. Other works include *La vida es sueño* (published 1636?: *Life is a Dream*), a baroque philosophical play which he also rewrote as an *auto*, and *El mágico prodigioso* (first performed 1637: *The Wonder-Working Magician*), a religious drama set in the reign of Diocletian. Edward *FitzGerald translated eight of his plays (1853, 1865). Roy *Campbell's translation of *El médico de su honra* (written 1633 or earlier), a play about the apparently justified murder of a falsely suspected wife, was published as *The Surgeon of his Honour*. See Melveena McKendrick, *Theatre in Spain 1490–1700* (1989).

CALDWELL, Erskine (1903–1987) American novelist, short story writer, and reporter, born in Georgia. Caldwell is best known for his fictional portraits of poor whites in the deep South characterized by a humorous, often grotesque attention to their sexual behaviour. *Tobacco Road* (1932) and *God's Little Acre* (1933) are his most famous works in this mode. In the 1930s Caldwell began a series of collaborations with the photographer Margaret Bourke-White, producing books of reportage like *You Have Seen their Faces* (1937) and *Say! Is This the U.S.A.?* (1941).

Caleb Williams (*Things as They Are, or The Adventures of Caleb Williams*) A novel by William *Godwin, published 1794. This work is remarkable as an early example of the propagandist novel, as a novel of pursuit, crime, and detection, and as a psychological study. It was designed to show 'the tyranny and perfidiousness exercised by the powerful members of the community against those who are less privileged than themselves'. A provocative preface to the original edition was withdrawn.

It is related in the first person by its eponymous hero. The first part of the book deals with the misdeeds of Tyrrel, an arrogant and tyrannical country squire, who ruins a tenant on his estate, Hawkins, for refusing to yield to one of his whims. He comes into conflict with the idealistic and benevolent Falkland, a neighbouring squire, knocks him down in public, and is shortly after found murdered. Suspicion falls on Falkland but is diverted to Hawkins and his son, who are tried and executed. From this time Falkland becomes eccentric and solitary. Caleb Williams, the self-educated son of humble parents, is appointed his secretary, and convinces himself that Falkland is in fact Tyrrel's murderer. The remainder of the book concerns Falkland's unrelenting persecution of Williams despite his devotion to his employer and refusal to betray his secret. Williams is imprisoned on a false charge of robbing his employer, escapes, but is tracked by Falkland's agents until, in despair, he lays a charge of murder against Falkland, is confronted with him, and, although he has no proof to offer, through his generosity and sincerity wins from the murderer a confession of guilt. Godwin's original ending was radically different; in it Falkland maintains his innocence and Williams ends, nearly demented, in jail. William *Hazlitt paid tribute to the power of the narrative when he wrote, 'no one ever began *Caleb Williams* that did not read it through'.

calendar The system according to which the beginning, length, and dates of the year are fixed. The Julian Calendar was introduced by Julius Caesar in 46 BC; the ordinary year has 365 days, and every fourth year is a leap year of 366 days, the months having the names, order, and length still retained. The Gregorian Calendar, introduced by Pope Gregory XIII in 1582, and adopted in Great Britain in 1752 (*see* CHESTERFIELD, PHILIP) brought the system into closer conformity with astronomical data. The Julian year of 365¼ days was 11 minutes 10 seconds too long, and this error amounted in 1752 to 11 days; accordingly, the British Calendar Act stipulated that 2 September would in that year be followed by 14 September, while century years were to be leap years only when exactly divisible by 400. The Act also formally recognized the beginning of the year as 1 January.

Calendar of Modern Letters (1925–7) A literary periodical, first a monthly, then a quarterly, edited by Edgell *Rickword, Douglas Garman, and Bertram Higgins. It published fiction by D. H. *Lawrence, *Pirandello, A. E. *Coppard, William *Gerhardie, and others; in its critical articles (some in a series called 'Scrutinies') it praised D. H. Lawrence and T. F. *Powys, faintly praised S. T. *Warner and others, condemned the 'non-combatant' and uncommitted critical attitudes of Edmund *Gosse and the grossness of Arnold *Bennett, found the products of *Bloomsbury to be on the whole frivolous and sentimental, and praised the critical approach of I. A. *Richards. *Towards Standards of Criticism: Selections from the Calendar of Modern Letters* was published in 1933 with an introduction by F. R. *Leavis, and **Scrutiny* upheld many of its attitudes.

Caliban In Shakespeare's *The *Tempest*, is described in the *folio 'Names of the Actors' as 'a salvage [savage] and deformed slave'. His name probably derives either from 'Carib' or 'cannibal'. Son of the witch Sycorax and the original possessor of Prospero's island, he is only semi-human, but has often been portrayed sympathetically in modern productions: the poetic qualities of his speeches and *postcolonial readings of the text have facilitated this.

'Caliban upon Setebos' A poem by Robert *Browning, included in **Dramatis Personae*. It is spoken by William *Shakespeare's character from *The *Tempest*, reimagined as a half-sympathetic creature, terrified of his god, Setebos, and condemned to brutality. The intellectual interest is in the poem's understanding of divinity as shaped by personal situation and experience. Condemned to a harsh life, Caliban cannot imagine—except for a brief moment—a higher power than one that reflects his own circumstances. Browning responds imaginatively to *Feuerbach's argument that the Christian God is a projection of human identity. The poem initiated a rereading of the imperial politics of Shakespeare's play.

Calidore, Sir The Knight of Courtesy, the hero of Book VI of Edmund *Spenser's **Faerie Queene*. He pursues and chains the *Blatant Beast, and rescues Pastorella. One of John *Keats's earliest poems, the fragment 'Young Calidore is paddling o'er the lake' (1816), was inspired by him.

Calisto y Melibea *See* CELESTINA.

CALLAGHAN, Morley (1903–90) Canadian novelist of Irish Catholic descent, born and educated in Toronto, proponent of what is termed colonial modernism. After the publication of his first novel, *Strange Fugitive* (1928), he travelled to Paris, where in 1929 he renewed contact with Ernest *Hemingway, whom he had met while working for the *Toronto Star*; his experiences there are recorded in *That Summer in Paris* (1963), with portraits of Scott *Fitzgerald and other expatriate Americans. He published short stories and several novels, and is best remembered for the novel triptych: *Such is my Beloved* (1934), in which Father Dowling, an idealistic young priest, generously but unwisely befriends two prostitutes; *They Shall Inherit the Earth* (1935); and *More Joy in Heaven* (1937), about a bank robber turned 'prodigal son'. These works share a noticeably spare, simple prose and narrative style, and a religious concern with the redemption of the ordinary.

CALLIL, Carmen *See* VIRAGO PRESS.

CALLIMACHUS (*c*.310/305–*c*.240 BC) Perhaps the finest of *Hellenistic poets and a scholar who worked in the Library at Alexandria. Of his many poems only six hymns, 60 epigrams, and a number of fragments survive. He was much admired by the Roman poets *Catullus, *Propertius, and *Ovid: Catullus imitated his poem on the 'Lock of Berenice'. A difficult author, Callimachus found few English readers until the 17th century: Thomas *Stanley, Richard *Bentley, and his nephew Thomas Bentley did much editorial work on his poems, and translations were made from the mid-18th century, for example by William *Dodd. He was imitated by Mark *Akenside in his 'Hymn to the Naiads'. One of his epigrams served as a model for W. J. *Cory's 'They told me Heraclitus...', and material of a mythological sort drawn from his hymns can be found in Alfred *Tennyson's *'Tiresias' and Robert *Bridges's *Prometheus the Firegiver.*

CALVERLEY, Charles Stuart (1831–84) Poet and translator (born Blayds, assumed Calverley from 1852). He became a barrister of the Inner Temple, but his career was hindered by a serious accident to the brain. He became known under the initials C.S.C. as a writer of light verse, parodies, and translations: a serious translation of *Theocritus was issued in 1869; *Verses and Translations* appeared in 1862, *Fly Leaves* in 1872.

CALVIN, Jean (1509–64) French theologian and reformer. His name derives from Calvinus, the Latinized form of Cauvin. Born in Noyon, Picardy of a well-to-do middle-class family, he studied canon and civil law, became interested in Greek and Hebrew, and by 1533 was giving signs of commitment to the doctrines of the Reformers (*see* REFORMATION). In 1536 he published the first edition of his *Institutio Christianae religionis* in Basle, and settled in Geneva, establishing moral and political ascendancy over that city in 1541. In addition to continuous revisions of his *Institutio* (the French version was published in 1541), he produced a succession of influential pamphlets, sermons, commentaries, and letters. The *Institutio* was conceived as a defence of the Reformed Faith. It repudiated scholastic methods of argument in favour of deductions from biblical authority and the moral nature of man, and it advocated the doctrines of sin and grace—with the associated doctrine of predestination derived from St Paul—at the expense of salvation by works. Calvin was an unswerving opponent of the power of bishops, favouring the voice of independent congregations. His ideas had a major influence in 16th- and 17th-century England. The clarity, conciseness, energy, and austerity of his use of the vernacular mark a significant advance in the development of French prose. See T. H. L. Parker, *John Calvin* (1975).

CALVINO, Italo (1923–85) Italian novelist, short story writer, journalist, and critic. His first work, *Il sentiero dei nidi di ragno* (1947: *The Path to the Spiders' Nests*), which deals with the resistance against Fascism, is a leading example of *neorealism. His subsequent works range widely over links between literature and science in *Le cosmicomiche* (1965; rev. 1984: *Cosmicomics*) and *Ti con zero* (1967: *Time and the Hunter*); fantasy, myth, and utopias in *Le città invisibili* (1972: *Invisible Cities*); the Tarot in *Il castello dei destini incrociati* (1973: *The Castle of Crossed Destinies*); experimental narrative in *Se una notte d'inverno un viaggiatore* (1979: *If on a Winter's Night a Traveller*); and the punctilious description of minute fragments of life, *Marcovaldo ovvero le stagioni in città* (1963: *Marcovaldo, or The Seasons in the City*), *Palomar* (1983: *Mr Palomar*). His fantasy trilogy *I nostri antenati* (*Our Ancestors*) is composed of three allegorical novels: *Il visconte dimezzato* (1952: *The Cloven Viscount*); *Il barone rampante* (1957: *Baron in the Trees*), which plays with the 'reality' of Samuel *Richardson and Henry *Fielding; and *Il cavaliere inesistente* (1959: *The Non-existent Knight*), which draws ironically on Renaissance chivalrous epic. His critique of neo-capitalism emerges in such novels as *La speculazione edilizia* (1957: *A Plunge into Real Estate*). His inventive ironic fantasies are comparable to those of Jorge *Borges, and he was deeply interested in folklore and *fairy stories, collected and published in his *Fiabe italiane* (1956: *Italian Folktales*). From 1967 to 1979 he was resident in Paris where he came into contact with Roland *Barthes, George *Perec, and the *OuLiPo movement. In 1985 he was invited to deliver the Charles Eliot Norton lectures, but died before the end of the series. These were published posthumously as *Lezioni americane: sei proposte per il prossimo millenio* (1988: *Six Memos for the Next Millenium*). *See also* MAGIC REALISM. See M. McLaughlin, *Italo Calvino* (1998).

CAMARA LAYE (1928–80) Guinean novelist. He is noted in particular for *L'Enfant noir* (1953; *The Dark Child*—later *The African Child*—trans. James Kirkup, 1954), a largely autobiographical account of childhood and adolescence in Africa, which explores the psychological and emotional consequences of the encounter with a modernized, Western world.

Cambell (Cambello) The name given by Edmund *Spenser in *Faerie Queene*, IV. iii, to Cambalo, whose tale he borrows from the 'Squire's Tale' of 'Dan *Chaucer*, well of English undefyled', and completes. Cambell is brother of Canacee, for whom there are many suitors. It is arranged that the strongest of these, three brothers, shall fight with Cambell and the lady be awarded to the victor. Two of the brothers are defeated: the contest between the third, Triamond, and Cambell is undecided, each wounding the other. They are reconciled by Cambina, Triamond's sister; Canacee is awarded to Triamond and Cambell marries Cambina. Canacee's magic ring in the 'Squire's Tale' reappears in the *Faerie Queene*, with the power of healing wounds.

Cambridge Bibliography of English Literature The major printed bibliographical reference work in this field of scholarship, often referred to as *CBEL*. It first appeared as a set of four volumes edited by F. W. Bateson in 1940, followed by a supplement (ed. George Watson, 1957). It was succeeded by the *New Cambridge Bibliography of English Literature* (*NCBEL*) in five volumes including an index (ed. G. Watson and I. R. Willison, 1969–77). A third edition was inaugurated with the appearance in 2000 of volume iv (ed. Joanne Shattock), covering the 1800–1900 period, but was subsequently abandoned.

Cambridge Platonists A group of Anglican thinkers who had close connections with Cambridge University and tried to promote a rational form of Christianity in the tradition of Richard *Hooker and *Erasmus. The group included Benjamin Whichcote (1609–83), appointed provost of King's College by Parliament (1644) and dispossessed at the Restoration (1660). His writings, mostly sermons and letters, were published posthumously. Posthumous publication was the fate also of the only volume (*Select Discourses*, 1660) produced by Whichcote's pupil John Smith (1618–52): Matthew *Arnold said that his sermon 'On the Excellency and Nobleness of True Religion' contained all that candidates for ordination needed to know outside of the Bible. Henry More (1614–87) remained all his life a fellow of Christ's College, refusing promotion. His early poetry in *Psychodia Platonica* (1642) has some remarkable as well as some remarkably awkward passages. His prose works (eleven were published during his lifetime) are profound, complex, overloaded with learning, and their interpretation is made difficult by More's conflicting attitudes. He attacked superstition but had himself a keen taste for the occult; he wanted to simplify religion so that all could understand it, but was bitterly opposed to the emotional fervour that had most appeal for the uneducated; at one time he was full of praise for *Descartes, later he censured him as a materialist. Ralph Cudworth (1617–88), master successively of Clare Hall (1645) and Christ's College (1654), had a more lucid style and a more logical mind, and his major work, *The True Intellectual System of the Universe* (1678), must be regarded as the group's most detailed manifesto. Another fellow of Emmanuel College often included in the group was Nathaniel Culverwell (d. 1651), but his outlook differed from that of the rest, being more Calvinist and Aristotelian.

The aims of the group were to combat materialism, which was finding a forceful exponent in Thomas *Hobbes, and to reform religion by freeing it from fanaticism and controversy. Drawing inspiration from *Plato and *Plotinus, they maintained that Sense reveals only appearances, Reality consists in 'intelligible forms' which are 'not impressions printed on the soul without, but ideas vitally protended or actively exerted from within itself'. They held furthermore that Revelation, the Rational Order of the Universe, and human Reason were all in harmony, so that to search for Truth was to search for God. They rejected the Calvinist doctrine that human nature was deeply corrupt, capable of salvation only through the action of a Divine Grace granted to some and withheld from others, and saw Man as 'deiform', able to advance towards perfection through Reason and the imitation of Christ. Reason for the Cambridge Platonists was not just power of critical thought, but to function effectively had to result in virtuous behaviour. Truth and Goodness were inseparable.

These doctrines were presented in a rhetorical, quotation-laden, often long-winded late Renaissance manner which has masked their revolutionary character, but it is evident that they prepared the way for the *Deism of the 18th century. The odd fact that Cudworth's daughter was one of John *Locke's patrons was in a way symbolic.

Cambridge University Press Books were first printed at Cambridge in 1521–3 by John Siberch (Johann Lair von Siegburg), a friend of *Erasmus. In 1534 *Henry VIII granted the university a charter authorizing the printing of books there, but the first university printer, Thomas Thomas, was not appointed until 1583. The undertaking was opposed by the *Stationers' Company as an infringement of their monopolies, but the university finally vindicated its rights. The Press's activities developed under the influence of

Richard *Bentley (1662–1742) when the present system of control by a Syndicate, or committee of senior academics, was instituted. The Press evolved from the original system by which licensed printers did some work for the university, through a partnership with a dynasty of printer-publishers (the Clays), to full control, by the Syndicate and its permanent staff, of its own large printing-house and worldwide publishing business, issuing schoolbooks, textbooks, works of learning and reference, journals, Bibles, and prayer books as part of the university's charitable function of fostering 'education, learning, religion, and research'. With a history of continuous activity since 1584, the Press claims to be the oldest printer-publisher in England, perhaps in the world. It has been a notable publisher of books on scientific, literary, classical, historical, and bibliographical subjects, as well as of journals such as *Shakespeare Survey* and of editions of authors like George *Beaumont and John *Fletcher, Jonathan *Swift, Samuel *Richardson, and D. H. *Lawrence. Among the most distinctive of Cambridge's publications is the great range of collaborative histories first planned by Baron *Acton (Ancient History, Medieval History, Modern History) and extended since his death to cover such subjects as the History of the Book in Britain, Literary Criticism, and the English Language. There is a three-volume history of the Press by David McKitterick (1992–2004).

Cambyses, King A tragedy (*c.*1568–9) by Thomas *Preston, which illustrates the transition from the morality play to historical tragedy. It is founded on the story of Cambyses (king of Persia) in *Herodotus; its grandiloquence became proverbial and is referred to in 1 **Henry IV*, II. v: 'I must speak in passion, and I will do it in King Cambyses' vein.' Among the characters are three comic villains, Ruff, Huff, and Snuff, who appear again in the *Martin Marprelate controversy in the course of John Lyly's **Pap with an Hatchet*.

CAMDEN, William (1551–1623) Antiquary and historian, educated at Christ's Hospital, St Paul's School, and at Oxford (where he knew Philip *Sidney) at Magdalen College, Broadgates Hall, and Christ Church. In 1593 he was appointed headmaster of Westminster School; one of his pupils was Ben *Jonson, who said that he owed Camden 'All that I am in arts, all that I know'. He made tours of antiquarian research throughout England, publishing his **Britannia* in 1586. The entertaining miscellany of antiquarian material *Remains of a Greater Work Concerning Britain* first appeared in 1605. He published *Annales...Regnante Elizabetha...ad Annum 1589*, a civic history of the reign of *Elizabeth I in 1615; the second part was published posthumously in 1625 and both parts translated into English in 1625–9. Camden founded a chair of ancient history in Oxford.

Camden Society Founded in 1838 in honour of William *Camden, for the purpose of publishing documents relating to the early history and literature of the British Empire. In 1897 it was amalgamated with the *Royal Historical Society.

Camelot The seat of King Arthur's court, is said by Sir Thomas *Malory to be Winchester. It has variously been identified with Camelford in Cornwall or South Cadbury in Somerset, and John *Leland says he found traces of Arthur in Queen's Camel in Somerset which (he says) was previously called Camelot. The scholar R. S. Loomis claims it is a fusion of Avalon, the location of Arthur's last battle, and Caerleon in South Wales. See Alan Lupack, *The Oxford Guide to Arthurian Literature and Legend* (2005).

CAMERON, Julia Margaret (1815–79) Photographer, born in Calcutta, into an artistic and well-connected family. Educated in France, she moved to England in 1848 when her husband Charles Hay Cameron retired. She had many friends in the literary world, and though her career as a photographer was short (twelve years) her portraits of Thomas *Carlyle, Alfred *Tennyson, Benjamin *Jowett, Anne Thackeray *Ritchie, and many others are renowned. One of the most celebrated is of her niece Julia, Mrs Herbert Duckworth, later the wife of Leslie *Stephen and mother of Virginia *Woolf. She lived from 1860 till 1875 at Freshwater, Isle of Wight, and many of her photographs were designed to illustrate poetic works, notably her neighbour Tennyson's; she was also fond of allegorical and symbolic subjects which she composed in a style strongly influenced by the *Pre-Raphaelites. Unconventional and striking in dress and manner, she was described by Lady Ritchie as 'a woman of noble plainness'.

CAMERON, Norman (1905–53) Poet, born in India of Scottish parents. He was educated in Edinburgh and at Oriel College, Oxford, worked (1929–32) as an education officer in Nigeria, then (after staying in Majorca with Robert *Graves) returned to England, where he worked for an advertising agency. During and immediately after the war (until 1947) he worked in government propaganda with the British forces in Italy and Austria. His poems were published in periodicals during the 1930s, principally in *New Verse*, and his first collection was *The Winter House* (1935). *The Collected Poems of Norman Cameron* appeared in 1957, with an introduction by Graves, and *Collected Poems and Selected Translations* in 1990. His poems are brief, lucid, and concentrated, built usually on a single image or parable: Dylan *Thomas wrote that a poem by Cameron 'moves around one idea, from one logical point to another, making a full circle'.

CAMERON, Verney Lovett (1844–94) The first European to cross Africa from east to west; he recorded the exploit in *Across Africa* (2 vols, 1877). The son of a parson, he joined the Royal Navy and served with the anti-slave trade patrol off East Africa before leading a *Royal Geographical Society expedition to help David *Livingstone, thought to be somewhere in the middle of the continent. He met only Livingstone's corpse but went on westwards across the Congo Basin to Benguela.

Short paragraphs, a racy style, and a serious concluding message made *Across Africa* popular. Cameron's impact on

Leopold II's ambitions was significant but his subsequent travels and advocacies had only a limited influence on official Britain. Much more successful were a series of adventure stories in book form and in the *Boy's Own Paper*, often based on his own experiences. His biography by W. R. Foran appeared in 1937.

Camilla*, or A Picture of Youth* A novel by Fanny *Burney (1796). The author called it her 'grand ouvrage', not a novel but a *work*, and it has a more overtly moral character than her earlier novels. At the centre lies the relationship between the lively and beautiful Camilla Tyrold and her eligible, but cool and judicious, suitor Edgar Mandlebert. The eventual marriage is delayed over five volumes by intrigues, contretemps, and misunderstandings, designed to exhibit the virtues and failings of Camilla's character or to illustrate similar difficulties in the lives of her sisters, and her exotic, selfish cousin Indiana Lynmere. The book contains some lively characterization, especially in minor characters such as the grotesque tutor Dr Orkborne, the fop Sir Sedley Clarendel, and Camilla's uncle Sir Hugh Tyrold. It was dedicated to the queen and published for an unusually distinguished list of subscribers, which included Ann *Radcliffe, Hannah *More, and Jane *Austen.

CAMÕES, Luís de (*c.*1524–1580) In pre-modern times sometimes Camoens, Portuguese poet and dramatist, best known for his *epic *Os Lusíadas* (1572: *The Lusiads*). He probably acquired his vast knowledge of classical and Italian literature at court. He wrote the epic while serving in India and the Far East, between 1553 and *c.*1569. It thus became the first great work of European literature to have been written outside Europe, and some of its intellectual freedom is due to Camões's absence from the constricting atmosphere at home. The poem recounts the first voyage to India (1497–9) in the context of the history of Portugal. The principal inspiration is *Virgil, but Camões's erudition was wide-ranging and the poem became the model of the learned epic in early modern Europe. Some of the moments of greatest poetic tension occur when historical characters, like Vasco da Gama, the commander of the Portuguese fleet, enter the classical supernatural world. Examples are the encounter in Canto 5 with the threatening giant Adamastor, who symbolizes the geographical unknown, and the Isle of Venus (Cantos 9–10), in which the returning voyagers are rewarded sexually and also, by a process of Platonic ascent, by a vision of the universe and of the future. There have been some fifteen translations into English, including those by Sir Richard *Fanshawe in the 17th century and Sir Richard *Burton in the 19th. Camões's reputation has suffered greatly from the association of his work with the ideals of imperialism. In the post-imperial age, however, he seems much more a poet of doubt, whose principal concern was the preservation of artistic integrity.

Campaspe A prose comedy by John *Lyly, published 1584 as *Alexander, Campaspe and Diogenes*. Alexander the Great loves his Theban captive Campaspe, gives her freedom, and engages Apelles to paint her portrait. Apelles and Campaspe fall in love, and when the portrait is finished Apelles spoils it so as to have a reason for further sittings. Alexander suspects the truth and by a trick makes him reveal it. He surrenders Campaspe to Apelles and returns to his wars, saying, 'It were a shame Alexander should desire to command the world, if he could not command himself.' The play includes the lyric 'Cupid and my Campaspe played | At cards for kisses...' The story of Alexander, Campaspe, and Apelles is told in *Pliny the Elder's *Natural History*, 35. 10.

CAMPBELL, John W. (1910–71) American editor and writer, born Newark, New Jersey. Beginning as a writer of epic space operas and (as 'Don A. Stuart') stories such as the elegiac 'Twilight' (1934) and 'Who Goes There?' (1938)—adapted for film as *The Thing* (1951, 1982)—Campbell became editor of the American magazine **Astounding Stories* in 1937. From then until his death he was one of the most influential editors in *science fiction. Among writers he discovered, or encouraged, were Isaac *Asimov, Robert A. *Heinlein, Theodore *Sturgeon, and A. E. *Van Vogt. Asimov credits him with fully articulating his 'three laws of robotics'. In later years, his opinionated editorials and support for pseudo-science such as Dianetics, 'reactionless-drive' machines, and ESP alienated some, but his work with *Astounding*, and the *fantasy magazine *Unknown* (1939–43) revolutionized the genre. See Albert I. Berger, *The Magic That Works: John W. Campbell and the American Response to Technology* (1994).

CAMPBELL, Joseph (1879–1944) Irish poet, who published some of his works under his Irish name, Seosamh MacCathmhaoil. Born in Belfast, he spent some years in London as secretary of the Irish National Literary Society. He supported the Republican cause in the Irish Civil War (1922–3), and was interned in Dublin. In 1925 he emigrated to the USA, where he became a pioneer of Irish studies. Many of his lyrics and ballads are based on legend and folklore; his collections include *The Gilly of Christ* (1907) and *The Mountainy Singer* (1909). He wrote the words of the Belfast anthem 'My Lagan Love' to a melody supplied by Herbert Hughes (1882–1937). The monologues of *Irishry* (1913) and the rueful, newly sophisticated lyrics composed in the months before his fatal heart attack on the remote County Wicklow farm to which he retired in 1939 have an enduring appeal. *Poems* (1963) was edited by Austin *Clarke.

CAMPBELL, Ken (1941–) Actor, director, and writer, born in Ilford. His interest in the bizarre and surreal resulted in co-founding the Science Fiction Theatre of Liverpool following his introduction to *science fiction by Brian *Aldiss. *Illuminatus!* (1976) was an epic romp through conspiracy theories lasting 8½ hours; *The Warp* (1980) lasted 22 hours. Other productions included adaptations of H. P. *Lovecraft's *The Case of Charles Dexter Ward* (1978) and Douglas *Adams's *The Hitchhiker's Guide to the Galaxy* (1979). Campbell also performs in his own one-man shows.

CAMPBELL, Ramsey (1946–) *Horror novelist and short story writer born in Liverpool. His early published work, written in his teens, bears the stamp of H. P. *Lovecraft, but Campbell soon developed his own approach characterized by a sly and subtle undermining of his characters' perceptions of reality. *The Face That Must Die* (1979) shows a grimness intensified and counterpointed by the protagonist's puns—a technique used more subtly in *The Count of Eleven* (1991). Lovecraftian awe returns in *The Darkest Part of the Woods* (2003). See S. T. Joshi, *Ramsey Campbell and Modern Horror Fiction* (2001).

CAMPBELL, Roy (1901–57) Author, born in Durban, Natal, and educated at Durban Boys' High School and, briefly, Natal University. He came to England in 1918 hoping to gain entry to Oxford but was unsuccessful. In 1924 he published, to great acclaim, *The Flaming Terrapin*, an exuberant allegorical narrative of the Flood, in which the terrapin represents energy and rejuvenation. Returning to South Africa (1924–7), he founded with William *Plomer a satirical literary magazine, *Voorslag* ('Whiplash', 1926–7), which he and Plomer wrote largely by themselves until joined by Laurens *van der Post. In 1928 he published *The Wayzgoose*, a satire on South African life. Now living in Provence, he published *Adamastor* (1930), and in 1931 *The Georgiad*, a long, biting attack on the *Bloomsbury Group. *Flowering Reeds* (1933), a book of gentler lyrics, was followed in 1934 by his first autobiography, *Broken Record*, a swashbuckling narrative of adventure and blatantly Fascist opinions. In 1935 he became a Roman Catholic. His next book of verse, *Mithraic Emblems*, appeared in 1936, and in 1939 a long poem, *Flowering Rifle*, a noisily pro-Fascist work which brought him much opprobrium. However, during the Second World War he fought with the British army in East Africa, and in 1941 published *Sons of the Mistral*, a selection of his best poems. *Light on a Dark Horse* (1951), a second autobiography, helped propagate his reputation for showy self-promotion. He did much translation in the course of his life, chiefly from French and Spanish. See P. Alexander, *Roy Campbell* (1982).

CAMPBELL, Thomas (1777–1844) Son of a Glasgow merchant, educated at Glasgow University and closely associated with the founding of the University of London (now University College London) in the late 1820s. He published *The *Pleasures of Hope* in 1799, **Gertrude of Wyoming* in 1809, *Theodric, and Other Poems* in 1824, and *The Pilgrim of Glencoe, and Other Poems* in 1842. He was very popular in his own day, in large part for his war songs, 'The Battle of Hohenlinden', 'The Battle of the Baltic', and 'Ye Mariners of England'; and for his ballads, such as 'The Soldier's Dream', 'Lord Ullin's Daughter', and 'Lochiel's Warning'.

CAMPION, St Edmund (1540–81) He left his fellowship at St John's College, Oxford, in 1570, travelling to Ireland and Douai. He joined the Jesuits in 1573 and, after time in Rome and Eastern Europe, returned to England in 1580, was arrested in 1581, sent to the Tower, examined under torture, and executed. Beatified in 1886, he was canonized in 1970. Evelyn *Waugh published a life of him (1935).

CAMPION, Thomas (1567–1620) Poet, musician, and theorist, educated at Peterhouse, Cambridge, and Gray's Inn; he studied medicine in middle age, receiving an MD from the University of Caen in 1605. Five songs by him were appended to the unauthorized **Astrophel and Stella* in 1591; in 1595 he published his Latin *Poemata*. *A Booke of Ayres* (1601) was a collaboration with Philip Rosseter. Campion's *Observations in the Art of English Poesie* (1602) defended classical metres against 'the vulgar and unarteficiall custome of riming'. The treatise is illustrated with his own poems, such as 'Rose-cheekt *Lawra*, come'. Between about 1613 and 1617 Campion published four *Bookes of Ayres*, mostly settings of his own poems, and, with John Coprario, *Songs of Mourning* for Prince Henry (1613). In the early years of James I's reign he wrote a number of court masques. See *The Works of Thomas Campion*, ed. W. R. Davis (1967).

campus novel A novel set on a university or polytechnic campus; usually written by novelists who are also (temporarily or permanently) academics; notable examples include Kingsley *Amis's **Lucky Jim* (1954), David *Lodge's *Changing Places* (1975), Malcolm *Bradbury's **The History Man* (1975), and Howard *Jacobson's *Coming from Behind* (1983).

CAMUS, Albert (1913–60) French novelist, playwright, and essayist. He was born in Algeria, which provides the setting for many of his works. His first and most successful novel *L'Étranger* (1942: *The Outsider*), in which the young white Algerian narrator Meursault recounts his killing of an Arab, and his essay *Le Mythe de Sisyphe* (1942: *The Myth of Sisyphus*) established him as a philosopher of the 'absurd' nature of the human condition. While careful to distance himself from the *existentialism of Jean-Paul *Sartre, he continued to explore the human condition in fiction (*La Peste*, 1947: *The Plague*; *L'Exil et le royaume*, 1957: *Exile and the Kingdom*), plays (*Caligula*, 1945; *Les Justes*, 1949; *see also* Absurd, Theatre of the), and several adaptations for the stage, including one from William *Faulkner's *Requiem for a Nun* (1956). He was awarded the *Nobel Prize for Literature in 1957. See O. Todd, *Camus* (1997).

Canaan Ancient region in the Near East, the land flowing with milk and honey promised to the Jews in the Old Testament, reached by crossing the river Jordan. In Puritan and evangelical literature, ranging from John *Bunyan to gospel songs, it represents eternal life, and the language of Canaan is that spoken by the godly.
See Bible.

Candide A hugely successful philosophical tale by *Voltaire, published in 1759. It recounts the adventures of its innocent young hero, Candide, brought up in the home of Baron Thunder-ten-Tronckh in Westphalia, where he is much influenced by his tutor Pangloss, an incurable Optimist and a follower of

*Leibniz who believes that 'all is for the best in the best of all possible worlds'. Driven from home because of his love for the baron's daughter Cunégonde, Candide ends up on a journey which takes him from Europe to South America, including Eldorado, and back again. The grotesque misfortunes that befall all the characters provide witty and devastating satires of religion, politics, and philosophy. Candide is eventually re-united with Cunégonde: he has lost his wealth and she her beauty, but they marry, and settle down with Pangloss and their other travelling companions to cultivate their garden.

CANETTI, Elias (1905–94) Novelist and playwright, born in Bulgaria of a Spanish- and German-speaking Jewish family. He was educated largely in Zurich and Frankfurt, and gained a doctorate in chemistry at the University of Vienna. Fleeing Nazism, he emigrated to Paris in 1938 and London, where he finally settled, in 1939. His best-known work, a novel, was published as *Die Blendung* in 1935 and in English translation as *Auto da Fé* in 1946. Canetti's sociological study of crowd behaviour *Masse und Macht* (1960) appeared as *Crowds and Power* in 1962. He also published plays, essays, and three volumes of autobiography: *Die gerettete Zunge* (1977), published in English as *The Tongue Set Free* (1979); *Die Fackel im Ohr* (1980) as *The Torch in my Ear* (1989); and *Das Augenspiel* (1985) as *The Play of the Eyes* (1990). For a time he was a close friend of Iris *Murdoch, with whom he had an affair. He was awarded the *Nobel Prize for Literature in 1981.

CANNING, George (1770–1827) Tory statesman and author, educated at Eton College and Christ Church, Oxford. He was appointed foreign secretary in 1822 and prime minister in 1827. Apart from his political speeches (published 1828), he is remembered in a literary connection as a founder of and contributor of brilliant parody and satire to the **Anti-Jacobin*, the chief object of which was to ridicule the Whigs and radicals of the 1790s. He was also a frequent and influential contributor to the **Quarterly Review*. His *Poems* were published in 1823.

canon A body of approved works, comprising either (i) writings genuinely considered to be those of a given author; or (ii) writings considered to represent the best standards of a given literary tradition.

'Canon's Yeoman's Tale, The' *See* CANTERBURY TALES, 22.

Canterbury Tales, The Geoffrey *Chaucer's most celebrated but unfinished work, extending to 17,000 lines in prose and verse of various metres (though the predominant form is the rhyming couplet). The General Prologue describes the meeting of 29 pilgrims in the Tabard Inn in Southwark. Detailed pen-pictures are given of 21 of them, vividly described but perhaps corresponding to traditional lists of the orders of society, clerical and lay (see J. Mann, *Chaucer and Medieval Estates Satire*, 1973). The host (*see* BAILLY, HARRY) proposes that the pilgrims should shorten the road by telling four stories each, two on the way to Canterbury and two on the way back; he will accompany them and award a free supper on their return to the teller of the best story. The work is incomplete; only 23 pilgrims tell stories, and there are only 24 stories told altogether ('Chaucer', as pilgrim, tells two). In the scheme the stories are linked by narrative exchanges between the pilgrims and by prologues and epilogues to the tales; but this aspect of the work is also incomplete. The final ordering of the stories is uncertain; the evidence of the manuscripts and of geographical references is conflicting, as is the scholarly interpretation of that evidence. The order that follows is that of the Ellesmere Manuscript, followed in the best complete edition of Chaucer, *The Riverside Chaucer* (ed. L. D. Benson *et al.*, 2008).

(1) 'The Knight's Tale', a shortened version of the *Teseida* of *Boccaccio, the story of the love of Palamon and Arcite (told again in Shakespeare's *The *Two Noble Kinsmen*), prisoners of Theseus, king of Athens, for Emelye, sister of Hippolyta, queen of the Amazons, whom Theseus has married. The rivals compete for her in a tournament. Palamon is defeated, but Arcite, the favourite of Mars, at the moment of his triumph is thrown and injured by his horse through the intervention of Venus and Saturn, and dies. Palamon and Emelye, after prolonged mourning for Arcite, are united.

(2) 'The Miller's Tale', a ribald story of the deception, first of a husband (a carpenter) through the prediction of a second flood, and secondly of a lover who expects to kiss the lady's lips but kisses instead her 'nether ye [*eye*]'. He avenges himself on her lover for this humiliation with a red-hot ploughshare. The Tale has been said to be a parody of *courtly love.

(3) 'The Reeve's Tale' is a *fabliau about two clerks who are robbed by a miller of some of the meal which they take to his mill to be ground, and who take their vengeance by sleeping with the miller's wife and daughter. It is an obvious rejoinder to the miller's tale of the duping of a carpenter (the reeve, manager of an estate, had once been a carpenter).

(4) 'The Cook's Tale' of Perkyn Revelour only extends to 58 lines before it breaks off. This is another ribald fabliau which ends with the introduction of a prostitute. *The Tale of *Gamelyn*, not by Chaucer, is introduced for the cook in some manuscripts.

(5) 'The Man of Law's Tale' is the story of Custance, daughter of a Christian emperor of Rome, who marries the sultan of Syria on condition that he become a Christian and who is cast adrift in a boat because of the machinations of the sultan's jealous mother. It is a frequently told medieval story, paralleled by the romance **Emaré* and by John *Gower's Constance story in *Confessio Amantis*, II. 587 ff. Chaucer's is based on a passage in the early 14th-century Anglo-Norman Chronicle by Nicholas *Trivet.

(6) 'The Wife of Bath's Tale' is preceded by an 856-line prologue in which the Wife condemns celibacy by describing her life with her five late husbands, in the course of which Chaucer draws widely on the medieval antifeminist tradition, especially on Jean de Meun's *La Vielle* (the Duenna) in the **Roman de la Rose*. The Tale that follows is the story of 'the loathly lady' (paralleled by Gower's 'Tale of Florent' in *Confessio Amantis*, I. 1396ff., and by the romance *Weddynge of Sir Gawen and Dame Ragnell*, edited in D. B. Sands, *Middle English Verse Romances*, 323–47) in which a knight is asked to answer the question, 'what do women most desire?' The correct answer, 'sovereignty', is given to him by a hideous old witch on condition that he marry her; when he does she is restored to youth and beauty.

(7) 'The Friar's Tale' tells how a summoner (an official in an ecclesiastical court) meets the devil dressed as a yeoman and they agree to share out what they are given. They come upon a carter who curses his horse, commending it to the devil; the summoner asks the devil why he does not take the horse thus committed to him and the devil replies that it is because the commendation does not come from the heart. Later they visit an old woman from whom the summoner attempts to extort twelve pence, whereupon she commends *him* to the devil. The devil carries him off to hell because her curse was from the heart. The story is widely attested in popular tradition. It is clear that the friar tells it to enrage the pilgrim summoner, who interrupts the narrative and rejoins with a scurrilous and discreditable story about a friar.

(8) 'The Summoner's Tale' parodies contemporary theological disputes, telling of a greedy friar who undertakes to divide a deathbed legacy amongst his community; he receives a fart and has to devise an ingenious stratagem to divide it with perfect justice.

(9) 'The Clerk's Tale', which the poet tells us he took from *Petrarch, was translated into Latin by the latter from the Italian version of Boccaccio in *The *Decameron* (Day 10, Tale 10). Boccaccio was the first writer (in 1353) to take the story from popular currency, and there are several versions of the story in Italian, Latin, and French (Chaucer's version is rather more dependent on a French prose version than on Petrarch's Latin). The story tells of patient Griselda and her trials by her husband, the Marquis Walter. Chaucer's version has more hints of criticism of the relentless husband than any of his predecessors (except Boccaccio, whose narrator frowns on Gualtieri's 'strange desire' to try his wife's obedience).

(10) 'The Merchant's Tale', in which the merchant, prompted by the tale of Griselda's extreme obedience, tells his 'Tale' of January and May, the old husband with his young wife, and the problems with obedient fidelity involved in this relationship. January ignores the good advice of Justinus in favour of the time-serving opinion of Placebo and marries May. When he goes blind, she makes love to her suitor Damyan in a pear tree. Pluto mischievously restores January's sight at this point, but his consort, Proserpine, inspires May to explain that the restoration of his sight was brought about by her activities in the pear tree and that this had been their purpose. Critics have argued about the relative proportions of mordancy and humour in the tale; see E. Talbot Donaldson in *Speaking of Chaucer* (1970). There are parallels to the various sections of the story in French, Latin, Italian, and German.

(11) 'The Squire's Tale', of Cambuscan, king of Tartary, to whom on his birthday an envoy from the king of Arabia brings magic gifts, including a ring for the king's daughter Canacee, which enables her to understand the language of birds. A female falcon tells Canacee the story of her own desertion by a tercelet (a male hawk). The tale is incomplete but it seems likely that Chaucer meant to finish it, judging from the fact that there is no suggestion that it is unfinished in the laudatory words of the franklin that follow it. Edmund *Spenser would later use this tale as his point of departure in Book IV of *The *Faerie Queene*.

(12) 'The Franklin's Tale', of Dorigen, wife of Arveragus, who in her husband's absence attempts to escape the attentions of her suitor, the squire Aurelius, by making her consent depend upon an impossible condition, that all the rocks on the coast of Brittany be removed. When this condition is realized by magic, the suitor, from a generous remorse, releases her from her promise. Chaucer states that the tale is taken from a *'Breton Lay', but if this is true, the original is lost. There are several parallels in medieval literature, of which the closest is Boccaccio's *Il filocolo*, Question 4. See N. R. Havely, *Chaucer's Boccaccio* (1980).

(13) 'The Physician's Tale' tells of Virginia who, at her own request, is killed by her father to escape the designs of the corrupt judge Apius. The original source is *Livy's *History*, and this is what Chaucer cites, though his version seems to rely principally on the *Roman de la Rose*, ll. 5589–658, by Jean de Meun.

(14) 'The Pardoner's Tale' (a pardoner is a licensed seller of papal indulgences, promising remission of punishment for sins) follows a prologue in which he declares his own covetousness, and takes covetousness as its theme, relating it to other sins: drunkenness, gluttony, gambling, and swearing. Three rioters set out to find Death, who has killed their companion; a mysterious old man tells them they will find him under a particular tree, but when they get there they find instead a heap of gold. By aiming to cheat each other in possessing the gold they kill each other. The character of the pardoner in the prologue here is related to Faus-Semblant (False-Seeming) in Jean de Meun's part of the *Roman de la Rose*, ll. 11065–972. There are many analogues for the tale, in Latin, Italian, and German.

(15) 'The Shipman's Tale.' There is a similar story in *The Decameron* (Day 8, Tale 1). The wife of a miserly merchant asks the loan of a hundred francs from a priest to buy finery. The priest borrows the sum from the merchant and hands it to the wife, and the wife grants him her favours. On the merchant's return from a journey the

priest tells him that he has repaid the sum to the wife, who cannot deny receiving it.

(16) 'The Prioress's Tale' tells of the murder of a child by Jews because he sings a Marian hymn while passing through their quarter and of the discovery of his body because of its continued singing of the hymn after death. There are many parallels for the story.

(17) 'Chaucer's Tale of Sir Thopas' is a witty and elegant parody of the contemporary romance, both in its subject and in the insubstantiality of its *tail-rhyme form. Its targets are no doubt general; but it can perhaps be taken to have special reference to the heroes it catalogues (VII. 898–900): Horn Child, the legend of Ypotys, *Bevis of Hampton, *Guy of Warwick, the unidentified Pleyndamour, and **Libeaus Desconus*. It is closest, it has been argued, to the last of these.

(18) When the Host interrupts the tale of Sir Thopas, Chaucer moves to the opposite extreme with a heavy prose homily, 'The Tale of Melibeus'. This story of the impetuous Melibeus and his wise wife Prudence dates from Italy in the 1240s, when the story was written in Latin prose for his third son by Albertano of Brescia. Chaucer's immediate source was the 1336 version in French prose by Renaud de Louens.

(19) 'The Monk's Tale' is composed of a number of tragedies of persons fallen from high estate, taken from different authors and arranged on the model of Boccaccio's *De Casibus Virorum Illustrium*. The tale is in eight-line stanzas.

(20) 'The Nun's Priest's Tale' is related to the French cycle of Renart (*see* REYNARD THE FOX), telling of a fox that beguiled a cock by praising his father's singing and was in turn beguiled into losing him by pausing to boast at his victory. The mock-heroic story is full of rhetoric and exempla, and it is one of the most admired of the Tales. The fable is familiar, but the parallels to Chaucer's version are not very close. The famous ironic ending invites the reader to 'take the morality' of the Tale, in spite of its apparent lightness of substance, on the grounds that St Paul says that everything is written in order to teach us something.

(21) 'The Second Nun's Tale', in *rhyme-royal, is perhaps translated from the life of St Cecilia in *The *Golden Legend* of Jacobus de Voragine. It describes the miracles and martyrdom of the noble Roman maiden Cecilia and her husband Valerian.

(22) 'The Canon's Yeoman's Tale' is told by a character who joins the pilgrims at this late stage with his master, the dubious canon, whose alchemical skills the yeoman praises. The first 200 lines of the tale tell of the Alchemist's arcane practice and its futility, before proceeding to the tale proper, which tells of how an alchemical canon (who is *not* his master, he protests) tricks a priest out of £40 by pretending to teach him the art of making precious metals. The dishonesty of the alchemists was much discussed and condemned in the 14th century; there is a close analogue to Chaucer's story in one of the *Novelle* of Giovanni Sercambi.

(23) 'The Manciple's Tale' is the fable of the tell-tale crow, told by many authors from *Ovid in *Metamorphoses* (2. 531–62) onwards. Phebus (Phoebus) has a crow which is white and can speak. It reveals to Phebus the infidelity of his wife (nameless in Chaucer, but Coronis in Ovid and later writers) and Phebus kills her in a rage. Then, in remorse, he plucks out the crow's white feathers, deprives it of speech, and throws it 'unto the devel', which is why crows are now black. A very similar version of the story is told in Gower's *Confessio Amantis* (III. 768–835), and there are other examples by Guillaume de *Machaut and in the **Ovide moralisé* (*c.*1324). As well as these, there is a story from *The *Seven Sages of Rome* which does not name Phebus and which exchanges the fates of wife and bird, as well as some sententious parallels from *Boethius and Jean de Meun.

(24) 'The Parson's Tale' which concludes the work (and was no doubt meant to, despite the incompleteness of the *Tales*) is a long prose treatise, ostensibly on Penitence but dealing at most length with the *seven deadly sins. The two principal sources are Raymund de Pennaforte's *Summa* (1220s) for the sections on Penitence, and Guilielmus Peraldus' *Summa Vitiorum* (*c.*1250s) for the seven deadly sins. Most manuscripts have 'The Parson's Tale' leading straight into the closing 'Retracciouns' in which Chaucer, or his narrator (the voice is uncertain), takes leave of his book. He asks forgiveness of God for his 'translacions and enditynges of worldly vanities', including 'The Tales of Caunterbury, thilke that sownen into [i.e. tend towards] synne'. But this rhetorical conclusion need not be read as a revocation of his work by the poet; following St *Augustine's *Retractationes*, many medieval works end by distancing the writer from the non-spiritual elements in his work: the Author's Epilogue in *The Decameron* and Chaucer's *Troilus* are other familiar examples. See H. Cooper, *The Canterbury Tales* (1989).

canto A subdivision of a long narrative or epic poem, employed in the works of Edmund *Spenser (the first to apply the term in English), Lord *Byron, Ezra *Pound, and many others.

Canu Llywarch Hen (The Song of Old Llywarch) A cycle of 9th- or 10th-century Welsh poems in which Llywarch laments the indignities of age and urges his 24 sons to seek glory in his name. All 24 die in the attempt. The monologue and dialogue poems are in the early three-line variant of the *englyn* stanza (a four-line strict *metre form used for single-stanza poems in later Welsh tradition). They may originally have had their place in a saga with connecting prose narrative.

Canute (Cnutr) A Dane who was king of England 1016–35. The legend of his failing to repel the sea is told by Holinshed,

VII. xiii, after *Henry of Huntingdon (who may have invented it) and Geffrei *Gaimar.

Canute, The Song of A famous early English poetic ballad fragment allegedly composed and sung by the king as he rowed past Ely, and recorded by a monk in the *Chronicles of Ely* in 1166.

Can You Forgive Her? A novel by Anthony *Trollope, published 1864–5, the first in the *Palliser series. Alice Vavasor, spirited and independent, is engaged to the 'paragon' John Grey, but irrationally rejects him in favour of her disreputable cousin George Vavasor. She extricates George from his financial and personal difficulties, and works to further his political ambitions. Nevertheless, George is ruined, and sets off for America, pausing only to make an attempt on the life of John Grey. Grey renews his courtship of Alice, who accepts him.

These difficulties are described alongside an account of the early married life of Lady Glencora Palliser, who, despite the virtues of her aristocratic husband Plantagenet, still loves the worthless Burgo Fitzgerald. She is tempted to elope with him, but is saved by the timely arrival of her husband, who takes her out of harm's way by embarking on a lengthy foreign tour, at the expense of his own political plans. His sacrifice results in an uneasy marital reconciliation.

The novel combines Trollope's interests in the dynamics of politics and courtship, subtly exploring the divided motives of characters who struggle to reconcile personal inclination and ambition with the demands of duty, honour, and good sense.

ČAPEK, Karel (1890–1938) Czech novelist and dramatist, the son of a doctor; educated at the universities of Paris, Berlin, and Prague. He and his brother Josef Čapek (1887–1945) began to write plays together *c.*1910. The best known of their joint works is *The Insect Play* (1921), a satire on human society and totalitarianism. Čapek's best-known independent work was *R.U.R.* ('Rossum's Universal Robots') (1920, first English performance 1923). The concept of the robot (Czech 'robota', meaning drudgery) opened up a flexible vein of *science fiction, and added a word to the English language. In Čapek's play the robots, having acquired human emotions, rebel against their servile status and destroy their masters. Other plays include *The Makropulos Affair* (1923), a play about longevity with some similarity to George Bernard *Shaw's *Back to Methuselah* (which Čapek had not at the time read) in which he arrives at conclusions in his own view diametrically opposed to Shaw's. Čapek also wrote *scientific romances, such as *The Manufacture of the Absolute* (1923) and *War with the Newts* (1936); a trilogy of more realistic novels, *Hordubal*, *The Meteor*, and *An Ordinary Life* (1933–4); and travel books and essays, including *Letters from England* (1923).

CAPELL, Edward (1713–81) Shakespearian commentator. His edition of Shakespeare in ten volumes (1768) was the first to be based on complete and careful collations of all the old copies, and his arrangement of the lines has been influential. His *Commentary, Notes and Various Readings to Shakespeare*, begun in 1774, was published in three volumes in 1783. Capell was responsible for the first full scholarly discussion of Shakespeare's sources, and for the first attempt to establish the relationship between the *folios and quartos; he supported the authenticity of the three parts of **Henry VI*, **Titus Andronicus*, **Love's Labour's Lost*, and *The *Taming of the Shrew*. He was attacked by *Malone and *Steevens, but his sound judgement makes his edition of lasting value.

CAPGRAVE, John (1393–1464) An Augustinian friar who spent most of his life in the friary at King's Lynn. He wrote a number of theological and historical works in Latin. In English he wrote lives of St Gilbert of Sempringham and St Catherine of Alexandria, and a small body of poetry. His most significant English work is his *Chronicle* of English history up to 1417, which is marked by simplicity and lucidity of style. See *John Capgrave's Abbreviation of Chronicles*, ed. P. J. Lucas (EETS, 1983).

CAPOTE, Truman (1924–84) American author, born in New Orleans, whose work ranges from the light-hearted story of playgirl Holly Golightly in *Breakfast at Tiffany's* (1958) to the grim investigation *In Cold Blood* (1966), a 'non-fiction novel' or work of *faction, in which Capote recreated the brutal multiple murder of a whole Kansas family by two ex-convicts, and traces the lives of the murderers to the moment of their execution. His unfinished novel *Answered Prayers* was published in 1985 and his previously lost first novel *Summer Crossing* in 2005.

CARACTACUS (*fl.* AD 50–1) Properly Caratacus, chief leader of the resistance to the Roman invasion of Britain in 43. For a period he led the Silures in south Wales. He was defeated by the Romans and then betrayed by Cartimandua, queen of the Brigantes. He was taken a prisoner to Rome in 51, where according to *Tacitus his noble spirit so pleased the emperor Claudius that he freed him. He figures in John *Fletcher's **Bonduca* and William *Mason's *Caractacus*, and provides the theme of a cantata by *Elgar.

Carcanet Press A small press established in South Hinksey, Oxford, in 1969 by poet, editor, and novelist Michael Schmidt (1947–): it moved to Manchester in 1971. It has published a wide and important range of new poetry in English and translation, as well as reviving neglected classics, and since 1981 has also published works of fiction.

CARD, Orson Scott (1951–) American author, born Richland, Washington; he uses his Mormon heritage in the 'Alvin Maker' and 'Homecoming' *science fiction and *fantasy novels. *Ender's Game* (1985) begins his best-known series: the hero, brought up a child soldier to fight an alien race, questions his victory. With its sequel *Speaker for the Dead* (1986), it won the *Hugo award. *Pastwatch* (1996), presents an *alternate history of the discovery of America in which the mistakes of the past are redeemed by time-travellers.

Cardenio A lost play, twice recorded as having been acted by the King's Men at court in 1613, and ascribed to Shakespeare and John *Fletcher in a bookseller's list of 1653. *Theobald in his successful tragicomedy *Double Falsehood* (1728) claimed to have 'revised and adapted' a play 'written originally by W. Shakespeare'. He did not include it in his edition of Shakespeare, which however also omitted other plays in which he believed Shakespeare to have had a hand. In 1770 a newspaper reported that 'the original manuscript' was 'treasured up in the Museum of Covent Garden playhouse'; the theatre, including its library, was destroyed by fire in 1808. Presumably Shakespeare's play, like Theobald's, was based on the story of Cardenio and Lucinda in *Don Quixote* (Pt 1, chs 24–8); Cardenio is the Ragged Knight, who, driven mad by the loss of his loved Lucinda, haunts the Sierra Morena, and is eventually reunited with her. Some of the motifs of Theobald's play recall Shakespeare's late plays, though the dialogue seems un-Shakespearian.

CARDINAL, Marie (1929–2001) French novelist, born in Algeria. Author of a large number of best-selling texts, including *Au pays de mes racines* (1980: *In the Country of my Roots*), in which she explores her feelings about her native Algeria, she is best known for her widely translated *Les Mots pour le dire* (1975: *The Words to Say It*), a remarkable and ground-breaking feminist autobiographical novel describing her childhood in Algeria, her difficult relationship with her mother, and the successful psychoanalysis that enabled her to become a writer.

Cardinal, The A tragedy by James *Shirley, acted 1641, printed 1652. This was the first play Shirley wrote for the King's Men, and both he and his contemporaries thought it his best. It is strongly reminiscent of *Jacobean tragedy, featuring a diabolical cardinal, masquers who turn out to be murderers, poison, and attempted rape.

CARDUCCI, Giosuè (1835–1907) Italian poet and classicist, winner of the *Nobel Prize (1906). His poetry celebrates Italy's classical heritage at the expense of Romanticism and the church. His early hymn to Satan ('A Satana', 1863) is republican in spirit, but he was to become poet laureate in middle age. Some of his best poems are in *Rime nuove* (1887: *New Rhymes*); *Odi barbare* (1877–93: *Barbarian Odes*), based on classical quantitative metre, and *Rime e ritmi* (1899: *Rhymes and Rhythms*).

Careless Husband, The A comedy by Colley *Cibber (1704). Sir Charles Easy neglects his wife and carries on an intrigue with her maid Edging and with Lady Graveairs. Discovering that his wife is aware of his infidelities, he is moved to reconciliation by her tolerance and virtue. The coquette Lady Betty Modish is manoeuvred into accepting the honourable Lord Morelove (contrasted with the boastful Lord Foppington, played by Cibber himself) by a plot to excite her jealousy. In his dedication, Cibber claims that he has set out to avoid coarseness and to imitate the conversation of the polite world.

Caretaker, The A play by Harold *Pinter, performed and published in 1960. One of Pinter's characteristically enigmatic dramas, it is built on the interaction of three characters, the tramp Davies and the brothers Aston and Mick. Aston has rescued Davies from a brawl and brought him back to a junk-filled room, in which he offers Davies a bed and, eventually, an ill-defined post as caretaker. The characters reveal themselves in inconsequential dialogue and obsessional monologue. Davies is worried about his papers, the blacks, gas leaks, and getting to Sidcup; Aston reveals that he has suffered headaches ever since undergoing electric shock treatment for his 'complaint'; Mick, the youngest, is alternately bully, cajoler, and materialist visionary, with dreams of transforming the room into a fashionable penthouse. In the end both brothers turn on Davies and evict him. The dialogue is at once naturalistic and surreal; the litany of London place names (Finsbury Park, Shepherd's Bush, Putney) and of decorator's jargon (charcoal-grey worktops, teak veneer) serves to highlight the no man's land in which the characters in fact meet.

CAREW, Thomas [pron. Carey] (1594/5–1640) Poet, son of a master in chancery. He was educated at Oxford University and became secretary to the diplomat Sir Dudley Carleton (1574–1632) at Venice and subsequently at The Hague. He won the favour of Charles I, was appointed to an office at court, and received an estate from him. His elegy for John *Donne was published with Donne's poems in 1633, his masque *Coelum Britannicum* (with settings by Inigo *Jones) was performed before the king in 1634, and his *Poems* appeared in 1640. He was a close friend of Sir John *Suckling and one of the best known of the *Cavalier poets; his works include many graceful, witty, and often cynical songs and lyrics, and several longer poems, including the erotic 'A Rapture', and 'To Saxham', a country-house poem in the genre of Ben *Jonson's 'To Penshurst', by whom, with Donne, he was much influenced. The standard edition of his work is by R. Dunlap, 1949.

CAREY, Peter (1943–) Australian novelist, born at Bacchus Marsh, Victoria, educated at Geelong Grammar School. After working for advertising agencies in Melbourne and London, Carey moved to Sydney in 1974 and New York in 1989; he now holds dual American and Australian citizenship. 'She Wakes' (1967) was Carey's first published short story, two earlier novels remaining unpublished. His critical reputation was established with two volumes of short stories, *The Fat Man in History* (1974) and *War Crimes* (1979), and the novel *Bliss* (1981), which won the Miles Franklin Prize (Australia's most prestigious award for a work of literature) and was made into a feature film (1985). Throughout his long career Carey has shown a fascination with the relationship between storytelling and truth, often indicated in titles like *30 Days in Sydney: A Wildly Distorted Account* (2001). Although much of his writing is grounded in Australian idiom and responds to that country's history, he has successfully 'translated' these for an international audience, witnessed by his *Booker Prize-winning novels *Oscar and Lucinda* (1988, film 1997) and *True History of the Kelly Gang* (2001). These are prismatic narratives which speak of colonial history to general readers and, perhaps in a different way, to critics fascinated by Carey's games with authenticity and authority. Other major Carey novels include *Illywhacker* (1985), featuring 139-year-old narrator Herbert Badgery; *Jack Maggs* (1997), winner of the Commonwealth Writers' Prize, which reconfigures Charles *Dickens's **Great Expectations* from the point of view of the convict Magwitch, and *Theft: A Love Story* (2006), shortlisted for several major awards. Carey's 2004 novel *My Life as a Fake* plays with themes and characters of the Ern Malley hoax, in which poets James McAuley and Harold Stewart submitted pseudo-modernist poems to the journal *Angry Penguins* under the name of 'deceased garage mechanic' 'Ern Malley'. The poems were published with great fanfare but the fallout from the exposure of the hoax included the trial of journal editor Max Harris for obscenity, and the debilitation of technically experimental writing in Australia. This novel perhaps best exemplifies Carey's key themes: that the truths of great literature are at once profound and fraudulent, but writers, publishers, and readers alike are swept up in a search for those truths; these searches enact our most compelling and extravagant desires. See Bruce Woodcock, *Peter Carey* (2003); Andreas Gaile (ed.), *Fabulating Beauty: Perspectives on the Fiction of Peter Carey* (2005).

CARLE, Eric (1929–) Prolific American author/illustrator, born Syracuse, New York, trained in Stuttgart, Germany. Carle uses collage, hand-painted papers, and die-cut pages as in *The Very Hungry Caterpillar* (1969), in which the Caterpillar 'eats' through pictures of food. The Eric Carle Museum of Picture Book Art opened in Amherst, Massachusetts in 2002.

CARLETON, William (1794–1869) Novelist and story writer, born into an impoverished Irish-speaking Roman Catholic family in Tyrone. *Traits and Stories of the Irish Peasantry* (1830–3) appeared shortly after his conversion to Protestantism. Like much of Carleton's work, *Traits* mixes didactic, naturalistic, *Gothic, and melodramatic elements. *Fardorougha, the Miser* (1839) and *The Black Prophet* (1847), a bleak story of the potato famine, are perhaps the best known of his novels. The violently contradictory responses of Carleton's writing to the social and political problems of 19th-century Ireland have elicited much attention from critics.

CARLISLE, Richard (1790–1843) Radical publisher and freethinker. A Tory in his youth, who burnt Tom Paine in effigy, he became a radical publisher who spent six years in prison from 1819 for selling Paine's deistical *The *Age of Reason*. In prison he founded his most notable journal, *The Republican*.

CARLYLE, Alexander (1722–1805) Nicknamed 'Jupiter' because of his stature. He was educated at the universities of Edinburgh, Glasgow, and Leiden. A minister at Inveresk until his death, and a leader of the Scottish 'Broad Church' party, he wrote an interesting autobiography (printed 1860) referring to notable figures of the *Scottish Enlightenment.

CARLYLE, Jane Baillie Welsh (1801–66) Letter writer, born in Haddington, East Lothian, the daughter of a doctor; educated privately and later at Miss Hall's school, Edinburgh. She showed considerable powers both of intellect and of character while still at school, and in 1821 was introduced by her former tutor Edward Irving to Thomas *Carlyle. Together and by correspondence she and Carlyle studied German literature, he effectively taking on the role of tutor, then of lover; they were married in 1826. Though much of her energy during her married life was devoted to domestic chores and to the humouring and protection of a temperamental husband, she is remembered as one of the best letter writers in the English language, witty, caustic, and observant, and as a literary hostess who impressed all who met her. Her vast circle of friends, acquaintances, and correspondents included the Italian patriot Giuseppe Mazzini (1805–72), Robert *Browning, Alfred *Tennyson, John *Forster, and Geraldine *Jewsbury (who spent much time with Jane Carlyle during her husband's years of obsession with Lady Ashburton), but many of her best letters were written to her relatives in Edinburgh and Liverpool and, most notably, to Thomas himself, with whom she corresponded copiously during their temporary separations. Her kindness and generosity are as remarkable as her wit; one of her most famous letters, about the loneliness of her life at Craigenputtock, was written to cheer a dissatisfied schoolmistress in Carlisle who aspired to be a writer (Letter to Mary Smith, Jan. 1857). Her subjects include personalities, travels, books, and, notably, her servants; she commented, 'I think, talk, and write about my servants as much as Geraldine [Jewsbury] does about her lovers.' See Rosemary Ashton, *Thomas and Jane Carlyle: Portrait of a Marriage* (2002); *Jane Carlyle: Newly Selected Letters*, ed. K. J. Fielding and D. Sorenson (2003).

CARLYLE, Thomas (1795–1881) Historian, biographer, and essayist, born at Ecclefechan, in Dumfriesshire, the son of a stonemason; his parents were serious, industrious, and devout, and belonged to a Dissenting branch of the Presbyterian Church. Carlyle, intended by them and by himself for the ministry, was educated at Annan Academy and at the University of Edinburgh, where, affected by the legacy of the *Scottish Enlightenment, he abandoned this resolve; he taught for a while at Annan and Kirkcaldy and then took to literary work, tutoring and reviewing. He studied German literature; his life of *Schiller appeared in the **London Magazine* in 1823–4 and was separately published in 1825; his translations of *Goethe's *Wilhelm Meister's Apprenticeship* and *Wilhelm Meister's Travels* appeared in 1824 and 1827 respectively, the latter being included in his anthology of selections from German authors,

German Romance (4 vols, 1827). In 1826 he married Jane Welsh (see above) and after two years in Edinburgh they moved for financial reasons to her farm at Craigenputtock, an isolated dwelling on the lonely moors of Nithsdale. 'Signs of the Times', an attack on *Utilitarianism, appeared in 1829 in the **Edinburgh Review*; **Sartor Resartus* followed in **Fraser's Magazine* in 1833–4, a highly idiosyncratic and personal work which showed his great debt to German philosophy and literature. In 1834 the Carlyles moved to Cheyne Row, Chelsea, where he worked on his *History of the *French Revolution*, which appeared in 1837; the manuscript of the first volume was accidentally used to light a fire while on loan to John Stuart *Mill, but with characteristic perseverance Carlyle rewrote it. This work, somewhat to his own surprise, established Carlyle's reputation, and he from this time onward strengthened the position that made him known as 'the Sage of Chelsea'. His series of lectures, *On *Heroes, Hero-Worship and the Heroic in History*, delivered in 1840 and published in 1841, attracted glittering and fashionable audiences, and taught him to distrust (and indeed to abandon) his own blend of 'prophecy and play-acting'; it also brought him and his wife many new and influential friends. In *Chartism* (1839) and *Past and Present* (1843) Carlyle applied himself to what he called 'the Condition-of-England question', attacking both laissez-faire and the dangers of revolution it encouraged, castigating an economic and political climate where Cash Payment had become 'the sole nexus between man and man', and manifesting with more passion than consistency a sympathy with the industrial poor which heralded the new novels of social consciousness of the 1840s (see Elizabeth *Gaskell and Benjamin *Disraeli). His evocation in *Past and Present* of medieval conditions at the time of Abbot Samson provided a new perspective on machinery and craftsmanship that was pursued by John *Ruskin and William *Morris, but Carlyle, unlike some of his followers, turned increasingly away from democracy towards the kind of feudalism which he saw expressed in the rule of the 'Strong Just Man'. His 'Occasional Discourse on the Nigger Question' (1849) and *Latter-Day Pamphlets* (1850) express his anti-democratic views in an exaggerated form. His admiration for *Cromwell was expressed in his edition of *Oliver Cromwell's Letters and Speeches* (2 vols, 1845), and for *Frederick the Great in a lengthy biography, some fourteen years in preparation, which appeared in 1858–65, 6 vols. A more modest and, to 20th-century tastes, more readable work, a life of his friend John *Sterling (with some remarkable reminiscences of S. T. *Coleridge), appeared in 1851.

Jane Carlyle died in 1866, a blow which he said 'shattered my whole existence into immeasurable ruin', and he thereafter wrote little of importance. He gave her papers and letters in 1871, with ambiguous instructions, to his friend and disciple J. A. *Froude, who published them after Carlyle's death, in 1883; Froude also published Carlyle's *Reminiscences* (1881) and a four-volume biography (1882–4). These posthumous publications caused much controversy, largely by breaking the conventions of Victorian *biography (against which Carlyle had himself fulminated) to suggest marital discord and sexual inadequacy on Carlyle's part.

Carlyle's influence as social prophet and critic, and his prestige as historian, were enormous during his lifetime. George *Eliot in the *Leader* (1855) wrote, 'there is hardly a superior or active mind of this generation that has not been modified by Carlyle's writings', and he was later described by W. B. *Yeats in his *Autobiography* as 'the chief inspirer of self-educated men in the 'eighties and early 'nineties'. In the 20th century his reputation waned, partly because his trust in authority and admiration of strong leaders were interpreted as foreshadowings of Fascism. His highly individualistic prose, which had always presented difficulties, became more obscure with the lapse of time; his violent exclamatory rhetoric, his italics and Teutonic coinages, and his eccentric archaisms and strange punctuation were already known by the late 1850s as 'Carlylese'; Harriet *Martineau described him as 'the greatest mannerist of the age', and William *Aytoun ridiculed him, along with the *Spasmodics, for 'dislocating language'. But many of his coinages have become accepted as part of the language, and his work continues to attract scholars and biographers. The major Duke-Edinburgh collected edition of his letters (1970–), with Ian Campbell, Aileen Christianson, and David Sorensen acting as senior editors, proceeds; see also Fred Kaplan, *Thomas Carlyle: A Biography* (1993).

Carmarthen *See* BLACK BOOK OF CARMARTHEN.

CARNELL, E. J. (Edward John) (1912–72) Born in London; editor and literary agent highly influential in British *science fiction. His early years were involved in science fiction fandom, and he became editor of a *fanzine, *Novae Terrae*, which he renamed **New Worlds*. In 1946 it became a professional magazine, the most important British science fiction magazine of the next two decades. Carnell encouraged numerous writers, including Brian *Aldiss, J. G. *Ballard, and Michael *Moorcock, who would become prominent in science fiction's *New Wave. He left *New Worlds* and its stablemate *Science Fantasy* in 1964 to concentrate on the *New Writings in sf* anthologies.

carnivalesque A term coined by the Russian critic Mikhail *Bakhtin to describe various manifestations of popular humour and cultural resistance to the restraints of official hierarchies. The institution of carnival itself provides a model for understanding some of the more playful effects of literature, principally in the novel and drama. According to this view, some kinds of literary *comedy are rooted in folk traditions of mockery directed at the church and other authorities.

carol Originally a ring-dance used in celebrations; thence a song, normally in rhymed stanzas with a repeated chorus. It had acquired religious associations, especially with Christmas festivities, by about 1500. The first known collection of *Christmasse Carolles*, now mostly lost but including the Boar's Head Carol, was printed by Wynkyn de *Worde in 1521.

CARPENTER, Edward (1844–1929) Socialist, poet, and anthologist, educated at Cambridge, where he became a fellow of Trinity Hall and worked with F. D. *Maurice. In 1874 he abandoned his fellowship and orders and moved north, working for some years as University Extension lecturer before settling at Millthorpe, near Chesterfield, where he pursued, by precept and example, his own version of socialism and communal fellowship. In this, he took inspiration from *Thoreau, John *Ruskin, and William *Morris. He wrote and lectured in support of varied progressive causes (sexual reform, women's rights, clean air, anti-vivisection, industrial reorganization). His lifestyle and private middle-class revolt (expressed by sandals, vegetarianism, overt homosexuality, praise of manual labour and the working man) became an important symbol of liberation for many, including E. M. *Forster. His long poem *Towards Democracy* (published in four parts, 1883–1902) expressed, among his many publications, his millenarian sense of the cosmic consciousness and 'spiritual democracy', and of the march of humanity towards 'freedom and joy'; both manner and content were much inspired by Walt *Whitman and the **Bhagavad-gītā*. His autobiography, *My Days and Dreams*, was published in 1916. See C. Tsuzuki, *Edward Carpenter, Prophet of Human Fellowship* (1980); S. Rowbotham, *Edward Carpenter: A Life of Liberty and Love* (2008).

CARR, J. L. (James Joseph Lloyd) (1912–94) Novelist, children's writer, and independent publisher, born and educated in Yorkshire, and at Dudley Training College. His works include *A Season in Sinji* (1968, a cricket story); *The Harpole Report* (1972); *How Steeple Sinderby Won the FA Cup* (1975); and *The Green Children of the Woods* (1976). *A Month in the Country* (1980; successfully filmed in 1987, with a screenplay by Simon *Gray) is a short novel set in the summer of 1920: the narrator Birkin, a war survivor, is engaged in restoring a wall painting in the village church at Oxgodby, where he meets another survivor who is camping out in the next meadow while seeking to discover a 14th-century tomb. *The Ballad of Pollock's Crossing* (1985), set in the 1920s, takes a young Yorkshire schoolteacher to the American Midwest, where he challenges what was then the American orthodoxy of Indian history.

CARR, Marina (1964–) Dramatist, brought up in Co. Offaly and educated at University College, Dublin. Carr's vivid and extreme plays typically adapt Greek prototypes to rural Irish settings, and deploy a theatrical dialect based on the speech of the Irish midlands. Her works include *Portia Coughlan* (1996), *Ariel* (2002)—a political satire based on the *Iphigeneia story—and the bleak, bitter *Woman and Scarecrow* (2006).

CARR, Terry (1937–87) American writer and editor, born in Oregon, whose 'The Dance of the Changer and the Three' (1968) is one of *science fiction's most powerful descriptions of alienness. As editor/anthologist from the 1960s he developed most of the important science fiction writers of the period.

CARRINGTON, Dora (1893–1932) Painter, diarist, and letter writer, born in Hereford, educated at Bedford High School: she studied art at the Slade School in London where her work was much admired by C. R. W. Nevinson (1889–1946) and Mark Gertler (1891–1939), both of whom became infatuated with her. It was not until her extraordinarily vivid diaries and charmingly illustrated letters were posthumously edited for publication by David *Garnett (1970) that she became known to the general public. That book told the story of her mysterious and passionate love for the homosexual Lytton *Strachey, after whose death she committed suicide. There is a biography (1989) by Gretchen Gerzina; two books on her art, one by her brother Noel Carrington (1978), the other by Jane Hill (1994); and a film called *Carrington* (1995) by Christopher *Hampton.

CARROLL, Jonathan (1949–) American novelist and screenwriter, born in New York; resident in Vienna. His work touches on *fantasy and *horror, even *magic realism, without collapsing into definable genre. In *Bones of the Moon* (1987) and *Outside the Dog Museum* (1991) realistic and supernatural elements interweave.

CARROLL, Lewis Pseudonym of Charles Lutwidge *Dodgson.

Carry On films Began with *Carry on Sergeant* (1958), but their characteristic tone of bawdy innuendo emerged in *Carry On Nurse* (1959), the popularity of which led to 29 variations on similar themes, up to the final *Carry On Columbus* (1992). Their stock company of seasoned comedians originally included Kenneth Williams, Sid James, and Hattie Jacques. Cheerfully irreverent, they draw on the techniques of *parody and *farce.

CARSON, Ciaran (1948–) Irish poet, translator, novelist, and musician, born in Belfast and educated at Queen's University, Belfast, where he is Seamus Heaney professor of poetry. From *The Irish for No* (1987) onwards, his poetry uses complex, digressive narratives, influenced by Carson's Irish-speaking background and his knowledge of traditional music and story, to explore history, memory, and the layered maps of Belfast life from the 17th century to the post-1968 *Troubles. *Breaking News* (2003) offers a spiky commentary on the West's implication in Middle Eastern violence from the Crimean War to the present, while *For All We Know* (2008) is a cryptic, fugue-like sonnet sequence on the progress of a love affair.

The vernacular flair that distinguishes Carson's poetry also informs such novels as *Shamrock Tea* (2001) and his versions of *Dante's *Inferno* (2002) and Brian *Merriman's *Midnight Court* (2005). His *Collected Poems* appeared in 2008.

CARSWELL, Catherine (1879–1946) Née Macfarlane, Scottish journalist, novelist, and biographer, born in Glasgow. She was dismissed from her job on the *Glasgow Herald* in 1915 for reviewing D. H. *Lawrence's *The *Rainbow* and with Lawrence's encouragement went on to complete her sexually frank autobiographical novel *Open the Door!* (1920). Her fictionalized *Life of Robert Burns* (1930) caused outrage in Scotland but is now considered a classic of literary biography.

CARTER, Angela (1940–92) Novelist and short story writer, born in Eastbourne and educated at Bristol University. Her work, imbued with a keen sense of the macabre and the wittily surreal, draws heavily on symbolism and themes derived from traditional fairy tales and folk myths. Her first two books, a volume of poetry (*Unicorn*, 1966) and a thriller (*Shadow Dance*, 1966), were followed by *The Magic Toyshop* (1967, filmed 1986), which associated her with the tradition of *magic realism and won the John Llewellyn Rhys Memorial Prize. *Several Perceptions* (1968) gained the Somerset Maugham Award. Succeeding novels—*Heroes and Villains* (1969), set in the aftermath of nuclear conflict, *Love* (1971), and *The Infernal Desire Machines of Dr Hoffman* (1972)—further displayed a fascination with neo-Gothic settings, often infused with a keen feminist sensibility. After *Fireworks: Nine Profane Pieces* (1974) her next novel, *The Passion of New Eve* (1977), was centrally concerned with feminist issues, as was a later cultural study, *The Sadeian Woman* (1979). *Nights at the Circus* (1984), about a female Victorian circus performer, Fevvers, who can fly, confirmed Carter's status as an outstanding literary fabulist, while her ability to evoke and adapt the darker resonances of traditional forms of *fantasy was brilliantly deployed in *The Bloody Chamber and Other Stories* (1979), which contains one of her best-known reworkings of traditional material, 'The Company of Wolves' (based on the story of Little Red Riding Hood), filmed in 1984. Her last novel, *Wise Children* (1991), was a rumbustious extravaganza, packed with Shakespearian analogies and allusions, about two theatrical dynasties. She translated the fairy tales of Charles *Perrault (1977) and, in collaboration with the artist Michael Forman, produced a retelling of 'Sleeping Beauty' and other fairy-tales (1982). She also compiled *The Virago Book of Fairy Tales* (1990; 2nd vol., 1992); *Black Venus* (1985) is a collection of short stories. A selection of critical writings, *Expletives Deleted*, was published posthumously in 1992. A posthumous collection of stories and sketches, *American Ghosts and Old World Wonders*, appeared in 1993.

CARTER, Elizabeth (1717–1806) Scholar and poet, born in Deal, daughter of the Revd Nicholas Carter, who educated her with her brothers in Latin, Greek, and Hebrew. With a persistence praised by Virginia *Woolf in *A *Room of one's Own*, she also acquired French, Italian, Spanish, German, Portuguese, and Arabic. Her father knew Edward *Cave, who published her early work in the **Gentleman's Magazine* and in 1738 issued her poems as a volume. Samuel Johnson, who thought very highly of her as a scholar, invited her to contribute to the **Rambler*, for which she wrote numbers 44 and 100. Her painstaking translation of *Epictetus (1758), printed by Samuel *Richardson, gained her a European reputation. Her *Poems on Several Occasions* appeared in 1762. She chose independence rather than marriage, and was an energetic correspondent and member of the *Blue Stockings who did much to raise the status of women intellectuals.

CARTER, Lin (1930–88) American novelist and editor born St Petersburg, Florida. His own fiction pastiches Edgar Rice *Burroughs and Robert E. *Howard, but as editor and anthologist, reviving important figures like Lord *Dunsany and popularizing *Tolkien, his influence on modern fantasy was immense.

CARTER, Martin (1927–97) Poet, born in Georgetown and educated at Queen's College, Guyana. In 1975 he spent a year at Essex University as poet in residence, the longest time spent away from his homeland. With his stirring and influential volume about political oppression, *Poems of Resistance* (1954), he established an international reputation. Other volumes include *Jail Me Quickly* (1964), *Poems of Succession* (1977), and *Poems of Affinity* (1980).

CARTLAND, Barbara *See* HISTORICAL FICTION.

CARTWRIGHT, Jim (1958–) Dramatist, born in Farnworth, educated at Harper Green Secondary Modern School; Farnworth is the impoverished Lancashire town that inspired his first play, *Road* (1986), a series of brash, lively sketches evoking a turbulent night in a run-down working-class community. This was followed by *Bed* (1989), about Britain's forgotten elderly; *Two* (1989), about life in a pub; *The Rise and Fall of Little Voice* (1994), about a mother's exploitation of her reclusive daughter's talent for mimicry; a raucously poetic portrait of sexual chaos and pain, *I Licked a Slag's Deodorant* (1996); *Hard Fruit* (2000); and *Prize Night* (2000). He has written extensively for television, and wrote and directed *Johnny Shakespeare* (BBC, 2007).

CARTWRIGHT, Justin (1945–) Novelist and screenwriter, born in South Africa, educated at Witwatersrand University and Trinity College, Oxford. His three novels featuring a journalist and film-maker, Tim Curtiz—*Interior* (1988), *Look at It This Way* (1990), and *Masai Dreaming* (1993)—survey, often sardonically, manners and mores in Africa and Europe. *In Every Face I Meet* (1995), set in London at the time of Nelson Mandela's release, and *Leading the Cheers* (1998) and *The Promise of Happiness* (2004), both of which contrast attitudes and assumptions on either side of the Atlantic, display to particularly good effect his satiric wit and acute alertness to contemporary social detail. *The Song Before It Is Sung* (2007) fictionalizes the relationship between Sir Isaiah Berlin (1909–97) and Adam von Trott (1909–44), the Prussian aristocrat involved in a plot to assassinate Hitler. *This Secret Garden* (2007) is a memoir of Oxford.

CARTWRIGHT, William (1611–43) Oxford scholar, preacher, poet, and dramatist, one of the 'sons' of Ben *Jonson. His most successful play, *The Royal Slave*, was performed before Charles I in 1636, and revived by professional players at Hampton Court at the queen's request. The 1651 edition of his works, *Comedies, Tragicomedies, with Other Poems*, was prefaced by over 50 commendatory verses from fellow Royalists.

CARVER, Raymond (1939–88) American short story writer and poet, born in Clatskanie, Oregon. His first collection of poetry, *Near Klamath*, was published in 1968. This was followed by *Winter Insomnia* (1970) and *At Night the Salmon Move* (1976). Although he claimed that he would like to be remembered as a 'poet and short-story writer and occasional essayist—in that order', it is for his short stories that he became best known. He came to prominence with the publication in 1976 of his first collection, *Will You Please Be Quiet, Please?* This was followed by three other collections, *What We Talk About When We Talk About Love* (1981), *Cathedral* (1983), and *Elephant* (1988). Like the stories of Richard *Ford and Tobias *Wolff, with whom he shares the label of *'dirty realism', his work deals powerfully with unremarkable, glamourless small-town lives, described in pared-down, simple prose. Carver continued to write poetry through the 1980s, publishing *Where Water Comes Together with Other Water* in 1985 and *Ultramarine* the following year, as well as *Fires* (1983), a volume which combined his poetry and short stories and a selection of his essays. He completed his last collection of poetry, *A New Path to the Waterfall* (1989), shortly before his death in 1988. An edition of his collected poems, *All of Us*, was published in 1996.

CARY, Elizabeth, Viscountess Falkland (1585–1639) Poet, playwright, and translator, the only child of the lawyer Sir Lawrence Tanfield (*c.*1551–1625), born in Burford Priory, Oxford. A self-taught linguist, she had mastered five languages before marriage at 15 to Henry Cary, later Lord Falkland, to whom she bore eleven children. Secretly embracing *Roman Catholicism, she separated from Falkland in 1625, was subsequently disinherited by her father, and died of consumption, in loneliness and want. Acquainted with the literary circle of Mary Herbert, countess of *Pembroke, she wrote hymns, poems, and translations from French, Spanish, Latin, and Hebrew, many of which are now lost, and *The Tragedy of Mariam* (1613), the first known play in English by a woman. The drama raises Mariam, the 'shrew' wife of Herod, to tragic status, and reflects Cary's own life, in the complex acrimony between dictatorial husband and dissident wife, and in its theme of society's destruction of women abdicating the private sphere for a public or published role. Her *History of Edward II* (*c.*1627) is the first English history play by a woman. Her daughter, a Benedictine nun, wrote her mother's biography. See Heather Wolfe, *Elizabeth Cary* (2001).

CARY, Henry Francis (1772–1844) Educated at Oxford, an assistant librarian at the British Museum from 1826 to 1837. He translated Dante's **Divina commedia*, producing with his translation the first Italian text of Dante to be printed in England. The *Inferno* appeared in 1805, and together with the *Purgatorio* and the *Paradiso* in 1814. *Coleridge praised 'the severity and learned simplicity' of Cary's diction, and the work became well known. He wrote a series of appreciative articles (collected in 1846) on the early French poets, then little regarded, in the **London Magazine*.

CARY, Joyce (1888–1957) Novelist, born in Londonderry. He was educated at Clifton College and Oxford, and studied art in Edinburgh and Paris. He took part in the Balkan War (1912–13), joined the Nigerian political service in 1913, and served with the Nigerian regiment in the Cameroons campaign, 1915–16. In 1920 he returned to England and devoted himself to writing. His early 'African' novels, *Aissa Saved* (1932), *An American Visitor* (1933), *The African Witch* (1936), and *Mister Johnson* (1939), show with shrewd sympathy the relations between Africans and their British administrators. His major work consists of two trilogies: *Herself Surprised* (1941), *To Be a Pilgrim* (1942), and *The Horse's Mouth* (1944), chiefly concerned with the life of the bohemian artist Gulley Jimson; and *Prisoner of Grace* (1952), *Except the Lord* (1953), and *Not Honour More* (1955), a study of politics. The major theme of the novels, which exhibit a vast range of characters, is the need for individual freedom and choice. Two further novels are studies of childhood: *Charley is my Darling* (1940) and the semi-autobiographical *A House of Children* (1941). Cary also wrote political studies, such as *Power in Men* (1939) and *The Case for African Freedom* (1941); poetry, including *Marching Soldier* (1945) and *The Drunken Sailor* (1947); a study in aesthetics, *Art and Reality* (1958); short stories, such as *Spring Song and Other Stories* (1960); and an unfinished novel with a religious theme, *The Captive and the Free* (1959). A biography by J. W. Noble appeared in 1973.

CARY, Lucius *See* FALKLAND, LUCIUS.

CARY, Mary (b. *c.*1621) From 1651 known as Mary Rande. A Londoner during the English revolution, she was one of the most formidable intellectuals of the Fifth Monarchist movement, who constructed a systematic programme of radical social reform (including wage ceilings, postal service, and stamp tax) for the millennium, which she expected to begin in 1701. She maintained the equal right of women 'saints' to speak on public matters, and spoke for the poor and oppressed. Her most important works are *The Little Horn's Doom and Downfall* (1646), which predicts the fall of Charles I, the utopian *A New and More Exact Map* (1651), and *Twelve Proposals* (1653).

CARYLL, John (1625–1711) Diplomatist and secretary to Mary of Modena (1658–1718), the queen consort of James II. He was the author of a tragedy, *The English Princess, or The Death of Richard III* (1667), and a comedy, *Sir Salomon* (1670). His nephew, also John Caryll (?1666–1736), was a friend and correspondent of Alexander *Pope, to whom he suggested the subject of *The *Rape of the Lock*.

CASANOVA, Giacomo (1725–98) Italian autobiographer. In the course of an adventurous life throughout Western Europe he wrote a number of historical works in Italian, but his reputation rests on his *Mémoirés (Histoire de ma vie)* written in French and posthumously published in 12 volumes (1826–38). These are primarily an account of an extraordinary succession of sexual encounters, but they also provide an intimate portrait of the manners of the age and achieve considerable psychological consistency.

CASAUBON, Isaac (1559–1614) French classical scholar, born in Geneva of Huguenot refugee parents; professor of Greek at the Academy of Geneva, 1582–96; professor of classical letters at the University of Montpellier, 1597–9; sub-librarian at the Royal Library in Paris, 1605–10. From 1610 until his death he lived in London, receiving a pension from James I and becoming naturalized in 1611. Casaubon published critical editions and commentaries on the works of a number of ancient authors, chiefly Greek, including *Theophrastus (1592) and the Hellenistic writer of the 2nd century AD, Athenaeus (1597). He planned a major work of church history in the form of a criticism of the 'Annals' of the Italian Roman Catholic Baronius, but only the first volume (*De Rebus Sacris et Ecclesiasticis Exercitationes XVI ad Baronii Annales* 1614) was finished when he died. He left a diary in Latin of his daily activities, the *Ephemerides*. There is a life of Casaubon by Mark *Pattison (1875). It has been suggested that Casaubon lent his name to George *Eliot's fictional scholar the Revd Edward Casaubon, in **Middlemarch*.

Case is Altered, The An early comedy by Ben *Jonson, performed *c.*1597/8 by the boy actors of the Children of Blackfriars, printed 1609, possibly the result of collaboration with Henry Porter (d. 1599) or Anthony *Munday (who is, however, satirized in it as Antonio Balladino). Its main plot, involving complicated identity-swapping and the revelation that the Milanese Count Ferneze's slave is his long-lost son, draws on *Plautus' *The Captives*, and its farcical sub-plot, involving the attempts made by the clowns Juniper, Onion, and Christophero to steal the daughter and the treasure of the supposed beggar Jacques de Prie, derives from Plautus' *The Pot of Gold*. The play seems to have been published without Jonson's permission, for he omitted it from the folio of his works.

CASLON, William (1692–1766) The first English typefounder to make a complete range of roman and italic types of his own design, besides cutting Greek and exotic scripts. From the mid-1720s his types began to supersede those imported from abroad in English printing, and they are still in use. His foundry was carried on by his descendants until 1874.

'Castaway, The' A poem by William *Cowper, written 1799, published 1803, based on an incident from Captain *Anson's *Voyage round the World* (1748). Cowper depicts with sympathetic intensity the suffering of a seaman swept overboard to drown. Mr Ramsay in Virginia Woolf's **To the Lighthouse* is given to declaiming its closing lines.

CASTELNUOVO-TEDESCO, Mario (1895–1968) Italian composer, whose prolific output contains a high proportion of Shakespearian works, including two operas and twelve overtures, predominantly linked to the comedies. He set many English poets, including John *Keats, P. B. *Shelley, Alfred *Tennyson, and Christina *Rossetti, but the *33 Shakespeare Songs* (1921–5) and the set of *28 Shakespeare Sonnets* (1944–7) are among his most substantial and original vocal works. His chamber opera *The Importance of Being Earnest* (1962) is based on Oscar *Wilde.

CASTELVETRO, Ludovico (1505–71) Italian scholar and critic from Modena, best known for his commentary on Aristotle's **Poetics* (1570, 1576), which included a Greek text, an Italian translation, and a critical discussion. His views on the *unities, more rigid than Aristotle's own, had considerable influence on the development of neo-classical theory.

CASTIGLIONE, Baldassare (1478–1529) Italian courtier, diplomat, humanist, and author in a variety of genres. His best-known work is *Il libro del cortegiano* (1528), translated into English as *The Courtyer* (1561) by Sir Thomas *Hoby. The four books of this work purport to record a series of conversations at the court of Urbino in 1507. In the work Castiglione draws on the humanist dialogue form, handbooks for the education of princes, and the writings of *Cicero and *Quintilian. Each book centres on a particular theme: the qualities necessary for the ideal courtier (I); how to practise these qualities (II); the court lady (III); the relationship of courtier and prince (IV); the book concludes with a celebration by *Bembo of Neoplatonic ideas of love. Among the most important of the courtier's attributes are the qualities of 'grazia' and 'sprezzatura'—or the art of performing difficult tasks with no apparent effort. *Il cortegiano* rapidly became extremely popular throughout Europe, spawning translations, imitations, and a whole genre of books of manners. For its influence in England see Henry Howard, earl of *Surrey, Sir Thomas *Wyatt, Philip *Sidney, Edmund *Spenser, and *Shakespeare; and later W. B. *Yeats. See also J. W. Woodhouse, *Baldassare Castiglione: A Reassessment of the Courtier* (1978); P. Burke, *The Fortunes of the Courtier* (1995).

Castle Dangerous A novel by Walter *Scott, published 1831. Both the plotting and writing show the effects of the paralytic strokes which Scott had already suffered in 1831 and which were to kill him a year later. In spite of this, there are passages of the old brilliance in his story of the 13th-century Scottish War of Independence and the taking of Castle Douglas by Robert the Bruce.

Castle of Indolence, The A poem in *Spenserian stanzas by James *Thomson (1748). According to Thomson's friend Patrick Murdoch (d. 1774), the poem grew out of 'a few detached stanzas, in the way of raillery on himself and some of his friends', originally written in 1733 (*Works*, 1762). The first of the two cantos describes the castle of the wizard Indolence, into which he entices weary pilgrims who sink into torpor amidst luxurious ease; Thomson includes sketches of himself, his patron George *Lyttelton, Murdoch, and John Armstrong. The inmates become diseased and languish in a dungeon. The second canto describes the conquest of the castle by the efficient and energetic Knight of Industry. *Wordsworth praised the poem's harmonious verse and pure diction.

Castle of Otranto, The Novel by Horace *Walpole (1764), published anonymously, with an elaborate preface describing the author as 'Onuphrio Muralto', a medieval Italian canon. Prince Manfred of Otranto has a devoted wife, Hippolita; a son, Conrad; and a daughter, Matilda. At his wedding to Isabella of Vicenza, Conrad is crushed by a vast, black-plumed helmet from the nearby statue of Alfonso the Good. A bold young man in the crowd is accused of causing Conrad's death and imprisoned beneath the helmet. Manfred determines that he must have an heir and declares that he will divorce Hippolita and marry Isabella, who escapes through a gloomy vault with the assistance of the mysterious young man. Manfred is confronted by Friar Jerome, who gives Isabella sanctuary in his nearby monastery. The young man is discovered to be Theodore, the son of Jerome, now revealed as the count of Falconara. Theodore finds Isabella in an eerie forest cave, and wounds her father, Frederic, whom he mistakes for an enemy. At the castle Jerome confirms that Theodore's mother was the daughter of Alfonso. Manfred stabs a woman he believes to be Isabella, only to find he has killed his daughter. Distraught, he reveals that his grandfather poisoned Alfonso in order to gain Otranto. He and Hippolita retire to monastic penitence, and Isabella marries Theodore, the rightful prince. Subtitled 'A Gothic Story' in its second edition, the book established several key *Gothic conventions: ghosts, vaults, living statues, mysterious appearances, and a psychology of extreme emotion.
See PIRANESI.

Castle of Perseverance, The A *morality play in 3,700 lines, dating from the first quarter of the 15th century, one of the group (the others are **Mankind* and **Wisdom*) known as Macro plays from their 18th-century owner. It is the earliest surviving complete morality. A huge play, divided into four parts, it is of interest as an exhaustive compendium of such morality features as a battle between vices and virtues, a mixture of allegorical (Backbiter) and diabolical (Belyal) figures, and the enactment of Death and Judgement; but it is also highly significant in the history of English theatre, largely because of a diagrammatic representation of the Castlemound as 'Theatre in the Round' which its staging requires. There is an edition by P. Happé in *Four Morality Plays* (1979); see also R. Southern, *The Medieval Theatre in the Round* (2nd edn 1975).

Castle Rackrent A novel by Maria *Edgeworth, published 1800. This work may be regarded as the first fully developed *historical novel and the first true *regional novel in English. Set, according to the title page, 'Before the year 1782', the characters, the life of the country, and the speech are unmistakably Irish. It is a brief, high-spirited work, narrated in his old age by the devoted Thady Quirk, steward to three generations of Rackrents. This racy character, for whom the Rackrents could do no wrong, was based (the author wrote) on her father's steward John Langan, who 'seemed to stand beside me and dictate'. The rattling narrative begins with the wild life of the hard-drinking Sir Patrick, 'inventor of raspberry whisky', who lived before Thady's time. He was succeeded by the litigious and debt-ridden Sir Murtagh, a skinflint who died of a fury. His brother Sir Kit, who inherits, brings to the castle his unfortunate English Jewish wife, who has 'never seen a peat-stack or a bog' and who, after many arguments over sausages, diamonds, and other matters, is shut up in the castle for seven years, until her gambling husband is killed in a duel. Meanwhile the cunning young lawyer Jason Quirk, Thady's son, is gathering more and more of the family's affairs into his hands. The next heir, Sir Condy, is an ardent, extravagant politician, who tosses a coin to decide whether to marry the rich Isabella Moneygawl or the pretty Judy M'Quirk. He marries Isabella and, keeping lavish open house in their tumbledown castle, they finally exhaust the last resources of the Rackrents. When the bailiffs arrive Isabella flees and Jason Quirk is found to own almost everything. The castle is sold and Condy amuses himself by feigning death at his own wake. When he eventually dies Isabella contests the property, but Jason (who is hated by the countrymen but admired by his father) emerges as a 'high gentleman with estates and a fortune'.

Miss Edgeworth wrote the book without her father's knowledge, and it is one of the few he did not 'edit'. The second half, relating to Sir Condy, was not written until two years after the first.

catachresis A rhetorical term for the misapplication of a word or phrase with seeming disregard for its ordinary denotation or grammatical function, as in *Milton's 'blind mouths'. The term is most often applied to strikingly illogical metaphors such as Hamlet's 'I will speak daggers to her'.

Catch-22 A comic, satirical, surreal, and apocalyptic novel by Joseph *Heller, originally entitled *Catch-18*, published in 1961, which describes the ordeals and exploits of a group of American airmen based on a small Mediterranean island during the Italian campaign of the Second World War, and in particular the reactions of Captain Yossarian, the protagonist. The title of the novel has passed into the language to describe a situation of deadlock, composed of two mutually exclusive sets of conditions. Heller conflates the war situation and the paranoia of McCarthy's America to produce an absurdist sequence of episodes which invert common-sense presumptions about reality.

catharsis A Greek word for 'purification' or 'purgation', which has long been a significant but much-debated concept in the theory of *tragedy, since Aristotle invoked it in his **Poetics*, where he writes that tragedy should succeed in 'arousing pity and fear in such a way as to accomplish a catharsis of such emotions'. Aristotle here seems to be responding to *Plato's view that poetic drama improperly fed the passions by a counter-suggestion that on the contrary it helped to cleanse and release them. The concept has been redefined by generations of critics, including Ludovico *Castelvetro, John *Milton, G. E. *Lessing, Johann Wolfgang von *Goethe, and Arthur *Schopenhauer.

CATHER, Willa Sibert (1876–1947) American novelist, born in Virginia, but brought up in Nebraska, and educated at the University of Nebraska-Lincoln. After a period of teaching and journalism, during which she published her first book of poems, *April Twilights* (1903), and a book of short stories, *The Troll Garden* (1905), she worked on the staff, then as editor, of *McClure's Magazine* in New York (1906–12). Her first novel, *Alexander's Bridge* (1912), was followed by *O Pioneers!* (1913), about a Swedish immigrant family struggling to establish itself in the Nebraskan prairies; *The Song of the Lark* (1915), a study of the professional dedication of an opera singer; and *My Antonia* (1918), the story of an immigrant girl from Bohemia, settled in Nebraska, narrated by her childhood friend Jim Burden. Cather's range and complexity are further demonstrated in *The Professor's House* (1925), which contrasts the middle-aged disillusion of Professor St Peter with his memories of his favourite student, whose discovery of an ancient New Mexican cliff city is recorded in Book II of the novel; New Mexico also provides the vividly pictorial setting for another major work, *Death Comes for the Archbishop* (1927), a historical novel based on the French Catholic mission of Father Latour. Her other works include two studies of the dangers and rewards of unconventionality: *My Mortal Enemy* (1926), in which Myra Henshawe lives to regret her runaway marriage and fallen fortunes, and *Lucy Gayheart* (1935), the story of a music student caught in the tension between the values of her home town and the values of the artistic world. The dual impulse towards exploration and cultivation, towards art and domesticity, towards excitement and safety, is a constant theme in Cather's work. She records her own debt to another pioneer, Sarah Orne *Jewett, in *Not under Forty* (1936). See James Woodress, *Willa Cather: Her Life and Art* (1982).

Catherine A novel by W. M. *Thackeray, published serially in **Fraser's Magazine*, 1839–40. Thackeray took the outline of the story of the murderess Catherine Hayes from the **Newgate Calendar*, and deliberately made his novel as grim and sordid as possible, in reaction against the popular 'Newgate novels' of Edward *Bulwer-Lytton, Harrison *Ainsworth, and others. However, the lively ironic characterization of the heroine and two invented characters, her seducer Galgenstein and his companion Corporal Brock, transcend the original intention.

CATHERINE, St (1347–80) Dominican lay sister, ascetic, and author. From 1370 she became increasingly involved in both religious and political issues in Italy, urging in particular the return of the papacy from Avignon to Rome. Almost 400 of her letters survive, including at least one to Sir John Hawkwood urging him to take part in the crusade to recapture the Holy Land which she was promoting. She is also the author of the *Dialogo della divina provvidenza* (1377–80: *A Treatise of Divine Providence*). Canonized in 1461, she was named a Doctor of the church in 1970.

CATHERINE II, THE GREAT (Empress Ekaterina Alekseevna) (1729–96) Russian empress, born Sophia Augusta Fredericka of Anhalt-Zerbst in Stettin, Pomerania. Arriving in Russia in 1744, she converted to Orthodoxy on her betrothal to Grand Duke Pavel Petrovich, who as Peter III acceded to the Russian throne in 1761. In June 1762 she was proclaimed empress in her own right after a palace coup. Her husband's subsequent murder (for Horace *Walpole, she was always 'Catherine Slay-Czar') and the succession of (increasingly young) favourites throughout her long reign, the most significant of whom was Prince Potemkin, were to bring a reputation for ruthlessness and sexual depravity that vied with her just claims to the title of 'Great'. Her solid achievements throughout her reign of 34 years lay in the fields of education, especially for (noble) women, culture (publishing, theatre, the arts), social welfare, provincial and town administration. Declaring in her famous *Grand Instruction* to her 1767 Legislative Commission that 'Russia is a European country', she promoted the westernizing policies of her great predecessor *Peter I and earned the approbation of such as *Voltaire (whose library she purchased) and *Diderot, whom she invited to Russia in 1773. She established a society (1768) for the translation of classical and modern European works, which included Sir William *Blackstone's *Commentaries*, the histories of William Robertson (1721–93), and novels by Henry *Fielding and Jonathan *Swift. As grand duchess, she had been advised by the British ambassador to learn English and read English plays, but her English remained rudimentary and she read her admired Fielding and Laurence *Sterne in German versions, as subsequently she did William *Shakespeare. A royal *Blue Stocking, Catherine took an active part in literature, initiating a vogue for satirical journals, modelled on the **Spectator*, and composing a number of plays that included ambitious productions written 'without rules, in imitation of Shakespeare' and two adaptations (*Merry Wives* and *Timon of Athens*). Strongly Anglophile in her cultural tastes, Catherine led the Russian vogue for English *landscape gardening on her estates near St Petersburg, invited a number of British gardeners as well as painters and engravers to her court, and commissioned, for instance, the famous 'Frog' dinner service from Josiah Wedgwood (1730–95). When diplomatic relations with Britain worsened during the Russo-Turkish War of 1787–91, she became the subject of numerous caricatures by James *Gillray, Thomas *Rowlandson, and Isaac Cruikshank (1756–1810) which inevitably emphasized her alleged sexual proclivities. With her death there came a flood of biographies, several negative and influenced by strongly Russophobe productions emanating from France, but others, notably by William Tooke (1777–1863) (five editions 1798–1800), striving to give a balanced account of her reign. She attracted her first woman biographer in Mary Hays (1760–1843), anxious to provide in her *Female Biography* (1803) 'a memorial of those women, whose endowments, or whose conduct, have reflected lustre upon the sex', and she has been followed by a veritable flotilla of biographers, mainly female, up to the present. See John T. Alexander, *Catherine the Great Life and Legend* (1989); Anthony Cross, *Catherine the Great and the British* (2001).

Catiline A Roman tragedy by Ben *Jonson, performed 1611, based principally on *Sallust's *Catiline*. Like **Sejanus* it represents Jonson's wish to treat Roman history with scholarly accuracy, an aim that involved incorporating large portions of *Cicero's Orations in its text. Jonson called it a 'dramatic poem', and adopts the Senecan apparatus of an introductory ghost and a classical chorus. The plot portrays the events of the year 63 BC. Catiline, secretly encouraged by Caesar and Crassus, organizes a conspiracy to overthrow the existing government. Cicero summons the Senate and accuses Catiline, who leaves Rome and joins the army raised by his adherents at Faesulae, but falls in a decisive engagement with the government forces. The first performance was a notorious failure, as Jonson noted in an angrily defensive preface to the printed text.

CATNACH, James (1792–1841) A publisher in Seven Dials, London. He issued at a very low price a large number of *chapbooks, *ballads, and *broadsides, many of them about crimes, highwaymen, and executions, which throw much light on his period.

Cato A tragedy by Joseph *Addison (1713). It deals with the death of Cato the republican, who commits suicide rather than submit to the dictator Caesar; the devotion of Juba, Cato's Numidian ally, to Cato's daughter Marcia, adds some emotional interest. Samuel *Johnson described it as 'rather a poem in dialogue than a drama', but in its day it was enormously successful, partly because of political claims made for it by opposing parties. Alexander *Pope wrote the prologue.

CATO, Marcus Porcius (95–46 BC) of Utica, statesman, otherwise known as Cato the younger to differentiate him from his great-grandfather. A Roman model of republican and *Stoic integrity, he committed suicide at Utica in Africa rather than surrender to Julius *Caesar. His daughter Porcia married Marcus *Brutus. He is included in *Plutarch's lives, is a hero of *Lucan's *Pharsalia*, and is the subject of Joseph *Addison's play **Cato*. His name is associated with liberty in Trenchard and Gordon's *Cato's Letters* (1720–23), widely read in revolutionary America.

CATULLUS, Gaius Valerius (*c*.84–*c*.54 BC) One of the most versatile of Roman poets, whose single verse collection, containing a mixture of 116 love poems, elegies, and satirical epigrams, ranges from the witty to the mournful and the delicate to the obscene. He was among the first to introduce into Latin the mannered style of the *Hellenistic school, particularly *Callimachus. Many of his poems explore the extremes of his affair with Lesbia. His work remained virtually unknown during the Middle Ages, but after a manuscript of his poems had come to light at Verona in the 14th century interest multiplied dramatically. Individual poems (on kisses, sparrows, the death of his brother) as well as his themes and moods were much imitated. There are notable English examples by Thomas *Campion, Ben *Jonson, Robert *Herrick, Richard *Lovelace, Lord *Byron, Leigh *Hunt, Walter Savage *Landor, Alfred *Tennyson, and Ezra *Pound, and a complete translation by C. H. *Sisson. See *Catullus in English*, ed. Julia Haig Glasser (2001).

CAUSLEY, Charles (1917–2003) Poet, born in Launceston, Cornwall, where he was educated and where, after six wartime years in the Royal Navy, he became a teacher. He spent the rest of his life in Cornwall, and Cornish topography and themes are central to his work. His first collection of verse, *Farewell, Aggie Weston* (1951), was followed by many others, including *Survivor's Leave* (1953), *Johnny Alleluia* (1961), *Secret Destinations* (1984), and *A Field of Vision* (1988). His *Collected Poems 1951–2000* appeared in 2000. His understanding of children is expressed in various collections of children's stories and anthologies of verse. His poetry is marked by a powerful simplicity of diction and rhythm, and shows the influence of popular songs and, notably, the ballad tradition. Innocence is a recurrent theme, and his admiration for John *Clare is the direct inspiration of several poems. Religious and seafaring images, often interwoven, are also characteristic. In many ways outside the poetic movement of his times, he was nevertheless hugely admired by such contemporaries as Philip *Larkin, Ted *Hughes, and Seamus *Heaney. He also published two verse plays, *The Gift of a Lamb* (1978) and *The Ballad of Aucassin and Nicolette* (1981).

CAUTE, David (1936–) Novelist and historian, born in Alexandria and educated at Wellington College and Oxford. His first novel, *At Fever Pitch* (1959), was followed by many more which range in theme from *The Decline of the West* (1966), an epic of postcolonial power struggle, violent conflict, and race/sex relations, set in French West Africa, to *Veronica, or The Two Nations* (1989), a story spanning the post-war period of a boy's incestuous and damaging passion for his half-sister. Caute's political studies include *The Fellow-Travellers: Intellectual Friends of Communism* (1973; rev. 1988) and *Under the Skin* (1983), an account of the collapse of white Rhodesia. *Fatima's Scarf* (1998) is a carefully researched novel set in the Yorkshire town of 'Bruddersfield' (a coinage borrowed from J. B. *Priestley) which explores the complex responses of the Muslim community in Britain and beyond to the publication of Salman *Rushdie's *Satanic Verses*, and the public debates surrounding the issue.

CAVAFY, Constantine (1863–1933) Poet, born in Alexandria of Greek parents from Constantinople. His father, who died in 1870, was a partner in an export firm with branches in England and Alexandria, and Constantine was at school in England between the ages of 9 and 16. On the collapse of the family business the Cavafys returned to Alexandria, where Constantine spent the rest of his life, living quietly with his mother, then alone, and working for many years as clerk in the Ministry of Public Works. He published two privately printed pamphlets of verse, in 1904 and 1910, and later distributed his work to friends in broadsheets; his local reputation grew, but recognition from the English-reading world was achieved largely through the influence of E. M. *Forster, who met him in Alexandria in 1917 and maintained a long friendship and correspondence. His poems, all fairly short, are both lyrical and colloquial, ranging from the personal confession to the dramatic monologue, and in subject matter treating historical themes and characters (Julian the Apostate, Mark Antony, the fall of Constantinople) with great verve and originality, homosexual themes with frankness, and contemporary Alexandrian café life with realism and a strong sense of place. There have been several translations, including versions by J. Mavrogordato (1951), Rae Dalven (1961), and E. Keeley and P. Sherrard (1975). See Michael Haag, *Alexandria: City of Memory* (2005).

CAVALCANTI, Guido (1260?–1300) Poet, a significant influence on the development of the *dolce stil nuovo and the early poetry of *Dante, who describes him in the dedication of the *Vita nuova* as his most important friend. He was exiled from Florence for political reasons in 1300 and died soon after. His poetry is complex in both themes and style, and characterized by Cavalcanti's interests in philosophy and psychology. Cavalcanti is referred to in Dante's *Inferno* X. 58 and is the protagonist of Boccaccio's *Decameron* VI. 9. Dante Gabriel *Rossetti translated, and Ezra *Pound produced versions of, some of the poems. His influence can also be found in T. S. *Eliot. See M. A. Cirigliano (trans.), *Complete Poems* (1992).

Cavaliers A name given to supporters of Charles I in the Civil War, derived from the Italian for horseman or knight. 'Cavalier lyrics' is the term applied to lyrics by Thomas *Carew, Richard *Lovelace, John *Suckling, and Robert *Herrick, all of whom were influenced by Ben *Jonson.

CAVE, Edward (1691–1754) Son of a Rugby cobbler who became a London printer and publisher. As 'Sylvanus Urban' he founded the **Gentleman's Magazine*, to which Samuel *Johnson contributed parliamentary sketches. Cave also published the **Rambler*. On his death Johnson published in the magazine 'The Life of Edward Cave' (1754).

CAVENDISH, George (1494–in or before 1562?) A gentleman of Thomas Wolsey's household, and author of a remarkable biography of the cardinal (*The Life and Death of Cardinal Wolsey*), in which with much art he contrasts the magnificence of the cardinal's life with his subsequent disgrace, and indicates 'the wondrous mutability of vain honours...And the tickle trust to worldly princes'. First printed in 1641, it previously circulated in manuscript.

CAVENDISH, Margaret *See* NEWCASTLE, MARGARET CAVENDISH, DUCHESS OF.

Cave of Mammon *See* MAMMON.

CAXTON, William (1415/24–1492) Born in Kent, a merchant and the first English printer. After apprenticeship in London he worked for approximately 30 years in the Low Countries, where he translated the first book printed in English, the *Recuyell of the Historyes of Troye*, and translated and printed *The Game and Playe of the Chesse*. The first major work published from his Westminster press was *The *Canterbury Tales* (*c*.1476). His version of *Malory was regarded as authoritative before the discovery of the Winchester Manuscript by W. F. Oakeshott (1934). Caxton's translations, calculated to appeal to Burgundian tastes among English readers, influenced the development of 15th-century prose style. See *Caxton's Prologues and Epilogues*, ed. W. J. B. Crotch (EETS OS 176, 1927; repr. 1957); N. F. Blake, *Caxton and his World* (1969); N. F. Blake, *William Caxton and Literary Culture* (1991); *Caxton's Own Prose*, ed. N. F. Blake (1973); G. D. Painter, *William Caxton: A Quincentenary Biography* (1977).

CECIL, David (Lord Edward Christian David Gascoyne) (1902–86) Scholar and biographer, educated at Eton College and Christ Church, Oxford, and Goldsmiths' professor of English literature at Oxford, 1948–69. His many works include a life of Melbourne (2 vols, 1939, 1954), *Two Quiet Lives* (1948; studies of Thomas *Gray and Dorothy *Osborne), *The Cecils of Hatfield House* (1973), and *A Portrait of Jane Austen* (1978).

Cecilia, St Early Christian martyr and patron saint of music, celebrated in odes for St Cecilia's Day (22 November), written by John *Dryden and W. H. *Auden among others, with music by Henry *Purcell, George Frideric *Handel, and Benjamin *Britten.

Cecilia *or Memoirs of an Heiress* Fanny *Burney's second novel (1782). Cecilia Beverley inherits a large fortune on condition that her future husband takes her name. She lives with a succession of guardians: Harrel, a gambler, who, failing in his attempt to exploit his ward, kills himself; the vulgar and avaricious Briggs; and the Hon. Compton Delvile, a man of implacable family pride. Cecilia and his son Mortimer fall in love, but old Delvile is furious at the idea that his son should exchange his name for Cecilia's. The marriage is further thwarted by the apparently friendly Monckton, who hopes to win Cecilia and her fortune when his wife dies. Monckton's treachery is exposed; Cecilia, who has been driven to madness by her tribulations, marries Mortimer; old Delvile is reconciled to the match. The novel was much admired by Edmund *Burke, and Samuel *Johnson praised the 'general power of the whole'.

CELAN, Paul (1920–70) Pseudonym of Paul Anschel, poet, born in then Romania of a Jewish family, who wrote in German. Both his parents died in an extermination camp, and he was interned for two years in a Romanian labour camp. He settled in Paris in 1950 where he finally ended his life by suicide. His poems have been translated by Michael *Hamburger: see the selection *Poems* (1980) with an introduction by Hamburger; see also *Selected Poems and Prose of Paul Celan*, trans. John Felstiner (2000). His most celebrated poem *Todesfuge* (*Death Fugue*), which interweaves by means of quasi-musical motifs German and Jewish experience of a death camp, challenges Theodor *Adorno's famous remark on the barbarity of writing poetry after Auschwitz. John *Banville explores fictionally the meeting between Celan and Martin *Heidegger in *Todtnauberg*, a radio play of 2006 commissioned by the BBC.
See HOLOCAUST.

Celestina, *or The Tragi-Comedy of Calisto and Melibea* A Spanish novel in dialogue written by Fernando *de Rojas. The first known edition appeared *c.*1499, in 16 acts, and a later version, in 1502, in 21 acts. The authorship of Act I and some later additions is disputed. The work has had several stage adaptations. A dark comedy of ambiguous moral intention, it marks an important development in the literary history of Spain and of Europe. James *Mabbe, its English translator, observed, 'some part of it seemeth somewhat more obscene than may suit with a civil style'. It is a gripping work, one of the first to present love and desire in the context of everyday life, and realistically reproduces contemporary street language laced with popular sayings. Its characters are vividly depicted as deceitful and self-deceiving: Calisto, a young gentleman of birth and fortune; Melibea, a modest young lady; Celestina, a cunning, greedy, and wise ex-prostitute who may also be a witch; Pármeno and Sempronio, Calisto's randy braggart servants; and Elicia and Areúsa, two whores. Calisto meets Melibea by chance and, while professing love, is consumed with lust for her, but she modestly rejects his advances. On the advice of one of his servants he turns to the aged go-between Celestina, who deflects Melibea from the path of virtue and brings about a general catastrophe. Celestina is murdered by Pármeno and Sempronio for withholding their promised share of the reward that she has received from Calisto, and they are executed for their crime. Calisto falls to his death after one of his clandestine sexual encounters with Melibea, and, to the despair of her unwitting parents, she commits suicide. An excellent and racy, if exuberantly diffuse, translation into English prose, *The Spanish Bawd*, was made by Mabbe, and published in 1631. The early part of *Celestina* was translated into English verse by John *Rastell, provided with a happy ending, and published, about 1525, as *A new commodye in englysh in maner of an enterlude*, better known as *An Interlude of Calisto and Melebea*. It is one of the first English dramatic works to approach true comedy. See Ian Michael *et al.*, *Context, Meaning, and Reception of Celestina: A Fifth Centenary Symposium* (2000).

CÉLINE, Louis-Ferdinand (1894–1961) Pseudonym of Louis-Ferdinand Destouches, French novelist. His first novel, *Voyage au bout de la nuit* (1932: *Journey to the End of the Night*), describing the experiences and opinions of an unsavoury and truculent slum doctor during and after the First World War, earned him the reputation of a right-wing misanthrope. His later novels, including *Mort à crédit* (1936: *Death on the Installment Plan*), *D'un château à l'autre* (1957: *From One Castle to Another*), and *Nord* (1960: *North*), are particularly notable for their unconventional narratives, the nightmare power of his vision, and the extravagant resourcefulness of his language.

CELLINI, Benvenuto (1500–71) An important Florentine goldsmith and sculptor, and author of an extremely vivid autobiography, considered amongst the greatest ever written. Begun in 1558, and abandoned in 1562, it was first published in 1730. Translated into English by Thomas Roscoe (1791–1871) in 1822, and by John Addington *Symonds in 1888, it also inspired an opera by *Berlioz (1837). Cellini combined the characters of artist and ruffian; he was arrogant, passionate, violent, and vainglorious. His autobiography gives vivid descriptions of his relationships with Renaissance popes and princes alongside an account of his working life, and recounts events, including the Sack of Rome (1527), in which he took part. He also wrote treatises on goldsmithing and sculpture, translated by C. R. Ashbee (1899).

Celtic literature Other than between Irish and Scottish Gaelic, there was little sense of common ground or purpose in the literature of the Celtic languages (Welsh, Cornish, Breton and the two major divisions of Gaelic) before the series of 'Celtic Revivals' that began in the 18th century and culminated with Matthew *Arnold and W. B. *Yeats a hundred years later. Common themes can nonetheless be seen in the writings collected by Kenneth Jackson in *A Celtic Miscellany* (1951) and in Arthurian materials that had expanded to a pan-European tradition. The postulation of a distinctively 'Celtic Note' in Arnold's *On the Study of Celtic Literature* (1866), following Ernest *Renan, was widely challenged in the 20th century, not least on the basis of its stereotyping in the interest of imperial ideology. See J. T. Koch and J. Carey, *The Celtic Heroic Age* (1994); Seamus *Deane, *Celtic Revivals* (1985).

Celtic Twilight, The A collection of stories by W. B. *Yeats, published 1893, illustrating the mystical belief of the

Irish in the world of fairies, ghosts, and spirits. It has since become a generic phrase (slightly ironical) for the whole *Irish Revival in literature.

Cenci, The A verse tragedy by P. B. *Shelley, largely written at Livorno, in summer 1819, published 1819 and 1821. The melodramatic plot is taken from the true story of Beatrice Cenci, who was tried and executed for the murder of her father, Count Francesco Cenci, at Rome in 1599. Shelley was attracted by the themes of incest and atheism: the play concentrates on the Iago-like evil of the count and the inner sufferings of Beatrice. Shelley claimed to have been influenced by the dramatic style of *Calderón, but in fact the play is indebted to William *Shakespeare for much of its construction and language: Beatrice's great speech on the prospect of death, 'So young to go | Under the obscure, cold, rotting, wormy ground!' (V. 4), is based on Claudio's in **Measure for Measure* (III. i). Surprisingly, Shelley hoped for a popular theatrical success at Drury Lane or Covent Garden; the play was eventually produced in Paris in 1891.

censorship In various forms has overshadowed English literature since the early 16th century, at first under statutory attempts to control the spread of printing through the monopoly of the *Stationers' Company, and subsequently through separate provisions for the official vetting of plays. Early censorship was directed chiefly against potentially heretical or seditious publications, and those satirizing public figures, as with the anonymous *Martin Marprelate pamphlets of 1588–9. The unpredictable dangers of public performance were addressed from 1581 by a licensing system in which new plays had to be presented for approval to the master of the *revels, a functionary in the lord chamberlain's office. A further Parliamentary Act of 1606 provided for fines to be charged against actors using blasphemous oaths, a measure that led to the expurgation of older plays when revived. Control of printed material was increasingly evaded by anonymous *pamphleteering in the 17th century, and encountered protest from writers, notably in *Milton's unlicensed pamphlet **Areopagitica* (1644). Under Parliamentary rule, theatres were closed between 1642 and 1660, after which the lord chamberlain's department resumed stage licensing. Printed publications were again restricted by the Licensing Act of 1662, but Parliament declined to renew its powers in 1695, thereby opening the way to the emergence of the modern newspaper. Further controls on theatre were imposed in response to anti-government satires by John *Gay and Alexander *Pope: the Licensing Act of 1737 confined spoken drama (as distinct from musical theatre and mime) in London to the *Drury Lane, Covent Garden, and Haymarket theatres while giving new statutory powers to the lord chamberlain to censor plays before performance; these powers were later extended nationally by the Theatres Act of 1843. Unlicensed theatres found ways to circumvent such restrictions, while some playwrights resorted to the publication of unperformed *closet drama. In the 19th century, a succession of statutes attempted to control pornographic books and prints: the Vagrancy Act 1824, the Obscene Publications Act 1857, and the Customs Consolidation Act 1876; but literature was affected more by self-censorship practised by publishers and by the powerful *circulating libraries. From the 1890s, playwrights used private performances in theatre clubs as a means to circumvent censorship. In the early 20th century, Victorian legislation was misused to suppress works of literary value, notably D. H. *Lawrence's *The *Rainbow* and Radclyffe *Hall's *The Well of Loneliness*, and to confiscate imported copies of James *Joyce's **Ulysses*. Protests from writers amid a public climate of liberalization led to a revised Obscene Publications Act (1959) which allowed literary merit as a defence: in a famous test case in 1960, *Penguin Books was acquitted of obscenity charges over its unexpurgated reprint of Lawrence's **Lady Chatterley's Lover*. Soon after, the lord chamberlain's censorship of plays was abandoned (1968). Since then, most literary censorship has been indirect and private rather than official, taking the form of intimidation against writers, publishers, or theatres by populist newspapers, by libel lawyers, or by religious pressure groups. The lord chamberlain's licensing archive is held in the British Library. See Nicholas de Jongh, *Politics, Prudery & Perversions* (2000); Richard Dutton, *Mastering the Revels* (1991).

CENTLIVRE, Susanna (?1669–1723) Dramatist and poet. She was one of the *The Nine Muses* (1700) who wrote elegies on John *Dryden's death. Her early life apparently involved two short-lived marriages and an acting career in breeches roles. Her first play, *The Perjured Husband* (1700), appeared under the name Susanna Carroll, taken from her second husband. She wrote eighteen further plays, chiefly comedies of intrigue and manners, the last being *The Artifice* (1722). *The Gamester* (1705) was her greatest early success. In 1707 she married Joseph Centlivre, 'yeoman of the mouth' (cook) to Queen Anne. *The *Busie Body* (1709) became a stock play; *The Wonder: A Woman Keeps a Secret* (1714), dedicated to the new king, George I, later provided David *Garrick with one of his most successful parts; and *A Bold Stroke for a Wife* (1718) was also frequently revived. She reviewed her career with irony in the poem *A Woman's Case* (1720). An ardent Whig, she was a friend of George *Farquhar, Richard *Steele, and Nicholas *Rowe, with whom she collaborated on a tragedy, *The Cruel Gift* (1716). Her mockery of Catholicism, and involvement in Edmund *Curll's campaigns against Alexander *Pope, earned her a place in *The *Dunciad*. See F. P. Lock, *Susanna Centlivre* (1979).

Cent nouvelles nouvelles A collection of often licentious French tales about such characters as deceived husbands, wily wives, and cunning clerics, loosely modelled on Boccaccio's **Decameron*, and composed by an anonymous writer between 1456 and 1461 for Philip, duke of Burgundy. The tales are told by members of the Burgundian court, including the duke himself.

Certain Sonnets 32 sonnets and poems by Philip *Sidney first printed in editions of *The *Arcadia* (1598). The last two sonnets, incorrectly used by 19th-century editors to conclude

Astrophel and Stella, are rejections of secular love, the second beginning

'Leave me ô Love, which reachest but to dust,
And thou my mind aspire to higher things:
Grow rich in that which never taketh rust:
What ever fades, but fading pleasure brings.'

CERVANTES SAAVEDRA, Miguel de (1547–1616) The great Spanish novelist and dramatist, born in Alcalá de Henares of an ancient but impoverished family, and wounded, losing for life the use of his left hand, at the battle of Lepanto (1571). He was taken by pirates in 1575, and spent the next five years as a prisoner at Algiers. The remainder of his life was, for the greater part, occupied with a struggle to earn a livelihood from literature and humble government employment. He was an agent responsible for provisioning the Armada against England and was twice imprisoned in Spain. His first attempt at fiction was a pastoral romance, *La Galatea* (1585), which was followed by his masterpiece, **Don Quixote*, of which the first part was dated 1605 (although probably published in 1604), the second 1615. He also wrote a number of plays (sixteen of which survive), a collection of highly accomplished short stories, *Novelas ejemplares* (1613: *Exemplary Stories*), and a tale of adventure, *Persiles y Sigismunda*, published posthumously in 1617. John *Fletcher drew largely on these last two for the plots of his plays. See P. E. Russell, *Cervantes* (1985).

CÉSAIRE, Aimé (1913–2008) Poet, dramatist, and politician born on the French Caribbean island of Martinique. With Léon Damas (1912–78) and Léopold Sédar *Senghor, whom he met in Paris in the 1930s, he developed the *Négritude movement, laying the foundation for *postcolonial literature and theory. His most influential work, *Cahier d'un retour au pays natal* (1939; *Return to my Native Land*, trans. Émile Snyder, 1968), is a passionate portrait of Martinique and an exhilarating call for the oppressed of colonialism to rise up against the status quo.

Chabot, The Tragedy of By George *Chapman, revised by John *Shirley, written 1611–22, published 1639. The last of Chapman's plays on recent French history, it is based on *Les Recherches de la France* by Étienne Pasquier (1529–1615). Its hero, the high-principled admiral Philip de Chabot, dies of wounded honour when falsely accused of treason.

CHADBOURN, Mark (1960–) Born Derbyshire; author of detailed and richly symbolic *fantasy novels, often using Celtic mythology as a springboard. His 'contemporary' novella *The Fairy Feller's Master Stroke* (2002) is based upon the painting by Richard *Dadd.

'Chaldee MS, The: A Translation from an Ancient Chaldee Manuscript', published in **Blackwood's Magazine* 1817. The article, purporting to be an ancient manuscript and written in pseudo-biblical prose, describes the conflict between the two Edinburgh publishers William *Blackwood and Archibald *Constable (owners, respectively, of *Blackwood's* and the **Edinburgh Review*), and contains many venomous descriptions of well-known Edinburgh figures. Its publication created a furore. Although anonymous, the piece was conceived by James *Hogg, who later admitted he supplied 'the kernal', and was principally composed by John *Wilson and John *Lockhart, who, according to Hogg, were the 'young lions of Edinburgh' who added the 'devilry'. Blackwood had to pay damages, but the circulation of 'Maga' rose.

CHALKHILL, John (?1595–1642) Author of two poems in Izaak *Walton's *The *Compleat Angler* and a pastoral poem, *Thealma and Clearchus*, prepared for publication by Walton in 1683 (which states on its title page that Chalkhill was a friend of Edmund *Spenser, though his dates make this impossible). Other poems and letters by Chalkhill, owned by a Derbyshire family, were acquired by the Pierpont Morgan Library in 1979, and incorporated into his *Works*, ed. Charles Ryskamp and Scott D. Westrem (2000).

CHALLONER, Richard (1691–1781) Roman Catholic religious writer, born near Lewes, Sussex. Educated at the English College in Douai, France, he was ordained priest, and published over 60 works, the most influential being his spiritual handbook *The Garden of the Soul* (1740) and his modernized version of the Rheims–Douai Bible (1749–50). He narrowly escaped the anti-Catholic Gordon riots of 1780.
See BIBLE.

CHAMBERLAYNE, Edward (1616–1703) Tutor to the duke of Grafton (1663–90; the illegitimate son of Charles II) and to Prince George of Denmark (1653–1708; the prince consort of Queen Anne), and author of *Angliae Notitia, or The Present State of England* (1669), a handbook of social and political conditions which met with extraordinary success and was enlarged by his son John Chamberlayne (1668/9–1723).

CHAMBERLAYNE, William (1619–89) A physician at Shaftesbury in Dorset, who fought on the Royalist side at the battle of Newbury. He published a play, *Love's Victory* (1658), a verse romance in five books, *Pharonnida* (1659), and a poem celebrating the Restoration, *England's Jubilee* (1660). The poet Robert *Southey said he owed *Pharonnida* 'many hours of delight'.

CHAMBERS, Aidan (1934–) Children's writer, critic, and publisher, born in Chester-le-Street, County Durham; he completed teacher training in London. *Postcards from No-Man's Land* won the Carnegie Medal (1999); *Dance on my Grave* (1982) explores homosexuality; *Breaktime* (1978) is a ground-breaking, postmodern novel. Influential books on education include *The Reluctant Reader* (1969) and *Tell Me: Children, Reading and Talk* (1993). With his wife Nancy he runs the Thimble Press, publishers of the children's literature journal *Signal* (1970–2005). He co-founded Turton and Chambers to publish translated children's books.

CHAMBERS, Sir E. K. (Edmund Kerchever) (1866–1954) Shakespearian scholar and dramatic historian, educated at Marlborough and Corpus Christi College, Oxford; he worked for the education department of the Civil Service (1892–1926). He contributed to the **Academy* and the **Athenaeum* and in 1904–5 was dramatic critic of the *Outlook* and the *Academy*. His major works of dramatic history, which began as 'a little book about Shakespeare', grew into the monumental *The Medieval Stage* (2 vols, 1903), *The Elizabethan Stage* (4 vols, 1923), and *William Shakespeare: A Study of Facts and Problems* (2 vols, 1930). His scholarly achievements are the more remarkable for being the fruits of his spare time. As well as editions of all Shakespeare's plays for the Red Letter Shakespeare and an important lecture on 'The Disintegration of Shakespeare' (1924) he published *Arthur of Britain* (1927), a synthesis and reassessment based on available evidence; biographies of S. T. *Coleridge (1938) and Matthew *Arnold (1947); editions of *Donne, *Milton, Francis *Beaumont, and John *Fletcher, among others; and the *Oxford Book of Sixteenth Century Verse* (1932).

CHAMBERS, Ephraim (?1680–1740) of Kendal, educated at Heversham grammar school; he published his *Cyclopaedia*, the first true English encyclopedia, in 1728. It was on a more comprehensive scale than John Harris's *Lexicon Technicum* (1704), and had some influence on *Johnson's *Dictionary*.

CHAMBERS, Robert (1802–71) Scottish writer and publisher, born and educated in Peebles, who founded with his brother William the firm of W. and R. Chambers, Edinburgh, and wrote and issued a number of books on Scottish history, biography, and literature. He established **Chambers's Journal* in 1832. His firm issued *Chambers's Encyclopaedia* (1st edn 1859–68). His anonymous *Vestiges of the Natural History of Creation* (1844) proposed a theory of biological evolution produced by the action of universal and progressive natural law. Though found odious by churchmen and incompetent by scientists, *Vestiges* was immensely influential in popularizing an evolutionary view of nature, and appears to have had a particular impact upon Alfred *Tennyson.

CHAMBERS, R. W. (Raymond Wilson) (1874–1942) Born in Staxton, Yorkshire; he graduated from University College London (1894), and was afterwards librarian and Quain professor there (1922–41). His scholarly interests extended from Old English to the Renaissance. His most celebrated works are studies of **Widsith* (1912) and **Beowulf* (1921); *On the Continuity of English Prose from Alfred to More* (1932); *Thomas More* (1935); and *Man's Unconquerable Mind* (1939), a collection of essays. He was president of the Philological Society in 1933 and served as honorary director of the *Early English Text Society from 1938. He died at Swansea after evacuation to Wales in the Second World War. A memorial lecture to him was endowed at the University of London; the first lecture, on Chambers, was given in 1951 by C. J. Sisson.

Chambers's Journal (originally *Chambers's Edinburgh Journal*) One of the most popular of the 19th-century journals of literature, science, and the arts, founded by Robert *Chambers in 1832. It changed its name in 1854, and survived until 1938.

CHAMISSO, Adelbert von (1781–1838) German zoologist and poet, chiefly remembered for his story *Peter Schlemihls wundersame Geschichte* (1814: *The Strange Story of Peter Schlemihl*) whose hero sells his shadow to a devil figure, a mysterious man in a grey coat, and becomes an outcast. Thomas *Pynchon's *V* has a character who is called a Schlemihl.

CHAMOISEAU, Patrick (1953–) Novelist, playwright, and theoretician, born on the French Caribbean island of Martinique. Representing a third generation of Martinican writers after Aimé *Césaire and Édouard *Glissant, Chamoiseau distanced himself from both by developing the notion of *créolité*. *Éloge de la créolité* (1989; *In Praise of Creoleness*, trans. Mohamed B. Taleb, 1990), co-written with Jean Bernabé and Raphaël Confiant, argues that Caribbean identity is defined by plurality and hybridity. His novels, including *Texaco* (1992; English trans. Rose-Myriam Réjouis and Val Vinokurov, 1997), explore the complex identity of Martinique by interweaving French and Creole and drawing on local traditions of oral storytelling.

Champion, The A journal opposed to Sir Robert Walpole (1676–1745), written largely by Henry *Fielding, from 1739 to 1740. In its columns Captain Hercules Vinegar, his wife, and their two sons discourse in essays, sermons, sketches, mock trials, and letters, on the political, social, literary, and domestic questions of the time.

Chances, The A play by John *Fletcher, written *c.*1617, printed 1647. The plot is based on one of *Cervantes's *Novelas ejemplares*; the 'chances' are the coincidences by which Constantia and the duke of Ferrara, who are eloping, are involved in complications from which they are rescued by Don John and Don Frederick, two Spanish gallants, Dame Gillian their landlady at Bologna, and Peter Vecchio, a wizard. Popular after the Restoration, it was adapted by the second duke of *Buckingham (1682, directed by Laurence Olivier at Chichester in 1962), whose version was successfully adapted by David *Garrick.

CHANDLER, Arthur Bertram (1912–84) Novelist. Born in Aldershot, he became an Australian citizen. His years in the merchant navy provided structures for over 40 *science fiction novels where exploration and trade feature highly and the romance and dangers of the seas are translated into space.

CHANDLER, Raymond (1888–1959) American writer of thrillers and detective stories, born in Chicago but brought up from the age of 7 in England, where he was educated at Dulwich College. He returned to America in 1912 and settled in California, where he worked for an oil company before embarking on a career as a writer. Many of his early stories were published in the 1930s in *Black Mask*, a magazine founded in 1920; his first novel, *The Big Sleep* (1939), introduced his detective narrator, cool, attractive, wise-cracking, lonely tough guy Philip Marlowe, who owes something to Chandler's admiration for Dashiell *Hammett. Chandler's 1945 essay 'The Simple Art of Murder' is one of the classic commentaries on the genre. Later works include *Farewell, my Lovely* (1940), *The High Window* (1942), *The Lady in the Lake* (1943), and *The Long Goodbye* (1953). All of his novels have been filmed and Chandler himself worked in Hollywood in the 1940s and 1950s, producing an original screenplay, *The Blue Dahlia* (1946). Chandler's unfinished novel was completed by the novelist Robert B. Parker and published as *Poodle Springs* in 1989. His work strongly influenced post-war crime writers like Ross *Macdonald.

CHANG, Jung (1952–) Chinese-born writer, educated in Sichuan University and the University of York, subsequently resident in London. Her popular and influential *Wild Swans: Three Daughters of China* (1992) traces the history of modern China through the life-stories of her grandmother, mother, and herself. Ten million copies have been sold. *Mao: The Unknown Story* (2005), co-written with her husband, the historian Jon Halliday, is a controversial biography of Mao Zedong.

Changeling, The A tragedy by Thomas *Middleton and William *Rowley, printed 1653, but acted at the Phoenix playhouse in 1622. Beatrice, daughter of the governor of Alicante, is ordered by her father to marry Alonzo de Piracquo. She falls in love with Alsemero, and to avoid the marriage employs the villain De Flores, whom she detests but who loves her, to murder Alonzo. To her horror, De Flores claims sex with her as his reward. Beatrice is now to marry Alsemero. To conceal the fact that she is no longer a virgin, she persuades her maid Diaphanta to take her place on the wedding night; and to remove a dangerous witness, De Flores then kills the maid. The guilt of Beatrice and De Flores is revealed to Alsemero, and they are brought before the governor, whereupon they take their own lives. The title of the play comes from the subplot, in which Antonio disguises himself as a crazy changeling in order to get access to Isabella, wife of a madhouse keeper. The main plot is taken from John Reynolds's *God's Revenge against Murder* (1621).

CHANNING, William Ellery (1780–1842) American Unitarian clergyman, who exercised a marked influence on American intellectual life, and is considered a forerunner of the *Transcendental Club. His *Remarks on American Literature* (1830) calls for a literary Declaration of Independence. His many pamphlets on slavery, pacifism, social questions, etc. are included in his collected *Works* (6 vols, 1841–3). His nephew, also William Ellery Channing (1818–1901), poet and Transcendentalist, with Ralph Waldo *Emerson founded *The *Dial* in 1840 and wrote the first biography of Henry *Thoreau, *Thoreau, The Poet-Naturalist* (1841). His first volume of verse, *Poems* (1843), was followed by several others including the book-length poem *The Wanderer* (1871). Thoreau referred to Channing's poetic style as 'sublime-slipshod'.

Chanson de Roland See ROLAND; CHANSONS DE GESTE.

chansons de geste Epic poems in Old French, written mainly between the late 11th and the early 14th centuries, about the heroic deeds of broadly historical figures, usually drawn from the Carolingian era (*see* CHARLEMAGNE). Most of the surviving *chansons de geste* are anonymous, with the notable exceptions of *Aimeri de Narbonne* and *Girart de Vienne* from the late 12th century, which are attributed to Bertrand de Bar-sur-Aube. In the prologue to *Girart de Vienne*, Bertrand de Bar-sur-Aube defines three groups of *chanson de geste* on the basis of their protagonists: first, those dealing with Charlemagne and his knights; secondly, those dealing with Charlemagne's rebellious vassals; and thirdly, those dealing with William of Orange. Though these categories are not watertight, they nevertheless suggest how the representation of historical events in the *chansons de geste* offered the means of exploring the stresses within contemporary feudal society: in *Raoul de Cambrai*, for instance, the social fabric is in a state of disintegration as powerful factions within France fight each other under a powerless king; and in the *Chanson de Guillaume* and, perhaps most famously, the *Chanson de Roland* (*see* ROLAND), which is the most translated of all Old French texts, we witness some of the strains caused by the impact of the Crusades. The only parallel English poems are those concerned with Charlemagne, such as the fragmentary Middle English *Song of Roland* (*see* FERUMBRAS, SIR; OTUEL, SIR), though traces of the genre can be found in Edmund *Spenser's **Faerie Queene*. See S. Kay, *The 'Chansons de geste' in the Age of Romance* (1995).

Chanticleer The cock in **Reynard the Fox*, and in Chaucer's 'The Nun's Priest's Tale' (*see* CANTERBURY TALES, 20) as Chauntecleer.

chapbook A small pamphlet of ballads, folk tales, nursery rhymes, or popular romances such as **Bevis of Hampton* and **Guy of Warwick*, circulated cheaply in the provinces by pedlars and chapmen from the 17th to 19th centuries. They were illustrated with wood-blocks, and normally consisted of 16 pages octavo or 24 pages duodecimo. Novels like **Robinson Crusoe* were often drastically abridged as chapbooks. James *Boswell and Samuel *Johnson fondly remember reading chapbook romances as children.

Chapel, Children of the *See* PAUL'S, CHILDREN OF.

CHAPLIN, Charlie (1889–1977) Actor and film-maker; he emerged from poverty to make a career in the London music halls. After extensive vaudeville touring in the United States, Mack Sennett first filmed him in 1914, and he quickly became a noted attraction in a series of short comedies, playing a mischievous tramp-like character. His astonishing international success enabled him to open his own studio in 1921 and control every aspect of his subsequent work. Each Chaplin film became a global event, from *The Kid* (1921) and *The Gold Rush* (1925) to *The Circus* (1928) and *City Lights* (1931). Resisting the development of sound technologies, until his anti-fascist *The Great Dictator* (1940) demanded speech, Chaplin continued to command worldwide admiration and influence artists in many media. A lifelong progressive, he was refused re-entry into the USA in 1952 and moved to Switzerland. An *Autobiography* in 1964, together with David Robinson's definitive 1985 biography, were the basis of Richard Attenborough's faithful biographical film *Chaplin* (1992).

CHAPLIN, Sid *See* REGIONAL NOVEL.

CHAPMAN, George (?1559–1634) Author and translator, born near Hitchin, in Hertfordshire. Though his work displays much learning, it is not certain that he had a university education. Some of his young manhood was spent as a soldier in the Netherlands. After more than a decade as a professional playwright he began to pursue courtly patrons, with limited success, and turned to his major work of freely translating *Homer, completed in 1616. Minor works of translation occupied him until his death, which seems to have been in poverty.

Chapman's earliest published works were non-dramatic poems: *The Shadow of Night* (1594), a pair of complex *Neoplatonic poems on night and day; *Ovid's Banquet of Sense* (1595), an allegorical account of *Ovid's courtship of Corinna; and his completion of Marlowe's **Hero and Leander* (1598). He went on to write many plays, some of them lost, for both public and private companies, but constantly suffered financial problems. Eight comedies, mostly satirical and topical, survive: *The Blind Beggar of Alexandria* (1596; pub. 1598), *An Humorous Day's Mirth* (1597; pub. 1599), *All Fools* (1599; pub. 1605), *May-Day* (1601–2; pub. 1611), *Sir Giles Goosecap* (1602), *The *Gentleman Usher* (1602–3; pub. 1606), *The Widow's Tears* (1604; pub. 1612), and **Monsieur D'Olive* (1605; pub. 1606). He collaborated with *Jonson and John *Marston on a further comedy, **Eastward Ho*, in 1605, which led to a short period of imprisonment for Jonson and Chapman because of its anti-Scottish satire.

The tragedies consist of two two-part plays, **Bussy D'Ambois* (1603–4; pub. 1607–8) and *The *Revenge of Bussy D'Ambois* (1610–11; pub. 1613), *The Conspiracy of Charles, Duke of *Byron* and *The Tragedy of Byron* (1607–8; pub. 1608), and one single play, **Caesar and Pompey* (1604; pub. 1631). *The Tragedy of *Chabot* (1611–12; pub. 1639) appears to be a Chapman tragedy revised by James *Shirley. Chapman also collaborated with John *Fletcher, Jonson, and *Massinger in writing *The *Bloody Brother* (*c.*1616; pub. 1639). The first of his Homeric translations, *Seven Books of the Iliads of Homer*, appeared in 1598 with a dedication to the earl of Essex complaining of poverty; twelve books of the **Iliad*, dedicated to Prince Henry, appeared in *c.*1609; the complete *Iliad* and **Odyssey* were published together in 1616 as *The Whole Works of Homer, Prince of Poets*. Jonson praised Chapman (along with Fletcher) as second only to himself as a writer of *masques, though all that survives is *The Memorable Masque* (1613), presented in the Middle Temple and Lincoln's Inn to celebrate the marriage of Princess Elizabeth.

Chapman is a serious, scrupulous, and intellectual writer, not always easy to understand; in modern times his plays have had more appeal to readers than to theatregoers, and even his literary reputation has often sprung from peripheral associations rather than direct knowledge. *Keats's sonnet beginning 'Much have I travelled in the realms of gold' has commended Chapman's Homer to generations of readers who have not themselves 'looked into' it. He was long the favourite candidate for the 'rival poet' referred to in Shakespeare's **Sonnets*. His complete plays and poems were edited by T. M. Parrott (1910, 1914), and individual plays have appeared in the Revels Plays and other series. P. Bartlett edited the *Poems* (1941) and Allardyce Nicoll the Homer (1957); editions of the comedies and the tragedies were produced under the general editorship of Allan Holady in 1970 and 1987. Among critical studies is *George Chapman's Major Tragedies*, by A. R. Braunmuller (1992).

CHAPMAN, Guy *See* JAMESON, STORM.

CHAPMAN, John (1821–94) The son of a Nottingham druggist and shopkeeper. Apprenticed to a watchmaker, he was educated at the local Pestalozzian Institute, where he heard lectures by Robert *Owen and other reformers. He moved to London early in life and established himself as a publisher and editor. He published George *Eliot's translation of Strauss in 1846, and she stayed in his home and literary headquarters at 142 Strand in 1851; in the same year he purchased the **Westminster Review*, of which she became assistant editor, and for which she wrote regularly. Chapman edited the *Review* continuously for 43 years until his death. A strikingly handsome man and a notorious philanderer, married to a wife considerably older than himself, Chapman was a conspicuous figure in literary London; Thomas *Carlyle, commending him to Robert *Browning in 1851, wrote that he had 'real enthusiasm (tho' a soft and slobbery) in him'. He qualified as a physician in 1857 and wrote various medical works, but appears to have been something of a quack. He died in Paris. His diaries for 1851 and 1860 survive, which, edited by G. S. Haight as *George Eliot and John Chapman, with Chapman's Diaries* (1940), shed considerable light on both their personalities. See also Rosemary Ashton, *142 Strand: A Radical Address in Victorian London* (2006), a study of the circle of writers who gathered round Chapman in his home on the Strand in the 1840s and 1850s.

Chapman and Hall A publishing company founded in 1830 at 186 Strand, London, by Edward Chapman (1824–80) and William Hall (1801?–47). It owed much of its success to its early association with Charles *Dickens (**Pickwick Papers* having originated in a suggestion from Hall) and published many distinguished and popular authors, including Thomas *Carlyle, Charles *Kingsley, Elizabeth *Gaskell, and Anthony *Trollope. George *Meredith was for a time literary director, and Arthur Waugh, father of Evelyn *Waugh, became chairman and managing director in 1902 and wrote a history of the firm (*A Hundred Years of Publishing*, 1930).

CHAPONE, Hester (1727–1801) Née Mulso, born at Twywell, Northamptonshire. She educated herself despite early discouragement and wrote her earliest dated poem 'To Peace. Written during the Late Rebellion. 1745' when only 18. In London she became a member of the *Blue Stockings, and knew Samuel *Johnson, who admired her poetry, particularly 'To Stella', a poem against love and in praise of the calm joys of friends. She married John Chapone in 1760, who unfortunately died in 1761; thereafter, she lived alone in London, publishing *Letter Written on the Improvement of the Mind* (1773) to much applause. *Miscellanies in Verse and Prose* followed in 1775. Johnson invited her to contribute to the **Rambler*, of which no. 10 is partly hers. Her works were highly regarded and went into many editions. Although 30 years younger, she was a particular friend of Samuel *Richardson, who called her 'little spit-fire' and with whom she discussed his female characters; Mary *Delany asserted that Hester Chapone was the model for one or two of Richardson's heroines. Her *Works* and *Posthumous Works* appeared in 1807.

Characters of Shakespeare's Plays Essays by William *Hazlitt, published 1817. They comment not only upon Hamlet, Macbeth, and other protagonists, but also upon the distinctive qualities of each major drama, and more generally upon the 'magnanimity' of Shakespeare's imagination. Especially notable is the essay on *Coriolanus*, which considers the affinities between poetic imagination and political power. Hazlitt rebukes Samuel *Johnson for his unimaginative treatment of Shakespeare, and attempts a more flexibly sympathetic appreciation.

character-writing Books of 'characters' were popular in the 17th century, and many were based, though some loosely, on *Theophrastus, translated by Isaac *Casaubon in 1592 and by John Healey (1585?–1616?; printed 1616, but previously circulated). The first was published in 1608 by Joseph *Hall, followed by Thomas *Overbury in 1614, the *Satirical Essays, Characters and Others* of John Stephens (*fl.*1611–17) in 1615, the *Certain Characters and Essays of Prison and Prisoners* (1618) by Geffray Minshull (bap. 1594, d. 1668), John *Earles's *Microcosmography* (1628), *Whimzies* (1631) by Richard Brathwaite (1587/8–1673), and others. The 'characters' gave generalized but detailed descriptions of the behaviour and appearance of a class or type; they were on the whole short, succinct, pointed, and less discursive than the essay, also a popular literary form of the period. *La Bruyère's much-admired 'Characters' (1688) were translated into English in 1699. See B. Boyce, *The Theophrastan Character in England to 1642* (1947); C. N. Greenough, *A Bibliography of the Theophrastan Character in English* (1947).

'Charge of the Light Brigade, The' A poem by Alfred *Tennyson, first published in the *Examiner* in 1854 only weeks after the famous charge (25 October 1854) at Balaclava, near Sebastopol, during which, owing to a misunderstood order, 247 officers and men out of 637 were killed or wounded. The poem, drawing heavily on newspaper reportage, half-turned an error into a heroic affirmation.

CHARKE, Charlotte (1713–1760) Actress and cross-dresser, youngest daughter of Colley *Cibber. Educated in a manner 'sufficient for a son', she displayed an early fondness for masculine dress and pursuits such as shooting. She took to the stage, often in masculine roles, and in opposition to her implacable father. Her 'mad pranks' and varied career as waiter, pastrycook, farmer, and strolling player are vividly described in her *Narrative of the Life of Mrs Charlotte Charke* (1755).

CHARLEMAGNE (742–814) King of the Franks (768) and crowned by Pope Leo III as emperor of the West (800), the son of Pepin the Short. He and his *Paladins are the subject of numerous **chansons de geste*, of which the *Chanson de Roland* is the most famous (*see* ROLAND). Of the three groups of French *chansons de geste* concerned with Charlemagne, only the first, the *geste du roi*, is represented in English, in such romances as **Otuel, Sir *Ferumbras*, and *The Sege of Melayne*. As well as being the subject of romances, Charlemagne is of significance in English literature for the tradition of learning he established at his court (led by the Northumbrian *Alcuin) which King *Alfred copied a century later. See M. Becher, *Charlemagne* (English trans. D. S. Bachrach, 2003).

CHARLES, duc d'Orléans (1394–1465) French poet, nephew of the French king Charles VI. Captured at the battle of Agincourt in 1415, he was held prisoner in England until 1440, during which time he wrote poetry. On his return to France he established his court at Blois, where he cultivated poets and artists. He wrote numerous chansons, ballades, and *rondeaux, using the fixed forms as a means of striking self-exploration. A large number of English poems, many of which are versions of Charles's French lyrics, are also probably to be attributed to him.

CHARLETON, Dr Walter (1619–1707) Fellow of the *Royal Society. His *Chorea Gigantium* (1655) attempted to demonstrate that Stonehenge was a Danish coronation site and prompted one of John *Dryden's finest early poems, 'To my Honoured Friend, Dr Charleton' (1663), in which Royalist, scientific, commercial, patriotic, and religious sentiments are subtly interwoven.

CHARNAS, Suzy McKee (1939–) American author, born in New York and resident in New Mexico. *Walk to the End of the World* (1974) is a *dystopia where women have been blamed for the collapse of civilization. *Motherlines* (1978), its sequel, offered a feminist alternative and *The Furies* (1994) a tentative conclusion. *The Vampire Tapestry* presents the relationships between a vampire (an anthropologist at a university) and the humans among whom he lives. Short fiction, including the award-winning 'Boobs', is collected in *Stagestruck Vampires* (2004). *My Father's Ghost* (2002) is a memoir of her father.

CHARRIÈRE, Isabelle de (1740–1805) Dutch-born novelist, dramatist, poet, and letter writer who spent her later life in Switzerland. She corresponded with James *Boswell, after making his acquaintance during his visit to the Netherlands in 1763–4, and knew David *Hume, whom she met while staying in England in 1766–7, when she was also presented at court. She is best known for her epistolary novels *Lettres neuchâteloises* (1784: *Lettres from Neuchâtel*) and *Lettres écrites de Lausanne* (1785: *Letters from Lausanne*), which scrutinize the workings of class and gender in provincial Swiss communities (the latter was translated into English in 1799), and *Lettres de Mistriss Henley* (1784), a story of a woman in an unhappy marriage. See C. P. Courtney, *Isabelle de Charrière* (1993).

CHARTIER, Alain (*c.*1385–*c.*1435) French poet and prose writer. His most famous poem was *La Belle Dame sans mercy* (1424), a story of unrequited love in 800 *octosyllabic lines; an English translation, falsely ascribed to *Chaucer, appeared in *c.*1526. His most famous prose work, the *Quadrilogue invectif* (1422), is a bitter attack on the divisions within French society and a passionate appeal for national unity. His Latin prose work *De Vita Curiali*, a disillusioned account of court life, was translated into English by William *Caxton.

Chartist movement A chiefly working-class political movement between 1837 and 1848, which arose as a result of the *Reform Bill of 1832, which had excluded the working classes from political rights for lack of the necessary property qualification. Their six-point 'People's Charter' consisted of: Universal Suffrage, Vote by Ballot, Annually Elected Parliaments, Payment for Members of Parliament, Abolition of the Property Qualification, and Equal Electoral Districts. The movement had an enormous following but failed through poor leadership, though the points eventually became law between 1860 and 1914, except for Annually Elected Parliaments. The movement was alluded to by novelists of the mid-19th century who were concerned with the *condition of England question, in particular Benjamin *Disraeli in **Sybil*, and Charles *Kingsley in **Alton Locke*; and also by Thomas *Carlyle in his essay 'Chartism'. The Chartists themselves also produced much literature, including the documentary accounts of Samuel *Bamford, and many short-lived periodicals sprang up (the *Northern Star*, the *Chartist Circular*, the *Star of Freedom*, the *Red Republican*, and others). Chartist poets and novelists, some of them writing in prison, included master bootmaker Thomas Cooper (1805–92), author of the lengthy and ambitious *The Purgatory of Suicides* (1853), a 'working man's epic' in Spenserian stanzas, who was imprisoned for 'incitement to riot'; Ebenezer *Elliott of Sheffield, the so-called 'Corn Law Rhymer'; Ernest Jones (1819–68/9?), orator and publisher, and author of an unfinished novel *De Brassier*; Thomas Martin Wheeler, author of *Sunshine and Shadow*, published in 37 parts in the *Northern Star* (1849–50); wood-engraver William James Linton (1812–97); and textile worker Gerald Massey (1828–1907) whose *Original Poems and Chansons* appeared in 1847. See Martha Vicinus, *The Industrial Muse: A Study of Nineteenth Century British Working Class Literature* (1974); D. Thompson, *The Chartists* (1984); *An Anthology of Chartist Poetry*, ed. P. Scheckner (1989); Malcolm Chase, *Chartism: A New History* (2007).

CHARYN, Jerome (1937–) American novelist who was born in New York and has constantly returned to that city for his subjects. The influence of Vladimir *Nabokov, John *Hawkes, and others persuaded Charyn that he could 'hallucinate' (his term) his way into material unconnected with his personal experience. He weaves his way in and out of different genres producing fiction dealing with the internment of Japanese Americans (*American Scrapbook*, 1969), a Gypsy narrative (*Eisenhower, my Eisenhower*, 1971), and a postmodern pastiche of an academic journal in *The Tar Baby* (1973). Bogged down by intricate fantasies in the 1970s, Ross *Macdonald offered Charyn a new direction for his fiction and he subsequently produced a series of novels centred on a New York detective Isaac Sidel. Charyn's second great love has been film: 'I've been a film theorist all my life,' he has stated. In 1989 he published a study of American film culture, *Movieland*. In 1988 he began dividing his time between Paris and New York. In Paris he began experiments with graphic novels and teaching film theory at the American University.

Chaste Maid in Cheapside, A By Thomas *Middleton, written 1613, printed 1630, one of the most popular and frequently reprinted of his comedies. The play centres on the attempt of the dissolute Sir Walter Whorehound to pass off his mistress as his niece and marry her to the foolish son of Yellowhammer, a rich goldsmith, while Whorehound himself is to marry Yellowhammer's daughter Moll. The first part of the plot succeeds, but the second fails. Moll and her resourceful young lover Touchwood finally succeed in evading their parents and marrying.

CHATEAUBRIAND, François-René, vicomte de (1768–1848) One of the major figures of early French Romanticism. Born at Saint-Malo and educated at Dol-de-Bretagne and Rennes, he spent some years in preparation for the priesthood at Dinan, before achieving celebrity with *Le Génie du Christianisme* (1802: *The Genius of Christianity*), a work of Christian apologetic which accompanied and contributed to the post-revolutionary religious revival in France. It argues with great eloquence for the emotional and imaginative appeal of religion to the deepest human instincts. 'Of all the religions that have ever existed the Christian religion is the most poetical, the most favourable to freedom, art and letters; the modern world owes all to it, from agriculture to the abstract sciences.' From this work Chateaubriand extracted two fragments, inspired in part by his stay in America (1791), which he published separately: *Atala* (1801; trans. 1802), the tragic romance, set in Louisiana, of the Indian maiden Atala and her lover Chactas; and *René* (1805; trans. 1813), the story of a young European devoured by a secret sorrow (his temperament and early circumstances resemble the author's) who flies to the solitudes of America to find solace for profound melancholy and unsatisfied longings. Both had a wide and enthusiastic reception. *Les Martyrs* (1809; trans. 1812) is a prose epic of early Christianity. *Mémoires d'outre-tombe* (1849–50: *Memoirs from Beyond the Grave*), his posthumously published autobiography, now regarded as his most accomplished work, gives a penetrating and brilliantly written account of the author's life against the varied background of an age of political upheaval. Between 1793 and 1800 Chateaubriand lived in exile in England, mainly in London, where he published an *Essai sur les révolutions* (1797: *Essay on Revolutions*). Under Louis XVIII he returned to London in 1822 as French ambassador. He translated **Paradise Lost* as *Le Paradis perdu* (1836).

CHATTERJEE, Upamanyu (1959–) Indian novelist, member of the generation of Indian writers in English who turned the new prominence of Indian writing in English to rich profit following Salman *Rushdie's remarkable success with *Midnight's Children* (1981). Born in Patna, Bihar, he also formed with Amitav *Ghosh and others part of a late 20th-century blossoming of Bengali writers in English. Drawing on his officer experience in the prestigious Indian Administrative Service, Chatterjee's acclaimed, best-known work, his first novel *English, August* (1988), offers a comic-ironic portrait, informed by Hindu myth, of the ennui and self-disgust attendant upon this highly sought-after job. Other work includes the novels *The Last Burden* (1993) and *Weight Loss* (2006).

CHATTERTON, Thomas (1752–70) Posthumous son of a Bristol schoolmaster, educated at Colston's School. He left school aged 14 and was apprenticed to an attorney. In 1768 he published in *Felix Farley's Bristol Journey* a passage of pseudo-archaic prose, the original of which he claimed to have discovered in a chest in St Mary Redcliffe. This attracted the attention of local antiquaries, for whom he provided fake documents and pedigrees. He had already written some poems purporting to be the work of an imaginary 15th-century Bristol monk, Thomas Rowley, a friend of William Canynge, a Bristol merchant. He also fabricated correspondence between the two and other background documents. He offered some of the poems to James *Dodsley in December 1768; Dodsley had published Thomas *Percy's **Reliques*, greatly stimulating interest in early poetry. In March 1769 Chatterton sent Horace *Walpole a treatise on painting 'bie T. Rowleie', which Walpole briefly accepted as authentic. The only Rowleian piece published in Chatterton's life was 'Elinour and Juga', which appeared in May 1769. In April 1770 he went to London, writing home 'in high spirits', and claiming 'great encouragement' from publishers; four months later (still only 17 years old) he took a fatal overdose of arsenic, probably accidentally. He wrote journalism and poetry, much of it satirical and political, before he died. The Rowleian 'An Excelente Balade of Charitie' was completed in London. The Rowley poems were published in 1777 by Thomas Tyrwhitt, with an appendix challenging their authenticity, which was further impugned by Thomas *Warton and Edmond *Malone. Chatterton's death, then treated as suicide, had a powerful effect on the *Romantic imagination; S. T. *Coleridge's first published poem was a 'Monody' on him, William *Wordsworth called him 'the marvellous Boy, The sleepless Soul that perished in his pride', John *Keats dedicated **Endymion* to his memory, and he features prominently in P. B. *Shelley's **Adonais*. Henry Wallis's famous painting of *The Death of Chatterton* (1856) was much admired by John *Ruskin. See E. H. W. Meyerstein, *The Life of Thomas Chatterton* (1930); *The Complete Works of Thomas Chatterton*, ed. D. S. Taylor and B. B. Hoover, 2 vols (1971); N. Groom (ed.), *Thomas Chatterton and Romantic Culture* (1999).

CHATWIN, Bruce (1940–89) Travel writer and novelist, born in Sheffield. After Marlborough College, he had an impressive career at Sotheby's, then studied archaeology at Edinburgh University. He travelled widely, developing a long-lasting interest in nomads. In the early 1970s he worked on the *Sunday Times Magazine*. His first book, *In Patagonia* (1977), an imaginative blend of fact and fiction, history, biography, anecdote, and geography, expanded the concept of *travel writing (though he disliked the label), giving to what many felt was becoming a moribund literary form a new energy and seriousness. His inventiveness and mixing of genres characterizes much of his work. *The Viceroy of Ouidah* (1980) is a fictionalized account of a real-life slave trader. *On the Black Hill* (1982) is a novel that tells the story of reclusive twin brothers on the Welsh–English border. *Patagonia Revisited* (1986) was written with Paul *Theroux. *The Songlines* (1987) has Chatwin linking Aboriginal stories of the land with his theories of nomadism. *Utz* (1988) is a study of a collector of Meissen porcelain in Prague. A selection of miscellaneous writings, compiled before Chatwin's death from an Aids-related illness, was published posthumously in 1989 as *What Am I Doing Here*. Another posthumous collection, *Anatomy of Restlessness*, was published in 1996. *Photographs and Notebooks* appeared in 1993 and was followed by *Winding Paths*, a further volume of photographs, in 1999, the same year as *Bruce Chatwin*, Nicholas *Shakespeare's biography.

CHAUCER, Geoffrey (*c.*1340–1400) Poet, the son of John Chaucer, a London vintner. Between *c.*1357 and 1360 he was a retainer in the household of Elizabeth, countess of Ulster, wife of Prince Lionel, afterwards duke of Clarence. In 1359 he was in France with Edward III's army, was taken prisoner, and ransomed. By 1366 he was married to Philippa, possibly the daughter of Sir Paon Roet of Hainault and the sister of *John of Gaunt's third wife, Katherine Swynford. Philippa died in 1387 and Chaucer enjoyed Gaunt's patronage throughout his life. He held many positions at court, and in the king's service, and he travelled abroad on numerous diplomatic missions. As well as missions to France, he made a journey to Genoa and Florence in 1372–3, in the course of which he may have encountered the works of *Boccaccio, *Petrarch, and *Dante. He was sent on to France and Lombardy in 1378. In 1374 he was appointed controller of customs in the port of London and leased his house over Aldgate. He was knight of the shire for Kent in 1386 and may have lived in Kent for most of the rest of his life. Between 1389 and 1391 he was clerk of the king's works. His last official position was that of deputy forester in the King's Forest at North Petherton in Somerset (1390s). He was buried at the entrance to the Chapel of St Benedict in Westminster Abbey, where a monument was erected to him in 1556: this was the origin of Poets' Corner. His son Thomas had a daughter, Alice, whose third husband was William de la Pole (1396–1450), later duke of Suffolk. His writings develop from an early period of French influence (culminating in *The *Book of the Duchess*, *c.*1368–72), through his 'middle period' of both French and Italian influences (including *The *House of Fame* after 1374 and the mature Italian-influenced works, of which the most important is **Troilus and Criseyde*, complete by 1388), to the last period of most of *The *Canterbury Tales* and his short lyrics. His prose works include a translation of *The Consolation of Philosophy* by *Boethius (*Boece*) and *A Treatise on the Astrolabe*, written to 'little Lewis', probably the poet's other son. There are portraits of Chaucer in the Ellesmere Manuscript (now in the Huntington Library); in the manuscript of *Troilus and Criseyde* in Corpus Christi College, Cambridge; and in Thomas *Hoccleve's *The Regement of Princes*, beside lines 4,995–6 (in several manuscripts: the best dates from Hoccleve's time, British Library Harley 4866, edited by Furnivall for EETS ES 72). See D. A. Pearsall, *The Life of Geoffrey Chaucer: A Critical Biography* (1992); P. Boitani and J. Mann (eds.), *The Cambridge Chaucer Companion* (1986); Douglas Gray (ed.), *The Oxford Companion to Chaucer* (2003).

CHAUDHURI, Amit (1962–) Indian writer in English, distinguished by his crystalline miniaturist style, who grew up in Bombay (Mumbai), but was born in Calcutta (Kolkata), where most of his fiction is set. *A Strange and Sublime Address* (1991) described the gradual awakening to life of a young writer-to-be in a vibrant Calcutta household. *Afternoon Raag* (1993) found its narrator studying at Oxford and remembering his earlier Bombay life. *Freedom Song* (1998) returned to Calcutta to follow the interconnected lives of three Bengali families, observed with the contemplative humanity that is Chaudhuri's trademark. These novels won, respectively, the Betty Trask Prize and Commonwealth Writers' Prize for Best First Book, the Southern Arts Literature Prize and Encore Award for best second novel, and the Los Angeles Times Book Prize. His fourth novel, *A New World* (2000), winner of India's Sahitya Akademi Award, dwells on the daily lives of a man and his young son on vacation with his ageing parents in Calcutta in the aftermath of a bitter custody battle. *Real Time*, a book of short stories, appeared in 2002, and *D. H. Lawrence and 'Difference': Postcoloniality and the Poetry of the Present*, a post-structuralist study of D. H. *Lawrence as a writer of 'difference', in 2003. He has contributed fiction, poetry, and reviews to numerous publications including the *Guardian*, the *London Review of Books*, and the *New Yorker*. He edited *The Picador Book of Modern Indian Literature* (2001). His poetry has been published in *St. Cyril Road and Other Poems* (2005).
See ANGLO-INDIAN LITERATURE.

CHAUDHURI, Nirad (1897–1999) Indian man of letters and travel writer, born in east Bengal, India, his upbringing moulded by the Hindu revivalism that characterized the early 20th-century Bengal Renaissance, a cultural nationalist movement in which Rabindranath *Tagore and Sri Aurobindo (1872–1950) also played a part. His first book, *The Autobiography of an Unknown Indian* (1951), a cultural history more 'national' than 'personal', dedicated to 'the memory of the British Empire in India', almost immediately plunged the writer into controversy. This lengthy work makes frank, subjective observations on what it describes as the struggle of 'civilisation', brought in by successive waves of conquest, against an inhospitable environment in India, 'in which the destiny of the British rule in India became necessarily involved'. *A Passage to England* (1959), an account of a five-week visit to England, further confirms Chaudhuri's views as an Anglophile circumspect about the decline of high culture in the land of his birth. Other works include *The Continent of Circe* (1966) and *The Intellectual in India* (1967). Despite his controversial opinions, Nirad Chaudhuri's robust yet supple deployment of the English language as a medium for the expression of an Indian sensibility has assured him recognition as a foremost 20th-century Indian writer in English.

Cheap Repository Tracts A series of over one hundred entertaining moral tales, ballads, sermons, and Bible stories published by the Cheap Repository press (1795–8), many of which are by the *evangelical writer Hannah *More. Counter-revolutionary, they aim at teaching the poor to accept the authority of church, government, and social hierarchy but they can also be seen as morally radical in their concern with developing the religious and rational capacities of the lower classes, especially women. More (like Mary *Wollstonecraft) argued that a more rational system of education would allow women to take up their duties as responsible citizens.

CHEEVER, John (1912–82) American novelist, whose sophisticated, ironic novels and short stories (many published in the **New Yorker*) satirize affluent suburban New England life, and have gained a growing following in England. His novels include *The Wapshot Chronicle* (1957), *The Wapshot Scandal* (1964), *Bullet Park* (1969), and *Falconer* (1977). He was awarded the *Pulitzer Prize for fiction in 1979 for *The Stories of John Cheever*. His *Letters* were published in 1987, edited by his son Benjamin Cheever. His daughter Susan Cheever has published novels, a memoir of her father (*Home before Dark*, 1985), and *American Bloomsbury* (2006), a biographical study of Louisa May *Alcott, Ralph Waldo *Emerson, and their contemporaries.

CHEKE, Sir John (1514–57) Fellow of St John's College, Cambridge, tutor to Edward VI, and first Regius professor of Greek at Cambridge. He was imprisoned by Queen Mary, 1553–4. An eminent classical and biblical scholar (translating much from Greek and English into Latin), he wrote little in the vernacular, but helped promote a simple style of English prose. John *Milton refers to him ('O soul of *Sir John Cheek*') in Sonnet XI, 'A Book was writ of late'.

CHEKHOV, Anton Pavlovich (1860–1904) Russian dramatist and short story writer, born in Taganrog. As a medical student in Moscow (1879–84) he began writing short pieces for comic magazines, attracting the attention of the literary world. The earliest examples of his mature stories are 'The Steppe' (1888) and 'A Boring Story' (1889). Other masterpieces followed: 'Ward Six' (1892), 'My Life' (1896), 'Ionych', and the trilogy 'The Man in a Case', 'Gooseberries', and 'About Love' (all 1898), 'The Lady with the Little Dog' (1899), 'Darling' (1899), and 'The Bishop' (1902). Chekhov's first successful full-length plays were *Ivanov* (1888) and *The Wood Demon* (1889) and his fondness for farce was reflected in several one-act plays such as *The Bear* (1888) and *The Proposal* (1889). In 1890 he unexpectedly embarked on an arduous journey across Siberia to the prison island of Sakhalin that resulted in a sociological study, *Journey to Sakhalin* (1895). His status as a dramatist rests on his four late plays. Although the 1896 St Petersburg premiere of his innovatory *The Seagull* (1895) was a disaster, the play was triumphantly revived in the 1898 inaugural season of the *Moscow Arts Theatre, founded by Konstantin Stanislavsky (1863–1938) and Vladimir Nemirovich-Danchenko (1858–1943). It was followed by *Uncle Vanya* (1900), *Three Sisters* (1901), and *The Cherry Orchard* (1904), a comedy written in the last stages of the tuberculosis that had ravaged his health for over a decade. In 1901 Chekhov married the Art Theatre actress Olga Knipper (1868–1959). Vsevolod Meyerhold (Meierkhold) (1874–1940) also appeared in the Art Theatre's Chekhov productions, and his later anti-naturalistic productions of the plays were probably closer to the intentions of a playwright who had always chafed at Stanislavskian naturalism. The first English productions of his plays were a staging of *The Seagull* in Glasgow in 1909 by George Calderon (1868–1915) and the Incorporated Stage Society's 1911 London production of *The Cherry Orchard*. E. M. *Forster, Virginia *Woolf, J. M. *Murry, and especially Katherine *Mansfield were among early admirers. Katherine Mansfield's stories are held to be the main channel through which his work influenced England, and her letters are full of expressions of her sympathy for him. G. B. *Shaw wrote **Heartbreak House* as a tribute to him. Chekhov's work is characterized by its subtle blending of naturalism and symbolism, dispassionate objectivity; and a sensitive combination of comedy, tragedy, and pathos. Since 1903 most of his work has been translated. The first major translation is that by Constance *Garnett, *The Tales of Tchehov* (1916–22) and *The Plays of Tchehov* (1923–4). The major modern translation is that by Ronald Hingley, *The Oxford Chekhov* (9 vols, 1964–80). An excellent modern version of the plays is by Michael *Frayn, *Plays* (1993). See also Patrick Miles (ed.), *Chekhov on the British Stage* (1993) and Donald Rayfield, *Anton Chekhov: A Life* (1997).

CHÉNIER, André-Marie (1762–94) French poet, born in Constantinople of mixed French and Greek parentage. He played an active part as a political journalist during the French Revolution, was arrested in March 1794, and died on the guillotine. His poetry remained unpublished in his lifetime, but the example of his life and death made a considerable impression on subsequent generations; the first collected edition of his poems, in 1819, gained wide popularity, exercising an influence on the *Romantic and *Parnassian movements. His poetry reveals his affinities with the classical world, particularly with the elegiac verse of the *Greek *Anthology*, and his involvement in the social and political issues of the revolution.

CHERRY-GARRARD, Apsley (1886–1959) Antarctic explorer, born in Bedford, heir to two landed English families and son of a major-general. He was educated at Winchester College and Oxford University. In 1910 he accompanied Robert Falcon *Scott to the Antarctic as assistant zoologist, editing the expedition's newspaper, the *South Polar Times*. Edward Wilson (1872–1912) chose him and 'Birdie' Bowers (1883–1912) to sledge 67 miles in winter darkness to collect emperor penguin eggs. He was in a support party for Scott's last race for the pole, and was one of those who discovered Scott's body ten months later. He wrote *The Worst Journey in the World* (1922), drawing on the diaries of Scott, Wilson, and Bowers, while convalescing from war injuries sustained in Flanders. It became a classic of Antarctic adventure, contributing to the mix of heroism, tragedy, and understated British grit that caught the popular imagination in the post-war world.

CHERRYH, C. J. (Carolyn Janice) (1942–) American *science fiction and *fantasy novelist, born in St Louis; noted for novels exploring the history of a universe dominated by rival commercial alliances. Examples include *Downbelow Station* (1981) and *Cyteen* (1988), both of which have won *Hugo awards. Traditional science fiction elements of space habitats, alien planets, and conflicts are increasingly set in a detailed historical and anthropological context. The 'Rusalka' fantasy series (1989–91) draws upon Russian mythology.

CHESNUTT, Charles (1858–1932) African American novelist, short story writer, and political activist, who was born in Cleveland, Ohio. A formative figure in the development of *African American literature, Chesnutt established himself with stories like 'The Goophered Grapevine' (1887), which describe black folk culture on the Southern plantations before the Civil War. His 1899 collection of 'conjure stories' *The Conjure Woman* further develops this interest. After he gave up court reporting Chesnutt produced three novels exploring the racial politics of the South: *The House behind the Cedars* (1900), *The Marrow of Tradition* (1901), and *The Colonel's Dream* (1905). *Post-Bellum—Pre-Harlem* (1931) is part autobiography, part reflections on how African American writing had evolved.

CHESTERFIELD, Philip Dormer Stanhope, fourth earl of (1694–1773) Statesman and writer. He was ambassador at The Hague 1728–32, lord lieutenant of Ireland 1745–6, and secretary of state 1746–8. He was a friend of Alexander *Pope, John *Gay, and John *Arbuthnot. He was opposed to Sir Robert Walpole (1676–1745), and wrote political tracts, but is chiefly remembered for his 'Letters' to his natural son Philip Stanhope (1732–68), which were written almost daily from 1737 onwards. These consist of instruction in etiquette and the worldly arts, and became after publication (by the son's widow in 1774) a handbook of aristocratic manners. The young man's shyness is addressed by advice about deportment (laughter occasions 'a shocking distortion of the face' and should be avoided), conversation, and approaches to women (described as 'children of larger growth'). Although widely admired, the letters attracted criticism for their cynical advocacy of superficial 'good breeding'; Samuel *Johnson declared that they 'teach the morals of a whore and the manners of a dancing-master' and William *Cowper described their author as 'Graybeard corrupter of our listening youth'.

Johnson had addressed the 'Plan' of his *Dictionary* to Chesterfield, but the appeal for patronage was neglected, perhaps unintentionally; just before publication of the *Dictionary*, Chesterfield wrote two papers in the *World* commending it. On 7 February 1755 Johnson addressed to him a celebrated letter, bitterly denouncing this overdue notice. Chesterfield used to show the letter, admiringly, to visitors. See *The Letters of Philip Dormer Stanhope*, ed. Bonamy Dobrée, 6 vols (1932).

CHESTERTON, G. K. (Gilbert Keith) (1874–1936) Author, born in London and educated at St Paul's School and, briefly, University College London and then at the Slade School of Fine Art, London. He made his name in journalism (according to him 'the easiest of all professions'), taking a controversial, anti-imperial, pro-Boer line on the Boer War. He would write regularly for the press for the rest of his life. His first published novel, *The Napoleon of Notting Hill* (1904), a fantasy of the future in which London is plunged into a strange mixture of medieval nostalgia and street warfare, displayed the full range of his political sympathies, glorifying the little man, revelling in the colour and romance of 'Merry England', and attacking big business, technology, and the monolithic state. These themes echo through his fiction, which includes his most accomplished novel, *The Man Who Was Thursday: A Nightmare* (1908), an alarming but rollicking fantasy with a surreal anarchist background which attacks *fin-de-siècle* pessimism, and his many volumes of short stories, of which the best known are those which feature Father Brown, an unassuming East Anglian Roman Catholic priest, highly successful in the detection of crime by intuitive methods, who first appears in *The Innocence of Father Brown* (1911); Chesterton himself became a Roman Catholic in 1922. In addition, he published several volumes of verse; his most characteristic poems (with some exceptions, such as 'The Donkey', from *The Wild Knight*, 1900, and 'Lepanto', from *Poems*, 1915) tend to celebrate the Englishness of England, the nation of Beef and Beer, e.g. 'The Secret People' (1915) and 'The Rolling English Road' (1914). Chesterton also wrote literary criticism, including works on Robert *Browning (1903), Charles *Dickens (1906), and George Bernard *Shaw (1910), and many volumes of political, social, and religious essays, including *Heretics* (1905), on contemporary writers, *Orthodoxy* (1908), and *The Everlasting Man* (1925); also an *Autobiography* (1936). Much of Chesterton's vast output has proved ephemeral, but his vigour, idiosyncrasies, optimism, puns, and paradoxes celebrate the oddity of life and the diversity of people and places with a peculiar and at times exhilarating zest. See Michael Coren, *Gilbert: The Man Who Was G. K. Chesterton* (1989).

CHESTRE, Thomas *See* Sir Launfal.

CHETTLE, Henry (*c*.1560–1603/7) Printer, pamphleteer, and dramatist. The son of a London dyer, he was apprenticed to the printer Thomas East and was for a time a partner with William Hoskins and John Danter in a printing business. Chettle may have had a hand in the compilation as well as in the printing of some literary works from the press, including the first quarto of **Romeo and Juliet* (1597); in 1596 he contributed prefatory letters to works by Thomas *Nashe and Anthony *Munday, identifying himself as being involved in their printing. Although in the satirical pamphlet *Kind-Heart's Dream* (?1593) he denied that **Greene's Groat's-worth of Wit* (1592), published after Robert *Greene's death, was his, there is strong evidence that it was in fact written by Chettle. By 1598 he was an established author of comedies for the stage and is listed in Philip *Henslowe's diary in association with 49 plays, 36 written in collaboration with authors such as John *Day, Thomas *Dekker, Thomas *Heywood, Ben *Jonson, Munday, and John *Webster, and thirteen on his own. Only a few of these collaborative plays were printed: these include two plays about Robert, earl of Huntingdon (1601), with Munday, *Patient Grissil* (1603) with Dekker and William Haughton, and *The Blind-Beggar of Bednal-Green* (1659) with Day. Chettle may well have had a considerable hand in the collaborative play of *Sir Thomas More*, which survives in manuscript. The only extant play for which he alone is known to be responsible is *The Tragedy of Hoffman* (*c*.1603), which was first printed 1631, but not then attributed to Chettle. It deals with the story of a Danish pirate who is executed and the revenge and execution of his son. He also published *England's Mourning Garment*, an elegy on *Elizabeth I, in 1603. There is a life by Harold Jenkins (1934).

Chevy Chase, The Ballad of One of the oldest of the English ballads; it probably dates in its primitive form from the 15th century. Its subject is the rivalry of the neighbouring families of Percy and Douglas, heightened by the national quarrel between England and Scotland. Percy, earl of Northumberland, has vowed to hunt for three days across the Scottish border 'maugre the doughty Douglas'. The two parties meet and fight, there is great slaughter on both sides, and both Percy and Douglas are killed (cf. **Otterbourne, The Battle of*). The ballad is quoted and discussed by Joseph *Addison, who admired its 'majestic simplicity' and compared it to Virgil, in the **Spectator* (nos 70 and 74, May 1711). It is included in Percy's **Reliques*.

CHEYNE, George (1672–1743) Doctor, educated at Aberdeen and Edinburgh universities. He later established a practice in Bath. John *Gay called him 'Cheyne, huge of size' in 1720 and in *The English Malady* (1733), a treatise on depression, Cheyne described his former obesity, which he cured with a rigorous diet, and his mental collapse *c.*1705, which he treated with religious study. This work, with several other medical treatises, recommended moderation and self-control and emphasized the moral duty to maintain one's own health. Alexander *Pope consulted Cheyne on dietary matters and asked him to convey his admiration of **Pamela* to Cheyne's friend Samuel *Richardson.

chiasmus A figure of speech by which the order of the words in the first of two parallel clauses is reversed in the second, e.g. 'He saved others; himself he cannot save.'

Chicano literature is the writing of Hispanic Americans, mainly of Mexican ancestry, which dates back to 1848, when parts of the south-west were annexed by the USA. The 1960s saw a renaissance in this area and the appropriation of the notion of Aztlan (originally denoting an Aztec homeland) to mean an ideal state of unification. See the anthology *Literatura Chicana, 1965–1995* (1997); Julio A. Martinez and Francisco A. Lomeli, *Chicano Literature: A Reference Guide* (1985).

Childe Harold's Pilgrimage A poem in Spenserian stanzas by Lord *Byron, of which the first two cantos appeared in 1812, Canto III in 1816, and Canto IV in 1818. The poem describes the travels, experiences, and reflections of a self-styled and self-exiled pilgrim, Childe Harold, whose wanderings correspond in many ways to Byron's own, although Byron denied that he identified himself with Harold, and wrote in an addition to his preface (1813) that the pilgrim 'was never intended as an example'—rather, he was 'a modern Timon, perhaps a poetical Zeluco'. Harold, a melancholy, defiant outcast, is the first of a series of histrionic *Byronic heroes: his character reappears, with little significant development, in *The *Corsair*, **Manfred*, and other works. The first two cantos describe how the wanderer, sated with his past life of sin and pleasure, finds distraction by travel: he journeys through Portugal, Spain, the Ionian Islands, and Albania, interspersing his evocations of the glorious scenery with diatribes against the Convention of Cintra ('Britannia sickens, Cintra! at thy name'), with an eleven-stanza description of the bloody sport of bull fighting, and (Canto II) with a savage attack on Lord Elgin, the 'last dull spoiler', for his pillage of the Greek antiquities. He salutes Albania and its wild, martial, and exotically garbed people, then once more laments the lost liberty of Greece. In Canto III, written six years later, the pilgrim, still 'wrung with the wounds that heal not', travels to Belgium, the Rhine, the Alps, and Jura: Stanza XXI introduces his celebrated passage on the battle of Waterloo, 'There was a sound of revelry by night...' Later stanzas (LXXVI–CVIII) pay tribute to 'wild Rousseau, The Apostle of affliction' and to Edward *Gibbon, 'Sapping a solemn creed with solemn sneer; The lord of irony'. In Canto IV, dedicated to his friend and travelling companion John *Hobhouse, he abandons the device of the pilgrim and speaks directly, in a long meditation on time and history, on Venice and *Petrarch, on Ferrara and *Tasso, on *Boccaccio and Florence, and on Rome—'Oh Rome! my country! city of the soul! The orphans of the heart must turn to thee...' The canto concludes with a passionate invocation of 'the deep and dark blue Ocean', 'the image of eternity'. The poem enjoyed great success. After the publication of Cantos I and II in March 1812 Byron wrote, 'I awoke... and found myself famous.' Later, however, he claimed that he came to dislike it as 'the false exaggerated style of youth'. The author's copious notes pursue many of the themes of the poem with wit and indignation.

Childe Roland In an old Scottish ballad, a son of King Arthur. His sister, Burd Ellen, is carried away by the fairies to the castle of the king of Elfland. Aided by the instructions of Merlin, Childe Roland enters the castle and rescues his sister. 'Child Rowland to the dark tower came, His word was still "Fie, foh, and fum, I smell the blood of a British man"' (Shakespeare, **King Lear*, III. iv). J. O. *Halliwell (*Nursery Rhymes*) thinks that Shakespeare is quoting from two different compositions, the first line from a ballad on Roland, the second and third from the story of Jack the Giant-Killer.

'Childe Roland to the Dark Tower Came' A poem by Robert *Browning, published in **Men and Women* (1855). The title derives from a fragment of song recited by Edgar in **King Lear*. A knight-in-training crosses a nightmare landscape in search of the Dark Tower (or has been deceived into doing so; it is not clear which); he eventually reaches the Tower and blows his horn defiantly at its foot. The poem ends with the title phrase, and there is no indication of what happens next. Because the story is told by the knight himself, the poem's form raises insoluble problems of interpretation. The monologue is both satisfying as a Gothic dream narrative and disturbing as an impenetrable allegory—of life, of art, or of both. Browning refused to explain the poem, saying simply that it had come to him as a dream. 'Thamuris marching' in **Aristophanes' Apology* makes an intriguing comparison with this episode of an anti-romance.

CHILDERS, Erskine (1870–1922) Writer and political activist. Born in London and educated at Haileybury College and Trinity College, Cambridge, where he argued against Irish Home Rule, he was from 1895 to 1910 a clerk in the House of Commons. He served in both the Boer War and the First World War before settling in Ireland in 1919, by now wholly committed to the goal of Irish independence. In 1921 he was appointed director of publicity for the Irish Republican Army and in 1922 he was court-martialled and shot by a Free State firing squad. As a writer he is remembered for *The Riddle of the Sands* (1903), often described as the first example of *spy fiction, a novel about two British yachtsmen sailing in the Baltic who discover German preparations for an invasion of England. See J. Ring, *Erskine Childers* (1996).

Children of the Chapel of Paul's *See* PAUL'S, CHILDREN OF.

children's literature *See introductory essay* pp. 23–31.

children's literature in translation *See* TRANSLATION FOR CHILDREN.

CHILLINGWORTH, William (1602–44) A scholar and fellow of Trinity College, Oxford. He became a Roman Catholic and went to Douai in 1630, but renounced Catholicism in 1634. He was one of the literary coterie that gathered round Viscount *Falkland at Great Tew, and was the author of the controversial work *The Religion of Protestants a Safe Way to Salvation* (1638).

Chimes, The A Christmas book by Charles *Dickens, published 1845. It is the story of a nightmare or vision in which Toby Veck, porter and runner of errands, under the influence of the goblins of the church bells and a dish of tripe, witnesses awful misfortunes befalling his daughter, a vision happily dissipated at the end; together with some social satire on justices, aldermen, and the like, in the persons of Sir Joseph Bowley and Mr Chute.

Chips with Everything *See* WESKER, ARNOLD.

chivalric/romance epic Terms used to describe the narratives, on mainly Arthurian and Carolingian subjects, which developed in Italy from the fourteenth century and reached their apogee in the poems of *Boiardo, *Ariosto, and *Tasso. Chivalric epic combines the martial and religious motifs of epic with the ideals of chivalry and *courtly love typical of romance, hence the hybrid term. In Italy chivalric epics were written almost exclusively in the stanzaic form of **ottava rima*. Both the content and the metre were influential on Edmund *Spenser and Lord *Byron.

CHOPIN, Kate (1850–1904) Née O'Flaherty, American novelist and short story writer, the daughter of an Irish immigrant father and Creole mother; she was born in St Louis, Missouri, and brought up in a largely female household. She married Oscar Chopin, a Creole, and went to live in New Orleans, Louisiana, spending her summers at Grand Isle, a fashionable resort off the south coast. Her husband died in 1882, leaving her with six children to support. After paying off his debts, she returned to St Louis and began to write, using as material her memories of New Orleans and of Cane River, the latter providing material for three collections of short stories and her first novel *At Fault* (1890). She was originally acclaimed as a 'local colourist', but has posthumously won recognition for *The Awakening* (1899), which tells the story of Edna Pontellier, married to a successful Creole business man, and leading a life of leisure which she finds vaguely dissatisfying. She commits adultery with one young man, while believing herself in love with another, and on the last page swims naked out to sea and presumably drowns. It was considered scandalous and morbid, and, discouraged by its hostile reception from writing more full-length fiction, Chopin turned to poems, essays, and short stories until her death from a brain haemorrhage.

choriamb A four-syllable metrical *foot with the first and last syllables stressed. The choriambic *metre is found in Greek choruses and was favoured in Latin by *Horace, but is very rarely used in English as the basis for whole lines: even *Swinburne's 'Choriambics' (1875) combines it with other feet.

CHRÉTIEN DE TROYES (*fl.* 1165–80) France's greatest writer of Arthurian *romance, the author of five major verse narratives in the second half of the 12th century, written in octosyllabic rhyming couplets and intended to be read aloud at court: *Erec and Enide* (*c.*1170); *Cligés* (*c.*1176); *Lancelot*, or *Le Chevalier de la charrette* (*c.*1177–81); *Yvain*, or *Le Chevalier au lion* (*c.*1177–81); and *Perceval* or *Le Conte du Graal* (1181–90), which he never completed. Two lyric poems in the style of the *troubadours are also known to be by him, and these, together with the time he spent at the court of *Marie de Champagne, suggest that he was familiar with the poetry and precepts of *courtly love. While generally supportive of chivalric values, he adopts in his poems a gently comic perspective on courtly conventions. He had an important influence on all subsequent Arthurian literature, including English, inspiring continuators, imitators, and adapters: the English romance *Iwain and Gawain* is in fact a loose translation of his *Yvain*. Twentieth-century English translations include those by W. W. Comfort (1914), who omits the *Perceval*, and D. D. R. Owen (1987). See J. J. Duggan, *The Romances of Chrétien de Troyes* (2001).

'Christabel' A poem by Samuel Taylor *Coleridge, published 1816. The poem is unfinished. The first part was written at Nether Stowey in 1797, the second at Keswick in 1800;

Coleridge made plans for Part III but found himself unable to continue with it. It is a medieval romance of the supernatural, written in what is sometimes referred to as 'Christabel metre'—that is, in four-foot couplets, mostly iambic and *anapaestic, used with immense variety, so that the line length varies from seven syllables to eleven. Christabel, praying at night in a wood for her betrothed lover, discovers the fair Geraldine in distress and takes her to the castle of her father, Sir Leoline. Geraldine claims to have been abducted from her home by five warriors, and to be the daughter of Leoline's estranged friend Sir Roland of Vaux. She shares Christabel's chamber, and bewitches her as they lie in one another's arms. In the morning she meets Leoline, who vows reconciliation with her father and vengeance on the 'reptile souls' of her abductors. Christabel, who has seen Geraldine's true malignant serpentine nature, is at first silenced by the spell placed upon her, but manages to implore her father to send Geraldine away, although she can offer no explanation for this plea. Leoline, offended by his daughter's insult to a guest, turns from her to Geraldine. So the poem ends. Though the poem does not yield up any clear allegorical meaning, the imagery throughout is sexually charged, and in thematic terms it has often been seen as connected with the corruption and seduction of innocence. To Coleridge's disappointment, Wordsworth did not include the poem in the second edition of the *Lyrical Ballads*. Coleridge's sources have been traced by A. Nethercot, *The Road to Tryermaine* (1939).

Christ and Satan An Old English poem of 729 lines in three sections, found in the *Junius Manuscript. Like many of the poems in this manuscript, it was once erroneously attributed to *Cædmon. The subjects of the three sections are: Satan's passionate and plangent lament for his fall from heaven; the *Harrowing of Hell; and the temptation of Christ by Satan, which ends with the condemnation of Satan by Christ and his banishment to hell.

Christian Morals *See* BROWNE, THOMAS.

Christian Year, The *See* KEBLE, JOHN.

CHRISTIE, Dame Agatha (1890–1976) Detective novelist, born and brought up in Torquay. She was educated at home, and in 1914 married Archibald Christie. During the First World War she worked as a hospital dispenser, which gave her a knowledge of poisons invaluable when she started writing *detective fiction. Her marriage broke up in 1926, and in 1930 she married the archaeologist Max Mallowan, whom she accompanied on his excavations of sites in Syria and Iraq. Her first detective novel, *The Mysterious Affair at Styles* (1920), introduced Hercule Poirot, the Belgian detective who appeared in many subsequent novels (her other main detective being the elderly spinster Miss Marple). In the next 56 years she wrote 66 detective novels, among the best of which are *The Murder of Roger Ackroyd* (1926), *Murder on the Orient Express* (1934), *Death on the Nile* (1937), *Ten Little Niggers* (1939), and *Sparkling Cyanide* (1945). She also wrote six novels under the pseudonym Mary Westmacott, two self-portraits (*Come Tell Me How You Live*, 1946; *An Autobiography*, 1977), and several plays, including *The Mousetrap*, first performed in London in 1952 and still running more than half a century later. Her prodigious international success seems due to her unrivalled and prolific ingenuity in contriving plots, sustaining suspense, and tantalizing and misdirecting the reader. See R. Barnard, *A Talent to Deceive* (1980); C. Osborne, *The Life and Crimes of Agatha Christie* (1982, revised edn 1999).

CHRISTINA OF MARKYATE (*c.*1096–after 1145) Recluse and prioress of Markyate (Hertfordshire), the subject of a remarkable anonymous *Life*. When young she made a vow of virginity which she maintained even after a forced marriage. She was kept in confinement, but eventually escaped, finding refuge first in Flamstead and subsequently at a hermitage in Markyate. In 1123, after the annulment of her marriage, she founded a community at Markyate, and made her monastic profession (*c.*1131), later acquiring a reputation as a visionary. See *The Life of Christina of Markyate*, trans. C. H. Talbot, rev. Samuel Fanous and Henrietta Leyser (2008).

CHRISTINE DE PISAN (*c.*1364–*c.*1431) French poet and scholar, born in Venice, and considered to be the first woman of letters in France. Author of courtly ballades and rondeaux, she is best known for her feminist works, including the *Epistre au dieu d'amours* (1399: *Epistle to the God of Love*), an eloquent denunciation of the anti-feminist attitudes of Jean de Meun (*see* ROMAN DE LA ROSE), *La Cité des dames* (1404–5: *The City of Ladies*), in which she constructs an ideal city peopled by the great women of history and legend, and *Le Livre des trois vertus* (1405: *The Book of the Three Virtues*), which explores women's duties. A number of English translations of her work appeared in the late 15th and early 16th centuries, and several new translations appeared in the late 20th century. See C. C. Willard, *Christine de Pizan* (1984).

Christis Kirk on the Green A Scottish poem of the late 15th or early 16th century from the *Bannatyne Manuscript, in nine-line stanzas with a 'bob', or short tag, after the eighth line, describes the rough fun, dancing, and love-making of a village festival or 'wappinshaw'. Two additional cantos were composed by Allan *Ramsay.

Christmas Carol, A A Christmas book by Charles *Dickens, published 1843. Ebenezer Scrooge, a miserly old curmudgeon, receives on Christmas Eve a visit from the ghost of Marley, his late partner in business, and encounters a series of visions of the past, present, and future, including one of what his own death will be like unless he mends his ways. He wakes up on Christmas morning a changed man. He sends a turkey to his ill-used clerk Bob Cratchit, positively enjoys subscribing to Christmas charities, and generally behaves like the genial old fellow that he has become. One of Dickens's most enduringly popular works, the book has been the subject of numerous adaptations on stage, screen, and television.

Christmas-Eve and Easter-Day A poem by Robert *Browning, published 1850. The poem is in two parts, in *octosyllabic metre, with an irregular rhyme scheme. The first part, 'Christmas-Eve', in the form of a narrative combining realistic and visionary elements, accepts that denominational religion is an imperfect medium for divine truth, but emphasizes the need to choose the best method of worship according to one's understanding. The second part, 'Easter-Day', in the form of an imagined dialogue, examines the difficulties of holding to the Christian faith at all, and argues that the condition of doubt is essential to the existence of human faith. The poem, the first to appear after Browning's marriage, shows the influence of E. B. *Browning's strong intellectual and emotional engagement with religious polemic, acting on Browning's own Nonconformist upbringing.

CHRISTOPHER, John (1922–) Pen-name of Christopher Samuel Youd, born in Lancashire, for his *science fiction for adults and children. *The Death of Grass* (1956) is a bleak novel of environmental disaster. The 'Tripods' sequence (1967–68) inaugurated his successful career as a writer for children.

Christ's Hospital The most famous of the Blue-Coat or charity schools, was founded in London under a charter of Edward VI as a school for poor children, in buildings that before the dissolution had belonged to the Grey Friars. S. T. *Coleridge, Charles *Lamb, Leigh *Hunt, and Edmund *Blunden were educated there.

Christ's Tears over Jerusalem A tract by Thomas *Nashe, published 1593. Nashe presents himself as a religious reformer, applying Christ's prophecy of the fall of Jerusalem as a warning to sinful London to repent. With his usual vigour, he analyses the vices and abuses of contemporary society.

Christs Victory, and Triumph *See* FLETCHER, GILES, THE YOUNGER.

chronicle play A type of drama popular in the 1590s and the early 17th century, in which scenes from the life of a monarch or famous historical character were depicted. Examples are Shakespeare's **Henry V* and **Henry VIII*, the *Sir Thomas *More* play, and Thomas *Dekker and John *Webster's *Sir Thomas Wyatt*.

Chrononhotonthologos (1734) A burlesque of contemporary dramatic absurdities by the singer and dramatist Henry Carey (1687–1743) under the pseudonym 'Benjamin Bounce'. 'The Most Tragical Tragedy that ever was Tragediz'd by any Company of Tragedians', the play chronicled with joyous brevity the melodramatic fate of the eponymous king of Queerummania.

CHRYSOSTOM, St John (*c*.347–407) A Greek Father of the Church, born and educated at Antioch in Syria. In 398 he became bishop of Constantinople, where he preached so eloquently against the vices of the city and its empress Eudoxia that he was condemned by a packed synod and banished. His name means 'Golden-mouth', in tribute to his eloquent preaching; in his voluminous sermons and biblical commentaries he stressed the ascetical and moral element in religion and the need for personal study of the Scriptures. His writings were much admired by Restoration Anglicans such as Gilbert *Burnet. See J. N. D. Kelly, *Golden Mouth* (1995).

CHUDLEIGH, Lady Mary (1656–1710) née Lee, author, born in Winslade, Devon. At the age of 17 she married George Chudleigh. She corresponded with Mary *Astell, whose *Some Reflections on Marriage* prompted her poem, *The Ladies Defence* (1701); in it Melissa argues robustly with three prejudiced men about the nature of marriage, obedience, and the advantages of female education. Her *Poems on Several Occasions* (1703), 'the innocent amusements of a solitary life', was followed by some pious *Essays upon Several Subjects in Verse and Prose* (1710). See *The Poems and Prose of Mary, Lady Chudleigh*, ed. Margaret Ezell (1993).

Church of England Though there has been an organized church in England since the 4th century, the name refers to the institution established by law following Henry VIII's breach with Rome in 1532. The monarch became head of the church, the monasteries were dissolved and their wealth appropriated, and the authority of the papacy was repudiated. The church took its distinctive shape in the reign of Edward VI under the direction of Thomas *Cranmer, with its own liturgy, *The Book of *Common Prayer*; Articles of Religion (originally Forty-Two, the Thirty-Nine Articles received their final form in 1571); two books of Homilies (1547, 1571), i.e. sermons to be read in churches; and the Authorized Version of the *Bible (1611). Although Protestant in doctrine, the Church of England retained many Catholic features in its ceremonies and vestments and retained government by bishops, and it was regarded by Puritans as incompletely reformed. Its principles were strongly defended by Richard *Hooker in *Of the *Laws of Ecclesiastical Politie*. During the Civil War many of the distinctive features of the Church of England were abolished by Parliament, but the church was restored together with the monarchy in 1660. It remains the officially established Christian church in England.
See PROTESTANTISM; PURITANISM; REFORMATION; ROMAN CATHOLICISM.

CHURCHILL, Caryl (1938–) Playwright, born in London and educated in Montreal and at Lady Margaret Hall, Oxford. Most of her plays, predominantly radical and feminist in tone, have been performed at the *Royal Court Theatre:

they include *Owners* (1972); *Light Shining in Buckinghamshire* (1976); *Cloud Nine* (1979), a comedy in two acts, the first exploring sexual repression in Victorian Africa, the second set in London in 1979 and exploring contemporary sexual identity; **Top Girls* (1982); **Serious Money* (1987); *Mad Forest* (1990), about the Romanian revolution; *The Skriker* (1994); *Blue Heart* (1997); and *This Is a Chair* (1997). She continues to surprise audiences with her most recent work: a darkly comic allegory about ethnic cleansing, *Far Away* (2001), was followed by *A Number* (2002), about the implications of human genetic cloning, and then by *Too Drunk to Say I Love You* (2006), a savage critique of contemporary US foreign policy.

CHURCHILL, Charles (1732–64) Poet, educated at Westminster School (where his friends included William *Cowper and George *Colman) and, briefly, St John's College, Cambridge. He was ordained priest in 1756, succeeding his clergyman father as curate of St John's, Smith Square, in 1758. His poverty was alleviated by the publication of *The *Rosciad* and *The Apology* (1761), which also brought him into the worldly circle of John *Wilkes, for whom he edited the **North Briton* and whose opponents he attacked in verse. *The Prophecy of Famine* (1763) is a mock-pastoral satire on Lord Bute, John *Home, and other Scots. Other targets were Tobias *Smollett (*The Author*, 1763) and William *Hogarth (*Epistle to William Hogarth*, 1763). *The Duellist* (1764) attacks Samuel Martin (1714–88), who had wounded Wilkes in a duel; *The Candidate* (1764) lambasts the earl of Sandwich (1718–92); *The Times* (1764) decries aristocratic vices, especially sodomy. *Gotham* (1764) jokingly installs Churchill as monarch of an ideal state. Churchill died at Boulogne on his way to visit Wilkes in France. His admirers included James *Boswell, despite Churchill's anti-Scottish prejudice and his attacks on Samuel *Johnson, and Lord *Byron. See W. C. Brown, *Charles Churchill: Poet, Rake, and Rebel* (1953); *The Poetical Works of Charles Churchill*, ed. D. Grant (1956).

CHURCHILL, Sir Winston (1874–1965) Statesman, writer, and prime minister. Born at Blenheim Palace, Oxfordshire, and educated at Harrow School and the Royal Military College, Sandhurst, he entered the army in 1895 and served in India, Egypt, and the Sudan. He was present as a war correspondent during the Boer War and first entered Parliament in 1900. He went on to serve in many capacities, including under-secretary of state for the colonies, 1906–8; president of the Board of Trade, 1908–10; home secretary, 1910–11; first lord of the Admiralty, 1911–15; secretary of state for war, 1918–21; for the colonies, 1921–2; chancellor of the Exchequer, 1924–9; prime minister, 1940–5 and 1951–5. Among his publications are: *The Story of the Malakand Field Force* (1898); *London to Ladysmith via Pretoria* (1900); *Ian Hamilton's March* (1900); *Savrola* (1900), his only novel; *Lord Randolph Churchill*, 2 vols (1906–7); *My African Journey* (1908); *Liberalism and the Social Problem* (1909); *The World Crisis*, 4 vols (1923–31); *My Early Life* (1930); *Marlborough*, 4 vols (1933–8), *War Speeches 1940–5* (1946); *The Second World War*, 6 vols (1948–53) and *A History of the English-Speaking Peoples*, 4 vols (1956–8). He was awarded the *Nobel Prize for Literature in 1953. See R. S. Churchill and M. Gilbert, *Winston S. Churchill*, 8 vols (1966–88).

CHURCHYARD, Thomas (?1523–1604) Author, at one time page to Henry Howard, earl of *Surrey. He lived a wandering life, partly as a soldier in Scotland, Ireland, France, and the Low Countries, partly as a hanger-on of the court and the nobility. His earliest known work dates from *c.*1552. Between 1560 and 1603 he published a multitude of broadsheets and small volumes in verse and prose, several containing autobiographical pieces and notices of current events. His best-known works are *Shore's Wife* (1563) in the **Mirror for Magistrates*, and the *General Rehearsal of Wars* (1579), in which he made use of his own experience as a soldier. Spenser in his **Colin Clouts Come Home Againe* refers to Churchyard as 'old *Palemon*...That sung so long untill quite hoarse he grew'.

CIBBER, Colley (1671–1757) Actor and author, son of Caius Cibber the sculptor, educated at Grantham School. He became an actor in 1690. His first play, *Love's Last Shift* (1696), introduced Sir Novelty Fashion, a comic fop role later transformed into Lord Foppington in Sir John *Vanbrugh's sequel *The Relapse*; such figures were Cibber's speciality as an actor. He went on to write many plays and adaptations, notably the successful comedies *She Would and She Would Not* (1702), *The *Careless Husband* (1704), and *The Lady's Last Stake* (1707), and an enduring adaptation of Shakespeare's **Richard III* (1700). *The Non-juror* (1717), a comedy based on *Molière's *Tartuffe*, provoked a satirical pamphlet by Alexander *Pope, partly in revenge for Cibber's abuse of the *Scriblerian comedy *Three Hours after Marriage*; Cibber had become a theatrical manager, first at the Haymarket, then at Drury Lane. A loyal Whig, he was appointed poet laureate in 1730, to general derision. He attracted many enemies by his indomitable egocentricity, and as a writer was more concerned with theatrical effect than with literary intelligence, but his plays were admired by Tobias *Smollett and Horace *Walpole. His disarmingly insouciant *An Apology for the Life of Mr Colley Cibber, Comedian* (1740) presents a vivid picture of the theatrical life of the time rather than autobiography as such: his infamous children Theophilus (*see* Cibber, T.) and Charlotte (*see* Charke) scarcely feature. The book was vengefully satirized by Henry *Fielding in **Shamela* and elsewhere; its brazen vanity gave Pope an excuse to install Cibber as the hero of the revised **Dunciad*, an elevation to which he responded with some damaging anecdotes about Pope's earlier life. See H. Koon, *Colley Cibber: A Biography* (1986); *An Apology for the Life of Colley Cibber, Comedian*, ed. J. M. Evans (1987).

CIBBER, Theophilus (1703–58) Son of Colley *Cibber, educated at Winchester College. He joined his father's theatrical company in 1720, with some success, but his wild temper and extravagant habits provoked much scandal. In 1734 he married Susanna Maria Arne (1714–66), sister of Thomas *Arne; she became with his encouragement a distinguished tragic actress, but he also encouraged for mercenary reasons her relationship with a well-to-do lover, William Sloper, as revealed, in detail, in the disastrous lawsuit of 1738 which derailed his career. He struggled along in minor roles, exploiting the family name and writing plays and memoirs until he was drowned on the way to an engagement at the Smock Alley Theatre, Dublin.

CICERO, Marcus Tullius (106–43 BC) Sometimes referred to as Tully, the supreme Latin orator and prose writer. Born into a wealthy family in Arpinum, he studied law, rhetoric, and philosophy at Rome and Athens. He delivered his first speech in 81, and became famous in 70 by prosecuting Verres, the extortionate governor of Sicily. Praetor in 66, and consul in 63, at the earliest permitted age, he had a brilliant career for a 'new man'. As consul, he repressed the insurrection planned by *Catiline, executing his associates without trial. For this he was temporarily exiled in 58, but returned the following year. Thereafter, he regularly overemphasized his own achievements and popularity. He aspired to be a leading statesman, but the conquests of Pompey and *Caesar eclipsed civilian achievements. When civil war came, in 49, he reluctantly took Pompey's side. After Pompey's defeat Cicero was pardoned by Caesar, whose advances he rebuffed, and whose assassination he welcomed. Believing, injudiciously, that he could manage young Octavian, and hating Mark Antony, he rushed into a last burst of political activity. At Antony's insistence, Cicero was killed, and his severed head and hands were nailed to the Rostra (the orators' platform in the Roman Forum).

In the intervals of public life Cicero was a prolific writer. His works include a large number of speeches; treatises on rhetoric, notably *On Oratory*, *Brutus*, and *The Orator*; collections of letters to Atticus and other friends; and philosophical dialogues on politics, ethics, epistemology, and religion, such as *Of Old Age*, *Of Friendship*, *Of Duties*, *Tusculan Disputations*, and *The Nature of the Gods*. He was an important transmitter of Greek philosophy, especially *Stoicism, to Rome, and the creator of a Latin philosophical vocabulary. His influence on thought and expression from the Middle Ages to the 19th century was enormous. His letters were the model for the Latin epistles of Petrarch and Erasmus. His rhetorical works, rediscovered in the 15th century, and his philosophical dialogues were essentials of humanist education. The long tradition of reading Cicero as an honorary Christian was challenged in the 18th century, particularly by David *Hume. See Elizabeth Rawson, *Cicero: A Portrait* (rev. 1983); also Robert *Harris's *Imperium* (2006), a lively fictionalized account of the early years of Cicero's career

CID, the (*c.*1030–1099) The national hero of Spain in whose story history and myth are entangled. Born Rodrigo Díaz, probably at Vivar (Burgos), and known in his lifetime as 'Cid Campeador' ('Seyd', lord; 'Campeador', champion), he rose to fame through military prowess in the service of the future Sancho II of Castile against fellow Christian princes and Moors. Having incurred the jealousy of Alfonso VI, king of León-Castile, he was banished and became a mercenary, fighting at times for Christians, at others for Moors. His principal feat was the capture in 1094 of Valencia from the Moors after a siege of nine months. He died after doing all he could for some five years to consolidate his hold on Valencia and its hinterland. In myth he has been transformed into a paragon of knightly and Christian virtue, and patriotic zeal. His achievements are narrated in the early 13th-century *Poema de mio Cid: Poem of the Cid* (the sole surviving full-length Spanish *epic poem, consisting of some 3,700 lines), in Spanish chronicles of the 14th century, and in numerous ballads. The chronicles relating to him were translated by Robert *Southey (1808). The Cid is the subject of *Corneille's most famous play. His wife was called Ximena. See Richard Fletcher, *The Quest for El Cid* (1991).

cinema became the dominant mass entertainment medium of the 20th century within a decade of the pioneering 'moving picture' displays in 1894–6 by Thomas Edison (1847–1931) in New York, Louis (1864–1948) and Auguste (1862–1954) Lumière in Paris, and Robert Paul (1869–1943) in London. Amid the topical and anecdotal subjects of early programmes, adaptations of literary and especially stage works soon appeared. Paul and Edison filmed single scenes from contemporary drama in 1896, while William *Shakespeare and Charles *Dickens were popular early sources. Tableaux from *King John* by the actor-manager Beerbohm Tree (1852–1917) were filmed in 1899 by Biograph and Paul produced a multi-scene *Scrooge*, based on a popular stage version of *A *Christmas Carol*, in 1901. Biblical subjects, especially the life of Christ, and traditional *fairy stories were also popular before 1910, providing opportunities for trick effects to represent miracles and magic. Georges Méliès (1861–1938) became the most famous producer of trick-based fantasies, including several loosely based on Jules *Verne's novels.

From around 1913, leading authors started to become involved in cinema, with a sophisticated Danish adaptation of Gerhart *Hauptmann's *Atlantis* in 1913 and *d'Annunzio lending his name to the ancient world spectacle *Cabiria* (1914). From Britain, Arthur Conan *Doyle, Rudyard *Kipling, and Rider *Haggard enjoyed early screen success, although meretricious authors also prospered. Thomas *Dixon's lurid melodrama *The Clansman* provided the basis of Civil War epic *The Birth of a Nation* (1915) by D. W. Griffith (1875–1948), the success of which helped cement the global domination of American producers. Few authors managed to retained any control over the adaptation of their work—George Bernard *Shaw was an exception, refusing permission until the sound era—but many benefited from selling rights, especially to the Hollywood studios. Works by popular writers such as *Dumas, Lew Wallace (1827–1905; **Ben-Hur*), the Polish novelist Henryk Sienkiewicz (1856–1916), Baroness *Orczy, Edgar *Wallace, and the Spanish novelist Vicente Blasco Ibáñez (1867–1928; *The Four Horsemen of the Apocalypse*) have been frequently refilmed, making them classic in a new 'intermedial' sense.

While most writers since the mid-20th century have had some involvement with cinema, either working on scripts or having their works adapted, the relationship was traditionally considered fraught, with Scott *Fitzgerald the most celebrated of many supposed casualties of Hollywood. However, Graham *Greene pioneered a new relationship with cinema, writing such original screenplays as *The Third Man*, and scripting many of his own stories and novels, as Paul *Auster continues to do, while Harold *Pinter developed a respected parallel career scripting the works of others. More recently, playwrights such as Sam *Shepard, David *Mamet, Christopher *Hampton, and Stephen *Poliakoff have also become directors of their own films.

CINZIO (Giambattista Giraldi) (1504–73) Born at Ferrara, the author of the *Hecatommithi* (1565), or 'hundred tales', told after the manner of Boccaccio's *Decameron* by ten ladies and gentlemen sailing to Marseilles after the Sack of Rome in 1527. Some of these were incorporated by Painter in his *Palace of Pleasure*, providing the plots of Shakespeare's *Othello* and *Measure for Measure*, and of plays by *Beaumont and *Fletcher and James *Shirley. His nine tragedies and his treatise on tragedy had a decisive influence on the development of 16th-century drama in Italy; his first and most famous play, *Orbecche* (1541), showing divine retribution on the royal house of Persia, was closely modelled on *Seneca's *Thyestes*, and was full of Senecan blood and horrors. Mario *Praz claims in *The Flaming Heart* (1958) that 'Cinthio provides the link between the Senecan tyrant and the Elizabethan villain', but P. R. Horne in *The Tragedies of Giambattista Cinthio Giraldi* (1962) questions this view.

Circe *See* ODYSSEY.

circulating libraries Commercial libraries from which books could be borrowed for a fee. Some booksellers lent books in this way in the 1660s, but the first regular example in Britain appears to have been Allan *Ramsay's, founded in Edinburgh about 1725. The bookseller William Bathoe (d. 1768) claimed his was the 'original circulating library' in London. By 1800 some 200 were in operation. Such libraries stimulated the production of books, particularly of novels, though popular reading was often considered improper: Sir Anthony Absolute declares, in Sheridan's *The *Rivals*, 'A circulating library...is an evergreen tree of diabolical knowledge.' *Mudie's Lending Library, opened in London in 1852, exercised a powerful censorship: George *Moore, whose novels were refused by Mudie's, denounced the company in *Literature at Nurse, or Circulating Morals* (1885). Such censorship was extended in the 20th century to writers such as H. G. *Wells and D. H. *Lawrence. The other large circulating libraries were those of the 19th-century bookselling firm W. H. Smith and Son, and 'Mrs Boot's Booklovers' Library', which was established by the Nottingham retail chemist Jesse Boot (1850–1931) in his larger provincial outlets. By about 1970 circulating libraries had been replaced by local public libraries.

citizen comedy An early 17th-century type of play, usually set in contemporary London and dealing with the common life of the middle classes. Ben *Jonson's **Bartholomew Fair* and Thomas *Middleton's *A *Chaste Maid in Cheapside* are examples of the genre.

Citizen of the World, The By Oliver *Goldsmith, a collection of letters purporting to be written by or to Lien Chi Altangi, a Chinese traveller in London. They appeared as *Chinese Letters* in John *Newbery's *Public Ledger* between January 1760 and August 1761, and were published in book form, with additions, in 1762. The letters comment with innocent surprise on the absurdities of English life and manners. The best-known characters are the 'Man in Black', a covert philanthropist, and 'Beau' Tibbs, an affected nonentity who claims acquaintance with the great and whose wife talks of countesses while washing shirts.

City Heiress, The A comedy by Aphra *Behn produced in 1682, displaying Behn's Royalist sympathies. A 'seditious knight' Sir Timothy Treat-All and his nephew Tim Wilding are rivals for the hand of an heiress, Charlot. Wilding triumphs by various stratagems including the offer of the throne of Poland, which Sir Timothy accepts.

City Madam, The A comedy by Philip *Massinger, acted 1632, printed 1658. The wife and daughters of London merchant Sir John Frugal have become proud and extravagant, and he decides to teach them a lesson. He pretends to retire to a monastery, leaving his property to his brother Luke, an ostensibly reformed wastrel. Luke treats the family, apprentices, and debtors with great harshness, but Sir John, and the two suitors his proud daughters have rejected, return disguised as Indians and expose his hypocrisy.

'City of Dreadful Night, The' *See* THOMSON, JAMES (1834–82).

City Wit, The, *or The Woman Wears the Breeches* A comedy by Richard *Brome, printed 1653, one of the best of Brome's comedies. Crasy, a young citizen, who has been ruined by his generous and easy-going disposition, contrives, with the aid of his servant Jeremy, who passes himself off as the rich widow Tryman, to avenge himself on his various persecutors, including his wife, her would-be lovers, her mother Mrs Pyannet Sneakup, his malignant brother-in-law, and the pedant Sarpego.

'Civil Disobedience' *See* THOREAU, HENRY.

Civil Wars between the Two Houses of Lancaster and York, The An *epic poem in eight books by Samuel *Daniel. The first four books (published 1595) cover English history from the Conquest to Richard II, the remainder (1609) from the Wars of the Roses to Edward IV.

CLAIRMONT, Claire (1798–1879) Daughter of Mary Clairmont, William *Godwin's second wife. She accompanied Mary Wollstonecraft Godwin, her stepsister, on Mary's elopement with P. B. *Shelley, and in spite of pursuit remained with them on the Continent, thus giving rise to many of the calumnies directed against Shelley. She returned to London with the Shelleys in 1816, fell in love with Lord *Byron, and when he went to Switzerland induced the Shelleys to follow him with her. Byron's daughter Allegra was born to her in 1817. In 1818 Byron demanded the baby, offering to acknowledge and educate her. Strongly against her will, and against the advice of Shelley, Claire surrendered the child. Much to her distress, in 1821 Byron placed the child in a convent near Ravenna, where she died of a fever in the following year. Claire's subsequent life was spent in Russia, Italy, and Paris. See *The Journals of Claire Clairmont* (1968) and *The Clairmont Correspondence*, 2 vols (1995), both ed. M. K. Stocking.

CLANCHY, Kate (1965–) Poet, born in Glasgow and educated at Edinburgh and Oxford. Her first book *Slattern* (1995) was acclaimed for its melodious yet taut language, and acute observation, often drawn from her experience as a schoolteacher in the East End of London. It includes a series of love poems remarkable for their lucid description of female desire and hurt. In *Samarkand* (1999) she addresses a greater range of issues, using longer forms to explore masculine violence, national identity, fulfilment in love, grief, and, in the sequence 'The New Home Cabaret', the meaning of 'home'. *Newborn* (2004) is a sequence of poems exploring the delights and difficulties of pregnancy, birth, and caring for a baby.

Clandestine Marriage, The A comedy by George *Colman the elder and David *Garrick (1766). Lovewell, clerk to the London merchant Mr Sterling, secretly marries his employer's younger daughter Fanny. The father has arranged a mercenary marriage between his elder daughter and Sir John Melvil, nephew of Lord Ogleby; but when Ogleby and Melvil arrive at Sterling's house, Melvil reveals his passion for Fanny. Mrs Heidelberg, Mr Sterling's sister, orders Fanny to be removed from the house; in despair she applies to Ogleby, who mistakes her inarticulate confession for a declaration of love for himself. When Lovewell is discovered in Fanny's bedroom, Ogleby successfully intervenes on the couple's behalf and all is forgiven. The play's blend of comic situation and warm sentiment was immediately and enduringly popular, despite a brief rift between the collaborators when Garrick declined the role of Ogleby.

CLANVOWE, Sir John (*c.*1341–*c.*1391) Diplomat and member of the king's household; possibly born in Hergest, Hereford, and died near Constantinople. Allegedly one of the *Lollard Knights, and author of the pacifist and puritanical work *The Two Ways*. He was a friend of *Chaucer, and he may also have been the author of *The *Cuckoo and the Nightingale, or The Boke of Cupide*, an elegant debate-poem in 290 lines which was included by W. W. *Skeat in his *Chaucerian and Other Pieces*. The manuscript ends *Explicit Clanvowe*, which, it was once thought, might refer to a Thomas Clanvowe (d. 1410), possibly a son. *Wordsworth translated it, and it was viewed in the 19th century as 'one of the prettiest things in Medieval Literature'. See *The Works of Sir John Clanvowe*, ed. V. J. Scattergood (1975) (*The Two Ways* and *The Cuckoo and the Nightingale*); K. B. McFarlane, *Lancastrian Kings and Lollard Knights* (1972).

Clapham Sect The name given in 1844 by Sir James *Stephen to a group of evangelical Anglicans, centred on Clapham, Surrey, from 1792 to 1815, who were known at the time as the Saints. Members included William *Wilberforce, Zachary Macaulay (father of T. B. *Macaulay), Granville Sharp (1735–1813), and the Thornton family, ancestors of E. M. *Forster, who described them in *Marianne Thornton* (1956). Hannah *More was a close associate. They were active philanthropists, involved in the reformation of manners and the founding of missionary and Bible societies; their greatest achievement was the abolition of the slave trade (1807).

CLARE, St (1194–1253) Founder of the first order of Franciscan nuns, also known as the Poor Clares. She spent her whole life in Assisi, where she was influenced by St Francis, who became her friend. Three of the stories in the *Fioretti* (*The Little Flowers of St Francis*) concern St Clare and her order.

CLARE, John (1793–1864) Poet, the son of a labourer, born in Helpstone, Northamptonshire, a neighbourhood to which he remained deeply attached, where he worked as hedge-setter and day labourer. In 1820 he published *Poems Descriptive of Rural Life and Scenery*, and in the same year married Martha Turner, having parted from his first love, Mary Joyce, a sorrow which troubled him throughout his life. His highly successful first volume brought him a transient fame and was followed by *The Village Minstrel* (1821), *The *Shepherd's Calendar* (1827), and *The Rural Muse* (1835). In 1832 he left his native cottage for Northborough, only 4 miles away, but the move, to one so deeply attached to place, was disturbing, and reinforced the theme of loss in his work. In 1837 he was admitted as insane to an asylum in High Beach, Epping. He escaped in 1841, walking home to Northamptonshire in the delusion that he would there be reunited with Mary, to whom he thought himself married. He was once more certified insane, and spent the rest of his life in Northampton General Asylum, where he was allowed much freedom and rewrote some of Lord *Byron's most notable works (he claimed that 'I was Byron and Shakespeare formerly. At different times…I'm different persons'). The declining sales of his work may have contributed to his mental troubles, for by the 1830s the vogue for rural poetry and 'ploughman' poets such as Robert *Burns and Robert *Bloomfield was passing; and Clare's work remained little read until the later 20th century, when various new editions of his poetry, autobiographical prose, and letters made it available once more, together with much previously unpublished work. Clare is now recognized as a poet of great truth and power; his much-anthologized asylum poems have perhaps tended to obscure the real nature of his gifts, and recently more attention has been paid to his highly personal evocations of landscape and place. His best poetry demonstrates a complex sensibility and fine organization, and has been variously read as laments for lost love and talent, for the death of rural England, or for lost innocence. Ronald *Blythe labelled Clare 'England's most articulate village voice' and many poets, including Edmund *Blunden, Geoffrey *Grigson, and Cecil *Day-Lewis, have written of their admiration for his work and contributed towards his fuller recognition. The standard scholarly edition, gen. ed. Eric Robinson, appeared in nine volumes between 1984–2003 and the best life is Jonathan Bate, *John Clare: A Biography* (2003). *The Letters of John Clare*, ed. M. Storey, was published in 1985. See also J. Barrell, *The Idea of Landscape and the Idea of Place 1730–1840: An Approach to the Poetry of John Clare* (1972).

CLARENDON, Edward Hyde, earl of (1609–74) Politician and historian, educated at Magdalen Hall (now Hertford College), Oxford, and the Middle Temple; he mixed as a young man with poets and intellectuals including Ben *Jonson, Edmund *Waller, John *Selden, and Viscount *Falkland's circle at Great Tew. He entered Parliament in 1640, becoming one of Charles I's chief advisers. As Prince Charles's guardian he followed him into exile in Jersey, where he began his *History*. At the *Restoration he returned as lord chancellor and played a leading role in reorganizing the country, but fell out of favour, partly through military setbacks in the Second Dutch War. He was impeached in 1667 for, among other things, flagrant breaches of habeas corpus, and fled to France, where he spent his last years completing his *True Historical Narrative of the Rebellion and Civil Wars in England* (printed under his son's supervision 1702–4) and writing his autobiography (1759). He died at Rouen. His daughter Anne Hyde had in 1660 married the future James II. The Clarendon Building at Oxford was built from the profits of his *History*.

Clarissa, *or The History of a Young Lady* An *epistolary novel by Samuel *Richardson, published 1748 (for 1747)–1749, in eight volumes. About one-third of the work (which is in all over a million words) consists of the letters of Clarissa to Anna Howe and of Lovelace to John Belford, but there are over twenty correspondents in all, displaying many points of view and variations in style. Lovelace, a dashing rake, is courting Arabella Harlowe, the elder sister of Clarissa. The Harlowes are an acquisitive, ambitious, 'narrow-souled' family, and when Lovelace transfers his affections to Clarissa they decide that she must marry the wealthy but repulsive Solmes. When she refuses she is locked up and humiliated. Lovelace, representing himself as her deliverer, persuades her to escape, under his protection, to London. He establishes her in a superior brothel, which she supposes to be respectable lodgings. She unwaveringly resists his advances and he is both enraged and attracted by her intransigence. She is fascinated by his charm and wit, but distrusts him and refuses his eventual proposals of marriage. In his growing insistence, Lovelace interferes with her letters, deceives her over a supposed emissary from her family, violently assaults her, and cunningly ensnares her after her escapes. He claims to believe her resistance is no more than prudery and that, once subdued, she will prove no more chaste than other women. He is tormented by the question 'Whether her frost be frost indeed? Whether her virtue be principle?' (vol. v, Letter 31). To Clarissa chastity represents identity itself, and the climax of her tragedy comes when Lovelace, abetted by the women of the house, drugs and rapes her, an event he reports in one of the shortest letters of the work: 'And now, Belford, I can go no farther. The affair is over. Clarissa lives' (vol. v, Letter 32). Clarissa loses grip of her reason. Cut off from family, friends, and even correspondence, she escapes, only to find herself trapped in a debtors' prison. She is rescued by Belford, a reformed character, who looks after her with affectionate care. Clarissa recovers her sanity, but almost ceases to write, and her long decline and Christian preparation for death are reported largely in letters by Belford. After her death her cousin, Colonel Morden, kills Lovelace, already overwhelmed by remorse, in a duel.

The novel was in one sense a work in progress, and many members of Richardson's circle offered suggestions and advice, not least to try to convince Richardson to engineer a final marriage between Clarissa and Lovelace, a suggestion which he dealt with, alongside other objections and criticisms, in an extensive postscript and in a series of further revisions and commentaries. Despite its prolixity, the novel was resoundingly acclaimed for its emotional power, unprecedented psychological minuteness, and its (apparently) unmediated access to private thought. Even Henry *Fielding, who had so cruelly ridiculed Richardson's **Pamela*, wrote a letter of enthusiastic praise to his former enemy. See *Clarissa*, ed. Angus Ross (1986).

CLARK, Kenneth, Lord (1903–83) Author, art historian, and public official; educated at Winchester College (where he aspired to be an artist) and Trinity College, Oxford, where he turned to art history. His first book, *The Gothic Revival* (1928), was a pioneering study of the movement. Other publications include **Leonardo da Vinci* (1939) and *The Nude: A Study of Ideal Art* (1953). He was director of the National Gallery from 1934 to 1945. His television series *Civilisation* (broadcast 1969) reached a worldwide audience.

CLARK, William *See* Lewis, Meriwether.

CLARK-BEKEDEREMO, John Pepper (1935–) Founder and editor of *The Horn*, which first published the work of Wole *Soyinka and Christopher *Okigbo. Educated at Ibadan, Nigeria, Clark-Bekederemo, influenced by modernist poets, reshaped English prosody to fit African experience in his plays and poetry *A Reed in the Tide* (1965) and *Casualties* (1970).

CLARKE, Arthur C. (1917–2008) Prolific and popular writer of *science fiction, born in Minehead, Somerset but resident in Sri Lanka since 1956. He was knighted in 2000. His great technical expertise in the realm of aeronautics and astronautics is manifested both in his fiction, which includes *Childhood's End* (1953), *The City and the Stars* (1956), and *Imperial Earth* (1975), in his many non-fiction works, and his script for Stanley Kubrick's **2001: A Space Odyssey* (1968) (adapted into a novel). After joining the British Interplanetary Society in 1934 he popularized space travel: his 1946 paper on geosynchronous satellites as relays first described a technique which revolutionized telecommunications. However, it is the tension between this enthusiasm and the visionary, even mystical vein in stories like 'The Sentinel' (1951) and 'The Star' (1955) (see *The Collected Stories of Arthur C. Clarke* (2001)) and the ambiguous utopias in several of his novels that strengthens his fiction. Here, he acknowledged the influence of Olaf *Stapledon. He was a patron of the *Science Fiction Foundation and funded the Arthur C. Clarke Award for best science fiction novel published in Britain. See Neil McAleer, *Odyssey: The Authorised Biography of Arthur C. Clarke* (1992).

CLARKE, Austin (1896–1974) Irish poet, verse dramatist, and broadcaster, born in Dublin, and educated at Belvedere College and University College, Dublin, where he lectured briefly in the English department. He worked for fifteen years in London as a journalist and book reviewer, returning to Dublin in 1937. While his early poetry is influenced by W. B. *Yeats and the *Celtic Twilight, it is informed by an unusually scholarly command of Gaelic sources. Much of his later work is satirical, attacking the collusion between church and state in mid-century Ireland. Clarke's versification is subtle and complex, finding its most original expression in the ornate historical re-creations of *Pilgrimage and Other Poems* (1929), in the austerely confessional *Night and Morning* (1938), and in the bulky, strikingly various *Flight to Africa and Other Poems* (1963). Clarke was also greatly interested in verse drama; he founded the Dublin Verse-Speaking Society in 1938, which developed into the Lyric Theatre Company and performed many of his own plays. He wrote three prose romances and two autobiographies, *Twice round the Black Church* (1962) and *A Penny in the Clouds* (1968). His *Collected Plays* were published in 1963 and his *Collected Poems* a few weeks after his death in 1974.

CLARKE, Charles Cowden- (1787–1877) The son of John *Keats's enlightened schoolmaster John Clarke, and a close friend of the poet. Keats's 'Epistle to Charles Cowden-Clarke' is full of affection and gratitude. Cowden-Clarke lectured frequently between 1834 and 1856 on William *Shakespeare and general literature, and many of his lectures were published. With his wife Mary Victoria Cowden-*Clarke he produced editions of Shakespeare, George *Herbert, and other poets. Also with his wife he wrote *Recollections of Writers* (1878), a lively and valuable collection of reminiscences of their close friends Keats, Charles *Lamb, Mary *Lamb, Leigh *Hunt, Douglas *Jerrold, and Charles *Dickens. See Richard Altick, *The Cowden Clarkes* (1948).

CLARKE, Gillian (1937–) Welsh poet, born in Cardiff and educated at University College, Cardiff. She was editor of the *Anglo-Welsh Review* from 1975 to 1984 and co-founder, in 1990, of the Taliesin Trust, responsible for the writers' centre Ty Newydd in Gwynedd, she has combined her literary interests with living on an organic farm in Ceredigion. Her main collections of verse are *Letter from a Far Country* (1982), *Letting in the Rumour* (1989), *The King of Britain's Daughter* (1993), *Five Fields* (1998), and *Making the Beds for the Dead* (2004). Her *Collected Poems* appeared in 1997. Clarke's work combines a sense of human implication in the cycle of the seasons with an awareness of Welsh history, language, and mythology. Sensuous and understated, her poems have a strong political dimension; their long-standing concern with issues of gender and ecology has been shadowed in recent work by apprehensions of post-9/11 global crisis.

CLARKE, John Cooper *See* PERFORMANCE POETRY.

CLARKE, Marcus (1846–81) Novelist, journalist, and dramatist, famed for the enduringly popular convict epic *For the Term of his Natural Life*. Born in London, Clarke was friends with G. M. *Hopkins and his brother Cyril before emigrating to Victoria, Australia in 1867. *His Natural Life* was serialized in the *Australian Journal* (1870–72) and has been widely reprinted: most modern editions use the revised version, published as a novel in 1874, and the longer title (after 1882). Protagonist 'Rufus Dawes'—Richard Devine—is wrongly transported to Tasmania, thence to the even more horrific Norfolk Island. In the past half-century critics have suggested that Clarke also made significant contributions to history, criticism, journalism, the short story, and theatre, where his work spanned opera, pantomime, and drama. His journalism forms a rich archive on colonial life in Melbourne. See Brian Elliott, *Marcus Clarke* (1958); Andrew McCann, *Marcus Clarke's Bohemia* (2004).

CLARKE, Mary Victoria Cowden- (1809–98) The joint author, with her husband Charles Cowden-*Clarke, of *Recollections of Writers*, and the author of the *Complete Concordance to Shakespeare*, published in monthly parts in 1844–5. She also published an autobiography, *My Long Life* (1896). See Richard Altick, *The Cowden Clarkes* (1898).

CLARKE, Samuel (1675–1729) Clergyman, educated at Caius College, Cambridge, where he studied and defended Newtonian natural science. Clarke's principal published work was *A Demonstration of the Being and Attributes of God* and *A Discourse Concerning the Unchangeable Obligations of Natural Religion* (1705–6), the published version of his two sets of *Boyle Lectures, delivered 1704–5. He emphasized the scientific and rational basis of religion, and was regarded by some clergy as insufficiently supportive of the divinity of Christ and the doctrine of the Trinity.

CLARKE, Susanna (1959–) Nottingham-born author who published a number of well-received *fantasy stories before the novel *Jonathan Strange & Mr Norrell* (2004). Its wry precision and detailed evocation of English magic in an alternative 19th century made it a best-seller and *Hugo winner.

CLARKSON, Laurence (1615–67) A pamphleteer whose spiritual autobiography *The Lost Sheep Found* (1660) charts his progress through many religious affiliations; from his Church of England boyhood in Lancashire he became Anabaptist, Seeker, Ranter, and finally *Muggletonian, suffering imprisonment for his views. His tracts, written with originality, force, and feeling, shed an interesting light on the adventurous and speculative ideas of the age: in *A Single Eye All Light, No Darkness* (1650), he argued that all things, even sin, are from God: 'What act soever is done by thee in light and love, is light and lovely, though it be that act called adultery.'

classicism, classic, and **classical** are terms used in several shifting and at times overlapping senses. A 'literary classic' is a work considered first-rate or excellent of its kind, and therefore fit to be used as a model or imitated; and this sense now applies as much to modern works and to those of a 'romantic' tendency as it does to the works of Greek and Roman ('classical') antiquity formerly known simply as 'the classics'. Similarly the term 'classical' itself has been applied to later literary periods: the 17th century, for instance, being regarded as the classical age of French and Spanish drama. Classicism denotes a particular commitment to and celebration of the lasting value of the Greek and Roman heritage, usually accompanied by or implying some disparagement of subsequent literary achievements and traditions. This critical position commonly favours such values as harmony, proportion, balance, decorum, and restraint, deploring the less regulated products of the vernacular modern literatures. While classicism is a critical position or unstated aesthetic preference, the applied imitation of Greek and Roman models in poetic and dramatic practice, along with the critical justification for such imitation, is more usually known as *neo-classicism, this being an important movement that flourished in England, and more powerfully in France, in the 17th and 18th centuries. The flourishing of *Romanticism in the first half of the 19th century, itself partly a revolt against neo-classical culture (although not usually against ancient poetry), provoked a more polemical phase of classicism led successively by Matthew *Arnold, the American critic Irving Babbitt (1865–1933), and T. S. *Eliot. It also promoted general discussion of the distinctions between opposed classical and romantic principles in literature, in which classical values are held to be those of order and respect for tradition, while the contrary romantic values are those of individualism, spontaneity, and inspiration.

CLAUDEL, Paul (1868–1955) French Catholic poet and dramatist. He spent many years abroad as a diplomat (1893–1936), mostly in the United States, South America, and the Far East, and his poems and plays draw heavily on the cultures he experienced there. He established a distinctive poetic voice, the so-called *verset claudélien*, free verse written for declamation and drawing on biblical and liturgical techniques of repetition, which was admired by W. H. *Auden. His major plays, ranging from the Symbolist *Tête d'or* (1890: *Golden Head*) via *L'Annonce faite à Marie* (1912: *Tidings Brought to Mary*) to *Le Soulier de satin* (1929: *The Satin Slipper*; perf. 1943), inspired by Japanese theatre, exerted a strong influence on the following generation of dramatists, though English-speaking directors have evidently struggled with them.

CLAUDE LORRAIN (1600–82) Landscape painter from Lorraine, who worked mainly in Rome. He was the first artist to be inspired by the Roman Campagna and its legends. Many 18th-century English travellers on the *Grand Tour were impressed by Claude's elegiac landscapes, bringing examples of his pictures and engravings back to England, where they influenced perceptions of the natural world. Poets like James *Thomson (1700–48) and John *Dyer frequently invoke Claude's name to suggest a *Virgilian serenity. Landscape gardeners emulated Claude's compositions, which were important to the theory of the *picturesque. Enthusiasts came to regard the Lake District as though it were a sequence of pictures by Claude and many carried a 'Claude glass', a blackened convex mirror which 'composed' the landscape into a view by Claude. Romantic poets responded intensely to the elusive beauty of Claude's later works, such as *The Enchanted Castle*, which moved both William *Hazlitt and John *Keats. See Marcel Roethlisberger, *Claude Lorrain: The Drawings* (1968); and *Claude Lorrain: The Paintings* (1979).

CLAUDIAN (Claudius Claudianus) (AD *c.*370–*c.*404) The last great classical Latin poet, was born in Alexandria and became court poet to the emperor Honorius in Rome; it is assumed that he remained a pagan. His short *epic *The Rape of Proserpina* influenced Edmund *Spenser's account of the garden of Proserpina (*Faerie Queene*, II. vii. 52) and was translated in 1617 by Leonard Digges (1588–1635). There was no complete English translation of his poems until 1817. See Harold Isbell, *The Last Poets of Imperial Rome* (1971).

CLAVELL, John (1603–42) A highwayman, condemned to death and then pardoned (1627). He published a metrical autobiography, *Recantation of an Ill-Lead Life* (1628), which begins '*Stand and Deliver* to your observation | Right serious thoughts', and proceeds to describe the highway law and organization of thieves. *The Soddered Citizen*, a comedy of which he was reputed author, was performed by the King's Men *c.*1630.

CLAVERHOUSE, Graham of *See* GRAHAM OF CLAVERHOUSE.

Claverings, The A novel by Anthony *Trollope, published 1867. Harry Clavering is a gentleman-engineer who becomes engaged to his master's daughter, steady Florence Burton. Julia Brabazon, an old flame, returns to London newly widowed after marrying the dissipated Lord Ongar for money. Harry is called in to protect her from the machinations of the sycophantic Sophie Gordeloup and the scheming Count Pateroff, and Lady Ongar offers to renew their old engagement, but Harry remains true to Florence. He gets his reward when his rich relations die in a fishing accident, and he becomes heir to the Clavering fortunes. The novel is characteristic of Trollope's interest in loyalty and temptation in courtship and marriage, complicated by questions of money and inheritance.

Cleanness (*or Purity*) An alliterative poem in 1,812 lines from the second half of the 14th century, the only manuscript of which is the famous Cotton Nero A. X which is also the sole manuscript of **Pearl*, **Patience*, and *Sir *Gawain and the Green Knight*. It deals with three subjects from the Scriptures and is hardly more than a vigorous paraphrase of them: the Flood, the destruction of Sodom and Gomorrah, and the fall of Belshazzar. It has some passages of great power, such as the denunciation of Sodom and the description of the destruction of Babylon. Modern critical practice usually treats the four poems in the manuscript as the work of a single author, regarding *Cleanness* as the earliest on grounds of quality (*Pearl* comes first in the manuscript). There is an edition by J. J. Anderson (1977); see also *The Poems of the Pearl Manuscript*, ed. Andrew Malcolm and Ronald Waldron (4th edn, 2002).

CLEAVER, Eldridge (1935–98) African American essayist and political activist born in Arkansas. He became a member of the Black Panther Party and his book of essays *Soul on Ice* (1967) became a key document for the *Black Arts Movement. He spent much of the 1970s abroad in Algeria and other countries. His *Postprison Writings and Speeches* were collected in 1969 and *Soul on Fire* (1978) gives a memoir of his life in exile.

CLELAND, John (1710–89) Novelist, educated at Westminster School. From 1728 he worked in the East India Company in Bombay (Mumbai), returning at the request of his father in 1740. **Memoirs of a Woman of Pleasure*, completed while Cleland was imprisoned for debt and published 1748–9, made his publisher a fortune, but Cleland received only 20 guineas. Both men were convicted of publishing an obscene work, and Cleland produced an expurgated version. His later fiction includes *Memoirs of a Coxcomb* (1751), *The Surprises of Love* (1764), and *The Woman of Honour* (1768). He wrote three unperformed plays, two medical works, many book reviews and pieces of political journalism, and three philological studies on aspects of Celtic languages (1766–9).

CLEMENS, S. L. *See* TWAIN, MARK.

CLEMO, Jack (Reginald John) (1916–94) Poet, born at St Austell, Cornwall, the son of a clay-worker. From childhood he suffered from poor eyesight and, subsequently, deafness, eventually becoming completely blind. He came to critical notice with his novel *Wilding Graft* (1948), which was admired by T. F. *Powys. His poetry includes *The Map of Clay* (1961), with an introduction by Charles *Causley, and *The Echoing Tip* (1971), which evoke with a kind of visionary grimness the tormented landscapes of the clay pits and express his own Calvinist faith. *Broad Autumn* (1975) was followed by *The Bouncing Hills* (1983), *The Shadowed Bed* (a novel, 1986), *A Different Drummer* (1986), *Selected Poems* (1988), and *Approach to Murano* (1992). He also wrote two volumes of autobiography, *Confessions of a Rebel* (1949) and *The Marriage of a Rebel* (1980).

CLEOPATRA (69–30 BC) Queen of Egypt, famous as the lover of Julius *Caesar and Mark Antony. She committed suicide following the death of Antony to avoid humiliation by her conqueror Octavian (later the emperor Augustus). Her story was told by *Plutarch in his life of Marcus Antonius, and retold among others by *Shakespeare, John *Dryden in **All for Love*, Sarah *Fielding, and George Bernard *Shaw, who focuses unusually on her relationship with Caesar.

Cleopatra A tragedy in blank verse by Samuel *Daniel, published 1594. It is on the Senecan model, and deals with the story of Cleopatra after the death of Antony. Octavius Caesar tries to persuade her to leave the monument that she had built, in order that he may have her to grace his triumph. Pretending to yield, she asks permission first to sacrifice to the ghost of Antonius. After the performance of the rites, she dines with great magnificence, and by her order a basket of figs is brought her which contains an asp. With this she kills herself. Her son Caesarion about the same time is murdered at Rhodes and the race of the Ptolemies becomes extinct.

clerihew A humorous verse form invented by Edmund Clerihew *Bentley, consisting of two rhymed but metrically clumsy couplets, with the first line referring to a well-known person, e.g.

> Sir James Jeans
> Always says what he means;
> He is really perfectly serious
> About the Universe being Mysterious.

'Clerk's Tale, The' *See* CANTERBURY TALES, 9.

CLEVELAND, John (1613–58) Poet. A schoolmaster's son, born in Loughborough, he became a tutor at St John's College, Cambridge, and was an active Royalist in the Civil War. His poems took metaphysical wit to an extreme, and were highly popular (with 25 editions between 1647 and 1700).

His elegy on Edward King (Milton's *Lycidas) announces that, now King has drowned, 'Neptune hath got an university'. Samuel *Johnson admired his best-known satire 'The Rebel Scot' for the couplet 'Had Cain been Scot, God would have changed his doom | Not forced him wander, but confined him home'. But John *Dryden thought he offered merely 'common thoughts in abstruse words'. Twentieth-century interest in political satire has revived his reputation. An edition by Brian Morris and Eleanor Withington appeared in 1967.

CLIFFORD, Lady Anne, countess of Pembroke, Dorset, and Montgomery (1590–1676) Diarist, sole surviving child of George, the third duke of Cumberland. She was tutored by Samuel *Daniel and acted in *masques at *James I's court including Daniel's *Tethys' Festival* (1610). She fought a long battle to establish her right to the Clifford estates, commissioning a portrait triptych by Jan van Belcamp (now in Appleby Castle) to celebrate her victory in 1649. Her letters and diaries (1603–16) chronicle her campaign and her stormy marriages to the earl of Dorset (d. 1624) and Philip Herbert, earl of Pembroke (1584–1650). She also left a 'day book', an intimate record of her old age as matriarch, landowner, and sheriff in Westmorland. Vita *Sackville-West, herself debarred from the inheritance of Knole by her sex, edited *The Diary of Lady Anne Clifford* (1923); see also Richard T. Spence, *Lady Anne Clifford* (1997).

CLIFFORD, Martin Pseudonym of Charles *Hamilton.

CLIVE, Caroline Archer (Mrs Clive) (1801–73) Poet and novelist, born in Shakenhurst, Worcestershire, and largely home educated. She wrote chiefly under the initial 'V'. Her first volume of poems, *IX Poems by V* (1840), attracted high praise, and her reputation was consolidated by her powerful novel *Paul Ferroll* (1855) (the name was one she had previously used as her *nom de plume*). Here, the hero murders his wife who had prevented him from marrying the woman he loved, escapes suspicion, and marries his true love, who, after eighteen years of happy marriage, dies of shock when Paul Ferroll voluntarily confesses his crime in order to save innocent suspects. *Paul Ferroll*, with its challenges to morality, was a forerunner of the *sensation novel. *Why Paul Ferroll Killed his Wife* (1860) followed. The victim of a number of incapacitating accidents during her life, Clive was interested, like Dinah *Craik, in representing the consequences of infirmity: she was accidentally burned to death while writing in her library.

Clockmaker, The *See* HALIBURTON, THOMAS.

Clockwork Orange, A A novel by Anthony *Burgess, published in 1962. Set in the near future, Alex recounts his life from the age of 15 as leader of a gang of thugs to his emergence from State Jail 84F after a period of experimental aversion therapy, which has left him unable to enjoy his former pleasures of rape, assault, and listening to Beethoven while indulging in fantasies of crime. Written in what Alex calls 'nadsat', a highly inventive mix of Russian, neologisms, and archaisms, the novel conjures up a *dystopian world of youth violence and institutional manipulation in which Alex comes to see himself as a victim. The disturbingly brilliant film version by Stanley Kubrick (1971) omitted a final chapter in which Alex looks back at his youth, and provoked wide controversy. Amid claims that it had provoked copycat violence, Kubrick withdrew the film from distribution in Britain, and it did not reappear until 2000, after his death.

Cloister and the Hearth, The A novel by Charles *Reade, published 1861. The story is set in the 15th century. Gerard, the son of a trader living in Tergou in the Netherlands, is destined to enter the church, but falls in love with Margaret Brandt, whose father is an impoverished scholar suspected of sorcery. They become engaged, but the burgomaster Ghysbrecht, together with Gerard's scheming brothers and his outraged father, prevent the marriage and succeed in having the young man imprisoned. He contrives to escape and finds Margaret, but is relentlessly pursued and has to leave the Netherlands. He travels through Germany and Burgundy to Italy, encountering many dangers and hardships and meeting all conditions of men, from bishop to beggar, in palace, monastery, road, and tavern: the richness and complexity of detail is intended to assist the sense of 'reality' sought by the author. While he is in Italy Gerard hears of Margaret's death; not realizing the news is a trick, he throws himself into a desperate world of gambling, drinking, and women. Margaret meanwhile has given birth to his son and lives in wretchedness at his loss. Eventually sickened by his life, Gerard renounces the world, takes his vows as a Dominican monk, and in the guise of Father Clement travels slowly back to the Netherlands. He is overjoyed to find Margaret alive, but agonized at his predicament, for his love for her is as strong as ever. Because of his son he allows himself to return to her and is accepted as the vicar of Gouda. The pain of his struggles to remain true to his vows slowly subsides, and he and Margaret achieve a peace in which passion is subsumed in the love of God. However, when she is dying, both confess to each other the strength of their human love. Their son, the end of the story indicates, is the future philosopher *Erasmus.

The novel was based on Reade's short story 'A Good Fight' (published in *Once a Week* in 1859), in which the fight refers to the struggle against sexual feeling, a theme common in Reade's work. The novel arose from his discovery, in 'a musty chronicle' (the *Colloquia* and the letters of Erasmus), of the story of Erasmus' father, an obscure cleric. *The Cloister and the Hearth* was Reade's most celebrated novel, and though his work always divided critical opinion, many judged it to be among the greatest historical fictions of the 19th century.

closet drama A dramatic poem intended for reading or recitation in private rather than for staged performance, a closet in this sense being a private study. Notable examples in English include John *Milton's **Samson Agonistes*. Many writers turned to this form in the 18th and 19th centuries, faced with *censorship of public spoken drama, among them

Lord *Byron (e.g. his *Manfred) and P. B. *Shelley in his *Prometheus Unbound.

Cloud of Unknowing, The A mystical prose work in the tradition of apophatic ('negative') theology associated with Pseudo-Dionysius, possibly from the north-east Midlands, dating from the late 14th century, and one of the most admired products of the Middle English mystical tradition. Its contemporary popularity is indicated by its survival in seventeen manuscripts; the author was presumably a priest, though no more certain identification of him has resulted from the many recent speculations about him. Other works have been plausibly attributed to him: *The Book of Privy Counselling*, *The Epistle of Prayer*, and *Deonise Hid Divinite*; it is likely that three other works linked with the *Cloud* in the various manuscripts are also by him: *Benjamin Minor*, *The Epistle of Discretion of Stirrings*, and *Of Discerning of Spirits*. See P. Hodgson (ed.), *The Cloud of Unknowing and Related Treatises on Contemplative Prayer* (1982); trans. A. C. Spearing (2001).

Cloud-cuckoo-land (Nephelococcygia) An imaginary city built in the air in *The Birds* of *Aristophanes.

CLOUGH, Arthur Hugh (1819–61) Poet, son of a Liverpool cotton merchant, pupil at Rugby School under Thomas *Arnold, and scholar at Balliol College, Oxford; he received a second-class degree in 1841 and told Dr Arnold, 'I have failed'. He became a fellow of Oriel College, Oxford, but resigned when he felt unable to sign the Thirty-Nine Articles. He took a post at University Hall, London; then (1852–3) spent several months in Boston, America, mostly working on his translation of *Plutarch's Lives* (pub. Boston, 1857), before returning to England to marry and become an examiner in the Education Office.

His earliest poems (late 1830s to early 1840s), collected in *Ambarvalia* (1849), demonstrate his facility and experimentation with metre. *The Bothie of Tober-na-Vuolich* (1848), originally entitled *The Bothie of Toper-na-fuosich*, is a poem in English hexameters about a student reading party in Scotland. Philip falls in love with Elspie, a peasant who represents 'work, mother earth, and the objects of living', and at the end of the poem the couple move to New Zealand. His friend Matthew *Arnold said the poem had 'freshness, life...the true Homeric ring'.

Amours de voyage (mostly written 1849; pub. **Atlantic Monthly*, 1858) is similar in form, but *epistolary. Claude, travelling in Rome at the time of the siege, is paralysed by 'terrible notions of duty', unable to form political commitments, and troubled by his impulse to court Mary, the daughter of a middle-class English family also travelling in Italy. *Dipsychus* (published posthumously, 1865), is a Faustian dialogue set in Venice in which a tempting spirit and an anti-heroic youth (possibly two aspects of the same mind) debate moral and religious subjects whilst wandering the city. The best known of Clough's shorter poems, sharply contrasted, are 'Say not the struggle nought availeth' and the satirical 'The Latest Decalogue', both written early but published posthumously in *Poems* (1862), with a Memoir by Francis Turner *Palgrave. Critics long considered Clough's life and work inconclusive, but his powerful conviction of the efficacy of doubt as a positive, productive condition has gradually been recognized. See Anthony Kenny, *Arthur Hugh Clough: A Poet's Life* (2005).

Club, the A dining society founded in 1764 by Samuel *Johnson, at the suggestion of Joshua *Reynolds. It met at the Turk's Head, Soho. The nine original members included Oliver *Goldsmith and Edmund *Burke; elected later were Thomas *Percy, George *Colman, David *Garrick, James *Boswell, Charles *Fox, George *Steevens, Richard Brinsley *Sheridan, and Edmond *Malone.

CLUNE, Frank (1893–1971) Australian writer. Born in inner Sydney and educated at local Catholic schools, Clune left home at 15 to roam the world. Settling down as an accountant on his second marriage, he wrote his first autobiography, *Try Anything Once* (1933), in hospital. It recounted his adventures as a newsboy, bush labourer, US army deserter, seaman, bootlegger, Gallipoli veteran, vaudevillian, and mouse-trap salesman. An immediate success, it launched Clune as a best-selling author of another 58 books. He specialized in sensational and romantic histories (usually with P. R. Stephensen (1901–65) as collaborator) and speedily written travel books, tracing his Australian journeys as an itinerant tax consultant, and later his tourist trips overseas. In these and in radio broadcasts, his enthusiasms, humour, forthright opinions, and vernacular style contributed to his persona as an unpretentious but proud Australian. His work promoted tourism within Australia and stimulated interest in colonial history.

CLUTE, John (1940–) Born in Toronto; author and critic resident in Britain since 1969, married to the artist Judith Clute. As reviewer and encyclopedist, co-editing *The Encyclopedia of Science Fiction* (2nd edn 1993) and *The Encyclopedia of Fantasy* (1997), he is one of the most influential authorities on *science fiction and *fantasy. He has published the novels *The Disinheriting Party* (1977) and *Appleseed* (2001). See Farah Mendlesohn (ed.), *Polder: A Festschrift for John Clute and Judith Clute* (2006).

COBB, Richard Charles (1917–96) Historian and autobiographer, educated at Merton College, Oxford, professor of modern history at Oxford 1973–84. Most of his works deal with French history and sociology and provide an evocative, eclectic portrayal of French life and culture; they include *Reactions to the French Revolution* (1972), *Death in Paris 1795–1801* (1978), and *Promenades* (1980). *Still Life* (1983), a memoir of his childhood in Tunbridge Wells, was followed by *A Classical Education* (1985), *People and Places* (1985), and *Something to Hold Onto* (1988).

COBBETT, William (1763–1835) Author, the son of a farmer near Farnham, Surrey, and self-educated; he enlisted as a soldier and served in New Brunswick from 1784 to 1791.

He obtained his discharge, brought an accusation of embezzlement against some of his former officers, and in 1792 retired, first to France then to America, to avoid prosecution. There he published in 1796 *The Life and Adventures of Peter Porcupine*, a provocatively pro-British work, and in 1801 his *Works*, critical of America. He returned to England in 1800, and became an anti-radical journalist, founding and writing the **Political Register* from 1802. Soon, however, as a result of what he observed, his views began to change, and from about 1804 he wrote more and more positively in the radical interest, suffering two years' imprisonment for his attack on flogging in the army. He published Parliamentary Debates, afterwards taken over by *Hansard, and *State Trials*; wrote an entertaining English grammar (1817); and a number of books on economic subjects. At the same time he was farming in Hampshire and later in Surrey. From 1817 to 1819 he was again in America. The reflections assembled in 1830 as **Rural Rides* began to appear in the *Political Register* from 1821. His *History of the Protestant 'Reformation' in England and Ireland* appeared in 1824; his *Advice to Young Men* in 1829. He became MP for Oldham in 1832. Throughout his life he was an avid reader and a prolific writer. He wrote with perspicuity and vigour on behalf of the common people, in a prose style commended by William *Hazlitt as 'plain, broad, downright English', and he produced without artifice (particularly in *Rural Rides*) an engaging and idiosyncratic portrait of himself. There are biographies by G. D. H. Cole (1924) and R. Ingrams (2005). See also *Selected Writings*, ed. L. Nattrass, 6 vols (1998).

COCKAYNE, Steve (1951–) Born in London; *fantasy writer, formerly a BBC cameraman. His *Wanderers and Islanders* (2002), *The Seagull Drovers* (2003), and *The Iron Chain* (2004) are set in a fantasy land which unsettlingly mirrors our own, where magicians and technologies combine.

COCKBURN, Alison (1713–94) Née Rutherford, Scots poet and songwriter, born in Fairnalee, Selkirkshire, whose lively soirées brought together most of the literary talent of 18th-century Edinburgh. She was friendly with David *Hume, was admired by Robert *Burns, and was on close terms with the family of Walter *Scott, to whom she was distantly related. She wrote one of the well-known versions of 'The Flowers of the Forest'.
See ELLIOT.

COCKBURN, Catharine (?1674–1749) Née Trotter. She began her literary career with a novella published in 1693; her tragedy *Agnes de Castro* was performed at the Theatre Royal, Drury Lane, probably in 1695. She corresponded with William *Congreve and George *Farquhar and wrote three further tragedies and one comedy; her last play was performed in 1706. In 1702 she published an essay in defence of John *Locke, the first of several works on religion and philosophy, including one in defence of Samuel *Clarke. Her prose works, letters, and occasional poems were edited, with her best-known play, *Fatal Friendship*, by Thomas Birch (1751).

COCKBURN, Claud (1904–81) Journalist and novelist, great-grandson of Henry *Cockburn; he was born in Beijing and educated at Keble College, Oxford. Resigning as New York correspondent for *The *Times* in 1933, he set up his own newsletter, *The Week*, which he continued to run while writing for the *Daily Worker* from 1936. His Spanish Civil War reportage was criticized by George *Orwell in *Homage to Catalonia*. After moving to Youghal, Co. Cork, in 1946 he contributed articles to **Punch* and became a regular columnist for the **Daily Telegraph* and the *Irish Times*. He was guest editor of *Private Eye* during the Profumo scandal in 1963. His best-known novel, *Beat the Devil* (1951), was made into a film of the same name by John Huston. His memoirs were collected as *I Claud* (1967).

COCKBURN, Henry Thomas, Lord Cockburn (1779–1854) Scottish author and judge, born in the Edinburgh area and educated at Edinburgh University. He shared with Francis *Jeffrey the leadership of the Scottish bar for many years. His *Memorials of his Times* (1856) gives a vivid account of literary circles in Edinburgh, and includes descriptions of Henry *Brougham, Lord Francis *Jeffrey, John *Wilson, Sydney *Smith, and the founding of the **Edinburgh Review*. His *Life of Jeffrey* was published in 1852.

Cock Lorell's Boat A popular verse satire of the early 16th century in which representatives of various trades take ship and sail through England. The captain of the boat is Cock Lorell, a tinker and probably a historical figure. It provides an interesting picture of contemporary low life.

Cockney School A term apparently first used in **Blackwood's Magazine* in October 1817, when John *Lockhart and his associates began a series of attacks 'On the Cockney School of Poetry'. Leigh *Hunt was the chief target, but William *Hazlitt and John *Keats were also objects of frequent derision. The Londoners, all of relatively humble origin, were contrasted with the great writers, all of whom 'have been men of some rank'. Hunt was particularly singled out for his 'low birth and low habits'. The virulence of the attacks, which described the writers as 'the vilest vermin' and of 'extreme moral depravity', was sustained over several years, and included the famous assault on Keats's **Endymion* in 1818. After his death Keats was described as a man 'who had left a decent calling [i.e. pharmacy] for the melancholy trade of Cockney-poetry'.

COCTEAU, Jean (1889–1963) French poet, novelist, dramatist, film director, and critic. He was prominently associated with *modernism in literature, art, music, ballet, and the cinema, collaborating with many of the leading figures in Europe, such as Diaghilev, Picasso, and *Stravinsky. He produced numerous volumes of poetry; novels, including *Le Grand Écart* (1923: *The Great Divide*; English trans. 1925) and *Les Enfants terribles* (1929: *The Terrible Children*; English trans. 1930, 1955); several sketches for ballets, including *Parade* (1917);

films, such as *La Belle et la bête* (1945: *Beauty and the Beast*); and plays, including *Orphée* (1926: *Orpheus*; English trans. 1933) and *La Machine infernale* (1934: *The Infernal Machine*; English trans. 1936), a reworking of the *Oedipus myth.

codex A manuscript with papyrus or parchment pages bound in book form in the ancient and medieval worlds. This crucial Roman invention replaced texts written on scrolls, which were far more difficult to search, and was the ancestor of the printed book.

COE, Jonathan (1961–) Novelist and biographer, born in Birmingham and educated at Trinity College, Cambridge. His early novels, *The Accidental Woman* (1987), *A Touch of Love* (1989), and *The Dwarves of Death* (1990), are short, playful, and experimental. *What a Carve Up!* (1994), which takes its name from a blackly comic film of the 1960s, satirizes the rampant materialism of the 1980s by focusing on the morally repugnant Winshaw family. Coe's other novels are *The House of Sleep* (1997); *The Rotters' Club* (2001), which chronicles, with painfully funny precision, the coming of age of four Birmingham schoolboys in the 1970s; its sequel, *The Closed Circle* (2004), which tracks the progress of the characters through a further twenty-five years; and *The Rain Before It Falls* (2007). He has also written biographies of Humphrey Bogart, James Stewart, and the novelist B. S. *Johnson.

Coelebs in Search of a Wife A novel by Hannah *More, published 1809. The book, which was immensely successful, consists of a collection of sharp social sketches and moral precepts, informed by More's ardent evangelicalism. The episodes are strung together by the hero's search for a wife, who must possess the qualities stipulated by his departed parents.

COETZEE, J. M. (John Maxwell) (1940–) Novelist and academic, born in Cape Town and educated at the university there and at the University of Texas, where he received his doctorate. He has held academic posts in both the USA and South Africa; in 2006 he took Australian citizenship, having settled in Adelaide. His self-reflexive, allusive, and disorienting fiction problematizes power relations and language itself. His first book, *Dusklands* (1974), contains two linked novellas, one concerning the American involvement in Vietnam, the other about an 18th-century Boer settler. *In the Heart of the Country* (1977) focuses on the meditations of an embittered Afrikaner woman. *Waiting for the Barbarians* (1980), a powerful allegory of oppression, was followed by the *Booker Prize-winning *Life and Times of Michael K* (1983), in which a gardener tries to take his ailing mother back to her home in the country as South Africa is torn by civil war; *Foe* (1986) interacts with the world of **Robinson Crusoe*; *Age of Iron* (1990) is a compelling story of a woman dying from cancer which links her with the diseased state. *The Master of Petersburg* (1994) is set in 1896, and follows the exiled *Dostoevsky back to St Petersburg where he becomes entangled in a web of intrigue. *Disgrace* (1999, Booker Prize, the first writer to win it twice) is the painful story of a middle-aged professor of English in post-apartheid South Africa charged with sexual harassment who seeks refuge on his daughter's farm in the Eastern Cape; the reader's expectations are dismantled in an ethically disorienting situation. *Elizabeth Costelloe* (2003) is similarly disconcerting as a narrative becomes a vehicle for lectures on animal rights. The protagonist of *Slow Man* (2005), an elderly Australian amputee who falls in love with his nurse, is visited by the previous novel's Elizabeth Costelloe. *Diary of a Bad Year* (2007) destabilizes boundaries by including the essays on political themes of an elderly writer who is preoccupied by his beautiful neighbour. Coetzee has published autobiography, essays, interviews, and literary criticism. He was awarded the *Nobel Prize for Literature in 2003.

coffee houses were first introduced in the time of the Commonwealth; the first recorded in England was in Oxford in 1650 (mentioned by Anthony *Wood), and the first in London was in 1652, in St Michael's Alley, off Cornhill, at the Sign of Pasqua Rosee. They were much frequented in the 17th and 18th centuries for political and literary discussions, circulation of news, etc. Among the most celebrated coffee and chocolate houses were the Bedford (Covent Garden, a favourite with actors), Button's (Russell Street, Covent Garden, popular with Joseph *Addison and his circle), Don Saltero's (Cheyne Walk, founded by a one-time servant of Sir Hans Sloane (1660–1753)), Garraway's (Change Alley, Corn Hill, a meeting place for stockjobbers in the days of the South Sea Company), the Grecian (Essex Street, off the Strand, frequented by members of the *Royal Society), Slaughter's (St Martin's Lane, a favourite of William *Hogarth and other artists), White's (a chocolate house in St James's), and Will's (Bow Street, frequented by authors, wits, and gamblers, and particularly associated with John *Dryden). Their decline during the 18th century has been in part attributed to the increasing popularity of clubs, such as the *Club, the *Kit-Cat Club, and the Brothers Club, founded in 1711 by Viscount *Bolingbroke. There is a description of coffee houses in T. B. *Macaulay's *History of England*, ch. III. See also Aytoun Ellis, *The Penny Universities* (1956); B. Lillywhite, *London Coffee Houses* (1963).

COKE, Sir Edward (1552–1634) English jurist, called to the bar in 1578. By favour of William Cecil (Lord *Burghley), he became recorder of London in 1592 and attorney-general in 1594, and represented the Crown at the trials of *Essex and Southampton (1600–1), Walter *Ralegh, and the Gunpowder Plot conspirators (1605). He became chief justice of the Common Pleas in 1606, coming into conflict with *James I about the jurisdiction of the common law courts. In 1613 he became chief justice of the King's Bench and a member of the Privy Council, but disagreements with the king continued, and in 1616 he was dismissed by the Council. Coke's *Reports* (1600–15) were the first textbook of early modern law. The first book of the *Institutes*, known as 'Coke upon Littleton' (1628), is a legal encyclopedia; the last three books (1641) form the basis of modern British constitutional law.

COLBURN, Henry (1784/5–1855) A highly successful publisher who founded the **New Monthly Magazine* in 1814 and the **Literary Gazette* in 1817, and who published the fashionable and profitable novels of Lady *Morgan and Theodore *Hook. He was the first to publish John *Evelyn's *Diary*, in 1818, and Samuel *Pepys's newly deciphered *Diaries* in 1825. In 1830 he went into partnership with Richard *Bentley and together they published a successful series of Standard Novelists (1835–41). His shameless advertising methods were controversial, but he died a very rich man.

Cold Comfort Farm (1932) The first novel of Stella Gibbons (1902–89), a witty and highly successful parody of a certain strain of doom-laden rural primitivism in English fiction. In passing, Gibbons makes fun of both Thomas *Hardy and D. H. *Lawrence, but her primary target is the fiction of Mary *Webb. Flora Poste, a sophisticated young lady 'possessed of every art and grace save that of earning her own living', goes to stay with distant relatives, the Starkadders, in the fictional village of Howling, Sussex. From the priapic Seth and his adoring mother Judith to the hellfire preacher Amos and the matriarchal Aunt Ada Doom, who once saw 'something nasty in the woodshed' and can't forget it, the Starkadders are consumed by dark emotions and terrible intrigues. Flora sets out to apply common sense to their problems and to introduce them to the realities of the modern world.

COLERIDGE, Hartley (1796–1849) The unworldly eldest son of Samuel Taylor *Coleridge, who inherited many of his father's gifts, including verbal eloquence, but achieved little, losing his Oxford fellowship for intemperance and failing as a schoolmaster. In 1833 he published *Poems, Songs and Sonnets* (the sonnets of which were much praised), and in the same year his unfinished *Biographia Borealis*, retitled *Worthies of Yorkshire and Lancashire* in 1836. He contributed to **Blackwood's Magazine*, the **London Magazine*, and other literary journals, and in 1840 published his edition, with brief biographies, of Philip *Massinger and John *Ford. His *Essays and Marginalia*, edited by his brother Derwent, were published posthumously in 1851. He spent his childhood and the latter part of his life in the Lake District, where he died. He is the subject of two important poems by his father, *'Frost at Midnight' and 'The Nightingale'.

COLERIDGE, Mary (1861–1907) Poet, the great-great-niece of S. T. *Coleridge, born in London and largely home educated; she published her first volume of verse, *Fancy's Following*, with the encouragement of Robert *Bridges in 1896, and a second, *Fancy's Guerdon*, in 1897. Two sonnets, 'True to myself am I' and 'Go in the deepest, darkest dead of night', have been much anthologized. Her first novel, a lively and fantastical romance, *The Seven Sleepers of Ephesus* (1893), was praised by R. L. *Stevenson but achieved little success; her second, *The King with Two Faces* (1897), a historical romance centring on Gustavus III of Sweden, was well received. She contributed extensively to various journals, such as the **Monthly Review* and the **Cornhill Magazine*. In 1900 she published *Non Sequitur*, a collection of spirited and ironic essays; her unpublished works appeared as *Gathered Leaves* in 1910.

COLERIDGE, Samuel Taylor (1772–1834) Poet, critic, and philosopher of *Romanticism. Youngest son of the vicar of Ottery St Mary, Devon, he was destined for the church. A temperamental, dreamy child, he was sent away after his father's early death to Christ's Hospital school, London, where his precocious classical reading and powers of 'inspired' talk (which never left him) attracted a circle of young admirers, including Leigh *Hunt and the future essayist Charles *Lamb. At Jesus College, Cambridge (1792–4), a brilliant career in classics was diverted by French revolutionary politics, heavy drinking, and an unhappy love affair, which led Coleridge to enlist in desperation in the 15th Light Dragoons under the name of Comberbache. He was bought out under an 'insanity' clause by his brother, but did not take a degree.

In the summer of 1794 an undergraduate walking tour through Oxford brought him the passionate friendship of Robert *Southey, and together they invented *Pantisocracy, a scheme to set up a commune in America. Coleridge now published his first poetry in the **Morning Chronicle*, a series of sonnets to eminent radicals including William *Godwin and Joseph *Priestley. To finance Pantisocracy, he and Southey gave political lectures in Bristol and collaborated on a verse drama, *The *Fall of Robespierre* (1794); they also simultaneously courted and married two sisters, Sara and Edith Fricker. After quarrelling with Southey over money and politics, Coleridge retired with Sara to a cottage at Clevedon, where their first son Hartley, named after the philosopher David *Hartley, was born (*see* COLERIDGE, HARTLEY). Here Coleridge edited a radical Christian journal, *The *Watchman*, which ran for ten issues; and published *Poems on Various Subjects* (1796), which included the 'Monody on the Death of Chatterton' and 'The Eolian Harp'. He considered entering the Unitarian ministry (*see* UNITARIANISM) and preached throughout the West Country; he also took opium in periods of sickness and depression.

In June 1797 Coleridge walked to Racedown, Dorset, where he met *Wordsworth and his sister Dorothy. The intense friendship that sprang up between the three shaped their lives for many years and proved one of the most creative partnerships in English Romanticism. It was based on a mutual love of poetry, critical discussion, and hill walking; and an impassioned response to the political and social problems of the age. Between July 1797 and September 1798 they lived and worked intimately together; the Coleridges at Nether Stowey, Somerset, and the Wordsworths two miles away at Alfoxden, on the edge of the Quantock hills, where they were visited by Lamb, William *Hazlitt, and others. Here Coleridge wrote a moving series of blank verse 'conversation' poems, addressed to his friends: 'Fears in Solitude', 'This Lime Tree Bower my Prison', 'The Nightingale', and *'Frost at Midnight'. He also composed his celebrated opium-vision *'Kubla Khan'. At Wordsworth's suggestion, Coleridge wrote *The Rime of the *Ancient Mariner*, which recounts a nightmare sea voyage with powerful metaphysical overtones; and started three other ballads, including *'Christabel', a tale of spiritual seduction set in a medieval castle. A selection from their work appeared as the *Lyrical Ballads* (1798), intended as an 'experiment' in English poetry, which, after a poor critical reception, achieved a revolution in literary taste and sensibility.

Disenchanted with political developments ('France: An Ode'), Coleridge now turned towards Germany, where he spent ten months (1798–9), partly in the company of the Wordsworths, studying *Kant, *Schiller, and *Schelling. Returned to London, he translated Schiller's verse play *Wallenstein*, engaged in journalism for Daniel *Stuart of the **Morning Post*, and first began to plan a great work on metaphysics. In 1800 he moved to the Lake District with the Wordsworths, but his marriage was increasingly unhappy and he had fallen disastrously in love with Wordsworth's future sister-in-law Sara Hutchinson, as recorded in 'Love' (1799) and other 'Asra' poems. His use of opium now became a crippling addiction. Many of these difficulties are examined in the brilliant and emotional *'Dejection: An Ode' (1802). During these years he also began to compile his *Notebooks* daily meditations on his life, writing, and dreams, which have proved among his most enduring and moving works. In 1804 Coleridge went abroad alone, the first of many attempts to restore his health and remake his career: he worked for two years as secretary to the governor of wartime Malta, and later travelled through Sicily and Italy. In 1807 he separated from his wife and went to live again with the Wordsworths and Sara Hutchinson at Coleorton, Leicestershire: here Wordsworth first read him 'The Poem to Coleridge' which became *The *Prelude*. In 1808, though ill, Coleridge began his series of Lectures on Poetry and Drama, which he continued sporadically over the next decade to audiences including John *Keats and Lord *Byron, and which as his *Shakespearean Criticism* introduced new concepts of 'organic' form and dramatic psychology. In 1809–10 he wrote and edited with Sara Hutchinson's help a second periodical, the **Friend*, 'a literary, moral, and political weekly paper' that ran for 28 issues: it contains the seeds of all his mature philosophic criticism. The intellectual effort, combined with the struggle against opium, shattered his circle of friends: Sara left for Wales, Dorothy grew estranged, he quarrelled irrevocably with Wordsworth. Coleridge fled to London, where between 1811 and 1814 he was on the verge of suicide, sustained only by his friends the Morgans, who took him to live in Calne, Wiltshire. Nevertheless he continued lecturing and journalism, and his play **Remorse*, a melodrama of the Spanish Inquisition, had a *succès d'estime* at Drury Lane (1813). After a physical and spiritual crisis at the Greyhound Inn, Bath, in the winter of 1813–14, Coleridge achieved a rebirth of his Christian beliefs, openly admitted his opium addiction, submitted himself to a series of medical regimes, and began slowly to write again. To this period belong the touching prose 'commentary' printed in the margins of the 'Mariner'; his essay 'on the Principles of Genial Criticism', adapted from Kant; and his **Biographia Literaria* (1817), a major work of poetic criticism, philosophy, and autobiography.

In the spring of 1816 Coleridge found permanent harbour in the household of Dr James Gillman, a surgeon living at Highgate, London, where he remained for the rest of his life. His by now almost legendary reputation among the younger Romantics was assured by *Christabel and Other Poems* (1816), which included for the first time 'Kubla Khan', and 'The Pains of Sleep'; it was published partly through Byron's influence. *Sibylline Leaves*, the first edition of his collected poems, was published in 1817 and expanded in 1828 and 1834; *Zapolya* in 1817. He became the centre of a new circle of young disciples: Thomas *Carlyle christened him 'the Sage of Highgate', and Lamb—who dedicated the **Essays of Elia* to him—described him as 'an Archangel a little damaged'.

His remaining prose works had a more openly social and religious slant: his two *Lay Sermons* (1816, 1817) were addressed to the 'Higher' and 'Middle' classes on questions of reform and moral responsibility. A final three-volume edition of *The Friend* added his 'Treatise on Method', originally written as an introduction to the *Encyclopaedia Metropolitana*, which makes a Baconian attempt to explain the growth of knowledge itself. His **Aids to Reflection* (1825) had a fruitful influence on John *Sterling, Charles *Kingsley, and the young Christian Socialists; while his *Church and State* (1830), a short monograph on the concept of a national 'Culture' and the 'clerisy' responsible for it, was taken up by Matthew *Arnold and John Henry *Newman. Coleridge also gave lectures on general literature and philosophy, which have survived in the form of notes and shorthand reports.

These later works develop Coleridge's leading critical ideas, concerning Imagination and Fancy; Reason and Understanding; Symbolism and Allegory; Organic and Mechanical Form; Culture and Civilization. The dialectical way he expresses them is one of his clearest debts to German Romantic philosophy, and represents a decisive counter-attack against British *Utilitarianism. His final position is that of a Romantic conservative and Christian radical, who strangely foreshadows much of the spiritual 'anxiety' of European *existentialism. He also wrote some haunting late poems, 'Youth and Age', 'Limbo', 'Work without Hope', and 'Constancy to an Ideal Object'. He died of heart failure at 3 The Grove, Highgate. The last echoes of his inspired conversation were captured in *Table Talk* (1836).

Coleridge has been variously criticized as a political turncoat, a drug addict, a plagiarist, and a mystic humbug, whose wrecked career left nothing but a handful of magical early poems. But the shaping influence of his highly imaginative criticism is now generally accepted, and his position (with his friend Wordsworth) as one of the two great progenitors of the English Romantic spirit is assured. Nothing has re-established him as a creative artist more than the modern editions of his *Letters* (6 vols, 1956–71), and his *Notebooks* (4 vols, 1957–90). There is a religious and metaphysical dimension to all his best work, both poetry and prose, which has the inescapable glow of the authentic visionary.

The Collected Works of Samuel Taylor Coleridge (23 vols, 1970–2002) contains all of Coleridge's writings apart from his notebooks and letters. Modern biographies include those by E. K. *Chambers (1938), Walter Jackson Bate (1968), and Richard *Holmes, 2 vols (1989, 1998). Hazlitt's superb essay 'On my First Acquaintance with Poets' (1823) is indispensable.

COLERIDGE, Sara (1802–52) Daughter of Samuel Taylor *Coleridge. Born at Greta Hall, Keswick, she grew up largely without her father in the company of Robert *Southey and his family and of the *Wordsworths. Home educated, she was, in Wordsworth's words, 'remarkably clever'; she read widely and acquired six languages. She married her cousin Henry Nelson Coleridge, and after his death continued with the labour of editing and annotating her father's papers, which she performed with such skill that much of her work still stands. In 1822 she translated Dobrizhoffer's Latin *Account of the Abipones* and in 1825 the *Memoirs* of the Chevalier Bayard. *Pretty Lessons for Good Children* appeared in 1834, and in 1837 her long prose narrative 'Phantasmion', set in the Lake country of her childhood and relating in the manner of a fairy-tale the story of Phantasmion and Iarine. She was greatly esteemed in London literary society, and was the friend of Thomas *Macaulay, the *Carlyles, and Aubrey *de Vere, among many others. The lively and engaging *Memoir and Letters*, published by her daughter in 1873, provides much information on the literary and personal lives of the Coleridges, the Wordsworths, and the Southeys. She appears, with Dora Wordsworth and Edith Southey, in Wordsworth's poem 'The Triad' (1828).

COLET, John (1467–1519) One of the principal Christian Humanists of his day in England. Born in London to wealthy parents, he studied at Oxford and Cambridge universities, and in Italy, and lectured at Oxford on the New Testament from about 1495 to 1505, *Erasmus being in his audience. As dean of St Paul's (1505) he founded and endowed *St Paul's School, writing for it a Latin grammar for which William *Lily, the first high master, wrote the syntax; later known as the Eton Latin Grammar, it became a standard school textbook. Although he was unwilling to publish in print, he was a famous preacher and lecturer; he has been seen as a precursor of the *Reformation. He first came to notice with his lectures on the Epistles of St Paul at Oxford in 1497–8 which draw on Florentine *Neoplatonism from *Plotinus to Pseudo-*Dionysius to *Pico della Mirandola. A friend of Erasmus and Thomas *More, he was a vitriolic and powerful opponent of *scholasticism, of ecclesiastical abuses, and of foreign wars. There is a biography by J. H. Lupton (1887), who also edited his expositions of the New Testament.

COLETTE, Sidonie Gabrielle (1873–1954) French novelist. Having achieved success in the music hall of the 1890s, she established her reputation as a writer with *Chéri* (1920) and *La Fin de Chéri* (1926: *The Last of Chéri*), narratives evoking the tragic passion of a young man and an older woman. The short, intense *récits* which she made her speciality include *La Maison de Claudine* (1922: *Claudine's House*), *Le Blé en herbe* (1923: *Young Shoots*), *Sido* (1929), *La Naissance du jour* (1932: *Dawn*), *Le Képi* (1943), and *Gigi* (1943). Inspired by her own life, they express a sensibility shaped by the style of the *belle époque* and informed by a sensual responsiveness to the world of nature and childhood. She has been widely translated into English, notably by Janet Flanner, Enid Macleod, Roger Stenhouse, and Antonia *White. See J. Thurman, *Secrets of the Flesh: A Life of Colette* (1991).

Colin Clout The pastoral name adopted by Edmund *Spenser in *The *Shepheardes Calender* and **Colin Clouts Come Home Againe*. Colin Clout is also the name of a rustic in John *Gay's *The *Shepherd's Week*.
See also COLLYN CLOUT.

Colin Clouts Come Home Againe An allegorical pastoral written by Edmund *Spenser on his return to Kilcolman after his visit to London of 1589–91, published 1595. It was dedicated to Walter *Ralegh 'in part of paiment of the infinite debt in which I acknowledge my selfe bounden unto you, for your singular favours and sundrie good turnes shewed to me at my late being in England'. The poem describes in allegorical form how Ralegh visited Spenser in Ireland and induced him to come to England 'his *Cynthia* to see'—i.e. the queen. After a charming description of the sea voyage, the poet tells of the splendour of the queen and her court and the beauty of the ladies who frequent it. Then follows a bitter attack on the court's envies and intrigues. The poem ends with a definition of true love and a tribute to Colin's proud mistress *Rosalind.

Colleen Bawn, The [meaning 'the fair girl'] A play adapted in 1860 by Dion *Boucicault from a novel, *The Collegians*, by Gerald *Griffin.

COLLIER, Jane (1715–55) Satirist, born near Salisbury, educated by her clergyman father. In London she became a member of Samuel *Richardson's circle, offering advice on **Clarissa* and perhaps collaborating with her companion Sarah *Fielding on an experimental dialogue-novel, *The Cry* (1754). *An Essay on the Art of Ingeniously Tormenting* (1753) was a spoof conduct manual in the manner of Jonathan *Swift's *Directions to Servants*; it outlines an ironic 'system for the practice of tormenting your friends', and perceptively documents the psychology of power in personal relationships. It reappeared in six editions of 1804–11, and may have influenced Jane *Austen.

COLLIER, Jeremy (1650–1726) A clergyman who refused to swear the oath to William and Mary and was outlawed in 1696 for publicly absolving on the scaffold two of those found guilty of plotting to assassinate William III. He is chiefly remembered for his *Short View of the Immorality and Profaneness of the English Stage* (1698), in which he attacked John *Dryden, William *Wycherley, William *Congreve, Sir John *Vanbrugh, Thomas *D'Urfey, and Thomas *Otway, complaining particularly of profanity in stage dialogue and mockery of the clergy. Congreve and D'Urfey were prosecuted, Thomas *Betterton and Anne *Bracegirdle were fined, and several of the poets replied, though not very effectively. Although the kind of play to which Collier objected continued to flourish, notably in the work of Congreve, Vanbrugh, and George *Farquhar, its days were numbered, and Collier contributed towards the climate that produced the 'reformed' drama of Colley *Cibber and his successors. *See* RESTORATION. Collier published a learned *Ecclesiastical History of Great Britain* in 1708–14.

COLLIER, John (1901–80) Born London; poetry editor of *Time and Tide* during the 1920s and 1930s, but remembered as a novelist and writer of fantastic stories combining satire with the macabre and the supernatural. His best-known novel is *His Monkey Wife* (1930), describing the marriage between a repatriated explorer and his pet chimpanzee. In 1935 he moved to America and made his living as a Hollywood screenwriter. *The John Collier Reader* (1972) is an anthology of his major stories with an introduction by Anthony *Burgess.

COLLIER, John Payne (1789–1883) Antiquary, whose achievements first received public attention with *The History of English Dramatic Poetry to the Time of Shakespeare: And Annals of the Stage to the Restoration* (1831) which contained valuable new documentary information but was contaminated with his own fabrications, the first of his insidious literary frauds. He dedicated the *History* to the duke of Devonshire (then lord chamberlain), who showed his appreciation by entrusting to him his library and making him his literary adviser. He was also given free access to Lord Ellesmere's manuscripts at Bridgewater House. In 1840 he founded the Shakespeare Society for which he published many rare works including *The Memoirs of Edward Alleyn* (1841); as director of the Society many rare documents were made available to him on which he based his researches and forgeries. But it was his falsifications of the marginal corrections of the so-called Perkins Folio (a second *folio of Shakespeare's plays dated 1632, with a possibly forged signature of Thomas Perkins on its cover) that finally brought him discredit.

Doubt was cast on the nature and extent of Collier's frauds by D. Ganzel in a biography, *Fortune and Men's Eyes* (1982).

COLLIER, Mary (?1690–1762) Poet, born near Midhurst, Sussex; taught to read by her parents. She earned a living by 'Washing, Brewing and such labour'. Her poem *The Woman's Labour: An Epistle to Mr. Stephen Duck* (1739) robustly defended the industry of rural women like herself against *Duck's aspersions in *The Thresher's Labour* (1730). Collier's *Poems on Several Occasions* (1762), which included an elegy on Duck and a poem on the marriage of George III, was published at Winchester with strong support from local subscribers; it was prefaced by 'Remarks of the Author's life, drawn by herself'.

COLLINS, An (*fl.* 1640s–1650s) Poet, unknown except for a volume of religious verse (*Divine Songs and Meditations*) bearing her name, published in London in 1653. It seems from the poems and prefatory material that she lived in the country, suffered chronic ill health, was middle aged, and had no children. She wrote during the English Civil War but her precise religious and political affiliations are elusive. Her poems use innovative forms and much biblical reference, especially to the Song of Songs (*see* BIBLE), and include a verse paraphrase of Ecclesiastes 12. There is an edition by Sidney Gottlieb, 1996, from the sole surviving copy, in the Huntingdon Library, California.

COLLINS, Anthony (1676–1729) Philosopher and freethinker, born at Isleworth, Middlesex, and educated at Eton College and King's College, Cambridge. In 1703 he became intimate with John *Locke. His debate on immortality with Samuel *Clarke in 1707–8 established his reputation as a leading freethinker. *A Discourse of Free-Thinking* (1713), his best-known work, drew angry replies from, among others, Richard *Bentley, George *Berkeley, Benjamin *Hoadly, and, in *Mr C...s Discourse...Put into Plain English* (1713), from Jonathan *Swift. Collins's classic defence of determinism, *A Philosophical Inquiry concerning Human Liberty* (1717), was republished by Joseph *Priestley in 1790. In 1720 he collaborated with Trenchard and Gordon on the anticlerical periodical the *Independent Whig*. In *Grounds and Reasons of the Christian Religion* (1724) he contested the Messianic prophecies. Overtly or covertly, Collins attacked arguments for the existence of God and nearly every part of Christian theology, and his rhetorical strategies in some ways anticipated those of David *Hume.

COLLINS, Merle (1950–) Born and educated in the Caribbean. She left Grenada after the American invasion, completing her doctorate in London. She has published three collections of poetry, two novels, and a book of short stories. Her expression of resistance to any kind of colonialism is wittily idiomatic.

COLLINS, Wilkie (1824–89) Novelist, elder son of the painter William Collins (1788–1847), who was born and lived for most of his life in the Marylebone district of London. Educated at private schools in London, he claimed he learned far more of significance in Italy, where he travelled with his family as a boy, 1836–8. He worked briefly for a tea-importer, and was called to the bar. Though he never practised as a lawyer, his fascination with legal processes is evident throughout his fiction. His first published book was a biography of his father (1848), followed by his only historical novel, *Antonina* (1850). His second novel, **Basil* (1852), was admired by Charles *Dickens, who employed Collins as a writer for **Household Words*. The two writers became personal friends and occasional collaborators, and Collins's third novel, *Hide and Seek* (1854), is his most Dickensian work. With the publication of his fifth and most successful full-length novel, *The *Woman in White* (1860), Collins became a popular writer of intricately plotted stories of mystery, suspense, and crime, though his work continued to attract condemnation for sensationalism (*see* SENSATION, NOVEL OF). His portrayal of attractive but transgressive women such as Magdalen Vanstone in **No Name* and *Lydia* Gwilt in **Armadale*, now considered a significant feature of his work, was particularly attacked. His four novels of the 1860s, *The Woman in White*, *No Name* (1862), *Armadale* (1866), and *The *Moonstone* (1868), are his most important works. Collins suffered from severe attacks of a rheumatic illness which caused him great pain, only relieved by the use of opium. One of his worst attacks occurred while he was writing *The Moonstone*, and he made use of the effects of opium in the plot of the novel. It used to be considered that Collins's opium habit, and the loss of Dickens's constructive criticism after 1870, led to a disastrous decline in the quality of his writing. However his explorations of the darker side of Victorian society and his interest in abnormal physiology and psychology are now seen as innovative, and recent critical re-evaluation has found much of interest in later 'novels with a purpose' such as *Man and Wife* (1870), *The Law and the Lady* (1875), and his anti-vivisection novel *Heart and Science* (1883). Collins had a lifelong interest in the theatre, and five of his original plays were produced, as well as a number of theatrical adaptations of his novels, of which *Man and Wife* and *The New Magdalen*, both produced in 1873, were the most successful. The only play for which he is now remembered is *The Frozen Deep* (1857), written for Dickens's amateur company, with Dickens playing the lead, and his other plays have not been revived or reprinted. Collins's private life was as much a cause of scandal as his fiction. He never married, but from 1859 lived openly with Caroline Graves, a widow from a working-class background. The romantic story that she was the original 'woman in white' is unlikely to be true. In 1868 he began another liaison with Martha Rudd, the daughter of a farm labourer, who had worked as a servant. By her he had two daughters and a son. Caroline Graves left Collins in 1868, but returned to him two years later, and remained with him for the rest of his life, though his relationship with Martha Rudd (known as Mrs Dawson) also continued until his death. Recent biographies by William Clarke, *The Secret Life of Wilkie Collins* (1988), and Catherine Peters, *The King of Inventors* (1991), contain new information. See also Andrew Gasson, *Wilkie Collins: An Illustrated Guide* (1998); Sue Lonoff, *Wilkie Collins and his Victorian Readers* (1982); Jenny Bourne Taylor, *In the Secret Theatre of Home: Wilkie Collins, Sensation Narrative, and Nineteenth Century Psychology* (1988); *The Public Face of Wilkie Collins: The Collected Letters*, ed. William Baker, Andrew Gasson, Graham Law, and Paul Lewis, 4 vols (2005).

COLLINS, William (1721–59) Poet, son of a Chichester hatter, educated at Winchester College (where he met Joseph *Warton) and Oxford University. Collins published his *Persian Eclogues* (1742) while an undergraduate. He moved to London in the 1740s, where he met James *Thomson, John *Armstrong, and Samuel *Johnson, and embarked on many abortive literary enterprises. His *Odes on Several Descriptive and Allegoric Subjects* (1746, dated 1747) made little initial impression; the volume includes his 'ode to Evening' and odes to Pity, Fear, and Simplicity (*see* ODE). His ode on the death of James Thomson appeared in 1749, and in 1750 he presented a draft of his *Ode on the Popular Superstitions of the Highlands* (published 1788) to John *Home. Thereafter he suffered increasingly from depression, and wrote nothing. His poems were collected by John Langhorne in 1765. Johnson commented on his harshness and obscurity as well as his 'sublimity and splendour' (**Lives of the English Poets*); later poets responded to his lyrical intensity and to his conception of poetry as visionary and sacred. See *The Poems of Thomas Gray, William Collins, Oliver Goldsmith*, ed. Roger Lonsdale (1969); P. L. Carver, *The Life of a Poet: William Collins* (1967).

COLLIS, John Stewart (1900–84) The son of an Irish solicitor, who was, like his brother Maurice Stewart Collis (1889–1973), a writer of biographies and other works, but is remembered largely for *While Following the Plough* (1946) and *Down to Earth* (1947; published as one volume, *The Worm Forgives the Plough*, 1973), works inspired by the years he spent working as a farm labourer in Dorset and Sussex during the Second World War. His autobiography, *Bound upon a Course* (1971), brought him belated recognition as a pioneer in the ecological movement, who wrote with imagination and authenticity of rural life.

COLLODI, Carlo (1826–90) Pen-name of Carlo Lorenzini, journalist, political activist, and author of plays, novels, memoirs, and children's books. He is best known for *Le avventure di Pinocchio* (1883: *The Adventures of Pinocchio*) which first appeared in serial form in the *Giornale per i bambini* (*The Children's Newspaper*). The first English translation appeared in 1892 and it has remained popular ever since. The film by Walt *Disney (1940) sentimentalizes the original story.

Collyn Clout A poem by John *Skelton, satirizing ecclesiastical abuses (*c.*1521–2).
See COLIN CLOUT.

COLMAN, George, the elder (1732–94) Playwright and theatre manager, son of the British envoy at Florence, educated at Westminster School, where he met Charles *Churchill and William *Cowper, and Christ Church, Oxford. With Bonnell Thornton (1725–68) he wrote the magazine *The Connoisseur* (1754–6). David *Garrick produced his comic afterpiece *Polly Honeycombe* in 1760 and his comedy *The Jealous Wife* in 1761. Colman and Garrick produced a theatrical newspaper, *The St. James's Chronicle*, as well as collaborating on *The *Clandestine Marriage* (1766). Colman managed Covent Garden Theatre, 1767–74, and the Haymarket, 1777–89; he was elected to Samuel *Johnson's *Club in 1768. He produced adaptations of *Shakespeare and *Jonson, translated the comedies of *Terence into blank verse (1765), and edited Francis *Beaumont and John *Fletcher (1778).

COLMAN, George, the younger (1762–1836) Son of George Colman, the elder (1732–94) born in London and educated at Westminster School and the universities of Oxford and Aberdeen. He made his name with the musical romantic comedy **Inkle and Yarico* in 1787, which was followed by other sentimental and humorous operettas. Among many other dramatic works, *The Iron Chest* of 1796 is a dramatization of **Caleb Williams* by William *Godwin. Colman's comedy of contemporary life, *The Heir-at-Law* (1797), became famous for the character of Dr Pangloss, a greedy, pompous pedant. *John Bull* (1803) contains a sketch of the supposed British character in Job Thornberry.

Colonel Jack, *The History and Remarkable Life of Colonel Jacque, Commonly Call'd* A novel by Daniel *Defoe (1722). The narrator, in some ways a masculine version of **Moll Flanders*, relates how he was abandoned by his parents and became (like Moll) a pickpocket. To abandon this risky profession, he enlists, but deserts to avoid serving in Flanders. He is kidnapped, sent (again like Moll) to Virginia, and sold to a planter. Promoted to the role of overseer, his 'humane' management of the slaves results in increased production and he is freed, to acquire much wealth as a planter in his own right. On his return to Britain he has a series of unfortunate matrimonial adventures, which culminate in penitent prosperity.

COLONNA, Vittoria (1490–1547) Italian poet, widely praised by her contemporaries, including *Sannazar, *Castiglione, *Bembo, *Tasso, and *Michelangelo, for the sonnets of her *Rime spirituali* (1540). The first hundred sonnets mourn the premature death of her husband, the marquis of Pescara, and others treat philosophical themes in an austere style that reflected her Calvinist sympathies. Her *Canzoniere* (*Songbook*) was published in 1544. She is mentioned by Sir John *Harington in his translation of **Orlando furioso* (Canto XXXVII). See *Rime*, ed. A. Bullock (1982).

colophon [from Gk κολοφών, summit, 'finishing touch'] A note or device (sometimes emblematic), placed at the end of a book or manuscript. It may contain the work's title, its scribe's or printer's name, and the date and place of printing; now the publisher's imprint, or logotype, usually found on the book's title page and often on its spine.

COLUM, Padraic (1881–1972) Irish poet, dramatist, and novelist, born in Co. Longford, whose work brought a realistic corrective to the *Irish Revival's portrayal of rural life. He won the praise of Ezra *Pound and the friendship of James *Joyce. Most of the lyrics for which Colum is remembered appeared in his first collection, *Wild Earth* (1907; expanded 1916). In 1914 he emigrated to the USA, where he collected Hawaiian folklore for the government. Colum was the author of 'She Moved through the Fair', perhaps the most famous Irish song of his time. With his wife Mary he wrote a memoir, *Our Friend James Joyce* (1958). His *Collected Poems* appeared in 1953. See Zack Bowen, *Padraic Colum: A Biographical Critical Introduction* (1970).

COLUMBA, St (Columcille) (*c.*521–597) Born in north-west Ireland and the founder of the monasteries of Iona and Durrow. He went to Scotland in 563 and settled in Iona, from which the conversion of Scotland and Northumbria by the Celtic church proceeded. His reputation rests on achievements in ecclesiastical organization which considerably outlived him. The book of his life and miracles was written by *Adomnan of Iona and it has been edited and translated by R. Sharpe (1995).

COLVIN, Sir Sidney (1845–1927) Critic of art and literature, educated at Trinity College, Cambridge, Slade professor of fine art at Cambridge 1873–85, director of the Fitzwilliam Museum in 1876, and keeper of the department of prints and drawings at the British Museum 1883–1912. Besides contributing many articles on the history and criticism of art to periodicals, he published several books including lives of W. S. *Landor (1881) and John *Keats (1887). He was honorary secretary of the Society of Dilettanti, 1891–6, and corresponded with some of the most eminent intellectuals of his day (see E. V. Lucas, *The Colvins and their Friends*, 1928). He edited the Edinburgh edition of R. L. *Stevenson's works (1894–7) and *The Letters of R. L. Stevenson* (1899 and 1911) and in 1895 published the *Vailima Letters* written to him by Stevenson, 1890–94.

COMBE, William (1741–1823) Author, born in London and educated at Eton College. He published a number of metrical satires, including *The Diaboliad* (1776) and many other works in prose and verse, including *The Devil upon Two Sticks in England* (1790) and *The Microcosm of London* (1808). He is particularly remembered for the verses that he wrote to accompany Thomas *Rowlandson's coloured plates and drawings of the adventures of 'Dr Syntax'. The first of these works, *The Tour of Dr Syntax in Search of the Picturesque*, a parody of the popular books of picturesque travels of the day, and particularly of the works of William *Gilpin, appeared in Rudolph *Ackermann's *Poetical Magazine* in 1809, and in 1812 as a book which went into many editions. Dr Syntax is the grotesque figure of a clergyman and schoolmaster, who sets out during the holidays, on his old horse Grizzle, to 'make a tour and write it', and meets with a series of absurd misfortunes. This was followed in 1820 by *The Second Tour of Dr Syntax in Search of Consolation* (for the loss of his wife) and in 1821 by *The Third Tour of Dr Syntax in Search of a Wife*. The three Tours were collected in 1826. Combe also wrote the letterpress for Rowlandson's *The English Dance of Death* (1815–16), *The Dance of Life* (1816), and *Johnny Quae Genus* (1822), another Syntax story.

Comédie humaine, La *See* BALZAC, HONORÉ DE.

comedy is a capaciously varied dramatic genre with several recognized sub-genres, divided by George *Meredith and others between the 'low' forms reliant upon physical clowning (*farce, *pantomime, *burlesque) and the 'high comedy' of elegant wit and dramatic *irony (as in the 'comedy of manners' set in fashionable society, or the 'romantic comedy' involving the tribulations of young lovers). The broadest sense of the term extends beyond theatre to the comic effects produced by some kinds of narrative verse and of prose fiction, from the

*fabliaux of *Chaucer to the novels and tales of P. G. *Wodehouse. In its principal dramatic sense, comedy is loosely defined as that kind of play in which, by contrast with *tragedy or *melodrama, the audience enjoys a relaxed superiority over the characters, and expects a happy and often festive conclusion to the action. The main line of English comedy derives from the Graeco-Roman 'New Comedy' of *Menander, *Plautus, and *Terence, which represents stock fictitious characters (misers, braggarts, young lovers) in amusing and happily concluded adventures. The *mystery plays and *interludes of the later Middle Ages include some farcical episodes, but are not held to be comedies. The first fully developed comedies in English date from the mid-16th century: **Ralph Roister Doister* and **Gammer Gurton's Needle* in verse, and **Supposes* in prose. In the late 16th and early 17th centuries the leading English exponents were *Shakespeare, in such romantic comedies as *A *Midsummer Night's Dream*, **As You Like It*, **Much Ado About Nothing*, and **Twelfth Night*, and Ben *Jonson in such plays as **Volpone* and *The *Alchemist*, which employ *satire in his so-called 'comedy of humours'. After the reopening of the theatres in 1660, the wittily irreverent comedy of manners flourished in a phase now known as Restoration comedy, in the plays of William *Congreve, William *Wycherley, Sir George *Etherege, Sir John *Vanbrugh, Aphra *Behn, and George *Farquhar. The 18th century witnessed the rise of the more respectably subdued form known as 'sentimental' comedy, along with popular burlesques and pantomimes; Richard Brinsley *Sheridan's *The *School for Scandal* and Oliver Goldsmith's **She Stoops to Conquer* are the classic comedies of that age. The 19th century is not noted for outstanding comedies until the advent of Oscar Wilde with *The *Importance of Being Earnest* and other plays. In the 20th century the major innovators were George Bernard *Shaw, with a new kind of intellectual comedy, and Noël *Coward in his elegantly structured comedies of manners; other notable practitioners of that age include Somerset *Maugham, Joe *Orton, and Alan *Ayckbourn. See Andrew Stott, *Comedy* (2004).
See also TRAGICOMEDY.

Comedy, The Divine *See* DIVINA COMMEDIA.

Comedy of Errors, The A comedy by *Shakespeare, acted at Gray's Inn 1594, first printed in the first *folio (1623), based mainly on *Plautus' *Menaechmi*.

Syracuse and Ephesus are enemies, and any Syracusan found in Ephesus is executed unless he can pay a ransom of 1,000 marks. Egeon, an old Syracusan merchant, has been arrested in Ephesus. He explains that he had identical twin sons, each named Antipholus, attended by two slaves called Dromio, also identical. Having in a shipwreck been separated, with the younger son and one Dromio, from his wife and the other son and slave, Egeon had never seen them since. The younger son (Antipholus of Syracuse) on reaching manhood went (with his Dromio) in search of his brother and mother and disappeared. After searching for five years, Egeon has now arrived in Ephesus.

The duke, moved by this tale, gives Egeon till evening to find his ransom. Now, the elder Antipholus (Antipholus of Ephesus), with his Dromio, has been living in Ephesus since the shipwreck and is married. Antipholus of Syracuse and the other Dromio have arrived there that very morning. Each twin is still identical with his brother, which gives rise to the comedy of errors. Antipholus of Syracuse is summoned home to dinner by Dromio of Ephesus; he is claimed as husband by Adriana, wife of Antipholus of Ephesus, who is kept out of his own house because he is supposed to be already inside. Antipholus of Syracuse falls in love with Luciana, his brother's wife's sister. Antipholus of Ephesus is confined as a lunatic, and Antipholus of Syracuse hides from his brother's jealous wife in a convent.

Evening comes and Egeon is led to execution. As the duke proceeds to the place of execution, Antipholus of Ephesus appeals to him for redress. Then the abbess of the convent presents Antipholus of Syracuse, also claiming redress. The simultaneous presence of the two brothers explains the misunderstandings. Egeon recovers his two sons and his liberty, and the abbess turns out to be his lost wife Emilia.

COMENIUS, John Amos (Jan Komenský) (1592–1670) Moravian educational reformer; he completed his studies in Heidelberg in 1614 and was ordained in 1618. He gained European fame in 1631 with the publication of *Janua Linguarum Reserata*, published in England as *The Gates of Tongues Unlocked and Opened*. In 1637 Samuel *Hartlib published *Conatuum Comenianorum Praeludia* (in 1639 as *Pansophiae Prodromus* and in 1642 in English as *A Reformation of Schools*). Comenius visited London in 1641, where he wrote *Via Lucis*, then travelled in northern and middle Europe, finally settling in Amsterdam, where he wrote his last great work, *De Rerum Humanorum Emendatione Consultatio Catholica*, much of which was presumed lost until 1934 and which was published in its entirety in 1966. His *Orbis Sensualium Pictus*, with a Latin and German text, appeared in 1658, and was published in English in 1659 as *Comenius's Visible World*, the first schoolbook consistently to use pictures in the learning of languages. He believed in a system of universal wisdom, and his most lasting contribution was as an educational thinker.

COMESTOR, Petrus (d. 1179) From Troyes in Champagne, named 'the feeder' because of his voracity in studying books. He was the author of a *Historia Scholastica*, a collection of scriptural narratives with commentary which was very popular throughout the Middle Ages in a French translation, and was one of the first of the very many commentators on the *Sententiae* of *Peter Lombard. He became chancellor of the University of Paris in 1164. His work was familiar to *Chaucer, and *Dante places him among the Doctors of the church in the heaven of the sun (*Paradiso*, XII. 134) as 'Pietro Mangiadore'.

Comical Revenge, The, *or Love in a Tub* A comedy by Sir George *Etherege, acted 1664. The main plot, in heroic couplets, deals with the rivalry of Lord Beaufort and Colonel

Bruce for the hand of Graciana, happily resolved when Bruce marries Aurelia instead. In the comic sub-plot, in prose, the libertine Sir Frederick Frolick's French valet Dufoy is confined in a tub, by his fellow servants, under the influence of opium. There is also a foolish country knight, Sir Nicholas Cully, and two sharpers, Palmer and Wheedle. It was a great hit and often revived, though Samuel *Pepys, who saw it in 1666, thought it 'silly'.

comics, comic strips These flourished from the end of the 19th century with *Ally Sloper's Half-Holiday* (1884–1923) widely acknowledged as the publication that established the form, although comic strips had appeared earlier in papers such as *The Graphic* (1869–1932); Edwin John Brett's *The Boys of England* (1866–99); and *Funny Folks* (1874–94). Ally Sloper was a sharp, gin-drinking, working-class anti-hero, the first regular character in the comic world. The form flourished in such publications as *Comic Cuts* (1890–1953), *Chips* (1890–1953), *The Gem* (1907–39), and *The Magnet* (1908–40; *see* HAMILTON, CHARLES). They also featured in boys' adventure comics such as *Adventure* (1921–61), *Wizard* (1922–63), and *Hotspur* (1933–59), finding new life in the *Beano* (1938–) and *Dandy* (1937–), both still flourishing with many of their original characters. *Rainbow* (1914–56) was the first coloured comic designed exclusively for children. There was a sustained battle between the subversively entertaining and the morally improving: *Rupert Bear, in the *Daily Express*, was on the side of the angels, as was Dan Dare in the *Eagle*. The founding of *Eagle* in 1950 by Lancashire vicar Marcus Morris was directly prompted by the growing infiltration of American horror comics; the original series ended in 1969, but Dan Dare survives in *2000 AD*. The publishers' self-regulating Comic Book Code was introduced in 1954; recently its guidelines have regularly been transgressed. Some *picturebook makers, notably Raymond *Briggs, have drawn on the visual grammar of comic books. See Scott McCloud's *Understanding Comics* (1993).

'Coming of Arthur, The' One of Alfred *Tennyson's **Idylls of the King* published 1869. It describes the newly crowned Arthur's first meeting with Guinevere, and their marriage.

Coming Race, The A novel by Edward *Bulwer-Lytton, published 1871. The narrator describes his visit to a subterranean race of superior beings that long ago took refuge, possibly from the biblical flood, in the depths of the earth. There they have evolved a highly sophisticated civilization, with the aid of a form of energy called Vril, which has great powers of destruction as well as great utility. Much of the novel is devoted to a satiric account of the narrator's own democratic society, of which he is initially proud, and to praise of the underground society, which has no war, no crime, and no inequality, and where women are stronger than men and free to choose their own mates. This involves the narrator in some embarrassing situations with his host's daughter Zee; he convinces her that he would never be happy in her world, and she returns him to the upper earth, aided by her mechanical Vril-powered wings. 'Love is swifter than Vril' is one of her more romantic statements. He is left to prophesy the death of the human race at the hands of 'our inevitable destroyers'. The sublime subterranean landscapes recall the paintings of John *Martin, whose work Bulwer-Lytton much admired. A memory of this early and influential example of *science fiction lingers in the trade name of the product 'Bovril', derived from 'Vril'.

commedia dell'arte A popular, unscripted form of comedy, which developed in Italy in the sixteenth century and flourished there until the 18th century. *Commedia dell'arte*, so called to distinguish it from literary, scripted *commedia erudita*, was performed by troupes of professional actors and was characterized by stock roles and minimal scenarios which actors amplified by improvisation and shared experience. Some if not all the actors wore masks, and in time the names of certain characters became stereotypes, in particular the servants Harlequin, Pulcinella, and Colombine, and the ridiculous old man Pantaloon. In Italy *commedia dell'arte* was superseded by the theatrical reforms of Carlo *Goldoni, but its influence continued in England in pantomime and puppet shows. See also K. and L. Richards, *The Commedia dell'arte: A Documentary History* (1990).

Common Prayer, The Book of The official service book of the *Church of England since the *Reformation, prescribing the structure of the Christian year, services for morning and evening prayer and for communion, matrimony, baptism, etc., and the texts of the *Bible to be read and *psalms to be sung throughout the year. It has had a huge impact on writers in English. The text evolved in stages. The first and second books of Edward VI (1549 and 1552) were largely compiled by Thomas *Cranmer, partly from earlier Latin service books. The wording of Cranmer's collects (short prayers spoken by the minister) and general prayers have entered the language, for example 'the devices and desires of our own hearts', 'whose service is perfect freedom', 'lighten our darkness'. The Prayer Book was revised under Elizabeth I (1559), reissued with minor changes under James I (1604), and a revised version was forced on the Scots in 1637 and then withdrawn. It was detested by the *Puritans, and in 1645 during the Civil War it was abolished. Under Charles II it was restored with further revisions (1662), and this has remained the official Prayer Book. A revised book agreed by the church was rejected by Parliament in 1928. Alternative forms in modernized language were then agreed: the Alternative Service Book (1980) has been replaced by the collection called Common Worship (2000), but without the official status of the 1662 Prayer Book. Supporters find modernized versions easy to understand; detractors regret the downgrading of the Prayer Book's literary qualities. See G. J. Cuming, *A History of Anglican Liturgy* (2nd edn 1982).

Commonwealth of Oceana, The (1656) A republican utopia by James *Harrington. Dedicated to Oliver *Cromwell, it recommends a two-chamber system, elections ('through the suffrage of the people given by the ballot') that would replace one-third of the executive annually, and a redistribution of landed property by an agrarian law limiting land holdings. Other proposals include an elected *poet laureate and a National Theatre. '*Oceana*' is England and the Archon, 'Olphaus Megalator', is Cromwell. Harrington expresses admiration for the republics of Greece and Rome, the Venetian republic, and *Machiavelli, 'the only politician of later ages'. He meant *Oceana* to be a reply to Thomas *Hobbes's **Leviathan*. David *Hume described it as 'the only valuable model of a commonwealth that has yet been offered to the public'.

COMMYNES, Philippe de (1447–1511) French chronicler. He served in a diplomatic capacity under Charles, duke of Burgundy, and subsequently under Louis XI and Charles VIII of France. His *Mémoires*, composed between 1489 and 1498, were first published in 1524–8, and deal with the reign of Louis XI and Charles VIII's Italian expedition. They were first translated into English by Thomas Danett (1596), and were the inspiration for Walter *Scott's **Quentin Durward*.

comparative literature An academic discipline in which literary works and traditions of more than one nation or language are studied, thus permitting fuller understanding of international literary movements and affiliations. By contrast with nationally or linguistically defined disciplines such as 'English literature', comparative literature ranges freely across frontiers in search of cross-cultural influences and correspondences. The name does not imply any obligation to compare different national literary traditions. The discipline has been more favoured by American and European universities than by British. Distinguished practitioners have included René Wellek (1903–95) and George *Steiner.

complaint A poetic form derived from the Latin *planctus*, bewailing the vicissitudes of life (as in Thomas *Hoccleve's *Complaint*) or addressed to a more particular end (such as *Chaucer's 'Complaint to his Purse'). The form is particularly common in poems up to the Renaissance; thereafter the terms *'elegy' and 'lament' were used.

Complaint of Buckingham, The A poem by Thomas *Sackville, contributed by him to the 1563 edition of *A *Mirror for Magistrates*. After his rebellion against Richard III, Henry Stafford, duke of Buckingham, takes refuge with a dependant, Humfrey Banastair. Banastair betrays him to the king and Buckingham is executed. As his corpse lies on the ground it raises its head and heaps curses on Banastair and his children.

'Complaint of Rosamund' A poem by Samuel *Daniel in *rhyme royal appended to *Delia*.

Compleat Angler, The, *or The Contemplative Man's Recreation* A discourse on fishing by Izaak *Walton, first published 1653, second, enlarged edition 1655, fifth edition with a continuation by Charles *Cotton, 1676. Piscator (a fisherman), Auceps (a fowler), and Venator (a hunter) debate during a fishing expedition along the river Lea. There are instructions for catching and cooking fish, also interludes of verse, angling anecdotes, moral reflections, and snatches of mythology and folklore. Walton's sources include *The Treatise of Fishing with an Angle* (*The Book of St Albans*, 1496) and an anonymous book, *The Art of Angling* published in 1577, of which the only known copy surfaced in 1954. Walton's idyllic, deeply nostalgic celebration of his 'calm, quiet, innocent recreation' has become a classic, attracting readers not usually interested in fish or books, and is one of the most frequently reprinted texts in English literature.

Complutensian Polyglot Bible, the *See* XIMÉNEZ DE CISNEROS, CARDINAL FRANCISCO.

COMPTON, D. G. (David Guy) (1930–) Born in London; author of crime and *science fiction novels. *The Continuous Katherine Mortenhoe* (1974) portrays media surveillance of a dying woman for the titillation of an audience. *Justice City* (1994) fuses the characteristics of a crime thriller with science fiction.

COMPTON-BURNETT, Dame Ivy (1884–1969) Novelist, born Pinner, Middlesex, and educated privately, at Addiscombe College, Sussex, and then at Royal Holloway College, London University (1902–6). She published her first, George *Eliot-inspired, novel, *Dolores*, in 1911, but recognition arrived with her second, *Pastors and Masters* (1925). This and other early works, such as *Brothers and Sisters* (1929) or *More Women Than Men* (1933), reveal an affinity with the brittle, deflationary wit and occasional satirical exuberance of Evelyn *Waugh and Anthony *Powell. But her highly condensed and abstracted novels, composed almost entirely in dialogue, were so unlike anyone else's that their impact was often compared to that of *Post-Impressionism in painting. They are generally set in the 1880–1914 period, in large, gloomy, generally dilapidated country houses full of servants, children, and dependent relatives. Each family is ruled in almost complete isolation from the outside world by a more or less tyrannical parent or grandparent: hence the consistently high rate of domestic crime ranging from matricide, incest, and child abuse to bigamy and fraud. Dame Ivy held that 'nothing is so corrupting as power', and her inward-looking, self-contained, and heavily monitored households provided her with an ideal environment in which to examine the misuse of power together with the violence and misery that follow. During the First World War she lost a brother on the Somme and two of her sisters committed suicide. When she eventually recovered from the protracted physical and emotional breakdown that ensued, she found herself increasingly preoccupied with the eruption of passionate and disruptive forces smouldering beneath the smooth surface of a deceptively calm and well-ordered society. In 1919 she began a lifelong relationship with Margaret Jourdain (1876–1951). *A House and Its Head* (1935), *A Family and a Fortune* (1939), and *Manservant and Maidservant* (1947) are perhaps the most outstanding of Compton-Burnett's twenty novels. She was appointed CBE in 1951 and DBE in 1967. See H. Spurling, *Ivy When Young: The Early Life of I. Compton-Burnett 1884–1919* (1974); H. Spurling, *Secrets of a Woman's Heart: The Later Life of I. Compton-Burnett 1920–1969* (1984).

COMTE, Auguste (1798–1857) French philosopher, in early life secretary to Claude-Henri de *Saint-Simon, with whom he shared the conviction that throughout history the mind and political institutions had evolved in close relation, and that a new phase of mental development had been entered. Comte's six-volume *Cours de philosophie positive* (1830–42: *Lectures on Positive Philosophy*) frames a general system of human conceptions as they had developed to their existing state. The four-volume *Système de politique positive* (1851–4: *System of Positive Politics*) gives a fuller treatment of political philosophy and its applications. Human knowledge, Comte argued, passed of necessity through three successive phases: the theological, the metaphysical, and the positive. This was the 'Law of the Three States' and it applied to the historical progress of the mind and to the development of the individual mind alike. The positive or scientific state, which had been attained but not brought to completion, was the 'normal' or final state of humanity. It was characterized by the abandonment of the search for absolute causes and the recognition of the 'laws of succession and relation' that govern phenomena as the true object of knowledge.

Comte intended to bring the science of social phenomena, sociology, into its final, positive, state and so lay the foundations of a social and political system proper to the age of industry. Temporal power was to be vested in a self-perpetuating elite of industrial chiefs. A separate spiritual authority would be established in the form of a priesthood with the duty of imparting the truths of positive philosophy and their practical consequences, and of administering a religion of Humanity (conceived as a Great Being composed of those men and women, past, present, and to come, whose lives had been, were, or would be devoted to human welfare). The influence of women on the feelings was to be foregrounded, in order to foster altruism, the basis of Comtean morality, expressed in the motto: 'Live for Others'.

Comte's principal English followers were Frederic *Harrison, E. S. Beesly, J. H. Bridges, and Richard Congreve. The *Cours de philosophie positive* was condensed, with the author's approval, in English translation by Harriet *Martineau (*The Positive Philosophy of Auguste Comte*, 2 vols, 1853); the *Système de politique positive* was translated by Harrison, Bridges, and others as *The System of Positive Polity* (4 vols, 1875–7). G. H. *Lewes provided an exposition of the leading ideas of the *Cours* in *Comte's Philosophy of the Sciences* (1853), and the fiction of his partner George *Eliot reflects Comte's influence. John Stuart *Mill gave a critical account of Comte's thought in *Auguste Comte and Positivism* (1865); *Lettres inédites de John Stuart Mill à Auguste Comte* was published in Paris in 1899. See also POSITIVISM.

***Comus,** A Maske Presented at Ludlow Castle, 1634: on Michaelmasse Night, before the Right Honorable John Earl of Bridgewater, Lord President of Wales* By John *Milton, first printed, anonymously and untitled, 1637. Written at the suggestion of Milton's friend, the composer Henry *Lawes, to celebrate the earl of Bridgewater's elevation to the presidency of Wales and the Marches, it portrays the abduction and enchantment of Bridgewater's 15-year-old daughter Lady Alice by the evil sorcerer Comus, son of Bacchus and Circe, the failure of her brothers (aged 9 and 11) to rescue her, and her eventual release by Sabrina, goddess of the river Severn. An Attendant Spirit, disguised as a shepherd, is sent from on high to protect the young aristocrats, and ensures that they are returned to Ludlow and presented to their parents at the end. See C. C. Brown, *Milton's Aristocratic Entertainments* (1985).

CONAN DOYLE *See* DOYLE, ARTHUR.

conceit An elaborate metaphor comparing two apparently dissimilar objects or emotions, often with an effect of shock or surprise. The *Petrarchan conceit, much imitated by *Elizabethan sonneteers and both used and parodied by Shakespeare, usually evoked the qualities of the disdainful mistress and the devoted lover, often in highly exaggerated terms; the *metaphysical conceit, as used by John *Donne and his followers, applied wit and ingenuity to, in the words of Samuel *Johnson, 'a combination of dissimilar images, or discovery of occult resemblances in things apparently unlike', e.g. Donne's famous comparison of two lovers to a pair of compasses.

Conchubar (Conchobar) [pron. Conachoor] In the Ulster cycle of Irish mythology, king of Ulster.
See also CUCHULAIN; DEIRDRE.

Conciliation with America, On By Edmund *Burke, speech made in the House of Commons on 22 March 1775, in a last effort to find a peaceful solution to the quarrel with the American colonies. Burke argues that force is inapplicable to the 'fierce spirit of liberty' prevailing in the English colonies. He shows that it would be impossible or inexpedient to change this spirit or to prosecute it as criminal and therefore proposes that Parliament must comply with it as necessary. American representation in Parliament is impracticable, but Burke resolves the taxation problem by proposing grants by the local legislatures.

concrete poetry A term used to describe a kind of experimental poetry developed in the 1950s and flourishing in the 1960s, which dwells primarily on the visual aspects of the poem (although two other forms of concrete poetry, the kinetic and the phonetic, have also been distinguished). An international movement was officially launched at the National Exhibition of concrete art in São Paulo in 1956; a Brazilian 'Pilot Plan' or manifesto, published in 1958, stated that 'concrete poetry begins by being aware of graphic space as structural agent'. Concrete poets experiment with typography, graphics, the 'ideogram concept', computer poems, collage, etc., and in varying degrees acknowledge influence from Dada, Hans Arp (1886–1966), Kurt Schwitters (1887–1948), Kazimir Malevich (1878–1935), and other visual artists. Ian Hamilton *Finlay, one of the leading Scottish exponents, expressed his own affinity with 17th-century *emblems and poems such as George *Herbert's 'Easter Wings', which use the shape as well as the sense of a poem to convey meaning. Edwin *Morgan, also a Scot, has written a variety of concrete poems, which were criticized by some devotees of the form as being 'too verbal'. Mary Ellen Solt in 'A World Look at Concrete Poetry' (*Hispanic Arts*, 1/3–4, 1968) declares that 'the concrete poet seeks to relieve the poem of its centuries-old burden of ideas, symbolic reference, allusion and repetitious emotional content'. Others claim a less radical role, pointing to Herbert, William *Blake, Lewis Carroll (C. L. *Dodgson), Ezra *Pound's use of Chinese characters, and E. E. *Cummings as evidence of a long tradition of typographical experiment. See Emmett Williams (ed.), *An Anthology of Concrete Poetry* (1967).

CONDELL, Henry *See* HEMINGES, JOHN.

CONDER, Charles *See* ART NOUVEAU.

CONDILLAC, Étienne Bonnot, abbé de (1714–80) French philosopher. Reacting against *Descartes and influenced by the empiricism of *Locke, his major works, notably the *Essai sur l'origine des connaissances humaines* (1746: *Essay on the Origin of Human Knowledge*) and the *Traité des sensations* (1754: *Treatise on Sensations*), both of which were translated into English in the 1770s, explore how human beings acquire their ideas through sensation and how simple ideas are linked, through language, by association. See I. F. Knight, *The Geometric Spirit: The Abbé de Condillac and the French Enlightenment* (1968).

condition of England A phrase coined by Thomas *Carlyle in the opening words of *Past and Present* (1843) to describe the social and political inequalities in what Benjamin *Disraeli, in *Sybil* (1845), was to term the 'Two Nations of England, the Rich and the Poor'. It formed the subject matter of social investigators and writers of government 'blue books', and of *social problem novelists, and developed the question asked by Carlyle in *Chartism* (1839): 'Is the condition of the English working people wrong; so wrong that rational working men cannot, will not, and even should not rest quiet under it?' *See also* CHARTIST MOVEMENT.

CONDON, Richard (1915–96) American novelist, born in New York. His second novel, *The Manchurian Candidate* (1959) remains his best-known work for its combination of brainwashing with a satire on Senator McCarthy, subsequently made into a film in 1962 (starring Frank Sinatra and Laurence Harvey), and 2004. Condon combined conspiracy with satire in his novels, *Winter Kills* (1984) being an investigation narrative into the assassination of President Kennedy.

CONDORCET, Jean-Antoine-Nicolas, marquis de (1743–94) French philosopher, mathematician, and revolutionary politician. A friend of the **Philosophes*, he wrote widely on constitutional reform, the abolition of the slave trade, and women's rights. His best-known work is his posthumously published *Esquisse d'un tableau historique des progrès de l'esprit humain* (1795: *Sketch for a Historical Picture of the Progress of the Human Mind*), a philosophical history of scientific progress which presents the Enlightenment and French Revolution as the penultimate epoch in the history of humankind. See D. Williams, *Condorcet and Modernity* (2004).

coney-catching *See* ROGUE LITERATURE.

Confessio Amantis *See* GOWER, JOHN.

confessional poetry A term principally applied to the self-revealing style of writing and use of intimate subject matter adopted and pioneered in America by Robert *Lowell (*Life Studies*, 1959): other writers in the tradition have included John *Berryman, Anne *Sexton, and Sylvia *Plath. A new wave of confessional writing in prose occurred in the 1980s and 1990s when a vogue for *autobiographical material, family history, and frank memoirs coincided in Britain with a new sense of male interest in domestic and psychological matters hitherto regarded as predominantly female terrain: this resulted in 'New Man' writing by Blake *Morrison, Nick *Hornby, and others. See *'lads' literature, for a related and reactive variant of the phenomenon.

Confessions of a Justified Sinner *See* PRIVATE MEMOIRS AND CONFESSIONS OF A JUSTIFIED SINNER.

Confessions of an English Opium Eater By Thomas *De Quincey, published 1822 (enlarged version 1856). The first of his books, De Quincey's study examines his own opium addiction and its psychological effects tracing how childhood and youthful experiences are transformed, under the influence of opium, into symbolical and revealing dreams. The central experience for subsequent dream-formations was his childhood loss of his sister, duplicated by the disappearance of the 15-year-old prostitute Ann, who befriended him during his months of homeless near-starvation in London. The euphoric reveries of the early stages of his addiction and the appalling nightmares of the later stages are described in sonorous and haunting prose, and the work, first appearing in the **London Magazine* in 1821, conferred instant literary fame on

De Quincey. In 1856 he greatly extended the *Confessions* for a collected edition of his works, but thereby blunted its effect.

Confidence-Man, The A cryptic novel by Herman *Melville, published in 1857, which employs the term 'confidence-man', coined after a notorious 1849 case, to denote trickery and deception. The novel, which describes the tricks and deceptions practised by the devil on the passengers of a Mississippi steamboat, has continued to baffle critics.

Congregationalism Otherwise known as Independency or Separatism, the system of church government based on the autonomy of individual 'gathered churches', with the right to choose their own pastors, outside the control of the established *Church of England. Independent churches grew in the late 16th century and were increasingly harassed in the early 17th, resulting in the emigration of some members to New England, where Congregationalism became the dominant religious and cultural force. The Independents, who were deeply unsympathetic to the *Presbyterian view of church government, were the victors in the Civil War. Their principles were enshrined in the Savoy Declaration of 1658. At the *Restoration they were persecuted, along with the Presbyterians, *Baptists, and *Quakers. Following the Act of Toleration of 1689, with the legal recognition of Protestant Dissent from the Church of England, the Congregationalists came to have an increasing impact on wider religious and literary culture. In the 18th century Congregationalism was heavily influenced by Calvinistic *Methodism, and increasingly at odds with rational Dissent and *Unitarianism. The most influential Congregationalist writer is undoubtedly Isaac *Watts.

See CHURCH OF ENGLAND; PROTESTANTISM; PURITANISM.

CONGREVE, William (1670–1729) Dramatist, born near Leeds, to a gentry family. His father being commander of the garrison at Youghal, he was educated at Kilkenny school and Trinity College, Dublin, at both of which he was a fellow student of Jonathan *Swift. He entered the Middle Temple, but gave up law for literature, publishing a novel of intrigue, *Incognita* (1691). In 1693 he achieved fame with his comedy *The Old Batchelour*, written with some help from John *Dryden and Thomas *Southerne. Of his other comedies, *The *Double Dealer* was published in 1694, **Love for Love* in 1695, and *The *Way of the World* in 1700. In these plays Congreve studied the social pressures on love and marriage, demonstrating an amused tolerance for (male) sexual libertinism, and providing some sharply intelligent and witty female roles. His one tragedy, *The *Mourning Bride*, was produced in 1697. In 1696 he published a letter to John *Dennis, 'Concerning Humour in Comedy', and in 1698 replied to the attack made on him in the *Short View* of Jeremy *Collier. After 1700 he wrote little for the stage, apart from an opera, *Semele*; he held several government posts, was a member of the *Kit-Cat Club, and enjoyed the friendship of Swift, Richard *Steele, and Alexander *Pope, who dedicated his translation of the **Iliad* to him. He collected his own *Works* in 1710; his final poem, *Letter to Cobham*, containing a meditative account of himself in retirement, appeared in 1728. *Voltaire visited him late in life. He left the bulk of his estate to Henrietta, duchess of Marlborough, of whose daughter he was perhaps the father. He also left a bequest to the actress Anne *Bracegirdle, another close female associate. He was buried in Westminster Abbey. See *The Works of William Congreve*, ed. D. F. Mckenzie, 2 vols (2008).

Coningsby A novel by Benjamin *Disraeli, published 1844. In the preface to the Hughenden edition of his novels in 1870 Disraeli declares that his ambition in the trilogy *Coningsby–*Sybil–*Tancred* was to describe the influence of the main political parties on the people, and to indicate how their condition might be improved. His theme is that the Crown must govern justly and the church inspire. His purpose was consciously political, and he chose the novel as the most effective means of influence on public opinion. *Coningsby* celebrates the new Tories of the 'Young England' set, whose opposition to Whiggery and concern at the treatment of the poor and the injustice of the franchise is strongly reflected in the narrative.

The high-spirited Coningsby is orphaned, and sent to Eton College by his wealthy grandfather Lord Monmouth, who represents the old type of oppressive Tory aristocrat. There Coningsby becomes the friend, and saves the life of Oswald Millbank, who is the son of an energetic Lancashire manufacturer, detested by Monmouth. At Cambridge and thereafter Coningsby develops political and social ideals far removed from those of his grandfather, and falls in love with Oswald's sister Edith. His behaviour so angers Monmouth that when the old man dies Coningsby finds he has been disinherited. He has to forgo his life of affluence and set to work in the Inns of Court. Gradually Millbank, who had been opposed to Coningsby's marriage to his daughter, realizes the young man's worth; he helps him to stand for Parliament and sees him returned. Edith and Coningsby are married and Coningsby's fortunes are restored.

The vigorous portrait of Lord Monmouth is based on Lord Hertford, who was also the model for W. M. *Thackeray's Lord Steyne. Sidonia, the wise old Jew who appears also in *Tancred*, reflects aspects of Lord Rothschild; and Rigby, possibly the most unpleasant of all Disraeli's characters, is based on John *Croker. *Coningsby* was immensely successful and came to be regarded as a manifesto for Young England.

CONNOLLY, Cyril (1903–74) Writer and journalist. Born in Coventry, he was educated at Eton College and Balliol College, Oxford. After a short spell as a tutor in Jamaica, he became a journalist and critic. He was literary editor of the *Observer* 1942–3, and was for many years a weekly reviewer for the *Sunday Times*. In 1939, with Stephen *Spender, he founded **Horizon* and edited it until it closed in 1950. His only novel, *The Rock Pool* (Paris, 1936; London, 1947), is a satiric extravaganza with echoes of Ronald *Firbank and Evelyn *Waugh; it describes the adventures of a young literary stockbroker in Trou-sur-Mer, an artistic expatriate colony on the French Riviera. His other works include *Enemies of Promise* (1938), which contains an autobiographical section, 'A Georgian

Boyhood', vividly recalling his schooldays; *The Unquiet Grave* (1944), subtitled 'A Word Cycle' and published under the pseudonym of Palinurus (the drowned pilot of the *Aeneid*), which largely consists of aphorisms and reflections; and various collections of essays (*The Condemned Playground*, 1945, which displays his gift for parody; *Previous Convictions*, 1963; *The Evening Colonnade*, 1973, and others). Connolly's favourite themes include the dangers of early success and the hazardous lure of literary immortality, but he also celebrated the ephemeral pleasure of food, wine, and travel. He was appointed CBE in 1972. See J. Lewis, *Cyril Connolly: A Life* (1997).

CONQUEST, Robert (1917–) Poet, critic, and historian, educated at Winchester College and Magdalen College, Oxford. He edited the important anthology **New Lines* (1956), widely seen as proselytizing on behalf of the new *Movement school of poets, which included Philip *Larkin, who was an admirer of Conquest's own poetry. Conquest's publications include *Poems* (1955), *Between Mars and Venus* (1962), and *Arias from a Love Opera* (1969); *New and Collected Poems* appeared in 1988.

Conquest of Granada by the Spaniards, The In two parts (Pt I produced in December 1670, Pt II in January 1671; both published 1672). Written in resounding rhyming couplets, this ten-act heroic extravaganza by John *Dryden depicts the troubled but finally fortunate loves of the noble if impulsive Almanzor and the Moorish beauty Almahide. With its ample cast of characters, including the vividly drawn *femme fatale* Lyndaraxa, and its epic setting against the background of the Spanish reconquest of Granada torn by the tribal rivalry between the Abencerragos and the Zegrys, the play was an artistic success and a huge box-office hit. As such it became the main target of the duke of *Buckingham's and others' burlesque in *The Rehearsal*, in which its high-blown verse and its larger-than-life hero were savagely satirized.

CONRAD, Joseph (Józef Teodor Konrad Korzeniowski) (1857–1924) Novelist and short story writer, born of Polish parents in the Russian-dominated Ukraine. His father's political sympathies caused the family to be exiled to Vologda in northern Russia, where Conrad's mother died when he was 7. After their return to Poland his father also died and Conrad was taken under the wing of his uncle Tadeusz Bobrowski, who was to be a continuing influence on his life. From an early age he longed to go to sea and in 1874 he went to Marseilles, embarked on a French vessel, and began the career as a sailor which was to supply so much material for his writing. In 1886 he became a British subject and a master mariner. In 1894, after twenty years at sea, he settled in England; a bequest from Bobrowski enabled him to devote himself to fiction; in 1896 he married Jessie George, by whom he was to have two sons. His first novels, *Almayer's Folly* (1895) and *An Outcast of the Islands* (1896), both set in the Malay archipelago, are rich in exotic description; *The Nigger of the 'Narcissus'* (1897) presents a leaner narrative, and **Lord Jim* (1900) a more complex combination of popular forms and literary style. The sea continued to supply the setting for most of his novels and short stories. His narrative technique is characterized by breaks in time-sequence and, in several works, a frame narrator, Marlow. His richly textured narrative prose sometimes bears traces of French idioms and Polish constructions.

He collaborated with Ford Madox *Ford on *The Inheritors* (1900) and *Romance* (1903), but disagreements subsequently brought their association to an end. *Typhoon* (1903) was followed by a major work, **Nostromo* (1904), an imaginative novel which again explores one of Conrad's chief preoccupations—man's vulnerability and corruptibility. In the novella *'Heart of Darkness' (1899 in *Blackwood's Magazine*; 1902 in *Youth*), Conrad had carried this issue to a terrifying conclusion. *The *Secret Agent* (1907) and *Under Western Eyes* (1911) are both novels with political themes, the latter set in Switzerland and Russia and centred on the tragedy of the student Razumov, caught up in the treachery and violence of revolution. Although warmly supported by Eve *Garnett and the literary agent J. B. Pinker, and praised by many influential men of letters, Conrad's work was generally ill received by critics and public, and he was plagued with money problems. It was only with *Chance* (1913) that Conrad achieved popular and financial success; the story of Flora de Barral, lonely daughter of a crooked financier, this novel combines the attractions of a sea background with the theme of romantic love and more female interest than is usual with Conrad. His other major works include *Youth* (1902), *The Mirror of the Sea* (1906), *Victory* (1915), *The Shadow-Line* (1917), *The Rescue* (1920), and *The Rover* (1923). Conrad's autobiography, *A Personal Record*, appeared in book form in 1912 and his unfinished novel *Suspense* was published in 1925.

By the time of his death, Conrad was well established in the literary world as one of the leading *modernists; a decline of interest in the 1930s was followed by increasing scholarly and critical attention, pioneered in part by a study in 1941 by M. C. Bradbrook, and by an essay in the same year by F. R. *Leavis in **Scrutiny* (later reprinted in *The Great Tradition*) in which Conrad is placed 'among the very great novelists in the language'. While early critics saw the works up to 1897 as an apprenticeship, and those after 1911 as a decline, recent criticism has taken the later novels more seriously. See F. R. Karl, *Joseph Conrad: The Three Lives* (1979); Z. Najder, *Joseph Conrad: A Chronicle* (1983); John Batchelor, *Joseph Conrad: A Critical Biography* (1994). Conrad's *Collected Letters* are being edited by F. Karl and L. Davies (7 vols to date, 1983–2005).

Conscious Lovers, The Richard *Steele's last comedy, based on the *Andria* of *Terence, performed 1722. Bevil is betrothed to Lucinda, daughter of Mr Sealand. But he loves Indiana, an orphan whom he has honourably supported. He tells Lucinda his feelings about the marriage, but offends his friend Myrtle, who loves Lucinda. He is challenged to a duel, but declines, the folly of duelling being a favourite theme of Steele's. Indiana is revealed as a lost daughter of Mr Sealand,

and she marries Bevil; Myrtle gains Lucinda. The play was a success and influenced the development of sentimental comedy in England.

consonance is the repetition of end or medial consonants, as in 'blank' and 'think', or 'The curfew to*lls* the kne*ll* of parting day' (Thomas *Gray's 'Elegy').

CONSTABLE, Archibald (1774–1827) A Scottish publisher, born in Carnbee, Fife, whom Walter *Scott described as 'of uncommon importance to literature'. He was an expert in antiquarian books, yet he also possessed a flair for choosing contemporary authors and he published most of Scott's early work. He established the highly successful **Edinburgh Review* in 1802, paying his contributors handsomely, and bought the **Encyclopaedia Britannica* in 1812. Yet in 1826 he went bankrupt, heavily involving Scott in his debts. He was an enthusiast for the new concept of cheap books, and in 1827 established Constable's Miscellany, a series of volumes on literature, art, and science.

CONSTABLE, Henry (1562–1613) Poet and theological writer. Educated at St John's College, Cambridge; around 1591, he embraced Roman Catholicism, and withdrew to Paris. He published *Diana*, a volume of sonnets, in 1592; it was republished in 1594 with additions by other poets. A supporter of James VI, he returned to London in 1603, was imprisoned several times, left the country in 1610, and died at Liège. Some of his poems (edited by Joan Grundy in 1960) are preserved in two important manuscripts; they also appeared in various collections, among others in **Englands Helicon*. Many of his sonnets are modelled on or translated from sonnets by the French poet Philippe Desportes (1546–1606).

CONSTABLE, John (1776–1837) Landscape painter, born at East Bergholt, Suffolk, the son of a miller. His works develop from the tranquillity of the early exhibited landscapes (*The Haywain*, 1821) to the sombre drama of *Hadleigh Castle* (1829). Constable's relationship with the Romantic poets has been much discussed by scholars; he is linked to them by his feeling for the simplest facts of nature and by his sense of their moral power. Yet Constable disliked the Lake District, where he met William *Wordsworth and S. T. *Coleridge in 1806, and his tastes were generally more traditional—for William *Cowper and Thomas *Gray, whose **Elegy Written in a Country Church-Yard* he illustrated, and for James Thomson's *The *Seasons* and Robert *Bloomfield's *The Farmer's Boy* (1802)—and lines from these works sometimes accompanied his pictures. Constable was a friend of Joseph Farington (1747–1821), of John Thomas *Smith, of Sir George *Beaumont, and of Charles Leslie (1794–1859). See Charles Leslie, *Memoirs of the Life of John Constable*, ed. Jonathan Mayne (1980); and ROMANTICISM.

Constance (1) a princess in a story in the **Canterbury Tales* (*see* CANTERBURY TALES, 5) and John *Gower's *Confessio Amantis*; (2) in *Shakespeare's **King John*, the mother of Arthur.

CONSTANT, Benjamin (Henri-Benjamin Constant de Rebecque) (1767–1830) French novelist, political philosopher, and politician, born at Lausanne of a family of French Protestant origins, who had his university education at Oxford (briefly), in Germany, and at Edinburgh. He was intermittently in Paris after 1795 and held office under the Consulate, but went into exile in 1803. From Hanover he published the anti-Napoleonic pamphlet 'De l'esprit de conquête et de l'usurpation' (1813). His political career in the Liberal opposition begins after the Restoration of the Bourbon dynasty. Constant is remembered for the political and religious treatises *De la religion considérée dans sa source, ses formes et ses développements* (5 vols, 1824–31), but much more for the literary masterpiece *Adolphe* (first published in London in 1816), a short novel of psychological analysis reflecting at some points his own liaison with Mme de *Staël. His *Journaux intimes*, first published in 1895, appeared in a complete edition in 1952; his *Cahier rouge*, recounting the first twenty years of his life, in 1907, and *Cécile*, the fragment of an autobiographical novel, in 1951. *See also* CHARRIÈRE, ISABELLE DE.

Constant Couple, The, *A Trip to the Jubilee* A farcical comedy by George *Farquhar, produced 1699, which was very successful owing chiefly to the amusing character of Sir Harry Wildair, 'an airy gentleman, affecting humorous gaiety and freedom in his behaviour'. It had a less successful sequel in *Sir Harry Wildair* (1701).

CONSTANTINE, David (1944–) Poet, born in Salford, fellow in German at the Queen's College, Oxford. *A Brightness to Cast Shadows* (1980) and *Watching for Dolphins* (1983) introduced a poet of rare lyric intensity. Learned but direct, Constantine offers a world lit by the supernatural, drawing on classical and Romantic traditions and standing at their intersection in 'Watching for Dolphins' itself, a poem of the longing for transcendence. The epic *Caspar Hauser* appeared in 1994, followed by *The Pelt of Wasps* (1998), *Something for the Ghosts* (2002), and a *Collected Poems* (2005). Constantine has also translated the *Selected Poems* of Friedrich *Hölderlin (1996). Other publications include a novel and a non-fiction book, *Early Greek Travellers and the Hellenic Ideal* (1984).

CONSTANTINE, Storm (1956–) *Fantasy author, born in Stafford; author of the 'Wraeththu' fantasy sequence beginning with *The Enchantments of Flesh and Spirit* (1987), which tapped into Gothic fascinations with androgynous sexuality and religious mythology: the 'grigori' in *Stalking Tender Prey* (1995) are fallen angels.

contact zone A term used by the North American literary theorist Mary Louise Pratt (1948–) to refer to spaces 'where cultures meet, clash and grapple with each other, often in contexts of highly asymmetrical relations of power'. The expression is intended to emphasize the range of ways in which people, usually from a position of disadvantage, imaginatively contest others' versions of themselves. Pratt invites her readers to reconsider situations which are often assumed to be either examples of one-sided conquest (such as the imperial frontier) or harmoniously bound by the shared idioms and values of a homogeneous community (such as the Western classroom). The term is widely used by scholars interested in linguistic, religious, economic, sexual, and other exchanges in colonial and postcolonial contexts, from the first contacts of Europeans with indigenous peoples, to the interpersonal dynamics of public spaces marked by significant inequalities or discrimination. See *Imperial Eyes* (1992); 'Arts of the Contact Zone', *Profession*, 91 (1991).

Contarini Fleming: *A Psychological Romance* A novel by Benjamin *Disraeli, published 1832. Despite its lack of popular success, this was Disraeli's favourite novel. It was the last in the group **Vivian Grey–Alroy–Fleming*, although it was published before *Alroy.* In the preface to the 1845 edition of his novels, Disraeli describes how in this book he attempted to provide a complete picture of the development of a poet. In making his hero the son of both Saxon and Venetian lineage, living in 'a northern court', Disraeli attempts to show the effects on character of North and South. Contarini is an impetuous, handsome boy, rebellious at school, from which he runs away. His kindly father sends him to a university, and then introduces him to society, where his wit and moody brilliance bring him great success. But society palls and, after various wild adventures in the northern forests, he finds his way to Venice, the home of his mother's family, where he is captivated by the beauty of the city and where he meets his cousin Alceste, whom he marries. She dies within a year and to calm his grief he again takes up his travels, before returning to an estate near Naples, where he intends to lead a solitary life in 'the study and creation of the beautiful'. The influence of *Goethe's *Wilhelm Meister* and of the *'Byronic' hero is evident.

Contemporary Review Founded in 1866 and edited for many years by Sir Percy Bunting (1836–1911). It covered religious, political, and literary subjects; in 1955 it incorporated the **Fortnightly Review*, and now deals largely with current affairs.

CONWAY, Anne, Viscountess (d. 1679) Metaphysical writer and friend of the philosopher and theologian Henry More (1614–87; *see* CAMBRIDGE PLATONISTS). Her posthumous *Principles of the Most Ancient and Modern Philosophy* (Latin 1690, English 1692) influenced *Leibniz.

COOK, David (1940–) Novelist, actor, and television playwright, born in Preston. He began his career as an actor after training at the Royal Academy of Dramatic Art. His first novel, *Albert's Memorial* (1972), concerns the tragicomic friendship between widowed Mary and homosexual Paul: this was followed by *Happy Endings* (1974) about the relationship between a 12-year-old boy and a schoolteacher. *Walter* (1978) is the story of a well-intentioned and sensitive young man with severe learning difficulties trying to cope with the challenges of work, institutional life, and his mother's death: *Winter Doves* (1979) is a sequel in which Walter escapes to freedom with his friend June. Other works include *Sunrising* (1984), a historical novel set in poverty-stricken rural middle England and London in the 1830s; *Missing Persons* (1986), *Crying out Loud* (1988), and *Second Best* (1991), about a single man's attempt to adopt a 10-year-old boy. Cook's work displays a deep and humane sympathy with the disadvantaged, the sexually marginalized, and those with mental or learning problems. A TV adaptation of *Walter* with Ian McKellen in the title role was chosen to launch Channel 4 in 1982.

COOK, Eliza (1818–89) Poet. Born in London and largely self-educated, she began writing verse at an early age. Her first volume, *Lays of a Wild Harp* (1835), appeared when she was 17. Encouraged by early success, she began contributing regularly to periodicals including the *Weekly Dispatch*, in which her most popular poem 'The Old Armchair' first appeared in 1837. Her poems were characterized by an unaffected domestic sentiment and sympathy with the poor and marginalized which appealed to a wide popular audience. She conducted *Eliza Cook's Journal*, which supported programmes for social reform for women and the working classes, from 1849, but her failing health caused its demise in 1854. Her complete poetical works were published in 1870.

COOK, James (1728–79) The son of a Yorkshire agricultural labourer, he had limited formal schooling, yet he revealed more of the world to Europeans than any other explorer. Apprenticed to a Whitby shipowner, he spent ten years on North Sea colliers before joining the navy in 1755. The Admiralty recognized his gift for navigation in his charts of the St Lawrence and Newfoundland, and entrusted him with three great voyages into the Pacific. The first (1768–71), on the *Endeavour*, made astronomical observations for the *Royal Society at Tahiti, and then searched for the conjectured South Land. Cook circumnavigated New Zealand and 'discovered' Australia's east coast, mapping over 5,000 miles of previously uncharted coastline. His dietary experiments combating scurvy, the ethnographic observations, and the vast collection of hitherto unimagined animal and plant life made the voyage a high point of *Enlightenment science. John *Hawkesworth turned the journals of Cook and Joseph *Banks, the botanist, into a narrative in 1773, taking many liberties but achieving immense commercial success. Cook's own unpretentious journal was published in 1893.

His second voyage on the *Resolution* (1772–5) finally proved no great South Land existed, criss-crossed the South Pacific as far south as the Antarctic ice, and demonstrated the value of the chronometer of John Harrison (1693–1776) solving the nagging problem of determining longitude. In his final voyage

(1776–80) he added the Sandwich (Hawaiian) Islands to the sum of European knowledge, and then set out to find a North-West Passage, mapping the coast from Nootka Sound to the Bering Strait. Returning to Hawaii, he was killed by locals in February 1779. His later journals were published in 1777 and 1784. Generally considered humane and unassuming, Cook was genuinely disturbed by the effects his voyages would have on the Pacific, but was also criticized for allowing himself to be treated as a god. The published journals and tales that circulated informally promoted the ideas of the noble savage and a South Sea paradise. They provided source material for philosophy, for the new discipline of anthropology, and for literature, including S. T. *Coleridge's 'Ancient Mariner'. J. C. Beaglehole has edited the journals and written an authoritative biography (published in 1974).

COOKSON, Catherine (1906–98) Novelist, born in Jarrow, educated at St Peter and St Paul's Roman Catholic School at Tyne Dock, Jarrow, and at night school. Her many novels often celebrate life in her native Tyneside. She was the illegitimate daughter of a domestic servant and tells the story of her own childhood in her memoir *Our Kate* (1969). Her novels are romantic but also realistic, featuring strong and resourceful heroines: one of her most popular characters was 'Mary Ann', who featured in a long series. Her works were outstandingly popular, as her high *Public Lending Right ratings demonstrated, and she was a generous benefactor to the arts and literary causes.

'Cook's Tale, The' *See* CANTERBURY TALES, 4.

Coole Park Co. Galway, home of Lady *Gregory, famous as the headquarters of the *Irish Revival. Summer home of W. B. *Yeats for nearly twenty years, it was the subject of many of his poems, notably 'In the Seven Woods', 'Coole Park, 1929', and 'Coole Park and Ballylee, 1931'. Guests who carved their names on its famous autograph tree (a copper beech) included G. B. *Shaw, J. M. *Synge, W. B. Yeats, Jack B. *Yeats, Augustus *John, G. W. *Russell (Æ), and Douglas *Hyde. The house, described by Lady Gregory in *Coole* (1931; enl. 1971), was pulled down in 1941.

COOLIDGE, Susan (1835–1905) Pen-name of Sarah Chauncy Woolsey, American children's writer of *family stories, born in Cleveland, Ohio; educated at the Select Family School for Young Ladies in New Hampshire. Remembered for *What Katy Did* (1872) and its four sequels (1873; 1886; 1888; 1890) about Katy Carr, her family and friends. In the best-known first volume, impulsive, storytelling, tomboy Katy injures her back falling from a swing and is confined to bed where she attends 'the School of Pain' under the guidance of her invalid Cousin Helen, emerging as a feminine, domesticated young woman.

COOPER, Lady Diana (Viscountess Norwich) (1892–1986) Née Manners, actress and hostess, remembered as the model for characters in works by Arnold *Bennett and Evelyn *Waugh. She published three volumes of memoirs, *The Rainbow Comes and Goes* (1958), *The Light of Common Day* (1959), and *Trumpets from the Steep* (1960).

COOPER, James Fenimore (1789–1851) American novelist, born in New Jersey. He spent his youth partly on the family estate at Cooperstown on Otsego Lake (New York), partly in the merchant marine (after dismissal from Yale University), partly in the American navy. He then settled down as a country proprietor and writer of novels. His second book *The Spy* (1821), a stirring tale of the American Revolution, brought him into prominence. *The Pioneers* (1823) was the first of his best-known group of novels, *Leather-Stocking Tales*, called after the deerskin leggings of their hero, pioneer scout Natty Bumppo (alias 'Deerslayer', 'Pathfinder', or 'Hawkeye') who acted as intermediary between the Indian and European characters. The series continued with *The Last of the Mohicans* (1826), *The Prairie* (1827), *The Pathfinder* (1840), and *The Deerslayer* (1841). They deal with adventures of the frontier and give a vivid picture of American Indian and pioneer life, earning Cooper the credit of being the 'American Walter *Scott'. From 1826 to 1833 Cooper travelled in Europe, and on his return published several highly critical accounts of European society, including *England, with Sketches of Society in the Metropolis* (1837); this was violently attacked in Britain, notably by John *Lockhart. Cooper was, however, also deeply critical of American democracy, and expressed his conservative opinions directly in *The *American Democrat* (1838) and fictionally in *Homeward Bound* and *Home as Found* (both 1838). His many other works include *The History of the Navy of the United States* (1839). A collection of *Letters and Journals* (6 vols, ed. J. F. Beard) appeared in 1960–8. Mark *Twain humorously attacked his lack of verbal precision in 'Fenimore Cooper's Literary Offences' (1895).

COOPER, Mary (d. 1761) London-based printer 1742–61, who published three landmark books for children: *The Child's New Play-Thing* (1742), and two collections of nursery rhymes: **Tommy Thumb's Pretty Song Book* (vol. i, none survive, date unknown; vol. ii, *c.*1744) containing many still-famous verses.

COOPER, Susan (1935–) Children's writer and playwright, born in Burnham, Buckinghamshire, educated at Somerville College, Oxford, where she was the first female editor of *Cherwell*. She moved to the USA in 1963. Her fantasy quintet, 'The Dark is Rising', beginning with *Over Sea, Under Stone* (1965), is based on Arthurian and Celtic legends and the search by the 'Old Ones' for the grail and other symbols of 'the light'. *The Grey King* won the Newbery Medal (1975). Cooper has won awards for TV scripts; *Dreams and Wishes* (1996) is a key collection of essays.

COOPER, William (1910–2002) Pseudonym of Harry Summerfield Hoff, novelist, who taught physics in a Leicester school before the war, during which period he published novels under his own name. After the war he embarked on a career in government service, and the Civil Service features in much of his work, as it does in that of his colleague C. P. *Snow. His most influential novel, *Scenes from Provincial Life* (1950), was hailed as seminal by writers of the 1950s, who also chose provincial, anarchic but ambitious, lower-middle-class heroes, and a low-key realist tone. It was followed in 1961 by *Scenes from Married Life*, and in 1982 by *Scenes from Metropolitan Life*, originally written as the middle volume of the trilogy. In these novels Joe Lunn narrates his own story, from his schoolmaster days in a provincial city when his mistress Myrtle is trying to marry him, through the post-war years in London when he is trying to marry Myrtle, to his successful marriage to schoolmistress Elspeth. A sequel, *Scenes from Later Life*, appeared in 1983 and another, *Scenes from Early Life*, in 1990. *Immortality at Any Price* was published in 1991.

Cooper's Hill *See* DENHAM, SIR JOHN.

COOVER, Robert (1932–) American novelist, born in Charles City, Iowa. Like John *Barth, he has tended to avoid realism in favour of more experimental narrative forms. His first novel, *The Origin of the Brunists* (1966), describes how the survivors of a mining accident form a religious cult and *The Public Burning* (1977) presents the execution of the Rosenbergs as a ludicrous national spectacle with walk-on parts by Richard Nixon and others. His 1992 essay 'The End of Books' caused a stir and was followed by Coover co-founding the Electronic Literature Association in 1999. Coover's interest in film has been demonstrated in his short story collection *A Night at the Movies* (1987) and his 2002 novel *The Adventures of Lucky Pierre: The Director's Cut*. His screenplay *After Lazarus* was published in 1980.

COPE, Wendy (1945–) Poet, born in Kent; she read History at St Hilda's College, Oxford, trained as a teacher at Westminster College, Oxford, and taught in London primary schools before becoming television columnist for the **Spectator* (1986–90). A gifted parodist, her first collection of poetry, *Making Cocoa for Kingsley Amis* (1986), was an instant popular success and established her as a skilfully subversive humorist, in the line of John *Betjeman. She employs traditional verse forms to satirical purpose, especially when directed at the sexual psychology of men, about which she can be both scathing and understanding, if always deflationary. Her relatively sparse output of original poetry includes *Serious Concerns* (1992), whose title registers a change of mood, and *If I Don't Know* (2001), in which domesticity unpredictably becomes a preoccupation. Her many other publications include two collections for children.

COPERNICUS (1473–1543) Latinized form of the surname of Nicolas Koppernik, astronomer, native of Torun, Poland, who propounded in his *De Revolutionibus* (1543) the theory that the planets, including the earth, move in orbits round the sun, in opposition to *Ptolemy's earlier geocentric theory. A cleric as well as an astronomer and a lawyer, Copernicus was a canon of Frauenberg Cathedral and was also attached to the Church of the Holy Cross in Breslau. Far from objecting to his theory, the Catholic Church urged him to publish, and he dedicated his book to Pope Paul III. Opposition began only when heliocentrism was treated as fact rather than hypothesis.

Cophetua, King A legendary king in Africa, who cared nothing for women until he fell in love with a beggar maid 'all in gray'. He married her and together they lived 'a quiet life during their princely reign'. The tale is told in one of the ballads included in Percy's **Reliques*, where the maid's name is given as Penelophon. Shakespeare, in **Love's Labour's Lost* (IV. i), gives it as Zenelophon. There are other references to the story in Shakespeare's **Romeo and Juliet* (II. ii) and 2 **Henry IV* (V. iii), in Jonson's **Every Man in His Humour* (III. iv), and in *Tennyson's 'The Beggar Maid' (1842); it was the subject of a well-known painting by Edward *Burne-Jones (1884).

COPLAND, Robert *See* HIGH WAY TO THE SPITAL HOUSE.

COPPARD, A. E. (Alfred Edgar) (1878–1957) Author of short stories and poetry, born in Kent. The son of a tailor, he had many jobs before he moved to Oxford in 1907 in order to work as a clerk. He became a full-time writer in 1919. His first collection of short stories, *Adam and Eve and Pinch Me* (1921), established his name and led to much encouragement, including that of Ford Madox *Ford. His first book of verse, *Hips and Haws*, appeared in 1922, and thereafter he produced a book of stories or verses almost every year until the early 1950s. The first part of an autobiography, *It's Me, O Lord!*, was published posthumously in 1957. The deceptive simplicity of Coppard's stories conceals a widely admired technical skill; many of the most characteristic tales are set in robust country backgrounds, and display a deep sympathy for the oddity and misfit.

COPPE, Abiezer (1619–72) A *Ranter, preacher, mystic, and pamphleteer, famed for his eccentric behaviour (he preached naked in the streets of London, denouncing the rich); his two *Fiery Flying Rolls* (1649) are charged with fervour and compassion, and are written in a highly original poetic prose described by Christopher *Hill (*The World Turned Upside Down*, 1972) as 'unlike anything else in the seventeenth century'. In 1650 these pamphlets were burned as blasphemous, by order of Parliament. Imprisoned at Newgate, Coppe partially recanted. He practised medicine after the *Restoration in Surrey, as 'Dr Higham'.

copyright While there had been protection for certain kinds of publishing monopoly since the early days of printing, and while payments to authors, or 'copy money', notionally recognized a form of author's copyright, the first definition of copyright as such in Britain was 'An Act for the encouragement of Learning, by vesting the copies of printed books in the authors or purchasers of such copies during the times therein mentioned' (1709), which stipulated that from 10 April 1710 an author of a printed book, or the publisher who had bought the rights, should have the right to publish that book for 21 years; for an unpublished book, the period was 14 years. Thereafter the right reverted to the author for a further 14 years. A few authors, such as Alexander *Pope, exploited the possibilities of this provision adroitly, but it was slow to affect authors' earnings. Additionally, publishers argued that the statute did not affect their 'perpetual' rights to property in classic authors such as *Shakespeare and *Milton, which had been bought and sold for generations. It was not until a landmark decision of 1774 that publishers lost this right. Since then the law has been continuously developed, on an international scale; the last major British revision was the Copyright, Designs and Patents Act 1988. Copyright is not infinite: broadly speaking, and with many variations, copyright in Europe and the USA lasts until 70 years after the author's death. In addition, the law provides for works to be used without permission in a range of special circumstances, including the quoting of limited extracts for purposes of criticism, review, research, or private study, or for teaching. *Copinger and Skone James on Copyright*, 15th edn (2004), by Kevin Garnett, Gillian Davies, and Gwilym Harbottle, has a chapter on the history of copyright.

copyright libraries *See* LEGAL DEPOSIT LIBRARIES.

Coral Island, The (1858) R. M. *Ballantyne's story for boys about how Ralph, Peterkin, and Jack take over a Pacific island, face hostile tribes and pirates, and eventually claim the territory for the queen. Admired by Robert Louis *Stevenson and William *Golding, it encapsulates the empire-building ethos of its period.

coranto or current of news, the name applied to periodical news-pamphlets issued between 1621 and 1641 (their publication was interrupted 1632–8) containing foreign intelligence taken from foreign papers. They were one of the earliest forms of English journalism, and were followed by *newsbooks.
See NEWSPAPERS.

CORBETT (Corbet), **Richard** (1582–1635) Poet, the son of Vincent Corbet, a Surrey gardener, of whom Ben *Jonson said in an elegy, 'His mind as pure and neatly kept | As were his nourseries…' Richard was educated at Westminster School and Christ Church, Oxford, and became chaplain to James I and, later, bishop first of Oxford, then of Norwich. He was generous, witty, and eloquent, and his poetry—*Certain Elegant Poems* (1647) and *Poetica Stromata* (1648)—ranges from the entertaining traveller's story of 'Iter Boreale' and the ironical verses on 'The Distracted Puritan' to the charming little poem 'To his son, Vincent Corbet' on his third birthday. His best-known poem is probably 'A Proper New Ballad, entitled The Fairies' Farewell' which begins 'Farewell rewards and fairies'. He also addressed some amusing lines to Thomas *Coryate after the latter's return from a journey in Europe. He pronounced the funeral oration for Sir Thomas *Bodley. An edition of his poems, edited by J. A. W. Bennett and H. R. Trevor-Roper, was published in 1955.

CORELLI, Marie (1855–1924) Pseudonym of Mary Mackay, novelist. She was the illegitimate daughter of George Mackay, well-known Scottish journalist and songwriter, and Mary Mills, his servant. She was educated at home, and then at a convent school in France. She studied music and attempted a career as a pianist and singer, turning to fiction at the age of 30 with her first novel, *A Romance of Two Worlds* (1886), which was followed by many more romantic melodramas. She hypnotized her public with her inventive narrative fluency and exuberantly irrational theories on anything from morality to radioactive vibrations. She achieved outstanding success and very high sales at the turn of the century, William *Gladstone and Oscar *Wilde being among her admirers. Critics, however, were always scornful, and her popularity declined long before her death. Her other novels include *Barabbas* (1893), *The Sorrows of Satan* (1895), *The Mighty Atom* (1896), *The Master Christian* (1900), *Temporal Power* (1902), *The Young Diana* (1918), and *The Secret Power* (1921). Though her eccentric egotism and pseudo-mystical religiosity attracted much mockery, she was an influential figure in the development of the occult as a prevalent theme in the fiction of her day.

CORIAT, Thomas *See* CORYATE, THOMAS.

Coriolanus A play by Shakespeare first printed in the first *folio (1623), in which, before the late insertion of **Troilus and Cressida*, it seems to have been placed first of the tragedies. It was probably Shakespeare's last tragedy, written about 1608. Its main source is *North's version of *Plutarch's 'Life of Caius Martius Coriolanus'. The opening scene, in which Menenius Agrippa tells the citizens of Rome a fable of the body's members rebelling against itself, was a popular Renaissance allegory of the state.

Caius Martius, a proud Roman general, fights with great courage in a war against the Volscians, and captures the town Corioli, receiving the surname Coriolanus. On his return it is proposed to make him consul, but his outspoken contempt of the Roman rabble makes him unpopular, and the tribunes of the people have no difficulty in securing his banishment. He goes to his old enemy the Volscian general Aufidius, is received with delight, and leads the Volscians against Rome to revenge himself. He reaches the walls of the city, and the Romans send old friends of Coriolanus to propose terms, but in vain. Finally his mother Volumnia, his meek wife Virgilia, her friend Valeria, and his son come to beg him to spare the city and he yields to the eloquence of his mother, suspecting that by so doing he has signed his own death warrant. He makes a treaty favourable to the Volscians, but Aufidius turns against him, accusing him of treachery, and with the help of fellow conspirators publicly kills him.

CORKERY, Daniel (1878–1964) Critic, dramatist, novelist, short story writer, and politician. Corkery taught at a primary school in his native Cork for many years before being appointed professor of English at University College there in 1931. The melancholy realism of his autobiographical novel *The Threshold of Quiet* (1917) and of the story collections *A Munster Twilight* (1916) and *The Stormy Hills* (1929) counters what he considered the misrepresentation of national life by the 'alien' Protestant elite who led the *Irish Revival. Corkery is remembered chiefly for two vivid, partisan works of criticism, *The Hidden Ireland* (1924) and *Synge and Anglo-Irish Literature* (1931).

CORMIER, Robert (1925–2000) Born Leominster, Massachusetts. Initially a journalist, he became notorious as the leading neo-realist writer for young adults in the USA. In *The Chocolate War* (1975) he subverted the *school story by having his brave protagonist be defeated and humiliated by corrupt boys and teachers. In *After the First Death* (1979) the teenage victims of a hijack are killed. Cormier felt that 'there are enough books with happy endings', and so tried 'to write warnings for what's waiting out there'. His later work, such as *Frenchtown Summer* (1999), was less controversial.

CORNEILLE, Pierre (1606–84) French dramatist, author of 32 plays. Born into a family of magistrates, he studied law and practised in Rouen until 1630, when he turned decisively to writing plays. He began by writing comedies, including *La Galerie du Palais* (1632?) and *La Place Royale* (1633–4), which are notable for their evocation of modern urban life and the love affairs of respectable young people. He also wrote tragicomedies, enjoying his first great success both in France and in England with *Le Cid* (1637; trans. John Rutter, 1637), inspired by Spanish drama (*see* CID, THE), which caused such a scandal on account of its unconventionalities, including an adverse judgement by the *Académie Française, that he rewrote it and called it a tragedy. It is in Corneille's hands that seventeenth-century tragedy develops into the form that we recognize today: the desire to create an illusion of reality on stage was served, most notably, by the observation of the *unities. Corneille also makes tragedy a site of intense psychological conflict. *Horace* (1640) dramatizes a conflict between domestic and patriotic imperatives; *Cinna* (1641) explores the tensions between justice and mercy; and *Polyeucte* (1643) presents the dilemma of a Christian martyr caught between the desire for glory and the pursuit of love. Corneille's world is a heroic one, where characters do what they are supposed to do, not what they want to do; but it is nevertheless a heroism behind which lurks the reality of human beings' mixed motives. Corneille exerted a powerful influence on the English dramatists of the *Restoration, particularly John *Dryden, thanks to important translations by Katherine *Philips (the 'matchless Orinda') and Charles *Cotton.

Cornelia A tragedy translated by Thomas *Kyd from a *Senecan play by Robert Garnier, published 1594; reissued in the following year as *Pompey the Great, His Fair Cornelia's Tragedy.* Cornelia is the daughter of Metellus Scipio and wife of Pompey the Great. Pompey, after the battle of Pharsalus, is killed on the way to Egypt. Scipio assembles new forces, but is defeated by Caesar at Thaspus in Africa and again at sea, and stabs himself. The play largely consists of Cornelia's lamentations for her misfortunes.

CORNFORD, Frances (1886–1960) Poet, born in Cambridge where she spent most of her life. She published several volumes of verse but is best known for her *triolet 'To a Fat Lady Seen from a Train', with its curiously memorable lines

> 'O why do you walk through the fields in gloves,
> Missing so much and so much?
> O fat white woman whom nobody loves'.

Her *Collected Poems* appeared in 1954. She was a granddaughter of Charles *Darwin and the mother of John *Cornford.

CORNFORD, John (1915–36) Poet and political activist, son of Frances *Cornford, born Cambridge and educated at Stowe School and Trinity College, Cambridge (1933–6). From the early 1930s he was heavily involved with radical politics and the Communist Party of Great Britain and in 1936 he is said to have been the first Englishman to enlist against Franco in the Spanish Civil War; he was killed in action in the same year. His poems had been published in various periodicals and were collected with miscellaneous prose pieces, mainly political, in *John Cornford: A Memoir*, ed. Pat Sloan (1938). See *John Cornford: Collected Writings*, ed. Jonathan Galassi (1988); P. Stansky and R. Abrahams, *Journey to the Frontier* (1966).

Cornhill Magazine (1860–1975) A literary periodical of consistently high quality which began with William *Thackeray as editor and specialized in the serialization of novels. Anthony Trollope's **Framley Parsonage* was succeeded by the novels of, among others, Elizabeth *Gaskell, Wilkie *Collins, Charles *Reade, George *Eliot, and Thomas *Hardy. Many poems of Alfred *Tennyson, Robert *Browning, and Algernon *Swinburne first appeared in it, as well as work by John *Ruskin, George *Macdonald, and another of its editors, Leslie *Stephen. It continued to provide an outlet for the work of numerous major writers, creative and critical, in the 20th century, ceasing publication in 1975.

Corn Law Rhymer *See* ELLIOTT, EBENEZER.

CORNWALL, Barry (1787–1874) Pseudonym of Brian Waller Procter. He practised as a solicitor and barrister in

London, and was made a commissioner in lunacy. He began to contribute to the *Literary Gazette* in 1815 and became a friend of Leigh *Hunt, Charles *Lamb, and later Charles *Dickens. Under his pseudonym he enjoyed great popular success, particularly as a writer of songs and lyrics. His *Dramatic Scenes* (1819) was praised by Lamb, and his poem *Marcian Collona* (1820), a verse tale of madness and passion, was well received. In 1821 William *Macready successfully produced Cornwall's one drama, *Mirandola*. His *English Songs* appeared in 1832, and he also wrote biographies of Lamb and Edmund *Kean. A. C. *Swinburne wrote exceptional elegies on his death. His daughter Adelaide Ann *Procter was also a writer.

coronach A lament or dirge, in the Highlands of Scotland or Ireland: a 'wailing together'. A lyric by Walter *Scott in *The *Lady of the Lake* and the traditional ballad 'The Bonnie Earl o' Moray' are said to be instances of the form.

Corridors of Power, The *See* SNOW, C. P.

Corsair, The A poem by Lord *Byron, published 1814. Conrad, a pirate chief, a *'Byronic' character of many vices but with the virtue of chivalry, receives warning that the Turkish pacha is preparing to descend upon his island. He takes leave of his beloved Medora, arrives at the pacha's rallying point, and introduces himself as a dervish escaped from the pirates. However, his plans go amiss, and he is wounded and taken prisoner, but not before he has rescued Gulnare, the chief slave in the pacha's harem, from imminent death. She falls in love with him, and finally brings him a dagger with which he may kill the pacha in his sleep. Conrad revolts from such an act, whereupon she herself kills the pacha and escapes with Conrad. When they arrive at the pirate island Conrad finds Medora dead from grief at the reported killing of her lover. Conrad disappears and is never heard of again: but see *Lara.

CORSO, Gregory *See* BEAT AND BEAT GENERATION.

CORTÁZAR, Julio (1914–84) Argentine novelist, short story writer, poet, critic, and essayist; educated at the Mariano Acosta teacher training college in Buenos Aires, but lived mainly in France from 1951 (French citizenship 1981). He was a major figure in the *Boom of Latin American literature and is best known for his self-regarding, playful, and metaphysical novel *Rayuela* (1963: *Hopscotch*), in which the reader chooses the sequence in which to read its chapters, and whether to include a number of optional chapters (*see* INTERACTIVE FICTION). Influenced by the French *Surrealists, the visual arts, jazz, and English-language writers of the macabre (especially Edgar Allan *Poe), Cortázar published several collections of short stories (e.g. *Bestiario*, 1951: *Bestiary*; and *Todos los fuegos el fuego*, 1966: *All Fires the Fire*), which include fantastic tales. Much of his work (e.g. collage fiction, miscellanies) challenges divisions between genres. The Cuban Revolution instantly transformed his politics, his support for it and for the Nicaraguan Revolution being evident in much of his subsequent writing (e.g. *Alguien que anda por ahí*, 1977: *Someone Round Here*; and *Nicaragua tan violentamente dulce*, 1983: *Nicaragua, so Violently Sweet*), but he remained an independent thinker torn between aesthetics and political commitment. He translated **Robinson Crusoe* and **Little Women* into Spanish, as well as G. K. *Chesterton, Edgar Allan Poe, André *Gide, and Marguerite *Yourcenar. See Peter Standish, *Understanding Cortázar* (2001).

CORTÉS, Hernán (1485–1547) The Spanish conqueror of the Aztec empire. He entered the capital, Tenochtitlán (later to be Mexico City), in 1519. It was not he but *Núñez de Balboa who was the first European to gaze on the Pacific (see John *Keats's sonnet 'On First Looking into Chapman's Homer').

CORVO, Baron *See* ROLFE, FREDERICK.

CORY, William Johnson (1823–92) Educationist and poet, assistant master at Eton College, 1845–72. On leaving he changed his name from Johnson to Cory. He published various educational works, but is best remembered for his volume of poems *Ionica* (1858), and in particular for the translation that it contains of the epigram of Heraclitus of Halicarnassus by *Callimachus, 'They told me Heraclitus, they told me you were dead.' He also wrote the 'Eton Boating Song', published 1865. His letters and journals were edited by F. Warre-Cornish (1897).

CORYATE, Thomas (?1577–1617) Travel writer, the son of a rector of Odcombe, and educated at Winchester School and Gloucester Hall, University of Oxford. After a period of employment as an entertainer at the court of Prince Henry, he travelled in 1608 through France, Italy, Switzerland, Germany, and the Netherlands, mainly on foot. In 1611 he published a long narrative of his travels entitled *Coryats Crudities*. A shorter sequel, *Coryats Crambe*, was published later the same year. In 1612 he set out overland to India, travelling through Constantinople, Palestine, and Mesopotamia, and reaching Agra in 1616. He died at Surat in 1617. Some of his letters from the East are included in a compilation called *Thomas Coriate Traveller for the English Wits: Greeting*. Coryate wrote in an extravagant and euphuistic style (*see* EUPHUES), and was well known as an eccentric and amusing character; there are many references to him in 17th-century literature.

COTGRAVE, Randle (*c*.1569–1653) Author of a famous French–English dictionary published 1611. He was a scholar of St John's College, Cambridge. He had a wide knowledge not only of French and French literature, but of the slang of the day and also of natural history. Sir Thomas *Urquhart relied largely upon his dictionary for the translation of *Rabelais.

'Cotter's Saturday Night, The' A poem by Robert *Burns, published 1786, which somewhat uneasily blends demotic *Scots and neo-classical English in its celebration of a lowly 'scene' of the type from which 'old Scotia's grandeur springs'. The domestic descriptions are in Scots, while the moralizing commentary is in English.

COTTLE, Joseph (1770–1853) A Bristol bookseller, who published the **Lyrical Ballads* and other work by *Wordsworth, *Coleridge, and Robert *Southey. He was the author of a poem, 'Malvern Hills', published 1798, and edited with Southey the works of Thomas *Chatterton in 1803.

COTTON, Charles (1630–87) Poet and translator, of Beresford Hall, Staffordshire. He was the son of Charles Cotton (d. 1658), a close friend of Sir Henry *Wotton, John *Donne, John *Selden, and other writers. The younger Charles was himself a friend of Richard *Lovelace and of Izaak *Walton. He wrote the dialogue between Piscator and Viator which forms the second part in the fifth edition of *The *Compleat Angler* (1676), and published in 1664 *Scarronides*, a mock-heroic burlesque of *Virgil (which Samuel *Pepys found 'extraordinary good'), and in 1665 a burlesque of *Lucian. His translation of *Montaigne, closer but less colourful than John *Florio's, appeared in 1685. His *topographical poem *The Wonders of the Peak* (1681) celebrates the beauties and curiosities of the Peak District (the seventh wonder being Chatsworth). Cotton's love of his native landscapes and particularly of 'fair Dove, princess of rivers' is also expressed in many of his *Poems on Several Occasions* (1689). William *Wordsworth and S. T. *Coleridge both admired his work, making particular mention of 'Ode upon Winter' and 'The Retirement'. Cotton also wrote love poems, some addressed to his first wife Isabella, sister of Colonel Hutchinson (*see* HUTCHINSON, Lucy). His poems were edited by J. Buxton in 1958.

COTTON, Sir Robert Bruce (1571–1631) Educated at Westminster School and Jesus College, Cambridge, an antiquary and collector of manuscripts and coins. He gave the free use of his library to Francis *Bacon, William *Camden, Walter *Ralegh, John *Selden, John Speed (?1552–1629), James *Ussher, and other scholars, and sent a gift of manuscripts to the Bodleian Library on its foundation. He joined the Parliamentary party and published various political tracts. The Cottonian Library, largely composed of works rescued from the dissolved monasteries, was left to the nation by Sir John Cotton (1621–1701), grandson of Sir Robert; it was placed in Essex House, then in Ashburnham House, where it suffered severely from fire in 1731. It was removed to the British Museum in 1753 and is now in the British Library. It includes the *Lindisfarne Gospels and other splendid biblical manuscripts such as the Codex Purpureus, the manuscript of **Beowulf*, and the famous manuscript that includes **Pearl* and *Sir *Gawain and the Green Knight*.

Count Robert of Paris A novel by Sir Walter *Scott, published 1831, the year before the author's death. This was one of the **Tales of my Landlord*, 4th series, the last of the Waverley novels. It was written in ill health and betrays the decline of his powers. The novel, set in the 11th-century First Crusade, is somewhat rambling, but also has examples of grotesqueries unparalleled elsewhere in his work.

Country Wife, The (the title is an indecent pun) A comedy by William *Wycherley, published and probably first performed 1675. The two main characters are Horner, a libertine, who spreads the rumour that he is impotent, so as to get access to married women, and the innocent Margery Pinchwife, who comes to London with her jealous husband, and is seduced by Horner, to their mutual satisfaction. Its sexual explicitness created a scandal even in its own day, and from 1753 to 1924 it was considered too indecent for performance, being replaced by David *Garrick's cleaned-up version, *The Country Girl* (1766).

Courier An evening newspaper of high reputation in the early part of the 19th century, under the management of Daniel *Stuart. *Coleridge, *Wordsworth, Charles *Lamb, and Robert *Southey were among its occasional contributors, and John *Galt was at one time its editor.

courtesy literature As a distinct literary genre teaching courtiers and others good manners and morals, was imported into England through works such as *Castiglione's *Il cortegiano* (translated by Sir Thomas *Hoby in 1561), Giovanni della Casa's *Il galateo* (translated by Robert Peterson in 1576), and Stefano Guazzo's *La civil conversatione* (Bks I–III translated by George *Pettie in 1581; Bk IV by Bartholomew *Yonge in 1586). Henry *Peacham's *The Compleat Gentleman* (1622) was one of the most popular native examples of this type of writing.

COURTHOPE, William John (1842–1917) Editor, critic, and poet, educated at Harrow School and Corpus Christi and New College, Oxford. He became a Civil Service commissioner and professor of poetry at Oxford. His important contributions to English literature include the last five volumes of the standard edition of *Pope's works, including a life (1871–89), and a *History of English Poetry* (1895–1910). Among his other works were *Ludibria Lunae* (1869), a satirical *burlesque on women's rights, *Paradise of Birds* (1870), and *The Country Town and Other Poems* (1920).

courtly love The term 'amour courtois' was popularized by the French scholar Gaston Paris (1839–1903) in 1883 in an essay on the *Lancelot* of *Chrétien de Troyes, to describe the conception of love developed by the *troubadours in the 12th century, which had become the central theme of lyric and epic poetry in France and Germany by 1200. Its relation of lover to adored lady is modelled on the dependence of feudal follower on his lord; the love itself was a religious passion, ennobling, ever unfulfilled, and ever increasing. The common (though not universal) requirement of non-fulfilment meant that the love was usually premarital or extra-marital. A code of practice for courtly lovers, *De Arte Honeste Amandi* (*c.*1185), was written by *Andreas Capellanus, who may have been a chaplain at the court of *Marie de Champagne. Though the poetry of the troubadours is the first definable occurrence of the phenomenon in Western Europe, many aspects of courtly love are older and have affinities with the poetry of *Ovid and with the religious terminology of love used by Arabic writers. The writing of this kind of poetry had spread to northern France and to the German **Minnesänger* and epic by 1200; the most influential works in the 13th century were the **Roman de la Rose* (Guillaume de Lorris, *c.*1230, and Jean de Meun, *c.*1275), and the lyric poems of the *dolce stil nuovo in Italy; Guido Guinicelli, *Cavalcanti, and *Dante's *Vita nuova*. The influence of courtly love is found in many places in medieval and Renaissance English literature, such as in the Harley Lyrics (in London, British Library, MS 2253) and in some of *Chaucer's poetry. See P. Dronke, *Medieval Latin and the Rise of the European Love-Lyric* (1968); R. Boase, *The Origin and Meaning of Courtly Love* (1977); B. O'Donoghue, *The Courtly Love Tradition* (1982).

Court of Love, The An early 15th-century allegorical poem in 1,442 lines of *rhyme royal, once doubtfully attributed to *Chaucer and included by W. W. *Skeat in his *Chaucerian and Other Pieces*, published as vol. vii of his large edition of Chaucer (pp. 409–47). It is in the tradition of the **Roman de la Rose*, describing the visit of the poet to the Court of Venus and the love scenes he saw portrayed there, ending with a May Day concert of birds when they sing descants on the opening words of psalms. It claims to be the work of 'Philogenet of Cambridge, clerk'.

Covenanters 17th-century Scottish *Presbyterians who supported the National Covenant (1638) to defend their religion, especially those extremists who fought violently against the reimposition of bishops in the Church of Scotland after the Restoration. They are described from opposing viewpoints in Walter *Scott's **Old Mortality* and John *Galt's *Ringan Gilhaize*.

COVENTRY, Francis (1725–54) Educated at Eton College and Magdalene College, Cambridge; from 1751 vicar of Edgware. He wrote *The History of Pompey the Little: or The Life and Adventures of a Lap-Dog* (1751), a vividly comic satire based on the life of a dog 'born a.d. 1735 at Bologna in Italy, a Place famous for Lap-Dogs and Sausages'. Pompey passes from one owner to another, through diverse social classes; Lady Mary Wortley *Montagu declared the book 'a real and exact representation of Life as it is now acted in London'. An edition by R. A. Day appeared in 1974.

COVERDALE, Miles (1488–1568) Translator. He studied at Cambridge University, was ordained priest in 1514, and adopted Lutheran views. He translated at Antwerp, apparently in the pay of Jacob van Meteren, the *Bible and *Apocrypha from German and Latin versions with the aid of William *Tyndale's New Testament. His translation was first printed perhaps at Cologne; a modified version was issued in 1537. Coverdale also superintended the printing of the Great Bible of 1539 (*see* BIBLE, THE ENGLISH). He was bishop of Exeter in 1551–3, and was allowed to leave England in 1554 after Queen Mary's accession. He was in England again in 1559, published his last book, *Letters of Saintes*, in 1564, and was rector of St Magnus, London Bridge, from 1563 to 1566. His collected works, which include translations of theological tracts and German hymns, were published in 1844–6. If he was in fact (which has been questioned) the translator of the version of the Bible attributed to him, he is entitled to the credit for much of the noble language of the Authorized Version, and in particular for the Prayer Book version of the Psalter.

COWARD, Sir Noël (1899–1973) Actor, dramatist, lyricist, and composer, born Teddington, Middlesex, and schooled erratically. His first play was performed in 1917, *The Young Idea* was staged in 1922, but he achieved fame with *The Vortex* (1924), in which he himself appeared as Nicky Lancaster, a cocaine addict tormented by his mother's adulteries. More characteristic of his talent are his comedies *Fallen Angels* (1925), *Hay Fever* (1925, about the eccentric, theatrical, guest-confusing, self-regarding Bliss family), *Private Lives* (1930, about two disastrous interconnected second marriages), *Design for Living* (New York, 1933; London, 1939, about a successful *ménage à trois*), *Blithe Spirit* (1941), which features the hearty medium Madame Arcati, and Elvira, a predatory ghost, and *Present Laughter* (1942). The smart sophistication, technical accomplishment, and convention-defying morality of these pieces captured the public of the day, but another and more sentimental side of Coward was revealed in his patriotic works (*Cavalcade*, 1931) and wartime screenplays such as *Brief Encounter* (1944) and *This Happy Breed* (1942). After the war Coward continued to write prolifically; his plays were less well received, to his own surprise, and he was outspoken in his contempt for the new *kitchen sink plays of the 1950s and for the 'pretentious symbolism' of Samuel *Beckett. In 1963, a revival of *Private Lives* at Hampstead Theatre Club precipitated a new wave of interest in Coward's work and many more revivals, including prestige productions at the *National Theatre. Coward was knighted in 1970 and died in Jamaica. He also published volumes of verse, short stories, a novel (*Pomp and Circumstance*, 1960), and two volumes of autobiography, *Present Indicative* (1937) and *Future Indefinite* (1954). *The Noël Coward Diaries* (1982, ed. G. Payn and Sheridan Morley) are an entertaining fund of theatrical gossip, criticism of fellow playwrights, and admiring comments on the royal family. See Philip Hoare, *Noel Coward: A Biography* (1995).

COWLEY, Abraham (1618–67) Poet, the posthumous son of a London stationer, King's scholar at Westminster

School, and scholar and fellow of Trinity College, Cambridge. His precocity is shown by 'Pyramus and Thisbe', a verse romance written when he was 10 years old, and 'Constantia and Philetus', written two years later (both included in *Poetical Blossoms*, 1633). *Love's Riddle*, a pastoral drama, and *Naufragium Joculare*, a Latin comedy, appeared in 1638. On the outbreak of the Civil War Cowley left Cambridge for Oxford, where he contributed to the Royalist cause by writing a satire, *The Puritan and the Papist* (1643), and a political epic, *The Civil War*. Book I of *The Civil War* was published in 1679; the remainder of the work was presumed lost until discovered and edited in 1973. In 1644 he left Oxford for Paris, where he was in the service of the courtier Henry Jermyn (bap. 1605, d. 1684) at the court of Henrietta Maria. In 1654 he returned to England, apparently as a Royalist spy, and was imprisoned briefly in 1655; however, his conduct at this time, together with various remarks in the preface to *Poems* (1656), gave rise to doubts in certain quarters about his continuing loyalty to the Royalist cause. At the Restoration he was disappointed in his expectation of a reward for his services, though the earl of St Albans and the duke of Buckingham combined to provide him with a competence. He spent the last years of his life in retirement, at Barnes and later Chertsey. On his death Charles II bestowed on him the epitaph 'That Mr Cowley had not left a better man behind him in England'. He is buried in Westminster Abbey. His principal works, besides those mentioned above, are *The Mistress* (1647), a collection of love poems; 'Miscellanies' in *Poems* (1656); also in the same collection 'Davideis', an epic on the biblical history of David, and 'Pindaric Odes' (*see* ODE), in which he introduces the irregular ode imitated by John *Dryden and others; *Ode, upon the Blessed Restoration* (1660); and *Verses on Several Occasions* (1663). His prose works, marked by grace and simplicity of style, include *A Proposition for the Advancement of Learning* (1661), *The Visions and Prophecies Concerning England* (1661), and some 'Essays', notably one 'Of my Self' containing interesting particulars of his early life (first published in *The Works*, 1668). His plays include *The Guardian* (1650), written to entertain the prince of Wales on his visit to Cambridge in 1642, which he later revised as *Cutter of Coleman Street* (1663). Cowley's life was written by his friend and literary executor Thomas *Sprat and is prefixed to *The Works* (1668).

COWLEY, Hannah (1743–1809) Née Parkhouse, dramatist, daughter of a Devon bookseller. Her comedies include *The Runaway* (1776), sent anonymously to David *Garrick who mounted it with great success in 1776, *The *Belle's Stratagem* (1780), and *A Bold Stroke for a Wife* (1783). Cowley wrote two tragedies (one of them, *Albina*, provoking a bitter row with Hannah *More over alleged plagiarism), and corresponded in verse as 'Anna Matilda' with Robert Merry (*see* DELLA CRUSCANS).

COWLEY, Malcolm (1898–1989) American editor and literary critic, born in Pittsburgh. Cowley began his career as a journalist, living in Paris 1921–3 where he became an important member of the *Lost Generation of expatriate writers. On his return to the USA he wrote poetry and became a close friend of Hart *Crane. He helped found the left-wing League of American Writers in 1935 and edited *The New Republic* from 1929 to 1944. He is best known for his memoirs of literary life, notably *Exile's Return* (1934) and *The Dream of the Golden Mountains* (1980).

COWPER, Richard (1926–2002) Novelist, pseudonym of John Middleton Murray, Jr, born in Bridport, Dorset. He published early novels as 'Colin Murray', but is best known for the transformed Englands of his *science fiction, especially the 'White Bird of Kinship' sequence beginning with *The Road to Corlay* (1978).

COWPER, William (1731–1800) Poet, son of the rector of Great Berkhamsted, Hertfordshire. He was educated, and bullied, at a private school and at Westminster School, where he was a contemporary of Charles *Churchill, and read widely in classical literature. He was called to the bar in 1754, but never seriously practised. Sensitive and hypochondriac by nature, he began to suffer from severe depression, exacerbated by his thwarted relationship with his cousin Theadora; when called for examination for a disputed clerkship in the House of Lords he broke down completely and attempted suicide. Thereafter he was subject to periods of acute melancholia, feeling himself cast out from God's mercy; as he put it in his autobiographical 'Memoir' (*c.*1767; pub. 1816), 'conviction of sin and expectation of instant judgement never left me'. He spent eighteen months in the Collegium Insanorum of the poet and doctor Nathaniel Cotton (1705–88) at St Albans. In 1765 he became a boarder (in his own words, 'a sort of adopted son') in the home of the Reverend Morley Unwin at Huntingdon, and on Morley's death moved with Mary, his widow, to Olney. There he came under the influence of John *Newton, the evangelical curate, with whom he wrote *Olney Hymns* (published 1779); his contributions include 'God moves in a mysterious way' and 'Oh, for a closer walk with God'. Under social pressure he became engaged to Mrs Unwin, but in early 1773 suffered a period of intense depression, making further suicide attempts; he was so convinced of his complete exclusion from the Christian communion that he never prayed or entered a church again. Recovering through activities such as gardening, the keeping of pet hares, and carpentry, he wrote a series of moral satires in couplets ('Table Talk', 'The Progress of Error', 'Truth', 'Expostulation', 'Hope', 'Charity', 'Conversation', and 'Retirement') which were published in 1782 with several shorter poems (including 'Verses Supposed to be Written by Alexander Selkirk'). In the same year he wrote *'John Gilpin', and in 1783–4 his best-known long poem *The *Task* (1785), both subjects suggested by a new friend, Lady Austen. The volume in which these appeared also contained 'Tirocinium', a vigorous attack on public schools. In 1786 he moved with Mrs Unwin to Weston Underwood, where he wrote various poems published after his death, including the unfinished 'Yardley-Oak', the verses 'On the Loss of the Royal George', 'To Mary', and 'The Poplar-Field', as well as further poems promoting the abolition of the slave trade. His translation of *Homer into blank verse, published by subscription in 1791, was a deliberate, and unsuccessful, attempt to oust the translation of Alexander *Pope from public favour. In 1791 he reluctantly engaged to edit the poems of John *Milton for his kinsman, the radical publisher Joseph *Johnson. The edition, which was abandoned in 1793, brought him into the circle of William *Hayley, who tried to encourage Cowper's labours, secured him a pension, and assisted in the care of Mrs Unwin, who eventually died in 1796. 'The *Castaway', written shortly before Cowper's own death, was a final expression of isolation and helplessness. Cowper's letters were published posthumously, in 1803–4, alongside a sympathetic biography by Hayley which advanced the poet's reputation. The poems are often quoted by sympathetic characters in Jane *Austen's fiction, and *Wordsworth, whose own blank verse was influenced by Cowper's, admired especially 'Yardley Oak'. Robert *Southey's 15-volume edition (1835–7) made Cowper a Victorian classic. See *The Poems of William Cowper*, ed. J. King and C. Ryskamp, 3 vols (1980–95); *The Letters and Prose Writings of William Cowper*, ed. J. D. Baird and C. Ryskamp, 5 vols (1979–86); J. King, *William Cowper: A Biography* (1986).

Cox and Box See BURNAND, SIR FRANCIS; FARCE.

CRABBE, George (1754–1832) Poet, born in Aldeburgh, Suffolk. He was apprenticed to a doctor and during that time, in 1775, he published *Inebriety*, a derivative but vigorous poem on the evils of drink. During his apprenticeship he met Sarah Elmy (the 'Mira' of his poems and journals), whom he married ten years later. He then began to practise as the parish doctor in Aldeburgh, meanwhile writing, reading, and studying botany. In 1780 he determined on a career in writing and went to London, where he became almost destitute before he was generously befriended by Edmund *Burke. On Burke's advice, and with his literary help, he published *The Library* (1781), a poem in the manner of *Pope containing the author's reflections on books and reading. Burke introduced Crabbe to influential friends, including Charles *Fox, Joshua *Reynolds, and Samuel *Johnson, and encouraged him to take orders. In 1781 he became curate at Aldeburgh, then from 1782 to 1785 was chaplain to the duke of Rutland at Belvoir, where he found stimulating company and leisure for writing. In 1783, after advice and revision from Burke and Johnson, he published *The *Village*, a poem in heroic couplets which established his reputation and made plain his revulsion from the conventions of the *pastoral and the myth of the Golden Age, painting instead a grim, detailed picture of rural poverty and of a blighted, infertile landscape, described with a botanist's precision.

In the same year he married Sarah Elmy, and in 1785 published a satirical poem on the contemporary press, *The Newspaper*. A long interval followed, during which he published nothing of importance, although he wrote and destroyed several unpublished novels, and during which he held (1789–1814) a living at Muston, Leicestershire, from which he was absent 1792–1805, living in Suffolk. In 1807 appeared a volume containing his previous works, some new shorter poems, 'The *Parish Register' (which revealed his gift as a narrative poet), and another, atypical, narrative in 55 eight-line stanzas, 'Sir Eustace Grey', set in a madhouse, in which Sir Eustace relates the tale of his guilt (he had killed his wife's lover in a duel) and his subsequent demented hallucinations. Alethea Hayter, in *Opium and the Romantic Imagination* (1968), relates the peculiarly vivid dream descriptions to Crabbe's opium-taking, a habit he had adopted in 1790 on a doctor's recommendation.

In 1810 he published *The *Borough*, a poem in 24 'letters' in which he illustrates the life of a country town (based on Aldeburgh), and which includes the tales of *'Peter Grimes' and *'Ellen Orford'. This was followed in 1812 by **Tales in Verse*. In 1813 Sarah died at Muston, after a depressive illness, and Crabbe began to visit London more frequently. In 1814 he was appointed vicar of Trowbridge, and in 1819 published **Tales of the Hall*, a series of varied stories. He visited Walter *Scott in Edinburgh in 1822 and became his friend. He died in Trowbridge and much unpublished work was found, some of which (for instance 'The Equal Marriage' and 'Silford Hall') was published in a collected edition in 1834; later discoveries appeared in *New Poems*, ed. A. Pollard (1960). The standard edition of the poems is by N. Dalrymple-Champneys and A. Pollard, 3 vols (1988). Crabbe's *Selected Letters and Journals*, ed. T. C. Faulkner and R. L. Blair, appeared in 1985.

Throughout the upheaval represented by the *Romantic movement, Crabbe persisted in his precise, closely observed, realistic portraits of rural life and landscape, writing mainly in the heroic couplets of the *Augustan age, and attempting to

> paint the cot
> As Truth will paint it, and as Bards will not. (*The Village*)

Lord *Byron called him 'Nature's sternest painter yet the best', Scott called him 'the English Juvenal', and he was the favourite poet of Jane *Austen. See *The Life of George Crabbe by his Son* (1834, with the *Poetical Works*, and 1947 with an introduction by Edmund *Blunden); T. Bareham, *George Crabbe* (1977).

CRACE, Jim (1946–) Novelist, born in Hertfordshire, worked in Botswana and the Sudan, and as a freelance journalist, before publishing his first book *Continent* in 1986. Set in an imaginary seventh continent, it established his characteristic fictional mode of bold excursions into fantasy combined with crisp precision of prose and concrete detail. Some of his novels such as *The Gift of Stones* (1988), *Signals of Distress* (1994), and *Quarantine* (1997), a reimagining of desert life in the 1st century, one of whose main characters is Christ, hark back to a semi-mythologized past. Others such as *Arcadia* (1992) and *The Pesthouse* (2007) portray *dystopian future worlds.

Craftsman A weekly journal started in December 1727 by the satirist Nicholas Amhurst (1697–1742), to which Henry St John, Viscount *Bolingbroke, contributed 'Remarks upon the

History of England' (September 1730–May 1731), his 'Dissertation upon Parties' (1733) and other essays. The Whig politician William Pulteney, earl of Bath (1684–1764), was another leading contributor. The journal chiefly promoted political opposition to Sir Robert *Walpole.

CRAIG, Gordon (1872–1966) Artist, actor, wood-engraver, writer, and stage designer, born in Stevenage, Hertfordshire, the son of Edward William Godwin and Ellen *Terry; he chose his own name, Craig, from the island Ailsa Craig. He began his career as an actor, then edited *The Page* (1898–1901), a periodical in which he published his own woodcuts. After directing in London he moved to the Continent, where he developed his avant-garde, anti-realist stage and lighting designs; in 1905 in Berlin he became the lover of the dancer Isadora Duncan (1878–1927), one of his many liaisons, who bore him a child. In the same year he published his first book, *The Art of the Theatre*, which was further expanded as *On the Art of the Theatre* (1911); several other works on the same subject followed, including *Towards a New Theatre* (1913). In 1908 in Florence he founded a theatre magazine, *The Mask*, which he edited (with a wartime interlude) until 1929. His radical ideas on design and stagecraft had considerable influence in both Europe and America, and his wood engravings contributed to a revival of the art. His memoirs of his early years, *Index to the Story of my Days*, were published in 1957.

CRAIK, Dinah Maria (1826–87) Née Mulock, a prolific writer of novels, poems, children's books, fairy-tales, essays, and short stories. Born in Hartshill, Staffordshire, she received some education at Brampton House School, near Newcastle-under-Lyme, but was already helping her mother to run a small private school at the age of 13. Later, she studied languages and drawing at the School of Design, Somerset House. The death of her mother led her unstable father to abandon the family in 1845, and she turned to writing to earn a living. A novel, *The Ogilvies* (1846), was followed by **Olive* (1850), which describes the struggles of a deformed girl to win respect and affection. These works established her name, but she wrote nine further novels before **John Halifax, Gentleman* (1856), the great and prolonged success for which she is chiefly remembered. In 1857, she published *A Woman's Thoughts about Women* (1857), and many of her subsequent works examine the difficulties and opportunities of women's changing situation in the Victorian period. Her short stories were collected under the title *Avillion* in 1853 and her *Collected Poems* appeared in 1881. See Sally Mitchell, *Dinah Mulock Craik* (1983).

CRANE, Hart (1899–1932) American poet, born in Ohio. He published two volumes of verse, *White Buildings* (1926) and *The Bridge* (1930), the latter an obscure but powerful work which explores the 'Myth of America', with many echoes of Walt *Whitman; its national symbols include Brooklyn Bridge itself, invoked in its Proem, and such historical and legendary characters as Columbus, *Rip Van Winkle, and Pocahontas, who, the poet explains, is the 'mythological nature-symbol chosen to represent the physical body of the continent, or the soul'. Crane was an alcoholic, and committed suicide by jumping from a steamer in the Caribbean after spending some time in Mexico. His *Complete Poems and Selected Letters and Prose*, ed. B. Weber, appeared in 1960, and his correspondence with Yvor *Winters was published in 1978.

CRANE, Stephen (1871–1900) American novelist, journalist, and short story writer, born in New Jersey, the son of a Methodist minister. He worked as a journalist in New York before attempting to publish his first novel, *Maggie: A Girl of the Streets* (1893), which was too grim to find a readership. His next work, *The Red Badge of Courage* (1895), a study of an inexperienced soldier (Henry Fleming) and his reactions to the ordeal of battle during the American Civil War, although based on no personal experience of war was hailed as a masterpiece of psychological realism, and Crane found himself working as a war reporter in Mexico, Cuba, and Greece. He settled in England (where his novel had been even more warmly greeted than in the USA) in 1897, already ill with tuberculosis; he developed a close friendship with Joseph *Conrad (to whose work his own was compared as an example of literary *Impressionism), and met many other literary figures, including H. G. *Wells. His collected works were published from 1969 to 1976.

CRANE, Walter (1845–1915) Designer, illustrator, painter, and writer; born in Liverpool. Crane is most famous for his coloured picture-books for children and for his flower books; some of these he wrote himself. He cherished ambitions as a philosophical painter and poet, and developed the themes of his allegorical pictures—*The Roll of Fate* (1882), *The Bridge of Life* (1884)—in accompanying poems. His most elaborate verse, *The Sirens Three*, was published in the *English Illustrated Magazine* (1885), with his own decorations. Crane, deeply influenced by William *Morris, played an important role in the Arts and Crafts movement; he was convinced of the value of the crafts and of good design and discussed his belief in *The Claims of Decorative Art* (1892). In the 1880s he became a socialist, and created many designs, cartoons, and verses for the socialist cause. His lectures on art education were published as *The Bases of Design* (1898) and *Line and Form* (1900).

Cranford A novel by Elizabeth *Gaskell, published serially in **Household Words*, 1851–3. *Cranford*, a series of linked sketches of life among the ladies of a quiet country village in the 1830s, is based on Knutsford in Cheshire where Elizabeth Gaskell spent her childhood. It centres on the formidable Miss Deborah Jenkyns and her gentle sister Miss Matty, daughters of the former rector. Drama is provided by the death of the genial Captain Brown, run over by a train when saving the life of a child, the panic caused in the village by rumours of burglars, the surprising marriage of the widowed Lady Glenmire with the vulgar Mr Hoggins, the village surgeon, the failure of a bank which ruins Miss Matty, and her rescue by the fortunate return from India of her long-lost brother Peter. *Cranford* used to be valued chiefly for its loving portrayal of the old-fashioned customs and 'elegant economy' of a delicately observed group of middle-aged figures in a landscape; more recently, critical attention has turned to its subtle representations of the emotional and practical dynamics of women's lives.

CRANMER, Thomas (1489–1556) Archbishop of Canterbury; educated at Jesus College, Cambridge, of which he became a fellow. In 1529, he argued in support of *Henry VIII in his divorce from Catherine of Aragon, was appointed to the archbishopric in 1533, and maintained the king's claim to be the supreme head of the Church of England. He promoted the Bible in the vernacular; supervised the production of the first prayer book of Edward VI, 1549; prepared the revised prayer book of 1552; and drafted the 42 Articles of religion (afterwards reduced to 39) in the same year. To meet the need for suitable sermons, he contributed to and probably edited the first book of **Homilies* issued in 1547. In Queen Mary's reign he was imprisoned, condemned for heresy, and, in 1556, degraded from his ministry. He signed six documents admitting the pope's supremacy and the truth of all Roman Catholic doctrine except transubstantiation; he was burned at the stake, repudiating these admissions, on 21 March 1556 at Oxford, holding his right hand (which had written his recantation) steadily in the flames, that it might be the first burnt, saying 'This hand hath offended'. His chief title to fame is that of being the principal author of the English liturgy. John *Foxe tells his story vividly in his **Acts and Monuments*; there is a modern life by Diarmaid MacCulloch (1996).

CRASHAW, Richard (1612/13–49) Poet. He lost both mother and stepmother before he was 9, and his father, a Puritan preacher and devotional writer, fiercely antagonistic towards the Catholic Church, died in 1626. He was educated at Charterhouse and Pembroke Hall, Cambridge, where he came under the influence of High Church friends including Nicholas *Ferrar, whom he visited at *Little Gidding. From 1635 to 1643 he was a fellow at Peterhouse. He became a Catholic convert *c.*1645 and fled to Paris, where his friend Abraham *Cowley persuaded Queen Henrietta Maria to interest herself on his behalf. Through her influence he moved to Italy, first as attendant on Cardinal Palotta, then in 1649 in a minor post at the Santa Casa of Loreto, where he died shortly after. He published a book of sacred Latin epigrams in 1634. His principal work *Steps to the Temple* (1646; 2nd edn 1648) was a collection of religious poems influenced by Giambattista *Marino and the Spanish mystics. The secular section, the *Delights of the Muses*, contains 'Music's Duel', a paraphrase of the Latin of Strada, about a musical contest between a lute-player and a nightingale, and 'Wishes. To his (Supposed) Mistress' ('Who'er she be | That not impossible she'). A posthumous collection, *Carmen Deo Nostro* (1652), has variant versions of some of the poems, several of which exist both in Latin and English. His best-known poems are 'The Weeper', about Mary Magdalen, and those addressed to St *Teresa of Ávila. He was a painter and musician as well as a poet. His baroque, Counter-Reformation sensuousness daringly challenges decorum and was routinely condemned, in the past, as 'excessive' or 'repulsive' by insular critics. His poems were edited by G. W. Williams, 1974. See M. F. Bertanesco, *Crashaw and the Baroque* (1971); R. V. Young, *Richard Crashaw and the Spanish Golden Age* (1982); J. R. Roberts (ed.), *New Perspectives on the Life and Art of Richard Crashaw* (1990).

CRAWFORD, Robert (1959–) Poet, critic, and anthologist, born at Bellshill, Lanarkshire; he studied English at the universities of Glasgow and Oxford, moving on to become professor of modern Scottish literature at St Andrews. His first collection of poems, *A Scottish Assembly*, appeared in 1990, along with *Sharwaggi*, a joint volume in *Scots with W. N. Herbert. Later books include *Masculinity* (1996), *The Tip of my Tongue* (2003), and *Full Volume* (2008). Crawford's good-humoured yet sharp poetry explores questions of national, cultural, and gender identity, while also celebrating the domestic and the personal with tenderness and speculative wit. His work is marked by an interest in specialist vocabularies, particularly those derived from technology. *Devolving English Literature* (1992; 2000) has been perhaps the most influential of his many critical studies. *Scotland's Books*, a spirited and individual history of Scottish literature, appeared in 2007.

Creed, the Apostles', the Athanasian, the Nicene The creeds are fundamental statements of Christian doctrine, particularly the Trinity. Originally required of candidates for baptism, they came to be recited as part of the liturgy of Catholic and Protestant churches.

CREELEY, Robert (1926–2005) American poet and prose writer, and one of the *Black Mountain group; he edited (1954–7) the *Black Mountain Review*. His verse tends to use tighter metrical forms, to be more personal, less rhetorical than that of associates like Charles *Olson, with whom he had an extended correspondence. His *Collected Poems* was published in 2006. Creeley also wrote a number of novels, including *The Gold Diggers* (1954/1965) and *The Island* (1963). His *Collected Prose* was published in 1984.

CREEVEY, Thomas (1768–1838) Diarist. He was educated in Hackney and at Queens' College, Cambridge, and served as Whig MP for Thetford and Appleby. *The Creevey Papers* (ed. Sir Herbert Maxwell, 1903) consist of letters and diary extracts, and describe the people and society of the Georgian era. See also *Creevey's Life and Times*, ed. J. Gore (1934).

Creole is used as a noun or an adjective of both people and language. The word may derive from *criar*, 'to breed' in Spanish. In the West Indies it is used of people of African or European descent born or naturalized in the Caribbean. A creole language develops from pidgin, which is used between people with no common language and discards the inessentials of the original language. Creole languages were once associated with slavery and regarded as inferior but are now used in literature and the media, and are seen to have a particular cultural history and expressive vitality.

CRESSWELL, Helen (1934–2005) Prolific children's author, born and educated in Nottingham and then King's College London. Her books often feature families, including the Bagthorpes (1978–2001) and the Lizzie Dripping books (1972–4; 1991). All her stories are wryly realistic. Cresswell successfully adapted Edith *Nesbit's and Enid *Blyton's books for television.

CRÈVECŒUR, Michel-Guillaume de (1735–1813) American prose writer, known as J. Hector St John de Crevecœur, born at Caen in France. He emigrated to Canada and served under Montcalm, then moved south, landing at New York in 1759 and taking American citizenship in 1765. He then settled in Orange County, New York State, where for several idyllic years he farmed, until the revolution obliged him to flee to Europe. These years were the basis of his famous work, much admired by the Romantics, *Letters from an American Farmer* (pub. London, 1782), which describe rural life and customs; the third essay, 'What is an American?', describes the nation idealistically as a cultural melting-pot and defines the American as a 'new man, who acts upon new principles'. D. H. *Lawrence commented on his role as myth-maker in *Studies in Classic American Literature* (1923), and described him as the 'emotional prototype' of the American (as distinct from Benjamin *Franklin, 'the real practical prototype').

CRICHTON, James ('The Admirable') (1560–82) Scottish polymath, poet, and adventurer, educated at the University of St Andrews, who served in the French army, travelled in Italy, and died in a brawl in Mantua. His colourful career is recounted by Sir Thomas *Urquhart and provides the subject of a historical novel by Harrison *Ainsworth. J. M. *Barrie's play *The Admirable Crichton* concerns a manservant marooned with his less gifted employers on a desert island.

CRICHTON, Michael (1942–2008) Popular novelist, film-maker, and creator of television series, who often engaged with scientific, medical, and social issues of wide concern. Born in Chicago, Crichton studied medicine and published his first *science fiction novel, *The Andromeda Strain* (1969), while still a student. Filmed in 1971, this established a pattern of 'techno-thrillers', projecting current scientific knowledge into melodramatic fantasy, while often sounding a cautionary note. Appropriately, his subjects were often biological, from the virulent extraterrestrial disease of his first novel to the deadly self-reproducing nano-particles of *Prey* (2002) and a warning against genetic patenting in *Next* (2006). His best-known creations are the long-running hospital-based television series *ER* (1994–2009) and the screenplay for *Jurassic Park* (1993), which portrayed spectacular dinosaurs recreated from prehistoric DNA. Crichton has also generated controversy, notably in *Rising Sun* (1994), apparently attacking Japanese business culture, and *State of Fear* (2004) questioning alarm over climate change, both interpretations that he denied.

Cricket on the Hearth, The The third of Charles *Dickens's five Christmas Books, published 1846. John Peerybingle, carrier, and his younger wife, Dot, are a happy couple, although the venomous old Tackleton, who is about to marry the young May Fielding, throws suspicion on Dot's sincerity. This suspicion appears to be confirmed when an eccentric old stranger comes to live with the Peerybingles and is discovered by John, metamorphosed into a bright young man by the removal of his wig, in intimate conversation with Dot. By the fairy influence of the Cricket on the Hearth John is persuaded to pardon her offence, which he attributes to the incompatibility of their ages and temperaments. But there turns out to be no need for forgiveness, for the young man is an old friend, the lover of May Fielding, believed dead, who has turned up just in time to prevent her marrying Tackleton. Among the other characters are Caleb Plummer and his blind daughter Bertha, the toymakers; and Tilly Slowboy, the Peerybingles' loving and incompetent nanny. The book was a great popular success, with the highest sales figures of all Dickens's Christmas Books.

CRIMP, Martin (1965–) Playwright, born in Kent, who read English at St Catherine's College, Oxford. He wrote fiction before being employed by the Orange Tree Theatre in south London, the venue for his early theatrical work, including *Dealing with Clair* (1988). Writer in residence at the *Royal Court from 1997, it was that year that his *Attempts on her Life* was produced there and brought him to real prominence. The play abandons character identification and narrative continuity in favour of a series of short scenes that cause the audience to question what might be signified by the title. His *Fewer Emergencies* (2005) was also produced at the Royal Court. Firmly established as a major playwright, he has also produced significant versions of works by *Ionesco, *The Chairs* (1997) for Theatre de Complicité, and *Rhinoceros* (2007).

Criterion (1922–39) An influential literary periodical launched as a quarterly and edited by T. S. *Eliot; *The *Waste Land* appeared in its first issue. It became the *New Criterion* in 1926, and in 1927, briefly, the *Monthly Criterion*, but then reverted to its original title and quarterly publication. It included poems, essays, short stories, and reviews, and published work by Ezra *Pound, William *Empson, W. H. *Auden, Stephen *Spender, Geoffrey *Grigson, etc.; it also introduced the work of Marcel *Proust, Paul *Valéry, Jean *Cocteau, and other European writers. Eliot disowned any particular programme, claiming that his magazine represented a 'tendency', 'toward something which, for want of a better name, we may call classicism'. It enjoyed immense literary prestige until it closed in 1939 under the pressure of what Eliot described as 'a depression of spirits' induced by 'the present state of public affairs'. See Jason Harding, *The Criterion* (2002).

Critic, The, *or a Tragedy Rehearsed* A comedy by Richard Brinsley *Sheridan, produced 1779. Modelled on Buckingham's *The *Rehearsal*, *The Critic* is an exuberant burlesque of contemporary tragic drama. Mr Puff, an enterprising purveyor of literary wares and the author of a ludicrously bombastic and sentimental tragedy, 'The Spanish Armada', invites Dangle and Sneer, two inept theatre critics, and Sir Fretful Plagiary (a caricature of Richard *Cumberland) to a rehearsal of his play. The drama introduces Sir Walter *Ralegh and other historical figures alongside Tilburina, who complicates the plot with her love for Don Ferolo Whiskerandos, a Spanish prisoner. The rehearsal is comically plagued by the solemn discussions of the author and his guests as well as the queries and mistakes of prompters and stagehands. The play has also been taken as a covert satire on governmental passivity in the face of a resurgent Spanish invasion threat.

Critical Dictionary of English Literature, A, *from the Earliest Accounts...to the Middle of the Nineteenth Century* By Samuel Austin Allibone (1816–89), first published in the USA in 1858 and in London in 1859. In the editor's words, 'the fruits of many years of anxious research and conscientious toil', this vast work, the first of its kind on a comprehensive scale, includes biographical entries for 30,000 authors and entries for an even greater number of books. The aim was to direct the public to 'the Best Works of the Best Authors', and each book of any note is described with generous extracts from contemporary reviews and other critical writing. The interpretation of 'English Literature' is wide, as the 'Best Books' for doctors, lawyers, merchants, or farmers were also included. The work was highly successful, with a new edition in 1871, and two supplements in 1891.

Critical Quarterly A literary review founded in 1959 and edited at that time by C. B. Cox and A. E. Dyson. From the beginning it published both criticism and creative writing. Latterly, under the editorship of Colin MacCabe, it has continued this tradition, while also becoming more oriented towards cultural studies more generally, including film and television, and literary theory. Contributors have included Philip *Larkin, Donald *Davie, D. J. *Enright, William *Empson, and Seamus *Heaney.

Critical Review A journal founded in 1756 to oppose the liberal **Monthly Review.* Until 1763 it was edited by Tobias *Smollett. Apart from commentary on public affairs, it reviewed a wide range of books. Oliver *Goldsmith began writing for it in 1759; Samuel *Johnson reviewed Goldsmith's *The *Traveller* there in 1764.

criticism, schools of *See* DECONSTRUCTION; FEMINIST CRITICISM; MARXIST LITERARY CRITICISM; MYTH CRITICISM; NARRATOLOGY; NEW CRITICISM; NEW HISTORICISM; POSTMODERNISM; PRACTICAL CRITICISM; PSYCHOANALYTIC CRITICISM; SOCIALIST REALISM; STRUCTURALISM. *See also* ARCHETYPE.

CROCE, Benedetto (1866–1952) Italian philosopher, historian, and critic. His aesthetics and criticism, published in his journal *La critica* from 1903 to 1944, were profoundly influential in Italy before the Second World War. His most influential work is *Estetica come scienza dell'espressione e linguistica generale* (1902: *Aesthetics as the Science of Expression and General Linguistics*). Central to all phases of his thought is the concept of art as a 'lyrical intuition'. His earliest work was on the culture of Naples especially in the baroque period, but his best-known criticism is *Breviario di estetica* (1913), *Poesia popolare e poesia d'arte* (1933: *Popular Poetry and Literary Poetry*), his essay on *Ariosto, Shakespeare, Corneille* (1920); and *La poesia* (1936: *Poetics*). His historical works include *La storia come pensiero e come azione* (1938: *History as Thought and as Action*), which asserts that history is always the history of freedom.

CROCKETT, S. R. *See* KAILYARD SCHOOL.

CROKER, John Wilson (1780–1857) Tory MP, secretary to the Admiralty, and a regular contributor to the **Quarterly Review*, in which he made very plain his Tory and Anglican stance, even in his literary reviews, and for which he acted as an important link with circles of political power. Known for his bitter opposition to most of the younger writers of his day, he became (and has remained) notorious for his criticism of John Keats's **Endymion* in 1818. P. B. *Shelley (in his preface to **Adonais*) and Lord *Byron (in his jingle 'Who killed John Keats?') established the belief, still quoted, that Croker's review hastened the death of the poet. Yet Croker's views on *Endymion*, although blinkered and ungenerous, were considerably more temperate than those of John *Lockhart in **Blackwood's Magazine*, and there is some justice in his comments on the diction and versification of Keats's early work. Croker was a painstaking scholar, and an expert on the 18th century. His books include *An Intercepted Letter from Canton* (1804), a satire on Dublin society; a reliable edition of Boswell's *Life of Samuel *Johnson*, in 1831, and in the same year *Military Events of the French Revolution of 1830*. He was a much-hated man, caricatured in three contemporary novels: Thomas Love Peacock's **Melincourt* (1817); Lady *Morgan's *Florence Macarthy* (1818); and Disraeli's **Coningsby* (1844); and was detested 'more than cold boiled veal' by his lifelong enemy Thomas *Macaulay. It appears that he was the originator of the political term 'Conservative', which first appeared in an article of his in the *Quarterly Review* in January 1830. *The Croker Papers*, published 1884, cover his political life 1808–32 and are of considerable historical interest.

CROKER, Thomas Crofton (1798–1854) Irish antiquarian, born in Cork, who worked in the Admiralty in London, and was probably the first collector to regard national and folk stories as examples of literary art. *Researches in the*

South of Ireland appeared in 1824; *Fairy Legends and Traditions in the South of Ireland*, which delighted Walter *Scott and was very successful, in 1825–8; *Legends of the Lakes* in 1829; and *Popular Songs of Ireland* in 1839. These works, together with Croker's many contributions to literary and antiquarian journals, provide a rich source of information on Irish folklore.

CROLY, George (1780–1860) Born in Dublin, educated at Trinity College, Dublin, and rector of St Stephen's Walbrook. He was author of *Paris in 1815* (1817), a work which owes much to Lord *Byron's **Childe Harold*; *Catiline* (1822), a tragedy; *May Fair* (1827), a satire; and *Salathiel* (1829), a romance of the legendary Wandering Jew. *Marston* followed in 1846, a romance to which the French Revolution and the Napoleonic Wars provide the background. He contributed to **Blackwood's Magazine*, and published numerous other narrative and romantic poems, as well as religious and historical works Lord Byron in **Don Juan* refers to Croly as 'the Revd Rowley Powley'.

CROMEK, Robert Hartley (1720–1812) Engraver. He appears also to have been a shifty literary speculator who made many enemies, notably William *Blake. He published *Reliques of Burns* in 1808, and in 1810 a volume of *Select Scottish Songs* by Robert *Burns. In the same year he published *Remains of Nithsdale and Galloway Song*, much of which consisted of the poems of Allan *Cunningham, which the author had disguised as ancient songs. It seems probable that Cromek knew of and ignored the deception. Blake expressed his enmity in the couplet, 'A petty, sneaking knave I knew | O! Mr Cr——, how do ye do?'

CROMPTON, Richmal (1890–1969) Born Bury, Lancashire; read classics at Royal Holloway College. Crompton's 41 books for adults have been eclipsed by her *'William' stories, the first of which was 'Rice-Mould' (1919) for *Home Magazine*. Until the 1940s, the stories, first collected in *Just William* (1922) were directed at adults; Crompton used the stories to satirize middle-class, middle England. Characteristic is 'Aunt Arabella in Charge' (*William the Pirate*, 1932) in which A. A. *Milne's Christopher Robin is mercilessly lampooned. The stories have been filmed and televised and gained new life through Martin Jarvis's radio adaptations. See Mary Cadogan, *Richmal Crompton: The Woman behind William* (1986).

CROMWELL, Oliver (1599–1658) Soldier, politician, general, and from 1653 to 1658 lord protector, the subject of innumerable contemporary pamphlets, satires, odes, and panegyrics. Andrew *Marvell's 'An Horatian Ode upon Cromwell's Return from Ireland', written in 1650, and his *The First Anniversary of the Government under his Highness the Lord Protector* (1655) are notable expressions of balanced admiration for Cromwell's 'active star'; 'If these the times, then this must be the man.' John *Milton, who was Latin secretary to the newly formed Council of State from 1649, appealed to him in the sonnet 'Cromwell, our chief of men' as the defender of conscience and liberty, and Edmund *Waller (his cousin) wrote in praise of his government and foreign policy. Sir William *D'Avenant's opera *The Cruelty of the Spaniards in Peru* (1658) and *The History of Sir Francis Drake* (1659) were intended to support Cromwell's war against Spain. After his death Cromwell was variously depicted by writers and historians as honest patriot, 'frantic enthusiast' (David *Hume), corrupt hypocrite, and true Englishman: Thomas *Carlyle in his lecture on the 'Hero as King' (1840) and his *Letters and Speeches of Oliver Cromwell* (1845) praised him as a Puritan hero, God-sent to save England, grappling 'like a giant, face to face, heart to heart, with the naked truth of things'.

CRONIN, A. J. (Archibald Joseph) (1896–1981) Novelist, born in Cardross, Scotland, and educated at Dunbarton Academy; he studied medicine at Glasgow University, then practised as a doctor in South Wales and London for some years before devoting himself, after the success of his first book, *Hatter's Castle* (1931), to an extremely successful career as a novelist whose works reached an even wider audience through film and television. His best-known novels are *The Stars Look Down* (1935) and *The Citadel* (1937). He lived in the USA from 1939 to 1945 and subsequently in Switzerland.

CROSS, Gillian (1945–) Children's writer, born in London and educated at Somerville College, Oxford, and Sussex University. Cross has produced over 40 books, from the televised comedy-thriller *The Demon Headmaster* (1982) to the challenging examination of families, fatherhood, and terrorism *Wolf* (1990), which won the Carnegie Medal.

CROSSLEY-HOLLAND, Kevin (1941–) Poet, translator from Old English, and children's writer, born in Buckinghamshire and educated at Bryanston School and St Edmund Hall, Oxford. His collections include *The Rain-Giver* (1972), *Time's Oriel* (1983), *Waterslain* (1986), and *The Language of Yes* (1996). His *Selected Poems* was published in 2001. His translations include *The Battle of Maldon and Other Old English Poems* (1965), *Beowulf* (1968), *Storm and Other Old English Riddles* (1970), *The Exeter Book Riddles* (1978), and *The Old English Elegies* (1988). Although he has travelled widely and his spells abroad are reflected in his subjects, the strongest pull in his work is towards the landscape and interwoven history and legend of East Anglia, where he has spent much of his life—its maltings, granaries, and woodlands, but most particularly the 'marsh, mud, creeks, shifting sand' of its coastline. His works for children, many based on East Anglian folk tales and Norse myths, include *Havelock the Dane* (1964) and *The Wildman* (1976). His prize-winning 'Arthur' trilogy opened with *The Seeing Stone* (2000) and closed with *King of the Middle March* (2003). He has also written libretti from his own works, notably with composer Nicola LeFanu (1947–).

crossover books A term that came to prominence in the 1990s, used to describe books such as J. K. *Rowling's 'Harry Potter' series and Philip Pullman's **His Dark Materials* trilogy, originally published for children but also successful with adults. The term is recent, the phenomenon is not: many

19th-century books, including those by G. A. *Henty and Frances Hodgson *Burnett, appealed to dual audiences. In the later 20th century, the popularity of fantasy blurred literary and audience distinctions; Richard *Adams's best-selling *Watership Down* (1972) was issued with different covers for adults and children, now a common feature of crossover books.

Crotchet Castle A satire by Thomas Love *Peacock, published 1831. The story assembles a group of theorists at a country house: Mr Skionar (who resembles Samuel Taylor *Coleridge), Mr MacQuedy (a Scottish economist who suggests J. R. MacCulloch), Mr Chainmail (who wants to revive the Middle Ages, possibly based on the historian Samuel Rush Meyrick, 1783–1848), and others. The Revd Dr Folliott, though more amiable and learned than Peacock's previous clerics, is also mocked for his bigoted conservatism. The dinner-table conversations at Crotchet Castle turn on the clash between Folliott's Toryism and MacQuedy's progressivism. The guests take a journey by river and canal to Wales, reminiscent of a trip Peacock took up the Thames with P. B. *Shelley in 1815. In Lady Clarinda, Peacock supplies the most spirited and cynical of his heroines. She has a foil in the romantic Susannah Touchandgo, who retires to a simple life in Wales after her father, a banker, absconds. The book ends with an assault by the mob on Mr Chainmail's 12th-century castle, an ironic comment on the more visionary schemes to solve the troubles of the age of reform.

CROWE, Catherine *See* GHOST STORIES.

CROWLEY, Aleister (1875–1947) Occultist and writer, born Leamington Spa and educated, briefly, at both Malvern College (1891–2) and Tonbridge School (1892) before entering Trinity College, Cambridge, in 1895. Crowley dedicated himself to esoteric studies from 1897 and left Cambridge without taking a degree. He combined a wildly peripatetic existence (in Mexico, Asia, and elsewhere) with a regular stream of occultist publications (such as *The Book of Lies*, 1913) and reached the peak of his notoriety in 1923 when a newspaper denounced him as 'the wickedest man in the world' following the sensational publication of his *Diary of a Drug Fiend* (1922). See Martin Booth, *A Magick Life: The Biography of Aleister Crowley* (2000).

CROWLEY, John (1942–) American novelist, born in Maine; who began with *science fiction in novels like *Engine Summer* (1979) but whose *Little, Big* adapted the structure of Faerie constructed by 'Lewis Carroll' (*see* DODGSON, CHARLES) in *Sylvie and Bruno* (1889) to contemporary New York. John *Clute calls it, for its theme and sense of story, a masterpiece of modern *fantasy. A later sequence, beginning with *Aegypt* (1987), develops the conceit of a 'secret history' of the world by drawing upon Giordano *Bruno's Hermeticism.

CROWNE, John (?1640–?1703) Playwright, probably the son of an emigrant to Nova Scotia, where he appears to have spent some of his youth. A prose romance, *Pandion and Amphigenia* (1665), was followed by his first comedy, *The Country Wit* (1675), containing the character of Sir Mannerly Shallow, subsequently developed into *Sir Courtly Nice in the play of that name (1685). He wrote several other comedies, a court masque, *Calisto* (1675), and eleven tragedies, including the two-part rhymed *The Destruction of Jerusalem* (1677), *Thyestes* (1681), and *Caligula* (1698). The success of the tragedies is said to have owed much to expensive and elaborate scenery. He was part-author, with John *Dryden and Thomas *Shadwell, of *Notes and Observations*, a satirical attack on *The Empress of Morocco* by Elkanah *Settle. Although Crowne was a favourite of Charles II, John *Dennis said that he had 'a mortal aversion to the court'; he himself claimed in his later years that his plays were 'successful, and yet clean'.

CRUDEN, Alexander (1701–70) Compiler of a concordance (an index of words and passages) of the King James *Bible, social campaigner, and reputed madman. Born and educated in Aberdeen, he aspired to the ministry, but was incarcerated as a lunatic by the family of his first love who feared he had discovered her incestuous relationship with her brother. This episode was used by enemies as evidence for further incarcerations in London. His experience of madhouses, related in *The London Citizen Exceedingly Injured* (1739), helped raise consciousness of their abuses and the plight of the unjustly accused. In later life he campaigned for reform of Newgate prison and, less practically, for moral reform of the nation.

The *Complete Concordance* (1737) included the Apocrypha and much miscellaneous but sometimes fanciful information now usually omitted (see e.g. 'serpent'). It became a standard reference work, as did his *Verbal Index to Milton's Paradise Lost* (1741).

Cruelty, Theatre of A phrase associated with French director Antonin *Artaud, and introduced to Britain during the 1960s through the work of Peter *Brook and critic and director Charles Marowitz (1934–), who chose the name for their experimental theatre group in homage to Artaud: the most celebrated production of the movement was Brook's version of Peter *Weiss's *Marat/Sade*. The emphasis of this style of theatre was as much on gesture and movement as on text.

CRUIKSHANK, George (1792–1878) Illustrator and caricaturist, son of Isaac Cruikshank, also a caricaturist. His vast amount of work was largely in political caricature, but among the books he illustrated were: Robert *Burns's 'The Jolly Beggars' in 1823; the *German Popular Stories* of Jacob and Wilhelm *Grimm in 1824–6; William *Cowper's *John Gilpin* in 1828; William *Rhodes's *Bombastes Furioso* in 1830; Daniel *Defoe's **Robinson Crusoe* in 1831; **Sketches by Boz* in 1836, which began a long association with Charles *Dickens including the illustrations to *Oliver Twist in 1837; Walter *Scott's *Waverley in 1836–9; W. H. *Ainsworth's The Tower of London in 1840; W. M. *Thackeray's Legend of the Rhine in 1845; Harriet Beecher *Stowe's *Uncle Tom's Cabin in 1853. In 1835 he became the editor of The Comic Almanack, a predecessor of *Punch.

Cry, the Beloved Country (1948) Is a novel by Alan Paton (1903–88), who was national president of the South African Liberal Party until it was declared illegal in 1968. The novel begins with the departure of the Reverend Stephen Kumalo from his impoverished homeland at Ndotasheni, Natal, for Johannesburg, in search of three members of his family including his son Absalom. Absalom has murdered the son of a white farmer, James Jarvis. Absalom is convicted and condemned to death, and Kumalo returns home with Absalom's pregnant wife. The novel ends with the reconciliation of Jarvis and Kumalo, and Jarvis's determination to rise above tragedy by helping the poor black community. It became a best-seller. Paton said it was 'a book with a message'.

C.S.C. *See* CALVERLEY, CHARLES.

Cuala Press A *private press founded in 1902 at Dundrum, Co. Dublin, by Elizabeth and Lily Yeats, sisters of W. B. *Yeats, to stimulate local crafts and employment. It was originally called the Dun Emer Press, changing its name in 1908, and it flourished as the Cuala Press until late 1946, publishing work by such Irish writers as Yeats, J. M. *Synge, Oliver *Gogarty, Lady *Gregory, and by Ezra *Pound, John *Masefield, and Rabindranath *Tagore. The press was revived by Anne and Michael Yeats, the children of W. B. Yeats, in 1969.

Cubism A movement in art pioneered by Pablo Picasso (1881–1973) and Georges Braque (1882–1963) between about 1907 and 1914. In its first phase, sometimes referred to as 'Analytic Cubism', forms were broken down for examination, and the multiple facets of objects splayed out as if seen from many points simultaneously. 'Synthetic Cubism', which emerged in 1912, involved a shift in emphasis from fragmentation to accumulation, with collage (or *papier collé*) becoming an important technique. Cubism was ground-breaking in its abandonment of fixed perspective and in its decisive move away from illusionistic representation, renegotiating the relationship between the three-dimensional world and the two-dimensional picture plane. It was also a radical investigation of the relationship between signs and their referents (*see* STRUCTURALISM). Using a limited vocabulary of objects (guitar, bottle, newspaper, pipe), Cubist artists explored the capacity for signs and referents to become interchangeable, or to generate further referents. It is partly for this reason that Cubism was closely allied to poetry, particularly to the work of *Mallarmé, *Rimbaud, and *Apollinaire. Gertrude *Stein developed a form of Cubist prose, and her writing influenced, in turn, the development of Cubist painting.

Cuchulain [pron. Cuhoolin] Hero of the Ulster cycle of Irish mythology, the ward of Conchubar, king of Ulster. His birth was miraculous, and he showed his prowess at an early age. While still a child he killed the watchdog of the smith Culain and undertook to take the dog's place, whence his name was changed from Setanta to Cuchulain ('Culain's hound'). Among the feats which won him the love of many women was his single-handed defence of Ulster against Queen Medb (pron. Maeve) and her Connaughtmen. Cuchulain is said to have lashed himself to a rock so he could die facing his enemies. Some of the legends about him were translated by Lady *Gregory (*Cuchulain of Muirthemne*). He figures in James *Macpherson's Ossianic poems and in many of the poems and plays of W. B. *Yeats. Cuchulain has been adopted as an icon both by Irish nationalists and Ulster loyalists.

Cuckoo and the Nightingale, The *See* CLANVOWE, SIR JOHN.

CUDWORTH, Ralph *See* CAMBRIDGE PLATONISTS.

CUGOANO, Ottobah (*c.*1757–?1803) Sold into slavery from present-day Ghana to the Caribbean. Freed, he settled in London, becoming active in abolitionist circles, meeting William *Blake, and collaborating with Olaudah *Equiano. His book *Thoughts and Sentiments on the Evils of Slavery* (1787) is a radical denunciation from a Christian perspective.
See SLAVERY.

CULLEN, Countee (1903–46) African American poet, who was an important figure in the *Harlem Renaissance. His first collection, *Colour* (1925), celebrated blackness and a second, *The Black Christ* (1929), caused some controversy for its appropriation of Christian imagery. Cullen's only novel was *One Way to Heaven* (1932).

CULPEPER, Nicholas (1616–54) Apothecary, Puritan, and republican. He conducted a campaign against the monopoly of the College of Physicians, and in 1649 published an English translation of the College's *Pharmacopoeia*, thus making its contents available for the first time to the poor who could not afford doctors' fees. Both this work and his *The English Physician Enlarged, or the Herbal* (1653) sold in vast quantities, but his infringement of the monopoly made him many enemies and he was the object of much slander and abuse.

cultural materialism *See* NEW HISTORICISM.

Culture and Anarchy A sequence of essays by Matthew *Arnold, published as a book in 1869, adapted from his 1867 lecture 'Culture and its Enemies' and from *Cornhill Magazine* articles (1868) responding to critics. This work sets out Arnold's central arguments about the place in modern society of 'culture', presented as the enlightened 'study of perfection' and as the harmonious development of human capacities. Responding to the fierce conflicts of 1866–7 over franchise reform, Arnold laments the aggressively partisan attitudes of the landed 'Barbarians', the lower-class 'Populace', and especially the 'Philistine' middle class, whose suspicion of state power, notably in the realm of education, he regards as dangerously self-defeating. He accuses the Philistines of blind complacency and of overemphasizing the value of 'Hebraism' (essentially Protestant moral vigilance) at the expense of the equally vital tradition of 'Hellenism' (the Renaissance and Enlightenment cultivation of beauty and truth for their own sakes); and he proposes that the task of the few devotees of culture is to act as a sceptical corrective to those imbalanced vested interests.

CULVERWEL, Nathaniel *See* CAMBRIDGE PLATONISTS.

CUMBERLAND, Richard (1732–1811) Dramatist, grandson of Richard *Bentley, educated at Westminster School, where he met William *Cowper, George *Colman, and Charles *Churchill, and Trinity College, Cambridge. He wrote several comedies, of which *The *West Indian* and *The Jew* (1794) were the most successful. He also wrote tragedies; three novels; a book on Spanish painting; periodical essays; religious and autobiographical poems; and *Memoirs* (1806). *See also* CRITIC.

CUMMINGS, Bruce Frederick (1889–1919) Diarist and biologist, born in Barnstaple, Devon, who wrote a diary under the pseudonym of W. N. P. Barbellion, *The Journal of a Disappointed Man*. It was published in 1919 with an introduction by H. G. *Wells, who called it a 'specimen, carefully displayed and labelled' of 'recorded unhappiness'. He clearly intended publication, and modelled his work partly on the diary of Marie *Bashkirtseff. The last entry was made on 21 October 1917, after which 'Barbellion's' death was recorded. In fact Cummings survived to see his own work published, and his *A Last Diary* (1920) covers the last two years of his life.

CUMMINGS, E. E. (Edward Estlin) (1894–1962) American poet, born in Cambridge, Massachusetts, and educated at Harvard University. His first book, *The Enormous Room* (1922), an account of his three-month internment in a French detention camp in 1917, won him an immediate international reputation for its brilliant prose and its iconoclastic views. In 1923 appeared *Tulips and Chimneys*, the first of twelve volumes of poetry, thanks to the help of his close friend John *Dos Passos. Strongly influenced by the English Romantic poets and Gertrude *Stein, the early poems attracted attention more for their experimental typography and technical skill than for their considerable lyric power; the frankness of his vocabulary and the sharpness of his satire also created some scandal. In *Eimi* (1933), a typographically difficult but enthralling journal of a trip to Russia, he broke in disillusion from his earlier socialist leanings, and thenceforth his work reflected his increasingly reactionary social and political views. His later lyrics, on the other hand, achieved a greater depth and simplicity. His other works include essays, plays, and *Tom* (1935), a satirical ballet based on Harriet Beecher Stowe's **Uncle Tom's Cabin*. His *Complete Poems: 1904–1962* was published in 1991.

CUNNINGHAM, Allan (1784–1842) Poet, born in Dumfriesshire and largely self-educated, apprenticed to his brother as a stonemason. An avid reader, he walked in Robert *Burns's funeral procession and became a friend of James *Hogg. Cunningham profited from the vogue for *primitivism by disguising his poems as old Scottish songs, many of which were published by R. H. *Cromek as *Remains of Nithsdale and Galloway Song* (1810). When Cunningham went to London, Cromek introduced him to Sir Francis Chantrey, whose secretary he became. He was soon a frequent contributor to the **London Magazine* and to **Blackwood's Magazine*. He published *Traditional Tales of the English and Scottish Peasantry* (1822); *The Songs of Scotland* (1825); *Lives of the Most Eminent British Painters, Sculptors, and Architects* (1829–33); and an edition of Burns (1834). Several of his songs, such as 'A wet sheet and a flowing sea' and 'Hame, hame, hame', which were very popular in his lifetime, are still anthologized.

CUNNINGHAME GRAHAM, Robert Bontine (1852–1936) Adventurer, writer, and political radical, son of a Scottish laird and a half-Spanish mother; educated at Harrow School and in Brussels. During a varied career Cunninghame Graham was a rancher in Argentina, a traveller, mainly in South America, but also in North Africa and Spain; a socialist Liberal MP (1886–92), and parliamentary candidate (in 1892) for the Scottish Labour Party, of which he was co-founder. He was elected president of the National Party of Scotland in 1928. His publications include volumes of Latin American history, several stories of Scotland, and travel books, including *Mogreb-el-Acksa* (1898), which inspired the play *Captain Brassbound's Conversion* by George Bernard *Shaw. His book *A Vanished Arcadia: Being Some Account of the Jesuits in Paraguay 1607–1767* (1901) inspired the 1986 film *The Mission*. Ford Madox *Ford and Joseph *Conrad were among his literary friends.

Cupid Son of *Venus and winged god of love (Eros in Greek), whose arrows usually represent unsatisfied desire. Depictions in classical, medieval, and Renaissance literature vary from the naughty but dangerous child to the powerful divine force capable of transforming the human devotee. Philip *Sidney's **Astrophel and Stella* illustrates the first, Edmund *Spenser's **Colin Clout* the second. Cupid has continued to represent the power of erotic love in countless literary texts.

Cupid and Campaspe *See* CAMPASPE.

Cupid and Psyche The allegorical centrepiece of the *Golden Ass* of *Apuleius, in which the author blends a familiar folk tale with a Hellenistic epyllion (a short erotic epic) which has some of the trappings of a philosophical myth. Psyche (meaning 'soul'), is beloved by *Cupid, who visits her nightly, but remains invisible, forbidding her to attempt to see him: one night she takes a lamp and looks at him as he sleeps, and agitated by his beauty lets fall a drop of hot oil on his shoulder. He departs in wrath, leaving her solitary and remorseful. Like the hero of the novel in which her tale is set, Psyche has forfeited her happiness through misplaced curiosity, and has to regain it through painful wanderings. Many elements of the story—the magic palace, the enchantress (Venus) to whom the hero (Cupid) is in thrall, the tasks the heroine has to perform, and the animals that aid her—belong to the world of the folk tale. Apuleius' story has been retold by many later writers, including William *Browne, Shackerley *Marmion, Mary *Tighe, William *Morris, Walter *Pater, and C. S. *Lewis. John *Keats's 'Ode to Psyche' owes a debt to it.

Cure for a Cuckold, A A comedy by John *Webster and William *Rowley, possibly with Thomas *Heywood, written 1624/5, printed 1661. It deals with the love affairs of two couples, Bonville and Annabel, and Lessingham and Clare; and contains a notable duel scene on Calais sands.

Curious Incident of the Dog in the Night-time, The (2003) *Crossover book by Mark *Haddon told as an account by 15-year-old Christopher Boone, who suffers from Asperger's Syndrome, of how he solves the mystery of who killed his neighbour's dog.

CURLL, Edmund (1683–1747) Bookseller notorious for instant biographies, seditious pamphlets, piracies, and pornography. In 1728 he was pilloried and fined for publishing the political *Memoirs* of John Ker and *Venus in the Cloister, or The Nun in her Smock*. He enraged Jonathan *Swift with his 'Key' to *A *Tale of a Tub* and unauthorized *Miscellanies*. Alexander *Pope drugged him with an emetic in 1716 and ridiculed him in *The *Dunciad*. In 1735 Pope manoeuvred Curll into publishing an unauthorized edition of his letters, in order to promote an 'authentic' edition. See Paul Baines and Pat Rogers, *Edmund Curll, Bookseller* (2007).

CURNOW, Allen (1911–2001) New Zealand poet and critic, born in Timaru. From 1937 to 1988 he wrote a weekly satirical poetry column under the pen-name of 'Whim Wham', in the *Christchurch Press* and then the *New Zealand Herald*, commenting on world issues and New Zealand politics, as well as more light-hearted topics. He joined the English department of the University of Auckland in 1951 and taught there until 1976. From an early stage he was seen to be an important figure in the creation of a truly New Zealand poetry. His first significant book, *Not in Narrow Seas* (1939), was followed by several others in the 1940s; and his editing of *A Book of New Zealand Verse* (1945; rev. 1951) and then *The Penguin Book of New Zealand Verse* (1960) was both influential and controversial. An increasingly prolific and audacious writer, from the 1970s he was recognized not only as his country's leading poet but as a poet with an international reputation, receiving the Queen's Gold Medal for Poetry in 1989. A number of collected and selected volumes are drawn on in *Early Days Yet: New and Collected Poems 1941–1997* (1997), with a final volume *The Bells of St Babel's: Poems 1997–2001* published in 2001.

Cursor Mundi A northern poem dating from *c.*1300, surviving in seven manuscripts of about 24,000 short lines, supplemented in most of them by another 6,000 or so lines of devotional material. The poem covers mankind's spiritual history from the Creation to the Last Judgement, divided into Seven Ages. It is derived from various late 12th-century Latin pseudo-histories made up of saints' lives, apocryphal legends, and biblical material. It has been edited by R. Morris (EETS os, 7 vols, 1874–93).

CURTIS, Tony (1946–) Welsh poet, born in Carmarthen and educated at University College, Swansea, whose collections include *Album* (1974), *Taken for Pearls* (1993), *Heaven's Gate* (2001), and *Crossing Over* (2007). His celebrations of family life, golf, and the landscape of Pembrokeshire are increasingly shadowed by an awareness of war and macrocosmic misery.

CURZON, Robert, fourteenth Baron Zouche (1810–73) Travel writer and collector of manuscripts, educated at Charterhouse and at Christ Church, Oxford. His *A Visit to Monasteries in the Levant* (1849) is a record of his travels to Mount Athos, Greece, Palestine, and Egypt in search of manuscripts, a number of which he purchased and removed to Britain. His other works include *An Account of the Most Celebrated Libraries of Italy* and *Armenia*, both published in 1854.

CURZON OF KEDLESTON, George Nathaniel, Marquess (1859–1925) First son of Baron Scarsdale of Kedleston Hall, Derbyshire. He attended Eton College and Balliol College, Oxford, entered Parliament in 1886, travelled widely, and wrote several books on the Orient, including *Persia and the Persian Question* (1892) and *Tales of Travel* (1923). As viceroy of India (1899–1905) he was an effective if inflexible reformer. He established the Archaeological Survey of India and saved the Taj Mahal from destruction. Twice married to American heiresses, he thrived on pomp and power. He was foreign secretary (1919–22) but was devastated not to become prime minister.

CUSK, Rachel (1967–) Novelist and critic. She was born in Canada, and read English at New College, Oxford. *Saving Agnes* (1993, Whitbread First Novel Award) is an eloquent and witty account of the frustrations and disappointments of an insecure Oxford-educated young woman, and her efforts towards salvation. Widely acclaimed for their prose style and perceptive interpretation of domestic life, her subsequent novels include *The Temporary* (1995); *The Country Life* (1997), a bizarre comic novel about a woman who leaves London to become an au pair in the country; and *The Lucky Ones* (2003). *In the Fold* (2005) and *Arlington Park* (2006) are concerned with the dubious morality of the English middle class. In 2003, **Granta* named Cusk among the Best of Young British Novelists. *A Life's Work* (2001) is an unsentimental, often bleak memoir about becoming a mother.

Custom of the Country, The A tragicomedy by John *Fletcher and Philip *Massinger, composed between 1619 and 1622; derived from the *Persiles y Sigismunda* of *Cervantes. *Dryden thought it more bawdy than any Restoration play, and *Pepys declared it 'of all the plays that ever I did see, the worst—having neither plot, language, nor anything in the earth that is acceptable' (2 January 1667).

Count Clodio, an Italian governor, claims his *droit de seigneur* ('the custom of the country') from Zenocia on her marriage to Arnoldo; she, Arnoldo, and Arnoldo's brother Rutilio escape by sea, but Zenocia is captured by a Portuguese captain and placed in service in Lisbon with Hippolita, who falls in love with Arnoldo and seeks Zenocia's destruction. There is an elaborate sub-plot involving Rutilio, his adventures in a brothel, and a duel. An adaptation by Nicholas Wright was performed by the Royal Shakespeare Company in 1983, and the play was given a staged reading at the *Globe Theatre in 1998.

Custom of the Country, The A witty and satiric novel by Edith *Wharton, published in 1913, in which a beautiful, energetic, destructive, and ambitious American, Undine Spragg, works her way to wealth and power through a succession of marriages.

CUTHBERT, St (*c*.635–687) Bishop of Lindisfarne. In 651, he entered the monastery of Melrose, of which he became prior. He later became prior of Lindisfarne, but received a vocation to the solitary life, and retired to the small island of Farne. In 684, at a synod held under St Theodore, archbishop of Canterbury, Cuthbert was selected for the see of Lindisfarne. After two years, feeling death approaching, he retired to the solitude of his island, and died in his cell on 20 March (his feast day) 687. His body, which was said to have remained for many years in a state of incorruption and was carried away by the monks when they were driven by the Danes from Lindisfarne, was finally buried in Durham Cathedral. His life is comparatively well documented in prose and poetry, one extended account appearing in *The *Ecclesiastical History of the English People* by *Bede.

CUTLER, Ivor *See* PERFORMANCE POETRY.

cyberpunk A term coined in the 1980s to describe the work of *science fiction writers like William *Gibson and Bruce *Sterling, who championed its cause in his *fanzine *Cheap Truth* and edited perhaps the definitive anthology, *Mirrorshades* (1986) also containing Pat *Cadigan and John *Shirley. The term itself derives from 'cybernetic'—signifying the human–machine flow of information through body modifications, computer connections, and virtual reality systems—and 'punk', particularly the rebellious youth culture derived from the punk-rock music scene. Perhaps the definitive texts were Gibson's short stories and his first novel *Neuromancer* (1984), in which a semi-criminal 'console cowboy' engages physically with the 'consensual hallucination' of cyberspace. However, earlier science fiction such as Alfred *Bester's *Tiger! Tiger!* (1956) and John *Brunner's *The Shockwave Rider* (1975) was influential in attitude or theme, as was the language of William *Burroughs filtered through *New Wave science fiction, and the tone of *noir movies and *hardboiled crime writers. Cyberpunk was quickly adopted as an emblem for postmodernism for its iconoclastic approach to both genre boundaries and lifestyle, but while it brought an energetic freshness to science fiction, later writers became dissatisfied with its masculine limitations and focus upon the street at the expense of the wider economy.

cyborg A term derived from 'cybernetic organism' to signify a fusion of human and machine. In *science fiction, this allows a rich range of explorations of the sense of uncanniness as we confront an Other. Deirdre, in C. L. *Moore's 'No Woman Born' (1944), who has her brain inserted into a metal body, inspires unease because of her and her companions' questions about her identity. Is she still human? Or female? Other fictions, such as Cordwainer *Smith's 'Scanners Live in vain' (1950) and Frederik *Pohl's *Man Plus* (1976), explore the deliberate creation of cyborgs to cope with hostile environments such as space.

Cymbeline A play by *Shakespeare, first published in the first *folio of 1623. It may have been written in 1610/11; Simon *Forman saw a performance, perhaps at the *Globe, probably in April 1611. He refers to its heroine as Innogen, not Imogen as printed in the folio, and this form is adopted by the Oxford and other editors. Its sources are *Holinshed, *A *Mirror for Magistrates*, and perhaps Boccaccio's **Decameron* (*see also* PHILASTER). Though included among the tragedies in the folio, it is now generally classified as a 'romance', and is more highly regarded than it was by Samuel *Johnson, who said that 'To remark the folly of the fiction, the absurdity of the conduct, the confusion of the names and manners of different times, and the impossibility of the events in any system of life, were to waste criticism upon unresisting imbecility, upon faults too evident for detection, and too gross for aggravation.' The play was much loved in the 19th century, however; *Tennyson died with a copy of it on the coverlet of his bed. G. B. *Shaw wrote an altered version of the long fifth act, published in 1938 under the title *Cymbeline Refinished*.

Innogen, daughter of Cymbeline, king of Britain, has secretly married Leonatus Posthumus, a 'poor but worthy gentleman'. The queen, Innogen's stepmother, determined that her clownish son Cloten shall marry Innogen, reveals the secret marriage to the king, who banishes Posthumus. In Rome Posthumus boasts of Innogen's virtue and makes a wager with Giacomo that if he can seduce Innogen he shall have a diamond ring that Innogen had given him. Giacomo is rejected by Innogen, but by hiding in her bedchamber he observes details of her room and her body which persuade Posthumus of her infidelity, and he receives the ring. Posthumus orders his servant Pisanio to kill Innogen; but Pisanio instead provides her with male disguise, sending a bloody cloth to Posthumus to convince him of her death. Under the name Fidele Innogen becomes a page to Belarius and Cymbeline's two lost sons, Guiderius and Arviragus, living in a cave in Wales. Fidele sickens and is found as dead by the brothers, who speak the dirge 'Fear no more the heat o'th'sun'. Left alone she revives, only to discover at her side Cloten's headless corpse, which she believes, because of his borrowed garments, to be that of her husband Posthumus. A Roman army invades Britain; Innogen falls into the hands of the general Lucius and becomes his page. The Britons defeat the Romans, thanks to the courage of Belarius and his two sons, aided by the disguised Posthumus. However, Posthumus, pretending to be a Roman, is subsequently taken prisoner. Lucius pleads with Cymbeline for the life of Fidele/Innogen: moved by something familiar in her appearance, he spares her life and grants her a favour. She asks that Giacomo be forced to tell how he came by the ring he wears. Posthumus, learning from this confession that his wife is innocent but believing her dead, is in despair till Innogen reveals herself. The king's joy at recovering his daughter is intensified when Belarius restores to him his two lost sons, and the scene ends in a general reconciliation. Tennyson described Posthumus' words to Innogen on being reconciled with her, 'Hang there like fruit, my soul, | Till the tree die!', as 'the tenderest lines in Shakespeare'.

Cymodoce A sea nymph, one of the Nereids in Greek mythology. Cymodoce is the name of Marinell's mother in Edmund *Spenser's **Faerie Queene* (IV. xii). A. C. *Swinburne's 'Garden of Cymodoce' in *Songs of the Springtides* (1880) is the island of Sark.

CYNEWULF Probably a Northumbrian or Mercian poet of the 9th or early 10th century. Modern scholarship restricts attribution to him of four extant poems, all of which end with his signature in runes. They are *Juliana* (the life of a virgin martyr) and *Christ II* in the *Exeter Book (the last is a poem on the Ascension, placed between poems on the Incarnation and on the Last Judgement, the three together also often treated as a composite poem, *Christ*); and *The Fates of the Apostles* (of slightly more doubtful attribution than the others) and *Elene*, the story of the finding of the Cross by St Helena, the mother of the Roman emperor Constantine, in the *Vercelli Book. Together these constitute a formidable poetic corpus of material and stylistic variety. See S. A. J. Bradley (trans.), *Anglo-Saxon Poetry* (1982); Earl R. Anderson, *Cynewulf* (1983); *Juliana*, ed. R. Woolf (1955); *Elene*, ed. P. O. E. Gradon (1958).

Cynthia (1) a name for Artemis or Diana, from Mount Cynthus in Delos, where Artemis was born, and used poetically to denote the moon; (2) the name given by the Roman poet *Propertius to his mistress; (3) deriving from (1), a name used by Edmund *Spenser (in **Colin Clouts Come Home Againe*), Walter *Ralegh, and others to denote *Elizabeth I as virgin moon goddess.

Cynthia's Revels An allegorical comedy by Ben *Jonson, performed 1600 by the Children of the Chapel at the *Blackfriars Theatre, printed 1601. The play satirizes court vices represented by characters with Greek names signifying their failings. Courtiers and ladies assemble for revels ordained by the goddess Cynthia (representing *Elizabeth I) and all drink from the Fountain of Self-Love (the play's sub-title). They perform in *masques, devised by the wise poet Crites, in which each character impersonates his complementary virtue. With the aid of *Mercury, sent by Jove to purge the court, Crites exposes the masquers, and as penance they go on a pilgrimage to drink the waters of Mount Helicon, the fountain of truth. Various characters have been tentatively identified with Robert Devereux, second earl of *Essex, Lucy, countess of Bedford (*c.*1581–1627), Jonson's patron, and his rival playwrights John *Marston and Thomas *Dekker. As usual in plays acted by boys, who were also choristers, there are numerous songs, including 'Queen and huntress, chaste and fair', one of Jonson's most famous.
See Paul's, Children of.

Cypresse Grove, A *See* Drummond of Hawthornden.

CYRANO DE BERGERAC (1619–55) French soldier, dramatist, and novelist, author of the intellectually daring (and therefore posthumously published) *L'Autre Monde* (*The Other World*), which prefigures modern *science fiction. His colourful and controversial life is the subject of a highly successful play by Edmond *Rostand.

D

DABYDEEN, David (1956–) Guyanese-born poet and novelist, educated at Cambridge and at University College London. Recurrent themes in Dabydeen's poetry include an exploration of slavery and indentureship, the cultural denigration and dislocation resulting from colonialism, and the power of language to redeem. *Slave Song* (1984) is notable for its innovative use of Guyanese rural Creole; the poems are accompanied by a 'translation' and commentary in Standard English highlighting the cultural power relationships between the two forms of language. *Turner* (1994) uses language that approaches Standard English and exhibits a sensuous lyrical beauty in contrast to the harshness and vulgarity of language in *Slave Song*. This long poem takes the submerged African head in J. M. W. *Turner's painting *The Slave Ship* (1840) as its starting point and negotiates the problems of history and identity the Middle Passage represents, exploring the creative as well as dislocating aspects inherent in this experience. Dabydeen's first novel, *The Intended* (1991), refers to Joseph *Conrad's 'Heart of Darkness' and is set in multicultural south London, following the learning experiences of a clever Guyanese schoolboy; *Disappearance* (1993) is narrated by a West Indian engineer working in a Kentish village, and *The Counting House* (1996) is a migrants' story set in the 19th century. *A Harlot's Progress* (1999) imagines the life of the black boy in William *Hogarth's series of pictures; *Our Lady of Demerara* (2004) is a quest novel. Dabydeen has written extensively on cultural diversity and postcolonial issues, and teaches at the University of Warwick.

DACIER, Anne (*c*.1651–1720) Née Lefebvre, French translator and woman of letters. Best known for her prose translation of Homer, which was in turn translated by John Ozell, she was the most celebrated Hellenist of her day.

DACRE, Charlotte (?1782–1825) The pseudonym of Charlotte Byrne, née King, under which name she published erotically charged *Gothic fictions. Also a poet, writing as 'Rosa Matilda' for the **Morning Post* (a London daily newspaper), Dacre published with her sister Sophia her first volume of verse, *Trifles of Helicon* (1798), republishing her own contributions to that volume as Charlotte Dacre in *Hours of Solitude* (1805). Heavy with repressed desire, the poems reputedly influenced Lord *Byron's **Hours of Idleness* (1807), although he later satirized her (as 'Rosa Matilda') in **English Bards and Scotch Reviewers* (1809). *The Poetical Register* for 1811 scorned her poetic efforts thus: 'Rosa Matilda' is 'lamentably deficient in taste and judgement' and would, 'we think, have acted more wisely had she excluded from her collection nearly one half of her poems'. She also published in 1805 a notorious Gothic novel, *The Confessions of the Nun of St. Omer*, which was followed in 1806 by **Zofloya, or The Moor*, the fiction by which she is best known today.

dactyl A trisyllabic metrical *foot in which the first syllable only is stressed. The dactylic *hexameter was the line of Greek epic verse; but continuous dactylic *metre is rare in English: Alfred Tennyson's 'The *Charge of the Light Brigade' (1854) employs truncated dactylic *dimeters, Thomas *Hardy's 'The Voice' (1914) dactylic *tetrameters.

DADD, Richard (1817–86) English painter, who is best known for his fairy pictures (*see* FAIRY STORIES) filled with meticulous, tiny detail. They follow Joshua *Reynolds, Henry *Fuseli, and Joseph Noel Paton (1821–1901) in illustrating scenes from *A *Midsummer Night's Dream* and *The *Tempest*. Dadd went mad in 1843 and murdered his father; he spent the rest of his life in Bethlehem Hospital and in Broadmoor. His most famous work is *The Fairy Feller's Master-Stroke* (1855–64); a manuscript poem by Dadd (dated 1865) explains its subject in detail. See Patricia Allderidge, *The Late Richard Dadd* (1974).

DAFYDD AP GWILYM (*c*.1315–*c*.1350) Welsh poet, probably born in Ceredigion and educated in the monastery at Strata Florida there. Though of noble lineage, he became a professional poet, travelling through Wales to give performances of his work. Of great formal variety and technical resourcefulness, his poems marry European conventions (notably that of *courtly love) to indigenous modes. Dafydd perfected the seven-syllable *cywydd* metre that would dominate Welsh art poetry for centuries. The formality of his poetry is tempered by colloquialism and by a frequently punning linguistic playfulness. His work can be simultaneously amorous and religious and is infused throughout by a strong sense of personality. See Richard Loomis (ed.), *Dafydd ap Gwilym: The Poems, Translation and Commentary* (1982).

Dagon The national deity of the ancient *Philistines, whose temple Samson pulled down (Judg. 16: 23–30; 1 Sam. 5: 1–5). See Milton's **Paradise Lost*, I. 456–66, and **Samson Agonistes*.

D'AGUIAR, Fred (1960–) Poet and novelist, born in London, and brought up as a child in Guyana: he returned to school in Britain aged 12, and studied at the universities of Kent and Warwick. He has written three volumes of poetry, *Mama Dot* (1985), which explores his early life in Guyana, *Airy Hall* (1989), and *British Subjects* (1993), which closely examines British and transcultural identity and contains a sequence called 'Frail Deposits', dedicated to Wilson *Harris, about a return trip to Guyana. His novels are *The Longest Memory* (1994), an intense, lyrical, brutal evocation of the life of Whitechapel, an 18th-century plantation slave in Virginia; *Dear Future* (1997), whose title refers to the letters its clairvoyant child protagonist writes to the future; and *Feeding the Ghosts* (1997), about the voyage of a slave ship returning from Africa, the captain of which throws his sick slaves overboard and is held to account by a survivor. The protagonist of *Bethany Bettany* (2003) is a 5-year-old girl whose mother hands her over to her dead father's family; she becomes a scapegoat for all their resentments. D'Aguiar's stage play *A Jamaican Airman Foresees his Death* was staged at the *Royal Court in 1995. *Bill of Rights* (1998) is a long poem on the theme of the 1978 Jonestown massacre/mass suicide in Guyana; *Bloodlines* (2000) is a narrative poem in rhyming verse about a black slave and her white lover.
See SLAVERY.

DAHL, Roald (1916–1990) Short story writer, novelist, and children's writer, born of Norwegian parents in Llandaff, Wales, educated at Repton School, Derbyshire. He describes his unhappy schooldays in the autobiographical *Boy* (1984) and his career in the RAF and with Shell in *Going Solo* (1986). His first collection of stories, *Over to You* (USA 1946, UK 1947) drew on his wartime experiences as a fighter pilot. While assistant air attaché in Washington in 1942, he negotiated unsuccessfully with Disney to film his story *The Gremlins*, which became his first book (1943/4). He established a reputation as a writer with a penchant for the macabre and the 'cruel tale': major collections include *Someone Like You* (USA 1953, UK 1954), *Kiss Kiss* (1960), and *Switch Back* (1974). Many of his stories were dramatized for television and subsequently republished as *Tales of the Unexpected* (1979). Dahl also wrote film scripts, including two books by Ian *Fleming, *You Only Live Twice* (1967) and *Chitty Chitty Bang Bang* (1968). In 1961 he published his first novel for children, *James and the Giant Peach* (UK 1967), followed by the phenomenally successful *Charlie and the Chocolate Factory* (1964, UK 1967). Fundamentally a didactic tale in which the bad children are horribly punished and the good child extravagantly rewarded, the book was filmed, in a version that Dahl disliked, as *Willie Wonka and the Chocolate Factory* (Mel Stuart, 1971, with Gene Wilder). It was filmed again in 2005 (Tim Burton, with Johnny Depp).

Dahl became the world's most successful children's writer in the 1970s and 1980s with books such as *The BFG* (1982)—which included the queen as a character—and *Matilda* (1988), many of which have been filmed and/or adapted for the stage. His books have been widely criticized for misogyny (*The Witches*, 1983), racism (the 'oompa-loompas' in *Charlie and the Chocolate Factory* were originally portrayed as black pygmies), and, generally, for violence and right-wing views. The later stages of his career benefited from a partnership with the illustrator Quentin *Blake. There is an 'unauthorized' biography by Jeremy Treglown (1994) and a museum and story centre in Great Missenden, Buckinghamshire.

DAHLBERG, Edward (1900–77) American novelist and prose writer, born in Boston. His first novel, *Bottom Dogs* (1929), was published with an introduction by D. H. *Lawrence and is an example of proletarian fiction like his other early novels *From Flushing to Calvary* (1932) and *Those Who Perish* (1934). *Do These Bones Live?* (1941) is an extended meditation on the American literary heritage of Edgar Allan *Poe and others. Dahlberg later published two autobiographies, *Because I Was Flesh* (1964) and *The Confessions of Edward Dahlberg* (1971).

Daily News Founded by Charles *Dickens in 1845 as a Liberal rival to the **Morning Chronicle*; the first issue appeared on 21 January 1846. Dickens himself edited the paper for seventeen numbers only, then handed over to John *Forster. Among its notable contributors and members of staff were Harriet *Martineau, Andrew *Lang, George Bernard *Shaw, H. G. *Wells, Arnold *Bennett, and the eminent war correspondent Archibald Forbes (1839–1900). It became the *News Chronicle* in 1930, having absorbed the *Daily Chronicle*, and survived under this title until 1960.

Daily Telegraph Founded in 1855, the first London daily paper to be issued at a penny. Its enterprising character and colourful style proved so successful that for a time it enjoyed a larger circulation than any other English newspaper. In its early days, with Thornton *Hunt as assistant editor, its political views were radical. After a period of decline in the early 20th century, circulation recovered in the 1930s; in 1937 the **Morning Post* was incorporated. The *Sunday Telegraph* was added in 1961. Among famous members of its staff have been G. A. *Sala, Sir Edwin *Arnold, Edward Dicey (1832–1911), and Sir William Deedes (1913–2007; the model for Evelyn *Waugh's character William Boot, in his 1938 Fleet Street novel *Scoop*).

Daisy Miller One of Henry *James's most popular stories, published 1879, dramatized by James (1883). Daisy Miller travels to Europe with her wealthy, commonplace mother, and in her innocence and audacity offends convention and seems to compromise her reputation. She dies in Rome of malaria. She is one of the most notable and charming of James's portrayals of 'the American girl'.

DALRYMPLE, Sir David, Lord Hailes (1726–92) Scottish lawyer, historian, and antiquary, a friend of James *Boswell, Samuel *Johnson, and Horace *Walpole. His two-volume *Annals of Scotland* (1776, 1779) was admired by Johnson for its empirical methodology and directness of address. An enthusiastic admirer of ancient Scottish poems and ballads, he edited the *Bannatyne Manuscript and corresponded with Thomas *Percy, for whose *Reliques* he provided texts.

DALRYMPLE, William (1965–) Historian, travel writer, and journalist born in Scotland, educated at Ampleforth College and at Trinity College, Cambridge. Dalrymple's books, many of them on India, include *In Xanadu* (1989), *City of Djinns* (1993), *From the Holy Mountain* (1997), *The Age of Kali* (1998), *White Mughals* (2002), and *The Last Mughal* (2006). Characterized by their deep historical research and elegant prose, his works have placed him at the forefront of a new generation of British travel writers. His mature writings challenge Samuel P. Huntington's 'clash of civilizations' theory and the orthodoxies of the 'war on terror' by focusing on the history of coexistence of Islam and Christianity and on the productive but often forgotten exchanges between them. Dalrymple, who divides his time between Delhi and London, has also written and presented television and radio programmes, including the television series 'Indian Journeys'.

Damascus, road to *See* PAUL, ST.

Damoetas A pastoral name for (1) a shepherd in the *Idylls* of *Theocritus and the *Eclogues* of *Virgil; (2) a base herdsman who has become a royal favourite in Philip *Sidney's **Arcadia*; (3) an old shepherd (possibly representing a Cambridge academic) in John *Milton's **Lycidas*.

Damon A shepherd singer in *Virgil's eighth *Eclogue*; a name adopted by poets for a rustic swain. Cf. *Epitaphium Damonis*, *Milton's Latin elegy on his friend Diodati.

Damon and Pythias A rhymed play by Richard *Edwards, acted at court and at Lincoln's Inn during the Christmas season of 1564–5, printed 1571. Damon and Pythias, Pythagorean Greeks, visit Syracuse, and Damon is arrested on a false charge of conspiring against Dionysius, the tyrant of Syracuse, who orders his execution. Damon is given two months to return home to settle his affairs, Pythias offering himself as security for his return. Damon is delayed and arrives when Pythias is about to be put to death. They contend which shall be executed, each striving to save the other. Dionysius, impressed with their mutual loyalty, pardons Damon and asks to be admitted to their brotherhood. In the original legend it is Phintias (of which 'Pythias' is a corruption), not Damon, who is sentenced, and Damon goes bail for him.

DAMPIER, William (1652–1715) Buccaneer and explorer, the son of a tenant farmer from Somerset. Apprenticed a seaman at 18, he graduated to buccaneering in Spanish America, and eventually made three circumnavigations of the globe. His lively accounts of his adventures, particularly *A New Voyage round the World* (1697) and *A Voyage to New Holland* (1703, 1709), set the vogue for exploration narratives as entertainment and inspired fictional works. He participated in expeditions that marooned and rescued Alexander *Selkirk, the model for **Robinson Crusoe*. His extended description of Aboriginal Australians—the first—stereotyped them for centuries as 'the miserablest People in the world'. While his scientific interest in plants and peoples was new, and his commentaries on ocean currents and prevailing winds had lasting value, he displayed vestiges of older enthusiasms for 'marvels'. His career was marred by accusations of brutality and drunkenness and he died in poverty.

DANA, Richard Henry (1815–82) Son of the poet and journalist Richard Henry Dana (1787–1879), born in Massachusetts. In 1834, he broke off his education at Harvard to embark as a common sailor, hoping to recover from 'a weakness of the eyes'. The ensuing voyage, from Boston around Cape Horn to California, was described in *Two Years before the Mast*. Published anonymously in 1840, it gives a vivid and moving account of his adventures, and of the harsh working conditions endured by sailors in this period, and is now regarded as a classic of sea literature.

Dance of Death (danse macabre, danse macabré) Gave expression to the sense especially prominent in the 15th century (perhaps as a consequence of the plague and the preaching of the mendicant friars) of the ubiquity of Death the leveller. The Dance appears to have first taken shape in France, as a mimed sermon in which figures typical of various orders of society were seized and hauled away each by its own corpse (not, as later, by the personification of Death). The earliest known painting of the Dance, accompanied by versified dialogues between living and dead, was made in 1424 in the cemetery of the Innocents in Paris, and the German artists (including Hans *Holbein) who later depicted it appear to have drawn inspiration from French sources. The origin of the word *macabre* or *macabré* has been the subject of many conjectures, such as that the latter is a corruption of Old French *Macabé*, to refer to a mystery play in which the Apocryphal killing of the Maccabees by Antiochus was represented.

DANE, Clemence (1888–1965) Pseudonym of Winifred Ashton, novelist and playwright, born in London; she worked as a teacher and actress before turning to writing. Her experiences as a teacher in a girls' school are reflected in her first novel, *Regiment of Women* (1917), which explores a lesbian relationship. Her first play, *A Bill of Divorcement* (1921), enjoyed a popular success never quite matched by her later plays, which include *Will Shakespeare* (1921), a blank verse drama, and *Wild Decembers* (1932), about the *Brontës.

DANGAREMBGA, Tsitsi (1959–) Film director and writer, born in Zimbabwe, and educated there and in Britain. Her novel *Nervous Conditions* (1988) challenges colonial and Shona patriarchy. Its opening line, 'I was not sorry when my brother died', defies the gendered role expected of the narrator, Tambudzai; she inherits her brother's education but it familiarizes her with a range of female nervous conditions. She recognizes that men control the traditional and the modernizing Rhodesian world. A second novel, *The Book of Not* (2006), continues Tambu's personal liberation struggle, which takes place during her country's violent guerrilla war.

Daniel An Old English poem of 764 lines, in the *Junius Manuscript. It paraphrases the Old Testament Book of Daniel. See R.T. Farrell (ed.), *Daniel and Azarias* (1974).

Daniel, Book of *See* BIBLE.

DANIEL, (Charles) Henry Olive (1836–1919) Scholar, fellow, and provost of Worcester College, Oxford, remembered for his lifelong interest in printing. In 1874, he established a private press—a precursor of the larger revival in fine printing—at Oxford, where he used the *Fell types and handmade paper, producing some fine examples of typography, including plays and poems of Robert *Bridges. A memorial volume, *The Daniel Press 1845–1919* (1921–2), was compiled by his friends.

DANIEL, Samuel (?1562–1619) Poet and historian. He entered Magdalen Hall, Oxford, in 1579, and after visiting Italy, where he met the pastoral poet *Guarini, he became tutor to William Herbert, third earl of Pembroke (1580–1630), and later to Lady Anne *Clifford, daughter of the countess of Cumberland. In 1592 he published *Delia*, a collection of sonnets inspired by *Tasso and Philippe Desportes (1546–1606), to which was appended the *'Complaint of Rosamund'. Edmund *Spenser mentioned him by name in **Colin Clouts Come Home Againe*. Daniel quickly made the transition to tragedy, his next work being **Cleopatra* (1594), a Senecan tragedy closely related to *Antonius* by the countess of *Pembroke, itself translated from Garnier in 1590. *Musophilus: Containing a General Defence of Learning* appeared in 1599. In 1603 he welcomed *James I's accession with a *Panegyric Congratulatory*, and published his verse 'Epistles' and *A Defence of Rhyme*, the last being a reply to Thomas *Campion's *Observations in the Art of English Poesy.* His career as a court poet developed with his masques and plays, *The Vision of the Twelve Goddesses* (1604), *The Queen's Arcadia* (1606), *Tethys' Festival* (1610), and *Hymen's Triumph* (performed 1614, published 1615). Early in 1604 he became licenser for the Children of the Queen's Revels, but he renounced this lucrative office in April 1605. This may have been because of the row caused by his second tragedy, **Philotas*, performed in the autumn of 1604, which was held—perhaps justly—to allude closely and sympathetically to the rebellion of the earl of *Essex in 1600. Daniel affixed an 'Apology', claiming that any resemblance to the Essex affair was purely coincidental, when the play was published in 1605. His position at court then seems to have recovered. His weightiest work was his **Civil Wars*, a verse epic on the Wars of the Roses. Four books appeared in 1595, and the complete eight books in 1609. A prose history of England from the Romans to Edward III, *The Collection of the History of England*, was his last work. Ben *Jonson called Daniel 'a good honest Man...but no poet'; other contemporaries valued him, such as William *Browne, who called him 'Well-languaged *Daniel*'. In later times his greatest admirers have been in the Romantic period. Charles *Lamb, William *Wordsworth, and S. T. *Coleridge were among those who read him appreciatively, the last finding his style and language as 'pure and manly' as Wordsworth's own. The bibliographical complexity of Daniel's texts, combined with a decline in admiration for his plain manner, may account for the lack of any complete edition of his works since Alexander *Grosart's of 1885–96.

Daniel Deronda George *Eliot's last novel, published 1876. Gwendolen Harleth, high-spirited, confident, and self-centred, marries Henleigh Grandcourt, an arrogant, selfish, and cold-hearted man of the world, for his money and his position, to save her mother, sisters, and herself from destitution, in spite of the fact that she knows of (and has indeed met) Lydia Glasher, who has had a long-standing affair with Grandcourt, and children by him. She rejects Mrs Glasher's appeals and threats, and suffers in consequence in terms of guilt and a sense of her husband's increasing power over her. In her misery she comes increasingly under the influence of Daniel Deronda, who becomes her spiritual adviser. He is an idealistic young man whose own parentage is involved in mystery; it is gradually revealed that he is not, as he had assumed, an illegitimate cousin of Grandcourt, but the son of a Jewish singer of international renown. This discovery strengthens his bonds with Mirah, a young Jewish singer whom he has saved from drowning, and her brother Mordecai, an intellectual Jewish nationalist. Gwendolen's husband is drowned at Genoa, in a manner that leaves her feeling partly guilty for his death; she confesses to Deronda, but discovers to her initial despair that he is to marry Mirah and devote himself to the Jewish cause and the founding of a Jewish national home. Notable among the minor characters is Klesmer, the musician, who persuades Gwendolen that her talent as a singer, though acceptable in an amateur, would not repay training, thus unwittingly pushing her towards her disastrous marriage. One of the themes of the novel is the nature of professional and artistic dedication, explored through Gwendolen's dilettante expectations, Klesmer's seriousness and insistence on constant application, Mirah's acceptance of a hard-working but less than illustrious career, and the passionate and self-glorifying commitment of Deronda's mother, who sacrificed her own child to her success.

The Jewish plot was condemned by critics, by Henry *James (*Daniel Deronda: A Conversation*, 1876) for being 'at bottom cold', and by F. R. *Leavis (*The Great Tradition*, 1948) as 'embarrassingly fervid'. Recent critical approaches have been more sympathetic to the scope of the novel's complex fusion of political and psychological interests.

D'ANNUNZIO, Gabriele (1863–1938) Italian novelist, playwright, and poet. A nationalist favouring the reclamation of territory from Austro-Hungarian rule, he is best remembered for his occupation of Fiume (1919–21) following Italy's failure to secure territories in the Balkans after the First World War. His novel *Il piacere* (1889: *The Child of Pleasure*) is important to European *decadence. His later novels, which include *Trionfo della morte* (1894: *Triumph of Death*) and *Il fuoco* (1900: *The Flame of Life*), were strongly influenced by the ideas of *Nietzsche. Some of his plays were set to music, one in French, *Le Martyre de Saint Sébastien* (1911), by Claude *Debussy, and *Parisina* (1913) by Pietro Mascagni (1863–1945). *La figlia di Iorio* (1904: *Iorio's Daughter*), set in his native Abruzzi, is significant among his plays, while his poetry is strongly represented in *Alcyone* and in *Maia*, part of the four-volume collection *Laudi* (1904: *Praises*). As a poet he was influenced by *Symbolism and the *Pre-Raphaelites. His prose style was admired by James *Joyce. See J. R. Woodhouse, *Gabriele d'Annunzio: Defiant Archangel* (1998).

DANTE ALIGHIERI (1265–1321) Poet, was born at Florence of a Guelf family. The circumstances of his early life are obscure, but in 1277 he was formally betrothed to his future wife, Gemma Donati, and in 1289 he took part in military operations against Arezzo and Pisa. During this early period of his life he fell in love with the girl whom he celebrates under the name of *Beatrice in the *Vita nuova* and the **Divina commedia*. When she died, in 1290, Dante was grief-stricken and sought consolation in the study of philosophy. In 1295 he became active in the political life of Florence. In June 1300 he was among the municipal priors who banished the leaders of the White and Black Guelf factions, and in October 1301 he was one of the three envoys sent to Rome to negotiate with Boniface VIII. During his absence the Blacks seized power and Dante, whose sympathies were with the Whites, became the victim of political reprisals. He spent the rest of his life in exile in various parts of northern Italy. He died at Ravenna, where he had for some years found refuge.

The precise dating of Dante's works remains a matter for debate. The first in order of composition (apart from his earliest lyric poems) was the *Vita nuova*, written in the period 1290–4, in which Dante brings together 31 poems, most of them relating to his love for Beatrice. A linking prose narrative tells the story of his love and interprets the poems from the standpoint of one who has come to see his beloved as the instrument of his spiritual salvation. There is a translation by Dante Gabriel *Rossetti (1861). The *Convivio*, or *Banquet*, is an unfinished philosophical work, planned as a series of fourteen treatises, each in the form of a prose commentary on one of Dante's own *canzoni*. The four completed treatises, written between 1304 and 1308, draw on numerous philosophical sources, but principally on *Aristotle. The Latin treatise *De Vulgari Eloquentia*, begun shortly before the *Convivio*, is also unfinished. The completed part consists of an enquiry into the form of vernacular language most suitable for lofty poetry, followed by the beginning of a discussion of the technique of the *canzone*. It is a pioneering work of historical linguistics. The *Monarchia*, written sometime between 1309 and 1319, is a Latin treatise on the universal empire and the relations between emperor and pope. It is very uncertain when Dante began his masterpiece, the *Divina commedia*. It was probably begun between 1306 and 1308, and was finished just before his death. The *Fiore*, an adaptation into Tuscan poetry of the **Roman de la Rose*, and the *Detto d'amore* are often attributed to the young Dante.

DANZIGER, Nick (1958–) Photojournalist and travel writer, born in London. He went to school in Switzerland and studied at Chelsea Art School. He travelled overland to China in 1984 on a Winston Churchill Memorial Trust Fellowship, a journey which involved crossing Afghanistan disguised as a mujahed during a Soviet offensive, and the subject of *Danziger's Travels* (1987). Its sequel, *Danziger's Adventures* (1992), is a collection of shorter pieces, juxtaposing accounts of news assignments to Tehran, Kabul, Kurdistan, and Tijuana alongside deadpan evocations of Danziger's more public appearances as a now-successful author on book tours, and of speaking engagements on cruise ships. Jack *London was the inspiration for *Danziger's Britain* (1997), an investigation of poverty in the United Kingdom.

Daphnaïda An elegy by Edmund *Spenser closely modelled on Geoffrey *Chaucer's **Book of the Duchess*.
See ALCYON.

Daphnis and Chloe A Greek pastoral romance written by an otherwise unknown 'Longus' perhaps in the 2nd or 3rd centuries AD. It describes in formal style the wakening of passion in its two protagonists. *Amyot's translation into French made it a popular text; Angel Day translated Amyot's version (1587), and there were several translations from the Greek in the 17th and 18th centuries. George *Moore produced a modern version in 1924, and the story provided the subject of a ballet with music by Ravel and choreography by Fokine, composed for Diaghilev and first performed in 1912.

DA PORTO, Luigi (1485–1529) Italian soldier, poet, and writer of novelle; his most famous work is the story of Romeo and Giulietta, subsequently elaborated by *Bandello, on whose version *Shakespeare drew for his **Romeo and Juliet*. Da Porto's source is Masuccio Salernitano's *Novellino*, but the choice of names for the protagonists, the setting in Verona, and the double tragedy of their deaths are Da Porto's innovations.

Dares Phrygius A Trojan priest mentioned in the **Iliad* (5. 9). He was supposed to have been the author of an account of the fall of Troy of which a Latin prose version is extant. This work, *De Excidio Troiae*, dating probably from the 5th century AD, provided, together with the complementary history of *Dictys Cretensis, the only detailed account of the Trojan War available in the medieval West. Everything written about Troy before the middle of the 17th century was to some extent dependent, directly or indirectly, on the narratives of Dares and Dictys.

Darkness at Noon A novel by Arthur *Koestler, published 1940, translated from German. It deals with the arrest, imprisonment, trial, and execution of N. S. Rubashov in an unnamed dictatorship over which 'No. 1' presides. Koestler describes Rubashov as 'a synthesis of the lives of a number of men who were victims of the so-called Moscow trials', and the novel did much to draw attention to the nature of Stalin's regime.

DARLEY, George (1795–1846) Poet, born in Dublin, the eldest of the seven children of a merchant, and educated at Trinity College, Dublin. He settled in London in 1821, and earned his living by writing textbooks on mathematics and as dramatic critic for the **London Magazine* and later as art critic for *The *Athenaeum*; he was a forerunner in the English rediscovery of early Italian painting. His first published poem was *The Errors of Ecstasie* (1822). *Sylvia*, a pastoral drama which was the most successful of his works in his own lifetime, followed in 1827. Many of his lyrics were published in magazines, the best known being *Syren Songs*, 'Serenade of a Loyal Martyr' (which may have influenced George *Meredith's 'Love in the Valley'), and 'It is not Beauty I demand', a 17th-century pastiche which F. T. *Palgrave included in his *Golden Treasury* under the impression that it was a genuine Caroline poem. Darley also published two historical plays, *Thomas à Becket* and *Ethelstan*. His finest work was his unfinished *Nepenthe*, privately printed 1835, an allegory of the imagination in excesses of joy or melancholy, partly inspired by John *Milton, P. B. *Shelley, and John *Keats, but containing some remarkable lyrics and passages of wild fantasy and highly skilled versification.

Darley suffered all his life from a severe stammer, which cut him off from most social activities, and he also had recurring headaches, probably some form of migraine. He never married, and his life was reclusive, but his friends—who included Charles *Lamb, Henry *Cary, John *Clare, Allan *Cunningham, Monckton *Milnes, and Thomas *Carlyle—admired him as an amiable, high-minded, and unjustly neglected poet, though he made some enemies by his virulent dramatic criticism. See C. C. Abbott, *The Life and Letters of George Darley* (1928); *Selected Poems of George Darley*, ed. Anne Ridler (1979).

DARTON family A prominent publishing dynasty associated particularly with the development of publishing for children, established by William Darton (1755–1819), who set up as an engraver, printer, and stationer in 1787. F. J. Harvey Darton (1878–1936) wrote the seminal history *Children's Books in England: Five Centuries of Social Life* (1932).

DARWIN, Charles (1809–82) Naturalist and author, born at Shrewsbury, grandson of Erasmus *Darwin, and educated at Edinburgh University and Christ's College, Cambridge. He embarked in 1831 with Robert *Fitzroy as naturalist on the *Beagle*, bound for South America, returned in 1836, and published in 1839 his *Journal of Researches into the Geology and Natural History of the Various Countries Visited by H.M.S. Beagle*. His great work *On the *Origin of Species by Means of Natural Selection* appeared in 1859. Darwin had received from Alfred Russel *Wallace a manuscript containing a sketch of his theory. Building upon the Uniformitarian geology of Charles Lyell (1797–1875), which supposed a very great antiquity for the earth and slow, regular change, Darwin argued for a natural, not divine, origin of species. In the competitive struggle for existence, creatures possessing advantageous mutations would be favoured, eventually evolving into new species. In the 'survival of the fittest' (a phrase coined by Herbert *Spencer, but accepted by Darwin) organic descent was achieved by natural selection, by analogy with the artificial selection of the stockbreeder. An orthodox Anglican as a young man, Darwin became an agnostic, seeing no higher moral or religious ends in evolution, only chance and necessity. Other evolutionists, such as Wallace and Spencer, by contrast, identified evolution with progress. Darwin's book gave rise to intense opposition, but found distinguished supporters in T. H. *Huxley, Lyell, and Sir Joseph Hooker (1817–1911); the reverberation of his ideas can be seen throughout the literature of the second half of the 19th century. In *The Descent of Man* (1871) Darwin discussed sexual selection, and argued that man too had evolved, from the higher primates, whereas Wallace made man a partial exception to this rule. Despite religious and humanist fears, evolutionism in general quickly won acceptance, but natural selection, Darwin's evolutionary mechanism, foundered for want of an adequate theory of inheritance until the rediscovery of Mendelian genetics, which led to the emergence of the modern evolutionary synthesis in the 1920s. A dedicated naturalist, Darwin also wrote extensively on barnacles, earthworms, and orchids, and was a pioneer observer of animal behaviour. *The Life and Letters of Darwin*, edited by his son Francis Darwin, appeared 1887–8, and several further volumes of letters have also been published. The Darwin Correspondence Project, based in Cambridge, has undertaken the process of making his extensive correspondence available online; see http://www.darwinproject.ac.uk; see also A. Desmond and J. Moore, *Darwin: The Life of a Tormented Evolutionist* (1991). For an account of the profound impact of his work on 19th-century fiction, see Gillian Beer, *Darwin's Plots* (1983).

DARWIN, Erasmus (1731–1802) Physician, natural philosopher, and poet, educated at Chesterfield School, St John's College, Cambridge, and Edinburgh. From 1756 he was a physician at Lichfield, where he established a botanical garden. After publishing research papers in *Philosophical Transactions* (*see* ROYAL SOCIETY), he embodied the botanical system of *Linnaeus (whose works he translated) in *The Loves of the Plants* (1789). This became Part II of *The Botanic Garden* (1791), of which Part I was 'The Economy of Vegetation'. The poem, supplemented by notes on many scientific and industrial matters, expounds an embryonic theory of evolution. It was targeted by George *Canning and John Hookham *Frere in 'The Loves of the Triangles', in the **Anti-Jacobin* in 1798. In his prose *Zoonomia* (1794–6), *Wordsworth's source for the story of Goody Blake, Darwin expounds the laws of organic life, normal and pathological, on evolutionary principles. His final didactic poems were *Phytologia*, on agriculture (1800), and *The Temple of Nature*, on the origins of society (1803). Anna *Seward published *Memoirs* of him in 1804, and his grandson Charles *Darwin, whose theories owe some initial impetus to his grandfather's controversial views, published an essay on his work in 1879. See Desmond King-Hele, *Erasmus Darwin: A Life of Unequalled Achievement* (1999).

DARWISH, Mahmoud (?1942–2008) Palestinian-born poet, who worked as a journalist in Haifa before moving to Cairo, Beirut, and Paris. He has published several volumes of poetry, mostly of national and political protest, sympathizing with the poor and dispossessed: a selection translated from the Arabic by Ian Wedde and Fawwaz Tuqan was published in 1973, followed by *The Music of Human Flesh* (1980, trans. D. Johnson-Davies) and *Sand and Other Poems* (1986, trans. Rana Kabbani). *The Adam of Two Edens: Selected Poems* appeared in 2001.

DAS, Kamala (1934–2009) Indian poet and novelist, born in Kerala, south India, into a literary household where both her mother and her grandparents were prominent Malayali poets. Das, bilingual in English and Malayalam, writes her poetry only in English, though it is distinguished by its freedom from Western literary influences and grammatical forms. Prominent for her intimate, outspoken exploration of Indian women's sexuality and domestic oppression, she created controversy with her autobiography *My Story* (1976) and its portrait of her early entrapment in an oppressive marriage. Her volumes of poems include *Summer in Calcutta* (1965), *The Descendants* (1967), and *The Old Playhouse and Other Poems* (1975). In 1984 she was awarded the Sahitya Akademi Prize for the first volume of her *Collected Poems*, and in 1985 the Asian World Prize for literature.

DASENT, Sir George Webbe (1817–96) Born in the West Indies and educated at Magdalen Hall, Oxford. He spent four years in Stockholm from 1841 studying Scandinavian literature and northern mythology. In 1845 he joined the staff of *The *Times* and in 1853 became professor of English literature at King's College London. He was an important figure in the popularization of Scandinavian literature and the interpretation of Icelandic sagas, publishing many translations. Among his publications are *Prose, or the Younger Edda* (1842), dedicated to Thomas *Carlyle, who had encouraged him, the *Grammar of the Icelandic or Old Norse Tongue* (1843), *Popular Tales from the Norse* (1859), and *The Story of Burnt Njal* (1861).

DAUDET, Alphonse (1840–97) Popular French novelist. Influenced by *naturalism, he is best known for his portrayal of life in his native Provence in *Lettres de mon moulin* (1869: *Letters from my Windmill*), which has been repeatedly translated into English, and as the creator of Tartarin, the ambitious and cowardly *provençal* character whose comic exploits are related in *Tartarin de Tarascon* (1872), *Tartarin sur les Alpes* (1885), *La Défense de Tarascon* (1886), and *Port-Tarascon* (1890). Daudet's other novels include the semi-autobiographical *Le Petit Chose* (1868: *Young What's His Name*) and *Numa Roumestan* (1881), which compares *méridional* and Parisian life. See M. Sachs, *The Career of Alphonse Daudet* (1965).

D'AVENANT, Sir William (1606–68) Playwright, poet, and theatre manager, born and educated in Oxford, rumoured to be the natural son of William *Shakespeare. His first play, *The Tragedy of Albovine*, was printed in 1629 but probably never performed; *The Cruel Brother* was performed in 1627, printed 1630. In 1630–32 he was gravely ill with syphilis, a subject referred to in his own works and in the jests of others; his first play on his recovery was probably his comic masterpiece *The *Wits*, performed 1633, printed 1636. In 1638 he succeeded to Ben *Jonson's pension as unofficial *poet laureate, then actively supported Charles I in the Civil War and was knighted by him in 1643 at the siege of Gloucester. In 1645 he visited Paris, where he met Thomas *Hobbes, to whom he addressed his *Preface* (1650) to **Gondibert* (1651). He was imprisoned in the Tower in 1650–52, and is said to have been saved by John *Milton. With *The *Siege of Rhodes* (1656) he simultaneously evaded the ban on stage plays and produced one of the earliest English operas (but *see also* FLECKNOE, RICHARD), with an entertainment that combined music and instruction. After the *Restoration he and Thomas *Killigrew the elder obtained patents from Charles II giving them the monopoly of acting in London; his charter for the Duke's House, Lincoln's Inn, was later transferred to Covent Garden. Among the innovations of the period were movable scenery and the use of actresses. In conjunction with John Dryden, D'Avenant adapted various of Shakespeare's plays to suit the taste of the day, among them *The *Tempest* (1667); he is satirized with John *Dryden in Buckingham's *The *Rehearsal*. His poems and songs (which include 'The lark now leaves his wat'ry nest') were edited by A. M. Gibbs in 1972.

DAVENPORT, Guy (1927–2005) American writer, painter, and translator, born in South Carolina. His best-known essay collection is *The Geography of the Imagination* (1981), and he also published several volumes of poetry. But he became known mainly for his short stories which deploy a wide range of verbal registers and narrative collage effects; his first volume was *Tatlin!* (1974), followed by *Da Vinci's Bicycle* (1979) and *Eclogues* (1981). The last of these uses classical literature as a base, and Davenport's varied output includes his translations of Archilochos, Sappho, and others. Like Donald *Barthelme, he was interested in the visual arts, including printing and book design, and he prepared a special edition of Canto CX for Ezra *Pound's 80th birthday. He experimented with typography and graphics in a number of his works.

DAVID *Bible poet and second king of Israel (reigned *c.*1010–*c.*970 BC). A figure of immense importance for Judaism and Christianity as the greatest king, creator of *Jerusalem as the capital of the nation, recipient of the covenant originally made with Abraham, and ancestor of Jesus, David has fascinated writers as a supremely noble and devastatingly human figure, and as an archetypal poet, 'the sweet psalmist of Israel' (2 Sam. 23: 1).

A youngest son and shepherd boy, he is anointed king by Samuel while Saul still reigns. His music soothes Saul's troubled spirit, and his skill with the sling overcomes the Philistine champion, Goliath. War between Saul and David ends when Saul and his son Jonathan die in battle with the Philistines. His lament for them is a high point of biblical poetry ('How are the mighty fallen!', 2 Sam. 1: 27). While he unites and strengthens the kingdom, his personal and family life disintegrates. The turning point is his adultery with Bathsheba, whose husband Uriah he has killed in battle.

He is traditionally the author of the *Psalms, many of which have been connected with incidents in his life. See 1 Samuel to 1 Kings 2, also 1 Chronicles 10–29.

David and Fair Bethsabe, The Love of King A play in blank verse by George *Peele, *c.*1581–94, printed 1599. Its sources are mainly scriptural, offering a highly poeticized account of King *David's seduction of Bethsabe (Bathsheba) and the death of his son Absalon.

David Copperfield A novel by Charles *Dickens, published 1849–50. 'Of all my books,' wrote Dickens, 'I like this the best.' It has always been a favourite with a wide public, and has been filmed and adapted for television on numerous occasions. The most autobiographical of Dickens's novels, it was the first to be written as a first-person narrative, showing how the young David learns to govern 'the first mistaken impulse of the undisciplined heart'. David Copperfield is born at Blunderstone (of which the original is the village of Blundeston) in Suffolk, soon after the death of his father. His mother, a gentle, weak woman, marries again, and the hypocritical cruelty of her second husband, Mr Murdstone, and his sister Jane Murdstone drives her to an early grave. Young Copperfield, who has proved recalcitrant, is sent to school, where he is bullied by the tyrannical headmaster Creakle, but makes two friends in the fascinating Steerforth and the good-humoured plodding Traddles. A period of menial employment in London, where he lives a life of poverty and misery, is enlivened by his acquaintance with the impecunious Mr Micawber. He runs away and walks penniless to Dover to throw himself on the mercy of his aunt Betsey Trotwood, an eccentric old lady who had renounced all interest in him from his birth because he had been born a boy instead of a girl. He is kindly received and given a new home, which he shares with an amiable lunatic, Mr Dick, whose attempts to complete a memorial regarding his affairs are continually frustrated by the intrusion of King Charles's head. Copperfield continues his education at Canterbury, living in the house of Miss Trotwood's lawyer, Mr Wickfield, whose daughter Agnes, a sweet and high-minded girl, exerts a powerful influence on the rest of his life. He then enters Doctors' Commons, being articled to Mr Spenlow. Meanwhile, he renews his friendship with Steerforth and, ignorant of his true character, introduces him to the family of his old nurse, Clara Peggotty, married to *Barkis the carrier. The family consists of Mr Peggotty, a Yarmouth fisherman, his nephew Ham, and the latter's cousin Little Em'ly, whom Ham is about to marry. Mr Peggotty also shares his home with the widow Mrs Gummidge, and patiently endures her peevish laments for her forlorn condition. Steerforth induces Em'ly to run away with him, producing intense misery in the Peggotty household. Mr Peggotty sets out to find her, following her through many countries, and finally recovering her after she has been cast off by Steerforth. The latter's crime also brings unhappiness to his mother and to her protégée Rosa Dartle, who loves Steerforth with all the suppressed violence of a passionate nature. The tragedy finds its culmination in the shipwreck and drowning of Steerforth, and the death of Ham in trying to save him.

Meanwhile Copperfield, blind to the affection of Agnes Wickfield, marries Dora Spenlow, a pretty empty-headed child, and becomes a celebrated author. Dora dies after a few years of married life and Copperfield, at first disconsolate, awakens to a growing appreciation and love of Agnes. Her father has fallen into the toils of a villainous and cunning clerk, Uriah Heep, who under the cloak of fawning humility has acquired complete control over him, reduced him to the verge of imbecility, and nearly ruined him. Uriah also aspires to marry Agnes. But his misdeeds are exposed by Micawber, employed as his clerk, with the assistance of Traddles, now a barrister. Uriah is sent to prison for life. Copperfield marries Agnes, and Mr Peggotty, with Em'ly and Mrs Gummidge, prospers in Australia, where Mr Micawber, relieved of his debts, appears finally as a respected colonial magistrate.

'Davideis' *See* COWLEY, ABRAHAM

DAVID-NÉEL, Alexandra (1868–1969) French traveller and writer, who studied Eastern religion and philosophy at the Sorbonne. David-Néel spent many years in the East, notably between 1911–25 and 1937–46, supported financially by Philippe Néel, whom she had married in Tunis in 1904 but from whom she separated soon afterwards. She met with the thirteenth Dalai Lama in 1912, the first Western woman to do so. In 1914–16 she stayed in a spiritual retreat in Sikkim with a young monk, Aphur Yongden, who became her lifelong travelling companion and whom she adopted in 1925. The most famous of her journeys was to Lhasa, which she visited disguised as a pilgrim in 1924, at a time when it was closed to foreigners. David-Néel immersed herself in the dialects and religion of Tibet. Her writings helped stimulate Western interest in Eastern spirituality and influenced, among others, the *Beat writer Allen *Ginsberg.

David Simple, The Adventures of, *In Search of a Real Friend* Novel by Sarah *Fielding (1744), described in the preface (by the author's brother, Henry *Fielding) as an exploration of 'the Mazes, Windings, and Labyrinths' of the heart. David discovers that his younger brother has defrauded him of his inheritance. Horrified by this deceit, he sets out on a quest to see if he can find a true friend. Everywhere he encounters self-seeking, hypocrisy, and dishonesty. Eventually he meets Cynthia, who has been excluded from her share of her father's fortune, and a brother and sister, Valentine and Camilla, whose stepmother has alienated their father's affection from them. The four friends live together in trusting companionship; David marries Camilla and Valentine marries Cynthia. In the sombre *Volume the Last* (1753) both couples suffer financial disasters and remorseless victimization; by the end only Cynthia and one of David's children survive.

DAVIDSON, Avram (1923–93) American author born in New York who combined *science fiction with erudite and witty *fantasy, often playing with *alternate worlds such as that of *The Phoenix and the Mirror* (1969), where the medieval image of the poet Virgil as a magician is true.

DAVIDSON, John (1857–1909) Poet, dramatist, and journalist. Born in Renfrewshire and briefly educated at the University of Edinburgh, Davidson was a schoolmaster in Scotland from 1872 to 1889. From 1890 to 1907 he worked in London, contributing to the **Yellow Book* and joining the *Rhymers Club. Davidson had already written several verse plays, but became well known through *Fleet Street Eclogues* (1893) and its successor *Ballads and Songs* (1894), both of which highlighted his gift for ballads and verse narrative. His best-known monologue is the lively and satirical 'Thirty Bob a Week'. Between 1901 and 1908 he wrote a series of 'Testaments', expounding in verse his materialistic and rebellious philosophy, and an unfinished dramatic trilogy, *God and Mammon* (1907–8). His death by drowning was a suspected suicide. Davidson later influenced T. S. *Eliot, who admired his urban imagery, and Hugh *MacDiarmid. See John Sloan, *John Davidson, First of the Moderns* (1995).

DAVIDSON, Robyn (1950–) Australian travel writer born in Queensland. Davidson's first book, *Tracks* (1980), recounts her 1,700-mile journey across the desert interior of Australia and her discomfort with the celebrity that resulted. *Desert Places* (1996) describes a sojourn with Rajasthani nomads. A collection of travel and autobiographical articles, *Travelling Light*, appeared in 1989, and a novel, *Ancestors*, in 1990. Davidson edited *The Picador Book of Journeys* (2001).

DAVIE, Donald (1922–95) Poet and critic, born in Barnsley, and educated at Barnsley Holgate Grammar School and at Cambridge, where he was much influenced by the ethos of F. R. *Leavis and the Cambridge English school; he describes his ambiguous feelings towards this heritage in his memoirs, *These the Companions* (1982). His critical work *Purity of Diction in English Verse* (1952) expressed many of the anti-Romantic, anti-bohemian ideals of the *Movement and of his fellow contributors to **New Lines*. His volumes of poetry include *Brides of Reason* (1955), *A Winter Talent* (1957), *Essex Poems* (1969), and *In the Stopping Train* (1977); two volumes of collected poems appeared in 1972 (1950–70) and 1983 (1971–83). His poems are philosophical, speculative, and erudite, manifesting a mind that (in his own phrase) 'moves most easily and happily among abstractions', yet they also vividly evoke the various landscapes of his travels and academic appointments, from Ireland to California, from Essex to Italy, and show a marked rejection of the English provincialism which characterized some of his friends from the Movement. Davie also wrote on Walter *Scott (1961), Ezra *Pound (1964), Thomas *Hardy (1972), and others, and adapted the *Pan Tadeusz* of Adam *Mickiewicz in *The Forests of Lithuania* (1959). A further *Collected Poems* appeared in 2002.

DAVIES, Edward (Celtic Davies) (1756–1831) Antiquarian, poet, dramatist, and clergyman whose *Celtic Researches* (1804) and *The Mythology and Rites of the Celtic Druids* (1809) took issue with some of the wilder enthusiasms of Iolo Marganwg (Edward *Williams), though without questioning the fundamentals of his druidism.

DAVIES, Idris (1903–53) Welsh poet, born in Rhymney, Monmouthshire, who worked as a collier before entering Loughborough College, where he trained as a teacher. He published two book-length sequences, *Gwalia Deserta* (1938) and *The Angry Summer* (1943), along with the miscellaneous *Tonypandy and Other Poems* (1945). Almost all his work is concerned with the plight of the industrial valleys of south Wales during and after the General Strike of 1926. It represents the most sustained British attempt to create a popularly accessible socialist poetry. The extent to which it should be described as faux-naïf is debatable. See *The Complete Poems of Idris Davies*, ed. Dafydd Johnston (1994).

DAVIES, John (*c.*1564–1618) of Hereford, poet and writing-master. He published several volumes of verse, epitaphs, *epigrams, and so on, including *Microcosmos* (1603), *The Muses' Sacrifice*, containing the famous 'Picture of an Happy Man' (1612), and *Wit's Bedlam* (1617). Some of his epigrams, most of which are contained in *The Scourge of Folly* (1611), are valuable for their notices of Ben *Jonson, John *Fletcher, and other contemporary poets.

DAVIES, Sir John (1569–1626) Poet and lawyer. Born in Wiltshire, he was educated at Winchester College and the Queen's College, Oxford, and the Middle Temple. In 1603, he was appointed solicitor- and attorney-general for Ireland, and was made lord chief justice of the King's Bench, in 1626, but died before taking up this office. His *Orchestra, or A Poeme of Dauncing*, published in 1596, describes the attempts of the suitor Antinous to persuade Penelope to dance with him, giving a long account of the antiquity and universality of dancing. The *Hymnes of Astraea* and *Nosce Teipsum* both appeared in 1599: the latter, written in *quatrains, is a philosophical poem on the nature of man and the nature and immortality of the soul. His *Epigrammes* ('Middleborough' [?London], *c.*1599) and *Gullinge Sonnets* (in manuscript) reflect his keen, satirical interest in the contemporary scene. His poems were edited by Robert Krueger in 1975.

DAVIES, Sir Peter Maxwell (1934–) Composer. Born and educated in Manchester, where he experimented with modernist compositional techniques alongside early English polyphony. His opera *Taverner* (1968) explored the political life of the composer John Taverner (1490–1545); *Eight Songs for a Mad King* (1969) gave expression to George III's insanity. In 1971 Davies settled on Orkney where he has developed a softer and clearer style, making use of local landscapes, history, and mythology, particularly in association with George Mackay *Brown. Davies's opera *The Martyrdom of St Magnus*, which inaugurated the St Magnus Festival in Kirkwall Cathedral in 1976, was based on Brown's novel *Magnus*, and many works from the Orkney period, such as the opera *The Lighthouse* (1980), use Brown's words or show his influence. Davies has written many works for young performers and has had a prominent role in music education; he was knighted in 1987 and made master of the queen's music in 2004.

DAVIES, Rhys (1901–78) Prolific Welsh writer, born in the Rhondda Valley, whose novels include *The Withered Root* (1927), *Jubilee Blues* (1938), and *The Black Venus* (1944). The best of Davies's many short stories are admired for their Chekhovian objectivity and implicit homoeroticism.

DAVIES, Robertson (1913–95) Canadian novelist, playwright, and critic, born in Thamesville, Ontario (the fictional Deptford). The family later moved to Kingston, Ontario (the fictional Salterton). Davies was educated at Upper Canada College, Toronto, Queen's University, Kingston, and Balliol College, Oxford, where he took his B.Litt. degree in 1938. For a time he acted with a provincial theatre company and then taught and acted at the Old Vic in London. There he met Brenda Matthews, whom he married in 1940. After returning to Canada he became literary editor of *Saturday Night* in Toronto and, in 1942, joined the editorial staff of the Peterborough *Examiner*, owned by his father, becoming joint owner and editor in 1946. In 1960 he was appointed professor of English at the University of Toronto and in 1963 became the first master of the university's Massey College. Between 1943 and 1953 he had written regular columns for the *Examiner* and other papers under the pseudonym Samuel Marchbanks, and these pieces were collected as *The Diary of Samuel Marchbanks* (1947), *The Table Talk of Samuel Marchbanks* (1949), and *Samuel Marchbanks' Almanack* (1967). *A Voice from the Attic* (1960) contains, amongst other pieces, review articles published in *Saturday Night* from 1953 to 1959. Further reprinted journalism can be found in *The Enthusiasms of Robertson Davies* (1979) and *The Well-Tempered Critic* (1981), both edited by Judith Skelton Grant. Davies has been an important figure in Canadian drama, as both playwright and critic. His Oxford thesis was published in 1939 as *Shakespeare's Boy Actors*, which formed the basis of his successful junior course-book *Shakespeare for Young Players* (1942). His topical one-act plays for adults include *Overlaid* (1948) and *Hope Deferred* (published in 1949 in *Eros at Breakfast and Other Plays*). Amongst the best of his full-length plays are *Fortune, my Foe* (1949), *At my Heart's Core* (1950), *A Jig for the Gypsy* (1954), *Hunting Stuart* (written in 1955; pub. 1972), and *General Confession* (written 1956; pub. 1972). It is, however, as a writer of fiction that he has achieved international eminence. His principal work as a novelist is contained in three extensive trilogies: the Salterton Trilogy—*Tempest-Tost* (1951), *Leaven of Malice* (1954), and *A Mixture of Frailties* (1958), which won the Leacock Award for Humour—a sequence of urbane comedies of manners; the Deptford Trilogy, usually considered the best of the three—*Fifth Business* (1970), *The Manticore* (1972), and *World of Wonders* (1975)—which moves towards the mode of fictional autobiography; and the Cornish Trilogy—*The Rebel Angels* (1981), the Booker-shortlisted *What's Bred in the Bone* (1985), and *The Lyre of Orpheus* (1988)—which marks a further shift of focus, this time towards satirical 'anatomies'. A collection of eighteen ghost stories, originally read at Massey College's Christmas celebration between 1963 and 1980, was published as *High Spirits* in 1982. *The Cunning Man* (1995) follows the consequences of the death of a priest who collapses and dies while celebrating Holy Communion.

DAVIES, Thomas (?1712–85) Actor and bookseller, educated at Edinburgh. According to his friend Samuel *Johnson, he was driven from the stage by Charles *Churchill's attack on his delivery in *The *Rosciad*. He introduced James *Boswell to Johnson in his bookshop in Russell Street, Covent Garden, on 16 May 1763. He appears frequently in Boswell's *Life of Johnson*, and Johnson contributed some information for his lively biography of David *Garrick (1780). He also published *Dramatic Miscellanies* (1785).

DAVIES, W. H. (William Henry) (1871–1940) Poet and autobiographer, born at Newport, Monmouthshire, Wales. He went as a young man to America, where he spent several poverty-stricken years. He lost a leg in an accident there, an experience recounted in a few laconic paragraphs in his *The Autobiography of a Super-Tramp*, published in 1908 with a preface by George Bernard *Shaw, who did much to encourage him and who interested himself in Davies's first volume, *The Soul's Destroyer and Other Poems* (1905). Davies was also supported, and assisted financially, by many other friends, especially Edward *Thomas. His best-known poems, such as 'Leisure', record his child-like response to the natural world. In 1923 he married Helen, a girl much younger than himself, and he tells the story in *Young Emma*, eventually published in 1980. *The Complete Poems* appeared in 1963, and Jonathan Barker edited *Selected Poems* (1985). See Richard Stonesifer, *W. H. Davies* (1963).

DAVY, Sir Humphry (1778–1829) Professor of chemistry at the Royal Institution, who greatly advanced knowledge of chemistry and magnetism and invented the miner's safety-lamp. As a young boy he assisted his friend Joseph *Cottle, Wordsworth's publisher, in correcting the proofs of **Lyrical Ballads*. His collected works, prose and verse, with a memoir by his brother, were published in 1839–40. Among these is a brief dialogue, *Salmonia, or Days of Fly-Fishing, by an Angler*

(1828), reminiscent of Izaak *Walton. Davy was a friend of Walter *Scott and there is a pleasing account in John *Lockhart's *Life of Scott* of his visits to Abbotsford.

DAVYS, Mary (1674–1732) Novelist, who moved from Dublin to London, York, and then Cambridge, where she opened a coffee shop. Her novels include the autobiographical travel story *The Fugitive* (1705, later expanded as *The Merry Wanderer*); *The Reform'd Coquet* (1724, with Alexander *Pope and John *Gay among the subscribers), whose sober hero disguises himself to protect the flighty heroine; *Familiar Letters* (1725), epistolary courtship exchanges with political commentary; and *The Accomplish'd Rake* (1727), a harshly satirical account of a 'modern fine gentleman'. One comedy, *The Northern Heiress* (1716), was performed; another, *The Self-Rival*, was published in her two-volume *Works* (1725).

DAY (Daye), **John** (1521/2–1584) The foremost English printer of the early part of the reign of *Elizabeth I. He published Protestant devotional books under Edward VI and was briefly imprisoned by Queen Mary; later he held lucrative monopolies for the *Psalms in metre, the catechism, and the ABC, printed the first church music book in English (1560), and, from 1563, undertook the huge task of the early editions in English of John *Foxe's **Acts and Monuments* (or *Book of Martyrs*). For Matthew *Parker, he used specially made type to print Old English characters for the first time.

DAY, John (*c.*1574–*c.*1640) Playwright, expelled after a few months from Gonville and Caius College, Cambridge, in 1592 for stealing a book. From 1598 to 1603 he wrote regularly for the Admiral's Men in collaboration with playwrights including Henry *Chettle, Thomas *Dekker, and William Haughton (d. 1605). His only surviving play from this period is *The Blind-Beggar of Bednal-Green* (1600; printed 1659), a collaboration with Chettle. He may be the 'John Day, yeoman' who was pardoned on a claim of self-defence for killing the playwright Henry Porter in 1599. His satire *The Isle of Gulls*, suggested by Philip Sidney's **Arcadia*, appeared in 1606, and *Law-Tricks* and *Humour out of Breath* in 1608. In 1607 he collaborated with George *Wilkins and William *Rowley on *The Travels of the Three English Brothers*, acted at the Red Bull. He emerges again as a collaborator on lost plays from 1620 to 1623. His best work, *The Parliament of Bees*, appeared perhaps in 1607, although the earliest extant copy is of 1641. It is an inventive dramatic allegory or masque, containing a series of 'characters' of different bees with their virtues and vices, and ending with Oberon's Star Chamber, where he judges the offenders, the wasp, the drone, and the humble bee. Day's works were collected by A. H. Bullen (1881); some are reprinted elsewhere.

DAY, Thomas (1748–89) Radical pamphleteer and author of the influential children's book *The History of Sandford and Merton* (3 vols, 1783–9), intended to illustrate the doctrine that people may be made good by reason and instruction. It consists of a series of episodes in which the rich and objectionable Tommy Merton is contrasted with the upright and tender-hearted Harry Sandford, a farmer's son; eventually Tommy is reformed. Day also wrote *The History of Little Jack* (1787), about a young wild boy suckled by goats. Day was a friend of the educational theorist Richard Edgeworth (*see* EDGEWORTH, MARIA).

DAY-LEWIS, Cecil (C. Day Lewis) (1904–72) Poet, born in Ireland, the son of a Church of Ireland minister; the family moved to England in 1905. He was educated at Sherborne School and Wadham College, Oxford, where he was befriended by Maurice Bowra and became friends with W. H. *Auden, with whom he edited *Oxford Poetry* (1927), Louis *MacNeice, and Stephen *Spender (they have been called the 'MacSpaunday' group, or the *Pylon School). He worked for some years as a schoolmaster and was politically active during the 1930s, writing for the *Left Review*, supporting the *Left Book Club, and speaking at meetings. He joined the Communist Party in 1936, and in 1937 edited a socialist symposium, *The Mind in Chains*, with contributions from Edward *Upward, Charles *Madge, Rex *Warner, and others. These preoccupations are not reflected in his earliest verse (such as *Beechen Vigil*, 1925), but become apparent in *Transitional Poem* (1929), *From Feathers to Iron* (1931), and *The Magnetic Mountain* (1933), all of which have a strong revolutionary flavour, prophesying a new dawn. The poor reception of *Noah and the Waters* (1936), a verse morality play about the class struggle, may have encouraged him to turn to the more pastoral themes of his later years. He moved to Devon in 1938, turned to the work of Thomas *Hardy, and translated Virgil's **Georgics* (1940). Yet *Overtures to Death* (1938) and *Poems in Wartime* (1940) also reflect obvious political concerns, and he worked for some time for the Ministry of Information. From this time he became an establishment figure (having already endured mockery from Geoffrey *Grigson for joining the Book Society Committee in 1937). He delivered the Clark Lectures in Cambridge in 1946 (*The Poetic Image*, 1947), broadcast frequently, gave recitals, sat on committees, judged awards, and had a senior role at Chatto and Windus.

During the 1930s he also embarked, under the pseudonym of 'Nicholas Blake', on a successful career as a writer of *detective fiction. His first work in this genre, *A Question of Proof* (1935), introducing his Audenesque detective Nigel Strangeways, was followed by many others. *The Friendly Tree* (1936) was the first of three largely autobiographical novels. He produced more translations too, of Paul *Valéry (1946), and Virgil again (*The *Aeneid*, 1952; *The Eclogues*, 1963). His collections of verse included *An Italian Visit* (1953), which records a journey with Rosamond *Lehmann, who had become his mistress. He eventually left his wife Mary for Jill Balcon, who became his second wife in 1951, and settled in London. He was professor of poetry at Oxford from 1951 to 1956, the first poet of distinction to hold the post since Matthew *Arnold, although Day-Lewis's literary reputation does not now rival that of Auden or MacNeice. In 1968 he was appointed *poet laureate. His autobiography, *The Buried Day*, was published in 1960, and *The Complete Poems of C. Day-Lewis* in 1992.

See Sean Day-Lewis, *C. Day-Lewis* (1980); Peter Stanford, *C. Day-Lewis* (2007).

DEACON, William Frederick (1799–1844) Journalist, poet, and parodist, educated at Cambridge. He is principally remembered today for *Warreniana* (1824), a collection of parodies which imagines the leading writers of the day, Walter *Scott, Lord *Byron, and William *Wordsworth amongst them, writing advertising copy for the blacking manufacturer Robert Warren. He spent most of the latter part of his life as a journalist for the *True Sun*.

DEANE, Seamus (1940–) Irish poet, scholar, and novelist, born in Derry and educated at St Columb's College, Derry, and Queen's University, Belfast (in both of which he was a contemporary of Seamus *Heaney), and at Cambridge. He has been a professor at University College, Dublin, and at the University of Notre Dame. Through such works as *Celtic Revivals* (1985) and *Strange Country: Modernity and Nationhood in Irish Writing since 1790* (1997), Deane has been a driving force behind the intellectualization and politicization of Irish literary criticism. He was the general editor of the ambitious and controversial three-volume *Field Day Anthology of Irish Writing 550–1988* (1991). In his poetry and in *Reading in the Dark* (1996), his delicately realized autobiographical novel, Deane focuses on the political and social landscape of Northern Ireland, showing sectarian violence and enmities as a lethal undercurrent to the domestic world.

Death's Jest-Book *See* BEDDOES, THOMAS LOVELL.

De BERNIÈRES, Louis (1954–) Novelist, born in London, educated at Bradfield College and the University of Manchester. After working as an English teacher in Colombia, he published three novels set in an imaginary South American country—*The War of Don Emmanuel's Nether Parts* (1990), *Señor Vivo and the Coca Lord* (1991), and *The Troublesome Offspring of Cardinal Guzman* (1992)—which mingle *magic realism with political satire and are much indebted to the fiction of *García Márquez. *Captain Corelli's Mandolin* (1994), the historical romance with which he achieved greatest success, takes place on the Greek island of Cephallonia during the Second World War. *Birds without Wings* (2004), which chronicles the destruction of an initially peaceful, mixed Christian and Muslim community, is set in Turkey during the First World War. *Red Dog* (2001) is a collection of canine short stories.

DEBUSSY, Claude (1862–1918) French composer, two of whose *Préludes* for piano claim English inspiration—*La Danse de Puck* (Book 1, 1910) and *Hommage à S. Pickwick* (Book 2, 1913). The only English poet he set was Dante Gabriel *Rossetti, whose 'The *Blessed Damozel' provided the text for an early cantata, *La Damoiselle élue* (1888): a second, a translation by Pierre Louÿs of 'Willowwood' (1900), was never published. Debussy planned an opera from **As You Like It*, but shelved it in favour of Maurice *Maeterlinck's *Pelléas et Mélisande* (1902). In 1890 he began a symphonic work on *The Fall of the House of Usher* (now lost), later writing three separate libretti for an opera on the subject, never developed beyond sketches. Debussy planned but did not complete another opera based on a Poe story, *The Devil in the Belfry*.

decadence Associated with the French decadent (renamed symbolist) movement of the 1880s, which included the poets Paul *Verlaine and Stéphane *Mallarmé and the novelist Joris-Karl *Huysmans (*À rebours*, 1884), the concept was applied in the English *fin-de-siècle* to literature, art, and culture characterized by extreme *aestheticism and perversity in style or subject matter. The most characteristic decadent works in England are Oscar *Wilde's *The Picture of Dorian Gray* (1890) and *Salome* (1894); the poetry of Ernest *Dowson and Arthur *Symons; and the art of Aubrey *Beardsley.
See also MODERNISM; SYMBOLISM.

Decameron, The Giovanni *Boccaccio's masterpiece, a collection of 100 tales told over a period of ten days (hence the title). The stories have many different sources, including both Mediterranean folklore and contemporary society. They are contained within a frame narrative (cornice), an innovative feature. This relates how seven young women and three young men flee Florence during the Black Death and take refuge in the countryside, where they entertain themselves by telling these tales. *The Decameron* has been called a 'mercantile epic' and a 'commedia umana'. Many tales concern the merchant classes, and the work as a whole deals with perennial human themes: love, lust, fortune, virtue, and vice. They also treat contemporary Italy—the clergy, trade, the role of women. *The Decameron* celebrates especially 'ingegno'—quick-wittedness, as the best instrument for success in all walks of life. The work had much influence on English literature, notably on *Chaucer (presumably indirectly, through a translation: Chaucer nowhere mentions Boccaccio in any of his works); sixteen of the tales were incorporated in William Painter's **Palace of Pleasure*. John *Keats and *Tennyson both produced versions of individual tales. The first English version of *The Decameron* (1620) has been attributed to *Florio. See *The Decameron*, trans. and introd. G. H. McWilliam (1995).

de CAMP, L. Sprague (1907–2000) Fantasy author, born in New York. *Lest Darkness Fall* (1941) and *The Incompleat Enchanter* (1941), written with Fletcher *Pratt, fused *fantasy with *alternate history. Among later novels were completions of stories by Robert E. *Howard, of whom he wrote a biography.

Decline and Fall First novel of Evelyn *Waugh, published to great acclaim in 1928. It follows the hapless career of the unworldly Paul Pennyfeather, whose trousers are removed during a dining club's drunken rumpus but who is sent down from Scone College, Oxford, for 'indecent behaviour' all the same. He becomes a schoolmaster at Llanabba Castle, where he encounters, among others, the dubious, bigamous, and irrepressible Captain Grimes, and Beste-Chetwynde, a pupil whose glamorous mother Margot eventually carries him off to the dangerous delights of high society. They are about to be married when Paul is arrested and subsequently imprisoned for Margot's activities in the White Slave trade, a sentence he bears stoically on the grounds that 'anyone who has been to an English public school will always feel comparatively at home in prison'; however, Margot arranges his escape, and he returns, unknown but under his own name, to resume his studies at Scone.

Decline and Fall of the Roman Empire, The History of the By Edward *Gibbon, volume i of the first (quarto) edition published 1776, volumes ii and iii 1781, and the last three volumes 1788. This monumental work falls into three divisions: from the age of Trajan and the Antonines to the subversion of the Western Empire; from the reign of Justinian in the East to the establishment of the second or German Empire of the West, under *Charlemagne; from the revival of the Western Empire to the taking of Constantinople by the Turks. It thus covers a period of about thirteen centuries, and comprehends such vast subjects as the establishment of Christianity, the movements and settlements of the Teutonic tribes, the conquests of the Muslims, and the Crusades. It traces, overall, the connection of the ancient world with the modern. Gibbon's prose is cool, lucid, and enlivened by ironic wit, much of it controversially aimed at the early church and the credulity and barbarism that overwhelmed the noble Roman virtues he admired. J. B. Bury's editions (1896–1900, 1909–14, 1926–9) are supplemented with notes incorporating subsequent research. See also the edition by David Womersley, 3 vols (1994).

deconstruction An approach to the reading of literary and philosophical texts that casts doubt upon the possibility of finding in them a definitive meaning, and that traces instead the multiplication (or 'dissemination') of possible meanings. A deconstructive reading of a poem, for instance, will conclude not with the discovery of its essential meaning, but with an impasse ('aporia') at which there are no grounds for choosing between two radically incompatible interpretations. According to deconstruction, literary texts resist any process of interpretation that would fix their meanings, appearing to 'undo' themselves as we try to tie them up. The basis for this apparently perverse approach to reading lies in a certain view of the philosophy of language, and specifically of the status of writing, as developed since 1966 by the French philosopher Jacques *Derrida, and by his American followers at Yale and elsewhere, including Paul *de Man. On this view, derived from a critical reassessment of Ferdinand de *Saussure, meaning can never be fully 'present' in language, but is always deferred endlessly—as when one may look up a word in a dictionary, only to be given other words, and so on ad infinitum. While speech gives the illusion of a fixed origin—the presence of the speaker—that can guarantee the meaning of an utterance, writing is more clearly unauthenticated and open to unlicensed interpretation. Derrida's alarmingly simplified account of the history of Western philosophy since *Plato proposes that the dominant metaphysical tradition, in its deep suspicion of writing, has repeatedly tried to erect a fixed point of reference (a 'transcendental signified' such as God, Reason, absolute truth, etc.) outside the promiscuous circulation of signifiers, one that could hold in place a determinate system of truths and meanings. The project of deconstruction, then, is not to destroy but to unpick or dismantle such illusory systems, often by showing how their major categories are unstable or contaminated by their supposed opposites. In philosophical terms, deconstruction is a form of relativist scepticism in the tradition of Friedrich *Nietzsche. Its literary implications are partly compatible with the *New Criticism's rejection of the *'intentional fallacy' or any notion of the author fixing a text's meanings, as they are with New Critical interest in paradox as a feature of poetry; but they go further in challenging the claims of any critical system to possess 'the meaning' of a literary (or any other) work. In some forms of deconstruction, notably that of de Man, literary texts are held to be more honest than other writings, because they openly delight in the instabilities of language and meaning, through their use of figurative language for instance. The deconstructive style of literary analysis commonly emphasizes this through puns and word-play of its own. Exemplary deconstructive readings may be found in Paul de Man, *Allegories of Reading* (1979), John Hillis Miller, *Fiction and Repetition* (1982), and Barbara Johnson, *The Critical Difference* (1980).
See also STRUCTURALISM.

DEE, John (1527–1609) Mathematician and astrologer. Educated at St John's College, Cambridge, he became a fellow of Trinity, where the stage effects he introduced into a performance of *Aristophanes' *Peace* procured him his reputation of being a magician, which was confirmed by his erudition and practice of crystallomancy, alchemy, and astrology. He wrote *Monas Hieroglyphica* (1564); a preface to the first English translation of Euclid (1570); and *General and Rare Memorials Pertayning to the Perfect Arte of Navigation* (1577). A profoundly learned scholar and hermeticist, he was greatly interested in antiquities, geography, and exploration, travelling much in Europe. He was also a sham: his conversations with angels were published in 1659. Philip *Sidney and Sir Edward *Dyer were among those who consulted him. Many books survive from his remarkable library, and he left personal biographical notes in printed tables of astronomical data (ephemerides), which James *Halliwell published as Dee's diary (1842). There is a life by Benjamin Wolley (2001).

DEEPING, Warwick (1877–1950) A student of medicine at Cambridge and subsequently in practice as a doctor before becoming a prolific and successful novelist. He caught the popular imagination with *Sorrell and Son* (1925): inspired by his experiences in the First World War, the novel tells the story of a wounded ex-officer who takes a menial job to pay for his son's private education, where he will not be exposed to 'class hatred' or 'the sneers of the new young working-class intellectuals' in the social war that Sorrell anticipates.

Deerbrook A novel by Harriet *Martineau, published in 1839; her only venture into domestic realism. Focusing on middle-class life in the small community of Deerbrook, the novel describes the experiences of two orphaned sisters, Hester and Margaret Ibbotson, who move to Deerbook from Birmingham. The malicious gossip and misunderstanding that permeate village life are vividly described, and the novel's exploration of changing social conditions for women, the rise of the professions, and the potential for happiness and unhappiness for both men and women in marriage look forward to the interests of Charlotte *Brontë, Elizabeth *Gaskell, and George *Eliot.

defamiliarization The process by which literary works unsettle readers' habitual ways of seeing the world. According to the literary theories of S. T. *Coleridge in **Biographia Literaria* (1817), of P. B. *Shelley in **Defence of Poetry* (1840), and of several modern *formalist critics, it is a distinctive feature of literature, especially poetry, that it tears away what Shelley called the 'veil of familiarity' from the world, making us look at it afresh. The concept of 'estrangement' (*ostranenie*) developed by the Russian theorist Viktor Shklovsky (1893–1984) has influenced modern restatements of the case.

Defence of Poetry, A An essay by Philip *Sidney written in 1579–80. Stephen *Gosson's *Schoole of Abuse*, dedicated to Sidney in 1579, may have helped to stimulate the composition of the *Defence*, but Sidney's chief aim was probably to write an English vindication of literature to match the many recently written on the Continent in Italian, French, and Latin. Two editions of the work appeared posthumously in 1595: one, published by William Ponsonby, bore the title *The Defence of Poesie* and the other, published by Henry Olney, *An Apologie for Poetrie*. Most modern editors have preferred the first title both because Ponsonby was the official publisher of Sidney's remains and because Sidney in the opening paragraph speaks of being moved 'to make a pitiful defence of poor poetry'.

Sidney expounds the antiquity of poetry in all cultures, 'whose milk by little and little enabled them to feed afterwards of tougher knowledges'. He demonstrates its superiority to philosophy or history as a means of teaching virtue. After defining and distinguishing the 'parts, kinds, or species' of poetry, vindicating each in turn, he digresses to England: he sees contemporary poetry as having reached a low ebb, with little to be admired since Geoffrey *Chaucer, but affirms with prophetic confidence that major poetry in every genre, including drama, can be written in the English language. *A Defence of Poetry* is remarkable for the lightness of Sidney's style and the catholicity of his examples, often drawn from experience: 'I never heard the old song of Percy and Douglas that I found not my heart moved more than with a trumpet; and yet is it sung but by some blind crowder, with no rougher voice than rude style.' (*See* CHEVY CHASE.) The poetic qualities of the essay in themselves illustrate the power of imaginative writing: 'Nature never set forth the earth in so rich tapestry as divers poets have done; neither with so pleasant rivers, fruitful trees, sweet-smelling flowers, nor whatsoever else may make the too much loved earth more lovely. Her world is brazen, the poets only deliver a golden.'

'Defence of Poetry, A' An essay by P. B. *Shelley, written at Pisa 1821, first published 1840. It was begun as a light-hearted reply to his friend Thomas Love *Peacock's magazine article 'The *Four Ages of Poetry', which humorously argued that the best minds of the future must turn to economic and social sciences, rather than poetry. In vindicating the role of poetry in a progressive society, and defending the whole notion of imaginative literature and thinking (not just 'poetry') within an industrial culture, Shelley came to write his own poetic credo with passionate force and conviction. Against a background of classical and European literature, he discusses in some detail the nature of poetic thought and inspiration; the problems of translation; the value of erotic writing; the connections between poetry and politics; and the essentially *moral* nature of the imagination—an emphasis he drew from S. T. *Coleridge.

Throughout, Shelley associates poetry with social freedom and love. He argues that the 'poetry of life' provides the one sure response to the destructive, isolating, alienating, 'accumulating and calculating processes' of modern civilization. There are superb literary evocations of the Greeks, *Dante, and John *Milton. The essay is not a regular treatise. It draws on many of Shelley's earlier prefaces and essays, notably *A *Philosophical View of Reform*. Though diffuse in places, it frequently sharpens to epigrammatic point: 'the great instrument of moral good is the imagination'; 'the freedom of women produced the poetry of sexual love'; and the famous peroration, ending 'Poets are the unacknowledged legislators of the world'—which must be read in context and which echoes in part the argument of Imlac in Samuel *Johnson's **Rasselas*.

de FILIPPO, Eduardo (1900–84) Italian playwright and actor, who draws on Naples, his native city, for his themes, characters, and language. His major plays are: *Filumena Marturano* (1946: *Filumena*), *Le bugie hanno le gambe lunghe* (1947: *Lies Have Long Legs*), *La grande paura* (1948: *The Great Fear*), *Sabato, domenica, lunedì* (1959: *Saturday, Sunday, Monday*).

DEFOE, Daniel (1660–1731) Author, born in London, the son of James Foe, a tallow chandler. He changed his name to Defoe from *c.*1695, after his first bankruptcy. He attended Morton's academy for Dissenters at Newington Green with a view to becoming a Dissenting minister, but by the time he married Mary Tuffley in 1683/4 he was established as a hosiery merchant in Cornhill; the competing demands of trade and religion colour his early fictions. Defoe travelled in France,

Spain, the Low Countries, and possibly Italy and Germany, and he was absorbed by travel and *travel literature throughout his career. He took part in Monmouth's rebellion, and in 1688 joined the advancing forces of William III. His first important work was *An Essay upon Projects* (1697), followed by *The True-Born Englishman* (1701), an immensely popular satirical poem attacking the prejudice against a king of foreign birth. In 1702 appeared *The Shortest Way with Dissenters*, in which Defoe, himself a Dissenter, impersonated the kind of High Tory who demanded the savage suppression of Dissent; for this he was fined, imprisoned (May–November 1703), and pilloried. While in prison he wrote his *Hymn to the Pillory*, a mock-Pindaric ode which was sold in the streets to sympathetic crowds. Meanwhile various business projects (the breeding of civet cats, marine insurance, a brick and tile works) had come to grief. Defoe was rescued by Robert *Harley, who arranged for his release and employed him as a secret agent; between 1703 and 1714 Defoe travelled around the country, testing the political climate, especially in Scotland on the eve of the Union (1707). Defoe wrote many pamphlets for Harley, and in 1704 began *The *Review*, a lively and highly opinionated survey of contemporary events and issues. Certain anti-Jacobite pamphlets in 1712–13 led to his prosecution by the Whigs and to a brief imprisonment. He now started a new trade journal, *Mercator*, in place of the *Review*. In 1715 he was convicted of libelling Lord Annesley (by implying that he was a *Jacobite); he escaped punishment through the intervention of Townshend, the Whig secretary of state, and thereafter infiltrated several Tory journals as a government agent. He wrote several manuals on family relationships, from *The Family Instructor* (1715) onwards. He turned to fiction late in life: **Robinson Crusoe* and its sequel the *Farther Adventures* appeared in 1719. The next five years saw the appearance of several fictions: *Captain *Singleton* (1720); **Moll Flanders*, *A Journal of the *Plague Year*, and **Colonel Jack* (1722); **Roxana*, **Memoirs of a Cavalier*, and *A New Voyage round the World* (1724). His *Tour through the Whole Island of Great Britain*, a guidebook in three volumes (1724–6), is a vivid account of the state of the country, gleaned from his travels (and some books). His last principal works were on social and economic matters: *The Complete English Tradesman* (1726), *Augusta Triumphans* (1728), *A Plan of the English Commerce* (1728), and *The Complete English Gentleman*, not published until 1890. He died in hiding from creditors in Ropemaker's Alley, Moorfields, and was buried in Bunhill Fields cemetery. Defoe's influence on the evolution of the English novel was enormous, though he would not have recognized 'the novel' as a label for what he was writing. His background in trade and commerce colours his prose with realistic, material detail, and the fictions are characterized by overarching narrative schemes of redemption through energetic work, pragmatic accumulation, and intelligent opportunism, as well as an intense imaginative identification with his protagonists, who are all outcasts of some sort and who all tell their own stories. Defoe produced some 250 books, pamphlets, and journals, almost all of them anonymously or pseudonymously, though bibliographic work by P. N. Furbank and W. R. Owens (see their *Critical Bibliography of Daniel Defoe*, 1998) has substantially reduced the number of works attributed to him. See Maximillian E. Novak, *Daniel Defoe: Master of Fictions* (2001).

De FOREST, John William (1826–1906) American novelist and historian, born in Connecticut, who did military service in the Civil War. He wrote a number of military memoirs and novels, and is remembered for *Miss Ravenel's Conversion from Secession to Loyalty* (1867), an early piece of Civil War realism.

Deformed Transformed, The An unfinished poetic drama by Lord *Byron, written in 1822 and published in 1824. Arnold, a hunchback, is reviled and rejected by his mother for his deformity: he resolves on suicide, but is prevented by a stranger, who offers to change his shape and summons up Caesar, Alcibiades, and others as models. Arnold chooses the form of Achilles, but retains his own name: the stranger takes on Arnold's form and follows him as his servant. They take part in the Sack of Rome in 1527, where Arnold distinguishes himself. The fragment ends with the opening chorus of Part III, in praise of peace. This version of the Faust legend is in part a meditation by Byron, born with a club-foot, on the inspirational effects of disfigurement: 'deformity is daring. | It is its essence to o'ertake mankind.'

Degaré, Sir A metrical romance in 1,073 lines of short couplets from the early 14th century in a south Midland dialect, one of the Middle English *Breton lays. Degaré, son of a princess of Brittany who has been raped by a knight, is abandoned in a forest with a purse of money, a letter of directions, and a pair of gloves which are to fit the lady that he is to marry. The poem recounts Degaré's prowess in the course of his searches for his parents. The lady that the gloves fit is, in the event, his own mother, who recognizes him with joy as her son immediately after their wedding ceremony and before its consummation. Rosemary Woolf makes the interesting suggestion that the romance may be a medievalizing of *Oedipus, as *Sir *Orfeo* is of *Orpheus. The name is probably a corruption of 'l'esgaré', 'the lost one' (apparently punned on in line 214, 'almost lost it is'), and is thought to be the origin of 'Diggory'. See editions by W. H. French and C. B. Hale, *Middle English Metrical Romances* (1930), and in *Medieval English Romances*, Part II, ed. A. V. C. Schmidt and N. Jacobs (1980).

DEIGHTON, Len *See* SPY FICTION.

Deirdre The heroine of the tale of 'The Fate of the Sons of Usnach' (pron. 'Usna'), one of the 'Three Sorrowful Stories of Erin'. She was the daughter of Fedlimid, harper to King *Conchubar (pron. Conachoor) of Ulster, and Cathbad the druid prophesied that her beauty would bring banishment and death to heroes. Conchubar destined her for his wife and had her brought up in solitude. But she accidentally saw and fell in love with Naoise (or Naisi; pron. 'Neesha'), the son of Usnach, who with his brothers carried her off to Scotland. They were lured back by Conchubar and treacherously slain, and Deirdre took her own life. See Lady *Gregory, *Cuchulain of Muirthemne*, and the dramas on Deirdre by G. W. *Russell (Æ), J. M. *Synge, and W. B. *Yeats.

Deirdre of the Sorrows *See* SYNGE, JOHN MILLINGTON; DEIRDRE.

Deism ('natural religion') The belief in a Supreme Being as the source of finite existence, with rejection of revelation and the supernatural doctrines of Christianity. The Deists, who came into prominence at the end of the 17th and during the 18th century (the word in English dates from the 1680s), were much influenced by the views of Lord *Herbert of Cherbury, often known as 'the father of Deism'. They include Charles Blount (1654–93), John *Toland (author of *Christianity Not Mysterious*, 1696), Matthew Tindal (1657–1733, author of *Christianity as Old as the Creation*, 1730), Anthony *Collins (author of *A Discourse of Freethinking*, 1713), Thomas Chubb (1679–1747), and the third earl of *Shaftesbury. John *Locke, who rejected the label of Deist, nevertheless contributed significantly to the movement with his *Reasonableness of Christianity* (1695). One of the most cogent refutations was by Joseph *Butler in his *Analogy of Religion* (1736), in which he argues that natural religion is no more credible and acceptable than revealed religion.

'Dejection: An Ode' An autobiographical poem by Samuel Taylor *Coleridge, first published in the *Morning Post*, 1802. Originally composed as a much longer verse letter to his beloved 'Asra' (Sara Hutchinson), it describes the loss of his poetical powers, the dulling of his responses to Nature, the breakdown of his marriage, and the paralysing effect of metaphysics (or opium). Paradoxically, this is achieved in verse of great emotional intensity and metrical brilliance. *Wordsworth partly answered it in his *'Intimations of Immortality' ode.

DEKKER, Thomas (?1572–1632) Probably of Dutch descent, he was born and mainly lived in London, which he evokes vividly in his writings. He was repeatedly imprisoned for debt, briefly in 1598–9 and from 1612 for nearly seven years; the six prison chapters added in 1616 to his prose work *Lanthorn and Candle-Light* (first version 1608), and *Dekker his Dream* (1620), evoke his experiences of imprisonment. Despite this he is held to have been of a cheerful, good-natured temperament. He was engaged by Philip *Henslowe about 1595 to write plays (over 40 of which are now lost) in collaboration with Michael *Drayton, Ben *Jonson, John *Webster, and others.

*The *Shoemakers' Holiday* and **Old Fortunatus*, comedies acted in 1599, were published in 1600. Having been ridiculed, jointly with John *Marston, by Jonson in his **Poetaster*, he retorted in **Satiromastix*, a play produced in 1601. His other principal plays are *The *Honest Whore*, of which Part I, in collaboration with Thomas *Middleton, appeared in 1604 and Part II, written 1604/5, in 1630; **Patient Grissil* (1603), written in collaboration with Henry *Chettle and William Haughton (d. 1605): and *The *Witch of Edmonton*, written in collaboration with John *Ford and William *Rowley in 1621, first published 1658. He also collaborated with Webster in **Westward Ho* (written 1604; pub. 1607) and **Northward Ho* (written 1605; pub. 1607), with Middleton in *The *Roaring Girl* (written *c.*1605; pub. 1611), and with Massinger in *The *Virgin Martyr* (written 1620; pub. 1622). His tragicomedy *Match Me in London*, written 1604/5, was published in 1631. Dekker also wrote pageants, tracts, and pamphlets. His pamphlet *The Wonderful Year* (1603) is a poignant description of London during the plague of that year; it was used by Defoe for his *Journal of the *Plague Year*. *News from Hell* (1606) is an imitation of Thomas *Nashe; *The *Gull's Horn-Book* (1609) is a satirical book of manners with interesting information about theatres.

Dekker's work is remarkable for its vivid if romantic portrayal of London life, both domestic and commercial, for its sympathy with the oppressed, including animals tortured for man's amusement, and for its prevailing cheerfulness, though E. D. Pendry in an introduction to a selection of prose works (1967) stresses that he could be tough and bitter as well as whimsical. His dramatic works were edited by F. T. Bowers in 4 vols (1953–61).

DELAFIELD, E. M. (1890–1943) The pen-name of Edmée Elizabeth Monica Dashwood, née de la Pasture (hence the *nom de plume*), novelist and journalist. Born at Aldrinton, Sussex, and educated privately and at various schools, she published over thirty novels, her first, *Zella Sees Herself*, appearing in 1917. Her most popular novel remains *The Diary of a Provincial Lady* (1930), a gentle satire of a middle-class country life; *Thank Heaven Fasting* (1932) is also noteworthy. See V. Powell, *The Life of a Provincial Lady* (1988).

de la MARE, Walter (1873–1956) Author, born in Kent, and educated at St Paul's Cathedral Choir School. From the age of 16, until 1908, he worked, unhappily, for an oil company. His *Songs of Childhood* appeared in 1902, under the name of Walter Ramal, but attracted little notice. *The Listeners* (1912) was his first successful book of poetry, and its eerie title poem is still widely remembered:

> 'Is there anybody there?' said the Traveller,
> Knocking on the moonlit door;
> And his horse in the silence champed the grasses
> Of the forest's ferny floor.

With the story *The Three Mulla-Mulgars* (1910) and the poems of *Peacock Pie* (1913) he made his name as a children's writer. His work is frequently concerned with childhood, littleness, the outsider, and mystery, often with an undercurrent of melancholy. In his celebrated novel *Memoirs of a Midget* (1921), he describes the world of the minute Miss M. He was an accomplished author of shorter fiction, and his tales of the supernatural (including 'Seaton's Aunt' and 'All Hallows') are subtle and powerful examples of the genre (*see* GHOST STORIES). *Come Hither* (1923) was a widely admired anthology for children. *Collected Rhymes and Verses* was first published in 1944, and *The Collected Poems* in 1979. See Theresa Whistler, *Imagination of the Heart* (1993).

DELANE, John Thadeus (1817–79) Educated at King's College London and Magdalen Hall, Oxford, the famously shrewd and energetic editor of *The *Times* (1841–77)—a position he took on at the age of 23. He was caricatured by Anthony Trollope in *The *Warden* as 'Tom Towers'.

DELANEY, Shelagh (1939–) Playwright, who was born in Salford, left school at 16, and is known for *A Taste of Honey*, which she wrote when she was 17 after seeing Terence *Rattigan's play *Variations on a Theme*. It was presented by Joan *Littlewood in 1958 and was hailed as a landmark in the new school of *'kitchen sink' realism, a movement partly inspired by reaction against the drawing-room drama of Rattigan and Noël *Coward. In 1961, a British film adaptation (starring Rita Tushingham) appeared. Much of her subsequent work was written for the cinema and television, including *Charley Bubbles* (1968) and *Dance with a Stranger* (1985).

DELANY, Mary (1700–88) Née Granville, from a Tory family; she became a friend and correspondent of Jonathan *Swift, and married his friend Patrick *Delany in 1743. She knew many literary figures, including Alexander *Pope, Edmund *Burke, and Horace *Walpole. She was a *Blue Stocking hostess, and a favourite at court, where she introduced Fanny *Burney. Her *Autobiography and Correspondence* (1861–2, 6 vols, ed. Lady Llanover) gives a spirited account of her literary and social life.

DELANY, Patrick (?1685–1768) Irish clergyman and writer, friend of Jonathan *Swift and husband of Mary *Delany. He published *Observations upon Lord Orrery's Remarks on the Life and Writings of Dr Jonathan Swift* (1754), a series of letters, signed 'J.R.', in an attempt to correct what he describes as Orrery's 'very mistaken and erroneous accounts' of Swift's life and character.
See BOYLE, JOHN.

DELANY, Samuel Ray (1942–) American author, teacher, and critic, born in New York. *The Jewels of Aptor* (1962) was followed by a number of *science fiction novels in which Delany challenged the boundaries of generic forms like space opera and *sword and sorcery. *Babel-17* (1966) and *The Einstein Intersection* (1967) draw upon linguistics and mythology; *Dhalgren* (1975), and *Nevèrÿon* (1979) and its sequels also consider cities, civilization, and sexuality: the latter theme explored to extreme lengths in the non-science fiction *The Mad Man* (1994) and *Hogg* (1995). The *Nevèrÿon* series adds mock-scholarly apparatus to emphasize the narrative's sense of reflection and recursiveness. Delany's fiction, and the encouragement he gave to others, opened science fiction for greater engagement with questions of race and sexual orientations. Short fiction is collected in *Aye, and Gomorrah* (2003). He has published an autobiography, *The Motion of Light in Water* (1988), and numerous collections of criticism.

de la RAMÉE, Marie Louise *See* OUIDA.

DELEDDA, Grazia (1871–1936) Italian novelist and winner of the *Nobel Prize (1926). She is, with *Verga, a major writer of **verismo*. Her best novels, drawn from her Sardinian background, are *Elias Portolu* (1903: *The Woman and the Priest*; English trans. 1928, introduction by D. H. *Lawrence), *Canne al vento* (1913: *Canes in the Wind*), *Cenere* (1903: *Ashes*), and an autobiographical novel, *Cosima* (1937).

DELEUZE, Gilles (1925–95) French philosopher whose thought is defined by movement, displacement, difference, and multiplicity. His collaboration with the anti-Freudian psychoanalyst Félix Guattari in the 1970s produced the two-volume study *Capitalisme et schizophrénie* (*Anti-Oedipus*, trans. Robert Hurley, Mark Seem, and Helen R. Lane, 1977), which examines the impact of the dynamic, disruptive power of capitalism on the individual. Like the multiple and non-hierarchical (or 'rhizomic') growth he theorizes in the second volume of the study, *Mille Plateaux* (1980: *A Thousand Plateaus*), Deleuze's own thought has spread across a wide range of disciplines in the arts, humanities, and social sciences, from film studies to urban geography. His two-volume study of *cinema, *L'Image-mouvement* (1983: *The Movement-Image*) and *L'Image-temps* (1985: *The Time-Image*), which explores the changing way in which it represents space, movement, and time, has been particularly influential.

DELILLO, Don (1936–) American novelist, born and brought up in the Bronx, New York. Like Thomas *Pynchon, he employs black comedy and the language of science to deal with themes of paranoia and consumerism. His first book, *Americana* (1971), is a road novel in which a television executive attempts to impose meaning on his experiences by filming them. This was followed by *End Zone* (1972), which mixes American football with metaphysics, and *Great Jones Street* (1973), a satirical exploration of the world of a disaffected rock star. There are echoes of Jorge Luis *Borges and Laurence *Sterne in *Ratner's Star* (1976), a sprawling fable about scientific understanding and the nature of fiction. Subsequent works exhibit greater sophistication of subject matter and technique. *Players* (1977) deals with language, terrorism, and the sterility of affluent urban lives. *Running Dog* (1978), a spy thriller and satire of consumerism, concerns the search for a pornographic film shot in Hitler's Berlin bunker. *The Names* (1982) concerns a murderous sect, and *White Noise* (1984) is an environmental disaster story narrated by the professor of Hitler studies at a Midwestern university. His version of the Kennedy assassination, *Libra* (1988), focuses on the role of Lee Harvey Oswald in shaping the American psyche. Both *Mao II* (1991), a postmodern tale of celebrity, terrorism, and the behaviour of crowds, and *Underworld* (1997), a multi-layered secret history of the Cold War, examine the significance of spectacular events and media imagery in shaping the development of memory, history, and mass psychology. *Falling Man* (2007) ties its narrative to the destruction of the World Trade Center's twin towers in New York on 11 September 2001.

de LINT, Charles (1951–) Canadian writer, born in Bussum, the Netherlands; author of a distinctive urban *fantasy drawing upon local and European folklore. *The Onion Girl* (2001) sensitively counterpoints a story of sexual abuse and the faerie otherworld which acts as both metaphor and setting for the protagonists.

DELIUS, Frederick (1862–1934) Composer, born in Bradford and educated at the International College, Isleworth, and at Leipzig, where he met Edvard Grieg. Delius was of German descent and lived his mature life in France, where he met Gabriel Fauré and Maurice Ravel, but his music, especially in orchestral forms such as *Brigg Fair: An English Rhapsody* (1907) and *On Hearing the First Cuckoo in Spring* (1912), has folk elements and a late Romantic nostalgia which suggest strong English roots. His stage works are not based on English texts: *A Village Romeo and Juliet* (1901) is after Gottfried Keller. But he set P. B. *Shelley (*Three Songs*, 1891) and Alfred *Tennyson (*Maud*, 1891; *The Splendour Falls on Castle Walls*, 1925). Walt *Whitman's poetry lies behind *Sea Drift* (1904), *Songs of Farewell* (1930), and *Idyll: Once I Passed through a Populous City* (1932). Other notable literary settings include Ernest *Dowson (*Songs of Sunset*, 1906–7, and *Cynara*, begun 1907, completed 1929) and W. E. *Henley (*A Late Lark*, 1925). Delius contracted syphilis in Paris in 1895 and later became blind and paralysed: after completing the incidental music for James *Flecker's *Hassan* (1920–23), he dictated his music to Eric Fenby, whose *Delius as I Knew Him* (1936) recounts this arduous labour of love.

DELL, Floyd (1887–1969) American novelist, playwright, and journalist, born in Illinois but based for most of his life in New York. Serving initially as an essayist and reviewer in Chicago, he moved to New York in 1913 to write poetry, short stories, and prose sketches; a selection of these pieces was published as *Love in Greenwich Village* (1926). His novel *Moon-Calf* (1920) describes the development of a young writer.

DELLA CASA, Giovanni (1503–56) Poet and churchman who became papal ambassador to Venice and was involved in the first attempt by the church to impose an Index of Forbidden Books (1549). He is best known for his treatise on manners, *Il Galateo ovvero dei costumi* (1558), which became an international best-seller. The first English translation, by Robert Peterson (*fl.* 1562–1606), appeared in 1576. Della Casa also wrote a considerable corpus of lyric poetry in the Petrarchan tradition and some pornographic verse. See R. Pine-Coffin (trans.), *Galateo or the Book of Manners* (1958).

Della Crusca One of the best known of the learned *academies, it was established in Florence in 1582, with the principal object of standardizing the Italian language. The first edition of its dictionary appeared in 1612. Members of the Academy, especially Lionardo Salviati (1540–89), were prominent in the famous literary polemics in the 1580s over the rival merits of the poems of *Ariosto and *Tasso.

Della Cruscans A poetic coterie led by Robert Merry (1755–98), who produced sentimental and highly ornamented verse towards the end of the 18th century. After a wandering and varied career, Merry lived in Florence from 1784 to 1787 as a member of the *Della Crusca academy. With Hester *Thrale Piozzi and others he produced in 1785 a *Miscellany*, in which he signed his work 'Della Crusca'. Merry returned to England and began contributing salon verses to fashionable newspapers to which a number of pseudonymous poets replied, amongst them 'Anna Matilda' (Hannah *Cowley) and 'Laura Matilda' (Mary *Robinson). Their effusions were collected in the *British Album* in 1790, a volume which proved very successful until the publication in 1791 of William *Gifford's *The Baviad*, a savage satire on the Della Cruscans, followed by *The Maeviad* in 1795, part of which was also directed against them.

DELONEY, Thomas (d. in or before 1600) Silk-weaver and writer; he may have been born and educated in Norwich: he was certainly able to translate from Latin. He wrote broadside ballads on popular subjects, including three on the defeat of the Armada in 1588: a collection of ballads, *The Garland of Good Will*, was entered in the Stationers' Register in 1593. He is now best known for his four works of prose fiction, originally published between 1597 and 1600 and which long remained popular: *Jack of Newberie*; *The Gentle Craft* and *The Gentle Craft: The Second Part*; and *Thomas of Reading*. His fiction celebrates the virtues and self-advancement of hard-working craftsmen, especially in the cloth trade, and has been much admired in modern times for its effective use of dialogue. *The Gentle Craft* includes the story of Simon *Eyre, the shoemaker's apprentice who became lord mayor and founder of Leadenhall, which was adapted by Thomas *Dekker in *The *Shoemakers' Holiday*. There is an edition of the fiction by M. E. Lawlis (1961).

Delphic oracle The most famous oracular seat of the god Apollo, who slew the monstrous Python there. Delphi, also called Pytho, is a striking site on the slopes of Mount Parnassus, traditionally the haunt of the Muses. The Pythian Games, second in rank to the Olympics, were held in the third year of each Olympiad; twelve Pythian Odes by *Pindar survive. The Pythia, a priestess, having purified herself in the Castalian spring, uttered the oracles in a trance; they were interpreted for those consulting the oracle by her prophet/priests. *Herodotus and, later, *Plutarch quote many Delphic oracles with respect. The gnomic motto 'Know yourself', carved on the walls of Apollo's temple, was thought characteristically Delphic. The oracle was closed by the Christian emperor Theodosius in AD 390.

DEL REY, Lester (1915–1993) American writer, pseudonym of Leonard Knapp, born in Saratoga, Minnesota. He is the author of numerous *science fiction stories and novels, of which his robot story 'Helen O'Loy' (1938) is perhaps his best known. His fourth wife, the editor Judy-Lynn, headed the imprint Del Rey Books, which he continued after her death in 1986.

de MAN, Paul (1919–83) American critic, born in Antwerp, and educated in engineering at the Université Libre de Bruxelles. After an unsuccessful career in publishing, he emigrated to the USA in 1948, and studied at Harvard before following an academic career at Cornell, Johns Hopkins, and Yale universities. His major works, *Blindness and Insight* (1971), *Allegories of Reading* (1979), and *The Rhetoric of Romanticism* (posthumous, 1984), examine the figurative nature of literary language and the gulf between language and meaning. He transformed academic analysis of literary *Romanticism by discarding the accepted view that Romantic poetry reconciles the human mind with nature; on the contrary, he argued, it reveals and laments the impossibility of such reconciliation. The leading American exponent of *deconstruction, he explored with notable rigour the ways in which literary works paradoxically undermine their apparent meanings. Four years after his death, articles he had written during the German occupation of Belgium (one of them tainted by anti-Semitic remarks) were rediscovered. Opponents of deconstruction seized upon these as evidence of a supposed moral deficiency in a critical method practised 40 years later by de Man and his—mostly Jewish—associates. Posthumous works include *The Resistance to Theory* (1986). See Martin McQuillan, *Paul de Man* (2001).

DEMOCRITUS (b. *c.*460 BC) Greek philosopher, born in Abdera; with his teacher Leucippus founded ancient atomism; he wrote on ethics (and other subjects) as well as physics. He was called the 'laughing philosopher' for his advocacy of 'cheerfulness' (*euthumia*); only fragments of his writings remain. The key to his atomism is that everything happens by necessity, probably interpreted in terms of forces of repulsion and attraction between atoms, themselves the absolutely uncuttable (*atoma*) building blocks of the world. Atomism was subsequently adopted by *Epicurus in the Hellenistic period, by *Lucretius in the Roman; then revived in the 17th century by the French philosopher Pierre Gassendi (1592–1655).

Demogorgon Supposedly the primeval god of classical myth, first named in late antiquity through a scribal error. He appears in *Boccaccio's *Genealogia Deorum*, Ariosto's **Orlando furioso*, Spenser's **Faerie Queene* (I. v. 22, IV. ii. 47), and Milton's **Paradise Lost* (II. 965). He is a prominent figure in P. B. *Shelley's **Prometheus Unbound*; his name may have attracted Shelley because it is supposedly compounded of 'demos' (people) and 'gorgo' (Gorgon, the name of three female monsters).

de MORGAN, William Frend (1839–1917) Potter and novelist, educated at University College London. At first he devoted his attention to art and in particular to the production of stained glass and glazed pottery, working for a time in association with his friend William *Morris; he published two treatises on the craft of pottery. He was particularly successful with decorative tiles, but ill health brought this pursuit to an end, and at the age of 67 he embarked somewhat casually on the writing of fiction, his first and best novel, *Joseph Vance* (1906), proving to his astonishment a great success. It is the rambling but entertaining tale of a drunken builder's son befriended by a middle-class family, who graduates from Oxford University and becomes an engineer and inventor. This was followed by several others; the last two, *The Old Madhouse* (1919) and *The Old Man's Youth* (1921), left unfinished on his death, were skilfully completed by his widow, the artist Evelyn de Morgan. See A. M. D. W. Stirling, *William de Morgan and his Wife* (1922).

Demos A novel by George *Gissing, published anonymously in three volumes in 1886 by Smith, Elder. The densely political plot reflects Gissing's views on the failure of socialism. The proletarian agitator Richard Mutimer unexpectedly inherits a fortune, and builds a utopian community, New Wanley. He marries the middle-class Adela Waltham, who then finds the hidden will that dispossesses him. Mutimer's subsequent scheme to encourage saving by the working class is defrauded, and he is stoned to death by a mob. Adela marries the true heir, aristocratic Hubert, and Wanley improbably reverts to its pre-industrialized state. William *Gladstone was briefly thought to be the novel's author. Its poet-cum-politician Westlake is based on William *Morris.

DEMOSTHENES (384–322 BC) Leading Athenian orator and politician who tried to unite the Greeks against the territorial ambitions of Philip II of Macedon. Sixty-one of his orations survive. He became a rhetorical and libertarian model both in antiquity and in the Renaissance and 18th century. His *Philippics* were imitated by *Cicero in his attacks on Mark Antony; *Plutarch paired his life with Cicero's; *Quintilian and *Longinus analysed his methods. Thomas *Wilson, who translated his *Philippics* (1570), said that they were 'most nedefull to be redde in these daungerous dayes, of all them that loue their countries libertie'. In 'Of Eloquence' (1742) David *Hume lamented, 'It would be easy to find a Philip in modern times; but where shall we find a Demosthenes?'

DENHAM, Sir John (1615–69) Born in Dublin and educated at Trinity College, Oxford. A Royalist, he was forced to surrender Farnham Castle, of which he was governor, in 1642, fled to the Continent in 1648, and was appointed king's surveyor at the *Restoration as a reward for his loyalty. His tragedy *The Sophy*, set in the Turkish court, was performed in 1641, and he also published occasional verses, satires, and a free translation from *Virgil (*The Destruction of Troy*, 1656). He is chiefly known for *Cooper's Hill* (piratically published 1642 and revised in later editions), an early and influential example of the *topographical poem, describing scenery around his home at Egham, Surrey. John *Dryden called it 'the exact standard of good writing'. He went mad after his 18-year-old second wife became the duke of York's mistress. She died, it was rumoured, poisoned by a cup of chocolate.

Denis Duval W. M *Thackeray's last, unfinished, novel, published in the **Cornhill Magazine* 1864. The story begins in Rye, in the second half of the 18th century. The narrator, Denis Duval, grows up in a colony of French Protestant refugees. A French noblewoman, Mme de Saverne, escapes from the persecution of her husband and comes to England with the help of the sinister Chevalier de la Motte, who was intended to become the villain of the novel. She takes refuge with her old nurse, Denis's mother, and Denis falls in love with her little daughter Agnes. Denis has to leave home and go to sea after he has exposed the smuggling activities of his grandfather and the treasonable behaviour of de la Motte. The fragment ends at this point. Thackeray intended Denis to rescue Agnes from the machinations of de la Motte after a series of adventures at sea.

DENNIS, John (1657–1734) Son of a saddler, educated at Harrow School and Caius College, Cambridge. He was a poet and dramatist, but is best known for his criticism, which combines respect for *neo-classical theory with a passion for the *sublime. His critical works (ed. E. N. Hooker, 2 vols, 1939–43) include *The Advancement and Reformation of Modern Poetry* (1701), *The Grounds of Criticism in Poetry* (1704), and *An Essay on the Genius and Writings of Shakespeare* (1712). His tragedies include *Appius and Virginia* (1709), Alexander *Pope's mockery of which (in his **Essay on Criticism*) started a feud, their interchanges including Pope's *Narrative of Dr Robert Norris* (1713) and Dennis's *Remarks upon Mr Pope's Homer* (1717). Dennis also features as 'Sir Tremendous' in the Scriblerian **Three Hours after Marriage* (1717). Pope did assimilate some of Dennis's critical comments, and shortly before Dennis's death wrote a prologue for a benefit performance.

DENNIS, Nigel (1912–89) Novelist, playwright, journalist, and critic, born in Surrey, but educated abroad, in Southern Rhodesia and Germany. He worked for many years in America, where his first novel, *Boys and Girls Come out to Play* (1949), is largely set. His best-known work is *Cards of Identity* (1955), a satiric fantasy set in an English country house, which comments harshly but with much incidental comedy on post-war social change and insecurity and the ease with which the human personality can be controlled. *A House in Order* (1966) is a more abstract treatment of the problem of identity in which the imprisoned narrator, confined to a greenhouse, tries to ignore the world at war outside by cultivating his own garden. Dennis also published three plays and several critical works, and was for some time co-editor of **Encounter.*

Deor An Old English poem from the 9th or 10th century in the *Exeter Book, of 42 lines divided into seven unequal sections and containing the refrain 'that passed; so can this'. Deor seems to be a minstrel who has fallen out of favour and consoles himself by considering the past misfortunes of others such as Wayland the Smith, Theodoric, and Hermanric. It is one of the group of poems in the Exeter Book referred to as 'elegies', short poems whose theme is usually the transience and unreliability of the world, sometimes (though not in *Deor*) ending with a Christian consolation. See edition by Kemp Malone (4th edn, 1966).

De QUINCEY, Thomas (1785–1859) Journalist and author, second son of a linen merchant, born in Manchester and educated at schools in Bath and Winkfield, ending at Manchester Grammar School, from which he ran away to the homeless wanderings in Wales and London which he was to describe in **Confessions of an English Opium Eater.* He afterwards went to Worcester College, Oxford, and—having made the acquaintance of *Coleridge and *Wordsworth—settled at Grasmere in the cottage formerly occupied by the Wordsworths. In 1804, while at Oxford, he had begun to take opium, and from 1812 he became an addict. In 1817 he married Margaret Simpson, daughter of a local farmer, by whom he had eight children, and in the following year, having by then exhausted his private fortune, he started to earn a living by journalism. *Confessions of an English Opium Eater*, by which he made his name, was published in 1822. For the next 30 years he earned a precarious living, mainly in Edinburgh, by tales, articles, and reviews, mostly in **Blackwood's Magazine* and *Tait's*, including *Klosterheim* (1832), *Recollections of the Lake Poets* (1834–9), 'Sketches...from the Autobiography of an English Opium Eater' (1834–41, later entitled *Autobiographic Sketches*), 'Suspiria de Profundis' (1845), and 'The English Mail Coach' (1849). A collected edition of his works, *Selections Grave and Gay*, was started under his supervision in 1853, and occupied him until his death.

Since nearly all De Quincey's work was journalism, written under pressure to support his family, it is more remarkable for brilliant tours de force such as 'On the Knocking on the Gate in "Macbeth"', 'On Murder Considered as One of the Fine Arts', and 'The Revolt of the Tartars' than for sustained coherence. Eclectic learning, pungent black humour sometimes degenerating into facetiousness, a stately but singular style distinguish his writing. His impressionistic reminiscences both of his own childhood and of his literary contemporaries are memorably vivid. His greatest, though never completed, achievement was his psychological study of the faculty of dreaming in 'Suspiria de Profundis' and 'The English Mail Coach', in which he traced—25 years before Freud was born—how childhood experiences and sufferings are crystallized in dreams into symbols which can form and educate the dreamer's personality, and can also give birth to literature, either as poetry or as 'impassioned prose', as De Quincey called his own climaxes of imagery. *The Opium-Eater* (1981) is a biography by G. Lindop, who also edited *The Works of Thomas De Quincey*, 21 vols (2000–03).

DERRIDA, Jacques (1930–2004) French philosopher, born to a Jewish family in Algiers, who studied in Paris at the École Normale Supérieure, where he taught from 1964 to 1984. He also held visiting professorships at several American universities. Following the publication in 1967 of *De la grammatologie* (*Of Grammatology*) and *L'Écriture et la difference* (*Writing and Difference*), he exerted a huge influence upon literary theory as the founder of *deconstruction, a subtly and often playfully sceptical approach to the relations between language and meaning, which was adopted by Paul *de Man and others as a method for exploring problems of literary criticism. Among his later works are *Glas* (1974), on *Hegel and *Genet; *La Carte postale* (1980: *The Post Card*), on *Freud and *Lacan; *Spectres de Marx* (1993: *Spectres of Marx*); and a collection of eulogies, *Chaque Fois unique, la fin du monde* (2003: *Each Time Unique, the End of the World*). See J. Powell, *Jacques Derrida* (2006).

'Der wilde Jäger' *See* WILD HUNTSMAN.

DESAI, Anita (1937–) Novelist and short story writer, born in India and educated in Delhi; her father, D. N. Mazumdar, was of the Bengal elite, her mother German. Despite her sense of writing as an outsider to India though 'feeling Indian', Desai's elegant and lucid novels vividly evoke the atmosphere, society, and landscapes of her native land, and are noted for their delicate portrayal of the inner lives of women. Her work includes *Fire on the Mountain* (1977), *Fasting, Feasting* (1999), and, possibly her finest novel, *Clear Light of Day* (1980), the story of a fragmenting family set within a nation in turmoil. *Games at Twilight* (1978) and *Diamond Dust* (2000) are collections of short stories, and her writing for children includes the prize-winning *The Village by the Sea* (1982). Desai has three times been shortlisted for the Booker Prize. Other work includes *In Custody* (1984), *Baumgartner's Bombay* (1988), and *Journey to Ithaca* (1995). Desai has spent the latter part of her life in the United States, where she is John E. Burchard professor of writing at MIT.
See also POSTCOLONIAL LITERATURE; DESAI, KIRAN.

DESAI, Kiran (1971–) Indian novelist in English, who has spent a significant part of her life in the USA. She is the daughter of the novelist Anita *Desai, whom she cites as among her strongest sources of inspiration. The self-professed follower of an aesthetic of 'messiness' and fragmentariness, rather than order and symmetry, Kiran Desai published her first novel, *Hullabaloo in the Guava Orchard*, a pastiche reworking of R. K. *Narayan's *The Guide*, to wide acclaim in 1998. She was the winner in 2006 of the Man Booker Prize that three times eluded her mother for her multi-layered second novel, a study in transnational migration and rootlessness, *The Inheritance of Loss* (2006).

DESANI, G. V. (Govindan Vishnoodas) (1909–2000) Indian writer, born in Nairobi, Kenya; he lived in Britain during the Second World War, where he became a regular lecturer and broadcaster. His prose poem *Hali* (1950) was published with a preface by E. M. *Forster, but he is known principally for his inventive avant-garde novel *All about H. Hatterr* (1948), in which Hatterr, son of a European merchant seaman and 'an Oriental, a Malay Peninsula-resident lady, a steady non-voyaging non-Christian human', seeks wisdom from the seven sages of India. This was revised and republished in 1972 with an introduction by Anthony *Burgess. His hybrid and 'dazzling, puzzling, leaping prose' has been described by Salman *Rushdie (*Indian Writing, 1947–1977*, 1997) as 'the first genuine effort to go beyond the Englishness of the English language' and has been an important influence on a range of *postcolonial writers, Peter *Carey and M. G. Vassanji (1950–), as well as Rushdie himself. Desani spent some years in India working for the *Illustrated Weekly of India*, and the later part of his career as a professor at the University of Texas. A collected volume of stories was published in 1990.
See ANGLO-INDIAN LITERATURE.

DESCARTES, René (1596–1650) French philosopher and mathematician. After a period of travel, in 1629 he decided to devote himself to philosophy and settled in the Netherlands, where he remained until 1649, when he accepted an invitation to visit Sweden, where he died. His main works are: *Discours de la méthode* (1637: *Discourse on the Method*), *Méditations philosophiques* (published in Latin in 1641, in French in 1647: *Philosophical Meditations*), *Principes de la philosophie* (published in Latin in 1644, in French in 1647: *The Principles of Philosophy*), and *Les Passions de l'âme* (1649: *Passions of the Soul*). The influence of these on European thought has been considerable. Philosophically his starting point is the problem of certainty posed by *Montaigne's radical scepticism: in other words, the need for a method that establishes reliable propositions. Rejecting the accumulated preconceptions of the past through a process of systematic doubt, he proposes to reconstruct the whole of philosophy on the basis of certain self-evident truths, including notably the existence of the self in consciousness, the famous 'cogito ergo sum' ('I think, therefore I am'). From this basis he attempts to deduce the existence of God as guarantor of the reliability of the perceptible world, and thus of its susceptibility to scientific analysis. As a mathematician (he made major contributions to algebraic notation and coordinate geometry), he considered mathematical reasoning to be applicable to the whole of science. Although his astronomical theories were demolished by Isaac *Newton, his reduction of matter to the quantifiable has remained fundamental to science. In epistemology and ethics, his rigorous mind–body dualism has similarly been immensely influential. See S. Gaukroger, *Descartes* (1995).

DESCHAMPS, Eustache (*c.*1340–*c.*1404) French poet. A disciple of Guillaume de *Machaut, he wrote a vast number of ballades and the first treatise on poetry in French (*L'Art de dictier*, 1392), as well as moralizing poems, including the unfinished misogynistic *Le Miroir de mariage*. He addressed one of his 'Balades de moralitez' to *Chaucer, whom he styled a 'grant translateur'.

Deserted Village, The Poem by Oliver *Goldsmith (1770), evoking the idyllic pastoral life of Auburn, 'loveliest village of the plain', in its former state of prosperous stability, now ruined; the poem deplores the growth of trade, the demand for luxuries, and the mercantile spirit which have ruthlessly depopulated such villages and driven 'a bold peasantry, their country's pride' to emigration. James *Boswell ascertained that the last four lines were contributed by Samuel *Johnson. Because the poem appears to lament a personal loss, Auburn was long identified with Lissoy, where Goldsmith spent much of his childhood, but it is clearly a composite portrait, drawn from his anxiously researched observations of the declining English countryside. Goldsmith's idealized descriptions of a happy rural community provoked Crabbe's protest in *The *Village*.

Despair The most potent temptation to assail the Christian pilgrim; appears in Edmund *Spenser's **Faerie Queene*, I. ix, as an aged cavern-dweller whose call to suicide has a narcotic mellifluousness. Despair was understood to be the unforgivable 'sin against the Holy Ghost'. In John *Bunyan's **Pilgrim's Progress*, he appears as Giant Despair, resident of Doubting Castle, where he imprisons Christian and Hopeful. Great-heart kills him in Part II.

Desperate Remedies The first of Thomas *Hardy's published novels; appeared in 1871. The plot is influenced by the fashionable themes of the novel of *sensation. Cytherea Gray, who loves and is loved by Edward Springrove, becomes lady's maid to Miss Aldclyffe. The contrivances of Miss Aldclyffe, the discovery that Edward is already engaged, and the need to support a sick brother drive Cytherea to marry Aeneas Manston, Miss Aldclyffe's villainous and illegitimate son, whose first wife is supposed to have died in a fire. Once married, Cytherea discovers that Edward is free from his engagement and that Aeneas's wife is probably still alive. Ingenious investigations reveal that Aeneas murdered his first wife in order to gain Cytherea. He hangs himself in his cell and the lovers are united.

Destiny A novel by Susan *Ferrier, published 1831. The earnest evangelical tone of the book almost overwhelms the sense of comedy shown in her other novels. The story relates, in a complex plot, the fortunes of the various members of the Malcolm family: Glenroy, a Highland chief, married to the London-bred Lady Elizabeth Waldegrave, who finds the conditions of Scottish life so intolerable she leaves him; Glenroy's poor but worthy cousin Captain Malcolm, and his son Ronald; another cousin, the misanthrope Inch-Orran, who disappoints Glenroy by leaving his estate to Ronald and his father; Glenroy's nephew Reginald, who becomes engaged to Edith, the chief's daughter, then jilts her to marry her half-sister; and Ronald, who disappears after a shipwreck in order to leave his father in possession of the Inch-Orran property, and returns, after years away, to marry the jilted Edith.

de TABLEY, Lord *See* WARREN, JOHN BYRNE LEICESTER.

detective fiction Crime has been a staple of storytelling since its beginnings, and misdirection of the reader, leading to striking revelations at a late crisis point, has equally had its special position in fiction. The classic English detective novel marries the two elements. The founding father of the genre was actually an American, Edgar Allan *Poe, whose three detective stories from the 1840s ('The Murders in the Rue Morgue', 'The Mystery of Marie Roget', and 'The Purloined Letter') strikingly anticipate many of its main features. English writers followed him in creating detectives who were remote from the common herd, creatures of pure ratiocination, emotional hermits who observed but did not participate in the hurly-burly of life around them. The fact that the steely logic of Poe's detective, Auguste Dupin, often leads him to conclusions that border on the absurd does not seem to have worried most readers.

Around mid-century there were other fictional detectives, such as Charles Dickens's Inspector Bucket (**Bleak House*, 1853) and Wilkie Collins's Sergeant Cuff (*The *Moonstone*, 1868), who were apparently more homely and engaging, but it was Poe's model which won the day. This was largely the result of Conan *Doyle's creation of Sherlock Holmes. Holmes and his comrade Dr Watson first appeared in *A Study in Scarlet* (1887) but the enormous popularity of the characters really began when the *Strand Magazine* started to publish Holmes short stories in 1891. Traces of the stereotypes of brilliant detective and dependable but dull-witted associate, initiated by Poe and carried on by Doyle, can be found in characters from Agatha *Christie's Hercule Poirot and Captain Hastings to Inspector Morse and Sergeant Lewis in the novels of Colin Dexter (1930–). Conan Doyle's success was the result of his mastery of the short story, packing each one he wrote with observation, conflict, and sharply dramatized character-types. This success, the huge sums a Holmes story commanded, and the large market offered by the plentiful magazines of the time attracted hordes of followers and imitators in the late Victorian and Edwardian periods. Most of these writers are nearly forgotten today but some, often those with thriving careers in other literary fields, created memorable detectives. Arthur *Morrison's Martin Hewitt also appeared in stories published in the *Strand*, Baroness *Orczy's Old Man in the Corner featured in several volumes of short stories, and G. K. *Chesterton's meek but insightful Roman Catholic priest Father Brown proved to be perhaps the detective who escaped the shadow of Holmes most successfully.

After the First World War public taste shifted away from the short story to the novel-length tale. The so-called Golden Age is often said to have been inaugurated by *Trent's Last Case* (1913) by E. C. *Bentley but it was led by a quartet of women writers who are still widely read today: Agatha Christie, Dorothy L. *Sayers, creator of the aristocratic Lord Peter Wimsey, Margery *Allingham, and Ngaio *Marsh. All four were productive, consistent, and unembarrassed by the idea they were satisfying a need for entertainment. Christie in particular gave the public a stream of ingenious and satisfying puzzles whose solutions habitually left her readers feeling agreeably fooled. Other writers, such as R. Austin Freeman (1862–1943), the Anglophile American John Dickson Carr (1906–77), a specialist in so-called 'locked-room' mysteries, and Gladys Mitchell (1901–83), made their own contributions to the Golden Age.

After the Second World War the conventions and artifice of the Golden Age might have seemed increasingly irrelevant, but they proved surprisingly resilient, not least because most of its leading practitioners were still going strong. Allingham wrote many of her best novels, including her masterpiece *The Tiger in the Smoke* (1952), after the war. Christie continued to publish fiction into the 1970s, Marsh and Mitchell into the 1980s. Other novelists, such as Edmund Crispin (1921–78), creator of the eccentric academic Gervase Fen, and J. I. M. *Stewart, writing under the pseudonym of Michael Innes, appeared to revitalize the traditional form. Some writers in the 1950s preferred to aim for greater realism, specializing in believable studies of the murderous mind or of everyday situations into which murder erupts. Julian *Symons and Michael Gilbert (1912–2006) wrote in this realistic vein but could also produce enjoyable fiction in a variety of styles.

In the late 1960s and 1970s, just as the Golden Age practitioners were coming to the ends of their careers, a further generation re-established the English detective novel as a popular force with new readers. Both P. D. *James and Ruth *Rendell wrote novels in the whodunnit tradition, though Rendell gave the impression of regarding these as the lesser part of her output, and James disguised the vital surprise element in a massive and intricate narrative plan with accretions of realistic detail. Neither would have anything to do with the Never-never-shire settings of some of the Golden Age writers. James's Inspector Dalgliesh, though, is a traditional outsider, a reputable poet, shy of emotional involvements, while Rendell can produce masterpieces of reader misdirection in the Christie tradition. Both writers' novels have been regularly transferred to television, and the success of these series, and of Dexter's Morse, has boosted the popularity of modern crime fiction as a whole.

Most writers of detective fiction today strive to marry the whodunnit tradition with a realistic surface and treatment. Private detectives are the exception rather than the rule and many writers have pushed their British policemen in the direction of the tougher American police procedural genre. Another tendency has been to move the scene of the crimes not only out of the fantasy England portrayed in so many of the Golden Age novels but also out of the capital that has been the setting for so many stories since the days of Holmes and Watson. London is still home to many detectives but crime does seem to be migrating to the regions. Pascoe and Dalziel, the police duo created by Reginald Hill (1936–), may operate in the entirely fictional Mid-Yorkshire force but the background against which Hill sets what have become his increasingly ambitious narratives is recognizably the real county. Yorkshire also provides the backdrop for the fiction of Peter Robinson (1950–), creator of Inspector Banks. Scotland, and more specifically Edinburgh, is the setting in the novels of Ian *Rankin, whose books featuring the maverick policeman Inspector Rebus began with *Knots and Crosses* (1987) and have included *Black and Blue* (1997), *The Falls* (2001), and *The Naming of the Dead* (2006). It sometimes seems as if every major British city now has its own fictional detective. Nottingham plays a major role in the novels of John Harvey (1938–), Manchester in many of those by Val McDermid (1955–), and Portsmouth in the work of Graham Hurley (1946–). All these writers use their chosen milieu with a strong sense for the urban landscape and its moulding of people. Other British writers have travelled abroad to find a setting for their fiction. Michael *Dibdin's Aurelio Zen novels take place in a variety of Italian cities from Venice to Naples; Alexander McCall Smith (1948–) has used an African setting (Botswana) to great effect in his books featuring the female investigator Precious Ramotswe.

The vigour and variety of British crime writing today are more impressive than ever. Studies of the mind of a criminal are frequent, still led by Ruth Rendell and her alter ego Barbara Vine (the pseudonym she created for a number of novels, beginning with *A Dark-Adapted Eye* in 1986). Minette Walters (1949–) has covered something of the same terrain in her novels, beginning with *The Ice House* in 1992, and so too have Frances Fyfield (1948–) and the journalists Nicci Gerrard (1958–) and Sean French (1959–), writing together under the pseudonym of Nicci French. Comedy crime fiction, popular since at least the 1920s, has been reinvented with a blacker hue by writers like Christopher Brookmyre (1968–) and Colin Bateman (1962–). Historical crime has also made a strong comeback. The Brother Cadfael novels of Ellis Peters (1913–95) began this trend but many others have followed in their wake. The Falco novels of Lindsey Davis (1949–), which take place in ancient Rome, the Victorian-era fiction of Anne Perry (1938–), and the books of C. J. Sansom (1952–), set amidst the dangers of Henry VIII's court, are notable examples of this thriving sub-genre. P. C. Doherty (1946–), under his own name and many pseudonyms, including Paul Harding, Michael Clynes, and Anna Apostolou, has made a speciality of the Middle Ages but has also diversified into ancient Egypt and ancient Greece.

The conventions of detective fiction have also been adopted by children's authors, and detective fiction for younger readers, including the 1928 novel *Emil and the Detectives* by Erich Kästner (1899–74), the title story of Richmal *Crompton's *William the Detective* (1935), *The Falcon's Malteser* (1986) by Anthony Horowitz (1956–), and Philip *Pullman's Sally Lockhart novels, has proved enduringly popular. Many of Enid *Blyton's tales feature her young protagonists in successful pursuit of criminals and spies.

The continuing success of the detective novel in all its many forms is much in evidence both in bookshop sales and in library loans. The future vitality of the genre seems in no doubt.

See also SENSATION.

deus ex machina [Latin for 'a god from the machine'] A god in Greek drama swung in by a crane to resolve a problem in the plot, especially in *Euripides; more generally an unexpected event or intervention in a narrative, introduced to resolve a difficult situation.

de VERE, Aubrey Thomas (1814–1902) Poet, born in Co. Limerick, Ireland, the son of Sir Aubrey de Vere (1788–1846, himself a poet), educated at Trinity College, Dublin. He came early under the influence of William *Wordsworth and

S. T. *Coleridge and had many friends in the literary world, including Alfred *Tennyson, Sir Henry *Taylor, the *Brownings, and John *Ruskin; in 1851, in the footsteps of his friend J. H. *Newman, he was received into the Roman Catholic Church. His voluminous works include *The Waldenses, or The Fall of Rora, with Other Poems* (1842); *English Misrule and Irish Misdeeds* (1848), which displays Irish sympathies, as do many of his works; and *Recollections* (1897). He is the subject of a memoir (1904) by Wilfrid Ward.

de VERE, Edward *See* OXFORD, EDWARD VERE.

DEVEREUX, Robert *See* ESSEX, ROBERT DEVEREUX.

Devil Is an Ass, The A comedy by Ben *Jonson, acted by the King's Men 1616, printed 1631. Pug, a minor devil, is sent to London by Satan to try his hand at iniquity for a day, and becomes servant to Fitzdottrel, a foolish country squire, who is targeted by various cheats, including Meercraft, a 'projector', who lures him with a scheme for draining the fens, and two gallants Wittipol and Manly, who have designs on his wife. Her virtue wins them over, however, and they rescue Fitzdottrel from his entanglements. Pug, utterly outclassed by human wickedness, lands up in Newgate, and persuades Satan to take him back to hell.

'Devil's Thoughts, The' A satirical poem by Samuel Taylor *Coleridge and Robert *Southey, published 1799, describing the devil going walking and enjoying the sight of the vices of men. The poem was imitated by Lord *Byron in his 'Devil's Drive', and by P. B. *Shelley in his 'Devil's Walk'.

DEWEY, John (1859–1952) American philosopher, one of the leaders of the Pragmatist school, and educationist, born in Vermont. His chief works are: *Critical Theory of Ethics* (1891), *Studies in Logical Theory* (1903), *Democracy and Education* (1916), *Human Nature and Conduct* (1922).

DEWEY, Melvil (1851–1931) American librarian who invented the Dewey decimal system of library classification.

DEXTER, Colin *See* DETECTIVE FICTION.

Dial, The (1) (1840–44) The literary organ of the American Transcendental movement (*see* TRANSCENDENTAL CLUB), of which Margaret *Fuller was editor; she was succeeded by Ralph Waldo *Emerson. It contained contributions by Henry *Thoreau. (2) (1889–97) (nos 1–5) A literary and artistic periodical edited in London by Charles *Ricketts and Charles Shannon. The 'Dial Group' also included T. S. *Moore and Lucien Pissarro (1863–1944). (3) (1880–1929) A literary monthly founded in Chicago, which moved in 1918 to New York. In its last decade it was one of the most important international periodicals, publishing work by T. S. *Eliot, W. B. *Yeats, D. H. *Lawrence, Ezra *Pound, E. E. *Cummings, Conrad *Aiken, and many others. Scofield Thayer was editor from 1925. It was expensively printed and paid well; Cyril *Connolly described it as 'the most successful of eclectic magazines, rich, discerning'.

Dial of Princes, The The title of the translation, published in 1557, by Sir Thomas *North of *El relox de principes* by Antonio de Guevara (*c.*1481–1545).

Diana of the Crossways A novel by George *Meredith, published 1885. Diana is based on the writer Caroline *Norton, whose husband had tried to divorce her. After the family's protests Meredith included a note that the work 'is to be read as fiction'. The beautiful and impulsive Irish girl Diana Merion marries Mr Warwick, a man incapable of understanding the remarkable qualities of his wife. Her innocent indiscretions arouse his jealousy and he brings an action for divorce, citing Lord Dannisburgh (drawn from Melbourne), which he loses. Percy Dacier, a rising young politician, falls in love with Diana, but when she is about to live with him, openly and rashly, the dangerous illness of her friend Lady Dunstane recalls her sense of duty and propriety. Dacier perseveres, but just as she is on the point of joining him he discovers that an important political secret which he had confided to her has been passed to a London newspaper. When she admits her indiscretion he leaves in a fury and marries a young heiress. Diana's husband dies and she eventually recovers from her heartache to wed her faithful adorer Thomas Redworth, who, without being brilliant, has the wit and understanding to appreciate her. Crossways, the name of Diana's house, reflects an emphasis on a historical turning point in marital and sexual politics. The novel became one of Meredith's most popular works.

DIAPER, William (1685–1717) Poet, born in Somerset, author of *Nereides, or Sea-Eclogues* (1712), in which the speakers are mermen and mermaids: Jonathan *Swift found them 'very pretty' and tried to promote Diaper's church career. He also wrote *Dryades* (1712) and a *topographical poem, 'Brent', the parish in Somerset where he was curate from 1709 (printed 1754). The poem describes vividly the damp Somerset levels, where rabbits took to the water with ducks, and all food allegedly tasted of frog. He translated two books of Oppian's *Halieuticks*, a Greek didactic poem on fish and fishing (pub. 1722). See *Complete Works*, ed. D. Broughton (1952).

diaries, diarists The tradition of diary-keeping in England seems to date from the 17th century. The motives of the earlier diarists are unknown, but an awareness that they were living in turbulent times may have inspired the most celebrated of diarists, Samuel *Pepys, whose raucous, candid, superbly vivid diary of the years 1660–69 is both an intimate personal record and an expansive portrait of London life, and John *Evelyn, whose *Diary* covers a much longer period and offers careful reflection on the events it describes. *The Diary of Ralph Josselin, 1616–83*, ed. Alan Macfarlane (1976), gives an engaging portrait of the domestic life, illnesses, and religious attitudes of a clergyman-farmer in Essex. There are many Nonconformist diaries, including those of the ex-communicant Oliver Heywood (1630–1702), published in four volumes (1881–5), and the Presbyterian Peter Walkden (1684–1769). The *Journal* of John *Wesley is perhaps the finest example in this tradition. Jonathan *Swift's flirtatious letter-diary *Journal to Stella* (covering the years 1710–13) demonstrates the cross-fertilization of epistolary and diary-writing traditions. Explicit self-awareness emerges in the licentious *London Journal* of James *Boswell, written for his friend John Johnston, and unpublished until 1950. By the late 18th century diary-keeping was commonplace, and authors frequently intended publication, as did Fanny *Burney, whose first diary (1767) was addressed to Nobody 'since to Nobody can I be wholly unreserved'. Celebrity diaries made popular reading: Lord *Byron's friend Thomas *Moore instructed his executors to publish Byron's *Journal* (1818–41) to 'afford the means of making some provision for my wife and family'. The early 18th-century art world was prolifically documented in the diaries of Joseph Farington (who missed scarcely a day between 1793 and 1821) and Benjamin Robert *Haydon, whose last entry records his suicide. Much loved for its ordinariness rather than for well-known names, James *Woodforde's diary documents forty-five years in the life of a Norfolk parson, while the journals of Dorothy *Wordsworth, long valued for the light they shed on William, are now justly feted for their intense evocation of landscape and the literary life of the Wordsworth household. Major Victorian examples of the genre include the lively and frank diaries of the country clergyman Francis *Kilvert, and those of *Victoria herself.

The flourishing tradition of political diaries began with the *Memoirs* (1821–60) of Charles *Greville, clerk to the Privy Council, which were criticized for indiscretion when published between 1874 and 1887. Twentieth-century diarists made a virtue of indiscretion, and have also benefited from post-Freudian self-analysis. The diaries of diplomat Harold *Nicolson and the urbane parliamentarian and socialite Henry 'Chips' Channon (1897–1958), the latter edited by Robert Rhodes James from a massive 30 volumes in 1967, are as noteworthy for their colourful gossip as for their historical records.

Twentieth-century literary diarists, with widely contrasted styles and purposes, include Arnold *Bennett, Evelyn *Waugh, and Noël *Coward. Virginia *Woolf used her diary as an alternative space where she could experiment with different versions of her self and her writing in ways which would feed into her fiction; she also filled it with wicked portraits, much gossip, and incisive commentary on contemporary events. Architectural historian James Lees-Milne (1908–97) published twelve highly praised sharp and anecdotal volumes principally describing upper-class and country-house life. The late 20th-century vogue for sexual candour is exemplified in the *Diaries* (1986, ed. John Lahr) of the homosexual playwright Joe *Orton. Recently the practice of writing diaries for virtually immediate publication has become routine in both politics and the arts: notable examples are the *Diaries* (1993) of politician Alan Clark (1928–99); *Peter *Hall's Diaries* (1983, ed. John Goodwin); and *The Roy Strong Diaries 1967–87* (1997), by art historian and arts administrator Sir Roy Strong (1935–). Comic fictional diaries were popular in the 1880s, the most celebrated example being the *Grossmiths' *The Diary of a Nobody* (1892), and have recently been successfully revived with *The Secret Diary of Adrian Mole, aged 13¾* by Sue *Townsend (1982: originally created for the *BBC) and Helen *Fielding's *Bridget Jones's Diary* (1996).

Diarmid (Diarmait Ó Duibhne) A member of the Fianna (*see* FENIAN CYCLE) who elopes with *Grainne, wife of *Finn, and is eventually left to die by Finn on the slopes of Ben Bulben.

Diary of a Nobody, The By George and Weedon *Grossmith, published 1892. Charles Pooter's diary covers fifteen months of his life in the early 1890s. His entries, describing the events of his life with his wife Carrie in Brickfield Terrace, Holloway, reveal in affectionate and comic detail the society of anxious gentility in which he lives. Pooter emerges as worthy, deferential, and acutely sensitive to minor humiliations, such as those he suffers at the Mansion House reception or the Volunteer Ball. The wide variety of people who impinge upon him include his son, the 'fast' young Lupin, and his shocking fiancée Daisy Mutlar; the revered superior, Mr Perkup; the fashionable spiritualist, Mrs James of Sutton, who unsettles Carrie; the noisy Gowing, the fatuous Padge, cheeky errand boys, and tiresome servants. Text and illustrations reveal fascinating contemporary background, including details of clothes, the plaster antlers and splayed fans of the decor, the new fad for the bicycle, the fashion for imitations of Sir Henry *Irving, and the slang and popular songs of the time. Hilaire *Belloc asserted that Pooter was 'an immortal achievement', and most readers have agreed.

DIBDIN, Charles (1745–1814) Performer and songwriter, remembered for the sea songs 'The Lass that Loved a Sailor' and 'Tom Bowling'. He wrote many comic operas and afterpieces, of which *The Waterman* (1774), populated by working-class London characters, was the most successful. Having fallen out with several theatrical managers, he sustained himself through one-man musical 'table entertainments', which allowed free rein to his abilities as singer and character actor. He wrote a musical tour through Britain illustrated with his own paintings (1801–2), and an autobiography, *The Professional Life of Mr Dibdin* (4 vols, 1803), in which he describes his relations with David *Garrick.

DIBDIN, Michael (1947–2007) Crime novelist, born in Wolverhampton and brought up in Northern Ireland, educated at the University of Sussex and the University of Alberta, Canada. Before becoming a full-time writer, he taught English in Perugia, and much of his best work—such as his accomplished pastiche mystery *A Rich Full Death* (1986), and his eleven Aurelio Zen novels, from *Ratking* (1988) to *End Games* (2007)—is set in Italy. *The Last Sherlock Holmes Story*

(1978) resurrected the London of *Jack the Ripper. *Dirty Tricks* (1991) is a blackly satiric comedy about Oxford. *The Dying of the Light* (1993) reworks the conventions of the country-house whodunnit to disturbing effect. His tense thriller, *Dark Spectre* (1995), combines 'police procedural' features with depiction of rootless lives in North America. Mordant wit, narrative verve, sardonic social and psychological penetration, trenchant pessimism, and vividly knowledgeable evocation of place distinguish all Dibdin's fiction.
See also DETECTIVE FICTION.

DIBDIN, Thomas Frognall (1776–1847) Nephew of Charles *Dibdin, educated at Oxford, a renowned bibliographer and librarian to the second Earl Spencer at Althorp. Dibdin published *An Introduction to the Knowledge of Rare and Valuable Editions of the Greek and Latin Classics* (1802), and, in 1809, his *Bibliomania* ('a bibliographical romance'), which did much to stimulate interest in old books and rare editions. Dibdin became secretary of the bibliophiles' *Roxburghe Club on its foundation in 1812. *A Bibliographical, Antiquarian, and Picturesque Tour in France and Germany* was published in 1821, and his *Library Companion* in 1824. In his *Bibliophobia* (1832) he comments with surprise on the respectful manner of the publisher John *Murray to his authors, and examines the depressed state of the book trade. *Reminiscences of a Literary Life* followed in 1836, and his *Bibliographical, Antiquarian, and Picturesque Tour in the Northern Counties of England* in 1838.

DICK, Philip K. (Kindred) (1928–82) Born in Chicago; writer of philosophical *science fiction who has had a profound influence on both science fiction and theories of *postmodernism. Beginning with magazine short stories in 1952, Dick created a body of work which spanned the spectrum of science fiction, from disposable trash to parodic art. An increasing body of scholarship now argues which is which. His early novel *Time out of Joint* (1959) explores consensus reality (the thought that reality is what exists, or what we can by consensus agree seems to exist), a question which troubled Dick through the *alternate history *The Man in the High Castle* (1962) and the *Gnostic *Ubik* (1969) to *Valis* (1981). *We Can Build You* (1972; written 1962; pub. in magazine form 1969), *The Simulacra* (1964), and especially *Do Androids Dream of Electric Sheep?* (1968; filmed as *Blade Runner* 1982) articulate ideas about authenticity later developed by the philosopher Jean *Baudrillard. Much of his science fiction, and the non-science fiction unpublished in his lifetime, is also a sympathetic depiction of 'ordinary' small-town people. Dick's own marital, health, and psychological problems shaped his work. Various explanations of his 1974 'breakdown' are described triumphantly in the comic *Valis*, whose protagonist 'Horselover Fat' is a thinly disguised Dick (who also appears). See Lawrence Sutin, *Divine Invasions: A Life of Philip K. Dick* (1989).

DICKENS, Charles (1812–70) Novelist, born in Portsmouth, the son of a clerk in the navy pay office. His early boyhood, spent in Chatham, was happy, and he attended a competent private school in Chatham. This was followed by a period of intense misery during which his father was imprisoned for debt in the Marshalsea and he himself (aged 12) worked in a blacking warehouse. These painful experiences inspired much of his fiction, notably the early chapters of **David Copperfield*. He then worked as an office boy, studied shorthand, and became reporter of debates in the Commons for the **Morning Chronicle*. He contributed to the *Monthly Magazine* (1833–5), the *Evening Chronicle* (1835), and other periodicals. These articles, subsequently republished as **Sketches by Boz, Illustrative of Every-Day Life and Every-Day People* (1836–7), attracted much attention. An approach from *Chapman and Hall led to the publication in twenty monthly numbers (beginning April 1836) of *The Posthumous Papers of the Pickwick Club*, published in volume form in 1837 (*see* PICKWICK PAPERS). After a slow start the series achieved immense popularity, and Dickens, with his young wife Catherine Hogarth, embarked on a promising future, courted by publishers, admired by the public, and befriended by celebrities. On Christmas Day 1836 he met John *Forster, who became a lifelong friend, and his biographer.

In 1837 (a year overshadowed by the death of his much-loved sister-in-law Mary) **Oliver Twist* began to appear in monthly numbers in **Bentley's Miscellany*, a new periodical of which Dickens was the first editor. It was followed by **Nicholas Nickleby*, also in monthly numbers. In 1840 a new weekly was launched, written wholly by Dickens, called **Master Humphrey's Clock*; it was originally intended to carry short sketches as well as instalments of the full-length novels *The *Old Curiosity Shop* (1840–41) and his long-deliberated **Barnaby Rudge* (1841). The novels proved so popular that the linking by 'Master Humphrey' was dropped. In 1842 he and his wife visited America, where he was rapturously received. His first impressions were favourable, but disillusion followed and his *American Notes* (1842) caused much offence in America, as did his portrayal of American stereotypes in **Martin Chuzzlewit* (1843–4). While in America he advocated international copyright and the abolition of slavery.

The sales of *Martin Chuzzlewit* were disappointing, but the demands of the public and his own growing family were met by the success of *A *Christmas Carol* (1843), the first of a series of Christmas books (*The *Chimes*, *The *Cricket on the Hearth*, *The Battle of Life*, and *The *Haunted Man*), works described by him as 'a whimsical sort of masque intended to awaken loving and forebearing thoughts'. In 1844 he paid a long visit to Italy, which produced 'Pictures from Italy' contributed to the **Daily News*, a new radical paper founded by Dickens in 1846 and briefly edited by him. He began **Dombey and Son* (1848) during a visit to Switzerland in 1846. In 1850 he started the weekly periodical **Household Words*; in 1859 it was incorporated into *All the Year Round*, which he continued to edit until his death. In this he published much of his later writings, including the Christmas stories that replaced the Christmas books. *David Copperfield* appeared in monthly numbers in 1849–50; **Bleak House* in 1852–3; and *A Child's History of England* (a work which manifests his own historical bias: his heroes were Alfred and Cromwell) appeared irregularly, 1851–3. **Hard Times* appeared in 1854, **Little Dorrit* in 1855–7, *A *Tale of*

Two Cities in 1859, *Great Expectations in 1860–61, and *Our Mutual Friend in 1864–5.

During these years of intense productivity he also found time for his large family, for a vast circle of friends, and for philanthropic enterprises, at times combined with his passion for amateur theatricals; it was a fund-raising performance of Wilkie *Collins's *The Frozen Deep* in 1857, in aid of Douglas *Jerrold's family, that introduced him to the young actress Ellen Ternan. His admiration for her further strained his deteriorating relationship with his wife, and he and Catherine separated in 1858. He defied scandal, protested his own innocence (and that of his sister-in-law Georgina, for many years his devoted housekeeper, whose name gossip had also linked with his), and continued to appear in public, distracting himself from domestic sorrow by throwing his restless energy into public readings of his own works. These, though immensely successful, were physically and emotionally exhausting. He revisited America in 1867–8, delivered a series of readings there, and on his return continued to tour the provinces. He died suddenly in 1870, leaving unfinished his last novel, *The *Mystery of Edwin Drood*.

Dickens captured the popular imagination as no other novelist had done and, despite murmurs against his sensationalism and sentimentality and his inability to portray women other than as innocents or grotesques, he was also held in high critical esteem, admired by contemporaries as varied as Queen *Victoria and *Dostoevsky. His popularity and fame proved durable, but it was not until the 20th century that he began to attract academic attention; see in particular George *Orwell, 'Charles Dickens', in *Inside the Whale* (1940), Humphry *House, *The Dickens World* (1941), and Edmund *Wilson, 'Dickens: The Two Scrooges', in *The Wound and the Bow* (1941). Later criticism has tended to praise the complexity of the sombre late works at the expense of the high-spirited humour and genius for caricature traditionally labelled 'Dickensian'. A series of distinguished illustrators inseparably connected with his work, including Hablot K. *Browne ('Phiz'), John *Leech, George *Cruikshank, George Cattermole, and Samuel Luke Fildes, meant that he had a significant impact on the visual culture of the period. He collaborated with Wilkie Collins in various stories which appeared in *Household Words*. See John Forster, *The Life of Dickens* (1872–4); Edgar Johnson, *Charles Dickens: His Tragedy and Triumph* (1952); Paul Schlicke, *The Oxford Reader's Companion to Dickens* (1999); Peter Ackroyd, *Charles Dickens* (2002). A collected edition of Dickens's *c.*14,000 letters, instigated by Humphry House, was published in twelve volumes under the general editorship of Madeline House, Graham Storey, and Kathleen Tillotson (1965–2002).

DICKENS, Monica (1915–92) Novelist, great-granddaughter of Charles *Dickens, born in London, educated at St Paul's Girls' School, and the Central School of Speech Training and Dramatic Art. Her works of fiction included the best-selling *One Pair of Hands* (1939), based on her experiences as a cook and general servant, *One Pair of Feet* (1942), reflecting her years as a wartime nurse, and *My Turn to Make the Tea* (1951), which drew on her time as a reporter on a local newspaper. She continued to incorporate first-hand experiences into her novels with *No More Meadows* (1953) and *Kate and Emma* (1964), which arose from her involvement with the National Society for the Prevention of Cruelty to Children, while her work for the Samaritans (the first American branch of which she founded in 1974) produced *The Listeners* (1970). She moved to America on her marriage to an American naval commander, but returned to England in 1985 after his death.

DICKENSON, John (*c.*1570–1635/6) Minor Elizabethan writer and government official. His *Arisbas* (1594) is a *euphuistic romance and *The Shepheardes Complaint* (?1596), written in English *hexameters with connecting prose passages, is reminiscent of Philip *Sidney's *Arcadia. His *Greene in Conceipt* (1598), reviving Robert *Greene from his grave, tells the 'Tragique Historie of faire Valeria of London'.

DICKINSON, Emily (1830–86) American poet, born in Amherst, Massachusetts, the daughter of a successful lawyer. She was educated at Amherst Academy (1834–47) and Mount Holyoake (1847–8); during her early years she was lively, witty, and sociable, but from her mid-twenties she gradually withdrew into an inner world, eventually refusing to leave her home, although she maintained intimate correspondences with people she never saw face to face. Her emotional life remains mysterious, despite much speculation about possible disappointed love affairs. She wrote poetry from girlhood onward, but only seven poems out of nearly 2,000 are known to have been published during her lifetime, and those appeared anonymously and much edited. She at one stage actively sought publication, but her contemporaries found her work bewildering, and she appears to have accepted her lot as an unrecognized writer. From *c.*1858 she assembled many of her poems in packets of 'fascicles', which were discovered after her death; a selection, arranged and edited by Mabel Loomis Todd and T. W. Higginson, appeared in 1890. Full publication was delayed by family difficulties, but eventually other editions and volumes of letters appeared, restoring her individual punctuation and presentation. At first regarded as an eccentric minor poet, she is now considered a major writer of startling originality. Her work presents recurrent themes—a mystic apprehension of the natural world, a preoccupation with poetic vocation, fame, death, and immortality—and is expressed in a rhetoric and language of her own, cryptic, elliptical, and at times self-dramatizing and hyperbolic. Her imagery reflects an intense and painful inner struggle over many years; she refers to herself as 'the queen of Calvary', and her verse is full of allusions to volcanoes, shipwrecks, funerals, storms, imprisonments, and other manifestations of natural and human violence. See R. B. Sewall's biography (2 vols, 1974).

DICKINSON, Goldsworthy Lowes (1862–1932) Scholar, humanist, and historian, born in London and educated at Charterhouse and, from 1881, at King's College, Cambridge, where he became a fellow (1887). He spent much of his life as teacher and mentor there. He wrote on

Hellenism, Plato, and the Socratic method: see, in particular, *The Greek View of Life* (1896), *The Meaning of Good* (1901), and *A Modern Symposium* (1905). He was also much interested in China: his *Letters from John Chinaman* (1901) preceded his only visit to that country in 1912. He was deeply shocked by the outbreak of the First World War—he reflected on the period in *The International Anarchy, 1904–1914* (1926)—and subsequently became involved in the work of the League of Nations, the concept of which he had helped to initiate, and the name of which he may have coined.

DICKINSON, Peter (1927–) British writer born in Northern Rhodesia (now Zambia), best known for his work for children, although he has published detective stories and *science fiction for adults, including the *alternate history *King and Joker* (1976). Achieving success with the 'Changes' trilogy (1968–71) and *The Blue Hawk* (1976), a *fantasy, Dickinson has also published novels such as *Tulku* (1979) and *AK* (1990) with historical or contemporary themes. *Eva* (1988) uses the device of a girl whose body is replaced by a chimpanzee's to explore issues from exploitation to evolution; theories about human evolution are also explored in *A Bone from a Dry Sea* (1992) and *The Kin* (1998).

DICKSON, Gordon Rupert (1923–2001) American *science fiction writer, born in Edmonton, Canada; much of whose fiction from *Dorsai!* (1959) onwards incorporates a detailed but unfinished cycle tracing humanity's cultural and genetic evolution into space, exploring a range of ethical issues. Only the science fiction (historical and contemporary novels were planned) was completed, but the flavour of medieval knighthood is taken up by the *fantasy *The Dragon and the George* (1976) and its sequels.

diction The aspect of literary style determined by choice of vocabulary: for example, a recurrent adoption of archaic words, or a preference for words derived from Latin, or simply a marked avoidance of colloquial words, may characterize a given diction. For the controversy on artificial diction in English poetry, *see* POETIC DICTION.

dictionary In the late 16th century it became clear that the division between two levels of English, 'learned' or 'literary', as opposed to 'spoken' or 'popular', necessitated glossaries of the kind previously available for Greek, Latin, or French. Robert Cawdrey's *Table Alphabeticall...of Hard Usuall English Wordes* (1604), containing about 3,000 words, might be called the first English dictionary; Henry Cockeram's *English Dictionarie* (1623) translates hard words to easy as well as easy to hard. The first major English dictionary was Nathan *Bailey's *Universal Etymological English Dictionary* (1721), which had more entries than its famous successor by Samuel *Johnson (1755). Johnson's *Dictionary* was a great landmark in English lexicographical history; Johnson illustrates his words in practice, and attempts to indicate the connotations of words, as well as offering their exact meaning. A number of 19th-century dictionaries attempted to develop these empirical techniques, which culminate in perhaps the greatest dictionary of any modern language, *The *Oxford English Dictionary* (1884–1928). The *OED* attempts to give a full history of the development of all English words since the 12th century, with full illustrative quotations, ordered according to the principal distinct senses of the word. *Roget's *Thesaurus*, in effect a dictionary of semantically linked words, first appeared in 1852. Noah *Webster's *American Dictionary of the English Language* (1828) became definitive in successive editions, but has been controversial in its later revisions for its refusal to discriminate between 'good' and 'bad' English by identifying supposedly inferior categories of words, such as 'slang', or 'obscene'. Specific dictionaries of jargon, slang, dialect, and technical terms (such as law) began to emerge in the 18th century with dictionaries of criminal argot, and have continued to develop as linguistic forms change. Most modern dictionaries have an online form, and linguists now tend to use concordances based on vast digitized bodies of text ('corpora') as arbiters of meaning. See J. A. H. Murray, *The Evolution of English Lexicography* (1900); J. R. Hulbert, *Dictionaries, British and American* (1955); T. Starnes and G. E. Noyes, *The English Dictionary from Cawdrey to Johnson* (1946); Thomas Finkenstaedt, *Ordered Profusion* (1973); Robert Burchfield, *Studies in Lexicography* (1987); Tom McArthur, *Living Words* (1988).

Dictionary of National Biography, The Designed and published by George *Smith, begun in 1882 with Sir Leslie *Stephen as editor. It included in its original form biographies of all national notables from earliest times to 1900. The work has been continued by the publishing of supplements at ten-year intervals. Stephen was succeeded in the editorship by Sir Sidney *Lee. Their names appear jointly on the title pages of vols xxii–xxvi (1890), and Lee's name alone from vol. xxvii till 1911. In 1917 the *DNB* was transferred to *Oxford University Press. The 1912–21 volume was edited by H. W. C. Davis and J. R. H. Weaver; 1922–30 by J. R. H. Weaver; 1931–40 by L. G. Wickham Legg; 1941–50 by L. G. Wickham Legg and E. T. Williams; 1951–60 by E. T. Williams and Helen Palmer; 1961–70 by E. T. Williams and C. S. Nicholls; 1971–80 and 1981–5 by Lord Blake and C. S. Nicholls; 1986–90 by C. S. Nicholls. A complete revision, now known as the *Oxford Dictionary of National Biography* (*ODNB*), was published in 2004, in an edition extending over 60 volumes and containing 56,646 biographies. Its editor, Professor Colin Matthews, died in 1999 and was succeeded by Professor Brian Harrison, then in 2004 by Dr Lawrence Goldman. It is also available in an online version which is updated twice yearly.

Dictys Cretensis (of Crete) Supposed author of a diary of the Trojan War which exists in Latin. In the preface, written in the 4th century AD, Lucius Septimius claims that he translated the work from a Greek version prepared for Nero from a Phoenician original. Dictys claims to have been present at the siege of Troy as a companion of the Cretan Idomeneus. Like the narrative of *Dares Phrygius his diary is probably a fabrication, but the two were the chief sources of medieval Trojan legends.

Diddler, Jeremy The chief character in James Kenney's farce *Raising the Wind* (1803). Jeremy's habit of continually borrowing small sums which he does not pay back probably gave rise to the present sense of the verb 'diddle'—to cheat or deceive.

DIDEROT, Denis (1713–84) French philosopher and man of letters. The son of a prosperous artisan, he became a leading member of the *Enlightenment. He began by translating the earl of *Shaftesbury (1745), and thereafter maintained his interest in English culture, publishing an influential appreciation of Samuel *Richardson (1761). He also wrote two sentimental plays on bourgeois domestic subjects, *Le Fils naturel* (1757: *The Natural Son*) and *Le Père de famille* (1758: *The Family Father*), which put into practice his innovative ideas on drama, influenced by George *Lillo; he also adapted Edward Moore's domestic prose tragedy *The *Gamester.* He developed a scientific empiricism and materialism which stimulated the originality of his thought: his *Pensées sur l'interprétation de la nature* (1754: *Thoughts on the Interpretation of Nature*), for example, anticipated evolutionary ideas on the nature and origin of life. In 1746 he assumed what became, in effect, a twenty-year editorship of the **Encyclopédie*. He is best known today, however, for three remarkably 'modern' novels, none of which he published in his lifetime: *La Religieuse* (*The Nun*), written in 1760, first published in 1796, and translated into English in 1797, the story of a young woman forced to become a nun; *Le Neveu de Rameau* (*Rameau's Nephew*), begun *c.*1760 and first published in 1804 in *Goethe's German translation; and *Jacques le fataliste* (*Jacques the Fatalist*), begun *c.*1773 and much influenced by Sterne's **Tristram Shandy* in its experimental form. See P. N. Furbank, *Diderot* (1992).

DIDION, Joan (1934–) American essayist and novelist, graduate of the University of California, Berkeley, known for her uncompromising depictions of contemporary American society, in collections of essays such as *Slouching towards Bethlehem* (1968), in which California of the 1960s comes to represent the decline in seriousness of the USA and the world. This was followed by *The White Album* (1979) and *Sentimental Journeys* (1993), where her laconic prose and sense of cultural despair are employed to scrutinize three American cities. She has published four novels which deal with the difficulties faced by women in a patriarchal society: in *Play It as It Lays* (1970) the main character has a mental breakdown; in *The Book of Common Prayer* we see the collapse of a mother–daughter relationship. Following a visit to San Salvador in 1973 she wrote *Salvador* (1983), describing the repressive political regime. This was followed by *Miami* (1987), where she traced the attempts of marginalized Hispanic communities to become integrated into society. Her moving memoir *The Year of Magical Thinking* (2005) documents her grief and struggle in the year following the sudden death of her husband and her daughter's illness.

Dido *See* AENEID.

Dido Queen of Carthage, The Tragedy of Published 1594 as written by Christopher *Marlowe and Thomas *Nashe, though Nashe's hand in it is disputed, as is its place in the chronology of Marlowe's works. Performed by the Children of the Queen's Chapel, it is closely based on Virgil's **Aeneid* (Bks 1, 2, and 4), depicting Dido's failure to persuade Aeneas to stay with her in Carthage and her subsequent suicide.

DIDSBURY, Peter (1945–) British poet, born in Fleetwood, Lancashire. He studied English and Hebrew at Oxford and later trained as an archaeologist. Closely associated with Douglas *Dunn and Sean *O'Brien in the 1970s, his work first appeared in Dunn's anthology *A Rumoured City* (1982), which carried a preface by Philip *Larkin. Didsbury's knowledgeable, eccentric, digressive, and often humorous voice is, however, more reminiscent of postmodernists such as John *Ashbery. His collections of poetry are *The Butchers of Hull* (1982), *The Classical Farm* (1987), *That Old Time Religion* (1994), and *Scenes from a Long Sleep: New and Collected Poems* (2003).

DI FILIPPO, Paul (1954–) American writer born in Rhode Island, Providence. *The Steampunk Trilogy* (1995) is an example of his energetic and inventive *science fiction; the short stories collected in *Ribofunk* (1996) expand the concerns of *cyberpunk to focus upon biological themes and nanotechnology.

DIGBY, Sir Kenelm (1603–65) Author, diplomatist, naval commander (who defeated the French and Venetian fleets in Scanderoon harbour (now İskenderun, Turkey), 1628), and one of the first members of the *Royal Society; he discovered the necessity of oxygen to the life of plants, but less scientifically believed in the curing of wounds by 'powder of sympathy'. In 1625 he secretly married the celebrated beauty Venetia Stanley (1600–33), and he gives an account, under disguised names, of his wooing in his *Private Memoirs* (published 1827); her situation is said to have provided the plot of James *Shirley's *The Wedding*, and her death in 1633 was lamented by Ben *Jonson, William *Habington, and others. He published a criticism of Sir Thomas *Browne's **Religio Medici* in 1643, and wrote 'Of Bodies' and 'Of the Immortality of Man's Soul' in the same year. A life by R. T. Petersson appeared in 1956.

Digby Plays Three late *mystery plays from East Anglia, probably dating from the early 16th century, bearing on them the name or initials of Myles Blomefylde (1525–1603), a collector of books from Bury St Edmunds. These plays are outcrops from the mystery cycles, found with non-literary material in

Digby MS 133. They are *Mary Magdalen*, *The Conversion of St Paul*, and *The Killing of the Children of Israel*; all of them, but especially *Mary Magdalen*, have considerable literary and theatrical interest. They have been edited by D. C. Baker, J. L. Murphy, and L. B. Hall, Jr (EETS os 283, 1982).

DILKE, Sir Charles Wentworth (1843–1911) Writer and politician, educated at Trinity Hall, Cambridge. He became MP for Chelsea in 1868 and held offices under William *Gladstone. He inherited the proprietorship of *The *Athenaeum* and **Notes and Queries* on his father's death in 1864. In 1885 he married the art historian Emilia Pattison (née Emilia Francis Strong, 1840–1904, author of *Claude Lorrain*, 1884; *The Shrine of Death*, 1886; and other works), who was the widow of Mark *Pattison. His connection with a divorce scandal contributed to the decline of his political and literary career. See D. Nicholls, *The Lost Prime Minister: A Life of Sir Charles Dilke* (1995).

dime novels The name for cheap (a dime is 10 cents), popular stories in America. The term, sometimes used for story magazines as well as novels, was first used in 1860 and thereafter was applied to series published in the late 19th and early 20th centuries. The format changed but these works were the precursors of the modern paperback. A collection of dime novels is housed at Stanford University.

dimeter A verse line with only two stressed syllables. *See also* METRE.

DINESEN, Isak (1885–1962) Pseudonym of Karen von Blixen-Finecke, née Karen Dinesen, short story writer and memoirist, who was born on the family estate at Rungstedlund, north of Copenhagen, and educated first in Switzerland, then at the Academy of Art, Copenhagen. Her father, Wilhelm Dinesen, a soldier, writer, and landowner, committed suicide when she was 10. She started publishing stories when she was 22, but it was the publication of *Seven Gothic Tales* (1934), her densely woven stories which work through suggestion and metaphor rather than direct fantasy or horror, which made her reputation. Her next book, *Out of Africa* (1937; filmed by Sydney Pollack in 1985), is her most famous and is her memoir of the seventeen years she spent in British East Africa, later Kenya, first as the wife of Baron Bror von Blixen-Finecke, and then on her own. The memoir refers to a world that is lost and its tone is coloured by that and her personal losses; it also documents the redemptive power of nature, and her respect for African culture, however mediated through a colonial vision. She contracted syphilis from Bror after the first year of marriage; they were separated in 1921 and divorced in 1925. Dinesen met her lover Denys Finch Hatton, a big game hunter, during this period; his death in 1931 and the failure of her coffee plantation forced her return to Denmark. During the 1940s and 1950s she continued to develop the techniques of the storytelling tradition in tales such as 'Babette's Feast', of which a Danish film appeared in 1987. Though Danish, Blixen wrote her work first in English.

DIODATI, Charles (d. 1638) Italian doctor's son, schoolfellow of John *Milton at St Paul's and closest friend; Milton addressed to him Latin *elegies 1 and 6 and an Italian *sonnet, and mourned him in the *pastoral *Epitaphium Damonis* (?1640). See D. C. Dorian, *The English Diodatis* (1950).

DIODORUS SICULUS (1st century BC) A Sicilian Greek historian, author of a universal history from the mythical past to 60 BC. Poggio Bracciolini's Latin translation of the first five books, which give an account of Egypt, Assyria, and early Greece, was published in 1472 and widely read in the 16th and 17th centuries. John *Skelton translated this version into English in the 1580s.

DIONYSIUS THE PSEUDO-AREOPAGITE (5th century AD) Greek author of an important collection of Neoplatonic mystical writings who attributed his work to the 1st-century Dionysius the Areopagite, converted by St *Paul at Athens (Acts 17: 34). His four treatises, *The Celestial Hierarchy*, *The Ecclesiastical Hierarchy*, *The Mystical Theology*, and *On the Divine Names*, were translated into Latin by *Scotus Eriugena and strongly influence the whole medieval mystical tradition. The 14th-century mystical prose work *Deonise Hid Divinite* (EETS os 231, 1949, ed. P. Hodgson) is founded on him, as its name suggests, and John *Colet later drew on him for his lectures in Oxford 1497–8.

'Dipsychus' A poem by A. H. *Clough.

dirty realism The name given to a kind of American fiction of the 1970s and 1980s characterized by a sparse narrative style. Exemplars of this mode are Raymond *Carver, Richard *Ford, and Tobias *Wolff. *Granta* published a collection of dirty realism in 1983.

DISCH, Thomas M. (1940–2008) American novelist and poet born in Des Moines, Iowa. His often dystopian *science fiction includes *Camp Concentration* (1968), a story of enhanced intelligence for military purposes, and *334* (1972), a prescient description of a near-future New York. The *Gothic flavour of *Black Alice* (1968), written with John T. *Sladek, and *Clara Reeve* (1975) (as Leonie Hargreave) intensifies with the horror modes of *The Businessman* (1984) and *The MD* (1991). 'The Brave Little Toaster' (1980), written as a children's story, was adapted as a film in 1987. Collections of poetry include *Yes, Let's: New and Selected Poems* (1989).

DISKI, Jenny (1947–) Novelist and critic, born in London. After a difficult childhood, some of it spent in institutional care, she studied anthropology at University College London, a discipline which informs much of her fiction. Her first novel, *Nothing Natural* (1986), describes a single mother trapped in a sadomasochistic relationship, while *Rainforest* (1987) is an ecological drama partly set in Borneo. *Then*

Again (1990), set in 14th-century Poland, and *The Dream Mistress* (1996) continue to investigate sexual roles, extreme states of consciousness, and Jewish identity. *Only Human* (2000) and *After These Things* (2004) retell the biblical stories of Abraham and his family. She is a regular and pungent contributor to the *London Review of Books*, collecting her journalism in *Don't* (1998) and *A View from the Bed* (2003). *Skating to Antarctica* (1997), *Strangers on a Train* (2002, winner of the J. R. Ackerley Prize), and *On Keeping Still* (2006) are idiosyncratic travel books.

DISNEY, Walt (1901–66) American film producer, screenwriter, and entrepreneur, born in Chicago. A pioneer of animation films, one of his first successes was the 'Oswald the Lucky Rabbit' series of the 1920s, closely followed by the debut of Mickey Mouse in *Steamboat Willie* (1928) and of Donald Duck in 1934. By the Second World War, Disney's cartoon characters had become household names. In the post-war period Disney helped the FBI maintain surveillance over labour union organizers and in the late 1940s he conceived the idea of an amusement park, which eventually materialized in the Disneyland complex in Orlando, Florida. The latter was constructed by Walt Disney Productions, which was also responsible for further cartoons, educational films, and a TV show in the 1950s. More an institution than an individual, Disney received the Congressional Gold Medal in 1968. See Steven Watts, *The Magic Kingdom: Walt Disney and the American Way of Life* (2001).

DISRAELI, Benjamin, first earl of Beaconsfield (1804–81) Politician, prime minister, and novelist. The oldest son of Isaac *D'Israeli, Benjamin attended private schools in and near London, but acquired much of his education in his father's library. At 17 he was articled in Lincoln's Inn but was more interested in his father's literary world, attempting many literary forms (including epic, verse tragedy, and satire) before settling on fiction. **Vivian Grey*, his extravagant first novel, was published anonymously in 1826, its success and notoriety encouraging him to provide a continuation in 1827. In the same year he published a political satire, *Popanilla*. Between 1828 and 1831 he travelled in Spain and Italy, and he made much use of these journeys, and subsequent travels in Albania, the Levant, and Egypt, in future novels. In 1831 he published *The Young Duke*, with a dashingly Byronic hero. This was followed by **Contarini Fleming* (1832) and *Alroy* (1833), a highly coloured *oriental historical romance spiced with cabbalistic lore. The burlesque 'Ixion in Heaven' was published in 1833. In 1834, he published *The Infernal Marriage*, a light political satire; *The Rise of Iskander*, set in warring Albania; *The Revolutionary Epic*, his one serious attempt at poetry; and *A Year at Hartlebury*, an anonymous novel, written with his sister Sarah. *A Vindication of the English Constitution* (containing ideas developed later in **Coningsby* and **Sybil*) followed in 1835; and the *Junius-inspired *Letters of Runnymede*, together with *The Spirit of Whiggism*, in 1836. Disraeli's experiences in high society are reflected in his next novels. *Henrietta Temple* is an exploration of young love, begun in 1834, during Disraeli's affair with Lady Henrietta Sykes. *Venetia*, also a love story, set in the 18th century but drawn partly from the lives of P. B. *Shelley and Lord *Byron, is more restrained. Both were published in 1837, the year in which Disraeli entered Parliament as member for Maidstone. *Count Alarcos*, an abortive attempt at verse drama set in 13th-century Spain, was published in 1839, but was not performed until 1868.

Disraeli's parliamentary career flourished, and for a while his political and literary interests worked together. The trilogy which is now most often remembered, *Coningsby* (1844), *Sybil* (1845), and **Tancred* (1847), was written to influence public opinion, and they may be regarded as the first truly political (*'condition of England') novels in English. They owe much to Blue Book enquiries of the day, and to personal observations made during a tour of the north of England in 1844. The first two, concerned with the conditions of the rural and urban poor, were particularly successful, and foreshadowed future social legislation. In them, Disraeli spoke for the 'Young England' party of which he had become a recognized leader. In 1852 Disraeli published *Lord George Bentinck: A Political Biography*, in tribute to his late friend and colleague, whom he had succeeded as leader of the Tory party in 1848, and who had supported him in his courageous stand for the removal of the civil and political constraints which prevented Jews from entering Parliament. He published no more novels for more than twenty years, as his political career intensified, culminating in his appointment as prime minister, briefly in 1868, and then in 1874.

**Lothair* appeared in 1870, and the first collected edition of the novels, with an illuminating preface by Disraeli, was published in the same year. **Endymion* (1880), his last completed novel, for which he was offered the enormous sum of £10,000, was set in the period of his youth. He died without completing the intriguing *Falconet*, which attempted a satirical portrait of Gladstone in Joseph Falconet, a brilliant but humourless young MP from Clapham. Politically astute, vigorous, and compassionate, Disraeli's novels reveal much of lasting significance about the literary and political culture of his day. See Michal Flavin, *Benjamin Disraeli: The Novel as Political Discourse* (2005).

D'ISRAELI, Isaac (1766–1848) The father of Benjamin *Disraeli, descended from a Jewish family from the Levant who had settled in Italy. He had hoped to become a creative writer, but instead turned largely to literary history. In 1791 he published the first volume of *Curiosities of Literature*, the last volume of which appeared in 1834. It was the first of several discursive and entertaining collections. His most remarkable and original work was *The Literary Character* (1795), in which he attempts to identify the qualities of temperament common to creative writers. Lord *Byron's annotations and encouragement led to an expanded version of the book. *Calamities of Authors* followed in 1813, *Quarrels of Authors* in 1814. His study in five volumes of *The Life and Reign of Charles I* appeared in 1828–30, and *Amenities of Literature* in 1840. He also published several novels and essays, and his works were much read and enjoyed, notably by Byron, who found them both amusing and instructive.

dissociation of sensibility A phrase coined by T. S. *Eliot in his essay 'The Metaphysical Poets' (1921) to describe a separation of thought from feeling in English poetry since the mid-17th century. Whereas John *Donne and the other 'metaphysical' poets were capable of a 'direct sensuous apprehension of thought', Eliot argued, *Milton, John *Dryden, and their successors, especially the Victorian poets, suffered from a general malaise of 'the mind of England' in which thought and feeling were cultivated separately. The argument was not supported in convincing detail, and the causes of the supposed dissociation—religious, scientific, or political—never clearly identified; but Eliot's conception of English poetic history as a process of psychic and linguistic disintegration was endorsed by Ezra *Pound, F. R. *Leavis, and the American *New Critics, who sometimes referred to the phrase.

diurnals *See* NEWSBOOKS.

Dives and Pauper A lengthy prose dialogue from 1405–10 in which a rich man requests doctrinal instruction about the Ten Commandments from his poor interlocutor, possibly a friar. See Priscilla Barnum's edn, EETS os 275, 280, 323 (1976–2004).

Divina commedia The greatest work of *Dante, comprising the *Inferno*, the *Purgatorio*, and the *Paradiso*, in *terza rima* (lines of eleven syllables, arranged in groups of three and rhyming *ababcbcdc*).

The *Inferno* is a description of hell, conceived as a graduated conical funnel, to the successive circles of which the various categories of sinners are assigned. The *Purgatorio* is a description of Purgatory, a mountain rising in circular ledges, on which are the various groups of repentant sinners. At the top of the mountain is the earthly paradise, where Dante encounters *Beatrice. In his visit to hell and Purgatory, Dante has for guide the poet *Virgil, and there he sees and converses with his lost friends or former foes. The *Paradiso* is a vision of a world of beauty, light, and song, where the poet's guide is Beatrice. The poem is not only an exposition of the future life, but a work of moral instruction, full of symbolism and allusions based on Dante's wide knowledge of philosophy, astronomy, natural science, and history.

Dante's name first occurs in English in *Chaucer, and that of Beatrice in Philip *Sidney; Dante was read and admired in the 17th century by John *Milton, Jeremy *Taylor, and Sir Thomas *Browne, among others. The first acknowledged translation was by the artist Jonathan Richardson in 1719, a blank verse version of the famous Ugolino episode (*Inferno*, Canto XXXIII), which remained a favourite with translators, including Thomas *Gray; it was also the subject of one of William *Blake's illustrations. However, Dante was by no means always highly regarded or even read in the 18th century; Horace *Walpole in a letter to William *Mason (25 June 1782) referred to him as 'extravagant, absurd, disgusting, in short a Methodist parson in Bedlam'. His reputation rose in the 19th century with the admiration of Lord *Byron, P. B. *Shelley, Thomas *Carlyle, and others, and with the enthusiasm of political refugees such as Ugo *Foscolo and Gabriele Rossetti (1783–1854), father of Dante Gabriel *Rossetti. See Paget Toynbee, *Dante in English Literature from Chaucer to Cary*, 2 vols (1909); A. Milbank, *Dante and the Victorians* (1998). In the 20th century he profoundly influenced T. S. *Eliot; Eliot's essay *Dante* (1929) and the many references and quotations in his poetry brought Dante to the attention of a new readership. Eliot particularly praises his universality, his 'visual imagination', and his power to make 'the spiritual visible'.

Among well-known translations are those of Henry *Cary (1805–14, blank verse); Henry Wadsworth *Longfellow (1867, blank terzine, or stanzas of three lines); P. H. Wicksteed (1899, prose); H. F. Tozer (1904, prose); G. L. Bickersteth (1932–55, *terza rima*); Laurence *Binyon (1933–43, *terza rima*); J. D. Sinclair (1939–46, prose); Dorothy *Sayers (1949–62, *terza rima*); C. H. *Sisson (1980, unrhymed verse); and A. Mandelbaum (1980–84, unrhymed verse). For a detailed account of Dante's translators, see G. F. Cunningham, *The Divine Comedy in English*, 2 vols (1965–6).

DIXON, Ella Hepworth (1857–1932) Daughter of William Hepworth Dixon, editor of *The *Athenaeum*. A prolific journalist, who briefly edited *The English-Woman*, she published collections of short comic sketches about finding a husband (*My Flirtations*, 1892), short stories (*One Doubtful Hour*, 1904), and a notable *New Woman novel, *The Story of a Modern Woman* (1894), Dealing with sexual double standards and the struggles of women in the literary market-place, it stresses the importance of solidarity between women in the modern world. The novel contains satirical portraits of the *Yellow Book circle and Oscar *Wilde (she wrote for his magazine, *Woman's World*). Dixon's autobiography, *As I Knew Them*, appeared in 1930. See V. Fehlbaum's *Ella Hepworth Dixon* (2005).

DIXON, Richard Watson (1833–1900) Clergyman, poet, and historian, born in London and educated at Pembroke College, Oxford, where he became the intimate friend of Edward *Burne-Jones and William *Morris. He was closely involved in the *Pre-Raphaelite movement before marriage and ordination distanced him from his early life. He became a minor canon in Carlisle in 1868 and published, despite difficulties of access to libraries, an important *History of the Church of England from the Abolition of the Roman Jurisdiction* (1878–1902). His contemplative poetry found discriminating admirers, including Robert *Bridges and G. M. *Hopkins. His long narrative poem *Mano* (1883), set in the year AD 999 as the world awaits the millennium, recounts in **terza rima* the adventures of Mano, a Norman knight. Many of his poems, including those written about European locations, consider natural phenomena and human behaviour from a moral perspective.

DIXON, Thomas, Jr (1864–1946) American minister, playwright, and novelist, born in Shelby, North Carolina. He grew up during Reconstruction, his father joined the Ku Klux Klan, and at university he befriended president-to-be Woodrow Wilson. A qualified lawyer, Dixon ran in North Carolina politics briefly, then was ordained a Baptist minister in 1886. Angered by the representation of Southerners in a dramatization of **Uncle Tom's Cabin*, he began writing novels, producing *The Leopard's Spots* (1902), *The Clansman* (1905), and *The Traitor* (1915). All celebrate the South before the Civil War, describe African Americans as racial inferiors, and present Reconstruction as a betrayal. The stage version of *The Clansman* became the basis of D. W. Griffith's 1915 film *The Birth of a Nation*. Dixon knew Griffith well and was active for a time in film-making. His 1916 novel *Fall of a Nation* continues the theme of national decline. See Anthony Slide's biography, *American Racist* (2004).

DNB *See* DICTIONARY OF NATIONAL BIOGRAPHY.

DOBELL, Sydney Thompson (1824–74) Poet. Born at Cranbrook, Kent, and educated at home, he published in 1850 *The Roman*, a dramatic poem inspired by sympathy with oppressed Italy which had some success, and in 1854 *Balder*, one of the most extensive productions of the *Spasmodic school. This lengthy dramatic poem, of which only the first part was completed, describes the inner turmoil and aspirations of a young poet, who has taken his bride and baby daughter to live in 'a tower gloomy and ruinous' while he plans his great work. His search for the ultimate experience of death is rewarded by the death of his baby in mysterious circumstances; his wife Amy goes mad; and finally, unable to witness her sufferings, Balder kills her. Balder's destructive egoism so shocked readers that Dobell prefaced a second edition with an explanation, claiming that his hero was not held up for admiration, but as a warning. In 1855 Dobell published (jointly with Alexander *Smith) *Sonnets on the War* and in 1856 *England in Time of War*, which contains the ballad with the refrain 'O Keith of Ravelston' ('A Nuptial Eve'), much admired by D. G. *Rossetti.

DOBSON, Henry Austin (1840–1921) Poet and essayist, born at Plymouth, Devon, and educated at Beaumaris Grammar School and at Strasbourg. He entered the Board of Trade, where he served from 1856 to 1901, with Edmund *Gosse as close friend and colleague. He was an accomplished writer of light verse, with a particular fondness for French forms such as the *triolet and the *rondeau. Many of his best-known poems evoke the courtly elegance of French society of the 18th century as portrayed, notably, by *Watteau. His collections include *Vignettes in Rhyme* (1873), *Proverbs in Porcelain* (1877), and *At the Sign of the Lyre* (1885). He was a significant figure in the late Victorian reassessment of the 18th century and his works on this included the prose biographies of William *Hogarth (1879), Richard *Steele (1886), Oliver *Goldsmith (1888), Horace *Walpole (1890), Samuel *Richardson (1902), and Fanny *Burney (1903). Under the title of *Four Frenchwomen* (1890) he published essays on Charlotte Corday, Madame Roland, the Princesse de Lamballe, and Madame de *Genlis. He also published three series of *Eighteenth Century Vignettes* (1892/4/6), besides several volumes of collected essays.

Doctor, The A miscellany by Robert *Southey, published 1834–47 (7 vols). It consists of a series of essays and observations on a great variety of subjects, reflecting Southey's wide range of reading and interests. It differs from a commonplace book in that the articles are connected, somewhat loosely, by the story of an imaginary Dr Dove of Doncaster and his horse Nobs. It is an original and often humorous work, which was never finished, and is chiefly renowned for containing the nursery story of 'Goldilocks and the Three Bears'.

Doctor Angelicus Thomas *Aquinas; **Doctor Invincibilis** William of *Ockham; **Doctor Irrefragibilis** *Alexander of Hales; **Doctor Mirabilis** Roger *Bacon; **Doctor Subtilis** *Duns Scotus.

Dr Doolittle (1920) The first in a series of books by Hugh *Lofting about a vet who can speak to animals. The doctor practises in the idyllic world of Puddleby-on-the-Marsh, and despite accusations of racism he and the animal characters, including Polynesia the parrot, Gub-Gub the pig, and the two-headed Pushmi-Pullyu, have remained popular. Rex Harrison (1967) and Eddie Murphy (1998) have starred in film versions.

Dr Faustus, The Tragical History of A drama in blank verse and prose by Christopher *Marlowe, published 1604 and, in a radically different version known as the 'B-text', 1616. Its date of composition is uncertain; the earliest known performance was by the Lord Admiral's Men in 1594. It is perhaps the first dramatization of the medieval legend of a man who sold his soul to the devil, and who became identified with a Dr Faustus, a necromancer of the 16th century. The legend appeared in the *Faustbuch*, first published at Frankfurt in 1587, and was translated into English as *The History of the Damnable Life and Deserved Death of Doctor John Faustus*. Marlowe's play follows this translation in the general outline of the story, though not in the conception of the principal character, who from a mere magician becomes a man thirsting for infinite power, ambitious to be 'great Emperor of the world'.

Faustus, weary of the sciences, turns to magic and calls up Mephistopheles, making a compact to surrender his soul to the devil in return for 24 years of life; during these

Mephistopheles shall attend on him and give him all he demands. Then follow a number of scenes in which the compact is executed, notable among them the calling up of Helen of Troy, where Faustus addresses Helen in the well-known line: 'Was this the face that launched a thousand ships...' Faustus's anguish as the hour for the surrender of his soul draws near is poignantly depicted. The play differs greatly from the *Faust* of *Goethe both in its end and in the conception of Faustus's character. It has been the most frequently performed of Marlowe's plays in modern times.

Dr Jekyll and Mr Hyde, The Strange Case of A short novel by Robert Louis *Stevenson, published 1886. Dr Jekyll, a physician conscious of the mixed good and evil in his own nature, and fascinated by the idea of the advantage that would arise if these two elements could be separated, discovers a drug by means of which he can create for himself a personality that manifests all his base instincts. This persona, repulsive in appearance, he assumes from time to time and calls Mr Hyde, and in it he gives rein to his vicious impulses. Hyde is an embodiment of pure evil. It gradually gains the greater ascendancy, and commits a horrible murder. Jekyll now finds himself from time to time involuntarily transformed into Hyde, while the drug loses its efficacy in restoring his original form and character. On the point of discovery and arrest he takes his own life. The novel's vivid exploration of the duality of human nature made it an immediate success, and its popularity has endured. Stage, film, and televison adaptations have been numerous, and the phrase 'Jekyll and Hyde' has entered the language as an expression of a divided personality.

DOCTOROW, Cory (1971–) Canadian author and journalist, born in Toronto. His *science fiction novel *Down and Out in the Magic Kingdom* (2003) is set in a post-scarcity future where even death is obsolete. *Someone Comes to Town, Someone Leaves Town* (2005) is a surreal urban *fantasy.

DOCTOROW, E. L. (Edgar Laurence) (1931–) American novelist, born in New York, who began his career as a script reader for Columbia pictures. Hi first novel, *Welcome to the Hard Times* (1960), reworks the western as a semi-philosophical treatise. *The Book of Daniel* (1971) is a fictionalized account of the Rosenberg trial and has much in common with Robert *Coover's *The Public Burning* (1977). His most commercially successful novel, *Ragtime* (1975), blends real-life figures of the early 20th century with a cast of emblematic Jewish and African American characters. Subsequent work focuses on the Great Depression and its aftermath and includes *Loon Lake* (1980), *World's Fair* (1985), and *Billy Bathgate* (1989). *The Waterworks* (1994) centres on life in 19th-century New York. *The March* (2005) describes Sherman's march to the sea (1864–5) in the American Civil War. His essays were published as *Creationists* (2006).

Doctor Thorne A novel by Anthony *Trollope, published 1858, the third of the *'Barsetshire' series. Dr Thorne's brother seduced the sister of a Greshambury stonemason, Roger Scatcherd, and was killed by him. Dr Thorne adopts Mary, the child of this liaison, conceals the circumstances of her birth, and introduces her to the best local circles. There she meets and falls in love with Frank Gresham, heir to the Greshambury estate. The estate is heavily mortgaged, and the leading creditor happens to be Sir Roger Scatcherd, the former stonemason, who has now served his prison term, married, and made money as a railway contractor. It seems necessary for Frank to marry money, and he half-heartedly sets about courting the wealthy Miss Dunstable. Sir Roger Scatcherd dies of drink and his dissipated son Louis quickly follows him, leaving the Scatcherd fortunes without an heir. Thorne reveals Mary's true identity and, as Scatcherd's next of kin, she inherits. The marriage with Frank can now proceed. The temporizing of the grandiloquent de Courcys in the marriage market forms the secondary plot of the novel, a comedy heightened by the Lady Amelia's marriage to the family lawyer Mr Gazebee. The plot of *Doctor Thorne*, one of Trollope's most enduringly popular novels, was suggested to the author by his brother Thomas Trollope.

Doctor Who *science fiction television series (originally for children, but with a strong adult following) which started in 1963, running until 1989. It was successfully revived in 2005. Its hero, the time-traveller known only as 'The Doctor', has adventures which take him through time and space. Gradually a back-story of sorts has emerged, with the device of 'regeneration' used every time the lead actor departs. It is one of the iconic British science fiction programmes.

documentary film Emerged in Britain during the 1930s as a distinctive kind of non-fiction *cinema, inspired equally by the romantic ethnography of Robert Flaherty (1884–1951), by *Russian film-makers' montage techniques, and by the European avant-garde. John Grierson (1898–1972) gathered a group of young intellectuals, including Humphrey *Jennings, Basil Wright (1907–87), Edgar Anstey (1907–87), Len Lye (1901–80), and Harry Watt (1906–87), who, together with W. H. *Auden, Benjamin *Britten, and others, became known as the 'documentary movement', producing such imaginative sponsored films as *Night Mail*, *Housing Problems*, and *Song of Ceylon*. Enlightened commercial sponsorship gave many post-war film-makers their first opportunity to tackle social themes, while *television later became the major patron of documentary, with its distinctive unobtrusive filming style sometimes known as 'cinéma vérité' or 'fly on the wall'.

DODD, William (1729–77) A popular preacher and royal chaplain whose debts led him to forge a bond in the name of his former pupil, the fifth earl of Chesterfield. Despite the efforts of Samuel *Johnson and others to secure a reduced sentence, he was hanged. Johnson wrote a sermon, known as *The Convict's Address*, for Dodd to preach in Newgate. His writings include *The Beauties of Shakespeare* (1752) and *Thoughts in Prison* (1777).

DODDRIDGE, Philip (1702–51) *Congregational minister and celebrated academy tutor. His most influential publications were *The Rise and Progress of Religion in the Soul* (1745); *The Family Expositor, or A Paraphrase and Version of the New Testament* (1739–56); *Some Remarkable Passages in the Life of Col. James Gardiner* (1747), the reformed rake and colonel of dragoons who was killed at Prestonpans and figures in Walter Scott's **Waverley*; and, posthumously, his *Hymns* (1755) and academy *Lectures* (1763). Of the hymns, 'O God of Jacob', 'O happy day', 'Hark the glad sound!', and 'Ye servants of the Lord' have long remained popular.

DODGSON, Charles Lutwidge (1832–98) Celebrated under his pseudonym Lewis Carroll, the third in a family of eleven children of considerable literary and artistic interests; they produced family magazines which display Dodgson's love of parody, acrostics, and other word games and puzzles; he later invented many educational board games and published books of puzzles. Born in Daresbury, Cheshire, he was educated at Rugby School and Christ Church, Oxford, where he became a lecturer in mathematics in 1855. His most famous work, **Alice's Adventures in Wonderland* (1865), originated in a boat trip with the young daughters of H. G. Liddell, Lorina, Alice, and Edith; it was for Alice that he expanded an impromptu story into book form. *Through the Looking-Glass and What Alice Found There* followed in 1871: both volumes were illustrated by John *Tenniel. One reviewer attributed the success of these works to the fact that, unlike most children's books of the period, they had no moral and did not teach anything. Despite difficulties with word-play, they have been translated into most world languages.

Dodgson's other works include *Phantasmagoria and Other Poems* (1869), *The Hunting of the Snark* (1876), and *Sylvie and Bruno* (1889, vol. ii, 1893, both parts expanded from a short story, 'Bruno's Revenge', published in *Aunt Judy's Magazine*, 1867). The most valuable of his various mathematical treatises is his light-hearted defence of Euclid, *Euclid and his Modern Rivals* (1879). Dodgson was also a keen amateur photographer, with a particular interest in photographing little girls, whose friendship he valued highly; he also took some striking portraits of *Tennyson's sons. His diaries were edited by R. L. Green (2 vols, 1953), his letters by M. N. Cohen with R. L. Green (2 vols, 1979), and there are lives by Anne Clark (1979), Morton N. Cohen (1995), and Donald Thomas (1996).

DODINGTON, George Bubb (1691–1762) Career politician and diarist. Dodington was a patron of writers such as Edward *Young; James *Thomson dedicated 'Summer' (from *The *Seasons*) to him, and Henry *Fielding did the same with **Jonathan Wild*. Dodington is probably the caricature patron 'Bufo', 'fed with soft Dedication all day long', of Alexander *Pope's *Epistle to Dr Arbuthnot*. See *The Political Journal of George Bubb Dodington*, ed. J. Carswell and L. A. Dralle, 2 vols (1965).

DODSLEY, Robert (1703–64) Publisher who began writing poems while a footman, including *Servitude* (1729) and *The Muse in Livery, or The Footman's Miscellany* (1732). Encouraged by fashionable patrons, in 1735 he set up as a bookseller (with Alexander *Pope's help) in Pall Mall; his brother James (1724–97) became a partner and eventually succeeded him. He wrote several plays, including *The Toyshop: A Dramatic Satire* (1735), a musical afterpiece, *The Blind Beggar of Bethnal Green* (1741), and a tragedy, *Cleone* (1758). He published major work by Pope, Samuel *Johnson, Edward *Young, Oliver *Goldsmith, Thomas *Gray, Mark *Akenside, and William *Shenstone. His *Select Collection of Old Plays* (12 vols, 1744) and *A Collection of Poems, by Several Hands* (1748–58) were important embodiments of, and influences on, mid-18th-century taste. He was the prime instigator of Johnson's *Dictionary*, and in 1758 founded *The *Annual Register*. See Harry Solomon, *The Rise of Robert Dodsley* (1996).

dolce stil novo Poetic style exemplified in the lyric poetry of *Dante's *Vita nuova* and that of fellow Florentine poets, especially *Cavalcanti. The phrase was coined by Dante in the **Divina commedia* (*Purgatorio* XXIV). The style emphasizes personal inspiration and experience of love, harmony between content and style, smoothness of diction and metre, and the praise of the lady as a heaven-sent being. This model for poetry particularly appealed to the *Pre-Raphaelites, who added their own interpretations and elaborations.

DOLCI, Danilo (1924–97) Italian writer and social activist, involved in particular in campaigns in Sicily against poverty, deprivation, and the Mafia. He gained an international reputation for his stand on these issues, described in *Inchiesta a Palermo* (1956; *Poverty in Sicily*) and *Banditi a Partinico* (1960: *Bandits at Partinico*), and was admired by Aldous *Huxley. See *Poverty in Sicily*, trans P. D. Cummins, introd. Aldous Huxley (1959).

'Dolores' A poem in *anapaests by A. C. *Swinburne, included in *Poems and Ballads* (1866). One of his most notorious works, it addresses Dolores, 'Our Lady of Pain', in a profane hymn to perverse and cruel sensual delights, and contains some of his most parodied lines (e.g. 'the lilies and languors of virtue' and 'the raptures and roses of vice'). It clearly shows Swinburne's obsession with erotic pain and the image of a 'splendid and sterile' *femme fatale*, and, with other poems in the volume ('Faustine', 'Anactoria', 'Les Noyades', 'Laus Veneris', etc.), understandably provoked violent abuse. It was also much admired by many, including John *Ruskin, who is said to have exclaimed during a recitation, 'How beautiful! How divinely beautiful!'

Dolorous Stroke The stroke dealt by Balyn to King Pellam in Book II of Malory's **Morte Darthur* (in 'The Knight with the Two Swords', the second book in the first of the *Works* in Vinaver's edition). It causes the devastation of three kingdoms and the deaths of the people in Pellam's castle, and *Merlin prophesies that its disastrous effect will only be cured by the achievement of the Grail by *Galahad. Merlin links in an obscure way this slight narrative event with the whole decline of the world of *Arthur, and the story is the starting point of the anthropological investigation in J. L. Weston's *From Ritual to Romance* (1920).

Dombey and Son, *Dealings with the Firm of* A novel by Charles *Dickens, published 1847–8. When the story opens Mr Dombey, the frigid head of the shipping house of Dombey and Son, has just been presented with a son and heir, Paul, and his wife dies. The father's love and ambition are centred in the boy, an odd, delicate, prematurely old child, who is sent to Dr Blimber's school, under whose strenuous discipline he sickens and dies. His death moved the nation nearly as much as the death of Little Nell in *The *Old Curiosity Shop,* though later chapters were seen by many as a disappointment. Dombey neglects his devoted daughter Florence, and the estrangement is increased by the death of Paul. Walter Gay, a good-hearted youth in Dombey's employment, falls in love with her, but is sent to the West Indies by Dombey, who disapproves of their relationship. He is shipwrecked and believed drowned. Dombey marries again—a proud and penniless young widow, Edith Granger—but his arrogant treatment drives her into the arms of his villainous manager Carker, with whom she flies to France. They are pursued, Carker meets Dombey in a railway station, falls in front of a train, and is killed. The effect of the railways on English life and the changing landscape is a dominant theme in the novel. The house of Dombey fails; Dombey has lost his fortune, his son, and his wife; Florence has been driven by ill treatment to fly from him, and has married Walter Gay, who has survived his shipwreck. Thoroughly humbled, Dombey lives in desolate solitude till Florence returns to him, and at last finds the way to his heart. Other notable characters in the book include Solomon Gills, the nautical instrument-maker and uncle of Gay; his friend Cuttle, the genial old sea captain; Susan Nipper, Florence's devoted servant; Toots, the innocent and humble admirer of Florence; Joe Bagstock, the gouty retired major; and 'Cousin Feenix', the good-natured aristocrat.

DOMETT, Alfred (1811–87) Remembered as a friend of Robert *Browning, who lamented his departure for New Zealand in 1842 in his poem 'Waring'. Domett remained in New Zealand until 1871, and was briefly prime minister there; on his return Browning encouraged the publication of his long poem about Maori life, *Ranolf and Amohia: A South-Sea Day Dream* (1872). Their correspondence was edited in 1906 by F. G. Kenyon.

DONAGHY, Michael (1954–2004) Poet, born in New York, educated at Fordham University and the University of Chicago, where he edited the *Chicago Review* and founded an Irish traditional music group. He lived for many years in London. *Shibboleth* (1988) introduced a restless imagination bringing impressive formal skills to bear on a wide-ranging subject matter, from the anecdotal to the philosophical. Musical themes are central to Donaghy's work, and in the sequence 'O'Ryan's Belt' (*Errata*, 1993) issues of identity underlie the precarious survival of songs from forgotten musicians. His writing is also provocatively inhabited by a range of attention-seeking, buttonholing monologuists. *Dances Learned Last Night: Poems 1975–1995* appeared in 2000, and a posthumous volume, *Safest*, was published in 2005.

DONALDSON, Stephen (1947–) American author, born Cleveland, Ohio; he spent most of his childhood in India. He is author of the multi-volume *fantasy series 'The Chronicles of Thomas Covenant, the Unbeliever' starting with *Lord Foul's Bane* (1977), in which the hero Covenant, diagnosed with leprosy, finds himself in a fantasy world reminiscent of *Tolkien's Middle Earth, but refuses to believe the truth of his experiences. The story has been taken up with *The Runes of the Earth* (2004). Donaldson's taste for the epic is shown in his five-volume *science fiction 'Gap' series, described as a reworking of *Wagner's 'Ring' cycle.

DONATUS, Aelius (4th century AD) A grammarian who taught at Rome and had St *Jerome among his pupils. He was the author of two Latin grammars, *Ars Minor,* for beginners, and *Ars Maior,* a more advanced work, which served as the basis of later works. A 'donet' or 'donat' meant in English an introductory Latin grammar, and hence an introduction to any art or science (e.g. **Piers Plowman*, B-text, V. 205).

Don Carlos A tragedy by Thomas *Otway, in rhymed verse, produced 1676. Philip II, king of Spain, having married Elizabeth of Valois, who had been betrothed to his son Don Carlos, is jealous of their mutual affection. Inflamed by the scheming of Ruy Gomez and his wife, the duchess of Eboli, he comes to believe that they are lovers; he causes the queen to be poisoned and Don Carlos takes his own life, the king discovering too late their innocence.

DONIZETTI, Gaetano (1797–1848) Italian opera composer. His *Lucia di Lammermoor* (1835) intensifies the dark passions of Walter Scott's dramatic novel *The *Bride of Lammermoor* (1819). Scott's **Kenilworth* (1821) was filtered through two French stage adaptations, Victor *Hugo's *Amy Robsart* and Eugène Scribe's *Leicester,* before Donizetti wrote *Elisabetta al Castello di Kenilworth* (1829; libretto by Tottola). Felice Romani's libretto for *Parisina* (1833) uses the events of Lord *Byron's poem as a framework, but in *Marino Falieri* (1835) the primary source is a play by the French author Casimir Delavigne. *Il diluvio universale* (1830) is based partly on Lord Byron's **Heaven and Earth* (1822) and Francesco Ringhieri's *Il diluvio* (1788).

Don Juan According to a Spanish story apparently first dramatized by *Tirso de Molina in *El burlador de Sevilla* (*The Seville Deceiver*), and subsequently by *Molière in *Le Festin de pierre* (*Dom Juan, or The Stone Banquet*), and by *Mozart in *Don Giovanni*, he was Don Juan Tenorio, of Seville. Having seduced an aristocratic lady, he is surprised by her father, whom he kills in a duel. Seeing a statue of the father erected over his tomb, Juan jestingly invites it to dine with him. The statue takes up the invitation, seizes Juan, and delivers the unrepentant rake to hell. Don Juan is the proverbial licentious, heartless, and, in some versions, impious seducer. This legendary figure has inspired countless reworkings in a variety of genres. Among them are plays by Thomas *Shadwell (*The Libertine*), Carlo *Goldoni, Alexander *Pushkin, Henry de *Montherlant, and George Bernard *Shaw (*Man and Superman*), as well as a poem by Lord *Byron. For Robert *Browning's Don Juan see **Fifine at the Fair*. Derek *Walcott's *The Joker of Seville* (1978) is an adaptation of *The Seville Deceiver* based on Roy *Campbell's blank verse translation.

Don Juan An unfinished epic satire in **ottava rima* by Lord *Byron, published 1819–24. Don Juan, a young gentleman of Seville, is sent abroad by his mother at the age of 16, in disgrace after an intrigue. His ship is wrecked and the passengers take to the long-boat. After many tribulations, in the course of which first Juan's spaniel and then his tutor are eaten by the crew, Juan is cast up on a Greek island. He is restored to life by Haidée, the daughter of a Greek pirate, and the pair fall in love. The father, who is supposed dead, returns, finds the lovers together, and captures the fighting Juan, who is put in chains on one of the pirate's ships. He is then sold as a slave in Constantinople to the sultan's wife, who has fallen in love with him. He arouses her jealousy and is threatened with death, but escapes to the Russian army, which is besieging Ismail. Because of his gallant conduct he is sent with dispatches to St Petersburg, where he attracts the favour of the empress Catherine, who sends him on a political mission to England. The last cantos (the 'English cantos') of the unfinished work are taken up with a satirical description of social conditions in England and with the love affairs of Juan. Don Juan himself is a charming, handsome young man, who delights in succumbing to the beautiful women he meets, but his character is little more than the connecting thread in a long social comedy, a poetical novel, of satirical fervour and wit. The first two cantos were ill received by the critics, who called them 'an insult and an outrage' and 'a filthy and impious poem', but the work became increasingly successful with the general public and was much admired by *Goethe, who translated a part of it. With **Beppo* Byron had found in *ottava rima* a new form for his new voice, and he adopted it for *Don Juan*. He told his publisher, John *Murray, 'I *have* no plan...the Soul of such writing is its licence...', but he did undoubtedly intend a longer work than the one which was cut short by his death, after sixteen cantos and a fragment of a seventeenth. He wished the poem to be 'a little quietly facetious upon everything'. Almost every serious passage is abruptly punctured; as William *Hazlitt wrote, after the 'intoxication' comes 'the splashing of the soda-water'. The outspoken wit and satire are especially directed at hypocrisy in all its forms, at social and sexual conventions, and at sentimentality. There are many attacks on the objects of Byron's scorn, among them *Southey, *Coleridge, *Wordsworth, *Wellington, Lord Londonderry, and many others. The poet told Lady *Blessington in 1823 that 'there are but two sentiments to which I am constant—a strong love of liberty, and a detestation of cant'. Both sentiments receive full expression in the poem.

DONLEAVY, J. P. (James Patrick) (1926–) Novelist, born in Brooklyn, USA, of Irish parents, educated at Trinity College, Dublin, and an Irish citizen since 1967. He is best known for *The Ginger Man* (1955), a comic and bawdy account, much influenced by James *Joyce, of Sebastian Dangerfield's adventures as a law student in Dublin. His other novels include *A Singular Man* (1964), *The Beastly Beatitudes of Balthazar B* (1968), *The Destinies of Darcy Dancer, Gentleman* (1977), *Schultz* (1979), *Leila* (1983), *Are You Listening Rabbi Löw* (1987), and *That Darcy, That Dancer, That Gentleman* (1990). He has also written several plays, including *Fairy Tales of New York* (1960) and various stage adaptations of his own novels. *The History of the Ginger Man*, an autobiography, was published in 1993.

DONNE, John (1572–1631) Poet and clergyman, related on his mother's side to Sir Thomas *More, born in London into a Catholic family, his uncle Jasper Heywood (1535–98) being the leader of the Jesuit mission in England. His father, a prominent member of the London Ironmongers' Company, died when Donne was 4, and six months later his mother married a Catholic physician, Dr John Syminges. Educated at home by Catholic tutors, Donne went at the age of 11 to Hart Hall, Oxford (now Hertford College), popular with crypto-Catholics. Catholicism debarred him from taking a university degree and also from any public career. In 1589–91 he may have travelled on the Continent, to Catholic Italy and Spain. In 1592 he was admitted to Lincoln's Inn. A portrait of this date bears a Spanish motto, *Antes muerto que mudado* (Sooner dead than changed), proclaiming his loyalty to Catholicism. However, in 1593 his younger brother Henry died in Newgate, having been arrested for harbouring a Catholic priest. This may have influenced Donne's decision to renounce the Catholic faith. *Satire III* may reflect this moment of crisis. He sailed as a gentleman volunteer with *Essex to sack Cadiz (1596) and with Walter *Ralegh to hunt the Spanish treasure ships off the Azores (1597). His poems 'The Storm' and 'The Calm' commemorate these voyages. On his return he became secretary to Sir Thomas Egerton (1540–1617), lord keeper of the great seal, having met Egerton's son while serving with Essex, and as Egerton's secretary he witnessed Essex's abortive coup and execution. He forfeited his chance of a civil career when late in 1601 he secretly married Lady Egerton's ward Ann More, the 14-year-old daughter of a wealthy Surrey landowner, whom he met in York House, Egerton's London residence. He was dismissed from Egerton's service and briefly imprisoned. For fourteen years he tried to find employment, depending on the charity of his wife's relations and living with his ever-growing family in a cottage at Mitcham. In 1612 he moved to a London house owned by his patron, Sir Robert Drury (1575–1615) of Hawstead, Suffolk, whom he had accompanied on his continental travels. In honour of Sir Robert's dead child Elizabeth, whom Donne had never met, he wrote his extravagant *Anniversaries*. Other friends and patrons in these years were Sir Walter Chute, with whom Donne went to the Continent in 1605–6, Sir Henry Goodyer, Donne's closest friend at court, to whom he wrote weekly, Lucy, countess of Bedford, for whom he probably wrote at least some of the Holy Sonnets, Magdalen Herbert (mother of George *Herbert), for whom he wrote *La Corona*, and Sir Robert Ker, Viscount Rochester, to whom he offered his services in the Essex divorce case. Despite Ker's good offices, *James I considered Donne unfit for confidential employment and urged him to enter the Church, which he did in 1615. James made him a chaplain-in-ordinary and forced Cambridge (which regarded him as a careerist) to grant him a DD. In the Church Donne held several livings and the divinity readership at Lincoln's Inn. His wife died in 1617 at the age of 33, after giving birth to their twelfth child (the sonnet 'Since she whom I loved' commemorates her), and the following year Donne went as chaplain to the earl of Doncaster in his embassy to the German princes. His 'Hymn to Christ at the Author's Last Going into Germany', full of apprehension of death, was written before this journey. In 1621 he procured the deanery of St Paul's. One of the most celebrated preachers of his age, he died on 31 March 1631, having first, as his earliest biographer Izaak *Walton records, had his portrait drawn wearing his shroud and standing on a funeral urn, as if rising from the dead.

His earliest poems, the Satires and Love Elegies, belong to the 1590s. His unfinished satirical epic 'The Progress of the Soul' bears the date 1601, and some of his Holy Sonnets were probably written in 1609–11. His 'Songs and Sonnets' are, however, largely undatable. Donne's prose works include *Pseudo-Martyr* (1610), denigrating Catholics who had died for their faith, and *Ignatius his Conclave*, a scabrous satire on the Jesuits (1611). *Biathanatos*, the first English defence of suicide (to which Donne confessed he was tempted), could not be published until after his death. His *Essays in Divinity* (1651) were composed in preparation for his ordination and the *Devotions* (1624) were assembled in less than a month from notes made during a near-fatal fever. His sermons appeared after his death in three volumes, *LXXX Sermons* (1640), *Fifty Sermons* (1649), and *XXVI Sermons* (1660). These were edited by his son John and based on texts which Donne himself prepared from his rough preaching notes during two periods of rest in the country in 1625 and 1630. His poems were collected by his son John and published in 1633 (2nd, enlarged, edn 1635). See R. C. Bald, *John Donne: A Life* (1970); J. Carey, *John Donne: Life, Mind and Art* (1981; 2nd edn 1990); *Elegies and Songs and Sonnets* (ed. H. Gardner, 1965); *Divine Poems* (ed. H. Gardner, 1952; 2nd edn 1978); *Satires, Epigrams and Verse Letters* (ed. W. Milgate, 1967); *Epithalamions, Anniversaries and Epicedes* (ed. W. Milgate, 1978); *Paradoxes and Problems* (ed. H. Peters, 1980); *Ignatius is Conclave* (ed. T. S. Healy, SJ, 1969); *Essays in Divinity* (ed. E. M. Simpson, 1952); *Devotions upon Emergent Occasions* (ed. A. Raspa, 1987); *Sermons* (ed. G. R. Potter and E. M. Simpson, 10 vols, 1953–62).
See also METAPHYSICAL POETS.

DONNELLY, Ignatius (1831–1901) American writer and politician, born in Philadelphia; he popularized theories about Atlantis and the authorship of *Shakespeare's plays. Of his speculative novels, *Caesar's Column* (1890), a *dystopian account of a visit to New York City in 1988, is the best known.

Don Quixote de la Mancha A comic romance by Miguel de *Cervantes, dated 1605 (although probably published 1604), a second part appearing in 1615. Cervantes initially gave his work the form of a burlesque of the ballads and romances of chivalry (*see* AMADIS OF GAUL; PALMERIN OF ENGLAND), which were already beginning to lose their popularity. But he soon ceased to write mere burlesque, as the character of his hero developed and deepened, and his work acquired the richness and profundity that have made it one of the most popular classics ever written. Don Quixote, a poor gentleman of La Mancha, a man of gentle and amiable disposition and otherwise sane, has had his wits disordered by inordinate devotion to the tales of chivalry, and imagines himself called upon to roam the world in search of adventures on his old nag Rocinante, and clad in rusty armour, accompanied by a squire in the shape of the rustic Sancho Panza, a curious mixture of shrewdness and credulity, whom he lures with the prospect of the governorship of the island of Barataria. Quixote seeks to conform to chivalric tradition by electing a beautiful damsel, one who in fact is a strapping peasant girl from a neighbouring village, to be the mistress of his heart. To him she is known as Dulcinea del Toboso, an honour of which she is entirely unaware. To the disordered imagination of the knight the most commonplace objects assume fearful or romantic forms, and he is consequently involved in absurd adventures, as in the famous episode (I. 8) when he tilts at windmills, imagining them to be giants. Finally one of his friends, Sansón Carrasco, in order to force him to return home, disguises himself as a knight, defeats Don Quixote in armed combat, and requires him to abstain for a year from chivalrous exploits. This period Don Quixote resolves to spend as a shepherd, living a pastoral life, but, falling sick on his return to his village, after a few days he dies. The plot also contains several lengthy digressions, including the 'Tale of *Inappropriate Curiosity' and the story of Cardenio and Lucinda. After the appearance of the first part of *Don Quixote*, a continuation was issued by a writer who styled himself Alonso *Fernández de Avellaneda, a forgery with which Cervantes ironically engages in his own second part. The book was translated into English by Thomas Shelton (fl. 1598–1629) in 1612 and 1620, by John Phillips (1631–1706?), nephew of John *Milton, in 1687, and in the 18th century by at least Peter *Motteux and Tobias *Smollett. John Rutherford's Penguin Classic version appeared in 2000. *Don Quixote* supplied the plots of several 17th-century English plays, and inspired and continues to inspire innumerable imitations (*see* LENNOX, CHARLOTTE, for an example). Its underlying theme, the confrontation of illusion with reality, prefigures a topic that has been a staple of later fiction; its comic irony, multiple perspectives, and metafictional elements (e.g. its use of parody, its series of unreliable narrators, its characters' awareness of themselves as literary figures, and its general literary playfulness) have proved seminal. See P. E. Russell, *Cervantes* (1985); introduction to Rutherford's translation.

Don Sebastian A tragicomedy by John *Dryden, produced 1689, published 1691. Dryden's first play after the (for him) disastrous Glorious Revolution, it is full of complicated political allusion. King Sebastian of Portugal, brave, pious, and a victim of foreign usurpation, represents the deposed Catholic James II. His conqueror, the tyrant Muley Moloch, perhaps represents the new king, William, and is killed in a revolt. The comic sub-plot, involving the Mufti and Mustapha, ridicules James II's enemies, the Anglican clergy and the London mob. The discovery that Sebastian's marriage to Almeyda is incestuous (leading to their noble renunciation of each other and their thrones) perhaps warns William's supporters that past wrongs will catch up with them.

DOOLITTLE, Hilda (1886–1961) American poet and novelist, who wrote as 'H.D.' Born in Bethlehem, Pennsylvania, and educated in Philadelphia's (Society of) Friends Central High School and Bryn Mawr College, in 1911 she followed her friend Ezra *Pound to Europe, where both became leading members of the *imagist movement. She married Richard *Aldington in 1913, but the marriage was not a success. She began a long-standing relationship with the writer *Bryher (Winifred Ellerman) in 1919. Her several volumes of poetry, from her first, *Sea Garden* (1916), to her last, the quasi-epic *Helen in Egypt* (1961), show a deep involvement with classical mythology, a mysticism in part influenced by her Moravian ancestry, a sharp, spare use of natural imagery, and interesting experiments with **vers libre*. With Bryher she founded the film journal *Close Up* (1927–33) and from their Swiss base made a number of experimental films including *Borderline* (1930). She also published several novels, including *Bid Me to Live* (1960), a *roman à clef* about her *Bloomsbury years, and *Tribute to Freud* (1965), an account of her analysis by Sigmund *Freud in 1933. Her *Collected Poems* were published in 1984 and a restored version of her memoir *The Gift* in 1998. Throughout her writings she explored the nature and limits of vision.

Doomsday Book (Domesday Book) 'The Book of the day of assessment'; the name since the 12th century of the record of the great inquest or survey of the lands of England made by order of William the Conqueror in 1086. It contains records of the ownership, area, and value of lands, and of the numbers of tenants, livestock, and so on. The manuscript is in the National Archives in Kew, London.

DORÉ, Gustave (1832–83) French illustrator and caricaturist, who became well known in London both for his illustrations of the *Bible (1866) and for his drawings and engravings of London life, done in 1869–71, which appeared in *London* (1872) by Blanchard Jerrold (1826–84). They show many aspects of the city, but dwell on the picturesque clutter and squalor of the poorer districts. Doré also did a series of steel engravings (1868–9) for Alfred *Tennyson's **Idylls of the King*, and illustrated S. T. *Coleridge's **Ancient Mariner* in 1875, and the works of *Dante, *Balzac, *Ariosto, *Rabelais, *Cervantes, and others. For many years his works were on permanent exhibition at the Doré Gallery in Bond Street, which opened in 1867. The 'agreeable terror' of his illustrations appealed to generations of children. A life by Blanchard Jerrold was published in 1891.

Doric A dialect of classical Greek spoken in the Peleponnese, the southern Aegean, and Sicily and other Greek colonies. The choruses in Greek tragedy, *Pindar's odes, and *Theocritus' eclogues were written in a heightened literary form of Doric. In English the term was associated with pastoral (hence John *Milton calls **Lycidas* 'a doric lay') and came to mean 'rustic'. In the 18th and 19th centuries it was applied to the language of Northumbria and the Scottish Lowlands, and now mainly refers to that of Aberdeen and the north-east of Scotland.

DORN, Edward (1929–1999) American poet, born in Illinois, who was a member of the *Black Mountain group, hence the use of open form in his poetry. An important early volume, *Geography* (1965), testifies to his preoccupation with place. He lived in England during this period, becoming a close friend of Jeremy *Prynne. His major work was the long poem *Gunslinger* (1968–89), which makes ironic use of the myth of the West to explore the nature of power. His novel *By the Sound* appeared in 1971.

DOROTHEA, St A Christian martyr who suffered in the persecution under Diocletian (*c.*304). Her story forms the subject of *The *Virgin Martyr* by Philip Massinger and Thomas Dekker, and an early poem by Gerald Manley *Hopkins.

DORSET, earl of *See* SACKVILLE, CHARLES; SACKVILLE, THOMAS.

DORSEY, Candas Jane (1952–) Canadian author and editor, born in Edmonton. Her story '(Learning About) Machine Sex' (1988) applies a feminist sense of poetic metaphor to the conventions of *cyberpunk. This careful touch also appears in novels such as *Black Wine* (1997) and *A Paradigm of Earth* (2001).

DOS PASSOS, John Roderigo (1896–1970) American novelist, born in Chicago and educated at Harvard University, who served in Europe during the First World War as a member of the ambulance service. His first important novel, *Three Soldiers* (1921), which has war as its subject, was followed by many others, as well as poetry, essays, travel writings, memoirs, and plays, which include *The Garbage Man* (1925), *Airways Inc.* (1929), and *Fortune Heights* (1933), published in 1934 as *Three Plays*. He is chiefly remembered for his novels *Manhattan*

Transfer (1925), a collective portrait in hundreds of fictional episodes of life in New York City, and *U.S.A.* (1938), a trilogy composed of *The 42nd Parallel* (1930), *1919* (1932), and *The Big Money* (1936). *U.S.A.* tries to capture, through a diversity of fictional techniques, the variety and multiplicity of American life in the first decades of the 20th century; it presents various interlocking and parallel narratives, against a panoramic collage of real-life events, snatches of newsreel and popular song, advertisements, and so on with a commentary by the author as 'The Camera Eye'; cinematic montage was one innovation Dos Passos tried in these works. In 1938 Jean-Paul *Sartre declared him to be the 'greatest writer of our time'. Despite the fact that he produced a number of historical studies and continued to write novels after the Second World War, his reputation declined, as he appeared to move towards the political right.

DOSTOEVSKY, Fedor Mikhailovich (1821–81) Russian prose writer, born in Moscow. He studied from 1838 to 1843 at the St Petersburg Military Engineering Academy. His first published work, a translation of *Balzac's *Eugénie Grandet*, appeared in 1844, followed by his first original work, *Poor Folk* (1846), *The Double* (1846), *White Nights* (1848), and other short prose pieces. In April 1849 Dostoevsky was arrested as a member of the socialist Petrashevsky Circle, organized by Mikhail Petrashevsky (1821–66). Reprieved from a death sentence at a macabre mock execution, he was sent to the Omsk penal settlement for four years, to be followed by five years as a private soldier in Semipalatink. During his Siberian imprisonment he underwent a religious conversion, rejecting the progressive ideas of his early years, and replacing them by deep faith in the Russian Orthodox Church and the spiritual values of the common people. After his return from Siberia in December 1859 he regained literary prominence with *Notes from the House of the Dead* (1860–61), a fictional portrayal of penal servitude, and the novel *The Insulted and the Injured* (1861) that refuted utopianism. Both appeared in the journal *Time* (1862–3) which Dostoevsky founded with his brother Mikhail. The same year he travelled abroad, visiting England, France, Germany, and Italy. His views on Western Europe, revealing his xenophobia and Russian chauvinism, are recorded in *Winter Notes on Summer Impressions* (1863). In London, which he describes as 'Baal', centre of world capitalism, he saw the Crystal Palace of the 1862 World Exhibition, an image used to express the corruption of the modern scientific world in *Notes from Underground* and other works. His horror at the poverty of Whitechapel and the prostitutes of the Haymarket was reflected in his later work. In London he also visited Alexander *Herzen (Aleksandr Ivanovich Gertsen) and Mikhail Bakunin (1814–76). Dostoevsky made further trips abroad throughout the 1860s. His reputation is based on the series of brilliant works which followed, *Notes from Underground* (1864), *Crime and Punishment* (1866), *The Idiot* (1868), *The Devils* (1872), *An Adolescent* (1875; also translated as *A Raw Youth*), and *The Brothers Karamazov* (1880). They reveal extraordinary powers of character analysis, and show Dostoevsky to be a significant and powerful thinker. Dostoevsky admired William *Shakespeare, Walter *Scott, Lord *Byron, and in particular Charles *Dickens, who had been known and translated in Russia since the 1830s. In his Omsk prison Dostoevsky read *The *Pickwick Papers* and **David Copperfield*. His letters and notebooks are full of references to Dickens, and they share an interest in the city, children, crime, and the suffering of the innocent. *Notes from the House of the Dead* was translated into English in 1881, and many of Dostoevsky's novels appeared in English in the 1880s. Robert Louis *Stevenson was an early admirer, claiming in 1886 that *Crime and Punishment* was 'the greatest book I have read in ten years'. Its influence on **Dr Jekyll and Mr Hyde* (1886) is apparent, but in general the response of late 19th-century England to Dostoevsky was cool. The main impact of his work in England followed the appearance of Maurice *Baring's *Landmarks in Russian Literature* (1910), J. M. *Murry's *Fyodor Dostoevsky* (1916), and especially the translations by Constance *Garnett (1912–20). For a literary and cultural biography see Joseph Frank's five-volume study *Dostoevsky* (1977–2002), and for British perspectives, W. J. Leatherbarrow (ed.), *Dostoevsky and Britain* (1995).

Double Dealer, The A comedy by William *Congreve, produced 1693, published 1694. The Double Dealer is Maskwell, who is employed by the passionate and promiscuous Lady Touchwood to break off the match between Lord Touchwood's heir Mellefont and Cynthia, daughter of Sir Paul Plyant. He succeeds, but Lord Touchwood overhears a conversation between Maskwell and Lady Touchwood which reveals their plot to him, and all is put right. The action of the play takes place in Lord Touchwood's house in the three hours after dinner on the night before Mellefont and Cynthia's wedding day. Congreve's second play, it was snubbed by critics and public.

Double Marriage, The *See* MASSINGER, PHILIP.

DOUCE, Francis (1757–1834) Antiquary and book-collector. Although his *Illustrations of Shakespeare* (1807) was a pioneering collection of contemporary material, his most lasting achievement was his personal collection of books, manuscripts (including the famous illuminated 'Douce Apocalypse'), and coins, which he bequeathed to the Bodleian Library, Oxford.

DOUGHTY, Charles Montagu (1843–1926) Born in Suffolk, educated at Caius College, Cambridge, principally remembered for his remarkable record of *Travels in Arabia Deserta*, carried out in 1876–8. The book, of more than 1,000 pages, was first published in two volumes in 1888, republished in 1921 with an introduction by T. E. *Lawrence, and widely read in Edward *Garnett's abridged version, *Wanderings in Arabia* (1908). Respected by scholars for its knowledge of Arabia and of the Bedouin, and an inspiration to later travellers to Arabia, it is notable for its extraordinary style. Doughty disapproved of 'Victorian prose', and mingled his own with Chaucerian and Elizabethan English, Latin, and Arabic. His equally eccentric volumes of verse, which include the epic *The Dawn in Britain* (6 vols, 1906), *Adam Cast Forth* (1908), and *Mansoul, or The Riddle of the World* (1920), are now largely forgotten.

Douglas A romantic tragedy in blank verse by John *Home, based on the ballad 'Gill Morrice', and first performed in Edinburgh in 1756, where it outraged those who believed it improper for a clergyman to write for the stage. David *Hume and Adam *Smith supported it, the former saluting its improvement on 'the unhappy barbarism' of Shakespeare.

Old Norval, a shepherd, brings up the infant son of Douglas, supposed dead by his mother, now Lady Randolph. Young Norval saves Lord Randolph's life, and is reunited with his mother, only to be killed through the machinations of Randolph's heir Glenalvon; his mother in despair hurls herself (offstage) from a cliff.

DOUGLAS, Lord Alfred (1870–1945) Poet, born near Worcester, third son of the ninth marquess of Queensbury. Educated privately and at Winchester College (1884–8), he entered Magdalen College, Oxford, in 1889, but left without taking a degree. He met Oscar *Wilde in 1891 and it was to him that Wilde addressed his letter from prison, *De Profundis*. Douglas translated Wilde's *Salome* from French to English (1894) and wrote various defensive accounts of his relationship with him, including *Oscar Wilde and Myself* (1914) and the less extreme *Oscar Wilde: A Summing up* (1940). He also published around twenty volumes of minor verse: *The City of Soul* (1899), *Sonnets* (1899), and *Lyrics* (1935) perhaps reveal him at his best. He converted to Roman Catholicism in 1911 and his *Autobiography* appeared in 1929. See H. M. Hyde, *Lord Alfred Douglas: A Biography* (1984).

DOUGLAS, the Black (Sir James Douglas) (d. 1330) In 1319, in the days of Robert Bruce and Edward II, invaded England and plundered the northern towns and villages. He three times destroyed an English garrison in his castle of Douglas, thereby earning his nickname and inspiring Walter Scott's **Castle Dangerous*.

DOUGLAS, Gawin (Gavin) (*c*.1476–1522) Scottish poet and bishop of Dunkeld, third son of Archibald, fifth earl of Angus. He wrote an allegorical dream poem, *The Palice of Honour* (*c*.1501; pub. *c*.1535), dedicated to James IV, and a translation of the *Aeneid* (*Eneados*, 1513; printed 1553). He was one of the first to draw the distinction between *Scots and 'Inglis', and, unlike many of his contemporaries, wrote only in the vernacular. As a churchman, he was critical of *scholasticism, a position that complemented the humanism evident in his poetry. Ezra *Pound admired him, saying that 'he gets more out of Virgil than any other translator', and there is evidence that his version was used by the earl of *Surrey and Thomas *Sackville. His works were edited by John Small of Edinburgh in 1874, and his shorter poems by P. J. Bawcutt (1967); Bawcutt has also published *Gavin Douglas: A Critical Study* (1976).

DOUGLAS, Keith (1920–44) Poet, born in Tunbridge Wells and educated at Edgeborough School, Guildford, and Christ's Hospital School, London. In 1938 he entered Merton College, Oxford, where Edmund *Blunden was his tutor. His verses began to appear in periodicals in the 1930s, but the only volume published in his lifetime was *Selected Poems* (1943). He enlisted in 1940, was killed in Normandy in June 1944, and is inevitably remembered largely as a war poet, whose descriptions of wartime Cairo and desert fighting and whose contemplations of death ('Simplify me when I'm dead') show a rapidly maturing energy and simplicity of diction. His vivid experimental narrative of desert warfare, *Alamein to Zem Zem*, was published posthumously in 1946 and was edited by Desmond Graham in 1979. Graham has also edited Douglas's *Complete Poems* (1978), prose (1985), and letters (2000). See also D. Graham, *Keith Douglas, 1920–1944: A Biography* (1974).

DOUGLAS, Norman (1868–1952) Novelist and essayist, educated at Yarlet Hall, Uppingham School, and the Karlsruhe *Gymnasium*, who spent much of his life abroad, principally in Italy. He is chiefly remembered for his travel books about Capri, Tunisia, and Calabria, published as *Siren Land* (1911), *Fountains in the Sand* (1912), and *Old Calabria* (1915), and for his novel *South Wind* (1917), which celebrates the pleasures of the hedonistic life on the island of Nepenthe. In the 1920s and 1930s he was a well-known figure in the expatriate literary community of Florence, where his account of his quarrel with D. H. *Lawrence, *D. H. Lawrence and Maurice Magnus: A Plea for Better Manners*, was published in 1924.

DOUGLASS, Frederick (Frederick Augustus Washington Bailey) (1818–95) Abolitionist, orator, editor, statesman, and autobiographer, born a slave in Maryland. Douglass speculated that his father may have been a white man, possibly his mother's owner. He was sent to Baltimore, aged 12, where the wife of his owner taught him to read, and escaped from a later cruel owner in 1838. The abolitionist William Lloyd Garrison (1805–79) was a major influence on him, and encouraged him to tell his story in meetings. Douglass became a leader of the abolitionist movement. His autobiography, *Narrative of the Life of Frederick Douglass, an American Slave*, was published in 1845 to huge acclaim, and led to tours of Great Britain and Ireland. It is the most influential and significant account of a slave's life ever published. Douglass later began an anti-slavery newspaper, *The North Star*, advised President Lincoln during the American Civil War, and held several government offices. See *Frederick Douglass: Autobiography*, ed. Henry Louis Gates (1994).
See also SLAVERY.

'Douglas Tragedy, The' A ballad included in Walter Scott's **Minstrelsy of the Scottish Border*, the story of the carrying off of Lady Margaret by Lord William Douglas. They are pursued by her father and seven brothers, who are killed in the ensuing fight. Douglas dies of his wounds and she does not survive him.

DOVE, Rita (1952–) American poet, born in Akron, Ohio. Her collections include *The Yellow House on the Corner* (1980), *Thomas and Beulah* (1986), *Grace Notes* (1989), and *Mother Love* (1995), a powerful lyrical exploration in varied fourteen-line stanzas of the resonance of the Demeter/Persephone myth, rich in classical allusion, personal emotion, and contemporary colouring. She has also published a novel, *Through the Ivory Gate* (1992). She was the US poet laureate 1993–5.

Dove Cottage A short distance from the north-east shore of Grasmere, taken by *Wordsworth and his sister at the end of 1799. They occupied it till the end of 1807. It was subsequently the home of Thomas *De Quincey. It is now owned by the Dove Cottage Trust and is a centre for Lake District tourism and Wordsworthian scholarship.

DOW, Alexander (1735/6–1779) Born in Perthshire; he served in Bengal as an army officer in the East India Company. In 1768 he published *Tales Translated from the Persian of Inatulla of Delhi*, a series of stories in the *oriental mode, and translated two volumes of a Persian *History of Hindostan* (third volume, 1772). His verse tragedies *Zingis* and *Sethona* were staged in 1769 and 1774.

DOWDEN, Edward (1843–1913) Scholar and critic, born in Cork and educated at Queen's College, Cork, and Trinity College, Dublin, where he became professor of English literature in 1867. He was a noted Shakespearian scholar and made his reputation with the publication of *Shakspere: A Critical Study of his Mind and Art* (1875), which influenced future approaches to Shakespearian biography. This was followed by *Shakspere* (1877), a primer, and editions of single plays. He wrote other volumes of criticism, a life of P. B. *Shelley (1887), short biographies of Robert *Southey, Robert *Browning, and *Montaigne, and published editions of Edmund *Spenser and other English poets.

DOWIE, Ménie Muriel (1867–1945) Novelist and travel writer. Her articles, short stories, and verse began to appear in the late 1880s, mostly unsigned or under pseudonyms, including 'Princess Top-Storey' and 'Judith Vermont', but she made her name with her travel book *A Girl in the Karpathians* (1891). A collection of essays, *Women Adventurers* (1893), followed, then a novel, *Gallia* (1895), whose frank treatment of sexual relations established her as a leading *New Woman writer. She wrote two further novels: *The Crook of the Bough* (1898) and *Love and his Mask* (1901). Her short stories, published in the **Yellow Book* and **Chambers's Journal*, were collected as *Some Whims of Fate* (1896), and her *Country Life* column was reprinted as *Things about our Neighbourhood* (1903). She withdrew from the literary scene after her scandalous divorce from Henry Norman in January 1903 and emigrated to the United States in 1941.

DOWLAND, John (1563–1626) English composer and lutenist. On failing to receive one of the vacant posts of lutenist to Queen Elizabeth in 1594, perhaps because of Catholic sympathies, he travelled abroad, visiting various German and Italian courts. He returned to England in 1597, when he issued *The First Booke of Songes or Ayres of Fowre Partes with Tableture for the Lute*, the earliest and most popular book of its kind. Richard *Barnfield's sonnet 'If music and sweet poetry agree' celebrates Dowland's success. But on the death of his patron, Dowland returned abroad and from 1598 to 1606 he was lutenist at the court of Christian IV of Denmark. *The Second Booke of Songs or Ayres* (1600) and *The Third and Last Booke of Songs* (1603) were published during this absence; after his return to England he brought out a fourth collection of songs, more penitential in character, *A Pilgrimes Solace* (1612). By now Dowland was famous as a lute composer all over Europe, above all for the widely disseminated song 'Flow, my teares' (1600), later arranged for instruments as the *Lachrymae* pavan. In 1612 Dowland was at last appointed lutenist to James I, though he appears to have written little of importance after this date. Some of his song texts are by courtly amateurs like Sir Fulke *Greville or Sir Edward *Dyer, and there is an occasional poem by John *Donne or George *Peele. Most have texts by unknown authors, some perhaps by Dowland himself. He referred to himself punningly as 'Semper Dowland, semper dolens' (always Dowland, always doleful) and the best of his songs are in tragic vein: in 'Sorrow, stay' and 'In darknesse let mee dwell', words, melody, and lute accompaniment are fused in an exceptional singleness of conception. See Diana Poulton, *John Dowland* (2nd edn, 1982).

DOWLING, Terry (1947–) Born in Sydney, New South Wales; Australian writer, mostly of short stories, often featuring linked characters in a future version of Australia, as in *Rynosseros* (1990) or *Twilight Beach* (1993). *Basic Black: Tales of Appropriate Fear* (2006) is a collection of dark *fantasy stories.

DOWSON, Ernest (1867–1900) Poet, born in Lee, Kent, the son of well-to-do but later impoverished parents. After erratic schooling he went in 1886 to The Queen's College, Oxford, where he read widely and made many friends, including Lionel *Johnson, but left without taking his degree. He assisted with his father's dwindling docking business, and established himself in the London society of Aubrey *Beardsley, Richard *Le Gallienne, Oscar *Wilde, and their friends. He contributed poems to the **Yellow Book*, the **Savoy*, and the anthologies published by the *Rhymers Club, and in 1891 met 'Missie', Adelaide Foltinowicz, a girl of 12, who later became an important symbol of lost love and innocence in his verse. He enjoyed a widely varied literary and social life between drawing rooms, taverns, and the Café Royal, Regent Street. His feelings for the Roman Catholic Church, into which he was received in September 1891, appear to have been as much aesthetic as religious. His father was now suffering from advanced tuberculosis, and died (possibly by suicide) in 1894; within months his mother hanged herself. Dowson's stories *Dilemmas* appeared in 1895, and at about that time he began to move restlessly between London, France, Ireland, and back again, living an ever wilder and more intemperate life. The first of his two books of poetry, *Verses* (containing his celebrated 'Non Sum Qualis Eram', better known as 'Cynara'), appeared in 1896, and his second, *Decorations* (half of which consists of his experiments with 'prose poems'), in 1899. His one-act verse play *The Pierrot of the Minute* was published in 1897.

The poems, which display much variety in stanza and prosody, group themselves chiefly into love poetry, including 'Cynara'; devotional poems, of which 'Nuns of the Perpetual Adoration' and 'Carthusians' are perhaps the most successful; poems of the natural world, such as 'Breton Afternoon'; and above all poems of ennui and world-weariness, such as the well-known 'Vitae Summa Brevis' ('They are not long, the days of wine and roses'), 'To One in Bedlam', and several translations and adaptations of *Verlaine. There is a life by M. Longaker (1944, rev. 1967); a volume of *Reminiscences* (1914) by his friend and fellow poet Victor Plarr; and his *Letters*, ed. D. Flower and H. Maas (1967).
See also ART FOR ART'S SAKE.

DOYLE, Arthur Conan (1859–1930) Writer, the son of an artist and draughtsman, Charles Doyle, and nephew of the illustrator Richard *Doyle. Educated at Stonyhurst and Edinburgh, he became a doctor and practised at Southsea, 1882–90. He is chiefly remembered for his widely celebrated creation of the subtle, hawk-eyed detective Sherlock *Holmes, whose brilliant solutions to a wide variety of crimes began in *A Study in Scarlet* (1887), continued through a long line of stories, chiefly in the *Strand Magazine*, and were collected in *The Adventures of Sherlock Holmes* (1892), *The Memoirs of Sherlock Holmes* (1894), *The Hound of the Baskervilles* (1902), and other works. His friend and foil, the stolid Dr Watson with whom he shares rooms in Baker Street, attends him throughout most of his adventures (*see* DETECTIVE FICTION). Doyle also wrote a long series of historical and other romances, which he believed to be superior to his 'Holmes' stories. Notable among them are *Micah Clarke* (1889), *The White Company* (1891), *The Exploits of Brigadier Gerard* (1896), the first of many 'Gerard' tales, *Rodney Stone* (1896), and *The Lost World* (1912). In 1902 Doyle wrote an influential pamphlet, 'The War in South Africa', which was much translated; and later many books on public themes, including a long history of the Flanders campaign in the First World War. His one-act play *Waterloo* provided Sir Henry *Irving in 1894 with one of his most successful parts. In 1926 Doyle published his *History of Spiritualism*, one of several books he wrote on the subject. His interest in fairies is a connection with the work of his uncle Richard Doyle, who illustrated many *fairy stories. See Andrew Lycett, *The Man Who Created Sherlock Holmes* (2007).

DOYLE, Sir Francis (1810–88) Poet, fellow of All Souls, and professor of poetry at Oxford, who published several volumes of verse, which include the patriotic military ballads 'The Loss of the Birkenhead' and 'The Private of the Buffs'.

DOYLE, Richard (1824–83) Illustrator, born in London, the son of the caricaturist John Doyle (1797–1868) and uncle of Arthur Conan *Doyle. He worked for **Punch* and designed the cover (with Mr Punch, Toby, and a margin of nymphs, goblins, and satyrs) that lasted from 1849 to 1956. He illustrated chiefly *fairy stories, including John *Ruskin's *The King of the Golden River* (1851) and William *Allingham's *In Fairyland* (1870), and also some of Charles *Dickens's Christmas Books; and published books of annotated drawings, including *The Foreign Tour of Brown, Jones and Robinson* (1854), whose comic adventures in England and on the Rhine he had depicted in *Punch*.

DOYLE, Roddy (1958–) Novelist, born in Dublin and educated at University College there, whose 'Barrytown trilogy' describes the adventures and misadventures of the Rabbitte family on Dublin's northside. In *The Commitments* (1987) Jimmy organizes a band to bring 'soul to the people'; in *The Snapper* (1990) his sister Sharon has an illegitimate baby; and in *The Van* (1991) Jimmy Sr struggles to survive unemployment and goes share in a chip van with his friend Bimbo. The dialogue is lively, contemporary, authentic, the scene setting minimal, and the large Rabbitte family portrayed with affection and sympathy. *Paddy Clarke Ha Ha Ha* (1993, *Booker Prize) vividly evokes the childhood world of a 10-year-old boy, whose life is overshadowed by the breakdown of his parents' marriage. *The Woman Who Walked into Doors* (1997) is the tough, sombre first-person narrative of an alcoholic mother of four, widowed when her violently abusive husband is shot by the Gardaí during an armed robbery. The emergence of the protagonist from alcoholism is chronicled in a sequel, *Paula Spencer* (2006). *A Star Called Henry* (1999) and *Oh, Play That Thing* (2004) trace the comic adventures of Henry Smart through a series of historical scenarios, including the Easter Rising in Dublin and the Jazz Age in Chicago. The stories of *The Deportees* (2007) focus on immigration and multiculturalism in Celtic Tiger Ireland.

Drab Term used first by C. S. *Lewis in *English Literature in the Sixteenth Century* to denote poetry and prose of the later medieval period until the early Renaissance: 'a period in which, for good or ill, poetry has little richness either of sound or images'. Although Lewis claimed that he did not use the term disapprovingly, it has generally been employed to characterize Tudor works which are unappealing to a modern ear. Typically, 'Drab' poets preferred strongly rhythmical verse forms such as *poulter's measure, making use of alliteration and of poetic 'fillers' such as 'eke', and employing few Latinate words. An example from **Tottel's Miscellany* illustrates these features:

'I know under the grene the serpent how he lurkes.
The hammer of the restles forge I wote eke how it wurkes.
I know and can by roate the tale that I would tel:
But oft the wordes come furth awrie of him that loueth wel.'

Yet many so-called 'Drab' writers, especially Sir Thomas *Wyatt and the earl of *Surrey, have been much admired. T. S. *Eliot admired the Tudor translators of *Seneca's plays, editing the *Tenne Tragedies* in 1927; and many other 'Drab' translations were of crucial importance for the later Renaissance in England, such as Sir Thomas *Hoby's version of *Castiglione's *Courtier* (1561) and Arthur *Golding's of *Ovid's *Metamorphoses* (1567).

DRABBLE, Dame Margaret (1939–) Novelist, born in Sheffield, and educated at the Mount School, York, and Newnham College, Cambridge. The novelist and critic A. S. *Byatt is her sister, and Drabble's first novel, *A Summer Birdcage* (1963), was a first-person account of the relationship between two young graduate sisters. It was followed by *The Garrick Year* (1964), which draws upon her brief career as an actor with the Royal Shakespeare Company. Her early novels deal primarily with the dilemma of educated young women caught by the conflicting claims of maternity, sexuality, and intellectual and economic aspiration. They include *The Millstone* (1965), the story of a young unmarried mother, which won the John Llewellyn *Rhys Prize; *Jerusalem the Golden* (1968), about the social ambitions of a girl who comes to London from the north of England, which won the James Tait Black Memorial Prize; *The Needle's Eye* (1972), in which an heiress takes voluntary poverty upon herself (*Yorkshire Post* Book Award); and *The Middle Ground* (1980), which tells the story of a journalist who comes to doubt her feminist creed. Later novels have a broader canvas, a more ironic relationship with traditional narration, and a wider interest in documenting social change: *The Ice Age* (1977) is a *condition of England novel that documents the effects of the oil crisis on social attitudes, while a trilogy of novels comprising *The Radiant Way* (1987), *A Natural Curiosity* (1989), and *The Gates of Ivory* (1991) follows the fortunes of three women friends through the social and political changes in Britain in the 1980s, moving in the third volume to war-torn Cambodia. *The Witch of Exmoor* (1996) is a mordant family chronicle inspired by a premiss borrowed from John Rawls (1921–2002), while *The Peppered Moth* (2004) traces a Yorkshire family through several generations. Later novels include *The Sea Lady* (2006), while her non-fiction includes *A Writer's Britain* (1979) and biographies of Arnold *Bennett (1974) and Angus *Wilson (1995). From 1979 to 2006 she was editor of *The Oxford Companion to English Literature*, seeing it through its 5th and 6th editions; she was awarded the DBE in 2008. She is married to the biographer Michael *Holroyd.

Dracula A novel by Bram *Stoker, published 1897, the most famous of all tales of vampirism. The story is told through the diaries of a young solicitor, Jonathan Harker, his fiancée Mina, her friend Lucy Westenra, and Dr John Seward, the superintendent of a large lunatic asylum at Purfleet, in Essex. It begins with Harker's journey to Count Dracula's eerie castle in Transylvania, in connection with the count's purchase of Carfax, an ancient estate adjoining Dr Seward's asylum. After horrifying experiences as an inmate of the castle, Jonathan makes his way to a ruined chapel, where he finds 50 great wooden boxes filled with earth recently dug from the graveyard of the Draculas, in one of which the un-dead count is lying, gorged with blood. These boxes are shipped to Whitby and thence to Carfax. Dracula disembarks at Whitby in the shape of a wolf, having dispatched the entire ship's crew en route, and proceeds to vampirize Lucy who, despite multiple blood transfusions and the occult precautions of Dr Seward's old teacher Professor Van Helsing, dies drained of blood but remains un-dead until staked through the heart. The rest of the book tells of the attempt to save Mina from Dracula's insidious advances and of the search for the boxes of earth, his only refuge between sunrise and sunset. All but one of these are neutralized with fragments of the Host. The last, with Dracula in it, is followed by Van Helsing and the others back to Transylvania where, after a thrilling chase, the count is beheaded and stabbed through the heart, at which his body crumbles to dust.

The sinister but glamorous figure of Dracula has been the subject of many films, including F. W. Murnau's silent *Nosferatu* (1922) and Tod Browning's early talkie *Dracula* (1931). Stoker's novel, reflecting as it does contemporary thinking on the cultural role of women, sexuality, immigration, colonialism, and disease, has attracted much recent academic interest, while its prominence within popular culture is undiminished, and film, television, and stage adaptations continue to proliferate.

DRAKE, Sir Francis (1540–96) Buccaneer, born near Tavistock, Devon, of yeoman stock but with useful family connections to Sir John *Hawkins, whom he joined in the slave trade and piracy. Several voyages from Plymouth to the Caribbean made Drake's fortune. In 1577 he set out to plunder Spanish settlements in the Pacific, and then sailed west to complete the first English circumnavigation of the world. He returned in 1581 to a knighthood and popular renown, bought Buckland Abbey, served as mayor, and was elected to Parliament. Under a commission from Elizabeth he plundered Santiago, Vigo, and Cartagena and in 1587 attacked Cadiz. As vice-admiral, he commanded a division of the English fleet against the Armada, and in 1589 joined Sir John Norris in plundering Corunna. Drake died on an unsuccessful expedition to the West Indies with Hawkins. He made dashing individual raids but was distrustful and uncertain as a leader, disregarded orders, and creamed off treasure for himself. He figured in *Hakluyt and *Purchas, and became the flamboyant hero of many legends, not least the story that he was playing bowls on Plymouth Hoe when the Armada was sighted. Originally the Spanish rather than the English promoted Drake as the foremost of the Elizabethan 'sea-dogs', but English writers came to celebrate him—inaccurately—as a staunchly Protestant founder of British naval supremacy. Henry *Newbolt wove Drake's achievements into the public-school ideal in his popular poem 'Drake's Drum' (1895). See Harry Kelsey, *Sir Francis Drake* (1998).

Dramatic Idyls A volume of six poems, by Robert *Browning, published 1879. After the publication of a sequel (*see* DRAMATIC IDYLS, SECOND SERIES), the collection was called 'Dramatic Idyls, First Series'. The spelling 'Idyl' differentiated the poems from *Tennyson's 'Idylls'. The poems are among the finest of Browning's later period, particularly 'Ivàn Ivànovitch', a story based on a Russian folk tale of a woman who threw her children to the wolves in order to save her own life. The collection has a notable unity of tone, and focuses on human behaviour in conditions of extreme stress.

Dramatic Idyls, Second Series A volume of six poems by Robert *Browning, published 1880 and influenced by the success of the 1879 volume (*see* DRAMATIC IDYLS). Although the collection does not have the unity of the first series, it demonstrates Browning's continuing interest and vitality in the dramatic monologue form, notably in 'Clive'.

dramatic irony An effect produced by discrepancies between a character's misperception of his or her situation and the audience's fuller knowledge of that character's true destiny. **Macbeth* provides an example in Duncan's cheerful speech on arriving at Macbeth's castle, where his murder has already been planned. When found in a *tragedy, this is sometimes called 'tragic irony'. The device is also found in narrative works, as in the climactic eleventh chapter of Joseph Conrad's *The *Secret Agent*, when Verloc summons his wife for marital intimacy, unaware that she is murderously enraged upon discovering his complicity in her brother's death.

Dramatic Lyrics A collection of poems by Robert *Browning, published in 1842 as no. III of **Bells and Pomegranates*. Browning's publisher, Edward *Moxon, persuaded him to vary the format of the series, which had been intended to consist solely of plays. The collection included some of Browning's best-known poems, such as 'My Last Duchess', 'Porphyria's Lover', and 'The Pied Piper of Hamelin'.

dramatic monologue A poem presented as though spoken not by the poet but by a single imagined or historical person, usually to an imagined auditor: the speaker or 'persona' is thus dramatized, often ironically, through his or her own words. The early masters of this modern form in English are Robert *Browning (as in 'My Last Duchess', 1842, and 'Fra Lippo Lippi', 1855) and Alfred *Tennyson (as in *'Ulysses' and 'St Simeon Stylites', both 1842). From the 20th century the most celebrated example is T. S. Eliot's 'The Love Song of J. Alfred *Prufrock' (1917); poets of the later 20th century who favoured the form include Carol Ann *Duffy and Andrew *Motion. See Elizabeth A. Howe, *The Dramatic Monologue* (1996).

Dramatic Romances and Lyrics A collection of poems by Robert *Browning, published 1845 as no. VII of **Bells and Pomegranates*. Many of the poems were revised before publication in consultation with Elizabeth Barrett *Browning, whom Browning was courting at the time. The collection included some of Browning's best-known poems, such as 'How They Brought the Good News from Ghent to Aix', 'The Lost Leader', and 'The Flight of the Duchess'.

Dramatis Personae A collection of poems by Robert *Browning, published 1864. A few had been published previously, but most were new. They were marked by Browning's grief after the death of his wife (*see* BROWNING, ELIZABETH BARRETT) in 1861, and by his searching examination of the relation of human to divine love, especially as it concerns the nature of belief. A striking unity of theme and structure makes the collection an intermediate stage in Browning's development between **Men and Women* and *The *Ring and the Book*. Several of the poems are anthology favourites—notably 'Rabbi Ben Ezra' and 'Prospice'—but the heart of the collection is the long dramatic monologues such as 'A Death in the Desert', *'Caliban upon Setebos', and 'Mr Sludge, "the Medium" '.

Drapier's Letters, The A series of pamphlets published by Jonathan *Swift in 1724. A patent for supplying copper coins for use in Ireland had been granted to an ironmaster, William Wood, after he bribed the duchess of Kendall, one of George I's mistresses. In 1723 the Irish Houses of Parliament protested against the transaction, and Swift was incensed by this scarcely disguised piece of shabby profiteering. Writing in the character of a plain-dealing Dublin draper, he published a series of five letters in which he prophesied economic ruin to the Irish if 'Wood's halfpence' were admitted into circulation. The fifth was addressed to the retired Irish politician and writer Viscount Molesworth. The government was forced to abandon the project and compensate Wood; Swift, whose authorship of the pamphlets was an open secret, became an Irish national hero. Two further Drapier letters, written at the same period, were published in 1735.

DRAYCOTT, Jane (1954–) British poet, born in London; she studied English in London and Bristol. Strongly influenced by medieval dream poetry, she is also indebted to Gerard Manley *Hopkins, whom she admires for 'his furious effort of expression, the choreography of his rhythms and aural precision'. Draycott's acute awareness of sound sees her frequently using extended sentences in which meaning proliferates and echoes, allying her work with that of her contemporaries Medbh *McGuckian and Alice *Oswald. Her full-length collections include *Prince Rupert's Drop* (1999), *Tideway*, an illustrated poem about the Thames (2002), and *The Night Tree* (2004).

DRAYTON, Michael (1563–1631) Poet, born at Hartshill, in Warwickshire. His early life was spent in the service of Sir Henry Goodyer (1534–95), who introduced him to Lucy, countess of Bedford (1581–1627). His friends included John *Stow, William *Camden, Ben *Jonson, William *Drummond, William *Browne, George *Wither, and possibly William *Shakespeare. He died in comparative poverty, but was buried in Westminster Abbey, where Lady Anne *Clifford paid for his monument. He was a prolific writer, and frequently revised and republished earlier works. His first publication, *The Harmony of the Church* (1591), comprised paraphrases from the Old Testament and Apocrypha. The nine *Spenserian pastorals of *Idea: The Shepherd's Garland* (1593) include praise of *Elizabeth I and a lament for the death of Sir Philip *Sidney.

Idea's Mirror (1594), a 64-sonnet sequence, continued the pastorals' lovelorn theme. In its final version, entitled *Idea* (1619), it included the famous sonnet 'Since there's no help, come let us kiss and part'. His poems on legendary and historical figures began in about 1594 with *Piers Gaveston*, followed by *Matilda* (1594), an epic poem in rhyme royal, *Robert, Duke of Normandy* (1596), and *Mortimeriados* (1596), a long poem on the Wars of the Roses, later revised as *The Barons' Wars* (1603). *England's Heroical Epistles* (1597) was modelled on *Ovid's *Heroides*, consisting of twelve pairs of verse letters in heroic couplets exchanged by lovers from English history, such as Henry II and Fair *Rosamond, and Edward IV and Jane Shore. Another Ovidian poem was *Endimion and Phoebe* (1595), which acknowledges help Drayton received from Thomas *Lodge. *The Owl*, a satire, perhaps reflecting Drayton's failure to thrive at *James I's court, appeared in 1604, and *Odes* in 1606. This collection included 'To the Virginian Voyage' and 'To the Cambro-Britons and their Harp' and his 'Ballad of Agincourt', which opens with the lines 'Fair stood the wind for France | When we our sails advance'. He later wrote a narrative poem on the same subject, *The Battle of Agincourt* (1627), publishing in the same volume *The Miseries of Queen Margaret*, **Nimphidia*, *The Court of Faery*, a wholly original and delightful epic of fairyland, and the interesting epistle to Henry Reynolds 'Of Poets and Poesie'. Drayton's largest project, the great topographical poem on England, **Poly-Olbion*, took many years and appeared in two parts, 1612 and 1622. Philip *Henslowe's diary shows that he also collaborated on plays but none has survived. His *Works* have been definitively edited in six volumes by J. W. Hebel, K. Tillotson, and B. H. Newdigate (1931–41; rev. 1961). See B. H. Newdigate, *Michael Drayton and his Circle* (1961); J. R. Brink, *Michael Drayton Revisited* (1990).

Dream of Gerontius, The *See* NEWMAN, JOHN HENRY.

Dream of John Ball, A A historical socialist fantasy by William *Morris, published in *Commonweal* (Nov. 1886–Jan. 1887, in volume form 1888). It takes the form of a dream in which the narrator is carried back to the time of the early stages of the *Peasants' Revolt in 1381; he encounters the 'hedge-priest' John Ball, and in their final night-long dialogue Morris both satirizes the 19th-century present and offers hope for a future when men 'shall see things as they verily are' and rise in successful protest against their exploitation.

Dream of the Rood An Old English poem of 156 lines, found in the 10th-century *Vercelli Book, in three parts: a description of the poet's vision of the cross and the address to him by the cross describing the Crucifixion (paralleled in part by the Northumbrian runic inscriptions on the 8th-century *Ruthwell Cross in Dumfriesshire); a homiletic address to the dreamer by the cross; and a declaration of faith and confidence in heaven by the dreamer himself. There has been much argument about the coherence of the poem; it seems likely that, as it stands, it was composed in one piece, drawing on an earlier cross *prosopopoeia related to the tradition of riddles in Old English and Latin. The poem is greatly admired for the devotional simplicity of its first, narrative section, and for the ingenious web of imagery upon which it is constructed. There are editions by B. Dickins and A. S. C. Ross (rev. 1963) and M. Swanton (1970).

DREISER, Theodore (1871–1945) American novelist, born in Indiana, the son of a Catholic German family, and brought up in semi-poverty. He left his family at the age of 15 for Chicago, and after various jobs became a journalist, meanwhile writing his first novel, *Sister Carrie* (1900), a powerful account of a young working girl's rise to the 'tinsel and shine' of worldly success. His supporter and friend H. L. *Mencken thought *Sister Carrie* a poorly balanced narrative and it was withheld from circulation by its publishers, who were apprehensive about Dreiser's frank and amoral treatment of Carrie's sexuality and ambition, and he continued work as a hack journalist until the greater success of *Jennie Gerhardt* (1911), again a novel of a working girl's betterment through liaisons. This was followed by the first parts of a trilogy about an unscrupulous business magnate, Frank Cowperwood (*The Financier*, 1912; *The Titan*, 1914; *The Stoic* was published posthumously in 1947). *The 'Genius'* (1915) is a study of an artist, with much autobiographical material. *An American Tragedy* (1925) is the story of Clyde Griffiths, son of unworldly, evangelist parents, who escapes from them to the life of a bell-boy in a Kansas City hotel; he moves to New York State to work in a collar factory, and when his girlfriend Roberta becomes pregnant he drowns her, possibly accidentally, and is tried and condemned to death; the narrative was based on an actual 1906 homicide. Dreiser's many other works include *Dreiser Looks at Russia* (1928, written after travels in Russia), *Tragic America* (1931), and *America Is Worth Saving* (1941), which express the growing faith in socialism that replaced the nihilistic naturalism and pessimism of his earlier works. Dreiser made unsuccessful attempts to break into the Hollywood film industry and became involved in a costly lawsuit against Paramount for their 1931 adaptation of *An American Tragedy.* See Jerome Loving's biography, *The Last Titan* (2005).

DREYFUS, Alfred (1859–1935) A captain in the French army, subject of a notorious judicial miscarriage. In 1894 an unsigned official letter, addressed to the German military attaché in Paris and listing a number of documents which were to be sent to him, was stolen from the German embassy and handed to the French Ministry of War. The similarity of the handwriting to that of Dreyfus, a Jew who held an appointment at the ministry, led to his arrest, trial, and sentence to imprisonment for life on Devil's Island off the coast of Guiana. In 1896 Colonel Picquart of the secret service came upon evidence indicating that the true criminal was a Major Esterhazy. But opposition involving the use of forgery, intimidation, and a violent anti-Semitic press campaign was raised against a retrial. In the course of this controversy Émile *Zola published his famous letter, entitled 'J'accuse', in the newspaper *L'Aurore* (January 1898), and was condemned in consequence to a year's imprisonment. Dreyfus was pardoned by the government in 1899 after a second trial had reaffirmed his guilt. It was not until 1906 that the second verdict was quashed by the Court of Appeal, and Dreyfus reintegrated into the army. The controversy gave rise to the term *Dreyfusard*, to signify a supporter of the innocence of Dreyfus. Extracts from the papers of Colonel Schwartzkoppen, the German military attaché in Paris at the time, confirming Esterhazy's guilt, appeared in 1930.

DRINKWATER, John (1882–1937) A prolific poet, dramatist, critic, and actor, born in Leytonstone, Essex. He attended Oxford High School and then worked as an office clerk before becoming an actor and co-founding, in 1907, the Pilgrim Players, which later became the Birmingham Repertory Theatre. He was the author of seventeen plays, including *Abraham Lincoln* (1918), *Oliver Cromwell* (1921), *Mary Stuart* (1921), and a successful comedy, *Bird in Hand* (1927). In 1903, he had also turned to poetry, and his work appeared in all five volumes of **Georgian Poetry*, and in the journal *New Numbers* (1914). His nine volumes of verse include *Swords and Ploughshares* (1915), *Olton Pools* (1916), *Tides* (1917), and *Summer Harvest* (1933). He also wrote stories and plays for children, and produced critical studies of, among others, Lord *Byron, *Cromwell, William *Morris, Samuel *Pepys, *Shakespeare, and A. C. *Swinburne. *Inheritance* (1931) and *Discovery* (1932) are two volumes of an unfinished autobiography.

DROESHOUT, Martin (1601–*c.*1650) Engraver of the portrait of Shakespeare on the title page of the first *folio (1623). *Schoenbaum says: 'How he obtained the commission we do not know—perhaps his fee was as modest as his gifts'; see *William Shakespeare: A Documentary Life* (1975).

drolls (droll-humours) In Commonwealth days when stage plays were forbidden, farces or comic scenes adapted from existing plays or invented by the actors, produced generally at fairs or in taverns. A few drolls, which are supposed to have been adapted and performed by an actor named Robert Cox, were published in 1655, but most were published after the Restoration by the bookseller and writer Francis Kirkman (1632–?1680) in *The Wits, or Sport upon Sport* (two parts, 1662, 1673). 'Bottom the Weaver', which was published separately in 1661, is described on the title page as having been 'often publicly acted by some of his majesty's comedians, and lately, privately, presented by several apprentices for their harmless recreation'. It is not known how many of the other drolls achieved performance.

DRUMMOND OF HAWTHORNDEN, William (1585–1649) Poet, laird of Hawthornden, Midlothian. He was educated at Edinburgh University and studied law in Bourges and Paris. His European travels familiarized him with the work of poets in many languages, including *Du Bartas, *Ronsard, *Tasso, and *Marino. His *Poems* (1616) mourn the death of his fiancée Mary Cunningham. *A Cypress Grove* (1623) counsels against fear of death. He also wrote satires and hymns, pamphlets and verses in support of Charles I, and a history of Scotland 1423–1524 (1655). He corresponded with Michael *Drayton, and in the winter of 1618/19 was visited by Ben *Jonson. His record of their Conversations is an unparalleled feast of literary gossip. The Hawthornden Prize, the oldest British literary prize (established in 1919), was named after Drummond of Hawthornden. See *Poetry and Prose*, ed. R. H. Macdonald (1976).

DRURY, Allen (1918–98) American novelist born in Houston. He served as a Senate correspondent and published a series of novels about Washington politics, notably *Advise and Consent* (1959).

Drury Lane, London So called from the Drury family, who had a large house there from Tudor times. The Theatre Royal, Drury Lane, was originally a cockpit, converted into a theatre in the time of *James I. It was rebuilt by Thomas *Killigrew (1612–83), to whom Charles II granted a patent in 1662, again by Sir Christopher *Wren in 1674, and again in 1812, when the reopening was celebrated in **Rejected Addresses*. Junius Brutus Booth (1796–1852), David *Garrick, Sarah *Siddons, John Philip *Kemble, and Edmund *Kean are among the famous actors who have appeared there. In the 19th century it was the great house of Christmas pantomimes, and after the Second World War many successful American musicals were staged there, including *Oklahoma!* (1947) and *South Pacific* (1951), both by Rodgers and Hammerstein, and *My Fair Lady* (1958, adapted from G. B. Shaw's **Pygmalion*).

DRYDEN, John (1631–1700) Poet and playwright, the eldest of fourteen children of Puritan landowning gentry in Aldwinkle, Northamptonshire, educated at Westminster School under Richard Busby (1606–95) and at Trinity College, Cambridge. He was an assistant to Oliver *Cromwell's secretary of state John Thurloe (bap. 1616, d. 1668), and processed at Cromwell's funeral with Andrew *Marvell and John *Milton. At his father's death he inherited a small estate, but supported himself mainly by his writing. His *Heroic Stanzas* (1658) on Cromwell's death was followed by poems applauding Charles II's return: *Astraea Redux* and *To His Sacred Majesty.* Other poems were addressed to Sir Robert Howard, the earl of *Clarendon, Walter *Charleton, and the royal mistress Lady Castlemaine (bap. 1640, d. 1709). His **Annus Mirabilis* (1667), a spectacular poem commemorating the English defeat of the Dutch at sea and the fire of London, led to his appointment as *poet laureate (1668), but most of his early writing was for the stage and included several rhymed heroic plays, *The Indian Queen* (1664, in collaboration with Sir Robert Howard), *The Indian Emperor* (1665, which has the Mexican ruler Montezuma as subject), **Tyrannic Love* (1669), and *The Conquest of Granada* in two parts (1670). He also wrote comedies, *The Wild Gallant* (1663), *The Rival Ladies* (1664), *Sir Martin Mar-all* (1667, in collaboration with the duke of *Newcastle), *An *Evening's Love* (1668), and a radical adaptation of *The *Tempest* (1667, with Sir William *D'Avenant). He was most original, however, with his tragicomedies, *Secret Love* (1667), **Marriage-à-la-Mode* (1672), *The Assignation* (1672), and a second *Shakespeare adaptation, **Troilus and Cressida* (1679). All these plays, together with the operatic adaptation of **Paradise Lost*, under the title *The State of Innocence, and Fall of Man* (unperformed, pub. 1667), and the immensely successful *Oedipus* (1678, with Nathaniel *Lee), reveal Dryden's considerable interest in philosophical and political questions.

He was the first of the very few English authors who have published an influential body of literary criticism and of even fewer for whom criticism was an art. **Of Dramatick Poesy* (1668), comparing French and English drama, was followed by *A Defence of an Essay* (1668), the preface to *An Evening's Love* (1671), *Of Heroic Plays* (1672), *Heads of an Answer* (to Thomas *Rymer, *c.*1677, pub. 1711), and *The Grounds of Criticism in Tragedy*, prefixed to *Troilus and Cressida* (1679). **Aureng-Zebe* (1675) was his best rhymed heroic play. The prologue, however, denounces rhyme in serious drama, and his next tragedy, **All for Love* (1678), based on Shakespeare's **Antony and Cleopatra*, was in blank verse. In assessing his Elizabethan predecessors, Shakespeare, *Jonson, and John *Fletcher, Dryden was torn between feeling that they were not as gentlemanly as Restoration writers and an awareness of their power. His eminence as critic and dramatist left him vulnerable to attack. He was represented as Bayes in *The *Rehearsal* (1671) by *Buckingham, and physically assaulted in 1679, possibly at the instigation of *Rochester. His principal opponent was Thomas *Shadwell, whom he ridiculed in **Mac Flecknoe* (*c.*1676, pub. 1682). Other poems in which he develops his critical principles include many witty and imaginative prologues and epilogues, and poems about, or addressed to, fellow writers and artists, notably Nathaniel Lee, the earl of Roscommon, John *Oldham, William *Congreve, and Godfrey *Kneller.

The constitutional crisis of the late 1670s and early 1680s saw Dryden's emergence as a formidable Tory polemicist. His contribution to the political debate included plays, especially *The *Spanish Friar* (1680), *The Duke of Guise* (1682, written with Lee), and the operatic *Albion and Albanius* (1685); his celebrated satires **Absalom and Achitophel* (1681), *The *Medal* (1682), and a number of lines for Nahum *Tate's *The Second Part of Absalom and Achitophel* (1682), as well as a host of partisan prologues and epilogues. His interest in religion was also heightened at this time. In **Religio Laici* (1682) he offers a defence of the Anglican *via media*. However, following the accession of James II Dryden became a Catholic and wrote *The *Hind and the Panther* (1687) in support of his new co-religionists. At the death of Charles II he attempted a *Pindaric ode, *Threnodia Augustalis* (1685), the first of several poems in this form, notably *To the Pious Memory of Mrs Anne Killigrew* (1686), *A Song for Saint Cecilia's Day* (1687), 'An Ode, on the Death of Mr Henry Purcell' (1696), and *Alexander's Feast* (1697), which was later incorporated into **Fables, Ancient and Modern* (1700).

In 1689 he refused the oath of allegiance to the new government, lost his court offices and income, and returned to the theatre with **Don Sebastian* (1689), **Amphitryon* (1690), *Cleomenes* (1692), and *Love Triumphant* (1694). However, he was tired of the theatre and turned to the politically less compromising work of translation, his extraordinary sweep and versatility taking in small selections from *Theocritus and *Horace, and more substantial passages from *Homer, *Lucretius, *Persius, *Juvenal, *Ovid, *Boccaccio, and *Chaucer, as well as the whole of *Virgil. In many of these translations he made frequent but subtle allusions to his *Jacobite principles. He also returned to criticism, notably in preface to the *Sylvae* (1685), 'A Discourse Concerning the Original and Progress of Satire' (1693), Dedication to *Examen Poeticum* (1693), and Dedication of the *Aeneis* (1697). His culminating achievement as translator was *Fables, Ancient and Modern*, to which 'The Secular Masque' (1700) was a coda. He was buried in Westminster Abbey. (*See also* RESTORATION.)

Other works by Dryden include: Plays: *Amboyna* (1673, a tragedy), **Mr Limberham* (1679, a sexually explicit comedy), and a dramatic opera, *King Arthur* (1691). Poems: 'Upon the Death of Lord Hastings', about a schoolmate who died of smallpox (1649), *Britannia Rediviva* (1688), and *Eleonora* (1696). *The Poems of John Dryden*, ed. P. Hammond and D. Hopkins (4 vols, 1995–2000) is the Longman's Annotated English Poets edition with invaluable notes and summaries of criticism. See also *Dramatic Works*, ed. M. Summers (6 vols, 1931–2); *Of Dramatic Poesy, and Other Critical Essays*, ed. G. Watson (2 vols, 1962); *Letters*, ed. C. E. Ward (1942); J. A. Winn, *John Dryden and his World* (1987); J. and K. Kinsley (eds), *Dryden: The Critical Heritage* (1971).

dub, dub poetry Dub is an instrumental remix of a reggae recording, often involving reverberation, echo, and other electronic effects, used as a backing track for improvisation or 'toasting'. Dub poetry, which is often forthright in its political and social commentary, is performed over a dub backing track or using the rhythms of reggae music. Both forms developed in Jamaica and Britain in the 1970s. Though essentially designed for live performance, dub poetry has become increasingly available in printed form. Notable exponents include Linton Kwesi *Johnson and Benjamin *Zephaniah.

Du Bartas, Guillaume de Saluste, seigneur (1544–90) French poet. He published a number of moral epics, including *Judith* (1574; English trans. 1584), but his most famous work was the creation epic *La Semaine* (1578; complete English trans. by Josuah *Sylvester, *Devine Weekes and Workes*, 1605). Partly because of his Protestant convictions, he was more influential in England than in France: Edmund *Spenser, Sir Philip *Sidney, and *Milton were familiar with his work, either in the original or through translation; it was praised by Samuel *Daniel, Michael *Drayton, Thomas *Lodge, and John *Marston, but John *Dryden found it 'abominable fustian'.

du BELLAY, Joachim (*c.*1522–1560) French poet. A member of the *Pléiade, he published *La Défense et illustration de la langue française* (1549: *The Defence and Illustration of the French Language*), advocating French as a poetic language, and the first French sonnet sequence, *L'Olive* (1549–50). He spent the years 1553–7 in Rome, and on his return to France published two further sequences, *Les Antiquités de Rome* and *Les Regrets*. At the end of the 16th century, English translations of selections of Du Bellay's poetry include those by Sir Arthur *Gorges and Samuel *Daniel, and Edmund *Spenser's version of the *Antiquités* as *Ruines of Rome* appeared in the *Complaints* of 1591. G. K. *Chesterton famously translated the sonnet from *Les Regrets* in which Du Bellay contrasts Rome with his native Anjou.

Dubliners A volume of short stories by James *Joyce, published in 1914. Focusing on life in Dublin, the stories follow a pattern of childhood, adolescence, maturity, and public life, culminating with the longest, 'The Dead', frequently described as 'the finest short story in English'. Joyce intended them to be a 'chapter of the moral history [of Ireland]', set them in Dublin 'because that city seemed to [him] the centre of paralysis', and wrote them in what he called 'a style of scrupulous meanness'. Because of Joyce's frankness and his insistence on publishing without deletion or alteration, he found himself in the first of what would be several battles with publishers who refused to print his work without excisions, as well as the focus of a brief campaign for freedom to publish (in the pages, for example, of *The *Egoist*).

Du BOIS, William Edward Burghardt (1868–1963) African American author, social reformer, and activist, who helped found the National Association for the Advancement of Coloured People, 1910. Among his many historical and sociological studies, *The Souls of Black Folk* (1903) is a collection of essays describing 'life within the Veil', which criticizes Booker T. *Washington for being insufficiently militant about black rights. He published his autobiography, *Dusk of Dawn*, in 1940; and a trilogy of novels about American racism: *The Black Flame* (1957), *Mansart Builds a School* (1959), and *Worlds of Colour* (1961). He became increasingly radical and anti-imperial during his long career, and in the year before his death moved to Ghana and became a citizen of that country.

Du BOS, Jean-Baptiste, abbé (1670–1742) Diplomat, historian, critic, and secretary of the *Académie Française from 1722 until his death. He was a friend of Pierre *Bayle, whose philosophical scepticism he found increasingly congenial, and of John *Locke, whose **Essay Concerning Human Understanding*, in Coste's French translation, he helped to publicize at the beginning of the century. His *Réflexions critiques sur la poésie et sur la peinture* (*Critical Reflections on Poetry and Painting*) was published in Paris in 1719 and in an English translation in 1748. For at least 50 years it was the most influential work of its kind in Europe. Among French writers who owed much to it were *Voltaire and later Hippolyte *Taine, while in Britain David *Hume followed Du Bos closely in his essay 'Of the Standard of Taste' (1757). Du Bos's eclectic work was a temperate defence of the moderns in the debate between the ancients and the moderns. His views are focused on six main questions: the nature of poetic or pictorial beauty; the relations between beauty and conformity to rules; how the arts influence each other; the qualities needed by great artists; how artistic reputations are established; and why some ages seem to be more artistically fertile than others. Du Bos argues that the arts are valued for the pleasure they are designed to provide; those best able to judge are not critics, scholars, or fellow artists, but the public, who rely on their inner conviction or sixth sense. The main task of reason is to justify the verdicts already delivered by sentiment, by identifying features of a work which cause pleasure. Genuine sentiment is immune to specious reasoning. Du Bos also holds that taste is influenced more by physical than social factors, as can be seen by the effects of age and physiology. Later writers sought to examine Du Bos's unanalysed notion of pleasure, and the respective roles of thought and feeling, or reason and sentiment, in the experience, appreciation, and judgement of art.

Duchess of Malfi, The By John *Webster, written 1612/13, printed 1623. The story is taken from one of *Bandello's novelle, through Painter's **Palace of Pleasure*, and also shows the influence of Sidney's **Arcadia*.

The Duchess, a high-spirited and high-minded widow, reveals her love for the honest Antonio, steward at her court, and secretly marries him, despite the warnings of her brothers, Ferdinand, duke of Calabria, and the cardinal, and immediately after informing them that she has no intention of remarrying. Their resistance appears to be induced by consideration for their high blood, and by, as Ferdinand later asserts, a desire to inherit her property; there is also a strong suggestion of Ferdinand's repressed incestuous desire for her. The brothers place in her employment as a spy the cynical ex-galley-slave Bosola, who betrays her to them; she and Antonio flee and separate. She is captured, and subjected by Ferdinand and Bosola to fearful mental tortures, including the sight of the feigned corpse of her husband and the attendance of a group of madmen; finally she is strangled with two of her children and Cariola, her waiting-woman. Retribution overtakes the murderers: Ferdinand goes mad, imagining himself a wolf ('A very pestilent disease...they call lycanthropia'); the cardinal is killed by the now remorseful Bosola, and Bosola by Ferdinand. Bosola has already killed Antonio, mistaking him for the cardinal. The human tenderness of the scenes between the duchess, Antonio, and their children; the pride and dignity of the duchess in her suffering ('I am Duchess of Malfi still'); and individual lines such as the celebrated 'Cover her face: Mine eyes dazzle: she died young' have long been admired, but until recently critics have been less happy about the overall structure, the abrupt changes in tone, and the blood bath of the last act. There have been many revivals, emphasizing T. S. *Eliot's point that Webster's 'verse is essentially dramatic verse, written by a man with a very acute sense of the theatre' (1941).

DUCK, Stephen (1705–56) Farm labourer and poet, born in Wiltshire. Almost entirely self-educated, through reading the **Spectator* and John *Milton, he took to writing verse. His poem *The Thresher's Labour* (1730) is a realistic portrayal of the unremitting toil of the labourer's life. Duck was taken up by several notable patrons, including Queen Caroline, who made him a yeoman of the guard in 1733 and keeper of her grotto, Merlin's Cave, in 1735. In 1746 he took holy orders; ten years later he drowned himself in despair. His *Poems on Several Occasions* (1736) included a biography by Joseph *Spence.

du DEFFAND, Marie de Vichy, marquise (1697–1780) A French literary hostess, whose salon was frequented by *Montesquieu, *d'Alembert, and others, and who became blind in later life. Horace *Walpole was her close friend, and a large number of her letters to him survive (ed. Helen Wrigley Toynbee, 1912); Walpole's letters to her were destroyed at his request.

DUDLEY, Robert, earl of Leicester (1532/3–88) Courtier and favourite of *Elizabeth I. Uncle of Philip *Sidney, he was a notable patron of writers and poets, including Edmund *Spenser. His personal power and ambitions provoked much hatred and a tradition of literary attacks, the most famous of which are *Leicester's Commonwealth* (1584) and, later, Walter *Scott's **Kenilworth*.

Duenna, The Comic opera by Richard Brinsley *Sheridan, produced with great success in 1775. It incorporates many popular song tunes. Don Jerome plans to marry his daughter Louisa to the rich Isaac, but she loves the poorer Antonio. Discovering that the duenna is acting as an intermediary between the lovers, he dismisses her, and imprisons Louisa. The women exchange places and Louisa escapes; Isaac is duped into marrying the duenna, and the lovers are united.

Duessa In Edmund *Spenser's **Faerie Queene*, the daughter of Deceit and Shame, Falsehood in general; in Book I she signifies, in particular, the Roman Catholic Church, and in V. ix, *Mary Queen of Scots.

DUFFY, Carol Ann (1955–) Poet, born in Glasgow. She moved to Staffordshire as a child, and graduated in philosophy from Liverpool University in 1977. Since then she has worked as a freelance writer in London and Manchester. Her debut collection, *Standing Female Nude* (1985), announced her interest in the *dramatic monologue, frequently using the voices of outsiders—the dispossessed, the insane, and those, especially women, ignored by history. Her interest in the speaking voice led her to the demotic and to a supple, distinctive grammar with frequent use of short sentences, italics, and slang. In *Selling Manhattan* (1987) her subtle rhythms marked by assonance and internal rhymes began to be used in more personal verse and in love poems as well as monologues; 'Wearing her Pearls', with its intricate preoccupations with class, sexuality, and obsession, is outstanding, and justly well known. The themes of nostalgia, desire, loss, and memory, the search for 'first space and the right place', begun in that volume came to predominate in *The Other Country* (1990) and *Mean Time* (1993), which contain several much-anthologized love poems and lyrics, as well as Duffy's characteristic satire, politics, and narrative. Her subsequent volumes *The World's Wife* (1999), *Feminine Gospels* (2002), and *Rapture* (2005) brought her critical acclaim and also a form of popularity beyond the usual reach of poets. All are also poetic sequences in which central preoccupations—marriage, women's experience, and the intensity of love and its ending—are reflected in different perspectives and varied forms. *The World's Wife*, in particular, which—extraordinarily for a volume of contemporary poetry—became a best-seller, employs the dramatic monologue of Duffy's earlier work in newly ironic and satiric modes: each poem is spoken in the 'voice' of the imagined female partner of one of the acclaimed men of history or mythology, usually to deflationary and sometimes to devastating effect. *New Selected Poems* appeared in 2004. In 2009, Duffy became the first woman to be appointed poet laureate. She is also the author of children's books, including *The Good Child's Guide to Rock N Roll* (2003), and a playwright. See Deryn Rees-Jones, *Carol Ann Duffy* (2002).

DUFFY, Maureen (1933–) Writer, born in Worthing, Sussex, educated at Trowbridge High School, Wiltshire, and King's College London. She has published plays, poetry, and non-fiction, but is perhaps best known as a novelist. Her first novel, *That's How It Was* (1962), is a moving autobiographical account of her working-class childhood. It was followed by many others, some of which deal frankly with the subject of homosexuality, notably *The Microcosm* (1966), set in London's lesbian community. In *Love Child* (1971), which describes a woman's affair from her child's point of view, the gender of both the narrator and the lover is undisclosed. *Wounds* (1969), *Capital* (1975), and *Londoners* (1983) form a London trilogy, the last of them a sardonic but poignant view of the writer's lot in the contemporary bedsitter land of Earl's Court in which once again the sex of the narrator is left intentionally ambiguous. Later novels include the science fiction *Gor Saga* (1981), which reflects her concern for animal rights (outlined in a handbook, *Men and Beasts*, 1984), and *Illuminations* (1991), about a woman who translates the letters of an 8th-century nun. *Restitution* (1998) is a post-*Holocaust novel, set in England and Berlin, exploring themes of family guilt, genetic heritage, and existential freedom. Her poetry includes *The Venus Touch* (1971), *Evesong* (1975), *Memorials of the Quick and the Dead* (1979), and *Collected Poems 1949–84* (1985). Among her plays are *A Nightingale in Bloomsbury Square* (1974), about Virginia *Woolf, and a trilogy based on Greek myths: *Rites* (1969), *Solo* (1970), and *Old Tyme* (1970). Her works of non-fiction include biographies of Aphra *Behn (*The Passionate Shepherdess*, 1977) and *Purcell (1994), and *The Erotic World of Faery* (1972).

DUGDALE, Sir William (1605–86) Antiquary, author of *The Antiquities of Warwickshire* (1656), a topographical history that set new standards of fullness and accuracy for the genre and inspired, amongst others, Anthony *Wood. His *Monasticon Anglicanum*, written in collaboration with Roger Dodsworth (bap. 1585, d. 1654), an account of the English monastic houses, appeared in three volumes (1655–73). In 1658 he published his *History of St Paul's Cathedral*, and in 1662 *The History of the Embanking and Draining of Divers Fens and Marshes*, which incidentally gives much information of antiquarian and historical interest. He also wrote *Origines Judicales* (1666), a history of English laws, law courts, and kindred matters, and *The Baronage of England* (1675–6).

DUHIG, Ian (1954–) Poet, born in London to émigré Irish Catholic parents, educated at Leeds University, a former worker with the homeless. Duhig is a learned, witty, and eclectic poet, versed in the Irish language (see, for example, 'According to Dineen') and Irish history, drawn to the arcane and absurd, full of rococo allusion, conceit, and pastiche. *The Bradford Count* (1991) features monologues by David *Livingstone and a depressed medieval monk. *The Mersey Goldfish* (1995) was followed by *Nominies* (1998), an ambitious and emotionally complex collection, which includes ballads of destitution and history, as well as the blackly comic 'The Ballad of Freddie the Dolphin'. Some poems of *The Lammas Hireling* (2003) witness to a newly chastened directness.

DUJARDIN, Édouard *See* SYMBOLISM; STREAM OF CONSCIOUSNESS.

Duke of Milan, The A tragedy by Philip *Massinger, written *c.*1621, printed 1623, one of his earliest independent plays and a popular one. It is based on the story of Herod and Mariamne as told by *Josephus.

Lodovico Sforza, duke of Milan, has, in the war between the emperor Charles and the king of France, allied himself with the latter. On their defeat, he goes to surrender to Charles, but, fearing for his life, leaves a written instruction with his wicked favourite Francisco to put his beloved wife Marcelia to death if he himself is killed. Francisco, seeking to corrupt Marcelia in revenge for the dishonouring of his own sister Eugenia by Sforza, reveals the existence of the warrant to her, but fails to move her chastity and only incenses her against the duke, so that on his return after a reconciliation with Charles she receives him coldly. This, coupled with accusations from various quarters of his wife's intimacy with Francisco, makes the duke suspicious of her. Francisco now tells Sforza that Marcelia made amorous advances to him, which so angers the duke that he stabs her to death; dying, she reveals the truth, leaving her husband distracted with remorse. Francisco flees, then returns to court disguised as a Jewish doctor, and promises to restore Marcelia to life. He is discovered and tortured, but not before he succeeds in poisoning the duke.

Duke's Children, The A novel by Anthony *Trollope, published 1880, the last in the *'Palliser' series. Glencora, the duchess of Omnium, encourages Frank Tregear, a young Conservative with little fortune, in his suit to her daughter Lady Mary Palliser, but after the death of the duchess Tregear has no one to plead his cause with the Liberal duke, and the match is broken off. Meanwhile the duke is anxious at the behaviour of his eldest son and heir, Lord Silverbridge. Sent down from Oxford as a result of his wild behaviour, Silverbridge immerses himself in London club life, and becomes well known for his interest in horse racing. He becomes part-owner, with the unsavoury Major Tifto, of a racehorse waggishly named 'The Prime Minister', and loses £70,000 betting on its performances in the Derby and St Leger. The duke pays his son's debts and hints that marriage might help him to settle down, whereupon Silverbridge admits his involvement with an impoverished but well-born cousin of Tregear's, Lady Mabel Grex, who is herself in love with Tregear, though she knows she can never afford to marry him. Tregear finds a seat in Parliament, finally convincing the duke of his political and personal integrity. The duke sanctions his marriage to Lady Mary, and is prepared to encourage Silverbridge's marriage to Lady Mabel, when he discovers that his son has fallen in love with the brilliant American Isabel Boncassen. He finds it hard to reconcile himself to the idea of a wedding between a future duke of Omnium and a girl whose family has risen from obscurity in two generations, even though Mr Boncassen is a respected scholar, but Silverbridge's determination and Isabel's charm make him give way gracefully in the end. Lady Mabel, a character of tragic dimensions, is left to solitary disappointment. The novel combines political interests with Trollope's characteristic concern with the role of loyalty and inheritance in courtship. It also reflects his changing views of American culture, and of parent–child relationships.

DUMAS, Alexandre ('Dumas *fils*') (1824–95) Influential French dramatist. His first venture into the theatre, *La Dame aux camélias* (1852: *The Lady of the Camelias*), a play about the doomed love of the reformed courtesan Marguerite Gautier for the respectable Armand Duval, was an enormous success and was turned into an opera, *La Traviata*, by *Verdi. Thereafter Dumas *fils* turned to the writing of social-problem dramas, including *Le Demi-monde* (1855: *The Half-World*), *Le Fils naturel* (1858: *The Natural Son*), *Les Idées de Madame Aubray* (1867: *The Ideas of Madame Aubray*), and *La Femme de Claude* (1873: *The Wife of Claude*).

DUMAS, Alexandre ('Dumas *père*') (1802–70) French novelist and playwright. A pioneer of the Romantic theatre in France, his popular, swift-moving, historical dramas include: *Henri III et sa cour* (1829: *Henry III and his Court*), *Antony* (1831), *La Tour de Nesle* (1832: *The Tower of Nesle*), and *Kean* (1836), about the colourful life of the actor Edmund *Kean. But he is best known as a novelist. In 1844 he published both *Le Comte de Monte-Cristo* (*The Count of Monte-Cristo*), a masterpiece of mystery and adventure which describes the vengeance of Edmond Dantès, falsely accused as a Bonapartiste conspirator in 1815 and imprisoned for many years in the Château d'If, and *Les Trois Mousquetaires* (*The Three Musketeers*), about the adventures of d'Artagnan, who comes from Gascony to Paris in the reign of Louis XIII to join the king's musketeers, and shares the exploits of three of them, Athos, Porthos, and Aramis; both works were translated into English almost immediately and have remained popular ever since. Dumas *père* continued d'Artagnan's adventures in *Vingt ans après* (1845: *Twenty Years Later*) and *Le Vicomte de Bragelonne* (1848–50: *The Vicount of Bragelonne*). The action of his other novels is set in the Wars of Religion in 16th-century France (e.g. *La Reine Margot*, 1845: *Queen Margot*), the late 18th century, and the Revolution (e.g. *Le Collier de la reine*, 1849–50: *The Queen's Necklace*; *La Comtesse de Charny*, 1852–5: *The Countess of Charny*). Dumas *père* also wrote numerous books of travel, 22 volumes of *Mémoires* (1852–5), several children's stories, and a *Grand Dictionnaire de cuisine* (1872, posthumous: *Dictionary of Cuisine*).

du MAURIER, Dame Daphne (1907–89) Novelist, born in London, the granddaughter of George *du Maurier. She was educated privately and it was while living alone in Cornwall during the winter of 1929–30 that she wrote her first novel, *The Loving Spirit* (1931), which was an immediate success. Two more novels followed in quick succession, but it was her frank memoir of her father (*Gerald*, 1934) that encouraged her to develop her powerful narrative skill and evocation of atmosphere: the result was *Jamaica Inn* (1936), another triumph. Married in 1932 to Major Frederick 'Boy' Browning, she was obliged to accompany him to Egypt when he was posted there. She became desperately homesick, and this unhappy period produced *Rebecca* (1938), a study in jealousy based on her own feelings towards a former fiancée of her husband's. She wrote ten more novels, including *Scapegoat* (1957), two plays, several collections of short stories, and three biographies, but *Rebecca* (turned into a film in 1940, as were seven more of her novels and stories, most notably *Hitchcock's *The Birds* (1963)) remained her finest work. It has brought her enduring fame, even though she believed it overshadowed the rest of her oeuvre. See Margaret *Forster, *Daphne du Maurier* (1993).

du MAURIER, George (1834–96) Artist and writer, born in Paris. He was the father of actor-manager Gerald du Maurier (1873–1934), and grandfather of the novelist Daphne *du Maurier. He spent his childhood in Paris and London, and in 1856 and 1860 studied art in Paris and Antwerp. He contributed to **Punch* and other periodicals and illustrated editions of Elizabeth *Gaskell, George *Meredith, Thomas *Hardy, and Henry *James, among others. In 1865 he began to write humorous verse, including 'The History of the Jack Sprats', and a parody of William *Morris's ballads, 'The Legend of Camelot', with mock *Pre-Raphaelite illustrations. In 1891 he published his first novel, *Peter Ibbetson*, largely based on his early childhood in Paris, and turning on two supernaturally related dreams. His next novel, **Trilby*, for which he is still remembered, appeared in 1894; its vast fame and success continued for many years. *The Martian*, a story based on school life, appeared posthumously in 1897.

dumb show A piece of silent action or stage business, especially in the Elizabethan and Jacobean theatre, where speech is expected but not actually delivered. These shows, such as the one before the play scene in **Hamlet* or Revenge's in *The *Spanish Tragedy*, suggest by mime and symbolism what is shortly to take place and its meaning.

DUNBAR, William (?1460–1513/30) Prolific Scottish poet and priest, an MA of St Andrews University (1479). Although much of Dunbar's life remains obscure, it is known that in 1500 he was awarded a royal pension and that he was a priest by 1504. In 1503, he wrote 'The Thrissill and the Rois', a political allegory in *rhyme royal, the Rose representing Margaret Tudor, who married James IV (the 'Thistle') in that year; in about 1507 he also wrote 'The Goldyn Targe', the 'Lament for the Makaris', and 'The Tretis of the Tua Mariit Wemen and the Wedo', as well as numerous minor pieces. He also wrote 'To Aberdein', celebrating Queen Margaret Tudor's entry into the town in 1511. The 'Tua Mariit Wemen and the Wedo' (widow), a visionary dialogue in which the three interlocutors relate their experiences of marriage, is a satire on marriage reminiscent of Chaucer's Wife of Bath's prologue in the **Canterbury Tales*. 'The Goldyn Targe' is a substantial allegory recalling *Chaucer and *Lydgate, in which the poet, appearing in a dream before the court of Venus, is wounded by the arrows of Beauty in spite of the shield ('targe') of Reason. In 'The Dance of the Sevin Deidly Synnis' (*c.*1507) the poet in a trance sees the fiend Mahoun call a dance of unrepentant outcasts, who are characterized with great vigour. The 'Lament for the Makaris' may also relate to the tradition of the *Dance of Death. It is a powerful elegy for the transitoriness of things, with its refrain '*Timor mortis conturbat me*' ('the fear of Death disturbs me'), and in particular for the deaths of Dunbar's fellow poets (the 'makaris', or 'makers', are 'poets'), including Geoffrey *Chaucer, John *Gower, and Robert *Henryson. Dunbar's satirical energy and Rabelaisian humour are particularly well displayed in 'The *Flyting of Dunbar and Kennedie'. His poems, some of which are preserved in the *Asloan and *Bannatyne manuscripts, are written in a range of high and low styles, the two sometimes provocatively juxtaposed within one poem. See *The Poems of William Dunbar*, ed. P. Bawcutt (1998); P. Bawcutt, *Dunbar the Makar* (1992); R. D. S. Jack, *The Poetry of William Dunbar* (1997).

DUNCAN, Robert *See* BLACK MOUNTAIN POETS.

Dunciad, The A *mock-epic satire by Alexander *Pope. A three-book version was published anonymously in 1728; in 1729 Pope published *The Dunciad Variorum*, which added notes, indexes, and essays to the poem. In this material Pope simultaneously parodied the ponderous apparatus of scholarly editions and provided evidence to support his own position. The *New Dunciad*, a fourth book, was published in 1742, and a final complete version in 1743. The poem had its roots in the activities of the *Scriblerus Club, but the criticisms of Pope's edition of *Shakespeare contained in Lewis *Theobald's *Shakespeare Restored* (1726), and the coronation of George II in 1727, prompted Pope to finish and publish it. Theobald was the hero of the poem in its earlier form, but in the final version Colley *Cibber was enthroned in his place. The satire is directed against 'Dulness' (characterized as a goddess in Swift's **Battle of the Books*, and here defined as a set of intellectual qualities by Pope in a note to I. 15 of the four-book version). In the course of the poem all the authors who had incurred Pope's enmity are pictured in humiliating situations that grotesquely parody epic conventions. In Book I, the hero, a struggling and incompetent writer, is carried off by the goddess and anointed king in the place of Laurence *Eusden, the deceased poet laureate. In Book II, the coronation is celebrated by ceremonial games: a race between booksellers, including Edmund *Curll, for the phantom of a poet; a pissing contest (Curll again); a mud-diving exercise; and finally a test for the critics, to determine whether they can hear the works of two authors without sleeping. But presently spectators, critics, and all fall fast asleep. In Book III the king, slumbering with his head on the lap of the goddess, is transported to the Elysian shades, where, under the guidance of Elkanah *Settle, he sees visions of the past and future triumphs of the empire of Dulness over the theatres and the court. In the last book these prophecies are brought to fruition; the sciences and universities are subjugated to Dulness, and the ancient empire of night and chaos (by allusion to **Paradise Lost*) is restored. The poem was enormously controversial and generated much protest and vehement responses from those it attacked. See *The Dunciad: In Four Books*, ed. Valerie Rumbold (1999); and *The Dunciad (1728) & The Dunciad Variorum (1729)*, ed. Rumbold (2007).

Dun Cow, Book of the The earliest extant vernacular Irish manuscript, of late 11th-century origin. Now fragmentary, it contains 37 texts, including tales of *Cuchulain, an Irish version of the *Historia Brittonum* (*see* NENNIUS), and an annotated version of *Amra Coluim Chille*, an early 7th-century elegy for St Columcille (*Columba).

DUNLAP, William (1766–1839) American dramatist, sometimes called the 'Father of American Theatre'; born in Perth Amboy, New Jersey, but lived most of his life in New York. He wrote many plays, with varying success, and attempted to introduce European drama into America. His *History of the American Theatre* (1832) was the first of its kind in the USA.

DUNMORE, Helen (1952–) Poet, novelist, and children's writer, born in Yorkshire and educated at the University of York. Her poetry collections include *The Apple Fall* (1983), *The Sea Skater* (1986), *Short Days, Long Nights* (1991), and *Glad of These Times* (2007). Her first adult novel, *Zennor in Darkness* (1993), set in Cornwall in 1917, featured D. H. *Lawrence and his wife Frieda amongst its leading characters. It was followed by *Burning Bright* (1994), *A Spell of Winter* (1995, winner of the Orange Prize for women's fiction), *Talking to the Dead* (1996), *Your Blue-Eyed Boy* (1998), and *With your Crooked Heart* (1999), all marked by richly textured writing and an eerie sense of place which matches their mysterious plots, often concerned with long-buried family secrets and betrayals. *The Siege* (2001) silhouetted ordinary lives against the backdrop of the siege of Leningrad. *Mourning Ruby* (2003), an exploration of loss and grief, focused on the accidental death of a child. *House of Orphans* (2006) is set in Finland in the early years of the 20th century. *Counting the Stars* (2008) recreates the obsessional love affair between the Roman poet *Catullus and his mistress Clodia. *Love of Fat Men* (1997) and *Ice Cream* (2000) are collections of short stories.

DUNN, Douglas (1942–) Scottish poet and critic, who became professor of English at St Andrews University in 1991. He was born at Inchinnan, Renfrewshire, and educated at Renfrew High School, the Scottish School of Librarianship, and the University of Hull. After graduating he worked in the Brynmor Jones Library at Hull under Philip *Larkin, whose influence has been detected in the blackly humorous vignettes of working-class life in Dunn's first collection, *Terry Street* (1969). *The Happier Life* (1972), *Love or Nothing* (1974), *Barbarians* (1979), and *St Kilda's Parliament* (1981) move beyond the urban realism of the first volume, and are marked by an increasingly historicized perspective and a growing interest in metrical and stanzaic variety. Dunn returned to Scotland in 1984 and the following year published the award-winning *Elegies*, on the death of his wife from cancer. *Northlight* (1988) and *Dante's Drum-Kit* (1993) further expand his temporal, geographical, and technical range. *The Donkey's Ears*, a narrative of the Russo-Japanese War in the **In Memoriam* stanza, appeared in 2000 along with *The Year's Afternoon*, a collection of reflective lyrics. He has published two volumes of short stories, *Secret Villages* (1985) and *Boyfriends and Girlfriends* (1995). He is the editor of *The Faber Book of Twentieth-Century Scottish Verse* (1992) and *The Oxford Book of Scottish Short Stories* (1995). *Essays* (2003) offers a selection of his criticism.

DUNN, Nell (1936–) Novelist and playwright, educated in a convent school, which she left at the age of 14. Her early novels, *Up the Junction* (1963) and *Poor Cow* (1967; filmed, Ken Loach, 1968), showed a keen ear for working-class dialogue and an uninhibited approach to female sexuality. Other works include *My Silver Shoes* (1996), which continues the story of the heroine of *Poor Cow* in middle age. Dunn's best-known play, *Steaming* (1981), is a comedy with an all-female cast set in a Turkish bath; other dramatic works with a darker edge include *The Little Heroine* (1988) and *Sisters* (1994).

DUNSANY, Edward Plunkett, eighteenth Baron (1878–1957) London-born Anglo-Irish aristocrat, friend of W. B. *Yeats and Oliver St John *Gogarty, and patron of Francis *Ledgwidge. His first book of mythological tales, *The Gods of Pegana* (1905), was illustrated by S. H. Sime (1867–1941), whose weird *fin-de-siècle* drawings were to accompany such subsequent fantasies as *The Book of Wonder* (1912) and *The King of Elfland's Daughter* (1924). Dunsany's first play, *The Glittering Gate*, was performed at the *Abbey Theatre in 1909; like much of his later dramatic work it shows the influence of *Maeterlinck. His short plays were popular with the Little

Theatre movement in America, and his full-length *If* was a success in London in 1921. The popular 'Jorkens' stories, beginning with *The Travel Tales of Mr Joseph Jorkens* (1931), show a talent for realism. Dunsany also wrote novels, essays, poetry, and memoirs. See Mark Amory, *Lord Dunsany* (1972).

DUNS SCOTUS, John (*c.*1265–1308) The 'Doctor Subtilis', a Scottish Franciscan who entered the order at Dumfries in 1278–9. He lectured on the *Sententiae* of *Peter Lombard at Oxford, Paris, and Cambridge universities. He was among those expelled from Paris by Philip the Fair in 1303. After further time at Oxford and Paris, he died at Cologne on 8 November 1308. It was long thought that he had produced two series of commentaries on the *Sententiae*: the *Reportata Parisiensia*, based, as its informal title indicates, on reported versions of his lectures, and the unfinished *Opus Oxoniense* or *Ordinatio*, which he had partially prepared for dissemination. However, the uncertainty of the states in which the manuscripts of his work survive, combined with the extreme sophistication of his thought, make detailed understanding of his systematic beliefs a challenge. His principal significance in the history of *scholasticism is that he drove the first wedge between theology and philosophy (a split which widened throughout the 14th century), with his emphasis on the separation between God as necessary Being from all contingent Beings, and the impossibility of arguing from the latter to the former. Although this emphasis, together with his associated Augustinian-Franciscan stress on faith and will rather than reason, distinguishes his thought from the synthesis of the Dominican *Aquinas, like the latter he incorporated a good deal of *Aristotle into his metaphysics. He was much influenced too by Arabic philosophers, especially *Avicenna, with their emphasis on Being as the metaphysical object. He straddles the line between 13th-century system-building and 14th-century scepticism, and his work was an important influence on William of *Ockham among others. The word 'dunce', first in the sense of 'a maker of impossibly ingenious distinctions', derives from him; some of his formal metaphysical distinctions were referred to by G. M. *Hopkins in his development of a poetic psychology. A Vatican edition of Scotus' works is in progress; until its completion, the edition by L. Vivès in 26 vols (1639; repr. 1891–5) is generally used.

DUNSTAN, St (d. 988) Distinguished Benedictine monk and archbishop of Canterbury. His education in the vicinity of Glastonbury was influenced by the presence of Irish pilgrims. He was a favourite with King Athelstan, but his piety made him unpopular at court. His kinsman Ælfheah (Elphege), who became bishop of Winchester in 934, persuaded Dunstan to take monastic vows and ordained him as a priest. He was restored to favour by King Edmund, who appointed him abbot of Glastonbury (*c.*940–46). Supported by King Eadred (who succeeded in 946), he incurred the disfavour of his successor, King Eadwig, and retired to Flanders (956). Edgar recalled him and archbishop of appointed him bishop of Worcester (957), bishop of London (959), and archbishop of Canterbury (960). Dunstan restored and reformed English monasteries and contributed to the integration of the Danes. He averted civil war by crowning Edward the Martyr (975), and foretold to King Ethelred the Unready the national calamities that would occur because of Edward's murder. See N. Ramsay, M. Sparks, and T. Tatton-Brown (eds.), *St. Dunstan: His Life, Times and Cult* (1992).

DUNTON, John (1659–1733) A publisher and bookseller who between 1691 and 1697 issued the **Athenian Gazette* (afterwards *Athenian Mercury*), dealing with philosophical and scientific matters, and incorporating a quiz in the form of questions sent in by readers. He also wrote many political pamphlets and *The Life and Errors of John Dunton* (1705).

DURAS, Marguerite (1914–96) French novelist, screenwriter, playwright, and film director, born in Indo-China. She used her own experience as source material, and, while her early works were traditional, after 1950 she more or less abandoned conventional narrative, her work becoming more experimental and employing some of the techniques of the **nouveau roman*. In *L'Amant* (1984: *The Lover*), for which she won the Prix Goncourt, she returns to the autobiographical material first explored in *Un barrage contre le Pacifique* (1950: *A Barrage against the Pacific*). Intensely passionate and deeply personal, it is widely seen as her most significant novel, although it may be for her screenplay for Alain Resnais's *Hiroshima mon amour* (1959: *Hiroshima, my Love*) that she is more widely remembered.

DURCAN, Paul (1944–) Irish poet, born in Dublin and educated at University College, Cork. Durcan is an acclaimed public reader of his work. Powered by parallelism, refrains, and startling transitions, his monologues are gleeful, painful, learned, and populist. Many of his poems are satires on the constriction of Irish life by prejudice and authority, often religious in origin ('Irish Hierarchy Bans Colour Photography'). *The Berlin Wall Café* (1985) laments marital break-up in a series of simultaneously lacerating and cartoon-like narrative lyrics. *Daddy, Daddy* (1990) and *The Laughter of Mothers* (2007) address tragicomic elegies and love poems to the poet's father and mother respectively, while commenting mordantly on the relationship of gender to nationality. Durcan's greatest originality lies in his gift for sceptical, humane fantasy ('The Haulier's Wife Meets Jesus on the Road near Moone'). He was Ireland professor of poetry from 2005 to 2007 (a cross-border academic chair established in 1998 to mark the international standing of Irish poets and to commemorate the achievement of Seamus *Heaney in winning the Nobel Prize for Literature in 1995). See *A Snail in my Prime: New and Selected Poems* (1993); *The Art of Life* (2004).

DÜRER, Albrecht (1471–1528) German painter and engraver, the son of a Hungarian goldsmith who settled in Nuremberg. His friendship with the great humanist scholar Willibald Pirkheimer (1470–1530) stimulated his interest in the new learning of the *Renaissance and he made two journeys to Italy, introducing to northern Europe the ideals and forms he encountered there. His most famous engravings, and those which have most literary influence, are *Knight, Death and the Devil* (1513) and *Melencolia I* (1514). In 1636 Thomas Howard, earl of Arundel, a passionate collector of Dürer, bought the Pirkheimer library with many books illuminated by the artist. The northern Renaissance aroused little enthusiasm in 18th-century England, but interest revived in the 19th century. James *Thomson's *City of Dreadful Night* contains a long description of *Melencolia*, which in turn reappears in Rudyard *Kipling. John *Ruskin, D. G. *Rossetti, and George *Eliot all admired him. See E. Panofsky, *The Life and Art of Albrecht Dürer* (1943).

D'URFEY, Thomas (1653–1723) A French Huguenot by descent, familiarly known as Tom Durfey, who wrote a large number of songs, tales, satires, melodramas, and farces. A friend of Charles II and James II, he was still writing in the reign of Queen Anne, and was one of the most familiar figures of the day, given to singing his own songs in public. His comedies include *Madame Fickle* (1676), *The Virtuous Wife* (1679), and the more sentimental *Love for Money* (1691). He was attacked by Jeremy *Collier and replied in a comedy, *The Campaigners* (1698), with an unrepentant prose preface. His works include many adaptations: **Bussy D'Ambois*, **Cymbeline* (as *The Injured Princess*), and a three-part dramatization of **Don Quixote* (1694–6) with music by Henry *Purcell. His *Wit and Mirth, or Pills to Purge Melancholy* (6 vols, 1719–20) is a collection of songs and ballads.

DURHAM, Edith (1863–1944) Travel writer and anthropologist, educated at Bedford College and the Royal Academy of Arts. After the death of her father and a long period nursing her mother, Durham travelled in the Balkans over two decades from the late 1890s. Her seven books on the region include *High Albania* (1909). Her work has been regarded as possessing anthropological value, and she served on the Council of the Royal Anthropological Institute, but her pro-Albanian views attracted criticism.

DURKHEIM, Émile (1858–1917) French sociologist. His significance rests on his attempt to establish modern sociology as a science. His studies of criminality (*De la division du travail social*, 1893: *On the Division of Work in Society*), of suicide (*Le Suicide*, 1897), and of the social (rather than supernatural) origins of religion (*Les Formes élémentaires de la vie religieuse*, 1912: *The Elementary Forms of Religious Life*) served to mark out the field and to determine the nature of the sociological fact. In 1898 he founded *L'Année sociologique* (*The Sociological Year*), the first sociological review.

DURRELL, Lawrence (1912–90) Poet, novelist, and travel writer, born in India; he returned to England in his late teens, and thereafter travelled widely, living in Paris in the 1930s, and then for much of his life in the eastern Mediterranean. Although he began to write and publish when very young, his work made little impact for some years. He was first recognized as a poet: his collections include *A Private Country* (1943), *Cities, Plains and People* (1946), and *The Tree of Idleness* (1955). His *Collected Poems* appeared in 1960. His first novel of interest, *The Black Book*, heavily influenced by Henry *Miller, was published in Paris in 1938, but did not appear in Britain until 1973. Publication of *Justine* (1957), the first volume of his *Alexandria Quartet*, finally brought Durrell fame: *Balthazar* and *Mountolive* followed in 1958, and *Clea* in 1960. Set in Alexandria during the period just before the Second World War, the first three novels cover roughly the same period of time and the same events, with characters bound together in a web of political and sexual intrigue, while *Clea* advances the action in time. Durrell's later novels include *Tunc* (1968), *Nunquam* (1970), and the volumes known collectively as the *Avignon Quintet* (*Monsieur*, 1974, *Livia*, 1978, *Constance*, 1982, *Sebastian*, 1983, and *Quinx*, 1985). His best-known travel books are his three 'island' books, *Prospero's Cell* (1945), based on his pre-war years in Corfu; *Reflections on a Marine Venus* (1953), based on his experiences as information officer in Rhodes, 1945–6; and *Bitter Lemons* (1957), an account of three years spent on Cyprus. There is a biography (1998) by Ian MacNiven. Lawrence Durrell's brother, the zoologist Gerald Malcolm Durrell (1925–95), was also a writer, well known for his popular accounts of animal life and his own zoo on Jersey: titles include *The Overloaded Ark* (1953), *My Family and Other Animals* (1956), and *A Zoo in my Luggage* (1960).

DÜRRENMATT, Friedrich (1921–90) Swiss-German dramatist, novelist, and essayist. He considered tragedy impossible in the present age where tragic guilt or responsibility could only be collective, not individual. Thus he advocated comedy as a more appropriate dramatic form. His own dark comedies tend to parody the conventions of tragedy and have elements of the grotesque. His plays, though *Der Besuch der alten Dame* (1956: *The Visit*, 1958) and *Die Physiker* (1962: *The Physicists*, trans. James *Kirkup, 1963) are the best known, include adaptations of Shakespeare's **King John* (1968) and **Titus Andronicus* (1970). He explored the idea of using popular literary forms for serious purposes in his *detective fiction, which became well known in English through *The Judge and the Hangman* (1952: *Der Richter und sein Henker*, 1952), *Suspicion* (1954: *Der Verdacht*, 1953), and *The Pledge* (1959: *Das Versprechen*, 1958). The latter was made into a successful film (directed by Sean Penn) starring Jack Nicholson, Helen Mirren, and Vanessa Redgrave in 2001. Dürrenmatt has also written many radio plays, and critical and philosophical essays, as well as theoretical works on theatre. See K. S. Whitton, *The Theatre of Friedrich Dürrenmatt* (1980).

Dutch Courtesan, The A comedy by John *Marston, acted at Blackfriars by boy actors of the Queen's Revels *c.*1604, printed 1605. Young Freevill, about to marry Beatrice, determines to break off his connection with Franceschina, a torrid Dutch courtesan. He introduces her to his repressed Puritan friend Malheureux, who quickly becomes infatuated. She agrees to gratify his passion if he will murder Freevill, and bring, as proof, a ring given to Freevill by Beatrice. Freevill consents to help him; a pretended quarrel is arranged, Freevill disappears, and Malheureux takes the ring to Franceschina, who quickly informs the authorities of Malheureux's crime.

He is arrested and sentenced to death. At the last moment young Freevill appears, and begs forgiveness for the deceit he used to cure his friend's infatuation. Franceschina is condemned to be whipped and jailed. The play proved popular and was revived and adapted during the Restoration.

DYCE, Alexander (1798–1869) Scholar, who edited many works of Shakespeare and his contemporaries. His editions include the works of George *Peele (1828 and 1829–39), Thomas *Middleton (1840), *Beaumont and *Fletcher (1843–6), Christopher *Marlowe (1850), John *Ford (1869), Robert *Greene (1831, 1861), and John *Webster (1830, 1857). As well as producing a full edition of Shakespeare's works (1857, 1864–7) he was the first editor of *Sir Thomas *More* (1844). He left his valuable collection of books and manuscripts to the Victoria and Albert Museum.

DYCK, Sir Anthony Van *See* VAN DYCK, SIR ANTHONY.

DYER, Sir Edward (1543–1607) Poet, educated either at Broadgates Hall or Balliol College, Oxford, and the Inner Temple. He was introduced at court by Robert *Dudley, earl of Leicester, taking part in the queen's entertainment at Woodstock (1575) and being one of the 'happy blessed Trinitie' with Philip *Sidney and Sir Fulke *Greville. Few authentic poems have survived ('*My mind to me a kingdom is', is probably by the earl of *Oxford): those which do show him to be a rather old-fashioned courtly poet. One of the best of his surviving poems, 'The lowest trees have tops', was set by John *Dowland in 1603. There is an account of his life and works by R. M. Sargent (2nd edn, 1968).

DYER, Geoff (1958–) Writer of fiction and non-fiction, born in Cheltenham. His first, Brixton-based novel, *The Colour of Memory* (1989), was followed by *The Search* (1993), in which a man is asked to track down a woman's husband. *Paris Trance* (1998), Dyer's third novel, is set in the French capital. Dyer's enthusiasm for his chosen subjects is the link between his non-fiction works: *Ways of Telling* (1986), a critical study of the work of John *Berger, *But Beautiful: A Book about Jazz* (1991), *The Missing of the Somme* (1994), and *Out of Sheer Rage: In the Shadow of D. H. Lawrence* (1997).

DYER, George (1755–1841) Educated at *Christ's Hospital and Emmanuel College, Cambridge, usher at Dedham Grammar School and later at a school in Northampton. He published his *Poems* in 1792, and various critical essays from time to time. He is remembered as a friend of Charles *Lamb, who writes of him as a gentle and kindly eccentric. He is the subject of Lamb's essay 'Amicus Redivivus' in *The Last Essays of Elia*, which describes how Dyer, departing from Lamb's cottage in Islington, marched absent-mindedly into the nearby river and disappeared. His rescue and resuscitation are affectionately described.

DYER, John (1699–1757) Welsh poet, born at Llanfynydd, educated briefly at Westminster School. He studied law, then painting (taught by Alexander *Pope's friend Jonathan Richardson (1667–1745)), and met writers such as Richard *Savage and Aaron *Hill. His *topographical poem in tetrameter couplets, *Grongar Hill* (1726), describes the scenery along the river Tywi. His *Ruins of Rome* (1740) was based on a tour to Italy. In 1741 he became a clergyman. He also farmed, and his poem *The Fleece* (1757) is enlivened by early industrial as well as pastoral landscapes. Samuel *Johnson scorned *The Fleece* for its prosaic subject: 'How can a man write poetically of serges and druggets?' But *Wordsworth admired it greatly, addressed a sonnet to Dyer, and in his notes to *The *Excursion* commented, 'He wrote at a time when machinery was first beginning to be introduced, and his benevolent heart prompted him to augur from it nothing but good.'

DYLAN, Bob (1941–) Born Robert Allen Zimmerman in Duluth, Minnesota, American singer, influenced by the folk style of Woody *Guthrie, for the early part of his career playing acoustic guitar. In the 1960s he became successful as a songwriter, partly following the method of Pete Seeger (1919–), and gave concerts with Joan Baez (1941–) to support the civil rights movement, achieving fame with songs like 'Blowin' in the Wind'. In the mid-1960s Dylan moved over to rock and roll, producing the album *Blonde on Blonde* (1966) which combined his styles up to that point. Dylan subsequently continued to expand his musical repertoire and in 2006 started work as a radio DJ. In 1971 he published a *stream-of-consciousness novel, *Tarantula*, acted in Sam Peckinpah's film *Pat Garrett and Billy the Kid* (1973), and in 2004 brought out his autobiography, *Chronicles: Volume I*. In 2008, he was awarded a 'Special Citation' from the *Pulitzer Board for 'his profound impact on popular music and American culture'. See Howard Sounes's biography, *Down the Highway* (2001).

dystopia a term coined to convey the opposite of Utopia. The dystopian mode, which projects an unpleasant or catastrophic future, is frequently used by *science fiction writers.

E

EAGLETON, Terry (1943–) Literary critic. Born in Salford to an Irish working-class family, he studied there at De La Salle College, then read English at Trinity College, Cambridge. Under the influence of Raymond *Williams, he joined the latter as fellow of Jesus College (1964–9), becoming active in the Catholic wing of the New Left. At Oxford as fellow of Wadham College (1969–89), he published his first notable works, *Myths of Power* (on the *Brontës, 1975), *Marxism and Literary Criticism* (1976), and the ambitious theoretical work influenced by *structuralist Marxism, *Criticism and Ideology* (1976). In such early works he aimed to develop a *Marxist criticism upon bases provided by Bertolt *Brecht and other continental thinkers. His later work, from *Walter Benjamin* (1981) onwards, displays a new flexibility and lively wit, especially in parodic summaries of modern intellectual traditions, as in the widely admired *Literary Theory* (1983) and in *The Ideology of the Aesthetic* (1990). As Warton professor of English literature at Oxford (1992–2001) and later as professor of cultural theory at Manchester (2001–), his work has repeatedly satirized the assumptions of contemporary 'postmodern' thought, in *Ideology* (1991), *The Illusions of Postmodernism* (1996), and *After Theory* (2003). A prolific author, he has also published comic fiction (*Saints and Scholars*, 1987); drama (*Saint Oscar*, about Oscar *Wilde, 1989); a remarkable memoir, *The Gatekeeper* (2001); a range of critical studies of *Shakespeare, Samuel *Richardson, the theory of *tragedy, and Irish literature; and a philosophical essay, *The Meaning of Life* (2008).

Ealing Studios Produced a series of comedies, from *Hue and Cry* (1947) to *The Ladykillers* (1955), which have come to be regarded as expressing distinctive British post-war values, such as resentment of overbearing authority, community feeling, and an opportunism bordering on the anarchic or criminal. Other key 'Ealing comedies' include *Passport to Pimlico, Whisky Galore*, and *Kind Hearts and Coronets* (all 1949) and *The Lavender Hill Mob* (1951), all produced under the leadership of Michael Balcon, with a small group of writers, directors, and editors often collaborating in line with the studio's motto, 'team spirit'. George Perry (1981) and Charles Barr (1993) have written on the place of the comedies within the studio's wider output.

EARLE, John (?1601–65) Character writer, a member of Viscount *Falkland's circle at Great Tew, who became tutor to Prince Charles in 1641, served him as chaplain during his exile in France, and after the *Restoration became bishop of Worcester, then Salisbury, in which roles he defended persecuted Nonconformists. *Microcosmography* (1628) was a collection of character sketches, chiefly by his hand, based on the model of *Theophrastus, though some of them are responses to the harsher and more satiric 'characters' of Sir Thomas *Overbury (e.g. his 'Good Old Man', compared with Overbury's 'Old Man'). He analyses varied social and moral types, ranging from the cook to the upstart country knight, with wit, sympathy, and insight.
See CHARACTER-WRITING.

Early English Text Society Founded in 1864 by F. J. *Furnivall, with support from W. W. *Skeat and others, to publish Early and Middle English texts. Much of its early history is undocumented. The Society, which is supported by subscription, continues to publish regularly, with over 475 volumes listed in its current catalogue.

Early Irish lyric poetry A term that usually refers to the more epigrammatic among the poems produced in Old Irish after the introduction of the Roman alphabet by Christian missionaries in the 5th century AD. Many of the lyrics were written by monks in the margins of the illuminated manuscripts produced in Irish monasteries in Ireland, Britain, and Europe, and they reflect the asceticism of monastic culture. Characteristically cast in syllabic *quatrains, they were the first European art poems to use rhyme, a feature that may have been borrowed from Latin hymns or from the marching songs of the later Roman Empire. The extent of their debt to the pre-Christian oral literature of Ireland is unclear, though it has been conjectured that their vivid renderings of the natural world reflect the monks' insistence on writing out of doors in repudiation of the pagan poets' practice of composing in darkened rooms. The 'steelpen exactness' ascribed to the lyrics by Flann *O'Brien has been an ideal of English-language poets in Ireland from Austin *Clarke to Ciaran *Carson and Paul *Muldoon.

Earthly Paradise, The A poem by William *Morris, published 1868–70, consisting of a prologue and 24 tales, in Chaucerian metres. The prologue tells how a company of Norsemen, fleeing from the pestilence, set sail in search of the fabled Earthly Paradise 'across the western sea where none grow old'. They are disappointed in their quest and return after long wanderings, 'shrivelled, bent and grey', to a 'nameless city in a distant sea' where the ancient Greek gods are still worshipped. They are hospitably received and there spend their remaining years. Twice in each month they meet their hosts at a feast and a tale is told, alternately by one of the elders of the city and one of the wanderers. The tales of the former are on classical subjects (Atalanta, Perseus, the Apples of the Hesperides, etc.), those of the latter from Norse and other medieval subjects, including 'The Lovers of Gudrun', a version of the *Laxdaela saga*. Between the tales are interpolated lyrics describing the changing seasons, and the whole work is prefaced by an apology which contains some of Morris's best-known (and in a sense most misleading) lines, in which he describes himself as 'the idle singer of an empty day', 'born out of my due time'. Although the plan of the work owes a debt to *The *Canterbury Tales*, it is almost entirely static, and its narrators undifferentiated.

East Lynne A *sensation novel by Ellen *Wood (Mrs Henry Wood), published 1861. It tells the story of Isabel Vane, a refined lady who, finding herself unprotected in the world, marries Archibald Carlyle, a rising lawyer. Her marriage is unsatisfying, and she imagines that her husband loves a neighbour, Barbara Hare. In a moment of undisciplined passion, she runs away with Sir Francis Levison, an unscrupulous seducer, who abandons her and the child born from their illegitimate union. Having divorced Isabel, and mistakenly assumed her to have been killed in a railway accident, Archibald marries Barbara. Isabel, rendered unrecognizable by disfigurement resulting from the accident, returns to the household to act as a governess to her own children, to watch helplessly as her delicate son dies. Worn down by remorse and sorrow, she too dies, after being recognized and forgiven by her worthy but ponderous husband. The novel was a phenomenal best-seller, and was rapidly adapted for the popular stage, where it persisted for many years as staple of the repertoire (the line 'Dead! Dead! And never called me mother!' belongs to a stage version, not the novel). More recently, it has attracted notice for its analysis of changing social conditions, and for the ambivalence of its treatment of Isabel, who is the object of both vigorous condemnation and heartfelt sympathy from the narrator.

EASTMAN, Max (1883–1969) American literary critic and political activist, born in New York State. He was active in the Greenwich Village community and edited the left-wing journal *The Masses* (1913–18). His critical works include *The Enjoyment of Poetry* (1913) and *Art and the Life of Action* (1934).

Eastward Ho A comedy by George *Chapman, Ben *Jonson, and John *Marston, printed 1605, having been performed by the Children of the Revels at the Blackfriars. A passage derogatory to the Scots (III. iii) gave offence at court, and Chapman and Jonson were imprisoned, but released on the intercession of powerful friends. The play is particularly interesting for the light it throws on London life of the time. Like Thomas Dekker's **Shoemakers' Holiday*, it gives a sympathetic picture of a tradesman.

The plot contrasts the careers of the virtuous and idle apprentices, Golding and Quicksilver, of the goldsmith Touchstone; and the fates of his two daughters, the modest Mildred, who marries the industrious Golding, and the immodest Gertrude who, in order to ride in her own coach, marries the penniless adventurer Sir Petronel Flash. Golding soon rises to the dignity of a deputy alderman, while Sir Petronel, having sent off his lady in a coach to an imaginary castle of his and filched her dowry, sets off for Virginia, accompanied by the prodigal Quicksilver, who has robbed his master. They are wrecked on the Isle of Dogs, and brought before Golding, the deputy alderman. After some days in prison, where their mortifications lead them to repent, they are released at Golding's intercession. The play has had successful modern revivals, especially by the Royal Shakespeare Company in 2002.

EBERHARDT, Isabelle (1877–1904) Author, born in Geneva, to an aristocratic German-Russian mother and the family tutor, an Armenian-born Orthodox priest turned anarchist. Eberhardt, who had been taught Arabic by her father, moved with her mother in 1897 to Algeria, where both converted to Islam. Most of Eberhardt's remaining years were spent in North Africa, through which she often travelled disguised as an Arab man, enjoying the greater freedom this gave her. She married an Arab soldier in 1901. Her fascination with Islam and with nomadism, her cross-dressing, sexual promiscuity, and early death (in a flash flood) have engaged new generations of readers. English translations of her posthumously published collections of writings include *In the Shadow of Islam* (1993) and *The Passionate Nomad: The Diary of Isabelle Eberhardt* (1987). A volume of her short stories, *The Oblivion Seekers and Other Writings* (1975), was translated by Paul *Bowles. Annette Kobak published a biography in 1988.

EBERHART, Richard (1904–2005) American poet, born in Austin, Minnesota. He began publishing with *A Bravery of Earth* (1930) and maintained a prolific output of works which shun experiment in favour of accessibility. He also wrote a number of verse plays including *The Apparition* (1951).

Ecclesiastes *See* BIBLE.

Ecclesiastical History of the English People, The The most famous work by *Bede, complete by 731 and widely known. It is a five-book Latin history from the invasion of Julius *Caesar to an account of the state of the country in 731. Book I narrates *Augustine's mission to England; Book II continues until the conversion of the north; Book III ends with the Synod of Whitby; Book IV concludes with the death of *Cuthbert; and Book V takes events to 731. The *History*'s sources include patristic literature, Eusebius, Gregory of Tours, Gildas, and *Orosius, and it is characterized by a vivid and engaging narrative style, being the source of famous stories such as the conversion of Edwin, the miracle of *Cædmon, and the layman Dryhthelm's visions of the next life. It was later translated into Old English. See the revised edition in English and Latin by B. Colgrave and R. A. B. Mynors (1991).

ECKHARD, Johannes (?1260–1327) Known as 'Meister Eckhard', a German Dominican who was conferred doctor by Boniface VIII but was later summoned before the bishop of Cologne and obliged to recant some of his opinions. He is regarded as the founder of German mysticism and one of its greatest exponents. See English trans. by J. M. Clark included in his *Meister Eckhart: An Introduction* (1957).

eclogue A short *pastoral poem, usually in the form of a dialogue between shepherds, but sometimes a soliloquy. In Latin the term could denote any short poem, but it became associated especially with *Virgil's pastoral poems in imitation of *Theocritus, which he called *bucolica* but which have long been renamed the *Eclogues*. The classic English examples are the twelve eclogues of Edmund Spenser's *The *Shepheardes Calender*.

Eclogues, The By Alexander *Barclay, written *c*.1513–14, interesting as the earliest English *pastorals, anticipating Edmund *Spenser. The five eclogues, printed between *c*.1518 and *c*.1530, are moral and satirical in character, dealing with such subjects as the evils of a court life and the happiness of the countryman's lot. They are modelled upon *Mantuan and the *Miseriae Curialium* of *Piccolomini.

ECO, Umberto (1932–) Italian semiologist, novelist, and essayist. His critical works include: *Thema: omaggio a Joyce* (1958: *Themes: Homage to Joyce*, tape with music by Luciano Berio), *La struttura assente* (1968: *The Absent Structure*), *Le forme del contenuto* (1971: *The Forms of Content*), *A Theory of Semiotics* (1975), *Opera aperta* (1962: *The Open Work*), *The Search for the Perfect Language* (1995), and *Serendipities* (1998). His historical mystery novel *Il nome della rosa* (1981: *The Name of the Rose*), concerning a series of murders in a medieval monastery, was an international best-seller and was subsequently filmed with Sean Connery in the role of the 'detective', Brother William of Baskerville. His other novels are *Il pendolo di Foucault* (1988: *Foucault's Pendulum*), *L'isola del giorno prima* (1994: *The Island of the Day before*), *Baudolino* (2000), and *La misteriosa fiamma della regina Loana* (2004: *The Mysterious Flame of Queen Loana*). His essays and journalistic pieces, many of which first appeared in the Italian weekly *L'espresso*, have been published in several collections including *Faith in Fakes* (1983) and *How to Travel with a Salmon and Other Essays* (1994). He has influenced the development of European semiotics (*see* SAUSSURE, FERDINAND DE) and has a long-standing interest in aesthetics, for which see *Art and Beauty in the Middle Ages* (1959; English trans. 1986) and *The Aesthetics of Thomas Aquinas* (1970; English trans. 1988).

Edda An Old Norse name of uncertain meaning given to a 13th-century poetic manual written by *Snorri Sturluson, known as the Prose, Younger, or Snorra Edda. The same name was applied in the 17th century to a manuscript collection of poems, the Poetic or Elder Edda. The Prose Edda is divided into a prologue and three parts: the 'Gylfaginning', or Deluding of Gylfi, a series of mythological stories in the form of a dialogue between one Gylfi and the Norse gods; the 'Skáldskaparmál', or Poetic Diction, in which Snorri illustrates the elaborate diction of *skaldic verse, retelling many myths and legends; and the 'Háttatal', or List of Metres, a long poem each strophe of which exemplifies a different Norse metre. Snorri's work is valuable for the stories it enshrines, the verses it has preserved, and Snorri's own gifts as a storyteller. The Poetic Edda was compiled in about 1270, but some of the poems in it undoubtedly belong to a much earlier age. The poems fall into two groups: heroic lays about legendary Germanic heroes such as Sigurör and Helgi; and mythological lays, such as the Völsunga saga, a history of the Norse gods from creation to apocalypse, and the Hávamál, the words of the High One, Oðinn. W. H. *Auden wrote free translations of many Eddaic lays. See *The Prose Edda of Snorri Sturluson*, trans. J. I. Young (1954); *The Poetic Edda*, i: *Heroic Poems*, ii: *Mythological Poems*, ed. U. Dronke (1969–97, parallel trans.); *Norse Poems* by W. H. Auden and P. B. Taylor (1981); E. O. G. Turville-Petre, *Origins of Icelandic Literature* (1953).

EDDISON, E. R. (Eric Rucker) (1882–1945) Born in Adel, Yorkshire; writer and civil servant who drew upon a wide variety of classical, mythological, and Renaissance sources for his *fantasy, beginning with *The Worm Ourobouros* (1922) in which his hero Lessingham is transported to Mercury to witness an epic conflict. Subsequent novels, *Mistress of Mistresses* (1935), *A Fish Dinner in Memizon* (1941), and the uncompleted *The Mezentian Gate* (1958), are set in that world's Valhalla, Zimiamvia, where a complex dance of identities ensues.

EDDY, Mary Baker Glover (1821–1910) American writer and evangelist, born at Bow, New Hampshire. She expounded the doctrine of Christian Science in *Science and Health with Key to the Scriptures* (1875); the Christian Science Association was formed in 1876, and in 1879 the Church of Christ, Scientist was founded.

EDEL, Leon (1907–1997) Literary critic and biographer, born in Pittsburgh, Pennsylvania, and educated at McGill University, Montreal, and the Université de Paris. He taught at several universities, including New York University and the University of Hawaii. He is renowned for his five-volume biography of *Henry *James*, *Henry James: A Biography* (1953–72), the second and third volume of which won both the Pulitzer Prize and National Book Award. He also wrote a study of James Joyce (1947) and a memoir, *The Visitable Past* (2000).

EDEN, Emily (1797–1869) Novelist, painter, and traveller, daughter of William Eden, first Baron Auckland. When her brother George Eden was appointed governor general of India in 1835, she accompanied him. *Up the Country* (1866) describes, through letters, her travels with her brother from Kolkata

(Calcutta) to Shimla; *Portraits of the People and Princes of India* (1844) is a collection of her paintings, the importance of which is increasingly recognized. Two posthumous volumes of letters have been published, *Letters from India* (1872) and a collection of her letters edited by her great-niece Violet Dickinson in 1919. Her novels *The Semi-detached House* (1859, anon.) and *The Semi-attached Couple* (1860, by 'E.E.') deal with fashionable society; their plots and characterization owe much to Jane *Austen and are a valuable record of the social life of the time. Both the novels and letters have been republished by the *Virago Press.

Eden, garden of The mythical garden planted by God, as described in Genesis chs 2–3, containing the tree of life and the tree of knowledge of good and evil, and watered by four rivers. God puts Adam in the garden to keep it, and creates Eve from Adam's rib. In the story of the Fall, one of the most powerful myths of Western culture, God forbids them to eat of the tree of knowledge on pain of death; Eve, tempted by the serpent, eats the fruit, followed by Adam, so God expels them from the garden to endure labour and mortality. The yearning for the return to a prelapsarian Edenic state (i.e. Eden before the Fall) has parallels with the classical myth of the return of the Golden Age, the first of the *Four Ages. The fullest literary depiction of Eden is in John Milton's **Paradise Lost*.

EDGAR, David (1948–) Dramatist, born in Birmingham, and educated at Oundle School. He studied drama at Manchester University, after which he worked as a journalist in Bradford and wrote political plays for a touring theatre company, the General Will. His early work included *Dick Deterred* (1974), a pastiche melodrama about Richard Nixon and the Watergate scandal. *Destiny* (1976), a play about Fascism in British society, was produced by the Royal Shakespeare Company. He came to general prominence in 1980 with his hugely successful eight-hour adaptation of Dickens's **Nicholas Nickleby*. *Maydays* (1983), the first play by a contemporary dramatist to be staged by the RSC at the Barbican Theatre, dealt with the post-war decline of socialism. His work also includes *Entertaining Strangers* (1985), set in 19th-century Dorchester, on which he worked with community playwright Ann *Jellicoe; *That Summer* (1987), about the British miners' strike of 1985; and three plays about Eastern Europe around and after the time of the collapse of the Soviet Empire, *The Shape of the Table* (1990), *Pentecost* (1994), and *The Prisoner's Dilemma* (2001). He has also written for radio and television and in 1991 adapted Robert Louis *Stevenson's *The Strange Case of *Dr Jekyll and Mr Hyde* for the *National Theatre. In 2003, *Continental Divide* considered the history of the relationship between mainstream and alternative politics in the USA; and *Playing with Fire* (2005) revisited the territory of *Destiny* with its documentary-like concern with racial tension in Britain.

EDGEWORTH, Maria (1768–1849) Novelist, the eldest daughter of the first wife of Richard Lovell Edgeworth (1744–1817), a wealthy Irish landlord of a large estate in Co. Longford, who was to marry three more wives after the death of Maria's mother in 1773 and to father in all 22 children. He was an eccentric, radical, and inventive man, deeply interested in the practical applications of science and in education: his friends included Erasmus *Darwin, Anna Laetitia *Barbauld, and Thomas *Day. His influence on Maria was profound; he frequently 'edited' her work (which involved cutting, correcting, and occasionally contributing passages), managed her literary career, and imparted to her many of his own enthusiasms. They wrote together *Practical Education* (1798), a treatise which owes much to *Rousseau, although its tone is less theoretical.

Edgeworth spent her infancy in Ireland, received some schooling in England, and when she was 15 returned to live the rest of her life with her family in Ireland. Her first publication was *Letters to Literary Ladies* (1795), a plea for women's education. From then on she wrote prolifically for some 40 years and established a high reputation. She visited London in 1803, when she was feted by the literary world, meeting, among others, Lord *Byron, Sydney *Smith, Joanna *Baillie, and Henry Crabb *Robinson. She visited Walter *Scott at *Abbotsford in 1823, and he returned the visit in Ireland in 1825. He greatly admired her work, described her as 'the great Maria', and acknowledged his debt to her Irish novels in the preface to his 'Waverley' edition of 1829. Jane *Austen sent her a copy of **Emma* and later admirers included Thomas *Macaulay, W. M. *Thackeray, John *Ruskin, and *Turgenev.

Edgeworth appears to have initiated, in **Castle Rackrent*, both the first fully developed *regional novel and the first true historical novel in English (*see* HISTORICAL FICTION), pointing the way to the historical/regional novels of Scott. Her writings fall into three groups: those based on Irish life (considered her finest), *Castle Rackrent* (1800) and *The *Absentee* (first published in *Tales of Fashionable Life* in 1812) together with **Ormond* (1817); those depicting contemporary English society, such as *Belinda* (1801–2), commended by the heroine of **Northanger Abbey*, *Leonora* (1806), *Patronage* (1814), and *Helen* (1834); and her many popular lessons and stories for and about children, including *The Parent's Assistant* (1796–1800), *Moral Tales* (1801), *Popular Tales* (1804), and *Harry and Lucy Concluded* (1825). Marilyn Butler has written the standard biography, *Maria Edgeworth* (1972), and is general editor of *The Works of Maria Edgeworth* (12 vols, 1999–2003).

Edinburgh Review (1802–1929) A quarterly periodical, established by Francis *Jeffrey, Sydney *Smith, and Henry *Brougham, and originally published by Archibald *Constable. It succeeded immediately in establishing a prestige and authority which (shared with the **Quarterly Review*) lasted for over a century. Thomas *Carlyle described it as 'a kind of Delphic oracle'. Under the influence of its first editor, Jeffrey, its politics became emphatically Whig, but although it was anxious for reform in many spheres an effort was made to hold a balanced view. Only a section of the journal was reserved for literature, but the views expressed there were highly influential and the few books selected for review were very fully considered. Jeffrey perceived the genius of John *Keats, but his veneration for 18th-century literature led him to notorious and scathing denouncements of William *Wordsworth, S. T. *Coleridge, and Robert *Southey as the 'Lake School'. Lord *Byron's satirical 'English Bards and Scotch Reviewers' (1809) was in part an attack on the *Edinburgh Review*, which had published Brougham's hostile response to **Hours of Idleness*. Between Jeffrey's resignation in 1829 and the demise of the *Review* in 1929 contributions were published from almost all the major writers and critics of the 19th and early 20th centuries.

EDRIC, Robert (Gary Edric Armstrong) (1956–) Novelist, born in Sheffield, educated at Hull University. After publishing two novels—*Winter Garden* (1985) and *A New Ice Age* (1986)—under his own name of G. E. Armstrong, he has produced a series of intensely individual works under the pseudonym of Robert Edric. Three of them—*Cradle Song* (2003), *Siren Song* (2004), and *Swan Song* (2005)—comprise a present-day crime noir trilogy. Almost all the others—among which *The Earth Made of Glass* (1994), set in 17th-century East Anglia, *Elysium* (1995), set in 19th-century Tasmania, and *Gathering the Water* (2006), set in Victorian Yorkshire, particularly stand out—are *historical novels of remarkable power, written with terse accomplishment and acutely sensitive to cruelty and damage.

education, literature of Before the 17th century educational writing sought mainly to improve the classical curriculum (Roger *Ascham's *The Schoolmaster*, 1570), but calls for broader purposes in education came from John *Milton (*A Small Tractate on Education*, 1650) and John *Locke (*Some Thoughts Concerning Education*, 1693). Richard Lovell Edgeworth (1744–1817) and Maria *Edgeworth's *Practical Education* (1798), influenced by Jean-Jacques *Rousseau, concerned the education of both sexes from infancy onwards, and had sections on moral development as well as on grammar and arithmetic. In the late 18th and 19th centuries much influential writing on education, particularly by Nonconformists, centred on the irrelevance of the classical curriculum and the need for a secular, scientific, and technological education. Such aims were expressed by Joseph *Priestley (*Essay on a Course of Liberal Education for a Civil and Active Life*, 1765), William *Godwin (*Enquiry Concerning Political Justice*, 1793), Jeremy *Bentham (*Chrestomathia*, 1816), John Stuart *Mill, Herbert *Spencer, and T. H. *Huxley. Supporters of a liberal education based on the classics included Thomas and Matthew *Arnold and John Henry *Newman (*On the Scope and Nature of University Education*, 1852). Influential works on women's education included those of Mary *Wollstonecraft and Erasmus *Darwin's *Plan for the Conduct of Female Education in Boarding Schools* (1797). Thomas *Paine's *Rights of Man* (Pt II, 1792) included a plan to finance the education of all up to the age of 14. Robert *Owen's *A New View of Society* (1814) and Robert Dale Owen's *An Outline of the System of Education at New Lanark* (1824) explained their theories: discussion rather than rote learning, avoidance of rewards and punishments. Competing theories and systems of education proliferated throughout the 19th century, often associated with political and religious movements. Polemical works like William Lovett's *Chartism: A New Organisation of the People* (1840) and William *Morris's *A Factory as It Might Be* (1884) included vigorously argued sections on the reform of education.

The progressive education movement of the early 20th century often focused on manner rather than content. W. B. Curry (*The School and a Changing Civilization*, 1934) and A. S. Neill (*Hearts Not Heads in the School*, 1944; *Summerhill*, 1960) set out ideas for education based on mutual trust between children and adults. Curry, like Karl Mannheim (*Man and Society*, 1940; *Diagnosis of our Time*, 1943), saw education as a way towards a free and peaceful society. *The Aims of Education* (1929) by A. N. Whitehead (1861–1947) emphasizes the role of activity in the acquisition of ideas. Child-centred ideas influenced state education, though these were based on Swiss psychologist Jean Piaget's ideas about child development rather than those of Neill and Curry. (See *Children and their Primary Schools* (HMSO, 1967), known as the 'Plowden Report'.) In 1969 C. B. Cox and Brian Dyson edited *Fight for Education: A Black Paper*, first in a series of 'Black Papers' which alleged falling standards and blamed child-centred methods.

The debate focused in the 1950s and 1960s on class inequality (B. Jackson and D. Marsden, *Education and the Working Class*, 1962; A. H. Halsey et al., *Origins and Destinations*, 1980) but from the 1970s ethnicity and gender became important issues: see *How the West Indian Child Is Made Educationally Subnormal in the British School System* (B. Coard, 1971), which stimulated further research, and *Feminism, Education and Social Justice* (1993, ed. M. Arnot and K. Weiner). As girls have increasingly overtaken boys in educational success, attention has focused on boys' problems in schools (see D. Epstein, *Failing Boys? Issues in Gender and Achievement*, 1998).

Edward An old Scottish ballad of domestic tragedy, included in Percy's **Reliques* and beginning: 'Why, does your brand sae drop wi' blude, Edward, Edward?'

Edward II A tragedy in blank verse by *Marlowe probably first performed 1592, published 1594. It deals with the recall by Edward II, on his accession, of his lover, Piers Gaveston; the revolt of the barons and the capture and execution of Gaveston; the period during which Spenser (Hugh le Despenser) succeeded Gaveston as the king's favourite; the estrangement of Queen Isabella from her husband; her rebellion, supported by her lover Mortimer, against the king; the capture of the latter, his abdication of the crown, and his murder in Berkeley Castle. The play was an important influence on Shakespeare's **Richard II*. It has been frequently performed in modern times, and there is a film by Derek *Jarman.

Edward III, The Reign of King A historical play written entirely in verse, based mainly on Lord *Berners's translation (1535) of *Froissart's *Chronicles*. Published anonymously in 1596, it could date from any time between 1588 and 1595. In recent times it has been attributed with increasing confidence, at least in part, to Shakespeare, and is included, for example, in the second edition (2005) of the Oxford *Complete Works*.

The first two acts are concerned mainly with the dishonourable wooing of the countess of Salisbury by the king, who is finally brought to a sense of shame by her determination to kill herself if he persists. The rest is occupied with the French wars. Scenes ii and iii, involving the wooing of the countess, are those most likely to have written by Shakespeare.

EDWARDS, Amelia B. *See* GHOST STORIES.

EDWARDS, Dic (1953–) Playwright, born in Cardiff and educated at the University of Wales. His first plays, *Late City Echo* (1981), about the firemen's strike, *At the End of the Bay* (1982), *Canned Goods* (1983), and *Looking for the World* (1986), were produced at the Sherman Theatre, Cardiff, and the last of these, set in Greece during the Colonels' junta, announced an increasing preoccupation with global politics. In *Utah Blue* (1995), he brought his intensely poetic style to bear on the case of the murderer Gary Gilmore: 'Death came down the chimney at Christmas and death lit up the Christmas tree.' *Astrakhan (Winter)* was produced in 2005; in the same year Edwards collaborated on an opera, *Manifest Destiny*, with the composer Keith Burstein. He has worked with young people for many years on a Theatre in Education project at Spectacle Theatre in south Wales. *The Pimp*, a play about *Baudelaire, was produced in 2006.

EDWARDS, Dorothy (1914–1982) Born in Teddington, Middlesex, writer for the BBC. Her autobiographical stories about 'My Naughty Little Sister' were broadcast on *Listen with Mother*, a radio programme she helped to devise, from 1950, first appearing in book form in 1952. Nine more books about the same character followed.

EDWARDS, Jonathan (1703–58) American minister and writer, born in Connecticut, the philosopher and formidable preacher who provoked the religious revival in New England known as the 'Great Awakening'. In his *Treatise Concerning Religious Affections* (1746) he nicely discriminated between the state of grace and the state of worldliness; and a theological dispute led to his dismissal from the charge of the church of Northampton, Massachusetts, in 1750. He was then for six years a missionary to the Native Americans. His principal philosophical work was *A Careful and Strict Enquiry into the Modern Prevailing Notions of...Freedom of Will* (1754), in which he attacked from a predestinarian standpoint the *Arminian view of liberty. His *Personal Narrative* (*c.*1740) describes his experience of conversion. His essay 'Images or Shadows of Divine Things' is an important statement of *Protestant typology. Yale University Press have published the definitive edition of his writings under the general editorship of Harry S. Stout; see *The Works of Jonathan Edwards*, 26 vols (1957–2008).

EDWARDS, Monica (1912–98) Born in Belper, Derbyshire; she received little formal education. Remembered for appealing pony stories, beginning with *Wish for a Pony* (1947), first in the linked Romney Marsh (1947–69) and Punchbowl Farm (1947–67) series, she also wrote career novels, non-fiction, and the film script for *Dawn Killer* (1958).

EDWARDS, Richard (1525–66) of Corpus Christi College and Christ Church, Oxford, master of the Children of the Chapel Royal, 1561–6. He composed *Palamon and Arcite* (now lost) for Queen Elizabeth's entertainment at Oxford, 1566. Her Majesty was amused. *The Excellent Comedy of...*Damon and Pithias* (performed at court and at Lincoln's Inn, 1564–5; printed 1571) is his only surviving play. He was the compiler of the *Paradise of Dainty Devices*, published posthumously (1576).

Edwin Drood, The Mystery of Charles *Dickens's final novel. Six of the planned twelve instalments were published in 1870, but Dickens died before completing the book. The fathers of Edwin Drood and Rosa Bud, both widowers, have before their deaths betrothed their young children to one another. The orphan Rosa has been brought up in Miss Twinkleton's school at Cloisterham (Rochester), where Edwin, also an orphan, has an uncle, John Jasper, the precentor of the cathedral, to whom he is devoted and who appears to return the devotion. It is understood that the two young people are to marry as soon as Edwin comes of age, although this very understanding has been fatal to love between them. Jasper, a sinister and hypocritical character, gives Rosa music lessons and loves her passionately, but inspires her with terror and disgust. Two more orphans appear, the twins Neville and Helena Landless. Neville and Edwin at once become enemies, for Neville admires Rosa and is disgusted at Edwin's unappreciative treatment of her. This enmity is secretly fomented by Jasper and there is a violent quarrel between the young men. On the last of Edwin's periodical visits to Cloisterham before the time of his anticipated marriage, Rosa and he recognize that this marriage will not be for their happiness and break off the engagement. That same night Edwin disappears under circumstances pointing to foul play and suggesting that he has been murdered by Neville Landless, a theory actively supported by Jasper. But Jasper receives with uncontrollable symptoms of dismay the intelligence that the engagement of Edwin and Rosa had been broken off before Edwin's disappearance, and this betrayal of himself is noted by Mr Grewgious, Rosa's eccentric, good-hearted guardian. Neville is arrested but, as the body of Edwin is not found, is released untried. He is ostracized by public opinion and is obliged to hide himself as a student in London. The remainder of the text is occupied with the continued machinations of Jasper against Neville and his pursuit of Rosa, who in terror of him flies to her guardian in London; with the counter-moves prepared by Mr Grewgious, assisted by the amiable minor canon Mr Crisparkle and a new ally, the retired naval officer Mr Tartar; also with the proceedings of the mysterious Mr Datchery, directed against Jasper. Of the solution or catastrophe intended by the author no hint exists, beyond those which the fragment itself contains, and the statement as to the broad lines of the plot given by John *Forster. There have been many conjectures, turning mainly on two points: whether Edwin Drood had in fact been murdered or had miraculously survived; and the identity of Datchery. It has been suggested, for instance, that Datchery was Drood himself, or Tartar, or Grewgious, or Grewgious's clerk Bazzard, or Helena Landless, in disguise. There have been several attempts at continuations, from *John Jasper's Secret* (1871–2) by H. Morford and others, to recent versions such as one by Leon Garfield (1980) and another contained in *The Decoding of Edwin Drood* (1980) by C. Forsyte.

EGAN, Greg (1961–) Australian novelist, born in Perth, Western Australia; his fiction draws upon mathematics and computer science to explore virtual realities and posthumanism. *Diaspora* (1997) posits a future where much of humanity has downloaded itself to become computer software. The implications regarding the nature of consciousness, gender, and moral goals are skilfully explored. Egan's fiction is the hardest of *hard science fiction, but exhilarating in its ambition.

EGAN, Pierce, the elder (*c.*1772–1849) Novelist and sports journalist. He was the author of *Boxiana*, 4 vols (1812–29), a history of pugilism, and the hugely successful *Life in London* (1820–21), illustrated by Robert and George *Cruikshank, which details the adventures of Corinthian Tom and his country cousin Jerry and is interesting for the light it throws on the manners of the Regency and for its ingenious use of slang. In 1824 Egan began a weekly paper, *Pierce Egan's Life in London*, which subsequently merged with the sporting journal *Bell's Life*. His son, also Pierce Egan (1814–80), was associated with him in several of his works, and wrote a number of novels.

EGERTON, George (1859–1945) The pen-name of Mary Chavelita Dunne, short story writer, born in Australia of Irish-Welsh parentage and brought up in Ireland. Her adventurous early life took her to America and Norway, where she fell briefly in love with Knut *Hamsun, whose novel *Hunger* she later (1899) translated. She was married twice, first to Egerton Tertius Clairemonte (d. 1901), then to a theatrical agent, Reginald Golding Bright (1874?–1941). Her first volume of short stories, *Keynotes* (1893), published by John Lane (1854–1925) with a cover by Aubrey *Beardsley, created something of a sensation with its echoes of Scandinavian realism and portraits of the *New Woman. Her later works were: *Discords* (1894), *Symphonies* (1897), *Fantasies* (1898), *The Wheel of God* (1898), *Rosa Amorosa* (1901), and *Flies in Amber* (1905). See T. de Vere White, *A Leaf from the Yellow Book* (1958).

EGGERS, Dave (1970–) American writer, editor, and publisher, born in Boston; he attended the University of Illinois. His widely praised memoir *A Heartbreaking Work of Staggering Genius* (2000) was followed by the novels *You Shall Know our Velocity* (2002) and *What Is the What* (2006), and a collection of short stories, *How We Are Hungry* (2004). In 1998 he founded McSweeney's publishing house, which produces a quarterly literary magazine.

Egoist Originally the *New Freewoman: An Individualist Review*, founded by Harriet Shaw *Weaver and Dora *Marsden. It published articles on modern poetry and the arts, and from being a feminist paper became, under the influence of Ezra *Pound and others, a mouthpiece for the *imagist poets. It ran from 1914 to the end of 1919, first fortnightly and then monthly, with Richard *Aldington as assistant editor, followed by T. S. *Eliot in 1917. Marsden and Weaver succeeded each other as nominal editors and it was due to Weaver that James *Joyce's **Portrait of the Artist as a Young Man* was published serially in the magazine in 1914–15. See Bruce Clarke, *Dora Marsden and Early Modernism* (1996).

Egoist, The A novel by George *Meredith, published 1879. The Egoist is Sir Willoughby Patterne, rich and handsome, with a high position in the county, but blind to his own arrogance and to the needs of the women he loves. Laetitia Dale, an intelligent young woman but past her first bloom, has loved him for many years, and his vanity has been flattered. But the dashing Constantia Durham is a greater prize, and she accepts his proposal. However, she soon discerns Sir Willoughby's limitations and elopes with the officer Harry Oxford, bringing Willoughby his first bewildering humiliation. Soon he discovers the qualities he requires in Clara Middleton, the daughter of an elderly scholar (said to be a sketch of Meredith's first father-in-law, Thomas Love *Peacock), whose passion for wine overwhelms even his affection for his daughter. Clara, bewitched by Willoughby's charm and surroundings, becomes engaged to him, but rapidly perceives his intention of directing and moulding her; her attempts to free herself from the engagement form the main theme of the book. Clara envies but cannot emulate Constantia's escape, and Willoughby struggles frantically against an incredible second jilting. Clara is meanwhile seeing more and more of Vernon Whitford, a poor and earnest young scholar (based on Leslie *Stephen), who lives at Patterne and is tutor to young Crossjay, son of a poor relation, an officer of the marines. The spirited Crossjay is finally the means of Clara's release, for he unintentionally overhears Willoughby seeking a way out of his humiliation by proposing to Laetitia Dale, a proposal which she, with sad dignity, refuses. So Willoughby finds himself trebly mortified. However, his persistence finally wins the reluctant Laetitia, and Clara marries Vernon Whitford. The sharply compressed dialogue of the last chapters is among Meredith's most brilliant.

egotistical sublime A phrase coined by John *Keats to describe his version of *Wordsworth's distinctive genius. Wordsworth possesses imaginative self-obsession, a 'devouring egotism', in contradistinction to *Shakespeare, 'who was the least of an egoist that it was possible to be'. *See* NEGATIVE CAPABILITY.

Eikon Basilike, *the Portraiture of His Sacred Majesty in his Solitudes and Sufferings* A book of which Dr John Gauden (1605–62), bishop of Worcester, claimed authorship. Long supposed to be the meditations of Charles I, it was published ten days after his execution, 30 January 1649, and appealed so strongly to popular sentiment that 47 editions of it were published. Parliament thought it necessary to issue a reply, John *Milton's *Eikonoklastes* (1649); 'Eikon Basilike' means 'royal image' and 'Eikonoklastes' 'image breaker'. *Eikonoklastes* takes the *Eikon* paragraph by paragraph in an effort to refute it, and also vigorously attacks the 'miserable, credulous and deluded' public. Gauden's claim, which was not made known until 1690, is considered in F. F. Madan's *A New Bibliography of the Eikon Basilike* (1950).

eisteddfod Originally a formal gathering of Welsh professional poets, the first of which may have been held in Cardigan in 1176, now a competitive festival covering a wide range of cultural practices. The structure and procedures of the modern bardic establishment, the *gorsedd*, were concocted in the late 18th century by Iolo Marganwg (Edward *Williams). The ceremony of chairing the winning poet became an integral part of the local, regional, and school eisteddfodau held throughout Wales since the 19th century, and of the national youth eisteddfod. The week-long National Eisteddfod, held annually in the first week of August, alternately in venues in north and south Wales, is the most important. Prose, drama, music, dance, arts and crafts, and a host of fringe activities have been added to the traditional poetic contests. Since the introduction of a 'Welsh-only' rule in 1937 'the National' has become the most important cultural event in the calendar for Welsh speakers of all ages.

E.K. *See* KIRKE, EDWARD.

ekphrasis A verbal description of or meditation upon a non-verbal artistic work, usually a painting or sculpture. Classic instances in English poetry include Keats's *'Ode on a Grecian Urn' (1820) and *Auden's 'Musée des Beaux Arts' (1939). Prose works sometimes include ekphrastic description, as in chapter XIX ('The Cleopatra') of Charlotte Brontë's **Villette* (1853).

Elaine The name (variously spelt), in Malory's **Morte Darthur*, of several ladies whose identities sometimes overlap: (1) Elaine Le Blank, the daughter of Sir Bernard of Astolat and known as the Fair Maid of Astolat (*Tennyson's Shalott), who falls in love with Launcelot and dies for love of him (*see* LAUNCELOT OF THE LAKE); (2) Elayne the Fair or Sans Pere (Peerless), the daughter of King Pelles and the mother, by Launcelot, of *Galahad; (3) Elayne the sister of Morgawse and Morgan le Fay in the opening pages of Malory; (4) Elayne the wife of King Ban and mother of Launcelot; (5) Elayne the daughter of King Pellinore.

élan vital A phrase coined by Henri *Bergson to describe the vital impulse which he believed directed evolutionary growth.

Elder Brother, The A drama by John *Fletcher, written *c.*1625, probably with Philip *Massinger, who completed it *c.*1635 (after Fletcher's death). The story was suggested in part by Sir Thomas *Overbury's Theophrastan 'character' of 'An Elder Brother' (1614).

Lewis, a French lord, proposes to marry his daughter Angelina to one of the sons of Brisac, a country gentleman. Charles, Brisac's studious heir, declines marriage. Brisac proposes that Angelina should marry the younger brother, Eustace, and that Charles should give up the bulk of his inheritance to Eustace, who eagerly falls in with the suggestion. The plan is almost executed when Charles sees Angelina and they fall in love. Eustace, a poor-spirited courtier, is routed, and after various complications the lovers are united.

ELDRIDGE, David (1973–) Playwright born in Romford, Essex, and educated at Exeter University. He premiered at the Bush Theatre in London with *Serving it Up* (1996), had a considerable success with *Festen*, his adaptation of the cult film, in 2004, and followed this up with *Incomplete and Random Acts of Kindness* in 2005. In 2006, his *Market Boy* played at the *National Theatre in London, offering a savagely comic take on Margaret Thatcher's Britain and its consequences in the context of a London street market, and featuring a brief appearance by the Iron Lady herself.

ELEANOR OF AQUITAINE (*c.*1122–1204) The granddaughter of the first troubadour whose work survives, Guilhem IX of Aquitaine, and inheritor of the kingdom of Aquitaine, married for her inheritance by Louis VII of France in 1137. She had two daughters with him before their divorce (on grounds of their consanguinity, which had been pointed out with disapprobation by St *Bernard of Clairvaux) in 1152. She was immediately remarried to Henry Plantagenet of Anjou, the future Henry II of England, to whom she bore eight children, including the future *Richard I (b. 1157) and, the youngest, the future King John (b. 1166). After the death of Henry II in 1189 she was regent of England in the absence of her son Richard until his death in 1199. She was an immensely influential patron of the arts, particularly in her patronage of the development of courtly poetry in Poitiers, a function carried on by her daughter with Louis, *Marie de Champagne. Among others she brought the troubadour Bernart de Ventadorn (*fl.* 1170s) to Poitiers, perhaps fuelling troubadour influence on more northerly French poetry.

elegiac In the modern sense, characteristic of an *elegy, thus solemnly mournful. The *quatrain of iambic *pentameters rhyming *abab* is sometimes known as the elegiac stanza after its use by Thomas *Gray in his **Elegy Written in a Country Church-Yard*. Applied to ancient Greek verse, however, the term denotes a verse form employing *hexameters and pentameters paired as couplets.

Elegiac Sonnets Verses by Charlotte *Smith, published in several editions between 1784 and 1797. Poems of sensibility, they offer acute descriptions of nature and the poet's reaction to it, whilst demonstrating the mournful tone evident elsewhere in Smith's work in striking 'the chords of the melancholy lyre'. They were greatly admired by *Wordsworth.

elegy A formal poetic lament for the death of a friend, a fellow poet, or a public figure; or in a broader sense, a solemnly reflective poem. A third sense, derived from the Greek *elegiac couplet, survives in the naming by John *Donne of many of his poems as Elegies because written in couplet form. The modern mournful sense predominates from the 17th century, when Milton's *'Lycidas' (1638) established the most influential model of the fully elaborated English *pastoral elegy, a form attempted earlier by *Spenser in *'Astrophel' and later imitated by P. B *Shelley in **Adonais* (1821, on the death of *Keats) and by Matthew *Arnold in *'Thyrsis' (1866, on the death of A. H. *Clough). In this form, the conventions derived from the Greek tradition of *Theocritus, *Moschus, and *Bion provide for a formal invocation of a Muse, the pretence that the poet and the person mourned are both shepherds, accusations of negligence against guardian nymphs, the plucking of flowers for the funeral bier, and signs of Nature herself grieving for the mourned one as for a favourite. The major 19th-century instance of Tennyson's **In Memoriam A.H.H.* (1850) is sometimes called an elegy but is better classed as a sequence of lyric lamentations on loss and the phases of grieving. The most admired English elegy of the 20th century is *Auden's 'In Memory of W. B. Yeats' (1939), which deliberately inverts or disappoints pastoral conventions. In the second sense, there are numerous sombre poetic meditations on mortality and loss that have been referred to as elegies, beginning with those Old English poems known as the *Exeter Book Elegies (e.g. *The *Wanderer, The *Seafarer*), and including such later works as Arnold's 'Dover Beach' (1867); the best known among those entitled as elegies, commonly referred to as 'Gray's Elegy', is Thomas *Gray's **Elegy Written in a Country Church-Yard* (1751). See Peter Sacks, *The English Elegy* (1985).

Elegy Written in a Country Church-Yard Poem in quatrains by Thomas *Gray, published 1751, but begun earlier. The churchyard is identified with that of Stoke Poges, a village where Gray had family and where he was eventually buried. The poem situates the speaker alone in the churchyard at night, reflecting on the obscure destinies of the villagers who lie buried ('Full many a flower is born to blush unseen') but drawing comfort from the safety that obscurity granted them. The poem concludes by imagining a sympathetic but puzzled villager reacting to the death of the melancholy and unknown author.

Elene *See* CYNEWULF.

'Elephant in the Moon, The' *see* BUTLER, SAMUEL ('HUDIBRAS').

ELGAR, Sir Edward (1857–1934) English late Romantic composer. The Malvern hills were his spiritual home and much of his music was written for the Three Choirs Festivals. The manuscript of the bright overture *Cockaigne* (1901) bears a rueful quotation from **Piers Plowman*, 'meteless and moneless on Malverne hilles'. The concert overture *Froissart* (1890) is a generalized tribute to chivalry; the symphonic study *Falstaff* (1913) has a precise programme based on the Falstaff of the **Henry IV* plays. The so-called *Enigma Variations* (1899) offers character portraits of friends through variations on a theme purporting to lie under an unplayed popular melody, never satisfactorily identified. Elgar set for chorus various texts by *Longfellow before *The Dream of Gerontius* (1900), a lushly poignant setting of sections of John Henry *Newman's poem, established him as a major figure in English oratorio. For *The Apostles* (1903) and *The Kingdom* (1906) Elgar (a Catholic) made his own selection of biblical texts. *The Music Makers* (1912) is an autobiographically inflected setting of Arthur *O'Shaughnessy's 'Ode'. Works like *Fringes of the Fleet* (poems by Rudyard *Kipling) and *The Spirit of England* (1915–17, Laurence *Binyon), with the popular success of 'Land of hope and glory' (words by A. C. *Benson) and the *Pomp and Circumstance* marches, suggest a populist patriotism, but the instrumental works of the immediate post-war period testify to a darkly regretful mood. Elgar was appointed master of the king's music in 1924 and created baronet in 1931. See M. Kennedy, *Portrait of Elgar* (3rd edn, 1987).

ELGIN, Suzette Haden (1936–) American author and linguist, born in Missouri; also founder of the Science Fiction Poetry Association. *Native Tongue* (1984) and its sequels drew upon feminist theories in considering a 'women's language' developed as a means of protection and identification.

Elia *See* ESSAYS OF ELIA.

ELIOT, George (1819–80) The pen-name of Mary Ann, later Marian, Evans, novelist, born in Chilvers Coton, Warwickshire, the youngest surviving child of Robert Evans, agent for the estates of the Newdigate family of Arbury Hall; educated at Mrs Wallington's school in Nuneaton, and the Misses Franklin's school in Coventry. In her girlhood she was particularly close to her brother Isaac, from whom she was later estranged. Her early evangelicalism did not withstand the influence of Charles Bray, a freethinking Coventry manufacturer (a development which temporarily alienated her father), but she remained strongly affected by religious concepts of love and duty. Her works contain many affectionate portraits of Dissenters and clergymen. She pursued her education rigorously, reading widely, and devoted herself to completing a translation of D. F. *Strauss's *Life of Jesus*, which appeared without her name in 1846. In 1850 she met John *Chapman, and became a contributor to the **Westminster Review*; she moved to 142 Strand, London, in 1851, as a paying guest in the Chapmans' home, where her emotional attachment to him proved an embarrassment. She became assistant editor to the *Westminster Review* in 1851, and in the same year met Herbert *Spencer, for whom she also developed strong feelings which were not reciprocated, though the two remained friends. In 1854 she published a translation of Ludwig *Feuerbach's *Essence of Christianity*; she endorsed his view that religious belief is an imaginative necessity for man and a projection of his interest in his own species, a heterodoxy of which the readers of her novels only gradually became aware. At about the same time she joined G. H. *Lewes in a union without marriage (he could not divorce his wife) that lasted until his death; they travelled to the Continent in that year and set up house together on their return. He was to be a constant support throughout her working life and their relationship, although its irregularity caused her much anxiety, was gradually accepted by their friends. 'The Sad Fortunes of the Rev. Amos Barton', the first of the **Scenes of Clerical Life*, appeared in **Blackwood's Magazine* in 1857, followed by 'Mr Gilfil's Love-Story' and 'Janet's Repentance'; these at once attracted praise for their domestic realism, pathos, and humour, and speculation about the identity of 'George Eliot', who was widely supposed to be a clergyman or possibly a clergyman's wife. She began **Adam Bede* (1859) in 1858; it was received with great enthusiasm and at once established her as a leading novelist. *The *Mill on the Floss* appeared in 1860 and **Silas Marner* in 1861. In 1860 she visited Florence, where she conceived the idea of **Romola*, and returned to do further research in 1861; it was published in the **Cornhill Magazine* in 1862–3. John Blackwood, son of William *Blackwood, was unable to meet her terms; by this time she was earning a considerable income from her work. **Felix Holt, the Radical* appeared in 1866. She travelled in Spain in 1867, and her dramatic poem *The Spanish Gypsy* (conceived on an earlier visit to Italy, and inspired by Tintoretto) appeared in 1868. **Middlemarch* was published in instalments in 1871–2 and **Daniel Deronda*, her last great novel, in the same way in 1874–6. She was now at the height of her fame, and widely recognized as the greatest living English novelist, admired by readers as diverse as *Turgenev, Henry *James, and Queen *Victoria. In 1878 Lewes died. Her **Impressions of Theophrastus Such*, a collection of moral essays and character sketches, appeared in 1879, and in 1880 she married the 40-year-old John Walter Cross, whom she had met in Rome in 1869 and who had become her financial adviser. The marriage distressed many of her friends, but brought the consolation of a congratulatory note from her brother Isaac, who had not communicated with her since 1857. She died seven months later.

After her death her reputation declined somewhat, and Leslie *Stephen indicated much of the growing reaction in an obituary notice (1881) which praised the 'charm' and autobiographical elements of the early works, but found the later novels painful and excessively reflective. Virginia *Woolf defended her in an essay (1919) which declared *Middlemarch* to be 'one of the few English novels written for grown-up people', but critics like David *Cecil and Oliver Elton continued to emphasize the division between her creative powers and supposedly damaging intellect. In the late 1940s a new generation of critics, led by F. R. *Leavis (*The Great Tradition*, 1948), introduced a new respect for and understanding of her mature works; Leavis praises her 'traditional moral sensibility', her 'luminous intelligence', and concludes that she 'is not as transcendently great as Tolstoy, but she *is* great, and great in the same way'.

As well as the novels for which she is remembered, she wrote various poems, including 'O may I join the choir invisible' (1867), 'Agatha' (1869), *Brother and Sister* (1869), a sonnet sequence recalling her happy childhood, 'The Legend of Jubal' (1870), and 'Armgart' (1871); also the novellas 'The Lifted Veil' (1859) and 'Brother Jacob' (1864). Her letters and journals were edited by Cross, 3 vols (1885); her complete letters were edited by G. S. Haight, 9 vols (1954–78), who also wrote a life (1968). *A Writer's Notebook 1854–1879* and *Uncollected Writings* were edited by Joseph Wiesenfarth (1981). See also Rosemary Ashton, *George Eliot: A Life* (1996).

ELIOT, T. S. (Thomas Stearns) (1888–1965) A major figure in English literature from the early 1920s until his death. He was born at St Louis, Missouri, and educated at Harvard, the Sorbonne, and Merton College, Oxford, where he pursued a doctoral thesis on the philosopher F. H. Bradley begun at Harvard. In 1914 he met Ezra *Pound, who encouraged him to settle in England; in June 1915 he married Vivien Haigh-Wood, and in the same month his poem 'The Love Song of J. Alfred Prufrock' appeared (also with Pound's encouragement) in **Poetry*. Eliot taught briefly during the war, then in 1917 began to work for Lloyds Bank; from 1917 he was also assistant editor of the **Egoist*. His first volume of verse, *Prufrock and Other Observations* (1917), was followed by *Poems* (1919), hand-printed by Leonard and Virginia *Woolf at the *Hogarth Press; the two volumes struck a new note in modern poetry, satiric, allusive, cosmopolitan, at times lyric and elegiac. The influence of French poetry, particularly Jules *Laforgue, is apparent; it is even more prominent in the poems from the period 1909–17 edited by Christopher *Ricks as *Inventions of the March Hare* (1996).

In 1922 Eliot founded a new quarterly, the **Criterion*; in the first issue appeared, with much éclat, *The *Waste Land*, which established him decisively as the voice of a disillusioned generation. Eliot's criticism, first published in the *Egoist*, the **Athenaeum*, the **Times Literary Supplement*, and the *Criterion*, altered the literary landscape. He helped to establish the reputations of Elizabethan and Jacobean dramatists and poets, particularly the *metaphysical poets, and to diminish the authority of *Milton and the Romantics. By changing the canon, he created an environment in which *modernist innovations could be treated seriously. *The Sacred Wood* (1920), his first collection of criticism, contained the influential essays 'Tradition and the Individual Talent', in which he argues for the impersonality of poetry; 'Hamlet and his Problems', in which he applied the phrase *'objective correlative' to poetic and dramatic creation; and 'Ben Jonson', which asserted the merits of Jonson's 'flat' characterization. 'The Metaphysical Poets' (1921), in which Eliot argued that the modern poet 'must be *difficult*', and must be more comprehensive and allusive in order 'to force, to dislocate if necessary, language into his meaning', was collected in *Homage to John Dryden* (1924), and in the *Selected Essays* (1932).

In 1925 Eliot left Lloyds and became a director of Faber and Faber, where he built up a list of poets (including Ezra Pound, Herbert *Read, W. H. *Auden, Stephen *Spender, and George *Barker; *see also* FABER BOOK OF MODERN VERSE) which represented the mainstream of the modern movement in poetry in England: from this time he was regarded as a figure of great cultural authority, whose influence was more or less inescapable. In 1926 he delivered the Clark Lectures in Cambridge, later edited by Ronald Schuchard as *The Varieties of Metaphysical Poetry* (1993).

In 1927 Eliot became a British subject and a member of the Anglican Church; his pilgrimage towards his own particular brand of High Anglicanism may be charted in his poetry through 'The Hollow Men' (1925), with its broken declarations of faith, through 'The Journey of the Magi' (1927) and 'Ash-Wednesday' (1930), to its culminating vision in **Four Quartets* (1935–42). His prose also shows the same movement; for example, the title essay of *For Lancelot Andrewes* (1928) praises tradition, prayer, and liturgy, and points away from 'personality' towards hierarchy and community, and in the preface to this collection he describes himself as a 'classicist in literature, a royalist in politics, and Anglo-Catholic in religion'. The same preoccupation with tradition continued to express itself in his critical works.

In the 1930s Eliot began his attempt to revive poetic drama. *Sweeney Agonistes* (1932), an 'Aristophanic fragment' which gives, in syncopated rhythms, a satiric impression of the sterility of proletarian life, was followed by a pageant play, *The Rock* (1934), *Murder in the Cathedral* (1935), *The Family Reunion* (1939), and three 'comedies': *The Cocktail Party* (1950), *The Confidential Clerk* (1954), and *The Elder Statesman* (1959). These last were not wholly successful attempts to clothe profound ideas in the garb of a conventional West End play. Eliot's classic book of verse for children, *Old Possum's Book of Practical Cats* (1939), which reveals the aspect of his character that claimed the influence of Edward *Lear, achieved a considerable stage success in a musical adaptation, *Cats*, in 1981.

Eliot was equally influential as critic and poet, and in his combination of literary and social criticism may be called the Matthew *Arnold of the 20th century. After the more purely literary essays referred to above, Eliot turned increasingly to examine the relations of culture and society. This trajectory may be traced in *The Use of Poetry and the Use of Criticism* (1933), *After Strange Gods* (1934), *The Idea of a Christian Society* (1939), and *Notes towards the Definition of Culture* (1948).

Eliot's poetic and critical influence, immense in his lifetime, waned notably in the 1980s and 1990s. Some English-language poets rejected modernism altogether as a false path. Of those sympathetic to it, many found the modernism of Ezra Pound and William Carlos *Williams, in some cases mediated by the *Black Mountain poets, a more adaptable model than the modernism of Eliot. For critics, the idea of postmodernism was most readily established by criticizing the authoritarianism and conservatism of modernism, and Eliot, as the exemplary modernist poet, suffered. More specifically, Eliot's poetry and prose were criticized for their misogyny and anti-Semitism, the latter most notably by Anthony Julius.

Eliot was formally separated from his first wife (whose ill health, both physical and mental, had caused him much misery) in 1932–3; she died in 1947. In 1948 he was awarded the *Nobel Prize for Literature and the OM. He married his second wife, Valerie Fletcher, in 1957. As Valerie Eliot she edited the drafts of *The Waste Land* (1971), and one volume of Eliot's letters (1988). See also Peter *Ackroyd, *T. S. Eliot* (1984).

elision The suppression of a vowel sound or syllable in order to maintain metrical regularity, usually at the start of a word, as in 'Th'expense'; when found within a word (e.g. 'heav'n'), it is known as syncope.

Eliza, The Journal to By Laurence *Sterne, discovered 1851 and published 1904. The *Journal*, more correctly known as the *Bramine's Journal*, was kept April to July 1767. It documents with deliberate pathos Sterne's love for Elizabeth Draper, wife of an official of the East India Company, whom Sterne met briefly before she returned to India. The first instalments of the *Journal*, sent to Eliza, were lost. At the time of its writing Sterne was also engaged on the more humorous *A *Sentimental Journey*, in which Eliza also features. The *Journal* is partly written under the persona of 'Yorick'.

ELIZABETH I (1533–1603) A daughter of *Henry VIII and Anne Boleyn, and queen of England from 1558 to 1603. Among her favourites at court were Robert *Dudley, earl of Leicester, Christopher *Hatton, and, for a time, Walter *Ralegh and the earl of *Essex: her chief minister was *Burghley. She was celebrated by the greatest poets of her age, including Edmund *Spenser, Ralegh, Sir John *Davies, and *Shakespeare in his and John *Fletcher's *Henry VIII* and probably in *A *Midsummer Night's Dream*, under such names as *Cynthia, Diana, Astraea, and *Gloriana (with many allusions to her semi-mythological role as Virgin Queen), and has been the subject of innumerable plays, novels, romances, and biographies. Her portrait was painted by such artists as Nicholas *Hilliard, Marcus Gheeraerts the elder (*c.*1520/1–*c.*1586), and the younger (1561/2–1636), and Isaac Oliver (*c.*1565–1617). Musicians paid tribute to her in contemporary collections such as Thomas *Morley's *Madrigales: The Triumphs of Oriana* (1601). During her progresses, civic receptions, and court entertainments—especially those prepared for the anniversary of her accession to the throne on 17 November, which was celebrated with challenges and tilting—she was entertained by writers such as Richard *Mulcaster, Philip *Sidney, George *Gascoigne, Edward *Dyer, John *Lyly, George *Peele, and Henry *Lee.

Roger *Ascham supervised part of her education: she learned Greek and Latin, French and Italian, as well as to write a fine italic hand. She was famed for her ready wit and for the stirring eloquence called forth in, for example, her speech at Tilbury on the approach of the Spanish Armada, her various addresses to Parliament, such as her 'Golden Speech' in 1601, her numerous letters, and her prayers. She also wrote poetry, which was highly praised by her courtiers and by George *Puttenham, who used one of her few undisputed works ('The doubt of future foes', on the conspiracies of *Mary Queen of Scots) as an example of rhetoric in his *Art of English Poesy.* Her verses include a dozen or so undisputed lyrics and epigrams, various doubtful attributions, and translations from *Boethius, *Horace, and *Plutarch. There is a selection from her writings edited by Steven W. May (2004).

Elizabethan literature A name often applied to the literature produced in the reigns of *Elizabeth I and the first Stuarts. *See also* DRAB; GOLDEN.

ELKIN, Stanley (1930–95) American novelist and short story writer, born in New York. Elkin completed a Ph.D. at the University of Illinois on William *Faulkner's fiction, which influenced his preference for rapid, colloquial narrative voices. He began publishing short stories in the 1960s, the first collection being *Criers and Kibitzers, Kibitzers and Criers* (1961). His first novel, *A Bad Man* (1967), was well-received and Elkin went on to describe the life of a radio character in *The Dick Gibson Show* (1971) and new American sales methods in *The Franchiser* (1976). Despite a long struggle with multiple sclerosis, Elkin's fiction belongs in the post-war generation which produced grotesque black humour narratives. Like Philip *Roth, he was also influenced by the techniques of stand-up comedians.

'Ellen Orford' One of the tales in Crabbe's *The *Borough.* It tells the story of a courageous woman, who, after a neglected childhood, is seduced and abandoned. Her child turns out to be an idiot, her husband dies, and his death is followed by the deaths of their children. She becomes a teacher but blindness forces her to retire, and she finds consolation in her trust in God. She appears in Benjamin *Britten's *Peter Grimes.*

ELLIOT, Jean (Jane) (1727–1805) Third daughter of Sir Gilbert Elliot of Minto, author of the most popular version of the old lament for the Scots killed in the battle of Flodden (1513), 'The Flowers of the Forest', beginning 'I've heard them lilting at our yowe-milking'. Written *c.*1763, published in 1769, and republished by David *Herd in 1776, it is her only surviving work. Another version, less clearly related to Flodden, was written by Alison *Cockburn.

ELLIOTT, Ebenezer (1781–1849) Poet. Born near Rotherham, Yorkshire, he became a master founder in Sheffield, and is remembered as the 'Corn Law Rhymer'. In 1829 he published *The Village Patriarch,* in which Enoch Wray, an old blind mason, reflects on rural life and the bitter poverty brought about by cruelty and injustice. Thomas *Carlyle, writing in the *Edinburgh Review* in 1832, found great interest in the poem, and 'a manful tone of reason and determination'—but nevertheless urged Elliott to abandon poetry for prose. *Corn Law Rhymes* (1830) is a collection of plain poems which employ both satire and pathos in fiercely condemning the Bread Tax. The book was immensely successful, at a time when sales of poetry were very low. His collected works were published in 1846 and contemporary interest in working-class culture has revived a significant readership for him.

ellipsis The leaving out from a sentence words necessary to express the sense completely.

ELLIS, A. E. (1920–2000) The pseudonym of Derek Lindsay, author of *The Rack* (1958), a novel—much indebted to Thomas *Mann's *The Magic Mountain* (1924)—set in a sanatorium in the French Alps after the Second World War, where the orphaned Paul Davenant remains for over two years.

ELLIS, Alice Thomas (1932–2005) Pseudonym of Anna Haycraft, novelist and editor; she was born in Liverpool, but grew up in Wales and was educated at Bangor Grammar School. Her parents attended the Church of Humanity (*see* COMTE, AUGUSTE) but she converted to Roman Catholicism at the age of 19. After attending Liverpool College of Art, she was briefly a postulant in a Liverpool convent. Her first two novels, *The Sin Eater* (1977) and *The Birds of the Air* (1980), won Welsh Arts Council Awards, while *The 27th Kingdom* (1982) was shortlisted for the *Booker Prize. Set in a small Welsh rural community, *Unexplained Laughter* (1985) is characteristic in its wit, economy, elegance, and sense of the otherworldly. A trilogy of novels comprising *The Clothes in the Wardrobe, The Skeleton in the Cupboard,* and *The Fly in the Ointment* appeared between 1987 and 1990. Her works of non-fiction include *A Welsh Childhood* (1990), collected volumes of her *Spectator* column 'Home Life', two co-authored books on juvenile delinquency, and *Serpent on the Rock* (1994), a stout defence of Catholic orthodoxy.

ELLIS, George (1753–1815) One of the talented group who, with George *Canning and John *Frere, founded and contributed to *The *Anti-Jacobin* in 1797. His *Poetical Tales by Sir Gregory Gander* appeared in 1778, and he contributed to the collection of Whig political satires, *Criticism on the Rolliad,* published in the *Morning Herald and Public Advertiser* in 1784. His most important works were his translations and selections from Middle English verse: *Early English Poets* (1801) and *Specimens of Early English Romances in Metre* (1805).

ELLIS, Henry Havelock (1859–1939) Writer and sexologist, born in Croydon, Surrey. He spent some early years studying and teaching in Australia. He returned to London in 1879 and eventually qualified as a physician, although he occupied himself mainly with literary pursuits. These included reviewing, translating, and editing the unexpurgated Mermaid Series of Elizabethan dramatists (1887–9) and the Contemporary Science Series. In 1884 he became an intimate friend of Olive *Schreiner, who shared his progressive ideas on sexuality, the subject with which he is most closely identified; other friends included Edward *Carpenter, Arthur *Symons, and the American advocate of birth control, Margaret Sanger (1879–1966). His 'new marriage' to the equally progressive (and primarily lesbian) Edith Lees (1861–1916) was not wholly successful. *Sexual Inversion* (1897), with J. A. *Symonds, the first in his influential and sexually liberating *Studies in the Psychology of Sex* (1897–1910), was the first serious study of homosexuality to be published in Britain; subsequent volumes in the series were published in America, for censorship reasons. His works included: *The New Spirit* (1890); *Affirmations* (1898); *The Dance of Life* (1923); and his autobiographical *My Life* (1939) as well as many other volumes on the psychology of sex, marriage, censorship, and social hygiene. He attracted many followers, but unlike *Freud, with whom he corresponded, he never developed a wholly consistent, scientific system of thought. See P. Grosskurth, *Havelock Ellis* (1980).

ELLISON, Harlan (1934–) American short story and television scriptwriter, born in Cleveland, Ohio. He edited the *Dangerous Visions* anthology (1967) for which he called for taboo-breaking stories that extended the boundaries of *science fiction; a practice he has consistently and inventively followed in his own work (such as 'I Have No Mouth, and I Must Scream' (1967)), which he prefers not to label by genre. This work, together with *Dangerous Visions* and its sequel, largely set the tone for the *New Wave in America. His stories are collected in *The Essential Ellison* (1991).

ELLISON, Ralph Waldo (*c.*1913–1994) African American novelist and essayist, born in Oklahoma City. He is mainly remembered for his novel *Invisible Man* (1952), which tells the story of a young African American travelling to New York from the South and trying to make his way there. The Surrealism of this novel owes a debt to Ellison's friend Richard *Wright and makes complex use of Ellison's interest in jazz and blues. For some forty years Ellison worked intermittently on a second novel, which was finally assembled from his papers by John F. Callahan and published as *Juneteenth* in 1999. Ellison's essays on American culture were published in a number of volumes, starting with *Shadow and Act* (1964); his *Collected Essays* appeared in 2003.

ELLMANN, Richard (1918–87) Scholar and biographer, born in Michigan and educated at Yale University and Trinity College, Dublin. In 1970 he became Goldsmiths' professor of English literature at Oxford; during his career he also taught at Harvard, Yale, Emory, and Chicago universities. His publications include *Yeats: The Man and the Mask* (1948, rev. 1979) and several works on *Joyce, including notably his monumental and revelatory biography *James Joyce* (1959, rev. 1982), which made an influential contribution to new ideas about the art of *biography. He also edited (with Robert O'Clare) *The Norton Anthology of Modern Poetry* (1973) and the *New Oxford Book of American Verse* (1976). His *Oscar Wilde*, which won a Pulitzer prize, appeared in 1987. A Festschrift in his honour, *Omnium Gatherum: Essays for Richard Ellmann*, was published in 1989.

ELLROY, James (1948–) American novelist and short story writer, born in Los Angeles, which has remained the setting for his crime novels, although in 1995 he moved to Kansas City. His mother was murdered in 1958, an event which Ellroy finally confronted in his memoir *My Dark Places* (1996). After years of delinquency, Ellroy started writing crime fiction, partly under the stimulus of Raymond *Chandler and Ross *Macdonald's work, commencing with *Brown's Requiem* (1981). He went on to produce a trilogy focusing on the detective Lloyd Hopkins: *Blood on the Moon* (1984), *Because the Night* (1984), and *Suicide Hill* (1985). Then followed a quartet of novels based in Los Angeles, starting with *The Black Dahlia* (1987), which deals with a notorious 1947 murder in that city. Ellroy's fiction is characterized by its rapid, complex plots, graphic violence, and the involvement of his protagonists in the sexual and criminal action. *American Tabloid* (1995) marked a new departure in moving away from Los Angeles and engaging with the plots of rival agencies and racketeers during the Kennedy years; the novel was the first in a trilogy on the American underworld.

ELLWOOD, Thomas (1639–1713) Quaker and poet, whose comment to John *Milton, 'Thou hast said much here of paradise lost, but what hast thou to say of paradise found?', suggested the subject of **Paradise Regained*. His *History of the Life of Thomas Ellwood* (1714) vividly recounts his conversion and sufferings.

'Eloisa to Abelard' A heroic epistle by Alexander *Pope, published 1717, retelling the tragic love of Héloïse and *Abelard; in her Gothic seclusion of 'grots and caverns', Héloïse remains unable to renounce for God the memory of 'unholy joy'. The poem was regarded as one of Pope's most imaginative ventures.

ELSTOB, Elizabeth (1683–1756) Self-taught pioneer in Old English studies, born in Newcastle-upon-Tyne, sister of William Elstob (1673–1715), a fellow of University College, Oxford. She published *An English-Saxon Homily on the Birthday of St Gregory* (1709) and *The Rudiments of Grammar for the English-Saxon Tongue* (1715), the first Old English grammar in modern English. Impoverished by William's death, she abandoned her projects, setting up a school in Evesham, then becoming governess to the duchess of Portland's children.
See also HICKES, GEORGE.

ELTON, Ben (1959–) English playwright, novelist, and scriptwriter. As a stand-up comedian and co-writer of television comedies such as *Blackadder* and *The Young Ones* he was one of the most influential entertainers of the 1980s, pioneering a style of articulate, politically acute comedy which subsequently filtered down into the work of many young novelists. His own early novels *Stark* (1989), *Gridlock* (1991), and *This Other Eden* (1993) were commercial rather than critical successes, but *Popcorn* (1996) was widely acclaimed. A coruscating attack on Hollywood's glorification of violence, it also found an afterlife, like its successor *Blast from the Past* (1998), as a successful West End play. He has subsequently written or collaborated on a number of stage musicals, including *The Beautiful Game* (2000). He has continued to publish popular fiction, often addressing topical issues; in 2000 he wrote and directed a film adaptation of his novel *Inconceivable* (1999), on the trauma of infertility, as *Maybe Baby* (2000).

ÉLUARD, Paul (1895–1952) French poet, leading exponent of *Surrealism from 1919 to 1938. He collaborated with Max Ernst on *Les Malheurs des immortels* (1922: *The Misfortunes of the Immortal*) and with André *Breton on *L'Immaculée Conception* (1930: *The Immaculate Conception*). Among his volumes of Surrealist poetry are *Les Dessous d'une vie ou la pyramide humaine* (1926: *The Underpinnings of a Life, or The Human Pyramid*), *Capitale de la douleur* (1926: *Capital of Pain*), *L'Amour, la poésie* (1929: *Love, Poetry*), *La Vie immédiate* (1932: *The Immediate Life*), *La Rose publique* (1934: *The Public Rose*), and *Les Yeux fertiles* (1936: *The Fertile Eyes*). He broke with the Surrealist movement in the late 1930s, and joined the Communist Party in 1942. He became one of the leading writers of the French Resistance (*Poésie et vérité*, 1942: *Poetry and Truth*; *Au rendez-vous allemand*, 1944: *To the German Rendezvous*).

ELYOT, Kevin (1951–) Playwright, born in Birmingham, educated at Bristol University. The first of his plays about modern homosexual love, loss, and betrayal was *Coming Clean* (1982). *My Night with Reg* (1994) was a comedy of homosexual affection composed in three short movements, each section divided by a period of time and a death. In *The Day I Stood Still* (1998), Elyot experimented further with time shifts in charting the unrequited passion of a music-loving loner in north London. Other work includes versions of *Ostrovsky's *Artists and Admirers* (1992) for the Royal Shakespeare Company, Wilkie *Collins's *The *Moonstone* (1996) for BBC television, and the plays *Mouth to Mouth* (2001), *Forty Winks* (2004), *And Then There Were None* (2005), and (for Channel 4) *Clapham Junction* (2007).

ELYOT, Sir Thomas (*c.*1490–1546) Humanist and diplomat, a friend of Thomas *More and perhaps of *Erasmus. His *Boke Named the Governour* (1531) is a work on education and politics which displays the influence of the classics, and of *Plato in particular. Elyot probably owed his appointment as ambassador to Charles V to the book, which was popular throughout the century and was alluded to by T. S. *Eliot in **Four Quartets*. He wrote a number of other works, including *The Doctrinall of Princis* (*c.*1533), translated from Isocrates, *The Castell of Helthe* (*c.*1537), an important manual promoting the theory of the *humours, and Platonic dialogues and compilations from the *Fathers of the church. His translations did much to popularize the classics. His Latin–English *Dictionary* (1538) was the first book published in England under that title. There is a life by S. E. Lehmberg (1960).

ELYTIS, Odysseus (1911–96) Greek poet. Born in Heraklion, Crete, he was educated in Athens and at the Sorbonne. He became associated with the so-called 'Thirties Generation' of poets, including George *Seferis, who were much influenced by Paul *Éluard and other members of the French *Surrealist movement. His most famous poem, *To Axion Esti* (1959; trans. Edmund Keeley and George Davidis, 1974), is divided into three sections: 'The Genesis' introduces an innocent first person who, in 'The Passion', is witness to the horrors of the Second World War; in 'The Gloria', despite the destruction he has witnessed, he expresses his excitement at discovering he is still able to find beauty in the world. Like much of his work, the *Axion Esti* combines a vivid sense of Greece's history and cultural heritage, sacred and secular, with a very personal perspective. Elytis's approach to the Greek language is original, and often favours flourishes of sound, rhythm, and image over meaning which is frequently opaque or elusive. He published seventeen volumes of poetry, numerous translations, and two volumes of critical essays. He was awarded the *Nobel Prize in 1979. The first complete collection of his poetry in English was published in 1997.

Emaré A mid-14th-century verse romance of 1,035 lines in a north-east Midland dialect, written in 12-line tail-rhyme stanzas. It is a *Breton lay (on the grounds that its introduction says it is) on the model of the repeatedly told Constance story; the name 'esmaré' could be a variant of the French word for 'tried', 'troubled'. The area of origin of the only manuscript might suggest a connection with the version of the story told by Nicholas *Trivet earlier in the 14th century; he was the first to call the heroine Constance. Emaré, like Constance, is repeatedly cast adrift, in this case first by order of her unnatural father and later by her mother-in-law, as was traditional in the story. At the end she is reunited with her lost son and penitent husband. It has been edited by W. H. French and C. B. Hale, in *Middle English Metrical Romances* (1930), ll. 421–55.

emblem book In its widest sense, an emblem is a visual representation carrying a symbolic meaning: hence, W. B. *Yeats's 'tower | Emblematical of the night' ('Dialogue of Self and Soul'). Most often, however, the word refers to a genre of verbal-pictorial art which is particularly associated with the Renaissance. One source of this genre was the belief that Egyptian hieroglyphics had been symbols rather than part of a language; this view was derived from the *Hieroglyphics* of Horapollo (or Horus Apollo), a Greek manuscript discovered in 1419, which was generally thought to be the work of an Egyptian in the 2nd or 4th century AD. Other important sources were the **Physiologus* and the epigrams of the *Greek *Anthology*.

The first emblem book, the *Emblematum Liber* of Andrea Alciati (1492–1550), was published in 1531. Each emblem consists of a motto, a symbolic picture, and an explanatory set of Latin verses called an epigram. This format was followed by most other emblem books. All three parts of an emblem contribute to its meaning: e.g. Alciati's picture of a bee-hive in a helmet, together with the motto *Ex bello pax* and the explanatory epigram, means that the weapons of war may be turned into the works of peace. Writers often borrowed one another's pictures and wrote new verses which reinterpreted them. In *A Theatre for Voluptuous Worldlings* (1569) Edmund *Spenser translated verses from *Petrarch and Joachim *Du Bellay which had been used for a Dutch emblem book, but the translation was printed without the original woodcuts. The earliest English emblem book to contain illustrations as well as verses was Geoffrey Whitney's (1548?–1600/01) *A Choice of Emblemes* (1586), which distinguished three categories: natural, historical, and moral. The 17th century produced many religious emblem books, of which the most famous English example was Francis *Quarles's **Emblems* (1635). The children's figures of these emblem books represent Divine Love (God) and Earthly Love (Man); they have been derived from the Cupid figures of earlier love emblems. George *Wither published *A Collection of Emblemes*, also illustrated (1634–5).

The poetry of some religious poets of the period, such as George *Herbert and Henry *Vaughan, is sometimes described as emblematic, though their books were not illustrated. John *Bunyan also wrote an emblem book without pictures, *A Book for Boys and Girls* (1686). By then the form had largely gone out of fashion; it enjoyed something of a revival in the Victorian period.

Emblems A book of short devotional poems by Francis *Quarles, first published 1635 and much reprinted; it was adapted from two Jesuit emblem books, *Typus Mundi* (1627) and Herman Hugo's *Pia Desideria*. The poems are in various metres, each based on some scriptural text, and some in the form of dialogues (e.g. between Eve and the Serpent, between Jesus and the Soul, and between the Flesh and the Spirit). The engravings are mostly by William Marshall (*fl.* 1617–48).

EMECHETA, Buchi (1944–) Nigerian novelist, born near Lagos, the daughter of a railway porter. She left her country at the age of 20 with four small children and moved to London. She obtained a degree in sociology at the University of London and wrote autobiographical novels, *In the Ditch* (1972) and its sequel, *Second-Class Citizen* (1974), published in one volume as *Adah's Story* (1983). Succeeding novels, *The Bride Price* (1976), *The Slave Girl* (1977), and *The Joys of Motherhood* (1979), deal with the position of women in Nigerian society, contesting stereotypical and idealized images of femininity, though Emecheta is wary of being categorized as a feminist. In 1980 she returned to Nigeria as a visiting professor at Calabar University, an experience which influenced her novel *Double Yoke* (1982). Also published in 1982 was *Destination Biafra*, a fictional account of the Nigerian civil wars which draws on the experiences of family and friends. *Gwendolen* (1989) focuses on the subject of child abuse and cultural isolation; *The Rape of Shavi* (1983) and *The New Tribe* (2000) engage with the politics of diasporic experience. Emecheta's autobiography, *Head above Water*, was published in 1986; she also writes for children.

EMERSON, Ralph Waldo (1803–82) American philosopher and poet, born in Boston, the son of a *Unitarian minister. He was educated at Harvard University, studied theology, was ordained, and became a pastor in Boston, but resigned because he felt unable to believe in the sacrament of the Lord's Supper. He departed in 1832 for Europe, and in 1833 visited England, where he met S. T. *Coleridge, William *Wordsworth, and Thomas *Carlyle; the latter became a lifelong friend and correspondent. On his return to America Emerson embarked on a career as lecturer, evolving the new quasi-religious concepts developed in the *Transcendental Club, which found written expression in his essay *Nature* (1836). Emerson, like his friend Carlyle, became revered as a sage and his 1837 Harvard address, 'The American Scholar', urged America to assert its intellectual independence of Europe. *The *Dial*, founded in 1840, was edited by Emerson from 1842 to 1844, and published many of his poems. His first volume of essays (1841) contains 'Self-Reliance', 'Compensation', and 'The Over-Soul', which proposes a mystic Unity 'within which every man's particular being is contained and made one with all other'. His second *Essays* (1844) contains 'The Poet', in which he declares: 'America is a poem in our eyes', a view given poetic expression by his devoted disciple Walt *Whitman. In 1845 Emerson delivered the lectures later published in 1850 as *Representative Men*; these studies of *Plato, *Swedenborg, Napoleon, and others owe something to Carlyle's concept of the Hero. In 1847 he revisited England on a lecture tour, and his *English Traits* (1865), a perceptive study of the English national character, won him more readers. On his return to America he was actively engaged in the anti-slavery campaign, and continued to lecture and write. Of his many later works, mention should be made of his moving tribute to his friend and follower Henry *Thoreau (1862), whom he describes as a 'born protestant'. A definitive edition of Emerson's *Collected Works*, ed. R. E. Spiller *et al.* (1971–), is in progress from Harvard University Press, which has also published a sixteen-volume edition of the *Journals and Miscellaneous Notebooks* (1960–82).

Emigrants, The: *A Poem in Two Books* A political poem by Charlotte *Smith, published 1793. It is dedicated to William *Cowper, who commented upon a draft of the poem. Smith, who had welcomed the 'demolition of regal despotism in France', argues that the errors of the émigré clergymen and nobility who had fled to Britain were being repeated in that country. She nonetheless condemns 'the dreadful scenes which have been enacted in France', notably the September massacres and the execution of Louis XVI.

Eminent Victorians A biographical work by Lytton *Strachey published in 1918. This group biography, with chapters on Cardinal Henry Manning (1808–92), Florence *Nightingale, Dr Thomas *Arnold of Rugby School, and General Charles Gordon (1833–85), is also a critique of the Victorian age. Strachey's irreverent approach to his subjects is intended to mark his separation from his Victorian predecessors, who are characterized as pompous and evangelical. His attention to style and the construction of a well-paced narrative—which are more important to him than accurate research—also established a new form of biography. His approach to biography is radically anti-heroic, seeing his subjects as locked within the assumptions and limitations of their age.

Emma A novel by Jane *Austen, begun 1814, published 1816. Emma, a clever, pretty, and self-satisfied young woman, is the daughter, and mistress of the house, of Mr Woodhouse, an amiable old fusspot. Her former governess and companion, Anne Taylor, beloved of both father and daughter, has just left them to marry a neighbour, Mr Weston. Missing Miss Taylor's companionship, Emma takes under her wing Harriet Smith, parlour-boarder at the school in the neighbouring village of Highbury. Harriet, a pretty, pliant girl of 17, is the daughter of unknown parents. Emma's active mind sets to work on schemes for Harriet's advancement, but her interfering and injudicious attempts lead in the end to considerable mortification. She first prevents Harriet from accepting an offer of marriage from Robert Martin, an eligible young farmer, as being beneath her. This tampering greatly annoys Mr Knightley, the bachelor owner of Donwell Abbey, who is Emma's brother-in-law and one of the few people able to see that she has faults. Emma has hope of arranging a match between Harriet and Mr Elton, the young vicar, only to find that Elton despises Harriet and has the presumption to aspire to her own hand. Frank Churchill, the son of Mr Weston by a former marriage, an attractive but thoughtless young man, now comes to visit Highbury. Emma first supposes him in love with herself, but presently thinks that Harriet might attract him, and encourages her not to despair. This encouragement, however, is misunderstood by Harriet, who assumes it is directed, not at Frank Churchill, in whom she has no interest, but at the great Mr Knightley himself, with whom Emma is half unwittingly in love. Emma then suffers the double mortification of discovering, first, that Frank Churchill is already engaged to Jane Fairfax, niece of Miss Bates, who lives in the village; and second, that Harriet has hopes, which appear on the surface to have some foundation, of supplanting her in Mr Knightley's affections. However, Knightley in the end proposes to the humbled and repentant Emma, and Harriet is happily consoled with Robert Martin.

The novel is among Austen's most accomplished works, fully realizing her own recommendation of '3 or 4 families in a Country Village' as 'the very thing to work on'. Minor characters include the vulgar Mrs Elton, with her frequent references to her 'caro sposo' and her brother-in-law's seat at Maple Grove, and the garrulous old maid Miss Bates, who becomes the occasion of one of Emma's educational moments at the celebrated outing to Box Hill when Emma is reprimanded by Mr Knightley for making a joke at Miss Bates's expense.

EMPEDOCLES (*c.*492–*c.*432 BC) Greek scientist, philosopher, and advocate of democracy who lived in Acragas (Agrigentum) in Sicily. Only about 450 lines survive from his poem *On Nature*, which was an important model for *Lucretius. He was responsible for demonstrating the existence of air, used experimentation in medicine, and taught that the universe was in a state of unending change thanks to the contrary action of Love, which united the four elements, earth, air, fire, and water, and Strife, which drove them apart. Legends accumulated round his name: he was supposed to work miracles, controlling the winds and raising the dead, and to have met his death plunging into the crater of Etna. The opposition of Love and Strife is an important principle in Edmund *Spenser's **Faerie Queene*, IV. The philosopher's death is the subject of *Hölderlin's draft plays *The Death of Empedocles* (1797–1800), and Matthew *Arnold's poem **Empedocles on Etna* (1852).

Empedocles on Etna A dramatic poem by Matthew *Arnold, published anonymously 1852. Arnold portrays the philosopher *Empedocles, said to have committed suicide by throwing himself into the crater of Etna, on the verge of his last act: his physician friend Pausanias tries to cheer him, accompanied by songs from the unseen Wordsworthian harp player Callicles. Empedocles expresses his intellectual doubts, dismissing the reassuring platitudes of religion and philosophy; man's yearning for joy, calm, and enlightenment is in itself no proof that these things exist or can be attained. He turns Pausanias away, grieves over his own 'dwindling faculty of joy', concludes that he is man no more, but 'a naked, eternally restless mind', and finally, in a kind of triumph, concluding that at least he has been ever honest in his doubts, hurls himself to his death.

EMPSON, Sir William (1906–84) Poet and critic. He was born to a landowning family at Yokefleet, Yorkshire, and educated at Winchester College and Magdalene College, Cambridge, where he studied mathematics, then English under I. A. *Richards. He developed his undergraduate essays into *Seven Types of Ambiguity* (1930), a widely admired and influential study of metaphor, verbal nuance, and multiple meanings in poetry. A fellowship at Magdalene was abruptly terminated when condoms were found in his rooms, after which he taught in universities in China and Japan, eventually settling in 1953 as professor of English at Sheffield. His criticism includes *Some Versions of Pastoral* (1935), *The Structure of Complex Words* (1951), and *Milton's God* (1961), the latter being notable for its attacks on Christianity as a sadistic cult of torture. Empson's poetry, collected in *Poems* (1935), *The Gathering Storm* (1940), and the revised *Collected Poems* (1955), makes use of analytical argument and imagery drawn from modern physics and mathematics; a technical virtuoso, he offered (in his own words) 'a sort of puzzle interest', and employed metaphysical conceits and linguistic, metrical, and syntactical complexities. Among several posthumously published volumes is *Using Biography* (1984), a spirited attack on the *New Criticism's neglect of the biographical element in literary interpretation. The standard biography is by John Haffenden, 2 vols (2005–6).

EMSHWILLER, Carol (1921–) Born in Michigan; American writer of fabulist *science fiction and *fantasy such as *Carmen Dog* (1988) and *The Secret City* (2007). *The Start of the End of It All* (1990) collects short fiction. She is the widow of the illustrator and film-maker Ed Emshwiller.

Encounter A political, cultural, and literary review, founded in 1953, and originally edited by Stephen *Spender and Irving Kristol (1920–); subsequently by Melvin J. Lasky (1920–2004), Frank *Kermode, Anthony *Thwaite, Nigel *Dennis, and others. D. W. Brogan, in an anthology selected from its first ten years, described it as 'a *journal de combat*...the organ of protest against the *trahison des clercs*', and its political tone at this period reflected some of the Anglo-American anti-Soviet spirit of the Cold War. But it was also the vehicle for Nancy *Mitford's celebrated formulation of the 'U' and 'Non-U' concept (1955), and C. P. *Snow pursued the *two cultures controversy in its pages (1959–60). It has also published poetry by Robert *Lowell, Sylvia *Plath, Theodore *Roethke, W. H. *Auden, Philip *Larkin, Kingsley *Amis, and others, and articles by major authors including Arthur *Koestler, Karl *Popper, and V. S. *Naipaul.

Encyclopaedia Britannica Early precursors of the *EB* include the *Cyclopaedia* (1728) of Ephraim *Chambers, and the great French **Encyclopédie*. *Encyclopaedia Britannica* was first issued by a 'Society of Gentlemen in Scotland' in numbers (1768–71), edited by William Smellie, a printer. It was a dictionary of the arts and sciences. The second edition (10 vols, 1777–84) added history and biography; the third (15 vols, 1788–97) and the fourth (20 vols, 1801–10) continued the expansion. It was taken over by Constable in 1812, and sold after the failure of that publishing house in 1826. After some further editions it passed to Cambridge University for the publication of the landmark 11th edition (28 vols, 1910–11). Since the 14th edition (1929), a system of continuous revision has replaced the making of new editions; it appeared on CD-ROM in 1998 and is now published online.

Encyclopédie, L' A dictionary of universal knowledge published between 1751 and 1772 in seventeen volumes of text and eleven volumes of plates. Conceived originally as a translation of Ephraim *Chambers's *Cyclopedia*, it grew under the editorship of *Diderot and d'*Alembert into something much bigger and more subversive. With articles written by the leading intellectuals of the age, including *Voltaire, *Montesquieu, *Rousseau, *Buffon, and Jacques Turgot (1727–81), it attempted both to provide an account of the current state of knowledge and to 'change the general way of thinking'. It thus embodied the ideas and aspirations of the *Enlightenment. Its attacks on superstition and credulity attracted the hostility of church and state. Despite or because of this hostility, it was a huge success, with over 4,000 subscribers to the first edition.

ENDE, Michael (1929–95) German writer and theatre director; born in Garmisch, Germany, he achieved success with *The Neverending Story* (1979: trans. into English 1983). Bastian's discovery of a book describing his journey within the *fantasy world he enters produces a text which literally comments upon itself.

ENDÔ, Shûsaku (1923–96) Japanese novelist, who became a Roman Catholic at the age of 11. He later studied French literature in France. The gap between Christian and traditional Japanese morality became his main theme. *The Sea of Poison* (1957) explores Japanese war guilt from a Christian perspective. *Silence* (1966) is about Portuguese missionaries in 16th-century Japan and the slaughter of the Japanese Christians.

Endymion (Disraeli) The last of Benjamin *Disraeli's novels, published 1880. Set between *c.*1830 and the early 1850s, it vividly describes the political and social scene of that time, including the antagonism between Whig and Tory, the power of the great political hostesses, the *Tractarians, railway mania, the *Chartists, and the story of Louis Napoleon as 'Florestan'. Lord Palmerston appears as the engaging Lord Roehampton; Lady Jersey as the relentless Zenobia; Bismarck as Ferroll, Cardinal Manning (1808–92) as Penruddock, Rothschild as Mr Neuchatel, while William *Cobbett and Richard Cobden (1804–65) combine in Job Thornberry. W. M. *Thackeray (in revenge for his *Codlingsby*) is satirized as St Barbe. Endymion, a sweet-natured boy, is the twin of the fiery, ambitious Myra. Their father is a rising politician, his social status underwritten by the expectation of a great inheritance, and of soon achieving cabinet rank. When neither materializes he kills himself, leaving his family impoverished. Endymion obtains a clerkship at Somerset House, and after Myra has rejected Penruddock, she obtains a place as companion to the daughter of a kindly Jewish banker. Myra's beauty and wit bring her social success, and she marries Lord Roehampton, who finds the retiring Endymion a place as secretary to a cabinet minister. Endymion becomes deeply interested in the plight of the poor, and in Manchester becomes a friend of Job Thornberry, a bold young radical and political economist. Throughout the novel there are rumblings of social unrest, and reports of incendiaries. Eventually Endymion is persuaded by Myra, and by Lady Montfort (whom he loves), to enter Parliament. After the death of Lord Roehampton Myra marries the exiled Florestan and goes to live abroad. Endymion marries Lady Montfort. On the death of the prime minister Endymion is asked to form the next government, and Myra visits him in his triumph.

Endymion (Keats) A poem in four books, by John *Keats, written 1817, published 1818. The poem tells, with a wealth of epithet and invention, the story of Endymion, 'the brain-sick shepherd-prince' of Mount Latmos, who falls in love with Cynthia, the moon, and descends to the depths of the earth to find her. There he encounters a real woman, Phoebe, and giving up his pursuit of the ideal he falls in love with her. She, however, turns out to be none other than Cynthia, who, after luring him, weary and perplexed, through 'cloudy phantasms', bears him away to eternal life. The poem includes in Book I the well-known 'Hymn to Pan', and in Book IV the roundelay 'O sorrow'. Its most famous line is its first, 'A thing of beauty is a joy forever'.

In his preface Keats describes the poem as 'a feverish attempt, rather than a deed accomplished'. Rich in luxuriant imagery, the allegory, which is sometimes obscure, appears to represent the poet pursuing ideal perfection, and distracted from his quest by human beauty. The work was violently attacked in the **Quarterly Review* and in **Blackwood's Magazine*, in which John *Lockhart attacked its 'calm, settled, imperturbable drivelling idiocy'.

Endymion, the Man in the Moon An allegorical prose play by John *Lyly, acted at court by Paul's Boys, 1588, published 1591. Endymion abandons Tellus (the earth) in consequence of a hopeless passion for Cynthia (the moon). Tellus conspires with the witch Dipsas against Endymion, who is sent to sleep for 40 years. Cynthia breaks the spell and releases Endymion with a kiss. The dramatic element is slight, the allegory perhaps relating to the rivalry between *Elizabeth I (Cynthia) and *Mary Queen of Scots (Tellus), and the favour of Elizabeth for Leicester (Endimion).

ENGELS, Friedrich (1820–95) German philosopher, the son of a factory owner who supervised his father's business in Manchester. He wrote influential essays on the social and political conditions in Britain in the 1840s, including *The Condition of the Working Class in England* (1845), in which he praised Thomas *Carlyle as the only British writer to take account (in *Past and Present*, 1843) of the atrocious working conditions of the urban poor. Engels collaborated with Karl *Marx, whom he helped to support when the latter settled in London in 1849, in writing *The German Ideology* (1845–6, but not published until 1932), a critique of German philosophy as lacking in social application; the *Manifesto of the Communist Party* (1848); and their great work, *Das Kapital*, the third volume of which Engels completed after Marx's death (vols i–iii, 1867/84/94).

Much has been extrapolated about Engels's views on literary theory from two letters, both written to aspiring novelists: in the first, written to Minna Kautsky in 1885, he says he is by no means opposed to literature designed to further social or political ideas (*Tendenzpoesie*), but that he believes 'the thesis must spring forth from the situation and action itself, without being explicitly displayed'. The second, written in English to Margaret Harkness in 1888 on receipt of a copy of her proletarian novel *A City Girl*, criticizes her work for being 'not quite realistic enough...Realism, to my mind, implies, besides the truth of detail, the truthful reproduction of typical characters under typical circumstances....In *City Girl*, the working class appears as a passive mass, incapable of helping itself...': but he reiterates that 'the more the opinions of the author remain hidden, the better the work of art'. These letters have been taken both to justify and to oppose the necessity for political commitment in art.

See MARXIST LITERARY CRITICISM.

ENGLAND, George Allan (1877–1936) American writer, born in Nebraska; active in American magazines from 1909, publishing stories and serials exploiting popular anxieties such as invasions (*Darkness and Dawn* (1914), collecting three serials involving a couple resuscitated in a devastated America) and the implications of air travel. *The Air Trust* (1915) warns against the possibility of the monopoly of the air by capitalist cartels.

Englands Helicon A miscellany of lyrical and pastoral poetry of the Elizabethan age published by John Flasket in 1600, with additions in 1614, including pieces by Sir Philip *Sidney, Edmund *Spenser, Michael *Drayton, Robert *Greene, Thomas *Lodge, Walter *Ralegh, Christopher *Marlowe, George *Peele, Anthony *Munday, and others; edited by H. E. Rollins (1935).

Englands Parnassus A collection of extracts from contemporary poets, by Robert Allott (*fl.* 1599–1600), published in 1600.

English Association Founded in 1906 to promote the teaching and advanced study of the English language and of English literature, it mounts conferences and publishes journals, including *English* and *Essays and Studies*. Past presidents include John *Galsworthy, I. A. *Richards, and Rebecca *West. Since 1993 it has been based at Leicester University and in 2006 it was incorporated by royal charter.

English Bards and Scotch Reviewers A satirical poem by Lord *Byron in heroic couplets, published 1809. Angered by Henry *Brougham's contemptuous criticism of his **Hours of Idleness* in the **Edinburgh Review*, Byron responded with this witty and spirited attack on Francis *Jeffrey, Robert *Southey, William *Wordsworth, S. T. *Coleridge, and Walter *Scott. He also poured patrician mockery on the 'doggrel' and 'childish prattle' of many of the minor poets and poetasters (William *Bowles, Joseph *Cottle, and many others) of the Romantic movement, while upholding and defending those (e.g. William *Gifford, George *Crabbe) who continued to sustain the classical traditions of John *Dryden and Alexander *Pope. It is a fine piece of invective, filled with woundingly memorable insults.

Englishman's Magazine (1831–3) An ambitious literary monthly, edited by Edward *Moxon, which published poems, criticism, and essays, as well as notes on drama, music, and art. It published the work of the unknown young Alfred *Tennyson, as well as that of Thomas *Hood, Charles *Lamb, Leigh *Hunt, John *Clare, A. H. *Hallam, and others. It vigorously supported William *Wordsworth and the *Cockney School, defending them against *Blackwood's*, the **Quarterly*, and similar journals. Unusually for the time, more than half the contributions were signed. The *Englishman's Magazine* seems to have been killed by John *Wilson's scathing comments in *Blackwood's* on Hallam's article proclaiming the genius of Tennyson.

English Review A periodical founded in 1908 through the inspiration of a group of writers including Joseph *Conrad, H. G. *Wells, and Eve *Garnett, with the purpose, in the words of its first editor, Ford Madox *Ford (then Hueffer), of 'giving imaginative literature a chance in England'. It was backed at first by Arthur Marwood, the 'heavy Yorkshire squire' and friend of Ford, from whom Ford drew many of the characteristics of Christopher Tietjens in *Parade's End*. The period of Ford's editorship, from December 1908 to February 1910, was one of great distinction: he published work by established writers such as Arnold *Bennett, John *Galsworthy, Henry *James, and H. G. Wells, and by newcomers such as D. H. *Lawrence and Wyndham *Lewis, amongst others. However, the *Review* ran into financial difficulties, and Ford was replaced by Austin Harrison, the editor until 1923. The title merged with the *National Review* in 1937.

English Stage Company An organization founded in 1956 by George Devine (1910–66) to present modern plays and encourage new dramatists; its home was the *Royal Court Theatre, London. It established itself with the success of John *Osborne's *Look Back in Anger* (1956), and it subsequently produced important new work by Osborne, Arnold *Wesker, John *Arden, Edward *Bond, Christopher *Logue, David *Storey, Joe *Orton, Ann *Jellicoe, N. F. *Simpson, Samuel *Beckett, Christopher *Hampton, Heathcote Williams (1941–), David *Hare, E. A. Whitehead (1933–), Brian *Friel, Athol *Fugard, Mustapha Matura (1939–), Caryl *Churchill, Howard *Barker, Howard *Brenton, and others.
See also KITCHEN SINK DRAMA.

English Traveller, The A romantic drama by Thomas *Heywood, written *c.*1624, printed 1633, with two plots, one tragic, one comic. Geraldine, returning from his travels, finds that the lady he loves has been married to Wincot, an old gentleman to whom he is under obligations. He and the lady bind themselves to marry after Wincot's death. But Geraldine finds that his treacherous friend Delavil has seduced Wincot's wife. When her guilt is exposed she dies in contrition and despair. The comic sub-plot is borrowed from the *Mostellaria* of *Plautus: a prodigal son wastes his father's substance during the latter's absence abroad, the father returns unexpectedly, the son's resourceful servant postpones discovery of the prodigal's doings, and all ends in pardon and reconciliation.

enjambment (enjambement) The continuation of the sense and grammatical construction of a verse line or couplet into the next without a punctuated pause, thus de-emphasizing the line-ending. The opposite effect, where the end of a line coincides with the end of a sentence or clause, is called end-stopping.

Enlightenment A term (originally the German *Aufklärung*) used to describe a scientific and rational ethos, including freedom from superstition and religious intolerance, observable in much of 18th-century Europe. The movement derives from thinkers such as John *Locke, the third earl of *Shaftesbury, and Isaac *Newton, though it was never a thoroughgoing cultural phenomenon in England. *Voltaire, *Rousseau, *Condorcet, and *Buffon were associated with the Enlightenment, as was one of its great monuments, *L'*Encyclopédie*. The **Encyclopaedia Britannica* was in part a product of the distinct intellectual movement sometimes described as the *Scottish Enlightenment, which featured such thinkers as Adam *Ferguson, David *Hume, and Adam *Smith. The American Declaration of Independence is in some senses a classic Enlightenment document. In his **Rights of Man* Thomas *Paine was much influenced by Enlightenment political ideals, and many other English writers echoed educational or egalitarian ideas associated with the movement, including William *Godwin, P. B. *Shelley, Erasmus *Darwin, Mark *Akenside, and the *Edgeworths, though the course of the French Revolution tainted its idealism. William *Blake subscribed to the political energies unleashed by the Enlightenment, but decried what he saw as the 'single vision' of Newtonian materialism; *Romanticism was in part a revolt against such pure rationality. See Roy Porter, *The Enlightenment* (2nd edn, 2000).

ENNIUS, Quintus (239–169 BC) Known as the father of Roman poetry, author of *tragedies, *satires, and *epic. He introduced the *dactylic *hexameter and many Homeric devices to Latin poetry. His *Annales*, an epic poem in eighteen books, told the story of the expansion of Rome from the fall of Troy to the present. It was admired by and influenced later Roman poets, but only fragments totalling about 550 lines have survived. John *Dryden mentions him a number of times in his critical essays, stressing *Virgil's debt to him and comparing him to Geoffrey *Chaucer.

Enoch Arden A narrative poem by *Tennyson, published 1864; the story was suggested by his friend Thomas *Woolner. Enoch Arden, Philip Ray, and Annie Lee are children together in a little seaport town; both boys love Annie, but Enoch wins and marries her. They live happily for some years, until Enoch is compelled through temporary adversity to go as boatswain in a merchantman. He is shipwrecked, and for more than ten years nothing is heard of him; Annie, consulting her Bible for a sign, puts her finger on the text 'Under the palm tree', which, after a dream, she interprets to mean that he is in heaven. She marries Philip, who has long watched over her.

Tennyson then turns to Enoch on his desert island, which is contrasted with the 'dewy meadowy morning-breath of England' for which he yearns. He is rescued and returns home, but when he discovers that Annie has remarried does not reveal himself, resolving that she shall not know of his return until after his death. The last lines—'And when they buried him the little port | Had seldom seen a costlier funeral'—are provocative, echoing the curiously ambiguous attitude to Providence which pervades the whole poem.

Enquiry Concerning Political Justice A philosophical treatise by William *Godwin, published February 1793, which established him as the chief proponent of British radicalism. Godwin attacks the 'brute engine' of government for systematically oppressing individual liberty in the name of law and order. He envisages instead a social and benevolent anarchism, based upon the belief that men act according to reason, that reason teaches benevolence, and that rational creatures can live peaceably without laws and institutions, including that of marriage, which is rooted in property law.

Enquiry into the Present State of Polite Learning, An Treatise by Oliver *Goldsmith, published 1759. It examines the causes of the decline of 'polite learning' from ancient times, through the Dark Ages, to its present state in Europe. He attributes the alleged decay in England to the low status of the writer, driven to hack-work for the booksellers through lack of *patronage; also to the lack of comic spirit among poets, the restrictive conditions of the theatre, and the malign detractions of critics. His attack on theatrical managers offended David *Garrick, and it was toned down for the second edition (1774).

ENRIGHT, Anne (1962–) Novelist and short story writer, born in Dublin and educated at Trinity College, Dublin, and the University of East Anglia. Enright's sometimes surreal fictions bring a tart wit to their exploration of the dynamics of family life. The stories of *The Portable Virgin* (1991) were followed by the novels *The Wig my Father Wore* (1995), *What Are You Like?* (2000), and *The Pleasure of Eliza Lynch* (2002). *The Gathering* (2007), a darkly comic excavation of the childhood secrets underlying the suicide of an alcoholic whose siblings assemble for his funeral, won the Man *Booker Prize. *Making Babies* (2004) is a wry autobiographical reflection on motherhood, and *Taking Pictures* (2008) a further collection of stories.

ENRIGHT, D. J. (Dennis Joseph) (1920–2002) Poet, born in Leamington and educated at Leamington College and Downing College, Cambridge. He taught English literature for 25 years, mainly in the East; many of his poems are set in Japan, Egypt, Singapore, and Germany, and concern cultural differences and misunderstandings, themes which he also explored in various critical essays and in his autobiographical *Memoirs of a Mendicant Professor* (1969). His first collection of verse, *The Laughing Hyena and Other Poems* (1953), was followed by several others, including *Bread rather than Blossoms* (1956), *Addictions* (1962), *Sad Ires* (1975), *A Faust Book* (1979; a sequence of poems on the *Faust legend), *Under the Circumstances* (1991), and *Old Men and Comets* (1993). His *Collected Poems*, with new poems, appeared in 1981 (new edn 1987). He also published novels for children (*The Joke Shop*, 1976; *Wild Ghost Chase*, 1978; *Beyond Land's End*, 1979) and other prose works, including *The World of Dew: Aspects of Living in Japan* (1955), *Insufficient Poppy* (1960, a novel), and works of criticism, including *Man Is an Onion* (1972, collected reviews and essays). His anthology *Poets of the 1950s* (1955) brought together many of the poets to appear in Robert *Conquest's **New Lines*, and in his preface to his anthology *The Oxford Book of Contemporary Verse 1945–1980* (1980) he reasserted the claims of 'the poetry of civility, passion, and order' against those of the confessional mode, as written by Robert *Lowell, John *Berryman, and others. His own work was predominantly detached and ironic in tone (although by no means impersonal) and wide-ranging in its subject matter. He also edited *The Oxford Book of Death* (1983) and *The Oxford Book of the Supernatural* (1994). *By-blows: Uncollected Poems* (1996) was followed by *Collected Poems, 1948–1998* (1998).

Entail, The A novel by John *Galt, published 1823, a satire on the corrupting effects of greed. Claud Walkinshaw, a successful packman, cruelly disinherits his eldest son in favour of his second, who is a half-wit. Walkinshaw is thereby enabled to recover the ancestral property of his family. The disastrous consequences of his act recoil upon himself, and on his children and grandchildren. As a study in obsession the book is powerful, and it was admired by Lord *Byron.

envoy (envoi) [French, 'a missive'] A final half-*stanza, in the same *metre as the preceding full stanzas, found in certain medieval French verse forms adapted by English poets, principally the *ballade and the *sestina. In the ballade form, the envoy is conventionally addressed to a nobleman or powerful patron.

ENZENSBERGER, Hans Magnus (1929–) German poet, essayist, polemicist, and commentator, who studied at several universities including Freiburg and Paris. A cosmopolitan, challenging, and thought-provoking writer, his works have been widely translated. The first English selection was *Poems for People Who Don't Read Poems* (1968, trans. Michael *Hamburger, Jerome Rothenberg, and the author), which contained work from his early German volumes 1959–64. *Der Untergang der Titanic* (1978: trans. by the author as *The Sinking of the Titanic*, 1981) was written during and after a stay in Cuba: its 32 cantos interweave his Cuban experience with life in Berlin and with cultural, political, and historical speculation about the foundering of Western civilization. Other volumes include *Mausoleum* (1975, prose poems) and *Zukunftsmusik* (1991: *Music of the Future*). *Selected Poems* (trans. M. Hamburger) appeared in 1994. *Ach Europa! Wahrnehmungen aus sieben Ländern mit einem Epilog aus dem Jahre 2006* (1987), which is a species of travel writing, appeared in English as *Europe, Europe:*

Forays into a Continent in 1989, and his novel *Wo warst du, Robert* (1998) as *Where Were You, Robert* in 2000. His poetic work is remarkable for its humane engagement, its direct, powerful, and resonant language, its wide range of historical and cultural reference, and its accessibility, and has reached a large readership in many countries.

Eōthen *See* KINGLAKE, ALEXANDER WILLIAM.

epanalepsis A rhetorical figure in which the same word is repeated at the beginning and end of a sentence or clause, as in 'Bold was the challenge and he himself was bold' (*Spenser) or 'Common sense is not so common' (*Voltaire).

'EPHELIA' Pseudonym of a female lyric poet, possibly attached to the *Restoration court. Lady Mary Villiers (1622–85) is among suggested identifications, though the question of authorship remains uncertain. Ephelia's *Female Poems on Several Occasions* (1679) are chiefly pastoral and amatory, addressed to 'Strephon' and written with technical panache. The poet, who praises fellow female poets *Orinda and Aphra *Behn, laments male inconstancy and adapts pastoral and courtly conceits to the mortifying position of an unrequited female lover in a male world.

epic Originally a lengthy poem recounting in elevated style the exploits of a legendary hero or heroes, especially in battles or voyages. This is also known as a heroic poem. In modern times the term is sometimes extended to certain prose works, especially to large-scale historical novels. In the poetic sense, the major examples in English are John *Milton's **Paradise Lost*, unusual in its biblical subject, and the Old English **Beowulf*. Others include the *alliterative **Morte Arthure*, while John *Keats's **Hyperion* is an unfinished attempt at an epic poem. English literature is somewhat richer in its tradition of *mock-epic poems (e.g. Alexander *Pope's **Dunciad*, Lord *Byron's **Don Juan*), which make fun of the classical epic conventions derived from *Homer and *Virgil.

Epicene, or The Silent Woman A comedy by Ben *Jonson, acted by the Children of the Queen's Revels 1609–10, printed 1616. Morose, an old bachelor pathologically averse to noise, proposes to disinherit his nephew Sir Dauphine Eugenie, by marrying and producing children, provided he can find a silent woman. Cutbeard, his barber, finds one called Epicene. After the wedding she turns into a loquacious shrew, and Morose's agony is increased when Dauphine and his friends arrive with a rowdy party of guests, including henpecked Captain Otter, his Amazonian wife, the Collegiate Ladies (a coterie of domineering women), and two cowardly, boastful knights. Frantic, Morose accepts Dauphine's offer to rid him of Epicene for £500 a year and the reversion of his property—whereupon Dauphine pulls off Epicene's wig revealing that, unknown to everyone else, including the audience, she is a boy. John *Dryden thought this play the most perfectly plotted of all comedies.

epic simile An extended simile comparing one complex action with another, for example the charge of an army with the onset of storm clouds, elaborated at such length as to become digressive. Sometimes called a Homeric simile after its frequent use by *Homer, it was imitated by *Virgil and in English by *Milton.

EPICTETUS (mid-1st to 2nd century AD) *Stoic philosopher, said to have been a freedman. He taught first in Rome and then in Nicopolis. He wrote nothing himself; his teachings were compiled in Greek by his disciple the historian Arrian as the *Discourses* and *Encheiridion* (Manual), or summary of his principles. Epictetus held health, pleasure, possessions to be of no account. Virtue alone mattered, and that resided in the will which should direct man to abstain and endure. The *Manual* was translated by John Healey (1610), and the complete works by Elizabeth *Carter (1758). Epictetus' principal English disciple was the third earl of *Shaftesbury. *See* MARCUS AURELIUS ANTONINUS.

EPICURUS (341–270 BC) The founder of the school of philosophy that bears his name. After teaching in various places he settled finally in Athens, where his school was known as the Garden. Some fragments of his prolific writings survive, but his ideas are perhaps best studied in the *De Rerum Natura* of *Lucretius. Epicurus adopted the atomic theory of *Democritus but postulated an indeterminacy in the movement of his atoms which allowed him to believe in free will. In ethics he regarded the absence of pain—*ataraxia* or peace of mind—as the greatest good. Conventional moralists tended to describe him as a contemptible pleasure-seeker (hence the term 'epicure'), but his life had been marked by rigorous abstinence from greed, lust, and anger, a fact which made Sir Thomas *Browne defend his reputation (**Pseudodoxia*, VII. 17). Surviving texts by and about Epicurus were translated by Walter *Charleton in *Epicurus's Morals* (1656). Epicureanism in a modified form found its high priest in the French exile Charles de Saint-Denis *Saint-Évremond, for whose translated essays John *Dryden wrote an appreciative preface (1692). David *Hume identified himself with Epicurus' views of religion in his first *Enquiry, Natural History of Religion*, and *Dialogues*.

epigram Originally an inscription, usually in verse, for example on a tomb; hence a short poem ending in a witty turn of thought; hence a pointed or antithetical saying.

Epigrams, The A collection of poems by Ben *Jonson, printed 1616, including 'Inviting a Friend to Supper', 'On my First Son', 'The Famous Voyage', and addresses to John *Donne and *James I.

epiphany Used in a Christian context to refer to the revelation of Christ to the Gentiles in the persons of the Magi (Matt. 2: 1–12), but adapted by James *Joyce in *Stephen Hero*, an early draft of *A *Portrait of the Artist as a Young Man*, where Stephen considers compiling 'a book of epiphanies. By an epiphany he meant a sudden spiritual manifestation, whether in the vulgarity of speech or of gesture or in a memorable phase of the mind itself. He believed that it was for the man of letters to record these epiphanies with extreme care, seeing that they themselves are the most delicate and evanescent of moments' (ch. 25). A number are 'record[ed]' in **Dubliners*, and at one point in **Ulysses* Stephen Dedalus recalls his 'epiphanies on green live leaves, deeply deep'. There are similar moments of blinding insight in a number of poems by W. B. *Yeats, such as 'Vacillation', and the fleeting but intense revelations experienced by characters in Virginia *Woolf's **Mrs Dalloway* and **To the Lighthouse* are equally epiphanic. Forty epiphanies noted down by the young Joyce have been published in his *Poems and Shorter Writings*, ed. R. Ellmann, A. Walton Litz, and J. Whittier-Ferguson (1991).

Epipsychidion An autobiographical poem by P. B. *Shelley, written at Pisa in 1821 and published there anonymously in the same year. Composed in couplets of breathless energy, the poem celebrates Shelley's lifelong search for the eternal image of Beauty, in the earthly form of his various wives, mistresses, and female friends: notably Harriet Westbrook, Mary *Shelley, Claire *Clairmont, and Emilia Viviani—to whom the work is addressed: 'In many mortal forms I rashly sought | The Shadow of that idol of my thought.' Though drawing on the courtly love and planetary imagery of *Petrarch and *Dante, the work is passionately sexual as well as platonic: it ends with an invitation to Emilia to elope to 'an isle under Ionian skies, | Beautiful as a wreck of Paradise'. There is an attack on conventional marriage, 'the dreariest and longest journey', and praise of 'Free' or 'True' Love. Yet despite its blaze of amorous rhetoric, the poem is partly also a study of the creative process itself. The title remains a puzzle: perhaps from the *epi-psyche*, the 'soul out of my soul', or beloved; or perhaps with ironic reference to the *epithalamium*, the conventional marriage song. A close biographical reading reveals much sly humour.

Epistles, Pauline *See* PAUL, ST.

Epistles to Several Persons Four ethical poems addressed to friends by Alexander *Pope, published 1731–5; the collective title 'Moral Essays' was added later by Pope's editor William *Warburton. Epistle I (1734), addressed to Viscount Cobham, sets forth the difficulties in judging human character and finds the solution in the discovery of the 'ruling passion'. Epistle II (1735), addressed to 'a Lady' (Martha Blount), deals with the characters of women and includes a gallery of unstable noblewomen, disguised under code names, and affectionate praise for Martha's own perfections. Epistle III (1733), to Lord Bathurst, deals with the abuse of riches, arguing that neither the miser nor the prodigal derives happiness from them. The famous character of the 'Man of Ross', who uses riches wisely, is counterbalanced by the disastrous fate of 'Sir Balaam'. Epistle IV (1731), to Lord Burlington, also discusses riches, giving instances of the tasteless use of wealth in architecture and gardening, and promoting the civic use of wealth. Pope intended the four poems to comprise the last part of his 'opus magnum', a 'system of ethics in the Horatian way', but this ambitious project was never completed. See Miriam Leranbaum, *Alexander Pope's 'Opus Magnum', 1729–1744* (1977).

Epistolae Obscurorum Virorum (*Epistles of Obscure Men*) Published 1515–17, an anonymous collection of letters in mock-medieval Latin purporting to be written by various bachelors and masters in theology to Ortuinus Gratius, a famous opponent of the new learning, in which they incidentally expose themselves to ridicule and to scurrilous charges. The letters are attributed principally to Ulrich von Hutten (1488–1523), soldier, humanist, and supporter of Martin *Luther, and were written in connection with the celebrated *Reuchlin–Pfefferkorn controversy.

epistolary novel A story written in the form of letters, or letters with journals, usually presented by an anonymous author masquerading as 'editor'. The first notable example in English, written entirely in epistolary form, was a translation by Roger L'Estrange from the French of the anonymous *Letters of a Portuguese Nun* (1678). In 1683 Aphra *Behn published *Love-Letters between a Nobleman and his Sister*, and many similar tales of illicit love followed. Thus when Samuel *Richardson, the first master of the form, came to write **Pamela* (1741) he felt a duty to rescue the novel from a doubtful reputation. The immediacy of the epistolary form lends itself to intense subjective analysis, but also to charges of implausible absurdity (fully exploited by Henry Fielding in his parody, **Shamela*). Between the 1740s and about 1800, when the form chiefly flourished, it was employed not only by Richardson but by Tobias *Smollett, Robert *Bage, and Fanny *Burney, among many others. After 1800 the form fell into almost complete disuse, although its effects were adapted to verse in A. H. *Clough's *Amours de voyage* (1858). Among modern attempts at revival, William *Golding's *Rites of Passage* (1980) provides an interesting variation in the form of an epistolary journal.

'Epithalamion' A hymn by Edmund *Spenser, probably in celebration of his marriage with Elizabeth Boyle in 1594. The poem was printed with the **Amoretti* in 1595. Its beauty of composition has always been much admired, and in 1960, Kent Hieatt (in his *Short Time's Endless Monument*) demonstrated that its 24 stanzas represent the hours of Midsummer Day.

epithalamium (epithalamion) A poem celebrating a wedding, and conventionally sung on the bridal night. Edmund Spenser's *'Epithalamion' (1595) is the classic English model. There are others by Philip *Sidney, Ben *Jonson, Andrew *Marvell, John *Dryden, P. B *Shelley, and W. H. *Auden.

eponymous Name-giving; a term applied in literary contexts to a real or fictitious person whose name provides the title of a work. Thus Emma Woodhouse is the eponymous heroine of Jane Austen's novel *Emma.*

EQUIANO, Olaudah (1745–97) Writer of the most influential early slave narrative, *The Interesting Narrative of the Life of Olaudah Equiano, or Gustavus Vassa, the African, Written by Himself* (1789). Its elegant expression itself makes the case against assumptions about African savagery, and reveals the barbarism of the European slave trade.
See SLAVERY.

ERASMUS, Desiderius (*c.*1467–1536) Great Dutch humanist, born at Rotterdam. Under pressure of his guardians he became an Augustinian monk, but thanks to the protection of the bishop of Cambrai was allowed to leave the cloister and travel extensively in Europe. He came more than once to England, where he was welcomed by the great scholars of the day, Thomas *More, John *Colet, and William *Grocyn, and was induced by St John *Fisher to lecture at Cambridge on Greek from 1511 to 1514. He was a friend and patron of Hans *Holbein, whom he introduced to More, and by whom he was painted several times. He received from Archbishop Warham (?1450–1532) the benefice of Aldington in Kent and, on resigning it, a pension which was continued until his death. His principal works were a new edition of the Greek New Testament (1516), followed by Latin paraphrases (1517–24); *Encomium Moriae* (*The Praise of Folly,* 1511, a satire written at the suggestion of More, principally directed against theologians and church dignitaries); *Enchiridion Militis Christiani* (1503, a manual of simple piety according to the teaching of Jesus Christ, which was translated perhaps by William *Tyndale into English, and also into other languages); *Institutio Christiani Principis* (*Education of a Christian Prince*); the vivid and entertaining *Colloquia* and letters furnishing autobiographical details and pictures of contemporary life, which were drawn upon by Charles Reade in *The *Cloister and the Hearth* and by Walter Scott in **Anne of Geierstein*. His *Adagia* (1500), a collection of Latin and Greek proverbs traced to their source with witty comments, one of the first works of the new learning, was much used by *Rabelais and by many English writers. His many editions and translations of the Bible, early Christian authors, and the classics revolutionized European literary culture. Erasmus prepared the way for the *Reformation, and at first sympathized with the movement. However, he refused to intervene either for or against Martin *Luther at the time of the Diet of Worms, although invoked by both sides. He urged moderation, distanced himself from Luther's violence and extreme conclusions, and at a later stage (1524, in his tract on 'Free Will') entered into controversy with him. The standard edition of the letters of Erasmus (11 vols, 1906–47) was edited by P. S. and H. M. Allen; see also Lisa Jardine, *Erasmus, Man of Letters: The Construction of Charisma in Print* (1993).

ERCELDOUNE, Thomas of (*fl.* late 13th century) Also called the Rhymer and Learmont, mentioned in two Scottish charters from the late 13th century. The reputation of this shadowy figure as a prophet derives largely from the 14th-century romance *Thomas of Erceldoune* and the ballad *Thomas the Rhymer.* He is said to have predicted the death of Alexander III, king of Scotland, and events in the life of William Wallace; and he is the traditional source of many (fabricated) oracles.

ERDRICH, Louise (1954–) Native American novelist and poet, a member of the Anishinaabe nation, born in Minnesota and brought up in North Dakota where her parents taught at the Bureau of Indian Affairs school. Her first writings were poems and short stories, some in collaboration with her then husband Michael Dorris (1945–97). Her first novel, *Love Medicine* (1984), set the keynote for her fiction, which incorporates Native American storytelling techniques through multiple narrators and time-jumps. *The Beet Queen* (1986) was attacked by Native writer Leslie Marmon Silko as being too preoccupied with technique. Most of Erdrich's fiction has been set in North Dakota. After her divorce she shifted her subject to contemporary Minneapolis with *The Antelope Wife* (1998), but *Last Report on the Miracle at Little No Horse* (2001) marked a return to her favoured terrain. She has published a number of poems dealing with cultural conflict (e.g. *Jacklight,* 1984) and also a number of stories for younger readers.

Erewhon [pron. e-re-whon, an anagram of 'nowhere'] A satirical novel by Samuel *Butler, critical of socialism and Darwinism, published anonymously 1872. The narrator (whose name is revealed in **Erewhon Revisited* as Higgs) crosses a range of mountains and comes upon the undiscovered country of Erewhon. He is first thrown into jail, where he is helped by his beautiful girl jailer, Yram. On his release he is lodged with Mr Nosnibor (Robinson) and his family. In this society morality is equated with health and beauty, and crime with illness. The Unborn select their parents, who have to endure their selection. The Musical Banks produce a currency which is venerated but not used. The development of machinery, which had threatened to usurp human supremacy, had led to civil war and is now forbidden. The country is ruled by so-called philosophers and prophets, whom Higgs sees to be merely faddists and fanatics. Threatened with prosecution for contracting measles, Higgs announces that he will visit the air god and end the terrible drought; with Nosnibor's daughter Arowhena, he escapes in a balloon to England, where they marry. Written over a period of ten years, the story had its origin in Butler's article 'Darwin among the Machines', published in New Zealand in 1863.

Erewhon Revisited A sequel to **Erewhon*, by Samuel *Butler, published 1901. John, the son of Higgs and Arowhena, is the writer of this account of his father's return to Erewhon. After twenty years Higgs finds that his ascent in the balloon has become that of a god, the Sunchild, in a sun-chariot, his conversation has become the basis of sacred texts, a temple has been built to him at Sunchildiston, and that the new religion is organized by two cynical exploiters, Professors Hanky and Panky. Once again Higgs's life is threatened, but again he escapes and, after further bewildered wanderings in Erewhon, returns, half unhinged, to England.

Eric, or Little by Little *See* FARRAR, F. W.

ERIGENA *See* SCOTUS ERIUGENA, JOHN.

Erl-King The German *Erlkönig*; subject of a famous ballad by *Goethe (1782). The name derives from a Danish word meaning king of the elves, but Goethe may have associated the word with *Erle* or alder tree. In the ballad, introduced into England by Matthew *Lewis's translation, he is a sinister figure who lures a child to his death. Lewis brought it to the notice of Walter *Scott, who also produced a translation. Goethe's ballad was the basis of one of Franz *Schubert's best-known settings (1816). Erl-King is also the subject of a *'ghost' story by the Dublin writer John Connolly which was broadcast by the BBC in 2000.

ERNAUX, Annie (1940–) French writer whose autobiographical texts depict the radical changes affecting post-war French society. Ernaux draws on the work of the sociologist Pierre *Bourdieu to situate her trajectory in a broader social context. Thus, the narrative of estrangement from her working-class father in *La Place* (1984: *A Man's Place*), as she makes her way through the education system and becomes a teacher, exemplifies a phenomenon with which, as the popularity of her work in France and abroad suggests, many post-war generations can identify.

ERVINE, St John (1883–1971) Playwright and novelist, born to deaf mute parents in Protestant east Belfast, who traded an early Irish nationalist enthusiasm for an increasingly vehement unionism. Many of his early plays (including *Mixed Marriage*, 1911; *The Magnanimous Lover*, 1912; and *John Ferguson*, 1915) were performed at the *Abbey Theatre, of which he was a controversial manager, and dealt with themes of religious conflict in Ulster. Having lost a leg while fighting on the Western Front, he settled in England, where he became drama critic for the *Observer* and achieved West End success with *The First Mrs Fraser* (1929) and other popular comedies. He also published several novels, and studies of C. S. *Parnell (1925), General Booth (1934), and G. B. *Shaw (1956).

eschatology In Christian writing the four last things, death, judgement, heaven, and hell.

ESENIN, Sergei Aleksandrovich (1895–1925) Russian poet from a village in Riazan province who enjoyed great success in pre-revolutionary literary salons with his poems of peasant life. He moved to Moscow in 1912, met Aleksandr *Blok in 1915, and published his first collection of poetry in 1916. He greeted the October Revolution of 1917 as a revival of peasant Russia, joined a group of peasant poets led by Nikolai Kliuev (1887–1937), but later mourned the demise of traditional rural life. He was briefly associated with the Imaginists, who were influenced by Italian *Futurism more than by Ezra *Pound and *imagism. His second wife (1922) was the dancer Isadora Duncan, with whom he visited the United States. His last years were characterized by disillusionment, drunkenness, and excess, and he committed suicide in Leningrad, writing his last poem in his own blood. A selection of his poetry was translated by Geoffrey Thurley as *Confessions of a Hooligan* (1973).

Esmond *See* HISTORY OF HENRY ESMOND, ESQUIRE.

Essay Concerning Human Understanding A philosophical treatise on the nature of mind by John *Locke, published 1690. In Book I Locke rejects the doctrine of 'innate ideas', maintaining that all knowledge is based on experience. The objects of understanding are termed *ideas*, and Book II provides an account of the origins of our ideas in the observation of the 'qualities' of external objects or of the internal operations of the mind such as sensation or reflection. A number of simple ideas being constantly found to go together, the mind is led to suppose a substratum for them, and this we call *substance*, but we have no other idea of its nature. We are equally ignorant of spiritual substance, the substratum of the operations of the mind: we do not even know whether material and spiritual substance are the same or different. In Book III Locke discusses language. He holds that words have meaning insofar as they stand for ideas in the mind; distinguishing between 'real' and 'nominal' essence, he argues that terms for natural kinds (e.g. 'gold', 'horse') can express only nominal essences or sets of ideas; they cannot latch on to the real essences or hidden constitutions of the things themselves. Book IV defines knowledge as the perception of the agreement or disagreement of ideas. Knowledge in matters of real existence is limited to two certainties, of our own existence, by intuition, and of the existence of God, by demonstration. We have a lesser degree of certainty of the existence of finite beings outside us. If the mind perceives nothing but its own ideas, how can we know that they agree with the things themselves? Locke advances various arguments for the possibility of knowledge about real things, but points out that such knowledge is narrowly limited. Accordingly there are very few certain propositions to be made concerning substances; a perfect science of natural bodies is unattainable. Knowledge at once general and real must be, not of the relations of ideas to reality, but of ideas to each other, as in mathematics. See the edition by P. H. Nidditch (1979).

Essay on Criticism A didactic poem in heroic couplets by Alexander *Pope, published anonymously 1711. It provides a set of flexible rules for the humane conduct of criticism, and discusses the authority of ancient and modern writers on the subject. The poem contains much satirical comment on the kinds of critic who ignore proper models. It was praised by Joseph *Addison, and contains some of Pope's most quoted lines, but provoked violent hostility from John *Dennis.

Essay on Man A philosophical poem in heroic couplets by Alexander *Pope, published 1733–4. It consists of four epistles addressed to *Bolingbroke, whose fragmentary philosophical writings have some influence on the poem's doctrine. Its objective is to prove that the scheme of the universe is the best conceivable, in spite of appearances of evil, and that our failure to see the perfection of the whole is due to our limited vision. 'Partial Ill' is 'universal Good', and 'self-love and social' are both directed to the same end. The epistles deal with man's relations to the universe, to himself as an individual, to society, and to happiness. It commanded considerable respect among Pope's contemporaries, though its orthodoxy was later questioned, and Samuel *Johnson disapproved of its complacent optimism and lack of philosophical knowledge. Pope's assertion that 'Whatever is, is right' anticipates the motto of Pangloss in *Voltaire's *Candide*.

Essay on the Learning of Shakespeare, An (1767) By the scholar Richard Farmer (1735–97). Farmer argued, controversially, that Shakespeare's apparent knowledge of ancient history, themes, and motifs could be more plausibly explained by studying the many translations available to him than by reference to some supposed classical education.

Essays, The By Francis *Bacon, first published in 1597, together with the 'Christian Meditations' and 'Of the Colours of Good and Evil'; it consisted of ten essays, in extremely bare style. The sentences were printed separately, marked with a paragraph sign, giving them the status of aphorisms—separate, succinct observations, drawn from experience in the realm of public life. The second edition (1612) contained 38 essays, in a more varied style, and on a wider range of topics. In this collection Bacon began to fill a gap he had drawn attention to in his *Advancement of Learning* (1605)—the lack of concrete knowledge of the different 'natures and dispositions' of human beings, and how they were affected by psychological and social factors (such as gender, health, social standing, physical appearance). The final version, now called *Essays or Counsels, Civil and Moral* (1625), included 58 essays, filling in more of these gaps in treating both 'civil' or public life, and the behaviour of private individuals. Bacon's approach varies greatly from essay to essay, and within each essay the topic is regarded from several different viewpoints, juxtaposing systematic analysis with brilliant aperçus. The styles used range from the detached and laconic to the passionately engaged, especially when expressing his moral beliefs. Samuel *Johnson said that the *Essays* were 'the observations of a strong mind operating upon life; and in consequence you find what you seldom find in other books'.

Essays and Reviews A controversial collection of essays on religious subjects from a *Broad Church standpoint published in 1860. Among them were Mark *Pattison's 'Tendencies of Religious Thought in England 1688–1750' and Benjamin *Jowett's 'On the Interpretation of Scripture'. The other essayists were the Revd H. B. Wilson (editor), Frederick Temple, Rowland Williams, Baden Powell, and C. W. Goodwin. A meeting of the bishops, urged on by Samuel Wilberforce, in 1861 denounced the book for its liberalism. The collection represented an important challenge to traditional biblical authority, all the more shocking to its first readers because it came from within the church.

Essays in Criticism The title of Matthew *Arnold's two major collections of literary essays, the first published in 1865, the second posthumously in 1888 (a third collection of minor pieces appeared under the same title in 1910). The first series includes 'The Function of Criticism at the Present Time'; the second, the important essay 'The Study of Poetry'. The title was adopted by the academic literary periodical founded at Oxford by F. W. Bateson in 1951 as a competitor to the influential Cambridge journal **Scrutiny*.

Essays of Elia, The Miscellaneous essays by Charles *Lamb, of which the first series appeared in the **London Magazine* between 1820 and 1823, and as a separate volume (1823). *The Last Essays of Elia* was published in 1833. Lamb adopted the name Elia, which was that of a former Italian clerk at the South Sea House, ostensibly to save the embarrassment of his brother John, who worked at that same place, but also for literary reasons. The essays are all cast as if written by Elia, but they are not reliably autobiographical, even when seeming so. The fanciful, old-fashioned character of the narrator is maintained throughout. He is, in Lamb's words, 'a bundle of prejudices' with a strong liking for the whimsical, the quaint, and the eccentric. The tone is never didactic or seriously philosophical, and the more disturbing aspects of life are avoided. The style is very literary and carefully wrought, filled with archaisms and with echoes of Lamb's master Laurence *Sterne. Among the best-known essays were: 'Some of the Old Benchers of the Inner Temple'; 'Christ's Hospital'; 'The South Sea House'; 'Mrs Battle's Opinions on Whist'; 'Dream Children'; and 'A Dissertation on Roast Pig'.

ESSEX, Robert Devereux, second earl of (1565–1601) Courtier and soldier, the godson and later the stepson of Robert *Dudley, earl of Leicester. Educated at Trinity College, Cambridge, he was regarded as the natural successor to Philip *Sidney, whose widow he married in 1590. Despite a fierce rivalry with Walter *Ralegh during the 1580s, a period of intense and lucrative favour in the 1590s culminated in his dispatch to Ireland in March 1599 to suppress Tyrone's rebellion. William *Shakespeare referred in **Henry V* (V. Chorus 29–34) to the return of 'the General of our gracious Empress', but in fact Essex's return was sudden and ignominious. He came back without leave, having panicked at his lack of success, and after almost a year of house arrest he made an abortive attempt at rebellion in the City of London in February 1601. On the eve of the revolt, Essex's supporters commissioned a special performance at the Globe Theatre by Shakespeare's company of what was probably his **Richard II*. Essex was executed on 25 February, the episode casting a dark shadow over the last eighteen months of Elizabeth's reign.

Essex was closely involved with Francis *Bacon and his elder brother Anthony (1558–1601), who kept him informed of political affairs and gathered political intelligence for him. Francis Bacon wrote an accession day entertainment for Essex and letters of advice to the earl of Rutland on his behalf. Essex addressed his *Apologie*, which circulated widely in manuscript and was printed in 1603, to Anthony Bacon. A literary patron of some discernment, involved with, among others, Edmund *Spenser, Fulke *Greville, and George *Chapman, Essex himself wrote poems, of which a dozen or so have survived. Almost immediately after his death, his life became or was suspected of being the stuff of heroic and tragic writing in works such as Samuel *Daniel's *Philotas* (performed 1605). Lytton *Strachey's *Elizabeth and Essex* (1928) is a highly coloured and highly readable fictionalization; Paul E. J. Hammer has written the most detailed account of Essex's political career up to 1597 (1999); and Steven W. May has edited his poems in *The Elizabethan Courtier Poets* (1991).

ESTE family Ruling house of Ferrara, from the 13th century to the end of the 16th, and of Modena and Reggio until the 19th century. Members of the family appear in Dante's *Inferno* (XII) and *Purgatorio* (V). In the course of the Renaissance members of the family, especially **Isabella d'Este** (1474–1539), were important patrons of the arts. Among those who enjoyed their patronage were *Boiardo, *Ariosto, *Cinzio, and *Tasso. The family regularly married into the ruling houses of Europe; **Mary of Modena**, wife of James II, was an Este.

Esther Waters A novel by George *Moore, published 1894. It is the story of the life of a religiously minded working-class girl, driven from home at 17 by a drunken stepfather. She finds a job at Woodview, the house of the Barfields, where a racing stable is kept. There she is seduced by a fellow servant and deserted. She has to leave her place, though kindly treated by her employer Mrs Barfield. Then follows a poignant tale of poverty, hardship, and humiliation: the lying-in hospital, service as wet-nurse, other miserable situations, even the workhouse, in the mother's brave struggle to rear her child. Her seducer re-enters her life, marries her, and makes a good husband. But he is a bookmaker and publican; exposure to weather at the races ruins his health and trouble with the authorities over betting at his public house causes the latter to be closed. He dies, leaving his wife and son penniless. Finally Esther returns to Woodview, where she finds peace with Mrs Barfield, now a widow, living alone and impoverished in a corner of the old house. The book's sexually explicit scenes made it controversial, and circulating libraries (*see* MUDIE, CHARLES) would not stock it; nevertheless, it became Moore's most successful novel.

ESTIENNE (in Latin **Stephanus**) The name of a family of French printers and scholars. Henri Estienne (d. 1520), of a Provençal family, came to Paris in 1502 and founded a printing house. His son Robert (1503–59) was printer to Francis I, and printed a number of important works and compiled the best Latin dictionary of the time, *Thesaurus Linguae Latinae* (1532). He was a Protestant, and in 1551 was exiled to Geneva. His son Henri Estienne (1531–98) spent most of his life at Geneva, where he printed for the republic, but also visited France, Italy, Flanders, and England: an ardent Hellenist, he printed works of Greek authors and compiled a *Thesaurus Graecae Linguae* (1572).

ETCHISON, Dennis (1943–) American writer of fictions of psychological *horror, frequently with Californian settings; born in Stockton, California. He began by publishing in *science fiction magazines. *Talking in the Dark* (2001) is a selection drawn from four previous collections.

ETHEREGE (Etheredge), **Sir George** (1636–91/2) Playwright. He was apprenticed to a lawyer, and probably travelled to France with his father, where he may have seen some of *Molière's early comedies. In his first play, *The *Comical Revenge, or Love in a Tub*, performed in 1664, the serious parts are in rhymed couplets, but the lively, realistic comic parts, in prose, are often cited as showing William *Congreve and Oliver *Goldsmith the way to an English comedy of manners. In London he belonged to the circle of wits that included Sir Charles *Sedley and Sir John *Rochester. His second play, **She Would if She Could*, was performed in 1668, and in the same year he travelled to Turkey as secretary to the ambassador Sir Daniel Harvey, returning in 1671. His best play, *The *Man of Mode, or Sir Fopling Flutter*, in which Dorimant is modelled on Rochester, was a tremendous hit in 1676. He married a wealthy widow and was knighted, *c.*1680, and was an envoy of James II in Ratisbon (Regensburg), 1685–9. His *Letterbook* recording his stay and his nonchalant attitude to his duties was edited by S. Rosenfeld (1928) and by Fredric Bracher (1974). He died in Paris, a *Jacobite exile. His polished and fashionable comedies were savagely attacked as immoral and coarse by the more genteel generation of Sir Richard *Steele.

ethnographic allegory A form of *allegory identified by the influential anthropologist and cultural critic James Clifford (1945–), who argued that non-fictional writings which purport to offer accurate accounts of real places are—just as much as more imaginative works—'inescapably allegorical'. In order to make sense of other cultures, ethnographers and travel writers tend to describe them in terms of myths or other explanatory schemes familiar to their readers. Perhaps the most enduring ethnographic allegories are those which invoke an idyllic paradise uncorrupted by civilization, or its opposite: a barbaric, violent world which has yet to receive its benefits. Allegories of salvage, which present themselves as attempts to document a dying race or culture or species before it disappears, have become increasingly common since the late 18th century. See James Clifford, 'On Ethnographic Allegory', in James Clifford and George E. Marcus (eds), *Writing Culture* (1986).

Ettrick Shepherd A name given to James *Hogg.

Eugene Aram A novel by Edward *Bulwer-Lytton, published 1832. It is the story of a schoolmaster, driven to murderous crime by poverty, who is later tormented by remorse. The same subject suggested Thomas *Hood's poem 'The Dream of Eugene Aram'.

Eulenspiegel, Till A German peasant of the early 14th century whose jests and practical jokes form the subject of a collection of satirical tales; one of these incidents features in Chaucer's 'Summoner's Tale' (see CANTERBURY TALES, 8). The earliest surviving printed edition, in High German, was published in Strasbourg in 1515, and there were early translations into English, Czech, Danish, Flemish, French, Latin, Polish, and Swedish. In England Till was known as Owlglass; an abridged translation into English by William Copland was published as *A Merye Jest of a Man that Was Called Howleglas* (*c*.1555). Several references in Ben *Jonson and John *Taylor assume a familiarity with Owlglass as prankster.

Euphues A prose romance by John *Lyly, of which the first part, *Euphues: The Anatomy of Wit*, was published in 1578, and the second, *Euphues and his England*, in 1580. Although very popular and regularly reprinted, their plots are very slender and really just a peg on which to hang the fashionable discourses, conversations, letters, mainly on the subject of love, and the witty language, which so appealed to contemporary readers.

In the first part Euphues, a young Athenian, visits Naples, where he makes the acquaintance of Philautus, an Italian, and a friendship develops between them. Nonetheless Euphues proceeds to oust Philautus from the affections of Lucilla, to be in turn ejected by one Curio. Euphues and Philautus, after upbraiding one another, unite in holding Lucilla 'as most abhominable', and part friends, Euphues returning to Greece and leaving behind him a pamphlet of advice to lovers, which he terms 'A cooling Carde for Philautus'.

In part two Euphues and Philautus travel to England, where their adventures are less entertaining than at Naples. They are largely concerned with the love affairs on which Philautus embarks, in spite of Euphues' advice to use circumspection in his dealings with English ladies; much space is occupied by a discussion on such questions as 'whether in love be more required secrecie or constancie'. Finally, Euphues is recalled to Greece. From Athens Euphues addresses a letter to the ladies of Italy, 'Euphues' Glasse for Europe', in which he describes England, its institutions, its ladies, its gentlemen, and its queen; and a final letter of general advice from Euphues to Philautus completes the work.

Euphues is famous for its distinctive style, to which it has given the name 'euphuism'. Its principal characteristics are the heavy use of antithesis, which is pursued regardless of sense, and emphasized by alliteration and other devices; and of allusions to historical and mythological personages and to natural history drawn from such encyclopedic writers as *Plutarch, *Pliny, and *Erasmus. Walter *Scott satirized euphuism in the character of Sir Piercie Shafton in *The *Monastery* and Charles *Kingsley defended *Euphues* in **Westward Ho!*

Euphues' Golden Legacy *See* ROSALYNDE.

euphuism *See* EUPHUES.

EURIPIDES (*c*.480s–*c*.407/406 BC) Greek tragedian. Nineteen of *c*.90 plays survive, ten as a collection of selected plays with ancient commentaries: *Alcestis*, *Medea*, *Hippolytus*, *Andromache*, *Hecuba*, *The Trojan Women*, *The Phoenician Women*, *Orestes*, *The Bacchae*, and *Rhesus*, and nine others as part of what was probably a complete collection: *Helen*, *Electra*, *The Children of Heracles*, *Heracles*, *The Suppliant Women*, *Iphigenia in Aulis*, *Iphigenia in Tauris*, *Ion*, and *Cyclops*. The plays of Euripides are characterized by an ambivalent attitude towards religious myths, which he sometimes seems to deploy purely for their dramatic potential (*see* DEUS EX MACHINA). He is also unusually successful in his characterization of extreme emotion, particularly that of women, for example Phaedra's passion for her stepson Hippolytus and Medea's murderous jealousy.

*Petrarch ranked him next to *Homer, and George *Buchanan took him as a model for his two Latin plays. Milton's **Samson Agonistes* was the first English tragedy to show his influence. John *Dryden praised his depiction of human behaviour, and P. B. *Shelley translated his satyr play *Cyclops*. William *Morris sentimentalized *Medea* in *The Life and Death of Jason* and *Alcestis* in *The *Earthly Paradise*. Robert *Browning's **Balaustion's Adventure* and **Aristophanes' Apology* contain striking interpretations respectively of *Alcestis* and *Heracles*. Influential 20th-century translations include those by Gilbert *Murray (now dated), Rex *Warner, and Richmond Lattimore (1906–84). Many modern writers have drawn on Euripides' plots, for example T. S. *Eliot on *Alcestis* in *The Cocktail Party*. Wole *Soyinka has produced a notable version of *The Bacchae*, and elements of this story have appeared in many other works, including William *Golding's *Lord of the Flies*. *See* AESCHYLUS; POETICS; SOPHOCLES; see also P. E. Easterling (ed.), *The Cambridge Companion to Greek Tragedy* (1997).

Europe: *A Prophecy* A poem by William *Blake, printed 1794 at Lambeth, in which he portrays the oppression of Albion during the 1,800-year sleep of Enitharmon, the female principle, and the approach of the French Revolution, symbolized by her son, the terrible Orc, the spirit of revolt.

Eurydice *See* ORPHEUS.

EUSDEN, Laurence (1688–1730) Educated at Trinity College, Cambridge, taking holy orders in 1714. He contributed to the **Spectator* and the **Guardian* and celebrated various Whig nobles in verse. In 1718 he was, controversially, made poet laureate. Pope refers to his notorious drinking habits in *The *Dunciad* and elsewhere.

Eustace Diamonds, The A novel by Anthony *Trollope, published 1873, the third in the *'Palliser' series. The unscrupulous Lizzie Eustace marries for money and, when Sir Florian Eustace dies, she not only inherits the family estates at Portray, but pockets the family diamonds as well, despite the demands of the Eustace lawyers that they be returned. She looks for support to her cousin and legal adviser Frank Greystock, but when his engagement to the demure governess Lucy Morris proves too durable, she turns to the stuffy Lord Fawn. Fawn proposes, but stipulates that the necklace must be returned to the Eustace estate. Lizzie retires to Portray, and assembles a curious collection of house-guests, including dashing Lord George de Bruce Carruthers, who becomes her third suitor, and the fashionable preacher Mr Emilius, who becomes her fourth. When Lizzie and her entourage set off southwards, Lizzie's bedroom is robbed at Carlisle. The thieves get away with the casket but not the jewels, which Lizzie has extracted for safe keeping. The police are suspicious, and when Lizzie is robbed a second time she is unable to conceal her trickery. Lord Fawn drops her immediately, Frank Greystock stops procrastinating and marries Lucy Morris, Lord George disappears, and Lizzie is compelled to marry Mr Emilius—without, as it will turn out, sufficiently enquiring into his shady past. The novel, which was popular, was influenced by Wilkie *Collins's treatment of crime and detection.

Evangelical Revival, the A label loosely given to several mid-18th-century religious awakenings in England, Wales, Scotland, and the American colonies, characterized by irregular open-air and itinerant preaching, societies, meetings, hymn singing, conversions, the reading and writing of religious experiences, and the publishing and distribution of materials among members. Opponents dismissed such phenomena as 'enthusiasm', or fanatical and superstitious self-delusion. Knowledge of different aspects of the movement and the activities of its leaders on both sides of the Atlantic was aided by popular magazines such as *The Christian History.* Key figures include Jonathan *Edwards, Howell Harris (1714–73), George *Whitefield, and John and Charles *Wesley. Its main literary productions were accounts of revival, such as Edwards's *Faithful Narrative* (1737), spiritual biographies and autobiographies, letters, and hymns. See D. Bruce Hindmarsh, *The Evangelical Conversion Narrative: Spiritual Autobiography in Early Modern England* (2005).
See also METHODISM.

Evangelists, the Four The authors of the four Gospels, Matthew, Mark, Luke, and John.
See BIBLE.

Evan Harrington A novel by George *Meredith, published 1861; a study of the nature of a gentleman, with autobiographical elements.

EVANS, Caradoc (1878–1945) Welsh writer, born David Evans near Llanfihangel-ar-Arth in Carmarthenshire, whose attacks on Nonconformist piety earned him the nickname 'best hated man in Wales' and the public enmity of David Lloyd George. After more than a decade as a draper's assistant in Carmarthen, Barry, Cardiff, and London, Evans became a journalist in 1906, eventually acting as editor of *Cassell's Weekly* and *T.P.'s Weekly.* With their reductive parodies of Welsh syntax and idiom and their presentation of religion as a cover for greed and lust, the stories of *My People* (1915) caused a major controversy in Wales, which Evans gleefully joined in a series of letters to the *Western Mail. Nothing to Pay* (1930), a gloomy portrait of a miserly draper, is the most admired of his novels. See John Harris (ed.), *Fury Never Leaves Us: A Miscellany of Caradoc Evans* (1985).

EVANS, Christopher (1951–) *science fiction author and schoolteacher, born in south Wales, who co-edited (with Robert *Holdstock) anthologies of British science fiction in the late 1980s. His most critically acclaimed novel, *Aztec Century* (1993), is an *alternate history in which the Aztecs have conquered Britain.

EVANS, Margiad (Peggy Eileen Whistler) (1909–59) Novelist, short story writer, and poet, born in Uxbridge. She spent much of her life on the Welsh Marches near Ross-on-Wye, and the divided loyalties and latent violence of borders—between genders as well as territories—are explored in *Country Dance* (1932), first and most famous of her four novels. *Autobiography* (1943), a compilation of essays and other writings, communicates a sense of intense inner life through its close attention to the natural world, while *A Ray of Darkness* (1952) dispassionately describes the onset of epilepsy, a symptom of the brain tumour that would cause the author's early death. Her stories are collected in *The Old and the Young* (1948).

EVANS, Mary Ann *See* ELIOT, GEORGE.

EVARISTO, Bernardine (1959–) Born in London of Nigerian and British parentage. Her novels include *Blonde Roots* (2008). Evaristo's work crosses national, historical, and generic boundaries: the Sudanese protagonist of her novel-in-verse *The Emperor's Babe* (2001), set in Londinium in 211, has an affair with the Roman emperor Septimius Serverus, himself an African. She also writes for the theatre and for radio, and has collaborated with jazz musicians.

Eve *See* EDEN, GARDEN OF.

Evelina *or A Young Lady's Entrance into the World* *epistolary novel by Fanny *Burney, published anonymously 1778. Sir John Belmont, disappointed of the fortune he expected to receive with his wife, abandons her and their child Evelina, who is brought up by a guardian. Visiting a friend in London, Evelina is introduced into society and falls in love with Lord Orville. She is much mortified by her comically vulgar relatives, and the ominous attentions of a persistent suitor, Sir Clement Willoughby. Belmont is asked to receive Evelina as his daughter, but insists that his daughter has been in his care since infancy, upon which it is discovered that his wife's nurse had passed her own child off as his daughter. Evelina is recognized as his heir, and marries Orville. The novel enjoyed huge success, numbering among its admirers Samuel *Johnson, Edmund *Burke, Edward *Gibbon, and Richard *Sheridan; it influenced Jane *Austen's fiction.

EVELYN, John (1620–1706) Diarist and author, born at Wotton House, Surrey, into a family that owed its wealth mainly to gunpowder production, and educated at Balliol College, Oxford, and the Middle Temple. After briefly joining the Royalist army he travelled abroad, returning to settle with his wife at Sayes Court, Deptford, in 1652, where he designed a famous garden. A virtuoso of extremely wide cultural interests, he was a founder member of the *Royal Society, and wrote on a range of topics that included theology, politics, horticulture, architecture, navigation, commerce, engraving, and cookery. Among his friends were Jeremy *Taylor and Samuel *Pepys. He published in 1661 *Fumifugium, or The Inconvenience of the Air and Smoke of London Dissipated*, the first book on air pollution in London; and in 1664 his influential *Sylva, or Discourse on Forest Trees*, intended to encourage landowners to plant trees for the British navy. He is chiefly remembered for his *Diary*, first published in 1818 and in a full and authoritative edition by E. S. de Beer in 1955 (6 vols). It covers most of his life, describing his travels abroad, his contemporaries, disasters such as the plague and the fire of London, the rebuilding of St Paul's Cathedral by Christopher *Wren (Evelyn had introduced Wren to the woodcarver Grinling Gibbons (1648–1721)), and court life and scandal (which he deplored), as well as reflecting his cultural and artistic interests, and is an invaluable record of the period. He appears not to have composed regularly day by day, but some time after the event. His diary is less spontaneous and personal than Samuel Pepys's, but more multifarious in its interests, as well as reflecting a more serious and cultivated mind. His *Life of Mrs Godolphin* was first printed in 1847. A keen bibliophile, he amassed a library of some 4,000 books and 900 pamphlets, many of them uniformly bound and bearing his motto *Omnia explorate, meliora retinete* ('Explore everything, keep the best') from 1 Thessalonians 5: 21.
See DIARIES.

Evening's Love, An *or The Mock Astrologer* A comedy by John *Dryden, produced 1668, published 1671. Combining elements of Spanish intrigue comedy and fast-moving farce with sexually explicit language, it proved a great commercial success. The plot, borrowed from Madeleine de *Scudéry, *Corneille, Philippe Quinault (1635–88), *Molière, and others, concerns the exploits of two English Cavaliers, Wildblood and Bellamy, in Madrid at carnival time. Bellamy pretends to be an astrologer, and both men gain Spanish wives. Wildblood's spirited mistress Jacinta tests him in the guise first of a Moor and then of a Mulatta, forgiving and marrying him though he fails to remain faithful on both occasions. The preface is among the most stimulating of Dryden's critical essays, defending drama as entertainment, and replying to charges of plagiarism.

'Eve of St Agnes, The' A narrative poem in Spenserian stanzas by John *Keats, written 1819, published 1820. The poem is set in a remote period of time, in the depths of winter. Madeline has been told the legend that on St Agnes's Eve maidens may have visions of their lovers. Madeline's love, Porphyro, comes from a family hostile to her own, and she is herself surrounded by 'hyena foemen, and hot-blooded lords'. Yet he contrives to steal into the house during a ball on St Agnes's Eve, and with the aid of old Angela is secreted in Madeline's room, where he watches his love prepare for sleep. When she wakes from dreams of him, aroused by his soft singing, she finds him by her bedside. Silently they escape from the house, and fly 'away into the storm'. With its rich and vivid imagery, its heightened atmosphere of excitement and passion, the poem is among Keats's most successful works.

Ever Green, The *See* RAMSAY, ALLAN.

Evergreen Review, The A New York-based journal, running from 1957 to 1973, which published works by the *Beat Generation and avant-garde writing from Europe. It was an important forum for experimental writing; see *The Evergreen Review Reader 1957–1966* (1994) and *The Evergreen Review Reader 1967–1973* (1999).

'Everlasting Gospel, The' *See* BLAKE, WILLIAM.

EVERSON, William (1912–94) American poet based in San Francisco and Oakland, who was an important figure in the San Francisco Renaissance. He began publishing poetry with *These Are the Ravens* (1935) and was known as Brother Antoninus during his years as a Dominican (1951–69). He remained fascinated by the poems of Robinson *Jeffers, about which he published critical studies in 1968 and 1988. Jeffers helped shape Everson's visionary stance. He also worked closely with Kenneth *Rexroth.

Everyman A popular morality play of *c.*1509–19, in 921 lines, almost certainly derived from its Dutch close counterpart *Elckerlijc*. Everyman is summoned by death and, in the last hour of his life, he discovers that his friends Fellowship,

Every Man in His Humour A comedy by … performed by the Lord Chamberlain's Men 1598, with William *Shakespeare in the cast, printed 1601. In his folio of 1616 Jonson published an extensively revised version, with the setting changed from Florence to London, and the characters given English names, which make the play's class bias more apparent. In the latter version Kitely, a jealous merchant with a young wife, is paid out for his jealousy and made a fool of by his brother-in-law Wellbred and a crowd of riotous but harmless gallants. The comic characters include Bobadill, a boastful cowardly soldier, Matthew, a 'town gull' and poetaster, Stephen, a 'country gull', and the mischievous servant Brainworm. The misunderstandings are cleared up at the end by the shrewd and kindly Justice Clement. Jonson added a prologue to the folio version giving an exposition of his dramatic theory.

Every Man out of His Humour A comedy by Ben *Jonson, acted by the Lord Chamberlain's Men at the newly built *Globe Theatre 1599, printed 1600. The play parades a variety of characters dominated by particular 'humours', or obsessive quirks of disposition: Macilente, a venomous malcontent; Carlo Buffone, a cynical jester; the submissive Deliro and his domineering wife Fallace; Fastidious Brisk, an affected courtier devoted to fashion; Sordido, a miserly farmer, and his son Fungoso, who longs to be a courtier; Sogliardo, 'an essential clown, enamoured of the name of a gentleman'; and Puntarvolo, a self-important knight, who wagers that he, his dog, and his cat can travel to Constantinople and back. By means of various episodes, such as Macilente's poisoning of Puntarvolo's dog and Brisk's imprisonment for debt, each character is eventually driven 'out of his humour'. Two judicious onlookers, Mitis and Cordatus, oversee the action throughout, and provide a moral commentary. An opening debate includes an explanation of Jonson's theory of humours.

Everyman's Library A series of reprints of world literary masterpieces founded in 1906 by Joseph Dent (1849–1926) and first edited by Ernest Rhys (1859–1946). The first title to appear was James *Boswell's *Life of *Johnson*. The series is currently published by Knopf in the USA and Weidenfeld and Nicolson in the UK.

EVTUSHENKO, Evgenii Aleksandrovich (1933–) Russian poet, born in Zima in southern Siberia and educated in Moscow. He travelled extensively and enjoyed international recognition as a prominent writer of the post-Stalin Thaw generation, who defended *modernism and protested against censorship. His first volume of verse appeared in 1952; the long autobiographical poem *Zima Railway Station* (1956) established … popularity. This was followed by *Babii Yar* (literally, 'the … cliff', 1961), a poem evoking the Nazi wartime … Jews near Kiev and tackling the dangerous … anti-Semitism. His poem 'Stalin's Heirs' … commitment to de-Stalinization pol… *Letter to Esenin* (1965), hailing … *Autobiography* (1963) … published in Paris. … for publication of the works of … campaigned … and … *Collected Poems, 1952–1990* (1991).

EWART, Gavin (1916–95) Poet; born in London, educated at Wellington College and Christ's College, Cambridge. He contributed to Geoffrey *Grigson's *New Verse* when he was 17; his first volume, *Poems and Songs*, appeared in 1939. After the war he worked for many years as an advertising copywriter before becoming, in 1971, a full-time freelance writer. His second volume, *Londoners*, followed his first after a long interval, in 1964, and after that he published several volumes of poetry, mainly of light, comic, satiric, and erotic verse which shows the influence of W. H. *Auden: these include *Pleasures of the Flesh* (1966), *Or Where a Young Penguin Lies Screaming* (1977), *All my Little Ones* (1978), and *More Little Ones* (1982). *The Collected Ewart 1933–1980* (1980) was followed by *The New Ewart: Poems 1980–1982* (1982), *Capital Letters* (1983), *Late Pickings* (1987), *Selected Poems 1933–1988* (1988), *Penultimate Poems* (1989), and *Collected Poems 1980–1990* (1991). He also edited the *Penguin Book of Light Verse* (1980) and *Other People's Clerihews* (1983), and was himself a master of the *limerick, the *clerihew, and the occasional verse.

EWING, Juliana Horatia (1841–85) Born in Ecclesfield, Yorkshire, writer of children's stories, whose inventive and unsentimental tales brought her much success and admiration, including from Edith *Nesbit and Rudyard *Kipling. Most of her work first appeared in *Aunt Judy's Magazine*, edited by her mother, Margaret Gatty. Her many publications present events as seen through the eyes of a young child; the most enduring include *Jackanapes* (1879), a touching soldier-story illustrated by Randolph *Caldecott; *A Flat Iron for a Farthing* (1872); and *Lob-Lie-by-the-Fire* (1874). There is a life by Gillian Avery (1961).

Examiner, The (1) A Tory periodical started by *Bolingbroke in August 1710; Jonathan *Swift took charge in October (nos 14–46), and was succeeded by Delarivier *Manley in 1711. It engaged in controversy with Richard *Steele's **Guardian* and Joseph *Addison's *Whig Examiner*, and lasted, with interruptions, until 1716. (2) A reformist weekly periodical, established by John and Leigh *Hunt in 1808, closing in 1881. Under Hunt it supported the work of P. B. *Shelley, John *Keats, Charles *Lamb, and William *Hazlitt. It was often bitterly attacked by Tory journals such as the **Quarterly Review* and

Blackwood's Magazine for its radical litera... disrespect towards the prince regent.

Excalibur A corrupt form... ...ory, *Geoffrey of Monmouth... ...steel', but the drew out of a sto... ...ed to the Irish *Caladbolg* which was giver... ...gendary sword. According to Mal- Bk I). Malo... was mortally wounded in the last battle, he Welsh f... (ba... Sir Bedevere to throw Excalibur into the lake. A hand rose from the water, took the sword, and vanished.

Excursion, The A poem in nine books by William *Wordsworth, published 1814. This is the middle section of a projected three-part poem 'on man, on nature and on human life', of which this part alone was completed. The whole work was to have been entitled 'The Recluse', 'as having for its principal subject the sensations and opinions of a poet living in retirement'. It was planned in 1798, when Wordsworth was living near *Coleridge at Alfoxden. *The *Prelude* was originally intended to be the introduction to the first part of 'The Recluse'.

The poet, travelling with the Wanderer, a philosophic pedlar, meets the pessimistic Solitary, the source of whose despondency is found in his want of religious faith and lack of confidence in the virtue of man. He is reproved with gentle and persuasive argument. The Pastor is then introduced, who illustrates the harmonizing effects of virtue and religion through narratives of people interred in his churchyard. They visit the Pastor's house, and the Wanderer draws his general and philosophic conclusions from the discussions that have passed. The last two books deal in particular with the industrial expansion of the early part of the century, and the degradation that followed in its train. The poem ends with the Pastor's prayer that man may be given grace to conquer guilt and sin, and with praise for the beauty of the world about them. Book I contains 'The Story of Margaret' or 'The *Ruined Cottage', originally written as a separate poem. The poem was famously castigated in a review by Francis *Jeffrey which begins, forthrightly, 'This will never do'.

exegesis *See* BIBLICAL COMMENTARIES.

'Exequy, An' *see* KING, HENRY.

Exeter Book One of the most important manuscripts containing Old English poetry, given by Bishop Leofric (d. 1072) to Exeter Cathedral, where it still remains. It contains many of the most admired shorter poems, such as *The *Wanderer, The *Seafarer, *Deor, *Widsith*, 'The *Ruin', *'Wulf and Eadwacer', *The *Wife's Lament, The *Husband's Message*, and *Resignation*, as well as a famous collection of riddles and some longer poems of a religious nature, notably **Guthlac, Christ, The *Phoenix*, and *Cynewulf's *Juliana*. Many of these are translated

...*axon* ...pp and E. V. K. ...S. Mackie, EETS 104 and ...J. Muir (1994).

...xistentialism A European philosophical tendency that flourished in the mid-20th century, although partly prefigured in the 19th by Søren *Kierkegaard and Friedrich *Nietzsche, achieving some influence upon English writers in the 1950s and 1960s. It was not a school with an agreed doctrine, but a broad current with divergent atheist and Christian versions, Martin *Heidegger and Jean-Paul *Sartre leading the former camp, Gabriel *Marcel the latter. It emphasized individual uniqueness, freedom, and responsibility in opposition to various forms of determinism, its name deriving from the principle that 'existence precedes essence': that is, human choices are not dictated by a determining essence or fixed human nature. The most influential literary exponents of this position were Sartre and Albert *Camus, whose impact can be felt especially in the early poems of Thom *Gunn and in the novels of Iris *Murdoch (who wrote a study of Sartre) and John *Fowles. Independently of such influences, the writings of W. H. *Auden from the 1940s onward echo idiosyncratically the themes of Christian existentialism.

Exodus A 590-line poem in Old English, based on the biblical story; it is contained in the *Junius Manuscript and may be early, possibly dating from the 8th century. Once erroneously attributed to *Cædmon, it contains a vigorous description of the destruction of the Egyptians in the Red Sea. The narrative departs considerably from the letter of the biblical narrative, and discussion of the poem has centred mostly on possible explanations for its allusive structure and the fact that it draws material from various parts of the Bible. The poem has been edited by P. J. Lucas (1977).

Exodus *See* BIBLE.

Experience, Songs of *See* SONGS OF INNOCENCE.

Expressionism A term coined in the early 20th century to describe a movement in art, then in literature, the theatre, and the cinema, characterized by boldness, distortion, and forceful representation of the emotions. One of its earliest manifestations was in the group of German painters Die Brücke ('the Bridge'), formed in Dresden in 1905 and influenced by Vincent Van Gogh (1853–90) and Edvard Munch (1863–1944): a later group was Der blaue Reiter ('the Blue Rider', from the title of a painting by the Russian painter Wassily Kandinsky, 1866–1944), formed in 1911, which was more concerned with the evocative qualities of colour and pattern, unrelated to content. In the theatre the term has been associated with the works of Ernst *Toller, August *Strindberg, and Frank *Wedekind. The epitome of Expressionism in German cinema was Robert Wiene's *The Cabinet of Dr Caligari* (1919). Expressionism flourished principally in Germany in the wake of a revival of interest in the writings of Friedrich *Nietzsche and took little root in Britain, though Wyndham *Lewis and *Vorticism have some affinities with it, and traces of its influence can be found in the verse dramas of W. H. *Auden and Christopher *Isherwood.

EYRE, Simon (*c.*1395–1458) A draper who became lord mayor of London (1445), was a generous benefactor of the city, and built Leadenhall as a public granary and market. John *Stow describes his career; he figures in Thomas *Deloney's *The Gentle Craft* and in Thomas *Dekker's *The *Shoemakers' Holiday.*

EZEKIEL, Nissim (1924–2004) One of India's best-known poets, born into an Indian Jewish family, and educated in Bombay (Mumbai) and at Birkbeck College, London. Editor, art critic, lecturer, playwright, translator, ironic social commentator, Ezekiel helped to create a fruitful literary climate for a whole generation of Indian poets writing in English and is recognized as having played an important part in naturalizing the English language to the Indian situation. The discipline, precision, and critical range of his work remain an enduring influence. His eight volumes of poetry include *A Time to Change* (1952), *The Unfinished Man* (1960), and *The Exact Name* (1965).

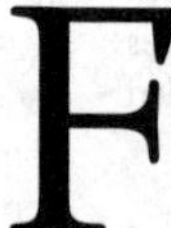

FABER, Michel (1960–) Novelist and short story writer, born in The Hague and brought up in Australia, where he studied at the University of Melbourne. He has lived in Ross-shire, Scotland since 1993. Faber's unsettling, frequently mischievous stories are collected in *Some Rain Must Fall* (1998), *The Fahrenheit Twins* (2005), and *The Apple: New Crimson Petal Stories* (2006). He has published two novellas, *The Hundred and Ninety-Nine Steps* (2001) and *The Courage Consort* (2004). *Under the Skin* (2000) is a novel about farming humans for alien consumption, and *The Crimson Petal and the White* (2002) a Victorian family saga centred on the life of Sugar, a prostitute.

Faber Book of Modern Verse, The An anthology published in 1936, edited by Michael *Roberts, which did much to establish the reputations of a rising generation, including W. H. *Auden, Louis *MacNeice, William *Empson, and Dylan *Thomas, and to create a lineage for the previous generation of modernists. In his introduction, Roberts traces the influences of Arthur Hugh *Clough, Gerard Manley *Hopkins (himself well represented), and the French *symbolists on modern poetry, defines the 'European' sensibility of such writers as T. S. *Eliot, Ezra *Pound, and W. B. *Yeats, and offers a persuasive apologia for various aspects of *modernism which the reading public had resisted, identifying them as an apparent obscurity compounded of condensed metaphor, allusion, intricacy of ideas, and verbal play. The poet, he declared, 'must charge each word to its maximum poetic value': 'primarily poetry is an exploration of the possibilities of language.' See Janet Adam Smith, 'Mr Eliot's Proposal', *TLS*, 18 June 1976.

FABIAN, Robert *See* FABYAN, ROBERT.

FABIUS (Quintus Fabius Maximus) (d. 203 BC) Nicknamed *Cunctator* (delayer); appointed dictator after the Carthaginian general Hannibal's crushing victory over the Romans at Lake Trasimene (217 BC). He carried on a defensive campaign of attrition. Hence the expression 'Fabian tactics' and the name of the Fabian Society (founded 1884), dedicated to the gradual introduction of socialism.

fable A term most commonly used in the sense of a short story devised to convey some useful moral or other didactic lesson about human manners and behaviour, but often carrying with it associations of the marvellous or the mythical, and frequently employing animals or inanimate objects as characters. *Aesop's fables and the *'Reynard the Fox' series were well known and imitated in Britain by *Chaucer, Robert *Henryson, and others, and *La Fontaine was imitated by John *Gay. *Mandeville's *The Fable of the Bees*, Jonathan Swift's **Gulliver's Travels*, and George Orwell's **Animal Farm* may be described as satirical fables. The form is found in many countries, notably in the ancient but still influential *Panchatantra* in India, the source of several European fables. Fables enjoyed something of a vogue in the 1920s and 1930s, in works by T. F. *Powys, David *Garnett, John *Collier, and others, and they have always been popular in *children's literature.

Fables, Ancient and Modern By John *Dryden, published 1700. Verse paraphrases of tales by *Ovid, *Boccaccio, and Geoffrey *Chaucer are interspersed with poems of Dryden's own, and together with the preface, in itself one of the most important examples of Dryden's criticism, they compose themselves into an Ovidian and Catholic meditation on the place of nature, sex, and violence in the flux of history.

fabliau A short tale in verse, almost invariably in *octosyllabic couplets in French, mostly dealing with incidents of ordinary life from a comic point of view. The fabliau was an important element in French poetry in the 12th and 13th centuries. In English, it has come to be applied loosely to tales with a sexual element, such as *Chaucer's tales of the Miller, the Summoner, and the Pardoner in the **Canterbury Tales*. See M. J. S. Schenck, *The Fabliaux* (1987); J. Hines, *The Fabliau in English* (1993).

FABYAN (FABIAN), Robert (d. 1513) Chronicler, sheriff of London in 1493. He reworked various sources into *The Newe Cronycles of England and Fraunce*, a compilation extending from the arrival of Brutus in England (*see* BRUT) to the death of Richard III (first printed 1516; ed. Sir Henry Ellis, 1811). His chronicles are of importance with respect to the history of London, and were several times brought up to date.

faction A term coined *c.*1970 to describe fiction based on and mingled with fact, at first applied particularly to American works of fiction such as *In Cold Blood* (1966) by Truman *Capote and *The Armies of the Night* (1968) by Norman *Mailer. The genre has continued to flourish, as the *historical novel has gained new seriousness: works such as Thomas *Keneally's *Schindler's Ark* (1982), based on documentary evidence, interviews, and

research, may be classified as fiction or non-fiction; it was classified as fiction in Australia and the UK, but published as non-fiction under the title *Schindler's List* in the USA.
See GONZO JOURNALISM.

Faerie Queene, The The greatest work of Edmund *Spenser, of which the first three books were published 1590, and the second three 1596.

The general scheme of the work is proposed in the author's introductory letter addressed to Walter *Ralegh and dated '23. Ianuary. 1589'. By the Faerie Queene the poet signifies Glory in the abstract and *Elizabeth I in particular (who also figures under the names of *Britomart, *Belphoebe, Mercilla, and *Gloriana). Twelve of her knights, the 'patrons' or examples of twelve different virtues, each undertake an adventure, on the twelve successive days of the queen's annual festival; an account of their origins was to have been given in the last of twelve books. Prince Arthur symbolizes 'magnificence', in the Aristotelian sense (says the author) of the perfection of all the other virtues (he must have meant not 'magnificence' but 'magnanimity', or 'gentlemanliness'). Arthur has a vision of the Faerie Queene and, determining to seek her out, is brought into the adventures of the several knights and carries them to a successful issue. This explanation, given in the letter to Ralegh, does not appear from the poem itself, for the author starts at once with the adventures of the knights; the poem does not conform to his scheme.

Of the six books Spenser published in his lifetime, the subjects are: I, the adventures of the *Redcrosse Knight of Holiness (the Anglican Church), the protector of the virgin *Una (truth, or the true religion), and the wiles of *Archimago and *Duessa; II, the adventures of Sir *Guyon, the Knight of Temperance, his encounters with *Pyrochles and Cymochles, his visit to the Cave of *Mammon and the House of Temperance, and his destruction of *Acrasia and her Bower of Bliss (Canto X of this book contains a chronicle of British rulers from *Brut to Elizabeth), III, the legend of Chastity, exemplified by Britomart and Belphoebe; IV, the legend of Triamond and *Cambell, exemplifying Friendship, together with the story of Scudamour and *Amoret; V, the adventures of *Artegall, the Knight of Justice, in which allegorical reference is made to various historical events of the reign of Elizabeth I: the defeat of the Spaniards in the Netherlands, the recantation of Henry IV of France, the execution of *Mary Queen of Scots, and the administration of Ireland by Lord Grey de Wilton; VI, the adventures of Sir *Calidore, exemplifying Courtesy. There is also a fragment on *Mutabilitie, being the sixth and seventh cantos of the legend of Constancie, which was to have formed the seventh book. This fragment, first published in 1609, contains a charming description of the seasons and the months.

Modelled to some extent on *Ariosto's **Orlando furioso*, *The Faerie Queene* is, with Philip *Sidney's **Arcadia*, one of the great achievements of Elizabethan literature. The poem's complex allegory (political, religious, moral, personal) is varied throughout, and its chief beauties lie in particular episodes and descriptions, such as those of the Cave of Mammon (Bk II), the marriage of Thames and Medway (Bk IV), or Calidore's vision of the Graces on Mount Acidale (Bk VI). The poem is written in the stanza invented by Spenser (and since used by James *Thomson, John *Keats, P. B. *Shelley, and Lord *Byron), in which a ninth line of twelve syllables (*alexandrine) is added to eight lines of ten syllables, rhyming *ababbcbcc*.

FAINLIGHT, Ruth (1931–) Poet and translator, born in New York, for many years resident in England. In her first collection, *Cages* (1966), her distinctively cool, ironic, yet not dispassionate voice spoke clearly: it shows some affinity with the tone of Robert *Graves, whom she and her husband Alan *Sillitoe knew in their early years in Majorca. Fainlight also knew Sylvia *Plath, and is the dedicatee of Plath's famous poem 'Elm'. *Cages* was followed by such volumes as *To See the Matter Clearly* (1968), *The Region's Violence* (1973), *Sibyls and Others* (1980), and *Sugar-Paper Blue* (1997). Her *Selected Poems* was published in 1995, and *Moon Wheels* in 2006. Her topics are both domestic and global: she combines the personal and the austerely detached, and excels at the uncanny casual moment of recognition. She has also published short stories and translations from the Portuguese, and has written opera libretti.

FAIRFAX, Edward (?1568–1635) Yorkshire scholar and gentleman, remembered for his translation of *Tasso's **Jerusalem Delivered* as *Godfrey of Boulogne Done into English Heroical Verse* (1600). An edition by K. M. Lea and T. M. Gang was published in 1981.

Fair Maid of Perth, The A novel by Walter *Scott, published 1828, the second of the *Chronicles of the Canongate*. Set at the end of the 14th century, it is chiefly remembered for its study of constitutional cowardice. It tells of the attempt to end the discord caused by the enmity of clans Chattan and Quhele by mortal combat of 30 picked champions on each side before the king. The hero of the story, Henry Smith, seeks an opportunity to face Conachar, chief of Clan Quhele, his rival for the love of the Fair Maid, Catharine Glover. Conachar combines a hot temper with cowardice. In the battle, he is protected by his foster-father, Torquil, who, with his eight sons, stands between him and danger until all are dead; left to face Smith, he runs away. The battle, and the subplot of the assassination of the king's heir, the duke of Rothesay, make this one of the most violent of Scott's novels.

Fair Maid of the West, The, *or A Girl Worth Gold* A comedy of adventure by Thomas *Heywood, in two parts, Part I *c.*1600, Part II *c.*1630, both printed 1631. The first part opens with a vivid scene at Plymouth, where the earl of *Essex's expedition is about to sail for the Azores (1597), and gallant Master Spencer unluckily kills a man in defence of Bess Bridges, 'the flower of Plymouth'. He has to fly the country, but provides for Bess by giving her the Windmill Tavern at Fowey, which she runs with spirit and decorum. Meanwhile Spencer, who has sailed to the Azores, is wounded to the point of death in trying to stop a quarrel. He sends a message to

Bess, bidding her adieu and making over all his property to her. Bess employs part of this to fit out a privateer, in which she sets sail to bring home his body. Instead she rescues Spencer himself, who has recovered and been captured by Spaniards. After many adventures, leading as far as Morocco, Bess is finally united with her lover. The first part makes a breezy and entertaining melodrama, but Part II is less effective, with more extreme coincidences and incidents.

***Fair Penitent,* The** Blank verse tragedy by Nicholas *Rowe, produced 1703, adapted from Philip *Massinger and Nathan *Field's *The *Fatal Dowry.* The play held the stage into the 19th century. The character of Lothario has become proverbial, and was Samuel *Richardson's model for Lovelace in **Clarissa*. Lothario was later played by David *Garrick; Sarah *Siddons was notable as Calista, the 'fair penitent'. Samuel *Johnson said of it that 'there is scarcely any work...at once so interesting by the fable, and so delightful by the language', though he also noted that the heroine's penitence has more to do with detection than guilt.

Fair Quarrel, A A comedy by John *Middleton and William *Rowley, written 1614–16?, published 1617. The mother of Captain Ager is insulted by a fellow officer, and a duel is arranged. Ager tells his mother about the accusation; at first she indignantly denies it, but then, in order to prevent the duel, admits her guilt. Ager refuses to fight, and is branded by his adversary as a coward. Having now what he considers an adequate reason, he fights and defeats his enemy. They are reconciled and all ends well.

fairy stories These have existed in the oral tradition of all cultures, but were recognized as a distinct literary genre at the time of the publication of the stories of Charles *Perrault. Many earlier literary works (including those of *Chaucer, *Boccaccio, *Malory, *Spenser, *Straparola, and Giambattista *Basile), had featured fairies and tales of the supernatural, but it was in the last two decades of the 17th century that a new vogue for the written fairy-tale was established. Many women were instrumental in developing what have come to be known as fairy-tales as distinct from stories about fairies and fairy lore such as Spenser's *The *Faerie Queene* (1590; 1596). Perrault's cousin Marie-Jeanne l'Héritier de Villandon (1664–1734; *Œuvres meslés*, 1695) and her friend Henriette-Julie de Castelnau, comtesse de Murat (1670–1716), both published stories. Marie-Catherine Le Jumel de Barneville, comtesse d'*Aulnoy, produced well-known tales featuring disguise, shape-changing, cross-dressing, and beast-husbands (*Les Contes des fées*, 1696): these were quickly translated into English (some appearing in 1699; 3 vols, 1721–2) and remained popular well into the 19th century.

Translated story collections from other cultures, notably the **Arabian Nights*, reinforced the popularity of fairy stories. During the 18th century, fairy stories flourished, both in versions from the French, and in home-grown popular forms, despite protests from some educationalists that they were unwholesome and immoral. During the 19th century, historians of folklore, notably the *Grimm brothers and Andrew *Lang, established the fairy story as a respectable subject for research, introducing many new tales to the British canon; in the same period T. C. *Croker was making an important collection of Irish folk tales, and *Andersen's stories were appearing in Danish. Sir John Rhŷs collected stories in *Celtic Folklore, Welsh and Manx* (1901; repr. 1980); J. M *Barrie's **Peter Pan* is one of the most enduring original stories with fairy characters.

The 20th century witnessed the rise of psychoanalytic, anthropological, feminist, and ideological studies of fairy stories, including by Sigmund *Freud, Carl *Jung, and James *Frazer. Bruno Bettelheim's classic work *The Uses of Enchantment: The Power and Importance of Fairy Tales* (1978) argues that the stories offer children a valuable tool for psychological growth and adjustment. Jack Zipes has written extensively about their role in acculturating children and their ability to function as memes, carrying cultural information. Key surveys of the genre include *The Ocean of Story* (1928) by Norman Penzer; Russian structuralist and narratologist Vladimir Propp's *Morphology of the Folk Tale* (1928; trans. 1968); Carol Ann *Duffy's *The Erotic World of Faery* (1972); and Marina *Warner's *From the Beast to the Blonde* (1994).

The late 20th century saw a revival of interest in the adult fairy-tale: A. S. *Byatt, Angela *Carter, Italo *Calvino, and Salman *Rushdie have all used the genre to remarkable effect, but a familiarity with fairy story also discreetly underlies many more conventional narratives. Fairy stories for children continue to be published through the whole range of the market, from popular mass market versions of old favourites to sophisticated and handsomely illustrated adaptations by well-known authors.

Faithful Shepherdess, The A pastoral tragicomedy in verse by John *Fletcher, written probably in 1607 or 1608, printed not later than 1610. The address to the reader includes a classic definition of tragicomedy. The action takes place at night in the woods of Thessaly, and revolves around the central figure of the faithful shepherdess Clorin, who has dedicated herself to the memory of her dead love. Thenot is in love with her, or rather with the image of her fidelity, for when she pretends to accept him, he spurns her. Other characters in the amorous round include Amaryllis, who loves Thenot, who in turn loves Amoret; the wanton Chloe and the coy Daphnis; and the Sullen Shepherd, who intervenes by transforming Amaryllis into the form of Amoret. With the aid of magic herbs, a satyr, and the god of the river, all is happily resolved.

FALCONER, William (1732–70) Son of a wig-maker, author of a nautical dictionary and of *The Shipwreck* (1762; rev. 1764, 1769), a poem in three cantos recounting the wreck of a ship on the coast of Greece. Falconer, himself a seaman, escaped this wreck, but eventually drowned at sea.

FALKLAND, Lucius Cary, second Viscount (1610–43) Politician and writer; he inherited the manor of Great Tew,

Oxfordshire, in 1625, where he became the centre of a cultivated circle including George *Sandys, John *Earle, Sidney *Godolphin, William *Chillingworth, and *Clarendon. Ben *Jonson, Sir John *Suckling, Abraham *Cowley, and Edmund *Waller all celebrated him in verse. Devout, rational, liberal, and pacifist by temperament, he sided with the parliamentary opposition at first, but could not accept the abolition of episcopacy. Appointed secretary of state by Charles I in September 1642, he fought at Edgehill and Gloucester and was killed at Newbury. He wrote verses and theological works including a *Discourse of Infallibility* (1646) defending reason in religion and opposing narrow dogmatism.

FALKNER, John Meade (1858–1932) Novelist, antiquary, and topographical writer, born at Manningford Bruce, Wiltshire. He went to school in Dorchester and Weymouth before attending Marlborough College and then Hertford College, Oxford, from which he graduated in 1882. Falkner rose to a senior position with a firm of Newcastle armaments manufacturers, and later (1921) became honorary librarian to the dean and chapter at Durham. He compiled handbooks to *Oxfordshire* (1894) and *Berkshire* (1902), as well as a *History of Oxfordshire* (1899), but is chiefly remembered for his three novels: *The Lost Stradivarius* (1895), a tale of the supernatural set largely in Oxford and Naples; *Moonfleet* (1898), a swift-moving historical romance involving smuggling; and *The Nebuly Coat* (1903), an antiquarian tale dealing with a church threatened by collapse. He also wrote poetry, a volume of which was published in 1933. See Kenneth Warren, *John Meade Falkner, 1858–1932: A Paradoxical Life* (1995).

Fall *See* BIBLE; EDEN, GARDEN OF.

Fall of Robespierre, The A radical drama written in 1794 by Samuel Taylor *Coleridge, who wrote Act I, and Robert *Southey, who wrote Acts II and III.

FALLOWELL, Duncan (1948–) Born in London and educated at Oxford University, novelist and travel writer. His sexually frank works include the innovative, gay travel books *One Hot Summer in St Petersburg* (1994) and *Going as Far as I Can* (2008), which is set in New Zealand.

False One, The A drama attributed to John *Fletcher, in which Philip *Massinger may also have had a share, performed 1621, printed 1647.

The play deals with the joint occupation of Egypt's throne by Ptolemy and his sister Cleopatra; the treacherous murder of Ptolemy by Septimius, 'the False One'; and Caesar's entanglement by the charms of Cleopatra.

Falstaff, Sir John A character in Shakespeare's *1* and *2* **Henry IV* and *The *Merry Wives of Windsor.* In the first play, Shakespeare seems originally to have named him after his historical original, the Wyclifite Sir John *Oldcastle, but to have been compelled to change the name after the play had been performed but before it was printed, after protests from Oldcastle's descendants, the Lords Cobham. The original name is restored in the Oxford *Complete Works.*

To Samuel *Johnson Falstaff is 'unimitated, unimitable', a 'compound of sense and vice', and he is the subject of an important critical essay by Maurice *Morgann. His orgins lie in the stock figure of the *Vice, together with some elements of the *miles gloriosus*, the 'boastful soldier' of Roman comedy. He is fat, witty, a lover of sack, and skilful at turning jokes on him to his own advantage—'I am not only witty in myself, but the cause that wit is in other men' (*2 Henry IV,* I. ii). In *1 Henry IV* he is shown as the drinking companion of Prince Harry, or Hal, and expects advancement when Harry becomes king. Harry humours him, allowing him to give his own version of the Gadshill encounter with the men 'in buckram', to mimic his father, Henry IV, and even to take credit for Hotspur's death at the battle of Shrewsbury. In *2 Henry IV* he is seen little with Harry, but is portrayed as old, ill, and unscrupulous in his financial dealings with Mistress Quickly and with his old friend Master Justice Shallow, from whom he borrows £1,000. His embodiment of anarchy is suggested in his confrontation with the lord chief justice (I. ii). On succeeding to the throne Harry, now Henry V, rejects him in the speech beginning 'I know thee not, old man. Fall to thy prayers', which Falstaff explains by assuring his friends that he will be sent for privately. In **Henry V,* however, Mistress Quickly tells us that 'the King has killed his heart' (II. i), and she later describes his death, in a tavern, in a speech which includes the famous line (as emended by *Theobald) 'his nose was as sharp as a pen, and a babbled of green fields'. The Falstaff of *The Merry Wives of Windsor* is a different figure, whose attempts to mend his fortunes by wooing two citizens' wives simultaneously end in his discomfiture in Windsor Forest. It is this Falstaff who is the subject of at least nine operas, including *Vaughan Williams's *Sir John in Love* (1929). *Elgar's symphonic study *Falstaff* (1913) is based on the Henry plays, while Verdi's opera *Falstaff* (1893) draws on both the Henry plays and *The Merry Wives of Windsor.* Falstaff is also the hero of an exuberant novel (1976) of that name by Robert *Nye.

family stories A genre popular in children's publishing since the 19th century. Initially, as in Mary *Sherwood's *The History of the Fairchild Family* (1818), books depicted nuclear families where the father 'stood in place of God'. Charlotte *Yonge was a major exponent of the genre, influencing writers such as Louisa M. *Alcott and Edith *Nesbit. Subsequently families were not invariably depicted as secure or perfect; by the late 20th century, portrayals of dysfunctional families had become common. Nevertheless, even in the broken/single-parent homes of contemporary writers such as Jacqueline *Wilson, the ideal of the family remains strong.

FANSHAWE, Anne, Lady (1625–80) Née Harrison, wife of Sir Richard *Fanshawe. She shared her husband's travels, and her affectionate *Memoirs,* written between 1674 and 1676, were first printed in 1829: 'whatever was real happiness, God gave it me in him.'

FANSHAWE, Sir Richard (1608–66) Poet, translator, diplomat, born in Hertfordshire and educated at Jesus College, Cambridge. He was a supporter of the Royalist cause, as was his wife Anne *Fanshawe, whom he married in 1644. After the *Restoration he served as ambassador in Portugal, then Spain, where he died. His first published work was a translation of *Guarini's *Il pastor fido* (*The Faithful Shepherd*, 1647): a reissue of this the following year contained some of his own poems, including a delightful ode urging the pleasures of country living, some accomplished *Spenserian stanzas, and sonnets from the Spanish, translated with much elegance. A selection from *Horace (1652) was followed by the *Lusiads* of *Camões (1655), which he prepared in retirement during the Civil War.

fantasy fiction During the second half of the 20th century fantasy fiction has become one of the most commercially successful literary genres. In one sense this is unsurprising. English literature containing elements of the fantastic is as old as the literature itself, including works like **Beowulf*, with fire-spewing dragon and man-eating ogres, *Sir *Gawain and the Green Knight*, with its enchantresses, Malory's *Le *Morte Darthur*, Spenser's *The *Faerie Queene*, or Shakespeare's **Midsummer Night's Dream* and *The *Tempest*, with their respective enchanted swords, knights, fairies, and wizards. The literature of the fantastic draws on a seemingly inexhaustible reservoir of concepts from the age-old, international, and pre-literary genre of the folk tale, or tale of wonder.

Literature of the fantastic may, however, be distinguished from fantasy fiction, a genre in some respects decisively modern. Readers in a period dominated by science and rationalism tended to accept the low rating given to fantasy and the fantastic by practitioners of the realistic novel, marginalizing fantasy into a form for satire, diversion, and above all for children. Major writers within this marginal/non-adult mode include George *MacDonald and Lewis *Carroll. Fantasy fiction, however, began to win a kind of autonomy as authors followed the late romances of William *Morris in creating imaginary otherworlds. Lord *Dunsany's short stories, beginning with *The Gods of Pegana* (1905), gave a major lead, although his influential novel *The King of Elfland's Daughter* did not appear until 1924. The location of Dunsany's fictions is often impossible to determine. At times set in a 'dreamworld' or on the borders of Faerie, they could also be set in earth's forgotten past or unknown future. All these locations, as used by later fantasy authors, liberate the reader from the constraints of the known while keeping a plausible inner coherence. The reader accepts the rules set up by the fiction, ignoring, or relishing, the contrast with everyday reality.

Fantasy fiction continued to be developed by writers such as E. R. *Eddison or Mervyn *Peake. Both these were, however, isolated figures. Fantasy fiction as genre began to create a readership for itself with the appearance of schools of writers, aware of each other's work, in (usually) monthly magazines in the USA.

The first of these was the group centred on **Weird Tales*, which included H. P. *Lovecraft, Robert E. *Howard, and Clark Ashton *Smith. Of these Lovecraft expanded Dunsany's 'imaginary mythologies', while Smith created a series of imaginary lands in far past or far future. Howard, perhaps, had the most generic influence, through his creation of the character Conan the Barbarian. *'Sword and sorcery' has remained prolific ever since, with Fritz Leiber (1910–92) and Michael *Moorcock among its most interesting exponents.

The other major early fantasy magazine was *Unknown*, which lasted for 39 issues between 1939 and 1943. *Unknown* took up the challenge of relating fantasy to the world of logic and science. Its authors typically worked from the premiss that magic could have been developed into a controllable technology, used in parallel with, or replacing, conventional science, in some parallel universe. 'Worlds where magic works' were created in *Unknown* by Robert *Heinlein and in particular by the 'Incomplete Enchanter' series of L. Sprague *de Camp and Fletcher *Pratt, where modern scientists move into the worlds of mythology or the romance settings of Spenser or *Ariosto. Fantasy fiction in the manner of *Unknown* is a highly rationalized and even argumentative mode.

The greatest influence within the fantasy genre, however, was another maverick, J. R. R. *Tolkien. His first published fantasy, *The Hobbit* (1937), was for children, but its three-volume successor *The *Lord of the Rings* (1954–5) attracted a mass adult readership and inspired generations of imitators. Tolkien's knowledge of Old English and Old Norse recreated the world of Germanic folk tale, with its dwarves, elves, trolls, and wizards, as a consistent and coherent whole. To this he added creatures of his own invention, such as hobbits; a complete mythology, chronology, and cartography; and a compelling story. Later authors followed him in recognizing the need to create other worlds whose complexity outruns the immediate needs of plot. Among the most significant of his followers are Stephen R. *Donaldson, David Eddings (1931–), and Robert *Jordan.

The continuing production of high-quality 'children's literature', or writing for young adults, such as Ursula K. *Le Guin's original 'Earthsea' sequence or the work of Diana Wynne *Jones, has also been important. So too has the revival, often by feminist authors such as Angela *Carter, of the traditional form of the *fairy-tale. The continuing ability of fantasy writers to write comically is best exemplified by the Discworld books of Terry *Pratchett. The first volume, *The Colour of Magic* (1983), parodied generic fantasy, but the series went on to create a world of its own. The feedback effect of role-playing games based upon fantasy scenarios has resulted in the intensifying (but also the manipulation) of stereotypes. A more recent trend came and went as the *New Weird, but the fruitful collision of modes is more generally exemplified by the highly detailed work of China *Miéville.

Reasons for the popular appeal of fantasy fiction no doubt include discontent with everyday life, openly voiced in Le Guin's *The Beginning Place* (1980). Fantasy has, however, also shown itself ready to deal with questions of contemporary importance, in particular, the nature and origins of evil. T. H. *White declared that the theme of his Arthurian fantasy *The Once and Future King*, written for the most part between 1938 and 1941, was to find 'an antidote to war'. This theme is powerful in the work of several of the authors mentioned above. Fantasy fiction has shown itself capable of dealing with topics which seem outside the range of the traditional realist novel, and speaks for and to a contemporary mass audience whose taste it has itself created. See Brian Attebery, *Strategies of Fantasy* (1992); John Clute and John Grant (eds), *The Encyclopedia of Fantasy* (1997).

FANTHORPE, U. A. (Ursula Askham) (1929–2009) Poet, born in Kent, and educated at St Anne's College, Oxford. A latecomer to writing, she was a teacher at Cheltenham Ladies' College and a hospital receptionist: that experience lies behind her first volume, *Side Effects* (1978). Other collections include *Standing To* (1982), *Safe as Houses* (1996), and *Queuing for the Sun* (2003). Her *Collected Poems* was published in 2004. Her poetry is lucid and accessible; her tone is both wry and lyrical, and her subject matter ranges from the classical to the historical and the domestic. She is also expert in the use of *dramatic monologue.

fanzines A term coined by *science fiction fan Russ Chauvenet in 1941 to describe the amateur magazines, published by fans for each other, in which much early bibliographical and critical discussion appeared. The word is now used to describe fan-produced publications in other fields.

FARAH, Nuruddin (1945–) Somali novelist. He says that 'I write because a theme has chosen me: the theme of Africa's upheaval and societal disorganisation. And I write in order to recover my missing half.' The sense of loss comes from spending over twenty years in exile from his native Somalia. Farah was born in Baidoa, attended Qur'ānic primary and secondary school, and went to Punjab University in Chandigarh. His work in Somali was censored and he left Somalia for Britain in 1974. He has lived in Italy, Los Angeles, Bayreuth, the Gambia, Khartoum, Kampala, and Jos. A cosmopolitan polyglot, his focus is always on Somalia, though the forms of the novels alter to suit the theme. *From a Crooked Rib* (1970) takes as its protagonist an uneducated woman who seeks gender equality in a world governed by a cruel patriarchy; Ebla's horror of infibulation recurs in Farah's later work. Characters reappear from book to book, creating for the reader a sense of family which Farah uses as a microcosm of the state. *A Naked Needle* (1976) was followed by three trilogies, the first *Variations on the Theme of an African Dictatorship. Sweet and Sour Milk* (1979) explores how a repressive regime operates as Loyaan tries to unravel the mystery of his twin's death. Medina, the protagonist in *Sardines* (1981), is packed in the state's tin by the regime but finds a way of resisting conformity. In *Close Sesame* (1983) the benign Muslim grandfather Deeriye unites faith with political commitment. In the second trilogy, *Blood in the Sun, Maps* (1986) presents two opposing concepts of national and individual identity, Hilaal's bounded and Misra's hybrid. *Gifts* (1993) and *Secrets* (1998) end the process with which *Maps* begins. *Territories* (2000) was followed by the first two parts of a new trilogy, *Links* (2005) and *Knots* (2007).

farce A form of popular comedy with its distant roots in the improvisations which actors introduced into the text of medieval religious dramas (the word is derived from French *farce*, literally 'stuffing'). Later forms include the *interludes performed in the 15th and 16th centuries, and the classical farce of *Molière, whose works were freely adapted by British dramatists. The 19th-century middle-class French farce, as practised by Eugène Labiche (1815–88), Georges Feydeau (1862–1921), and Georges Courteline (1858–1929), has also proved popular in adaptation. In England, the full-length home-grown farce emerged in the 19th century: Morton's **Box and Cox* was a famous if isolated example, and *Pinero also wrote several, including *The Magistrate* (1885), *The Schoolmistress* (1886), and *Dandy Dick* (1887). *Gilbert and Sullivan's farcical comic operas belong to the same period. *Charley's Aunt* (1892) by Brandon Thomas (1856–1914), a comedy with an excellent opportunity for cross-dressing (an Oxford undergraduate impersonates his own rich Brazilian aunt), is still frequently performed. The term 'farce' is now generally used to cover a form of theatre which employs ridiculous situations, mistaken identities, split-second timing, and marital misadventures (hence the term 'bedroom farce'): later exponents include Ben Travers (1886–1980), whose celebrated 'Aldwych farces' included *A Cuckoo in the Nest* and *Rookery Nook*, both 1926; Ray Cooney (1932–), who wrote many plays for actor-manager Brian Rix at the Whitehall; Alan *Ayckbourn, Michael *Frayn, Joe *Orton, and Tom *Stoppard. Dario *Fo is notable among those who have used the farce for serious political purposes. Television has produced a new genre of serial and surreal farce in the Monty Python series and John Cleese's popular hotel comedy *Fawlty Towers*, which has generated many imitators.

Far from the Madding Crowd A novel by Thomas *Hardy, published 1874. The title is a quotation from Gray's **Elegy Written in a Country Church-Yard*. The theme, in this and other novels by Hardy, is the contrast of a patient and generous love with unscrupulous passion. The plot was more complex and dramatic than anything Hardy had previously attempted, and the book quickly achieved a wide popularity, which has endured. The shepherd Gabriel Oak serves the young and spirited Bathsheba Everdene, owner of the farm, with unselfish devotion. She depends on his support, but cannot regard him as a suitor. Another of her admirers is a neighbouring farmer, Boldwood. The dashing Sergeant Troy loves one of Bathsheba's servants, Fanny Robin, but after a fatal misunderstanding deserts her, and she eventually dies in childbirth in the workhouse. Troy has meanwhile captivated and married Bathsheba, but soon begins to neglect and ill-treat her. When he hears of Fanny's death he disappears, and is thought to have been drowned. Farmer Boldwood, now obsessed with Bathsheba, gives a party at which he pledges Bathsheba to marry him some time in the future. Troy reappears at the party and Boldwood, driven to madness by his reappearance, shoots him. Boldwood is tried and pronounced insane. Gabriel and Bathsheba are at last married. Hardy made a stage version of the novel, produced by the Hardy Players in Dorchester in 1924. Later adaptations for radio, theatre, and cinema, including a successful film with Julie Christie, Terence Stamp, and Alan Bates (1967), have been numerous.

FARJEON, Eleanor (1881–1965) Born in London into a highly literary Hampstead family; she received little formal education. Her career as a children's writer began with *Nursery Rhymes of London Town* (1916); her reputation was established with *Martin Pippin in the Apple Orchard* (1921; not originally intended for children), which she followed with many volumes of poems, plays, fantasies, and stories and *A Nursery in the Nineties* (1935), reminiscences of her childhood. She lived in Sussex, which features in her writing, and was a close friend of and wrote about Edward *Thomas. See Eileen Colwell, *Eleanor Farjeon* (1961).

FARLEY, Paul (1965–) Poet and occasional radio dramatist, born in Liverpool; educated at the Chelsea School of Art and Design. His first collection, *The Boy from the Chemist is Here to See You* (1998), was welcomed for its formal dexterity, evocation of place, and often deadpan humour. *The Ice Age* (2002) and *Tramp in Flames* (2006) saw him continuing to evoke and transform vivid childhood memories against the backdrop of an increasingly dreamlike cityscape. His study of the Liverpool film-maker Terence Davies (1945–) draws extensively on his own experience of growing up in the 1960s and 1970s.

FARMER, Philip José (1918–2009) American *science fiction and *fantasy author, born in Terre Haute, Indiana; *To your Scattered Bodies Go* (1971) and its sequels envisage all humanity resurrected on the shores of a huge river. *Tarzan Alive* (1972) is part of a playful series of metafictional 'biographies' connecting the heroes of genre fiction.

Farmer's Boy, The See Bloomfield, Robert.

FARQUHAR, George (1677–1707) Playwright, born in Londonderry, educated at Trinity College, Dublin. He had become an actor by 1696 but gave up the stage after accidentally wounding a fellow player. He moved to London and began writing comedies: *Love and a Bottle* (1698); *The Constant Couple* (1699); *Sir Harry Wildair*, its sequel (1701); *The Inconstant* (based on John *Fletcher's *The Wild Goose Chase*) and *The Twin Rivals* (1702); *The Stage Coach*, with Peter *Motteux (1704); and after a brief military career, *The *Recruiting Officer* (1706) and *The *Beaux' Stratagem* (1707). A present of 20 guineas from the actor-manager Robert Wilks (*c*.1655–1732) enabled the impoverished Farquhar to complete this last play, staged just before he died. He also wrote a novella, *The Adventures of Covent Garden* (1698), and *Love and Business* (1702), consisting of letters and poems, including a self-portrait. See *The Works of George Farquhar*, ed. S. S. Kenny, 2 vols (1988).

FARRAR, F. W. (Frederic William) (1831–1903) Philosopher and theologian, eventually dean of Canterbury, born in India, educated at King William's College, Isle of Man, King's College London, and Cambridge, where he became a fellow of Trinity College. While a master at Harrow School, he published the enormously successful *Eric, or Little by Little* (1858), a partly autobiographical **school story* about 12-year-old Eric Williams, who is bullied and corrupted at school despite the efforts of his noble friend Edwin Russell. Following Edwin's death—and that of Eric's younger brother—the dissipated boy runs away to sea where he is badly treated but morally saved. His reputation restored, he makes a good death surrounded by his former schoolmates. As well as many works of theology, Farrar also wrote *Julian Home: A Tale of College Life* (1859) and *St Winifred's, or The World of School* (1862).

FARRELL, J. G. (James Gordon) (1935–79) Novelist. Born in Liverpool, the son of an accountant, he was educated at Rossall School and Brasenose College, Oxford, where, in his first term, he contracted poliomyelitis. He later travelled widely in America, Europe, and the East. His first novel, *A Man from Elsewhere* (1963), was set in France, his second, *The Lung* (1965), describes the experiences of a polio victim, and *A Girl in the Head* (1967) the desultory adventures of Count Boris Slattery in an English seaside town called Maidenhair. His first substantial novel, *Troubles* (1970), is set in Ireland, in the decaying Majestic Hotel, just after the First World War, against a background of Sinn Fein violence. *The Siege of Krishnapur* (1973, *Booker Prize) deals with the events of the Indian Mutiny, in a characteristically ironic and comic vein. *The Singapore Grip* (1978) moves closer to the epic, blending real and fictitious characters and describing the fall of Singapore to the Japanese, an event which Farrell portrays as a death-blow to the British Empire. His last three novels involved considerable historical research, and all reflect a sense of the end of the empire and the stubborn, at times heroic, at times stupid, refusal of his characters to recognize the course of history. His most vivid creation is Major Brendan Archer, courteous, faithful, and chivalrous, holding fast to his own code of civilized conduct in increasingly violent circumstances: he appears in *Troubles* and again in *The Singapore Grip*. Similarly, the sardonic, kindly, rationalist Dr McNab from *The Siege* reappears in *The Hill Station* (1981), which was left unfinished when Farrell was accidentally drowned, shortly after moving from London to Ireland.

FARRELL, James Thomas (1904–79) American naturalist novelist, Chicago-born, and best known in Britain for his trilogy about Studs Lonigan, a young Chicago Catholic of Irish descent. *Young Lonigan* (1932) describes his boyhood, *The Young Manhood of Studs Lonigan* (1934) his desultory career as house painter, small-time crook, and so on, and *Judgement Day* (1935) his unemployment during the Depression and early death from a heart condition aggravated by poor living.

Fascism Italian political movement and later political party, founded in 1919 in reaction to the disaffection following the post-war political settlement. It is principally associated with Benito Mussolini (1883–1945), who seized power in 1922, establishing the Fascist regime which lasted until Mussolini's downfall in summer 1943 following the Allied landings in Sicily. Though totalitarian in its aims and operations, at least until the alliance with Nazi Germany (1938) the regime did not consistently demand ideological conformity from the literary establishment. In its early years Fascism attracted the support of Filippo *Marinetti, Giuseppe *Ungaretti, and Luigi *Pirandello. Writers generally considered anti-Fascist include Vasco Pratolini (1913–91), Ignazio *Silone, and Elio *Vittorini. The nationalist element of Fascism led to the promotion of the cult of writers as diverse as *Dante and *d'Annunzio.

fashionable novel ('silver-fork school') A class of novel, popular *c.*1825–50, which held up for admiration the lives of the wealthy and fashionable. Theodore *Hook was one of the leaders of this popular school of writing. William *Hazlitt, in his essay on 'The Dandy School' (**Examiner*, 1827), castigates the narrow superficiality of such novels which encourage the reader, he feels, only to 'the admiration of the folly, caprice, insolence, and affectation of a certain class'. Edward *Bulwer-Lytton (whose own **Pelham* was a celebrated example) held that the genre was influential in the paradoxical sense that its effect was ultimately to expose 'the falsehood, the hypocrisy, the arrogant and vulgar insolence of patrician life'. M. W. Rosa, in *The Silver-Fork School* (1936), discusses the work of Susan *Ferrier, Thomas *Lister, Benjamin *Disraeli, Plumer *Ward, Catherine *Gore, and others, and argues that the school 'culminated in a single great book—*Vanity Fair*'. See A. Adburgham, *Silver Fork Society: Fashionable Life and Literature from 1814 to 1840* (1983).

FAST, Howard Melvin (1914–2003) American novelist, born in New York, who joined the Communist Party in 1944 and was jailed in 1950 for contempt of Congress. Although he had started publishing earlier, in this period he wrote *Spartacus* (1951), his famous novel about the Roman slave revolt. Fast renounced communism and in 1957 published his memoir on the Communist Party, *The Naked God*. The son of a Ukrainian Jewish family, Fast turned to these subjects in his later novels, which included *The Crossing* (1971) and *The Immigrants* (1977). He also published a number of science fiction stories (*A Touch of Infinity*, 1973) and under the pen-name E. V. Cunningham published the Masao Masuto Mysteries (1967–84). His autobiography *Being Red* came out in 1990.

FASTOLF, Sir John (1380–1459) Distinguished soldier and benefactor of Magdalen College, Oxford. He was the patron of William Worcester, who wrote the *Boke of Noblesse*, and stepfather of Stephen Scrope, who translated *Christine de Pisan's *Epistle of Othea*. He appears in the *Paston Letters. Shakespeare's Falstaff owes nothing to Fastolf beyond his name. *1* **Henry VI* presents Fastolf as a coward who betrays Talbot and is stripped of his Garter; however, the real Talbot's case against Fastolf was unsuccessful.

Fatal Curiosity, The Blank verse tragedy by George *Lillo, successfully produced by Henry *Fielding in 1736. Old Wilmot, under stress of poverty and urged by his wife, murders a stranger who has deposited a casket with them, only to find the victim is his son, supposed lost in a shipwreck. The plot is archetypal and appears in many literatures; Lillo's version influenced the German 'fate-drama', and Albert *Camus used it in *Le Malentendu* (1945).

Fatal Dowry, The A tragedy by Philip *Massinger and Nathan *Field, acted *c.*1616–18, printed 1632. The play is based on one of the *controversiae* (or imaginary legal disputes) of Seneca the elder. Charalois's father, marshal of the duke of Burgundy, dies in debt, and his creditors refuse to allow his body to be buried. Charalois goes to prison, with his friend Romont, to secure the release of the body. Rochfort, ex-president of the parliament, touched by Charalois's piety and Romont's honesty, procures their release, and arranges the marriage of his daughter Beaumelle with Charalois. She is found by Romont exchanging kisses with her former lover, the fop Novall. Charalois, at first incredulous, also discovers Beaumelle and Novall together, and kills Novall in a duel. Rochfort condemns Beaumelle, and Charalois stabs her. But the father then accuses Charalois of ruthlessness. Charalois is tried for the murder of Novall and Beaumelle and acquitted, but is killed by a friend of Novall, who in turn is killed by Romont. Nicholas Rowe's *The *Fair Penitent* is founded on this play.

Fatal Marriage, The, *or The Innocent Adultery* A tragedy by Thomas *Southerne, performed 1694. Biron, having married Isabella against his father's wish, is sent by him to the siege of Candy and reported killed. His widow is repudiated by the father and brought to misery. During seven years she is courted by Villeroy, and finally, from gratitude for his devotion and urged by Carlos, Biron's younger brother, she marries him. Biron, who has all this time been a captive, now returns and reveals himself to Isabella. Carlos, it now appears, had known that Biron was alive, but had concealed his knowledge, wishing to oust him from the succession. For the same reason he had urged the marriage of Isabella, in order finally to ruin her and her son in his father's estimation. Carlos waylays and mortally wounds Biron. Isabella, already overwhelmed by the situation in which she finds herself, kills herself. The guilt of Carlos is exposed. The play is founded on Aphra *Behn's novel *The Nun, or The Perjured Beauty* but, unlike Behn's heroine, Southerne's Isabella is portrayed as a helpless victim, 'born to suffer' and condemned by fate to 'a long line of woe'. The role was originally played by Elizabeth

*Barry with great effect, and was subsequently played by many leading actresses, including Susanna *Cibber (1714–66), Sarah *Siddons, and Fanny *Kemble. The play was revived by David *Garrick in 1757 as *Isabella, or The Fatal Marriage*.

Father and Son Memoir by Edmund *Gosse of his relationship with his father, Philip Henry Gosse, published in 1907. His mother died early and his father, a member of the Plymouth Brethren, was, though a noted naturalist, at odds with Darwin. The book documents Gosse's unhappy struggle as he gradually rejects his father's religious beliefs.

Fathers of the church The early Christian writers, a term usually applied to those of the first five centuries. Sometimes the Greek and Latin Fathers are distinguished, the former including Clement of Alexandria (*c*.150–*c*.215), the first to apply *Platonic philosophy to the exposition of Christianity, *Origen, Athanasius (*c*.296–373), the scourge of *Arianism, Basil the Great (*c*.330–79), Gregory Nazianzen (329/30–398/90), and *Chrysostom; the latter Tertullian (*c*.160–*c*.225), who was hostile to classical learning, Cyprian (d. 258), *Jerome, Ambrose (*c*.339–97), who introduced hymns into the Roman church, *Augustine, *Gregory (Pope Gregory I), and *Bernard.

FAULKNER, (originally Falkner) William (1897–1962) American novelist, born in Mississippi, where he spent most of his life; the history and legends of the South provided material for his greater books. After a desultory education and working at various odd jobs, while working as a journalist in New Orleans he met Sherwood *Anderson, who encouraged him to write his first novel, *Soldier's Pay* (1926). This was followed by others, including *Sartoris* (1929), the first of the series in which he describes the decline of the Compson and Sartoris families, representative of the Old South, and the rise of the crude and unscrupulous Snopes family. The principal setting of these novels is 'Jefferson'—a composite picture of several Mississippi towns—in the mythical Yoknapatawpha County. *The Sound and the Fury* (1929) is a narrative tour de force in which Faulkner views the decline of the South through several eyes, most remarkably those of Benjy Compson, a 33-year-old 'idiot'. *As I Lay Dying* (1930) is equally distinguished, and demonstrates Faulkner's comic as well as his tragic vision, in his account of the death of poor white Addie Bundren, and of her children's grotesque attempts to fulfil her wish to be buried in Jefferson. He made his name, however, not with these but with a more sensational work, *Sanctuary* (1931). *Light in August* (1932) and *Absalom, Absalom!* (1936) confirmed his reputation as one of the finest of modern novelists. Other important works include *The Hamlet* (1940), *Intruder in the Dust* (1948), and several volumes of short stories, collected in 1950. In the 1930s and 1940s he worked in Hollywood and collaborated with Howard Hawks on the adaptation of Ernest *Hemingway's novel *To Have and Have Not* (1944) as well as on *The Big Sleep* (1946). *Faulkner's MGM Screenplays* was published in 1982. He was awarded the *Nobel Prize in 1949. See Joseph Blotner, *Faulkner: A Biography* (1974).

FAULKS, Sebastian (1953–) Novelist and journalist, born in Berkshire, educated at Emmanuel College, Cambridge. His first novel was *A Trick of the Light* (1984), but his reputation rests chiefly on a series of skilfully researched novels in which fictional individuals are caught up in large historical events. His 'French trilogy' comprises *The Girl at the Lion d'Or* (1988), which in describing a tragic love affair in rural France encompasses French politics during the 1930s; the hugely popular *Birdsong* (1993), which recreates the world of sappers on the Western Front in the First World War; and *Charlotte Gray* (1998), in which the eponymous heroine joins the SOE (Special Operations Executive) in order to look for her lover, a pilot who has gone missing in Nazi-occupied France. *On Green Dolphin Street* (2001) is set largely in America during the Cold War era, while later novels such as *Human Traces* (2005), set in the 19th century, and *Engleby* (2007), set in the 1970s, explore mental illness. His non-fiction includes a volume of pastiches, *Pistache* (2006), and *The Fatal Englishman: Three Short Lives* (1996), biographical essays, linked by a common theme of the self-destructive impulse, of the painter Christopher Wood (1901–30), the pilot and author Richard *Hillary, and the journalist Jeremy Wolfenden (1934–65). In 2008, he published a pastiche James Bond adventure novel, *Devil May Care*.

Faust As a figure of legend, the dissatisfied scholar who concludes a pact with the devil which finally costs him his soul. The legend, possibly based on a historical figure, originated in 16th-century Germany and appears for the first time in a *chapbook of 1587. The story was swiftly translated and used by Christopher *Marlowe in **Dr Faustus*. In Germany the story gradually dwindled to a subject for puppet theatre and received no treatment of comparable poetic stature until it was taken up again by *Goethe. The poetic drama *Faust* grew into a lifetime's work: a fragment was published in 1790, but it saw completion in two parts, the first published in 1808, the second in the year of his death, 1832. Goethe's treatment marks a radical revision of the original theme; the pact takes the form of a wager, and at the end of *Part II*, with the hero 100 years old, *Mephistopheles fails to win his soul. It was, however, *Faust, Part I* which made the greater impact in 19th-century England. It too marked a significant revision of the legend as the drama revolves around Faust's love affair with Gretchen. The work was viewed as potentially offensive to English taste, and the first translations omitted the 'offensive' matter, but in 1822 P. B. *Shelley's translations of the scenes concerned appeared in Leigh *Hunt's *The Liberal*. Lord *Byron was a great admirer of Goethe, and the work's influence can be detected in **Manfred*. Byron was in turn greatly admired by Goethe, and in *Part II* Byron figures as Euphorion, the doomed offspring of Faust and Helen of Troy. It seems to have been Goethe's version which was responsible for the modern revival of the legend, and there have been many literary treatments of the theme since. Heinrich *Heine attempted a version, as did Thomas *Mann in his novel *Doktor Faustus* (1948), and Robert *Nye's novel *Faust* (1980) also returns to the theme. In music, Charles *Gounod's operatic treatment (*Faust*, 1859) is based on Goethe, but there is even a modern rap version by the jazz violinist and composer Leroy Jenkins (1932–2007). It can be said that the notion of a 'Faustian Pact' has entered popular consciousness.

Faustus, Doctor See Dr Faustus.

Fawn, The See Parasitaster.

Feast of Fools A medieval festival originally of the sub-deacons of the cathedral, held about the time of the Feast of the Circumcision (1 January), in which the humbler cathedral officials burlesqued the sacred ceremonies. A lord of the feast was elected, styled bishop, cardinal, abbot, etc., according to the locality. (*See also* fool.) The Feast of Fools had its chief vogue in the French cathedrals, but there are a few English records of it, notably in Lincoln Cathedral and Beverley Minster. See E. K. *Chambers, *The Mediaeval Stage* (1903).

FEAVER, Vicki (1943–) Poet, born in Nottingham and educated at the universities of Durham and London. *Close Relatives* (1981) introduced Feaver's characteristic style: deceptively plain language enlivened by taut rhythms and suddenly enlarged by boldly imaginative metaphors. *The Handless Maiden* (1994) is more clearly feminist in theme, and more emphatic in its use of myth and biblical narrative, both as metaphor and in *dramatic monologues such as 'Circe' and the celebrated 'Judith'. *The Book of Blood* (2006) engages in forms of what has been called the 'domestic gothic', suggesting affinities with the work of Stevie *Smith; as in Smith, too, violence of various kinds is never far away.

FEDERMAN, Raymond (1928–) French-born American novelist and critic, who emigrated to the USA and completed a doctorate on Samuel *Beckett at the University of California (Los Angeles), published in 1965 as *Journey into Chaos: Samuel Beckett's Early Fiction*. As a child, Federman was hidden in a closet by his mother to avoid deportation to the concentration camps by the Nazis, a traumatic experience to which he gave expression in the trilingual volume *The Voice in the Closet* (1989). Federman has produced playful *postmodern texts which, as he puts it in his 1993 collection of essays *Critifiction*, 'challenge the traditional bases of both cultural and aesthetic judgement'. His novels never allow readers to forget the fictiveness of the work and frequently experiment with typography, as in *Double or Nothing* (1971) and *Take It or Leave It* (1976). Another constant in his works has been authorial reference, with play on his name (penman, l'homme de la plume). *My Body in Nine Parts* (2005) is a prose self-anatomy. In 1967 he published his first (bilingual) volume of poems, *Among the Beasts*, and he has also written a number of plays, which were collected as *The Precipice & Other Catastrophes* (1999). Federman was active in the *Fiction Collective and promoted experimental fiction in his edited collection *Surfiction* (1975; expanded 1981). See the 1998 casebook, *Federman from A to X-X-X-X*.

FEIFFER, Jules (1929–) American cartoonist, novelist, and dramatist, who was born in New York. His cartoons ran in the *Village Voice* (1956–97) and made major satirical statements on contemporary America; for example, his first collection *Sick, Sick, Sick* (1958) engaged with fears of nuclear war and helped establish Feiffer's characteristic black humour. Among his plays, *Little Murders* (1968) deals with the random violence of New York life. His novels include *Harry the Rat Man with Women* (1963) and *Ackroyd* (1977). He has written a number of screenplays and stories for children.

FEINSTEIN, Elaine (1930–) Poet, novelist, translator, and biographer, born in Bootle and educated at Newnham College, Cambridge. Her first volume of poetry, *In a Green Eye*, appeared in 1966. Others include *Badlands* (1986), *Daylight* (1997), and *Gold* (2000). Her work is feminist, prominently preoccupied with European Jewish experience and family life, and influenced by American modernism. She has also published biographies whose subjects include the poets *Pushkin, *Tsvetaeva (whom she has translated), *Akhmatova, D. H. *Lawrence, and Ted *Hughes. In the latter two she focuses on the relationships between these male writers and the various women in their lives. *Collected Poems and Translations* appeared in 2003. Her novels, which, despite some experiment, are primarily realistic, include *The Circle* (1970), *Children of the Rose* (1975), *The Shadow Master* (1979), and *Loving Brecht* (1992); again, Jewish experience is a major subject.

FEIST, Raymond Elias (1945–) American *fantasy writer, born in Los Angeles; his 'Riftwar' series, beginning with *Magician* (1982), is set in a world originally devised as a *fantasy role-playing game. Most of his work is post-*Tolkien fantasy, although *Faerie Tale* (1988) puts our world and Faerie into collision.

Félibrige A literary movement founded in 1854 by seven *Provençal poets under the leadership of Frédéric Mistral (1830–1914) to foster a renaissance of Provençal writing. Its most memorable products are Mistral's vernacular epics *Mireio* (1859) and *Calendau* (1867). It has served as an inspiration to a number of more recent movements favouring dispossessed languages and cultures.

Felix Holt, the Radical A novel by George *Eliot, published 1866. Set in 1832 in Loamshire, it vividly evokes the political ferment and corrupt electioneering tactics of the times. Harold Transome arrives home after many years in the East to inherit the family estate on his elder brother's death, and startles his family by standing as a Radical candidate. He is good-natured and intelligent, but his political convictions are not incompatible with buying beer for the local workers to secure their support. His character is strongly contrasted with that of Felix Holt, austere, idealistic, and passionate, who although educated has chosen the life of an artisan, and aims to stir his fellow workers to a sense of their own worth and destiny. The heroine, Esther, who supposes herself to be the daughter of old Lyon, the Independent minister, has an innate love of refinement, and when Felix chastises her for her frivolity she gains a new consciousness, and gradually falls in love with him. A complex chain of events reveals that Esther is in fact the heir to the Transome estate; Harold woos her, from motives not entirely mercenary, and Esther is forced to choose between his worldly attractions, and poverty with Felix, who has been imprisoned for his rash but innocent involvement in a riot. She renounces her claim to the estate and chooses Felix. It is finally revealed to Harold (the reader having known from the beginning) that he is not his father's son, but the son of the hated lawyer Jermyn; the account of the years of suffering of the proud and lonely Mrs Transome, subjected in secrecy to a man she no longer respects, ever fearful of her son's discovery, befriended only by her faithful servant Denner, is often considered the most powerful feature of the novel.

FELL, Dr John (1625–86) Dean of Christ Church, Oxford, and bishop of Oxford, and an early promoter of the *Oxford University Press, to the development of which he greatly contributed. Fell was author of a critical edition of Cyprian (1682), and edited with many arbitrary alterations the *Historia Universitatis Oxoniensis* of Anthony *Wood. He is the subject of the well-known epigram beginning 'I do not love you, Dr Fell', a translation by Thomas *Brown of *Martial, *Epigrams*, I. 32.

FELL, Margaret (1614–1702) An early leader of the Society of *Friends, converted by George *Fox in 1652 during his stay at her home, Swarthmore, in Cumberland, which became the Friends' administrative centre. She was of gentry origin, a powerful character and an organizer of genius, who coordinated the growing movement, wrote copiously on religious and political issues, interceded personally with Charles II on behalf of persecuted Friends, and suffered grievous imprisonments in the 1660s. She became the first to express the Friends' peace principles in 1660, and claimed full spiritual equality for women in *Women's Speaking Justified* (1666). After the death of her first husband, Judge Thomas Fell, she married Fox in 1669, but chiefly lived and travelled apart from him, continuing her radical activities into her eighties. See M. M. Ross, *Margaret Fell: Mother of Quakerism* (1984 edn); B. Y. Kunze, *Margaret Fell and the Rise of Quakerism* (1994); S. Davies, *Unbridled Spirits* (1998).

FELLTHAM, Owen (?1602–68) Essayist and poet. He published a series of moral essays, *Resolves* (*c.*1620), when 18 years old, contributed to *Jonsonus Virbius* (*see* JONSON, BEN), famously called Charles I 'Christ the Second', and published a *Brief Character of the Low Countries* (1652).

Female Quixote, The, *or The Adventures of Arabella* A novel by Charlotte *Lennox (1752). Arabella is a young, beautiful, and female version of *Cervantes's Quixote. The daughter of a marquis, growing up in a remote castle with a passion for reading chivalric romances, with no 'correction' from reality, she assumes that all men are her slaves, potential abductors, or ravishers; innocent men are constantly thrown into confusion by her impassioned accusations. After many ludicrous events at home, she travels, with her devoted cousin Mr Glanville and others, to Bath and London, where her misreading of the world causes great perplexity, a duel, and illness. An elderly clergyman reclaims her from the powerful fantasy through which she has apparently mastered her environment, and she duly marries her patient protector Glanville. Samuel *Richardson and Samuel *Johnson offered suggestions towards the writing of the novel, which was warmly reviewed by Henry *Fielding.

Female Tatler, The Light satirical periodical which began on 8 July 1709 under the editorship of 'Phoebe Crackenthorpe, a lady that knows everything', in rivalry with Richard *Steele's the **Tatler.* From issue 53 it was 'written by a society of ladies'; it closed in March 1710. The actual authorship is not known.

feminine rhyme *See* RHYME.

feminist criticism A modern tradition of commentary and polemic devoted to the analysis of women's literary work, and of their representation in literature. The beginnings of this movement are to be found in the journalism of Rebecca *West from about 1910. More influential as founding documents are the essays of Virginia *Woolf, notably *A Room of one's Own* (1929), and Simone de *Beauvoir's book *Le Deuxième Sexe* (1949; *The Second Sex*, 1953). In its developed form, the tradition was reborn amid the cultural ferment of the post-1968 period, especially in the United States. The misogynist or belittling attitudes of male critics and novelists were subjected to ironic scrutiny in Mary Ellmann's *Thinking about Women* (1968) and to iconoclastic rage in Kate Millett's *Sexual Politics* (1970), the latter work berating D. H. *Lawrence and Norman *Mailer in particular. Many feminist academics continued the investigation into stereotyped representations of female characters. Examinations of the offences of male writers tended to give way in the later 1970s to woman-centred literary histories seeking to trace an autonomous tradition of women's literature and to redeem neglected female authors. Influential examples of such work in America were Ellen Moers, *Literary Women* (1976), Elaine Showalter, *A Literature of their Own* (1977), and Sandra M. Gilbert and Susan Gubar, *The Madwoman in the Attic* (1979). By the beginning of the 1980s, feminist criticism was becoming more self-critical and internally differentiated: the mainstream of American feminist criticism eschewed 'male' literary theory and saw its own purpose as the affirmation of distinctly female 'experience' as reflected in writing; but black-feminist and lesbian-feminist critics objected that their own experiences were being overlooked.

Meanwhile the value of 'experience' as a clue to women's writing was doubted by feminists allied to *Marxist criticism, *psychoanalytic criticism, and post-*structuralism especially but not exclusively in Britain and France. One such school, led by the French writers Julia *Kristeva, Hélène Cixous, and Luce *Irigaray, sought to define an *écriture féminine* (for which 'feminine writing' would be a misleading translation) on the basis of a psychological 'politics' of language itself: if language belongs not to women but to a masculine social order, the distinctive female literary strategy will be to subvert it with bodily, even orgasmic, pulsations. British feminist criticism, although drawing upon both American and French approaches, has usually been more historical and sociological. Feminist criticism has thus become a varied field of debate rather than an agreed position. Its substantial achievements are seen in the readmission of temporarily forgotten women authors to the literary *canon, in modern reprints and newly commissioned studies by feminist publishing houses such as the *Virago Press (1977) and the Women's Press (1978), in anthologies and academic courses. See Gill Plain and Susan Sellers (eds.), *A History of Feminist Literary Criticism* (2007).

FÉNELON, François de Salignac de la Mothe (1651–1715) French theologian and man of letters. Appointed archbishop of Cambrai in 1695, he wielded considerable influence at court. For his pupil the duc de Bourgogne, Louis XIV's grandson, he wrote *c.*1695 *Télémaque*, a pedagogical romance based on Telemachus' voyage in the **Odyssey* and intended to teach the skills and virtues of the enlightened monarch; but Louis XIV saw the work as a critique of his regime, and Fénelon was disgraced. However, he went on to enjoy a reputation as a precursor of the *Enlightenment, and *Télémaque* was frequently reprinted and translated in the 18th century.

Fenian cycle Also known as the Fionn cycle and the Ossianic cycle, a body of stories and verses featuring *Finn, son of Cumhal, and his band of 3rd-century hunter warriors, the Fianna (or Fenians). The early tales were set in Munster and Leinster, but as they spread throughout the Gaelic world they absorbed details of other localities: James *Macpherson's **Fingal* appears to have been based on later Highland ballad versions. Pagan and Christian values confront each other in the 12th-century monastic compilation *Acallam na Seanórach* (*The Colloquy of the Elders*) through the debates between Finn's long-lived son *Oisín and St *Patrick.

FENN, Lady Eleanor (Ellenor) (1743–1813) Writing primarily as 'Mrs Teachwell' for the printer-publisher John Marshall, a popular, prolific, Norfolk-based writer best known for *Cobwebs to Catch Flies* (*c.*1873). Although childless, like many women writers of her day, she was interested in and experimented with new ways to instruct children.

FENN, George Manville (1831–1909) Born in London, and largely self-educated. He is remembered as a prolific writer of boys' adventure stories, often serialized in periodicals such as the *Boy's Own Paper*, beginning with *Hollowdell Grange* (1867). Fenn also wrote a biography of his friend G. A. *Henty (1907).

FENTON, James (1949–) Poet, essayist, and journalist, born in Lincoln, educated at Magdalen College, Oxford. He has worked as a political journalist for the *New Statesman*, as a freelance correspondent in Indo-China, as theatre critic of the *Sunday Times* and as chief book reviewer for *The *Times*, and as a columnist for the **Guardian*. Elected professor of poetry at Oxford in 1994, he published his lectures as *The Strength of Poetry* in 2001. The main stylistic influence on his work is W. H. *Auden. His first collection, *Terminal Moraine* (1972), displayed an imagination hungry for stimulus of all kinds, from politics to anthropology and horticulture. *The Memory of War and Children in Exile: Poems 1968–1983* (1983) is similarly eclectic in its inspiration and exuberant in execution, although several pieces, grounded in his experiences as a reporter, display sombre authority in the contemplation of war and its aftermath: 'A German Requiem' is outstanding in its portrayal of post-war German 'forgetting'. *Manila Envelope* (1989) was published from the Philippines, where he was working as a correspondent: it expresses panic and desperation as nonsense verse. A collection of his reportage from Vietnam, Korea, and the Philippines, including his celebrated eyewitness account of the fall of Saigon, was also published in 1989 as *All the Wrong Places: Adrift in the Politics of Asia*. *Out of Danger* appeared in 1993, and his *Selected Poems* was published in 2006. Both disclose a delight in popular forms of verse; and Fenton is a brilliant reciter, from memory, of his own work. In a prolific career he has also worked as a librettist, translator, and anthologist, and published extensively on both gardening and painting, including *Leonardo's Nephew: Essays on Art and Artists* (1995).

FERBER, Edna (1885–1968) American novelist and playwright, whose many works have been praised for their documentary realism. She began her career as a journalist and later served as a war correspondent in the Second World War. Several of her works were adapted for stage or screen; for example, the novel *Show Boat* (1926) formed the basis for Jerome Kern's 1927 musical, and *Cimarron* (1930) was adapted by Louis Sarecky for his 1931 film. Several of her works deal with Oklahoma life, *Giant* (1952) with the rich of Texas.

Ferdinand Count Fathom, *The Adventures of* A novel by Tobias *Smollett, published 1753. In the 'Dedication' Smollett outlines his theory of the novel as 'a large diffused picture' dominated by a central figure surrounded by various groups and episodes. In these *Adventures* the monstrous figure of Ferdinand is contrasted with the noble Count de Melvil and his son, with whom he is brought up. Actually the son of a camp-follower of Marlborough's army, Ferdinand uses his social position, talents, and charm to win social, sexual, and economic success as 'Count Fathom' in Vienna and London. In Bristol he is caught cheating at cards and imprisoned. Freed by young Melvil, his attempts to continue his career are repeatedly thwarted and he disappears, faintly remorseful, from the story, which then relates, with increasing sentiment and many frissons of horror, the misfortunes and eventual union of young Melvil and his love Monimia.

FERGUSON, Adam (1723–1816) Philosopher, born in Perthshire; he succeeded David *Hume as Advocates' librarian in 1757, and was successively professor of natural philosophy, moral philosophy and 'pneumatics', and mathematics at Edinburgh. He was a member of the *Select Society and co-founder of the *Royal Society of Edinburgh. In *The Morality of Stage-Plays Seriously Considered* (1757), he defended John *Home's **Douglas*. *An Essay on the History of Civil Society* (1767) was a pioneer work in political sociology; it contained a discussion 'Of the History of Literature', which argues that poetry is a more natural form of literary expression than prose, and that literature develops better during periods of social activity than in leisure and solitude. *The History of the Progress and Termination of the Roman Republic* (3 vols, 1783) was praised by Edward *Gibbon. Ferguson's *Principles of Moral and Political Science* (2 vols, 1792) was based on his long teaching career.

FERGUSON, Sir Samuel (1810–86) Poet, antiquarian, and lawyer, born in Belfast and educated at Trinity College, Dublin, who was a key influence on the *Irish Revival. His many translations and works based on Gaelic legend include *Lays of the Western Gael* (1865); *Congal* (1872), an 'epic' poem on the last stand of Irish paganism against Christianity; the long narrative poem 'Conary'; and a retelling of the legend of *Deirdre (both 1880). He published a magisterial elegy on the nationalist leader Thomas Davis in 1845 and a striking dramatic monologue on the Phoenix Park murders ('At the Polo-Ground') four decades later. *Ogham Inscriptions in Ireland, Wales, and Scotland*, his most important antiquarian work, appeared in 1887. See Robert O'Driscoll, *An Ascendancy of the Heart: Ferguson and the Beginnings of Modern Irish Literature in English* (1976).

FERGUSSON, Robert (1750–74) Scottish poet, born in Edinburgh, who abandoned his studies at St Andrews to become a copying clerk in his native city. His early poems, imitations of William *Shenstone and other English authors, were published in Ruddiman's *Weekly Magazine* in 1771. 'The Daft Days', one of the 35 *Scots works on which his reputation rests, appeared there in January 1772. *Poems* (1773) collected 27 English and nine Scots poems. The posthumous *Poems on Various Subjects* (1779), made up largely of material published in the *Weekly Magazine* in the months after the appearance of the 1773 volume, inspired Robert *Burns to 'emulating vigour': 'Leith Races' foreshadows 'The *Holy Fair', while 'The Farmer's Ingle' provides a notably unsentimental prototype for 'The *Cotter's Saturday Night'. Fergusson vividly evokes the street life, taverns, and amusements of Edinburgh, and mocks the established literary world in his attacks on Henry *Mackenzie (in the English 'The Sow of Feeling') and Samuel *Johnson. 'Auld Reekie', an ambitious satire on Edinburgh in octosyllabic couplets, was left unfinished. In 1773 he developed manic-depressive symptoms, and he died shortly after his removal to Bedlam. The standard two-volume edition of his works, with a life, was edited by M. P. McDiarmid (1954–6).

Ferishtah's Fancies A volume of poems by Robert *Browning, published 1884. The main part of the collection consists of twelve poems focused on the thought and actions of an imaginary Persian sage, Ferishtah. Browning's non-Christian speaker probed moral problems, asking questions about belief, and testing the relationship between different forms of moral system. The volume was a significant contribution to the later Victorian interest in Islamic thought.

FERLINGHETTI, Lawrence (1920–) American *Beat poet. Although born in New York, he was the mainstay of the San Francisco Renaissance. In 1953 he co-founded City Lights Books (named after the Charlie *Chaplin film), a publishing house and bookstore that specialized in Beat poetry. He was arrested in 1956 for publishing Allen *Ginsberg's *Howl* and wrote a full account of the trial ('Horn on Howl') for the **Evergreen Review* (1957). His own work includes poetry collections such as *A Coney Island of the Mind* (1958) as well as two volumes of plays. Unlike many of his contemporaries he disapproved of the Beats' emphasis on the self and argued for a more directly political project with which they could be aligned. He was a fervent supporter of the Cuban Revolution and most famously composed the poem 'One Thousand Fearful Words for Fidel Castro' after his visit there in 1960. That same year he published a brief prose narrative, *Her*, and in 2001 published *Love in the Days of Rage*, a novel set in 1968 Paris. He described *Americus I* (2004) as 'part documentary, part public pillow-talk, part personal epic'.

FERMOR, Sir Patrick Leigh (1915–) Travel writer, educated at the King's School, Canterbury. In 1933 Fermor set off on foot for Constantinople, a journey recounted many years later in *A Time of Gifts* (1977) and *Between the Woods and the Water* (1985). The first two instalments of a projected trilogy, these highly acclaimed books cover Fermor's wanderings from, respectively, the Hook of Holland to Hungary, and from Transylvania to the Danube. After leaving Constantinople, Fermor continued to live and travel in the Balkans and Greece. During the German occupation of Crete he lived for more than two years disguised as a shepherd and captured the commander of the German forces in Crete, an episode which became the basis of a film, *Ill Met by Moonlight* (1956). After the war Fermor became director of the British Institute in Athens. His first travel book, *The Traveller's Tree* (1950), and his novella, *The Violins of Saint-Jacques* (1953), are both set in the French Caribbean, whilst *A Time to Keep Silence* (1957) explores monastic life in Europe. *Mani* (1958) and *Roumeli* (1966) describe the southern Peloponnese and northern Greece, offering an erudite account of local customs and dialect, and a lively evocation of village life. He has also published *Three Letters from the*

Andes (1991), based on letters to his wife. Fermor has been much praised as a prose stylist, although his lyricism can sometimes seem excessive; at its best, however, his work combines infectious enthusiasm, a powerful sense of place, and a highly informed historical imagination. He was knighted in 2004.

FERNÁNDEZ DE AVELLANEDA, Alonso The name assumed by the Spanish author of the spurious Part II of **Don Quixote*, published in 1614. *Cervantes's own Part II appeared the following year, alluding ironically to Fernández de Avellaneda's sequel.

FERRAR, Nicholas (1592–1637) Educated at and fellow of Clare College, Cambridge, a member of Parliament and active in the affairs of the Virginia Company. In 1625 he retired to *Little Gidding, an estate belonging to his mother, and established there with his brother, his brother-in-law John Collett, and their families a religious community based on Anglican principles. Ferrar wrote little himself, but was a close friend of George *Herbert, who on his deathbed entrusted to him the manuscript of his poems *The Temple*, published 1633.

FERRERS, George *See* MIRROR FOR MAGISTRATES.

Ferrex and Porrex *See* GORBODUC.

FERRIER, James Frederick (1808–64) Scottish philosopher, nephew of Susan *Ferrier; he was born in Edinburgh and educated at Edinburgh University and Magdalen College, Oxford. He studied German philosophy at Heidelberg and was successively professor of civil history at Edinburgh (1842–5) and of moral philosophy and political economy at St Andrews (1845–64). His idealistic philosophy, connected with that of George *Berkeley, is developed in *The Institutes of Metaphysic* (1854) and *Lectures on Greek Philosophy and Other Philosophical Remains* (mostly published in **Blackwood's Magazine*, 1838–43, and in volume form 1866). The principal positions of his philosophy are two: first, that 'Along with whatever any intelligence knows, it must, as the ground or condition of its knowledge, have some cognisance of itself.' Nor can it know itself except in relation with objects. Mind and matter, per se, are unknowable. Secondly, that we can be ignorant only of what is capable of being known. From these positions he argues that it is necessary to 'conceive a supreme intelligence as the ground and essence of the Universal whole'. In substance, Ferrier's conclusions closely resemble those of *Hegel, though reached independently and from a different starting point. Thomas *De Quincey said that Ferrier produced 'German philosophy reflected through a Scottish medium'.

FERRIER, Susan (1782–1854) Novelist, born in Edinburgh, the daughter of a lawyer friend of Walter *Scott. She was educated at home. Ferrier was the author of three widely read novels with largely Scottish settings: **Marriage* (1818), *The *Inheritance* (1824), and **Destiny* (1831). Her work combines a firmly moral didacticism with shrewd social observation. In later life she became increasingly religious and renounced her literary career.

Ferumbras (or *Firumbras*), ***Sir*** A Middle English metrical romance of 10,540 short lines related to the French Charlemagne romances *Fierabras* and the *Destruccion de Rome*. It is one of the more artistic of the English romances of 'the *matter of France', and more distinguished than the version known from its 19th-century owner as the 'Fillingham Firumbras' (ed. M. I. O'Sullivan, EETS OS 198, 1935). The story tells of the capture by Ferumbras, the son of the sultan of Babylon, of Rome and the Holy Relics, of his combat and later friendship with Oliver, and of the conversion to Christianity of Ferumbras and his sister Floripas. The two become friends of Roland, Oliver, and Charlemagne, and Floripas marries Guy of Burgundy. The same story is told in *The Sowdone of Babylon*, a version from about 1400 of a lost French romance. See S. J. Herrtage's edn (EETS ES 34, 1879; repr. 1966).

festivals, literary These now play a significant role in the promotion of literature around the world. Britain's first post-war literary festival, a small-scale local occasion which aimed to bring writers and readers together, took place in Cheltenham in 1949. A Writers' Conference attached to the well-established Edinburgh Festival of music and drama in 1962 was attended by Stephen *Spender, Muriel *Spark, Lawrence *Durrell, Rebecca *West, Angus *Wilson, and others, and achieved notoriety through lively debates on drugs and homosexuality as well as books. Since then, scores of festivals have sprung up across the country, usually offering a week or fortnight of events, including readings, lectures, book signings, and writing workshops. In Britain, festivals range from the truly international to those such as the Lancaster LitFest (est. 1978), which seek primarily to promote local writing. Others concentrate on poetry (the Aldeburgh Poetry Festival) or drama (the Royal Court Young Writers Festival). Among the most popular are the Edinburgh Book Festival (est. 1983) and the Hay-on-Wye Festival (est. 1988), which—like the Sunday Times Oxford Literary Festival (est. 1997)—attract sponsorship from national newspapers. Other well-established festivals include Ways with Words, held annually at Dartington Hall in Devon, Southwold in Suffolk, and Keswick in Cumbria, and the Ilkley Festival in Yorkshire, launched by W. H. *Auden in 1973. Literary festivals especially grew in number and prominence during the 1980s when their potential as effective publicity and marketing tools became apparent. Many authors are now expected to make appearances on the festival circuit when their books are published. Outside Britain major festivals include the Harbourfront International Festival of Authors in Toronto (est. 1979) and the Melbourne Writers Festival (est. 1990). Elsewhere, as at the Adelaide Festival of Arts or the New Yorker Festival, a book festival is part of a larger celebration of the arts. Writers are now prepared to travel far to attend these events: India's first international literary festival was the New Delhi Kitab (2006) arranged by Liberatum, an organization whose other arts and literature festivals take place in different—and usually exotic—locations: Marrakech, Petra, and St Petersburg.

FEUCHTWANGER, Lion (1884–1958) German novelist and playwright. Born of a Jewish family in Berlin, he is best known as the author of *Die hässliche Herzogin* (1923: *The Ugly Duchess*) and *Jud Süss* (1925: *Jew Süss*), a historical novel set in 18th-century Germany. On Hitler's seizure of power he was expatriated and lived in France until interned by the Vichy government. Subsequently he escaped to the USA, where he settled in Hollywood. *Jew Süss*, in a translation by Willa and Edwin *Muir (1927), was highly praised by Arnold *Bennett in his *Evening Standard* column ('a complete picture of a complex social organism'), and became a best-seller. In 1924 he collaborated with Bertolt *Brecht on an adaptation of Christopher *Marlowe's *Edward II* and in Hollywood on Brecht's own drama *Die Gesichte der Simone Machard* (1943: *The Visions of Simone Machard*). Feuchtwanger appears as a character in Christopher *Hampton's play *Tales from Hollywood* (1983).

FEUERBACH, Ludwig (1804–72) German philosopher and critic of the Bible, a disciple of *Hegel. Feuerbach's most influential work was *Das Wesen des Christentums* (1841: *The Essence of Christianity*), in which he asserted that Christianity is a man-created myth, satisfying man's need to imagine perfection: 'Man, by means of the imagination, involuntarily contemplates his inner nature; he represents it as out of himself. The nature of man, of the species…is God.' George Eliot, who translated the work into English in 1854, wrote that she agreed with Feuerbach's religion of humanity, and her novels show the influence not only of Feuerbach's thought but also of his application of religious terms to a secular philosophy. Feuerbach's style of materialism was criticized by *Marx in his *Theses on Feuerbach* (1845).

FICHTE, Johann Gottlieb (1762–1814) German philosopher, a pupil of Immanuel *Kant, from whose dualism he subsequently dissented. He became professor of philosophy at Jena in 1794, but was accused of atheism and dismissed. He subsequently lectured in Erlangen and Berlin. Though his philosophical system grew out of Kant's, it has the distinguishing feature that the thinking self, or *ego*, is seen as the only reality. This *ego*, in defining and limiting itself, creates the *non-ego*, the world of experience, as its opposite, the medium through which it asserts its freedom. He expounded this doctrine of 'subjective idealism' in his principal work, *Wissenschaftslehre* (1794: *Doctrine of Knowledge*), which greatly influenced German *Romanticism. Shocked by the humiliation of Prussia and its army by Napoleon in 1806–7, he became increasingly interested in the idea of nationhood, and sought reality, not in the *ego* but in the notion of a divine idea lying at the base of all experience, of which the world of the senses is the manifestation. His *Reden an die deutsche Nation* (1814: *Speeches to the German Nation*) attempted to foster a patriotic sense of German nationhood among his contemporaries under foreign occupation. Samuel Taylor *Coleridge studied his work in the context of German idealism and makes critical observations in **Biographia Literaria*. Fichte's view of history as the biography of its heroes greatly influenced Thomas *Carlyle, particularly in the latter's lectures *On *Heroes, Hero-Worship and the Heroic in History* (1841), as did his idealism. In **Sartor Resartus*, Carlyle uses Fichte's idea of the world of Appearances as a garment under which lies the essence or Divine Idea.

FICINO, Marsilio (1433–99) Italian humanist and philosopher, and a highly influential exponent of Platonism. He translated into Latin many important works of *Plato and the *Neoplatonists (e.g. Porphyry, *Plotinus, Proclus, and *Dionysius the Pseudo-Areopagite), sought to establish an essential harmony between Platonism and Christianity, and under the patronage of first Cosimo and then Lorenzo de *Medici was the leader of a 'Platonic Academy' at Florence. His views influenced *Reuchlin and *Colet and were an inspiration to many English poets, including Philip *Sidney and John *Milton.
See MEDICI.

Fiction Collective An independent American writers' collective, founded in 1973 by Jonathan Baumbach (1933–), Ronald *Sukenick, and others, whose purpose was to bypass commercial publishing restrictions by giving innovative and experimental novelists more control over the production of their works. Authors published included Russell Banks (1940–) and Gerald *Vizenor. In 1989 the press was reorganized and renamed Fiction Collective 2 (FC2).

FIEDLER, Leslie Aaron (1917–2003) American literary critic and novelist, best known for his 1960 study *Love and Death in the American Novel*, which argued that American fiction had a distinct *Gothic tradition (hence its obsession with death) and was incapable of dealing with adult sexuality. Fiedler opposed the *New Criticism, drawing instead on Sigmund *Freud for his critical writings. The latter were not confined to literature, as witness *Freaks: Myths and Images of the Secret Self* (1978). His collected essays were published in 1972 (5 vols). From the 1970s onwards Fiedler's interests drew him to popular culture and *science fiction, and his study *Olaf Stapledon: A Man Divided* appeared in 1978. Fiedler also wrote a number of novels, the first being *Nude Croquet* (1957), which caused some controversy over its sexual content.

FIELD, Michael Poet and dramatist, pseudonym of Katharine Bradley (1846–1914) and her niece Edith Cooper (1862–1913). Bradley, born in Birmingham and educated in Paris and at Newnham College, Cambridge, became deeply attached to her invalid sister's daughter Edith (born in Kenilworth). They attended University College, Bristol, together in the late 1870s, studying classics and philosophy. Bradley published first under the pseudonym of Arran Leigh; together she and Cooper adopted the name 'Michael Field' with the publication of *Callirrhoë; Fair Rosamund* (1884). They produced more than twenty volumes of verse drama and poetry. Their best-known work draws sensuously and erotically on pagan classical themes: their most respected collections are *Long Ago* (1889), which retells the story of *Sappho, and *Sight and Song* (1892), which pairs their poems with paintings viewed on their frequent European travels. Bradley and Cooper were significant figures in London's literary and artistic culture; friends included Charles Shannon (1865–1937) and Charles *Ricketts (who also illustrated their work), Robert *Browning, Oscar *Wilde, and George *Meredith. In 1907 the poets converted to Roman Catholicism: Bradley's confessor was the poet and priest John Gray (1866–1934). While critics have debated the nature of Bradley and Cooper's relationship, from the late 20th century onwards they have been widely regarded as pioneering lesbian poets. See Emma Donoghue, *We Are Michael Field* (1998).

FIELD, Nathan (1587–1619/20) Actor and dramatist, educated at St Paul's; forced into service of the Children of the Chapel Royal, a theatre company; probably succeeded William *Shakespeare as actor and shareholder in the King's Men, *c.*1616. He wrote two comedies, *A Woman Is a Weathercock* (1609), which shows the influence of Ben *Jonson and includes a parody of a speech in *The *Spanish Tragedy*, and *Amends for Ladies* (1610). Later he collaborated with a number of other dramatists, including John *Fletcher and Philip *Massinger, and is best known for his share of Massinger's *The *Fatal Dowry*.

FIELDING, Helen (1958–) Novelist, born in Morley, West Yorkshire; she attended Wakefield Girls' High School and read English at St Anne's College, Oxford. Her experiences as a television journalist and maker of documentaries in Africa for the charity Comic Relief inspired her first novel, *Cause Celeb* (1994). But it was *Bridget Jones's Diary* (1996), a lively 'chick lit' novel emerging from her columns in *The Independent* and the *Daily Telegraph* about the romantic misadventures of a 30-something 'singleton' and her friends in London, that brought her widespread readership (and spawned numerous imitations). *Bridget Jones: The Edge of Reason* (1999) continued both the story and Fielding's technique of underpinning her present-day comedy with situations and characters from Jane *Austen's fiction.

FIELDING, Henry (1707–54) Playwright, journalist, novelist, and lawyer, son of a colonel, born at Sharpham Park, Somerset, the house of his maternal grandfather. His mother died when he was 11, and when his father remarried Henry was sent to Eton College. There he made lifelong friends of George *Lyttelton, who was to become a generous future patron, and of the future statesman William Pitt the elder. At 19 he attempted to elope with an heiress, but failing in this settled in London, earning his living as a dramatist, with the encouragement of his cousin Lady Mary Wortley *Montagu. *Love in Several Masques* was successfully performed in 1728 at Drury Lane. In the same year he became a student at Leiden, where he remained about eighteen months, greatly enlarging his knowledge of classical literature. Returning to London he recommenced his career as a dramatist, and between 1730 and 1737 wrote some 25 dramas, mostly farces and satires, and including two adaptations of *Molière, *The Mock Doctor* and *The Miser*. In 1730 three of his plays were performed: *The Author's Farce*, a satire on the writing profession; *Rape upon Rape*, a denunciation of the practices of the law; and **Tom Thumb* (published in a revised form the following year as *The Tragedy of Tragedies, or The Life and Death of Tom Thumb the Great*), a burlesque of the turgid tragedies of the day. William *Hogarth designed the frontispiece, beginning a long and close association. *Don Quixote*, a tribute to *Cervantes, appeared in 1734. In that year Fielding married Charlotte Cradock, the model for Sophia in **Tom Jones* and for the heroine of **Amelia*. His improvidence led to long periods of poverty, from which he was periodically relieved by his friend Ralph *Allen. In 1736 Fielding took over the management of the New Theatre, for the opening of which he wrote *Pasquin*, targeting various religious and political abuses. But *The Historical Register for 1736* was fiercer political satire than the government of Sir Robert Walpole (1676–1745) would tolerate, and the Licensing Act of 1737, introducing censorship by the lord chamberlain, ended Fielding's theatrical career. He entered the Middle Temple and was called to the bar in 1740. In 1739–40 he wrote most of the anti-Jacobite periodical the **Champion*. In 1740 Samuel Richardson's **Pamela* enjoyed tremendous popular success; Fielding expressed his contempt in the parody **Shamela*. In 1742 the novel **Joseph Andrews*, also partly designed as a riposte to Richardson, brought him £185 11*s*. In 1743 Fielding published by subscription three volumes of *Miscellanies*, which included some essays, the Lucianic *A *Journey from this World to the Next*, and a ferocious satire, *The Life of *Jonathan Wild the Great*, in part directed at Walpole. In 1744 his wife died, and for a while he wrote little except a preface to his sister Sarah's novel **David Simple*, and some journalism, particularly the *True Patriot* and the *Jacobite's Journal*. In 1747 he caused some scandal by marrying his wife's maid Mary Daniel. With the support of Lyttelton, he was appointed JP for Westminster in 1748 and at once joined battle with the 'trading justices' who imposed and embezzled fines. In 1749 **Tom Jones* was enthusiastically received by the general public, though Samuel *Richardson, Tobias *Smollett, and Samuel *Johnson criticized it heavily. In the same year Fielding's legal jurisdiction was extended to the whole county of Middlesex, and he was made chairman of the quarter sessions of Westminster. From his court in Bow Street he continued his struggle against corruption and lawlessness and, with his blind half-brother and fellow magistrate Sir John Fielding, strove to establish new standards of honesty and competence on the bench. He wrote several influential legal enquiries and pamphlets, including *An Enquiry into the Causes of the Late Increase of Robbers* (1751). **Amelia* (1751) sold the best of all his novels. He returned to journalism in 1752 with the *Covent-Garden Journal*, and published in 1753 an exhaustively detailed *Proposal for Making*

Effective Provision for the Poor. But his gout and asthma were now so far advanced that he had to use crutches, and in 1754, in hope of improvement, he set off with his wife and daughter for Portugal, dying near Lisbon in October. The *Journal of a Voyage to Lisbon* (1755) describes the journey in unsparing detail.

Fielding characterized himself as 'the founder of a new province of writing' and Walter *Scott commended him for his 'high notions of the dignity of an art which he may be considered as having founded'. His highly plotted 'comic epics in prose' interpret the lure of psychological intensity offered by Richardson's epistolary method as a delusive self-indulgence and instead link the emerging novel form with the humour of *Lucian, *Cervantes, and Jonathan *Swift. See M. C. Battestin, *Henry Fielding: A Life* (new edn, 1993). The *Wesleyan Edition of the Works of Henry Fielding* (1967–) is in progress.

FIELDING, Sarah (1710–68) Novelist, sister of Henry *Fielding, born in Dorset and educated in Salisbury. For much of her life she lived quietly in and around London, where she became part of Samuel *Richardson's circle, and later near Bath. She contributed small items to Henry's work before publishing in 1744 her own best-known novel, *The Adventures of *David Simple*, a psychologically focused 'Moral Romance', with (in its second edition) a preface by her brother. *Familiar Letters between the Principal Characters in David Simple* followed in 1747, and in 1753 the sombre *Volume the Last*. Her *The Governess* (1749) was the first English school story written for children. She was almost certainly the author of *Remarks on Clarissa* (1749). With Jane *Collier she published *The Cry* (1754), an unusual dialogue between Portia (the Solo) representing integrity, and an audience (the Chorus) representing ignorant malice. The parallel of author against critic is implied throughout. The heavily researched *The Lives of Cleopatra and Octavia* (1757) presents a series of dramatic monologues in which the subtle self-seeking of Cleopatra is contrasted with the honesty of Octavia. *The History of the Countess of Dellwyn* (1759) traces the disastrous relationship of an old husband and a young wife, and includes some thoughts on literary mimesis. The light-hearted epistolary novel *History of Ophelia* (1760) relates the adventures of an ingenuous young woman constantly astonished by the unquestioned conventions of society. A successful translation of *Xenophon's *Memoirs of Socrates, with the Defence of Socrates before his Judges* appeared in 1762.

Fifine at the Fair A poem in alexandrine couplets by Robert *Browning, published 1872. The speaker is Don Juan, who is strolling with his wife Elvire near Pornic in Brittany, where a fair is being held. Attracted by the gypsy dancer Fifine, Don Juan discusses with Elvire the nature of his feelings, contrasting the ephemeral nature of desire with the dull permanence of love. This initial theme gives rise to a series of absorbing variations on the interconnected topics of knowledge, identity, and authenticity in life and art. The poem's interest in the casuistry of an over-wrought self-consciousness, and the text's unusually bitter tone, take their origin in part from Browning's dismay in the mysterious aftermath of his quarrel with Lady Ashburton, which began in 1869 with, it seems, a failed proposal of marriage (whether from him to her or vice versa is uncertain) and was still apparent in 1871; Fifine represents Lady Ashburton in this interpretation, and Elvire, Elizabeth Barrett (*see* BROWNING, ELIZABETH BARRETT). But the autobiographical context is transcended in a poem which innovatively tests Byronic models of masculinity in a different emotional environment. Browning told his friend Alfred *Domett that the poem was 'the most metaphysical and boldest he had written since *Sordello*' but it is now the provocative debate about the sexual politics of the poem, and its fascination with the intellectual shape of an angular mind, which attract readers.

FIGES, Eva (1932–) Novelist and feminist, born in Berlin, educated at Kingsbury Grammar School and Queen Mary College London. She came to England in 1939, and during the 1960s belonged to a circle of 'experimental' writers which also included B. S. *Johnson, Alan Burns (1929–), and Ann Quin (1936–73). Her novels are poetic and fragmented, her preferred form the *interior monologue. They include *Winter Journey* (1967), *Days* (1974), *Waking* (1981), *Ghosts* (1988), *The Tree of Knowledge* (1990), a fictionalized biography of John *Milton's wife, and *Nelly's Version* (2002), an eerie study of amnesia. *Patriarchal Attitudes* (1970) and *Sex and Subterfuge: Women Writers to 1850* (1982) were influential works of *feminist social and literary criticism. Her memoirs *Tales of Innocence and Experience: An Exploration* (2004) and *Journey to Nowhere* (2008) recall her experiences as a refugee.

FILMER, Sir Robert (*c.*1590–1653) A defender of the divine right of kings. His *Patriarcha, or The Natural Power of Kings*, written ?1638, published 1680, was attacked and ridiculed by John *Locke in his first *Treatise of Government* (1690). He also opposed the witch-hunting mania.

Film Society The Society enabled artists, intellectuals, and progressives in London to see a wide range of international cinema that was otherwise banned from exhibition by Britain's draconian film *censorship. Launched in 1925, with Roger *Fry, J. M. Keynes (1883–1946), George Bernard *Shaw, H. G. *Wells, and Virginia *Woolf among its founder members, and run by the future producer Ivor Montagu and Iris Barry, the society showed predominantly German and *Russian films, but also included popular science and *animation in its wide-ranging programmes, which continued until the late 1930s. A national, and eventually international, network of film societies followed and continues.

Filostrato A poem in **ottava rima* on the story of Troilus and Cressida, by *Boccaccio (1335), of special interest as the source of Chaucer's **Troilus and Criseyde*.

FINE, Anne (1947–) OBE, FRSL, born in Leicester, educated at the University of Warwick. The second children's laureate (2001–3), she has written over 50 books, beginning with *The Summer House Loon* (1978). These are often comic, but feature pragmatic approaches to personal and social problems. Fine has won numerous awards for her children's books, including the Carnegie Medal for both *Goggle Eyes* (1990) and *Flour Babies* (1993); both were adapted for television. *Madame Doubtfire* (1987) was filmed as *Mrs Doubtfire* with Robin Williams (1993). Fine has written six well-received adult novels, including *Raking the Ashes* (2005).

Fingal, *an Ancient Epic Poem, in Six Books: Together with Several Other Poems, Composed by Ossian, the Son of Fingal. Translated from the Galic Language* (1762) and *Temora, an Ancient Epic Poem, in Eight Books* (1763) These extended narratives in poetic prose, which purported to be translated from ancient Gaelic epic originals, were in the main the original work of James *Macpherson, though they were based loosely on *Fenian ballads current in his native Highlands. Macpherson transforms the legendary Irish hero *Finn or Fionn into the Scottish Fingal, ignores key episodes and characters in the original tales (including *Grainne, Finn's faithless wife, and her lover *Diarmid, who do not appear at all), and brings together Fingal and Cuthullin (the Irish *Cuchulain) who according to tradition were separated by more than two centuries. Morven, Fingal's kingdom in the north-west of Scotland, is Macpherson's invention. Fingal is pictured by Macpherson as fighting both the Norwegians and the Romans under Caracalla—'Caracul, King of the World'. The enormous impact of Macpherson's work is indicated by the fact that even Edward *Gibbon took the trouble to discuss it, writing of 'the tenderness, the elegant genius of Ossian', and contrasting the 'untutored Caledonians, glowing with the warm virtues of nature' with 'the degenerate Romans, polluted with the mean vices of wealth and slavery'. *Fingal* accorded more comprehensively even than the **Iliad* or the **Odyssey* with 18th-century ideas about *primitivism, the *sublime, and *sentiment—as well it might, since it was composed under their influence. Hugh *Blair bestowed upon it such epithets as 'grand...pathetic...serious...grave...wild and romantic...sublime and tender'. See Howard Gaskill (ed.), *The Poems of Ossian and Related Works* (1996).

FINLAY, Ian Hamilton (1925–2006) Scottish poet, graphic artist, and sculptor, born in Nassau in the Bahamas and brought up in Scotland. He became widely known in the 1960s as a leading figure in the *concrete poetry movement, and published a series of handsome and innovative pamphlets, slim volumes, and postcard poems in association with his own Wild Hawthorn Press and other small presses. His creation of Little Sparta, a sculpture garden at Dunsyre, south of the Pentland Hills, is celebrated for its combinations of nature, word, image, and artefact, and its reconciliation of the classical with the modern. See *The Dancers Inherit the Party: Early Stories, Plays and Poems* (2004).

Finn (Fionn) The principal hero of the *Fenian cycle. Finn MacCoul has been thought a historical figure by some authorities, though most regard him as mythical. He was the son of Cumhal and father of *Oisín (Ossian), and is supposed to have lived in the 3rd century AD, a contemporary of King Cormac Mac Airt. The king appointed him chief of the Fianna, a military body composed of men of exceptional strength and prowess, of whose heroic or romantic deeds there are countless tales. Finn was chosen as their leader not for surpassing physical qualities, but on account of his wisdom, generosity, and truthfulness. He is said to have perished in a fight with mutinous Fenians in 283.
See also DIARMID; FINGAL; GRAINNE.

Finnegans Wake The final, notoriously obscure, wondrously perplexing work of James *Joyce, laboured over for seventeen years and published in 1939. It defies synopsis and provokes exegesis in equal measure. Written in a unique style which makes abundant use of puns and portmanteau words (using at least 40 languages besides English) and a very wide range of allusion, it has yet to be fathomed and probably never will be. Whether it is a consummate, many-layered epic or a colossal leg-pull has been debated from the beginning. The central theme of the work is the cyclical pattern of history, of fall and resurrection, inspired by Giambattista *Vico's *La scienza nuova*. This is presented in the story of Humphrey Chimpden Earwicker, a Dublin publican, and the book is apparently a dream-sequence representing the stream of his unconscious mind through the course of one night. Alongside its endless puzzles it contains passages of great lyrical beauty and much humour.

FINNEY, Jack (1911–95) American author, born in Milwaukee; best known for *The Body Snatchers* (1955), filmed 1956 and 1978 as *Invasion of the Body Snatchers*, where alien spores create duplicate 'pod-people'. It has been variously interpreted as dramatizing fears of communism or American conformity.

Finnsburh, The Fight at Known as 'The Finnsburh Fragment', to distinguish it from the 'Finnsburh Episode' in **Beowulf*; a 48-line fragmentary poem in Old English dealing with part of the tragic tale of Finn and Hildeburh, a later part of which is sung by the *scôp* in *Beowulf*, ll. 1063–159. An attempt is made to heal the long-standing feud between the Danes and the Frisians by the marriage of the Frisian king Finn to Hildeburh, the sister of Hnaef who is king of the Half-Danes. After a period of peace, the feud breaks out again in a battle at Finn's court and Hnaef is killed, as is his nephew, the son of Finn and Hildeburh: the beginning of that battle is the subject of the fragment. After an uneasy winter truce, during which the Danes have to remain as guests of Finn, the slayer of their leader, the Danes, led by Hengest, gain vengeance by killing Finn when the spring comes. The fragment is included by F. Klaeber in his edition of *Beowulf* (1922; rev. and supplemented up to 1950).

FINZI, Gerald (1901–56) English composer, of the school of Gustav *Holst and Ralph *Vaughan Williams. He made major choral settings of poems by Thomas *Traherne, Henry *Vaughan, and William *Wordsworth (**Intimations of Immortality*, 1950) and solo settings from John *Milton, William *Shakespeare, Christina *Rossetti, and Thomas *Hardy. He also publicized the work of Ivor *Gurney.

FIRBANK, Ronald (1886–1926) Novelist, born in London, son of Sir Joseph Thomas Firbank, MP (1850–1910), and grandson of Joseph Firbank (1819–86), a wealthy, self-made railway contractor; he derived from the latter an income which enabled him to travel extensively throughout his life and to pay for the publication of most of his own work. He spent two terms at Uppingham School in 1900, but his education was largely private until he went to Trinity Hall, Cambridge, in 1906, where he took no examinations, but met R. H. *Benson, who received him into the Roman Catholic Church in 1907. He had already published a volume of Oscar *Wilde-influenced stories in 1905 and in 1906 he worked on *The Artificial Princess* (published posthumously in 1934). But his career as a novelist really took off (creatively, rather than in terms of public recognition) with the appearance of *Vainglory* in 1915. This was followed by *Inclinations* (1916); *Caprice* (1917, the story of the spectacularly brief and dazzling theatrical career of the daughter of a rural dean); *Valmouth* (1919, set in a spa dominated by an erotic and manipulative black masseuse); *Santal* (1921, set in North Africa); and *The Flower beneath the Foot* (1923). A play, *The Princess Zoubaroff*, was published in 1920. The first of his novels to be financed by a publisher, not by himself, was *Prancing Nigger* (1924), which appeared under that title in America, and under his own preferred title, *Sorrow in Sunlight*, in Britain; set in the West Indies, 'with a brilliant background of sunlight, sea, and as tropical' as he could make it, it describes the social aspirations and adventures of a black family, the Mouths. (In this novel he himself appears, characteristically, as the name of an orchid, 'a dingy lilac blossom of rarity untold'.) His last finished work, *Concerning the Eccentricities of Cardinal Pirelli* (1926), appeared shortly after his death, from a disease of the lungs, in Rome. *The New Rythum and Other Pieces* was published in 1962 and includes a very early work, *Lady Appledore's Mésalliance*, and chapters from an unfinished novel, set in New York, on which he was working when he died. Dandy, aesthete, exotic, and homosexual, Firbank received little encouragement as a writer during his lifetime (except from the *Sitwells), but nevertheless succeeded in creating a distinctive 'Firbankian' style, in both his life and works. His use of dialogue, his idiosyncratic ellipses, his highly coloured fantasies, and his intense concentration of language and image are now seen as truly innovative. Those who show traces of his influence include Evelyn *Waugh, Ivy *Compton-Burnett, William *Gerhardie, Anthony *Powell, and Muriel *Spark. See Brigid *Brophy, *Prancing Novelist* (1973).

Fir Bolg Legendary early invaders of Ireland, according to tradition of an Iberian tribe, who were driven into Arran, Islay, and the Hebrides by the *Milesians.

FIRDAUSĪ (Ferdosi), **Abū l-Qāsim** (*c.*940–1020) Persian poet and author of the *Shahnama* (*Shahnameh*), 'The Book of Kings', a vast epic of some 60,000 couplets, composed over a period of 35 years. The *Shahnama* is the earliest and still the most popular masterpiece of Persian literature. It recounts the history of the kings and heroes of Persia from legendary times down to and including the Sassanian period (226–651). Though every hemistich, or half-line of verse, has the same metre and the style is simple, Firdausī is adept at varying his phrasing to match the theme and mood of each episode. The *Shahnama* had a profound impact on wider Persian culture, some of the finest miniature paintings illuminating its major manuscripts.

There have been many partial translations into English from 1785 (by Joseph Champion) to the present day (by Dick Davis), almost all in abbreviated form. However, the epic is known to English readers principally through Matthew *Arnold's telling of one of its many vivid incidents, the story of *'Sohrab and Rustum'.

First Part of the Contention of the Two Famous Houses of York and Lancaster *See* Henry VI.

FISHER, St John (*c.*1469–1535) Theologian and martyr, educated at Michaelhouse (absorbed in Trinity College, 1546), Cambridge, of which he became a fellow. He became the first Lady Margaret professor of divinity, chancellor of the university, and bishop of Rochester, 1504, and was president of Queens' College, Cambridge, 1505–8. He was a patron of *Erasmus and induced him to lecture on Greek at Cambridge from 1511 to 1514. He wrote three treatises against the Lutheran Reformation and was committed to the Tower for refusing to swear to the Act of Succession. The pope did not improve his chances of escape from death by sending him a cardinal's hat while he was in prison. Fisher was deprived, attainted, and beheaded for refusing to acknowledge *Henry VIII as supreme head of the church. His Latin theological works were published in 1597; his English works, edited by J. E. B. Mayor, appeared in 1876. His English prose style showed a great advance, in point of rhetorical artifice and effect, on that of his predecessors. He was canonized in 1935 and is commemorated on 22 June. There is a life by M. Dowling (1999).

FISHER, Roy (1930–) Poet, born in Birmingham and educated at Birmingham University. Since retiring from the American Studies department at Keele University in 1982 he has lived in the Peak District as a freelance writer and semi-professional jazz pianist. Pluralist in spirit and style, his poetry is notoriously difficult to pigeonhole. It has polarized the opinions of poets like Donald *Davie and Eric Mottram (1924–95): the first seeing it as rooted in a middle English, social-democratic realism; the second as avant-garde, international modernism. What Sean *O'Brien calls the 'intensely paradoxical' nature of his work remains pointedly unresolved by the poet. He has described himself both as 'a 1905 Russian Modernist' and as 'a Romantic'. A brief overview of major volumes attests to this heterogeneity: *City* (1961) combines burlesque, imagist, and lyrical poetry with paragraphs of prose varying from the documentary to the surreal; *Ten Interiors with Various Figures* (1966) is a sequence of hybrid verse and prose; *The Ship's Orchestra* (1967) is a Cubist prose-poetry novella; *The Thing about Joe Sullivan: Poems 1971–1977* (1978) includes free verse sequences and lyrics which have invited comparisons to the *Black Mountain school and to *jazz poetry's syncopations and rhapsodic improvisations; *The Furnace* (1986) is a short epic that superimposes the industrial West Midlands onto the landscape of his new home in north Staffordshire; and *Birmingham River* foregrounds a voice-over (both a satire and a celebration) for a television documentary on the city. As a whole, the work marries a playful, self-conscious, heterodox postmodern aesthetic to a very English ironic cultural criticism. It rarely remains bound by genre and includes numerous collaborations with visual artists, notably Tom *Phillips. His oeuvre dramatizes the efforts of a culture to understand its own complex, mutable psychogeography. It demonstrates a deep concern for the moral and political implications of the processes of perception and representation, rare amongst experimental writing in being so tangibly rooted in place and time. *The Long and the Short of it: Poems 1955–2005* (2005) is the most comprehensive collection. See also John Kerrigan and Peter Robinson (eds), *The Thing about Roy Fisher: Critical Studies* (2000).

FISHER, Vardis (1895–1968) American novelist born in Idaho, who wrote a series of historical novels about the Old West. These include *Tale of Valour: A Novel of the Lewis and Clarke Expedition* (1960) and *The Mothers: An American Saga of Courage* (1965), about the 1840s Donner party of migrants who resorted to cannibalism. In 1943 he began publishing his Testament of Man series which ran to twelve volumes and received a mixed reception.

FitzBoodle, George Savage One of W. M. *Thackeray's pseudonyms. As the narrator of the *FitzBoodle Papers*, published in **Fraser's Magazine* 1842–3, FitzBoodle, a bachelor clubman, tells the story of his own amorous misadventures.

FITZGERALD, Edward (1809–83) Poet and translator. FitzGerald, whose parents owned estates in England and Ireland, was the third son in a family of eight and was born in Suffolk, where he spent most of his life. He was educated at the King Edward VI Grammar School, Bury St Edmunds, and Trinity College, Cambridge. He never engaged in any profession or made any extended travels, but often visited London. His quirky but engaging personality made him much beloved by many close friends, who included W. M. *Thackeray, Alfred and Frederick *Tennyson, and Thomas *Carlyle. He lived for sixteen years in a cottage on his family's estate at Boulge, and for the last 23 years of his life he was based in Woodbridge. In these years he spent much time sailing with Lowestoft fishermen off the Suffolk coast. His first published book (1849) was a biography of the Quaker poet Bernard Barton, whose daughter he afterwards married; the middle-aged couple were incompatible and separated after a few months. In 1851 he published *Euphranor: A Dialogue on Youth* and later he produced translations of plays by *Calderón, *Aeschylus, and *Sophocles, a collection of aphorisms, and a selection of George *Crabbe's poetry. His only celebrated work is his free translation of *The *Rubáiyát of Omar Khayyám* (1859). His other translations from Persian included Attar's *Bird Parliament* and Jami's *Salaman and Absal*. He was a prolific and delightful letter writer, whose anecdotes of his literary friends have been a gold mine to biographers. His *Collected Letters*, which had previously appeared in selected versions, was published in 1980, ed. A. M. and A. B. Terhune.

FITZGERALD, F. Scott (Francis Scott Key) (1896–1940) American novelist and short story writer, born in Minnesota and educated at Princeton University, where he befriended Edmund *Wilson. His first novel, *This Side of Paradise* (1920), made him instantly famous; shortly after its publication he married the glamorous Zelda Sayre, and together they embarked on a life of high living, big spending, and party-going, seeing themselves as representative figures of the 'Jazz Age'. His stories chronicled the mood and manners of the times, including his fantasy of extravagance, 'The Diamond as Big as the Ritz'. *The Beautiful and Damned* (1922), a novel about a wealthy, doomed, and dissipated marriage, was followed by *The Great Gatsby* (1925), widely considered his finest work. This is the story of shady, mysterious financier Jay Gatsby, who harbours a romantic and destructive passion for Daisy Buchanan. The story is narrated by the innocent outsider Nick Carraway, who observes from a distance as adultery, hard drinking, fast driving, and finally murder take their toll. More short stories followed, and Zelda's only novel, *Save Me the Waltz*, appeared in 1932, but by this time she and Scott were suffering from mental breakdown and from the effects of their violent lives. *Tender is the Night* (1934, but later in various revised versions) records, through the story of American psychiatrist Dick Diver and his schizophrenic wife Nicole, his own sense of impending disaster. This novel's description of wealthy expatriates on the Riviera was not well received in the America of the Depression, and Fitzgerald's own 'crack-up' accelerated, as Zelda failed to recover: he died in Hollywood, of a heart attack, after working as a screenwriter, leaving his last novel, *The Last Tycoon* (originally *The Love of the Last Tycoon*), unfinished. It appeared in 1941, and was followed by a posthumous collection, *The Crack-Up* (1945). Fitzgerald was constantly drawn to the glamour of Hollywood, where he worked at different points, but also feared that film might supersede the novel. His assignments included *Three Comrades* (1937–8; screenplay published 1978) and *Cosmopolitan (Babylon Revisited)* (1940; screenplay published 1993). See Matthew J. Bruccoli's biography *Some Sort of Epic Grandeur* (1981; rev. 2002). The Cambridge University Press edition of Fitzgerald's works is establishing reliable texts.

FITZGERALD, Penelope (1916–2000) Novelist and biographer, only daughter of the essayist and humorist

E. V. Knox, 'Evoe' (1881–1971). She was born in Lincoln and educated at Wycombe Abbey and Somerville College, Oxford. In 1941 she married Desmond Fitzgerald (d. 1976). Her first book was a biography of the *Pre-Raphaelite painter Edward *Burne-Jones (1975), which was followed by two composite biographies, one of her father and his three brothers (1977), and one of the poet Charlotte *Mew and her circle (1984). Fitzgerald's first novel, *The Golden Child* (1977), written to divert her husband during his last illness, is a murder mystery involving an exhibition of Egyptian treasures in a London museum. Other novels, all gently perceptive comedies of manners drawing on her own experiences, followed. *The Bookshop* (1978) is set in a fictional East Anglian town in the late 1950s. *Offshore* (1979) is about life among a group of houseboat owners on the Thames during the 1960s and won the *Booker Prize for fiction. *Human Voices* (1980) is a story of the BBC during the Second World War and *At Freddie's* (1982) is set in a West End stage school. She had by this time, in her own words, 'finished writing about the things in my own life, which I wanted to write about', and her last four novels used historical settings. *Innocence* (1986) takes place in 1950s Italy; *The Beginnings of Spring* (1988) is the story of an Englishman, living in Moscow just before the start of the First World War, whose wife suddenly leaves him; and *The Gate of Angels* (1990) is a love story set in Edwardian Cambridge. *The Blue Flower* (1996) recreates the life of the German Romantic poet Novalis (F. L. *Hardenberg). Her final book, *The Means of Escape* (2000), is a collection of short stories.

FITZRALPH, Richard (*c.*1295–1360) Born in Dundalk, Ireland, and educated at Oxford University; he died in Avignon. He became chancellor of Oxford (1333) and archbishop of Armagh (1347), and was later known as 'Armachanus'. He attacked the friars and, arraigned before the pope at Avignon in 1357 to defend his opinions, he wrote the *Defensio Curatorum*. Regarded as the spokesman of the secular clergy against friars, he wrote a treatise against the friars' doctrine of obligatory poverty, *De Pauperie Salvatoris*, in which he discussed 'dominion' or 'lordship', his view on the subject similar to that later adopted by *Wyclif. See K. Walsh, *A Fourteenth-Century Scholar and Primate: Richard Fitzralph in Oxford, Avignon and Armagh* (1981).

Fitzrovia A term which describes both the area north of Oxford Street in London's West End and its bohemian habitués between the mid-1920s and about 1950. Centred at first on the Fitzroy Tavern, on the corner of Charlotte Street, Fitzrovia, in the words of Augustus John (1878–1961), was 'the Artist's Quarter, its only rival being Chelsea' (*Finishing Touches*, 1964). Its focus then moved, according to Julian Maclaren-Ross (*Memoirs of the Forties*, 1965), to The Wheatsheaf. Dylan *Thomas, William *Empson, Wyndham *Lewis, George *Orwell, Roy *Campbell, and Patrick *Hamilton were all to a greater or lesser extent Fitzrovians.

FITZROY, Vice-Admiral Robert (1805–65) Hydrographer (or ocean-mapper) and meteorologist, born at Ampton Hall, Suffolk, and educated at Harrow School and the Royal Naval College, Portsmouth. His first command was the *Beagle* charting the southernmost coasts of South America. Charles *Darwin joined his 1831–6 voyage around the world; FitzRoy published his account of the voyage in 1839. He entered Parliament in 1841 and was appointed governor of New Zealand in 1843, but his conciliatory policies to the Maori met opposition and his high-handed financial policies were clumsy. Dismissed in 1845, he returned to England and pioneered weather forecasting and storm warnings, publishing his *Weather Book* in 1863. After being reprimanded for exceeding his instructions, he cut his own throat.

F.J. *The Pleasant Fable of Ferdinando Jeronimi and Leonora de Valasco* Usually referred to, from its running title, as *The Adventures of Master F.J.*; a novella by George *Gascoigne, supposedly translated 'out of the Italian riding tales of *Bartello*', but probably his own invention. It concerns the love affair between F.J., a Venetian, and the lady of the house where he is staying in Lombardy. The love affair is pursued and discussed in a large number of letters and poems; after enjoying Leonora's favours for a time, F.J. is supplanted by her secretary, and returns to Venice. The novella exists in two versions: the first, printed in *A Hundreth Sundrie Flowres* (1573), is set in the north of England, is frankly erotic, and has every appearance of being a *roman à clef*; the second, printed in *The Posies of George Gascoigne* (1575), is more fully Italianate and has been to some extent expurgated.

Flashman The sadistic bully in *Tom Brown's Schooldays* by Thomas *Hughes, revived in a series of humorous novels by George MacDonald *Fraser. *See also* HISTORICAL FICTION.

FLATMAN, Thomas (1637–88) Educated at Winchester College, and New College, Oxford, much esteemed as a painter of miniatures; he also wrote poetry. *Poems and Songs* (1674) contains 'A Thought of Death', 'Death, a Song', and 'The Dying Christian to his Soul', the last of which was imitated by Alexander *Pope.

FLAUBERT, Gustave (1821–80) Major French novelist, born in Rouen, the second son of a physician. His first novel, *Madame Bovary* (1857), the sardonic tragedy of life in provincial Normandy, is notable for its rigorous psychological development, its impersonal narrative method, its irony, and its highly worked style; it was translated into English in 1886 by Eleanor Marx-Aveling, daughter of Karl *Marx, and has attracted and perplexed translators in equal measure ever since. Ancient Carthage is minutely recreated in Flaubert's next novel, *Salammbô* (1862), for which he undertook detailed researches. Charting the love life of the provincial student Frédéric Moreau against the backdrop of events in Paris between 1840 and 1851, *L'Éducation sentimentale* (1869: *Sentimental Education*) is a masterpiece, though relatively little translated since the first rendering in 1898. His three stories, *Trois Contes* (1877: *Un Cœur simple* (*A Simple Heart*), *La Légende de Saint-Julien l'Hospitalier* (*The Legend of St Julian Hospitator*), *Hérodias*), are set respectively in his own period, in the Middle Ages, and in biblical antiquity; they were first translated in 1903 by G. B. Ives. The metaphysical *Tentation de Saint-Antoine* (1874: *The Temptation of St Anthony*), part poem, part prose narrative, exercised Flaubert over more than 25 years; it was translated in a poetically archaic way by Lafcadio *Hearn in 1910. The unfinished and posthumously published *Bouvard et Pécuchet* (1881), relating the various projects and experiments of two retired copying clerks, was to form 'a sort of farcical critical encyclopaedia'. The publication of Flaubert's letters (4 vols, ed. J. Bruneau, 1973–98), with their searching reflections on the art of fiction and the life of the novelist, has crowned his reputation as the exemplary artist. See G. Wall, *Flaubert* (2001).

FLAXMAN, John (1755–1826) English neo-classical sculptor and draughtsman. Flaxman was steeped in the writings of Johann *Winckelmann, and his linear style is influenced by Greek vases and classical reliefs. He designed many funerary sculptures, the most famous being the monument to the earl of Mansfield in Westminster Abbey (1793–1801). He studied in Rome (1787–94), and here created a series of illustrations to the **Iliad* and the **Odyssey* (Alexander *Pope's translation, pub. 1793) which won him an immense reputation throughout Europe. His illustrations to Dante's **Divina commedia* (1793), commissioned by Thomas *Hope, were praised by *Goethe (1799). Flaxman maintained a lifelong friendship with William *Blake; the two artists influenced one another, and Blake engraved Flaxman's illustrations to *Hesiod in 1817. He was created professor of sculpture at the Royal Academy in 1810, and his lectures were published posthumously in 1829. See David Irwin, *John Flaxman* (1979).

FLECKER, James Elroy (1884–1915) Poet and playwright, of Jewish descent, born in Cheltenham, educated there at Dean Close School, then Uppingham School, and afterwards at both Oxford and Cambridge. At Trinity College, Oxford, he was influenced by the last flowering of the *Aesthetic movement. During a career in the consular service, which further emphasized his love of the East, he produced several volumes of lyrical romantic verse. His collections include *The Bridge of Fire* (1907), *Forty-Two Poems* (1911), and his best-known collection, *The Golden Journey to Samarkand* (1913). He also published *The Grecians* (1910), a dialogue on education, and an experimental, highly individual novel, *The King of Alsander* (1914). Flecker died of tuberculosis in Switzerland. The work for which he is possibly best remembered is a play, *Hassan* (1922). His other play, *Don Juan*, was published in 1925. See John Sherwood, *No Golden Journey* (1973).

FLECKNOE, Richard (d. ?1678) A lay brother, said to have been a Roman Catholic priest, a writer with an interest in experimental forms, many of whose works were published privately. His *Miscellanea* (1653) includes a defence of the stage (in his 'Discourse upon Languages') and a lament for the theatres silenced under the Commonwealth. His *Ariadne* (1654) is probably the first English opera, though the music (which he composed himself) is lost; its preface, which discusses the use of recitative and the art of writing words for music, shows that he was familiar with current developments in Italy. His *Love's Dominion* (1654), a pastoral with songs, was performed privately on the Continent, and acted after the Restoration under the title *Love's Kingdom*. Its reputation for insipidity, and Andrew *Marvell's earlier satire ('Flecknoe, an English priest at Rome', ?1645), suggested to John *Dryden his attack on Thomas *Shadwell, **Mac Flecknoe*.

FLEMING, Ian (1908–64) Journalist, thriller writer, and bibliophile, educated at Eton College and the Royal Military Academy, Sandhurst; subsequently he worked for Reuters and as foreign manager of Kemsley newspapers. His first novel, *Casino Royale* (1953), introduced the suave hero James *Bond, who subsequently appeared in a series of Cold War adventures with exotic settings, including *Live and Let Die* (1954), *Diamonds Are Forever* (1956), *From Russia with Love* (1957), *Goldfinger* (1959), and *On Her Majesty's Secret Service* (1963), which launched an even more popular film series with *Dr No* (1962). His children's story *Chitty Chitty Bang Bang* (1964), filmed in 1968, became a spectacular stage musical in 2000. There are biographies by John Pearson (1966) and Andrew Lycett (1996). *See also* SPY FICTION.

FLEMING, Peter (1907–71) Journalist and travel writer, brother of Ian *Fleming, educated at Eton College and Christ Church, Oxford, where he read English. He wrote regularly for the **Spectator* (in later years as 'Strix') and *The *Times*, but is remembered largely for his travel books, which include *Brazilian Adventure* (1933), an irreverent account of a search party in the Mato Grosso; *One's Company* (1934), which followed a trip to China to report on the conflict between nationalists and communists; and *News from Tartary* (1936), an account of an overland journey from Peking (Beijing) to Kashmir undertaken with the Swiss traveller Ella Maillart. Fleming served in intelligence and other roles during the Second World War, after which he settled into a family estate in Oxfordshire with the actress Celia Johnson, whom he had married in 1935. He later wrote a number of history books as well as continuing his journalistic career.

Fleshly School of Poetry *See* ROSSETTI, DANTE GABRIEL; BUCHANAN, ROBERT WILLIAMS.

FLETCHER, Giles, the elder (1546–1611) Poet and diplomat, educated at Eton College and King's College, Cambridge, of which he became a fellow, 1568; after leaving Cambridge and marrying, he went on missions to Scotland and Germany. He was sent as envoy to Russia in 1588 and published *Of the Russe Common Wealth*, a pioneering account of Russian government, in 1591. His *Licia, or Poemes of Love*

(1593) is notable both for being one of the first sonnet sequences to follow the publication of **Astrophel and Stella* (1591) and for having a dedication in which he sets out his belief that 'a man may write of love, and not be in love, as well as of husbandry, and not go to plough'. He was the uncle of John *Fletcher and father of Giles and Phineas *Fletcher. His English works were edited by Lloyd E. Berry (1964).

FLETCHER, Giles, the younger (?1586–1623) Poet, younger son of Giles *Fletcher the elder, educated at Westminster School and Trinity College, Cambridge, where he was reader in Greek; then he became rector of Alderton, Suffolk. His best-known poem, *Christ's Victory, and Triumph in Heaven, and Earth, over, and after Death* (1610), is an allegorical work in four cantos dealing respectively with a dispute between Justice and Mercy, the Temptation, the Passion, and the Resurrection and Ascension. It influenced John *Milton's *Paradise Regained*, where Satan's fall from the pinnacle, which has no biblical authority, may reflect the similar fall of Fletcher's tempter Presumption. His works and those of his brother Phineas *Fletcher were edited by F. S. Boas, 2 vols (1908–9).

FLETCHER, John (1579–1625) Playwright, born at Rye in Sussex, where his father Richard (subsequently chaplain at the execution of *Mary Queen of Scots and bishop of Bristol and of London) was then minister. John Fletcher was nephew of Giles *Fletcher the elder and cousin of Giles *Fletcher the younger and Phineas *Fletcher. He was educated at Corpus Christi College, Cambridge, and, after his father's death (in debt and under royal displeasure) in 1596, was left to make his own way in the world. Little is known of his early life; about 1606 he began to write plays in collaboration with Francis *Beaumont, with whom he enjoyed a close personal and professional relationship. Before his death of the plague, he produced some fifteen plays with Beaumont, and around sixteen as sole author. He collaborated with Philip *Massinger, William *Rowley, Thomas *Middleton, Ben *Jonson, George *Chapman, *Shakespeare, and others in the writing of many further works. The chronology of his plays, and the extent of his collaborations, are exceedingly difficult to determine with any precision. Dates given below are mostly approximate dates of first performance.

The principal plays of which Fletcher was probably sole author are: *The *Faithful Shepherdess*, 1608–9; *The *Woman's Prize*, 1609–11; **Valentinian*, 1610–12; *Monsieur Thomas*, a comedy, 1610–13; *Wit without Money*, a comedy, 1614; *The Mad Lover*, 1616; *The *Chances*, 1617; *The *Loyal Subject*, 1618; *Women Pleased*, a comedy, 1618; *The *Humorous Lieutenant*, 1619; *The *Wild Goose Chase*, 1620–21; *The Pilgrim*, a comedy, 1621; *The Island Princess*, a romantic comedy, 1621; *A Wife for a Month*, a romantic drama, 1624; **Rule a Wife and Have a Wife*, 1624.

Plays certainly or probably by Beaumont and Fletcher are: *Cupid's Revenge*, a tragedy based on material in the second book of Sidney's **Arcadia*, 1607–8, printed 1615; **Philaster*, 1608–9; *The Coxcomb*, a romantic comedy, 1608–10; *The Captain*, a comedy, 1609–11; **Bonduca*, 1609–14; *The *Maid's Tragedy*, 1610; *A *King and No King*, 1611; *Four Plays in One*, four short plays (two founded on *Boccaccio, one on *Bandello, one an allegory about false and true friends), *c.*1613 (possibly with collaboration from Nathan *Field); *The Scornful Lady*, 1613, printed 1616; **Thierry King of France*, 1613, printed 1621 (with Beaumont and Massinger); *The Honest Man's Fortune*, 1613, printed 1647; *The Knight of Malta*, a tragicomedy, 1618, printed 1647; *Love's Cure* (later rewritten by Massinger, printed 1647).

The following plays are probably by Fletcher and some other dramatists: *Love's Pilgrimage* and *The Double Marriage*, comedies, printed 1647; *Sir John Van *Oldenbarnavelt*, performed 1619; *The *Custom of the Country*, 1619; *The *False One*, 1621; *The Little French Lawyer*, 1621; *The Laws of Candy*, printed 1647; *The *Spanish Curate* and *The *Beggar's Bush*, both performed 1622. In all the above Fletcher certainly or probably collaborated with Massinger. The romantic drama *The *Lovers' Progress*, performed 1623, was later revised by Massinger. *The Maid in the Mill* was written by Fletcher and Rowley, 1623. *The *Elder Brother*, printed 1637, is thought to have been written by Fletcher and revised by Massinger. *The Fair Maid of the Inn*, 1626, was probably the result of a collaboration between Fletcher and Massinger, possibly with assistance from Jonson, John *Webster, and Rowley. *The Nice Valour*, a comedy, printed 1647 (which contains the lyric 'Hence all you vain delights', which suggested Milton's *'Il Penseroso'), was probably by Fletcher and Middleton. *The *Bloody Brother, or Rollo, Duke of Normandy* (performed *c.*1616) is by Fletcher, Jonson, Chapman, and Massinger. *The Noble Gentleman*, a comedy, acted 1626, is probably by Fletcher, possibly with Beaumont or Rowley. Fletcher also collaborated with Shakespeare in *The *Two Noble Kinsmen*, **Henry VIII*, and the lost **Cardenio*.

The attribution of various plays in the Beaumont and Fletcher canon by use of versification and idiom tests was pioneered by F. G. Fleay, in 'On Metrical Tests as Applied to Dramatic Poetry' (1874), and his successors in the field include E. H. C. Oliphant (*The Plays of Beaumont and Fletcher*, 1927); C. Hoy ('The Shares of Fletcher and his Collaborators in the Beaumont and Fletcher Canon', in *Studies in Bibliography*, 1956–7, 1958–62); and B. Hensman, *The Shares of Fletcher, Field, and Massinger in Twelve Plays of the Beaumont and Fletcher Canon* (1974). There is a scholarly edition of the works under the general editorship of F. Bowers, 10 vols, 1966–96; more accessible editions of individual plays are available in series such as the Revels Plays and the new Mermaids.

FLETCHER, Phineas (1582–1650) Poet, elder son of Giles *Fletcher the elder, educated at Eton College and King's College, Cambridge, and rector of Hilgay, Norfolk. Like his brother Giles *Fletcher the younger, he was a poet of the Spenserian school. His parallel poems in Latin and English, *The Locusts, or Apollyonists* (1627), attack the Jesuits, and contain a diabolical conclave that may have influenced John *Milton. *The Purple Island* (1633) is an ingenious allegorical account of the human body and mind. The same volume contains *Piscatory Eclogues*, featuring fisher boys on the banks of the Cam. *Britain's Ida* (1628), published as Edmund *Spenser's, may be his. The works of Phineas and his brother

Giles Fletcher were edited by F. S. Boas, 2 vols (1908–9); see also Dinah *Craik's novel *John Halifax, Gentleman*, where the narrator is named 'Phineas Fletcher'.

FLINDERS, Matthew (1774–1814) Navigator and hydrographer (or ocean-mapper), born at Donington, Lincolnshire, son of a surgeon. Attending local schools, he was 'induced to go to sea...from reading *Robinson Crusoe*'. A budding naval career, including service under William Bligh (*see* BOUNTY), took him to Sydney in 1795, where he explored the coastline. With George Bass he established that Van Diemen's Land was an island, publishing his careful surveys in 1801 and attracting the attention of Sir Joseph *Banks. Charged with a well-equipped scientific expedition to systematically survey the coast of New Holland, he was first to circumnavigate the continent and largely completed its mapping, but when returning to Britain he was detained by the French governor of Mauritius for six years. In 1804 he was first to suggest the name Australia for the continent. Back in London he completed *A Voyage to Terra Australis* under Banks's supervision. It was published the day before he died.

Flodden (Floddon) **Field** The battle of Flodden, in Northumberland, fought on 9 September 1513, when Thomas Howard, *earl of Surrey, on behalf of *Henry VIII (then in France), defeated James IV of Scotland, the latter being killed on the field along with some 10,000 of his followers. It was made the subject of poems, of rejoicing or lament, on both sides of the border. John *Skelton's 'Against the Scots' is a song of exultation of the English victory, and several English ballads appeared. On the Scottish side there is the beautiful lament 'The Flowers o' the Forest', of which the most popular version is by Jean *Elliot: *see also* COCKBURN, ALISON. The battle is described in the sixth canto of Walter *Scott's *Marmion: A Tale of Flodden Field*.

Flood *See* BIBLE.

FLORENCE OF WORCESTER (d. 1118) A monk of Worcester, formerly but incorrectly regarded as the author of the *Chronicon ex Chronicis* from its beginning to 1117, when it was continued by other hands to its end in 1295. A modern view regards the *Chronicon* as the work of John of Worcester. Florence, praised in an obituary (1118), was possibly involved in compiling the material of the *Chronicon* up to 1117. See A. Gransden, *Historical Writing in England c.550-c.1307* (1974).

Florimell In Edmund *Spenser's *Faerie Queene*, Books III and IV, the type of chastity and virtue in woman. She is in love with the knight Marinell, who 'sets nought' by her. She takes refuge from her pursuers in the sea and is imprisoned by Proteus. Finally, Marinell's heart is touched by the expressions of grief in her complaint, and Neptune orders Proteus to release her.

FLORIO, John (*c*.1553–1626) Writer, translator, and teacher of languages, son of an Italian Protestant refugee, born in London and educated at Magdalen College, Oxford. After a spell as tutor to the earl of Southampton he was reader in Italian to Anne of Denmark, wife of James I (1603), and groom of the privy chamber from 1604. His interesting collections of Italian–English dialogues, *First* and *Second Fruits*, were followed in 1598 by an Italian dictionary entitled *A World of Words*; it was revised and augmented as *Queen Anna's New World of Words* (1611). His most important work was his translation from *Montaigne: *Essays or Moral, Politic and Military Discourses* (1603, 1613). Not only did Florio make Montaigne's work available in English, but he displayed great resourcefulness and ingenuity in the process of translation. Florio's friends included Samuel *Daniel and Ben *Jonson, and some have thought that Shakespeare ridiculed him in *Love's Labour's Lost*. Certainly Shakespeare drew on Florio's version of Montaigne, in *The *Tempest* and elsewhere. Florio has also been suggested as the earliest translator of the *Decameron*. There is a book on him by F. A. *Yates (1934); see also M. Wyatt, *The Italian Encounter with Tudor England: A Cultural Politics of Translation* (2005).

Floris and Blancheflour A Middle English metrical romance in 1,083 lines from the first half of the 13th century, based on a 12th-century French original and surviving in four later manuscripts, all of which lack the opening lines. Floris and Blancheflour are brought up together: he is the son of a Saracen king and she the daughter of a Christian lady who has been captured and brought to the king's court. They fall in love and Blancheflour is banished. Floris sets off to find her, equipped with a precious cup and a magic ring which prove instrumental in his finding her and their ultimate marriage by consent of the emir. The story, which has analogues in the *Arabian Nights* and other works, is the subject of *Boccaccio's *Filocolo*. The English romance is one of the most popular of its genre. See editions by A. B. Taylor (1927) and in D. B. Sands, *Middle English Verse Romances* (1966).

Florizel In Shakespeare's *The *Winter's Tale*, the prince of Bohemia who falls in love with the rustic Perdita. 'Florizel' was the name adopted by George IV, when prince of Wales, in his correspondence with Mary *Robinson, the actress, with whose performance as Perdita he had been captivated.

Floure and the Leaf, The A 15th-century allegory in 595 lines of *rhyme royal, formerly but erroneously attributed to Geoffrey *Chaucer. The followers of the flower and the leaf were the two parties in the mannered, courtly debates on love in the French poetry of writers such as *Deschamps. In the English poem, the poet wandering in a grove sees the white company of knights and ladies of the leaf (Diana, goddess of chastity) and the green company of the flower (Flora), 'folk that loved idleness' and had delight 'of no businesse but for to hunt and hauke and pley in medes'. It has the charm of its tradition, and it was modernized by John *Dryden in his *Fables Ancient and Modern*. There is an edition by D. A. Pearsall (1990).

FLUDD, Robert (1574–1637) Educated at St John's College, Oxford, and on the Continent; he became a fellow of the Royal College of Physicians in 1609, and had a successful practice. He entered the debate on the authenticity of the *Rosicrucian texts with his defence, *Apologia*, in 1616, and was deeply interested in Hermeticism and *Neoplatonism, which he held to be of greater authority than *Aristotle and *Galen. His views on the universe as macrocosm–microcosm attracted much controversy, but despite his own mystical views on the circulation of the blood, he was the first to defend William *Harvey's *De Motu Cordis*. The standard biography is by J. B. Craven, 1902; see also A. G. Debus, *The English Paracelsians* (1965); F. A. *Yates, *The Rosicrucian Enlightenment* (1972). Hilary *Mantel's novel *Fludd* (1989) draws on Fludd's life.

flyting [from the Old English *flītan*, to quarrel or dispute] A verse contest in insults, practised in particular by the Scottish poets of the early 16th century but present in Old English and Old Norse literature. The most famous example is the 'Flyting of *Dunbar and Kennedie'.

FO, Dario (1926–) Italian playwright, actor, director, and political activist, born in Varese in northern Italy. He has written and produced many classical *farces and comedies, often in collaboration with his wife, Franca Rame: many of these have been performed worldwide in various adaptations and translations. Well known among them are *Morte accidentale di un anarchico* (1970: *Accidental Death of an Anarchist*, 1979), inspired by a 1969 bomb explosion in Milan and the subsequent death in police custody of innocent suspect Pino Pinelli; *Non si paga, non si paga!* (1974: *Can't Pay, Won't Pay*); and *Clacson trombette & pernacchi* (1981: *Trumpets and Raspberries*, 1984), a comedy which uses a mistaken identity ploy to explore political corruption and the workings of the Fiat corporation. Fo was awarded the *Nobel Prize in 1997. See T. Behan, *Dario Fo: Revolutionary Theatre* (2000).

focalization The technical term in modern *narratology for the adoption of a limited 'point of view' from which the events of a given story are witnessed, usually by a character within the fictional world. Unlike the 'omniscient' perspective of traditional stories, which in principle allows the narrator privileged insight into all characters' secret motives and the ability to recount simultaneous events in different places, a focalized narrative constrains its perspective within the limited awareness available to a particular witness, to whom the thoughts of other characters remain opaque. As seeing differs from telling, such a focalizing observer is not necessarily the narrator of the story, but may be a character in an account given by a third-person narrator: this method of using a 'centre of consciousness' within the fictional world is associated especially with Henry *James, but has been widely adopted by other novelists.

FOGAZZARO, Antonio (1842–1911) Italian novelist and essayist. His humour and powers of characterization are at their best in *Piccolo mondo antico* (1895: *The Little World of the Past*), set north of Lake Lugano during the last ten years of Austrian rule, and reflecting the author's Catholic preoccupations. Owing to his unorthodoxy two of his novels, *Il santo* (1905: *The Saint*) and *Leila* (1910), were placed on the *Index Expurgatorius*, as containing passages to be deleted or altered before the works could be approved for reading by Roman Catholics.

FOLENGO, Teophilo (1491–1544) An Italian Benedictine monk and writer in several genres. Under the pseudonym 'Merlin Coccai' he wrote a long burlesque-heroic poem, *Baldus (Opus Macaronicum)*, in *macaronic Latin *hexameters. Its hero is Baldus, who has for followers the giant Fracassus and the cunning Cingar. Folengo's admiration for, and burlesquing of, the Italian romance epic tradition is also a feature of his *Orlandino*. Folengo's influence is evident in *Rabelais. *See* CHIVALRIC/ROMANCE EPIC.

folios and quartos, Shakespearian Shakespeare's earliest published plays (like other early books) are referred to as folios or quartos according to the folding of the printed sheets and therefore the size of the book. Folios, being printed from sheets that have been folded once, are large and tall; quartos, printed from sheets folded twice, are smaller and squarer.

Of about 750 copies of the first folio printed between February 1622 and November 1623 and sold, probably for fifteen shillings each unbound, by the *Jaggards, some 230 survive in various states of preservation, 80 or so in the Folger Shakespeare Library and twelve in Meisei University, Tokyo. Fragments of an incinerated copy are preserved in a glass case in Philadelphia. A second folio was issued in 1632, containing 'An Epitaph on…Shakespeare' by *Milton, his first published poem. A third folio was issued in 1663, whose second impression of 1664 contained *Pericles* and six apocryphal plays; the fourth and last folio was published in 1685. Thirty-six plays, eighteen printed for the first time, were arranged by *Heminges and Condell into sections of comedies, histories, and tragedies for the first folio. It was dedicated to the brothers William Herbert, earl of Pembroke, and Philip Herbert, earl of Montgomery, and contains the *Droeshout portrait and a list of 'the Principal Actors in all these Plays', together with commendatory verses by contemporaries including Ben *Jonson.

During his lifetime eighteen of Shakespeare's plays were published in quartos, some of them with reprints, and *Othello* appeared in 1622. Following A. W. *Pollard's analysis, it used to be thought that over half of those quartos were 'bad' ones, that is, that their texts are extremely corrupt as a result of their reconstruction from memory by a member, or members, of their cast. Thus, the first edition (Q1, or the first quarto) of *The Merry Wives of Windsor* (1602) is probably based on the recollections of the actor who played the part of the Host. Some 'bad' quartos, for example *The First Part of the Contention* (1594) and *The True Tragedy of Richard Duke of York* (1595), were once thought of as source plays (for *2* and *3* **Henry VI*); similarly the quarto *The Taming of a Shrew* (1594) has been thought of as 'bad' and the folio text, *The *Taming of the Shrew*, as 'good'. In two cases, **Romeo and Juliet* (1597) and **Hamlet* (1603), 'good' second quartos were soon issued (in 1599 and 1604–5 respectively) to correct the 'bad' first quartos. The nature and number of these 'bad' (or 'short') quartos have been much disputed and theories about their origins have included the possibility that they derive from shorthand accounts taken down by members of the theatrical company or of the audience, that they represent authorial first drafts, and that they represent shortened or altered versions of the play made for various circumstances, such as provincial touring. It is increasingly thought that even 'bad' quartos may preserve authoritative theatrical readings.

Textual criticism and bibliography have largely been concerned with establishing relationships between the 'good' quartos (in some cases the 'bad' ones as well) and their versions in the first folio, to determine on which text an editor is to base his edition. In trying to establish this relationship scholars have mainly sought to determine the nature of the copy which the printers used. The chief types of copy which have been distinguished are: (1) 'foul papers', that is an original authorial draft, as in Q1 of *A *Midsummer Night's Dream* (1600); (2) a fair scribal copy, as in the folio text of *The *Tempest*; (3) a prompt copy from the theatre, as in the folio text of **As You Like It*; (4) a memorial text, as discussed above; and (5) a reconstructed text, that is one based on an early quarto but where some kind of manuscript copy has also been used, as in the case of the folio text of **Richard III*. There is still much disagreement about the nature of these categories and to which ones the plays in their various quarto and folio versions belong.

The fullest accounts of the first folio are W. W. *Greg's *The Shakespeare First Folio* (1955); C. *Hinman's *The Printing and Proof-Reading of the First Folio of Shakespeare* (1963)—see also his Norton Facsimile of F (1968; 2nd edn, 1996); and Anthony James West's *The Shakespeare First Folio* (vols i (2002) and ii (2003) of a projected four volumes have appeared so far). Sixteen facsimiles of quartos were issued in the Oxford Shakespeare Quarto Facsimiles series, ed. W. W. Greg and C. Hinman (1939–75), and the series has been continued by the *Malone Society. Stanley Wells, Gary Taylor, John Jowett, and William Montgomery, *William Shakespeare: A Textual Companion* (1987) provides a valuable introduction to the subject.

folk song A song or ballad, usually without identifiable author, handed down orally from generation to generation, evolving through the modifications of individual performers, often existing in different forms in different parts of the country. In the mid-18th century Thomas *Percy's fashionably edited collections of ballads were concerned mainly with the poetry, but interest in the music was stimulated. The end of the 19th century saw an immense increase of activity in the collection, transcription, and publication of folk songs, driven by an anxiety about the effects of industrialization and urbanization on rural culture. The Folk-Song Society was founded in 1898, and Cecil *Sharp's Folk Dance Society followed in 1911; the two were amalgamated in 1932. The composers Percy *Grainger, Gustav *Holst, Ralph *Vaughan Williams, and George *Butterworth all derived inspiration from folk song.

Fomorians The sea-giants of Gaelic mythology. They are represented as more ancient than the gods (the *Tuatha Dé Danann), and as having been ousted by them and destroyed at the battle of Moytura (C. Squire, *Mythology of the British Islands*, 1905).
See also BALOR.

FONTANE, Theodor (1819–98) German travel writer and novelist. His travel writing includes an account of his first summer in London (*Ein Sommer in London*, 1854). He is best known for the novels *Frau Jenny Treibel* (1892), an ironic criticism of middle-class hypocrisy and small-mindedness, and *Effi Briest* (1895), a socially critical novel of adultery, made into an acclaimed film by R. W. Fassbinder. In his handling of the theme Fontane has been compared to Gustave *Flaubert and Lev *Tolstoy. He had an abiding interest in ballad and folk poetry, and was an ardent admirer of Robert *Burns and Walter *Scott. He translated a number of traditional ballads, such as 'Edward, Edward', into German, as well as contemporary street ballads which he encountered during his stay as an official correspondent in London (1855–59), and Alfred *Tennyson's 'Charge of the Light Brigade'.

FONTENELLE, Bernard le Bovier (1657–1757) French man of letters. The nephew of *Corneille, he was a man of wide learning whose critical approach paved the way for the *Enlightenment. His best-known works include the *Nouveaux Dialogues des morts* (1683: *New Dialogues of the Dead*), indebted to *Lucian of Samosata but thoroughly modern in their sceptical assessment of received ideas, and the *Entretiens sur la pluralité des mondes* (1686: *Conversations on the Plurality of Worlds*), a popular introduction to contemporary scientific ideas which was translated into English by Aphra *Behn as early as 1688.

fool A character appearing in various forms in English drama, most notably in the works of Shakespeare and his contemporaries. The fool has a variety of origins, from the medieval court jester to the licensed clown of the *Feast of Fools. He has numerous incarnations in Shakespeare: as the simpleton (the clown in *The *Winter's Tale*), the rogue (Autolycus, also in *The Winter's Tale*), and the wise court jester (the Fool in **King Lear*), licensed to speak freely, however satirically or disrespectfully. He is also related to the Arlecchino of the **commedia dell'arte*.

Richard *Tarlton was the most famous comic actor of his day, known for his talent for improvised doggerel; he played the main comic parts in the Queen's Company of players until his death in 1588. In Shakespeare's company the fools' parts were played by William *Kemp until his retirement *c.*1599, when he was replaced by Robert Armin, a more subtle actor for whom Shakespeare probably wrote the more complex parts of Feste in **Twelfth Night* and the Fool in *King Lear*. These actors were closely associated with the parts they played, and Kemp's name appeared in the place of the characters' in early printings of *Romeo and Juliet* and *Much Ado about Nothing*. See D. Wiles, *Shakespeare's Clown* (1987).

Fool of Quality, The A novel in five volumes by Henry *Brooke, published in Dublin 1765–70 and in London 1766–70. Harry Clinton, the Fool of Quality, is the second son of the earl of Moreland; the narrative follows his education, growth, and manhood. The most important adult in his world is not his decadent father but his merchant uncle, Mr Clinton (sometimes Fenton), whose enlightened views on Harry's education (much influenced by *Rousseau's *Émile* and John *Locke's *On Education*) guide the boy's growth into a wise and generous adult. Clinton is more than a merchant, since he carries a hint of kingly or even divine power. Harry is protected from calamity largely by his innocence, but Clinton possesses an omnipotence which enables him to rescue the unfortunate, such as Hammel Clement and his family, from disaster and destitution; and a philosophy which reconciles human wretchedness with divine providence. The various episodes, much interrupted by literary and philosophical digression and by discussions between the author and a 'friend' on the text itself, fluctuate between extremes of euphoria and despair, and the tone of the narration is held at a high level of tearful, ecstatic, or nostalgic sensibility. The book appealed greatly to John *Wesley and to Charles *Kingsley (who found it 'more pure, sacred and eternal than anything since the *Faerie Queene*', and who drew on it for his own novel **Yeast*); both produced new editions of it.

foot A metrical unit of two, three, or (very rarely) four syllables.
See METRE.

FOOTE, Samuel (1721–77) Actor and dramatist, educated at Worcester College, Oxford, but sent down in 1740 without a degree. His stage debut was in the role of Othello, and he acted in many stock plays, but his real talent was for comic mimicry: in 1747 he produced *Diversions of the Morning*, a successful revue caricaturing several prominent actors. There followed a series of comic pieces and puppet shows, including *Taste* (1752), *The Minor* (1760), *The Patron* (1764), and *The Nabob* (1772), all satirizing contemporary personalities (including some of Foote's friends). Foote's leg was amputated in 1766, after a fall from a horse, but he continued to act with a specially made wooden leg. Foote was often embroiled in literary feuds with writers like Henry *Fielding and Charles *Churchill, and other victims of his ruthless impersonations. He was accused of sodomy in 1776 and, though acquitted, died within a year.

FORBES, Rosita (1890–1967) Traveller and writer, born at Riseholme Hall, Lincolnshire. Her first marriage, to Colonel Ronald Foster Forbes in 1911, ended in divorce six years later. After serving as an ambulance driver in the First World War, she travelled extensively and developed an interest in the Arab world. Her several travel books include *The Secret of the Sahara: Kufara* (1921), which recounted her journey, disguised as a Muslim, across the Libyan desert with Egyptian explorer Ahmad Hassanein, whose role she understated; *From Red Sea to Blue Nile* (1925); and *Conflict: Angora to Afghanistan* (1931). Forbes married Colonel Arthur Thomas McGrath in 1921 and visited the Yemen, again in disguise, the following year. She visited South America with her husband in 1931, and Afghanistan in 1936. She published two volumes of autobiography, *Gypsy in the Sun* (1944) and *Appointment with Destiny* (1946).

FORD, Ford Madox (formerly Ford Hermann Hueffer) (1873–1939) Novelist and editor, the son of Dr Francis Hueffer, a music critic of *The *Times*, and grandson of the *Pre-Raphaelite painter Ford Madox Brown; he was deeply affected by his Pre-Raphaelite inheritance, and expressed ambiguous feelings towards it in both critical and fictional works. His first published works were *fairy stories, beginning with *The Brown Owl* (1891). In 1894 he eloped with and married Elsie Martindale, an act which was prelude to a turbulent emotional life. In 1898 he met Joseph *Conrad and they collaborated in various works including the novels *The Inheritors* (1901) and *Romance* (1903); for some years they worked in happy intimacy, united by their faith in 'the novel as a work of Art', although from 1901 their relationship deteriorated: Ford's own published recollections of it are revealing but not reliable. During a diverse and productive literary career Ford published over 80 books, both fiction and non-fiction. He developed his own theory of 'Impressionism' in the novel and non-fictional prose, applied to great effect in *The Soul of London* (1905), a vivid portrait of the fabric and life of the city. In 1908 Ford embarked on two significant enterprises, an affair with the glamorous and emancipated novelist Violet *Hunt, which was to involve him in scandal and in complex, unsuccessful divorce proceedings; and the founding of the **English Review*, which he edited for fifteen months, with much éclat but also with much financial and personal stress.

In 1915 Ford published what he himself regarded as his finest achievement, his 'one novel', *The *Good Soldier*, and in the same year enlisted in the army: he was invalided home from France in 1917 and changed his name from Hueffer to Ford in 1919. The war inspired a volume of poems (1918), sketches, and propaganda pieces written for his friend Charles Masterman; also, more significantly, his other major work of fiction, now known as *Parade's End* (or sometimes, after its hero, as the 'Tietjens' tetralogy), which was published in four parts between 1924 and 1928. Ford began writing it in France, which became his home in 1922. In Paris in 1924 he founded the *Transatlantic Review*, in which he published work by *Joyce, *Pound, Gertrude *Stein, E. E. *Cummings, and others. During his last years, which were spent in France and America, he published further novels, notably *The Rash Act* (1933), several volumes of autobiography and reminiscence (including *Return to Yesterday*, 1931, and *It Was the Nightingale*, 1933), and a final characteristically personal and ambitious volume of criticism, *The March of Literature* (1938). He died in Deauville. As a writer he has been more studied than read, a neglect due partly, perhaps, to the diversity of his output, and partly to his own unsettled emotional and eccentric personality, which has somehow obscured the outlines of his achievements; as an editor he has long been regarded as a highly influential figure whose devotion to literature and ready appreciation of originality and quality in others (*see* MODERNISM) did much to shape the course of 20th-century writing. See Max Saunders, *Ford Madox Ford: A Dual Life* (2 vols, 1996).

FORD, John (1586–after 1639) Playwright, born in Devon of a landed family, and admitted to the Middle Temple in 1602. He probably spent many years there, since he is called 'Master John Ford, of the Middle Temple' as late as 1638. His earliest work was non-dramatic (1606–20), but he appears to have written all or a substantial part of around twenty plays, some of them lost. Between 1621 and 1625 he collaborated with Thomas *Dekker and others in at least five plays including *The *Witch of Edmonton*. After 1625 Ford probably worked alone. His chief plays are *The *Lover's Melancholy* (1629), **Love's Sacrifice* (1633), **'Tis Pity She's a Whore* (1633), *The *Broken Heart* (1633), **Perkin Warbeck* (1634), and *The Lady's Trial* (1639). Ford's plays are predominantly concerned with courage and endurance in suffering. He explores melancholy, torture, incest, delusion, but always seriously and objectively, through 'the distinct personal rhythm in blank verse which could be no one's but his alone' (T. S. *Eliot). He is described in William Heminges's 'Elegy on Randolph's Finger': 'Deep in a dump Jack Ford alone was got | With folded arms and melancholy hat.'

There is as yet no modern complete edition; single plays are available in a number of series including the Revels Plays and New Mermaids.

FORD, Mark (1929–) Poet and critic, born in Nairobi and educated at various international schools, Oxford, and Harvard. From 1991 to 1993 he was visiting lecturer at Kyoto University and subsequently became professor of English at University College London. A D.Phil. in contemporary American poetry preceded his editing of two anthologies of New York School poetry, *The New York Poets* (2004) and *The New York Poets II* (2005), and a book-length interview with John *Ashbery (2003). It is with this poet that his own work is most often aligned. Two collections, *Landlocked* (1992) and *Soft Sift* (2001), entwine witty, erudite, emotionally complex discourses in self-conscious ways that recall Ashbery's work. He incorporates a much broader variety of cultural influences than this, however. Some of these are explored in his eclectic collection *A Driftwood Altar: Essays and Reviews* (2005). Other engaging critical work includes *Raymond Roussel and the Republic of Dreams* (2000).

FORD, Richard (1796–1858) Educated at Winchester College and Trinity College, Oxford, author of *A Handbook for Travellers in Spain* (1845), in which country he lived between 1830 and 1834. Ford was a connoisseur of Spanish art and, through articles for the *Quarterly Review* and other periodicals, was largely responsible for introducing English readers to Velázquez.

FORD, Richard (1944–) American novelist and writer of short stories, born in Jackson, Mississippi. He is best known for his novel *The Sportswriter* (1986), followed by *Independence Day* (1995) and *The Lay of the Land* (2006). These novels, wistfully lyrical and sharply realistic by turns, tell the story of Frank Bascombe, novelist turned eponymous sportswriter, who by the second novel has quit his job and moved into the real-estate market. Ford is the author of three other novels, including *The Ultimate Good Luck* (1981). His story collections, which include *Rock Springs* (1987) and *Women with Men* (1997), have been associated with *dirty realism and frequently compared with the work of contemporaries like Raymond *Carver.

FOREST, Antonia (1915–2003) Novelist, born in Hampstead, London, educated at University College London; her thirteen rich and complex novels (1948–82) combine elements of *school and *family novels and *historical fiction. All but one of her books feature the Marlow family, sometimes in the Elizabethan period, sometimes in the mid-20th century.

Forest, The A collection of miscellaneous short poems, odes, epistles, and songs, by Ben *Jonson, printed in the folio of 1616, including 'To Penshurst' and the songs 'Drink to me only with thine eyes' and, from **Volpone*, 'Come, my Celia, let us prove'. The title was suggested by Latin *silva*, which can mean both 'collection' and 'wood'.

FORESTER, C. S. (Cecil Scott) (1899–1966) The pen-name of Cecil Lewis Troughton Smith, novelist, principally remembered for his seafaring novels set during the Napoleonic Wars, featuring Horatio Hornblower, introduced in 1937 in *The Happy Return*, and rising by degrees over subsequent volumes to the rank of admiral. Forester gives an account of his own creation in *The Hornblower Companion* (1964). His other works include *Brown on Resolution* (1929) and *The African Queen* (1935; filmed 1951, with a screenplay by James *Agee).

formalism A term applied, usually pejoratively, to any creative performance in which technique or manner seems to have been cultivated at the expense of substance; or to critical approaches that disregard the subject matter of a work in favour of discussing its formal or stylistic features. More positively, formalism as a critical principle may be defended as a way of understanding art or literature primarily through its techniques rather than as a mere vehicle for personal expression or for moral and political doctrines. Formalism thus exists in continuous dispute with a range of biographical, social, and religious modes of criticism that show more interest in the 'message' of an art than in the medium. Just as in literary *modernism a 'formalist' emphasis on creative technical experiment is prominent, so in modern literary criticism formalism has been a powerful principle, notably in the *New Criticism of the mid-20th century. Outside the English-speaking world, the most important such critical tradition has been that of the *'Russian formalists'—a label applied to two groups of linguistic and literary scholars active in St Petersburg and Moscow in the period 1915–30, led by Roman Jakobson (1896–1982) and Viktor Shklovsky (1893–1984). Repudiating the mainly psychological and historical methods of previous Russian critics, they inaugurated a new 'scientific' approach to literature that focused upon the linguistic 'devices' and conventions—from metre to plot structure—by which literature distinguishes itself from ordinary uses of language. They thus attempted to arrive at an objective account of 'literariness' through formal linguistic analysis, and of its principal effects through the concept of *defamiliarization. Stalin's suppression of intellectual life led to a recantation by Shklovsky in 1930, but Jakobson had earlier emigrated to Czechoslovakia, where he helped to found in 1926 the Prague Linguistic Circle, which became a major link between Russian formalism and the emergence of the broader *structuralist movement. Meanwhile in Russia the arguments of the formalists had influenced, partly through strong disagreement, the work of *Bakhtin and his group. In the West, the work of Shklovsky and his associates, Boris Tomashevsky, Boris Eikhenbaum, and Vladimir Propp, was rediscovered in the 1960s; Propp's work in particular encouraged the development of *narratology. See Peter Steiner, *Russian Formalism* (1984).

FORMAN, Simon (1552–1611) Physician and astrologer, a picturesque character who left voluminous notebooks of great interest to social historians and others. In his *Book of Plays* (preserved in a manuscript in the Bodleian Library, Oxford) he records and comments on visits to performances of Shakespeare's **Macbeth* and *The *Winter's Tale* at the Globe Theatre in 1611, and to **Cymbeline* at an unnamed playhouse.

FORREST, Leon (1937–97) African American novelist who was born in Chicago and from 1965 to 1973 worked as a journalist. His first three novels were edited by Toni *Morrison, then working at Random House. *The Bloodworth Orphans* (1977) was respectfully received, although Forrest's work has been criticized for its complexity. *Divine Days* (1992) is akin to James *Joyce in its scale and brief time-span, and concerns a playwright who can hear and incorporate the voices of others into his narrative. In addition to fiction, Forrest wrote two musical libretti: *Re-Creation* (1978) and *Soldier Boy, Soldier* (1982). Despite endorsements from Saul *Bellow and others, Forrest's work has only slowly been recognized.

FORREST-THOMSON, Veronica (1947–75) British poet and critic. She was born in Malaya, grew up in Glasgow, and studied English at Liverpool, before moving to Cambridge. Her doctoral thesis, 'Poetry as Knowledge: The Use of Science by Twentieth-Century Poets', was supervised first by J. H. *Prynne and later by Graham Hough. Forrest-Thomson held academic posts in Leicester and Birmingham and her critical book *Poetic Artifice: A Theory of Twentieth-Century Poetry* was published in 1974. In it she explores the relationship between the language of ordinary experience and poetic language which 'must work to create its alternative imaginary orders'. Forrest-Thomson was briefly married to the critic Jonathan Culler. Her poetry was greatly influenced by William *Empson, Ludwig *Wittgenstein, Roland *Barthes, and other writers of the Tel Quel group in France. Collections include *Identi-Kit* (1967), *Language Games* (1971), and, posthumously, *On the Periphery* (1976). A revised *Collected Poems* was published in 2008.

Fors Clavigera: *Letters to the Workmen and Labourers of Great Britain* By John *Ruskin, issued monthly from January 1871 to March 1878, then at irregular intervals: two numbers appeared in 1880, four in 1883, the last three in 1884. *Fors Clavigera* was a sustained challenge, deliberate and serious, to the supporters of a capitalist economy. The obscurity of the title, and extraordinary diversity of subject matter, suggest how little he wished to ingratiate himself with the working classes. He analyses the letters of 'clerks, manufacturers and other' in the 'Notes and Correspondence' section as mercilessly as the writings and speeches of his more famous enemies; only the painter James *Whistler sued for libel. Ruskin's tactics were demonstrative rather than discursive. He delivers lessons in 'the principles and plans of political economy' by setting events from contemporary history and his own immediate experience against the nobler human possibilities expressed in literature and art. *Fors Clavigera*, which attracted a wide and disparate readership, became the mouthpiece of Ruskin's utopian Guild of St George. See *Fors Clavigera*, ed. D. Birch (2000).

FORSTER, E. M. (Edward Morgan) (1879–1970) Novelist, essayist, and short story writer, born in London, the only child of Edward Morgan Forster, architect, who died in 1880, and Alice 'Lily' Whichelo (1855–1945). His boyhood was dominated by women, among them his influential great-aunt Marianne Thornton; on her death in 1887 she left him £8,000 in trust. His happiest childhood years (1883–90) were spent at Rooksnest, Stevenage, a house he evokes in **Howards End*. He was a boarder (1890–93) at Kent House preparatory school, Eastbourne, and on leaving it he and his mother moved to Tonbridge, Kent, where Forster attended Tonbridge School; he later claimed to have been deeply unhappy there. In 1897 he went to King's College, Cambridge, where he found congenial friends; the atmosphere of free intellectual discussion, and a stress on the importance of personal relationships inspired partly by the philosopher G. E. Moore (1873–1958), was to have a profound influence on his work. In 1901 he was elected to the *Apostles and largely through them was later drawn into closer contact with *Bloomsbury. A year of travel in Italy and a cruise to Greece followed, providing rich material for a number of stories and his first and third novels, in which the attitudes of English tourists abroad, thoroughly repressed, *Baedekers in hand, clinging to English *pensioni*, and suspicious of anything foreign, are satirized. On his return from Greece he began to write for the new *Independent Review*, launched by a group of Cambridge friends, led by G. M. *Trevelyan; in 1904 it published his first short story, 'The Story of a Panic'. In 1905 he completed *Where Angels Fear to Tread*, which was published the same year, and spent some months in Germany as tutor to the children of Elizabeth *von Arnim. In 1906, now established with his mother in Weybridge, he became tutor to Syed Ross Masood (1889–1937), a striking and colourful Indian Muslim patriot, for whom Forster developed an intense affection. *The Longest Journey* appeared in 1907, *A *Room with a View* in 1908, and *Howards End*, which established Forster as a writer of importance, in 1910. The following year he published *The Celestial Omnibus*, a collection of short stories, mostly pastoral and whimsical in tone and subject matter, and in 1912–13 he visited India for some months. In 1913 a significant visit to the home of Edward *Carpenter resulted in his writing *Maurice*, a novel with a homosexual theme which he circulated privately; it was published posthumously in 1971. This novel did not, as he had hoped, open a new vein of creativity, and the outbreak of war further impeded his career. He worked for a while at the National Gallery, then went to Alexandria in 1915 to work for the Red Cross; his *Alexandria: A History and a Guide* was published somewhat abortively in 1922 and reprinted in revised form in 1938. In Alexandria he met the Greek poet C. P. *Cavafy, whose works, on his return to England in 1919, he helped to introduce; an essay on Cavafy appears in Forster's *Pharos and Pharillon* (1923). In 1921–2 he revisited India, working as personal secretary for the maharaja of the native state of Dewas Senior for several months. The completion of *A *Passage to India*, which he had begun before the war, was overshadowed by the death of his closest Egyptian friend, Muhammad al-Adl, but when the novel appeared in June 1924 it was highly acclaimed. Forster's fears that this would be his last novel proved correct, and the remainder of his life was devoted to a wide range of literary activities; over many years he took a firm stand against censorship, involving himself in the work of *PEN and the National Council for Civil Liberties (forerunner of today's Liberty organization), of which he became the first president in 1934. In 1927 he delivered the Clark Lectures at Cambridge, printed the same year as *Aspects of the Novel*; his tone in these was in his own words 'informal, indeed talkative', and they contain the celebrated comment, 'Yes—oh dear yes—the novel tells a story.' F. R. *Leavis, representing the new school of Cambridge criticism, found the lectures 'intellectually null', but they were a popular success, and King's offered him a three-year fellowship and, in 1946, an honorary fellowship and a permanent home. In 1928 *The Eternal Moment*, a volume of pre-1914 short stories, whimsical and dealing with the supernatural, appeared, and in 1930 he met a policeman named Bob Buckingham with whom he was to enjoy a close and sustaining relationship for the rest of his life. He wrote two biographies, *Goldsworthy Lowes *Dickinson* (1934) and *Marianne Thornton* (1956). *Abinger Harvest*, essays named after Abinger Hammer, the Surrey village in which Forster inherited a house in 1924, appeared in 1936; *Two Cheers for Democracy* came out in 1951 and *The Hill of Devi*, a portrait of India through letters and commentary, in 1953. Between 1949 and 1951 he worked with Eric Crozier (1914–94) on the libretto for Benjamin *Britten's opera *Billy Budd*. He spent his last years in King's College, and was awarded the OM in 1969. *Maurice* was followed by further posthumous publications: *Albergo Empedocle and Other Writings* (1971); *The Life to Come and Other Stories* (1972); *Arctic Summer and Other Fiction* (1980); and *The Prince's Tale and Other Writings* (1999). Five of Forster's novels have been turned into successful feature films. See biographies by P. N. Furbank, 2 vols (1977–8) and Nicola Beauman, *Morgan* (1993).

FORSTER, John (1812–76) Biographer and historian, educated at Newcastle Grammar School, University College London, and the Inner Temple, and called to the bar in 1843. He became drama critic for the *True Sun* in 1832, and then editor of *Foreign Quarterly Review*, 1842–3, *Daily News*, 1846, and *The Examiner*, 1847–55. He was engaged in 1835 to Letitia *Landon, but married Eliza Colburn, the wealthy widow of the publisher Henry *Colburn, in 1856. He was the literary associate and close friend of Leigh *Hunt, Charles *Lamb, Walter Savage *Landor, Edward *Bulwer-Lytton, and Charles *Dickens. From 1837 on he read in manuscript everything Dickens wrote. His popular literary biographies include *Life and Adventures of Oliver Goldsmith* (1848; rev. 2 vols, 1854), *Landor* (2 vols, 1869), *Dickens* (3 vols, 1872–4), and the first volume of a scholarly life of Jonathan *Swift (1875). He is recognized as the first professional biographer of 19th-century England.

FORSTER, Margaret (1938–) Novelist and biographer, born in Carlisle and educated at Somerville College, Oxford. Her first success was *Georgy Girl* (1965; film script with Peter *Nichols 1966), the story of an ordinary girl keen to sample the delights of the Swinging Sixties. Several comedies of contemporary manners followed, but later novels darkened in tone. *Mother Can You Hear Me?* (1979) is a sombre evocation of motherhood, portrayed through three generations of the same family; *Have the Men Had Enough?* (1989) a painful and angry account of old age and dementia. Forster's other fiction includes *Lady's Maid* (1990), *Mother's Boys* (1994), *The Memory Box* (1999), *Keeping the World Away* (2006), and *Over* (2007). Biographical works include lives of Elizabeth Barrett *Browning and Daphne *du Maurier. *Hidden Lives* (1995) and *Precious Lives* (1998) are poignant family memoirs. Forster is married to the author and journalist Hunter Davies (1936–).

Forsyte Saga, The A sequence of five texts by John *Galsworthy, first published in one volume in 1922. The saga comprises three novels, *The Man of Property* (1906), *In Chancery* (1920), and *To Let* (1921), and two interludes, 'Indian Summer of a Forsyte' (1918), and *Awakening* (1920), which together trace the declining fortunes of three generations of the Forsyte family. Among other things, Galsworthy lays bare the urbane brutality and blinding materialism which underpin the 'full plumage' of upper middle-class family life. In *The Man of Property*, Soames Forsyte, a successful solicitor, the nephew of 'old Jolyon', lives in London surrounded by his prosperous old uncles and their families. He marries the penniless Irene and builds a country house for her, Robin Hill; when she falls in love with its architect, Bosinney, Soames reasserts what he regards as his proprietorial rights and rapes her. Bosinney is killed in a street accident and Irene returns to Soames. *In Chancery* describes the growing love of young Jolyon, Soames's cousin, for Irene; Irene's divorce from Soames and her happy marriage with Jolyon; and the birth of their son Jon. Meanwhile Soames marries Annette Lamotte and they have a daughter, Fleur. In *To Let*, Fleur and Jon fall in love; Jon's father feels compelled to reveal the past of Irene and Soames, and the agonized Jon, in spite of Fleur's Forsyte determination, rejects her. She marries Michael Mont, and when young Jolyon dies Irene leaves to join Jon in America. The desolate Soames learns that his wife is having an affair with a Belgian, and discovers that Irene's house, Robin Hill, is empty and to let. *The Forsyte Saga* was serialized in 26 episodes for BBC television in 1967 and proved a phenomenal success. It was also adapted by Granada in 2002 as an ITV mini-series, but to rather less acclaim.

FORSYTH, Frederick *See* SPY FICTION.

FORT, Charles (1847–1932) American journalist and author, born in Albany, New York; whose collections of scientific anomalies including *The Book of the Damned* (1919) influenced numerous *science fiction writers with their iconoclastic scepticism and as sources of ideas. *The Outcast Manufacturers* (1906) is an underrated novel. 'Fortean' phenomena are events which seem to challenge the boundaries of accepted scientific knowledge, and the *Fortean Times* (founded as *The News* in 1973, and renamed in 1976) investigates such phenomena.

FORTESCUE, Sir John (*c*.1397–1479) English constitutional lawyer. A Lancastrian supporter, he was pardoned by Edward IV. His principal works were *De Natura Legis Naturae* (1461–3), distinguishing absolute from constitutional monarchy; a treatise in English on *The Difference between an Absolute and a Limited Monarchy*; *De Laudibus Legum Angliae* (1468–71); and *On the Governance of England* (1470s; ed. C. Plummer, 1885). He recanted Lancastrian views in *A Declaration* (1471–3). See *Works*, ed. Lord Clermont (2 vols, 1869).

Fortnightly Review (1865–1934) An influential and respected literary periodical, which retained its high standard throughout its existence. Despite its title, it was from November 1866 onwards a monthly. The contents were miscellaneous, but the *Review* is largely remembered for its literary value. Almost all numbers ran a serialized novel; the first contained a chapter of Anthony *Trollope's *The Belton Estate* and a part of Walter *Bagehot's *The English Constitution*. Positivist and anti-orthodox, the first editor, G. H. *Lewes, and his successor John *Morley published work by *Thackeray, George *Eliot, Matthew *Arnold, T. H. *Huxley, George *Meredith, D. G. *Rossetti, Leslie *Stephen, Walter *Pater, and Thomas *Hardy, among others. The editor from 1894 to 1928, W. L. Courtney, published Henry *James, George *Gissing, Rudyard *Kipling, and H. G. *Wells. In 1934 it changed its name to the *Fortnightly*, under which title it survived until 1954. It was then incorporated in the **Contemporary Review*.

Fortunes of Nigel, The A novel by Walter *Scott, published 1822. The novel is set in 17th-century London and tells the story of a young Scots nobleman, Nigel Olifaunt, who comes to claim repayment of a debt owed to his father by the king, James VI and I. The king's portrait is one of the book's highlights, as are those of the other historical characters and the vivid descriptions of Alsace drawn by Scott from his reading of the Elizabethan and Jacobean dramatists.

FORWARD, Robert L. (1932–2002) American physicist and *hard science fiction writer; born in Geneva, New York. A solar system in *Rocheworld* (1990) is reached by the kind of light-sail propulsion system Forward was devising for actual space programmes.

FOSCOLO, Ugo (1778–1827) Italian poet, tragedian, and critic. He was the first modern Italian poet of exile, and the writer of his generation who was most sensitive to the crisis of his age. In 1797 he wrote an ode to Bonaparte as Liberator, but when later that year Napoleon's Treaty of Campoformio handed over Venetian independence to the Austrians, Foscolo was bitter at the betrayal. Nevertheless he fought with the French throughout Napoleon's occupation of northern Italy. In 1804, with the plan to invade England, he was stationed in northern France where he fell in love with an Englishwoman, by whom he had a daughter, 'Floriana'. After Napoleon's defeat and the reoccupation of northern Italy by the Austrians in 1814, Foscolo went into exile, first in Switzerland; then, from 1816, in London where, tended by his daughter, he was to die in poverty. He wrote tragedies in imitation of *Alfieri and intensely lyrical neo-classical sonnets (1802). In the first Romantic Italian novel, *Ultime lettere di Jacopo Ortis* (1802; rev. 1814: *Last Letters of Jacopo Ortis*), inspired by Goethe's *Werther* (*see* WERTHERISM), the hero chooses suicide, having lost both his love and his political hopes after the Treaty of Campoformio. His greatest work is *Dei sepolcri* (1807: *Of Sepulchres*), a 295-line poem influenced by Thomas *Gray. This poem deals with the tension between the modern poet's prophetic 'interrogation' of history and his exile from the society with which he is at odds. In his last years Foscolo contributed critical essays—notably on *Dante, *Petrarch, and *Tasso—to the **Edinburgh Review*, which brought him into contact with Francis *Jeffrey, with whom he corresponded on literary matters; to the **Quarterly Review*; and to the **New Monthly Magazine*. He died in Turnham Green, London. See G. Cambon, *Ugo Foscolo: Poet of Exile* (1981).

FOSTER, Roy (Robert Fitzroy) (1949–) Historian and biographer, born in Waterford and educated at Newtown School and Trinity College, Dublin. He became Carroll professor of Irish history at Hertford College, Oxford, after teaching at Birkbeck College, London. Foster is a noted historian of Ireland and has published many essays as well as *Modern Ireland 1600–1972* (1992). He has also published biographies of Charles Stewart *Parnell (1979) and Lord Randolph Churchill (1981). His most significant biography is the two-volume *W. B. Yeats: A Life*, published in 1997 and 2003, for which he was awarded the James Tait Black Memorial Prize.

FOUCAULT, Michel (1926–84) French philosopher, literary critic, and historian. His early work, notably *Folie et déraison: histoire de la folie à l'âge classique* (1961: *Madness and Civilization*), *Les Mots et les choses* (1966: *The Order of Things*), *L'Archéologie du savoir* (1969: *The Archaeology of Knowledge*), and *Surveiller et punir: naissance de la prison* (1975: *Discipline and Punish*), is devoted to the history of institutions (scientific, medical, penal, etc.) and the discourses on which their power is founded (*see* STRUCTURALISM). It expresses a libertarian distrust of the ways in which modern institutions regulate knowledge and submit people to the control of 'experts'. His later work includes a three-volume history of sexuality, left incomplete at his death: *La Volonté de savoir* (1976: *The Will to Knowledge*), which argues that sex became controlled by medical discourse in the 19th century, *L'Usage des plaisirs* and *Le Souci de soi* (both 1984: *The Use of Pleasure* and *The Care of the Self*). He had a strong influence on American historical and literary studies, notably *New Historicism and the work of Edward *Said. See D. Macey, *The Lives of Michel Foucault* (1993).

FOULIS, Robert (1707–76) By trade originally a barber. With his brother Andrew he visited Oxford and France in 1738–40, collecting rare books, which were sold to fund a new business as bookseller and then printer in Glasgow. He was associated with Glasgow University, printing their first Greek book (1743) and the 'immaculate' *Horace (1744); he also worked closely with the professor of moral philosophy there, Francis *Hutcheson. The Foulis brothers issued nearly 600 books, many of them ambitious large-scale projects, including the folio *Homer (1756–8) and **Paradise Lost* (1770). See Philip Gaskell, *A Bibliography of the Foulis Press* (2nd edn, 1986).

Four Ages In *Ovid's *Metamorphoses*, history has declined inexorably from the perfect Golden Age through the Silver and Bronze Ages to the miserable Iron Age when Astraea, goddess of justice, leaves the earth. The return of Astraea and the recovery of the Golden Age is an important literary motif from *Virgil to John *Dryden.

'Four Ages of Poetry, The' A literary essay by Thomas Love *Peacock, published 1820. It makes ironic use of the argument advanced by 18th-century cultural historians such as Johann *Winckelmann, that as society progresses, poetry deteriorates in inevitable stages. P. B. *Shelley's reply, *A *Defence of Poetry*, takes Peacock's charges seriously, and argues that poetry in modern times continues to play an important social role, through advocating the ideal and stimulating the life of the mind.

FOURIER, Charles (1772–1837) French social reformer. Persuaded that the competitive principles of civilization had created unhappiness by establishing inequality of wealth and repressing human passions, Fourier advocated a system of social reorganization, generally known as *Fouriérisme*, to ensure cooperation in the interests of personal and collective harmony. To this end he proposed the regrouping of society into phalansteries, housing communities of about 1,620 members. Each phalanstery was to be a cooperative enterprise providing for the subsistence of all its members, and dividing its remaining revenues among them according to capital invested, labour, and talent. The internal organization of the phalanstery would allow for variety of occupation and a large measure of sexual freedom. Much admired by followers of *Surrealism, Fourier's major works are *Théorie des quatre mouvements* (1808: *The Theory of the Four Movements*), *Traité de l'association domestique agricole* (1822: *Treatise on Domestic Agricultural Association*), and *Le Nouveau Monde industriel* (1829–30: *The New Industrial World*). See J. Beecher, *Charles Fourier* (1987).

Four Quartets A poem in four parts by T. S. *Eliot, published as a whole in New York in 1943. The first part, 'Burnt Norton', was the final poem in *Collected Poems 1909–35* (1936); 'East Coker', 'The Dry Salvages', and 'Little Gidding' first appeared in the *New English Weekly* in 1940, 1941, and 1942 respectively, and were then published separately in pamphlet form by Faber and Faber.

The four quartets represent the four seasons and the four elements; the imagery of the first centres on a Cotswold garden, that of the second round a Somerset village (from where Eliot's own ancestor had departed in 1669 for the New World), the third mingles the landscapes of Missouri and New England, the landscapes of Eliot's youth; and the fourth was inspired by the landscape and history surrounding St John's Church, Little Gidding, Cambridgeshire. But all are concerned with time past and time present: 'Little Gidding', for example, interweaves the wartime London of the Blitz with the England of *Julian of Norwich. These were the first of Eliot's poems to reach a wide public (they were seen as a unifying force in the war years), and they succeeded in communicating in modern idiom the fundamentals of Christian faith and experience. For a discussion of their composition, see H. Gardner, *The Composition of Four Quartets* (1978); for cultural contextualization, see Steve Ellis, *The English Eliot* (1991), and John X. Cooper, *T. S. Eliot and the Ideology of Four Quartets* (1995).

Four Sons of Aymon *See* AYMON.

fourteener A verse line of fourteen syllables, usually in iambic *metre and so with seven stresses. Such lines were favoured by some English poets in the 15th and 16th centuries, and slightly later but more notably by George *Chapman in his translation of the **Iliad*.

Four Zoas, The A symbolic poem by William *Blake, originally entitled *Vala*, written and revised 1795–1804, described by John Beer (*Blake's Humanism*, 1968) as 'a heroic attempt to write the first psychological epic'. It presents characters familiar from Blake's earlier symbolic works (Urizen, Los, Orc, and others), elaborating his cosmic mythology in a framework of a 'Dream of Nine Nights'; this framework was possibly suggested by Edward Young's **Night Thoughts*, which Blake was illustrating at the same period. The Four Zoas appear to represent the four human faculties, once united, but then at war with one another until the final radiant vision of joy and peace when the eyes of the Eternal Man 'behold the depths of wondrous worlds'.

FOWLER, Henry Watson (1858–1933) Lexicographer and grammarian, born in Tonbridge, Kent, and educated at Rugby School and Balliol College, Oxford; joint author, with his brother Francis George Fowler (1870–1918), of *The King's English* (1906) and *The Concise Oxford Dictionary of Current English* (1911), and sole compiler of *The Pocket Oxford Dictionary* (1924) and *A Dictionary of Modern English Usage* (1926), which soon came to be regarded as both authoritative and indispensable.

FOWLER, Karen Joy (1950–) American novelist, born in Bloomington, Indiana; she uses the contrast between *science fiction and realism to rich effect. *Sarah Canary* (1991) offers several interpretations of 'Sarah's' identity. *The Jane Austen Book Club* (2004) explores the relationships of members of a discussion group.

FOWLES, John (1926–2005) Novelist, educated at Bedford School and New College, Oxford, where he read French. He worked as a schoolteacher before embarking on a career as a full-time writer. His first novel, *The Collector* (1963), a psychological thriller, consists largely of the laconic first-person narration of a repressed clerk and butterfly collector who kidnaps a female art student. This was followed by *The Magus* (1966; rev. 1977), a novel mostly set on the Greek island of 'Phraxos', where a British schoolmaster is drawn into a series of elaborate psychological games in which reality and illusion become increasingly difficult to differentiate. *The French Lieutenant's Woman* (1969) takes place largely in Lyme Regis in 1867 and is notable for Fowles's extensive use of authorial commentary and for the alternative endings he provides. *Daniel Martin* (1977) is a long, semi-naturalistic, semi-experimental account of a screenwriter and his relationships with Hollywood, capitalism, art, and his sister-in-law; *Mantissa* (1982) is an erotic fantasy in which a novelist hospitalized with amnesia imagines encounters with Erato, Muse of love poetry. Fowles's last novel to be published, *A Maggot* (1985), reworks a real-life 18th-century murder mystery to take in contemporary documents, erotic obsession, religious mania, and magic and the supernatural. His non-fiction includes *The Aristos* (1965), an idiosyncratic exposition of his 'personal philosophy', and *The Tree* (1979), which explores the influence of the natural world on his life and on his writing. Two volumes of *Journals* have so far been published (2003 and 2006), one of them posthumously. There is a biography by Eileen Warburton (2002).

FOX, Caroline (1819–71) Diarist, of an old Quaker family, born at Falmouth, whose *Memories of Old Friends* (1882, ed. Horace N. Pym: extracts from journals and letters which cover the years 1835–71) contains vivid recollections of John *Sterling, the *Carlyles, Elizabeth Fry, the Coleridges, and other eminent Victorians. Her turn of mind was predominantly serious and reflective, but she could also be very entertaining, as her account of an evening in 1842 with the Carlyles discussing *Swedenborg bears witness. A selection of her journals, *Caroline Fox 1835–1871*, ed. Wendy Monk, was published in 1972.

FOX, Charles James (1749–1806) Whig politician, one of the managers of the proceedings against Warren Hastings (1732–1818), and a constant opponent of William Pitt the elder. He was noted for learning and charm but also for his malign influence over the prince of Wales. He became a member of Samuel Johnson's *Club (1774).

FOX, George (1624–91) Son of a Leicestershire weaver and founder of the Society of *Friends, or Quakers. He had no formal schooling, but was apprenticed to a shoemaker and a shepherd. He left home in 1643 in search of enlightenment. A charismatic crowd-puller, he taught that the inner light of the Spirit, not ordination, gave both men and women the right to preach, and that the faithful might worship in the fields, not 'steeple-houses' (churches). He opposed violence, oath-taking, and marks of social rank such as titles and hat-doffing. For these views he was often imprisoned. His travels, mostly on foot, extended to Ireland, Barbados, New England, the Netherlands, and Germany, and included many spiritual enlightenments, such as his vision of souls coming to Christ on Pendle Hill in 1652. He married Margaret *Fell, a widow, in 1669. His *Journal*, revised by a committee under the superintendence of William *Penn and published in 1694, is one of the great visionary works of world literature. There is a biography, *First among Friends*, by H. Larry Ingle (repr. 1996). See also Christopher Hill, *The World Turned Upside Down* (1972).

FOX, William Johnson (1786–1864) Independent *Unitarian preacher, orator, journalist, drama critic, and editor. He was influential in a literary context for his association with the *Monthly Repository*, originally a Unitarian periodical, but which under his ownership and editorship (from 1831) encouraged and published many progressive writers of the day, including Robert *Browning, Harriet *Martineau, and

John Stuart *Mill. He sold it in 1836 to his friend and protégé R. H. *Horne. He continued to write and speak extensively and effectively on public matters, and in 1847 became MP for Oldham.

FOXE, John (1516/17–87) Martyrologist, born at Boston, Lincolnshire, and educated at Oxford University, where he became a fellow of Magdalen College but resigned his fellowship in 1545, being unwilling to conform to the statutes in religious matters. In 1554 he retired to the Continent, and issued at Strasbourg his *Commentarii Rerum in Ecclesia Gestarum* (the earliest version of what was to become his *Acts and Monuments*). He was employed at Basle as a proof-reader for various printers and especially for Johann Oporinus, who published Foxe's allegorical verse drama *Christus Triumphans* (1556), his appeal to the English nobility on religious toleration (1557), and the first issue of the new version of his Protestant martyrology *Rerum in Ecclesia Gestarum...Commentarii* (1559). On his return to England he was ordained priest by Grindal in 1560, and in 1564 joined John *Day, the printer, who in 1563 had issued the English version of the *Rerum in Ecclesia Gestarum...Commentarii* as *Acts and Monuments*, popularly known as the *Book of Martyrs*. Becoming a canon of Salisbury in 1563, he objected to contributing to the repairs of the cathedral. He preached his much-reprinted *Sermon of Christ Crucified* at Paul's Cross in 1570. His edition of Cranmer's canon laws *Reformatio Legum Ecclesiasticarum* appeared in 1571. He was buried in St Giles Cripplegate. Four editions of the *Acts and Monuments* (1563, 1570, 1576, and 1583) appeared in the author's lifetime; of the posthumous editions, that of 1641 contains a memoir of Foxe, attributed to his son Simeon.

FRAME, Janet Paterson (1924–2004) New Zealand writer, born in Oamaru of Scottish parentage, educated at Otago University. She trained as a teacher but, after misdiagnosis as a schizophrenic, spent several harrowing years undergoing treatment, an experience that coloured her work. Her first book, *The Lagoon* (1952), a collection of stories, was followed by a novel, *Owls Do Cry* (1957, published in Britain in 1961), in which many circumstances of her life are mirrored. Other novels, which exhibit her gifts as a stylist, include *The Rainbirds* (1968) and *The Carpathians* (1988). She published three volumes of autobiography—*To the Island* (1982), *An Angel at my Table* (1984), and *The Envoy from Mirror City* (1985). These were made into a film by Jane Campion under the title of the second volume. Two further collections of short stories were published as *The Reservoir and Other Stories* (1966) and *You Are Now Entering the Human Heart* (1983). A volume of poetry, *The Pocket Mirror*, appeared in 1967.

Framley Parsonage A novel by Anthony *Trollope, published in volume form 1861, fourth in the *'Barsetshire' series. Serialized in the newly founded **Cornhill Magazine* (January 1860–April 1861, with illustrations by John Everett *Millais), the novel became Trollope's first popular success. Mark Robarts is an ambitious young clergyman. At the age of 26 Lady Lufton helped him to the comfortable living at Framley, but he becomes involved with the unreliable Whig member of Parliament Mr Sowerby of Chaldicotes. Robarts rashly guarantees some bills for Sowerby. As an indirect gesture of gratitude Sowerby pulls strings to acquire for Robarts a prebendary stall at Barchester, but makes no attempt to pay the bills when they fall due. Sowerby is by this time in considerable financial difficulty and, after an abortive attempt to marry the money of the patent-medicine heiress Miss Dunstable, his career ends in ruin. Mark Robarts becomes liable for the full amount of the debts and has to appeal to his original patron, Lady Lufton.

This is doubly embarrassing for the Luftons, as young Lord Lufton has fallen in love with Robarts's sister Lucy. At first Lady Lufton vehemently opposes the match, and hopes to interest her son in Griselda Grantly, daughter of the archdeacon. Griselda, however, marries the wealthy Lord Dumbello, and Lady Lufton and Lucy are thrown together by the illness of Mrs Crawley, wife of a neighbouring clergyman. In nursing her Lucy shows her true worth, and Lady Lufton removes her opposition to the match. Mark Robarts's debts are paid as a gesture of goodwill. The proud, impoverished curate Mr Crawley makes his first appearance in this novel.

FRANCE, Anatole (1844–1924) Pseudonym of Jacques-Anatole-François Thibault, French novelist and man of letters. As writer, journalist, and editor he became a leading figure in French literary life from about 1890. His first successful novel, *Le Crime de Sylvestre Bonnard* (1881: *The Crimes of Sylvestre Bonnard*), was followed by *La Rôtisserie de la reine Pédauque* (1893: *The Queen Pedauque*) which, with its companion volume *Les Opinions de M. Jérôme Coignard* (1893: *The Opinions of Jérôme Coignard*), offers a pastiche of life in 18th-century France. Social and political satire dominate the four novels which introduce the observant and disenchanted provincial professor M. Bergeret and which together form the *Histoire contemporaine* (1897–1901: *Contemporary History*). *L'Île des pingouins* (1908: *Penguin Island*) gives an allegorical and satirical version of the evolution of human society. His most significant novel is *Les Dieux ont soif* (1912: *The Gods Will Have Blood*), a study of fanaticism during the French Revolution. The collections of his short stories—variously exotic, philosophical, and satirical—include *L'Étui de nacre* (1892: *Mother of Pearl*) and *Le Puits de Sainte-Claire* (1895: *The Well of St Clare*). France provided a fictionalized account of his childhood and early years in *Le Livre de mon ami* (1885: *My Friend's Book*), *Pierre Nozière* (1899), *Le Petit Pierre* (1918: *Little Pierre*), and *La Vie en fleur* (1922: *The Bloom of Life*). His contemporary success was such that there was an English complete works published in many volumes between 1908 and 1928. He was awarded the *Nobel Prize for Literature in 1921.

Francesca da Rimini *See* PAOLO AND FRANCESCA.

FRANCIS (François) **DE SALES, St** (1567–1622) Bishop of Geneva and spiritual writer, born in Savoy and educated in Paris and Padua. He was famed in his lifetime for converting Calvinists and ministering to the poor. His best-known works, *An Introduction to the Devout Life* and *Treatise on the Love of God*, were frequently translated into English.

FRANCIS OF ASSISI, St (Giovanni Francesco Bernardone) (1181/2–1226) A wealthy young man, he experienced a spiritual crisis, after which he lived in solitude and prayer, devoting himself to the relief of the poor, the sick, and lepers. He was joined by disciples for whom he drew up the first Rule of St Francis in 1209. He preached in Italy, and went to the Holy Land and Spain. The special emphases of his teaching were poverty and love of nature. Two years before his death, he is said to have discovered on his body the stigmata, the marks made by the nails of Christ's crucifixion. Two 13th-century biographies of him were written, by St Bonaventure and by Thomas of Celano. The *Fioretti de San Francisco* (*Little Flowers of St Francis*) is a 14th-century Italian narrative, partly legendary, of the doings of St Francis and his first disciples. He occurs with St Dominic, the founder of the Dominicans, in *Dante's *Paradiso*, XII. See Regis J. Armstrong *et al.* (eds), *Francis of Assisi: Early Documents* (1999–2001).

FRANK, Anne (1929–45) Born in Germany; she fled to the Netherlands from Nazi persecution with her family in 1933. *The Diary of a Young Girl*, first published in English in 1952, describes Anne's life in hiding in Amsterdam during the German occupation. The family were betrayed in 1944 and Anne died in Bergen-Belsen concentration camp. The Diary is an important work in the literature of the *Holocaust, although its reception has been viewed by some critics as inappropriately humanist and universalizing. The subsequent stage and screen adaptations of the Diary have become central to the American cultural consciousness of the Holocaust.

FRANK, Pat (1907–64) Pseudonym of Harry Hart Frank, American novelist. Born in Chicago, he spent most of his life in Florida, which provides the setting for his best-known novel, *Alas Babylon* (1959). This describes the struggle to survive a nuclear war between the USA and the Soviet Union in a small Florida town. Frank's first novel was *Mr Adam* (1946), the story of the only intact male after a nuclear disaster renders all other men sterile. He served in the Office of War Information and then as a domestic journalist, constantly keeping politics in the forefront of his writing. *Hold Back the Night* (1952) draws on his experiences of the Korean War and *Forbidden Area* (1956; UK title *Seven Days to Never*) describes the attempted subversion of the USA by brainwashed Soviet agents.

Frankenstein, *or The Modern Prometheus* A *Gothic tale of terror by Mary *Shelley, published 1818. In her preface she records that she, P. B. *Shelley, and Lord *Byron had spent the wet summer of 1816 in Switzerland reading German ghost stories; all three agreed to write tales of the supernatural, of which hers was the only one to be completed. She also records that the original concept came to her in a half-waking nightmare.

Technically an *epistolary novel, told through the letters of Walton, an English explorer in the Arctic, the tale relates the exploits of Frankenstein, an idealistic Genevan student of natural philosophy, who discovers at the University of Ingolstadt the secret of imparting life to inanimate matter. Collecting bones from charnel-houses, he constructs the semblance of a human being and gives it life. The creature, endowed with supernatural strength and size and terrible in appearance, inspires loathing in whoever sees it. Lonely and miserable (and educated in human emotion by studies of *Goethe, *Plutarch, and *Paradise Lost*), it turns upon its creator, and, failing to persuade him to provide a female counterpart, eventually murders his brother, his friend Clerval, and his bride Elizabeth. Frankenstein pursues it to the Arctic to destroy it, but dies in the pursuit, after relating his story to Walton. The monster declares that Frankenstein will be its last victim, and disappears to end its own life. This tale inspired many film versions, and has been regarded as the origin of modern *science fiction, though it is also a version of the myth of the noble savage, portraying a nature essentially good corrupted by ill treatment. It is also remarkable for its description of nature, which owes much to the Shelleys' admiration for *Wordsworth, *Coleridge, and in particular *The Rime of the *Ancient Mariner*. The novel has been interpreted as a warning about human presumption, as a prophecy of the ramifications of unfettered scientific enquiry, and as a critique of the solipsism of (male) *Romanticism. The book is sometimes read, controversially, in personal terms of Shelley's troubled experience of motherhood, even as a veiled attack on her husband as an inadequate parent.

FRANKLIN, Benjamin (1706–90) Political writer and autobiographer, born in Boston, Massachusetts, the son of a tallow chandler, largely self-educated. He was apprenticed at the age of 12 to his half-brother, a printer, to whose *New England Courant* he contributed, but they later quarrelled and he moved to Philadelphia. In 1724 he travelled to England, hoping to buy equipment for his own printing press, and worked in a London printing house for some months, returning to Philadelphia in 1726. Four years later he set up his own press, from which he issued the *Pennsylvania Gazette*, and became prosperous. He acquired a wide reputation by his occasional writings, especially *Poor Richard's Almanack* (1733–58), the best known of American *almanacs, which followed the British pattern of mixing practical information with satiric prognostications, aphorisms, proverbs, etc. He was active as a public figure, founding the American Philosophical Society and the academy that became the University of Pennsylvania, and he also became well known for his practical interest in natural philosophy. His experiment with lightning and electricity, using a kite, was famous, and he also invented the Franklin stove and a new kind of clock. In 1757 he travelled to England as agent for the colonies, where he mixed widely in intellectual society (his friends including Edmund *Burke, David *Hume, Adam *Smith, William *Strahan, and Joseph *Priestley) and contributed to the controversies that caused the breach with England. He returned home in 1774 and, after helping to draft the Declaration of Independence, travelled to France as ambassador, where he was enthusiastically welcomed. Upon his return in 1785 he continued to be active in public affairs, and signed the Constitution as a member of the Federal Constitutional Convention. His *Autobiography*, which he began to write in England, in 1771, and which breaks off with an account of his return to England in 1757, was published in England in 1793 (translated from the French), in America in 1818. Franklin's prose was much admired in England; Francis *Jeffrey (1806, *Edinburgh Review*) praised its 'force and clearness', and William *Lecky (*History of England in the Eighteenth Century*) described it as 'always terse, luminous, simple, pregnant with meaning, eminently persuasive'. D. H. *Lawrence, however, deplored 'middle-sized, sturdy, snuff-coloured Doctor Franklin' and his orderly thrift: 'He tries to take away my wholeness and my dark forest, my freedom' (*Studies in Classic American Literature*, 1923). See biography by Edmund Morgan, *Benjamin Franklin* (2003).

FRANKLIN, Sir John (1786–1847) Arctic explorer, and author of two *Narratives* (1823 and 1828) of voyages to the Polar Sea. His final voyage of discovery in *Erebus* and *Terror* in search of the North-West Passage began in 1845. After nothing was heard of his progress, numerous relief expeditions were sent out, including one organized by his widow. Through Inuit testimony and the discovery of artefacts and human remains, they established that all 129 members had died. Their fate, including claims of survival cannibalism, continues to exert a powerful fascination.

FRANKLIN, Miles *See* BULLETIN.

'Franklin's Tale, The' *See* CANTERBURY TALES, 12.

FRASER, Lady Antonia (1932–) Née Pakenham, biographer, broadcaster, anthologist, and writer of mystery stories, educated at St Mary's Convent, Ascot, and Dragon School, Oxford, before graduating from Lady Margaret Hall, Oxford. She married Harold *Pinter in 1980. Her readable and scholarly biographies include lives of *Mary Queen of Scots (1969), Oliver *Cromwell (1973), and *James I of England (1974). Her female detective Jemima Shore was introduced in *Quiet as a Nun* (1977), and has since appeared in several mystery novels and in a television series. Amongst Fraser's other books are *The Gunpowder Plot: Terror and Faith in 1605* (1997) and *Marie Antoinette: The Journey* (2001). She received a CBE in 1999.

FRASER, George MacDonald (1925–2008) Novelist and screenwriter, born in Carlisle, educated at Carlisle Grammar School and Glasgow Academy; he joined the army in 1943, served in North Africa and Burma (about which he wrote an admired memoir, *Quartered Safe Out Here*, 1992), and subsequently worked as a journalist before becoming a full-time author. Short story collections such as *McAuslan in the Rough* (1974) comically recall his army experiences. He also published *historical fiction such as *Black Ajax* (1997). But his most celebrated achievement is his sequence of rumbustiously satiric novels (and three stories published as *Flashman and the Tiger*, 1999) which debunk Victorian imperialism by chronicling the privately disreputable but publicly acclaimed military career of the cowardly bully Harry *Flashman, a character from Thomas Hughes's **Tom Brown's Schooldays*. From *Flashman* (1969) to *Flashman on the March* (2005), meticulous historical research and a remarkable flair for capturing period slang combine with narrative gusto in portraying the farcically outrageous escapades of his caddish and lecherous anti-hero. Fraser's additional career as a screenwriter is documented in his book of reminiscences *The Light's on at Signpost* (2002).

Fraser's Magazine (1830–82) A general and literary Tory journal of high standing, founded by William *Maginn and Hugh Fraser, which provided competition for **Blackwood's Magazine*. Unlike *Blackwood's*, the **Edinburgh Review*, or the **Quarterly Review* it was not owned by a publisher of books, and prided itself that it could not therefore be accused of partisanship in its reviews. Among notable contributors were James *Hogg, S. T. *Coleridge, Robert *Southey, Thomas Love *Peacock, Thomas *Carlyle, Harrison *Ainsworth, W. M. *Thackeray, and John *Ruskin. The magazine's early interest in fiction (it serialized a number of Thackeray's early works) receded in the 1840s. J. A. *Froude was editor from 1860 to 1874, but the journal had by then declined in influence and reputation.

Fraternity of Vagabonds, The A tract written and printed by John Awdely (*c.*1532–1575), published in 1565 in two parts: the first dealing with thieves' cant and the devices beggars use to excite compassion, the second with the methods employed by well-dressed impostors.

FRAUNCE, Abraham (?1559–?1592/3) Educated at Shrewsbury School and St John's College, Cambridge. With Philip *Sidney's patronage he was a follower of Peter *Ramus in logic, rhetoric, and dialectic. His most interesting work, *The Arcadian Rhetoric* (1588), illustrates rhetorical tropes with examples from Sidney's **Arcadia*, side by side with Torquato *Tasso, Guillaume de Saluste *Du Bartas, and Juan *Boscán de Almogáver). Other works include *The Lawyers' Logic* (1588), *The Countess of Pembroke's Emanuel* (1591), and *The Countesse of Pembroke's Yvychurch* (1591).

FRAYN, Michael (1933–) Novelist and playwright, educated at Kingston Grammar School and Emmanuel College, Cambridge. He worked for some years as a humorous columnist for the **Manchester Guardian*, then for the **Observer*, and has published ten novels, including *The Russian Interpreter* (1966), *Towards the End of the Morning* (1967, a comedy of Fleet Street life), *Headlong* (1999), and *Spies* (2002). His stage comedies include *Alphabetical Order* (1975), again with a background of journalism; *Donkeys' Years* (1976), based on a college reunion; *Noises Off* (1982), a farce of theatre life; and he has produced versions of virtually all of the plays of Anton *Chekhov. *Benefactors* (1984), whilst still a comedy, signalled a move into a more serious phase in his playwriting. *Copenhagen* (1998), a tense, lucid drama about the unexplained meeting in 1941 in Occupied Denmark of German physicist Werner Heisenberg and his Danish mentor Niels Bohr, was followed by *Democracy* (2003), a play set in 1960s Berlin. He is also the author of a book of philosophical reflections, *The Human Touch: Our Part in the Creation of a Universe* (2006).

FRAZER, J. G. (Sir James George) (1854–1941) Scottish anthropologist and classical scholar. He was born in Glasgow and educated at the university there, but spent most of his life in Cambridge, where he studied from 1874 and was fellow of Trinity from 1879. One of the founders of modern anthropology, he did much to popularize this field of study, although his methods (he relied on secondary sources, including questionnaires sent to missionaries around the world) and many of his conclusions have been superseded. *The Golden Bough* (1890; expanded in 12 vols, 1906–15) is a vast and enterprising comparative study of the beliefs and institutions of mankind, offering the thesis that man progresses from magical through religious to scientific thought. Its discussion of fertility rites, the sacrificial killing of kings, the dying god, and the scapegoat figure caught the literary imagination, and its influence may be seen more lastingly in the works of D. H. *Lawrence, T. S. *Eliot, Ezra *Pound, and Naomi *Mitchison, and in the principles of *myth criticism, than in the works of later anthropologists (beyond the avowedly Frazerian early 20th-century 'Cambridge Ritualist' group). Frazer's many other works include *Totemism and Exogamy* (1910) and *Folklore in the Old Testament* (1918), and he also published extensive commentaries on Pausanias (1898) and the *Fasti* of *Ovid (1929). There is a life by Robert Ackerman (1987).

FREDERIC, Harold (1856–98) American novelist and journalist, who was born in Utica, New York, and is best known for his novel *The Damnation of Theron Ware* (1896; UK title *Illumination*). This centres on the treatment of a *Methodist minister and reflects the materialist priorities of Reconstruction in the period following the Civil War. Apart from his other novels and romances, Frederic served as London correspondent for the *New York Times* (1884–98).

FREDERICK THE GREAT, of Prussia (1712–86) Ruled as king from 1740 until his death. He was an able administrator and military commander, as well as a man of considerable culture. By his resistance to Austrian ambitions and victories in the Seven Years War he greatly enhanced Prussian power. Frederick fostered strong links with the French Enlightenment, and for a time he and *Voltaire were mutually admiring correspondents. He despised the German language, preferring both to speak and write in French. Several of his poems were published in London with great success. He was the subject of a biography by Thomas *Carlyle, entitled *The History of Frederick II of Prussia Called Frederick the Great* (6 vols, 1858–65), in which he is described as 'a questionable hero' who nevertheless was able to emerge from a 'century opulent in accumulated falsities'.

free indirect style A way of narrating characters' thoughts or utterances that combines some of the features of third-person report with some features of first-person direct speech, allowing a flexible and sometimes ironic overlapping of internal and external perspectives. Free indirect style (a translation of French *style indirecte libre*) dispenses with tag-phrases ('she thought', etc.), and adopts the idiom of the character's own thoughts, including indicators of time and place, as *She'd leave here tomorrow,* rather than 'She decided to leave that place the next day'. The device was exploited by some 19th-century novelists such as Jane *Austen and Gustave *Flaubert, and has since been widely adopted.

FREEMAN, Edward Augustus (1823–92) Historian and controversialist. Endowed with private means, which he supplemented by regular writing for the *Saturday Review,* he spent much of his life in the study of medieval and ancient history, but he was handicapped by wordiness and a marked aversion to public libraries, a trait shared by many Victorian scholars (e.g. Thomas *Carlyle, Henry *Buckle). His best-known work is his gigantic *History of the Norman Conquest*, 5 vols (1867–79), and its sequel on *The Reign of William Rufus*, 2 vols (1882). Here his Whig belief in the excellence of the British constitution as it had developed from the Conquest was at odds with his deep affection and respect for Anglo-Saxon culture, which also led him to write in a curiously archaic style, rejecting Latin derivations wherever possible. In his hands, therefore, the events of 1066 emerge as a happy tragedy. He was capable of close friendships (for instance with William *Stubbs and J. R. *Green), but he was guilty of almost paranoid hatreds which are not rationally explicable, particularly for Charles *Kingsley and J. A. *Froude. His aversion to blood sports involved him in public controversy with Anthony *Trollope, and all his work is infected with anti-Semitism and a violent though selective xenophobia.

FREEMAN, Mary Eleanor Wilkins (1852–1930) American novelist and short story writer. Born in Randolph, Massachusetts, she wrote mostly about rural life in New England. Like Sara Orne *Jewett, she produced local colour fiction which describes the waning of *Puritanism, for example in her first collections *A Humble Romance* (1887) and *A New England Nun* (1891). In addition she wrote a number of short stories for children, the best known being *Goody Two-Shoes* (1883).

free verse A term loosely used from the early years of the 20th century to describe many forms of irregular, syllabic, or unrhymed verse, freed from the traditional demands of *metre; also known as *vers libre*. Some 19th-century poets, notably William *Blake and Walt *Whitman, practised kinds of free verse, but its widespread adoption was encouraged by

Ezra *Pound and his *imagist associates, while their contemporaries T. S. *Eliot, D. H. *Lawrence, and Edith *Sitwell were also notable, and in their time controversial, for their free verse poems.

FRENCH, Marilyn (1929–2009) American novelist and feminist writer, born in New York, whose first book was on James *Joyce (*The Book as World: James Joyce's Ulysses*, 1976). It was, however, *The Women's Room* (1977) which brought her fame; this was the first exploration of her central fictional theme: the institutionalized assumptions of male dominance which put women automatically at a disadvantage. *The Bleeding Heart* (1980) continues this concern in dramatizing the conflict between the protagonist and her overbearing lover. French produced a number of attacks on sexism including *The War against Women* (1992) and *From Eve to Dawn: A History of Women in Three Volumes* (2002). *Beyond Power* (1985) is a collection of her essays. Her last novel, *The Love Children* (2009), returns to the American 1960s.

***French Revolution, The:** A History* The historical work by which Thomas *Carlyle established his reputation, written in London 1834–7, published 1837. In three volumes ('The Bastille', 'The Constitution', and 'The Guillotine'), it opens with the death of Louis XV in 1774, covers the reign of Louis XVI, the period which included the assembly of the States General, the fall of the Bastille, the Constituent and Legislative Assemblies, the flight of the king to Varennes, the Convention, the trial and execution of the king and queen, the reign of terror, and the fall of Robespierre, and extends to 5 October 1795, when Bonaparte quelled the insurrection of the Vendémiaire, the title of the last chapter being 'The Whiff of Grapeshot'. A work of great descriptive power, it draws on the imaginative resources of fiction and poetry to present a notable gallery of portraits (Mirabeau, Lafayette, Danton, Robespierre) and a series of impressive set pieces. It was greatly admired by Charles *Dickens, and was in part the inspiration of *A *Tale of Two Cities*.

FRENCH-SHELDON, May (1847–1936) Travel writer and explorer, born in Beaver, Pennsylvania. A minor literary figure in London in the 1880s, she was inspired by the example of her friend H. M. *Stanley to undertake in 1891 a three-month trek to Mount Kilimanjaro, in present-day Tanzania. Her experiences and discoveries were recounted in *Sultan to Sultan: Adventures among the Masai and Other Tribes of East Africa* (1892), which became a best-seller on both sides of the Atlantic. In 1903, she travelled to the Belgian Congo (today, the Democratic Republic of Congo) at the behest of the campaigning newspaper editor W. T. *Stead. Her mission was to investigate allegations of colonial atrocities in the region, but she confounded the hopes of her employer by claiming to discover no evidence of any brutality towards the native population. In later life she lectured widely in the USA, where her reputation as a female explorer made her a heroine to many women in the 1910s and 1920s.

FRENEAU, Philip Morin (1752–1832) The 'poet of the American Revolution', and miscellaneous writer, editor, and journalist, born in New York and educated at the College of New Jersey (later Princeton University). He lived for a while (1775–8) in the West Indies, where he wrote poems inspired by the tropical atmosphere and landscape, and in 1780 during the Revolutionary War was captured by the British, an experience which prompted the bitter satire of his poem *The British Prison-Ship* (1781), one of his many attacks on the British. His not wholly prosperous career as a writer was interspersed with periods at sea as a ship's master (1784–90 and 1803–7). His first collection of verse, *Poems* (1786), was followed by various volumes of essays, poems, etc., and he wrote widely for newspapers and periodicals, some of which he also edited. His verse ranged from the satirical and patriotic to works such as 'The Wild Honey Suckle' (1786), a nature poem of delicacy and sensitivity which heralds *Romanticism.

FRERE, John Hookham (1769–1846) Educated at Eton College and Caius College, Cambridge. He was a friend of George *Canning, a Tory MP, and an official of the Foreign Office, who occupied many important positions at home and abroad. While at Eton Frere wrote a translation of **Brunanburh*, and was one of the founders of *The Microcosm* periodical (1786–7). He contributed some accomplished satirical verse to *The *Anti-Jacobin*, including most of 'The Loves of the Triangles' (a parody of Erasmus *Darwin). He was one of the founders of the **Quarterly Review* in 1809, and an adviser to John *Murray the publisher. He is, however, chiefly remembered as the inspirer of the style, stanza, and idiom of Lord *Byron's **Beppo* and **Don Juan*. In the Italian verses of *Pulci he found a verse form and a colloquial voice which he felt could be adapted to English, and in 1817 he published the first two cantos of his mock epic *Prospectus and Specimen of an Intended National Work…by William and Robert Whistlecraft… Relating to King Arthur and his Round Table*. It gave *Byron what he wanted, and he describes *Beppo* as 'in or after the excellent manner of Mr Whistlecraft'. Frere also published lively metrical versions of *Aristophanes: *The Frogs* (1839) and *The Acharnians, The Knights*, and *The Birds* in 1840.

FREUD, Esther (1963–) Novelist, born in London, whose first novel, *Hideous Kinky* (1992), draws on her experience as a child in Morocco with her hippie mother. She has published five more novels, similarly simple in style and autobiographical in nature, of which the most recent is *Love Falls* (2007).

FREUD, Sigmund (1856–1939) Born of Jewish parents at Freiberg in the present day Czech Republic, and famous as the founder of psychoanalysis. For most of his adult life he lived and worked in Vienna, but in 1938, following Nazi Germany's

annexation of Austria, he fled and settled in London. His account of the dynamics of mental life evolved from his early study of clinical neuroses, and he developed his ideas in an extensive series of essays and volumes, from his famous work on dreams (1900) and the development of sexuality in children (1905) to late works applying his insights to questions of society and religion in the 1920s and 30s. Though the therapeutic benefits of psychoanalysis are disputed, psychoanalytic ideas have had a profound and lasting effect on literature itself, on criticism, and on literary and cultural theory. In an elegy on Freud, W. H. *Auden observed that his ideas had become a 'climate of opinion', and it is true that many of Freud's concepts, often in simplified or vulgarized form, have entered educated and even common discourse—e.g. Oedipus complex, repression, the death instinct, penis envy, narcissism, 'Freudian' slips, *phallic symbolism (about which he was sceptical), and his formulation of mental structure as a division between 'Id, the Ego, and the Superego'. Freud's thinking was deeply influenced by literary sources, and on occasions he was tempted to write directly on literary topics. Some of these pieces, such as his essay on 'The Uncanny', have been seminal. Though bizarrely converted to Looney's claims for the earl of *Oxford as the author of *Shakespeare's plays, Freud wrote interestingly on **Macbeth*, *The *Merchant of Venice*, and **King Lear*, while his ideas on **Hamlet* as manifesting the Oedipus complex were developed by Ernest Jones and others. Given that general 'climate of opinion' Auden speaks of, precise instances of Freud's influence on literature are hard to determine. Franz *Kafka was acutely aware of his ideas, and it seems indisputable that D. H. *Lawrence and James *Joyce were touched by the Freudian climate, though both disavowed any influence. The significance for both biographers and novelists of Freud's stress on the formative experiences of childhood is obvious, and in *Elizabeth and Essex* (1928) Lytton *Strachey produced what is possibly the first consciously Freud-oriented biography; its many successors include Leon Edel's life of Henry *James. Freud's works were made available in English by James Strachey, Lytton's brother, in the *Standard Edition of the Complete Psychological Works of Sigmund Freud* (24 vols, 1953–73; currently being revised). Whatever the status of psychoanalysis as science, Freud himself is a writer of great distinction and his works belong to world literature. See R. Clark, *Freud: The Man and the Cause* (1980); P. Gay, *A Godless Jew: Freud, Atheism, and the Making of Psychoanalysis* (1987); G. Frankland, *Freud's Literary Culture* (2000).
See PSYCHOANALYTIC CRITICISM.

Friar Bacon and Friar Bungay, *The Honourable History of* A comedy in verse and prose by Robert *Greene, written *c.*1589, acted by 1594. It is partly based on a prose romance, *The Famous History of Friar Bacon* (*c.*1555?), surviving only in an edition of 1627. An anonymous sequel of uncertain date, *John of Bordeaux*, survives only in manuscript. Bacon with the help of Friar Bungay makes a head of brass, and, conjuring up the devil, learns how to give it speech. It is to speak within a month, but 'if they heard it not before it had done speaking, all their labour should be lost'. After watching day and night for three weeks, Bacon hands over the duty to his servant Miles and falls asleep. The head speaks two words, 'Time is'. Miles, thinking his master would be angry if waked for so little, lets him sleep. The head presently speaks again, 'Time was'; and finally, 'Time is past', when it falls down and breaks. Bacon awakes, and heaps curses on Miles's head.

'Friar's Tale, The' *See* CANTERBURY TALES, 7.

FRIEL, Brian (1929–) Irish playwright, born Omagh, Co. Tyrone, and educated at St Patrick's College, Maynooth. Friel began as a short story writer and his continuing interest in direct narration is reflected in the monologues in *Faith Healer* (1979) and *Molly Sweeney* (1994). His plays are shadowed by his childhood as a member of the minority Catholic community in Northern Ireland. His characteristic concern with the gulf between experience and its public representation is explored in psychological terms in his first international success, *Philadelphia, Here I Come!* (1964), in which different actors play the protagonist's social and private selves. Such later plays as *The Freedom of the City* (1973), the much-revived *Translations* (1980), and *Making History* (1988) pursue this theme in explicitly political terms. A film version of *Dancing at Lughnasa* (1990), featuring Meryl Streep and Michael Gambon, appeared in 1998. Friel has adapted works by *Chekhov and *Turgenev.

FRIEL, George (1910–75) Scottish novelist, born in Glasgow and educated at the University of Glasgow. His novels include *The Boy who Wanted Peace* (1964), *Grace and Miss Partridge* (1969), and the widely admired *Mr Alfred, MA* (1972), a portrait of a disaffected bachelor schoolteacher. His short stories were collected in 1992 as *A Friend of Humanity*.

Friend A weekly periodical edited and largely written by Samuel Taylor *Coleridge in the Lake District, 1809–10. It was the first to publish early sections of Wordsworth's **Prelude*. In its final three-volume book form of 1818, Coleridge transformed it into a substantial series of interlinked essays 'to aid in the formation of fixed principles in politics, morals, and religion, with literary amusements interspersed'. Vol. i contains a notable defence of 'free communication' in the press; vol. ii attacks Jacobin theories of the 'Rights of Man'; vol. iii expounds the 'Principles of Method'.

Friends, Society of A religious society founded in 1648–50 by George *Fox, distinguished by faith in the Inner Light, the spiritual equality of men and women, refusal of oaths, plain egalitarian dress, language, and manners, and antagonism to paid clergy and forms of worship. The movement was regarded as subversive by both the Protectorate and the restored monarchy, and heavily persecuted. Each member was also a minister, and the message was carried to the Netherlands, Rome, America, and Turkey. Margaret *Fell first declared the peace principle for which Friends are famous at the Restoration, when a quietist ethic succeeded the revolutionary phase.

Quakerism encouraged literacy among people of all ranks. Six hundred and fifty Friends published 3,853 documents before 1700, 82 of the authors being women. The Society has pioneered social reform. Its nickname 'Quakers' reflected the derisive public reaction to the 'quaking' convulsions of early Friends when seized by the power of the Inner Light.
See also PENN, WILLIAM; NAYLER, JAMES; BARCLAY, ROBERT.

Friendship's Garland A satirical collection of essays in letter form by Matthew *Arnold, originally printed in the **Pall Mall Gazette*, published 1871. The principal imaginary correspondent is a Prussian, Arminius, Baron von Thunder-ten-Tronckh (a descendant of a character in Voltaire's **Candide*). Through him Arnold expresses his mockery of the English *Philistine as represented by Bottles, a wealthy manufacturer; of narrow Liberal reform as represented by the 'deceased-wife's -sister' Act; of the **Daily Telegraph* and its naive patriotism, and of English foreign and educational policy. Arminius believes in the application of 'Geist' or 'Intelligence', which the English persistently undervalue, and teases 'poor Arnold' for his supposed 'infatuation about everything English'.

FRISCH, Max (1911–91) Swiss-German playwright, diarist, and novelist, also a qualified architect. His best-known plays are *Biedermann und die Brandstifter* (originally written for radio: *The Fire-Raisers*, 1958) and *Andorra* (1961). The first is a satire on the helplessness of the bourgeoisie in the face of danger and the impotence of art as warning. *Andorra* is a powerful parable on the evil which results from the creation of human scapegoats. The novel *Homo Faber* (1957; English trans. 1959) concerns the fate of the rational hero, an engineer, unable to control the events of his life as coincidences which defy explanation pursue him like tragic Furies; it was made into an English-language film, starring Sam Shepard, by Volker Schlöndorff in 1991. His novella *Blaubart* (1982) was translated into English (1983) and published in paperback as *Bluebeard* by Penguin.

FROISSART, Jean (1337–after 1404) French chronicler and poet. He travelled widely in Western Europe, collecting material for his future histories. In 1361 he was received in England by Edward III, and visited Scotland. In 1366 he accompanied the Black Prince to Bordeaux, and in 1368 the duke of Clarence to Milan. He revisited England in 1394–5. His chronicles record the chivalric exploits of the nobles of England and France from 1325 to 1400. They were translated into English by John Bourchier (Lord *Berners) in 1523–5. As author of lively personal *lais* and ballades he influenced *Chaucer.

FROST, Robert Lee (1874–1963) American poet, born in San Francisco. He was taken at the age of 10 to the New England farm country of which his poetry was to be so deeply expressive. He spent some time at both Dartmouth College and Harvard University, but left to teach, edit a country paper, learn to make shoes, and to farm. In 1912 he came to England with his wife and family, where he published his first volumes of poems, *A Boy's Will* (1913) and *North of Boston* (1914), which contains 'Mending Wall' and 'The Death of the Hired Man'; he met the *Georgian poets, and formed a particularly close and fruitful friendship with Edward *Thomas, whom he was to describe as 'the only brother I ever had'. Upon his return to New England in 1915 he settled in New Hampshire and continued to write poetry, supporting himself by successive teaching appointments in several colleges. His volumes include *Mountain Interval* (1916), which contains 'Birches' and 'The Road Not Taken'; *New Hampshire* (1923); *Collected Poems* (1930); *A Witness Tree* (1942); and *In the Clearing* (1962). He established himself as one of the most popular of 20th-century American poets, admired for the blend of colloquial and traditional in his verse, and hailed as a fitting heir, in his response to the natural world, of William *Wordsworth and Ralph Waldo *Emerson; his dramatic monologues and pastorals have been particularly popular. But beneath his country lore and wisdom lay a more troubled, combative, at times destructive spirit, both in his life and work, expressed in such poems as 'Fire and Ice' (1923) and 'Bereft' (1928), which led to Lionel *Trilling's praise of him, on the occasion of his 85th birthday, as a 'poet of terror'. Frost recited his poem 'The Gift Outright' at the 1961 inauguration of President Kennedy. *The Notebooks of Robert Frost* were published in 2007.

'Frost at Midnight' A blank verse poem by Samuel Taylor *Coleridge written at Nether Stowey, Somerset, in February 1798. Addressed to his sleeping child Hartley *Coleridge, it meditates on the poet's own boyhood, and magically evokes the countryside, ending on a note of rare and thrilling happiness. It is possibly the finest of Coleridge's series of 'conversation' poems.

FROUDE, James Anthony (1818–94) Historian and biographer, born in Dartington, son of the archdeacon of Totnes, youngest of eight children, five of whom died of tuberculosis along with his mother, by the time he was 3. Educated at Westminster School and Oriel College, Oxford, he was familiar with the *Oxford Movement but became alienated from it, and having been ordained a deacon in 1845, increasingly found relations with organized religion untenable. His religious doubts and sexual frustrations led to a controversial autobiographical novel, *The Nemesis of Faith* (1849). It was publicly burned by William Sewell (1804–74), brother of Elizabeth *Sewell, who like Froude was a fellow of Exeter College. Obliged to resign his fellowship, Froude left for London, where he maintained himself by journalism; he wrote for several of the reviews, and edited **Fraser's Magazine* 1860–74. He then fell under the influence of Thomas *Carlyle, and became one of his most faithful companions; he shared with Carlyle the desire to dramatize history through its significant actors, and to treat the Reformation as a key turning point in English history, ensuring the precedence of the state over the church. His *History of England from the Death of Cardinal Wolsey to the Defeat of the Spanish Armada* (12 vols, 1856–70) was a distinguished work of scholarship on which all subsequent Tudor studies rest, and he was the first English historian to make a thorough and systematic use of archive material in the manner laid down by the German historian Leopold von Ranke (1795–1886). He was also the first to publicize and glorify the deeds of the Elizabethan seamen, a topic to which he returned in his Oxford lectures on *English Seamen in the Sixteenth Century* (1892–4; pub. 1895). All his books were highly successful, even his collected essays, *Short Studies in Great Subjects* (4 vols, 1867–83); though he was criticized, particularly by the Oxford High Church, for his partisan treatment of the English Reformation and his attempt to rehabilitate Henry VIII, he achieved popularity and esteem. Later the accuracy of his scholarship was unjustly attacked by E. A. *Freeman, whose charges seem to have been accepted by professional historians, especially when Froude went on to publish a slipshod history of 18th-century Ireland (2 vols, 1872–4). In his later years he attracted controversy; his American lecture tour in 1872 was cut short by Irish nationalist agitation, his attempt to intervene in South African politics in 1874–5 provoked a storm, and even his visit to the West Indies in 1886–7 had political repercussions. But this was nothing to the uproar which greeted his *Reminiscences* of Carlyle (1881) and his *Letters and Memorials* of Jane Welsh *Carlyle (1883), where, writing according to Carlyle's principles, he exposed, along with his intellectual achievements, the failings of his marriage. Many contemporary readers interpreted his frank approach as a betrayal of Carlyle's memory; nevertheless, his impact on the work of future biographers was considerable. In 1892 he accepted the Regius chair of modern history at Oxford, an appointment which met with a mixed reception. He was a brilliant public speaker and his lectures attracted large audiences, but he died after only two years in the post. See Julia Markus, *J. Anthony Froude: The Last Great Undiscovered Victorian* (2005).

FROUDE, R. H. (Richard Hurrell) (1803–36) Tractarian and poet, brother of J. A. *Froude, educated at Oriel College, Oxford, where he became a fellow. He was intimate with John Henry *Newman, with whom he collaborated in the early stages of the *Oxford Movement. He contributed three of the *Tracts for the Times* and wrote poems contained in **Lyra Apostolica*. His *Remains* (1838–9), including strictures on the Reformers, aroused public hostility against the movement.

FRY, Christopher (1907–2005) Born in Bristol of Quaker stock. He worked as schoolmaster, actor, and theatre director before making his name as a playwright with works that were hailed in the late 1940s as a sign of a new renaissance of poetic drama; his mystical and religious plays, including *A Sleep of Prisoners* (1951), were frequently compared to those of T. S. *Eliot, though the theatre-going public tended to prefer the ebullient optimism and exuberant word-play of his comedies, e.g. *A Phoenix Too Frequent* (1946, based on *Petronius), *The Lady's Not for Burning* (1949, set in the Middle Ages), and *Venus Observed* (1950, a romantic chateau comedy). *The Dark is Light Enough* (1954) was less successful; the vogue for poetic drama proved short-lived and *Curtmantle* (1962), about Thomas *Becket, struck critics as dated.

FRY, Roger (1866–1934) Art critic and painter, born in London of a Quaker family, educated at Clifton College and King's College, Cambridge, where he read natural sciences and was a member of the *Apostles. He became art critic of the **Athenaeum* in 1901, helped to establish the *Burlington Magazine* in 1903, and from 1906 to 1910 was employed by the Metropolitan Museum of Art in New York. On his return to England he organized two highly influential and controversial exhibitions of *'Post-Impressionist' paintings (a term he coined himself) at the Grafton Galleries in 1910 and 1912, and his collected essays (*Vision and Design*, 1920; *Transformations*, 1926) were also instrumental in spreading enthusiasm for modern French painting. He was closely associated with the *Bloomsbury Group, and his biography was written by Virginia *Woolf (1940). See Frances Spalding, *Roger Fry: Art and Life* (1999).

FRYE, Northrop (1912–91) Canadian critic. Born in Sherbrooke, Quebec, he studied at Victoria College, University of Toronto, and, after ordination in the United Church of Canada, at Oxford. Returning to Toronto as a lecturer, he wrote *Fearful Symmetry* (1947), an influential defence of William *Blake's allegorical system. His most important book is *Anatomy of Criticism* (1957), which redirected American literary theory away from the 'close reading' of *New Criticism and towards the larger meanings of literary genres, modes, and archetypes. Rejecting critical evaluation in favour of a value-free literary science, Frye elaborates here a comprehensive map of the literary 'universe' in a boldly schematic series of classifications. His early work did much to redeem the genre of *romance, the subject of his later book *The Secular Scripture* (1976). He wrote three books on *Shakespeare, two collections of essays on Canadian literature, and the more ambitious work *The Great Code: The Bible and Literature* (1982), among many other writings. His emphasis on the deeper 'codes' or generic structures under the surface of literature foreshadowed the later turn to *structuralism in literary studies. There is a life by Joseph Adamson (1993).

Fudge Family in Paris, The A satire by Thomas *Moore, published 1818, and inspired by 'those groups of ridiculous English who were at that time swarming in all directions throughout Paris' after the restoration of the Bourbons. It takes the form of letters written by or to various members of the Fudge family when visiting France, and includes inane descriptions of Paris by the mindless Fudge children, and pompous, sycophantic letters from their father to the British foreign secretary, Castlereagh. Fusing social Horatian satire with liberal politics, Moore attacks post-Napoleonic European politics, the Holy Alliance, and British mistreatment of Ireland.

FUGARD, Athol (1932–) South African playwright, actor, and director born in Middlesburg, the son of a small shipowner; he was brought up in Port Elizabeth and educated there and at Cape Town University. He moved in 1958 to

Johannesburg, where he worked for some time as clerk to the Native Commissioner's Court, an experience which sharpened his awareness of racial tension and inequality, the subject of much of his drama. His plays include *The Blood Knot* (1961; pub. 1963), about the fraught relationship of two coloured brothers; *Boesman and Lena* (1968; pub. 1969), a sombre work figuring a derelict middle-aged couple of Coloured migrant workers, whose presence as they set up their shelter on the open stage has a symbolic quality akin to that of the characters of Samuel *Beckett; *Sizwe Bansi is Dead* (1972; pub. 1974, written with John Kani and Winston Ntshona), based on the problems created by the pass laws; *A Lesson from Aloes* (1980; pub. 1981), which contrasts the political attitudes of an Afrikaner, his wife, and their Coloured friends; and *'Master Harold'...and the Boys* (1982; pub. 1983), an autobiographical play portraying the relationship between a white teenager and two black family servants, 'the boys'. Fugard's career has been complicated by the politics of racialism; he was in 1962 active in encouraging a boycott of South African theatre by overseas English-speaking playwrights, insisting that plays should be performed before non-segregated audiences, but later modified this attitude in view of the complexities of a situation which his own works vividly evoke. *The Island* (1973), co-written with Kani and Ntshona, was performed at the National Theatre in London in 2000 by Kani and Ntshona in their original parts as two prisoners, partly for a generation no longer aware of the political significance of Robben Island. Later plays such as *Sorrows and Rejoicings* (2002) and *Exits and Entrances* (2004) are memory plays; Fugard's only novel, *Tsotsi* (1980), was made into a successful film in 2005. The plays often take place on an almost bare stage and depend on the mesmeric power of the dialogue.

Fulgens and Lucrece A late 15th-century *interlude by Henry Medwall (*fl.* 1486), regarded as the earliest known purely secular play in English. It has been edited by G. Walker in *Medieval Drama* (2000).

FULLER, John (1937–) Poet and novelist, son of Roy *Fuller, born in Kent and educated at New College, Oxford; fellow of Magdalen College, Oxford, from 1966. His first volume of poetry was *Fairground Music* (1961); others include *Cannibals and Missionaries* (1972), *The Illusionists* (1980), *Stones and Fires* (1996), and *The Space of Joy* (2006). His poems are diverse in range and material, extending from lyrics to pastiche verse epistles, from sonnets to unrhymed monologues, from humoresques to grave meditations. In collaboration with James *Fenton he published a collection of comic poems, *Partingtime Hall*, in 1987. A *Collected Poems* appeared in 1996. He is a lifelong advocate of W. H. *Auden, on whom he has published an indispensable *Commentary* (1998). His novels include *Flying to Nowhere* (1983), a fantasy about a 16th-century abbot who thinks he has discovered the seat of the soul, *The Burning Boys* (1989), and *A Skin Diary* (1997).

FULLER, Margaret (1810–50) American author and feminist, born in Massachusetts, whose name is associated with the activities of the New England *Transcendental Club; she helped to found *The *Dial*, which she edited for two years (1840–42), and in the same period (1839–44) conducted a series of conversations or seminars for educated women in Boston. One of the products of these discussions was her influential feminist tract *Women in the Nineteenth Century* (1845), which argues that woman as a spiritual being should be liberated from male-imposed social restrictions. In 1844 she moved to New York, where she wrote for Horace Greeley's *New York Tribune*, and in 1846 she went to Europe and settled in Italy, where she married one of the followers of the patriot Mazzini (1805–72), the Marquis Ossoli. Sailing from Livorno to America in 1850, she and her husband were drowned when their ship was wrecked just short of its destination. Her *Memoirs* (1852) were edited by Ralph Waldo *Emerson, W. H. Channing, and J. F. Clarke. She is said to have suggested the character of the magnetic and passionate Zenobia in Nathaniel *Hawthorne's *The *Blithedale Romance*.

FULLER, Roy (1912–91) Poet and novelist, born near Oldham, the son of a director of a rubber-proofing company. He was educated at Blackpool High School, and then became a solicitor, working for many years for a building society. During the 1930s he contributed to left-wing literary magazines, including *New Verse*, and his first volume, *Poems* (1939), shows the influence of W. H. *Auden and Stephen *Spender. This was followed by several collections of poetry: *Collected Poems 1936–1961* (1962), with work from several previous volumes, forms a link between the poets of the 1930s and the poets of the *Movement, in its lucid, ironic, detached tone, and its formal accomplishment. His later volumes, which include *From the Joke Shop* (1975) and *The Reign of Sparrows* (1980), while displaying an equal interest in technique, frequently strike a more personal note, particularly in the many sardonic reflections on old age and the ageing process. Fuller also published several novels, including, notably, *Image of a Society* (1956), which is a portrait of personal and professional conflicts in a northern provincial building society, narrated in a low-key, naturalistic, yet ironic manner. He was professor of poetry at Oxford, 1968–73, and *Owls and Artificers* (1971) and *Professors and Gods* (1973) are collections of his Oxford lectures. He also published three volumes of memoirs, *Souvenirs* (1980), *Vamp till Ready* (1982), and *Home and Dry* (1984).

FULLER, Thomas (1608–61) Clergyman and historian, born at Aldwinkle St Peter's in Northamptonshire and educated at Queens' and Sidney Sussex colleges, Cambridge. He became rector of Broadwindsor, Dorset, in 1634, and shortly before the Civil War was made a preacher at the Savoy. A moderate Royalist, he followed the war as chaplain to Sir Ralph Hopton (bap. 1596, d. 1652) and during his travels conceived the idea of 'a more exact collection' of the worthies of England. After the Restoration he became 'chaplain in extraordinary' to the king. He published *The History of the Holy War* (i.e. of the Crusades) in 1639; *The *Holy State and the Profane State* in 1642; **Good Thoughts in Bad Times* in 1645 (followed by two sequels); *A Pisgah-Sight of Palestine*, a topographical and historical work, in 1650. His *The Church-History of Britain; with the History of the University of Cambridge* (1655), which covers from the birth of Christ to the execution of Charles I, was criticized (by Peter *Heylyn, among others) for its 'puns and quibbles' and its 'trencher-jests', but was widely read and enjoyed. *The History of the Worthies of England*, his best-known and most characteristic work, appeared after his death in 1662, and was the fruit of much research; in his own words, 'My pains have been scattered all over the land, by riding, writing, going, sending, chiding, begging, praying, and sometimes paying too, to procure manuscript material.' Charles *Lamb referred to him as 'the dear, fine, silly, old angel', and he was much admired by S. T. *Coleridge. His writings are marked by a lively and eccentric curiosity, by 'fantastic caprices' (Leslie *Stephen), and by a fondness for aphorisms.

Furies *See* ORESTEIA.

FURNIVALL, Frederick James (1825–1910) Philologist and reformer, educated at University College London and Trinity College, Cambridge. He began his career as a barrister, but soon devoted his great energy to educational, philological, and literary pursuits. He was from 1847 a member of the Philological Society, and became its secretary; in 1861 he became editor of the proposed New English Dictionary which developed into the **Oxford English Dictionary*. He founded the *Early English Text Society (1864), the Chaucer Society (1868), the Ballad Society (1869), the New Shakspere Society (1873), the Wyclif Society (1881), the Browning Society (1881), and the Shelley Society (1886), and himself edited many texts. A friend of John *Ruskin and Charles *Kingsley, Furnivall was also a leader in the movement for popular education, supported women's rights, and taught grammar at the Working Men's College founded in 1854.

FURPHY, Joseph *See* BULLETIN.

FUSELI, (Füssli), Henry (1741–1825) Swiss artist who came to England in 1764. After studying in Rome (1770–78) he settled in London. Fuseli's works show the powerful attraction of Edmund *Burke's ideas of the *sublime, and he was fascinated by the supernatural and the darkest of human passions. Fuseli drew his subjects from *Shakespeare, *Milton, *Dante, *Ossian, and other poets. He made brilliant contributions to John *Boydell's Shakespeare Gallery, and his famous painting *The Nightmare* (1782) was known throughout Europe. Fuseli, who began his career as a translator, was a learned artist who shone in literary and artistic society in London. Though both William *Hazlitt and S. T. *Coleridge despised his nightmare fantasy, William *Blake, a constant friend, admired him greatly. Blake engraved some of Fuseli's designs and Fuseli wrote the preface to Blake's edition of Robert *Blair's *The Grave*. Mary *Wollstonecraft suffered from an obsessive passion for Fuseli. See P. A. Tomory, *The Life and Art of Henry Fuseli* (1972).

FUST, Johann (d. 1467) German goldsmith. He financed *Gutenberg's experiments in printing, but the partnership between them was dissolved probably in 1455 and Fust carried on with his son-in-law Peter Schöffer. Their Latin Psalter of 1457 is the first to bear a printer's imprint and date. Robert *Browning wrote a dialogue, 'Fust and his Friends' (in **Parleyings with Certain People*).

Futurism A 20th-century avant-garde movement in Italian art, literature, and music, founded by Filippo *Marinetti in 1909 in Paris. Its programme, outlined in the *Futurist Manifesto*, was to break with the past and its academic culture and to celebrate technology, dynamism, violence, and power. In language and in poetry it advocated the destruction of traditional syntax, metre, and punctuation in the name of the 'free word'. The *Manifesto of Futurist Painting* (1910), by Giacomo Balla, Umberto Boccioni, Carlo Carrà, Luigi Russolo, and Gino Severini, advocated a new art which represented nature in a dynamic state. Futurist painting was first seen in Britain at the Sackville Gallery in 1912 and was accompanied by wild readings from Marinetti. Roger *Fry gave the movement a cautious welcome, and their work had a strong influence on Wyndham *Lewis, T. E. *Hulme, Ezra *Pound, Ford Madox *Ford, and the British *Vorticist movement, though in publications such as **Blast* (1912–15) the Vorticists tried to make clear distinctions between the Italian version of Futurism and its British counterpart. The friendship of C. W. R. Nevinson (1889–1946) with Marinetti led to an exhibition, 'The Post-Impressionist and Futurist Exhibition', in 1913 in which Nevinson put into practice many of Marinetti's ideas. D. H. *Lawrence was hugely impressed by the Futurist project and in 1914 planned to write an article on the subject. Though this did not materialize, the influence of Futurism can be clearly seen in **Women in Love* (begun 1913, pub. 1920), most especially in the ideas that he attributes to the sculptor Loerke. The movement petered out during the 1930s after Marinetti's incorporation into Fascist academic culture. See Marjorie Perloff, *The Futurist Movement* (2003); Richard Humphreys, *Futurism* (1999).
See MAIAKOVSKY, VLADMIR VLADIMIROVICH, for Russian Futurism.

FYGE (later Egerton), **Sarah** (1670–1723) Poet, born in London, daughter of a physician. In 1686 her poem *The Female Advocate*, written in response to Robert Gould, was published, causing her father to send her to live in the country with relatives. She was also married, reluctantly, to an attorney, who died *c.*1695. In 1700 she published a number of poems on the death of John *Dryden. The deficiencies of her second marriage, to a clergyman, Thomas Egerton, were revealed in a scandalous and unsuccessful divorce case of 1703, in which she accused her husband of cruelty and he accused her of adultery and theft. In that year Fyge published *Poems on Several Occasions*, which contains several poems lamenting the conventions that bind women and others celebrating her love for 'Alexis', a friend of her first husband. Delarivier *Manley caricatured her tangled attachments in *The New Atalantis* (1709).

G

GABORIAU, Émile (1832–73) French writer of crime fiction, considered to be the first practitioner in France of the *roman policier.* He created two famous characters, the professional detective Monsieur Lecoq and the amateur Le Père Tabaret. Gaboriau's best-known works are *L'Affaire Lerouge* (1866: *The Lerouge Affair*), *Le Crime d'Orcival* (1867: *Orcival's Crime*), *Le Dossier No. 113* (1867: *File No. 113*), *Monsieur Lecoq* (1869), and *Les Esclaves de Paris* (1869: *The Slaves of Paris*).

Gabriel One of the archangels, who foretold the birth of John the Baptist to Zacharias and of Jesus to Mary (Luke 1: 11–20, 26–38). In Islam he is Jibril, the angel who revealed the *Qur'ān to Muhammad. Milton makes him 'Chief of the angelic guards' (**Paradise Lost*, IV. 550).

GADBURY, John *See* ALMANACS.

GADDA, Carlo Emilio (1893–1973) Italian novelist. His most important novels are *Il castello di Udine* (1934: *The Castle of Udine*), a memoir of his experience in the First World War; *Adalgisa* (1944), a critique of contemporary Milanese society; and the unfinished *Cognizione del dolore* (1963, written 1938–41: *The Cognizance of Sorrow*). Also unfinished is *Quel pasticciaccio brutto de via Merulana* (1957: *That Dreadful Mess on the Via Merulana*), which uses the conventions of the thriller to dissect Roman society under *Fascism. That his two major works are incomplete is not accidental: in *Cognizione* the relationship between the protagonist and his mother is irresolvable, and *Pasticciaccio* stops short of revealing the murderer. His style is remarkable for its grotesquerie, its implicit use of European philosophy, and its pastiches of different languages and dialects. See M. Bertone and R. S. Dombrowski, *Carlo Emilio Gadda: Contemporary Perspectives* (1998).

GADDIS, William (1922–98) American novelist, born in New York and educated at Harvard University where he briefly edited the *Harvard Lampoon*. The hero of his enormous first novel *The Recognitions* (1955) is Wyatt Gwyon, who has abandoned his training as a priest to become a forger of Old Masters. The book offers an extended satirical meditation on the lack of authenticity in contemporary culture. For *J.R.* (1975) Gaddis told his story of an 11-year-old stock-market dealer entirely in fractured, frequently comic dialogue revealing the protagonist's blatant opportunism. The smaller-scale *Carpenter's Gothic* (1985), as its title suggests, located in an isolated old house, and *A Frolic of his Own* (1994) both satirize America's obsession with litigation using more accessible methods than his first novels. The posthumous *Agape Agape* (2002) is the monologue of an elderly man meditating on value in art and incorporating comments on the player piano which had been an enduring interest of Gaddis's. *The Rush for Second Place* (2002) gathers Gaddis's uncollected pieces.

GAIMAN, Neil (1960–) *Science fiction and *fantasy author, born in Portchester, England, now resident in Minnesota. His fantasy novels, short stories, screenplays, children's books, and comic book scripts consistently explore aspects of storytelling. The 'Sandman' comic book 'A Midsummer Night's Dream', based on *Shakespeare's play, won the World Fantasy Award for short fiction. After collaborating with Terry *Pratchett on *Good Omens* (1990) he published novels, such as *Neverwhere* (1996), *American Gods* (2001), and *Coraline* (2002); graphic novels, often in collaboration with the artist Dave McKean; and various collections of short stories. All are marked by an erudite sensitivity to the dark undercurrents of folklore and the potential for humour in fantasy and *horror. His *The Graveyard Book* (2008), a novel for children, won the 2009 Newbery Medal.

GAIMAR, Geffrei (*fl.* *c.*1136–7) Author of the earliest extant work of history in a French vernacular, *L'Estoire des Engleis*, an Anglo-Norman romance history in octosyllabic rhymed couplets covering the period from the Anglo-Saxon settlements to the death of William Rufus. An earlier section, beginning (like *Geoffrey of Monmouth's contemporary *History*) with the fall of Troy, has been lost. *L'Estoire* contains the story of Havelok, corresponding to the Anglo-Norman *Le Lai d'Haveloc*. Gaimar was probably a secular clerk of Norman blood. His patron was Constance, the wife of Ralph FitzGilbert of Lincolnshire and Hampshire, areas in which Gaimar displays particular interest. See *L'Estoire des Engleis*, ed. A. Bell (Anglo-Norman Texts Society, 1960); English trans. by T. D. Hardy and C. T. Martin (Rolls Series, 1888–9).

GAINSBOROUGH, Thomas (1727–88) Portrait and landscape painter; after training in London he returned to his native Suffolk (1748). He painted landscapes and small portrait groups in landscape settings, including the famous *Mr and Mrs Andrews* (*c.*1748). From 1774 he worked in London where he became a fashionable portrait painter. His varied landscapes included rococo idylls, seascapes, and pictures of mountain grandeur—in 1783 he planned a visit to the Lakes. The 'fancy pictures', Arcadian rustic themes like the *Peasant Girl Gathering Sticks*, led on to the sentiment of early *Romanticism. Gainsborough, in both style and temperament, is quite unlike his rival Joshua *Reynolds, although Reynolds's *Fourteenth Discourse* is a fine appreciation of his art. Gainsborough's biographer William Jackson wrote that he 'avoided the company of literary men [and]...detested reading'. See Malcolm Cormack, *The Paintings of Thomas Gainsborough* (1991).

Gai saber The title of a 13th-century society in Toulouse which devoted itself to a consideration and cultivation of the courtly *troubadour idea of 'jois', 'exaltation'.

Galahad, Sir (The Haute Prince) In *Malory, the son (by enchantment) of *Launcelot and *Elaine, daughter of King Pelles. He is predestined by his immaculate purity to achieve the Siege Perilous (*see* ROUND TABLE) and the *Grail, after the vision of which he dies in ecstasy.

GALDÓS, Benito Pérez *See* PÉREZ GALDÓS, BENITO.

Galehaut (Galehault) **of Surluse and the Long Isles** An important character in the story of the love of Launcelot and Guinevere as described in the early 13th-century French prose *'Vulgate' cycle. He was a friend of Launcelot who demanded tribute from Arthur; he introduced the lovers but became jealous of the queen's influence over Launcelot. He is famous as the Galeotto in *Dante's episode of Paolo and Francesca (*Inferno*, V. 137). *Malory wrongly calls him 'the Haute Prince' through a confusion with the similar name *Galahad.

GALEN (Claudius Galenus) (AD *c.*129–*c.*200) Perhaps the most influential of ancient physicians. He is reputed to have written some 500 treatises in Greek, several of which have survived. Translated into Latin during the 11th and 12th centuries, his writings dominated the development of medieval medicine, and in the 16th century he was also esteemed as an exponent of scientific method. Thomas *Linacre translated six of his works and there are references to him in *Chaucer, Francis *Bacon, and Sir Thomas *Browne.

Galeotto *See* GALEHAUT OF SURLUSE AND THE LONG ISLES.

GALIGNANI, Giovanni Antonio (1757–1821). With his English wife Anne Parsons (1776–1822) he established an English bookshop and circulating library in Paris *c.*1799, and in 1814 founded a newspaper, *Galignani's Messenger*, which had a wide circulation among English residents on the Continent. The paper was continued by his sons John Anthony (1796–1873) and William (1798–1882), who were born in London. As publishers in Paris they issued reprints of English books, and guides to Paris, Switzerland, and so on. A famous bookshop of this name still stands on the rue de Rivoli in Paris.

GALILEO GALILEI (1564–1642) Italian astronomer and physicist, born in Pisa of a Florentine family. In 1604 he demonstrated that unequal weights drop with equal velocity, an observation apocryphally said to be based on the dropping of weights from the leaning Tower of Pisa. In 1609 he assembled a telescope on the basis of reports of such an instrument in the Netherlands, and so discovered the moons of Jupiter, the phases of Venus, the configuration of the moon, and the stars invisible to the naked eye, all of which were described in *Sidereus Nuncius* (1610: 'Starry Messenger'). His two principal works were *Dialogo sopra i due massimi sistemi del mondo* (1632), in which Copernicanism is shown to be superior to the Ptolemaic cosmology, and *Discorsi intorno a due nuove scienze* (1638), an exposition of the mathematics of moving bodies. Galileo's publications led him into conflict with the Inquisition; in 1616 he was forbidden to teach Copernican cosmology and in 1634 he was compelled to repudiate it and sentenced to life imprisonment, commuted to house arrest. (The story of his muttering 'eppur si muove'—'yet it does move'—after his recantation is also apocryphal.) Milton records his meeting with Galileo in *Areopagitica* and recalls the 'optic glass' of 'the Tuscan artist' in *Paradise Lost*, Book I.

GALLAGHER, Stephen (1954–) Born in Salford; screenwriter, novelist, and television director known for suspense, supernatural dramas, and *science fiction (he wrote two series of *Doctor Who* in the early 1980s). He adapted his novel *Chimera* (1982) for television.

GALLAND, Antoine (1646–1715) French translator and orientalist. His *Mille et une nuits* (1704–17) was the first translation into a European language of the Arabic *Thousand and One Nights* (*see* ARABIAN NIGHTS ENTERTAINMENTS). It was quickly translated into English, and it subsequently influenced, amongst others, Joseph *Addison, Richard *Steele, William *Beckford, S. T. *Coleridge, Alfred *Tennyson, and Charles *Dickens.

galliambics Verses written in imitation of a *metre used by *Callimachus in Greek and by *Catullus in Latin. Requiring lines of sixteen syllables or more with awkwardly paired stresses, it is unusually difficult to reproduce this metre in English. Alfred *Tennyson's 'Boädicea' (1864) is a rare attempt.

GALLOWAY, Janice (1956–) Scottish novelist and short story writer, born in Kilwinning, Ayrshire, and educated at Glasgow University, who worked as a teacher before becoming a full-time writer in 1989. *The Trick is to Keep Breathing* (1990), a typographically experimental study of mental breakdown on a bleak housing estate, was followed by two further novels, *Foreign Parts* (1994) and *Clara* (2002), the latter an exploration of the life of the pianist Clara Wieck, wife of Robert *Schumann. *Blood* (1991) and *Where You Find It* (1996) collect brief fictions which combine social observation with a dark sense of the uncanny. She has also written poems and a libretto on Mary *Shelley (*Monster*, 2002, with music by Sally Beamish).

GALSWORTHY, John (1867–1933) Novelist and dramatist, born at Kingston Hill, Surrey, and educated at Harrow School and New College, Oxford. He was called to the bar in 1890, but a chance meeting with Joseph *Conrad in 1893, and the strong influence of his future wife, turned him to writing. His first volume of stories, *From the Four Winds*, appeared in 1897, and in 1898 he brought out his first novel, *Jocelyn*. There followed another novel, *Villa Rubein* (1900), and a further volume of stories, *Man of Devon* (1901), in which the Forsyte family makes its first appearance. All four books were published under the pseudonym John Sinjohn. In 1905 he married his cousin's wife, with whom he had been living for ten years. *The Island Pharisees* (1904), the first novel he published under his own name, revealed his abiding interest in the effects of poverty and the constraints of convention. It was much praised and other novels followed, including *The Country House* (1907), *Fraternity* (1909), and *The Dark Flower* (1913). The first of the Forsyte novels, *The Man of Property*, appeared in 1906, followed by *In Chancery* (1920) and *To Let* (1921), which, together with two interludes, appeared collectively as *The *Forsyte Saga* in 1922. The second part of the Forsyte chronicles, containing *The White Monkey* (1924), *The Silver Spoon* (1926), *Swan Song* (1928), and the two interludes 'A Silent Wooing' and 'Passers By', was published as *A Modern Comedy* in 1929. In 1931 Galsworthy followed the immense success of the Forsyte books with a further collection of stories, *On Forsyte Change*.

Galsworthy began his dramatic career in 1906 with *The Silver Box*—a play about theft in which he employed a favourite device of 'parallel' families, one rich and one poor. This was the first of a long line of plays on social and moral themes. His reputation as a dramatist became firmly established with *Strife* (1909), an examination of men and managers in industry, which was followed by *Justice* (1910), in which a minor felon is ground down by the cruel majesty of the law; the play was part of Galsworthy's long campaign against the practice of solitary confinement. His later plays include *The Skin Game* (1920), tracing the rivalry between a nouveau riche manufacturer and an aristocrat; *Loyalties* (1922); and *Old English* (1924). Posthumous publications included *Collected Poems* (1934) and, in 1935, *The End of the Chapter*, consisting of *Maid in Waiting* (1931), *Flowering Wilderness* (1932), and *Over the River* (1933), relating the family history of the Charwells, cousins of the younger Forsytes. Galsworthy was awarded the *Nobel Prize for Literature in 1932; he was already an OM (1929), and received many other honours. See James Gindin, *John Galsworthy's Life and Art* (1987).

GALT, John (1779–1839) Scottish novelist, born in Irvine, Ayrshire, where he attended the local grammar school. His family moved to Greenock when he was 9, and he was employed as a clerk there before moving to London in 1804. While travelling in Europe in 1809 he met Lord *Byron, of whom he published a biography in 1830. From 1824 to 1827 he was secretary of the Canada Company, and spent three years in Canada from 1826, founding the town of Guelph (nearby Galt is named after him) and building a road between Lake Huron and Lake Erie. As a result of intrigues by his enemies he returned to England heavily in debt. He moved back to Greenock in 1834. Galt wrote poetry, drama, historical fiction, biography, memoirs, and travel books, but is chiefly remembered for the studies of rural life in western Scotland he thought of as 'theoretical histories' rather than novels: *The *Ayrshire Legatees* (1821), **Annals of the Parish* (written 1813, published 1821), *The *Entail* (1823), *The *Provost* (1822), and *The Member* (1832). At their best these bring a ground-breaking subtlety and irony to first-person narration, and acutely render social and historical change.

GALTON, Sir Francis (1822–1911) Remembered for work on heredity and his advocacy of eugenics; initially made his mark as an explorer. Born near Spearbrook, Birmingham, he was a child prodigy, but nevertheless failed educationally. Then in 1850–52 his not very remarkable travels in south-west Africa, recorded in *Tropical South Africa* (1853), earned him his FRS and a medal from the *Royal Geographical Society. He inaugurated the Society's 'Hints to Travellers' booklets. These and his own more discursive *The Art of Travel* (1855) helped to popularize a serious approach to travel and recording information.

Galton could be intolerant and insensitive and caused more than one crisis at the RGS, with which he broke his connection over its proposed admission of women as fellows. Galton began a novel at the end of his life but then suppressed it. Undoubtedly a genius with an enormous output of scientific papers, his place in British intellectual history remains problematic.

Game at Chess, A A satirical comedy by Thomas *Middleton, produced 1624, when it was acted for a record run of nine performances at the Globe until suppressed by the authorities. Six different transcripts in manuscript survive.

It deals allegorically with the rivalry of England and Spain (the White House and the Black House) and the project of the 'Spanish Marriage' (1623), the failed plan for Prince Charles to marry the Spanish infanta in 1623. The play places on stage the sovereigns of the two countries, Charles, prince of Wales, Buckingham, and the Spanish ambassador *Gondomar, and represents the discomfiture of the Black House. The play, reflecting the popular dislike of the Spanish match, was enthusiastically received, but gave great offence to the Spanish ambassador and to *James I.

Gamelyn, The Tale of A verse romance of the mid-14th century in 898 lines of couplets. It survives in 25 manuscripts, including some of *The *Canterbury Tales*, where it is usually assigned to the Cook, although there is no evidence that Chaucer himself intended to use it. Gamelyn is the youngest of three brothers whose father leaves them his property in equal shares, but whose eldest brother cheats him of his entitlement. Like Orlando in **As You Like It* (which is related to it via Thomas Lodge's *Rosalynde*), Gamelyn overthrows the court wrestler and flees to the forest, from where he wages a successful campaign to recover his birthright. The story also has striking affinities with the legends of *Robin Hood and has been edited by Stephen Knight and Thomas H. Ohlgren in *Robin Hood and Other Outlaw Tales* (1997).

Gamester, The A comedy by John *Shirley, acted 1633, printed 1637. This was one of Shirley's most popular plays, adapted (and sentimentalized) by Charles *Johnson in 1712 as *The Wife's Relief* and by *Garrick in 1758 as *The Gamesters*. Its main plot is taken from the **Heptameron* of Marguerite of Navarre.

Wilding, the title character, tells his wife of his intention to make love to his ward, her relation Penelope, and makes an assignation with the girl. Mrs Wilding takes Penelope's place; Wilding, who has just lost heavily to his friend Hazard, sends him in his place as a way of paying his debt. When husband and wife compare notes, he is appalled at the revelation of the double bed-trick. To conceal his disgrace, he arranges for Hazard to marry Penelope; it then turns out that everyone's honour has been preserved anyway, so he has cheated himself twice. There is a romantic sub-plot, and a comic one featuring young Barnacle, a citizen's son who wants to learn the art of being a 'roaring boy'. *The Gamester* is also the title of a play by Susannah *Centlivre and of a tragedy by Edward *Moore.

Gammer Gurton's Needle The second English comedy in verse (the first being **Ralph Roister Doister*), published 1575, having been acted 1566, at Christ's College, Cambridge. Its authorship has been attributed either to John Still, fellow of Christ's College, or to William Stevenson, also a fellow of the college and one of its leading spirits in dramatic activities.

It is written in rhymed long doggerel, and deals farcically with the losing and finding of the needle used to mend the garments of Hodge, Gammer Gurton's man. The other characters, besides Hodge and the Gammer, are Tib and Cock, their maid and boy; Diccon the Bedlam; Dame Chat and Doll, her maid; Master Bailey and his servant Scapethrift; Doctor Rat the curate; and Gyb the cat. The mischievous Diccon persuades the Gammer that Dame Chat has taken the needle; a quarrel follows and Doctor Rat is called in, but gets his head broken. Finally Hodge becomes acutely aware that the needle is in the seat of his breeches. The play includes the famous old drinking song with the refrain: 'Back and side go bare, go bare, both foot and hand go cold: | But belly god send thee good ale enough, whether it be new or old.'

Ganelon In the *Charlemagne romances and the *Morgante maggiori* of *Pulci, the traitor who schemes for the defeat of the rearguard at Roncesvalles (*see* ROLAND). He appears in *Dante's *Inferno* (XXXII. 122) and *Chaucer's 'Nun's Priest's Tale' (**Canterbury Tales*, 20).

GARAMOND, Claude (d. 1561) French typefounder, noted for his elegant roman types, inspired by one cut for *Aldus Manutius in 1495, and for his 'Grecs du roi', the Greek type he cut for Francis I for use by *Estienne, the king's printer.

GARCÍA LORCA, Federico (1898–1936) Spanish poet and dramatist, born in Fuente Vaqueros, near Granada. He spent his first eleven years in the region. Such immersion in the language and ways of the Andalusian countryside profoundly influenced his sensibility. In Granada he began writing poetry, became an excellent pianist, and studied law without much enthusiasm at the university. Lorca's early prose and poetry is pervaded with intense erotic anxiety and anticlerical anger, and shows that by 1918 he was aware of being homosexual. In 1921 he published a selection of verse, *Libro de poemas* (*Book of Poems*), in Madrid, where for several years he lived sporadically at the famous, Europe-oriented students' residence (La Residencia de Estudiantes), and became close friends with Luis Buñuel (1900–83) and Salvador Dalí (1904–89). He celebrated Dalí in a distinguished ode. In 1927 he staged *Mariana Pineda* and published his second volume of poems, *Canciones* (*Songs*). His *Romancero gitano* (*Gypsy Ballads*) firmly established his reputation as a poet the following year. Tired of his 'gypsy myth', depressed, and by then within the orbit of *Surrealism, Lorca fled to New York in 1929, where he produced the anguished compositions published posthumously as *Poeta en Nueva York* (1940: *Poet in New York*), wrote a film script, *Viaje a la luna* (*Trip to the Moon*), written in 1929, and began a revolutionary play, *El público* (*The Audience*), which back in Spain he described as ' *explicitly* homosexual'. In 1932, following the proclamation of a new Spanish Republic, he was appointed director of Madrid University's touring theatre, La Barraca, with which he took Spanish classical plays out into the provinces and widened his experience of practical stagecraft. Unable to stage *The Audience* and its successor, *Así que pasen cinco años* (1931: *When Five Years Pass*), he developed his rural vein in the tragedies *Bodas de sangre* (*Blood Wedding*, performed 1933) and *Yerma* (performed 1934) with which he shot to fame as a dramatist; the former was translated by Ted *Hughes. *Llanto por Ignacio Sánchez Mejías* (1934: *Lament for Ignacio Sánchez Mejías*), written for a friend who was a bullfighter, is one of the finest elegies in the Spanish language. *Doña Rosita la soltera* (*Doña Rosita the Spinster*, performed 1935) expresses Lorca's desolate view of Granada. His last play, *La casa de Bernarda Alba* (*The House of Bernarda Alba*), was completed just before his return to the city in July 1936 and the outbreak of the Spanish Civil War: it was published posthumously in 1945. He was murdered by the Fascists in August 1936. See Ian Gibson, *Federico García Lorca: A Life* (1989).

GARCÍA MÁRQUEZ, Gabriel (1927/8–) Colombian novelist, born in the Caribbean backwater of Aracataca, and a key figure in the *Boom. He was educated at the Liceo Nacional at Zipaquirá, near Santa Fe de Bogotá, and never completed his university law degree. After beginning his lifelong journalistic career, he went to Europe for the Liberal Colombian newspaper *El espectador* and in 1955 published his first novel, *La hojarasca* (*Leaf Storm*); it introduces the isolated fictional town of Macondo, which more famously became the setting for his *Cien años de soledad* (1967: *One Hundred Years of Solitude*), written in Mexico and recounting the lives of several generations of the Buendía family. In this exuberant, tragicomic novel of *magic realism, a style which García Márquez popularized, a deadpan narrator adopts the voice of a rural Caribbean storyteller, relating in closely observed detail a series of plausible and marvellous events which provide a history of Colombia seen from below. The author has long supported the Cuban Revolution; the novel has a strong political dimension. Known primarily as a magic realist, García Márquez's work is in fact constantly experimental, from his realist novella *El coronel no tiene quien le escriba* (1958: *No One Writes to the Colonel*) to the complex novel of dictatorship *El otoño del patriarca* (1975: *The Autumn of the Patriarch*), and the fictional investigation of a murder in *Crónica de una muerte anunciada* (1981: *Chronicle of a Death Foretold*). In 1985 he published *El amor en los tiempos del cólera* (*Love in the Time of Cholera*), an examination of love, memory, and old age, in the form of a popular romance. His later work includes *El general en su laberinto* (1989: *The General in his Labyrinth*), a re-creation of Simón Bolívar's final days, *Del amor y otros demonios* (1994: *Of Love and Other Demons*), and *Memoria de mis putas tristes* (2004: *Memories of my Melancholy Whores*). García Márquez is a master of both the wide-ranging saga, and the spare short story in which much is left unsaid. He has published several collections of stories, among them *Los funerales de la Mamá Grande* (1962: *Big Mama's Funeral*) and *Doce cuentos peregrinos* (1992: *Strange Pilgrims*). His work is influenced by writing in English, especially that of William *Faulkner, Ernest *Hemingway, James *Joyce, and Virginia *Woolf, while he has inspired writers like Salman *Rushdie and Angela *Carter. He was awarded the *Nobel Prize for Literature in 1982; *Vivir para contarla* (*Living to Tell the Tale*), the first volume of his autobiography, appeared in 2002.

GARCILASO DE LA VEGA (?1501–36) Spanish poet and friend of Juan *Boscán de Almogáver; the names of the two poets are coupled in Lord *Byron's **Don Juan* (I. 95). His sonnets, eclogues, and odes inaugurated the Golden Age of Spanish poetry.

GARDAM, Jane (1928–) Novelist and short story writer, born in Coatham, North Yorkshire, educated at Saltburn High School for Girls and Bedford College, London. Some of her books are written for teenagers but have attracted adult readers as well. *Bilgewater* (1976) is a journey of enlightenment through the snares of adolescence, whose dangers Gardam portrays with extraordinary insight, as she does in *A Long Way from Verona* (1971), a comic novel set in the wartime Yorkshire of her own childhood. Although Gardam's work is very English in feel, her first volume of stories for adults, *Black Faces, White Faces* (1975), is set in Jamaica, while *Old Filth* (2004, winner of the Orange Prize) describes the long-term psychological effects on an unsuccessful international lawyer of being sent 'home' to England as a child by his Raj parents. She received the Whitbread Novel Award for *The Queen of the Tambourine* (1991). Her collections of stories include *The Sidmouth Letters* (1978) and *Showing the Flag* (1989).

Garden of Cyrus, The By Sir Thomas *Browne, the companion piece to **Hydriotaphia*, published 1658; treats of the occurrence of the quincunx (:·:) or lozenge and the number five in man-made objects, primarily the plantations of the ancients, and then their buildings, other artefacts, and customs, in plants, in animals, and in traditional philosophy and theology. He chooses his 'bye and barren theme' partly to please the dedicatee, an ardent horticulturist, partly because 'Paradise succeeds the Grave'. By intertwining many heterogeneous observations he playfully demonstrates his ability to elaborate and digress.

GARDNER, Erle Stanley (1889–1970) American writer of crime fiction. Born in Massachusetts, he spent most of his life in California, the setting for most of his novels. Trained as a lawyer, Gardner began publishing crime and mystery stories in magazines in the 1920s. In 1933 he began his long-running series of 82 narratives of Perry Mason, a lawyer-cum-detective, which combined crime investigation with courtroom dramas. At first narrated in the *hardboiled style of the inter-war period, Gardner's novels later softened their tone and were adapted for the *Perry Mason* television series 1957–66. See Dorothy B. Hughes, *Erle Stanley Gardner: The Case of the Real Perry Mason* (1978).

GARDNER, John (1933–82) American novelist, born in Batavia, New York; his *Grendel* (1971) retells the story of *Beowulf through the monster's voice. *The Sunlight Dialogues* (1972) opposes different viewpoints of America; other works, such as *Mickelsson's Ghosts* (1982), use supernatural or fantastic images without wholeheartedly embracing them.

'Gareth and Lynette' One of Tennyson's **Idylls of the King*, published 1872. It describes Gareth's disguise as a scullion at court, and his winning of Lynette through his rescue of her besieged sister Lyonors.

Gareth of Orkney, Sir The third son of King Lot of Orkney and Arthur's sister Morgawse. He conceals his identity at Camelot, works in the kitchen, and is nicknamed by Kay 'Beaumains' ('Fair hands'). The fourth of *Malory's eight *Works* (ed. Vinaver) is named *Sir Gareth of Orkney* and the book (VII in *Caxton) narrates Gareth's encounters with Lyonet and her sister, his future wife, Lyonesse, whom he rescues from Ironsyde. Malory's exact source is unknown. *See also* 'GARETH AND LYNETTE'.

GARFIELD, Leon (1921–96) Born in Brighton, where he briefly studied art. Garfield is an excellent but underestimated writer of what he called 'that old-fashioned thing, the family novel'—heavily atmospheric adventures set in the 18th and 19th centuries, owing something to *Smollett and *Dickens, notably in *Black Jack* (1968). His self-consciously inventive style is best seen in his series of novellas, *Garfield's Apprentices* (1976–8), and his adaptation of Greek myths (with Edward Blishen), *The God Beneath the Sea* (1970), awarded the Carnegie Medal. He wrote the scripts for *Shakespeare: The Animated Tales* (BBC, 1992–4).

Gargantua *See* Rabelais, François.

GARIBALDI, Giuseppe (1807–82) Italian revolutionary, general, politician, writer, and international celebrity. He began his political career with the Young Italy movement and took part in Mazzini's uprising (1834). From 1848 he was closely involved in the establishment of a united Italy. His most famous exploit in this context was the expedition of the Thousand to liberate Sicily and the Italian south (1860), for which he re-formed his Italian Legion of Redshirts. He wrote three semi-autobiographical novels drawing on his military experiences, of which the first, *Clelia*, appeared simultaneously in English (*The Rule of the Monk*, 1870). Garibaldi's travels took him to North and South America, as well as England, which he visited on four occasions, the last in 1864. Among his many English admirers were *Gladstone, Lord Shaftesbury (1801–85), *Tennyson, and the future King Edward VII. See L. Riall, *Garibaldi: The Invention of a Hero* (2007).

GARIOCH, Robert (1909–81) The pen-name of Robert Garioch Sutherland, Scottish poet, born in Edinburgh and educated at Edinburgh University. He spent three years from 1942 as a prisoner of war in Italy and Germany, an experience recalled in the self-deprecating prose of *Two Men and a Blanket* (1975). He worked as a schoolmaster in London and Edinburgh until his retirement in 1964. Garioch is known principally for his *Scots poems, which are at once more idiomatic and more formally continuous with earlier practice—particularly that of Robert *Fergusson—than those of Hugh *MacDiarmid and Goodsir *Smith. *Selected Poems* (1966) was his first full-scale collection, though he had published a number of pamphlets over the previous two decades. Later volumes include *The Big Music* (1971) and *Doktor Faust in Rose Street* (1973). His poetry is witty, satirical, and amusing, with an underlying pessimism. His many verse translations—of *Pindar, George *Buchanan, *Belli, *Apollinaire, and others—made almost as notable a contribution to the 20th century's refurbishment of Scots as his shrewd and laconic original work. See *Collected Poems* (2004).

GARLAND, (Hannibal) Hamlin (1860–1940) American novelist, born in West Salem, Wisconsin, remembered for his portraits of life in the Midwest. *Main-Travelled Roads: Six Mississippi Valley Stories* (1891) remains his best-known work, which established him as an important practitioner of realism in his fiction. In addition to stories and essays (*Crumbling Idols* (1894) collects his essays on art), Garland published many novels and an autobiography, *A Son of the Middle Border*, in 1917. He also published studies of prairie life and of the Native Americans in his chosen region, winning the 1922 Pulitzer Prize for biography. See Joseph B. McCullough, *Garland* (1978).

GARNER, Alan (1934–) OBE, born in Congleton, Cheshire; educated at Manchester Grammar School and, for a time, Magdalen College, Oxford. Garner has some claim to be the most distinguished writer for children of the 20th century. He began with two fantasies, *The Weirdstone of Brisingamen* (1960) and *The Moon of Gomrath* (1963), based on an eclectic mixture of Norse and Celtic mythology. Thereafter his books have been marked by extensive scholarly study of folklore, language and dialect, anthropology, and other fields, typified by *The Owl Service* (1967), based on a tale from the fourth branch of the collections of Welsh legends *The *Mabinogion*. This story of a trio of contemporary teenagers doomed to relive a legendary love-triangle was the first book to win both the Guardian Award and the Carnegie Medal. *Red Shift* (1973), which involves three parallel stories (Roman soldiers in savage surroundings, a Civil War massacre, and a contemporary teenage romance), pushed at the boundaries of the children's book in terms of both its sometimes brutal content and its highly oblique and sophisticated style. Garner turned to naturalism with *The Stone Book Quartet* (1976–8), intricate and stylistically intense novellas depicting the coming of age of boys in four generations of the Garner family; one of the reiterated themes is the steady decline in standards of craftsmanship and personal integrity. The remarkable reconstruction of rural Cheshire in these stories is revisited in the first and fourth parts of Garner's first novel for adults, *Strandloper* (1996). Based on a true story, the novel, intensely realistic and mystical by turns, follows William Buckley, who is transported from Cheshire to Australia, where he escapes, becomes a shaman with a tribe of Aborigines, and returns home. Another adult novel, *Thursbitch* (2003), again uses the Cheshire setting as a driving force and, in the manner of *Red Shift*, involves linked stories from different eras.

Garner has published many retellings of British folktales; his essays and talks are collected in *The Voice that Thunders* (1997). Neil Philip's *A Fine Anger* (1981) is a detailed study of his early work.

GARNETT, Constance (1861–1946) Née Black, translator from Russian, born in Brighton and educated at Newnham College, Cambridge. She married Edward *Garnett in 1889 and with the encouragement of their Russian friends soon began to learn Russian. She paid her first visit to Russia in 1893, when she met *Tolstoy. Her first translation, *Goncharov's *A Common Story*, was published in 1894 and her career as a translator finished 71 volumes and 40 years later with *Turgenev's *Three Plays* (1934). On the way she had brought to the

British public the major works of *Chekhov, *Dostoevsky, *Gogol, *Tolstoy, and Turgenev, a Herculean achievement, fully recognized by her contemporaries. Joseph *Conrad, D. H. *Lawrence, Arnold *Bennett, and H. E. *Bates are among those who would have echoed Katherine *Mansfield, writing to Constance in 1921, that 'the younger generation owe you more than we ourselves are able to realise. These books have changed our lives, no less.' See Richard *Garnett, *Constance Garnett: A Heroic Life* (1991).

GARNETT, David (1892–1981) Novelist and critic, born in Brighton, Sussex, and educated at University College School, London. He studied botany for some years at the Royal College of Science and was a conscientious objector and farm labourer during the First World War before opening a bookshop in Soho. Soon afterwards he turned to writing and his first novel, *Lady into Fox* (1922), an enigmatic fable about a young wife transformed into a vixen, had considerable success, winning both the Hawthornden and James Tait Black Memorial prizes for 1923. This was followed by another fable, *A Man in the Zoo* (1924), about a thwarted lover who donates himself as a specimen of *Homo sapiens* for exhibition in the zoo. *The Sailor's Return* (1925) describes the conflict between a sailor, his black African wife, and the Dorset villagers among whom they settle. Other novels, such as *Aspects of Love* (1955), made into a successful musical by Andrew Lloyd Webber, appeared sporadically from then on. Garnett also wrote a biography, *Pocahontas, or The Nonpareil of Virginia* (1933, *see* SMITH, CAPTAIN JOHN), the semi-fictional *Beany-Eye* (1935), and three volumes of autobiography, *The Golden Echo* (1953), *The Flowers of the Forest* (1955), and *The Familiar Faces* (1962). In addition he edited *The Letters of T. E. *Lawrence* (1938) and *The Novels of Thomas Love *Peacock* (1948).

GARNETT, Edward (1868–1937) Son of Richard *Garnett and husband of Constance *Garnett. He published several volumes, including novels, plays, and critical works, but is chiefly remembered as publisher's reader for several successive firms, the last of which was Jonathan Cape. In this role he encouraged and advised many of the most important writers of the period, amongst them Joseph *Conrad, D. H. *Lawrence, Dorothy *Richardson, E. M. *Forster, and W. H. *Hudson.

GARNETT, Eve (1900–91) Artist and children's writer. Born in Worcestershire, Garnett studied at the Royal Academy schools and exhibited at the Tate Gallery. She illustrated Evelyn Sharp's *The London Child* (1927), which moved her to produce a book of drawings, *'Is it Well with the Child?'* (1938). *The Family from One End Street* (1937; Carnegie Medal), which attempted sympathetically to portray working-class characters (Mr Ruggles is a dustman, his wife a washerwoman), has been accused of being patronizing, but is perhaps better seen as ahead of its time. There are two sequels. See Terence Molloy, *Eve Garnett: Artist, Illustrator, Author* (2002).

GARNETT, Richard (1835–1906) The son of Richard Garnett (1789–1850), linguist, philologist, and from 1838 assistant keeper of printed books at the British Museum. The younger Richard also worked at the British Museum, where his erudition became legendary; he was superintendent of the Reading Room from 1875, a post from which he resigned in 1884 to become chief editor of the library's first printed catalogue. He published several volumes of original and translated verse and several biographies, and edited many works, including *Relics of Shelley* (1862). He is best remembered as a writer for his collection of pagan tales *The Twilight of the Gods* (1888), some of which originally appeared in the **Yellow Book*.

See also GARNETT, CONSTANCE; GARNETT, EDWARD.

GARRICK, David (1717–79) Actor and dramatist, born in Hereford, the son of a recruiting officer, and educated in Lichfield. He accompanied Samuel *Johnson, briefly his tutor, to London, and set up with his brother in the wine trade before turning to the stage. His mythological burlesque *Lethe* was performed at Drury Lane in 1740, and in 1741 he appeared as an actor at Ipswich in Thomas Southerne's **Oroonoko*. He then made a successful London debut as Richard III, a key role, and subsequently proved his abilities in both comic and tragic parts. He wrote a number of farces, including *The Lying Valet* (1741), *Miss in her Teens* (1747), *A Peep behind the Curtain* (1767), and *Bon Ton, or High Life above Stairs* (1775). He adapted and produced several Shakespeare plays, and collaborated with George *Colman the elder in *The *Clandestine Marriage* (1766). In 1747 he became a partner in the management of Drury Lane. He made his last appearance in 1776, when he sold his patent share to Richard Brinsley *Sheridan and two others for £35,000. In 1769 he organized a grand 'Shakespeare Jubilee' at Stratford-upon-Avon, but lost over £2,000 when heavy rain forced him to cancel most of the three-day event. He did however stage a dramatic procession of Shakespeare characters, *The Jubilee*, successfully. Garrick was also a keen collector of early play texts. In 1773 he was elected a member of Johnson's *Club. Garrick's brilliance as an actor was celebrated in Churchill's **Rosciad* (1761) and contemporaries responded warmly to his imaginative identifications with his characters. He was painted by many artists, including Sir Joshua *Reynolds, William *Hogarth, Thomas *Gainsborough, and John Zoffany (1733–1810). See G. W. Stone and G. M. Kahrl, *David Garrick: A Critical Biography* (1979); *The Letters of David Garrick*, ed. D. M. Little and G. M. Kahrl, 3 vols (1963).

Garrick Club Founded in 1831 as a club in which 'actors and men of education and refinement might meet on equal terms'. Its original premises were at 35 King Street, London. Richard *Barham, the count d'*Orsay, and Samuel *Rogers were among its first members. It was much frequented by W. M. *Thackeray, and possesses a famous collection of portraits of actors and actresses and theatrical memorabilia.

GARTH, Sir Samuel (1660/61–1719) Physician and member of the *Kit-Cat Club, knighted in 1714. His *The Dispensary* (1699), a *mock-epic poem ridiculing the opposition of apothecaries to the establishment of a dispensary to offer discounted medical supplies to the poor, influenced his friend Alexander *Pope's **Rape of the Lock*. He had also advised Pope on his *Pastorals*. Garth wrote the epilogue to Joseph *Addison's **Cato*, and a *topographical poem, *Claremont* (1715), in the vein of **Windsor-Forest*.

GASCOIGNE, George (?1534/5–77) Soldier and poet, from a prominent Bedfordshire family. He may have been educated at Cambridge, entered Gray's Inn in 1555, spending more than ten years there, and was at court. In 1561 his marriage to the already-married Elizabeth Boyes, mother of the poet Nicholas *Breton, initiated a series of legal and financial difficulties, culminating in a spell in debtors' prison in Bedford in 1570. Between 1572 and 1574 he was a soldier in the Netherlands, spending four months as a prisoner of the Spanish. His poems and plays were published during his absence, supposedly without his authority, as *A Hundred Sundry Flowers* (1573); on his return he brought out a corrected and augmented edition under the title of *The Posies of George Gascoigne* (1575). In the last two years of his life he achieved some success as a court poet.

Many of Gascoigne's works were contained in *The Posies*: a variety of secular and devotional verse, including 'The Delectable History of Dan Bartholmew of Bath'; a verse account of his adventures in the Netherlands, 'The Fruits of War', dedicated to Lord Grey de Wilton; two plays written for performance at Gray's Inn in 1566, **Supposes*, a prose comedy based on *Ariosto's *I suppositi*, and **Jocasta*, a blank verse tragedy purportedly based on **Euripides*, but actually translated from Lodovico Dolce; a strange Chaucerian novella of sexual intrigue, *The Adventures of Master *F.J.*; and *Certain Notes of Instruction Concerning the Making of Verse or Rhyme in English*, a pithy and pioneering account of English versification. Gascoigne's other works include *The Glass of Government: A Tragical Comedy* (1575), *The Drum of Dooms Day* (1576), and *The *Steel Glass: A Satire* (1576). Gascoigne had been involved in the entertainments put on for *Elizabeth I by the earl of *Leicester at Kenilworth in July 1575. On 1 January 1576 Gascoigne presented her with an illustrated autograph manuscript of his translations into Latin, Italian, and French of the anonymous *Tale of Hemetes the Heremyte*, which had been part of the royal entertainments at Woodstock in September 1575. Gascoigne's achievement has been overshadowed by the later Elizabethan poets who followed in his path, such as Edmund *Spenser, Christopher *Marlowe, and Philip *Sidney; but he was an innovator in a wide variety of literary forms. The two versions of *The Adventures of Master F.J.* and the poem 'Gascoigne's Woodmanship', which relates his pursuit of a deer to his quest for patronage, are the only examples of his works to have commanded much modern interest. His *Hundred Sundry Flowers* were edited by G. W. Pigman III (2000), and there is a study by Gillian Austen (2008).

GASCOIGNE, Sir William (?1350–1419) Appointed lord chief justice of the King's Bench in 1400 by Henry IV; he appears in that capacity in Shakespeare's **Henry IV*. Shakespeare follows *Holinshed's apparently apocryphal story (told in Thomas *Elyot's *Governor*) that Prince Harry struck Gascoigne when he was chief justice for attempting to arrest one of the prince's unruly followers, whereupon Gascoigne arrested the prince himself. Harry, when Henry V, praises Gascoigne when confirming him in office for this fearless and even-handed administration of justice. See *1 Henry IV*, III. ii, and *2 Henry IV*, v ii.

GASCOYNE, David (1916–2001) Poet, born in Harrow, educated at Salisbury Choir School and Regent Street Polytechnic, where he met George *Barker. He published his first volume, *Roman Balcony* (1932), aged 16, and, in 1935, *A Short Survey of Surrealism*, which established him as a champion of that movement and a writer unusually aware of European literature. He translated many of the French Surrealists, and his own work shows the influence of writers such as Paul *Éluard, Guillaume *Apollinaire, and Tristan Tzara (1896–1963). Gascoyne's work includes *Man's Life Is his Meat* (1936), *Hölderlin's Madness* (1938), and *Night Thoughts* (1956), a long poem commissioned by the BBC. After a fallow period occasioned partly by ill health Gascoyne began writing again in later life, and taking stock of earlier unpublished material. The results include *Paris Journal 1937–39* (1979), *Selected Poems* (1994), and *Selected Verse Translations* (1996).

GASKELL, Elizabeth (Mrs Gaskell) (1810–65) Novelist, daughter of William Stevenson, a Unitarian minister and later a treasury official and journalist. Born in London, she was brought up by her aunt in Knutsford, Cheshire (the original of 'Cranford' and of 'Hollingford' in **Wives and Daughters*). She was educated at the school of the Byerley sisters, first in Barford, Warwickshire, and then in Stratford-upon-Avon. In 1832 she married William Gaskell, minister at the Cross Street Unitarian Chapel in Manchester; they had four daughters and a son who died in infancy. As a distraction from her sorrow at his death she wrote her first novel, **Mary Barton* (1848). It won the attention of Charles *Dickens, at whose invitation much of her work was first published in **Household Words* and *All the Year Round*. Her other full-length novels were **Cranford* (1853), **Ruth* (1853), **North and South* (1855), **Sylvia's Lovers* (1863), and **Wives and Daughters* (1866), which was left unfinished when Gaskell died suddenly of heart failure at the Hampshire house she had just bought for her husband's retirement. She also wrote the first and most celebrated biography of Charlotte *Brontë—which caused a furore because it contained some allegedly libellous statements which had to be withdrawn—and many vivid short stories and novellas, including the fine *Cousin Phillis* (1864).

Gaskell was an active humanitarian, and in several of her novels she argued for the need for social reconciliation, for better understanding between employers and workers, between the respectable and the outcasts of society. She was a keen observer of human behaviour and speech, among both industrial workers in Manchester and farming and country-town communities, and a careful researcher of the background and technicalities of her novels. She had a natural gift for storytelling, although she was at first rather uncertain in plot creation and given to melodramatic devices. She was a beautiful and much-liked woman, at ease in any company, and a devoted wife and mother, with many friends who included (besides Charlotte Brontë) John *Ruskin, Monckton *Milnes, the *Carlyles, Charles *Kingsley, Charles Eliot *Norton, Mary Howitt (1799–1888) and her husband William (1792–1879), Madame Mohl (1793–1883), and Florence Nightingale (1820–1910). Her relations with Dickens were chiefly professional, as their characters were not congenial: on one occasion, exasperated by her resolute refusal to take instruction as a contributor, he exclaimed to his sub-editor: 'If I were Mr G. Oh Heaven how I would beat her!' Her contemporaries classed her as a novelist with the Brontës and George *Eliot, but although *Cranford* has always remained a favourite with the general reader her other novels were underrated in critical esteem for many years after her death. The subtlety and innovation of her writing has now led to her being acknowledged as a major novelist. See Jenny Uglow, *Elizabeth Gaskell: A Habit of Stories* (1993); *The Works of Elizabeth Gaskell*, ed. Joanne Shattock *et al.* (2006).

GASKILL, Bill (1930–) Theatre director, born in Shipley, Yorkshire. He was artistic director of the *Royal Court 1965–72, where he directed first productions of work by such writers as John *Arden, Edward *Bond, and David *Hare. A strong supporter of Bertolt *Brecht, he introduced several of his plays to Britain. From 1963, he was a director, with Laurence Olivier (1907–89), of the newly formed *National Theatre at its Old Vic home, and in 1974 he co-founded the Joint Stock Company with David Hare and Max *Stafford-Clark. In 1990 he published *A Sense of Direction*.

GASS, William H. (1924–) American novelist, critic, and academic, born in Fargo, North Dakota. He studied philosophy at university, an interest which fed into the formal experimentation of his fiction. *Omensetter's Luck* (1966) was his first novel, a comparatively realist portrayal of Ohio life. *Willie Masters' Lonesome Wife* (1968) combines experiments with photographs and typography. Gass's writings on the novel and the nature of representation include *Fiction and the Figures of Life* (1970) and *Habitations of the Word* (1984).

GAUDEN, Dr John (1605–62) Reputed author of *Eikon Basilike*.

GAUDIER-BRZESKA, Henri (1891–1915) French sculptor and draughtsman, who came to London in 1910, where he became associated with avant-garde artists and writers. His most brilliantly accomplished works are his pen and pencil line drawings, some of which were published in *Rhythm*. Gaudier, with Wyndham *Lewis and Ezra *Pound, founded the *Vorticist group in 1914, and contributed a Vorticist history of sculpture to the first issue of *Blast* which exalts the energy and intensity of primitive art and condemns the ideals of the Greeks and the Renaissance. Gaudier enlisted in the French army in 1914 and was killed in action. Pound, who stressed that Gaudier had given him 'a new sense of form' and of 'planes in relation', republished several of his writings in *Gaudier-Brzeska: A Memoir* (1916). See Paul O'Keefe, *Gaudier-Brzeska* (2004).

GAUTIER, Théophile (1811–72) French poet, novelist, critic, and journalist. He was an admirer of Victor *Hugo, and played a prominent role in the Romantic movement in the 1830s (his *Histoire du romantisme* (*History of Romanticism*) appeared in 1874). He was closely associated with the doctrine of *l'art pour l'art* (*'art for art's sake'), expounded in the preface to his novel *Mademoiselle de Maupin* (1835). His best-known collection of poems is *Émaux et camées* (1852: *Enamels and Cameos*), which exercised considerable influence on the *Parnassians. He had a long career in journalism, and wrote widely on travel, art, ballet, and the theatre.

GAVIN, Jamila (1941–) Born in India; she studied at Trinity College of Music, London. Gavin's books for children reflect her Anglo-Indian background, Britain's multicultural society, and her interest in history. The Surya Trilogy (1992–7) features partition; *Kamla and Kate* (1983) is about a mixed-race friendship; *Coram Boy* (2000) depicts the 18th-century trade in orphans.

Gawain (Walwain), **Sir** The eldest of the four sons of King Lot of Orkney and Arthur's sister Morgawse. His wife, in some stories, was Dame Ragnell and their son was Ginglain, the Fair Unknown (*Libeaus Desconus); in some sources, he also had two natural sons. In the Arthurian legends he is prominent from the first 12th-century stories in which he is the leading knight, courageous, pure, and courteous, and generally a contrast in this respect to Sir Kay. He is particularly prominent in French romances until the 14th century. In later versions his excellence is surpassed by that of Launcelot and his character becomes harsher, more ruthless, and often philandering; thus, in the *Queste del Saint Graal*, he does not achieve the Grail Quest. In *Geoffrey of Monmouth he is Arthur's ambassador to Rome; in *Malory he becomes at the end the bitter enemy of Launcelot, who has accidentally killed Gawain's beloved younger brothers Gaheris and Gareth, and also Agravain, who betrayed the affair between Launcelot and Guinevere. Gawain is killed when Arthur lands at Dover before the final battle with Mordred. He is related to Gwalchmei, the sun god of Welsh mythology, and elements of this relation surface in many stories about Gawain; in Malory too there is allusion to Gawain's strength waxing and waning with the sun. The most celebrated single adventure of Gawain is the one described in *Sir *Gawain and the Green Knight*. In Malory his characterization varies according to the source being followed; for example, his status is not very high in *The Book of Sir Tristram de Lyones* (the fourth of the eight *Works* ed. by Vinaver), but he is a great and memorably conflicted character in the eighth, the *Morte Arthur Saunz Guerdon*. See Thomas Hahn (ed.), *Sir Gawain: Eleven Romances and Tales* (1995).

Gawain and the Green Knight, Sir A greatly admired alliterative poem in the north-west Midlands dialect, believed to date from the second half of the 14th century, the only manuscript of which is the famous Cotton Nero A. X which is also the sole manuscript of **Pearl*, **Patience*, and **Cleanness*. It is in 2,530 lines in long-lined alliterative stanzas of varying length, each ending with a *'bob and wheel'. The poem is divided into four 'fitts', or narrative divisions:

Fitt 1: Arthur and his court are seated at a New Year's feast in Camelot waiting for a marvel when a huge green man enters, bearing an axe and a holly bough. He challenges a knight to cut off his head on condition that the knight agrees to have his own head cut off a year hence. Gawain accepts the challenge and cuts off the green knight's head; to the astonishment of all, the knight picks it up and rides away.

Fitt 2: A year later Gawain sets off to keep his side of the bargain. After riding through grim landscapes in wintry weather, Gawain comes upon a beautiful castle where he is graciously received. The lord of the castle, Bertilak de Hautdesert, makes an agreement with Gawain that each day he will hunt in the fields and Gawain in the castle; at the end of the day they will exchange spoils.

Fitt 3: For three consecutive days, the lord hunts and Gawain, famous for his skill and prowess in love, is amorously approached by the beautiful lady of the castle, who gives him one kiss on the first day, two on the second, and on the third day three kisses and a girdle which has magic properties that will save his life. Each evening Gawain exchanges the kisses with his host for the animals slain in the hunt; but on the third evening he keeps the girdle (thus breaking his bargain), to protect him in the imminent meeting with the green knight.

Fitt 4: Gawain is directed to the green knight's chapel where he kneels to receive his blow. Twice the knight feints at him, and the third time he makes a cut in Gawain's neck. Then he explains that he is Bertilak, and that his existence as the green knight has been caused by the enchantment of Morgan le Fay, who also lives at Hautdesert, and who is related to Gawain through Arthur's bloodline. Morgan's plan was to use the green knight's appearance at Camelot to cause Guinevere to die of fright. The cut in Gawain's neck was sustained because of his infidelity in keeping the girdle. Gawain bitterly curses his failing and the snares of women; but the green knight applauds him and, on Gawain's return to Camelot, Arthur's courtiers declare that they will all wear a green girdle for Gawain's sake. The poem's closing words, 'Hony Soyt Qui Mal Pence', may connect it with the founding of the Order of the Garter. The elegance of the narrative, as well as the vivid language of the poem, are universally admired, and this is agreed to be one of the greatest and most enigmatic poems in Middle English.

See J. R. R. *Tolkien, E. V. Gordon, and N. Davis (eds) (2nd edn, 1967). Simon *Armitage and Bernard *O'Donoghue, two distinguished poets, have produced new translations; Armitage in 2006, O'Donoghue in 2007.

GAY, John (1685–1732) Poet and dramatist. Born and educated at Barnstaple, apprenticed for a time to a London silk mercer. In 1708 he published, with Aaron *Hill's encouragement, a burlesque poem, *Wine*, and in 1711 an essay, *The Present State of Wit*. *Rural Sports* (1713) is a *georgic poem similar in some of its darker aspects to his friend Alexander *Pope's **Windsor-Forest*, and *The Fan* (1713) is reminiscent of the mock-heroic style of *The *Rape of the Lock*. *The *Shepherd's Week* (1714), dedicated to *Bolingbroke, ridiculed the simplicity of the pastorals of Ambrose *Philips. After an early failure (*The Wife of Bath*, 1713), Gay's satirical farce *The What D'ye Call It* was produced successfully in 1715. **Trivia*, an urban georgic poem, appeared in 1716. With Pope and John *Arbuthnot he wrote a controversial satirical comedy, *Three Hours after Marriage*, in 1717. His poem in *ottava rima* 'Mr Pope's Welcome from Greece', written *c.*1720 and first published in 1776, celebrated his friend's completion of the *Iliad* translation; it gives a vivid picture of the members of the *Scriblerus Club and of many other contemporary figures. Gay speculated unwisely in South Sea funds with the substantial proceeds of his *Poems* (1720) and his hopes of advancement under the new king (never very realistic given his literary allegiances) were disappointed. He had been intermittently helped in his early career by patrons such as the earl of Burlington and the duke of Chandos, and eventually he became an inmate of the household of the duke of Queensberry. The first series of his popular *Fables*, illustrated with plates, appeared in 1727, but greater success came in 1728 with *The *Beggar's Opera* and its sequel **Polly*, which was banned from the stage but sold well on publication in 1729. He also wrote the libretti of *Handel's *Acis and Galatea* (pub. 1732) and *Achilles*, an opera produced posthumously at Covent Garden in 1733. He died of a sudden fever and was buried in Westminster Abbey; his own epitaph was: 'Life is a jest, and all things show it; | I thought so once, and now I know it.' The duke of Queensberry attended to various posthumous publications, including a second series of more overtly political *Fables* (1738). See Gay's *Poetry and Prose*, ed. V. A. Dearing and C. E. Beckwith, 2 vols (1974); *Dramatic Works*, ed. John Fuller, 2 vols (1983); David Nokes, *John Gay: A Profession of Friendship* (1995).

gay and lesbian literature A comparatively modern concept, although homosexual themes, occasionally explicit but more often coded, have been apparent in the literature of most cultures and countries almost from the outset, as in the Babylonian epic *Gilgamesh* (*c.*1700 BC). Although often bowdlerized by translators and editors, classical texts such as *Plato's *Symposium*, the *Greek *Anthology*, and

*Ovid's *Metamorphoses* provided models for later writers. *Shakespeare's *sonnets (1609), the first 126 of which are addressed to a young man, also caused editorial difficulties: John Benson (d. 1667) republished them in 1640, leaving out some sonnets altogether and regendering the pronouns of others. Other early texts, often drawing for their depiction of the various shades of male friendship upon *Theocritus' *Idylls* and the second of *Virgil's *Eclogues*, include Edmund Spenser's **Shepheardes Calender* (1579), Christopher Marlowe's **Edward II* (1594), and the poems of Richard *Barnfield.

With the exception of the fragmentary literary remains of *Sappho, lesbian writing lacks these strong classical precedents. Apart from extraordinary early figures like 'the English Sappho', Katherine *Philips, lesbian literature was born among the 'ephemera' in which women privately wrote down their affections for each other: letters, diaries, commonplace books. Among the most celebrated of these are the diaries of Eleanor Butler (?1739–1829) and Anne Lister (1791–1840).

The influence of bisexual libertines such as the earl of *Rochester (1647–80) and the marquis de *Sade (1740–1814) looms over the Gothic novel, notably William Beckford's **Vathek* (1786) and Matthew Lewis's *The *Monk* (1796), but homosexual literature proper dates from the late 19th century, expressing the newly pathologized concept of homosexuality as a lifelong condition. Although the trials of Oscar *Wilde, in which he was cross-examined about his work as well as his life, caused an anti-homosexual backlash in literature, the ironic and melancholy poems about doomed youths in A. E. *Housman's *A Shropshire Lad* (1896) found a strong echo in the poetry of the First World War, notably that of Siegfried *Sassoon and Wilfred *Owen. Virginia Woolf's **Orlando* (1928) and the novels of Ronald *Firbank (1886–1926) effected a transition from 1890s decadence to camp modernism, but the difficulties of confronting contemporary homosexuality and lesbianism in a straightforward manner remained: E. M. *Forster felt unable to publish *Maurice*, written in 1913, 'until my death and England's', while Radclyffe *Hall's *The Well of Loneliness* (1928) was successfully prosecuted for obscenity. The mid-century produced much didactic, often apologetic fiction in which a central character was used to represent homosexual people in general. Many such novels ended in death, as Christopher *Isherwood noted while writing *A Single Man* (1964), which is arguably the first mainstream 'gay novel' in that it challenged prejudice head-on and without special pleading. Another novelist who did much to present homosexual characters as part of ordinary society was Angus *Wilson, while writers such as Maureen *Duffy and Brigid *Brophy often took a more oblique or experimental approach.

In poetry W. H. *Auden tended to omit third-person pronouns from his love lyrics, but younger poets such as Thom *Gunn, Carol Anne *Duffy, and Mark Doty (1953–) were able to be more forthright. The latter two were part of a new generation of writers who in the 1970s emerged from the women's and gay liberation movements. Others include Edmund *White, Armistead *Maupin, Adam *Mars-Jones, Alan *Hollinghurst, Jeanette *Winterson, David Leavitt (1961–), and Sarah Waters (1966–). While some of these authors' books were set in specifically homosexual milieux, and others addressed specific issues such as Aids, the widespread popularity in particular of Maupin's *Tales of the City* series and Waters's historical novels suggested gay and lesbian literature had finally merged with the mainstream, a notion confirmed when Hollinghurst's homosexually explicit *The Line of Beauty* won the Man *Booker Prize in 2004. Gay and lesbian studies and 'queer theory' are now part of academe.

gazette [from Italian *gazzetta*] Apparently so called from the coin of that name, which may have been the sum paid either for the paper itself or for the privilege of reading it (*OED*). The *gazzetta* was a news-sheet first published in Venice about the middle of the 16th century, and similar news-sheets (*see* CORANTO; NEWSPAPERS) appeared in England from the 17th century, giving news from foreign parts.

gazetteer A geographical index or dictionary. A work of this kind by the historian Laurence Echard (bap. 1672, d. 1730) bore the title *The Gazetteer's or Newsman's Interpreter; Being a Geographical Index* (1693), intended for the use of 'gazetteers' or journalists.

GEDDES, Alexander (1737–1802) Catholic priest, linguist, and biblical scholar, born in Rathven, Aberdeenshire, and educated at the Scots College in Paris. His 'Dissertation on the Scoto-Saxon Dialect', which appeared in the *Transactions of the Society of Antiquaries of Scotland* (1792), discusses the theory and practice of the *Scots language, and complains of the new vogue for introducing 'low words and trite proverbial phrases' instead of seeking the 'genuine Scottish idiom'.

GEE, Maggie (1948–) Novelist, born in Poole, Dorset, and educated at Somerville College, Oxford. Her fiction, often formally innovative and experimental, has addressed social and political issues from racism to climate change and includes *The Burning Book* (1983), *Grace* (1988), *Lost Children* (1994), *The White Family* (2002), and *My Cleaner* (2005).

GELLHORN, Martha (1908–98) American journalist and novelist, born in St Louis, Missouri, mainly remembered for her war dispatches. She began her career as a journalist in the late 1920s, then reported on the Depression in the USA before becoming a foreign correspondent in the 1930s. She reported extensively on the Second World War and other conflicts, publishing a selection of her dispatches as *The Face of War* (1959). From 1940 to 1945 she was married to Ernest *Hemingway and she produced a number of travelogues and novels including *The Lowest Trees Have Tops* (1967). See Caroline Moorhead, *Martha Gellhorn: A Life* (2003).

GELLIUS, Aulus (b. AD 125/8) Roman man of letters, the author of a miscellany in twenty books, *Noctes Atticae* ('Attic Nights'), which contains extracts from many authors, anecdotes, and short discussions on a variety of topics. Several of the stories in William Painter's *Palace of Pleasure* are taken from Gellius. A complete English translation was made in 1795 by William Beloe (1758–1817).

GEMMELL, David (1948–2006) Born in London; journalist who turned to novel writing with *Legend* (1984): a successful career as an author of heroic *fantasy followed. Later novels explored ancient history, with the third of the 'Troy' sequence (2005–7) completed by Gemmell's wife Stella after his death.

Generydes A late Middle English romance surviving in two forms: 10,000 short rhyming lines and 7,000 lines of *rhyme royal, perhaps from the first part of the 15th century. After Generydes' exile, Clarionas cures and marries him. It has been edited by W. A. Wright (EETS os 1878; repr. 2001).

Genesis *See* BIBLE.

Genesis An Old English poem of 2,396 lines in the *Junius Manuscript, previously attributed hypothetically to *Cædmon. Lines 235–851 are an interpolated section (usually called 'Genesis B') translated from a continental Saxon original which deals in a dramatic and vivid manner with the Fall of the Angels (the title of this excerpt in Sweet's *Anglo-Saxon Reader*). It has often been suggested that this section may have been the Old English poem on the subject that *Milton knew and that it may therefore have been a seminal influence on **Paradise Lost*. There are also some echoes of it in the early poems of W. H. *Auden. See *ASPR* (Anglo-Saxon Poetic Records) 1, ed. G. P. Krapp (1931); see also *The Later Genesis*, ed. B. J. Timmer (1948).

Genesis and Exodus A Middle English poem in just over 4,000 lines of rhyming couplets, written about the middle of the 13th century in an east Midlands dialect, with notable spelling variations, and believed to originate in Norfolk. It relates scriptural history from the Creation to the death of Moses in popular form, based partly on the Bible but mostly, as in episodes such as the accidental killing of Cain, on the *Historia Scholastica* of Petrus *Comestor. The poem, particularly in its early sections, has a lively vigour. It has been edited by O. Arngart (Lund Studies in English 36, 1968).

GENEST, John (1764–1839) Educated at Westminster School and Cambridge, cleric, and author of *Some Account of the English Stage from the Restoration in 1660 to 1830*, 10 vols (1832), an accurate and comprehensive work of reference.

GENET, Jean (1910–86) French dramatist and novelist. Much of his work is marked by his experiences as a convicted criminal in the earlier part of his life, notably his autobiographical *Journal du voleur* (1949; *The Thief's Journal*, 1954), and novels such as *Notre-Dame des fleurs* (1944; *Our Lady of the Flowers*, 1948) and *Miracle de la rose* (1946; *Miracle of the Rose*, 1965). His experimental plays include *Les Bonnes* (1946; *The Maids*, 1954), about two resentful maids; *Le Balcon* (1956; *The Balcony*, 1957), which is set in a brothel; and *Les Nègres* (1958; trans. 1960), written for black actors before a white audience. He is the subject of Jean-Paul *Sartre's *Saint Genet, comédien et martyr* (1952; *Saint Genet, Actor and Martyr*, 1964). See Edmund *White, *Genet* (1993).

GENLIS, Stéphanie-Félicité du Crest, Madame de (1746–1830) French educationalist and novelist. She is best known for her moral stories for children, *Les Veillées du château* (1784: *Tales of the Castle*), which were translated into English in 1785.

GENTLE, Mary (1956–) Born in Eastbourne; writer of increasingly genre-blurring *fantasy and *science fiction. *White Crow* (2003) collects stories and novels 1989–94 which, featuring the same characters in various settings, draw heavily on Renaissance Hermeticism (*see* HERMES TRISMEGISTUS). *Ash* (2000) and *Ilario* (2006) are *alternate histories.

Gentleman Dancing-Master, The A comedy by William *Wycherley, probably performed 1671, published 1673, loosely based on a play by *Calderón de la Barca. Hippolita, a clever girl, tricks her father Mr Formal by pretending her wooer, young Gerrard, is her dancing master, thus escaping marriage to the Frenchified fop and rich city heir Monsieur de Paris. There was a New York revival in 2005.

Gentleman's Journal A periodical edited by Peter Anthony *Motteux from 1692 to 1694, containing the news of the month and miscellaneous prose and poetry. It was the germ of the modern magazine (*see* PERIODICAL).

Gentleman's Magazine (1731–1914) A periodical founded by Edward *Cave under the pseudonym 'Sylvanus Urban'. It constituted a 'monthly intelligencer', a well-illustrated digest of interesting news, essays, anecdotes, and information, and a record of publications, from the daily and weekly news-sheets and journals. Cave's appears to be the first use of the word 'magazine' to describe a journal. Soon original contributions had largely replaced news compilations and the magazine began to include serious works of criticism, essays, history, and poetry. Samuel *Johnson was a regular contributor and had some influence on the management of the *Magazine*. His parliamentary reports evaded the official ban on such publications by claiming to emanate from 'Lilliput', though he was anxious about the extent to which he had fictionalized speeches. John *Nichols was an effective editor from 1792 to 1826, but the magazine ceased to be the leading periodical it had been under Cave.

Gentleman Usher, The A tragicomedy by George *Chapman, probably acted *c.*1602–3, printed 1606. The Duke Alphonso and his son Vincentio are both in love with Margaret, daughter of Earl Lasso. The daughter loves Vincentio, who is ordered into exile. Margaret in despair disfigures herself with a poisonous ointment. The remorseful duke gives up Margaret, who because of her disfigurement refuses to marry Vincentio. The doctor cures her, solving the difficulty. The play's name is taken from the usher, Bassiolo, a vain steward, possibly based on Malvolio in Shakespeare's **Twelfth Night*, who acts as go-between for the lovers and is made to look ridiculous.

GEOFFREY DE VINSAUF (*fl. c.*1208–13) English author of *Poetria nova* ('The new poetics'), an influential medieval textbook; most probably two prose treatises, *Documentum de Modo et Arte Dictandi et Versificandi* and *Summa de Coloribus Rhetoricis*; and several poems. In 'The Nun's Priest's Tale' (**Canterbury Tales*, VII. 3347) *Chaucer's narrator unfavourably compares his lament for the downfall of a cockerel with the skill displayed by Geoffrey in his apostrophizing of the Friday ('O Veneris lacrimosa dies!') on which Richard I died.

GEOFFREY OF MONMOUTH (Gaufridus Monemutensis) (d. 1154/5) Probably a canon of the church of St George in Oxford Castle. He was appointed bishop of St Asaph in 1151. In his greatly influential *Historia Regum Britanniae* ('History of the Kings of Britain', complete by 1139) he purports to give an account of the kings who dwelt in Britain since before the Incarnation of Christ, extending over a period of 1,900 years, from Brutus (*see* Brut), the great-grandson of Aeneas, to Cadwallader, 'and especially of Arthur and the many others who succeeded him'. He drew on *Bede and *Nennius, on British traditions, and on a romantic imagination which has been deemed responsible for, among other things, the creation of Leir, the origin of **King Lear.* Whatever its veracity, the longevity and clarity of his writing contributed substantially to the popularity of the Arthurian legends. The *Historia* was translated into Anglo-Norman by Geffrei *Gaimar and *Wace, and into English verse by *Laȝamon and by *Robert of Gloucester; its translation into French was a major factor in the dissemination of Arthurian legends because of the hegemony of French courtly literature. Geoffrey's Section V is *The Prophecies of Merlin*, which also circulated separately and was possibly one of his earliest writings. The *Vita Merlini*, a Latin poem, has also been attributed to him. There is a translation by Lewis Thorpe (1966) and a discussion by J. J. Parry and R. A. Caldwell in R. S. Loomis (ed.), *Arthurian Literature in the Middle Ages* (1959).

GEORGE, Henry (1839–97) American writer on political economy, born in Philadelphia, who advocated the nationalization of land and a 'single tax' on its increment value. Although not himself a socialist, he considerably influenced the British socialist movement, speaking out against land peonage, or bonded labour, in Ireland and Scotland. George Bernard *Shaw heard him speak in 1882, and claimed that at that point 'the importance of the economic basis dawned' on him. H. G. *Wells bought a sixpenny paperback copy of George's best-selling *Progress and Poverty* (1879) when a young man in Midhurst and records its 'fermenting influence' upon his mind. His complete works were published in ten volumes in 1904 and the Robert Schalkenbach Foundation established to promote understanding of George.

George Barnwell, The History of, *or The London Merchant* A prose tragedy by George *Lillo, produced 1731, based on a popular ballad. A young apprentice, Barnwell, is seduced by the heartless Sarah Millwood, who encourages him to rob his employer and murder his uncle. For this crime both are executed, he penitent and she defiant. The play was frequently performed as a moral warning to apprentices. It was admired by Alexander *Pope, though Oliver *Goldsmith mocked it as a 'Tradesman's Tragedy' for its commercial focus. The play had a European impact and was commended and imitated by G. E. *Lessing and *Diderot.

Georgian Poetry A series of five volumes of verse published between 1912 and 1922, planned by Rupert *Brooke, Harold Monro (1879–1932), who published it at his Poetry Bookshop, and Edward *Marsh, the editor. The early volumes were widely influential and successful, bringing a fresh vision and manner into the tired poetry of the time. Writers represented in the first volume included Rupert *Brooke, W. H. *Davies, John *Masefield, D. H. *Lawrence, Walter *de la Mare, Lascelles *Abercrombie, Gordon Bottomley (1874–1948), and John *Drinkwater. Later volumes contained the work of Edmund *Blunden, Robert *Graves, Ralph *Hodgson, Isaac *Rosenberg, and Siegfried *Sassoon. However, the poems of quality were fewer in the volumes of 1919 and 1922. Several poets objected to being identified as 'Georgian', and the term soon acquired a pejorative sense. Ezra *Pound, T. S. *Eliot, and the *Sitwells attacked the entire series, but some of the poets represented have maintained high reputations. See Robert H. Ross, *The Georgian Revolt* (1967).

Georgics, The (written 36–29 BC) *Virgil's substantial second poem, loosely modelled on *Hesiod's *Works and Days.* The poem is ostensibly a farmer's guide (the title means 'husbandry'). The first book tackles agriculture; the second, trees, especially the olive and grape; the third, cattle and horses; the fourth, bee-keeping and honey. Virgil bases the appeal of rustic life on its frugal simplicity and the satisfactions of hard work. It is an aesthetic and moral vision, a nostalgic picture of what Italian country life might still have to offer, emphasizing the vital importance of peace, long banished by the horrors of civil war (1. 463–514). Incidental panegyrics stud the *Georgics*, and the third book opens with a glorification of Octavian (Augustus) and Rome (3. 1–48). Other notable passages describe the zones of the earth; the zodiac; the sinister omens at Caesar's murder; the unique excellence of Italy; and the tale of *Orpheus and Eurydice (4. 315–558).

The poem was much admired and imitated in the 18th century, for example in *Windsor-Forest* and *The *Seasons*. There are important translations by John *Dryden and Cecil *Day-Lewis. See John Chalker, *The English Georgic* (1969).

'Geraint and Enid' One of Tennyson's **Idylls of the King*, first published under this title in 1886. It originally formed with 'The Marriage of Geraint' a single idyll, published in 1859 as 'Enid' and divided in 1873. Geraint, suspecting his wife's virtue, subjects her to various trials, from which she emerges patient and triumphant.

GERARD, Alexander (1728–95) Clergyman and philosopher, professor of moral philosophy and logic at Marischal College, later professor of divinity at King's College, Aberdeen. He published two studies which contributed to the development of aesthetic theory: *An Essay on Taste* (1759, augmented 1780) and *An Essay on Genius* (1774).

GERARD, John (*c.*1545–1612) Herbalist and superintendent of Lord *Burghley's gardens. He was author of the celebrated *Herbal, or General History of Plants* (1597), largely adapted from the *Stirpium Historiae Pemptades Sex* of the Flemish scholar Rembert Dodoens (1517–85). A revised edition of the *Herbal* was published by the apothecary Thomas Johnson (*c.*1595–1644) in 1633. The work gives a description of each plant, the localities in which it is found, and its medical virtues (correcting superstitions, e.g. about the mandrake); discusses nomenclature; and contains a large number of beautiful woodcuts, many of which had appeared in a recent continental work on the subject.

GERAS, Adèle (1944–) Born in Jerusalem, educated at Roedean School and St Hilda's College, Oxford. A prolific novelist and poet for children and adults, her work spans genres, periods, and forms and includes several works about Jewish experience and folk tales, *school stories, and recently novelized retellings of *Homer.

GERHARDIE (originally Gerhardi)**, William Alexander** (1895–1977) Born of English parents in St Petersburg, Russia. Educated there until 1912, he served with the Royal Scots Greys and in the British embassy at Petrograd (1916–18) during the First World War, then with the British military mission in Siberia. He then attended Worcester College, Oxford, where he wrote his first novel, *Futility: A Novel on Russian Themes* (1922), and the first English book on Anton *Chekhov (1923). His next novel, *The Polyglots* (1925), is perhaps his best-known work, the bizarre narrative of a wildly egocentric young officer who on a military mission in the Far East comes into contact with a highly eccentric Belgian family, the Vanderflints; the intermingling of comedy and tragedy, of events of historical significance and the utmost human triviality, of Belgians, British, Russians, and Japanese, creates an oblique, lyrical, inconsequential world which is characteristic of Gerhardie, and largely autobiographical in content. Other novels include *Pending Heaven* (1930), *Resurrection* (1934), and *Of Mortal Love* (1936). *Meet Yourself as You Really Are* (1936, written with Prince Leopold of Loewenstein) is an interesting early example of *hypertext: it consists of a questionnaire which leads along many different interactive paths to self-knowledge. His autobiography *Memoirs of a Polyglot* appeared in 1931, and in 1940 a historical study, *The Romanovs*, the last book he published during his lifetime. For the rest of his days he lived increasingly as a recluse, planning novels but not writing them. *God's Fifth Column*, Gerhardie's biography of the age 1890–1940, edited by Michael *Holroyd and Robert Skidelsky, was published in 1981. His name was spelt Gerhardie for the first time on the revised Collected Edition of his works, published in ten volumes in the early 1970s. See Dido Davies, *William Gerhardie: A Biography* (1990).

***Germ,** Thoughts towards Nature in Poetry, Literature and Art* A periodical of which the first issue appeared on 1 January 1850. Edited by W. M. *Rossetti, it was the organ of the *Pre-Raphaelite Brotherhood, and ran for four issues, the last appearing on 30 April 1850; the last two were renamed *Art and Poetry, Being Thoughts towards Nature*. It contained work by D. G. *Rossetti (including 'The *Blessed Damozel' and 'Hand and Soul'), Christina *Rossetti, Coventry *Patmore, Ford Madox Brown (1821–93), William Bell *Scott, and others. It provided a brief but significant platform for the aims and ideals of the early years of the Brotherhood and was credited by W. M. Rossetti as the inspiration behind William *Morris's continuation of Pre-Raphaelite impetus in the **Oxford and Cambridge Magazine* (1856).

GERNSBACK, Hugo (1884–1967) Born Gernsbacher, American publisher and editor. Born in Luxembourg, Gernsback emigrated to the USA in 1904 to establish several businesses exploiting the new technology of radio, including the magazine *Modern Electrics*, in which he serialized his novel *Ralph 124C 41+* (1911–12), a utopian melodrama of what he was to call 'scientifiction'. In 1926, he launched *Amazing Stories*, the first English-language magazine dedicated to scientifiction (later *science fiction), which he promoted as a didactic and inspirational, even prophetic form, after the examples of Jules *Verne, Edgar Allan *Poe, and H. G. *Wells, all of whom were extensively reprinted in *Amazing*. 'Extravagant fiction today: cold fact tomorrow' was its slogan. Losing control of *Amazing* in 1929, he continued to publish magazines. Gernsback's influence upon later science fiction is controversial; he popularized the form but arguably he also trivialized it. See Gary Westfall, *The Mechanics of Wonder* (1998).

Gerontius, The Dream of See NEWMAN, JOHN HENRY.

Gertrude of Wyoming A poem by Thomas *Campbell, in Spenserian stanzas, published 1809. The poem, which was immensely popular, centres on a historical event, the destruction of the settlement of Wyoming in Pennsylvania by a force of Indians under the Mohawk Brandt, and the death of Gertrude, the newly married wife of Sir Henry Waldegrave. Campbell later withdrew the charge of cruelty against Brandt.

Gerusalemme liberata See JERUSALEM DELIVERED.

Gesta Romanorum A collection of stories, each with an attached moralization, in Latin, probably compiled in England in the late 13th century. There are about 165 manuscripts of the Latin versions, and the work's popularity is shown by the existence of 15th-century versions in many European languages and by its influence on later medieval writers such as *Boccaccio, *Chaucer, *Hoccleve, and *Lydgate. See S. J. Herrtage (ed.), *Early English Versions of the Gesta Romanorum* (EETS ES 33, 1879; repr. 1962).

Ghismonda (previously **Sigismonda**) In Boccaccio's **Decameron* (Day 4, Tale 1), daughter of Tancred, prince of Salerno. Her father, having discovered her love for his squire Guiscardo, killed the latter and sent his heart in a golden cup to Ghismonda, who took poison and died. The father, repenting his cruelty, caused the pair to be buried in the same tomb. The story is the subject of John *Dryden's 'Sigismunda and Guiscardo', and of Robert Wilmot's **Tancred and Gismund*. James *Thomson's *Tancred and Sigismunda* (1745) deals with a different story.

GHOSH, Amitav (1956–) Indian author and academic, born in Calcutta (Kolkata) and educated at the University of Delhi and Oxford; resident in New York. *The Shadow Lines* (1988), a novel exploring the effect upon a family of the partition of Bengal, won the Indian Sahitya Akademi Award. *The Calcutta Chromosome* (1996) won the Arthur C. Clarke Award for best *science fiction novel. Its use of the World Wide Web in near-future Calcutta as a tool for exploring a secret history involving early research into the malaria parasite parallels later novels' concern for the intertwined history of individuals and cultures.

ghost stories The genre comprises short stories or, less commonly, novels or novellas that treat the power of the dead to return to the world of the living. Their ghosts take many forms, from the recognizably human to the fearfully alien. They may be insubstantial wraiths, or corporeal creatures with the ability to inflict physical harm. Or they may never reveal themselves at all, relying instead on an ability to infect and control the minds of the living, or to achieve their ends through inanimate objects—a pair of gloves, a car, even a saucepan.

Ghost stories are a comparatively recent phenomenon. It is true that the dead frequently rise again in classical and early modern literature—as in *Chaucer's 'Nun's Priest's Tale', when Chanticleer the cock tells how the ghost of a murdered man revealed the circumstances of his death to his sleeping companion ('And truste wel, his dreem he foond ful trewe'; but the literary ghost story represents the supernatural differently. Before the 19th century, the ghosts are less important than the information they reveal; and though they excite fear and wonder, their introduction is not designed to unsettle. In the literary ghost story, the ghost is central, and the arousal of fear is the story's primary purpose. There are certainly benevolent ghosts in the literature; but in the most memorable stories the supernatural presence is malevolent.

Literary ghost stories were largely a Victorian creation, part of a wider engagement with the unseen and the uncanny—like the enthusiasm for spiritualism—that challenged the prevailing forces of secularism and science. The author often posed as the detached reporter or recorder of events, as in *The Night-Side of Nature* (1848) by Catherine Crowe (1790–1876), a popular collection of tales and incidents claiming to be based on actual experiences.

The ghost story's immediate literary predecessors were the short stories and fragments common in English magazines during the late 18th and early 19th centuries, but Victorian ghost stories were quite different in character and intention from their Gothic forerunners. Where early *Gothic fiction had been largely unconcerned with either historical detail or present realities, Victorian writers of ghost stories usually set supernatural incidents in solid everyday settings, which made their violations of normality all the more convincing. There is a parallel here with *sensation fiction, a literary vogue of the 1860s and 1870s, in which criminality lurks beneath the normality of domestic life.

An early example of a story which struck a new and distinctly anti-Gothic note was Walter *Scott's 'The Tapestried Chamber' (1828). The story takes place in a castle, but it is an English castle, 'rich in all the bizarrerie of the Elizabethan school', set in a real English landscape in the recent past. Such characteristics became fully developed in the stories of Sheridan *Le Fanu, who created the strongest body of short ghost fiction in the Victorian period. Le Fanu gave his most effective stories credible settings and characters and created ghosts that induced physical fear—like the famous spectral monkey in 'Green Tea' (1869). His first collection, *Ghost Stories and Tales of Mystery* (1851), made little impact at the time, but it began the Golden Age of the Victorian ghost story, and for the next twenty years or so ghost stories were produced in abundance, helped by a boom in magazine publishing during the 1860s. It was in the pages of monthlies such as *Temple Bar*, *Tinsley's*, **Belgravia*, and *All the Year Round* (owned and edited by Charles *Dickens) that the Victorian ghost story flourished, with Christmas numbers offering a seasonal opportunity to satisfy a growing public taste for tales of the supernatural. Dickens himself was responsible for one of the most anthologized of all ghost stories, 'The Signalman' (1866), though his role as popularizer of Christmas and its association with the telling of ghost stories was of far greater importance. Many writers of magazine ghost stories were women, amongst them Amelia B. Edwards (1831–92), whose famous story 'The Phantom Coach' first appeared in *All the Year Round* in 1864; Mary Elizabeth *Braddon, author of 'The Cold Embrace' (1860) and 'Eveline's Visitant' (1867), both published in *Belgravia*; Rhoda *Broughton (*Tales for Christmas Eve*, 1873); and Mrs

J. H. Riddell (1832–1906: *Weird Stories*, 1882). The same dominance continued through the 1890s and into the 20th century, with writers such as 'Vernon *Lee' (*Hauntings*, 1890), Edith *Wharton (*Tales of Men and Ghosts*, 1910), Violet *Hunt (*Tales of the Uneasy*, 1911), Marjorie *Bowen (*Curious Happenings*, 1917), and May *Sinclair (*Uncanny Stories*, 1923), amongst others, contributing notably to the genre's development.

Le Fanu's heir, and the great exponent of the factualizing narrative, in which ancient objects and historical and bibliographical references are used to reinforce a sense of actuality and provide a conduit between past and present, was M. R. *James. His antiquarian ghost stories, the first of which, 'Canon Alberic's Scrap-Book', was published in 1895, drew on his own formidable learning and were so convincing that some readers believed them to be factual accounts. His four collections, beginning with *Ghost Stories of an Antiquary* in 1904, were built on solid Victorian foundations but were far from offering a conventional view of the supernatural. James excelled at conveying physical horror. His ingeniously plotted stories, some of which drew on themes from English and Scandinavian folklore, typically portrayed safe and ordered worlds invaded by terrifying agents of unappeasable supernatural malice. James's style was emulated by a number of younger contemporaries, some of whom had known him personally, including E. G. Swain (1861–1938: *The Stoneground Ghost Tales*, 1912), R. H. Malden (1879–1951: *Nine Ghosts*, 1943), and A. N. L. Munby (1913–74: *The Alabaster Hand*, 1949). Contemporary authors influenced by M. R. James include Ramsey *Campbell and Susan *Hill, whose richly atmospheric novel *The Woman in Black* (1983) has been successfully adapted for both the stage and television.

If M. R. James is the master of the direct ghost story, in which the intrusion of the supernatural is objective and incontrovertible, Henry *James created, in *The *Turn of the Screw* (1898), a potent reinterpretation of Victorian conventions, which begins with a deliberately Dickensian evocation—ghost stories told round the fire at Christmas—but goes on to blur the boundary between subjective and objective phenomena. Similarly ambiguous stories include 'How Love Came to Professor Guildea' (in *Tongues of Conscience*, 1900) by Robert *Hichens and 'The Beckoning Fair One' (in *Widdershins*, 1911) by Oliver Onions (1873–1961). Uncertainty also characterizes the ghost stories of Walter de la Mare (e.g. 'Out of the Deep', in *The Riddle*, 1923); more recently, the enigmatic stories of Robert Aickman (1914–81), in *Powers of Darkness* (1966), *Cold Hand in Mine* (1975), and other collections, fuse traditional elements of ghost fiction with oblique narrations that are concerned not with appearance and consistency, but with 'the void behind the face of order'.

The 20th century was prolific in ghost stories. The first 30 years of the century saw the rise of specialist ghost story writers such as Algernon *Blackwood (*The Listener*, 1907); W. F. Harvey (1885–1937: *Midnight House*, 1910); E. F. *Benson (*The Room in the Tower*, 1912); A. M. Burrage (1889–1956: *Some Ghost Stories*, 1927); and H. Russell Wakefield (1888–1964: *They Return at Evening*, 1928). Like their Victorian predecessors, these writers show us ordinary men and women confronted by mysteries that are beyond nature and reason. Ghost stories continue to be written and read, their resilience and adaptability testifying to the tenacity of what Virginia Woolf called 'the strange human craving for the pleasure of feeling afraid'. See Julia Briggs, *Night Visitors: The Rise and Fall of the English Ghost Story* (1977); J. Sullivan, *Elegant Nightmares: The English Ghost Story from Le Fanu to Blackwood* (1978); E. F. Bleiler, *The Checklist of Science Fiction and Supernatural Fiction* (1978); M. Cox and R. A. Gilbert (eds.), *The Oxford Book of English Ghost Stories* (1986, 1989); Richard Dalby (ed.), *The Virago Book of Ghost Stories* (2006).

Giaour, The A poem by Lord *Byron, published 1813. Eight editions of the work appeared in the last seven months of that year, and its length was increased from 685 to 1,334 lines. The story is of a female slave, Leila, who loves the Byronic Giaour (the term refers to an infidel), and is in consequence bound and thrown in a sack into the sea by her Turkish lord, Hassan. The Giaour avenges her by killing Hassan, then in grief and remorse banishes himself to a monastery.

GIBBINGS, Robert (1889–1958) Wood-engraver and book designer. From 1924 to 1933 he was director of the *Golden Cockerel Press where he employed many notable engravers including Eric *Gill. His most popular work, in which he combined his skills as writer, topographer, and illustrator, was his series of eight 'river books', which began with *Sweet Thames Run Softly* (1940) and concluded in 1957 with *Till I End my Song*.

GIBBON, Edward (1737–94) Historian, born in Putney. He was a sickly child and his education at Westminster School and at Magdalen College, Oxford, was irregular and by his own account 'unprofitable'. He became a Catholic convert at the age of 16, and was sent to Lausanne by his father, where he was reconverted to Protestantism, subsequently losing faith altogether. There he continued to read voraciously, as he had done since boyhood, his 'blind and boyish taste' for exotic history maturing into serious study of French and Latin classics. He also became attached to Suzanne Curchod (later Madame *Necker, mother of Madame de *Staël), but his father persuaded him to break off the engagement and he returned to England in 1758. In 1761 he published his *Essai sur l'étude de la littérature*, of which an English version appeared in 1764. From 1759 he served as a captain in the Hampshire Militia until he left again for the Continent in 1763; it was in Italy, while 'musing amid the ruins of the Capitol', that he formed the plan of *The History of the *Decline and Fall of the Roman Empire*. He settled in London in 1772, and entered Parliament in 1774, voting steadily for Lord North and receiving a minor post in return; he rarely spoke in debates. He was elected to Johnson's *Club in 1774; he seems not to have been close to Johnson personally, but Edmond *Malone valued his companionship. James *Boswell always resented the 'artful infidelity' of the *History* and was hostile to its author. In 1776 the first volume appeared and was generally favourably received, especially by figures in the *Scottish Enlightenment, but Gibbon's ruthlessly sceptical chapters on the growth of Christianity provoked much criticism, to which he replied in 1779 in *A Vindication of Some Passages in the XVth and XVIth Chapters*. The second and third volumes appeared in 1781, but were less warmly received; he himself suspected he had become prolix through 'superfluous diligence'. He retired to Lausanne in 1783 to complete the work; the last three volumes appeared in 1788. He returned to England and lived in the home of his friend the earl of Sheffield, who put together Gibbon's remarkable *Memoirs* from various drafts, publishing them in 1796 with his *Miscellaneous Works*. See *The Letters of Edward Gibbon*, ed. J. E. Norton, 3 vols (1956), and two volumes of biography by P. B. Craddock (1982, 1989).

GIBBON, Lewis Grassic (1901–35) The pen-name of James Leslie Mitchell, novelist, born near Auchterless, Aberdeenshire, and educated at Arbuthnott School and (stormily and briefly) at Mackie Academy, Stonehaven. He worked as a journalist in Aberdeen and Glasgow before joining the Royal Army Service Corps in 1919; from 1923 to 1929 he was a clerk in the RAF. His experience of travel with the forces resulted in such works written under his own name as *The Calends of Cairo* (1931), and the novels *Stained Radiance* (1930) and *Spartacus* (1933). He wrote prolifically but with little financial success, encouraged by H. G. *Wells, Hugh *MacDiarmid, and others, and published books on exploration and anthropology, but is now remembered principally for his trilogy *A Scots Quair*. Its constituent novels *Sunset Song* (1932), *Cloud Howe* (1933), and *Grey Granite* (1934) relate the life of Chris Guthrie from girlhood on her father's farm, through three marriages, the First World War, and the Depression, to her son's commitment to the Communist Party, and reflect the author's Diffusionist view of history. All three were published under the name of Grassic Gibbon, taken from Mitchell's mother's maiden name, and are written in a powerful, idiosyncratic, and ingenious lyrical idiom which can be read as English by the general reader and as *Scots by the reader familiar with the old language and literature of the Lowlands; the narrator shares his heroine's mixture of love and hatred for their ancestral land, 'the red clay of the Mearns', and the plot abounds in lurid and violent incident. *Sunset Song* was hailed as the first really Scottish novel since John *Galt, though many objected to its raw frankness. Mitchell died of a perforated ulcer in Welwyn Garden City, where he had been living since 1931. There is a life by I. S. Munro (1966). An unfinished novel, *The Speak of the Mearns*, was published in 1982.

GIBBONS, Orlando (1583–1625) English composer and court musician. After some years as a chorister at King's College, Cambridge, Gibbons became a gentleman of the Chapel Royal and later its senior organist, as well as organist of Westminster Abbey. He wrote much instrumental and sacred vocal music, publishing with William *Byrd and John *Bull *Parthenia* (1613), a collection of keyboard music, and contributing seventeen tunes to George *Wither's *The Hymnes and Songs of the Church* (1623). His one book of secular vocal works, *The First Set of Madrigals and Mottets, Apt for Viols and Voyces* (1612), is serious in tone, and includes poems like Walter *Ralegh's 'What is our life', and 'Oh! deare heart' (attributed to John *Donne). 'The Silver Swanne', one of the best known of all English *madrigals, is in this collection.

GIBBONS, Stella *See* COLD COMFORT FARM.

GIBBONS, Thomas (1720–85) Congregational minister and biographer, born in Swaffham Prior and educated at dissenting academies in London. Of his many works the most important are his biography of Isaac *Watts (1780) and his edited collection of a wide range of women's lives, *Memoirs of Eminently Pious Women*, 2 vols (1777; considerably expanded in 1815), prefaced by an essay on the education of daughters.

GIBSON, W. W. (Wilfrid Wilson) (1878–1962) Poet, born in Hexham, Northumberland. He moved to London in 1912, where he met Edward *Marsh, to whose **Georgian Poetry* he contributed, and Rupert *Brooke, who made him one of his heirs. The four issues of *New Numbers* (1914) had featured Gibson and Brooke, along with Lascelles *Abercrombie and John *Drinkwater. Gibson published many volumes of verse, much of it dealing with northern rural themes, and his experiences in the First World War inspired several shorter, sharper battle pieces, such as 'Breakfast'. By *Collected Poems, 1905–25* (1926), his popularity was already waning.

GIBSON, William (1948–) American-Canadian writer. Born in South Carolina, USA, but resident in Canada since 1968, Gibson was one of the writers whose work began to be defined as *cyberpunk in the early 1980s. He coined the now common term 'cyberspace' (for the 'virtual space' linking computer networks, or more loosely the World Wide Web) in his story 'Burning Chrome' (1982), later refining it in the influential novel *Neuromancer* (1984), popular among adopters of computer technology and theorists of postmodern culture. It won several awards, including the *Hugo. He co-wrote, with Bruce *Sterling, the *alternate history novel *The Difference Engine* (1990). Subsequent novels, such as *Pattern Recognition* (2003) and *Spook Country* (2007) have, without deserting the subject matter of information hunting among media-savvy sub-cultures, moved much closer to the shape of contemporary fiction. It has been said that Gibson's future has been in the same place, but the real world has travelled towards it.

GIDE, André (1869–1951) French novelist, essayist, critic, and dramatist. His fiction, interesting both for its formal experimentation and its teasing exploration of sexuality and morality, includes a number of short novels, notably *L'Immoraliste* (1902; *The Immoralist*, 1930), *La Porte étroite* (1909; *Strait is the Gate*, 1924), and *La Symphonie pastorale* (1919; *The Pastoral Symphony*, 1931), as well as two longer novels, *Les Caves du Vatican* (1914; trans. as *Lafcadio's Adventures*, 1928) and *Les Faux-monnayeurs* (1925; *The Counterfeiters*, 1928), all of which were translated by Dorothy *Bussy, Lytton *Strachey's sister and Gide's friend. He also wrote a number of autobiographical works, including *Si le grain ne meurt* (1926; *If it Die…*, 1935), which describes his revolt against his Protestant upbringing, and his *Journal* for the years 1889 to 1949 (trans. 1947–51). He was awarded the *Nobel Prize for Literature in 1947. His recorded disillusion with the Soviet Union, which he visited in 1936, was edited by Enid Starkie from his *Retour de l'U.R.S.S.* (1936) and *Retouches à mon retour* (trans. as *Afterthoughts: A Sequel*, 1938) for inclusion in *The God that Failed: Six Studies in Communism* (1950).

GIFFORD, William (1756–1826) Satirist and editor, born in Ashburton, Devon, the son of a glazier and himself a shoemaker's apprentice. He was sent with the help of a friendly surgeon to Oxford, after which he became tutor to the son of Lord Grosvenor. He published in 1791 and 1795 two satires, *The Baviad* and *The Maeviad*, the first directed against the *Della Cruscan school of poetry, and the second divided between the Della Cruscans and the contemporary drama. In 1797–8 he was editor of *The *Anti-Jacobin*, where he encouraged the parodic talents of the youthful George *Canning and John Hookham *Frere. In 1809 he was appointed the first editor of the **Quarterly Review*, a post he held until 1824. His ultra-Toryism led him to attack some of the circle around Leigh *Hunt and the *'Cockney School'; he attacked William *Hazlitt personally and published John *Croker's virulent attack on Keats's **Endymion*. He was, much to the wrath of the journal's principal contributors such as Robert *Southey, an interventionist editor; among many instances, he wholly altered the warm tone of Charles *Lamb's essay on Wordsworth's *The *Excursion*. He was satirized in turn by Hunt in *Ultra-Crepidarius* (1823) and was the subject of *ad hominem* attacks by Hazlitt in 'A Letter to William Gifford, Esq.' (1819) and *The *Spirit of the Age*. Gifford translated the satires of *Juvenal (1802) and of *Persius (1821), and edited the works of Philip *Massinger, Ben *Jonson, John *Ford, and James *Shirley. A short autobiography is prefixed to the 1827 edition of Juvenal. See J. Strachan, *Gifford and the Della Cruscans*, vol. iv of *British Satire 1785–1840* (2003).

GILBERT, Sir William Schwenck (1836–1911) Dramatist, educated at King's College London. He worked as a clerk at the Privy Council office, studied law at the Inner Temple, and practised as a barrister without great success; in later life he became a justice of the peace. In 1861 he began contributing regular columns of comic verse, with his own illustrations, to the magazine *Fun*; this was the beginning of the **Bab Ballads* (first collected under this title in 1869). Here he sketched out his fantasy world, turning the odd into the ordinary, calling it 'Topsy-Turvydom', a phrase picked up in the title of Mike Leigh's film about Gilbert and *Sullivan, *Topsy-Turvy* (1999). The ballads were popular across a wide social range, though Gilbert had a low opinion of this part of his own work: 'I am a doggerel bard', runs the refrain in one of them. Encouraged by T. W. *Robertson, he turned his verbal dexterity and talent for absurd plotting to drama, beginning with *Dulcamara* (1866), a burlesque based on *Donizetti's opera *L'elisir d'amore*. Several other light, parodic stage works followed. *The Palace of Truth* (1870) is a poetical fantasy based on a novel by Madame de *Genlis and influenced by the fairy work of James *Planché; *The Princess* (1870) is a 'respectful perversion' of *Tennyson's poem. The verse play *Pygmalion and Galatea* (1871) was a popular success; *The Wicked World* (1873), a controversial sex comedy. A burlesque version of the latter, transformed to political satire, *The Happy Land* (1873), was produced in collaboration with Gilbert Arthur *À Beckett. Gilbert also adapted Dickens's **Great Expectations* for the stage (1871) and wrote social problem dramas such as *Charity* (1874). But his strength was topical light verse, making clever use of rhyme and metre, and in 1869 he met Sullivan, whose talent for musical parody and pleasing melody was perfectly suited to Gilbert's verse. Their first collaboration was *Thespis* (1871), in which a group of actors usurp the places of the Olympian gods. In 1874 Gilbert met the impresario D'Oyly Carte, for whom he and Sullivan wrote *Trial by Jury* (1875), which began their series of light operas (*see* GILBERT AND SULLIVAN OPERAS). Carte leased the old Opéra Comique for their productions and in 1881 built the Savoy Theatre especially for the D'Oyly Carte company. The collaboration lasted for over twenty years, though after *The Gondoliers* (1889) there was a rift resulting from a business transaction. *Utopia, Limited* (1893) healed the breach. *The Grand Duke* (1896), the only unsuccessful Savoy opera, was the last. Gilbert continued writing plays and operas without Sullivan; among them the travesty of **Hamlet, Rosencrantz and Guildenstern* (1891), *Fallen Fairies* (1909), with music by Edward German, and *The Hooligans* (1911), his last play. Gilbert used the profits from his plays to build the Garrick Theatre. He was knighted in 1907, and died of a heart attack while attempting to rescue a young woman who had fallen into his lake. See J. W. Stedman, *W. S. Gilbert: A Classic Victorian and his Theatre* (1996).

Gilbert and Sullivan operas Series of comic operas with librettos by Sir W. S. *Gilbert and music by Sir Arthur *Sullivan. The plots turn on stock romance incidents and cheerfully lampoon the social establishment. The operas are: *Trial by Jury* (1875); *The Sorcerer* (1877); *HMS Pinafore* (1878), a huge success in America; *The Pirates of Penzance* (1879, New York; 1880, London); **Patience* (1881); *Iolanthe* (1882); *Princess Ida* (1884), a satire on female education suggested by Tennyson's *The *Princess*; *The Mikado* (1885), set in Japan; *Ruddigore* (1887), a mock melodrama; *The Yeomen of the Guard* (1888), their own favourite; *The Gondoliers* (1889); *Utopia, Limited* (1893), a highly political satire; and *The Grand Duke* (1896).

Gil Blas *See* LESAGE, ALAIN-RENÉ.

GILCHRIST, Anne (1828–85) Née Burrows, daughter of upper-class parents who encouraged her education, and the wife of Alexander Gilchrist (1828–61), author of a *Life of Etty* (1855) and a life of the then largely unrecognized William *Blake, on which he was working when he died. She finished it, and it was published in 1863; it made a considerable contribution to the awakening of interest in Blake's work in the late 19th century. Anne Gilchrist was friendly with the *Carlyles, and with William Michael *Rossetti (also an admirer of Blake), who imparted to her his admiration for Walt *Whitman. She corresponded passionately with Whitman (who occasionally replied), wrote appreciations of his work, and visited him in America in 1876–9. She also wrote a life of Mary *Lamb (1883) and various articles and sketches. See *Anne Gilchrist: Her Life and Writings*, ed. H. H. Gilchrist (1887).

GILDAS (*fl.* 5th–6th centuries AD) A British historian who wrote *De Excidio et Conquestu Britanniae* ('On the ruin and conquest of Britain'), a Latin account of the history of Britain followed by a castigation of contemporary rulers and priests. He gives a providential reading of events, using the Bible and patristic sources. Despite being factually unreliable in some respects, his account of the impact of the Anglo-Saxons was an influential source for historians from *Bede onwards. *Geoffrey of Monmouth mentions his 'excellent book' in the first sentence of his *Historia Regum Britanniae*.

gilded age, the The period of expansion and reconstruction in the USA after the American Civil War when much new wealth was created. The phrase was coined by Mark *Twain and Charles Dudley Warner (1829–1900) in their novel *The Gilded Age: A Tale of Today* (1873), which satirizes the cynical boosterism of the period.

GILFILLAN, George (1813–78) A Scottish Dissenting minister, literary critic, and editor, who for a brief period in the mid-19th century exercised considerable influence, particularly as the champion of the *Spasmodic school. He was befriended by Thomas *Carlyle, who found his prose 'full of fervour, and crude, gloomy fire—a kind of opium style'. His *A Gallery of Literary Portraits* ran to three series, 1845, 1850, 1854, with essays on the Spasmodics, Thomas *Macaulay, Carlyle, etc., and he also edited many volumes of minor British poets, with notes and memoirs.

GILL, Eric (1882–1940) Stone-carver, engraver, and typographer, who cut lettering and designed types, among them Perpetua and Gill Sans-serif. Born in Brighton, Sussex, he settled in Ditchling in 1907, where a community of craftsmen and artists began to gather round him; David *Jones was there for four years from 1921. In 1913 Gill became a Roman Catholic, and worked for some years from 1914 on a commission to carve the Stations of the Cross for Westminster Cathedral. His statue of Prospero and Ariel carved on site on Broadcasting House in Upper Regent Street is a well-known landmark. From 1924 he was associated with the *Golden Cockerel Press, for which his illustrated books included *The Four Gospels* and Chaucer's **Troilus and Criseyde*. Gill wrote essays, pamphlets, and books on art, sculpture, and typography, proclaiming the religious basis of art, the validity of craftsmanship in the machine age, and the body's holiness (many of his early works were erotic and his own sexual life was highly unorthodox); his works include *Art-Nonsense and Other Essays* (1929), *The Necessity of Belief* (1936), and an *Autobiography* (1940). A life by Fiona MacCarthy was published in 1989.

GILLRAY, James (1757–1815) Caricaturist. He used his mordant wit and political independence to expose the vices of Parliament and the royal family, and his vicious caricatures of Napoleon helped to rouse the patriotism of the country in the face of threatened invasion.

GILMAN, Charlotte Perkins (1860–1935) Writer and feminist, born in Connecticut. Her father abandoned the family and, unable to support themselves, they were helped by aunts, one of whom, on the father's side, was Harriet Beecher *Stowe. Gilman had only four years' schooling and was mostly self-taught. In 1884 she married Charles Walter Stetson and had one daughter. She suffered from post-partum depression; separation and divorce, socially frowned on, nevertheless saved her mental health. Her experience is recorded in her most famous short story, 'The Yellow Wallpaper' (1892), a disturbing first-person account of domestic entrapment, exacerbated by Dr Weir Mitchell's oppressive 'rest cure'. In Gilman's story, madness can be read as a reasonable response to intolerable treatment. Gilman became active in the feminist movement and was a prolific writer and advocate for the necessity of women's economic independence. Her treatises include *Women and Economics* (1898), *Concerning Children* (1900), and *The Home: Its Work and Influence* (1903). She edited her own magazine, *The Forerunner*, for seven years, in which she published her own fiction, including her utopian novel *Herland* (1911). Her autobiography, *The Living of Charlotte Perkins Gilman*, was published posthumously in 1935. See Anne J. Lane, *To Herland and Beyond: The Life of Charlotte Perkins Gilman* (1990).

GILPIN, William (1724–1804) Born near Carlisle, son of an artist, educated at the Queen's College, Oxford. He entered the church, and taught at Cheam School, Surrey, where he introduced enlightened educational principles. In 1777 he became vicar of Boldre, in the New Forest. Gilpin travelled extensively in Britain in his holidays and defined and popularized the notion of the *picturesque as a means of appreciating nature. His fashionable writings, beginning with *Observations on the River Wye* (1782), did much to form taste for the landscapes of *Romanticism in literature, art, gardening, and travel, helping to promote the Lake District and the Highlands as destinations for picturesque tourism. He expounded his theoretical principles in *Three Essays: On Picturesque Beauty; On Picturesque Travel; and On Sketching Landscape* (1792). He also published religious works and biographies, and was parodied by William *Combe as 'Dr Syntax'. See Malcolm Andrews, *The Search for the Picturesque* (1989).

GILROY, Paul (1956–) Social theorist. He completed his Ph.D. at the Centre for Contemporary Cultural Studies where, studying with Stuart *Hall, he contributed to the collective publication *The Empire Strikes Back* (1982). His books include *There Ain't No Black in the Union Jack* (1987), *The Black Atlantic* (1993), and *After Empire* (2004).

GINSBERG, Allen (1926–97) American *Beat poet born in New Jersey and educated at Columbia University, New York. He took the democratic spirit of Walt *Whitman and applied it to his own experiences of homosexuality and madness. In 1954 he met the poet Peter Orlovsky (1933–), who became his lifelong partner. Ginsberg's major poems *Howl* (1956) and *Kaddish* (1960) are composed according to the dictates of breath and are both declamatory laments for an America which has disowned marginalized figures like Trotskyites, Wobblies (i.e. Industrial Workers of the World, an international union), Hell's Angels, Junkies, Queers. His empathy for the outcast made him an ideal figurehead for the counter-culture of the 1960s and he wrote and campaigned tirelessly against the Vietnam War, in support of the drugs LSD and cannabis, and in defence of such contemporaries as Abbie Hoffman (1936–89), Timothy Leary (1920–96), and William *Burroughs. His later work, *Mind Breaths* (1978) and *Plutonium Ode and Other Poems* (1982), displays less of the urgency of his earlier work, yet still maintains a confessional tone wherein his most private concerns are addressed as a statement about the nation. Along with Ann Waldman (1945–) he founded the Jack Kerouac School of Disembodied Poetics at the Naropa Institute in Boulder, Colorado. See Michael Schuhmacher, *Dharma Lion: A Biography of Allen Ginsberg* (1994).

GINZBURG, Eugenia (Evgenia) (1904–77) Writer, born in Moscow to Jewish parents who later moved to Kazan. She studied at Kazan University and became a teacher and journalist. Her memoir *Journey into the Whirlwind* (1967) documents her suffering and resilience during her long imprisonment (1937–55) under Stalin.

GINZBURG, Natalia (1916–91) Née Levi, Italian novelist and autobiographer. Ginzburg studied at Turin University and opposed *Fascism. After the war she combined writing with editing; in 1983 she was elected to the Italian Parliament. She wrote, amongst other autobiographical books, *Lessico famigliare* (1963), translated as *Family Sayings* (1967).

GIORGIONE DA CASTELFRANCO (1476–1510) Venetian painter, to whom very few pictures, including the Castelfranco altarpiece, the *Three Philosophers*, and *The Tempest* (*c.*1504), are universally attributed. Yet his importance has been recognized since *Vasari; he introduced a new kind of painting, often of enigmatic, pastoral subjects, where figures are caught in a poignant, dreamy mood. John *Ruskin in **Modern Painters* ('The Two Boyhoods') compared him with *Turner. In the later 19th century literary interest in Giorgione was intense. Prominence was given to the *Fête champêtre* (*c.*1510), also known as the *Concert champêtre*, now commonly attributed to *Titian. It shows two well-dressed male courtiers making music with naked women in a landscape, and was evoked by D. G. *Rossetti's sonnet 'For a Venetian Pastoral by Giorgione' (1850; rev. 1870). Giorgione's work, or at least his special style, inspired Walter *Pater's 'The School of Giorgione' (1877), first published in the second edition of *The Renaissance* with its celebrated dictum, 'All art constantly aspires to the condition of music.'

GIOTTO DI BONDONE (*c.*1267–1337) The most celebrated of the early Italian painters, whose art marks a turning away from Byzantine tradition to the clear space and dignified human figures of Renaissance art; his undisputed works are frescos in the Arena Chapel at Padua (1303–13) and in the Peruzzi and Bardi chapels in Sta Croce, Florence. Giotto was the first artist to be celebrated by literary men in his own day; praised by *Dante, *Boccaccio, and *Petrarch, and his epitaph written by *Poliziano, he was seen as the start of a new artistic era and rapidly became a legendary figure. Yet there followed a long period of neglect, until the late 19th century when he was admired by John *Ruskin, followed by Roger *Fry and Bernard *Berenson. E. M. Forster, in *A *Room with a View*, wittily describes a scene in Sta Croce, where his heroine looks for Giotto's 'tactile values'—a phrase made famous by Berenson's essay *The Florentine Painters of the Renaissance* (1896).

GIOVANNI, Nikki (1943–) African American poet, born in Knoxville, Tennessee. She began publishing her poems during the period of the civil rights and Black Power movements, her first volume being *Black Feeling, Black Talk* (1967). Among her later work, *Shimmy Shimmy Like my Sister Kate* (1996) looks back to the *Harlem Renaissance. Other poems draw on spirituals. In 2007 the Cleveland Karamu Theatre presented a play celebrating her life and work.

Gipsies Metamorphosed, The A masque by Ben *Jonson, performed before James I 1621, printed 1640. It is the most elaborate of his masques, and unusual in its assigning of principal parts to members of the court. The chief event is the telling of the king's fortune by the Gypsy captain, a part taken by the duke of Buckingham (1592–1628).

GIRALDUS CAMBRENSIS (Gerald of Wales) (?1146–*c.*1220/23) Writer and ecclesiastic, a native of Pembrokeshire and of Anglo-Norman and Welsh descent. He studied at Paris in the 1160s and again 1176–9. In 1184 he entered the service of Henry II as a royal clerk. After about twelve years he retired from court and spent several further years studying in Lincoln. As a churchman he had a stormy career. He was archdeacon of Brecon, and twice (1176 and 1198) a nominee for the see of St David's, but was rejected, first by Henry II in 1176, then by the archbishop of Canterbury in 1198. He appealed to Rome, sought Welsh support, was outlawed, fled abroad, and was imprisoned before being reconciled to the king and archbishop. He was buried at St David's. His works include *Topographia Hibernica*, an account of the geography, fauna, marvels, and early history of Ireland; *Expugnatio Hibernica*, a narrative of the partial conquest of Ireland, 1169–85, *Itinerarium Cambriae*, a description of the topography of Wales; *Gemma Ecclesiastica*, a charge to the clergy of his district; *De Rebus a se Gestis*; and saints' lives. See *Giraldi Cambrensis Opera*, ed. J. S. Brewer *et al.* (repr. 1964–6); *The Historical Works of Giraldus Cambrensis*, ed. T. Wright (1905); R. Bartlett, *Gerald of Wales* (1982).

GIRAUDOUX, Jean (1882–1944) French diplomat, novelist, and playwright; his first novel, *Suzanne et le Pacifique* (*Suzanne and the Pacific*), was published in 1921. In 1928 the novel *Siegfried et le Limousin* (1922: *Siegfried and the Man from Limousin*) was successfully adapted for the stage. Thereafter the theatre became the most suitable medium for Giraudoux's gifts of irony and paradox; his plots are frequently stylized and modernized versions of biblical or classical legend. His plays include *Amphitryon 38* (1929), *Judith* (1931), *La Guerre de Troie n'aura pas lieu* (1935; trans. 1955 by Christopher *Fry as *Tiger at the Gates*), *Ondine* (1939), and *Pour Lucrèce* (1953; trans. by Fry as *Duel of Angels*, 1958).

GIRODIAS, Maurice (1920–90) Founder of the *Olympia Press.

GISBORNE, Maria (1770–1836) Née James. She refused William *Godwin, and married John Gisborne in 1800. She and her husband were close friends of P. B. *Shelley. They lent him their Italian villa when they were in England, and in 1820 he published his buoyant 'Letter to Maria Gisborne', written to London from the workshop of the villa.

Gismond of Salerne *See* TANCRED AND GISMUND.

GISSING, George Robert (1857–1903) Novelist, born in Wakefield, Yorkshire, son of a pharmaceutical chemist. Following his father's death when he was 13, he was sent to a Quaker boarding school in Cheshire, from where he obtained a scholarship to Owens College (now the University of Manchester). Caught stealing from the college locker rooms to support a parentless girl, Nell Harrison, he was sentenced to one month's imprisonment. On his release, he set sail for America where he worked as a teacher and photographer's assistant and sold his first short stories to Chicago papers, some of which were later collected in *Brownie* (1931) and *Lost Stories from America* (1992). In 1877, Gissing returned to London, and married Nell. It was an unhappy marriage, largely due to her chronic alcoholism. They were separated by 1882, and Nell died in 1888. Gissing supported himself with private tuition (Frederic *Harrison's two sons were among his pupils), while establishing his literary reputation with a series of novels with London settings and proletarian themes: *Workers in the Dawn* (1880), *The Unclassed* (1884; rev. 1895), **Demos* (1886), *Thyrza* (1887; rev. 1891), and *The Nether World* (1889). He turned with less success to provincial settings for *Isabel Clarendon* (1886) and *A Life's Morning* (1888). He himself believed that the most characteristic part of his work was 'that which deals with a class of young man distinctive of our time—well-educated, fairly bred, but *without* money'. After a trip to Italy, he turned away from working-class subjects to write *The Emancipated* (1890; rev. 1893), **New Grub Street* (1891), his acknowledged classic, and *Born in Exile* (1892). In 1891, he entered into another unhappy marriage, with Edith Underwood, a stonemason's daughter. They had two sons, but parted in 1897, and in 1902 she was sent to an asylum. Gissing turned to the Woman Question in *The *Odd Women* (1893), **In the Year of Jubilee* (1894), and *The Whirlpool* (1897). Though never highly successful, he began to earn more money with *Denzil Quarrier* (1892), and a series of shorter one-volume novels: *Eve's Ransom, Sleeping Fires, The Paying Guest* (1895), and *The Town Traveller* (1898). He was also commissioned to produce short stories, collected in *Human Odds and Ends* (1898), and *Charles Dickens: A Critical Study* (1898). George *Meredith had been an early supporter of Gissing's work; Gissing also met Thomas *Hardy and became friendly with W. H. *Hudson and H. G. *Wells. In 1898, Gissing met Gabrielle Fleury, with whom he fell in love. Unable to obtain a divorce, Gissing moved to France and entered into a common law union with Gabrielle. Subsequent works are the novels *The Crown of Life* (1899) and *Our Friend the Charlatan* (1901); the travel book *By the Ionian Sea* (1901); an abridgement of John *Forster's *Life of Dickens* (1903); and a fictionalized version of his own memories and reflections, *The Private Papers of Henry Ryecroft* (1903), which won him many admirers. Gissing died of lung disease in the village of Ispoure in southern France. Posthumously published were *Veranilda* (1904), a classically set romance, *Will Warburton* (1905), *The Immortal Dickens* (1925), *Notes on Social Democracy* (1968), and the short story collections *The House of Cobwebs* (1906), *The Sins of the Fathers* (1924), and *A Victim of Circumstances* (1927). Gissing's notebooks and diary have been published; also nine volumes of his *Letters* (completed 1997). Morley Roberts wrote the affectionate but inaccurate portrait *The Private Life of Henry Maitland* (1912); see Jacob Korg's critical biography (1963).

GITTINGS, Robert (1911–92) Poet and biographer, born in Portsmouth, the son of a naval surgeon, and educated at Jesus College, Cambridge. His first volume of poetry, *The Roman Road and Other Poems* (1932), was followed by several volumes of poems and plays, and a *Collected Poems* (1976). His biographical works include *John Keats* (1968) and a two-volume life of Thomas *Hardy (1975, 1978); and *The Nature of Biography* (1978; based on lectures delivered at the University of Washington). With his biographer wife Jo (Joan Grenville) Manton he wrote *Claire Clairmont and the Shelleys*, published posthumously in 1992.

GIULIO ROMANO (?1499–1546) Italian mannerist painter and architect, and the most important of *Raphael's pupils;

his most famous works were created for Federigo Gonzaga at Mantua and include the Palazzo del Te (begun 1526)—where the frescos in the Sala dei Giganti and the witty, erotic decoration of the Sala de Psiche are most notable—and decorations in the Ducal Palace. Giulio is the only Renaissance artist mentioned by William *Shakespeare, who apparently thought that he was a sculptor: in *The *Winter's Tale* (v. ii) he mentions 'that rare Italian master, Julio Romano'. *Aretino wrote obscene verses to accompany engravings made after pornographic drawings by Giulio; 'Aretine's pictures' are mentioned by Ben *Jonson, John *Donne, and Alexander *Pope, who perhaps knew them by repute.

GLADSTONE, William Ewart (1809–98) The great Liberal statesman, born in Liverpool, the son of a prosperous tradesman; he was educated at Eton College (where one of his close friends was Arthur *Hallam) and at Oxford, where he distinguished himself as an orator, although it took him some time to determine on a career as politician rather than churchman. He is remembered in literary history for his *Studies on Homer and the Homeric Age* (1858), a subject further dealt with in his *Juventus Mundi* (1869) and *Homeric Synchronism* (1876). He firmly maintained his belief in a personal *Homer and 'a solid nucleus of fact in his account of the Trojan war', and, like Thomas *Arnold and J. H. *Newman, sought to justify classical studies as the basis of a Christian education. *The Gladstone Diaries*, ed. M. R. D. Foot and H. C. G. Matthew, 14 vols (1968–94), shed new light on his complex personality, particularly his zeal for rescuing prostitutes. The diaries (which are for the most part restrained and factual) also illustrate Gladstone's literary tastes; he read his own verses, **Marmion*, and **Lalla Rookh* to his wife immediately after their marriage, was given to reading Tennyson's *The *Princess* and *Guinevere* to his rescue cases, and found Harrison *Ainsworth's *Jack Shepherd* 'dangerous' reading for the masses. His long and critical review of Mary *Ward's *Robert Elsmere* (1888) helped to ensure the book's enormous success. See H. C. G. Matthew, *Gladstone: 1809–98* (1995).

GLANVILL, Joseph (1636–80) Clergyman and philosopher, educated at Exeter College and Lincoln College, Oxford. He was rector of the abbey church at Bath, and held other benefices. He attacked the scholastic philosophy in *The Vanity of Dogmatizing* (1661), a work that contains the story of 'The *Scholar-Gipsy'. He defended belief in the pre-existence of souls in *Lux Orientalis* (1662) and belief in witchcraft in *Saducismus Triumphatus* (1681).

GLASGOW, Ellen Anderson Gholson (1873–1945) American novelist, born in Richmond, Virginia, where she spent most of her life, and which formed the setting of much of her work. She was an admirer of Thomas *Hardy. Her best-remembered novels are *Barren Ground* (1925), a narrative of survival in adversity, and *The Sheltered Life* (1932). A supporter of women's suffrage, she was drawn to Fabianism. She attempted a realistic portrayal of the social and political conflicts of her native region, perceived through a sharp, informed, at times lyrical, and somewhat isolated sensibility. *The Woman Within* (1954) is a posthumously published autobiography. See Susan Goodman, *Ellen Glasgow: A Biography* (2003).

Glastonbury In Somerset; its abbey was said to have been founded by Joseph of Arimathea, according to the *Grail legends. The abbey pre-dates the 10th century. *William of Malmesbury, in his *De Antiquitate Glastoniensis Ecclesiae* (*c.*1140), suggests that it may have been one of the first Christianized areas in England, founded by French monks. *Giraldus Cambrensis tells the story of the discovery there by the monks of the bodies of Arthur and Guinevere in the 1180s, confirming the story of 'a certain Breton poet' who, according to Henry II, said they were buried there. This led to the identification of Glastonbury with *Avalon. It has been suggested that Henry II arranged the finding of Arthur's body to scotch the tradition that he would eventually return. The tradition of the foundation by Joseph of Arimathea advanced to the point in the 15th century when it was claimed by Henry Lovelich that he had been buried there. See J. A. Robinson, *Two Glastonbury Legends* (1926); R. S. Loomis, *The Grail from Celtic Myth to Christian Symbol* (1963).

Glatysaunt Beast The creature in Sir Thomas *Malory's **Morte Darthur* later allegorized by Edmund *Spenser as the *'blatant beast' of vicious discourse. 'Glatysaunt' is from an Old French term meaning 'barking', referring to the dogs carried in the beast's belly. In Malory it is pursued by Palomydes the Saracen.

GLENDINNING, Victoria (1937–) Née Seebohm, biographer and novelist, born in Sheffield and educated at Somerville College, Oxford. She became an editorial assistant on the *Times Literary Supplement* in 1974. She is the author of *A Suppressed Cry* (1969), a portrait of her great-aunt Winnie Seebohm (1863–85), one of the first students to attend Newnham College, Cambridge, and her Quaker family: the research for this inspired her historical novel *Electricity* (1995). Other works include lives of Elizabeth *Bowen (1977), Edith *Sitwell (1981), Vita *Sackville-West (1983), Rebecca *West (1987), Anthony *Trollope (1992), Jonathan *Swift (1998), and Leonard *Woolf (2006). Twice winner of the Whitbread Prize for biography, she was awarded a CBE in 1998.

Gli ingannati Comedy produced (1532) by the Accademia degli Intronati, Siena (*see* ACADEMIES). The plot was later taken up by *Shakespeare and forms the basis of his **Twelfth Night*.

GLISSANT, Édouard (1928–) Novelist, poet, playwright, and essayist born on the French Caribbean island of Martinique. Like his elder compatriot Aimé *Césaire, Glissant has engaged critically with the culture and history of the island. However, he is strongly critical of the notion of *Négritude put forward by Césaire and others. In *Discours* *antillais* (1981: *Caribbean Discourse*), he asserts the need to articulate a specifically Caribbean cultural identity, rather than a universal, and more abstract, black identity laying claim to African roots.

Globe Theatre The *Burbages' theatre on Bankside in Southwark, erected in 1599 with materials from the old Theatre on the north side of the river. It was a large polygonal building, thatched, with the centre open to the sky. The thatch caught fire in 1613, when a theatrical cannon misfired as the king entered in *All is True* (*Henry VIII), and the whole building was destroyed. It was rebuilt—tiled—in 1614 and demolished in 1644. Shakespeare had a share in the theatre and acted there. Shakespeare's Globe, which opened in 1996 close to the original site of the Globe, includes a full-sized reconstruction of the theatre, built in oak and using Elizabethan construction techniques, based on excavations carried out on Bankside: the driving force behind the building of this new theatre, opened by Elizabeth II in 1997, was the American actor-director Sam Wanamaker (1919–93).

Gloriana One of the names under which *Elizabeth I is figured in literature during her reign and particularly in Edmund *Spenser's **Faerie Queene*. The name was also used as the title of the opera composed by Benjamin *Britten for the coronation of Elizabeth II (1953), with a libretto by William *Plomer.

GLOVER, Richard (1712–85) Politician and poet. His blank verse epic *Leonidas* (9 books, 1737; 12 books, 1770) promoted the opposition to Sir Robert Walpole (1676–1745), and brought him fame. His ballad 'Admiral Hosier's Ghost' (1740) similarly undermined Walpole's policy towards Spain; the poem was included in Percy's **Reliques*. Glover also wrote *London, or The Progress of Commerce* (1739). His play *Boadicia* was acted by David *Garrick's company in 1753; *Medea* (1761) received occasional performances. At his death he left a sequel, *Jason* (1797); a 30-book epic, *The Athenaid* (1788); and *Memoirs* (1813) of his time as MP for Weymouth, 1761–85.

GLYN, Elinor (1864–1943) Née Sutherland, born on Jersey and educated privately, author of many sensational romantic novels, of which the best known is *Three Weeks* (1907), a notorious success, which features illicit passion in Venice on a tiger skin. As exotic as her characters in appearance, she and adaptations of her works achieved outrageous success in Hollywood in the 1920s. See Joan Hardwick, *Addicted to Romance* (1994).

Gnosticism [from the Greek 'gnosis', knowledge] A Christian heresy of the 2nd century AD. Gnostic teaching distinguished between a perfect and remote divine being and an imperfect demiurge who had created suffering. Gnosticism was long known only through hostile early Christian sources, but in 1945 key Gnostic texts, notably the Gospel of Thomas, were found at Nag Hammadi in Egypt. See A. D. Nuttall, *The Alternative Trinity: Gnostic Heresy in Marlowe, Milton, and Blake* (1998).

Go-Between, The A novel by L. P. *Hartley (1953); filmed in 1970, starring Julie Christie and Alan Bates.

'Goblin Market' A poem by Christina *Rossetti, published 1862. The fairy-tale plot, described in short, irregularly rhymed verses, concerns two sisters, Lizzie and Laura, tempted by goblins selling forbidden fruit. Laura yields, eats, and sickens, pining for more yet unable to hear the goblins' market-song. To save her sister, Lizzie braves their temptations while refusing to eat herself, reviving Laura by feeding her juices that the furious goblins smeared on Lizzie's skin. 'Goblin Market' has repeatedly been marketed for child readers, but late 20th-century readings also highlight its eroticism and interpret it in terms of religion, female sexuality, and commodity culture.

GODBER, John (1956–) Playwright and theatre manager, born in Yorkshire, and educated at Bretton Hall College and Leeds University. His major breakthrough came with *Bouncers* (1983), the first version of which dates from 1977 and which has been revived in numerous revised versions since. His mixture of poeticized colloquial dialogue with physical theatre is best seen in *Up 'n' Under* (1984), in which a small cast enact an entire rugby match on stage. A short teaching career now over, he had taken over the Hull Truck Company, for whom he has produced a stream of popular comedies, drawing from his own and the local community's interests: amongst these *Teechers* (1987) stands out. He is a prolific writer and, after Alan *Ayckbourn, the most frequently produced of his contemporaries.

GODDEN, Rumer (1907–98) Novelist and children's writer, born in Eastbourne, Sussex, and educated at Moira House School there. She spent her childhood in India, later returning to open a mixed-race dance school in Calcutta (Kolkata). Her novels include *Black Narcissus* (1939), about life in a Himalayan convent (filmed, 1946); *The River* (1946), set in India, and *The Greengage Summer* (1958; filmed 1961), about children discovering the sexual intensity of the adult world. Several of her children's books feature dolls, notably *The Doll's House* (1947) in which one doll attempts to kill another and a third dies attempting a rescue. *The Diddakoi* (1972) displays her interest in outsiders, while *Thursday's Children* (1984) is among several books featuring the world of dance. The autobiographical *Two under the Indian Sun* (1966) was written with her sister. She was appointed OBE in 1993.

GODFREY OF BOUILLON *See* BOUILLON, GODEFROI DE; FAIRFAX, EDWARD.

Gododdin, Y Long poem about the history of Celtic Britons, or Brythons, which celebrates an expedition by a force of

300 Celtic warriors from the Firth of Forth to Catraeth (probably Catterick in Yorkshire), where they fell to the overwhelming numerical superiority of their Anglo-Saxon foes. The poem, attributed to the survivor Aneirin, takes the form of a series of elegies, mostly for individual warriors, and tells how Mynyddawg Mwynfawr, king of the Gododdin people, assembled his force from various quarters of Britain and feasted them for a year at Din Eidyn (taken by most scholars to be Edinburgh) before setting off for Catraeth. The poem appears to have a temporal setting near the year 600, though the manuscript source dates from the 13th century. See K. H. Jackson, *'The Gododdin': The Oldest Scottish Poem* (1969); J. T. Koch, *'The Gododdin of Aneurin': Text and Context from Dark-Age North Britain* (1997).

GODOLPHIN, Sidney (1610–43) Poet and Royalist, a friend of Viscount *Falkland and described by Sir John *Suckling as 'little Sid'. He was killed at the battle of Chagford, Devon. His poems, not collected during his life, were edited by W. Dighton (1931). Thomas Hobbes dedicated **Leviathan* to Godolphin's brother Francis.

GODWIN, William (1756–1836) Journalist, philosopher, and novelist. Educated at the Hoxton Dissenting Academy, he later rejected the church, becoming an atheist and political radical. His major work, **Enquiry Concerning Political Justice*, ostensibly a reply to Edmund *Burke's **Reflections on the Revolution in France* (1790), envisions a better society, founded in a belief in the moral perfectibility of mankind, the notion that men act according to reason, that reason teaches benevolence, and that therefore rational creatures can live in harmony without laws and institutions, including property laws and marriage. Leading radicals and poets gravitated to Godwin's work, which seemed the only sensible reaction to the irrational course the revolution had taken under Robespierre. William *Wordsworth shared for a time Godwin's faith in the power of individual thought, before turning from a creed that devalued emotion.

During the treason trials of 1794 Godwin was at the height of his powers, writing *Cursory Strictures on the Charge Delivered by the Lord Chief Justice Eyre*, a successful, logically argued defence of twelve radicals accused of high treason, including John Horne *Tooke and Thomas *Holcroft. A novelist of note, Godwin published, also in 1794, the first of six psychological fictions, **Caleb Williams*, a compelling psychological mystery (adapted for the stage as *The Iron Chest*) in which the characters transcend the Godwinian rationalism they were intended to illustrate, lending the work emotional insight and power. There followed **St Leon* (1799), a tale of domestic affections (featuring a portrait of Mary *Wollstonecraft, whom he had married in 1797, and misunderstood by reviewers as an attack on marriage); *Fleetwood* (1805); *Mandeville* (1817); *Cloudesley* (1830); and *Deloraine* (1833). There also appeared a four-volume *Life of Geoffrey Chaucer* (1803).

Wollstonecraft shared Godwin's, faith in logic and rationality but opposed his atheism. Immediately following her death in 1797 (shortly after the birth of their daughter, the future Mary *Shelley) Godwin published his *Memoirs of the Author of a Vindication of the Rights of Woman* (1797), a loving and candid account of her life. His revelations of Wollstonecraft's love affairs and suicide attempts unintentionally scandalized the public, sullying her reputation for decades to come. Godwin subsequently married Mary Jane Clairmont, whose daughter by her first marriage, Claire *Clairmont, bore a daughter, Allegra, to Lord *Byron. M. Philp has edited *Collected Novels and Memoirs of William Godwin* (8 vols, 1992), and *Political and Philosophical Writings of William Godwin* (7 vols, 1993). See also P. H. Marshall, *William Godwin* (1984).

GOETHE, Johann Wolfgang von (1749–1832) Germany's most celebrated poet, also a dramatist, novelist, and scientist. Born in Frankfurt am Main, he studied at Leipzig and in 1775 he was invited to the court of Weimar by the duke, Karl August, and remained there for most of his life. He took on ministerial duties and was raised to the nobility in 1782. His Italian journey (1786–8) marked a turning point in his life. On his return he was able to devote more time to his literary work and scientific investigation of nature. He undertook studies in geology, comparative anatomy, botany, and even optics: convinced that Isaac *Newton was in error, he evolved a theory of light as one and indivisible, expounded in the *Farbenlehre* (1810: *Treatise on Colour*). Though wrong about the physical nature of light, his ideas on colour are of interest and were valued by the painter J. M. W. *Turner.

In England Goethe initially gained a reputation as a dangerously immoral writer: his first novel, *Die Leiden des jungen Werthers* (1774: *The Sorrows of Young Werther*), translated into most European languages, caused outrage for its supposed defence of suicide. (*See* WERTHERISM.) The reputation was slow to dissipate. During the revolutionary and Napoleonic period, most German writers were viewed with suspicion, but Walter *Scott was enthused by Goethe's drama of the Middle Ages *Götz von Berlichingen mit der eisernen Hand* (1773) and attempted a translation in 1799 (an adaptation for the English stage was made by John *Arden under the title *Iron Hand* in 1965). Goethe's most celebrated work in England, the first part of *Faust* (1808), only compounded his reputation as a dangerously immoral and irreligious writer. (*See* FAUST.) *Wordsworth was unable to see beyond this, and even S. T. *Coleridge, who made some exquisite translations of individual lyrics, was apparently deterred by it and declined a commission by the publisher John *Murray to translate the work. Hostile attitudes to Germany abated swiftly after the defeat of Napoleon by the Anglo-Prussian alliance. The first translation of *Faust*, with the 'offensive' parts omitted, appeared in 1820, and an anonymous translation of 1821, *Faustus: From the German of Goethe*, was controversially reissued in 2008 as the work of Coleridge. Lord *Byron, who was greatly admired by Goethe and returned the sentiment, relished the work's challenge to the timidity of prevailing taste, and P. B. *Shelley published a translation of the suppressed scenes in Leigh *Hunt's *The Liberal* in 1822. But Goethe's most influential advocate in the first half of the 19th century was Thomas *Carlyle, who translated two novels—*Wilhelm Meisters Lehrjahre* (1795–6) as *Wilhelm Meister's Apprenticeship* in 1824 and its sequel *Wilhelm Meisters Wanderjahre* (1821) as *Wilhelm Meister's Travels* in 1827—and also published an important series of laudatory essays. In *Sartor Resartus*, Carlyle went on to extol Goethe as 'the Wisest of our Time'. Carlyle's new emphasis was a conscious effort to overturn the view of Goethe as a pernicious figure and, in an age of doubt and growing secularism, to establish literature as a source of spiritual and moral authority. Carlyle's view of Goethe set the tone for his reception in England for much of the century, and established him as a figure of immense stature and one impossible to ignore. George Henry *Lewes's excellent biography (*The Life and Works of Goethe*, 1855) offers a fuller and more balanced view than Carlyle's, and Goethe was significant to many writers of the time, including *Tennyson, George *Eliot—the denouement of *The *Mill on the Floss* may owe something to that of *Die Wahlverwandtschaften* (1809: *Elective Affinities*), and the chapter epigraphs of **Middlemarch* and **Daniel Deronda* are frequently quotations from Goethe—and above all Matthew *Arnold, who declared Goethe a major influence on his own work. In his essay on Heinrich *Heine in **Essays in Criticism* (1865) Arnold lauds Goethe as a liberator of humanity and a 'dissolvent' of the 'old European order'. It is striking that the Goethe who was valued in Victorian England was the 'sage' of Eckermann's *Gespräche mit Goethe in den letzten Jahren seines Lebens* (1837–48); surprisingly popular, too, was the much-translated bourgeois idyll *Hermann und Dorothea* (1798). Although the many translations of *Faust Part I* during the course of the century are evidence of the work's continuing appeal, the *Faust, Part II* (1832) was relatively coolly received: Arnold was dismissive. While the sexual frankness of the love episode in *Part I* made some mid-Victorian readers, including Arnold, uncomfortable, by the end of the century this was no longer a concern, and the work brought some solace to Oscar *Wilde in Reading gaol.

In the 20th century Goethe's influence and the urgency of what he had represented to the Victorians waned. T. S. *Eliot ranked Goethe with Dante and Shakespeare as one of the three great European poets, but the public utterance masked a private indifference shared, for example, by James *Joyce and D. H. *Lawrence. Nevertheless, the 20th century saw important translations of his work, notably Louis *MacNeice's version of *Faust Part I* (1951) and W. H. *Auden's co-translation of *Italienische Reise* (*Italian Journey*, 1962). David *Constantine has translated *Die Wahlverwandtschaften* (*Elective Affinities*, 1999), and in 2005 his eagerly awaited translation of *Faust I* replaced the dull version previously available in Penguin Classics. See N. Boyle, *Goethe: The Poet and the Age*, 3 vols (1991–).

GOGARTY, Oliver St John (1878–1957) Dublin writer, surgeon, and wit, and in early manhood a friend of James *Joyce, who caricatured him in **Ulysses* as 'stately, plump Buck Mulligan'. He published several novels and volumes of verse and a notable book of reminiscences, *As I Went Down Sackville Street* (1937). W. B. *Yeats, who included seventeen of his poems in *The Oxford Book of Modern Verse* (1936), rated his work highly.

Gogmagog According to *Geoffrey of Monmouth, a twelve-foot member of the tribe of giants who occupied Britain before the coming of Brutus (*Brut). He attacked Brutus and killed many settlers. Brutus told the avenging Britons to spare Gogmagog so that he could wrestle with Brutus' ally Corineus (a companion of Antenor who joined Brutus at the Pillars of Hercules). Corineus defeated him, throwing him to his death at sea. See Edmund *Spenser, **Faerie Queene* (III. ix. 50). The hills near Cambridge are called the Gogmagog Hills. The name was divided between two figures, Gog and Magog, which have been carried in the lord mayor's procession through the City of London from the 15th century. Wooden copies flanked the Guildhall's council chamber door in 1708: these were destroyed in the Second World War, and modern copies now stand in the west gallery.

GOGOL, Nikolai Vasilevich (1809–52) Russian prose writer and dramatist. Born in Ukraine, the setting for his early writings, he left for St Petersburg in 1828 in search of a literary career. He achieved success with his first collection of stories, *Evenings on a Farm near Dikanka* (1831–2), based on Ukrainian folklore. The Ukrainian theme continued in his collection *Mirgorod* (1835). Another collection, *Arabesques* (1835), introduced the contrasting theme of St Petersburg as urban fantasy. His brilliant St Petersburg stories, 'Nevsky Prospekt' (1835), 'Notes of a Madman' (1835), 'The Portrait' (1835), 'The Nose' (1836), and 'The Greatcoat' (1842), are set in a mad city where nothing is what it seems. In 1836 he wrote a play that became a cornerstone of the Russian classical repertoire; *The Government Inspector* is a savagely satirical picture of life in a provincial Russian town. From 1836 to 1848 Gogol lived mainly abroad, principally in Rome. During this period he was at work on his prose masterpiece, the comic epic *Dead Souls*; the first part was published in 1842, but in 1845, during a developing spiritual crisis, he burnt the drafts of the second part. In 1847 he published a moral treatise, the *Selected Passages from Correspondence with Friends*, to almost universal rebuke from his friends. He sought solace in a pilgrimage to Jerusalem in 1848, but in vain. On his return he continued *Dead Souls*, but, in despair at his failure to imbue it with the intended moral content, he burnt the manuscript of Part II after adopting a regime of total fasting and prayer during Lent 1852. He died ten days later.

Gogol's prose is characterized by extraordinary imaginative power and linguistic originality. He was an admirer of William *Shakespeare, Henry *Fielding, Thomas *De Quincey, Walter *Scott, and particularly Laurence *Sterne, who may have influenced him. 'The Portrait' was translated into English in 1847, in **Blackwood's Magazine*. The most complete early translation is by Constance *Garnett, *Collected Works* (1922–7), revised by Leonard J. Kent (1969). See also Robert Maguire, *Exploring Gogol* (1994).

Golagros and Gawain A 15th-century Scottish poem of 1,362 lines in thirteen-line alliterative stanzas, first printed in a pamphlet in Edinburgh in 1508, and having some structural similarities to *The *Awntyrs of Arthure* in that it falls into two parts. It is loosely based on the French prose *Perceval* and concerns a journey made by Arthur and his knights to the Holy Land. There are two episodes, both demonstrating the courtesy of Gawain: in the first, Kay churlishly and Gawain courteously ask for hospitality; in the second Arthur unwisely lays siege to the stronghold of Golagros and Gawain fights in single combat against the latter, ending with Golagros's defeat and reflections on the vagaries of fortune. But the poem's main topic is the codes of chivalry, which it addresses confidently, with rich lexical and descriptive detail. See the edition by Thomas Hahn in *Sir Gawain: Eleven Romances and Tales* (1995).

GOLD, Michael (1893–1967) American novelist, born in New York, whose Lower East Side was the setting for his novel *Jews without Money* (1930), which has become a classic of proletarian realism. Gold helped found the left-wing journal *New Masses* and became an active member of the Communist Party.

Golden A term used by C. S. *Lewis in the introduction to *English Literature in the Sixteenth Century* (1954) to distinguish the literature of the later Elizabethan period from its predecessors in the *'Drab' age. In the Golden period, Lewis argued, 'for a few years nothing more is needed than to play out again and again the strong, simple music of the uncontorted line and to load one's poem with all that is naturally delightful'. The period may be seen as running roughly from John *Lyly's **Euphues* (1579) to the death of *Elizabeth I in 1603. All the major works of Edmund *Spenser, Philip *Sidney, and Christopher *Marlowe fall within this period, as does much of *Shakespeare's writing. The term suggests a certain bright, innocent, repetitive beauty, perhaps exemplified in such poems as Thomas *Campion's:

'There is a garden in her face,
Where roses and white lillies grow;
A heav'nly paradise is that place,
Wherein all pleasant fruits do flow.'

The term's limited applicability will be realized when it is remembered that **Hamlet*, **Dr Faustus*, and much of John *Donne's poetry were among the works written within the period of so-called 'Golden' poetry.

Golden Ass, The *See* APULEIUS.

Golden Bowl, The The last completed novel of Henry *James, published 1904. It describes a triangular love intrigue between an impoverished Italian prince, a rich American heiress, and her friend. The novel represents one of James's most sophisticated experiments with a limited point of view, and multiple symbolism in the golden bowl of the title.

Golden Cockerel Press A *private press founded in 1920 at Waltham St Lawrence, Berkshire, by Harold (Hal) Taylor (1893–1925), and taken over in 1924 by Robert *Gibbings (1889–1958), wood engraver, illustrator, and writer of travel books. Eric *Gill designed type for the Golden Cockerel Press and was associated with it from 1924, producing wood engravings for its books; he was responsible for one of its most celebrated productions, *The Four Gospels* (1931).

Golden Grove, The *See* TAYLOR, JEREMY.

Golden Legend, The A medieval manual of ecclesiastical lore, including lives of saints, commentary on church services, and homilies for saints' days. A version in English of this compilation from various sources was published by *Caxton in 1483 and was his most popular production, often reprinted. One of its most important sources was the *Legenda Aurea* in Latin by Jacobus de Voragine (1230–98), an Italian Dominican friar who became archbishop of Genoa. Caxton's version was edited by F. S. Ellis (3 vols, 1892; Temple Classics, 1900); selections ed. G. V. O'Neill (1914).

Golden Treasury *See* PALGRAVE, FRANCIS TURNER.

GOLDING, Arthur (1535/6–1606) Translator into English of Latin and French works, including *Ovid's *Metamorphoses* (1565, 1567), *Caesar's *Gallic War* (1565), the Roman historian Justin's abbreviation of Trogus Pompeius (1564), and *A Work Concerning the Trueness of the Christian Religion* (1587) by Philippe de Mornay (1549–1623), which had originally been undertaken by Philip *Sidney. His translations are clear, faithful, and fluent; his popular and influential version in *fourteeners of *Ovid was known to William *Shakespeare.

GOLDING, Sir William (1911–93) Novelist, born in Cornwall and educated at Marlborough Grammar School and Brasenose College, Oxford. He worked as an actor with small theatre companies; then became a teacher before serving as a naval rating, and as lieutenant in command of a rocket ship, during the war. After the war he returned to teaching, and began writing in 1948. He had published a volume of lyric verse, *Poems*, in 1934 but his acclaimed and highly influential first novel, **Lord of the Flies*, in which the decline into savagery of schoolboys marooned on a tropical island becomes a parable illustrating his belief that 'man produces evil as a bee produces honey', did not appear until 1954. *The Inheritors* (1955), which portrays Neolithic man's extermination of his gentler ancestors, continues Golding's concern with human corruption, a theme further explored in subsequent novels, *Pincher Martin* (1956), *Free Fall* (1959), *The Spire* (1964), *The Pyramid* (1967), and *Darkness Visible* (1979). Remarkable for its strikingly diverse settings in time and place, and for its ability to view life from unfamiliar perspectives, Golding's fiction (much influenced by the classical Greek literature he loved) concentrates on isolated individuals or small groups under extreme pressures and, from this, produces suspenseful fables of intense allegorical power. A play, *The Brass Butterfly*, was published in 1958, and a collection of three novellas, *The Scorpion God*, in 1971. There are two volumes of essays, *The Hot Gates* (1965) and *A Moving Target* (1982). He was awarded the *Nobel Prize in 1983, and his novel *The Paper Men* (1984), about the pursuit of a world-famous English novelist by an American academic, reflects his discomfort at finding himself increasingly in the public eye. *Close Quarters* (1987) and *Fire down Below* (1989) complete his master-work, a trilogy (published as *To the Ends of the Earth*, 1991), begun with *Rites of Passage* (*Booker Prize) in 1980. Set on a decrepit ship sailing from England to Australia in Napoleonic times, it demonstrates, along with his customary fabular and narrative skills, his considerable talent for ironic comedy. *The Double Tongue*, a novel of ancient Greece left in draft at his death, was published in 1995. He was knighted in 1988. See John Carey, *William Golding: The Man who wrote Lord of the Flies* (2009).

GOLDMAN, Emma (1869–1940) Anarchist activist, born in Lithuania. She campaigned in the USA for workers' rights, birth control, and other causes. She was deported to Russia in 1919 and in 1931 published her autobiography *Living my Life*.

GOLDONI, Carlo (1707–93) The most important Italian dramatist of the 18th century and one of the greatest of all Italian playwrights. He wrote some 250 pieces for the theatre including 150 comedies, in Italian, Venetian dialect, and French. He was also responsible for reforming the Italian theatrical tradition through the introduction of wholly scripted drama in place of improvised **commedia dell'arte*. Most of his plots are based on everyday life; he also satirizes the aristocracy and contemporary fashions. He spent the last 30 years of his life in Paris. His best-known plays, which continue to be regularly performed both in Italy and in England, include: *Il servitore di due padroni* (1745: *The Servant of Two Masters*), *La vedova scaltra* (1748: *The Clever Widow*), *La locandiera* (1752: *The Mistress of the Inn*), *Le smanie per la villeggiatura* (1761: *Pining for Vacation*), *Le baruffe chiozzotte* (1762: *The Chioggia Scuffles*), and *Il ventaglio* (1763: *The Fan*). His *Pamela* is derived from Samuel *Richardson's novel. See *Three Comedies*, trans. C. Bax *et al.* (1979); *The Holiday Trilogy*, trans. A. Oldcorn (1994).

GOLDSMITH, Oliver (?1728–74) Writer, son of an Anglo-Irish clergyman, born probably at Pallas, Co. Longford. He spent much of his childhood at Lissoy, and is thought to have drawn on his memories of it when writing *The *Deserted Village*. He was educated at Trinity College, Dublin, and graduated in 1750; rejected for ordination, he went to Edinburgh, where he studied medicine but took no degree. He studied in Leiden, and during 1755–6 wandered about France, Switzerland, and Italy, reaching London destitute in 1756, where he supported himself precariously as a physician in Southwark and as an usher in Peckham. He began a literary career as reviewer for Ralph Griffith's **Monthly Review*, a notable early piece being a favourable review of Edmund *Burke's *Enquiry into...the *Sublime and Beautiful*; Burke was to become a close friend. In 1759 appeared his first substantial work, *An Enquiry into the Present State of Polite Learning in Europe*. He met Thomas *Percy, who was to become a loyal friend and his biographer. He contributed to many periodicals (the *Busy Body*, the **Critical Review*, the *Ladies' Magazine*), and during October and November 1759 published his own, *The Bee*. He wrote for Tobias *Smollett's *British Magazine*, and for John *Newbery's new *Public Ledger* he wrote his 'Chinese Letters', subsequently republished as *The *Citizen of the World*; he may also have written the nursery tale 'Goody Two-Shoes'. Around 1761 he met Samuel *Johnson; he became one of the original members of the *Club, and was painted by Joshua *Reynolds. Johnson remained his friend and champion, and in 1762 sold for him the (possibly unfinished) manuscript of *The *Vicar of Wakefield* to Newbery, thereby saving him from arrest for debt. Goldsmith wrote many biographies, compilations, translations, and abridgements: these include lives of *Voltaire (1761), Beau *Nash (1762), Thomas *Parnell (1770), and *Bolingbroke (1770), an abridgement of *Plutarch (1762), a *History of England in a Series of Letters from a Nobleman to his Son* (1764), a *Roman History* (1769), and a *Grecian History* (1774). His poem *The *Traveller* (1764) earned him more solid literary respect; it was much admired by Johnson and Charles *Fox among others. Goldsmith's first comedy, *The *Good-Natur'd Man*, was rejected by David *Garrick but produced at Covent Garden in 1768; **She Stoops to Conquer* (1773) was a more spectacular success. Goldsmith's views on comedy were contained in an essay in the *Westminster Magazine* entitled 'A Comparison between Laughing and Sentimental Comedy' (1773); his own plays marked a return to the witty form. Goldsmith's best-known poem, *The Deserted Village*, was published in 1770; his lighter verses include the unfinished **Retaliation* (1774) and the posthumously published *The Haunch of Venison* (1776), written to thank his patron Lord Clare for a gift of game. His eight-volume *History of the Earth and Animated Nature* (1774), also published posthumously, was adapted from *Buffon, *Linnaeus, and John *Ray, among others, and inventively portrays 'tygers' in Canada, and squirrels migrating on bark boats in Lapland, fanning themselves along with their tails. James *Boswell's **Life of Johnson* represents Goldsmith as jealous, extravagantly dressed, improvident, and naive, but also as tender-hearted, simple, and generous. He was regarded with much affection; Johnson, in his Latin epitaph, stated that he adorned whatever he touched, and Johnson also wrote an epitaph for him in Greek. He never married, and his relationship with Mary Horneck, his 'Jessamy bride', remains mysterious. The 1801 *Miscellaneous Works* contain Percy's biographical memoir; other biographies include those by John *Forster (1848) and Ralph M. Wardle (1957). See *The Collected Works of Oliver Goldsmith*, ed. A. Friedman, 5 vols (1966); *The Collected Letters of Oliver Goldsmith*, ed. K. C. Balderston (1928).

GOLDSTEIN, Lisa (1953–) American writer, born in Los Angeles; she uses a variety of backgrounds for her *fantasy novels, from the Central European village of *The Red Magician* (1982) to Elizabethan London in *Strange Devices of the Sun and Moon* (1993). *The Alchemist's Door* (2002) features the Elizabethan occultist John *Dee.

Goliard, Goliardic *See* GOLIAS.

Golias (Goliardus) The mythical patron whose name is found attached in English manuscripts of the 12th and 13th centuries to Latin poems of a satirical and profane kind, the most famous of these being the so-called 'Apocalypse of Golias', for which no certain evidence of authorship can be claimed. According to F. J. E. Raby (*A History of Secular Latin Poetry in the Middle Ages*; 2 vols, 1934), the conception of Golias as 'Bishop' or 'Archpoet' is a myth, largely of English creation. The 'Goliards' are, it seems, to be linked with Golias, the biblical Goliath of Gath, the symbol of lawlessness and of evil, though the original derivation may have been from 'gula' (throat), on account of their supposed gluttony. The famous 'Goliardic' measure or 'Vagantenstrophe' appears to have passed from secular into religious verse.

GOLLANCZ, Sir Victor (1893–1967) Publisher; nephew of Sir Israel Gollancz (1864–1930), he founded his own firm in 1927, publishing writers including Ford Madox *Ford and George *Orwell, and in 1936 the *Left Book Club. He was well known for his progressive views, his resistance to *Fascism, his 'Save Europe Now' movement in 1945 to relieve starving Germany, and his opposition to capital punishment; these were reflected in his firm's publications.

GONCHAROV, Ivan Aleksandrovich (1812–91) Russian novelist and travel writer, born in Simbirsk. A state bureaucrat 1835–67, he served from 1855 as official censor. In 1852–5 he journeyed round the world on a diplomatic mission to Japan. The resulting account, *The Voyage of the Frigate Pallada* (1858), translated by N. W. Wilson (1965), reflected his acerbic impressions of the exotic, and of England and British colonialism. He wrote three novels: *A Common Story* (1847), translated by Constance *Garnett (1894), *Oblomov* (1859), translated by David Magarshak (1959), and *The Precipice* (1869), translated by M. Bryant (1915). Oblomov, the typically lethargic Russian nobleman of his comic masterpiece, is a universal archetype of man whose escapist dreams conflict with reality. See Milton Ehre, *Oblomov and his Creator* (1973).

GONCOURT, Edmond de (1822–96) and **Jules de** (1830–70) French authors, brothers, who wrote in close collaboration. Their earliest interests were art criticism, in which field they published several works (including the important *L'Art du dix-huitième siècle* (*Eighteenth-Century Art*), 1859–75), and French social history. From 1851 they wrote novels, painstakingly documented studies which they regarded as a form of contemporary social history. *Sœur Philomène* (1861), *Germinie Lacerteux* (1864), and *Madame Gervaisais* (1869) are among the best known. Their *écriture artiste*, an impressionistic, highly mannered style, elaborate in syntax and vocabulary, is well exemplified in *Manette Salomon* (1867), a novel of artist life. Some years after Jules's death, Edmond returned to novel writing with, for example, *Les Frères Zemganno* (1879: *The Zemganno Brothers*). The famous *Journal des Goncourt* is a richly detailed record of literary life in Paris between 1851 and 1896. Several volumes were published, omitting many passages likely to shock or give offence, during Edmond de Goncourt's lifetime; a complete edition appeared between 1956 and 1959. The Académie Goncourt, founded under the will of Edmond de Goncourt in 1902, is a society of ten writers which meets annually to award the most celebrated of France's literary prizes, the Prix Goncourt.
See also NATURALISM.

Gondal *See* ANGRIA AND GONDAL.

Gondibert An uncompleted romantic *epic by Sir William *D'Avenant, published 1651, consisting of some 1,700 quatrains. It is a tale of chivalry, set in Lombardy; but the author declares himself bored with the poem before its complex plot is resolved. D. F. Gladish in his 1971 edition describes it as 'a poetic museum of seventeenth-century literature and theory'.

GONDOMAR, Don Diego Sarmiento de Acuña, marquis de (1567–1626) The Spanish ambassador in the reign of James I. He was the enemy of Sir Walter *Ralegh, and caused Thomas *Middleton to be imprisoned for his play *A *Game at Chess*.

Gongorism A Latinate diction and style introduced into Spanish literature in the 16th century by the poet Luis de Góngora y Argote (1561–1627), a style akin to Euphuism in England and Marinism in Italy (*see* EUPHUES; MARINO, GIAMBATTISTA). Góngora was a poet of genius. His *Soledades* (*Solitudes*) were translated by E. M. Wilson (1931), encouraged by F. R. *Leavis and T. S. *Eliot.

gonzo journalism A phrase coined in 1970 about the work of Hunter S. *Thompson and subsequently applied to writing which combines fact and fiction, often in a flamboyant way.
See FACTION.

Good Friday The annual commemoration of Jesus' crucifixion, two days before Easter Day, celebrating his resurrection.
See BIBLE.

GOODKIND, Terry (1948–) American writer, born Omaha, Nebraska; author of post-Tolkien *fantasy. *Wizard's First Rule* (1994) began a long and successful series. Goodkind has suggested that he is influenced by the philosophy of Ayn *Rand, using fantasy to explore the morality behind his stories.

GOODMAN, Paul (1911–72) American novelist and essayist born in New York. He began writing in the 1930s but his major output dates from the 1950s. A self-described anarchist, Goodman became associated with the counter-culture, though he criticized the New Left in *New Reformation* (1970). *Growing up Absurd* (1960) combines autobiography with critiques of American society. Goodman was a prolific essayist and short story writer, *The Collected Stories* (1978–80) running to four volumes. His novels include *Parents' Day* (1951), which deals with paedophilia, and *The Empire City* (1959), an ironic portrait of New York.

Good-Natur'd Man, The A comedy by Oliver *Goldsmith, produced 1768. Honeywood is an open-hearted but credulous young man, who gives away to the importunate what he owes to his creditors. His uncle Sir William Honeywood decides to have him arrested for debt to show him who are his true friends. Young Honeywood is in love with Miss Richland, a lady of fortune, and she with him, but he is too diffident to propose to her. Instead he recommends to her the suit of Lofty, a government official to whom he believes himself indebted for the release from arrest which is actually secured by Miss Richland. Honeywood, cured of his folly, is united with her. A sub-plot turns on a love affair between Leontine, the son of Croaker, Miss Richland's doleful guardian, and Olivia; these two are also united through the intervention of Sir William. The character of Croaker was based on Suspirius in the **Rambler* no. 59, according to James *Boswell. The theme of excessive generosity was treated several times by Goldsmith and, according to Thomas *Davies, he himself, 'rather than not relieve the distressed, would borrow'. In the preface Goldsmith attacked 'genteel comedy' and praises the comedy of 'nature and humour'.

Good Soldier, The A novel by Ford Madox *Ford published in 1915. Generally considered Ford's finest technical achievement, it consists of the first-person narration of American John Dowell (an archetypally unreliable narrator), who relates the history of relationships that begin in 1904, when he and his wife Florence meet Edward and Leonora Ashburnham in a hotel in Nauheim, Germany. The two couples form a foursome, and meet regularly. In August 1913 the Ashburnhams take their young ward Nancy Rufford to Nauheim with them, and Florence commits suicide. Later that year the Ashburnhams send Nancy to India (where she goes mad) and Edward also commits suicide. Subsequently, Dowell becomes Nancy's 'male sick nurse' and Leonora remarries. The substance of the novel lies, apparently, in Dowell's growing understanding of the intrigues that lay behind the orderly Edwardian façade both couples had presented to the world; the carefully plotted time-scheme (orchestrated round the fatal date of 4 August, Florence's wedding day and death day, but settled on by Ford well in advance of 4 August 1914, the date on which Britain declared war on Germany) introduces the 'facts' (that Edward and Florence had been lovers, that both Edward and Dowell were in love with Nancy and Nancy with Edward) in an apparently casual, haphazard way that lends plausibility to an essentially melodramatic tale. The frequent time shifts show an affinity with Ford's one-time collaborator Joseph *Conrad.

Good Thoughts in Bad Times A collection of reflections by Thomas *Fuller, published 1645 at Exeter, where Fuller was living as chaplain to the Royalist army officer Sir Ralph Hopton (bap. 1596, d. 1652). It was followed in 1647 by *Good Thoughts in Worse Times*, and in 1660, at the Restoration, by *Mixed Contemplations in Better Times*. The work consists of meditations on his own shortcomings, observations of passages of Scripture, and applications of historical incidents and anecdotes to current events, and is marked by his characteristic good humour.

GOOGE, Barnabe (1540–94) Poet and translator, educated briefly at Christ's College, Cambridge; he was a kinsman of Lord *Burghley and pursued a career at court. He published *Eclogues, Epitaphs, and Sonnets* (1563; ed. J. M. Kennedy, 1989), and translations, including *Four Books of Husbandry* (1577) by Conrad Heresbach (1496–1576). He took an interest in Spanish writing, and his eclogues are important as being, with Alexander *Barclay's, the earliest examples of pastorals in English.

GOONAN, Kathleen Ann (1952–) American writer, born in Cincinnati; former teacher whose writing career began with *Queen City Jazz* (1994)—the first of a *science fiction series dealing with the human effects of nanotechnology. *War Times* (2007) considers *alternate histories of the Second World War.

Gorboduc, *or Ferrex and Porrex* One of the earliest of English tragedies, of which the first three acts are by Thomas Norton (1530/32–84) and the last two by Thomas *Sackville. It was acted in the Inner Temple Hall on Twelfth Night 1561. The play is constructed on the model of a Senecan tragedy, and the subject is taken from the legendary chronicles of Britain.

Gorboduc and Videna are king and queen, and Ferrex and Porrex are their two sons. The dukes of Cornwall, Albany, Logres, and Cumberland are the other chief characters. Ferrex and Porrex quarrel over the division of the kingdom. Ferrex is killed by Porrex, and Porrex is murdered in revenge by his mother. The duke of Albany tries to seize the kingdom and civil war breaks out. There is no action on the stage, the events being narrated in blank verse. Sidney praised the play in his **Defence of Poetry* as being 'full of stately speeches and well-sounding phrases'.

The legend of Gorboduc is told by *Geoffrey of Monmouth, and figures in Spenser's *The *Faerie Queene* (II. x. 34 and 35), where Gorboduc is called Gorbogud.

GORDIMER, Nadine (1923–) South African novelist and short story writer, awarded the *Nobel Prize for Literature in 1991. Most of her work is concerned with the political situation in her native land; her protests against apartheid and censorship are outspoken. Her collections of stories include *The Soft Voice of the Serpent* (1952), *Six Feet of the Country* (1956), *Friday's Footprint* (1960), *Livingstone's Companions* (1971), *Jump* (1991), and *Loot* (2003); her novels include *A Guest of Honour* (1970), in which an English colonial administrator returns to the complexities of a newly independent African country from which he had been previously expelled for his sympathies with the black population; *The Conservationist* (1974, joint winner of the *Booker Prize); *Burger's Daughter* (1979), which describes the personal and political heritage of Rosa Burger, whose communist father had died in prison; and *July's People* (1981), a novella set in the future, in which a white family on the run from civil war find themselves dependent on their black servant. Later novels include *A Sport of Nature* (1987) and *My Son's Story* (1990). *None to Accompany Me* (1994), focusing on the period leading up to democratic elections in South Africa, appeared after the release of Nelson Mandela in 1990 and his election as president of South Africa in 1994; it was followed by *The House Gun* (1998), which investigates a post-apartheid crime, with a black lawyer defending a white murderer. *The Pickup* (2001) continues Gordimer's exploration of the legacy of mistrust in interracial relationships. *Get a Life* (2005) focuses on a new threat to South Africa, the exploitation of its fragile ecosystem. *The Essential Gesture* (1988) and *Writing and Being* (1997) are collections of essays in which Gordimer states that 'nothing I say here will be as true as my fiction'.

GORDON, Lyndall (1941–) Academic and biographer, born in South Africa and educated at Cape Town and Columbia University. She taught at St Hilda's College, Oxford, and subsequently remained in the university as a research fellow. Her work includes *Eliot's Early Years* (1977) and its sequel, *Eliot's New Life* (1999), later revised as one book, *T. S. Eliot: An Imperfect Life* (1999); *Virginia Woolf: A Writer's Life* (1984), which won the James Tait Black Memorial Prize; *Charlotte Bronte: A Passionate Life* (1994); *A Private Life of Henry James: Two Women and his Art* (1998); and *Vindication: A Life of Mary Wollstonecraft* (2005). *Shared Lives* (1992) is her memoir of women's friendship in 1950s South Africa.

GORE, Catherine (Mrs Charles Gore) (1799–1861) Née Moody, born either in London or East Retford, Nottinghamshire, and educated at home. A novelist of the *silver-fork school, she published about 70 novels between 1824 and 1862, many anonymously; they include *Mothers and Daughters* (1830), *Mrs Armytage, or Female Domination* (1836), *Cecil, or The Adventures of a Coxcomb* (1841), and *The Banker's Wife, or Court and City* (1843). She also wrote several plays and many short stories. Her lively novels, with their marked interest in titled ladies and fashionable life, were parodied by W. M. *Thackeray in 'Lords and Liveries', one of *Mr Punch's Prize Novelists*.

GORGES, Sir Arthur (*c*.1557–1625) Courtier and poet, educated at Oxford. From 1580 a gentleman pensioner at court, he was Walter *Ralegh's cousin and close friend. His grief for the death of his young wife Douglas Howard was depicted by Edmund *Spenser in *Daphnaïda* (1591). Gorges's love poems, 'Vanities and Toys of Youth', remained in manuscript until edited with his other poems, including an elegy on Prince Henry, 'The Olympian Catastrophe' (1612), by H. E. Sandison (1953). Among his other works are a powerful rendering of *Lucan's epic *Pharsalia* (1614) into rhyming tetrameters; and a translation of Francis *Bacon's *Wisdom of the Ancients* (1619).

Gorgon *See* PERSEUS.

GORKY, Maxim (Aleksei Maksimovich Peshkov) (1868–1936) Russian prose writer and playwright, born in Nizhnii Novgorod. His rough upbringing is recollected in *My Childhood* (1913–14). *Among People* (1915) and *My Universities* (1923) describe experiences as a drifter along the Volga from the age of 11. His acquaintance with itinerant workers gave authority to his early studies of their futile protests, 'Makra Chudra' (1892), 'Chelkash' (1895), 'The Song of the Falcon' (1895), and 'Twenty-Six Men and a Girl' (1899). They were followed by colourful novels describing dissidents in the commercial world, *Foma Gordeev* (1900) and *The Three of Us* (1901). Militant proletarian heroes appeared in early plays, *The Petit-Bourgeois* (1902) and the internationally acclaimed *The Lower Depths* (1904). Obliged to leave Russia after the 1905 revolution, he lived mainly on Capri. In exile he wrote *Mother* (1907), a novel about a mother whose son's arrest prompted her to embrace his socialism. Lenin welcomed the novel as an inspiration for the proletarian cause. Gorky, however, showed a detachment from contemporary issues in plays, *Summer Folk* and *Children of the Sun* (both 1905), and prose works, 'Okurov Town' (1910) and *The Life of Matvei Kozhemiakin* (1911). His interest in 'God-building' as a substitute for socialism was explored in his first-person novel *Confession* (1908). Allowed home to Russia in 1913, he returned to Capri in 1923 on grounds of ill health after disagreements with Lenin. There he wrote *The Artamonov Business* (1925), chronicling three generations of a merchant family, and embarked on his unfinished epic *The Life of Klim Samgin*.

Persuaded back to the USSR as a literary figurehead in 1928, he became the first president of the Writers' Union in 1934 and an advocate of *Socialist Realism. His own works, however, revealed his inability to engage with Soviet reality. The circumstances of his death remain mysterious. A ten-volume translation of Gorky's *Collected Works* was published in Moscow 1978–83. Barry P. Scherr, *Maxim Gorky* (1988) is a critical biography.

Gormenghast *See* PEAKE, MERVYN.

Gospels *See* BIBLE.

GOSSE, Sir Edmund William (1849–1928) Critic, librarian, and man of letters, the son of Philip Henry Gosse (1810–88), eminent zoologist and member of the Plymouth Brethren of fundamentalist Christians, his relations with whom he describes (not always reliably) in *Father and Son* (1907). This is in Gosse's own words 'the record of a struggle between two temperaments, two consciences and almost two epochs', as well as a moving and amusing study of an individual childhood. Gosse went to London from Devon in 1867 to work as a transcriber at the British Museum. In 1875, the year of his marriage, he became a translator at the Board of Trade. He saw himself as a poet and made early acquaintance with the *Pre-Raphaelites. *Swinburne became a close friend. When Gosse applied for the post of Clark lecturer at Cambridge in 1883, he was able to give *Tennyson, Robert *Browning, and Matthew *Arnold as referees. A great deal of his early critical work was devoted to Scandinavian literature and he was the first to introduce Henrik *Ibsen's name to England. A successful lecture tour of America in 1884–5 was followed by an attack by John Churton Collins (1848–1908) on his published lectures *From Shakespeare to Pope*, an indictment of his carelessness which shadowed the rest of his life.

Gosse's books include lives of Thomas *Gray (1882), William *Congreve (1888), P. H. Gosse (1890), John *Donne (1899), Jeremy *Taylor (1904), Coventry *Patmore (1905), Ibsen (1907), and Swinburne (1917), as well as collections of poems and critical essays. He introduced André *Gide to England and was honoured by the *Académie Française for his services to the literature of France. His close friends included R. L. *Stevenson, Henry *James, and Thomas *Hardy. From 1904 he was librarian of the House of Lords and exercised considerable power and influence: H. G. *Wells dubbed him the 'official British man of letters'. He was writing regularly for the *Sunday Times* until his death. A biography by Ann Thwaite appeared in 1984.

GOSSON, Stephen (1554–1624) Author, educated at Corpus Christi College, Oxford. His plays are not now extant, but were ranked by Francis *Meres among 'the best for pastorall'; however, he soon became a leader of the Puritan attacks on plays and players. His *School of Abuse* (1579) was dedicated to Philip *Sidney, as was a romance, *The Ephemerides of Phialo*, to which he appended *An Apology of 'The School of Abuse'* (both also 1579). Whether or not he was 'scorned' by Sidney as Edmund *Spenser claimed in a letter to Gabriel *Harvey, his *School of Abuse* helped to stimulate Sidney to write his **Defence of Poetry*. Thomas *Lodge replied more directly to Gosson in *A Defence of Stage Plays*, provoking a reply from Gosson in *Plays Confuted in Five Actions* (1582). Gosson's attacks on the stage were edited by A. F. Kinney under the title *Markets of Bawdrie* (1974).

Gotham A village near Nottingham famed for its inhabitants' simplicity. The origins of the tradition are obscure, but there is a reference to it in the Towneley *mysteries, and related stories appeared in a collection, the *Merie Tales of the Mad Men of Gotam Gathered Together by A.B.*, of which a 1630 edition survives. A reprint of a copy (probably 1565) was published in 1965, ed. S. J. Kahrl. Washington *Irving introduced the name as a sobriquet for New York (*Salmagundi*, 1807–8). Gotham was most readily recognized in the late 20th century as the skyscraper city of the exploits of the famous comic strip hero Batman, created in the 1930s by Bob Kane (d. 1998). Batman and his friend Robin first lived in a Gothic mansion on the outskirts of the city, but they moved into a penthouse in the city in the 1960s.

See also CHURCHILL, CHARLES.

Gothic fiction A mode of narrative fiction dealing with supernatural or horrifying events and generally possessed of a claustrophobic air of oppression or evil. Frightening or horrifying stories of various kinds have been told in all ages, but the literary tradition confusingly designated as 'Gothic' is a distinct modern development in which the characteristic theme is the stranglehold of the past upon the present, or the encroachment of the 'dark' ages of oppression upon the 'enlightened' modern era. In Gothic romances and tales this theme is embodied typically in enclosed and haunted settings such as castles, crypts, convents, or gloomy mansions, in images of ruin and decay, and in episodes of imprisonment, cruelty, and persecution. The first important experiment in the genre, written half in jest, was Horace Walpole's *The *Castle of Otranto* (1764, subtitled *A Gothic Story* in the 2nd edn, 1765), which tells a pseudo-Shakespearian tale of a family curse that eliminates the princely dynasty of the usurper Manfred in 12th-century Italy, foiling his incestuous attempt to marry his dead son's fiancée.

The great vogue for Gothic novels occurred in Britain and Ireland in the three decades after 1790, culminating in the appearance of Charles Maturin's **Melmoth the Wanderer* (1820). During this period, the leading practitioner of the new genre was Ann *Radcliffe, whose major works *The Romance of the Forest* (1791), *The *Mysteries of Udolpho* (1794), and *The *Italian* (1797) were decorous in their exhibitions of refined sensibility and of virtue in distress. *Udolpho* in particular established the genre's central figure: that of the apprehensive heroine exploring a sinister building in which she is trapped by the aristocratic villain. Radcliffe's formula was followed by numerous clumsy plagiarists in the popular market for *chapbooks and 'shilling shockers', but she also inspired a few more talented imitators. Of these, the most striking is Matthew *Lewis, whose novel *The *Monk* (1796) cast aside Radcliffe's decorum in its sensational depictions of diabolism and incestuous rape.

The term 'Gothic' in this context means 'medieval', and by implication barbaric. In the late 18th century it was applied loosely to the centuries preceding the enlightened Protestant era that began with the Glorious Revolution of 1689. Radcliffe, Lewis, and Maturin set their novels in the Catholic countries of southern Europe in the 16th and 17th centuries, alarming their readers with tales of the Spanish Inquisition and of villainous, hypocritical monks and nuns. While drawing upon the imaginative liberties of greater English writers of the 'Gothic' age—principally *Shakespeare's use of ghosts and omens, and *Milton's portrait of Satan—the Gothic novelists deplored the cruelty and arbitrary power of barons and monks, and mocked the superstitious credulity of the peasants. In this sceptical Protestant attitude to the past, they differ significantly from the genuinely nostalgic medievalism of A. W. N. *Pugin and other advocates of the later *Gothic Revival in architecture. Radcliffe in particular was careful to distance herself from vulgar belief in ghosts or supernatural marvels, by providing rational explanations for the apparitions and nocturnal groans that frighten her heroines.

Some of Radcliffe's contemporaries and immediate successors managed to achieve comparable effects of apprehension and claustrophobia in novels with more modern settings: William Godwin in **Caleb Williams* (1794), his daughter Mary *Shelley in **Frankenstein, or The Modern Prometheus* (1818), and the Scottish writer James Hogg in *The *Private Memoirs and Confessions of a Justified Sinner* (1824) all evoked powerful unease without employing medieval trappings. Although each of these three novels includes prominent prison scenes, the principal strength is the evocation of psychological torment, guilt, self-division, and paranoid delusion. There are some grounds for excluding these works from the strictest definitions of Gothic fiction, but they are nonetheless commonly grouped with the work of Radcliffe, Lewis, and Maturin.

By the 1820s, the Gothic novel had given way to the more credible historical novels of Walter *Scott, its clichés by now provoking less terror than affectionate amusement, as in Jane Austen's parody **Northanger Abbey* (1818). Some of the tales of terror published by **Blackwood's Magazine* and its London rival the **New Monthly Magazine*, however, retained the Gothic flavour in more concentrated forms, and John *Polidori's story 'The Vampyre' (1819) launched the powerful new Gothic subgenre of vampiric fiction, which commonly expresses middle-class suspicion of the decadent aristocracy. From these sources the first master of American Gothic writing, Edgar Allan *Poe, developed a more intensely hysterical style of short Gothic narrative, of which his story 'The Fall of the House of Usher' (1839) is the classic model. Since Poe's time, the strong tradition of American short story writing, from Nathaniel *Hawthorne to Joyce Carol *Oates, has frequently resorted to Gothic themes and conventions.

In English and Anglo-Irish fiction of the Victorian period, the Gothic influence is pervasive, not just among minor authors such as Edward *Bulwer-Lytton and Bram *Stoker but among some major figures: the novels of the *Brontë sisters are strongly Gothic in flavour, Charlotte Brontë's **Villette* (1853) being a late example of the overtly anti-Catholic strain in this tradition. Charles *Dickens favoured such settings as prisons and gloomy houses, while his characterization employs a Gothic logic that highlights cursed families and individuals who are paralysed by their pasts: the significantly named Dedlock family in **Bleak House* (1852–3) and Miss Havisham in **Great Expectations* (1860–61) are among the best-known examples, but similar emphases prevail throughout his oeuvre. Somewhat closer to the spirit of the original Gothic novels are the so-called *sensation novels of the 1860s, notably Wilkie Collins's *The *Woman in White* (1860), and Sheridan Le Fanu's **Uncle Silas* (1864), which is descended directly from Radcliffe's *Udolpho* in its use of the imprisoned heiress. Le Fanu's ghost stories and tales of terror, along with those of Elizabeth *Gaskell and others, are also significant contributions to the Victorian Gothic tradition. The last decades of the Victorian period witnessed a curious revival of Gothic writing by Irish- and Scottish-born authors in which the haunted house seemed to give way to the possessed body, as in Robert Louis Stevenson's *The Strange Case of *Dr Jekyll and Mr Hyde* (1886), Oscar *Wilde's *The Picture of Dorian Gray* (1890), and Stoker's vampire classic **Dracula* (1897). At the turn of the century, more traditional Gothic settings and effects are found in such mystery stories as Henry James's *The *Turn of the Screw* (1898), which again refers back to *Udolpho*, and Arthur *Conan Doyle's *The Hound of the Baskervilles* (1902).

In the first part of the 20th century the Gothic tradition was continued principally by writers of ghost stories, such as M. R. *James and Algernon *Blackwood, and by *fantasy writers, of whom Mervyn *Peake is the most distinctive. A major exception in the realm of higher literary achievement is the work of William *Faulkner, which renews and transcends the Gothic genre in its preoccupation with the doomed land-owning dynasties of the American South. The English writer Daphne *du Maurier meanwhile opened a new vein of popular Gothic romance with **Rebecca* (1938), which revived the motif of the defenceless heroine virtually imprisoned in the house of a secretive master figure, inspiring countless formulaic imitations in the popular paperback market. The Hollywood cinema did even more to grant Gothic narrative a favoured place in the popular imagination, through its various adaptations of *Dracula*, *Frankenstein*, and other literary works.

Gothic settings and character-types reappear regularly as part of the repertoire of serious fiction. The novels and stories of Angela *Carter, notably *The Magic Toyshop* (1967) and *The Bloody Chamber & Other Stories* (1979), showed how Gothic images of sexuality and domestic confinement could be used imaginatively to explore the concerns of contemporary feminism. In the 1980s, several of the finest novels in English were clearly derived from the Gothic tradition: Graham *Swift's *Waterland* (1983) and Toni Morrison's **Beloved* (1987), for example, both encapsulate their larger tragic and historical themes within the convention of the dreadful family secret and the haunted house. American writers specializing in Gothic fiction at the end of the 20th century included the English-born novelist Patrick *McGrath, whose *The Grotesque* (1989) and later works display a mood of macabre humour, the hugely popular *horror writer Stephen *King, and the vampire romancer Anne *Rice, who also has a cult following associated with the 'Goth' youth sub-culture.

The critical fortunes of Gothic writing since Walpole's time have swung intermittently between derision of its hoary clichés and enthusiasm for its atmospheric, psychologically suggestive power. From either side, the Gothic tradition is usually considered a junior or marginal rival to the mainstream of fictional *realism. Walpole inaugurated the tradition in the hope that the lifelike solidity of realism might be reconciled with the imaginative range of romance. It fell to his greater successors—the Brontë sisters, Dickens, and Faulkner—to fulfil this promise. See D. Punter, *The Literature of Terror* (1980; rev. edn, 1996); C. Baldick (ed.), *The Oxford Book of Gothic Tales* (1992); F. Botting, *Gothic* (1996).

See also GHOST STORIES.

Gothic Revival A revival of the Gothic style of architecture and design that began in the late 18th century with a new romantic interest in the medieval, and produced Horace *Walpole's Strawberry Hill and William *Beckford's Fonthill. This was followed in the 19th century by a more scholarly study of Gothic, expressed in the works of A. W. N. *Pugin and John *Ruskin. The widespread adoption of the Gothic style transformed English towns and cities. Major buildings and churches throughout the country from the Houses of Parliament down adopted this style. Such architects as William Butterfield (1814–1900), G. E. Street (1824–81), and Gilbert Scott (1811–78) had many less successful imitators. Kenneth *Clark's

The Gothic Revival, first published 1928, reprinted 1950, signalled a new interest in Victorian architecture, which would be championed with more conviction by John *Betjeman.

GOTLIEB, Phyllis (1926–) Canadian poet and novelist, born in Toronto; pioneer of Canadian *science fiction since *Sunburst* (1964), which tells of a group of telepathic mutant children. Subsequent novels include *Violent Stars* (1999) and *Birthstones* (2007). *The Works* (1978) is a collection of poetry.

GOUDGE, Elizabeth (1900–84) Born in Wells, Somerset, educated at Reading University Art School; a prolific writer remembered for her works for children, especially *The Little White Horse* (1946), about Maria Merryweather who meets a unicorn. The book's combination of fantasy and reality is characteristic of Goudge's best work.

GOULD, Nat (Nathaniel) (1857–1919) Journalist and novelist, born in Manchester; from 1884 he spent eleven years in Australia, and his first book, *The Double Event* (1891), was published while he was there. Most of his vivid and extraordinarily popular novels (he published about 130) were concerned with horse racing. He also wrote two books of Australian life, *On and Off the Turf in Australia* (1895) and *Town and Bush* (1896).

GOUNOD, Charles François (1818–93) French composer, of whose operas the most famous is *Faust* (1859), based on *Goethe's text. His opera *Roméo et Juliette* (1867) rapidly gained a European audience: the libretto, by Barbier and Carré, stays close to William *Shakespeare's drama, and the music is sensitive and passionate. Gounod's four-year stay in England (1870–74) produced many settings of poems in English by George *Wither, Edmund *Waller ('Go, lovely rose'), Henry Wadsworth *Longfellow, *Wordsworth, Charles *Kingsley, Thomas *Hood, Alfred *Tennyson, Lord *Byron, P. B. *Shelley, Francis *Palgrave, and Cecil Frances *Alexander ('There is a green hill far away'). A few Scottish *folk songs also appeared. *Ave Maria*, an adaptation of the first prelude from J. S. *Bach's *Well-Tempered Clavier*, has proved an enduringly popular song.

GOWER, John (d. 1408) Poet, of a gentry family who owned land in Kent. He probably lived in Kent throughout the first half of his life. He may have been trained in the law, but certainly from 1398 (and possibly earlier) to his death he lived at the priory of St Mary Overie in Southwark, devoted to his writing. He was married in 1398, and was blind by about 1400. He was a friend of Geoffrey *Chaucer and (jointly with Ralph *Strode) the dedicatee of **Troilus and Criseyde* (see V. 1856).

Gower produced a considerable body of poetry in three languages. In French he wrote his *Cinkante Balades* (written in *Anglo-Norman and presented to Henry IV *c.*1400) and his first large-scale work, the *Mirour de l'omme*, an allegory written *c.*1376–9 in about 32,000 lines of octosyllabics in twelve-line stanzas, concerned with fallen man, his virtues and vices. His second major work was the Latin *Vox Clamantis* (completed after 1381), an *apocalyptic poem of seven books in 10,265 lines of elegiac couplets, dealing with politics, kingship, and ecclesiastical abuses. The Latin *Cronica Tripertita* (1399–1400) is a critical account of the reign of Richard II. In English Gower wrote 'In Praise of Peace' in 55 stanzas of *rhyme royal, as well as his principal work, the *Confessio Amantis*. This exists in three versions from the 1390s, the earliest of which is the most commonly attested amongst the 49 manuscripts. In his revision of the *Confessio* (in the early 1390s, while Richard II was still on the throne) he removed the praises of King Richard at its conclusion and dedicated the final version to Henry of Lancaster (later Henry IV). The poem is over 33,000 lines long, containing 141 stories in octosyllabic couplets, handled with metrical sophistication and considerable skill. The framework of the poem is the confession of a lover, Amans, to Genius, a priest of Venus; the confessor helps to examine the lover's conscience and narrates exemplary stories of behaviour and fortune in love, organized under the headings of the *seven deadly sins and drawing widely on classical sources (most prominently *Ovid) and medieval romance. There are eight books: one for each sin, and one which gives an encyclopedic account of philosophy and morals. The poem is as interesting for its prologue and epilogue, and for its exchanges between the priest and lover, as it is for the narratives themselves. When the lover has been entirely forgiven of his sins and his grasp of the ethics of love is complete, the confessor tells him that he is too old for love and disappears. The lover sees the reason in this and returns home, a conclusion which has been seen as a comment on the inordinate extent of his apprenticeship in the self-perfecting of *courtly love. Several of the exemplary tales are paralleled by stories in *The *Canterbury Tales* and other works of Chaucer: the story of Florent (I. 1407–861) corresponds to 'The Wife of Bath's Tale' (*CT*, 6); Constance (II. 587–1612) to 'The Man of Law's Tale' (*CT*, 5); Phebus and Cornide (III. 768–835) to 'The Manciple's Tale' (*CT*, 23); Pyramus and Thisbe (III. 1331–494) to Chaucer's 'Legend of Thisbe' (*The *Legend of Good Women*, II. 706–923); Ceix and Alceone (IV. 2927–3123) to *The *Book of the Duchess* (ll. 62–220); Tarquin and his son Aruns (VII. 4593–5123) to the 'Legend of Lucrece' (*Legend of Good Women*, V. 1680–885). 'Jason and Medea' (V. 3247–4222) and some of the shorter stories ('Narcissus', I. 2275–358; 'Canace and Machaire', III. 143–336; 'Rosiphilee', IV. 1245–446) are slight masterpieces of the classical narrative. Up to the 17th century almost every writer who praised Chaucer coupled his name with Gower's (see C. F. E. Spurgeon, *500 Years of Chaucer Criticism and Allusion*, 1925, vol. i) and he speaks the prologue to William *Shakespeare's **Pericles*, which is partly based on Gower's 'Apollonius of Tyre' (*Confessio Amantis*, VIII. 271–2008). See *Works* (French, Latin, and English), ed. G. C. Macaulay (1899–1902); trans. of *Vox Clamantis* in E. W. Stockton, *The Major Latin Works of John Gower* (1962); *Confessio Amantis*, ed. Russell Peck with Latin translations by Andrew Galloway (2003–6); Sian Echard (ed.), *A Companion to Gower* (2004).

Grace Abounding to the Chief of Sinners, or *The Brief Relation of the Exceeding Mercy of God in Christ to his*

Poor Servant John Bunyan (1666) A Puritan conversion narrative by John *Bunyan, testifying to the focal events in his journey to assurance of salvation. Its pastoral purpose was to comfort his flock at Bedford during his imprisonment. The author bound himself to the Puritan 'plain style', for 'God did not play in convincing of me…I may not play in relating'. It tells of his joining the Bedford church, call to the ministry, and trials, and describes his anguished oscillation between suicidal despair and contrite reassurance, bearing witness to the volatile moods ('up and down twenty times in an hour') which typified Puritan experience. External events (military service in the Civil War, marriage, etc.) are subordinate to inner and spiritual events, as Bunyan struggles against the lure of church bells, the doctrines of the *Ranters, Sabbath recreations, dancing, swearing, and blaspheming—even against envy of toads and dogs as being exempt from God's wrath.

GRAFFIGNY, Françoise d'Issembourg d'Happoncourt, Madame de (1695–1758) French novelist and playwright. Her epistolary novel *Lettres d'une Péruvienne* (1747: *Letters from a Peruvian Princess*), about a kidnapped Inca princess in Paris, quickly became a European best-seller; it was translated into English four times between 1748 and 1774.

GRAFTON, Richard (*c.*1511–1573) Chronicler and printer. As printer to Edward VI, Grafton produced the 1549 edition of the *Book of Common Prayer. Always interested in national history, he and John *Stow had scholarly quarrels over the subject. Grafton's own *A Chronicle at Large* (1568) was used by William *Shakespeare.

GRAHAM, R. B. Cunninghame *See* CUNNINGHAME GRAHAM, ROBERT BONTINE.

GRAHAM, W. S. (William Sydney) (1918–86) Scottish poet, born and brought up at 1 Hope Street, Greenock (an address that deeply amused him); he studied structural engineering at Stow College, Glasgow, before winning a bursary to pursue a literature course at Newbattle Abbey, then a newly founded college for adult education, in 1938. After a long nomadic period in Ireland, Scotland, England, and the United States, he settled in Cornwall in 1954. The poems in *Cage without Grievance* (1942), *Seven Journeys* (1944), and *2ND Poems* (1945—the title is a punning dedication to his wife Nessie Dunsmuir) are often said to resemble those of Dylan *Thomas, though they lack the acoustic force and syntactical discipline of the Welsh poet's work. *The White Threshold* (1949), a breakthrough volume, makes use of marine images drawn from Graham's youth on the Clyde estuary and includes the serene, verbally playful meditation 'Listen. Put on Morning'. The long title poem of *The Night-Fishing* (1955) resourcefully deploys the metaphor of a herring fishing expedition to explore the poet's struggle with language and vocation. *Malcolm Mooney's Land* (1970) and *Implements in their Places* (1977) bring a new lucidity and inventiveness to Graham's characteristic preoccupation with solipsism, community, and communication. In addition to the bravura title sequence and such companion pieces as 'What is the Language Using Us For' and 'Language Ah Now You Have Me', *Implements* includes the haunted elegy 'Loch Thom' and the teasing dramatic monologue 'Johann Joachim Quantz's Five Lessons'. *New Collected Poems* (2004) makes canonical a number of hitherto fugitive lyrics which further establish Graham's almost unique status in 20th-century verse as a poet who waited to the end of a long career to discover the full range and depth of his gift.

GRAHAM of Claverhouse, John (*c.*1648–1689) 'Bonnie Dundee', first viscount, a Royalist officer employed by the Scottish Privy Council in executing the severities of the government in Scotland during the reigns of Charles II and James II. In 1688, when James 'forsook his own cause', Graham's life was in danger even in Scotland; he determined to raise the Highlands for James (after the manner of his collateral, Montrose, in 1644) and was killed at the moment of victory in the battle of Killiecrankie. He figures prominently in Walter Scott's **Old Mortality*; see also William *Wordsworth's sonnet 'In the Pass of Killiecranky' (written 1803; pub. 1807).

GRAHAME, Kenneth (1859–1932) Author, born in Lasswade, Scotland. Following his mother's death in 1864, he lived with his grandmother at Cookham Dene, attending St Edward's School in Oxford. He entered the Bank of England in 1879 and was appointed secretary in 1898, one of the youngest holders of this position. Grahame contributed to the *National Observer* and the **Yellow Book*, encouraged by W. E. *Henley, who published many of the essays which later appeared in *Pagan Papers* (1893). Six of the 'papers' describe the life of a family of five orphans, whose activities later appeared in *The Golden Age* (1895) and its continuation, *Dream Days* (1898). Their sharp, authentic vision of childhood and the shrewd observations of the narrator were widely praised, notably by Algernon *Swinburne, influenced writers such as Edith *Nesbit, and brought Grahame great success. *The *Wind in the Willows*, based partly on bedtime stories and letters to his son, owed some of its success to praise by Theodore Roosevelt, who recommended it to the publisher, Charles Scribner.

Grail, the Holy In Arthurian legend, a symbol of perfection sought by the knights of the *Round Table. In the latest development of the legend it is identified as the cup of the Last Supper in which Joseph of Arimathea caught the blood of the crucified Christ and which, in some versions, he brought to north Wales or Glastonbury at the end of his wanderings. The legend has a long history, drawing on Celtic elements as well as Middle Eastern ones, and it is most familiar in English in the version of Sir Thomas *Malory which is mostly an abridgement of the stories contained in three of the romances of the early 13th-century French prose 'Vulgate' cycle. R. S.

Loomis notes that, in spite of its long history, the ten principal versions of the legend were written in a period of about 50 years, between 1180 (*Chrétien de Troyes) and 1230 (Gerbert). As well as Chrétien's *Perceval* or *Conte del Graal* and the Vulgate versions, there is a third major version in that period, the *Parzival* of *Wolfram von Eschenbach (*c.*1205), which was the inspiration for Richard *Wagner's *Parsifal*. Von Eschenbach's and Chrétien's story, in which Perceval is the successful quester, may be regarded as related to the original and more 'authentic' Grail myth which later accumulated layers of Christian meaning until, by Malory's time, it was very far removed from its archetype.

In Malory's *Tale of the Sankgreal* (the sixth of Vinaver's eight *Works*) *Launcelot fathers *Galahad on *Elaine, the daughter of the Grail King *Pelles. On the feast of Pentecost Galahad is brought to the Round Table and seated at the Siege Perilous; the Grail appears, accompanied by lightning, but the knights cannot see it. Led by *Gawain they set off in search of it. Launcelot fails in the quest, despite several glimpses, because of the sin of his amour with *Guinevere; Gawain gives up the quest. Three knights distinguished by great purity, Galahad, Bors, and Perceval, come to the castle of Corbenic where they have a vision of Christ and receive the Eucharist from him; they take the Grail from him and carry it to Sarras. Galahad dies in ecstasy; Perceval becomes a monk and dies two months later; Bors returns and reports their adventures in Camelot, in particular telling Launcelot of the eminence of his son Galahad.

The origins and motivation of the Grail have been explained in three principal ways: (1) as a Christian legend from the first, which altered only in detail through its history; (2) as a pagan fertility ritual related to the devastation and redemption of the land of King Pellam—a connection made briefly by Malory (*see* DOLOROUS STROKE; see J. L. Weston, *From Ritual to Romance* (1920); this is an interpretation important in literary history but no longer accepted by critics); (3) as a Celtic story, already mythological in Irish, transmitted through Welsh (*see* MABINOGION) and Breton to the French romance tradition and gradually Christianized (Loomis). There is disagreement as to whether a fairly coherent myth has been constructed out of disparate elements (Vinaver), or an originally coherent myth has been obscured by misunderstandings and mistranslations of elements (Loomis). Loomis believes that the horn of plenty (*cor*) of Celtic myth has been misinterpreted as the body (*cors*) of Christ, and that the phrase *San Grael* (Holy Grail, derived possibly from the Latin word for dish) has been wrongly divided as *Sang real* (royal blood, for the Eucharist). It is likely that the symbol was effective, in the Middle Ages as now, as a 'heap of broken images' (T. S. *Eliot) whose obscurity made it particularly apt as the object of a romance quest, a genre whose creators were constantly in search of difficult tasks. See R. S. Loomis, *The Grail from Celtic Myth to Christian Symbol* (1963); A. Lupack, *The Oxford Guide to Arthurian Literature and Legend* (2005).

GRAINGER, James (?1721–66) Born in Duns, educated at Edinburgh, physician and miscellaneous writer. He emigrated to the West Indies in 1759. His didactic poem *The Sugar-Cane* (1764) was well reviewed, though Samuel *Johnson commented, 'One might as well write "The Parsley-bed, a Poem", or "The Cabbage-garden, a Poem".'

GRAINGER, Percy (1882–1961) Australian composer and pianist. He settled in London in 1901 as a concert pianist and in 1905 became a member of the English Folk-Song Society; he was an active collector of *folk songs, working with Ralph *Vaughan Williams and Cecil *Sharp and introducing the wax cylinder phonograph to record his discoveries. He was also interested in Danish folk song. He came to prominence as a composer with *Molly on the Shore* (1907) and *Handel in the Strand* (1911–12), and he made many folk-song settings, although his most famous work, *Country Gardens* (1919), based on a morris dance sent to him by Sharp, is actually a variant of the tune 'The *Vicar of Bray'. Grainger also made a great many settings of Rudyard *Kipling in different forms.

Grainne (Grania) In the legends relating to the Irish hero *Finn, the daughter of King Cormac. Finn, though a great warrior and hunter, was unfortunate in love. He sought to marry Grainne, but she fell in love with Finn's nephew Diarmid O'Duibhne (*see* DIARMID) and eloped with him. The long story of their flight and Finn's unsuccessful pursuit ends in Finn's temporary acceptance of the situation; but Finn finally causes the death of Diarmid.

GRAMSCI, Antonio (1891–1937) Founder of the Italian Communist Party (1921) and, through his ideas on culture, an important factor in its appeal. Born in Sardinia, son of a minor civil servant, he read literature and philology at Turin University. Elected to Parliament in 1924, he was arrested in 1926 and sentenced to twenty years in jail by the Fascist Special Tribunal; he died from illnesses contracted in prison. His *Quaderni del carcere* (1948–51: *Prison Notebooks*) deal with philosophy, history, culture, folklore, literature, language, and the role of the intellectuals. They include his theatre criticism, and journalism for *Ordine nuovo* (*New Order*), which he founded. His letters from prison are a classic of Italian prose.

GRAND, Sarah (1854–1943) The pseudonym of novelist Frances Elizabeth Bellenden McFall, née Clarke. In 1890, after nearly twenty years of marriage, she left her surgeon husband and son to pursue her writing career. She achieved sensational success with *The Heavenly Twins* (1893), which attacked sexual double standards in marriage and dealt frankly with the dangers of syphilis and the immorality of the Contagious Diseases Acts. The novel launched her on a public career as a *New Woman (a phrase she was said to have coined in 1894); she lectured and wrote extensively on the need for sexual equality. *The Beth Book* (1897), a semi-autobiographical novel, describes with much spirit (and occasional lapses into melodramatic absurdity) the girlhood, disillusioning marriage, literary aspirations, and eventual independence of its heroine. See Gillian Kersley, *Darling Madame: Sarah Grand and Devoted Friend* (1983).

Grandison, Sir Charles, The History of A novel by Samuel *Richardson, published 1754. For many years Richardson had been thinking of the portrayal of a 'Good Man', to balance his female creations in **Pamela* and **Clarissa*. He was also anxious to avoid the controversy which attended his earlier fictions, and as a result Sir Charles is an unlikely paragon of honour, wisdom, and virtue, suitable for a conduct manual. The novel is once more epistolary in form, but lacks the direct emotional immediacy of the earlier fictions, as well as the sense that the act of writing itself has symbolic power for oppressed women. The novel ranges more widely in scene, plot, and character, but is set more exclusively in the aristocratic society of which Richardson had little personal knowledge and which features as morally suspect in his female-centred novels. The beautiful Harriet attracts the unwelcome attentions of Sir Hargrave Pollexfen, a weakened version of *Clarissa*'s Lovelace. He has her abducted, and after the failure of a secret marriage ceremony she is carried off into the country. Sir Charles, hearing her cries, rescues her and they fall in love. He must, however, fulfil an obligation to go to Italy, where he has previously become involved with an Italian aristocrat, Clementina Porretta. Religious differences have kept them apart. Clementina's unhappiness has deranged her mind, and her parents, now prepared to accept any terms for the cure of their daughter, summon Sir Charles to Italy. As she recovers, however, Clementina reaffirms that she cannot marry a heretic (Protestant), and Sir Charles, released, returns to England to marry Harriet. Three months later Clementina arrives, declaring that she wishes to become a nun but that her parents wish her to marry another suitor. Her parents and suitor then appear, but Sir Charles is able to arrange everything to everyone's satisfaction, and Harriet, he, and Clementina swear eternal friendship. The book was very popular, and Jane *Austen dramatized scenes from it for family performance: see *Jane Austen's 'Sir Charles Grandison'*, ed. Brian Southam (1980), and the edition of the novel by Jocelyn Harris (1972).

Grand Tour Beginning as informal diplomatic training for Elizabethan courtiers, the Grand Tour reached its heyday in the mid-18th century: a leisurely journey of two or three years through Western Europe, during which the sons of the aristocracy completed a classical education, refined their manners, and learned the ways of the world before taking their place in society. The conventional route took the young traveller, usually accompanied by a harried tutor or 'bear-leader', through Paris into Italy (the glories of ancient Rome were being excavated at Herculaneum and Pompeii), often returning via Switzerland, the Rhine, and the Low Countries. Stimulated by the *Enlightenment's emphasis on empirical observation, the poor quality of English universities, and a sense that the Continent was more sophisticated, it served the social function of cementing the aristocracy within and across national borders, providing expensively acquired cultural capital to a small elite. The tour was intended to combine pleasure and instruction: sexual adventures were as much anticipated as connoisseurship and sightseeing.

Tourists returned with souvenirs: collections of antiquities, portraits by Pompeo Batoni (1708–87) and Rosalba Carriera (1675–1757), cityscapes by Canaletto (1697–1768), Panini (1691–1765), and *Piranesi. They also introduced to England a taste for the Palladian villa and the Claudian garden (*see* PALLADIANISM; CLAUDE LORRAIN). Some simply had their xenophobia confirmed. Many accounts of tours survive: journals and sketchbooks were expected outcomes of the educational purpose. Richard Lassells's *Voyage* (1670) first used the term. Some, such as Joseph *Addison's *Remarks on Several Parts of Italy* (1705), took on features of the *guidebook. For the quality of writing, and a new subjectivity, the letters of Thomas *Gray and Horace *Walpole (on their tour in 1737–41) and accounts by James *Boswell, Edward *Gibbon, and William *Beckford stand out. Tobias *Smollett's *Travels through France and Italy* (1766) was a particularly cantankerous account, satirized in Laurence *Sterne's **Sentimental Journey* (1768).

Scholars disagree about whether the true Grand Tour survived beyond 1789, despite remaining a cliché for the tourism industry. By the 1760s fashionable 'macaronis' returning from Italy were increasingly lampooned by a more assertive and patriotic English taste. The Tour began to lose its cachet as middle-class travellers took part and more adventurous aristocrats were esteemed for less conventional travels. *Romanticism redirected the traveller's attention to the natural, the sublime, the unexpected, and the subjective response, though Grand Tourists themselves came to appreciate Alpine scenery and melancholy ruins. With continental travel opening up after 1815, and becoming easier with railways and package tours, the experience was very different, and the increasingly confident middle class found less that would improve them. However, in North America and Australasia the belief in the improving tour of Europe as necessary for the cultural elite lingered well into the 20th century.

GRANGE, John (b. 1556/7) Educated at the Queen's College, Oxford, and the Inns of Court; he attended the Roman Catholic seminary at Douai. His romance of erotic intrigue *The Golden Aphroditis* (1577) is comparable to George *Gascoigne's *Adventures of Master *F.J.* Largely made up of speeches, moral discourses, letters, and poems, it describes the courting of Lady A.O. (who turns out to be the daughter of Diana and Endymion) by Sir N.O.

Grania *See* GRAINNE.

GRANT, Joan (1907–89) Pen-name of Joan Marshall Kelsey, born in London; occultist and writer whose 'far memory' in *Winged Pharaoh* (1937) claimed to describe a previous incarnation as an Egyptian priestess. Subsequent books recalled Renaissance Italy or pre-Columbian America. They influenced a school of occultist *fantasy.

GRANT, John (1949–) Pen-name of Paul Le Page Barnett, Scottish editor, novelist, and compiler of reference books. A prolific writer of *fantasy gamebooks in the early 1990s, he also wrote more ambitious works such as *Albion* (1991) and *The World* (1992). He co-edited, with John *Clute, the *Encyclopedia of Fantasy* (1997) and was technical editor of the 1993 2nd edition of the *Encyclopedia of Science Fiction. The Far-Enough Window* (2002) is a witty, modern version of the Victorian fairy-tale.

Granta A Cambridge University undergraduate periodical started in 1889 and taking its title from an old name for the river Cam. An early editor was R. C. (Rudolph Chambers) Lehmann, later a regular writer for *Punch* and the father of the novelist Rosamond *Lehmann and the poet and publisher John *Lehmann. In the 1950s and 1960s, *Granta* was edited as a literary magazine devoted to publishing poetry and fiction by students at the university, including Michael *Frayn, Sylvia *Plath, and Ted *Hughes. After some years of financial difficulties and intermittent publication, it was relaunched in 1979 by a group of postgraduates which included Bill Buford, who edited it for sixteen years as, in his own words, 'an international paperback magazine of contemporary fiction and cultural journalism'. In 1995, Ian Jack took over as editor. He was succeeded in the post by Jason Cowley in 2007. Since 1979, many highly acclaimed writers, including Saul *Bellow, Angela *Carter, Peter *Carey, Raymond *Carver, Nadine *Gordimer, Milan *Kundera, Gabriel *García Márquez, Edmund *White, and Jeanette *Winterson, have contributed to *Granta*. Issues of the magazine have regularly followed a particular theme (travel, autobiography, London, the sea) and these have been amongst the most successful. In 1983, the magazine published a list of twenty 'Best of Young British Novelists'. Including Martin *Amis, Pat *Barker, Julian *Barnes, Kazuo *Ishiguro, Ian *McEwan, and Salman *Rushdie, the list proved to be remarkably prescient of future success, and *Granta* has twice (in 1993 and 2003) repeated the exercise of choosing such a list. The magazine also has a book publishing imprint named Granta Books.

GRANVILLE-BARKER, Harley (1877–1946) Born in London, where his mother taught elocution. He became an actor at the age of 14, and quickly gained recognition. From 1904 to 1907 he directed with brilliant success at the *Royal Court Theatre, producing *Shakespeare, many classics, and the work of moderns (such as *Galsworthy, and his own *The Voysey Inheritance*, 1905), and above all establishing the reputation of George Bernard *Shaw. His own play *Waste* was banned in 1907 by the Lord Chamberlain. In 1910 he produced his own *The Madras House* and Galsworthy's *Justice* at the Duke of York's; then in 1912 two productions, *The *Winter's Tale* and **Twelfth Night*, which revolutionized the presentation of Shakespeare. An apron stage, simple settings, an authentic text, and swift continuity of action were new to critics and public, and not until a similar production of *A *Midsummer Night's Dream* in 1914 did Barker meet with any general acclaim. In the same year he produced a version of Thomas *Hardy's *The Dynasts*, which was a failure, and he spent much of the years 1914–18 producing in New York. After the war he retired from the stage (and hyphenated his name), but in 1919 became president of the new British Drama League, and in 1923 began his Prefaces to the new *Players' Shakespeare*. The project was abandoned, but Granville-Barker continued with his Prefaces, of which he eventually published five series between 1927 and 1947, covering ten plays. These intelligent studies broke new ground in presenting the producer's rather than the scholar's point of view. Among other writing, lectures, and broadcasts he published *On Dramatic Method* (1931); *On Poetry in Drama* (1937); and *The Use of Drama* (1946).

graphic novels Term used to distinguish longer, more complex single works of sequential art conceived or developed as a unified work, from periodical comic books. The term was first popularized on the cover of *A Contract with God* (1978) by Will Eisner (1917–2005) and was used to reposition a new wave of more 'mature' comic writers in the 1980s, such as Alan *Moore and Dave Gibbons (1949–) in *Watchmen* (1987), or Neil *Gaiman in the 'Sandman' series, reprinted in album form, which aimed at the wider appeal of the French *bande dessinée* and Japanese *manga*. It was applied especially to more sophisticated works such as *Maus* (1991) by Art Spiegelman (1948–) or *The Tale of One Bad Rat* (1996) by Bryan Talbot (1952–), as well as the 'adult' work of Raymond *Briggs such as *Where the Wind Blows* (1982). For some it distinguishes books like these, or *Jimmy Corrigan* (2000) by Chris Ware (1967–), which won the *Guardian* First Book Award, from the more 'juvenile' market of superhero comic books. For others it is simply a marketing tool which includes album collections of the very same 'comic book' material.

GRASS, Günter (1927–) Prolific German novelist, essayist, and outspoken democratic socialist, born in Danzig, now Gdańsk in Poland. His long, often humorous, fantastic, and narratively innovative novels display a virtuoso linguistic vitality and invention. *Die Blechtrommel* (1959: *The Tin Drum*), *Hundejahre* (1963: *Dog Years*), *Der Butt* (1977: *The Flounder*), *Das Treffen in Telgte* (1979: *The Meeting at Telgte*), *Die Rättin* (1986: *The Rat*), *Unkenrufe* (1992: *The Call of the Toad*), *Ein weites Feld* (1995: *Too Far Afield*), and *Im Krebsgang* (2002: *Crabwalk*) are in their various ways concerned with the burden and the right remembering of Germany's past. The political dimension of his work—and his stance towards German unification in 1989 in particular—has often proved controversial, but after the award of the *Nobel Prize for Literature in 1999 he enjoyed the status of Germany's conscience. In consequence, his belated disclosure in the autobiography *Beim Häuten der Zwiebel* (2006: *Peeling the Onion*) that his military service in the last months of the war had been in an SS regiment caused uproar. Attacked and vilified on all sides, he was defended by Salman *Rushdie, in whose defence Grass had spoken at the time of *The Satanic Verses* controversy in 1989.

GRAVES, Alfred Perceval (1846–1931) Born in Dublin, an inspector of schools in various parts of England, 1875–1910, who published many volumes of lyrics and Irish and Welsh songs, and an autobiography, *To Return to All That* (1930). He composed the popular 'Father O'Flynn' and 'My Love's an Arbutus'. He was the father of the poet Robert *Graves.

GRAVES, Richard (1715–1804) Novelist, poet, and translator, educated at Pembroke College, Oxford, where he met William *Shenstone, a lifelong friend. Graves was rector of Claverton, near Bath, from 1749 to his death. He was also a friend of Ralph *Allen, and taught the young Thomas *Malthus at his rectory school. His novel *The Spiritual Quixote, or The Summer's Ramble of Mr Geoffry Wildgoose* (1773) ran into several editions. Wildgoose, his head turned by religious controversy, abandons his estate to travel through the West Country and to the Peak District, challenging everywhere the 'enthusiasm' of new Methodists such as George *Whitefield, with ludicrous results. Graves's other novels include *Columella* (1779), based on the life of Shenstone; he published *Recollections of William Shenstone* in 1788.

GRAVES, Robert (1895–1985) Poet and novelist, son of A. P. (Alfred Perceval) *Graves, born in London and educated at Charterhouse; he joined the army in 1914 and his first poetry appeared (with the encouragement of Edward *Marsh) while he was serving in the First World War (*Over the Brazier*, 1916; *Fairies and Fusiliers*, 1917); his poems also appeared in *Georgian Poetry*. In 1918 he married, and in 1919 went to St John's College, Oxford, to read English, though he left without taking a degree, later successfully submitting a critical work, *Poetic Unreason and Other Studies* (1925), as a thesis for a B.Litt. In 1926, accompanied by his wife and a new acquaintance, Laura *Riding, he went briefly to Egypt as professor of literature. He was to live and work with Riding in Majorca, then Brittany, until 1939, publishing various works in collaboration with her, including *A Survey of Modernist Poetry* (1927). He spent the Second World War in England, then returned to Majorca in 1946 with his second wife, Beryl Hodge, and settled there permanently. Graves's output was prodigious; he wrote many volumes of poetry, essays, fiction, biography, and works for children, and published many free translations from various languages. He saw himself primarily as a poet, and wrote some of his prose reluctantly, for financial reasons, but much of it is of lasting quality. His powerful autobiography, *Goodbye to All That* (1929), which describes his unhappy schooldays and the horrors of the trenches, and gives a frank account of the breakdown of his first marriage, is an outstanding example of the new freedom and passionate disillusion of the post-war generation. He wrote many novels, most of them with a historical basis; they include *I, Claudius* and *Claudius the God* (both 1934), narrated in the imaginatively and idiosyncratically conceived persona of the Emperor Claudius; *Antigua, Penny, Puce* (1936), a barbed tale of sibling rivalry; and the controversial *The Story of Marie Powell, Wife to Mr Milton* (1943). Notable amongst his non-fiction works is *The White Goddess: A Historical Grammar of Poetic Myth* (1948), which argues that true poets derive their gifts from the Muse, the primitive, matriarchal Moon Goddess, the female principle, once dominant but now disastrously dispossessed by male values of reason and logic. This has influenced several subsequent poets, notably Ted *Hughes. Graves's often unorthodox interpretation of myth may also be seen in his *The Greek Myths* (1955), *The Hebrew Myths* (1963, with R. Patai), and other works. A personal mythology also manifests itself, although not to the point of obscurity, in much of his poetry. His volumes of verse appeared regularly over the years, and his *Collected Poems* (1955) confirmed a worldwide reputation; *The Complete Poems in One Volume*, edited by Beryl Graves and Dunstan Ward, was published in 2000. Since his early days, when he rid himself of tendencies towards Georgian poetic diction, Graves (partly through voluntary exile) avoided identification with any school or movement, speaking increasingly with a highly individual yet ordered voice in which lucidity and intensity combine to a remarkable degree. His love poetry, some of his best-known and most distinctive work, is at once cynical and passionate, romantic and erotic, personal and universal. He also wrote ballads, songs for children, dramatic monologues, narratives, and poetic anecdotes; his technique is not experimental, but the classical precision of his verse is rarely archaic. Graves received many honours, and refused many. He was professor of poetry at Oxford from 1961 to 1966, and various of his essays and lectures have been published in *Poetic Craft and Principle* (1967), *The Crane Bag and Other Disputed Subjects* (1969), and other works. See Martin Seymour-Smith, *Robert Graves: His Life and Work* (1982).

graveyard poets Term applied to 18th-century poets who wrote melancholy, reflective works, often set in graveyards, on the theme of human mortality. Examples include Thomas *Parnell's 'Night-Piece on Death' (1721), Edward Young's **Night Thoughts* (1742), Robert *Blair's *The Grave* (1743), and Thomas *Gray's **Elegy Written in a Country Church-Yard* (1751).

GRAY, Alasdair (1934–) Scottish novelist, playwright, and painter, born in Glasgow, and educated at the Glasgow School of Art. He worked as an art teacher, muralist, and theatrical scene-painter, and had some success as a radio and television dramatist in the 1960s and 1970s. The dual narrative of his first novel, *Lanark: A Life in Four Books* (1981), mirrors Glasgow with the nightmarish Unthank, and the experiences of the growing Duncan Thaw with those of the alienated adult Lanark. The book, which had been in gestation for more than twenty years, established Gray as a leading figure in contemporary Scottish writing. *Unlikely Stories, Mostly* (1983), a collection of elaborately illustrated shorter works, was followed by *1982, Janine* (1984), an investigation of personal and political inadequacy mediated through the sadomasochistic fantasies of a depressed electrical engineer. Among the most warmly received of his subsequent works have been *Poor Things* (1992), a pastiche of the Victorian mystery novel, and *Old Men in Love* (2007), both of which employ multiple narratives and feature Gray himself in the role of semi-fictional editor. Gray's interest in the status of the book as artefact is vindicated in his handsomely designed *Book of Prefaces* (2000), a collection of introductory essays and verses by great English, Irish, Scottish, and American writers from the 7th century to the present, with glosses by the editor and a range of contemporary authors from Roger Scruton to Iain Crichton *Smith. Other works include the novellas *The Fall of Kelvin Walker* (1985) and *McGrotty and Ludmilla* (1990), both reworkings of earlier dramatic material; *Something Leather* (1990), which advertised itself as an attempt to combine 'the amenities of a novel with the varieties of a short story collection'; and *A History Maker* (1994), a futuristic tale set in the 23rd-century Scottish borders.

GRAY, David (1838–61) Scottish poet, born in Duntiblae, Kirkintilloch, the son of a handloom weaver, and educated at the University of Glasgow. Befriended by Robert *Buchanan and Monckton *Milnes, he was struck by consumption; he lived just long enough to see the proofs of *The Luggie and Other Poems* (1862), the title poem of which is a blank verse celebration of the river Luggie. The sonnets he wrote while approaching death have many echoes of John *Keats, whom he greatly admired.

GRAY, John Henry (1866–1934) Poet, born in Woolwich of a Nonconformist background. He became a Roman Catholic, was ordained in 1901, and spent many years as rector of St Peter's in Edinburgh. He was a friend of Oscar *Wilde, who encouraged the publication of his first volume of poetry, *Silverpoints* (1893), which contained translations from Paul *Verlaine and Stéphane *Mallarmé. He published other volumes of poetry, booklets of devotional verse, and a surreal novel, *Park: A Fantastic Story* (1932), set in the future. His long poem 'The Flying Fish' first appeared in *The *Dial* in 1896, and was republished in *The Long Road* (1926). A life by Brocard Sewell, *In the Dorian Mode*, was published in 1983.

GRAY, Simon (1936–2008) Playwright, director, and novelist, educated at Westminster School, Dalhousie University, Halifax, Nova Scotia, and Trinity College, Cambridge. He is best known for his plays about the problems and contradictions of middle-class and academic life, many of which show a clear debt to his Cambridge years: these include *Butley* (1971), *The Common Pursuit* (1984; the title an oblique tribute to F. R. *Leavis), and *Hidden Laughter* (1990). His novels include *Little Portia* (1967), inspired by his time as a language teacher in Cambridge, as was his play *Quartermaine's Terms* (1981). He has also written accounts of his career and theatrical involvement: *Fat Chance* (1995) tells the disastrous story of the production and collapse of his play about espionage, *Cell Mates* (1995). He has frequently collaborated with Harold Pinter, and in 2004 Pinter directed Gray's *The Old Masters*, a play concerned with artistic provenance and its significance. In the same year, Gray published a frank and comic account of his life, *The Smoking Diaries. Little Nell*, a play about *Dickens and his mistress Ellen Ternan, was produced in 2007.

GRAY, Thomas (1716–71) Poet, born in London, the son of a scrivener or professional scribe. He was educated at Eton College, with Horace *Walpole, and at Peterhouse, Cambridge. He accompanied Walpole on a tour of France and Italy in 1739–41, but they quarrelled and returned home separately. In 1741 Gray's father died, leaving the family financially insecure. In 1742 Gray moved to Cambridge, where he was to live, apart from travels and visits, for the rest of his life, first at Peterhouse, then from 1756 at Pembroke College; in 1741–2 he began to write English rather than Latin poetry, including *Ode on a Distant Prospect of Eton College* (1747), the first of his works to appear in print. In June 1742 his Etonian friend the poet Richard West died, prompting Gray's tributary 'Sonnet on the Death of West'. Reconciled with Walpole in 1745, the following year Gray showed him some of his poetry, including the beginning of his **Elegy Written in a Country Church-Yard* (1751); in 1750 he completed the elegy at Stoke Poges, where his mother and aunt had lived since 1742. The cat celebrated in 'Ode on the Death of a Favourite Cat' (1748) was Walpole's. In 1754 Gray finished his Pindaric ode, *The *Progress of Poesy*, and in 1757 a second Pindaric ode, *The *Bard*, both remarkably ambitious and intense; both were published by Walpole in 1757, the first works printed by the Strawberry Hill Press. He was offered the laureateship on the death of Colley *Cibber in that year, but declined. He turned to antiquarian studies and *'picturesque' travels in Scotland and the Lake District. New discoveries of Old Norse and Celtic poetry prompted Gray to produce various imitations, including 'The Fatal Sisters' and 'The Descent of Odin' (written 1761; pub. 1768). In 1768 he was made professor of modern history at Cambridge. After his death, William *Mason constructed an edition of Gray's poems with accompanying 'Memoirs' out of Gray's papers, including his *Journal* of his visit to the Lakes. This was a model for *Boswell's **Life of Johnson*, but involved some falsification of the materials. See *Correspondence of Thomas Gray*, ed. P. Toynbee and L. Whibley, with additions by H. W. Starr, 3 vols (1971); Robert Mack, *Thomas Gray: A Life* (2000). The standard editions of the poems are by H. W. Starr and J. R. Hendrickson (1966) and Roger Lonsdale (with William *Collins and Oliver *Goldsmith, 1969).

Great Awakening Though sometimes applied to other periods, this phrase initially describes the religious revival of the mid-18th century in the USA, most famously showing itself through the writings of Jonathan *Edwards.

Great Expectations A novel by Charles *Dickens, which first appeared in *All the Year Round* 1860–61, in volume form 1861. It describes the development of the character of the narrator, Philip Pirrip, commonly known as 'Pip', a village boy brought up by his tyrannical sister, the wife of the gentle blacksmith Joe Gargery. He is introduced to the house of Miss Havisham, who, half-crazed by the desertion of her lover on her bridal night, has brought up the girl Estella to use her beauty as a means of torturing men. Pip falls in love with Estella, and aspires to become a gentleman. Money and expectations of more wealth come to him from a mysterious source, which he believes to be Miss Havisham. He goes to London, and in his new mode of life meanly abandons the devoted Joe Gargery, a humble connection of whom he is now ashamed. Misfortunes come upon him. His benefactor proves to be an escaped convict, Abel Magwitch, whom he, as a boy, had helped; his great expectations fade away and he is penniless. Estella marries his sulky enemy Bentley Drummle, by whom she is cruelly ill treated. Taught by adversity, Pip returns to Joe Gargery and honest labour, and is finally reunited with Estella, who has also learnt her lesson. Other notable characters in the book are Joe's uncle, the impudent old impostor Pumblechook; Jaggers, the skilful Old Bailey lawyer, and his good-hearted clerk Wemmick; and Pip's friend in London, Herbert Pocket. John *Forster's life of Dickens suggests that the author originally devised a less happy ending to the story, which he altered in deference to the advice of Edward *Bulwer-Lytton. The novel's powerful exploration of complex cultural and psychological conflicts has secured an enduring popularity, and a high critical reputation.

Greaves, Sir Launcelot, The Adventures of Novel by Tobias *Smollett, published 1762. Smollett's shortest novel, this was written in episodes (some of them while in prison for libel in 1760) for Smollett's periodical *British Magazine*, and thus stands as an early model for serial fiction, in which form it was praised by Oliver *Goldsmith. Launcelot is handsome, learned, and good, but when the book opens he is unfortunately crazed by the loss of Aurelia, who has been compelled to break with him by her vindictive uncle. Together with his absurd cowardly squire Crabshaw, and his horse Bronzomarte, Launcelot undertakes a quixotic life of knight errantry, warring against the enemies of virtue and reason. During his adventure on the road between London and York he is involved in many brawls in the cause of justice; he is trapped and abducted; embroiled in a violent election; challenged to a tournament; denounced by the misanthropic charlatan Ferret; and thrown into the prison of the atrocious Judge Gobble. After a terrible period in a madhouse, Launcelot recovers and Aurelia is at last restored to him. The imitation of *Cervantes works as a satiric device against the corrupt society Launcelot encounters; his 'reason' exposes social 'madness'.

GREEN, Henry (1905–73) Novelist, pseudonym of Henry Vincent Yorke, born near Tewkesbury, Gloucestershire, and educated at Eton College and Magdalen College, Oxford. The first of his nine novels, *Blindness* (1926), was published during his first year as an undergraduate and had been written while he was still at school; his second, *Living* (1929), in marked contrast, describes life on a factory floor in Birmingham, and is based on his own experiences working for the family firm H. Pontifex and Sons; he himself rose from the shop floor to become managing director, and the novel vividly records working-class idiom. It also manifests the idiosyncrasies of prose—dropped articles, sentences without verbs, a highly individual use of colloquial language in both narrative and dialogue—which contribute to his work's distinctive quality. *Party Going* (1939), describing a group of rich, idle young people, delayed at a London railway station in fog, has strong symbolic suggestions in an apparently trivial narrative. This was followed by his autobiographical *Pack my Bag: A Self-Portrait* (1940) and further novels: *Caught* (1943); *Loving* (1945), one of his most admired works, which describes life above and below stairs in an Irish country house during wartime, with a notable portrait of the butler, Raunce (*see* 'BIG HOUSE' FICTION); *Back* (1946); *Concluding* (1948); *Nothing* (1950); and *Doting* (1952); the latter two written almost wholly in dialogue. Although he liked to describe himself as 'a business man whose pastime was romancing over a bottle to a good band', he was a highly conscious and original artist, who has always commanded more admiration from fellow writers than from the common reader. See Jeremy Treglown, *Romancing: The Life and Work of Henry Green* (2000).

GREEN, John Richard (1837–83) Educated at Magdalen College School and at Jesus College, Oxford, where he was unhappy and did badly. After a spell as a curate in the East End of London he took to journalism, contributing frequently to the **Saturday Review*. He is best known for his *Short History of the English People* (1874), dedicated to William *Stubbs and Edward *Freeman, who encouraged his career as a historian. This work, which was immensely popular, was remarkable for its broad approach, vigorous style, generosity of outlook, and attention to the social, economic, and intellectual aspects of national history. Green aimed to chart 'the growth...of the people itself' and to produce an account in which 'Aidan and Bede would claim more space than the wars of the Anglo-Saxon kingdoms'. It was enlarged in *The History of the English People* (1877–80).

GREEN, Matthew (1697–1737) Poet. He appears to have had Quaker connections, and was employed at the Customs House; his only literary friend was Richard *Glover, to whom he left his manuscripts. His posthumous poem *The Spleen* (1737) advises on melancholy and recommends in fluent octosyllabics a simple country life; Green imagines 'a farm some twenty miles from town' where he could live (with occasional visits to London) on 'two hundred pounds half-yearly paid'.

GREEN, Thomas Hill (1836–82) Born near Ferrybridge, Yorkshire, educated at Rugby and Balliol College, Oxford. He was a fellow of Balliol 1866–78 (the first not to be ordained into the Church of England), and was appointed White's professor of moral philosophy in 1878. Green's philosophical publications began with a criticism of *Locke, *Hume, and *Berkeley in the form of two very full introductions to a new edition of Hume's *Treatise of Human Nature*. Mary *Ward pays tribute to his persistent influence in her sympathetic portrait of him as Henry Grey in *Robert Elsmere* (1888); she quotes from his *The Witness of God, and Faith: Two Lay Sermons* (1883) and describes him as one who held 'a special place in the hearts of men who can neither accept fairy tales, nor reconcile themselves to a world without faith'. See *The Collected Works of T. H. Green*, ed. P. P. Nicholson, 5 vols (1997).

GREENAWAY, Kate (1846–1901) Born in London, educated at Heatherley's and the Slade School; she wrote and illustrated children's books and magazines, designed Christmas cards, and exhibited pictures of attractive children playing picturesquely. Her reputation was established when the influential printer Edmund Evans produced *Under the Window* (1878) for Routledge. This collection of rhymes for children which she both wrote and illustrated became an instant best-seller. She thereafter produced nine of her own books (1880–89) and a series of almanacs (1883–95), and illustrated others' work including Robert *Browning's *The Pied Piper of Hamelin* (1888). Her innocent vision of childhood was admired by John *Ruskin, with whom she corresponded.

Greenaway's influence extends beyond her illustrations: her pictures of pretty children in old-fashioned clothes playing in idyllic gardens permeated culture, from fashion and design to the very meaning of childhood. See M. H. Spielmann and G. S. Layard, *Kate Greenaway* (1905); R. Engen, *Kate Greenaway: A Biography* (1981).
See also PICTUREBOOKS.

GREENAWAY, Peter (1942–) Film-maker, who emerged as a creator of complex and enigmatic feature films with *The Draughtsman's Contract* (1982), having made shorter avant-garde films for twenty years, often with *postmodern literary, visual, and musical associations. Among his most significant features are a savagely neo-Jacobean revenge drama, *The Cook, the Thief, his Wife and her Lover* (1989), and a phantasmagoric treatment of *The *Tempest* in *Prospero's Books* (1991), in which John Gielgud speaks all the characters' lines and narrates. Originally trained as a painter, Greenaway is prolific in many forms, including large-scale exhibitions and installations. He collaborated with the painter Tom *Phillips on *A TV Dante* (1989), presenting the first eight cantos of the *Inferno*, and has written many opera libretti, one of which has been composed by Louis Andriessen. Running through his work is the mythic figure of Tulse Luper, ostensibly an ornithologist, who has figured in a variety of films and exhibitions.

GREENE, Graham (1904–91) Novelist and playwright, educated at Berkhamsted School, where his father was headmaster, then at Balliol College, Oxford; a book of verse, *Babbling April* (1925), was published while he was still at Oxford. He joined the Roman Catholic Church in 1926, married in 1927, and was from 1926 to 1930 on the staff of *The *Times*, which he left in order to attempt to make a living as a writer. His first three novels (1929–31), which he later disclaimed, made little impression, but *Stamboul Train* (1932) sold well and was followed by many increasingly successful novels, short stories, books of reportage and travel, plays, children's books, etc. Greene describes his own early years in *A Sort of Life* (1971), which gives a vivid impression of a manic-depressive temperament tempted by deadly nightshade and Russian roulette, and a literary imagination nourished by influences as diverse as Stanley *Weyman, Marjorie *Bowen, and Robert *Browning. Greene remarked that 'if I were to choose an epigraph for all the novels I have written, it would be from *Bishop Blougram's Apology*:

> Our interest's on the dangerous edge of things,
> The honest thief, the tender murderer,
> The superstitious atheist...'

His pursuit of danger (despite quieter interludes, e.g. as literary editor on the **Spectator* and *Night and Day*) dominated much of his life and travels, as described in his second volume of autobiography, *Ways of Escape* (1980). His novels include *England Made Me* (1935); *The Power and the Glory* (1940); *The Heart of the Matter* (1948); *The End of the Affair* (1951; a wartime love affair with strong religious-supernatural touches modified by Greene himself in a later version); *The Quiet American* (1955, set in Vietnam); *A Burnt-out Case* (1961, set in a leper colony in the Congo); *The Honorary Consul* (1973, set in Argentina); and *The Human Factor* (1978, a secret service novel). Other works of fiction he classed as 'entertainments': these include *Brighton Rock* (1938, paradoxically the first novel in which critics detected a strong Catholic message, not surprisingly, in view of the fact that it introduces what was to be his central concept of 'the appalling strangeness of the mercy of God'); *The Confidential Agent* (1939); *Loser Takes All* (1955); and *Our Man in Havana* (1958). *The Third Man* (1950), also described as an entertainment, was originally written as a screenplay and filmed (1949) by Carol Reed (1906–76; *see* EXPRESSIONISM). Greene's plays include *The Living Room* (1953), *The Potting Shed* (1957), and *The Complaisant Lover* (1959). He also published travel books, describing journeys in Liberia (*Journey without Maps*, 1936), Mexico (*The Lawless Roads*, 1939), and Africa (*In Search of a Character: Two African Journals*, 1961). His *Collected Essays* appeared in 1969. His range as a writer is wide, both geographically and in variations of tone, but his preoccupations with moral dilemma (personal, religious, and political), his attempts to distinguish 'good-or-evil' from 'right-or-wrong', and his persistent choice of 'seedy' (a word which he was to regret popularizing) locations give his work a highly distinctive and recognizable quality, while his skilful variations of popular forms (the thriller, the detective story) have brought him a rare combination of critical and popular admiration. There is a biography by Norman Sherry (3 vols, 1989, 1994, 2004).

GREENE, Robert (1558–92) Author and playwright, born in Norwich, educated at St John's College and Clare College, Cambridge (1575–83), and incorporated MA at Oxford (1588). From about 1585 he lived mainly in London. Although he liked to stress his university connections, his literary persona was that of a feckless drunkard, who abandoned his wife and children to throw himself on the mercies of tavern hostesses and whores; writing pamphlets and plays was supposedly a last resort when his credit failed. He is said to have died of a surfeit of Rhenish wine and pickled herrings, though it was more likely to have been plague, of which there was a severe outbreak in 1592. Greene was attacked at length by Gabriel *Harvey in *Four Letters* (1592) as the 'Ape of *Euphues' and 'Patriarch of shifters'; in the same year, Thomas *Nashe defended him in *Strange News*, acknowledging Greene to have been a drunkard and a debtor, but claiming that 'He inherited more virtues than vices.' Greene's 38 or so publications, progressing from moral dialogues to prose romances, romantic plays, and finally realistic accounts of underworld life, bear out Nashe's assertion that printers were only too glad 'to pay him dear for the very dregs of his wit'. The sententious moral tone of his works suggests that his personal fecklessness and reported deathbed repentance may have been largely a pose.

Among the more attractive of his romances are the *Lylyan sequel *Euphues his Censure to Philautus* (1587); **Pandosto* and *Perimedes the Blacksmith* (1588); and **Menaphon* (1589). Among his 'repentance' pamphlets are *Greene's Mourning Garment*, *Greene's Never Too Late* (1590), and the attributed **Greene's Groat's-Worth of Wit* (1592). *Greene's Vision* (1592) is a fictionalized account of his deathbed repentance in which he receives advice from Geoffrey *Chaucer, John *Gower, and King Solomon. The low-life pamphlets include *A Notable Discovery of Coosenage* (1591) and three 'coney-catching' pamphlets in the same years 1591–2. His eight plays were all published posthumously. The best known are *Orlando furioso* (1594), **Friar Bacon and Friar Bungay* (1594), and **James the Fourth* (1598), of which there are editions by J. A. Lavin and N. Sanders.

Greene is renowned for his connections with William *Shakespeare. The attack on him in **Greene's Groat's-Worth of Wit* as an 'upstart crow, beautified with our feathers' is the first reference to Shakespeare as a London dramatist; and his *Pandosto* provided Shakespeare with the source for *The Winter's Tale*. The voluminousness of Greene's works and the supposed profligacy of his life have caused him to be identified with the typical university wit who becomes an Elizabethan hack-writer; he probably provided a name and a model for the swaggering Nick Greene in Virginia *Woolf's *Orlando* (1928). Greene's works were edited in 15 volumes by Alexander *Grosart (1881–6).

Greene's Groat's-Worth of Wit, *Bought with a Million of Repentance* A prose tract attributed to Robert *Greene, but edited and probably written by Henry *Chettle, published in 1592.

It begins with the death of the miser Gorinius, who leaves the bulk of his large fortune to his elder son Lucanio, and only 'an old groat' to the younger, Roberto (i.e. the author's persona), 'wherewith I wish him to buy a groat's-worth of wit'. Roberto conspires with a courtesan to fleece his brother, but the courtesan betrays him, subsequently ruining Lucanio for her sole profit. The gradual degradation of Roberto is then narrated, and the tract ends with the curious 'Address' to his fellow playwrights Christopher *Marlowe, Thomas *Lodge, and George *Peele, urging them to spend their wits to better purpose than on the making of plays. It contains the well-known passage about the 'upstart crow, beautified with our feathers', the '**Johannes Fac Totum*', who 'is in his own conceit the onely Shake-scene in a country', which probably refers to William *Shakespeare as a non-graduate dramatist newly arrived in London.

GREENLAND, Colin (1954–) Novelist, born in Dover. His works of *fantasy and *science fiction include the inventive neo-space operas *Take Back Plenty* (1990) and *Harm's Way* (1993). *Finding Helen* (2003) is a contemporary novel with fantastic elements. *The Entropy Exhibition* (1983) is a study of the *new wave.

GREENLAW, Lavinia (1962–) Poet and novelist, born in London and educated at Kingston Polytechnic and the Courtauld Institute. Her first volume of poems, *Night Photograph* (1993), includes poems on scientific subjects whose combinations of precision and wonder are indebted to Elizabeth *Bishop. *A World Where News Travelled Slowly* (1997) and *Minsk* (2003) refine her characteristically taut style, returning often to matters of difficult communication, travel, restlessness, and a hypersensitivity to changes of internal and external weather. More recent works include *Thoughts of a Night Sea* (photographs by Garry Fabian Miller; 2003), and the memoir *The Importance of Music to Girls* (2007). *Mary George of Allnorthover* (2001) and *An Irresponsible Age* (2006) are novels.

Green-sleeves The name of an inconstant lady who is the subject of a ballad; its earliest surviving complete form was published in 1584. The ballad, and the tune to which it was sung, became and remain very popular; both are mentioned by William *Shakespeare in *The Merry Wives of Windsor*, II. i and V. v.

GREENWELL, Dora (1821–82) Poet and essayist, who published seven volumes of poetry 1848–71, of which *Carmina Crucis* (1869), described by her as 'roadside songs with both joy and sorrow in them', was particularly admired. An evangelical Anglican who led a largely secluded life, her longer prose works were on religious subjects, but her essays covered a variety of social causes including women's education, child labour, and the education of the disabled. In this latter cause she edited a series of stories for children urging decent treatment for 'imbeciles'. She was a friend of Josephine Butler, met Elizabeth Barrett *Browning, and corresponded with Christina *Rossetti: John *Whittier wrote the introduction to the US edition of one of her prose works.

GREENWOOD, Walter (1903–74) Novelist and dramatist, born in Salford and educated at the local council school. He is chiefly remembered for his classic novel of life in a northern town during the Slump, *Love on the Dole* (1933; dramatized 1934; filmed 1941), into which he funnelled his own experience of poverty, deprivation, and unemployment. He wrote nine further novels, several plays, a book of short stories, and a volume of autobiography, *There Was a Time* (1967).

GREER, Germaine (1939–) Australian scholar and journalist. She was born in Melbourne, the daughter of an insurance executive, and educated at the universities of Melbourne, Sydney, and Cambridge, where she completed a Ph.D. thesis on Shakespearian comedy. While teaching at the University of Warwick (1968–72), she published her first book, *The Female Eunuch* (1970), a classic of modern feminist argument; this was followed by *The Obstacle Race* (1979), a discussion of the difficulties of women painters, and of their critical neglect; *Sex and Destiny* (1984); and other sociological works, along with the literary study *Shakespeare* (1986). *The Madwoman's Underclothes* (1986) is a collection of essays and occasional pieces (1968–85); *Daddy We Hardly Knew You* (1989) is a family memoir; *The Change* (1991) discusses the menopause; and *The Whole Woman* (1999) reconsiders the progress of feminism. She returned to academic life at Newnham College, Cambridge (1989–97), and published *Slip-Shod Sibyls: Recognition, Rejection and the Woman Poet* (1995), a challenging view of women poets, known and little known, which does not spare what Greer sees as their failings as writers. Later work includes *The Boy* (2003), a study of male beauty in art. There is an unauthorized biography by Christine Wallace (1997).

GREG, Sir Walter Wilson (1875–1959) Scholar and bibliographer, educated at Harrow School and Trinity College, Cambridge, where he was friends with R. B. *McKerrow. His first substantial publication (1900) was a finding-list of English plays written before 1700 which was the beginning of his monumental *A Bibliography of the English Printed Drama to the Restoration* (1939–59). In 1906 he founded, and was general editor of (1906–39), the *Malone Society. His edition of Philip *Henslowe's Diary and Papers (1904–8) is an outstanding example of his palaeographical abilities and his knowledge of Elizabethan theatrical history, which he further developed in later works. Greg pioneered the New Bibliography, raising scholarly standards by his constructive reviews, and applying his skill in palaeography and textual criticism to editions of manuscript plays, notably *Sir Thomas *More* (1911), and in his other works, including *Dramatic Documents from the Elizabethan Playhouses* (1931) and *English Literary Autographs, 1550–1650* (1925–32). In his last and most fruitful years he published a remarkable parallel-text edition of *'Doctor Faustus' 1604–1616* (1950), and important accounts of *The Editorial Problem in Shakespeare* (1942), *The Shakespeare First Folio* (1955), and *Some Aspects and Problems of London Publishing between 1550 and 1650* (1956).

GREGG, Percy (1836–89) Born in Bury St Edmunds; author and political journalist among whose novels *Across the Zodiac: The Story of a Wrecked Record* (1880) was one of the first novels to imagine a voyage to another planet by means of a spaceship. Its antigravity propulsion may have influenced H. G. *Wells's 'cavorite'. The Mars reached by the spaceship is an ambiguous *utopia, scientifically advanced, but socially menacing. *Interleaves* (1875) is a book of poetry: other poetry collections were published as by Lionel H. Holdreth.

GREGORY, Augusta, Lady (1852–1932) Née Persse, born at Roxborough, Co. Galway; dramatist, folklorist, and literary patron. She married the former MP and governor of Ceylon Sir William Gregory, of nearby *Coole Park, in 1880, and was widowed in 1892. A leading figure in the *Irish Revival, she assisted W. B. *Yeats and Edward *Martyn in the foundation of the *Irish Literary Theatre, forerunner of the *Abbey Theatre, for which she became playwright, director, and patent holder. She helped popularize Irish legends with her translations *Cuchulain of Muirthemne* (1902) and *Gods and Fighting Men* (1904), and Irish folklore with *Poets and Dreamers* (1903), *A Book of Saints and Wonders* (1906; enl. 1907), and *Visions and Beliefs in the West of Ireland* (1920). Gregory's Gaelic-derived idiom (often called 'Kiltartanese') and knowledge of folklore were assets in her collaboration with Yeats on several plays including *Cathleen ni Houlihan* (1902), of which she wrote at least half, and *The Unicorn from the Stars* (1908). The best known of her many one-act plays are *Spreading the News* (1904) and *The Rising of the Moon* (1907). *Our Irish Theatre* (1913) is her partisan account of the Abbey's early years. Gregory's stance as a cultural nationalist culminated in her fight for the return to Ireland of 39 French Impressionist pictures collected by her nephew Sir Hugh Lane, who drowned in the sinking of the *Lusitania* in 1915 leaving an unwitnessed codicil to his will, a campaign she partly recorded in *Hugh Lane's Life and Achievement* (1921). Adapted versions of the sonnets she wrote during her 1882–3 affair with Wilfrid Scawen *Blunt were published by Blunt under his own name as 'A Woman's Sonnets' in 1892. Gregory's collected works are published in the Coole Edition (1970–82), ed. Colin Smythe.

GREGORY, Robert (1881–1918) Artist. The son of Sir William and Lady Augusta *Gregory, he designed sets for early *Abbey Theatre productions. He joined the Royal Flying Corps in 1916 and was killed in action. W. B. *Yeats wrote several commemorative poems about him, including 'An Irish Airman Foresees his Death' and 'In Memory of Major Robert Gregory'.

GREGORY I, St (Gregory the Great) (*c.*540–604) One of the greatest of the early popes (from 590), a reformer of monastic discipline and a prolific writer whose works include the *Cura Pastoralis* (*see* ALFRED), the *Dialogues*, and famous collections of letters and sermons. He sent *Augustine of Canterbury to England. *Bede (*History*, II. i) writes that, seeing Anglo-Saxon boys for sale in the slave market at Rome, he remarked: 'Not *Angli* but *Angeli*, if they were Christians.' The story that he delivered the emperor Trajan from hell by his prayers, touched by his humility and justice, is mentioned by *Aquinas, by *Dante more than once, and by Langland (**Piers Plowman*, B XI. 140ff.). See *Dialogues*, trans. O. J. Zimmerman (1959, repr. 1977); R. A. Markus, *Gregory the Great and His World* (1997).

GREGORY OF TOURS (*c.*540–594) Bishop of Tours, whose *Historia Francorum* is the chief authority for the early Merovingian period of French history. He places in 520 the raid against the Frisian territory of the Franks by a Scandinavian leader 'Chochilaicus' (in Latin) who has been identified with the Geatish king Hygelac in **Beowulf*; the raid is mentioned in *Beowulf* at lines 1207, 2357, 2503, and 2912. Gregory's identification provides the only historical corroboration for any character or event in the poem.

Gregynog Press A *private press founded in 1923 at Gregynog Hall, Powys, Wales, and endowed by the sisters Gwendoline (1882–1951) and Margaret (1884–1963) Davies as part of their plan to establish an arts and crafts centre. In addition to fine printing, it excelled in craft bindings, and survived until 1941. It was revived in 1974 as 'Gwasg Gregynog'.

Grendel *See* BEOWULF.

GRENFELL, Julian (1888–1915) Poet, educated at Eton College and Balliol College, Oxford. He loved hunting and games, and joined the regular army in 1910. In 1914, he was sent to France with the Royal Dragoons, where he won the DSO but was killed in May 1915. The day after his death, his celebrated poem 'Into Battle' appeared in *The *Times*, and it is for this much-anthologized poem that he is usually remembered. See Nicholas *Mosley, *Julian Grenfell* (1976).

GREVILLE, Charles Cavendish Fulke (1794–1865) Politician and man of public affairs, who was for many years clerk to the Privy Council. From 1820 to 1860 he kept a detailed diary of his life in the inner circles of politics and power. He was the friend and trusted confidant of both Whigs and Tories, and includes in his work many lively portraits of friends and colleagues, such as the duke of *Wellington and Lord Palmerston. His *Memoirs* were first edited and published in 1874–87; see also the edition by Lytton *Strachey and Roger Fulford, 8 vols (1938).
See DIARIES.

GREVILLE, Sir Fulke, first Baron Brooke (1554–1628) Courtier and writer, educated at Shrewsbury School, where he was an exact contemporary of his close friend Philip *Sidney, and at Jesus College, Cambridge. From the mid-1570s he was at court, where he served as secretary to the principality of Wales, treasurer of the navy, and chancellor of the exchequer. Francis *Bacon and Samuel *Daniel were among his friends. In 1621 he was created Baron Brooke and granted Warwick Castle and Knowle Park by *James I. He was murdered by a servant, Ralph Heywood, who then killed himself. An elegy on Sidney was published in *The Phoenix Nest* (1593), but most of his writings were published posthumously in *Certain Learned and Elegant Works* (1633). They include a sonnet sequence *Caelica*, which is serious, high-minded, and unadorned, like most of his productions. His two Senecan tragedies *Mustapha* (published 1609) and *Alaham* were written, in their earliest versions, before the fall of *Essex in February 1601, and are severe, moral studies of political power. His neo-Stoic *Letter to an Honourable Lady* belongs to 1589, the verse *Treatise of Monarchy* to about 1600, and his major prose work, *A Dedication to Sir Philip Sidney*, was probably begun in 1610. Greville was a compulsive reviser, however, and many works survive in variant versions. Often he seems to change his mind about his central theme or purpose. The *Dedication to Sir Philip Sidney* is as much about his own political ideals and disappointments as about his friend's career, and in its printed version (1652, as *The Life of Sir Philip Sidney*) it incorporates judgements of *Elizabeth I, whose biography he planned to write. His best-known lines, from the Priests' Chorus in *Mustapha*, epitomize much of his thought:

> 'Oh wearisome condition of humanity!
> Born under one law, to another bound:
> Vainly begot, and yet forbidden vanity,
> Created sick, commanded to be sound.'

His *Poems and Dramas* were edited by Geoffrey *Bullough (1939); *The Remains* by G. Wilkes (1965); the *Life of Sir Philip Sidney* by D. Nowell Smith (1907); *Prose Works* by J. Gouws (1986). There are biographies by R. A. Rebholz (1971), Joan Rees (1971), and C. H. Larson (1980). See also Richard Waswo, *The Fatal Mirror* (1972).

GREY, Zane (1872–1939) American novelist, born in Zanesville, Ohio, who is remembered for his many novels of the Old West. His reading of Owen *Wister's *The Virginian* (1902) suggested this subject to him and from 1908 onwards Grey produced many *westerns. One of the most famous was *Riders of the Purple Sage* (1912), about a tyrannical Mormon community in Utah. Grey also published a number of essays and books on hunting and fishing.

GRIEG, David (1969–) Scottish playwright, born in Edinburgh, raised in Nigeria, and educated at Bristol University. In 1990 he co-founded the Suspect Culture theatre group in Glasgow. Grieg was brought to prominence by *Europe* (1994), a play exploring the aftermath of the collapse of the Soviet Union, set on an unlocated station at which no train ever stops. He has had more than thirty-five plays produced, including *The Cosmonaut's Last Message to the Woman He Once Loved in the Former Soviet Union* (1999), *San Diego* (2003), and *The American Pilot* (2005).

GRIFFIN, Gerald (1803–40) London-based Irish dramatist, novelist, and poet, born in Limerick, who repudiated literature to become a Christian Brother. His best-known works are the novel *The Collegians* (1829), in which young Cregan, tempted by wealth and beauty, permits the murder of his humble country wife; and the song 'Aileen Aroon'. Dion *Boucicault's *The Colleen Bawn* is an adaptation of *The Collegians*. *Gisippus*, Griffin's blank verse classical drama, was produced at Drury Lane in 1842. See John Cronin, *Gerald Griffin: A Critical Biography* (1978).

GRIFFITH, Elizabeth (1727–93) Actress and playwright, born in Glamorgan. Her most successful plays were *The Double Mistake* (1766) and *The School for Rakes* (1769). She wrote several *epistolary novels, and published *A Series of Genuine Letters between Henry and Frances*, based on materials from her own courtship, in 1757.

GRIFFITH, George (1857–1906) Pen-name of George Chetwynd Griffith-Jones, *science fiction writer born in Plymouth. His popular magazine serials such as *The Angel of the Revolution* (1893) prefigured H. G. *Wells as stories of the apocalyptic future shaped by flight. *A Honeymoon in Space* (1900) imagined space travel.

GRIFFITH, Nicola (1960–) *Science fiction writer, born in Yorkshire, resident in the USA, whose first novel, *Ammonite* (1993), explored a single-gendered world. Her next novel, *Slow River* (1994), won the Science Fiction Writers of America's Nebula award. Later novels, including *Always* (2007), are crime fiction.

***Griffith Gaunt**, or Jealousy* A novel by Charles *Reade, published 1866. The story is set in the 18th century. Griffith Gaunt, an impoverished gentleman of Cumberland, wishes to marry Kate Payton, a spirited young Roman Catholic. She prefers another suitor, George Neville, but when Griffith loses his inheritance for her sake she accepts him, hoping for a contented marriage without undue submission. After some happy years, Griffith begins to drink heavily, and does not notice Kate's disguised but growing passion for her new spiritual director, Father Leonard. When he finds Kate and the priest walking together at a time when Kate is supposed to be ill in her room, he attacks Leonard with demonic violence and the terrified Kate renounces her love. Griffith gallops away, and in his fever is nursed by Mercy Vint, an innkeeper's daughter, whom he later bigamously marries. He briefly returns home to fetch some money, and the frenzied Kate tries to stab him. He escapes, but a disfigured body is later found in a mere and Kate is tried for murder. Mercy Vint walks miles with her child to save Kate. Eventually Kate and Griffith are happily reconciled, Mercy marries Kate's old suitor Neville, and the four live as neighbours, ostracized but happy in their good works. The novel, based on a story by Wilkie *Collins, was unusually frank for its time and Reade was prosecuted in a case in which Charles *Dickens ('as a husband and father') refused to help defend him. Reade's interest lay clearly not only in the theme of jealousy, both male and female, but in Kate's sexuality.

GRIFFITHS, Ann (1776–1805) Née Thomas, Calvinistic Methodist hymn-writer from Llanfihangel-yng-Ngwynfa, Montgomeryshire, whose 30 hymns are considered among the greatest religious poems in Welsh and whose life and work feature as an emblem of lost cultural integrity in the poetry of R. S. *Thomas.

GRIFFITHS, Trevor (1935–) Playwright, born and educated in Manchester. After university and National Service, he became involved with the Campaign for Nuclear Disarmament. His plays are all vitally concerned with socialist politics and history and, after an apprenticeship in the fringe, his *The Party* (1973) was staged at the *National Theatre, a play revisiting the political events of May 1968 in Paris, with Laurence Olivier in a lead role. He regards television as the most effective political medium, and his *Comedians* (1975) drew on the television series of that name to look at a group of aspiring comedians attending evening class. In 1971 he had provided the screenplay for Warren Beatty's *Reds*. In 1992, *The Gulf between Us* took a very critical stance on the Gulf War, and *Thatcher's Children* (1993) looked at the effects of Thatcherism on a generation born as Margaret Thatcher came into office.

GRIGSON, Geoffrey (1905–85) Poet and critic; born in Cornwall, educated at St Edmund Hall, Oxford, and editor of many publications, including the influential *New Verse* (1933–9), which he founded. His first volume of poetry, *Several Observations* (1939), was followed by others, including *Under the Cliff* (1943), *The Isles of Scilly* (1946), *Collected Poems 1924–1962* (1963), *Angles and Circles* (1974), and *History of Him* (1980). Much of his work celebrates his native Cornwall, and his collections of essays, which contributed to his reputation as a fierce controversialist, include *The Harp of Aeolus* (1947) and *The Contrary View* (1974). He also edited selections of work by William *Barnes (1950), John *Clare (1950), Walter Savage *Landor (1964), Charles *Cotton (1975), and others, and his eclectic reading is expressed in several Faber anthologies.

GRIMALD, Nicholas (1519/20–*c.*1562) Of Christ's College, Cambridge, and Oxford, chaplain to Bishop *Ridley. He wrote two Latin plays and contributed 40 poems to Richard *Tottel's *Miscellany* which he may have edited. In 1556, he published a translation of *Cicero's *De Officiis*; his Latin paraphrase of *Virgil's *Eclogues* appeared in 1591. He was admiringly commemorated in an elegy by Barnabe *Googe.

GRIMBALD (Grimbold), **St** (d. ?901) A monk of St Bertin at Saint-Omer, the details of whose life are uncertain. King *Alfred summoned him to England for the promotion of learning and acknowledges him as one of his teachers in the preface to the *Regula Pastoralis*. A *Life of Grimbald* survives in the *c.*1300 breviary of Hyde Abbey, Winchester.

GRIMM, Jacob Ludwig Carl (1785–1863) and **Wilhelm Carl** (1786–1859) German brothers who pioneered the study of German philology, law, mythology, and folklore. They are chiefly known in Britain for their collection of fairy-tales, *Kinder- und Hausmärchen* (1812–15), translated into English by Edgar Taylor with illustrations by George *Cruikshank in 1823 as *German Popular Stories*. The brothers regularly revised the collection (popularly known as 'Grimms' Fairy Tales') until 1858, increasingly directing them at children by removing bawdy material and inserting or intensifying Christian content. The pair also began the German etymological dictionary *Deutsches Wörterbuch*, the German equivalent of the **OED*, in 1852. The work was continued by others and completed in 1960. Jacob formulated 'Grimm's Law' of the mutation of consonants.

GRIMWOOD, Jon Courtenay Born on Malta; British journalist and novelist who combines *science fiction and crime modes. His 'Arabesk' trilogy (2001–3) is set in an alternate future where the Ottoman Empire has survived. *End of the World Blues* (2006) oscillates between near and far futures.

Gringolet (Gryngolet) Gawain's horse, in *Chrétien de Troyes's *Erec et Enide* (l. 3935), *Le Chevalier à l'épée* (l. 226), and *Sir *Gawain and the Green Knight* (l. 597).

GRISHAM, John (1955–) Prolific writer of legal thrillers. Born in Arkansas, he practised law and politics in Mississippi while writing *A Time to Kill* (1988). *The Firm* (1991) became a best-seller and Tom Cruise starred in the 1993 film. Writing a novel every year, Grisham sold over 60 million books during the 1990s.

Groat's-Worth of Wit *See* GREENE'S GROAT'S-WORTH OF WIT.

Grobian [German *Grobheit*, rudeness] An imaginary personage often referred to by writers of the 15th and 16th centuries in Germany as a type of boorishness. Sebastian Brant in his *Narrenschiff* (*see* SHIP OF FOOLS) invented St Grobianus as typical of ill-mannered and indecent behaviour. In 1549 Friedrich Dedekind, a German student, wrote a poem in Latin elegiacs, *Grobianus, de Morum Simplicitate*, a burlesque of the generally uncivilized social conditions then prevailing in Germany, in the form of ironical advice on conduct given to a gallant. This was translated into German by Kaspar Scheidt, and into English, and suggested to Thomas Dekker his **Gull's Horn-Book*.

GROCYN, William (?1449–1519) Scholar, educated at Winchester School and New College, Oxford. He held various academic and ecclesiastical preferments, studying in Italy with Thomas *Linacre and Hugh *Latimer under *Poliziano and Demetrius Chalcondyles (1423–1511). A friend of *Erasmus, John *Colet, and Thomas *More, he was the first to lecture on Greek at Oxford.

GRONNIOSAW, Ukawsaw (*c.*1705–1775) Writer of the first account of an African being taken into slavery in English, *A Narrative of the Most Remarkable Particulars in the Life of James Albert Ukawsaw Gronniosaw, an African Prince Written by Himself* (1772). After his escape from slavery he lived in Colchester and Kidderminster. *See* SLAVERY.

GROSART, Alexander Balloch (1827–99) Editor remembered for his reprints of rare Elizabethan and Jacobean literature; between 1868 and 1896 he edited more than 130 volumes.

GROSSETESTE, Robert (*c.*1170–1253) Bishop of Lincoln and the first chancellor of Oxford University. He was the author of translations from the Greek, including *Aristotle's *Ethics* and the works of Pseudo-Dionysius (*see* DIONYSIUS THE PSEUDO-AREOPAGITE). Though closely connected with the Franciscans in thought, he remained a secular throughout his life. He was a prolific, influential figure in the development of the Augustinian philosophical tradition, and was largely responsible for the Oxford emphasis on the development of the natural sciences. Some of his writings tackle theological topics with originality; others develop his interest in experimental science, especially optics and mathematics. Influenced by the Platonic tradition in Arab philosophy, he developed his light-metaphysic in his work *De Luce*. See R. W. Southern, *Robert Grosseteste: The Growth of an English Mind in Medieval Europe*, 2nd edn (1992); James McEvoy, *The Philosophy of Robert Grosseteste* (1983).

GROSSMITH, George (1847–1912) and **Weedon** (1852–1919) Brothers whose father was a friend of Henry *Irving, the *Terry family, and other theatrical people. Both pursued successful theatrical careers. *The *Diary of a Nobody* (1892), which appeared in **Punch*, was written by both brothers, and illustrated by Weedon. Its popularity with a wide range of readership was immediate, and has not faltered. *See* DIARIES.

Grosvenor Gallery, the Bond Street, London For the exhibition of pictures of the modern school, erected by Sir Coutts Lindsay in 1876. It was especially associated for a time with the *Aesthetic movement. Bunthorne in *Gilbert and Sullivan's **Patience* describes himself as:

> A pallid and thin young man,
> A haggard and lank young man,
> A greenery-yallery, Grosvenor Gallery,
> Foot-in-the-grave young man.

The Gallery closed in 1890. See Susan P. Casteras, *The Grosvenor Gallery* (1996).

GROTE, George (1794–1871) Historian, politician, and banker, educated at Charterhouse, MP for the City of London, 1832–41. He took an active part in favour of the Reform movement (*see* REFORM BILLS), publishing a pamphlet on the subject in 1820 and another in 1831. Radical and atheist, he was much influenced by James *Mill and *Utilitarianism. He retired from Parliament in order to devote himself to historical work. His famous *History of Greece*, in eight volumes, on which he had been intermittently at work since 1823, was published in 1846–56, and achieved immediate success. It was for many years the standard work on the subject. Grote's other publications include studies of *Plato (1865) and *Aristotle (1872), and various papers and essays on philosophical and ethical subjects.

GROTIUS, Hugo (1583–1645) Dutch statesman, jurist, playwright, and poet. He was born at Delft, studied law at Orléans and Leiden, and became the leader of the bar at The Hague. He wrote in 1601 a sacred drama in Latin, *Adamus Exsul*, with which John *Milton was probably familiar when he wrote **Paradise Lost*. Grotius was on a deputation to London in 1613, but his intimacy with John van Oldenbarnavelt (1547–1619), who was executed for conspiracy against the state, led to his condemnation to life imprisonment. He escaped in a large box in which books were sent to him for the purpose of study, and took refuge in Paris. He became the ambassador of Queen Christina of Sweden at the French court, and died, after shipwreck, in her service. He wrote many works, including a Latin history of the revolt of the Netherlands. But his principal claim to fame is his great treatise of international law, the *De Jure Belli ac Pacis*, published in 1625. In the midst of the Thirty Years War (1618–48) he asserted in this work the principle of a rule of law binding upon nations in their relations with one another.

Group, the An informal association of writers, mostly poets, set up in London by Philip *Hobsbaum, with his then wife, poet Hannah Kelly, in 1955. A number of poems or a chapter of a novel (which had been previously distributed to other participants) would be read aloud by the author and discussed by all present. Members included Peter *Redgrove, Peter *Porter, Edward *Lucie-Smith, and George *MacBeth. An anthology of the Group's writings, edited by Hobsbaum and Lucie-Smith, appeared in 1963 (*A Group Anthology*). When Hobsbaum moved to Belfast he established a similar group there in 1963, usually known now as the 'Belfast Group'. Members included Seamus *Heaney, Michael *Longley, and Paul *Muldoon. From 1966, when Hobsbaum went to Glasgow, meetings were organized by Heaney. See Heather Clark, *The Ulster Renaissance: Poetry in Belfast 1962–1972* (2006).

Grub Street According to Samuel *Johnson's *Dictionary*, 'originally the name of a street near Moorfields in London, much inhabited by writers of small histories, dictionaries, and temporary poems, whence any mean production is called *grubstreet*'. It ran north–south for a quarter of a mile through the insalubrious parish of St Giles Cripplegate. The name was changed in 1830 to Milton Street (in honour of a builder). See Pat Rogers, *Grub Street* (1972).

Grub Street Journal A satirical literary newspaper, which ran for 418 weekly issues, 8 January 1730 to 29 December 1737. Its first editors were John Martyn and Richard Russel. Alexander *Pope (whose enemies were reviled as 'Knights of the Bathos') was suspected of having had a hand in it, but the connection has not been proved. Its targets included John *Henley's *Hyp-Doctor*, Lewis *Theobald, Colley *Cibber, and Edmund *Curll. See James T. Hillhouse, *The Grub Street Journal* (1928).

Gryll In Edmund *Spenser's *The *Faerie Queene* (II. xii. 86), the hog in *Acrasia's Bower of Bliss who objected greatly at being changed back into a man. The incident is based on a dialogue of *Plutarch, in which Gryllus is one of the Greeks transformed into swine by Circe.

Gryll Grange The last satirical novel of Thomas Love *Peacock, serialized 1860, issued as a book 1861. Mr Falconer, idealist and classicist, lives in a tower attended by seven virgins, but is persuaded to join a convivial house party at Gryll Grange, where he woos and wins Morgana Gryll. A second plot concerns the courtship of the scientific, outgoing Lord Curryfin, and the musical, meditative Alice Niphet. As part of the Christmas festivities they act an Aristophanic play which parodies the competitive examinations newly introduced into the Civil Service: Hannibal, Richard Cœur de Lion, and Oliver Cromwell are all failed. Urbane and polished, *Gryll Grange* upholds civilization, harmony, and completeness against the rising prestige of technology and religious asceticism.

Guardian, The (1) A periodical started by Richard *Steele on 12 March 1713, ceasing 1 October 1713. Major contributors included Joseph *Addison, Eustace Budgell (1686–1737), George *Berkeley, and Alexander *Pope, whose attack on Ambrose *Philips is no. 40, and whose essay on gardens is no. 173. It was opposed politically by the Tory **Examiner* and was succeeded by the *Englishman*. See *The Guardian*, ed. J. C. Stephens (1982). (2) A national daily newspaper, generally thought to represent centre-left political views, originally published (1821–1959) as the **Manchester Guardian*.

GUARINI, Giovanni Battista (1538–1612) Italian playwright, born at Ferrara, author of the pastoral drama *Il pastor fido* (1589–1602), written in emulation of *Tasso's *Aminta*. It had a considerable vogue in England in the 17th century, where it was translated many times; notably by Sir Richard *Fanshawe in 1647 as *The Faithfull Shepherd* (ed. W. F. Staton and W. E. Simeone, 1964). Guarini also wrote an influential defence of tragicomedy, the *Compendio della poesia tragicomica* (1601).

Gudrun (1) In the **Völsunga Saga* and in Morris's **Sigurd the Volsung*, daughter of the king of the Niblungs. (2) Heroine of the *Laxdaela saga* (*see* SAGA), who appears in Morris's version, 'The Lovers of Gudrun', in *The *Earthly Paradise*. (3) Gudrun Brangwen in D. H. Lawrence's **Women in Love*.

GUICCIARDINI, Francesco (1483–1540) Florentine historian and statesman, employed by the *Medici and the papacy. His *Storia d'Italia*, a history of Italy from 1492 to 1534, was translated into English (from a French version) by Sir Geoffrey Fenton, and is of lasting significance; passages from it were inserted in the second edition of *Holinshed's *Chronicles*. Both *Ralegh and Francis *Bacon knew the work well, and *Gibbon proclaimed it 'from the point of view of intellectual power, the most important work to have issued from an Italian mind'. The *Ricordi*, a collection of aphorisms, was also widely known.

guidebooks Specialized works providing advice, recommendations, and instructions for travellers, associated with the rise of mass tourism in the mid-19th century. However, literature had long provided impetus and determined itineraries for travel: religious texts for pilgrims; classical works for those on the *Grand Tour. Accounts of those travels could include information on routes, accommodation, dangers, cultural differences, and the everyday needs of the traveller. The fifth book of the *Liber Sancti Jacobi*, a mid-12th-century pilgrim's guide to Santiago de Compostela, is often regarded as the first guidebook with its wide-ranging and opinionated advice.

Modern guidebooks provided practical information in an accessible format with no stylistic pretensions. Mariana Starke (1761/2–1838) introduced a number of their conventions into *Letters from Italy* (1800), including suggested itineraries and a rating system of one, two, or three exclamation marks for paintings. Accommodating the surge in continental travel after 1815, a number of companies marketed uniform series of guidebooks covering a range of countries, updated on a regular basis. Those of Karl *Baedeker and John *Murray became so well known that they served as synonyms for guidebook. Formal and objective, they conveyed an aura of cultural authority and released the less affluent traveller from dependence on personal guides or package tours. The Murrays introduced the term 'handbook', and helped create the stereotype of the tourist with guidebook in hand, subservient to the star ratings by which they ticked off sights and decided their responses. The guidebook's practical purpose allowed other travel writing to become more self-consciously literary and personal, to allow full play to a *Romantic sensibility, and to disparage mass tourism.

In the 20th century, James Muirhead (1853–1934) and his brother Findlay (1860–1935) followed the tradition with their *Blue Guides* from 1918. They were particularly authoritative on art and architecture. The *Footprint* series began with South America (1924), and aimed at independent travellers with unusual destinations. The American Eugene Fodor (1905–91) updated his guides yearly from 1936, with more quirky comments on cultural difference. The more democratic American series—Arthur Frommer (1929–) began with *Europe on $5 a Day* (1957) and the Harvard students' *Let's Go* series followed in 1960—incorporated reader feedback. In the 1970s a number of 'anti-tourist' tourist guides appeared, catering for the emerging backpacking phenomenon, including *Lonely Planet* (Melbourne) from 1973, and *Rough Guides* (London) from 1982. Special-interest guides also proliferated. The internet has facilitated further interaction between guidebook content and reader comment, creating a sense of online community among travellers, but the convenient format and portability of the handbook ensures it remains popular.

GUIDO DELLE COLONNE A 13th-century Sicilian writer of Latin romances, influential author of the *Historia Destructionis Troiae,* which was in fact a prose version of a poem by *Benoît de Sainte-Maure, although Guido does not acknowledge this. His romance was used as a source in poems attributed to John *Barbour and *Huchown, and by John *Lydgate in his *Troy Book*, as well as several anonymous poems. The story of Troilus and Cressida, which Guido took from Benoît, proved to be a compelling, popular narrative developed by *Boccaccio, *Chaucer, Robert *Henryson, and later *Shakespeare.

Guignol The chief character in the popular French puppet show of that name, similar to the English Punch and Judy show: Guignol is a variant (from Lyons) of the character of Polichinelle, who became Anglicized as *Punch. The word Guignol is also used for the theatre where the show is performed. Grand Guignol is a term applied to a theatre presenting plays of a gruesome character.

GUILLAUME DE LORRIS *See* ROMAN DE LA ROSE.

GUILPIN, Everard (b. *c.*1572) Presumed to be the author of *Skialetheia, or A Shadow of Truth, in Certain Epigrams and Satires* (1598). The seven satires, which inveigh against contemporary vices, have suggestive affinities with those of John *Marston and John *Donne. *Skialetheia* has been edited by D. Allen Carroll (1974).

Guinevere The wife of King *Arthur in the Arthurian legend. The name figures in various forms: in *Geoffrey of Monmouth she is 'Guanhamara', of a noble Roman family, brought up in the household of Cador, duke of Cornwall. In the *Brut* of *Laȝamon she is 'Wenhaver', a relative of Cador; in *Sir *Gawain and the Green Knight* she is Wenore, Guenore, Gwenore, and Gaynor (the form also in *The *Awntyrs of Arthure*). The most widespread form of both her name and her story developed in the French tradition, in *Chrétien's *Lancelot* (1170s) and the related early 13th-century Prose *Lancelot* of the Vulgate cycle, where the queen Guenièvre is the lover of Lancelot, with disastrous consequences: Lancelot fails to achieve the *Grail, and in the final confrontation with Modred he arrives too late to save Arthur, finding that the queen has become a nun. This traces only the main tradition of Guinevere, from Chrétien to *Malory; there is also a more disreputable version of her as unfaithful and vengeful, reflected in such poems as **Sir Launfal*. But in this main tradition, the tragic love of Guinevere and Lancelot is one of the classics of *courtly love.

'Guinevere' One of Tennyson's **Idylls of the King*, published 1859. It describes Guinevere's growing repentance, her parting with Launcelot, her last meeting with Arthur, and her death as abbess of the nunnery of Almesbury.

Gulliver's Travels A satire by Jonathan *Swift, published 1726 as *Travels into Several Remote Nations of the World 'By Lemuel Gulliver'*. Much cloak-and-dagger secrecy surrounded the publication; its textual history is far from straightforward, and the widely varying editions published by Benjamin Motte (1726) and George Faulkner (1735) are difficult to reconcile. The idea of a satire in the form of a travel narrative probably emerged at the meetings of the *Scriblerus Club; in the *Memoirs of Scriblerus* the hero is described as visiting the same countries as Gulliver. In the first part, Gulliver, a surgeon on a merchant ship, relates his shipwreck on the island of Lilliput, the inhabitants of which are 6 inches high, everything on the island being on the scale of an inch to a foot compared with things as we know them. Because of this miniaturization, the pomp of the emperor, the civil feuds of the inhabitants, the war with their neighbours across the channel look ridiculous. By implication, the English political parties and religious denominations are satirized in the implacable feuds between the wearers of high heels and low heels, and in the controversy about whether to break eggs at the big or small end. In the second part Gulliver is accidentally left ashore on Brobdingnag, where the inhabitants are as tall as steeples, and everything else is in proportion. Here the king, after enquiring into the manners, government, and learning of Europe, tells Gulliver that he 'cannot but conclude the bulk of your natives to be the most pernicious race of little odious vermin that nature ever suffered to crawl upon the surface of the earth'.

The third part (which was written last) is occupied with a visit to the flying island of Laputa, and its neighbouring continent and capital Lagado. Apart from some political animus in relation to England's treatment of Ireland, the satire is here directed against men of science (especially members of the *Royal Society), historians, and projectors, with special reference to the South Sea Company, which had generated a speculative economic bubble that had burst in 1720. In Laputa Gulliver finds the wise men so wrapped up in their speculations as to be complete fools in practical affairs. At Lagado he visits the Academy of Projectors, where professors are engaged in extracting sunshine from cucumbers and similar absurd enterprises. In the Island of Sorcerers he is enabled to call up the great men of old, and discovers, from their answers to his questions, the deceptions of history. The Struldbruggs, a race endowed with immortality, so far from finding this a mark of special status, are the most miserable of mankind. In the fourth part Swift describes the country of the Houyhnhnms, or horses endowed with reason; their rational, clean, and simple society is contrasted with the filthiness and brutality of the Yahoos, beasts in human shape whose human vices Gulliver is reluctantly forced to recognize. So alienated is he from his own species that when he finally returns home he recoils from his own family in disgust. *Gulliver's Travels* was an immediate if scandalous success and was read (according to Alexander *Pope and John *Gay) 'from the cabinet council to the nursery'. Its use of a supposedly exotic setting to render the 'normal' conventions of society eccentric and strange, the radical instability of its central character, and its assault on the emergent form of the novel as represented by Daniel *Defoe have generated enormous amounts of discussion. Conversely, there have always been some readers who found themselves disturbed by the darkness of Swift's vision, particularly in the last book, which William *Thackeray described as 'furious, raging, obscene', and which Leslie *Stephen found 'painful and repulsive'.

Gull's Horn-Book, The A satire on fops and gallants by Thomas *Dekker, published 1609, parodying the *courtesy books of the period, and suggested by a German original (*see* GROBIAN). As a sociological document it reveals attitudes to leisure, luxury, and London's shifting population.

GUMILEV, Nikolai Stepanovich (1886–1921) Russian poet and critic, born in Kronstadt, and educated at Tsarskoe Selo, where in 1903 he met Anna *Akhmatova, to whom he was married from 1910 to 1918. His first book of poetry was published in 1905. In 1911 he founded the Guild of Poets, which brought together the members of the school of Russian *Acmeism, whose poetic ideals were clarity and precision. After serving as a volunteer with the Uhlans from 1914 he visited England in June 1917 and again in January–April 1918. He met Roger *Fry and Aldous *Huxley, and visited Lady Ottoline *Morrell at Garsington Manor in June 1917. He also met G. K. *Chesterton and during an air raid made a 'mad' speech suggesting that countries should be ruled by poets and offering Chesterton the crown of England. He became acquainted with many writers associated with Alfred *Orage's *The New Age*, which frequently published translations from and articles about Russian writers. He returned to Russia in 1918 and taught creative writing in Petrograd. On 3 August 1921 he was arrested for alleged participation in a pro-monarchist plot, and was executed later that month. His last collection of poetry, *The Pillar of Fire*, widely acknowledged as his finest, appeared between his arrest and execution. *The Pillar of Fire: Selected Poems* (1999) contains translations of his work by Michael Basker and Richard McKane.

GUNN, Neil (1891–1973) Scottish novelist, short story writer, and playwright, born and brought up in Caithness. His first novel *The Grey Coast* (1926), short stories, and several of his plays contemplate Highland life in decline but *Morning Tide* (1931) introduces more Gunnian characteristics: a sensuous lyricism, remarkable evocations of childhood and of the sea, and a hard-won confidence in humankind. Two historical novels followed: *Sun Circle* (1933), about a Viking invasion, and *Butcher's Broom* (1934), a powerful testament to the Highland Clearances. The modernist *Highland River* (1937) maps the life of its hero, Kenn, on to his experience of the river of his childhood. *The Silver Darlings* (1941) is set in Caithness immediately after the Napoleonic Wars, synthesizing folk song, historical detail, acute psychological observation, and symphonic recurrences of almost supernatural experiences. *Young Art and Old Hector* (1942) explores the shared experience of a child and an old man. In *The*

Green Isle of the Great Deep (1944) the duo return, but to a dystopian Celtic heaven. *The Serpent* (1943) and *The Key of the Chest* (1945) scrutinize homespun values more critically, while *The Silver Bough* (1948) and *The Well at the World's End* (1951) gently satirize those who wish to observe 'primitive communities'. The thriller *Bloodhunt* (1952) and the metaphysical *The Other Landscape* (1954) envisage rehabilitation after violence. *The Atom of Delight* (1956), Gunn's last book, analyses incidents in the first two decades of his life.

GUNN, Thom (1929–2004) Poet, born in Gravesend, the son of journalists, and educated at Trinity College, Cambridge, where he was a contemporary of Ted *Hughes. His first volume of poems, *Fighting Terms* (1954), earned critical acclaim for combining vigorous contemporaneity with learned metrical verse. After leaving Cambridge, he followed his lifelong partner Mike Kitay to California, taking up a Creative Writing fellowship at Stanford University. His second collection, *The Sense of Movement* (1957), shows the distinct influence of Yvor *Winters, whom he met at Stanford. It retains Gunn's characteristic tensions of theme and style, however, marrying Winters's rationalist precision to treatments of American pop culture (notably the motorcycle rebel). In 1960 he settled permanently in San Francisco, and embarked upon a full-time career as a writer. *My Sad Captains* (1961) is a consciously transitional volume: the first half reasserting Winters's 'technique of comprehension', only for the second to introduce a more open syllabic style which would inform all of his subsequent work. *Moly* (1971) is predominantly the result of LSD experiences in the late 1960s, prompting a seemingly counter-intuitive return to formal metrics. A much more angst-ridden volume, *Jack Straw's Castle* (1975), is based on a recurrent nightmare. With the explicit treatment of his homosexuality in *The Passages of Joy* (1982), his critical reputation reached its lowest ebb. He was characterized by some as a rigorous intellectual poet who had descended into hippyish frivolity. His rehabilitation came with *The Man with Night Sweats* (1992), a frank and moving series about friends who were victims of AIDS, acknowledged as an exemplary poetic response to the epidemic. The *Collected Poems* (1993) contains all but the work of *Boss Cupid* (2000), his final volume of 'survivor' poems. His celebration of men of action (and violence), his gallery of heroes (ranging from Elvis Presley to Caravaggio), together with his rational, laconic, colloquial manner provide an interesting synthesis of the English *Movement and elements of American *Beat poetry. Collections of occasional prose include *The Occasions of Poetry: Essays in Criticism and Autobiography*, ed. Clive Wilmer (1982), and *Shelf Life* (1993).

GUNNING, Susannah (?1740–1800) Author of six novels before her marriage in 1768. Some very public difficulties concerning her daughter's marriage in 1791 were referred to by Horace *Walpole as 'the Gunningiad', but also led to a resumption of her novelistic career, and a poem, *Virginius and Virginia* (1792).

GURDJIEFF, Georgei Ivanovitch (?1874–1949) Esoteric thinker and teacher, son of a Greek father and Armenian mother, born at Alexandrople, just inside Armenia on the Turkish frontier. He claimed to have spent his youth travelling in Central Asia, India, and Tibet with a company of fellow seekers acquiring occult knowledge. In 1910 he appeared in St Petersburg practising as a healer with theosophical leanings, and in 1914 met Peter Demianovich *Ouspensky, who became his principal disciple and recorded his teaching in *In Search of the Miraculous* (1950). He moved to the Caucasus during the revolution, then via Constantinople and Berlin to France, where he set up the Institute for the Harmonious Development of Man at Fontainebleau, where Katherine *Mansfield died in 1923. His ideas influenced Aldous *Huxley (*After Many a Summer*, 1939, and *The Doors of Perception*, 1954) and Christopher *Isherwood. Alfred *Orage, editor of the *New Age*, was a disciple, and followed him to Fontainebleau in 1922. A powerful and hypnotic personality, often labelled as a charlatan, Gurdjieff insisted that his knowledge was more a method than a doctrine, and could only be acquired by initiates through discipline and self-observation.

GURNAH, Abdulrazak (1948–) Novelist, critic, and academic, born in Zanzibar, became a teacher at the University of Kent. His novels, some of them shortlisted for major prizes, nearly all engage with questions of cultural identity, betrayal, guilt, and displacement which affect both immigrants and the communities in which they settle, disturbing the view that ethnicity is peculiar to migrants. *Desertion* (2005) traces the transition within an East African coastal community from the colonial period to independence, and within a Muslim family from a claustrophobic but densely textured world to the narrator's arid experience in contemporary Britain.

GURNEY, Ivor (1890–1937) Poet and composer, born in Gloucester, the son of a tailor. He studied composition under Sir Charles Villiers *Stanford at the Royal College of Music from 1911. In the First World War he served on the Western Front, from 1915 to 1917, and suffered a bullet wound, before being gassed at Passchendaele. He published two volumes of verse, *Severn and Somme* (1917) and *War's Embers* (1919). His *Five Elizabethan Songs* appeared in 1920. He wrote two A. E. *Housman cycles, *Ludlow and Teme* and *The Western Playland* (1919), and set six poems by Edward *Thomas, *Lights Out* (1918–25), amid several other such projects. After the war Gurney began studying with Ralph *Vaughan Williams, but became increasingly unsettled, at times sleeping rough, and taking night walks back to Gloucestershire from London. He was committed to a mental institution in 1922, and spent the rest of his life in care, dying in the City of London Mental Hospital. He had continued to compose and to write poetry, producing altogether nearly 300 songs and 1,700 poems. Selections from the poetry were published by Edmund *Blunden (1954), and Leonard Clark (1973). Interest in his verse—with its memories of the war, its evocations of Gloucestershire, and descriptions of his own mental state—continued to grow, and

P. J. *Kavanagh edited some 300 items as Gurney's *Collected Poems* (1982); further selections have continued to appear. See also Gurney's *Collected Letters*, ed. R. K. R. Thornton (1991); Michael Hurd, *The Ordeal of Ivor Gurney* (1978).

GUTENBERG, Johann (*c.*1400–1468) The inventor of printing with movable type. Born at Mainz, he learned printing skills in Strasbourg, where he lived from 1434. Returning to Mainz in 1444, he borrowed money from Johann *Fust (*c.*1400–1466) in 1448, founding a press with him. Fust dissolved the partnership acrimoniously in 1455, taking possession of the equipment and stock. Books published up to 1455 cannot be assigned certainly to Gutenberg or Fust or Fust's son-in-law Peter Schöffer (*c.*1425–1503), but the 42-line Latin Bible (the 'Gutenberg Bible'), printed at Mainz in 1454, is usually attributed to Gutenberg. See Albert Kapr, *Johannes Gutenberg* (trans. 1996).

GUTHLAC, St (d. 714/15) A young nobleman of Mercia who reacted against his military life and became a hermit at Crowland (or Croyland) in Lincolnshire. Æthelbald, king of Mercia, had a church built over his tomb, which later became the abbey of Crowland. The Latin *Vita Sancti Guthlaci* (*c.*740) was written by Felix of Croyland not long after his death, in the tradition of Latin saints' lives such as Evagrius' *Vita Sancti Antonii*. There is a late Old English prose version from Mercia. Two adjacent poems in Old English, found in the *Exeter Book, known as *Guthlac A* and *Guthlac B*, are distinguished from each other in style and in the degree of their dependence on Felix: B is much more closely copied from him and is written in a more elaborate, Cynewulfian style than A. The poems used to be attributed to *Cynewulf and they are thought to date originally from the late 9th century. See J. Roberts (ed.), *The Guthlac Poems of the Exeter Book* (1979).

GUTHRIE, Woody (Woodrow Wilson) (1912–67) American folk singer, born in Okemah, Oklahoma. He travelled around the USA during the Depression, producing *Dust Bowl Ballads* in 1939. His autobiography *Bound for Glory* appeared in 1943. Despite failing health, Guthrie featured in the folk revival of the 1960s, influencing singers like Pete Seeger (1919–) and Bob *Dylan. See Joe Klein, *Woody Guthrie: A Life* (1980).

Guy Mannering A novel by Walter *Scott, published 1815, the second of the **Waverley* novels. The story, set in the 18th century, narrates the fortunes of Harry Bertram, son of the laird of Ellangowan in Dumfriesshire, who is kidnapped as a child and carried to the Netherlands at the instigation of a dishonest lawyer, Glossin. Ignorant of his parentage, he joins the army, and serves with distinction under Colonel Guy Mannering. Bertram loves Julia, Mannering's daughter. Glossin, who has seized the Ellangowan estate, is alarmed by the possibility that Bertram may learn the secret of his parentage. He and his ally Hatteraick plot to kill Bertram but are foiled, not least because of the efforts of an old Gypsy, Meg Merrilies. They are captured and Hatteraick, after murdering Glossin, kills himself. Bertram is restored to his property and reconciled with Mannering, and marries Julia. The novel was hugely successful and went through eleven editions during Scott's lifetime.

Guy of Warwick Popular verse romance of about 1300, based on an Anglo-Norman original, occurring in four manuscripts ranging from 7,000 to 12,000 lines. Guy is the son of Siward, steward of Rohand, earl of Warwick. He performs many exploits in order to win the hand of the earl's daughter Fenice, rescuing the emperor of Germany's daughter, fighting the Saracens, and slaying the Soldan (sultan). On his return to England he is honourably received by King Athelstan and marries Fenice, but goes back to the Holy Land. He returns to England and fights the Danish giant Colbrand, slays the Dun Cow of Dunsmore, and vanquishes a winged dragon in Northumberland. He becomes a hermit and is fed by Fenice, who does not recognize him until he sends her his ring from his deathbed. The romance served as a patriotic rallying-poem because of its celebration of Athelstan's resistance to the Danes. The legend was versified by John *Lydgate (*c.*1450). The Beauchamp earls claimed descent from Guy. See edition by J. Zupitza (3 vols, EETS ES 42, 49, 59, 1883–91).

GUYON, Madame (1648–1717) French *mystical writer, imprisoned for her *quietist teaching. She was defended by her correspondent *Fénelon and criticized by *Bossuet. She had several English and Scottish followers in the 18th century, including the religious polemicist George Garden (1649–1733), George *Cheyne, and the Jacobite writer Chevalier (Andrew Michael) Ramsay (1686–1743). William *Cowper translated some of her poems, and John *Wesley abridged her autobiography.

Guyon, Sir The knight of Temperance and hero of Book II of Edmund *Spenser's **Faerie Queene*. His various exploits, the conquest of *Pyrochles, the visit to the cave of *Mammon, the capture of *Acrasia, and the destruction of her Bower of Bliss, are related in II. v-xii.

Guzmán de Alfarache A Spanish *picaresque romance (Pt I: 1599; Pt II: 1604), the second of its kind (the successor of **Lazarillo de Tormes*) by Mateo Alemán (1547–*c.*1614). It was translated by James *Mabbe into English (as *The Rogue*) in 1622 and published with an introductory poem by Ben *Jonson. Guzmán is by turns scullion, thief, gentleman, beggar, soldier, and page.

GWYN, Eleanor ('Nell') (1650–87) Actress and royal mistress, reared in her mother's bawdy-house; she became an orange-seller in the theatre and at 14 went on the stage. When she retired, aged 21, she was the most famous actress of her time. She was Charles II's mistress and bore him two sons.

H

HABINGTON, William (1605–54) Poet and playwright, of an old Catholic family, educated at Saint-Omer and Paris. He married Lucy Herbert, daughter of the first Baron Powis, and celebrated her in *Castara* (1634, anon.), a collection of love poems. A later edition (1635) contained in addition some elegies on a friend, and the edition of 1640 a number of sacred poems. He also wrote a tragicomedy, *The Queen of Aragon* (1640). His poems were edited by Kenneth Allott (1948), with a life.

HADDON, Mark (1962–) Novelist and poet, born in Northampton, educated at Uppingham School and Merton College, Oxford. After publishing many books for children, including the 'Agent Z' and 'Baby Dinosaur' series, he achieved wide acclaim and won the Whitbread Book of the Year Award with his first adult novel, *The Curious Incident of the Dog in the Night-Time* (2003), a remarkable tour de force written from the point of view of a boy with Asperger's Syndrome. His second adult novel, *A Spot of Bother*, followed in 2006. A collection of poems, *The Talking Horse and the Sad Girl and the Village under the Sea*, appeared in 2005.

Hades The name given in classical mythology to both the god of the underworld (Roman Pluto), the husband of Persephone (Proserpina), and the underworld itself, guarded by the monstrous dog Cerberus. Odysseus' visit to the underworld (**Odyssey*, 11) is echoed in the Hades episode in **Ulysses*. The underworld to which Aeneas descends (**Aeneid*, 6) encompasses both the Elysian Fields of the blessed and Tartarus, the place of punishment. In the New Testament the Greek term Hades is usually translated as Hell, as in the story of Dives and Lazarus (Luke 16).

HADFIELD, Jen (1978–) Poet, born to an English father and Canadian mother in Cheshire and educated at Edinburgh University. Her poems reflect her travels in Canada and her domicile on the Shetland island of Burra. Combining startling metaphor with dialect and an inventively transgressive syntax, they explore the natural world, frequently from animal perspectives. A debut collection, *Almanacs* (2005), was followed by *Nigh-No-Place* (2008), which won the T. S. Eliot Prize.

HĀFIZ, Shams ad-dīn Muhammad of Shiraz (d. *c.*1390) Greatest of the Persian lyric poets. His poems, mainly lyrical odes (*ghazals*), are collected together in his *Divan*. He sings of the sorrows of love, wine, and beauties of nature, with a mystic tone and depth of language and feeling that make him unique. The poems are most commonly treated as mystical, less often as mundane, which points to a balance within them. However, any one single approach does less than justice to the poet's obvious joy in the subtle weaving of imagery and allusion in ways open to more than one interpretation.

Sir William *Jones was the first to translate one of Hāfiz's *ghazals* into English, and since then there has been a plethora of translators, Gertrude *Bell (1897) and Richard *Le Gallienne (1905) being the best known. Arthur Arberry (1905–69) produced the most acute of the 20th-century interpretations (1947 and 1954). There is a new complete translation of the *ghazals* by Peter Avery (2007). R. W. *Emerson also translated two *ghazals* from a German translation.

See also SA'DĪ.

HAGGARD, Sir Henry Rider (1856–1925) Novelist, sixth son of a Norfolk squire. He went, aged 19, for six years to South Africa to serve as secretary to the governor of Natal; his first book *Cetywayo and his White Neighbours* (1882) was an attack on Britain's South African policies. He achieved fame with his spellbinding novels of exotic adventure; the most celebrated of these—*King Solomon's Mines* (1886) and *She* (1887)—were set in Africa, and vividly convey the fascination he found in its landscape, wildlife, tribal society, and mysterious past. Rudyard *Kipling and Andrew *Lang were close friends of his, and he had a worldwide readership which included *Jung, who used *She* as a striking example of the anima concept, or the expression of a feminine inner personality. Haggard's novels have remained enduringly popular and several have been filmed. His autobiography, *The Days of my Life*, appeared in 1926, and there is a biography by Morton Cohen (1960).

hagiography Lives of the saints, sometimes including martyrology, lives of the martyrs. Originally written and collected by monks in the early and medieval churches, such collections of lives were also made of post-*Reformation saints, for example *Puritans and *Quakers. *See* FRIENDS, SOCIETY OF. The term is often now used to condemn uncritical biography.

haiku A lyric verse form of Japanese origin, composed in unrhymed lines of five, seven, and five syllables (thus seventeen in all), and encapsulating a single impression of a natural scene or object at a particular season (e.g. by reference to blossom or melting snow). It arose in the 16th century and achieved classical expression in the work of Bashō (1644–94). At first the opening stanza in a sequence, the haiku became established as an independent form in the 19th century. Western poets of the early 20th century, notably the school of *imagism, admired its indirect evocation of feeling through natural images, and encouraged its now widespread use in English.

Hajji Baba of Ispahan, The Adventures of See MORIER, JAMES JUSTINIAN.

HAKLUYT, Richard [pron. Haklit] (1552–1616) Geographer and travel writer who greatly influenced overseas enterprise and the development of English prose writing. From Herefordshire, he attended Christ Church, Oxford, and took orders but interested himself principally in geography. Experience in the 1580s as chaplain at the embassy in Paris demonstrated that England lagged behind continental rivals in overseas activities. He devoted the rest of his life to promoting colonial projects, especially in America, translating accounts of voyages and travels, writing about English enterprises, collecting existing accounts in English by others, and encouraging Elizabethan 'sea dogs' to write about their experiences. He produced some 25 travel works. *Divers Voyages Touching the Discoverie of America* (1582) and an edition of *Peter Martyr's *De Orbe Novo* (1587) were notable early works but in 1589 came *The Principall Navigations, Voiages and Discoveries of the English Nation*, of which a facsimile and indexed edition was published by the *Hakluyt Society (1965). A much-enlarged version in three volumes, *The Principal Navigations, Voiages, Traffiques and Discoueries of the English Nation*, came in 1598–1600. Hakluyt also produced memoranda for the government, notably his 'Discourse of Western Planting' of 1584. His efforts coincided with a slump in European demand for English textiles, encouraging interest in alternative overseas markets. Hakluyt popularized the exploits of men like Sir Hugh Willoughby (d. ?1554), Sir John *Hawkins (1532–95), Sir Francis *Drake, Sir Humphrey Gilbert (1537–83), and Martin Frobisher (1535–94). He gave practical help and advice to Sir Walter *Ralegh, was consulted by the key government figures, Sir Francis Walsingham (*c.* 1532–90) and Robert Cecil (1563–1612) and in 1601 became an adviser to the newly formed East India Company (whose ships carried copies of *Principal Navigations* as essential equipment), while his advocacy did much to inaugurate Britain's long endeavour to find a North-West Passage to India.

Hakluyt's friends included eminent writers and poets such as Philip *Sidney, Edward *Dyer, William *Camden, Richard Harvey (1552?–1616), Richard *Mulcaster, Thomas *Nashe, and Michael *Drayton. His rewards were comfortable preferments in the church but his legacy was a wonderful collection of vigorous writings in English which have constantly been reproduced and anthologized for 400 years, as in the twelve-volume edition of *Principal Navigations* in 1903–5, the 'Everyman' edition of 1907, or the useful Oxford 'World's Classics' selection of 1958. After his death, Hakluyt's papers came into the hands of Samuel *Purchas.

Hakluyt Society Named after Richard *Hakluyt and founded by the geographer W. D. Cooley in 1846 to publish 'rare and valuable Voyages, Travels, and Geographical Records'. In practice, the texts are historical, emanating from any source, if necessary translated into English, and each is edited by an expert. Henry Yule's *Cathay and the Way Thither* (1866) set a standard of scholarship the Society has striven to maintain in the 350 or more volumes issued since 1846. The first series of 100 editions ended in 1898. The second, of 190, included such key texts as the standard English version of *The Travels of Ibn Battuta*, while an 'Extra Series' is notable for *The Journals of Captain James Cook*. In the 21st century, the Society's larger-format third series continues to feature definitive editions of historical texts on travel, exploration, and the resulting cultural encounters. See www.hakluyt.com for a complete list.

HALDEMAN, Joe (1943–) American *science fiction writer, born in Oklahoma; he drew upon his service in Vietnam for *The Forever War* (1976), the story of a centuries-long interstellar war. *Forever Free* (1999), using the same protagonists, might be said to consider the dissatisfaction of war veterans. Haldeman also used his experiences for the non-science fiction *1968* (1995). *The Hemingway Hoax* (1990) is a skilful piece of *alternate history.

HALE, Kathleen (1898–2000) Writer and artist born in Lanarkshire, Scotland, educated at Reading University, remembered for her sixteen children's books about Orlando, a 'marmalade' cat, and his family, beginning with *Orlando's Camping Holiday* (1938). The stories were adapted for BBC Radio *Children's Hour*. There is an autobiography (1996). She was appointed OBE in 1976.

HALÉVY, Élie (1870–1937) French social and political historian, author of *Histoire du peuple anglais au XIXe siècle* (*History of the English People in the Nineteenth Century*), a study of political, economic, and religious change in England after 1815. Having dealt with the period 1815–41 in three volumes (1913–23), Halévy went on to write a further two (1926–32) on the years 1895–1915 before turning his attention to the middle of the century. His last work (1946), on the years 1841–52, was published after his death.

HALEY, Alex (1921–92) African American writer, born in Ithaca, New York, co-author of *The Autobiography of Malcolm X* (1965). *Roots: The Saga of an American Family* (1976) claimed to trace his ancestry to Kunta Kinte, who had been brought from Gambia to the province of Maryland in 1767, to be sold as a slave. It was extremely successful, though he later admitted that passages had been taken from the novelist and anthropologist Harold Courlander (1908–96). In 1977 *Roots* was made into a very popular and influential TV mini-series. *Queen: The Story of an American Family* (1993) investigated another part of Haley's family and was completed after his death.

half-rhyme *See* RHYME.

HALIBURTON, Thomas Chandler (1796–1865) Born at Windsor, Nova Scotia, Canada; he became a judge of the supreme court of the province. As a writer he became known for his *The Clockmaker, or The Sayings and Doings of Samuel Slick, of Slickville* (1836; London, 1837), a satirical and humorous work of fiction published anonymously which had a great vogue in England. It was followed by other works in the same series, including *The Attaché, or Sam Slick in England* (1843–4), designed to stimulate political reform through the satirical observations of the character Sam Slick, a Yankee from Ohio. He spent the last years of his life in England. See V. L. O. Chittick, *Thomas Chandler Haliburton: A Study in Provincial Toryism* (1924).

HALIFAX, George Savile, marquess of (1633–95) Politician and writer, a powerful influence in the court of Charles II, known for the moderation and avoidance of extremes he advocates in his *Character of a Trimmer* (1688). He was an anti-Catholic, but in a famous House of Lords debate he successfully opposed the Exclusion Bill of his uncle the earl of *Shaftesbury, which would have debarred the future James II (a Catholic) from the throne. His *Letter to a Dissenter* dissuades Nonconformists (who, like Catholics, were excluded from public office) from the extreme step of throwing in their lot with James's court party. He is the 'Jotham' of John *Dryden's *Absalom and Achitophel*. His other works include *The Anatomy of an Equivalent* (1688), *A Lady's New Year's Gift, or Advice to a Daughter* (1688), and *A Character of King Charles II* (printed with *Political, Moral, and Miscellaneous Reflections* in 1750).

Hali Meiðhad 'Holy Maidenhood' A letter on virginity from the West Midlands, written *c*.1220s. It occurs in two manuscripts which also contain *Sawles Warde* and one or more members of the group of saints' lives known as the *Katherine Group. Vigorously written in an accomplished style, very reminiscent of that of *Ancrene Wisse*, its exaltation of virginity and hostility to marriage is extreme. There is an edition by B. Millett (EETS 284, 1982).

HALL, Edward (1497–1547) Educated at Eton College and King's College, Cambridge, author of a chronicle glorifying the House of Tudor entitled *The Union of the Two Noble and Illustre Families of Lancaster and York*. First published posthumously in 1548 by Richard *Grafton, it was prohibited by Queen Mary. Hall's *Chronicle* is interesting for the account it gives of the times of *Henry VIII and the vivid description of his court and of the Field of the Cloth of Gold. It was used by William *Shakespeare as a source in his early history plays.

HALL, Joseph (1574–1656) Anglican bishop, religious writer, and satirist, educated at Ashby-de-la-Zouch and Emmanuel College, Cambridge. He was successively bishop of Exeter (1627) and Norwich (1641), but was ejected in 1643 when the Parliamentarians did away with bishops. At Cambridge he published two volumes of satires, *Virgidemiarum* (1597, 1598), and a satirical description of London disguised as a travel narrative, *Mundus Alter et Idem* (1605?; English translation by John Healy 1608). His were not, as he claimed, the first English satires; Thomas *Lodge's *Fig for Momus* had appeared in 1593. But Hall's *Characters of Virtues and Vices* (1608) is the first English example of Theophrastan *character-writing, and his *Three Centuries of Meditations* (1606–9), quarried from his sermons, offered a Protestant alternative to the influential Catholic mode of Ignatian meditation. A favourite of *James I, he was sent three times on royal embassies abroad; and was employed as a controversialist by the king and later by William *Laud. His *Humble Remonstrance* (1640 and 1641), defending the rule of bishops, drew a reply from the syndicate of Puritan ministers who wrote under the acronym *Smectymnuus. John *Milton joined in this controversy on the Puritan side, virulently attacking Hall and expressing disgust at his early satires. Hall's collected works fill ten volumes, and he is famous for his plain, Senecan prose style. Thomas *Browne attended him in his last illness. See F. Huntley's *Biographical and Critical Study* (1979); Richard McCabe, *Joseph Hall: A Study in Satire and Meditation* (1982).

HALL, Sir Peter (1930–) Director of plays, operas, and films. He was born in Suffolk and educated at St Catharine's College, Cambridge. From 1955 to 1959 Hall ran the important Arts Theatre in London, where he directed the British premiere of *Waiting for Godot* in 1955. He founded the Royal Shakespeare Company in 1960, laying great emphasis on intelligent verse speaking, and was director of the *National Theatre from 1973 to 1988. His production of Christopher *Marlowe's *Tamburlaine* opened the new Olivier auditorium there. He then started his own theatre company, and in 2005 revived *Godot* as a touring production. He has shaped post-war British subsidized theatre and applied the same classical rigour to Samuel *Beckett, Harold *Pinter, and Edward *Albee as to Stratford Shakespeare, where his joint production, with John Barton, of the history cycle *The Wars of the Roses* (1963) remains a modern landmark. His *Diaries* were published in 1983.

HALL, Radclyffe (1880–1943) Pseudonym of Marguerite Radclyffe-Hall, novelist and poet, born in Bournemouth and educated erratically before briefly attending King's College, London. Between 1906 and 1915 she published five volumes of verse, and she went on to write seven novels: *The Forge* (1924), *The Unlit Lamp* (1924), *A Saturday Life* (1925), and the double prize-winning *Adam's Breed* (1926) being the first four. Her restrained yet open treatment of lesbianism in *The Well of Loneliness* (1928) occasioned a trial for obscenity. It was banned and an appeal refused; it only became legally available in the UK in 1949. Her final novels are *The Master of the House* (1932) and *The Sixth Beatitude* (1936). See Diana Souhami, *The Trials of Radclyffe Hall* (1998).

HALL, Stuart (1932–) Born in Jamaica and educated there and at Oxford University. A leading theorist of black Britain, he founded the *New Left Review*, and was director of Birmingham's Cultural Studies Centre, then a professor of sociology at the Open University. His books include *Questions of Cultural Identity* (1996).

HALLAM, Arthur Henry (1811–33) Scholar and critic, educated at Eton College and Trinity College, Cambridge, where he became a close friend of Alfred *Tennyson and after his early death the subject of Tennyson's **In Memoriam* (1855). He was a young man of promise, an Italian scholar, and an admirer of the Romantic poets. His *Remains*, edited by his father Henry *Hallam in 1834, contain poetry, philosophy, and criticism.

HALLAM, Henry (1777–1859) Historian, and the father of Tennyson's friend Arthur *Hallam, educated at Eton College and Oxford. He became a barrister and a commissioner of stamps. He spent some ten years on the preparation of his first published work, *A View of the State of Europe during the Middle Ages* (1818), in which he attempts 'a comprehensive survey of the chief circumstances that can interest a philosophical enquirer'. Hallam's best-known work, the *Constitutional History of England* (1827), to the death of George II, was hugely influential: it was continued by Sir T. E. May. In 1834 Hallam edited, with a memoir, the verse and prose of his son Arthur (*see* HALLAM, ARTHUR HENRY). His last important work was *An Introduction to the Literature of Europe during the Fifteenth, Sixteenth, and Seventeenth Centuries* (1837–9), which covers not only creative literature but classics, mathematics, theology, science, and philosophy.

HALLIWELL, James Orchard (later James Orchard Halliwell-Phillipps) (1820–89) Shakespearian scholar. He entered Trinity College, Cambridge, in 1837 where he had unlimited access to the locked-up manuscripts. After seventeen volumes went missing, he transferred to Jesus College. He was elected a fellow of the *Royal Society before he was 19 and was a founder member of the Shakespeare Society. In 1842 he married Henrietta, daughter of Sir Thomas *Phillipps, whose surname he later added to his own. He made important discoveries in the Stratford records, incorporating them into his biographical studies of Shakespeare. He published a *Life of William Shakespeare* (1848, etc.), *Observations on the Shakespearean Forgeries at Bridgewater House* (1853), on the John Payne *Collier controversy, *A Dictionary of Old English Plays* (1860), and *Outlines of the Life of Shakespeare* (1881–7), which became a primary source for subsequent 19th-century Shakespeare biographies. He edited the *Works* of Shakespeare (16 vols, 1853–65) and some 150 volumes, mainly of 17th-century literature (some in collaboration with Thomas *Wright), and did much work for the *Percy Society, notably editing *The Nursery Rhymes of England* (1842–6), a pioneering study which remained standard until that of the *Opies, and for the *Camden Society.

HALL-STEVENSON, John (1718–85) Educated at Jesus College, Cambridge, where he met Laurence *Sterne, who may have based Eugenius in **Tristram Shandy* and *A *Sentimental Journey* on him. He owned the half-ruinous Skelton Castle, in Yorkshire, where he hosted a group of rakish literary friends, 'the Demoniacs', including Sterne. He published *Fables for Grown Gentlemen* (1761), *Crazy Tales* (1762), and other often bawdy verse. His *Works* (1795) include a frontispiece depicting his 'Crazy Castle'.

hamartia *See* POETICS.

HAMBURGER, Michael (1924–2007) Poet and translator, born in Berlin of a German family which emigrated to England in 1933, and educated at Oxford. His volumes of poetry include *Flowering Cactus* (1950), *Weather and Season* (1963), which contains 'In a Cold Season', on the trial of the Nazi war criminal Adolf Eichmann, *Ownerless Earth* (1973), *Roots in the Air* (1991), and *Late* (1997). His poems characteristically combine a European and an English naturalist sensibility. His many distinguished translations include versions of Hugo von *Hofmannsthal (1961), and the *Poems and Fragments* of Friedrich *Hölderlin (1966). An important critical book, *The Truth of Poetry*, was published in 1968; his autobiography, *A Mug's Game*, in 1983; and his *Collected Poems 1941–1994* in 1995. See Peter Dale, *Michael Hamburger in Conversation* (1998).

HAMILTON, Anthony (Antoine) (*c.*1646–1720) Third son of Sir George Hamilton (1607–79), and brother-in-law of the comte de Gramont (1621–1707). Hamilton wrote the *Mémoires de la vie du comte de Gramont* (*Memoirs of the Life of the Comte de Gramont*), published anonymously at Cologne in 1713. These entertaining memoirs are an important source for the social history of the period. They were edited (in French) by Horace *Walpole and translated into English (with many errors) by Abel *Boyer in 1714; and this translation, revised and annotated by Walter *Scott, was reissued in 1811. A new translation was made in 1930 by Peter *Quennell, with an introduction and commentary by C. H. Hartmann. The first part, dealing with Gramont's life on the Continent down to the time of his banishment from the French court, was probably dictated by Gramont to Hamilton. The second, relating to the English court, appears to be Hamilton's own work.

HAMILTON, Charles (1876–1961) Born in Ealing, London; his education did not extend beyond school. His first boys' story was published when he was 17; eventually he became the world's most prolific author of juvenile fiction, regularly writing in excess of 70,000 words a week. He wrote under many pen-names; best known were 'Frank Richards' of the *Magnet* (1908–40) and 'Martin Clifford' of the *Gem* (1907–39). The *Magnet* published his *school stories about Greyfriars School, whose pupils included Billy Bunter; after the *Magnet*'s closure the stories reappeared in book form, on television, and in the theatre. George *Orwell, writing in **Horizon* (1939), objected to the snobbery, insularity, dated slang, and tedious style of this exclusively male world, but Hamilton's spirited reply conceded nothing. See Hamilton's *The Autobiography of Frank Richards* (1952) and Mary Cadogan's life (rev. 2000).

HAMILTON, Elizabeth (1756–1816) Novelist, born in Belfast, but domiciled mainly in Scotland. Her novels *Translations of the Letters of a Hindoo Rajah* (1796) and *Memoirs of Modern Philosophers* (1800) satirized contemporary radicals like William *Godwin. *The Cottagers of Glenburnie* (1808) portrays manners and economy in rural Scotland. Hamilton also wrote tracts on female education, and an autobiographical fragment.

HAMILTON, Ian (1938–2001) Poet, editor, biographer, and essayist, educated at Darlington Grammar School and Keble College, Oxford. He published collections of poetry, *The Visit* (1970), *Returning* (1976), and *Fifty Poems* (1988); other works include *The Little Magazines* (1976); a life of Robert *Lowell (1983); and *In Search of J. D. Salinger* (1988), a compelling account of the difficulties he encountered in writing about his elusive subject, which he describes as 'a kind of **Quest for Corvo*, with *Salinger as quarry'. This investigation led to *Keepers of the Flame: Literary Estates and the Rise of Biography* (1992), in which he discusses historical, legal, and ethical questions associated with the growing interest in literary biography. He edited the *New Review* (1974–9) and *The Oxford Companion to Twentieth Century Poetry in English* (1994). *Walking Possession* (1994) collects essays and reviews 1968–93.

HAMILTON, Patrick (1904–62) Playwright and novelist. Born near Brighton, Sussex, he had an erratic education; after leaving Westminster School at the age of 15 he worked for a time as a repertory actor; his several successful plays include *Rope* (1929) and *Gas Light* (1939), both thrillers, and *The Duke in Darkness* (1943), a historical drama. His novels include *Craven House* (1926), the story of the inmates of a boarding house; the 'London trilogy' collected as *Twenty Thousand Streets under the Sky* (1935), which deals with the interlocking lives of Bob, a waiter, Jenny, a prostitute, and Ella, a barmaid; *Hangover Square* (1941), a thriller set in Earls Court dealing with George Harvey Bone's fatal passion for destructive Netta; and *The Slaves of Solitude* (1947), also set in a boarding house, which centres on the wartime experiences of the quiet spinster Miss Roach. Hamilton's particular gift is for describing, in the words of J. B. *Priestley, 'a kind of No-Man's-Land of shabby hotels, dingy boarding-houses and all those saloon bars where the homeless can meet'. All the novels show a preoccupation with the perils and pleasures of drinking, and Hamilton's Marxism is expressed in his compassion for the hopelessness of his characters' lives. See Sean French, *Patrick Hamilton: A Life* (1993).

HAMILTON, Peter F. (1960–) Born in Rutland; *science fiction novelist who moved from near-future England and global warming in *Mindstar Rising* (1993) to epic space opera in *The Reality Dysfunction* (1996) and subsequent novels. Extended life, nanotechnology, and genetic manipulation are explored against vast clashes of cultures.

HAMILTON, William, of Bangour (1704–54) Scottish *Jacobite patriot and poet, who commemorated the battle of Gladsmuir in an ode and fought at Culloden. He is chiefly remembered for his song 'The Braes of Yarrow' ('Busk ye, busk ye, my bony bony bride'), published in Allan *Ramsay's *Miscellany*.

HAMILTON, Sir William (1730–1803) British envoy at Naples from 1764, where his embassy became a centre of cultural activity. Hamilton's *Campi Phlegraei* (1776) recorded his observations on Vesuvius and other volcanoes. In 1791 he married Emma Hart, later mistress of Nelson. His friends included William *Beckford and Horace *Walpole, and one of his collections of vases and coins, sold to the British Museum in 1771, formed the core of its department of classical antiquities.

HAMILTON, Sir William Rowan (1805–65) Irish mathematician whose fame rests principally on his discovery of the science of quaternions, a higher branch of calculus. He was also a poet, and friend and correspondent of William *Wordsworth, S. T. *Coleridge, Maria *Edgeworth, and other literary figures.

Hamlet A tragedy by *Shakespeare, probably written by 1601: it was registered as 'lately acted' in July 1602. A short text probably reconstructed from memory by actors was published 1603 and a good text, almost twice as long, 1604–5. The *folio text (1623) adds passages not in the second quarto, and omits others. References by Thomas *Nashe, Thomas *Lodge, and others show that a play on the same subject (now lost) preceded Shakespeare's; it was presumably a source. His chief non-dramatic source was *Saxo Grammaticus' narrative in his *Historiae Danicae*, as retold by Belleforest in his *Histoires tragiques*.

Old Hamlet, king of Denmark, is recently dead, and his brother Claudius is now king, having married his widow Gertrude. Young Hamlet, returning from university at Wittenberg, learns from his father's ghost that Claudius murdered him by pouring poison into his ear, and is commanded to avenge the murder without injuring Gertrude. Hamlet warns his friend Horatio and the guard Marcellus (who have also seen the apparition) that he intends to feign madness, and swears them to secrecy. Immediately after his famous speech of deliberation beginning 'To be, or not to be' (III. i) he rejects Ophelia, whom he has loved, while spied on by Claudius and Ophelia's father Polonius. He welcomes a troupe of visiting players, and arranges a performance of a play ('the Mousetrap') about fratricide, which Claudius breaks off, in apparently guilty and fearful fury, when the player Lucianus appears to murder his uncle by pouring poison into his ear. Hamlet refrains from killing Claudius while he is at prayer, but stabs

through the arras in his mother's closet, killing the old counsellor Polonius, before reproaching his mother for her affection for Claudius. Claudius sends Hamlet to England with sealed orders that he should be killed on arrival. Hamlet outwits him, however, returning to Denmark, having arranged the deaths of his old friends Rosencrantz and Guildenstern, who were his uncle's agents. During Hamlet's absence Ophelia has gone mad with grief from Hamlet's rejection of her and her father's death, and is found drowned. Her brother Laertes, having returned from France, is determined to avenge his sister's death. Hamlet and Laertes meet in the graveyard where Ophelia is to be buried, and fight in her grave. Claudius arranges a fencing match between Hamlet and Laertes, giving Laertes a poisoned foil; an exchange of weapons results in the deaths of both combatants. Gertrude drinks a poisoned cup intended for her son, and the dying Hamlet succeeds in killing Claudius. Fortinbras, prince of Norway, whose military heroism has been alluded to throughout the play, appears fresh from wars with Poland and gives Hamlet a military funeral.
See also OBJECTIVE CORRELATIVE.

HAMMETT, Dashiell (1894–1961) American writer of *detective fiction, whose tough, realistic works (*Red Harvest*, 1929; *The Maltese Falcon*, 1930; *The Glass Key*, 1931; *The Thin Man*, 1932; etc.), based in part on his own experiences as a detective in San Francisco, created a vogue for *hardboiled heroes and seedy locales. Many of his stories were filmed, and he worked as a Hollywood screenwriter, before falling foul of the McCarthy witch-hunt and being imprisoned for 'un-American activities' in 1951. He was a long-standing companion of the playwright Lillian *Hellman (1905–84), whom he met in 1930. A novel by Joe Gores based on his life was filmed in 1982. There is also a life by Diane *Johnson (1983).

HAMMICK, Georgina (1939–) Novelist and short story writer, born in Hampshire and educated at schools in England and Kenya before attending the Académie Julian, Paris, and the Salisbury School of Art. The author of two volumes of short stories, *People for Lunch* (1987) and *Spoilt* (1992), and a novel, *The Arizona Game* (1996), she explores emotional terrain with acuity and an ironic wit which illuminates the dark corners of relationships. Her faithfulness to language and shades of meaning is evident throughout her work. She is one of five poets in *A Poetry Quintet* (1976) and edited an anthology, *The Virago Book of Love and Loss* (1992).

HAMPTON, Christopher (1946–) Playwright, screenwriter, and translator, born in the Azores, and educated at New College, Oxford. His first play, *When Did You Last See my Mother?* (1966), was followed by *Total Eclipse* (1968), based on the tormented relationship of Paul *Verlaine and Arthur *Rimbaud. *The Philanthropist* (1970) is an elegant and epigrammatic comedy, whose title alludes to *Molière's *Le Misanthrope*. *Savages* (1972) is a political and ecological drama set in the Amazon, protesting against genocide and other atrocities in Brazil. *Treats* (1976) is a provoking study of sexual behaviour, responding to the rising tide of feminist orthodoxy; *Tales from Hollywood* (1982) describes the lives of the German literary refugees and their attempts to survive in Hollywood in the 1930s. Hampton has also made many translations and stage and screen adaptations of works by Malcolm *Bradbury, George *Steiner (*The Portage to San Cristobal of A.H.*, 1982), Joseph *Conrad, Graham *Greene, and Henrik *Ibsen. He adapted *Laclos's *Les Liaisons dangereuses* for both stage (1985) and screen (1989). Most of his original work is marked by an ironic, good-humoured, and humane detachment, though paradoxically he is also strongly drawn to the *modernist experiments and violent visions of Conrad: he is at home both with the epic and with West End drawing-room satire.

HAMSUN, Knut (1859–1952) Norwegian novelist, poet, and dramatist, born Knut Petersen in central Norway. He is best known for his novel *Hunger* (1890), set in Christiania (now Oslo), in which his narrator suffers the state of semi-starvation which Hamsun himself had endured during ten years of hardship and work as a labourer in Norway and the USA; its nervous, hallucinatory quality and abrupt, vivid prose made a considerable impact, and he followed its success with many other works of fiction, including *Mysteries* (1892), *Pan* (1894), *Victoria* (1898), *Under the Autumn Star* (1906), *Wanderer Plays on Muted Strings* (1909), *Growth of the Soil* (1917), and *Wayfarer* (1929). He was awarded the *Nobel Prize for Literature in 1920, and continued to write almost to the end of his life, although he alienated many of his followers by his support of Hitler during the Second World War. The influence of his early work was, however, great; Isaac *Singer has stated that 'the whole modern school of fiction in the twentieth century stems from Hamsun' ('Knut Hamsun, Artist of Skepticism', preface to translation by Robert Bly, 1967). *Hunger* was originally translated by George *Egerton (1899).

HAND, Elizabeth (1957–) American writer, born in San Diego. *Winterlong* (1990) began a *science fiction sequence whose baroque elements were succeeded by darker concerns, such as artistic obsession in the *Pre-Raphaelite era in *Mortal Love* (2004). *Bibliomancy* (2003) collects four novellas which show Hand's skill with the fantastic, rather than simple *fantasy.

HANDEL, George Frideric (1685–1759) Composer of German birth who settled in London at the age of 27 and became a naturalized Englishman fifteen years later. He scored a spectacular triumph with *Rinaldo* (1711), which was written to an Italian text in the manner of *opera seria*. His earliest setting of English words, a short cantata by John Hughes, dates from the same period. The masque *Acis and Galatea* (1718) was written for performance at Cannons, the seat of Lord Carnarvon (later duke of Chandos, hence Handel's 'Chandos Anthems'); the libretto was by John *Gay, and Gay's friends Alexander *Pope and John *Arbuthnot may have had a hand in *Esther* (?1720), probably also written for

Cannons. A version of *Esther* revised by Samuel Humphreys was given in London in 1732, with professional adult singers replacing the Children of the Chapel Royal who had sung the original version that year. By this time Gay's *Beggar's Opera* had begun to dampen the craze for the heroic operas that Handel had been producing through the 1720s, and Handel was encouraged by the success of *Esther* to embark on his series of 'oratorios or sacred dramas', starting with *Deborah* and *Athalia* (1733). *Saul* (1739), and immediately after it *Israel in Egypt* (1739), both had texts by Charles Jennens, who also provided the composer with the anthology from Old and New Testaments which he called *Messiah* (1742). *Samson* (1743) was adapted from *Milton's poem, and *The Occasional Oratorio* (1746) from Milton and *Spenser. Jennens was librettist for *Belshazzar* (1745), but was then succeeded as Handel's main collaborator by Thomas Morell, who wrote most of the remaining oratorio texts, including *Judas Maccabaeus* (1747), *Theodora* (1750), and *Jephtha* (1752). Of the secular odes, *Alexander's Feast* (1736), an adaptation of John *Dryden, was followed by *Ode for St Cecilia's Day* (1739), also from Dryden. Handel's setting of *L'Allegro, il Penseroso e il Moderato* (1740–41), is based on Milton's two poems, with a third section by Jennens, in praise of moderation. *Semele* (1743) is a setting of a *Congreve text originally designed for music, with some additional lines from Pope's *Pastorals*.

Handlyng Synne By *Mannyng of Brunne, a treatise in octosyllabic couplets, begun in 1303 and based on the French *Manuel des pechez* by William of Wadington. It deals with sin under various headings: the Ten Commandments, the seven deadly sins, sacrilege, and the sacraments, culminating with penance. Each sin is illustrated by a story and the value of the work lies in Mannyng's narrative vigour. His most familiar and often anthologized story is 'The Dancers of Colbek', which tells of some churchyard revellers, including the priest's daughter, who would not stop dancing, and whom the priest therefore cursed, condemning them to dance incessantly for a year. At the end of the year the priest's daughter drops dead. There is an edition by F. J. *Furnivall (EETS OS 119 and 123, 1901 and 1903) and one by Idelle Sullens (1983).

Hand of Ethelberta, The A novel by Thomas *Hardy, published 1876. As the author suggests in his preface, this is 'a somewhat frivolous narrative'. Ethelberta is among the numerous offspring of Chickerel, a butler. She marries the son of the house where she is governess, and is soon left a widow at 21. Her spirited efforts to maintain her social position, while concealing her relationship with the butler (and yet helping her brothers and sisters), account for most of the story. She finally secures a wicked old peer for a husband, while her faithful admirer, the musician Christopher Julian, is left to marry her sister Picotee.

HANLEY, James (1901–85) Novelist, short story writer, and playwright, born in Dublin but brought up in Liverpool from 1908. He attended a local school before joining the merchant navy at the age of 12; his subsequent experiences were often incorporated into his fiction. His debut novel, *Drift*, and his first volume of short stories, *The German Prisoner*, both appeared in 1930. The following year he issued his second novel, *Boy* (1931), about sexual violence on board a ship, by private subscription, but when the book was published in a mass market edition in 1934 it was prosecuted for obscenity. Hanley did not allow it to be republished during his lifetime. The lives of the Dublin poor were portrayed in *The Furys* (1935), *Secret Journey* (1936), and *Our Time Is Gone* (1940). His many other novels include *Captain Bottell* (1933), *Quartermaster Clausen* (1934), *Hollow Sea* (1938), *The Ocean* (1941), *Sailors' Song* (1943), *The Closed Harbour* (1952), and *A Woman in the Sky* (1973). Further volumes of short stories include *Men in Darkness* (1931), *People Are Curious* (1938), and *A Walk in the Wilderness* (1950). A volume of autobiography, *Broken Water*, was published in 1937 and another, *No Directions*, followed in 1943. See John Fordham, *James Hanley: Modernism and the Working Class* (2002).

Hansard The official reports of the proceedings of the Houses of Parliament. The government printer Luke Hansard (1752–1828) published *Journals of the House of Commons* (1774–1828); his son, Thomas Curson Hansard (1776–1833), published parliamentary Reports from 1809, putting his name to the title page from 1829. In 1909 the name lapsed; it was restored in 1943. *Hansard* is now a publication of HM Stationery Office, appearing in print daily and weekly, and online.

hardboiled A term signifying a matter-of-fact, understated style of describing violence characteristic of American crime fiction since the 1920s. One of its earliest exemplars was Dashiell *Hammett and the term is also linked with *noir fiction. See Bill Pronzini and Jack Adrian (eds), *Hard-Boiled* (1995).

***Hard Cash:** A Matter of Fact Romance* A *sensation novel by Charles *Reade, published 1863 (published in serial form as *Very Hard Cash*). Reade's polemical and sometimes graphically violent novel attacks mid-Victorian Britain's poorly regulated asylum system through two main plot strands. The first concerns Alfred Hardie, whose father Richard wrongfully incarcerates him in a lunatic asylum in order to conceal a banking fraud. He escapes only when a fellow inmate sets the institution on fire. A second plot involves genuine insanity, when Richard Dodd, a sea captain ruined by Hardie's fraudulent scheme, is driven mad by his loss. Dodd also appears in Reade's *Love Me Little, Love Me Long* (1859). Reade concludes the novel with a request for information regarding the wrongful committal of sane persons—a request which eventually led to Rosina Bulwer-Lytton's *A Blighted Life* (1880).

HARDENBERG, Friedrich Leopold von (1772–1801) Known as 'Novalis', German Romantic poet and novelist, author of poems religious, mystic, and secular. In *Hymnen* *an die Nacht* (1800: *Hymns to the Night*), he laments the death of his young fiancée Sophie von Kuhn. The unfinished novels *Heinrich von Ofterdingen* (1802) and *Die Lehrlinge zu Sais* (1802: *The Disciples at Sais*), which show the influence of *Fichte's idealism, are his most acclaimed prose works. Novalis, who was the subject of an enthusiastic essay by Thomas *Carlyle in the *Foreign Review* (1829), had a powerful influence on German poets and artists, as well as on Giacomo *Leopardi and on a later generation of English poets, including James *Thomson, who translated his 'Hymns to Night' (pub. 1995, ed. Simon Reynolds). Penelope *Fitzgerald's novel *The Blue Flower* was based on his life: the title image of 'die blaue Blume', taken from *Heinrich von Ofterdingen*, is a symbol of the transcendental longing characteristic of German *Romanticism.

hard science fiction A term describing a form of *science fiction in which scientific information and thinking is fundamental to the story and the aim is to be as accurate (or plausible) as possible. Encouraged by John W. *Campbell, its exponents include Arthur C. *Clarke, Robert L. *Forward, and Stephen *Baxter.

Hard Times A novel by Charles *Dickens, published 1854. Thomas Gradgrind, a citizen of Coketown, a northern industrial city (based on impressions of Preston, which Dickens visited in 1854), is a misguided exponent of *utilitarianism, an 'eminently practical man', who believes in facts and statistics and brings up his children Louisa and Tom accordingly, ruthlessly suppressing the imaginative sides of their nature. He marries Louisa to Josiah Bounderby, a manufacturer 30 years older than herself. Louisa consents partly from the indifference and cynicism engendered by her father's treatment, partly from a desire to help her brother, who is employed by Bounderby and who is the only person she loves. James Harthouse, a young politician without heart or principles, comes to Coketown and, taking advantage of her unhappy life with Bounderby, attempts to seduce her. The better side of her nature is awakened by this experience, and at the crisis she flees for protection to her father, who in turn is awakened to the folly of his system. He shelters her from Bounderby and the couple are permanently separated. But further trouble is in store for Gradgrind. Tom has robbed his employer's bank, and though he contrives for a time to throw suspicion on a blameless artisan, Stephen Blackpool, he is finally detected and hustled out of the country. Notable minor characters include Sleary, the proprietor of a circus, and Cissy Jupe, whose father had been a performer in his troupe, whose generous hearts are contrasted with the harshness of Gradgrind's regime; also Mrs Sparsit, Bounderby's venomous housekeeper.

Condemned by T. B. *Macaulay for its 'sullen socialism', the novel was not greatly popular in its day, but later gained a considerable reputation, partly through the admiration of George Bernard *Shaw (who published a preface, 1912) and F. R. *Leavis (*The Great Tradition*, 1947), who saw Dickens in this work 'for once possessed by a comprehensive vision'.

HARDY, Thomas (1840–1928) Novelist and poet, born at Higher Bockhampton, near Dorchester in Dorset, son of a stonemason, whose family had known better days. His father taught Hardy the violin and his mother greatly encouraged his early interest in books. He attended school in Dorchester and at 16 was articled to John Hicks, a local architect. At the age of 22 he went to London, where he worked for the architect Arthur Blomfield, pursued a hectic London life, and also found time for extensive reading. During this time he lost the religious faith which had once led him to consider holy orders. He returned home in 1867 to continue architectural work in Dorchester, and began his first (unpublished) novel, *The Poor Man and the Lady*. At this time he probably fell in love with Tryphena Sparks, a relative aged 16. The history of his relationship with her, and of her relationship with Hardy's friend Horace Moule, continues to be the subject of speculation. In 1868 he was sent on an architectural mission to St Juliot, Cornwall, where he met the rector's sister-in-law, Emma Gifford. His first published novel, **Desperate Remedies*, appeared in 1871, to be followed by **Under the Greenwood Tree* (1872), *A *Pair of Blue Eyes* (1873), and **Far from the Madding Crowd* (1874). The success of the last enabled him, in 1874, to give up architecture for writing, and to marry Emma Gifford. The marriage soon produced intolerable strains, but it also produced, after Emma's death in 1912, some of Hardy's most moving poems. Between 1874 and the publication of **Jude the Obscure* in 1895 Hardy wrote twelve other novels (see below), as well as many short stories and poems. He and Emma travelled in Europe and Hardy spent several months of nearly every year in London. In 1885 they moved into Max Gate, near Dorchester, a forbidding house, to Hardy's own design. During this time Hardy greatly enjoyed the admiration of London's literary and aristocratic society and complained of reviewers' views on his 'pessimism' and 'immorality', culminating in what he chose to see as the bitterly hostile reception of **Tess of the D'Urbervilles* in 1891 and *Jude the Obscure* in 1895. He gave up the writing of fiction (which he had always regarded as inferior to poetry) and began to assemble his first volume of verse, *Wessex Poems* (1898). His successive collections, ending with *Winter Words* in 1928, were received without enthusiasm, except by a discerning few. In 1912 Emma died and in 1914 Hardy married Florence Dugdale. She, together with the terrier Wessex, did much to protect Hardy from the adulation of his admirers. Public honours fell upon him, among them the OM, honorary degrees from Cambridge and Oxford, a visit from the prince of Wales, the gold medal of the *Royal Society of Literature. Among the pall-bearers at his funeral in Westminster Abbey were J. M. *Barrie, John *Galsworthy, Edmund *Gosse, A. E. *Housman, Rudyard *Kipling, and George Bernard *Shaw.

The underlying theme of many of the novels, the short poems, and the epic drama *The *Dynasts* is, in Laurence *Binyon's words, 'the implanted crookedness of things'; the struggle of human beings against the indifferent force that rules the world and inflicts on them the sufferings and ironies of life and love. Hardy's sharp sense of the humorous and absurd finds expression largely in the presentation of the rustic characters in the novels. Most of the poems and novels reveal Hardy's attention to the natural world, consciousness of the multiplicities of human identities, and comic ironies.

Hardy's novels and short stories, according to his own classification, fall into three groups; most of them are described separately under their titles:

Novels of Character and Environment: **Under the Greenwood Tree* (1872); **Far from the Madding Crowd* (1874); *The Return of the Native* (1878); *The *Mayor of Casterbridge* (1886); *The *Woodlanders* (1887); *Wessex Tales* (1888); **Tess of the D'Urbervilles* (1891); *Life's Little Ironies* (1894); **Jude the Obscure* (1896, in the edition of the *Works* of that year).

Romances and Fantasies: *A *Pair of Blue Eyes* (1873); *The *Trumpet Major* (1880); **Two on a Tower* (1882); *A Group of Noble Dames* (1891); *The *Well-Beloved* (published serially 1892; revised and reissued 1897).

Novels of Ingenuity: **Desperate Remedies* (1891); *The *Hand of Ethelberta* (1876); *A Laodicean* (1881).

A Changed Man, The Waiting Supper, and Other Tales (1913) is a reprint of 'a dozen minor novels' belonging to the various groups.

Hardy published eight volumes of poetry: *Wessex Poems* (1898); *Poems of the Past and Present* (1902); *Time's Laughing-stocks* (1909); *Satires of Circumstance* (1914); *Moments of Vision* (1917); *Late Lyrics and Earlier* (1922); *Human Shows* (1925); *Winter Words* (1928). The *Collected Poems* (1930), published posthumously, contain over 900 poems of great variety and individuality, yet consistent over more than 60 years in attitudes to life and fate. Probably the most remarkable are in the group of poems written in recollection of his first wife ('Poems of 1912–13' in *Satires of Circumstance*). Hardy disliked, to use his own words, 'the jewelled line' of poetry that did not, to his mind, follow the patterns of speech. He experimented with rhythms and verse forms, avoiding facile flow. Gosse, Blunden, and Lytton *Strachey were of the small band who greatly admired his poetry, but not until long after his death did it begin to receive general critical acclaim. Philip *Larkin is among the most conspicuous of 20th-century poets to have found Hardy enabling.

Hardy published over 40 short stories, most of which were collected in *Wessex Tales* (1888); *A Group of Noble Dames* (1891); *Life's Little Ironies* (1894); and *A Changed Man*...(1913). The stories vary considerably in content, form, and style, and in many cases demonstrate a high degree of skill, but Hardy's reputation in this field has never approached his reputation as a novelist or poet.

The Dynasts, a vast work in blank verse and prose, occupied him for many years, and was published in three volumes, 1904, 1906, and 1908. He wrote one other poetic drama, *The Famous Tragedy of the Queen of Cornwall* (1923).

Recent studies include a two-volume life by Robert *Gittings (*Young Thomas Hardy*, 1975; *The Older Hardy*, 1980); John Bayley, *An Essay on Thomas Hardy* (1978); Michael Millgate, *Thomas Hardy* (1982); Ralph Pite, *Thomas Hardy: A Guarded Life* (2006); Claire Tomalin, *Thomas Hardy: The Time-Torn Man* (2006).

HARDYNG, John (*c.*1378–*c.*1464) Author of *The Chronicle of John Hardyng* in verse, written between the years 1440 and 1457. The *Chronicle* covers the period from Brutus (*see* BRUT) to 1437 and argues the claims of English kings (in the interests of Henry V and Henry VI) to overlordship of Scotland. A second version revises the work in the Yorkist interest, expunging the earlier eulogy of Henry V and declaring Henry VI to be 'of small intelligence'; this is perhaps the (dubious) authority for that prevailing view of him. It was edited by H. Ellis (1812; repr. New York, 1974); see A. Gransden, *Historical Writing in England II* (1982).

HARE, Sir David (1947–) Dramatist and director, born in St Leonard's, Sussex, educated at Jesus College, Cambridge. After some time in fringe theatre, during which he co-founded (with Tony Bicat) the Portable Theatre Company, he became resident dramatist at the *Royal Court Theatre in London in 1970–71. *Slag* (1970), *The Great Exhibition* (1972), *Knuckle* (1974), and *Teeth 'n' Smiles* (1976) marked him out as a powerful and original talent with a keen eye for both the iniquities of social privilege and the contradictions of radical idealism. In *Plenty* (1978), Hare provides a metaphor of the economic and ideological decline of post-war Britain through the experiences of Susan Traherne, a former courier in Occupied France who seeks in vain for an outlet for her wartime idealism. In 1984, he became an associate director at the *National Theatre where he directed *Pravda* (1985), a political satire concerning two national newspapers, co-written with Howard *Brenton, with whom he had previously collaborated on *Brassneck* (1973). Also at the National, his acclaimed trilogy of plays on British institutions began with *Racing Demon* (1990), about the Church of England. This was followed by *Murmuring Judges* (1991), a critique of the British criminal justice system, and *The Absence of War* (1993), about the Labour Party. *Amy's View* (1997) charts the antagonism over two decades of ageing actress Esme Allen and her daughter Amy's partner Dominic, Esme representing the 'Death of the Theatre' and he the destructive 'Rise of the Media': the play ends on a note of defiant faith in the redeeming power of art. Hare continues to be active in theatrical life, appearing in his own account of a visit to Israel and Palestine, *Via Dolorosa* (1998), even as his own *The Blue Room* was playing elsewhere in London. In 2003 and 2004 he acknowledged the growing strength of the docu-drama movement with his *The Permanent Way*, a devised piece questioning Britain's railway system post-privatization, and *Stuff Happens*, in which Tony Blair and George Bush are shown as they move towards the decision to invade Iraq. His is a unique voice in the British theatre.

HARE, Julius Charles (1795–1855) Author and Anglican clergyman, born at Valdagno, Italy; educated at Charterhouse School and Trinity College, Cambridge. He was elected fellow in 1818 and became a close friend of the scientist and philosopher William Whewell (1794–1866). With his brother Augustus William Hare (1792–1834, biographer and compiler of travel books), he published the popular *Guesses at Truth* (1827), a collection of observations on philosophy, religion, literature, language, and related subjects. He translated (with Connop *Thirlwall) *Niebuhr's important *History of Rome* (1828–42), which was vehemently attacked for its scepticism in the *Quarterly Review, prompting the translators to publish a *Vindication of Niebuhr's History* (1829). He edited (with Thirlwall) the *Philological Museum* (1832–3), which attempted to introduce the neglected new continental philology of Jacob *Grimm. His edition of John *Sterling's *Essays and Tales* (1848) highlighted Sterling's religious doubts; it was countered in Thomas *Carlyle's *Life of John Sterling* (1851). Hare's most significant influence lay in his role as advocate of German literature and scholarship.

HARINGTON, James *See* HARRINGTON, JAMES.

HARINGTON, Sir John (1560–1612) Courtier, translator, and writer, godson of *Elizabeth I; he was educated at Eton College and King's College, Cambridge. Supposedly at the queen's command, he translated *Ariosto's *Orlando furioso* (1591), retaining the *ottava rima* of the original and providing *A Preface or rather Brief Apology of Poetry*, closely related to Philip Sidney's *Defence of Poetry*, and interesting, often gossipy notes referring to such figures as his own pet dog Bungy, who is also depicted on the book's title page. Though Ben *Jonson claimed 'that John Harington's *Ariosto*, under all translations was the worst', it has been read and enjoyed for generations, its modern readers including Anthony *Powell. Harington's next work, *A New Discourse of a Stale Subject, Called the Metamorphosis of Ajax* (1596), a proposal for the introduction of water closets, was an ill-judged bid for royal favour; together with other satires and epigrams it led to a period of exile from court. In 1599 Harington accompanied the earl of *Essex to Ireland, and was deputed by him to appease the queen's anger on his return, without success. His letters and miscellaneous writings were collected in Henry Harington's *Nugae Antiquae* (1769–75); N. E. McClure edited his letters and epigrams (1930); Robert McNulty edited the *Orlando furioso* (1972); E. S. Donno *The Metamorphosis of Ajax* (1962); and S. Cauchi the translation of *Virgil's *Aeneid Bk VI* (1991). There is a study by J. Scott-Warren (2001). The lasting interest of Harington's writings lies in his lively personality and ability to record detailed impressions of his world. He gives, for instance, an account of a visit to the queen a few weeks before her death, in which she said to him, 'When thou dost feel creeping time at thy gate, these fooleries will please thee less.'

HARLAND, Henry (1861–1905) American author who wrote several novels about Jewish immigrant life under the pseudonym of Sidney Luska. Born in Brooklyn, and educated at the College of the City of New York and (briefly) at Harvard divinity school, he settled in London in 1889, where he became in 1894 editor of the **Yellow Book*. He proved an enterprising and capable editor, publishing the work of established figures like Henry *James alongside that of controversial writers, including John *Davidson and Arthur *Symons. He published several novels during his London period, among them the popular *The Cardinal's Snuff-Box* (1900), which reflected his conversion to Roman Catholicism in 1898. His early death in San Remo, Italy, resulted from the tuberculosis which shadowed his later years.

Harleian manuscripts A collection of manuscripts made by Robert *Harley, first earl of Oxford, and augmented by his son Edward, the second earl (1689–1741). The library contained 50,000 books, 350,000 pamphlets, and over 7,000 volumes of manuscripts, including early biblical texts in Greek, Latin, and Hebrew, texts of classical authors and church Fathers, papal bulls and registers, charters, deeds, and state papers. The books were bought for £13,000 by Thomas *Osborne in 1741 (*see* HARLEIAN MISCELLANY); Parliament paid £10,000 for the manuscripts, forming in 1753 one of the foundation collections of the *British Museum. The manuscripts are now in the *British Library.

Harleian Miscellany, The A selection of tracts from the library of Edward Harley (1689–1741), son of Robert *Harley. It was edited by William *Oldys, and published (8 vols, 1744–6) by Thomas *Osborne; Samuel *Johnson wrote the introduction.

Harlem Renaissance The flourishing of *African American literature and culture, centred on the Harlem district of New York, which took place in the 1920s and 1930s. Among the anthologies produced in this period, Alain Locke's *The *New Negro* (1925) helped promote a new ethnic pride. The movement included mutual help within the community as well as assistance by white patrons including Carl Van Vechten (1880–1964). Developments in the theatre led to the first staging of a play by an African American on Broadway in 1925, and landmark works of the decade included Jean *Toomer's *Cane* (1923). The new poets included Countee *Cullen and Langston *Hughes, whose 1926 essay 'The Negro Artist and the Racial Mountain' promoted the exploitation of cultural links with Africa. From the late 1920s onwards more novels appeared by figures such as Jamaica-born Claude McKay, Nella Larsen, and Hughes which all explored the complexities of urban life. James Weldon *Johnson and Zora Neale *Hurston began their careers in this period, researching into anthropology as well as producing their own poetry and fiction. The Harlem Renaissance was a formative period in African American literature, laying down a body of work which would be used and developed by later writers.

HARLEY, Robert, first earl of Oxford (1661–1724) Tory statesman, chief minister in the last four years of Queen Anne's reign. He oversaw Daniel *Defoe's secret government missions, 1703–14. He frequented the *Scriblerus Club, and several verse invitations to him by Alexander *Pope and Jonathan *Swift survive. Harley was impeached in 1715 but released in 1717; Pope's commendatory *Epistle to Oxford* dates from 1722. He acquired a great library, which his son Edward augmented; *see* HARLEIAN MANUSCRIPTS; HARLEIAN MISCELLANY.

Harley Lyrics A collection of 32 Middle English lyrics that have been collected with other material in Latin and French in the manuscript Harley 2253, from Ludlow, Shropshire (though the poems are thought to be originally from various parts of the country), dated to the 1340s. The lyrics are on both secular and religious themes and this collection is particularly valued because it preserves the only surviving versions of the secular poems, including 'Alysoun', 'Lenten ys come with love to toune', 'Blow, Northerne Wynd', 'Wynter wakeneth al my care', and 'The Man in the Moon'. The poems are varied and highly sophisticated with respect to theme, diction, and literary form. They have been edited by G. L. Brook (1956); N. P. Ker edited a facsimile of the manuscript (EETS os 255, 1965).

Harlot's Progress, The See HOGARTH, WILLIAM.

HARNETT, Cynthia (1893–1981) London-born writer and illustrator who studied at Chelsea School of Art and is remembered for her six vivid and well-researched historical novels for children—*The Great House* (1949), *The Wool-Pack* (1951; winner of the *Carnegie Medal), *Ring out Bow Bells!* (1953), *Stars of Fortune* (1956), *The Load of Unicorn* (1959), and (with the illustrator Gareth Floyd) *The Writing on the Hearth* (1971). Harnett's books feature the lives of ordinary children growing up during momentous events in the 14th to the 18th centuries.

Harper's Monthly Magazine Founded in 1850 by Harper & Brothers of New York, at first to reproduce in America the work of distinguished English contributors to serials like Charles *Dickens, W. M. *Thackeray, and Edward *Bulwer-Lytton. It subsequently became more American in character, publishing work by Herman *Melville, William Dean *Howells, Sarah Orne *Jewett, and others. From 1900 to 1925 it was known as *Harper's New Monthly Magazine*, and subsequently as *Harper's Magazine*.

Harper's Weekly (1857–1916) An illustrated political and literary journal, published in New York, best known for its engravings and woodcuts. It serialized novels by Charles *Dickens, Elizabeth *Gaskell, and others, and later published work by Rudyard *Kipling, Henry *James, and Arthur Conan *Doyle.

HARPSFIELD, Nicholas (1519–75) Educated at Winchester College and New College, Oxford. A lawyer by training, he attached himself to Cardinal Reginald Pole (1500–58), but was imprisoned in the Fleet, 1562–74. As well as controversial works and a history of the English church, he completed (*c.*1556–7) an important life of Sir Thomas *More, first published in full in 1932.

HARRINGTON (Harington), **James** (1611–77) Political philosopher, born in Northampton of an ancient family, and educated at Trinity College, Oxford, where he took no degree; he subsequently travelled on the Continent, and attended the court of the elector palatine. During the Civil War he attended Charles I in his captivity (1647–8), and a tradition (through John *Aubrey and Anthony *Wood) was established that his deep personal devotion to the monarch plunged him into years of profound melancholy on his execution; some have seen this as one of the impulses behind his great republican work *The *Commonwealth of Oceana* (1656). Harrington also wrote several tracts in defence of this work, and other political works (*The Prerogative of Popular Government*, 1657–8; *The Art of Law-Giving*, 1659; *Aphorisms Political*, 1659) expounding concepts including republicanism, the ballot, rotation of officers, and indirect election. In 1659 he founded the Rota, a *coffee-house academy which met for political discussion, the first of its kind in England. In 1661 he was arrested and imprisoned on a charge of treason, defended himself ably, and was later released, but by this time his health was in decline, and little is known of the remaining years of his life. Harrington has never been considered a great stylist (David *Hume described his prose as 'altogether stiff and pedantic') but he had many admirers, including William *Wordsworth and S. T. *Coleridge, and his shrewd historical analysis and political projections have increasingly attracted attention. See *The Political Works of James Harrington*, ed. J. G. A. Pocock (1977).

HARRINGTON, Sir John See HARINGTON, SIR JOHN.

HARRIOT (Hariot), **Thomas** (1560/61–1621) Mathematician, astronomer, and polymath. He was employed by Sir Walter *Ralegh as an expert, especially in navigation and cartography, went on the 1585–6 expedition to Virginia, and later assisted over the 1595 Guiana expedition. His *A Briefe and True Report of the New Found Land of Virginia* (1588), an early example of an economic survey, was printed by *Hakluyt. It shows sympathetic understanding of the local Algonquian and, incidentally, promoted tobacco. From 1591, Harriot's scholarship was supported by Henry Percy, earl of Northumberland. He corresponded with Kepler and is thought to have influenced *Descartes, but his failure to publish and the probably unfair association of his name with atheism and necromancy spoilt his reputation; the judge at Ralegh's trial in 1603 referred to 'that devil Harriot' and Thomas *Kyd claimed that Christopher *Marlowe had been an intimate. Modern scholars have found Harriot's papers fruitful for research.

HARRIS, 'Frank' (really James Thomas) (1856–1931) Author and editor. Born in Galway, he went to America at the age of 14, then travelled on the Continent before settling in London, where he edited the *Evening News* (1883–6), the **Fortnightly Review* (1886–94), and, most significantly, the **Saturday Review* (1894–8), in which he published, among others, G. B. *Shaw (as a drama critic), H. G. *Wells, and Max *Beerbohm, all of whom left vivid recollections of him. As an editor he had great flair, though his extrovert arrogance made him as many enemies as friends; Wells described him as 'too loud and vain...to be a proper scoundrel', but a scandalous reputation gathered round him, occasioned by his fight against Victorian prudery, by his decreasingly respectable role as editor (of such periodicals as the *Candid Friend, Vanity Fair,* and *Hearth and Home*), and by his sexually boastful, explicit (and unreliable) memoirs, *My Life and Loves* (4 vols, 1922–7). His other publications include volumes of short stories, some influenced by *Maupassant and *Balzac; *The Bomb* (1908), a novel about socialist-anarchism set in Chicago; a play, *Mr and Mrs Daventry* (performed 1900; pub. 1956), based on a plot which he bought from his friend Oscar *Wilde; and lives of Shakespeare, Wilde (1918), and Shaw (1931). He advertised himself with characteristic bravado as the greatest Shakespearian of his day, and his highly personal reading of Shakespeare in *The Man Shakespeare and his Tragic Life-story* (1909), though derided by scholars, had a considerable impact. Harris remains an enigmatic and controversial figure, whose personality continues to attract attention and whose real achievements tend to be obscured by his persistent and self-destructive self-aggrandizement. There is a lively biography by his one-time admirer and employee Hugh *Kingsmill, published 1932. See also Philippa Pullar, *Frank Harris* (1975).

HARRIS, Joel Chandler (1848–1908) American journalist and author, born at Eatonton, Georgia, with a strong interest in the myths, customs, dialects, and idioms of black Americans, which he reproduced in his famous 'Uncle Remus' series, from *Uncle Remus: His Songs and Sayings* (1880) to *Uncle Remus and the Little Boy* (1910). Originally published in the *Atlanta Constitution* newspaper, these consist of trickster folk tales featuring a variety of animals, with cunning Brer Rabbit as hero, told by 'Uncle Remus', an elderly former slave, to a little boy and interspersed with comments on many other subjects.

HARRIS, John (1820–84) Cornish poet and miner, born at Bollenowe, near Camborne, who published several volumes of poetry celebrating his native landscapes, including *Lays from the Mine, the Moor and the Mountains* (1853) and *A Story of Carn Brea* (1863). *Songs from the Earth*, a selection (1977), has an introduction by D. M. *Thomas which saw a 'Romantic visionary quality which breathes life into an Augustan vocabulary'.

HARRIS, Robert (1957–) Novelist and journalist, born in Nottingham, educated at Edward VII College, Melton Mowbray, and Selwyn College, Cambridge; he worked for BBC television, as political editor of the *Observer*, and as a political columnist for the *Sunday Times* and the *Daily Telegraph*. His early books, such as *Selling Hitler* (1986), an account of the forged Hitler diaries, were lively, informed non-fiction. In 1992, he began a full-time and highly successful fictional career with *Fatherland*, an *alternate history novel in which the Third Reich survives into the 1960s. *Enigma* (1995), set in Bletchley Park during the Second World War, and *Archangel* (1998), peering back from 1990s Russia to the terrors of the Stalin era, continued his concern with totalitarian menace. *Pompeii* (2003), another fast-paced thriller, was silhouetted against the eruption of Vesuvius in AD 79. It was followed by *Imperium* (2006), the first novel in a projected trilogy about Marcus Tullius *Cicero, in which Harris's fascination with politics and his interest in the Roman world combine. *The Ghost* (2007), a sardonic novel about the perilous ghostwriting of the memoirs of a recently retired British prime minister, reflects, like much of his fiction, his keen admiration for George *Orwell and Graham *Greene.

HARRIS, Wilson (1921–) Guyanese-born novelist, educated at Queen's College, Georgetown, British Guiana, where he qualified and subsequently worked as a land surveyor before coming to England in 1959. His 'Guyana Quartet' consists of *Palace of the Peacock* (1960), *The Far Journey of Oudin* (1961), *The Whole Armour* (1962), and *The Secret Ladder* (1963). Later works include *The Waiting Room* (1967), *The Age of the Rainmakers* (1971), and *The Tree of the Sun* (1978). The Carnival trilogy consists of *Carnival* (1985), *The Infinite Rehearsal* (1987), and *The Four Banks of the River of Space* (1990). *Jonestown* (1996) describes the mass suicide of the followers of cult leader Jim Jones. It was followed by *The Dark Jester* (2001), *The Mask of the Beggar* (2003), and *The Ghost of Memory* (2006). His fiction is experimental in form, built on a complex, poetic structure, interweaving history, mythology, and the contemporary world. *See also* POSTCOLONIAL LITERATURE.

HARRISON, Frederic (1831–1923) Positivist and writer, educated at King's College School, London, and Wadham College, Oxford, professor of jurisprudence and international law to the Inns of Court (1877–89), and from 1880 to 1905 president of the English Positivist Committee, formed to disseminate the doctrines of Auguste *Comte. He was the author of many works on historical, political, and literary subjects, and attracted the censure of Matthew *Arnold in **Culture and Anarchy* for his challenging remarks on culture: 'The man of culture is in politics one of the poorest mortals alive. For simple pedantry and want of good sense no man is his equal', a view which roused Arnold to his own defence of the meaning of culture. His long and active career as a polemicist led to many literary connections; in 1880 he engaged the young George *Gissing (then unknown) as a tutor, and he published work on Alfred *Tennyson, John *Ruskin, and John Stuart *Mill.

HARRISON, Harry (1925–) American *science fiction writer, born in Stamford, Connecticut; celebrated for his humorous 'Stainless Steel Rat' series, which first appeared in **Astounding* (1957), and other spoofs of science fiction's conventions. *Make Room! Make Room!* (1966), filmed as *Soylent Green* (1973), is among his more serious and thoughtful satires.

HARRISON, M. John (1945–) *Science fiction and *fantasy writer, born in Warwickshire; first published in **New Worlds* magazine. His fiction covers most areas of the fantastic, as well as realist fiction such as *Climbers* (1989). Much of his early work was marked by a struggle to overcome the generic conventions of science fiction and fantasy by introducing darker reflections of contemporary life. *Light* (2002) is science fiction space opera that revisits the territory of his urban fantasy/horror novels and stories (collected in *Things That Never Happen*, 2002). See Mark Bould and Michelle Reid (eds), *Parietal Games* (2005).

HARRISON, Tony (1937–) Poet, born in Leeds, and educated at Leeds Grammar School and Leeds University, where he read Classics. Memories of his working-class childhood and family life, and the difficulties of class mobility, provide the material for much of his poetry, although his work also reflects his experiences of Africa, the Soviet Union, and America, and he can be a powerful love and erotic poet. His first volume was *The Loiners* (1970); others include *Continuous* (1981), *V* (1985), written during the miners' strike of 1984–5, which was the first of his 'film poems', broadcast by Channel 4 in 1987, *A Cold Coming: Gulf War Poems* (1992), and *Under the Clock* (2005). Among what he calls his 'theatre works' are versions of *Molière's *The Misanthrope* (1973), *Racine's *Phèdre* (*Phaedra Britannica*, 1975), the **Oresteia* (1981), and Victor *Hugo's *The Prince's Play* (1996); his 'film poems' include *The Blasphemers' Banquet* (1989) and *The Shadow of Hiroshima* (1995). All of his work shows great facility in rhyme and a skilful adaptation of colloquial speech. *Collected Poems* and *Collected Film Poetry* appeared in 2007. Harrison is renowned for his independent voice and impassioned commentary on public affairs.

HARRISON, William (1535–93) Born in London and educated at St Paul's and Westminster schools and Christ Church, Oxford, rector of Radwinter in Essex and canon of Windsor. A friend of such scholars as Gabriel *Harvey and John *Stow, Harrison's main interest was in writing chronologies of the history of the world and of English history: these remain in manuscript. He was the author of the admirable *Description of England* and the translator of John *Bellenden's Scottish version of *Boece's *Description of Scotland*, both included in *Holinshed's *Chronicles*. There is a study by G. J. R. Parry (1997).

Harrowing of Hell A semi-dramatic poem of 250 lines in octosyllabic couplets from about 1250, based on the legend that Christ descended into hell to lead out the souls condemned there by Adam's sin. The legend derives from the account in the Apocryphal Gospel of Nicodemus. There are also versions in Old and Middle English prose, in **Piers Plowman*, and in the *mystery plays. In the poem a narrative introduction is followed by speeches by Christ, Satan, the doorkeeper of hell, and some of the souls in hell. Christ reproves Satan and claims Adam; Satan replies that he will win one of mankind on earth for every soul released. But Christ breaks down the door, binds Satan, and frees his servants. See W. H. Hulme (ed.), *The Middle English Harrowing of Hell and Gospel of Nicodemus* (EETS ES 100, 1907).

Harry Potter *See* POTTER, HARRY.

Harry Richmond, The Adventures of A novel by George *Meredith, published 1871. This began as 'an autobiographical study', and its early sections describe Meredith's schooldays near Petersfield in some detail. Still more deeply autobiographical is the novel's consideration of the father–son relationship. Richmond Roy is the son of an actress and a mysterious royal personage. Although flamboyant and romantic, he is only an indigent teacher of singing, once employed by Squire Beltham of Riversley, one of whose daughters he carried off and married. She shortly dies, and young Harry, their son, is dramatically captured by his father from his grandfather's house. Here the narrative adroitly switches to the first person, and the rest of the story is related by Harry. The conflict between his father and grandfather, and his father's obsessive determination to marry him well, are important themes in the book. Harry loves his tempestuous father, but eventually realizes that he must escape the 'dreadful devotion' of his parent. Richmond Roy lives a life of splendour in the courts of petty German princes, interrupted by periods in a debtors' prison. At one of these courts Harry and the beautiful Princess Ottilia fall in love. The outrageous manoeuvres of Harry's father to settle the unlikely match, and the humiliations to which Harry is exposed, are related with much comic-grotesque detail. Harry also encounters the fascinating Gypsy Kioni in one of the novel's many *picaresque and implausible sub-plots, but in the end marries an English girl, Janet Ilchester, as his grandfather had long wished. Roy dies melodramatically in the last chapter, perishing in the flames of Riversley Grange while seeking to save Harry's ever-loyal Aunt Dorothy.

HARSENT, David (1942–) Poet, born in Devon; he left school at 16 to work in a bookshop. His first volume, *A Violent Country*, was published in 1969, and others have included *Dreams of the Dead* (1977), *Mister Punch* (1984), *News from the Front* (1993), *A Bird's Idea of Flight* (1998), *Marriage* (2002), and *Legion* (2005). His *Selected Poems 1969–2005* was published in 2007. His early work is characteristically short-lined, free verse, ruminative, imagistic, and melancholic, and prominently preoccupied with human and sexual relationships and with mortality. This poetry was of the kind favoured by Ian *Hamilton, editor of *The Review* and the *New Review*, which published Harsent. Later work, however, developed a greater extensiveness and range by employing a longer line and experimenting with versions of poetic sequence—in which Harsent was always interested—and of narrative. 'Marriage', for instance, is a sequence written in the voice of the painter Pierre Bonnard which meditates, profoundly and involvingly, on his relationship with Maria Boursin, his long-time partner and model and eventual wife; the poem ramifies with implication and includes some extraordinary notations of privacy and mutuality. 'Legion' runs a desolating and dreadful descant on modern warfare. Although no actual war zone is specified, Harsent's knowledge of Bosnia obviously lies behind and underwrites the sequence, and it contains unforgettable images of brutalized vulnerability, as though great journalism is being given an altogether original density and focus—such as, for instance, the picture of a 'raw recruit' crawling out from a mound of corpses to charge at a machine-gun emplacement 'armed with only a shovel, with only a trowel, with only a toothpick, with only his teeth'. Harsent has translated the work of the Bosnian poet Goran Simic. He also writes crime thrillers under a pseudonym, and wrote the libretto for Harrison *Birtwistle's opera *Gawain* (1991), based on the medieval poem *Sir *Gawain and the Green Knight*.

HARTE, Bret (1836–1902) Author and poet, born at Albany, New York, and taken to California at 18, where he saw something of mining life. He worked on newspapers and periodicals in San Francisco, to which he contributed the short stories which made him famous. Notable among these were 'The Luck of Roaring Camp' (1868) and 'The Outcasts of Poker Flat', which were included in *The Luck of Roaring Camp and Other Sketches* (1870). His humorous-pathetic verse includes 'Plain Language from Truthful James' (1870), often referred to as 'The Heathen Chinee'. He collaborated briefly with Mark *Twain. Harte served as American consul at Krefeld in Germany (1878–80) and at Glasgow (1880–85), after which he lived in England. He is best remembered as pioneer local colourist in his early works. See Axel Nissen, *Bret Harte: Prince and Pauper* (2000).

HARTLEY, David (1705–57) Philosopher and doctor, educated at Bradford Grammar School and Jesus College, Cambridge. As a practising physician he published work on smallpox and stones in the bladder. In his *Observations on Man, his Frame, his Duty and his Expectations* (1749) he repudiated the view of the third earl of *Shaftesbury and Francis *Hutcheson that the 'moral sense' is instinctively innate in us, and attributed it rather to the tendency of ideas which have occurred together to recall one another. From this association of the ideas of pain and pleasure with certain actions, Hartley traces the evolution of the higher pleasures out of the lower, until the mind is carried to 'the pure love of God, as our highest and ultimate perfection'. The psychological doctrine was founded on an attempt to find Newtonian principles in the operation of the mind, notably in the theory of physical 'vibrations' or 'vibratiuncles' in the 'medullary substance' of the brain. This mechanistic theory of the processes of the imagination was popularized by Joseph *Priestley in *Lectures on Oratory and Criticism* (1777) and other works and influenced the development of aesthetic theory up to the time of S. T. *Coleridge, who named his first son Hartley in honour of the philosopher.

HARTLEY, L. P. (Leslie Poles) (1895–1972) Novelist. He was the son of a solicitor who became the director of a brickworks, and he spent his childhood at the family home, Fletton Towers, near Peterborough. He was educated at Harrow School and Balliol College, Oxford. He began his literary career as a writer of short stories and as a fiction reviewer; his stories were published as *Night Fears* (1924) and *The Killing Bottle* (1932); *Simonetta Perkins*, a novella set in Venice (where Hartley spent much of his time) describing a young Bostonian's adventure with a gondolier, appeared in 1925. His first full-length novel, *The Shrimp and the Anemone* (1944), was followed by *The Sixth Heaven* (1946) and *Eustace and Hilda* (1947), the last being the title by which the trilogy is known: the first volume is a powerfully evocative account of a childhood summer by the sea in Norfolk, at the end of which Eustace unexpectedly inherits a small fortune, and the two subsequent volumes take him through fashionable Oxford undergraduate life to Venice and the Continent, as he struggles with his complex, intense relationship with his elder sister Hilda. Hartley's best-known novel is *The *Go-Between* (1953), narrated in the first person by an elderly man recalling in 1952 the events of the hot summer of 1900, when, staying with a school friend in a Norfolk country house for the holidays, he innocently carried letters between the friend's sister and the local farmer with whom she was having an affair. As the story progresses, it becomes clear that this distant holiday has marked him for life. The portrayal of leisurely Edwardian England, with its cricket matches, bathing parties, and lurking social embarrassments, is masterly. The novel's opening sentence, 'The past is a foreign country: they do things differently there,' is often quoted. Hartley's other novels include *A Perfect Woman* (1955); *The Hireling* (1957), which takes up the recurrent theme of dangerous inter-class sexual relationships in its story of the widowed Lady Franklin and her friendship with her driver; *The Brickfield* (1964); and *The Love-Adept* (1969).

HARTLIB, Samuel (d. 1662) Reformer and writer, born in Elblag, Poland, and educated at Königsberg and Cambridge universities; he settled in England to escape religious persecution. Influenced by Francis *Bacon's progressive thinking, he became, during the Commonwealth, the centre of a circle of intellectuals, several from humble origins, interested in scientific, educational, social, and agrarian reform. He brought John *Comenius to England, was a patron of Robert *Boyle, and a friend of John *Milton, who addressed his *Of Education* (1644) to him. His utopia, *A Description of the Famous Kingdom of Macaria*, was published in 1641. Among his projects was a state-funded 'Office of Address', a kind of precursor of the internet, which would collect information from thinkers and practitioners of all kinds and distribute it for the common good. His vast archive, now in Sheffield University, was published on CD-ROM in 1995. See Charles Webster, *The Great Instauration: Science, Medicine and Reform 1626–1660* (1975).

HARVEY, Gabriel (1552/3–1631) Writer and scholar, eldest son of a Saffron Walden rope-maker, educated at Christ's College, Cambridge. Elected a fellow of Pembroke Hall, he became Edmund *Spenser's friend and probably his tutor. The poet addressed his sonnet 'Harvey, the happy above happiest men' to him. Harvey benefited from the patronage of Sir Thomas Smith (1513–77), whom he commemorated in a series of Latin elegies *Smithus* (1578), which may have influenced the form of Spenser's 'Teares of the Muses'. After a brilliant but troubled academic career, mainly concerned with rhetoric, Ramism (*see* RAMUS, PETER), civil law, and Latin poetry, Harvey turned his interests towards the court and the vernacular. He figures as Hobbinol in Spenser's *The *Shepheardes Calender* (1579). In his exchange of *Letters* with Spenser (1580) he indicated the difficulties of writing English verse in classical metres, but also delivered his judgement of *The *Faerie Queene*, as it then existed, as '*Hobgoblin* run away with the Garland from Apollo'. He was in trouble with the university and the government for these *Letters*, which included satirical verses on the earl of *Oxford, but was protected by the earl of *Leicester, for whom he worked for a time. His attack on the dying Robert *Greene in *Four Letters* (1592) provoked Thomas *Nashe's stinging replies which Harvey's *Pierces Supererogation* (1593) did not mitigate. With his old-fashioned humanist values and often awkward prose style Harvey came off worse in the controversy, and spent the last 30 years of his life in retirement at Saffron Walden, probably practising medicine.

Harvey's extraordinarily wide range of interests is reflected in the marginalia beautifully written in the books he owned. Many of these survive and record penetrating comments and notes on rhetoric, mathematics and navigation, politics, astrology, medicine, his contemporaries, and literature, including references to William *Shakespeare and to his friends Philip *Sidney and Spenser. His English works were edited by A. B. *Grosart (1884–5) and there is a study by V. F. Stern (1979).

HARVEY, Sir Paul (1869–1948) Scholar and diplomat, educated at Rugby School and New College, Oxford. He was orphaned at an early age, and the first stages of his distinguished career were watched over with interest by Henry *James and Lady Augusta *Gregory, both friends who had known him since boyhood. He was the compiler of *The Oxford Companion to English Literature* (1932), the first of the Oxford *Companions*, the idea for which originated in a suggestion from Kenneth Sisam at the *Oxford University Press in 1927–8, and wrote most of the entries himself. It was conceived as a reference book on the lines of *Brewer's *Dictionary of Phrase and Fable*, to contain English authors, plots of their works, and characters; foreign authors commonly quoted; legendary characters; a little classical background; and allusions, such as 'The Wise Men of Gotham'. Somewhat to Harvey's dismay, the project grew to include literary terms, periodicals, social clubs, etc., and the pressure of work obliged him to concede that he could not on the average deal with more than three five-act plays a day 'and to do this is a burden; the shorter the article, the greater the labour of condensation'. The result of his labours was a much-loved and idiosyncratic volume, with a very wide range of reference and some masterly plot summaries, which went through four editions. The volume was updated by Dorothy Eagle after his death, and was succeeded by a new edition (ed. Margaret Drabble) in 1985. Harvey went on to compile the *Oxford Companions* to *Classical Literature* (1937) and *French Literature*, completed by Janet E. Heseltine (1959).

HARVEY, William (1578–1657) Doctor and scientist, born in Folkestone; educated at King's School, Canterbury, Caius College, Cambridge, and the University of Padua, where he studied under the anatomist Hieronymus Fabricius (1537–1619). He practised in London, became influential in the College of Physicians, and acted as physician to *James I and Charles I. His career was disrupted by the Civil War. At the battle of Edgehill he took care of the royal children, reading to them under a hedge. When Charles moved the court to Oxford, Harvey was made warden of Merton College, but he had to retire to London under the Commonwealth. His discovery of the circulation of blood (or, as some argue, rediscovery, since the Spanish physician Michael Servetus, burned at the stake as a heretic in 1553, had anticipated him, without his knowing it) was announced in 1616, and published in *De Motu Cordis* (1628; English trans. 1653). In embryology, he hypothesized the existence of a mammalian egg and dissected many deer from the royal parks in hopes of finding it. His incomplete *De Generatione* (1651; trans. 1653) was published by his disciple George Ent (1604–89). He left an endowment to the Royal College of Physicians for an annual oration (still given) and founded the Harvey Grammar School in Folkestone (still flourishing). The doctor-poet Henry *Vaughan makes use of the imagery of Harveian circulation, as does the philosopher Henry More (1614–87). Harvey's ideas also influenced Sir Thomas *Browne.

HARY'S *Wallace* A famous Scottish epic poem celebrating the deeds of Sir William *Wallace, written by Hary (Harry; *c.*1440–*c.*1492). Although the poem was written in the 1470s, the earliest extant version, now in the National Library of Scotland, was written in 1488 by John Ramsay, the scribe of John *Barbour's *The Bruce*. The poem consists of *c.*12,000 lines in heroic couplets. Hary is not concerned about balance: Wallace is presented throughout as a committed hero of great valour, in contrast to his English opponents. Although vivid and of great literary value and energy, the poem is not a reliable history of its hero's life, since some of the episodes it narrates have no basis in fact, or have been heavily embroidered. The rewriting of the poem in 1722, by William Hamilton of Gilbertfield, angered Robert *Burns. The poem has been edited by M. P. McDiarmid, 2 vols, Scottish Text Society 4–5 (1968–9).

HAŠEK, Jaroslav (1883–1923) Czech writer, born in Prague, remembered for his creation of the character of 'the good soldier Švejk' (or Schweik), a subversive, irreverent, opportunistic figure, a 'wise fool', who appeared in several narratives, most notably in the long rambling work bearing his name, published 1921–3. Hašek's works have been translated into English by Cecil Parrott.

HATHAWAY, Anne (1555/6–1623) She married *Shakespeare in November 1582. Her family home, a farmhouse known as 'Anne Hathaway's cottage', is still to be seen in Shottery, on the edge of Stratford-upon-Avon.

HATTON, Sir Christopher (*c.*1540–1591) Said to have attracted the attention of *Elizabeth I by his graceful dancing (alluded to by Sheridan, *The *Critic*, II. ii). He became her favourite, receiving grants of offices and estates (including Ely Place, now the site of Hatton Garden). Hatton was lord chancellor, 1587–91, and chancellor of Oxford University, 1588. The friend and patron of Edmund *Spenser, Thomas *Churchyard, and Barnaby *Rich, he wrote Act IV of **Tancred and Gismund*.

Haunted Man and the Ghost's Bargain, The A Christmas book by Charles *Dickens, published 1848. Redlaw, a learned chemist, is haunted by memories of sorrow and injustice. He is visited by an evil spirit, who tempts him to think that he is cursed by these memories, and makes a bargain by which he will forget them, on condition that he communicates this power of oblivion to everyone he meets. He discovers with horror that forgetfulness blots out from his own life and the lives of those about him (in particular the delightful Tetterbys) gratitude, repentance, compassion, and forbearance. He prays to be released from his bargain, which is effected by the influence of the angelic Milly Swidger.

HAUPTMANN, Gerhart (1862–1946) German dramatist. His first play, *Vor Sonnenaufgang* (1889: *Before Sunrise*), was the first work of *naturalism to be performed on the German stage. His most important naturalist play, *Die Weber* (1892: *The Weavers*), depicts the uprising of Silesian weavers which had taken place in 1844. Notable for the use of dialect, the direct dramatization of class conflict, and the eschewing of an individual hero, it was greatly admired by Lenin. Like Henrik *Ibsen and August *Strindberg, Hauptmann began to move towards a new symbolic drama, but returned from time to time to a more realist style. His narrative works, of which the two novellas of 1888, *Bahnwärter Thiel* (*Signalman Thiel*) and *Fasching* (*Shrovetide*), are the outstanding examples, are dark naturalistic tales with some symbolic elements in the manner of Émile *Zola. He won the *Nobel Prize for Literature in 1912. Hauptmann was much admired by James *Joyce, who translated two of his plays and described *The Weavers* as a masterpiece: 'a little immortal thing'.

Havelok the Dane, The Lay of A late 13th-century romance in 3,000 lines of rhyming octosyllables. There is an Anglo-Norman version, the anonymous *Lai d'Haveloc*, which resembles the 800-line account in Anglo-Norman at the beginning of Geffrei *Gaimar's *Lestoire des Engleis*. The dispossessed Havelok, prince of Denmark, marries Goldeboru, the dispossessed daughter of King Athelwold of England. Havelok is brought up by the fisherman Grim and becomes kitchen-boy in the household of Godrich, Goldeboru's treacherous guardian. His noble origins are twice revealed, once to Grim and once to Goldeboru, by a mystical light shining over his head. At the end all three return to Denmark, defeat and hang Havelok's usurping guardian Godard, and reclaim the throne. The story has parallels with events in English and Norwegian history: Havelok has been etymologically identified with Anlaf Cuaran, the son of a Viking chief Sihtric, king of Northumberland in 925, who was defeated with King Constantine of Scotland in 937 at *Brunanburh; but most of its material and themes are legendary. It is one of the most admired of all Middle English romances because of its narrative coherence and the sustained interest of its action. The manuscript was discovered by accident in the Bodleian Library and has been edited by Donald B. Sands in *Middle English Verse Romances* (1966) and Ronald B. Herzman *et al.* in *Four Romances of England* (1999).

HAVERGAL, Frances Ridley (1836–79) Poet and hymn-writer, educated briefly at schools in London, Worcester, and Germany. She was a gifted musician who spent much of her life with the poor. Her many published volumes were collected as *Poetical Works* (1884); her autobiography was issued in 1880. 'Take my life and let it be' remains her best-known hymn.

HAWES, Stephen (*c.*1474–*c.*1511) A poet in the tradition of *Chaucer and *Lydgate, groom of the chamber to Henry VII. His **Passetyme of Pleasure* was first printed by Wynkyn de *Worde, 1509. His *Example of Vertu*, an allegory of life spent in pursuit of purity, was printed by de Worde in 1512. Other works include *The Conversion of Swearers* and *The Comfort of Lovers*. See W. E. Mead (ed.), *The Pastime of Pleasure*, EETS os 173 (1928).

HAWKER, R. S. (Robert Stephen) (1803–75) Clergyman and poet, educated at Pembroke College, Oxford, and from 1834 vicar of Morwenstow in Cornwall; much of his poetry was inspired by Cornish landscape and legend, and by the frequent shipwrecks off the dangerous coast of his parish. He was an isolated and eccentric figure, though the portrait drawn in Sabine *Baring-Gould's *The Vicar of Morwenstow* (1875) has been modified by Piers Brendon's *Hawker of Morwenstow* (1975). He was the author of 'The Song of the Western Men', first published anonymously in 1825; based on an old Cornish ballad, it has the refrain: 'And shall Trelawney die?' He published various volumes of poetry, including in 1864 part of a projected long blank verse Arthurian poem, *The Quest of the Sangraal*, which has passages of visionary power attributed by some to his opium addiction.

HAWKES, John (Clendennin Talbot Burne) (1925–98) American novelist, born in Stamford, Connecticut, who produced a series of surreal novels starting with *The Cannibal* in 1949. Hawkes consistently avoided conventional means of representation, making his narrators notoriously unreliable, and in works like *The Lime Twig* (1961) drew on nightmare to evoke the criminal world of London. He spent much of his life teaching at Brown University.

HAWKESWORTH, John (1720–73) Schoolmaster and writer of miscellaneous essays, plays, stories, and general journalism. With the assistance of his friends Samuel *Johnson and Joseph *Warton, he successfully conducted the

Adventurer, a bi-weekly successor to Johnson's **Rambler*, 1752–4. He produced a reliable edition of Jonathan *Swift, with a biography (6 vols, 1755), and in 1766 an edition of Swift's letters. His highly successful *Almoran and Hamet* (1761) is an *oriental tale. Untrammelled by space or time, Almoran can change into any shape to pursue his strange, and often supernatural, adventures among magnificent heroes and base villains. Hawkesworth edited and annotated various journals, including those of James *Cook and the explorer Philip Carteret (1733–96), for his *Account of the Voyages...in the Southern Hemisphere* (1773), a popular success which however proved controversial for its editorial interventions, challenges to theological orthodoxy, and sympathetic account of the sexual freedom of the Pacific Islanders. See J. L. Abbott, *John Hawkesworth: Eighteenth-Century Man of Letters* (1982).

HAWKINS, Sir Anthony Hope (1863–1933) Barrister and author. Educated at Marlborough College, St John's School, Leatherhead, and Balliol College, Hawkins was called to the bar in 1887. He gave up the law after the success of *The *Prisoner of Zenda* (1894), published under the pseudonym 'Anthony Hope'. A sequel, *Rupert of Hentzau*, followed in 1898. Hawkins published several other novels and plays, and *The Dolly Dialogues* (1894), reprinted from the *Westminster Gazette*, which is a series of light-hearted conversations featuring a flirtation between Samuel Carter, a bachelor, and Dolly Foster, who in chapter 5 marries Lord Mickleham.

HAWKINS, Sir John (1532–95) Naval commander and merchant, who led expeditions to West Africa and the Caribbean, slave trading and privateering. Later he intrigued against Spain, and was MP for Plymouth and treasurer of the navy, driving reforms that assisted against the Armada. In 1569 he published a brief account of his 1567–8 voyage.

HAWKINS, Sir John (1719–89) Lawyer and magistrate who devoted his life to music and literature. In 1760 he published an edition of Izaak Walton's **Compleat Angler*, praised by his friend Samuel *Johnson, who, however, found him 'a most unclubbable man': indeed, Hawkins left the *Club, of which he had been a founder member. But Johnson made him an executor, and Hawkins wrote a detailed biography (1787), later overshadowed by James *Boswell's. He also edited Johnson's works (15 vols, 1787–9). His scholarly *General History of the Science and Practice of Music* (5 vols, 1776) appeared in the same year as, and was seen as the rival of, Charles *Burney's history. Hawkins was knighted in 1772. His daughter Laetitia-Matilda published a book of family memoirs in 1823–4. See B. H. Davis, *A Proof of Eminence: The Life of Sir John Hawkins* (1973).
See also MUSIC.

HAWKWOOD, Sir John (d. 1394) A famous military commander whose considerable achievements feature in chronicles from England, France, and Italy, including those of *Froissart. As a *condottiere*, he was the leader of the body of English mercenaries known as the White Company and fought for one Italian city or another, and for pope or prince, from 1360 to 1390. He concluded his career as commander in chief of the Florentine forces, and died at Florence. His body was returned to England. Paolo Uccello painted a commemorative equestrian portrait of him in 1436.

HAWTHORNE, Nathaniel (1804–64) American novelist and short story writer, born at Salem, Massachusetts. He was a descendant of members of a Puritan family notorious for their persecution of the so-called Witches of Salem. Hawthorne (who adopted this spelling of the family name) spent a solitary childhood with his mother, a widowed recluse, during which he read widely; he was educated at Bowdoin College, Brunswick (with Henry Wadsworth *Longfellow), then returned to Salem, where he began to write stories and sketches and published a novel, *Fanshawe* (1828), at his own expense. His stories began to appear in periodicals and were collected in *Twice-Told Tales* (1837) and later volumes, including *Mosses from an Old Manse* (1846) and *The Snow-Image and Other Twice-Told Tales* (1851). He also wrote some lasting works for children, including *A Wonder Book* and *Tanglewood Tales* (1852 and 1853, stories from Greek mythology). He was, however, slow to earn his living as a writer; he was employed for some time as measurer at the Boston custom house (1839–41), then spent in 1841 several months at the Brook Farm community, an experience on which he based *The *Blithedale Romance* (1852), a novel which conveys his mixed response to the *Transcendentalists. He married in 1842 and settled in Concord; from 1846 to 1849 he was surveyor of the port of Salem. He lost his post through a change of administration, and then wrote *The *Scarlet Letter* (1850), a classic enquiry into the nature of American Puritanism and the New England conscience, and *The *House of the Seven Gables* (1851), a study in ancestral guilt and expiation. In 1850 he met Herman *Melville, who greatly admired his work, and wrote an enthusiastic review comparing him to the Shakespeare of the tragedies. From 1853 to 1857 Hawthorne served as American consul at Liverpool; he then spent two years in Italy, which provided the setting and inspiration for *The *Marble Faun* (1860), returning in 1860 to Concord, where he spent his last years. *Our Old Home*, sketches of his life in England, appeared in 1863. Hawthorne has long been recognized as a moralist and allegorist much preoccupied with the mystery of sin, the paradox of its occasionally regenerative power, and the compensation for unmerited suffering and crime. The dark side of his writing was recognized by Melville but described as fanciful in Henry *James's 1879 study of Hawthorne for the 'English Men of Letters' series. The Centenary Edition of Hawthorne's Works (Ohio State University Press, 1962–95) runs to 23 volumes. See Brenda Wineapple, *Hawthorne: A Life* (2003).

HAY, J. MacDougall (1881–1919) Scottish preacher whose novel *Gillespie* (1914) brings an apocalyptic intensity to its portrayal of the impact of an entrepreneur on a rural community. Hay was the father of the multilingual poet George Campbell Hay (1915–84).

HAYDN, Joseph (1732–1809) Austrian composer, prolific in all genres. After becoming known throughout Europe, Haydn made two triumphant concert tours to London, in 1791–2 and 1794–5, at the invitation of the music promoter Johann Peter Salamon (hence the 'London' symphonies). He was befriended by Charles *Burney, and patronized by the prince of Wales. Performances of *Handel's oratorios in Westminster Abbey stimulated Haydn to write *Die Schöpfung* (*The Creation*, 1798), to a text compiled from Genesis and Books VII and VIII of **Paradise Lost*, translated into German by Baron van Swieten. The success of this encouraged Haydn to compose *Die Jahreszeiten* (1801) with a text (again by van Swieten) from James Thomson's *The *Seasons*. Haydn also made some 125 arrangements with instrumental accompaniment of Scottish and Welsh folk songs: after his return to Vienna he made another 250 of these for the Scottish publishers Whyte and Thomson.

HAYDON, Benjamin Robert (1786–1846) Historical painter, born in Plymouth, Devon, best known for his posthumously published *Autobiography and Journals* (selections ed. Tom *Taylor, 1853; complete text in 5 vols, ed. W. B. Pope, 1960, 1963). Haydon, son of a bookseller, had some success with his large paintings of biblical and classical subjects, but quarrelled with most of his patrons, fell into debt, and finally committed suicide. His vigorous advocacy helped to secure the Elgin Marbles for the British Museum, and his pioneering theories on art education, industrial design, and state patronage of the arts, expressed in his *Lectures on Painting and Design* (1846), had much influence. He was a friend of John *Keats, William *Wordsworth, William *Hazlitt, Leigh *Hunt, Mary Russell *Mitford, and Elizabeth Barrett *Browning, and his vivid and vehement journals contain many interesting anecdotes and pen portraits of his contemporaries. His outrageous personality has interested many novelists, notably Charles *Dickens, who used him (combined with Leigh *Hunt) as the model for Harold Skimpole in **Bleak House*, and Aldous *Huxley, whose Casimir Lypiatt in *Antic Hay* is based on Haydon. See David Blayney Brown, *Benjamin Robert Haydon* (1996).

HAYLEY, William (1745–1820) A prolific poet, whose most ambitious works, *The Triumphs of Temper* (1781) and *The Triumphs of Music* (1804), were ridiculed by Lord *Byron as 'Forever feeble and for ever tame', but were nevertheless popular. In 1805 his *Ballads on…Animals* was illustrated by William *Blake, who was at that time his friend and protégé, although the two were not always in sympathy. He was a close friend of William *Cowper, whose *Life* he published in 1803; he also published lives of John *Milton (1804) and George *Romney (1809). Robert *Southey commented that 'Everything about that man is good except his poetry.' He was nonetheless offered the laureateship in 1790, but declined it.

HAYTER, Alethea (1912–2006) Historian and biographer, born in Egypt and educated at Downe House School and Lady Margaret Hall, Oxford. She worked for the British Council (1945–71). Her writing includes *A Sultry Month* (1965), and *The Wreck of the Abergavenny* (2002), a study of the effect of catastrophe on other lives, including William *Wordsworth's, whose brother was captain.

HAYWARD, Abraham (1801–84) Essayist, educated at Blundell School, Tiverton. He was called to the bar in 1832. Author of *The Art of Dining* (1852), his gastronomic dinners in his chambers were famous for their distinguished company which included John *Lockhart and Thomas Babington *Macaulay. Some of his essays and reviews including *More about Junius* (1868), a vigorous attack on the Franciscan theory of *'Junius', and an account of the life and work of John Stuart *Mill (1873) provoked acute controversy. His articles appeared in the leading periodicals of his day and many were collected in five volumes of *Biographical and Critical Essays* (1858–74). He also published biographical and legal works and a translation of Goethe's **Faust*. Two volumes of his correspondence edited by H. E. Carlisle were published, 1886.

HAYWARD, Sir John (?1564–1627) Historian, educated at Pembroke College, Cambridge, the author of various works in which he emulated the style of the great Roman historians. His *First Part of the Life, and Reign of Henry IV* (1599), dedicated to *Essex, gave offence to *Elizabeth I and led to his imprisonment. His other chief works were the *Lives of the III Normans, Kings of England* (1613), the *Life and Reign of King Edward VI* (1630), and *The Beginning of the Reign of Queen Elizabeth* (1636).

HAYWOOD, Eliza (?1693–1756) Actress, playwright, and novelist, whose work has recently become the subject of strong critical interest. She wrote four plays, and acted into middle age. Her first novel, *Love in Excess* (1719), explored the complications of desire in a layered, complex narrative. *Fantomina* (1725) imagined the doomed sexual freedom of a masquerading woman. One of her novels libelled Martha Blount (1690–1762), and in revenge Alexander *Pope included in *The *Dunciad* a damaging portrait of Haywood as a 'Juno of majestic size', complete with 'two babes of love' (illegitimate novels), won as a trophy by the bookseller Edmund *Curll. Haywood's later fictions were still contentious: *The Adventures of Eovaai* (1736) was a political satire, and *Anti-Pamela* (1741) satirized Samuel *Richardson's success. But *The History of Miss Betty Thoughtless*, a novel of female education and reform, escaped the censures incurred by her earlier scandalous fictions and had considerable influence. Haywood conducted a notable periodical, the *Female Spectator*, 1744–6.

HAZLITT, William (1778–1830) Critic, *theatre critic, and essayist, born in Maidstone, the son of a *Unitarian minister of Irish birth who sympathized with the American Revolution. His infancy was passed in Ireland and in New England, his youth in the Shropshire village of Wem. He attended the New Unitarian College at Hackney, London, absorbing *Enlightenment philosophy and radical politics. He refused to enter the ministry, entertaining hopes of becoming a philosopher or, like his brother John, a painter. The influences of S. T. *Coleridge, *Wordsworth, and Charles *Lamb turned him away from painting and towards writing, although he deplored the Lake Poets' betrayal of their early radicalism. Hazlitt's first books were philosophical studies: *An Essay on the Principles of Human Action* (1805), which disputes *Hobbes's account of self-interested motives, and a polemic against *Malthus, *A Reply to the Essay on Population* (1807). *The Eloquence of the British Senate* (1807) contains studies of contemporary political leaders. He married Sarah Stoddart in 1808, settling near Salisbury. Four years later, he moved to London and launched his career as a public lecturer, political journalist, and critic of painting, drama, and poetry, writing for the **Morning Chronicle*, for Leigh Hunt's **Examiner*, and for the **Edinburgh Review*. His book **Characters of Shakespeare's Plays* appeared in 1817, as did *The Round Table*, containing general essays such as 'On Gusto'. In the following year he published his theatre reviews as *A View of the English Stage*, and gave two series of literary lectures at the Surrey Institution, the first of which was attended by *Keats and published as **Lectures on the English Poets* (1818); its sequel was *Lectures on the English Comic Writers* (1819). His *Political Essays* (1819) include remarkable studies of Edmund *Burke, whom he honoured as a man of genius while abhorring his political conservatism. *Lectures Chiefly on the Dramatic Literature of the Age of Elizabeth* (1820) was followed by a two-volume collection of general essays, *Table Talk* (1821–2).

Meanwhile his personal affairs were thrown into turmoil by an obsessive infatuation with his landlord's daughter, Sarah Walker; in the deluded hope of marrying her, he divorced his wife in 1822. **Liber Amoris* (1823), his confessional account of this episode, damaged his public reputation. After taking Isabella Bridgewater as his second wife in 1824 he produced two of his best works, *The *Spirit of the Age* (1825) and *The *Plain Speaker* (1826). Lesser works of this period are the collection of aphorisms, *Characteristics* (1823), and *Notes of a Journey through France and Italy* (1826). His last years were spent on his four-volume *Life of Napoleon Buonaparte* (1828–30). He died in Soho, and is buried in St Anne's churchyard. Posthumous works include *Literary Remains* (1836), containing two of his most striking essays, 'My First Acquaintance with Poets' and 'The Fight'.

Hazlitt is now acknowledged as an original master of English prose in the 19th century and as a serious rival to Coleridge in the value of his critical writings. His prose style is variable, moving from the pugnacious to the seductive, from allusive subtlety to democratic plainness, but always stamped with personality and passion. He revived the art of the essay, and brought new psychological and political insight into literary criticism. Devoted to the ideals of the French Revolution, he nonetheless grasped the imaginative force of conservatism, whether in *Shakespeare or in Walter *Scott and *Wordsworth; this tension between rational enlightenment and the power of 'genius' animates much of his work. The standard edition is the *Complete Works* (ed. P. P. Howe, 21 vols, 1930–34). See also D. Wu, *Selected Writings of William Hazlitt*, 9 vols (1998). The standard biography is S. Jones, *Hazlitt: A Life* (1989). See also D. Bromwich, *Hazlitt: The Mind of a Critic* (1983); Tom *Paulin, *The Day-Star of Liberty* (1998).

HAZLITT, William Carew (1834–1913) Bibliographer, grandson of William *Hazlitt. Among his works are a *Hand-Book to the Popular Poetical and Dramatic Literature of Great Britain* (1867), four series of *Bibliographical Collections and Notes* (1876–1903), and memoirs of his grandfather (1867). His editorial work included *English Proverbs and Proverbial Phrases Collected from the Most Authentic Sources* (1869, for which H. G. *Bohn accused him of plagiarism), *Letters of Charles Lamb* (1886), reprints of Hazlitt, Robert *Herrick, and Sir John *Suckling, and a translation of *Montaigne. His *Confessions of a Collector* appeared in 1897. Samuel *Schoenbaum described him as 'unreliable' and 'an antiquarian bumbler'.

HAZZARD, Shirley (1931–) Novelist and short story writer, born in Sydney, Australia. Her work at the United Nations headquarters in New York 1951–61 provided material for her satirical linked short stories, *People in Glass Houses* (1967). She had already published a short story collection, *Cliffs of Fall* (1963), and *The Evening of the Holiday* (1966), a novel exploring the fruitful theme of northern Europeans in Italy. *The Bay of Noon* (1970), set in Naples just after the Second World War, pursues this theme. It is in Hazzard's dense, multi-layered survey of the post-war world *The Transit of Venus* (1980) that her preoccupations with ideas, politics, and complex human emotions reach their fullest expression. It follows the loves and careers of Australian sisters Caro and Grace, along with the British working-class astronomer Ted Tice, from post-war England through ensuing decades. Hazzard's concerns are enacted in the interplay of a large cast, while secrets, loss, and death provide a tragic dimension.

H.D. Initials used as pseudonym by Hilda *Doolittle.

HEAD, Bessie (1937–86) Born in South Africa to a 'white' mother and 'black' father under apartheid classification; brought up in a foster family and educated in a mission school, she lived as a refugee in Botswana from the age of 26. Her major work was written and set in Botswana, though *The Cardinals*, published posthumously (1993), was written in South Africa. *When Rain Clouds Gather* (1968) addresses the rural community's ability to survive economic hardship and the autocracy of their chief, while *Maru* (1971) and *A Question of Power* (1973) present a young woman's struggle against racism and sexism in the Botswana community. The latter novel, with its autobiographical rendering of psychological breakdown, also turns back to the remembered effects of apartheid. In her later, less introspective phase, Head's stories *The Collector of Treasures* (1977) develop the themes gleaned from social history and interviews with villagers, which were published later as *Serowe: Village of the Rain Wind* (1981). *A Bewitched Crossroad* (1984) augments fact with fiction in order to counter the European version of Botswana's past.

Additional stories and essays, early and late, have been collected in *Tales of Tenderness and Power* (1989) and *A Woman Alone* (1990). Overall, Head's major interest is in envisioning an Africa free of inherited and imported oppressions, hospitable to European thinking yet strongly enough informed with communal rural traditions to resist the social breakdown and materialism of postcolonial life. The small selection of her letters hitherto published in *A Gesture of Belonging* (1991) reflects a life that was often lonely, funded by meagre royalties and refugee subsidies. Today, her pioneering, deeply engaged narratives have earned her an international reputation. See Gillian Stead Eilersen, *Bessie Head: Thunder behind her Ears* (1995).

Headlong Hall A satire by Thomas Love *Peacock, published 1816, the first of the series of books in which Peacock adapts the Socratic dialogue as a tool for satirizing contemporary culture. Mr Foster the optimist, Mr Escot the pessimist, Mr Jenkinson the status-quo-ite, Dr Gaster, a gluttonous cleric, Mr Milestone, a landscape gardener, and many others gather at the Welsh country house of Squire Headlong to eat, drink, and discuss the arts. In the central comic episode, Mr Milestone blows up part of the grounds in order to achieve the smooth effect preferred by his real-life prototype, Humphry Repton. The debates of the philosophers enact the clash between the optimism of *Condorcet and William *Godwin and the pessimism of *Malthus.

See also PICTURESQUE.

HEANEY, Seamus (1939–) Irish poet, born near Castledawson in south Londonderry and educated at St Columb's College, Derry, and Queen's University, Belfast. The most prominent of the poets who emerged from Northern Ireland in the 1960s and 1970s, he lectured for a time at Queen's before moving south of the Irish border in 1972, living first in Co. Wicklow and then settling in Dublin. He has been Boylston professor of rhetoric and oratory at Harvard and Oxford professor of poetry. He was awarded the *Nobel Prize for Literature in 1995. Heaney's early poetry in *Death of a Naturalist* (1966) is rooted in the farmland of his youth, and communicates a strong physical sense of environment in vividly mimetic language. The denser, more poignant and self-conscious lyrics of *Wintering Out* (1972) and *North* (1975) brood on the cultural and historical implications of words, exploring their use and history in the context of the unfolding crisis in Northern Ireland. Later volumes are notably various in style and attitude and are characterized by a suspicion as well as a celebration of the rhetorical resourcefulness that marks Heaney off from his British and Irish contemporaries. The stately elegizing of *Field Work* (1979), the self-lacerating confessionalism of *Station Island* (1984), the cerebral parable spinning of *The Haw Lantern* (1987), the visionary meditations of *Seeing Things* (1991)—a book as airy as Heaney's debut volume was earthy—and the formal plenitude and moral rigour of *The Spirit Level* (1996) exemplify a self-renewing energy that has evoked comparisons with W. B. *Yeats. The award-winning *District and Circle* (2006) at once summarizes the achievement of a lifetime and recasts it in a self-deprecatingly minor key. As a critic as well as a poet and translator, Heaney has responded not only to the Irish and English traditions (and their problematic interface) but also to poetry from Scotland, Wales, the USA, Eastern Europe, and classical antiquity. At once broad in its aesthetic sympathies and stringent in its sense of the social responsibilities of literature, his criticism argues for the relevance of poetry in an unjust world. Among Heaney's major translations are *Sweeney Astray* (1983), *Beowulf* (1999), and stage versions of *Philoctetes* (*The Cure at Troy*, 1990) and *Antigone* (2004). *Opened Ground* (1998) and *Finders Keepers* (2002) provide generous compilations respectively of his poetry and criticism.

HEARD, Gerald (1889–1971) Writer and broadcaster, born in London and educated at Sherborne School, Dorset, and Gonville and Caius College, Cambridge. He shot to prominence following the publication of *The Ascent of Humanity* (1929) and became a notable figure both in London intellectual circles and nationally, through his role as a science and current affairs commentator with the BBC. He was hailed as 'one of the most penetrating minds in England' by E. M. *Forster and 'the cleverest man in the world' by Evelyn *Waugh, but his most obvious influence was on Aldous *Huxley, whose writings in the 1930s are clearly indebted to *The Social Substance of Religion* (1931), *The Source of Civilization* (1935), and other works by Heard. He emigrated to the USA in 1937 and continued to publish regularly.

HEARN, Lafcadio (1850–1904) Writer, born on the Greek island of Levkas, of Irish-Greek parentage, and educated in England. In 1869 he left penniless for the United States. He worked as a journalist in Cincinnati and incurred scandal by cohabiting with a black woman, Alethea Foley. Hearn translated from the French, and his own works show the influence of the exoticism of Pierre Loti (1850–1923), Charles *Baudelaire, and Théophile *Gautier. In 1877 he moved to New Orleans, where he remained for several years, and about which he wrote much, contributing to the popular image of that city. In 1889 he was sent by *Harper's Weekly* to the West Indies. He lived in Martinique, an experience that resulted in *Two Years in the French West Indies* (1890) and a novel, *Youma: The Story of a West-Indian Slave* (1890). In 1890 he went to Japan, where he spent the rest of his life, becoming a naturalized Japanese. He married a Japanese woman, took the name of Yakumo Koizumi, and adopted Japanese dress, though he never mastered the language. He taught at a school in Matsue, and from 1896 to 1903 lectured on English literature at the Imperial University, Tokyo. In several works, including *Glimpses of Unfamiliar Japan* (1894), *Out of the East* (1895), and *Japan: An Attempt at Interpretation* (1904), he affectionately evokes the landscapes, mythology, and customs of his adopted country.

HEARNE, Thomas (1678–1735) Antiquary and bibliographer, the 'Wormius' of Pope's **Dunciad*. Educated at St Edmund Hall, Oxford, he compiled *Reliquiae Bodleianae* (1703) and edited many historical chronicles such as John *Leland's

Itinerary and William *Camden's *Annales*. As a nonjuror, refusing to swear allegiance to William and Mary after the Glorious Revolution of 1688, he could not take high office, but he recorded Oxford life and scholarship from the Bodleian Library; his notebooks appeared as *Remarks and Collections of Thomas Hearne*, ed. C. E. Doble *et al.*, 11 vols (1885–1921).

'Heart of Darkness' A tale by Joseph *Conrad, serialized in 1899 in **Blackwood's Magazine*, and published, with other narratives, in book form in 1902. On board a boat anchored peacefully in the Thames the narrator, Marlow, tells the story of his journey on another river. Travelling in Africa to join a cargo boat, Marlow grows disgusted by what he sees of the greed of the ivory traders and their brutal exploitation of the natives. At a company station he hears of the remarkable Mr Kurtz who is stationed in the very heart of the ivory country and is the company's most successful agent. Leaving the river, Marlow makes an arduous cross-country trek to join the steamboat which he will command on an ivory-collecting journey into the interior, but at the Central Station he finds that his boat has been mysteriously wrecked. He learns that Kurtz has dismissed his assistant and is seriously ill. The other agents, jealous of Kurtz's success, hope that he will not recover, and it becomes clear that Marlow's arrival at the Inner Station is being deliberately delayed. With repairs finally completed Marlow sets off on the two-month journey towards Kurtz. The river passage through the heavy motionless forest fills Marlow with a growing sense of dread. The journey is 'like travelling back to the earliest beginnings of the world'. Ominous drumming is heard and dark forms glimpsed among the trees. Nearing its destination the boat is attacked by tribesmen and a helmsman is killed. At the Inner Station Marlow is met by a naive young Russian sailor who tells Marlow of Kurtz's brilliance and the semi-divine power he exercises over the natives. A row of severed heads on stakes round the hut give an intimation of the barbaric rites by which Kurtz has achieved his ascendancy. Ritual dancing has been followed with human sacrifice and, without the restraints imposed by his society, Kurtz, an educated and civilized man, has used his knowledge and his gun to reign over this dark kingdom. While Marlow attempts to get Kurtz back down the river Kurtz tries to justify his actions and his motives: he has seen into the very heart of things. But dying his last words are: 'The horror! The horror!' Marlow is left with two packages to deliver, Kurtz's report for the Society for Suppression of Savage Customs, and some letters for his Intended. Faced with the girl's grief Marlow tells her simply that Kurtz died with her name on his lips. This short novel has become one of the most discussed texts in *postcolonial literary studies: it also inspired Coppola's post-Vietnam film *Apocalypse Now* (1979).

Heart of Midlothian, The A novel by Walter *Scott, published 1818 as the second series of **Tales of my Landlord*, loosely based on two historical events: the riots in Edinburgh, in which John Porteous, commander of the Edinburgh City Guard, was dragged from the Edinburgh Tolbooth ('the Heart of Midlothian') and hanged by a mob, and the story of Isobel Walker whose pardon for child murder, for which she had been sentenced to death, was obtained by her sister Helen. In the novel, the riot is engineered by George Staunton, to release his lover Effie Deans, who is imprisoned in the Tolbooth and falsely accused of child murder. Effie refuses to escape, stands trial, and, since her sister Jeanie refuses to perjure herself to save her, is condemned to death. Jeanie sets out on foot for London to plead for her life and, after various vicissitudes, secures her sister's pardon from Queen Caroline. Effie's child later unwittingly becomes his father's assassin.

Scott had given a picture of the sterner, crueller side of strict *Presbyterianism two years earlier in **Old Mortality*; in this novel, the rigid tenets of Davie Deans, father of Jeanie and Effie, are seen through more compassionate eyes. Jeanie inherits his unbending rectitude, but demonstrates the heights to which it can rise through love.

HEATH-STUBBS, John (1918–2006) Poet, educated at Worcester College for the Blind and the Queen's College, Oxford, where his first published poems appeared in *Eight Oxford Poets* (1941, ed. Sidney *Keyes and Michael Meyer). He described himself as a traditionalist in literature, though believing that traditional values can only be maintained at the price of continual change and flexibility. His inspiration came chiefly from ancient Greece, Rome, Alexandria, classical myth, Christian legend, and works of art and scholarship, and his poetry included translations from the 14th-century Persian poet *Hāfiz and Giacomo *Leopardi. These interests may appear to set him apart from much of the poetry of his time, but he was also a poet of the contemporary megalopolis, and he combined traditional forms with a flexible free verse. His first volume was *Wounded Thammuz* (1942); others include *The Blue-Fly in his Head* (1962), *Artorius* (1972), a poem on Arthurian legend, *Sweet-Apple Earth* (1993), and *Pigs Might Fly* (2005). He was also a literary critic: *The Darkling Plain* (1950) is a study of Victorian Romantic poetry, and his *Literary Essays*, edited by A. T. Tolley, was published in 1998, as was his *Collected Poems 1943–1987*. He published an autobiography, *Hindsights*, in 1993.

HEAT-MOON, William Least (1939–) Writer, of English, Irish, and Native American (Osage Nation) ancestry, born William Trogdon in Kansas City, and educated at the University of Missouri-Columbia, where he gained a Ph.D. and taught English. He is the author of three non-fiction books chronicling travels, lives, and landscapes in often overlooked parts of the United States: *Blue Highways: A Journey into America* (1982) recounts a 13,000-mile journey by van along minor roads through rural areas and small towns; *PrairyErth (A Deep Map)* (1991) is a study of Chase County, Kansas; and *River Horse: The Logbook of a Boat across America* (1999) describes a four-month waterway journey from the east coast to the west, often in the wake of earlier explorers, including Meriwether *Lewis, whose writing style Heat-Moon has admired.

Heaven and Earth A poetic drama by Lord *Byron, published in *The* **Liberal*, 1822. Like its predecessor **Cain*, it is subtitled 'A Mystery', and questions God's choice to create only to destroy. The story, suggested by Genesis ch. 6, tells of the marriage of rebel angels and mortal women: Japhet, son of Noah, loves Anah, but she and her sister Aholibamah are carried away by their immortal lovers, the spirits Azaziel and Samiasa. The drama ends as the flood sweeps over the earth, and Japhet remains upon a rock as the Ark floats towards him.

HEBER, Reginald (1783–1826) Clergyman, poet and hymn-writer, educated at Oxford; in 1822 he became bishop of Calcutta. His works include *Poems and Translations* (1812); an edition of the works of Jeremy *Taylor (1822), and his *Life* (1824); various hymns of his own authorship, including 'Brightest and best of the sons of the morning', 'From Greenland's icy mountains', and 'Holy, holy, holy' in 1827; *Narrative of a Journey through India* (1828); and his *Poetical Works* (1841).

HEBER, Richard (1777–1833) Half-brother of Reginald *Heber, a devoted bibliophile; he travelled widely to collect his library of 150,000 volumes, and edited *Persius and other classical authors. He is the 'Atticus' of T. F. *Dibdin's *Bibliomania*.

Hebrew Melodies A collection of short poems by Lord *Byron, some written during the early days of his marriage, published 1815. Many are on scriptural subjects, but some are love songs and lyrics: the volume was published by Jewish composer Isaac Nathan (?1791–1864) who arranged some to traditional Hebrew melodies. The poems include 'She walks in beauty' and 'The Assyrian came down like the wolf on the fold'.

HECHT, Anthony (1923–2004) American poet, born in New York, whose volumes include *The Hard Hours* (1967), *The Venetian Vespers* (1979), and *The Transparent Man* (1989). He saw combat in Europe in the Second World War, which fed into his poetry, and later formed a friendship with W. H. *Auden, about whom he published a critical study, *The Hidden Law* (1984). Many of his poems evoke an intense experience of Europe, often linked to a restrained and poignant *confessional mode. He taught poetry at the University of Rochester from 1967 to 1985.

HECHT, Ben (1894–1964) American screenwriter and novelist, born in Racine, Wisconsin. He began his career as a reporter for the *Chicago Daily News* and participated in the Chicago Renaissance along with the poet and novelist Maxwell Bodenheim (1891–1954). His many stories include *A Thousand and One Afternoons in Chicago* (1922) and he published *A Jew in Love* (1931) among other novels. In the 1920s he moved to Hollywood and became a prolific writer of screenplays, including those for *Underworld* (1928) and *A Farewell to Arms* (1957). During the Second World War Hecht became a campaigner for Hitler's Jewish victims and for the establishment of the state of Israel. See William MacAdams, *Ben Hecht* (1989).

Hector *See* ILIAD.

HEGEL, Georg Wilhelm Friedrich (1770–1831) German philosopher. His first important work was *Phänomenologie des Geistes* (1807: *Phenomenology of Spirit*), followed by his *Logik* (1812–16), and later by the *Philosophie des Rechts* (1820: *Philosophy of Right*), embodying his political views. Endeavouring to overcome the Kantian dualism of nature and spirit, Hegel argues that all difference presupposes a unity, that a definite thought cannot be separated from its opposite, that the idea of fullness, for example, cannot be separated from that of emptiness, that they are identical in difference. Duality and unity are blended in consciousness and the boundaries between mind and matter set aside. Hegel's central idea is the dialectic of thesis–antithesis–synthesis, which he applied to the problem of historical evolution as represented by the *Weltgeist* or World Spirit. His dialectical method was adopted by political thinkers of both right and left, those who supported authoritarian rule in Prussia in the 19th century and those, like Ludwig *Feuerbach, Karl *Marx, and Friedrich *Engels, who advocated reform and revolution. Though extravagantly praised by Matthew *Arnold, Hegel does not appear to have greatly influenced his ideas and is treated with some levity in **Friendship's Garland*. However, Hegel's view of history was significant for Walter *Pater, and he enjoyed a vogue in philosophical circles in England, particularly at Oxford, in the 1880s and 1890s.

HEGLEY, John *See* PERFORMANCE POETRY.

HEIDEGGER, Martin (1889–1976) German philosopher, educated at Freiburg Jesuit Seminary and Freiburg University. Heidegger was primarily concerned with the question of being; in his formulation, he dealt with the question 'what is "is"?' Heidegger used the word *Dasein* to refer to specifically human modes of being; *Dasein* is, for him, self-conscious and involves not only Being but also the very Question of Being. In his most famous work *Sein und Zeit* (1927: *Being and Time*, 1962), he studies *Dasein* in relation to time, asking how Being deals with its temporality, including the fear of being 'thrown into Being'. Heidegger believed that Being can only be articulated through language; he defined as 'poetry' that language capable of doing this, language which is responsive to Being. For Heidegger, the representation of things estranges us from the things themselves; in his famous example of Van Gogh's painting of a pair of peasant shoes he describes how the act of estranging us from the shoes themselves serves to show us their essential 'shoeness'. His work arose as much out of literary as philosophical tradition, and although Heidegger's writing is often abstruse, and despite the backlash against him due to his sympathies—never unambiguously disavowed—with Nazism, his writings had enormous influence on 20th-century thought and literary theory. In *Todtnauberg* (a radio play of 2006, named after Heidegger's mountain retreat in the Black Forest) John *Banville explores fictionally the meeting between Paul *Celan, a victim of Nazism, and the philosopher. Heidegger was one of the founders (with Hans-Georg Gadamer) of *hermeneutic criticism, and a crucial influence for 20th-century *existentialism (especially Jean-Paul *Sartre). His work was a starting point for Jacques *Derrida's development of *deconstruction and also significant, more recently, for the nascent 'ecopoetics'. A collection of his work on the nature of thought, language, and poetry has been translated as *Poetry, Language, Thought* (1971). See George Steiner, *Heidegger* (1978).

Heimskringla A series of short sagas making up a history of the kings of Norway from mythical times to the year 1177, written by *Snorri Sturluson. It is of more value for its high literary quality than for its historicity, although it is basically reliable and its political analyses are illuminating. It has a bearing on English history, as it covers the reign of the Danish king *Canute (Cnutr) and describes Viking expeditions to England. Its title is taken from its opening words, 'Kringla heimsins'—'orb of the world'. See *The Olaf Sagas from Heimskringla*, trans. S. Laing (1914, etc.).

HEINE, Heinrich (1797–1856) German poet, born of Jewish parents in Düsseldorf. He studied law at the universities of Bonn, Göttingen, and Berlin. Disappointed in his hopes of a liberal regime in Germany after the defeat of Napoleon, he moved in 1831 to Paris, remaining there for the rest of his life. His political works earned him a reputation as a radical, but he was most famous as a poet. His early lyric poetry, collected in the *Buch der Lieder* (1827: *Book of Songs*), is characterized by effusively romantic emotion combined with sharp self-mockery and deflating irony. It became one of the most widely read and influential books of poetry in Germany. The satirical travel sketches in his *Reisebilder* (1826–31: *Travel Pictures*), and his savage and witty attacks on German thought and literature in *Zur Geschichte der Religion und Philosophie in Deutschland* (1834: *On the History of Religion and Philosophy in Germany*) and *Die romantische Schule* (1836: *The Romantic School*), brought him notoriety in Germany where his works were officially proscribed in 1835. He renewed his onslaught in two satirical mock epics, *Atta Troll* (1843) and *Deutschland: Ein Wintermärchen* (1844), which were greatly admired by *Marx. In 1848 he became paralysed by spinal tuberculosis and was bedridden for the rest of his life. He left a moving and witty record of the final years in his 'mattress grave' in *Romanzero* (1851) and *Gedichte 1853 und 1854*. George *Eliot wrote appreciative essays on his works. In **Essays in Criticism*, 1st series (1865), Matthew *Arnold acclaimed Heine as an embodiment of the modern spirit and as a force for liberation. A. E. *Housman acknowledged Heine as an important technical influence on his verse form. See J. L. Sammons, *Heinrich Heine: A Modern Biography* (1979).

HEINLEIN, Robert Anson (1907–88) American *science fiction writer, born in Butler, Missouri; he began publishing science fiction after leaving the navy: his first story, 'Lifeline' (1939), was for **Astounding*, and he was one of John W. *Campbell's great successes, providing both a mature voice and inventive fiction. 'All You Zombies' (1959) is one of science fiction's most remarkable time-travel ideas. Many of his early stories linked into a loose 'future history', including the collection *The Past through Tomorrow* (1967). A series of successful children's science fiction novels in the 1950s was succeeded by *Starship Troopers* (1959), whose political libertarianism and support for the military made it increasingly controversial. The sexual radicalism of *Stranger in a Strange Land* (1961) gave it a cult following in the mid-1960s. Subsequent novels such as *Farnham's Freehold* (1964) and *The Moon is a Harsh Mistress* (1966) reflected his enthusiasm for the 'competent man', but an increasingly strident narrative voice emerged in novels such as *'The Number of the Beast'* (1980). Although his political ideas were very different, Heinlein resembled H. G. *Wells in that he created the rules for his successors.

Heir of Redclyffe, The A novel by Charlotte *Yonge, published 1853. This novel, illustrating the contrast between real and apparent virtue, is the story of the cousins Guy and Philip Morville. Guy, the heir of a baronetcy and an ancient house, is hot-tempered but generous; Philip a much-admired prig. Philip passes on ill-founded suspicions about Guy and succeeds in thwarting his marriage to his guardian's daughter Amy, but Guy's character, refined by Christian discipline, is eventually vindicated and he marries Amy. On their honeymoon they find Philip ill with fever; Guy nurses him, catches the fever, and dies, whereby the now repentant Philip inherits Redclyffe. A product of Yonge's devotion to Tractarian principles, *The Heir of Redclyffe* was extremely popular. Profits from the novel, donated to Bishop Selwyn of New Zealand, helped to finance a new missionary schooner, *The Southern Cross*.

He Knew He Was Right A novel by Anthony *Trollope, published 1869. Louis Trevelyan, on a visit to the Mandarin Islands, marries Emily Rowley, daughter of the governor. The couple return to England, where Trevelyan is troubled by visits from the governor's old friend, the ageing philanderer Colonel Osborne. Osborne enjoys the sensation he creates, and continues to call; Emily's pride adds to her husband's jealousy. A separation follows, and Bozzle, a private detective, becomes the only mediator between the couple. Trevelyan abducts his son and removes him to Italy. In time Emily pursues them, finding her husband in a state of mental breakdown. They are partly reconciled, but Trevelyan dies soon after his return to England. The Italian scenes allow Trollope to caricature the transatlantic feminism of Miss Wallachia Petrie and to marry the English aristocrat Mr Glascock to the charming American Caroline Spalding. The novel also contains the story of old Aunt Stanbury of the cathedral close at Exeter, with her protégés, particularly her nephew Hugh, whose engagement to Emily's sister Nora temporarily angers her. The novel's strength, however, lies in its exploration of the destructive power of sexual jealousy in the disintegrating marriage of Louis and Emily Trevelyan.

Helen of Troy Wife of Menelaus, king of Sparta, abducted by Paris, son of Priam, king of Troy; she was, as first told in the **Iliad*, the cause of the Trojan War, 'the face that launched a thousand ships' (**Dr Faustus*). She has come to epitomize variously love, beauty, and disastrous irresponsibility, in works from **Troilus and Cressida* to W. B. *Yeats's 'When Helen lived' and 'No second Troy'.

Heliand, The An Old Saxon paraphrase in alliterative verse of the New Testament, dating from the 9th century.

HELIODORUS *See* AETHIOPICA.

Hellas A lyrical drama by P. B. *Shelley written at Pisa in late 1821, the last work to be published in his lifetime, 1822. Based in form on the *Persians* of *Aeschylus, it was inspired by news of the Greek War of Independence against the Turkish Empire, and dedicated to their national leader, Prince Mavrocordato, whom Shelley had known at Pisa.

The action, 'a series of lyric pictures', is set at Constantinople, where the Turkish Sultan Mahmud receives a number of messengers reporting the insurrection, and prophesying Greek victory. Shelley uses visionary figures—Christ, Mahomet, Ahasuerus the Wandering Jew, and the phantom of Mahomet II—to explore a cyclical philosophy of history. But the main interest lies in the choruses, composed like songs for opera, and concluding with the celebrated poem 'The world's great age begins anew'. Shelley's preface, his last great appeal for political liberty in Europe, remains a classic statement of English philhellenism: 'We are all Greeks.'

Hellenistic A term applied to Greek art and history between the death of *Alexander the Great (323 BC) and that of Cleopatra (31 BC), which meant the absorption of the last Greek kingdom by Rome. In the visual arts, it denotes an interest in small scale and realism, and in non-classical subjects: children, old women, artisans. In literature, Hellenistic works are characteristically short, with highly wrought finish and learned content, written for the cultured reader, not the multitude. Hellenistic style is epitomized in the poems of *Callimachus and *Theocritus. Much work, in all the arts, continued to be produced on a large scale and in a traditional manner; but the new style—at first controversial and defended in polemical writings by Callimachus—won the critical battle. It was again controversial in Rome in the 1st century BC, and was explicitly defended, against unnamed attackers, by *Catullus, *Virgil, and *Propertius.

HELLER, Joseph (1923–99) American novelist, born in New York. He served as a bombardier in the air force during the Second World War, an experience which resurfaced in his first novel, **Catch-22* (1961), a satire on the absurdity of war and McCarthyism which brought him instant fame and which has since become a classic of *black humour fiction. A sequel, *Closing Time*, appeared in 1994. His second novel, *Something Happened* (1974), is the domestic tragicomedy of a middle-aged New York executive, Bob Slocum, and *Good as Gold* (1979) a surreal and comic satire about Jewish New York and Washington politics. *God Knows* (1984), a monologue spoken by the biblical King *David, was followed by *Picture This* (1988), on Rembrandt and *Aristotle. Heller published an autobiographical memoir, *Now and Then*, in 1998.

HELLMAN, Lillian (1905–84) American dramatist, screenwriter, librettist, and writer of memoirs, born in New Orleans. She was for many years the partner of Dashiell *Hammett, and with him was accused of 'un-American activities' during the McCarthy period. Her plays include *The Children's Hour* (1934), set in a girls' school, in which two teachers are accused by a malicious pupil of having a lesbian relationship, and lose the libel action they take against her grandmother; *The Little Foxes* (1939), a family melodrama set in 1900 in the deep South; and *Watch on the Rhine* (1941), an anti-Nazi war drama set near Washington. Other works include *Pentimento: A Book of Portraits* (1973), an account of friendships with various people, including 'Julia', filmed as *Julia* (1977), with Vanessa Redgrave.

HÉLOÏSE *See* ABELARD, PETER.

HELVÉTIUS, Claude Arien *See* PHILOSOPHES.

HEMANS, Felicia (1793–1835) Née Browne, a prolific and popular poet, sometimes outselling even Lord *Byron. She was born in Liverpool, and educated at home, but spent much of her adult life in north Wales, moving to Dublin in 1831, to be with her brother, where she died. From the publication of her first volume, *Poems* (1808), when she was 15 and living in north Wales with her mother and sister, her poetry exhibits a remarkable range of subject and style. *Poems* deals with subjects common in 18th-century women's verse—events in family life, apostrophes to genius, hope, and mirth, etc.—but also includes some political and patriotic poems, celebrating English military heroism (her two brothers were in the army, which is the justification for treating of this apparently unfeminine subject). Thus 'To my Younger Brother, on his Entering the Army' follows 'To Patriotism'. In 1812 she married Captain Hemans, an army veteran, from whom she lived apart from 1818, though they had five sons, whom she supported through her writing. *The Domestic Affections* (1812) values an emollient domesticity in the context of war, apparent in the title poem, which links patriotism to a middle-class domestic ideology of empire and home. *Welsh Melodies* (1822) treats of local history, landscape, and legend; and **Records of Woman* (1828) evokes legendary, historical, and literary women. The volume is dedicated to Joanna *Baillie, a strong influence on Hemans, as was William *Wordsworth, to whom she wrote several miscellaneous poems. *Records* participates in the feminization of history through the celebration of heroic women and turbulent passions at the same time that it emphasizes the calming force of the love of home. Hemans made many translations from the Portuguese and published in 1818 *Translations from Camõens and Other Poets*. Her best-known poem, 'Casabianca', beginning 'The boy stood on the burning deck', appeared in *The Forest Sanctuary* (2nd edn, 1829). Later works include *Songs of the Affections* (1830), *Hymns on the Works of Nature, for the Use of Children* (1833), *Songs and Hymns of Life* (1834), and *Poetical Remains* (1836). See G. Kelly (ed.), *Felicia Hemans* (2002).

HEMINGES (Heminge), **John** (1566–1630), and **CONDELL, Henry** (d. 1627) Fellow actors of Shakespeare and joint compilers of the first *folio of his plays (1623). A monument in their memory was erected in Love Lane, London.

HEMINGWAY, Ernest (1899–1961) American short story writer and novelist, born in Illinois, the son of a doctor. After working as a Kansas City reporter he served in 1918 as a volunteer with an ambulance unit on the Italian front, where he was wounded, then worked as a reporter for the Toronto *Star*. His journalism, an important source of income throughout his career, has been collected in *By-Line* (1967) and *Dateline: Toronto* (1985). He settled in Paris among the American expatriate literary group, where he met Ezra *Pound and Gertrude *Stein, described in his posthumously published *A Moveable Feast* (1964). Following their advice, he published *In our Time* (1925), a *modernist sequence of vignettes alternating with stories. *The Sun Also Rises* (1926; in Britain, as *Fiesta*, 1927) catches the post-war mood of disillusion of the *Lost Generation through its portrayal of expatriates in Europe. *A Farewell to Arms* (1929), the story of a love affair between an American lieutenant and an English nurse during the war on the Italian front, demonstrated a similar laconic and understated style. Among his short stories, the collections *Men without Women* (1927) and *Winner Take Nothing* (1933) are especially notable. He celebrated bull fighting in *Death in the Afternoon* (1932) and big game hunting in *The Green Hills of Africa* (1935). He actively supported the Republicans during the Spanish Civil War, helping to make the 1937 film *The Spanish Earth*. *For Whom the Bell Tolls* (1940) is set against this background. He was a war correspondent in Europe in the Second World War. In his later years he lived mostly in Cuba, where his passion for deep-sea fishing provided the setting for his most successful later work, *The Old Man and the Sea* (1952), a parable-novella about man's struggle against nature. He was awarded the *Nobel Prize in 1954 and wrote little thereafter; he shot himself in July 1961, having been seriously ill for some time. Posthumous publications include *The Dangerous Summer* (1985) and *The Garden of Eden* (1987). See Carlos Baker, *Hemingway* (1968).

hendecasyllabic Having eleven syllables to a verse line, as in much Italian and Spanish verse, and in a Latin *metre used by *Catullus and imitated in some poems by *Tennyson and by *Swinburne. The English iambic *pentameter, normally of ten syllables, becomes hendecasyllabic when it uses an extra syllable.

HENDERSON, Zenna (1917–83) American *science fiction writer, born Tucson, Arizona; author and schoolteacher best known for her stories later collected as *Pilgrimage: The Book of the People* (1961) and *No Different Flesh* (1966), poignant and telling episodes of how aliens, wrecked on Earth in 1950s America, survive and hide their paranormal powers.

hendiadys [from the Greek words meaning 'one by means of two'] A figure of speech by which a single complex idea is expressed by two words joined by a conjunction, e.g. 'sound and fury' for 'furious sound'.

Hengist and **Horsa** The traditional leaders of the Jutes who, according to *Bede (*History*, I. 15), landed at Ebbsfleet in 449 and were given by *Vortigern the Isle of Thanet for a dwelling place. Horsa was killed in battle against Vortigern in 455, but Hengist was the progenitor of a line of Kentish kings through his son Æsc.

HENLEY, W. E. (William Ernest) (1849–1903) Poet, critic, and journalist. Born and educated in Gloucester, he suffered from boyhood from tubercular arthritis and had a foot amputated; to save the other he went to Edinburgh in 1873 and placed himself under Joseph Lister's care. His 'Hospital Sketches', first published in the *Cornhill Magazine* in 1875, are a striking poetic record of this ordeal; as is his best-known poem, the defiant 'Invictus'. While in hospital he met Robert Louis *Stevenson, who became a close friend. They collaborated on four unsuccessful plays in the 1880s and Stevenson acknowledged Henley as an inspiration for Long John Silver in *Treasure Island*. Henley's most important role was as a courageous and independent editor of the *Magazine of Art* (1881–6), the *Scottish* (later *National*) *Observer* (1888–94), and the *New Review* (1895–8); publishing important work by Thomas *Hardy, Rudyard *Kipling, Stevenson, W. B. *Yeats, Henry *James, and H. G. *Wells, among others. He produced numerous other literary works: these include *A Book of Verses* (1888), *The Song of the Sword and Other Verses* (1892), *London Voluntaries* (1893), and *For England's Sake* (1900). A powerful and flamboyant personality, he had considerable influence on the literary scene in late Victorian London.

HENRI, Adrian (1932–2000) Poet and painter, born in Birkenhead and educated at the University of Durham, where he studied Fine Art. He settled in Liverpool in 1957, and during the 1960s was known (with Roger *McGough and Brian *Patten) as one of the *'Liverpool poets'; from 1967 to 1970 he led the poetry/rock group 'Liverpool Scene'. His own collections of poetry include *Tonight at Noon* (1968), *City* (1969), *From the Loveless Motel* (1980), *Penny Arcade* (1983), and *Collected Poems 1967–1985* (1986).

Henry IV, King, *Parts 1* and *2* Historical plays by *Shakespeare, written and performed about 1597. Part 1 was printed in quarto 1598, Part 2 1600. The chief sources are the chronicles of Edward *Hall and *Holinshed, and Samuel *Daniel's historical poem *The *Civil Wars*. The contemporary popularity of the plays on the stage was recorded by Leonard Digges (printed 1640 but written before 1635):

> let but Falstaff come,
> Hal, Poins, the rest, you scarce shall have a room,
> All is so pestered.

They are still frequently performed.

The subject of Part 1 is the rebellion of the Percys, assisted by Douglas and in concert with Mortimer and Glyndŵr; and its defeat by the King and Prince Harry (or Hal), prince of Wales, at Shrewsbury (1403). *Falstaff (originally named *Oldcastle) first appears in this play. The prince of Wales associates with him, and Poins, Bardolph, and Peto, in their disreputable life. Poins and the prince contrive that the others shall set on some travellers at Gadshill and rob them, and then be robbed by themselves. The plot succeeds, and leads to Falstaff's well-known fabrication to explain the loss of the booty, and his exposure. At the battle of Shrewsbury, Prince Harry kills Hotspur in single combat, and then discovers Falstaff feigning death. He mourns him with the words 'I could have better spared a better man.' After Harry's exit Falstaff resourcefully claims credit for having slain Hotspur.

Part 2 deals with the rebellion of Archbishop Scrope, Mowbray, and Hastings; while in the comic sub-plot the story of Falstaff's doings is continued, with those of the prince, Pistol, Poins, Mistress Quickly, and Doll Tearsheet. Falstaff, summoned to the army, falls in with Justices Shallow and Silence in the course of his recruiting, and borrows £1,000 from Shallow. Henry IV dies, reconciled to his son, and Falstaff hurries from Gloucestershire to London to greet the newly crowned king, who rejects him in the speech beginning 'I know thee not, old man. Fall to thy prayers', banishing him from his presence but allowing him 'competence of life'.

Henry V, King A historical drama by *Shakespeare, written, as the reference to *Essex in Ireland (V, Chorus, 30–2) indicates, in the spring or summer of 1599. It was printed in 1600 from what may be a memorial reconstruction, which omits the Choruses; the first *folio text (1623) is based on Shakespeare's own papers. Its chief sources are the chronicles of Edward *Hall and *Holinshed. The play has been popular in times of national crisis, as in the film version made in 1944 with Laurence Olivier as Henry. Kenneth Branagh's 1989 film (which he directed and in which he played the leading role) presented a harsher and more questioning view of the play.

The play opens with the new King Henry astonishing clergy and courtiers by his piety and statecraft. The archbishop of Canterbury demonstrates, in the long 'Salic Law' speech, Henry's claim to the throne of France. The dauphin sends a mocking gift of tennis balls, in a reference to Henry's wild youth, giving the king an immediate pretext for invasion. Henry unmasks the three traitors, Scrope, Grey, and Cambridge, and sets out for France; he captures Harfleur, and achieves a resounding victory at Agincourt (1415), a battle for which he prepares his soldiers in the 'Crispin Crispian' speech. Comic relief is provided by the old tavern companions of *Falstaff, who have fallen on hard times, and by some of Henry's soldiers, especially the pedantic but courageous Welsh captain Fluellen. The new, patriotic, comic characters symbolically defeat the old when Fluellen compels the braggart Pistol to eat a leek (V. i). The last act is given to Henry's wooing of Katherine of France.

Henry VI, King, *Parts 1, 2,* and *3* Sections of a historical tetralogy (completed by **Richard III*) by *Shakespeare written between 1590 and the summer of 1592. Part 1 was not published until the first *folio (1623), but Part 2 was published anonymously in 1594 under the title 'The First Part of the Contention betwixt the Two Famous Houses of York and Lancaster...', and Part 3 in 1595 as 'The True Tragedy of Richard Duke of York, and the Death of Good King Henry the Sixth'. These titles are restored in the Oxford Complete Works. Shakespeare's authorship of the plays, especially of Part 1, was doubted throughout the 18th and 19th centuries, on the grounds that they were unworthy of him. In the 20th century, however, although scholars have made increasingly confident claims for his sole authorship, others have argued that parts of the plays were written in collaboration, especially that most of the first act of *1 Henry VI* was by Thomas *Nashe. Reference to 'an upstart crow' in **Greene's Groat's-Worth of Wit* used to be taken as evidence of plagiarism, but is now generally read as merely the malice of a rival dramatist. The plays' chief sources are the chronicles of Edward *Hall and *Holinshed.

Part 1, opening with the funeral of Henry V, deals with wars in France in which the gallant Talbot is a powerful leader on the English side, and the witchlike *Joan of Arc, 'La Pucelle', on the French. After a series of encounters Talbot, together with his valiant son John Talbot, is killed near Bordeaux. A crucial scene in the Temple Garden establishes the opposition of Plantagenet and York in the subsequent wars through the plucking of red and white roses. In the fifth act the earl of Suffolk arranges a marriage between the young Henry VI and *Margaret of Anjou, daughter of the king of Naples, vowing ominously to rule king, queen, and kingdom.

Part 2 shows Henry's marriage to Margaret. The giving of Anjou and Maine to her father as a price for her marriage angers *Humphrey, duke of Gloucester, the lord protector; his wife Eleanor is banished as a witch (II. iii) and he is arrested on a charge of high treason, against the king's better judgement, and murdered. Suffolk is banished and, after a touching farewell to Queen Margaret, murdered by pirates on the Kent coast. Richard, duke of York, pretender to the throne, stirs up Jack *Cade to rebellion: after considerable success, Cade is eventually killed by Alexander Iden, a Kentish gentleman. The final act concerns the battle of St Albans (1455), in which Somerset is killed, a victory for the Yorkists.

Part 3 opens with Henry's attempt to buy peace by making the duke of York his heir, thus disinheriting his son by Margaret. Savagery and strife proliferate, however; Margaret, enraged and eloquent, instigates the murder of the boy Rutland, York's youngest son, by Clifford, and the mock coronation and murder of York himself, who addresses to her the line that Robert *Greene was to parody, 'O tiger's heart wrapped in a woman's hide!' Clifford is killed at the battle of Towton, which also includes a scene symbolic of the horrors of civil war in which a son who has killed his father encounters a father who has killed his son. Henry VI is captured and Edward (IV) declared king; he marries the dowerless widow Elizabeth Grey, though previously promised to Bona, the French king's sister. Richard, duke of Gloucester (later Richard III), emerges as an ambitious schemer. Warwick, a powerful supporter of the Lancastrian side, is killed at Barnet by King Edward; the battle of Tewkesbury is a decisive victory for Edward, and Margaret's young son (also an Edward) is killed in cold blood by Edward, Richard, duke of Gloucester, and George, duke of Clarence. King Henry, imprisoned in the Tower, is murdered by Richard. After much neglect, the plays came into their own in the later 20th-century theatre.

Henry VII, The History of the Reign of By Francis *Bacon, published in 1622. An innovatory historiographer, Bacon rejects in this work the medieval chronicle form and the idea of history as the theatre of God's providence. He follows *Machiavelli and *Guicciardini in concentrating on political events, but fuses their focus on powerful individuals with *Tacitus' emphasis on underlying causes and motives. He uses the standard historical sources—the *Anglicae Historiae Libri XXVI* (1534; rev. edn 1555) of Polydore *Vergil, and Edward *Hall's *The Union of the Two Noble and Illustre Families of Lancastre and York* (1548)—but emphasizes the importance of the king's personality. His weak dynastic claims accounted, Bacon suggests, for the insecurity that made him 'a dark prince, and infinitely suspicious', as well as prompting the counter-claims of Lambert Simnell and Perkin Warbeck (this episode was the source for John *Ford's play **Perkin Warbeck*).

HENRY VIII (1491–1547) King of England, from 1509. His book *A Defence of the Seven Sacraments*, directed against Martin *Luther's teaching, was printed in 1521 and presented to Pope *Leo X, who conferred on Henry the title 'Defender of the Faith'. Henry was also an accomplished musician and poet, and several of his compositions survive, including 'Pastime with good company', 'Alas, what shall I do for love?', and 'O my heart and O my heart'. His lyrics deal with courtly and chivalric themes, with one known exception, the sacred composition 'Quam pulcra es' (see J. Stevens, *Music and Poetry in the Early Tudor Court*, 1961). Hans *Holbein was painter at Henry's court, and drew and painted many of his circle, as well as the king himself. Henry's private life has been the subject of numerous dramas and works of fiction, including a play by William *Shakespeare and John *Fletcher, and he is popularly remembered for his six wives, who were, successively, Catherine of Aragon (m. 1509), Anne Boleyn, mother of *Elizabeth I (m. 1533), Jane Seymour (m. 1536), Anne of Cleves (m. 1539), Catherine Howard (m. 1540), and Catherine Parr (m. 1543). His life was written by Lord *Herbert of Cherbury.

Henry VIII A historical drama originally acted as 'All is True'. *Shakespeare has been claimed as its sole author, but it is usually held that he was responsible for less than half of it, the remainder being written by John *Fletcher, whose hand in it was originally suggested by *Tennyson. On one of its earliest performances, in June 1613, the firing of cannon resulted in the burning down of the *Globe Theatre.

It deals with the fall and execution of the duke of Buckingham; the question of the royal divorce (vividly depicting the dignified resignation of Queen Katherine); the pride, fall, and death of Cardinal Wolsey; the advancement and coronation of Anne Boleyn; the triumph of Cranmer; and the christening of the Princess Elizabeth.

The chief sources of the play are *Holinshed's *Chronicles* and Foxe's **Acts and Monuments* (or *Book of Martyrs*).

HENRY OF HUNTINGDON (*c.*1088–*c.*1157) Archdeacon of Huntingdon, compiler at the request of Bishop Alexander of Lincoln of a *Historia Anglorum*, which in its latest form extends to 1154.

HENRY, James (1798–1876) Classicist, physician, and poet, born in Dublin and educated at Trinity College, Dublin, who spent more than twenty years from 1846 travelling on foot through Europe to collate manuscripts of the **Aeneid* and meet fellow *Virgil scholars. The opening part of the first volume of his *Aeneidea* appeared in 1873, but the rest of this ground-breaking five-volume work of textual analysis, exegesis, and interpretation remained unpublished until after his death. Henry is chiefly remembered today for his dry, resolutely atheistical poetry, a selection of which was edited by Christopher Ricks in 2002. See J. B. Lyons, *Scholar and Sceptic* (1985).

HENRY, O. (1862–1910) Pseudonym of William Sydney Porter, American short story writer, born in North Carolina. He had a chequered early career, which included a term in prison for embezzlement (1896). He began to write short stories in prison, based on his observations of life, and published the first of his many collections, *Cabbages and Kings*, in 1904. His stories, generally comic and ingenious, have been accused of being mannered by H. L. *Mencken and others, though since 1919 the O. Henry Award has been given annually for exceptional short stories. See David Stuart, *O. Henry: A Biography* (1986).

HENRYSON, Robert (d. ?1490) Poet; he studied at Glasgow University and was possibly a schoolteacher in Dunfermline. He belongs to a group known until recently, and misleadingly, as 'Scottish *Chaucerians'. Chaucer's work is better understood as, at most, an imaginative starting point for Henryson's independent and subtle poetry. Together with William *Dunbar, he is one of the most prominent of the 15th-century Scottish poets. His most important poems are *The *Testament of Cresseid*, a moralizing sequel to Chaucer's **Troilus and Criseyde* that narrates the fortunes of

Cresseid after her betrayal of Troilus, and the *Morall Fabillis*, in which Henryson provocatively calls into question the relationship between beast fables and their ostensible morals. One of the distinctive characteristics of Henryson's poetry, in addition to its resourceful handling of diction and register, is its ability to evoke pathos while acknowledging the intransigence of morality and mortality. See *Poems*, ed. Denton Fox (1981); Douglas Gray, *Robert Henryson* (1979).

HENSHER, Philip (1965–) Novelist and journalist, educated at the universities of Oxford and Cambridge, who worked for some years as a clerk in the House of Commons. His 1996 novel *Kitchen Venom* is of interest in containing an early fictional portrayal of Prime Minister Margaret Thatcher. *The Mulberry Empire* (2002) is a *historical novel set largely in 19th-century Afghanistan.

HENSLOWE, Philip (*c.*1557–1616) He built the *Rose Theatre on Bankside in 1587, and thereafter was involved in theatrical affairs as financier, manager, and owner until his death. With his stepson-in-law Edward *Alleyn he was involved in the affairs of several important companies of actors, notably the Lord Admiral's Men, and in the building of the Fortune and *Hope theatres. Most of the dramatists of the period, apart from Shakespeare, at some time wrote for his companies. His *Diary* (ed. R. A. Foakes and R. T. Rickert, 1961) contains a mass of information about theatrical life, and about dramatists and their methods of writing plays.

HENTY, G. A. (George Alfred) (1832–1902) Journalist and novelist born in Trumpington, Cambridge; educated at Westminster School. While a soldier in the Crimea he became a war correspondent, subsequently covering campaigns in Italy, Abyssinia, Ashanti, Spain, India, and in Paris during the Commune. He wrote several novels for adults before achieving fame as the author of stories for boys, mainly based on military history. *Out in the Pampas* (1868) was followed by some 70 other books, sometimes at the rate of three or four a year. Most ran to several editions; among the best remembered are *Under Drake's Flag* (1883), *With Clive in India* (1884), and *The Lion of St Mark's* (1889). The didactic influence, conveyed largely through the manly characters of the heroes, is supported by strong narrative and an appearance of historical fidelity. There is a biography (Guy Arnold, *Held Fast for England: G. A. Henty, Imperialist Boys' Writer*, 1980) and a bibliographical study (Peter Newbolt, *G. A. Henty, 1832–1902: A Bibliographical Study of his British Editions*, 1996).

HENZE, Hans Werner (1926–) Prolific German composer with wide literary interests. The solo cantata *Whispers from Heavenly Death* (1948) is from Walt *Whitman. Among Henze's many operas are two with libretti by W. H. *Auden and Chester Kallman, *Elegy for Young Lovers* (1961) and *The Bassarids* (1966), and *Moralities* (1968), a set of three scenic cantatas with texts by Auden after *Aesop. Henze's *Royal Winter Music* I (1976) is a sonata for guitar in which each movement explores a character from Shakespeare. The large-scale stage work *We Come to the River*, described as 'actions for music' with a text by Edward *Bond, was written for the Royal Opera House, Covent Garden (1976). Henze has set several other pieces by Bond.

Heptaméron, L' A collection in French of 72 tales of love (originally intended as 100, but unfinished) by Marguerite de Navarre (1492–1549), sister of King Francis I. The tales, which depict love as a serious and sometimes tragic passion, are linked by the fiction that the narrators are travellers detained in an inn by a flood. The name *Heptaméron*, or 'seven days', was first given to the collection in 1559, on the analogy of Boccaccio's **Decameron*.

Hera *See* JUNO.

HERACLITUS OF EPHESUS (*fl. c.*500 BC) One of the formative figures in Greek philosophy, commonly associated with the idea that 'everything is in flux'. 'Fluxing' afterwards became associated with weeping: hence Heraclitus becomes 'the weeping philosopher', as opposed to the 'laughing' *Democritus. More accurately he is 'obscure', preferring to express himself in aphorisms; more than 100 survive. He may or may not (implicitly) have denied the law of contradiction—the compresence or state of concurrent existence (somehow) of opposites was evidently important to his thinking about the world; fire too was central, either as fundamental substance, or as a symbol of flux (or as both).

Herbal, The, *or General History of Plants* *See* GERARD, JOHN.

Her Benny A novel by the Methodist author Silas K. *Hocking, published in 1879. Set in Liverpool, it vividly describes the struggles of two street children to survive in the face of poverty and neglect. It proved enduringly popular, was translated into several languages, and sold a million copies in Hocking's lifetime. Anne Dalton adapted the book for the stage in 1993, and her play has been regularly revived.

HERBERT, Sir A. P. (Alan Patrick) (1890–1971) Writer and politician, born at Leatherhead, Surrey, and educated at Winchester College and New College, Oxford. His works include *The Secret Battle* (1919), a stirring account of the horrors of war which was received with acclaim; *Misleading Cases in the Common Law* (1927), which ridiculed some absurdities in court procedure; *A Book of Ballads* (1949); and *Independent Member* (1950), describing his experiences as MP for Oxford University (1935–50). Herbert campaigned for several causes, such as reform in the divorce laws (a theme treated in *Holy Deadlock*, 1934), reform in English spelling (in *What a Word*, 1935), improving authors' rights, changes in the obscenity laws, and water-buses on the Thames. *Riverside Nights* (1926;

a revue) and his best-known novel *The Water Gipsies* (1930) reflect his affection for the Thames. He was knighted in 1945. See Reginald Pound, *A. P. Herbert: A Biography* (1976).

HERBERT, Frank (1920–86) American *science fiction writer, born in Tacoma, Washington. *Dune* (1965) became one of the best-selling science fiction novels of the period, thanks in part to its detailed evocation of the ecology of the desert-planet Arrakis/Dune, which tapped into the growing concern for environmental issues. Several sequels followed, elaborating on its Messianic themes and political intrigues. David Lynch's film of *Dune* (1984) associated Herbert's name with this one work, although *Whipping Star* (1970) and *Hellstrom's Hive* (1973) are also successful novels.

HERBERT, George (1593–1633) Poet, fifth son of Sir Richard and Magdalen Herbert and younger brother of Lord *Herbert of Cherbury, born in Montgomery into a prominent family. His father died when he was 3 and in 1608 his mother, the patron of John *Donne, remarried Sir John Danvers (1584/5–1655), who was twenty years her junior. Educated at Westminster School where he was named king's scholar, and Trinity College, Cambridge, Herbert published his first poems (two sets of memorial verses in Latin) in a volume mourning Prince Henry's death in 1612. But he had already, according to his earliest biographer, Izaak *Walton, sent his mother at the start of 1610 a New Year's letter dedicating his poetic powers to God and enclosing two sonnets ('My God, where is that ancient heat towards thee?' and 'Sure, Lord, there is enough in thee to dry'). In 1616 he was elected a major fellow of Trinity, and in 1618 appointed reader in rhetoric. In 1620 he became public orator at the university. He seems at this period to have been keen on making the acquaintance of the great, and conscious of his distinction of birth. Francis *Bacon and Donne were among his friends, and the public oratorship introduced him to men of influence at court. Although he was obliged, by the terms of his fellowship, to take holy orders within seven years, he seems to have gravitated towards a secular career, leaving his university duties to be performed by proxies. In 1624, and again in 1625, he represented Montgomery in Parliament. This fairly brief experience of worldly ambition seems, however, to have disillusioned him. He was ordained deacon, probably before the end of 1624, and installed in 1626 as a canon of Lincoln Cathedral and prebendary of Leighton Bromswold in Huntingdonshire, near *Little Gidding, where Nicholas *Ferrar, whom Herbert had known at Cambridge, had recently established a religious community. Once installed, Herbert set about restoring the ruined church at Leighton. His mother died in 1627, and his *Memoriae Matris Sacrum* was published in the volume containing Donne's commemoration sermon. In March 1629 Herbert married his stepfather's cousin, Jane Danvers, and they adopted two orphaned nieces of Herbert's. He became rector of Bemerton, near Salisbury, in April 1630, being ordained priest the following September. In his short priesthood he gained a reputation for humility, energy, and charity. He was also a keen musician, and would go twice a week to hear the singing in Salisbury Cathedral which was, he said, 'Heaven upon earth'. He died of consumption shortly before his 40th birthday. When he realized he was dying he sent his English poems to his friend Ferrar with instructions to publish them, if he thought they might 'turn to the advantage of any dejected soul', and otherwise to burn them. *The Temple*, containing nearly all his surviving English poems, was published in 1633, *Outlandish Proverbs* (a collection of foreign proverbs in translation) in 1640, and Herbert's prose picture of the model country parson, *A Priest to the Temple*, in 1652, as part of *Herbert's Remains*. His translation of Luigi Cornaro's *Trattato de la vita sobria* appeared in 1634, and his 'Brief Notes' on Juan de Valdés's *Hundred and Ten Considerations* in 1638. He told Ferrar that his poems represented 'a picture of the many spiritual conflicts that have passed betwixt God and my soul'. They were much admired in the 17th century, and thirteen editions of *The Temple* came out between 1633 and 1679. In the 18th century Herbert went out of fashion, though John *Wesley adapted some of his poems for hymns. The Romantic age saw a revival, and the appreciative notice in S. T. Coleridge's *Biographia Literaria* (1817) enhanced Herbert's reputation. Modern critics have noted the subtlety rather than the simplicity of his poems, seeing them as an attempt to express the ultimately ineffable complications of the spiritual life. The precise nature of Herbert's relationship to Calvinism has also generated debate. See *The English Poems of George Herbert* (ed. Helen Wilcox, 2007); Amy M. Charles, *Life* (1977); J. R. Roberts's *Annotated Bibliography of Modern Criticism* (2nd edn, 1988); A. D. Nuttall, *Overheard by God* (1980).

HERBERT, Mary *See* PEMBROKE, MARY HERBERT.

HERBERT, Zbigniew (1924–98) Polish poet and essayist, born in Lvov, whose predominantly political poetry has appeared in English as *Selected Poems* (1968; repr. 1985, trans. Czesław *Miłosz and Peter Dale Scott) and in another selection by John and Bogdana Carpenter (published 1977), who also translated his collection *Report from the Besieged City*, which appeared in English in 1985. His last collection, *The Epilogue of the Storm*, appeared in 1998. *The Collected Poems 1956–1998* was published in 2007.

HERBERT of Cherbury, Edward, Lord (1582–1648) Elder brother of George *Herbert, born at Eyton-on-Severn, Shropshire, into one of the foremost families of the Welsh border. In 1596, aged 14, he was enrolled as gentleman commoner at University College, Oxford. That year his father died, and Herbert became ward of Sir George More (1553–1632; later John *Donne's father-in-law). At 16 he was married to his cousin Mary, daughter of Sir William Herbert of St Julians, heiress to her father's estates in England, Wales, and Ireland. By the time he was 21 the couple had had, he reports, 'divers children', of whom none survived him. He was created knight of the Bath in 1603. His adventures are recounted by Herbert in his *Life*, a remarkable document, not least for its unabashed presentation of its author's martial valour, success with women, truthfulness, sweetness of breath, and other virtues. He aspired to a career in public service and spent much of the time from 1608 to 1618 in France, getting to know the French aristocracy and court. He also travelled in Italy and served under the prince of Orange in the Low Countries, fighting at the siege of Juliers (1610). He offered, he says, to decide the war by single combat with a champion chosen by the enemy, but the challenge was declined. In 1619 he became ambassador to France, on Buckingham's recommendation. His most famous philosophical work, *De Veritate*, was published in Paris in 1624. To attract royal notice he wrote, in 1630, *The Expedition to the Isle of Rhé*, which tries to justify Buckingham's calamitous generalship, and in 1632 he began a history of *Henry VIII's reign, published in 1649. At the outbreak of the Civil War he retired to Montgomery Castle and declined to become involved. The castle was threatened by Royalists in 1644, and he admitted a Parliamentary garrison in exchange for the return of his books, which had been seized. He moved to his London house and dedicated himself to philosophy, supplementing his *De Veritate* with *De Causis Errorum*, on logical fallacies, and *De Religione Laici*, both published in 1645, and writing besides *De Religione Gentilium*, one of the earliest works of comparative theology, and his autobiography (begun in 1643). In 1647 he visited Pierre Gassendi (1592–1655) in Paris. Herbert's *De Veritate* postulates that religion is common to all men and that, stripped of superfluous priestly accretions, it can be reduced to five universal innate ideas: that there is a God; that he should be worshipped; that virtue and piety are essential to worship; that man should repent of his sins; and that there are rewards and punishments after this life. It gained him the title of father of English *Deism, and was widely read in the 17th century, earning the attention and disagreement of Marin Mersenne (1588–1648), Gassendi, René *Descartes, and John *Locke. Herbert also wrote obscure and metrically contorted metaphysical poetry, evidently influenced by his friend Donne, and some tender and musical love lyrics (*see* METAPHYSICAL POETS). See *Life*, ed. S. Lee (1886; rev. 1906), and ed. J. M. Shuttleworth (1976); *Poems English and Latin*, ed. G. C. Moore Smith (1923); *De Veritate*, ed. and trans. M. H. Carré (1937); *De Religione Laici*, ed. and trans. H. R. Hutcheson (1944); R. D. Bedford, *The Defence of Truth* (1979).

HERBST, Josephine (1892–1969) American writer born in Sioux City, Iowa. In 1922 she moved to Germany, then Paris to join the expatriate writers' circle there, including Ford Madox *Ford and Ernest *Hemingway. Among her novels, she produced a historical trilogy: *Pity is Not Enough* (1933), *The Executioner Waits* (1934), and *Rope of Gold* (1939).

Hercules (Greek Herakles) Mythical Greek hero and demigod. His twelve labours included cleansing the Augean stables, bringing back the apples of the Hesperides, and descending to the underworld to capture Cerberus. He came to represent both a Stoic hero and in Christian allegory a type of Christ. The choice of Hercules between the paths of virtue and pleasure, as told in *Xenophon's *Memorabilia*, was a favourite topos in Renaissance and 18th-century art, literature, and music.

HERD, David (1732–1810) Edinburgh-based law clerk and antiquary, born in Marykirk, Kincardineshire, who in 1769 produced a collection of mainly *Scots songs, which appeared in a two-volume revised version in 1776 as *Ancient and Modern Scottish Songs, Heroic Ballads, Etc*. Herd carefully collated unitary versions of his texts from a variety of sources, and later made his manuscripts available to Robert *Burns, for whom they provided the basis for several songs.

HERDER, Johann Gottfried (1744–1803) German philosopher and critic. Born at Mohrungen in East Prussia, he studied theology at Königsberg. Inspired by Thomas *Percy's *Reliques*, he was an ardent collector of folk song, publishing two volumes of *Volkslieder* (1778–9). In this and in his admiration for James *Macpherson's *Ossian* and for *Shakespeare, about whom he wrote an enthusiastic essay in *Von deutscher Art und Kunst* (1773: *On German Art*), he exercised a profound influence on the young *Goethe. He is notable also as an investigator of problems of language in *Über den Ursprung der Sprache* (1772: *On the Origin of Language*) and as a philosopher of history. In *Ideen zur Philosophie der Geschichte der Menschheit* (1784–91: *Ideas towards a Philosophy of the History of Mankind*) he espoused an understanding of cultural development as a process of cyclical, quasi-organic evolution rather than simple linear progress.

Hergest, Red Book of *See* MABINOGION.

hermeneutics A term for the theory of interpretation, employed at first in biblical scholarship, but then also more generally in the humanities and social sciences. In modern literary theory and related fields, the term refers to a philosophical tradition, predominantly German, in which certain general problems of interpretation arise. It originates in the lectures of the theologian Friedrich Schleiermacher (1768–1834), who proposed that comprehension of the grammatical sense of a text was insufficient without a larger intuitive grasp of the author's intention. The philosopher Wilhelm Dilthey (1833–1911) later developed the implications of this idea, and formulated the problem of the 'hermeneutic circle': that we cannot understand any part of a text or of a historical period without understanding the whole, yet we cannot understand the whole without understanding its parts. His answer to the conundrum is that we reconcile part and whole through successively adjusted provisional understandings or intuitive projections. In the philosophical tradition of Martin *Heidegger and his followers, hermeneutics reaches far beyond mere interpretation, as 'understanding' is held to precede its objects. In modern literary theory, a return to hermeneutic problems is found in *Validity in Interpretation* (1967) by E. D. Hirsch (1928–) which distinguishes between a work's determinate 'meaning' and its variable 'significance', and in various alternatives to his view. An especially influential modern hermeneuticist was the French philosopher Paul Ricœur (1913–2005), who noted a distinction between the religious 'hermeneutics of the sacred', which seeks to restore an original meaning that has become obscured, and the modern 'hermeneutics of suspicion', which seeks (as in *Marx and *Freud) a concealed meaning behind misleading appearances. See Peter Szondi, *Introduction to Literary Hermeneutics* (1995).

Hermes *See* MERCURY.

Hermes Trismegistus The 'thrice great Hermes' of Milton's *'Il Penseroso', the name given by Neoplatonists and devotees of mysticism and alchemy to the Egyptian god Thoth, identified with the Greek god Hermes, and regarded as the author of all mystical doctrines. From the 3rd century onwards the name was applied to the author of various Neoplatonic writings, including *On the Divine Intelligence*. This work, translated by *Ficino (*c.*1490) into Latin and by John Everard (1650) into English, made a notable impact on 16th- and 17th-century writers, such as Thomas *Vaughan, Sir Thomas *Browne, and the *Cambridge Platonists. In 1614 Isaac *Casaubon established that the Hermetic writings, far from being ancient, were actually later than *Plato, though many ignored his findings. See Frances Yates, *Giordano Bruno and the Hermetic Tradition* (1964); D. P. Walker, *The Ancient Theology* (1972).

Hermsprong, *or Man as He Is Not* (1796) Robert *Bage's final and most popular novel. Hermsprong, who has been brought up among Native Americans (an indication of natural virtue), arrives in England via revolutionary France, and finds himself in the conventional aristocratic circle of the gouty Lord Grondale and the sycophantic clergyman Dr Blick. Hermsprong's lack of social vices, and his radical views on the equality of women and the class divisions of society, produce many comic situations. Eventually he is discovered to be the rightful heir of Lord Grondale, whose daughter he marries. Other notable characters are Maria Fluart, a feminist in the *Wollstonecraft mode, whose wit and intelligence defeat the designs of the ageing Grondale, and the sardonic narrator Gregory Glen.

Hero and Leander The tragic story of Leander's love for Hero, the priestess of Aphrodite: he is drowned while swimming to her at night across the Hellespont, and she then in despair throws herself into the sea. This story has been the subject of poems by Christopher *Marlowe (completed by George *Chapman) and by Thomas *Hood, and of a burlesque by Thomas *Nashe in his *Lenten Stuff*.

HERODOTUS (5th century BC) Author of the earliest Greek history. He describes Egypt, Cyrene, and Babylon, apparently as an eyewitness. His main subject is the wars between the Greeks and the Barbarians (i.e. the Persians), but before reaching it he describes in detail the Persian empire, Egypt, Scythia, and the early history of Athens and Sparta. This helps to make the events of Xerxes' invasion and defeat intelligible within a human and divine pattern. Herodotus combines ethnography, geography, folk tale, anecdote, military history, and politics. He was criticized for credulousness and fabulousness, even in ancient times, but his methods of research and verification constituted the first recognizable form of history in the modern sense. Indeed, the term 'historiē' or 'learning by enquiry', which is what he calls his work, has come to mean 'history' as we understand it. See Carolyn Dewald and John Marincola (eds), *The Cambridge Companion to Herodotus* (2006).

Heroes, Hero-Worship and the Heroic in History, On A series of lectures on the role of heroes in history by Thomas *Carlyle, published 1841. Influenced by German thinking, particularly the work of the German philosopher Johann Gottlieb Fichte (1762–1814), Carlyle establishes a version of history as 'the biography of great men'. None of Carlyle's heroes was born into the ruling classes, but demonstrated their pre-eminence through the qualities they shared of faith, sincerity, leadership, and a belief in social justice. Carlyle has six categories of hero—as Divinity, Prophet, Poet, Priest, Man of Letters, and King—and chooses as exemplars *Dante, William *Shakespeare, Martin *Luther, John *Knox, Samuel *Johnson, Jean-Jacques *Rousseau, Robert *Burns, Oliver *Cromwell, and Napoleon Bonaparte (1769–1821). Carlyle argues that people need to worship heroes and that some men show leadership, not through force, but through being endowed with divine purpose.

heroic poetry Another term for *epic poetry.

heroic verse (heroic line) The *metre used in the heroic (i.e. *epic) poetry of a given language: in English since the 16th century the iambic *pentameter, in French the *alexandrine, in Italian the *hendecasyllabic line, in Greek and Latin the dactylic *hexameter.

HERRICK, Robert (1591–1674) Poet, seventh child of Nicholas Herrick, a prosperous goldsmith who migrated to London from Leicester, and of Julian, daughter of a London mercer, William Stone, whom Nicholas married in 1582. In November 1592, sixteen months after Robert's birth, and two days after making his will, Herrick's father fell to his death from a fourth-floor window in his London house. Suicide was suspected, but being 'moved with charity' the queen's almoner did not confiscate the Herrick estate for the Crown, as was usual with suicides. There is no record of Robert attending school, but the family was wealthy and the classical bent of his poetry makes it likely he had a grammar-school education. In 1607 he was apprenticed to his uncle Sir William Herrick, goldsmith, a man of mark who was MP for Leicester, owned land in thirteen counties, and had been knighted in 1605. Herrick's earliest datable poem was written about 1610 to his brother Thomas on his leaving London to farm in Leicestershire ('A Country Life: To his Brother M. Tho. Herrick'). 'To my dearest Sister M. Mercy Herrick' must also have been written before 1612. In 1613, having obtained release from his apprenticeship, he entered St John's College, Cambridge, as a fellow commoner, a status reserved for sons of wealthy families, which entailed double fees and privileges such as dining at high table. He lived lavishly at university and, despite his private income, frequently sent to his uncle William for additional funds. College friends included Clipseby Crew (knighted 1620) to whom he addressed several poems including the outstanding 'Nuptial Song'. Herrick moved to Trinity Hall, graduating BA in 1617, MA in 1620. In 1623 he was ordained priest. He evidently mixed with literary circles in London, particularly the group around Ben *Jonson, and was well known as a poet by 1625 when the antiquary Richard James (bap. 1591, d. 1638) in 'The Muses' Dirge' ranked him beside Jonson and Michael *Drayton. Friends included Phineas *Fletcher, William *Browne, John *Selden, Richard *Corbett, Mildmay Fane (second earl of Westmorland), and William and Henry *Lawes. In 1627 he was one of the army chaplains on the duke of Buckingham's disastrous expedition to the Isle of Rhé, in aid of the Protestants of La Rochelle. In reward for his services he received the living of Dean Prior, a village deep in the south Devon countryside, taking up the living in September 1630. Repelled by the barren isolation of rural life at first, he developed, as his poems show, a feeling for folk customs and festivals like May Day and Harvest Home, which appealed partly because the Puritans tried to suppress them. He also made friends among the country gentry, writing poems to their daughters. He left Dean Prior for a period, without permission from his bishop, and lived in Westminster with Tomasin Parsons, daughter of a musician and 27 years younger than Herrick, by whom he may have had an illegitimate daughter. An ardent loyalist, Herrick was ejected from his living by Parliament in 1647 and returned to London, where the following year his poems *Hesperides*, together with his religious poems *Noble Numbers*, were published. During the Commonwealth he probably subsisted on the charity of his relations and in 1660 was reinstated at Dean Prior where he remained for the rest of his life, writing, apparently, no more poems, and being buried in an unmarked grave in the churchyard. Herrick's secular poems are mostly exercises in miniature, very highly polished (as comparison with surviving earlier versions shows) and employing meticulous displacements of syntax and word order so as to give diminutive, aesthetic grace to the great chaotic subjects—sex, transience, death—that obsess him. He is one of the finest English lyric poets, and has a faultless ear. His religious poems have generally been derided as childish, but more recent scholarship has seen them as part of a calculated 17th-century Anglican attempt to idealize childhood in face of the Puritan emphasis on original sin. See *Works*, ed. L. C. Martin (1956); *Complete Poetry*, ed. J. Max Patrick (1963); G. W. Scott, *Robert Herrick* (1974); L. S. Marcus, *Childhood and Cultural Despair* (1978); M. Swann, *Curiosities and Texts: The Culture of Collecting in Early Modern England* (2001).

HERSEY, John (1914–93) American novelist and journalist, born in Tientsin, China, primarily remembered for his report on the dropping of the first atomic bomb, *Hiroshima* (1946), which has become a classic of modern reportage. His other works include *The Wall* (1950), a novel set in the Warsaw ghetto.

HERVEY, James (1714–58) Anglican clergyman, who became a Methodist when a student at Oxford, though his Calvinist beliefs later led to a breach with John *Wesley. His *Meditations and Contemplations* (1746–7) and *Theron and Aspasio* (1755), in which he attempted to combine the language of Puritan meditation with that of the **Spectator* and *Shaftesbury's *Moralists* and drew heavily on *Milton and Edward *Young, were extremely influential in the *Evangelical Revival, although critically derided, and had enormous sales.

HERVEY, John, Baron Hervey of Ickworth (1696–1743) Whig courtier and poet. As vice-chamberlain (from 1730) he exercised great influence over Queen Caroline. He collaborated with Lady Mary Wortley *Montagu in response to attacks from Alexander *Pope, who satirized him in prose and verse, from 1732 onwards, as 'Lord Fanny', an idle versifier. The famous 'Sporus' portrait of the *Epistle to Dr Arbuthnot* is the most inventive, acute, and powerful of the attacks. Hervey also appears in other works under the names Narcissus and Adonis; his effeminacy was a particular target. Some of Hervey's poems appeared in Robert *Dodsley's *Collection of Poems by Several Hands* (1748–58). His carefully polished *Memoirs of the Reign of George II* (first edited by J. W. *Croker, 1848) give a vivid picture of the intrigues of court life. See also the edition by R. Sedgwick (3 vols, 1931), and R. Halsband, *Lord Hervey: Eighteenth-Century Courtier* (1973).

HERZEN, Alexander (Aleksandr Ivanovich Gertsen) (1812–70) Russian revolutionary thinker and writer, born in Moscow, the son of a wealthy nobleman. From his youth he was interested in political, social, and philosophical questions, and was drawn to the French utopian socialism of Henri de *Saint-Simon and Pierre-Joseph *Proudhon. His involvement in radical politics led to two periods of internal exile. During the second period in 1841 he began his ideological novel *Who Is To Blame?*, eventually published in 1847. That year he emigrated, at first to Italy, France, and Switzerland, finally settling in London in 1852. The failure of the revolutions of 1848 and the turbulence of his private life deeply affected his political outlook. His disillusionment—described in *From the Other Shore* (1850) and *Letters from France and Italy* (1855)—led him to elaborate a more nationalistic and agrarian kind of socialism, based on the Russian peasant commune. In London he established the first Free Russian Press (1853) and published his almanac the *Polar Star* (1855–68). Prompted by Nikolai Ogarev (1813–77) who arrived in London in 1856, Herzen founded the influential *Bell* (1857–67). Smuggled into Russia, it advocated radical reform and emancipation of the serfs. His outstanding work is his unfinished and heterogeneous memoir *My Past and Thoughts* (1855–69), translated in six volumes by Constance *Garnett (1924–7), in which personal recollections are interwoven with the development of his political ideology and philosophical speculations. See Edward Acton, *Alexander Herzen and the Role of the Intellectual Revolutionary* (1979).

HESIOD (*fl.* 700 BC) One of the earliest Greek poets. The *Theogony* contains a very influential account of the origins of the world and the genealogy of the gods, for which the poet claims inspiration from the *Muses. *Works and Days* gives a picture of a farmer's life that was to serve *Virgil for a model in the **Georgics*; hence George *Chapman entitled his translation *The Georgics of Hesiod*. The first complete English translation was published by Thomas Cooke (1703–56) in 1728; he was subsequently known as 'Hesiod' Cooke. John *Flaxman's illustrations to Hesiod were engraved by William *Blake. See Hesiod, *Theogony; Works and Days*, trans. M. L. West (1978).

Hesperides *See* HERRICK, ROBERT.

HESSE, Hermann (1877–1962) German Swiss author of several mystical novels which attracted a revival of interest in Germany, Britain, and America in the 1960s–1970s. *Siddhartha* (1922) is rooted in Hesse's study of Indian religions and describes the quest of two Hindu friends for spiritual and sexual fulfilment; it was later adopted as a *New Age cult book. *Der Steppenwolf* (1927) came into vogue with the cult of 'the outsider' initiated in part by Colin *Wilson. The latter reflects Hesse's interest in double personalities (a legacy of *Romanticism also connected with Hesse's interest in psychoanalysis). *Narziss und Goldmund* (1930) is a Surrealist work set in the Middle Ages and *Das Glasperlenspiel* (*The Glass Bead Game*, 1943), Hesse's last novel, envisages a philosophical utopia under the control of a quasi-monastic elite, and was based on the novel *Die Lehrlinge zu Sais* (1802) by Friedrich Leopold von *Hardenberg (known as Novalis). As a result of his cosmopolitan and pacifist views his books were banned in Germany in 1943. He was awarded the *Nobel Prize for Literature in 1946.

hexameter In English, either (1) an iambic verse line with six stressed syllables (*see* METRE), as found in the final line of the Spenserian *stanza and sometimes as the basis of whole *sonnets (e.g. the opening sonnet of Philip Sidney's **Astrophel and Stella* sequence) or even of longer poems (e.g. Robert Browning, **Fifine at the Fair*), and commonly called an *alexandrine after the twelve-syllable French line; or (2) an imitative transposition into English stress patterns of the classical dactylic hexameter, which was the line of Greek and Latin *epic poetry among other forms. In Greek and Latin verse, the dactylic hexameter comprised five dactyls followed by a spondee or trochee, with possible substitution of a spondee for any of the first four dactyls. Several poets have attempted English imitations of this line, most notably A. H. *Clough in *The Bothie of Tober-na-Vuolich* (1848), and in the late 20th century Peter *Reading.

Hey for Honesty, Down with Knavery A comedy attributed to Thomas *Randolph, printed 1651. The play is a free adaptation of *Aristophanes' *Plutus*, with allusions to current events and recent plays, including mentions of *Falstaff and *Hamlet's ghost. The moralistic action concludes with Chremylus, 'an honest decayed gentleman', recovering his wealth, and Plutus, the blind god of wealth, recovering his sight and marrying Honesty.

HEYLYN, Peter (1600–62) An Anglican controversialist and writer of ecclesiastical history, whose works include a defence of William *Laud (*Cyprianus Anglicus*, 1668), histories of the *Reformation (1661) and *Presbyterianism (1670), and a *Cosmography* (1652).

HEYWOOD, John (?1497–?1580) Author, probably born in London. He married Elizabeth Rastell, niece of Sir Thomas *More. Under *Henry VIII he was a singer and player on the virginals. He was much favoured by Queen Mary, and on her death escaped persecution for his Catholic faith by withdrawing to Malines, and afterwards to Antwerp and Louvain. He published *interludes, substituting the human comedy of contemporary types for the instructive allegory of the *morality; but he used narrative and debate rather than plot and action. His principal works were *The Four PP* (first printed ?1544), *The Play of the Weather* (1533), in which Jupiter listens to conflicting opinions as to the kind of weather to be supplied, and *A Play of Love* (1534). He may also have been the author of *The Pardoner and the Friar* and *Johan Johan the Husband, Tyb his Wife and Sir John the Priest*. Heywood wrote a dialogue called *Witty and Witless*, collections of proverbs and epigrams, and a long satirical poem, *The Spider and the Fly* (1556).

HEYWOOD, Thomas (1573–1641) Dramatist and poet, a Lincolnshire man, and a student at Cambridge. He was writing and probably acting for Philip *Henslowe's Admiral's Men from 1596, and later became a leading dramatist of Queen Anne's and Lady Elizabeth's Men at the Red Bull and Cockpit theatres. He claimed to have had at least a hand in over 200 plays, many of which are lost; he was immensely versatile, though his chief strength lay in domestic drama. His best plays are *A *Woman Killed with Kindness* (acted 1603; printed 1607), *The *Fair Maid of the West* (1601–2?; 1609?), and *The *English Traveller* (*c.*1604). His other chief plays were *The Four Prentices of London* (acted *c.*1600; printed 1615), ridiculed in Francis *Beaumont's *The *Knight of the Burning Pestle* (1607?); *Edward IV* (two parts, printed 1599); *The Rape of Lucrece* (printed 1608); *The Royal King and the Loyal Subject* (printed 1637), and *The Wise Woman of Hogsdon* (*c.*1604; printed 1638). *The Golden Age* and *The Brazen Age* (both printed 1611), *The Silver Age* (printed 1613), and *The Iron Age* (two parts, printed 1632) are a panoramic dramatization of classical mythology. His *An Apology for Actors* (*c.*1608; printed 1612) is the best Jacobean summary of traditional arguments in defence of the stage, and has some good anecdotes. In his epistle to the printer, Heywood complains about William *Jaggard's inclusion of two poems from it in the 1612 edition of *The *Passionate Pilgrim*, ascribed to *Shakespeare. He also translated *Sallust and published poems (including *The Hierarchy of the Blessed*

Angels, 1635), translations, and pageants for seven lord mayor's shows. Two plays, *The Captives* (1624) and *The Escapes of Jupiter* (a mildly erotic cut version of the *Golden* and *Silver Ages*), survive in his own hand. There is no modern complete edition of his works.

Hiawatha, The Song of American narrative poem in unrhymed trochaic *tetrameter (*see* METRE), by Henry Wadsworth *Longfellow, published 1855, reproducing Native American stories which centre in the life and death of Hiawatha, reared on the shores of Lake Superior. He marries Minnehaha ('laughing water'), and after various adventures departs for the Isles of the Blest to rule the kingdom of the Northwest Wind. Longfellow took his information from the ethnographer Henry Rowe Schoolcraft (1793–1864). The poem's incantatory metre and novel subject matter made it immensely popular, and attracted many parodies by George A. Strong (1832–1912) and others.

HICHENS, Robert Smythe (1864–1950) Novelist and short story writer, born in Kent, and educated at Clifton College, Bristol; remembered for *The Green Carnation* (1894), published anonymously, which satirized the aesthetes and Oscar *Wilde, and for the best-selling *The Garden of Allah* (1904), a romance of the desert set in North Africa.

HICKES, George (1642–1715) The leader of the great generation of Anglo-Saxon scholars which included the *Elstobs, Humfrey *Wanley, and Edmund Gibson (1669–1748). He published the first Anglo-Saxon grammar in 1689. The climax of his work was the monumental *Linguarum Veterum Septentrionalium Thesaurus*, or the 'Treasury of the Northern Tongues' (1703–5), a comparative grammar of Old English and the related Germanic tongues, produced through much collaboration. Its examination of the manuscript sources of Anglo-Saxon history had a deep influence upon the study of the Old English past. See D. C. Douglas, *English Scholars* (1939).

HIGDEN, Ranulf (d. 1364) A Benedictine monk of St Werburgh's, Chester. His popular Latin prose *Polychronicon* is a universal history surviving in over 100 manuscripts, translated by *John of Trevisa in 1387 and printed by William *Caxton in 1482. Higden also wrote sermons and treatises on preaching.

HIGGINS, Aidan (1927–) Novelist, born in Celbridge, Co. Kildare, and best known for *Langrishe, Go Down* (1966), an extension of the Irish *'big house' genre, which sets the decline of a once powerful family of Catholic landowners in the context of the larger European malaise of the 1930s through its depiction of the affair between Imogen Langrishe and an egotistical German student. Other novels include the somewhat sprawling *Balcony of Europe* (1972), concerned with the fortunes of an expatriate community in 1960s Andalusia, and *Bornholm Night Ferry* (1983), a melancholy erotic variation on the *epistolary novel. Higgins has also produced some striking travel writing. His three autobiographies are collected in *A Bestiary* (2004). *Flotsam and Jetsam* (1996) gathers his shorter fiction.

HIGGINS, Matthew James (1810–68) Known as 'Jacob Omnium'; born at Benown Castle in Co. Meath, Ireland; educated at Eton College and New College, Oxford. Higgins was a prominent journalist who contributed to *The *Times*, **Punch*, and the **Cornhill Magazine*. His campaigning articles, which often exposed abuses of social and public life, brought him into contact with W. M. *Thackeray, who dedicated his **Adventures of Philip* to Higgins. His *Essays on Social Subjects* was published in 1875.

HIGGINSON, Thomas Wentworth (1823–1911) American writer born in Cambridge, Massachusetts. Trained as a pastor, Higginson served in the Civil War and describes his experiences in *Army Life in a Black Regiment* (1870). He became Emily *Dickinson's correspondent and mentor, and published biographies of Margaret *Fuller, Henry Wadsworth *Longfellow, and James Greenleaf *Whittier. His works were collected as *The Magnificent Activist* (2000).

HIGHSMITH, Patricia (1921–95) Writer of mixed German and English-Scots parentage, educated at Barnard College at Columbia University, New York. Her stylish crime novels have a distinctively black humour: the best known, including *The Talented Mr Ripley* (1956), *Ripley under Ground* (1971), and *Ripley's Game* (1974), feature her amoral anti-hero, the leisure-loving amateur villain Tom Ripley, resident in France. *The Price of Salt*, a novel with a lesbian theme and a happy ending, was published pseudonymously (under the name of Claire Morgan) in 1952, and appeared under her own name in 1990, retitled *Carol*. Her last novel, *Small g: A Summer Idyll*, about a bohemian café in Zurich, was published in 1995.

High Way to the Spittle House, The A tract printed and adapted from a French work by Robert Copland (*fl.* 1505–47), describing the beggars and other types of the poorer classes who visit St Bartholomew's Hospital in London. Taking the form of a dialogue between the author and the hospital's porter, it throws a vivid light on the poverty prevailing in the early 16th century.

HILL, Aaron (1685–1750) Poet, dramatist, and theatre manager, educated at Westminster School. His varied output includes the libretto for *Handel's *Rinaldo* (1711), an influential theatrical periodical, *The Prompter*, which he edited (1734–6) with William Popple (1701–64), and an unfinished epic poem, *Gideon* (1749). Having travelled widely, he wrote a history of the Ottoman Empire (1709). He criticized Alexander *Pope's edition of Shakespeare in his bi-weekly *Plain Dealer* and was satirized in *The *Dunciad* and elsewhere; he responded in *The Progress of Wit* (1730). His circle included Eliza *Haywood,

Edward *Young, Richard *Savage, John *Dyer, and Charles *Churchill; *A Collection of Letters, Never Before Printed* (1751) contains letters by Pope and James *Thomson to Hill. His commercial concerns include the production of beechnut oil, harvesting timber on Speyside, and a vineyard at Plaistow. Samuel *Richardson promoted an edition of his *Works* (1753) to assist his daughters, Urania, Astrea, and Minerva. See C. Gerrard, *Aaron Hill: The Muses' Projector 1685–1750* (2003).

HILL, Christopher (1912–2003) Marxist historian, educated at St Peter's School, York, and Balliol College, Oxford, where he was a fellow, then (1965–78) master. During the war he was commissioned in the Oxford and Bucks Light Infantry, then became a major in the Intelligence Corps, seconded to the Foreign Office. As a historian he transformed the accepted view of the 17th century, seeing it as essentially the century of revolution. His many books include *Puritanism and Revolution* (1958), *The Intellectual Origins of the English Revolution* (1965; rev. 1986), and *The World Turned Upside Down: Radical Ideas during the English Revolution* (1972), which provides a lively introduction to the prose of many of the lesser known and radical writers of the period, including Laurence *Clarkson, Abiezer *Coppe, William *Walwyn, Gerrard *Winstanley, and the anonymous author of **Tyranipocrit Discovered*. He also edited the works of Winstanley, and wrote studies of Oliver *Cromwell (*God's Englishman*, 1970), John *Milton (*Milton and the English Revolution*, 1977), John *Bunyan (*A Turbulent, Seditious and Factious People: John Bunyan and his Church*, 1988), and *The English Bible in 17th Century England* (1993).

HILL, Eric (1927–) OBE, Known for his many popular *movable and picture books about Spot the dog, beginning with *Where's Spot* (1983). Hill was born in Holloway, London, and left school early, thereafter working in a cartoon studio and advertising agencies where he acquired skills in graphic design.

HILL, Geoffrey (1932–) Poet, born in Bromsgrove and educated at Keble College, Oxford. His first volume of poetry was *For the Unfallen* (1959), followed by *King Log* (1968), *Mercian Hymns* (1971), which consists of prose poems celebrating Offa, 'a presiding genius of the West Midlands', and *Tenebrae* (1978). His early works show the influence of William *Blake and A. E. *Housman; his language is rich and complex, and much given to ambiguity, and his themes are predominantly historical and religious. His long poem *The Mystery of the Charity of Charles Péguy* (1983) is a densely allusive meditation on the life, faith, and death of the French poet *Péguy. Hill's *Collected Poems* was published in 1994. *Canaan* (1996), published after a long period of poetic silence, is a volume in which distinct poetic sequences are interwoven; it mulls over the political and religious history of England, and denounces what it takes to be the corruption of recent public life. It has been followed, in rapid succession, by several further sequences, including *The Triumph of Love* (1998), *The Orchards of Syon* (2002), and *Without Title* (2006). Hill's literary criticism is assembled in *Collected Prose* (2007), and a *Selected Poems* appeared in 2006. His version of Henrik *Ibsen's *Brand* was produced at the *National Theatre in 1978. See Andrew Michael Roberts, *Geoffrey Hill* (2004).

HILL, Selima (1945–) Poet, born in London, educated at New Hall, Cambridge, where she read Moral Sciences. Her first volume was *Saying Hello at the Station* (1984), and others include *The Accumulation of Small Acts of Kindness* (1989), a sequence charting a young woman's journey through mental breakdown and recovery, *Violet* (1997), *Bunny* (2001), and *Red Roses* (2006). Hill's work is varied in style, tone, and form, and she is prolific; but, throughout, her singular poetic landscape invests the everyday with wild flights of imagination, often through her signature use of surreal, extended similes. Her subject matter prominently includes difficulties in childhood and family relationships, Catholicism, sexual abuse, the otherness of animals, and the erotic.

HILL, Susan (1942–) Novelist, born in Scarborough, Yorkshire, who published her first novel, *The Enclosure* (1961), while still a student at King's College, London. Among her best-known novels are *I'm the King of the Castle* (1970), a dark investigation of childhood which won the Somerset *Maugham Award; *Strange Meeting* (1971), which drew upon the work of Wilfred *Owen and Siegfried *Sassoon; and *The Bird of Night* (1972), which won the Whitbread Award. Hill's sensitivity to atmosphere and the physical environment is used to good effect in *The Woman in Black* (1983), a Victorian ghost story later adapted for a hugely successful stage play, *The Mist in the Mirror* (1992), and *The Man in the Picture* (2007). *Mrs de Winter* (1993) is a sequel to Daphne du Maurier's **Rebecca*. Her short stories are collected in *The Albatross* (1971) and her radio plays in *The Cold Country* (1975). She has also written several books for children.

HILLARY, Richard (1919–43) RAF fighter pilot who was horribly wounded and disfigured in combat in 1940, underwent painful and lengthy surgery, and died in a flying accident. He is remembered as a writer for his vivid account of his wartime experiences, *The Last Enemy* (1942). See David Ross, *Richard Hillary: The Definitive Biography of a Battle of Britain Fighter Pilot and Author of The Last Enemy* (2004).

HILLIARD, Nicholas (*c.*1547–1619) Miniaturist, patronized by *Elizabeth I from the early 1570s and later by *James I. His portraits of the queen and of courtiers and his miniatures, which often bear inscriptions and emblems, played a part in the ceremonies of love at the Elizabethan court; his *An Unknown Youth Leaning against a Tree amongst Roses* (London, Victoria and Albert Museum) suggests the delicate beauty of the Elizabethan lyric whereas his *Young Man against Flames* (also V&A) is charged with strong erotic power. Hilliard was the first British painter who won widespread fame and was accepted as an equal by a cultivated society; he was eulogized by contemporary poets, including Henry *Constable and John *Donne. Between 1589 and 1603 he wrote a treatise, the *Art of*

Limning, influenced by Leon Battista Alberti (1404–72), and *Castiglione's *Book of the Courtier*; Hilliard argues that limning is a noble art, 'fittest for gentlemen'. The treatise mentions an artistic discussion with Sir Philip *Sidney, and a conversation about shadow with Elizabeth I. Hilliard found the more prosaic court of James I less stimulating, and his art declines after 1600.

HILTON, James (1900–54) Novelist and screenwriter, born in Leigh, Lancashire, and educated at The Leys school, Cambridge, and Christ's College, Cambridge (1918–22). He was a prolific novelist, but is remembered principally for *Lost Horizon* (1933), set in the Tibetan lamasery of Shangri-La (the origin of this term) where the inmates enjoy extended youth, and *Good-bye Mr Chips* (1934), a novella about a schoolmaster. Both became successful films. From 1936 Hilton became a highly paid Hollywood screenwriter, and he died in California.

HILTON, Walter (*c.*1343–1396) Augustinian canon of Thurgarton, Nottinghamshire, the author of a prose work in two books, concerning prayer and contemplation, known as *The Scale of Perfection*, written in English and translated into Latin; and of *Mixed Life*, which considers how a lay person's devotional life might be regulated. Hilton wrote a number of Latin epistles and two further treatises, on images and angels' song, are attributed to him. It is likely that he knew *The *Cloud of Unknowing*.

HIMES, Chester (1909–84) African American writer, born in Jefferson City, Missouri. He served a prison spell for armed robbery and in the 1950s moved permanently to Paris in the company of James *Baldwin and Richard *Wright. His first novel, *If He Hollers Let Him Go* (1945), depicts the life of a black shipyard worker during the Second World War, and in 1957 he began publishing a detective series with *A Rage in Harlem*. These novels centre on two New York City detectives called Coffin Ed Johnson and Gravedigger Jones, and draw partly on the style of Dashiell *Hammett. Himes's two autobiographies are *The Quality of Hurt* (1973) and *My Life of Absurdity* (1976). See James Sallis, *Chester Himes: A Life* (2002).

Hind and the Panther, The A poem by John *Dryden, published 1687. Dryden became a Catholic in 1685, and the poem attempts to reconcile Anglican and Catholic political interests, while defending Catholic doctrine. The first part represents religious sects as different beasts, and in particular the Catholic Church and the Church of England as the Hind and the Panther. The second part explores arguments about church authority and transubstantiation, issues full of political as well as religious implications. The third part, constituting half the poem, recommends a political alliance between both Churches and the Crown against Whigs and Dissenters. It contains two celebrated fables, that of the swallows and that of the doves. However, the balance of the latter, and so of the whole poem, may have been upset by James II's Second Declaration of Indulgence, which appealed to Dissenting Protestant sects over the heads of the Anglican establishment.

HINMAN, Charlton (1911–77) A modern pioneer in the study of Shakespeare's texts. His two-volume *The Printing and Proof-Reading of the First Folio* (1963) offers a detailed analysis of how the first *folio was printed, based on a close comparison of 55 copies of the first folio in the Folger Library aided by a machine of his own invention, the Hinman Collator. His work showed how the shares of individual compositors who set up the type in different sections may be distinguished and characterized.

Hippolyta A queen of the Amazons given in marriage to *Theseus by *Hercules, who had conquered her and taken away her girdle, the achievement being one of his twelve labours. She had a son by Theseus called *Hippolytus. According to another version she was slain by Hercules, and it was her sister Antiope who was the wife of Theseus. She and Theseus frame the action in *Shakespeare's *A *Midsummer Night's Dream*.

Hippolytus A son of *Theseus and *Hippolyta. The fatal passion of Phaedra for her stepson Hippolytus is the subject of *Racine's *Phèdre*.

His Dark Materials *fantasy *crossover trilogy (1995–2000) by Philip *Pullman. *Northern Lights* (1995; filmed as *The Golden Compass* 2007) was followed by *The Subtle Knife* (1997) and *The Amber Spyglass* (2000). The story, loosely based on **Paradise Lost*, is about Lyra Belacqua and Will Parry, who travel between worlds, unwittingly re-enacting the Christian Fall, thereby saving humans from an oppressive religious regime based on a defunct deity. In Lyra's world, each character is accompanied by a 'daemon', the soul manifested in animal form. Influenced by a wide variety of literary and non-literary sources, from the ideas of William *Blake to those of quantum physics, the trilogy has attracted many enthusiastic readers.

Historia Ecclesiastica Gentis Anglorum *See* ECCLESIASTICAL HISTORY OF THE ENGLISH PEOPLE.

historical fiction The origins of the British historical novel can be traced back as far as the Elizabethan period and even to the medieval *romances of chivalry, but a convenient generic starting point is Horace Walpole's *The *Castle of Otranto* (1764). *Otranto* patented many of the conventional devices of the *Gothic–historical tale, but it was the success, half a century later, of Walter *Scott's 25 Waverley novels (1814–32) which established the historical novel as a dominant style of fiction. The variety of Scott's historical settings is remarkable, ranging from the early 'Scottish novels' (e.g. *The *Heart of Midlothian*, 1818; **Rob Roy*, 1817), through the English Middle Ages (**Ivanhoe*), medieval France (**Quentin Durward*,

1823), the Middle East of the Crusades (*The *Talisman*, 1825), and even the Roman Empire (**Count Robert of Paris*, 1831).

For most of the Victorian period the historical novel retained its status as the most respected of fiction's genres. Deferring to 'the author of *Waverley*', all the great Victorian novelists tried their hand at the form, from W. M. *Thackeray with *The *History of Henry Esmond* (1852) and Charles *Dickens with *A *Tale of Two Cities* (1859) to George *Eliot with **Romola*. The Victorians admired a number of historical novels which are rarely read today, including W. H. *Ainsworth's *Rookwood* (1834), Edward *Bulwer-Lytton's *The Last Days of Pompeii* (1834), Charles Reade's *The *Cloister and the Hearth* (1861), Charles *Kingsley's *Hereward the Wake* (1866), and R. D. *Blackmore's tale of 17th-century Devon, **Lorna Doone* (1869).

Towards the end of the 19th century, a number of novelists explored the romantic potential of the genre, notably Robert Louis *Stevenson with adventure tales such as **Kidnapped* (1886) and dark studies in psychology such as *The *Master of Ballantrae* (1889). Henry Rider *Haggard's large output of adventure novels included many with a historical setting, from *Eric Brighteyes* (1890, describing Viking raids and exploration) to *Montezuma's Daughter* (1893, last years of the Aztec Empire). At the same time (partly as a result of the Education Act of 1870) there was a huge market in 'manly' historical yarns for boys, often with a strong imperialist tendency. The most famous exponent of this kind of fiction was G. A. *Henty.

Although he had high hopes for the historical fiction over which he laboured (such as *Sir Nigel*, 1906), Arthur Conan *Doyle discovered to his chagrin that readers preferred Sherlock Holmes. More successful historical novelists of the first decades of the 20th century included Jeffrey Farnol (1878–1952), author of *The Broad Highway* (1910) and *The Amateur Gentleman* (1913), Rafael Sabatini (1875–1950), creator of Scaramouche and Captain Blood, and Baroness *Orczy, whose 1905 novel *The Scarlet Pimpernel* introduced Sir Percy Blakeney, the apparently effete Englishman who was, in reality, the daring saviour of French aristocrats from the revolutionary guillotine.

Historical fiction retained its popularity throughout the 20th century. Georgette *Heyer began publishing her 'Regency romances' in the 1920s and many are still in print more than thirty years after her death. Drawing on the nautical-historical novel pioneered by Captain Frederick *Marryat a century earlier, C. S. *Forester launched his Hornblower sequence (set in the Napoleonic Wars) in 1937. Other writers, such as Douglas Reeman (1924–), also writing under the name of Alexander Kent, and, most notably, Patrick O'Brian (1914–2000), with his series of novels featuring the early 19th-century naval captain Jack Aubrey and his friend the physician Stephen Maturin, have followed in his wake. Mary *Renault's novels of ancient Greece, including *The King Must Die* (1958), *The Mask of Apollo* (1966), and *Fire from Heaven* (1969), provided vivid portraits of figures both from legend, like *Theseus, and from history, like *Alexander the Great. Eleanor Hibbert (1906–93) employed a series of pseudonyms that included 'Jean Plaidy', 'Victoria Holt', and 'Philippa Carr' to publish well over a hundred romantic novels set in a variety of historical eras.

The 1960s and 1970s saw writers of all kinds continuing to visit the past for their subject matter. New directions in historical fiction were indicated by John *Fowles's Victorian romance crossed with French *nouveau roman*, *The French Lieutenant's Woman* (1969). J. G. *Farrell published a number of serio-comic novels about British colonial rule, including *Troubles* (1970) and the *Booker Prize-winning *The Siege of Krishnapur* (1973). George Macdonald *Fraser's Flashman series, the first of which appeared in 1969, took the schoolboy villain of **Tom Brown's Schooldays* (1857), invented a scandalous post-Rugby career for him, and provided a sequence of episodes from his supposed memoirs.

Writers or readers have not lost their taste for historical fiction in recent decades. Bernard Cornwell (1944–) is best known for the Sharpe books, set in the Napoleonic Wars, but has also written novels set during the Dark Ages, the Hundred Years War, and the American Civil War; Philippa Gregory (1954–) has published a series focusing on the Boleyn family in Tudor England; Robert *Harris has set thrillers in ancient Rome; and Ken Follett (1949–) had a major best-seller with *The Pillars of the Earth* (1989), the story of the building of a fictional medieval cathedral.

Over the last twenty years, the Booker Prize has several times been won by historical novels, including A. S. *Byatt's *Possession* (1990), Barry *Unsworth's *Sacred Hunger* (1992), and Pat *Barker's *The Ghost Road* (1995), the last volume of a trilogy of books set during the First World War, and many of the most imaginative and ambitious of contemporary novelists have chosen to work, either regularly or occasionally, with historical subjects. Peter *Ackroyd has resurrected the London of the past in novels such as *Hawksmoor* (1985) and *The House of Doctor Dee* (1993); Rose *Tremain's *Restoration* (1989) and *Music & Silence* (1999) are both set in the 17th century; Lawrence Norfolk's (1963–) *Lemprière's Dictionary* (1991) and *The Pope's Rhinoceros* (1996) mingle esoteric historical erudition with complicated and picaresque narratives; Beryl *Bainbridge has written novels about Scott's Antarctic voyages (*Birthday Boys*, 1991), the Crimean War (*Master Georgie*, 1998), and Samuel *Johnson (*According to Queeney*, 2001); and Sarah *Waters (1966–) has built a reputation on novels set in the Victorian era, including *Tipping the Velvet* (1998) and *Fingersmith* (2002). Nearly two centuries after Scott initiated the historical novel as a genre the form is still full of vigour.

History of Henry Esmond, Esquire, The A historical novel by W. M. *Thackeray, set during the reign of Queen Anne, published 1852. Esmond, who tells his own story, mainly in the third person, is the (supposedly illegitimate) son of the third Viscount Castlewood, who dies at the battle of the Boyne. A serious, lonely boy, he lives at Castlewood House under the protection of the fourth viscount, his father's cousin, and his young wife Rachel. Rachel and her husband have two children, Frank, the heir, and Beatrix, a beautiful but wilful girl. The Castlewoods become estranged after Rachel catches smallpox, inadvertently brought to the household by Henry, and loses much of her beauty. The wicked Lord Mohun attempts to seduce Rachel, and Castlewood is killed in the resulting duel. On his deathbed he reveals to Henry that he is in fact the legitimate heir, but Henry keeps silent for the sake of Rachel and her son. He is imprisoned for a year for his involvement in the duel, for which Rachel bitterly reproaches him, and on his release fights in the war of the Spanish Succession. On a visit to England, he is reconciled to Rachel, who secretly loves him. But Henry is captivated by Beatrix, who is too ambitious to consider a man with no fortune or position in society. Beatrix becomes engaged to the duke of Hamilton, who fights a duel with Mohun, in which both are killed. Beatrix and her brother Frank, now the fifth viscount, are ardent Jacobites, and Esmond plots with them to restore James Edward Stuart, the Old Pretender, to the throne. At the moment when he should be in London the Pretender is at Castlewood, 'dangling after Trix', and the plot fails. Esmond, disillusioned with Beatrix and the Jacobite cause, marries Rachel and they emigrate to Virginia. The later history of the family in America and England is told in *The *Virginians*.

History of the Rebellion and Civil Wars *See* CLARENDON, EDWARD HYDE.

Histriomastix *See* PRYNNE, WILLIAM.

HITCHCOCK, Sir Alfred Joseph (1899–1980) Film director, born in Leytonstone in east London and educated by Jesuits; he began working in *cinema as a designer in 1920, and directing in 1925. *The Lodger* (1927) established a reputation for creating high tension in everyday surroundings and drawing spectators into intense identification with ambiguous characters. Always technically ambitious, he converted an originally silent *Blackmail* (1929) into the British industry's first 'talkie', and was considered Britain's leading director before moving to Hollywood to make Daphne *du Maurier's *Rebecca* (1940) and remaining based there for the rest of his career. Exacting in his demands on collaborators, his more than 40 elaborate psychological thrillers defined an atmosphere still widely known as 'Hitchcockian', and several, including *Vertigo* (1958), are considered among the greatest of all films. Hitchcock was knighted shortly before his death in 1980. Among numerous biographies and career studies, the book-length interview by the film-maker François Truffaut (1932–84), *Hitchcock/Truffaut* (1967), holds a special place for its wit and insight.

HOADLY, Benjamin (1676–1761) Born at Westerham, Kent, bishop successively of Bangor, Hereford, Salisbury, and Winchester, a Low Church divine much in favour with the Whigs and Queen Caroline. His famous sermon 'The Nature of the Kingdom or Church of Christ' (1717), arguing that the church is to be identified with the kingdom of heaven and that all forms of church government are without biblical authority, initiated the Bangorian controversy. His critics, who saw him as undermining the authority of the church, included William *Law. Hoadly wrote a life of his friend the theologian Samuel *Clarke.

HOBAN, Russell (1925–) American *fantasy and *science fiction writer, born in Lansdale, Pennsylvania; resident in London. In 1959 he wrote the first of over 50 children's books, the best known being *The Mouse and his Child* (1967). Hoban's fables for adults suggest the strategies of *magic realism in their bizarre but internally consistent worlds. *The Lion of Boaz-Jachin and Jachin-Boaz* (1973) draws on Sumerian mythology. *Turtle Diary* (1975) was filmed (1985) with a screenplay by Harold *Pinter. The myths, rituals, and language of the post-nuclear holocaust society in *Riddley Walker* (1980) are debased versions of our own. *Pilgermann* (1983) is a complex allegory set during the First Crusade of 1098. *Mr Rinyo-Clacton's Offer* (1998), a tale of damnation with echoes of the *Faust legend, is set in a strangely transformed London. *Linger Awhile* (2006), a *Pygmalion-like fable about the resurrection of a 1950s actress, is also set in London. Hoban wrote the libretto for Harrison *Birtwistle's opera *The Second Mrs Kong* (1994).

HOBB, Robin (1952–) Pen-name of American *fantasy and *science fiction author Margaret Astrid Lindholm Ogden, born in California. As Megan Lindholm she wrote fantasy novels such as *The Wizard of the Pigeons* (1986). *Assassin's Apprentice* (1995), as Hobb, began a series of more epic works marked by a strong sense of political conflict.

HOBBES, Thomas (1588–1679) Philosopher, born at Malmesbury and educated at Magdalen Hall, Oxford. For a great part of his life he was in the service of the Cavendish (*see* NEWCASTLE) family, and in 1647 was appointed mathematical tutor to the prince of Wales (later Charles II). In the 1620s he translated some of Francis *Bacon's essays into Latin, and took down his thoughts from his dictation. On three occasions he travelled on the Continent with pupils, met *Galileo, Pierre Gassendi (1592–1655), *Descartes, and the French mathematician Marin Mersenne (1588–1648), and became, with the exception of Bacon, the first English intellectual to gain a European presence and reputation. On his return to England he submitted to the Council of State in 1652, and was pensioned after the Restoration. He was intimate with William *Harvey, Ben *Jonson, Abraham *Cowley, John *Aubrey, Edmund *Waller, and Sidney *Godolphin.

As a philosopher Hobbes resembles Bacon in the utilitarian importance that he attaches to knowledge. Nature and man are the objects of his enquiry. But unlike Bacon he regards science as essentially deductive, and takes geometry as the model of scientific method. He attached great importance to the definition of words and used rigorous definition to show that many popular ideas are nonsense (the idea of a 'free subject', for example). He was a materialist, regarding sensation as the basis of all knowledge and the motion of material particles as the cause of all sensation. Our appetites are our reactions to external motions, and are directed by self-preservation. Man is essentially selfish. What seem unselfish actions are motivated by the selfish wish to alleviate the pain of compassion. Being selfish, man, left to himself, would engage in perpetual conflict, and life would be 'solitary, poor, nasty, brutish and short'. To prevent this, Hobbes's political philosophy, expounded in *De Corpore Politico* (1650, originally *Elements of Law*), *De Cive* (Latin 1642, English 1651), and **Leviathan* (English 1651, definitive Latin text 1668), is in effect a defence of totalitarianism, asserting that the state must have absolute power, taking precedence over conscience and matters of faith and doctrine. This brought him into general disfavour on both political and religious grounds. Hobbes's philosophical works include *Human Nature* (1650), *De Corpore* (Latin 1655, English 1656), and *De Homine* (1658). He published the first English translation of *Thucydides in 1629, a translation of *Homer in quatrains (1674–5), and a sketch of the Civil Wars, *Behemoth, or The Long Parliament* (1680), which was suppressed. His reply to Sir William *D'Avenant's dedication of **Gondibert*, published in 1650, expresses his literary theory. He believes poetry 'should avert men from vice and incline them to virtuous and honourable actions', holds that imagination is decayed memory, and ridicules the notion of inspiration and the poetic invocation of the Muse. His prose, seemingly plain and direct, exhibits a masterly understanding of rhetoric, a weighted use of metaphor, and sustained irony, as in *Leviathan*, chapter 47, which comes close to equating religion with a belief in fairies. On this and other grounds he was often branded an atheist. His complete works were edited by Sir William Molesworth (1839–45), and his *Correspondence* by Noel Malcolm (1994). See J. W. N. Watkins, *Hobbes's System of Ideas* (1965); M. M. Goldsmith, *Hobbes's Science of Politics* (1966); S. Shapin and S. Shaffer, *Leviathan and the Air Pump* (1995); Q. Skinner, *Reason and Rhetoric in the Philosophy of Hobbes* (1996); N. Malcolm, *Aspects of Hobbes* (2002).

Hobbit, The, *or There and Back Again* (1937) The first published excursion by *Tolkien into 'Middle Earth', an intricately realized other world. Hobbits are the bucolic residents of 'the Shire', based on the pastoral Midlands. The reluctant hero, Bilbo Baggins, is drawn into a quest for dragon's gold in wild lands by the magician Gandalf, in the course of which he acquires a magic ring which is central to Tolkien's epic, *The *Lord of the Rings*. The book was a forerunner of the late 20th-century vogue for fantasy, and achieved worldwide popularity in the 1960s.

HOBHOUSE, John Cam (1786–1869) A politician, and close friend of Lord *Byron, one of whose executors he became. His *Imitations and Translations from the Ancient and Modern Classics* (1809) contains nine poems by Byron, with whom he travelled in Europe; his *Journey through Albania* (1813) describes the same journey that appears in Byron's **Childe Harold*. In 1818 he produced the 'Historical Illustrations' to Canto IV of that poem, and the canto is dedicated to him. He was an adviser to John *Murray, who published most of Byron's work, and he ensured that Byron's *Memoirs* were burnt immediately after the poet's death. His *Recollections of a Long Life* (1865) contains much material relating to Byron.

HOBSBAUM, Philip (1932–2005) Poet and critic, born in London but brought up in the north of England, and educated at Downing College, Cambridge, prominently by F. R. *Leavis. He was the founder of the *Group, first in London and later in Belfast, whose members at different times included Peter *Redgrove, Michael *Longley, and Seamus *Heaney. His books include *The Place's Fault* (1964) and *Women and Animals* (1972). See Heather Clark, *The Ulster Renaissance: Poetry in Belfast 1962–1972* (2006).

HOBSON, Thomas (1545–1631) A Cambridge carrier, who 'sickened in the time of his vacancy, being forbidden to go to London by reason of the plague'. John *Milton wrote two epitaphs on him, and his name survives in the phrase 'Hobson's choice', which refers to his custom of letting out his horses in rotation, and not allowing his customers to choose among them. See the **Spectator*, 509.

HOBY, Sir Thomas (1530–66) Translator, educated at St John's College, Cambridge; from 1547 to 1555 he made frequent visits to the Continent and his notebook covering the years 1551–64, with interesting accounts of Italy, was published by the *Camden Society (1902). In 1552–3, while staying in Paris, he translated *Castiglione's *Il cortegiano*, as *The Courtier*, though it was not published until 1561. It became immediately popular, even being translated into Latin in 1577, and was an important influence on such writers as Edmund *Spenser, Ben *Jonson, and *Shakespeare. It was edited by Walter Raleigh (1900) and V. Cox (1994).

HOCCLEVE (Occleve), **Thomas** (*c.*1367–1426) Apart from John *Lydgate the most significant named English poet of the 15th century. He was a clerk in the office of the privy seal and some of his poetry claims to describe (not without literary artifice) the events of his own life, as in 'La Male Regle de Thomas Hoccleve' (1405–6), the prologue to *The Regiment of Princes* (1411–12), and in two poems from the late sequence known as the *Series* (1420s): 'The Complaint' and 'The Dialogue with a Friend'. Hoccleve's poetry also includes translations from *Christine de Pisan and other French sources. Long regarded as a poor imitator of Geoffrey *Chaucer, whom he mentions with admiration, Hoccleve has recently enjoyed a critical renaissance: additional influences from **Piers Plowman* and John *Gower have been recognized in his work and he is now seen as a significant contributor to the complex literary culture of his time. Ed. in two EETS volumes (ES 61 and 73, by F. J. *Furnivall and Sir Israel Gollancz, rev. A. I. Doyle and J. Mitchell, 1970, and ES 72, 'The Regiment of Princes', etc. by F. J. Furnivall, 1897); *Thomas Hoccleve's Complaint and Dialogue*, ed. J. A. Burrow, EETS OS 313 (1999).

HOCKING, Silas K. (Kitto) (1850–1935) Novelist and *Methodist minister, born in Cornwall and educated in local grammar schools, who wrote fifty books, including *For Light and Liberty* (1890), *A Son of Reuben* (1894), *For Such is Life* (1896), and *Who Shall Judge* (1910). Hocking's didactic but compassionate novels made him one of the most popular authors of his generation. His most enduringly celebrated book is **Her*

Benny (1879), a story of street children set in Liverpool, which sold more than a million copies in his lifetime. He published an autobiography, *My Book of Memory*, in 1923.

HODGSON, Ralph (1871–1962) Poet, born in County Durham, the son of a coal merchant, and brought up in the south, where his lifelong love and observation of the natural world took root. His first volume, *The Last Blackbird*, appeared in 1907, but his reputation was not established until 1917, when he published *Poems*, a volume which contains one of his most ambitious, visionary works, 'A Song of Honour'. Hodgson was much encouraged by friends such as Walter *de la Mare, Siegfried *Sassoon, and T. S. *Eliot, as well as by Edward *Marsh who published some of his work in **Georgian Poetry*. *Collected Poems* was published in 1961.

HODGSON, William Hope (1877–1918) Born in Essex; writer of supernatural and *horror fiction whose first novel, *The Boats of the Glen Carrig* (1907), was coloured by his days as a seaman. His visionary *Gothic novel *The House on the Borderland* (1908) explores physical and spiritual cosmologies. In the epic *The Night Land* (1912) the far future of a doomed humanity is depicted in language reminiscent of medieval romances. *Carnacki the Ghost-Finder* (1913) collects stories involving a 'psychic detective'.

HOFFMAN, Eva (1945–) Born in Poland to Jewish parents who survived the Holocaust in hiding in the Ukraine. She emigrated to Canada in 1958. Her works, including *Lost in Translation* (1989), *Exit into History* (1993), *Shtetl* (1997), and *After Such Knowledge* (2004), explore identity, memory, and dislocation.

HOFFMANN, Ernst Theodor Amadeus (1776–1822) German Romantic, music critic, minor composer, and writer. Born in Königsberg, where he studied law, he began as a writer of fiction only in his thirties. During the last fourteen years of his life he produced two full-length novels, *Die Elixiere des Teufels* (1815–16: *The Devil's Elixir*) and the unfinished *Lebensansichten des Kater Murr* (1819–21: *The Life and Opinions of Murr the Cat*), in addition to some fifty stories and novellas. His shorter works, collected mainly in the *Fantasiestücke* (1814–15), *Nachtstücke* (1816–17), and *Die Serapionsbrüder* (1818–21), include *Der goldne Topf* (*The Golden Pot*) and *Der Sandmann* (*The Sandman*), on which Delibes's comic ballet *Coppélia* is loosely based. Hoffmann's fiction is marked by extravagant and frequently macabre fantasy of great psychological fascination and depth. *Freud's celebrated essay *Das Unheimliche* (1919: *The Uncanny*) was among the first of many interpretations of *The Sandman*. His life provided the inspiration for Offenbach's *Tales of Hoffmann* while the story *Nußknacker und Mäusekönig* was the basis of *Tchaikovsky's ballet *The Nutcracker*.

HOFMANN, Michael (1957–) Poet and translator, son of German novelist Gert Hofmann (1931–93), born in Freiburg and educated in the United States and England. He came to England in 1961, studied English at Oxford and Cambridge, and later settled in London. He is bilingual, and his extensive translations include work by Franz *Kafka, Rainer Maria *Rilke, Bertolt *Brecht, Joseph *Roth, and the contemporary German poet Durs Grunbein (b. 1962). His own volumes of poetry are *Nights in the Iron Hotel* (1983), *Acrimony* (1986), Part II of which, 'My Father's House', is a powerful and moving sequence to his father, that 'indulgent patriarch', *Corona, Corona* (1993), and *Approximately Nowhere* (1999), which returns to the subject of his father. His poems, both European and American in manner and content, dwell on themes of travel and displacement, often invoking contemporary landscapes of casual urban disorder and disconnection. A collection of his criticism, *Behind the Lines*, appeared in 2001.

HOFMANNSTHAL, Hugo von (1874–1929) Austrian poet, dramatist, and essayist, born in Vienna where he studied law and Romance literature. His celebrated *Brief des Lord Chandos* (1902: *The Chandos Letter*), fictionally addressed to Francis *Bacon, expresses his sense of a crisis in language as inadequate to meaning or thought and marks a turning away from the linguistic opulence of his *fin-de-siècle* works. The new direction in his writing is evident in *Das gerette Venedig* (1905), a version of Thomas *Otway's **Venice Preserved*, and *König Ödipus* (1907). *Jedermann* (1911: *Everyman*), a modernization of the old morality play, was written for the Salzburg Festival and prefigures *Das Salzburger grosse Welttheater* (1922: *The Great Salzburg World Theatre*). The First World War destroyed the social world of the Austro-Hungarian monarchy, and his later plays include the wittily nostalgic comedy *Der Schwierige* (1921: *A Difficult Man*) and his last play *Der Turm* (1925: *The Tower*), a tragedy, which completed his development towards the idea of literature as carrying a social and religious message. He wrote the libretti for six of Richard *Strauss's operas, including *Der Rosenkavalier* (1911) and *Ariadne auf Naxos* (1912); his correspondence with Strauss (1926) is of both literary and musical interest.

HOGARTH, William (1697–1764) British painter and engraver. Born in London, he was apprenticed to a goldsmith and began engraving *c.*1720. In 1726 he designed twelve large engravings for Samuel Butler's **Hudibras*; his earliest paintings were conversation pieces, and he also painted portraits. In 1732 *The Harlot's Progress* introduced his 'modern moral subjects'; it was followed by *The Rake's Progress* (1733–5) and *Marriage à la Mode* (1743–5). This highly original genre consisted of a series of paintings, popularized through engravings, which tell a story that is topical, erotic, spiced with contemporary portraits, and yet comments with humanity and passion on social and political vices and corruption. Hogarth's later engravings, the *Industry and Idleness* series (1747) and the prints *Beer Street* and *Gin Lane* (1750–51), are coarser, and their harsher morality is aimed at a mass market. Hogarth also published a work on aesthetics, *The Analysis of Beauty* (1753), in which he defined the serpentine 'line of beauty'.

His series of engravings were immensely successful and immediately inspired numerous plays and novels; his success was such that his work was pirated and he was instrumental in obtaining the passage of 'Hogarth's Act' (1735) protecting the copyright of engravers. Henry *Fielding became Hogarth's friend and collaborator in the early 1730s; in his preface to *_Joseph Andrews_ (1742) he describes Hogarth as a 'Comic History-Painter', defending him against critics who attacked his work as mere caricature or burlesque. Fielding, and later Tobias *Smollett, compared characters and scenes in their novels to the prints of Hogarth. Laurence *Sterne was another friend and admirer, and his *_Tristram Shandy_ (1759–67) shows the influence of Hogarth's aesthetics. The artist aroused less interest in the late 18th century but his popularity soared in the early 19th century, with essays by William *Hazlitt and Charles *Lamb that emphasized his literary qualities. Both Charles *Dickens and W. M. *Thackeray admired and were influenced by him; Dickens, in the preface to *_Oliver Twist_, writes that he had never met 'the miserable reality' of low-life London except in Hogarth. No other British painter has had such close connections with literature; Hogarth's _Portrait of the Painter and his Pug_ (1745) shows his aggressive image resting on volumes of William *Shakespeare, John *Milton, and Jonathan *Swift and lays claim to his place within a British artistic tradition. See R. E. Moore, _Hogarth's Literary Relationships_ (1948); Jenny Uglow, _Hogarth_ (1997).

Hogarth Press Founded in 1917 by Leonard *Woolf and Virginia *Woolf at their home, Hogarth House, Richmond, Surrey, mainly as a hobby. Their earliest publications included Katherine *Mansfield's _Prelude_ (1918), Virginia Woolf's _Kew Gardens_ (1919), and T. S. *Eliot's _Poems_ (1919). Their policy was to publish new and experimental work; they also published translations of Maxim *Gorky, Anton *Chekhov, Lev *Tolstoy, Fedor *Dostoevsky, Ivan *Bunin, Rainer Maria *Rilke, and Italo *Svevo. In addition, they were the first to introduce the work of Robinson *Jeffers, J. C. *Ransom, and E. A. *Robinson into England. Until 1923 they operated on a subscription basis. In 1924 they moved to Tavistock Square, where John *Lehmann became assistant (1931–2), and then part-owner (1938–46). Between 1917 and 1946 the Press published 525 titles, including pamphlets on psychoanalysis, politics, aesthetics, economics, and disarmament. In 1947 Lehmann's share in the Press was bought by Chatto and Windus. Since 1987, the Hogarth Press has been an imprint of Random House.

HOGG, James (1770–1835) Scottish poet and novelist, born at Ettrick Hall, a remote farm in the Ettrick Forest, and forced by poverty to become a cowherd at the age of 7. Eventually rising to the position of shepherd (hence the nickname 'the Ettrick Shepherd'), he taught himself to read and write and published a poem in the _Scots Magazine_ in 1794. _Scottish Pastorals_ (1801) made little impact but in 1802 he met Walter *Scott while the latter was touring the Selkirk area collecting songs for *_Minstrelsy of the Scottish Border_. In 1807, with Scott's backing, he published _The Mountain Bard_, a collection of original ballads, along with a treatise on sheep diseases. Both were financially successful. He moved to Edinburgh in 1810, and in 1813 made his name with _The *Queen's Wake_, becoming friends with Lord *Byron, William *Wordsworth, Robert *Southey, John *Murray, and other literary figures. He was on the board of *_Blackwood's Magazine_, to which he frequently contributed, notably to the *'Chaldee MS' and the *_Noctes Ambrosianae_ (where he is depicted as the buffoonish 'Shepherd'). Granted a farm in Yarrow in 1816, he lived there for most of his remaining years. His modern reputation rests mainly on the novels _The Three Perils of Man_ (1822), _The Three Perils of Woman_ (1823), and _The *Private Memoirs and Confessions of a Justified Sinner_ (1824), none of which was highly regarded in his lifetime. Other important works include _The Domestic Manners and Private Life of Sir Walter Scott_ (1834), the three-volume _Tales of the War of Montrose_ (1835), and an edition of Robert *Burns (with William Motherwell, 1834–5). His death elicited one of Wordsworth's last great poems, 'Extempore Effusion'. See Karl Miller, _Electric Shepherd: A Likeness of James Hogg_ (2003).

HOGG, Thomas Jefferson (1792–1862) Educated at Oxford with P. B. *Shelley and sent down with him on the publication of their *'Necessity of Atheism'. He was one of the circle of Shelley, Thomas Love *Peacock, and other friends who about 1820 referred to themselves as 'The Athenians'. In 1832 he contributed reminiscences of Shelley at Oxford to the *_New Monthly Magazine_, and these later formed a part of his _Life of Shelley_ (1858). Peacock, in his _Memorials of Shelley_, felt obliged to question and revise many of Hogg's observations.

HOGGART, Richard (1918–) Scholar and writer, brought up in Leeds and educated at Leeds University. He has held many academic and public appointments, and was Warden of Goldsmiths' College, London, 1976–84. His interest in literature, education, mass media, and working-class culture was expressed in his influential and partly autobiographical work _The Uses of Literacy_ (1957), which became a founding text of cultural studies, a new academic discipline that Hoggart helped to establish by founding the Centre for Contemporary Cultural Studies at the University of Birmingham in 1964. His later works include literary-critical essays, observations on contemporary culture (_The Way we Live Now_, 1995), and three volumes of memoirs, _A Local Habitation_ (1988), _A Sort of Clowning_ (1990), and _An Imagined Life_ (1992).

HOLBACH, Paul-Henri, Baron d' _See_ PHILOSOPHES.

HOLBEIN, Hans, the younger (1497/8–1543) German painter, born in Augsburg; by 1515 he was in Basle, where he designed woodcuts for the publisher Johannes Froben (_c._1460–1527) and met *Erasmus. In 1516 he made a series of marginal drawings in Erasmus' _The Praise of Folly_ and painted Erasmus several times. His religious paintings include the unflinchingly realistic _Dead Christ_ (1521); _c._1525 he designed a series of woodcuts, _The Dance of Death_. Erasmus recommended Holbein to Sir Thomas *More, and he spent the years 1526–8 in England, probably staying at More's house in Chelsea; he painted the friends and patrons of Erasmus and More and his family. Holbein settled in England in 1532, when Thomas *Cromwell seized on his potential as a court painter. His drawings and paintings of the period include many literary figures—Sir Thomas *Wyatt, the earl of *Surrey, Sir Thomas and Lady *Elyot, and Sir Philip Hoby (1505–58), friend of *Titian and *Aretino. Holbein created the massive, overpowering image of *Henry VIII; contemporaries were 'abashed and annihilated' before the mural painting of the king and his parents at Whitehall Palace (1537; destroyed; part of the cartoon is in the National Portrait Gallery). The 19th century was fascinated by his *Dance of Death*: Charles *Dickens bought a set in 1841; and Willa *Cather took from it the title of *Death Comes for the Archbishop*. See Jane Roberts, *Hans Holbein* (2005).

HOLCOT, Robert (*c.*1290–1349) A Dominican, perhaps born in Northamptonshire. He studied and taught at Oxford University from *c.*1326 to 1334 and taught at Cambridge University *c.*1334–6. Theologically, he was a follower of William of *Ockham at least in his insistence on human free will, opposing Thomas *Bradwardine. His prolific output included commentaries on Scripture and the *Moralitates Historiarum*, a series of stories that influenced the **Gesta Romanorum*. Holcot typifies clerical humanism in his enthusiasm for classical as well as theological literature.

HOLCROFT, Thomas (1745–1809) Successively stable-boy, shoemaker, actor, radical activist, and author. He was largely self-educated, a militant atheist, and believed fervently in man's capacity for self-improvement. His varied and energetic life is described in his *Memoirs* (edited and completed by his friend William *Hazlitt), which contain reminiscences of Samuel *Foote and Charles *Macklin, and later accounts of radical associates such as William *Godwin and John Horne *Tooke. He was acquitted in the treason trials of 1794, not least because of Godwin's pamphlet in support of the defendants, 'Cursory Strictures'. He wrote a number of comic and sentimental plays, of which the best known was *The Road to Ruin* (1792); also several novels, including *Anna St Ives* (1792) and *The Adventures of Hugh Trevor* (1794), both of them influenced by Godwin's radical philosophy, but less successful as literature than **Caleb Williams*. After the hostile reception of his play *Knave or Not?* in 1798, Holcroft, plagued by debt, moved to Hamburg, then Paris, returning to England in 1802; he died in London after a long illness, during which he dictated a large part of his *Memoirs*. See *The Novels and Selected Plays of Thomas Holcroft*, ed. W. Verhoeven, 5 vols (2007).

HÖLDERLIN, Friedrich (1770–1843) German poet and friend of *Hegel and *Schelling. He suffered from insanity from 1802. His only novel, *Hyperion* (1797, 1799), is an *epistolary work set in contemporary Greece. He wrote poems on classical subjects, in which he expressed a hopeless, romantic yearning for ancient Greek harmony with nature and beauty in classical verse forms. His works have been finely translated by Michael *Hamburger (1966).

HOLDSTOCK, Robert (1948–) Born in Hythe, Kent; author of *science fiction and, with *Mythago Wood* (1984) and sequels, *fantasy exploring *archetypes of place and character. *Celtika* (2001) began a series linking Merlin with Greek myths.

HOLINSHED, Raphael (*c.*1525–1580?) Historian, from a Cheshire family and said by Anthony *Wood to have been a 'minister of God's word'. He came to London early in the reign of *Elizabeth I, and was employed as a translator by Reyner *Wolfe, the printer and publisher. While working for him he planned the *Chronicles* (1577), which are known by his name, but were written and compiled by several people. They form the first authoritative vernacular and continuous account of the whole of English national history. The *History of England* was written by Holinshed himself. The *Description of England*, a vivid and humorous account of English towns, villages, crops, customs, etc. of the day, was written by William *Harrison. The *History and Description of Scotland* and the *History of Ireland* were translations or adaptations, and the *Description of Ireland* was the work of Richard Stanyhurst (1547–1618) and Edmund *Campion. A few passages in the *History of Ireland* offended the queen and her ministers, and were expunged. The *Chronicle* was reissued, with continuations, edited by John Hooker (alias Vowell; 1527–1601), in 1587, and politically offensive passages removed. This second edition was widely used by William *Shakespeare and by other dramatists.

HOLLAND, Philemon (1552–1637) Master of the free school at Coventry from 1628, celebrated for his translations of *Livy (1600), *Pliny's *Natural History* (1601), *Plutarch's *Moralia* (1603), *Suetonius (1606), the 4th-century Roman historian Ammianus Marcellinus (1609), William *Camden's **Britannia* (1610), and *Xenophon's *Cyropaedia* (1632). His knowledge of Greek and Latin was accurate and profound, and his renderings are made in vivid, familiar, and somewhat ornamented English.

Holland House, Kensington, London Built at the beginning of the 17th century for the administrator Sir Walter Cope (1553?–1614), who called it 'Cope Castle', it passed into the possession of the courtier Henry Rich (bap. 1590; son of Penelope *Rich), first earl of Holland, who was executed in 1649. In 1767 it was acquired by Henry Fox, first Baron Holland (1705–74), who entertained Horace *Walpole and the wit and politician George Selwyn (1719–91) there. In the time of his grandson, the third baron (1773–1840), Holland House became a great political, artistic, and literary centre. Many celebrated writers, including R. B. *Sheridan, Thomas *Moore, Thomas *Campbell, Samuel *Rogers, T. B. *Macaulay, George *Grote, Charles *Dickens, and W. M. *Thackeray, were received there. Joseph *Addison, who had married the widow of one of the earls of Warwick and Holland, died at Holland House in 1719.

HOLLINGHURST, Alan (1954–) Novelist, born in Gloucestershire, educated at Magdalen College, Oxford, whose sexually explicit yet elegantly conceived and written work has done much to bring gay fiction into the mainstream. His first novel, *The Swimming-Pool Library* (1988), is narrated by a young Oxford graduate, who saves the life of an octogenarian aristocrat and is subsequently asked to write his memoirs. Culturally allusive, the book explores with *Firbankian panache the dangers and pleasures of the homosexual world. The narrator of *The Folding Star* (1994) travels to an unnamed Belgian town (based on Bruges), where he develops a romantic and erotic obsession with one of his private pupils. The novel interweaves the life of an ancient and silent city with his memories of his youth and with the story of a celebrated Belgian symbolist *fin-de-siècle* painter who had himself suffered a sexual obsession. *The Spell* (1998) describes the affairs of four gay men and their friends in London clubs and at drug-fuelled weekends in a beautifully evoked Dorset countryside. Hollinghurst's concern with the aesthetics of style and artifice achieves its fullest expression in *The Line of Beauty* (2004). Set in the Thatcherite 1980s, with Aids beginning to cut a swathe through the gay community, it is *Jamesian in both concept and style and tells the story of a comparative innocent caught up in the corrupting world of a Tory MP, whose family virtually adopts and then rejects him. It won the Man *Booker Prize in 2004.

Hollywood novel A term designating novels set in the American movie capital, which take the film business as their subject. Nathanael *West's *The Day of the Locust* (1939) is the most famous example. See Anthony Slide, *The Hollywood Novel* (1995).

HOLMES, Oliver Wendell (1809–94) American writer, born at Cambridge, Massachusetts, trained in medicine but achieving fame through his literary works. His reflective essays, *Autocrat of the Breakfast-Table*, appeared in 1858, followed by *The Professor at the Breakfast-Table* (1860), *The Poet at the Breakfast-Table* (1872), and *Over the Tea-Cups* (1891). He also wrote novels (*Elsie Venner* (1861) deals with genetic inheritance), poems, and memoirs of Ralph Waldo *Emerson and John Lothrop *Motley. He also wrote much light and occasional verse. See Edwin P. Hoyt, *The Improper Bostonian* (1979).

HOLMES, Richard (1945–) Biographer, born in London and educated at Downside School and Churchill College, Cambridge. In 1974 his first major biography, *Shelley: The Pursuit*, appeared to great acclaim and won a Somerset Maugham Award. This was followed by other works including the semi-autobiographical *Footsteps: Adventures of a Romantic Biographer* (1985), which broke new ground in its account of Holmes's personal experiences and travels in the course of pursuing, sometimes unsuccessfully, subjects who included Gérard de *Nerval and R. L. *Stevenson: this influential work was instrumental in creating a more personal approach to the art of *biography, in which the narrator feels able to intrude his or her own thoughts and feelings. *Dr Johnson and Mr Savage* (1993) was another unorthodox work, exploring the relationship of the two poets, and their early days of poverty together in London, and seeking to reinterpret Samuel *Johnson's attitude to Richard *Savage. His two-volume biography of S. T. *Coleridge, *Early Visions* (1989), which won the Whitbread Book of the Year, and *Darker Reflections* (1998), winner of the Duff Cooper Prize, is a magisterial, and deeply sympathetic account, written with sensitivity, colour, and passion. His *Sidetracks: Explorations of a Romantic Biographer* (2000) continues the personal reflections of *Footsteps*. *The Age of Wonder* (2008) concentrates on the lives of William Herschel (1738–1822) and his sister Caroline, exploring the influence of scientific discovery on the great Romantic writers.

Holmes, Sherlock Famous fictional detective created by Arthur Conan *Doyle.

Holocaust, literature of the The racialized mass murder committed by the Nazis during the Second World War has been the subject of a great variety of written work, ranging from diaries, testimonies, and memoirs, to fiction, poetry, and drama. *Diaries are often seen as most authentically concerned with the events they describe: both personal diaries, and those written in ghettos by self-styled archivists (for instance, Emmanuel Ringelblum's *Notes from the Warsaw Ghetto* (1958) and David Sierakowiak's *Five Notebooks from the Lódz Ghetto* (1996): neither writer survived). Immediately after the war Holocaust writing was not popular; Elie Wiesel was unable to find a publisher for his long, Yiddish account of Auschwitz, *And the World Was Silent*, which was eventually published in French as a slim volume entitled *Night* in 1958. However, Anne *Frank's *Diary of a Young Girl*, published in English in 1952, did much to increase public interest in the Holocaust. The trial of Adolf Eichmann in 1961 also added to general knowledge of the Holocaust (*see* ARENDT, HANNAH). Sylvia *Plath, most notably in poems such as 'Daddy' and 'Lady Lazarus', was one of the first non-survivors to write about the Holocaust, to the chagrin of critics such as George *Steiner who saw these poems as enlisting an unprecedented tragedy to prop up personal angst. Others have seen her work, like that of Geoffrey *Hill and Randall *Jarrell, as the effort of a poet to represent a historicized subjectivity. Among the canonical works written in the first decades after the war Primo *Levi's *If This Is a Man* (1960) is probably the best known, and his essays, particularly *The Drowned and the Saved* (1988), have contributed to his high reputation. Very quickly a tradition among survivor-writers arose for generic and narrative experimentation in order to represent the Holocaust: André Schwarz Bart's novel *The Last of the Just* (1960) draws upon Jewish tradition to represent Auschwitz in magic realist vein; while Piotr Rawicz's nightmarish black comedy *Blood from the Sky* (1964) describes life in hiding in Nazi-occupied Ukraine. Jiri Weil's allegorical novel *Life with a Star* (1989) renders the Nazi occupation of Prague without naming any of the different groups of protagonists; Jakov Lind's 1966 novel *Landscape in Concrete* is a Kafkaesque portrayal of a German soldier who 'only follows orders'; while Aharon Appelfeld's novels (*Badenheim 1939*, 1990; *To the Land of the Reeds*, 1994) are stylized accounts of the Holocaust years which imply but do not describe the facts of mass murder. Both Ida Fink (*A Scrap of Time*, 1989) and Louise Begley (*Wartime Lies*, 1991) have published fictionalized autobiographies of their experiences in hiding during the war: written by survivors, these works gain from the leeway of novelization. The work of non-Jewish survivors has also been characterized by formal and generic experimentation; such writers include Charlotte Delbo, a French political prisoner whose memoir *Auschwitz and After* (1995) considers the problem of memory and subjectivity, and Tadeusz Borowski, a Polish political prisoner whose blackly comic fictionalized vignettes in *This Way for the Gas, Ladies and Gentlemen* (1976) disconcertingly describe the life of a guard in Auschwitz. Such experimentation exists alongside a tradition of 'documentary fiction', in which the techniques of the novel are combined with eyewitness accounts or other historical material. Such works include Jean-François Steiner's *Treblinka* (1967) and Anatolii Kuznetsov's *Babi Yar: A Document in the Form of a Novel* (1970). This tendency not to trust outright invention continues even in works written more than 50 years after the Holocaust: Thomas *Keneally's *Schindler's Ark* (1982) is described as *'faction', while even novels which take the Holocaust simply as the trigger for fiction, such as William *Styron's *Sophie's Choice* (1979), Martin *Amis's *Time's Arrow* (1991), and D. M. *Thomas's *The White Hotel* (1981), all draw upon historical sources. Critical reactions to anything but the most scrupulously factual and respectful novels by non-survivors about the Holocaust have tended to be explosive—see for instance the response to Rolf Hochhuth's 1964 play *The Deputy*, about the role of Pope Pius XII in the Holocaust; by contrast, the poetic approach of Anne Michaels's prize-winning novel *Fugitive Pieces* (1996) was seen by many to be appropriate to its subject, although others judged it to be over-aestheticized. Poetry has not been as popular a medium for representing the Holocaust, although the poetry of the survivor Paul *Celan is a striking exception. *The Poems of Paul Celan*, trans. Michael *Hamburger (1988, 1994), is a collection of elliptical, powerful lyrics, and his 'Death Fugue' is, alongside Nelly Sachs's 'O the chimneys' (*Selected Poems*, 1968), and Itzhak Katznelson's long poem *Song of the Murdered Jewish People* (1980), the best-known poetic treatment of the subject. As the Holocaust recedes further in time, the work of the generations after is growing in importance. The '1.5 generation', the child survivors, are represented by Georges *Perec and Raymond *Federman, both highly experimental writers. Art Spiegelman's *Maus* (1986, 1991) is the most celebrated work of the second generation; others include a range of memoirs (Anne Karpf, *The War After*, 1996; Helen Epstein, *Where She Came From*, 1997; Eva *Hoffman, *After Such Knowledge*, 2004) and novels by Thane Rosenbaum and Melvin J. Bukiet. The best-known third-generation Holocaust novels are Joseph Skibell's *Blessing on the Moon* (1997) and Jonathan Safran Foer's *Everything Is Illuminated* (2002). The 'generation after' in Germany is also concerned to address issues of memory arising out of the Holocaust; particularly notable here are the novels of W. G. *Sebald (*The Emigrants*, 1996; *Austerlitz*, 2001). Writing by and about other groups of victims has been far less extensive. In the case of the Gypsies, written records formed little part of their tradition (though see Alexander Ramati's documentary novel *And the Violins Stopped Playing*, 1989); and in the case of gay men, homosexuality remained illegal until the 1970s in Germany and Austria (see Heinz Heger's *The Men with the Pink Triangle*, 1980, and Martin Sherman's fictional 1979 play *Bent*, which takes the events of the Nazi persecution as an allegory for identity politics).

HOLROYD, Michael de Courcy Fraser (1935–) Author and biographer, born in London and educated at Eton College. His first book was a critical biography of Hugh *Kingsmill, which was followed by a two-volume life of Lytton *Strachey (*The Unknown Years*, 1967; *The Years of Achievement*, 1968), a work which greatly contributed to a revival of interest in the *Bloomsbury Group and to a new interest in the art of *biography, and which incidentally achieved a remarkable recovery of the personality of Strachey's friend and companion the painter Dora *Carrington. Other works followed, including a major two-volume biography of Augustus *John (1974, 1975). His biography of George Bernard *Shaw was published in four separate volumes: *The Search for Love* (1988), *The Pursuit of Power* (1989), *The Lure of Fantasy* (1991), and *The Last Laugh* (1992). In *Basil Street Blues* (1999), a memoir, he turns his biographer's gaze on his own family and his younger self, which he followed up with *Mosaic* (2004) which further explores family secrets and takes the form of a detective story. He has also published a collection of essays about biography and autobiography, *Works on Paper: The Craft of Biography and Autobiography* (2002). *A Strange Eventful History: The Dramatic Lives of Ellen Terry, Henry Irving and their Remarkable Families* (2008) is a collective biography, which tells the story of a complex theatrical dynasty with skill and verve.

HOLST, Gustav (1874–1934) English composer, taught by Sir Hubert *Parry and Sir Charles Villiers *Stanford at the Royal College of Music, where he met Ralph *Vaughan Williams, his closest musical friend. Holst's early works, including a Walt *Whitman setting, *The Mystic Trumpeter* (1904), show traces of Richard *Wagner, but he became involved in the *folk-song movement and was attracted to the Elizabethan composers and Henry *Purcell, influences audible in *The Hymn of Jesus* (1917), a setting from the apocryphal Acts of St John, and *Four Songs for Voice and Violin* (1916–17), on medieval texts. Later choral settings include a setting of Whitman's *Ode to Death* (1919) and the *First Choral Symphony* (1924), to poems of John *Keats. His friend Robert *Bridges supplied the text for *Seven Partsongs* (1926) and the *Choral Fantasia* (1930). Holst also set poems by *Tennyson, Thomas Lovell *Beddoes, and Thomas *Hardy. Holst had written the *Saint Paul's Suite* (1913) for the school where he taught (the *Brook Green Suite*, 1933, was for the same institution), but came to prominence as an orchestral composer with his persistently popular *The Planets* (1918). His orchestral rhapsody *Egdon Heath* (1927) is headed with a quotation from Hardy's **Return of the Native*. Holst wrote libretti for three of his operas: *Savitri* (1909), an unusual one-act chamber opera reflecting his interest in Hindu philosophy; *The Perfect Fool* (1923); and *At the Boar's Head* (1925), in which the tavern scenes from both parts of **Henry IV* were set to traditional folk songs and country dances. *The Wandering*

Scholar (1930) has a libretto by Clifford Bax (1886–1962) after Helen *Waddell.

HOLT, Tom (1961–) Born in London; best known for his humorous *fantasy fiction, although he has also written historical novels. *Expecting Someone Taller* (1987) teams an incompetent young man with gods trying to make sense of the modern world: a mould successfully exploited in over twenty succeeding novels.

HOLTBY, Winifred (1898–1935) Novelist, born at Rudston, Yorkshire, and educated at Queen Margaret's School, Scarborough, and Somerville College, Oxford. She broke off her studies to serve with the Women's Army Auxiliary Corps, an experience which led her to devote much time to lecturing on international questions, before returning to Somerville in 1919. She was an ardent feminist and a prolific journalist, and published several novels, the best known of which is her last, *South Riding*, published posthumously in 1936. Set in Yorkshire, it is at once the story of enterprising headmistress Sarah Burton and a portrait of a whole community. Her other novels include *Anderby Wold* (1923), *The Crowded Street* (1924), *The Land of Green Ginger* (1927), and *Mandoa, Mandoa!* (1933). She also published several works of non-fiction, including the first book-length evaluation of Virginia *Woolf (1932). See Vera *Brittain, *Testament of Friendship* (1940); Marion Shaw, *The Clear Stream* (1999).

HOLUB, Miroslav (1923–98) Poet and scientist, born in Pilsen, Czechoslovakia, equally famed internationally for his poetry and work in the field of immunology. Holub began publishing poetry in 1958 and was first introduced to English readers when *Selected Poems* (1967) was published in the Penguin Modern European Poets series. *Although* (1971) and *Notes of a Clay Pigeon* (1977) followed in Britain, with two selections, *The Fly* (1987) and *On the Contrary* (1984), appearing in the 1980s. Collected English translations were finally published in *Poems Before & After* (1990), after a delay arising from opposition from the Czech authorities. *Before* refers to the stifling pre-1968 climate, and the poems from this period are often expressed allegorically in lean, free forms suffused with Holub's mordant wit. The poems of *After* show a movement to more expansive and dramatic structures, including the puppet poems of *Interferon, or On Theatre* (1986) which provide an absurdist vehicle for Holub's political satire. His subsequent collections are *Vanishing Lung Syndrome* (1990), *Supposed to Fly* (1996), and *The Rampage* (1997). Prose works include *The Dimension of the Present Moment* (1990) and *The Jingle Bell Principle* (1990).

'Holy Fair, The' A poem by Robert *Burns, published 1786, in which the poet humorously contrasts the conviviality of the folk assembled for a Mauchline prayer meeting with the puritanical exhortations of their spiritual leaders. The poem is the central text in a tradition of sardonic Scots celebrations of public festivity that stretches from *'Christis Kirk on the Green' and 'Peblis to the Play' through Robert *Fergusson's 'Leith Races' to 'Donegore Hill' by James Orr (1770–1816; *see* RHYMING WEAVERS) and Robert *Garioch's satire on the Edinburgh Festival, 'Embro to the Ploy'.

'Holy Grail, The' One of Alfred Tennyson's **Idylls of the King*, published 1869, in which Sir Percivale, now a monk, describes the quest of the Holy *Grail, and the differing degrees of failure of himself, Bors, Gawain, and Launcelot.

Holy Living *See* TAYLOR, JEREMY.

Holy State and the Profane State, The By Thomas *Fuller, published 1642, the most popular of his works during his life, a mixture of *character-writing, essays, and 30 short biographies; the characters include, for example, 'The Good Widow', 'The Good Merchant', and 'The True Gentleman'.

Holy War, The A Puritan prose allegory by John *Bunyan, published 1682, which narrates how Diabolus gets possession of the city Mansoul, and how King Shaddai sends his own son Emmanuel to free it.

'Holy Willie's Prayer' A *dramatic monologue by Robert *Burns, written in 1785 and circulated privately in the poet's lifetime, in which the Mauchline Kirk elder Willie Fisher (1737–1809) is overheard at his prayers, unwittingly revealing himself as a drunken and adulterous hypocrite. The poem is often interpreted as an assault on the doctrine of predestination.

HOME, Daniel Dunglas (1833–86) A spiritualistic medium, whose séances in England in 1855 and subsequent years were attended by well-known people including Robert *Browning, who, unlike his wife, remained sceptical (see his 'Mr Sludge, "The Medium"'). He published *Incidents of my Life* (1863, 1872).

HOME, John (1722–1808) Scottish playwright and clergyman, born in Leith and educated at Edinburgh University, who succeeded Robert *Blair as minister of Athelstaneford, and later became secretary to Lord Bute and tutor to the prince of Wales. His friends included Adam *Smith, William *Collins, and David *Hume (his cousin). His first tragedy, *Agis*, was initially rejected by David *Garrick, but **Douglas* was performed to much acclaim at Edinburgh in 1756, and at Covent Garden in 1757. His later tragedies were less successful. James *Macpherson produced his first 'translation' at his instigation in 1759 and Home remained a firm believer in the authenticity of 'Ossian'.

Homecoming, The A play by Harold *Pinter, performed and published 1965. A dark Freudian family drama, the play presents the return to his north London home and ostentatiously womanless family of Teddy, an academic, and his wife of six years, Ruth, once a photographic model. The patriarch, Mac, a butcher, is alternately violent and cringing in manner, and the other two sons, Lenny and Joey, in a very short time make sexual overtures to Ruth, who calmly accepts them; by the end of the play Teddy has decided to leave her with the family, who intend to establish her as a professional prostitute. The tone is dark, erotic, and threatening; the shocking and the banal are sharply juxtaposed throughout. Ruth's acceptance of her role as mother, mistress, and possibly breadwinner for her new family, and her rejection of her husband, are intricately connected with the enigmatic figure of the long-dead mother, Jessie, who is both reviled and idolized by her survivors.

HOMER (supposedly 8th century BC) A biography was invented for 'Homer' in later antiquity, but in reality the name stands simply for the two great epic poems, the **Iliad* and the **Odyssey*. Nothing is known of the original singer/poet or poets, although it is assumed that some unknown individual must have given each poem a coherent shape and unity, from a mass of pre-literate heroic song. We do not know when or where the epics were first committed to writing. They are in an artificial dialect, containing elements from different periods and different dialects of Greek. These two epics were always regarded as the supreme creations of Greek literature, and their critical pre-eminence was confirmed in *Aristotle's *Poetics*. Other early epics were sometimes ascribed to Homer, but none enjoyed comparable prestige, and none survives. Traditionally Homer was blind, like the singer Demodocus in the *Odyssey*. Many cities claimed to be the birthplace of the blind bard; Chios was the strongest claimant, on the strength of the **Homeric Hymn to Apollo*. They are set in the distant past, in the age of heroes, and specifically concern the legendary Trojan War, associated with the end of the Mycenean age (13th century BC). Ptolemy II of Egypt (308–246 BC) collected manuscripts of the poems and assembled scholars in the Library of Alexandria, who set to work to produce an agreed and satisfactory text of Homer. The work done under him and his successors by scholars such as Aristarchus is the basis of our modern texts. Homer's reputation survived in the Middle Ages even in the Latin West where his works were unknown. Serious British interest in the poems began in the 17th century with George *Chapman's translation, the 'Chapman's Homer' of Keats's famous sonnet, and Thomas *Hobbes's version. The blind *Milton associated himself with Homer; Alexander *Pope in the preface to his translation of the *Iliad* extolled his poetic fire; James *Macpherson's 'Ossian' prepared the ground for F. A. Wolf's theory that the *Iliad* consisted of bardic lays woven together. Matthew *Arnold's *On Translating Homer* indicates the worship the poet still inspired in cultivated Victorians. See Jasper Griffin, *Homer* (1980); Robert Fowler (ed.), *The Cambridge Companion to Homer* (2004).

Homeric Hymns, The A collection of 33 ancient Greek hymns of unknown authorship, addressed to gods such as Demeter, *Apollo, Hermes, Aphrodite, and *Zeus, and a major source of myths relating to them. They were composed by various poets (not including *Homer) from the 8th to the 6th centuries BC. George *Chapman included his translation in *The Crown of All Homer's Works* (1624?). P. B. *Shelley translated seven of them and drew on the form for his 'Hymn to Intellectual Beauty'. Thomas Love *Peacock, Alfred *Tennyson, and A. C. *Swinburne are all indebted to them in particular poems. See *The Homeric Hymns*, trans. Michael Crudden (2002).

Homilies, Books of A title applied in the Church of England to two books of homilies (i.e. sermons), published 1547 and 1563, appointed to be read in the churches. The contents of the second Book of Homilies are listed in Article 35 of the Thirty-Nine Articles in the Book of *Common Prayer.

HONE, Joseph Maunsell (1882–1959) Literary scholar and biographer, born in Dublin and educated at Wellington School and Cambridge University. He published many fine press editions of Irish writers as well as writing *The Life of George Moore* (1938) and, most famously, *W. B. Yeats, 1865–1939* (1942).

HONE, William (1780–1842) Born in Bath, radical author and bookseller, who published numerous political satires, parodies, and pamphlets, many illustrated by George *Cruikshank. Their most notable collaborations are *The Political House that Jack Built* (1819), *The Queen's Matrimonial Ladder* (1819), *The Man in the Moon* (1820), and *A Slap at Slop* (1822). Hone was prosecuted, unsuccessfully, for blasphemy on account of his *Political Litany* (1817). He published his *Every-Day Book*, which was dedicated to Charles *Lamb and praised by Walter *Scott and Robert *Southey, in 1826–7 and his *Table-Book* in 1827–8. See M. Wood, *Radical Satire and Print Culture 1790–1822* (1994); B. Wilson, *The Laughter of Triumph* (2006).

Honest Whore, The A play by Thomas *Dekker in two parts, both written *c.*1604/5, of which the first was printed 1604, the second 1630. It appears from *Henslowe's diary that Thomas *Middleton collaborated in writing the first part.

In Part I Count Hippolito, meeting Bellafront, and discovering that she is a harlot, reproaches her bitterly for her way of life and converts her to honesty. She falls in love with Hippolito, who rejects her and marries Infelice, daughter of the duke of Milan. Bellafront marries Matheo, who had caused her downfall.

In Part II the converted Bellafront is the devoted wife of the worthless Matheo, who, to pay for his vices, is prepared to see her return to her old way of life. Hippolito, now falling in love with her, tries to seduce her. She stoutly resists, and is finally rescued by her father, Orlando Friscobaldo. The play's painful nature, strengthened by powerful scenes in Bedlam and Bridewell, is alleviated by the admirable character Orlando Friscobaldo, and by the comic sub-plot, dealing with the eccentricities of the patient husband Candido, the linen draper.

HOOD, Thomas (1799–1845) Poet and journalist, born in London, the son of a bookseller, assistant editor of the **London Magazine*, 1821–3, and the friend of Charles *Lamb, William *Hazlitt, Thomas *De Quincey, and other literary men. He edited various periodicals: *The Gem* (1829), the *Comic Annual* (1830), the **New Monthly Magazine* (1841–3), and *Hood's Magazine* (1843). He and John Hamilton *Reynolds published *Odes and Addresses to Great People* (1825), a series of satires and parodies which sold well. He wrote much humorous and satirical verse, often making use of his remarkable skill with puns, but his satire lacked bite. Lamb, recognizing this lack, and referring to Hood's attempts to do in verse for London what William *Hogarth had done with engraving, called him 'our half-Hogarth'. His serious poems include 'The *Song of the Shirt', which was immensely successful; 'The *Bridge of Sighs', and 'The Dream of Eugene Aram', the first about a suicide by drowning, the second about a murder; 'The Last Man'; 'The Plea of the Mid-summer Fairies' (which includes 'I remember, I remember'); and shorter pieces, such as 'The Death-bed'. He wrote a comedy, *York and Lancaster*, and in *Hood's Own* (1839) published a lively account of an assembly at the Lambs' house. He received a Civil List pension not long before his death.

HOOD, Thomas, the younger (1835–74) A talented humorous writer and artist, known as Tom Hood, the son of Thomas *Hood. The first of his illustrated books, *Pen and Pencil Pictures*, was published in 1857. He became editor of *Fun* in 1865, in which year he published the most successful of his six novels, *Captain Master's Children*. In 1867 he founded *Tom Hood's Comic Annual*, which continued after his death. He wrote and illustrated many children's books; his collected verse, *Favourite Poems*, was published in 1877.

HOOK, Theodore Edward (1788–1841) Wit, satirist, musician, practical joker, writer of light verse and dramas, and a prolific and popular novelist. Hook had a facility for improvisation, rapid composition, and easy—if ephemeral—brilliance. He was a successful editor of the Tory newspaper *John Bull*, to which he contributed both acidulous invective and scurrilous satire. Imprisoned for debt in the 1820s, after his release he became the most successful writer of 'silver-fork novels', portraying the doings of the fashionable world. As a former friend of the prince of Wales, Hook had known high society well, and his novels were read in large numbers by those aspiring to social fashion. Among his various novels, *Sayings and Doings* (1824–8), *Maxwell* (1830), *Gilbert Gurney* (1836), and *Gurney Married* (1838) were all successful. Their principal interest today, however, is to the literary and social historian.
See also FASHIONABLE NOVEL.

HOOKER, Richard (1554–1600) Theologian and philosopher, the son of poor parents, educated through the help of patrons at Exeter Grammar School and Corpus Christi College, Oxford. Following an Oxford career as college fellow and deputy professor of Hebrew, he was subsequently master of the Temple Church in London, subdean of Salisbury, and rector of Boscombe in Wiltshire and of Bishopsbourne in Kent, where he died. His fame rests on his great prose classic, the defence of the *Church of England as established in *Elizabeth I's reign entitled *Of the *Laws of Ecclesiastical Politie*. Books I–IV were published in 1593, Book V in 1597, Books VI and VIII in 1648, and Book VII in 1662. Other works were issued at Oxford in 1612–14. The influential biography by Izaac *Walton (1666) is delightful but often inaccurate. Hooker's admirers have included William *Chillingworth, John *Locke, S. T. *Coleridge, and John *Keble, who edited his works.

HOPE, A. D. (Alec Derwent) (1907–2000) Australian poet, born New South Wales, and educated at the universities of Sydney and Oxford. His first collection, *The Wandering Islands* (1955), was followed by *Poems* (1960), *Collected Poems 1930–1965* (1966; rev. 1972), and other volumes, but much of his work was written and published before his first book appeared. His work is technically accomplished, witty, and allusive, abounding in references to the Bible and classical mythology: he pays homage to Lord *Byron, S. T. *Coleridge, W. B. *Yeats, and other colleagues in the trade. He displays a formidable command of traditional verse forms, and his salute to **ottava rima* in 'A Letter from Rome' (1958) hits a characteristic informal ironic note, but he also explores more sombre themes, often with a detached gravity: see for example 'The Death of the Bird' (1948) on a last migration, or 'Meditation on a Bone' (1956), on scholarship and passion.

HOPE, Anthony Pseudonym of Sir Anthony Hope *Hawkins (1863–1933).

HOPE, Christopher (1944–) South African-born poet, children's writer, short story writer, and novelist, educated at the universities of Witwatersrand and Natal, who moved to London in 1975, where he worked for a while as a teacher before becoming a full-time writer. His first volume of poetry, *Cape Drives* (1974), evokes the landscapes and racial tensions of South Africa: it was followed by a novel, *A Separate Development* (1980), the story of Harry Moto, a white teenage South African outsider who ends up in jail writing his memoirs, and *In the Country of the Black Pig* (poems, 1981). Hope's output is varied in subjects and settings: other titles include *Kruger's Alp* (1984), a historical satire about the aftermath of the Boer War; *My Chocolate Redeemer* (1989), set in France; *Learning to Fly* (1990, short stories); *Serenity House* (1992), which deals with the legacy of the Holocaust as Max Montfalcon awaits death in an old people's home in north London; and *Me, the Moon and Elvis Presley* (1997), a novel about post-apartheid problems. *My Mother's Lovers* (2006) is a generically flexible novel, with elements of thriller and autobiography, and a wide geographical and satirical scope.

HOPE, Thomas (*c.*1770–1831) A man of great wealth, architect, art historian, and traveller, and the author of the once popular novel *Anastasius*, published in 1819 and at first attributed to Lord *Byron, who, indeed, wished he had written it. It tells, at considerable length, the story of a brave but unscrupulous Greek who travels in the Middle East and becomes involved in a variety of escapades. It is possible that the story influenced the later cantos of **Don Juan*.

Hope Theatre On Bankside, Southwark, built in 1613 by Philip *Henslowe as a bear-garden, with a movable stage on which plays could be performed. Jonson's **Bartholomew Fair* was acted there in 1614.

HOPKINS, Gerard Manley (1844–89) Poet and priest, born in Stratford, Essex, the eldest of nine children in the High Anglican, artistically minded home of Kate and Manley Hopkins. He attended Highgate School, where he showed academic and artistic promise, 'nervous grace', and distinctive independence. In his final years he won the school poetry prize for 'The Escorial' and had another poem published in the national journal *Once A Week*. In 1863 he went up to Balliol College, Oxford, as an exhibitioner. The 'star of Balliol' was tutored by Benjamin *Jowett, T. H. *Green, and (very briefly) Walter *Pater, among others. He developed a lasting friendship with Robert *Bridges and was a lively, social, and artistic undergraduate. Yet he was increasingly drawn to self-discipline, restraint, and religion, and anxious about his attraction to young men, particularly Bridges's cousin Digby Dolben, a schoolboy, poet, and devotee of Roman Catholicism. Dolben's accidental death in 1867 left Hopkins distraught. Hopkins's quest for security and religious certainty led him to convert to Roman Catholicism, with John Henry *Newman's guidance, in 1866. In 1867 he completed his degree (a double first), then taught for a year at Newman's Oratory School, Birmingham. In 1868 he entered the Society of Jesus (Jesuits). His preparation, or 'formation', included life as a novice (Roehampton, 1868–70), as 'scholastic', in preparation for the priesthood (Stonyhurst, 1870–73), as 'regent', working in a Jesuit ministry (professor of rhetoric, Roehampton, 1873–74), and as 'theologian' (St Beuno's in north Wales, 1874–77, where he also learned Welsh). Although Hopkins was strongly attracted to the strictness and self-suppression of Jesuit rule, he also found conformity difficult. Believing that poetry and priesthood were irreconcilable, he burnt his poems on becoming a Jesuit (though he sent copies to Bridges for safe keeping) but continued to write and record his brilliantly detailed observations of nature in his journals. After eight years his creativity was revived by a disaster at sea and he produced the astonishingly innovative poem 'The *Wreck of the Deutschland' (1875): its rejection by the Jesuit periodical *The Month* spelled the end of his hopes for acceptance as a Jesuit poet. Following ordination in 1877, Hopkins had a peripatetic pastoral career. Frequent transfers were necessitated by Jesuit policy, short-staffing in parishes and schools, and his own shortcomings as preacher, administrator, and teacher. He worked in Chesterfield and London before being sent to Oxford, 1878–9; next came postings to industrial Liverpool (1880–81) and Glasgow, both of which he hated, before he resumed teaching at Roehampton and Stonyhurst. In 1884 he was appointed to the chair of Greek and Latin at University College, Dublin. By this time he had been through eleven postings in eight years and at this 'third remove' from homeland, family, and friends, he experienced desolation and anguish. He died of typhoid in June 1889.

Hopkins's earliest poems express a Keatsian sensuousness, a Ruskinian zest for natural detail, and a distinctive flair for aural and rhythmic effects. Oxford texts such as 'Heaven-Haven' and 'Easter Communion' trace his desire and need to convert. While studying for ordination, inspired by 'God's grandeur' in Wales, he composed a remarkable series of experimental sonnets including 'The Wind-hover', 'Spring', and 'Pied Beauty'. Aesthetic and moral questions intensify in subsequent poems such as 'Henry Purcell' and 'Binsey Poplars'. Exiled in Dublin, he composed the 'terrible sonnets' such as 'Carrion Comfort', 'No worst, there is none', and 'Spelt from Sibyl's Leaves'; poems which have become classic representations of psychic despair and fragmentation. But he was also inspired to write further poems glorifying God and Nature, 'That Nature is a Heraclitean Fire' and 'To R.B.' In his journals and letters Hopkins developed highly personal theories of natural essence and expressiveness and of metre, and coined the terms 'inscape', 'instress', and *'sprung rhythm', respectively, to define them. 'Inscape' refers to 'the individual or essential quality of the thing' or 'individually-distinctive beauty of style'. 'Instress' is the force or energy which sustains an inscape; it originates in the Creator and is felt by the responsive perceiver (a concept claimed to relate to the theologian *Duns Scotus and his idea of *haecceitas*, or 'thisness', which Hopkins greatly admired). 'Sprung rhythm' is distinguished from regular or 'running rhythm' (with its regular metrical feet) because it involves writing and scanning by number of stresses rather than by counting syllables. Surviving prose writings, including journals, letters, and sermons, articulate Hopkins's profound responsiveness to nature and beauty, his acumen as a literary critic and theorist of prosody, his playful wit, devoted friendliness, and spiritual and theological insights. Removed from the literary scene, he engaged avidly with contemporary developments and corresponded with writers, including the poets Coventry *Patmore and R. W. *Dixon, one of his former teachers. He was also deeply influenced by the visual arts, keenly admiring the *Pre-Raphaelites. His own artistic talents were encouraged by studies of John *Ruskin and by family members; two of his brothers became illustrators. In later years he explored musical theory and composition.

Hopkins's poetic fame was posthumous and gradual. Bridges became the guardian of the manuscripts after his death. Doubting how the public would respond, he published a few poems in anthologies but delayed a full edition until 1918. It sold poorly, and it was not until the second edition in 1930, read and admired by the critic F. R. *Leavis and poets W. H. *Auden, Stephen *Spender, and R. S. *Thomas, that Hopkins achieved recognition. T. S. *Eliot was persuaded to publish excerpts from the letters and notebooks in the **Criterion*, cementing Hopkins's reputation as a proto-modernist poet. It was only in the late 20th century that he was re-examined as a major Victorian poet, who provided some of the greatest expressions of faith and doubt and produced perhaps the most formally and linguistically innovative poetry of his period.

See *Poetical Works of Gerard Manley Hopkins*, ed. Norman H. Mackenzie (1990); *Journals and Papers*, ed. Humphrey House and Graham Storey (1959); *Sermons and Devotional Writings*, ed. Christopher Devlin (1959); *Selected Letters*, ed. Catherine Phillips (1990). The major biographies are by R. B. Martin (1991) and Norman White (1992).

HOPKINS, Matthew (d. 1647) The witch-finder, said to have been a lawyer at Ipswich and Manningtree. He initiated many prosecutions, and procured a special judicial commission under which 60 women were hanged in Essex in one year, and many in Norfolk and Huntingdonshire. His *The Discovery of Witches* was published in 1647. See C. L'Estrange Ewen, *Witch Hunting and Witch Trials* (1929); Keith Thomas, *Religion and the Decline of Magic* (1971); Robin Briggs, *Witches and Neighbours* (1996).

HOPKINSON, Nalo (1960–) Canadian author of *science fiction and *fantasy, born in Jamaica. *Brown Girl in the Ring* (1998) and *Midnight Robber* (2000) draw upon the richness of Caribbean culture and its storytelling techniques. She has also edited several anthologies of *postcolonial science fiction.

HORACE (Quintus Horatius Flaccus) (65–8 BC) Roman poet. His father, an emancipated slave, gave him a good education and was remembered by Horace with gratitude (*Satires*, I. 6). Ambitiously, he joined *Brutus' army as military tribune; defeat meant the confiscation of his inherited property. A friend of *Virgil, he was taken up by *Maecenas, to whom he addressed several poems, and who gave him the Sabine farm much celebrated in the poems. In the 30s, Horace wrote *Satires* and *Epodes*, in which good humour and self-deprecation contend with anger and some calculated obscenity. His greatest work is his lyric *Odes* (Books 1–3 23 BC, Book 4 8 BC), in the metres of such archaic Greek poets as Alcaeus, *Sappho, and *Anacreon. They are written with exquisite verbal art and a sophisticated sensibility. His verse *Epistles*, their informal manner suggesting a relaxed and charming personality, allow readers to feel that they know Horace as a man. *The Art of Poetry* resonates with influential phrases: 'in medias res' (in the midst of things), 'ut pictura poesis' (as painting so poetry). English satire from Thomas *Wyatt to Alexander *Pope's *Imitations* derives much of its manner and aims from Horace. The writers of formal *odes, Andrew *Marvell and John *Dryden in particular, are also indebted to him. More surprisingly, Rudyard *Kipling was a great admirer and actually composed a 'Fifth Book of Horace's Odes'. Notable translators include Christopher *Smart. See *Horace in English*, ed. D. S. Carne-Ross and Kenneth Hayes (1996); Stephen Harrison (ed.), *The Cambridge Companion to Horace* (1977).

Horatian ode *See* ODE.

Horizon A literary magazine founded in 1939 by Cyril *Connolly, Stephen *Spender, and Peter Watson, which ran from 1940 to 1950. Subsidized by Watson, it was edited throughout by Connolly, and published works by George *Orwell, Auberon *Waugh, Laurie *Lee, W. H. *Auden, and Geoffrey *Grigson, amongst others. See Michael Shelden, *Friends of Promise* (1989).

HORMAN, William (1457–1535) Fellow of New College, Oxford, and headmaster of Winchester College and Eton College, of which he became vice-provost. He was the author of *Vulgaria*, a lively collection of Latin sentences, reflecting the contemporary world, for boys to learn. It was printed in 1519 by Richard Pynson (1448–1529), by Wynkyn de *Worde (1530), and for the Roxburghe Club (ed. M. R. *James, 1926).

HORNBY, Nick (1957–) Novelist and autobiographer, born in Redhill, Surrey, and educated at Cambridge. *Fever Pitch* (1992), his hugely successful memoir about his years as a supporter of Arsenal football club, opened the floodgates for a new genre of male *confessional writing. This was followed by two comic novels, *High Fidelity* (1995) and *About a Boy* (1998), which both explored the emotional confusions and immaturity of a certain kind of white middle-class Englishman. *How to Be Good* (2001) was a change of direction inasmuch as the narrator of this story involving guilty adultery, the break-up of a marriage, and the desire to assuage a troubled social conscience is a woman. *A Long Way Down* (2005) extracts poignant comedy from four characters who come together through failed attempts at suicide. *See* LADS' LITERATURE.

Horn Childe A northern verse romance from the period 1290–1340. The plot is similar to that of **King Horn* though different in some details. Horn is a prince in the north of England who flees with his teacher and companions to the south where a king's daughter, Rimnild, falls in love with him. Two of Horn's companions betray the lovers to the king, and Horn flees to Wales and Ireland, taking Rimnild's magic ring with him. After ridding Ireland of pagans, he returns to England, is revenged on his companions, and marries Rimnild. *Horn Childe* is probably the romance referred to in 'Sir Thopas' (*see* CANTERBURY TALES, 17). It was edited by Maldwyn Mills (1988).

HORNE, John *See* TOOKE, JOHN HORNE.

HORNE, Richard Henry (Hengist) (1802–84) Poet and dramatist, educated at Sandhurst; he served in the Mexican navy, and, in his own words, 'took up scribbling' when he was 30. He made his name with *Orion*, an allegorical epic which he published in 1843 at a farthing 'to mark', he said archly, 'the public contempt into which epic poetry had fallen'. The poem deals with the myth of Orion, portrayed as 'a Worker and a Builder for his fellow men', and contrasted with Akinetos, the 'Great Unmoved', or Apathy. It was much praised by Thomas *Carlyle, G. H. *Lewes, and Edgar

Allan *Poe, who found it 'one of the noblest, if not the very noblest poetical work of the age'; contemporary reviewers compared it not unfavourably with *Keats's *Hyperion* and *Endymion*. Horne wrote several blank verse tragedies, influenced by John *Webster, and adapted various plays for the stage, including *The *Duchess of Malfi*. He contributed many articles to *Dickens's *Daily News* and *Household Words*, published other volumes of verse, and in 1852, in the midst of the gold fever, went to Australia where he stayed until 1869. His varied adventures there are described in the autobiographical preface to his *Australian Facts and Prospects* (1859). From 1839 he corresponded with Elizabeth Barrett *Browning (whom he first met in 1851), and he published two volumes of her letters to him (1877). She collaborated with him in his *A New Spirit of the Age* (1844). See Anne Blaine, *The Farthing Poet* (1968).

HORNIMAN, Annie (1860–1937) Theatre patron and manager, born in London into a Nonconformist family of wealthy tea merchants. With a legacy from her Quaker grandfather, she provided the financial assistance that allowed W. B. *Yeats and the Irish National Theatre Society to establish a permanent home in the *Abbey Theatre, Dublin, in 1904. Her greatest achievement was as founder of the Manchester Repertory Company at the Gaiety Theatre, Manchester, in 1908, where she was a pioneer supporter of the 'new drama' of Henrik *Ibsen and G. B. *Shaw.

HORNUNG, E. W. (Ernest William) (1866–1921) Novelist, born Middlesborough, who spent four years at Uppingham School, and is remembered as the creator of Raffles, public-school man, gentleman burglar, and cricketer, who appeared in the best-selling thrillers *The Amateur Cracksman* (1899), *The Black Mask* (1901), *A Thief in the Night* (1905), and *Mr Justice Raffles* (1909), narrated by his admiring assistant Bunny. See George *Orwell, 'Raffles and Miss Blandish', in *Horizon* (1944).
See also DETECTIVE FICTION.

HOROVITZ, Michael (1935–) Poet, performance artist, and editor, born in Frankfurt. He emigrated to England with his family as a child, and was educated at Brasenose College, Oxford. He was one of the earliest British exponents of the counter-culture and *Beat Generation, editing important anthologies of new work for *New Departures* including *Children of Albion: Poetry of the 'Underground'* (1969), organizing many poetry readings and events (including the celebrated poetry festival at the Royal Albert Hall in June 1965), and encouraging many young poets, whose work appears in *Grandchildren of Albion* (1997).

horror Horror and the supernatural or 'weird' tale have been with us, in one form or another, for as long as literature has existed. Mary *Shelley's *Frankenstein* (1818), Robert Louis Stevenson's *Strange Case of *Dr Jekyll and Mr Hyde* (1886), and Bram Stoker's *Dracula* (1897) are landmarks in horror, but so, too, it could be argued, are certain plays by *Shakespeare, Christopher *Marlowe, and John *Webster. But the horror/*fantasy tradition goes back further, to the monster in *Beowulf*, the most important poem in Old English, dating from the 10th century, and indeed beyond to the bloody visions of *Sophocles (496–406 BC) and others. More directly influential on the horror/fantasy fiction of the 20th century was *Romanticism and the *Gothic, in particular the 'delightful horror' that Edmund *Burke finds in the infinite; the richly iconic figure of the vampire; the and the macabre short stories of Edgar Allan *Poe. H. P. *Lovecraft is probably the most influential horror writer of the first half of the 20th century, thanks partly to his own evocations of personal anxiety, cosmic awe, and terror, and his championing of writers like M. R. *James, Arthur *Machen, and Algernon *Blackwood. Horror as a publishing category is sometimes problematic, largely because many potential readers are put off by the name. Robert *Aickman preferred to call his horror tales 'strange stories'. Ramsey *Campbell, on the other hand, has never shied away from the term 'horror', and he is Britain's most respected living writer of the mode. If there is a ghetto mentality, one horror writer who has smashed his way out of it to head the world's best-seller lists is Stephen King (1947–). His study *Danse Macabre* (1981) intelligently describes the various effects attainable in horror. In the USA, Dennis Etchison (1943–), Peter *Straub, Poppy Z. Brite (1967–), Steve Rasnic Tem (1950–), and British-born Clive *Barker, among others, consistently produce notable work; in the UK, a new generation of horror writers has grown up reading the subtly weird stories and novels of Campbell (who also edited an outstanding, intelligent anthology in *New Terrors*), Aickman, and M. John *Harrison. In the 1980s and 1990s the most notable new writers of horror/fantasy included Joel Lane (1963–), Michael Marshall Smith (1965–), Mark Morris (1963–), Conrad Williams (1969–), Kim *Newman, Christopher Fowler (1953–), and Graham Joyce (1954–). Certain anthologies such as Nicholas Royle's *Darklands* and *Darklands 2*, Stephen Jones and David Sutton's *Dark Terrors* series, Stephen Jones's *The Mammoth Book of Best New Horror*, and Ellen Datlow and Terri Windling's *The Year's Best Fantasy and Horror* have encouraged these new writers to develop a voice at the same time as continuing to support veterans such as John Burke (1922–), Basil Copper (1924–), and Ronald Chetwynd-Hayes (1919–2001). Although there may always be a (limited) market for their splatter-filled tales (Shaun Hutson (1958–) and James Herbert (1943–) have both been moving away from trademark graphic horror towards thrillers), it is with regard to the subtler, more imaginative writers that it may be true to say that of the popular genres, horror is arguably the one that runs closest to the literary mainstream and most interestingly subverts it. While much fiction categorized as horror touches on the fantastic or the supernatural, extremes of psychological or physical horror can be seen in more realistic genres, such as the fascination for stories of serial killers like the Hannibal Lector of Thomas Harris (1940–) where the horrific intrudes into the everyday world as fearsomely as any vampire.

HOSKYNS, John (1566–1638) Born in Herefordshire and educated at Winchester College, New College, Oxford, and the Middle Temple, a lawyer and poet who enjoyed a high reputation for wit and learning. He is best known for his *Directions for Speech and Style,* drawn on by Ben *Jonson in his *Timber, or Discoveries,* but not published in full until 1935 (ed. H. H. Hudson). The *Directions* were written around 1599; most of Hoskyns's examples are drawn from Philip *Sidney's **Arcadia,* but he also makes interesting use of other contemporary authors.

HOSPITAL, Janette Turner (1942–) Novelist and short story writer, born in Melbourne, Australia, who studied at the University of Queensland and at Queen's University, Canada. She has taught in universities in Australia, Canada, the USA, and the UK. *The Ivory Swing* (1982) won the Canadian Seal First Novel Award. Since then she has published *The Tiger in the Tiger Pit* (1983), *Borderline* (1985), *Charades* (1988), *The Last Magician* (1992), and *Oyster* (1996). Her allusive, lyrical prose and intricate narratives have been much admired. The theme of dislocation—both cultural and emotional—is recurrent in her work, as is the damage wrought by secrecy, and the ways in which the past influences and can discolour the present. She elaborates these themes in her collections of short stories, *Dislocations* (1986) and *Isobars* (1990). Her *Collected Stories* (including seven previously uncollected) appeared in Australia in 1995.

HOSSEINI, Khaled (1965–) Tajik novelist and doctor, born in Afghanistan, educated at Santa Clara University and the University of California, San Diego; now an American citizen. His first novel, *The Kite Runner* (2003; filmed 2007), which treats the recent history of Afghanistan and the experience of emigration to America through the events in the life of the young boy Amir and his father, was an international best-seller. It was followed by *A Thousand Splendid Suns* (2007), the story of Laila and Mariam, two Afghan women whose lives become closely connected, which was also notably successful.

HOTSON, Leslie (1897–1992) Canadian scholar and literary detective who specialized in the minute examination of Shakespeare's life and times. He made important discoveries (including vital material relating to Christopher *Marlowe's death), but many of his theories and conclusions about Shakespeare's works have not gained widespread acceptance.

HOUELLEBECQ, Michel (1958–) Controversial French novelist and poet whose work engages with some of the dominant preoccupations of the late 20th and early 21st centuries: the impact of neo-liberalism on human relationships and identity (*Extension du domaine de la lutte,* 1994: *Whatever*); religious fundamentalism (*Plateforme,* 2001); and cloning (*La Possibilité d'une île,* 2005: *The Possibility of an Island*). Following the publication of *Plateforme,* and an interview in which he was critical of Islam, Houellebecq was tried for (and later acquitted of) inciting racial hatred.

HOUGHTON, Baron *See* MILNES, MONCKTON.

Hours of Idleness A collection of poems by Lord *Byron, published 1807. The first of Byron's works for general rather than private publication, these poems show a wide variety of attitudes, from the light to the sentimental and the solemnly nostalgic, and hint at the tone and technical range of his mature work. But their quality is uneven and the volume was bitterly attacked by Henry *Brougham in the **Edinburgh Review* as 'so much stagnant water'. Byron responded in **English Bards and Scotch Reviewers.*

HOUSEHOLD, Geoffrey (1900–88) Novelist, educated at Clifton College and Magdalen College, Oxford, and the author of many successful adventure stories in the tradition of John *Buchan. The most characteristic (including his best known, *Rogue Male,* 1939, and its sequel *Rogue Justice,* 1982) pit a sporting, well-bred, lonely adventurer against the forces of darkness in the modern world (e.g. Nazis and Nazi agents), and depend on the suspense of pursuit and revenge. Other titles include *Watcher in the Shadows* (1960) and *Dance of the Dwarfs* (1968).

Household Words A weekly periodical started in 1850 by Charles *Dickens, and incorporated in 1859 into *All the Year Round,* which he edited until his death. Priced at twopence, it was aimed at a large audience, and achieved a weekly circulation of 40,000. It carried contributions from well-known writers such as Elizabeth *Gaskell, Charles *Reade, and Edward *Bulwer-Lytton, established the reputation of Wilkie *Collins, and published poems by the young George *Meredith and Coventry *Patmore, as well as much of Dickens's own work. Although its attacks on the abuses of the day (poor sanitation, slums, factory accidents) were radical and persistent, its subject matter was varied and entertaining.

House of Fame, The An unfinished dream-poem by Geoffrey *Chaucer, possibly composed *c.*1374–*c.*1385. There are three books, in 2,158 lines of *octosyllabics; it is believed to be Chaucer's last poem in that French form. The poem remains enigmatic and it is uncertain what its purpose or extent would have been (though the poem says that the third book is in fact the final one).

After a sceptical prologue on dreams and the invocation to the god of sleep, Book I has its narrator fall asleep and dream that he is in a Temple of Glass where he sees depicted Aeneas and Dido (based on **Aeneid,* 4); the dream moves on to deal more briefly with other parts of the *Aeneid.* At the end of Book I the poet sees an eagle who alights by him and is his guide through the House of Fame in Book II (initially suggested, perhaps, by *Fama,* Rumour, in *Aeneid,* 4. 173 ff.). The eagle explains in ponderous terms the arbitrary workings of Fame and the book ends with a vision of the world (ll. 896–1045). The eagle departs and at the beginning of Book III Chaucer enters the Palace of Fame (Rumour) where he sees the famous of both classical and biblical lore. Eolus, ruler of the winds, blows a trumpet to summon up the various celebrities who introduce themselves in categories reminiscent of the souls in Dante's *Divina commedia*, which Chaucer parodies throughout this poem. Towards the end comes a vision of bearers of false tidings: shipmen, pilgrims, pardoners, and messengers, whose confusion seems to be about to be resolved by the appearance of 'A man of gret auctorite...' when the poem ends. Poetic responses to the work were made by John *Lydgate (in *The Temple of Glas*), Gawin *Douglas, and John *Skelton. See J. A. W. Bennett, *Chaucer's Book of Fame* (1968); S. Delaney, *Chaucer's House of Fame* (1972); P. Boitani, *Chaucer and the Imaginary World of Fame* (1984); *The Riverside Chaucer*, ed. L. D. Benson *et al.* (2008).

'House of Life, The' A sequence of 101 sonnets by Dante Gabriel *Rossetti, begun in the 1850s and published in two parts in *Poems* (1870) and *Ballads and Sonnets* (1881). They have been considered both a record of Rossetti's grief for his dead wife, and a commentary on his passion for William *Morris's wife Jane. Critics have debated whether the sonnets' obscurity results from Rossetti's use of private symbols, or whether their shifting representations of body and soul offer a meditation on relations between sign and referent (in *structuralist theory), language and thought, and master–slave dynamics in sexual, or gendered, expression. The obscurity also reflects the quality of writing. Walter *Pater remarked that in these sonnets 'Life is a crisis at every moment', and 'The Fleshly School of Poetry' (1871), an article by Robert *Buchanan, cited the work in its vehement attack on the perceived moral depravity of Rossetti's poetry.

House of the Seven Gables, The A novel by Nathaniel *Hawthorne, published 1851. It deals with the problem of hereditary guilt, unmerited misfortune, and unexpiated crime, through the story of the Pyncheon family, suffering from generation to generation from the curse of old Maule, the dispossessed owner of the Pyncheon property. An important part in the purging of this curse is played by a young daguerrotypist. The novel's semi-allegorical treatment of the theme of the 'transmitted vices of society' is characteristic of Hawthorne, and manifests his acute sensitivity about his own Puritan ancestry.

HOUSMAN, A. E. (Alfred Edward) (1859–1936) Poet and scholar, educated at Bromsgrove School and St John's College, Oxford. While at university he formed a passionate attachment to his contemporary Moses Jackson, who became an important inspiration of his later verse. The brilliant Housman failed his final examinations and became a clerk in the Patent Office in London, during which time he worked on *Propertius, *Ovid, *Juvenal, and other classical authors, publishing articles when he could. In 1887 Jackson emigrated to India, then married, and soon afterwards the anguished Housman (who had not written verse since his schooldays) began to compose poetry. In 1892 he was appointed a professor of Latin at University College London, where he began to produce his definitive edition of Manilius (1903–30). In 1896 he published, at his own expense, *A Shropshire Lad*, a series of 63 spare and nostalgic verses, based largely on *ballad forms, and mainly set in a half-imaginary Shropshire, a 'land of lost content', and often addressed to, or spoken by, a farm-boy or a soldier. Many of the poems had been written in the early months of 1895, which happened to be the time of the Oscar *Wilde trial. Housman made the barest profit from the publication, but Richard *Le Gallienne found the verse of 'exquisite simplicity', and another reviewer noted its 'heart-penetrating quality'; public indifference slowly gave way to interest, and sales mounted steadily. During the years of the First World War *A Shropshire Lad* became hugely popular. In 1911 Housman was appointed professor of Latin at Cambridge, and lived thereafter at Trinity College. At a time when Jackson was ill (he would die in 1923), Housman published *Last Poems* (1922), whose 41 poems met with great acclaim. In 1933 he gave his well-known lecture 'The Name and Nature of Poetry', which was published in the same year. In 1936 *More Poems* appeared, from work in the notebooks; eighteen further poems were printed in Laurence *Housman's *A.E.H.* (1937), and *Collected Poems* appeared in 1939. *The Letters of A. E. Housman* was published in 1971, edited by Henry Maas, and a new, much larger edition in 2007, edited by Archie Burnett, who also edited *The Poems of A. E. Housman* (1997). Housman is the principal character in Tom *Stoppard's play *The Invention of Love* (1997). See Richard Perceval Graves, *A. E. Housman* (1979); Norman Page, *A. E. Housman* (1983).

HOUSMAN, Laurence (1865–1959) Writer and dramatist, brother of A. E. *Housman, educated at Bromsgrove School. He then went to art school in London, and would later write art criticism for the **Manchester Guardian* as well as illustrating a number of books. He published many stories, for both children and adults, and wrote much on feminism and on socialist and pacifist themes. Among his works were volumes of somewhat derivative poems, including *Green Arras* (1896) and *Spikenard* (1898); *An Englishwoman's Love-Letters* (1900), which enjoyed some notoriety and was widely parodied; and several successful novels, among them a political satire, *Trimblerigg* (1924), directed against David Lloyd George. His first play, *Bethlehem*, was performed in 1902. Some of his plays on controversial topics, such as *Pains and Penalties* (1911), were banned. *The Little Plays of St Francis* (1922), together with further plays on the same theme and on St Clare, were well received and much performed for many years. *Angels and Ministers* (1921), consisting of gently mocking scenes laid in the court of Queen Victoria, were collected with further royal playlets into *Victoria Regina* (1934). When the lord chamberlain's ban on the impersonation of members of the royal family was lifted in 1937 the play enjoyed great success. In 1937 Housman published both an autobiography, *The*

Unexpected Years, and *A.E.H.*, a volume containing a valuable memoir of his brother.

HOVE, Chenjerai (1956–) Born in Zimbabwe though now living in exile; he describes his country as 'a big wound'. His collections of poetry are *Up in Arms* (1982), *Red Hills of Home* (1985), *Rainbows in the Dust* (1998), and *Blind Moon* (2003). He writes in Shona, but is best known for his novels in English, *Shadows* (1991), *Ancestors* (1996), and the award-winning *Bones* (1988), exploring the role of women in the Zimbabwean liberation struggle.

HOWARD, Elizabeth Jane (1923–) Novelist and short story writer, born in London, actress and model before becoming a full-time writer. Her third marriage, dissolved in 1983, was to Kingsley *Amis. Well crafted and strongly evocative of place and time, her novels of English middle-class life include *The Beautiful Visit* (1950), *After Julius* (1965), and *Getting It Right* (1982). *The Light Years* (1990), *Marking Time* (1991), *Confusion* (1993), and *Casting Off* (1995) form the saga of the Cazalet family from 1937 to the post-war period. *Mr Wrong* (1975) is a collection of her stories. Her many plays for television include an adaptation of *After Julius*. Her autobiography, *Slipstream*, appeared in 2002.

HOWARD, Henry *See* SURREY, HENRY HOWARD.

HOWARD, Robert E. (1906–36) Born in Texas, prolific American author of stories of numerous genres (*fantasy, *horror, *historical, *western, and *detective fiction) for American 'pulp' magazines. He is best known for 'Conan the Barbarian', whose colourful adventures in a mythic past helped to define the sub-genre of *sword and sorcery.

Howards End *'Condition of England' novel by E. M. *Forster, published 1910. On the one hand are the Schlegel sisters, Margaret and Helen, and their brother Tibby, who care about ideas, civilized living, music, literature, and conversation with their friends; on the other, the Wilcoxes, Henry and his children Charles, Paul, and Evie, who are concerned with the business side of life and distrust emotions and imagination. Helen Schlegel is drawn to the Wilcox family, falls briefly in and out of love with Paul, and thereafter reacts away from them. Margaret becomes more deeply involved. She is stimulated by the very differences of their way of life and acknowledges the debt of intellectuals to men of business like Henry. Eventually, she marries him, to the consternation of both families, and her love and steadiness of purpose are tested by the ensuing strains and misunderstandings, which include the revelation that Helen has been made pregnant by Leonard Bast, a young, married, lower-class, but intellectually aspiring clerk whom the Schlegels had briefly befriended. Her marriage cracks but does not break. In the end, torn between her sister and her husband, she succeeds in bridging the mistrust that divides them. Howards End, where the story begins and ends, is the house that belonged to Henry Wilcox's first wife, Ruth, and is a symbol of human dignity and endurance. Yet just beneath Forster's suite of contrasts, more thorny irresolutions are felt, and it is these which are often as absorbing for today's reader.

HOWELL, James (?1593–1666) Historian, political writer, and poet; of Welsh descent, he held diplomatic and administrative posts under Charles I and was imprisoned in the Fleet as a Royalist, 1643–51; at the *Restoration he became historiographer royal. His *Dodona's Grove* (1640) is a political allegory, and in 1642 he published his entertaining *Instructions for Foreign Travel*. A violently anti-Scots pamphlet, *A Perfect Description of the Country of Scotland*, reprinted in the **North Briton*, 31, was attributed to him, but its authorship is disputed. Howell wrote many other works, including poems and historical pamphlets, but is chiefly remembered for his *Epistolae Ho-Elianae: Familiar Letters Domestic and Foreign* (1645–55), reprinted many times, ed. J. Jacobs (1890–92). These letters to correspondents, most of whom are imaginary, were written largely during his imprisonment; their intimate 'back-stairs' view of history had a lasting appeal, and W. M. *Thackeray wrote of them, 'Montaigne and Howell's *Letters* are my bedside books...I like to hear them tell their old stories over and over again.'

HOWELL, Thomas (*fl.* 1568–81) Minor Tudor poet patronized by the Herbert family. His *Devices* (1581) contains the earliest printed reference to Philip *Sidney's **Arcadia*.

HOWELLS, William Dean (1837–1920) American novelist, born in Ohio; he began life as a printer and journalist. He was American consul at Venice, 1861–5, an experience reflected in his *Venetian Life* (1866) and *Italian Journeys* (1867). He was sub-editor of the **Atlantic Monthly*, 1866–71, and chief editor 1871–81, and was associate editor of **Harper's Magazine*, 1886–91, to which periodicals he contributed many articles on literary subjects. He pioneered the promotion of realism in American fiction and, among his many novels, *The Rise of Silas Lapham* (1885) portrays the pursuit of commercial and social success and *A Hazard of New Fortunes* (1890) is a semi-autobiographical exposé of social hypocrisy. His works of criticism and reminiscence include *Criticism and Fiction* (1891), *My Literary Passions* (1895), *Literary Friends and Acquaintances* (1900), and *Literature and Life* (1902). He also wrote several dramas. He was a leading American man of letters of his age, and did much to encourage Henry *James and other writers. The Selected Edition of Howells' works by Indiana University Press includes his *Selected Literary Criticism*, 3 vols (1993). See Susan Goodman and Carl Dawson, *William Dean Howells: A Writer's Life* (2005).

Howleglass *See* EULENSPIEGEL, TILL.

HOYLE, Sir Fred (1915–2001) Born Bingley, Yorkshire; astronomer (knighted 1972), who wrote *science fiction novels alone and with his son Geoffrey. In *The Black Cloud* (1957), his first novel, a living gas-cloud surrounds Earth. *October the First is Too Late* (1966) explores concepts of time.

HRABAL, Bohumil (1914–97) Novelist, born in Brno, Czechoslovakia. He trained as a lawyer but was unable to practise under communist rule. His writing career began only in his late forties, with *Dancing Lessons for the Advanced in Age* (Czech 1964; English 1995), the reminiscences of a nostalgic roué, unfolding in a single sentence more than 100 pages long. *Closely Observed Trains* (Czech 1965; English 1968) is a tragicomic novella about a young railway worker in Nazi-occupied Czechoslovakia. The Oscar-winning film version, directed by Jiri Menzel, brought Hrabal to international notice, but he was then unable to publish in his own country for many years. *Too Loud a Solitude* (Czech 1980; English 1990), the charming fictional memoirs of a book-pulper, preceded *I Served the King of England* (Czech 1982; English 1989), the life story of a self-interested waiter, which ranges over most of pre- and post-war European history. He also published shorter pieces, including *The Death of Mr Baltisberger* (Czech 1966; English 1975) and *The Little Town Where Time Stood Still* (Czech 1982; English 1993).

HROTSVITHA (Roswitha) (*fl.* 10th century) A Benedictine abbess of Gandersheim in Saxony, who wrote plays loosely modelled on *Terence for the use of her convent, an example of the survival of classical influence in the Middle Ages.

HUBBARD, L. Ron (Lafayette Ronald) (1911–86) American author and founder of the Church of Scientology, born Nebraska; he published widely in American pulp magazines, especially stories of *science fiction and *fantasy. After his success with the psychotherapy programme 'Dianetics', which became the Scientology religion, he abandoned fiction to return with *Battlefield Earth* (1982), and sequels.

hubris *See* POETICS.

HUCHOWN of the Awle Ryale (*fl.* 14th century) Apparently a northern alliterative poet mentioned by Andrew Wyntoun (*c.*1350–*c.*1423), *c.*1400, who claims that 'He made the gret Gest of Arthure | And the Anteris of Gawane, | The Epistill als of Suete Susane'. These poems have been tentatively identified as, respectively, the alliterative **Morte Arthure, The *Awntyrs of Arthure*, and *The Pistyl of Susan*. Huchown has been identified with the Sir Hugh Eglinton mentioned in William *Dunbar's 'Lament for the Makaris' (l. 53).

Huckleberry Finn, (The) Adventures of A novel by Mark *Twain, published in 1884 as a sequel to *The Adventures of *Tom Sawyer* (1876), and generally accepted as one of the great works of American fiction. Narrated by Huck Finn, it describes the flight of Huck from well-meant attempts to 'sivilise' him, and from his feckless father, down the Mississippi where he eventually rejoins Tom Sawyer. He is accompanied by a runaway slave Jim, whose bid for freedom he supports, despite the inner promptings of a 'conscience' telling him he is stealing the rightful property of Jim's owner ('All right, then, I'll go to hell'). Huck's simplicity is used by Twain to reveal the absurdities of a family feud and the hypocrisies of shore society. His account has become a classic of vernacular narrative. The novel has continued to provoke controversy over its representation and designation of African Americans.

Hudibras A satire in three parts, each containing three cantos, written by Samuel *Butler (1613–80). Part I, dated 1663, appeared in December 1662, Part II, dated 1664, was published 1663, and a revised version of both parts came out in 1674. Part III was published 1680. Its narrative form is that of a mock romance, derived from **Don Quixote*, in which a grotesque Presbyterian knight, Sir Hudibras, and his sectarian squire Ralpho set out on horseback and encounter a bear-baiting mob who, after a comic skirmish, imprison them in the stocks. In the second part a widow, whom Hudibras hopes to marry for the sake of her property, agrees to release them on condition that the knight undergoes a whipping for her sake. They visit Sidrophel, a charlatan posing as an astrologer, whom Hudibras assaults and leaves for dead. In Part III Hudibras returns to the widow and claims that he has fulfilled his promise to whip himself, but is interrupted by a gang which he mistakes for Sidrophel's supernatural agents. They cudgel him and force him to confess to his iniquities. He consults a lawyer, who advises him to write love letters to the widow in order to inveigle her in her replies. The second canto of Part III has no connection with the rest of the poem but consists of an account of political events between the death of Oliver *Cromwell and the restoration of Charles II and a dialogue between two politicians, one of them modelled on the first earl of *Shaftesbury. The loose narrative framework of the poem allows Butler ample opportunity to digress; in fact the digressions form the substance of the poem. They deal with academic pedantry, the theological differences between the Presbyterians and independent sectarians, Aristotelian logic, the Hermetic philosophy, the politics of the Civil War period, the ethics of oath-breaking, witchcraft, alchemy, astrology, and the nature of marriage. *Hudibras* is profoundly learned, but Butler treats all erudition with contempt. His most powerful satirical weapon is his style, the deliberately cumbersome octosyllabic metre and comic rhymes of which render absurd every subject to which they are applied.

Hudibrastic In the style of Samuel Butler's **Hudibras*; in octosyllabic couplets and with comic rhymes.

HUDSON, W. H. (William Henry) (1841–1922) Born near Buenos Aires, the son of poor American parents who had moved to the Argentine to farm. His education was haphazard and he ran wild on the family ranch. Rheumatic fever at 15 disabled him for the outdoor life he had intended, and his lifelong interest in birds intensified. He collected specimens for the Smithsonian Institution, began to publish stories and articles on natural history in English and Argentine journals, and in 1874 came to London, where he remained for the rest of his life. He became a British subject in 1900. In 1885 he published *The Purple Land*, a series of stories set in South America. A standard work, *Argentine Ornithology*, of which Hudson was part-author, appeared in 1888. Alfred Russel *Wallace praised *The Naturalist in La Plata* (1892), the first of Hudson's books to enjoy some success. Hudson's *British Birds* was published in 1895. *Idle Days in Patagonia*, an engaging work of travel and natural lore, appeared in 1893, and in 1900 *Nature in Downland*. His novel **Green Mansions* (probably the best known of his books) was published in 1904. *A Shepherd's Life*, which some hold to be his finest book, appeared in 1910. *Adventures among Birds* (1913) was much praised, and the joyful account of his boyhood, *Far Away and Long Ago* (1918), received great acclaim. Another standard work, *Birds of La Plata*, appeared in 1920. New editions of Hudson's earlier books now began to be issued, and his collected works were published in 24 volumes in 1922–3. By the time of his death he was generally recognized as a masterly, often poetic writer on the natural world.

HUGH OF LINCOLN, LITTLE ST (?1246–55) A child supposed to have been crucified (27 August 1255) by a Jew named Copin or Jopin at Lincoln, after having been starved and tortured (for differing lengths of time in different versions of the story). A confession to this effect was extracted from Copin by John of Lexington. The body is said to have been discovered in a well and buried near that of Robert *Grosseteste in the cathedral, and to have been the cause of several miracles. The story, a frequent theme for medieval poets, and often related with strong anti-Semitic overtones, is mentioned by Chaucer ('The Prioress's Tale', *see* CANTERBURY TALES, 16) and by Marlowe in *The *Jew of Malta*. See also the ballad of 'The Jew's Daughter' in Percy's **Reliques*.

HUGHES, Langston (1902–67) African American writer, born in Joplin, Missouri, who lived in Harlem after 1947. A leading figure in the *Harlem Renaissance, Hughes applied blues and jazz techniques in his poetry from *The Weary Blues* (1926) onwards. He wrote a number of plays and novels, though from his fiction the five volumes of Simple stories (1950–65), presenting Jesse B. Semple as the spokesman for urban black America, were most successful. Hughes published two autobiographical volumes, *The Big Sea* (1940) and *I Wonder as I Wander* (1956). He was a vigorous campaigner against racism throughout his career and in the 1930s was drawn to the social promise of communism. Hughes's *Collected Works* have been issued by the University of Missouri Press in sixteen volumes (2001–3). See Arnold Rampersad, *The Life of Langston Hughes* (1986).

HUGHES, Richard Arthur Warren (1900–76) Writer of Welsh descent, born in Surrey and educated at Charterhouse and Oxford. In 1924, Hughes wrote *Danger*, the first original radio play commissioned by the *BBC, and he gained fame with his first novel, *A High Wind in Jamaica* (1929), an unsentimental story of a family of children sent from Jamaica to England and captured by pirates. Another seafaring novel, *In Hazard*, appeared in 1938 but Hughes published very little in the next two decades. In 1961, he broke a long silence with *The Fox in the Attic*, the first volume of a planned historical sequence charting the rise of Nazism. Opening just after the First World War, it mingles real and fictional characters, both German and British, and ends with Hitler's Munich putsch of 1923. A second volume, *The Wooden Shepherdess*, appeared in 1973 but the sequence was incomplete when Hughes died.

HUGHES, Shirley (1927–) OBE, prolific children's author-illustrator, born in West Kirby, Wirral, trained at Liverpool Art School and the Ruskin School of Drawing and Fine Art, Oxford. Initially a book illustrator, her first picture book, *Lucy and Tom's Day* (1961), established Hughes as the chronicler of suburban life for children, notably with her 'Alfie' series. She has twice won the Kate Greenaway Medal, for *Dogger* (1977) and *Ella's Big Chance* (2004), and received the Eleanor Farjeon Award in 1984. She has published a non-fiction work: *A Brush with the Past 1900–1950* (2005), and an autobiography: *A Life in Drawing* (2002).

HUGHES, Ted (1930–98) Poet, born in west Yorkshire, educated at Pembroke College, Cambridge, where he met Sylvia *Plath, whom he married in 1956. As a boy he spent much time on shooting and fishing expeditions with his brother, and his obsession with animals and his sense of the beauty and violence of the natural world appear in his first volume, *The Hawk in the Rain* (1957). This was followed by *Lupercal* (1960), *Wodwo* (1967), several books of children's verse, and *Poetry in the Making* (1967), a perennially popular book of essays, for children, on poetry. *Crow* (1970) is a sequence of poems introducing the central symbol of the crow, partly inspired by a meeting with the American artist Leonard Baskin. Hughes retells the legends of creation and birth through the dark vision of predatory, mocking, indestructible Crow, 'screaming for blood' amidst 'the horror of creation'. Other volumes include *Cave Birds* (1975), *Season Songs* (1976), and *Moortown* (1979), the last of these containing the sequence 'Prometheus on his Crag', written in Iran in 1971, on his expedition with the stage director Peter *Brook, during which he also wrote *Orghast*, a play in an invented language. Hughes also published plays for children and various versions of classical and modern European drama, and edited several anthologies. *Remains of Elmet* (1979), with photographs by Fay Godwin, celebrates the landscapes of his youth in the Calder valley, which he describes as 'the last ditch of Elmet, the last British kingdom to fall to the Angles'; *River* (1983), with photographs by Peter Keen, is a sequence of poems invoking riverside and river life. Together these volumes constitute arresting examples of the renewed vogue for *topographical poetry that arose in the environmentally conscious second half of the 20th century. Hughes's stress on the physical, animal, and subconscious is in marked contrast to the urbane tone of the *Movement, and his poetry, hailed as vital and original, has also been described as excessively violent. He was appointed *poet laureate in 1984. Later volumes include *Wolfwatching* (1989), *Rain-Charm for the Duchy and Other Laureate Poems* (1992), and *Birthday Letters* (1998), a sequence describing his relationship with Plath. The huge *Collected Poems*, edited by Paul Keegan, appeared in 2003. *Shakespeare and the Goddess of Complete Being*, which capped his lifelong involvement with Shakespeare, was published in 1992, and *Winter Pollen*, a collection of critical prose, in 1995. *Tales from Ovid* (1997) offers free verse translations from *Ovid's *Metamorphoses*, and Hughes's extensive work as a translator, which included a sustained devotion to the contemporary poetry of Eastern Europe, was confirmed by the posthumous publication of *Selected Translations*, ed. Daniel Weissbort (2006). See Neil Roberts, *Ted Hughes: A Literary Life* (2006).

HUGHES, Thomas (1822–96) Novelist, educated at Rugby School and Oriel College, Oxford. He was a barrister and Liberal MP, and, under the influence of Frederick Denison *Maurice, devoted much energy to movements for social reform, especially working men's education. He is remembered as the author of the extraordinarily successful novel *Tom Brown's Schooldays* (1857, by 'An Old Boy'), which evokes the Rugby of his youth and his veneration for its headmaster, Dr Thomas *Arnold. Hughes condemned, in the character of the tyrannical *Flashman, the bullying prevalent in public schools of the day, and advocated a form of what came to be known as 'muscular Christianity', which attempted to combine Christian principles with physical courage, self-reliance, love of sport, school loyalty, and patriotism, a mixture that had much impact on the public-school ethos. Its detractors found it philistine, and indeed there are few mentions in the novel of any intellectual pursuits. Nevertheless, its vigour did much to establish the popularity of the *school story as a literary genre. The sequel, *Tom Brown at Oxford* (1861), is less engaging. Hughes wrote several biographies and memoirs and one other novel (*The Scouring of the White Horse*, 1859), and published various sermons and addresses, including *The Manliness of Christ* (1879), which attacks the view that Christianity is a religion for the timid and fearful. There is a life by E. C. Mack and W. H. G. Armytage (1953); see also N. Vance, *The Sinews of the Spirit: The Idea of Christian Manliness in Victorian Literature and Religious Thought* (1985).

HUGO, Victor-Marie (1802–85) Poet, novelist, and dramatist, the leading figure of the Romantic movement in France. Elected to the *Académie Française in 1841, he came late to active political life, being elected to the Assembly in 1848. He spent the years 1851–70 in exile, the greater part of the time in Guernsey. He returned to Paris in 1870 and was again chosen as a deputy, later becoming a senator of the Third Republic. Hugo is one of the masters of French poetry, to which he brought a new freedom of subject, style, and versification. His many collections include *Odes et poésies diverses* (1822), *Odes et ballades* (1826), *Les Orientales* (1829), *Les Feuilles d'automne* (1831: *Autumn Leaves*), *Les Chants du crépuscule* (1835: *Songs of Twilight*), *Les Voix intérieures* (1837: *Inner Voices*), *Les Rayons et les ombres* (1840: *Sunlight and Shadows*), and *Le Rhin* (1842: *The Rhine*). His daughter and her husband were drowned in 1843, and a long silence followed. *Les Châtiments* (*Punishments*), a violent satire against Napoleon III, written in exile, appeared in 1853. Spiritual and cosmic themes come to the fore in *Les Contemplations* (1856). The poems of *La Légende des siècles* (1859, 1877, 1883: *The Legend of the Centuries*) compose an epic and prophetic treatment of history, of which the posthumously published *La Fin de Satan* (1886: *The End of Satan*) and *Dieu* (1891: *God*) were intended to form the final parts. Hugo's determinedly anti-classical and sumptuously historical plays include *Cromwell* (1827), the preface to which became a manifesto of the French Romantic movement; *Hernani* (1830), set in 16th-century Spain, the first two performances of which infamously took place amidst the vociferous manifestations of the partisans and opponents of the new drama; and *Ruy Blas* (1838), set in 17th-century Spain but presenting parallels with the Bourbon monarchies of 1789 and 1830. Hugo's novels were also hugely successful in France and in England, most obviously *Notre Dame de Paris* (1831) and *Les Misérables* (1862), but also *Les Travailleurs de la mer* (1866: *The Toilers of the Sea*), set in Guernsey, and *Quatrevingt-treize* (1874: *Ninety-Three*), set in the counter-revolutionary Vendée. See G. Robb, *Victor Hugo* (1997).

Hugo award For achievement in *science fiction; named after Hugo *Gernsback, and presented at annual World Science Fiction Conventions.

HUIZINGA, Johan (1872–1945) Dutch historian, chiefly known in Britain for four books, *Homo Ludens* (1938; trans. 1949), *Erasmus of Rotterdam* (1924; trans. 1924), *In the Shadow of Tomorrow* (1935; trans. 1936), and *The Waning of the Middle Ages* (1919; trans. 1924). The last of these is the best known, a cultural history that, in opposition to Jacob *Burckhardt's model of a cultural shift, emphasizes the continuity of the medieval tradition.

HULME, T. E. (Thomas Ernest) (1883–1917) Poet, essayist, and (in his own phrase) 'philosophic amateur', born in Endon, Staffordshire; educated at Newcastle-under-Lyme High School and St John's College, Cambridge, and University College London. His reaction against *Romanticism and advocacy of the 'hard dry image' influenced *imagism. His essay 'Romanticism and Classicism' defines Romanticism as 'spilt religion', and predicts a new 'cheerful, dry and sophisticated' poetry; similarly, in the visual arts, he predicted the triumph of precise, abstract geometric form. (His friends included Jacob Epstein and Henri *Gaudier-Brzeska.) His own poems (of which only six were published in his lifetime) largely bear out his thesis; several of the handful that survive are short, provocative treatments of the subject of 'Sunset'. Hulme's contributions to Alfred *Orage's *New Age* included essays on Henri *Bergson, whom he also translated. He was killed in action during the First World War, and much of his work survived only in notebooks. The selection of his work edited by Herbert *Read, *Speculations* (1924), was influential, but Read did not attempt to date the manuscripts, an oversight which obscured Hulme's intellectual development; the *Collected Writings*, edited by K. Csengeri (1994), clarifies the chronology. Hulme's double role as conservative and *modernist had considerable influence on the development of 20th-century taste; T. S. *Eliot described him in 1924 as 'classical, reactionary and revolutionary...the antipodes of the eccentric, tolerant and democratic mind of the end of the century', and Hulme's stress on original sin and man's 'extraordinarily fixed and limited nature' finds echoes in Eliot's own work. See Robert Ferguson, *The Short Sharp Life of T. E. Hulme* (2002).

HUMBOLDT, Alexander von (1769–1859) German explorer and scientist, and brother of Wilhelm (see below). The published results of his expedition to South America and Mexico (translated into English, 1814–21) earned him an enormous celebrity—alluded to by Lord *Byron in **Don Juan*—and by linking natural history to environment his work was a vital source of inspiration to both Charles *Darwin and Alfred Russel Wallace (1823–1913). In anthropology he rejected all notions of racial superiority. His greatest work, *Kosmos* (1845–62), a description of the universe from celestial phenomena to the earth's biogeography, was translated into many languages and has claims to be the most important work of popular science ever published.

HUMBOLDT, Wilhelm von (1767–1835) German writer, philologist, diplomat, and educationalist. He introduced educational reforms in Prussia in the early 19th century, his particular achievement being the founding of the University of Berlin (since 1945 named after him) on liberal and humanistic principles. Students' education was to be based on the study of the classical languages; universities were to be autonomous; and students were to be free to move from one university to another to complete their degrees. Matthew *Arnold wrote approvingly of Humboldt's reform in *Schools and Universities on the Continent* (1868).

HUME, David (1711–76) Philosopher, born and educated in Edinburgh. He spent three years (1734–7) in private study in France, and in 1739 published anonymously his **Treatise of Human Nature*, a sceptical account of the workings of the mind, which sold poorly. His *Essays Moral and Political* (1741–2) was more popular. *A Letter from a Gentleman to his Friend in Edinburgh* (1745) includes Hume's defence of his *Treatise* when he contended unsuccessfully for the moral philosophy chair at Edinburgh, against the opposition of Francis *Hutcheson and William Wishart (*c.*1692–1753). He reworked his *Treatise* as *Philosophical Essays Concerning Human Understanding* (1748), better known under its 1756 title, *Enquiry Concerning Human Understanding*, and *Enquiry Concerning the Principles of Morals* (1751). In 1752 Hume published his *Political Discourses*, which made him famous on the Continent. He was appointed Advocates' librarian in Edinburgh, subsequently surrendering the stipend to the blind poet Thomas *Blacklock. In 1754 appeared the first volume of his *History of Great Britain*, followed by further volumes in 1757, 1759, and 1762; the work became immensely popular in Britain and abroad, earning the praise of Edward *Gibbon and *Voltaire. *Four Dissertations*, dedicated to John *Home, was published in 1757, after suppression of controversial essays on suicide and immortality. From 1763 to 1765 Hume was secretary to the embassy in Paris, where he was well received by literary society. He brought *Rousseau to England, but Rousseau's suspicious nature led to a quarrel, Hume's account of which was published in 1766. James *Boswell visited Hume on his deathbed, hoping that his scepticism would crumble at the approach of death: it did not. After his death, his friend Adam *Smith published his brief autobiography with a eulogy (1777). Hume's religious views were highly contentious in their day, incurring the special wrath of Samuel *Johnson, who praised James *Beattie's weak refutation of Hume's sceptical argument that the evidence for miracles is inferior to the evidence for the 'laws of nature' established by uniform experience. Hume's *Dissertation* on 'The Natural History of Religion' (1757) further undermined orthodoxy by deriving religion from psychological processes; the *Dialogues Concerning Natural Religion* (1779) conclude merely 'that the cause or causes of order in the universe probably bear some remote analogy to human intelligence'. Hume's writings on politics and history show a strong interest in human character and motivation. Though a believer in civil liberties, and an opponent of 'divine right', he rejected the social contract theory of obligation as historically unrealistic; Hume favoured an explanation based on custom and convenience. His closest ally on political and economic matters was Adam *Smith. Hume wrote little directly about literature, despite his own polished literary style, but he was friendly with the poet James *Thomson, and expressed a strong preference for the classicism of John *Milton and Alexander *Pope, against the wildness of *Shakespeare. See Ernest C. Mossner, *The Life of David Hume* (2nd edn, 1980); *The Letters of David Hume*, ed. J. Y. T. Greig (1932); *New Letters of David Hume*, ed. R. Klibansky and E. C. Mossner (1954).

Humorous Lieutenant, The A comedy by John *Fletcher, acted *c.*1617–19. Prince Demetrius is in love with Celia, a captive. His father Antigonus, king of Syria, also falls in love with her and, during his son's absence at the wars, tries to seduce her, but she remains faithful to Demetrius. On Demetrius' return from victory, Antigonus informs him that Celia is dead and, while Demetrius shuts himself up in despair, tries to win her by a love potion. But the plot fails, and finally Celia's virtue and loyalty persuade the king to give her up to his son.

The title is taken from an eccentric lieutenant, suffering from an infirmity which stimulates him to wonderful deeds of courage in war. When cured, his courage fails him; and it comes again when he is deceived into thinking himself sick once more. By accident he drinks the potion intended for Celia, and falls ludicrously in love with the king.

humours Comedy of, a term applied especially to the type of comic drama written by Ben *Jonson, where a 'humour' is the embodiment in one of the characters of some dominating individual passion or propensity. The principal humours, whose balance was thought to determine a man's nature, were blood, phlegm, choler, and melancholy or black choler.

HUMPHREY, duke of Gloucester (1390–1447) Youngest son of Henry IV, distinguished soldier and patron of men of letters including John *Lydgate and John *Capgrave. During the minority of Henry VI, from 1422, Humphrey was appointed protector and acted as regent, 1420–21 and periodically until 1431, in place of his brother, the duke of Bedford, who was frequently abroad in the French wars. Politically he was naively ambitious and quarrelsome. He read Latin and Italian literature, and he promoted Italian humanism in England. He collected books from his youth and gave the first books for a library at Oxford; still named after him is the oldest part of the Bodleian Library, which was built to house his bequest in the 15th century. He married Jacqueline of Bavaria late in 1422 (Lydgate wrote a ballad to celebrate the wedding), but he abandoned her in Burgundy in 1425 in favour of Eleanor Cobham, and the marriage was annulled in 1428. He married Eleanor before 1431; in the 1440s she was repeatedly tried for witchcraft (it seems that she did experiment with black magic), and she was finally imprisoned on the Isle of Man in 1446. Humphrey and Eleanor appear in Shakespeare's history plays.

HUMPHREYS, Emyr (1919–) Welsh novelist and poet, born in Prestatyn and educated at the University College of Wales, Aberystwyth. His 23 novels include *Hear and Forgive* (1952), *A Toy Epic* (1958; a Welsh version, *Y Tri Llais*, appeared the same year), *Outside the House of Baal* (1965), *Unconditional Surrender* (1996), *The Shop* (2005), and a septet, running from *National Winner* (1971) to *Bonds of Attachment* (1991). Humphreys has described his work both as an attempt to 'show the Welsh condition as a microcosm of the human condition', and as an effort to create 'the Protestant novel', an exploration of the responsibility of the individual to transmit good through history. With its complex narrative patterns and its fusion of traditional realism with lyricism, his fiction can be enjoyed without reference to its underlying obsessions. *The Taliesen Tradition* (1983) meditates on the ways literature has influenced Welsh identity over the centuries. *Collected Poems* appeared in 1999.

Humphry Clinker, The Expedition of *Epistolary novel by Tobias *Smollett (1771). It presents, in the words of Walter *Scott, 'the various effects produced upon different members of the same family by the same objects'. Nearly two-thirds of the letters are either from Matthew Bramble to his friend and doctor Lewis, or from Jery Melford (Bramble's nephew) to his Oxford friend Phillips. Others are from Bramble's sister Tabitha to her housekeeper; from Bramble's niece Lydia to her friend Letty; and from the comically semi-literate Winifred Jenkins, Tabitha's servant, to Molly, a maid at the hall. The narrative follows a journey from Wales to London, to Scotland and back again. The letters begin in Gloucester. At Clifton, Lydia meets Wilson, apparently an actor, but Jery prevents him from pursuing her. They travel to Bath, which enchants Lydia, but which Bramble denounces as 'a sink of profligacy and extortion'. On the journey to London, the destitute Humphry is engaged as a postilion; his Methodism outrages Bramble, but his female relations reconcile him to Humphry's simple sincerity. At Harrogate they encounter a reformed Count Fathom (from **Ferdinand Count Fathom*). At Durham they meet the Scot Lismahago, who tells of his exotic history among Native Americans, capturing Tabitha's affections. In Scotland Bramble recovers his health; after Edinburgh, which disgusts them by its filth, they enjoy the cleanliness of Glasgow and an Arcadian interlude by Loch Lomond. On the return journey, their carriage overturns in a river, and Humphry rescues Bramble, whose natural son he is shortly afterwards proved to be. Wilson meanwhile is revealed as the son of Bramble's old friend Dennison. The marriages of Wilson and Lydia, Humphry and Winifred, and Lismahago and Tabitha seal a general improvement in happiness and mutual understanding between the characters, though Jery remains sceptical and unattached.

HUNT, John (1775–1848) The brother of Leigh *Hunt. He was a courageous and enterprising publisher who was prosecuted, threatened with legal actions, and fined many times. In 1805 he founded a short-lived paper, *The News*, then in 1808 he and his brother established the very successful **Examiner*, a general weekly independent paper devoted to liberal and reforming causes, which ran for many years and was frequently threatened with actions for libel. In 1810 he started a quarterly, *The *Reflector* (with Leigh as editor), in which several essays by Charles *Lamb appeared, but it ran for only four numbers. He was prosecuted in 1811 for an article against military flogging and was successfully defended by Henry *Brougham. However, in 1813 he and Leigh were both sentenced to two years' imprisonment in separate jails and fined £500 apiece for a libel on the prince regent. Both men refused a guarantee to abstain from further attacks on the prince. In 1815–17 John published those essays of his brother and of William *Hazlitt which were collected as *The Round Table* (1817). Hazlitt, in dedicating his *Political Essays* of 1819 to John Hunt, described him as 'the tried, steady, zealous and conscientious advocate of the liberty of his country'. He was the publisher and Leigh the editor of the short-lived but brilliant **Liberal*, founded in 1822, in which Lord *Byron published *The *Vision of Judgement*, a work which had been refused by Byron's publisher, John *Murray. John was prosecuted for 'a seditious libel' on the late king, but Byron's executors settled the costs and the fine of £100. In the same year John published in *The Liberal* all the later cantos of **Don Juan* (from Canto VI), which Murray had again refused. The *Literary Examiner*, founded in 1823, was short-lived, and in the same year John's long collaboration with his unbusinesslike brother, who owed him large sums, ended in unhappy litigation.

HUNT, Leigh (1784–1859) Writer, publisher, and editor, born at Southgate, the son of a poor clergyman. Hunt received his schooling as a charity boy at *Christ's Hospital. His first collection of poems, *Juvenilia*, appeared in 1801. In 1808 he founded and edited, with his brother John *Hunt, the radical journal **The Examiner*, the first of many journals he was to initiate. He was to write poetry and drama, but the bulk of his large output was in the form of essays on a wide variety of subjects, many of which were published in his journals. *The *Reflector*, in which he published Charles *Lamb's essays on William *Shakespeare and William *Hogarth, appeared in 1810. In 1813 he and his brother were fined £500 and sentenced to two years' imprisonment for a libel in *The Examiner* on the prince regent. While in jail he was allowed to have his family with him, to continue to write and edit *The Examiner*, and to receive visits from friends, who included Lord *Byron, Thomas *Moore, the *Lambs, Jeremy *Bentham, James *Mill, and Henry *Brougham. In 1816 he printed John *Keats's early sonnet 'O Solitude' in *The Examiner*, and began his vigorous and lifelong support of Keats, P. B. *Shelley, and the *Romantic poets; his name was linked with that of Keats and *Hazlitt in attacks on the so-called *Cockney School. He published his influential poem *The *Story of Rimini*, dedicated to Byron, in the same year. His verses appeared in *Foliage* (1818) and in 1819 he published his poems *Hero and Leander* and *Bacchus and Ariadne*. In the **Indicator* in 1821 he published Keats's *'La Belle Dame sans Merci'. In *The *Liberal*, founded jointly with Byron, there appeared in 1822 *The *Vision of Judgement*, and in the three subsequent numbers works by Byron, Shelley, Hazlitt, Hunt, *Hogg, and others. His critical account of the co-founder of *The Liberal* in *Lord Byron and Some of his Contemporaries* (1828) was generally seen as ignoble and was mercilessly satirized by Moore's 'The Living Dog and the Dead Lion'. *The Companion*, a magazine which contains some of Hunt's best work, appeared in 1828, his *Tatler* in 1830–32, and his *London Journal* in 1834–5. *Captain Sword and Captain Pen* (1835) is an effective threnody on the horrors of war. 'Abou Ben Adhem' (probably, with 'Jenny kissed me', Hunt's best-known poem) was published in an anthology, the *Book of Gems* (1838). Hunt's play *A Legend of Florence* (1840), a semi-Elizabethan tragedy, was produced at Covent Garden and was well received: he wrote several others without success. In the same year he published an edition of Restoration dramatists. In 1844 appeared his *Poetical Works* and *Imagination and Fancy*, in which he usefully compares painting and poetry; in 1846 an anthology, *Wit and Humour*, and *Stories from Italian Poets*; in 1847 (the year in which he received a Civil List pension) appeared *Men, Women, and Books*; in 1848 *A Jar of Honey from Mount Hybla* and *The Town*, an evocation of London; in 1850 a lively *Autobiography*, much admired by Thomas *Carlyle and others; in 1851 *Table Talk*; in 1853 *The Religion of the Heart*; in 1855 *The Old Court Suburb*, essays on Kensington, and a bowdlerized edition of *Beaumont and *Fletcher. Hunt's essays, although much influenced by the essayists of the previous century, were not moral in principal intent. His aim was to convey appreciation and enjoyment ('to reap pleasure from every object in creation'), and his pleasure in literature, drama, music, and friendship is agreeably infectious.

Hunt was a brave and outspoken radical during the Regency, and a poet whose contemporary importance has recently been positively reassessed. His gift for detecting talent, from Keats to *Tennyson, and his determined support for it, made him an invaluable editor. His sunny, optimistic nature is sketched in the early character of Skimpole in **Bleak House*; *Dickens denied the later knavery of Skimpole had anything to do with Hunt. See *The Selected Writings of Leigh Hunt*, 6 vols, ed. R. Morrison and M. Eberle-Sinatra (2003); A. Holden, *The Wit in the Dungeon: The Life Of Leigh Hunt* (2005); N. Roe, *Fiery Heart: The First Life of Leigh Hunt* (2005).

HUNT, Thornton Leigh (1810–73) Journalist and editor, born in London, the eldest son of Leigh *Hunt. He was, with George Henry *Lewes, joint founder of *The *Leader*, and in 1855 joined the staff of the new **Daily Telegraph*, of which he became the virtual editor. His prolonged relationship with Lewes's wife Agnes, who bore him four children, was the indirect cause of the unorthodoxy of the union of Lewes with George *Eliot.

HUNT, Violet (1866–1942) Novelist and literary hostess, born in Durham city and educated at Notting Hill and Ealing High School and then Kensington Art School. She was for some years the companion of Ford Madox *Ford. A flamboyant feminist, a supporter of women's suffrage, and a friend of H. G. *Wells, Henry *James, Rebecca *West, Ezra *Pound, Joseph *Conrad, Wyndham *Lewis, D. H. *Lawrence, and many others in the literary world, she published seventeen novels (including *The Maiden's Progress* (1894), *A Hard Woman* (1895), *The Human Interest* (1899), and *White Rose of Weary Leaf* (1908), often regarded as her best), short stories, an autobiography, *The Flurried Years* (1926), and a biography of Elizabeth *Siddal. See Joan Hardwick, *An Immodest Violet* (1990).

HUNT, William Holman (1827–1910) Painter and founder member of the *Pre-Raphaelite Brotherhood. Many of his most famous paintings, such as *The Scapegoat* (1854) and *The Light of the World* (1851–3), have strong religious themes, though he also painted literary and historical subjects from William *Shakespeare, Alfred *Tennyson, John *Keats, and Edward *Bulwer-Lytton. His autobiographical *Pre-Raphaelitism and the Pre-Raphaelite Brotherhood* (1905) provided a full but biased history of the movement. See Judith Bronkhust, *William Holman Hunt* (2006).

HUNTER, Evan (1926–2005) American writer, born Salvatore Albert Lombino in New York, who began writing under the pen-name of Evan Hunter and then adopted that name. Among his many novels, *The Blackboard Jungle* (1954) achieved fame for its depiction of high school life. Hunter also wrote a number of screenplays (including Alfred *Hitchcock's *The Birds*) but is also remembered for the crime fiction he published under the name of Ed McBain, especially his 87th Precinct series, set in New York, which began in 1956. Hunter's other pen-names included Curt Cannon and Richard Marsten.

HUNTER, Sir William Wilson (1840–1900) Historian and novelist, born in Glasgow, educated there and in Paris and Bonn. He entered the Indian Civil Service in 1862. He was a man of broad cultural interests and was author of several notable works on Indian historical subjects, including *Annals of Rural Bengal* (1868), *Orissa* (1872), *The Imperial Gazetteer of India* (1881), the novel *The Old Missionary* (1895), which documents life in India in the early 19th century, and *The Thackerays in India* (1897). He had completed only two volumes of his *History of British India* (1899–1900) at his death.

HUNTINGDON, Selina Hastings, countess of (1707–91) Founder of the group of Calvinistic Methodists known as 'Lady Huntingdon's Connexion' and of Trevecca College in Breconshire (later Cheshunt College). A warm supporter of George *Whitefield, she quarrelled with John *Wesley over doctrine. She was frequently satirized, for example in Francis *Coventry's *Pompey the Little* and Richard *Graves's *Spiritual Quixote*.

Huon of Bordeaux The hero of a French 13th-century **chanson de geste*. He has the misfortune to kill Charlot, son of *Charlemagne, in an affray, not knowing who his assailant is. He is thereupon condemned to death by the emperor, but reprieved on condition that he will go to the court of Gaudisse, amir of Babylon, bring back a handful of his hair and four of his teeth, kill his doughtiest knight, and kiss Esclarmonde his daughter. By the help of the fairy Oberon, Huon achieves the adventure. The work was translated by Lord *Berners and printed in about 1515. Huon's adventure is the theme of *Weber's opera *Oberon*.

HURD, Richard (1720–1808) Clergyman and scholar, son of a Staffordshire farmer, educated at Emmanuel College, Cambridge, and bishop successively of Lichfield and Worcester. He produced an edition of *Horace's *Ars Poetica* (1749) and *Epistola ad Augustum* (1751), adding to the second his 'Discourse Concerning Poetical Imitation'. His *Moral and Political Dialogues* appeared in 1759, with dialogues between, for example, Abraham *Cowley (whose *Works* he edited in 1772) and Thomas *Sprat. Hurd's *Letters on Chivalry and Romance* (1762) was an important reassessment of Elizabethan literature: Hurd was sympathetic to *Spenser, arguing that the 'Gothic' was more poetic than the 'Grecian', and that *neo-classical rules were inappropriately applied to romances, which were composed on different but equally artistic principles. His view that 'what we have lost is a world of fine fabling' was echoed and developed by Thomas *Warton. Hurd was a friend and correspondent of William *Warburton, William *Mason, and Thomas *Gray.

HURDIS, James (1763–1801) Clergyman and poet. He published *The Village Curate: A Poem* (1788), in the style of William *Cowper, later his friend, and *The Favourite Village* (1800), an account of the Sussex landscapes of his childhood. He also edited Michael *Drayton's *English Heroic Epistles* (1788). Hurdis was professor of poetry at Oxford in 1793.

HURSTON, Zora Neale (1891–1960) African American novelist, folklorist, journalist, and critic, born in Eatonville, Florida, the first incorporated all-black town in America. She worked her way through university, where she studied cultural anthropology. She was a prolific writer during the 1920s and 1930s, prominent in the *Harlem Renaissance: her works include *Mules and Men* (1935), a study of black American folklore in the South; the novel for which she is best known, *Their Eyes Were Watching God* (1937); plays, short stories, and *Dust Tracks on a Road* (1942), an autobiography. Writers such as Alice *Walker and Toni *Morrison acknowledge their debt to her. See Robert E. Hemenway, *Zora Neale Hurston: A Literary Biography* (1977).

Husband's Message, The An Old English poem of 53 lines in the **Exeter Book*, one of the group usually called 'elegies'. Its ostensible form is a message to a woman from her husband who has had to leave his own country because of a feud, telling her of his prosperity in another land and asking her to join him. The text of the poem is the inscription itself which bears the message, and it is sometimes thought to be the continuation of the riddle (no. 60, the Reed) which it follows in the Exeter Book. It has also, not too implausibly, been interpreted in a religious sense, perhaps as an address from Christ to the church. Ed. and trans. R. Hamer, in *A Choice of Anglo-Saxon Verse* (1970); ed. R. F. Leslie in *Three Old English Elegies* (1961).

HUSTON, Nancy (1953–) Canadian novelist and essayist who moved to Paris in 1973, studying for a Ph.D. under the supervision of Roland *Barthes. Although born in anglophone Canada, Huston writes in French and translates her own work into English. Her first novel, *Les Variations Goldberg*, was published in 1981. As a writer positioning herself between two languages, and exploring the resulting impact on identity and subjectivity, she has clear affinities with Samuel *Beckett, evoked in *Limbes/Limbo: hommage à Samuel Beckett* (2000, bilingual edition).

HUTCHESON, Francis (1694–1746) Irish Presbyterian clergyman and philosopher, born in Co. Down and educated at Glasgow University. Shortly after taking up a clerical appointment in Armagh in 1719 he opened a Dissenting academy in Dublin. While there he wrote a series of aesthetic, moral, and political essays for the Dublin and London press, in addition to two books, *An Inquiry into the Original of our Ideas of Beauty and Virtue* (1725) and *An Essay on the Nature and Conduct of the Passions and Affections with Illustrations on the Moral Sense* (1728), both subsequently revised. He was made professor of moral philosophy at Glasgow in 1729, a position he retained until his death. His *System of Moral Philosophy* was published in 1755 with a biography by William Leechman. A protégé of Robert Molesworth, Hutcheson introduced the civic humanist tradition into higher education: he trained a generation of students, among them Adam *Smith, in the Whig philosophy of personal liberty and government restraint, and his progressive views on social justice, representative government, colonial autonomy, and the rejection of slavery were influential among Scots émigrés to America. In ethics he developed the ideas of the third earl of *Shaftesbury on the moral sense into a fully-fledged system. He saw a close relation between aesthetic and moral perception, by which we come to be aware of providentially designed order. We have a 'moral sense of beauty in actions and affections' which is stimulated by contemplating benevolence directed at another person. Virtue is identical with benevolence insofar as it gives disinterested pleasure, that action being best which aims at the greatest happiness of the greatest number. This view anticipates *Utilitarianism. Hutcheson was instrumental in helping to establish the publishing and printing business of the *Foulis brothers.

HUTCHINSON, Lucy (1620–after 1675) Poet and biographer, daughter of the administrator Sir Allen Apsley (1566/7–1630), and wife of John Hutchinson (1615–64). She was the author of *Memoirs of the Life of Colonel Hutchinson*, which she wrote after his death to preserve his memory for her children; it is a classic account of the state of the country at the outbreak of civil war and of the conflict in the vicinity of Nottingham, told from the point of view of the radical Puritan high gentry. John Hutchinson held Nottingham for Parliament as governor, signed the king's death warrant, was imprisoned at the Restoration, and saved from execution partly through his wife's intervention. Her narrative was first published in 1806 (ed. J. Hutchinson), with a brief 'Fragment' of her own life, in which she records with satisfaction that she 'out-stripped' her brothers in intellectual achievement. Her mastery of the grand sweep as well as the fine nuance of history is at odds with her grief-stricken disavowal of autonomy as her husband's mere 'mirror' and 'shadow'. She also translated Lucretius' *De Rerum Natura*, and wrote a biblical poem entitled *Order and disorder, or, The world made and undone, being meditations upon the creation and fall, as it is recorded in the beginning of Genesis*, of which the first five cantos appeared anonymously in 1679; see *Order and Disorder*, ed. D. Norbrook (2001), which makes the complete text available. See also *Memoirs of the Life of Colonel Hutchinson*, ed. N. H. Keeble (1995).

HUTCHINSON, R. C. (Ray Coryton) (1907–75) Novelist, educated at Oriel College, Oxford; he worked for some years in the advertising department of Colman's at Norwich before becoming a full-time writer. His works include *The Unforgotten Prisoner* (1933), a powerful portrayal of revenge and conciliation in the aftermath of the First World War, seen partly through the sufferings of young Klaus, half English and half German, a victim of the conflicts of his parents and of his country; *Testament* (1938), set in Russia at the time of the revolution; *The Stepmother* (1955); and *Rising* (1976), a *historical novel set in South America.

Hutchinsonians (1) The followers of **Mrs Anne Hutchinson** (1591–1643), who emigrated from England to Massachusetts, where she founded an antinomian sect (rejecting the rule of moral law), was banished from the colony, and was eventually massacred by Native Americans at Hell Gate, New York county, with all but one of her family. (2) The followers of **John Hutchinson** (1674–1737), whose chief work, *Moses's Principia* (1724), maintained that Hebrew was the primitive language of mankind and the key to all knowledge. It was written as an attack on Isaac *Newton's *Principia*, and is thought to have influenced Christopher *Smart.

HUTTEN, Ulrich von *See* EPISTOLAE OBSCURORUM VIRORUM.

HUTTON, Richard Holt (1826–97) Editor, critic, and theologian, educated at University College London, prepared for the *Unitarian ministry at Manchester New College. He became joint editor with his friend Walter *Bagehot of the *National Review* (1855–64). From 1861 until his death he was joint editor of *The *Spectator*, and under his control the journal wielded great influence. His works, most of which show his theological inclinations, include *Essays, Theological and Literary* (1871), a volume on John Henry *Newman (1891), *Criticisms on Contemporary Thought* (1894), and *Aspects of Religious and Scientific Thought* (1899). See M. Woodfield, *R. H. Hutton, Critic and Theologian* (1986).

HUXLEY, Aldous Leonard (1894–1963) Born in Godalming; grandson of T. H. *Huxley and brother of Julian Huxley. His mother died when he was 14, and when he was 16 at Eton College he developed serious eye trouble which prevented any possibility of a scientific career. He recovered sufficiently to read English at Balliol College, Oxford. During the war he met Lady Ottoline *Morrell: she and other literary figures were to appear, not always to their own satisfaction, in his early satirical novels. By 1919 he had already published three volumes of verse; a volume of stories, *Limbo* (1920), was followed by *Crome Yellow* (1921), a country-house satire which earned him a reputation for brilliance and cynicism, and much offended Lady Ottoline. During the 1920s and 1930s Huxley and his wife Maria lived in Italy, then France; during this period he wrote much fiction, including *Mortal Coils* (1922, stories; includes 'The Gioconda Smile'); *Antic Hay* (1923, set mostly in post-war London's nihilistic bohemia); *Those Barren Leaves* (1925, set in Italy); and *Point Counter Point* (1928), in which was a portrait of his friend D. H. *Lawrence. *Brave New World* (1932), his most enduringly popular work, attacked the utopian scientifically managed futures of H. G. *Wells and satirized mass culture. It was followed by *Eyeless in Gaza* (1936). Huxley's literary reputation deteriorated when he left in 1937 for California, partly for the sake of his eyes, partly to promote (in company with Gerald *Heard) his new belief in absolute pacifism. He continued to write in many genres: novels include *After Many a Summer* (1939), *Ape and Essence* (1948), another, darker, *dystopia, and *Island* (1962), an optimistic utopia. Other works include essays, historical studies, travel works, and *The Devils of Loudon* (1952), a study in sexual hysteria. He became deeply interested in mysticism and parapsychology; *The Doors of Perception* (1954) and *Heaven and Hell* (1956) describe his experiments with mescalin and LSD. *Brave New World Revisited* (1958) examines the original novel in the light of the evolution of the post-war world towards or away from his earlier prophecies.

Although *Brave New World* has an assured place as a classic, Huxley's other novels have proved difficult to 'place' as literature. Their mixture of satire and earnestness, of apparent brutality and humanity, have led some to dismiss them as smart and superficial, a symptom rather than an interpretation of a hollow age; others have seen them as brilliant and provocative 'novels of ideas' written by a man who was not by nature a novelist. See David Bradshaw, *The Hidden Huxley* (1994); N. Murray, *Aldous Huxley: An English Intellectual* (2003).

HUXLEY, T. H. (Thomas Henry) (1825–95) Scientist. He studied at Charing Cross Hospital and was assistant surgeon on HMS *Rattlesnake*, 1846–50. His surveys of marine life on the Australian Barrier Reef appeared as papers for the *Royal and Linnean Societies (*see* Linnaeus, Carl von), he was elected FRS in 1851, and in 1854 became professor of natural history at the Royal School of Mines. He wrote extensively on specialist subjects, but was also widely known and admired as a lecturer to lay audiences, often of working men; he aimed to avoid 'technical dialect' and had a gift for explaining complicated scientific points in language that was generally intelligible. His views on religion, education, philosophy, and evolution, and on man's newly conceived place in the universe (e.g. in *Evidence as to Man's Place in Nature*, 1863, *Evolution and Ethics*, 1893, and other essays), had a profound impact on 19th-century thought. He was a friend of Charles *Darwin, and an influential though discriminating supporter of his theories, once describing himself as 'Darwin's Bulldog'. He coined the word 'agnostic' to describe his own philosophical position, which he expounded at the *Metaphysical Society and in the **Nineteenth Century*. A vigorous though courteous disputant, he engaged in controversy with Richard *Owen, William *Gladstone, and other critics of evolutionary theory. His *Collected Essays* were published in 1893–4, his *Scientific Memoirs* in 1898–1903, and his *Life and Letters*, edited by his son Leonard, in 1900–03. See S. L. Lyons, *Thomas Henry Huxley: The Evolution of a Scientist* (1999).

HUYSMANS, Joris-Karl (1848–1907) French novelist. After a number of early novels in a naturalistic vein (e.g. *Marthe: histoire d'une fille*, 1876: *Marthe: The Story of a Whore*; *En ménage*, 1881: *Home Life*), he adopted another mode in *À rebours* (1884: *Against the Grain*, 1922, trans. J. Howard; *Against Nature*, 1959, trans. R. Baldick), the work for which he is now chiefly remembered. Introducing the neuraesthenic aristocrat Des Esseintes, who turns his back on the world as he finds it to create a world of sensuousness and artifice within which to cultivate extremes of self-awareness, *À rebours* has been regarded as a manual of the extravagant *aestheticism of the *fin-de-siècle*. It was much admired by Oscar *Wilde, who introduces it into *The Picture of Dorian Gray* as the 'yellow book' given to Dorian by Lord Henry Wotton. Huysmans's later work includes four novels which follow the spiritual progress of the central character Durtal towards Roman Catholicism: *Là-bas* (1891: *Down There*), *En route* (1895), *La Cathédrale* (1898: *The Cathedral*), and *L'Oblat* (1903: *The Oblate*).

HYDE, Douglas (1860–1949) Irish writer, language activist, and cultural nationalist, whose 1892 lecture on 'The Necessity of De-Anglicizing Ireland' provided an ideological blueprint for the *Irish Revival. Born near Castlerea, Co. Roscommon, and educated at Trinity College, Dublin, Hyde became the first professor of Modern Irish at University College, Dublin, in 1909 and the first president of Ireland in 1938. He published verse in Irish in the 1880s under the pen-name *An Craoibhín Aoibhinn* ('Delightful little branch'). He founded the Gaelic League in 1893 and was its president until 1915 when he resigned in disapproval of its increasing politicization. His English translations in *Love Songs of Connacht* (1893) powerfully influenced the idioms of the Revival. In 1901 Hyde's *Casadh an tSúgáin* ('The Twisting of the Rope') became the first professionally produced play in Irish.

HYDE, Edward *See* Clarendon, Edward Hyde.

Hyde Park A comedy by James *Shirley, acted 1632, printed 1637. This comedy seems to have been written for the annual opening of the park, and it exploits the topical appeal of its subject. The fourth act features horse racing; when *Pepys saw a revival of the play after the Restoration, horses were actually led across the stage. Apart from the local colour, there is a plot about the return of a long-lost husband in disguise; another plot, sometimes seen as a foreshadowing of *Restoration comedy, is the courtship of the witty Carol and her equally witty suitor Fairfield, culminating in what is probably the earliest example of a 'proviso scene' (i.e. a scene of premarital negotiation) such as Congreve was to develop more fully in *The *Way of the World*.

Hydriotaphia (*Urn Burial*) By Sir Thomas *Browne, published with *The *Garden of Cyrus*, 1658. A sceptical meditation on human pomp in magnificent baroque prose, inspired by some burial urns excavated in Norfolk. It has been admired by many writers, including James *Joyce, Virginia *Woolf, and Jorge Luis *Borges.

Hymenaei A marriage masque by Ben *Jonson, performed at Whitehall on Twelfth Night 1606, and printed in that year, with the theme of union. The marriage was that of the earl of Essex and Lady Frances Howard, the murderer of Sir Thomas *Overbury. It ended in scandal and divorce.

hymns The Greek *hymnos* means a 'song of praise', honouring gods or heroes, and it is used in this sense by English poets such as P. B. *Shelley ('Hymn to Intellectual Beauty'). In the Christian tradition, hymns are songs of worship, sung by congregation and choir. They are often based on the Bible but, unlike canticles such as the 'Magnificat' or 'Nunc Dimittis', they are not settings of biblical texts. Hymn singing was revived in 16th-century Germany by the Lutherans, and some of the earliest English hymns were written for Dissenting churches: Isaac *Watts, an Independent minister, published *Hymns and Spiritual Songs* in 1707. Hymns were also increasingly popular among evangelicals, as with Charles *Wesley's *Hymns and Sacred Poems* (1739), and *Olney Hymns* (1779), a collaboration between William *Cowper and John *Newton. Typically, these hymns resemble *ballads in their four-line verses and simple metres. Before 1820, only the singing of *psalms was permitted in the Church of England. After this date, there was a great revival of Anglican hymnody, leading to **Hymns Ancient and Modern* (1860), edited by Sir Henry Baker (1821–77), which included new compositions (by Cecil Frances *Alexander and John Henry *Newman) and translations from Latin hymns. In the *Yattendon Hymnal* (1899), edited by Robert *Bridges, and *The English Hymnal* (1906), edited by Sir Percy Dearmer (1867–1936) and *Vaughan Williams, folk melodies were frequently employed, as hymn singing was connected to ideas of Englishness.

Hymns Ancient and Modern A major collection of hymns for the Church of England, first published in 1860, ed. (Sir) Henry Baker (1821–77). William Henry Monk (1823–89) joined him for the full music edition—with tunes for each hymn—in 1861. The original inflection, revealing the influence of the Anglo-Catholic historian and translator John Mason *Neale, was *Tractarian. With the revised 1875 edition, the text's appeal was broadened and it became essential to Anglican hymnody, though its Tractarian roots were always discernible. Subsequent editions have included *Hymns Ancient and Modern New Standard* (1983). Among many hymns established in the repertoire through the Victorian editions were Neale's 'Blessed city, heavenly Salem' ('Christ is made the sure foundation') and 'O come, O come Emmanuel' and Baker's 'O praise ye the Lord!' For generations of Anglican writers, texts from *Hymns Ancient and Modern* were a significant literary resource.

hypallage [from a Greek word meaning 'exchange'] A transference of epithet, as 'Sansfoy's dead dowry' for 'dead Sansfoy's dowry' (*Spenser).

hyperbole Exaggeration for rhetorical emphasis, as in the colloquial 'it took me ages to get here'. Found in various literary uses, hyperbolic expression is especially characteristic of inflated or bombastic styles of dramatic speech, as often in the plays of *Marlowe and *Shakespeare, for example 'His legs bestrid the ocean' (*Antony and Cleopatra*).

Hyperion:** A Fragment* and ***The Fall of Hyperion Fragments of epic poems by John Keats written 1818–19. *Hyperion* was published 1820, *The Fall of Hyperion* not until 1850. In 1818 Keats gave up the effort to finish *Hyperion*, then began to recast it as *The Fall of Hyperion*, but again the effort was abandoned.

In the first version, written as direct narrative, the tremendous figure of the fallen *Saturn, conquered by Jove, mourns the loss of his kingdom and debates with his fallen fellow Titans, in their craggy lair, how he may regain his kingdom. They conclude that only the magnificent Hyperion, who is still unfallen, will be able to help them. In Book III the golden Apollo, god of music, poetry, and knowledge, speaks to the goddess Mnemosyne of his inexplicable anguish; then, at the moment of his deification, the fragment ends. In the second version, the poet is in a luxuriant garden, where he drinks an elixir, which induces a vision. He finds himself in a vast domed monument, then proceeds with pain and difficulty to climb the stair to the shrine of the priestess Moneta. Together they find the agonized fallen Saturn, and with Mnemosyne and Thea they speak to him of his pain and loss. In despair he leaves with Thea to comfort his fellow Titans, while the poet and Moneta watch the magnificent, but much troubled, Hyperion blaze into the west. The precise meaning of the allegory is not always clear, but both poems have as their general theme the nature of poetry and the nature and development of the poet. It is not known why Keats abandoned what was to have been his great work, but one of his fears, expressed in a letter to his friend John Hamilton *Reynolds, was that his writing was too Miltonic.

hypertext An interlinked group or network of texts, usually digital texts written and read on computers and connected through the activation of keywords that lead the reader from one block of text (lexia) to another, either on the World Wide Web (from 1990) or on a CD-ROM disk. The term was coined by Theodor H. Nelson in 1965, with reference to the possibility of linking computerized texts and (as 'hypermedia') sounds and moving images too. It came also to be applied to the general realm of such textual connections, including, retrospectively, those of print culture too, both intratextual (indexes, contents tables, cross-references) and intertextual (citations, bibliographies, catalogues). Paperback 'gamebooks' for young readers, such as the *Fighting Fantasy* series, flourished in the 1980s: these were essentially hypertext stories in print. In 1987 Apple Computer released HyperCard, a hypertext reading and authoring programme included with every Apple Macintosh computer sold. The world community of hypertext readers and authors expanded rapidly, expanding still further with the growing use of the Web in the 1990s. The hypertext structure enabled by the standard HTML (hypertext mark-up language) feature of Web linkage came to be exploited by some American writers in the 1990s, especially at Brown University, Rhode Island, bringing into being a distinctive body of electronic literature known as hypertext fiction or hyperfiction, in which the reader assembles the elements of the story by navigating among variously linked lexia. Among the best-known such works are Michael Joyce's (1945–) *Afternoon: A Story* (1990), Stuart Moulthrop's (1957–) *Victory Garden* (1992), Shelley Jackson's (1963–) *Patchwork Girl* (1995), and Mark Amerika's (1960–) *Grammatron* (1997). The first three of these were published on CD-ROM by Eastgate Systems in its Storyspace software; the last on the Web as an openly accessible work. A common feature of these works is their self-conscious *metafictional play with the hypertext principle of connection itself, the new form becoming a thematic concern of the story. At the same time some academic literary theorists, notably George P. Landow in his book *Hypertext* (1992), along with established novelists such as Robert *Coover in his 1992 article 'The End of Books', saw the advent of hypertext in post-*structuralist terms as a liberation of readers from old cultural hierarchies and 'linear' determinism into unbounded participatory *intertextuality. Discussion of hypertext by theorists and creative writers alike in the 1990s often displayed a utopian tendency to greet the multi-linearity and potential interactivity (*see* INTERACTIVE FICTION) of hypertext as the dawn of a more democratic literary millennium, despite an evidently persistent demand from most readers for immersion in continuous narratives produced by skilled storytellers. At the turn of the 21st century, increasingly sophisticated hypermedia programmes and computer games tended to eclipse this nascent literary tradition in favour of predominantly visual narratives. An evolution from written lexia to the use of visual elements is evident in, for example, *Grammatron* and in Talan Memmot's (1964–) innovative and characteristically metafictional *Lexia to Perplexia* (2000). See George P. Landow, *Hypertext 3.0* (2006), and the online periodical *Electronic Literature Collection* inaugurated in 2006 (http://collection.eliterature.org).

Hypnerotomachia Poliphili: *The Strife of Love in a Dream* Italian romance attributed to Francesco Colonna (1433–1527). The work is written in a hybrid language, and is highly allegorical and densely packed with references to classical and Middle Eastern archaeology, mythology, magic, and folklore. The linguistic difficulties and cultural demands it poses make it virtually unreadable and its interpretation remains problematic. It was the first vernacular book printed by *Aldus Manutius (1499) and contains a notable series of woodcut illustrations to the text. See *The Strife of Love in a Dream*, trans. J. Godwin (1999).

hypotaxis [from Greek, 'subjection'] The frequent use of relative and dependent clauses (subordination), as in 'When I came, then I saw, and, having seen, I conquered'. The adjectival form is 'hypotactic'.
See also PARATAXIS.

I

iamb, iambic pentameter *See* METRE.

IBSEN, Henrik (1828–1906) Norwegian poet and dramatist, generally acknowledged as the founder of modern naturalistic drama. His first successes, *Brand* (1866) and *Peer Gynt* (1867), were 'dramatic poems', and established his reputation in Scandinavia, but it was over twenty years before the work of Edmund *Gosse and William *Archer (and later the support of Thomas *Hardy, William *James, G. B. *Shaw, and others) won him recognition as a major dramatist in England. In 1872 Gosse wrote a review of *Poems* of the unknown Ibsen and zealously promoted his work. In the same year Archer read Ibsen's *Emperor and Galilean*, and his translation of *The Pillars of Society* was used for the first performance of Ibsen in England in 1880 (a single matinée), which was largely ignored. By the end of the 1880s Archer's translations were bringing Ibsen to the attention of the reading public, and in 1889 a long review of Ibsen's work by Gosse in the **Fortnightly Review* was followed by a highly successful production of Archer's translation of *A Doll's House* (1889), a play which attacked the oppression of women in marriage. In 1890 Shaw delivered a lecture to the Fabian Society (published in 1891 as *The Quintessence of Ibsen*) which championed Ibsen as a fearless moral pioneer. In 1891 a single performance of *Ghosts* (1881) and a commercial production of *Hedda Gabler* (1890) provoked public outrage; in 1893 a production of *The Master Builder* was condemned by critics but supported by the public. In the course of the next ten years Ibsen became established in England as a major dramatist and an important influence, both through Archer's translations of Ibsen's prose dramas and through productions of many of the plays. In 1900 the *Fortnightly Review* contained an enthusiastic review of *When We Dead Awaken* (1899) by the 18-year-old James *Joyce, who became a lifelong admirer.

Ibsen's earlier plays (such as *Ghosts* and *An Enemy of the People*, 1882) were concerned largely with social and political themes, but the last six (*The Wild Duck*, 1885; *Rosmersholm*, 1886; *The Lady from the Sea*, 1888; *The Master Builder*, 1892; *Little Eyolf*, 1894; and *John Gabriel Borkman*, 1896) are more deeply concerned with the forces of the unconscious, and were greatly admired by *Freud. At the end of his life Ibsen commented that he was 'more of a poet and less of a social philosopher than people...suppose', and also declared that his interest was not so much in women's rights as in human rights. Ibsen created new attitudes to drama, and is credited with being the first major dramatist to write tragedy about ordinary people in prose. The quality of his dialogue, and his discarding of traditional theatrical effects, demanded a new style of performance. All his great prose dramas are now in the standard English-language repertoire, and *Peer Gynt* is also frequently revived; there have been many translations since Archer's, including versions by Una Ellis-Fermor, Michael Meyer, Robert Farquharson Sharp, James Walter McFarlane, and Peter Watts, and stage adaptations include those by Arthur *Miller, John *Osborne, Christopher *Fry, Ann *Jellicoe, Geoffrey *Hill, and Christopher *Hampton. There are biographies by M. Meyer (3 vols, 1967–71) and R. Ferguson (1996).

Ida, Princess The heroine of Alfred Tennyson's *The Princess*, which is the basis of the *Gilbert and Sullivan operetta *Princess Ida*.

Idea A sonnet sequence by Michael *Drayton, first published as *Idea's Mirror* in 1594, then much revised and expanded. It includes the famous Sonnet 61, 'since there's no help, come, let us kiss and part'.

***Idea:** The Shepherd's Garland* *See* DRAYTON, MICHAEL.

Idea of a University, The *See* NEWMAN, JOHN HENRY.

'Idiot Boy, The' A poem by *Wordsworth, first published in **Lyrical Ballads* (1798). One of the most characteristic and controversial of the poet's early works, it takes as hero the idiot son of a poor countrywoman, Betty Foy, who is sent off on horseback by night to fetch the doctor for a sick neighbour. He is so long gone that his mother sets out to seek him, and finds him at last by a waterfall, whither the pony has wandered freely through the moonlight, to the boy's delight. The neighbour recovers and sets out to meet mother and son, and all three are happily reunited; the boy's description of his adventures, 'The cocks did crow to-whoo, to-whoo, And the sun did shine so cold', fittingly illustrate Wordsworth's intention of 'giving the charm of novelty to things of everyday'. Wordsworth ably defended his choice of subject matter (which offended many) in a letter to John *Wilson, June 1802, attacking the 'false delicacy' of his detractors, and praising the natural humanity of the poor: 'I have indeed, often looked upon the conduct of fathers and mothers of the lower classes of society towards idiots as the great triumph of the human heart.'

Idler, The A series of just over 104 papers, mostly by Samuel *Johnson, published in the *Universal Chronicle, or Weekly Gazette*, 15 April 1758 to 5 April 1760. These papers are more lightweight and relaxed than those of the **Rambler.* They include the well-known sketches of Dick Minim, the critic, of Mr Sober (Johnson himself), and Jack Whirler (John *Newbery the publisher). Twelve were by other writers, including three by Joshua *Reynolds and three by Thomas *Warton the younger. The title was later adopted for a monthly journal edited by Jerome K. *Jerome and Robert Barr, 1892–1911.

idylls *See* ECLOGUE.

Idylls of the King A series of twelve Arthurian poems by Alfred *Tennyson, written mostly between 1855 and 1874, although the poet continued to revise it for the rest of his life. *'Morte d'Arthur', composed in 1833 after A. H. *Hallam's death, was incorporated into 'The Passing of Arthur'. The project occupied Tennyson over many years, during which he studied *Malory, *The *Mabinogion*, *Laȝamon, and other sources of Arthurian legend. In 1855–6 he began writing the first Idyll, to become *'Merlin and Vivien', which he followed with 'Enid', later divided into 'The Marriage of Geraint' and *'Geraint and Enid'. The first four were published in 1859 as 'Enid', 'Vivien', 'Elaine', and *'Guinevere' and constituted, with many revisions, approximately half the final version. They were extremely successful, selling 10,000 copies in six weeks. In 1869 followed 'The Coming of Arthur', 'The *Holy Grail', *'Pelleas and Ettarre', and 'The Passing of Arthur'. 'The Last Tournament' was published in the **Contemporary Review* in 1871, then, with *'Gareth and Lynette', in 1872. *'Balin and Balan', written 1872–4, did not appear until 1885. The sequence as now printed first appeared in 1891.

The *Idylls* present the story of *Arthur, from his first meeting with Guinevere to the ruin of the realm in the 'last, dim, weird battle of the west'. The focus of most of the poems, however, is on other characters' stories, each offering a picture of the realm. The adultery of Guinevere and Lancelot may be a force that destroys the bright hopes of Camelot and the idealism of the Round Table, but both Victorian and subsequent critics have pointed out that the poem (almost despite itself) cannot sustain such blame. A. C. *Swinburne commented ironically on the fact that 'our Laureate should find in the ideal cuckold his type of the ideal man', and Gerard Manley *Hopkins, noting something untrustworthy in the poems' plot and voice, suggested that a better title might be 'Charades from the Middle Ages'. Tennyson, however, wrote that 'there is an allegorical or perhaps rather a parabolic drift in the poem', which later critics have sought to elucidate in relation to aesthetics, politics (especially imperial endeavours and the efficacy of violence), gender constructions, and Christian morality.

IGNATIUS (Íñigo) LOYOLA, St (1491–1556) Founder of the Society of Jesus, born near Azpeitia in the Basque country; he became page to the royal treasurer of Castile, Juan Velázquez de Cuéllar, who oversaw his military education. Fighting for the viceroy of Navarre, he was wounded at the siege of Pamplona (1521), and thereafter devoted himself to religion. He undertook a pilgrimage to the Holy Land in 1523, returning via Venice and Lombardy to Barcelona, where he began to study Latin before attending the universities of Alcalá de Henares and Salamanca. He then pursued his studies at Paris, acquiring a circle of fellow students around whom he would build the Society of Jesus (Jesuits). Bound by vows of chastity, poverty, obedience, and submission to the Pope, they obtained papal authorization for their Society in 1540. The object of this disciplined spiritual army was to support the Catholic Church in its conflict with the 16th-century reformers and to propagate the faith. St Francis *Xavier and other missionaries carried on the latter work in parts of the world far from Europe. From the early 1550s, the Jesuits increasingly turned their attention to education. Loyola's *Spiritual Exercises*, a manual of devotion and of rules for meditation and prayer, was published in Rome in 1548.

Ignoramus A Latin farce by George Ruggle (1575–1622). Acted at Cambridge before *James I in 1615, it adapts an Italian comedy by Giambattista della Porta (*c.*1535–1615), and ridicules the recorder of Cambridge, Francis Brackyn, who had already been mocked in the last part of *The *Parnassus Plays*.

Igraine Mother of *Arthur, conceived after *Uther Pendragon, disguised as her husband, lay with her.

Iliad An epic poem traditionally by *Homer, regarded by the Greeks as their supreme literary creation. It is set in the tenth year of the Trojan War, fought by the Achaeans under Agamemnon in order to recover *Helen, his brother Menelaus' wife. The Achaeans' best warrior, Achilles, refuses to fight out of rage with Agamemnon. When his great friend Patroclus is killed by the Trojan champion Hector, Achilles returns to battle and kills Hector beneath the walls of Troy. He then refuses to give up the body for burial, until old King Priam is brought through the night by the god Hermes, to beg for the body of his son. We know that what will immediately follow will be the death of Achilles and the fall of Troy, foreshadowed in the poem but not narrated. The heroes know that they cannot avoid what is destined by the gods. This heroic ethos is strongly challenged in **Paradise Lost*. There are important 18th-century translations by Alexander *Pope and William *Cowper, and many 20th-century ones, e.g. Richmond Lattimore (1951; verse) and Martin Hammond (1987; prose). See M. W. Edwards, *Homer, Poet of the Iliad* (1987).
See also ODYSSEY; LOGUE, CHRISTOPER.

'Il Penseroso' A poem in rhymed octosyllabics (with a ten-line prelude) by John *Milton, written ?1631, printed 1645. The title means 'the contemplative man'. The poem is an invocation to the goddess Melancholy, bidding her bring Peace, Quiet, Leisure, and Contemplation. It describes the pleasures of the studious, meditative life, of tragedy, epic poetry, and music. It had a considerable influence on the meditative *graveyard poems of the 18th century, and there are echoes in Alexander *Pope's *'Eloisa to Abelard', and later *Gothic works. It is a companion piece to *'L'Allegro'.

imagery A collective term for the references to perceptible things or actions found within a literary work, usually those evoked by *metaphors and *similes; these are commonly assumed to involve mental pictures or 'images', but may also rely on other sense-impressions such as imagined sounds or flavours. The term is found in critical writings by John *Dryden and Samuel *Johnson, but has been more often applied since the 1930s, when critical analysis of the recurrent imagery (e.g. horticultural, maritime, meteorological, culinary) found in a poem or play, and especially in the plays of *Shakespeare, was used as a clue not only to the work's underlying theme but sometimes also to the author's typical preoccupations or mental universe. This approach was pioneered in Shakespearian studies by G. Wilson Knight in *The Wheel of Fire* (1930) and by Caroline Spurgeon in *Shakespeare's Imagery and What it Tells Us* (1935).

Imaginary Conversations of Literary Men and Statesmen By Walter Savage *Landor, published 1824–9, followed by *Imaginary Conversations of Greeks and Romans*, published 1853. The conversations are between characters from classical times to the 19th century; some are dramatic, some idyllic, some satirical. There are some 150 dialogues. Their quality is somewhat uneven, for Landor's own passionate and often prejudiced views tend to obtrude. *Wordsworth observed that the dialogues between classical characters, such as that between Cicero and his brother, were often the best.

imagism A movement of English and American poets, which flourished from around 1910 to 1917, and derived in part from the *aesthetic philosophy of T. E. *Hulme. Its first anthology, *Des imagistes* (1914), edited by Ezra *Pound, had eleven contributors, including Richard *Aldington, Hilda *Doolittle (known as 'H.D.'), Ford Madox *Ford, Amy *Lowell, James *Joyce, Pound, and William Carlos *Williams. Some of D. H. *Lawrence's poems of this period may also be described as imagist. The characteristic products of the movement are more easily recognized than defined: they tend to be short, often close to Japanese forms, composed of short lines of musical cadence rather than metrical regularity, avoiding abstraction and treating the image with a hard, clear precision rather than with overt symbolic intent (Pound said that 'the natural object is always the adequate symbol'). Amy Lowell succeeded Pound as spokesperson of the group, and was responsible for several imagist anthologies.

Imitation of Christ *See* THOMAS À KEMPIS.

IMLAH, Mick (1956–2009) Scottish poet, born in Aberdeen and educated at Magdalen College, Oxford. He was editor of *Poetry Review* from 1983 to 1986 and worked for the **Times Literary Supplement* from 1992. He published two collections, *Birthmarks* (1988) and *The Lost Leader* (2008), the latter an ambitious assembly of meditations and monologues on Scottish political and cultural history. He co-edited the *New Penguin Book of Scottish Verse* (2000) with Robert *Crawford.

IMLAY, Gilbert (1754–1828) American author, who lived for a time in Kentucky and in 1792 published his *Topographical Description of the Western Territory of North America*, a pastoral account which incorporates attacks on slavery. In 1793 he published *The Emigrants*, an early frontier novel presenting utopian images of America. In 1793 while in Paris, he met Mary *Wollstonecraft and began a liaison which she recorded in her letters from Scandinavia.

***Importance of Being Earnest, The:** A Trivial Comedy for Serious People* A play by Oscar *Wilde, first performed at the St James's Theatre, London, on 14 February 1895. Wilde's most dazzling and epigrammatic work, it describes the courtships of two young men-about-town, John Worthing (Jack) and Algernon Moncrieff (Algy). Jack becomes engaged to Algy's cousin, Gwendolen Fairfax, who believes Jack's name is Ernest; meanwhile, Algy is in love with Jack's ward, Cecily Cardew. Both young men lead double lives: in order to escape the country, Jack has invented a wicked brother Ernest whom he must visit in the city, where he himself goes by that name; Algy has also created a fictitious character, the sickly Bunbury, whose ill health requires a visit whenever he wishes to avoid engagements in town (particularly those with his formidable aunt Lady Bracknell). After many confusions of identity, during which we discover that Cecily's governess, Miss Prism, had once mislaid Jack as a baby in a handbag at Victoria Station, it is revealed that Jack and Algy are in fact brothers, and that Jack's name is indeed Ernest. All objections to both matches are thus overcome, and Gwendolen's desire to marry a man named Ernest is satisfied, so all ends happily.

Impressionism The name derisively given (from a painting by Monet called *Impression: soleil levant*) to the work of a group of French painters who held their first exhibition in 1874. Their aim was to render the effects of light on objects rather than the objects themselves. Claude Monet (1840–1926), Alfred Sisley (1839–99), and Camille Pissarro (1831–1903) carried out their ideals most completely. Auguste Renoir (1841–1919) reacted against the spontaneity of the movement in the early 1880s, while Paul Cézanne (1839–1906) became increasingly interested in an analysis of form that led to Cubism. The term is used by transference in literature to indicate an emphasis on subjective impressions over objective facts. A theory of literary Impressionism was developed by Ford Madox *Ford in his 1913 essay 'On Impressionism' and put into practice in his novel *The *Good Soldier* (1915).

Impressions of Theophrastus Such, The A volume of essays by George *Eliot, published 1879. Most of the eighteen essays are character studies loosely based on the model of *Theophrastus; the author writes in the character of the bachelor son of a Tory Midlands country parson, himself a Londoner, and reflects on various contemporary types, such as the carping and arrogant Lentulus and the ever-youthful though ageing Ganymede. The last chapter echoes **Daniel Deronda* in its defence of Jewish nationalism and its attack on various manifestations of anti-Semitism.

imprimatur Official permission or licence for a book to be printed. During the reigns of Charles I and Charles II books had to be licensed before publication. This system (attacked by John Milton in **Areopagitica*) ended in 1695.
See L'ESTRANGE, SIR ROGER.

Improvisatrice, The A long narrative poem by Letitia Elizabeth *Landon ('L.E.L.'), published 1824. Set in Italy, it recounts the doomed love of a beautiful young female minstrel and artist, the Improvisatrice of the poem's title, for the impossibly handsome, raven-haired, pale-cheeked youth, Lorenzo, with whom she is infatuated, loving him, in her own words, 'wildly'. Though he is drawn to her, he does not declare his love, and, sensing his inconstancy, she wastes away with grief. When she is on the brink of death, Lorenzo returns to claim her as his own, explaining that his wife (whom he married out of duty because of a childhood betrothal, and whom he loved as a dear friend) died following their wedding. But the Improvisatrice has sunk too low and Lorenzo's love fails to rescue her from an untimely demise.

The tale of the Improvisatrice is related in her own words, but is intermixed throughout with other episodes, such as 'Sappho's Song', 'A Moorish Romance', 'The Hindoo Girl's Song', that call forth similar scenes of doomed love affairs and female suffering, portending the Improvisatrice's own fate. The device of the interpolated narratives allows the Improvisatrice's individual tale to become every woman's story, and the whole can be read as a lament for, but also a vindication of, erotic and passionate female love.

Jonathan Wordsworth in his 1996 edition of the poem suggests that Landon writes from books and from heightened imagination, seldom from experience. Indeed, the plot of *The Improvisatrice* carries strong echoes of Madame de *Staël's influential French romance *Corinne* (1807), a novel about a beautiful female artist—a poet—living in Italy, who dies grief-stricken, when her lover rejects her for a more conventional woman. *Corinne* is notable as a literary work that imagines what life for a female poet or imaginative artist might be like, and Landon takes up this theme in *The Improvisatrice*, her most important and best-known work.

In a Glass Darkly A collection of stories by Sheridan *Le Fanu, published 1872. They claim to be cases from the papers of 'Dr Martin Hesselius, the German Physician'—the first of a long line of psychic investigators in English literature. Of the five stories the best known are 'Green Tea', featuring a malignant monkey, and 'Carmilla', a powerful and much-anthologized tale of a female vampire which antedates Bram Stoker's **Dracula* by 25 years and was adapted by Carl Dreyer in his film *Vampyr* (1932).

'Inappropriate Curiosity, The Tale of' An episode in **Don Quixote* (I. 33–5) set in Florence, which provided the plot of several English 17th-century dramas (e.g. Aphra *Behn, *The Amorous Prince*; Thomas *Southerne, *The Disappointment*; John Crowne (*c*.1641–1712), *The Married Beau*). Anselmo, having married the beautiful Camila, urges Lotario to test her virtue. Lotario, at first reluctant, yields to the constant pressure of his friend. Camila's eventual seduction encourages the licentiousness of her maid Leonela, which leads to the discovery of her mistress's infidelity, the death of Anselmo and, indirectly, that of Lotario, while Camila retires to a convent where she soon dies.

INCHBALD, Elizabeth (1753–1821) Née Simpson, a novelist, dramatist, and actress, and a close friend of William *Godwin until his marriage with Mary *Wollstonecraft. She is chiefly remembered for her two prose romances, *A *Simple Story* (1791) and **Nature and Art* (1796), both of which display skill in character and narration and illustrate her faith in natural upbringing (*see* PRIMITIVISM); and her play **Lovers' Vows* (1798), which retains its fame as the drama enacted by the Bertram family in Austen's **Mansfield Park*. Her most successful play was *I'll Tell You What*, produced in 1785. She edited *The British Theatre*, a large collection of plays, both old and new, in 1806–9.

'Inchcape Rock, The' A ballad by Robert *Southey, written 1796–8, published 1802. Because the rock, off the Firth of Tay, was dangerous to mariners, the abbot of Arbroath, or Aberbrothock, fixed a warning bell upon it. A piratical character, Sir Ralph the Rover, in order to plague the abbot, cuts the bell from its float and later, on his homeward way, is wrecked upon the rock.

incunabula (incunables) Books printed before the 16th century, from the Latin word for 'swaddling clothes' or 'cradle', hence 'infancy'.

Index Librorum Prohibitorum The list of books (not authors, as sometimes thought) that Roman Catholics were forbidden to read. Rules for the formation of this list and of the related *Index Expurgatorius* (an authoritative specification of the passages to be expunged or altered in works Roman Catholics might otherwise read) were drawn up by the Council of Trent in 1564. Successive editions of the *Index Librorum Prohibitorum* were published from time to time, but were largely obsolete by the 18th century. Both indexes were abolished in 1966.

Indicator (1819–21) A periodical established and edited by Leigh *Hunt. It was non-political and devoted to literary matters. Hunt and his friends, notably William *Hazlitt and Charles *Lamb, thought it his happiest venture in periodical publishing. It published the work of the young poets, including John Keats's *'La Belle Dame sans Merci'*, and introduced much foreign literature. Although short-lived, it sold well.

Indo-European The name applied to the great family of cognate languages (formerly called Indo-Germanic and Aryan) spoken over most of Europe and extending into Asia as far as northern India. Much of the energy of the 19th-century comparative philologists was devoted to illustrating the connections between these groups of languages of which fourteen are distinguished by W. B. Lockwood in *A Panorama of Indo-European Languages* (1972). See J. P. Mallory, *In Search of the Indo-Europeans* (1989).

Inferno, of Dante *See* DIVINA COMMEDIA.

INGELOW, Jean (1820–97) Poet, born in Boston, Lincolnshire. Educated at home, she published volumes of verse, many stories for children (including *Mopsa the Fairy*, 1869), and adult prose fiction; her best-known poems are 'Divided', a poem of lost love, and 'The High Tide on the Coast of Lincolnshire, 1571', both in *Poems* (1863). She was acquainted with many major artists and writers of the period including John *Ruskin and Henry Wadsworth *Longfellow.

INGLIS, Esther (1571–1624) Huguenot scribe who worked in Scotland producing a large number of manuscripts which she presented to royal and aristocratic patrons. She was able to write in a wide variety of scripts, producing coloured illustrations and decorations to accompany her texts. These were largely compilations and translations, but included some original works of her own, as well as dedicatory poems. Some of her manuscripts took the form of miniature books and were supplied with embroidered bindings.

Ingoldsby Legends, The *See* BARHAM, R. H.

INGS, Simon (1965–) Born Hampshire; journalist and writer of post-*cyberpunk *science fiction such as *Hot Head* (1992). *The Weight of Numbers* (2006) moves away from science fiction to the narratives—revolutionary war, the space programme—of the late 20th century.

Inheritance, The A novel by Susan *Ferrier, published 1824. The novel relates, in an improbably complex but humorous plot, the fortunes of Gertrude St Clair, granddaughter of the earl of Rossville and heiress to his estate. On the death of her father (who had been repudiated by the earl) she and her mother are admitted to Rossville Castle and encounter the earl, a conceited tyrant. Gertrude falls in love with her fascinating cousin Colonel Delmour and after the earl's death becomes engaged to him, to the despair of all who care for her, and in particular of another cousin, Edward Lyndsay, who loves Gertrude with self-effacing humility. A vulgar American now comes forward and claims to be Gertrude's father. It is revealed that the ambitious Mrs St Clair, despairing of children, has adopted the daughter of a servant and passed her off as her own. Gertrude, having lost title and fortune, is abandoned by Colonel Delmour, and the faithful Edward Lyndsay gradually wins her love. Miss Pratt, a garrulous spinster, is a memorable character in this lively and vigorous novel.

inkhorn A term originating in the 16th century, applied to excessively literary, bookish, or pedantic language: *see* WILSON, THOMAS, for an example.

Inkle and Yarico A romantic musical comedy by George *Colman the younger, first staged 1787. The young Londoner Inkle, improbably saved from cannibals on a voyage to Barbados by the beautiful native girl Yarico, has to decide between fidelity to her and a wealthy marriage to Narcissa, the governor's daughter; he chooses the latter and is punished for his ingratitude. Robert *Burns, on seeing Elizabeth Kemble (1762/3–1841) as Yarico in Dumfries in 1794, wrote, 'At Yarico's sweet notes of grief | The rocks with tears had flowed.' The plot is based on a story in *The *Spectator* (no. 11), which had been versified by Frances Thynne Seymour, the duchess of Somerset (1699–1754), as 'The Story of Inkle and Yarrico' (1738). *See* PRIMITIVISM.

Inklings An informal literary discussion group which met in Oxford from the 1930s to the 1960s, and read aloud original compositions by its members. The group's driving force was C. S. *Lewis, who borrowed the name from a short-lived undergraduate literary society founded at University College in 1931, and it was in his rooms at Magdalen College that the Inklings originally met. Later meetings took place in Oxford pubs, notably the Eagle and Child. Members included J. R. R. *Tolkien, who read versions of his works *The Hobbit* and *The Lord of the Rings* to the group, the novelist Charles *Williams, the philosopher Owen Barfield (1898–1997), and the scholar and theatre producer Nevill Coghill (1899–1980). The Inklings, friends and associates rather than members of a club with recognized rules and regulations, were united by their enthusiasm for traditional narrative fiction and fantasy literature. See Humphrey Carpenter, *The Inklings* (1978).

In Memoriam A.H.H. A poem by Alfred *Tennyson, written between 1833 and 1850 and published anonymously in the latter year. The poem was written in memory of Arthur Henry *Hallam, a young man of great promise and an intimate friend of Tennyson, who died at Vienna aged 22. In stanzas of four octosyllabic lines rhyming *abba*, it is divided into 132 sections of varying length. Not a single elegy but a group of lyrics, it documents the changing moods of the author's bereavement, and expresses his anxieties about change, evolution, and immortality, the last a subject which continued to perturb him deeply. The epilogue is a marriage song on the occasion of the wedding of Tennyson's youngest sister Cecilia to Edmund Lushington; Hallam had been engaged to another sister, Emily. A critical and popular success (G. H. *Lewes referred to it as 'the solace and delight of every house where poetry is loved'), it was widely regarded as a message of hope and an affirmation of faith. But T. S. *Eliot commented in 1936: 'It is not religious because of the quality of its faith, but because of the quality of its doubt. Its faith is a poor thing, but its doubt is a very intense experience. *In Memoriam* is a poem of despair, but of despair of a religious kind.' Recent critical approaches have considered Tennyson's interest in the spoken word and in science, and the alleged homoerotic element of the elegy.

Inn Album, The A poem of approximately 3,000 lines, in blank verse, by Robert *Browning, published 1875. Browning originally intended to write a play on the subject, but changed his mind to avoid competing with Alfred *Tennyson's forthcoming *Queen Mary*. The poem has affinities with drama in its use of long passages of dialogue, but the whole is more like a short novel.

The story is based on the career of a famous Regency rake, Lord de Ros, but was influenced by the trial of the Tichborne Claimant which had just ended, and it has a contemporary setting. It is an intricate melodrama, involving a spendthrift aristocrat, his cast-off mistress, his wealthy young protégé and dupe, and the pure young girl to whom the younger man has cynically become engaged; it concludes with blackmail, suicide, and murder. At another level this sensational tale of social and psychological corruption, treated with the satirical realism of **Red Cotton Night-Cap Country*, may be read as a bleak fable of the dualism of human art, its self-destructive combination of ideal and material elements.

INNES, Michael The pseudonym of J. I. M. *Stewart.

Innisfail (Inishfallen) [from Irish *Inis fáil*] 'Island of destiny', a poetic name for Ireland.

Innocence, Songs of *See* SONGS OF INNOCENCE.

Innocents Abroad, The A satirical account by Mark *Twain, published 1869 (in England, 1870, as *The New Pilgrim's Progress*), of a cruise on the *Quaker City* to the Mediterranean with a company of Americans in 1867. Through its humour, the work, originally published as travel letters in New York and Californian newspapers, makes many serious points about tourist practices and the writing of travel experiences.

inscape, instress *See* HOPKINS, GERARD MANLEY

Intelligencer *See* L'ESTRANGE, SIR ROGER.

intentional fallacy A phrase coined by the American *New Critics W. K. Wimsatt, Jr (1907–75), and Monroe C. Beardsley (1915–85) in an essay of 1946 to describe the common assumption that an author's declared or assumed intention in writing a work is a proper basis for deciding upon the work's meaning or value. These critics argued that once a work is published, it has an objective status and that its meanings belong to the reading public. Any surmise about the author's intention thus has to be tested against the evidence of the text itself.

interactive fiction A term encompassing a range of experimental approaches to fictional form and the writing process. Formal developments range from text-based role-playing games to *hypertext novels, and include material published in both print and electronic media. The defining feature of this work is that the author relinquishes to the reader a degree of control over the text, opening it to a range of readings. Notable examples include B. S. *Johnson's *The Unfortunates* (1969), which consisted of a box of 27 unbound sections, with only the beginning and end segments designated by the author, and Milorad Pavic's *Dictionary of the Kazars* (1988), a pastiche reference book in the form of three dictionaries representing separate cultural traditions, which enabled a linear reading, random consultation, or the tracing of themes and events across the texts. Developments in *hypertext, CD-ROM, and World Wide Web (WWW) technologies enabled further exploration of the relationship between author and reader. New forms of interactive authorship have been made possible by the development of the MOO—a computer-based technology (Multiple User Dungeons, Object-Oriented) enabling individual users to create imaginary spaces, roles, and personalities.

interior monologue An extended representation in prose or verse of a character's unspoken thoughts, memories, and impressions, rendered as if directly 'overheard' by the reader without the intervention of a summarizing narrator. The device is distinguished from the *dramatic monologue by the fact that the thoughts are unspoken. Many modern poems make use of this convention, and it is widely employed in modern fiction, notably in the deliberately incoherent *'stream-of-consciousness' style adopted by Dorothy *Richardson, James *Joyce, and others.

interludes Plays performed at court, in the halls of the nobles, at the Inns of Court, and in colleges, generally but not exclusively by professional actors, dealing with a short episode and involving a limited number of characters. Interludes were sometimes performed by villagers, as we know from 'Pyramus and Thisbe' in *A *Midsummer Night's Dream*. Their vogue was chiefly in the 15th and 16th centuries. They succeeded *morality plays in the history of drama, and are not always clearly distinguishable from them. The characters are still frequently allegorical, but the comic or farcical element is more prevalent, and they are shorter than the moralities. There are good examples by John *Heywood, John *Rastell, and Henry Medwall (d. 1502). The origin of the name is obscure. The *Oxford English Dictionary* speaks of interludes as 'commonly introduced between the acts of long mystery-plays or moralities'; some scholars find the probable origin in the fact that interludes were 'occasionally performed in the intervals of banquets and entertainments'. E. K. *Chambers gives reasons for questioning both these explanations. He interprets *interludium* not as a *ludus* (or entertainment) in the intervals of something else, but as a *ludus* carried on between two or more performers, and as primarily applicable to any kind of dramatic performance. See T. W. Craik, *The Tudor Interlude* (1958).

intertextuality The sum of relationships between and among writings. This modern critical term, coined by Julia *Kristeva, usually covers the range of ways in which one 'text' may respond to, allude to, derive from, mimic, parody, or adapt another. The concept has been used in various ways under the influence of *structuralism and post-structuralism, often in reaction against the *New Criticism and its assumption that a literary work is a self-contained object. The idea that poems are made from other poems has been proclaimed by Northrop *Frye, Roland *Barthes, and Harold *Bloom, among others. See Graham Allen, *Intertextuality* (2000).

Interzone Established 1982 by a collective including John *Clute, Colin *Greenland, and David *Pringle; now the longest-running British *science fiction magazine. Edited and published solely by Pringle from issues 25 to 193, it spearheaded a revival in British science fiction and *fantasy, publishing stories by Stephen *Baxter, Eric *Brown, Greg *Egan, Gwyneth *Jones, and Kim *Newman, as well as Brian *Aldiss, J. G. *Ballard, Barrington J. *Bayley, and Brian *Stableford, together with newer writers from Britain, the USA, and Europe.

In the Year of Jubilee A novel by George *Gissing, published 1894, and in a censored American version 1895. The novel describes a group of young upper- and lower-middle-class people at the time of Queen Victoria's Golden Jubilee in 1887. The superficially educated Nancy Lord falls in love with Lionel Tarrant; after a sexual encounter in a seaside resort, they have to marry. Nancy's father dies before learning of their marriage, leaving a will that prohibits Nancy from marrying before she is 30. Lionel's inheritance also disappears; after separation and hardship, the Tarrants are finally reconciled, but live separately in London. Gissing's heavy irony condemns, but is resigned to, the emergent mass culture portrayed in the novel.

'Intimations of Immortality from Recollections of Early Childhood' The 'Great Ode' of William *Wordsworth, composed 1802–4/6, published 1807. It is Wordsworth's most profound and memorable exploration of the significance of the intensity of childhood experience of the natural world (which suggests to him a state of pre-existence), of its gradual fading into 'the light of common day', and of the consolations of maturity, where man can still retain 'shadowy recollections' of former glory, and can still have sight, if only by glimpses, 'of that immortal sea which brought us hither'. The poem ends with a moving affirmation of the poet's faith in the powers of the philosophic mind and the human heart. The tone throughout is tentative rather than dogmatic, and Wordsworth was later to insist that he used the concept of pre-existence (which had both a popular and a Platonic basis) not as a philosopher but as a poet, using his own peculiarly vivid childhood recollections of 'a splendour in the objects of sense' and his conviction of personal immortality.

Invisible Man A surreal and claustrophobic novel by American writer Ralph *Ellison, published in 1952, which describes the experiences of a young African American in New York, drawing partly on Richard *Wright's *Native Son*. It has a dense style packed with multiple allusions.

Invisible Man, The A *scientific romance by H. G. *Wells, published 1897, about a scientist who fatally stumbles upon the secret of invisibility.

IONESCO *See* ABSURD, THEATRE OF.

Iphigeneia In Greek mythology the daughter of the royal couple Agamemnon and Clytemnestra. In one version of her story she was sacrificed by her father at Aulis, in order to appease the goddess Artemis and ensure that winds would take the Greek fleet to Troy; in another she was secretly saved by Artemis and became her priestess at Tauris. Different versions are told in the **Oresteia*, two plays by *Euripides, *Racine's *Iphigénie*, and two operas by the composer Christoph Willibald von Gluck (1714–87).

Ipomadon A Middle English romance, from the French of Hue de Rotelande (*c.*1190). There are three, independent English versions: one in prose; one in 8,890 lines of twelve-line, *tail-rhyme stanzas, thought to be from Yorkshire of the late 14th century; and a condensed version in rhyming couplets in a 15th-century manuscript. Ipomadon is a prince of Apulia who wins by his exploits (mostly in disguise) the love of the disdainful duchess of Calabria. See Rhiannon Purdie's edn (EETS os 316, 2001).

IRELAND, John (*c.*1440–1495) Theologian and public servant; he studied at St Andrews and then at Paris, where he supported the controversial nominalist theology associated with the thought of William of *Ockham. His surviving works include two books of his Commentary on the Sentences of *Peter Lombard (1480s), a treatise *On Penance and Confession* (1484) in the *Asloan Manuscript, and *The Meroure of Wyssdome* (completed 1490), a substantial treatise in Middle Scots in which he praises Geoffrey *Chaucer for his treatment of divine foreknowledge in **Troilus and Criseyde*. See *The Meroure of Wyssdome*, ed. C. Macpherson, F. Quinn, and C. Macdonald, 3 vols (1926–90).

IRELAND, William Henry (1777–1835) Remembered chiefly as a forger of Shakespeare manuscripts. He began his audacious series of deceptions at the age of 17, when he was working in a lawyer's office with easy access to old parchment, deeds, and antiquated forms of writing. An exhibition of his forgeries of poems and deeds, arranged in 1794 by his innocent and excited father, wholly deceived the general public, and James *Boswell kissed the parchments. A facsimile edition was published in 1795, and other works, including the plays *Vortigern and Rowena* and *Henry II*, made their appearance. However, strong doubts were expressed, Charles *Kemble's production of *Vortigern* was jeered, and in 1796 Edmond *Malone published *An Inquiry into the Authenticity of Certain Miscellaneous Papers*. In the same year Ireland admitted to the forgeries, and embarked on a more conventional literary career. He published two volumes of poems, then in 1808 *The Fisher Boy*, which, like Robert *Bloomfield's earlier *Farmer's Boy*, satisfied the fashion for tales of rural life. *The Sailor Boy* (1809) relates the rise of humble Dick to be a captain at Trafalgar. In 1815 he produced *Scribbleomania*, a satirical collection of entertaining but frequently inaccurate descriptions of his contemporaries.

Irene Samuel *Johnson's only play, a verse tragedy begun in 1736, and performed nine times (with David *Garrick's support) in 1749. The story, from Richard *Knolles, concerns Irene, a Greek slave loved by the emperor Mahomet, whose courtiers fear her influence over him. To show his self-command, he kills her. Originally, the event took place onstage, but the first-night audience reacted badly and the death was moved offstage. Johnson was disappointed by the play's mixed reception.

IRIGARAY, Luce (1932–) Belgian feminist philosopher, psychoanalyst, and linguist. Having trained with Jacques *Lacan in the 1960s, Irigaray emerged as a trenchant critic of the Western philosophical tradition in general, and the dominant—and largely male-authored—psychoanalytic models of female sexuality in particular. Her work since the 1970s, including *Ce sexe qui n'en est pas un* (1977: *This Sex Which Is Not One*), has set out to articulate different ways of conceptualizing female sexuality, gender, and identity which foreground multiplicity and fluidity.

Irish Literary Theatre Founded by W. B. *Yeats, Lady *Gregory, and Edward *Martyn in 1899 to encourage Irish drama. The theatre employed English professional actors. It dissolved in acrimony after the departure of Martyn and the failure of the Yeats and George *Moore collaboration *Diarmuid and Grainne* in 1901.

Irish Revival A movement in Irish cultural nationalism which began in the last quarter of the 19th century and flourished in ambiguous alliance with political nationalism until a few years after the establishment of the Irish Free State in 1922. Among the books which fostered the revival were translations and retellings of Irish legend, folklore, and poetry, such as Samuel *Ferguson's *Lays of the Western Gael* (1865), and histories, such as Standish O'Grady's *History of Ireland* (1880) and Douglas *Hyde's *Literary History of Ireland* (1899). Repeated attempts by W. B. *Yeats and others to found a national theatre issued in the setting up of the *Abbey Theatre company. Plays by Yeats, J. M. *Synge, G. B. *Shaw, and Sean *O'Casey made the Abbey famous. Meanwhile the poetry of Yeats and the prose work of George *Moore, James *Joyce, and many others established the new literary stature of Irish writing.

Irish Texts Society Founded in 1898 to promote the study of Irish literature. The Society publishes annotated texts in Irish with English translations and commentaries.

IRVING, Sir Henry (1838–1905) Actor, originally John Henry Brodribb. Born at Keinton Mandeville, Somerset, Irving spent his early years in Cornwall, moving to London (where he was educated at the City Commercial School) at the age of 11. After a long theatrical apprenticeship, much of it spent in provincial theatres, he achieved fame as an actor for his performance in *The *Bells* (1871–2), and afterwards scored successes in a large number of Shakespearian and other parts, his impersonation of *Tennyson's Becket being one of his chief triumphs. His management of the Lyceum Theatre in association with Ellen *Terry, 1878–1902, was distinguished, and he revived popular interest in Shakespeare. He was romantic, intelligent, and charismatic, but with mannered speech and movement. His impact on the conventions of theatrical production was profound; he established, for instance, the practice of darkening the auditorium in order to focus attention on the stage.

IRVING, John Winslow (1942–) American novelist, born in Exeter, New Hampshire. From 1967 to 1972, and again from 1975 to 1978, he was an assistant professor of English at Mount Holyoke College. His serio-comic novels, which display great individuality of style and imagination, began with *Setting Free the Bears* (1968), about two young men on a motorcycle tour of Austria who plot to free all the animals in the Vienna Zoo. This was followed by *The Water-Method Man* (1972) and *The 158-Pound Marriage* (1974). These made little impact, but with *The World According to Garp* (1978), the comic biography of a writer, he achieved international success. After this came *The Hotel New Hampshire* (1981) and *The Cider House Rules* (1985). *My Movie Business* (2000) describes the movie adaptation of the latter novel. *A Son of the Circus* (1994) describes an expatriate Parsi surgeon who returns to India and becomes involved in the repercussions of two murders committed twenty years earlier. *Trying to Save Piggy Sneed*, published in 1993, is a collection of short stories. *Until I Find You* (2005) is a *picaresque account of a young Canadian actor's experiences.

IRVING, Washington (1783–1859) Born in New York; trained as a lawyer, he turned to a literary career, writing for various newspapers, and publishing, with his brother William Irving (1766–1821) and friend James K. Paulding (1779–1860), a series of whimsical and satirical essays and poems, *Salmagundi* (1808). This was followed by his burlesque *A History of New York from the Beginning of the World to the End of the Dutch Dynasty*, by 'Diedrich Knickerbocker'. In 1815 he visited Britain, making the acquaintance of Walter *Scott, John *Murray, and others. Encouraged by Scott, he published *The Sketch Book* (1819–20), essays and tales under the pseudonym 'Geoffrey Crayon, Gent.' This work, which contains picturesque sketches of English life and American adaptations of German folk tales (including *'Rip Van Winkle' and 'The Legend of *Sleepy Hollow'), made him a celebrity in both continents. It was followed by *Bracebridge Hall* (1822), which features Squire Bracebridge, an old-fashioned country gentleman. Some of his subsequent works were inspired by his period as diplomatic attaché in Spain (1826–9), including *Legends of the Alhambra* (1832). He served as secretary to the US legation in London (1829–32), and returned to America in 1832 to an enthusiastic welcome as the first American author to have achieved international fame. His later works include *The Crayon Miscellany* (1835), *Astoria* (1836; an account of John Jacob Astor's development of the fur trade), and his monumental five-volume life of George Washington (1855–9). His *Complete Works*, in 30 volumes, were published by the University of Wisconsin Press (1969–82). See Mary Weatherspoon Bowden, *Irving* (1981).

IRWIN, Robert (1946–) British writer and specialist in Arabic studies whose fiction occasionally explores the *fantastic connotations of his source material, as in *The Arabian Nightmare* (1983). *Exquisite Corpse* (1995) is set amidst the Surrealist movement of the 1930s.

Isabella (1) In *Orlando furioso*, daughter of a Saracen king of Spain, loved by the Scottish prince Zerbino. After his death she fell into the power of *Rodomont, and to protect her honour tricked him into killing her. (2) In Kyd's **Spanish Tragedy*, wife to Hieronimo. (3) Queen to Marlowe's **Edward II*. (4) The heroine of Shakespeare's **Measure for Measure*.

'Isabella, or The Pot of Basil' A narrative poem by John *Keats, written 1818, published 1820.

The poem is based on a story in Boccaccio's **Decameron*. The worldly, ambitious brothers of Isabella intend that she shall marry a nobleman. When they discover her love for the humble Lorenzo they lure him away, murder him, and bury his body in a forest. His ghost then appears to Isabella and tells her where he is buried. With the help of her old nurse she finds his body, severs the head, and places it in a pot with a plant of basil over it. Her brothers, observing how she cherishes the plant, steal the pot, discover the mouldering head, and fly, conscience-stricken, into banishment. Pathetically Isabella mourns her loss, pines away, and dies. The poem reflects a contemporary fashion for the macabre, and Charles *Lamb pronounced it the best work in the volume of poems of 1820, but Keats himself very soon came to dislike it.

Isaiah *See* BIBLE.

Iseult of the White Hands In Arthurian legend, daughter of the ruler of Brittany, with whom *Tristram falls in love and whom he marries after his banishment by King Mark. But Iseult of Brittany does not succeed in replacing *Iseult the Fair; in one version, when Tristram is dying, he sends for his first Iseult by ship; if she is on the ship on its return from Ireland it is to fly a white flag: if not a black one. The white flag is flown; but Iseult of the White Hands tells Tristram it is black, whereupon he dies.

Iseult the Fair Daughter of the king of Ireland in Arthurian legend. She is the lover of *Tristram (Tristan) who is sent by his uncle, King Mark of Cornwall, to bring her as his wife. This is the great classic of doomed love, since Tristram is the slayer of her uncle Marhaus and they are fated to fall in love by erroneously drinking a love potion meant for Mark and Iseult on their wedding night. A jealous Mark eventually murders Tristram.

ISHERWOOD, Christopher (1904–86) Writer, born at High Lane, Cheshire, the son of an army officer who was killed in the First World War. He made the acquaintance of W. H. *Auden at preparatory school and became a friend of Edward *Upward at Repton School before they both went up to Corpus Christi College, Cambridge. His first novels, *All the Conspirators* (1928) and *The Memorial* (1932), show the influence (as he acknowledged) of E. M. *Forster and Virginia *Woolf; his own voice is first most distinctly audible in *Mr Norris Changes Trains* (1935) and *Goodbye to Berlin* (1939), works which reflect his experiences of living in Berlin, 1929–33, where he supported himself by giving English lessons. They were planned as part of a long novel, to be entitled *The Lost*, which was never written, and are largely autobiographical in manner and content. The first is a novel about a conman and double agent, the corrupt, seedy, emotional, and engaging Arthur Norris, and his adventures in the criminal and political underworld; the second is a series of sketches, of which the best known is 'Sally Bowles' (published independently in 1937). Sally is a cabaret artist of more beauty, eccentricity, and wit than talent; her bohemian enterprises were successfully dramatized in 1951 by John Van Druten as *I Am a Camera*, turned into a stage musical in 1966 as *Cabaret*, and made into an award-winning film of the same name in 1972. Both novels give a vivid portrait of Germany on the eve of Hitler's rise to power. Isherwood travelled widely in Europe after leaving Berlin, went to China with Auden in 1938, and in 1939 went with him to America; Isherwood became an American citizen in 1946. During the 1930s he collaborated with Auden in the writing of *The Dog beneath the Skin* (1935), *The *Ascent of F6* (1936), and several other works, and wrote the semi-autobiographical *Lions and Shadows* (1938), in which his friends appear under fictitious names. After settling near Hollywood, where he worked as a scriptwriter, he became interested in Hindu philosophy and Vedanta, influenced partly by Aldous *Huxley and Gerald *Heard, and edited various works on the subject (for example, *Vedanta for the Western World*, 1945) and translated the **Bhagavad-gītā* (1944, with Swami Prabhavananda) and other Hindu classics. Novels written in America include *Prater Violet* (1945), about his experiences in Hollywood, *Down There on a Visit* (1962), and *A Single Man* (1964), now regarded by many as his most important work of fiction; *Kathleen and Frank* (1971) is a memoir of his parents, and *Christopher and his Kind* (1977) is a frank account of his homosexual life in the 1930s. See Peter Parker, *Isherwood: A Life* (rev. edn, 2005).

ISHIGURO, Kazuo (1954–) Novelist, born in Nagasaki, who came to England in 1960, read English and philosophy at the University of Kent, and studied creative writing on the postgraduate course run by Malcolm *Bradbury at the University of East Anglia. His first three novels—*A Pale View of Hills* (1982), about a Japanese widow who has moved to England after the bombing of Nagasaki; *An Artist of the Floating World* (1986), in which a delicately skilled Japanese artist is coarsened by collusion with his country's militarism in the 1930s; and *The Remains of the Day* (1989), a subtle portrait of a butler tainted by unquestioning service to a British aristocrat of Fascist sympathies—comprise a kind of trilogy about the disorientations caused by the Second World War. Each features a diffident narrator and they are much concerned with doubt. More experimental, Ishiguro's next three novels are riddled with mystery. *The Unconsoled* (1995) is a Kafkaesque story of a musician's disorienting experiences in a teasingly unidentified European country. *When We Were Orphans* (2000), in which a 1930s detective investigates his parents' disappearance in Shanghai, works surreal variations on the 'Golden Age' whodunnit genre (*see* DETECTIVE FICTION). *Never Let Me Go* (2005) takes a *science fiction scenario and turns it into a haunting fable in which Ishiguro's talents for resonant understatement, sinister suggestiveness, and unsettling obliquity combine with his powers of sympathetic characterization and his preoccupation with exploitation and lives maimed by oppressive milieux to particularly powerful and moving effect. *The Remains of the Day* (which won the 1989 *Booker Prize) was made into an acclaimed film. Ishiguro has written two original screenplays, *The Saddest Music in the World* (2003) and *The White Countess* (2005).

ISIDORE OF SEVILLE (*c.*560–636) Archbishop of Seville and enormously influential through his *Etymologiae*, the earliest medieval encyclopedia in twenty books, which argues that the natures of things can be derived from their names. This work was an authority until at least the 14th century.

Island, The A poem by Lord *Byron, published 1823. The poem, a mixture of romance and humour, is based on the story of the mutiny on HMS **Bounty*, and idolizes nature at the expense of society.

Island in the Moon, An An untitled burlesque fragment by William *Blake, written *c.*1784–5, first printed in 1907. It is a satirical portrait of scientific and cultural dilettantism and pretension, interspersed with songs (some of them bawdy); its characters include 'Sipsop the Pythagorean' and 'Inflammable Gas', the latter probably inspired by Joseph *Priestley.

Island of Dr Moreau, The A *scientific romance by H. G. *Wells, published 1896. It is an evolutionary fantasy about a shipwrecked naturalist who becomes involved in an experiment to 'humanize' animals by surgery. The theme was developed by Brian *Aldiss.

Isumbras, Sir Extremely popular verse romance in 804 lines of twelve-line *tail-rhyme stanzas, from the north-east Midlands, popular before 1320 and mentioned in **Cursor Mundi*. It is a variant on the story of St Eustace, of Eastern origin. Isumbras is strong, handsome, and prosperous, but also proud and arrogant. A bird sent by God offers him the choice of suffering in youth or old age, and he chooses the former. He loses his wife, children, and possessions, and suffers for 21 years among the Saracens. But he bears all patiently, and at the end of that period an angel tells him that his sins are expiated and he is restored to his family and possessions. Its moral theme is typical of 14th-century tail-rhyme romances. See Harriet Hudson (ed.), *Four Middle English Romances* (2nd edn, 2006).

Italian, The A Gothic novel by Ann *Radcliffe, published 1797. The tale recounts the romance between an Italian nobleman and his love, Ellena di Rosalba, whose manipulative mother opposes the match and enlists the help of the vicious monk Schedoni. A Satanic archetype, Schedoni's malevolent presence dominates the novel's powerful psychological and political symbolism. Also notable for its sublime landscapes and swiftly paced narrative, *The Italian* holds a major place in the history of the development of *Gothic fiction.

Ithaca *See* ODYSSEY.

Ivanhoe A novel by Walter *Scott, published 1819. The story deals, somewhat anachronistically, with the antagonism in England between Saxon and Norman during the reign of Richard I. The hero, Wilfred of Ivanhoe, disowned by his father Cedric the Saxon because of his love for Cedric's ward, the lady Rowena, has joined King Richard on crusade; Prince John, taking advantage of the king's absence, endeavours to seize the throne himself. The story hinges on two main episodes: the tournament at Ashby-de-la-Zouche where Ivanhoe, returned in disguise, and supported by an equally disguised Richard, defeats all challengers, including the Templar Sir Brian de Bois-Guilbert, and the siege of Sir Reginald Front-de-Bœuf's castle of Torquilstone to which he and Bois-Guilbert have carried off Isaac the Jew and his daughter

Rebecca. The main plot thereafter concerns the passion of the Templar for Rebecca, and her resistance to his dishonourable advances. Bois-Guilbert dies in combat with Ivanhoe, who, reconciled to his father, marries Rowena; Rebecca, suppressing her love for Ivanhoe, leaves England with her father.

The first of Scott's novels to deal with an English, rather than Scottish subject, *Ivanhoe* is also one of his best constructed. In Rebecca, the beautiful Jewess, he produced a heroine as virtuous and strong-minded as Jeanie Deans (**Heart of Midlothian*), but with all the graces which Jeanie lacked, and had the resolution to deprive her of the conventional happy ending. The novel was a great success, the first edition selling out within the week.

IYER, Pico (1957–) Travel writer, essayist, and novelist, born in Oxford of Indian parents; he grew up in England and California, and was educated at Eton College, and Oxford and Harvard universities. Iyer, who spends much of his time in Japan, has described himself as 'a multinational soul on a multinational globe', folding up and carrying his self around as if it were an overnight bag. Much of Iyer's writing concerns itself with travel in a globalized world. He has commented that what he most likes about travel is the way that it makes him rethink his assumptions, sending him back a different person. Iyer has written for several magazines and journals, including *Time* and the *London Review of Books*. His books, which many believe have revitalized travel writing with a postmodern sensibility, include *Video Night in Kathmandu* (1988) and *Global Soul* (2000).

J

JACK OF NEWBERY (Newbury) (d. 1520) John Winchcombe, alias John Smallwood, a clothier from Newbury, whose wealth inspired the authors (including Thomas *Deloney) of chapbooks and other stories. According to legend he led 100 or 250 men, equipped at his own expense, at the battle of *Flodden Field (1513) and entertained *Henry VIII and Catherine of Aragon at his house.

JACKSON, Shirley (1916–65) American author, born in San Francisco, who became notorious in 1948 after the publication of her macabre short story 'The Lottery' in the *New Yorker*. She subsequently wrote innovative novels of the supernatural, including *The Haunting of Hill House* (1959).

JACKSON, Thomas (1783–1873) *Methodist minister, editor, and biographer, born near Market Weighton, Lincolnshire, the son of an agricultural labourer. He was largely self-taught. After serving as an itinerant preacher for twenty years, he spent the next twenty years as the influential editor of the principal Wesleyan Methodist magazines, and almost another twenty as theological tutor at Richmond College. His main publications are his editions of John *Wesley's *Works* (1829–31), still the best until the completion of the Abingdon edition; the *Life* (1841) and *Journal* (1849) of Charles *Wesley; *The Lives of Early Methodist Preachers* (1837–8; 4th expanded edn, 1871–3); and his *Recollections of my Own Life and Times* (1873).

Jack Straw An enigmatic figure possibly to be identified with Wat Tyler, the doomed leader of insurgents from Essex in the Peasants' Revolt of 1381. He is mentioned in Geoffrey *Chaucer's 'The Nun's Priest's Tale' (*see* CANTERBURY TALES, 20), and is the subject of an anonymous play of 1593, *The Life and Death of Jack Straw*.

Jack the Ripper The name given to a murderer who, between 1888 and 1891, killed and eviscerated several prostitutes (at least five, possibly more) in the Whitechapel area of London. Attempts to guess his identity have included a Harley Street surgeon, a mad midwife, a Russian anarchist, the duke of Clarence (1864–92), and J. K. *Stephen. He has been the subject of many novels and films, including Mrs Belloc Lowndes's *The Lodger* (1913) and Colin *Wilson's *Ritual in the Dark* (1960), in which he appears as a homosexual sadist, and his presence is also felt in the works of Peter *Ackroyd and Iain *Sinclair. See Philip Sugden, *The Complete History of Jack the Ripper* (2002).

Jack Wilton, The Life of *See* UNFORTUNATE TRAVELLER.

Jacobean In literary terms, applies to writing of the period of *James I of England, who succeeded Elizabeth I in 1603: most commonly used of 'Jacobean tragedy'.
See MIDDLETON, THOMAS; TOURNEUR, CYRIL; WEBSTER, JOHN; REVENGE TRAGEDY.

Jacobin Originally a name of the French friars of the order of St Dominic, so called because the church of Saint-Jacques in Paris was given to them and they built their first convent near it. From them the name was transferred to the members of a political club established in 1789, in Paris, in the old convent of the Jacobins, to maintain extreme democratic and egalitarian principles. It was applied in a transferred sense to sympathizers with their principles, and about 1800 became a nickname for any radical political reformer.

Jacobite Term used to describe supporters of James II of England (1633–1701), his son James (1688–1766), and Charles Edward Stuart (1720–88), especially after the Hanoverian accession of 1714. The most significant military 'risings' occurred in 1715 and 1745; the crushing of the latter at Culloden (1746) by troops under the duke of Cumberland (1721–65) ended Jacobite hopes. Alexander *Pope had some Jacobite sympathies, but unlike his friends Viscount *Bolingbroke and Francis *Atterbury was not an activist. The Jacobite defeat was lamented in many later songs, such as those of Carolina *Nairne, and depicted in novels such as *Waverley*.

JACOBS, Harriet (1813–97) African American writer, born into slavery in Edmonton, North Carolina. In 1835 she escaped and found employment for a time with the poet and editor N. P. Willis (1806–67). In 1861 she published *Incidents in the Life of a Slave Girl* under the pseudonym of Linda Brent. The narrative has since become a classic account of the sexual exploitation of female slaves.
See SLAVERY.

JACOBSON, Dan (1929–) Novelist and critic; born in Johannesburg, but for many years settled in England, where he taught at University College London. His first volume of stories was appropriately titled *A Long Way from London* (1958), and early novels such as *The Trap* (1955) and *The Price of Diamonds* (1957) were set in South Africa. Later novels include *The Confessions of Joseph Baisz* (1977) and *The Rape of Tamar*

(1970), based on the biblical story. *Her Story* (1987), set both in the future and at the time of the Crucifixion, also pursued religious themes, while *All for Love* (2005) is a historical novel based on a royal scandal of the Hapsburg Empire. The autobiographical *Time and Time Again* (1985) won the J. R. Ackerley Prize, while *Heshel's Kingdom* (1998) vividly and movingly re-examines the question of Jewish history and destiny through a quest for Jacobson's grandfather, a Lithuanian rabbi.

JACOBSON, Howard (1942–) Novelist, born in Manchester and educated at Downing College, Cambridge. His first novel, *Coming from Behind* (1983), a *campus satire set in a Midlands polytechnic, was followed by *Peeping Tom* (1984), which similarly mixed erudite farce and erotic mishap, and *Redback* (1987), which takes its narrator to Australia, also the subject of a volume of travel writing, *In the Land of Oz*, published the same year. Later novels, such as *The Making of Henry* (2004) and *The Act of Love* (2008), have been more blackly comic explorations of the Jewish experience in Britain and of the battle between the sexes. *The Mighty Walzer* (1999) is a funny and poignant coming-of-age story, set in the Jewish community of 1950s Manchester, about a boy entering the dangerous territory of adolescence armed only with a champion's skill at table tennis.

Jacob's Room Third novel by Virginia *Woolf, published in 1922. It takes the form of a **Bildungsroman*, but rather than being tightly focused on the development of Jacob Flanders from childhood to young manhood, Woolf's protagonist is largely viewed from afar or through the eyes of others or simply eludes the narrator's gaze altogether, thus perfectly conveying the novel's central theme of loss. It is an elegy for both Woolf's brother Thoby Stephen, who died in 1906, and the legions slaughtered in the First World War. The novel commences with Jacob lost on a beach in Cornwall; moves to his native Scarborough; disregards his schooldays at Rugby altogether; and portrays him at Cambridge behaving utterly inconsequentially. After university he works less than avidly as a lawyer in London, has affairs, and then travels abroad. He returns to London and in a brief final chapter we learn that he has been killed in the war. It was the first of Woolf's novels to be published by the *Hogarth Press and every page resounds with the freedoms such autonomy entailed.

JAGGARD, William (*c.*1568–1623) and **Isaac** (1595–1627) London printers and principal publishers of the Shakespeare first folio (*see* FOLIOS AND QUARTOS).

JAGO, Richard (1715–81) Poet and clergyman, educated with William *Shenstone (a friend whose letters he later edited) at Solihull School and at University College, Oxford. In 1767 he published *Edge-Hill*, a *topographical poem in four books describing, with historical, moral, and scientific digressions, the views from that hill at morning, noon, afternoon, and evening. He published poems in Robert *Dodsley's *Collection of Poems* (1748–58), and his collected *Poems*, with a biography, appeared in 1784.

JAKOBSON, Roman *See* FORMALISM; STRUCTURALISM.

JAMES I (1394–1437) King of Scotland. In 1406, he was captured by an English ship while on his way to France. He was detained in England until 1424, but was well educated and became part of Henry IV's household; he was a captive at the same time as another famous literary hostage, *Charles d'Orléans. In 1424 he married Lady Joan Beaufort, the granddaughter of *John of Gaunt, who is the heroine of James's famous Boethian and semi-autobiographical poem *The *Kingis Quair*, which he may have composed on his return to Scotland, and in which he acknowledges the authority and influence of *Chaucer and *Gower. He was assassinated at Perth by Sir Robert Graham (*see* SHIRLEY, JOHN (*c.*1366–1456)). The authorship of *The Kingis Quair* has been doubted, but there seems no good reason to deny it to James. See E. W. M. Balfour-Melville, *James I, King of Scots 1406–37* (1936).

JAMES I (James VI of Scotland) (1566–1625) King of England 1603–25, and son of *Mary Queen of Scots. His belief in witchcraft, expounded in his *Demonology* (1597), may have influenced William *Shakespeare's **Macbeth*. He is reputedly the author of *True Lawe of Free Monarchies* (1598), a reply to the argument of George *Buchanan in his *De Jure Regni* that the king is elected by and responsible to the people. His *Basilikon Doron* (1599), precepts on the art of government, disastrous as it turned out, was addressed to his son, the future Charles I. He also wrote a polemic against tobacco-smoking (1604), theological works, poetry in Scots, Latin, and English, translations of *Du Bartas and *Lucan, and a treatise on the rules for writing *Scots poetry. He was the target of the 1605 Gunpowder Plot. The courtier Sir Anthony Weldon (bap. 1583, d. 1648) said he was called 'the wisest fool in Christendom'.

JAMES, Alice (1848–92) Diarist, only daughter of Henry James, Sr, and Mary Walsh, and sister of William *James, philosopher, and Henry *James, novelist. She shared the family regime of private education and accompanied her brothers on trips to Europe but was not, like them, sent away to school; instead she was expected to cultivate domestic virtues. Failing to marry, Alice made a career out of illness. From 1889 she kept a diary, commenting on current affairs and people she met, creating for herself the role of an author, if not a public career as such. She also wrote many letters to friends and family. Her diary was published in 1964. See Jean Strouse, *Alice James: A Biography* (1982).

JAMES, C. L. R. (Cyril Lionel Robert) (1901–89) Historian, novelist, Marxist theorist, and cricket enthusiast, born near Port of Spain, Trinidad. His many works include *Minty Alley* (1936), a realist novel describing the intrigues amongst the mixed-race lodgers in a West Indian boarding house, seen largely through the eyes of 20-year-old Haynes, who has moved in from a more educated background. *The Black Jacobins* (1938) is a significant study of the revolution led by Toussaint *Louverture in Haiti; *Beyond a Boundary* (1963) is a memoir focusing on politics and cricket.

JAMES, George Payne Rainsford (1799–1860) Novelist and historical writer. Born in London, the son of a doctor, he was educated at the Revd William Carmalt's school at Putney. Lord *Byron nicknamed him Little Devil because of his exuberant personality. He travelled widely, served in the Napoleonic Wars, held various diplomatic posts, and was appointed historiographer royal by William IV. Influenced by Walter *Scott he wrote numerous romantic novels, biographies, and popular historical works, including *Richelieu* (1829), *Darnley* (1830), and *Life of Edward the Black Prince* (1836). W. M. *Thackeray parodied him as 'the solitary horseman' in his burlesque *Barbazure, by G. P. R. Jeames, Esq.* for the lone rider who was a frequent beginning to his romances. Widely celebrated in his day, he is now little read.

JAMES, Henry (1843–1916) American novelist, born in New York. His father, Henry James, Sr, wrote on questions of theology and was a follower of *Swedenborg. His elder brother William *James was a distinguished philosopher. After a desultory education in New York, London, Paris, Geneva, and the Harvard law school, Henry James settled in Europe in 1875. From 1865 he was a regular contributor of reviews and short stories (the *Complete Tales* were published in twelve volumes by Rupert Hart-Davis, 1962–4) to American periodicals and owed much to his friendship with William Dean *Howells. For more than twenty years he lived in London, and in 1898 moved to Lamb House, Rye, where his later novels were written. He at first chiefly concerned himself with the impact of the older civilization of Europe upon American travellers, and to this period belong his novels **Roderick Hudson* (1876), *The American* (1877), the novella **Daisy Miller* (1879), and **Portrait of a Lady* (1881). He next turned to a more exclusively English stage in *The Tragic Muse* (1890), *The Spoils of Poynton* (1897), *What Maisie Knew* (1897), and *The Awkward Age* (1899), in which he analysed English character with extreme subtlety, verging at times on obscurity. From this period dates *The *Turn of the Screw* (1898), an ambiguous narrative by a governess of the 'possession' of the two children in her charge. In his last three great novels, *The *Wings of the Dove* (1902), *The *Ambassadors* (1903), and *The *Golden Bowl* (1904), he returned to the 'international' theme of the contrast of American and European character, expressing his narrative through nuanced prose geared to the perspectives of his main characters. His two unfinished novels, *The Ivory Tower* and *The Sense of the Past*, were published in 1917. For the revised New York Edition of his fiction, 26 vols (1907–17), James wrote a series of prefaces, published in 1934 as *The Art of the Novel*, edited by R. P. *Blackmur. In his critical essays James concentrated on the 19th-century novel, singling out George *Eliot and *Balzac ('the master of us all') for special praise. He also published several volumes of travel sketches (*Portraits of Places*, 1883; *A Little Tour in France*, 1884; etc.), see *Collected Travel Writings*, 2 vols (Library of America, 1993); and wrote a number of plays, of which the few that were acted were not successful (*Complete Plays*, 1949). Nevertheless, James made attempts throughout his career to apply the techniques of the theatre in his fiction. For the English Men of Letters series he wrote a life of Nathaniel *Hawthorne (1879); and in *The American Scene* (1906) published a record of the impressions produced on him by a visit to America after an absence of nearly twenty years. *A Small Boy and Others* (1913), *Notes of a Son and a Brother* (1914), and *The Middle Years* (1917) are autobiographical volumes, collected as his *Autobiography* in 1956. In 1915 James became a British subject, and in 1916 was awarded the Order of Merit. His *Literary Criticism* (2 vols) was published in 1984 by the Library of America. Leon *Edel's five-volume biography (1953–72) takes a *Freudian approach.

JAMES, M. R. (Montague Rhodes) (1862–1936) Medievalist, palaeographer, and biblical scholar, born near Bury St Edmunds, successively provost of King's College, Cambridge, and (from 1918) of Eton College. His memoirs, *Eton and King's*, were published in 1926. He edited works by Sheridan *Le Fanu, whom he greatly admired, and himself wrote several volumes of distinguished *ghost stories, many with East Anglian settings, including 'Oh, Whistle, and I'll Come to You, my Lad', which appeared in *Ghost Stories of an Antiquary* (1904). *More Ghost Stories of an Antiquary* appeared in 1911, followed by *A Thin Ghost and Others* (1919), *A Warning to the Curious* (1925), and his collected ghost stories in 1931. See Michael Cox, *M. R. James: An Informal Portrait* (1983).

JAMES, P. D. (Phyllis Dorothy) Baroness James of Holland Park (1920–) Crime writer, born in Oxford, educated at Cambridge Girls' High School, worked as a hospital administrator, and in the Home Office, where she became involved with forensic investigations. Her first novel, *Cover her Face* (1962), introduced Adam Dalgleish, a police detective (and poet) who went on to appear in most of her mystery novels from *A Mind to Murder* (1963) to *The Private Patient* (2008). A female private detective, Cordelia Gray, features in *An Unsuitable Job for a Woman* (1972) and *The Skull beneath the Skin* (1982). Often set on the coast of East Anglia or Dorset and in isolated or semi-closed communities, James's crime novels make sophisticated use of the conventions of 'Golden Age' *detective fiction, of which she is an acute admirer, to engage with themes of guilt, shame, cruelty, and retribution.

Characteristically, her books, plotted with bravura intricacy, combine the neatness of the whodunnit genre with less tidily resolvable moral and emotional quandaries. She has also written a psychological thriller, *Innocent Blood* (1980), and a dystopian novel, *The Children of Men* (1992). Her autobiography, *Time to Be in Earnest*, appeared in 1999. She was made a life peer in 1991.

JAMES, William (1842–1910) American philosopher, born in New York, the elder brother of Henry *James. He was at first a student of art and then a teacher of physiology, but turned his attention to psychology. He pioneered the study of psychology at Harvard University and numbered among his students W. E. *Du Bois and Gertrude *Stein. His views are embodied in his *Principles of Psychology* (1890), where he coined the expression *stream of consciousness, now widely used as a literary term. He opposed philosophical idealism, preferring empiricism, and took a pluralistic approach to the world, as demonstrated in *Varieties of Religious Experience* (1902) and *A Pluralistic Universe* (1909). His 1896 essay 'The Will to Believe' shifts religion away from the truth of beliefs to the psychology of the believer. James himself held to a belief in a larger spiritual universe and included psychic phenomena in his researches. See Linda Simon, *Genuine Reality: A Life of William James* (1999).

JAMESON, Anna Brownell (1794–1860) Writer, feminist, traveller. Born in Dublin, she began adult life as a governess. Friendship with the *Kembles, and a long visit to Germany, brought her into contact with literary society, and she became a close friend of the *Brownings, of Mary Russell *Mitford, and eventually of the *Carlyles. She first attracted attention in 1826 with *A Lady's Diary* (later retitled *The Diary of an Ennuyée*), describing a visit to Italy. She produced many highly respected works of art history and criticism, biography, theology, history, travel, social comment, and general essays, some of which exhibited a strong interest in the position and education of women. Her *Winter Studies and Summer Rambles* (1838), an account of her visit to Canada, is an important work in early Canadian literature. The work for which she is now chiefly remembered is *Characteristics of Women* (1832, later known as *Shakespeare's Heroines*), dedicated to Fanny Kemble, and illustrated with her own etchings. *Shakespeare she saw as 'the Poet of Womankind', whose heroines display all the aspects and complexities of womanhood. She divides the 25 heroines of her book into four groups: the characters of intellect, such as Portia; those of passion and imagination, such as Viola; those of the affections, such as Desdemona; and those from history, such as Cleopatra and Lady Macbeth. In preparation Anna Jameson read Samuel *Johnson, William *Hazlitt, S. T. *Coleridge, Charles *Lamb, and other major critics, as well as relevant European and Greek drama, and thoroughly investigated the sources of the histories. Although she makes little attempt to relate character to context, her interpretations, many of which are very detailed, were considered illuminating, and the work was received with considerable respect, Gerard Manley *Hopkins placing her among the most eminent of Shakespeare's critics. See the biography by Clara Thomas, *Love and Work Enough* (1967).

JAMESON, Storm (1891–1986) Writer, born in Whitby, the daughter of a sea captain, and educated at Leeds University; her first novel, *The Pot Boils* (1919), was followed by many other works of fiction, including *Women against Men* (1933, stories), *Company Parade* (1934), *Love in Winter* (1935), and *None Turn Back* (1936), the last three forming a trilogy. She also published poems, essays, and biographies, and several volumes of autobiography, including *Journey from the North* (1969), describing her time during the Second World War as president of *PEN. Her second husband was the historian and author Guy Chapman (1889–1972), remembered for his vivid personal account of trench warfare in France, *A Passionate Prodigality* (1933).

James the Fourth, The Scottish History of A play by Robert *Greene, published posthumously 1598. In spite of the title, this is a fictionalized romantic comedy, framed by the comments of Oberon, king of fairies. James, king of Scots, marries the English princess Dorothea, but loves Ida, daughter of the countess of Arran. Dorothea is faithful to the king, disguising herself as a man when she learns that he seeks her life; she is wounded, but is reconciled to the king after Ida has married the English lord Eustace. Minor characters include *Machiavellian counsellor Ateukin and the affectionate dwarf Nano.

JAMIE, Kathleen (1962–) Scottish poet and travel writer, born in Renfrewshire, and brought up at Currie, near Edinburgh. An Edinburgh University philosophy graduate, she has taught creative writing at the University of St Andrews since 1999. The bulk of her early verse is collected in *Mr and Mrs Scotland Are Dead: Poems 1980–1994* (2002). Jamie's poetry is marked by a deepening lyricism and a slowly, almost reluctantly unfolding interest in Scottish themes and language. *Jizzen* (1999), a volume of interrelated poems broadly concerned with birth and childhood, includes a number of delicate lyrics in *Scots. The focus of *The Tree House* (2004) is on the natural world, apprehended in its quietness and vulnerability rather than its savagery. She has published two prose works, *The Golden Peak: Travels in North Pakistan* (1992; reissued as *Among Muslims*, 2002) and *Findings* (2005), a collection of autobiographical meditations on nature.

JAMIESON, John (1759–1838) Scottish clergyman, antiquarian, and lexicographer, born in Glasgow and educated at the University of Glasgow, who in 1808 produced the two-volume *Etymological Dictionary of the Scottish Language*, celebrated for its precision of definition and range of quotation.

Jane Eyre A novel by Charlotte *Brontë, published 1847. The heroine, a penniless orphan, has been left to the care of her aunt Mrs Reed. Harsh treatment rouses her defiant spirit, and a passionate outbreak leads to her consignment to Lowood School (based on the Clergy Daughters' School at Cowan Bridge, which the author herself briefly attended). There, consoled for the severity of the regime by the kindness of the superintendent Miss Temple and a fellow orphan, Helen Burns, who dies in Jane's arms of consumption, she spends some miserable years, eventually becoming a teacher. On Miss Temple's marriage she obtains a post as governess at Thornfield Hall to Adèle, the ward of Mr Rochester, a

*Byronic hero of grim aspect and sardonic temper. Rochester, despite Jane's plainness, is fascinated by her sharp wit and independence, and they fall in love. After much resistance she agrees to marry him, but on the eve of their wedding her wedding veil is torn by an intruder who Rochester assures her is a servant, Grace Poole, but who is the next day revealed to be his mad Creole wife Bertha, confined to the upper regions of the Hall for years, whose unseen presence has long disturbed Jane. The marriage ceremony is interrupted by Mrs Rochester's brother from the West Indies and, despite Rochester's full confession and pleadings with Jane to stay with him, she flees. After nearly perishing on the moors, she is taken in and cared for by the Revd St John Rivers and his sisters Mary and Diana. It emerges that they are her cousins, and that Jane has inherited money from an uncle; the legacy is equally divided between the four. Under pressure from the earnest appeals and strong personality of the dedicated Rivers, she nearly consents to marry him and share his missionary vocation in India, but is prevented by a telepathic appeal from Rochester. She returns to Thornfield Hall to find the building burned, and Rochester blinded and maimed from his attempt to save his wife from the flames. She marries him, and in the last chapter we learn that his sight is partially restored.

The novel's exceptional emotional and narrative power quickly made it a success, though, despite its strict adherence to conventional moral standards, it was considered by many to be unsuitable for young ladies. Additional scandal attended the publication of the second edition, which Charlotte dedicated to W. M. *Thackeray, unaware that he too had a wife certified as insane. More recently its strong sexual undercurrents have led to *Freudian interpretations encouraged by the author's frequent use of dream imagery, while Jane's spirited independence has attracted the attention of feminist critics; see S. Gilbert and S. Gubar, *The Madwoman in the Attic* (1979). The story of the first Mrs Rochester became the basis of *Wide Sargasso Sea*, a novel by Jean *Rhys.

JANOWITZ, Tama (1957–) American novelist, born in San Francisco, then resident in New York, whose fiction has been associated with Brett Easton Ellis (1964–) and others for its streetwise humour. Her first novel was *American Dad* (1981) but she achieved wider fame with her stories *Slaves of New York* (1986).

JARMAN, Derek (1942–94) Painter, writer, and film-maker, who became a 'queer' activist following his own HIV diagnosis in 1986. After studying literature and painting at London University, Jarman's first career was in set design for ballet and opera, which led to design for Ken Russell's films *The Devils* (1971) and *Savage Messiah* (1972). Subsequently, although continuing to exhibit as a painter, most of his work was in film, often shot informally in 8 mm. His first feature, *Sebastiane* (1976), with subtitled Latin dialogue and overt homosexuality, created a sensation, as did *Jubilee* (1977), a *dystopian punk view of contemporary England. Two Shakespeare films, *The *Tempest* (1979) and a dramatization of Shakespeare's *sonnets in *The Angelic Conversation* (1985), combined Jarman's literary interests with his acute sense of contemporary style, while *Caravaggio* (1986) and *Wittgenstein* (1993) portrayed the painter and the philosopher as gay heroes. In addition to published diaries, there is a compendious biography by Tony Peake (1999).

JARRELL, Randall (1914–65) American poet and critic, born in Nashville, Tennessee; he taught for many years in various colleges, and his one novel, *Pictures from an Institution* (1954), satirizes life in a progressive women's college. He published several volumes of poetry, from his first, *Blood for a Stranger* (1942), to *The Lost World*, published posthumously in 1966 with a memoir by his friend Robert *Lowell. His critical writings on contemporary poetry were collected in *Poetry and the Age* (1953). See William H. Pritchard, *Randall Jarrell: A Literary Life* (1990).

JARRY, Alfred *See* ABSURD, THEATRE OF THE.

Jaws A best-selling first novel by Peter Benchley, about a man-eating shark terrorizing an American seaside community, which set a new box-office record when filmed in 1975, making $100 million during its initial US release, and so launching the modern summer 'blockbuster'. Mechanical sharks, daring marine photography, dramatic music, and fine performances, notably by Robert Shaw as an Ahab-like sailor (*see* MOBY-DICK), combined to make Steven Spielberg's film a modern classic, launching his career as the pre-eminent director of lucrative popular spectacle.

jazz poetry A genre presaged in the USA by Vachel Lindsay (1879–1931) with his incantatory ballads 'General William Booth' (1913), 'The Congo' (1914), *The Daniel Jazz* (1920), and so on; and then by Langston *Hughes, who was probably the first to pitch his verse in conjunction with musicians in the late 1930s. The fusion was developed in the 1950s by Kenneth *Patchen, Kenneth *Rexroth, Amiri *Baraka (adopted name of black militant writer Everett Le Roi Jones), and the poets of the American *Beat Generation; and in Britain from the mid-1950s to the 1980s by Christopher *Logue, Roy *Fisher, Michael *Horovitz, Pete Brown (1940–), Spike Hawkins (1942–), and others. Various permutations of primarily non-academic, often regional, entertainers and singer-songwriters have proliferated since, with the punk-rock, post-punk, and 'new wave' voices of John Cooper Clarke (b. 1949), Paul Weller (b. 1958) of the band The Jam, and the Rastafarian and reggae-cadenced contributions of Anglo-Jamaican poets such as James *Berry, E. K. *Brathwaite, Linton Kwesi *Johnson, and Benjamin *Zephaniah.
See PERFORMANCE POETRY.

JEA, John (1773–1816) Born in what is now Nigeria and sold as a child, with his family, into slavery in New York. His autobiography *The Life, History, and Unparalleled Sufferings of John Jea, the African Preacher* (1811) describes his gradual conversion to Christianity, disastrous marriage, and missionary activity.

JEAN DE MEUN *See* Roman de la Rose.

Jean Paul An abbreviation frequently used in the 19th century of the name of Johann Paul Friedrich *Richter.

JEFFERIES, Richard (1848–87) Writer and naturalist, the son of a Wiltshire farmer. He attended a preparatory school in Sydenham, Kent, and subsequently a number of small private schools in Swindon, but much of his education was acquired through his own eager reading. He began his literary career as a local reporter in Wiltshire, and was soon writing copiously, including novels (which had no success), works of natural history and country life, and essays in journals and magazines. The books for which he is remembered combine his love of the natural world with a poetic apprehension and individuality of thought which blur the usual literary distinctions. He first attracted attention with *The Gamekeeper at Home: Sketches of Natural History and Rural Life* (1878), published first in the **Pall Mall Gazette*. This, together with *Hodge and his Masters* (1880), appears to have influenced Thomas *Hardy's article of 1883 on 'The Dorsetshire Labourer'. For these books, as for most of his others, Jefferies relied greatly on 'field notebooks', where he entered his meticulous observations on the life of the countryside. *Wild Life in a Southern County*, in which the author, sitting on a Wiltshire down, observes in ever widening circles the fields, woods, animals, and human inhabitants below him, was published with success in 1879, as was *The Amateur Poacher*. *Wood Magic* (1881), in which a solitary boy lives in a magical world of speaking wild animals, was followed in 1882 by **Bevis: The Story of a Boy*, an evocation (for both adults and children) of his country childhood (*see* children's literature). The book for which he was probably best known, *The Story of my Heart*, tracing the growth of his unorthodox beliefs, caused some scandal on its publication in 1883. *After London*, a savage vision of the future, in which London is a poisonous swamp inhabited by cruel dwarfs, followed in 1885, as did a much-reprinted collection of essays, *The Open Air*. Published in the year of his death, *Amaryllis at the Fair*, though lacking narrative, contains in Iden an impressive portrait of Jefferies's father. Jefferies's early death was a result of long-standing tubercular illness. See S. J. Looker and C. Porteous, *Richard Jefferies* (1965); there is also a life (1909) by Edward *Thomas.

JEFFERS, Robinson (1887–1962) American poet, born in Pittsburgh. He travelled widely with his parents and later settled, with his wife Una, at Carmel on the Californian coast, where they lived in seclusion. The scenery of the redwood and seashore inspires much of his works, and one of his dominant themes is what he called 'Inhumanism'—the insignificance of man, contrasted with the vast, merciless, enduring processes of nature and the animal kingdom; the hawk provides one of his most strikingly recurrent symbols. After two minor volumes he made his name with *Tamar and Other Poems* (1924), of which the title poem is a tragic narrative of family passion and incest in a wild Californian setting; this was followed by other volumes, many of them of a similar pattern—a long narrative, together with shorter lyrics, including *The Women at Point Sur* (1927). Jeffers numbered among his friends Edgar Lee *Masters and D. H. *Lawrence. He suffered a lapse in popularity due to his wartime espousal of an attitude of isolationism, expressed in 'The Eye'. He had a stage success with his adaptation of *Euripides' *Medea* in 1947 and his collected poems were published in 2001. See Melba Berry, *The Stone Mason of Tor House* (1966).

JEFFERSON, Thomas (1743–1826) Third president of the USA, born in Virginia, and main author of the Declaration of Independence. Among his literary interests was an enthusiasm for the poetry of *Ossian. In 1787 he published *Notes on the State of Virginia*, where he attacked the cruelties of Christianity and slavery, though he was himself a slave owner and believed African Americans to be racially inferior. William Wells *Brown's 1853 novel *Clotel* engages with the belief that Jefferson had children by his slave Sally Hemmings.

JEFFREY, Francis, Lord (1773–1850) Educated at Edinburgh and Glasgow universities, a Whig who became a Scottish judge and an MP. He is remembered in a literary connection as the founder, with Sydney *Smith, of the **Edinburgh Review* in 1802, as its editor until 1829, and as a stern but judicious critic of the writers of his day. Although he was often severe (and was challenged to a duel by Thomas *Moore), he nevertheless wrote appreciatively of many writers, including George *Crabbe, Walter *Scott, Lord *Byron, and, most notably, John *Keats, in whose *Poems* of 1820 he discerned genius. William *Hazlitt thought him an admirable editor, perceptive and just, with 'a great range of knowledge, an incessant activity of mind'. His critical blind spot was an inability to understand William *Wordsworth—his review of *The *Excursion* in 1814 begins: 'This will never do'—and this led to a series of attacks on 'a *sect* of poets' designated as 'The *Lake Poets'.

Jekyll and Hyde *See* Dr Jekyll and Mr Hyde.

JELLICOE, Ann (1927–) Playwright and director, born in Middlesbrough, Yorkshire, educated at Pollam House, Darlington, and Queen Margaret's School, Yorkshire; trained as an actress at the Central School of Speech and Drama. She was associated for some years with the *English Stage Company, which put on the play which made her name, *The Sport of my Mad Mother* (1958), an experimental drama about a London street gang. This was followed by *The Knack* (1962) and *Shelley* (1965). She has also written plays for children and drama-documentaries on historical themes performed by the local West Country community, including *The Reckoning* (1978), set in Lyme Regis and based on the 1685 Monmouth Rebellion. A pioneer in community theatre, in 1985 she worked with David *Edgar on his community play *Entertaining Strangers* in Dorchester, and in 1987 published her handbook, *Community Plays: How to Put Them On*.

JENKINS, Robin (1912–2005) Scottish novelist, born in Flemington, Lanarkshire, and educated at Glasgow University, whose many novels explore issues of morality and self-deception in the context of a materialistic understanding of society. His best-known works include *The Cone-Gatherers* (1955), *The Changeling* (1958), *A Very Scotch Affair* (1968), and *Fergus Lamont* (1979). Many of his novels deal with the depressed west of Scotland of the author's childhood and early manhood, but some—notably *Some Kind of Grace* (1960) and the strongly anti-imperialist *The Holy Tree* (1969), set respectively in Afghanistan and Borneo—reflect his mid-career experience as a teacher and employee of the British Council in Asia.

JENNINGS, Elizabeth (1926–2001) Poet, born in Boston, Lincolnshire, of a Roman Catholic family, and educated at St Anne's College, Oxford. She worked as a library assistant, in advertising, and in publishing, while publishing her early collections of poetry, *Poems* (1953), *A Way of Looking* (1955), and *A Sense of the World* (1958). She was somewhat arbitrarily associated with the *Movement, through Robert Conquest's inclusion of some of her work in **New Lines* (1956), but her subsequent volumes of verse (e.g. *Recoveries*, 1964; *The Mind has Mountains*, 1966) are highly personal and confessional accounts of mental breakdown and hospital treatment, very far removed in tone from the laconic detachment of the more representative Movement poets. Her *Collected Poems* were published in 1967 (revised and extended 1987) and she subsequently published several more volumes, including *Lucidities* (1970) and *Moments of Grace* (1979), which manifest her quiet and sensitive control of, and openness towards, experiences of suffering, loneliness, friendship, and religious faith. Other volumes include *Celebrations and Elegies* (1982), *Extending the Territory* (1985), *Tributes* (1989), *Times and Seasons* (1992), and *Familiar Spirits* (1994). She also published two volumes of prose, *Every Changing Shape* (critical essays, 1961) and *Christianity and Poetry* (1965).

JENNINGS, Humphrey (1907–50) Film-maker, painter, and writer, widely considered the leading figure in British *documentary film of the 1930s and 1940s, also active in *Surrealism and co-founder with Charles *Madge in 1937 of *Mass Observation, the influence of which is apparent in his *Spare Time* (1939). Jennings's wartime films, *Listen to Britain* (1942), *Fires Were Started* (1943), and *A Diary for Timothy* (1945), combine stirring patriotism with a wry view of war's incongruity. His last films, *Dim Little Island* (1949) and *Family Portrait* (1950), reflected on Britain's post-war prospects before a fatal accident on location in Greece cut short his career. A collage text on the impact of the Industrial Revolution, *Pandaemonium*, appeared posthumously and Kevin Jackson's fine biography (2004) explores his Cambridge cultural milieu, including close friendship with William *Empson.

'Jenny' A poem by D. G. *Rossetti, first published 1870, although he had worked on it for many years and continued to do so. It was among the poems buried with his wife Lizzie in 1862 and later exhumed. The speaker describes a night spent with a prostitute, golden-haired Jenny; as she sleeps, he meditates on her position as a fallen woman and implicitly on his own status as her client. It is a controversial study of Victorian sexual attitudes, which offended those like R. W. *Buchanan who thought Rossetti's work too sensual. Fallen women were favourite subjects with the *Pre-Raphaelites, as in Rossetti's painting *Found* and Holman *Hunt's *The Awakening Conscience*.

JENYNS, Soame (1704–87) MP, essayist, and poet, whose *Free Enquiry into the Nature and Origin of Evil* (1757) elicited a scathing attack from Samuel *Johnson in the *Literary Magazine*. Jenyns justified suffering as necessary within the 'scale of Being' and ignorance as the 'opiate' of the poor, recalling the moral philosophy of Alexander Pope's **Essay on Man*. Johnson attacked the facile optimism of these views. Jenyns's epitaph on Johnson was reprinted, and reproved, by James *Boswell.

jeremiad A prophetic warning or lament of a country's moral or social degradation, alluding to the biblical books of Jeremiah and Lamentations predicting and lamenting the fall of *Jerusalem to *Babylon.

JEROME, St (Hieronymus) (331/*c.*342–420) Church Father, and *Bible translator. Born at Stridon in Croatia, Jerome studied and was baptized in Rome, where he was later secretary to Pope Damasus (382–5). An ascetic, he had previously spent four or five years as a hermit in Syria, where he learnt Hebrew. From 386 to his death, he lived in Bethlehem, ruling the monastery, studying, and translating. A literary man as well as a Christian, he was the unsurpassed master of Latin among the *Fathers of the church.

Commissioned by Damasus to make a new Latin translation of the Bible, he followed the Hebrew text for the Old Testament rather than the Septuagint Greek favoured by his contemporaries, and translated it more literally than he would have a secular text. Though opposed, his work became the *Vulgate or common translation, the official Bible of the Roman Catholic Church. See J. N. D. Kelly, *Jerome* (1975).

JEROME, Jerome K. (Klapka) (1859–1927) Novelist, dramatist, and journalist, born in Walsall, Staffordshire, and educated at what was later renamed Marylebone Grammar School, London. He became an actor and published a volume of humorous pieces about the theatre, *On the Stage—and Off* (1885), and another collection of light essays, *Idle Thoughts of an Idle Fellow* (1886); *Barbara*, the first of his many plays, was produced in the same year. He achieved lasting fame with *Three Men in a Boat* (1889), the comic story of three young men and their dog who take a rowing holiday on the Thames. *Three Men on the Bummel*, describing a tour in Germany (which Jerome visited in 1898–9), appeared unsuccessfully in 1900, and in 1902 he published *Paul Klever*, an autobiographical novel. Another of his well-received plays is *The Passing of the Third Floor Back* (1908). There is a life by J. Connolly (1982).

JERROLD, Douglas William (1803–57) Playwright, novelist, and journalist; the son of an actor-manager. He briefly attended schools in Sheerness and Southend, served in the navy, was apprenticed to a printer, and became dramatic author of the Surrey Theatre before making his name in the theatre with *Black-Ey'd Susan* (1829), founded on John *Gay's ballad; other successful plays included *Fifteen Years of a Drunkard's Life* (1828), *The Rent Day* (1832), and *The Prisoner of War* (1842). He was a friend of Charles *Dickens. In his later years Jerrold turned to journalism; he was associated with **Punch* from its beginnings and became a regular contributor, writing several serial works, including liberal political articles signed 'Q', and *Mrs Caudle's Curtain Lectures* (issued as a book in 1846), a comic series which greatly added to the journal's popularity. From 1845 he ran *Douglas Jerrold's Shilling Magazine* and from 1846 *Douglas Jerrold's Weekly Newspaper*. He wrote several novels and his studies of *Men of Character* (1838) were illustrated by W. M. *Thackeray.

Jerusalem Also known as Zion, Sion, Salem, the City of *David (a phrase also used for Bethlehem), and the Holy City; often thought of particularly as God's dwelling place, his 'holy hill of Zion' (Psalm 2: 6). As the site of the Jewish Temple, the passion and crucifixion of Jesus, and Muhammad's ascension to heaven, Jerusalem is the holy city of three religions, important both as a place and as a symbol. After Babylon had destroyed it (587/6 BC) and exiled the Jewish people, ideal visions of a new Jerusalem, together with new heavens and a new earth, became a potent symbol of hope and promise (see e.g. Isaiah 65: 17–25, Revelation 21). Notable literary images of the new Jerusalem include 'the heavenly Jerusalem', the object of Christian's pilgrimage in Bunyan's **Pilgrim's Progress*, and Blake's **Jerusalem*.

***Jerusalem:** The Emanation of the Giant Albion* A prophetic poem by William *Blake, written and etched 1804–20. (It is not to be confused with the poem beginning 'And did those feet…', commonly known as 'Jerusalem', which appears at the beginning of Blake's **Milton*.) After a preface in which he defends his use of free verse ('Poetry Fetter'd Fetters the Human Race'), Blake proceeds to personify England as the fallen giant Albion, and to summon him to the 'awakening of Eternal Life'. The poem ends with a 'fourfold vision' of regeneration, 'rejoicing in Unity in the Four Senses' and in the 'forgiveness of Sins which is Self-Annihilation'.

Jerusalem Delivered (*Gerusalemme liberata*) A poem by *Tasso, published without his consent 1580, in authorized form 1581. Tasso later rewrote the poem, giving it a more regular structure and a more austere moral tone, and changing the title to *Gerusalemme conquistata*. The new work, published 1593, is generally considered inferior to the original.

The poem is an *epic of the First Crusade, with the addition of romantic and fabulous elements. By the side of Godfrey of Bouillon, the leader of the Christian host besieging Jerusalem, and other historical characters, we have the romantic figures of Sofronia and her lover Olindo, who are prepared to face martyrdom to save the Christians in the beleaguered city; the warlike Clorinda, who is beloved by Tancred the Norman, and killed by him unwittingly; and Armida, the niece of the king of Damascus, who lures the Christians to her enchanted gardens. Rinaldo, prince of Este (an imaginary personage, introduced as a way of extolling the author's patron), rescues the prisoners of Armida, and Armida falls in love with him. By her enchantments they live happily together until Rinaldo is summoned away to help the army by defeating the devil-enchanted wood. He takes part in the capture of Jerusalem, and at last is reconciled with a repentant Armida. The poem was translated into English in 1594 by Richard Carew (1555–1620), and in 1600 by Edward *Fairfax as *Godfrey of Bulloigne*. Spenser's description of Acrasia's Bower of Bliss (**Faerie Queene*, II. xii) was modelled on the gardens of Armida, and the poem considerably influenced *Milton and others (*see* TASSO, TORQUATO).

Jessica's First Prayer A novel for children and newly literate readers by Hesba *Stretton, first published in *Sunday at Home* (1866). It tells the story of a neglected girl, one of the impoverished 'street arabs' for whose welfare Stretton campaigned vigorously, who is eventually rescued from poverty and adopted by a coffee-stall keeper. It sold two million copies in her lifetime. It was in part an attack on the hypocrisy of prosperous church and chapel congregations who ignored the plight of the poor, but its vivid descriptions of deprivation, and its optimistic conclusion, gave it a wide appeal. It was widely translated, and was for a while (by order of Tsar Alexander II) compulsory reading in all Russian schools.

jest book literature Collections of 'merry tales', 'quick answers', and 'pleasant conceits' popular throughout the 16th and 17th centuries and later. Their authorship was often ascribed to witty writers such as John *Skelton and George *Peele or to famous jesters such as John *Scoggin and Robert Armin. The genre is related to the apophthegm (a pithy, practical saying) and adage (a proberbial saying), popularized by *Erasmus, and to *rogue literature, and can be detected in some early fiction, for example in the opening of Thomas *Nashe's *The *Unfortunate Traveller*.

JETER, K. W. (Kevin Wayne) (1950–) American author of *science fiction and *horror, born in Los Angeles. *Morlock Night* (1979) is a sequel to H. G. *Wells's *The Time Machine*. Known for *Dr Adder* (1984), he has also written sequels to the Ridley Scott film *Blade Runner* (1982).

JEWETT, Sarah Orne (1849–1909) American novelist and short story writer, born in Maine. She was inspired when young by Harriet Beecher *Stowe's novel set in Maine, *The Pearl of Orris Island* (1862), to write about her native region of New England, and began her career by publishing short stories in the **Atlantic Monthly*. Her volumes include *Deephaven* (1877), *A Country Doctor* (1884), *A White Heron* (1886; short stories), and *The Country of the Pointed Firs* (1896), which describes daily life in a decaying Maine seaport town. Her precise, realistic, subdued portraits of ordinary people and her sense of community and place bear witness to her admiration for Gustave *Flaubert. Willa *Cather records her debt to her in *Not under Forty* (1936). See Paula Blanchard, *Sarah Orne Jewett* (1994).

Jew of Malta, The An ironical tragedy in blank verse by Christopher *Marlowe, performed about 1592, not published until 1633. The governor of Malta decides that the Jews of the island should pay the tribute demanded by Turkey. Barabas, a rich Jew who resists the edict, has his wealth impounded and his house turned into a nunnery. In revenge he embarks on an orgy of slaughter, killing his daughter Abigail's lover among others, and poisoning Abigail. He betrays Malta to the Turks and, as a reward, is made its governor. He now plots to use a collapsible floor to destroy the Turks at a banquet, but is himself betrayed and hurled through this same floor into a cauldron, where he dies. The prologue to the play is spoken by 'Machevil', and Barabas is one of the prototypes for unscrupulous *Machiavellian villains in later Elizabethan and Jacobean drama. His praise of gold and precious stones as 'Infinite riches in a little room' is often quoted. The play has been successfully revived in modern times.

JEWSBURY, Geraldine Endsor (1812–80) Novelist, journalist, and intimate friend of the *Carlyles. Born in Manchester, the daughter of a cotton manufacturer and his artistically inclined wife, she was educated at the Misses Darbys' boarding school, near Tamworth. Her brilliant wit and conversation made her house in Manchester, and later in London, a centre for such eminent visitors as the Carlyles, J. A. *Froude, T. H. *Huxley, John *Ruskin, D. G. *Rossetti, and Connop *Thirlwall. Besides contributing numerous articles and reviews to the **Athenaeum*, the **Westminster Review*, and other journals, and acting as a 'literary adviser' for Richard Bentley (it was on the basis of her recommendation that he published Ellen *Wood's **East Lynne*), she wrote six novels, including *Zöe* (1845), *The Half Sisters* (1848), and *Marian Withers* (1851), and two stories for children. Heavily influenced by her admiration of Thomas Carlyle and George *Sand, the central subject of Jewsbury's forthright and often controversial fiction is the limitation—educational, financial, and emotional—of middle-class women's lives. She never married, but was involved in several intensely emotional entanglements with men. Jewsbury destroyed all the letters to her from Jane Carlyle, except for one which was published in Mrs Annie Ireland's *Life of Jane Welsh Carlyle* (1891); it was the wish of both women that their letters be destroyed.

JEWSBURY, Maria Jane (1800–33) Poet, and sister of Geraldine *Jewsbury; born in Measham, Leicestershire, and educated at Miss Adams's school in Shenstone, Staffordshire, she was the daughter of a cotton manufacturer and kept house for him in Manchester after her mother's death. In 1832 she married W. K. Fletcher, a chaplain with the East India Company. She published poetry and essays, contributed to the *Manchester Courier* and the **Athenaeum*, and was a close friend of the *Wordsworths. Her most remarkable work was perhaps the 'Oceanides', a poem which she wrote on her voyage out to India, 1832–3, and which was published in twelve sections in *The Athenaeum*; the poem vividly celebrates the stages and changing moods of the voyage. She died of cholera not long after her arrival.

JHABVALA, Ruth Prawer (1927–) Novelist, born in Germany, the daughter of a Polish Jewish solicitor; she came to England in 1939 as a refugee and was educated in London. In 1951 she married a Parsi Indian architect, and subsequently lived for 24 years in India, where she wrote several novels including *Esmond in India* (1958), *A New Dominion* (1973), and *Heat and Dust* (1975, *Booker Prize), all of which reflect her mingled affection for and discomfort with her adopted country and, pitched from the vantage point of double exile, show intimate knowledge of the lives of both Indian and European families. She published volumes of short stories and wrote several original screenplays, including *Shakespeare-Wallah* (1965), the story of a troupe of travelling actors, and screen adaptations of E. M. Forster's *A *Room with a View* and **Howards End*, both produced by Merchant-Ivory, for which she won Academy Awards. In 1975 she moved to New York, where her novel *In Search of Love and Beauty* (1983) and numerous later works are set.

jig 'An afterpiece in the form of a brief farce which was sung and accompanied by dancing', popular in the Elizabethan and Jacobean theatre. Few survive, but there are numerous references to them in contemporary literature and both William *Kemp and Richard *Tarlton performed them with great success. Compare *Hamlet's comment on Polonius: 'he's for a jig, or a tale of bawdry, or he sleeps' (II. ii. 503–4). There is a study, *The Elizabethan Jig*, by C. R. Baskervill (1919); see also C. J. Sisson, *Lost Plays of Shakespeare's Age* (1936).

JOAN OF ARC, St (1412–31) Jeanne d'Arc, or more correctly Jeanne Darc, as it was spelt in all contemporary documents, the daughter of Jacques Darc, a farmer of Domrémy in the valley of the Meuse, an illiterate girl who contributed powerfully to liberate France from the English in the reign of Charles VII. Inspired, she claimed, by the voices of Sts Michael, Catherine, and Margaret, her mission was a double one, to raise the siege of Orléans, and to conduct Charles to his coronation at Rheims. She accomplished these tasks and then wished to return home; but she yielded to the demands of the French patriots and was taken prisoner by the Burgundians, who handed her over to the English. But it was a French court of ecclesiastics (with the help of the Inquisition) who sentenced her as a heretic, and the English who burned her at Rouen. She was canonized in 1920. She appears in Shakespeare's *1 *Henry VI*, and is the subject of *Voltaire's *La Pucelle*, a tragedy by *Schiller, a poem by Robert *Southey, and a drama by Jean *Anouilh. George Bernard *Shaw's play *Saint Joan* was successfully revived at the National Theatre in 2007. See Marina *Warner's *Joan of Arc: The Image of Female Heroism* (1981) for a discussion of St Joan's changing function as national and political symbol.

Job *See* BIBLE.

Jocasta A tragedy in blank verse, translated from an Italian adaptation of the *Phoenissae* of *Euripides, by George *Gascoigne and Francis Kinwelmarshe, included in Gascoigne's *Posies* (1575).

Jocoseria A volume of ten poems of various lengths and metres by Robert *Browning, published 1883. The collection is consciously a miscellany. Browning borrowed the title from Otto Melander's book of jokes and stories (1597) to suggest its lightweight character, though several of the poems ('Donald', 'Cristina and Monaldeschi', 'Ixion') do not bear out this judgement. The volume contains the much-parodied lyric 'Wanting is—what?', an exquisite miniature on the notion of art as a form of desire.

Johannes Factotum 'John Do-everything', a Jack-of-all-trades, a would-be universal genius. The phrase, as also *Dominus Factotum, Magister Factotum*, and the corresponding Italian *fa il tutto*, is found in the 16th century. It occurs in **Greene's Groat's-Worth of Wit*, attacking *Shakespeare for 'being an absolute *Johannes Fac Totum*', who 'is in his own conceit the onely Shake-scene in a country'.

JOHN, St *See* BIBLE; EVANGELISTS.

JOHN, Augustus (1878–1961) OM, painter, born at Tenby, the son of a solicitor, and trained at the Slade School. He made his name with his accomplished drawings and etchings, and was later celebrated as a perceptive portraitist. His autobiography, *Chiaroscuro* (1952), contains many anecdotes about writers whom he met or knew as friends (including Oscar *Wilde, G. B. *Shaw, James *Joyce, and Wyndham *Lewis), and he also painted some remarkable portraits of literary figures, including W. B. *Yeats, Shaw, Dylan *Thomas, T. E. *Lawrence, Ronald *Firbank, and Joyce. Michael *Holroyd's two-volume biography (1974–5) gives a full account of John's flamboyant personality and unorthodox domestic life, and suggests various fictitious characters who were partly based on John, including Struthers in D. H. *Lawrence's **Aaron's Rod*, Albert Sanger in *The Constant Nymph* by Margaret Kennedy (1896–1967). Gulley Jimson in Joyce *Cary's *The Horse's Mouth*, and the younger Strickland in Somerset *Maugham's *The Moon and Sixpence*. His sister Gwen John (1876–1939), who also studied at the Slade, was a painter of distinction.

John Bull, The History of A collection of pamphlets by John *Arbuthnot, the first of which, *Law is a Bottomless Pit*, appeared on 6 March 1712. They characterized the War of Spanish Succession under coded satirical stories, designed to promote the peace negotiations of Robert *Harley's administration. John Bull represents England: 'an honest plain-dealing fellow, choleric, bold, and of a very inconstant temper...very apt to quarrel with his best friends, especially if they pretend to govern him...a boon companion, loving his bottle and his diversion.' Other characters are Nicholas Frog (the Dutch), Lord Strutt (Philip of Spain), Lewis Baboon (Louis XIV of France), and Humphrey Hocus, an attorney (the duke of Marlborough). See the edition by A. W. Bower and R. A. Erickson (1976).

John Bull's Other Island An ironic description of Ireland deriving from Leon Paul Blouet's *John Bull and his Island* (1884) and used by G. B. *Shaw as the title of a play written at the request of W. B. *Yeats for the opening of the *Abbey Theatre. Yeats declined to stage the play, however, and it opened instead at the Court Theatre in London in November 1904 to great success.
See IRISH LITERARY THEATRE.

John Buncle Esq., The Life and Opinions of A novel by Thomas *Amory (2 vols, 1756, 1766). The eccentric Buncle sets out on a journey through the magnificent landscapes of northern England. He comes upon small centres of civilized culture, encountering beautiful, learned women, seven of whom (with the intervention of successive deaths) he marries: Miss Spence, with 'the head of Aristotle, the heart of a primitive Christian, and the form of Venus de Medicis', is typical. The book otherwise consists of eloquent digressions on religious, scientific, and literary subjects. William *Hazlitt found 'the soul of Rabelais' in the book.

'John Gilpin, The Diverting History of' Popular poem by William *Cowper, published anonymously in 1782 in the *Public Advertiser*, and reprinted in the same volume as *The *Task* (1785). John Gilpin, a 'linen-draper bold' of Cheapside, tries to ride to the Bell at Edmonton for his wedding anniversary party, but a bolting horse carries him ten miles beyond it. Lady Austen told Cowper the story to amuse him, and he rapidly turned it into a ballad.

John Halifax, Gentleman A novel by Dinah *Craik published 1856. The story, set between the Bredon Hills in Worcestershire and the provincial town of Tewkesbury, tells of the orphan John, who finds employment with the tanner Abel Fletcher. He is befriended by Abel's weakling son Phineas Fletcher (the name recalls the 17th-century poet Phineas *Fletcher), improves his position, and marries the book's heroine, Ursula March. Phineas's narrative function as an onlooker, the constantly loving observer of his friend's trials and successes, contributes to the emotional density and complexity that makes the novel more than a conventional rags-to-riches story. Despite setbacks and sorrows, including the death of his much-loved blind daughter and the restlessness of his younger children, John dies a prosperous and universally respected man. His status as 'gentleman' is earned not by birth and wealth but by his own Christian integrity and worth. The book's thoughtful analysis of the transfer of cultural and economic power from the aristocracy to the commercial middle classes made it immensely successful in both England and America, and it ran into numerous editions over many years. It was one of the first novels to give a heroic role to a tradesman, and helped to break down the suspicion of fiction among Nonconformist readers. Long after Craik's death American tourists would visit the 'Halifax country' of Tewkesbury.

JOHN OF GAUNT (1340–99) Duke of Lancaster, the fourth son of Edward III and father of Henry IV, named from his birthplace, Ghent. He was effectively regent during the early years of the young Richard II's reign and afterwards his bitter enemy. He supported John *Wyclif for a while and was patron of *Chaucer, whose *The *Book of the Duchess* is believed to commemorate the death of Gaunt's wife Blanche in 1369. He is a major figure in *Shakespeare's **Richard II*.

JOHN OF SALISBURY (late 1110s–1180) Churchman and outstanding humanist scholar; he was born in Old Sarum and studied at Paris under *Abelard. He was secretary to Theobald, archbishop of Canterbury, and subsequently to St Thomas *Becket, with whom he was exiled when the latter temporarily fell into disfavour with Henry II. He wrote a life of Becket and of St *Anselm, arguing for the canonization of both. Ultimately he became bishop of Chartres in 1176. Among his many works, the principal items are the influential *Polycraticus* (or *De Nugis Curialium*), on the vanities of the court and miscellaneous questions on philosophy, and the *Metalogicon*, a defence of the seven liberal arts which conveys his respect for great authors and argues for the value of a liberal education. See *Polycraticus*, ed. C. C. J. Webb (1909); *Metalogicon*, ed. J. B. Hall and K. S. B. Keats-Rohan (1991).

JOHN OF THE CROSS, St (Juan de la Cruz) (1542–91) Educated by the Jesuits and at Salamanca, a Spanish friar of the Carmelite order and a major figure of the Counter-Reformation. Encouraged by St *Teresa of Ávila, he became a joint founder of the Discalced (or Barefoot) Carmelites, and she was a considerable influence on his spiritual understanding and grasp of practical affairs. He was imprisoned in Toledo in 1577 for his reformist views, an experience which inspired some of his finest mystical writing. Fewer than 1,000 lines of his poetry survive, but they are among the greatest in the Spanish language: particularly his *Cántico espiritual* (*Spiritual Canticle*), most of which was composed in prison; his *Nocha oscura* (*The Dark Night*), composed shortly afterwards; and *Llama de amor viva* (*The Living Flame of Love*), written *c.*1583–4. He writes of the stages of union of the soul with God, and of the ecstasy of that union, in a language both erotic and spiritual, and of an exceptional power, grace, and intensity. A selection of his poems was translated by Roy *Campbell (1951) and his collected works by K. Kavanaugh and O. Rodríguez (1991). See Colin Thompson, *St John of the Cross: Songs in the Night* (2002).

JOHNS, 'Captain' W. E. (William Earl) (1893–1968) Born in Bengeo, Hertfordshire; Johns was an RAF bomber pilot in 1918. His criticism of government armaments policy lost him his editorship of *Popular Flying* and *Flying* in 1939, but his fictional flying hero, *Biggles, was such a successful RAF recruiting device he was asked to produce a female equivalent—Joan Worralson (*Worrals of the WAAF*, 1941)—and Gimlet King (*King of the Commandos*, 1943) for the army. Johns wrote 169 books.

JOHNSON, Amryl (1944–2001) Poet, born in Trinidad; she moved to Britain as a child. Graduating from Kent University, she quickly established herself as a poet and skilled performer with *Long Road to Nowhere* (1985), *Gorgons* (1992), and *Calling* (2000). *Sequins for a Ragged Hem* (1988) is a Caribbean travelogue.

JOHNSON, B. S. (Bryan Stanley) (1933–73) Novelist, poet, and film-maker, born in Hammersmith, London. After graduating from King's College London he published seven novels, each highly adventurous in form. *Travelling People* (1963) is a lightweight novel of comic misadventures, each chapter written in a different style; *Albert Angelo* (1964) vividly evokes the London of its era, and has holes cut through the pages to provide a 'flashforward' to future events. *Trawl* (1967) and *The Unfortunates* (1969) are autobiographical pieces, the latter consisting of unbound sections presented in a box. (*See* INTERACTIVE FICTION.) *House Mother Normal* (1971), *Christie Malry's Own Double Entry* (1973), and *See the Old Lady Decently* (1975) continue his passionate crusade to break free of the confines of the neo-Dickensian novel. Johnson's work has an emotional candour and directness unusual in a so-called 'experimental' writer; the same qualities are to be found in his two volumes of poetry. He committed suicide at the age of 40. See *Like a Fiery Elephant* (2004), a biography by J. *Coe.

JOHNSON, Charles R. (Richard) (1948–) African American novelist, born in Evanston, Illinois, who was active as a cartoonist in the 1960s before publishing his first novel, *Faith and the Good Thing*, in 1974. In 1995 he aroused controversy by seeming to criticize Alice *Walker in his introduction to his *Oxherding Tale*. Apart from his novels, in 1988 he published *Being and Race: Black Writing since 1970*, and in 1997 edited the collection *Black Men Speaking*. He has written screenplays and his essays and articles were collected in *I Call Myself an Artist* (1999).

JOHNSON, Diane (1934–) American novelist and biographer, born in Illinois. Her ironic and observant novels, many of which have a hint of thriller suspense, include *Fair Game* (1965); *The Shadow Knows* (1972), about a woman pursued and victimized; and *Persian Nights* (1987), set in Persia on the eve of revolution, seen through the eyes of an innocent American abroad. *Le Divorce* (1997), *Le Mariage* (2000), and *L'Affaire* (2003) are a trilogy of manners with a violent undertow, set in Paris. She co-wrote the screenplay for *The Shining* (1980) by Stanley Kubrick (1928–99), and has also written an innovative feminist life of Mary Ellen Peacock (1821–61), wife of George *Meredith (*Lesser Lives*, 1972), and a life of Dashiell *Hammett (1983).

JOHNSON, James Weldon (1871–1938) African American writer and civil rights activist, born in Jacksonville, Florida. He trained as a lawyer and served as US consul in South America in the early 1900s. In 1912 he published (anonymously) *The Autobiography of an Ex-Coloured Man*, describing the masked identity of a young African American in a white world. Between 1916 and 1930 he served as leader of the National Association for the Advancement of Coloured People (NAACP). Johnson was a prominent figure in the *Harlem Renaissance, a productive poet, and a researcher into anthropology, publishing several collections of spirituals. He published an autobiography, *Along This Way*, in 1934. See Eugene Levy, *James Weldon Johnson: Black Leader, Black Voice* (1976).

JOHNSON, Joseph (1738–1809) A radical bookseller and publisher of St Paul's Churchyard, who encouraged and published many writers, including *Wordsworth (*Descriptive Sketches*, 1793), Anna Laetitia *Barbauld, William *Cowper, Erasmus *Darwin, and Mary *Wollstonecraft. He held literary dinners over the shop, where his guests included William *Blake, Henry *Fuseli, William *Godwin, Joseph *Priestley, and Thomas *Paine. From 1788 to 1799 he published the scientific and literary monthly the **Analytical Review*. Although his shop served as an important meeting place, he himself had the reputation of a retiring and self-effacing man.

JOHNSON, Linton Kwesi (1952–) Poet, performer, and reggae artist; born in Jamaica, he came to England in 1963 to join his mother who had emigrated two years earlier, and was educated in south London and Goldsmiths' College, where he studied sociology. His first books of poems, *Voices of the Living and the Dead* (1974) and *Dread Beat an' Blood* (1975), introduced his characteristic voice of disaffected dissent, with bleak and powerful lyrics. He coined the term *'dub poetry' to describe the way reggae DJs blend music and verse. Later volumes of verse and albums include *Forces of Victory* (1979) with its influential 'Sonny's Lettah', condemning 'suspicion laws', *Bass Culture* (1980), *Inglan Is a Bitch* (1980), *Making History* (1984), and *Mi Revalueshanary Fren* (2002). His work (*Tings an' Times*, CD, 1991, and *More Time*, CD, 1998, with its haunting single 'Liesense Fi Kill') continues to show a strong political commitment to the cause of black rights.

JOHNSON, Lionel Pigot (1867–1902) Poet, critic, and essayist, educated at Winchester College and New College, Oxford. He became an influential man of letters, and one of the notable Catholic converts of his day. A perceptive supporter of Thomas *Hardy, his *The Art of Thomas Hardy* (1894) was among the first full-length studies to appear. His *Poems* appeared in 1895, *Ireland and Other Poems* in 1897, and *Post Liminium*, a posthumous collection of essays, in 1911. He was a member of the *Rhymers Club and a friend of W. B. *Yeats, who much admired his poetry; there is an account of his personality and decline into alcoholism in Yeats's *Autobiographies*.
See ART FOR ART'S SAKE.

JOHNSON, Pamela Hansford (1912–81) Critic and novelist, the granddaughter of Henry Irving's treasurer, brought up in Clapham, where she attended Clapham County Girls Grammar School. The district is evoked in several of her many works, from her first novel, *This Bed thy Centre* (1935), to her last, *The Bonfire* (1981). In 1950 she married C. P. *Snow. She is most widely known for her 'Dorothy Merlin' trilogy, a satire on the pretensions of literary life, which consists of *The Unspeakable Skipton* (1959), *Night and Silence, Who is Here* (1962), and *Cork Street, Next to the Hatter's* (1965).

JOHNSON, Richard (*fl.* 1592–1622) Author of *The Most Famous History of the Seven Champions of Christendome* (1596–7), a widely read chivalric romance, which influenced Edmund *Spenser; *The Nine Worthies of London* (1592); two collections of ballads (1612; 1620), the second of which refers to plays by *Shakespeare; *Tom a Lincoln*, an Arthurian romance (*c.*1599; earliest surviving edition 1631); and the *jest book *Pleasant Conceits of Old Hobson* (1607).

JOHNSON, Robert (*c.*1583–1633) Court lutenist. From 1607 he composed music for songs in plays, including **Cymbeline*, *The *Winter's Tale*, and *The *Tempest*: 'Full fathom five' and 'Where the bee sucks' are his best-known settings. He also composed for plays by Thomas *Middleton, John *Webster, Ben *Jonson, and Francis *Beaumont and John *Fletcher.

JOHNSON, Samuel (1709–84) Writer, born at Lichfield, son of a bookseller. At the age of 3 he was brought to London to be touched for the king's evil (scrofula) by Queen Anne; the illness seriously affected his sight, but he was from an early age an avid reader. He was educated at Lichfield Grammar School and Pembroke College, Oxford, where he spent fourteen months, 1728–9, but took no degree. He worked briefly and unhappily as an under-master at Market Bosworth, then moved to Birmingham, where he contributed essays (none of which survive) to the *Birmingham Journal*, and translated and abridged from French an account (originally in Portuguese) of Father Lobo's *Voyage to Abyssinia* (1735). In the same year he married Elizabeth Porter, a widow twenty years his senior, and started a private school at Edial, near Lichfield. This was not a success; Johnson's lack of a degree and convulsive mannerisms hindered his prospects as a teacher, and in 1737 he set off with one of his few pupils, David *Garrick, to London. Having contacted Edward *Cave, he began regular contributions to the **Gentleman's Magazine*, writing prefaces, essays, poems, Latin verses, biographies, and, most notably, his *Parliamentary Debates*, which were widely accepted as authentic speeches by the great politicians of the day. In 1738 he published his poem **London*, based in part on his friendship with the poet Richard *Savage, whose nocturnal wanderings he often shared during this period of poorly paid hack-work; his *Life of Mr Richard Savage* (1744) is a vivid evocation of the pitfalls of *Grub Street. It was subsequently included in his **Lives of the English Poets*. In *Marmor Norfolciense* (1739), Johnson attacked Robert Walpole (1676–1745), and his *Compleat Vindication of the Licensers of the Stage* (1739) was an ironic 'defence' of the Stage Licensing Act of 1737 by which Walpole's government suppressed Henry *Brooke's *Gustavus Vasa*. In 1743–4 he was employed, with William Oldys (1696–1761), on the **Harleian Miscellany.* His *Miscellaneous Observations on the Tragedy of Macbeth* (1745) brought him the praise of William *Warburton. In 1747 Johnson issued the 'Plan' of his Dictionary (*see* JOHNSON'S DICTIONARY), on which he had already started work at his new home in Gough Square; he dedicated the plan to the earl of *Chesterfield. In 1749 he published *The *Vanity of Human Wishes*, the first work to bear his own name, and in the same year Garrick produced his tragedy **Irene*, written in 1736 at Edial; while not particularly successful on stage, it brought him almost £300. In 1750 he started the **Rambler*, a periodical written almost entirely by himself. His wife died in 1752, a loss which caused him intense and prolonged grief. From March 1753 to March 1754 Johnson contributed regularly to John *Hawkesworth's *Adventurer*; in 1754 his biography of his old employer Cave appeared in the *Gentleman's Magazine*. His *Dictionary* was published in 1755, after nine years of labour; it firmly established his reputation, and also brought him, just before publication and through the support of the librarian and antiquary Francis Wise (1695–1767) and Thomas *Warton, the Oxford degree he had failed to achieve earlier. He continued to write essays, reviews, and political articles for various periodicals, and during 1758–60 wrote the **Idler* papers. In 1759 appeared his only extended fiction, **Rasselas*. In 1762 Johnson was relieved from hack-work by a Crown pension of £300 a year. The following year he met his biographer, James *Boswell, in the bookshop of his friend Thomas *Davies.

By this point Johnson was one of the most eminent literary figures of his day, the centre of a circle of distinguished figures like Joshua *Reynolds, Edmund *Burke, and Oliver *Goldsmith. The *Club was founded in 1764 to hold regular meetings of such men; later members included Garrick, Charles James *Fox, and Boswell. Although Johnson himself was a fervent Tory, he was on friendly and intimate terms with several well-known Whigs, even managing, when Boswell engineered a meeting, to be civil to the radical John *Wilkes. In 1765 he met the *Thrales, in whose town and country houses he found comfort and companionship. Later that year his edition of Shakespeare, on which he had been at work for some years, appeared; in the last months he received assistance from George *Steevens, who also helped with later revisions. The value of Johnson's edition lies in the sanity and sensitivity of its notes; the preface is one of his finest works of critical prose. He returned to politics, this time on the government side, with four political pamphlets: *The False Alarm* (1770), against Wilkes; *Thoughts...Respecting Falkland's Islands* (1771); *The Patriot* (1774); and *Taxation No Tyranny* (1775), on the question of American taxation and representation: Johnson supported taxation as warmly as he opposed slavery. In 1773 he travelled with Boswell to Scotland and the Hebrides, a journey recorded in his **Journey to the Western Islands of Scotland* (1775) and Boswell's *Journal of a Tour to the Hebrides* (1785); in 1774 he visited north Wales with the Thrales, and in 1775 went with them to Paris, his only visit to the Continent; his diaries of these trips appeared in 1816. In 1777 he undertook, at the request of a number of booksellers, to write *The Lives of the English Poets*, the crowning work of his old age (1779–81). In 1784, saddened by his estrangement from Mrs Thrale, he died at his house in Bolt Court and was buried in Westminster Abbey.

Johnson's reputation rests not only on his works but also on Boswell's record of his powerful conversation, his eccentricities and opinionated outbursts (against Scots, Whigs, Americans, and actors), his interest in the supernatural, and many other aspects of his large personality. Johnson had no children, but accepted into his house many dependants, such as his wife's friend, the blind Anna Williams, and Robert Levet, an unlicensed, alcoholic doctor who worked with the poor and whose death in 1782 prompted Johnson's famous elegy 'On the Death of Dr Levet'. Johnson was always generous with literary support for other writers, including a surprising number of women writers (Charlotte *Lennox, Elizabeth *Carter, and Fanny *Burney among them). His profound but melancholy religious faith is revealed also in his *Prayers and Meditations* (1785). *Anecdotes of the Late Samuel Johnson*, by Mrs Piozzi, formerly Mrs Thrale, appeared in 1786, a year before Sir John *Hawkins's biography (1787). Modern biographies include one by John *Wain (1974). The first large-scale edition of his *Works* was undertaken by Hawkins (11 vols, 1787); the Yale edition of his works, begun in 1958, reached its eighteenth planned volume in 2005. Johnson's letters, many of which were included in Boswell's biography, have been edited by Bruce Redford (5 vols, 1992–4).

See also JOHNSON, THE LIFE OF SAMUEL.

JOHNSON, Terry (1955–) Playwright and theatre director, born in Middlesex and educated in Birmingham. *Insignificance* (1982), like much of his later work, is peopled with real characters: the play evokes a (fictional) meeting between Marilyn Monroe, Albert Einstein, Joe DiMaggio, and Senator McCarthy in a New York hotel room in 1953. This was followed in 1984 by *Unsuitable for Adults*, the first of his trilogy of plays examining the relationship between the British and their comic icons. The serious questions raised by these plays are belied by the comedy, which often extends to pure slapstick or farce. In *Hysteria* (1993), Sigmund *Freud and Salvador Dali are thrown together in the London consulting room of the former, in what turns out to be a nightmarish reincarnation of a Freudian case history, with, towards the end, a three-dimensional, living manifestation of a Dali painting. Johnson continued his series on British comedy with *Dead Funny* (1994), and completed it in 1998 with *Cleo, Camping,*

Emmanuelle and Dick, a behind-the-scenes look at the making of four *'Carry On' films. His dedication to opening up new vistas on stage was further explored in *Hitchcock Blonde* (2003), which included a re-creation of the shower scene from *Hitchcock's film *Psycho*, though *Piano/Forte* (2006) largely retreated back into domestic comedy. He has directed extensively at the *Royal Court Theatre, and at the *National Theatre.

Johnson, The Life of Samuel By James *Boswell, published in 1791. Boswell informed *Johnson in 1772 of his intention to write his life, and had been collecting materials for this purpose as part of his journal since their first meeting in 1763. After Johnson's death in 1784 he set to work arranging and adding to his 'prodigious multiplicity of materials', a task which involved him in great labour, perplexity, and vexation, though he received invaluable help from Edmond *Malone, who also edited revised versions after Boswell's death. Despite early criticism of its monumentality and occasional triviality, and some modern scepticism about its method, Boswell's *Johnson* remains the most celebrated biography in the English language. Boswell learned much from Johnson's own expertise in biography, and brought to the task boundless curiosity and persistence. His portrait is vivid and intimate, a 'Flemish picture' including letters, anecdotes, and much conversation, and full of trifling incidents as well as significant events. Boswell's skill in stage-managing encounters (as with John *Wilkes, or Johnson's old fellow collegian, the modest Oliver Edwards, 1711–91) adds greatly to the work's liveliness. The edition by G. B. Hill (6 vols, 1887) was revised by L. F. Powell (1934–64). See also *The Correspondence and Other Papers of James Boswell: Relating to the Making of the Life of Johnson*, ed. Marshall Waingrow (1969). Two volumes of a projected four-volume edition of *James Boswell's Life of Johnson: An Edition of the Original Manuscript*, ed. Marshall Waingrow, Bruce Redford, and Elizabeth Goldring, have appeared (1994, 1999).

'Johnson's Dictionary' (*A Dictionary of the English Language*) By Samuel *Johnson, published 1755. In 1746 Johnson contracted with Robert *Dodsley and other booksellers to write an English dictionary, for a fee of £1,575. A 'Plan' and dedication to *Chesterfield appeared in 1747. Johnson's object was to produce 'a dictionary by which the pronunciation of our language may be fixed, and its attainment facilitated; by which its purity may be preserved, its use ascertained, and its duration lengthened'. Working with six assistants in newly rented premises in Gough Square, London, Johnson wrote definitions of over 40,000 words, illustrated with about 114,000 literary quotations from Philip *Sidney onwards. Five editions were published in his lifetime, and the work remained without rival until the **Oxford English Dictionary*. Its monumental authority is occasionally sweetened with playful definitions such as *lexicographer*, 'a writer of dictionaries, a harmless drudge'. See A. Reddick, *The Making of Johnson's Dictionary 1746–1773* (1990).

JOHNSTON, Arthur (*c.*1579–1641) Scottish physician, poet, translator, and editor, born at Caskieben, Aberdeenshire, and educated at Aberdeen, probably at King's College. His Latin translation of the Psalms, undertaken at the behest of William *Laud, appeared in 1637, the same year as his anthology *Delitiae Poetarum Scotorum*. He is remembered mainly for his Latin verse in elegiac couplets.

JOHNSTON, Jennifer (1930–) Novelist, daughter of playwright Denis Johnston (1901–84), born in Dublin and educated at Trinity College there. Her work employs a spare, delicate prose to explore Irish political divisions, focusing on relationships that promise to defy barriers of caste, class, and age but typically end in catastrophic surrender to historical imperatives. *The Gates* (1973) extends the elegiac tendencies of the 'big house' genre, and yet works towards an ambiguously optimistic conclusion. *Shadows on our Skin* (1977) and *The Railway Station Man* (1984) probe the moral ambiguities of the violence of the Northern Irish *Troubles in settings in or around Derry, where Johnston settled in the 1970s. *The Invisible Worm* (1991) portrays a woman trapped in a sterile marriage and a large seaside house, while *Two Moons* (1998) is a cross-generation novel of retrospect, love, and ageing, and *Foolish Mortals* (2007) an unsentimental comedy of family life in contemporary suburban Dublin.

JOHNSTONE, Charles (?1719–1800) Novelist, educated at Trinity College, Dublin. To supplement his legal practice in London he wrote *Chrysal, or The Adventures of a Guinea* (4 vols, 1760–65). 'Chrysal' is the spirit of gold in the guinea, whose progress from hand to hand, through six different countries, links a series of sharp satirical episodes. Further novels included *The History of Arsaces, Prince of Betlis* (2 vols, 1774), an *oriental tale which expresses covert sympathy with the American colonists in their struggle for independence. In 1782 Johnstone travelled to Calcutta (Kolkata), where he remained as a journalist and later as a newspaper proprietor.

JOLLEY, Elizabeth (1923–2007) Australian novelist, poet, and playwright, born in Birmingham. She moved to Western Australia in 1959 with her family. Her first book was not published until 1976; it was followed by three short story collections, eleven novels, two non-fiction works, and several radio plays. Her writing is characterized by a recurring sense of alienation and displacement, its source revealed in the semi-autobiographical trilogy *My Father's Moon* (1989), *Cabin Fever* (1990), and *George's Wife* (1993). Here as in other novels the tone is one of deep sadness, with the protagonist, Vera, experiencing intense loneliness. The structure is musical, employing repetitions, recurring moods, and images to build a resonant symbolism. Many of her earlier novels combine dark comedy, often centred on eccentricity and bizarre behaviour in characters who are invariably outsiders, with *Gothic plots and surprises.

Jonah *See* BIBLE.

Jonathan Wild the Great, The Life of Novel by Henry *Fielding, published as the third volume of his *Miscellanies*, 1743. Wild begins a flamboyant criminal career under the direction of the corrupt sheriff's officer Mr Snap, whose shrewish daughter he marries. After becoming an expert pickpocket, Wild organizes a gang of thieves, whose booty he sells at huge profit; he lives in style, dressing finely as a gentleman, and cunningly keeping himself beyond the reach of the law. He ensnares Heartfree, an innocent jeweller and model of domestic happiness, by having him robbed, imprisoned as a bankrupt, and eventually condemned for theft. He also has Mrs Heartfree abducted to the Netherlands, after which she is subjected to a series of threatening sexual advances. At length, Wild's embittered gang turn on him, and in a foolish confusion over a piece of lace, he is committed to Newgate. Heartfree is exonerated and his wife returns unharmed, but Wild is condemned, meeting death with his customary swagger by stealing a corkscrew from the chaplain. Like *The *Beggar's Opera*, the novel was loosely based on the notorious thief-taker Jonathan Wild (?1682–1725), but as with the play, it was really a satire: Wild is, with forceful irony, held up for admiration in his practice of the 'virtues' of hypocrisy, manipulation, and greed, and the figure of the Great Man among thieves and cheats is constantly compared with the Great Man in public life, with Sir Robert Walpole (1676–1745) (actually a subscriber to the *Miscellanies*) a particular target.

JONES, David (1895–1974) Poet and artist, born in Kent, educated at the Camberwell Art School and the Westminster School of Art; his father gave him his strong sense of identity with Wales, although he lived there only from 1924 to 1927. He served in the trenches throughout the First World War, an experience significant for all his work. In 1921 he became a Roman Catholic and in 1922 began a long association with Eric *Gill. He produced engravings, watercolours, and drawings. The Welsh **Mabinogion*, the *'matter of Britain', the Bible, and the Roman Catholic liturgy provide much of the material and the background for his poetry. In 1927 he began *In Parenthesis*, an epic work of mixed poetry and prose on the subject of the war, published in 1937. The personal story and terrible sufferings of Private John Ball are related to the long history of war, and embedded in Welsh legend and the work of *Malory. In 1952 Jones published *The Anathemata*, a complex work of poetry and prose, part chronicle, part incantation, celebrating in richly allusive language the ancient 'matter of Britain'. *The Sleeping Lord and Other Fragments* (1974) is a collection of pieces of a projected work centred on the Crucifixion, the residue of which was published as *The Roman Quarry* (1981). *Wedding Poems*, written in 1940, appeared in 2002. Jones was also a mythographer and writer on aesthetics: his essays are collected in *Epoch and Artist* (1959) and *The Dying Gaul* (1978). See Thomas Dilworth, *The Shape of Meaning in the Poetry of David Jones* (1988).

JONES, Diana Wynne (1934–) Born in London, educated at St Anne's College, Oxford. Her many inventive, complex, and funny *fantasy books for children and adults display wide reading of canonical texts, myths, and legends: *The Homeward Bounders* (1981) uses the Prometheus legend; *Castle in the Air* (1990) draws on the **Arabian Nights*. Jones's books often involve multiple parallel worlds as in those about a magician known as the Chrestomanci, beginning with *Charmed Life* (1977); all celebrate the power of storytelling. *Howl's Moving Castle* (1986) was made into an anime film (Hayo Miyazaki, 2004).

JONES, Gayl (1949–) African American writer and critic, born in Lexington, Kentucky, who began publishing stories and poems in the 1970s. Her first novel, *Corregidora* (1975), treats domestic abuse, a theme which recurs in *Eva's Man* (1976). Her poetry and prose draw on the patterns of blues and jazz, and in 1991 she published a study of the vernacular, *Liberating Voices: Oral Tradition in African American Literature*.

JONES, Glyn (1905–95) Welsh poet, short story writer, and novelist, born in Merthyr Tydfil, Glamorgan, the setting of much of his fiction and of his rumbustious poem 'Merthyr'. *The Blue Bed* (1937) and *The Water Music* (1944) contain his most influential stories. He drew on his experience of teaching in Cardiff primary schools in *The Dream of Jake Hopkins* (1944), a long poem for radio, and *The Learning Lark* (1960), his second novel. His third novel, *The Island of Apples* (1965; rev. 1992), mingles urban realism with Arthurian romance in its depiction of the pains of adolescence. *The Dragon Has Two Tongues* (1968), a seminal account of Welsh writing in English, contains vivid portraits of Dylan *Thomas, Idris *Davies, and others. Jones offered his own idiosyncratic résumé of his career in the anthology *Goodbye, What Were You?* (1994). *Collected Poems* appeared in 1996 and *Collected Stories* in 1999.

JONES, Gwyn (1907–99) Welsh short story writer, novelist, anthologist, and Norse scholar, born in New Tredegar, Monmouthshire, and educated at University College, Cardiff, where he was professor of English from 1954 to 1975. He founded the *Welsh Review* in 1939. His translation of the **Mabinogion* (with Thomas Jones) appeared in 1948, and his acclaimed *History of the Vikings* twenty years later. His longer works of fiction include *Times Like These* (1936), set in the Welsh valleys during the Depression, and the historical novels *A Garland of Bays* (1938) and *The Walk Home* (1962). He edited the *Oxford Book of Welsh Verse in English* (1977). See *Collected Stories* (1997).

JONES, Gwyneth (1952–) Children's writer, and author of *science fiction and *fantasy for adults, born in Manchester, educated at Sussex University. Her fiction for children, including the ghost story *King Death's Garden*, is published under the name Ann Halam. Her first adult novel, *Divine Endurance* (1984), manipulated science fiction ideas skilfully (she is also an acute critic of the field). This sense of the form and subject matter of science fiction is best seen in the 'Aleutian' trilogy beginning with *White Queen* (1991), whose imagined aliens demonstrate the fluidity of our ideas of identity and gender.

JONES, Henry Arthur (1851–1929) Born in Buckinghamshire, he left school at 12, and worked as a draper's assistant and commercial traveller before his first play was staged in Exeter in 1878. He made his name in London with a melodrama, *The Silver King* (1882), written in collaboration with Henry Herman. As a young man he was greatly encouraged by G. B. *Shaw and Max *Beerbohm. A friend and contemporary of Arthur *Pinero, Jones was a prolific playwright, who did much to re-establish serious themes in the theatre. His finest work included *The Case of Rebellious Susan* (1894), *The Liars* (1897), *Mrs Dane's Defence* (1900), and *The Lie* (1923). Jones also promoted the cause of serious English drama through articles and speeches, and fought for the abolition of censorship. William *Archer judged Jones the most popular playwright of the 1890s, but his popularity, like that of Pinero, faded in the 20th century.

JONES, Inigo (1573–1652) Architect, stage designer, painter, mathematician, and man of letters, whose depth of knowledge of Roman and Italian art and of Renaissance theory was new in England, and whose revolutionary buildings brought the classical style to this country. Little is known of his early career; he travelled abroad some time between 1598 and 1604, and again in 1613–14, when he developed a deep admiration for *Palladio, met the Italian architect Vincenzo Scamozzi (1548–1616), and copied ancient Roman monuments. In 1615 he became surveyor of the king's works; his most famous buildings are the Queen's House, Greenwich (1616–18 and 1629–35), and the Banqueting Hall, Whitehall (1619–22), both lucid, classic, harmonious buildings with crisp detail which mark a turning point in English architecture. Jones's career as a designer of *masques opened in 1605, and many of his drawings for costume and scenery—influenced by his European counterparts, among them the stage designer and architect Bernardo Buontalenti (1536?–1608) and the printmaker and etcher Jacques Callot (1592?–1635)—survive. A stormy but fruitful collaboration with Ben *Jonson began in 1605 with *The Masque of Blackness*, and lasted until 1630/31; their quarrel about the rival claims of the visual arts and literature was also long-standing, and became notorious. Later Jones worked with other poets, producing with Thomas *Carew, in *Coelum Britannicum* (1634), perhaps the most brilliant of later Caroline masques. Jones's fame in England soared between 1710 and 1760, when, with Palladio, he became one of the heroes of the Palladian movement, revered by Lord Burlington and Alexander *Pope. Many of his designs were published in two folio volumes, edited by William *Kent (1727). See S. Orgel and R. Strong, *Inigo Jones: The Theatre of the Stuart Court* (1973).

JONES, James (1921–77) American novelist who served in Hawaii during the Second World War and subsequently drew on this experience for his best-selling novel *From Here to Eternity* (1951). A war trilogy was completed by the publication of *The Thin Red Line* (1962) and *Whistle* (1978).

JONES, Leroi *See* BARAKA, AMIRI.

JONES, Mary (d. 1778) Poet. She lived in Oxford with her clergyman brother, who was chanter of Christ Church. She learned French and Italian and may have worked as a governess. Her ballad 'The Lass of the Hill' was a popular success in 1742. She was close to a number of aristocratic families with court connections, who eventually organized a strong subscription list of about 1,400 people for her *Miscellanies in Prose and Verse* (1750). When the volume went on public sale in 1752 it was very favourably reviewed in the **Monthly Review* by the editor and bookseller Ralph Griffiths (1720?–1803). Later Griffiths invited her to become a reviewer, an exceptional offer for a woman writer; she declined gracefully. Among her literary acquaintances were Charlotte *Lennox, Thomas *Warton, and Samuel *Johnson, who called her 'the Chantress'. Her verse, presented in the modes made familiar by Alexander *Pope and Jonathan *Swift, is witty, sociable, and self-mocking.

JONES, Russell Celyn (1955–) Welsh writer, born in London and raised in Swansea. His novels are *Soldiers and Innocents* (1990), about an army officer who turns deserter and goes on the run with his child; *Small Times* (1992), which charts a romance between a petty thief and a successful actress; *An Interference of Light* (1995), describing a homosexual affair in a Welsh mining community; and *The Eros Hunter* (1998), a gripping crime thriller set in contemporary London. All of these books are notable for their pungent, laconic prose and rueful interrogation of masculine values, with a particular emphasis on fathers and sons.

JONES, Sir William (1746–94) A distinguished orientalist, radical Whig, and lawyer, educated at Harrow School and University College, Oxford. In the 1770s he became friends with Samuel *Johnson, Edward *Gibbon, and Edmund *Burke; he was elected to the *Club in 1773. Jones learned Arabic, Persian, and Sanskrit, and was a pioneer of comparative philology, publishing *Poems, Consisting Chiefly of Translations from the Asiatick Languages* (1772), *The Moâllakát* (1782), from Arabic, and *Sacontala, or The Fatal Ring: An Indian Drama* (1789). In 1783 Jones was knighted, and made a judge in the Bengal Supreme Court; he contributed extensively to the journal *Asiatick Researches* (1788–94). He had considerable influence on the oriental themes of Romantic poets such as *Byron, *Southey, and Thomas *Moore. His works were edited by Lord Teignmouth (6 vols, 1799) and his letters by G. Cannon (2 vols, 1970). See G. Cannon, *The Life and Mind of Oriental Jones* (1990).

JONG, Erica (1942–) American novelist, born in New York, who achieved fame with her first book, *Fear of Flying* (1973), a sequence of explicit sexual episodes delivered in a wisecracking style. In addition to her novels, which include *Fanny* (1980), a pastiche *picaresque, she has published a number of books of poetry and essays. *The Devil at Large* (1993) is a study of Henry *Miller, *Fear of Fifty* (1994) a midlife memoir, and *Seducing the Demon* (2007) a series of reflections on the writer's life.

JONSON, Ben (Benjamin) (1572/3–1637) Dramatist, poet, scholar, and writer of court *masques. He was of Border descent, but was born in or near London, the posthumous son of a clergyman. Educated at Westminster School under William *Camden, he worked as a bricklayer in his stepfather's employ, saw military service in Flanders, where he boasted that he killed an enemy champion in single combat, and joined a strolling company of players for whom he acted the part of Hieronimo in *The *Spanish Tragedy*, a play for which he wrote additional scenes in 1601–2. In 1597 he began to work for Philip *Henslowe's companies as player and playwright, and was imprisoned for his share in *The Isle of Dogs*, a 'very seditious and slanderous' satire now lost (*see* SWAN THEATRE). In 1598 he killed a fellow actor in a duel, but escaped hanging by pleading benefit of clergy, being branded instead on his thumb as a felon. He became a Roman Catholic during imprisonment, but returned to Anglicanism twelve years later. His first important play, **Every Man in His Humour*, with William *Shakespeare in the cast, was performed by the Lord Chamberlain's Company at the Curtain in 1598, and **Every Man out of His Humour* at the Globe in 1599. **Cynthia's Revels* (1600) and **Poetaster* (1600–1, attacking Thomas *Dekker and John *Marston) were performed by the Children of the Queen's Chapel. His first extant tragedy, **Sejanus*, was given at the Globe by Shakespeare's company, 1603; his first court masque, *The Masque of Blackness*, written to accommodate Queen Anne's desire to appear as a negress, was given on Twelfth Night, 1605. In that year he was imprisoned, and in danger of having his nose and ears slit, for his share in **Eastward Ho*, and gave evidence to the Privy Council concerning the Gunpowder Plot. Then followed the period of his major plays: **Volpone*, acted at both the Globe and at Oxford and Cambridge universities, 1605–6; **Epicene, or The Silent Woman*, 1609–10; *The *Alchemist*, 1610; and **Bartholomew Fair*, 1614. In 1612–13 he was in France as tutor to Walter *Ralegh's son, who is reputed to have wheeled him dead drunk around the town in a wheelbarrow, and in 1618–19 he journeyed on foot to Scotland, where he stayed with William *Drummond of Hawthornden, who recorded his matchlessly frank and scandalous conversations about fellow authors and others.

Though not formally appointed the first *poet laureate, the essentials of the position were conferred on Jonson in 1616, when a pension was granted to him by *James I. In the same year he published a folio edition of his *Works*, which raised the drama to a new level of literary respectability, received an honorary MA from Oxford University, and about this date became lecturer in rhetoric at Gresham College in London. He was elected chronologer of London in 1628. After *The *Devil Is an Ass* (1616), he abandoned the public stage for ten years, and his later plays, *The *Staple of News* (1626), *The *New Inn* (1629), *The *Magnetic Lady* (1631), and *A *Tale of a Tub* (1633), show a relatively unsuccessful reliance on allegory and symbolism; John *Dryden called them his 'dotages'. From 1605 onwards Jonson was constantly producing masques for the court, with scenery by Inigo *Jones. He introduced the 'antimasque', an antithetical, usually disorderly, prelude to the main action which served to highlight by contrast the central theme of political and social harmony. There are examples of this in *The Masque of Queens* (1609), *Love Restored* (1612), *Mercury Vindicated from the Alchemists at Court* (1616), *Pleasure Reconciled to Virtue* (1618, which influenced John *Milton's **Comus*), and *Neptune's Triumph for the Return of Albion* (1624). After *Chloridia* (1631), his collaboration with Jones ended with a famous quarrel, which Jonson treated in several vituperative poems, concerning the priority of words to mere spectacle. His last masques were produced in 1633–4. His non-dramatic verse includes his *epigrams (among them tender and moving epitaphs on his first daughter, Mary, and first son, Benjamin) and *The *Forest*, printed in the folio of 1616. *The Underwood* and a translation of *Horace's *Ars Poetica* were printed in 1640. His chief prose works are *The English Grammar* and *Timber, or Discoveries*, printed in 1640.

During the reign of James I Jonson's literary prestige and influence were unrivalled. He presided over a literary circle which met at the *Mermaid Tavern, and later in the Apollo Room of the Devil and St Dunstan Tavern, where his *leges convivales* or 'social rules' were inscribed over the mantelpiece. His friends included Shakespeare, whom he loved 'on this side idolatry', John *Donne, Francis *Bacon, George *Chapman, Francis *Beaumont, John *Fletcher, Sir Robert *Cotton, and John *Selden, and among the younger writers (who styled themselves the 'sons' or 'tribe of Ben') Richard *Brome, Thomas *Carew, William *Cartwright, Sir Kenelm *Digby, Viscount *Falkland, Robert *Herrick, Thomas *Randolph, and John *Suckling. His chief patrons were the *Sidney family, the earl of Pembroke, Lucy, countess of Bedford, and the duke and duchess of Newcastle. He suffered a stroke in 1628, after which he was perhaps permanently bedridden until his death in August 1637. He was buried in Westminster Abbey under a tombstone bearing the inscription 'O rare Ben Jonson', and celebrated in a collection of elegies entitled *Jonsonus Virbius* (1638). As a man Jonson was arrogant and quarrelsome, but fearless, warm-hearted, and intellectually honest. His reputation declined sharply from about 1700, as Shakespeare's, with whom he was inevitably compared, increased. It revived in the 20th century, thanks partly to the comprehensive edition of C. H. Herford and P. and E. Simpson (11 vols, 1925–52), vols i and ii of which contain the standard biography. See Anne Barton, *Ben Jonson, Dramatist* (1984); R. L. Harp (ed.), *The Cambridge Companion to Ben Jonson* (2000).

JORDAN, Dorothy (1761–1816) Née Phillips, actress, born near Waterford, Ireland, who made her first stage appearance in 1779 in Dublin under the name of Miss Francis. She came to England and adopted the name of Mrs Jordan, under which she appeared as Calista in *The *Fair Penitent* at Leeds in 1782. She made her debut at Drury Lane as Peggy in David *Garrick's *The Country Girl* in 1785, and took many parts there, at the Haymarket, and at Covent Garden, Lady Teazle in *The *School for Scandal* being one of her finest roles. Her last London performance was in 1814 and her final stage appearance at Margate in 1815. She was much praised by William *Hazlitt, Charles *Lamb, Leigh *Hunt, and others. She was for many years mistress of the duke of Clarence (William IV), and bore him ten children. She went to France in 1815 and died at Saint-Cloud. See Claire *Tomalin, *Mrs Jordan's Profession: The Actress and the Prince* (1994).

JORDAN, Neil (1950–) Irish novelist and successful international film director and screenwriter. After a collection of stories, *Night in Tunisia* (1976), and first novel, *The Past* (1979), he wrote and directed *Angel* (1982), a poignant thriller set in troubled Northern Ireland. *The Company of Wolves* (1984), imaginatively adapted from Angela *Carter's story, furthered his reputation and led to the major success of *Mona Lisa* (1986). Sexual ambiguity is a feature of Jordan's most distinctive films, *The Crying Game* (1992) and *Breakfast on Pluto* (2005), the latter based on a novel by Patrick *McCabe, whose *The Butcher Boy* Jordan also filmed in 1997. Among many other films, his Graham *Greene adaptation *The End of the Affair* (1999) is notable.

JORDAN, Robert (1948–2007) American *fantasy writer, pen-name of James Oliver Rigney, Jr, born in Charleston, South Carolina; author of the hugely popular 'Wheel of Time' fantasy series beginning with *The Eye of the World* (1990). The twelfth and final volume was unfinished at the time of his death.

JOSEPH, Jenny (1932–) Poet, born in Birmingham and educated at St Hilda's College, Oxford. Her first collection, *The Unlooked-for Season*, appeared in 1960. This was followed by *Rose in the Afternoon* (1974), which contains her extremely popular poem 'Warning', about projected defiantly bad behaviour in old age. Other collections include *The Thinking Heart* (1978), *Persephone* (1980), which is a narrative in both poetry and prose, *Beyond Descartes* (1983), and *Ghosts and Other Company* (1995). She employs fable, dramatic monologue, and myth to illuminate with unromantic precision a recognizable but not always comfortable everyday world. A *Selected Poems* appeared in 1992. Recent work includes *Led by the Nose* (2002), a book on smells experienced by the gardener, and *Extreme of Things* (2006). She is also a writer of children's books.

Joseph Andrews, The History of the Adventures of, *and of his Friend Mr Abraham Adams* A novel by Henry *Fielding (1742). The title page proclaims that the story is told in the manner of *Cervantes, and in an important preface Fielding relates his innovative 'comic romance' to classical forms. His object is to defend what is good by displaying the Ridiculous, which arises from Affectation, and ultimately from Vanity and Hypocrisy. The work begins as a parody of Samuel Richardson's **Pamela*, with Joseph as Pamela's brother and 'Mr B.' appearing as young Booby. Joseph is in service with Sir Thomas and Lady Booby. After Sir Thomas's death Lady Booby makes amorous advances to Joseph, and when he rejects them he is dismissed. Beaten and robbed on the road, he is taken to an inn where he encounters his old mentor, the vigorous but unworldly Parson Adams. Joseph's beloved, the illiterate milkmaid Fanny, is rescued by Adams from an attack in a wood, and the three travellers support each other through the perilous hinterland of an England run by corrupt justices, vicious squires, hypocritical clergymen, and cheating innkeepers. Eventually they are given hospitality by Wilson, a country gentleman, whose life story clearly echoes much of Fielding's own experience. The party returns at last to Booby Hall, where a further sequence of comic misadventures reveals that Joseph is the long-lost son of Wilson, and Fanny is Pamela's sister. Joseph and Fanny are married, and Adams is rewarded with a handsome living.

Joseph of Arimathea According to Matthew 27: 57–60, Joseph donated his own tomb for Christ's burial. For the legend of Joseph and the Grail, *see* GRAIL; GLASTONBURY. According to fable, St Philip sent twelve disciples, led by Joseph, into Britain to preach Christianity. They founded at Glastonbury the first primitive church, which developed into Glastonbury Abbey. Here Joseph was buried. Medieval treatments of his legend include Robert de *Boron's *Joseph d'Arimathie* and an English alliterative poem, ed. David Lawton (1983).

JOSEPHUS, Flavius (*c.*37–*c.*100) Jewish historian and Roman sympathizer who wrote in Greek for a Gentile audience. He obtained the favour of Vespasian by foretelling that he would one day become ruler of the Roman Empire. He was present at the siege and destruction of Jerusalem in 70, went to Rome with Titus, became a Roman citizen, and devoted himself to writing. His *History of the Jewish War* describes the Jews' struggle with Rome, much of it from his own experience. His *Jewish Antiquities* is a history of the Jews from the Creation down to the beginning of the revolt against Rome in 66; it includes a brief account of the death of Jesus which may have been added by a Christian author. There are English translations of his works by Thomas *Lodge, Sir Roger *L'Estrange, and William Whiston (1667–1752).

JOSIPOVICI, Gabriel (1940–) Novelist, playwright, and critic, born in Nice, and educated at Victoria College, Cairo, and Oxford University. His critical works include *The World and the Book* (1971), in which he discusses writers ranging from *Rabelais to Saul *Bellow, *The Lessons of Modernism* (1977), and an examination of the Bible, *The Book of God* (1988). His fiction is innovative and experimental, and includes *The Inventory* (1968), in which a man takes an inventory of the belongings of a dead man; *Words* (1971); *Migrations* (1977); *Moo Park* (1994); *Now* (1998), which consists almost entirely of dialogue; *Goldberg: Variations* (2002); and *Everything Passes* (2006). *The Singer on the Shore*, a collection of essays and reviews, was published in 2006. See Monika Fludernik, *Echoes and Mirrorings: Gabriel Josipovici's Creative Oeuvre* (2000).

Journey from This World to the Next, A Published in the second volume of *Miscellanies* by Henry *Fielding (1743). The tale purports to have been found in an almost indecipherable manuscript, left in an attic by someone now departed to the West Indies. The soul leaves the body in its lodgings in

Cheapside and finds itself, guided by Mercury, in a stagecoach with other souls. At the door of Elysium the underworld judge Minos dictates who shall be permitted to enter; the generous and the honest are favoured, whatever their rank, while the cruel and hypocritical are rejected. In the Elysian Fields heroes and writers of antiquity converse animatedly with *Shakespeare, *Milton, *Dryden, *Addison, and Fielding's own *Tom Thumb. The spirit of Julian the Apostate appears and narrates his adventures in several guises: slave, Jew, courtier, statesman. The last section, Anne Boleyn's confessional story, is plausibly ascribed to Sarah *Fielding.

Journey to the Western Islands of Scotland, A By Samuel *Johnson, published January 1775. It is a personal narrative of the tour undertaken by James *Boswell and Johnson from August to November 1773 in Scotland and the Hebrides. Boswell gives an account of the journey in his *Journal of a Tour to the Hebrides* (1785). Johnson said that he dealt 'more in notions than facts', and the book sets out his response to Scottish history, culture, and landscape, including current economic and political issues such as emigration, the subjugation of the clan system, the mapping of the Highlands in the wake of the *Jacobite risings, and the consequent pressures on a vanishing oral culture. On publication the book aroused the wrath of James *Macpherson because of its contemptuously sceptical comments on the authenticity of 'Ossian', and other Scots were offended by Johnson's uncompromising views of their country. See the edition by J. D. Fleeman (1985).

Jovial Crew, A, *or The Merry Beggars* A romantic comedy by Richard *Brome, produced 1641. Oldrents, a kindly country squire, is saddened by a Gypsy's prediction that his two daughters will be beggars. Springlove, an honest vagabond whom Oldrents has made his steward, is seized each spring with a desire to return to his wandering life, and rejoins the beggars whom Oldrents entertains in his barn. Oldrents's daughters decide to join the beggars for a frolic, with their two lovers, this giving effect to the Gypsy's prediction. Meanwhile Justice Clack's niece has run away with the Justice's clerk, and they too fall in with the beggars. The search for the runaways, and the apprehension of the beggars, give occasion for comic scenes, and all ends well. The play, Brome's masterpiece, is highly original in its picture of Oldrents's compassion for the poor and Springlove's longing for a vagabond life.

JOWETT, Benjamin (1817–93) Born in Camberwell, London, and educated at St Paul's School and Balliol College, Oxford. A legendary figure in Victorian Oxford, famed for his 'cherubic chirp', long silences, and occasional devastating rudeness. He was professor of Greek from 1855 and master of Balliol College from 1870. A Broad Churchman in the tradition of Thomas *Arnold, he outraged Tractarians with the common sense of his *Epistles of Paul* (1855), was nearly charged with heresy over his contribution to **Essays and Reviews* (1860), and helped to abolish religious tests for university degrees (1871). His translations of *Plato (1871), *Thucydides (1881), and Aristotle's **Poetics* (1885), criticized by scholars, pleased the public. He held that the purpose of university education was the personal development of each student and hoped more particularly to form future statesmen. As Herbert Asquith, Sir Alfred Milner, Sir Edward Grey, and George Nathaniel *Curzon were among his pupils, he may be regarded as a founding father of Edwardian England.

JOYCE, Graham (1954–) Novelist, born near Coventry; his fiction crosses the boundaries between *science fiction, *fantasy, and realism. Often, as in *The Facts of Life* (2002) or *Limits of Enchantment* (2005), a detailed sense of place is linked to an equally strong supernatural atmosphere.

JOYCE, James (1882–1941) Writer, born at West Rathgar, Dublin, and educated (1888–91) at the Jesuit boarding school Clongowes Wood College, near Clane, Co. Kildare, and, from 1893, at the Jesuit day-school Belvedere College, Dublin, and subsequently at the Royal University of Ireland (1898–99) and at University College, Dublin (1899–1902). A good linguist, from an early age, he read and studied widely, and in 1901 wrote a letter of profound admiration in Dano-Norwegian to Henrik *Ibsen. Other early influences included Gerhart *Hauptmann, *Dante, George *Moore, and W. B. *Yeats, who was to treat him with considerable personal kindness. Dissatisfied with the narrowness and bigotry of Ireland, as he saw it, Joyce went to Paris for a year in 1902, where he lived in poverty, wrote verse, and discovered the novel *Les Lauriers sont coupés* (1888) by Édouard Dujardin (1861–1949), which he was later to credit as the source of his own use of *interior monologue. He returned to Dublin in 1903 for his mother's death, stayed briefly in the Martello tower of **Ulysses* with Oliver *Gogarty, then left Ireland more or less for good with Nora Barnacle (1884–1951), the woman with whom he spent the rest of his life, whom he had first met in 1904 when she was a hotel chambermaid, and who would bear him a son and a daughter. They lived at Trieste for some years, where Joyce taught English at the Berlitz school, before moving in 1915 to Zurich; after the war they settled in Paris. His first published work was a volume of verse, *Chamber Music* (1907), followed by **Dubliners* (1914), a volume of short stories published after great delays and difficulties, culminating in his final visit to Ireland in 1912, when the sheets were destroyed through the prospective publisher's fear of libel. When the stories at last appeared they were greeted with enthusiasm by Ezra *Pound, in a review in *The *Egoist*; Pound's friendship and support greatly encouraged Joyce's career and reputation. Another important ally gained at this period was the independently wealthy Harriet Shaw *Weaver, business manager and then editor of *The Egoist*, and a lifelong benefactress of Joyce. Difficulties also attended the performance and publication of Joyce's play *Exiles*: it was published in 1918, staged unsuccessfully the same year in Munich, and first performed in London by the Stage Society in 1926. *A *Portrait of the Artist as a Young Man*, a largely autobiographical work, was published serially in *The Egoist*, 1914–15 (part of a first draft, *Stephen Hero*, appeared in 1944), and in one volume in 1916 (New York) and 1917 (London). With strong backing from Yeats and Pound, Joyce received a grant from the *Royal Literary Fund in 1915, and shortly after that a grant from the Civil List. Yet, despite these cash injections and growing recognition of his genius, he continued to struggle against poverty, and also suffered from increasing eye trouble; a severe attack of glaucoma in 1917 led to years of pain and several operations. He was also much tormented in later years by his daughter's severe mental illness. Instalments of **Ulysses* first appeared in the **Little Review* (March 1918–December 1920), and it was first published in its entirety in Paris on 2 February 1922, Joyce's 40th birthday. It was received as a work of consummate power and stupendous scale by writers as diverse as T. S. *Eliot, Ernest *Hemingway, and Arnold *Bennett; others (Virginia *Woolf, for example) were less admiring at first. The first UK edition appeared in 1936. Another small volume of verse, *Pomes Penyeach*, was published in 1927, and his second great work, **Finnegans Wake*, extracts of which had already appeared as 'Work in Progress', was published in its complete form in 1939. Joyce's books have prompted a vast mass of critical commentary in many languages and the global interest in his writings shows no sign of cooling. See Richard Ellmann, *James Joyce* (1959; new and rev. edn, 1983).

JOYCE, Patrick Weston (1827–1914) Irish antiquarian, born in Ballyorgan, Co. Limerick, and educated at Trinity College, Dublin, author, among other works, of *Irish Names of Places* (1869–1913), *A Grammar of the Irish Language* (1878), *Old Celtic Romances* (1879, 1894, from which Alfred *Tennyson drew his 'Voyage of Maeldune'), and a *Social History of Ireland* (1903–20), all highly influential in the *Irish Revival. He also published *Irish Peasant Songs* (1906) and contributed folk songs to Petrie's *Ancient Music of Ireland*.

Jude the Obscure A novel by Thomas *Hardy, originally printed in abridged and bowdlerized form in **Harper's New Monthly Magazine* (1894–5, as *Hearts Insurgent*), then in the 1895 edition of his works. In the author's words, it describes 'a deadly war waged between flesh and spirit'. Jude Fawley, a young Wessex villager of exceptional intellectual promise, is encouraged by the schoolmaster Phillotson, and conceives the ambition of studying at Christminster (which represents Oxford). But he is trapped into marriage by the coarse, handsome barmaid Arabella Donn, who feigns pregnancy to win him, and shortly afterwards deserts him. He moves to Christminster, working as a stonemason and continuing his studies, hoping one day to be admitted to the university, the vision of which still haunts him. He meets his cousin, Sue Bridehead, a hypersensitive young woman who works in a shop selling ecclesiastical ornaments. They fall in love, despite efforts on both sides to avoid one another. Sue, in what appears to be a fit of desperate masochism, suddenly marries Phillotson, who had long been interested in her. She is driven from him by physical revulsion, and flies to Jude; they begin to live together in Christminster, but do not consummate their love until Arabella reappears on the scene. Jude, who had been planning to enter the priesthood as a licentiate, as a substitute for his thwarted intellectual ambitions, is now doubly defeated. He and Sue become free to marry, but Sue shrinks from the step, partly because of her apprehension that a conventional union will destroy love, and partly from a superstitious fear that the Fawley family is doomed to marry unhappily: she compares the family to the house of Atreus, and Jude compares it to the house of Jeroboam, an interchange which reflects the theme of Hellenism and Hebraism prominent throughout the novel.

Under the pressure of poverty and social disapproval their relationship deteriorates, and tragedy overtakes them in the death of their children: the eldest, 'Old Father Time', son of Jude and Arabella, hangs the two babies and himself, leaving a note saying, 'Done because we are too menny.' In an agony of remorse and self-abasement, Sue returns to Phillotson and the church, and Jude, deeply shocked by her abandoning of her freethinking principles, begins drinking heavily (a weakness to which he had always been susceptible) and is tempted back by Arabella. He dies wretchedly, not yet 30, and his last words are: 'Wherefore is light given to him that is in misery, and life unto the bitter in soul?'

The novel's provocative views on sexuality and marriage caused an uproar, and the **Pall Mall Gazette* set the tone by castigating it as 'dirt, drivel and damnation'; even Hardy's friend Edmund *Gosse found it 'grimy' and 'indecent'. Hardy describes in the preface to the 1912 edition how the work was 'burnt by a bishop—probably in his despair at not being able to burn me'. The hostile reception of the book was one of several reasons why Hardy wrote no more fiction. Nevertheless, this unremittingly pessimistic novel has since become one of Hardy's most frequently studied and widely celebrated works.

Judith A 350-line poem in Old English, fragmentary at the beginning, found in the **Beowulf* manuscript. The poem corresponds to about the last quarter of the Apocryphal Book of Judith. It describes the banquet in the Assyrian camp, the bringing of Judith to the drunken Holofernes, her beheading of him and escape, and the defeat and flight of the Assyrians. The language of the poem is opulent and its battle description is celebrated. See the edition by M. Griffith (1997).

'Julian and Maddalo: A Conversation' A poem partly in dialogue form by P. B. *Shelley, written at Venice and Este in 1818, published 1824. It is the most naturalistic of Shelley's long poems, deliberately opposed to the 'idealism' of his dramas.

Julian (Shelley) and Count Maddalo (Lord *Byron) ride and boat through 'bright Venice', discussing problems of free will, progress, and religious belief. They visit a 'Maniac', confined in elegant rooms in an island asylum, whose tortured and confused monologue shows how superficial their arguments have been. The Maniac, partly based on *Tasso and partly on Shelley himself, has suffered some profound 'wrong' in love. His presence deepens and darkens the terms of the debate: he provides 'the text of every heart'. A little child, based on Claire Clairmont's baby Allegra, is also introduced to show the powers of innocence and good, though the outcome of the 'conversation' is not entirely optimistic. This is one of Shelley's most subtle studies of human affection and hopes. It is composed in fluent, almost chatty couplets, with marvellous evocations of the deserted Venetian lido and twinkling lagoon. It powerfully influenced Robert *Browning's *dramatic monologues.

JULIAN OF NORWICH (1342–after 1416) A recluse attached to the church of St Julian at Norwich. *Revelations of Divine Love* (the modern title) describes visions revealed to her during an illness in 1373 and her reflections on them. The *Revelations* exist in a Short and a Long version (the latter, written sometime after 1393, incorporates subsequent revelations from 1388 and 1393). T. S. *Eliot quotes from her in 'Little Gidding' (*Four Quartets*): 'Sin is Behovely, but | All shall be well, and | All manner of thing shall be well.' See *The Writings of Julian of Norwich*, ed. Nicholas Watson and Jacqueline Jenkins (2006); *Revelations of Divine Love*, trans. C. Wolters (1973).

Julius Caesar A Roman tragedy by *Shakespeare, probably written and performed 1599, not printed until the first *folio (1623). Its major source is Thomas *North's translation of *Plutarch's *Lives*. The play seems to have been popular in its own time.

It begins with the events of the year 44 BC, after Caesar, already dictator, has returned to Rome from a successful campaign in Spain, amidst fears that he will allow himself to be crowned king. Distrust of Caesar's ambition gives rise to a conspiracy against him among Roman lovers of freedom, notably Cassius and Casca; they win Brutus to their cause. The conspirators murder Caesar in the senate house. Antony, Caesar's friend, stirs the people to fury against the conspirators by a skilful speech at Caesar's funeral. Octavius, nephew of Julius Caesar, Antony, and Lepidus, united as triumvirs, oppose the forces raised by Brutus and Cassius. The quarrel and reconciliation of Brutus and Cassius, with the news of the death of Portia, wife of Brutus, provide one of the finest scenes in the play (IV. iii). Brutus and Cassius are defeated at the battle of Philippi (42 BC), and kill themselves.

Jumpers A comedy by Tom *Stoppard performed and published 1972. The play's central character is a professor of moral philosophy, George Moore, who shares with the Cambridge philosopher G. E. Moore (1873–1958) not only his name but also his intuitionist ethics. The physical acrobatics of the jumpers of the title parallel the 'verbal gymnastics' of Moore's lengthy speeches, which are brilliantly witty parodies of academic philosophy.

JUNG, Carl Gustav (1875–1961) Swiss psychiatrist, whose professional career began at the Burghölzli mental hospital in Zurich. Impressed by the work of *Freud on dreams, he sought to apply psychoanalytic ideas to the treatment of schizophrenia. Between 1907 and 1912 he worked in close collaboration with Freud but then broke with him to found his own school of 'Analytical Psychology'. Like Freud, Jung was not only the founder of a school of psychology which lives on today but also introduced into psychology many terms, such as 'complex', 'collective unconscious', 'extrovert'–'introvert', *'archetype', and 'individuation', which have entered general educated discourse. Jung wrote extensively on topics far outside the normal field of psychology, such as religion, mythology, and alchemy, where he could apply his ideas on symbolism and archetypes. His influence has been commensurately wide, not least in the area of literary criticism. J. B. *Priestley made use of his ideas in *Literature and Western Man*, while *Archetypal Patterns in Poetry* (1934) by Maud Bodkin (1875–1967) is directly derived from Jung. His influence on the idea of archetypal criticism in the work of Northrop *Frye (1912–91) is plain. The mythographer Joseph Campbell (1904–87), whose work on the figure of the hero is itself important in literary studies, was greatly indebted to Jung. Alex Aronson's *Psyche and Symbol in Shakespeare* (1972) is an interpretation of Shakespearian drama in terms of Jungian psychology. Hermann *Hesse made use of Jung's concepts in his novels, and Jung himself wrote an essay on Joyce's **Ulysses*. Arthur *Koestler too has made use of Jungian ideas, while the physicist Wolfgang Pauli (1900–58), the art historian Herbert *Read, and the composer Michael *Tippett have all acknowledged their debt to Jung. His work and ideas were of special importance to Ted *Hughes.

Jungle Book, The (1894), and ***The Second Jungle Book*** (1895) Fifteen stories by Rudyard *Kipling about India, seven featuring the feral boy, Mowgli, who is educated by Baloo the bear and Bagheera the panther in 'the law of the jungle'. The best-known non-Mowgli story may be 'Rikki-Tikki-Tavi', about the fight between a mongoose and cobras. 'Toomai of the Elephants' was filmed as *Elephant Boy* (Flaherty and Korda, 1937), and the Mowgli stories were filmed as *The Jungle Book* in 1942 (Zoltan Korda) and 1994 (Steven Sommers) as well as loosely adapted to make the popular animated film by Disney (1967).

JUNIUS The pseudonymous author of a series of letters that appeared in the **Public Advertiser*, January 1769–January 1772, denouncing, with bitter scorn, the policies of the duke of Grafton, Lord North, and many other government figures, along with George III. Junius also took an active part on behalf of John *Wilkes, and his arguments in favour of the freedom of the press and the liberties of the subject are of a classic Whig kind. The name is from the Roman republican hero Lucius Junius Brutus. Both before 1769 and after 1771 political letters under similar pseudonyms, which have been traced to the same hand, appeared in the newspapers. The letters were much reprinted and attracted much attention, hostile and otherwise, including some responses from Samuel *Johnson. An 'authorized' edition of the letters appeared in 1772. The identity of Junius has never been definitely established, and many candidates were suggested at the time and later, including Edward *Gibbon, Edmund *Burke, Richard *Glover, and Wilkes himself. The most plausible candidate, on linguistic and political grounds, is Sir Philip Francis (1740–1818), chief clerk in the war office 1762–72 and later an ally of Burke against Warren Hastings (1732–1818). Francis had been at St Paul's

School with Henry Sampson Woodfall (1739–1805), the publisher of the letters, and there is a great deal of circumstantial evidence pointing to his authorship, though it has not been conclusively proved. See *The Letters of Junius*, ed. J. Cannon (1978); F. Cordasco and G. Simonson, *Junius and his Works* (1986).

JUNIUS, Francis (François Du Jon) (1591–1677) Philologist and antiquary, born at Heidelberg, a friend of John *Milton, and librarian and tutor in the household of Thomas Howard, fourteenth earl of Arundel (1585–1646). His *Etymologicum Anglicanum* (1743) was used by Samuel *Johnson. He gave Anglo-Saxon manuscripts, including the so-called *Cædmon Manuscript (*see* JUNIUS MANUSCRIPT), to the Bodleian Library, and to the *Oxford University Press materials for printing in Gothic, Runic, Anglo-Saxon, and Roman founts. He published an edition of Cædmon in 1655.

Junius Manuscript One of four major manuscripts containing Old English poetry, named after the editor Francis *Junius who printed it at Amsterdam in 1655, calling it 'Cædmon the monk's poetical paraphrase of Genesis, etc.' The biblical poetry in the manuscript (**Genesis A and B*, **Exodus*, **Daniel*, and **Christ and Satan*) continued to be associated with *Cædmon for some time, but it is unconnected with him. See editions by G. V. Krapp and E. V. Dobbie, *Anglo-Saxon Poetic Records*, vol. i (1931), and in facsimile by Sir Israel Gollancz (1863–1930) (British Academy, 1927).

Juno The principal Roman goddess (Hera in Greek), sister and wife of *Jupiter, and associated with marriage. In the **Aeneid* she is the great enemy of Aeneas and the Trojans.

Juno and the Paycock *See* O'CASEY, SEAN.

Jupiter (Zeus in Greek) Also called Jove, in Roman mythology king and father of the gods and brother and husband of *Juno. In the **Aeneid* he ensures that Aeneas fulfils his destiny as founder of the future city of Rome. His sexual encounters, often in disguise, with mortals of both sexes could be disastrous for them, as it was for Danaë, Leda, and Callisto; the youth Ganymede on the other hand became his cupbearer. His best-known human offspring was *Hercules, born to Alcmena. These stories, several of which are told in *Ovid's *Metamorphoses*, were often referred to in Renaissance literature, for example in Christopher *Marlowe's *Hero and Leander*.

JUVENAL (Decimus Iunius Iuvenalis) (*fl.* AD 100) The greatest Roman satiric poet, author of sixteen satires, the last one incomplete. Nothing definite is known about his life. In Satire 1, a friend urges that writing satire is too dangerous; Juvenal replies that it is hard not to write satire in Rome, but he will attack only those who are safely dead. Satire 3, translated by Samuel *Johnson as *London*, is a bitter tirade on the misery of being poor in Rome. The lengthy Satire 6 is an onslaught on women as extravagant, cruel, false, lecherous. Satire 10, also translated by Johnson, reveals with grim irony the vanity of human wishes. The earlier Satires are unsurpassed in their expression of hatred and disgust; their caustic style is often contrasted with that of the urbane and witty Horace. Other English imitators include Joseph *Hall and John *Oldham. John *Dryden edited and wrote in part a translation of Juvenal to which he prefixed his long discourse on satire, and his influence on Alexander *Pope and Jonathan *Swift is also strong. See Kirk Freudenburg (ed.), *The Cambridge Companion to Roman Satire* (2005).

K

KAFKA, Franz (1883–1924) German-speaking Jewish novelist, born in Prague, where he studied law. Kafka worked as an official in an insurance company until forced to retire by tuberculosis. None of his three novels was completed to his satisfaction, and all were published posthumously: *Der Prozess* (1925: *The Trial*), *Das Schloss* (1926: *The Castle*), and the fragment *Amerika* (1927). Among the best-known short works are the stories 'Das Urteil' (1913: 'The Judgement'), 'Die Verwandlung' (1915: 'The Metamorphosis'), and 'In der Strafkolonie' (1919: 'In a Penal Colony'). Like the novels they display a tendency to fable and parable and explore themes of existential alienation and guilt. Much of his work was translated into English by Edwin and Willa *Muir, beginning with *The Trial* in 1930. W. H. *Auden declared Kafka 'the voice of the 20th century', and while the voice and vision are inimitable, their influence has been extensive and profound. Those touched by his work include writers as various as Milan *Kundera, Joseph *Heller, Vladimir *Nabokov, and *García Márquez. *The Trial* was made into a film by Orson *Welles in 1963. Ted *Hughes's *Wodwo* contains a poem entitled 'Kafka' and a story in his manner, and Alan *Bennett's TV play *The Insurance Man* (1986) features Kafka as a character. Kafka also left a large body of letters and diaries of exceptional interest for the insights they offer into his complex and tortured personality. The word 'Kafkaesque' has entered the language to signify a strange, baffling, nightmarish, or anxiety-ridden reality characteristic of that depicted in his work.

Kailyard school [from 'Kail-yard', cabbage patch] A term applied to a group of Scottish writers who exploited a sentimental and romantic image of small-town life in Scotland; the vogue lasted from the 1880s to the end of the 19th century. Leading exponents were J. M. *Barrie (in such books from his early career as *Auld Licht Idylls*, 1888, and *A Window in Thrums*, 1889), 'Ian Maclaren' (John Watson, 1850–1907), and S. R. Crockett (1859–1914). Crockett's *The Stickit Minister* (1893) and Maclaren's *Beside the Bonnie Brier Bush* (1894) won a wide international readership. The Kailyard idyll was ferociously challenged by George Douglas *Brown's *The House with the Green Shutters* (1901) and J. MacDougall *Hay's *Gillespie* (1914) but still retained enough popular appeal in Scotland to earn further furious rebuff in the poetry of Hugh *MacDiarmid in the 1920s and the fiction of Lewis Grassic *Gibbon a decade later.

KAISER, Georg (1878–1945) German dramatist. A prolific and inventive writer, author of some 60 plays, he was banned by the National Socialist regime and emigrated, moving to Switzerland. *Die Bürger von Calais* (1914: *The Burghers of Calais*), *Gas I* (1918), and *Gas II* (1920) are regarded as leading examples of German Expressionist theatre (*see* EXPRESSIONISM).

Kama Sutra *See* BURTON, SIR RICHARD.

KANE, Sarah (1971–99) Playwright, brought up in Essex and educated at the universities of Bristol and Birmingham. Her first play, *Blasted* (1996), performed at the *Royal Court, was a violent drama, in which events in a Leeds hotel room suddenly explode into a European battleground of extreme violence. The play brought her overnight success and notoriety. In a short period before her death by suicide, she produced a body of work that has seen her acclaimed as a major playwright. *Phaedra's Love* (1997) was followed by *Cleansed* (1998), and *Crave* (1998), in which four unnamed characters create a series of interlinking dialogues on, amongst other things, sexual abuse and obsessional love. Her *4.48 Psychosis*, which is much more than the suicide note its title suggests, was produced posthumously in 2000.

KANT, Immanuel (1724–1804) German idealist philosopher, born and educated at Königsberg in Prussia. His major contributions to philosophy began with *Critique of Pure Reason* (1781), followed by *Prolegomena to Any Future Metaphysics* (1783), *Fundamental Principles of the Metaphysic of Ethics* (1785), *Metaphysical Rudiments of Natural Philosophy* (1786), the second edition of the *Critique of Pure Reason* (1787), the *Critique of Practical Reason* (1788), and the *Critique of Judgement* (1790). His *Religion within the Boundaries of Pure Reason* (1793) called down on him government censure. His philosophy was subsequently developed and profoundly modified by *Fichte, *Schelling, and *Hegel. In Britain, Kant's critique of empiricism was greatly valued by S. T. *Coleridge, who made extensive use of his ideas in 'An Essay on Genial Criticism' (1814) and elsewhere. More generally, Kantian ideas filtered through to Thomas *De Quincey, William *Hazlitt, and P. B. *Shelley. Kant also exercised a considerable influence on Thomas *Carlyle, though his reception of Kant's thought was a quirkily individual one. Today Kant is acknowledged as a philosopher of the highest importance. His work remains widely studied and highly influential. See Roger Scruton, *Kant* (1982).

KAPUR, Manju (1958–) Indian novelist in English, educated in India and Canada, professor in English at Miranda

House, Delhi. She is the practitioner of a quietist, conversational prose style tracking the generational unfolding of Indian family life, interested in both continuity and change. Awarded the Commonwealth Prize for Best First Novel (Eurasia region), *Difficult Daughters* (1998) is at once a **Bildungsroman* and a family saga in which conflicts between tradition and modernity mirror schisms in the Indian nation at Partition. *A Married Woman* (2003) is a path-breaking narrative of homoerotic self-awakening, and *Home* (2006) unhurriedly follows the history across three generations of a joint family running a cloth business in Delhi's busy Karol Bagh.

KARAMZIN, Nikolai Mikhailovich (1766–1826) Russian man of letters, born near Simbirsk; he spent most of his career in Moscow. In 1789 he embarked on extensive travels through Europe which included a visit to London. On returning, he edited the *Moscow Journal* (1791–2), in which appeared the first of his influential *Letters of a Russian Traveller* (full translation by Andrew Kahn, 2003) and important short stories, 'Poor Liza' and 'Natalia, the Boyar's Daughter'. Prolific and wide-ranging, Karamzin was poet and prose writer, essayist and critic, journalist and editor, translator and creator of a new 'language of feeling'. In 1803 he was appointed imperial historiographer and immersed himself in his *History of the Russian State* (12 vols, 1818–29), which was unfinished at his death. Karamzin greatly admired English literature, particularly the plays of William *Shakespeare (translated *Julius Caesar*, 1787), the poetry of Alexander *Pope, Edward *Young, and James *Thomson (translated *The Seasons*, 1787–8), the prose of Laurence *Sterne, and the writing of the 'Historical Triumvirate of Britain', Edward *Gibbon, David *Hume, and William Robertson (1721–93). He himself was the first Russian writer to gain any reputation in Britain through translations (via German) of his stories and letters (1803–4) and mentions in travel accounts. See A. G. Cross, *N. M. Karamzin* (1971).

Katherine Group The name given to five Middle English works of devotional prose found together in manuscript Bodley 34, dating from *c.*1190–1225: *Seinte Marherete, Seinte Iuliene, Seinte Katerine, *Sawles Warde*, and **Hali Meiðhad*. They come from Herefordshire or Shropshire, and their common language is also, for the most part, shared with **Ancrene Wisse*: three of these texts appear with a version of it in a British Library manuscript. Their language, from a transitional period of English, is distinctive and interesting, and their style is lively and often colloquial, with vivid details of illustration. The three saints' lives are all concerned with heroic virgins who were frequently exalted in medieval writings: St Catherine of Alexandria, St Juliana of Nicomedia, and St Margaret of Antioch, who were all believed to have suffered from the persecutions of Diocletian in the first decade of the 4th century. The most celebrated English life of one of these saints is the Old English *Juliana* by *Cynewulf. See N. R. Ker, *Facsimile of MS Bodley 34* (EETS 247, 1960); *The Katherine Group*, ed. S. R. T. O. d'Ardenne (1977); S. R. T. O. d'Ardenne and E. J. Dobson, *Seinte Katerine* (EETS ss 7, 1981); S. R. T. O. d'Ardenne, *The Liflade and te Passiun of Seinte Iuliene* (EETS 248, 1961); F. M. Mack, *Seinte Marherete* (EETS 193, 1934).

KAUFFER, E. (Edward) **McKnight** (1890–1954) American-born artist and illustrator, who settled in England in 1914, and won great praise for his posters and commercial designs, notably for the London Transport Board and the Great Western Railway: Arnold *Bennett (*Evening Standard*, 1928) wrote that he had 'changed the face of London streets' and that his success 'proves that popular taste is on the up-grade'. He also illustrated various works by T. S. *Eliot, including the 'Ariel Poems' series (1927–31). He moved back to America in 1940 and died in New York. See Mark Haworth-Booth, *E. McKnight Kauffer* (1979).

KAVANAGH, Julia (1824–77) Novelist, born in Thurles, Ireland, educated at home. She spent much of her youth in France, which gave her an insight into French life and character that she conveyed faithfully in her novels and tales. Her father, an unsuccessful writer, abandoned the family in 1844; Kavanagh subsequently supported herself and her mother Bridget (her lifelong companion) with her own literary work. Of the novels the best known were *Madeleine* (1848), *Nathalie* (1850), and *Adèle* (1858). Then followed *French Women of Letters* (1862) and *English Women of Letters* (1863), highly praised series of biographical sketches. *Forget-me-nots* (1878) is a collection of short stories. Kavanagh's novels, popular and respected, usually figure spirited and independent heroines. *Nathalie*, which describes the experiences of a passionate young schoolmistress in northern France who marries an older man, has been identified as an influence on Charlotte Brontë's *Villette*. The two novelists had corresponded, and met in London in 1850. Kavanagh published *The Pearl Fountain*, a collection of fairy stories written with her mother, in 1876.

KAVANAGH, P. J. (Patrick Joseph) (1931–) Poet and novelist, born in Worthing and educated at Merton College, Oxford. His first volume of poetry was *One and One* (1960). Others include *Edward Thomas in Heaven* (1974), *An Enchantment* (1991), and *Something About* (2004); his *Collected Poems* was published in 1992. His novels include *A Happy Man* (1972), *Rebel for Good* (1980), and *Only by Mistake* (1986). *The Perfect Stranger* (1966) is a hauntingly memorable account of his life up to the sudden death of his first wife Sally, daughter of Rosamond *Lehmann, in 1958. He edited the *Collected Poems of Ivor Gurney* (1982; rev. edn, Ivor 2004; *see* Gurney, Ivor). A collection of his journalistic columns, *A Kind of Journal*, appeared in 2003.

KAVANAGH, Patrick (1905–67) Poet who moved post-Yeatsian Irish poetry decisively away from the *Irish Revival's concern with the past towards everyday themes and colloquially based language. He was born in Co. Monaghan, the son of a small farmer and shoemaker; after some years of farming he went to Dublin in 1939 and embarked on a literary career as journalist and poet. His works include *Ploughman and Other Poems* (1936), *A Soul for Sale* (1947), *Tarry Flynn* (1948, a semi-autobiographical comic novel), and *Come Dance with Kitty Stobling* (1960), a volume distinguished by a series of debonair, deceptively ramshackle sonnets. His best-known work is probably *The Great Hunger* (1942), a long cinematic poem contrasting the experience of its impoverished protagonist, Patrick Maguire ('locked in a stable with pigs and cows forever', and suffering from sexual and intellectual hunger), with the idealizations of rural life in both the drama of *Abbey Theatre and the rhetoric of nationalist politicians. Kavanagh later repudiated the tragic pessimism of *The Great Hunger* in favour of the comic vision of his 1950s lyrics. A definitive *Collected Poems* appeared in 2004. See also *A Poet's Country: Selected Prose* (2002); Antoinette Quinn, *Patrick Kavanagh: A Biography* (2001).

KAWABATA, Yasunari (1899–1972) Japanese novelist. After an initial modernist period, Kawabata developed a fascination with death, eroticism, and traditional Japanese aesthetics. A well-known early book is *Izu Dancer* (1926). *Snow Country* (1948) is another classic. Kawabata became the second Asian writer (after Rabindranath *Tagore) to win the *Nobel Prize for Literature, in 1968. He committed suicide four years later.

KAY, Guy Gavriel (1954–) Canadian *fantasy writer, born in Saskatchewan. After helping to edit J. R. R. *Tolkien's posthumous *Silmarillion*, Kay wrote novels that increasingly fused *fantasy with historical 'versions' of, for example, the Byzantine Empire (*Sailing to Sarantium*, 1998); worlds which seem like analogues of ours.

KAY, Jackie (1961–) Scottish poet, dramatist, and fiction writer, educated at the University of Stirling and now a professor of creative writing at Newcastle University. A version of her adoption at birth by Glaswegian parents is told in *The Adoption Papers* (1991) in the voices of the adoptive mother, the birth mother who remembers the absent Nigerian father, and the daughter as she grows up. Kay's novel *Trumpet* (1998) traces the revelation, after the death of the mixed race jazz musician Joss Moody, that 'he' was a woman, destabilizing racial and gender boundaries. Her collections of short stories, *Why Don't You Stop Talking* (2002) and *Wish I Was Here* (2006), similarly disrupt readerly expectations. Her volumes of poetry, *Other Lovers* (1993), *Off Colour* (1998), *Life Mask* (2005), *Darling: New and Selected Poems* (2007), and *Red, Cherry Red* (2007), are witty and imaginatively empathetic. She has written poetry and fiction for children, including the novel *Strawgirl* (2002).

KAYE-SMITH, Sheila (1887–1956) Novelist, born in Sussex, where she spent all her life. Her successful *regional novels are precisely located, principally on the Kent–Sussex border, and include *Starbrace* (1909) and *Joanna Godden* (1921). Hers was the genre of novel satirized by Stella Gibbons in **Cold Comfort Farm* (1932).

KAZAN, Elia (1909–2003) Greek-American film and theatre director, born Elias Kazanjoglou in Constantinople. In 1913 his family emigrated to New York, an experience on which he based his film and novel *America, America* (1963). His later novels *The Arrangement* (1967) and *The Anatolian* (1983) further explore the lives of Greek Americans. In the 1930s Kazan worked in the New York Group Theatre with figures like Clifford *Odets and briefly joined a communist cell. His theatre activities continued with productions of plays by Arthur *Miller and Tennessee *Williams. From the 1940s onwards he was active in Hollywood, directing *On the Waterfront* (1954) among other films. Controversially, he named names during the House Un-American Activities Committee's investigation of communist activities in the movies, which he describes in his autobiography *Elia Kazan: A Life* (1988). See Richard Schickel, *Elia Kazan: A Biography* (2005).

KAZANTZAKIS, Nikos (1883–1957) Greek writer and philosopher, born in Crete and educated at the University of Athens and later in Paris, where he studied under the philosopher Henri Bergson (1859–1941). Kazantzakis's prolific output includes essays, plays, poetry, novels, travel books, and translations. His massive *epic poem *The Odyssey: A Modern Sequel* (1938) offers contemporary reflections on the experiences of Odysseus, while *The Last Temptation of Christ* (1951; a controversial film adaptation, directed by Martin Scorsese, was released in 1988) explores the humanity revealed in the ministry of Jesus. *Zorba the Greek* (1946; filmed 1964), Kazantzakis's best-known work, is the story of the friendship that develops between the uneducated but irrepressible Zorba, and the visiting writer and intellectual who employs him.

KEAN, Edmund (1787/90–1833) An actor of uncertain parentage whose adventurous childhood gave rise to innumerable legends. He was befriended by various guardians, including Moses Kean, a mimic and ventriloquist, and worked on stage as infant prodigy and strolling player before achieving fame in 1814 as Shylock in *The *Merchant of Venice*, a performance recorded by William *Hazlitt. He was a great tragic actor, whose numerous successful roles included Richard III, Hamlet, Othello, Macbeth, Lear, and *Marlowe's *Jew of Malta*. *Dumas *père* wrote a play based on his colourful life which was subsequently adapted by Jean-Paul *Sartre (1954). His son Charles John Kean (1811–68) was also an actor, and manager of the Princess's Theatre, 1851–9.

KEANE, Molly (1904–96) Novelist and playwright, born in Co. Kildare, into a leisured Anglo-Irish world (her mother was the dialect poet 'Moira O'Neill'). She was educated by governesses and spent a brief period at boarding school. At the age of 17 she wrote her first novel, choosing the pseudonym M. J. Farrell (after a public house) to hide her literary life from her sporting friends. Between 1928 and 1952 she published ten further novels, including *Devoted Ladies* (1934), *The Rising Tide* (1937), and *Two Days in Aragon* (1941). She also wrote successful plays (with the actor, writer, and producer John

Perry, 1906–c.1994) such as *Spring Meeting* (1938) and *Treasure Hunt* (1949). Chronicling Anglo-Irish values, especially the thrill of the chase, both sporting and sexual, her work is characterized by a detailed evocation of place and a bitter-sweet flavour. An underlying awareness of the cruelties, snobberies, and evasions of the decaying Anglo-Irish milieu is most notably articulated in *Good Behaviour* (1981). Published under her own name and written after a long silence subsequent to her husband's death, the novel brought her work to a new audience. *Time after Time* (1983) and *Loving and Giving* (1988) followed. She also published *Nursery Cooking* (1985, illustrated by Linda Smith).

KEATING, Geoffrey (Seathrún Céitinn) (c.1580–c.1644) Irish priest, historian, and poet whose *Foras Feasa Éirinn (Compendium of Knowledge about Ireland)* offers a systematic narrative of Irish history, culture, and values from the Creation to the establishment of the Anglo-Norman colony. Known as 'the Herodotus of Ireland', Keating is regarded as one of the greatest prose stylists in Irish. Of Norman descent (his name is a corruption of 'Fitzstephen'), he aimed both to counter hostile representations of Ireland by such British writers as *Giraldus Cambrensis and Edmund *Spenser and to illustrate the unity of interest of indigenous Gaels and Old English (Catholics of Norman or English stock). Keating's eloquent Counter-Reformation preaching brought him to the attention of the authorities and he reputedly planned *Foras Feasa* while a fugitive in a cave in the Glen of Aherlow. He also wrote theological treatises and notably sophisticated poems, both political and amorous.

KEATLEY, Charlotte (1960–) Playwright, born in London, and educated at the universities of Manchester and Leeds. She is best known for *My Mother Said I Never Should* (1987), a play that traces the changes in women's lives through four generations of the same family. It is a play in which the male family members never appear on stage, and one that makes startling use of its non-chronological, non-linear structure.

KEATS, John (1795–1821) Poet, the son of the manager of a livery stables in Moorfields, who died when he was 8; his mother remarried, but died of tuberculosis when he was 14. The oldest of the family, he remained deeply attached to his brothers George and Tom and to his sister Fanny. He was well educated at Clarke's school, Enfield, where he began a translation of the *Aeneid*, and in 1810 was apprenticed to an apothecary-surgeon. His first efforts at writing poetry appear to date from 1814, and include an 'Imitation of Spenser'; Keats's school friend Charles *Cowden-Clarke recorded the profound effect of his early reading of *Spenser. In 1815 Keats cancelled his fifth year of apprenticeship and became a student at Guy's Hospital; to the same year belong 'Ode to Apollo' and 'Hymn to Apollo'. In 1816 he was licensed to practise as an apothecary, but in spite of precarious finances abandoned the profession for poetry. In 1816 he also met Leigh *Hunt, who published in the same year in his **Examiner* Keats's poem 'O Solitude', and in the course of a survey of young poets in the same journal included Keats's sonnet 'On First Looking into Chapman's Homer'. Keats met P. B. *Shelley and Benjamin *Haydon, began to plan **Endymion*, and wrote 'I stood tiptoe upon a little hill' as a first effort towards that poem. His first volume of poems was published in March 1817. It included, among sonnets, epistles, and miscellaneous poems, 'I stood tiptoe' and 'Sleep and Poetry'. There were at first some pleasing reviews, but public interest was not aroused and sales were meagre; and in the autumn came the first of John *Lockhart's harsh attacks in **Blackwood's Magazine*, labelling Keats and his associates as members of the so-called *Cockney School. He finished the first draft of *Endymion* and during the winter of 1817–18 saw something of *Wordsworth and *Hazlitt, both of whom much influenced his thought and practice. In December Haydon gave his 'immortal dinner', whose guests included Wordsworth, Charles *Lamb, and Keats. *Endymion*, dedicated to Thomas *Chatterton, whom Keats greatly admired, was published in the spring of 1818, and *'Isabella, or The Pot of Basil' finished in May.

With his friend Charles Armitage Brown (1786–1842) Keats then toured the Lakes, spent July and August in Scotland, and made a brief visit to Northern Ireland. He had travelled frequently in southern England but he had never before seen scenery of rugged grandeur. It moved him deeply and he made full use of it when he came to write **Hyperion*. Bitter attacks on *Endymion* came in the autumn from Lockhart in *Blackwood's* and from the **Quarterly Review*. For the time being Keats concealed his pain and wrote to his brother George that, in spite of the reviews, 'I think I shall be among the English poets after my death', but his friends believed the wound was deep. Meanwhile his brother Tom was very ill and Keats spent much time with him. When Tom died in December Keats moved into his friend Brown's house in Hampstead, now known as Keats House. There, in the early winter, he met Fanny *Brawne, with whom he fell deeply in love, and with whom he remained in love until his death. During the course of the summer and autumn of 1818 his sore throats had become more frequent and persistent. Nevertheless September 1818 marked the beginning of what is sometimes referred to as his 'great year'; he began *Hyperion* in its first version, abandoning it a year later; he wrote, consecutively, *'The Eve of St Agnes', 'The Eve of St Mark', the 'Ode to Psyche', *'La Belle Dame sans Merci', *'Ode to a Nightingale', and probably at about the same time the *'Ode on a Grecian Urn', 'Ode on Melancholy', and 'Ode on Indolence'; *'Lamia Part I', 'Otho the Great' (in collaboration with Brown); the second version of *Hyperion*, called *The Fall of Hyperion*, *'To Autumn', and 'Lamia Part II'. During this year he was beset with financial problems, both his own and those of his friends and relations, and intensely preoccupied with his love for Fanny, to whom he became engaged. In the winter of 1819 he began the unfinished 'The Cap and Bells', but he became increasingly ill with tuberculosis and his great creative work was now over. His second volume of poems, *Lamia, Isabella, The Eve of St Agnes, and Other Poems*, was published in July 1820, and included, as well as the title poems, five odes, *Hyperion*, 'Fancy', and other works. The volume was generally well received, gaining much praise in some quarters, with criticism from *Blackwood's* much muted, but the sales were very slow. Shelley invited Keats to Italy and in September, after sorting out his copyrights and financial affairs, Keats set off with his friend Joseph *Severn. They did not go to the Shelleys but settled in Rome, where Keats died the following February.

Keats has always been regarded as one of the principal figures in the *Romantic movement, and his stature as a poet has grown steadily through all changes of fashion. *Tennyson considered him the greatest poet of the 19th century, and Matthew *Arnold commended his 'intellectual and spiritual passion' for beauty; in the 20th century he has been discussed and reconsidered by critics from T. S. *Eliot and F. R. *Leavis to Lionel *Trilling (*The Opposing Self*, 1955) and Christopher *Ricks (*Keats and Embarrassment*, 1974). His letters, published in 1848 and 1878, have come to be regarded with almost the admiration given to his poetry, to which many of them act as a valuable commentary. They show him an acute if forgivably inconsistent critic and include his central critical notions of the *egotistical sublime and *negative capability. He wrote fully and revealingly to Fanny Brawne, to his brothers and sister, to Shelley, Leigh Hunt, Haydon, Severn, and many others, mixing the everyday events of his own life with a lively and delicate interest in that of his correspondents, and displaying wit and high spirits as well as his profoundest thoughts on love, poetry, and the nature of man. T. S. Eliot described the letters as 'certainly the most notable and most important ever written by any English poet' (*The Use of Poetry and the Use of Criticism*, 1933). The major biographies are by W. J. Bate (1963), Robert *Gittings (1968), and Andrew *Motion (1997). The standard edition is J. Stillinger's *Poems of John Keats* (1982) but there are also excellent editions by M. Allott (1970) and J. Barnard (1973). See also C. Ricks, *Keats and Embarrassment* (1974); N. Roe, *John Keats and the Culture of Dissent* (1997).

KEBLE, John (1792–1866) Churchman and poet, educated at Corpus Christi College, Oxford. He became fellow and tutor at Oriel College (where John Henry *Newman and Edward *Pusey were also fellows) and professor of poetry at Oxford, 1831–41. His sermon on national apostasy in 1833 was considered the start of the *Oxford Movement, which he also supported by writing nine of the *Tracts for the Times*. Although a leading figure in Oxford intellectual life, he was personally unambitious, and from 1836 until his death was vicar of the country parish of Hursley. His volume of sacred verse *The Christian Year*, published anonymously in 1827, had an immense success and was widely admired, not only by Tractarians, but also by *evangelical and *Broad Church readers; intended as a guide to devotion and a commentary on the *Book of *Common Prayer*, it shows the influence of George *Herbert and, in its feeling for the natural world, of William *Wordsworth, and combines Keble's considerable scholarship with deep personal feeling. A second volume, *Lyra Innocentium*, followed in 1846. Charlotte Mary *Yonge was a pupil of his, and drew a vivid character sketch in *Musings over the Christian Year...with a Few Gleanings of Recollections of Keble* (1871). Keble also edited Richard *Hooker (1836), helped Newman with Richard Hurrell *Froude's *Remains*, contributed to **Lyra Apostolica*, and published a life of Bishop Thomas Wilson (1653–1755). Keble College, Oxford, was founded in his memory in 1870. There are lives by W. Lock (1893) and G. Battiscombe (1963).

KEILLER, Patrick (1950–) English film-maker, trained as an architect; he made avant-garde films before creating a distinctive form of fictionalized *documentary in *London* (1994) and *Robinson in Space* (1997), both narrated by Paul Schofield, which survey the changing face of, respectively, London and England, as seen by a jaundiced reincarnation of Daniel *Defoe's hero Robinson Crusoe.

Kells, Book of An 8th- to 9th-century manuscript of the Gospels, with prefaces, summaries, and canon tables; seven charters of the abbey of Kells have been added. Written in the formal bookhand termed Irish majuscule, it has magnificent illustrations consisting of intricate patterns made up of abstract and animal forms. It was probably completed at Kells after the sack of Iona in 806. Collated by James *Ussher in 1621, it was presented to Trinity College, Dublin, after the *Restoration.

KELLY, Hugh (1739–77) Playwright, born in Killarney, but came to London in 1760 and wrote for the *Court Magazine* and Charlotte *Lennox's *Ladies' Museum*. In 1767 a book of his essays, *The Babler*, was published by John *Newbery, for whose *Public Ledger* Kelly wrote between 1767 and 1772. His only novel was *Memoirs of a Magdalen* (1767). His *False Delicacy*, produced by David *Garrick in 1768, is a sentimental comedy in which comic mistakes arise from excessive delicacy; it was to some extent a rival to Goldsmith's *The *Good-Natur'd Man*. Kelly's most successful play was *The School for Wives* (1773). In 1774 he was called to the bar, but he continued to write for newspapers, attracting some hostility for his support of government policy.

KELMAN, James (1946–) Novelist, short story writer, and dramatist, born in Glasgow. He left school at 15 to become an apprentice compositor and later moved briefly to the United States, returning to Scotland and a succession of temporary jobs. The stories of *Not Not While the Giro* (1983) depict Scottish working-class life with terse humour and introduce the pared-back, multi-focal vernacular narrative style developed in the novels *The Busconductor Hines* (1984) and *A Chancer* (1985). *A Disaffection* (1989) offers a critique of the education system through its portrait of an alcoholic secondary teacher. The award of the *Booker Prize to *How Late It Was, How Late* (1994) caused outrage in genteel quarters of the London press, both because of the novel's deployment of expletives and its sympathetic presentation of the alienation of its protagonist, an unemployed building worker and petty criminal who comes round after a drinking binge to find himself blind and in police custody. Other works include three collections of stories, *Greyhound for Breakfast* (1987), *The Burn* (1991), and *The Good Times* (1998); and *Hardie and Baird and Other Plays* (1991). The novels *Translated Accounts* (2001) and *You Have to Be Careful in the Land of the Free* (2004) are set respectively in an unnamed *dystopia and in America, while *Kieron Smith, Boy* (2008) returns to the Glasgow of Kelman's childhood, which it unsentimentally evokes, giving a full expression to the author's uncompromising linguistic politics.

Kelmscott Press *See* MORRIS, WILLIAM.

KEMBLE, Charles (1775–1854) Actor, born in Brecon, south Wales, educated at the Jesuit college in Douai, France. Kemble was the son of a strolling actor-manager, Roger Kemble (1721–1802), and brother of Sarah *Siddons, John Philip *Kemble, Stephen Kemble, and other theatrical siblings; father of Fanny *Kemble and the scholar John Mitchell *Kemble. He was a leading actor for some 25 years, and became a respected member of London society. Handsome and elegant, he had a light voice, and his most successful roles were of young men, such as Mirabell in *The *Way of the World*, Mercutio, Orlando, Benedick, and, most especially, Romeo. His range was considerable in comedy and romance, but he did not often attempt tragedy.

KEMBLE, Fanny (Frances Anne) (1809–93) Daughter of Charles *Kemble, a beautiful and accomplished actress. She attended schools in Bath, Boulogne, and Paris, but was largely home educated. She first appeared under her father's management at Covent Garden in 1829, when she played Juliet to his Mercutio, achieving a success that saved his theatre from financial collapse. She played comedy and tragedy with equal success, and added most of the great roles to her repertoire, including Portia, Lady Macbeth, Beatrice, Lady Teazle in *The *School for Scandal*, Belvidera in **Venice Preserved*, and many others. After a tempestuous and unsuccessful marriage in America, she published *Journal of a Residence on a Georgian Plantation in 1838–1839* (1863), in which she recorded her hatred of the slavery she had witnessed in the American South. She published a volume of poems in 1844 and *Records of a Later Life* in 1882.

KEMBLE, John Mitchell (1807–57) Historian and philologist, elder son of Charles *Kemble, educated at Trinity College, Cambridge, where he was a member of the *Apostles and a friend of Richard *Trench, Richard Monkton *Milnes, and Alfred *Tennyson. He later studied in Germany, where he became a close friend of Jacob *Grimm and was converted to the new continental philology, which he supported on his return. His text of **Beowulf* (1833), dedicated to Grimm, aroused much controversy, and he did valuable work on the early history of England.

KEMBLE, John Philip (1757–1823) Eldest brother of Charles *Kemble. He achieved success as a tragic actor, and was particularly renowned in the roles of Coriolanus and Hamlet, in which part William *Hazlitt particularly admired him.

KEMP, Will (William) (*c*.1564–?1603) A comic actor and dancer, who acted in plays by *Shakespeare and Ben *Jonson. In 1599 he danced a morris dance from London to Norwich; his own account, *Kemp's Nine Days Wonder*, was published in 1600. See David Wiles, *Shakespeare's Clown* (1987).

KEMPE, Margery (*c*.1373–*c*.1438) Daughter of John Brunham, once mayor of King's Lynn, Norfolk. She married John Kempe (*c*.1393) and had fourteen children. She abandoned conventional married life for religion, travelled throughout England, and went on pilgrimage to Jerusalem, Rome, Santiago de Compostela, and Wilsnack in Poland. The *Boke* that now bears her name was produced in collaboration with two scribes, and details her visions and social experiences, some aspects of which are explicitly authenticated by the scribe mediating the narrative. The *Boke* relates the reactions she provoked from various English clergy, resulting in a complex picture of religious life in England at this time. See S. B. Meech and H. E. Allen (eds) (EETS os 212, 1940).

KEN, Thomas (1637–1711) Educated at Winchester College and fellow of New College, Oxford, who became bishop of Bath and Wells. His works of devotional prose and verse include *The Practice of Divine Love* (1685), the extremely popular *A Manual of Prayers for the Use of Scholars of Winchester College* (1674), and some well-known hymns, including 'Awake, my soul, and with the sun'. His works were collected by W. Hawkins in 1721.

KENDALL, May (1861–?1943) Satirist, poet, and essayist. She published a collection of satirical poems and essays entitled *That Very Mab* (1885); a volume of poems, *Dreams to Sell* (1887); and a collection of stories, *Songs from Dreamland* (1894). She lived in Yorkshire.

KENEALLY, Thomas (1935–) Prolific Australian novelist, born in Sydney. His ebullient account of his youth, *Homebush Boy* (1995), recounts his passion for G. M. *Hopkins and his decision to enter the priesthood. Quitting his training, Keneally worked as a teacher and clerk, publishing his first novel, *The Place at Whitton*, in 1964. *Bring Larks and Heroes* (1967), on a young soldier's experience of convictism, and *Three Cheers for the Paraclete* (1968), about a priest's collision with his superiors, both won the Miles Franklin Award. *The Survivor* (1969) and *A Dutiful Daughter* (1971) examine family relationships, the latter with an innovative second-person narrative, but Keneally returned to historical themes in *The Chant of Jimmie Blacksmith* (1972), made into a successful film (1978); *Blood Red, Sister Rose* (1974), about *Joan of Arc; and *Confederates* (1979). War, notably the Second World War—in which Keneally's father served—recurs in novels ranging from *The Fear* (1965) to *The Widow and her Hero* (2007). His most celebrated work is *Schindler's Ark* (1982; *Schindler's List* in the USA), which won the *Booker Prize and has been widely translated. The book, which tells of German industrialist Oskar Schindler, who risked his life to save Jews in Poland, was filmed by Steven Spielberg as *Schindler's List* (1993), winning BAFTA and Academy awards for Best Film. Keneally's later work includes the novels *Woman of the Inner Sea* (1992), *A River Town* (1995), *An Angel in Australia* (2002), and *The Tyrant's Novel* (2003), and the memoir *Searching for Schindler* (2007). Other non-fiction includes *Towards Asmara* (1988), on war in Eritrea, and *The Commonwealth of Thieves* (2005), on the founding of white Australia, as well as biographies of Abraham Lincoln, Dan Sickles, and Des Hasler. His travel writing includes *Now and in Time to Be: Ireland and the Irish* (1991), and *The Place Where Souls Are Born* (1992), on the American south-west. He is a lifetime republican—see *Our Republic* (1993)—and was made an Australian National Living Treasure in 1997.

Kenilworth A novel by Walter *Scott, published 1821. The novel is a celebration of the glories of the Elizabethan age. The fact that the plot is riddled with anachronisms did nothing to impair its popularity with the public; published in the year of the coronation of George IV, the story of *Elizabeth I and her favourite Leicester and of the betrayal and murder of Leicester's wife Amy Robsart caught the national mood. *Shakespeare, *Spenser, and *Ralegh all appear, and the climax of the novel is the great pageant at Kenilworth in July 1575.

KENNEDY, A. L. (Alison Louise) (1965–) Scottish writer, born in Dundee and educated at the University of Warwick. Her bleak, pessimistic, but distinctive fiction includes both volumes of short stories, such as *Original Bliss* (1997), and novels like *So I Am Glad* (1995), *Everything You Need* (1999), and *Day* (2007).

KENNEDY, Walter (?1455–?1518) A Scottish poet from a powerful family, the rival (ostensibly, and probably in reality) of William *Dunbar in 'The *Flyting of Dunbar and Kennedie' and mentioned by him in his 'Lament for the Makaris' as being on the point of death. The few poems by him that survive are extant in the *Asloan and *Bannatyne manuscripts and the *Maitland Folio. See J. Schipper (ed.) in *Denkschriften der kaiserlichen Akademie der Wissenschaften*, 48 (1902).

kenning A poetic compound made up of two or more nouns standing for another noun, occurring in ancient Germanic languages, notably Old Norse (Icelandic) and Old English. *Snorri Sturluson gives the authoritative discussion in his **Edda*. Strictly defined, it must be metaphorical, the poetic compound being literally distinct from its components. Thus, 'man' has been represented as 'tree-of-the-storm-of-Othinn': Othinn is god of battle and 'tree' (straight and upright) is a common element in 'person' kennings. 'Woman' is 'fir-tree-of-the-ember-of-the-wave': Gunnar throws the Nibelungs' treasure into the Rhine; the glowing ember in the water is gold, which this person (fir-tree) wears as decoration. Some Old English kennings are metonymic and thus not literally distinct: 'swanroad', 'whaleroad', and 'gannet's bath' (sea); 'voice-bearers' (people).

KENT, William (1685–1748) Painter, architect, decorator, and landscape gardener, best known through his association from 1719 with his major patron, the *Palladio enthusiast the third earl of Burlington (1694–1753). His imaginative, informal, and Arcadian garden designs, the archetype for the English *landscape garden, were highly influential and praised by his peers, including Horace *Walpole, who recognized Kent's originality. The best known, although subsequently altered, was the garden at Stowe. Although an indifferent painter, he has the distinction of being the earliest painter of medieval subjects, including paintings of Henry V (*c*.1730) commissioned by Queen Caroline, wife of George II. See Tim Mowl, *William Kent: Architect, Artist, Designer, Opportunist* (2006).

KERMODE, Sir Frank (1919–) Literary critic, born in Douglas, Isle of Man. He studied at the University of Liverpool, and served in the Royal Navy in the Second World War. He held a succession of academic posts at the universities of Newcastle, Reading, Manchester, Bristol, London, and Cambridge, resigning in 1982. His critical studies have alternated between the English Renaissance—beginning with an edition of *The *Tempest* (1954)—and 20th-century literature, in which he has championed the works of Wallace *Stevens and Ford Madox *Ford. His most influential early books are *Romantic Image* (1957), which demonstrates continuities between late Romantic and early modernist uses of enigmatic symbols, and *The Sense of an Ending* (1967), which explores the ways in which narrative fiction makes sense of linear time. Through his editorship of the Fontana Modern Masters series of books on modern thinkers and his seminars on literary theory at University College London, he helped to inject fresh currents of European thought into literary studies in Britain. His later books include *The Classic* (1975), *The Genesis of Secrecy* (1979), *Essays on Fiction* (1983), *An Appetite for Poetry* (1989), *Shakespeare's Language* (2000), and a memoir, *Not Entitled* (1997). He was knighted in 1991.

KEROUAC, Jack (1922–69) American novelist, born in Lowell, Massachusetts, of French Canadian parents, and educated at Columbia University. His first novel, *The Town and the City* (1950), was written under the influence of Thomas *Wolfe. He achieved fame with *On the Road* (1957) where, thinly disguising himself as Sal Paradise, he describes his cross-county excursions with his friend Neal Cassady (1926–68; Dean Moriarty in the book). Written in a free-flowing confessional prose, the novel was composed on a continuous paper roll: see *On the Road: The Original Scroll* (2007), which restores deleted passages. The work became a classic of the *Beat movement, and further books like *The Subterraneans* (1958) and *The*

Dharma Bums (1958) continued in this autobiographical mode, the latter based on his friendship with the poet Gary *Snyder. In his essays 'Essentials of Spontaneous Prose' (1953) and 'Belief & Technique for Modern Prose' (*Evergreen Review, 1959), he outlined a philosophy of writing that refused all revision and was more akin to the free association and improvisation of jazz. He attempted to practise these principles in his poetry (*Mexico City Blues* (1955), etc.). His later years were spent in alcoholic decline, a process that effectively alienated him from the group he helped to define. See Gerald Nicosia, *Memory Babe* (1994).

KERR, Judith (1923–) Children's writer, born in Berlin; she fled to England via Switzerland and France in the 1930s when her Jewish journalist father attracted the attention of the rising Nazi party. The story of her adjustment to life in Paris and London and her education as an art student at the Central School of Arts and Crafts is told in the fictionalized autobiographical trilogy *Out of the Hitler Time* (1971–8), beginning with *When Hitler Stole Pink Rabbit*. Kerr is also known for her many picture books about Mog the cat and her family, and *The Tiger Who Came to Tea* (1968).

KESAVAN, Mukul *See* ANGLO-INDIAN LITERATURE.

KESEY, Ken (1935–2001) American novelist, born in La Junta, Colorado, who volunteered to participate in the CIA-backed MK-ULTRA programme of experimentation with LSD and other drugs at a Stanford hospital. This formed the basis for his first novel, *One Flew over the Cuckoo's Nest* (1962), which presents the mental ward of a hospital as a surreal form of prison. In 1964 Kesey joined with Neil Cassady (*see* KEROUAC, JACK) and other friends to travel round America in a school bus. These 'Merry Pranksters' are described in Tom *Wolfe's *The Electric Kool-Aid Acid Test* (1968). Kesey's later works include the miscellanies *Kesey's Garage Sale* (1972) and *Demon Box* (1986), as well as a screenplay, *The Further Inquiry* (1995).

KESSON, Jessie (1916–94) Née MacDonald, Scottish novelist and radio playwright, born in the Inverness workhouse and raised partly in an orphanage near Skene, Aberdeenshire, who was encouraged to write by Nan *Shepherd. Her work includes the novels *The White Bird Passes* (1958), *Glitter of Mica* (1963), and *Another Time, Another Place* (1983), which was made into an award-winning film; and *Where the Apple Ripens and Other Stories* (1985).

KEYES, Sidney (1922–43) Poet, born in Dartford, Kent. He was brought up largely by his grandfather, whom he commemorates in several poems, and was educated at Dartford grammar school and Tonbridge School, Kent, where he began to write poetry, and at the Queen's College, Oxford, where he became friendly with John *Heath-Stubbs, and edited, with Michael Meyer (1921–2000), *Eight Oxford Poets* (1941), which contains some of Keyes's own work. His first collection, *The Iron Laurel*, appeared in 1942; in the same year he joined the army. His second, *The Cruel Solstice*, appeared in 1943, after his death in Tunisia on 29 April 1943; this collection was awarded the Hawthornden Prize posthumously in 1944. His *Collected Poems*, with a memoir by Meyer, appeared in 1945; rev. 1989. See John Press, *Sidney Keyes* (2005).

KIBERD, Declan (1951–) Critic and theorist of Irish literature. Born in Leopold Bloom's Eccles Street in Dublin (*see* ULYSSES), Kiberd attended primary school in Clontarf, where he was taught by John *McGahern. He was educated at Trinity College, Dublin, winning the Gold Medal in both English and Irish and later (1977–9) becoming a lecturer in Irish. He has been professor of Anglo-Irish literature at University College, Dublin, since 1997. His widely influential *Inventing Ireland* (1995) and *Irish Classics* (2000) bring *postcolonial perspectives and rhetorical flair to bear on a broad range of Irish writing.

Kidnapped* and *Catriona [Gaelic for Catherine and pronounced Catreena] A novel and its sequel by Robert Louis *Stevenson, published 1886 and 1893. The central incident in the story is the murder of Colin Campbell, the 'Red Fox' of Glenure, the king's factor on the forfeited estate of Ardshiel: this is a historical event. Young David Balfour, impoverished on the death of his father, goes for assistance to his uncle Ebenezer, a miserly villain who has illegally taken control of the Balfour estate. Having failed to murder David, Ebenezer has him kidnapped on a ship to be carried off to the Carolinas. On the voyage Alan *Breck is picked up from a sinking boat. He is 'one of those honest gentlemen that were in trouble about the years forty-five and six', a *Jacobite who 'wearies for the heather and the deer'. The ship is wrecked on the coast of Mull, and David and Alan travel together. They witness the murder of Colin Campbell, and suspicion falls on them. After a perilous journey across the Highlands they escape across the Forth, and the novel ends with the defeat of Ebenezer and David's recovery of his inheritance. *Kidnapped* was a popular success, but its sequel, *Catriona*, was less well received. It is concerned with the unsuccessful attempt of David Balfour to secure the acquittal of James Stewart of the Glens, who is falsely accused, from political motives, of the murder of Colin Campbell; with the escape of Alan Breck to the Continent; and with David's love affair with Catriona Drummond, daughter of the renegade James More.

KIERKEGAARD, Søren Aabye (1813–55) Danish philosopher and theologian, born in Copenhagen, educated at the University of Copenhagen. Although he is now chiefly remembered as having initiated existentialist trends in modern philosophy (e.g. *Concluding Unscientific Postscript*, trans. W. Lowrie and D. F. Swenson, 1941), he also wrote on religious, psychological, or literary subjects (e.g. *The Concept of Dread* and *Fear and Trembling*, both trans. W. Lowrie, 1944). His satirical gifts are demonstrated in his essay on *The Present Age* (trans. A. Dru, 1962), reminiscent of Thomas *Carlyle's polemics. His various writings have common features: a distrust of dogma and an emphasis on particularity; an imaginative concern with the forms under which human character and motivation manifest themselves; and a passionate belief in the value of individual choice, rather than passive acquiescence in established opinions and norms. His insistence on personal decision, unmediated by artificial reasoning, lay at the root of his rejection of *Hegel. He saw in Hegelianism a philosophy which obliterated, in the name of metaphysical demonstrations, the subjective commitment and 'risk' in every valid act of faith. To all such speculative attempts to conceal or explain away what is central to human existence as genuinely understood and known, Kierkegaard opposed the concept of authentic choice, which stakes everything on a belief which cannot be proved, but which is maintained in the face of all intellectual uncertainty. This idea finds expression in the religious sphere, but it also applies to other kinds of experience, including the ethical. Some of Kierkegaard's most penetrating psychological observations occur in his descriptions of the 'leap of faith' and in his analyses of the state of 'dread' (*Angst*) which precedes and accompanies it. The emphasis on freedom as a condition which both fascinates and repels links his philosophical ideas and the doctrines of his existentialist successors. His ideas have influenced literary figures as diverse as W. H. *Auden, Franz *Kafka, Rainer Maria *Rilke, and John *Updike. *See* EXISTENTIALISM; see also Alastair Hannay, *Kierkegaard: A Biography* (new edn, 2003).

'Killigrew, Mrs Anne, To the Pious Memory of' *See* DRYDEN, JOHN.

KILLIGREW, Henry (1613–1700) Brother of Thomas *Killigrew the elder, educated at Christ Church, Oxford, the author of one play, *The Conspiracy* (1638). He was the father of Anne Killigrew (1660–85; *see* DRYDEN, JOHN).

KILLIGREW, Thomas, the elder (1612–83) Playwright and theatre manager. He was page to Charles I; groom of the bedchamber and a favourite companion of Charles II. With Sir William *D'Avenant he held the monopoly of acting in *Restoration London. He built a playhouse on the site of the present Theatre Royal Drury Lane, in 1663, and was master of the revels in 1679. His most popular play, *The Parson's Wedding*, a bawdy farcical comedy, was first performed 1640/41 and printed in 1664 with his other plays, which include *The Princess, The Prisoners, Claracilla*, and *Thomaso, or The Wanderer* (in two parts), on the last of which Aphra *Behn based her successful adaptation *The Rover. Cecilia and Clorinda*, a tragicomedy in two parts, is based on a subject from *Artamène, ou le Grand Cyrus* by Madeleine de *Scudéry.

KILLIGREW, Sir William (?1606–95) Brother of Thomas *Killigrew the elder, a court official under Charles I and Charles II and author of *Selindra* and *Ormasdes, or Love and Friendship*, tragicomedies, and *Pandora*, a comedy, published in 1664; and of *The Siege of Urbin*, a tragicomedy, published in 1666.

Killing No Murder A pamphlet ironically dedicated to Oliver *Cromwell, 'the true father of your country; for while you live we can call nothing ours, and it is from your death that we hope for our inheritances'; it advocates his assassination. It was written by the Leveller Edward Sexby (d. 1658) and printed in 1657 in the Netherlands. The name on the title page is that of William Allen, who had been one of Cromwell's Ironsides. See O. Lutaud, *Des révolutions d'Angleterre à la révolution française: le tyrannicide et Killing No Murder* (1973).

'Kilmeny' The subject of the 13th bard's haunting supernatural song in *The *Queen's Wake* by James *Hogg. The girl Kilmeny goes up the glen, does not return, and is mourned for dead. At last she comes back. She had been carried away from the troubles of men to 'ane land of love, and ane land of lychte', from which she had a vision of war and sin in the world below. She asked to return to tell her friends what she had seen, and she returns transformed and sanctified; but after a month and a day she disappears and passes again to another world.

KILNER, Dorothy (1755–1836) and **Mary Ann** (1753–1831) Sisters-in-law living in Stratford, Essex, who wrote popular children's stories, often using an anthropomorphized animal or object as narrator, as in Dorothy's *Life and Perambulation of a Mouse* (*c*.1783) and Mary Ann's *The Adventures of a Pin-Cushion* (*c*.1780).

KILROY, Thomas (1934–) Irish playwright, born in Callan, Co. Kilkenny, and educated at University College, Dublin. He was professor of modern English at University College, Galway, from 1978 to 1989. Kilroy's plays include *The Death and Resurrection of Mr Roche* (1969), which explores the relationship between conventionality and repression in Irish middle-class life; *Talbot's Box* (1979), a sympathetic portrait of the ascetic Dublin labourer Matt Talbot (1856–1925); and *Double Cross* (1986), a study of the mutually mirroring careers of two Irish Catholics, Brendan Bracken, Winston *Churchill's wartime minister of information, and William Joyce, the Nazi propagandist ('Lord Haw-Haw'). He has also written *The Secret Fall of Constance Wilde* (1997) and *The Shape of Metal* (2003), along with resourceful Irish domestications of Anton Chekhov (*The Seagull*, 1981) and Henrik Ibsen (*Ghosts*, 1989). *The Big Chapel*, a novel on violent contention between liberal and conservative Catholics in post-Famine rural Kilkenny, appeared in 1971.

KILVERT, Francis (1840–79) Diarist, educated privately in Bath and at Wadham College, Oxford. He became a rural curate in Wiltshire, then Radnorshire, before he became vicar of Bredwardine, Herefordshire, in 1877. He is remembered for his lively and humane diary, kept with no thought of publication, from 1870 until his death; it was first published in a three-volume selection edited by William *Plomer (1938–40), and has become a classic of its kind. His wife, whom he married only five weeks before his death, destroyed large portions of it, but enough is left to provide a full portrait of the author and the remote and beautiful region of the Welsh borders where he lived and worked. Two encounters of great importance to him were with the niece of *Wordsworth, who told him that her uncle 'could not bear the act of writing', and with William *Barnes, 'the great idyllic Poet of England'.

Kim A novel by Rudyard *Kipling, published 1901. Kimball O'Hara, the orphaned son of a sergeant in an Irish regiment, spends his childhood as a vagabond in Lahore, until he meets an old lama from Tibet and accompanies him in his travels. He falls into the hands of his father's old regiment, is adopted, and sent to school, resuming his wanderings in his holidays. Colonel Creighton of the Ethnological Survey notices his aptitude for secret service ('the Great Game'), and he embarks on the work under the directions of the native agent Hurree Babu. While still a boy he distinguishes himself by capturing the papers of a couple of Russian spies in the Himalayas. The book presents a vivid picture of India, its teeming populations and diverse religions, and the life of the bazaars and the road.

KINCAID, Jamaica (1949–) Novelist and short story writer, born Elaine Potter Richardson in Antigua; now resident in America. Her fiction arises from anger about slavery and its postcolonial traces, particularly in the experience of girls and their mothers. *At the Bottom of the River* (1983) is a volume of short stories which begins an exploration of the mother–daughter relationship; her first novel, *Annie John* (1985), set in Antigua, explores the fierce vicissitudes of a daughter's love for her mother and her homeland. *Lucy* (1990) describes a girl leaving Antigua for America, and *The Autobiography of my Mother* (1996) is a first-person narrative in which a woman looks back on her troubled life, crossing generic boundaries between fiction and autobiography as Kincaid does in *My Brother* (1997). *A Small Place* (1988) is a scintillatingly savage attack on Western tourism in Antigua, which is seen as a second wave of colonialism implicating corrupt local politicians. Non-fictional work includes *My Garden (Book)*, a series of meditations on gardening, and *Talk Stories* (2001), a collection of Kincaid's pieces for **New Yorker*'s 'Talk of the Town', written when she first came to the United States from Antigua (1978–83).

Kind Heart's Dream A pamphlet by Henry *Chettle, registered December 1592, noteworthy for its allusion to William *Shakespeare.

Kind of Loving, A A novel by Stan *Barstow.

KING, Francis Henry (1923–) Prolific novelist, short story writer, and critic, born in Switzerland, and brought up partly in India, educated at Shrewsbury School. As a conscientious objector, he worked on the land during the Second World War, then studied at Balliol College, Oxford, where he published his first three novels while still an undergraduate. He worked for the British Council (1949–63), mainly in Italy, Greece, and Japan, which provided settings for several of his novels, notably *The Dividing Stream* (1951), *The Firewalkers* (1956), and *The Custom House* (1961). His work is marked by cool, ironic detachment and a close analysis of human motivation, particularly in some of its less admirable aspects. *A Domestic Animal* (1970) was the subject of a libel action, itself turned to good fictional account in *The Action* (1978). Other compelling novels include *Act of Darkness* (1983), set in India but based on the Constance Kent murder case, but perhaps his finest achievements are his volumes of short stories, *The Brighton Belle* (1968) and *Hard Feelings* (1976).

KING, Henry (1592–1669) Poet, educated at Westminster School and Christ Church, Oxford. He became bishop of Chichester and was the friend of John *Donne and Izaak *Walton. He published poems sacred and profane, an unauthorized volume appearing in 1657. His best-known poem is 'An Exequy to his Matchless Never to be Forgotten Friend', written for his wife Anne who died in 1624. An edition of his poems, with a life (ed. M. Crum), appeared in 1965.

KING, Jessie *See* ART NOUVEAU.

KING, Stephen (1947–) American *horror and *fantasy writer, born in Portland, Maine; the state is the location for much of his fiction. Initially, after *Carrie* (1974), he wrote as Richard Bachman—a clash of identities exploited in *The Dark Half* (1989). In *The Stand* (1978) he shows ordinary Americans in physical and metaphysical confrontation; other themes include relationships between writers and audiences (*Misery*, 1987), and childhood friendships ('The Body', 1982, filmed as *Stand by Me*, 1986). The final volumes of the 'Dark Tower' sequence (1982–2004), set in a world built from the myths of popular culture, are touched by reflections on a near-fatal accident in 1999. In 2003 King was awarded the National Book Foundation Medal for Distinguished Contribution to American Letters.

KING, William (1663–1712) Educated at Westminster School and Christ Church, Oxford, an advocate at Doctors' Commons, a High Church Tory, and a writer of burlesques, satires, and light verse, much of which was published anonymously. In his *Dialogues of the Dead* (1699) he joined Charles Boyle (1674–1731) in the attack on Richard *Bentley (*see* BATTLE OF THE BOOKS). Other works include *The Transactioneer* (1700, a satire on Sir Hans *Sloane), and *The Art of Cookery, in Imitation of Horace's Art of Poetry* (1708). His poverty in later life was noted sympathetically by John *Gay and Jonathan *Swift.

King Alisaunder An early 14th-century romance in 8,034 lines of short couplets, based on the late 12th-century Anglo-Norman *Roman de toute chevalerie* (ed. B. Foster and I. Short,

1976–7). It is based on a legend according to which Alexander was not the son of Philip of Macedon but of the Egyptian king Nectanabus, who tricked Philip's wife by magic into sleeping with him. The poem relates the birth and youth of Alexander, his succession to Philip's throne, conquest of Carthage and other cities, and wars with Darius. The poem then narrates his perils and conquests in the Far East (describing the geography and wonders of those regions), his seduction by Candace, and death by poison. It is written in a lively verse and flexible metre that make it a compelling example of the genre. See G. V. Smithers (ed.) (EETS os 227, 1952, and 237, 1957).

King and No King, A A tragicomedy by Francis *Beaumont and John *Fletcher (probably largely by Beaumont), performed 1611, printed 1619; it was one of their most successful dramas.

The erratic Arbaces, king of Iberia, has defeated Tigranes, king of Armenia, in single combat, concluding a long war. Arbaces offers his prisoner freedom if he will marry his sister Panthea, who has grown to womanhood during his long absence, but Tigranes loves Spaconia, an Armenian lady. However, when Tigranes and Arbaces meet Panthea, they are so smitten by her beauty that they both fall violently in love with her. Panthea appears to return Arbaces' incestuous passion; all seems set for sin and tragedy when, in the last act, the lord protector of the kingdom, Gobrias, confesses that Arbaces is in fact his own son, therefore 'no king', and Panthea the true queen of Iberia. Arbaces and Panthea react to this news with joy and are united; Tigranes regrets his infidelity, is reunited with Spaconia, and released. Comic relief throughout is provided by Bessus, a cowardly captain in Arbaces' army, reminiscent of Paroles in **All's Well That Ends Well*, a play which has other similarities of plot and tone.

Dryden, in **Of Dramatick Poesy*, praises the play for its theatrically effective denouement, and for the complex character of Arbaces ('that strange mixture of a man', derived, he supposes, from the extravagances of Alexander the Great).

King Charles's head A phrase taken from Mr Dick's obsession in **David Copperfield*, now used to describe any recurrent and irrational obsession.

King Horn An early surviving English verse romance in 1,545 lines, dating from the late 13th century. The story is substantially the same as that of the later **Horn Childe*. In this version, Horn, the son of the king and queen of Suddene, is turned adrift by invading Saracens and falls in love with Rymenhild, the daughter of the king of Westernesse. Horn's companion Fikenhild betrays the lovers, has Horn banished to Ireland, and marries Rymenhild himself. After heroic deeds in Ireland, Horn returns to Westernesse in disguise and makes himself known to Rymenhild. Finally, having recovered his land of Suddene, he kills Fikenhild and marries Rymenhild, who becomes his queen. This romance exemplifies many traditional motifs typical of the genre. See Rosamund Allen (1984) and Ronald B. Herzman *et al.* (eds), in *Four Romances of England* (1999).

Kingis Quair, The ('The King's Book') A poem of 1,379 lines, arranged in 197 stanzas of 'lynis sevin', or *rhyme royal (so called because of its employment in this king's poem, but previously used in Chaucer's **Troilus and Criseyde* and elsewhere). It is attributed to *James I of Scotland and may have been written about the time of his marriage (1424) to Lady Joan Beaufort, the poem's heroine, when his long period as a prisoner in England was drawing to a close, or on his return to Scotland. The poem survives in a single manuscript in the Bodleian Library. The author acknowledges the authority of both *Chaucer and *Gower. *Boethius' *Consolation of Philosophy* is also an important influence, the royal prisoner reflecting on the workings of Fortune after he has read this book. He sees a beautiful lady walking in the garden below, and is smitten with love. He visits the empire of Venus and the palace of Minerva, goddess of wisdom; he speaks with the goddess Fortuna, and finally is assured by Venus of the ultimate success of his suit. See Linne Mooney and Mary-Jo Arn (eds), in *The Kingis Quair and Other Prison Poems* (2005).

King John A historical drama written in a first version before 1536, by John *Bale.

King John, The Life and Death of A historical play by *Shakespeare, probably based on an anonymous play, *The Troublesome Reign of John King of England* (1591), though the latter may be a derivative rather than a source. Shakespeare's play was probably written about 1596. It was first printed in the *folio of 1623. The play, with some departures from historical accuracy, deals with events in King John's reign, principally with the tragedy of young Arthur, ending with the death of John at Swinstead Abbey. It is striking that it makes no mention of Magna Carta. The play's tragic quality, the poignant grief of Constance, Arthur's mother, and political complications are relieved by the wit and gallantry of the Bastard, supposed son of Falconbridge, actually the son of Richard Cœur-de-Lion.

KINGLAKE, Alexander William (1809–91) Educated at Eton College and Trinity College, Cambridge. He published anonymously in 1844 *Eōthen: or Traces of Travel Brought Home from the East*, an account of a journey undertaken in the Middle East some ten years earlier. It gives a lively description of his travels, recording his reactions to, for example, the desert, the Holy Land, an encounter with Lady Hester *Stanhope, and the plague in Cairo. The book was an instant success; his friend Eliot *Warburton said it evoked 'the East itself in vital actual reality', and its familiar tone has been compared with that of Sterne's **Sentimental Journey*. Other critics, however, have criticized Kinglake's often sweeping dismissals of the supposedly inert, uncreative 'oriental' mind, and of Middle Eastern culture generally. He later produced a history of the Crimean War (1863–87), having accompanied the British army to the Crimea in 1854.

King Lear A tragedy by *Shakespeare, dating from 1604–5, performed at court 1606. The quarto printed in 1608 (reprinted 1619) is now thought to have been badly printed from Shakespeare's original manuscript, and the text of the first *folio (1623) appears to represent a revision from a few years later. The Oxford *Complete Works* presents texts edited from each version. The play's sources include a chronicle play, *King Leir* (performed 1594, printed 1605), the *Chronicles* of *Holinshed, and *A *Mirror for Magistrates*. The Gloucester sub-plot derives from Sidney's **Arcadia*.

Lear, king of Britain, a petulant and unwise old man, has three daughters: Goneril, wife of the duke of Albany; Regan, wife of the duke of Cornwall; and Cordelia, for whom the king of France and duke of Burgundy are suitors. Intending to divide his kingdom among his daughters according to their fondness for him, he demands professions of love from them. Goneril and Regan claim extravagant affection, and each receives one-third of the kingdom. Cordelia, disgusted with their hollow flattery, says she loves him according to her duty, neither more nor less. Infuriated, Lear divides her portion between his other daughters, with the condition that he shall be maintained by each daughter in turn, with 100 knights. Burgundy withdraws his suit for Cordelia, and the king of France accepts her without dowry. The earl of Kent, taking her part, is banished. Goneril and Regan reveal their heartless character by grudging their father the maintenance that he had stipulated for, until, enraged, he rushes out of doors in a storm. The earl of Gloucester shows pity for the old king, and is suspected of being in league with the French, who have landed in England. His eyes are put out by Cornwall, who receives a death-wound in the struggle. Gloucester has been turned against his son Edgar by Edmund, Edgar's illegitimate brother. Edgar takes the disguise of a lunatic beggar (Tom o'Bedlam), and tends his father till the latter's death. Lear, whom rage and ill treatment have driven mad, is conveyed to Dover by the faithful Kent in disguise, where Cordelia receives him. Meanwhile Goneril and Regan have both turned their affections to Edmund. Embittered by this rivalry, Goneril poisons Regan, and takes her own life. The English forces under Edmund and Albany defeat the French, and Lear and Cordelia are imprisoned. Gloucester, reconciled with Edgar, dies offstage. Edmund is fatally wounded by Edgar in a duel; his last-minute reprieve for Lear and Cordelia comes too late to save Cordelia's life, and she is hanged. Lear dies from grief. Kent, Albany (who took no part in Goneril's cruel treatment of Lear), and Edgar are left to restore order, and Edgar accepts responsibility for the kingdom.

KINGSLEY, Charles (1819–75) Novelist and social reformer, born at Holme in Devon, where his father was curate-in-charge; educated at Helston Grammar School, Cornwall, King's College London, and Magdalene College, Cambridge. He became curate and subsequently, in 1844 (the year of his marriage to Frances Grenfell), rector of Eversley in Hampshire. His blank verse drama *The Saint's Tragedy*, published in 1848, treats the conflict between natural sexuality and asceticism, a persistent theme in his work. Influenced by Frederick Denison *Maurice and the writings of Thomas *Carlyle, he was seriously interested in the movement for social reform, while condemning the violent policies of the *Chartists. He contributed, over the signature 'Parson Lot', to *Politics for the People* in 1848, and to its successor, *The Christian Socialist*, in 1850–51.

His first novel, **Yeast*, was serialized in **Fraser's Magazine* in 1848, and published in book form in 1851; **Alton Locke* appeared in 1850. Both are reforming novels, concerned with the sufferings of the working classes. A visit to Germany in 1851 inspired his first historical novel, *Hypatia, or New Foes with Old Faces*, published in *Fraser's* in 1851 and in book form in 1853; set in 5th-century Alexandria, it exalts the Greek Neoplatonic philosopher Hypatia who was torn to pieces in AD 415 by a mob of infuriated Christians, and condemns the ignorant fanaticism of the Alexandrian monks. It had a mixed reception; many complained of its violence, its anachronisms, and its emphasis on Hypatia's nakedness at death; and J. H. *Newman's *Callista* was written in part to correct its hostile portrait of the early church. His next novel, *Westward Ho!* (1855), was inspired by the patriotism with which he greeted the Crimean War. Its vehement anti-Catholicism and bloodthirsty narrative shocked some readers, but delighted more. **Two Years Ago* (1857) returns to the theme of social reform and *Hereward the Wake* (1866) is a historical novel based on the exploits of the legendary outlaw, in Kingsley's version the son of Leofric of Mercia and Lady Godiva, who attempts to save England from the Normans.

Other works include *The Heroes* (1856), in which he tells for young readers the stories of Perseus, Theseus, and the Argonauts, and *The *Water-Babies* (1863), also for the young. The latter displays his profound and sympathetic interest in underwater and seashore life, as does his earlier work *Glaucus, or The Wonders of the Shore* (1855), which contains several tributes to his friend and fellow naturalist Philip Gosse, father of Edmund *Gosse. Much of his poetry was soon forgotten, but his songs and ballads remained popular. These include 'Airly Beacon' and 'The Sands of Dee', and some of his lines, such as 'Be Good, sweet maid, and let who can be clever' (quoted in *Two Years Ago*) and 'For men must work and women must weep', from 'The Three Fishers', became proverbial. Kingsley also wrote many tracts, and published lectures and sermons. His *At Last* (1871) is a record of a long-desired visit to the West Indies.

Kingsley became a respected figure, who gained towards the end of his life (as professor of modern history at Cambridge, 1860–69, and as canon of Chester and Westminster) public and indeed royal approval, but he remained the centre of controversy. His leanings towards polemics were damagingly displayed in his celebrated confrontation with Newman, initiated by his review in *Macmillan's Magazine* (January 1864) of J. A. *Froude's *History of England*, vols vii and viii; in this he misrepresented Newman's sermon on 'Wisdom and Innocence' in support of his own statement that 'Truth for its own sake has never been a virtue of the Roman clergy.' Newman's crushing rejoinder appeared in the form of his *Apologia*, and he was widely considered the victor of the exchange.

Kingsley was a keen sportsman who was tender to animals, a champion of the working man who despised black people, a muscular Christian who wrote much (like his friend Thomas *Hughes) of the virtues of 'manliness' and who nevertheless held an unusually explicit physical passion for his wife, an admirer of physical prowess who himself suffered from an acute stammer and occasional nervous breakdowns. His complex personality and vigorous fiction represent some of the central paradoxes of his age, and he continues to interest readers. See R. B. Martin, *The Dust of Combat* (1959); Susan Chitty, *The Beast and the Monk* (1974); Brenda Colloms, *Charles Kingsley* (1975).

KINGSLEY, Henry (1830–76) Novelist, younger brother of Charles *Kingsley, born at Barnack, Northamptonshire, where his father was rector, and brought up at Clovelly, in Devon, and in Chelsea. He was educated at King's College School, London, and at Worcester College, Oxford, which he left without taking a degree. From 1853 to 1858 he was in Australia, at the gold diggings and as a trooper in the Sydney Mounted Police. His Australian experiences inspired two of his best novels, *Geoffry Hamlyn* (1859) and *The Hillyars and the Burtons* (1865), which were influential in Australia. After his return to England in 1858 he married his cousin Sarah Haselwood and lived at Wargrave, Berkshire, making a precarious living as a novelist and journalist. For a time he was editor of the *Edinburgh Daily Review*, and was its correspondent at the Franco-Prussian War.

Ravenshoe (1862), the best known of his 21 books, is a story of inheritance in a Roman Catholic family in Devon, and includes Crimean War scenes. Kingsley's strongest novels contain lively descriptions of landscape in England and Australia, engrossing accounts of storms and cyclones, attacks and alarms, and well-observed character sketches. His plots are less impressive, and he was unduly preoccupied by his ideal of the virile 'English gentleman'. Kingsley, an impulsive, convivial, but insecure man, was a friend of Matthew *Arnold, A. C. *Swinburne, Lewis *Carroll (Dodgson), and Anne Thackeray *Ritchie. His late relations with his brother Charles were soured by frequent requests for loans. See W. H. Scheuerle, *The Neglected Brother: A Study of Henry Kingsley* (1971).

KINGSLEY, Mary Henrietta (1862–1900) Niece of Charles *Kingsley. She was largely self-educated, and cared for her parents until their death in 1892. Influenced by the ethnological work of her father, George Henry Kingsley, she made her first journey to West Africa in 1893, returning in 1894. *Travels in West Africa* (1897) is a lively account of her travels and ethnological researches, written in an engaging and witty style, including positive views of the people and landscape, and recommending to British rulers a closer understanding of African culture. *West African Studies*, with further ethnological observations and political reflections, appeared in 1899. Kingsley went to South Africa in 1900 to nurse Boer prisoners of war, and died at Simonstown of enteric fever.

KINGSMILL, Hugh (Hugh Kingsmill Lunn) (1889–1949) Anthologist, biographer, literary critic, novelist, and parodist, educated at Harrow School and Oxford University, whose lives of Matthew *Arnold (1928), Charles *Dickens (1935), and D. H. *Lawrence (1938) gave him a reputation for iconoclasm. He also wrote a life of Frank *Harris (1932), with whom he had worked in 1912 on *Hearth and Home*. His other works include *The Return of William Shakespeare* (1929, a fictional fantasy with some perceptive literary criticism), and *The Progress of a Biographer* (1949, collected literary criticism). See Michael *Holroyd, *Hugh Kingsmill: A Critical Biography* (1964); *The Best of Kingsmill*, ed. Holroyd (1970).

KING-SMITH, Dick (1922–) Best-selling British author of *animal stories. Born in Bitton, Gloucestershire, he was a soldier, farmer, and teacher before becoming an author. His stories combine realism with anthropomorphism (his animals talk), celebrating animals' ingenuity and the nature of language. *The Sheep-Pig* (1983) was filmed as *Babe* (1995).

King Solomon's Mines A novel by Henry Rider *Haggard, published in 1885. It describes an expedition into uncharted regions of Africa, led by Sir Henry Curtis, who is hoping to find his brother, who was lost as he searched for the legendary mines of King Solomon. Captain John Good, the celebrated hunter Allan Quatermain, and a dignified black man, Umbopa, make up the rest of the party. After many blood-chilling adventures, they encounter the murderous King Twala, who rules with the help of an ancient and evil witch, Gagool. Umbopa is revealed as Ignosi, the rightful king, and after a fierce battle Twala is killed, and Ignosi assumes his throne. Gagool is compelled to lead the party to the concealed diamond mines, but treacherously attempts to trap them there. The heroic black girl Foulata, who loves Captain Good, dies in defeating Gagool, and the adventurers contrive to escape, with enough diamonds to make them wealthy for life. They succeed in rescuing Curtis's brother on their return to England. Tightly constructed and vigorously written, the book became an instant best-seller, and has been filmed several times. The complex thinking it reveals on issues of race, gender, adventure, and empire has attracted much recent scholarly attention.

KINGSTON, Maxine Hong (1940–) Academic and writer, born to Chinese immigrant parents in Stockton, California, the first child in her family to be born in the USA. Her father was a poet and scholar but could only get menial jobs in California; her mother trained as a midwife. The immigrant community she grew up in influenced Kingston's writing. She studied at Berkeley University. Her book *The Woman Warrior: Memoir of a Girlhood among Ghosts* (1976) mixes memoir and storytelling and was followed by *China Men* (1980). Her book *The Fifth Book of Peace* (2003) reflects her lifelong commitment to pacifism and writing.

KINGSTON, W. H. G. (William Henry Giles) (1814–80) London-born, highly prolific, and popular writer of stories for boys, covering adventures in all continents, at sea, in history, at school, and elsewhere. A strong patriotic and didactic message is evident in his writing.

KINSELLA, Thomas (1928–) Irish poet and translator, born in Inchicore, Dublin, and educated at University College, Dublin. He relinquished a senior position in the Irish Civil Service for an appointment at the University of Southern Illinois in 1965, moving to Temple University, Philadelphia, in 1970. Kinsella's grave, elegant work from *Another September* (1958) to *Nightwalker and Other Poems* (1968) was widely hailed as the most ambitious Irish poetry since the death of W. B. *Yeats. Under the influence of Jungian psychology and American poetry, notably that of Ezra *Pound, he abandoned the large stanza forms and sometimes ponderous tones of his early poetry to produce a series of elaborately interconnected free verse meditations on origins, growth, memory, and decay. Some of the most vivid writing from the series is contained in *New Poems 1973*, *One and Other Poems* (1979), and *Blood and Family* (1988). His acclaimed translation of the ancient Irish epic *The Táin* (*see* TÁIN-BÓ-CUAILNGE) appeared in 1968 and his dual language *An Duanaire: Poems of the Dispossessed* (with Seán Ó Tuama) in 1981. His *New Oxford Book of Irish Verse* (1986) was criticized for nationalist bias. Kinsella's work subsequent to *Collected Poems* (2001) includes *Marginal Economy* (2006) and *Man of War* (2007).

KIPLING, Rudyard (1865–1936) Author and poet, born in Bombay (Mumbai), son of John Lockwood Kipling, author and illustrator of *Beast and Man in India* (1891), and Alice Kipling, sister-in-law of Edward *Burne-Jones. He was brought to England in 1871, where he spent five years living unhappily with a family in Southsea with his younger sister, separated from his parents, a period recalled with bitterness in his short story 'Baa, Baa, Black Sheep' (1888) and his novel *The Light That Failed* (1890). From 1878 to 1882 he attended the United Services College, Westward Ho!, later depicted in his schoolboy tales *Stalky & Co.* (1899). From 1882 to 1889 he worked as a journalist in India; many of his early poems and stories were originally published in newspapers or for the Indian Railway Library, and were later collected under various titles, which include *Departmental Ditties* (1886), *Plain Tales from the Hills* (1888), *Soldiers Three* (1890, in which the three soldiers are the three privates Learoyd, Mulvaney, and Ortheris), and *Wee Willie Winkie* (1890). In 1889 he came to London, where he achieved instant literary celebrity, aided by W. E. *Henley's publication in his *Scots Observer* of many of the poems ('Danny Deever', 'Mandalay', etc.) later collected as *Barrack-Room Ballads* (1892). In 1892 he married Caroline Balestier, sister of his American agent Charles Balestier (1861–91) (with whom he had written *The Naulahka*, 1892); from 1892 to 1896 the Kiplings lived on Balestier homeground at Brattleboro, Vermont. In 1896 they returned to England, settling finally at 'Bateman's' in Sussex in 1902, though Kipling continued to travel extensively, spending much time in South Africa, which he first visited in 1900 during the Boer War, where he had his first sight of warfare. Widely regarded as unofficial poet laureate, he refused many honours; in 1907 he was the first English writer to receive the *Nobel Prize.

Kipling's output was vast and varied, and has been variously judged. His early tales of the Raj, praised for their cynical realism, were compared to those of *Maupassant, but his growing reputation as the poet of empire cut both ways. His poem 'Recessional', written for Jubilee Day 1897, was acclaimed for catching the mood of the moment, but the mood changed. Kipling retained his popularity with the common soldier and reader, and his verse has added many phrases to the language (including 'the white man's burden'), but he was increasingly accused of vulgarity and jingoism in *aesthetic and anti-imperialist circles. His fluent versification, with its powerful echoes of *hymns and *ballads, and his use in both prose and verse of colloquial speech, impressed many but alienated others; even such admirers as Henry *James, W. B. *Yeats, and T. S. *Eliot were uneasy about the nature of his art. Nevertheless, the extent and force of his literary impact, particularly in relation to Britain's imperial aspirations, has never been in doubt, and his critical reputation has revived in recent years. His most uncontroversial achievements are perhaps his tales for children (principally *The *Jungle Book*, 1894; *Just So Stories*, 1902; *Puck of Pook's Hill*, 1906; and *Rewards and Fairies*, 1910) and his picaresque novel of India **Kim*. His autobiographical fragment *Something of Myself* was published in 1937, and there are biographies by C. Carrington (1955), Angus *Wilson (1977), Lord Birkenhead (1978), and Andrew Lycett (2000).

KIRK, Robert *See* SECRET COMMONWEALTH OF ELVES.

KIRKE, Edward (1553–1613) A friend of Edmund *Spenser and Gabriel *Harvey, educated at Pembroke Hall and Caius College, Cambridge. He may have written the preface, the arguments, and the commentary to Edmund *Spenser's **Shepheardes Calender* (1579), under the initials 'E.K.' The question of E.K.'s identity remains unresolved.

KIRKUP, James (1918–2009) Poet, translator, and travel writer, born in South Shields and educated at Durham University. His volumes of poetry include *A Correct Compassion* (1952), whose well-known title poem celebrates the precision of a surgical operation, *The Descent into the Cave* (1957), *Paper Windows* (1968), *A Bewick Bestiary* (1971), and *The Authentic Touch* (2006). In 1977 his poem 'The Love that Dares to Speak its Name' (which deals with the Roman centurion's homosexual fantasy about the dead Christ) became the subject of the first prosecution for blasphemous libel for over 50 years, and as a result the editor of *Gay News*, the periodical which published the poem, was fined and given a suspended prison sentence. Kirkup's autobiographical *The Only Child* (1957) is an evocative account of a working-class northern childhood, and he has also published many books on Japan, and translated works by Friedrich *Dürrenmatt, Henrik

*Ibsen (with Christopher *Fry), Paul *Valéry, and others. He has also published very frank memoirs detailing his literary and homosexual adventures (*A Poet Could Not But Be Gay*, 1991; *Me All Over*, 1993).

Kit-Cat Club Founded in the early 18th century by leading Whigs, and involving writers such as Richard *Steele, Joseph *Addison, William *Congreve, Sir Samuel *Garth, and Sir John *Vanbrugh. It originally met at the tavern kept by Christopher Cat, whose mutton pies were called 'Kit-cats'. The club subsequently convened at the publisher Jacob *Tonson's house at Barn Elms, where Sir Godfrey *Kneller's 'Kit-Cat' portraits of the members, painted to fit a special gallery, were displayed. Some 40 of these survive in the National Portrait Gallery.

kitchen sink drama A term applied in the late 1950s to the plays of writers such as Arnold *Wesker, Shelagh *Delaney, and John *Osborne, which portrayed working-class or lower-middle-class life, with an emphasis on domestic realism. These plays were written in part as a reaction against the drawing-room comedies and middle-class dramas of Noël *Coward and Terence *Rattigan, and also undermined the popularity of the verse drama of T. S. *Eliot and Christopher *Fry. Kenneth *Tynan was a principal advocate of this new group of writers.

KITCHIN, Clifford Henry Benn (1895–1967) Novelist and barrister, educated at Exeter College, Oxford, whose great gifts as a chess player, bridge player, pianist, author, and investor of an inherited fortune led his close friend L. P. *Hartley to describe him as 'the most talented man I have ever known'. His early novels, *Streamers Waving* (1925) and *Mr Balcony* (1927), were witty and allusive, with a strong element of fantasy; the later ones, such as *The Birthday Party* (1938) and *The Secret River* (1956), were works of settled accomplishment. He also wrote several *detective stories, including the well-known *Death of my Aunt* (1929).

KLEIST, Heinrich von (1777–1811) German poet, dramatist, essayist, and writer of novellas. Born into a military family, he served in the Revolutionary Wars. He resigned his commission in 1799 and studied science, mathematics, and philosophy at Frankfurt an der Oder in preparation for a career in the Prussian Civil Service which he initially abandoned in favour of his vocation as a writer. His reading of *Kant in 1801, which left him with a troubled sense of the unknowable nature of existence, was the occasion of a personal crisis which persisted intermittently until his death by suicide. Unrecognized in his lifetime, Kleist is best known in Britain for his dramas *Prinz Friedrich von Homburg* (1821), a production of which with Tom Courtenay in the title role inaugurated Manchester's Royal Exchange Theatre in 1976, and the comedy *Der zerbrochne Krug* (1811: *The Broken Jug*), versions of which have been made by John *Banville and Blake *Morrison. David *Constantine published an annotated translation of Kleist's best-known plays, stories, and essays as *Selected Writings* (1997). Kleist's stories were greatly admired by Ted *Hughes. The essay *Über das Marionettentheater* (1810: *On Marionette Theatre*), with its anecdote about an untrickable fencing bear, made a profound impression on Philip *Pullman.

KLEMPERER, Victor (1881–1960) Academic and diarist, born to a Jewish family; he studied at the universities of Munich, Geneva, Paris, and Berlin. He kept a diary from 1933, published to acclaim in 1995, in which he bore witness to the daily humiliation and terror of life for Jews in Nazi Germany.

KLOPSTOCK, Friedrich Gottlieb (1724–1803) German poet, famous in his lifetime for his odes and the religious epic *Der Messias* (*The Messiah*), of which the first three cantos were published in 1748 and the last in 1773. It was directly inspired by Milton's **Paradise Lost* and is marked by Pietistic religious sentiment. His fame spread to England, and William *Wordsworth and S. T. *Coleridge sought out 'the venerable father of German poetry' at Hamburg during their visit to Germany in 1798.

KNELLER, Sir Godfrey (1646/9–1723) Portrait painter born in Lübeck, trained in the Netherlands and Italy; he arrived in England in 1676. His immensely successful career at the English court spans the reigns of five monarchs; he was knighted in 1692 and made a baronet in 1715. Joseph *Addison's poem on his picture of George I surveys his portraits of earlier rulers, but he also painted the 'beauties' of the court, admirals, generals, and literary figures. Kneller's finest achievements are the *Kit-Cat series (1702–17). Outstanding are the portraits of John *Dryden (*c.*1698) and Matthew *Prior (1700). Kneller, a neighbour of Alexander *Pope at Twickenham, knew most of the leading literary figures of the day. He was flattered by poets, among them Dryden, Prior, and John *Gay.

Knickerbocker Magazine Founded in New York City in 1833, under the editorship of Charles Fenno Hoffman (1806–84). Until it was discontinued in 1865, the *Knickerbocker* numbered many of the foremost American writers among its contributors, including James Fenimore *Cooper, Washington *Irving, and Henry Wadsworth *Longfellow.

KNIGHT, Charles (1791–1873) Born in Windsor, the son of a bookseller; he became an influential publisher and writer who did much to introduce the sale of cheap books. Though his own formal education had been limited, he was committed to making knowledge available to the poor; and helped to create, from the 1820s onwards, an entirely new class of reader. He was publisher to the 'Society for the Diffusion of Useful Knowledge', for whom he produced the *Penny Magazine*, the *Penny Cyclopaedia*, and other works, including 'The Library of Useful Knowledge'. In his *Autobiography of an Artisan* (1847), Christopher Thomson described how he went without sugar in his tea in order to afford the *Penny Magazine*. In 1825 Knight published his *Library of Entertaining Knowledge* and in 1842 his *Store of Knowledge*. His popular illustrated history of London appeared between 1841 and 1844, when his series 'Weekly Volumes', containing contributions from Harriet *Martineau, was published; in 1842 and 1844 his biographies of William *Shakespeare, of whose works he had produced a popular pictorial edition (1839–41), and William *Caxton; and in 1856–62 *The Popular History of England*. His *Passages of a Working Life* (1864–5) contains valuable information about the writers and the publishing trade of his time.

KNIGHT, William Payne *See* PICTURESQUE.

Knight of the Burning Pestle, The A comedy now thought to be the unaided work of Francis *Beaumont, but formerly generally attributed to Beaumont and John *Fletcher; it was probably performed 1607–8, and was printed (anonymously) 1613. Though it failed when first acted, it is the most successful of Beaumont's plays, a high-spirited comedy of manners, and a burlesque of knight errantry and of such fabulous and patriotic plays as Thomas *Heywood's *The Four Prentices of London* and *The Travels of the Three English Brothers* by John *Day, William *Rowley, and George *Wilkins. It has clear echoes of **Don Quixote*, in both attitude and incident, and satirizes the middle-class taste for such improbable romances as **Palmerin of England*.

It takes the form of a play-within-a-play: a grocer and his wife, members of an audience about to watch a drama called *The London Merchant*, interrupt the prologue to insist that their apprentice Rafe have a part. He therefore becomes a Grocer Errant, with a Burning Pestle portrayed on his shield, and undertakes various absurd adventures, including the release of patients held captive by a barber, Barbarossa. These are interspersed with the real plot, in which Jasper, a merchant's apprentice, woos, and after much opposition wins, his master's daughter Luce. Modern editions include one for the Revels Plays by S. P. Zitner (1984).

'Knight's Tale, The' *See* CANTERBURY TALES, 1.

KNOLLES, Richard (?1550–1610) Author of *The General History of the Turks* (1603), which was much admired by Samuel *Johnson (who took from it the plot of his **Irene*), and also by Lord *Byron, who credited it with inspiring the 'oriental colouring' of his poetry.

KNOWLES, James Sheridan (1784–1862) After trying the army, medicine, and teaching, he became an actor and verse dramatist, and was described by the **Edinburgh Review* in 1833 as 'the most successful dramatist of the day'. His *Virginius* was produced at Covent Garden with Charles *Kemble and William *Macready in 1820; *Caius Gracchus* in 1823 (1815 Belfast); *William Tell* in 1825. His greatest success was *The Hunchback*, produced in 1832; *The Wife*, with prologue and epilogue by Charles *Lamb, followed in 1833, and in 1837 his highly successful *The Love Chase*. His friend William *Hazlitt described Knowles as 'the first tragic writer of his time', and he was the recipient of many of the letters in Hazlitt's **Liber Amoris*.

KNOWLES, Sir James Thomas (1831–1908) Editor, architect, and friend of Alfred *Tennyson. He published in 1862 *The Story of King Arthur and his Knights* from Malory's **Morte Darthur*. He founded the *Metaphysical Society, became editor of the **Contemporary Review* in 1870, and in 1877 founded the **Nineteenth Century*.

KNOX, John (*c*.1514–1572) Scottish religious reformer, born in Haddington and educated at the University of St Andrews. Ordained in the late 1530s, he began preaching for the reformed religion at St Andrews in 1547 and consequently spent two years in captivity on a French galley. In 1551 he became chaplain to Edward VI, leaving England for Europe in 1554 after the accession of Mary Tudor. He met *Calvin at Geneva, and was pastor of the English congregation at Frankfurt am Main, 1554–5. He toured Scotland for a year from August 1555 but judged it too dangerous to remain, and lived in Geneva from 1556 to 1559, finally returning home as leader of the reformers in the latter year. In 1558 he published his *First Blast of the Trumpet against the Monstrous Regiment of Women* ('Regiment' having the older sense of 'rule, magisterial authority' and referring to the English reign of Mary Tudor and the Scottish regency of Mary of Guise). The *First Book of Discipline* (1559), of which Knox was part-author, advocated a national system of education for Scotland ranging from a school in every parish to the three universities. His *Treatise on Predestination* was published in 1560, the year he was appointed minister at St Giles' Cathedral in Edinburgh. His *History of the Reformation in Scotland* (1587) contains a dramatic account of the return of Mary Queen of Scots to Scotland, of his interviews with her, and of his fierce denunciations from the pulpit of St Giles'.

KNOX, Ronald (1888–1957) Writer and Roman Catholic priest, born at Kibworth, Leicestershire, and educated at Eton College and Balliol College, Oxford. He was received into the Church of Rome in 1917 and *A Spiritual Aeneid* (1918) describes his conversion. Knox was an extremely prolific writer and he produced many theological works, published a new translation of the Bible (1945–9), and acquired a wide reputation as journalist and broadcaster. He also wrote six detective stories, including *The Viaduct Murder* (1926) and *Double Cross Purposes* (1937). *Let Dons Delight* (1939), a work for which he himself had a particular affection, uses a dream framework to describe, through conversations in an imaginary Oxford senior common room at 50-year intervals, the process of specialization and fragmentation that he saw as leading to the loss of a common culture. He became a close friend of Evelyn *Waugh, who wrote his official biography (1959); see also Penelope *Fitzgerald, *The Knox Brothers* (1977).

KOCH, Kenneth (1925–2002) American poet and playwright, born in Cincinnati, a prominent member of the *New York School. He collaborated with Frank *O'Hara and John *Ashbery, and taught poetry at all levels. He also wrote a number of (mostly brief) experimental plays. See Koch's *The Art of Poetry* (1996).

KOESTLER, Arthur (1905–83) Writer, born in Budapest and educated there and at the University of Vienna. In 1931 he joined the Communist Party (he left it in 1938) and travelled in the Soviet Union. He was imprisoned under Franco during the Spanish Civil War and after his release he came to England, where his *Spanish Testament* appeared in 1937. His publications manifest a wide range of political, scientific, and literary interests, and include **Darkness at Noon*, published to great acclaim in 1940; *Scum of the Earth* (1941), based on his experiences in a French concentration camp; *Arrival and Departure* (1943); *The Yogi and the Commissar* (1945); and *Thieves in the Night* (1946). Koestler became a British citizen in 1948. His later non-fiction includes *The Ghost in the Machine* (1967), which reflected his growing interest in parapsychology. He also wrote two celebrated volumes of autobiography, *Arrow in the Blue* (1952) and *The Invisible Writing* (1954). See David Cesarini, *Arthur Koestler: The Homeless Mind* (1998).

Koran *See* QUR'ĀN.

KORDA, Sir Alexander (Sándor László Kellner) (1893–1956) Film director and producer, born to a Jewish family in rural Hungary, the eldest of three sons (brothers Zoltan and Vincent often worked with him). Journalism led to reviewing films, from which he graduated to directing, in Budapest 1914–19, then in Vienna and Berlin, before working in Hollywood from 1927 to 1930. Returning to Europe, Korda settled in London. *The Private Life of Henry VIII* (1933), starring Charles Laughton, was successful on both sides of the Atlantic, and set the pattern for Korda's shrewd populism as a producer. Spectacular adaptations of H. G. *Wells's *Things to Come* and *The Man Who Could Work Miracles* followed, together with three outings for Baroness *Orczy's Scarlet Pimpernel, a cycle of 'imperial' films that included Edgar *Wallace's *Sanders of the River* (1935) and A. E. W. *Mason's *The Four Feathers* (1939), and an aborted adaptation of Robert *Graves's *I, Claudius* (1937). Knighted in 1942, Korda was close to Winston *Churchill and active in wartime propaganda.

KOSINSKI, Jerzy (1933–91) Polish-American novelist, born Josek Lewinkopf in Łódź, who emigrated to America in 1957. He published two sociological works under the pseudonym Joseph Novak, then his first novel, *The Painted Bird*, in 1965. This surreal account of a young boy's experience of the Second World War was later charged with plagiarism, as were other works. *Being There* (1971) was made into a film (1979) starring Peter Sellers. His essays are collected in *Passing By* (1992). He committed suicide in 1991. See James Park Sloan, *Jerzy Kosinski: A Biography* (1996).

KOTZEBUE, August von (1761–1819) German dramatist and diplomat in Russian service, author of a large number of sentimental plays which enjoyed a considerable vogue in England during the 1790s. His *Menschenhass und Reue* (1789) was a great success for Richard Brinsley *Sheridan who brought it out in 1798 as *The Stranger.* The play tells the story of a separated couple, a seduced wife and husband who in consequence has become misanthropic, the wife's repentance, and their eventual reconciliation. **Lovers' Vows*, made famous by Jane Austen's **Mansfield Park*, was adapted by Mrs Elizabeth *Inchbald from Kotzebue's *Das Kind der Liebe* (1790). Sheridan adapted *Die Spanier in Peru* (1797) as *Pizarro.* Kotzebue's assassination by a nationalist student in 1819 led to the introduction of the Karlsbad decrees and severe political repression in Germany.

'Kraken, The' A short poem by Alfred *Tennyson, published in *Poems, Chiefly Lyrical* (1830). It describes the mythical sea monster mentioned in Pontoppidan's *Natural History of Norway* (1755), sleeping in the depths of the sea 'his ancient, dreamless, uninvaded sleep', and waiting only to rise and die; Christopher Ricks (*Tennyson*, 1972) describes it as an example of the poet's 'pained fascination with the thought of a life which somehow is not life at all'.

KRISTEVA, Julia (1941–) Bulgarian critical theorist, psychoanalyst, and writer. Having moved to Paris in 1966 to pursue her academic career, she quickly gravitated towards the research groups on critical theory and semiotics led by Roland *Barthes. She went on to make a substantial contribution to contemporary thinking about the relationship between language, subjectivity, and desire. Her early essays, collected in *Séméiotiké: recherches pour une sémanalyse* (1969: *Desire in Language: A Semiotic Approach to Literature and Art*, 1980), were instrumental in bringing the work of the Russian linguistic philosopher Mikhail *Bakhtin to the attention of a Western audience. Her engagement with *Lacanian psychoanalysis in works such as *La Révolution du langage poétique* (1974: *Revolution in Poetic Language*) saw her formulate an account of *modernist writing, including that of James *Joyce, which traces its disruptiveness to its staging of the collision between the prelinguistic libidinal energy of the individual, and the linguistic structures into which that energy must be channelled. In 1990, Kristeva published her first novel, *Les Samouraïs* (*The Samurai*), a portrait of the Parisian intelligentsia which can be seen as a response or sequel to *Les Mandarins*, Simone de *Beauvoir's account of the intellectual scene in Liberation Paris.

KRYLOV, Ivan Andreevich (1769–1844) Russian fabulist, born in Moscow; he received little formal education and began work as a humble government clerk. Moving to Petersburg in 1782, he began to dabble in literature, writing comedies and comic operas and editing a satirical periodical, *Spirits' Correspondence* (1789–90). Two further satirical journals, the *Spectator* (1792) and the *St Petersburg Mercury* (1793–4), incurred the wrath of the censors and led him to quit the capital. A decade later and back in Petersburg, he turned to the *fable, a classical form that proved an ideal vehicle for his vigorous language, earthy humour, pungent wit, and sound common sense. Between 1809 and 1843 he published nine volumes of fables, mostly original, but about a third imitated and adapted from *Aesop and *La Fontaine. Many lines have become proverbial. He enjoyed the love of his Russian public, who dubbed him 'Grandfather Krylov', and he was immortalized in the famous statue (1855) by Klodt that stands in Petersburg's Summer Garden. All his fables have found at least one English translator. His first translator, who knew him personally, was John Bowring (1821), but it was the prose versions by William *Ralston (four increasingly enlarged editions between 1869 and 1883) that ensured his popularity with English readers. Other translations have appeared at regular intervals but the witty and skilled verse translations by Bernard Pares (1926) are by far the most successful. See A. G. Cross, 'The English and Krylov', *Oxford Slavonic Papers* (1983), with full list of translations.

'Kubla Khan: A Vision in a Dream' A poem by Samuel Taylor *Coleridge, published 1816. In 1797, while living near the Wordsworths in Somerset, Coleridge took opium and fell asleep when reading a passage in *Purchas his Pilgrimage* (*see* PURCHAS, SAMUEL) relating to the Khan Kubla and the palace that he commanded to be built. He claimed that on awaking he was conscious of having composed in his sleep two or three hundred lines on this theme, and eagerly began to set down the lines that form this fragment. He was then unfortunately interrupted by 'a person…from Porlock', and, on returning to his task an hour later, found that almost the entire remainder of the poem had slipped from his memory. The poem has no narrative line, but consists of a series of potent visionary images, suggesting themes of eternity and change. Alph, the sacred river, flung up in a tremendous fountain, connects Khan's 'stately pleasure dome', great caverns, and the 'sunless sea'. Within the gardens of the pleasure dome are growth and sunlight and colour. There are hints of death and war, the vision of a damsel with a dulcimer, and of the frenzy of the poet who has drunk 'the milk of Paradise'. Coleridge thought the poem a 'psychological curiosity' and vigorously defended poetic images 'just on the vestibule[s] of Consciousness'. J. L. Lowes, in *The Road to Xanadu* (1927), traces the varied sources of Coleridge's imagery. See also A. Hayter, *Opium and the Romantic Imagination* (1968).

KUNDERA, Milan (1929–) Czech novelist, born in Brno, and educated in Prague, where he later taught at the Institute for Advanced Cinematographic Studies. He lost his post after the Russian invasion in 1968, and in 1975 settled in Paris. His first novel, *Zert*, was published in 1967 (*The Joke*, trans. 1969). His other novels include *The Farewell Party* (1972; trans. 1977) and *The Book of Laughter and Forgetting* (1979; French 1979; English 1980), a semi-fictional, semi-autobiographical evocation of the cultural, political, and sexual life of post-war Europe, seen partly through Kundera's own eyes, partly through those of several of the 'two or three new fictional characters baptized on earth every second'. Other novels include *Life is Elsewhere* (1973; French 1973; English 1986), in which the central characters are an aspiring poet and his mother, and *The Unbearable Lightness of Being* (1985; French 1984; English 1985), a classic of *magic realism. *Laughable Loves* (1969; trans. 1974) is a collection of stories. From 1993, he has published in French rather than Czech. Much of this work has been translated into English by Linda Asher. Recent fiction includes *La Lenteur* (1993; *Slowness*, 1995), *L'Identité* (1997; *Identity*, 1998), and *Ignorance* (2000; trans. 2002).

KUPPNER, Frank (1951–) Scottish poet, born in Glasgow, whose collections include *A Bad Day for the Sung Dynasty* (1984), *Ridiculous! Absurd! Disgusting!* (1989), and *A God's Breakfast* (2004). *A Concussed History of Scotland* (1990) and *Something Very Like Murder* (1994) are radically different exercises in innovative and idiosyncratic prose.

KUREISHI, Hanif (1954–) CBE Playwright, novelist, and screenwriter, born in south London to an English mother and Pakistani father, and educated at King's College London. His screenplays include the highly successful *My Beautiful Laundrette* (1986), *Sammy and Rosie Get Laid* (1987), *The Mother* (2003), and *Venus* (2006). His first novel, *The Buddha of Suburbia* (1990, adapted for television in 1993), is narrated by the bisexual Karim Amir, and offers a comic panorama of multicultural London life, with sex, party-going, and yoga—where Muslim patriarchal attitudes coexist with Karim's acting ambitions and his friend's rock-star success in New York. He wrote and directed the film *London Kills Me* (1991), set in west London. Other works include the novel *The Black Album* (1995), dealing with race and religion, and *Love in a Blue Time* (short stories, 1997). The film *My Son the Fanatic* (1998), based on one of these stories, portrays the conflict between a liberal northern immigrant taxi-driver and his fundamentalist son. *Intimacy* (1998), a confessional novella narrated by a man who leaves his partner and sons, as Kureishi had done, was filmed by Patrice Chereau in 2001.

KYD (Kid), Thomas (1558–94) Dramatist, born in London. He was educated at Merchant Taylors' School, London, whose headmaster was Richard *Mulcaster; he may have worked for a time as a scrivener. He wrote (now lost) plays for the Queen's Men, *c.*1583–5, and was in the service of an unknown lord, 1587–93. He was associated with Christopher *Marlowe, with whom he shared a room in 1591, and whose 'atheistical' writings led to Kyd's suffering a period of torture and imprisonment in 1593. His **Spanish Tragedy* (*c.*1587) was published anonymously in 1592. The play proved exceptionally popular on stage and had passed through eleven printed editions by 1633. The only work published under his name was a translation of Robert Garnier's *Cornelia* (1594), reissued in 1595 as *Pompey the Great, his Faire Cornelia's Tragedy. The First Part of Hieronimo* (printed 1605) is probably a *burlesque adaptation of a fore-piece to *The Spanish Tragedy.* Other works Kyd is likely to have written are a lost pre-Shakespearian play on the subject of Hamlet, *The Householder's Philosophy* (a prose translation from *Tasso), and *The Tragedy of Solyman and Perseda* (printed 1592).

L

'La Belle Dame sans Merci' A ballad by John *Keats, written 1819, published 1820, which describes a knight fatally enthralled by an elfin woman. Although Keats himself spoke of it lightly, critics and biographers have written of it at length, many concurring with Robert *Graves (*The White Goddess*, 1948) that 'the Belle Dame represented Love, Death by Consumption...and Poetry all at once'. It was much admired by the *Pre-Raphaelites, and William *Morris asserted that 'it was the germ from which all the poetry of his group had sprung'.

La Belle Dame sans mercy (1424) is the title of a poem by Alain *Chartier; its translation into English (*c*.1526) was attributed at one time to *Chaucer, but is now thought to be the work of Sir Richard Ros.

LA BRUYÈRE, Jean de (1645–96) French satiric moralist, author of *Les Caractères ou les mœurs de ce siècle* (1688; *The Characters, or The Manners of the Age*, 1699). The work, consisting of short portrait sketches revealing human corruption, was published as an appendage to La Bruyère's translation of the *Characters* of *Theophrastus from which it derives its method. It was immediately successful on publication, and has been widely admired by such writers as Gustave *Flaubert, André *Gide, and Marcel *Proust.
See also CHARACTER-WRITING.

LA CALPRENÈDE, Gauthier de Costes, sieur de (*c*.1610–1663) French dramatist and novelist. Between 1635 and 1642 he wrote six tragedies and three tragicomedies, some on subjects from English history (e.g. *Le Comte d'Essex*, 1637). From 1643 until his death he wrote a series of quasi-historical romances which enjoyed great international success: *Cassandre* (10 vols, 1644–50), trans. Sir Charles Cotterell (1667), centres on the life of the daughter of Darius, wife of Alexander the Great; *Cléopâtre* (12 vols, 1647–56), trans. R. Loveday *et al.* (1652–9), describes the adventures of the daughter of Antony and Cleopatra; and *Pharamond* (12 vols, 1661–70), first four vols trans. John Davies (1662), narrates the loves of the first French kings for the Cambrian princess Rosemonde.

LACAN, Jacques (1901–81) French psychoanalyst who reformulated *Freudian models of the unconscious and underlined the fundamental role played by language in the formation of human identity. For Lacan, humans are defined and driven principally by desire. He explores the consequences for the psyche when it is incorporated into the 'symbolic order', the pre-existing social structures which are mediated for the most part by language, and desire becomes subject to regulation as a result. Learning to speak is at once a necessity and a tragedy for Lacan, as it permits the socialization of the infant at the cost of an irredeemable sense of lack, which we try to mask by investing in the domain of the 'imaginary', a mis-recognition of the self as unified and stable. Lacan's rethinking of identity in terms of lack and instability has had a substantial impact on disciplines across the humanities and social sciences, including political science, film studies, and queer theory. However, it has also been subject to extensive critique, not least from feminist scholars such as Luce *Irigaray, who have taken issue with his account of female sexuality and desire. See M. Bowie, *Lacan* (1991).

LACLOS, Choderlos de (1741–1803) French novelist. His masterpiece *Les Liaisons dangereuses* (1782: *Dangerous Liaisons*), influenced by Samuel *Richardson's epistolary novels, records the seductions of Valmont, aided by his accomplice Madame de Merteuil. In its teasingly ambiguous depiction of aristocratic moral and sexual mores, it remarkably combines the searching psychological analysis of 17th-century drama, the assumptions of 18th-century philosophical sensationalism, and intimations of demonic Romantic revolt. It has been translated numerous times and was successfully adapted by Christopher *Hampton for both stage (1985) and screen (1989).

lads' literature Often abbreviated to 'lad lit'; writing from the 1990s onward which reflects the tastes and preoccupations of young men. The male equivalent of 'chick lit', 'lad lit' emerged in the wake of the identification of the social phenomenon of the 'New Lad', a hedonistic consumer of drink and drugs, unashamed of his obsessions with sport, cars, and women and apparently unaffected by feminist demands for a more mature masculinity. Magazines such as *Loaded* provided the New Lad with much of his reading matter but there are also key texts in hardcovers. Nick *Hornby's *Fever Pitch* (1992) and *High Fidelity* (1995) show football and record collecting functioning as a means for men to discuss their feelings; John King's *The Football Factory* (1996) and *Headhunters* (1997) offer vicarious insights into the world of football hooligans; Tony Parsons's (1953–) *Man and Boy* (1999) reveals a New Lad struggling to grow up.

Lady Audley's Secret A *sensation novel by Mary *Braddon, published in 1862. The complex story revolves round the sinister scheming of the beautiful but mysterious Lucy Graham, newly married to the respectable Sir Michael Audley, after having worked as a governess. Sir Michael's nephew Robert Audley begins to suspect that the charming Lucy is not what she seems after the sudden and unexplained disappearance of his friend George Talboys, who has been searching for his wife Helen after returning from a long absence in Australia. His investigations reveal that Helen and Lucy are one and the same woman, and that she has married Sir Michael bigamously. Lady Audley's increasingly desperate and wholly unscrupulous struggles to avoid exposure and disgrace in the face of Robert's relentless pursuit end with the revelation that, as she confesses, she is mad—this is her secret. She ends her life incarcerated in a lunatic asylum. The racy and absorbing plot, and Lucy's defiantly unrepentant wickedness, fascinated the novel's first readers, and it became a best-seller. Its ambivalent handling of female identities and domestic values has attracted much recent critical notice.

Lady Chatterley's Lover Novel by D. H. *Lawrence (privately printed, Florence, 1928; expurgated version, 1932; full text, 1960). Constance Chatterley is married to Sir Clifford, who is confined to a wheelchair through injuries suffered in the First World War. She has an unsatisfying affair with a playwright followed by a passionate love relationship with gamekeeper Oliver Mellors. She becomes pregnant, goes to Venice with her sister partly to obscure the baby's parentage, but returns and tells her husband the truth, spurred on by the knowledge that Mellors's estranged wife Bertha has been stirring scandal in an effort to reclaim him. The novel ends with the temporary separation of the lovers, as they hopefully await divorce and a new life together. Lawrence's frank descriptions of sex and his uncompromising use of four-letter words caused the book to be unpublishable until 1960, when *Penguin Books were prosecuted for obscenity and acquitted, a victory which had a profound effect on both writing and publishing in subsequent decades.

Lady of May, The A short pastoral entertainment, first published in 1598, by Philip *Sidney. It consists of a dispute between a shepherd and a forester for the hand of the rustic May Lady, and was performed for *Elizabeth I when she visited the earl of *Leicester at his hunting lodge at Wanstead, Essex, in 1578. The character of the pedantic schoolmaster Rombus may have suggested that of Holofernes in William *Shakespeare's **Love's Labour's Lost*.

Lady of Pleasure, The A comedy by James *Shirley, acted 1635, printed 1637. In the central plot, Aretina, Lady Bornwell, is cured of thoughtless hedonism by her husband. In the sub-plot Celestina, a 16-year-old widow, attempts to cure the otherwise unnamed Lord A of his apparent misogyny. The comic third plot concerns the dissolute Master Frederick, clownish suitors, a dandy, and a bawd. The play's intrigue, fashionable conversation, focus on social deportment, and switch from amorality to a moral ending anticipate the *Restoration comedy of manners.

'Lady of Shalott, The' A poem by Alfred *Tennyson, published 1832, much revised for the 1842 *Poems*. It tells the story of an enchanted weaver who leaves her tower after falling in love, only to die. An allegory of the artist's remoteness from human life, a contemplation of art's relationship with the real, of the 'femininity' of the poet, even of the political plight of handloom weavers, the poem has sustained a diversity of critical views. It was widely illustrated (e.g. by J. W. Waterhouse, 1849–1917), and set to music, during the Victorian period.

Lady of the Lake In the Arthurian legends, a rather shifting supernatural character. In *Malory she gives Arthur the sword Excalibur, but when she asks for the head of Balyn as payment, Balyn strikes off her head, for which deed he is banished from the court. Also called the Lady of the Lake (in Malory 'chief' lady, suggesting more than one) is Nimiane (Nymue and, probably by scribal misreading, Vivien), the wife of Pelleas, who loves Merlin, whom she tricks into revealing his magic arts and then imprisons in a tower of air in the forest of *Broceliande from which he never escapes. In Malory she is said to have accompanied the three queens who bore Arthur away by ship after his death. In Celtic origin she may derive from Morgan, the archetypal lake lady.

Lady of the Lake, The A poem in six cantos by Walter *Scott, published 1810. The action takes place chiefly on and around Loch Katrine in Perthshire, and involves the wooing of Ellen Douglas, the lady of the title and daughter of the outlawed Lord James of Douglas: she is courted by various suitors, including a mysterious wandering huntsman-knight whom she ferries to the island in the lake. After various adventures and skirmishes, this personage is revealed at court, as Ellen seeks her father's pardon, to be King James V himself. The lively narrative evokes Highland scenery and manners, and contains various poetic interludes, including the *coronach (Canto III) 'He is gone on the mountain' and the ballad (Canto IV) 'Alice Brand', which tells the story of Alice's lost brother, transformed by the Elf King into a hideous dwarf, and redeemed by his sister's courage. The poem was immensely popular, and inspired several composers, including *Schubert and *Rossini.

Lady Susan A novel by Jane *Austen, written probably 1793–4, published 1871, from an untitled manuscript dated 1805: the manuscript is a fair copy, and the date of composition is discussed by B. C. Southam, *Jane Austen's Literary Manuscripts* (1964). It is Jane Austen's only *epistolary novel, although her first version of **Sense and Sensibility*, called *Elinor and Marianne*, was also in letter form.

The story consists of letters, written chiefly between the kindly Mrs Vernon and her mother Lady de Courcy, and between Lady Susan and her London friend Mrs Johnson.

The events occur mainly at Churchill, the country house of the Vernons. Lady Susan, the widow of Mr Vernon's brother, is beautiful, selfish, and unscrupulous. She has had to leave the house of the Mainwarings, where both Mr Mainwaring and his sister's suitor Sir James Martin have fallen in love with her. At Churchill she meets Reginald de Courcy, Mrs Vernon's brother, young and gullible, who also succumbs to her superficial charms. Lady Susan's 16-year-old daughter Frederica is terrorized by her mother, and becomes so distraught when learning of her mother's plan to marry her off to Sir James Martin that she begs Reginald de Courcy to intercede for her. The story then breaks off and the author appends a 'Conclusion', informing the reader that Lady Susan herself married Sir James Martin; that Frederica went to live at Churchill and would in time marry Reginald; and that 'this correspondence [i.e. the novel]...could not, to the great detriment of the Post Office revenue, be continued any longer'.

LA FARGE, Oliver (1901–1963) American novelist and anthropologist, born in New York, best remembered for his 1929 novel *Laughing Boy*, an examination of the interaction of American and Native cultures in the south-west.

LAFAYETTE, Marie-Madeleine de La Vergne, comtesse de (1634–93) French novelist. The centre of a select circle in Paris which included Madame de *Sévigné and *La Rochefoucauld, she wrote four historical novels, one of which in particular, *La Princesse de Clèves* (1678; trans. 1679), had a decisive influence on early modern prose fiction, both by its remarkable concision (in sharp contrast to the immense romances of *Scudéry and *La Calprenède) and by its psychological acuteness. The novel dissects the married heroine's overwhelming passion for another man and offers teasingly ambiguous insights into a society obsessed with appearances. Her posthumously published *Histoire de Madame Henriette d'Angleterre* (1720) was translated by Ann Floyd (1722).

LA FONTAINE, Jean de (1621–95) French poet, author of *Fables*, published in twelve books between 1668 and 1694. He draws in part on the familiar fables of *Aesop and Phaedrus, but he also explores the limits of the genre, rejecting facile didacticism in favour of thought-provoking little comedies, written in remarkably agile irregular verse, which rarely offer up a simple lesson. Some of the *Fables* were translated as early as 1693 by John *Dennis, followed by Bernard de *Mandeville's versions in *Aesop Dress'd* (1704); in the 20th century, Marianne *Moore's complete translation (1954) is a distinguished example of one poet giving voice to another.

LAFORGUE, Jules (1860–87) French poet, prominent in the development of **vers libre*, author of *Les Complaintes* (1885: *Complaints*), *L'Imitation de Notre-Dame la Lune* (1886: *Imitation of Our Lady of the Moon*), and the posthumously published *Derniers Vers* (1890: *Final Verse*). The characteristic tone of his poetry is one of ironic self-deprecation. He was an important influence on the early work of T. S. *Eliot, and on the poetry of Ezra *Pound (see Canto *CXVI*). *Three of his poems were translated by* Hart *Crane (1922). He also published a collection of short stories, *Moralités légendaires* (1887: *Legendary Moralities*).

LAING, R. D. (Ronald David) (1927–89) Author, poet, psychoanalyst, born in Glasgow. He studied medicine at Glasgow University. His works include *The Divided Self* (1960), *Sanity, Madness and the Family* (1964), and *The Politics of Experience and the Bird of Paradise* (1967). *Knots* (1970) is a collection of poem-pattern-dialogues revealing the 'knots, tangles...impasses, disjunctions' of various forms of what he describes as human bondage. His radical ideas on madness, family dynamics, and care in the community made a considerable impact on the counter-culture of the 1960s, and his work has continued to exert an influence. Mary Barnes, one of his patients at his experimental therapeutic centre, Kingsley Hall, was the subject of a play by David *Edgar.

Lake Poets, Lake School Terms applied to Samuel Taylor *Coleridge, Robert *Southey, William *Wordsworth, and sometimes to Thomas *De Quincey, who lived in the Lake District at the beginning of the 19th century. The expression 'Lake School' seems first to have appeared in the **Edinburgh Review*. Lord *Byron makes play with the term, and in the dedication to **Don Juan* (1819) refers slightingly to 'all the Lakers'. In his *Recollections of the Lake Poets* De Quincey denies the existence of any such 'school'.

Lallans *See* Scots.

Lalla Rookh A series of *oriental tales in verse connected by a story in prose, by Thomas *Moore, published 1817. The first of the tales is written in heroic couplets, the others in stanzas of varied metre. The work enjoyed immense popularity, and went into twenty editions by 1840.

The frame story tells of the journey of Lalla Rookh ('Tulip Cheek'), the daughter of the emperor, from Delhi to Kashmir, to be married to the king of Bucharia. On the way she and her train are diverted by four verse tales told by Feramorz, a young Kashmiri poet, with whom she falls in love and who turns out, on her arrival, to be the king of Bucharia himself. A series of accidents on the way throws the pompous chamberlain Fadladeen into a bad temper, which he vents in pungent criticisms of the young man's verse, in the style of the **Edinburgh Review*.

'L'Allegro' A poem in rhymed octosyllabics with a ten-line prelude by John *Milton, written ?1631, printed 1645. The Italian title means 'the cheerful man', and this idyll is an invocation to the goddess Mirth to allow the poet to live with her, first amid the delights of pastoral scenes, then amid those of 'towered cities' and the 'busy hum of men'. It is a companion piece to *'Il Penseroso'.

LAMARCK, Jean Baptiste de Monet, chevalier de (1744–1829) French naturalist. He advanced the view that species were not unalterable, and that the higher and more complex forms of life were derived from lower and simpler forms; that environment and new needs led to new actions and hence to organic modifications or the creation of new organs, and that these were transmitted to descendants. Charles *Darwin introduced Lamarckian ideas into later editions of his work, having retreated from his original position on natural selection.

LAMARTINE, Alphonse de (1790–1869) French poet and politician. His poetry, from the *Méditations poétiques (Poetic Meditations)* of 1820, established him as a leading figure in the French Romantic movement; he also produced many volumes of biography, memoirs, political and historical works, novels, and travel writing. His work, both literary and historical, was widely translated into English from the late 1820s. Other collections of poetry include the *Nouvelles Méditations poétiques* (1823: *New Poetic Meditations*), the *Harmonies poétiques et religieuses* (1830: *Poetic and Religious Harmonies*), and the *Recueillements poétiques* (1839: *Poetic Contemplations*); he also published two fragments of a projected epic poem, *Jocelyn* (1836) and *La Chute d'un ange* (1838: *The Fall of an Angel*), while in 1835 he published his account of a journey to Syria, Lebanon, and the Holy Land. In the provisional government of 1848 he served as minister of foreign affairs (*Trois Mois au pouvoir*, 1848: *Three Months in Power*), withdrawing from public life in 1851. His historical works include the *Histoire des Girondins* (1847: *History of the Girondins*) and the *Histoire de la Révolution de 1848* (1849: *History of the 1848 Revolution*).

LAMB, Lady Caroline (1785–1828) Daughter of the third earl of Bessborough. She married William Lamb, afterwards second Viscount Melbourne. In 1812, shortly after her marriage, she became infatuated with Lord *Byron, and about the same time began to show signs of serious mental instability. Her first novel, *Glenarvon*, published anonymously in 1816 after Byron had broken with her, is a *Gothic extravaganza, in which she herself is cast as the dashing Calantha and Byron as the fated, fascinating Glenarvon. The novel enjoyed a tremendous but brief *succès de scandale*. Her *Graham Hamilton* (1822) and *Ada Reis* (1823) are less well remembered today.

LAMB, Charles (1775–1834) Author and critic, born in London. His father, the Lovel of 'The Old Benchers of the Inner Temple' in his most notable work, the **Essays of Elia*, was the clerk to Samuel Salt, a lawyer, whose house in Crown Office Row was Lamb's birthplace and his home during his youth. He was educated at *Christ's Hospital, where he formed an enduring admiration for S. T. *Coleridge. After a few months at the South Sea House (*see* Essays of Elia), he obtained at 17 an appointment in the East India House, where he remained until his retirement in 1825. For a short time in 1795–6 he was mentally deranged, and the threat of madness became a shadow on his life. In 1796 his sister Mary, in a fit of insanity, killed their mother. Lamb undertook the charge of his sister, who remained liable to periodic breakdowns, and she repaid him with great sympathy and affection. They lived in London, which Lamb loved, then from 1823 in Islington, Enfield, and Edmonton, where he died.

Four sonnets of Lamb's appeared in 1796 in a volume of poems by Coleridge, who became a lifelong friend. In 1798 appeared *Blank Verse* by Charles Lloyd and Charles Lamb, which included the poem 'The Old Familiar Faces'. In the same year appeared the *Tale of Rosamund Gray and Old Blind Margaret*, a melodramatic, sentimental village tragedy, in which Rosamund meets a fate worse than death, then death itself. In 1802 Lamb published *John Woodvil* (at first called *Pride's Cure*), an ineffective tragedy in the Elizabethan style; and in 1806 his farce *Mr H* proved a failure at Drury Lane. With his sister he wrote *Tales from Shakespear* (1807), designed to make the stories of Shakespeare's plays familiar to the young; and also *Mrs Leicester's School* (1809), a collection of original stories. *The Adventures of Ulysses* (1808) was an attempt to do for the *Odyssey* what they had done for Shakespeare. In 1808 he published **Specimens of English Dramatic Poets Who Lived about the Time of Shakespeare*. Between 1810 and 1820 his literary output was not great. It includes the essays 'On the Tragedies of Shakespeare', which presents the characters of the tragedies as individual 'objects of meditation', stripped of their dramatic function; and an admiring analysis 'On the Genius and Character of Hogarth' in 1811. He wrote for Leigh *Hunt's **Reflector* and for the **Examiner*, and in 1814 contributed to the **Quarterly Review* an article (much altered by John *Gifford, the editor) on Wordsworth's *The *Excursion*, commending the originality of Wordsworth's genius, as well as his high seriousness. A collection of his miscellaneous writings in prose and verse appeared in 1818. From 1820 to 1823 Lamb was a regular contributor to the **London Magazine*, in which appeared the first series of essays known as *Essays of Elia*, published in a collected volume in 1823. The second series was published in 1833. Of his poems the best known are 'The Old Familiar Faces', the lyrical ballad 'Hester' (1803), and an elegy 'On an Infant Dying as Soon as Born' (1827). *Album Verses* (1830) includes many other lyrics and sonnets.

A. C. *Bradley regarded Lamb as the greatest critic of his century, but few would follow him quite so far. Lamb's literary criticism is scattered and small in volume. He had no interest in critical theory, and a poor sense of structure; as he wrote to William *Godwin: 'I cannot grasp at a whole.' But his sympathies were wide and his sensitivity acute; while careful always to approve moral worth he also enjoys 'an airing beyond the diocese of strict conscience', as into the then little read Jacobean or Restoration drama. His habit of brief but accurate characterization, and of generalized but perceptive comment (such as he employs in his *Specimens*) results in original and illuminating work. He was a prolific letter writer of great charm, wit, and quality, and many of his observations on literature are scattered throughout the letters. He was much loved, and his various homes were a meeting place for Coleridge, *Wordsworth, Leigh Hunt, William *Hazlitt, Robert *Southey, and other literary men. His *Letters* have been edited by E. W. Marrs (3 vols, 1975–8); see also the standard life by E. V. Lucas (1905) and W. F. Courtney, *Young Charles Lamb: 1775–1802* (1982).

LAMB, Mary (1764–1847) The sister of Charles *Lamb (under whose name the facts of her life will be found). She collaborated with her brother in writing for children the successful prose *Tales from Shakespear* (1807), and she wrote the greater part of *Mrs Leicester's School* (1809), a book of stories for children containing many autobiographical details, to which her brother contributed three tales.

LAMBERT, Constant (1905–51) English composer, conductor, and music critic, who studied at the Royal College of Music under Ralph *Vaughan Williams, 1922–5. He was a close friend of Peter *Warlock, and like William *Walton was a member of the *Sitwell circle, taking part in early performances of Walton's *Façade*; his best-known work, *The Rio Grande* (1928), is a jazzy setting for piano solo, chorus, contralto, and orchestra of a poem by Sacheverell *Sitwell. He also set *Eight Poems of Li-Po* (1926–9) and wrote a choral masque to words from Thomas *Nashe's 'pleasant comedy' *Summer's Last Will and Testament* (1936), and there is a version of *The Dirge from *Cymbeline*, 'Fear no more the heat of the sun' (1940). The ballet *Romeo and Juliet* (written for Diaghilev in 1926) is tangential to *Shakespeare: an actor and actress, rehearsing the play, themselves fall in love and eventually elope in an aeroplane. Lambert's controversial book *Music Ho!* (1934), subtitled 'A Study of Music in Decline', was enthusiastically acclaimed in its day and remains a classic of its period.

'Lamia' A narrative poem by John *Keats, written 1819, published 1820.The story was taken from Robert Burton's **Anatomy of Melancholy* and thence from Philostratus. Lamia, a sorceress, is transformed by Hermes from a serpent into a beautiful woman. She loves the serious young Corinthian Lycius, and he, spellbound by her beauty and believing her human, falls in love with her. They retire to her secret and sumptuous palace in Corinth. Here, not content with his happiness and against Lamia's wishes, Lycius orders a magnificent bridal feast and summons his friends. Among them, though uninvited, comes his old guide and mentor, the sage Apollonius, who pierces Lamia's disguise and calls her by her name. Her beauty withers, with a frightful scream she vanishes, and Lycius dies in a frenzy of grief. Keats wrote to his brother George that he believed the poem had 'a sort of fire in it' and that it would please a sensation-loving public. Interpretations of the work vary considerably, but it is clearly connected with Keats's persistent theme of the relationship between the real and the ideal.

LAMMING, George William (1927–) Novelist and poet, born in Barbados, who has also taught at Brown University, USA. His first novel, *In the Castle of my Skin* (1953), tells of a boy's adolescence in a small village in Barbados, and of his growing awareness of the colonial situation. *The Emigrants* (1954) describes the arrival in Britain of a group of West Indians. *Of Age and Innocence* (1958) and *Season of Adventure* (1960) are more optimistic works, set on the imaginary island of San Cristobal. *The Pleasures of Exile* (1960) is a collection of essays on Caribbean culture and politics. *Water with Berries* (1971) is a political allegory and *Natives of my Person* (1972) is a novel about 16th-century explorers.

LAMPEDUSA, Giuseppe Tomasi di (1896–1957) Sicilian aristocrat, author of a remarkable novel, *Il gattopardo* (1958: *The Leopard*), which describes the reactions of a noble Sicilian family to the political and social changes following Garibaldi's annexation of Sicily in 1860. A film version was made by Visconti (1963) with Burt Lancaster in the title role. See D. Gilmour, *The Last Leopard* (1988).

LANCASTER, Sir Osbert (1908–96) Writer, artist, cartoonist, and theatre designer, educated at Charterhouse and Lincoln College, Oxford. He is remembered for his many illustrated works which gently mock the English way of life: he was particularly good at country-house and upper-class architecture and mannerisms, but also had a sharp eye for suburbia. Titles include *Pillar to Post* (1938) and *Homes Sweet Homes* (1939), which record architectural history and fashion, and books based on Draynflete, the ancestral village of the Littlehampton family, which include *Draynflete Revealed* (1949) and *The Life and Times of Maudie Littlehampton* (1982).

Landfall The most important of New Zealand's literary periodicals, founded in 1947 as a quarterly.

LANDON, Letitia Elizabeth (1802–38) Poet and novelist, born and educated in London. Her poetry rivalled Felicia *Hemans's in popularity. Publishing from an early age under her initials 'L.E.L.' enabled her to assume the literary persona of an innocent, gentle, and devoted but rejected female lover, such that the initials themselves acquired a kind of feminine enchantment in the eyes of the reading public.

Between 1821 and her death, she wrote prolifically, contributing poems to literary reviews including the **Literary Gazette* (becoming head reviewer in 1824), and also supplying hundreds of love lyrics to gift books and annuals, including *The Keepsake* and *The Amulet*. She edited two such publications, *Fisher's Drawing Room Scrap Book* (1832–39) and *Heath's Book of Beauty* (1833), and from 1832 contributed poems and short stories to the **New Monthly Magazine*. She later wrote 'silver-fork' novels, society fictions popular in the period, namely, the triple-deckers *Romance and Reality* (1831), *Francesca Carrera* (1834), and *Ethel Churchill* (1837). Capitalizing on her periodical success, she published in 1824 her first volume of verse, *The *Improvisatrice*, which went through six editions in a year. A steady stream of further volumes followed, including *The Troubadour* (1825), *The Golden Violet* (1826), *The Venetian Bracelet* (1829), *The Vow of the Peacock* (1835), a collection of children's stories, *Traits and Trials of Early Life* (1836), and a play, *The Triumph of Luca*, published posthumously.

Landon's poetry replaces the emphasis on domestic and maternal love typical of Hemans's verse with a focus on erotic love and female suffering. Following the poetic tradition of sentiment made fashionable by the *Della Cruscans, she writes in a highly self-conscious, romantic vein about the suffering of the female lover and the female poet (the two themes merge in her work). Jerome McGann describes her poetry as the 'Art of Disillusion'.

Her unprotected position as a woman in the literary world gave rise to various vague scandals linking her name to William *Maginn and, less certainly, to Edward *Bulwer-Lytton, who appears with his wife Rosina in her novel *Romance and Reality* (1831). Such rumours caused her to break off her engagement to John *Forster, and she later married George Maclean, with whom she travelled to West Africa, where she died shortly afterwards in mysterious circumstances, either by suicide or accident, from swallowing prussic acid. See *Letitia Elizabeth Landon: Selected Writings*, ed. J. J. McGann and D. Reiss (1997).

LANDOR, Robert Eyres (1781–1869) Cleric and writer, youngest brother of Walter Savage *Landor. Born in Warwick, and educated at Worcester College, he was the author of five tragedies, including *The Count of Arezzi* (1823), which was attributed to Lord *Byron and enjoyed a brief success for that reason. He also published a poem, *The Impious Feast* (1828); a fantastic prose story, *The Fawn of Sertorius* (1846); and *The Fountain of Arethusa* (1848), dialogues between two modern explorers and famous men of classical times, comparable with Walter Savage Landor's **Imaginary Conversations*.

LANDOR, Walter Savage (1775–1864) Poet and author, educated at Rugby and at Trinity College, Oxford, where he was expelled. An intractable temper involved him in trouble throughout his life. As a young man he fought as a volunteer in Spain against the French. In 1795 he published a miscellany of verses, *Poems*, and in 1798 an epic poem in seven books, *Gebir*. In 1802 followed *Poetry by the Author of Gebir*, and in 1806 another collection of poems, *Simonidea*. In 1811 he married Julia Thuillier. A dramatic tragedy, *Count Julian*, followed in 1812, but was never staged. In the same year Landor's intemperate 'Commentary on the Memoirs of Mr Fox' had to be suppressed. In 1815 he began a long residence in Italy, which did not end until 1835, when he separated from his wife. **Imaginary Conversations of Literary Men and Statesmen* appeared 1824–9. In 1834 he published the light-hearted *Citation and Examination of William Shakespeare Touching Deer-Stealing*. **Pericles and Aspasia*, a full-length work which grew out of an imaginary conversation, appeared in 1836, and in 1837 *The *Pentameron*, in which *Boccaccio and *Petrarch discuss the poetry of *Dante. The trilogy *Andrea of Hungary, Giovanna of Naples*, and *Fra Rupert*, set in the 14th century, was published in 1839–40, and *The Hellenics*, a retelling in verse of various Greek myths, completed in 1847. In 1853 appeared *Imaginary Conversations of Greeks and Romans*. His work was much admired by Robert *Browning and many others. Boythorn in Dickens's **Bleak House* is a genial caricature of Landor. See M. Elwin, *Landor: A Replevin* (1958).

landscape gardening A 'natural' style of gardening, inspired by the paintings of *Claude Lorrain, and moving away from the geometric designs imitated from continental palace gardens. It was pioneered in England by Charles Bridgeman or Bridgman (*fl.* 1709–38), who worked on royal gardens and large country estates, including Stowe. His style passed to William *Kent, Kent's assistant Lancelot 'Capability' Brown (1716–83), and Humphry Repton (1752–1818), they continued to produce careful compositions emphasizing soft curves, water features, and the absence of regular lines. Repton is recommended to 'improve' the grounds of Sotherton in **Mansfield Park* (1814). Literary exponents of the shift in style include Alexander *Pope, who created his own five-acre garden at Twickenham and advised several of his landed friends on their estates, and William *Shenstone, whose much larger garden, the Leasowes, at Halesowen, became a tourist attraction. The movement was described approvingly in Horace *Walpole's *Essay on Modern Gardening* (1780).

LANDSEER, Sir Edwin Henry (1802–73) Painter, the son of an engraver. A visit to Walter *Scott in 1824 introduced him to the landscapes of Scotland, which featured prominently in his work. Professional and social success came rapidly to him; he enjoyed the favour of Queen *Victoria, and his friends included Charles *Dickens, W. M. *Thackeray, William Charles *Macready, and the Count d'*Orsay. Although he painted portraits, historical scenes (mostly from Scott), and, in his late days, some strange allegorical works, he is best remembered for his animal paintings, such as *The Monarch of the Glen* (1851) and *Dignity and Impudence* (1839).

LANE, Allen (1902–70) Publisher. He was born Allen Lane Williams, in Bristol, and took the name Allen Lane when he went to London to work at the Bodley Head for his distant cousin 'Uncle John' *Lane. With the foundation in 1935 of the *Penguin series, he became a pioneer in the paperback revolution in publishing. See Jeremy Lewis, *Penguin Special: The Life and Times of Allen Lane* (2005).

LANE, Edward William (1801–1876) Arabic scholar, who published in 1836 *An Account of the Manners and Customs of the Modern Egyptians*, a work of profound anthropological insight that is still of value, though it was savagely attacked in Edward *Said's *Orientalism* (1978). In 1838–40 he produced an expurgated translation of *The Thousand and One Nights* (or **Arabian Nights Entertainments*), which was much read, though later attacked by Sir Richard *Burton. In contrast, his *Selections from the Qur-án* (1843) had little impact. From 1843 to his death in 1876 he worked solely on his magnum opus, his *Arabic–English Lexicon*, using the great Arabic–Arabic dictionaries of medieval times as his authorities. At the time of his death the *Lexicon* was roughly three-quarters complete, and the final sections of the work were seen to the press by his nephew. Even in its unfinished state, and allowing for the fact that it does not cover modern Arabic, it remains the key dictionary for all serious Arabists.

The last of Lane's work to appear was *A Description of Egypt*, which Murray had promised to publish in 1831. It eventually was printed by the American University in Cairo Press in 2000.

LANE, John (1854–1925) *Fin-de-siècle* publisher who, with Charles Elkin Mathews, established the Bodley Head Press in 1887. Authors who appeared under its imprint included John *Davidson, Ernest *Dowson, Richard *Le Gallienne, John Addington *Symonds, and Oscar *Wilde. The firm gained a high reputation for the quality of its publications, and as publisher of the **Yellow Book* it became the centre of ferment in art and letters in the 1890s.

LANFRANC (*c.*1010–1089) Archbishop of Canterbury (1070–89). A celebrated teacher, he had preceded *Anselm as prior of Bec. He was a man of wide learning who worked successfully with William the Conqueror and rebuilt Canterbury Cathedral, which had been burnt down in 1067. See M. Gibson, *Lanfranc of Bec* (1978).

LANG, Andrew (1844–1912) Scottish folklorist, anthropologist, and man of letters, born at Selkirk, educated at St Andrews University and Balliol College, Oxford. He became a fellow of Merton College, but in 1875 left Oxford for London, becoming one of the most prolific writers of his day. His many volumes of poetry (the *Collected Poems* (4 vols) appeared in 1923), belles-lettres, imaginary letters and dialogues, and so on are now largely forgotten, as are his melodramatic novels, which include *The Mark of Cain* (1886) and *The Disentanglers* (1902). He collaborated with H. Rider *Haggard in *The World's Desire* (1891) and with A. E. Mason in *Parson Kelly* (1899). As a Greek scholar, Lang devoted himself largely to *Homer. He was one of the joint authors (with S. H. Butcher) of prose versions of the **Odyssey* (1879, preceded by his sonnet 'The Odyssey') and (with W. Leaf and E. Meyers) of the **Iliad* (1883). He wrote on the Homeric question, arguing with the unity of Homer. He also took part in the Baconian controversy (*see* SHAKESPEARE: AUTHORSHIP OF THE WORKS), favouring Shakespearian authorship, in *Shakespeare, Bacon and the Great Unknown* (1912).

Lang's first book on folklore, *Custom and Myth*, did not appear until 1884, but contained papers written and printed much earlier. *Myth, Ritual and Religion*, dealing chiefly with totemism (a belief system based on a mystical relation between an individual, or group, and an animal, or plant), was published in 1887, and *The Making of Religion* in 1899. *Freud's *Totem and Taboo* refers to Lang's work in this field. Lang is remembered for his own *fairy stories, which include *The Gold of Fairnilee* (1888, drawing on Scottish history and fairy lore) and *Prince Prigio* (1889) and *Prince Ricardo of Pantouflia* (1893), both set in the imaginary world of Pantouflia, and for his twelve collections of folk and fairy-tales, some in *translation. Each volume was named after a different colour, from *The Blue Fairy Book* (1889) to *The Lilac Fairy Book* (1910); they did much to stimulate interest in fairy-tales. In their compilation Lang was greatly aided by his wife, Leonora. He edited other collections including the **Arabian Nights* (1898); his *Tales of Troy and Greece* (1907) was long regarded as a children's classic.

LANGHAM (Laneham), **Robert** The name of the author of the printed letter describing some of the entertainments put on by the earl of *Leicester for *Elizabeth I's visit to Kenilworth in 1575. William *Shakespeare may have remembered the shows in *A *Midsummer Night's Dream* (II. i. 148–68) and Walter *Scott used the description in **Kenilworth*. The list of Captain Cox's books which 'Langham' gives is an important source for the titles of ballads, romances, and other popular contemporary literature. The ghost of Captain Cox appears again in Ben *Jonson's *Masque of Owls* (1624). There is an edition of the letter by R. J. P. Kuin (1983).

LANGHORNE, John (1735–79) Clergyman and poet, born near Kirkby Stephen and educated at Appleby, Cumbria. He worked as a tutor, took deacon's orders, and attended Clare College, Cambridge, without taking a degree. After a number of curacies Langhorne became in 1766 rector of Blagdon, Somerset. He began writing for the **Monthly Review* in 1761; an *oriental tale, *Solyman and Almena*, appeared in 1762. His *Genius and Valour: A Scotch Pastoral* (1763) defended the Scots against Charles *Churchill's *Prophecy of Famine*. He edited the works of William *Collins (1765) and, with his brother William (1721–72), translated *Plutarch's *Lives* (6 vols, 1770). His poem *The Country Justice* (1774–7), reflecting his experiences as a justice of the peace (from 1772), was much admired by William *Wordsworth.

LANGLAND, William (*c.*1325—*c.*1390) The supposed author of **Piers Plowman*, about whose identity and life very little is known for certain. A note (*c.*1400) in the Trinity College, Dublin, manuscript of the C-text states that a 'William de Langlond' was the son of Stacy de Rokayle of Shipton-under-Wychwood in Oxfordshire, and that this William wrote the poem. John *Bale states that he was born in Cleobury Mortimer, Shropshire, and separate evidence connects the Langlands, a prosperous family, with this area. He may possibly be identified with William Rokele, a priest who held a living in East Anglia. The poem in its various forms invites readers to think that 'Will', the dreamer ('Long Will' in the B-text), lived in London (Cornhill, more precisely, in the C-text), but that he had also lived in the Malvern district of the West Midlands.

Language Poets A movement beginning in the 1960s and continuing through the New York journal *L=A=N=G=U=A=G=E* (1978–82), whose practitioners foreground language and the production of meaning in their works. Its members include Ron Silliman (1946–), Barrett Watten (1948–), and Charles Bernstein (1950–), the latter co-editing with Bruce Andrews (1948–) *The L=A=N=G=U=A=G=E*

Book (1984). The movement draws partly on the practice of Gertrude *Stein.

langue d'oïl The language of northern France during the medieval period, so called to distinguish it from the *langue d'oc* (*see* PROVENÇAL), the distinction being based on the particle of affirmation: late Latin 'hoc ille' for 'yes' became 'o'il' in the north and 'oc' in the south. The distinction of language corresponded to a difference of culture and literature, the *langue d'oïl* being the literary medium of the *trouvères, the *langue d'oc*, or Provençal, that of the *troubadours. The dialects of the *langue d'oïl*, particularly Norman, Picard, and Francien (the language of the Paris region), each had some literary independence during the 12th and 13th centuries, but Francien gradually became the standard language, and is the ancestor of modern standard French.

LANIER (Lanyer), Emilia (1569–1645) Née Bassano, poet. A member of a large Italian family of musicians and instrument-makers living in London, she married a penurious civil servant, Alfonso Lanier, in 1592. Her collection of poems *Salve Deus Rex Judaeorum* (1611) is chiefly religious, but includes 'The Description of Cookham', a country-house poem celebrating the patronage of Margaret Clifford, countess of Cumberland (1560–1616), and her daughter Anne *Clifford. A very early example of the genre, the poem may pre-date Ben *Jonson's 'To Penshurst'. There is no proof to support A. L. Rowse's (1903–97) contention that Lanier was the dark lady of Shakespeare's sonnets. There is an edition of the poems by S. Woods (1993).

LANIER, Sidney (1842–81) American poet and musician, born in Macon, Georgia. After serving in the Confederate army during the Civil War, he devoted himself to poetry, in spite of ill health and poverty. He published his first *Poems* in 1877. His lyrical and metrically experimental verse, some of it in regional dialect, is strongly influenced by his knowledge and practice of music. He became a lecturer in English at Johns Hopkins University in 1879, and his critical writings include *The Science of English Verse* (1880). See Jack De Bellis, *Sidney Lanier* (1972).

Laodicean, A A novel by Thomas *Hardy, published 1881. Paula Power is a vacillating young woman, the Laodicean (i.e. a lukewarm or indecisive person) of the title. Faced with the ordeal of total immersion, according to her father's Baptist faith, she cannot take the plunge. She dithers between her love for George Somerset, a young architect, and Captain de Stancy, the heir of an ancient family which once owned the castle in which she now lives. She accepts the more romantic captain, but discovers in time a plot hatched by Willy Dare, de Stancy's illegitimate son, to blacken the character of George Somerset. She finally marries Somerset, her ancient castle is burned to the ground, and she remains a wavering Laodicean to the end.

Laokoon An influential essay in literary and artistic criticism by G. E. *Lessing, published 1766. It takes its title from the celebrated group of statuary disinterred at Rome in the 16th century representing Laocoön and his sons in the coils of serpents. Adopting this group and the Horatian formula 'ut pictura poesis' ('as is painting, so is poetry': *Horace, *Ars Poetica*, 361) as the initial subject of discussion, Lessing examines the grounds for the divergence in the treatment of the scene by the artist and by *Virgil who described it (*Aeneid* Bk 2), and develops the essential differences between the art of poetry and the plastic arts. The work was left unfinished but translated into English in 1853 by E. C. Beasley.

'Laon and Cythna' *See* REVOLT OF ISLAM.

Lara A poem by Lord *Byron, published 1814. Lara is in fact Conrad of *The *Corsair* returned to his domains in Spain accompanied by his page Kaled, who is his love, the slave Gulnare, in disguise. Lara lives, like other *Byronic heroes, aloof and alien, shrouded in mystery. He is, however, recognized as Conrad, and becomes involved in a feud in which he is finally killed, dying in the arms of Kaled.

LARDNER, Ring (1885–1933) American sports journalist and short story writer, born in Niles, Michigan. He began his career writing sports reports for the newspapers, then in 1916 published *You Know Me Al*, a collection of fictional letters by a baseball player. Lardner wrote a number of plays but is mainly remembered for his pioneering use of the vernacular in short story collections like *Gullible's Travels* (1917). He was a close friend of F. Scott *Fitzgerald and influenced the style of Ernest *Hemingway. See Jonathan Yardley, *Ring* (1977). His son Ring Lardner, Jr (1915–2000), was also a novelist and a member of the blacklisted Hollywood Ten, denied employment as a consequence of their political beliefs in the McCarthy era.

LARKIN, Philip (1922–85) Poet and novelist, born in Coventry and educated at King Henry VIII School, Coventry, and St John's College, Oxford, where he met Kingsley *Amis, who became a lifelong friend, and developed an interest in jazz which was later to produce a volume of essays, *All What Jazz* (1970). From 1943 he worked in various libraries before becoming librarian of the Brynmor Jones Library at Hull University. In his first book, *The North Ship* (1945), the poems were, by Larkin's own account, much influenced by W. B. *Yeats. In 1946 he published *Jill*, set in wartime Oxford, a novel that describes the undergraduate career of John Kemp, a working-class boy from Lancashire; 'Jill' is the fantasy sister he creates, who is transformed into a teasing reality. A second novel, *A Girl in Winter* (1947), relates a day in the life of refugee librarian Katherine Lind, working in a drab English provincial town, with a lengthy flashback to an abortive adolescent romance with a penfriend. Larkin's own poetic voice (with a new allegiance to Thomas *Hardy) became distinct in *The Less Deceived* (1955), where the colloquial bravura of a poem like

'Toads' is offset by the half-tones and somewhat bitter lyricism of other pieces; his name was at this time associated with the *Movement, and his work appeared in **New Lines* (1956). *The Whitsun Weddings* (1964) adds a range of melancholy urban and suburban provincial landscapes, a satiric sociological commentary, and more stoic wit, manifested in 'Toads Revisited', with its characteristic Larkinian conclusion: 'Give me your arm, old toad; Help me down Cemetery Road.' Many of the poems in *High Windows* (1974), notably 'The Old Fools', show a preoccupation with death and transience. In 'Annus Mirabilis' and 'Posterity' the poet ironically places himself as somewhat defiantly out of date; in the words of his fictitious American biographer: 'One of those old-type *natural* fouled-up guys.' Throughout his work, the adaptation of contemporary speech rhythms and vocabulary to an unobtrusive metrical elegance is highly distinctive. A controversial *Collected Poems* edited by Anthony *Thwaite, which printed Larkin's published and unpublished poems in chronological order, was published in 1988; a new version in 2003 reprinted the volumes as Larkin originally published them. Larkin also edited *The Oxford Book of Twentieth-Century English Verse* (1973). A volume of essays, *Required Writing*, was published in 1983 and *Further Requirements* in 2001. A *Selected Letters*, also edited by Thwaite, appeared in 1992. See Andrew Motion, *Philip Larkin: A Writer's Life* (1993).

LA ROCHEFOUCAULD, François de Marsillac, duc de (1613–80) French courtier, soldier, and moralist, author of *Réflexions ou sentences et maximes morales* (1665), usually known as *Maximes*. By the fifth (1678) edition, the *Maximes* consisted of 504 brief reflections which range widely over human nature and society, investigating and extending the sense of such traditional moral concepts as love, friendship, wit and folly, virtue and vice, happiness and misfortune. The epigraph to the collection, 'Our virtues are mostly vices in disguise', expresses one of its leading themes; another is the discovery of the springs of people's actions in their vanity, self-interest, desire for praise, and readiness to deceive themselves. The possibility of noble conduct and genuine worth is admitted, but most men and women are judged to be ruled by circumstances and their passions. There were several English translations of the *Maximes* in the 17th and 18th centuries, including one by Aphra *Behn, *Reflections on Morality or Seneca Unmasqued* (1685).

LAROUSSE, Pierre (1817–75) French grammarian, lexicographer, and encyclopedist. He edited and (in part) compiled the *Grand Dictionnaire universel du XIXe siècle* (1866–76), a vast encyclopedia which aimed to comprehend every department of human knowledge. In 1852 he founded, together with Augustin Boyer, the publishing house of Larousse, which continues to issue the dictionaries and reference works bearing its name.

La Saisiaz **and *The Two Poets of Croisic*** Two long poems by Robert *Browning, published 1878, the third and final such pairing in his work. *La Saisiaz* is a philosophical elegy prompted by the sudden death of a close friend of Browning's, with whom he had been holidaying in a chalet called 'La Saisiaz' near Geneva. It deals cautiously with questions about the immortality of the soul; a private poem, it contains little about the individual it mourns. *The Two Poets of Croisic* is lighter and more acerbic in tone than *La Saisiaz*: it tells of two obscure poets from the small village of Croisic in Brittany, each of the stories illustrating, in comic and grotesque vein, various follies of the life of letters. Its serious theme was the way in which art acts as a memorial for the dead.

LAS CASAS, Bartolomé de (?1474–1566) Spanish historian and bishop of Chiapas (Mexico), famous for his protest against the ill treatment by his countrymen of the native peoples of Spanish America, in his *Brevísima relación de la destrucción de las Indias*: *Short Account of the Destruction of the Indies* (written 1542 and dedicated to Philip II of Spain; first printed 1552). This work gave rise to the 'Black Legend' of Spanish barbarity which was exploited by Protestant propagandists in England and elsewhere. Las Casas also wrote a *Historia de las Indias*: *History of the Indies*, finished in manuscript in 1561, but unpublished until 1875–6.

LASKI, Marghanita (1915–88) Novelist, critic, and journalist, born in London but brought up in Manchester, and educated there and at Somerville College, Oxford. She was the niece of the political theorist Harold Laski (1893–1950). Her novels include *Little Boy Lost* (1949), *The Village* (1952), and *The Victorian Chaise Longue* (1953). She also wrote two books exploring mystical experiences, *Ecstasy* (1961) and *Everyday Ecstasy* (1980), and biographical studies of Jane *Austen and George *Eliot.

Last Chronicle of Barset, The A novel by Anthony *Trollope, published 1867, the last and one of the strongest of the *'Barsetshire' series. Josiah Crawley is accused of fraudulently acquiring a cheque for £20, and using it to pay off the debts resulting from his struggles to survive on his meagre curate's income. Proud and gloomy, Crawley broods over his wrongs, but he cannot remember the origin of the cheque and is committed for trial. The autocratic Mrs Proudie prejudges his case, and attempts to oust Crawley from his church. Matters are not finally cleared up in Crawley's favour until Dean Arabin's family are recalled from the Continent, whereupon Mrs Arabin explains her part in the muddle. At the close of the novel the Crawley fortunes brighten. Mr Crawley is presented with the fatter living of St Ewold's, and the archdeacon finally removes his opposition to the marriage of loyal Grace Crawley and his son Major Grantly. Interleaved with the matter of Crawley's cheque is the London life of Johnny Eames and his continuing love for Lily Dale despite his unfortunate flirtation with Madalina Demolines; and the deaths of Mrs Proudie and Mr Harding, once warden of Hiram's Hospital.

Last Days of Pompeii, The A historical novel by Edward Bulwer-*Lytton, published in 1834. It describes the events leading up to the destruction of the Roman city of Pompeii by the cataclysmic eruption of Mount Vesuvius in AD 79. The decadence of Roman culture is contrasted with early Christianity, and with the values of Greek and Egyptian civilization. Vivid and dramatic, the novel was widely read throughout the 19th century, and was subsequently adapted for the screen several times, most recently in a serialized version for television in 1984.
See also QUO VADIS?

Last Man, The A novel by Mary *Shelley, published 1826. A *dystopia, it portrays a late 21st-century world where humanity is destroyed by a plague. It contains a thinly veiled portrait of Lord *Byron in the character of Lord Raymond and is sometimes seen, like **Frankenstein*, as a critique of the destructive potential within Romantic idealism.

Last of the Mohicans, The: *A Narrative of 1757* A novel by James Fenimore *Cooper, published in 1826.

LATIMER, Hugh (*c.*1485–1555) Leading Protestant preacher and martyr. A farmer's son from Leicestershire, he was educated at Cambridge, took priest's orders, and gradually adopted *Protestant views, recommending the translation of the *Bible into English. He was accused of heresy, but had the support of Henry VIII and Anne Boleyn. He was appointed bishop of Worcester in 1535, and was a keen dismantler of images and promoter of preaching; he thought confiscated monastic wealth should be used for the poor. In 1539 he was forced to resign his bishopric. Under Edward VI he resumed his career, preaching his famous sermons 'On the Plough' in 1548. On Mary's accession in 1553 he was imprisoned with Nicholas *Ridley and Thomas *Cranmer, and with Ridley was condemned as a heretic and burnt at Oxford on 16 October 1555. His sermons, notable for their simple vernacular style and graphic illustrations, were published by the *Parker Society (1844–5).

LAUD, William (1573–1645) The son of a Reading cloth merchant, a scholar and later president of St John's College, Oxford. At Charles I's accession he was bishop of St David's, and was promoted successively to the sees of Bath and Wells and London, becoming archbishop of Canterbury in 1633. He encouraged the king's belief that he ruled by divine right, and, in his effort to impose uniformity on the Church of England, persecuted Puritans, Presbyterians, and sectarians, imposing harsh and humiliating punishments. In 1637 William *Prynne, John Bastwick (1593–1654), and Henry Burton (1578–1648) had their ears cut off and were branded on both cheeks for the crime of seditious libel. In the run-up to the Civil War he was accused of high treason and committed to the Tower. Tried and condemned in 1644, he was beheaded in January 1645. A few of his sermons were published in 1651, and a collected edition of his works in 1696–1700. A former chancellor of Oxford University, he gave some 1,300 manuscripts in eighteen different languages, and his collection of coins, to the Bodleian Library. See Hugh Trevor-Roper, *Archbishop Laud* (1940; 2nd edn, 1962).

LAUDER, William (d. 1771) Literary forger. Lauder was a classical scholar who interpolated in the works of the 17th-century Latin poets Masenius and Staphorstius extracts from a Latin verse rendering of **Paradise Lost* in order to suggest that Milton had plagiarized them. Samuel *Johnson wrote a preface for Lauder's original pamphlet and drafted an apology when the fraud was exposed by John Douglas (1721–1807).

Launcelot of the Lake, Sir The greatest and most romantic of the knights of the Round Table, son of King Ban of Benwick in Brittany, father of *Galahad by *Elaine Sans Pere (daughter of King Pelles), and the lover of *Guinevere. He is a relatively late development in the English Arthurian tradition, not appearing at length before the 14th century, although the story of his love for Guinevere is the subject of *Chrétien de Troyes's *Lancelot* (*c.*1170s) and of the early 13th-century French prose 'Vulgate' *Lancelot* (and there is a lost Anglo-Norman story earlier than these). His name, which probably has Welsh etymological connections, refers to a tradition that he was abducted at birth and brought up by a lake-lady, before being brought by a hermit to Arthur's court. Chrétien's romance *Lancelot*, or *Le Chevalier de la charrette*, is concerned exclusively with the love of Lancelot and Guinevere, presented faithfully as a *courtly love affair, to an extent that has been thought to be self-parodying by some critics. The main elements of the Launcelot story are found in the three romances of the French prose cycle: *Lancelot*; the *Queste del Saint Graal*; and the *Mort Artu* (for these, see ch. 22, 'The Vulgate Cycle', by Jean Frappier, in R. S. Loomis (ed.), *Arthurian Literature in the Middle Ages*, 1959). *Malory's treatment of Launcelot is closely based on this: Launcelot's love for the queen is again central; it is strained by his relations with Elaine the Fair Maid of Astolat, whose death ends Guinevere's jealousy. Their love is betrayed by *Agravain; the lovers flee to Launcelot's castle of Joyous Gard and, after a siege, the queen is restored to Arthur. Launcelot withdraws to Brittany where he is pursued by Arthur and Gawain; in the ensuing clash Launcelot injures Gawain. Arthur returns to Dover to fight the usurping *Mordred and Gawain is killed. Launcelot comes back to help the king, but arrives too late for the final battle in Cornwall in which both Arthur and Mordred die. He finds that Guinevere has become a nun, so he becomes a priest. On his death he is carried to Joyous Gard where visions suggest that he is taken to heaven. He is very prominent in Malory who stresses the tragedy of his imperfection (his relationship with the queen) which prevents his full achievement of the *Grail, though he has glimpses of it. Malory also makes much of his later bitter hatred by Gawain because of his killing of Gawain's brothers; the implacability of Gawain's hatred prevents Arthur from making a peace with Launcelot which might have enabled them to ally to defeat Mordred. See T. P. Cross and W. A. Nitze, *Lancelot and Guenevere* (1930; repr. 1970).

Laura (1) *See* PETRARCH. (2) The wife of Beppo in Byron's poem **Beppo*.

LAURENCE, Margaret (1926–87) Canadian novelist and short story writer, born in the prairie town of Neepawa, Manitoba (model for the fictional Manawaka). Her mother died when she was 4, and after her father's death in 1935 she was brought up by her stepmother (her natural mother's elder sister). She attended the local high school, at which she began to write stories, and studied at United College (now the University of), Winnipeg. In 1947 she married John Laurence, a civil engineer, whose work later took them to live in Africa for five years. Her time there inspired *A Tree for Poverty* (1954), a translated selection of Somali poetry; *The Prophet's Camel Bell* (1963), a memoir of her life in Somaliland; her first novel, *This Side Jordan* (1960), set in Ghana; a collection of stories set in West Africa, *The Tomorrow-Tamer* (1963); and a critical work on contemporary Nigerian dramatists and novelists, *Long Drums and Cannons* (1968). In 1962 she moved to England with her two children after separating from her husband, and it was at Penn in Buckinghamshire that she began the series of four books based on her home town, renamed Manawaka, for which she is now best known: *The Stone Angel* (1964); *A Jest of God* (1966), retitled *Now I Lay Me Down* for British publication, filmed as *Rachel, Rachel* (1968), and later reissued under that title; *The Fire-Dwellers* (1969); and *The Diviners* (1974). *A Bird in the House* (1970), a collection of linked short stories, is also part of the Manawaka sequence. She returned to Canada in 1974. *Heart of a Stranger* (1976) is a collection of essays. A draft of her memoirs, *Dance on the Earth*, edited by her daughter, was published in 1989.

LAUTRÉAMONT, comte de (1846–70) Pseudonym of Isidore Ducasse, French prose poet. Born in Montevideo, Uruguay, Lautréamont is best known for his six *Chants de Maldoror* (1868–69: *Songs of Maldoror*), a work which won the admiration of the *Surrealists for its nightmare vision of unbridled passion and cruelty.

LAVATER, Johann Kaspar (1741–1801) Swiss poet and theologian of Pietist tendency. He is mainly remembered as the founder of the 'science' of physiognomy, which attempted to systematize the deep-seated intuition that moral and intellectual character can be read from facial features. His copiously illustrated *Physiognomische Fragmente* (1775–8), which found several translators in England, including Thomas *Holcroft, brought him European celebrity. Henry *Fuseli's translation of Lavater's *Aphorisms on Man* (1788), his most famous work in English, was well known to William *Blake. Surprisingly, his reputation lingered on well into the 19th century when physiognomy metamorphosed into phrenology. Its later adherents included Captain *Fitzroy of the *Beagle*, and even the young George *Eliot.

Lavengro: *The Scholar, the Gypsy, the Priest* A veiled autobiography by George *Borrow, published in 1851. 'Lavengro' is a Romany term for 'wordsmith', and was a name given to Borrow in his youth by Ambrose Smith, who figures in the narrative as Lavengro's Gypsy friend Jasper Petulengro.

The work is presented as the story of Borrow's own restless life, though many of its elements are heavily romanticized. The hero's father is a soldier, and he follows him from post to post around Britain, striking up unconventional friendships. He becomes attached to a family of Gypsies, and meets tinkers, including the pugilistic Flaming Tinman, with whom he has a vividly described fight. Lavengro also develops an intellectual and literary life, and becomes expert in the comparative study of languages (though much of his scholarship is suspect). The book closes as Lavengro becomes involved with the Amazonian vagrant Belle Berners, a story which is resumed in *The *Romany Rye*. Vigorously written and packed with incident, *Lavengro* enjoyed lasting success.

LAVIN, Mary (1912–96) Short story writer and novelist, born to Irish immigrant parents in Massachusetts and brought up from the age of 9 in Ireland, where she was educated at University College, Dublin. Her first collection was *Tales from Bective Bridge* (1942), ten stories based in and around the village of Bective, Co. Meath. Subsequent collections include *The Long Ago* (1944), *The Becker Wives* (1946), *A Single Lady* (1951), and *The Shrine* (1977). Family relationships and domestic conflicts over class, religion, and property are recurrent issues, and are treated with irony and pathos. Some of Lavin's most memorable stories explore the psychology of widowhood through the character of Vera Traske. Her novels are *The House in Clewe Street* (1945), a three-generation family saga which explores the restrictions of small-town living, and *Mary O'Grady* (1950), which follows its protagonist from Tullamore in the early 1900s to Dublin. *A Likely Story* (1957) is a children's tale set in Bective.

LAW, William (1686–1761) Devotional writer, born at King's Cliffe in Northamptonshire, the son of a grocer, and educated at Emmanuel College, Cambridge. From 1711 to 1716 he was a fellow of Emmanuel and curate at Haslingfield, Cambridgeshire, but lost his fellowship after refusing to take the oath of allegiance to George I. From 1723 to 1737 he lived with the family of Edward Gibbon at Putney, for part of this time as tutor to his son, father of Edward *Gibbon the historian. In 1728 he was ordained a priest in the nonjuring church, which refused allegiance to the Hanoverian dynasty, believing that the Stuarts were the legitimate rulers of the United Kingdom. His early writings include brilliant attacks on Benjamin *Hoadly (1676–1761), Bernard de *Mandeville, and the religious writer Matthew Tindal (bap. 1657, d. 1733), but he is chiefly remembered for his devotional handbooks of this period, *A Practical Treatise upon Christian Perfection* (1726) and especially *A Serious Call to a Devout and Holy Life* (1729). Their uncompromising message is enlivened with satirical portraits of the lives of the godless rich, contrasted with idealized ones such as Ouranius the country priest and Miranda the charitable gentlewoman. In 1740 Law returned to King's Cliffe with two companions, one of them the

historian's aunt Hester, to live a life of charity, celibacy, prayer, reading, and writing. He had long been a student of *mysticism, but from the 1730s on he made a detailed study of Jacob *Boehme, whose influence is reflected in his most important later works, *The Spirit of Prayer* (1749–50) and *The Spirit of Love* (1752–4). The widespread influence of Law's writings was furthered by the many cheap abridgements published by his one-time disciple John *Wesley, even though the two quarrelled publicly over his theology. His friend and admirer John *Byrom versified passages from his works and kept detailed accounts of his reading and conversation in his diaries. See J. Hoyles, *The Edges of Augustanism: The Aesthetics of Spirituality in Thomas Ken, John Byrom and William Law* (1972).
See NONJURORS.

LAWES, Henry (1596–1662) and **William** (1602–1645) English composers. Henry became one of Charles I's musicians in 1631 and was widely recognized in his day as the most important songwriter after John *Dowland: his 433 songs include settings of Thomas *Carew (38), Edmund *Waller (16), Robert *Herrick (14), Sir John *Suckling, Richard *Lovelace, and Katherine *Philips. As a particular friend of *Milton, who later honoured him with a sonnet, he arranged the original performance of *Comus*, contributing the songs. His brother William, also a song composer, wrote much instrumental music and contributed to many stage works during the period immediately before the establishment of opera in England. He composed a large part of the music for the most sumptuous of English masques, John Shirley's *The *Triumph of Peace* (1634), and wrote incidental music for several of the masques of Ben *Jonson, Suckling, and Sir William *D'Avenant, among others, before being killed in crossfire near the besieged city of Chester, an event lamented by Herrick in *Hesperides*. Both brothers experimented with a declamatory 'recitative' style, facilitating the operatic developments of Matthew *Locke, John *Blow, and Henry *Purcell.

LAWLESS, Emily (1845–1913) Born in Co. Kildare, daughter of an Irish peer; she was author of the historical novels *Hurrish* (1886), an agrarian story set in Clare, and *Grania* (1892). She also wrote *With Essex in Ireland* (1890); *With the Wild Geese* (1902), a collection of austere, intellectually bracing poems; and a *Life of Maria Edgeworth* (1904).

LAWRENCE, D. H. (David Herbert) (1885–1930) Novelist and poet, born at Eastwood, Nottinghamshire, one of five children of a miner and an ex-schoolteacher. He was often ill as a child (he was later to develop tuberculosis) and grew up in poverty. His ill-suited parents quarrelled continually, and a passionate and deeply influential bond grew between Lawrence and his mother; she was determined to keep him out of the mines and encouraged him at school. With the help of a scholarship he attended Nottingham High School for three years, but at 15 was forced to give up his education, working for a short time as a clerk in a surgical goods factory before becoming a pupil-teacher. At this time he formed a close friendship with Jessie Chambers, a local farmer's daughter, the Miriam of *Sons and Lovers*. In 1906 he took up a scholarship at Nottingham University College to study for a teacher's certificate.

He was already writing poetry and short stories and he now began his first novel, *The White Peacock* (1911), which was followed by *The Trespasser* (1912). He taught for two years at an elementary school in Croydon, but after the death of his mother he became seriously ill and was advised to give up teaching. His first major novel, *Sons and Lovers* (1913), is an autobiographical account of these early years, though Lawrence later felt he had been unjustly harsh about his father. In 1912 he met Frieda Weekley (née von Richthofen), wife of his old professor at Nottingham. Six years older than Lawrence and mother of three children, she was dissatisfied with her marriage and suffocated by life in Nottingham. They fell in love and eloped to Germany. They were always on the move, always short of money, and their life together was passionate and stormy. Lawrence's nomadic life supplied him with material for much of his writing and he wrote four travel books of a very personal kind. He spent the war years in England and began to form friendships in literary and intellectual circles: Aldous *Huxley, David *Garnett, Lady Ottoline *Morrell, J. M. *Murry, Katherine *Mansfield, Richard *Aldington, and Bertrand *Russell (with whom he was later to quarrel bitterly). His next novel, *The *Rainbow* (1915), was seized by the police and declared obscene. He was outspoken in his criticism of the war and while living in Cornwall he and his German-born wife were persecuted as suspected German agents. His vision of life and of England darkened, and in 1919 he and Frieda left for Italy. He had finished his novel **Women in Love* in 1916 but was unable to find a publisher until 1920 in New York, and 1921 in London. In 1920 *The Lost Girl* (begun before the war) won the James Tait Black Memorial Prize, the only official honour he was to receive during his lifetime. *Aaron's Rod*, the first of several novels espousing strong male leaders, followed in 1922 and the same year he began his serious travels, to Ceylon and Australia and finally to America and Mexico. While in Australia he wrote *Kangaroo*, which appeared in 1923.

Lawrence's output was remarkable considering his unsettled life, his poor health, and his fraught relationship with Frieda. He lived in constant anxiety about money, struggling to publish a few stories and articles in various periodicals, and was sometimes helped by well-to-do friends or admirers. While in Mexico he began work on *The Plumed Serpent* (1926) and wrote many short stories and poems. In 1923 Frieda returned to Europe alone, and after an exchange of tug-of-war letters Lawrence joined her in England. But he was miserable there and early in 1924 they returned to New Mexico, to the Kiowa Ranch, where Lawrence had hoped to found Rananim, his ideal community. While on a visit to Old Mexico he fell desperately ill and was told that he was in an advanced state of tuberculosis, with two years to live. They returned to Italy, via England and Germany, settling first at the Villa Bernardo at Spotorno and finally near Florence at the Villa Mirenda. Here he finished **Lady Chatterley's Lover*, his last novel and the one that was to cause more furore than any other. It was privately printed in Florence in 1928; more than 30 years would pass before unexpurgated editions appeared in the United States and England. It had become clear that he was dying and Frieda took him first to Germany and then to France in a forlorn search for a cure. He died at Vence in the south of France on 2 March 1930.

It is difficult now to understand the outrage occasioned by Lawrence's work, which blinded many readers to its lasting value. He was a moralist, and sometimes a preacher; he believed that modern man was in danger of losing his ability to experience the quality of life. Passionately involved with his characters and the physical world of nature, he wrote of them with a fresh immediacy and vividness. Central to F. R. *Leavis's literary canon in the 1950s and 1960s, in the 1970s and 1980s he was often depicted as misogynistic and authoritarian; later critics have advanced more nuanced interpretations.

In his poems, written throughout his career, Lawrence wanted to be free of the weight of formalism but not, as he said, to 'dish up the fragments as a new substance'. At times uneven, his poetry always has the immediate and personal quality of his prose. His poetry was gathered in *Complete Poems* (3 vols, 1957). Other non-fiction works include *Movements in European History* (1921), *Psychoanalysis and the Unconscious* (1921), *Fantasia of the Unconscious* (1922), *Studies in Classic American Literature* (1923), and *Apocalypse* (1931). A scholarly edition of his letters, ed. J. T. Boulton, was published in eight volumes, 1979–2000; a selected edition appeared in 1996. The fullest account of his life is contained in the three-volume biography by John Worthen, Mark Kinkead-Weekes, and David Ellis (1991, 1996, 1997).

LAWRENCE, George Alfred (1827–76) Novelist, born at Braxted, Essex, educated at Rugby and Balliol College, Oxford. He was called to the bar but abandoned law for a literary career. His first and best-known novel, *Guy Livingstone* (1857), was an immediate and lasting success; its glorification of physical strength and questionable morality provoked criticism from those who objected to endowing the vigorous but unprincipled Livingstone with 'heroic qualities and social aplomb', but won applause from others for its lack of hypocrisy. A leading example of the 'muscular school', the novel represented a revolt against the comparable but very much more high-minded 'muscular Christianity' of the time, embodied by Thomas *Hughes and Charles *Kingsley. It set a fashion not only in literature (*'Ouida' was a notable disciple) but even in the mode of dress and behaviour of the young men of the period. *Sword and Gown* followed in 1859, and *Border and Bastille* in 1863, which describes Lawrence's adventures when he attempted to join the Confederate forces during the American Civil War, was captured by Northern authorities, and sent back to England. He continued producing successful novels almost every other year. *Guy Livingstone* was parodied by Bret *Harte in his 'Guy Heaveystone'.

LAWRENCE, T. E. (Thomas Edward) (1888–1935) Soldier and writer, born at Tremadoc, Caernarvonshire, and educated at Oxford High School and Jesus College, Oxford. His daring exploits in the Middle East during the First World War won him the confidence and admiration of the Arabs, and later made him, as 'Lawrence of Arabia', a figure of myth. His subsequent career was marked by mental breakdown, self-accusation, and anxiety about his legend; he enlisted in the RAF in 1922 as an aircraft hand under the name of John Hume Ross, and a year later joined the tank corps as T. E. Shaw. He later returned to the RAF, retiring from it shortly before he was killed in a motorcycle accident. *The Seven Pillars of Wisdom*, his account of the Arab Revolt, was printed for private circulation in 1926 (pub. 1935); a shortened version, *Revolt in the Desert*, was published in 1927. Winston *Churchill declared it one of 'the greatest books ever written in the English language'. His account of life in the RAF, *The Mint* by '352087 A/c Ross', appeared posthumously in 1936 (USA) and 1955 (UK). See L. James, *The Golden Warrior* (rev. edn, 1995).

LAWRENCE, Sir Thomas (1769–1830) Painter. His portraits are distinguished for their courtliness and social elegance. He painted portraits for the Waterloo Chamber at Windsor Castle of persons who took part in the defeat of Napoleon.

Laws of Ecclesiastical Politie, Of the By Richard *Hooker, a philosophical and theological treatise in eight books (Books I–IV 1593, Book V 1597, Books VI and VIII 1648, Book VII 1662). The work is a defence, written in a dignified and harmonious prose, of the position of the *Church of England against the attacks of the Puritans. Books I–IV deal with first principles: the first, which has been the most influential, is a philosophical discussion of the origin and nature of law in general, as governing the universe and human society, and of the distinction between laws of a permanent and of a temporary character; the second, third, and fourth deal with the assertion of the Puritan party that Scripture is the sole guide in determining the actions of a Christian and the form of church polity, and that the Anglican Church is corrupted with popish rites and ceremonies. The later books deal with questions of worship and governance. The fifth is a defence of the *Book of *Common Prayer*. The last three books do not represent work prepared by Hooker for the press; a finished version of these may have been destroyed. According to Hooker's original scheme, the incomplete Book VI was to have dealt with *presbyterianism. Book VII is a defence of the role of bishops, and Book VIII explores the nature of the king's supreme authority, both contentious topics in the 17th century. The *Laws* has been seen as the first major work on theology, philosophy, and political thought written in English. See *The Folger Library Edition of the Works of Richard Hooker*, ed. W. S. Hill (1977–98).
See PURITANISM.

LAWSON, Henry *See* BULLETIN.

lay A short lyric or narrative poem intended to be sung; originally applied specifically to the poems, usually dealing with matters of history or romantic adventure, which were sung by minstrels.

LAȜAMON (*fl.* 13th century) A priest of Areley Kings, Worcestershire. He wrote the *Brut*, a history of England from the legendary Brutus to *Cadwallader, drawing mostly on *Wace's French version of *Geoffrey of Monmouth's *Historia Regum Britanniae*. The *Brut* gives for the first time in English the story of Arthur and those of Lear, Cymbeline, and other figures prominent in later English literature. The poem is in 32,241 short lines, and, though written in early Middle English, mainly observes the later Old English alliterative half-line with occasional rhyme. It employs some of the epic formulas, such as eloquent similes, and stylistic features of Old English such as resourceful diction also contribute to this transitional poem's quality. There are two 13th-century manuscripts, both of which are in the edition by F. Madden (3 vols, 1847); see G. L. Brook and R. F. Leslie (eds), EETS os 250, 277 (1963, 1978).

Lay of the Last Minstrel, The A poem in six cantos by Walter *Scott, published in 1805. Scott's first important original work, it is a metrical romance in irregular stanzas (much of it in rhymed octosyllabics) put in the mouth of an ancient minstrel, the last of his race, who bewails the decline of his art and his nation as he tells a Border tale of feud and witchcraft and frustrated love set in the mid-16th century.

Lays of Ancient Rome A collection of poems by Thomas *Macaulay, published 1842, in which Macaulay takes episodes from Roman history (some from *Livy), including the defence of the bridge leading to Rome against the Tuscans ('Horatius'); 'The Battle of Lake Regillus'; and 'Virginia'. These ballads with their hypnotic rhythms and heroic patriotic attitudes were immensely popular though controversial in their popularization of history. Later editions included rousing poems from British history written in Macaulay's youth, first published in *Knight's Quarterly Magazine* (1823–4): these include 'The Battle of Naseby', 'Ivry', and 'Moncontour'. 'Epitaph of a Jacobite', a touching lament by a follower of James II, was written later, in 1847, and was subsequently included with the *Lays*.

Lazarillo de Tormes The first of the Spanish *picaresque romances, of uncertain authorship (earliest surviving edition 1554). It is the ironical fictional autobiography of the son of a miller, who lived on the banks of the Tormes, near Salamanca. The boy begins his career of wit and fraud as the guide of a blind man whose money and food he steals. He passes into the service of various poverty-stricken or rascally employers, and reaches the position of town-crier of Toledo. His career provides occasion for many satirical portraits of Spanish types. David Rowland's English translation was published in 1576.

LAZARUS, Emma (1849–87) American poet, born in New York, remembered for her 1883 poem 'The New Colossus'. Her poetry and other activities became more concerned with Judaism after she read George *Eliot's **Daniel Deronda*. See Esther Schor, *Emma Lazarus* (2006).

LEACOCK, Stephen Butler (1869–1944) Humorist, born near Winchester, Hampshire, of well-to-do parents, but brought up and educated in Canada, where he was for many years lecturer, then professor in political economy, at McGill University, Montreal. He wrote biographies of Mark *Twain (1932) and Charles *Dickens (1933), but is best known for his many volumes of collected humorous essays and stories; these include *Literary Lapses* (1910), *Nonsense Novels* (1911), *Sunshine Sketches of a Little Town* (1912), *Arcadian Adventures with the Idle Rich* (1914), and *Frenzied Fiction* (1918). J. B. *Priestley described his best work as 'balanced between cutting satire and sheer absurdity' (introduction to *The Bodley Head Leacock*, 1957).

Leader A weekly periodical started in 1850 by George Henry *Lewes and Thornton Leigh *Hunt, to which Lewes contributed satirical pieces and lively theatre reviews under the pseudonym of 'Vivian'. The staff included Herbert *Spencer and Alexander *Kinglake. It ran until 1866, in its later issues as *Saturday Analyst and Leader*.

LEAPOR, Mary (1722–46) Poet, born in Northamptonshire, the daughter of a gardener who worked first on the estate of Sir John Blencowe (1642–1726), then as a nursery gardener in Brackley. She was in early years discouraged from writing and 'overstudying'. She was in domestic service in several houses, one of which appears in the comic 'country house' poem *Crumble Hall*. Despite this lowly position, she produced a distinguished body of work which attracted the attention of Bridget Freemantle (1698–1779), a rector's daughter, who persuaded her to consider publication. Leapor died of measles before this plan was executed, but her *Poems upon Several Occasions* appeared in 1748 and 1751 with support from Samuel *Richardson and David *Garrick. Her work, which has been edited by Richard Greene and Ann Messenger (2003), is predominantly satiric in tone: its heroic couplets declare her admiration for Alexander *Pope, as do her sharply drawn and realized characters, but she also writes tellingly about her own position as a woman writer who runs the risk of being thought 'mighty proud' by her neighbours, and who has to endure the condescension of patrons less sensitive than Miss Freemantle ('Artemesia'). Her verses 'Upon her Play Being Returned to her, Stained with Claret' elegantly demonstrate both her good humour and her sense of her own worth.

LEAR, Edward (1812–88) Artist, traveller, and writer, born in Holloway, the twentieth child of a stockbroker, and brought up largely by his elder sister Ann. He worked as a zoological draughtsman until he came under the patronage of the earl of Derby, for whose grandchildren he wrote *A Book of Nonsense* (1845), with his own *limericks and illustrations. He travelled widely, and published accounts of Italy (1846), Albania and Illyria (1851), Calabria (1852), and Corsica (1870); he also visited and sketched Egypt, the Holy Land, Greece, and India. He settled in 1871 in San Remo and died there. His posthumous reputation as a watercolourist has risen steadily and as a writer he is remembered for his *nonsense verses, with their linguistic fantasies and inventiveness and their occasional touches of underlying melancholy. Lear suffered from epilepsy and depression, and despite many close friends (including *Tennyson's wife Emily) from loneliness. Later nonsense volumes were *Nonsense Songs, Stories, Botany and Alphabets* (1871), which contains 'The Owl and the Pussy-Cat' and 'The Jumblies'; *More Nonsense, Pictures, Rhymes, Botany etc.* (1871); and *Laughable Lyrics* (1877), with the Dong, the Yonghy-Bonghy-Bò, and the Pobble who has no toes. There are lives by Angus Davidson (1938) and Vivien Noakes (1968).

Lear, King *See* King Lear.

Leatherstocking Tales, The A sequence of novels by James Fenimore *Cooper published 1823–41, which centre on Natty Bumppo, a hunter and marksman given different names according to his role in each novel.

LEAVIS, F. R. (Frank Raymond) (1895–1978) Critic, born the son of a piano dealer in Cambridge, where he attended the Perse School. After war service as a stretcher-bearer in an ambulance unit, he studied history, then English, at Emmanuel College, Cambridge, going on to write a Ph.D. thesis on the development of English journalism. While a probationary Cambridge lecturer (1927–32) he married Queenie Roth (*see* Leavis, Queenie Dorothy), co-founded the journal **Scrutiny*, and wrote his first major book, *New Bearings in English Poetry* (1932), which, under the critical influence of T. S. *Eliot, lamented the feebleness of most late Victorian verse and identified a recent recovery in the poetic vigour of Gerard Manley *Hopkins, Edward *Thomas, Eliot, Ezra *Pound, and W. B. *Yeats. After these years of insecurity, he secured a college lectureship (1935), then fellowship at Downing College, where he taught until 1962, sending out many devoted students into the teaching profession as missionaries armed with his critical principles and cultural values. Among his early works, *For Continuity* (1933), *Culture and Environment* (1933, with Denys Thompson), followed by *Education and the University* (1943), stress the importance of creating within university English departments a discriminating intellectual elite whose task it would be to preserve the cultural continuity of English life and literature, a continuity he believed to be threatened by mass media, technology, and advertising. He soon became identified as a leading figure in a 'Cambridge school' of criticism, combining the 'close reading' of poetry advocated by I. A. *Richards with his own pessimistic diagnosis of modern cultural decline. His influential book *Revaluation* (1936) continued to reshape the main line of English poetry, tracing it through John *Donne and Alexander *Pope to Hopkins and Eliot, and aiming iconoclastic attacks at Edmund *Spenser, *Milton, and P. B. *Shelley. In the 1940s he turned his attention to fiction, notably in *The Great Tradition* (1948), in which he pronounces the great English novelists to be Jane *Austen, George *Eliot, Henry *James, and Joseph *Conrad, dismissing other major fiction (e.g. that of Henry *Fielding, Laurence *Sterne, Thomas *Hardy, and most of Charles *Dickens's work apart from **Hard Times*) in notoriously summary fashion. In later years he reversed his position on Dickens (see *Dickens the Novelist*, with Q. D. Leavis, 1970), and increasingly abandoned his earlier devotion to T. S. Eliot in favour of the contrary influence of D. H. *Lawrence, notably in the eulogistic *D. H. Lawrence: Novelist* (1955). His later essays appeared in *The Common Pursuit* (1952) and several subsequent collections. Throughout his career he cast himself as a persecuted outsider to the literary 'establishment', disparaged celebrated contemporary writers (e.g. the *Sitwells and Stephen *Spender) in offensively belittling terms, and engaged in bitter public disputes with rival critics. A notably ill-tempered public debate arose from his *Two Cultures? The Significance of C. P. *Snow* (1962). Nonetheless Leavis was granted grudging admiration even by his many injured adversaries for bringing a new urgency and moral seriousness into English criticism. See Ian MacKillop, *F. R. Leavis: A Life in Criticism* (1995).

LEAVIS, Queenie Dorothy (1906–81) Née Roth, scholar and critic, a draper's daughter born in Edmonton, where she attended Latymer School. She studied English at Girton College, Cambridge. Her orthodox Jewish family repudiated her upon her marriage (1929) to F. R. *Leavis, a Gentile. Her Ph.D. thesis, supervised in part by I. A. *Richards, was published as *Fiction and the Reading Public* (1932), a pioneering study in the sociology of literature which examines the contemporary commercial market in fiction in historical perspective. She worked 1932–53 as an unofficial sub-editor for **Scrutiny* while raising three children, also contributing many reviews and articles, notably on Jane *Austen. A strong influence upon her husband's work, she collaborated with him on *Dickens the Novelist* (1970). Her essays were reprinted posthumously in the three-volume *Collected Essays* (ed. G. Singh, 1983–9).

le Carré, John (1931–) Pseudonym of David John Moore Cornwell, who was educated at Oxford, taught briefly at Eton College, then joined the Foreign Office. His earliest novels were conventional thrillers. The first, *Call for the Dead* (1961), introduced the mild-mannered secret agent George Smiley, who appears in many of his later books. *The Spy Who Came in from the Cold* (1963), a Cold War thriller inspired by the Berlin Wall, brought le Carré immediate fame. Its successors, including *The Looking Glass War* (1965), *A Small Town in Germany* (1968), *Tinker, Tailor, Soldier, Spy* (1974), *Smiley's People* (1980), *The Little Drummer Girl* (1983), *The Russia House* (1989), and *The Night Manager* (1993), confirmed his reputation as a storyteller who could combine elaborate plotting and realistic detail with a moral complexity unusual in the genre. The ending of the Cold War persuaded le Carré to look beyond the East–West conflict for his plots. *Our Game* (1995) is set in the aftermath of the break-up of the Soviet Union; *The Constant Gardener* (2001) takes place in Africa against a backdrop of corruption in the pharmaceutical industry; *The Mission Song* (2006) tells the story of a Western-backed coup in the Congo.

LECKY, William Edward Hartpole (1838–1903) Historian, born in Co. Dublin; educated at Trinity College, Dublin. His *History of the Rise and Influence of Rationalism in Europe* (1865) was the first of his works to attract attention; it traces the progress of rationalism from religious dogmatism to tolerance. His *History of European Morals from Augustus to Charlemagne* (1869) was also widely read. The final volumes of his *History of England in the Eighteenth Century* (1878–92) address the history of Ireland, challenging J. A. *Froude's misstatements.

Le CLÉZIO, Jean-Marie (1940–) French novelist, born in Nice of a French mother and a Mauritian father who also held British citizenship. His first novel, *Le Procès-verbal* (1963: *The Interrogation*), was awarded the Prix Renaudot. Since then he has written some seventeen novels, and these are increasingly preoccupied with the themes of travel, nature, colonialism, and dislocation, such as *Désert* (1980: *Desert*), whose heroine, Lalla, leaves her native shanty town in Morocco for Marseilles, and the semi-autobiographical *Onitsha* (1991: trans. *Onitsha*, 1997), set in 1948, whose hero, Fintan, travels from France to Nigeria in search of his English father. Le Clézio was awarded the *Nobel Prize for Literature in 2008.

LECONTE de LISLE, Charles-Marie-René (1818–94) French poet and leader of the *Parnassians. He published a number of collections, including *Poèmes antiques* (1852: *Antique Poems*), *Poèmes barbares* (1862: *Barbaric Poems*), and *Poèmes tragiques* (1884: *Tragic Poems*).

Lectures on the English Poets A critical work by William *Hazlitt, delivered as public lectures in 1818 and published that year. The series begins with *Chaucer and *Spenser, concluding with *Wordsworth and *Coleridge. By contrast with these *Lake Poets, *Shakespeare is praised for his lack of egotism, and immersion in his characters. This view influenced the poetics of *Keats, who attended the lectures.

LEDGWIDGE, Francis (1891–1917) Irish poet, born in Slane, Co. Meath. He worked as a labourer and was befriended by Lord *Dunsany, who saw in his poems the promise of an authentic Irish rural voice, and wrote introductions for his three collections, *Songs of the Field* (1916), *Songs of Peace* (1917), and *Last Songs* (1918). Most of his poems are Keatsian lyrics of the countryside, although there are some that deal with Irish and Welsh mythology in a refreshingly un-Yeatsian manner. He is remembered chiefly for 'Lament for Thomas McDonagh' (*sic*) and the other elegies he wrote in Ebrington Barracks, Derry, for the executed poet-rebels of 1916. He was killed by a stray shell behind the lines near Ypres during the First World War.

LEE, Harper (1926–) American novelist, born in Alabama, a close friend of Truman *Capote. She is known for her 1960 Pulitzer Prize-winning novel *To Kill a Mockingbird*, which explores themes of racial injustice, courage, and childhood through the experiences of Scout Finch, a small-town tomboy. Widely celebrated and much studied, it is Lee's only novel. Lee was awarded the Presidential Medal of Freedom in 2007.

LEE, Harriet (1757–1851) Daughter of an actor, who ran a private school in Bath with her sister Sophia *Lee. She became both dramatist and novelist, but succeeded only as the latter. An *epistolary novel, *Errors of Innocence*, appeared in 1786; *Clare Lennox* in 1797; and her very successful *Canterbury Tales* (in part a collaboration with Sophia) in 1798, with three further volumes in 1805. The twelve stories of the *Tales*, told by travellers accidentally thrown together, include 'Kruitzner', on which Lord *Byron based his verse drama *Werner*, with acknowledgement. Her own adaptation of the story for the stage was briefly performed. She was a friend of Jane and Anna *Porter; of Sir Thomas *Lawrence, and of William *Godwin, who proposed to her in 1798.

LEE, Sir Henry (1533–1611) Master of the armoury, queen's champion, and ranger of Woodstock. Lee was closely involved in much Elizabethan pageantry and, around 1570, probably initiated the annual celebration of the queen's accession day (17 November) with tilts and allegorical devices, involving speeches, poetry, and music: some of these are reflected in Philip *Sidney's revised *Arcadia*. He played a part in the Woodstock entertainments of 1575 and 1592; on the second occasion the queen also visited one of Lee's houses at Ditchley. On his own retirement as queen's champion in 1590 the poem, which Lee may have written himself, 'His golden locks, Time hath to silver turned', was sung. The event was commemorated by George *Peele in his **Polyhymnia*. Lee appears in Walter *Scott's **Woodstock* and there is a life by E. K. *Chambers (1936).

LEE, Hermione (1948–) Critic and biographer, brought up in London and educated at the Lycée Français Charles de Gaulle, City of London School for Girls, and St Hilda's College, Oxford. Lee has taught at the universities of Liverpool, York, and Oxford. Her books include *The Novels of Virginia Woolf* (1977); *Elizabeth Bowen* (1981; rev. 1999); *Philip Roth* (1982); *Willa Cather: A Life Saved Up* (1989; rev. 2008); *Virginia Woolf* (1996); and *Edith Wharton* (2007). She has also published a collection of essays on biography and autobiography, *Body Parts: Essays on Life-Writing* (2005).
See BIOGRAPHY.

LEE, Laurie (1914–97) Writer, born in Gloucestershire and educated at Slad village school and Stroud Central School. He worked for some time in an office in Stroud before travelling in Europe from 1935 to 1939, and then worked in various film units, for the Ministry of Information and the Festival of Britain, among other employers. His volumes of poetry (*The Sun my Monument*, 1944; *The Bloom of Candles*, 1947; *My Many-Coated Man*, 1955) show a sensuous apprehension of the natural world, as does his best-known work, the widely popular *Cider with Rosie* (1959), a highly evocative and nostalgic account of his country boyhood in a secluded Cotswold valley. It describes a vanished rural world of home-made wine, village school, church outings, 'a world of silence…of hard work and necessary patience…of white roads, rutted by hooves and cartwheels, innocent of oil and petrol'; Lee described himself as a chance witness of 'the end of a thousand years' life'. The 'Rosie' of the title is a village girl who 'baptized [him] with her cidrous kisses' behind a haycock. A second autobiographical volume, *As I Walked out One Midsummer Morning* (1969), describes his departure from Stroud, his walk to London, and his months in Spain on the eve of the Spanish Civil War. *A Moment of War* (1991) is a sequel. His other works include screenplays, travel books, and an essay on the birth of his daughter, *The Firstborn* (1964). See Valerie Grove, *Laurie Lee: The Well-loved Stranger* (1999).

LEE, Nathaniel (?1649–92) Educated at Westminster School and Trinity College, Cambridge, a failed actor turned playwright, whose tragedies, marked by extravagance and passion, were long popular. They include *Nero* (1675), *Sophonisba* and *Gloriana* (1676), all in rhymed heroic couplets; his best-known tragedy, *The *Rival Queens* (1677), in blank verse; *Theodosius* (1680); and one of his most serious dramas, *Lucius Junius Brutus*, which was banned for its anti-monarchical speeches after only three performances. He collaborated with John *Dryden in *Oedipus* (1679) and *The Duke of Guise* (1682), and wrote one comedy, *The Princess of Cleve* (?1681), which is nearly as extreme as his tragedies. He lost his reason, was confined to Bedlam 1684–9, and died after a drinking bout. Several editions of his collected plays appeared in the 18th century, and an edition in 2 vols, ed. T. B. Stroup and A. L. Cooke, in 1954–5.

LEE, Sir Sidney (1859–1926) Editor and biographer, born Solomon Lazarus Levi. He was educated at City of London School and Balliol College, Oxford. He was a member of the editorial staff of *The *Dictionary of National Biography* from the beginning in 1882 and became joint editor in 1890 and sole editor from 1891. His publications include *Stratford-on-Avon from the Earliest Times to the Death of Shakespeare* (1885; new edn 1906), *Life of William Shakespeare* (1898; rev. edn 1925), which for many years was considered the standard biography, *Life of Queen Victoria* (1902), *Great Englishmen of the 16th Century* (1904), *Elizabethan Sonnets* (1904), *Shakespeare and the Modern Stage* (1906), *The French Renaissance in England* (1910), *Principles of Biography* (1911), *Shakespeare and the Italian Renaissance* (1915), and the *Life of King Edward VII* (1925–7).

LEE, Sophia (1750–1824) Daughter of an actor, who ran a private school in Bath with her sister Harriet *Lee. She had some success as both dramatist and novelist. Her play *The Chapter of Accidents* (1780) was frequently staged; and her first novel, *The Recess* (1783–5), a form of early *historical novel, sold well and was translated into French. A long ballad, *The Hermit's Tale*, followed in 1787, and a verse tragedy, *Almeyda, Queen of Grenada* (1796). She contributed to her sister's *Canterbury Tales* (1798), and published an *epistolary autobiographical novel, *The Life of a Lover* (1804).

LEE, Vernon (1856–1935) Born as Violet Paget; she grew up multilingual in Europe and spent most of her life in Italy. She was the sister of Eugene *Lee-Hamilton, and derived her pseudonym from his name. Influenced by Walter *Pater, and a contributor to the **Yellow Book*, she was the author of more than forty books and many essays. The subjects of her non-fiction include history, art, literary criticism, ethics, aesthetics, biography, and travel. She also wrote short and full-length fiction and drama. Her interest in psychology and her knowledge of German ideas in the discipline helped her develop—or at least introduce into English—a theory of the aesthetics of empathy. Lee's pacifism during the First World War contributed to the decline in her popularity and influence. Later scholars have helped restore her reputation, and her tales of the supernatural, including the enduringly popular *Hauntings* (1890), have often been reprinted. See Vineta Colby, *Vernon Lee: A Literary Life* (2003).

LEECH, John (1817–64) Caricaturist and illustrator, who formed a lifelong friendship with W. M. *Thackeray at Charterhouse; he was also a close friend of Charles *Dickens, whose *A *Christmas Carol* and other Christmas Books he illustrated. From 1841 until his death he contributed to **Punch* political cartoons and scenes of everyday middle-class life. He drew for a number of other magazines, and illustrated the works of Robert Smith *Surtees.

'Leech Gatherer, The' *See* 'Resolution and Independence'.

LEE-HAMILTON, Eugene (1845–1907) Poet, novelist, and half-brother of Violet Paget (alias Vernon *Lee). Raised in France and later entering Oriel College, Oxford, he left university without a degree in 1866 and was employed in the Foreign Office in 1869. He lived most of his life in Florence and, health permitting, hosted intellectual contemporaries including Edith *Wharton and Henry *James. Works such as *Imaginary Sonnets* (1888) and *The Sonnets of the Wingless Hours* (1894) demonstrate his skilful control of the sonnet form and use of dramatic impersonal voice. He published two novels and a metrical translation of *Dante's *Inferno* (1898).

Le FANU, Sheridan [pron. Léff-anew] (1814–73) Journalist, newspaper proprietor, and writer of novels and tales of mystery and the supernatural, who came of a well-educated Dublin family of Huguenot origins, connected by marriage with the Sheridans; his paternal grandmother was the sister of Richard Brinsley *Sheridan. After graduating at Trinity College, Dublin, Le Fanu was called to the bar, but never practised. By 1840 he had published a dozen or so stories (including 'A Strange Event in the Life of Schalken the Painter', rated by M. R. *James as 'one of the best of Le Fanu's good things') in the *Dublin University Magazine*, which had been founded in 1833 by a group of young Trinity College men with strong literary interests. From 1840 onwards he became increasingly involved in Irish journalism as editor of the *Warden* and owner or part-owner of that and other papers. His first two novels, *The Cock and Anchor* (1845) and *Torlogh O'Brien* (1847), were in the tradition of Walter *Scott and Harrison *Ainsworth; and it was not until 1861, three years after his wife's death, that his main output began with the serialization in the *Dublin University Magazine*, which he acquired in that year, of *The House by the Churchyard*. There followed *Wylder's Hand* (issued in book form in 1864), **Uncle Silas* (1864), *Guy Deverell* (1865), *The Tenants of Malory* (1867), *A Lost Name* (1868), *The Wyvern Mystery* (1869), *Checkmate* (1871), *The Rose and the Key* (1871), and *Willing to Die* (1873). In 1872 appeared the remarkable collection of stories entitled **In a Glass Darkly*.

Le Fanu was one of the best-sellers of the 1860s–1880s, but he then entered a period of what has been called 'unmitigated famelessness'. The later revival of interest dates from the publication in 1923 of *Madam Crowl's Ghost and Other Tales of Mystery*, a collection of forgotten tales by Le Fanu edited by M. R. James, who considered that Le Fanu 'stands absolutely in the first rank as a writer of *ghost stories'. Since then Le Fanu's reputation has steadily risen, and he is now recognized as the equal of Wilkie *Collins as a writer of mysteries, and as occupying a prominent place in the field of the sinister and the supernatural.

Left Book Club Publishing venture founded in 1936 by Victor *Gollancz and others. Modelled on commercial book club lines, its educational aim was to resist the rise of Fascism and Nazism by providing, as Gollancz wrote in the first issue of *Left Book Club News*, 'the indispensable basis of *knowledge* without which a really effective United Front of all men and women cannot be built'. In its heyday it had about 50,000 members. The vast majority of its publications were factual (though three novels and one play, *Waiting for Lefty*, 1937, by Clifford *Odets, were included), and the best-known title today is George *Orwell's *The Road to Wigan Pier* (1937), which appeared with an introduction by Gollancz warning readers against the second half of the book in which Orwell, he claimed, appeared as 'devil's advocate for the case against Socialism'. The Club was dissolved in 1948.

legal deposit libraries Under the terms of the Legal Deposit Libraries Act (2003), which superseded the Copyright Act of 1911 and the Irish Copyright Act of 1963, the six libraries in question (the British Library, London; the Bodleian Library, Oxford; the University Library, Cambridge; the National Library of Wales, Aberystwyth; the National Library of Scotland, Edinburgh, and Trinity College, Dublin) are entitled to receive free of charge a copy of every British or Irish publication. It is the responsibility of publishers to send publications directly to the British Library within a month of their appearance, but the other five libraries must make a written claim for them within a year of the date of publication via the Agency for the Legal Deposit Libraries. The legislation covers all printed works, including maps, printed music, journals, and newspapers.

LE GALLIENNE, Richard (1866–1947) Poet, novelist, and critic, of Channel Islands descent, born in Liverpool where he was an apprentice accountant for seven years. His first volume, *My Ladies' Sonnets and Other 'Vain and Amatorious' Verses*, was printed privately in Liverpool in 1887 and in 1888 he left for London. There he became attached to the *fin-de-siècle* group which centred on Aubrey *Beardsley; he was an original member of the *Rhymers Club with W. B. *Yeats, Oscar *Wilde, and Lionel *Johnson. He contributed to the **Yellow Book* and throughout the 1890s wrote verse and literary criticism; he published several romantic novels, including *The Quest for the Golden Girl* (1896); *The Romance of Zion Chapel* (1898); and *Young Lives* (1899), which describes the early London years of his first marriage (his first wife Mildred died of typhoid in 1894). *The Romantic '90s* (1926) is an account of this period. In 1901 he settled in the United States, returning to Europe in 1927 to spend his last years in the south of France.

Legend of Good Women, The Written by Geoffrey *Chaucer and of uncertain date, based on works including *Ovid's *Heroides*, and *Boccaccio's *De Claris Mulieribus*. The prologue survives in two versions, known as F (from Bodley MS Fairfax 16, the best of the MSS of this version) and G (from University Library Cambridge MS Gg 4.27). It opens with some famous lines in praise of the daisy (conforming to the tradition of 'Marguerite' poems in French) and continues with the rebuking of the sleeping narrator by the god of love because of his previous dispraise of women (another commonplace convention). The narrator vows to make amends by composing this work in praise of women celebrated for their fidelity in love, as directed by the queen of love, Alceste. The unfinished poem contains nine stories of famous women: *Cleopatra, Thisbe, Dido, Hypsipyle and Medea, Lucrece, Ariadne, *Philomela, Phyllis, and Hypermnestra. The poem is also significant for its being the first attested use of the heroic couplet in Chaucer. See H. Phillips and N. Havely, *Chaucer's Dream Poetry* (1997).

Legend of Montrose, A A novel by Walter *Scott, published 1819, in **Tales of my Landlord*, 3rd series. The novel is based on an episode in the earl of Montrose's campaign of 1644 to raise Scotland for Charles I against the Covenant forces of the marquis of Argyle. The love of Allan McAulay for the mysterious Annot Lyle is the main theme, but the most interesting part of the story is the character of Dugald Dalgetty, the pedantic mercenary who, like so many of his 17th-century compatriots, had served in the Thirty Years War and will fight for either king or Covenant, whichever pays best.

LE GUIN, Ursula (1929–) American novelist and short story writer, born in Berkeley, California. Her numerous works of *science fiction and *fantasy for both children and adults have been widely admired for their distinguished prose and their imaginative and thoughtful speculations. She creates her worlds with an anthropologist's eye for detail and ambiguity. Her works include the 'Hainish' sequence, beginning with *Rocannon's World* (1966), *Planet of Exile* (1966), and *City of Illusions* (1967). Most of her science fiction, including many of the stories in *The Birthday of the World* (2002), is set in the Hainish universe. Earthsea is the setting for her fantasy sequence: *A Wizard of Earthsea* (1968), *The Tombs of Atuan* (1971), and *The Farthest Shore* (1972), later expanded by *Tehanu* (1990), *The Other Wind*, and *Tales from Earthsea* (both 2001). *The Left Hand of Darkness* (1969), a *Hugo winner, imagines an androgynous species to consider issues of gender. *The Dispossessed* (1974) and *Always Coming Home* (1985) are thoughtful utopias. Other novels include *Malafrena* (1979), set in an imaginary European country, and *The Beginning Place* (1980), a realistic novel which touches, as does much of her occasional criticism, on why we need fantasy.

LEHMANN, John (1907–87) Poet, publisher, and editor, brother of Rosamond *Lehmann. He was educated at Eton College and Trinity College, Cambridge, where he became friendly with the poet Julian Bell (1908–37), nephew of Virginia *Woolf; from 1931 he was associated with the *Hogarth Press, and became managing editor in 1938. The press published his first book of poems, *A Garden Revisited* (1931), and several other volumes. His *Collected Poems 1930–63* appeared in 1963. Lehmann is probably best known as the editor of **New Writing* (1936–41) and of the **London Magazine* (1954–61). His three volumes of autobiography, *The Whispering Gallery* (1951), *I am my Brother* (1960), and *The Ample Proposition* (1966), record a life rich in literary friendships and activity, as do his several volumes of reminiscence and biography, which include works on the *Sitwells (1968), the Woolfs, and Rupert *Brooke (1980). See Adrian Wright, *John Lehmann: A Pagan Adventurer* (1998).

LEHMANN, Rosamond Nina (1901–90) Novelist, sister of John *Lehmann, born in Buckinghamshire. She was educated privately and at Girton College, Cambridge, and achieved a *succès de scandale* with her first novel, *Dusty Answer* (1927), which describes a girl's awakening into womanhood. Her second novel, *A Note in Music* (1930), also created a stir with its treatment of homosexuality. *Invitation to the Waltz* (1932) describes the impact on Olivia Curtis of her first dance; its sequel, *The Weather in the Streets* (1936), takes Olivia through a failed marriage, an adulterous love affair, and an abortion. *The Echoing Grove* (1953), a novel about the relationship of two sisters, was followed only after many years by *The Swan in the Evening: Fragments of an Inner Life* (1967). This short autobiography recalls her childhood, then describes the sudden death of her daughter in 1958 and her spiritual experiences which convince her of her daughter's survival after death. There is a biography by Selina Hastings (2002).

LEIBNIZ, Gottfried Wilhelm (1646–1716) German philosopher and mathematician, born at Leipzig, the founder of the Society (later Academy) of Sciences at Berlin. He discovered the infinitesimal calculus at about the same time as Isaac *Newton, but by a different method. As a philosopher he was inspired by René *Descartes, Benedict de *Spinoza, and Thomas *Hobbes, but broke away from Descartes's mechanical conception of the universe. Matter he regarded as a multitude of monads, each a nucleus of force and a microcosm or concentration of the universe. Admitting that the interaction of spirit and matter is inexplicable, he assumed a 'pre-established harmony' between them: the spirit is modified by final causes, bodies by efficient causes; the two series are brought together, like two clocks ticking in unison (the simile is *Voltaire's), by a harmony established from all time by God, the supreme monad and perfect exemplar of the human soul. Voltaire satirized his 'optimism' in **Candide*. His system is embodied in his *Théodicée* (1710) and *Monadologie* (1714), written in French. Leibniz was one of the chief forces in the German *Enlightenment.

LEICESTER, Robert Dudley, earl of (1532/3–88) The favourite of *Elizabeth I and uncle of Philip *Sidney. He figures in Walter *Scott's **Kenilworth* as the unfortunate Amy Robsart's husband.

LEIGH, Augusta (1784–1851) Half-sister of Lord *Byron, daughter of his father by the latter's earlier marriage to Lady Carmarthen. Augusta's relations with Byron have been the subject of much speculation, and it is probable that he was the father of her daughter Elizabeth Medora, born in 1814.

LEIGH, Mike (1943–) Writer and stage and film director, who has evolved a unique way of working in extended periods of intense improvisation and collaboration with actors. Raised in Salford, Lancashire, Leigh trained at RADA, the London International Film School, and the Central School of Art and Design. His work has the vivacity, humour, and social detail of a latter-day William *Hogarth or Charles *Dickens. His many plays now seem like a preparation for a prodigious output of television and feature films, although he returned to the stage in 2005 with *Two Thousand Years*, drawing for the first time on his Jewish background. His films range from the suburban repression of *Bleak Moments* (1971) to the inner-city anomie of *Meantime* (1983). *Abigail's Party* (1977), his best-known stage and television play, is a classic of social embarrassment. *Life is Sweet* (1990), the provocative, Dostoevskian *Naked* (1993), and the richly poignant *Secrets and Lies* (1996, winner of the Cannes Palme d'Or) are among the best British modern films; while *Vera Drake* (2005, Leone d'oro at Venice) returned to the world of his parents, a doctor and a midwife, in its sympathetic portrayal of a 1950s backstreet abortionist. *Happy-Go-Lucky* (2008), a portrait of a cheerful primary school teacher, is an uncharacteristically sunny film. Many of Leigh's plays and screenplays are in print. Michael Coveney's critical biography, *The World According to Mike Leigh*, appeared in 1996, and a collection of interviews was published in 2000.

LEIGHTON, Frederic, Lord (1830–96) Victorian classical artist, born at Scarborough, but educated on the Continent. In 1855 his *Cimabue's Celebrated Madonna Carried in*

Procession through the Streets of Florence (1855) was shown at the *Royal Academy. It was immensely successful, offered a real challenge to the native *Pre-Raphaelite Brotherhood, and was bought by Queen *Victoria. In the 1860s he made significant contributions to the new experimental 'aesthetic' painting, but in the 1870s began to occupy a more orthodox position in the art establishment, becoming president of the Royal Academy in 1878, and a peer in 1896. His interest in Florentine Renaissance subjects led to his commission to illustrate **Romola*. In Rome in the early 1850s he moved in the circle of Adelaide *Sartoris, and was to appear as the exuberant Mr Kiowski in her *A Week in a French Country House* (1867); he also met there Robert *Browning and W. M. *Thackeray. He appeared as Gaston Phoebus in Benjamin *Disraeli's **Lothair*, and as the public artist Lord Mellifont in Henry *James's story 'The Private Life' (1892). See L. and R. Ormond, *Lord Leighton* (1975).

Leinster, Book of An Irish manuscript of the 12th century, containing mythological, genealogical, and historical texts in prose and verse, including versions of **Táin-Bó-Cuailnge* and *The Fate of the Sons of Usnach* (*see* DEIRDRE).

L.E.L. Initials used as pseudonym by Letitia Elizabeth *Landon.

LELAND, John (*c.*1503–1552) The earliest of modern English antiquaries, educated at St *Paul's School and Christ's College, Cambridge. He studied at Paris, took holy orders, and by the 1530s was involved with the royal libraries, claiming he received a commission in 1533 to search monastic and collegiate libraries for old authors. Between *c.*1533 and 1543, he made tours through England, researching a great account of the 'history and antiquities of this nation', but the work remained a mass of undigested notes. By 1551 he was insane. Leland's *Itinerary* was first published at Oxford, in nine volumes, by Thomas *Hearne in 1710–12; and his *Collectanea* in six (1715). Leland claimed to have 'conserved many good authors, the which otherwise had been like to have perished', in the dissolution of the religious houses. There is an edition of the *Itinerary* by Lucy Toulmin Smith (1906–10).

LELY, Sir Peter (1618–80) British portrait painter, of Dutch origin, who is best known as the painter of the voluptuous beauties who graced the court of Charles II. He became principal painter to the king in 1661 and his style is a vulgarized version of Sir Anthony *Van Dyck's. Lely was a friend of Richard *Lovelace, who eulogized him in verse. Lely's poignant double portrait of *Charles I and the Duke of York* (1647) inspired Lovelace's poem 'See what a clouded majesty', which contains the somewhat unexpected praise: 'None but my Lilly ever drew a mind.' His most characteristic works are the *Windsor Beauties* (Hampton Court).

LEMON, Mark (1809–70) Magazine editor and playwright, born in London, educated at Cheam School. He was a founder, first joint editor, then editor of the comic weekly **Punch*, from 1841 until his death, and contributor to other periodicals. His shrewd and adventurous editorship, and his success in recruiting and retaining talented contributors, made a crucial contribution to the growing success of *Punch*. Lemon wrote prolifically for the stage, and performed in Charles *Dickens's private theatricals. He collaborated with Dickens in *Mr Nightingale's Diary* (1851), a one-act farce with both authors in the cast, but the friendship was interrupted in 1858 by his refusal to print Dickens's proclamation of his reasons for separating from his wife (the two men made up their quarrel in 1867). Lemon also wrote fairy-tales for children, and in his final years published several novels, of which *Falkner Lyle* (1866) was the most successful. See A. A. Adrian, *Mark Lemon: First Editor of Punch* (1966).

LEMPRIÈRE, John (*c.*1765–1824) Schoolmaster and classical scholar, educated at Pembroke College, Cambridge. As a young man he wrote the entertaining and influential *Bibliotheca Classica, or A Classical Dictionary Containing a Full Account of All the Proper Names Mentioned in Antient Authors* (1788), which has frequently been enlarged and revised and is still in use.

LENCLOS, Anne (1620–1705) Known as Ninon de Lenclos, a Frenchwoman noted for her beauty and intellect, which she retained into old age, depicted by Mademoiselle *Scudéry as 'Clarisse' in her *Clélie*. She had many famous lovers, and her salon was frequented by *Saint-Évremond, *Molière, and the young *Voltaire.

LENNOX, Charlotte (*c.*1730–1804) Née Ramsay, novelist and translator. She was born in Gibraltar, the daughter of an army officer, and spent some of her childhood in New York province. When she came to England she married badly, failed as an actress, and turned to a not very remunerative life as a writer. The unremarked *Poems on Several Occasions* (1747) was followed by her first novel, the autobiographical *Life of Harriot Stuart, Written by Herself* (1750). Her name was established by *The *Female Quixote* (1752), which was praised by Henry *Fielding. Her collection and translation of the sources of Shakespeare's plays appeared as *Shakespear Illustrated* (1752–3). *Henrietta* (1758), a novel concerned with female dependence, was dramatized as *The Sisters*, with an epilogue by Oliver *Goldsmith: it had one performance in 1769. David *Garrick produced her *Old City Manners* in 1775, with more success. Samuel *Johnson, who had celebrated her first novel with a party and a huge apple pie, remained a helpful friend and admirer of her work to his death, citing her under 'Talent' in his *Dictionary*. She was also aided by Samuel *Richardson. Her later novels were unsuccessful, and she turned to translating French texts; her poverty made her one of the early beneficiaries of the *Royal Literary Fund.

'Lenore' (1774) A celebrated ballad by the German poet Gottfried August Bürger (1747–94), based on the Scottish ballad 'Sweet William's Ghost'. Lenore is carried off on horseback by the spectre of her dead lover and is married to him at the graveside. It was translated by several hands including William *Taylor, whose version circulated in manuscript before its publication in 1796 in the **Monthly Magazine*. The ballad and Taylor's translation came to the attention of Walter *Scott who published, anonymously, a translation of his own the same year, as 'William and Helen' along with 'The *Wild Huntsman'. Its frisson of supernatural horror appealed to contemporary taste for the *Gothic, and it was greatly admired by P. B. *Shelley. As late as 1872 the ballad provided the programme for Joachim Raff's Fifth ('Lenore') Symphony and, aptly, is alluded to in the first chapter of Bram *Stoker's late Gothic **Dracula* (1897).

LEO X (Giovanni de' Medici) (1475–1521) Pope 1513–21, a patron of literature and art, notably of *Raphael. It fell to him to deal with the theses of *Luther, whom he excommunicated in 1521. It was he who gave *Henry VIII the title of 'Defender of the Faith'.

LEONARD, Elmore (1925–) American writer, born in New Orleans, and educated at the University of Detroit. He began his literary career writing *westerns, with a short story, 'Trail of the Apache', appearing in *Argosy* in 1951. Subsequent stories and novels became classic western films, including '3.10 to Yuma' (first filmed 1957, remade in 2007), 'The Tall T' (1957), and *Hombre* (1961), filmed in 1966 with Paul Newman. As the market for westerns declined, he turned to crime writing, producing many titles including *City Primeval* (1980), *Glitz* (1985), *Freaky Deaky* (1988), *Get Shorty* (1990), filmed with John Travolta in 1996, and *Rum Punch* (1992), filmed by Quentin Tarantino as *Jackie Brown* (1997). Admired for his terse dialogue, vividly observed locations, laconic wit, and short action scenes, he has been acclaimed as the heir to Dashiell *Hammett and Raymond *Chandler, and like them, an inspiration to film-makers.

LEONARD, Tom (1944–) Scottish poet, essayist, and polemicist, born in Glasgow, and educated at the University of Glasgow. Leonard's writings in prose and verse, sometimes with accompanying cartoons, focus on vernacular authenticity as a mode of resistance to hierarchies of power and aesthetic value. He is best known for the satirical poems in phonetically transcribed Glaswegian collected in *Intimate Voices: Selected Work 1965–1983* (1984) but has also published a good deal of verse in an English shorn of the customary comforts of rhyme, metrical regularity, and metaphor. His anthology *Radical Renfrew* (1990) uncovers a rooted tradition of egalitarian poetry in the west of Scotland, while his formally innovative biography *Places of the Mind* (1993) pays homage to one of the greatest figures in that tradition, James *Thomson ('B.V.'). See *Access to the Silence: Poems and Posters 1984–2004* (2004).

LEONARDO DA VINCI (1452–1519) Florentine painter, sculptor, musician, scientist, and thinker, who developed in his painting greater complexity in composition, chiaroscuro, and psychological insight than had ever been achieved before; his *sfumato* technique was deeply influential. *The Last Supper* (*c.*1495) and the *Mona Lisa* (*c.*1503) are perhaps the two most celebrated pictures in the Western tradition. In 1481/2 Leonardo went to Milan, and remained in the employ of Ludovico *Sforza until 1499; he was then in Florence, Rome, and Milan again, and finally in France, where he died near Amboise. In the 19th century the enigmatic charm of Leonardo's women mesmerized writers; Théophile *Gautier and the *Goncourt brothers pondered over the subtle smile of the *Mona Lisa*, the 'Gioconda smile'; in the second half of the century her beauty was seen as darker and tinged with evil, and was most powerfully evoked in a famous passage by Walter *Pater, in an essay which owes something to D. G. *Rossetti's early sonnet 'Our Lady of the Rocks' and to A. C. *Swinburne's descriptions of Fatal Women. Pater's 'Lady Lisa' popularized the Fatal Woman whose development has been outlined by Mario *Praz, and echoes of her fascination recur through Decadent poetry until she is parodied by Aldous *Huxley in 'The Gioconda Smile'.

leonine verse A form of Latin verse much used in the Middle Ages (for example in John *Gower's Latin poetry), consisting of hexameters, or alternate hexameters and pentameters, in which the last word rhymes with that preceding the caesura. The term is applied to English verse of which the middle and last syllables rhyme. It may be derived from the composer Léonin (Leoninus), who was active in the late 12th century.

LEOPARDI, Giacomo (1798–1837) The greatest Italian Romantic poet. His richly suggestive lyrics (*Canti*, 1831, 1845) were written between 1816 and 1837. In 1824 he turned his attention to philosophical prose, notably the ironical dialogues *Operette morali* (1827: *Moral Tales*). The 'cosmic pessimism' of his poems is often attributed to chronic illness, but it was also an intensely intellectual and even scholarly development. In his early thought, based on *Vico and the classics, poetry is given the task of recovering the freshness of the Greek response to nature. Later he was to see nature as purposeless, indifferent, or even cruel—the 'stepmother' of humanity; and he elaborated a Romantic poetics based on the tension between past and present, childhood innocence and adult awareness of insignificance, illusions and their loss. This gave rise to a wistful poetry of images he called 'vague', in that they evoke memory: the present is too precise to be beautiful. Both Ezra *Pound and Robert *Lowell produced versions of his poems.

LEPRINCE DE BEAUMONT, Jeanne-Marie (1711–80) French novelist and story writer, born in Rouen, France. She emigrated to England *c.*1745, working as a governess in the highest circles and, in 1756, publishing her influential four-volume *Magasin des enfants* (she produced the English translation, *The Young Misses Magazine*, 1757). Although she wrote numerous other texts, it is this for which she is remembered. The contents, in the form of conversations between a governess and her children, are both didactic and amusing; included in the text are two now-famous *fairy stories, 'Beauty and the Beast' and 'The Three Wishes', told specifically for young readers.

Le QUEUX, William Tufnell *See* SPY FICTION.

Lêr (Lir) In Gaelic mythology, the sea god, one of the *Tuatha Dé Danann; perhaps to be identified with the British sea god Llyr. He was the father of *Manannán. According to the story of 'The Fate of the Children of Lêr', one of the 'three sorrowful tales of Erin', Lêr had one daughter, Fionnuala, and three sons. These were changed into swans by their jealous stepmother Aoife, and condemned to spend 900 years on the seas and lakes of Ireland. Before the end of this period St Patrick arrived, the old gods were swept away, and the swans were able to return to their home. They were converted to Christianity and restored to human shape; but were now old people and soon died.

LERMONTOV, Mikhail Iurevich (1814–41) Russian Romantic poet, novelist, and dramatist, born in Moscow. Descended from a 17th-century Scottish mercenary in Russian service (George Learmont), Lermontov was himself a career army officer. He was twice exiled to the Caucasus, the first time as a result of government displeasure with his poem 'The Death of a Poet' (1837), commemorating Aleksandr *Pushkin, and he was killed there in a duel near Piatigorsk. Strongly influenced by Lord *Byron, the proud assertion of his poem 'No, I am not Byron' (1832) notwithstanding, Lermontov wrote lyric and narrative poetry on the themes of disillusionment, rebellion, and personal freedom. His verse melodrama, influenced by Alexandre *Dumas (1802–70), *The Masquerade* (1836), was heavily censored, and published in full only in 1873, but his prose masterpiece, the novel *A Hero of our Time*, appeared in 1840. First rendered into English in 1854, it has been much translated in the 20th century, most successfully by Paul Foote (1966). See also Laurence Kelly, *Lermontov: Tragedy in the Caucasus* (1977).

LESAGE, Alain-René (1668–1747) French novelist and playwright. Generally regarded as the first major writer in France to live entirely by his pen, he is best known as the author of two *picaresque novels: *Le Diable boiteux* (1707: *The Devil on Crutches*), which offers a series of satirical sketches of contemporary society, and the enormously successful *Histoire de Gil Blas de Santillane* (1715–35), which was translated by Tobias *Smollett in 1749 and which, with *Don Quixote* and *Rabelais, can be considered the greatest foreign influence on 18th-century English comic fiction. Lesage was also a prolific playwright, achieving greatest success with *Turcaret* (1709), a satire of an unscrupulous financier.

LESKOV, Nikolai Semenovich (1831–95) Russian prose writer, born in Orel province. Nephew of Alexander Scott, a Russianized British Protestant of the agricultural firm Scott and Wilkins, Leskov worked initially in estate management. This experience provided him with a keen ear for colloquial speech and the central themes of his writing, Russian provincial life and religious culture. His first journalistic work appeared in 1860 and his first major short story, 'The Musk-Ox', in 1863. His 'Lady Macbeth of the Mtsensk District' (1865) inspired *Shostakovich's opera of 1934. Leskov's masterpiece, the 'chronicle' *Cathedral Folk* (1872), explored Russian Orthodox piety, as did 'The Sealed Angel' and 'The Enchanted Wanderer' (both 1874). After 1875 Leskov, now sceptical of official Orthodoxy, wrote articles and stories examining radical non-Orthodox believers, including a study of the English evangelist Lord Radstock (1833–1913), 'Schism in High Society' (1876). In his most famous story, 'Lefty' (1881), a left-handed blacksmith outdoes English craftsmen by shoeing a steel flea they had presented to the tsar. See David Magarshak's translation *Selected Tales* (1961); Hugh McLean, *Nikolai Leskov* (1977).

LESSING, Doris (1919–) Née Tayler, novelist and short story writer, born in Persia (Iran) of British parents and brought up on a farm in Southern Rhodesia. She left school at 15 and worked in various jobs. After the break-up of her first marriage she became involved in radical politics. She remarried in 1945, but in 1949 left for England with her youngest child and the manuscript of her first novel to be published, *The Grass is Singing* (1950), the story of the relationship between a white farmer's wife and her black servant. From this period on she supported herself and her son by her writing. Her quintet *Children of Violence* (1952–69) is a *Bildungsroman*, tracing the history of Martha Quest from her childhood in Rhodesia, through post-war Britain, to an apocalyptic ending in 2000. Perhaps her best-known work is *The Golden Notebook* (1962), a lengthy and ambitious novel hailed as a landmark by the women's movement. Later novels, *Briefing for a Descent into Hell* (1971) and *Memoirs of a Survivor* (1975), enter the realm of 'inner space fiction', exploring mental illness and the breakdown of society. The sequence of five novels collectively entitled *Canopus in Argos: Archives* (1979–83) marks a complete break with traditional realism, describing the epic and mythic events of a fictional universe with a remarkable freedom of invention. In order to test the market for fiction by unknown writers, she submitted two far more conventional novels to her publishers under the pseudonym of Jane Somers. Initially turned down, *Diary of a Good Neighbour* (1983) and *If the Old Could* (1984) were eventually published and their authorship subsequently revealed. Other novels include *The Good Terrorist* (1985), describing the behaviour of a group of middle-class revolutionaries in a London squat, and *The Cleft* (2007), in which a Roman senator describes the creation of mankind through a study of a primitive society entirely populated by women. Two evocative volumes of autobiography, *Under my Skin* (1994) and *Waiting in the Shade* (1997), cover Lessing's life up until 1962, and many other works of fiction and non-fiction display her concern with politics, with the changing destiny of women, with a fear of technological disaster, her love of cats and her interest in *Sufism and the works of Idries *Shah. These themes are all explored in *Time Bites* (2004), a collection of essays which almost amounts to a further autobiography. Her *Collected Stories*, 2 vols (1978), show a similarly broad range of interests. In 2007, to her evident surprise, she was awarded the *Nobel Prize for Literature and devoted her acceptance speech to the importance of books and her concern that the internet was resulting in 'a fragmenting culture', replacing the 'great store of literature' that once produced a truly international community of readers.

LESSING, Gotthold Ephraim (1729–81) German critic and dramatist. Educated at Leipzig University, he became the literary adviser of the National Theatre at Hamburg (1765–9), and in 1770 librarian to the duke of Brunswick at Wolfenbüttel. As a dramatist his principal works were the contemporary comedy *Minna von Barnhelm* (1767), the social tragedy *Emilia Galotti* (1772), and the verse drama *Nathan der Weise* (1779), a plea for religious tolerance. *Miss Sara Sampson* (1755), the first significant domestic tragedy in German, was modelled on George *Lillo's **George Barnwell* (1731). His chief critical works include the *Briefe die neueste Litteratur betreffend* (1759–65: *Letters Relating to Recent Literature*) and the *Hamburgische Dramaturgie* (1767–9) which were instrumental in emancipating contemporary German theatre from French neo-classical taste and establishing Shakespeare and English drama as more congenial models. In so doing he paved the way for the theatre of *Goethe and *Schiller. S. T. *Coleridge, who planned but never executed a biography of Lessing, was one of his earliest English admirers, but his humane and liberal beliefs and his lucid prose style were valued in Victorian England by Thomas *Macaulay, George *Eliot, G. H. *Lewes, and Matthew *Arnold. Lessing's **Laokoon* (1766) on the limits of the several arts has been highly influential in aesthetics and was admired by James *Joyce.

L'ESTRANGE, Sir Roger (1616–1704) Journalist and pamphleteer, and an active Royalist, obliged to flee to the Continent in 1648. After the *Restoration he was appointed surveyor of printing presses and licenser of the press. He issued the *News* and the *Intelligencer* (1663–6) which were ousted by the *London Gazette* of Henry *Muddiman; also many political pamphlets, one of the earliest being a reply to John *Milton, *No Blind Guides* (1660). In his periodical the *Observator* (1681–7) he attacked the Whigs, Titus Oates (1649–1705), and Dissenters, often employing a lively dialogue form of question and answer; his prose is colloquial, forceful, and conversational. He was knighted by James II in 1685, but after the revolution was regarded by the Whigs as a grave threat to liberty, and was several times imprisoned; he thereafter supported himself by translations which include *The Visions of Quevedo* (1667), *Aesop's *Fables* (1692), and the works of *Josephus (1702).

letters and correspondence These are important autobiographical documents for both historians and literary critics. In the 16th and 17th centuries, letters were particularly associated with female writers and have provided a unique source of information about women's lives. Letters were written according to rhetorical exemplars such as *Erasmus' *De Conscribendis Epistolis* (1522) and the *English Secretorie* (1586) by Angell Day (*fl.* 1563–95). While laying down rules, Renaissance manuals also introduced the concept of the 'familial' letter and encouraged improvisation. However, the conventions of letter writing make it hard to establish letters simply as forms of self-expression; instead writers could construct themselves in many ways according to the occasion and the recipient, ranging between submission and authority. At the same time the practice of letter writing encouraged privacy, seclusion, and a withdrawal into a separate space and could be seen as establishing a material site for the creation of selfhood. In the 18th century the publication of letters began to confuse the letter's association with private space, even as epistolary novels such as Samuel *Richardson's *Pamela* and *Clarissa* drew on letters in order to explore their characters' interiority; paradoxically these novels also betray feminine privacy by exposing it. Mary *Wollstonecraft in her *Letters Written during a Short Residence in Sweden, Norway and Denmark* (1798) turns the use of the letter round, using the conventional role of the female letter writer to make astute political and philosophical comments, reflecting her belief that sympathy and reason should unite. John *Keats's letters, which T. S. *Eliot believed were 'certainly the most notable and most important ever written by any English poet', used the form as a vehicle for working out his aesthetics, eschewing a formal polemic for a mingling of literary insight with the everyday. For Elizabeth *Bishop, 20th-century American poet and another renowned letter writer, the letter had become an art form in itself. Emerging from her own situation of frequent travel, Bishop's letters suggest the principles of a modest and familiar art form which can juxtapose different things and make the inconsequent meaningful. Letters have had an important place within modern theoretical debate as a figure for the feminine or for the circulation of discourses where vehicle and meaning do not necessarily align. Just as the establishment of the Post Office manifested the need to regulate correspondence, it revealed the fact that letters can go astray. Letter writing displays an ideology and history connected with both the feminine and the public–private divide.

LEVER, Charles (1806–72) Born in Dublin, educated at Trinity College, Dublin. He qualified as a doctor and practised in Ireland. He became a prolific and successful novelist, writing chiefly of military and Irish life. His first novels, *Harry Lorrequer* (1839), *Charles O'Malley* (1841), and *Jack Hinton the Guardsman* (1843), were extremely popular, and in 1842 he gave up medicine for the editorship of the *Dublin University Magazine*. *Tom Burke of Ours* (1844) and a *historical novel, *The Knight of Gwynne* (1847), were notable among the stream of his racy, anecdotal works. In 1845 he left Ireland and eventually settled in Italy. *The Martins of Cro'Martin* (1847) provides a spirited portrait of life in the west of Ireland, and *The Dodd Family Abroad* (1852–4) an account of an English family's vicissitudes on the Continent. Lever's later novels, which were not written with the breakneck speed that characterized his earlier literary productions, were more thoughtfully constructed; *Sir Jasper Carew* (1855), *The Fortunes of Glencore* (1857), and *Lord Kilgobbin* (1872) are considered among the best of this period. Lever received much encouragement and advice from W. M. *Thackeray, and was admired by George *Eliot and Anthony *Trollope. See S. Haddelsey, *Charles Lever: The Lost Victorian* (2000).

LEVERTOV, Denise (1923–97) British-American poet, born in Ilford, Essex; she published the neo-Romantic *The Double Image* in 1947. In 1948 she moved to America where she held a variety of academic posts. She became a central figure in the *Black Mountain group, where she formed a friendship with Robert Duncan (1919–), and she maintained her modernist aims in an unceasing flow of volumes from 1958 to 1996. Her search for the mystic and for 'organic form' led her to use free verse as she addressed family relationships, the natural world, and politics, notably the Vietnam War. *The Sorrow Dance* (1967) and *Selected Poems* (1986) contain some of her best work. Her prose includes *The Poet in the World* (1973) and *New & Selected Essays* (1992).

LEVI, Carlo (1902–75) Italian writer and painter. His best-known work, *Cristo si è fermato a Eboli* (1945: *Christ Stopped at Eboli*), was rapidly translated into English and made a particular impact. It is based on his experience in southern Italy where he had been condemned to internal exile as an opponent of the *Fascist regime. It was subsequently turned into a film by Francesco Rosi (1979). His other works are: *L'orologio* (1950: *The Watch*), set in the uneasy period in Italian politics and society at the end of the Second World War; *Le parole sono pietre* (1955: *Words are Stones*) on Sicily; *Il futuro ha un cuore antico* (1956: *The Future Has an Ancient Heart*) on the Soviet Union; *La doppia notte dei tigli* (1959: *The Two-fold Night*) on Germany.

LEVI, Peter (1931–2000) Poet, translator, classical scholar, travel writer, and archaeologist, born in Ruislip, near London, and educated at Campion Hall, Oxford, where he was tutor and lecturer, 1965–77; he was a Jesuit priest from 1964 to 1977, when he resigned the priesthood. His first volume of poetry, *The Gravel Ponds* (1960), was followed by several others, including a *Collected Poems 1955–1975* (1976); his poems mingle imagery and themes from classical antiquity, British history and prehistory, Christianity, and domestic life. Notable among his translations is Pausanias' *Guide to Greece* (1971). A volume of autobiography, *The Flutes of Autumn* (1983), concludes with an eloquent tribute to David *Jones. Levi was professor of poetry at Oxford, 1984–2000.

LEVI, Primo (1919–87) Italian writer of memoirs, fiction, essays, and poetry, born in Turin. His greatest works are his first, *Se questo è un uomo* (1947: *If This is a Man*, 1960), his memoir of Auschwitz; *La tregua* (1963: *The Truce*, 1965), the story of his journey home, and the work which effectively launched his second career as a writer; and his last, *I sommersi e i salvati* (1986: *The Drowned and the Saved*, 1988), essays which return to Auschwitz, and to the question of what it means to be human. Levi took a degree in chemistry and, after the war, worked as an industrial chemist in Turin for 30 years. In 1943 he was captured as a partisan and sent as a Jew to Auschwitz. His scientific training and self-effacing nature made him an observant and objective witness. To these gifts he added clarity of expression, ironic humour, and metaphorical imagination, which are exemplified again in his 'chemist's autobiography', *Il sistema periodico* (1975: *The Periodic Table*, 1985), the work which consolidated his international reputation. He also wrote fiction in the form of short stories, including *La chiave a stella* (1978: *The Wrench*, 1987), and *Lilit* (1981: *Moments of Reprieve*, 1986); one full-length novel, *Se non ora, quando?* (1982: *If Not Now, When?* 1987); and two books of poetry (*Shema*, 1976, and *Ad ora incerta*, 1984: *Collected Poems*, 1988). He took his own life on 11 April 1987. See R. S. Gordon (ed.), *The Cambridge Companion to Primo Levi* (2007); I. Thomson, *Primo Levi: A Biography* (2003); C. Angier, *The Double Bond: Primo Levi: A Biography* (2003).
See HOLOCAUST.

Leviathan, *or The Matter, Form, and Power of a Commonwealth, Ecclesiastical and Civil* A treatise of political philosophy by Thomas *Hobbes, published 1651, Latin text 1668. Hobbes works out his political philosophy from first principles. Men, he argues, are selfish by nature, and their judgements of what is good and evil are subjective, so their disputes cannot be settled by reference to any absolute values. Consequently the state of nature would be one of perpetual warfare, and man's life would be 'solitary, poor, nasty, brutish and short'. To prevent this Hobbes lays down certain 'Laws of Nature', which are not what we understand by natural laws, but rather agreements that must be reached to make social life possible. These are: that every man should seek peace, and should be contented with as much liberty towards other men as he would allow them towards himself. This amounts to a contract or covenant, and the obligation to perform covenants is the third Law of Nature. From this Hobbes develops the case for political absolutism. For to enforce these covenants it is necessary to establish a central power, and so all men must enter into a contract to confer their individual powers on one man, namely, a sovereign, whose powers are inalienable. This will transform a multitude into a commonwealth. Once such a contract has come into being, subjects cannot lawfully change the form of government, and since the sovereign represents all his subjects he cannot commit an injustice. Since the aim of the commonwealth is peace, it will be right for the sovereign to introduce censorship of the press and curtail freedom of speech if he thinks peace is threatened. The sovereign power is indivisible; it cannot for instance be divided between king and Parliament. Further, since there can be only one sovereign power, it will be inadmissible for a subject to obey his conscience, or his church. The church must be subordinate to the state. The obligation of subjects to obey the sovereign is understood, however, to last only so long as the power by which he is able to protect them.

LEVINAS, Emmanuel (1906–95) French moral and religious philosopher. Influenced by both Talmudic scholarship and phenomenology, Levinas insists that philosophy should privilege ethics over ontology; or, as he puts it, 'ethics is first philosophy'. In *Totalité et infini* (1961: *Totality and Infinity*), his most influential analysis of the relationship between Self and Other, he underlines the role played by our encounter with the Other in triggering our moral consciousness.

LÉVI-STRAUSS, Claude (1908–) French anthropologist, born in Brussels and educated in Paris, taking degrees in law and philosophy. From 1934 to 1939 he taught at the University of São Paulo, Brazil, becoming interested in anthropology and pursuing some fieldwork in Amazonia. During the 1940s he taught in New York and worked at the French embassy in Washington. Returning to Paris, he taught at the École Pratique des Hautes Études, and then as the first professor of social anthropology at the Collège de France. His principal early works are the analysis of kinship systems in *Les Structures élémentaires de la parenté* (1949: *The Elementary Structures of Kinship*) and the autobiographical travelogue *Tristes tropiques* (1955: *The Sad Tropics*). *Le Totémisme aujourd'hui* and *La Pensée sauvage* (both 1962: *Totemism Today* and *Savage Thought*) are notable defences of the complex thinking practised by 'primitive' peoples. His major contributions to the analysis of myths appear in *Anthropologie structurale* (1958: *Structural Anthropology*), *Le Cru et le cuit* (1964: *The Raw and the Cooked*), and the four volumes of *Mythologiques* (1964–72). After Ferdinand de *Saussure, he has been the chief exponent of *structuralism in the 'human sciences', seeking the underlying codes, rules, or systems of meaning that can explain the workings of the human mind behind the variety of cultural appearances. His influence not just in anthropology but upon French philosophy, psychoanalysis, and literary theory has been extensive.

LEVY, Amy (1861–89) Poet and novelist. She was born in London and educated at Newnham College, Cambridge; her family was Jewish and she grew up observing Jewish practices, later maintaining sympathy with the Jewish community though ceasing to hold orthodox beliefs. Her collections are *Xantippe and Other Verse* (1881, of which the title poem is a dramatic monologue spoken by the allegedly shrewish wife of *Socrates), *A Minor Poet and Other Verse* (1884), and the posthumously published *A London Plane-Tree and Other Verse* (1889). In 1886 Levy visited Florence and met Violet Paget (Vernon *Lee), subsequently entering Lee's circle of friends, which included the poet Dorothy Blomfield (1858–1932) among other feminist scholars. Amid writing numerous essays, she produced two novels, *Romance of a Shop* and *Reuben Sachs* (both 1888). The latter tells the story of an Anglo-Jewish community, and was unfortunately misunderstood by reviewers, who overlooked the complexities of the novel's representations of Jewishness and, to Levy's dismay, saw the book as an attack on Jewish identity. Levy's third novel, *Miss Meredith*, appeared in 1889, but, suffering from depression, she committed suicide later that year.

LEVY, Andrea (1956–) Born in London to Jamaican parents. Her novels explore the experience of black British-born children in London. *Every Light in the House Burnin'* (1994) is set in the 1960s, and *Never Far from Nowhere* (1996) in the 1970s. *Fruit of the Lemon* (1999) tells the story of a black Londoner who visits Jamaica. *Small Island* (2004), which won the Orange, Whitbread, and Commonwealth Writers' prizes, depicts the post-war wave of Caribbean immigration often called the 'Windrush generation' after the SS *Empire Windrush*, the ship that brought 492 Jamaican immigrants to England in June 1948.

LEWES, George Henry (1817–78) A writer of extraordinarily varied interests and talents. Born in London, he received a desultory education in schools in London, France, and Greenwich, but did not attend university. He is best known as the partner and supporter of George *Eliot. When he met her in 1851, however, he already had behind him a varied career as comic dramatist, actor, essayist on subjects ranging from *Hegel's aesthetics (his was the first proselytizing article on the subject in England) to Spanish drama, and author of a novel in imitation of *Goethe, *Ranthorpe* (1847). He wrote one of the first books in English on Auguste *Comte's positivist philosophy (1853), and a popular history of philosophy from Francis *Bacon to Comte (*Biographical History of Philosophy*, 1845–6). His life with George Eliot, dating from 1854, could not be regularized because he had condoned the adultery of his wife Agnes with Thornton Leigh *Hunt; admirers of P. B. *Shelley, the Leweses believed in free love, and when Agnes bore the first of her four children by Hunt in 1850 Lewes registered the boy as his own. By the time he met George Eliot, he was estranged from Agnes, but could not divorce her.

Lewes's *Life of Goethe* (1855), which he researched with George Eliot's help in Weimar and Berlin in 1854–5, was a work of valuable scholarship. He turned his attention increasingly to science: his later works range from biological works like *Seaside Studies* (1858) and *The Physiology of Common Life* (1859) to his ambitious investigation of psychology, *Problems of Life and Mind* (1873–9), the last volume of which was completed by George Eliot after his death. George Eliot benefited not only from his encouragement of her talents but also from his intellectual interests, which influenced her own. See R. Ashton, *G. H. Lewes: A Life* (1991); *Versatile Victorian: Selected Critical Writings of George Henry Lewes*, ed. R. Ashton (1992).

LEWIS, Alun (1915–44) Poet, born in Glamorgan. He went to university at Aberystwyth and trained as a teacher before joining the army (after much hesitation) in 1940. His first volume of poems, *Raiders' Dawn*, appeared in 1942. In 1943 it was followed by a volume of stories, *The Last Inspection*, most of which deal with army life in England. His most anthologized poem, 'All Day it has Rained' (published 1941), refers to Edward *Thomas, to whom another of his most powerful poems is addressed. Lewis died in Burma. Many of Lewis's poems are concerned with isolation and death. Letters and stories were collected in *In the Green Tree* (1948). *Selected Poetry and Prose*, with a biographical introduction by Ian *Hamilton, appeared in 1966. Cary Archard edited his *Collected Stories* (1990) and *Collected Poems* (1994). *A Cypress Walk* (2006) is a collection of letters. See John Pikoulis, *Alun Lewis* (1984).

LEWIS, C. S. (Clive Staples) (1898–1963) Belfast-born literary scholar, critic, and novelist, educated at Malvern College and University College, Oxford, fellow of Magdalen College, Oxford (1925–54), and professor of medieval and Renaissance English at Cambridge. His critical works include *The Allegory of Love* (1936) and *English Literature in the Sixteenth Century* (1954). He is more widely known for his popular religious and moral writings, including *The Problem of Pain* (1940), *The Screwtape Letters* (1940), and *The Four Loves* (1960). *Out of the Silent Planet* (1938) is the first of three strongly Christian *science fiction novels, influenced by his friendship with J. R. R.*Tolkien and Charles *Williams.

In 1950 he began a series of seven 'Narnia' stories for children, beginning with *The Lion, the Witch, and the Wardrobe*. These feature Peter, Susan, Edmund, and Lucy Pevensie, and their adventures in the alternative world of Narnia, which is populated by creatures from myths, legends, and sagas, the most important of these being Aslan the lion, a divinity modelled on Christ. Although not straightforward allegories, they convey many of Lewis's ideas about Christianity. The Chronicles have been filmed for television (1990) and cinema (2005) and turned into a computer game; *The Lion, the Witch, and the Wardrobe* is regularly staged.

Surprised by Joy (1955) is his spiritual autobiography. 'The *Inklings', a group of his friends, met for many years to talk and read aloud their compositions. In 1956 he married American Helen Joy Davidman, who died in 1960. He wrote about their marriage in *A Grief Observed* (1961). Their relationship became the subject of a successful stage play and film, *Shadowlands* (1989), by William Nicholson. See Walter Hooper, *C. S. Lewis: A Companion and Guide* (1996).

LEWIS, Cecil Day *See* Day-Lewis, Cecil.

LEWIS, Gwyneth (1959–) Bilingual Welsh poet, born in Cardiff and educated at Girton College, Cambridge. She has published five collections of poetry in Welsh, in addition to her English collections *Parables and Faxes* (1995), *Zero Gravity* (1998), and *Keeping Mum* (2003). Her *Sunbathing in the Rain: A Cheerful Book on Depression*, a powerful account of her struggle with mental illness, appeared in 2002.

LEWIS, M. G. (Matthew Gregory) (1775–1818) Educated at Westminster School and Christ Church, Oxford, remembered as the author of *The *Monk* (1796), a scandalous *Gothic novel, from which his nickname 'Monk' Lewis was derived. Lewis was greatly influenced by German Romanticism, and wrote numerous dramas in its more histrionic manner. His verses (of which 'Alonzo the Brave and the Fair Imogine', which appears in *The Monk*, is probably the best known) had some influence on Walter *Scott's early poetry.

LEWIS, Meriwether (1774–1809) American explorer, who was born and educated in Virginia, and became an army captain in 1800. In 1801 he was appointed personal secretary to President Thomas Jefferson (1743–1826), under whose direction he led the forty-plus strong Corps of Discovery expedition, which explored the area of the Louisiana Purchase 1804–6. Lewis chose as his second in command his friend William Clark (1770–1838), a retired army captain. The expedition covered more than 8,000 miles in its western journey from St Louis to the Pacific and back again. While its quest for a direct water route to the Pacific failed, it succeeded in its other goals. It studied and described more than 300 plant and animal species, the geology and mineralogy of the regions, and the Native Americans whose first contact with whites this was and several groups of whom provided invaluable support (thanks in part to the presence of Sacagawea, a Shoshone, who, with her French Canadian fur trader husband, had been employed by the party). After the expedition Lewis was rewarded with 1,500 acres of land and, in 1807, with the governorship of the Louisiana Territory. Lewis's journals were published posthumously. A new thirteen-volume edition of the expedition's journals, edited by Gary E. Moulton, was published by the University of Nebraska Press in 2002 and online. The expedition and its accounts stimulated American interest in the west and helped establish its dominance in the region over rival European interests.

LEWIS, Norman (1908–2003) Travel writer and novelist, born in Enfield, north London, educated at Enfield Grammar School. His many travel narratives recount journeys through Indo-China and Burma (*A Dragon Apparent*, 1951; *Golden Earth*, 1952), the Mediterranean, India, and Cuba, and combine vivid evocation of place, lively storytelling, and acute political analysis. In 1968, a 12,000-word article in the *Sunday Times* entitled 'Genocide in Brazil' drew attention to the dubious practices of US missionaries in the region, and the near-extinction of the native population; it prompted an international outcry and led to the creation of the charity Survival International. (See Christopher *Hampton's play *Savages*.) Lewis is also the author of several novels, among them *The Day of the Fox* (1955), *The Volcanoes above Us* (1957), and *A Suitable Case for Corruption* (1984), and two autobiographical volumes, *Jackdaw Cake* (1985, later revised as *I Came, I Saw*) and *The World, the World* (1996).

LEWIS, Saunders (1893–1985) Welsh dramatist, poet, critic, literary historian, and cultural agitator, born in Wallasey and educated at the University of Liverpool. In the scale and impact of his exertions, Lewis is a Welsh counterpart to W. B. *Yeats in Ireland and Hugh *MacDiarmid in Scotland, though unlike them he committed his major work to a Celtic language. In 1925 he co-founded the Welsh Nationalist Party (later Plaid Cymru) and was involved in 1936 in the symbolic burning of building materials at an RAF bombing school on the Llŷn peninsula. His nineteen plays include the (English) comedy *The Eve of St John* (1921), the austere poetic tragedy *Siwan* (1956), set in the Welsh Middle Ages, and *Brad* (1958), an acute exploration of the ethical dilemma of the participants in the 1944 plot against Hitler. *Monica* (1930) is the more admired of his two novels. Though he published fewer than 60 poems, Lewis is regarded as one of the greatest masters of Welsh metrics. His horrified depictions of the industrialized valleys of south Wales recall his mentor Yeats alike in their magniloquence and their distaste for democracy. He continued to write plays, mostly for BBC radio and television, until his death. See *The Plays of Saunders Lewis*, trans. Joseph P. Clancy (4 vols, 1985–2002).

LEWIS, Sinclair (1885–1951) American novelist, born in Sauk Centre, Minnesota. After graduating from Yale he spent some years in journalism and published several novels, achieving his first success with *Main Street* in 1920. It describes with satirical realism the dullness of life in a small Midwestern town called Gopher Prairie. He strengthened his reputation with **Babbitt* (1922), the story of George Babbitt, a prosperous and self-satisfied house agent in the Midwestern town of Zenith, who comes to doubt the conventions of middle-class society, but is eventually reabsorbed after a period of defiance and ostracism. The term 'babbittry' denotes the qualities personified by this character. Among many other novels, *Arrowsmith* (1925) describes the career of a bacteriologist; *Elmer Gantry* (1927) takes a satiric view of Midwestern evangelism; and *Dodsworth* (1929) describes the marital relations of a middle-aged American industrialist and his adventures in Europe. *It Can't Happen Here* (1935) speculatively describes the establishment of totalitarianism in the USA. Lewis was awarded the *Nobel Prize in 1930. See Mark Schorer, *Sinclair Lewis: An American Life* (1961).

LEWIS, Wyndham (1882–1957) Novelist, critic, and artist, born in a yacht off the coast of Nova Scotia and educated at private schools before attending Rugby School for a year (1897–8); he then studied at the Slade School of Art (1898–1901), before spending the next seven years on the Continent. His first stories appeared in the **English Review* in 1909. He was a leader of the *Vorticist movement and, with Ezra *Pound, edited *Blast* (1914, 1915); Lewis's own *little magazine, *The Enemy*, appeared in three book-length issues, 1927–9, written largely by himself (with poems by Laura *Riding and Roy *Campbell). He served with the Royal Artillery in 1916–17, and his novels include the aggressively *modernist *Tarr* (1918; rev. 1928); *The Apes of God* (1930), an acerbic satire on London literary life; *The Revenge for Love* (1937); and *Self Condemned* (1957). His projected four-part work *The Human Age* (*The Childermass*, 1928; *Monstre Gai* and *Malign Fiesta*, both 1955) remained unfinished at his death. Important volumes of essays and criticism include *Time and Western Man* (1927), *The Lion and the Fox: The Role of Hero in the Plays of Shakespeare* (1927), and *The Writer and the Absolute* (1952). *Blasting and Bombardiering* (1937) and *Rude Assignment* (1950) are autobiographies. Although his criticism of the increasing hollowness and mechanization of 20th-century civilization had affinities with the ideas of Ezra Pound, T. S. *Eliot, and D. H. *Lawrence, his savage satirical attacks on his contemporaries (particularly the *Bloomsbury Group) and his praise of the pre-Führer Hitler (in *Hitler*, 1931) alienated him from many in the literary world, though he did repudiate his enthusiasm for the German dictator in *The Hitler Cult* (1939) and the pro-Jewish *The Jews, Are they Human?* (1939). He is not to be confused with D. B. Wyndham Lewis (1891–1969), the biographer and journalist who also wrote as *Beachcomber. See Paul O'Keeffe, *Some Sort of Genius: A Life of Wyndham Lewis* (2000).

LEYDEN, John (1775–1811) Scottish antiquary, physician, poet, and orientalist, who was equally inspired by Border ballads and the travels of Mungo *Park. He assisted Walter *Scott in **Minstrelsy of the Scottish Border* (1802), contributed to M. G. *Lewis's *Tales of Wonder* (1801), and in 1803 set off for India and the Far East. He died at Batavia, Java, having mastered many oriental languages and having set himself up somewhat prematurely as the antiquarian rival of William *Jones. Scott mourned his 'bright and brief career' in *The Lord of the Isles*, and contributed a memoir to the *Edinburgh Annual Register*, 1811, dwelling on his friend's colourful eccentricities. This was reproduced with Leyden's *Poems and Ballads* (1858, 1875). He published several treatises on oriental languages, and translated the *Malay Annals* (1821) and the *Commentaries of Baber* (1826).

Libeaus Desconus [a corruption of *le bel inconnu*, the fair unknown] A 14th-century romance in 2,232 lines of twelve-line, *tail-rhyme stanzas, surviving in six manuscripts. Gingelein, the son of Gawain, asks Arthur for knighthood and, since his name is unknown, he is knighted as *Li Beaus Desconus*. The poem describes his adventures leading to his marriage with the Lady of Sinadoune, his kinship to Gawain revealed through his ability to rescue her from enchantment. In *Chaucer's 'Sir Thopas' the knight's name is given simply as 'Sir Lybeux' (*see* CANTERBURY TALES, 17). *Malory's tale of *Gareth also has obvious affinities with the *bel inconnu* tradition. See M. Mills (ed.), EETS OS 261, 1969.

Libelle of Englyshe Polycye, The ('The Little Book of English Policy') A political poem of about 2,250 lines written *c.*1436, in which the author urges his countrymen to regard the sea as the source of national strength, discusses commercial relations with other countries, and emphasizes the importance of retaining Ireland, Calais, and Wales. The poem was included by Richard *Hakluyt, and it has been doubtfully attributed to Adam Moleyns or Molyneaux (d. 1450), clerk of the king's council. See T. Wright, *Political Poems and Songs... Edward III to Richard III* (Rolls Series vol. ii, 1861); best edn by F. G. Warner (1926).

Liberal, The (1822–4) A magazine of four issues only but of great brilliance. Conceived by P. B. *Shelley, the plan was carried out after his death by Lord *Byron and Leigh *Hunt from Pisa. Byron's *The *Vision of Judgement* first appeared in its pages, as did his *Heaven and Earth*, and much other work by Shelley, Hunt, William *Hazlitt, James *Hogg, and others. Libel problems with the *Vision*, and the incompatibility of Byron and Hunt, brought the magazine to an untimely close.

Liber Amoris, *or The New Pygmalion* An autobiographical prose work by William *Hazlitt, published anonymously in 1823. It records in letters and dialogues the frenzied infatuation Hazlitt conceived at the age of 43 for a 19-year-old girl, Sarah Walker, who waited at table in his London lodgings, and who eventually rejected him for another suitor. The fevered tone of the book, and its humiliating self-exposure, distressed Hazlitt's friends and gave ammunition to his various enemies, his anonymity having been seen through at once. Recent commentators are more likely to read the work less as about Hazlitt than about the confessional genre itself, the degree of self-irony and knowingness involved in its writing, and the extent to which it explores the permeability of the boundary between the public and private.

Liberty, On An essay by John Stuart *Mill, published 1859. In this hugely influential work, central to Victorian liberalism and continuously in print since its first publication, Mill attempts to define the proper relations between the individual and society. He argues that 'the sole end for which mankind are warranted, individually or collectively, in interfering with liberty of action of any of their number, is self-protection'. The individual is only answerable to society for conduct which affects others. The good of the individual, either physical or moral, is not a sufficient justification for the interference of society. 'Mankind are greater gainers by suffering each other to live as seems good to themselves, than by compelling each to live as seems good to the rest.'

libraries, public The first British public libraries were established under the Museum Act, in Canterbury (1847), Warrington (1848), and Salford (1850). A library service was begun in Brighton in 1850 by a private Act. The 1850 Public Libraries Act, piloted by William Ewart against stiff opposition, empowered borough councils in England and Wales (extended to Scotland in 1853, where growth followed a parallel but different course) with a population of 10,000 plus to spend a halfpenny rate on libraries and museums, thus establishing a principle although imposing severe restrictions in practice. In 1855 this was raised to a penny rate and the population limit was lowered to 5,000; in 1866 the population limit was removed. Norwich was the first authority to adopt the 1850 Act, but provided no services until 1857. Winchester was the first library opened under the Act, in 1851, followed the next year by Manchester, then Liverpool (by a special Act), Sheffield, and Birmingham. St Margaret and St John's at Westminster was London's only public library from 1857 until 1885, when another was opened in Wandsworth. Growth was slow at first, only 48 libraries being established before 1870, chiefly in England, but also in Wales and Scotland. Thereafter growth was faster, and by the turn of the century some 400 libraries had been set up. The supporters of the Public Libraries Acts hoped that they would encourage working people in refinement, thrift, and sobriety; opponents objected to the burden on the rates and expected the libraries to lead to idleness and discontent.

Public thrift was shamed by private generosity. By 1913 the American philanthropist Andrew Carnegie (1835–1919) had given £2m for public libraries and, through the Carnegie UK Trust set up in that year, he continued to give important and influential support. John Passmore Edwards (1823–1911) supported 24 libraries, chiefly in and around London and his native Cornwall. After the First World War, the Public Libraries Act of 1919 removed the rate limitation and extended library powers to the counties. By 1928, with the help of the Carnegie Trust, most counties had started a library service. The Mitchell Report (1924) and the Kenyon Report (1927) reflected an increasing interest in library development, and marked a stage in the development of libraries for all. Village reading rooms were set up, and library provisions were made for children. The Public Library service continued to grow despite being set back by the Depression of 1931–3, helped by the overall increase of local government spending on libraries between 1928 and 1939 (£1.8m to £3.2m). The growth of the county library service was a notable feature of the post-war years, until it was arrested by the recession of the early 1980s. Attempts have been made from the 1960s onwards to make libraries attractive as community centres, and to extend their activities to include exhibitions of art and photography, schemes for loaning both reproductions of and original works of art, poetry readings, and other community events; also to attract a larger readership of children through storytelling sessions, school visits, and comparable activities. The provision of information through electronic media has become an important feature of the recent work of libraries.

Library, The A bibliographical journal, published from 1889 to 1898 as the organ of the Library Association, and from 1899 to 1918 as an independent journal. In 1920 it was merged with the *Transactions* of the *Bibliographical Society, though retaining its original title.

libretto The Italian word for the 'little book' in which the text of an *opera (or oratorio) was printed, and hence the text itself. In England, opera developed from stage plays and masques, such as *The Siege of Rhodes*, by the experienced playwright Sir William *D'Avenant, so libretti were normally, to begin with, play texts. Occasionally later composers (Claude *Debussy, Richard *Strauss) have chosen to set stage plays more or less unadapted, but the practice is rare. Texts specifically written for opera cannot generally stand independent of the music that they inspire: Nahum *Tate's libretto for *Purcell's *Dido and Aeneas*, which has been much attacked for its naively florid imagery, nevertheless succeeded in provoking Purcell's musical imagination. Other early English librettists include Thomas *Shadwell, whose *Psyche* (1675, with music by Matthew *Locke) was adapted from *Molière, and John *Dryden, whose *Albion and Albanius* (1685) was set to music by Louis Grabu. Joseph *Addison's single attempt, *Rosamond*, met with a disastrous failure in Thomas Clayton's setting (1707). After the formal establishment of Italian opera in Britain with the arrival of *Handel, composers tended to set a text specially provided by a professional librettist such as Pietro Metastasio. English libretti survived in the form of the *ballad operas which followed John Gay's *The *Beggar's Opera*, though these were in effect straight plays interspersed with music. Nearer to the true libretto were the many comic opera texts produced by Isaac *Bickerstaff in the 1760s and 1770s, set mainly by Thomas *Arne and Charles *Dibdin. In the same vein is Richard Sheridan's *The *Duenna* (1775). In the 1870s the series of *Gilbert and Sullivan operas showed the potential for dedicated partnerships between librettists and composers, foreshadowing popular musical collaborations between lyricists and composers such as Rogers and Hammerstein.

Giuseppe *Verdi generally worked with a professional librettist, as in his brief but productive collaboration with Arrigo *Boito. Hector *Berlioz and Richard *Wagner wrote their own libretti, a practice which continued into the 20th century with Gustav *Holst and Michael *Tippett and many others. Thomas *Hardy, J. M. *Synge, A. P. *Herbert, Clifford Bax (1886–1962), J. B. *Priestley, and William *Plomer are among those writers who have provided texts for composers; W. H. *Auden, in his libretti for Benjamin *Britten, Stravinsky, and Hans Werner *Henze, established himself as an important writer in the form. Peter Maxwell *Davies and Harrison *Birtwistle have each worked closely with poets, and developed their own opera texts. James *Fenton contributed material to the libretto of the immensely successful musical adaptation of Victor *Hugo's *Les Misérables* (perf. UK 1985).

LICHTENBERG, Georg Christoph (1742–99) German scientist and thinker, born in Hessen, educated and later a professor at Göttingen. An important figure in the German *Enlightenment, he twice visited England, in 1770 and 1774–5, and was a guest at Kew of George III. He was an ardent admirer of English institutions and literature and a keen dramatic critic. His letters from England to his friends in Germany contain shrewd observations on the acting of David *Garrick, Charles *Macklin, and others, and throw an interesting light on contemporary English manners. He also published (1794–9) a commentary on William *Hogarth's engravings. His aphorisms, collected in nine volumes after his death (1800–05), are considered his finest literary achievement. See *Lichtenberg's Visits to England: As Described in his Letters and Diaries*, trans. and ed. M. L. Mare and W. H. Quarrell (1938).

LICKBARROW, Isabella (1784–1847) Poet, born in Kendal. Her most notable volume is her first, *Poetical Effusions* (1814), published 'to assist the humble labours of herself and her orphan sisters'. William *Wordsworth features on the volume's subscription list (as do Thomas *De Quincey and Robert *Southey), and her poetry shares the pleasure of her fellow Lake District poets in the natural world. Though sometimes melancholic, her tone lacks the air of despair evident in the work of her more famous predecessor Charlotte *Smith.

LIDDELL, Robert (1908–92) Novelist, travel writer, and critic, educated at Haileybury School and Corpus Christi, Oxford. He worked for a time in the Bodleian Library but his career was largely spent as a lecturer in Egypt and Greece. His fiction includes three novels which reflect the Mediterranean world he knew—*Unreal City* (1952, set in Alexandria towards the end of the Second World War), *The Rivers of Babylon* (1959), and *An Object for a Walk* (1966). His books on Greece, including *Aegean Greece* (1954) and *Mainland Greece* (1965), reveal his sympathetic insight into the country's past and present. Liddell also published a biography of the Greek Alexandrian poet *Cavafy (1974). In later life, he wrote of his friendship with novelists Elizabeth *Taylor and Ivy *Compton-Burnett in *Elizabeth and Ivy* (1986), and published a volume on the fiction of Barbara *Pym, a friend from 1930s Oxford.

Life in London *See* EGAN, PIERCE.

Life of Charlotte Brontë, The The only biography written by Elizabeth *Gaskell, published in 1857. Gaskell, who first read and admired **Jane Eyre*, met Charlotte *Brontë in 1850. Her biography commemorates her friend's life by making her the heroine of a romantic story where she overcomes difficult circumstances through the force of her personality and finds happiness in her marriage to Arthur Nicholls. Gaskell's achievement is to have drawn on personal letters and information, and to have found a form which privileges the private over the public; however, she also made Brontë's life far more conventional than in fact it was, suppressing information about Brontë's love for Constantin Heger (1809–96), a married man who was Brontë's teacher in Brussels. The biography also originally contained libellous material and had to be corrected and reissued.

life-writing A broad term for all forms of writing about lives, including autobiography, biography, memoirs, diaries, and letters, widely used since the 1970s. The inclusiveness of the term acknowledges the fluidity between genres, and the way that many works incorporate different elements or modes. For instance, Richard *Holmes's *Footsteps* (1985) is an autobiographical discussion of biography, outlining the challenges and dangers of his own chosen profession. Hermione *Lee's *Body Parts* (2005) is a series of essays about the problems of biography. The term also signals the expansion of self-reflection and reflection about lives beyond the literary mainstream and their use by groups, particularly women, working-class, gay, and black British writers, who felt themselves unrepresented within the canon. In the 1970s telling one's own story could be seen as an act of political empowerment or 'consciousness-raising', intended to challenge the official record, disclosing formerly repressed or unrecorded experience which was nevertheless shared by the group. Sheila Rowbotham's *Woman's Consciousness, Man's World* (1973) begins with a personal journey which is also seen as a political one; Anne Oakley in *Taking it Like a Woman* (1984) assumes that in writing about her own life, she is also representing the common plight of women. Within education, particularly the social sciences, 'life-writing' was seen as empowering students, allowing them to use their own lives as a source of knowledge and to recognize themselves as subjects within their own worlds. Autobiography and biography were also seen as important forms for historians and offered new forms of social history from the perspective of subjects who had previously been 'hidden from history'. From the 1970s, oral history, the recording of eyewitness participants, also became important and archives based on this material were established in university centres. In 1981 the *Mass Observation project (originally established in 1937) was housed at Sussex University. The academic study of life-writing is now a recognized area, promoting interdisciplinarity as it incorporates the use of life stories from many different fields.

LIGHTFOOT, John (1602–75) Biblical and rabbinic scholar, and from 1643 master of Catharine Hall, Cambridge. His best-known work is his series of *Horae Hebraicae et Talmudicae* (1658–78), which relates Jewish studies to the interpretation of the New Testament. He assisted Brian Walton (1600–61) with the Polyglot Bible.

Light Shining in Buckinghamshire (1) The title of an anonymous pamphlet issued by the Levellers, a radical political movement, in 1648, attacking monarchy and calling for equality of property. It was followed by a sequel, *More Light Shining in Buckinghamshire* (1649). *See* PAMPHLETEERING, ORIGINS OF. (2) The title of a play by Caryl *Churchill, staged in 1976 by Joint Stock at the Theatre Upstairs at the *Royal Court Theatre for the *English Stage Company.

LILBURNE, John (*c*.1614–1657) Pamphleteer and political agitator. He was brought before the Star Chamber in 1638 for printing an unlicensed book, and imprisoned; *A Work of the Beast* (1638) gives an account of his barbarous treatment. He fought with distinction in the Parliamentary army, but criticized the army officers and was repeatedly imprisoned; he was banished in 1652 but returned the following year. In 1655 he became a Quaker. He was associated with the Levellers, a radical political movement, and in his many pamphlets he speaks for the rights of the common man, describing his followers as 'clubs and clouted shoon', for God 'doth not choose many rich, nor many wise...but the fools, idiots, base and contemptible poor men and women in the esteem of the world'. However, he never advocated communism. He published pamphlets jointly with Richard *Overton and William *Walwyn. A life by P. Gregg was published in 1961.

'Lilli-Burlero Bullen-a-la!' An English approximation of the Irish *An Lile ba léir é, ba linn an lá* ('The Lily was clear, the day was ours'), a battle-cry attributed to the Irish Catholic insurgents of the 1641 rebellion. The phrase was used as the refrain of a satirical Williamite song on the appointment by James II of the Catholic earl of Tyrconnel as lord deputy of Ireland in 1687. The song, usually attributed to Thomas (later Lord) Wharton (1648–1715), is given in Thomas *Percy's **Reliques* and features in Orange Order parades up to the present. The employment (since 1955) of the tune as the signature of the BBC World Service's English-language news bulletin has been objected to on sectarian grounds, most notably by Robert *Graves.

LILLO, George (1691/3–1739) Playwright, probably the son of a London jeweller of Dutch descent. In 1730 he wrote a *ballad opera, *Silvia, or The Country Burial*, but it was *The History of *George Barnwell, or The London Merchant* (1731), based on a ballad story, that established his influence. His other plays include *The Christian Hero* (1735), and *The *Fatal Curiosity* (1736), produced by Henry *Fielding, who praised Lillo's work and personal ethos as evincing 'the Spirit of an old Roman, join'd to the Innocence of a primitive Christian'. Lillo may have been partially responsible for a tragedy on the subject of *Arden of Faversham, which surfaced in 1759. See *The Dramatic Works of George Lillo*, ed. James L. Steffenson (1993).

LILLY, William (1602–81) A noted astrologer, patronized by Elias *Ashmole and by leading members of the Long Parliament, who built up a highly successful London practice. His *Christian Astrology* (1647) is a classic study of astrological traditions and the first comprehensive astrological textbook published in English rather than Latin. Its republication in 1985 is credited with bringing about the renaissance of astrology in Europe and America. He specialized in horary astrology, the branch of astrology which attempts to answer questions by studying astrological charts calculated according to the exact time and place at which the question was asked, and published hugely popular prophetic almanacs yearly from 1644 until his death. His prediction of Charles I's defeat at Naseby in June 1645 established his reputation as England's leading astrologer. In 1648 the Parliamentarian leaders ordered him to attend the siege of Colchester to encourage the troops with prophecies of victory. His autobiography gives a fascinating insight into the world of 17th-century professional magic, and contains accounts of talismanic magic, crystal-gazing, and the invocation of spirits. His fortunes declined after the *Restoration and in 1666 he was called before a committee investigating the Great Fire, which he had predicted in 1652 and was accordingly suspected of deliberately starting. However, he was cleared. He was the model for Sidrophel in Butler's **Hudibras*. The case books recording his consultations survive among the Ashmole manuscripts in the Bodleian Library. See David Plant, *The Life and Work of William Lilly* (published online); Derek Parker, *Familiar to All, William Lilly and Astrology in the 17th Century* (1973); and his autobiography, *The History of my Life and Times*, ed. K. M. Briggs (1974).

LILY, William (?1468–1522/3) Friend of John *Colet and Sir Thomas *More, grandfather of John *Lyly, and a leader of the revival of Greek studies in England. Though married and a layman, he was made first high master of St *Paul's School. He contributed a short Latin syntax, with the rules in English, to the Latin grammar by Colet and *Erasmus, *c.*1513. This, with another grammar, was the basis of the work known as *Lily's Grammar*, long familiar to English schoolboys; compare the Latin lesson in William *Shakespeare's *The *Merry Wives of Windsor*, IV. i. On the history of his grammatical writings, see V. J. Flynn, in *Papers of the Bibliographical Society of America*, 37 (1943).

limerick A form of jingle, of which the first instances occur in *The History of Sixteen Wonderful Old Women* (1820) and *Anecdotes and Adventures of Fifteen Gentlemen* (*c.*1821), subsequently popularized by Edward *Lear in his *Book of Nonsense*. In the older form of limerick, as written by Lear, D. G. *Rossetti, and others, the first and last lines usually end with the same word, but in more recent examples, such as the following comment on George *Berkeley's philosophy by Ronald *Knox, and those written by W. H. *Auden, Gavin *Ewart, Ogden *Nash, Norman *Douglas, Robert *Conquest, and others, a third rhyming word is supplied:

There once was a man who said: 'God
Must think it exceedingly odd
If he finds that this tree
Continues to be
When there's no one about in the Quad.'

LINACRE, Thomas (*c.*1460–1524) Physician and classical scholar, educated at Oxford and a fellow of All Souls College. An MD of Padua, he became one of *Henry VIII's physicians. Later he was tutor to Princess Mary, for whom he composed a Latin grammar, *Rudimenta Grammatices* (1523?). He was largely instrumental in founding the College of Physicians in 1518. In addition to grammatical and medical works, he translated from the Greek, mainly from *Galen. Linacre College, Oxford (founded 1962), takes its name from Thomas Linacre.

Lindisfarne Gospels A manuscript of the four Gospels in the *Vulgate text, probably written in honour of the canonization of St *Cuthbert (698). The script is Anglo-Saxon majuscule and there are magnificent illuminations and decorative capitals. An Anglo-Saxon gloss was added in the late 10th century in Northumbrian dialect with a colophon stating that the text was written by Eadfrith, bishop of Lindisfarne 698–721, and naming the binder, the goldsmith who ornamented the binding, and the translator, Aldred of Chester-le-Street. See Janet Backhouse, *The Lindisfarne Gospels* (1981).

LINDSAY, Lady Anne *See* BARNARD, LADY ANNE.

LINDSAY, David (1876–1945) Scottish author born in Blackheath, London; best known for *Voyage to Arcturus* (1920), in which the protagonist Maskull embarks upon a visionary quest through a series of alternative philosophies embodied in the bizarre characters and landscapes of the planet Tormance. The novel influenced C. S. *Lewis's *Out of the Silent Planet* (1938) and Harold *Bloom's *The Flight to Lucifer* (1979); its admirers include Philip *Pullman. Other works include *The Haunted Woman* (1922). *The Violet Apple* and *The Witch* (1975) were issued posthumously. See Bernard Sellin, *The Life and Works of David Lindsay* (1981); J. B. Pick *et al.*, *The Strange Genius of David Lindsay* (1970).

LINDSAY (Lyndsay), Sir David (*c.*1486–1555) Scottish poet and Lyon king-of-arms, and associated with the courts of both James IV and James V. His first poem, 'The Dreme', written *c.*1528 but not printed till after his death, is an allegorical lament on the misgovernment of the realm, followed by an exhortation to the king. In 1530 he wrote the *Complaynt to the King*, in octosyllabic couplets, commenting on the improved social condition of the realm except as regards the church, lamenting that others have been preferred before him at court. The *Testament, and Complaynt, of our Soverane Lordis Papyngo* (finished 1530; printed 1538) combines advice to the king, put in the mouth of his parrot, with a warning to courtiers drawn from the examples of Scottish history, and with a satire on ecclesiastics in the form of a conference between the dying parrot and its 'Holye Executouris'. Lindsay's distinguished, reformist morality play, *Ane *Pleasant Satyre of the Thrie Estaitis*, was produced in Fife in 1552. Other poems by Lindsay include *The Tragedie of the Cardinale* (*c.*1547), *The Monarchie* (*Ane Dialog betwix Experience and ane Courteour, off the Miserabyll Estait of the Warld*) (1554), and the *Historie of Squyer Meldrum* (first extant edition of 1582), a verse romance on the career and exploits of a Scottish laird. See *Works*, ed. D. Hamer (Scottish Text Society, 3rd series, 1, 2, 6, 8, 1931–6); *Sir David Lyndsay: Selected Poems*, ed. J. Hadley Williams (2000); *Ane satyre of The Thrie Estaitis*, ed. R. J. Lyall (1989).

LINDSAY, Norman *See* BULLETIN.

LINDSAY, Robert (*c.*1532–*c.*1586) Of Pitscottie, author of *The Historie and Croniclis of Scotland* from the reign of James II, one of Walter *Scott's principal sources for the period.

LINDSAY, Vachel *See* CINEMA.

LINGARD, John (1771–1851) A Roman Catholic priest, author of *The Antiquities of the Anglo-Saxon Church* (1806); and, more importantly, of a *History of England* (1819–30), which was chiefly intended to emphasize the disastrous effects of the *Reformation. His idealized portrait of the Middle Ages influenced writers and thinkers as diverse as William *Morris and the founders of the *Oxford Movement.

LINKLATER, Eric (1899–1974) Novelist, playwright, and journalist. Born in Penarth, Wales, he was brought up in Aberdeen. His father came from the Orkney Islands; his mother was the daughter of a Swedish seaman. Linklater served as a sniper in the Black Watch during the First World War. After graduating MA at the University of Aberdeen in 1925 he worked for two years in Bombay (Mumbai) as assistant editor of the *Times of India* and then briefly as an academic in Aberdeen, Cornell, and Berkeley universities. His most popularly successful novel, *Juan in America* (1931), genially satirizes Prohibition-era America, as *Private Angelo* (1946) does post-Mussolini Italy. *Magnus Merriman* (1934), an ironic fictionalized treatment of his flirtation with Scottish nationalism, contains a notable portrait of Hugh *MacDiarmid ('Hugh Skene').

LINNAEUS, Carl von (1707–78) Latinized form of Carl von Linné, Swedish botanist and founder of the binomial system of plant classification according to genus and species. His international reputation was established in 1735 with the publication (in Latin) of *Systema Naturae*; the final form of his theory of plant classification is contained in the last edition of *Genera Plantarum* (1771). From 1741 he was professor of medicine and then botany at Uppsala, where he wrote several important travel books based on his Swedish field trips. The Linnean Society of London was founded in 1788, and the library and herbarium of Linnaeus are housed with other collections in Burlington House, Piccadilly.

LINTON, Eliza Lynn (1822–98) Née Lynn, novelist and journalist. Born in Keswick, she received no formal education, but read widely as a girl. She launched her London literary career with two historical novels (*Azeth the Egyptian*, 1846; *Amymone*, 1848), and also wrote for the **Morning Chronicle* (she was the first woman journalist in England to earn a fixed salary). Her third novel, *Realities* (1851), was widely condemned for its attack on conventional morality, and she did not publish another for fourteen years. She wrote extensively for popular periodicals, including Charles *Dickens's **Household Words* and later *All the Year Round*. Increasingly conservative, she became widely known for her anti-feminist pieces in the **Saturday Review*, collected as *The Girl of the Period* (1883), and was a vehement critic of the *New Woman. She published numerous successful novels of contemporary life, including *Rebel of the Family* (1880). Her posthumously published memoir *My Literary Life* (1899) contains a notably hostile portrait of George *Eliot.

LINTON, W. J. (1812–97) Wood-engraver, radical polemicist, and poet. He wrote about his craft (both its technical and artistic features) in works such as *Masters of Wood Engraving* (1889). In 1858 he married the novelist and journalist Eliza Lynn (*see* LINTON, ELIZA LYNN); they separated in 1867. He worked as an engraver for several important literary projects, including Edward *Moxon's edition of Alfred *Tennyson and George *Eliot's **Romola*. His own *Poems* appeared in 1895.

LINTOT, Barnaby Bernard (1675–1736) Bookseller, a rival to Jacob *Tonson, and publisher of several important works by John *Gay, George *Farquhar, Richard *Steele, Nicholas *Rowe, and especially Alexander *Pope, including *The *Rape of the Lock* and **Windsor-Forest*. He was the publisher for Pope's translation of *Homer. Pope caricatured his corpulence in Book II of *The *Dunciad*.

LIPPARD, George (1822–54) American novelist, born in Pennsylvania, who became a close friend of Edgar Allan *Poe. He wrote a series of historical romances but is remembered primarily for his sensational revelation of big-city vice in *The Monks of Monk Hall* (1844), also called *The Quaker City*. He acknowledged the influence of Charles Brockden *Brown on his writing. See David S. Reynolds, *George Lippard* (1982).

LIPSIUS, Justus (Joest Lips) (1547–1606) A Flemish humanist, who adopted the Lutheran faith while professor at Jena (1572–5), turned to *Calvinism when professor at Leiden (1579–91), and reverted to the Catholicism of his youth when he became professor at Louvain in 1592. His principal works were editions of *Tacitus and *Seneca, which contributed greatly to the development of neo-Stoicism, and a treatise on politics in which he advocated the suppression by fire and sword of religious dissidence.

Lir *See* LÊR.

Lisle Letters A collection of some 3,000 letters written to and from Arthur Plantagenet, Viscount Lisle (d. 1542; an illegitimate son of Edward IV), his family, and household, while he was lord deputy of Calais from 1533 to 1540. They give a vivid picture of the political and domestic life of the time; the originals are in the National Archives and were edited in six volumes by Muriel St Clare Byrne (1981), with a one-volume abridgement by B. Boland (1983).

Listener A BBC weekly magazine, of which the first number appeared on 16 January 1929, the last in 1991; it published reviews, broadcasts, essays, poetry, and so on. Its literary editor from 1935 to 1959 was J. R. *Ackerley, who attracted work from many distinguished writers. *The Music of What Happens: Poems from the Listener* (1981), edited by Derwent May (1930), poet and novelist, and literary editor from 1965, contains work by Stevie *Smith, Philip *Larkin, Peter *Porter, Ted *Hughes, Seamus *Heaney, and others.

LISTER, Thomas Henry (1800–42) The first registrar-general of England and Wales. He was a neglected but accomplished novelist, much influenced by Jane *Austen, whose tone he noticeably adopts and the names of whose characters he sometimes uses. Although they contain certain overdramatic incidents, *Granby* (1826), *Herbert Lacy* (1828), and *Arlington* (1832) are all shrewd and animated works, which describe with an ironic eye the aristocratic and upper-middle-class society of the time.

LISZT, Franz (1811–86) Hungarian composer, conductor, and pianist of exceptional virtuosity, a central figure in the

*Romantic movement. He made three concert tours to England, 1824–7, and wrote a 'paraphrase' for piano and orchestra on 'God Save the Queen' and 'Rule Britannia' (1841). His series of twelve 'symphonic poems' (1856–61), on such subjects as *Orpheus* and *Prometheus,* contains a *Mazeppa* after Lord *Byron and concludes with a **Hamlet*, originally planned as an overture to the play. There is a single delicate English setting, of Alfred *Tennyson's 'Go not, happy day'; a late choral work, *Die Glocken des Strasburger Münsters* (1875), is based on an episode from Henry Wadsworth *Longfellow's *Golden Legend.* When Liszt died, George Bernard *Shaw described him as 'a man who loved his art, despised money, attracted everybody worth knowing in the nineteenth century, lived through the worst of it, and got away from it at last with his hands unstained'.

Literary Culture and the Novel in the New Millennium *See introductory essay* pp. 1–8.

Literary Gazette (1817–62) A very successful journal founded by Henry *Colburn, with William Jerdan (1782–1869) as editor. It aimed at a very wide coverage of books, fine arts, and sciences, but most of the space was given to book reviews and long extracts from the works reviewed. Early contributors, in the days of its greatest success, included George *Crabbe, Mary Russell *Mitford, Barry *Cornwall, and Letitia Elizabeth *Landon.

literati A term introduced into English in 1624 by Robert *Burton to refer to the literate class in China, and later applied to the writers and readers of fashionable literature in other communities, often by contrast with the practical scientists, or virtuosi. The term is now often used to identify those who frequented the literary clubs and leading bookshops of 18th-century Edinburgh (including residents like Robert *Fergusson, Alison *Cockburn, James *Boswell, and Henry *Mackenzie, along with visitors like John *Gay, Daniel *Defoe, Oliver *Goldsmith, and Tobias *Smollett). It is more narrowly applied to a group of professional men, mostly lawyers and clergy, and supporters of the Moderate party in the Scottish Church, who deliberately cultivated an English writing style, both to make a cultural impact on London society and to cement the political union with England. They included the lawyers Henry Home (1696–1782) and James *Monboddo, the philosophers David *Hume and Adam *Smith, and the clerical coterie of Hugh *Blair, Alexander *Carlyle, Adam *Ferguson, John *Home, and William *Wilkie, several of whom were associated with the abortive first **Edinburgh Review.* Although their writings were primarily on history, philosophy, and the theory of criticism, many of them also supported the legalization and revival of the theatre, against strong Calvinist opposition. Hume in 1752 and James *Beattie in 1779 assisted the movement for stylistic 'improvement' by publishing collections of unacceptable 'Scotticisms'; and the actor-manager Thomas Sheridan (1719?–88) lectured to men's and women's classes on English elocution in 1761 under the auspices of the *Select Society.
See SCOTTISH ENLIGHTENMENT.

litotes A figure of speech in which an affirmative is expressed by the negative of the contrary, for example 'a citizen of no mean city', 'a not unhandsome man'; an ironical understatement.

Little Billee A humorous ballad of three sailors of Bristol, of whom Little Billee is the youngest. When provisions fail he narrowly escapes being eaten by the other two. *Thackeray wrote a version of the ballad. 'Little Billee' was the nickname of the hero of George Du Maurier's **Trilby.*

Little Black Sambo (1899) A best-selling picture book by Helen Bannerman (née Watson) (1862–1946), a Scot living in India, who sold the book to the publisher Grant Richards for £5. It became notorious as a supposed symbol of racism. Elizabeth Hay's *Sambo Sahib* (1981) details the controversy.

Little Dorrit A novel by Charles *Dickens, published in monthly parts, 1855–7. William Dorrit has been so long in the Marshalsea prison for debtors (where Dickens's own father was briefly imprisoned) that he has become the 'Father of the Marshalsea'. He has had the misfortune to be responsible for an uncompleted contract with the Circumlocution Office (a satirical portrait of government departments of the day, with their incompetent officials typified in the Barnacles). His lot is alleviated by the devotion of Amy, his youngest daughter, 'Little Dorrit', born in the Marshalsea, whose diminutive stature is compensated by her greatness of heart. Amy has a snobbish sister Fanny, a theatrical dancer, and a scapegrace brother, Tip. Old Dorrit and Amy are befriended by Arthur Clennam, the middle-aged hero, for whom Little Dorrit conceives a deep passion, at first unrequited. The unexpected discovery that William Dorrit is heir to a fortune raises the family to affluence. Except Little Dorrit, they become arrogant and purse-proud. Clennam, on the other hand, owing to an unfortunate speculation, is brought to the debtors' prison, and is found in the Marshalsea, sick and despairing, by Little Dorrit, who tenderly nurses him and consoles him. He learns the value of her love, but her fortune stands in the way of his asking her to marry him. The loss of it makes their union possible, on Clennam's release.

With this main theme is wound the thread of an elaborate mystery. Clennam has long suspected that his mother, a grimly puritanical paralysed woman, living in a gloomy house with a former attendant and present business partner, Flintwinch, has done some wrong to Little Dorrit. Through the agency of a stagy villain, Rigaud, alias Blandois, this is brought to light, and it becomes clear that Mrs Clennam is not Arthur's mother, and that her religious principles have not prevented her from suppressing a codicil in a will that benefited the Dorrit family.

There are a host of vivid minor characters, including the worthy Pancks, rent-collector to the humbug Casby; Casby's voluble daughter Flora Finching, the early love of Arthur Clennam; her eccentric relative 'Mr F's Aunt'; Merdle, the swindling financier, and Mrs Merdle, who 'piques herself on being society'; Affery, the villain Flintwinch's wife; 'Young John' Chivery, the son of the Marshalsea warder; and the Meagles and Gowan households.

Little Dorrit was heavily criticized on publication, largely for its sombre tone and complex plot, but later critics such as George Bernard *Shaw (his 'masterpiece among many masterpieces'), Lionel *Trilling, and Angus *Wilson have done much to reverse this judgement. Penetrating in its explorations of themes of imprisonment, hypocrisy, loyalty, and betrayal, it is now among the most widely admired of Dickens's novels.

Little Gidding A manor in Huntingdonshire where Nicholas *Ferrar and his family established, 1625–46, a religious community of some 40 members, following a systematic rule of private devotion, public charity, and study. The house was visited by Charles I, Richard *Crashaw, and George *Herbert. Joseph *Shorthouse's novel *John Inglesant* (1881) portrays its life vividly. It was raided by Cromwell's soldiers in 1646, and the community dispersed. T. S. *Eliot celebrates it in 'Little Gidding', one of the **Four Quartets*, and a record of its activities survives in *The Little Gidding Story Books*, five manuscript volumes bound by Mary Collett, part of which was printed in 1899 (ed. E. C. Sharland).

Little John Companion of *Robin Hood from early ballads and chronicles. A yeoman and archer, he figures in Walter Scott's **Ivanhoe*.

little magazines A term used to describe minority literary and artistic periodicals, possibly derived from one of the better known of such publications, the **Little Review*. Notable English 'little magazines' include the **London Magazine*, *New Verse*, *Poetry Review*, the **Review* and its successor the *New Review*, **Stand*, **Agenda*, *Poetry and Audience*, **PN Review*, *Areté*, *Printer's Devil*, and *Thumbscrew*.

Little Review An American monthly magazine founded in Chicago in 1914 by Margaret Anderson. In 1916 it came under the influence of Ezra *Pound, who was foreign editor from 1917 to 1919; it published W. B. *Yeats, Wyndham *Lewis, T. S. *Eliot, Ford Madox *Ford, and, notably, from 1918, chapters of James *Joyce's **Ulysses*. It later became a quarterly published from Paris (1924–9), edited principally by Jane Heap (1883–1964) and including work by Ernest *Hemingway, E. E. *Cummings, and Hart *Crane.

Little Women (1868) By L. M. *Alcott, based on the author's New England childhood and concerning the lives of Meg, Jo, Amy, and Beth March and their 'Marmee', while their father is serving as a chaplain in the Civil War. Recent criticism has found dark psychological undercurrents beneath its apparently cosy surface. One of the most popular of children's books, it has been filmed five times, and there have been many adaptations for television.

LITTLEWOOD, Joan (1914–2002) Director whose company, Theatre Workshop, had a strong influence on post-war British theatre. Born in south London, she trained at RADA, and at one time worked as a BBC radio producer. In 1936 Littlewood created a left-wing touring company, Theatre Union. Out of this evolved Theatre Workshop, which combined a radical social conscience with an exuberant musical style. Based at the Theatre Royal, Stratford East, from 1953, the company staged rare English and foreign classics, new works by Shelagh *Delaney and Brendan *Behan, and popular musicals by Lionel Bart. Littlewood's most celebrated production was *Oh, What a Lovely War!* (1963), a documentary satire counterpointing the grim statistics of First World War carnage with the affirmative popular songs of the period. In 1994 she published her idiosyncratic autobiography, *Joan's Book*. See Howard Goorney, *The Theatre Workshop Story* (1981); R. Leach, *Theatre Workshop: Joan Littlewood and the Making of Modern British Theatre* (2006).

LITTRÉ, Émile (1801–81) French scholar, philosopher, and lexicographer, who began work on his great dictionary of the French language in 1846. It was published in four volumes (1863–72), with a supplementary volume in 1877. The whole work was reprinted in 1950. Littré was a follower of Auguste *Comte, becoming the leading exponent of the positive philosophy after Comte's death, publishing *Auguste Comte et la philosophie positive* in 1863. In 1867 he founded with Grégoire Wyrouboff, the Russian positivist, the *Revue de philosophie positive*. Littré also edited and translated the works of *Hippocrates (1839–61) and wrote an *Histoire de la langue française* (1862).

liturgy A formal act of worship or church service, as opposed to private devotion, involving a prescribed form of words and ceremonies spoken and performed by the priest and sometimes by the congregation. In Christian churches the Christian year forms the basis of the liturgy, and in some medieval churches Latin liturgical drama based on stories from the life of Christ was enacted. Vernacular *mystery plays may have developed from these. The term was sometimes used as shorthand for the *Book of *Common Prayer*. Under Archbishop *Laud and again with the High Church revival in the 19th century, liturgy was particularly valued. It was deeply disliked by the *Puritans and their successors. Seventeenth-century poems on the passion of Christ, for example by Richard *Crashaw, or George *Herbert's 'The Sacrifice', owe a good deal to liturgical tradition, as does John *Keble's phenomenally successful *Christian Year* (1827). *See* PSALMS.

LIVELY, Penelope (1933–) Novelist and children's writer, born in Cairo, educated at St Anne's College, Oxford, where she read history. In 1957 she married Jack Lively, tutor in politics at St Peter's College, Oxford. The intrusion of the past upon the present is a recurrent theme in her graceful, alert fiction. She began by writing novels for children, including *The Ghost of Thomas Kempe* (1973), which won the Carnegie Medal. Her first adult novel, *The Road to Lichfield* (1977), was followed by *Treasures of Time* (1979), which brings past and present together through the figure of a distinguished archaeologist. *Moon Tiger* (1987), which won the *Booker Prize, presents the recollections of a dying woman, from her childhood just after the First World War to the 1970s. Her collected short stories were published in 1986 as *Pack of Cards*. There are two volumes of autobiography, *Oleander, Jacaranda* (1994) and *A House Unlocked* (2001), and an exercise in alternative autobiography, *Making it up* (2005).

Liverpool poets The name given to a group of three poets, Adrian *Henri, Roger *McGough, and Brian *Patten, who came together in the 1960s in the period of the Liverpool euphoria generated partly by the success of the *Beatles. They performed together, and published together in various periodicals and anthologies including *The Mersey Sound* (1967), *The Liverpool Scene* (1967), and *New Volume* (1983). The combined tone of their work was pop, urban, anti-academic, good-humoured, and vocal: poetry was conceived by them as a medium for public rather than private consumption, a *performance art.

Lives of the English Poets, The A work by Samuel *Johnson, originally entitled *Prefaces, Biographical and Critical, to the Works of the English Poets*, published 1779–81. Johnson was invited in 1777 by a deputation of London booksellers to provide biographical prefaces for an edition of the works of various English poets, from the period of John *Milton onwards, designed to rival cheap multi-volume collections published in Scotland. To the proposed selection Johnson added four minor poets (Sir Richard *Blackmore, Isaac *Watts, John *Pomfret, and Thomas Yalden (1671–1736)), making 52 in all. When the work was completed the prefaces were issued separately as *The Lives of the Most Eminent English Poets*, 4 vols (1781). The *Lives* contain much interesting biographical matter, particularly where Johnson knew the poet concerned, as in the case of Richard *Savage; but they are not always accurate by modern standards. Johnson's criticism was fearlessly idiosyncratic and much of it was at once controversial. His hostility towards Milton's republicanism and the obscurity of Thomas *Gray's Odes inspired particularly vociferous protest. He attacked the personal characters of the earl of *Rochester and Jonathan *Swift, and displayed no deference towards the work of gentlemen amateurs; his critique of the metaphysical style in his account of Abraham *Cowley became notorious. But the work is also marked by a deep appreciation of the achievements of poets in their personal and historical situations, and remains a classic in the history of critical taste and judgement. T. S. *Eliot ('Johnson as Critic and Poet', 1944) credited it 'with a coherence, as well as an amplitude, which no other English criticism can claim'. See the four-volume edition by Roger Lonsdale (2006).
See also BIOGRAPHY.

LIVINGSTONE, David (1813–73) Explorer and missionary, born in Blantyre, Lanarkshire, Scotland. He educated himself before training as a doctor and being ordained for the London Missionary Society. Arrived in South Africa in 1841, he married but found settled missionary life uncongenial, and embarked upon a series of expeditions northwards. The discovery of Lake Ngami in 1849 was followed by encounters with the Makololo in the Zambesi Valley who, in effect, sponsored his epic crossing of the continent in 1853–6 including his visit to the Victoria Falls. This attracted the attention of the *Royal Geographical Society who made Livingstone famous. *Missionary Travels and Researches* (1857) understandably became one of the most popular travel books ever. People and natural history are described in an expert but attractive way whilst Livingstone's serious moral purpose—to end the slave trade—becomes clear. The British government appointed him to lead an expedition from 1858 to 1863 using steamboats on the Zambesi to reach the interior. Livingstone proved a poor leader of either Europeans or Africans and little was achieved for the immediate benefit of local Africans. However, Lake Malawi and other important features were put on the map. Livingstone's second book, *Narrative of an Expedition to the Zambezi* (1865), was less appealing than his first. In 1866 he returned to Africa without European companions to report further on the slave trade and in the hope of solving the problem of the source of the Nile which many felt *Speke's discovery of Lake Victoria had not settled. His wanderings led to several relief expeditions but only Henry *Stanley reached him, in the famous encounter of October 1871. Livingstone had become obsessed with the idea reported by *Herodotus 2,200 years before that there existed a hill with the Nile's 'fountains', which he hoped to find. In fact, when he died in the swamps of Lake Bangweulu, he was at the sources of the Congo River. His mummified remains were brought to the coast by his African companions and subsequently buried in Westminster Abbey. Horace Waller edited his *Last Journals* (1874), cementing the image of a modern saint and martyr dying to save Africa from the ravages of the slave trade.

LIVY (Titus Livius) (59 BC–?AD 17) Roman historian whose great work related the history of Rome from its beginnings to 9 BC. Of its 142 books only 35 have survived, the best known of which give us the legendary history of early Rome and the second Punic War. Most of what now survives was recovered by *Petrarch. *Machiavelli wrote *Discourses on Livy*, and Philemon *Holland translated Livy into English (1600). Livy's stories of Rome's beginnings became an essential part of classical education, and provided material for Painter's **Palace of Pleasure* (1566–7) and George *Pettie's similar work of 1576, for *Shakespeare's **Rape of Lucrece* (1594), and later for Thomas Babington *Macaulay's **Lays of Ancient Rome* (1842).

LLWYD, Morgan (1619–59) Puritan poet and preacher, born in Cynfal Fawr in Merionethshire and educated at Wrexham Grammar School, whose *Llyfyr y Tri Aderyn* ('Book of Three Birds', 1653) is seen as one of the classics of Welsh prose.

Llyr *See* MABINOGION.

LOCHHEAD, Liz (1947–) Scottish poet and dramatist, born in Motherwell, Lanarkshire, and educated at the Glasgow School of Art. Her poems and plays employ a colloquially ironic idiom to explore such themes as the ambiguous role of women in working-class culture, historical responsibility, and the relationship between vocalization and cultural authority. Her plays include *Blood and Ice* (1982), based on the life of Mary *Shelley; a Scots adaptation of *Molière's *Tartuffe* (1985); *Mary Queen of Scots Got her Head Chopped Off* (1987); a version of the *Medea* of *Euripides (2000); and the romantic comedy *Good Things* (2006). Her mature poetry is collected in *The Colour of Black and White: Poems 1984–2003* (2003).

LOCKE, John (1632–1704) Philosopher, born at Wrington, Somerset, educated at Westminster School and Christ Church, Oxford. He held various academic posts at that university, and became physician to the household of the first earl of *Shaftesbury in 1667. He held official positions and subsequently lived at Oxford, then fled to the Netherlands in 1683 as a consequence of Shaftesbury's plotting for Monmouth; how far he was himself involved is not certain. In 1687 he joined William of Orange at Rotterdam; on his return to England he became commissioner of appeals and member of the Council of Trade. His last years were spent in Essex in the home of Sir Francis and Lady Masham, the latter being the daughter of Ralph Cudworth (1617–88), one of the *Cambridge Platonists.

Locke's principal philosophical work is the **Essay Concerning Human Understanding* (1690), a work which led John Stuart *Mill to call him the 'unquestioned founder of the analytic philosophy of mind'. Always critical of 'enthusiasm', he was originally opposed to freedom of religion, and never supported Catholic emancipation; but in his maturity he defended the rights of the Dissenters on both moral and economic grounds. He published three *Letters* on Toleration between 1689 and 1692; a fourth was left unfinished at his death. His defence of simple biblical religion in *The Reasonableness of Christianity* (1695), without resort to creed or tradition, led to a charge of *Socinianism, which Locke replied to in two *Vindications* (1695, 1697). He was also involved in an extensive pamphlet war with Edward Stillingfleet (1696–8) over the alleged compatibility of his *Essay* with Socinianism and *Deism.

Locke published in 1690 two *Treatises of Government* designed to combat the theory of the divine right of kings. He finds the origin of the civil state in a contract. The 'legislative', or government, 'being only a fiduciary power to act for certain ends, there remains still in the people the supreme power to remove or alter the legislative when they find the legislative act contrary to the trust reposed in them'. Throughout, Locke in his theory of the 'Original Contract' opposes absolutism; the first *Treatise* is specifically an attack on Sir Robert Filmer's *Patriarcha*. Although Locke in his early manuscripts was closer to Thomas *Hobbes's authoritarianism and continues to share with Hobbes the view that civil obligations are founded in contract, he strongly rejected Hobbes's view that the sovereign is above the law and no party to the contract. He published a volume on education in 1693, and on the rate of interest and the value of money in 1692 and 1695. The first edition of his collected works appeared in 1714. The Clarendon edition of his works, projected to be 30 volumes, was launched in 1975.

Locke's writings had an immense influence on the literature of succeeding generations, and he was very widely read. His *Thoughts Concerning Education*, concerned with practical advice on the upbringing of 'sons of gentlemen', were given to Samuel *Richardson's Pamela by Mr B—, and to his son by the earl of *Chesterfield, and their influence is seen in Jean-Jacques *Rousseau's *Émile* (1762); his view of the child's mind as a *tabula rasa*, and his distinctions between wit and judgement, were the subject of much discussion in the *Augustan age. The anti-philosophy jokes of the *Scriblerus Club demonstrate the currency of his ideas; Joseph *Addison was his champion in many essays. But perhaps his greatest literary influence was on Laurence *Sterne, who quotes him frequently in **Tristram Shandy*, and who was deeply interested in his theories of the random association of ideas, of the measuring of time, and the nature of sensation. On this subject, see Kenneth MacLean, *John Locke and English Literature of the Eighteenth Century* (1936). See *An Essay Concerning Human Understanding*, ed. Peter H. Nidditch (1975); *A Paraphrase and Notes on the Epistles of St Paul*, ed. Arthur W. Wainwright (2 vols, 1987); *The Correspondence of John Locke*, ed. E. S. De Beer (8 vols, 1976–89).
See also RESTORATION.

LOCKE, Matthew (*c.*1622–1677) The most eminent composer of the early *Restoration, prolific in many forms, but especially important as a producer of vocal and instrumental music for the stage; notable surviving examples include plays by Sir George *Etherege, Thomas *D'Urfey, Sir William *D'Avenant, and Elkanah *Settle, for whose *Empress of Morocco* (1673) he wrote a masque, 'Orpheus and Euridice'. His music for the 1659 revival of James *Shirley's masque *Cupid and Death* (for which the original music was written by Orlando *Gibbons's son Christopher) is interesting for its declamatory, recitative style of word setting, the essential feature upon which the future development of *opera was to depend. The music he wrote for D'Avenant's *The Siege of Rhodes* (1656), an early operatic experiment, is lost. His music for Thomas *Shadwell's *Psyche* (1675), based on a *tragédie-ballet* by *Molière, together with his contributions to Shadwell's version of *The *Tempest* (1674), appeared as *The English Opera* in 1675.

LOCKER-LAMPSON, Frederick (1821–95) Poet and bibliophile, born Locker, remembered for his light verse, included in *London Lyrics* (1857), *Lyra Elegantiarum* (1867, an anthology, which, in its preface, offers a description of **vers de société*, in which 'sentiment never surges into passion, and where humour never overflows into boisterous merriment'), and *Patchwork* (1879).

LOCKHART, John Gibson (1794–1854) Writer, biographer, and critic, born at Cambusnethan, educated at Glasgow University and Balliol College, Oxford. He was called to the Scottish bar, and became one of the principal contributors to *Blackwood's Magazine*. In 1817 he began a long series of attacks on, in particular, Leigh *Hunt, John *Keats, and William *Hazlitt, castigating them as the low-born *'Cockney School of Poetry' and treating their work with great harshness. He did, however, support William *Wordsworth and S. T. *Coleridge. In 1818 he translated Friedrich von *Schlegel's *Geschichte der alten und neuen Literatur* as *Lectures on the History of Literature, Ancient and Modern*, and he contributed several important articles on German literature to *Blackwood's* during the 1820s. From 1825 to 1853 he was editor of the *Quarterly Review*. His ferocity as a critic was reflected in his chosen nickname, 'The Scorpion'. He published a wide range of books. *Peter's Letters to his Kinsfolk* (1819) contains spirited sketches of life in Edinburgh and Glasgow. In 1821 he published *Valerius*, set in Rome under Trajan; in 1822 came his novel *Some Passages in the Life of Adam Blair*, a dark and disquieting story of a Scots minister. This was followed in 1823 by a conventional and popular romance, *Reginald Dalton*, and by his translations of *Ancient Spanish Ballads*. His *Life of Burns* appeared in 1828, and in 1837–8 his *Memoirs of the Life of Sir Walter Scott* (his father-in-law), which is comprehensive, methodical, and full of personal detail.

Locksley Hall A poem in trochaics by Alfred *Tennyson, published 1842, probably written 1837–8. It consists of a monologue spoken by a disappointed lover, revisiting the desolate moorland home by the sea where he had been brought up by an unsympathetic uncle, and where he fell in love with his cousin Amy. She returned his love, but, through family pressure, accepted another suitor. The narrator scorns the modern world of steamship and railway, and ends with an ambiguous acceptance of 'the ringing grooves of change'—a phrase that Tennyson wrote while under the temporary impression that the new railways ran in grooves, not on rails.

Locrine (Logrin) In *Geoffrey of Monmouth's *History* (II. 1–5), the eldest son of Brutus (*see* BRUT) and Ignoge. He rules over Loegria (*Logres), his inherited third of the kingdom. He abandoned his wife Gwendolen for Estrildis, later mother of his daughter Sabrina. A. C. *Swinburne wrote a play concerning him (*Locrine*, 1887).

Locrine, The Lamentable Tragedy of A play published in 1595, and included in the third Shakespeare *folio. The authorship is unknown. The play deals with the legend of *Locrine, king of England, his queen Gwendolen, and Estrildis.

LODGE, David (1935–) Critic and novelist, born in London and educated at University College London; he became professor of modern English literature at the University of Birmingham in 1976. Critical books such as *Language of Fiction* (1966), *Working with Structuralism* (1981), and *After Bakhtin* (1990) display his gift for lucid exposition, and he has done much to explain continental literary theory in Britain, while simultaneously expressing 'a modest affirmation of faith in the future of realistic fiction'. Written in keeping with that faith, many of his novels—*The British Museum is Falling Down* (1965), *Changing Places* (1975), *Small World* (1984), *Thinks...*(2001)—have academic settings. Others (*How Far Can You Go?*, 1980, and *Paradise News*, 1991) focus on changes and challenges faced by Roman Catholics in recent times. Lodge's talent for satiric comedy, advocacy of liberal values, and often masterly use of juxtaposition in the structuring of his narratives are especially well exhibited in *Nice Work* (1988), an elegant and entertaining 20th-century version of the Victorian *condition of England novel, which throws together a post-structuralist feminist academic and a Midlands industrialist of unreconstructed views. *Author, Author* (2004) fictionalizes the events of Henry *James's middle years, particularly his ventures into play writing. Lodge's own plays include *The Writing Game* (1990) and *Home Truths* (1998, reworked as a novella, 1999). His 2008 novel, *Deaf Sentence*, comically and sympathetically depicts a retired academic struggling with the trials of ageing.

LODGE, Thomas (1558–1625) Writer and doctor, son of Sir Thomas Lodge, lord mayor of London, educated at Merchant Taylors' School, London, and Trinity College, Oxford. He was a student of Lincoln's Inn in 1578 and seems to have converted to Roman Catholicism *c.*1580. In 1579–80 he published an anonymous *Defence of Poetry*, a reply to Stephen *Gosson's *School of Abuse*, and in 1584 *An Alarum against Usurers* (dedicated to Philip *Sidney), depicting the dangers that moneylenders present to young spendthrifts. Appended to it was a prose romance, *Forbonius and Prisceria*. *Scilla's *Metamorphosis*, an Ovidian verse fable, was published in 1589. In 1585 and 1586 Lodge may have sailed on a privateering expedition to the Terceras and the Canaries, and in 1591–3 to South America with the adventurer Thomas Cavendish (1560–92). On the earlier voyage he said he wrote his best-known romance, *Rosalynde* (1590), 'hatched in the storms of the ocean, and feathered in the surges of many perilous seas'. After four more prose romances he published *Phillis: Honoured with Pastoral Sonnets, Elegies, and Amorous Delights* (1593), including many poems adapted from Italian and French models, to which was appended 'The Complaint of Elstred', the story of King *Locrine's unhappy mistress. His play *The Wounds of Civil War* (1594), about Marius and Sulla, had been performed by the Lord Admiral's Men; he also wrote *A Looking Glass for London and England* (1594), in collaboration with Robert *Greene. No other plays by him are known. *A Fig for Momus* (1595) was a miscellaneous collection of satirical poems, including epistles addressed to Samuel Daniel and Michael *Drayton. *Wit's Misery, and the World's Madness: Discovering the Devils Incarnate of this Age* appeared in 1596, as did a remarkable romance, *A *Margarite of America*, written during the second voyage, under Cavendish, while they were near the Magellan Straits. Lodge left England in 1597 to study medicine at Avignon; he was incorporated MD at Oxford in 1602, and in the next year published *A Treatise of the Plague*. He completed two major works of translation: the works of *Josephus (1602), which was frequently reprinted, and of Lucius Annaeus

*Seneca (1614). His last work was a translation of the commentary on *Du Bartas (1621) by the French humanist Simon Goulart (1543–1628). Lodge is now mainly remembered for *Rosalynde* and for the lyrics scattered throughout his romances. His works were edited in four volumes by Edmund *Gosse (1883).

LOFFT, Capel (1751–1824) Barrister, reformer, and eccentric, who lived on his family estate near Bury St Edmunds and corresponded with many eminent literary figures. He published poems and essays, but is perhaps best remembered for his support of Robert *Bloomfield, whose poem *The Farmer's Boy* (1800) he edited (claiming to have made only 'occasional corrections...with respect to orthography and sometimes in the grammatical construction'). His son, also Capel Lofft (1806–73) and also somewhat eccentric, complained that his father's 'love of literature was excessive' in his own 'mental autobiography', *Self-Formation* (1837); he also wrote an *epic on *Chartism called *Ernest* (1839).

LOFTING, Hugh (1886–1947) Born in Maidenhead, Berkshire. A civil engineer who studied at the Massachusetts Institute of Technology (MIT), Lofting settled in New York in 1912. While fighting in France and Flanders, he was impressed by the animals' stoicism and the scanty care they received. His hero, *Dr Dolittle, was created in illustrated letters sent home to his children. Lofting published fourteen Dr Dolittle books, winning the Newbery Medal for *The Voyages of Dr Dolittle* in 1923. Films based on the series were made in 1967 (Richard Fleischer) with Rex Harrison, and in 1998 (Betty Thomas) with Eddie Murphy.

Logic, Ratiocinative and Inductive, A System of A treatise by John Stuart *Mill, published 1843, revised and enlarged in the editions of 1850 and 1872. Mill's *Logic* argues that all knowledge is derived 'from experience, and all moral and intellectual qualities principally from the direction given to the associations'. In attributing to experience and association our belief in mathematical and physical laws, he came into conflict with the intuitional philosophers, giving his own explanation 'of that peculiar character of what are called necessary truths, which is adduced as proof that their evidence must come from a deeper source than experience'. This conflict is further developed in Mill's *Examination of Sir William Hamilton's Philosophy*.

Logres In *Geoffrey of Monmouth's *History* (where it is called Loegria), the part of Brutus' kingdom assigned to his eldest son *Locrine, that is, England. It is the usual term for Arthur's kingdom in medieval romance from *Chrétien de Troyes onwards.

LOGUE, Christopher (1926–) Poet, playwright, and translator, born in Portsmouth. Living in Paris during the 1950s, he co-edited with Alexander Trocchi (1925–84) the short-lived but influential magazine *Merlin* (1952–5) which published work by Samuel *Beckett, Jean *Genet, and Pablo *Neruda. He was associated with the early years of the *English Stage Company, which put on several of his plays, including the *Brechtian musical *The Lily White Boys* (1960, with Harry Cookson). He was a pioneer in the *jazz poetry movement, and experimented with publishing his poems as Verse Posters. His volumes of poetry include *Wand and Quartet* (1953), *New Numbers* (1969), and *Ode to the Dodo: Poems from 1953–1978* (1981). A *Selected Poems* was published in 1996, and an autobiography, *Prince Charming*, in 1999. He is also widely known for his controversial, continuing versions of sections of *Homer's *Iliad*, collected as *Logue's Homer* in 2001, with further volumes succeeding.

Lohengrin The son of *Perceval, first mentioned in the *Parzival* (c.1205) of *Wolfram von Eschenbach, and in Wolfram's incomplete epic *Titurel*. Summoned from the Temple of the *Grail at Montsalvatsch, he is brought in a swan-boat to Antwerp. He marries Princess Elsa of Brabant on the condition that she does not ask what his race is; but she does, and the swan-boat returns him to his Grail vigil. The story is the subject of Richard *Wagner's opera (1850).

Lollards From Middle Dutch *lollaert*, 'mumbler', but also polemically associated with the Latin *lolium*, the tares of the parable in Matthew 13: 24–30. Commonly used since the 14th century to denote the followers of John *Wyclif, the word has recently come under renewed scrutiny on two accounts. First, some early usage clearly denotes something other than Wycliffism, as in the C-text of *Piers Plowman* where the term is used in connection with both the idle (including delinquent friars) and those privileged with prophetic insight ('lunatyk lollares'). Second, later examples suggest persistent imprecise usage, as in the false accusations made against Margery *Kempe.

Lollius An unknown author mentioned three times by Chaucer in connection with the Trojan War (*Troilus and Criseyde*, I. 394, V. 1653, and *The *House of Fame*, l. 1468), once regarded as a great puzzle, but no doubt correctly explained (by R. G. Latham in 1868) as a misreading of *Horace, *Epistles*, I. 2. 1: 'Troiani belli scriptorem, Maxime Lolli,...relegi', where 'Lolli' is the vocative for the addressee of the letter, not the *scriptor*. Lollius came by this misreading to be regarded as a writer on the Trojan War whose work, naturally, was missing and he thus provided a useful fiction as Chaucer's source. The *scriptor* referred to in Horace is Homer, and *Maxime* is the family name of *Lollius*.

London A poem in heroic couplets by Samuel *Johnson, published anonymously by Robert *Dodsley in 1738, in imitation of the Third Satire of *Juvenal, quotations from which appeared at the foot of the page. Alexander *Pope predicted its unknown author would soon be 'déterré' ('unearthed'). The poem reflects with bitter irony on London's vices and affectations, on the oppression of the poor, and the corruption of Sir Robert *Walpole's administration.

London, A Survey of See Stow, John.

LONDON, Jack (John Griffith) (1876–1916) American novelist, born in San Francisco. He grew up in poverty, scratching a living in various legal and illegal ways—robbing the oyster beds, working in a canning factory and a jute mill, serving aged 17 as a common sailor, and taking part in the Klondike gold rush of 1897. These experiences provided material for his works, and made him a socialist. He vigorously attacked capitalism and exploitation, while maintaining some markedly chauvinist and racist attitudes. *The Son of the Wolf* (1900), the first of his many collections of tales, is based upon life in the far north, as is the book that brought him recognition, *The Call of the Wild* (1903), which tells the story of the dog Buck, who, after his master's death, returns to the primitive world to lead a wolf pack. In the same year appeared *The People of the Abyss*, an emotive documentary based on some weeks spent in the slums of London's East End. Other tales of struggle, travel, and adventure followed, including *The Sea-Wolf* (1904), *White Fang* (1906, another tale with dog as hero), *South Sea Tales* (1911), and *Jerry of the South Seas* (1917). *The Iron Heel* (1908) is a novel about the class struggle, which prophesies a fascist revolution; *The Valley of the Moon* (1913) advocates a return to the land in an ideal community. One of London's most interesting novels is the semi-autobiographical *Martin Eden* (1909), which describes the struggles of the protagonist, a sailor and labourer, to acquire education and to become a writer. *John Barleycorn* (1913), also semi-autobiographical, is a record of London's own struggle against alcohol. He also wrote socialist treatises, autobiographical essays, and much journalism in his short but intensely active life. The Fitzroy Edition of his works (Arco 1962–8) runs to eighteen volumes. See Andrew Sinclair, *Jack: A Biography of Jack London* (1977).

London Assurance See Boucicault, Dion.

London Cuckolds, The A rollicking farce by Edward Ravenscroft (*fl.* 1671–97), first produced at the Dorset Gardens theatre in 1681 and annually revived on Lord Mayor's Day (9 November) for nearly a century. An adaptation by Terry *Johnson was performed at the National Theatre in 1998.

London Gazette See Oxford Gazette.

London Labour and the London Poor See Mayhew, Henry.

London Library Founded in 1841 by Thomas *Carlyle, with the support of many literary figures, including William *Gladstone, George *Grote, and Henry *Hallam. The manifesto, published on 15 February 1841, deplored the lack of libraries in London, and carried a quotation from Edward *Gibbon: 'The greatest city in the world is destitute of that useful institution, a public library.' It opened on 3 May 1841, in two rooms in Pall Mall, with a stock of 3,000 volumes and with John George Cochrane (1761–1852) as its first librarian. Initial subscribers included Charles *Dickens, Thomas *Macaulay, and William *Macready. It moved to its present premises in St James's Square in 1845, and continues to be much valued by its many members. See John Wells, *Rude Words: History of the London Library* (1991). *See also* libraries, public.

London Magazine (1) A periodical which ran from 1732 to 1785, founded in opposition to the **Gentleman's Magazine*. (2) A magazine of great brilliance (1820–29), established under the editorship of John *Scott on roughly the same miscellany plan as **Blackwood's Magazine*, except that it was non-political and gave a large proportion of its space to writers and books. Scott championed the work of the younger writers, including William *Wordsworth, Charles *Lamb, Thomas *De Quincey, John *Clare, Thomas *Hood, Thomas *Carlyle, and in particular the *'Cockney School' (John *Keats, Leigh *Hunt, and William *Hazlitt). But he was soon provoked into attacks on *Blackwood's*, which bitterly derided most of his writers, and he was killed in a duel in 1821 by J. H. Christie, its representative, who was later acquitted of murder. John *Taylor (1781–1864) then took over the editorship with the assistance of Hood; but, although the magazine continued successfully for another eight years, Taylor's habit of editorial interference angered his writers, and many, including Lamb and Hazlitt, withdrew their work; see J. Bauer, *The London Magazine 1820–29* (1953). (3) A monthly literary magazine founded in 1954 by John *Lehmann, and edited by him until 1961. It was welcomed in its first issue by T. S. *Eliot as a non-university-based periodical that would 'boldly assume the existence of a public interested in serious literature'. It aimed to avoid being 'narrowly British' or political in content; Lehmann (*The Ample Proposition*, 1966) writes that he aimed to create 'the London magazine, and not the Magazine of Oxford, or Cambridge, or Redbrick', and to reach Samuel *Johnson's 'common reader'. He was succeeded as editor by Alan *Ross, who enlarged the magazine's range to cover other arts, including photography.

London Mercury A monthly literary periodical founded in 1919 by J. C. *Squire, who edited it until 1934. Although its contributors included modernists and those sympathetic to experiment, including Aldous *Huxley, D. H. *Lawrence, and Edgell *Rickword, the dominant tone was set by Squire's editorials, which condemned 'anarchical cleverness', and by traditionalist contributors of fiction, poetry, and reviews, including Walter *de la Mare, G. K. *Chesterton, Hilaire *Belloc, W. H. *Davies, and Edward Shanks (1892–1953). In 1939 it was incorporated in *Life and Letters*.

London Prodigal, The A comedy published in 1605, attributed to Shakespeare in the title of the quarto edition of that year and included in the third and fourth *folios, but undoubtedly by some other, unidentified hand. The play is a comedy of London manners, and deals with the reclaiming of the prodigal young Flowerdale by the fidelity of his wife.

London Review of Books A literary and cultural review founded in 1979 and edited by Karl Miller (1931–), professor of modern English literature at University College London, in conscious emulation of the *New York Review of Books* (founded 1963) in both design and editorial approach. It has published critical essays and articles by many of the most prominent critics and scholars of the day, including Christopher *Ricks, John *Bayley, Frank *Kermode, A. J. P. *Taylor, David *Lodge, Sir Peter Medawar (1915–87), and Dan *Jacobson, and has published poems and fiction by Seamus *Heaney, Nadine *Gordimer, Gavin *Ewart, Douglas *Dunn, Tom *Paulin, Ted *Hughes, Peter *Redgrove, Derek *Walcott, and many others.

Loneliness of the Long Distance Runner, The A novella by Alan *Sillitoe.

LONGFELLOW, Henry Wadsworth (1807–82) American poet, born in Maine and educated at Bowdoin College, where he was the classmate of Nathaniel *Hawthorne. The offer of a professorship of modern languages at Bowdoin took him to Europe to study, 1826–9; after lecturing at Bowdoin he returned to Europe again to prepare for the post of professor at Harvard. His wife, travelling with him, died in the Netherlands in 1835. In 1836 he began his many influential years of teaching at Harvard.

His prose romance *Hyperion* (1839), a product of his bereavement, is the tale of a young man who seeks to forget sorrow in travel, a thread on which are hung philosophical discourses, poems, and legends. In the same year he published *Voices of the Night*, which includes his didactic pieces 'A Psalm of Life', 'Footsteps of Angels', and 'The Reaper and the Flowers'. *Ballads and Other Poems* appeared in 1841, with such well-known pieces as 'The Wreck of the Hesperus' and 'The Village Blacksmith'. In 1842 he met Charles *Dickens in America, and visited him in London later in the same year; on his voyage home he wrote *Poems on Slavery* (1842). By this time he was already one of the most widely read poets in America, and subsequent volumes confirmed this reputation. These include *The Belfry of Bruges and Other Poems* (1847); *Evangeline* (1849; a narrative poem in hexameters, set in Acadia, now Nova Scotia); *The Song of *Hiawatha* (1858); and *The Courtship of Miles Standish* (1858; another long hexameter narrative, based on a New England legend). In 1854 he resigned his professorship, but his creative life was tragically interrupted in 1861 by the death of his second wife, who was burned to death in a domestic accident. *Tales of a Wayside Inn* (1863, 1st series; with the rousing 'Paul Revere's Ride' and 'The Song of King Olaf') follows the form of the **Canterbury Tales*; a group of travellers, in the 'old-fashioned, quaint abode' of the inn, pass the evening by telling tales, directed by the landlord. Other 'Tales of a Wayside Inn' followed in 1872. See Newton Arvin, *Longfellow: His Life and Work* (1963).

LONGINUS (1st century AD) Supposed author of an important work on literary theory, known as 'Longinus *peri hypsous*' (*On the Sublime*). Traditionally ascribed to Dionysius Longinus or Cassius Longinus, the treatise is incomplete: probably we have two-thirds of the text. Longinus responds to Caecilius of Calacte, who had dealt unsatisfactorily with the subject of *hypsos* (sublimity), minimizing the element of *pathos* (emotion). Longinus rejects the technicalities of rhetorical theory: sublimity is 'the reflection of greatness of soul', not to be achieved by mere stylistic devices, and inseparable from emotion. Works which are uneven in quality and level, but which exhibit the highest qualities of intensity and imagination, are superior to 'faultless mediocrity'. The first English translation was published in 1652 by John Hall (bap. 1627, d. 1656), but Longinus' influence in England, felt in such writers as John *Dryden, Alexander *Pope, and Joseph *Addison, dates from the French translation by Nicholas *Boileau (1674). See *On Sublimity*, trans. D. A. Russell (1965). *See* SUBLIME.

Longinus ('Longeus' in *Malory) The traditional name of the Roman soldier who pierced with his spear the side of Christ at the Crucifixion. The lance in the *Grail legend is sometimes identified as his spear, as by Malory (*The Works of Sir Thomas Malory*, ed. E. Vinaver, rev. P. J. C. Field (3rd edn, 1990), 54). See R. S. Loomis (ed.), *Arthurian Literature in the Middle Ages* (1959).

LONGLEY, Edna (1940–) Née Broderick, poetry critic born in Dublin and educated at Trinity College there, where she met Michael *Longley, whom she later married. Longley taught for many years at Queen's University, Belfast, and later became professor emerita there. Daughter of a Scottish Presbyterian mother and an Irish Catholic father excommunicated for accepting the chair of mathematics at Trinity, she brings a subtly archipelagic imagination to bear on modern Irish and British poetry. Informed by a Yeatsian antipathy to abstraction, her work champions the aesthetic while insisting on the importance of the historical particularity out of which poems emerge. See *Poetry and Posterity* (2000).

LONGLEY, Michael (1939–) Irish poet, born to English parents in Belfast and educated at Trinity College, Dublin, where he studied classics. He is married to the critic Edna *Longley, with whom he shares a devotion, manifest in his work, to Edward *Thomas and Louis *MacNeice. The formalist command of *No Continuing City* (1969) was increasingly tempered by colloquialism and an undercurrent of unnerving fantasy in subsequent volumes. Longley's role as a celebrant of the ordinary has been challenged by the post-1968 *Troubles. Some of his most striking poems ('Wounds', 'The Linen Workers', 'The Butchers') explore the idea of home in relation to the despoliation of domesticity by political violence. Four collections from *Gorse Fires* (1991) to *Snow Water* (2004) bring an almost Japanese delicacy to their meditations on war, ageing, and the landscape of Co. Mayo. *Collected Poems* appeared in 2006. See F. Brearton, *Reading Michael Longley* (2006).

LONGMAN, Thomas (1699–1755) Bookseller, founder of the family firm of publishers, and one of the consortium behind Samuel *Johnson's *Dictionary.* His nephew's son Thomas Norton Longman (1771–1842) published work by William *Wordsworth, S. T. *Coleridge, and Walter *Scott, and became proprietor of the **Edinburgh Review.* The firm was absorbed by Pearson in 1968, but the imprint survives as a publisher of educational books. See Philip Wallis, *At the Sign of the Ship, 1724–1974* (1974).

LONSDALE, Frederick (1881–1954) Playwright, born Lionel Frederick Leonard, in St Helier, Jersey, the son of a seaman. His many successful, worldly, witty, and light-hearted drawing-room comedies include *Aren't We All?* (performed 1923), *The Last of Mrs Cheyney* (1925), and *On Approval* (1927). He also wrote musical comedies. See *Freddy Lonsdale* (1957) by his daughter Frances Donaldson.

Look Back in Anger A play by John *Osborne, first produced by the *English Stage Company at the Royal Court Theatre on 8 May 1956, published 1957. It proved a landmark in the history of the theatre, a focus for reaction against a previous generation (*see* KITCHEN SINK DRAMA), and a decisive contribution to the corporate image of the *Angry Young Man. The action takes place in a Midlands town, in the one-room flat of Jimmy and Alison Porter, and centres on their marital conflicts, which appear to arise largely from Jimmy's sense of their social incompatibility: he is a jazz-playing ex-student from a new university, working on a market sweet stall, she is a colonel's daughter. He is by turns violent, sentimental, maudlin, self-pitying, and sadistic, and has a fine line in rhetoric. The first act opens as Alison stands ironing the clothes of Jimmy and their lodger Cliff, as Jimmy reads the Sunday papers and abuses her and the 'Edwardian brigade' which her parents represent. In the second act the battle intensifies, as Alison's friend Helena attempts to rescue her from her disastrous marriage; Alison departs with her father, and Helena falls into Jimmy's arms. The third act opens with Helena at the ironing board; Alison returns, having lost the baby she was expecting, and she and Jimmy find a manner of reconciliation through humiliation and games-playing fantasy. In its use of social milieu, its iconoclastic social attitudes, and its exploration of sadomasochistic relationships, the play was highly influential.

Looking Backward: 2000–1887 A utopian novel by Edward *Bellamy, published in 1888.

LOOS, Anita (1888–1981) American screenwriter, novelist, and playwright, who began writing subtitles for D. W. Griffith in 1912. Best remembered for her classic comedy *Gentlemen Prefer Blondes* (1925), in which the ambitious Lorelei Lee from Little Rock, Arkansas, describes in faux-naïf prose her adventures and conquests: filmed by Howard Hawks in 1953 with Marilyn Monroe and Jane Russell.

LOPE DE VEGA *See* VEGA CARPIO, LOPE FÉLIX DE.

LORCA, Federico García *See* GARCÍA LORCA, FEDERICO.

Lord Jim A novel by Joseph *Conrad, published 1900. Jim is chief mate on board the *Patna*, an ill-manned ship carrying a party of pilgrims in Eastern waters. He is young, idealistic, and a dreamer of heroic deeds. When the *Patna* threatens to sink, the officers decide to save their own skins and escape in the few lifeboats; Jim despises them, but at the last moment, almost involuntarily, he jumps into a boat with them. The *Patna* does not sink and the pilgrims are rescued. What happens to Jim thereafter is related by an observer, Marlow. Jim, alone among the crew, remains to face the court of inquiry, disturbed at having abandoned his code of conduct. Condemned by the court and stripped of his papers, he tries to disappear, moving on whenever his past threatens to catch up with him. He searches for anonymity and the chance to redeem himself. Through Marlow's intervention Jim is sent to a remote trading station in Patusan. His efforts create order and well-being in a previously chaotic community and he wins the respect and affection of the people: for them, he becomes Tuan Jim ('Lord' Jim). He has achieved some sense of peace, but the memory of his jump is still with him. When Gentleman Brown and his gang of thieves arrive to plunder the village Jim begs the chiefs to spare them, pledging his own life against their departure. But Brown behaves treacherously and a massacre takes place. Jim feels he has only one course of action; rejecting the idea of flight, he delivers himself up to Chief Doramin, whose son was a victim of the massacre. Doramin shoots him and Jim willingly accepts this honourable death.

Lord of the Flies (1954) A novel by William *Golding. An aeroplane carrying a party of schoolboys crashes on a desert island. The boys' attempts, led by Ralph and Piggy, to set up a democratically run society quickly fail and the savagery which in Golding's work underlies man's nature takes over. Terror rules under the dictator Jack, and two boys are killed; it is only with the arrival of a shocked rescue officer that a mask of civilization returns. It is a savage reply to the naive optimism of R. M. *Ballantyne's *The Coral Island*.
See also BEELZEBUB.

Lord of the Rings, The J. R. R. *Tolkien's huge mythopoeic novel, which first appeared in three volumes in 1954–5. It tells the story of the heroic and finally successful struggle to destroy a powerful ring forged by the evil Sauron, selling a million copies in a 1965 pirated paperback edition in the United States and acquiring cult status among 1960s hippies, to the author's dismay. It inspired the influential role-play game *Dungeons and Dragons* (1974) and many other games and memorabilia, before New Zealand film-maker Peter Jackson took charge of bringing Middle Earth to the screen in 1995. *The Fellowship of the Ring* (2001), *The Two Towers* (2002), and *Return of the King* (2003), combining live action with digital effects, achieved massive commercial success, generally satisfying the novel's many fans and attracting countless new followers.

Lorna Doone A novel by R. D. *Blackmore, published 1869. This vivid and continuously popular story is set in the later 17th century on Exmoor, Devon, where an outlawed family, the Doones, and their retainers terrorize the surrounding countryside. They murder a farmer, father of the novel's hero John Ridd, a boy of 12 when the story starts. He secretly discovers the child Lorna, who has been kidnapped by the Doones, and they grow to love each other. John Ridd becomes a giant in height and strength, and is involved in adventures with the highwayman Tom Faggus, who marries his sister Annie, in the events leading up to Monmouth's rebellion. He rescues Lorna from the villainous Carver Doone during a superbly described blizzard. The Doones are eventually destroyed, Lorna turns out not to be a Doone but an heiress of noble family, and she and John are married; but Carver Doone shoots her at the altar. John avenges her, she recovers, and the story ends happily. The infamous Judge Jeffreys plays a part in the action, and John Ridd and Tom Faggus are also based on historical characters.

Lost Generation A phrase expressed by Gertrude *Stein to Ernest *Hemingway in his memoir *A Moveable Feast* (1964), describing the cynicism of American expatriates in Europe immediately after the First World War.

Lot King of Orkney in the Arthurian legends, the husband of Arthur's sister or half-sister *Morgawse. Their sons are *Gawain, *Agravain, Gareth, and Gaheris, as well as *Mordred in the earlier versions (before Arthur was made his unwitting, incestuous father). The feud between his family and Pellinore's is one of the running themes in *Malory.

Lothair A novel by Benjamin *Disraeli, published 1870, after his first term as prime minister (1868). Like the hero of **Tancred*, Lothair is a young man in search of the truth. He is a wealthy nobleman, left, on his parents' death, in the joint guardianship of Lord Culloden, a member of the Scottish Kirk, and the brilliant cleric Grandison, who adopts the Catholic faith and becomes a cardinal. A deep interest in the merits of the Anglican and Catholic faiths, and their shared background in Judaism, pervades the book. As Lothair comes of age in 1866, the forces of Garibaldi confront the papacy. The Catholics and the Italian patriots struggle and manoeuvre for control of the influential Lothair. Like *Endymion (in the novel of that name), Lothair is reflective rather than active and is much influenced by three women, the beautiful Catholic Clare Arundel, the charming Lady Corisande, and the stormy Italian patriot Theodora. Lothair joins Theodora in Italy, but she is killed at Viterbo and he is himself wounded at Mentana. Lothair continues to look for the 'cradle' of Christianity, and in Jerusalem the mystic Paraclete gives him a revelation of the origins of the faith. The cardinal and fellow prelates struggle to convert Lothair, but he resists, feeling that the fanaticism of both the Catholics and the Italian patriots is corrupting. He returns home, confirmed in his Anglicanism, and marries Lady Corisande.

Memorable characters include the artist Mr Phoebus, modelled on Frederic *Leighton, and Lord St Aldegonde, the aristocratic republican opposed to all privileges except those of dukes, and in favour of the equal division of all property except land. 'Lothair-mania' swept England, the USA, and Europe; a perfume, a racehorse, and a waltz were named after the hero. Although the book was poorly reviewed, sometimes for political reasons, the first edition sold out in two days and there were eight editions in 1870 alone.

LOUVERTURE, Toussaint (*c.*1743–1803) Addressed in a sonnet by William *Wordsworth, the leader of a slave revolt which began in 1791 in the French colony of Saint-Domingue and which has been acclaimed as the only successful slave uprising in history. For some years he administered the colony (which was eventually to achieve independence as Haiti) with great skill, but he was overcome by a military expedition sent out by Napoleon, and was transported to France, where he died in prison in the Jura mountains. He remained a hero to radical writers: Harriet *Martineau published a life in 1840, and C. L. R. *James described the Haitian revolution in *The Black Jacobins* (1938).

LOVE, Nicholas (d. 1423/4) Prior of the Carthusian House of Mount Grace, Yorkshire, author by *c.*1411 of *The Mirrour of the Blessed Lyf of Iesu Christ*, an accomplished prose translation of the *Meditationes Vitae Christi*, now known to be by Johannes de Caulibus, a Franciscan. The most important life of Christ to circulate in late-medieval England, it survives in over 50 manuscripts and several early printed editions and has been edited by M. G. Sargent (2005).

LOVECRAFT, H. P. (Howard Phillips) (1890–1937) American writer born in Providence, Rhode Island. Through his essay 'Supernatural Horror in Literature' (1927) and his own fiction in **Weird Tales* and elsewhere, he became the most influential figure in *horror fiction after Edgar Allan *Poe. Early stories were set in dreamworlds reminiscent of Lord *Dunsany. Others, such as 'The Colour out of Space' (1927) and the 'Cthulhu Mythos' tales, transform a strong sense of place into a cosmic awe and terror about what may intrude into it. Numerous collections include *The Call of Cthulhu* (1999). See S. T. Joshi, *A Dreamer and a Visionary* (2001).

Love for Love A comedy by William *Congreve, performed 1695. It was the first play put on in the new theatre in Lincoln's Inn Fields and was a huge success. The plot concerns the outwitting of curmudgeonly Sir Sampson

Legend by his son Valentine, an extravagant but basically honourable young man, Valentine's servant Jeremy, and the wealthy Angelica, with whom Valentine is in love. The characters in the farcical sub-plot are Valentine's younger brother Ben, a rough and stupid sailor, Miss Prue, an awkward country girl, daughter of the superstitious pantaloon Foresight, and Tattle, a half-witted beau.

Love in a Tub *See* COMICAL REVENGE.

LOVELACE, Richard (1618–57/8) Educated at Charterhouse School and Gloucester Hall, Oxford, the heir to great estates in Kent. Wealthy, handsome, and elegant, he was a courtier, and served in the Scottish expeditions of 1639. Having presented a 'Kentish Petition' to the House of Commons in 1642, he was thrown into the Gatehouse prison, where he is supposed to have written the song 'To Althea' ('stone walls do not a prison make'). He rejoined Charles I in 1645, and served with the French king in 1646. According to Anthony *Wood, his betrothed Lucy Sacheverell married another on a false report of his death. He was imprisoned again in 1648 and in prison prepared for the press his *Lucasta: Epodes, Odes, Sonnets, Songs etc.*, which includes the well-known lyric 'On Going to the Wars'. He died in extreme poverty. After his death his brother published his remaining verses, *Lucasta: Posthume Poems*. He wrote two plays, now lost. During the earlier part of the 18th century his work was entirely neglected, until Thomas *Percy reprinted two of his lyrics in his **Reliques* (1765), since when his reputation as a *Cavalier poet has steadily increased. His works were edited by C. H. Wilkinson (2 vols, 1925).

Lovel the Widower The story by W. M. *Thackeray, published in the **Cornhill Magazine*, 1860, with which he opened his new periodical. The story is told by Lovel's friend Mr Batchelor, who is more than half in love with the young governess Bessy Prior, who copes tactfully with Lovel's spoiled children, his interfering mother-in-law Lady Baker, her own greedy relatives, and her other suitors, who include the highly educated butler Bedford. Lady Baker discovers that Miss Prior once earned her living as a dancer in the theatre and orders her out of the house, but Lovel finally asserts himself and asks Bessy to marry him.

'Lover's Complaint, A' A 47-stanza poem in *rhyme royal appended to William *Shakespeare's *sonnets (1609), in which a nameless young woman, weeping beside a river, tells how she was seduced and abandoned. The attribution to Shakespeare has often been doubted. In 2007 Brian Vickers attributed it to John *Davies of Hereford.

Lover's Melancholy, The A romantic comedy by John *Ford, printed 1629. Palador, prince of Cyprus, has been betrothed to Eroclea, daughter of Meleander; but, to escape the schemes of Palador's father, she has been taken to Greece, where she has remained disguised as a boy. Meleander has been accused of treason, imprisoned, and driven to madness. Palador, after his father's death, is left in a state of hopeless melancholy. Eroclea returns to Cyprus as the page of Menaphon. Thamasta, cousin of the prince, falls in love with her in this disguise, and to escape her attentions Eroclea is obliged to reveal her identity. She is then restored to Palador; Meleander is released and cured; Thamasta marries Menaphon; and all ends happily. The play contains a version of Strada's contest of the lute player and the nightingale, which is also dealt with by Richard *Crashaw.

The conventional plot is the framework for Ford's analysis of love melancholy, strongly influenced by Robert Burton's **Anatomy of Melancholy*. The recognition scene between Palador and Eroclea contains some of Ford's finest poetry ('Minutes are numbered by the fall of sands, | As by an hourglass').

Lovers' Progress, The A romantic drama by John *Fletcher, acted 1623, revised 1634 as *The Wandering Lovers* by Philip *Massinger, printed 1647. Lidian and Clarangé, devoted friends, are both in love with Olinda. Clarangé lets it be believed that he is dead, and finally turns friar, in order to surrender Olinda to Lidian. The plot is complicated with another illustration of the conflict of love and friendship. Lisander loves the virtuous Calista, wife of his friend Cleander. Cleander is killed by a servant. The unwise but not criminal behaviour of Lisander and Calista makes them suspects, and they narrowly escape condemnation for the murder.

Lovers' Vows A play by Elizabeth *Inchbald, adapted from *Das Kind der Liebe* by August von *Kotzebue, acted 1798. The play is chiefly of interest because of the place it occupies in the story of Jane Austen's **Mansfield Park*. Baron Wildenhaim has in his youth seduced and deserted Agatha and married another woman. Agatha is reduced to destitution, in which state she is found by her son Frederic, who for the first time learns the story of his birth. To help his mother, he goes out to beg, chances upon his unknown father, and attempts to rob him. He is arrested, discovers who the baron is, reveals his own identity and his mother's, and finally, with the aid of the pastor Anhalt, persuades the baron to marry Agatha.

Love's Labour's Lost A comedy by *Shakespeare, probably written and performed about 1595, printed in quarto 1598. No major sources for it have been identified. It has often been felt to contain topical references (*see* *school of night), but none of these has been firmly established.

The king of Navarre and three of his lords have sworn to keep away from woman and to live studying and fasting for three years. The arrival of the princess of France on an embassy, with her attendant ladies, obliges them 'of mere necessity' to disregard their vows. The king is soon in love with the princess, his lords with her ladies, and the courting proceeds amidst disguises and merriment, to which the other characters contribute: Don

Adriano de Armado, the Spaniard, a master of extravagant language, Holofernes the schoolmaster, Dull the constable, Sir Nathaniel the curate, and Costard the clown. News of the death of the princess's father interrupts the wooing, and the ladies impose a year's ordeal on their lovers. The play ends with the songs of the cuckoo and the owl, 'When daisies pied and violets blue' and 'When icicles hang by the wall'.

Loves of the Angels, The A poem by Thomas *Moore, published 1823. The poem, founded on the *oriental tale of Harut and Marut and certain rabbinical fictions, describes the loves of three fallen angels for mortal women, and illustrates the decline of the soul from purity. The first angel loved Lea, and taught her the spell which opens the gate of heaven. At once she uttered it and rose to the stars. The second angel loved Lilis; he came to her in his full glory and she was burned to death. The third, Zaraph, loved Nama; they were condemned to live in imperfect happiness among mortals, but would ultimately be granted immortality. Moore's poem was both popular and controversial.

'Loves of the Triangles, The' A clever parody by George *Canning and John Hookham *Frere in the *Anti-Jacobin* in 1798 of Erasmus *Darwin's *The Loves of the Plants*. Darwin good-humouredly acknowledged its skill.

Love's Sacrifice A tragedy by John *Ford, printed 1633. Fernando, favourite of the duke of Pavia, falls in love with Bianca, the duchess. He declares his love, but is rejected. Presently, however, the duchess, in whom he has awakened a strong passion, comes to his room and offers herself to him, but warns him that she will not survive her shame, but take her own life before morning. Fernando masters his passion and determines to remain her distant lover. Fiormonda, the duke's sister, who has vainly pursued Fernando, discovers his feelings for Bianca, and seeks revenge. With the help of D'Avolos, the duke's wicked secretary, she stirs up the duke's jealousy, and a trap is laid for Fernando and Bianca. The duke finds them together, and kills Bianca. Realizing too late that she is innocent, he stabs himself, and Fernando takes poison in Bianca's tomb.

Less wide-ranging than *'Tis Pity She's a Whore*, the play's main theme is the folly of love, including the platonic love cult, fashionable at the Caroline court.

LOWELL, Amy (1874–1925) American poet, born in Massachusetts. Her first volume of poetry, *A Dome of Many-Coloured Glass* (1912), was relatively conventional; shortly thereafter she took up *imagism and in 1913–14 visited England, where she met Ezra *Pound, D. H. *Lawrence, 'H.D.' (Hilda *Doolittle), and other writers, becoming so active in it herself that Pound spoke of 'Amy-gism'. Her subsequent volumes, which include *Sword Blades and Poppy Seed* (1914), *Men, Women and Ghosts* (1916; which contains 'Patterns'), and *Can Grande's Castle* (1918), show her experiments in what she called 'polyphonic prose' as well as her allegiance to imagism. Her love of New England is expressed in two of her own favourite pieces, 'Lilacs' and 'Purple Grackles', published in *What's O'Clock* (1925). She became well known as a public figure through her lectures and readings in America. See Jean Gould, *Amy* (1975).

LOWELL, James Russell (1819–91) American writer, born in Cambridge, Massachusetts, and educated at Harvard University. He succeeded Henry Wadsworth *Longfellow as professor of French and Spanish at Harvard in 1855, and was American minister in Spain, 1877–80, and in England, 1880–85. He served as editor of the **Atlantic Monthly* and co-editor (with Charles Eliot *Norton) of the **North American Review*. His works include several volumes of verse, the satirical *Biglow Papers* (1848 and 1867, prose and verse), and memorial odes after the Civil War; also various volumes of essays, including *Among my Books* (1870) and *My Study Window* (1871). See Edward Wagenknecht, *Lowell* (1971).

LOWELL, Robert (1917–77) American poet, born in Boston, of venerable New England families. He was educated at Kenyon College, where he became friendly with Randall *Jarrell and John Crowe *Ransom, and where he encountered the *New Criticism methods of close textual analysis. In 1940 he married his first wife, the novelist Jean *Stafford, and became a fanatical convert to Roman Catholicism: his first volume of verse, *Land of Unlikeness* (1944), betrays the conflict of Catholicism and his Boston ancestry. He was jailed for six months during the Second World War as, in effect, a conscientious objector. His second volume, *Lord Weary's Castle* (1946), which contains 'The Quaker Graveyard in Nantucket' and 'Mr Edwards and the Spider', gained him recognition. He married his second wife, the writer Elizabeth Hardwick (1916–2007), in 1949. *The Mills of the Kavanaughs* (1951) has as its title poem a meditation by a Catholic widow, Anne Kavanaugh, reflecting on the past in her ancestral home in Maine; this was followed by *Life Studies* (1959), *For the Union Dead* (1964), *Near the Ocean* (1967), and volumes of translation, plays, and other works. He reached the height of his public fame during his opposition to the Vietnam War and support of Senator Eugene McCarthy, as his *Notebook 1967–1968* (1968) records; but he had long been suffering bouts of manic illness and heavy drinking, and a visit to Britain in 1970 increased the disorder of his private life. His highly personal, confessional volume of poetry *The Dolphin* (1973) caused scandal with its revelations of marital anguish and discord. He married the writer Caroline Blackwood (1931–96) in 1973, but later returned to America, where he died: *Day by Day* was published just before his death. A legendary figure in his lifetime, the label 'confessional' does not recognize Lowell's capacity to contextualize. See Paul L. Mariani, *Lost Puritan* (1996).

LOWNDES, William Thomas (1793–1843) Author of *The Bibliographer's Manual of English Literature* (1834) and *The British Librarian* (1839–42), important early bibliographical works. The former was revised and enlarged (1857–64) by Henry *Bohn.

LOWRY, Malcolm (1909–57) Novelist, born in Wallasey, near Liverpool, the fourth son of a wealthy cotton broker. On leaving school, he went to sea, travelling to the Far East. He returned to take a degree at St Catharine's College, Cambridge, graduating in 1932. In 1933 he published *Ultramarine*, a work indebted to *Blue Voyage* by his friend Conrad *Aiken, in whose autobiography *Ushant* (1952) he was to appear as Hambro. He travelled widely in Europe and the USA, settling in Mexico with his first wife Jan from 1936 to 1938; there he worked on *Under the Volcano*, his most important work, published 1947. Various manuscripts were meanwhile rejected. In 1940 he settled in Dollarton, British Columbia, with his second wife Margerie, a former film actress. His last years were spent in England, and he died 'by misadventure' in Sussex. He was a chronic alcoholic, as are many of his characters, and had severe problems in disciplining his work, which went through innumerable revisions, many with Margerie's help. His posthumous publications include *Hear Us O Lord from Heaven thy Dwelling Place* (1961), *Selected Poems*, ed. Earle Birney and M. B. Lowry (1962), *Dark as the Grave Wherein my Friend Is Laid* (1968), and *October Ferry to Gabriola* (1970). See Gordon Bowker, *Pursued by Furies* (1993), a biography; *Collected Letters*, ed. Sherrill Grace (1995–6).

LOY, Mina (1882–1966) Poet and artist, born Mina Gertrude Lowy in London, and educated at a progressive school in Hampstead and art schools in Munich and Paris. On moving to Italy in 1907 she became acquainted with F. T. *Marinetti and other *Futurists. The publication of her 'Love Songs' (in *Others*, 1915) caused, as William Carlos *Williams remarked, 'wild enthusiasm among free verse writers… and really quite a stir in the country at large'. Loy's work was noticed for its radical views and its innovative forms. Her *Psycho-Democracy: A Movement to Focus Human Reason on the Conscious Direction of Evolution* appeared in 1921; *Lunar Baedecker*, a landmark in *modernist poetry, in 1923; and her long autobiographical poem *Anglo-Mongrels and the Rose* between 1923 and 1925. She settled in New York in 1940 and became a naturalized American citizen in 1946. See Carolyn Burke, *Becoming Modern: The Life of Mina Loy* (1996).

Loyal Subject, The A drama by John *Fletcher, acted 1618. The duke of Muscovy is jealous of his late father's loyal general, Archas. He dismisses Archas, replacing him with an incompetent flatterer, Boroskie. The young Archas, son of the general, disguised as a girl (Alinda), serves Olympia, the duke's sister, wins her affection, and attracts the duke's love. When the Tartars invade and Boroskie feigns sickness, Archas is recalled and conquers. But Boroskie inflames the duke's suspicion of Archas. The troops show their devotion to Archas, who is carried off to torture. The infuriated troops attack the palace, and then march away to join the Tartars, but are brought back by Archas, fresh from the rack. The repentant duke marries Honora, daughter of Archas. The identity of Alinda is now revealed, and the young Archas is married to Olympia.

LUBBOCK, Percy (1879–1965) Critic and biographer, educated at Eton College and King's College, Cambridge. His works include *Earlham* (1922), an account of his own Norfolk childhood holidays; *Roman Pictures* (1923), which describes an English tourist's responses to Rome; *Shades of Eton* (1923), recollections of his schooldays; and *Portrait of Edith Wharton* (1947). He was a friend of Henry *James, and edited a selection of his letters (1920); also of A. C. *Benson, a selection from whose diary he edited (1926). His *The Craft of Fiction* (1921), which analyses the techniques of *Tolstoy, *Flaubert, James, and others, appears to have been closely studied by Graham *Greene, who describes it as an 'admirable primer' in *Ways of Escape* (1980).

LUCAN (Marcus Annaeus Lucanus) (AD 39–65) Roman poet, born in Córdoba, Spain, and nephew of *Seneca. Favoured by Nero, then estranged from him, Lucan joined Piso's conspiracy to depose Nero and was forced on its discovery to kill himself. His various works are lost, except the unfinished epic *Pharsalia* or *Bellum Civile*, in ten books, on the civil war between Caesar and Pompey. The first three books were published in 62/3; they contain fewer anti-imperial sentiments than the later books, apparently published posthumously. At first, Caesar and Pompey are morally equal, both guilty of overthrowing the republic. After the decisive battle of Pharsalus (Book 7), the balance changes. Pompey becomes a Stoic sage, superior to the cruel changes of Fortune, and far above Caesar, the daemonic wrecker. Another key figure is *Cato of Utica. Lucan's style, deliberately un-Virgilian, is dense, epigrammatic, and sombre. There are important translations by Arthur *Gorges, Thomas *May, and Nicholas *Rowe. See M. P. O. Morford, *The Poet Lucan* (1967).

LUCIAN (AD *c.*125–*c.*200) Of Samosata in Syria, rhetorician and writer of about 80 prose satires in Greek. Many of his works are dialogues where mythical or historical figures are placed in ridiculous situations, and the contrast between their traditional dignity and what they are made to say or do becomes a fruitful source of irony. Lucian was popular with the Renaissance humanists. Sir Thomas *More and *Erasmus put some of his dialogues into Latin, and Erasmus' mock encomium *The Praise of Folly* made his irony familiar to educated Europe. The first influential selected translation into English, by Francis Hickes (1565/6–1631), was published in 1634, with additions by his son Thomas (1598/9–1634). John *Dryden's 'Life of Lucian' (actually a critical assessment) was published with a four-volume complete translation by many hands (1710–11). Henry *Fielding much admired Lucian and imitated him in his *Journey from this World to the Next* (1743), though his plans for a translation came to nothing. The piece by Lucian that had perhaps the most influence was *The True History*: this claimed to describe a visit to the moon and inspired a long series of imaginary voyages, including Jonathan *Swift's **Gulliver's Travels* (1726) and Samuel *Butler's **Erewhon* (1872). See *Selected Dialogues*, trans. C. D. N. Costa (2006); Christopher Robinson, *Lucian and his Influence in Europe* (1979).

LUCIE, Doug (1953–) British dramatist, born in Chessington, Surrey, and educated at Worcester College, Oxford. His first play, *John Clare's Mad Nuncle* (1975), was followed by subsequent works which have been widely admired for their sardonic portrayal of Britain in the 1980s, a place and period he sees as corrupt, acquisitive, and callous. Key plays include *Hard Feelings* (1982), about bright young Londoners who harass the Jewish lodger of the flat they share; *Progress* (1984), which primarily concerns the pretension of modern liberals, among them a consciousness-raising group of 'non-sexist' men; and *Fashion* (1987), about the world of advertising. With *Grace* (1993), the satiric attack switched to born-again religion as represented by an American 'televangelist' whose attempt to set up his European headquarters in an English mansion was, surprisingly for Lucie, seen as menacing a Britain which, though morally damaged by the 'Thatcher years', still embodied some traditional decencies. His more familiar cynicism reasserted itself in the melodramatic *Gaucho* (1994), about a decent man who becomes a drugs smuggler, arms dealer, and international villain. Subsequent work includes *The Green Man* (2002) and *Pass It On* (2006).

LUCIE-SMITH, Edward (1933–) Poet and art critic, born in Jamaica. *A Tropical Childhood and Other Poems* appeared in 1961, and in the early 1960s Lucie-Smith was associated with the *Group, but since then has moved more towards literary journalism; his works include various editions of contemporary poetry, works of art history and criticism, a life of *Joan of Arc (1976), and *The Burnt Child* (autobiography, 1975). *Changing Shape: New and Selected Poems* was published in 2002.

Lucius (1) Supposedly the first Christian British king (in Edmund *Spenser's *The *Faerie Queene* (II. x. 53)). (2) Roman emperor who demands tribute from King *Arthur. In *Geoffrey of Monmouth's *History* he is slain when attacking Arthur. (3) Character in **Julius Caesar*. (4) **Timon of Athens*. (5) **Titus Andronicus*. (6) **Cymbeline*.

Luck of Barry Lyndon, The A satirical *historical novel by W. M *Thackeray, published in **Fraser's Magazine* 1844, republished under the title *Memoirs of Barry Lyndon, Esq., Written by Himself* (1856). It is the *picaresque story of an Irish adventurer who unconsciously reveals his villainy while attempting self-justification. Redmond Barry flees from Ireland after a duel, having been tricked into believing he has killed his opponent. He serves in the Seven Years War, first in the English, then in the Prussian, army. He is set to spy upon the chevalier de Balibari, who turns out to be his uncle Cornelius Barry. The two set up as card-sharpers, and Barry becomes a successful gambler and man of fashion. He marries a wealthy, foolish widow, the countess of Lyndon, and takes her name. He spends her fortune and ill-treats her and her son, showing affection only to his old mother and his own son Bryan, whom he indulges until the boy is killed in a riding accident. Finally the countess, with the help of her son Viscount Bullingdon, now grown up and no longer susceptible to his stepfather's bullying, is released from Barry's hold over her. Barry is forced to live abroad on a pension, and when left penniless after the countess's death ends his life miserably in the Fleet Prison, prematurely senile and cared for by his devoted old mother. The novel was filmed in 1975 by Stanley Kubrick.

Lucky Jim A novel by Kingsley *Amis.

Lucrece, The Rape of See RAPE OF LUCRECE.

Lucretia A legendary Roman heroine, whose story is told in *Livy's Book I. She was raped by Sextus Tarquinius, son of Tarquinius Superbus, king of Rome, and after urging her father and husband to avenge her she stabbed herself. As a result Lucius Junius Brutus, the king's nephew, led the revolt which resulted in the expulsion of the Tarquins from Rome and the establishment of the republic. In later literature and painting Lucretia and Brutus (ancestor of Marcus *Brutus) became models respectively of female and republican virtue. *See* RAPE OF LUCRECE.

LUCRETIUS (Titus Lucretius Carus) (99/94–55/51 BC) Author of the Latin hexameter poem in six books *De Rerum Natura* ('On the Nature of the Universe'). Almost nothing is known about him. His poem, addressed to Memmius, versifies and commends the philosophy of *Epicurus, which, it is argued, can rid the world of the evils of conventional religion and the superstition which inevitably accompanies it. The world is composed of atoms (*primordia*), falling forever through the void (*inane*), and by their interaction producing all things. This atomic theory, originated in the 5th century BC by Leucippus and *Democritus, is expounded with great energy and enthusiasm. Gods exist, but in blessed inactivity, not intervening in human life; civilization is the achievement of human effort. There are notable translations (in whole or in part) by Lucy *Hutchinson, John *Evelyn, John *Dryden, Thomas Creech (1659–1700), and C. H. *Sisson. His supposed madness and suicide are the subject of a poem, 'Lucretius', by *Tennyson. See Stuart Gillespie and Philip Hardie (eds), *The Cambridge Companion to Lucretius* (2007).

'Lucy poems' The name given to a group of poems by William *Wordsworth, most of which were written in Germany in the exceptionally cold winter of 1798–9. 'She dwelt among the untrodden ways' and 'Strange fits of passion have I known' were sent to S. T. *Coleridge in a letter, as was 'A slumber did my spirit seal'; 'Three years she grew in sun and shower' was written a little later, in the spring. All four were published in the *Lyrical Ballads of 1800. A fifth poem, 'I travelled among unknown men', was sent in a letter in 1801 to Mary Hutchinson (later Wordsworth's wife), and published in 1807. The poems are remarkable for their lyric intensity and purity, and the identity of Lucy has aroused much speculation; in 'Strange Fits of Passion' she appears to be identified with Dorothy *Wordsworth (who was with him in Germany), but in other poems she is presented as having died. In a letter to Thomas Poole (1766–1837), Coleridge reflected that, 'Most probably, in some gloomier moment he had fancied the moment in which his sister might die' (1799). The name Lucy is used in the ballad 'Lucy Gray', also written in Germany and published in 1800, where it is also associated with death and solitude.

Lud A mythical king of Britain, according to *Geoffrey of Monmouth's *History* (I. 17). He renamed the capital Caerlud (Lud's city) from which derives the name London.

LUKE, St *See* BIBLE; EVANGELISTS.

LULLY, Raymond (Ramon Llull) (1232/3–1315/16) A Catalan born in Majorca, who, after seeing visions of the crucified Christ, became a Franciscan, mystic, poet, and missionary to the Arabs. His philosophical *Great Art* attempted to unify all knowledge. He promoted the establishment of schools for missionary languages and obtained a decree for the foundation of chairs of Hebrew, Greek, Chaldean, and Arabic at various universities, including Oxford. Engaged on a missionary crusade in North Africa in his eighties, he died of wounds. Most of his writing was in Latin, but he was also the first great writer of poetry and prose fiction in Catalan. See Anthony Boner, *Doctor Illuminatus: A Ramon Llull Reader* (1993).

Luria A tragedy in blank verse by Robert *Browning, published 1846, together with *A *Soul's Tragedy*, as no. VIII of **Bells and Pomegranates*. It was written, Browning told Elizabeth Barrett *Browning, 'for a purely imaginary stage', and is set in the 15th century during the conflict between Florence and Pisa, though the actual episode is unhistorical. The plot concerns the fall of the noble-hearted Florentine commander Luria, a Moorish mercenary (Browning acknowledged the influence of **Othello*) who, at the height of his triumph, is falsely accused of plotting a coup against the republic. The failure of political idealism, consummated and transcended by a heroic death, relates the play to Browning's earlier poem **Sordello*.

LURIE, Alison (1926–) American novelist and critic, born in Chicago, and for some years a member of the English department at Cornell. Her sharply satiric and sociologically observant novels include *Love and Friendship* (1962), *Imaginary Friends* (1967), and *The War between the Tates* (1974), a campus novel involving student politics, teenage revolt, and marital anguish and infidelity. *Foreign Affairs* (1984) brings to England two Americans, middle-aged scholar of children's literature Vinnie Miner and handsome academic Fred Turner, where both find a kind of romance. *The Truth about Lorin Jones* (1988) is a novel of biographical quest, *Women and Ghosts* (1994) is a collection of short stories, and *The Last Resort* (1998) is a benign comedy of death and love set in Key West, Florida, where Jenny Walker, the hitherto docile wife of an ageing eco-celebrity professor, finds herself happily involved in a lesbian affair: it reintroduces characters from earlier novels, including the long-running literary critic L. D. Zimmern, who first appeared in *Real People* (1969). *Truth and Consequences* (2005) is a campus novel dealing with the effects of chronic pain on relationships and the creative process.

Lusiads, The *See* CAMÕES, LUIS DE.

LUTHER, Martin (1483–1546) German theologian and leader of the *Reformation in Germany. Born of humble family at Eisleben, he entered the Augustinian order in 1505. As a monk he visited Rome in 1510, and his experience there of ecclesiastical venality influenced his future career. Famously nailing his *Theses* to the door of the church at Wittenberg in 1517, he attacked the principle of papal indulgences, and as a consequence was the subject of a papal ban pronounced at the Diet of Worms (1521). He left the monastic order and married, and devoted himself to forming the League of Protestantism. His translation of the Bible became an influence on the German language as profound as the Authorized Version on English. Thomas *Cranmer's *Litany* (1544), the first instalment of the Prayer Book, contains a section which derives from a litany of Luther. His commentary on St *Paul's Letter to the Galatians (1535), translated into English several times between 1575 and 1644 and highly influential, was greatly praised by John *Bunyan. His popular hymn 'Ein' feste Burg' ('A fortress strong') has had many translators, including Thomas *Carlyle who devotes a chapter to Luther in *On *Heroes, Hero-Worship and the Heroic in History.* He is the subject of John *Osborne's play *Luther* (1961).

LUTTRELL, Henry (?1765–1851) Wit and member of the circle of political, literary, and artistic figures centred on *Holland House, owned by the third Baron Holland (1773–1840). He was the author of clever and lively verses, including *Advice to Julia* (1820), admired by Lord *Byron.

LUTTRELL, Narcissus (1657–1732) Annalist and bibliographer. His *Brief Historical Relation of State Affairs from September 1678 to April 1714* was published in 1857 (6 vols), after T. B. *Macaulay had drawn attention to the manuscript. His collection of pamphlets, annotated with the date of issue and thus forming a valuable historical resource, was dispersed but many of the items have been traced: see Stephen Parks, *The Luttrell File* (1999).

Luve Ron ('the Love Song') Mystical love poem in 210 lines by the Franciscan Thomas de Hales, written probably in the second part of the 13th century. It describes to a young woman novice Christ's love and the joy of mystical union with him. See R. Morris (ed.), in *An Old English Miscellany* (1872), EETS OS 49.

Lycidas A *pastoral elegy by John *Milton. Written 1637 and published the following year, it laments the death of Edward King (1612–37), who was at Christ's College, Cambridge, with Milton, and drowned while crossing from Chester Bay to Dublin when his ship struck a rock and sank in calm weather. Milton fills his poem with mythological allusions which, together with the pastoral machinery, has caused some to doubt its sincerity, among them Samuel *Johnson who condemned it as 'easy, vulgar, and therefore disgusting'. More usually it is hailed as the greatest elegy in the language. The passage in which St Peter condemns the venal clergy records young Milton's opinion of the state of the Church under Archbishop *Laud. Milton's working manuscript, with alterations and revisions, survives at Trinity College, Cambridge, and has been published in facsimile in the Columbia *Complete Works* and elsewhere.

LYDGATE, John (*c.*1370–1449/50) Poet, born in Lydgate, Suffolk, and admitted to the monastery of Bury St Edmunds *c.*1385. He was in Paris in *c.*1426, and was prior of Hatfield Regis in Essex (not continually resident) between 1423 and 1434; otherwise he spent nearly all his life in the monastery at Bury (in Lancashire; now a part of Greater Manchester). He is one of the most prolific of English poets, with a corpus of well over 100,000 lines. Up to the 17th century, Lydgate was almost invariably coupled for praise with Geoffrey *Chaucer and John *Gower. Joseph *Ritson's description of him as 'a voluminous, prosaick and drivelling monk' has been more typical of his critical reputation since then, but more recently he has received a more favourable critical reassessment, with both his shorter, occasional poems and his much longer works now seen as important components in the different aspects of Lancastrian literary culture, concerned as they were with matters such as civic culture, religious orthodoxy, and the political health of the realm. Some of his most important shorter works include *The Complaint of the Black Knight* (modelled on Chaucer's *The *Book of the Duchess*); *The Temple of Glas* (indebted to *The *House of Fame*); and the allegorical *Reason and Sensuality*. His longer works are the *Troy Book* (1412–20), a 30,000-line translation of *Guido delle Colonne commissioned by Prince Henry (later Henry V); *The Siege of Thebes* (1420–22), a pseudo-'Canterbury Tale' translated from a French prose version of the *Roman de Thebes*; *The Pilgrimage of Man*, translated from Deguileville (1426–28), which comprises 24,000 lines of octosyllabic couplets; and *The Fall of Princes* (completed by 1438/9), a translation in 36,000 lines of a French version of *Boccaccio's *De Casibus Virorum Illustrium*. See D. A. Pearsall, *John Lydgate* (1970); *John Lydgate: Poetry, Culture and Lancastrian England*, ed. Larry Scanlon and James Simpson (2006). There is a selection of *Poems*, ed. J. Norton-Smith (1966). See also *The Siege of Thebes*, ed. Robert R. Edwards (2001); *Troy Book: Selections*, ed. Robert R. Edwards (1998).

LYELL, Sir Charles *See* DARWIN, CHARLES; SCIENCE.

LYLY, John (1554–1606) Writer and dramatist, the grandson of William *Lily. He was educated probably at the King's School, Canterbury, then at Magdalen College, Oxford. He served as secretary to Edward de Vere, the earl of *Oxford, was MP successively for Hindon, Aylesbury, and Appleby (1589–1601), and supported the cause of the bishops in the *Martin Marprelate controversy in a satirical pamphlet, **Pap with an Hatchet* (1589). The first part of his **Euphues: The Anatomy of Wit* appeared in 1578, and the second part, *Euphues and his England*, in 1580. Its distinctive style came to be known as 'Euphuism'. Among Lyly's plays, all of which were written for performance by boy actors to courtly audiences, are **Campaspe* and *Sapho and Phao* (1584); **Endymion* (1591); *Gallathea* and **Midas* (1592); and *Mother Bombie* (1594, *see* BUMBY, MOTHER). The attractive songs in the plays, including such well-known lyrics as 'Cupid and my Campaspe played', were first printed in Blount's collected edition of 1632: it is doubtful to what extent they are by Lyly. Although *Euphues* was his most popular and influential work in the Elizabethan period, his plays are now admired for their flexible use of dramatic prose and the elegant patterning of their construction. R. W. Bond edited Lyly's works in 1902, and there is a good study of him by G. K. Hunter, *John Lyly: The Humanist as Courtier* (1962).

LYNDSAY, David *See* LINDSAY, DAVID.

LYOTARD, Jean-François (1924–1998) French philosopher who emerged as one of the most prominent thinkers of *postmodernism following the publication in 1979 of *La Condition postmoderne* (*The Postmodern Condition*). He defines postmodernism as a suspicion of the grand and totalizing narratives of progress dominating Western philosophical and political thinking since the *Enlightenment. In subsequent work, including *Le Différend* (1983: *The Differend*), Lyotard went on to explore the challenge to ethics and justice posed by a rejection of grand narratives, and the universalism they articulate.

Lyra Apostolica A collection of sacred poems contributed originally to the *British Magazine* and reprinted in a separate volume in 1836. The poems, 179 in all, appeared anonymously. The six authors were J. W. Bowden (1798–1844), Richard Hurrell *Froude, John *Keble, John Henry *Newman, Robert Wilberforce (1802–57), and Isaac *Williams, with Newman contributing the lion's share, including his best-known poem 'Lead, kindly light'. All the writers were associated with the *Oxford Movement.

lyric, lyric poetry The largest general class of poetry, the term usually being applied to short poems expressive of a poet's thoughts or feelings, and which could not be classed under another heading such as narrative or dramatic verse. As a broad genre, it includes such forms as the *sonnet, *ode, and *elegy, along with many other varieties deriving from popular song. The term originally referred to a Greek song to be accompanied on the lyre, either in solo performance or chorally, but later became associated with song-like poems uttered by a single speaker. The connection with music gradually weakened until it became only a conventional pretence in most 20th-century poetic practice, though the association has been revived in contemporary musical culture. In England lyric poems flourished in the Middle English period (in such manuscript collections as the *Harley Lyrics*), and attained exceptional sophistication in the songbooks and plays of the Elizabethan age, then among such early 17th-century poets as John *Donne and Robert *Herrick. A further revival is seen in the late 18th and early 19th centuries (*see* ROMANTICISM) with the lyric verse of William *Wordsworth, P. B. *Shelley, John *Keats, and Alfred *Tennyson. In the period from the late 19th century to the mid-20th, notable lyric poets include A. E. *Housman, W. B. *Yeats, Thomas *Hardy, and W. H. *Auden. See Scott Brewster, *Lyric* (2007).

Lyrical Ballads, *with a Few Other Poems* A collection of poems by William *Wordsworth and S. T. *Coleridge, of which the first edition appeared 1798, the second with new poems and a preface (known as the 1800 edition) January 1801, and a third in 1802. The book is a landmark of English *Romanticism and is often seen as the beginning of a new literary epoch. The poems were written largely in Somerset, and Coleridge, in the **Biographia Literaria*, describes the nature of their collaboration: 'it was agreed that my endeavours should be directed to persons and characters supernatural or at least romantic…Mr Wordsworth, on the other hand, was to propose to himself as his object, to give the charm of novelty to things of everyday.' Coleridge's contributions to the first edition were *The Rime of the *Ancient Mariner*, 'The Foster-Mother's Tale', 'The Nightingale', and 'The Dungeon'; Wordsworth's included ballads and narratives such as 'The Thorn', 'The *Idiot Boy', and 'Simon Lee, the Old Huntsman', and more personal poems such as 'Lines Written in Early Spring' and 'Lines Written a Few Miles above *Tintern Abbey'. They appeared with a brief 'Advertisement' by Wordsworth, stating his theory of *poetic diction and attacking the 'gaudy and inane phraseology of many modern writers'. His views were expanded in his important preface to the second edition, and enlarged again in 1802. The poems themselves, with their 'low' subjects and language and their alleged banality and repetitions, were much ridiculed, as was Wordsworth's confident and unperturbed maintaining of his own position. The second volume of the second edition added many of Wordsworth's most characteristic works, including the so-called *'Lucy poems', 'The Old Cumberland Beggar', and *'Michael: A Pastoral'.

Lyrical Tales A collection of narrative poems mixing didactic, *Gothic, and sentimental modes, by Mary *Robinson, published 1800, and, as the *British Critic* had it, 'the last poetical production of this celebrated, but unfortunate female'. The volume was influenced by the first volume of William *Wordsworth and S. T. *Coleridge's **Lyrical Ballads* (1798), notably in 'The Haunted Beach' which is indebted to *The Rime of the *Ancient Mariner.*

LYTTELTON, George, first Baron Lyttelton (1709–73) Politician and writer, an opponent of Sir Robert Walpole (1676–1745), and friend of Alexander *Pope, William *Shenstone, and Henry *Fielding, who dedicated **Tom Jones* to him. He was a notable literary patron and secured James *Thomson a pension; he was addressed in *The *Seasons* and contributed some lines to *The *Castle of Indolence*. He assisted Robert *Dodsley in editing the famous *Collection of Poems* (1748–58), to which he also contributed. His other works include *Dialogues of the Dead* (1760) and a history of Henry II (1767–71). He was caricatured by Tobias *Smollett as Scragg in **Peregrine Pickle*; Samuel *Johnson's dismissive 'Life' of him incurred the lasting hostility of Elizabeth *Montagu, who had contributed the last three of the *Dialogues*.

LYTTON, Edward Earle Lytton Bulwer *See* BULWER-LYTTON, EDWARD GEORGE EARLE LYTTON.

LYTTON, Edward Robert Bulwer, first earl of Lytton (1831–91) Poet, diplomat, and colonial administrator, son of Edward *Bulwer-Lytton, educated at Harrow School and Bonn. His childhood was overshadowed by the quarrels of his parents, and he relied much on the protective interest of his father's friend John *Forster, who encouraged his literary efforts. After a successful career in the diplomatic service he became viceroy of India (1876–80), where his 'Forward' policy aroused much opposition. He published several volumes of verse, at first under the pseudonym 'Owen Meredith'. *Clytemnestra, The Earl's Return, The Artist and Other Poems* (1855) was followed by *The Wanderer* (1858); both show talent, and the Wanderer's mildly *Byronic and lyrical continental adventures had some success. His later volumes, which include two long verse romances, seemed to some marred by prolixity and facile versification. His favourite, *King Poppy: A Story without End*, a fanciful and lengthy blank verse allegory, was circulated privately to his friends in 1875, revised over many years, and published in 1892. Lytton seems to have found his dual career as statesman and poet problematic, and to have sensed his own failure in the latter role: in 'Last Words of a Sensitive Second-Rate Poet', published in *Chronicles and Characters* (1868), the poor reception of which much distressed him, he writes, 'Talk not of genius baffled. Genius is master of man. | Genius does what it must, and Talent does what it can.' There is a critical biography by A. B. Harlan (1946).

M

MABBE, James (1572–?1642) Translator, educated at, and fellow of, Magdalen College, Oxford. He is remembered for his translations of Fernando de Rojas's **Celestina* and of *The Spanish Lady,* one of *Cervantes's 'Exemplary Novels'. Mabbe Hispanicized his name as 'Puede-Ser' (may-be).

Mabinogion, The Strictly, the first four Welsh tales contained in the collection of Lady Charlotte Guest (1812–99), made in 1838–49. The four are preserved in two Welsh manuscripts: The White Book of Rhydderch (1300–25) and The Red Book of Hergest (1375–1425). 'Mab' is the word for 'youth', but, even by the time of the medieval title, it is likely that the word meant nothing much more precise than 'story'. The original common element of the four stories was probably the hero Pryderi; as they survive their subjects are (1) Pwyll, the father of Pryderi; (2) Branwen, the daughter of Llyr and her marriage to the Irish king Matholwch; (3) Manawyddan, the son of Llyr and his association with Pryderi; (4) the death of Pryderi in battle with the nephews of Math who had cheated him. There is no mention of *Arthur in these four branches of the Mabinogion proper; but five of the other seven tales published by Guest from The Red Book of Hergest deal indirectly with him: *The Lady of the Fountain, Peredur, Geraint,* three romances from French originals; *Culhwch and Olwen*; and *The Dream of Rhonabwy*; the latter two native tales are perhaps the most appealing of the collection. The other two tales in Guest's collection are *The Dream of Macsen Wledig* and *Lludd and Llefelys.* See P. K. Ford (trans.), *The Mabinogi and Other Medieval Welsh Tales* (1977); S. Davies (trans.), *The Mabinogion* (2007); C. W. Sullivan (ed.), *The Mabinogi: A Book of Essays* (1996).

McALMON, Robert (1896–1956) American writer and publisher, born in Clifton, Kansas, who joined the American expatriate group in Paris after the First World War, founded the Contact editions, and published a number of books of poetry including *The Portrait of a Generation* (1928). His autobiography *Being Geniuses Together* appeared in 1938. See Sanford J. Smoller, *Adrift among Geniuses* (1975).

macaronic verse A term originally applied to a kind of humorous Latin verse of the 16th and 17th centuries in which words from a modern language (more often French or German than English) would be included with deliberately incongruous Latin endings; thus a kind of dog-Latin burlesque, of which there are some examples among the poems of *Skelton and of *Drummond of Hawthornden. It is now more commonly applied to any poem into which lines, words, or phrases from other languages are frequently introduced, such as T. S. Eliot's *The *Waste Land* or Ezra *Pound's *Cantos.*

MACAULAY, (afterwards Graham) **Catherine** (1731–91) Author of an unflinchingly republican *History of England* (8 vols, 1763–83). Samuel *Johnson, with whom she clashed on the issue of the American colonists, mocked her radical views, but she was admired in America, and in France, where a translation of her *History* appeared in 1791–2. Her *Letters on Education* (1790) and her response to Edmund Burke's **Reflections on the Revolution in France* led to a correspondence of mutual admiration with Mary *Wollstonecraft. See B. Hill, *The Republican Virago* (1992).

MACAULAY, Dame Rose (Emilie Rose Macaulay) (1881–1958) Author and journalist, born in Rugby, educated at Oxford High School, after a childhood in Italy, and at Somerville College, Oxford. Her novels include the boldly anti-war *Non-Combatants and Others* (1916), the satirical best-seller *Potterism* (1920), and *They Were Defeated* (1932), drawing on the life of Robert *Herrick. She published studies of John *Milton (1934) and E. M. *Forster (1938); travel books, *Fabled Shore* (1949) and *Pleasure of Ruins* (1953); and *Personal Pleasures* (1935), a volume of essays. *The World my Wilderness* (1950) and the idiosyncratic tragicomedy *The Towers of Trebizond* (1956) appeared after a decade in which she wrote no fiction, and her return to the Anglican faith from which she had been estranged through her love for the married novelist Gerald O'Donovan, who died in 1942. Her renewed faith was inspired partly by the Revd J. H. C. Johnson, her correspondence with whom was published after her death in two volumes of *Letters to a Friend* (1961–2).

MACAULAY, Thomas Babington (1800–59) Poet, politician, and historian, son of the philanthropic reformer Zachary Macaulay (1768–1838). Born in Rothley Temple, Leicestershire, and educated at Trinity College, Cambridge, he was called to the bar, but his essay on John *Milton for the **Edinburgh Review* in August 1825 brought him instant fame, and for the next twenty years he wrote many articles on historical and literary topics for the *Review.* In 1830 he entered Parliament as a Whig, first for Calne (Wiltshire), then for Leeds, and took an active part in the passing of the Reform

Bill. But in 1834, in order to achieve financial independence, he took up a post on the Supreme Council of India, where his Minutes on Law and Education had a decisive influence on the development of the sub-continent. On his return in 1838 he began to write a detailed history of England from the revolution of 1688. He was elected MP for Edinburgh in 1839 and again in 1852; he was a secretary at war 1839–41 and paymaster-general 1846–7. But by now his literary fame was such that everything he published was a 'dazzling success', beginning in 1842 with **Lays of Ancient Rome*. His collected *Essays Critical and Historical* (1843) sold steadily down the century. Lord *Acton called them 'A key to half the prejudices of our age'; but their urgent, declamatory style, their self-confidence and biting wit, endeared them to the reading public all over the world. His *History of England* (vols i–ii, 1849; vols iii–iv, 1855) was more restrained and deeply researched. Macaulay took an immense pride in the English constitution, and shared with many Victorians an exaltation at the material advances of the 19th century, under the shadow of the French Revolution. The purpose of the *History* was defensive—to demonstrate that revolution on the continental model was unnecessary in England because of the statesmanlike precautions taken in 1688. He used a wide range of manuscript sources with great skill. He also took an interest in social history, though this was focused on his largely superficial chapter III, on 'The Condition of England in 1685'. He acknowledged a great debt to Walter *Scott, evident in his habit of exploring on the ground all the places in which his narrative was set. His descriptive power was one of his great assets; another was his skill as a narrator. The *History* was one of the best-sellers of the century; it brought him wealth and, in 1857, a peerage. He at first intended to take the *History* up to 1830, but when he died in 1859 he had only reached 1697. Macaulay was always criticized for his philistinism and his overweening self-confidence; Lord Melbourne once said, 'I wish I was as cocksure of anything as Tom Macaulay is of everything.' But his literary brilliance disarmed hostility, and his popularity persisted throughout the 19th century, and beyond.

He was the subject of one of the strongest Victorian biographies, by his nephew Sir George *Trevelyan (1876). See also John Clive, *Thomas Babington Macaulay: The Shaping of the Historian* (1973), and Jane Millgate's literary study (1973). His letters have been edited by Thomas Pinney, 6 vols (1974–81).

McAULEY, Paul J. (1955–) *Science fiction writer, born in Gloucestershire; equally at home with the far futures of novels like *Eternal Light* (1991), and the grittier near futures of *Fairyland* (1995) or *Whole Wide World* (2001), whose themes include surveillance and bio-engineered life-forms.

McBAIN, Ed *See* HUNTER, EVAN.

Macbeth A tragedy by *Shakespeare, probably written and first performed at the *Globe in 1606, but not printed until the first *folio (1623). The relatively short text has often been thought to contain non-Shakespearian material, probably by Thomas *Middleton, who may have adapted as well as abbreviated the original play. Two songs certainly by him (from *The *Witch*) were added to the play. It may have been performed before James I, who had a strong interest in witches and was supposedly a descendant of Banquo.

Macbeth and Banquo, generals of Duncan, king of Scotland, returning from a victorious campaign against rebels, encounter three witches, who prophesy that Macbeth shall be thane of Cawdor, and king hereafter, and that Banquo shall beget kings though he be none. Immediately afterwards comes the news that the king has created Macbeth thane of Cawdor. Motivated by the prophecy and urged on by Lady Macbeth, Macbeth murders Duncan, who is visiting his castle. Duncan's sons Malcolm and Donalbain escape, and Macbeth becomes king. To defeat the prophecy of the witches regarding Banquo, he causes Banquo to be murdered, but his son Fleance escapes. Haunted by the ghost of Banquo, Macbeth consults the witches, and is told to beware of Macduff, the thane of Fife; that none born of woman has power to harm Macbeth; and that he never will be vanquished till Birnam Wood shall come to Dunsinane. Learning that Macduff has joined Malcolm, who is gathering an army in England, he surprises the castle of Macduff and causes Lady Macduff and her children to be slaughtered. Lady Macbeth sleepwalks and dies. The army of Malcolm and Macduff attacks Macbeth; passing through Birnam Wood every man cuts a bough and under these 'leavy screens' marches on Dunsinane. Macduff, who was 'from his mother's womb | Untimely ripped', kills Macbeth. Malcolm becomes king of Scotland.

MacBETH, George (1932–92) Poet, born in Lanarkshire, who read Classics at New College, Oxford. From 1955 to 1976 he produced programmes on poetry and the arts for the BBC, and he also edited various anthologies. He was a member of the *Group, and in the 1960s was associated with the vogue for poetry in performance. His early work was experimental, and at times macabre and violent in its preoccupations; later collections show (in his own words) fewer 'comic and performance and experimental elements'. His books include *A Form of Words* (1954), *The Colour of Blood* (1967), and *Trespassing: Poems from Ireland* (1991). A *Selected Poems*, edited by Anthony *Thwaite, was published in 2002. He also published novels.

Macbeth, Lady Ambitious wife of Macbeth in *Shakespeare's play. L. C. Knights's essay 'How many children had Lady Macbeth?' (1933) is a teasing riposte to the sort of biographical speculation favoured by A. C. *Bradley.

McCABE, Patrick (1955–) Irish novelist, born in Clones, Co. Monaghan, and educated at St Patrick's College, Drumcondra. His novels include *Music on Clinton Street* (1986), which charts the encroachment of American culture on 1960s and 1970s rural Ireland; *The Dead School* (1995), an account of the ultimately catastrophic dissension between a conservative teacher and a younger colleague; *Breakfast on Pluto* (1998), in which the transvestite Patrick 'Pussy' Braden escapes to London only to become involved in prostitution and IRA subversion; and *Winterwood* (2006). McCabe's macabre comedy of small town life has been called 'Bog Gothic'. Most critics agree that it finds its most memorable expression in *The Butcher Boy* (1992), a horrifying story told in the voice of Francie Brady, an engaging but disturbed and ultimately homicidal boy living a life of neglect and compensatory fantasy in an unnamed small town in Ireland.

McCAFFREY, Anne (1926–) American *fantasy and *science fiction writer, born in Cambridge, Massachusetts, resident in Ireland. Her 'Dragonriders of Pern' series, beginning with *Dragonflight* (1968), appealed to a wide audience by offering a science fiction version of the popular *fantasy motif of dragons—here seen as biologically engineered by humans isolated on a remote world. Among numerous other novels is *The Ship Who Sang* (1969), where a girl's brain and nervous system guides a starship, making her a *cyborg.

MacCAIG, Norman (1910–96) Scottish poet, born Norman McCaig in Edinburgh and educated at Edinburgh University, where he studied classics. He worked for many years as a schoolmaster, and afterwards as a lecturer at the University of Stirling. After a false start as an exponent of the New Apocalypse, a group of poets influenced by neo-Romantic anarchism who took their name from the anthology *The New Apocalypse* (1939), he emerged with *Riding Lights* (1955) as an elegant formalist with a keen visual sense and an agile 'metaphysical' wit. His most characteristic work, however, belongs to the 1960s and later, when he dispensed with regular forms and opted increasingly for short, unrhymed poems marked by an unusual blend of terseness and humour. The figurative daring and playfulness of MacCaig's lyrics are undercut by a stoic pessimism, and many of his finest poems are elegies or meditations on the extinction of consciousness. The poet ascribed the hard, witty clarity of his work to his classical training and Gaelic ancestry. A definitive *Poems* appeared in 2005.

McCARTHY, Cormac (1933–) American novelist, born in Rhode Island, who grew up in Tennessee. His first novels were respectfully received, though with some reservations about his subjects: *Child of God* (1974) was based on an actual necrophilia case. His famous Border Trilogy—*All the Pretty Horses* (1992), *The Crossing* (1994), *Cities of the Plain* (1998)—was based on journey narratives, centring on young male protagonists, and set in southern Texas and Mexico. *No Country for Old Men* (2005; the 2007 film adaptation won that year's Oscar for Best Picture) dramatizes the workings of the drugs cartels in the same region and *The Road* (2006) describes the travels of a father and son across a burnt American landscape.

MacCARTHY, Desmond (1877–1952) Literary journalist and drama critic, born in Plymouth, Devon, and educated at Eton College and Trinity College, Cambridge, where he became an *Apostle. He is remembered largely for his perceptive theatre criticism, some of it collected in *The Court Theatre* (1907), *Drama* (1940), and *Shaw* (1951). He was drama critic (from 1913) then literary editor (from 1920) of the *New Statesman*, and from 1928 to 1952 he reviewed weekly for the *Sunday Times*. He was also closely involved with *Life and Letters* from 1928 to 1934. See H. Cecil and M. Cecil, *Clever Hearts* (1990).

McCARTHY, Mary (1912–89) American writer, born in Seattle and orphaned at the age of 6. After graduating from Vassar College she worked as a drama critic, then taught for some years at Bard College and Sarah Lawrence College, experiences she used in her satirical *campus novel *The Groves of Academe* (1952), which describes the political persecutions of the McCarthy period. *The Group* (1963), a study of the lives and careers of eight Vassar girls, caused some stir when published in England because of its frank descriptions of contraception, breastfeeding, and so on. She published two volumes of reportage, *Vietnam* (1967) and *Hanoi* (1968), protesting against American involvement in Vietnam. She also published several volumes of essays and an autobiography, *How I Grew* (1987). Her second husband was Edmund *Wilson. See Carol Gelderman, *Mary McCarthy: A Life* (1990). Her correspondence with Hannah *Arendt was published in 1995.

McCAUGHREAN, Geraldine (1951–) Prolific London-born writer for children and adults, educated at Christ Church, Canterbury. Her output includes numerous retellings of classic texts, among them Greek mythology (1992), Shakespeare's plays (1994), Bunyan's **Pilgrim's Progress* (1999), and *Cyrano* (2006). Her novels for younger readers are often set in the past, whether medieval England (*A Little Lower Than the Angels*, 1987) or ancient China (*The Kite Rider*, 2001). She was commissioned to write a sequel to **Peter Pan*; *Peter Pan in Scarlet* appeared in 2006. Adult fiction includes *Fires' Astonishment* (1990) and *The Ideal Wife* (1997).

McCLURE, Michael (1932–) American poet, born in Kansas, who then moved to San Francisco, where he participated in the *Beat movement. He subsequently gave poetry readings and performances during the 1960s hippy counterculture. His 1965 play *The Beard*, about an imagined encounter between Billy the Kid and Jean Harlow, occasioned arrests for obscenity. Apart from his plays and poetry, McClure has also been an active songwriter, essayist, and journalist.

McCOY, Horace (1897–1955) American novelist, born in Tennessee, who moved to Los Angeles during the Depression. This supplied the location for his *hardboiled novels, the most famous of which are *They Shoot Horses, Don't They?* (1936), about a dance marathon, and *Kiss Tomorrow Goodbye* (1948). McCoy was also a screenwriter for different Hollywood studios.

McCULLERS, Carson (1917–67) American novelist and short story writer, born in Georgia, where most of her works are set. Her best-known novel is *The Heart Is a Lonely Hunter* (1940), exploring her recurrent subject of isolation. Other works include *Reflections in a Golden Eye* (1941), *The Member of the Wedding* (1946; dramatized by the author, 1950), a collection, *The Ballad of the Sad Café* (1951), of which the title story was dramatized by Edward *Albee in 1963, and her unfinished autobiography, *Illumination and Night Glare* (1999). Her work has been linked to Southern *Gothic. See Josyane Savigneau, *Carson McCullers* (2001).

MacDIARMID, Hugh (1892–1978) Best known of the numerous pseudonyms of Christopher Murray Grieve, Scottish poet and cultural agitator who on his return from service with the RAMC in the Great War became the prime instigator of the *Scottish Renaissance. A postman's son from Langholm, Dumfriesshire, MacDiarmid left teacher training college in Edinburgh without his qualification and made his living as a journalist on a series of local newspapers, settling in Montrose, Angus, in 1920, where he was employed until 1929 on the *Montrose Review*. He launched various literary and nationalist periodicals and became notorious for his iconoclastic 'Contemporary Scottish Studies' column in the *Scottish Educational Journal*. In 1928 he helped found the National Party of Scotland along with R. B. *Cunninghame Graham and Compton *Mackenzie. He moved to London in 1929, evidently in the hope of reaching a wider audience for his poetry which, despite winning the admiration of W. B. *Yeats and other important figures, had made little general impact outside Scotland. After the break-up of his marriage and a period of alcoholism he returned to Scotland and settled on the Shetland island of Whalsay in 1933 with Valda Trevlyn, a young Cornishwoman he had met in London, and their infant son. By now MacDiarmid had adopted the implacable communist politics he would retain to the end. In the years after the incomplete *Collected Poems* of 1962 brought belated recognition, he received a daily stream of pilgrims at his Lanarkshire cottage with startling modesty and courtesy.

MacDiarmid's poetry is unusually various in kind as well as quality. The compressed *Scots lyrics of *Sangschaw* (1925) and *Penny Wheep* (1926) marry Expressionist techniques and a bleak modern cosmology to traditional Scottish tropes and idioms, while the tragicomic monologue *A Drunk Man Looks at the Thistle* (1926) combines ruthless satire of received versions of Scottishness with love lyrics, meditations on the miseries of embodiment, and alternately sombre and exalted metaphysical speculations. The poetry of the early 1930s explores origins and evolution in relation both to the poet's own family and Dumfriesshire childhood and to the promise of an imminent mutation in consciousness, of which in *First Hymn to Lenin and Other Poems* (1931) it presents the Bolshevik leader as guarantor. MacDiarmid dropped Scots in favour of English after 1933. His most notable work in the latter language is 'On a Raised Beach' (composed 1933), a materialist recasting of the Romantic crisis ode to accommodate intimations that are overwhelmingly of mortality. *In Memoriam James Joyce* (1955) is the most carefully assembled of the long, prosaic 'poems of fact' which he claimed provided a necessarily post-lyrical response to the complexities of modernity. MacDiarmid's private letters, however, suggest that he felt that he had lost his lyric powers as a result of the domestic turbulence of the early 1930s. See *Complete Poems*, ed. Alan Riach (2 vols, 1993).

McDONAGH, Martin (1970–) Playwright born in Camberwell, London, to Irish parents. He came to prominence with *The Beauty Queen of Leenane* (1996), the first play of a trilogy set in Leenane, a remote small town in Connemara, and followed this with the Aran Trilogy, comprising *The Cripple of Inishmaan*, *The Lieutenant of Inishmore*, and *The Banshees of Inisheer* (1997–2001). The plays mix sardonic humour with dark, brooding meditations on life. In 2003, his macabre play *The Pillowman* further established his reputation as a major force in contemporary theatre.

MacDONALD, Alexander (*c.*1695–*c.*1770) Scottish Gaelic poet, born at Dalilea on Loch Shiel and educated at Glasgow University, who composed under the pseudonym Alasdair MacMhaighistir Alasdair. The first cousin of Flora MacDonald, heroine of the Jacobite cause, he was Gaelic tutor to Charles Edward Stuart, the Young Pretender, Stuart claimant to the thrones of England, Scotland, and Ireland, and wrote a journal of the 1745 uprising. His assertively titled *Ais-Eiridh na Sean Chánoin Albannaich* ('The Resurrection of the Ancient Scottish Language', 1751) was the first printed collection of secular verse in any variety of Gaelic. MacDonald's surviving poetry is voluminous, various, and rhetorically inventive, and draws on the classics and Scottish poetry in English and *Scots, as well as on Gaelic tradition. His most famous poem, 'Birlinn Chlann Raghnaill' ('Clanranald's Galley'), an almost 600-line account of a voyage from South Uist to Carrickfergus, is remarkable for its technical attention to the skills of seamanship and for its alternately delicate and powerful evocations of the natural world. It has been translated by Hugh *MacDiarmid (1935) and (in part) I. C. *Smith (1977).

MacDONALD, George (1824–1905) Born in Huntly, Scotland, educated at King's College, Aberdeen. MacDonald was briefly a Congregationalist minister. He published over 50 books, among them the novels *David Elginbrod* (1863) and *Robert Falconer* (1868), which helped to found the *'Kailyard school' of fiction. His two allegorical fantasies for adults, *Phantastes* (1858) and *Lilith* (1895), were influenced by his study of *Novalis and E. T. A. *Hoffmann and, with his children's books, strongly influenced C. S. *Lewis, Frances Hodgson *Burnett, and Maurice *Sendak. He edited *Good Words for the Young* 1870–72. MacDonald is primarily remembered for his fantasies for children, notably *At the Back of the North Wind* (1871) and *The Princess and the Goblin* (1872), both deeply symbolic, with elements of Christian mysticism. There are biographies by Greville MacDonald (1924) and William

Reaper (1987); see also *For the Childlike: George MacDonald's Fantasy for Children*, ed. Roderick McGillis (1992).

McDONALD, Ian (1960–) *science fiction writer, born in Manchester, now resident in Belfast. His work has increasingly assumed a global perspective: *River of Gods* (2004) and *Brasyl* (2007) are centred on India and Brazil respectively. *Chaga* (1995) and its sequels are among science fiction's most powerful reflections on colonialism.

MacDONALD, Ross (1915–83) Pseudonym of Kenneth Millar, American novelist, raised in Ontario, who spent most of his life in southern California, which supplies the setting for his many crime novels. The latter, commencing with *The Moving Target* (1948), mostly centre on Lew Archer, a streetwise private eye, and are narrated in a *hardboiled style deriving from Dashiell *Hammett and Raymond *Chandler. See Tom Nolan, *Ross Macdonald: A Biography* (1999).

MacDONALD, Sharman (1951–) Playwright, born in Glasgow and educated at Edinburgh University. She worked briefly for John *McGrath's 7:84 Company, before producing the play for which she is best known, *When I was a Girl I Used to Scream and Shout* (1984). It explores the relationship between a mother and daughter, a theme that was further mined in *When We Were Women* (1988). Subsequent work, *After Juliet* (1999) and *Broken Hallelujah* (2006), has been produced for the *National Theatre. Her fiction includes *The Beast* (1986) and *Night Night* (1988). She has also written radio plays (for the BBC) such as *Sea Urchins* and *Gladly my Cross Eyed Bear* (1999), and the libretto to *Hey Persephone!*, performed at Aldeburgh with music by Deirdre Gribbin (1998).

McELROY, Colleen J. (1935–) African American poet and travel writer, born in St Louis, Missouri. Her poetry collections include *Queen of the Ebony Islands* (1984) and *What Madness Brought Me Here* (1990). The innovative *A Long Way from St Louie* (1997) offers travel memoirs, organized thematically rather than chronologically.

McEWAN, Ian (1948–) Novelist and short story writer, born in Aldershot, educated at the University of Sussex and at the University of East Anglia, where he was the first graduate of the new creative writing department established by Angus *Wilson and Malcolm *Bradbury. His early books—the short story collections *First Love, Last Rites* (1975) and *In Between the Sheets* (1977), and two taut novels, *The Cement Garden* (1978; filmed 1993), a story of parentless siblings, and *The Comfort of Strangers* (1981; filmed 1990), a tale of sadomasochistic atrocity—show a fascination, often macabrely displayed, with the vulnerability of the immature. *The Child in Time* (1987), focusing on a couple whose young daughter is abducted, brings greater emotional depth and psychological complexity to its exploration of maturity and immaturity, as does *The Innocent* (1990; filmed 1993), set in Berlin during the early years of the Cold War. *Black Dogs* (1992) contrasts religious and rationalist responses to evil in the wake of the Second World War. In *Enduring Love* (1997; filmed 2004), which traces the repercussions of a helium balloon accident (rendered with bravura tension), McEwan's interest in science moves to the fore. *Amsterdam*, a black comedy about euthanasia, won him the 1998 *Booker Prize. Opening in the 1930s and exhibiting to particularly fine effect his skill at evoking period and place, *Atonement* (2001; filmed 2007) is a masterly study of the dangers of the literary imagination. *Saturday* (2005; filmed 2008), which takes place on the day of the 2003 mass demonstration in London against the impending war in Iraq, brilliantly inhabits the consciousness of a neurosurgeon faced with ethical dilemmas and personal challenges. *On Chesil Beach* (2007), an affecting short novel about a disastrous honeymoon night in 1962, exhibits McEwan's talent for resonant concision, exact and imaginative prose, and acute emotional, physical, psychological, and social attentiveness at its most subtle and compelling. He has also written a television play, *The Imitation Game* (1981), about the Bletchley Park code-breaking centre during the Second World War; the film screenplay, *The Ploughman's Lunch* (1983); and libretti for Michael Berkeley's anti-nuclear oratorio *Or Shall We Die?* (1982), and his opera about an ageing composer, *For You* (2008).

Mac Flecknoe, *or A Satire upon the True-Blue-Protestant Poet, T. S.* A *mock-epic poem by John *Dryden, published 1682, and in a definitive edition, 1684. The outcome of a series of disagreements, personal, professional, and critical, between Dryden and Thomas *Shadwell, the poem represents the latter as heir to the kingdom of poetic dullness, currently governed by the minor writer Richard *Flecknoe. It brilliantly exploits the crudity of Shadwell's farces (notably *The Virtuoso*) and critical writings; while the range of its allusions to 17th-century theatre demonstrates the complexity of Dryden's critical thought and, since he satirizes his own work (notably **Tyrannic Love*) as well as Shadwell's, his humility towards the tradition in which he was working. *Mac Flecknoe* was a vital inspiration for Pope's **Dunciad*.

McGAHERN, John (1934–2006) Irish novelist and short story writer, born in Dublin and educated at St Patrick's College, Drumcondra. All of his richly symbolic short stories and his novels, from *The Barracks* (1963) through the acclaimed *Amongst Women* (1990) to *That They May Face the Rising Sun* (2001), trace what one of his characters calls 'all the vivid sections of the wheel we watched so slowly turn, impatient for the rich whole that never came but that all the preparations promised'. Though the separate works focus on individuals trapped in situations over which they have little control—brutalized country children in the earlier fiction, middle-class urban professionals and marginalized Protestants in the short stories, ageing pensioners in the dark and lyrical final novel—McGahern's writing overall offers arguably the most panoramic view of post-independence Irish society yet attempted in literature. A startlingly Oedipal *Memoir* appeared in 2005.

McGONAGALL, William (*c.*1830–1902) Scottish poet, actor, and handloom weaver, who possessed celebrity status in Scotland for his legendary public readings of his topical verse. His unintentionally hilarious poems, usually featuring gloom and disaster, were ridiculed but also gained him an enviable reputation as the world's worst poet.

McGOUGH, Roger (1937–) OBE, poet and writer, born in Liverpool, and educated at St Mary's College and the University of Hull. He worked as a teacher before becoming a member of the music/poetry group the Scaffold (1963–73). Emphasis on *performance poetry became a hallmark of his style, and in 1967 he and the other *Liverpool poets, Brian *Patten and Adrian *Henri, published *The Mersey Sound*. This was followed by another group work, *The New Volume* (1983). He has written many volumes of poetry for both adults and children, as well as fiction and plays, distinguished by high spirits, wit, and accessibility: works include *Watchwords* (1969, poems), *In the Glassroom* (1976, poems), and *The Great Smile Robbery* (1982, children's fiction). *Selected Poems 1967–1987* (1989) was followed by a second selection, *You at the Back* (1991). McGough is also known for his anthologies of humorous verse for children and his translations of *Molière.

McGRATH, John Peter (1935–2002) Playwright and director, educated in Mold, Clwyd, and at Oxford University, whose first success was the play *Events while Guarding the Bofors Gun* (pub. 1966). He founded in 1971 the theatre group 7:84, through which he explored and expressed his belief in the possibility of a genuine working-class theatre, characterized by 'directness, comedy, music, emotion, variety, effect, immediacy', and often with a strong local or community interest (*A Good Night Out*, 1981). The group, which later divided into separate English and Scottish companies, presented plays by McGrath himself (including *The Cheviot, the Stag and the Black, Black Oil*, 1974; *Little Red Hen*, 1977; both dealing with Scottish politics) and by others, including John *Arden, Trevor *Griffiths, and Adrian *Mitchell. McGrath also wrote, directed, and produced extensively for film and television.

McGRATH, Patrick (1950–) Novelist, born in London. His father was a superintendent at Broadmoor, and McGrath grew up in the grounds of this institution, surrounded by the criminally insane. His early fiction tended towards the bizarre: *Blood and Water* (1988) is a sometimes lurid collection of short stories; *The Grotesque* (1989) a morally serious parody of English *Gothic fiction; and *Spider* (1990) tells of a schizophrenic's return to the scene of his brutal London childhood. Subsequent novels show him moving beyond the neo-Gothic genre. *Dr Haggard's Disease* (1993) and *Asylum* (1996) are both studies in romantic obsession, the latter telling of a psychiatrist who becomes infatuated with one of her husband's most dangerous patients. *Martha Peake* (2000) is *historical fiction, set in the dark underworlds of 18th-century London and America, *Port Mungo* (2004) the story of a turbulent relationship between two brilliant but dissolute artists.

McGUCKIAN, Medbh (1950–) Née McCaughan, Irish poet, born in Belfast and educated at Queen's University, Belfast, where she subsequently became a lecturer in creative writing. *The Flower Master* (1982; rev. 1993) is the first of eleven collections. Lyrical, beguiling, and slyly erotic, McGuckian's poetry delights in flux and in a refusal to settle into semantic finality. Many of her poems have a strongly intertextual character, and offer gnomic commentaries on issues raised by the (usually) unidentified writings they adapt. An engagement with Irish history, from an oblique nationalist perspective, is notable in *Shelmalier* (1998), a series of elegiac meditations on the 1798 rebellion, *Drawing Ballerinas* (2001), and *Had I a Thousand Lives* (2003). *The Currach Requires No Harbours* appeared in 2006.

McGUINNESS, Frank (1953–) Irish playwright and poet, born in Buncrana, Co. Donegal, and educated at University College, Dublin. An adolescence spent on the Irish border in the early years of the *Troubles may have been a crucial influence on McGuinness's presentation of communities isolated by conflict and violence. The vivid and angry *Factory Girls* (1982) deals with a group of women barricaded into a factory. *Observe the Sons of Ulster Marching towards the Somme* (1985) offers a Catholic writer's notably empathetic exploration of one of the key myths of Ulster Protestantism. The interest in sexual politics of these plays and of *Mary and Lizzie* (1989) and the Beirut-set *Someone Who'll Watch over Me* (1992) emerges as an explicit concern with issues surrounding gay identity in *Gates of Gold* (2002).

MACHADO, Antonio (1875–1939) Spanish poet. Following the largely symbolist texts of *Soledades, galerías, otros poemas* (1907: *Solitudes, Galleries, Other Poems*), his most famous collection, *Campos de Castilla* (1912: *Landscapes of Castile*), reflects on the poet's childhood in Seville, and the landscape of Castile, with its implications for the character and the future of his country. He published a volume of poetry, *Nuevas canciones* (1924: *New Songs*), before turning to prose, adopting a variety of pseudonyms to allow himself to explore more freely a variety of philosophical subjects and tones. Throughout his life he had been a spokesman for the Republican cause, and he died in France in flight from the Fascists. After his death his work was suppressed by Franco, not regaining prominence until the mid-1960s. His poems have inspired numerous English versions, including *Castilian Ilexes* (1963) by the poet Charles *Tomlinson and the scholar Henry Gifford (1913–2003).

MACHAUT, Guillaume de (*c.*1300–77) French musician and poet. He was prominent in the development of the *ballade and the *rondeau, and one of the most widely celebrated composers in the field of polyphonic songwriting. His poetry influenced Chaucer, particularly in *The *Book of the Duchess*.
See Marot, Clément.

MACHEN, Arthur (1863–1947) Welsh *fantasy and *horror writer; born in Caerleon, son of a clergyman; deeply influenced by his lonely childhood, the Welsh landscape, and local folklore. He left for London in 1880, and his work as a cataloguer of occult books introduced him to secret sects and societies (he later joined the Order of the Golden Dawn of which W. B. *Yeats and Aleister *Crowley became members). He translated *L'*Heptaméron* (1886) and *The Memoirs of *Casanova* (1894) and began writing the mystic, supernatural tales of rural and urban life for which he is best remembered, including *The Great God Pan* (1894), *The Hill of Dreams* (1907), and *The Three Impostors* (1895). He spent several years from 1901 as an actor and in 1910 joined the London *Evening News*, which led to his rediscovery and the publication in 1923 of the Caerleon Edition of his works. His short story 'The Bowmen' in the *Evening News* (Sept. 1914) was responsible for the legend of 'The Angels of Mons', said to have saved the retreating British forces. Other works include *Hieroglyphics* (1902, criticism), *Far off Things* (1922), and *Things Near and Far* (1923), both autobiographical.

MACHIAVELLI, Niccolò (1469–1527) Political theorist, dramatist, and historian of Florence, and perhaps the most notorious Italian writer outside Italy. After holding various offices, from 1498, in the restored Florentine republic and discharging various missions abroad, he was exiled on suspicion of conspiracy on the return of the *Medici in 1512, but was subsequently restored to some degree of favour. He turned his political experiences to advantage in his writings, which include the *Discorsi sopra la prima deca di Tito Livio* (written 1516–17; printed in 1531: *Discourse on the First Ten Books of Titus Livius*) on republican government, *Arte della guerra* (*The Art of War*, written 1517–20; English trans. 1560–62), and a history of Florence (*Istorie Fiorentine*, 1520–25; trans. 1595). His comedy *Mandragola*, probably written in 1518, is a cynical depiction of Florentine society. His best-known work is *Il principe* (written 1513, pub. 1532: *The Prince*), a treatise on statecraft by an acute observer of the contemporary political scene. Dedicated to the Medici duke of Urbino, its aim is to disseminate successful strategies for acquiring and maintaining political power. Machiavelli teaches that the lessons of the past (of Roman history in particular) should be applied to the present, and that the acquisition and effective use of power may necessitate unethical methods not in themselves desirable. In 1640 Edward Dacres published the first English translation of *The Prince*, but it was well known both by repute and in Italian and Latin editions throughout the previous century. It is repeatedly referred to in Elizabethan drama, and influenced the policy of Thomas Cromwell (?1485–1540), Robert Cecil (1563–1612), and the earl of *Leicester. It was appreciated critically by Francis *Bacon; exploited intelligently by Christopher *Marlowe; used guardedly in the Maxims of State wrongly attributed to Walter *Ralegh by John *Milton, who in 1658 published the collection as *The Cabinet-Council*. Selected maxims from *Il principe* were translated into French and refuted by Gentillet, a French Huguenot, in 1576; these appeared in an English translation, by Simon Paterick, in 1602.

In Elizabethan and Jacobean drama, Machiavellian villains and anti-heroes abound, appearing in many guises, as pander, atheist, poisoner, politician, miser, and revenger, and the name of Machiavelli himself is frequently invoked: for example by Gloucester, who resolved in *3 *Henry VI* 'to set the murtherous Machiavel to school' (III. ii. 193), by Flamineo in *The *White Devil*, who rejoices in 'the rare trickes of a Machivillian' (V. iii. 193), and in the prologue to *The *Jew of Malta* by the spirit of Machiavelli himself. There is a sketch of his character in George *Eliot's **Romola*.

McILVANNEY, William (1936–) Novelist, poet, and journalist, born in Kilmarnock, Ayrshire, the son of an ex-miner, and educated at Kilmarnock Academy and Glasgow University. His widely praised *Docherty* (1975), set in the fictional mining town of Graithnock in the first quarter of the 20th century, draws on his own family history. McIlvanney's work balances literary allusiveness with a socialist desire to widen the readership of fiction. The latter aspiration may lie behind his recourse to the detective genre in his three Inspector Jack Laidlaw novels (*Laidlaw*, 1977; *The Papers of Tony Veitch*, 1983; *Strange Loyalties*, 1991). Set mainly in Glasgow, these focus on Laidlaw's subversive outlook and the psychological, social, and political roots of crime. *The Big Man* (1985) is a parable of the break-up of working-class communities, while *The Kiln* (1996) continues the history of the Docherty family. *Weekend* (2006) plays a multi-layered, philosophical variation on the *campus novel.

MacINNES, Colin (1914–76) Novelist, the son of singer James McInnes (*sic*: Colin altered the spelling of his name) and Angela *Thirkell, brought up partly in Australia; on his return to England, after a period in art school and (during the war) the army, he embarked on a career as a writer and journalist. His first novel, *To the Victors the Spoils* (1950), was followed by *June in her Spring* (1952, set in Australia) and the novels for which he is best remembered, *City of Spades* (1957) and *Absolute Beginners* (1959). These describe teenage and black immigrant culture, and the new bohemian underworld of Notting Hill, coffee bars, jazz clubs, drink, and homosexuality. MacInnes called himself an 'anarchist sympathizer' and defended several of the causes of the 1960s, including Black Power and the writers of **Oz*. His relations with his mother were less than friendly: he despised her writing (a 'sterile, life-denying vision of our land': *New Statesman*, June 1963) and she cut him out of her will. See *Inside Outsider* (1983), a biography by T. Gould. *See also* BLACK BRITISH LITERATURE.

MACINTYRE, Duncan Ban (Donnchadh Bàn Mac an t-Saoir) (*c.*1723–1812) Scottish Gaelic poet, born at Druim Liaghart, Argyll, who fought on the Hanoverian side during the Jacobite uprising and worked thereafter as a gamekeeper for the earls of Breadalbane. In 1767 he moved to Edinburgh and enlisted in the city guard. Many of his songs and poems suggest the influence of Alexander *MacDonald. His best-known work, the long poem 'Moladh Beinn

Dòbhrainn' ('The Praise of Ben Doran'), reflects his intimacy with the rural Highlands and has been translated by Hugh *MacDiarmid (1940) and I. C. *Smith (1969).

McINTYRE, Vonda Neel (1948–) American *science fiction writer, born in Louisville, Kentucky; known for work for the *Star Trek franchise, but also a *Hugo winner for *Dreamsnake* (1978). *The Moon and the Sun* (1997), an *alternate history at the court of Louis XIV, combines her scientific background with meticulous historical research.

MACKAY, Shena (1944–) Novelist and short story writer, born in Edinburgh, brought up in Kent, and educated at Tonbridge Girls' Grammar School and Kidbrooke Comprehensive School. Her first two novellas, *Toddler on the Run* and *Dust Falls on Eugene Schlumberger*, were published together in 1964, when she was only 19. Subsequent novels, *Music Upstairs* (1965), *Old Crow* (1967), and *An Advent Calendar* (1971), established her mastery of comic narratives in which bizarre sequences of events often flow from tiny accidents, and a profound sympathy for her characters' damaged lives is apparent beneath offhand ironies. The often very ordinary settings of Mackay's fiction are transformed by ornately detailed prose in her collection of stories, *Babies in Rhinestones* (1983), and the novels *A Bowl of Cherries* (1984) and *Redhill Rococo* (1986, winner of the Fawcett Prize). *Dunedin* (1992) is partly set in New Zealand at the beginning of the 20th century, but also provides a hellish vision of contemporary suburban London. *The Orchard on Fire* (1996), a dark tragicomedy about childhood friendship, was shortlisted for the *Booker Prize. *The Artist's Widow* (1998), a satire on modern artistic values, is one of her most astringent novels. *Heligoland* (2003), centred on a group of people living in a modernist apartment block, is more utopian in feel. Mackay's full range is demonstrated in her *Collected Short Stories* (1994).

McKENDRICK, Jamie (1955–) Poet, born in Liverpool, educated at Nottingham University. Having taught in Italy, he is drawn to the Mediterranean, where 'the soul speaks Latin | with a Gothic slur'. *The Sirocco Room* (1991) and *The Kiosk on the Brink* (1993) are sardonic, anxious books whose promise is fulfilled in *The Marble Fly* (1997), *Ink Stone* (2003), and *Crocodiles and Obelisks* (2007), in which meditations on art and history mingle with bleak humour. McKendrick has developed a suggestive but economical idiom in which the ordinary sometimes warps into the uncanny. He has also edited the *Faber Book of Twentieth-Century Italian Poems* (2004).

MACKENZIE, Sir Compton (1883–1972) Author, born at West Hartlepool, Co. Durham, into a theatrical family, educated at St Paul's School, London, and Magdalen College, Oxford. He lived at various times on Capri, in the Channel Islands, and in Scotland. He was a prolific writer in all genres, although he is best remembered for his novels. The most notable include *Carnival* (1912), a grim story of Jenny, an actress and singer, who settles for the chorus-line and makes a ruinous marriage; and *Sinister Street* (2 vols, 1913–14), which presents in sexually frank terms a semi-autobiographical figure, Michael Fane, 'handicapped by a public school and university education', passing through school, Oxford, and low life in London. The novel transformed Mackenzie into a literary celebrity; Ford Madox *Ford found it 'the history of a whole class...during a whole period of life'; and F. Scott *Fitzgerald acknowledged its deep influence on his early work. In 1915 Mackenzie fought at Gallipoli and he subsequently published two volumes of war memoirs, *Gallipoli Memories* (1929) and *Greek Memories* (1932). After the war, his fiction included *Vestal Fire* (1927), a story of two cousins, Maimie and Virginia, who find their Anglo-Saxon attitudes loosening on the Mediterranean island of Sirene (really Capri), and become disastrously devoted to the scandalous Count Marsac, and *Extraordinary Women* (1928), a tale of lesbian entanglements, again set on Sirene. During 1937–45 appeared the six volumes of *The Four Winds of Love*, his most ambitious work, tracing the life of John Ogilvie, a pensive and individualistic Scot, from the time of the Boer War to the emergence of Scottish nationalism in 1945, a cause to which Mackenzie himself was devoted. *Whisky Galore* (1947), a fictional account of an actual wreck of a ship loaded with whisky on the Scottish island of Eriskay, was made into a highly successful film. *Thin Ice*, a sombre novel of homosexual scandal, appeared in 1956, and in 1963–71 the ten 'Octaves' of his popular and critically successful *My Life and Times*.

MACKENZIE, Henry (1745–1831) Scottish novelist, playwright, essayist, and lawyer, born in Edinburgh and educated at Edinburgh University, who was appointed comptroller of taxes for Scotland in 1779. His initially anonymous novel *The *Man of Feeling* (1771), in which the refined and gentle hero is presented in a series of loosely linked sketches, went through many editions and was translated into several European languages. It was greatly admired by Charles *Lamb and was one of Robert *Burns's 'bosom favourites'. In 1773 he published *The Man of the World*, in which the protagonist is by contrast a villain; and in 1777 *Julia de Roubigné*, an *epistolary novel. *The Prince of Tunis* (1773) was the first and most successful of his five plays. Mackenzie was chairman of the committee that investigated James *Macpherson's 'Ossian' and editor of the periodicals the *Mirror* and the *Lounger*, to both of which he also frequently contributed. *See* SENTIMENT.

MCKERROW, Ronald Brunlees (1872–1940) Bibliographer and editor, co-founder of the *Malone Society, 1906. He became joint secretary of the *Bibliographical Society, 1912, and in 1925 founded the *Review of English Studies*. His best-known works were an important edition of the works of Thomas *Nashe (1904–10) and *An Introduction to Bibliography for Literary Students* (1927).

MCKILLIP, Patricia Anne (1948–) American *fantasy writer, born in Salem, Oregon; novels including *The*

Forgotten Beasts of Eld (1974), *The Riddle-Master of Hed* (1976), and *Ombria in Shadow* (2002) possess an assured mastery of the fantasy form which have caused them to be described as modern classics.

McKINLEY, Robin (1952–) American *fantasy author, born Warren, Ohio, now resident in Britain. Her fiction, often for children or young adults, includes *Beauty* (1978), recasting the traditional fairy-tale, and *The Blue Sword* (1982). *Water: Tales of Elemental Spirits* (2001) was co-written with her husband Peter *Dickinson.

MACKINTOSH, Sir James (1765–1832) Educated at Aberdeen University, a doctor, philosopher, disputant, and barrister, and the author of the highly successful *Vindiciae Gallicae* (1791), a reasoned defence of the French Revolution. Mackintosh later recanted his views, in a lecture attended by a disapproving William *Hazlitt. He published a *Dissertation on the Progress of Ethical Philosophy* (1830) and wrote the first three volumes of a *History of England* (1830–31) for Lardner's *Cabinet Cyclopaedia*, as well as an unfinished *History of the Revolution in England in 1688* (1834).

MACKLIN (MacLaughlin), **Charles** (?1699–1797) Irish-born actor and playwright whose thoughtful playing of *Shylock, in 1741, brought a new standard of psychological realism to the stage. His most successful plays were the romantic comedies *Love à-la-Mode* (1759) and *The *Man of the World*, the latter performed in 1781 after a long delay because of its satiric prejudice against the Scots. He continued to act until a failing memory forced him to retire in 1789.

MACKMURDO, A. H. *See* ART NOUVEAU.

MACLAREN, Ian *See* KAILYARD SCHOOL.

MacLAVERTY, Bernard (1942–) Novelist and short story writer, born in Belfast, who worked as a laboratory technician before reading English at Queen's University, Belfast, and then moving to Scotland. He has published increasingly distinguished collections of stories—*Secrets* (1977), *A Time to Dance* (1982), *The Great Profundo* (1987), *Walking the Dog* (1994), and *Matters of Life & Death* (2006). Like these stories, his novels explore damage done by parochialism and bigotry in Northern Ireland. *Lamb* (1980) portrays a Christian Brother rescuing an abused boy from a reformatory. *Cal* (1983) depicts a reluctant IRA man drawn into a doomed affair with the widow of one of his victims. In *Grace Notes* (1997), a composer who has escaped the turmoil of Ulster comes to terms with the tormented history of her birthplace through her music. *The Anatomy School* (2001), an autobiographical-seeming account of a Catholic young man growing up in Belfast, gives a particularly fine display of MacLaverty's talents: exact rendering of place and period, beautifully caught (and sometimes very funny) dialogue, humane warmth, intensely credible characterization, and an ability to depict people penned in by hostile circumstances with an authenticity unmatched in Irish fiction since James Joyce's **Dubliners*. His work for film includes adaptations of *Cal* (1984) and *Lamb* (1986), and an original screenplay, *Hostages* (1993).

MACLEAN, Sorley (Somhairle MacGill-Eain) (1911–96) Scottish Gaelic poet, born on Raasay and educated on Skye and at the University of Edinburgh, where he studied English. He served in the signal corps from 1940 and was wounded at the battle of El Alamein. From 1956 until 1972 he was headmaster of Plockton high school, Ross-shire. *Dàin do Eimhir* ('Poems to Emer'), a sequence of 61 lyrics written in the late 1930s and published, in incomplete form, in 1943, pits love against public responsibility in the context of the threat of *Fascism. *An Cuilithionn* ('The Cuillin'), a long poem apostrophizing Hugh *MacDiarmid, to whose romantic Leninism it is indebted, was abandoned unfinished in December 1939. Maclean's lyrics of desert combat, like his magisterial meditations on the woods of Raasay and the cleared village of Hallaig, substitute humanist scepticism for the impassioned partisanship of his earlier work. In all its phases, his intricate, intensely musical poetry fuses aspects of oral tradition with an awareness of European history, literature, and politics. It has been translated by I. C. *Smith (*Eimhir*, 1971), Seamus *Heaney (*Hallaig*, 2002), and (with misleading blandness) by the poet himself. See *O Choille gu Bearradh/From Wood to Ridge: Collected Poems* (1999).

MacLEISH, Archibald (1892–1982) American poet and dramatist, born in Illinois and educated at Yale and Harvard universities. He was one of the American expatriates in Paris in the 1920s, and was strongly influenced by Ezra *Pound and T. S. *Eliot. His volumes of verse include *The Pot of Earth* (1924); *The Hamlet of A. MacLeish* (1928); *New Found Land* (1930); the narrative poem *Conquistador* (1932); and his *Collected Poems, 1917–1933* (1933). In 1938 he supplied the text for the documentary photo-volume *Land of the Free*. Among his verse dramas are *Panic* (1935), the anti-totalitarian *The Fall of the City* (1937), and the successfully staged *J.B.* (1958), an updating of the trials of Job. After his return to America at the end of the 1920s, MacLeish became an increasingly public figure, holding many important posts which brought him into conflict with the FBI; he was librarian of Congress (1939–44), assistant secretary of state (1944–5), and Boylston professor at Harvard (1949–62). See Scott Donaldson, *Archibald MacLeish: An American Life* (1992).

MACLEOD, Fiona Pseudonym of William *Sharp.

MacLEOD, Ken (1954–) Born in Stornoway; Scottish *science fiction writer noted for exploring libertarian and utopian ideas, especially in the 'Fall Revolution' series (1995–9), where his suspicion of artificial intelligence and 'green' rejection of technology is dramatized. *The Execution Channel* (2007) engages the post-9/11 world.

MACLISE, Daniel (1806–70) Irish portrait and history painter; he sketched Walter *Scott in 1825, when Scott was visiting Cork with Maria *Edgeworth. In 1827 he settled in London where he moved in literary circles and became a close friend of Charles *Dickens and of John *Forster; his well-known portrait of Dickens (1839) is in the National Portrait Gallery, London. He contributed a brilliant series of caricatures of celebrated authors to *Fraser's Magazine.*

Macmillan's Magazine A periodical founded in 1859, and edited successively by David *Masson (1859–68), George Grove (1868–83), John *Morley (1883–5), and Mowbray Morris (1885–1907). It was one of the first magazines to use signed articles only, and published a wide variety of material, including poetry, serialized fiction, and articles on politics and travel. Contributors included Alfred *Tennyson, Thomas *Hughes, Thomas *Hardy, Margaret *Oliphant, Frederick Denison *Maurice, and Henry *James.

MACMURRAY, John (1891–1976) Scottish moral philosopher and broadcaster, author of *The Self as Agent* (1957) and *Persons in Relation* (1961), who was born in Maxwellton, Kirkcudbrightshire, and educated at the University of Glasgow and Balliol College, Oxford. His work stresses the social dimension of experience and seeks to reconcile aspects of Marxism and Christianity. He is said to have been the model for Luke in Nan *Shepherd's *The Quarry Wood*. See J. E. Costello, *John Macmurray: A Biography* (2002).

McMURTRY, Larry (1936–) American novelist and screenwriter, born in Texas, which has remained the setting for most of his fiction. His most famous novels are *The Last Picture Show* (1966) and *Lonesome Dove* (1985), about western cattle drives. His *Berrybender Narratives* (2002–4) concern a hunting expedition in the Old West. Among his screenplays, the adaptation of Annie *Proulx's *Brokeback Mountain* (2005) won McMurtry an Oscar.

MacNEICE, Louis (1907–63) Poet and writer, born in Belfast and educated at Marlborough College and Merton College, Oxford, where he published a book of poems, *Blind Fireworks* (1929). After lecturing in classics at Birmingham University and Bedford College, London University, he joined the BBC Features Department in 1941. Meanwhile he had made several unsuccessful attempts at writing for the theatre, including *Station Bell* (1935) and *Out of the Picture* (1937); produced a fine verse translation of the *Agamemnon* (1936); and was becoming known as a poet through his contributions to *New Verse* and his *Poems* (1935). *Letters from Iceland* (1937) was written in collaboration with W. H. *Auden. Subsequent volumes of poetry include *The Earth Compels* (1938); *Autumn Journal* (1939), a long personal and political meditation on the events leading up to the Munich Agreement of September 1938 and generally considered his finest single work; *Plant and Phantom* (1941); *Springboard* (1944); *Holes in the Sky* (1948); *Autumn Sequel* (1954); and *The Burning Perch* (1963).

His early work revealed a technical virtuosity, a painter's eye for an image, humour, and an impulse towards making sense of what he later called the 'drunkenness of things being various' ('Snow'); suspicious of all rigid systems, whether political, religious, or philosophical, he worked to establish some pattern from life's flux. He used most of the classic verse forms, but his distinctive contribution was his deployment of assonance, internal rhymes, half-rhymes, and ballad-like repetitions. He was also renowned as an outstanding writer of radio documentaries and radio plays; these include *Christopher Columbus* (1944) and his most powerful dramatic work, *The Dark Tower* (1946). He also published a pseudonymous novel (*Roundabout Way*, 1932, by 'Louis Malone'), a book on W. B. *Yeats (1941), and a translation of an abridged version of *Goethe's *Faust* (1951); *Varieties of Parable* and a volume of autobiography, *The Strings are False*, both appeared posthumously in 1965. Although overshadowed in the 1930s and 1940s by Auden, and later by critical fashion, his reputation was revived by the publication in 1966 of his *Collected Poems*, edited by E. R. Dodds. See Jon *Stallworthy, *Louis MacNeice* (1995).

McPHERSON (MacPherson), **Conor** (1971–) Irish playwright and theatre and film director, born in Dublin and educated at University College, Dublin. His plays, featuring long monologues and sometimes marked by a *Gothic sense of the satanic and of the proximity of the dead to the living, explore themes of regret, anxiety, and self-delusion in the context of a rapidly modernizing Ireland. They include *This Lime Tree Bower* (1995), *The Weir* (1997), and *Shining City* (2004). *The Seafarer* (2006), in which a group of drunks meets to play cards on Christmas Eve, enjoyed major success on Broadway in 2007–8.

MACPHERSON, James (1736–96) Poet, born in Invertromie, Inverness-shire, the son of a farmer, and educated at King's College and Marischal College, Aberdeen, and at the University of Edinburgh. In 1758 he published *The Highlander*, a heroic poem in six cantos. In 1759 he met John *Home, at whose insistence he translated his first 'Ossianic' ballad; encouraged by Home and Hugh *Blair he then produced *Fragments of Ancient Poetry, Collected in the Highlands of Scotland, and Translated from the Galic or Erse Language* (1760). Rumours that a Gaelic epic existed fuelled the contemporary passion for *primitivism; urged on by his admirers, Macpherson travelled round the Highlands and Islands collecting materials for **Fingal: An Ancient Epic Poem, in Six Books* (1762). It claimed to be Macpherson's faithful translation of an epic by Ossian, the son of *Finn (or, in this version, Fingal), dating from some vague but remote period of early Scottish history. A second epic, *Temora* (1763), soon followed. These works created a sensation; patriotic Scots, delighted at the revelation of so rich a national treasure, praised them highly. David *Hume and Adam *Smith were at first convinced by them: Home and Blair remained so. Ossian's fame spread to the Continent, where *Klopstock, *Schiller, and *Goethe joined in the chorus of praise. Goethe quoted Ossian at length in *The Sorrows of Young Werther*, which, with Ossian, was to be one of the favourite works of Napoleon. Ossian also had an influence on national consciousness in Scandinavia: Macpherson was translated by the Danish writer Steen Blicher (1782–1848), and helped to inspire efforts to record the Finnish *Kalevala*. But at home doubts of the poems' authenticity sprang up almost at once, with Samuel *Johnson as the most formidable of sceptics; his enquiries during his tour of Scotland and remarks published in his **Journey to the Western Islands* (1775) were highly critical. A committee appointed after Macpherson's death, chaired by Henry *Mackenzie, investigated the matter and reported in 1805 that Macpherson had liberally edited Gaelic poems and inserted passages of his own, a view supported by subsequent scholarship. The immense popularity of the poetry survived the exposure of its origins; as late as 1866 Matthew *Arnold in his lectures on Celtic literature was defending its 'vein of piercing regret and sadness'. Macpherson's other works include a prose translation of the *Iliad* (1773) and a *History of Great Britain* (1775). He wrote in defence of Lord North's ministry, was MP for Camelford from 1780, and was buried in Westminster Abbey at his own expense. See Fiona Stafford, *The Sublime Savage: A Study of James Macpherson and the Poems of Ossian* (1988).

MACREADY, William Charles (1793–1873) Actor-manager, son of a provincial actor-manager, born in London and educated at Rugby School. He achieved a considerable reputation in the provinces before appearing at Covent Garden in 1816. By 1819 he was an established rival of Edmund *Kean, appearing regularly at both Covent Garden and Drury Lane; he was manager of both theatres at various times, where he sought to improve standards of production. He introduced new plays, and worked to restore Shakespeare's texts. In 1837 he appeared in *Strafford*, which Robert *Browning had written for him, and in 1838 in Lord *Byron's *Two Foscari*; but it was in the roles of Lear, Hamlet, and Macbeth that he won fame as a tragic actor. He knew some of the most important writers of his day and was a friend of Charles *Dickens. His last performance was as Macbeth in 1851 and Alfred *Tennyson wrote a sonnet to mark the occasion.

Macro Plays Three *morality plays (*The *Castle of Perseverance*, **Mankind*, and **Wisdom*) named after their 18th-century owner, Cox Macro (1683–1767). See *The Macro Plays*, ed. Mark Eccles (EETS 262, 1969).

MADAN, Judith Cowper (1702–81) Poet, from a powerful family; aunt of William *Cowper, and friend of Alexander *Pope, who encouraged her writing. Her response to Pope's *'Eloisa to Abelard', called 'Abelard to Eloisa', written in 1720, appeared in 1728; 'The Progress of Poetry', written *c.*1721, appeared in 1731. Much else remains unpublished.

MADGE, Charles (1912–96) Poet and sociologist, whose left-wing sympathies were manifested in his poetry (his first volume was *The Disappearing Castle*, 1937) and other work and writings. His second volume of verse, *The Father Found* (1941), was followed by a gap of 50 years until *Of Love, Time and Places* (1993), a selection from the earlier volumes together with more recent work. In 1937 with Humphrey Jennings and Tom Harrisson he founded *Mass Observation, a scheme which recruited hundreds of observers (including poets and novelists) to collect accurate sociological data about everyday life and popular culture. His first wife was the poet Kathleen *Raine.

Madoc A narrative poem by Robert *Southey, published 1805. Madoc is the youngest son of Owen Gwyneth, king of Wales (d. 1169). He leaves Wales and sails to a western land across the ocean where he founds a settlement and defeats the Aztecas. He returns home for a fresh supply of adventurers and tells his tale. After going back to the settlement in Aztlan, war breaks out again with the Aztecas. Madoc is ambushed and captured, chained by the foot to the stone of human sacrifice, and required to fight in succession six Azteca champions. After much fighting the Aztecas are finally defeated and migrate to another country. The poem gave its title to *Madoc: A Mystery* (1990) by Paul *Muldoon.

madrigal Originally a short amatory lyric, but used in musical terminology to describe a type of song for several voices, to secular words, usually sung by amateurs, without instrumental accompaniment. The madrigal reached England from Europe but was not widely disseminated until *Musica Transalpina* (1588), an anthology of 57 Italian madrigals with English texts; four other such volumes appeared in England between 1588 and 1598, with 45 more by 1627. Some composers, such as Thomas *Morley, stayed fairly close to the Italian model; others, such as John *Ward, Thomas *Weelkes, and John *Wilbye, adapted it to a more serious manner. In 1601 Morley brought out the collection *The Triumphes of Oriana*, a tribute to *Elizabeth I, with contributions by 23 musicians. Subsequent collections include those of Orlando *Gibbons (1612) and Thomas *Tomkins (1622), after which the form, already challenged by the dominance of the lute song, largely died out.

Mad World, my Masters, A A comedy by Thomas *Middleton, written 1604–7, printed 1608. In a complex plot of deceits and disguises, young Follywit plans to rob his wealthy grandfather, Sir Bounteous Progress, and Penitent Brothel tries to seduce the wife of the jealous Hairbrain. A courtesan, Gullman, the mistress of Sir Bounteous, contributes to both actions, and finally Follywit (who has married Gullman) finds himself fooled, bound to his grandfather's mistress. But she claims to be a reformed character, Sir Bounteous generously endows the young couple, and all ends reasonably happily.

MAECENAS (d. 8 BC) Wealthy friend of the emperor Augustus and patron of *Virgil, *Propertius, and particularly *Horace, to whom he gave his Sabine farm. His name has become the generic term for a generous patron of the arts.

MAETERLINCK, Maurice (1862–1949) Belgian poetic dramatist and essayist. He wrote in French, establishing himself as one of the leading figures in the *symbolist movement with his play *La Princesse Maleine* (1889; English trans. 1892). In 1892 *Pelléas et Mélisande* appeared (English trans. 1894), the work for which he is now chiefly remembered and the source of *Debussy's opera of the same name (1902). He also achieved great contemporary popularity with *L'Oiseau bleu* (1908; *The Blue Bird*, 1909) and was awarded the *Nobel Prize in 1911. He drew heavily on traditions of romance and *fairy-tale, and the characteristic tone of much of his drama is one of doom-laden mystery and timeless melancholy. He also produced a number of philosophical essays, including *La Vie des abeilles* (1901; *The Life of the Bee*, 1901) and *L'Intelligence des fleurs* (1907; *The Intelligence of Flowers*, 1907).

Maeve (Medb) [pron. Mayv] In the Ulster cycle, queen of Connaught.
See CUCHULAIN; TÁIN-BÓ-CUAILNGE.

magazine Originally a place where goods or weapons are stored. The **Gentleman's Magazine* described itself in its first number (1731) as 'a Monthly Collection to store up, as in a Magazine, the most remarkable Pieces' of 'humour or intelligence' published in the preceding month. The word was already in common use in book titles, as in Edward Hatton's *The Merchant's Magazine, or Tradesman's Treasury* (1695), but the success of the *Gentleman's* and the arrival of further journals such as the *London Magazine* (begun 1732) and the *Town and Country Magazine* (1769) confirmed the sense of 'magazine' as a periodical publication containing miscellaneous articles from various sources.

magic realism A term used to describe a style of modern fiction in which the recognizably realistic mingles with the unexpected and the inexplicable, and in which elements of dream, fairy story, or mythology combine with the everyday, often in a mosaic or kaleidoscopic pattern of refraction and recurrence. It has been most commonly applied to works by Latin American authors such as *García Márquez, Alejo Carpentier (1904–80), and Isabel *Allende, and sometimes also to those of Günter *Grass, Italo *Calvino, Milan *Kundera, and other European writers. In the 1970s and 1980s it was adopted in Britain by several of the most original younger fiction writers, including, notably, Salman *Rushdie, Angela *Carter, and Emma *Tennant, who reached beyond the limits of fictional *realism in order to draw upon the imaginative resources of *fable, folk tale, or *Gothic romance.

MAGINN, William (1793–1842) Irish satirist and journalist, born in Cork and educated at Trinity College, Dublin. He came to London in 1823, where he wrote under various pseudonyms including 'Ensign Morgan O'Doherty', in whose name he produced memoirs, anecdotes, and verses in English, Latin, and Greek for the **Literary Gazette* and other journals, but most notably for **Blackwood's Magazine*, to which he was an important and prolific contributor, notably in his parodic verse and in the **Noctes Ambrosianae*, in the devising of which he seems to have had some part. He became assistant editor of the *Evening Standard*, and in 1830 helped in the establishing of **Fraser's Magazine*, in which much of his best work, including 'Homeric Ballads' and 'A Gallery of Literary Characters', appeared. He was rumoured to have been the lover of L. E. *Landon. Maginn's wit and learning are evident in his parodies of Walter *Scott, S. T. *Coleridge, Thomas *Moore, Benjamin *Disraeli, Thomas *Carlyle, and many others. He wrote seriously and well on Shakespeare and others. Maginn was the original of Captain Shandon in Thackeray's **Pendennis*.

Magnetic Lady, The, *or Humours Reconciled* A comedy by Ben *Jonson, performed 1632, printed 1641. Lady Loadstone, the 'Magnetic Lady', who 'draws unto her guests of all sorts', has a niece Placentia, who is pursued by various suitors. After an argument between two of them, she goes into labour and gives birth. Her uncle, the usurer Sir Moth Interest, uses this as an excuse to seize her dowry. However, Compass, the play's hero, learns that Lady Loadstone's real niece is her waiting woman Pleasance, who had been exchanged with Placentia when the two were infants. He marries Pleasance, whom he loves, reveals her true identity, and receives her dowry. Placentia is married to the father of her child, Lady Loadstone's steward Needle, and Lady Loadstone marries Compass's brother Captain Ironside. Between the acts there is an interlude of debate about the theatre between a boy actor and two sceptical youths, Probee and Damplay.

Magnificence A morality play (*c.*1519) by John *Skelton. Magnificence, symbolizing a generous prince, is ruined by mistaken liberality and bad counsellors, but restored by Good-Hope, Perseverance, and other similar figures. The play was edited by Paula Neuss (1980).

Mahābhārata An ancient Hindu epic poem, written in Sanskrit, reputedly over 100,000 stanzas long, describing the war between two groups of cousins, the Pandavas and the Kauravas, unfolding and to some extent legitimizing the divine pre-existing order of the universe, or *dharma*. It dates in its earliest written forms to the 5th or 6th century BC, though it is presented as the creation of the god Vishnu who resonantly pronounced upon his great epic: 'What is found here, may be found elsewhere. What is not found here may not be found elsewhere.' The characters of the *Mahābhārata*, unlike those of Greek mythology, seem surprisingly modern in their questioning of destiny and tradition, especially the central figure of Draupadi, wife to all five Pandava brothers. The work was introduced to an English-speaking readership in 1785 when a section, the **Bhagavad-Gītā*, Krishna's rousing address to Arjuna on the battlefield of Kurukshetra, translated by Charles Wilkins, was published. Since then there have been numerous translations of sections of the poem, notably by Christopher *Isherwood and Swami Prabhavananda (1893–1976) (American edition, 1944; introduction by Aldous *Huxley). The *Mahābhārata* became well known in Britain with Peter *Brook's stage adaptation of 1985. Brook worked closely with French writer Jean-Claude Carrière (1931–), and their production attracted enormous public interest, sparking off lively debate about 'cultural appropriation' and British-South Asian identity. With its episodic and family-saga structure, the *Mahābhārata* has exerted an important influence on Anglo-Indian literature, including works by Salman *Rushdie and Shashi Tharoor (1956–), as well as on Indian film.

MAHFOUZ, Naguib (1911–2006) Egyptian author and Nobel laureate 1988. He wrote over 30 novels and several hundred short stories. The novels that brought him fame depicted life in the old quarters of Cairo in which he spent his early years. Foremost among these were *Midaq Alley* (1947), and the trilogy that was his masterpiece, *Palace Walk* (1956), *Palace of Desire* (1957), and *Sugar Street* (1957). In later novels his writing became more allegorical and symbolic. The first of these, *The Children of Gebelawi* (1959), was banned in Egypt because of its controversial treatment of religion and its use of characters based on Muhammad, Moses, and Jesus. Important later works include *The Thief and the Dogs* (1961), *Autumn Quail* (1962), *Small Talk on the Nile* (1966), *Miramar* (1967), *The Harafish* (1977), and *The Journey of Ibn Fattouma* (1983). He was little known outside the Arab world until he won the *Nobel Prize, but he has since become widely read in translation.

MAHON, Derek (1941–) One of the acclaimed poets to emerge from Northern Ireland in the 1960s. Born in Belfast and educated at Trinity College, Dublin, Mahon has lived in London and New York, as well as in the Irish Republic. His work blends a stylistic insouciance owing something to W. H. *Auden and Louis *MacNeice with a *Beckettian irony and despair. These qualities achieve a near perfect balance in 'A Disused Shed in County Wexford' (from *The Snow Party*, 1975), perhaps the most anthologized Irish poem of recent times. While the formality of early volumes like *Lives* (1972) and *The Hunt by Night* (1982) gave way to an unbuttoned, discursive mode in *The Hudson Letter* (1995) and *The Yellow Book* (1997), the award-winning *Harbour Lights* (2005) reveals an undiminished command of stanza and tone. Mahon has published many translations, mainly of French poetry and drama. See *Collected Poems* (1999).

MAHONY, Francis Sylvester (1804–66) Journalist, translator, and poet, born in Cork, best known by his pseudonym Father Prout, a Jesuit priest who admitted he had mistaken his vocation and left the order. He contributed many lively papers and poems to **Fraser's Magazine* and **Bentley's Miscellany*. These included translations from *Horace, Pierre-Jean de *Béranger, Victor *Hugo, together with mystifications in the form of invented 'originals' in French, Latin, and Greek for well-known poems by Thomas *Moore, Charles *Wolfe, and others. He travelled extensively, and was Paris correspondent for the *Globe*, 1858–66. The contributions to *Fraser's* were collected in 1836 as *The Reliques of Father Prout*.

MAHY, Margaret (1936–) Although a New Zealander, this highly respected, popular, and prolific writer for children and young adults has had a notable impact on readers, writers, and publishers in the UK, with seminal picture books such as *A Lion in the Meadow* (1969) and young adult novels including *The Changeover* (1984), all of which blur the boundaries between fantasy and reality in complex and satisfying ways.

MAIAKOVSKY, Vladimir Vladimirovich (1893–1930) Russian poet and dramatist, born in Georgia. In 1908 he joined the Bolshevik Party in Moscow where he was an art student (1908–14). While in prison after being arrested three times for revolutionary activities (1908–9), he began to write poetry. In 1910 he and a group of other painter-poets published the first Russian *Futurist collection, *A Trap for Judges*, and in 1912 signed the Futurist manifesto 'A Slap in the Face for Public Taste'. His first long poem, *A Cloud in Trousers* (1914–15), began a series of masterpieces on his main theme, impossible fate and impossible love. These poems, *The Backbone-Flute* (1916), *Man* (1918), *About That* (1923), and his lyrics were dedicated to the love of his life, Lili Brik, whom he had met in July 1915. Maiakovsky welcomed the revolution and expected the Futurists to provide the vanguard of the new state's art, but they found little favour with the communist authorities. More acceptable was his poster work for the ROSTA telegraph agency (1919–22). In 1923 Maiakovsky was one of the founders of LEF (the Left Front of the Arts) that was forced to disband in 1925. Although acting as an official ambassador for Soviet art in Europe and America after 1923, he increasingly reveals in his work a constant tension between the personal and the civic, between his revolutionary utopianism and his awareness of the persistence of bourgeois values. By the end of the decade Maiakovsky was in a state of crisis; his relationship with Lili Brik had soured, and he had fallen in love with an émigrée, Tatiana Iakovleva, who refused to return to Russia. His despair finds expression in his last unfinished poem, *At the Top of my Voice*, and two plays staged by Vesevolod Meyerhold (1874–1940), *The Bedbug* (1929) and *The Bath House* (1930). Both are hyperbolic, satirical onslaughts on the stifling of revolutionary values by entrenched philistinism. He shot himself on 14 April 1930. The suicide cast a shadow on his official reputation until Stalin's personal approval restored his standing. For English translations of Maiakovsky, see Herbert Marshall, *Mayakovsky* (1965); Max Hayward and George Reavey, *The Bedbug and Selected Poetry* (1960).

Maid Marian Originally a female figure in traditional May Day pageants. From the 16th century, she appears as the companion of *Robin Hood, the association having probably been suggested by the fact that he was also represented in the pageants. Her identity varies according to different versions of the legend.

Maid Marian A medieval romance by Thomas Love *Peacock largely written 1819, published 1822. It features *Robin Hood, *Maid Marian, Friar Tuck, and Prince John, while lampooning institutions such as the monarchy and the church in the post-Napoleonic era. The irreverent treatment of Prince John's government also mocks the idealized medievalism newly fashionable among conservative propagandists, artists, and historians. Peacock wrote *Maid Marian* at a time when he had fallen under the spell of the new Italian opera of *Rossini, Bellini (1801–35), and *Donizetti. Many scenes already seem cast as duets or quartets, and the book was later adapted as a popular operetta.

Maid of Honour, The A tragicomedy by Philip *Massinger, acted about 1621–2, published 1632, based on a story by *Boccaccio. The swashbuckling Bertoldo, a knight of Malta and half-brother of the king of Sicily, is in love with Camiola, but she refuses him because of the difference in their station and his knightly vow of celibacy. When he is taken prisoner by the Sienese, Camiola directs her wooer Adorni to carry the ransom to Bertoldo, and to require of him a contract to marry her. Adorni faithfully discharges his mission, but Aurelia, the duchess of Siena, falls in love with Bertoldo and he yields to her wooing. When they are on the point of being married, Camiola intervenes and pleads her cause. Everyone, including Aurelia, condemns Bertoldo's ingratitude; the marriage is broken off. Camiola enters a nunnery, and the repentant Bertoldo resumes his vocation as a knight of Malta.

Maid's Tragedy, The A tragedy by Francis *Beaumont and John *Fletcher, written ?1610, published 1619. Amintor, a gentleman of Rhodes, breaks his engagement to Aspatia at the king's request and marries Evadne instead, sister to his friend Melantius. On their wedding night, in a powerful confrontation, Evadne reveals that she is the king's mistress and refuses to sleep with him. Amintor agrees to present a mock marriage to the world, but later reveals the truth to Melantius, who passionately reproaches the penitent Evadne, and persuades her to murder the king. Meanwhile the desolate Aspatia laments her loss in some of the finest verse in the play (II. ii); her lines 'And the trees about me, | Let them be dry and leafless; let the rocks | Groan with continual surges; and behind me | Make all a desolation. Look, look, wenches!' were used by T. S. *Eliot as an epigraph to 'Sweeney Erect'; the speech is also quoted by Emily *Eden in *The Semi-detached House* (chapter 20). Aspatia disguises herself as her brother and provokes the reluctant Amintor to a duel. He wounds her; as she lies dying Evadne arrives, fresh from the king's murder, hoping to be pardoned by Amintor. He rejects her; she commits suicide; Aspatia reveals herself and dies; Amintor takes his own life. The last act of the play was rewritten by Edmund *Waller, with a happy ending in which Amintor marries Aspatia. Modern editions include one by T. W. Craik (1988).

MAILER, Norman (1923–2007) American novelist and essayist, educated at Harvard University, whose naturalistic first novel *The Naked and the Dead* (1948) was based on his experiences with the army in the Pacific. It was followed by other novels, including *Barbary Shore* (1951), *The Deer Park* (1955), and *An American Dream* (1965). *Advertisements for Myself* (1959) marked a turning point in mixing journalism, autobiography, political commentary, and fictional passages. *The Presidential Papers* (1963) and *The Armies of the Night* (1968) are his most famous works of political reportage. *The Executioner's Song* (1979), a lengthy account of a murderer, and his study of Lee Harvey Oswald (*Oswald's Story: An American Mystery*, 1995) use documentary methods. Mailer's exploration of themes of power has produced *Ancient Evenings* (1983), set in ancient Egypt, *Harlot's Ghost* (1991), a portrait of the CIA, and *The Castle in the Forest* (2007), an account of Hitler's youth. *The Gospel According to the Son* (1997) is a first-person account of the life of Jesus and *The Spooky Art* (2003) collects Mailer's essays on the art of writing. See Carl E. Rollyson, *The Lives of Norman Mailer* (1991).

MAIR (Major), **John** (*c*.1467–1550) Born in Gleghornie, near Haddington. He has been called 'the last of the schoolmen'. He studied at Cambridge and Paris, where he became doctor of theology. He lectured on scholastic logic and theology at Glasgow and St Andrews from 1518 to 1525, and then returned to Paris, where he was regarded as the most eminent exponent of medieval learning. He published between 1509 and 1517 a Latin *Commentary on the Sentences of Peter Lombard* and in 1521 a Latin *History of Greater Britain, both England and Scotland*, in which he showed himself in advance of his times by advocating the union of the two kingdoms. According to *Rabelais (II. vii), among the books found by Pantagruel in the library of St Victor was a treatise by Mair, *De Modo Faciendi Puddinos* ('On the art of making black-puddings').

Maitland Folio One of the most important and substantial collections of Scottish literature. It contains 182 poems, among which are works by William *Dunbar, Robert *Henryson, Gawin *Douglas, and 41 poems written by Sir Richard Maitland (1496–1586), the compiler of the miscellany. Ed. W. A. Craigie, 2 vols, Scottish Text Society 7, 20 (1919, 1927).

MAKIN, Bathsua (b. 1600, d. in or after 1675) Née Reginald, scholar, educationalist, and poet, and tutor to Princess Elizabeth, daughter of Charles I. Makin was the daughter of Henry Reginald (d. 1635), a schoolteacher, and was described by the diarist Sir Simon D'Ewes (1602–50) as 'the greatest scholler, I thinke, of a woman in England'. Her *Essay to Revive the Ancient Education of Gentlewomen* (1673) insists that the whole 'encyclopaedia of learning' be opened to women. Makin asserts that 'women are not such silly giddy creatures as many proud ignorant men would make them' but will become more malleable through education. The moderation of her claims may have been linked with a wish to dissociate herself from the 1670 translation of Cornelius *Agrippa's inflammatory feminist *Female Pre-eminence: or The Dignity* *and Excellence of that Sex, above the Male* by Henry Care (1646/7–1688).

MALAMUD, Bernard (1914–86) American novelist, born in Brooklyn, who began publishing his short stories in the 1940s. His first novel *The Natural* (1952) dealt with the life of a middle-aged baseball player and *The Assistant* (1957) draws on Malamud's own experiences of New York, but he is best known for *The Fixer* (1966), the story of a Jewish handyman in tsarist Russia just before the First World War, who is falsely accused of murder and turned into the scapegoat for anti-Semitic feeling in his neighbourhood. Other works include *A New Life* (1961), *The Tenants* (1971), *Dubin's Lives* (1979), and *God's Grace* (1982), a post-nuclear war narrative. Malamud's *Complete Stories* appeared in 1998 and the PEN/Malamud Award for proficiency in the short story was set up in 1988. See Philip Davis, *Bernard Malamud: A Writer's Life* (2007).

MALCOLM X (1925–65) African American campaigner for civil rights, born Malcolm Little in Omaha, Nebraska, who chose X to erase his slave name. He collaborated with Alex *Haley in writing his autobiography and was shot in 1965 by political opponents.

Malcontent, The A tragicomedy by John *Marston, and generally considered his best play, published 1604 (with additions by John *Webster), written not earlier than 1602. The central character is Altofronto, banished duke of Genoa, disguised as the malcontent Malevole; in this role he reveals to his successor Pietro that he is being deceived by his wife Aurelia, and watches over the attempts of the Machiavellian Mendoza to supplant Pietro, banish Aurelia, and marry Altofronto's own wife Maria. After much intrigue Altofronto reveals himself to the by now penitent Pietro, and the two expose Mendoza's villainy and regain their own wives. The plot resembles that of **Measure for Measure*, but the exposure of court corruption, lust, and greed is more harshly satiric, reflecting (in *Swinburne's view) 'the poet's own ambitions and dissatisfied intelligence'. Modern editions include one by T. W. Craik (1988).

Maldon, Battle of A 325-line poem in Old English, of uncertain date, incomplete at the beginning and the end, dealing with the battle fought in 991 at Maldon in Essex against Danish raiders. The Danes are drawn up by the river Pant (Blackwater), opposed by Byrhtnoth, ealdorman of Essex since 956, who rejects their demand for tribute. He is killed and the English defeated, partly because some of his men flee but perhaps also because of Byrhtnoth's 'ofermod', his excessive pride, in magnanimously yielding ground to the Danes. The poem's second half, in which Byrhtnoth's followers pledge their loyalty to their dead leader, is a powerful statement of fidelity and determination to avenge his death. The poem survives only in a transcript fortunately made by John Elphinston, under-keeper of the Cotton Library (*see* COTTON, SIR ROBERT BRUCE) because the manuscript was destroyed in the fire at the Cotton Library in 1731. It was edited by D. G. Scragg (1981).

MALLARMÉ, Stéphane (1842–98) French poet, leading figure in the *symbolist movement, one of the founders of modern European poetry, and more recently one of the heroes of *structuralism. His formidably dense verse has both lured and defied translators, beginning with Arthur *Symons. Two of his longer pieces, the icily poised *Hérodiade* (*c.*1864) and the sensuously textured *Prélude à l'après-midi d'un faune* (*c.*1865: *Prelude to the Afternoon of a Faun*), celebrate the hidden virtues of deferment and absence against the vulgarity of possession and plenitude. His pursuit of a perfection realizable only through renunciation of the actual demanded a new effort of language: the intensely wrought lyrics, sonnets, and elegies gathered in *Poésies* (1887) and *Vers et prose* (1893) attempt a science of suggestion through the exploitation of syntactical and metaphoric ambiguities and of the formal and aural properties of verse. These tendencies reach their culmination in *Un coup de dés jamais n'abolira le hasard* (1897: *A Throw of the Dice Will Never Eliminate Chance*), a poem which makes revolutionary use of typographical possibilities to suggest a musical score and to indicate what he called the 'prismatic subdivisions of the idea'. Claude *Debussy's *Prélude à l'après-midi d'un faune* (1894) was inspired by Mallarmé's *L'Après-midi d'un faune* (1876).
See also MAETERLINCK, MAURICE.

MALLET (Malloch), **David** (?1705–65) Scottish writer, author of a philosophical poem, *The Excursion* (1728), and a popular ghost ballad, 'William and Margaret'. He helped support Richard *Savage, and gained the friendship of Alexander *Pope. He collaborated with James *Thomson in the masque *Alfred* (1740), wrote a *Life of Francis Bacon* (1740), and edited *Bolingbroke's *Works* (5 vols, 1754). His most notable tragedy was *Elvira* (1763), which was admired by Edward *Gibbon.

MALLOCK, William Hurrell (1849–1923) Novelist, poet, and satirist, the nephew of Richard Hurrell and James Anthony *Froude, born at Cockington Court, Devon, and educated at Balliol College, Oxford. He is best known as author of *The New Republic: or Culture, Faith and Philosophy in an English Country House* (1877), a lively satire on English society and ideas, including a sympathetic portrait of John *Ruskin as Mr Herbert. Benjamin *Jowett, Matthew *Arnold, Walter *Pater, T. H. *Huxley, and John *Tyndall all appear under thin disguises. He also published poems, novels, and memoirs, including *A Human Document* (1892) which later became the basis of the artist Tom Phillips's collage *Humument* (1970). A High Anglican Tory, Mallock attacked socialism and the *Fabian Society in several studies of social and economic science, and was himself attacked by George Bernard *Shaw in the **Fortnightly Review* in April 1894.

MALONE, Edmond (1741–1812) Scholar, educated at Trinity College, Dublin. He came to London in 1777 and established himself as a writer and as a friend of Samuel *Johnson, Sir Joshua *Reynolds, Edmund *Burke, and others. In 1778 he published *An Attempt to Ascertain the Order in Which the Plays Attributed to Shakespeare Were Written*, in George *Steevens's edition of *Shakespeare, following this with his own edition (10 vols, 1790). He edited the works of Oliver *Goldsmith (1777) and Joshua Reynolds (1797–8), and the prose works of John *Dryden (1800). A member of the *Club, he helped James *Boswell prepare the *Journal of a Tour to the Hebrides* (1785) and the *Life of Samuel *Johnson* (1791), of which he edited the third to sixth editions (1799–1811). He exposed the forgeries of Thomas *Chatterton in 1782 and William Henry *Ireland in 1796. His work for a new edition of Shakespeare was completed and issued posthumously (21 vols, 1821) by James Boswell the younger. See P. Martin, *Edmond Malone, Shakespearean Scholar* (1995).

Malone Society Founded by Sir Walter *Greg and Ronald *McKerrow in 1906 in order to facilitate the study of early English drama by printing dramatic texts and documents. Its name is taken from Edmond *Malone.

MALORY, Sir Thomas (1415/18–1471) Author of *Le *Morte Darthur*. Although his identity was uncertain for a long time, he was identified by Eugène Vinaver as Sir Thomas Malory of Newbold Revel, Warwickshire, made knight before 1442. The *Morte Darthur* was written in prison and Malory of Newbold Revel was charged with crimes of violence, theft, and rape after 1450. For a Yorkshire identification see W. M. Matthews, *The Ill-Framed Knight* (1966). It was also proposed that Malory had been a hostage in France, because much of the work drew on a 'French book'. See P. J. C. Field, *The Life and Times of Sir Thomas Malory* (1993).

MALOUF, David (1934–) Australian poet and novelist, born in Brisbane of English and Lebanese parents, and educated at Brisbane Grammar School and the University of Queensland. His first volume of poems was published in 1970 and has been followed by several others, including *Neighbours in a Thicket* (1974) and *First Things Last* (1980). *Selected Poems 1959–1989* appeared in 1994. His semi-autobiographical novel *Johnno* (1975) is set in wartime Brisbane, while *An Imaginary Life* (1978) is a lyrical prose meditation on the last years of the Roman poet *Ovid. Other novels include *Harland's Half Acre* (1984), *The Great World* (1990), *Remembering Babylon* (1993), and *The Conversations at Curlow Creek* (1996), the last two both set in 19th-century Australia. *Antipodes* (1985), *Dream Stuff* (2000), and *Every Move You Make* (2006) are collections of short stories; *12 Edmondstone Street* (1985) is a selection of autobiographical essays.

MALRAUX, André (1901–76) French novelist, essayist, and art critic. Out of his experiences as a political activist, in China in the 1920s and in Spain during the Civil War, he wrote a number of novels on revolutionary themes, including *Les Conquérants* (1928; *The Conquerors*, 1929), *La Condition humaine* (1933; trans. under various titles: *Storm in Shanghai*, 1934; *Man's Fate*, 1934; *Man's Estate*, 1948), and *L'Espoir* (1937; *Days of Hope*, 1938; *Man's Hope*, 1938). His writings on art include *Les Voix du silence* (1951; *The Voices of Silence*, 1953). In 1967 his *Antimémoires* appeared (*Anti-memoirs*, 1968).

MALTHUS, Thomas (1766–1834) Educated at Cambridge, where he had a brilliant student career. He became curate of Albury in Surrey in 1798. In that year, provoked by William Godwin's **Enquiry Concerning Political Justice* of 1793, he published *An Essay on the Principle of Population*, in which he argued that population (growing geometrically) would soon increase beyond the means of subsistence (which grew only arithmetically), and that checks in the form of poverty, disease, and starvation were necessary. After he had collected a great deal of further information from travels in northern Europe, the *Essay* was heavily recast in a second edition of 1803; in this Malthus modified his conclusions, suggesting that the regulation of greed and sexual activity would act as more acceptable checks on population growth. His work was vigorously attacked by Godwin, William *Cobbett, William *Hazlitt, and others, but it exerted a powerful influence on social thought in the 19th century. Charles *Darwin declared in his *Life* that Malthus' *Essay* helped to point him towards his own theory of evolution.

MALZBERG, Barry Nathaniel (1939–) American author and editor, born in New York; his novels, including *Beyond Apollo* (1972) and *Herovit's World* (1973), are alienated encounters with the themes and tropes of *science fiction. *The Engines of the Night* (1982) collects his reflections upon the field.

MAMET, David (1947–) American playwright, born in Flossmoor, Illinois, and educated at colleges in Vermont and New York. His work is distinguished by its attention to the rhythms of blue-collar speech and the theme of how low-life criminality mirrors the world of big business. *American Buffalo* (1975) follows the bungled attempts of three petty crooks to pull off a robbery, while *Glengarry Glen Ross* (1983) adapts a similar plot to a bunch of real-estate salesmen. Often criticized for sexism, his work is unafraid to address crises in gender relations, with plays such as *Sexual Perversity in Chicago* (1974), which satirizes the vacuity of male sexual bravado. *Oleanna* (1992) dramatizes the misunderstandings between a professor and his student in a complex narrative of sexual harassment. He has written widely for the cinema, and has directed films of his own, including the highly acclaimed *House of Games* (1987). His most recent stage work includes a retelling of *Faustus* (2004), and *Romance* (2005), a courtroom farce. He has also written two novels, *The Village* (1994), a portrayal of hunting which recalls Ernest *Hemingway, and *The Old Religion* (1997), a fictional reconstruction of the lynching of a Jewish factory owner falsely accused of the rape and murder of a Southern white girl. His *The Wicked Son: Anti-Semitism,*

Self-Hatred and the Jews, a study of Jewish identity, was published in 2006.

Mammon, the cave of Described in Edmund *Spenser's *The *Faerie Queene* (II. vii). It is the treasure-house of the god of wealth, visited by Sir Guyon. In **Areopagitica*, John *Milton uses the example of Spenser making Guyon enter the cave of Mammon 'that he might see and know, and yet abstain'.

Manannán The son of *Lêr, a highly popular god of the old Gaelic pantheon, the subject of many legends and the patron of sailors and merchants. The Isle of Man was his favourite abode, and is said to take its name from him. There he has degenerated into a legendary giant, with three legs (seen revolving in the coat of arms of the island).

Manawyddan *See* MABINOGION.

Man Booker Prize for Fiction A prize founded (as the Booker-McConnell Prize for Fiction) in 1969, awarded annually to the best full-length novel published in the previous twelve months by an author from the Commonwealth or the Republic of Ireland writing in English; its aim is to stimulate the kind of public interest aroused in France by the Prix *Goncourt. (See Appendix 3 (*d*) for list of winners.) Originally financed by Booker, now part of the Iceland Group plc, and administered by the *Book Trust, the prize was renamed the Man Booker in 2002 when the investment company Man Group plc became the chief sponsors. The administration was taken over by a newly registered charity, the Booker Prize Foundation. The prize, now worth £50,000, is considered by many to be the most prestigious of all British book prizes and its winners can also expect to see a very large increase in the sales of their novels. In 1993, as part of the celebrations of 25 years of the prize, a so-called Booker of Bookers was awarded to Salman *Rushdie for his novel *Midnight's Children*, chosen as the best book to have won the prize in its first quarter of a century. In 2005, the Man Booker International Prize, a biennial award to a living writer of any nationality, intended to recognize his or her complete oeuvre, was established. The first recipient was the Albanian writer Ismail Kadare, the second the Nigerian Chinua *Achebe.

Manchester Guardian Founded in 1821 as a weekly, and in 1855 as a daily paper; the principal Liberal paper outside London, edited 1872–1929 by Charles Prestwich Scott (1846–1932). Its title was changed to the *Guardian* in 1959; since 1961 it has been published from London. The paper has retained its liberal values.

Manchester School The name first applied by Benjamin *Disraeli to the political party, led by Richard Cobden (1804–65) and John Bright (1811–89), who advocated the principles of free trade. It was afterwards extended to the party who supported those leaders on other questions of policy. 'Manchester policy' was used derisively to signify a policy of laissez-faire and self-interest. The 'Manchester School' of drama refers loosely to the playwrights associated with Miss *Horniman's Company of Actors at the Gaiety Theatre, Manchester, 1907–14, including Harold Brighouse (1882–1958), W. S. Houghton (1881–1913), and Allan Monkhouse (1858–1936).

'Manciple's Tale, The' *See* CANTERBURY TALES, 23.

MANDELSHTAM, Nadezhda (1899–1980) Writer, born in Saratov, who spent her early life in Kiev where she studied art. She shared the exile of her husband, Osip *Mandelshtam, under Stalin. After Osip's death in 1938 she lived on the run, having made it her mission to memorize and thus preserve his poetry. When she was eventually permitted to return to Moscow in 1964 she wrote and published her memoirs. The first volume, *Hope against Hope* (1970), details the last four harrowing years of her marriage whilst *Hope Abandoned* (1974) focuses on her own life as a widow. Both contain a pun in Russian as 'nadezhda' means hope.

MANDELSHTAM, Osip Emilevich (1891–1938) Russian poet, born into the family of a Jewish leather merchant in Warsaw and brought up in St Petersburg. He spent most of 1907–10 in Western Europe, particularly Paris, and then studied at St Petersburg University. His first poems appeared in 1910. In 1911 he joined the *Acmeist Guild of Poets with Anna *Akhmatova and Nikolai *Gumilev, and the poems of his first collection, *Stone* (1913), are marked by Acmeist brevity and clarity. He met Nadezhda Iakovlevna Khazina (1899–1980) in Kiev in 1919 and married her in 1922. His second collection, *Tristia* (1922), confirmed his status while considerably widening his range. During the early 1920s Mandelshtam came under increasing attack for being 'out of step' with the new Soviet age, and his ruminations on the subject produced such important poems as 'The Age' and 'The Slate Ode'. He wrote no new poems between 1925 and 1930, turning instead to prose. His third volume, *Poems*, and collections of prose and criticism appeared in 1928. In 1930 he made a long visit to Armenia, from which emerged *The Journey to Armenia*, a major prose piece (trans. Clarence Brown, 1980), his last work to be published in the Soviet Union for 30 years. His first arrest, in 1934, resulted from his recitation of his famous poem denouncing Stalin. Prison was followed by internal exile and attempted suicide. In exile he wrote his important late poetry the 'Voronezh Notebooks' (trans. Richard and Elizabeth McKane, 1996). He returned from exile in 1937, but was arrested again in 1938 and sentenced to five years' hard labour; he died of a heart attack on the way to the camps. His collected works were first published abroad; a volume of his poetry appeared in Leningrad in 1973. In the 1990s the full range of his work became available in Russia for the first time. The two volumes of memoirs by his widow Nadezhda *Mandelshtam, *Hope against Hope* (1970) and *Hope Abandoned* (1974), are not only the main source of information on the poet but also a powerful and harrowing description of the experience of 20th-century totalitarianism: her work was eventually published in Russia in the 1990s. Mandelshtam is now regarded as one of the major poets of the 20th century. He has been widely translated into English, notably by Clarence Brown and W. S. Merwin (*Selected Poems*, 1973) and by David McDuff (*Selected Poems*, 1983).

MANDEVILLE, Bernard (1670–1733) Moral philosopher, born in the Netherlands. He trained as a physician at Leiden, settled in London, and published *A Treatise of the Hypochondriack and Hysterick Passions* (1711; enlarged edition, 1730). His other prose works include *The Virgin Unmasked* (1709, 1714), an odd mix of advice manual and political speculation; *Free Thoughts on Religion, the Church and National Happiness* (1720), a defence of *Deism and an attack on clericalism; and *An Enquiry into the Origin of Honour* (1732), on the social effects of self-esteem and self-love. *A Modest Defence of Public Stews* (1724), recommending governmental regulation of brothels, is often assumed to be his, but the ascription is uncertain. Of his moral and satirical verse the best known is 'The Grumbling Hive, or Knaves Turn'd Honest' (1705), which was incorporated with prose supplements into *The Fable of the Bees, or Private Vices, Public Benefits* (1714; enlarged 1723). Mandeville here rejects the optimistic view of benevolent human nature put forward by *Shaftesbury, and argues that the mutual help on which society thrives like a colony of bees is due to personal acquisitiveness and the love of luxury: a 'virtuous' society, where only subsistence needs are satisfied, would lack both culture and trade and would collapse from want of employment. Mandeville's writing was admired by Daniel *Defoe, but his ironic use of the language of 'vice' and 'virtue' was attacked by William *Law, John *Dennis, Francis *Hutcheson, Isaac *Watts, and George *Berkeley (*Alciphron*, 1732); Mandeville himself responded to the last in *A Letter to Dion* (1732).

MANDEVILLE, Sir John Ostensible author of the book of *Travels* translated into many European languages after its first appearance in France *c.*1357, which survives in 22 versions, including prose and metrical English versions. Claiming to be a guide, both geographical and ethical, for pilgrims to the Holy Land, it is really a compilation from authors including William of Boldensele, Friar Odoric of Pordenone, and *Vincent of Beauvais, combining geography and natural history with romance and marvels, and famously featuring a supposed encounter between 'Mandeville' and the sultan of Egypt, who offers some sharp criticisms of backsliding Christians. It was an important influence on English writers from *Chaucer to *Shakespeare. M. C. Seymour has argued that the writer, whether of English or French nationality, may have been a Benedictine monk from Saint-Omer. Translated by C. W. R. D. Moseley (1983); metrical version ed. M. C. Seymour (EETS os 269, 1973).

Manfred A poetic drama by Lord *Byron, published 1817. Manfred, a Faustian figure, 'half-dust, half deity', lives alone in a castle in the Alps, tortured by guilt for 'some half-maddening sin'. He summons the spirits of the universe, who offer him everything except the oblivion he seeks. Eventually, overcoming his terror of death, he tries to hurl himself from an Alpine crag, but is dragged back by a hunter. He invokes the Witch of the Alps and reveals his sin—his incestuous love for his sister Astarte. He descends to the underworld, the Hall of Arimanes, and encounters a vision of Astarte, who promises him death on the morrow. Back in his castle an abbot begs him to repent, but he cannot. He denies the power of the demons who summon him, and when they vanish he dies.

Byron was deeply interested in the idea of supermen, halfway between gods and mortals, and was to return to the theme in **Heaven and Earth*. However, he was dissatisfied with *Manfred* and did not wish it to be performed, a wish which was ignored after his death. Aspects of the drama were satirized in **Nightmare Abbey* by Thomas Love *Peacock, but its power as an archetypal statement of romantic rebellion lived on, and inspired musical compositions by *Schumann, *Balakirev, and *Tchaikovsky.

MANGAN, James Clarence (1803–49) Irish poet, born in Dublin, whose life was plagued by poverty and alcohol. Under various pseudonyms he published prose and verse in newspapers and periodicals, many of his poems purporting to be translations from languages ranging from German to Turkish. His best-known works ('Dark Rosaleen', 'O'Hussey's Ode to the Maguire') play variations upon more subdued Gaelic prototypes in pursuit of an ecstatic, nationalist sublime. Some poems, such as 'Twenty Golden Years Ago' and 'The Nameless One', are querulously autobiographical, while others (e.g. 'Siberia') conflate psychological and political vistas to powerfully evoke famine and desolation. Mangan, who died of malnutrition, has for all his belatedness increasingly come to be seen as Ireland's greatest contributor to *Romanticism.

Manichaeism *See* GNOSTICISM.

Mankind A morality play in 914 lines from East Anglia, written *c.*1470–71, one of the group called *Macro Plays after their 18th-century owner (the others being **Wisdom* and *The *Castle of Perseverance*). Its principal theme is Sloth (*Accidia*), and it is notable for the variety of dramatic idioms which it employs, provocatively juxtaposing exhortations to good Christian conduct with obscenity and topical satire. It continues to be admired for its ingenious structure, its canny deployment of the demon Tutivillus, and its audacious mockery of legal and ecclesiastical languages. It was edited by G. A. Lester in *Three Late Medieval Morality Plays* (1981).

MANLEY, Delarivier (*c.*1670–1724) Writer, whose colourful life included a bigamous marriage with her cousin John Manley, some years as mistress of the warden of the Fleet Prison, John Tilly, and a final liaison with the *Jacobite printer and alderman John Barber. She wrote several plays and published many novels, including *The New Atalantis* (1709), a **roman à clef* which attacked various notable Whigs in sufficient detail for her to be arrested; the narrative of 'Delia' is autobiographical, as is *The Adventures of Rivella* (1714). Her early friendship with Richard *Steele foundered for financial and political reasons; in 1711 she succeeded Jonathan *Swift as editor of the Tory **Examiner* for a few numbers. Swift wrote of her (*Journal to Stella*, 28 Jan. 1712), 'she has very generous principles, for one of her sort; and a great deal of sense and invention; she is about forty, very homely, and very fat'. See F. Morgan, *A Woman of No Character: An Autobiography of Mrs. Manley* (1986).

MANN, Heinrich (1871–1950) German novelist, brother of Thomas *Mann. His early work includes some notable satirical novels directed against life and institutions in Wilhelmine Germany, such as *Professor Unrat* (1905) and *Der Untertan* (1918: *The Subject*), the former achieving fame as the basis of the film *Der blaue Engel* (1930: *The Blue Angel*) starring Marlene Dietrich. Of his later work the best known in England is the two-part historical novel *Young Henry of Navarre* and *Henry, King of France* (1935–8). More politically engaged than his brother in the period before 1918, his anti-nationalist and pacifist stance occasioned a rift between them. Like his brother, he emigrated from Nazi Germany, settling finally in America. He figures centrally as a character in Christopher *Hampton's *Tales from Hollywood* (1982).

MANN, Thomas (1875–1955) German novelist and essayist. Born in Lübeck, he emigrated from Nazi Germany, settled in America, and became a US citizen in 1944. He returned to Europe in 1952, settling in Switzerland. *Buddenbrooks*, a novel on the theme of the decay of a family, with strongly autobiographical features, appeared in 1901 and quickly made him famous. *Tonio Kröger* (1903), one of his most celebrated novellas, is, like so many of his works, about the nature of the artist. *Der Tod in Venedig* (1912: *Death in Venice*) presents the artist and artistic creation with the pervasive irony characteristic of much of his work and was the basis of an acclaimed film by Luchino Visconti (1971) starring Dirk Bogarde. Originally a man of rather conservative sympathies, as expressed in *Betrachtungen eines Unpolitischen* (1918: *Observations of an Unpolitical Man*), he caused surprise by quickly lending public support to the Weimar Republic. *Der Zauberberg* (*The Magic Mountain*) appeared in 1924, the 'Joseph' novels (in four parts) in 1933–43, during which time he also published his novel *Lotte in Weimar*, based on a brief episode in the life of *Goethe. As a *Nobel Prize-winner (1929) he enjoyed immense prestige in America, and his recorded wartime speeches were broadcast to Germany by the BBC. Constantly concerned with the character and role of the artist, particularly in what Mann saw as his culpable, even criminal, relation to society, he linked this theme with the problem of Nazism in *Dr Faustus* (1947). His last full-length novel derived from the *picaresque tradition: *Die Bekenntnisse des Hochstaplers Felix Krull* (1954: *The Confessions of the Confidence Trickster Felix Krull*).

mannerism A term used to describe any stylistic habit that becomes exaggerated or is carried to excess, but more specifically applied to the style of Italian art of *c.*1520–*c.*1600, between the High Renaissance and the baroque, in which powerful and disturbing effects are achieved by distorted or elongated figures, violent perspective, and unexpected colour harmonies. In literature, the term is applied to a variety of poetic styles involving far-fetched conceits, as with the Elizabethan sonneteers and the *metaphysical poets, and to some unusual prose styles such as that of John *Lyly in his **Euphues*.

MANNING, Frederic (1882–1935) Novelist and poet, born in Sydney and educated at home due to chronic asthma. He settled in England in 1903 and never returned to Australia. He published *The Vigil of Brunhild* in 1907, followed by *Scenes and Portraits* (1909) and *Poems* (1910). He served in the First World War as a private with the King's Shropshire Light Infantry, an experience which inspired his novel *The Middle Parts of Fortune*, published privately and anonymously in 1929 and reissued in 1977 with his full name; an expurgated version, *Her Privates We* by 'Private 19022', appeared in 1930. *The Middle Parts of Fortune* is a powerful account of camaraderie, military inefficiency, and squalor in and behind the trenches, seen through the detached eyes of Private Bourne (named after the Lincolnshire town which Manning made his home). Bourne's death in 1916 ends the narrative.

MANNING, Olivia (1908–80) Novelist, born in Portsmouth, educated at Portsmouth Grammar School. She published one novel before marrying a British Council lecturer, R. D. Smith, in 1939 and travelling with him to Bucharest. From there they went to Greece, Egypt, and Jerusalem, usually one step ahead of the Nazis. This experience inspired *The Balkan Trilogy* (*The Great Fortune*, 1960; *The Spoilt City*, 1962; *Friends and Heroes*, 1965) and *The Levant Trilogy* (*The Danger Tree*, 1977; *The Battle Lost and Won*, 1978; *The Sum of Things*, 1980). This six-novel sequence, with its refreshingly tart portrait of a marriage, is a major fictional response to the Second World War, encompassing several theatres of conflict and fielding a huge cast of vivid characters. Mainly focusing on refugee civilians, most notably Guy and Harriet Pringle, it partly shifts its viewpoint in the second trilogy to a young British officer serving in the desert. Manning wrote five other novels and two volumes of short stories.

MANNYNG, Robert, of Brunne (Bourne) in Lincolnshire (d. *c.*1338) Author of two works, the verse *Chronicle of England* (finished 1338) and **Handlyng Synne*, an adaptation in octosyllabic couplets of the Anglo-Norman *Manuel des péchés*. He was probably a member of the Gilbertine order. See *Handlyng Synne*, ed. Idelle Sullens (1983).

Man of Feeling, The A highly influential 'novel of *sentiment' by Henry *Mackenzie, published 1771. Supposedly found in a mutilated manuscript of unknown authorship, the story is fragmented, giving the effect of a series of brief, poignant episodes, with some humorous and ironic interludes. Harley, the man of feeling, travels to London and, though often cheated, demonstrates an unwavering benevolence and acute, tearful sensibility. He gives heartfelt but limited assistance to the downtrodden, reunites a prostitute with her father, rescues an old family friend, and returns home without achieving worldly success, dying as his beloved declares her love for him.

'Man of Law's Tale, The' *See* CANTERBURY TALES, 5.

Man of Mode, The A comedy by Sir George *Etherege, generally considered his best, and a classic of the *Restoration period, first performed at court in 1676. Richard *Steele denounced its immorality and the cruelty of its sexual politics in the **Spectator*, 65, and John *Dennis defended it. It has two interwoven plots. In one, rake and playboy Dorimant, who was modelled on John *Rochester, and first played by Thomas *Betterton, shakes off his mistress Mrs Loveit, seduces Belinda, and woos the heiress Harriet Woodvil. In the other Young Bellair outwits his father and marries Emilia. The fop Sir Fopling Flutter gives the play its title. Nicholas Hytner's modern-dress production at the *National Theatre in 2007 attracted wide attention.

Man of the World, The (1) A novel by Henry *Mackenzie, published 1773, with a villainous seducer as its hero, in contrast to his **Man of Feeling*. (2) A comedy by Charles *Macklin, performed 1781, adapted from his *The True Born Scotchman*, performed in Dublin in 1764. It had long been refused an English licence because of its satire on the Scots, though Macklin claimed that his intention was only to 'explode the reciprocal national prejudices that equally soured and disgraced the minds of both English and Scots men'.

Manon Lescaut *See* PRÉVOST, ANTOINE-FRANÇOIS.

MANSFIELD, Katherine Pseudonym of Kathleen Mansfield Beauchamp (1888–1923), writer, born in Wellington, New Zealand, and educated at Miss Swainson's school, Wellington, and at Queen's College school, London (1903–6). She went back to New Zealand to study music for two years, before returning to London in 1908: she never revisited her home country. In 1909 she became pregnant by a young musician, Garnet Trowell, married another man, George Bowden (they were divorced in 1918), but left her husband immediately after the ceremony and in time gave birth to a stillborn child in Bavaria, an experience that formed the background to her first collection of stories, *In a German Pension* (1911), most of which had been previously published in A. R. *Orage's *New Age*. In 1911 she met J. M. *Murry, whom she was to marry in 1918; he was editing **Rhythm*, to which, and to its successor the *Blue Review*, she contributed stories, many based on her New Zealand childhood. In 1915 she and Murry spent some weeks near Zennor, Cornwall, in strained proximity to their friends D. H. *Lawrence and his wife. In 1917 Mansfield was diagnosed with tuberculosis and from then on spent part of every year in the south of France or Switzerland. In 1918 'Prelude' was published by the *Hogarth Press; Mansfield enjoyed a close, tense, admiring friendship with Virginia *Woolf, hedged with mutual jealousy. After the publication of *Bliss and Other Stories* (1920) she was increasingly recognized as an original and experimental writer, whose stories were the first in English to show the influence of Anton *Chekhov, whom she greatly admired (and once, to her regret, plagiarized). *The Garden Party and Other Stories* (1922) was the third and last collection to be published in her lifetime and it was received with great acclaim. In that year she entered Le Prieuré, the institute at Fontainebleau, near Paris, run by the Greek-Armenian guru G. I. *Gurdjieff, hoping to regain spiritual and physical health; she died the following January. Her stories vary greatly in length and tone, from long, impressionistic, delicate evocations of family life ('At the Bay', 'Prelude') to short, sharp sketches such as 'Miss Brill'. Two collections were published posthumously (*The Dove's Nest*, 1923; *Something Childish*, 1924) as well as extracts from her journal. Four volumes of Mansfield's *Collected Letters*, ed. V. O'Sullivan and M. Scott, have been published, 1984–96. There is a life by Claire *Tomalin (1987). See also C. K. *Stead, *Mansfield: A Novel* (2004).

Mansfield Park A novel by Jane *Austen, begun 1811, published 1814. Sir Thomas Bertram of Mansfield Park, a stern but kind-hearted man, has two sons, Tom and Edmund, and two daughters, Maria and Julia. His wife, a charming, indolent woman, has two sisters: Mrs Norris, a near neighbour, who is spiteful and selfish, and Mrs Price, the wife of an impecunious officer of marines, with a large family of young children. To assist the Prices, Sir Thomas takes charge of their eldest daughter Fanny, a timid child of 9. In spite of her humble situation and the cruelty of Mrs Norris, Fanny, by her gentle and modest disposition, gradually becomes indispensable to the household. Her strength of character is shown when Sir Thomas leaves to take care of his plantations in Antigua, in the West Indies. Family discipline is considerably relaxed, forbidden private theatricals are mounted, and a flirtation begins between Maria Bertram, who is already engaged to marry Mr Rushworth, and Henry Crawford, the attractive, worldly brother-in-law of the parson of Mansfield. Against all this Fanny resolutely sets her face. Loving her cousin Edmund, she grieves to see him fascinated by the frivolous Mary Crawford, Henry's sister. Maria having become Mrs Rushworth, Henry turns his attention to Fanny, to his own and her astonishment falls in love with her, and proposes marriage. Fanny unhesitatingly rejects him, incurring the grave displeasure of Sir Thomas for what he regards as a piece of ungrateful perversity. During a visit paid by Fanny to her own home in Portsmouth matters come to a crisis. Henry, accidentally encountering Maria Rushworth again, runs away with her; and Julia elopes with a foolish and unsuitable suitor, Mr Yates. Mary Crawford's failure to condemn her brother's conduct, together with her aversion to marrying a clergyman (for Edmund has by now taken orders), opens Edmund's eyes to her true character. He turns for comfort to Fanny, falls in love, and they are married. As Marilyn Butler writes in her 1990 edition of the novel, 'Austen uses Fanny's emotional involvement with the people around her to explore the social and moral values by which she and they try to order their lives'.

MANTEL, Hilary (1952–) CBE, novelist, born in Glossop, Derbyshire, educated at Harrytown Convent, the London School of Economics, and Sheffield University. She describes the disintegration of her Roman Catholic family in *Giving up the Ghost* (2003), a memoir complemented by the volume of stories *Learning to Talk* (2003). At university she was active in left-wing politics, an interest that led her to write a novel set during the French Revolution, *A Place of Greater Safety*, which was not however published until 1992. Her first two novels, *Every Day is Mother's Day* (1985) and *Vacant Possession* (1986), were interlinked black comedies inspired by a job in social work. In 1977 Mantel went to live with her geologist husband in Botswana, and subsequently wrote *A Change of Climate* (1994) about missionaries who had worked in Africa. She and her husband later lived in Saudi Arabia, an experience which inspired her essay 'Last Months in Al Hamra' (Shiva *Naipaul Memorial Prize, 1987), and her novel *Eight Months on Ghazzah Street* (1988). *Fludd* (1989), set in a northern village in the 1950s, concerns a mysterious figure who might be a force for good or evil; it won the Winifred *Holtby, Southern Arts, and Cheltenham Festival prizes. Comparisons with Muriel *Spark, whose wit and psychological acuity Mantel shares, were confirmed by *An Experiment in Love* (1995), about the friendship between two girls through school and university, and *Beyond Black* (2005), set among psychics and more than living up to its title. *The Giant O'Brien* (1998) viscerally recreates the 18th-century London world of surgeons and body-snatchers. *Wolf Hall* (2009) depicts the life of the statesman Thomas Cromwell (1485–1540).

MANTUAN (Mantuanus) (1448–1516) Johannes Baptista Spagnolo, a Carmelite of Mantua who wrote Latin *eclogues. These were common grammar-school texts and influenced the *pastoral poetry of Alexander *Barclay and Edmund *Spenser. He is the 'good old Mantuan' quoted by Holofernes in *Love's Labour's Lost* (IV. ii).

manuscript publication The circulation of works in manuscript continued long after the introduction of printing to England. In addition to controversial political and religious works, authors allowed their literary productions to circulate among their friends and to be published in multiple copies by scribes or scriveners for various reasons. These included a fear of the so-called stigma of print among women writers and among noble and aristocratic ones, a desire to evade censorship or punishment for libellous, seditious, heretical, or pornographic works, and a wish to limit personal writings to an immediate coterie or circle of friends. Among those authors whose work circulated widely in handwritten copies were Thomas *Wyatt and the earl of *Surrey, Philip *Sidney (especially his translation of the Psalms, completed and revised by Mary Sidney (1561–1621)), Sir John *Davies, John *Donne (especially the *Songs and Sonnets* at the Inns of Court), Ben *Jonson (especially his poems), Francis *Bacon, Walter *Ralegh, William *Strode, Edmund *Waller, Katherine *Philips, and the earl of *Rochester.

All sorts of literary and non-literary works were copied, initially by an author and often by his or her friends, but the copying of texts was also undertaken by professional scribes. Ralph Crane (*fl.* 1589–1632) produced multiple manuscript copies of Thomas Middleton's politically scandalous *A *Game at Chess*; he also provided the manuscript copy from which other plays, including John *Webster's *The Duchess of Malfi* and plays by *Shakespeare in the first *folio, were first printed. The anonymous copyist known from his handwriting as the Feathery Scribe (*fl. c.*1625–40) made multiple copies of political, legal, and antiquarian works, perhaps at the rate of a penny-halfpenny per page. This sort of copying, probably organized by stationers who supplied paper, ink, and the works to be transcribed, seems sometimes to have taken place in scriptoria, whose distinctive products can be identified. Multiple copying was generally cheaper, quicker, and less subject to official attention than printing. The practice probably died out as a result of changes to *copyright law in the early 18th century. There are important studies of the subject by Harold Love, *Scribal Publication in Seventeenth-Century England* (1993), and Peter Beal, *In Praise of Scribes* (1998).

MANUTIUS, Aldus *See* ALDUS MANUTIUS.

MANZONI, Alessandro (1785–1873) Italian novelist, author of *I promessi sposi* (*The Betrothed*), a work of unique historical significance. In a long series of painstaking revisions from its first published version (1825–7) to its final form (1840–42), it strove to forge from Tuscan the literary Italian which, after the unification of Italy (1870), became the chief model of standard educated Italian. The novel is also remarkable for its powerfully characterized historical reconstruction of 17th-century Lombardy, under Spanish domination and ravaged by plague. The simple attempts of two poor silk-weavers to marry are used to explore the corrupt and oppressive rule of the Spaniards and, by implication, of the later Austrians. Manzoni also wrote two historical tragedies in verse, *Il conte di Carmagnola* (1820: *The Count of Carmagnola*) and *Adelchi* (1822), which deal with the relationship between oppressed and oppressors, and the role of divine providence in history; and two famous patriotic poems of the Risorgimento, 'Marzo 21' ('21 March') and 'Il cinque maggio' ('5 May'). After 1850 he rejected the novel as a genre, and wrote critical essays, in particular on language. He greatly admired Walter *Scott, and was the subject of a Requiem Mass by Giuseppe *Verdi. See S. B. Chandler, *Alessandro Manzoni: The Story of a Spirited Quest* (1974).

MAP, Walter (d. *c.*1209) From the Welsh borders; archdeacon of Oxford during the reign of Henry II and famous as the author of a partly serious, partly satirical, and always entertaining miscellany entitled *De Nugis Curialium*, 'Courtiers' Trifles', which survives in a single Oxford manuscript. The collection, begun *c.*1181–2 but never formally completed, includes stories in different genres, history and satire, as well as a disquisition inspired by but erroneously attributed to St *Jerome in early printed editions of his works: the *Dissuasio Valerii ad Rufinum de Non Ducenda Uxore* referred to by Chaucer in the 'Prologue to the Wife of Bath's Tale' (**Canterbury Tales*, III. 671). Some *Goliardic poems have also been doubtfully attributed to Map. See *De Nugis Curialium*, ed. and trans. M. R. James, rev. C. N. L. Brooke and R. A. B. Mynors (1983).

MAPANJE, Jack (1944–) Malawian poet, detained without trial for nearly four years in his native Malawi in 1987. He has lived in Britain since his release. His first collection of poetry, *Of Chameleons and Gods* (1981), was banned in Malawi. *The Chattering Wagtails of Mikuyu Prison* (1993), *Skipping without Ropes* (1998), *The Last of the Sweet Bananas* (2004), and *The Beasts of Nalunga* (2007) trace the growth of an incarcerated poet's mind, with anger, wry wit, and compassion.

MARBER, Patrick (1964–) Playwright, born in London, educated at Wadham College, Oxford; he worked as an alternative comic on stage and radio before becoming a playwright. His directed his first two plays, *Dealer's Choice* (1995), about a game of poker, and *Closer* (1997), a black comedy about sexual infidelities, at the *National Theatre. *Howard Katz* (2001) was less well received, though his updating of *Molière's *Don Juan* (1665), *Don Juan in Soho* (2006), was more successful.

Marble Faun, The A novel by Nathaniel *Hawthorne, published 1860 (in England as *Transformation*). It is the product of Hawthorne's two years in Italy. The scene is laid in Rome, and the title is taken from the resemblance of one of the principal characters, Count Donatello, to the Marble Faun of Praxiteles. Donatello is in love with the liberated young American art student Miriam, who is being persecuted by a mysterious stranger subsequently killed by Donatello. The narrative is one of Hawthorne's explorations of the nature of sin and guilt.

MARCEL, Gabriel (1889–1973) French Catholic *existentialist. Following Søren *Kierkegaard and Karl Jaspers (1883–1969), he repudiated abstraction, generalization, categorization, in favour of individual authenticity. From *Être et avoir* (1935: *To Be and To Have*) to *Le Mystère de l'être* (1951: *The Mystery of Being*), he argued that being is a concept that cannot be analysed, only recognized, and that man has to confront it not as a problem to be posed or conceived, but as an experience to be lived and explored.

MARCELLUS, Marcus Claudius (42–23 BC) Son of Octavia, nephew, son-in-law, and heir of the emperor Augustus. His premature death is described in a celebrated passage in *Virgil's **Aeneid* (Bk 6), echoed in John *Dryden's *Absalom and Achitophel* and 'To the Memory of Mr Oldham'.

Marco Polo *See* POLO, MARCO.

MARCUS AURELIUS ANTONINUS (AD 121–80) Roman emperor 161–80 and single-mindedly *Stoic philosopher, author of twelve books of personal 'meditations' written in Greek, heavily influenced by *Epictetus' *Discourses*. The *Meditations* hardly relate to Marcus' career as ruler and general; written at the end of his life, they focus on practical ethics, death, and man's relationship to state (Rome) and cosmos. The first printed edition dates from 1558, but before that Antonio de Guevara had published *Libro aureo del emperador Marco Aurelio* (1529), parts of which he falsely claimed to derive from Marcus; a French version of this was translated by John *Berners as *The Golden Boke of Marcus Aurelius* (1535), and by Thomas *North as the *Diall of Princes* (1557). Its popularity was more than matched by the later translations from the Greek (1634) by Méric Casaubon (1599–1671), and Jeremy *Collier (1701). The *Meditations* was an important text for the third earl of *Shaftesbury and Matthew *Arnold.

MARECHERA, Dambudzo (1952–87) Controversial novelist, playwright, and poet. Born in Zimbabwe, educated there and in Oxford without graduating, Marechera won the *Guardian* First Novel Prize with *The House of Hunger* (1978), a collection of short stories. In it he flouted the realist conventions and nationalist preoccupations of most African fiction as he did in his novel *Black Sunlight* (1980). Multiple genres are used in *Mindblast* (1984). *The Black Insider* (1990) and *Cemetery of Mind* (1992) appeared posthumously.

Marforio *See* PASQUIL.

MARGARET OF ANJOU (1430–82) The 'she-wolf of France', daughter of Reignier (or René), king of Naples, who is a dominant character in Shakespeare's *1, 2, and 3 *Henry VI* and **Richard III*. In *1* and *2 Henry VI* she is the mistress of Suffolk, though married to Henry. In *3 Henry VI* she becomes more aggressive, with her mocking and murder of York, and in *Richard III* she is a powerful prophet of doom. The historical Margaret remained in France after her defeat at the battle of Tewkesbury. When the plays are performed in sequence this becomes one of Shakespeare's most powerful female roles. Dame Peggy Ashcroft played Margaret memorably in John Barton's adaptation of the four plays as *The *Wars of the Roses* (1963). Margaret figures also in Walter Scott's **Anne of Geierstein*.

Margarite of America, A A prose romance by Thomas *Lodge published 1596, but written during his voyage to South America under Thomas Cavendish in 1591–3. It describes the tragic love of Margarite, daughter of the king of Muscovy, for the treacherous and violent Arsadachus, son of the emperor of Cusco, who eventually kills her, together with his wife Diana and their child. It is notable for its variety of visual spectacle and pageantry, its highly patterned poems and songs, and the unsparing savagery of many of the incidents. It was edited by H. D. Janzen (2005).

MARGUERITE OF NAVARRE *See* HEPTAMÉRON, L'.

Maria *See* WRONGS OF WOMAN.

'Mariana' (1830) and **'Mariana in the South'** (1832) Two poems by Alfred *Tennyson, suggested by Shakespeare's Mariana of 'the moated grange' in **Measure for Measure*. Both describe women waiting hopelessly for their lovers; the first inspired John Everett *Millais's painting of 1851, and the landscape of the second was drawn from Tennyson's journey with Arthur Henry *Hallam in 1832. Tennyson appears to have invented the stanza form.

MARÍAS, Javier (1951–) Spanish novelist, translator, and member of the Royal Spanish Academy, born and educated in Madrid. In addition to translations of Sir Thomas *Browne, Laurence *Sterne, and Joseph *Conrad, he has published a number of novels including *Todas las almas* (1989: *All Souls*), an academic comedy set in Oxford where he taught 1983–5, and *Corazón tan blanco* (1992: *A Heart so White*), a complex and carefully plotted novel of jealousy and passion, packed with *Shakespearian allusions. His major trilogy, *Tu rostro mañana: Your Face Tomorrow*, was completed in 2007. It centres on its narrator's involvement with a shadowy group connected to MI6, represented in Oxford by a retired don, Sir Peter Wheeler.

MARIE DE CHAMPAGNE Daughter of *Eleanor of Aquitaine and her first husband Louis VII of France, who became countess of Champagne in 1164 on her marriage to Count Henry, and regent there on his death in 1181. She set up at Troyes from the 1160s onwards a cultural centre modelled on that of her mother at Poitiers. Her most famous protégé was *Chrétien de Troyes who attributes to her the *sen* and *matière* of his *Lancelot* in the first lines of the poem. *Andreas Capellanus also claims to be her courtier.

MARIE DE FRANCE (*fl. c.*1180–89) A French poet resident in England, about whom little certain is known. She knew Latin and English. Three works have been attributed to her, most famously twelve *Lais*, a series of apparently Celtic stories told in Anglo-Norman couplets. It has also been claimed that she wrote *Espurgatoire*, a French version of the Latin *St Patrick's Purgatory*. As well as the famous *Lais*, some of which gave rise to versions in English (*see* BRETON LAYS), she wrote a collection of *Aesop's Fables which she called *Isopet* and which she says she translated from English. See *Lais*, ed. A. Ewert (1944), trans. Glyn S. Burgess and Keith Busby (1999).

Marinell *See* FLORIMELL.

MARINETTI, Filippo Tommaso (1876–1944) Italian dramatist, novelist, and poet, who launched *futurism in 1909. In his poems he anticipated the Dada technique of juxtaposing words without syntactical links. In his plays he abandoned verisimilitude and traditional methods of characterization and plot development. His innovations include the use of automatons; the simultaneous staging of unrelated actions; and the 'drama of objects', in which human interlocutors play no significant part. He shared with *Fascism the glorification of virility, nationalism, and war.

MARINO, Giambattista (1569–1625) Neapolitan poet, best known for his *Adone* (1623), a long poem on the love of Venus and Adonis. The term *marinismo* (or sometimes *secentismo*) denotes the flamboyant style of Marino and his 17th-century imitators, with its extravagant imagery, excessive ornamentation, and verbal conceits. Richard *Crashaw was profoundly influenced by Marino. See Mario *Praz, *Secentismo e marinismo* (1925); J. Mirollo, *The Poet of the Marvellous* (1963).

Marino Faliero, Doge of Venice A drama in blank verse by Lord *Byron, published 1821 and produced in the same year at Drury Lane, against its author's wishes. The play, based upon historical facts and inspired by Byron's 1816–17 period in Venice, is set in 1355. The elderly but vigorous Faliero, recently elected doge, is outraged by the inadequate punishment imposed upon a young patrician who has grossly insulted Faliero's young and innocent wife. In revenge Faliero joins a popular insurrection in an attempt to overthrow the constitution and its corrupt officers, but the plot is discovered, and he is executed, defiant to the last. This conspiracy was also the subject of a tragedy by A. C. *Swinburne, 1885.

Marius the Epicurean A philosophical novel by Walter *Pater, published 1885, and originally conceived as the first part of a trilogy intended to reconcile questions of religion, philosophy, and the beautiful. The incomplete *Gaston de Latour* (1888) was to have formed the second part of this trilogy. Pater describes the boyhood, education, and young manhood of Marius, a serious young Roman imbued with a 'morbid religious idealism'. With his friend Flavian (who, like so many of Pater's characters, dies young) he discovers the 'jewelled' delights of *Apuleius, in particular of the story of **Cupid and Psyche*, then progresses through the philosophies of *Heraclitus, Aristippus, and *Marcus Aurelius to Christianity. He dies more or less a martyr to save a Christian friend. The work is a vehicle for Pater's own reflections on pagan and Christian art and religion; T. S. *Eliot in his essay 'Arnold and Pater' (1930) quotes with approval A. C. *Benson's view that Pater's true interest was in the sensuous appeal and liturgical solemnities of religion, and concludes that the book documents an important historical moment in the process whereby 'religion became morals, religion became art, religion became science and philosophy'. The book was a significant influence on the *Aesthetic movement, and was especially important to the development of the work of Oscar *Wilde.

MARIVAUX, Pierre Carlet de Chamblain de (1688–1763) French playwright, novelist, and essayist. Between 1721 and 1724 he published the 25 numbers of *Le Spectateur français*, inspired by Addison's **Spectator*, and he went on to publish two *memoir-novels, *La Vie de Marianne* (1731–42: *The Life of Marianne*) and *Le Paysan parvenu* (1734–5: *The Fortunate Peasant*), the former long seen as a model for Richardson's **Pamela*. But he is best known for writing more than 30 comedies for the French and Italian actors in Paris. Marivaux takes the traditional comic device of the external obstacle to love (e.g. a stubborn father) and turns it into something internal, focusing on the psychological obstacles to the union of lovers.

Mark, King In Arthurian legend, the king of Cornwall and the husband of Isoud of Ireland, who is brought to Mark by her lover Tristram; in some versions Tristram is the son of Mark's sister Elizabeth. Various Tristram stories represent the king as nobly trusting, or as a treacherous coward.
See TRISTRAM AND ISOUD.

MARK, St *See* BIBLE; EVANGELISTS.

MARK, Jan (1943–2006) Born in Welwyn, Hertfordshire, educated at Canterbury College of Art, best known as a writer of novels and short stories for children and young people, though she was also a historian, critic, and anthologizer of children's literature, a creative writing teacher, and poet. Her first book, *Thunder and Lightnings* (1976), about friendship between two boys who share a passion for aeroplanes, immediately established her as an important writer for children. She moved between genres, constantly experimenting with forms and ideas, paying great attention to language and style, and never underestimating her readers.

MARKANDAYA, Kamala (1924–2004) British novelist, born and educated in India. *Nectar in a Sieve* (1954) established her as the first notable woman novelist in English from the Indian sub-continent. The impact of new economic and political forces on traditional Indian society is Markandaya's main theme in *A Silence of Desire* (1960), *Possession* (1963), *A Handful of Rice* (1966), and *The Coffer Dams* (1969). Her work introduced rural south India to the international literary stage. *The Nowhere Man* (1972) transports the clash of cultures to England, where Markandaya settled in the early 1960s following her marriage. *Two Virgins* (1973) marks a radical change, showing a more experimental style and more positive view of modernization. Her most ambitious novel is *The Golden Honeycomb* (1977)—a historical look at how the coming of Indian independence affected a native or princely state. *Pleasure City* (1982) provides a subtle view of a friendship between Rikki, a local fisher boy, and Tully, the representative of the multinational company which builds a modern holiday resort next to Rikki's village. The sensitive exploration of relations between Indians and Europeans is a hallmark of Markandaya's work.

MARKHAM, Mrs (*c.*1779–1837) Pseudonym of Elizabeth Penrose, who wrote textbooks for children including popular histories of England (1823) and France (1828) and accompanying sets of questions, all characterized by an inclusive tone and the omission of acts of cruelty. *Historical Conversations for Young Persons* (1836) took dialogue form.

MARKHAM, E. A. (Edward Archibald) (1939–2008) Poet, editor, and fiction writer; he was born on Montserrat in the Caribbean and came to England in 1956. His volumes of poetry include *Human Rites* (1984), *Living in Disguise* (1986), *Towards the End of a Century* (1989), *Misapprehensions* (1995), and *A Rough Climate* (2002). His work frequently returns without sentimental nostalgia to the theme of his Montserrat childhood and his grandmother's house. His short story collections include *Something Unusual* (1986), *Ten Stories* (1994), *Taking the Drawing Room through Customs* (2002), *Meet Me in Mozambique* (2005), and *At Home with Miss Vanesa* (2006). He became professor of creative writing at Sheffield Hallam University in 1997; a novel, *Marking Time*, appeared in 1999, and in 2006 he published a work of non-fiction, *Between Coleridge and Tommy Steele*.

MARKHAM, Gervase (?1568–1637) Writer on country pursuits, the art of war, and horsemanship; he also wrote plays and poems. His principal works on horses are *A Discourse of Horsemanship* (1593), *Cavelarice, or The English Horseman* (1607), *Markham's Method or Epitome* (?1616), and *Markham's Faithful Farrier* (1629). His chief work on country occupations, *A Way to Get Wealth* (1623), contains treatises on 'Cheap and Good Husbandry' (the management of domestic animals); 'Country Contentments' (hunting, hawking, fishing), with a section on the 'English Housewife' (cooking, dairying, physic); and agriculture and horticulture (these treatises had been separately published earlier). Other works include a poem about Sir Richard Grenville (1595) and *The English Arcadia* (prose, 1607). There is a bibliography by F. N. L. Poynter (1962).

MARLOWE, Christopher (1564–93) Poet and playwright, son of a Canterbury shoemaker, educated at the King's School, Canterbury, and Corpus Christi College, Cambridge. He became a BA in 1584, and MA, after some difficulty, in 1587. Though an excellent classicist, as his writings make clear, he seems to have been of a violent and at times criminal temperament. He was atheistic and probably homosexual, and was probably employed as a government spy. In 1589 he was involved in a street fight in which the poet Thomas *Watson killed a man. Early in 1592 he was deported from the Netherlands for attempting to issue forged gold coins. On 30 May 1593 he was killed by one Ingram Frizer (as Leslie *Hotson discovered) in a Deptford tavern after a quarrel over the bill; Marlowe was at the time under warrant to appear before the Privy Council on unknown charges. Thomas *Kyd and another friend, Richard Baines, testified after his death to his blasphemy and unconventional beliefs.

The chronology of his writings is disputed. Some of his plays were acted by the Lord Admiral's Men with Edward *Alleyn in leading roles. *The Tragedy of *Dido Queen of Carthage*, published in 1594, may have been written while he was still at Cambridge, possibly in collaboration with Thomas *Nashe. Part I of **Tamburlaine* was written not later than 1587, and Part II in the following year; it was published in 1590. The next plays may have been *The *Jew of Malta*, not published until 1633, and **Edward II*, published in 1594. The highly topical **Massacre at Paris*, which survives only in a fragmentary and undated text, and **Dr Faustus*, published 1604, may both belong to the last year of Marlowe's life. At various times he translated **Ovid's Amores*, published without date as *All Ovid's Elegies*, together with some of Sir John *Davies's 'Epigrams'; wrote two books of a humorously erotic narrative poem, **Hero and Leander*, which was completed by George *Chapman and published in 1598; made a fine blank verse rendering of *Lucan's First Book*, Book 1 of *Lucan's *Pharsalia*; and wrote the song 'Come live with me and be my love', published in *The *Passionate Pilgrim* (1599) and **Englands Helicon* (1600), with a reply by Walter *Ralegh. In spite of his violent life Marlowe was an admired and highly influential figure: within weeks of his death George *Peele paid tribute to him as 'Marley, the Muses' darling for thy verse'. *Shakespeare's early histories are strongly influenced by Marlowe, and he paid tribute to him in **As You Like It* as the 'dead shepherd'. Ben *Jonson referred to 'Marlowe's mighty line', and among others who praised him were Nashe, Chapman, Gabriel *Harvey, and Michael *Drayton. There are many modern editions of his plays and poems, and biographies by David Riggs (2004) and Park Honan (2005).

MARLOWE, Derek (1938–96) Novelist and screenwriter, born in Perivale, Middlesex, educated at Queen Mary College, London. His first novel, the spy thriller *A Dandy in Aspic* (1966), remains the best known of his nine novels, although his later work was more ambitious. *Do You Remember England?* (1972), his most autobiographical work, is both the story of a tragic love affair and a revealing picture of the idle rich at play. His fiction was characterized equally by an elegant style and a facility for Byzantine plotting. He spent his last ten years writing for television and in Hollywood, with a tenth novel left unfinished. His credits include two episodes of the classic Granada Television series *Adventures of Sherlock Holmes*, starring Jeremy Brett, in 1984–5.

Marmion: *A Tale of Flodden Field* A poem in six cantos by Walter *Scott, published in 1808. Marmion is a favourite of Henry VIII, proud and treacherous, who tires of one lover (a perjured nun, Constance of Beverley, who is walled up alive in a scene of Gothic horror) and pursues another, the wealthy Lady Clare. After much intrigue the action moves to Flodden, with stirring descriptions of the battle, during which Marmion is mortally wounded. The poem contains the Song of Lochinvar (Canto V).

MARMION, Shackerley (1603–39) Playwright, educated at Wadham College, Oxford. He served in the Netherlands, and joined Sir John *Suckling's expedition to Scotland in 1638. He wrote three plays, *Holland's Leaguer* (1632), *A Fine Companion* (1633), and *The Antiquary*, which show the influence of Jonsonian comedy and his own interest in Platonic love.

MAROT, Clément (1496–1544) French poet. He spent the greater part of his life in court service, and from 1527 was *valet de chambre* to Francis I. His Protestant sympathies led to arrest or exile on several occasions, and he spent some time in Italy and Geneva. He enjoyed great popularity in the 16th century, developed the *rondeau and *ballade, and introduced a number of new forms into French poetry, including the *elegy, the *eclogue, the *epigram, the *epithalamium, and (probably) the *Petrarchan sonnet. His translations of the Psalms were much admired by *Calvin, and were very frequently reprinted for some 200 years after his death.

Marprelate Controversy *See* MARTIN MARPRELATE.

MARQUAND, John P. (Phillips) (1893–1960) American novelist, born in Delaware, who produced a series of portraits of American society from the 1930s through to *Women and Thomas Harrow* (1958), his last novel. He also published a number of spy novels centring on the Japanese character Mr Moto.

MÁRQUEZ, Gabriel García *See* GARCÍA MÁRQUEZ, GABRIEL.

MARQUIS, Don (1879–1937) Illinois-born American journalist and writer of light verse, known for his creation of archy the cockroach, a *vers libre* bard writing in lower case (as he cannot manage the shift key), and his friend mehitabel the alley cat. These characters first appeared in the New York *Sun*, then in the New York *Herald Tribune* and *Collier's Weekly*, and in various collections from *archy and mehitabel* (1927) onwards.

Marriage A novel by Susan *Ferrier, published 1818. Lady Juliana, the foolishly romantic daughter of the earl of Courtland, elopes with a penniless young officer, Henry Douglas, who takes her to his Highland home, a gaunt, lonely house, where she is greeted by 'three long-chinned spinsters' and 'five awkward purple girls'. The dismay of the worldly Juliana, and the characters of the household and of the neighbouring gentry, are presented with liveliness and wit. Lady Juliana gives birth to twin daughters, the climax of her misfortunes. The couple move to London, and Henry eventually joins a regiment in India, permanently separating from his wife. Of the twins, Mary is brought up in Scotland, and grows into a plain but a wise and sensible girl. She rejects her mother's choice of a wealthy husband for her, marries happily, and settles in Scotland. Adelaide, her sister, marries an ageing duke, and eventually elopes with a man as heartless as herself. The novel, which Walter *Scott greatly admired, is clearly intended to commend prudent marriage.

Marriage-à-la-Mode A tragicomedy by John *Dryden produced 1672, published 1673. The main plot concerns a usurper's discovery that his daughter and his (lawful) predecessor's son have been secretly reared together in rural seclusion, and have fallen in love. The comic plot is a double intrigue involving two friends and their pursuit respectively of the wife of the one and the betrothed of the other. The counterpointing of these contrasting plots is particularly striking, especially as each ends anticlimactically, the lawful heir being restored to his throne in a stagy manner, and the adulterous lovers failing to consummate their affairs. The play contains some of Dryden's finest songs, and embodies the principles of comic writing outlined in his preface to *An *Evening's Love*.

Marriage of Heaven and Hell, The A prose work by William *Blake, etched *c.*1790–93, introduced by a short poem ('Rintrah roars and shakes his fires in the burden'd air'). It consists of a sequence of paradoxical aphorisms in which Blake turns conventional morality on its head, claiming that man does not consist of the duality of Soul=Reason and Body=Evil, but that 'Man has no Body distinct from his Soul... Energy is the only life, and is from the Body... Energy is Eternal Delight.' He proceeds to claim that *Milton's Satan was truly his Messiah, and that Milton 'was a true Poet and of the Devils party without knowing it', and to produce a series of 'Proverbs of Hell' ('Sooner murder an infant in its cradle than nurse unacted desires' being one of the most notorious), which also celebrate the holiness of the natural world. He then moves to a sequence of visionary encounters with angels and prophets, in the course of which he dismisses the writings of Emanuel *Swedenborg (whom he had greatly admired) as 'a recapitulation of all superficial opinions', accuses him of not having conversed sufficiently with Devils but only with Angels, and ends with an evocation of an Angel turned Devil 'who is my particular friend; we often read the Bible together in its infernal or diabolical sense...'. The aphorisms, both in form and content, resemble the paradoxes of George Bernard *Shaw, who greatly admired Blake and was much influenced by his doctrine of contraries; they were also adopted by those active in the counter-culture movement of the 1960s.

MARRYAT, Captain Frederick (1792–1848) London-born author, naval captain, and FRS. He first achieved fame for his sea stories, beginning with the partly autobiographical *The Naval Officer, or Scenes and Adventures in the Life of Frank Mildmay* (1829). Marryat resigned his commission in 1830 and thereafter supported himself by writing. Among his most successful works, *Peter Simple* (1834), *Jacob Faithful* (1834), and *Mr *Midshipman Easy* (1836), all set at sea, were followed by *Japhet in Search of a Father* (1836), about a foundling. With *Masterman Ready* (1841) he turned his attention to children's books, and it is chiefly for these he is remembered. *The Settlers in Canada* (1844) was followed by *The Children of the New Forest* (1847), a historical novel about the adventures of the four Beverley children, orphaned during the Civil War, who learn the arts of survival from a poor forester.

MARSDEN, Dora (1882–1960) Editor and suffragette, born in Yorkshire and educated at Manchester University. She became a prominent member of Emmeline and Christabel Pankhurst's Women's Social and Political Union, but resigned in 1910. The next year, she co-founded the *Freewoman*, becoming its editor. Contributors included H. G. *Wells and Rebecca *West. The *Freewoman* was relaunched as the *New Freewoman* in 1913, and then as *The *Egoist* in 1914. While she was editor, *The Egoist* began its serialization of James *Joyce's *A *Portrait of the Artist as a Young Man*. Later, Marsden wrote philosophy, of which, in 1928 and 1930, two volumes were published. See Bruce Clarke, *Dora Marsden and Early Modernism* (1996).

MARSH, Sir Edward Howard (1872–1953) Classicist, scholar, patron of modern poetry and painting, educated at Westminster School and Trinity College, Cambridge, a lifelong and eminent civil servant. An early champion of Henrik *Ibsen, he became a friend and executor of Rupert *Brooke, and between 1912 and 1922 edited five highly influential volumes of **Georgian Poetry*. He edited Brooke's *Collected Poems*, with a long memoir, in 1918; made many translations of classical and French authors, including *La Fontaine; and in 1939 published *A Number of People*, reminiscences of his many friends in the literary and political worlds. See C. Hassall, *Edward Marsh, Patron of the Arts* (1959).

MARSH, Dame Ngaio [pron. Ny-o] (1899–1982) Writer of *detective fiction, born at Christchurch, New Zealand. When young she worked as an actress and she devoted much time in later life to theatre in New Zealand, an interest reflected in many of her novels. Her hero, Chief Detective Inspector Roderick Alleyn, first appears in *A Man Lay Dead* (1934); other titles include *Vintage Murder* (1937), *Surfeit of Lampreys* (1941), *Died in the Wool* (1945), and *Final Curtain* (1947).

MARSHALL, Paule (1929–) African American writer, born in Brooklyn, whose first novel, *Brown Girl, Brownstones*

(1959), describes the lives of Barbadian immigrants in New York. Her subsequent works include *The Chosen Place, The Timeless People* (1969), set in the Caribbean.

MARS-JONES, Adam (1954–) Writer and critic, educated at Westminster School and Cambridge. His fiction includes two short story collections, *Lantern Lecture* (1981) and *Monopolies of Loss* (1992), which responds to the Aids epidemic, and a novel about an ailing gay man, *The Waters of Thirst* (1993). *Pilcrow* (2008) is the first part of a projected three-volume novel.

MARSTON, John (1576–1634) Poet and dramatist, whose mother was Italian. He graduated from Oxford in 1594, and joined his father, a lawyer, in the Middle Temple, where he maintained rooms until 1606. There he began to write satirical verse and plays for the new professional children's companies, playing at private indoor theatres. He took orders in 1609 and was incumbent of Christchurch, Hampshire, 1616–31. His *The Metamorphosis of Pygmalion's Image: And Certain Satires* and *The Scourge of Villainy* (both 1598) were published under the pseudonym Kinsayder, under which name he figures in *The Return from Parnassus* (*see* PARNASSUS PLAYS). Some of these satires were directed against literary rivals, including Bishop Joseph *Hall, and were burned by order of the archbishop of Canterbury in 1599. Marston's quarrel with Ben *Jonson resulted in his portrayal as Crispinus in **Poetaster*, but the two became friends again. His dramatic works were printed as follows: *The History of *Antonio and Mellida* (1602), of which *Antonio's Revenge* is the second part; *The *Malcontent* (1604), with additions by John *Webster; **Eastward Ho* (1605), a comedy, written with Jonson and George *Chapman; *The *Dutch Courtesan* in the same year; *The *Parasitaster, or The Fawn*, a comedy, and *Sophonisba*, a tragedy (both 1606); *What You Will* (1607), a comedy; and *The Insatiate Countess* (1613), a tragedy (possibly completed by William Barksted). The plays were edited by H. H. Wood (1934–9) (including the doubtfully assigned *Histriomastix*, 1610), the poems by A. Davenport (1961). There is a life by P. J. Finkelpearl (1969).

MARSTON, John Westland (1819–90) Dramatic poet and critic, who contributed to the **Athenaeum*, wrote several critical works, and more than a dozen plays, including the successful *The Patrician's Daughter*, performed at Drury Lane in 1842. His son Philip Bourke Marston (1850–87) published poems and short stories (*Collected Poems*, 1892). Their London home was a meeting place for many eminent friends in the theatrical and literary world, including Edmund *Kean, William *Macready, Charles *Dickens, A. C. *Swinburne, and D. G. *Rossetti.

MARTEL, Yann (1963–) Novelist and short story writer, born to Canadian parents in Salamanca, Spain; he grew up in various countries including Costa Rica, France, and Mexico, and studied philosophy at Trent University, Ontario. He made his debut with a collection of experimental stories, *The Facts behind the Helsinki Roccamatios* (1993), and a fantastic and partly autobiographical novel, *Self* (1996). But it was his second novel, *The Life of Pi*, a lively, ambitious fable about an Indian boy shipwrecked along with a Bengal tiger and other exotic animals, which won the 2002 *Man Booker Prize, that gained him wider readership and acclaim.

MARTIAL (Marcus Valerius Martialis) (AD 38/41–101/4) Roman epigrammatist of Spanish origin. He wrote about 1,500 epigrams, the best known published in twelve books; in their formal perfection they are indebted to the example of *Catullus. They are usually direct addresses to individuals and include celebrations of friendship and the country life, flattery of the emperor Domitian, and satirical and often obscene portraits of the inhabitants of contemporary Rome. Martial was much imitated by 17th-century poets, notably Ben *Jonson, Robert *Herrick, and Abraham *Cowley. Translations include Thomas *May's *Selected Epigrams* (1629) and Peter *Porter's *After Martial* (1972). See J. P. Sullivan and A. J. Boyle (eds), *Martial in English* (1996).

MARTIANUS CAPELLA (Marcian) (*fl.* 410–39) A North African writer, celebrated in the Middle Ages. He was the author of *De Nuptiis Philologiae et Mercurii* ('The Marriage of Mercury and Philology') in nine books of prose and verse. The first two deal with the wooing (in a wide, metaphorical sense) of Philology by Mercury, and the last seven are an allegorical encyclopedia of the seven liberal arts (consisting of grammar, rhetoric, and logic—the trivium; and arithmetic, geometry, astronomy, and music—the quadrivium). This allegorization, together with that of the contemporary *Prudentius, remained popular up to the Renaissance. Marcian is referred to by Geoffrey *Chaucer in 'The Merchant's Tale' (*see* CANTERBURY TALES, 10) and in *The *House of Fame*. Richard *Mulcaster is still using Martianus' method in his allegorizing of Philology in *The First Part of the Elementarie* (1582).

MARTIN, George R. R. (1948–)American novelist, editor, and television scriptwriter who has written numerous works of *science fiction and *fantasy. The complex 'Song of Ice and Fire' series (1996 onwards) is a fantasy of dynastic struggle influenced by the history of medieval Europe.

MARTIN, John (1789–1854) Painter, born near Hexham in Northumberland. His relationship with literature was close: he illustrated John *Milton's **Paradise Lost* (1823–7); he drew subjects from Thomas *Gray, Lord *Byron, and Mary *Shelley; he was admired by poets and writers. It has been suggested that his *Sadak in Search of the Waters of Oblivion* (1812) may have inspired a passage in John *Keats's **Hyperion*. P. B. *Shelley wrote a poem to accompany the engraving, published in 1828. William *Beckford took Martin to Fonthill (1823). Edward *Bulwer-Lytton enthused over his works, and his **Last Days of Pompeii* (1834) is indebted to Martin. Through his prints Martin became a widely popular artist; they were copied by both Branwell and Charlotte *Brontë, and Martin's fantastic cities influenced the imagery of their juvenilia: Martin himself plays Edward de Lisle of Verdopolis, painter of Babylon. Martin's paintings are the swansong of the taste for the Burkeian *sublime.

MARTIN, Sir Theodore (1816–1909) Poet, biographer, and translator, who was educated at Edinburgh University, practised as a solicitor in Edinburgh, and moved to London in 1846. He contributed, under the pseudonym *'Bon Gaultier', to *Tait's Magazine* and **Fraser's Magazine*, and collaborated with W. E. *Aytoun in the writing of the 'Bon Gaultier ballads', published in 1845. He also translated many works from German, Latin, Danish, and Italian, and wrote a life of Prince Albert, 5 vols (1875–80), and reminiscences of Queen *Victoria (*Queen Victoria as I Knew Her*, 1902).

Martin Chuzzlewit, The Life and Adventures of A novel by Charles *Dickens, published 1843–4; the last of Dickens's *picaresque tales. Martin, the hero, is the grandson of old Martin Chuzzlewit, a wealthy gentleman embittered by the greed of his family. The old man has reared Mary Graham, a young orphan, to look after him, and regards her as his daughter. Young Martin is in love with Mary; but the grandfather, perceiving his selfishness, repudiates him and gets him dismissed from his position as pupil to his cousin Mr Pecksniff, architect and arch-hypocrite. Martin, accompanied by the indomitably cheerful Mark Tapley as his servant, sails for America to seek his fortune. He goes as an architect to the fraudulent Eden Land Corporation, where he loses his money and nearly dies of fever (this part gave great offence in America). He then returns to England, his experiences having reformed his selfish attitudes. His grandfather has meanwhile established himself and Mary in Pecksniff's household and pretended to place himself under his direction, thus satisfying himself of Pecksniff's treachery. Pecksniff tries to bully Mary into marrying him. Old Martin exposes the hypocrite, restores his grandson to favour, and gives him Mary's hand. Pecksniff ends his days as a beggar.

A sub-plot concerns Jonas Chuzzlewit, the son of old Martin's brother, a character of extraordinary villainy. He murders his father (in intention if not in fact); marries Mercy Pecksniff and treats her brutally; murders the director of a bogus insurance company, by whom he has been deceived and blackmailed; is detected; and finally poisons himself.

The book contains many memorable minor characters: Tom Pinch, Pecksniff's gentle and loyal assistant, and his sister Ruth; Pecksniff's daughters Charity and Mercy (Cherry and Merry); and Mrs Gamp, the disreputable old nurse.

MARTIN DU GARD, Roger *See* ROMAN-FLEUVE.

MARTINEAU, Harriet (1802–76) Writer and journalist, born in Norwich; her childhood and youth were dogged by illness and poverty, and she was deaf throughout her adult life. She was largely home educated, but was much influenced by two years in a Unitarian school, and by a brief period in a Bristol boarding school run by her aunt. A devout Unitarian in youth, her first published work was *Devotional Exercises* (1823), from which time she wrote tirelessly for the rest of her life. She began to review for W. J. *Fox's *Monthly Repository*, then in 1830 won all three prizes in an essay competition set by the Unitarians. Between 1832 and 1834 she published a series of didactic stories, *Illustrations of Political Economy*, revealing both her passion for social reform and the influence of Jeremy *Bentham and John Stuart *Mill. The stories were immensely successful, as were her tales for Henry *Brougham's Society for the Diffusion of Useful Knowledge, and she became a literary celebrity, including among her friends Thomas *Malthus, Sydney *Smith, and Monckton *Milnes, as well as politicians who consulted her on economic and social matters. In 1834 she travelled in America, and supported the abolitionists at some personal risk. *Society in America* appeared in 1837, and her first novel, **Deerbrook* (always her favourite among her works), in 1839. *The Hour and the Man*, a fictional portrayal of Toussaint *Louverture, came out in 1840, and a book of children's stories, *The Playfellow*, in 1841. In 1845 she settled in the Lake District and became a friend of the *Wordsworths. She had by now repudiated her Unitarian faith, and indeed all religious belief. Her radical *History of the Thirty Years' Peace* was published in 1849, and her anti-theological *Laws of Man's Social Nature* in 1851. Her translation and condensation of Auguste *Comte, *The Philosophy of Comte*, appeared in 1853. For most of the rest of her life she continued energetically with her journalism, and wrote a book which appeared posthumously as *An Autobiographical Memoir*, containing many observations on public and literary figures of her day. On several occasions she refused the offer of a Civil List pension, feeling it would compromise her independence. See S. Hoecker-Drysdale, *Harriet Martineau: First Woman Sociologist* (1992); Valerie Sanders, *Reason over Passion: Harriet Martineau and the Victorian Novel* (1986); *The Collected Letters of Harriet Martineau*, ed. D. A Logan, 5 vols (2007).

MARTINEAU, James (1805–1900) Philosopher and theologian, brother of Harriet *Martineau, educated at Norwich Grammar School and Manchester New College, where, after working as a Unitarian minister at Dublin and Liverpool, he was appointed professor of moral philosophy in 1840; he was principal of the college from 1869 to 1885. He was an ardent upholder of the theist position, a powerful critic of materialism and naturalism, and was prompt to recognize the claims of the Darwinian philosophy of evolution. His chief books, mainly philosophical and religious works, were mostly published after his 80th year. These include *Types of Ethical Theory* (1885), *A Study in Religion* (1887), and *The Seat of Authority in Religion* (1890). He was joint editor of the *Prospective Review* (1845–54). See F. Schulman, *James Martineau: This Conscience-Intoxicated Unitarian* (2002).
See UNITARIANISM.

Martin Marprelate The name assumed by the authors of a number of anonymous pamphlets (seven survive) issued in 1588–9 from a secret press, containing attacks in a mocking, rollicking style on the bishops, and defending the *Presbyterian system of discipline. They were stimulated by the attempts of Archbishop Whitgift (1530–1604) to impose uniformity in liturgical practice and to promote royal supremacy and the authority of the Articles.

The Marprelate tracts are among the best prose satires of the Elizabethan age. Their titles (in abbreviated form) are: *The Epistle, The Epitome, Mineral and Metaphysical Schoolpoints, Hay Any Work for Cooper* (a familiar street cry, here alluding to Thomas Cooper, bishop of Westminster (1517–94)), *Martin Junior, Martin Senior,* and *The Protestation*. As well as ballads, rhymes, and plays, they provoked replies from such noted writers as John *Lyly and Thomas *Nashe; Richard and Gabriel *Harvey later became involved in the controversy. But the replies are on the whole less entertaining than the original pamphlets. Richard *Hooker's work eventually settled the matter for the church. Among the various suspected authors, the Welshman John Penry (1559–93) died in prison and the clergyman John Udall (1560–92/3) was executed. Their collaborator Job Throckmorton (1545–1601) denied his complicity at Penry's trial, and escaped punishment.

Martinus Scriblerus, Memoirs of the Extraordinary Life, Works and Discoveries of A prose satire, initiated by the *Scriblerus Club and written mainly by Alexander *Pope and John *Arbuthnot, the latter contributing particularly science-based material. It was printed in the second volume of Pope's prose works (1741). The story of Martinus' birth, christening, education, and travels offered many opportunities for burlesque on various forms of contemporary knowledge and study. The 'double mistress' episode, featuring a lawsuit about the sexual identity of conjoined twins, was often suppressed. Pope identified many of the notes and other mock-scholarly additions to *The Dunciad* as the work of Martinus Scriblerus, and other authors, such as Henry *Fielding, Richard Owen Cambridge (1717–1802), and George *Crabbe, used variants of the pseudonym. The work was edited by Charles Kerby-Miller (1950; repr. 1988).

MARTYN, Edward (1859–1923) Irish playwright, born into an aristocratic Catholic family in Tillyra Castle, Co. Galway, and educated at Christ Church, Oxford; he was one of the founders of the *Irish Literary Theatre, as well as an ardent supporter of Irish educational and musical activities. He was president of Sinn Fein from 1905 to 1908. His best-known plays are the *Ibsen-influenced *The Heather Field* (chosen along with W. B. *Yeats's *The Countess Cathleen* to open the Irish Literary Theatre in 1899) and *Maeve* (1899), a drama of Anglo-Irish antagonism. He is caricatured as 'dear Edward' in his cousin George *Moore's *Hail and Farewell*.

MARVELL, Andrew (1621–78) Poet and politician, son of the Revd Andrew Marvell (*c.*1584–1641), born at Winstead in Holderness, Yorkshire. In 1624 the family moved to Hull on his father's appointment as lecturer at Holy Trinity Church. Marvell probably attended Hull Grammar School. He matriculated at Trinity College, Cambridge, as a subsizar (an undergraduate receiving an allowance from the college) in December 1633, and graduated in 1639. In 1637 he had contributed Greek and Latin verses to a Cambridge volume congratulating Charles I on the birth of a daughter. His mother died in April 1638, his father remarrying in November. Around 1639 Marvell may have come under the influence of Roman Catholic proselytizers: according to one story he went to London with them and was fetched back by his father. In January 1641 his father was drowned while crossing the Humber, and soon after Marvell left Cambridge for London. Between 1643 and 1647 he travelled for four years in the Netherlands, France, Italy, and Spain, learning languages and fencing, and perhaps deliberately avoiding the Civil War (he said later that 'the cause was too good to have been fought for'). On his return from the Continent he apparently moved in London literary circles and had friends among Royalists. *An Elegy upon the Death of My Lord Francis Villiers* was published in 1648, and his poems to Richard *Lovelace ('his Noble Friend') and on the death of Lord Henry Hastings (1630–49) in 1649. In the early summer of 1650 he wrote 'An Horatian Ode upon Cromwell's Return from Ireland', and 'Tom May's Death'. From 1650 to 1652 Marvell tutored young Mary Fairfax, daughter of the Parliamentarian general, at Nun Appleton in Yorkshire, writing 'Upon Appleton House' and lyrics such as 'The Garden' and the Mower poems in the summer of 1651. In 1653 he wrote *The Character of Holland*, was appointed tutor to Cromwell's ward William Dutton, and moved to John Oxenbridge's house at Eton, where he wrote 'Bermudas'. In 1654 with 'The First Anniversary' (published 1655) he began his career as unofficial laureate to Oliver *Cromwell, and was appointed in 1657 Latin secretary to the Council of State (a post previously occupied by his friend and sponsor John *Milton, now blind). For eight months during 1656 Marvell was in Saumur with Dutton, where he was described as 'a notable English Italo-Machiavellian'. He mourned Cromwell in 'Upon the Death of His Late Highness the Lord Protector' (1658) and took part in the funeral procession. The following year (January) he was elected MP for Hull, and remained one of the Hull members until his death. At the *Restoration his influence secured Milton's release from prison.

From June 1662 to April 1663 Marvell was in the Netherlands on unknown political business, and in July 1663 he travelled with the earl of Carlisle as private secretary on his embassy to Russia, Sweden, and Denmark, returning in January 1665. His satires against the earl of *Clarendon were written and published in 1667. Later that year he composed his finest satire, 'Last Instructions to a Painter', attacking financial and sexual corruption at court and in Parliament, and took part in the impeachment of Clarendon. *The Rehearsal Transpros'd*, a prose work advocating toleration for Dissenters, which set new standards of irony and urbanity, appeared in 1672 (second part, 1673). Gilbert *Burnet called these 'the wittiest books that have appeared in this age', and Charles II apparently read them 'over and over again'. According to the report of government spies, Marvell (under the codename 'Mr Thomas') was during 1674 a member of a fifth column promoting Dutch interests in England, and in touch with Dutch secret agents. The second edition of **Paradise Lost* contained a commendatory poem by Marvell, and in his prose works he continued to wage war against arbitrary royal power. *Mr Smirk, or The Divine in Mode* and *A Short Historical Essay Concerning General Councils* (both 1676), and *An Account of the Growth of Popery and Arbitrary Government in England* (1677), were all Marvell's, though prudently published anonymously. The *London Gazette* offered a reward, in March 1678, for information about the author or printer of *An Account*. That August, however, Marvell died in his house in Great Russell Street from medical treatment prescribed for a fever. His *Miscellaneous Poems* appeared in 1681, printed from papers found in his rooms by his housekeeper Mary Palmer, who gave herself out to be his widow and signed the preface 'Mary Marvell' in order to get her hands on £500 which Marvell had been keeping for two bankrupt friends. This volume did not contain the satires (the authorship of some of which is still disputed): these appeared in *Poems on Affairs of State* (1689–97).

Famed in his day as patriot, satirist, and foe to tyranny, Marvell was virtually unknown as a lyric poet. It was not until after the First World War, with Sir Herbert Grierson's *Metaphysical Lyrics* and T. S. *Eliot's 'Andrew Marvell', that the modern high estimation of his poetry began to prevail. In the second half of the 20th century his small body of lyrics attracted much exegetical effort. His oblique and finally enigmatic way of treating quite conventional poetic materials (as in 'The Nymph Complaining for the Death of her Faun' or 'To his Coy Mistress') has especially intrigued the modern mind. See *Poems and Letters*, ed. H. M. Margoliouth, 3rd edn rev. P. Legouis and E. E. Duncan-Jones (2 vols, 1971); *Poems*, ed. N. Smith (2003); *Latin Poems*, ed. and trans. W. A. McQueen and K. A. Rockwell (1964); *The Rehearsal Transpros'd*, ed. D. E. B. Smith (1971); P. Legouis, *Andrew Marvell: Poet, Puritan, Patriot* (2nd edn, 1968); H. Kelliher, *Andrew Marvell: Poet and Politician* (1978); J. B. Leishman, *The Art of Marvell's Poetry* (1966).

MARX, Karl (1818–83) German philosopher, historian, political economist, and revolutionary activist. Born in Trier of Jewish descent, he studied philosophy and law at the universities of Bonn and Berlin. In 1842 he became editor of the *Rheinische Zeitung* at Cologne, but the paper was suppressed by the censor. He moved to Paris where he met Friedrich *Engels, initiating a lifelong collaboration. Expelled from Paris, he went to Brussels, but at the outbreak of the revolutionary movement of 1848 returned to Cologne, where, with Engels, he again conducted a newspaper, the *Neue Rheinische Zeitung*. His radical views caused him to be expelled, and he finally settled in London. After years of poverty and obscurity he became internationally known through his leading involvement in the First International Workingmen's Association of 1864 and defence of the Paris Commune (1871). His best-known works include *The Communist Manifesto* (with Engels, 1848) and *Das Kapital*, of which only the first volume was published in his lifetime (1867): two further unfinished volumes were edited by Engels and appeared after his death (1885 and 1894). His influence on the modern world, mediated by Marxism and its proponents, has been profound. Political revolutions in China, Russia, and many other countries were carried through in the hope of implementing communist ideals. Even when called into question or emphatically rejected, Marx's ideas have been widely absorbed. His materialist view of history, with its emphasis on economic issues such as ownership of the means of production and the central importance of the conflict between social classes, as well as his dialectical methodology, adapted from *Hegel, have been especially influential. In the turbulent inter-war years of the 20th century many European literary figures, including Bertolt *Brecht and *García Lorca, as well as British poets such as the young W. H. *Auden, Stephen *Spender, and Cecil *Day-Lewis, found their understanding of the modern world coloured by Marx's ideas. In historiography and the social sciences his influence continues to be widely felt; it is clearly reflected, for example, in the work of prominent historians such as E. J. Hobsbawm, Christopher *Hill, and E. P. *Thompson. Marx had relatively little to say about literature, and his own literary tastes were conservative: *Shakespeare, and the novels of Walter *Scott and Honoré de *Balzac were his favourite reading. Nevertheless, for many literary critics Marx's ideas have been crucial to their understanding of literary texts and literary history (*see* Marxist literary criticism). See S. S. Prawer, *Marx and World Literature* (1976).

Marxist literary criticism A critical tradition that approaches literature from the perspective of the 'historical materialism' developed by *Marx and *Engels; that is, as a changing form of material production that participates in and illuminates the processes of history. Neither Marx nor Engels bequeathed a critical or aesthetic theory, but they tended to disparage socialist writers of a propagandist type, and suggested that art is not tied directly to phases of economic development but has a certain autonomy. These principles are upheld in 'classical' Marxism, by Georgi Plekhanov (1856–1918), Leon Trotsky (1879–1940), and Georg Lukács (1885–1971), against tendencies in more mechanistic applications of Marxism to reduce art to its economic circumstances or to dismiss the bourgeois cultural heritage in favour of some purely 'proletarian' art. Of these, it was Lukács who eventually developed a consistent Marxist critical position, one that stressed the value of 19th-century *realism. In the Soviet Union under Stalin, the prescriptive policy of *Socialist Realism obstructed independent critical thinking, except in the then little-known *Bakhtin circle. The first significant Marxist criticism in the English-speaking world emerged within the doctrinaire constraints of Communist Party orthodoxy: Granville Hicks (1901–82) in the USA and the more imaginative Christopher Caudwell (Christopher St John Sprigg, 1907–37) in England assessed literature in terms of its usefulness as a weapon in the class struggle. The German Marxists Walter *Benjamin and Bertolt *Brecht provided more persuasive views of literature as a 'production' of new meanings rather than a mere reflection of history. In disagreement with Lukács, Brecht distrusted the 'illusionism' of realistic or naturalistic art, and claimed political value for his own kind of *modernist experiments. His influence was strong upon Roland *Barthes and other critics who brought about alliances among Marxist, *formalist, and post-*structuralist literary theory, usually of a kind that regards realism as inherently conservative. In the English-speaking world since 1968, the foremost Marxist critics have been Raymond *Williams, who discarded the traditional metaphor of economic 'base' and cultural 'superstructure', Terry *Eagleton, whose work since the 1970s has approached literature through the contradictions of 'ideology', and Fredric Jameson (1934–), who has developed from Lukács's work a broader system for the analysis of literary and cultural forms. Eagleton and Jameson have both employed Marxist methods to illuminate general problems of literary theory and the phenomenon of *postmodernism. Since the 1930s, elements of Marxist theory have variously been combined with those of other critical schools such as *psychoanalytic criticism, *feminist criticism, structuralism, and *deconstruction. See Terry Eagleton, *Marxism and Literary Criticism* (2nd edn, 2002).

Mary Barton: *A Tale of Manchester Life* Elizabeth *Gaskell's first novel, published 1848. The largely working-class cast of characters in this novel was then an innovation. The background of the story is Manchester in the 'hungry forties', and the acute misery of the unemployed mill-hands. Mary Barton is the daughter of the embittered John Barton, a trade unionist. She has attracted Henry Carson, son of one of the employers, and, flattered by his attentions and the hope of a grand marriage, has rejected her faithful admirer Jem Wilson, a young engineering worker. A group of workers, enraged by the failure of local mill-owners to take their suffering seriously, decide to kill Henry Carson. The lot falls on John Barton to do the deed. Suspicion falls on Jem Wilson when Carson is shot dead. Mary realizes her true love for Jem, and discovers that her father was the murderer. Her desperate efforts to save Jem without betraying her father are successful. John Barton finally confesses to the father of Henry Carson, is forgiven, and dies. Mary and Jem are married, and emigrate to Canada.

The book's views on industrial relations were attacked by both Tories and Manchester mill-owners, but it achieved a wide readership, and was admired by Charles *Dickens and Thomas *Carlyle. It has become one of the best known of the *'condition of England' novels from the 1840s.

'Mary Morison' one of Robert *Burns's earliest surviving song lyrics, published 1786, possibly addressed to Alison Begbie.

Mary Poppins P. L. *Travers's magical Edwardian nanny, who first appeared in 1934 (*Mary Poppins*), then in seven sequels to 1988. Where Travers's character has god-like powers, in the hugely successful Disney film (1964) and the London musical (2004), she is less mystic and egocentric.

MARY QUEEN OF SCOTS (Mary Stewart) (1542–87) Daughter of James V of Scotland and Mary of Guise; she married Francis II of France (1558), Lord Darnley (1565), and Bothwell (1567). Imprisoned by *Elizabeth I, she was beheaded on a charge of conspiring against her life. She figures as *Duessa in *The *Faerie Queene*, and in ballads with her four attendants, the *Queen's Maries. She appears in Walter *Scott's *The Abbot*, and in a tragedy by *Schiller (in which she and Elizabeth meet, as they did not in real life). James *Hogg celebrated her in *The Queen's Wake* (1813). She also features in three plays by A. C. *Swinburne, and a novel by Maurice Hewlett (1861–1923). Her story has been dramatized by Robert *Bolt in *Vivat! Vivat Regina!* (1970) and Liz *Lochhead in *Mary Queen of Scots Got her Head Chopped Off* (1987). There is a study by J. Wormald (1988).

masculine rhyme *See* RHYME.

MASEFIELD, John Edward (1878–1967) Poet, born in Herefordshire. His idyllic early childhood was vital to his later work, but in 1884 his mother died, and his father in 1890, so he was brought up by relatives who did not prove sympathetic. Warwick School was followed at the age of 13 by training for the merchant navy. In 1894 Masefield sailed for Chile, suffered acutely from sea-sickness, and was returned home. He sailed again across the Atlantic, but at the age of 17 jumped ship in New York and became a vagrant in America, taking what jobs he could find, reading voraciously, and writing verse. Back in England he began his prolific writing career, which included poetry, plays, novels, essays, children's stories, and, at the end of his life, memoirs. *Salt-Water Ballads* was received with interest in 1902: one of its dedicatees, a teacher eleven years older than himself, Constance de la Cherois Crommelin, became his wife. *Salt-Water Ballads* included 'I must to the seas again' (the line was altered to the more familiar 'I must go down to the seas again' for the musical setting by John *Ireland). *Ballads and Poems*, containing the poem 'Cargoes', appeared in 1910, but in this year he suffered a nervous crisis, only resolved when the first lines of *The Everlasting Mercy* (1911) came to him on a country walk: this narrative poem, with its account of the conversion of the rough Saul Kane, provoked indignation and admiration. *The Widow in the Bye Street* (1912) was another novel of Herefordshire low life, with a strong erotic theme, and *Reynard the Fox* (1919) was a rattling verse tale set in the rural world of Masefield's childhood. Meanwhile he had produced collections of shorter verse, as well as stories, novels, and plays: his *Collected Poems* (1923) sold in great numbers, as did the novels *Sard Harker* (1924), *Odtaa* (1926), *The Bird of Dawning* (1933), and his story for children *The Midnight Folk* (1927). In 1930 Masefield became *poet laureate, and in 1935 received the Order of Merit. He continued to write with energy, producing more volumes of poetry, the sea novels *Dead Ned* (1938) and *Live and Kicking Ned* (1939), and the autobiographical *So Long to Learn* (1952). A final luminous fragment of autobiography, describing his country childhood up to his mother's death, appeared in 1966 as *Grace before Ploughing*. See Constance Babington Smith, *John Masefield* (1978); Paul Binding, *An Endless Quiet Valley* (1998).

Mask of Anarchy, The A poem of political protest by P. B. *Shelley, written in response to the 'Peterloo Massacre' at St Peter's Fields in Manchester in August 1819, published 1832.

Composed at speed and in anger, the poem uses the popular *ballad form with immense power and sometimes surreal effect. The 'mask' is a pageant, or masquerade, of British political leaders—Castlereagh (1769–1822), Eldon (1751–1838), Sidmouth (1757–1844)—whom Shelley blames not only for the killing of eleven people and injuries to around 500 others at a public demonstration for parliamentary reform, but also for the general conditions of harshness and oppression in England: what he calls the 'triumph of Anarchy' (compare *The *Triumph of Life*). Anarchy rides on a horse: 'He was pale even to the lips, | Like Death in the Apocalypse.' His bloody progress is only prevented by Hope, 'a Maniac maid', who throws herself under the trampling hooves. The poem ends with a celebration of freedom, and Shelley's historic appeal for non-violent mass political protest in a great assembly of working people: 'Rise like lions after slumber | In unvanquishable number.'

masks *See* MASQUES.

MASON, A. E. W. (Alfred Edward Woodley) (1865–1948) Failed actor turned successful novelist, best remembered for *The Four Feathers* (1902), the story of Harry Feversham's heroism in redeeming himself from the accusation of cowardice in the eyes of three fellow officers and his beloved, Ethne Eustace. There are several film adaptations, notably the 1939 version (produced by Alexander Korda). His many other popular works include the series featuring Inspector Hanaud, which began with *At the Villa Rose* (1910).

MASON, William (1725–97) Poet and clergyman, educated at Hull Grammar School and St John's College, Cambridge. He was the friend and correspondent of Thomas *Gray, Richard *Hurd, William *Warburton, and Horace *Walpole. He edited *The Poems of Mr Gray, to which are Prefixed Memoirs of his Life and Writings* (1775), the biographical portion of which was an important model for James Boswell's *Life of *Johnson*. Mason's own work includes the tragedies *Elfrida* (1751) and *Caractacus* (1759), the latter clearly influenced by Gray's interest in *primitivism. Mason's blank verse *The English Garden* (4 books, 1771–81) expresses his enthusiasm for the *picturesque style of *landscape gardening.

masques (masks) Dramatic entertainments involving dances and disguises, in which the spectacular and musical elements predominated over plot and character. They were acted indoors by amateurs, though professional dancers and singers were sometimes employed too, and were designed to include their spectators in the action, sometimes simply by a concluding dance. As they were usually performed at court, often at very great expense, many have political overtones. They were perhaps of Italian origin, but assumed a distinctive character in England in the 16th and 17th centuries. Many of the leading poets and dramatists, Samuel *Daniel, Thomas *Campion, George *Chapman, and Thomas *Middleton, wrote masques, and they reached their highest degree of elaboration at the court of *James I where the queen, Anne of Denmark, had a penchant for masquing, and older courtiers complained of the consequent extravagance and loose behaviour, with court ladies exposing their breasts and other scandalous happenings. Ben *Jonson was pre-eminent as a writer of masques for James, and introduced the 'antimasque' as a comic and grotesque foil to the main spectacle. The architect Inigo *Jones designed the machinery or decoration (the 'Painting and carpentry' as Jonson scathingly dismissed them) for some of them. Jonson's *The Sad Shepherd*, John *Milton's *A Mask*, better known as **Comus*, and other such works often called masques can only be loosely assigned to the genre, and are closer to *pastoral dramas. See David Lindley (ed.), *Court Masques 1605–1640* (1995); David Bevington and Peter Holbrook (eds), *The Politics of the Stuart Court Masque* (1998).

Massacre at Paris, The A play by Christopher *Marlowe written *c.*1592. The undated first edition (*c.*1593/4) describes it as having been acted by the Admiral's Men. It is a short and poor text, probably representing a mangled version of what Marlowe wrote. A single leaf surviving in manuscript used to be thought to be a forgery by J. P. *Collier, but is now considered a genuine contemporary copy of part of one scene.

The play deals with the massacre of Protestants in Paris on St Bartholomew's Day, 24 August 1572 (an event witnessed by Philip *Sidney, who was staying in Paris at the time). Its most memorable character is the Machiavellian duke of Guise, whose high aspiring language seems to have influenced *Shakespeare in his early history plays. The massacre is depicted in a series of short episodes, a notable one being that in which the rhetorician *Ramus is killed after a verbal onslaught by the Guise on his emendations of Aristotle. The Guise himself is eventually murdered on the orders of Henry III. Leaping over seventeen years, the play concludes with the murder of Henry III and the succession of the (then) Protestant Henry of Navarre. It is difficult to tell whether the frequent comic effect of the play is authorially intended or is the result of the incompleteness of the text.

massacre of St Bartholomew *See* BARTHOLOMEW, MASSACRE OF ST.

MASSIE, Allan (1938–) Scottish novelist, critic, and editor of the *Edinburgh Review* (1982–4), born in Singapore, educated at Trinity College, Glenalmond, and Trinity College, Cambridge. One of the best historical novelists of his generation, he has also written books set in the present, including thrillers and love stories, while his first novel, *Change and Decay in All Around I See* (1978), was a comedy of manners. His Imperial Trilogy, *Augustus* (1989), *Tiberius* (1990), and *Caesar* (1993), was extended with *Antony* (1997) and *Caligula* (2004), and a second historical sequence, starting with *An Evening of the World* (2001), begins in the Dark Ages. *King David* (1995) has a biblical theme, while *The Ragged Lion* (1994) recreates the life of Walter *Scott. More recent history provided material for *A Question of Loyalties* (1989), looking back to the Vichy regime in 1940s France, and *The Sins of the Father* (1991), which is experimental in form and is set against the legacy of the Holocaust.

MASSINGER, Philip (1583–1640) Poet and playwright, born at Salisbury, and educated at St Alban Hall, Oxford. His father was the trusted agent of the Herbert family, and Massinger addressed various dedications and poems to the Herberts. He became the chief collaborator of John *Fletcher after the withdrawal of Francis *Beaumont, and on Fletcher's death in 1625 he became the principal dramatist of the King's Men. He was buried in Fletcher's grave at St Saviour's, Southwark (now Southwark Cathedral).

He is known to have written or shared in the writing of 55 plays. Of these 22 are lost. Of the extant plays fifteen are of his sole composition, sixteen were written in collaboration with Fletcher, and two in collaboration with others. Massinger's share in the Fletcher plays was given no acknowledgement in the Beaumont and Fletcher folios, but has been identified with reasonable confidence by modern scholars. He shared with Fletcher the writing of such plays as *The *Custom of the Country* (1619), *Sir John van *Oldenbarnavelt* (1619), *The Double Marriage* (1620), *The *Beggar's Bush* (1622), and *A Very Woman* (?1625) and with Fletcher and others collaborated in *The *Bloody Brother* (*c.*1616). With Thomas *Dekker he shared the writing of a religious play, *The *Virgin Martyr*, a work uncharacteristic of both men. With Nathan *Field he wrote *The *Fatal Dowry*, in which his high romantic seriousness blends strikingly with Field's satire.

He wrote only two social comedies, *A *New Way to Pay Old Debts* and *The *City Madam*. *A New Way* was a mainstay of the English stage in the late 18th and early 19th centuries, with the villainous Sir Giles Overreach providing a vehicle for the talents of a long line of actors including John Philip *Kemble and Edmund *Kean. Like several other of his plays, it has had modern revivals. Both comedies are inspired by Massinger's patrician contempt for the ambitions and affectations of the rising mercantile classes in the city. Two amusing and sophisticated but much more romantic comedies are *The Guardian* (1633) and his feminist play *The Picture* (1629).

Massinger wrote several excellent tragedies. The early **Duke of Milan*, a tragedy of jealousy, was followed by *The *Roman Actor*, his favourite play. It makes remarkable use of plays-within-the-play, and in the person of Paris the actor he was able to show something of his own prolonged difficulties with political censorship. Because of this censorship he was forced to do a complete rewriting of **Believe as You List*, perhaps his greatest tragedy. It is a powerful story of a returned nationalist leader failing to get support and being hounded by the imperial authorities. The remainder of his plays are in the Fletcherian vein of tragicomedy. These include *The *Maid of Honour*, *The *Bondman*, *The Renegado*, and *The Great Duke of Florence* (acted 1627; printed 1636).

The standard edition of Massinger's plays is by Philip Edwards and Colin Gibson (5 vols, 1976). There is a biographical and critical study by T. A. Dunn, *Philip Massinger* (1957).

MASSINGHAM, H. J. (Harold John) (1888–1952) Nature writer and ruralist, son of H. W. *Massingham, born in London and educated at Westminster School and the Queen's College, Oxford. He published many books reflecting his deep appreciation of the countryside and natural history; they include *Wold without End* (1932) and *The English Countryman* (1942).

MASSINGHAM, H. W. (Henry William) (1860–1924) Born at Norwich and educated at King Edward VI's School, Norwich; he was described by his friend G. B. *Shaw as 'the perfect master journalist'. He was the influential editor of the Liberal *Nation* from 1907 to 1923.

Mass Observation A network of lay correspondents formed in 1937 by the poet Charles *Madge and film-maker Humphrey *Jennings, with the anthropologist Tom Harrisson (1911–76). Conceived as an 'anthropology of ourselves', the movement provided valuable data on wartime morale and later consumer attitudes. Revived in 1981, its archive is held at the University of Sussex.

MASSON, David (1822–1907) Biographer, critic, journalist, born in Aberdeen and educated at Aberdeen Grammar School and Marischal College, Aberdeen; successively professor of English literature at University College London (1853) and Edinburgh University (1865). He is remembered for his *Life of Milton* (7 vols, 1859–94). He was a disciple of Thomas *Carlyle and became the founder and editor of **Macmillan's Magazine* (1859). His other works include biographies of William *Drummond of Hawthornden (1873) and Thomas *De Quincey (1881), editions of John *Milton, Oliver *Goldsmith, and De Quincey, and *Essays Biographical and Critical* (1856). His *Edinburgh Sketches and Memories* (1892), *Memories of London in the Forties* (1908), and *Memories of Two Cities* (1911) are accounts of literary circles in mid-century London and Scotland.

Master Humphrey's Clock A weekly founded by Charles *Dickens in 1840, originally intended as a miscellany which would contain a continuous narrative (*The *Old Curiosity Shop*) linked by the reminiscences of the narrator, Master Humphrey. This device was soon dropped, as was the periodical's title after the publication in weekly numbers of **Barnaby Rudge* (1841).

Master of Ballantrae, The: *A Winter's Tale* A novel by Robert Louis *Stevenson, published 1889. A powerful study of fraternal jealousy, this is the story of the lifelong feud between the master of Ballantrae, violent, unscrupulous, elegant, and courageous, and his brother Henry, at the outset a quiet, dull, honest young man. The master joins Prince Charles Edward in the 1745 rebellion, disappears after Culloden, and is believed dead. After many adventures the master returns, with a price on his head, to find that Henry has appropriated his place and his intended bride. He embarks on a course of persecution, first in Scotland then in America, which brings both brothers to a melodramatic grave in the Adirondack Mountains in the north-eastern region of New York, where Stevenson first conceived the story. The extravagant action and the hints of the supernatural are rendered more plausible by the dour character of the narrator, the loyal Ephraim Mackellar.

MASTERS, Edgar Lee (?1868–1950) American writer, born in Kansas, who is best known for his collection of poems *Spoon River Anthology* (1915), which consists of dramatic monologues spoken from beyond the grave by the inhabitants of a Midwestern cemetery. His biographical studies included volumes on Walt *Whitman and Mark *Twain.

MATHER, Cotton (1663–1728) American Presbyterian minister of Boston, Massachusetts, and voluminous writer, among whose works *Wonders of the Invisible World* (1693) celebrates the divine mission of the settlers in America. He was noted for the part he played in the Salem witchcraft trials of 1692, on which he commented in his best-known work, *Magnalia Christi Americana* (1702), a series of biographical and historical portraits. See Barrett Wendell, *Cotton Mather: A Biography* (1993).

MATHESON, Richard (1926–) American author of novels, short stories, and screenplays; born in New Jersey. The fusion of *science fiction and *horror in *I Am Legend* (1954: several times filmed), and the tension in stories like 'Duel' (1971: also filmed) influenced writers like Stephen *King.

MATHEWS, Harry (1930–) The only American member of *OuLiPo. His early fictions, such as *The Conversions* (1962) and *Tlooth* (1966), offer a compendium of eccentric narratives and sophisticated word-play. His recent novels, *Cigarettes* (1987) and *The Journalist* (1994), are just as inventive and bewildering, but explore more recognizable American contexts. In these works Mathews disguises the formal constraints underlying his plots and characters. Mathews has also written a number of shorter, more obviously experimental texts, such as 'Their Words, for You' (1977) which consists wholly of scrambled proverbs. Mathews's poetry (collected in *A Mid-Season Sky*, 1992) again employs rigid conventions as a means of embodying the surrealism of everyday life.

MATHIAS, Thomas James (?1754–1835) Clergyman and Tory satirist. He published anonymously in 1794 the first part of *The Pursuits of Literature*, a work which went through sixteen editions, in which he satirizes many contemporary authors, most of them radicals; other parts followed in 1797. A lover of Italy, he spent his last years at Naples.

matter A term derived from French *matière*, sometimes used by modern scholars to refer to medieval romances. It has its origins in the work of Jean Bodel (late 12th–early 13th century), a writer of *fabliaux* and *chansons de geste*. In the *Chanson de Saisnes*, he used phrases equivalent to 'matter of Rome', 'matter of France', and 'matter of Britain' to denote the subject matter of romances. The first category denoted stories from Greek and Roman mythology. The second category was concerned with Frankish events, and was used by Jean to refer specifically to romances concerned with the emperor *Charlemagne and his circle. The third category denoted Arthurian subject matter. These three categories are often used to denote a cycle of stories. Typical of the matter of Rome are stories about *Alexander the Great, a popular hero in the Middle Ages. The matter of France, which often celebrates conflicts between the Franks and the Saracens, includes *chansons de geste* that fall into sub-groups: that is, narratives pertaining to Charlemagne himself, other knights, and rebels, respectively. The *Chanson de Roland* is one of the best-known narratives from the first group. The matter of Britain contains the *Brut foundation myth and the Arthurian chronicle tradition pioneered by *Geoffrey of Monmouth. Scholars have recently gone further than Bodel, adding the term 'matter of England' to refer to romances concerned with English heroes or localized in England (such as *King Horn, *Havelok the Dane, *Bevis of Hampton, and *Athelstan). See the discussion in W. R. J. Barron, *English Medieval Romance* (1987).

MATTHEW, St *See* BIBLE; EVANGELISTS.

MATTHIESSEN, Peter (1927–) Travel writer, novelist, and naturalist. Educated at the Hotchkiss School, Connecticut, and Yale University, he co-founded the *Paris Review* in 1953, with George Plimpton, Donald Hall, and others. Matthiessen has since admitted that he was a CIA operative at this time, but claims that he soon left the agency. He is the author of several novels, including *At Play in the Fields of the Lord* (1965; subsequently filmed in 1991), the highly experimental *Far Tortuga* (1975), and *Killing Mr Watson* (1990). However, it is for his travel writing that he is best known. His many works in this genre include *The Cloud Forest* (1961), the National Book Award-winning *The Snow Leopard* (1978), and *Sand Rivers* (1981). They combine a strong environmentalist ethic and considerable scientific rigour with a sense of spiritual reverence and self-enquiry that derives from Matthiessen's interest in Zen Buddhism.

MATURIN, Charles (1780–1824) Novelist and dramatist, educated at Trinity College, Dublin. A Protestant of French Huguenot stock, he took holy orders and for a time kept a school. He was a curate at St Patrick's Cathedral, Dublin, and claimed that he became a writer because he had failed to progress as a clergyman. He was an important *'Gothic' novelist. He published *The Fatal Revenge* in 1807; *The Wild Irish Boy* in 1808; and *The Milesian Chief* in 1811. In 1816 his tragedy **Bertram* was successfully produced by Edmund *Kean at Drury Lane, on the recommendation of Walter *Scott and Lord *Byron. His next two tragedies, *Manuel* (1817) and *Fredolfo* (1819), failed. He then returned to novels, publishing *Women, or Pour et Contre* (1818) and his most memorable work, **Melmoth the Wanderer* (1820). The anti-Catholicism of this novel was made explicit in his *Five Sermons on the*

Errors of the Roman Catholic Church (1824). His last novel, *The Albigenses*, appeared in 1824.

Maud A poem by Alfred *Tennyson, published 1855, composed 1854, but springing from the germ of the lyric 'Oh! that 'twere possible', composed 1833–4. The poem is a monodrama in sections of different metres, in which the morbid narrator describes the progress of his emotions: first describing his father's death and his family's ruin, both contrived by the old lord of the Hall; then expressing his growing love for Maud, the old lord's daughter, and the scorn of her brother, who wishes her to marry a vapid 'new-made' lord. He secures a meeting with Maud, but they are interrupted and her brother is killed in the subsequent fight. He escapes abroad, goes mad; and finally reawakens to apparent hope in fighting in the Crimean War. The poem contains several of Tennyson's best-known lyrics ('I have led her home', 'Come into the garden, Maud'), but there was much debate on its first publication as to whether it was pro- or anti-war. Tennyson insisted that it was, first and foremost, *dramatic*, but the disagreements led him to refer to it as 'poor *Maud*'. It was always his favourite poem to read aloud.

MAUGHAM, W. Somerset (1874–1965) Writer and playwright, born in Paris and educated at King's School, Canterbury, and in Heidelberg, before training as a doctor in London; his first novel, *Liza of Lambeth* (1897), drew on his experiences of slum life during this period. It was followed by *Mrs Craddock* (1902) and *The Merry-Go-Round* (1904), but neither was a success. He achieved fame in 1907 with *Lady Frederick*, and in 1908 had four plays running in London. Primarily homosexual, he married in 1917 (dissolved 1929), but spent little time with his wife. More importantly, he had met Gerald Haxton (1892–1944) in 1914; in 1916 they set off for the South Seas together and further travels to China, Asia, and Mexico followed. In 1927 Maugham bought a house on the French Riviera, which became both a home for Haxton and himself and a meeting place for writers and politicians.

Maugham wrote over 30 plays, including *Our Betters* (1917); *Home and Beauty* (1919); *The Circle* (1921), the story of a young wife who elopes with a rubber planter from Malaya; *East of Suez* (1922); *The Constant Wife* (1926), in which a woman takes revenge on her unfaithful husband and departs for Italy with an old admirer; *The Sacred Flame* (1928); and the anti-war drama *For Services Rendered* (1932). His best-known novel, *Of Human Bondage* (1915), describes Philip Carey's lonely boyhood and subsequent experiences with a prostitute: Carey is burdened with a club foot just as Maugham had to struggle with a severe stammer. *The Moon and Sixpence* (1919) recounts the life of Charles Strickland, a Gauguinesque artist who neglects duty for art, and *The Painted Veil* (1925) is a tale of love and cholera in China which was as well received as *Cakes and Ale* (1930), a comedy about the good-natured wife of a grand old man of letters, Edward Driffield, whom many took to be based on the recently deceased Thomas *Hardy. *The Razor's Edge* (1944) takes a mystical turn, as its American hero learns the value of non-attachment in an Indian ashram. *A Writer's Notebook* (1949) consists of extracts from notes which Maugham had kept from the age of 18.

Maugham also wrote many successful short stories: 'Rain', set in Samoa (*The Trembling of a Leaf*, 1921), tells of the conflict between a life-affirming prostitute, Sadie Thompson, and a repressed missionary, while 'The Alien Corn' (*Six Stories in the First Person Singular*, 1931) is about a pianist who commits suicide when he realizes he will never transcend the second rate. In 1954 Maugham was created a Companion of Honour but claimed to take the view, expressed in his autobiography, *The Summing Up* (1938), that he stood 'in the very first row of the second-raters', an opinion which has been largely shared by critics. Nevertheless, much of his writing remains in print and many of his works have been adapted for television and the cinema, including three films of *The Painted Veil* (1934, 1957, and 2006). See Bryan Connon, *Somerset Maugham and the Maugham Dynasty* (1997).

MAUPASSANT, Guy de (1850–93) French short story writer and novelist, a member of the so-called 'groupe de Médan', the group of young writers supposedly influenced by Émile *Zola and *naturalism. He contributed *Boule de suif* (*Ball of Fat*) to *Les Soirées de Médan*, a collection of tales, narrating incidents from the Franco-Prussian War, intended to promote the ideals of the 'groupe de Médan'. His numerous stories typically deal with country folk or urban employees and civil servants, though other social groups (aristocrats, prostitutes, soldiers) also appear; many of these were reworked and appear in collections such as *La Maison Tellier* (1881: *The Tellier House*), *Miss Harriet* (1884), *Le Horla* (1887), and *L'Inutile Beauté* (1890: *Useless Beauty*), and they earned for him a reputation in the English-speaking world as the 'French Chekhov', with translations appearing as early as 1887. He also wrote six novels, of which the best known are *Une vie* (1883: *A Life*), *Bel-Ami* (1885), and *Pierre et Jean* (1888), which have also been much translated.

MAUPIN, Armistead (1944–) American writer, best known for a sequence of six comic novels depicting alternative lifestyles in *San Francisco: Tales of the City* (1978), *More Tales of the City* (1980), *Further Tales of the City* (1982), *Babycakes* (1984), *Significant Others* (1987), and *Sure of You* (1989). Beginning life as a daily newspaper serial, this joyous **roman-fleuve* about the inhabitants of a bohemian boarding house broke new ground in its high-spirited celebration of gay sub-cultures. Maupin was also one of the first writers to chronicle the Aids epidemic. *Maybe the Moon* (1992) was a more muted satire on hypocrisy in the film business

MAURIAC, François (1885–1970) French Catholic novelist. His best-known works, which powerfully explore the constraints of bourgeois convention, religion, and human frailty, are *Thérèse Desqueyroux* (1927), *Le Nœud de vipères* (1932: *Nest of Vipers*), and *Le Mystère Frontenac* (1933: *The Frontenac Mystery*), all of which were translated by Gerard Hopkins.

He also wrote poetry and plays, and enjoyed success as a high-profile journalist. He was awarded the *Nobel Prize in 1952.

MAURICE, F. D. (John Frederick Denison) (1805–72) Churchman and reformer, educated at Trinity Hall, Cambridge. He was ordained as an Anglican priest in 1834. *The Kingdom of Christ* (1838) was a plea for Christian unity. In 1840 he became professor of English literature and history at King's College London. His belief in the application of Christian principles to social reform gained him many followers; he became a leader of the Christian Socialist movement, which brought him into close contact with Charles *Kingsley. His *Theological Essays* (1835) presented his unorthodox views on Eternal Punishment and caused his dismissal from King's College. In 1854 he founded a Working Men's College, and was its first principal. In 1866 he became professor of moral philosophy at Cambridge. John *Ruskin regarded him as a fine mind lost to theology.

MAUROIS, André (1885–1967) Pseudonym of Émile Herzog, French author of *biography, whose subjects include P. B. *Shelley (*Ariel*, 1923, which appeared as the first *Penguin paperback in 1935), Benjamin *Disraeli (1927), Lord *Byron (1930), Ivan *Turgenev (1931), Marcel *Proust (1949), and George *Sand (1952). He also wrote histories of England (1937) and the United States (1948), as well as two novels which draw upon his experience with British troops during the First World War: *Les Silences du colonel Bramble* (1918: *The Silences of Colonel Bramble*) and *Les Discours du docteur O'Grady* (1922: *The Speeches of Dr O'Grady*).

MAWSON, Sir Douglas (1882–1958) Scientist and Antarctic explorer, born at Shipley, Yorkshire, son of a draper of old yeoman stock who migrated to Australia in 1884. He attended Fort Street School, Sydney, studied engineering, chemistry, and geology at the University of Sydney, and obtained a lectureship, later a chair, at the University of Adelaide. After geological surveys in Vanuatu, he joined Ernest *Shackleton's 1907 Antarctic expedition, climbing the Mount Erebus volcano and reaching the south magnetic pole. He rejected Robert *Scott's offer of a place in his ill-fated polar expedition, but organized his own Australasian Antarctic Expedition of 1911–14, widely recognized as scientifically the most valuable of all the early expeditions. Sledging in crevasse-infested George V Land, two companions were killed; his lone return trek, told in *The Home of the Blizzard* (1915), was an epic survival story. He led the British, Australian, and New Zealand Antarctic Research Expedition of 1929–31 which resulted in Australia's annexation of the largest portion of Antarctica. See Philip Ayres, *Mawson* (1999).

MAX MÜLLER, Friedrich (1823–1900) Philologist and mythographer, son of the Romantic German poet Wilhelm Müller. He came to England in 1846 and became a British subject. He was commissioned by the East India Company to bring out an edition of the Sanskrit *Rigveda* which was published in 1849–73, and was acknowledged for many years as a leading authority on Indian culture. He settled in Oxford in 1848 and was Taylorian professor of modern European languages from 1854 to 1868, and a curator of the Bodleian Library, 1856–63 and 1881–94. Max Müller delivered two remarkable courses of lectures on 'The Science of Languages' at the Royal Institution in 1861–4, and was professor of comparative philology at Oxford from 1868 until his death. He devoted much attention to comparative mythology and the comparative study of religions. His views on solar mythology interested a number of contemporary writers, including George *Eliot and John *Ruskin. A full edition of his works was published in 1903; see also Lourens P. van den Bosch, *Friedrich Max Müller: A Life Devoted to the Humanities* (2002).

MAXWELL, Gavin (1914–69) Writer, traveller, and conservationist, educated at Stowe School and Hertford College, Oxford, where he studied estate management. He is best remembered for *Ring of Bright Water* (1960), a poignant evocation of life on the remote Scottish coast and of his relationship with two semi-tame otters; his other works include travel writings and the autobiographical *The House of Elrig* (1965).

MAXWELL, Glyn (1962–) Poet and dramatist, born in Welwyn Garden City and educated at Oxford. Versatile and prolific, he followed his first collection *Tale of the Mayor's Son* (1990) with *Out of the Rain* (1992), and *Rest for the Wicked* (1995): he ranges from classical myth to contemporary satire and surreal speculation. Many of the poems in *The Breakage* (1998) dwell on the First World War. His novel *Blue Burneau* (1994) is a political fantasy set on an imaginary island. He has written several verse dramas, encouraged by Derek *Walcott, with whom he studied at Boston: three of them were published as *Gnyss the Magnificent* (1995). *Moon Country* (1996), written with Simon *Armitage, describes a journey to Iceland in the footsteps of W. H. *Auden and Louis *MacNeice. Recent work includes *Time's Fool: A Tale in Verse* (2000), *The Nerve* (2002), and *The Sugar Mile* (2005), a poem for many voices.

MAY, Julian (1931–) American *science fiction author, born in Chicago. Her fiction explores humanity's prehistory and myth. Her epic style in novels such as *The Many-Coloured Land* (1981) and *Intervention* (1987), as well as her more recent *Conqueror's Moon* (2003), crosses into that of *fantasy.

MAY, Thomas (1596–1650) Writer and historian, educated at Sidney Sussex College, Cambridge. He adopted the Parliamentary cause and was secretary for the Parliament (1646). He was the author of two narrative poems on the reigns of Edward III and Henry II, a history of the Long Parliament (1647), translations of *Virgil's *Georgics* and *Lucan's *Pharsalia* (which were praised by Ben *Jonson), two comedies, *The Heir* and *The Old Couple* (*c.*1620), and three tragedies on classical subjects. May seems to have hoped to succeed Jonson as laureate in 1637, and transferred his allegiance from court to Parliament when Sir William *D'Avenant obtained the post; this is why Andrew *Marvell, in 'Tom May's Death' (1681), writes of his 'Most servile wit and mercenary pen'.

MAYHEW, Henry (1812–87) Playwright, journalist, and social reformer, the son of a London solicitor, educated at Westminster School, from which he ran away. He was briefly articled to his father before becoming a dramatist and journalist. The first of his many plays and farces (some very successful) was *The Wandering Minstrel* (1834). In 1841 he was a co-founder and briefly a joint editor of **Punch*. He wrote many novels and stories, as well as books on science, religion, education, and travel, including works on Germany and the Rhine (where he briefly lived), and *The Boyhood of Martin Luther* (1865). But he is chiefly remembered for the philanthropic journalism to which he turned at the end of the 1840s; his remarkable series of 82 articles, couched as lengthy 'letters', in the **Morning Chronicle* were published with some alterations as *London Labour and the London Poor* (1851). His painstaking investigations into the plight of the poor revealed the extent to which starvation, disease, and transportation were daily horrors, and the work remains essential reading for those interested in the social conditions of the period. He performed similar work on the subject of prisons, publishing *The Criminal Prisons of London* (1862) and *London Children* (1874). His plain but harrowing descriptions, often using the words of those he spoke with, did much to stir the public conscience towards reform.

MAYNE, William (1928–) Born in Hull and educated at Canterbury Cathedral Choir School. The most distinctive stylist in British children's literature of the 20th century, Mayne produced over 100 books from *Follow the Footprints* (1954), including many subtle studies of family relationships, and distinguished fantasies such as *Earthfasts* (1967). *A Grass Rope* (1957) won the Carnegie Medal and *Low Tide* (1993) the Guardian Award. His literary reputation was damaged by his imprisonment for sexual assaults on children in 2004.

MAYNE-REID, 'Captain' Thomas *See* REID, 'CAPTAIN' THOMAS MAYNE.

Mayor of Casterbridge, The: *A Story of Character* A tragic novel by Thomas *Hardy, published 1886. Michael Henchard, a hay-trusser, gets drunk at a fair and sells his wife and child for five guineas to a sailor, Newson. When sober again he takes a solemn vow not to touch alcohol for twenty years. By his energy and acumen he becomes rich, respected, and eventually the mayor of Casterbridge. After eighteen years his wife returns, supposing Newson dead, and is reunited with her husband. She brings with her her daughter Elizabeth-Jane, and Henchard is led to believe that she is his child, whereas she is in fact Newson's. Through a combination of unhappy circumstances, and the impulsive obstinacy of Henchard, troubles accumulate. He quarrels with his capable young assistant in his corn business, Donald Farfrae. Mrs Henchard dies and Henchard learns the truth about the girl. Farfrae becomes his successful rival, both in business and in love, and marries Lucetta, whom Henchard had hoped to win. Soon Henchard's business is ruined, the story of the sale of his wife is revealed, and he takes again to heavy drinking. Farfrae now has Henchard's business, his house, and Lucetta, while Henchard works as a labourer in his yard. Eventually Farfrae becomes mayor, the office Henchard once held. His stepdaughter is his only comfort, then Newson returns and claims her and after Lucetta's death Farfrae marries her. Thus he possesses all that was once Henchard's. Henchard becomes lonelier and more desolate, and dies wretchedly in a hut on Egdon Heath.

Measure for Measure A tragicomedy by *Shakespeare, probably written in the summer of 1604, but not printed until the first *folio (1623). It seems that the version that has come down to us has undergone adaptation, probably by Thomas *Middleton. Its chief source is George *Whetstone's play *Promos and Cassandra*, itself based on a story in *Cinzio's *Hecatommithi*. It has often been categorized as a 'problem play' because of its concern with sexual and political morality and the complexity of its plot and themes.

The duke of Vienna, on the pretext of a journey to Poland, hands over the government to his virtuous-seeming deputy Angelo, who enforces strict laws against sexual licence which for the past fourteen years had been neglected. Angelo immediately sentences to death Claudio, a young gentleman who has made Julietta pregnant. Claudio's sister Isabella, who is a novice in a sisterhood of nuns, pleads with Angelo for her brother's life, urged on by Claudio's friend Lucio. Angelo responds to her pleas by offering to spare Claudio's life if she will sleep with him. Isabella refuses, and will not be persuaded even by the desperate entreaties of Claudio in prison. The duke, disguised as a friar, has made a visit of spiritual comfort to Claudio, and now devises a way of saving his life. Isabella is to agree to a midnight assignation with Angelo, but her place is to be taken by Mariana, who was betrothed to Angelo and still loves him. Mariana is first seen listening to the song 'Take, O, take those lips away'. This scheme is successful, but Angelo still proceeds with the order for Claudio's execution, though unknown to Isabella Claudio is saved by the substitution of the head of Ragozine, a pirate, who has died that night in the same prison. The duke lays by his disguise, simulates a return to Vienna, and pretends to disbelieve the complaints of Isabella and suit of Mariana, in favour of Angelo's hypocritical denial. When Angelo is forced to confess, both Mariana and Isabella plead for his life; Mariana is married to Angelo, Lucio to a whore, and the duke proposes marriage to the novice Isabella. She makes no reply. For the theory that Middleton adapted the text, see J. Jowett and G. Taylor, *Shakespeare Re-shaped, 1606–1623* (1993); G. Taylor, 'Shakespeare's Mediterranean *Measure for Measure*', in T. Clayton *et al.* (eds), *Shakespeare and the Mediterranean* (2004).

Medal, The A poem by John *Dryden, published 1682. The earl of *Shaftesbury, who is represented in **Absalom and Achitophel* and possibly in **Mr Limberham*, was acquitted of high treason in 1681, and a medal was struck to commemorate the event. Dryden's response includes savage attacks on Shaftesbury himself, the City, and the Commons. It predicts the constitutional instability which was to beset the country in the ensuing 30 years. Thomas *Shadwell and Samuel Pordage (1633–?91) both wrote replies.

MEDICI Family that were de facto rulers of Florence 1434–94, 1512–27; dukes of Tuscany from 1530 and grand dukes from 1569 to 1737. The earlier Medici were great patrons of art and literature, chief among them **Cosimo** (1389–1464) and **Lorenzo 'the Magnificent'** (*c.*1449–1492), founders of the Medicean or Laurentian Library. The latter, himself a poet, was father of Pope *Leo X, **Giovanni de' Medici**. **Cathérine de Médicis**, as she is known in France (1519–89), daughter of the grandson of Lorenzo the Magnificent, was consort of Henry II of France, and regent during the minority of Charles IX; her rule there was the source of much of the anti-Italian feeling embodied in the myth of the *Machiavellian politician. **Marie de Médicis** (1573–1642), niece of Francesco, the first grand duke, was consort of Henry IV of France from 1600 and regent 1610–17. There is a life of Lorenzo by William *Roscoe (1795).

MEE, Sir Arthur (1875–1943) Writer and editor. Born in Stapleford, Nottinghamshire, he left school at 14. He is remembered for the *Children's Encyclopedia*, which he conceived in 1919 and edited until his death. He also founded the *Children's Newspaper*, and wrote numerous instructional books and series about important figures and places.

MEHTA, Gita *See* ANGLO-INDIAN LITERATURE.

MEHTA, Ved Prakash (1934–) Indian writer and journalist (now an American citizen), born near Lahore, and educated at the Dadar School for the Blind in Bombay (Mumbai), Balliol College, Oxford, and at Harvard. His works include several studies of Indian life and autobiographical and biographical memoirs, including *Face to Face* (1957), *Daddyji* (1972), *Mamaji* (1979), *Vedi* (1982), *The Ledge between the Streams* (1984), *Sound-Shadows of the New World* (1986), and *The Stolen Light* (1989)—a series now collectively entitled *Continents of Exile. Fly and the Fly-Bottle* (1963) is a personal account of meetings with various British intellectuals, including Isaiah Berlin (1909–97), A. J. Ayer (1910–89), A. J. P. *Taylor, and Iris *Murdoch, originally published in the **New Yorker*, to which he was a regular contributor. *Delinquent Chacha* (1966), a comic novel, satirizes Indians indigenized to English life.

meiosis An understatement, sometimes ironical or humorous and intended to emphasize the size, importance, and so on of what is belittled. Except in *litotes, which is a form of meiosis, the use of meiosis is chiefly colloquial (e.g. 'He's doing all right out of it'; 'That must be worth a few bob').

Meistersinger A title taken in the 15th century by certain professional German poet musicians whose work could be either secular or religious in nature. They were often respected master craftsmen in ordinary trades such as weaving and shoemaking. Their craft, and they themselves, were governed by an elaborate set of guild rules, affectionately depicted in Richard *Wagner's opera *Die Meistersinger von Nürnberg* (1868). There were numerous 'schools' located in different cities and they flourished mainly in the first half of the 16th century. Their work represents a phase in the development of bourgeois literature away from the courtly *Minnesang* (*see* MINNESÄNGER).

MELANCHTHON (1497–1560) The Greek form of the name of Philip Schwartzerd, German humanist who was professor of Greek at Wittenberg University and one of the principal advocates of the *Reformation. In 1553 the government of Edward VI instructed Thomas *Cranmer to invite Melanchthon to a position at Cambridge University with a view to drawing up a confession of faith for the Protestant church. Possibly due to the accession of the Catholic Queen Mary the offer was not taken up.

'Melibeus, The Tale of' *See* CANTERBURY TALES, 18.

Melincourt, *or Sir Oran Haut-ton* A satire by Thomas Love *Peacock, published 1817. One of the most ambitious of Peacock's books, it has a more novelistic plot than the others, featuring the abduction and threatened rape of a rich young heiress, Anthelia Melincourt. The plot, which is indebted to Richardson's **Clarissa* and to Thomas *Holcroft's *Memoirs: Anna St Ives*, has strong feminist implications. Anthelia is rescued by a humorous variant on the Noble Savage, Sir Oran Haut-ton (*see* MONBODDO, JAMES BURNETT), an orang-utan whom the hero, Mr Sylvan Forester, has educated to everything except speech, and for whom he has bought a seat in Parliament. Sir Oran is affectionate and chivalrous and plays delightfully on the flute. His virtues show up the corruptions of 'advanced' society. Forester, whose idealist views resemble P. B. *Shelley's literary brand of radicalism, debates with Mr Fax, a Malthusian economist, such causes as rotten boroughs, paper currency, slavery, and the recent conservatism of the *Lake Poets. Provoked by an 1816 article by Robert *Southey in the **Quarterly Review*, Peacock censures Southey himself (Mr Feathernest), S. T. *Coleridge (Mr Mystic), William *Wordsworth (Mr Paperstamp), and William *Gifford, the editor of the *Quarterly* (Mr Vamp), as a group of political traitors.

Melmoth the Wanderer A novel by Charles *Maturin, published 1820. This work, which was praised by writers as diverse as W. M. *Thackeray, D. G. *Rossetti, and Charles *Baudelaire, is a powerful *Gothic novel. Melmoth, who has sold his soul for the promise of prolonged life, offers relief from suffering to each of the characters, whose terrible stories succeed one another, if they will take over his bargain with the devil. However, Stanton, imprisoned in the cell of a raving lunatic, Moncada, in the hands of the Inquisition, Walberg, who sees his children dying of hunger, and many other sufferers all reject the proposed bargain. After his trial Oscar *Wilde adopted the name Sebastian Melmoth.

melodrama A kind of sensational drama that flourished in the 19th century, noted for its simplified division of characters between the virtuous and the vicious and for its strong emotional impact in scenes of virtue in distress. Douglas *Jerrold's *Black-Ey'd Susan* (1829) and Dion *Boucicault's *The Colleen Bawn* (1860) are notable examples. This stage tradition had some influence upon 19th-century novels, especially those of Charles *Dickens, and on early 20th-century cinema. The term originally referred to musical plays of the kind performed in the unlicensed theatres (*see* CENSORSHIP) of the early 19th century.

MELVILLE, Herman (1819–91) American novelist and poet, born in New York City. After his father's business failure and death in 1832 Melville left school and was largely an autodidact, devouring *Shakespeare, the King James *Bible, and 17th-century meditative writers such as Sir Thomas *Browne, as well as the numerous historical, anthropological, and technical works which he used to supplement his experiences when he wrote. After sailing as a 'boy' on a packet to Liverpool in 1839, Melville shipped in 1841 on the whaler *Acushnet* for the South Seas, where he jumped ship, joined the US navy, and finally returned three years later to begin writing. The fictionalized travel narrative of *Typee, or A Peep at Polynesian Life* (1846) was Melville's most popular book during his lifetime. Like most of his works, *Typee* was published first in Britain, for prestige and to guard against piracy, and throughout his career Melville enjoyed a rather higher estimation in Britain than in America. After a well-received sequel, *Omoo: A Narrative of Adventures in the South Seas* (1847), the perfunctorily plotted *Mardi and a Voyage Thither* (1849), an allegorical romance with philosophical meditations, fared less well.

Having married the daughter of a Massachusetts chief justice in 1847, and with a mother, sisters, and eventually four children to support, Melville wrote the realistic sea stories *Redburn: His First Voyage* (1849) and *White-Jacket, or The World in a Man-of-War* (1850), which he considered potboilers. Inspired by the achievement of Nathaniel *Hawthorne, Melville changed his next sea tale into **Moby-Dick, or The Whale* (1851), a prose epic combining Shakespearian tragedy with encyclopedic sea lore. After the critical disaster of *Pierre, or The Ambiguities* (1852), a *Gothic romance and satire on the literary profession, Melville wrote anonymous magazine stories, among them *'Bartleby the Scrivener', and *'Benito Cereno', which were collected in *The Piazza Tales* (1856), and the historical novel *Israel Potter: His Fifty Years of Exile* (1855) about a neglected hero of the American Revolution. To recover from a breakdown he undertook a long journey to Europe and the Holy Land (depicted in the narrative poem *Clarel*, 1876). Sceptical and tormented, but unable to discard his Manichaean (*see* GNOSTICISM) view of God, Melville remarked while visiting Hawthorne in Liverpool in 1856, 'I have just about made up my mind to be annihilated.' *The *Confidence-Man: His Masquerade* (1857), a mordantly nihilistic satire of human gullibility, was Melville's last novel. After unsuccessful lecture tours, he worked as customs officer in New York harbour, where he wrote *Battle-Pieces and Aspects of the War* (1865), trenchant poems of disillusion with Civil War era America. Despite some revival of interest in Britain, Melville died virtually forgotten, with **Billy Budd, Foretopman* only being published in 1924. After long neglect, Melville's oeuvre is now recognized for its experiments in different genres and its exploration of metaphysical issues. See the definitive Northwestern-Newberry edition of Melville's works (1968–). Hershel Parker's *Herman Melville* (1996/2002) remains the seminal biography, supplemented by Jey Leyda's *The Melville Log* (1951).

memoir-novel An early form of the novel, purporting to be true, and often including diaries and journals, but in fact largely or wholly fictitious. The author appears, if at all, merely as 'editor' of another's memoirs. Daniel *Defoe, with **Robinson Crusoe* (1719) and **Moll Flanders* (1722), was the first English master.
See NOVEL.

Memoirs of a Cavalier A fictional military memoir generally ascribed to Daniel *Defoe, published 1724. The narrator, 'Col. Andrew Newport', travels in 1630 to Vienna, and accompanies the army of Ferdinand II, Holy Roman emperor, to the siege and sacking of Magdeburg. Under Gustavus Adolphus he participates in many battles of the Thirty Years War. Returning to England, he joins Charles I's army, first against the Scots, then against the forces of Parliament, being present at the battle of Edgehill, the relief of York, and the battle of Naseby. In *The Gathering Storm* (1948), Sir Winston *Churchill claimed to have adopted from the *Memoirs* his method of hanging 'the chronicle and discussion of great military and political events upon the thread of the personal experience of an individual'.

Memoirs of a Woman of Pleasure Often known as *Fanny Hill*, a novel by John *Cleland, published 1748–9. It was completed while Cleland was confined for debt in the Fleet Prison. The story of Fanny's misfortunes, her descent into prostitution, and her eventual recovery to a happy marriage is recounted in a lively, breathless style, as a vehicle for Cleland's absorbed examination of sexual desire, in both men and women, in its many varieties and in minute but always carefully euphemistic physiological detail. After being ruled obscene, the book was not published openly in Britain until the 1970s.

MENANDER (342/1–*c.*290 BC) Poet of the Attic New Comedy. Nearly a hundred titles are recorded. Papyrus discoveries—Menander was much read in Egypt—have restored one whole play, *Dyscolus* ('Mr Grumpy'), and substantial portions of *Epitrepontes* ('The Arbitration'), *Perikeiromene* ('He Cut her Hair off!'), *Sikyonius* ('The Man from Sicyon'), *Aspis* ('The Shield'), *Samia* ('The Girl from Samos'), and *Phasma* ('The Ghost'). His comedy renounces the boisterousness, fantasy, and obscenity of *Aristophanes. Menander was famous for truth to life: less in his plots, full of long-lost heirs and abducted daughters, than in his deft dialogue and psychologically perceptive characterization. His plays, popular classics in later antiquity, were fashionable in Rome, where *Plautus and *Terence translated and adapted some to Roman taste. *The *Importance of Being Earnest* is a last, brilliant, echo, complete with a lost-and-found baby. Another New Comedy staple, the *servus callidus*—the servant cleverer than his master—has proved persistent; examples include *Mozart's Figaro, or P. G. *Wodehouse's Jeeves.

Men and Women A collection of 51 poems by Robert *Browning, published in two volumes, 1855. The poems date from the period after Browning's marriage in 1846, and express a new-found energy and confidence—'poems of all sorts and sizes and styles and subjects', as he said, adding, 'I hope to be listened to, this time.' The volumes made their way slowly. The poems show Browning's mind at its most multitudinous and eclectic, ranging over history, art, philosophy, and religion; they include many of his most celebrated dramatic monologues, such as 'Fra Lippo Lippi', 'Bishop Blougram's Apology', 'Andrea del Sarto', and 'Cleon', whose effect is based on the fusion of an intensely realized situation, a powerful sense of personality, and a density of ideas. The collection also includes 'Love among the Ruins', and the challenging *'"Childe Roland to the Dark Tower Came"'. The collection closes with an address to Elizabeth Barrett *Browning, 'One Word More' (a phrase picked up during their correspondence in 1845–6).

Menaphon A popular prose romance with *interludes of verse by Robert *Greene, published 1589. Thomas *Nashe's preface to the first edition offered a satirical survey of contemporary literature.

The romance recounts the adventures of the princess Sephestia, shipwrecked on the coast of Arcadia. The convention of impenetrable disguise is taken to ridiculous lengths as Sephestia, disguised as Samela, is wooed simultaneously by her father and her teenage son, while herself carrying on a love affair with her (disguised) husband. Her fourth lover is the shepherd Menaphon of the title. Some charming lyrics, including the cradle song 'Weep not my wanton, smile upon my knee', diversify the intricate narrative.

MENCKEN, H. L. (Henry Louis) (1880–1956) American journalist and critic, born in Baltimore, who, through the pages of the *Smart Set* and the *American Mercury*, exercised a great influence on American taste, attacking its Puritanism and hypocrisy. He was influenced in his iconoclastic approach by Friedrich *Nietzsche and Mark *Twain. He strongly supported American writers like Theodore *Dreiser and Sherwood *Anderson, and in 1919 published *The American Language*, documenting its vigour from multi-ethnic sources. His essays were published as *Prejudices* in six series (1919–27). See Marion Elizabeth Rodgers, *Mencken: The American Iconoclast* (2005).

MENDELSSOHN(-BARTHOLDY), Felix (1809–47) German composer, whose most popular work is one of the most famous compositions inspired by Shakespeare, the incidental music to *A *Midsummer Night's Dream*. Mendelssohn read Shakespeare from an early age in the translations by *Schlegel, and wrote the overture at the age of 17 for performance at home. The remaining numbers, including the Scherzo, the Nocturne, and the Wedding March, were added for a stage performance in Berlin (1843). This remained Mendelssohn's only completed contribution to Shakespeare music; an early project for an opera on *The *Tempest* never came to fruition. Mendelssohn made many visits to Britain, the first of which included a trip to Scotland which inspired the overture *The Hebrides* and the 'Scottish' Symphony: the latter was dedicated to Queen *Victoria, who sang some of his songs, with the composer at the piano, in 1842. He also set a passage from **Fingal* (1847). Another outcome of his English connection was the oratorio *Elijah* (1846), modelled on *Handel and originally written to a German text. He wrote some anthems to English words, of which 'Hear my Prayer' (containing 'O for the wings of a dove') is the best known. There are settings of Walter *Scott, but few other songs with English words. The eight books of *Songs without Words* were staple repertoire for the Victorian amateur pianist.

MENEGHELLO, Luigi (1922–2007) Italian novelist and professor at the University of Reading. His novels *Libera nos a malo* (1963: *Free us from Evil*) and *I piccoli maestri* (1964: *The Outlaws*), and *Pomo pero* (1974: *Eeny Meeny*), a commentary on *Libera nos a malo*, mix fiction, autobiography, and social comment with memories, including of the Resistance against *Fascism. His extreme linguistic self-consciousness draws on a variety of stylistic registers and language (including English), making him one of the most original writers to have emerged from post-war Italy. His last work, *La materia di Reading* (1997), draws on his experiences as founder professor of the Department of Italian Studies in that university.

Menelaus *See* ILIAD.

MENEN, Aubrey Clarence (1912–89) Indo-Irish writer, born in London, educated at the University of London (1930–32). He worked as a dramatist and in radio (1934–6) before visiting India at the outbreak of the Second World War, where he spent the next years broadcasting for the Indian information service. Drawing on his experiences as an education officer in a remote part of India, Menen's first novel *The Prevalence of Witches* (1947), an argumentative satire of religion and imperialism, is set in the mythical Indian state of Limbo, an obscure outpost of the empire. Drawing comparisons with Aldous *Huxley, Anatole *France, and Evelyn *Waugh, Menen published several more novels, an autobiography, and semi-autobiographical essays, all with Chatto and Windus.

Menippean satire A form of humorous writing, lighter and less censorious than satire proper, and characterized by miscellaneous erudition in the comical treatment of philosophical and otherwise intellectual topics. The term derives from the 3rd-century Greek philosopher Menippus, whose works were known and imitated by later Roman authors but did not survive. Notable works in English to which the term has been applied include Robert Burton's **Anatomy of Melancholy* (1621) and Lewis Carroll's **Alice's Adventures in Wonderland* (1865).

Men's Wives Three stories by W. M. *Thackeray, which appeared in **Fraser's Magazine*, 1843. Cynical and satirical, they are concerned with different kinds of unhappy marriage, and the exploitation of one partner by the other. The longest and most fully developed story, 'The Ravenswing', concerns Morgiana Crump ('The Ravenswing'), who possesses beautiful hair and a wonderful singing voice, marries the profligate Captain Walker, and supports him by singing.

Mephistopheles A word of unknown origin, which appears first in the German *Faustbuch* of 1587 as 'Mephostophiles'. Mephistophilis is the name of the devil to whom Dr Faustus bargains away his soul in Christopher *Marlowe's tragedy. A 'Mephostophilus' is mentioned in *Shakespeare's **Merry Wives*. In Goethe's version of the legend Mephistopheles fails to win Faust's soul in the end.
See also FAUST.

MERCER, David (1928–80) Playwright, born in Wakefield, the son of an engine-driver. After attempts at various careers he achieved recognition with his trilogy of television plays *Where the Difference Begins* (1961), *A Climate of Fear* (1962), and *The Birth of a Private Man* (1963), published together as *The Generations* in 1964. The trilogy is primarily concerned with problems of left-wing political commitment; it opens in a Yorkshire working-class home, and ends with death on the Berlin Wall. Mental disturbance, alienation, class conflict, generation conflict (particularly between working-class father and educated son), and Marxism, both British and continental, are recurrent themes in many subsequent works for stage, screen, and television, which include *A Suitable Case for Treatment* (TV 1962; published in *Three TV Comedies*, 1966; filmed as *Morgan*, 1965); *After Haggerty*, staged and published in 1970, which has as protagonist a Marxist theatre critic; and *Shooting the Chandelier* (TV 1977; pub. 1978). One of the first English playwrights to engage fully with television, he also wrote *Providence* (1977) for the French film-maker Alain Resnais.

Merchant-Ivory A partnership between the Indian producer **Ismail Merchant** (1936–2005) and American director **James Ivory** (1928–), usually working with the German-born novelist Ruth Prawer *Jhabvala, which has been responsible for a distinguished series of literary *adaptations. Their early films, notably *Shakespeare-Wallah*, about an English theatre troupe, were mostly set in India, but their first Henry *James adaptation, *The Europeans* (1979), launched a series based on James and E. M. *Forster, including *The Bostonians*, *A Room with a View*, *Howard's End*, and *The Golden Bowl*. Other sources have included Jean *Rhys, for *Quartet* (1981), and Kazuo *Ishiguro, for *The Remains of the Day* (1993).

Merchant of Venice, The A comedy by *Shakespeare written 1596–7. It was printed in 1600, and this text was reprinted in the first *folio (1623). Its chief source is the first story of the fourth day in *Il pecorone*, Giovanni Fiorentino's collection of *novelle*. Other sources include Anthony *Munday's *Zelauto* and the **Gesta Romanorum*. In performance *Shylock, treated sometimes comically, sometimes tragically, has often become the central character. An adaptation by George Granville (1666–1735), *The Jew of Venice*, was the normal stage version from 1701 to 1741.

Bassanio, a noble but poor Venetian, asks his loving friend Antonio, a rich merchant, for 3,000 ducats to enable him to prosecute fittingly his suit of the rich heiress Portia at Belmont. Antonio, whose money is all employed in foreign ventures, undertakes to borrow the sum from Shylock, a Jewish usurer, whom he has rebuked for his extortions. Shylock agrees to lend the money against a bond by which, if the sum is not repaid at the appointed day, Antonio shall forfeit a pound of his flesh. By her father's will Portia is to marry the suitor who selects, from three caskets (one of gold, one of silver, one of lead), the one which contains her portrait. Bassanio makes the right choice—the leaden casket—and is wedded to Portia, and his friend Graziano to her maid Nerissa. News comes that Antonio's ships have been wrecked, that the debt has not been repaid when due, and that Shylock claims his pound of flesh. The matter is brought before the duke. Portia disguises herself as an advocate, Balthasar, and Nerissa as her clerk, and they come to the court to defend Antonio, unknown to their husbands. Failing in her appeal to Shylock for mercy, Portia admits the validity of his claim, but warns him that his life is forfeit if he spills one drop of blood, since his bond entitles him to nothing but flesh. Pursuing her advantage, she argues that Shylock's life is forfeit for having conspired against the life of a Venetian citizen. The duke grants Shylock his life, but gives half his wealth to Antonio, half to the state. Antonio surrenders his claim if Shylock will turn Christian and make over his property on his death to his daughter Jessica, who has run away and married the Christian Lorenzo and been disinherited; Shylock agrees. Portia and Nerissa ask as rewards from Bassanio and Graziano the rings that their wives have given them, which they have promised never to part with. Reluctantly they give them up, and are reproached accordingly on their return home. The play ends with news of the safe arrival of Antonio's ships.

'Merchant's Tale, The' *See* CANTERBURY TALES, 10.

Mercurius Aulicus *See* BERKENHEAD, SIR JOHN.

Mercurius Librarius, *or A Catalogue of Books* A booksellers' trade journal founded in 1668 by two stationers, John Starkey (*c.*1630–1690) and Robert Clavell (b. in or before 1633, d. 1711), described by Walter Graham (*The Beginnings of English Literary Periodicals*, 1926) as 'in a very limited sense... entitled to be regarded as the first literary periodical published in England'. It survived until 1709, and a reprint (as *Term Catalogue*), edited by Edward *Arber, was published in 1903. A second *Mercurius Librarius, or A Faithful Account of All Books and Pamphlets* began as a weekly in 1680, but does not seem to have lasted long.

Mercury (Greek Hermes) Son of *Jupiter and messenger of the gods to men, characterized by his snake-entwined staff (the *caduceus*) and his winged hat and sandals. He was associated variously with eloquence, trade, theft, and treachery. In *Virgil's **Aeneid* he is sent by Jupiter to tell Aeneas to abandon Dido. From the 17th century onwards his name has often been used in the title of newspapers and periodicals.

MEREDITH, George (1828–1909) Novelist. He had a precarious childhood in Portsmouth as the son of an impoverished, but flamboyant and extravagant, tailor who was widowed early—a background which Meredith was later at pains to conceal, although he made use of it in several of his novels. He was intermittently educated in Portsmouth and Southsea, and then with much success at the unusual school of the *Moravians at Neuwied in Germany. In London, after a period with a solicitor, he began his long literary career with 'Chillianwallah', a poem published in 1849. In the same year he married Mary Ellen Nicholls, the widowed daughter of Thomas Love *Peacock, and in 1851 paid for the publication of his own *Poems*, a volume he later disowned but which was praised by *Tennyson and Charles *Kingsley. *The Shaving of Shagpat* (1855), a series of *oriental fantasies about a vain, bewhiskered enchanter whose power resides in one hair on his head, was praised by the critics but did not sell well. In the same year he sat as the model for Henry Wallis's painting *The Death of Chatterton*. In 1857 his wife left him for Wallis, and *Farina*, a German burlesque reminiscent of *Shagpat*, appeared. His first major novel, *The *Ordeal of Richard Feverel*, was published in 1859; it sold poorly, its sexual frankness caused much scandal, and *Mudie's cancelled its order of 300 copies, but it brought praise in *The *Times* and the **Athenaeum*, as well as the friendship of Thomas *Carlyle and the *Pre-Raphaelites.

Meredith was now contributing to many periodicals, including the **Fortnightly Review*, in which **Evan Harrington* began to appear in 1860: the novel has many elements of autobiography, for its hero, like the author himself, is the son of a tailor. Meredith wished the book to be a popular success, and it is accordingly written in a relatively plain style. In 1860 he became a reader for *Chapman and Hall (a post he retained until 1894) and a regular compiler of news for the *Ipswich Chronicle*, a task he endured for eight years. **Modern Love* and *Poems of the Roadside* appeared in 1862. In 1864 he published *Emilia in England* (retitled *Sandra Belloni* in 1886) and married his second wife, Marie Vulliamy. *Rhoda Fleming* (1865), one of his shorter 'plain' works, is a regional novel with a farmer's daughter as its central character. *Vittoria*, a sequel to *Sandra Belloni*, began to appear in 1866, but was enlarged, after Meredith had spent a brief inactive period as a war correspondent in Italy, before its publication in book form in 1867: the novels trace the career of Emilia Sandra Belloni, a singer and the daughter of an Italian musician, first against an English backdrop, then in northern Italy during the failed revolution of 1848–9, led by Mazzini, who appears as a heroic figure. Few of these works brought much profit, but Meredith's reputation was growing steadily with the discerning public. *The Adventures of *Harry Richmond* (1871) brought some success, and the friendship of the influential Monckton *Milnes. A political novel, **Beauchamp's Career*, followed in 1876, and in 1877 Meredith delivered a lecture on 'The Idea of Comedy' which was published in 1897 and enjoyed a lasting reputation.

The novel for which he was chiefly celebrated, *The *Egoist*, appeared in 1879. *The Tragic Comedians*, a novella based on an episode in the life of the German socialist Ferdinand Lassalle, appeared in 1880 and *Poems and Lyrics of the Joy of Earth*, often held to include his best poetry, including the final version of 'Love in a Valley', in 1883. The only novel to meet with general popularity, though exhibiting the growing difficulty of Meredith's style, was **Diana of the Crossways*, which ran to three editions in 1885 alone, and a century later found a new lease of life with the critical approval of the feminist movement. Among other volumes of verse were *Ballads... of Tragic Life* (1887) and *A Reading of Earth* (1888): then came three more novels, *One of our Conquerors* (1891), Meredith's convoluted study of the woes that are in marriage and the minimal pleasures that may eventually be gained from it; *Lord Ormont and his Aminta* (1894), another study of unhappy marriage, with more exotic settings and a more aristocratic milieu than normal in Meredith's work; and *The *Amazing Marriage* (1895), his last novel and considered by some his most impenetrable. A collection of short stories, including the celebrated 'The Case of General Ople and Lady Camper', appeared in 1898, as did *Odes... of French History*; *A Reading of Life* followed in 1901 and *Last Poems* in 1909. *Celt and Saxon*, an unfinished story, was published posthumously in 1910, and a conversational comedy, *The Sentimentalists*, was produced in the same year.

By the time he died Meredith had written steadily for 50 years, had received the OM and an Oxford DCL, was president of the *Society of Authors, and had become a greatly revered man of letters, sought out by many younger poets and novelists, such as Henry *James, Thomas *Hardy, and Robert Louis *Stevenson. He himself felt he was a poet first and a novelist after, but that was not the verdict of his readers. His reputation stood very high well into the 20th century, with his perceptive portrayal of women, his narrative skill, and his incisive dialogue receiving most praise; but the deliberate intricacy of much of his prose (twisted, as Anthony *Trollope wrote, 'into curl-papers') defeats many modern readers, and for the last 50 years or so neither his poetry nor his novels have received any great popular or critical acclaim. See L. Stevenson, *The Ordeal of George Meredith* (1954); G. Beer, *Meredith: A Change of Masks* (1970).

MEREDITH, Owen Pseudonym of Edward Robert Bulwer *Lytton.

MERES, Francis (1565/6–1647) Educated at Pembroke College, Cambridge, and rector and schoolmaster at Wing, Rutland. He was author of *Palladis Tamia: Wit's Treasury* (1598), containing quotations and maxims from various writers. In it Meres reviewed 125 English writers from the time of Geoffrey *Chaucer to his own day, contrasting each English one with a similar Latin, Greek, or Italian author. Particularly notable are his list of twelve of William *Shakespeare's plays, including *Love's Labour's Won,* and of his 'sugared sonnets among his private friends', and his accounts of Robert *Greene's, George *Peele's, and Christopher *Marlowe's deaths. The section on 'Poetry', which Shakespeare himself may have read, was edited by D. C. Allen (1933).

MÉRIMÉE, Prosper (1803–70) French novelist, playwright, and writer of short fiction. One of the earliest of the French Romantic dramatists, he successfully passed off the six short plays of *Le Théâtre de Clara Gazul* (1825) as having been written by the imaginary Spanish actress of the title. Another hoax was *La Guzla*, a collection of supposed translations of Illyrian poetry, in reality his own inventions. *La Jacquerie* (1828) was a series of dramatic scenes of medieval life; *La Chronique du règne de Charles IX* (1829) a historical novel of the religious wars of the 16th century. Mérimée's short stories—he is a recognized master of the form—include 'Matteo Falcone' (1829), 'La Vision de Charles XI' (1829), 'La Vénus d'Ille' (1837), 'Colomba' (1840), 'Carmen' (1845), which inspired Bizet's opera, and 'Lokis' (1869). His *Lettres à une inconnue*, written to Mademoiselle 'Jenny' Dacquin, display his critical and ironic temperament.

MERLEAU-PONTY, Maurice (1908–61) French philosopher. With Jean-Paul *Sartre, co-editor of *Les Temps modernes*, he dominated French intellectual life in the period following the Second World War. Reacting against Cartesian idealism, he based his theory of knowledge on the relationship between consciousness and the world. His main work, *Phénoménologie de la perception* (1945: *Phenomenology of Perception*), attempts to do equal justice to the mind's constructive powers in perception and to the independence of the object of perception, arguing that the structure of consciousness is neither discernible from first principles nor dependent on causal mechanisms, but exhibited in the mind's actual encounters with the world.

Merlin A magician with analogues in several Celtic literatures, who most famously guides the destinies of *Arthur and his predecessor *Uther, though the range of activities attributed to him in his various incarnations extends far beyond this. His story is first set out by *Geoffrey of Monmouth in his *Vita Merlini* (*c.*1150), which draws on the story of Ambrosius as told by *Nennius. Merlin is born of a devil and a virtuous maiden and is named after his maternal grandfather. Although precocious and wilful, he is not malevolent as his father intended. He grows infatuated with Nimiane (Nimue or Vivien: *see* Lady of the Lake), who imprisons him in a forest of air in Broceliande where he dies. He is also credited with a series of prophecies, as in Geoffrey of Monmouth's *Prophetiae Merlini*. Most famously, he predicts to *Vortigern the triumph of the Britons over the Saxons, in this way interpreting the killing of a white dragon by a red one after the two creatures are released during the digging of the foundations of a citadel from which Vortigern is to fight the Saxons. In Geoffrey of Monmouth's *Historia Regum Britanniae*, Merlin aids Uther in the deceitful bed-trick by which he marries Igraine (Ygerna) and fathers Arthur. The Arthurian stories connected with him form a very important part of the whole tradition in French in the Middle Ages, particularly as transmitted by the (fragmentary) stories of Merlin by Robert de *Boron, the prose Vulgate *Merlin* and the *Suite du Merlin*. He also features prominently in the early tales of *Malory's *Morte Darthur*, and later in Alfred *Tennyson's 'Merlin and Vivien', one of his **Idylls of the King*. See R. S. Loomis (ed.), *Arthurian Literature in the Middle Ages* (1959).

'Merlin and Vivien' One of Tennyson's **Idylls of the King*, published 1859 as 'Vivien', retitled 1870. The wily Vivien, filled with hatred for Arthur and his court, seduces the aged Merlin and extracts his most precious secrets.

Mermaid Tavern A tavern that stood in Bread Street (with an entrance in Friday Street), London. It was frequented by Francis *Beaumont, John *Donne, Inigo *Jones, and others who may have included William *Shakespeare. According to Thomas *Coryate a 'Fraternity of Sirenaical Gentlemen' met there 'the first Friday of every month', but the membership of the 'club' is not clear. The tavern is celebrated by Beaumont in the fine lines ('Master Francis Beaumont to Ben Jonson'):

> 'What things have we seen
> Done at the Mermaid! heard words that have been
> So nimble, and so full of subtle flame
> As if that every one from whence they came
> Had meant to put his whole wit in a jest,
> And had resolved to live a fool the rest
> Of his dull life.'

John *Keats also wrote 'Lines on the Mermaid Tavern' beginning: 'Souls of poets dead and gone'.

MERRIL, Judith (1923–97) American-Canadian author, editor of *science fiction, and political activist; born New York, resident in Canada from 1968. Her novel *Shadow on the Heart* (1950) is, like her first published story 'That Only a Mother' (1948), a response to nuclear anxieties following the Second World War. Her 'Year's Best' anthologies (1957–68), gathered from non-genre sources, opened up new avenues. In championing higher standards she influenced science fiction's

*New Wave, introducing new British writers in the anthology *England Swings SF* (1968).

MERRILL, James (1926–95) American poet, born in New York, who began publishing in the 1940s. His regular visits to Greece led to an inclusion of local motifs in his work and in 1982 he published *The Changing Light at Sandover*, an extended collection of messages from Ouija séances. *The (Diblos) Notebook* (1965) is a short novel and in 1993 Merrill published an autobiographical memoir, *A Different Person*. See Alison *Lurie, *Familiar Spirits* (2000).

MERRIMAN, Brian (*c.*1749–1805) Irish-language poet, author of *Cúirt an Mheán Oíche* ('The Midnight Court'), a long satirical poem admired by W. B. *Yeats and translated by, among others, Ciaran *Carson, Seamus *Heaney (incomplete, *The Midnight Verdict*, 1993), Thomas *Kinsella, and Frank *O'Connor. Scholars have struggled to relate the vernacular gusto and libertarian fury of Merriman's famous poem (two other pieces attributed to him are short and undistinguished) to earlier tradition. The poem begins as a mock *aisling before proceeding to the court scene in which men are accused of the sexual neglect of women. The abolition of clerical celibacy is recommended before the women turn aggressively on the speaker, identified by a series of punning clues as Merriman himself.

MERRITT, A. (Abraham) (1884–1943) American writer and journalist, born in New Jersey, whose novels (initially serialized) include *The Moon Pool* (1919) and *The Ship of Ishtar* (1926). Their supernatural and lost-race motifs, and Merritt's ornate style, made them influential works of pulp-magazine *fantasy, frequently reprinted.

MERRY, Robert (1755–98) English poet and dramatist, educated at Rugby School and Christ's College, Cambridge, known as *'Della Crusca'. Resident in Florence in the mid-1780s, he adopted his pseudonym after the Florentine literary academy. Returning to England he became the centre of a poetic coterie (*see* DELLA CRUSCANS) which included Hannah *Cowley and Mary *Robinson and which was attacked as mawkish and sentimental by William *Gifford in *The Baviad* (1791). A supporter of the French Revolution, he published 'The Laurel of Liberty' (1790), one of the earliest works of English *Jacobinism and a poetic response to Edmund Burke's **Reflections on the Revolution in France* (1790). In the mid-1790s, he emigrated to the United States, where his drama *The Abbey of St Augustine* was successfully staged, and died in Baltimore in 1798.

Merry Devil of Edmonton, The A romantic comedy of unknown authorship, acted by the King's Men before 1604. Based on real events and popular in its time, it was registered for publication in 1607 and published anonymously six times between 1608 and 1656. It has occasionally been attributed to *Shakespeare. Charles *Lamb, who praised it highly, suggested Michael *Drayton as the possible author, and more recently Thomas *Dekker has been proposed.

The prologue presents Peter Fabel of Edmonton, a magician, who has made a pact with the devil. Its period has expired, and the fiend comes for Fabel. He is, however, tricked into sitting on a necromantic chair, where he is held fast and is obliged to give a respite. The play itself, in which the magical element is practically absent, deals with the attempt of Sir Arthur Clare and his wife to break off the match between their daughter Millicent and Raymond Mounchensey, and its defeat by the elopement of the young couple, aided by the kindly magician Fabel.

Merry Wives of Windsor, The A comedy by *Shakespeare, possibly written or adapted for the occasion of George Carey, Lord Hunsdon's installation as a knight of the Garter at Windsor on 23 April 1597. Various topical allusions have been discerned in the play, but the tradition that it was written at the request of *Elizabeth I for a play showing *Falstaff in love is documented no earlier than 1702 (by John *Dennis). The passage alluding to the Garter Feast is found only in the *folio text (1623), which is twice the length of the 'bad' quarto (1602); the latter appears to be based on a report of a less courtly performance.

Falstaff, in need of cash, decides to make love to the wives of Ford and Page, two gentlemen living at Windsor, because they control their husbands' purses. Nim and Pistol, the discarded followers of Falstaff, warn the husbands. Falstaff sends identical love letters to Mistress Ford and Mistress Page, who contrive the knight's downfall. At a first assignation at Ford's house, they hide Falstaff in a basket when the husband arrives, cover him with foul linen, and have him tipped into a muddy ditch. At a second assignation, they disguise him as the 'fat woman of Brentford', in which character he is soundly beaten by Ford. The jealous husband having also been twice fooled, the plot is now revealed to him, and a final assignation is given to Falstaff in Windsor Forest at Herne's Oak, where he is plagued and pinched by mock fairies and finally seized and exposed by Ford and Page.

The sub-plot concerns the wooing of Anne, Page's daughter, by Doctor Caius, a French physician, Slender, the foolish cousin of Justice Shallow, and Fenton, a wild young gentleman, whom Anne loves. Mistress Quickly, servant to Dr Caius, acts as go-between for the three suitors, and encourages them all. Sir Hugh Evans, a Welsh parson, interferes on Slender's behalf and is challenged by the bad-tempered Dr Caius, but hostilities are confined to the 'hacking' of the English tongue. At the final assignation with Falstaff in the forest, Page, who favours Slender, arranges that the latter shall carry off his daughter, dressed in white; while Mistress Page, who favours Dr Caius, arranges that he shall carry her off dressed in green. In the event both find themselves fobbed off with a boy in disguise, while Fenton has run away with and married the true Anne.

Messiah (1) An oratorio by George Frideric *Handel. (2) A religious epic (*Der Messias*) by Friedrich Gottlieb *Klopstock.

(3) A sacred eclogue by Alexander *Pope, published in the *_Spectator_ on 14 May 1712, fusing the prophetic style of *Virgil's fourth eclogue with the Messianic language of Isaiah.

metafiction A kind of fiction that openly draws attention to its own fictional status. Laurence *Sterne's _Tristram Shandy_ (1759–67) is the classic English example, while a notable later exercise in this form is John *Fowles's novel _The French Lieutenant's Woman_ (1969).

Metamorphoses See APULEIUS; OVID.

metaphor Description of one thing (or person, idea, feeling, action, etc.) in terms properly belonging to another, with the suggestion (rather than explicit likening, as in *simile) that they share some common quality, as in reference to a person as 'an angel' or to the act of 'devouring' a book. One of the most powerful of figurative expressions, it is also commonplace and in the case of so-called 'dead' metaphors (e.g. the 'branch' of a bank) may go almost unnoticed. Analysis of metaphors distinguishes a literal element (the 'tenor') from a figurative element (the 'vehicle'): in the hackneyed metaphor 'the ship of state', the state is the tenor, the ship the vehicle.

metaphysical poets Poets generally grouped under this label include John *Donne (who is regarded as founder of the 'school'), George *Herbert, Richard *Crashaw, Henry *Vaughan, Andrew *Marvell, and Thomas *Traherne, together with lesser figures like Edward *Benlowes, Lord *Herbert of Cherbury, Henry *King, Abraham *Cowley, and John *Cleveland. The label was first used (disparagingly) by Samuel *Johnson in his 'Life of Cowley' (written in 1777), where he identifies them as a 'race of writers' who display their learning, use far-fetched comparisons, and lack feeling. But Alexander *Pope partly anticipated Johnson when he spoke (Joseph *Spence's _Anecdotes_) of Cowley borrowing his 'metaphysical' style from Donne, and earlier John *Dryden had complained that Donne 'affects the metaphysics', perplexing the minds of the fair sex with 'nice speculations of philosophy'. Earlier still William *Drummond, probably with Donne in mind, censured poetic innovators who employed 'metaphysical ideas and scholastical quiddities'. The label is misleading, since none of these poets is seriously interested in metaphysics (except Herbert of Cherbury, and even he excludes the interest from his poetry). Further, they have in reality little in common: the features their work is generally taken to display are sustained dialectic, paradox, novelty, incongruity, 'muscular' rhythms, giving the effect of a 'speaking voice', and the use of elaborately extended metaphors, or 'conceits'. With the new taste for clarity and the impatience with figurative language that prevailed after the *Restoration, their reputation dwindled and, though their 'quaintness' earned some recognition from critics, their revival was delayed until after the First World War. When it came, however, it was dramatic: indeed, the revaluation of metaphysical poetry, and the related downgrading of the *Romantics and John *Milton, was the major feature of the rewriting of English literary history in the first half of the 20th century. Key documents in the revival were H. J. C. Grierson, _Metaphysical Lyrics and Poems of the Seventeenth Century_ (1921), and T. S. *Eliot's essay 'Metaphysical Poets', which first appeared as a review of Grierson's collection (_TLS_, 20 Oct. 1921). According to Eliot these poets had the advantage of writing at a time when thought and feeling were closely fused, before the *'dissociation of sensibility' set in about the time of John Milton. Their virtues of difficulty and tough newness were felt to relate them closely to the modernists—Ezra *Pound, W. B. *Yeats, and Eliot himself. Modern scholarship has followed Johnson's hint and related the English metaphysicals to *Marino, *Gongorism, and the European baroque generally. See Rosemond Tuve, _Elizabethan and Metaphysical Imagery_ (1947); J. E. Duncan, _The Revival of Metaphysical Poetry_ (1959); F. J. Warnke, _European Metaphysical Poetry_ (1961); L. Nelson, _Baroque Lyric Poetry_ (1961); J. M. Cohen, _The Baroque Lyric_ (1963); Colin Burrow (ed.), _Metaphysical Poetry_ (2006).

Metaphysical Society Founded in 1869 by Sir James *Knowles. It lasted until 1880 and brought together for discussion meetings most of the leaders of English thought of the period, of all shades of opinion, including T. H. *Huxley, John *Tyndall, Henry Manning (1808–92), William *Gladstone, and Alfred *Tennyson.

Methodism From its origins in the 1730s, this religious movement in its Wesleyan form grew to nine million members worldwide by 1900. In the 18th century it had two main branches: the Calvinistic Methodism of the followers in Wales of Howell Harris and in England of George *Whitefield and the countess of *Huntingdon, and the Arminian Methodism of the followers of the *Wesleys. Wesleyan Methodism was divided into local societies, preaching houses, and circuits, serviced by itinerant lay preachers, organized centrally by an annual conference, and directed by John Wesley. In its origins Methodism was a movement in the Church of England, but by the end of the 18th century both Calvinist and Arminian Methodists had separated from it, the former mostly to join *Congregationalists and *Baptists, the latter to set up the Methodist Church, which itself later split into separate bodies such as the Primitive Methodists. In the early 19th century the Welsh Calvinistic Methodists also formed a separate church. The various denominations had their own magazines and publishing outlets.
See JACKSON, THOMAS.

metonymy A figure of speech which substitutes a quality or attribute of something for the thing itself, as _the fair_ to mean 'the fair sex', _the deep_ to mean 'the deep sea', _the bench_ for the judiciary, or _Shakespeare_ to mean the works of Shakespeare. In such examples, metonymy works by a kind of conventional abbreviation. A closely related figure is that of synecdoche, in which a part is substituted for the whole (_per head_, to mean 'per person'), or a whole is substituted for a part (_Pakistan_, to mean the Pakistani cricket team).

metre The more or less regular pattern formed by the sequence of syllables that make up lines of verse. Poems in which the sound patterns are not perceptibly formed from similar groupings of syllables are regarded as non-metrical, and thus placed in the category of *free verse. The largest body of traditional English verse, however, observes some form of metrical regularity. The particular forms of such regularity vary from one language to another: in ancient Greek and Latin, lines of verse were made from fixed numbers of 'feet', a foot being a combination of syllables regarded as either long or short; while in French and in Japanese what is measured is simply the number of syllables that make up the line, without distinctions of length or stress. These metrical systems are known as 'quantitative' and 'syllabic' respectively. Verse written in English almost always employs a different principle, one that relies on a distinction perceived between stressed (•) and unstressed (○) syllables. English verse lines are measured either principally or wholly by the number of stresses (i.e. stressed syllables) they are expected to contain. They may also observe further regularities in the total number of syllables, stressed or unstressed, that each line may include. The two major tendencies or traditions of English verse metre may be differentiated according to whether this inclusive syllable-count applies.

The older of the two dominant English metrical systems counts only the number of stresses in a line, so allowing variation in the number of unstressed syllables. This 'accentual metre' was the standard metrical principle of Old English verse, and was still vigorous in 14th-century literature, for example in the works of *Langland and in *Sir *Gawain and the Green Knight*. Following the example of *Chaucer, poets in English since that time have usually counted their syllables and thus departed to some degree from the pure accentual principle. Accentual verse has continued to flourish, however, in a wide range of popular songs, *hymns, *ballads, and *nursery rhymes, and in revivalist experiments such as that of Gerard Manley *Hopkins.

The second English metrical system is known as the 'accentual-syllabic', because it counts both the number of stresses and the total number of syllables in a line, thus restricting the use of unstressed syllables. So, in the standard line of post-Chaucerian English verse, the iambic pentameter, we expect to find ten syllables, of which five are stressed; in the perfectly regular version of this line, the unstressed and stressed syllables will alternate so as to conclude with a stress (○ • ○ • ○ • ○ • ○ •):

If Winter comes, can Spring be far behind?

Such a pattern is an expectation, not a rule, and accentual-syllabic verse of any sophistication requires variety in the placing both of the stressed syllables and of the pause (*caesura) within the line. Given the restriction that accentual-syllabic metres place upon the use of unstressed syllables, they fall into two basic kinds, known as duple and triple. By far the more commonly used are the duple metres, in which stressed syllables alternate with single unstressed syllables, as in the iambic metre illustrated above. In triple metres, pairs of unstressed syllables alternate with the stresses, as in *Hardy's dactylic tetrameter (• ○ ○ • ○ ○ • ○ ○ • ○ ○):

Woman much missed, how you call to me, call to me

The predominance of the duple metres in English gives the use of triple metres the appearance of being a special or even comical device, as in the anapaestic metre of the limerick (○ • ○ ○ • ○ ○ •):

There was an Old Man in a tree

Of the two duple metres, the iambic, in which unstressed syllables are heard to precede the stresses, is the standard. The less commonly used trochaic metre gives the impression that the stresses precede the unstressed syllables (• ○ • ○ • ○ • ○):

Ye whose hearts are fresh and simple

Trochaic metre is unusual in that its regular form, illustrated in the tetrameter by *Longfellow above, is quite rare by comparison with an irregular (truncated, or 'catalectic') version in which the final unstressed syllable is not used, allowing the line to end with a stress (• ○ • ○ • ○ •):

Tyger, tyger, burning bright

Similar forms of truncation are found in the triple metres Setting aside the distinction between accentual and accentual-syllabic metres for a moment, the simplest description of the metre in a given line of verse is given by the number of stresses we expect it to include. In English, the two standard lines are the four-stress (tetrameter) and the five-stress (pentameter); in accentual-syllabic terms these standard lines may be described as octosyllabic and decasyllabic, if we take the use of duple metre for granted. The four-stress line is the older and the more persistent in all popular forms of verse and song, being easily compatible with the regularity of musical beats. It is also the natural line for accentual metres. The five-stress line has the effect of loosening or suppressing the assertive beat, and approximating itself to the rhythms of speech. Less frequently found as the regular basis of verse are the three-stress (trimeter) and two stress (dimeter) lines on the one hand, or the six-stress (*hexameter) and seven-stress (heptameter) lines on the other. Two-, three-, and six-stress lines find their usual place in verse forms that mix longer and shorter lines: the 'Burns stanza' employs dimeters for its fourth and sixth lines, the limerick for its third and fourth, while the Spenserian stanza has a hexameter as its final line.

The theory of metre, known as prosody or metrics, has been bedevilled by the survival of terminology and concepts derived from ancient Greek practice, despite the radical difference between Greek quantitative principles and English stress patterns. The ways in which stressed and unstressed syllables can be arranged in English verse have come to be named after the various kinds of Greek 'foot' they seem to resemble, when one mistranslates 'long syllable' as 'stressed syllable'. Many modern metricians regard the concept of the foot as a positive hindrance to the understanding of English metre and especially of accentual verse, but the names have stuck, and the analysis (scansion) of English lines as sequences of 'feet' is still attempted. Four principal kinds of metrical pattern in English are accordingly named after the *iamb* (○•), the *trochee* (• ○), the *anapaest* (○ ○ •), and the *dactyl* (• ○ ○). Two other feet are sometimes invoked in scansion of English verse: the *spondee* (• •) and the *pyrrhic* (○ ○); among several others that are of relevance to ancient Greek verse but only very rarely to English are the *amphibrach* (○ • ○), the *amphimacer* (• ○ •), and the *choriamb* (• ○ ○ •).

Understanding the metrical effects of English verse requires some appreciation of the many variations that poets can play upon a regular metrical pattern. In the case of the iambic pentameter, especially, the scope for such variation is so wide that completely regular lines like P. B. *Shelley's 'If Winter comes, can Spring be far behind?' will be outnumbered by irregular versions. The principal variant upon the standard pentameter involves what is (in traditional foot-based scansion) known as 'initial trochaic inversion' because the line starts with a stress but 'compensates' for this with an unstressed syllable (• ○ ○ • ○ • ○ • ○ •):

Far on the ringing plains of windy Troy

Similar inversions may be found in later positions in a line. Other permissible variations include the use of an unstressed syllable where a stress is expected, thus speeding up the line (e.g. ○ • ○ • ○ • ○ ○ ○ •):

A horse! a horse! My kingdom for a horse!

or the addition of an eleventh, unstressed syllable:

To be or not to be, that is the question

See P. Hobsbaum, *Metre, Rhythm and Verse Form* (1996); D. Attridge, *Poetic Rhythm: An Introduction* (1995); D. Attridge, *The Rhythms of English Verse* (1982).

Metropolis (1927) Film by Fritz Lang (1890–1976). Its images of a *dystopian city and its humanoid robot echo throughout *science fiction.

MEW, Charlotte Mary (1869–1928) Poet and short story writer, the daughter of a prosperous London architect, born in Bloomsbury where she spent most of her life. She was educated in Gower Street School and was an able musician. Her short story 'Passed' appeared in the **Yellow Book* in 1894, but she became well known with her first volume of poetry, *The Farmer's Bride* (1915). Her second, *The Rambling Sailor*, appeared posthumously in 1929. Mew's themes of solitariness, guilt, unworthiness, and Catholicism have a peculiar sense of a personality under pressure; her meditations on sexual identity (including homosexual) are fraught. In life, her love for May *Sinclair was only one of a number of unsuccessful romances. She killed herself in 1928. Mew's collected poems and prose were edited by V. Warner, 1981; see also Penelope *Fitzgerald, *Charlotte Mew and her Friends* (1984).

MEYNELL, Alice (1847–1922) née Thompson, poet and essayist whose first volume of poetry was *Preludes*, 1875. She was educated almost wholly by her father; her sister was, as Lady Butler, an important painter of battle scenes. Meynell's circle included Francis *Thompson, George *Meredith, and Coventry *Patmore and her volumes of verse included *Poems* (1893), *Later Poems* (1902), and *Last Poems* (1923); many of her most widely regarded poems deal with the theme of religious mystery. She is now also admired for her essays, introductions, and anthologies, which were freshly independent in approach and judgement. Her essays, published in the *National Observer*, the **Pall Mall Gazette*, the *Tablet*, and other periodicals, were collected under various titles, which include *The Rhythm of Life* (1893), *The Colour of Life* (1896), and *The Spirit of Place* (1899). There is a life by J. Badeni (1981).

MEYNELL, Sir Francis Meredith Wilfrid (1891–1975) Book designer, publisher, and journalist, the son of Wilfrid and Alice *Meynell. The founder and director of the *Nonesuch Press, he published his autobiography, *My Lives*, in 1971.

'Michael' A pastoral poem by William *Wordsworth, written and published 1800. A narrative in blank verse, it describes, with moving simplicity, the lonely life in Grasmere of the old shepherd Michael, his wife, and his beloved son Luke. Because of family misfortune Luke is sent away to a dissolute city, where he disgraces himself; he eventually disappears abroad. Michael dies in grief and the cottage and pasture become a ruin.

Michael, St Archangel and victor in the war in heaven over the dragon *Satan and his host (Revelation 12). Despite his minor role in the Bible, he became a major figure in Western art. In **Paradise Lost* his fellow archangel Raphael narrates the war in heaven, and Michael the history of the fallen human race.

Michaelmas Terme *See* MIDDLETON, THOMAS.

MICHELANGELO BUONARROTI (1475–1564) Florentine painter, sculptor, architect, and poet, who worked also in Rome, and whose artistic legacy includes some of the greatest works of the *Renaissance, including the *Pietà* (completed 1499; St Peter's, Rome) and the ceiling of the Sistine Chapel (1508–12). He also left around 300 poems and numerous letters. Amongst them are many love poems, full of Platonic imagery, to the beautiful Tommaso de' Cavalieri, whom he had met in 1532. Others, intensely spiritual, are addressed to Vittoria *Colonna. The poems of his later years express fears of sin and salvation.

Michelangelo's contemporaries idolized 'il divino Michelangelo' and his biography was written in his lifetime: *Vasari described him bringing to perfection the artistic tradition that had opened with Cimabue (*c.*1240–*c.*1302). Yet by the 1540s he came under attack: Pietro *Aretino, in a famous letter of 1545, poured scurrilous abuse on his character and work. Throughout the 17th and 18th centuries, classicists felt uneasy with his individuality and tended to favour *Raphael. A change took place in the late 18th century, when Joshua *Reynolds praised him in his last discourse, and his work was increasingly esteemed by followers of the *sublime. The writings and drawings of Henry *Fuseli and William *Blake, and of *Goethe, Delacroix, and *Stendhal in Europe, bear witness to a passionate admiration. In the late 19th century scholarly editions of the poems and letters were published. His homosexuality began to be stressed and an elaborately documented biography was written by J. A. *Symonds (1893).

MICHELET, Jules (1798–1874) French historian, keeper of the National Historical Archives (1831–52), professor at the

Collège de France (1838–51). His principal work, *L'Histoire de France* (vols i–vi, 1833–43; vols vii-xvii, 1855–67: *History of France*), is remarkable for its luminously eloquent style, its aim to recreate the complexity of the past, and for the part that the author attributes to geographical and racial factors in bringing about historical change. Michelet's fervent republicanism is evident in his other major work, *La Révolution française* (7 vols, 1847–53: *The French Revolution*). His monographs and shorter studies on historical subjects include *Les Jésuites* (1843, with Edgar Quinet: *The Jesuits*), *Du prêtre, de la femme, de la famille* (1845: *On the Priest, the Wife, the Family*), *Le Peuple* (1846: *The People*), and *La Femme* (1860: *Woman*).

MICHENER, James A. (Albert) (1907–97) American novelist, raised in Pennsylvania, who began his extensive output with *Tales of the South Pacific* (1947), set in the Second World War. His historical novels (*Hawaii*, 1959; *The Source*, 1965; etc.) were the fruit of painstaking research. *The World is my Home* (1992) is an autobiographical memoir. See John P. Hayes, *James A. Michener* (1984).

MICKIEWICZ, Adam (1798–1855) Polish poet, born near Nowogródek, and educated at the University of Wilno (now Vilnius), where he became involved in nationalist politics, was imprisoned, and then exiled in 1824 to Russia for five years by the Russian authorities. He subsequently lived in Dresden, Paris, and Rome, and died in Constantinople. His first collection of poems, published 1822, contained his poetic manifesto, an essay 'On Romantic Poetry'; in the same year he studied English and became a devoted admirer of Lord *Byron, whose struggles for freedom strongly influenced him. His passionately patriotic works include *Konrad Wallenrod* (1828), a narrative poem presenting in historical guise the enduring hostility between Russia and Poland, and *Dziady* (*Forefathers' Eve*), a complex and baffling work, of which the first part appeared in 1823, and the third and greatest in 1832. Part III is a poetic drama (unfinished), in which the central character, Gustav, awakens to political and prophetic consciousness; it is based on Mickiewicz's own political experiences at Wilno. *Pan Tadeusz* (1834) is an epic poem set in Lithuania on the eve of Napoleon's expedition to Russia in 1812: it was adapted by Donald *Davie as *The Forest of Lithuania* (1959).

Microcosm of London, The *See* ACKERMANN, RUDOLPH.

Microcosmographie *See* EARLE, JOHN.

Midas A prose play by John *Lyly, published 1592, on the legend of Midas, king of Phrygia.

Middle Ages A conventional but contestable term designating a notional period from the Roman decadence (5th century AD) and the end of classical culture proper to its widespread revival during the 'Renaissance' (*c.*1500), although several European countries experienced 'renaissances' within this period, particularly given the growth of vernacular literatures in the 12th–14th centuries. The 'Middle Ages' have been associated with the development of the universities and the rise of *scholasticism in the 12th and 13th centuries. The earliest use yet discovered of 'Middle Age' in English is in John *Foxe's *Actes and Monuments* (1570); there are corresponding Latin terms from the 16th century, such as *medium aevum, media aetas*.

Middlemarch: *A Study of Provincial Life* A novel by George *Eliot, published 1871–2. The scene is laid in the provincial town of Middlemarch, in the English Midlands, during the years of the agitation immediately preceding the first Reform Bill in 1832. The novel has a multiple plot, with several interlocking sets of characters. Dorothea, an ardent and idealistic young woman, under the negligent though affable care of her eccentric uncle, marries the elderly pedant Mr Casaubon, despite the doubts of her sister Celia, her neighbour and suitor Sir James Chettam (who later marries Celia), and Mrs Cadwallader, the rector's outspoken wife. The marriage proves unhappy. Dorothea realizes during a disastrous honeymoon in Rome that Casaubon's scholarly plans to write a great work, a 'Key to all Mythologies', are doomed, as are her own aspirations to share in her husband's intellectual life, and her respect for him gradually turns to pity. She is sustained by the friendship of Casaubon's young cousin Will Ladislaw, a lively, light-hearted young man, detested by Casaubon, who begins to suspect that Dorothea's feelings for him are questionable; his irritation is increased by his fear that he has acted justly but ungenerously to his impoverished kinsman. Shortly before he dies, with characteristic meanness, he adds a codicil to his will by which Dorothea loses her fortune if she marries Ladislaw.

Meanwhile, we follow the fortunes of Fred and Rosamond Vincy, son and daughter of the mayor of Middlemarch; the extrovert Fred, unsuitably destined to become a clergyman, is in love with Mary Garth, an unselfish young woman who is caring for her disagreeable and aged relative Mr Featherstone. Mary will not accept Fred unless he rejects his father's ambition that he should enter the church, and proves himself responsible and self-sufficient. Rosamond, the town's beauty, sets herself to win the hand of Tertius Lydgate, the ambitious and high-minded young doctor. She succeeds, but the marriage is wrecked by her self-centred materialism. Lydgate, finding himself in debt, reluctantly borrows money from Mr Bulstrode, a religious hypocrite. Lydgate's career is ruined when he is implicated in the death of Raffles, an unwelcome visitor from Bulstrode's shady past. Only Dorothea, now widowed, continues to believe in him, but she is deeply shocked to find Ladislaw and Rosamond together in compromising circumstances. Rosamond reveals that Ladislaw has not betrayed his love for Dorothea, and Dorothea renounces her inheritance to marry him. Fred Vincy becomes a steady young man, and marries Mary Garth. Lydgate is condemned to a lucrative but unfulfilling practice as a fashionable doctor, and dies with his early ambitions unfulfilled.

Throughout this wide-ranging and complex narrative, George Eliot analyses and comments upon the social, intellectual, and political upheavals of the period, contrasting the staunch Tory attitudes of Chettam and the Cadwalladers with the growing demand for Reform, unsatisfactorily espoused by the hapless Brooke, more effectively by Ladislaw, who becomes an 'ardent public man', and a member of Parliament, with Dorothea's support. The importance of marital loyalty is also a consistent theme, movingly reflected in Mrs Bulstrode's support of her husband after his disgrace.

George Eliot's reputation reached its height with *Middlemarch*, despite some complaints that the action was slow or the tone didactic. Its status as one of the greatest works of English fiction remains unquestioned.

MIDDLETON, Conyers (1683–1750) Combative Anglican clergyman of sceptical tendencies, fellow of Trinity College, Cambridge, fierce opponent of Richard *Bentley, and Protobibliothecarius (principal librarian) of the University Library. Elizabeth *Montagu and Sarah *Scott, his stepgranddaughters, were partly brought up in his household, and he was a friend of Lord *Hervey. His *Letter from Rome* (1729), on the Roman Catholic Church's debt to pagan ceremonies, provoked controversy; his very successful *Life of Cicero* (1741) made him rich. *A Free Inquiry into the Miraculous Powers* (1749), which attacked the authenticity of post-apostolic miracles, was widely criticized; Edward *Gibbon's claim that it was responsible for his own temporary conversion to Catholicism is now discredited.

MIDDLETON, Erasmus (bap. 1739, d. 1805) Church of England evangelical minister and biographer, one of six students expelled from St Edmund Hall, Oxford, in 1768 for *Methodist practices. He was staunchly Calvinist and hostile to Wesleyan Methodism. His main publication is *Biographia Evangelica, or An Historical Account of the Lives and Deaths of the Most Eminent and Evangelical Authors or Preachers*, 4 vols (1779–86).

MIDDLETON, Stanley (1919–2009) Novelist, born and educated in Nottingham where much of his fiction is set. Since the publication of *A Short Answer* (1958) and *Harris's Requiem* (1960), Middleton has produced more than forty novels, including *Terms of Reference* (1966), *Two Brothers* (1978), *Entry into Jerusalem* (1983), *Valley of Decision* (1985), *Against the Dark* (1998), *Love in the Provinces* (2002), and *Her Three Wise Men* (2008). His best-known novel, *Holiday*, the story of a middle-aged man attempting to escape the pains of the present by returning to the seaside resort where he was happy as a child, was joint winner of the *Booker Prize in 1974. Resistant to changes in literary fashion over five decades, Middleton has remained committed to the social realism that prevailed when he began his career, and all his novels chronicle the family lives and domestic difficulties of largely middle-class and middle-aged characters in the English Midlands.

MIDDLETON, Thomas (1580–1627) Poet and playwright, the son of a prosperous London bricklayer. He matriculated at Oxford but probably did not take a degree. His first published work was a long poem, *The Wisdom of Solomon Paraphrased* (1597), followed by other verses and prose pamphlets. By 1600 he was in London, 'daily accompanying the players', and by 1603 he was writing for Philip *Henslowe, working with John *Webster, Thomas *Dekker, William *Rowley, Anthony *Munday, and others; much of his work of this period is lost. He collaborated with Dekker in the first part of *The *Honest Whore* (1604) and wrote many successful comedies of city life, including *The Family of Love* (with Dekker?, written 1602; pub. 1608), *The *Roaring Girl* (with Dekker, written 1604–8?; pub. 1611), *Michaelmas Term* (written 1604–6; pub. 1607), *A Trick to Catch the Old One* (written 1604–7; pub. 1608), *A *Mad World, my Masters* (written 1604–7; published 1608), *A *Chaste Maid in Cheapside* (written 1613; pub. 1630), and *The Mayor of Queenborough* (written 1615–20; pub. 1661). *A *Fair Quarrel*, a tragicomedy written with Rowley (*c*.1615–16; pub. 1617), a play in a very different genre, discusses the ethics of duelling; *The Spanish Gipsy*, also with Rowley (and possibly John *Ford, written 1623; pub. 1625) is a romantic comedy based on two plots from *Cervantes. Other plays include *The *Witch* (written 1609–16; pub. 1778) and *Anything for a Quiet Life* (with Webster?, written ?1621); he probably revised Shakespeare's **Measure for Measure*, adapted **Macbeth*, collaborated on **Timon of Athens*, and was responsible for *A *Yorkshire Tragedy* (*c*.1605).

A writer of great versatility, Middleton wrote many pageants and masques for city occasions, and was appointed city chronologer in 1620. His political satire *A *Game at Chess* (written 1624; pub. 1625) created a furore, and caused him and the actors to be summoned before the Privy Council: it was described by T. S. *Eliot as 'a perfect piece of literary political art'. But Middleton is now best known for his two great tragedies, *The *Changeling* (with Rowley, written 1622; pub. 1653) and **Women Beware Women* (written 1620–27; pub. 1657). Both have been successfully revived on stage in recent years. Most scholars now also consider that *The *Revenger's Tragedy* (1607) is by Middleton (see D. J. Lake, *The Canon of Thomas Middleton's Plays*, 1975). A collaborative edition of the *Complete Works* prepared under the supervision of Gary Taylor and John Lavagnino, along with a companion volume, *Thomas Middleton and Early Modern Textual Culture*, appeared in 2007.

Midshipman Easy, Mr A popular novel by Frederick *Marryat, published 1836. Jack Easy is the son of a wealthy gentleman who brings his boy up to believe that all men are equal, a notion which gives Jack many problems as a midshipman. But he is heir to a fortune and this, together with his cheerful honesty and the help of his Ashanti friend Mesty, help him through his adventures. Hawkins, the bellicose chaplain, Mr Biggs the boatswain, and Mr Pottyfar, the lieutenant who kills himself with his own universal medicine, are notable among the ship's company.

Midsummer Night's Dream, A A comedy by *Shakespeare, written probably *c*.1594–5; printed in quarto in 1600 and 1619; reprinted with changes apparently deriving from performance in the first *folio. It is often thought to be associated with a courtly marriage but none has been successfully identified. There is no single source, but Shakespeare drew, among other authors, on *Chaucer, Arthur *Golding's translation of *Ovid, and *Apuleius' *Golden Ass*.

Hermia refuses her father Egeus' command to marry Demetrius, because she loves Lysander, while Demetrius has formerly professed love for her friend Helena, and Helena loves Demetrius. Under the law of Athens, Theseus, the duke, gives Hermia four days in which to obey her father; else she must suffer death or enter a nunnery. Hermia and Lysander agree to leave Athens secretly in order to be married where the Athenian law cannot pursue them, and to meet in a wood a mile outside the city. Hermia tells Helena of the project, and the latter tells Demetrius. Demetrius pursues Hermia to the wood, and Helena Demetrius, so that all four are there that night. This wood is the favourite haunt of the fairies.

Oberon and Titania, king and queen of the fairies, have quarrelled, because Titania refuses to give up to him a changeling Indian boy for a page. Oberon tells Robin Goodfellow (Puck), a mischievous sprite, to fetch him a certain magic flower, of which he will press the juice on Titania's eyes while she sleeps, so that she will fall in love with what she first sees when she wakes. Overhearing Demetrius in the wood reproaching Helena for following him, and wishing to reconcile them, Oberon orders Robin to place some of the love-juice on Demetrius' eyes, but so that Helena shall be near him when he does it. Robin, mistaking Lysander for Demetrius, applies the charm to him, and as Helena is the first person Lysander sees he at once woos her, enraging her because she thinks she is being mocked. Oberon, discovering Robin's mistake, now places some of the juice on Demetrius' eyes; he on waking also first sees Helena, so that both Lysander and Demetrius are now wooing her. The women quarrel, and the men go off to fight for Helena.

Meanwhile Oberon has placed the love-juice on Titania's eyelids. She wakes to find Bottom the weaver close by, wearing an ass's head (Bottom and a company of Athenian tradesmen are in the wood to rehearse a play for the duke's wedding, and Robin has put an ass's head on Bottom). Titania at once falls in love with him, and toys with his 'amiable cheeks' and 'fair large ears'. Oberon, finding them together, reproaches Titania for bestowing her love on an ass, and again demands the changeling boy, whom she in her confusion surrenders; whereupon Oberon releases her from the charm. Robin at Oberon's orders throws a thick fog about the human lovers, and brings them all together, unknown to one another, and they fall asleep. He applies a remedy to Lysander's eyes, so that when he awakes he returns to his former love. Theseus and Egeus appear on the scene, the runaways are forgiven, and the couples married. The play ends with the 'tragedy' of 'Pyramus and Thisbe', comically acted by Bottom and his fellow tradesmen, to grace these weddings and that of Theseus and Hippolyta.

MIÈVILLE, China (1972–) Author of *fantasy fiction, born in Norwich. His second novel *Perdido Street Station* (2000) fuelled the hybrid energy of the *New Weird, attacking the conservatism of fantasy on both political and literary grounds. Short stories are collected in *Looking for Jake* (2005).

MIGNE, Jacques-Paul (1800–75) French priest and publisher. He founded a printing house to make theological works available at moderate prices. His most famous publication was the *Patrologiae Cursus Completus*, comprising the *Patrologia Latina* (221 vols, 1844–64), the works of Latin ecclesiastical writers from the earliest known to Innocent III (d. 1216), and the *Patrologia Graeca* (161 vols, 1857–66), the writings of Christian Greeks down to the time of the Council of Florence (1438–9).

Milesians The people of Míl Espáine ('soldier of Spain'), who are said to have invaded Ireland about 1300 BC and driven the *Tuatha Dé Danann underground. They probably represent the first Gaelic inhabitants of the country.

Military Memoirs of Capt. George Carleton First published in 1728 as *The Memoirs of an English Officer*. It was once attributed to Daniel *Defoe, and to Jonathan *Swift, but it is probably a genuine memoir; evidence of a real officer named Captain Carleton was uncovered in the 1920s. The narrative covers his service in the Dutch wars of the 1670s and (in greater detail) with Lord Peterborough in Spain from 1705 until Carleton's capture in 1708. His five years as a prisoner yield many observations on Spanish life. The book was greatly admired by Samuel *Johnson, and Walter *Scott brought out a new edition of it in 1808.

MILL, James (1773–1836) Scottish historian, economist, and philosopher, born near Forfar, the son of a shoemaker. Educated for the ministry, he came to London in 1802 and took up journalism. His *History of British India* (1817) secured a well-paid post with the East India Company. Associated with Jeremy *Bentham and David Ricardo (1772–1823), whose views in philosophy and political economy he adopted, Mill published *Elements of Political Economy* in 1821, *Analysis of the Phenomena of the Human Mind* in 1829, and *Fragment on Mackintosh* in 1835. In the *Analysis*, David *Hartley's theory of association provides a psychological basis for Bentham's utilitarianism: associations may become inseparable, transforming what had merely been means into ends sought on their account, thus explaining the altruism of a self-seeking individual. The *Fragment on Mackintosh* responds to the attack on utilitarianism in James *Mackintosh's *Dissertation on the Progress of Ethical Philosophy*. Mill helped to found and contributed to the **Westminster Review*. The *Autobiography* (1873) of his son John Stuart *Mill gives a portrait of his austere personality.

MILL, John Stuart (1806–73) Philosopher and political economist, son of James *Mill, by whom he was rigorously educated from a very early age, and by whose influence he obtained a clerkship in the India House. He formed the

Utilitarian Society, which met during 1823–6 to read essays and discuss them, and in 1825 edited Jeremy *Bentham's *Treatise upon Evidence*. In 1826 an acute mental crisis caused him to reconsider his own aims and those of the Benthamite school; he found a new will to live in poetry, particularly in that of *Wordsworth, who brought him 'a greatly increased interest in the common feelings and common destiny of human beings'. In 1831 he met Harriet Taylor (1807–58), whom he saw constantly for the next twenty years and who was, in his view, the chief inspiration of his philosophy; they married in 1851, after her husband's death. His divergence from strict Benthamite doctrine is shown in his essays on 'Bentham' and 'Coleridge' (1838, 1840, *London and Westminster Review*) whom he describes as 'the two great seminal minds of England in this age'; and, later, in **Utilitarianism* (1861). In 1843 he published his *System of Logic* and in 1848 *Principles of Political Economy*. In 1859 appeared his essay *On *Liberty* and two volumes of *Dissertations and Discussions*, and in 1865 his *Examination of Sir William Hamilton's Philosophy*. Other works include *Thoughts on Parliamentary Reform* (1859), *Representative Government* (1861), *Auguste Comte and Positivism* (1865), his *Inaugural Address* on being installed rector of the University of St Andrews in 1867, and *The Subjection of Women* (1869). His engaging *Autobiography* (1873) describes his intellectual and moral development from his earliest years to his maturity. On the dissolution of the East India Company in 1858 he retired with a pension, and was independent MP for Westminster 1865–8. He passed most of the rest of his life in France, and died at Avignon. See Richard Reeves, *John Stuart Mill* (2007).

MILLAIS, Sir John Everett (1829–96) Painter. He began his career as child prodigy and finished as president of the Royal Academy (1896); he is best known as a founder member of the *Pre-Raphaelite Brotherhood. His *Lorenzo and Isabella* (1848–9), from John *Keats's poem, is one of the earliest Pre-Raphaelite works; the startling realism of his *Christ in the House of his Parents* (1849–50) was brutally attacked by Charles *Dickens in *Household Words* in 1850. *Ophelia* (1851–2), *Mariana* (1851), which was exhibited with lines from Alfred *Tennyson's poem, and the poignant, melancholy *Autumn Leaves* (1856) display his brilliant technique and fresh, precise detail. His portrait of his champion John *Ruskin was painted in Scotland in 1853; Millais fell in love with Effie Ruskin on this holiday and married her in 1855. Millais made a distinguished contribution to the revival of book illustration in the 1860s; he had contributed to Edward *Moxon's edition of Tennyson in 1857; he illustrated several of Anthony *Trollope's novels with sharply observed scenes from contemporary Victorian life and became a close friend of Trollope. He also became a friend of Dickens and drew him the day after the novelist's death. *Bubbles* (1886) became celebrated as a soap advertisement.

MILLAY, Edna St Vincent (1892–1950) American poet, born in Maine and educated at Vassar College. Her first volume, *Renascence and Other Poems* (1917), was followed by *A Few Figs from Thistles* (1920), which established her persona as a reckless, romantic, cynical, sexually frank *New Woman. This was followed by many other volumes, including dramatic pieces. Her *Collected Poems* were published in 1956. She was the first woman to receive the *Pulitzer Prize for poetry in 1923. Her impact on a whole generation was recorded by Dorothy *Parker and her poetry was praised by Thomas *Hardy. See Nancy Milford, *Savage Beauty* (2001).

Millenium Hall, A Description of *utopian novel by Sarah *Scott, published in 1762 and much reprinted thereafter. Through inset stories within a frame narrative, it assembles a cast of women who have made or found themselves independent of male control and have created a self-supporting philanthropic community devoted to the protection of the weak and unfortunate.

MILLER, Arthur (1915–2005) American playwright, born in New York and educated at the University of Michigan, where he began to write plays. He made his name with *All my Sons* (1947), an *Ibsenesque drama about a manufacturer of defective aeroplane parts, and established himself as a leading dramatist with *Death of a Salesman* (1949), in which a travelling salesman, Willie Loman, is brought to disaster by accepting the false values of contemporary society. This was followed by *The Crucible* (1952), in which the Salem witchcraft trials of 1692 are used as a parable for McCarthyism in America in the 1950s. *A View from the Bridge* (1955) is a tragedy of family honour and revenge, sparked by the presence in longshoreman Eddie's apartment of two illegal Italian immigrants; the lawyer Alfieri comments as chorus on the inevitability of the action. *The Misfits* (1961) is a screenplay written for his then wife Marilyn Monroe. *After the Fall* (1964) presents the semi-autobiographical figure of Quentin, seeking to comprehend the meaning of his own past relationships, and *The Price* (1968) contrasts the lives and opinions of two long-estranged brothers. Other plays include *The American Clock* (1980), *Playing for Time* (1981), *The Last Yankee* (1993), *Broken Glass* (1994), and *Mr Peters' Connections* (1998). In his last play, *Finishing the Picture* (2004), Miller returned to the subject of Monroe, exploring the troubled making of *The Misfits*. Miller has also published short stories, essays (*Theatre Essays*, 1971), a novel *Focus* (1945), and a number of travel photo texts. He published an autobiography, *Timebends*, in 1987. See Martin Gottfried, *Arthur Miller: A Life*(2003).

MILLER, Henry (1891–1980) American novelist and essayist, born in New York, who rejected university in favour of a bohemian life of odd jobs and intellectual, sexual, and literary enterprises. He left America for Paris in 1930, and his autobiographical novel *Tropic of Cancer* was published in Paris in 1934 by the Obelisk Press, the predecessor of the *Olympia Press, being a frank and lively account of an American artist's adventures in Paris. This, like many of Miller's works, was banned for decades in Britain and the USA for its sexual content. He was very influenced by *Surrealist writing and film, and experimented with Anaïs *Nin in composing dream narratives. He was also an admirer of D. H. *Lawrence and for a time worked closely with Lawrence *Durrell. *Tropic of Capricorn* (France 1939; USA 1962) was a companion volume to the first 'Tropic', being followed by *The Colossus of Maroussi* (1941), about Greece, *The Air-Conditioned Nightmare* (1945), reflections on Miller's return to America, and the *Rosy Crucifixion* trilogy: *Sexus* (1949), *Plexus* (1953), and *Nexus* (1960). In 1944 he settled in Big Sur, near Carmel, California, and despite continuing attacks from censors in various countries, including his own, he gradually became accepted as a major figure in the fight for literary and personal freedom, and a spiritual sage who greatly influenced the *Beat Generation. Miller's phallic eroticism was attacked by Kate Millett and other feminists. See Robert Ferguson, *Henry Miller* (1991).

MILLER, Hugh (1802–56) Geologist and journalist, born in Cromarty, Scotland. He left school at 16, renouncing university in order to become a stonemason, so that he could study in the winter close season. He published poetry (*Poems Written in the Leisure Hours of a Journeyman Mason*, 1829), but was more successful as journalist and as self-educated palaeontologist. From 1840 he edited the *Witness*, a radical and evangelical twice-weekly, contributing articles on subjects including rural poverty, geology, and foreign affairs. His books include the popular *The Old Red Sandstone, or New Walks in an Old Field* (1841), a vivid account of his excitement as he searched for fossils in the sandstone quarries. His autobiographical *My Schools and Schoolmasters* (1854) was also highly regarded. In *The Footprints of the Creator* (1849), an attack on Robert *Chambers's *The Vestiges of Creation*, Miller developed a religious view of evolution, arguing that evolutionary change was sudden, not gradual. He shot himself on Christmas Eve 1856, after recording 'a fearful dream'. See George Rosie, *Hugh Miller: Outrage and Order* (1981); L. Borley (ed.), *Hugh Miller in Context: Geologist and Naturalist, Writer and Folklorist* (2002).

MILLER, Walter Michael, Jr (1922–96) American *science fiction writer, born in Florida; his only completed novel, *A Canticle for Leibowitz* (1959), won a *Hugo award. Echoing the author's Catholicism, it powerfully explores the preservation and rebirth of knowledge in a new Dark Age following a nuclear holocaust.

'Miller's Tale, The' *See* CANTERBURY TALES, 2.

Mill on the Floss, The A novel by George *Eliot, published 1860. This is the most autobiographical of Eliot's novels. Tom and Maggie Tulliver, the principal characters, are the children of the honest but ignorant Mr Tulliver, miller of Dorlcote Mill on the river Floss. Tom is good-hearted, but unimaginatively conventional. Maggie in contrast is highly strung, intelligent, emotional, and, as a child, rebellious. From this conflict of temperaments, and from Maggie's frustrated sense of purpose, spring much of her unhappiness and the ultimate tragedy. Her deep love of her brother is thwarted by his lack of understanding, and she turns to the clever and sympathetic Philip Wakem, who is the deformed son of a neighbouring lawyer, for companionship. Unfortunately lawyer Wakem is the object of Mr Tulliver's dislike, which develops into hatred when Tulliver is bankrupted as a result of litigation in which Wakem is on the other side. Tom, loyal to his father, discovers the secret friendship of Maggie and Philip, and forbids their meetings: Maggie reluctantly complies. Her life becomes dreary and circumscribed, as she struggles to suppress her need for emotional and intellectual fulfilment. After Mr Tulliver's death, accelerated by a scene of violence in which he thrashes the lawyer, Maggie leaves the mill. Now a strikingly attractive young woman, she visits her cousin Lucy Deane at St Ogg's, who is to marry the handsome and agreeable Stephen Guest. Stephen, though faithful in intention to Lucy, is attracted by Maggie, and she by him. A boating expedition leads, partly by Stephen's design, partly by accident, to Maggie's being irremediably compromised; Stephen implores her to marry him, but she refuses. Her brother turns her out of the house, and the society of St Ogg's ostracizes her. She takes refuge with the loyal friend of her childhood, the packman Bob Jakins. Her mother stands by her; otherwise, only Lucy, Philip, and the clergyman Dr Kenn show sympathy. The situation seems without issue, but in the last chapter a flood descends upon the town, and Maggie courageously rescues Tom from the mill. There is a moment of recognition and reconciliation before the boat overturns, and both, locked in a final embrace, are drowned.

The portrayal of childhood, of provincial life, and the subsidiary characters of Mrs Tulliver's sisters, the strong-minded Mrs Glegg and the melancholy Mrs Pullett, with their respective spouses, pleased most contemporary critics, though the book was felt to lack the charm of **Adam Bede*; Maggie's lapse into passion, the character of the lightweight Stephen, and the relentless tragedy of the denouement alienated others. It is now one of the most widely read and admired of George Eliot's works.

Mills and Boon A British publishing company founded in 1908 by Gerald Mills and Charles Boon. Originally a publisher of general fiction (its early authors included P. G. *Wodehouse and Jack *London), its name has become synonymous with popular *romantic fiction. It launched the career of Georgette Heyer (1902–74) in the 1920s and, as the circulating libraries (*see* MUDIE, CHARLES) declined in the 1950s and paperback fiction became more popular, it published increasing quantities of light romances, doctor–nurse romances, and *historical fiction, selling not only in bookshops, but also in newsagents and, later, supermarkets. In association with the Canadian firm Harlequin, which acquired the company in 1971, Mills and Boon continues to publish a range of romantic titles.

MILMAN, Henry Hart (1791–1868) Poet and historian, educated at Eton College and Brasenose College, Oxford. He became incumbent of St Mary's, Reading, then professor of poetry at Oxford (1821–31) and dean of St Paul's (1849). He wrote a number of verse dramas, of which *Fazio* (1815), a neo-Jacobean tragedy set in Italy, proved successful on the stage; also a *Miltonic epic, *Samor* (1818), set in 5th-century Britain. His historical writings include *The History of the Jews* (1829) and *History of Latin Christianity*, 6 vols (1854–5).

MILNE, A. A. (Alan Alexander) (1882–1956) Born in Hampstead and educated at Westminster School and Trinity College, Cambridge. A prolific essayist and light versifier, he was assistant editor of **Punch* (1906–14), served in the Warwickshire regiment during the First World War, and published a fantasy, *Once upon a Time* (1915). He was a popular playwright, with plays such as *Mr Pim Passes By* (1919; pub. 1921), *The Truth about Blaydes* (1921; pub. 1922), and *Toad of Toad Hall* (1929), a dramatization of part of Kenneth Grahame's *The *Wind in the Willows*. Among his novels is a notable detective story, *The Red House Mystery* (1922). Milne's books for children include two collections of poems, *When We Were Very Young* (1924) and *Now We Are Six* (1927), typifying the 'beautiful child' fashion of the day. His books featuring toy animals belonging to his son Christopher Robin, *Winnie-the-Pooh* (1926) and *The House at Pooh Corner* (1928), were illustrated by E. H. *Shepard. To his annoyance, these overshadowed the rest of his work. See Ann Thwaite, *A. A. Milne: The Man behind Winnie-the-Pooh* (1990).

MILNES, (Richard) Monckton (1809–85) Later Baron Houghton, writer and politician; educated at Trinity College, Cambridge, where he became the friend of Alfred *Tennyson, Arthur *Hallam, and W. M. *Thackeray, the first of many close literary friendships, which included, most notably, A. C. *Swinburne (whom he greatly assisted), Richard *Burton, the *Brownings, Coventry *Patmore, and Walter Savage *Landor. He was a supporter of Florence *Nightingale, and for some years her suitor. In 1837 he became an MP and worked for various reforming causes, including the Copyright Act and the establishment of Mechanics' Institutes. He published his first volume of verse in 1838 and *Palm Leaves* in 1844, following these with works of biography, history, sociology, and material relating to James *Boswell. His major work was probably his *Life and Letters of Keats* (1848), a poet whom he consistently championed. He also did much to enhance the reputation of William *Blake, and in 1875 edited the works of Thomas Love *Peacock. His own collected *Poetical Works* appeared in 1876. His large collection of erotic books included the first serious collection of de *Sade. See J. Pope-Hennessy, *Monckton Milnes*, 2 vols (1950–52).

MIŁOSZ, Czesław (1911–2004) Polish poet, born on the Polish–Lithuanian borderland of Wilno (Vilnius). He was a leader of the Polish literary avant-garde in the 1930s, and prominent in the Resistance. After some years in the diplomatic service, he emigrated to America, settling in California, and teaching at Berkeley. His works include novels, volumes of essays, and *The Captive Mind* (1951), an apologia for his withdrawal from Poland. He also translated William *Shakespeare, John *Milton, and T. S. *Eliot into Polish. He was awarded the *Nobel Prize for Literature in 1980. *New and Collected Poems 1931–2001* was published in 2006. Miłosz's translations of modern Polish poets have been influential, and his own work has had great impact on, among others, Seamus *Heaney.

Milton A poem in two books by William *Blake, written and etched 1804–8, one of his most complex mythological works, prefaced by his well-known lines 'And did those feet in ancient time', commonly known as 'Jerusalem'. It uses the mythological and allegorical framework of his earlier poems and also develops Blake's own powerful and personal response to **Paradise Lost* and its author, which perplexed his imagination for years (*see* MARRIAGE OF HEAVEN AND HELL). Blake seems to suggest that he himself becomes permeated with the spirit of *Milton, who descends to earth in order to save Albion through the power of Imagination: the bizarre and the sublime mingle, as Blake describes the spirit of Milton entering his foot—'and all this Vegetable World appear'd on my left Foot | As a bright sandal form'd immortal of precious stones and gold. | I stooped down and bound it to walk forward through eternity'. Blake imagines himself carried from Lambeth to Felpham (in Sussex) by Los, where, walking in his cottage garden, he is visited by the Virgin Ololon, in search of Milton. The poem draws to an end with Milton's address to Ololon, in which he proclaims his mission of regeneration—'To cast off the rotten rags of Memory by Inspiration | To cast off Bacon, Locke and Newton from Albion's covering'—and prophesies the purging away by Jesus of the 'sexual garments' which hide 'the human lineaments'. The final section is an apocalyptic vision, in which Jesus 'wept and walked forth | From Felpham's Vale clothed in Clouds of blood', from which Blake returns to his 'mortal state' to hear the mounting lark. The mythology of the poem is obscure, but much of it clearly relates to the experiences of his time at Felpham, combining mystic vision and natural observation.

MILTON, John (1608–74) Poet, born in Bread Street, Cheapside, at the Sign of the Spread Eagle, the house of his father John Milton the elder, a scrivener (or professional copyist) and composer of music. He was educated at St *Paul's School, where he became friendly with Charles *Diodati, then at Christ's College, Cambridge, where he acquired the nickname 'the Lady of Christ's', and may have alienated his fellow students by, in his own words, 'a certain niceness of nature, an honest haughtiness'. He was briefly expelled, probably in 1626; he became BA in 1629, and MA in 1632. During his Cambridge period, while considering himself destined for the ministry, he began to write poetry, mostly in Latin. His first known attempt at English verse, 'On the Death of a Fair Infant', was probably written in 1628 on the death of his niece Anne Phillips, and 'At a Vacation Exercise' belongs to the same year. His first distinctively Miltonic work, 'On the Morning of Christ's Nativity', written at Christmas 1629, shows a baroque use of imagery and the love of resounding proper names apparent in his later work. A Latin elegy to Diodati tells his friend that the inspiration for this poem came to him on Christmas morning. His fragmentary 'The Passion' was probably written at Easter 1630, and *Arcades probably in 1632. 'On Shakespeare', his two epitaphs for Thomas *Hobson, the university carrier, and 'An Epitaph on the Marchioness of Winchester' belong to 1631. His twin poems, *'L'Allegro' and *'Il Penseroso', may have been written at Cambridge, or possibly at Hammersmith, where Milton the elder moved 1631/2: Milton himself on leaving Cambridge adopted no profession, but embarked on an ambitious course of private study at his father's home in preparation for a future as a poet; his Latin poem 'Ad Patrem' (?1634) thanks his father for his support. His 'masque' *Comus, published anonymously in 1637, was written, and performed at Ludlow, in 1634. In 1636 the Miltons moved to Horton, then in Buckinghamshire, where John pursued his studies in Greek, Latin, and Italian, devoting much time to the church *Fathers. In 1637 he wrote *Lycidas, a pastoral elegy, which dwells on fears of premature death, unfulfilled ambition, and wasted dedication. During the twenty years that elapsed between this and his composition of *Paradise Lost Milton wrote no poetry, apart from Latin and Italian pieces, and sonnets, among them 'On the Late Massacre in Piedmont', on his blindness ('When I consider how my light is spent'), on the death of his second wife ('Methought I saw my late espoused saint'), and addresses to Oliver *Cromwell, the Parliamentarian general Thomas Fairfax (1612–71), and the Puritan statesman Henry Vane (1613–62), and to Henry *Lawes (with whom he had collaborated on the *Arcades* and *Comus*) and his young friends and students Edward Lawrence (1633–57) and Cyriack Skinner (1627–1700). From 1638 to 1639 Milton travelled abroad, chiefly in Italy; he met Hugo *Grotius in Paris and *Galileo, still under official condemnation, at his villa just outside Florence.

While he was away, Diodati died, and on his return Milton commemorated him in the Latin elegy *Epitaphium Damonis*. He established himself in London and became tutor to his nephews Edward and John *Phillips. He appears at this time to have been contemplating an epic on an Arthurian theme. His attentions were now diverted by historical events to many years of pamphleteering and political activity, and to a tireless defence of religious, civil, and domestic liberties. In 1641 he published a series of five pamphlets against episcopacy, engaging in controversy with Bishops Joseph *Hall and James *Ussher, and displaying from the first (*Of Reformation in England and the Causes that Hitherto Have Hindered It*) a vigorous, colourful Ciceronian prose, and a keenly polemic spirit which could yet rise to visions of apocalyptic grandeur. *The Reason of Church Government* (1642) was the first to which he put his name; it was followed in the same year by *An Apology against a Pamphlet…against* *Smectymnuus, which contains interesting autobiographical details. In July 1642 Milton married Mary Powell, daughter of Royalist parents; he was 33, she 17. Within six weeks he consented to her going home to her parents at Forest Hill, near Oxford (the Royalist stronghold), on condition that she returned by Michaelmas. She did not do so, for reasons perhaps connected with the outbreak of the Civil War as well as personal antipathy and sexual incompatibility. Taking advantage of the breakdown in censorship, Milton published in 1643 *The Doctrine and Discipline of Divorce*, arguing among other points that a true marriage was of mind as well as of body, and that the chaste and modest were more likely to find themselves 'chained unnaturally together' in unsuitable unions than those who had in youth lived loosely. This pamphlet made him notorious, but he pursued his arguments in three more on the subject of divorce in 1644–5, including *Tetrachordon*, and also published in his own support a translation of Martin Bucer's views on the same theme. *Of Education*, addressed to his friend Samuel *Hartlib, appeared in 1644, as did his defence of the liberty of the press, *Areopagitica. During this period he became aware of his growing blindness; by 1652 he was to be totally blind. His wife rejoined him in 1645, and their first daughter Anne was born a year later: a second daughter Mary was born in 1648 and Deborah in 1652. A son, John, born 1651, died in infancy.

After the execution of Charles I, Milton published *The Tenure of Kings and Magistrates* (1649), arguing in general terms that a people 'free by nature' had a right to depose and punish tyrants, and attacking the *Presbyterians, whose belief in church discipline and state authority posed in his view a growing threat to freedom. He was appointed Latin secretary to the newly formed Council of State. He replied officially to *Eikon Basilike in *Eikonoklastes* (i.e. Image Breaker, 1649), and to *Salmasius in *Pro Populo Anglicano Defensio* (1651: *A Defence of the English People*), a work which created a furore on the Continent and was publicly burned in Paris and Toulouse; also to Du Moulin's *Clamor* (which he attributed to Alexander More, or Morus (1616–70)) in *Defensio Secunda* (1654), which contains some self-defensive autobiographical passages and reflections on his blindness. He was now assisted in his secretarial duties successively by G. R. Weckherlin (1584–1653), Philip Meadows (bap. 1626, d. 1718), and Andrew *Marvell. His first wife died in 1652, three days after the birth of their third daughter, and in 1656 he married Katherine Woodcock, then aged 28, who died in 1658, having given birth to a daughter who survived only a few months. He retained his post as Latin secretary until the *Restoration, having lived during most of this period at Petty France, Westminster. On the eve of the Restoration, he boldly published *The Ready and Easy Way to Establish a Free Commonwealth* (1660), a last-minute attempt to defend the 'Good old Cause' of republicanism and to halt the growing tide of Royalism and the 'defection of the misguided and abused multitude'. At the Restoration he went into hiding briefly, then was arrested, fined, and released: Sir William *D'Avenant and Marvell are said to have interceded on his behalf. He now returned to poetry and set about the composition of *Paradise Lost*; he had shown his nephews a sketch of lines from Book IV as early as 1642, and his notebooks show that he had earlier contemplated a drama on a similar theme. In 1663 he married his third wife, Elizabeth Minshull (who survived him by more than 50 years), and moved to what is now Bunhill Row, where he spent the remaining years of his life, apart from a brief visit to Chalfont St Giles in 1665, to avoid the plague, organized by his Quaker friend Thomas *Ellwood. *Paradise Lost* is said by John *Aubrey to have been finished in 1663, but the agreement for his copyright was not signed until 1667. *Paradise Regained was published in 1671 with *Samson Agonistes*: the composition dates of the latter have been much discussed, and the assumption that it was his last poem has been challenged. In these late years he also published various works written earlier in his life, including a *History of Britain* (1670), from legendary times to the Norman Conquest, and a compendium of *Ramus' *Logic* (1672). In 1673 appeared a second edition of his *Poems*, originally published in 1645, including most of his minor verse. His *A Brief History of Moscovia*, drawn from the *Hakluyt and *Purchas collections, appeared posthumously in 1682.

The State Papers that he wrote as Latin secretary (discovered in 1743) are mostly concerned with the routine work of diplomacy, but include an interesting series of dispatches, 1655–8, on the subject of the expulsion and massacre of the Protestant Vaudois by the orders of the prince of Savoy, who had commanded them to abandon their faith. These breathe the same indignation as the sonnet on the massacre, 'On the Late Massacre in Piedmont'. His theological treatise *De Doctrina Christiana*, based entirely on biblical citations, was first printed in 1825. It ridiculed the doctrine of the Trinity, justified polygamy as a Christian form of marriage, and argued that God was a material substance and that the soul died with the body. These unorthodoxies had made its publication during his lifetime impossible. His *Commonplace Book*, with interesting insights into his studies and plans for composition, came to light in 1874.

Milton died from 'gout struck in' (probably of renal failure associated with gout) and was buried beside his father in St Giles', Cripplegate. There are full biographies by David *Masson and W. R. Parker (2 vols, 1968; rev. 1996 by Gordon Campbell); and Barbara Lewalski (2000). See also *A Milton Chronology* (1997) by G. Campbell. His personality continues to arouse as much discussion as his works; as a man he has been variously presented as sociable, good-natured, and increasingly serene, as a domestic tyrant who bullied his daughters, as a strict Puritan, a misogynist, a libertine, and as a radical heretic. (See Christopher *Hill, *Milton and the English Revolution*, 1977.) As a writer, his towering stature was recognized early. Although appreciated as a master of polemical prose as well as of subtle lyric harmony, his reputation rests largely on *Paradise Lost*, which John *Dryden (who made a rhymed version of it) was describing by 1677 as 'one of the greatest, most noble and sublime poems which either this age or nation has produced'. William *Blake's dictum from *The *Marriage of Heaven and Hell* (1790) that Milton was 'a true Poet and of the Devil's party without knowing it' preceded the Romantic version, disseminated principally by P. B. *Shelley, which represented Satan the Arch-Rebel as the true hero of *Paradise Lost*, and its God as either dull or wicked. Critics such as C. S. *Lewis (*A Preface to Paradise Lost*, 1942) have endeavoured to dismiss this notion, but it continues to attract students and creative writers, including William *Empson (*Milton's God*, 1961). A different controversy, echoing the older complaints of Johnson and Addison, was brought into focus by T. S. *Eliot's attack, in 1936, in which he described Milton as one whose sensuousness had been 'withered by book-learning' and further impaired by blindness, and who wrote English 'like a dead language'. He modified these views later, but they were endorsed by F. R. *Leavis, who condemned the alleged rhythmic deadness, mechanical externality, and Latinate syntax of the later works. These charges were ably countered by Christopher *Ricks (*Milton's Grand Style*, 1963), who showed that Milton's verse, although powerful, is also subtle and suggestive. Modern readings have explored Milton's conflicting feelings in portraying gender (see J. Wittreich, *Feminist Milton*, 1987, and S. Davies, *John Milton*, 1991); and the complex stresses of his political affiliations (see *Surprised by Sin*, 1968; 2nd edn 1998, by Stanley Fish). See too D. Danielson (ed.), *The Cambridge Companion to Milton* (2nd edn 1999). The Columbia edition of the *Complete Works* (18 vols, 1931–8) and the Yale edition of the *Prose* (8 vols, 1953–82) are standard, and, for the poems, the Longmans edition by J. Carey and A. Fowler (1st edn 1968; 2nd edn of the *Shorter Poems* 1997 and of *Paradise Lost* 1998).

mime In modern usage, a term used to describe a kind of theatrical performance without words, in which meaning is conveyed by gesture and movement. As an art form it has flourished more on the Continent, in the work of such performers and writer-performers as Marcel Marceau (1923–2007) in France, than in England. The nearest significant counterpart in English traditions is the silent dramatic scene known as the *dumb show.

mimesis *See* POETICS.

Minnesänger ('minnesingers') German lyric poets of the late 12th to the 14th centuries, so called because chivalric love (*Minne*) was the principal subject of their poetry. They were influenced by the Provençal troubadours and the northern French trouvères. The *Minnesang* flourished during the years 1180–1220, known as the *Blütezeit*, after which it began to decline and evolve into *Meistergesang*. Some of the greatest *Minnesänger*—Hartmann von Aue, *Wolfram von Eschenbach, and Gottlieb von Strassburg—were also writers of epic. The other most admired exponents of the lyric are Reinmar von Hagenau, Heinrich von Morungen, and Walther von der Vogelweide. See Olive Sayce (ed.), *Poets of the Minnesang* (1967).
See COURTLY LOVE; MEISTERSINGER.

MINOT, Laurence The author (of whom almost nothing is known) of a series of spirited, patriotic war songs, written about 1352, concerning events of the period 1333–52 in the English wars against the Scots and French, such as Crécy, Halidon Hill, and the sieges of Berwick and Calais. The poems give some suggestion of what medieval warfare was like, but have little claim to literary distinction. See *The Poems of Laurence Minot 1333–1352*, ed. T. B. James and J. Simons (1989).

Minotaur The monstrous offpring of Pasiphaë's union with a bull sent from the sea by the god *Poseidon. He was kept in a labyrinth built by Daedalus for Minos, king of Crete and Pasiphaë's husband. Minos required the Athenians to send youths and maidens as tribute for the Minotaur to destroy. *Theseus with the help of Minos' daughter Ariadne slew the

Minotaur and escaped from the labyrinth. The story symbolizes destructive passion in *Racine's *Phèdre* and Ted *Hughes's *Birthday Letters*. It is retold by Mary *Renault, and is the subject of an opera by Harrison *Birtwistle with libretto by David *Harsent.

Minstrelsy of the Scottish Border A collection of *ballads compiled by Walter *Scott, published in two volumes in 1802 and expanded in four subsequent editions up to 1812. Scott divided his material into three sections: historical, romantic, and 'imitations'. Despite its title, the *Minstrelsy* included some works from the north-east of Scotland (notably **Sir Patrick Spens*, 1803 onwards). Scott had been collecting ballads since 1792 and was later aided by friends and advisers, including John *Leyden, James *Hogg, Robert *Surtees, and many old women (among them Hogg's mother) who kept alive the oral traditions. He also had recourse to a range of archival sources. The extent to which Scott altered and 'improved' the texts has been much discussed; recent scholarship suggests that it never amounted to the wholesale reconstruction on the basis of fragmentary remains of which he was long suspected. Scott's intention in presenting the ballads was avowedly patriotic: 'By such efforts, feeble as they are, I may contribute somewhat to the history of my native country; the peculiar features of whose manners and character are daily melting and dissolving into those of her sister and ally.' The *Minstrelsy* contains many well-known ballads, including 'The *Douglas Tragedy', 'The Twa Corbies', and *The *Wife of Usher's Well* (its first printing).

MIRRLEES, Hope (1887–1978) Novelist and poet born in Chiselhurst, Kent. 'Paris: A Poem' was published by Leonard and Virginia *Woolf's Hogarth Press (1919). She is best known for her third novel *Lud-in-the-Mist* (1926), a dark fairy-tale whose republication in 1970 helped spark the modern *fantasy renaissance.

mirror (mirour) As a literary term, based on the medieval Latin use of the word 'speculum' (e.g. *Speculum Historiale* of *Vincent of Beauvais or *Speculum Meditantis* of John *Gower, translated into French as *Mirour de l'omme*) to mean a true reflection or description of a particular subject, hence compendium. Thus there are titles such as *Mirrour of the Blessed Lyf of Iesu Christ* by Nicholas *Love, the *Mirrour of the World* (translated by William *Caxton from French), the *Mirror of Fools* (translation of the late 12th-century *Speculum Stultorum* by Nigel *Wireker), and, in the Renaissance, *A *Mirror for Magistrates*.

Mirror for Magistrates, A A work planned by George Ferrers (*c.*1510–1579), master of the king's pastimes in the reign of *Henry VIII, and William Baldwin (d. in or before 1563) of Oxford. In it various famous men and women, most of them characters in English history, recount their downfall in verse. The book was originally begun as a continuation of John *Lydgate's *The Fall of Princes*, itself based on *Boccaccio's *De Casibus*. After a suppressed edition (of 1554?) it first appeared in 1559, containing twenty tragedies by various authors. In the enlarged edition of 1563 Thomas *Sackville contributed the 'Induction', set in deep winter, in which Sorrow leads the poet to the realms of the dead, and the **Complaint of Buckingham*. Further editions, with more tragedies added, were published in 1571, 1574, 1575, 1578, 1587, and 1609/10. John Higgins (*c.*1544–*c.*1602), compiler of the 1574–87 additions, added complaints by figures from early or mythical British history, such as Locrinus, Elstride, and Cordila, as well as Roman history, such as Julius Caesar and Nero.

Though the *Mirror* may not seem to offer much to a modern reader, it was one of the major achievements of what C. S. *Lewis called the *'Drab Age', and provided source material for many major writers, including Edmund *Spenser, William *Shakespeare, Samuel *Daniel, and Michael *Drayton. The *Mirror* and its continuations were edited by L. B. Campbell (1938–46).

MIRSKY, D. S. (Prince Dimitrii Petrovich Sviatopolk-Mirsky) (1890–1939) Russian literary historian and critic, born in Gievka, the family estate in Ukraine, but educated in Moscow and St Petersburg. Emigrating in 1920, he taught Russian literature at the University of London from 1922 until his dismissal for his political views in 1932. He became the most influential interpreter of Russian literature to the British and his *A History of Russian Literature* (1926–7) and *Pushkin* (1926) are still widely read. In 1932, the 'comrade prince' returned to the Soviet Union, where he continued to publish on Russian and English literature, and to engage in literary polemics. His *The Intelligentsia of Great Britain* (1934), with its scathing appraisals of such as George Bernard *Shaw, H. G. *Wells, Bertrand *Russell, and D. H. *Lawrence, caused a scandal on its publication the following year in London. In 1937 Mirsky was arrested and sent to Siberia, where he died in a prison hospital near Magadan. See G. S. Smith, *D. S. Mirsky: A Russian-English Life* (2000).

Misfortunes of Elphin, The A satirical romance by Thomas Love *Peacock, published 1829. It ingeniously blends Welsh Arthurian legend, in which Peacock was expert, and political debate. Elphin is king of Ceredigion in western Wales, but the bulk of his territory has been engulfed by the sea, owing to the incompetence of Seithenyn, drunk in charge of the embankment meant to keep out the waves. The 'inundation of Gwaelod', in the generation before the main action, becomes an allegory for the French Revolution. Elphin succeeds to the diminished kingdom and is imprisoned by a powerful neighbour, from which he is rescued by his bard Taliesin. Seithenyn's celebrated drunken speech about the wall ('the parts that are rotten give elasticity to those that are sound'), imitating a speech made by George *Canning in 1822 in defence of the existing constitution, is perhaps Peacock's finest political parody. The book also contains the celebrated 'War Song of Dinas Vawr', in context a sly comment on political opportunism, and a clever bardic contest in which the current Romantic fashion for escapist themes is gently mocked.

MISHIMA, Yukio (1925–70) Japanese novelist. Although married, with children, Mishima produced work that is suffused with a strong homoerotic sensibility. His first—and some say his best—novel, *Confessions of a Mask* (1949), deals directly with homosexuality, as does *Forbidden Colours* (1954). Even his later, political activities, culminating in his ritual samurai-style suicide, reflect his aesthetic and sexual preoccupations.

misrule, king, lord, or abbot of At the end of the 15th and beginning of the 16th centuries, an officer appointed at court to superintend the Christmas revels. At the Scottish court he was called the 'abbot of unreason'. Lords of misrule were also appointed in some of the university colleges and Inns of Court.

MISTRAL, Frédéric *See* FÉLIBRIGE.

MISTRY, Rohinton (1952–) Indian writer, born in Bombay (Mumbai) but based in Canada since 1975. Mistry is a former bank clerk whose first book was *Tales from Firozsha Baag* (1987), a collection of linked short stories set among the Parsi residents of a Bombay apartment building. More the portrait of a whole community than a series of separate narratives, it paved the way for the novel *Such a Long Journey* (1991) in which the hero, Gustad Noble, works in a Bombay bank and becomes unwittingly involved in a scheme to divert funds into an illegal government account. Set against the backdrop of the creation of Bangladesh, it shows history as a juggernaut sweeping aside ordinary people's lives, a theme also treated in the more expansive *A Fine Balance* (1996). This heartbreaking account of poverty and thwarted ambition concerns two brothers working as tailors during the 1970s State of Emergency: by the end of the novel, official corruption and their own naivety have left them not just penniless but physically maimed. Mistry has been the recipient of numerous awards, including the Governor General's Award for Fiction, the Commonwealth Writers', Giller, and W. H. Smith prizes, and the Royal Society for Literature's Winifred Holtby Prize. All three of his novels so far have made the shortlist for Britain's *Man Booker Prize. The most recent of these, *Family Matters* (2002), deals with a down-at-heel Parsi family in 1990s Bombay as it struggles to cope with financial hardship and the burden of looking after a relative suffering from Parkinson's disease. The novel's characteristic Zoroastrian meditation on duty and the desire to pursue 'good thoughts, good words and good deeds' takes place against a backdrop of increasing communalism, leading to a denouement where the cost of personal and religious purism is vividly evoked. Unlike his countryman Salman *Rushdie, Mistry avoids magical realism, instead favouring a more low-key but equally mixed mode of storytelling, drawing on influences from the European novel and the oral heritage of Persia and South Asia, to weave his narratives of Indian life.

MITCHEL, John (1815–75) Irish nationalist and solicitor, born near Dungiven, Co. Londonderry, and educated at Trinity College, Dublin. He worked on the staff of *The *Nation* from 1845 to 1847, and then founded the more radical *United Irishman*. He was tried for sedition for his part in the rising of 1848, and transported to Tasmania to serve a fourteen-year sentence. In his *Jail Journal, or Five Years in British Prisons* (1854) he left a vivid account of his experiences. He escaped to America, where he again became editor of various papers, including the Richmond *Enquirer*, organ of the Confederate president Jefferson Davis. His work also includes a *Life and Times of Aodh O'Neill, Earl of Tyrone* (1845) and *The History of Ireland* (1869).

MITCHELL, Adrian (1932–2008) Poet, novelist, and playwright, born in London and educated at Oxford. Associated with the pacifism, protest, and free verse forms of underground poetry, he has always been an accessible poet, a reputation to which his popular readings have contributed. His collections include *Out Loud* (1969), *Ride the Nightmare* (1971), *For Beauty Douglas* (1981), *Love Songs of World War II* (1989), and *Greatest Hits* (1991). His novels include *If You See Me Comin'* (1962) and *Wartime* (1973), and his many plays and stage adaptations, which make considerable use of songs and lyrics, include a version of Peter *Weiss's *Marat/Sade* (1966) and *Tyger* (1971), based on the life and work of William *Blake. *Heart on the Left: Poems 1953–1984* was published in 1997, and it has been followed by *All Shook Up* (2000) and *The Shadow Knows* (2004).

MITCHELL, David (1969–) Novelist, born in Southport, educated at the University of Kent; he taught English in Japan. His fiction—from his first novel, *Ghostwritten* (1999), onwards—has been distinguished by virtuoso use of pastiche and bravura intertwining of widely diverse storylines, narrative voices, and geographical and historical settings. Two of his novels, *number9dream* (2001) and *Cloud Atlas* (2004), have been shortlisted for the *Man Booker Prize, and in 2003 he was named among *Granta*'s Best of Young British Novelists. Mitchell recalls his childhood in *Black Swan Green*, which appeared in 2006.

MITCHELL, Julian (1935–) Novelist, playwright, and screenwriter, educated at Winchester College and Wadham College, Oxford. His novels include *Imaginary Toys* (1961), *The White Father* (1964, set in Africa), and the more experimental *The Undiscovered Country* (1968). Mitchell then turned to the theatre and television, adapting the novels of Ivy *Compton-Burnett for the stage and achieving West End success with *Half-Life* (1977), a play about an ageing archaeologist, and *Another Country* (1981; pub. 1982; filmed 1984), set in a public school, which examines the pressures and conflicts that turned some of the young intellectuals of the 1930s towards

Marxism, and made one of them a potential spy. Later plays include *Francis* (1983), based on the life of *Francis of Assisi, and *After Aida* (1986); screenplays include a study of Oscar *Wilde, played by Stephen Fry (1998), and TV adaptations of Colin Dexter's 'Inspector Morse' Oxford *detective stories. In 2007, he wrote *Consenting Adults*, a play about the 1957 Wolfenden Report, which had recommended that 'homosexual behaviour between consenting adults in private should no longer be a criminal offence'.

MITCHELL, Margaret (1900–49) American novelist, educated at Smith College. Her best-selling and *Pulitzer Prize-winning novel *Gone with the Wind* (1936) was the only fiction she published in her lifetime (her romance *Lost Laysen*, written when she was 15, was published in 1996). The equally popular film, masterminded by producer David Selznick, was released in 1939. Set in Georgia during the American Civil War, *Gone with the Wind* is the story of headstrong Scarlett O'Hara, her three marriages, and her determination to keep her father's property of Tara at all costs, despite the vicissitudes of war and passion.

MITCHISON, Naomi (1897–1999) CBE, novelist and writer, born in Edinburgh and educated at the Oxford Preparatory (later the Dragon) School and the Society of Home Students (later St Anne's College), Oxford. Sister of the scientist J. B. S. Haldane (1892–1964), she married the future Labour politician G. R. Mitchison (1890–1970) in 1916. She wrote over 70 books, including *The Conquered* (1923), *The Corn King and the Spring Queen* (1931), a historical novel set in Greece and the eastern Mediterranean in 228–187 BC, *We have been Warned* (1935), *The Blood of the Martyrs* (1939), and *The Big House* (1950). Her non-fiction works, including three volumes of autobiography (*Small Talk*, 1973; *All Change Here*, 1975; *You May Well Ask*, 1979), reflect her commitment to the many progressive political and social causes to which she dedicated her life. See Jill Benton, *Naomi Mitchison* (1990).

MITFORD, Jessica Lucy (1917–96) CBE, Writer, journalist, and sister of Nancy *Mitford, born at Asthall Manor, Oxfordshire, and educated at home. Unlike her other sisters, Diana and Unity, who supported Hitler, she adopted left-wing views early in her life, and during the Spanish Civil War became a Republican sympathizer, eloped to Spain to join her cousin Esmond Romilly, and married him there in 1937: after his death (in 1941 in Hamburg) she married American lawyer Bob Treuhaft, and settled with him in California. Together they joined the Communist Party, and maintained a lifelong support of civil rights and other radical and sometimes unpopular causes. Her vivid and entertaining account of her early family life, *Hons and Rebels* (1960), was followed by many other works of polemic and biography, and by campaigning documentaries, ranging from *The American Way of Death* (1963), a spirited exposé of the funeral industry, to *The American Way of Birth* (1992), attacking childbirth technology. Her letters have been published as *Decca: The Letters of Jessica Mitford*, ed. Peter Y. Sussman (2006).

MITFORD, Mary Russell (1787–1855) Dramatist and writer, born at Alresford, Hampshire, educated at M. de Quentin's school in Chelsea, where she learned excellent French. Her father's extravagance and gambling compelled her to earn a living as a writer. She published a volume of verse in 1810, and was encouraged to continue writing by S. T. *Coleridge. Further volumes of poems appeared, and various essays in magazines, then in 1823 her drama *Julian*, with William *Macready in the title role, was produced successfully at Covent Garden, and was followed by the even more successful *Foscari* in 1826 and *Rienzi* in 1828. She wrote other historical dramas, but meanwhile, in 1824, she had begun a series of sketches and stories which made up **Our Village* (1832), the work for which she is remembered. This was followed by *Belford Regis* (1835), a portrait of Reading; *Country Stories* (1837); and *Recollections of a Literary Life* (1852). A novel, *Atherton, and Other Tales*, was published in 1854. Her fluent letters, to Charles *Lamb, Benjamin *Haydon, Richard Henry *Horne, John *Ruskin, Elizabeth Barrett *Browning, Walter Savage *Landor, and many others, reveal an intense enjoyment of people and places and a sunny, affectionate nature: they were published in a selection ed. A. G. L'Estrange (*Life of M. R. Mitford in a Selection from her Letters to her Friends*, 3 vols, 1870) and in *Letters of M. R. Mitford, 2nd Series*, ed. H. Chorley, 2 vols (1872). See also a life by V. Watson (1949).

MITFORD, Nancy (1904–73) Novelist, daughter of the second Lord Redesdale, educated largely at home; she published four novels, including *Wigs on the Green* (1935) satirizing the British Union of Fascists (of which her brother-in-law Oswald Mosley was leader), before her first popular success, *The Pursuit of Love* (1945). In this novel the sensible Fanny describes life with her six unruly Radlett cousins and their hapless parents, Aunt Sadie and irascible Uncle Matthew. That this eccentric family is based on Mitford's own is confirmed by her sister Jessica's autobiography *Hons and Rebels* (1960). *Love in a Cold Climate* (1949) is a sequel, chiefly concerned with unsuitable relationships in the family of some Radlett neighbours called Montdore. Several characters reappear in subsequent novels (*The Blessing*, 1951; *Don't Tell Alfred*, 1960). The appeal of Mitford's novels lies in their outrageous comedy, the reckless and incurable romanticism of many of the principals, and in the author's fine ear for upper-class locutions. *Noblesse Oblige* (1956, with A. S. C. Ross *et al.*) was a characteristic Mitford 'tease', provoking a widespread debate on class distinctions ('U' and 'Non-U') in vocabulary. Her journalism, *A Talent to Annoy* (1986), and a volume of witty *Letters* (1993), including many to her close friend and literary mentor Evelyn *Waugh, were edited by Charlotte Mosley. She settled in France in 1946 and wrote several popular illustrated historical biographies of French subjects: *Madame de Pompadour* (1954), *Voltaire in Love* (1957), *The Sun King* (1966). See Selina Hastings, *Nancy Mitford* (1985).

MO, Timothy (1950–) Novelist, born in Hong Kong, the son of a Chinese father and an English mother. His first novel, *The Monkey King* (1978), set in Hong Kong's business community, was followed by *Sour Sweet* (1982), about a Chinese family's move to London in the 1960s. It was shortlisted for the *Booker Prize and subsequently adapted by Ian *McEwan for a film (1988). His most ambitious work, *An Insular Possession* (1986), is set during the 19th-century opium wars between Britain and China. *The Redundancy of Courage* (1991), also shortlisted for the Booker, tells the story of a young Chinese hotelier in East Timor whose life is transformed by violent events. *Brownout on Breadfruit Boulevard* (1995) and *Renegade or Halo2* (1999), both published under Mo's own imprint, Paddleless Press, are set in the Philippines. The latter won the James Tait Black Memorial Prize.

Moby-Dick, *or The Whale* (1851) Novel by Herman *Melville, first published in Britain, as *The Whale*. Its 135 chapters exhibit an extraordinary variety of styles, from sailors' slang to biblical prophecy and Shakespearian rant. Inspired by his friend Nathaniel *Hawthorne to say 'NO! in thunder' to Christianity, Melville fused his narrator Ishmael's search for knowledge with the tragic quest narrative of Captain Ahab seeking revenge on the white whale that has bitten off his leg. The whaler, *Pequod*, is a male microcosm of a crew drawn from many nations. Melville interrupts the narrative with factual data, tales, soliloquies, and meditations on the whale. After a fierce three-day chase Moby-Dick destroys the *Pequod*. Ishmael survives the vortex, buoyed up on the harpooner Queequeg's coffin. The novel is written in a dense and allusive style, packed with biblical and other symbolism.

mock biblical A rhetorical strategy in which scriptural quotations, narratives, or figures are used for satirical ends. Mock-biblical satire rarely attacks the Bible itself, but appropriating the Bible in parody to satirize the secular world has a special force because scriptural texts cannot be wholly divorced from their authoritative context. John *Skelton's *Speke Parrot* (1552) is one of the earliest instances in English of biblical images used to satirize worldly affairs. During the *Reformation Lucas Cranach ('the elder'), working in consort with Martin *Luther, effectively deployed the mock biblical against Rome in satirical woodcuts. A cluster of writings surrounding the *Popish Plot trials of 1679 and the Exclusion crisis of 1681—most notably John *Dryden's **Absalom and Achitophel* (1681)—propelled the mock biblical into the mainstream of partisan political writing, and a flood of typological, political, and ecclesiastical satire followed. The mode was available to all parties: Jonathan Swift's *A *Tale of a Tub* (1704) boldly used a mock-biblical perspective from an Anglican point of view; Daniel *Defoe's *True-Born Englishman* (1701) and *Iure Divino* (1706) made free with sacred writings from a Dissenting angle; and one of Alexander *Pope's less august efforts, a smutty parody of *Sternhold and Hopkins's metrical psalmody, was published by Edmund *Curll as a 'Roman Catholick Version of the First Psalm'. Mock-biblical satire became part of the 18th-century journalistic stock-in-trade and figured prominently during the Excise crisis (1733), the 'Jew Bill' (1753), the 'prime ministry' of Bute (1761–3), the Westminster election of 1784, and other political events. Charles *Churchill's *Prophecy of Famine* (1763) and William Blake's *The *Marriage of Heaven and Hell* (1790–93) and *The Book of *Los* (1793) testify to the ongoing vitality of this satirical species. The fashion for pseudo-biblical 'Chapters', 'Chronicles', 'Books', and 'Lessons' inspired by Robert *Dodsley's *Chronicle of the Kings of England* (1740) and Horace *Walpole's *Lessons for the Day* (1742) culminated in the publication of 'The *Chaldee MS' (1817) in **Blackwood's Magazine*, to a storm of controversy. In the Romantic period, many of the most vibrant mock-biblical satires were found in the political prints of Thomas *Rowlandson, George *Cruikshank, and James Gillray (1756–1815).

mock epic (mock-heroic) A satirical form that generates humour through the presentation of low characters or trivial subjects in the lofty style of classical epic or heroic poems. It is similar in spirit and character to the *mock biblical. The disjunction between matter and manner (a petticoat likened to a warrior's shield, or a chamber pot regarded as a trophy) parodies the conventions of epic poetry and satirizes the people and events who appear to regard themselves in heroic light. Almost invariably a poem in heroic couplets, the mock epic typically employs elevated *poetic diction, focuses on a single 'heroic' incident, and incorporates selected elements from the machinery of classical epic: invocation to the Muse; the challenge; battles; boasting from the hero; games and other tests of prowess; perilous journeys; *epic similes; prayers and sacrifices to gods and goddesses, and their subsequent intervention; the visit to the underworld; and the vision of future glories. Although the mock-epic satirical poem, which flourished in the later 17th and 18th centuries, portrayed real characters and events (often thinly disguised) in contemporary and local settings, its literary ancestry may be traced back to classical antiquity. The pseudo-Homeric **Batrachomyomachia* ('Battle of the Frogs and Mice'), *Virgil's mock-heroic aggrandizing of the bees ('little Romans') in *Georgic* IV, and the pseudo-Virgilian *Culex* (in which a shepherd kills a gnat that has saved his life), though lacking any satirical design, supplied precedents for the display of trivial subjects comically elevated by the heroic manner, and for the heroic manner comically debased by trivial subjects. Later examples include Vida's *Scacchia Ludus* (1537), which describes a game of chess between Apollo and Mercury with the pantheon as spectators; Tassoni's *Secchia rapita* (1622), in which the citizens of Modena and Bologna, in the guise of epic heroes, make war over a stolen bucket; *Scarron's *Virgile travesti* (1648–52), and Charles *Cotton's creative adaptation, *Scarronides* (1664). *Boileau's *Le Lutrin* (1674, 1683), an accomplished medley of burlesque, farce, parody, and satire, in which two ecclesiastical dignitaries fight over the placement of a lectern, was widely influential in England. Dryden's **Mac Flecknoe* (1682), a demolition of his rival Thomas *Shadwell, and Sir Samuel *Garth's *The Dispensary* (1699), which satirically chronicles a dispute between the College of Physicians and the Company of Apothecaries over the dispensing of medication, are the most important mock-heroic poems between Boileau and Alexander *Pope, whose *Rape of the Lock* (1712, 1714) and **Dunciad* (1728, 1742–3) mark the high points of mock epic in English. Jonathan *Swift's *Battle of the Books*, though in prose, has some mock-epic features. After Pope, mock epic tended to abandon its epic machinery and learned allusion for more direct personal and political satire. Later examples include Paul Whitehead's *The Gymnasiad, or Boxing Match* (1744), R. O. Cambridge's *The Scribleriad* (1751), Christopher *Smart's *The Hilliad* (1753), Charles *Churchill's *Rosciad* (1761), Thomas *Chatterton's *Consuliad* (1770), and *The Lousiad* (1785 *et seq.*) of 'Peter Pindar' (John *Wolcot). See Ulrich Broich, *The Eighteenth-Century Mock-Heroic Poem* (1990); G. C. Colomb, *Designs on Truth: The Poetics of the Augustan Mock-Epic* (1992); Richard Terry, *Mock-Heroic from Butler to Cowper* (2005).

modernism Is manifold, resists neat definition, and is still expanding as previously neglected strains and texts are recognized and absorbed into the mix, but is perhaps best understood as an epoch of radical cultural upheaval which flourished predominantly in Europe and the USA from, arguably, around the last quarter of the 19th century to, no less debatably, around the start of the Second World War. It is also the catch-all term for the remarkable variety of contending groups, movements, and schools in literature, art, and music that flourished in Europe in particular during this period, such as *Symbolism, *Impressionism, *Post-Impressionism, *Aestheticism, *decadence, fauvism, Cubism, constructivism, *Expressionism, *imagism, *Vorticism, *Futurism, Dada, and *Surrealism. Collectively these movements represent modernist culture's uncompromising confrontation with and sense of severance from the conventions and tastes of both mass society and the governing elite and its determination to rebuild and renew the arts; the period is thus characterized by the issuing of manifestos, the proliferation of *'little magazines', and the rapid dissemination of avant-garde works and ideas. Conversely, it was also a time in which mass modernity and its cutting-edge technologies, such as telephony, electricity and aviation, were seen by some modernists to presage the new and more heroic world they longed for. In addition, modernists took a keen interest in the parallel revolutions that were taking place in physics, psychology, anthropology, and so on, and wrote about the modern city with either contempt or awe.

Focusing on the United Kingdom and Ireland, the modernist period was predominantly an age of renewal in poetry and the novel (rather than drama). The modernist novel may be seen as a reaction against 19th-century conventions of representation and narrative omniscience and is often non-chronological, with experiments in time such as sudden jumps, temporal juxtapositions, simultaneity, or a concern with duration (making a great deal occur within a small amount of text, or stretching a small amount of action over a large textual space) in evidence. Instead of upholding the realist illusion, major modernist novels, such as James *Joyce and Virginia *Woolf, break narrative frames or move from one level of narration to another without warning or foreground the reflexivity of their texts. Instead of plot events, there is an emphasis on characters' consciousness, memory, and perception (from around 1900, the ideas of the philosopher Henri *Bergson and the psychoanalyst Sigmund *Freud began to infiltrate modernist writing). Works are often oriented around a centre or centres of consciousness and are characterized by the use of such techniques as *free indirect style and *interior monologue. Authority is often vested in strangely limited third-person or unreliable first-person narrators, or there are multiple, shifting narrators. Instead of using closure and the fulfilment of reader expectations, or following genre conventions and formulas, as in a Victorian novel, modernist novels often work towards open endings and they make free use of ellipses, ambiguity, and complexity.

In British and Irish literature, the beginning of modernism is associated with *fin-de-siècle* movements such as *naturalism (through which the liberating impact of Émile *Zola was felt), Symbolism, decadence, and Aestheticism. Together with the theories of Walter *Pater, the work of Charles *Baudelaire, Jules *Laforgue, and Stéphane *Mallarmé had a profound influence on the British and Irish poets of the 1890s, such as Oscar *Wilde, Ernest *Dowson, Arthur *Symons, Lionel *Johnson, and W. B. *Yeats. Henrik *Ibsen, Gustave *Flaubert, Joris-Karl *Huysmans, and the Russians Ivan *Turgenev, Lev *Tolstoy, and Fedor *Dostoevsky, were important influences for such writers as Joyce, Woolf, D. H. *Lawrence, Ford Madox *Ford, and others, as well as the American Henry *James (naturalized as a British citizen in 1915) and the Polish-born Joseph *Conrad (naturalized in 1886). Realistic fiction writers from the late 1890s to the Edwardian period wrote about modern life and often portrayed subjects such as extreme poverty, sexual misadventure, or the remote reaches of the British Empire (e.g. Arnold *Bennett, John *Galsworthy, Henry Rider *Haggard, Rudyard *Kipling, Somerset *Maugham, H. G. *Wells, and Arthur *Morrison), but they were following the general lines of the Victorian novel and were neither innovative in technique nor experimental in language. But in the late 1890s the novels of Henry James and *'Heart of Darkness' (1899, 1902), by Conrad, signalled a new direction, becoming increasingly complex, dense, and ambiguous. In his 'late style', as it appears in *The *Wings of the Dove* (1902), *The *Ambassadors* (1903), and *The *Golden Bowl* (1904), James's writing is marked by convoluted, ultra-qualified sentences filled with parenthetical statements, self-interruptions, and indirection. Yet of the writers who began their careers in the late Victorian period, Conrad appears now to be the most roundedly modernist. His remarkable series of novels, *Heart of Darkness*, **Nostromo* (1904), *The *Secret Agent* (1907), and *Under Western Eyes* (1911), experiment with abrupt temporal and spatial shifts in the presentation of narrative information and with many long gaps in exposition or seeming digressions; they also employ a dense and shifting prose style characterized by ambiguity and repetition and by the use of multiple narrators and narrative frames. At the same time, all four works are engaged with key areas of *fin-de-siècle* anxiety: the corruption of imperialism and colonialism, urban chaos, political extremism, degeneration, and the inability to discover the truth. Joyce's career began with the deceptively rich naturalism of *Dubliners (1914), but in A *Portrait of the Artist as a Young Man (1916) he started to experiment with interior monologue and free indirect discourse (in which the style shifts to match the 'centre of consciousness' in focus, changing in complexity and reference as the character develops or the spotlight switches to another character). *Ulysses (1922) focuses on one day in the lives of two Dubliners, using a mixture of multiple narrators (including many different third-person narrative voices), interior monologue, *stream of consciousness, literary parodies, and numerous stylistic and technical changes. *Finnegans Wake (1939) is a multilingual, multiple-punning, endlessly intertextual novel which some critics have seen as the zenith of modernism. Woolf's major novels, *Jacob's Room (1922), *Mrs Dalloway (1925), *To the Lighthouse (1927), and The *Waves (1931), are all markedly experimental in technique and narrative structure, whereas D. H. Lawrence's modernism is most in evidence in *Sons and Lovers (1913), The *Rainbow (1915), and *Women in Love (1920). Tarr (1918; 1928) by Wyndham *Lewis is another important modernist novel.

Modernist poetry followed a similarly iconoclastic agenda, overthrowing conventional forms and moving towards fragmentation, free verse, complex allusion and patterning, and personal discourse, often purposefully obscure. These effects are most evident in the poetry of T. S. *Eliot and Ezra *Pound. Nevertheless, much British poetry of the modernist period is not modernist in this sense but self-consciously traditional in form and subject matter, especially the *Georgian poets (such as Rupert *Brooke, Edward *Thomas, J. C. *Squire, and John *Drinkwater) and the soldier-poets (Wilfred *Owen, Siegfried *Sassoon, Ivor *Gurney, and Isaac *Rosenberg). But it was three outsiders who were the most important figures in British modernist poetry: W. B. Yeats and the Americans Pound and Eliot. Pound was the greatest promoter of modernism in London, where he lived from 1908 to 1920. He declared the start of imagism with his own famous two-line poem 'In a Station of the Metro' and the publication of a group of poems by Hilda *Doolittle (H.D.) and Richard *Aldington. Pound's own poetry shifted from imitation of Robert *Browning and medieval forms, through imitation of Japanese poetic structures and the minimalist writing of imagism, to Vorticism, and, with the *Cantos* (on which he worked from 1915 to 1969), the epic poem. This extremely complex 'poem with history' is almost 800 pages long, and has many sections on Confucianism, 18th-century American history, Renaissance Italy, and elliptical personal memoirs. Making few concessions to the reader, it includes untranslated Chinese, Italian, Greek, Latin, French, and Provençal. T. S. Eliot published *Prufrock and Other Observations* in 1917, but his masterpiece is The *Waste Land (1922), which would go on to capture the largest audience of any single modernist poem.

Although there were many continuities with modernism in the 1930s, notably in the work of Samuel *Beckett, Jean *Rhys, Malcolm *Lowry, Elizabeth *Bowen, and Flann *O'Brien, many of the writers of that decade set themselves apart from the earlier modernists by their involvement with left-wing causes and the fight against *Fascism and Nazism: W. H. *Auden, Cecil *Day-Lewis, Stephen *Spender, and Louis *MacNeice are among the most important of these. When (if) modernism petered out and *postmodernism began has been contested almost as hotly as when the transition from Victorianism to modernism occurred.

See V. Kolocotroni, J. Goldman, and O. Taxidou (eds), *Modernism: An Anthology of Sources* (1998); L. Rainey (ed.), *Modernism: An Anthology* (2005); D. Bradshaw (ed.), *A Concise Companion to Modernism* (2003); D. Bradshaw and K. J. H. Dettmar, *A Companion to Modernist Literature and Culture* (2006); C. Baldick, *The Modern Movement* (2004).

Modern Love A poem by George *Meredith, published 1862. An intense, innovative work of 50 verses, each of sixteen lines, it is spoken by a narrator who painfully discovers the unreality of his ideas of women. The verses are connected as much by theme as by direct sequence of events. They unfold the disillusionment of passionate married love giving place to discord, jealousy, and intense unhappiness, ending in the separation and wreck of two ill-assorted lives, and the death by poison of the wife, the 'Madam' who has given way to the narrator's mistress, the 'Lady'. The sequence only obliquely registers Meredith's own unhappy experience in his first marriage to Mary Ellen Peacock, who died of kidney failure in 1861: the poems are extensive meditations on the imaginative and ethical implications of Darwinian evolution.

Modern Manners A satire in the manner of Alexander *Pope by Mary *Robinson, published 1793 under the pseudonym 'Horace Juvenal', criticizing contemporary fashionable life and literature.

Modern Painters By John *Ruskin, a work of encyclopedic range which filled five volumes: i, 1843; ii, 1846; iii and iv, 1856; v, 1860. It began as a defence of contemporary landscape artists, especially J. M. W. *Turner. Ruskin's plan was to show his artists' 'Superiority in the Art of Landscape Painting to all the Ancient Masters Proved by Examples of the True, the Beautiful and the Intellectual'. Volume i deals with the true. Turner had been accused of defying nature. For Ruskin he was the first painter in history to have given 'an entire transcript of the whole system of nature'. Knowledge is to be attained not from the traditions of 17th-century landscape but from direct observation of the facts of nature.

In vol. ii the logical framework of ideas was rapidly constructed. Beauty is perceived by the 'theoretic', i.e. contemplative, faculty (as opposed to the aesthetic, which is sensual and base). It consists of the varied manifestations, in natural forms, of the attributes of God. But Ruskin now wanted to write, not of 'party or person', but of the functions of all art. Two years' study of old art brought revelations: Tuscan painting and sculpture of the 13th and 14th centuries, Venetian Gothic architecture, and oil painting of the Renaissance. The outcome was that *Modern Painters* ii belies its title and exalts the 'great men of old time'.

In the third and subsequent volumes the earlier systematic treatment gives way to a looser structure. A detailed analysis of mountain beauty takes up most of *Modern Painters* iv, to Ruskin 'the beginning and the end of all natural scenery'. Part of Turner's greatness lies in his representation of the gloom and glory of mountains.

In *Modern Painters* v Ruskin concludes his investigation of natural beauty. The volume reflects a new interest in myth as a source of wisdom and instrument of interpretation. A history of *Invention Spiritual* from ancient Greece to the present ends in the defeat of man's spiritual and intellectual powers by the 'deathful selfishness' of modern Europe. Turner's greatness is finally revealed in his mythological paintings, which express despair at the triumph of mortifying labour over beauty. The work had an enormous impact on the visual sensibility of the 19th century, particularly its earlier, more radical volumes. These opened readers' eyes to the variety and splendour of nature and encouraged artists in the direction of a more accurate representation of the material world.

Modest Proposal, A, *for Preventing the Children of Poor People in Ireland, from Being a Burden to their Parents or Country; and for Making Them Beneficial to the Publick* (1729) A pamphlet by Jonathan *Swift in which an apparently well-meaning commentator suggests that the problem of Irish poverty would be solved by fattening the 'excess' children of the poor to feed the rich. 'A young healthy child, well nursed, is at a year old a most delicious, nourishing and wholesome food, whether stewed, roasted, baked or boiled, and I make no doubt that it will equally well serve in a fricassee or a ragout.' Swift imitates the style of the political economists of his time, and pursues the idea with a remorselessly sustained ironic logic.

MOIR, David Macbeth (1798–1851) Scottish doctor, born in Musselburgh, Midlothian, who signed himself *Δ*, Delta, published a number of volumes of poems, and contributed much prose and verse to **Blackwood's Magazine* and to many other periodicals. He is chiefly remembered as the author of *Mansie Wauch, Tailor in Dalkeith* (1828), which is an imaginary autobiography, in the manner of Moir's friend John *Galt, revealing a comically parochial view of the world, and satirizing the rising fashion for *autobiography. Moir also published works on medicine, and in 1851 *Lectures on Poetical Literature*.

MOLESWORTH, Mary Louisa (1839–1921) née Stewart. Born in Rotterdam, Molesworth initially wrote for both adults and children as 'Ennis Graham'. She is now remembered for juvenile fantasies such as *The Cuckoo Clock* (1877), which was influenced by George *MacDonald, works that blend fantasy and realism such as *The Carved Lions* (1895), and realistic, psychologically perceptive studies of childhood, typified by her first children's novel, *Carrots: Just a Little Boy* (1876). Walter *Crane frequently illustrated her books. See Jane Cooper, *Mrs Molesworth* (2002).

MOLIÈRE (1622–73) Pseudonym of Jean-Baptiste Poquelin, French comic playwright and actor. Son of a court furnisher, he was educated at the Jesuit Collège de Clermont, but at the age of 21 abandoned his studies in order to found a theatre troupe, the 'Illustre Théâtre'. From 1645 to 1658 the troupe toured the provinces, performing his own comedies (*L'Étourdi*, 1653: *The Scatterbrain*; *Dépit amoureux*, 1656: *Lovers' Tiff*) as well as plays by others. Returning to Paris he was granted by royal favour the use of the Théâtre du Petit-Bourbon. For the next fifteen years he played regularly before city and court audiences, his troupe being adopted by the king as the 'Troupe du Roi' in 1665. He was at once enormously popular and the object of professional and ecclesiastical malice. Equally gifted as actor, director, and playwright, he had a decisive influence on the evolution of French comedy by effectively bringing together the 'high' comedy of *Corneille, with its emphasis on the representation of polite society, and the 'low' comedy of farce, essentially laughter-provoking and particularly associated with the **commedia dell'arte*. His comedies often caused controversy precisely because they invite audiences to laugh at people who are conspicuously like themselves. Whether dealing with the conflicts between husbands and wives (*L'École des maris*, 1661: *The School for Husbands*; *L'École des femmes*, 1662: *The School for Wives*), between youth and age (*L'Avare*, 1669: *The Miser*), between artifice and nature (*Les Précieuses ridicules*, 1659: *The Ridiculous Précieuses*; *Les Femmes savantes*, 1672: *The Learned Ladies*), between piety and hypocrisy (*Le Tartuffe*, 1664), between professional and domestic life (*Le Malade imaginaire*, 1673: *The Imaginary Invalid*), between master and servant (*Sganarelle*, 1660; *Le Bourgeois gentilhomme*, 1660: *The Bourgeois Gentleman*), between nobleman and peasant (*Don Juan*, 1665), or even between moral rectitude and relativism (*Le Misanthrope*, 1666: *The Misanthrope*), he shows a heightened awareness of human beings' capacity to be ridiculous, self-deluding fools. His experience as a practising actor and director are reflected in the remarkable variety of his verbal and visual comic language, ranging from bawdy jokes to sophisticated linguistic game-play, from slapstick comedy to the kind of sophisticated stage action that provokes as much thought as laughter. His influence on English *Restoration comedy exceeded that of Ben *Jonson: dramatists like William *D'Avenant, John *Dryden, William *Wycherley, John *Vanbrugh, and Thomas *Shadwell quarried his plays for characters and situations. Of the innumerable modern translators and adapters of Molière, Ranjit Bolt (1959–), Christopher *Hampton, and Tony *Harrison stand out. A film based on his life, *Molière*, was released in 2007.

MOLINA, Tirso de *See* TIRSO DE MOLINA.

Moll Flanders, The Fortunes and Misfortunes of the Famous A novel by Daniel *Defoe, published 1722. 'Moll Flanders' is the criminal alias of the narrator, whose real name is never revealed. The story purports to be the edited autobiography of a woman born in Newgate prison and abandoned as a child when her mother is convicted of theft. She is brought up in the house of the compassionate mayor of Colchester. The story relates her seduction, her five subsequent marriages and other liaisons, and her visit to Virginia, where she finds her mother and discovers that she has unwittingly married her own brother. After leaving him and returning to England, she is gradually reduced to destitution and turns to crime to support herself. She becomes an extremely skilled pickpocket and shoplifter, but is eventually caught and condemned to death, then reprieved and, like her mother, transported to Virginia. She takes with her one of her former husbands, a highwayman. With the funds that each has amassed they set up as planters, and spend their last years in prosperity and ostensible penitence. The book draws on Defoe's wide interests in social and economic problems, as well as his strong religious sense of sin and redemption. It is sometimes considered the earliest true 'Newgate Novel'.

Moloch (Molech) The name of a Canaanite idol, to whom children were sacrificed as burnt offerings (Leviticus 18: 21 and 2 Kings 23: 10), represented by Milton (**Paradise Lost*, I. 392) as one of the chief of the fallen angels; hence applied to an object to which horrible sacrifices are made.

MOMADAY, Navarre Scott (1934–) Native American writer, born on the Kiowa reservation in Oklahoma, whose second publication, *House Made of Dawn* (1968), which received the *Pulitzer Prize for fiction, played a key role in the resurgence of *Native American literature. He works in a range of different genres: stories and poems (*In the Presence of the Sun*, 1992), Kiowa mythology (*The Way to Rainy Mountain*, 1996), and *Three Plays* (2007). *The Names* (1976) is a memoir. In 2007 he was awarded the National Medal of Arts by President George W. Bush.

Monastery, The A novel by Walter *Scott, published 1820. *The Monastery* followed the success of *Ivanhoe*, but did not equal its sales. Set in the abbey of Melrose (renamed Kennaquhair) in the Scotland of the early Reformation, it vividly describes the decline of the unreformed Catholic Church, but was the first of Scott's novels to be considered a failure. A sequel, *The *Abbot*, followed in 1820 with greater success.

MONBIOT, George (1963–) Travel writer, journalist, and environmental campaigner. Educated at Stowe School and Brasenose College, Oxford, he is the author of three investigative travel narratives, *Poisoned Arrows* (1989), *Amazon Watershed* (1991), and *No Man's Land* (1994); and of several works advocating political and environmental reform.

MONBODDO, James Burnett, Lord (1714–99) Scottish judge and pioneer in anthropology, who published *Of the Origin and Progress of Language* (1773–92) and *Ancient Metaphysics* (1779–99). An admirer of *Rousseau, he was deeply interested in primitive societies; he himself lived an eccentrically austere life, believing civilization caused corruption and degeneracy. Thomas Love *Peacock's character of Sir Oran Haut-ton, in **Melincourt*, derives from Moboddo's contention that the orang-utan represented 'the infantine state of our species'. He was mocked by Samuel *Johnson for his interest in the idea that primitive men might possess vestigial tails, but he was a respected figure in Scottish literary and intellectual life, and a member of the *Select Society.

Money A comedy by Edward *Bulwer-Lytton, successfully produced in 1840. Alfred Evelyn, private secretary to the worldly-wise Sir John Vesey, loves Clara Douglas, as poor as himself. She refuses him, not wishing to involve him in her own poverty. Alfred comes into a large fortune, and, stung by Clara's refusal, which he misinterprets, proposes to the ambitious Georgina, daughter of Sir John; but soon regrets the step. To test her affection, he pretends to be ruined. Georgina promptly transfers the promise of her hand to a rival suitor, while Clara comes forward to help Alfred. Thus released, and with earlier misconceptions removed, Alfred marries Clara.

Monk, The A *Gothic novel by Matthew *Lewis, published 1796. Ambrosio, the worthy superior of the Capuchins of Madrid, falls to the temptations of Matilda, a diabolical wanton who, disguised as a boy, has entered his monastery as a novice. Now utterly depraved, Ambrosio lusts after one of his penitents, pursues the girl with the help of magic and murder, rapes and finally kills her in an effort to escape detection. She is revealed to have been his sister. He is discovered, tortured by the Inquisition, and sentenced to death, finally compounding with the devil for escape from burning, only to be hurled by him to destruction and damnation. Although extravagant in its mixture of the supernatural, the terrible, and the indecent, the book contains scenes of great effect. It enjoyed considerable contemporary notoriety.

'Monk' Lewis The nickname of Matthew *Lewis, author of *The *Monk*.

'Monk's Tale, The' *See* CANTERBURY TALES, 19.

monody An *elegy or dirge presented as the utterance of a single speaker, as in Milton's *'Lycidas'. In ancient Greek usage, a monody was an *ode for a solo voice rather than a chorus.

MONRO, H. E. (Harold Edward) (1879–1932) Poet, chiefly remembered for his Poetry Bookshop which he founded in 1913 to publish poetry, to encourage its sale, and to promote poetry readings; and for publishing the series **Georgian Poetry*, edited by Edward *Marsh. He founded and edited the *Poetry Review*, among other journals and broadsheets, and wrote poetry himself; his *Collected Poems*, introduced by T. S. *Eliot, appeared in 1933. His poems 'Bitter Sanctuary' and 'Milk for the Cat' appear in many anthologies.

MONROE, Harriet *See* POETRY.

MONSARRAT, Nicholas (1910–79) Novelist, best remembered for his highly successful novel *The Cruel Sea* (1951), based on his wartime experiences at sea; his other works include *The Tribe that Lost its Head* (1956), about the struggle for independence in an African state, and two volumes of autobiography (1966–70).

Monsieur D'Olive A comedy by George *Chapman, published 1606, acted a few years before. The plot is conventional, but the play is enlivened by the remarkable character D'Olive, 'the perfect model of an impudent upstart', fluent, self-confident, good-humoured, witty, 'a mongrel of a gull and a villain'.

MONTAGU, Basil (1770–1851) Writer and lawyer, the son of John, fourth earl of Sandwich, and his mistress Martha Ray, the singer. He met William *Wordsworth in 1795, and became friendly with him, S. T. *Coleridge, and William *Godwin, sharing their youthful radical views; his young son, also Basil Montagu, lived with Wordsworth during their West Country period, and inspired the poem 'Anecdote for Fathers'. Montagu became a successful barrister and author. He published many legal and political works on such subjects as bankruptcy, copyright, and the death penalty; edited Francis *Bacon (1825–37); and in 1846 published a little volume of mock-heroic couplets, *Railroad Eclogues*, in which he describes the advent of the railways in rural England and the effects of speculation.

MONTAGU, Elizabeth (1720–1800) née Robinson, writer and literary hostess, a celebrated member of the *Blue Stockings. Her sister was the novelist Sarah *Scott. She married the wealthy grandson of the earl of Sandwich, and embarked on a life of well-funded literary patronage. Her receptions, begun in the early 1750s, were comparatively formal, with the guests ranged in a half-circle around their hostess. She told David *Garrick that, whatever their birth, wealth, or fame, 'I never invite idiots.' Fanny *Burney found her 'brilliant in diamonds, solid in judgement, and critical in talk'. She helped many young authors, such as James *Beattie and Richard *Price, with hospitality, encouragement, and money. Hannah *More called her 'the female Maecenas of Hill St', recalling *Horace's patron. She wrote the first three of George Lyttelton's **Dialogues of the Dead* (1760); in 1769 appeared her well-received *Essay on the Writings and Genius of Shakespeare*, refuting the strictures of *Voltaire. One of its few critics was Samuel *Johnson, who had earlier been impressed by her 'radiations of intellectual excellence', calling her 'Queen of the Blues'. She supported his blind friend Anna Williams with a pension, incurring his deep gratitude, but his comments on Lyttelton and others in *Lives of the English Poets* caused a breach between them.

MONTAGU, Lady Mary Wortley (1689–1762) née Pierrepont, writer, daughter of the fifth earl and first duke of Kingston. She had an early entry to social and literary life, writing verses while young and teaching herself Latin. In 1712 she secretly married Edward Wortley Montagu, and accompanied him in 1716 when he went to Constantinople (now known as Istanbul) as ambassador. She was deeply interested in this unfamiliar territory and gained access to several areas from which men were excluded; her 'Turkish Letters', written at the time, described many scenes previously unknown to Europeans, and explored her own ambivalent reactions to the Orient. On her return in 1718 she introduced the oriental practice of inoculation against smallpox, an illness by which she herself had been marked in 1715. She had become friendly with Alexander *Pope before her visit to Turkey; in 1716 Edmund *Curll piratically published three of her satirical *Court Eclogues* under the title *Court Poems*, leading to Pope's infamous revenge by emetic, at one level a kind of gallant gesture. His letters to her while she was away indicate a strong if self-mocking romantic fascination on his part. The reasons for their quarrel are not clear, but in later works he was to attack her under the name of 'Sappho' for her sexual incontinence and lack of cleanliness. She joined with Pope's enemy Lord Hervey (1696–1743) in the scornfully aristocratic *Verses Addressed to the Imitator of Horace* (1733), a 'witty fornication' which increased Pope's animosity and was in part the provocation for his *Epistle to Dr Arbuthnot* (1735). In 1737–8 she wrote an anonymous periodical, the *Nonsense of Common-Sense* (ed. R. Halsband, 1947), and in 1739 left England and her husband to live for nearly 23 years in France and Italy, spending ten years near Brescia and engaging in an unhappy affair with Francesco Algarotti (1712–64). She returned to England shortly before her death, at which point her 'Turkish Letters' were released for publication. For a time she was remembered principally for her erudite and entertaining letters, many of them written to her daughter, Lady Bute, during her European exile; *Voltaire praised them above those of Madame de *Sévigné. Her *Letters and Works*, ed. Lord Wharncliffe, appeared in 1837. R. Halsband edited the *Complete Letters* (3 vols, 1965–7), and he and I. Grundy edited *Essays and Poems; and Simplicity: A Comedy* (1977). See also Grundy's biography, *Lady Mary Wortley Montagu* (1999).

MONTAGUE, John (1929–) Irish poet, born in New York, and educated at St Patrick's College, Armagh, and University College, Dublin. He taught for many years at University College, Cork, and was the first Ireland professor of poetry (1998–2001). His early collections include *Poisoned Lands* (1961) and *The Rough Field* (1972), a long collage on the historical predicament of the Catholics of Ulster. *Tides* (1970) and *The Great Cloak* (1978) consist mainly of love poetry, to which Montague brings an eroticism rare in mid-century Irish verse. With its unemphatic rhythms and spare use of rhyme, Montague's work absorbs the example of William Carlos *Williams, Robert *Creeley, and other poets of his native America. He has published two collections of short stories, and two memoirs (*Company*, 2001; *The Pear is Ripe*, 2007). He edited *The Faber Book of Irish Verse* (1974). See *Collected Poems* (1995).

MONTAIGNE, Michel de (1533–92) French moralist and author of the *Essais*. The title Montaigne gave to his exceptionally original work was suitably extraordinary: in the 16th century 'essais' meant 'tests' or 'trials'; it had no connotations of literary genre, though it has acquired them since, and Montaigne is often regarded as the inventor of the modern 'essay'. Montaigne published the first two books of his *Essais* in 1580, and had them reprinted in a revised version in 1582; in 1588 he published an enlarged edition, containing the third book; and until his death he was working on a further, much-expanded edition, which was published posthumously in 1595. This complex textual history is an integral part of the *Essais*, for this work, which Montaigne presents as his self-portrait, actually shows us Montaigne rereading himself, having new thoughts and making new poetic elaborations on the basis of what he had thought and written earlier: the additions are part and parcel of Montaigne's portrait of himself as an individual subject to constant change. The individual chapters that make up the *Essais* cover a huge variety of topics (moral, historical, philosophical, political, religious), and in each we see Montaigne putting his own personal judgement to the test: his chapters are never presented as objective constructions of truth, but are subjective, the record of an individual exploring issues in a highly personal way. This personal voice was first translated into English by John *Florio in 1603, whose version of Montaigne's 'Des cannibales' is quoted by Gonzago in Shakespeare's *The *Tempest*. Florio's colourful translation, though frequently reissued in the 20th century, was eclipsed at the end of the 17th century by Charles *Cotton's more accurate rendering (1685–6), which remained popular until the late 19th century (*see* HAZLITT, WILLIAM CAREW). Other notable readers of Montaigne's work have been Robert *Burton, Sir Thomas *Browne, Jonathan *Swift, and Thomas Love *Peacock.

MONTALE, Eugenio (1896–1981) The greatest Italian poet of the 20th century, recipient of the *Nobel Prize (1975). He draws on an extreme range of language from the prosaic to the lyrical—from naval and biological terminology to the dialect of Genoa, his native city—and on all the strains in Italian literary tradition, recovering 'dead' words, coining new ones, and subjecting every word to intense multiplicity of meaning. This linguistic engagement means that he rejected the aloof 'Petrarchan' role for the poet, although his wariness of moral keys has often attracted the accusation of apoliticality. His main books of poems (now all included in the critical edition approved by him shortly before his death, *E.M.: l'opera in versi*, ed. F. Contini, 1980) are *Ossi di seppia* (1925: *Cuttle-Fish Bones*), *Le occasioni* (1939: *Occasions*), *La bufera e altro* (1956: *The Storm and Others*), *Satura* (1971), and *Diario del' 71 e del' 72* (1973: *Diary of 1971 and 1972*). His translations of Shakespeare, G. M. *Hopkins, W. B. *Yeats, and T. S. *Eliot are in *Quaderno di traduzioni* (1975: *Translator's Notebook*). He has been translated by Robert *Lowell and by Edwin *Morgan.

MONTEMAYOR, Jorge de (*c.*1519–1561) Portuguese poet and author who wrote mostly in Spanish. His principal work is *La Diana* (?1559), a prose pastoral interspersed with verses, in which he transferred Arcadia to the heart of Spain. It was extremely popular, was translated into several languages, and was influential in England. The English translation, *Diana*, was by Bartholomew *Yonge (1598); the episode of Felix and Felismena in Yonge's version is almost certainly the direct source of much of the plot of Shakespeare's *The *Two Gentlemen of Verona*. The scene is laid at the foot of the mountains of León and the pastoral is occupied with the misfortunes of Syrenus and Sylvanus, two shepherd lovers of the fair Diana, a shepherdess; and with the loves, transfers of affection, and disguises of various other shepherds and shepherdesses. Happiness is finally restored by the agency of enchanted potions. Two continuations were published: Alonso Pérez's *Segunda parte de la Diana*: *Second Part of Diana* (1563), which was condemned to the flames in **Don Quixote* (I. 6), and Gaspar Gil Polo's popular *Diana enamorada* (1564: *Enamoured Diana*); both were translated by Yonge.

MONTESQUIEU, Charles de Secondat, baron de (1689–1755) French political philosopher, historian, and novelist. A member of the lesser nobility of Guyenne, he trained as a lawyer and served as president of the Bordeaux *parlement*. He made his name as a writer with the publication of *Lettres persanes* (1721: *Persian Letters*; trans. John Ozell, 1722), in which the fictional correspondence of two Persian visitors to Paris provides a satirical review of French legal and political institutions. His masterpiece, *De l'esprit des lois* (1748: *On the Spirit of the Laws*; trans. Thomas Nugent, 1750), is concerned with both political constitutions (he favours a liberal constitutional monarchy on the English model) and the many other factors (moral and physical) which influence laws and behaviour. He lived in England during 1729–31, and he travelled in Western Europe in the company of Lord *Chesterfield.

MONTGOMERIE, Alexander (*c.*1543–1598) Scottish poet, born at Hazlehead Castle, Ayrshire, who was leader of the 'Castalian band' at James VI's court in Edinburgh. He was outlawed for Catholic partisanship in 1597, the year of publication of his principal work, *The Cherry and the Slae*, a searching allegorical investigation of the relative merits of high ambition and lowly contentment. His other poems are unusually various in form, theme, and tone. See *The Poems of Alexander Montgomerie*, ed. D. J. Parkinson (2000).

MONTGOMERY, James (1772–1854) Poet, editor, and hymn-writer. Born in Irvine, Ayrshire, and educated at the Moravian School near Pudsey (Yorkshire), he was editor of the *Sheffield Iris* in the 1790s and was twice imprisoned for publishing radical articles. He published *Prison Amusements* (1797), but made his name as a poet with *The Wanderer of Switzerland* (1806). He also published *The West Indies* (1809), *The World before the Flood. Greenland* (1819), and *The Pelican Island* (1827). His hymns include 'Hail to the Lord's Anointed' and 'Angels from the realms of glory'.

MONTGOMERY, L. M. (Lucy Maud) (1874–1942) Canadian writer remembered for her series beginning with *Anne of Green Gables* (1908), set on Prince Edward Island, where she was born—in Clifton, now New London. Emily, her other enduring heroine, also developed through a series, beginning with *Emily of New Moon* (1923). Both series are semi-autobiographical; Anne and Emily are complex, creative characters living on the margins of stunted worlds that they help to expand.

MONTGOMERY, Robert (1807–55) English poet and clergyman. He wrote on religious themes (*The Omnipresence of the Deity*, 1828; *Satan*, 1830) and also composed vitriolic social satire (*The Age Reviewed*, 1827). He was lampooned for his poetic pretensions in **Blackwood's Magazine* by John *Wilson and the techniques used to advertise his work were the subject of Thomas *Macaulay's withering attack in the **Edinburgh Review* for April 1830, which also declared that Montgomery's work 'bears the same relation to poetry which a Turkey carpet bears to a picture'. Despite these critical attacks, Montgomery's work enjoyed wide popularity.

MONTHERLANT, Henry de (1896–1972) French novelist and dramatist. Born of an aristocratic and Roman Catholic family, he showed himself receptive to the ideas of Maurice *Barrès, Gabriele *d'Annunzio, and André *Gide, evolving in his early novels—notably *Les Célibataires* (1934: *The Bachelors*)—an ideology of chivalric ardour and masculine disdain. His major plays, which include *La Reine morte* (1942: *The Dead Queen*), *Le Maître de Santiago* (1947: *The Master of Santiago*), *La Ville dont le prince est un enfant* (1951: *The City Where the Prince is a Child*), and *Port-Royal* (1954), exhibit his gifts for biting language and heroic intensity. His culminating work, the novel *Le Chaos et la nuit* (1963: *Chaos and Night*), evokes the austere isolation of an exiled Spanish anarchist. He travelled widely and sometimes dangerously during his early life. An extreme right-winger in politics, he consistently rejected modern French democracy. His work has been translated into English by T. Kilmartin and J. Griffin.

Monthly Magazine An influential radical publication founded in 1796 by Richard Phillips (1767–1840), a *Jacobin and a supporter of Thomas *Paine. Contributors included William *Godwin, Thomas *Malthus, William *Hazlitt, Robert *Southey, and William *Taylor. The magazine had an encyclopedic range, covering literature (including German, Spanish, and oriental literature), science, politics, and philosophy. Its first editor was Dr John *Aikin (to whom S. T. *Coleridge originally intended to send the **Ancient Mariner*); its last (in 1825) was John *Thelwall. The **Anti-Jacobin* was founded, in part, to oppose the views of the *Monthly*.

Monthly Review A periodical founded by the bookseller Ralph Griffiths (?1720–1803) in June 1749, the first literary review designed to give an account of all publications above the level of *chapbook. It was liberal in outlook, by contrast with its main rival, the conservative **Critical Review*. Several notable writers, including Arthur *Murphy, Richard Brinsley *Sheridan, Charles *Burney, and Oliver *Goldsmith, contributed, though Goldsmith's relationship with Griffiths seems to have been acrimonious. It ceased publication in 1844.

MONTROSE, James Graham, fifth earl and first marquis of (1612–50) Royalist and general; remembered as a poet for a few songs and epigrams, printed in *Memoirs of Montrose and his Times* (2 vols, 1856) by Mark Napier (1798–18), and since much anthologized, including 'My dear and only love' and lines said to have been written on his prison window the night before his execution in Edinburgh.

Moonstone, The A novel by Wilkie *Collins, published 1868. It was the last of his popular successes. The moonstone, an enormous diamond originally stolen from an Indian shrine, is given to an English girl, Rachel Verinder, on her 18th birthday, but disappears the same night. Under suspicion of stealing it are Rosanna Spearman, a hunchbacked housemaid, formerly a thief; a troop of Indian jugglers; Franklin Blake, Rachel's cousin; and Rachel herself. A detective, Sergeant Cuff, is called in to solve the mystery, and is aided by the house steward Gabriel Betteredge, principal narrator of the story, but thwarted by Rachel's reticence and by the suicide of Rosanna. It is eventually discovered that Franklin Blake was seen by Rachel to take the diamond, that at the time he was sleepwalking under the influence of opium, that it was taken from him by Rachel's other suitor, Godfrey Ablewhite, a sanctimonious hypocrite, and finally secured (by the murder of Ablewhite) and returned to the forehead of the statue from which it was stolen by the Indian jugglers, who were its disguised guardians. Widely admired as an early detective novel (T. S. *Eliot called it 'the first, the longest, and the best of modern English detective novels'), it has proved enduringly popular.

MOORCOCK, Michael (1939–) Born in London; one of the most prominent of *science fiction's *New Wave when he edited **New Worlds* from 1964 to 1971. A prolific and versatile writer, his own works include the continuing 'Elric' fantasies, beginning 1963, themselves part of a much-revised meta-sequence in which various heroes are aspects of an 'Eternal Champion'. Using 'Jerry Cornelius' (*The Final Programme*, 1969; *A Cure for Cancer*, 1971; *The English Assassin*, 1972; *The Condition of Muzak*, 1977), Moorcock adapted this mode of storytelling to more contemporary concerns. Cornelius' adventures have appeared since, notably in 'Firing the Cathedral' (2002). The 'Colonel Pyat' books, *Byzantium Endures* (1981), *The Laughter of Carthage* (1984), *Jerusalem Commands* (1992), and *The Vengeance of Rome* (2006), explore the development of *Fascism and the Jewish Holocaust through the unreliable memoirs of a self-deceiving Russian émigré snob, racist, charlatan, and cocaine addict. They are arguably Moorcock's masterpieces. The poignant and optimistic *Mother*

London (1988) celebrates the adaptability and vitality of London's people, landscape, history, and mythology through a dense non-linear narrative tracking the stories of a group of psychiatric outpatients from the Blitz to the 1980s. Other notable works include *Gloriana* (1978) and *King of the City* (2000).

MOORE, Alan (1953–) Comic-book writer, author of *Watchmen* (1986–7), *V for Vendetta* (1982–8), *From Hell* (1991–8), and *The League of Extraordinary Gentlemen* (1999–2000); stylistically and thematically challenging comic books later collected as *graphic novels. *Voice of the Fire* (1996) is a novel set in his native Northampton.

MOORE, Brian (1921–99) Novelist, born and educated in Belfast, the son of a Roman Catholic surgeon of strong Irish nationalist views. He emigrated in 1948 to Canada and subsequently moved to the USA. Some early potboilers were published pseudonymously. The first serious work under his own name was *Judith Hearne* (1955; published in the USA as *The Lonely Passion of Judith Hearne*, 1956), a poignant story of a lonely Belfast spinster who takes refuge in alcohol. His subsequent works, many of which deal with transatlantic migrations, include *The Feast of Lupercal* (1957, set in Belfast); *The Luck of Ginger Coffey* (1960, describing the misfortunes and daydreams of an Irish immigrant in Canada); *I am Mary Dunne* (1968, a first-person female narration set in America); *Catholics* (1972, a papal representative visiting an Irish religious community at some time in the future); and *The Mangan Inheritance* (1979, an American journalist in search of his Irish heritage and the poet J. C. *Mangan). Other works include *The Black Robe* (1983), a violent *historical novel set in 17th-century Quebec; *Lies of Silence* (1990), a novel of the *Troubles, in which a hotel manager finds himself in the hands of gunmen; and *The Magician's Wife* (1997), a historical novel set in France and Algeria in the 1850s. Critics have praised both the versatility of his subject matter and the economy and understatement of his style.

MOORE, C. L. (Catherine Lucille) (1911–87) American writer, born in Indianapolis. Although much of her work after 1940 was in pseudonymous partnership with her husband Henry Kuttner (1915–58), she has been acclaimed for her innovative *fantasy and *science fiction since 'Shambleau' (1933) in **Weird Tales*. 'Black God's Kiss' (1934) introduced the first female *sword and sorcery hero. The *cyborg in 'No Woman Born' (1944) highlights gender. *Black Gods and Scarlet Dreams* (2002) collects her 'Jirel of Joiry' and 'Northwest Smith' stories.

MOORE, Edward (1712–57) A linen draper turned author, who contributed to the **Gentleman's Magazine* and other periodicals, wrote some much-reprinted *Fables for the Female Sex* (1744) in imitation of John *Gay, and contributed to Robert *Dodsley's *Collection of Poems* (1748–58). Moore's first comedy, *The Foundling* (1748), was successfully staged with David *Garrick and Charles *Macklin in leading roles; despite some resonances of Richardson's **Pamela*, it was warmly praised by Henry *Fielding. Less popular was *Gil Blas* (1751), which took its plot from Tobias *Smollett's translation of *Lesage's *Gil Blas of Santillane* (IV. iii-vi) where a lady masquerades as a student in order to get acquainted with a young man, requiring a series of quick comic changes to maintain the dual role of lady and student. Moore's most successful play was a domestic prose tragedy, *The Gamester* (1753), an adaptation of Aaron *Hill's *The Fatal Extravagance* (1721): the weak hero Beverley becomes addicted to gambling and is lured to ruin and death by the villain Stukeley. This play was widely translated, and was adapted by Denis *Diderot. From 1753 to 1756 Moore edited and co-wrote the satirical periodical *The World*, which included Lord *Lyttleton, Horace *Walpole, and Lord *Chesterfield among its contributors.

MOORE, Francis *See* OLD MOORE.

MOORE, George (1852–1933) Irish novelist, born into an aristocratic Catholic family at Moore Hall in Co. Mayo; his father's racing stables provided background for his most successful novel, **Esther Waters*. He studied painting in Paris for some years and the knowledge of French writing he gained there stood him in good stead when, settling in England in 1881, he set about revitalizing the Victorian novel with naturalistic and, later, realistic techniques borrowed from *Balzac, *Zola, and the *Goncourts. His first novel, *A Modern Lover* (1883), set in artistic bohemian society, was banned by the *circulating libraries, confirming Moore in his battle against prudery and censorship. It was followed by *A Mummer's Wife* (1885, set in the Potteries); *Esther Waters* (1894); *Evelyn Innes* (1898) and its sequel *Sister Teresa* (1901). In his later novels, such as *The Brook Kerith* (1916), which unfolds the interwoven lives of Christ, St Paul, and *Joseph of Arimathea, and *Heloïse and Abelard* (1921), he aimed at epic effect. *Confessions of a Young Man* (1888), *Memoirs of my Dead Life* (1906), and *Hail and Farewell* (3 vols, 1911–14) are all autobiographical; the last is an important though unreliable source for the history of the *Irish Revival. Moore's decade in Ireland from 1901 issued in two seminal contributions to the Revival, the collection of stories *The Untilled Field* (1903) and the novel *The Lake* (1905), both influenced by *Turgenev. His collaboration with W. B. *Yeats in setting up the *Irish Literary Theatre ended in acrimony. The stories of *Celibate Lives* (1927) show the influence of *Flaubert, not only in subject but also in their careful reworking of earlier material. He lived at 121 Ebury Street in London from 1911 until his death, an object of pilgrimage for younger writers and admirers. See Adrian Frazier, *George Moore* (2000).

MOORE, John (1729–1802) Scottish surgeon, travel writer, and novelist, born in Stirling and educated at the University of Glasgow. He was appointed tutor to the duke of Argyll in 1772 and travelled extensively in Europe with his young charge, publishing in 1779 and 1781 highly successful, mainly epistolary accounts of his experiences there. *Zeluco* (1786), a didactic portrait of a vicious man, went through thirteen editions; *Edward* (1796), designed as a compensatory depiction of virtue, was less popular. In 1797 Moore produced a collected edition of Tobias *Smollett, his distant cousin, with a brief biography. His *epistolary novel **Mordaunt* was published in 1800. Moore was the father of Sir John *Moore of Corunna.

MOORE, Sir John (1761–1809) Lieutenant-general and son of John *Moore. He fought in the Peninsular War, and is the subject of the famous elegy by Charles *Wolfe.

MOORE, Marianne (1887–1972) American poet, born in Missouri. From 1925 to 1929 she was editor of *The *Dial*. Her first volume, *Poems* (1921), was followed by *Observations* (1924), *Selected Poems* (1935, with an introduction by T. S. *Eliot), *The Pangolin, and Other Verse* (1936), and other collections. Her *Collected Poems* appeared in 1951. Moore's early work was well known in Britain, being admired by I. A. *Richards. Combining urbanity with sophistication, her poems are composed with a strong sense of visual effect. In 'Poetry' she expressed the desire to create 'imaginary gardens with real toads in them'. She was a friend of the poet Elizabeth *Bishop, whose work she influenced. See Bernard F. Engel, *Marianne Moore* (1988).

MOORE, Thomas (1779–1852) Poet, songwriter, and biographer, born in Dublin, the son of a grocer. Although a Catholic, he was educated at Trinity College, Dublin (then largely a Protestant institution), where he befriended the Protestant patriot Robert Emmet, whose execution in 1803 is lamented in a series of more or less coded references throughout Moore's work. He studied law at the Middle Temple from 1799 and in 1801 published the mildly risqué *The Poetical Works of the Late Thomas Little* (under which pseudonym Lord *Byron refers to him in **English Bards and Scotch Reviewers*). In 1803 he was appointed admiralty registrar in Bermuda, a post which he briefly occupied before transferring it to a deputy. *Epistles, Odes, and Other Poems* (1806) was brought to general notice by the controversy surrounding Francis *Jeffrey's attack in the **Edinburgh Review*. From 1808 to 1834 Moore continued to add to his *Irish Melodies*, which established him as the national bard of Ireland. He was a good musician and a skilful writer of patriotic and characteristically melancholy songs, which he set to Irish tunes, mainly those collected by Edward Bunting in *Ancient Music of Ireland* (1796). Among his more famous songs are 'The harp that once through Tara's halls', 'The Minstrel Boy', and 'The Last Rose of Summer'. He acquired a European reputation with **Lalla Rookh* (1817). The satirical entertainment *The *Fudge Family in Paris* appeared in 1818. His deputy in Bermuda then defaulted, leaving Moore to meet a debt of £6,000. He left England for Italy, returning in 1822 when the debt had been paid. *The *Loves of the Angels* (1823) enjoyed a considerable vogue and caused some scandal. In 1824 he was prevailed upon to permit the burning of Byron's *Memoirs*, which the poet had entrusted to him five years previously. *Memoirs of Captain Rock, the Celebrated Irish Chieftain* (1824) blamed English misrule for Irish agrarian violence. Biographies of Richard Brinsley *Sheridan, Byron, and the Irish revolutionary Lord Edward Fitzgerald (1763–98) appeared respectively in 1825, 1830, and 1831, and *The Epicurean*, a novel about a Greek philosopher, in 1827. He was awarded a literary pension in 1835, and in the same year published *The Fudges in England*, a light satire on an Irish priest turned Protestant evangelist. His *History of Ireland* (1835–46) was not a success. Moore was awarded a Civil List pension in 1850.

Moore's *Letters* were edited by W. S. Dowden (2 vols, 1964); see also *The Journal of Thomas Moore*, ed. Peter *Quennell (1964).

MOORE, Thomas Sturge (1870–1944) Poet, wood-engraver, and illustrator, and brother of the philosopher G. E. Moore (1873–1958); he was a friend of Charles *Ricketts and the artist Charles Haslewood Shannon (1863–1937), and also of W. B. *Yeats, his correspondence with whom was published in 1953, and for whom he designed several books. His first volume of verse, *The Vinedresser and Other Poems* (1899), was followed by several others, and by various verse dramas, including *Tragic Mothers: Medea, Niobe, Tyrfing* (1920).

MOORE, Ward (1903–78) American writer, born in New York. After his first novel *Breathe the Air Again* (1942) he turned to *science fiction. *Bring the Jubilee* (1953) is a classic *alternate history, in which the Confederates win the American Civil War, and the narrator diverts the flow of history.

MOORHOUSE, Geoffrey (1931–) Born in Bolton, educated at Bury Grammar School; he worked as a journalist on the *Bolton Evening News* and, from the age of 27, on the **Manchester Guardian*, on which he became the chief features writer. He has written more than twenty books, including several travel naratives, among them *The Fearful Void* (1974) and *Apples in the Snow: A Journey to Samarkand* (1990). His works on India include *Calcutta* (1971), *To the Frontier* (1984), which won the Thomas Cook award for best travel book of the year, and *Om: An Indian Pilgrimage* (1993). He has also written histories of the Tudor period. He was elected a fellow of the Royal Society of Literature in 1982.

MORAES, Dom (1938–2004) Prolific, widely travelled Indian poet and writer. He was born in Bombay (Mumbai) and read English at Jesus College, Oxford. *A Beginning* (1957), his first book of poems, made him the youngest poet to win the Hawthornden Prize. His other volumes of poetry include *John Nobody* (1965) and *Bedlam and Others* (1967); his autobiographical memoir *My Father's Son* (1968) was hailed as a minor classic by Stephen *Spender. Moraes co-translated with Aryeh Sivan an anthology of *Modern Hebrew Peace Poetry* (1998).

morality plays Medieval allegorical plays in which personified human qualities are acted and disputed, mostly coming from the 15th century. They developed into the *interludes, from which it is not always possible to distinguish them, and hence had a considerable influence on the development of Elizabethan drama. They lost popularity with the development of naturalistic drama, but interest in them revived in the 20th century, prompted by a new interest in more mannered, pageant-like theatre, such as the Japanese *Nōh theatre and the plays of W. B. *Yeats and Bertolt *Brecht. Among the most celebrated English examples are **Everyman*; *Ane *Pleasant Satyre of the Thrie Estaitis* by Sir David *Lindsay; **Magnificence* by John *Skelton; *King John* by John *Bale; **Mankind*; and *The *Castle of Perseverance*. See P. Happé (ed.), *Four Morality Plays* (1979); G. Wickham (ed.), *English Moral Interludes* (1976).

MORAVIA, Alberto (1907–90) Pseudonym of Alberto Pincherle, a prolific writer of novels, short stories, and essays. He played a major part in shaping *neo-realism in Italian fiction after the Second World War, and in some of his writing reflects the influence of *existentialism and the French **nouveau roman*. His best novels are: *Gli indifferenti* (1929: *The Time of Indifference*), which portrays a middle-class society sick with a moral inertia which favoured the rise of *Fascism; *La Ciociara* (1957: *Two Women*), the most lyrical and complex of his novels, dealing with the close of the war, when Italy was occupied by both Germans and Allies, which was subsequently made into a film by De Sica (1960) starring Sophia Loren; and *La Noia* (1960: *The Empty Canvas*). Among his shorter novels, the best known is *Agostino* (1943). *La Romana* (1947: *The Woman of Rome*) and the highly esteemed *Racconti romani* (1957: *Roman Tales*) draw on the language and culture of Roman plebeians in order to criticize middle-class values. Other full-length novels, notably *Il conformista* (1951: *The Conformist*) and *1934* (1983), explore the psychosexual basis of politics. Moravia was film critic for the weekly *L'espresso* from 1955 until his death.

Moravians With its origins in pre-Reformation Bohemia, the Moravian Church developed in the 18th century in Germany as an offshoot of Lutheran Pietism and spread worldwide through its missionary activities. It had a marked impact on early *Methodism, despite the breach between the two movements. In 1722 Moravian refugees settled on the estate of the German religious reformer Count Zinzendorf (1700–60) in Saxony, forming a religious community called Herrnhut from which they soon sent out missionaries. John *Wesley met some of them on his voyage to Georgia in 1735–6 and visited Herrnhut in 1738, providing a very full account in his second *Journal*. The principal Moravian settlement in England, Fulneck, near Leeds, was founded in 1744. Moravians were required to write accounts of their religious experiences, and Moravian hymnody had its own distinctive language. Influential Moravians include the bookseller James Hutton (1715–95) and the hymn-writers John Cennick (1718–55) and James *Montgomery.

Mordaunt An *epistolary novel by John *Moore, published 1800, in which acquaintances of the gentleman traveller Mordaunt reveal their lives and character. Though the novel is mainly a satire of English manners, the letters from a French marquise in the central section allow Moore to explore his interest in revolutionary France.

Mordred (Modred) In Arthurian legends, the nephew of King *Arthur, the son of King Lot of Orkney and Arthur's sister *Morgawse or Morcades (sometimes Anna; *see* PENDRAGON). *Geoffrey of Monmouth makes him the son of Arthur and his sister by an illicit union; he is accordingly the brother or half-brother of *Gawain and his brothers. During Arthur's absence on a Roman war he seizes the queen (with her compliance, according to Geoffrey of Monmouth and his successors, such as *Laȝamon and *Wace) and the kingdom. In the final battle in Cornwall he is slain by Arthur but deals the king his death-blow. He is alluded to as a traitor in the **Divina commedia* (*Inferno*, XXXII. 61–2).

MORE, Hannah (1745–1833) Writer and philanthropist. She was educated at her sisters' boarding school in Bristol and studied French, Italian, Spanish, Latin, and mathematics. More came to London in 1774 and became friendly with David *Garrick, Edmund *Burke, Samuel *Johnson, Sir Joshua *Reynolds, Thomas *Percy, and Elizabeth *Montagu, whose *Blue Stocking salon she entered in 1775. Her tragedy *Percy* was successfully produced by Garrick in 1777. She was much admired by Horace *Walpole, who printed her ballad *Bishop Bonner's Ghost* at his press at Strawberry Hill in 1781. Her poem *Bas Bleu* (written 1782; pub. 1784) vividly describes the conversational charm of Blue Stocking society. Her well-meaning intervention on behalf of Ann *Yearsley in 1785 demonstrated a paternalist concern for the poor, which was further elaborated in a series of tracts: *Village Politics* appeared in 1793, in opposition to Thomas *Paine's *Rights of Man*, and in 1795–8 she published **Cheap Repository Tracts* (of which the best known is *The Shepherd of Salisbury Plain*), which sold 2 million copies in four years and led to the formation of the *Religious Tract Society in 1799. She was an active opponent of the slave trade and friend of William *Wilberforce. More's *Strictures on the Modern System of Female Education* (2 vols, 1799) appealed to those who found Mary *Wollstonecraft's views too aggressively radical. In 1809 she published a novel, or fictionalized conduct manual, **Coelebs in Search of a Wife*, a huge commercial success despite the strictures of Sydney *Smith in the **Edinburgh Review*. More's fervent piety ensured a ready audience, but latterly she was seen as a reactionary and from 1820 she withdrew from public life. See A. Stott, *Hannah More: The First Victorian* (2003).

MORE, Henry *See* CAMBRIDGE PLATONISTS.

MORE, Sir Thomas (St Thomas More) (1478–1535) Humanist and martyr, son of Sir John More, a judge, educated at St Antony's School, Threadneedle Street, London, and at Canterbury College (now Christ Church), Oxford. He was for a time in youth in the household of John Morton, archbishop of Canterbury (d. 1500), and it was probably from Morton's information that he derived his account of Richard III's reign and especially of the murder of the princes. Called to the bar, he had a brilliantly successful legal career. He devoted his leisure to literature, becoming intimate with John *Colet, William *Lily, Thomas *Linacre, and, in 1499, *Erasmus, who afterwards stayed frequently at his house. He entered Parliament in 1504. During an absence as envoy to Flanders he sketched his description (in Latin) of the imaginary island of **Utopia*, which he completed and published in 1516. He became master of requests and privy counsellor in 1517, being treated by *Henry VIII with exceptional courtesy during his residence at court. He was present at the Field of the Cloth of Gold, 1520, where he met the great Greek scholar Guillaume *Budé. He completed his *Dialogue*, his first controversial book in English (directed mainly against William *Tyndale's writings), in 1528. He succeeded Thomas Wolsey (1470/71–1530) as lord chancellor in 1529, but resigned in 1532 and lived for some time in retirement, mainly engaged in controversy with Tyndale and John Frith (1503–33).

Although willing to swear fidelity to the new Act of Succession, More refused to take any oath denying the pope's authority, or assume the justice of the king's divorce from Catherine of Aragon, 1534; he was therefore committed to the Tower of London with John Fisher (*c.*1469–1535), bishop of Rochester, who had assumed a similar position. During the first days of his imprisonment he prepared a *Dialogue of Comfort against Tribulation* and treatises on Christ's passion. He was indicted of high treason, found guilty, and beheaded in 1535. His body was buried in St Peter's in the Tower and, according to Thomas Stapleton, his head exhibited on London Bridge. The head was later buried in the *Roper vault in St Dunstan's, Canterbury.

More was a critic and a patron of art. During his first English visit in 1526–8, Hans *Holbein painted portraits of More and produced an evocative group portrait of his family in the house at Chelsea. More's other chief English works are his *Life of John Picus Earl of Mirandula* (printed by John *Rastell, *c.*1510), his *History of Richard the Third* (printed imperfectly in Richard *Grafton's *Chronicle* 1543, used by Edward *Hall, and printed fully by William Rastell (1508–65) in 1557), *The Supplication of Souls* (1529), *The Confutation of Tyndale's Answer* (1532), and *The Apology of Sir Thomas More* (1533). His English works were collected in 1557. His Latin publications (collected 1563 onwards) included, besides the *Utopia*, four of *Lucian's dialogues, epigrams, and controversial religious works. There is a pleasant description of More at Chelsea in the epistle of Erasmus to Ulrich Hutten (1488–1523), 23 July 1519. He was beatified by the Church of Rome in 1886, and canonized in 1935. Robert *Bolt's play about More, *A Man for All Seasons* (1960), was also made into a successful film. There is a life by Peter *Ackroyd (1998).

More, Sir Thomas A play based on Edward *Hall's *Chronicle* and biographies of *More, surviving in an incomplete transcript with additions in various hands (British Library, Harley MS 7368) which was submitted to Sir Edmund Tilney, master of the revels, probably about 1593. The scribe, Anthony *Munday, is likely to have been at least part-author of the original play. Tilney required major changes before granting permission to perform. The revisions (which may date from 1593–4 or 1603–4) are in five different hands, probably including those of Henry *Chettle, Thomas *Heywood, Thomas *Dekker, and a playhouse scribe known to have worked for both Strange's Men and the Admiral's Men. The fifth ('Hand D') has been claimed, with strong support, as Shakespeare's. If so, this is his only surviving literary manuscript. A scene of three pages, it depicts More, as sheriff of London, pacifying apprentices in a May Day rebellion against foreigners. *More* was first printed in 1844; there is a scholarly transcript in the *Malone Society reprints (1911; repr. 1961). There is an edition of the complete text in the second edition of the Oxford *Complete Works*. The first known professional performance was in London in 1954; it was seen at the Nottingham Playhouse in 1964, directed by Frank Dunlop, with Ian McKellen as More, and other revivals include one by the Royal Shakespeare Company in 2005.

MORGAN, Charles Langbridge (1894–1958) Novelist and dramatist, and from 1926 to 1939 dramatic critic of *The *Times*. His novels include *The Fountain* (1932), *Sparkenbroke* (1936), *The Judge's Story* (1947), and *The River Line* (1949, dramatized 1952). The last is set against a background of the French Resistance; Morgan's status as a writer has been and remains significantly higher in France than in Britain.

MORGAN, Edwin (1920–) Scottish poet, playwright, translator, and critic, born in Glasgow and educated at the University of Glasgow, where he later became a professor of English. He served in the Royal Army Medical Corps from 1940 to 1946 and was appointed 'Scots Makar' (national poet of Scotland) by the Scottish Executive in 2004. Morgan's poetry in the many volumes linking *The Vision of Cathkin Braes* (1952) to *A Book of Lives* (2007) is notably, even prodigiously various in form and manner, and is marked by an egalitarian spirit and an interest in the possibilities of science and technology. Sound poems and *concrete poems exist side by side with understated lyrics of homoerotic love and experimental deployments of traditional forms (*Glasgow Sonnets*, 1972; *The New Divan*, 1977). He has translated *Montale, *Neruda, and many others into English, and *Shakespeare and *Maiakovsky into Scots. The subtle and wide-ranging criticism collected in *Essays* (1974) and *Crossing the Border* (1990) shares the lightness of touch that characterizes his poetry. See *Collected Poems* (1996); *Cathures* (2002); *Collected Translations* (1996).

MORGAN, Lady (*c.*1776–1859) Née Sydney Owenson, prolific and very popular Irish novelist, poet, biographer, essayist, travel writer, satirist, and socialite, born in Dublin, the daughter of an actor, and friend of Thomas *Moore, Richard Lalor Sheil (1791–1851), and Richard *Sheridan. *The*

Wild Irish Girl (1806), the third of her ten novels, is central to the development of the national tale in Ireland. It called forth an imitation by Charles *Maturin, *The Wild Irish Boy* (1808). She was paid by her publisher £1,200 (a huge sum) for *Florence Macarthy* (1818), a serious novel on the subject of contemporary Ireland. Her travel studies, *France* (1817) and *Italy* (1821), the latter much admired by Lord *Byron but venomously attacked by John Wilson *Croker in the **Quarterly Review*, were also highly successful. In *The Mohawks* (1822), jointly authored with her husband, the royal physician Sir Charles, she attacked her Tory opponents, notably in the *Quarterly* and **Blackwood's Magazine*. See *The Wild Irish Girl*, ed. C. Connolly and S. Copley (2000).

MORGAN, William De *See* DE MORGAN, WILLIAM FREND.

Morgan le Fay Queen of *Avalon, the daughter of Arthur's mother Igerne and therefore his half-sister; she is derived from a figure in Welsh and Irish (the Morrigan) mythology, and has a curiously ambivalent attitude to Arthur. In *Malory she attempts to kill Arthur through the agency of her lover Sir Accolon, but she is also the leader of the queens who carry him away to cure his wounds. She is sometimes represented as the bitter enemy of *Guinevere (a tradition indicated by the end of *Sir *Gawain and the Green Knight*, where it is said that she instigated the beheading game to frighten Guinevere to death). *Geoffrey of Monmouth calls the fairy lady who takes Arthur off to Avalon Argante, but all later accounts (such as *Giraldus Cambrensis and the prose Vulgate cycles) call her Morgan. A related figure occurs in the **Orlando innamorato* and **Orlando furioso*, called 'Morgana' there and being a *Lady of the Lake. The term *Fata Morgana* (*fata* means 'fairy' in Italian) is given in Sicily to a vision traditionally seen at sea from the Calabrian coast.
See MORGAWSE.

MORGANN, Maurice (1725–1802) Holder of various government offices, and author of pamphlets on political questions such as slavery, adultery, and the French Revolution. His *Essay on the Dramatic Character of Sir John Falstaff* (1777), a classic of Shakespeare criticism, argues through close study of *1 *Henry IV* that *Falstaff is not a coward, and suggests that Shakespeare intended the audience to sympathize with the knight. A. C. *Bradley was much impressed by the work.

Morgante maggiore A poem by Luigi *Pulci which recast, with humorous additions and alterations, the popular epic *Orlando* (*see* ROLAND). Orlando (Roland) encounters three giants. He slays two and subdues the third, Morgante, converts him, and makes him his brother in arms. Together they embark on a series of adventures, in which they are joined by other knights of *Charlemagne, and briefly the half-giant Margutte. Lord *Byron translated the first canto; and there are translations by J. H. *Frere (*The Monks and Giants*, 1817) and J. Tusiani (*Morgante: The Epic Adventures of Orlando and his Giant Friend*, 1998).

Morgawse (Morcades) Half-sister of Arthur, the wife of King Lot of Orkney, and mother of *Mordred, *Gawain, *Agravain, Gareth, and Gaheris. She seems to be in some ways identical in origin with *Morgan le Fay; in later versions Arthur sleeps with her in disguise, thus begetting Mordred. She is called 'Anna' in *Geoffrey of Monmouth, though Anna is otherwise attested as Arthur's full sister.

MORIER, James Justinian (1782–1849) Diplomat, novelist, and travel writer, born in Smyrna, and educated at Harrow School. He joined the diplomatic service in 1807 and became attached to Sir Harford Jones's mission to Persia, during which he collected valuable information about the country. His account of these travels appeared in *A Journey through Persia, Armenia and Asia Minor to Constantinople in the Years 1808–1809* (1812); *A Second Journey through Persia* appeared in 1818. He retired from the Foreign Office in 1817 to devote his time to literature. Morier published a number of *oriental romances including the popular *The Adventures of Hajji Baba of Ispahan* (1824). Its sequel, *The Adventures of Hajji Baba in England* (1828), was less successful. His later works, including *Ayesha* (1834), did not reach the level of his earlier ones. In 1824 he was a founder member of the **Athenaeum*.

MORLEY, Henry (1822–94) Biographer and academic, educated in Germany and at King's College London. He turned from medicine to journalism, joined the staff of **Household Words* at Charles *Dickens's invitation, edited the **Examiner*, and devoted much of his career to the development of English literature as an academic subject. He became the first professor of English language and literature at University College London. He published biographies of Palissy the Potter (1852), Cardano (1854), and *Agrippa (1856), wrote *A First Sketch of English Literature* (1873) and eleven volumes of *English Writers* (1887–95), and edited cheap editions of English classics in Morley's Universal Library (1883–8) and Cassell's National Library (1886–92).

MORLEY, Lord, Henry Parker, tenth baron (1480/81–1556) Translator and courtier. After serving in the household of Lady Margaret Beaufort (1443–1509), he had a successful career at court, including diplomatic missions, under *Henry VIII and Queen Mary. Morley made translations from Latin and Italian, presenting them to his monarchs in manuscript as New Year's gifts. The earliest of these was a translation of *Petrarch's *Trionfi*, made in the 1520s but not printed until *c.*1555. After renderings of various classical lives and a tale from the Italian, his first appearance in print, an *Exposition and Declaration* of Psalm 94 (1539), was really a defence of Henry's position as head of the Church of England. It was followed by his version of the first 46 lives from *Boccaccio's *De Claris Mulieribus* (1543) and by devotional works. There is a study edited by M. Axton and J. P. Carley (2000).

MORLEY, John, first Viscount Morley of Blackburn (1838–1923) Educated at Cheltenham College and Lincoln College, Oxford. He began his literary career as a journalist, writing chiefly for the *Fortnightly Review*, of which he was editor (1867–82), and became a friend of George *Meredith and John Stuart *Mill; he was editor of the *Pall Mall Gazette* 1881–3. His literary achievements, chiefly biographical, include *Edmund Burke: An Historical Study* (1867), *Voltaire* (1872), *Rousseau* (1873), *On Compromise* (1874), *Burke* (1879), *The Life of Richard Cobden* (1881), *Oliver Cromwell* (1900), and *Life of Gladstone* (1903), and he edited the popular English Men of Letters series. He was a Liberal MP (1883–1908) and a close supporter of William *Gladstone; he was chief secretary for Ireland (1886 and 1892–5) and secretary of state for India (1905–10). From 1910 he was lord president of the council, but resigned at the outbreak of war.

MORLEY, Thomas (1557/8–1602) English composer, organist, and writer. He studied under William *Byrd, to whom he dedicated the important treatise *A Plaine and Easie Introduction to Practicall Musicke* (1597), the first work of its kind in the English language. He became organist of St Paul's and a gentleman of the Chapel Royal, and in 1598 he was granted the patent for music publishing previously held by Byrd. He appears to have been involved in spying on Catholics. Morley championed the Italian *madrigal, and actively developed its English counterpart. His first two publications, the *Canzonets, or Little Short Songs to Three Voyces* (1593) and the first book of *Madrigalls to Foure Voyces* (1594), contain the most original of his own work in this form, brightly Italianate in style yet finished with a Byrd-like seriousness. The two volumes of *Balletts to Five Voyces* and *Canzonets to Two Voyces* which followed in 1595 were largely free transcriptions of pieces by contemporary Italian composers, and were printed in both Italian and English—'Now is the month of maying', for example, appearing also as 'Se ben mi ch'ha bon tempo' (after Orazio Vecchi). Three further such volumes, containing madrigals for four, five, and six voices, appeared in 1597–8. Morley was the moving spirit behind *Madrigales: The Triumphes of Oriana* (1601), a collection of madrigals for five and six voices by 23 English composers. Most of Morley's madrigal texts are either from Italian originals or from anonymous sources, but his *First Book of Ayres... to the Lute* (1600) contains a setting of 'It was a lover and his lass' which is apparently the earliest Shakespeare setting to survive, though it is not known whether it was ever used in a production of **As You Like It*. Shakespeare and Morley lived for some time in the same London parish and the possibility of a connection between the two men has been much debated.

Morning Chronicle A Whig journal founded by the printer William Woodfall (1746–1803) in 1769, and successfully conducted by him for twenty years. It rose to importance after James Perry (1756–1821) became chief proprietor and editor in 1789. Its staff then included Richard Brinsley *Sheridan, Charles *Lamb, Thomas *Campbell, Sir James *Mackintosh, Henry *Brougham, Thomas *Moore, and David Ricardo (1772–1823). Perry was succeeded by John Black (1783–1855), scholar, Scotsman, and friend of James *Mill; John Stuart *Mill described Black as 'the first journalist who carried criticism and the Spirit of Reform into the details of English institutions... Black was the writer who carried the warfare into those subjects, and by doing so he broke the spell.' Both Mills were among his contributors, Charles *Dickens was one of his reporters, and W. M. *Thackeray his art critic. The *Chronicle* closed in 1862.

Morning Post A London daily newspaper founded in 1772. Under the management of Daniel *Stuart, Sir James *Mackintosh and S. T. *Coleridge were enlisted in its service, and Robert *Southey, William *Wordsworth, and Andrew *Young were also contributors. After a period of decline, it recovered its position under the direction of Peter Borthwick (1804–52) and his son Algernon Borthwick, Lord Glenesk (1830–1908). It was amalgamated with the **Daily Telegraph* in 1937.

MORPURGO, Michael (1943–) OBE, children's laureate 2003–5, prolific children's writer, born in St Albans, Hertfordshire, educated at King's College London. His *animal stories include *War Horse* (1982), an account of the First World War as experienced by a horse (staged by the National Theatre, 2007). *The War of Jenkins' Ear* (1993) is a *school story about new-boy Christopher, who thinks he is Christ on his Second Coming. *Private Peaceful* (2003), a *war story, criticizes the treatment of British soldiers in the First World War, and is a popular stage play. See Geoff Fox, *Dear Dr Morpingo: Inside the World of Michael Morpurgo* (2004).

MORRELL, Lady Ottoline (1873–1938) Literary hostess, born in London and educated by a governess. From 1907 she entertained a wide circle of literary and political celebrities at her Thursday evening gatherings at 44 Bedford Square, London, and continued her career as hostess and patron of the arts at Garsington Manor, Oxfordshire, between 1915 and 1927. Her friends and guests included Henry *James, Lytton *Strachey, Bertrand *Russell, Virginia *Woolf, T. S. *Eliot, W. B. *Yeats, D. H. *Lawrence, and Aldous *Huxley. Tall, striking, dazzlingly dressed, and eccentric, she appears as a character in several works of fiction by her protégés, most memorably as Hermione Roddice in Lawrence's **Women in Love* and as Priscilla Wimbush in Huxley's *Crome Yellow* (1921). She was deeply hurt by both portraits. Her *Memoirs*, edited by Robert Gathorne-Hardy, appeared in two volumes in 1963 and 1974. See Miranda Seymour, *Ottoline Morrell: Life on the Grand Scale* (rev. edn, 1998).

MORRIS, Jan (formerly James) (1926–) Travel writer, novelist, essayist, and popular historian, born in Somerset of Anglo-Welsh descent, educated at the Cathedral Choir School, Oxford, Lancing College, Sussex, and Christ Church, Oxford, author of more than 50 books. As James, Morris served as an army officer with the 9th Lancers 1942–7. From 1949 to 1951 he read English at Oxford. He then travelled widely, working as a correspondent for *The Times* and for the *Manchester Guardian* before turning freelance in 1961. He established his reputation with his scoop on the 1953 ascent of Mount Everest, which was announced on Coronation Day. In 1972 Morris underwent surgery to complete her gender reassignment. *Conundrum* (1974) is an account of her transsexuality. Of the many places Morris has written about, Oxford, Trieste, and Venice have especially influenced her. She announced that the well-received *Trieste and the Meaning of Nowhere* (2001) would be the last of her books. It was not. Probably her best-known work, however, remains the 'Pax Britannica' trilogy (*Pax Britannica*, 1968; *Heaven's Command*, 1973; *Farewell the Trumpets*, 1978), a sympathetic chronicle of the decay of British imperialism. Long resident in Wales, Morris is a champion of Welsh nationalism and culture.

MORRIS, Sir Lewis (1833–1907) Poet, born at Carmarthen and educated at Oxford. He contributed actively to the establishment of the University of Wales. He published several volumes of verse, imitative of Alfred *Tennyson; the most popular were *Songs of Two Worlds* (1871) and *The Epic of Hades* (1876–7). The latter, consisting of monologues by characters from Greek mythology, salutes Tennyson's *A Dream of Fair Women*.

MORRIS, William (1834–96) Writer, artist, and socialist reformer; born in Walthamstow and educated at Marlborough School and Exeter College, Oxford. Having been influenced by John *Ruskin's writing on art and architecture, he was articled to the architect G. E. Street (1824–81), and in 1858 worked with D. G. *Rossetti, Edward *Burne-Jones, and others on the frescos in the Oxford Union. He was one of the originators of the **Oxford and Cambridge Magazine* (1856), to which he contributed poems, essays, and tales. In 1858 he published *The Defence of Guenevere and Other Poems*, which contains much of his best work, including 'The Haystack in the Floods', 'Concerning Geffray Teste Noire', 'Shameful Death', and 'Golden Wings', poems notable for their medieval settings and their striking mixture of beauty and brutality. In 1859 he married Jane Burden (1839–1914), one of the most painted *Pre-Raphaelite 'stunners'; their home, Red House at Bexley, designed by Philip Webb (1831–1915), was an important landmark in domestic architecture. The failure to find suitable furniture for it led to the founding, together with Rossetti, Burne-Jones, Webb, Ford Madox Brown (1821–93), and others, of the firm of Morris, Marshall, Faulkner and Co. This firm produced furniture, printed textiles, tapestries, wallpapers, and stained glass; its designs brought about a revolution in public taste and remain popular. In the late 1860s Morris published *The Life and Death of Jason*, based on the legend of Jason and Medea, and *The *Earthly Paradise* (1868–70), which established him as a leading poet, though its length and archaic verse mean that it is now seldom read. In 1871 he moved to Kelmscott Manor and visited Iceland, which stimulated his interest in Icelandic heroic literature. His epic **Sigurd the Volsung* appeared in 1876; he also published translations from Icelandic with Eiríkr Magnússon. In 1877 he founded the Society for the Protection of Ancient Buildings. From this time on he turned increasingly towards political activity, joining the Social Democratic Federation in 1883 and shortly afterwards organizing a breakaway group as the Socialist League. He was to lecture and write for the cause with great energy. His later works, with the exception of two volumes of political poetry, were mainly in prose; the best known are *A *Dream of John Ball* (1888) and *News from Nowhere* (1891), both utopian socialist fantasies. He also wrote several historical romances set in the distant past of northern Europe. These include *The House of the Wolfings* (1889), *The Roots of the Mountains* (1890), *The Story of the Glittering Plain* (1890), *The Wood beyond the World* (1894), and his last work, *The Sundering Flood* (1898). All were published by the *Kelmscott Press, which he had founded in 1890, and for which he designed founts of type and ornamental letters and borders. The Press published Caxton's *The *Golden Legend* and an edition of Geoffrey *Chaucer, alongside many other works. Morris also translated numerous classical and medieval texts, including the *Aeneid* (1875) and the *Odyssey* (1887).

Morris's blend of political and aesthetic beliefs was important to the development of British socialism, and his lectures on art, architecture, and politics retain their force. See Fiona MacCarthy, *William Morris: A Life for our Time* (1994). His letters have been edited by Norman Kelvin (1984–96).

MORRIS, Wright (1910–98) American novelist, born in Nebraska, who began his career composing 'photo-texts' about the USA, resulting in *The Inhabitants* (1946) and others. Photography remained an interest throughout his life. His novels include *The Field of Vision* (1956) and *Plains Song: For Female Voices* (1980). He published three volumes of memoirs, collected as *Writing my Life* (1993), and *The Territory Ahead* (1958), a study of American literature.

morris dance An English folk dance since at least the 15th century, now commonly performed throughout the summer months. Morris, or 'morisco' ('Moorish') dancers (the name deriving from celebrations of the expulsion of the Moors from Spain) dress in striking, sometimes grotesque, uniforms, usually with bells attached to legs or arms. The rhythmic dances often involve the waving of handkerchiefs or clashing of sticks. See Cecil J. Sharp and H. C. MacIlwaine, *The Morris Book* (1907). *See* KEMP, WILL.

MORRISON, Arthur (1863–1945) Novelist, born in the East End of London, to working-class parents, whose *realist tales of East End life in London were first published in various magazines, and later collected as *Tales of Mean Streets* (1894). He is chiefly remembered for his novel *A Child of the Jago* (1896), which provoked a public debate about violence and the conditions of slum life in London.

MORRISON, Blake (1950–) Poet and novelist, born in Skipton, Yorkshire, and educated at Nottingham University and University College London. He worked as poetry and fiction editor of the *Times Literary Supplement* from 1978 to 1981, and has also been literary editor of both the *Observer* and the *Independent on Sunday.* He has published three volumes of poetry, *Dark Glasses* (1984), *The Ballad of the Yorkshire Ripper* (1987), and *Pendle Witches* (1996). A *Selected Poems* appeared in 1999. His non-fiction books include *And When Did You Last See your Father?* (1993), a candid memoir of his father and his responses to his death, which launched a genre of confessional autobiography; *As if* (1997), a response to the James Bulger murder trial, which draws on his own experience of parenthood as well as the month he spent covering the trial for a magazine; and *Things my Mother Never Told Me* (2002). His first novel, published in 2000, was *The Justification of Johann Gutenberg*, a portrait of the inventor of movable type; and a second, *South of the River*, appeared in 2007. He has also published critical studies of Seamus *Heaney (1982) and *The Movement: English Poetry and Fiction of the 1950s* (1980) (*see* MOVEMENT, THE), and a book for children, *The Yellow House* (1987). Morrison edited *The Penguin Book of Contemporary British Poetry* (1982) with Andrew *Motion.

MORRISON, Toni (1931–) African American novelist, born in Lorain, Ohio, educated at Howard University, where she later taught, and at Cornell. Before becoming a professional writer she worked in publishing, as an editor for Random House. Her novels deal with the historical experiences of African Americans within a white social and cultural environment. *The Bluest Eye* (1970) recounts a year in the life of Pecola Breedlove, a victim of rape by her father. Succeeding novels included *Sula* (1974), the story of two young black girls, one of whom leaves the small Ohio community of their birth and returns ten years later; *Song of Solomon* (1977); and *Tar Baby* (1981). **Beloved* (1987) was set in the 19th century and is the story of a runaway slave who kills her daughter rather than see her brought up to slavery (*see* SLAVERY); *A Mercy* (2008) continues her exploration of the profound traumas of slavery. Her other work includes *Jazz* (1992), and a study of the significance of African Americans in American literature, *Playing in the Dark: Whiteness and the Literary Imagination* (1992). She was the first African American woman to be awarded the *Nobel Prize for Literature in 1993. In the 1990s she became active in the Princeton Atelier, bringing students and artists together.

MORROW, James (1947–) American novelist and short story writer, born in Philadelphia. His *fantasy and *science fiction draws on theological metaphors; as in *Towing Jehovah* (1994), where God's body is discovered in the Atlantic. In *City of Truth* (1991) everyone tells the truth. *The Last Witchfinder* (2006) is a historical novel.

'Mortal Immortal, The' A short story by Mary *Shelley, published 1833. The story is narrated by the immortal Winzy, on his 323rd birthday. The student of the alchemist Cornelius Agrippa, he discovers an 'Elixir of Immortality'. Winzy marries the coquette Bertha who ages into a jealous crone, whilst the scholar remains unwrinkled. The 'old-hearted youth' describes how he 'lived on for many a year—alone, and weary of myself—desirous of death, yet never dying'. The story ends with his claim to have 'conceived a design by which I may end all'.

Morte Arthur, Le (The Stanzaic *Morte Arthur*) A late 14th-century poem from the north-west Midlands in 3,834 lines of eight-line rhyming stanzas surviving in one manuscript, and an important source (directly or indirectly) for the sections in *Malory leading up to and dealing with the death of Arthur, though it is clear that Malory was also using a French text. The poem narrates Launcelot's love affairs with Guinevere and the Maid of Astolat, Arthur's last battles, and the king's being borne away to Avalon. See *King Arthur's Death*, ed. L. D. Benson (1976); trans. Brian Stone, *King Arthur's Death* (1989).

Morte Arthure A 14th-century alliterative poem in 4,346 long lines, adapted by *Malory for his story of Arthur and Lucius. Correspondences with the *Roman de Brut* by *Wace suggest that, directly or indirectly, this or *Laȝamon's *Brut* may have been the poet's principal source. The poem may justifiably be regarded as the most powerful epic narrative in Middle English. Its subject matter corresponds roughly to Malory's first, second, and eighth romances (in Vinaver's numbering): the early exploits of Arthur, his European ventures, and the final battle with Modred. Malory, however, adapted the *Morte* so as to procure a victory for Arthur early in his cycle of adventures, rather than allowing his continental exploits to lead to his defeat and death at home (*see also* MORTE ARTHUR) as they do in this poem. It is among the most important Middle English poems, influencing *The *Awntyrs of Arthur*, *Hary's *Wallace*, and other works. See selections ed. J. Finlayson (1967); also *King Arthur's Death*, ed. L. D. Benson (1976); trans. Brian Stone, *King Arthur's Death* (1989). The poem is discussed by J. L. N. O'Loughlin in R. S. Loomis (ed.), *Arthurian Literature in the Middle Ages* (1959); see also T. Turville-Petre, *The Alliterative Revival* (1977).

'Morte d'Arthur' A poem by Alfred *Tennyson, written 1833–4, published 1842, subsequently incorporated in 'The Passing of Arthur' (1869), preceded by 169 lines and followed by 29, where it formed one of the **Idylls of the King*, though it continued to be published separately as well. Tennyson's first major Arthurian work, it describes the last moments of Arthur after the battle with Mordred's forces, and includes his elegy on the Round Table, delivered to Sir Bedivere: 'The old order changeth, yielding place to new. '

Morte Darthur, Le The title given to the cycle of Arthurian legends by Thomas *Malory, printed by William *Caxton in 1485. In 1934, W. F. Oakeshott discovered in Winchester College Library a manuscript without Caxton's division into

21 books and without several of his colophons. This manuscript, dividing the whole into eight parts, was used by Vinaver as the basis of his new edition of Malory. Though Malory refers throughout to a 'French book' as his source, it is clear that his sources were more various, and that sometimes he shelters under the supposed authority of French when in fact improvising. Vinaver divides the cycle into eight *Works* which he views as separate romances: (1) The Book of King Arthur, based largely on the *Suite du Merlin* (*see* MERLIN); (2) The Tale of Arthur and Lucius, based principally on the Alliterative English **Morte Arthure*; (3) The Tale of Sir Launcelot du Lake, mostly from two sections of the Prose *Lancelot* in the Vulgate cycle; (4) Sir Gareth of Orkney, the precise source of which is not known; (5) Tristram de Lyones, thought to be a translation of part of a lost 13th-century prose *Tristan* in French; (6) The Quest of the Holy Grail, principally from the prose Vulgate *Queste del Saint Graal* (*see* GRAIL); (7) Launcelot and Guinevere; and (8) The Morte Darthur, both based to a considerable degree on the French Vulgate *Mort Artu*, and the English stanzaic *Le *Morte Arthur*. Since the publication of Vinaver's three-volume edition in 1947, critics have debated whether Malory's work is to be regarded as a single book (see Lumiansky and Moorman below) or as eight Works (Vinaver), with a middle position adopted by C. S. *Lewis and by D. S. Brewer (see Bennett, *Essays on Malory* below). Although Vinaver's edition is now regarded as authoritative, the traditional view of Malory's work as a whole compounded of disparate parts (by analogy with the **Canterbury Tales* or cycles of *mystery plays) prevails. See *The Works of Sir Thomas Malory*, ed. E. Vinaver, rev. P. J. C. Field (3rd edn, 1990); in one volume as *Malory: Works* (2nd edn, 1971); Caxton's edition, ed. J. Cowen (Penguin, 2 vols, 1969); J. A. W. Bennett (ed.), *Essays on Malory* (1963); R. M. Lumiansky (ed.), *Malory's Originality* (1964); C. Moorman, *The Book of Kyng Arthur* (1965); T. Takimaya and D. S. Brewer (eds), *Aspects of Malory* (1982); E. Archibald and A. S. G. Edwards, *A Companion to Malory* (1996).

MORTIMER, John Clifford (1923–2009) Novelist, barrister, and playwright, formerly married to novelist Penelope *Mortimer. Well known for his opposition to censorship (he was defence counsel in the 1971 obscenity trial of the underground magazine *Oz*), Mortimer gained a wide readership for his stories about an eccentric defence barrister, Horace Rumpole, who appears in *Rumpole of the Bailey* (1978) and numerous subsequent volumes. Many of the stories have been adapted for television. Other works of fiction include *Paradise Postponed* (1985), a comic saga of English life from 1945 to the 1980s, and its sequels, *Titmuss Regained* (1990) and *The Sound of Trumpets* (1998); *Summer's Lease* (1988); *Dunster* (1992); and *Quite Honestly* (2005). His plays include *A Voyage round my Father* (1971), a powerful and poignant portrait of his blind barrister father. *Clinging to the Wreckage* (1982), *Murderers and Other Friends* (1994), and *The Summer of a Dormouse* (2000) are autobiographical.

MORTIMER, Penelope (1918–1999) Novelist, born in north Wales and educated at London University: her works, with their emphasis on frankness about female experience, contributed to the development of the woman's novel in the 1960s. They include *The Pumpkin Eater* (1962, her seventh book: filmed 1964, script by Harold *Pinter), *My Friend Says It's Bulletproof* (1967, which tackled the taboo subject of breast cancer), *The Home* (1971), *Long Distance* (1974), and *The Handyman* (1983). A volume of autobiography, *About Time*, appeared in 1979.

Mortimer his Fall Fragments of a tragedy by Ben *Jonson, printed in 1640, concerning the earl of Mortimer, the murderer of Edward II. Only the Argument and the opening speeches survive.

MORTON, H. V. (Henry Vollam) (1892–1979) Travel writer and journalist, born in Ashton-under-Lyne and educated at King Edward's School, Birmingham. He wrote for several newspapers, notably the *Daily Express*, on which he was a popular columnist during the 1920s. Appearing first as articles, *In Search of England* (1927) was an immediate success. Its focus on the countryside and historic towns contrasts with other influential inter-war travelogues that explore 'Englishness' such as those of J. B. *Priestley and George *Orwell. Similar preoccupations characterize its sequel, *The Call of England* (1928), and his books on Scotland (1929, 1933), Ireland (1930), and Wales (1932), while he also wrote extensively on London. Several books of biblically inspired travel in the Middle East followed in the late 1930s. Disillusioned by the post-war Labour government, in 1947 Morton emigrated to South Africa, the subject, along with Spain and Italy, of his later works.

MORTON, John Maddison (1811–91) Playwright, son of the playwright Thomas *Morton, educated in France. He wrote *farces and showed a special gift for adaptations from the French. His most successful piece was **Box and Cox* (1847); *Done on Both Sides* appeared in the same year.

MORTON, Thomas (?1764–1838) Dramatist. He entered Lincoln's Inn in 1784, and was the author of three successful comedies, *The Way to Get Married* (1796), *A Cure for Heartache* (1797), and *Speed the Plough* (1798). The last of these introduced the name and character of 'Mrs Grundy', and the conception of Grundyism as the extreme of moral rigidity.

MOSCHUS (*fl.* *c.*150 BC) A *pastoral poet of Syracuse, author of a short *epic *Europa*, and traditionally linked with *Theocritus and *Bion. The anonymous *Lament for Bion* was long wrongly ascribed to Moschus. There are echoes of it in John *Milton's Latin *Epitaphium Damonis*, and in his **Lycidas*, P. B. *Shelley's **Adonais*, and Matthew *Arnold's *'Thyrsis'.

Moscow Arts Theatre Founded in 1898 by the actor and theatre director Konstantin Stanislavsky (1863–1938) and the playwright and theatre director Vladimir Nemirovich-

Danchenko (1858–1943), with the aim of creating a repertory theatre which would provide the public with the best in classic and modern drama, and pursue the highest professional standards. Though its founders were soon forced to abandon their policy of offering cheap tickets, they succeeded in other aspects of theatre reform: the 'star system' was replaced by ensemble performance, artificial styles of acting gave way to a style based on psychological realism, and scenery, sound effects, and lighting were used to create an illusion of everyday reality on stage. They also promoted the role of the director as the figure whose ideas provided a single, unifying vision for a production.

The plays of Anton *Chekhov are particularly associated with the theatre; his play *The Seagull* was successfully revived by the theatre two years after its first disastrous production in 1896, leading to the rehabilitation of Chekhov's reputation as a dramatist. His work provided an ideal vehicle for its 'house style' of psychological realism, which encouraged the audience to identify with and experience a character's emotions, and promoted ensemble acting in which the psychological realist acting style helped to reveal the subtext of the characters' interactions. Another author closely connected with the theatre was Mikhail *Bulgakov, whose play *The Days of the Turbins*, a sympathetic portrayal of a family on the 'wrong' side in the revolution, was first performed in 1926 and became one of Stalin's favourites (it was revived on Stalin's orders in 1932).

The first visit to Britain of a company from the theatre took place only in 1958; Harley *Granville-Barker met Stanislavsky in 1914 to discuss plans to recreate an original Moscow Arts Theatre production in London, but war and revolution intervened. After 1917 the theatre's repertoire and realistic acting style made it a target for attacks from the left; Chekhov's plays were thought to be too sympathetic to the gentry and officer classes, and of little relevance to Soviet life. The theatre was protected by the Bolshevik state which designated it an academic theatre in 1921, and it continued to produce classics as well as new works. In 1932 it was renamed after the writer and dramatist Maxim *Gorky, and its realistic style was promoted as the only model for the rest of the Soviet theatre to follow, rather than the avant-garde experimentation of the 1910s and 1920s. In 1928 Chekhov's *The Cherry Orchard* returned to the repertoire, but now with the emphasis firmly on comedy rather than on an elegiac farewell to a previous era. By the time of its first visit to Britain in 1958, the theatre had come under attack at home for being out of touch with contemporary audiences. The theatre's reputation rests largely on the productions staged in its early years, and on Stanislavsky's theoretical writings on acting, which inspired the school of 'method acting' in the USA. See Nick Worrall, *The Moscow Arts Theatre* (1996).

MOSES Ancient Israelite leader and lawgiver in the *Bible; supposed author of the Pentateuch (the first five books of the Old Testament). Born an Israelite but found in the bulrushes and raised by Pharoah's daughter, he secured Pharoah's permission to lead the Israelites out of captivity through the ten plagues which culminated in the death of the firstborn, celebrated in the feast of the Passover (so named because the angel of death passed over the Israelites' houses). The exodus began with the crossing of the Red Sea, in which Pharoah's army drowned. The Israelites wandered forty years in the wilderness, saved from starvation by quails and manna, and given water when Moses struck the rock. God spoke directly to him from the burning bush and on Mount Sinai, where he dictated the Ten Commandments. See Exodus, Leviticus, Numbers, and Deuteronomy.

MOSLEY, Nicholas, third Baron Ravensdale (1923–) Novelist and biographer, educated at Eton College and Balliol College, Oxford. His highly intellectual, experimental, and metaphysical novels include *Accident* (1964) and *Impossible Object* (1968), both of which were filmed; *Natalie Natalia* (1971); and *Catastrophe Practice* (1979), a complex network of three plays with prefaces and a short novel, built on the mathematical 'catastrophe theory' of the 1970s, applied here to human relationships and identity. Other novels are *Imago Bird* (1980), *Serpent* (1981), and *Judith* (1986). His biographies include a life of Julian *Grenfell (1976) and a two-volume study of his father, *Rules of the Game: Sir Oswald and Lady Cynthia Mosley 1896–1933* (1982) and *Beyond the Pale: Sir Oswald Mosley 1933–1980* (1983). He won the Whitbread Prize for his much-praised panoramic novel *Hopeful Monsters* (1990).

MOSLEY, Walter (1952–) African American novelist, born in Los Angeles, a practitioner of the *hardboiled style. With *Devil in a Blue Dress* (1990) he began his Easy Rawlins series, centring on a Los Angeles private eye. He has also produced *science fiction novels like *Blue Light* (1998) and his non-fiction includes *Workin' on the Chain Gang: Shaking off the Dead Hand of History* (2000). *This Year You Write your Novel* (2007) is an advice volume to aspiring writers.

Mosses from an Old Manse (1846) A collection of tales and sketches by Nathaniel *Hawthorne. The Old Manse itself is the author's Concord home, and best known among the book's contents are 'Young Goodman Brown', 'Rappaccini's Daughter', and 'Roger Malvin's Burial'.

Mother Goose Traditional name for a narrator of *nursery rhymes and *fairy stories. She entered the English language through the frontispiece of Charles *Perrault's tales in 1729; the name was taken up by children's publisher John *Newbery and others, making her a well-known figure of folklore in Britain and North America. She appeared as a comic, wise, or bawdy old crone, wearing a witch's hat above her hooked nose and sharp chin. Frequently she rides or is a goose, sporting bonnet and spectacles. She has a long history in pantomimes and continues to feature in nursery rhyme books.

'Mother Hubberds Tale' ('Prosopopoia') A satire in rhymed couplets, by Edmund *Spenser, included in the volume of *Complaints* published in 1591. The ape and the fox, 'disliking of their evill | And hard estate', determine to seek their fortunes abroad, and assume the disguises first of an old soldier and his dog, then of a parish priest and his clerk, then of a courtier and his groom; their misdemeanours in these characters are recounted. Finally, they steal the lion's crown and sceptre and abuse the royal power, until Jove intervenes and exposes them. The poem is a satire on the abuses of the church and the evils of the court.

motion The name given to puppet plays in the 16th and 17th centuries. They originally dealt with scriptural subjects, but their scope was later extended. *Shakespeare in *The *Winter's Tale* (IV. iii) refers to a 'motion of the Prodigal Son', and there are references to 'motions' in Ben Jonson's **Bartholomew Fair, A *Tale of a Tub*, and **Every Man out of His Humour*.

MOTION, Sir Andrew (1952–) Poet and biographer, born in London, educated at Radley College and University College, Oxford. His first collection, *The Pleasure Steamers* (1978), was mostly lyrical in character and showed the influence of Philip *Larkin. *Secret Narratives* (1983) contains a sequence of short narrations told within an enigmatic context, and forms a contribution to the 'new narrative' poetry of the 1980s, whose practitioners also include James *Fenton. *Dangerous Play* (1984) contains an autobiographical prose piece, 'Skating', which is concerned with the accident, coma, and death of his mother, a preoccupation to which Motion has often returned. Other volumes include *Love in a Life* (1991), *Salt Water* (1997), and *Public Property* (2002). Both in his purely lyrical forms and in his more enigmatically narrative modes Motion is a poet of arrestingly limpid linguistic clarity: his deepest literary affinity is probably with Edward *Thomas, on whom he has written a critical book. Motion has also written biographies of Philip Larkin (1993) and John *Keats (1997) and has published novels, including *The Pale Companion* (1989) and *The Invention of Dr. Cake* (2003), and a memoir of his childhood, *In the Blood* (2006). *Selected Poems 1976–1997* appeared in 1998. Motion was appointed *poet laureate in 1999.

MOTLEY, John Lothrop (1814–77) American historian, born in Massachusetts, educated at Harvard, Göttingen, and Berlin universities. He was American minister to Austria, 1861–7, and to Great Britain, 1869–70. He is chiefly remembered as a historian and author of *The Rise of the Dutch Republic* (1855). This was followed by the *History of the United Netherlands* (1860–67) and *The Life and Death of John Barneveld* (1874). In addition to historical works he published *Merry Mount: A Romance of the Massachusetts Colony* in 1849.

MOTTEUX, Peter Anthony (1660–1718) Journalist and translator. Born in Rouen, he was among the Huguenots who fled to England after the revocation of the Edict of Nantes (1685). He edited and wrote much of the **Gentleman's Journal*, completed Sir Thomas *Urquhart's translation of Rabelais (1693–4), and published a free translation of **Don Quixote* (1700–03).

MOTTRAM, R. H. (Ralph Hale) (1883–1971) Writer, born in Norwich and educated there and at Lausanne, Switzerland. He worked as a bank clerk before establishing himself as a novelist with *The Spanish Farm Trilogy* (1927), a sequence of novels based on his own experiences during the First World War. It consists of the Hawthornden Prize-winning *The Spanish Farm* (1924), *Sixty-Four, Ninety-Four* (1925), and *The Crime at Vanderlynden's* (1926), and is set in northern France on the 'Ferme l'Espagnole' of Flemish-speaking, French-writing farmer Jerome Vanderlynden and his daughter Madeleine. Mottram authored 60 books, but none matched the success of his *Trilogy*.

Mourning Bride, The A tragedy by William *Congreve, produced 1697; it was his only attempt at tragedy, and was received with enthusiasm. Almeria, daughter of Manuel, king of Granada, has secretly married Alphonso, prince of the enemy state of Valencia. He is captured by Manuel. The discovery of his marriage to Almeria infuriates Manuel, who orders his immediate murder, and, further to punish his daughter, impersonates the captive in his cell, so that when she comes to save him he may mock her disappointment. He is by mistake killed instead, and decapitated. A revolt against Manuel releases the true Alphonso, and he and Almeria are reunited. The play contains celebrated lines such as 'Music has charms to soothe a savage breast', and 'Heaven has no rage, like love to hatred turned, | Nor hell a fury, like a woman scorned'.

'Mouse, To a, On turning up her Nest, with the Plough, November, 1785' A poem by Robert *Burns, which subtly cites the Bible and Samuel Johnson's **Rasselas* in its expression of tender, unsentimental concern for the unhoused rodent and, by extension, all earth's defenceless creatures.

movable books Picture books incorporating flaps, volvelles (movable dials), pop-up elements, or other devices that reveal hidden elements of a text, convert one image to another, or simulate action. Early examples include 18th-century harlequinades (adaptations of the *commedia dell'arte*); movable books came to prominence in the 19th century through publishers such as Dean and Son, Raphael Tuck, and Ernest Nister. The German Lothar Meggendorfer (1847–1925) was a leading practitioner. Recent exponents are Robert Crowther and the American Robert Sabuda. See Ann Montanaro, *Pop-up and Movable Books* (1993).

Movement, the A term coined by J. D. Scott, literary editor of the **Spectator*, in 1954 to describe a group of writers including Philip *Larkin, Donald *Davie, D. J. *Enright, John *Wain, Elizabeth *Jennings, and Robert *Conquest. Two anthologies (Enright's *Poets of the 1950s*, 1955, and Conquest's *New*

Lines, 1956) illustrate the Movement's predominantly anti-romantic, witty, rational, sardonic tone; its fictional heroes (notably Larkin's John Kemp in *Jill*, and Kingsley *Amis's Dixon in *Lucky Jim*) tended to be lower-middle-class scholarship boys. Definitions of its aims tended to be negative, and by 1957 its members began to disown it. It has, nevertheless, proved highly influential on later poets, and forms a constant reference point in debates about modern 'English' poetry. See Blake *Morrison, *The Movement* (1980).

MOXON, Edward (1801–58) A distinguished London publisher and bookseller, he was also a poet though Leigh *Hunt described him archly as 'a bookseller among poets, and a poet among booksellers'. Various volumes of his poems were published between 1826 and 1835, and his chief interest in publishing was in poetry. He was a close friend of Charles *Lamb, who introduced him to many contemporary writers and whose 'adopted' daughter, Emma Isola, he married. He set up his own business in 1830, when he proceeded to build a remarkable list which included P. B. *Shelley, John *Clare, William *Wordsworth, S. T. *Coleridge, Lamb, Hunt, Robert *Browning, Coventry *Patmore, and Henry Wadsworth *Longfellow, as well as Alfred *Tennyson, whose close friend he became and whose work he continued to champion and publish until his death. Hunt wrote that 'Moxon has no connection but with the select of the earth.' In 1831 he established the **Englishman's Magazine* in which he published much of the work of the writers he supported, and in which he defended them against the attacks of **Blackwood's*, and the **Edinburgh* and **Quarterly Reviews*. Apart from their literary qualities, his publications were famed for a high standard of typography and binding.

MOXON, Joseph (1627–91) Maker of globes and mathematical instruments, printer, and typefounder, born in Wakefield, the son of a printer. He wrote *Mechanic Exercises, or The Doctrine of Handy-Works Applied to the Art of Printing* (1683–4; ed. H. Davis and H. Carter, 3rd edn 2003), the first manual of printing and typefounding in any language, and probably the first English book to be published in serial parts.

MOZART, Wolfgang Amadeus (1756–91) Austrian composer and pianist. He visited London with his parents and sister when he was 8: he was received by George III, and systematically 'tested' by Daines Barrington, whose 'Account of a Very Remarkable Young Musician' appeared in the *Philosophical Transactions* of the *Royal Society, 1771. Mozart's first two symphonies were written in Ebury Row, and before he left London in July 1765 he presented to the British Museum his first vocal work, the unaccompanied motet 'God is our refuge'. Mozart never came to England again, nor did he set any more English words. Near the end of his life he was rumoured to have been working on a libretto based on *The *Tempest* by F. H. von Einsiedel, with revisions by F. W. Gotter, but no music survives. Mozart and his contemporary Salieri (1750–1825) appear as the principal characters in *Amadeus* by Peter *Shaffer.

'Mr Gilfil's Love-Story' *See* SCENES OF CLERICAL LIFE.

Mr Limberham, *or The Kind Keeper* A comedy by John *Dryden, produced 1679, published 1680. The play was banned by royal decree after three performances and has not been popular since, but Dryden nonetheless thought highly of it. The title role is possibly based on the earl of *Shaftesbury. Limberham is an impotent masochist, who is cuckolded by the oversexed hero Woodall, to whom every woman in the play succumbs. By implication the play attacks a sexually corrupt court, the blind hedonism of the nobility, and the hypocrisy of Dissenters.

Mr Scarborough's Family Anthony *Trollope's 45th novel, published in 1883 (Trollope died during its serialization). John Scarborough has gone through two marriage ceremonies, enabling him to pronounce his eldest son Mountjoy legitimate or illegitimate as he pleases. Hearing of Mountjoy's debts, he declares him illegitimate and names his calculating brother Augustus as heir. Augustus reveals his impatience to inherit, and, now on his deathbed, Scarborough again alters the will, reinstating Mountjoy. In the last pages of this dark novel Mountjoy returns to the moneylenders, and sets about mortgaging the property to the hilt.

Mrs Caudle's Curtain Lectures *See* JERROLD, DOUGLAS WILLIAM.

Mrs Dalloway Fourth novel by Virginia *Woolf, published 1925. The action is restricted to the events of one hot day in the middle of June 1923, punctuated by the chimes of Big Ben: one of the novel's key contrasts is between the oppressiveness of clock time and the unrestricted, time-defying freedom of the mind. It opens in Westminster as Clarissa Dalloway, wife of Richard Dalloway MP (both had appeared briefly in Woolf's first novel, *The Voyage Out*, 1915), sets off to buy flowers for her party that evening. Alive with the sights and sounds of the London scene yet interwoven with memories of Bourton, Clarissa's family home, where, aged 18, she refused to marry Peter Walsh, the narrative is handled with a technical confidence and bravura that herald a new phase in Woolf's mastery of the novel. Mrs Dalloway—51 years old, fashionable, worldly, wealthy, the 'perfect hostess'—is the public persona of Clarissa, a far more vulnerable woman who possesses a 'virginity preserved through childbirth' and who feels more at ease amongst the ebb and flow of London's streets. She is seen through the eyes not just of Walsh, returned after five years in India, but, among others, her girlhood friend Sally Seton, her daughter Elizabeth, and her daughter's tutor Doris Kilman. Mrs Dalloway's experience is also contrasted with that of the shell-shocked Septimus Warren Smith, who commits suicide by hurling himself from a window; news of his death intrudes upon Clarissa's party, brought by Sir William Bradshaw, the Harley Street specialist whom he had uselessly consulted on the advice of Dr Holmes. Woolf wanted the reader to make continuous connections between Clarissa and Septimus, and the similarities between the two characters proliferate as the novel draws to a close. She noted in her diary, 'I want to give life & death, sanity & insanity; I want to criticise the social system, & to show it at work, at its most intense', and in this she succeeds triumphantly. Along with **To the Lighthouse* (1927) it remains one of Woolf's most popular works.

Mrs Lirriper's Lodgings and ***Mrs Lirriper's Legacy*** Christmas stories by Charles *Dickens, which appeared in *All the Year Round*, 1863 and 1864. Mrs Lirriper lets lodgings in Norfolk Street, Strand, and her lodgers and past lodgers tell their stories.

Mucedorus, A Comedy of A play of uncertain authorship, published in 1598 with 'new additions' in the third edition, of 1610, which says that it was acted by the King's Men. The whole play and, less implausibly, the additions have sometimes been attributed to *Shakespeare.

Mucedorus, prince of Valencia, in order to discover the virtues of Amadine, daughter of the king of Aragon, disguises himself as a shepherd, saves her from a bear, and falls in love with her. Banished from her father's court, he next appears as a hermit, saves Amadine from a 'wild man', reveals his identity to her father, and is finally successful in his suit.

Much Ado About Nothing A comedy by *Shakespeare, written probably 1598–9, first printed 1600. Its chief sources are a novella by Matteo *Bandello and an episode in Ariosto's **Orlando furioso*. The play has always been popular in performance.

The prince of Aragon, with Claudio and Benedick in his suite, visits Leonato, duke of Messina, father of Hero and uncle of Beatrice. The witty Beatrice has a teasing relationship with the sworn bachelor Benedick. Beatrice and Benedick are each tricked into believing the other in love, and this brings about a genuine sympathy between them. Meanwhile Don John, the malcontented brother of the prince, thwarts Claudio's marriage by arranging for him to see Hero apparently wooed by his friend Borachio on her balcony—it is really her maidservant Margaret in disguise. Hero is publicly denounced by Claudio on her wedding day, falls into a swoon, and apparently dies. Benedick proves his love for Beatrice by challenging Claudio to a duel. The plot by Don John and Borachio is unmasked by the 'shallow fools' Dogberry and Verges, the local constables. Claudio promises to make Leonato amends for his daughter's death, and is asked to marry a cousin of Hero's; the veiled lady turns out to be Hero herself. Benedick asks to be married at the same time; Beatrice, 'upon great persuasion; and partly to save your life, for I was told you were in a consumption', agrees, and the play ends with a dance.

muckrakers Term coined by US president Theodore Roosevelt in 1906 to describe American writers attempting to expose abuses in commerce and politics. One of the most famous muckrakers was Upton *Sinclair.

MUDDIMAN, Henry (b. 1629) A pensioner at St John's College, Cambridge. He was authorized as a journalist by the Rump Parliament, at the request of General Monck (1608–70), in 1659, in which year he started the *Parliamentary Intelligencer* and *Mercurius Publicus*. He became the most famous of the 17th-century journalists, and his *newsletters in manuscript, sent twice a week to subscribers all over the kingdom, were an important political feature of the day. One of his principal rivals was Sir Roger *L'Estrange, whose papers, however, he drove from the field. In 1665, under the direction of his patron Sir Joseph Williamson (1633–1701), he started the **Oxford Gazette* (the predecessor of the *London Gazette*), the court being then at Oxford on account of the great plague.
See GAZETTE; NEWSPAPERS.

MUDIE, Charles (1818–90) The founder of Mudie's Lending Library (1842–1937). Mudie played a large part in the rise of the three-volume novel. Born in London, the son of a Scottish newsagent, he embarked on a career as bookseller, stationer, and lender of books in Bloomsbury. The lending proved so successful that he opened premises in Oxford Street in 1852, where the business prospered for many years, despite frequent complaints about Mudie's moral scruples in selecting his stock, which amounted, some claimed, to a form of censorship. George *Moore was a particularly outspoken adversary, publishing *Literature at Nurse, or Circulating Morals* in 1885. Nevertheless, Mudie remained popular for many years:

As children must have Punch and Judy
So I can't do without my Mudie.

See G. L. Griest, *Mudie's Circulating Library and the Victorian Novel* (1971).

MUGGERIDGE, Malcolm (1903–90) Journalist and broadcaster, born in Croydon and educated at Selwyn College, Cambridge. He published novels, plays, reportage, and memoirs, and from 1953 to 1957 was a successful editor of **Punch*, but is principally remembered as a pundit and controversialist. In his youth he shocked liberals and the left by his exposé of the Soviet Union (*Winter in Moscow*, 1934) and in later years, while remaining iconoclastic, he became a well-known television performer and an outspoken Christian apologist. His diaries were published in 1981 and there is a biography written by Richard Ingrams (1995).

Muggletonians A sect founded *c.*1651 by Lodowicke Muggleton (1609–98), a tailor, and his cousin John Reeve (1608–58), who claimed to be the 'two witnesses' of Revelation 11: 3–6. They denied the doctrine of the Trinity, and taught that matter was eternal and reason the creation of the devil.

MUHAMMAD (Mahomet) The founder of the Muslim religion. He was born at Mecca *c.*570, and, according to Muslim belief, he was called by the angel Gabriel *c.*610 to his role as a prophet. From time to time he imparted the revelations he received, and these became the *Qur'ān. After fierce opposition from the Meccans, he moved to Medina in 622 (the *hijra*). There he prospered both religiously, despite the opposition of local Jewish tribes, and on a secular level. After seven years of struggle Mecca surrendered, and by the time he died in 632 most of the Arabian peninsula had accepted his religious and political authority.

The first reasonably accurate, though unsympathetic, English account of Muhammad's life is in the *Preliminary Discourse* to the translation of the Qur'ān by George Sale (1697–1736), appearing in 1734. The next key assessment is that of Edward Gibbon (**Decline and Fall of the Roman Empire*, 1776–88, ch. L). In the 19th century, Thomas *Carlyle's lecture on Mahomet in *Heroes and Hero-Worship* (1840, lecture 2) had considerable vogue.

'Muiopotmos, or The Fate of the Butterflie' A mythological poem by Edmund *Spenser published among his *Complaints* (1591). It describes the destruction of the butterfly Clarion by the jealous spider Aragnoll, and contains the lines: 'What more felicitie can fall to creature, | Than to enjoy delight with libertie?'

MUIR, Edwin (1887–1959) Poet, son of a tenant farmer, born in Orkney, where he spent his childhood. His family moved to Glasgow when he was 14, and within five years both parents and two of his brothers were dead. While working as an office boy and clerk he turned to socialism and the philosophy of *Nietzsche. He began to write, and in 1913 he started contributing to Alfred Orage's **New Age*. In 1919, he married Willa Anderson (*see* MUIR, WILLA); they moved to London, where Muir became assistant to Orage, and underwent a course of psychoanalysis which profoundly affected his writing. In 1921 the Muirs went to Prague, and remained in Europe for four years, a period that later produced their collaborative translations from the German (notably, 1939–40, of Franz *Kafka). More importantly, it freed Muir's imagination as a poet. *First Poems* (1925) was followed by several other collections, including *Chorus of the Newly Dead* (1926), *The Labyrinth* (1949), and *Collected Poems, 1921–1951* (1952). Muir's poetry is mostly traditional rather than experimental in form, and much of his imagery is rooted in the landscapes of his childhood. A recurrent theme is the dream journey, and the narrative of the poet's own life lends itself naturally to the myth of an Eden threatened by various forms of catastrophe or expulsion. A sense of subdued menace lies beneath many of his quiet and orderly poems, which sometimes (as in his well-known piece 'The Horses') achieve a sense of the *Apocalypse. Muir also published three novels, a number of critical works, including *Scott and Scotland* (1936), and a highly evocative autobiography, published in 1940 as *The Story and the Fable* and revised as *An Autobiography* (1954). His wife's *Belonging: A Memoir* was published in 1968. See P. H. Butter, *Edwin Muir* (1966). Butter also edited *The Complete Poems* (1991).

MUIR, Kenneth (1907–96) Professor of English literature at Liverpool University (1951–74). He edited Sir Thomas *Wyatt's poems and letters; he also edited and wrote about many of Shakespeare's plays, and did much work on their sources.

MUIR, Willa (1890–1970) Née Anderson, Scottish novelist, translator, and essayist, born in Montrose, Angus, and educated at the University of St Andrews, who was the senior partner in her collaborative translations, with her husband Edwin *Muir, of *Kafka and others. Her novels *Imagined Corners* (1931) and *Mrs Ritchie* (1933) are set in a fictionalized Montrose ('Calderwick') and share a strong feminist awareness with such works of cultural criticism as *Women: An Inquiry* (1925) and *Mrs Grundy in Scotland* (1936). *Belonging* (1968) is an alternately rueful and tart memoir.

MUKHERJEE, Bharati (1940–) Indian American writer, born in Calcutta (Kolkata), who took up residence in America in the 1960s. Her fiction explores the nature of American identity, in her first novel, *The Tiger's Daughter* (1971), through the perspective of an illegal immigrant. *The Holder of the World* (1993) reverses the perspective by describing an American woman's experience of India. *The Tree Bride* (2004) starts in San Francisco and traces back a young Indian woman's relation to her family ancestors.

MULCASTER, Richard (1531/2–1611) Schoolmaster and writer, educated at Eton College, King's College and Peterhouse, Cambridge, and Christ Church, Oxford. He was the first headmaster of Merchant Taylors' School, London, where his pupils included Edmund *Spenser, Thomas *Kyd, Thomas *Lodge, and Lancelot *Andrewes, and he was later high master of St *Paul's School. He wrote two books on education, *Positions* (1581), dedicated to *Elizabeth I, and *The Elementary* (1582). Both books show his humanist interests and ideals, such as his suggestion that gentlewomen should be educated in school, though only up to the age of 13 or 14, and his stress on physical exercise, music, and vernacular literature, including the writing of English verse. Presumably the future poets who attended his school benefited from this last belief. He also published Latin and English verses on the queen's death (1603), and helped devise City shows and pageants.

MULDOON, Paul (1951–) Poet and librettist, born in Co. Armagh and educated at Queen's University, Belfast. He worked for BBC Northern Ireland before moving in 1985 to the USA, becoming a professor at Princeton. He was Oxford professor of poetry from 1999 to 2004. Muldoon's precocious *New Weather* (1973) marked him out as a distinctive new voice: ironic, allusive, knowing. By the appearance of *Quoof* (1983) he had established himself as one of the most verbally inventive poets of the post-war period. In *Madoc: A Mystery* (1990), the idealistic social philosophy of *Pantisocracy, as expounded by Samuel Taylor *Coleridge and Robert *Southey (author of the original **Madoc*), inspires a dazzling melange of allusions, correspondences, and fragmented storylines. *Hay* (1999) sustains a bewilderingly intricate architectonics of rhyme without weakening the subtle detail of its individual poems. 'Turkey Buzzards', from *Horse Latitudes* (2006), at once an exercise in rhetorical pyrotechnics and a touching elegy for the poet's sister, is one of many poems to suggest the seriousness impelling Muldoon's tirelessly playful approach to language. See *Poems 1968–1998* (2001); *The End of the Poem: Oxford Lectures* (2006).

MULGRAVE, earl of *See* SHEFFIELD, JOHN.

MÜLLER *See* MAX MÜLLER, FRIEDRICH.

MULOCK, Dinah Maria *See* CRAIK, DINAH MARIA.

Mum and the Sothsegger An incomplete alliterative poem (*c.*1409) of 1,751 lines, in a 15th-century British Library manuscript. Its idiom, range of concerns, dream vision, and wandering narrator clearly derive from William *Langland. Concerned with events in the early 15th century, it considers whether it is better to be Mum (as in 'keep mum') and to remain silent in evil days, or to speak unwelcome truths like the Sothsegger (Truth-teller). See Helen Barr (ed.), *The Piers Plowman Tradition* (1993).

mummers' play (St George play) A folk play evolved from the *sword-dance, widespread through England, Scotland, Ireland, and Wales. The play, in its characters and detailed action, varies in different localities, but the principal characters are St George (Sir George, King George, Prince George), the Turkish knight, Captain Slasher, and the Doctor. Different versions have given rise to a great variety of names for the minor personages. After a brief prologue, the fighting characters advance and introduce themselves, or are introduced, in boastful rhymes. A duel or several duels follow, and one or other of the combatants is killed. The Doctor then enters, and resuscitates the slain. Additional grotesque characters are then presented, and a collection is made. The central incident of the play is doubtless connected with the celebration of the death of the year and its resurrection in the spring. A celebrated description of mumming occurs in Book II, chs 4–6 of Thomas Hardy's *The *Return of the Native*, in which Eustacia Vye disguises herself as the Turkish knight, in the place of the lad Charley, in order to engineer a meeting with Clym Yeobright. See E. K. *Chambers, *The English Folk-Play* (1933).

MUNBY, Arthur Joseph (1828–1910) Poet, diarist, and lawyer, born in York and educated at St Peter's School, York, and Trinity College, Cambridge. He published various volumes of verse, including *Verses New and Old* (1865) and *Relicta* (1909), but is now chiefly remembered for his diaries and notebooks, used by Derek Hudson as the basis of his *Munby: Man of Two Worlds* (1972). These give an interesting picture of Victorian literary and social life; they also reveal Munby's obsession with working women and the story of his secret marriage to a domestic servant, Hannah Cullwick (1833–1909), which explain some of the allusions in his poems. See Diane Atkinson, *Love and Dirt: The Marriage of Arthur Munby and Hannah Cullwick* (2003).

Munchausen, Baron, *Narrative of his Marvellous Travels* By Rudolf Erich Raspe, published 1785. The original Baron Münchhausen is said to have lived 1720–97, to have served in the Russian army against the Turks, and to have been in the habit of grossly exaggerating his experiences. Raspe (1737–94) was a Hanoverian scholar who, when librarian at Cassel, stole gems from the Landgraf's collection, fled to England, and added to his diminishing resources by publishing in English a version of the baron's tall tales. This was translated into German, enlarged, and popularized by poet Gottfried August Bürger. The baron's fantastic adventures have inspired many films, including one directed by Terry Gilliam in 1988.

MUNDAY, Anthony (1560–1633) Hack-writer. He wrote or collaborated in a number of plays, and was ridiculed by Ben *Jonson as Antonio Balladino in *The *Case is Altered*. Among his plays are probably *Fedele and Fortuna* (*c.*1584) and *John a Kent and John a Cumber* (*c.*1589–90, dealing with a conflict between two wizards); he collaborated in the writing of *Sir Thomas *More* and in *The Downfall of Robert, Earl of Huntington* (printed 1601), followed by *The Death* of the same, dealing with the legend of *Robin Hood. Munday wrote ballads, which are lost, and as 'Shepheard Tonie' contributed several poems to **Englands Helicon* (1600). He also translated popular romances, including the **Palmerin* cycle (1581–1602), *Paladin of England* (1588), and **Amadis of Gaul* (?1590), and wrote City pageants from 1605. His experiences as a student at the English College in Rome during 1579 are the basis for his *The English Roman Life* (1582).

MUNRO, Alice (1931–) Canadian short story writer, born in Wingham, Ontario, where she grew up. She spent two years at the University of Ontario studying English literature and on her first marriage moved to British Columbia. In the early 1970s she returned to live in Ontario. Her collections, *Dance of the Happy Shades* (1968), *Who Do You Think You Are?* (1978), published in Britain as *The Beggar Maid*, and *The Progress of Love* (1986), won the prestigious Canadian Governor General's Award. Her other collections include *Friends of my Youth*, *Lives of Girls and Women* (1973), in which the stories are interlinked, *Open Secrets* (1994), *Hateship, Friendship, Courtship, Loveship, Marriage* (2001), *Runaway* (2004), and *The View from Castle Rock* (2006). Munro describes herself as writing about 'places where your roots are', in her case relatively poor, small-town southern Ontario, whose texture and unremarkable lives, especially women's, engage her imaginative sympathy. Tapping what she has termed her 'emotional reality', her writing is characterized by, above all, superb and precise mastery of the short story form; both lucid and compellingly mysterious, the stories combine poetic intensity and economy with the surprising scope and depth of a novel. She won the *Man Booker International prize in 2009.

MUNRO, H. H. (Hector Hugh) *See* SAKI.

MUNRO, Rona (1959–) Playwright, born in Aberdeen and educated at Edinburgh University. Her first produced plays, *Fugue* (1983) and *Piper's Cave* (1985), announced a writer who was fascinated by the poetic relationship of the landscape of her native Scotland and human, particularly female, struggle. *Iron* (2002), her most successful play, is about a mother and daughter attempting to forge a relationship, the former being imprisoned for the murder of her husband (and the daughter's father).

MURDOCH, Dame Iris (1919–99) Novelist and philosopher, born in Dublin of Anglo-Irish parents, and educated at Badminton School and Somerville College, Oxford. She worked for some time in the Civil Service, then lectured in philosophy in Oxford and London; her works on philosophy include *Sartre, Romantic Rationalist* (1953), *The Sovereignty of Good* (1970), and *Metaphysics as a Guide to Morals* (1992). In 1956 she married the literary critic John *Bayley, who later published two controversial books, *Iris* (1998) and *Iris and the Friends* (1999), describing her final years as a victim of Alzheimer's disease. In an influential essay, 'Against Dryness' (**Encounter*, Jan. 1961), she distinguished between what she called 'crystalline' novels (tightly structured, self-contained fictions, making much use of myth, allegory, and symbol) and a more open and relaxed type of writing, exemplified at its finest by the great 19th-century English and Russian novels. Most of her 26 novels fall within the former category, characteristically deploying elaborate patterning (often in the form of intricately choreographed sexual relationships) and characters who represent a philosophical or other concept. Among the best of these books are her first novel, the genially bohemian *Under the Net* (1954), and *A Severed Head* (1961; dramatized 1963 by J. B. *Priestley), an elegant satire wittily drawing on motifs from *Freud and Sir James *Frazer's *The Golden Bough*. *The Bell* (1958), a mellow, humane portrayal of a lay religious community in the Gloucestershire countryside, is the most impressive of her more naturalistic novels. Central to all her fiction is an insistence on the need to respect the shapelessness and contingency of life and to resist the impulse to impose self-pleasing or self-deceiving patterns on it. See Peter Conradi, *Iris Murdoch: A Life* (2001).

MURPHY, Arthur (1727–1805) Playwright, born in Ireland. He was a close friend of Samuel *Johnson from 1754, and introduced Johnson to the *Thrales in 1765. He was called to the bar in 1762, numbering Edmund *Burke among his clients. In addition to dramatic and political journalism, Murphy wrote some twenty farces, comedies, and tragedies, including adaptations of *Molière and *Voltaire; his better-known pieces include *The Way to Keep Him* (1760), **Three Weeks after Marriage* (1764), and *Know your Own Mind* (1777). He produced an edition of Henry *Fielding, with a biography, in 1762; a translation of *Tacitus (1793); and biographical essays on Johnson (1792) and David *Garrick (1801).

MURPHY, Dervla (1931–) Born in Lismore, Ireland, daughter of a local librarian with IRA sympathies. She often told of receiving an atlas and a bicycle for her tenth birthday and deciding then to cycle to India. She left school at 14 but caring for her invalid mother allowed only short cycling trips in Europe. In 1963, after her mother died, she cycled solo from Dublin to Delhi, and described her sometimes hair-raising adventures in *Full Tilt* (1965), the first of some 21 travel books on Africa, Asia, and South America. She travelled lightly, usually by bicycle, alone or with her young daughter born in 1968. Her books depict an intrepid adventurer, politically sensitive, especially on racial issues, regularly extricating herself from dangerous scrapes. She continued to cycle into her seventies, though, as in *Through Siberia by Accident* (2005), her plans sometimes went awry. *Wheels within Wheels* (1979) is an autobiography.

MURPHY, Pat (1955–) American *science fiction and *fantasy author, born in Spokane, Washington. *The City, Not Long After* (1988) explores post-holocaust San Francisco. *There and Back Again* (1999), *Wild Angel* (2001), and *Adventures in Time and Space with Max Merriwell* (2002) are more playful explorations of her chosen genres.

MURPHY, Richard (1927–) Irish poet, born in County Mayo, who spent his early childhood in Ceylon (Sri Lanka), and was educated at Magdalen College, Oxford. His poetry characteristically portrays the landscapes and seascapes of the west of Ireland; his publications include *Sailing to an Island* (1963) and the historical meditation *The Battle of Aughrim* (1968). Murphy's dry, classical, somewhat patrician style mediates powerful themes of social and sexual exclusion (see, for example, the sonnet sequence which gives its title to *The Price of Stone*, 1985), though he sometimes allows himself a more Romantic utterance ('Seals at High Island', 1974). His memoir *The Kick* (2003) includes vivid portraits of Theodore *Roethke, Ted *Hughes, Sylvia *Plath, and other writers. *Collected Poems* appeared in 2000.

MURPHY, Tom (1935–) Irish playwright, born in Tuam, Co. Galway. Murphy's work marries the dominant naturalistic strain of Irish drama with the poetic impulse that had characterized the plays of the early *Abbey Theatre. *A Whistle in the Dark* (1961) ferociously exposes the violence of family life, while *A Crucial Week in the Life of a Grocer's Assistant* (1969) offers an angry portrait of the constrictions and hypocrisies of small-town Ireland. The fantastical *The Morning after Optimism* (1971) and the anticlerical *The Sanctuary Lamp* (1975)—in which two socially excluded friends, one Irish and one English, overturn a confessional in a church—further explore the gap between ideals of liberated selfhood and the pressures of communal experience. The exuberant *The Gigli Concert* (1983) and the darker *Bailegangaire* (1985), the most acclaimed of Murphy's 25 plays, fuse realism with baroque dialogue, surreal comedy, and a yearning for transcendence.

MURRAY, Gilbert (1866–1957) Classical Greek scholar and translator, born in Sydney, New South Wales, and educated at Oxford. He became professor of Greek at Glasgow in 1889 and was Regius professor of Greek at Oxford 1908–36. His translations of *Euripides into English verse were widely performed, and he imbued his influential interpretations of Greek literature with his own secular liberalism.

MURRAY, Sir James (1837–1915) Lexicographer, the son of a clothier from Hawick, in the Scottish borders. He was educated at Cavers School, near his native village of Denholm, and at Minto School, but his great philological and antiquarian knowledge was acquired largely through his own efforts. He became a schoolmaster and moved to London in 1864, where he worked as a bank clerk before returning to his earlier profession at Mill Hill. Throughout these years he pursued his philological interests and made the acquaintance of many like-minded scholars, including W. W. *Skeat, Henry *Sweet, and Frederick *Furnivall; he became a member of the Philological Society, to which he delivered in 1868 papers later printed as *The Dialect of the Southern Counties of Scotland* (1873) which were received with much respect. In 1879, after lengthy negotiation and much hesitation, he was appointed editor of the **Oxford English Dictionary*, a monumental work which was to occupy the rest of his life. He laid down the lines on which the work was to be compiled, and persevered through many difficulties (some financial), resisting suggestions that the work be completed more rapidly. There is a detailed account of the dictionary's composition in *Caught in the Web of Words* (1977) by his granddaughter K. M. E. Murray, which also gives a vivid portrait of his industry, his high moral standards and sense of responsibility, and his happy family life. He was the father of eleven children, several of whom aided him considerably in the great work that dominated their early lives. See also S. Winchester, *The Meaning of Everything: The Story of the Oxford English Dictionary* (2003).

MURRAY, John (1778–1843) The son of John Murray I (1745–93), who founded the publishing house still in existence. The second John Murray was among those who, together with reviews such as the **Edinburgh* and the **Quarterly*, began to substitute for the dying system of personal patronage his own encouragement and commercial expertise. His publishing house became a social meeting place for many of the literary figures of his time, and it is probable that the plan for the founding of the Athenaeum club was devised in his rooms. With the help and encouragement of Walter *Scott he established the Tory *Quarterly Review* in 1809, and took a close interest in its management. He gave up the London agency of **Blackwood's Magazine* in protest at its attacks on the *Cockney School. He was the friend and publisher of Lord *Byron, who was his single most important author. *'Childe Harold' appeared under his imprint, as did most of Byron's other work. However, he was so apprehensive of the public reception of **Don Juan* that he published only the early cantos, and those without his imprint; the later cantos were published by John *Hunt, who also produced *The *Vision of Judgement*, which Murray had refused. Murray bought Byron's memoirs of 1818–21 from Thomas *Moore, and reluctantly consented to having them burned in his grate at Albemarle Street. His other authors included Jane *Austen, George *Crabbe, S. T. *Coleridge, Robert *Southey, Leigh *Hunt, and George *Borrow. The *Guide for Travellers on the Continent* (1820) by Mariana Starke (1761/2–1838) led to a long and profitable series of *guidebooks, several of which were written by John Murray III (1808–92). In the publishing slump of the late 1820s and 1830s Murray noted that 'the taste for literature is ebbing', and he sold his copyright of Jane Austen's novels.

The John Murray succession continued until the early 21st century, when the publisher was bought by Hodder Headline. The firm's archive was acquired by the National Library of Scotland in 2005.

MURRAY, Les (1938–) Australian poet, born in Nabiac, in the Manning River area of New South Wales. An austere childhood on an isolated dairy farm, darkened by the death of his mother in 1951, profoundly shaped Murray's views, particularly his hostility to elites. After interrupted schooling he matriculated to Sydney University in 1957, where he took numerous language courses but suffered personal crises. In 1962 he met and married Valerie Morelli, and subsequently worked as a translator at the Australian National University (Canberra); he converted to Roman Catholicism in 1964. The family travelled to Europe early in 1967, returning to Sydney in mid-1968; Murray graduated from Sydney in 1969. His first book of poems, *The Ilex Tree* (1965), was written in collaboration with Geoffrey Lehmann; Murray committing himself to writing full time in 1971. In 1985 he returned to live permanently in Bunyah, near where he had grown up, having established himself as a distinctive poetic voice, and outspoken critic and editor. At the heart of Murray's poetry is a profound response, expressing itself through a rich visual imagination and meticulously crafted language, to the Australian bush, and to the ideals and values of the pioneer settlers. He has produced more than twenty volumes of poems, among which are *The Weatherboard Cathedral* (1969), *Poems against Economics* (1972), *Lunch & Counter Lunch* (1974), *Ethnic Radio* (1977), *The People's Otherworld* (1983), *The Idyll Wheel: Cycle of a Year at Bunyah* (1989), *Dog Fox Field* (1990), *Translations from the Natural World* (1992), *Subhuman Redneck Poems* (1996), *Conscious and Verbal* (2000), *Poems the Size of Photographs* (2003), *The End of Symbol* (2004), and *Holy Cows* (2006). There are nearly a dozen 'collected' or 'selected' volumes, the most recent and largest of which is *Collected Poems: 1961–2002* (2002; 2006), dedicated, like all of his work since 1983, to 'the glory of

God'. Two verse novels, *The Boys Who Stole the Funeral* (1980) and *Fredy Neptune* (1998), have garnered considerable critical attention, while Murray's own criticism, essays, and other writings have been collected in *The Peasant Mandarin* (1978), *Persistence in Folly* (1984), *Blocks and Tackles* (1990), *The Paperbark Tree* (1992), *A Working Forest* (1997), and *The Quality of Sprawl: Thoughts about Australia* (1999). He is the editor of *The New Oxford Book of Australian Verse* and *The Anthology of Australian Religious Poetry* (both 1986). Murray was made a National Living Treasure of Australia in 1997 and in 1998 won the Queen's Gold Medal for Poetry. See Peter Alexander, *Les Murray: A Life in Progress* (2000).

MURRY, John Middleton (1889–1957) Editor and critic, born in Peckham of ambitious lower-middle-class parents. He made his mark while still an Oxford undergraduate as editor of the *modernist periodical **Rhythm* (1911–13), through which he met in 1912 Katherine *Mansfield, whom he was to marry in 1918. In 1914 he met D H. *Lawrence, whom he greatly admired. From 1919 to 1921 Murry was editor of the **Athenaeum*, in which he published an impressive range of writers, including Virginia *Woolf, T. S. *Eliot, and Paul *Valéry, and in which he himself attacked *Georgian poetry. In 1923, the year of his wife's death, he founded the **Adelphi*; although he was to marry again three times, he continued to dwell on her memory, editing her stories, letters, and journals. His many critical works include *Fyodor Dostoevsky* (1916), *The Problem of Style* (1922), *Countries of the Mind* (1922, 1931), and *Keats and Shakespeare* (1925). He also wrote many works of a semi-mystical nature, and became deeply interested in the concept of an ideal community (a concern dating back to his friendship with Lawrence) and in pacifism. Throughout his turbulent emotional and professional life he was attracted to the extreme and the romantic, seeing life as a spiritual search. His reputation as a critic declined in an age of specialization and professionalism, but he remains an important figure in literary history. See his autobiography, *Between Two Worlds* (1935), and the standard life by F. A. Lea (1959).

MUSAEUS (1) A legendary Greek poet, said to have been a pupil of *Orpheus. (2) A Greek poet, who perhaps lived about AD 500, the author of a poem on **Hero and Leander* which provided the groundwork for Christopher *Marlowe's poem of the same title. During the Renaissance the first, legendary Musaeus was sometimes assumed to have written what was in fact a late Greek poem. It was first translated into English, in 1645, by Sir Robert Stapylton (1607/9–1669).

Muses In Greek mythology there were nine Muses, daughters of Zeus and Memory, each patronizing a different art: Calliope (epic); Clio (history); Euterpe (music); Melpomene (tragedy); Terpsichore (dancing); Erato (lyric poetry); Polyhymnia (sacred poetry and rhetoric); Urania (astronomy); Thalia (comedy). They were associated with Mounts Helicon and Parnassus and the Pierian spring, and the god *Apollo was sometimes described as their leader. *Hesiod in the *Theogony* described himself as taught by them, and invocation of the Muse(s) to aid the poet, notably in *Homer and *Virgil, was a traditional formula of *epic. *In *Paradise Lost* Book VII John *Milton rejects Calliope for the Heavenly Muse Urania, identified with the Holy Spirit.

Muses Lookinge-Glasse, The A defence of the drama, in the form of a play, by Thomas *Randolph, printed 1638, in which Roscius, by presenting the extremes of virtue and vice in pairs, persuades two doubting Puritans that drama may promote moral good.

music, literature of The first important English contribution to musical literature was Thomas *Morley's *Plaine and Easie Introduction to Practicall Musicke, Set Down in Forme of a Dialogue* (1597; modern edn by R. A. Harman, 1952). The musical writings of the 17th century were mainly technical and instructional, as in the publications of John Playford (1622/3–1686/7), whose *Introduction to the Skill of Musicke* (1654) appeared in successive editions (one of them revised by Henry *Purcell) until 1730. Two exceptions are the chapter on music in Henry *Peacham's *Compleat Gentleman* (1622) and the idiosyncratic *Musick's Monument, or A Remembrancer of the Best Practical Musick, both Divine, and Civil, that Has Ever been Known, to Have Been in the World* (1676), by Thomas Mace (1612/13–?1706). Roger *North's treatises *The Musicall Grammarian* and *Memoires of Musick* remained in manuscript at his death in 1734; modern editions appeared in 1959 and 1990. North's individual approach to the theory and aesthetics of music was carried on in the controversial *An Essay on Musical Expression* (1752) by the composer Charles Avison (bap. 1710, d. 1770). The later 18th century saw the production of two monumental histories of music, by Charles *Burney and Sir John *Hawkins. The first volume of Burney's *A General History of Music from the Earliest Ages to the Present Period* appeared early in 1776, nine months before Hawkins's *A General History of the Science and Practice of Music*, complete in five volumes (also 1776); Burney's remaining three volumes came out in 1782 and 1789. Burney's *History* was based on extensive European field research, recounted entertainingly in *The Present State of Music in France and Italy* (1771) and *The Present State of Music in Germany, the Netherlands and the United Provinces* (1773). John Mainwaring's *Memoirs of the Life of the Late George Frederic Handel* (1760) was the first monograph devoted to a single composer, to be followed by Hawkins's *Corelli* (1777), and Burney's *Handel* (1785), issued in connection with the *Handel commemoration in Westminster Abbey (1784). Most of the important biographical work in the 19th century was done outside England, but growing interest in musical scholarship produced the four volumes of George Grove's *Dictionary of Music and Musicians* (1879–89), partly edited by Hubert *Parry; the *Dictionary* is now revised in a 29-volume edition (2001). The music reviews of George Bernard *Shaw were collected as *London Music in 1888–89 as Heard by Corno di Bassetto* (1937) and *Music in London* (3 vols, 1932); his major essay, *The Perfect Wagnerite*, came out in 1898. Another Wagnerian landmark, *A Study of Wagner*, was published the following year by William Roberts (1868–1959), under the pseudonym 'Ernest Newman'; his work on the subject culminated in a four-volume *Life of Richard Wagner* (1933–47). The revival of interest in early English music in the 20th century produced Edmund Fellowes's pioneering biographies of native composers, *Orlando Gibbons* (1925), *William Byrd* (1936), and *English Madrigal Composers* (1921), as well as several important studies by Peter *Warlock; other composers who have produced notable writings include Charles Villiers *Stanford, Constant *Lambert, Ralph *Vaughan Williams, Benjamin *Britten, and Michael *Tippett.

MUSIL, Robert Edler von (1880–1942) Austrian novelist, born in Klagenfurt. He trained as an engineer before studying philosophy and psychology at Berlin University. While still a doctoral student he published his first novel, *Young Törless* (1906), which was followed by various short works of fiction and two plays. During the First World War Musil served in the Austrian army. From 1924 he devoted his life to the work for which he is best known, the massive and unfinished novel *Der Mann ohne Eigenschaften* (1930–32). After Nazi Germany's annexation of Austria in 1938 he sought refuge in Switzerland. The novel appeared in English translation as *The Man without Qualities* (1953–60) and, despite its daunting scale, its ironic portrait of the society of imperial Austria is witty, urbane, and approachable. A new translation by S. Wilkins and B. Pike, published in 1995, includes much previously unseen, incomplete, and fragmentary material.

MUSSET, Alfred de (1810–57) French poet and playwright. His first published work was a free translation of Thomas De Quincey's **Confessions of an English Opium Eater* (1828). His career as a writer was enlivened by a notorious liaison with George *Sand in the 1830s. His most famous poems, *Souvenir* (1841), recalling a chance meeting with Sand in a theatre foyer, and *Les Nuits* (1835–7: *Nights*), explore the central Romantic motif of lost love. His most original achievements are his plays, in particular *Fantasio, On ne badine pas avec l'amour* (*Love Isn't to be Trifled With*), and *Lorenzaccio* (all 1834), which blend irony, fantasy, and psychological penetration. Even his liveliest work is seldom free from the melancholy and anxiety known as the *mal du siècle*.

'Mutabilitie Cantos' Name given to the fragmentary Book VII of Edmund *Spenser's **Faerie Queene*, consisting of two cantos only, first published with the 1609 folio edition of the poem. They describe the challenge of the Titaness Mutabilitie to the cosmic government of Jove. (The first canto includes the charming topographical fable of Faunus and Molanna, which reflects Spenser's affection for his Irish home.) The goddess Nature vindicates Jove's rule, displaying its orderly beauty in a procession of Seasons and Months, asserting finally that natural things 'are not changed from their first estate | But by their change their being doe dilate'. The cantos can be seen as an epilogue to *The Faerie Queene*, ending with the poet's prayer: 'O! that great Sabaoth God, graunt me that Sabaoths sight.'

MYERS, Frederic William Henry (1843–1901) Poet, critic, and inspector of schools, educated at Cambridge, where he spent much of his life. He published several volumes of poetry and critical essays; his essay on George *Eliot, first published in the *Century Magazine* in 1881 (and reprinted in *Essays Classical and Modern*, 1883), describes the celebrated incident in which she spoke to him of '*God, Immortality, Duty*', and declared 'how inconceivable was the *first*, how unbelievable the *second*, and yet how peremptory and absolute the *third*'. Myers's own childhood obsession with the possibility of survival after death led to his involvement with the *Society for Psychical Research, of which he was a founder; he was joint author (with Edmund Gurney and Frank Podmore) of *Phantasms of the Living* (1886), a two-volume work dealing largely with telepathy, which embodied the first results of the Society's labours. He was also a member of the Theosophical Society.

MYERS, John Myers (1908–88) Author of fiction and non-fiction about the American West; born in New York, resident of Arizona. The *fantasy *Silverlock* (1949) celebrates the literary imagination: its protagonist is shipwrecked on the shores of a 'Commonwealth' inhabited by the characters of legend and romance.

MYERS, L. H. (Leopold Hamilton) (1881–1944) Novelist, son of F. W. H. *Myers, born in Cambridge and educated at Eton College and, briefly, Trinity College, Cambridge. His first published work was a verse play, *Arvat* (1908). His novels are concerned with the problem of how human beings can live rightly in society if they exclude spirituality, which, to his mind, was an activity as natural as sex. Apart from *The Orissers* (1922), *The 'Clio'* (1925), and *Strange Glory* (1936), his novels are set in an imaginary 16th-century India: *The Near and the Far* (1929), *Prince Jali* (1931), *The Root and the Flower* (1935), and *The Pool of Vishnu* (1940); collected together under the title *The Near and the Far* in 1943 and generally considered to be his best works of fiction. Myers committed suicide by taking an overdose of veronal while suffering from depression.

'My mind to me a kingdom is' The first line of a poem on contentment, originally printed in William *Byrd's *Psalms, Sonnets, and Songs* (1588). Frequently referred to in the 16th and 17th centuries, it was often attributed to Edward *Dyer. It is more probably by the earl of *Oxford.

Mysteries of Udolpho, The A novel by Ann *Radcliffe, published 1794. The orphaned Emily St Aubert is carried off by her aunt's villainous husband Montoni to a remote castle in the Apennines, where her life, honour, and fortune are threatened and she is surrounded by apparently supernatural terrors. These are later explained as the result of human agency and Emily escapes, returns to France and, after further mysteries, is reunited with her lover Valancourt., The book was extremely popular, and plays an important part in Jane Austen's **Northanger Abbey*.

Mysterious Mother, The A *Gothic tragedy in blank verse by Horace *Walpole, printed at his press at Strawberry Hill in 1768. It deals with the remorse of a mother (the countess of Narbonne) for an act of incest committed many years before. When her son Edmund, who had been the unwitting partner of her crime, marries Adeliza (brought up as her ward, but in reality the child of their union) she takes her own life. The theme of incest shocked many of Walpole's readers but greatly interested Lord *Byron, who described the play as 'a tragedy of the highest order, and not a puling love-play'.

mystery plays A term conventionally used to denote biblical dramas popular in England from the 13th to the later 16th century. The term 'mystery', which is not contemporary, derives from the *mestier* (*métier* or trade) of their performers. 'Miracle plays', strictly, are enactments of the miracles performed by the saints, whereas the 'mysteries' enact the events of the *Bible from the Creation to the Ascension (and in some cases later). Their origin is much disputed; one of the earliest is the Anglo-Norman *Jeu d'Adam* (*see* ADAM), and there were cycles in many countries: France, Italy, Ireland, and Germany (surviving in the Oberammergau Passion Play). Though it is clear from their archives that many English towns had them, only three complete cycles survive—York, Chester, and Towneley (named after the owners of the manuscript)—as well as the N-town plays (so called because it is not known in which town they were performed). They are connected with the feast day of Corpus Christi (the Thursday after Trinity Sunday) which was declared in 1264 and first observed as a holy day in 1311. The various pageants (whose number varies from 25 in Chester to nearly 50 in York) were each assigned to a particular trade-guild, often with a humorous or macabre connection between the *métier* and the play: the York Shipwrights enact the story of Noah, for instance. Their great popularity in England from the time of *Chaucer to *Shakespeare is attested by those writers, among others. Their end was no doubt mainly caused by *Reformation distaste for images and religious pageantry (an attitude occasionally manifested earlier). As an early, popular form of theatre, they manifest energy, humour, resourceful stagecraft, and seriousness; their composers were anything but unlearned, as is clear from the group of six plays in the Towneley cycle assigned to a presumed author known as 'the Wakefield Master'. The latter's most celebrated play is the Second Shepherd's Play in which the Nativity is parodied by and collocated with a contemporary case of sheep stealing. It was not these plays so much as the moralities and *interludes which affected the development of Elizabethan drama. But they have had a considerable vogue since the 20th century, possibly owing to the interest in techniques such as alienation and popular, less articulated forms of drama (such as *Nōh plays from Japan); evidence of this is Benjamin *Britten's *Noye's Fludde*, and revivals of performances of the cycles, most notably at York.

Editions of the plays include: *The York Plays*, ed. Richard Beadle (1982); *The Chester Mystery Cycle*, ed. R. M. Lumiansky and David Mills, EETS SS 3 and 9 (1974, 1986); *The Towneley Plays*, ed. G. England and A. W. Pollard, EETS ES 71 (1897; repr. 1973); *The N-Town Play*, ed. Stephen Spector, EETS SS 11–12 (1991). P. Happé, *The English Mystery Plays* (1975) is a very useful selected edition, as is Greg Walker, *Medieval Drama: An Anthology* (2000). For discussion, see R. Beadle (ed.), *The Cambridge Companion to Medieval English Theatre* (1994).

mysticism In Christian thought this refers variously to attempts at union with or direct knowledge of God or Jesus achieved through contemplation, self-denial, visions, or trances. In some accounts this process is arduous and intellectual, in others it is instantaneous. It is often described in physical or emotional terms. Perhaps surprisingly, given the essential indescribability of the subject, there is a large literature of mystical theology and experience. Medieval English mystics include Richard *Rolle, *Julian of Norwich, Walter *Hilton, and Margery *Kempe. Despite *Protestant hostility to the assumptions of mysticism there has been much Protestant interest in *Roman Catholic mystics, such as *Thomas à Kempis, *Teresa of Avila, and St *John of the Cross. There have been notable Protestant mystics, such as Jacob *Boehme, who influenced William *Law, and Emanuel *Swedenborg, who impressed and then disgusted William *Blake. Mystical poets include W. B. *Yeats, T. S. *Eliot, and Geoffrey *Hill. See Evelyn Underhill, *Mysticism* (1911; frequently republished); Bernard McGinn, *The Presence of God: A History of Western Christian Mysticism*, 4 vols to date (1991–).

myth criticism An area of literary investigation and commentary that deals with the relations between 'myth'—in the positive sense of a traditional story—and literature, often drawing upon anthropology, psychology, and studies of folklore. Myth criticism is usually concerned to demonstrate that literary works draw upon a common reservoir of *archetypes or recurrent images, or that their narrative patterns repeat those of ancient myths or religious rituals, as in quests for sacred objects, or cycles of death and rebirth. Much *psychoanalytic criticism overlaps with myth criticism, not just in the tradition of Carl *Jung but in that of Sigmund *Freud, who interpreted literary texts as well as dreams and neurotic symptoms as echoes of the Oedipus myth. Jung, however, is the principal founder of the school of myth critics which flourished from the 1930s to the 1960s. An early study in this vein is *Archetypal Patterns in Poetry* (1934) by Maud Bodkin (1875–1967); other notable works are *Quest for Myth* (1949) by Richard Chase (1914–62), Robert *Graves's *The White Goddess* (1948), W. H. *Auden's *The Enchafèd Flood* (1951), and C. L. Barber's *Shakespeare's Festive Comedy* (1959). A more elaborate theoretical foundation for myth criticism was proposed by Northrop *Frye in his *Anatomy of Criticism* (1957). This tradition of literary study came under repeated attack for dealing only with the 'contents' of literary works and ignoring all questions of language and style; and it declined in the 1960s as new theoretical agendas redefined the relations between anthropological and literary study (*see* STRUCTURALISM). Some of its concerns survive in the writings of the American critic Leslie *Fiedler, and in the questions posed by the French anthropological philosopher René Girard (1923–), whose studies of scapegoating and sacrificial victims have excited interest among students of dramatic tragedy.

mythography The compilation and interpretation of myths, drawn on especially in the Renaissance period by poets and painters. *Ovid's *Metamorphoses* was a very important source of knowledge of classical myth; the stories were often given allegorical meanings by later Christian interpreters. The major Renaissance Latin handbooks—*Boccaccio's *De Genealogia Deorum*, the *Mythologiae* by Natalis Comes (1520–82)—were well known to English poets such as Ben *Jonson. John *Lemprière's *Classical Dictionary* was an important source for John *Keats, and the work of later mythographers like Friedrich *Max Müller, Andrew *Lang, Sir J. G. *Frazer, Carl *Jung, and Claude *Lévi-Strauss has been widely influential. Robert *Graves and Kathleen *Raine can be seen as eccentric modern exponents of mythography. See Jean Seznec, *The Survival of the Pagan Gods* (1961); Edgar Wind, *Pagan Mysteries in the Renaissance* (1958).

NABOKOV, Vladimir Vladimirovich (1899–1977) Russian-born novelist, poet, and literary scholar. The son of a leading member of the Cadet party and of the Kerensky government, Nabokov had published only a small volume of poetry when his family left Russia for Germany in 1919. After studying French and Russian literature at Trinity College, Cambridge (1919–23), Nabokov lived in Berlin (1923–37) and Paris (1937–40), writing mainly in Russian, under the pseudonym 'Sirin'. His early novels, like *Laughter in the Dark* (1932), tended to be black comedies and reflect his constant interest in the cinema. In 1940 he moved to the USA, working as a lecturer at Wellesley College (1941–8) and as professor of Russian literature at Cornell University (1948–59), experience which fed into his 1957 novel *Pnin*. From then on all his novels were written in English. The outstanding success of his novel *Lolita* (Paris 1955; USA 1958) enabled him to give up teaching and devote himself fully to writing in Montreux, Switzerland. He wrote a screenplay for Stanley Kubrick's film adaptation of *Lolita*, which was not accepted. Two other strong interests which influenced his fiction were chess and lepidoptery (the study of butterflies and moths). Nabokov's reputation for linguistic and formal inventiveness led him into controversy with his translation of Pushkin's *Eugene Onegin* (1964); *Pale Fire* (1962) is a fictitious translation and commentary. His autobiography *Speak, Memory* appeared in 1967 and his lectures on literature were published in four volumes (1980–83). See Brian Boyd, *Vladimir Nabokov*, 2 vols (1990–91).

NADEN, Constance (1858–89) Poet and philosopher. Born and educated in Birmingham, she was keenly interested in contemporary science and the work of Herbert *Spencer. Remembered for *A Modern Apostle* (1887), her witty and sceptical poems reflect her radical views and incorporate commentary on women's status, evolution, and social science.

NAIPAUL, Shiva (1945–85) Novelist and travel writer, born in Port of Spain and educated in Trinidad and at University College, Oxford. His first two novels, *Fireflies* (1970) and *The Chip-Chip Gatherers* (1973), were set in Trinidad. *North of South* (1978) is an account of a journey through Africa, and *Black and White* (1980) investigates the mass suicide in Guyana instigated by Jim Jones. Naipaul's third novel, *A Hot Country* (1983), is set in Cuyama, a fictitious South American state that much resembles Guyana. *Beyond the Dragon's Mouth* (1984) consists of fictional and travel pieces. *An Unfinished Journey* (1986) collects travel and personal memoirs, including 'My Brother and I', an essay on the author's relationship with his elder brother V. S. *Naipaul.

NAIPAUL, Sir V. S. (Vidiadhar Surajprasad) (1932–) Novelist and travel writer, born in Trinidad, educated at Queen's Royal College, Port of Spain, and University College, Oxford; he worked for the BBC before beginning his career as a writer engaged with colonial and postcolonial concerns. His first three books, *The Mystic Masseur* (1957), *The Suffrage of Elvira* (1958), and *Miguel Street* (short stories, 1959), are comedies about Trinidadian life. The tragicomic *A House for Mr Biswas* (1961), also set in Trinidad, portrays a man (modelled on Naipaul's father) thwarted from attaining independence. *Mr Stone and the Knights Companion* (1963), Naipaul's only novel located in London, was followed by *The Mimic Men* (1967), narrated by a failed politician on a fictitious Caribbean island. After *A Flag on the Island* (1967), a collection of stories set in the West Indies and London, his work—both fiction and reportage—becomes more overtly political and pessimistic. *In a Free State* (1971, *Booker Prize) explores problems of nationality and identity through linked narratives about displaced characters. *Guerrillas* (1975) depicts political and sexual violence in the Caribbean; *A Bend in the River* (1979) is an equally horrifying portrait of emergent Africa. Naipaul's predominantly gloomy view of postcolonial societies can also be seen in his travel and autobiographical books such as *The Middle Passage* (1962) and *A Way in the World* (1994), about the Caribbean; *An Area of Darkness* (1964) and *India: A Million Mutinies Now* (1990), about the sub-continent; *The Return of Eva Peron* (1980), his account of Argentina; and *Among the Believers: An Islamic Journey* (1981). His recurrent themes of political violence, homelessness, and alienation have invited comparisons with Joseph *Conrad. They further inform his autobiographical novel about a writer from Trinidad arriving in post-imperial Britain, *The Enigma of Arrival* (1987), and *Half a Life* (2001), his bitter novel about an Indian in London and Africa. Naipaul was knighted in 1990, and was awarded the *Nobel Prize in 2001. There is a biography by Patrick French, *The World Is What It Is* (2008).
See ANGLO-INDIAN LITERATURE; BLACK BRITISH LITERATURE; POSTCOLONIAL LITERATURE.

NAIRNE, Carolina, Baroness (1766–1845) Née Oliphant, born at Gask, Perthshire, the author of many spirited and well-known *Jacobite songs, including 'Will ye no come back again?' and 'Charlie is my darling'; also of humorous and pathetic ballads, such as 'The Laird of Cockpen' (suggested by an older song) and 'The Land o' the Leal'. She concealed her authorship during her lifetime, and her poems were collected and published as *Lays from Strathearn* in 1846.

NAPIER, John (1550–1617) Laird of Merchiston, near Edinburgh, educated at St Andrews. A mathematician and inventor, he devised logarithms, the nature of which he explained in his *Mirifici Logarithmorum Canonis Descriptio* (1614). His *Rabdologia* (1617) explains the use of numerating rods ('Napier's bones') and metal plates for effecting multiplications and divisions—the earliest form of calculating machine. He also invented the present notation of decimal fractions.

NARAYAN, R. K. (Rasipuram Krishnaswami) (1906–2001) Indian novelist writing in English; he was born in Madras and educated at the Collegiate High School in Mysore, where his father was headmaster, then at Maharaja's College, Mysore. He worked (very briefly) as a teacher, then as a journalist, before publishing his first novel, *Swami and Friends* (1935), in which he created the imaginary small and microcosmic Indian town of Malgudi, which he was to map out and populate in several succeeding novels, including *The Bachelor of Arts* (1937), *The English Teacher* (1945), *Mr Sampath* (1949), *The Financial Expert* (1952), *The Guide* (1958: winner of the Sahitya Akademi Award), *The Vendor of Sweets* (1967), *The Painter of Signs* (1977), *A Tiger for Malgudi* (1983), and *The Grandmother's Tale and Other Stories* (1993). His fictional world is peopled with characters—journalists, printers, professors, financial experts, lawyers, dreamers—portrayed with a gentle irony as they struggle to accommodate tradition with Western attitudes inherited from the British. Graham *Greene, who recommended his first novel for publication, compared the tragicomedy, pathos, and frequently disappointed aspirations of his characters to those of *Chekhov, and commented that Narayan's particular comic gift flourished in 'the strong framework of social convention'. His work is seen as falling into three phases or periods: an early autobiographical phase (up to the 1940s), a more complex middle period in which Malgudi is realized in all its rich detail, and a later phase (from the late 1960s) in which modernity comes to Malgudi. Though to a non-initiate his writing can appear tirelessly conversational and even superficial, its power resides precisely in its pacifist understatement and reticence, underpinned by strong spiritual beliefs. Narayan is rarely interested in current political or intellectual debates as such, but rather as the shaded-in background to the unfolding of his characters' lives. A counterbalance to the fantastical and fabulist trend in Indian writing (represented by G. V. *Desani, Salman *Rushdie, and others), Narayan's work has consistently defied comparison. His national and international reputation grew steadily across the final decades of his life and in 1982 he was made fellow of the American Academy and Institute of Arts and Letters. Characterizing his achievement, the renowned critic C. D. Narasimhaiah remarked that 'few writers have been more Indian'. Narayan's other publications include short stories (*An Astrologer's Day and Other Stories*, 1947; *Lawley Road*, 1956; *A Horse and Two Goats*, 1970; *Malgudi Days*, 1982) and a charming memoir, *My Days* (1975).
See ANGLO-INDIAN LITERATURE.

Narnia *See* LEWIS, C. S.

narratology The term applied since 1969 to the formal analysis of narratives. Although in principle applicable to ancient theories of storytelling such as *Aristotle's, the term is applied to the modern tradition, of which *Morphology of the Folktale* (1928) by the Russian scholar Vladimir Propp (1895–1970) is taken to be the founding work. Narratology rests upon certain basic distinctions between what is narrated (e.g. events, characters, and settings of a story) and how it is narrated (e.g. by what kind of narrator, in what order, at what time). Different narratological approaches pursue each of these questions. Investigations into the narrated materials commonly seek the elementary units that are common to all narratives: Propp's work on Russian folk tales proposed that there were no more than 31 such basic elements or 'functions', and that they always appeared in the same order. Likewise, the French narratologist A. J. Greimas (1917–92) proposed that there are only six basic roles (or 'actants') in stories: subject, object, sender, receiver, helper, and opponent. This kind of folkloric analysis has no necessary interest in literary technique. On the other hand, studies of narration, that is, how stories are told, have an obvious relevance to literary fictions. In this field, there is an English-speaking tradition of narratology, originating in the theory and practice of Henry *James, and codified in terms of narrative 'point of view' by his disciple Percy *Lubbock in *The Craft of Fiction* (1921); other notable early contributions were E. M. *Forster's *Aspects of the Novel* (1927) and Edwin *Muir's *The Structure of the Novel* (1928). More convincing than these works was *The Rhetoric of Fiction* (1961) by Wayne C. Booth (1921–2005), which introduced important new distinctions such as those between the real author and the 'implied author' of a novel, and between reliable and unreliable narrators. The most comprehensive analyses of the various kinds of possible narrator and narrative order appear in the works of the French narratologist Gérard Genette (1930–), especially his *Figures III* (1972; partly translated as *Narrative Discourse*, 1980). See Shlomith Rimmon-Kenan, *Narrative Fiction* (2nd edn, 2002).

Narrenschiff *See* SHIP OF FOOLS.

NASH, Ogden (1902–71) American writer of sophisticated light verse, born in Rye, New York, renowned for his puns, epigrams, elaborate rhymes, elaborate lack of rhymes, wildly asymmetrical lines, and other verbal fancies. His verse appeared in many collections from 1931 onwards. See Douglas M. Parker, *Ogden Nash* (2005).

NASH, Richard ('Beau') (1674–1761) Born at Swansea, educated at Carmarthen Grammar School and, briefly, at Jesus College, Oxford. He went to Bath in 1705, using his personal charm to promote a new code of etiquette and dress, and becoming the unquestioned autocrat of social interaction. Oliver *Goldsmith's anecdotal but psychologically astute biography of Nash (1762) was probably written without personal knowledge of its subject.

NASHE, Thomas (1567–*c*.1601) Writer, born in Lowestoft, Suffolk; he became a sizar of St John's College, Cambridge. By 1588 he had settled in London and by 1589 had his first publications: a preface to Robert *Greene's **Menaphon*, surveying the follies of contemporary literature, a theme expanded in *The Anatomy of Absurdity.* His hatred of Puritanism drew him into the *Martin Marprelate controversy, but it is not clear which of the unascribed anti-Martinist pamphlets were his work. In 1592 Nashe replied to the savage denunciations of Richard Harvey, astrologer and brother of Gabriel *Harvey, with **Pierce Penniless his Supplication to the Devil.* In the same year he avenged Gabriel Harvey's attack on Greene with *Strange News of the Intercepting Certain Letters.* A florid religious meditation, **Christ's Tears over Jerusalem*, dedicated to Elizabeth, Lady Carey (1552–1618), was published in 1593: an offensive passage about London led to his imprisonment. In the following year *The Terrors of the Night*, a discourse on dreams and nightmares, was dedicated to Carey's daughter, to whom he may have acted as tutor for a time.

*The *Unfortunate Traveller* also appeared in 1594, described in the dedication to the third earl of Southampton (1573–1624) as 'being a clean different vein from other my former courses of writing'. It is a mixture of *picaresque narrative, literary parody, and mock-historical fantasy. Nashe returned to satire with *Have with You to Saffron-Walden, or Gabriel Harvey's Hunt is up* (1596), to which Harvey replied; in 1599 John Whitgift (1530/31?–1604), archbishop of Canterbury, ordered the suppression of both writers' works. Nashe's lost satirical comedy *The Isle of Dogs* (1597) also led to trouble with the authorities, and though, unlike his collaborator Ben *Jonson, Nashe seems to have avoided a spell in prison, he was forced to flee London for Great Yarmouth. *Nashe's Lenten Stuff* (1599), a mock encomium of the red herring (or kipper), includes a burlesque version of the story of *Hero and Leander. In 1600 **Summer's Last Will and Testament* was published, though it had probably been written in the plague year of 1592–3, when the archbishop's household had moved to Croydon. Nashe had a share in Christopher *Marlowe's **Dido Queen of Carthage*, and probably other plays, including *1 *Henry VI* and ones now lost. He was amusingly satirized as 'Ingenioso', a Cambridge graduate who lost favour with his patrons and turned to satire, in the three **Parnassus Plays* (1598–1606). Mourned by Jonson, admired by Thomas *Dekker and Thomas *Middleton, Nashe's life and his writings, especially *The Unfortunate Traveller*, are full of interest. The entire works were edited by R. B. *McKerrow in 1904–10 and revised with corrections and additions by F. P. Wilson in 1958; see also a life by C. Nicholl, *A Cup of News* (1984).

Nasrudin A semi-legendary Turkish sage and folk hero, around whose name has gathered a body of jokes, stories, and anecdotes. They have been collected and translated many times: for recent versions, see *The Pleasantries of the Incredible Mulla Nasrudin* (1968) and *The Subtleties of the Inimitable Mulla Nasrudin* (1973) by Idries *Shah.

NATHAN, George Jean (1882–1958) American drama critic and polemicist, born in Fort Wayne, Indiana, and co-founder in 1924 with H. L. *Mencken of the *American Mercury.* He published many collections of theatre criticism and essays, including *The Popular Theatre* (1918), *The Critic and the Drama* (1922), and *Art of the Night* (1938), which show him as an early supporter of the works of Eugene *O'Neill.

NATION, Terry (1930–97) Television scriptwriter, born in Cardiff; best known for *Dr Who's adversaries, the 'daleks'. He also created *Survivors* (1975–7), where post-catastrophe anxieties of writers like John *Wyndham or George R. *Stewart were replayed for the 1970s, and *Blake's Seven* (1978–81).

Nation, The Irish weekly periodical founded by Thomas Davis (1814–45), Charles Gavan Duffy (1816–1903), and John Blake Dillon (1814–66) in 1842. It played a leading role in spreading the ideas of the radical Young Ireland movement and was suppressed by the government in 1848. A second series, begun the following year, ran almost to the end of the century but never equalled the influence of the first. Though remembered chiefly for the rousing ballads of Davis and others, *The Nation* was host to many different types of poetry and its reviews and articles covered not only the turbulent Irish politics of the day but a wide range of 19th-century literary and intellectual life.

National Anthem Various 17th-century tunes more or less resemble that of 'God Save the King'; the closest resemblance is that of a galliard composed by John *Bull. The words appear to date from the 1680s, but no author is known. The first recorded public performance of 'God Save the King' took place at Drury Lane Theatre on 28 September 1745, during the alarm caused by the *Jacobite invasion, and was prepared from a version in *Thesaurus Musicus*, a song collection of 1744, by Thomas *Arne, composer of *'Rule, Britannia'. It soon became customary to greet the king with the song when he entered a place of public entertainment, and during the reign of George III it was used as a political and patriotic signal in debates about the regency and the French Revolution. It was sung at the coronation banquet of George IV, confirming its popular status as 'National Anthem'. Many composers, including *Haydn, *Beethoven, *Liszt, and *Debussy, alluded to or wrote variations on the tune; political parodies of the words include the 'New National Anthem' written by P. B. *Shelley in 1819 after the Peterloo massacre, and the 'People's Anthem' (1848) of Ebenezer *Elliott, the Corn Law Rhymer.

National Theatre A three-auditorium complex on London's South Bank devoted to the spectrum of world drama. Initially proposed by a London publisher, Effingham Wilson, in 1848, the idea of a National Theatre Company only became a living reality at the Old Vic in 1963 under the direction of Laurence Olivier: its early successes included standard classics by *Shakespeare, George *Farquhar, Anton *Chekhov, and George Bernard *Shaw as well as new plays by Tom *Stoppard, Peter *Shaffer, and Peter *Nichols. In 1976 it moved into its South Bank home designed by Sir Denys Lasdun where, under the direction of Sir Peter *Hall, Sir Richard Eyre, Trevor Nunn, and Nicholas Hytner, it has provided an eclectic mixture of world drama, new writing, and popular musicals. Its repertoire has ranged from *Aeschylus and *Sophocles to Bertolt *Brecht and Sean *O'Casey but it has achieved particular success with new plays including the David *Hare trilogy, charting the decline of British institutions under Thatcherism, *The Madness of George III* and *The History Boys* by Alan *Bennett, *Arcadia* by Tom *Stoppard, *Angels in America* by Tony Kushner, and *Closer* by Patrick *Marber. It became officially known as the Royal National Theatre in October 1988.

Native American literature The body of work by indigenous American writers. In the writings of James Fenimore *Cooper, Mayne *Reid, and others, American Indians, as they were called, were usually depicted as picturesquely wild or part of the past history of America. Early converts to Christianity gave a voice to these groups. William Apess (1798–1839), for instance, produced one of the first autobiographies (*A Son of the Forest*, 1829) by a Native American. Later in the 19th century, the researches of the Smithsonian Institution and later of anthropologists like Alfred L. Kroeber (1876–1960; the father of Ursula *Le Guin, in whose works indigenous cultures figure prominently) began to record Native American cultural practices. The flourishing of this writing from *c.*1968 onwards has been called the Native American Renaissance, within which have featured writers like Louise *Erdrich, Leslie Marmon Silko (1948–), Navarre Scott *Momaday, and many others. As well as producing fiction, Gerald *Vizenor is a leading theoretician of the semiotics of 'indianness'. See A. Lavonne Brown Ruoff, *American Indian Literatures* (1990).

naturalism An international movement in prose fiction that flourished during the final third of the 19th century and the early years of the 20th; it achieved some influence also on the drama of the period. It developed the existing tradition of *realism in the direction of fully documented accuracy of representation of social and economic circumstances, with additional deterministic emphases on the supposed scientific 'laws' of human behaviour, understood to be governed by heredity and economic necessity. In France, Émile *Zola was the dominant practitioner of naturalism in prose fiction and the chief exponent of its doctrines. His novel *Thérèse Raquin* (1867), together with the *Goncourt brothers' *Germinie Lacerteux* (1865), are considered as marking the beginnings of the movement; its most substantial and important achievement in French fiction is the series of twenty novels written by Zola between 1871 and 1893 under the general title of *Les Rougon-Macquart*. Other French writers who shared, in a greater or lesser degree, the ideas and aims of naturalism are Alphonse *Daudet, Guy de *Maupassant, and, in his early fiction, Joris-Karl *Huysmans. In the English-speaking world, some of the ambitions and effects of naturalism are to be found echoed or adapted in novels of the 1890s and beyond, notably in George *Moore's *Esther Waters* (1894), Thomas Hardy's **Jude the Obscure* (1895), Somerset *Maugham's *Liza of Lambeth* (1897), Frank *Norris's *McTeague* (1899), Theodore *Dreiser's *Sister Carrie* (1900), and Arnold *Bennett's *Anna of the Five Towns* (1902), among many others. In the theatre, the term was applied to some realistic works written under the influence of Henrik *Ibsen, for example the plays of Gerhart *Hauptmann in Germany, but is more often used more generally in reference to the 'naturalistic', (i.e. faithfully lifelike) impressions made by certain acting styles and authentic stage furnishings or costumes. See David Baguley, *Naturalist Fiction* (1990).

Nature and Art A romance by Elizabeth *Inchbald, published 1796, the story of two contrasted brothers, William and Henry, and their equally contrasting sons. The story illustrates the wholesome effects of a natural and simple upbringing compared with the warping effects of civilization.

Nausicaa *See* ODYSSEY.

NAYLER, James (1616/17–60) A Quaker who had served in the Parliamentary army, converted by George *Fox in 1651. He describes 'being at the plough' and hearing a voice telling him 'Get thee out from thy kindred' (*Saul's Errand to Damascus*, 1654). His eloquence and tenderness of heart won him many disciples, especially disaffected women, with whom he challenged Fox for the leadership. His entry into Bristol on a donkey in 1656 accompanied by followers shouting 'Hosannah' brought him before the House of Commons on a charge of blasphemy, for which he was cruelly punished and imprisoned in Bridewell. Though he had split the movement, his contrite release in 1659 brought reconciliation with Fox. He wrote pamphlets of striking beauty and depth, especially *Milk for Babes* (published 1661). Quaker history blamed Nayler's fall on the women surrounding him, particularly Martha Simmons, but recent scholarship has recognized Nayler's disciples as casualties of complex historical conditions which refused females parity as leaders. See P. Mack, *Visionary Women* (1992); P. Crawford, *Women and Religion in England 1500–1720* (1993); S. Davies, *Unbridled Spirits* (1998).

NEALE, J. M. (John Mason) (1818–66) Scholar and hymn-writer, educated at Trinity College, Cambridge, who helped to found the Cambridge Camden Society. Distinct from the *Camden Society, and also known as the Ecclesiological Society, the society worked for the return of a medieval style in ecclesiastical arichitecture. He was author of *The*

History of the Holy Eastern Church (1847–73), and many hymns (some of them translations from Greek, medieval Latin, and Eastern sources), including 'O happy band of pilgrims', 'Art thou weary', and 'Jerusalem the Golden'. **Hymns Ancient and Modern* owes much to his inspiration.

NECKER, Suzanne (1739–94) Née Curchod, a Swiss woman, at one time engaged to Edward *Gibbon; she became the wife of Jacques Necker, the French financier and statesman. She was prominent in French literary circles of the period preceding the revolution. Her daughter became Germaine de *Staël.

NEDHAM (Needham), **Marchamont** (1620–78) Journalist, and chief author of *Mercurius Britanicus* (1643–6), the arch-enemy of the Royalist *Mercurius Aulicus* of Sir John *Berkenhead. His subsequent professional career showed shifting loyalties, and he was several times imprisoned. In 1660, after some years of considerable power as editor of *Mercurius Politicus*, he fled to the Netherlands, obtained a pardon, and returned to England, where he practised medicine and continued to write pamphlets. He was also the author of verses and a translation of John *Selden's *Mare Clausum* (1652). His prose was powerful, and John *Milton was not implausibly credited with some of his anonymous works.
See also NEWSPAPERS.

negative capability A phrase coined by John *Keats to describe his conception of the receptivity necessary to the process of poetic creativity, which draws on S. T. *Coleridge's formulation of 'Negative Belief' or 'willing suspension of disbelief'. In a letter to Benjamin Bailey (1791–1853; 22 Nov. 1817) Keats wrote, 'If a Sparrow come before my Window I take part in its existence and pick about the Gravel', and a month later (22 Dec. 1817) he wrote to his brothers George and Thomas defining his new concept: '*Negative Capability*, that is when man is capable of being in uncertainties, Mysteries, doubts, without any irritable reaching after fact and reason—'. Keats regarded Shakespeare as the prime example of negative capability, attributing to him the ability to identify completely with his characters, and to write about them with empathy and understanding; he contrasts this with the partisan approach of *Milton and the 'wordsworthian or egotistical sublime' (Letter to Richard Woodhouse (1788–1834); 27 Oct. 1818) of William *Wordsworth. However, he was ambivalent about his own attitude, and sometimes expressed admiration for the Miltonic approach; as Douglas Bush wrote in 1960, 'As artist he fluctuates—and is aware of his fluctuations—between belief in the poetic efficacy of a wise passiveness, and belief in the active pursuit of rational knowledge and philosophy.'

Négritude A term denoting a movement in literature that dates from the 1930s, deriving its impetus from French-speaking African and Caribbean writers. It sought to recover and define the richness of black cultural values in the face of the dominant values of European colonialism, emerging specifically as a protest against French colonial rule and the French policy of assimilation. Prominent members included the poet and essayist Léopold Sédar *Senghor, who became the first president of the Republic of Senegal in 1960; Aimé *Césaire, poet and dramatist from Martinique (*Cahier d'un retour au pays natal*, 1939: *Return to my Native Land*); and Léon Damas (1912–78), from French Guiana.

NEILSON, Anthony (1967–) Scottish playwright, whose work includes *Normal: The Düsseldorf Ripper* (1991), *The Wonderful World of Dissocia* (2004), *Realism* (2006), and *God in Ruins* (2007). Neilson, whose uncompromising plays characteristically explore conditions of mental instability or social alienation, came to notice through his identification with the 'In-yer-face' drama linked with the *Royal Court Theatre of the 1990s. See Aleks Sierz, *In-yer-face Theatre: British Drama Today* (2001).

NELSON, Robert (1656–1715) Devotional writer, *nonjuror, friend of John *Tillotson, and active early member of the *SPCK. His *Companion for the Festivals and Fasts of the Church of England* (1704), designed as an aid to the *Book of *Common Prayer*, and *Practice of True Devotion* (1708) were very popular until the mid-19th century.

NEMEROV, Howard (1920–91) American poet, born in New York, who was twice made national poet laureate. His first volume of poetry, *The Image of the Law*, appeared in 1947 and was followed by further collections, all working within traditional metric forms and showing the influence of Owen *Barfield. Nemerov also published a number of essays, short stories, and novels, including *The Homecoming Game* (1957).

Nemesis of Faith, The A controversial religious novel by James Anthony *Froude, published in 1849, describing the spiritual vicissitudes of its irresolute hero, Markham Sutherland; it was publicly burned in Oxford by William Sewell (1804–74), Anglican clergyman and fellow of Exeter College.

NENNIUS (*fl.* *c.*770–810) Mistakenly believed, on the basis of a single revision, to be the author or reviser of the *Historia Brittonum*. He may have been a pupil of Elfoddw, bishop of Bangor (d. 809). Composed in Wales *c.*829–30, the *Historia* is a collection of materials on the history and geography of Britain, and claims to give an account of the historical *Arthur who led the Britons against the Saxons in twelve battles (including Mount Badon). It is one of the sources on which *Geoffrey of Monmouth drew for his *Historia Regum Britanniae*. A mixture of legend and history, it is characterized by pride in the Celtic people of Britain and interest in its topography. See Nennius, *'British History' and 'The Welsh Annals'*, ed. and trans. J. Morris (1980).

neo-classicism In literature, the practice of imitating the great authors of Greek and Roman antiquity (notably its poets and dramatists) as a matter of aesthetic principle; and the acceptance of the critical precepts which emerged to guide that imitation. The more specific emulation of selected ancient Roman poets in early 18th-century England is known as Augustanism (*see* AUGUSTAN AGE).

Medieval writers had often used classical works for models, but *Petrarch in the 14th century was the first to do so because he considered it the only way to produce great literature; and where he led a host of later authors followed. The *epic, *eclogue, *elegy, *ode, *satire, *tragedy, *comedy, and *epigram of ancient times all found imitators, first in Latin, then in the vernaculars, and eventually practice was succeeded by precept. At the beginning of the 16th century the recovery of the previously neglected **Poetics* of Aristotle provoked an attempt to establish rules for the use of the ancient genres. The *Poetics* itself was repeatedly edited, translated, and supplied with commentaries, the most influential being the one by *Castelvetro (1570), and there also appeared a number of treatises on poetry, culminating in *Scaliger's controversial *Poëtice* (1561). These theoreticians imprisoned imitation within a rigid framework of rules, for which the flexibility of ancient practice offered little precedent. The most famous of their inventions was the observance of the dramatic *unities of time, place, and action, which won widespread support in 17th-century France, where Nicholas *Boileau, the most influential of neo-classicist critics, extended the scope of their prescriptions from drama to all other major genres. Until the last quarter of the 17th century neo-classicism had little influence in England. The imitation of classical models had been less common than on the Continent and, except for Ben *Jonson, no important writer had paid strict attention to the rules humanist critics had formulated. But after the appearance of Boileau's *L'Art poétique* (1674), and of Thomas *Rymer's *Tragedies of the Last Age Considered* (1678), John *Dryden and other playwrights began to take neo-classical theories more seriously. Translations and adaptations of *Corneille and *Racine enjoyed some popularity. Dryden produced **All for Love* (1678) as a neo-classical version of Shakespeare's **Antony and Cleopatra*, while Joseph *Addison's **Cato* (1713) has been called the only correct neo-classical tragedy in English; but ultimately the fashion was not to last. The usual excuse for the rules was that they helped writers to be true to nature. Alexander *Pope wrote,

> Those RULES of old *discover'd*, not *devis'd*,
> Are *Nature* still, but *Nature methodiz'd*,

and implicit in his view was the assumption that 'nature' consisted in what was generally true. But this assumption, advanced first by Scaliger and echoed much later by Samuel *Johnson, had never commanded unquestioning support, and what could be regarded as 'natural' was already coming to be seen no longer as absolute, but as historically conditioned. At the same time the inescapable presence of *Shakespeare in English literary culture provided a stubborn obstacle to the domestication of French neo-classical principles, the tension between them being already evident in Dryden's *Heads of an Answer to Rymer* (published posthumously in 1711). What undermined neo-classicism most decisively however in the later 18th century was the changing view of literary creation provoked by Boileau's translation (1674) of the treatise on the *Sublime then attributed to *Longinus. A cult of sublimity—greatness of conception and emotion—replaced the wish to produce a just representation of general reality, and the way to *Romanticism lay open.

Neoplatonism A philosophical and religious system, combining Platonic ideas with Persian, Indian, and Egyptian theology, developed in Alexandria in the 3rd century AD by *Plotinus, an Egyptian philosopher whose *Enneads* were edited by Porphyry (*c.*233–309). He taught that there is a supreme 'One' transcending all human concepts, from which the universe emanated. Plotinus' successor Iamblichus (*c.*245–325) posited the existence of innumerable lesser gods, demons, and other superhumans, who could give knowledge of the future and influence events. Proclus (412–85) introduced an order of 'henads' between the One and the universe, whom he identified with the classical Greek gods. Transcendence of the material world, the soul's return to the One at death, and the belief that evil has no existence but is simply the absence of good are other features of Neoplatonic thought. *Augustine's early attachment to Neoplatonism affected the development of Christianity, and in the Middle Ages Neoplatonic ideas also influenced Jewish cabbalists and Islamic and Sufi thinkers. From the 5th and 6th centuries Neoplatonism sometimes overlapped with *Gnosticism. In the Renaissance Neoplatonism was revived and variously refashioned by *Ficino, *Pico della Mirandola, *Agrippa, and *Paracelsus and tended to become associated with alchemy, Hermeticism, and magic. It influenced literature in a number of ways. The Neoplatonic theory that earthly love and beauty are images of spiritual absolutes, as expounded in Edmund *Spenser's *Hymns*, is common in love poetry. Prospero in *The *Tempest* is an example of a Neoplatonic magician who can raise spirits, and he had real-life counterparts in the 16th and 17th centuries. The Attendant Spirit or Daemon in Milton's **Comus* is Neoplatonic, as, on a humorous level, are the sylphs of *The *Rape of the Lock*. The attempt to bring together all systems of belief that maintained the power of spirit over matter appears in Thomas *Vaughan and in the writings of the *Cambridge Platonists. The Neoplatonist Thomas Taylor (1758–1835) was the first to translate Plotinus' works into English. Modern thinkers whom some regard as essentially Neoplatonic include Carl *Jung and Rudolf Steiner (1861–1925).

neo-realism A movement in the post-war Italian novel and film which may be seen as a continuation of **verismo*. While its narratives were naturalistic on the surface, the works were imbued with a lyrical populism that was occasionally sentimental and even owed something to the style of films made under *Fascism. As Fascism collapsed, the Resistance emerged as the theme of neo-realist novels by Beppe Fenoglio (1922–63), Elio *Vittorini, and the young Italo *Calvino, and of films by Rossellini (1906–77), whose *Roma città aperta* (1945: *Rome Open City*) is a classic of this genre. At the same time, neo-realism documented the lives of poor people in the underdeveloped south or struggling in northern cities: this strand is represented by the work of Carlo *Levi and Cesare *Pavese, and by the films of Vittorio De Sica (e.g. *Bicycle Thieves*, 1948), Ermanno Olmi, Francesco Rosi (1922–), and the young Luchino Visconti (1906–76).

Neo-Romanticism A movement in painting, literature, book illustration, film, and theatre from the late 1930s to the early 1950s. The term was first used in 1942 to designate figurative work by artists including Paul Nash (1889–1946), John Piper (1903–92), and Graham Sutherland (1903–80), who turned for inspiration to Samuel *Palmer and J. M. W. *Turner, and to the landscape vision of the *Romantic poets. Characterized by the powerful evocation of place, and allegiance to a distinctively English tradition, Neo-Romanticism flourished during the Second World War. John Piper's paintings of bombed churches incandescent against dark backdrops became some of the best-known images of wartime ruins. The new romantic spirit in painting was championed by Kenneth *Clark and by Herbert *Read, whose own poetry and prose returned repeatedly to the Wordsworthian theme of lost innocence. A younger generation of Neo-Romantics, inspired particularly by Sutherland, included Michael *Ayrton, John Minton (1917–57), and John Craxton (1922–). Their work tended to be more explicitly melancholic, and more concerned with individual psychic states than with the representation of landscape. This later vein of Neo-Romanticism found literary expression in the writing of the New Apocalypse group, which included Dylan *Thomas and Norman *MacCaig.

Neptune (Greek Poseidon) In classical mythology the powerful god of the sea and brother of *Jupiter. In the **Iliad* he opposes the Trojans, but in the **Odyssey* he repeatedly thwarts the Greek Odysseus on his voyage home, and in **Aeneid* Book 1 he calms the sea after *Juno raises a storm to wreck the Trojan ships. His violent desire for Leander inadvertently drowns the young man in Christopher *Marlowe and George *Chapman's *Hero and Leander*.

NERUDA, Pablo (1904–73) Pen-name of the Chilean poet Ricardo Eliecer Neftalí Reyes Basoalto, the son of a railwayman. The best-known 20th-century poet from Spanish America, Neruda was brought up in the southern Chilean town of Temuco, where his natural surroundings made an indelible impression on him. He did not complete his training in Santiago de Chile to teach French. He travelled widely in the diplomatic service from 1927 to the early 1940s (in South-East Asia, Argentina, Spain, and Mexico), and supported the Spanish Republic during the Spanish Civil War. Franco's victory was an enduring wound. After the Second World War he visited the USSR, China, and Eastern Europe. He had joined the Chilean Communist Party in 1945 and was elected that year to the Chilean Senate, remaining a political activist and poet thereafter. Having been appointed by the socialist president Salvador Allende as Chilean ambassador in Paris, he was awarded the *Nobel Prize for Literature in 1971. He died in Santiago de Chile shortly after Pinochet's coup. Neruda published over 40 astonishingly varied volumes of poetry. His first major collection, *Veinte poemas de amor y una canción desesperada* (1924: *Twenty Love Poems and a Song of Despair*), apparently a spontaneous outpouring of love, erotic desire, and melancholy, was the meticulously wrought product of a long poetic apprenticeship drawing upon *Romanticism and *Symbolism; it became the most popular collection of poetry ever written in Spanish. The first two volumes of his *Residencia en la tierra* (1933 and 1935: *Residence on Earth*), a tortured meditation on loneliness, transience, disintegration, and death expressed in experimental and sometimes hermetic verse, made him a leader of the avant-garde (*The *Criterion* reviewed some of the poems). Largely as a result of his experiences during the Spanish Civil War, Neruda's poetry became less introspective, and his left-wing politics shone through many of his collections. The most ambitious was an alternative history of Latin America, his epic *Canto general* (1950: *General Song*), much of which he wrote on the run from the Chilean police and which consolidated his reputation. Subsequent volumes ranged from endearing odes dedicated to simple objects like an onion or a pair of winter socks, to propaganda, autobiographical verse, and short, intensely personal, and often amorous, lyrics. See Adam Feinstein, *Pablo Neruda: A Passion for Life* (2004).

NERVAL, Gérard de (1808–55) Pseudonym of Gérard Labrunie, French poet and story writer, best known for his enigmatic sonnet sequence *Les Chimères* (1854: *Chimeras*) and his short story *Sylvie* (1853), about his love for three women. He also produced much journalism, and an account of a journey to the Middle East, *Le Voyage en Orient* (1851). Much of his later life was dominated by his struggle against mental instability, of which he gives an account in *Aurélia* (1855). The elusive, visionary quality of much of his work exercised an influence over the followers of both *Symbolism and *Surrealism.

NESBIT, E. (Edith) (1858–1924) Born in Kennington, London, educated at schools in France following the death of her father. Nesbit was central to the development of 20th-century children's literature, both in her tone of address and her social ideas. She was closely associated with the Fabian Society, notably with George Bernard *Shaw. Her first book of poetry, *Lays and Legends* (1886), was admired by Algernon *Swinburne and Rider *Haggard. She produced hack-work to support her family, including retellings of *Shakespeare (1897). *The Story of the Treasure Seekers* (1899) was her first successful children's book; in 1902 her *Five Children and It* appeared in the *Strand Magazine* and in book form. Nesbit's books remain popular: *Five Children and It* was adapted by Helen *Cresswell (BBC TV, 1991) and filmed in 1991 and 2004; *The Railway Children* (1906) was filmed in 1970, and adapted for television in 1957, 1968, and 2000.

NESVADBA, Josef (1926–2005) Czech psychiatrist and author, born in Prague; his sometimes satirical stories made him the best-known Czech *science fiction writer, other than Karel *Čapek, outside his own country. English collections include *Vampires Ltd.* (1964) and *In the Footsteps of the Abominable Snowman* (1970).

New Age A phrase and concept which became current in the 1960s ('the age of Aquarius', so called for astrological reasons). New Age thinking manifests itself in forms of oriental mysticism, in yoga, Zen Buddhism, and the cult of the guru and the ashram: Hermann *Hesse's *Siddhartha* was adopted as a key text, as were the writings of Lebanese mystic Kahlil Gibran (1883–1931) and those of Carlos Castaneda (?1925–98), who explored shamanistic practices and the use of drugs (peyote) in Mexico through the wisdom of 'Don Juan'. *Tolkien's *fantasies were also admired, and produced many imitations. The New Age found a home in Britain in ecological and spiritual communities (Findhorn, Arthurian cults associated with Glastonbury), and in the USA (notably in California) in various groups seeking spiritual and psychological self-help and self-realization. *The New Age* was also the title of a periodical edited by A. R. *Orage (1907–22), whose interest in *Gurdjieff has a connection with these later spiritual movements. Aldous *Huxley and Christopher *Isherwood may also be seen as links in a chain of continuing interest in heightened states of consciousness.

New Apocalypse A group of writers who flourished briefly as a group in the 1940s, united by a reaction against what they saw as the 'classicism' of W. H. *Auden. It was characterized by wild, turbulent, and at times surreal imagery. They described themselves as 'anti-cerebral', claiming a 'large, accepting attitude to life', invoked the name of D. H. *Lawrence, and approved of Dylan *Thomas. George *Barker, Vernon *Watkins, and Henry *Treece were associated with the movement.

New Atlantis, The An unfinished work by Francis *Bacon, posthumously published at the end of a volume containing his *Sylva Sylvarum, or A Natural History* (1627; some copies dated 1626). William Rawley (*c.*1558–1667), Bacon's chaplain and literary executor, called it a 'fable' devised to describe 'a college instituted for the interpreting of nature and the producing of great and marvellous works for the benefit of men, under the name of Salomon's House, or the College of the Six Days' Works'—alluding to the biblical account of the Creation. A hybrid, it begins with the narrative of a sea voyage in the Pacific, in which a ship gets blown off course into unknown waters near Peru, and lands on an island resembling the lost island of Atlantis, as described by *Plato in the *Timaeus* and *Critias*. A native explains to the travellers how a King Solamona had reigned there 'about 1900 years ago', and had set up a scientific research institute with the goal of discovering 'the knowledge of causes and secret motions of things; and the enlarging of the bounds of human empire, to the effecting of all things possible'. The 'Father' or director of the institute describes a wide range of laboratories for physical experiments at low temperatures, for conservation of food, medical research, biology and chemistry, optics and acoustics, each with the appropriate technologies. He also describes the personnel, hierarchically divided: collectors of scientific information, experimenters, theorists, and philosophers. The whole work expressed Bacon's forward-looking belief that scientific research could flourish only as a collective pursuit, and its vision had an inspiring effect in the mid-17th century, acknowledged by those associated with the *Royal Society such as Robert Hooke (1635–1703), William *Petty, John *Evelyn, Thomas *Sprat, and Joseph *Glanvill.

NEWBERY, John (1713–67) Bookseller, a pioneer publisher of children's books. Oliver *Goldsmith, who contributed the papers later gathered as *The *Citizen of the World* to Newbery's *Public Ledger*, may have written the much-imitated 'Goody Two-Shoes' for Newbery; 'the philanthropic bookseller' in *The *Vicar of Wakefield* is based on the publisher. Christopher *Smart, who married one of Newbery's stepdaughters, also worked for him. Samuel *Johnson introduces him affectionately as 'Jack Whirler' in the **Idler*. Newbery also dealt profitably in patent medicines.

NEWBOLT, Sir Henry (1862–1938) Barrister, poet, and man of letters, educated at Clifton and Corpus Christi College, Oxford, remembered principally for his rousing patriotic nautical ballads, which include 'Drake's Drum', published in *Admirals All and Other Verses* (1897). His other collections include lyrics and satires, and he also published novels, short stories, and *A Naval History of the War, 1914–18* (1920). He was benevolent and active in public life, and served on many committees, including that of the *Royal Literary Fund.

NEWBY, Eric (1919–2006) Travel writer, born in London and educated at St Paul's School. He worked in advertising, the fashion industry, and journalism (where he was the travel editor of the *Observer* from 1964 to 1973), but regularly took time out from all these jobs to pursue adventures, and misadventures, around the world. He is the author of more than twenty travel books, of which the best known is *A Short Walk in the Hindu Kush* (1958). They stand in the comic tradition of A. W. *Kinglake, Robert *Byron, and Evelyn *Waugh, with Newby usually depicting himself as a bumbling Englishman abroad, always somewhat out of his depth. The tone is more sombre and more moving, however, in *Love and War in the Apennines* (1971), probably Newby's best work, which recounts a period spent on the run as an escaped prisoner of war in Italy during the Second World War. He was appointed a fellow of the *Royal Geographical Society in 1973, and made a CBE in 1994.

NEWBY, P. H. (Percy Howard) (1918–97) Novelist and broadcaster, born in Sussex. He served as stretcher-bearer and then as a lecturer in Egypt during the Second World War. His first two novels, *A Journey to the Interior* (1945) and *Agents and*

Witnesses (1947), draw on his wartime experiences and broad knowledge of Egyptian society. Other works include *Something to Answer for* (1968), which won the first *Booker Prize, and *Feelings Have Changed* (1981), which gives an insight into his years with the Third Programme of the *BBC.

NEWCASTLE, Margaret Cavendish, duchess of (1623–73) Daughter of Sir Thomas Lucas, the second wife of William Cavendish, first duke of *Newcastle, whom she met in Paris during his exile. Her first volume of verse, *Poems and Fancies* (1653), which displays her interest in chemistry and natural philosophy, was followed by many other works, including plays, letters, and an affectionate, vivid, and informal biography of her husband (1667). Dismissed as 'mad, conceited and ridiculous' by Samuel *Pepys and as 'airy, empty, whimsical and rambling' by John *Evelyn's wife, she was nevertheless praised (and influenced) by Thomas *Hobbes, and both Charles *Lamb and Virginia *Woolf wrote of her with sympathy. Her intellectual curiosity was omnivorous, and she was one of the first women to attend a meeting of the *Royal Society. Her *autobiography, *A True Relation of my Birth, Breeding and Life*, was appended to her collection of fictions, *Nature's Pictures* (1656): here she diplomatically dismissed her writing as 'scribbling' but justified her forwardness in writing her own life on the grounds that 'Caesar, Ovid and many more' had done so. She regarded the female intelligence as distinguished by its fantastical quality, which she demonstrated by wearing outrageous fashions of her own devising. See E. Graham *et al.* (eds), *Her Own Life* (1989); Katie Whitaker, *Mad Madge* (2003).

NEWCASTLE, William Cavendish, first duke of (1592–1676) Husband of Margaret Cavendish, duchess of *Newcastle. He supported the king generously during the Civil War, and from 1644 lived abroad, often in much poverty, until the *Restoration. He was the author of several poems and plays, collaborating in the latter with James *Shirley, whose patron he was, and with John *Dryden and Thomas *Shadwell.

Newcomes, The A novel by W. M. *Thackeray, published 1853–5. Colonel Thomas Newcome is an unworldly soldier who has spent his career in India. His half-brothers Hobson and Brian are wealthy and pretentious. Having sent his son Clive to England to be educated, Colonel Newcome later returns from India, and indulgently allows Clive to study art. Clive loves Ethel, daughter of Sir Brian Newcome, but Ethel's ruthless brother Barnes and her grandmother Lady Kew want her to make a grand marriage. Though Ethel is independent-minded, she allows herself to become engaged first to her cousin Lord Kew, and then to the wealthy Lord Farintosh. Barnes's own disastrous marriage persuades her to remain single. Meanwhile Clive has been manoeuvred into marriage with a superficial girl, Rosey Mackenzie. Colonel Newcome's fortune is lost with the failure of a fraudulent bank, and the family is reduced to poverty. Rosey's discontented mother makes life so intolerable for the Colonel that he takes refuge in the Grey Friars almshouse, where he dies, in one of the most famously affecting scenes in Victorian fiction. Rosey also dies, and Thackeray allows the reader to assume that Clive and Ethel will marry. Certain aspects of Clive's character were suggested by Frederic *Leighton, whom Thackeray met in Rome. The novel is remarkable for its vituperative attacks on the cynicism and greed of the mid-Victorian marriage market.

New Criticism An important movement in American literary criticism in the period 1935–60, characterized by close attention to the verbal nuances of lyric poems, considered as self-sufficient objects detached from their biographical and historical origins. In reaction against the then dominant routines of academic literary history, the New Critics insisted that a poem should not be reduced to its paraphrased 'content', but understood in its own terms as a complex unity of verbal ironies, ambiguities, and paradoxes. They repudiated what they called the 'extrinsic' approaches to poetry—historical, psychological, or sociological—and cultivated an 'intrinsic' understanding of the actual 'words on the page', while defending poetry as a richer form of knowledge than that offered by scientific abstraction.

The early phase of the New Critical campaign was led by Southern poets and university teachers: J. C. *Ransom and his former student Allen *Tate, along with R. P. *Warren and Cleanth *Brooks, editors of the *Southern Review* (1935–42). The name applied to this movement comes from the title of Ransom's book *The New Criticism* (1941), which surveys the critical work of T. S. *Eliot, I. A. *Richards, and William *Empson in Britain, from which the New Critics clearly derived their inspiration. While Ransom and Tate formulated the theoretical principles, Brooks and Warren, notably in their textbook *Understanding Poetry* (1938), applied them to the teaching of literature in universities. More marginal contributions to the cause came from R. P. *Blackmur (*The Double Agent*, 1935) and Yvor *Winters (*Primitivism and Decadence*, 1937).

From 1939, when Ransom founded the *Kenyon Review* and Brooks published his *Modern Poetry and the Tradition*, the New Criticism made important headway in replacing 'extrinsic' approaches with critical analysis in the universities; notably at Yale, where a second wave of New Critical theory was represented by *Theory of Literature* (1949) by René Wellek (1903–95) and Austin Warren (1899–1986), and by *The Verbal Icon* (1954) by W. K. Wimsatt (1907–75). The latter work includes essays written with M. C. Beardsley (1915–85) on the critical 'fallacies' involved in judging a work according to its author's intentions (*see* INTENTIONAL FALLACY) or its readers' impressions. In this period, the most celebrated work of 'applied' New Criticism was Brooks's *The Well Wrought Urn* (1947).

By the late 1950s, New Criticism had become an academic orthodoxy which younger critics found to be not only inapplicable to genres other than lyric poetry but narrow in its exclusion of social and historical dimensions of literature. Nonetheless, some of its methods and strictures have survived as essential precautions against clumsy misreadings of poems.

NEWDIGATE, Sir Roger (1719–1806) Educated at Westminster School and University College, Oxford, MP successively for Middlesex and Oxford University, and founder of the Newdigate Prize at Oxford for English verse (1805).

Newgate Calendar, The The title was originally used to signify a simple list of convicts in Newgate prison in London, but about 1773 appeared *The Newgate Calendar, or Malefactors Bloody Register*, a five-volume biographical compilation of notorious criminals from 1700 to that date. Similar large-scale anthologies of crime appeared in the next 50 years under varying titles, including *The Malefactor's Register, or The Newgate and Tyburn Calendar* (1779, much reprinted). Andrew Knapp and William Baldwin, attorneys-at-law, issued *Criminal Chronology* (1809), *The Newgate Calendar* (1824–6), and *The New Newgate Calendar* (1826). Plots derived from the Calendars appear in novels by Harrison *Ainsworth (*Jack Sheppard* and *Rookwood*), Edward *Bulwer-Lytton (**Pelham* and **Eugene Aram*), and William Godwin (**Caleb Williams*), and in Thomas *Hood's poem 'The Dream of Eugene Aram'. William Thackeray's **Catherine* and Charles Dickens's **Oliver Twist* also derived material from the Calendars. See Rayner Heppenstall, *Reflections on the Newgate Calendar* (1975).

Newgate novel *See* AINSWORTH, WILLIAM HARRISON.

New Grub Street A novel by George *Gissing, published 1891. It describes the jealousies and intrigues of the literary world of his time, and the effect of poverty on artistic endeavour. The main theme is the contrast between the career of Jasper Milvain, the unscrupulous writer of reviews (who accepts the materialistic conditions of literary success), and those of more artistic temperaments. Among these are Edwin Reardon, author of two fine works, who is hampered by poverty, and the generous Harold Biffen, a poor scholar, author of the unsuccessful 'Mr Bailey, Grocer', a work which meticulously reflects the lives of 'the decently ignoble'. The literary world is represented in a multitude of characters, including the pedant Alfred Yule, made rancorous and sardonic by constant disappointment. Amy, Edwin's wife, leaves him in despair. Jasper is attracted to Yule's daughter and assistant Marian, who passionately loves him; but he proposes to her only when she inherits a legacy of £5,000. When this legacy vanishes, he shabbily withdraws, and marries Amy, the widow of Edwin, who was driven into an early grave by failure and the loss of his wife. Marian is left to a lifetime of unacknowledged drudgery in libraries. The sombre story ends with Jasper's success, the triumph of self-advertisement over artistic integrity. *New Grub Street* remains one of Gissing's most celebrated novels.

New Historicism A term applied to a trend in American academic literary studies in the 1980s that emphasized the historical nature of literary texts and at the same time (in contradistinction from 'old' historicisms) the 'textual' nature of history. As part of a wider reaction against purely formal or linguistic critical approaches such as the *New Criticism and *deconstruction, the New Historicists, led by Stephen Greenblatt (1943–), drew new connections between literary and non-literary texts, breaking down the familiar distinctions between a text and its historical 'background' as conceived in previous historical forms of criticism. Inspired by Michel *Foucault's concepts of discourse and power, they attempted to show in detail how literary works are entangled in the power relations of their time, not as secondary 'reflections' of any coherent world-view but as active participants in the continual remaking of meanings. New Historicism is less a system of interpretation than a set of shared assumptions about the relationship between literature and history, and an essayistic style that often develops general reflections from a startling historical or anthropological anecdote. Greenblatt's books *Renaissance Self-Fashioning* (1980) and *Shakespearean Negotiations* (1988) are the exemplary models. Other scholars of Renaissance (or 'early modern') culture associated with him include Jonathan Goldberg, Stephen Orgel, and Louis Montrose. The term has been applied to similar developments in the study of *Romanticism, such as the work of Jerome McGann and Marjorie Levinson. The journal *Representations* has been a prominent exhibitor of this school's work. While American New Historicism, following Foucault, tends to argue that literary dissent is harmlessly contained by 'power', the otherwise similar movement in Britain known as 'cultural materialism' parts company with it on this point, insisting that no ruling authority can neutralize every form of cultural subversion. The cultural materialists, such as Jonathan Dollimore, Catherine Belsey, and Alan Sinfield, although indebted to Foucault, are more closely aligned with *Marxist literary criticism, notably through the work of Raymond *Williams, and show a stronger interest in the adaptation, reproduction, and institutionalization of texts, especially those of Shakespeare. See John Brannigan, *New Historicism and Cultural Materialism* (1998).

New Inn, The, or *The Light Heart* A comedy by Ben *Jonson, performed in 1629 by the King's Men, printed 1631. Frances, the young Lady Frampul, invites some lords and gentlemen to make merry at the New Inn at Barnet. One of the guests, Lord Beaufort, falls in love with, and is promptly married to, the son of the innkeeper, who has been dressed up as a girl, while Frances falls in love with Lovel, a melancholy gentleman staying at the inn. In a succession of discovered identities it is learnt that the innkeeper's son really is a girl and, moreover, Frances's sister Laetitia; that the innkeeper is Frances's long-lost father; and that the son's old Irish nurse is the father's long-lost wife and Frances's mother. Jonson records in his dedication that the play was hissed at its first performance, but it was successfully performed by the Royal Shakespeare Company in 1987.

New Journalism The title of a 1973 collection edited by Tom *Wolfe and E. W. Johnson, since used to describe a mode of journalism which incorporates first-person narration, gives prominence to the reporter, and uses other novelistic strategies. Practitioners of this mode include Truman *Capote, Norman *Mailer, Joan *Didion, and Hunter S. *Thompson. *See* GONZO JOURNALISM.

NEWLAND, Courttia (1973–) A dramatist and fiction writer of Caribbean heritage, who says, 'Telling untold stories keeps me alive.' His novels include *The Scholar* (1997) and *Snakeskin* (2002). His recent works are a novella, *The Dying Wish* (2006), and a short story collection, *Music for the Off-Key* (2006).

New Lines (1956) An anthology edited by Robert *Conquest, containing work by himself, Elizabeth *Jennings, John Holloway (1920–99), Philip *Larkin, Thom *Gunn, Kingsley *Amis, D. J. *Enright, Donald *Davie, and John *Wain, poets associated with the *Movement. In his introduction Conquest attacked obscure and over-metaphorical poetry, presenting the claims of 'rational structure and comprehensible language'. *New Lines Volume II* (1963) added other poets including Anthony *Thwaite, Vernon *Scannell, and George *MacBeth.

NEWMAN, John Henry (1801–90) Theologian, cardinal, and writer, educated privately at Ealing and at Trinity College, Oxford. He became a fellow of Oriel College, Oxford, where he came in contact with John *Keble and Edward *Pusey and later with Richard Hurrell *Froude. In 1828 he was presented to the vicarage of St Mary's, Oxford, where his four o'clock Sunday sermons attracted much attention. In 1832 he went to the south of Europe with Froude, and with him in Rome wrote much of the **Lyra Apostolica*; 'Lead, kindly Light', which appeared in this collection, was composed during a passage from Palermo to Marseilles in 1833. In the same year he resolved with William Palmer (1803–85), Froude, and A. P. Perceval (1799–1853) to fight for the doctrine of apostolic succession and the integrity of the Prayer Book, and began *Tracts for the Times* (*see* OXFORD MOVEMENT). He was moving slowly towards the Roman Catholic Church, and in 1841 his celebrated *Tract XC*, on the compatibility of the Articles with Catholic theology, roused great opposition and brought the Tractarians under official ban. He retired to Littlemore in 1842, where he adopted a semi-monastic way of life; he had always favoured celibacy and argued in its defence. In 1843 he resigned the living of St Mary's, preaching his last sermon there in September of that year, and in 1845 he joined the Church of Rome, a move which shocked many of his fellow Tractarians, caused a rift with Keble and Pusey, and isolated him from his old Oxford life. He went to Rome in 1846 and was ordained; on his return in 1847 he established the Oratory in Birmingham. He was in Ireland as rector of the new Catholic University in Dublin, 1854–8; his lectures and essays on university education appeared in various forms from 1852, and finally as *The Idea of a University Defined and Illustrated* (1873). In these he maintained that the duty of a university is instruction rather than research, and to train the mind rather than to diffuse useful knowledge; he also defended theological teaching and the tutorial system. In 1864 appeared his *Apologia pro Vita Sua*, in answer to Charles *Kingsley, who had remarked in *Macmillan's Magazine*, misrepresenting Newman, that Newman did not consider truth a necessary virtue. The *Apologia* came out serially, and was not so entitled until it appeared in volume form. It is an exposition of his spiritual history, written with feeling, which displays his formidable powers of argument. It made a profound impression on many who did not agree with his religious convictions, including George *Eliot (who said it had 'breathed much life' into her). His poem *The Dream of Gerontius* (later set to music by Edward *Elgar) appeared in the *Month* in 1865, and in book form in 1866; it is a vision of a soul leaving the body at death, and includes the well-known hymn 'Praise to the Holiest in the height'. Newman hoped it would allow readers to *feel* the necessity of the doctrine of Purgatory. In 1870 he published *The Grammar of Assent*, an examination of the nature of belief, which argues that human beings reach certainties not through logic but through intuitive perception; the real universe is not logical, and the premisses of logic are not realities but assumptions. In 1879 Newman was created cardinal.

Newman also published two novels, both anonymously. *Loss and Gain* (1848) gives a portrait of the religious debate of Oxford at the period of the Oxford Movement; his protagonist, Charles Reding, undergraduate son of a clergyman, is gradually drawn towards the Roman Catholic Church, despite the efforts of friends, teachers, and advisers, many of whom are drawn with satiric wit; the alleged weaknesses of the opposition are set against the loneliness and sacrifice involved in Reding's conversion. *Callista* (1856) describes the persecution and martyrdom of a Christian convert, the sculptor Callista, in the 3rd century. Newman also published many volumes of sermons, lectures, lives of saints, and so on. Although he argued that most of his writing was prompted by occasion and duty, and that he found the process of writing painful 'like gestation or childbirth', many of his works have outlived the occasions that prompted them. There is a life by Ian Ker (1988); see also F. Turner, *John Henry Newman: The Challenge to Evangelical Religion* (2002).

NEWMAN, Kim (1959–) Author and film critic, born in London; his *alternate histories, including *Anno Dracula* (1992) and *Back in the USSA* (1997: co-written with Eugene Byrne), recast figures from history or popular culture. *Life's Lottery* (1999) encourages the reader's decisions to influence the plot.

New Monthly Magazine (1814–84) A periodical co-founded by Henry *Colburn and F. Schoberi, in opposition to the *Jacobin **Monthly Magazine*, whose 'political poison' it attacked in its early years. Under Thomas *Campbell, who took over the editorship in 1821, it became more literary in interest. Colburn's tendency to promote his own publications became less apparent, and much literary work of distinction appeared. Thomas *Talfourd wrote well on William *Wordsworth, Charles *Lamb, John *Keats, and others; and among other distinguished editors were Edward *Bulwer-Lytton (for three stormy years), Thomas *Hood, Theodore *Hook, and Harrison *Ainsworth.

New Negro Phrase in use from *c.*1895 onwards to describe the changing situation of African Americans, especially as re-examined by themselves. *The New Negro: An Appreciation* was the title of a 1925 study of race in America by Alain Locke. The *Harlem Renaissance was also known as the New Negro Movement.

newsbooks (diurnals) The successors of the *corantos in the evolution of the newspaper. Newsbooks consisting of one printed sheet (eight pages) and later of two printed sheets (sixteen pages) were issued during the period 1641–54, then gave place to the **Oxford* (later *London*) *Gazette*.
See also GAZETTE; NEWSPAPERS; BERKENHEAD, SIR JOHN; MUDDIMAN, HENRY; NEDHAM, MARCHAMONT.

News Chronicle *See* DAILY NEWS.

newsletters A term specially applied to the manuscript records of parliamentary and court news, sent twice a week to subscribers from the London office of Henry *Muddiman in the second half of the 17th century.

New Society A weekly periodical founded in 1962, edited by Timothy Raison, 1962–8, then by Paul Barker, 1968–86; merged with the *New Statesman* in 1988. It covered the social sciences, social policy, documentary reportage, and the arts, and reviewed books of a wide range of interest.

newspapers, origins of The direct ancestors of newspapers devoted to English news were the Dutch *corantos, *newsbooks dealing with foreign events. The first to appear in English was a single-sheet publication, *The New Tydings out of Italie Are Not Yet Com* (Amsterdam, 2 Dec. 1620), followed by a second number, *Corrant out of Italy, Germany &c* (Amsterdam, 23 Dec. 1620), printed by Joris Veseler for Dutch map-engraver Pieter van der Keere. The first English weekly of home news appeared in November 1641 (*Heads of Severall Proceedings in This Present Parliament*), shortly followed by various other publications, mostly of eight pages, for example Samuel Pecke's *A Perfect Diurnall*, Richard Colling's *Kingdomes Weekly Intelligencer*, Sir John *Berkenhead's *Mercurius Aulicus* edited from the Royalist headquarters in Oxford, *Mercurius Civicus*, which was the first to be illustrated with woodcuts, and, perhaps the most popular, *Mercurius Britanicus*, edited by Thomas Audley and the most professional journalist of the period, Marchamont *Nedham. Decreasingly efficient censorship and the stirring political climate stimulated demand for news, and by 1645 fourteen papers were on sale in English in London, including John Dillingham's *Moderate Intelligencer*. In 1647 appeared the pro-Royalist *Mercurius Pragmaticus*, edited by Nedham, John *Cleveland, and the minor poet Samuel Sheppard (*c.*1624–?1655); in 1648 the *Moderate*, edited by chief censor Gilbert Mabbott, became the first paper consistently to preach a radical programme. This period of rapid journalistic expansion also saw the birth of many unlicensed, short-lived, and counterfeit newsbooks, as well as the publication of literally thousands of pamphlets (*see* PAMPHLETEERING). The style of the newsbooks ranges from the baldly informative, through attempts at non-controversial objectivity, to the colourful, scurrilous, and highly polemical; Colling's prose was perhaps the most consciously literary, and his paper contains the only Interregnum newspaper reference to *Chaucer yet discovered. The thirst for information introduced many new readers to familiarity with the printed word and created a new class of professional journalist: the newsbooks introduced many of the ingredients of modern journalism, such as features, fillers, advertising, human-interest items, as well as news and political argument. This vigorous proliferation came to a sudden end in September 1649 when Parliament, irritated by the onslaughts of both radical pamphleteers and Royalist Mercuries, and anxious about public reaction to the massacre at Drogheda, passed a stringent printing law with heavy fines which effectively silenced all the licensed weeklies, while authorizing two new papers, one to deal with army news, the other with news from Westminster. Both were predictably cautious, as were other new publications that slowly surfaced, and a period of press docility followed, leaving Nedham with a virtual monopoly of information in his official sixteen-page *Mercurius Politicus* and its close relation the *Publik Intelligencer* (1650–60): Nedham, having offended various shades of political opinion, fled to the Netherlands in 1660. His place was taken by Henry *Muddiman, who started his career as spokesman for the revived monarchy in 1659 with the *Parliamentary Intelligencer*, later *Kingdomes Intelligencer*. In 1665 he founded the **Oxford Gazette*, the first real newspaper. See J. Frank, *The Beginnings of the English Newspaper 1620–1660* (1961).
See GAZETTE; L'ESTRANGE, SIR ROGER.

NEWTON, Sir Isaac (1642–1727) Scientist, born in Woolsthorpe, near Grantham; entered Trinity College, Cambridge, in 1661, remaining there until 1696, when he moved to London as master of the mint. He was elected Lucasian professor of mathematics at Cambridge in 1669 and became president of the *Royal Society in 1703. He was knighted in 1705. His major scientific works were *Philosophiae Naturalis Principia Mathematica* (1687), *Opticks* (1704), and *Arithmetica Universalis* (1707). Newton's ideas were diffused through popularizations such as Henry Pemberton's *View of Sir Isaac Newton's Philosophy* (1728); Newtonianism was the dominant philosophy of the *Enlightenment, influencing all fields of science, and finding its way into the poetry of Alexander *Pope, James *Thomson, and Edward *Young. Newton had few friends, but his vast correspondence kept together a band of dedicated disciples, some of whom were used as intermediaries in his debates with philosophical adversaries such as *Leibniz. Modern scholarship has not seriously affected his stature in the fields of mathematics, dynamics, celestial mechanics, astronomy, optics, natural philosophy, or cosmology. Newton was however attacked by Jonathan *Swift, in part over his role in assaying Wood's halfpence (*see* DRAPIER'S

LETTERS), and more fundamental opposition to Newtonian materialism came from *Goethe and William *Blake. Newton had in fact written more than two million words on alchemy; he was as steeped in the hermetic tradition as the mystical romantics, and the extent of his dedication to theology, biblical chronology, prophecy, and alchemy is now more fully appreciated. In these latter spheres, Newton is close in spirit to the *Cambridge Platonists.

NEWTON, John (1725–1807) Evangelical clergyman and former slave trader. His autobiography, *An Authentic Narrative* (1764), gives a vivid picture of his ordeals at sea and the beginning of his evangelical conversion. Only later did he support the abolition of the slave trade. He became curate of Olney, Buckinghamshire, in 1764 and with William *Cowper (on whom his powerful faith and at times overbearing personality had a profound influence) wrote *Olney Hymns* (1779), his most famous contribution being 'Amazing grace'. His publications include several collections of spiritual letters, notably *Cardiphonia* (1780). See D. B. Hindmarsh, *John Newton and the English Evangelical Tradition* (1996).
See also HYMNS.

New Wave science fiction Term (almost certainly echoing the late 1950s 'new wave' of French cinema) given to the *science fiction (or *speculative fiction) published under the editorship of Michael *Moorcock in *New Worlds* magazine (1964–71), and more generally to the work of various writers/editors, including Moorcock himself, Brian *Aldiss, J. G. *Ballard, Harlan *Ellison, Thomas M. *Disch, John *Sladek, Samuel R. *Delany, and Judith *Merril, dissatisfied with the standards and subject matter of contemporary science fiction. An editorial by Ballard emphasizing *inner* (psychological) rather than outer space was influential, while Moorcock and Ballard's championing of William *Burroughs emphasized experimentation, taboo-breaking, and wider literary ambitions. Many 'New Wave' writers, on both sides of the Atlantic, were creative offspring of the older tradition fuelled by the liberalities of the 1960s; others dissociated themselves from any concept of a 'movement'. 'New Wave' writing faded in the early 1970s, but had a lasting impact on science fiction.

New Way to Pay Old Debts, A A comedy by Philip *Massinger, acted probably in 1625–6, published 1633, perhaps the best known of his works. The play deals with the downfall of Sir Giles Overreach, a character based in part on the notorious extortioner Sir Giles Mompesson (1584–?1651). The rapacious Overreach, having taken the property of his prodigal nephew Frank Wellborn and reduced him to utter poverty, treats him contemptuously. Lady Allworth, a rich widow whose husband Wellborn had helped, agrees to pretend she is about to marry him. Overreach, deceived, changes his attitude and helps Wellborn. Tom Allworth, Lady Allworth's stepson and page to Lord Lovell, is in love with Overreach's daughter Margaret, who returns his love. Overreach is determined that his daughter shall marry Lord Lovell and become 'right honourable'. Lovell consents to help Allworth to win Margaret, and a trick is played on Overreach by which he promotes the marriage, thinking that Lord Lovell is to be the bridegroom. Overreach goes mad on discovering that he has been deceived, and cannot maintain his claim to Wellborn's property; he is sent to Bedlam. Wellborn receives a company in Lord Lovell's regiment, and Lovell marries Lady Allworth.

New Weird Term given to an amorphous literary movement focusing on *horror and *speculative fiction, dating (broadly speaking) from the 1990s. Like the *New Wave before it, many of whose figures, such as Michael *Moorcock and M. John *Harrison, acted as godfathers to the 'movement', the self-proclaimed New Weird was less a school than a way of describing very different writers united only in avoiding the conventional. China *Miéville's preference for 'weird' rather than 'science' or 'fantasy' fiction to describe his work suggests the hybridity harking back to H. P. *Lovecraft, or Arthur *Machen, whose influence certainly can be seen on Harrison. Harrison's use of the term 'bricolage' for his own techniques echoed Miéville's identification in 2003 of a group of writers deliberately dissolving the boundaries between the different categories of fantastic fiction. Michael Cisco (1970–) suggests that New Weird might simply be seen as a refusal to accept the boundaries between *general* and *genre* literature, noting the mention of writers like *Borges, *Calvino, and Angela *Carter among its 'practitioners'.

New Woman fiction A term used to describe late 19th-century writings which foreground the ideas and actions of the 'New Woman', a phrase said to have been coined by *Ouida when responding to Sarah *Grand's article 'The New Aspects of the Woman Question', 1894. Grand's own novels, like *The Heavenly Twins* (1893) and *The Beth Book* (1897), include many elements associated with this movement: attacks on sexual double standards; demands for better employment and educational opportunities for women; frankness about matters like venereal disease, contraception, and sex education; and questioning of traditional attitudes towards marriage and woman's place in the family and in relation to motherhood. The first example of the genre is probably Olive *Schreiner's **Story of an African Farm* (1883). Other significant contributors include Emma Francis *Brooke, Mona *Caird, Ella Hepworth *Dixon, George *Egerton, and Ménie Muriel *Dowie. Many novelists also published journalism dealing with further related issues within the growing women's movement of the period, such as rational dress and women's suffrage. Male writers also addressed similar themes, including Henrik *Ibsen, who made a substantial impact on the debate through London productions of *The Doll's House* (in 1889) and *Hedda Gabler* (in 1891), George *Gissing (*The Odd Women*, 1893), and Thomas *Hardy (*Jude the Obscure*, 1895). Less sympathetic fictional treatments came from both men (Grant *Allen, *The Woman Who Did*, 1895) and women, like Margaret *Oliphant, who wrote bitterly about the 'anti-marriage league' in 1896, or in the vehemently anti-feminist fiction and journalism of Eliza Lynn *Linton. See S. Ledger, *The New*

Woman: Fiction and Feminism at the Fin de siècle (1997); A. Heilmann, *New Woman Strategies* (2004).

New Worlds British *science fiction magazine which can be traced back to a 1930s fanzine *Novae Terrae* (later *New Worlds*), the last issues of which were edited by John *Carnell. In 1946–7 the title was used for a fiction magazine edited by Carnell, revived in 1949. Carnell was succeeded in 1964 by Michael *Moorcock, whose radical change of form and contents consolidated the sense of a *New Wave promised by Carnell's publication of J. G. *Ballard. The magazine formally ended in 1971 after 201 issues, although the name survived in a quarterly paperback and other irregular incarnations until 1997.

New Yorker An American weekly magazine founded in 1925 by Harold Ross (1892–1951). It is sophisticated, satirical, and urbane, and although famed for its humour has also published distinguished articles of reportage, such as, notably, 'Hiroshima' by John *Hersey, which occupied an entire issue in 1946. Writers and cartoonists associated with the magazine include James *Thurber, Ogden *Nash, S. J. *Perelman, and John *Updike.

New York School Phrase attached to a group of artists, poets, and less commonly musicians active in New York from the 1950s onwards. In painting, the rise of Abstract *Expressionism reflected a rejection of realism and experimentation with new compositional methods by Jackson Pollock (1912–56), Mark Rothko (1903–70), and others. The New York poets moved away from a *confessional style, experimenting with light, visual, and urban subjects partly influenced by *Surrealism. The most famous poets in the group include John *Ashbery, Kenneth *Koch, Frank *O'Hara, and James *Schuyler. See David Lehman, *The Last Avant-Garde* (1998).

NGUGI WA THIONG'O (1938–) Changed his name from James Ngugi when he stopped writing in English and began publishing in Gikuyu. Both decisions were motivated by his belief that writing in the language of the colonizer alienated Africans from their own culture. His essays on postcolonial politics have been as influential as his fiction and plays: *Homecoming* (1972); *Writers in Politics* (1981); *Barrel of a Pen* (1983); *Decolonising the Mind* (1986); *Moving the Centre* (1993); *Penpoints, Gunpoints, and Dreams* (1998). He was born in Kenya, where a State of Emergency was declared in 1952 because of the Mau Mau uprising, and educated at University College, Makerere, and at Leeds University. While he was teaching at the University of Nairobi his play in Gikuyu, translated as *I Will Marry When I Want* and co-written with Ngugi wa Mirii as a literacy project, was performed by a peasant cast to huge audiences in 1977; its licence was withdrawn and Ngugi was detained for a year, and was not reinstated in his academic post. *Detained: A Writer's Prison Diary* (1981) is a scathing attack on neocolonialism. Ngugi went into exile in 1982. In *The River Between* (1965), set around 1930, Waiyaki fails as a saviour who tries to reconcile cultural integrity and educational enlightenment. *Weep Not, Child* (1964), set during the Emergency, explores a child's perplexity as his intellectual ability provides him with schooling that makes him feel he has betrayed his family. *A Grain of Wheat* (1967) is stylistically more complex than the earlier novels, its dislocating shifts in perspective enacting for the reader the fragmentation of Kenyan society at the moment of independence. All the characters, Home Guards, District Officers and freedom fighters alike, are crippled by guilt; as General R says, 'No one will ever escape from his own actions.' *Petals of Blood* (1977), a modernist version of crime fiction, depicts a community's attempt to realize the dream of national identity in opposition to global capitalism. *Devil on the Cross* (1982), *Matigari* (1987), and *Wizard of the Crow* (2006) engage directly with Gikuyu orality.

Niamh [pron. Neev] In the second or southern cycle of Irish mythology, the daughter of *Manannán, the sea god. She fell in love with *Oisin, the son of *Finn, carried him off over the sea, and kept him with her for 300 years. She then let him return to his own country, mounted on a magic steed, but on condition that he should not set foot on earth. Oisin disregarded the caution, immediately lost his youth, and became a blind, decrepit old man.

Nibelung (Niblung, Niebelung) In the Norse *sagas and German **Nibelungenlied*, a mythical king of a race of dwarfs, the Nibelungs, who dwelt in Norway. The Nibelung kings and people also figure in William *Morris's **Sigurd the Volsung*.

Nibelungenlied A Middle High German epic poem of the early 13th century of unknown authorship. Its story is found in primitive shape in both forms of the *Edda where it is substantially the same as that told by William *Morris in **Sigurd the Volsung*. In the *Nibelungenlied*, however, the old legendary material is absorbed into the contemporary world of chivalry and differs in detail. Siegfried, son of Siegmund and Sieglind, king and queen of the Netherlands, having got possession of the Nibelung hoard guarded by Alberich, rides to woo Kriemhild, a Burgundian princess, sister of Gunther, Gernot, and Giselher. Hagen, their grim retainer, warns them against Siegfried, but the match is arranged, and the hoard is given to Kriemhild as marriage portion. Siegfried undertakes to help Gunther to win Brunhild, queen of Issland, by defeating her in trials of skill and strength, which he succeeds in doing. The double marriage takes place, but Brunhild remains suspicious, and Siegfried, called in by Gunther to subdue her, does so in Gunther's semblance and takes away her ring and girdle, which he gives to Kriemhild. The two queens quarrel, and Kriemhild reveals to Brunhild the trick that has been played on her. Hagen, who thinks his master's honour injured by Siegfried, treacherously kills the latter at a hunt. Kriemhild later marries Etzel (Attila), king of the Huns, and in order to avenge her husband and secure the hoard, which her brothers have seized and sunk in the Rhine, persuades them to visit Etzel's court. There they are set upon and overcome, but refuse to betray the hiding place of the hoard, and are slain. Hagen, the last survivor of the party who knows the secret, is killed by Kriemhild with Siegfried's sword; and Kriemhild herself is slain by Dietrich's knight Hildebrand. The poem, which recounts the death of all the major figures, is pervaded with a powerful sense of inevitable tragedy. *Der Ring des Nibelungen* is Richard *Wagner's version.

Nicholas Nickleby A novel by Charles *Dickens, published 1838–9. Nicholas, a high-spirited boy of 19, his mother, and his gentle sister Kate are left penniless on the death of his father. They appeal to his callous and grasping uncle, Ralph Nickleby, of whom Nicholas makes an enemy by his independent bearing. Nicholas is sent to work at Dotheboys Hall, where Wackford Squeers starves and maltreats 40 urchins under pretence of education. His special cruelty is expended on the half-witted Smike, left on his hands and employed as a drudge. The infuriated Nicholas thrashes Squeers and escapes with Smike, who becomes his devoted friend. He supports himself and Smike as an actor in the company of Vincent Crummles; he then enters the service of the benevolent Cheeryble brothers. Meanwhile Kate, apprenticed to Madame Mantalini, dressmaker, is exposed to the lecherous designs of Sir Mulberry Hawk, one of Ralph's associates. She is rescued by Nicholas, who breaks Sir Mulberry's head and makes a home for his mother and sister. Nicholas himself falls in love with Madeline Bray, the support of a selfish father. Ralph intends to marry Madeline to Gride, a revolting old money-lender. Ralph, whose hatred for Nicholas is intensified by the failure of his plans, knowing Nicholas's affection for Smike, conspires to remove the boy; his plots are thwarted with the help of Newman Noggs, his eccentric clerk, but nevertheless Smike declines, and eventually dies in Nicholas's arms. Confronted with ruin and exposure, and shattered by the discovery that Smike was his own son, Ralph hangs himself. Nicholas, befriended by the Cheerybles, marries Madeline, and Kate marries the Cheerybles' nephew Frank. Squeers is transported, and Gride is murdered. Episodic in structure and irrepressibly cheerful in tone, the novel is a vigorous example of Dickens's early work.

NICHOLS, Grace (1950–) Poet and children's writer, born in Georgetown, Guyana. In 1977 she moved to London and began a successful career as a travelling poet. Her first collection of poetry, *I Is a Long-Memoried Woman* (1983), established her reputation instantly as a Caribbean poet with a gift for wittily demonstrating the literary qualities of *Creole for exploring Caribbean history, folklore, and myth, including Amerindian, Aztec, and Inca civilizations. She has done this consistently in all her work including *The Fat Black Woman's Poems* (1984), *Lazy Thoughts of a Lazy Woman* (1989), *Sunris* (1996), and *Startling the Flying Fish* (2006). She has written one novel, *Whole of a Morning Sky* (1986). She is also a prolific writer of children's stories and poems.

NICHOLS, John (1745–1826) Printer and antiquary, editor and manager of the **Gentleman's Magazine* from 1792 until his death. In that role Nichols built up an invaluable collection of letters and documents, later published in nine volumes as *Literary Anecdotes of the Eighteenth Century* (1812–16), with further instalments in the eight-volume *Illustrations of the Literary History of the Eighteenth Century* (1817–58), the project being completed by his son. Nichols's *The Progresses and Public Processions of Queen Elizabeth* (4 vols, 1788–1821) was a source for Scott's **Kenilworth*. Nichols also published a vast history of Leicestershire, and a biography of William *Hogarth (1781); and edited various authors, including Jonathan *Swift.

NICHOLS, Peter (1927–) Playwright, born and educated in Bristol. He served with the RAF in the Far East, then returned to train and work as an actor and teacher before making his name with both stage and television plays. His works include *A Day in the Death of Joe Egg* (1967), in which schoolteacher Bri and his wife Sheila struggle to share the burden of their handicapped daughter Joe; *The National Health* (1969), a satirical hospital comedy which contrasts reality with soap opera; *Forget-Me-Not-Lane* (1971), a family drama set during the Second World War; *Privates on Parade* (1977, set in Malaya); and *Passion Play* (1980), a marital tragicomedy. *Feeling You're Behind* (1984) is an autobiography; see also *Peter Nichols: Diaries 1969–1977* (2000).

NICHOLS, Robert (1893–1944) Poet and playwright, born on the Isle of Wight and educated at Winchester College and at Trinity College, Oxford (1913–14), before enlisting in the Royal Field Artillery. His volumes of poems, *Invocation* (1915) and *Ardours and Endurances* (1917), were highly regarded; he appeared in **Georgian Poetry*, and was thought by some to be another Rupert *Brooke. But *Aurelia* (1920) was his last volume of lyrics, after which he taught at Tokyo Imperial University (1921–24), moved on to Hollywood, and concentrated on writing plays, where he believed his talent lay. However, *Guilty Souls* (1922), *Wings over Europe* (1932), and other dramas met with little success. *Such Was my Singing* (1942) contained fragments from two vast works, 'Don Juan Tenorio the Great' and 'The Solitudes of the Sun', neither of which was ever finished. See Anne and William Charlton, *Putting Poetry First: A Life of Robert Nichols* (2003).

NICHOLSON, Norman (1914–87) Poet, born in the working-class iron town of Millom, Cumberland, where he lived all his life (apart from a long spell in a sanatorium, suffering from tuberculosis, when he was in his late teens) and which became the theme of most of his work. He evokes its buildings, its dying industry, its people, its geology, and the surrounding rural landscape in several volumes of verse, including *Five Rivers* (1944), *The Pot Geranium* (1954), and *A Local Habitation* (1972), the title of which indicates the intense, precise rootedness of his poetry. His *Collected Poems* (ed. Neil Curry) appeared in 1994.

NÍ CHUILLEANÁIN, Eiléan (1942–) Poet and academic, born in Cork, now resident in Dublin, where she edits the poetry magazine *Cyphers* and works as a professor of English at Trinity College. Her austere, anecdotal, sometimes slyly humorous lyrics conjure an enigmatic world in which vividly rendered details assume the dimensions of parable or myth. *Acts and Monuments* (1972), her notably mature first collection, was followed by *Site of Ambush* (1975) and *The Rose Geranium* (1981). *The Magdalene Sermon* (1989) and *The Brazen Serpent* (1994) take their focus from ironic hagiographies and agnostic studies of the miraculous. Ní Chuilleanáin's gift for disarming, obliquely political epiphany reaches a new level of subtlety in *The Girl who Married the Reindeer* (2001).

Nicolette *See* AUCASSIN AND NICOLETTE.

NICOLSON, Sir Harold George (1886–1968) Biographer and critic, born in Tehran and educated at Wellington College and Balliol College, Oxford. The son of a diplomat, he himself joined the diplomatic service, and served in the Foreign Office during the war. He resigned from the diplomatic service in 1929. In 1935 he became an MP for the National Labour Party but lost his seat in 1945. He published critical and biographical works on Paul *Verlaine (1921), Alfred *Tennyson (1923), A. C. *Swinburne (1926), and George V (1952) and wrote on diplomacy in *Curzon* (1934) and in other lectures and essays. *Some People* (1927), where he produced a series of semi-fictitious sketches, based on his experiences of public school and the diplomatic service, is his most inventive work. His marriage to Vita *Sackville-West, which allowed them both to have other, same-sex relationships, is described in *Portrait of a Marriage* (1973) by his son Nigel Nicolson, who also edited his diaries, *The Harold Nicolson Diaries 1907–1963* (2004).

NÍ DHOMHNAILL, Nuala (1952–) Irish-language poet, born in Lancashire, and brought up partly by relatives in the Kerry Gaeltacht, who has won an international audience through translations into English and other languages. Educated at University College Cork, she spent seven years in Amsterdam and Ankara with her Turkish husband. Her collections include *An Dealg Droighin* (1981), *Feis* (1991), and *Cead Aighnis* (1999). Though rooted in Gaelic tradition, her voice is stubbornly contemporary in its feminist awareness, and can be by turns passionate, acerbic, lyrical, and satirical. *Pharaoh's Daughter* (1990) includes translations by, among others, Seamus *Heaney, Michael *Longley, and John *Montague. The Irish language sometimes functions in her work as a metaphor for a folkloric Otherworld: the title of *The Astrakhan Cloak* (1992), with English versions by Paul *Muldoon, plays on *aistriúchán*, Irish for 'translation'. Other bilingual collections include *The Water Horse* (1999), with Medbh *McGuckian and Eiléan *Ní Chuilleanáin, and *The Fifty Minute Mermaid* (2007), again with Muldoon. Ní Dhomhnaill was Ireland professor of poetry from 2002 to 2004.

Niebelung *See* NIBELUNG.

NIEBUHR, Barthold Georg (1776–1831) German historian and diplomat. The son of a distinguished Danish explorer, he was educated at Kiel and, in 1798, at Edinburgh where he studied physical science. The three-volume *Römische Geschichte (Roman History)*, originally delivered as lectures at the new University of Berlin, appeared between 1811 and 1832 and inaugurated a great period of German historical scholarship. Niebuhr, who devoted more attention to the development of social institutions than to individuals and events, was the first historian to deal with Roman sources in a rigorously questioning and critical spirit. Thomas *Arnold drew English attention to Niebuhr's work in the *Quarterly Review* in 1825, and his own *History of Rome* (1838–43) was heavily indebted to it. The two met at Bonn in 1830. The *History* was translated into English by Julius *Hare and Connop *Thirlwall in 1828–42.

NIETZSCHE, Friedrich Wilhelm (1844–1900) German philosopher, educated at Bonn and Leipzig universities. Appointed to a chair in classical philology at Basle when only 25, he resigned because of ill health in 1879 and, ten years later, suffered a mental breakdown from which he never recovered. In his first work, *Die Geburt der Tragödie* (1872: *The Birth of Tragedy*), he challenged accepted ideas about classical civilization, arguing that Greek tragedy was made possible only by the mingling of 'Apollonian' values of measure, reason, and harmony with irrational energies which he termed 'Dionysiac'. After his resignation from the professorship there followed a decade of extraordinary productivity. *Die fröhliche Wissenschaft* (1882: *The Gay Science*), with its famous assertion 'God is dead', was followed by *Also sprach Zarathustra* (1883–5: *Thus Spake Zarathustra*), *Jenseits von Gut und Böse* (1886: *Beyond Good and Evil*), *Zur Genealogie der Moral* (1887: *On the Genealogy of Morals*), and *Die Götzen-Dämmerung* (1889: *Twilight of the Idols*). Other works written in this decade were published during his illness or posthumously, when indeed the force of his work began to be fully registered. Nietzsche is considered by many to be among the most influential thinkers of modern times. By some the influence has been deemed baleful, and his reputation has suffered unfairly from guilt by association with Nazism. Despite the fact that Nietzsche's break with the formerly revered Richard *Wagner was in part caused by the composer's nationalism and anti-Semitism, some of his ideas —the 'Übermensch' (superman), 'the morality of the slave', 'the will to power', etc.—were seized upon by Nazi ideologues. More positively, his extensive influence may owe something to the fact that in his philosophical works, which have great literary quality, he is not a 'system builder'. Instead, at times playfully, he subjects the moral values of Christian civilization, its ethical and metaphysical foundations, to a rigorously sceptical and corrosive scrutiny. Apart from his influence in the areas of philosophy, psychology, and theology, Nietzsche's importance to literature is twofold. Diverse literary figures such as George Bernard *Shaw, D. H. *Lawrence, W. B. *Yeats, Thomas *Mann, and Rainer Maria *Rilke felt the impact of his thought, but so too has modern criticism. His method, with its sensitivity to the inescapably figurative nature of language, anticipates Jacques *Derrida and *deconstruction. See J. P. Stern, *A Study of Nietzsche* (1979).

NIGHTINGALE, Florence (1820–1910) Health reformer and writer, born in Florence and educated at home. Her family circumstances were comfortable, but she rejected a life of affluent leisure in order to work tirelessly to transform perceptions of nursing as a profession for women. She became famous for her campaign to improve conditions for the sick and wounded soldiers of the Crimean War (1853–6), largely undertaken through her work in the military hospital at Scutari. Her interests were not confined to nursing, and her *Suggestions for Thought to Searchers after Religious Truth among the Artizans of England* is a wide-ranging exploration of her views on religion. It was set in type and bound, in three volumes, in 1860, but remained unpublished in her lifetime. *Suggestions* included 'Cassandra', an impassioned essay on the confinements imposed on the lives of middle-class women of her generation, which was published by the feminist Ray Strachey (1887–1940) in 1928, and has become recognized as an important text in the history of feminism. Virginia *Woolf described it as 'shrieking aloud in agony' in *A *Room of one's Own*. The publication of her *Collected Works*, ed. Lynn McDonald and Gérard Vallée (2001–), is in progress, and is expected to extend to sixteen volumes. See Mark Bostridge, *Florence Nightingale* (2008).

Nightmare Abbey A satire by Thomas Love *Peacock, published 1818. The most literary of Peacock's satires, it mocks the modish gloom infecting contemporary literature: S. T. *Coleridge's German transcendentalism is the prime example, but Lord *Byron's self-dramatizing and P. B. *Shelley's esotericism are also ridiculed. In imitation of the opening of William *Godwin's novel *Mandeville* (1817), Mr Glowry's isolated house is staffed by servants with long faces and names like Diggory Deaths-head. He gives a house party attended by Mr Toobad, the millenarian pessimist, Mr Flosky (Coleridge), Mr Cypress (Byron), and Mr Listless, the common reader, who is currently immersed in depression. Two guests remain unfashionably cheerful, Mr Asterias the scientist and Mr Hilary, whose literary tastes come from the Greeks. Scythrop Glowry, the son of the house, a young writer who resembles P. B. Shelley, cannot decide between his frivolous cousin Marionetta and Mr Toobad's sybilline daughter Stella. Peacock seems to have intended to present, in amusing contemporary terms, the dilemma facing the young John *Milton in *'L'Allegro' and *'Il Penseroso'. In a classic comic denouement, in which the ladies are discovered to one another, Scythrop loses both. He briefly contemplates suicide in Werther's manner (*see* WERTHERISM), but calls instead for a bottle of Madeira.

Night Thoughts on Life, Death, and Immortality, The Complaint, or A poem of some 10,000 lines of blank verse, in nine books, by Edward *Young, published 1742–5. Amid gloomy meditations on life's vicissitudes, the poet laments the deaths of Lucia, Narcissa, and Philander, loosely identified as his wife, his stepdaughter, and her husband; he also addresses much reproof and exhortation to a young atheist, Lorenzo. The poem includes lines which have become proverbial, such as 'Procrastination is the thief of time' (I. 393); it was enormously popular in Britain and had considerable influence in Europe. The poem's piety and grandeur were praised by Samuel *Johnson, and its pathos by James *Boswell; William *Blake produced over 500 designs for a projected edition of 1795, but only one volume was published. *See also* GRAVEYARD POETS.

Nimphidia A fairy poem by Michael *Drayton, published in 1627, featuring Oberon, Puck, Queen Mab and her wooer Pigwiggin, a snail-shell coach, grasshoppers and earwigs as steeds, a cowslip as a place of assignation, and other miniature fairy accoutrements.

'Nimrod' *See* APPERLEY, CHARLES JAMES.

NIN, Anaïs (Angela Antolina Rosa Edelmira Nin y Culmell) (1903–77) Novelist and diarist, born in Neuilly, France, to the Spanish–Cuban composer Joaquin Nin and his Danish/French wife Rosa Culmell y Vigaraud, who was also a musician. When her parents separated in 1914 she moved to New York, abandoning formal education at the age of 16. She later studied psychoanalysis and was a patient of *Jung. She married Hugh Parker Guiler, a banker and later film-maker, in 1923, and they moved to Paris, where Nin met Henry Miller with whom she had a passionate affair; she later bigamously married Rupert Pole. She wrote Surrealist novels, including *House of Incest* (1936), the five-volume *Cities of the Interior* (1947–54; published in one volume in 1959), and erotica, published posthumously as *Delta of Venus* (1977). Her major work, however, was a seven-volume diary (1966–80) which she kept throughout her life, and which was republished in unexpurgated form after her death. It provides an account of the literary and artistic circle which she frequented, but is mostly celebrated as an intimate, interior exploration of female subjectivity and sexuality. See Deirdre Bair, *Anaïs Nin: A Biography* (1995).

Nineteen Eighty-Four A novel by George *Orwell, published 1949; a dystopian story of totalitarianism of the future and one man's hopeless struggle against it. Winston Smith, the hero, has no heroic qualities, only a wistful longing for truth and decency. But in a social system where there is no privacy and where having unorthodox ideas incurs the death penalty he knows he has no hope. His brief love affair ends in arrest by the Thought Police, and when, after months of torture and brainwashing, he is released, he makes his final submission of his own accord. The book is a warning of the possibilities of the police state brought to perfection, where power is the only thing that counts, where the past is constantly being modified to fit the present, where the official language, 'Newspeak', progressively narrows the range of ideas and independent thought, and where Doublethink becomes a necessary habit of mind. It is a society dominated by slogans—'War is Peace, Freedom is Slavery, Ignorance is Strength'—and controlled by compulsory worship of the head of the Party, Big Brother. The novel had an extraordinary impact, and many of its phrases and coinages (including its title) passed into the common language, although the precise implications of Orwell's warning (and it was a warning, rather than a prophecy) have been subjected to many different political interpretations.

Nineteenth Century A monthly review founded in 1877 by James *Knowles, who became its first editor after resigning his editorship of the **Contemporary Review.* Serious and intellectual in tone, it was more impartial in its attitude than the **Fortnightly Review,* bringing together in its pages the most eminent advocates of conflicting views; one of its celebrated controversies (1890–91) was that between William *Gladstone and T. H. *Huxley on the subject of the miracle of the Gadarene Swine. Other contributors included John *Ruskin, Beatrice *Webb, William *Morris, *Ouida, and Oscar *Wilde. *Tennyson, a friend of Knowles, provided a prefatory sonnet for the first issue, welcoming contributions from the faithful and from 'wilder comrades' seeking a harbour 'In seas of Death and sunless Gulfs of Doubt'. The venture proved successful and profitable, and Knowles continued as editor until his death in 1908. When the century of the title ended, the review added to its old title 'And After', and changed the whole title to the *Twentieth Century* in 1951. It finally ceased publication in 1972. See M. Goodwin (ed.), *Nineteenth Century Opinion* (1951), a selection from the years 1877–1901.

Nine Worthies 'Three Paynims, three Jews, and three Christian men', namely Hector of Troy, *Alexander the Great, and Julius *Caesar; Joshua, *David, and Judas Maccabaeus; *Arthur, *Charlemagne, and Godefroi de *Bouillon (Caxton, preface to *Le *Morte Darthur*). The list of worthies in Shakespeare's **Love's Labour's Lost,* v. ii, is not quite the same, for it includes Pompey and *Hercules.

Niobe Mother of many children who boasted of her superiority to the goddess Leto, who had only two, Apollo and Artemis (Diana). To punish her Apollo and Artemis slew all her children, and she was then transformed into a weeping rock. Her story is told in Homer's **Iliad,* Book 24, and *Ovid's *Metamorphoses,* Book 6. She became a symbol of grief. *Hamlet ironically describes Gertrude as 'Like Niobe, all tears'.

NIVEN, Larry (1938–) American *science fiction writer, born Los Angeles; usually identified with the *hard science fiction of novels like *Ringworld* (1970), set in his 'known space' universe. *The Magic Goes Away* (1977) is a *fantasy—where, however, magic is seen almost as a physical resource.

Njáls saga A prose epic written *c.*1280 but set nearly 300 years previously. It is generally considered the most distinguished of the Icelandic *sagas. An extremely rich and complex narrative, it falls into three parts. The first is concerned with Gunnar Hámundarson, who is a friend of Njáll, and it ends with his death. In the second part, Njáll's sons avenge his death, but after many adventures, they are burned alive, with their father, by their enemies. In the third section, their death is avenged in turn. Translated, with an introduction by Magnus Magnusson and Hermann Pálsson (1960).

Noah *See* BIBLE.

Nobel Prizes were established under the will of Alfred Bernhard Nobel (1833–96), a Swedish chemist distinguished in the development of explosives, by which the interest on the greater part of his large fortune is distributed in annual prizes for the most important discoveries in physics, chemistry, and physiology or medicine respectively, to the person who shall have most promoted 'the fraternity of nations' (the Nobel Peace Prize), and to the 'person who shall have produced in the field of literature the most outstanding work of an idealistic tendency'. The Bank of Sweden also awards (since 1969) an associated prize in economics. See Appendix 3 (*a*) for a list of winners.

Noctes Ambrosianae A series of dialogues, published in **Blackwood's Edinburgh Magazine* from 1822 to 1835. The series was devised by John *Lockhart, and bears some resemblance to his own *Peter's Letters to his Kinsfolk,* in which the setting, *Ambrose's Tavern, first appears. The speakers are largely based on real people, such as James *Hogg (the 'Shepherd') and John *Wilson ('Christopher North'). Wilson wrote more than half the 71 dialogues, but Lockhart, Hogg, and William *Maginn also contributed. The wide-ranging conversations present a romanticized and whimsical view of Scotland. See J. H. Alexander (ed.), *The Tavern Sages: Selections from the Noctes Ambrosianae* (1992).

NOEL, Roden Berkely Wriothesley (1834–94) Poet, the author of several volumes of verse, including *A Little Child's Monument* (1881), inspired by the death of his son Eric, and *Songs of the Heights and Deeps* (1885). His collected works were issued in 1902.

Nōh plays A form of ceremonial, ritualistic drama peculiar to Japan, slow, symbolical, and spiritual in character. The style originated in the 14th century, was perfected in the 15th, and flourished during the Edo or Tokugawa period (1603–1868). It has since been revived. The plays are short (one or two acts), in prose and verse, and a chorus contributes comments. The scenery and props are minimal, though the masks and costumes are often lavish. They were formerly acted only at the shōgun's court, five or six in succession, presenting a complete life drama, beginning with a play of the divine age, then a battle piece, a 'play of women', a psychological piece (dealing with the sins and struggles of mortals), a morality, and finally a congratulatory piece, praising the shōgun's lords and reign. The text was complemented by symbolic gestures, chanting, and music. About 200 Nōh plays are extant. Of these the most interesting are the psychological pieces, in which some type of human character or some intense emotion is taken as the subject. In various respects the Nōh plays are comparable with the early Greek drama. Both Ezra *Pound and W. B. *Yeats were much influenced by the Nōh theatre: in 'Certain Noble Plays of Japan' (1916), Yeats describes the impact of its ritual, simplicity, and stylization on his own plays.

noir French term ['black'] Used to describe American films and fiction of the 1940s and 1950s, which combine different genres and entrapping plot twists. The mode grows out of *hardboiled narratives.

NOLLEKENS, Joseph (1737–1823) Sculptor, born in London, the son of Antwerp-born painter Joseph Francis Nollekens ('Old Nollekens', 1702–48). His many busts of statesmen, aristocrats, and writers were lively, and his career was immensely successful. An eccentric figure, he is frequently mentioned in the literature of the period, and was a friend of Samuel *Johnson and Joshua *Reynolds. Fanny *Burney drew on him for the character of Briggs in **Cecilia*.

No Name A novel by Wilkie *Collins, published 1862. When her parents die, the spirited Magdalen Vanstone, a talented amateur actress, discovers that she and her sister Norah are both illegitimate and penniless. Their father's fortune goes to a cousin, Noel Vanstone, a querulous invalid. Norah works as a governess, but Magdalen is determined to have justice. With the help of an amiable rogue, Captain Wragge, she gets access in disguise to Noel Vanstone, and charms him into marrying her under an assumed name. His French housekeeper discovers and reveals the deception, and persuades him to alter his will, leaving his money in a secret trust. Vanstone dies, and Magdalen, disguising herself as a parlourmaid, penetrates the house of the trustee of his will to find the document which reveals the legatee. The money finally returns to the sisters through Norah's love match with Vanstone's heir. Magdalen marries a sea captain, and Wragge becomes rich through investing in a patent medicine. The novel is remarkable for its sympathetic portrayal of Magdalen, its energetic and unscrupulous heroine.

Nonesuch Press A publishing firm established in 1923 by Francis *Meynell, his wife Vera Mendel, and David *Garnett, for the production of books of high quality of content and presentation, at a moderate price. Not strictly a *private press, it shared many of the aims of the private presses. After closing in 1936, the imprint has been revived several times. See J. Dreyfus *et al.*, *A History of the Nonesuch Press* (1981).

nonjurors The name given to Church of England clergy and laymen in the 17th and 18th centuries who supported the Stuart succession and refused to take the oaths of allegiance to William and Mary after 1688 and to the Hanoverian Georges after 1714, thus excluding themselves from holding office. Notable nonjuring writers include Thomas *Ken, Charles Leslie (1650–1722), Jeremy *Collier, Robert *Nelson, Thomas *Hearne, William *Law, Charles Jennens (1700–73), and John *Byrom.

nonsense Usually in verse; has been associated with children because of its roots in nursery rhymes and singing games based on sound rather than sense. However, deliberate nonsense has undercurrents that are personal (as with Edward *Lear), or political (Dr *Seuss), or which may be the vehicle for complex intellectual games (as in Lewis *Carroll's *The Hunting of the Snark*, 1876). It may also be used for parody or to patronize audiences (as with George Farrow's *The Wallypug of Why*, 1895). Spike Milligan is a modern practitioner; there are studies by Elizabeth Sewell (1952), Wim Tigges (1988), and Jean-Jacques Lecercle (1994).

NOON, Jeff (1957–) Novelist and playwright, born in Manchester. Noon won the Arthur C. Clarke Award with *Vurt* (1993), lyrically fusing *cyberpunk and mythology. Subsequent novels and stories, collected in *Pixel Juice* (1998), use techniques adapted from modern club music to enrich the mix.

NORRIS, Frank (Benjamin Franklin) (1870–1902) American novelist, born in Chicago but brought up partly in San Francisco. The influence of *Zola and *naturalism is seen in his best work, which includes *McTeague* (1899), a tragic account of violence, greed, and treachery in San Francisco, in which McTeague, an unlicensed dentist, becomes both thief and murderer; and in his unfinished trilogy *The Epic of the Wheat*: the first two volumes, *The Octopus* (1901) and *The Pit* (1903), describe the raising of wheat in California and speculation on the Chicago wheat exchange. A projected third volume, *The Wolf*, to be set in famine-stricken Europe, was never written. See Joseph R. McElrath, Jr, and Jessie S. Crissler, *Frank Norris: A Life* (2006).

NORRIS, John (1657–1712) Poet and philosopher, born in Wiltshire, educated at Winchester College and Exeter College, Oxford, and a fellow of All Souls, Oxford, until his marriage in 1689. From 1692 until his death he was rector of Bemerton, Wiltshire (as George *Herbert had been). *A Collection of Miscellanies* (1687) contains poems, essays, and discourses; these were followed by several religious and philosophical works. He was the first to publish an account of John *Locke's **Essay Concerning Human Understanding*. Initially a friend of Lady Damaris Masham (1658–1708) and Locke, he quarrelled with them for reasons unknown. Mary *Astell published her correspondence with Norris as *Letters Concerning the Love of God* (1695). In philosophy he was a follower of the French philosopher Nicolas Malebranche (1638–1715), whose work develops the theories of *Descartes; his most important philosophical works are *An Account of Reason and Faith* (1697) and *An Essay towards the Theory of the Ideal or Intelligible World* (1701–4). His practical religious works, some abridged by John *Wesley, were well known throughout the 18th century. His poems were edited by A. B. *Grosart (1871).

NORTH, Christopher Pseudonym of John *Wilson (1785–1854).

NORTH, Roger (1651–1734) Youngest son of Dudley, fourth Baron North, and great-great-nephew of Sir Thomas *North. Educated at Jesus College, Cambridge, and the Middle Temple, he abandoned his career as a lawyer at the accession of William of Orange. In 1742–4 his son published his affectionate biographies of three of his brothers: Francis North (1637–85), keeper of the great seal; the merchant Sir Dudley North (1641–91); and John North (1645–83), master of Trinity College, Cambridge. North wrote extensively on politics, mathematics, estate management, etymology, history, law, and *music; much remains unpublished. See *Notes of Me: The Autobiography of Roger North*, ed. P. Millard (2000).

NORTH, Sir Thomas (1535–?1603) Translator, younger son of Edward North (*c.*1504–64), first Baron North; he perhaps studied at Peterhouse, Cambridge. He entered Lincoln's Inn, attended the court, was knighted in 1591, and pensioned by *Elizabeth I in 1601. He is famous for his translations, which include the **Dial of Princes* from Guevara's *El relox de principes* (1557), published with *The Famous Book of Marcus Aurelius, The Moral Philosophy of Doni*, from the Italian (1570, *see* BIDPAI), and *Plutarch's *Lives* from the French of Jacques *Amyot (1579), to which he made additions from other authors in 1595 and 1603. His Plutarch, written in noble and vivid English, was William *Shakespeare's chief source for classical history and had a great influence on Elizabethan prose.

North American Review (1815–1939) A Boston quarterly, later monthly periodical. Its editors included Charles Eliot *Norton, James Russell *Lowell, and Henry *Adams. Its contributors ranged from Ralph Waldo *Emerson and Washington *Irving to Henry *James and Mark *Twain.

North and South A novel by Elizabeth *Gaskell, published serially in **Household Words* 1854–5, in volume form 1855. It contrasts the values of rural southern England and industrial northern England, and is more conciliatory in its approach than the provocative **Mary Barton*. Margaret Hale is the daughter of a clergyman whose religious doubts force him to resign his Hampshire living and to move with his family to a sooty cotton-spinning northern city. Here, at a moment of conflict between workers and employers, Margaret meets the grim Mrs Thornton and her son, a stubborn manufacturer, whose lack of sympathy for the workers Margaret finds unattractive. She endangers herself to protect him from a mob of strikers; he misunderstands her motives and offers marriage, which she refuses. But when he suspects her of an intrigue with another man (in fact her brother, whom she has to shield as he is in danger of arrest), and shows his suspicion, she realizes that she loves him. After a series of misfortunes, Margaret and Thornton are finally united. Margaret, at first repelled by 'trade' and its practitioners, comes to respect the ideas and the family life of northern mill-hands and mill-owners.

Northanger Abbey A novel by Jane *Austen, begun 1798, sold to a publisher 1803, but not published until 1818, when it appeared posthumously with **Persuasion*. It is probably the earliest of her completed works. The novel satirizes popular tales of romance and terror, such as Ann *Radcliffe's **Mysteries of Udolpho*, and contrasts the improbabilities of *Gothic fiction with the normal realities of life. Catherine Morland, daughter of a well-to-do clergyman, is taken to Bath for the season by her friends Mr and Mrs Allen. Here she makes the acquaintance of Henry Tilney (son of the eccentric General Tilney) and his pleasant sister Eleanor. Catherine falls in love with Henry, and gains his father's approval, which is founded upon the exaggerated report of her parents' wealth given him by the foolish young John Thorpe, brother of Catherine's friend Isabella. Catherine is invited to Northanger Abbey, the medieval seat of the Tilneys. Somewhat unbalanced by her eager reading of Radcliffe's novels, Catherine imagines a mystery in which General Tilney is criminally involved with the death of his wife, and is mortified when her suspicions are discovered. She learns that the Gothic novel does not reflect real life: 'Charming as were all Mrs Radcliffe's works, and charming even as were the works of all her imitators, it was not in them perhaps that human nature, at least in the midland counties of England, was to be looked for.' General Tilney, having received a second report from John Thorpe as misleading as the first, representing Catherine's parents as extremely humble, packs her off back to her family and forbids Henry to have any further thoughts of her. Henry, disobeying his father, follows Catherine to her home, proposes, and is accepted. General Tilney's consent is obtained when his humour has been greatly improved by the marriage of his daughter Eleanor to a peer, and his discovery of the true financial position of Catherine's family. Interwoven with the main plot is the flirtation of Captain Tilney, Henry's elder brother, and the vulgar Isabella Thorpe, who is engaged to Catherine's brother; the consequent breaking of the engagement and rupture of the friendship between Catherine and Isabella; and Isabella's failure to secure Captain Tilney.

North Briton A weekly political periodical founded in 1762 by John *Wilkes, in opposition to the *Briton*, which Tobias *Smollett was conducting in the interests of the Scottish prime minister Lord Bute. Wilkes was assisted by Charles *Churchill. The *North Briton* purports to be edited by a Scotsman, who rejoices in the ousting of the English from power. In no. 45 (23 Apr. 1763) Wilkes attacked the king's speech and was imprisoned for libel. He was eventually discharged, and the use of general arrest warrants declared illegal, but no. 47 of the periodical did not appear until 1768; it ceased publication altogether in 1771.

Northern Lass, The A comedy by Richard *Brome, printed 1632. This is the earliest of Brome's extant plays, and was very popular. Sir Philip Luckless is about to marry the rich city widow Fitchow, when he receives a letter from Constance, the 'northern lass', reminding him of her love for him. Mistaking the writer for another, less reputable Constance, he disregards the letter and marries the widow, only to discover his mistake too late. The play concerns the schemes by which the widow is induced to agree to a divorce, while her foolish brother, whom she tries to marry to Constance, is fobbed off with an inferior substitute, and Luckless and the true Constance are united.

Northward Ho A comedy by John *Webster and Thomas *Dekker, written 1605, printed 1607. Greenshield, failing to seduce Mayberry's wife, takes her ring by force. To avenge himself, he shows the ring to her husband as evidence of her infidelity. Mayberry, helped by the little old poet Bellamont, a genial caricature of George *Chapman, becomes convinced of her innocence, and takes revenge on Greenshield and his accomplice Featherstone. The play was a good-humoured answer to the **Eastward Ho* of Chapman, Ben *Jonson, and John *Marston. Like **Westward Ho* it gives a vivid picture of the manners of the day.

NORTON, Andre (1912–2005) American *science fiction and *fantasy author, born in Cleveland, Ohio. Her numerous books, such as *Storm over Warlock* (1960) and *Catseye* (1961), introduced young people in the 1950s and 1960s to the central concerns of the genres. Their quality ensured a loyal readership. Her 'Witch World' fantasies, beginning with *Witch World* (1963), attracted a somewhat older audience. Later novels were collaborations with others, including Elizabeth Moon (1945–).

NORTON, Caroline (1808–77) Née Sheridan, poet, novelist, editor, and hostess: she was a granddaughter of Richard *Sheridan. She married the Hon. George Norton in 1827 and in 1836 became involved in a notorious divorce action (her husband unsuccessfully citing Lord Melbourne) and later in spirited and influential battles for the custody of her children and a revision of the laws relating to married women's property. Her high public profile and authorship of pamphlets such as *English Laws for Women in the Nineteenth Century* (1854) helped to secure new rights for Victorian women through the Infant Custody Act (1839) and the Matrimonial Causes Act (1857). Norton successfully supported her family by writing, publishing several volumes of *Byronic verse, including *The Undying One, and Other Poems* (1830), in which the title poem is a version of the legend of the Wandering Jew, and *A Voice from the Factories* (1836), a powerful poem on child labour. She also edited several best-selling *poetry annuals and produced stories, essays, and novels, including *Lost and Saved* (3 vols, 1863). She served as a model for the heroine of Meredith's **Diana of the Crossways* and also knew Benjamin *Disraeli, Charles *Dickens, W. M. *Thackeray, and Alfred *Tennyson.

NORTON, Charles Eliot (1827–1908) American art historian and man of letters, born in Cambridge, Massachusetts, and educated at Harvard University, where he was professor of fine arts from 1873 to 1898. His aim was, in his own words, to arouse in his countrymen 'the sense of connection with the past and gratitude for the efforts and labours of other nations and former generations'. He was joint editor of the **North American Review* (1864–8), and founder and co-editor of *The Nation* (1865). His many friends among English writers and artists included John *Ruskin, the *Brownings, and Thomas *Carlyle. See James C. Turner, *The Liberal Education of Charles Eliot Norton* (1999).

NORTON, Mary (1903–92) Born in London, educated at St Margaret's convent in Sussex; she acted at the Old Vic in 1925–6. Apart from her *'Borrowers' series, she also wrote *Bedknob and Broomstick* (1957), filmed by Disney in 1971, and *Are All the Giants Dead?* (1975).

Norval *See* DOUGLAS (by John Home).

NOSTRADAMUS (1503–66) French astrologer, whose enigmatic prophecies, cast in the form of rhymed quatrains grouped in sets of 100 and published under the title *Centuries* (1555, English trans. 1672), enjoyed widespread popularity during the Renaissance. Interest in his prophecies has proved persistent.

Nostromo A novel by Joseph *Conrad, published 1904. In an imaginary South American country, Costaguana, Charles Gould runs a silver mine of national importance in the province of Sulaco. He is married to Emilia, a woman of charm and intelligence. In a time of political unrest and revolution the dictator President Ribiera flees the country and the opposing factions struggle for control. Nostromo ('our man' or 'boatswain') is an Italian sailor, now Capataz de Cargadores, handsome, courageous, and a hero to all. When the silver from the mine is in danger of being seized by the rebel forces, Gould becomes obsessed with the idea of saving it. He enlists the help of Decoud, a cynical journalist, and of an older man, Dr Monygham, a fond admirer of Emilia, who was tortured under the previous regime; together they appeal to Nostromo. With great daring Decoud and Nostromo sail off with the silver. Their journey through the night, their collision with an enemy boat, and their eventual arrival at a nearby island where they bury the treasure are vividly described. Decoud is left on guard while Nostromo returns to Sulaco. Alone on the deserted island Decoud loses his mind and, after shooting himself, drowns, his body weighted with silver. The common assumption is that the silver was lost at sea and the temptation proves too much for Nostromo, who decides to steal it. His old friend Viola is appointed lighthouse keeper on the island and, unwittingly, guard for the silver. Nostromo trifles with Viola's two infatuated daughters, grows rich as he gradually pilfers the silver, and is finally shot when mistaken for an intruder. Mortally wounded, he sends for Emilia, and confesses his crime in the hope of absolution, but dies without revealing the whereabouts of the treasure; as the 'incorruptible' Emilia, appalled by the destruction it has caused and by Nostromo's miserable subjection to his obsession, declares: 'No one misses it now. Let it be lost forever.'

Notes and Queries A periodical founded in 1849 by William *Thoms, originally subtitled 'a medium of inter-communication for literary men, artists, antiquaries, genealogists, etc.' It was conceived as part academic journal, part correspondence column, where scholars could seek or exchange information. Still thriving, it is now largely literary in subject, and has moved closer to the conventional format of a scholarly journal, publishing longer contributions. Its motto was (until 1923) Captain Cuttle's 'When found, make a note of' (*see* DOMBEY AND SON).

nouveau roman ('new novel') A term applied to the work of a wide range of modern French novelists, including Nathalie *Sarraute, Claude Simon (1913–2005), Marguerite *Duras, Robert Pinget (1919–97), Alain *Robbe-Grillet, and Michel *Butor. What distinguishes these novelists is primarily their conviction that the traditional novel is inadequate. With its dependence on an omniscient narrator, the *nouveaux romanciers* argue, the traditional novel creates an illusion of order and significance which is denied by the reality of experience. The aim of the new novel is to foster change by dispensing with any technique which imposes a particular interpretation on events, or which organizes events in such a way as to endow them with a collective significance.

Nouvelle Héloïse, La *See* ROUSSEAU, JEAN-JACQUES.

Nouvelle Revue française, La A monthly review of literature, drama, and the other arts, founded in 1909 by a group that included André *Gide, the novelist Jean Schlumberger (1877–1968), and the actor and theatre director Jacques Copeau (1879–1949). A publishing enterprise associated with the review, the 'maison d'éditions de la nrf', was started soon afterwards. The *NRF* published a number of little-known writers later to become famous, including Paul *Valéry, Jean *Giraudoux, Paul *Claudel, Henry de *Montherlant, and François *Mauriac, and made efforts to introduce German, Russian, and English authors to French readers. Valéry Larbaud (1881–1957) delivered a celebrated lecture on Joyce's **Ulysses* in the bookshop of Adrienne Monnier (1892–1955), La Maison des Amis des Livres, on 7 December 1921, which appeared in the *NRF* in April 1922. Publication was interrupted during the First World War and ceased in 1943, to recommence in 1953 as *La Nouvelle Nouvelle Revue française*. In 1959 the original title was readopted, under which it continues to appear.

NOVALIS Pseudonym of F. L. *von Hardenberg.

Nova Solyma, the Ideal City, *or Jerusalem Regained* An anonymous Latin utopian romance, written in the time of Charles I, probably by the Puritan Samuel Gott (1614–71). It contains a notable scheme of education.

novel, rise of the The word 'novellae' was employed in the 16th century to describe the short tales of the **Decameron* and the **Heptameron*, and others like them. Used in a recognizably modern sense, the word 'novel' appears in England in the mid-17th century, when it was chiefly associated with romances of illicit love. For this reason the word 'history' was more often favoured to describe the long prose fictions of the 18th century which were the precursors of the modern novel. The novel form developed slowly, through the *memoir-novel and the *epistolary novel of the 16th and 17th centuries to the novel of the omniscient third-person narrator, which has dominated from the late 18th century to the present time. The chief novelists of the 18th century (Daniel *Defoe, Samuel *Richardson, Henry *Fielding, Tobias *Smollett, and Laurence *Sterne) developed the form so fully that by the early 19th century Jane *Austen could write (albeit with a hint of irony), in **Northanger Abbey*, that in the novel 'the greatest powers of the mind are displayed'. Form, style, and subject matter varied considerably, but by 1824 Walter *Scott could confidently define the novel as 'a fictitious narrative...accommodated to the ordinary train of human events', a definition which has proved durable. See Ian Watt, *The Rise of the Novel* (1957); Michael McKeon, *The Origins of the English Novel 1600–1740* (1987).

See also FASHIONABLE NOVEL; HISTORICAL FICTION; ORIENTAL NOVEL; SENTIMENT.

Novum Organum A Latin treatise on scientific method, which Francis *Bacon included in his *Instauratio Magna* (1620). This 'great renewal' of natural philosophy (which Bacon never completed) involved a systematic methodology, starting with fresh observation of natural phenomena, followed by carefully controlled experiments, to provide data from which scientific laws could be formulated. The 'new instrument' outlined here (the title alludes to the corpus of Aristotelian philosophy, known as the *Organon*) abandoned the main tool of logic, the syllogism, which Bacon criticized as a self-contained verbal procedure starting from propositions which were not based on experience. Instead, he recommended inductive reasoning, moving from specific observations to broader generalizations and theories, tested by the use of 'negative instances' (if 100 white swans are observed, the discovery of a single black one is enough to falsify the thesis that all swans are white).

Book I of the *Novum Organum* restates in the form of detached aphorisms Bacon's fundamental criticisms of science and his plans for its renewal. Calling for the direct observation of nature (rather than recycling *Aristotle's texts), Bacon was nonetheless aware of the possible distortions involved, brilliantly analysing the four 'Idols' (from the Greek εἴδωλα, illusions) to which human beings are prone. These are the Idols of the Tribe, Cave, Market Place, and Theatre: respectively, the distortions caused by sense perception, which are common to all; distortions caused by differences of temperament and education, arising from particular circumstances of each individual; distortions arising from the treacherous medium of language; and the illusions of philosophic systems, these systems being in Bacon's view like so many stage plays, representing imaginary worlds of the philosophers' own manufacture. In the more technical Book II Bacon gives a worked example of inductive method as applied to heat, using experimental data to construct tables of absence and presence, concluding that heat is a form of motion. Though Bacon's inductive method has been misrepresented as a purely mechanical procedure, it includes deductive elements arising from hypotheses, representing a substantial contribution to natural science.

NOYES, Alfred (1880–1958) Poet, educated at Oxford, who held violently anti-modernist views on literature. His books of verse include *Drake* (1908) and *Tales of the Mermaid Tavern* (1913). His poem 'The Highwayman' is still well known. He also wrote plays, novels, and an autobiography, *Two Worlds for Memory* (1953).

nunc dimittis 'now lettest thou thy servant depart in peace', the Latin version of the Song of Simeon after he has seen the child Jesus (Luke 2: 29–32). It forms part of Evensong in the *Book of *Common Prayer*. More generally it means a willingness to depart or a dismissal.

NÚÑEZ DE BALBOA, Vasco (1475–1519) Spanish discoverer and conquistador. He joined an expedition from the Caribbean island of Hispaniola to mainland Central America as a stowaway in 1510, and founded at Darién (Panama) the first permanent European settlement in the Americas. In 1513 it was he who was the first European to set eyes on the Pacific Ocean, not *Cortés, as John *Keats supposed when he wrote:

Or like stout Cortez when with eagle eyes
He stared at the Pacific—and all his men
Looked at each other with a wild surmise—
Silent, upon a peak in Darien.

'Nun's Priest's Tale, The' *See* CANTERBURY TALES, 20.

nursery rhymes Obscure in origin; mostly appear to date from the 17th century as part of the oral tradition. They include riddles, street cries, parodies, political satires, and singing games. Many collections have been illustrated, notably by Arthur Rackham (1923), Quentin *Blake (1983), and Michael Foreman (1990). The earliest printed version appears in *A Little Book for Little Children* (*c.*1702–12) by 'T.W.'; **Tommy Thumb's Pretty Song Book* (1744) is the first collection. James Orchard *Halliwell's *The Nursery Rhymes of England* (1842) is a seminal study; the definitive collection is the *Opies' *The Oxford Dictionary of Nursery Rhymes* (1951).

NYE, Robert (1939–) Novelist, poet, playwright, and critic, born in London and educated at Southend High School, which he left at 16. He began his career as a poet whose exuberant earlier work was collected in two volumes, *Juvenilia 1* (1961) and *Juvenilia 2* (1963). His first novel, *Doubtfire* (1967), shows the influence of James *Joyce, but he is best known for a sequence of pastiche biographies of characters from literature, folklore, and history, the first of which, *Falstaff*, was published in 1976. Others of these idiosyncratic fictional portraits are *Merlin* (1978), *Faust* (1980), *The Memoirs of Lord Byron* (1989), *Mrs Shakespeare* (1993), and *The Late Mr Shakespeare* (1998). Nye has also written radio and stage plays, and books for children. His short stories were collected as *Tales I Told my Mother* (1969) and *The Facts of Life* (1983). A *Collection of Poems 1955–1988* (1989) includes new poems and revised versions of early pieces.

Nymphidia *See* NIMPHIDIA.

nymphs In Greek mythology, beautiful female divinities who inhabited trees (dryads), fresh water (naiads), the sea (nereids), caves and mountains (oreads). Several of them figure in *Ovid's *Metamorphoses*. They were often pursued by gods, for example Arethusa by Alpheus, Daphne by *Apollo, or Syrinx by *Pan. Nymphs could be dangerous to human beings, for example Salmacis to Hermaphroditus, or Calypso to Odysseus. Edmund *Spenser, Andrew *Marvell, and John *Keats among other poets were fascinated by the longing for the unattainable that nymphs represented, sometimes known as nympholepsy.

NYREN, John (1764–1837) A famous early cricketer and cricket chronicler. He belonged to the celebrated Hambledon Club, which flourished in the late 18th century, and was a left-handed batsman of average ability and a fine fielder at point and mid-wicket. His recollections were published in *The Young Cricketer's Tutor* (1833), edited by John *Keats's friend Charles *Cowden-Clarke, which includes some history of the game, reminiscences of great matches and 'cricketers I have known', and advice on tactics.

OATES, Joyce Carol (1938–) American novelist, short story writer, poet, and critic, born in Lockport, New York, educated at Syracuse University and the University of Wisconsin. A former professor of English at the University of Detroit (a city which provides the setting for much of her work), she began teaching at Princeton in 1978. Oates is a prolific novelist whose fiction portrays intense individual experiences as frequently neo-*Gothic expressions of the dark and violent heart of American society. Her first novel was *With Shuddering Fall* (1964). Many others followed, regularly winning awards and several being set in her fictional Eden County in upstate New York. *Black Water* (1992), set on an island off the coast of Maine, is the story, told in 32 short episodes, of a young woman's meeting with a US senator at a beach party and her subsequent death by drowning. *Foxfire* (1993) is a powerful portrayal of a teenage girl-gang in upstate New York during the 1950s. *Blonde* (2000) chronicles the life of Marilyn Monroe. *What I Lived for* (1994) is about the public and private faces of a property millionaire and city councillor. Her many short stories have been collected in *By the North Gate* (1963), *Marriages and Infidelities* (1972), and *The Museum of Dr Moses* (2007) among other volumes. Apart from her poetry, selections of essays and critical writings can be found in *The Edge of Impossibility* (1971), *Contraries* (1981), and *Uncensored* (2005). Her monograph *On Boxing* was published in 1987 and *The Faith of a Writer* in 2003. Her 1973–82 *Journal* was published in 2007.

Obermann *See* SENANCOUR, ÉTIENNE PIVERT DE.

objective correlative A term used by T. S. *Eliot in his essay 'Hamlet and his Problems' (1919; included in *The Sacred Wood*, 1920). Eliot ascribes the alleged 'artistic failure' of Shakespeare's play **Hamlet* to the fact that Hamlet himself is 'dominated by an emotion which is inexpressible, because it is in *excess* of the facts as they appear...The only way of expressing emotion in the form of art is by finding an "objective correlative"; in other words, a set of objects, a situation, a chain of events which shall be the formula of that *particular* emotion.' The phrase was much cited in mid-20th-century criticism, often as a way of distancing modern poetic taste from the allegedly vague effusiveness of Victorian poetry.

Objectivism *see* ZHUKOVSKY, VASILII ANDREEVICH.

O'BRIEN, Edna (1930–) Irish novelist and short story writer, born and brought up in Tuamgraney, Co. Clare. After training as a pharmacist in Dublin, O'Brien moved to London in 1954. Her first novel, *The Country Girls* (1960), describes the girlhood of Caithleen Brady (Kate) and Bridget Brennan (Baba), who escape from their rural homes and repressive convent education to the 'crowds and lights and noise' of Dublin. The book was banned in Ireland and burned in Tuamgraney, winning O'Brien a scandalous celebrity that has survived the liberalization of Irish social mores. Kate and Baba continue their search for experience in *The Lonely Girl* (1962; repr. as *The Girl with Green Eyes*) and *Girls in their Married Bliss* (1963), following the author's career trajectory to London. O'Brien's subsequent novels include *A Pagan Place* (1971), the sombre reverie *Night* (1972), *Johnny I Hardly Knew You* (1977), *House of Splendid Isolation* (1994), and *The Light of Evening* (2006). *Down by the River* (1997) fictionalizes the plight of a teenage rape victim who fell foul of Ireland's draconian abortion laws in 1992, while *In the Forest* (2002) recreates the events surrounding a notorious 1994 triple murder in the author's native east Clare. O'Brien's lyrical descriptive powers and lack of inhibition have led to comparisons with *Colette. Her short story collections include *A Scandalous Woman* (1974), *Mrs Reinhardt* (1978), *Returning* (1982), and *Lantern Slides* (1990).

O'BRIEN, Flann (1911–66) Pseudonym of Brian Ó Nualláin, novelist, born at Strabane, Co. Tyrone, and educated at University College, Dublin. He worked for the Irish Civil Service and for many years contributed a satirical column to the *Irish Times* under the name 'Myles na Gopaleen'. His exuberant first novel, *At Swim-Two-Birds* (1939), operates on several levels of invention: the narrator, a Dublin student living with his uncle, offers variants of reality which include a naturalistic portrayal of student and lower-middle-class life; a 'novel-within-a-novel' written by 'eccentric author Dermot Trellis' and dealing with the legendary hero *Finn Mac Cool; and a layer of Irish folklore rendered as farce, featuring the Pooka, the Good Fairy, and so on. The effect is a multidimensional exploration of the nature of fiction, extending an Irish tradition that runs from Laurence *Sterne to James *Joyce. O'Brien's second novel, *An Béal Bocht* (1941), written in Irish, is a hilarious parody of autobiography from Irish-speaking regions (trans. *The Poor Mouth*, 1973). The best known of his other works is *The Third Policeman* (written 1940; pub. 1967), a darker, more disturbing testing of the limits of fiction than his debut. See Anthony Cronin, *No Laughing Matter: The Life and Times of Flann O'Brien* (1989).

O'BRIEN, Kate (1897–1974) Irish novelist, born in Limerick, and educated at University College, Dublin. She became a professional writer after the London success of her play *Distinguished Villa* (1926). *Without my Cloak* (1931) is a saga of the emergent Catholic Irish middle class. *The Ante-Room* (1934) and *Mary Lavelle* (1936) explore the conflict between erotic freedom and religious orthodoxy in the lives of sensitive young women. The latter novel is set in Spain, where O'Brien had worked as an au pair, and from where she would be barred after the publication of her travelogue *Farewell Spain* (1937). *That Lady* (1946), a forensic exposition of the injustices of patriarchy in the 16th century, also draws on her Spanish experience. *The Land of Spices* (1942) delicately portrays relationships in an isolated Irish convent. Like *Mary Lavelle*, it was banned in Ireland. O'Brien's other work includes *My Ireland* (1962) and the memoir *Presentation Parlour* (1963).

O'BRIEN, Sean (1952–) Poet and critic, born in London, brought up in Hull, and educated at Cambridge. His volumes include *The Indoor Park* (1983), *HMS Glasshouse* (1991), and *Downriver* (2001). *Cousin Coat: Selected Poems 1976–2001* appeared in 2002, and a version of *Dante's *Inferno* in 2006. A collection of essays on poetry, *The Deregulated Muse*, was published in 1998. O'Brien's poetry, colloquial yet at times formal, and characteristically driven by an unusual rhythm (often employing the *dactyl), evokes contemporary urban landscapes and popular culture, reinforced by strong literary and painterly allusions. The effect, often with sardonic political point, is of a slightly surreal, displaced, offbeat portrait of contemporary Britain.

O'BRIEN, Tim (1946–) American novelist, born in Minnesota, who writes mainly about the Vietnam War. His first book was *If I Die in the Combat Zone* (1973), which, like his later works, combines reportage with fictional narrative. *The Nuclear Age* (1985) deals with fears of nuclear war.

Ó BRUADAIR, Dáibhí (*c.*1625–1697) Irish poet, born in east Cork, whose 80 surviving poems bring a huge weight of learning and a mixture of *bardic and looser song metrics to bear on their commentary on the fluctuating and ultimately calamitous fortunes of the 17th-century Irish Gaelic world. By turns celebratory, comic, meditative, and savagely querulous, Ó Bruadair's work is the most various in Gaelic tradition. A small portion of it has been translated by James *Stephens, Thomas *Kinsella, and Michael Hartnett (1941–99).

Observator *See* L'ESTRANGE, SIR ROGER.

Observer, The A Sunday newspaper, founded by W. S. Bourne and first issued on 4 December 1791. In 1814 it was bought by William Innell Clement (1779/80–1852), who boosted its circulation through the use of woodcut illustrations for sensational events (e.g. the Cato Street conspiracy in 1820). It lost readers by siding with the North in the American Civil War, but revived in the 1870s with Julius Beer (1837–80) as proprietor and Edward Dicey (1832–1911) as editor. It was bought by Alfred *Harmsworth in 1905, and edited from 1905 to 1908 by Austin Harrison (1873–1928), then from 1908 to 1942 by James Louis Garvin (1868–1947). The paper passed in 1911 to William Waldorf Astor (1848–1919), and was edited from 1948 to 1975 by David Astor (1912–2001), who commissioned work from writers such as George *Orwell and Vita *Sackville-West. In 1993 the *Observer* was bought by the group owning the **Guardian*.

O'CASEY, Sean (John Casey) (1880–1964) Irish playwright, born in Dublin into a lower-middle-class Protestant family. His education was interrupted by poor eyesight and he left school at 14. He worked at a variety of jobs, spending nine years from 1903 as a labourer on the Great Northern Railway of Ireland, meanwhile learning Irish, joining the Gaelic League and the Irish Republican Brotherhood, and developing an enthusiasm for the theatre through amateur dramatics and the plays of *Boucicault. He became secretary of the Irish Citizen Army in 1913 but resigned long before the organization took part in the 1916 Rising. He began to publish articles, songs, and broadsheets under the name of Seán Ó Cathasaigh; his first plays were rejected by the *Abbey Theatre, but he received encouragement from Lady *Gregory, and *The Shadow of a Gunman* was performed in 1923, followed by *Juno and the Paycock* in 1924; they were published together as *Two Plays* (1925). *The Plough and the Stars* provoked nationalist riots at the Abbey in 1926. All three plays deal with the rhetoric and dangers of Irish patriotism, with tenement life, self-deception, and survival; they are tragicomedies in which violence throws into relief the blustering masculine bravado represented by Jack Boyle and Joxer Daly in *Juno*, and the heroic resilience of Juno, or Bessie Burgess in *The Plough*. O'Casey moved to England in 1926; his alienation from Ireland was confirmed by a rift with W. B. *Yeats and the Abbey over its rejection of *The Silver Tassie* (1928), an experimental anti-war play about an injured footballer, which introduced the *Expressionist techniques employed in his later works. These include *Within the Gates* (1933), *Red Roses for Me* (1942), *Cock-a-Doodle Dandy* (1949), and *The Bishop's Bonfire* (1955); although none achieved the popularity of his Abbey plays, O'Casey continued to arouse both controversy and admiration, on stage and off. He also published a series of flamboyant autobiographies, in six volumes, beginning with *I Knock at the Door* (1939) and ending with *Sunset and Evening Star* (1954). See Christopher Murray, *Sean O'Casey: Writer at Work* (2004).

Oceana *See* COMMONWEALTH OF OCEANA.

Ocean to Cynthia, The A poem by Walter *Ralegh reflecting on his shifting relationship with *Elizabeth I. The title plays on Ralegh's name (Walter/Water). Edmund *Spenser in **Colin Clouts Come Home Againe* (1595) referred to Ralegh's authorship of 'a lamentable lay...Of *Cynthia* the Ladie of the sea, | Which from her presence faultlesse him debard'. Ralegh may have written a longer poem or sequence of poems on this theme; what survives in Ralegh's autograph is a 522-line piece 'The 21th: and last booke of the Ocean to Scinthia' and a 22-line fragment 'the beginninge of the 22 boock, entreating of Sorrow'. Cf. Walter Oakeshott, *The Queen and the Poet* (1960).

OCKHAM, William of (*c.*1287–1347) Philosopher and theologian, born at Ockham in Surrey. He joined the Franciscans and studied at Oxford, where he wrote a Commentary (known as the *Ordinatio*) on the first book of the *Sentences* of *Peter Lombard. A version of his commentary on Books II–IV (*c.*1317–19) also survives. The writings produced in the early part of his career include several important commentaries on the works of Aristotle, and a substantial *Summa Logicae* (completed by 1324). His intellectual resourcefulness and originality made his ideas controversial. In 1324 he was summoned by the pope to Avignon to answer charges of unorthodoxy, but although his writings were scrutinized, his ideas were not condemned. In 1328 he fled from Avignon along with the Franciscan general, Michael of Cesena, having taken the side of the Spiritual Franciscans in their dispute with Pope John XXII. He was excommunicated. Thereafter he remained with the emperor Louis of Bavaria, concerned with the question of papal power until his death in Munich in 1347. Ockham was influential in the fields of theology, philosophy, and political theory. The logical axiom associated with him is 'Ockham's Razor', namely the principle that (in W. J. Courtenay's words) 'plurality ought not to be posited without necessity'. His argument that shared characteristics do not exist apart from individuals influenced the later medieval philosophical tradition known as nominalism. His political writings addressed the relationship between ecclesiastical and secular power. See *Philosophical writings*, trans. P. Boehner (1957), rev. S. F. Brown (1990); *Predestination, God's Foreknowledge, and Future Contingents*, trans. M. M. Adams and N. Kretzmann (New York, 1969); *Quodlibetical Questions*, trans. A. J. Freddoso, 2 vols (1990); *A Short Discourse on Tyrannical Government*, ed. A. S. McGrade and J. Kilcullen (1992); *A Letter to the Friars Minor and Other Writings*, ed. A. S. McGrade and J. Kilcullen (1995).

O'CONNOR, Flannery (1925–64) American novelist and short story writer, born in Georgia, whose works offer examples of Southern *Gothic. *Wise Blood* (1952) is a novel about a violent young religious extremist and *The Violent Bear It Away* (1960) also deals with fanaticism, as do many of her short stories, collected as *The Complete Stories* (1971). Elizabeth *Bishop described her work as 'clear, hard, vivid, and full of… more real poetry than a dozen books of poems'. *Mystery and Manners* (1969) collects her miscellaneous prose.

O'CONNOR, Frank (1903–66) Pseudonym of Michael Francis O'Donovan, versatile Irish writer best known for his short stories and his translations and interpretations of Gaelic literature. O'Connor was born and brought up in poverty in Cork, where he was an active Republican until after the Civil War (1922–3). His collections include *Crab Apple Jelly* (1944), *Traveller's Samples* (1951), and *Domestic Relations* (1957). Realistic and closely observed, his stories offer a portrait of the middle and lower classes of Ireland, and of the 'warm dim odorous feckless evasive southern quality' of his native Cork, which as a young man he had shocked by his productions of plays by *Ibsen and *Chekhov, and by his support of *Joyce. He also wrote two volumes of autobiography, *An Only Child* (1961) and *My Father's Son* (1969). His critical works include *The Lonely Voice: A Study of the Short Story* (1962). His translation of Brian *Merriman's *Midnight Court* (1945), like much of his fiction, was banned in Ireland.

octosyllabics Verse lines of eight syllables, usually iambic tetrameters (*see* METRE) and often paired in rhyming couplets.

Odd Women, The A novel by George *Gissing, published 1893. To escape her dreary life in a draper's, Monica Madden, impoverished by the death of her father, marries the tyrannical Edmund Widdowson. Wrongly suspected by him of adultery, she dies giving birth to his daughter. Three of Monica's sisters also die (of tuberculosis, suicide, and a boating accident); two more become respectively an alcoholic and foolishly religious. While containing a portrayal of an establishment that promotes women's independence, the novel is a relentlessly grim look at the prospects of England's half a million more women than men, the 'Odd Women' of the title.
See NEW WOMAN FICTION.

ode A lyric poem of some length and elevated style on a serious subject, often celebrating a special event or hymning the qualities of some person, deity, or abstract entity. Odes are generally classified as either Pindaric or Horatian, depending upon their stanzaic structure and tone. The Pindaric ode—which is typically passionate, visionary, and sonorous—is modelled on the lyrics of *Pindar. Designed to be sung and danced by the Greek chorus either at a public festival or in a theatre, these lyrics were written in complex *stanzas which mirror the pattern of the dance and have a three-part structure: dancing to the left, the chorus chanted the strophe; dancing to the right, they repeated the pattern in the antistrophe; standing still, they brought the intricate pattern to a close in the epode, which had a different length and arrangement.

Unlike Pindarics, the Horatian ode (named after *Horace) tends to be meditative, tranquil, and colloquial. Horatian odes almost always repeat a single stanzaic form, and are typically shorter than the more declamatory Pindaric ode. Among the best-known Horatian odes are *Marvell's 'An Horatian Ode upon Cromwell's Return from Ireland', Thomas *Gray's 'Ode on a Distant Prospect of Eton College', and Keats's *'To Autumn'.

The first outstanding imitation of Pindar was *Jonson's 'To the Immortal Memory…of…Sir Lucius Cary and Sir H. Morison' (1629), with the three parts renamed as 'turn', 'counter-turn', and 'stand'. This was a 'regular ode' in that it closely followed Pindar's scheme of all strophes and antistrophes conforming to one stanzaic pattern, and all epodes following another. The Pindaric ode gained popularity in English with the publication of Abraham *Cowley's *Pindarique Odes* (1656), which attempted to capture the spirit of Pindar, rather than furnish an exact translation. In this work and in his original Pindaric compositions, beginning with the 'Ode, upon the Blessed Restoration and Return of His Sacred Majesty' (1660), Cowley developed the 'irregular ode', which abandoned Pindar's stanzaic rules, each stanza now developing its own pattern of rhythm, rhyme, and number of lines.

*Dryden's odes, 'To the Pious Memory...of Mrs. Anne Killigrew' (1686), 'Ode in Honour of St Cecilia's Day' (1687), and 'Alexander's Feast, or The Power of Musique' (1697), added to the reputation of the irregular Pindaric. Promising the would-be poet a freedom from formal constraints, the irregular ode, with its lofty manner, prosodic liberty, and intensity of feeling, attracted many writers in the 18th century, producing some fine examples, notably William *Collins's 'Ode to Liberty' (1746). Writing regular Pindaric odes, *Congreve and Gray worked against the prevailing trend; Gray's 'The *Progress of Poesy' and 'The *Bard' are two of the finest such works in English. From the mid-18th century onwards, it often becomes more difficult and less useful to distinguish between the Pindaric and Horatian styles, as poems indebted to both traditions became increasingly common.

The Romantic poets produced a remarkable number of outstanding odes, including S. T. *Coleridge's 'Dejection: An Ode'; William Wordsworth's 'Ode: *Intimations of Immortality...'; P. B. *Shelley's *'Ode to the West Wind' and 'To a Sky-Lark'; and Keats's *'Ode to a Nightingale' and *'Ode on a Grecian Urn'. With a few notable exceptions, such as Alfred *Tennyson's 'Ode on the Death of the Duke of Wellington' (1852), the Pindaric ode was not congenial to Victorian sensibilities, nor was it revived with much success in the 20th century. One of the most successful modern examples of the form is Allen *Tate's 'Ode to the Confederate Dead' (1927, 1937). See Carol Maddison, *Apollo and the Nine: A History of the Ode* (1960); John D. Jump, *The Ode* (1974).

'Ode on a Grecian Urn' A poem by John *Keats, written 1819, published 1820. While he describes the pastoral scenes of love, beauty, and joy illustrated on the urn, the poet reflects on the eternal quality of art—though its 'Cold Pastoral' is not without its ambiguities—and the fleeting nature of human love and happiness. The last two lines are particularly well known and their meaning much debated: 'Beauty is truth, truth beauty,—that is all | Ye know on earth, and all ye need to know.'

'Ode to a Nightingale' A poem by John *Keats, written 1819, published 1820. Keats's friend Charles Armitage Brown (1787–1842) relates that a nightingale had nested near his house in Hampstead (now known as Keats House), and that one morning Keats sat under a plum tree in the garden composing his ode on 'some scraps of paper'. Briefly, the poem is a meditation on the immortal beauty of the nightingale's song and the sadness of the observer, who must finally—as the price of his humanity—accept sorrow and mortality.

'Ode to Autumn' *See* 'To Autumn'.

'Ode to the West Wind' A poem by P. B. *Shelley, 'chiefly written in a wood that skirts the Arno, near Florence' in October 1819, published 1820. The ode is a passionate invocation to the spirit of the West Wind, both 'Destroyer and Preserver'. It is composed in five sweeping stanzaic movements, each taking the form of a sonnet, but with complex musical patterns of internal rhyme and run-on lines, culminating in a breathless series of cries or questions. The symbolism is rich. The Wind is the seasonal force of renewal in Nature; it is also the power that produces self-sacrifice (even self-destruction) in personal life, the 'unextinguished' political hopes that drive continually over the 'unawakened Earth', and the very passion of creativity itself. Shelley's observations of wind, water, wood, cloud, and sky combine imagery which is simultaneously scientific, mythical, and even biblical. The effect is one of hope and energy, achieved through suffering and despair.

ODETS, Clifford (1906–63) American dramatist, born in Philadelphia. He was a founder member in 1931 of the Group Theatre, which followed the naturalistic methods of the *Moscow Arts Theatre, and his reputation was made when it performed his short play *Waiting for Lefty* (1935), about a taxi-drivers' strike. This was followed in the same year by two other dramas of social conflict, *Till the Day I Die*, about the German communists and the rise of the Nazis, and *Awake and Sing!*, portraying struggle and tragedy in a poor Jewish family in the Bronx. Later works include *Clash by Night* (1941), *The Big Knife* (1948, an attack on the corruptions of Hollywood), and *The Country Girl* (1950, first known in Britain as *Winter Journey*), about an alcoholic actor's marriage. See Margaret Brenman-Gibson, *Clifford Odets—American Playwright: The Years from 1906–1940* (1981: no second volume).

O'DONOGHUE, Bernard (1945–) Irish poet, born in Cullen, Co. Cork, and brought up there and in Manchester. A medievalist, he is a fellow of Wadham College, Oxford. His four main collections are *The Weakness* (1991), *Gunpowder* (1995), *Here Nor There* (1999), and *Outliving* (2003). He has also published critical books and a translation of *Sir *Gawain and the Green Knight* (2006). Many of his poems are set in the north Cork landscape of his childhood and are haunted by a sense of the dignity, fragility, and unknowability of ordinary people. The more recent work confronts themes of ageing and exile. See *Selected Poems* (2008).

Odyssey An epic poem traditionally ascribed to *Homer, which relates the adventures of Odysseus on his return home to Ithaca ten years after the Trojan War. The local youth, assuming his death, compete to marry his wife

Penelope, infesting the house and exhausting the royal resources. His son Telemachus sets out to find him. Odysseus, meanwhile, has adventures in unknown seas and lands. He is freed by *Zeus from the nymph Calypso, shipwrecked, allured by the Sirens' deadly song, attacked by six-headed Scylla, and nearly drowned in the whirlpool Charybdis. The young Princess Nausicaa, finding him naked on the Phaeacian shore, takes him to her father. He relates his encounters since Troy, with the Lotus-Eaters, Polyphemus the Cyclops, Aeolus, ruler of the winds, the cannibal Laestrygonians, the enchantress Circe, and the land of the dead, where he met Achilles. His men slaughtered the cattle of the Sun; heaven shipwrecked and drowned them. The second half of the narrative, following Odysseus' return to Ithaca, is slower and more realistic; with Telemachus' help, he kills the suitors and reclaims wife and realm. In the Renaissance and later, the wily Odysseus under his Latin name Ulysses became something of a philosopher, as in Alfred *Tennyson's monologue. The most ambitious reworking of the story is by James *Joyce. Translators include Alexander *Pope (1725–26), William *Morris (1887), and Richmond Lattimore (1965). See M. I. Finley, *The World of Odysseus* (2nd edn, 1977).

OË, Kenzaburo (1935–) Japanese author who was awarded the *Nobel Prize for Literature in 1994. His best-known work in the West is *A Personal Matter* (1964), the shocking, powerful, and frank account of a teacher's discovery that he has become the father of a seriously brain-damaged child.

OED *See* OXFORD ENGLISH DICTIONARY.

Oedipus *See* SOPHOCLES.

O'FAOLAIN, Julia (1932–) Novelist and historian, daughter of Sean *O'Faolain, born in London but brought up in Dublin. She has lived in Ireland, England, Italy, and the United States. Her fiction includes a collection of short stories and eight novels, among which are *Women in the Wall* (1975), set in 6th-century Gaul and examining the phenomenon of nuns voluntarily immuring themselves; *No Country for Young Men* (1980), about history's difficult legacy in contemporary Ireland's private and public life; *The Obedient Wife* (1982); *The Irish Signorina* (1984); and *The Judas Cloth* (1992), a sweeping saga reconstructing the controversial career of the 19th-century pope Pius IX.

O'FAOLAIN, Sean (1900–91) Irish novelist, short story writer, and public intellectual, born in Cork, the son of a police constable. He was educated at University College, Cork, was a member of the Irish Republican Army during the War of Independence (1919–21), studied at Harvard for three years from 1926, and taught for a time in London before returning to Ireland in 1933. From 1940 to 1946 he edited the literary periodical *The Bell*, and served as director of the Arts Council of Ireland for two years from 1957. His first collection, *Midsummer Night Madness and Other Stories*, appeared in 1932. Early novels, such as *Bird Alone* (1936), deal with the parochialism of Irish society and the betrayal of nationalist hopes. He published biographies of Constance Markiewicz (1934), Daniel O'Connell (1938), Eamon de Valera (1939), and Hugh O'Neill (1942), and an essayistic study, *The Irish* (1947). An autobiography, *Vive-moi!*, appeared in 1964, and *Collected Stories* in 1981. His best-known stories evoke frustrated lives, missed opportunities, characters limited by their environment (as he had felt himself to be by provincial Cork); later stories (*The Heat of the Sun: Stories and Tales*, 1966; *The Talking Trees*, 1971), like his warmly received novel *And Again?* (1979), tend to be dryer, more amusing, and more resilient in tone.

***Of Dramatick Poesy:** An Essay* By John *Dryden, published 1668, in the form of a dialogue between Eugenius (Charles *Sackville), Crites (Sir Robert Howard, 1626–98), Lisideius (Sir Charles *Sedley), and Neander (Dryden himself), who take a boat on the Thames on the day of the battle between the English and Dutch navies in June 1665, and discuss the comparative merits of English and French drama, and of the old and new in English drama. Largely concerned with justifying Dryden's current practice as a playwright, the essay contains historically interesting appreciations of William *Shakespeare, John *Fletcher, and Ben *Jonson.

O'FLAHERTY, Liam (1896–1984) Novelist, story writer, and political radical who was born on Inishmore in the Aran Islands. His first novel, *Thy Neighbour's Wife* (1923), published with the encouragement of Edward *Garnett, was followed by several others, including *The Assassin* (1928), *Skerrett* (1932), *Famine* (1937), and *Insurrection* (1950). His best-known work, *The Informer* (1925), was filmed by his cousin John Ford in 1935. O'Flaherty's short stories, collected in such volumes as *Spring Sowing* (1924) and *Two Lovely Beasts* (1948), portray rural themes in elemental terms and are notable for their presentation of life, or more often death, as seen from an animal's point of view. O'Flaherty published three volumes of flamboyant memoirs: *Two Years* (1930), *I Went to Russia* (1931), and *Shame the Devil* (1934). *Dúil*, a collection of short stories in his native Irish, appeared in 1953. See *The Letters of Liam O'Flaherty*, ed. A. A. Kelly (1996).

Ogier the Dane A hero of the *Charlemagne romances, identified with a Frankish warrior, Autgarius, who fought against Charlemagne and then submitted to him. According to the romances, he is hostage for his father Gaufrey of Dannemarch at Charlemagne's court. He is linked with a number of legends, some of which include him among the *Paladins. The connection with Denmark is doubtful; 'Dannemarch' perhaps signifies the marches of the Ardennes. Nevertheless, as Holger Danské he became the subject of Danish folk song, identified as a national hero who fought with the Ostrogoth Dietrich of Bern (*c.*500).

OGILBY, John (1600–76) Scottish author, topographer, and printer, who published verse translations of *Virgil, *Aesop, and *Homer; also maps, atlases, and *Road Books of England and Wales*, the last of which were constantly revised until they faded into Mogg's *Road Books*.

O'GRADY, Standish James (1846–1928) Novelist, translator, and cultural commentator whose vision of the grandeur of the Irish past and argument for the necessity of Anglo-Irish Protestant leadership of the Catholic masses were crucially influential on the development of the *Irish Revival. He remained an important controversialist in cultural and political affairs until his removal to the Isle of Wight, for health reasons, in 1918.

O'HAGAN, Andrew (1968–) Scottish novelist, born in Glasgow and educated at the University of Strathclyde, who works as a contributing editor on the **London Review of Books* and **Granta*. He came to prominence with *The Missing* (1995), a speculative, partly autobiographical history of missing persons in late 20th-century Britain. *Our Fathers* (1999), his first novel, criticizes tropes of Scottish nationhood through its portrayal of a brutal and alcoholic Glaswegian father. *Personality* (2003) fictionalizes the career of 1970s child-star Lena Zavarone, while *Be Near Me* (2006) depicts the trials of a sensitive and snobbish priest assigned to a working-class Ayrshire parish. *The Atlantic Ocean* (2008) is a collection of essays on Britain and America.

O'HANLON, Redmond (1947–) Travel writer, born in Dorset and educated at Marlborough and Merton College, Oxford. His main areas of academic interest are literature and natural history, as the title of his first book, *Joseph Conrad and Charles Darwin* (1984), suggests. These authors are key reference points in his accounts of hazardous journeys undertaken in Indonesia (*Into the Heart of Borneo*, 1984), Amazonia (*In Trouble Again*, 1988), and Central Africa (*Congo Journey*, 1996), in which the promise of an encounter between the scholarly self-deprecating English narrator and the last representative of a lost tribe or vanishing species is never quite fulfilled. O'Hanlon's originality lies in his comic evocation, through dialogue, of the often tense relationships between himself and his travel companions and guides, a feature which also characterizes *Trawler* (2003), an account of two weeks spent with the crew of a fishing boat in the North Sea.

O'HARA, Frank (1926–66) American poet, born in Baltimore, who became one of the leading members of the *New York School. He was an art critic, serving as assistant curator in the Museum of Modern Art, and incorporated painterly techniques in his poems. His first volume was *A City Winter* (1951) and subsequent collections included *Lunch Poems* (1966). He also published prints and other graphic texts. See Brad Gooch, *City Poet* (1993).

O'HARA, John (1905–70) American novelist, born in Pennsylvania, the son of a doctor. More than 200 of his sharp, satiric short stories were published in the **New Yorker*, and were later collected under many different titles, from *The Doctor's Son* (1935) onwards. His novels, which gained wide popularity with their toughness, frankness, and sophistication, include *Appointment in Samarra* (1934), set in the country club and cocktail belt; *Butterfield 8* (1935), which evokes the promiscuity, violence, and hard drinking of Manhattan under prohibition; and *Pal Joey* (1940; later a musical), told in the form of letters from a nightclub singer. O'Hara also wrote a number of plays and screenplays. See Geoffrey Wolff, *The Art of Burning Bridges* (2003).

Oisin (Oisín) [pron. Uh-sheen] Known also as Ossian (*see* MACPHERSON, JAMES; FINGAL), a legendary Gaelic warrior and bard, son of *Finn. He is said to have returned to Ireland after 300 years in Tír na nÓg (The Land of Youth) and found his countrymen diminished in stature and weakened, a myth usually interpreted in relation to the supplanting of paganism by Christianity.

OKARA, Gabriel (1921–) Born in the Ijaw region of Nigeria; he began to decolonize language before the end of the colonial period. Educated in Nigeria and the USA, he was on the editorial staff of *Black Orpheus* and believed that African ideas needed to be translated almost literally from their African language. His novel *The Voice* (1964) is a challenging transliteration using Ijaw phrasing and syntax: 'Who are you people be?' In *The Fisherman's Invocation* (1978) and *The Dreamer, his Vision* (2005) his poems are poised between Africa and Europe. Unpublished manuscripts were destroyed during the Nigerian Civil War (Biafran War) of 1967–70.

O'KEEFFE, John (1747–1833) Actor and dramatist, born in Dublin; he studied art at the Royal Academy there. He visited London in 1762 and became devoted to the theatre, acting in Dublin and elsewhere in Ireland. Having played Lumpkin in **She Stoops to Conquer*, he produced *Tony Lumpkin's Ramble through Cork* (1773) and *Tony Lumpkin in Town* (1774). After the success of *The Son-in-Law* (1779), O'Keeffe moved to London permanently and produced about 50 farces and musical plays, often playing on his Irish background. His best-known works are *The Castle of Andalusia* (1782); *The Poor Soldier* (1783), which had great success in America; and *Wild Oats*, a romp of much intelligence and wit, produced at Covent Garden in 1791, and successfully revived in 1976. O'Keeffe wrote the song 'I am a friar of orders grey' (from his opera *Merry Sherwood*, 1795). William *Hazlitt described him as 'the English Molière'.

OKIGBO, Christopher (1932–67) An outstanding poet capable of interweaving modernist European and Ibo aesthetics, who was killed when serving as a major in the Nigerian Civil War (Biafran War). His degree from Ibadan was in classics, his family was Roman Catholic, and his grandfather was a priest of the Ibo god Idoto; his verse represents a quest to ritualize and explore the complex strands of his own identity, evoking T. S. *Eliot's *The Waste Land*. The separately published *Heavensgate* (1962), *Limits* (1964), *Silences* (1965), and *Path of Thunder* (1968) are all included in the posthumously published *Labyrinths* (1971) and *Collected Poems* (1986).

OKRI, Ben (1959–) Novelist and poet, born in Lagos, and educated at the University of Essex. His first novel, *Flowers and Shadows* (1980), was followed by *The Landscapes Within* (1981), revised and reissued as *Dangerous Love* (1996). *The Famished Road* (*Booker Prize, 1991) is a poetic, colourful novel narrated by a 'spirit child', Azaro, which blends myth, harsh contemporary reality, and a strong and epic sense of African place: *Songs of Enchantment* (1993) and *Infinite Riches* (1998) are sequels. Other prose works include the mythic *Astonishing the Gods* (1995), *Arcadia* (2002), and *Starbook* (2007). *Incidents at the Shrine* (1986) and *Stars of the New Curfew* (1989) are collections of short stories. *An African Elegy* (1992) is a collection of poems and *Mental Fight* (1999) is an epic poem. Okri is known for his political and social concerns as well as for his distinctively glowing prose, often composed of short, arresting sentences, which move from closely observed detail to the visionary and strange. He has also written occasional verse on topical issues.

OLCOTT, Colonel H. S. *See* BLAVATSKY, MADAME ELENA PETROVNA.

Old Bachelor, The The first comedy of William *Congreve, produced 1693. The 'Old Bachelor' is Heartwell, who is tricked into marrying Silvia, Vainlove's ex-mistress. To his relief the marriage proves invalid because the parson was Vainlove's friend Bellmour in disguise. Meanwhile Bellmour is carrying on an intrigue with Laetitia, the young wife of Fondlewife. Other characters are Sir Joseph Wittol, a foolish knight, who marries Silvia, thinking her the wealthy Araminta; and his companion, the cowardly bully Captain Bluffe. In the end Bellmour marries Belinda, whom he has been courting, in spite of her affectations, but Vainlove, who loves women only as long as they refuse him, finds that Araminta will not yet agree to marry him.

OLDCASTLE, Sir John, Baron Cobham (d. 1417) After association with the so-called 'Lollard knights', he aroused suspicion of heresy (*c.*1410–11) through contacts with Bohemia. Although tried and imprisoned, he escaped and attempted a revolt. Recaptured and executed in 1417, he appears as Falstaff in the **Henry IV* plays by William *Shakespeare.

Oldcastle, The First Part of Sir John A play first printed in 1600, reprinted in 1619 as *Shakespeare's, and included in the third and fourth *folios of his plays. It is certainly not by him, though the historical John *Oldcastle seems to have been Shakespeare's original model for *Falstaff. It is a collaborative work in which Anthony *Munday and Michael *Drayton among others had a hand. The play deals with the proceedings in Henry V's reign against Oldcastle as the chief supporter of the Lollards.

Old Curiosity Shop, The A novel by Charles *Dickens, published as a separate volume 1841. It was originally intended to be fitted into the framework of **Master Humphrey's Clock* (1840–41), but this narrative was soon abandoned.

Nell Trent lives in the grotesque atmosphere of the old curiosity shop kept by her grandfather, whom she devotedly tends. Reduced to poverty, he has borrowed money from Daniel Quilp, a hideous dwarf and a monster of iniquity, and this money he secretly expends in gambling, in the vain hope of retrieving his fortunes. Quilp, who believes him a rich miser, discovers his mistake, and seizes the shop. The old man and the child flee and wander about the country, suffering great hardships and haunted by the fear of being discovered by Quilp, who relentlessly pursues them. They finally find a haven in a cottage by a country church. The grandfather's brother, returning from abroad and anxious to relieve their needs, has difficulty in tracing them. At last he succeeds, but Nell, worn out with her troubles, has just died, and the grandfather soon follows her.

The novel contains a number of lively minor characters. Besides the grotesque Quilp (drowned on the point of being arrested), there are his associates, the attorney Sampson Brass and his grim sister Sally; the honest Kit Nubbles, devoted to Little Nell, who incurs the hatred of Quilp and is nearly transported through his machinations; Mr and Mrs Garland, the kindly couple who befriend Kit; the facetious Dick Swiveller; 'the Marchioness', the half-starved drudge in the Brass household (she finally marries Dick); Codlin and Short, the Punch and Judy men, whom Little Nell and her grandfather accompany for a time in their wanderings; and Mrs Jarley, of the waxworks.

The death of Little Nell, in its day one of the most celebrated scenes in fiction, later became the focus of much of the reaction against Dickens's use of pathos.

Oldenbarnavelt, Sir John van A historical tragedy, probably by John *Fletcher and Philip *Massinger, successively written, censored, rewritten, and acted in 1619, within three months of the execution of its real-life central character. Ralph Crane's transcript of this remarkable play was discovered by A. H. Bullen among the manuscripts of the British Museum, and printed in his *Old English Plays* (1883, vol. ii). It deals with contemporary events in the Netherlands. Oldenbarnavelt, the great lawyer, disturbed by the growing power of Prince Maurice of Nassau and the army, conspires against him and raises companies of burghers in the towns to resist the army. The plot is discovered, the companies disarmed, and

Oldenbarnavelt's principal associates are captured. One of these, Leidenberch, confesses. Oldenbarnavelt, who by virtue of his great position is still left at liberty though suspect, reproaches him and tells him that death is the only honourable course left to him. Leidenberch, in remorse, takes his own life. The prince, who had counselled moderation, now convinced of the gravity of the conspiracy, advises severe measures. Oldenbarnavelt is arrested, tried, and executed. A transcript by T. H. Howard-Hill was published by the *Malone Society in 1980, and the play is printed in vol. viii (1992) of Fredson Bowers's edition of the plays in the Beaumont and Fletcher canon.

Old Fortunatus A comedy by Thomas *Dekker, written 1599, published 1600, based on a story contained in a German 'Volksbuch' of 1509 and dramatized by Hans *Sachs in 1553. The beggar Fortunatus, encountering Fortune, is offered the choice between wisdom, strength, health, beauty, long life, and riches, and chooses the last. He receives a purse from which he can at any time draw ten pieces of gold. He goes on his travels, in the course of which he secures the marvellous hat of the soldan of Turkey, which transports the wearer wherever he wishes to go. But at the height of his success Fortune steps in and puts an end to his life. His son Andelocia, refusing to learn from his father's fate and equipped with the purse and hat, has a series of adventures at the court of Athelstane, loses his talismans, and meets a miserable death.

OLDHAM, John (1653–83) Poet and translator, educated at St Edmund Hall, Oxford. He published several Pindaric *odes, but is chiefly remembered for his ironical *Satire against Virtue* (1679) and *Satires upon the Jesuits* (1681). He also translated and wrote imitations of *Juvenal, *Horace, *Bion, *Moschus, and Nicholas *Boileau. His *Poems and Translations* were collected in 1683. He died young of smallpox, and John *Dryden commemorated him and his verse in the well-known lines beginning 'Farewell, too little and too lately known'.

Old Manor House, The A novel by Charlotte *Smith, published 1794. Smith's most successful novel, fusing elements of realism, *romance, and the *Gothic, tells the love story of Orlando and Monimia against the background of the destiny of Rayland Hall, the old manor house. It contains a fine satirical portrait of Mrs Rayland, ridiculously proud of her ancestry.

OLDMIXON, John (?1673–1742) Whig historian and pamphleteer, who also wrote plays and poems. He published *The British Empire in America* (1708), *The Secret History of Europe* (1712–15, anonymously), and histories of England during the Stuart reigns (1729) and those of William III, Anne, and George I (1735–9). He attacked Jonathan *Swift, and Alexander *Pope, who returned fire in *Peri Bathous* and *The *Dunciad*. His *Memoirs of the Press* (1742) records the disappointments of his literary life.

OLD MOORE (Francis Moore) (1657–?1714) Astrologer, licensed physician, and Whig partisan, who had an astrological practice in Lambeth, later in Southwark. His *Vox Stellarum, an Almanac for 1698 with Astrological Observations* appeared in 1697. *Old Moore's Almanack* long outlived its creator, and sold extremely well throughout the 18th and 19th centuries. It still survives, thanks to its reputation for sensationalism and prophecy.
See ALMANACS.

Old Mortality A novel by Walter *Scott, published 1816 in **Tales of my Landlord*, 1st series. 'Old Mortality' is the nickname of Robert Paterson who, towards the end of the 18th century, travels through Scotland cleaning and repairing the tombs of the Cameronians, a sect of fanatical Covenanters who took up arms for their religion against Charles II. The novel, one of Scott's masterpieces, tells the story of young Henry Morton of Milnwood, a moderate Presbyterian of courage and integrity who, like many of Scott's heroes, finds himself drawn into a struggle which at first he only imperfectly understands, in which both sides are equally capable of bravery and fanaticism. The action takes place in the period between the uprising of the Covenanters at Drumclog and their defeat at Bothwell Bridge three weeks later, with a final section several years after.

OLDS, Sharon (1942–) American poet, born in San Francisco, who had a Calvinist upbringing, and whose collections have received many awards, notably the T. S. *Eliot Prize. *The Father* (1992) focuses on her father's death from cancer. Her work has drawn comparison with Walt *Whitman in its celebration of the body.
See also WICKS, SUSAN.

Old Vic Theatre (previously the Royal Victoria) A theatre in the Waterloo Road, London, long famous for its notable productions of Shakespeare's plays under the management of Lilian Baylis (1874–1937), who took it over in 1912, and, from 1963, for over ten years the home of the National Theatre Company.

Old Wife's Tale, The A play largely in prose by George *Peele, published 1595. The play is a satire on the romantic dramas of the time, the first English work of this kind. Two brothers are searching for their sister Delia, who is held captive by the magician Sacrapant. The brothers also fall into his hands. They are all rescued by the knight Eumenides aided by the ghost of Jack the Giant-Killer, grateful because the knight had borne the expense of Jack's funeral. The play is rich in songs and magical invocations.

OLIPHANT, Laurence (1829–88) Born in Cape Town of Scottish descent; after a desultory education and extensive travel with his parents, he became a barrister in Ceylon, where his father was chief justice. *A Journey to Khatmandu* (1852) and *The Russian Shores of the Black Sea* (1853–4) recount some of his adventures. He was secretary to Lord Elgin in Washington, Canada, and China; the latter is described in *A Narrative of the Earl of Elgin's Mission to China 1857–9* (1859). He acted as *The *Times* correspondent in Circassia during the Crimean and Franco-Prussian Wars. His novel *Piccadilly* (1870) satirizes London society. He was an MP during 1865–7, but fell under the influence of American 'prophet' Thomas Lake Harris (1823–1906), whose Brotherhood of New Life in New York state he joined, surrendering to him most of his property. His allegiance to Harris ended in 1882, in which year Oliphant and his wife founded a community for Jewish immigrants in Haifa.

OLIPHANT, Margaret (1828–97) Née Wilson, a prolific Scottish writer, author of more than 100 books and innumerable articles. Born in Wallyford, near Edinburgh, she was educated at home. Early widowed, she was compelled to write for an income, both for her own and for her brother's families. Throughout her life, she supported her family with her pen. In 1849 she published *Passages in the Life of Mrs Margaret Maitland*, a tale of Scotland which had an encouraging reception; *Caleb Field*, a historical novel, appeared in 1851; and among her many domestic romances *The Athelings* (1857) was probably the most interesting. In 1862 appeared her biography of the brilliant heretical preacher Edward Irving (1792–1834) and in 1891 a life of Laurence *Oliphant (no relation). Her 'Chronicles of Carlingford' proved her most lasting success. Carlingford is a quiet country town near London, and this series of novels (the most notable of which are *Salem Chapel*, 1863; *The Perpetual Curate*, 1864; *Miss Marjoribanks*, 1866; and *Phoebe Junior*, 1876) is set among the aristocracy, professional families, and tradesmen of the town. Religious themes predominate, but the books are sharp and humorous, and she became one of the most popular novelists of her generation. Her other most interesting group of books, *Stories of the Seen and Unseen*, all connected in some way with death and the experience of the soul, began with *A Beleaguered City* (1880) which was followed by *A Little Pilgrim* (1882) and others. Her astute *Literary History of England* (1882) earned much praise, but the continuing stream of undemanding romances and novels of domestic life brought little further success, and her family was shadowed by misfortune and loss (her children all predeceased her). Her long association with **Blackwood's* was commemorated in the posthumous *Annals of a Publishing House* (1897). Her autobiography (1899) describes the destructive necessity of having to write so much, and movingly records the domestic tragedies that haunted her life. See E. Jay, *Mrs Oliphant: A Fiction to Herself* (1995).

Olive A novel by Dinah *Craik, published in 1850. It tells the story of Olive Rothesay, a disabled girl, resented by her mother and slighted by her father, who struggles with adversity in order to become a successful artist. Having rejected the marriage proposal of her misogynistic tutor, she finally becomes the happy wife of her friend's widower, and the adoptive mother of his daughter. Like **Jane Eyre*, with which it shares many preoccupations, the novel describes a process of intellectual and emotional growth which allows a disadvantaged young woman to value herself, and then to be valued. It has recently attracted the attention of scholars interested in fictional representations of disability.

Oliver In the *Charlemagne cycle of legends, one of Charlemagne's *Paladins. He is the close friend of *Roland, with whom he has a prolonged and undecided single combat (the origin of their comradeship), and is his equal in bravery, but more prudent. At the battle of Roncesvalles he urges Roland to summon help by sounding his horn, but Roland postpones doing so till too late. Oliver's sister Aude is betrothed to Roland.

Oliver Twist A novel by Charles *Dickens, published 1837–8. Oliver Twist is the name given to a child of unknown parentage born in a workhouse and brought up under ruthless conditions. Bumble, the parish beadle, is especially callous. Here Dickens demonstrates his hostility to Benthamism, and to the provisions of the 1834 New Poor Law. Unhappily apprenticed to an undertaker, Oliver runs away, reaches London, and falls into the hands of a gang of thieves, ruled by the old Jew Fagin. The burglar Bill Sikes, his mistress Nancy, and 'the Artful Dodger', an impudent young pickpocket, are also members of the gang. He is temporarily rescued by the benevolent Mr Brownlow, but kidnapped by the gang, acting on behalf of the sinister Monks, who wants to ensure Oliver's degradation. Oliver is forced to accompany Bill Sikes on a burglary, is wounded, and encounters the kindly Mrs Maylie and her protégée Rose, who take him in. The good-hearted Nancy reveals to Rose that Monks knows about Oliver's parentage, and wishes all proof of it destroyed. Enquiry is set on foot. Nancy's action is discovered by the gang, and she is brutally murdered by Bill Sikes. A hue and cry is raised; Sikes, trying to escape, accidentally hangs himself. The rest of the gang are caught, and Fagin executed. Monks, discovered and threatened with exposure, confesses that he is the half-brother of Oliver, and has pursued his ruin, animated by hatred and the desire to retain the whole of his father's property. Rose is the sister of Oliver's unfortunate mother. Oliver is adopted by Mr Brownlow. Monks emigrates and dies in prison. Bumble ends his career in the workhouse over which he formerly ruled.

Dickens resented the implication that this work made crime glamorous, and in a preface to the third edition (April 1841) dissociated it from the popular *'Newgate novels' of the period, by Harrison *Ainsworth, Edward *Bulwer-Lytton, and others. It has remained among the most popular and widely known of his works, and television, stage, and film adaptations have been numerous.

Olivia The only novel written by Dorothy *Bussy, which she published anonymously in 1949 with the *Hogarth Press. Set in a girls' school, it depicts a lesbian relationship between two teachers and its impact on the pupils. Though Bussy denied it was autobiographical, it draws on her own experiences in the schools of Marie Souvestre both in France and England.

OLIVIER, Edith (1872–1948) Novelist, biographer, and country writer. Her novels include *The Love Child* (1927), *Dwarf's Blood* (1931), and *The Seraphim Room* (1932), all of which combine fantasy with social observation to unusual and often disconcerting effect. Her love of Wiltshire is recorded in a series of country books, and in her autobiography, *Without Knowing Mr Walkley* (1938). Though not young in the 1930s, she was a central figure in the group known as the Bright Young Things, forming close friendships with Rex Whistler (1905–44) and Cecil Beaton (1904–80).

OLSEN, Tillie (1912–2007) American writer, born in Nebraska, whose works explore a range of feminist issues. *Tell Me a Riddle* (1961) collects four short stories and *Yonnondio* (1974) is an unfinished novel which she started in the 1930s. Her influential non-fiction volume *Silences* (1978) explores writer's block and other topics.

OLSON, Charles (1910–70) American poet, born in Worcester, Massachusetts, who became the central figure among the writers at *Black Mountain College, North Carolina. Olson's theory of Objectism derives from the philosophy of A. N. Whitehead (1861–1947) and posits a perceptual field, whose consequences he outlined in the influential essay 'Projective Verse'. Olson began publishing poetry in the late 1940s but his major sequence was *The Maximus Poems*, which he worked on serially from 1953 until his death (complete edition published 1980), named after a 4th-century Phoenician mystic. The sequence combines myth, the history of migration, and New England lore centring on Gloucester, articulated through long poetical lines deriving from Walt *Whitman and Ezra *Pound. Olson's correspondence with Robert *Creeley was published in ten volumes (1980–96). See Tom Clark, *Charles Olson* (1991).

Olympia Press A Paris-based imprint founded in 1953 by Maurice Girodias (1920–90), son of writer and publisher Jack Kahane (1887–1939), owner of the Obelisk Press. It published many English-language literary and pornographic works then censored in England, some of which were pseudonymous, including books by Christopher *Logue and Alexander Trocchi (1925–84). Girodias also published Vladimir *Nabokov's *Lolita* (1955), William *Burroughs's *Naked Lunch* (1959), and work by Henry *Miller and British experimentalist Paul Ableman (1927–2006). Olympia Press eventually merged in the late 1960s with the US-based Grove Press.

O'MALLEY, Ernie (1897–1957) Irish revolutionary whose laconic guerrilla war memoir *On Another Man's Wound* (1936) was praised by John *McGahern and others. O'Malley conducted a number of close literary friendships, notably with Hart *Crane and Louis *MacNeice, who portrayed him as Aidan in *Autumn Sequel*. See Richard English, *Ernie O'Malley: IRA Intellectual* (1998).

Omar Khayyám, The Rubáiyát of A 'translation' by Edward *FitzGerald of the *rubais* or quatrains attributed to a 12th-century Persian poet. The 'translation' was first published anonymously in 1859; FitzGerald produced further editions, revised and with added quatrains, in 1868, 1872, and 1879. The work is in fact part translation, part inspired by the originals, and part invention. Sceptical of divine providence, suspicious of human grandeur, and concentrating on the pleasures of the fleeting moment, the poem includes felicitously phrased aphorisms which are among the most frequently quoted lines in English poetry.

ONDAATJE, Michael (1943–) Canadian poet and novelist, born in Sri Lanka. He moved to Canada in 1962, and was educated at the University of Toronto and at Queen's University, Kingston, Ontario; he taught English at the University of Western Ontario from 1967 to 1970 and then at Glendon College, York University, Toronto. He first came to critical notice as a poet with *The Dainty Monsters* (1967), and has continued to publish collections of his poetry, including *Rat Jelly* (1973), *There's a Trick with a Knife I'm Learning to Do* (1979), and *Handwriting* (1998). In *The Collected Works of Billy the Kid* (1970), a collage of poetry and prose and visual devices, he uses temporal dislocation and multiple viewpoints to present an amalgamation of history, fiction, and autobiography. *Coming through Slaughter* (1976) is a fictionalized life of the legendary jazz musician Charles 'Buddy' Bolden (1876–1931). In *Running in the Family* (1982), blurring the boundaries between autobiography and fiction, Ondaatje drew on his family's Sri Lankan past to produce 'not a history but a portrait or "gesture" '. *The English Patient* (1992), set at the end of the Second World War, focuses on an enigmatic Englishman, burnt beyond recognition in a plane crash, who is being tended by a nurse in a villa outside Florence; as his past emerges through his drifting memories, a multi-layered story of love, desire, and damaged lives unfolds. The novel won the *Booker Prize and was made into a hugely successful film (1996) directed by Anthony Minghella. Subsequent novels include *Anil's Ghost* (2000), a narrative set amidst the conflicts of contemporary Sri Lanka, and *Divisadero* (2007).

One Flew over the Cuckoo's Nest 1962 Novel by Ken *Kesey, set in the mental ward of an American hospital presided over by Big Nurse. Its surreal presentation of resistance to authority by the inmate McMurphy made it a classic of the counter-culture of the sixties. There was a stage version in 1963, and in 1975 it was made into a successful film, starring Jack Nicholson.

O'NEILL, Eugene (1888–1953) American dramatist, born in New York. He had a varied career (as seaman, gold prospector, journalist, and actor) before associating himself (1916) with the experimental Provincetown Players, which staged several of his early one-act plays, including *Bound East for Cardiff* (1916) and *The Moon of the Caribbees* (1918). His first big success was the full-length naturalistic drama *Beyond the Horizon* (1920), which was followed in the same year by his expressionistic *The Emperor Jones* (1920), a tragedy which describes the rise and fall of the black 'emperor' of a West Indian island, and *Anna Christie* (1921), a naturalistic study of a prostitute on the New York waterfront and her redemption. Among other important plays of this period were *The Hairy Ape* (1922), *All God's Chillun Got Wings* (1924), and *Desire under the Elms* (1924). O'Neill's criticism of contemporary materialistic values was powerfully and poetically expressed in *The Fountain* (1925), *The Great God Brown* (1926), *Lazarus Laughed* (1927), and *Marco Millions* (1927). He experimented with a *stream-of-consciousness technique in *Strange Interlude* (1928), and adapted the theme of the **Oresteia* to the aftermath of the American Civil War in his trilogy *Mourning Becomes Electra* (1931). *Ah! Wilderness* (1932) and *Days without End* (1934) were followed by a long absence from the stage, during which he was awarded the *Nobel Prize (1936) and worked on several plays, including *The Iceman Cometh* (1946), a lengthy naturalistic tragedy presenting a collection of down-and-out alcoholics in a Bowery saloon. His masterpiece, *Long Day's Journey into Night*, was written in 1940–41, and posthumously produced and published in 1956; it is a semi-autobiographical family tragedy, portraying the mutually destructive relationships of drug-addicted Mary Tyrone, her ex-actor husband James, and their two sons, hard-drinking Jamie and intellectual Edmund. Despite occasional lapses into melodrama and rhetoric, O'Neill's plays remain powerfully theatrical and original; he transcends his debt to *Ibsen and *Strindberg, producing an oeuvre in which the struggle between self-destruction, self-deception, and redemption is presented as essentially dramatic in nature. See John Patrick Diggins, *Eugene O'Neill's America* (2007).

onomatopoeia The formation of a word by an imitation of the sound associated with the object or action designated: as 'hurlyburly', 'buzz', 'creak'. The term is also applied to the use of a combination of words to evoke by sound a certain image or mood, the most frequently quoted example being Alfred *Tennyson's 'murmuring of innumerable bees'.

opera A staged dramatic performance in which music forms an essential part of the performance. It is normally on secular themes, is acted, and has scenery, features which distinguish it from oratorio. Conventionally, opera is characterized by recitatives (a kind of sung declamation), solo arias, duets, and choruses, sung to orchestral accompaniment. In opera, music is a fully integrated aspect of performance, whereas in the *masque, music is generally episodic and ornamental. Opera developed from experiments in the *stile recitativo* (the 'reciting style') made by a group of cultured intellectuals at the Medici court in Florence towards the end of the 16th century. *Orfeo* (1607), by Claudio Monteverdi (1567–1643), is sometimes regarded as the earliest true opera. The earliest attempts at opera in English were somewhat obstructed by the closing of the public theatres in the Interregnum, but the first English work that is normally regarded as an opera is *The Siege of Rhodes* (1656), of which the text was by Sir William *D'Avenant: the music, a collaboration between several composers, is lost. The first English example of which the music has survived is John *Blow's *Venus and Adonis* (*c*.1684), a genuine opera in miniature which preceded Henry *Purcell's *Dido and Aeneas* by some five years. Purcell's text was by Nahum *Tate, and fully-fledged operas were, in the 18th and 19th centuries, normally written to a specific *libretto rather than adapted from a stage play. Not all operas are sung throughout: the English *ballad opera of the 1730s and the comic operettas of *Gilbert and Sullivan in the 1890s have prose dialogue interspersed with songs. In the late 19th century English composers began attempting to revive opera as a serious form, and though Hubert *Parry's opera *Guenever* (1886), written under the dominating influence of Richard *Wagner, was not performed, and Edward *Elgar failed to complete his *Spanish Lady*, subsequent notable operas were produced by Gustav *Holst, Ralph *Vaughan Williams, and Frederick *Delius. The most successful English opera composer of the 20th century was Benjamin *Britten, who collaborated with W. H. *Auden and E. M. *Forster on several projects. Michael *Tippett, Peter Maxwell *Davies, and Harrison *Birtwistle have also continued the tradition. Opera has however more usually been associated with the European musical tradition of *Mozart and *Beethoven, and with specialist composers such as *Donizetti, *Rossini, Vincenzo Bellini (1801–35), *Puccini, and *Verdi. Claude *Debussy and Richard *Strauss are among the other composers of opera on themes from literature; the Russian tradition of literary opera includes *Tchaikovsky, *Stravinsky, *Prokofiev, and *Shostakovich.

OPIE, Amelia (1769–1853) Novelist and poet, and friend of Sydney *Smith, Richard Brinsley *Sheridan, Madame de *Staël, and many other writers. Born in Norwich, the daughter of a doctor and leading luminary in the town's literary society, she was brought up in the tradition of 'rational dissent'. She came to know William *Godwin and Mary *Wollstonecraft, though her politics lacked their overt radicalism. The suggestion that Godwin asked her to marry him is probably without foundation. In 1798 she became the wife of John Opie the Cornish painter. Her works include *The Father and Daughter* (1801); *Poems* (1802); *Simple Tales* (1806); a *Memoir* of her husband in 1809; *Valentine's Eve* (1816); *Madeline* (1822); and *Lays for the Dead* in 1833. After her husband's death she returned to Norwich from London and became a devout Quaker. She published several spiritual and moral works such as *Illustrations of Lying* (1825) and *Detraction Displayed* (1828). Her most notable fiction is **Adeline Mowbray*, suggested by the story of Mary Wollstonecraft. She was a copious novelist and poet, and was satirized by T. L. Peacock in **Headlong Hall* as Miss Poppyseed, 'an indefatigable compounder of novels'.

OPIE, Iona (1923–) and **Peter** (1918–82) Authors, folklorists, and collectors specializing in childhood who produced distinguished works including the *Oxford Dictionary of Nursery Rhymes* (1951), *The Lore and Language of Schoolchildren* (1959), and *Children's Games in Street and Playground* (1969). Edited anthologies include *The Oxford Book of Children's Verse* (1973). After Peter's death Iona published *The People in the Playground* (1993) and *Children's Games with Things* (1997).

OPPEN, George (1908–84) American poet, born in New Rochelle, New York, who became a member of the 1930s Objectivist group, which included William Carlos *Williams and Louis *Zukofsky. Oppen abandoned poetry to help in the fight against Fascism, returning to poetry after the Second World War and publishing *The Materials* (1962) among other volumes.

OPPENHEIM, E. Phillips *See* SPY FICTION.

ORAGE, Alfred Richard (1875–1934) Literary editor. From 1907 till 1922 he edited the political and literary weekly the *New Age*. Its contributors included Ezra *Pound and T. E. *Hulme. In 1931 he founded the *New English Weekly*. See Wallace Martin, *'The New Age' under Orage* (1967).

Ó RATHAILLE, Aodhagán (Egan O'Rahilly) (*c*.1670–1729) Born in Kerry, central figure in the *aisling tradition. Ó Rathaille's impassioned, intricately musical lyrics lament the fate of the aristocratic Gaelic order of Munster in the aftermath of the Williamite wars. They have been translated by James Clarence *Mangan, Frank *O'Connor, Seamus *Heaney, and others, and are cited in a variety of ways in the poetry of W. B. *Yeats, Hugh *MacDiarmid, and Thomas *Kinsella.

ORCZY, Baroness (Mrs Montague Barstow) (1865–1947) Hungarian-born novelist who lived from the age of 15 in London. She achieved best-seller status with her romantic novel *The Scarlet Pimpernel* (1905), the story of the League of the Scarlet Pimpernel, a band of Englishmen pledged to rescue innocent victims of the reign of terror in Paris. Its leader, Sir Percy Blakeney, outwits his opponents—in particular the wily Chauvelin—by means of his courage and ingenious disguises, at the same time concealing his identity from his friends in England. The success of the novel followed its success in a dramatized version, written by Orczy in collaboration with her husband. It was performed first in Nottingham in 1903, then, to great acclaim, in London in 1905. She wrote many other historical and romantic novels, including several sequels to *The Scarlet Pimpernel*.

Ordeal of Richard Feverel, The A novel by George *Meredith, published 1859. Meredith's first mature work, written just after the painful collapse of his first marriage, it exhibits his theory of 'comedy', and the growing luxuriance of his style. Its treatment of sexual themes meant that it was boycotted by *Mudie's Lending Library, limiting its early sales, and damaging Meredith's reputation. Sir Austin Feverel's wife runs off with a poet, leaving him with their son Richard. The obtuse Sir Austin devises a 'System' for Richard's education, which consists in keeping the boy at home (for schools are corrupting) and in trusting to authoritarian parental vigilance. The slow collapse of the 'System', and Richard's struggle for freedom and knowledge, form the underlying theme of the book. Richard and Lucy Desborough, a neighbouring farmer's niece, fall in love at first sight, and an idyllic courtship ends in the discovery of their attachment. Lucy lacks the birth Sir Austin requires for his son. His attempts to separate the young couple result in their secret marriage and the fury of the possessive Sir Austin. Ordered to await his father in London, Richard becomes entangled with a courtesan, while the predatory Lord Mountfalcon attempts to ensnare Lucy. Overcome with shame at his treatment of his wife, Richard hears that he is a father and that Lucy and Sir Austin are reconciled. But on returning he learns of the designs of Lord Mountfalcon; he challenges him to a duel and is seriously wounded. In the succeeding fever his confusions are stripped away and he is finally freed of his devouring father. These events overwhelm Lucy, who loses her mind and dies.

ORDERICUS VITALIS (1075–1142/3) Born near Shrewsbury of a Norman father and probably English mother, a monk of Saint-Évroul in Normandy. His Latin *Ecclesiastical History of England and Normandy* (written 1114–41), one of the standard authorities for the Norman period, covers events from the beginning of the Christian era down to 1141. His sympathies and interests are largely invested in English matters.

Oresteia, The A trilogy of plays by *Aeschylus. *Agamemnon* describes the return to Argos after the Trojan War of the victorious Agamemnon, brother of Helen's husband Menelaus, and his murder by his wife Clytemnestra, foretold by his captive, the prophetess Cassandra, daughter of King Priam of Troy. *The Libation Bearers* (*Choephoroe*) portrays the vengeance of the son and daughter of Agamemnon, Orestes and Electra: Orestes murders Clytemnestra and her lover Aegisthus, and is himself pursued by the Furies (Erinyes). The *Eumenides* shows the Furies in pursuit of Orestes, who is protected by the younger god Apollo. Orestes is tried, Athena, goddess of wisdom, delivers her casting vote on his behalf, and he goes free, released from the ancient blood vengeance: Athena reconciles the Furies to the new Law, and they are transformed into the Kindly Ones (Eumenides), who bless the city of Athens.

Other versions of the story appear in the works of *Sophocles (who wrote *Electra*) and *Euripides, and it reappears in many forms throughout Western literature; there are notable 20th-century dramatic versions by *T. S. Eliot (*The Family Reunion*, 1939), Eugene *O'Neill (*Mourning Becomes Electra*, 1931), and Jean-Paul *Sartre (*Les Mouches*, 1943).

Orfeo, Sir A metrical romance of the early 14th century in about 600 lines (the poem varies considerably in its three manuscript versions), identified in its prologue as a *Breton lay. It represents the story of Orpheus and Eurydice (*see* ORPHEUS) in a Celtic guise: Queen Heurodys is carried off to fairyland and pursued by King Orfeo whose melodious playing of his harp succeeds in bringing her back to the world of men. The Middle English version (to which Francis Child's ballad 'King Orfeo' is related) ends happily: the queen's return is permanent, and the steward left in charge of the kingdom by Orfeo during his absence passes the romance test of his fidelity. The poem is admired as one of the most charming and interesting of Middle English romances. It has been edited by A. J. Bliss (1954; rev. 1966).

oriental novel (oriental tale) A class of story set in the Middle or Far East, especially popular in the 18th century. Public interest in the Orient (encompassing Egypt, India, and Japan) as a zone of powerful fantasy was stimulated by Richard *Knolles's influential history of the Turks; by the translation into English in 1705–8 of the **Arabian Nights*; and by the translations of Sir William *Jones. Oriental parables developed from 18th-century periodical essays into short novels. Many of the tales (such as those of Alexander *Dow, John *Hawkesworth, James Ridley (1736–65), and Frances *Sheridan, and William *Beckford's **Vathek*) relate the flamboyant adventures of well-defined heroes and villains, often with supernatural intervention. Johnson's **Rasselas* uses a lavish oriental setting to promote a realistic moral fable. Later such locations were explored with ambiguous relish in poems such as Robert *Southey's *The Curse of Kehama* (1810), Thomas *Moore's **Lalla Rookh*, and Lord *Byron's *The *Corsair* and *The *Giaour*.

ORIGEN (*c.*184/5–*c.*253/4) A great Christian theologian and biblical critic in the Alexandrian school, and compiler of the famous *Hexapla* versions of the Old Testament. He studied under Ammonius, sometimes regarded as the founder of *Neoplatonism, and he is of great importance as the introducer of Neoplatonic elements into Christianity. His *Principles*, which were rejected by church orthodoxy, were translated by St *Jerome and quoted by St *Bernard, and he influenced the allegorical method of literary criticism developed by St *Augustine. See Jean Daniélou, *Origen*, trans. Walter Mitchell (1955).

Origin of Species, On the The great work of Charles *Darwin, published in 1859. Its full title was *On the Origin of Species by Means of Natural Selection, or the Preservation of Favoured Races in the Struggle for Life*.

ORIGO, Iris (1902–88) Née Cutting, historian and biographer. Her wealthy American father died in 1910, and mother and daughter then settled in Italy; Iris was mostly educated at home. In 1924 Iris married Marchese Antonio Origo. Among her twelve books in English are a biography of Giacomo *Leopardi (1935; rev. 1953); *War in Val d'Orcia* (1947), a vivid and moving account of wartime events in her part of Italy; *The Last Attachment* (1949), chronicling Lord *Byron's last years; and *The Merchant of Prato: Francesco di Marco Datini* (1957), a lively and meticulous study of a 14th-century merchant-banker. See Caroline Moorehead, *Iris Origo, Marchesa of Val d'Orcia* (2000).

Orinda *See* PHILIPS, KATHERINE.

Ó RÍORDÁIN, Seán (1916–77) Poet, born in Irish-speaking area of west Cork, and educated, as he mordantly observed, by tuberculosis. His ground-breaking debut *Eireaball Spideoige* ('A Robin's Tail', 1952) is at once deeply attuned to the traditions of Gaelic Munster and responsive—in rhythm as well as idiom—to the example of Gerard Manley *Hopkins and T. S. *Eliot. The lyrics of *Brosna* ('Firewood', 1964) are generally shorter and less disjunctive in style. Ó Ríordáin's is a poetry of tortured interiority, leavened by an impish wit. A Catholic sense of unworthiness coexists with religious doubt and scepticism with regard to the philosophical basis of the selfhood pursued in the poetry and in the partly published journal he kept from 1940 until his death. Ó Ríordáin has been translated by Ciaran *Carson, Patrick Crotty, Greg Delanty, and others.

Orlando furioso A poem by *Ariosto, published in its complete form in 1532, designed to exalt the house of *Este and its legendary ancestor Rogero (Ruggiero) and to continue the story of Orlando's love for Angelica begun by Boiardo in **Orlando innamorato*.

Saracens and Christians, in the days of *Charlemagne, are at war. The Saracens under Agramant, king of Africa, are besieging Charlemagne in Paris with the help of Marsilio, the Moorish king of Spain, and two mighty warriors, *Rodomont and Mandricardo. Angelica, who at the end of Boiardo's poem had been left by Charlemagne to the care of Namo, escapes. Orlando, chief of the Paladins, a perfect knight, invincible and invulnerable, hopelessly infatuated with Angelica, forgets his duty and pursues her. Angelica meets with various adventures, finally coming upon the wounded Moorish youth Medoro, whom she tends, falls in love with, and marries. They honeymoon in the woods. Orlando, arriving there by chance and learning their story, is seized with a furious and grotesque madness, and runs naked through the country, destroying everything in his path. He is finally captured by his own companions and miraculously cured of his madness and his love. In a conclusive battle of three against three on the island of Lampedusa he kills Agramant.

Although the madness of Orlando gives the poem its name, it is also concerned with the love of Rogero for Bradamante, a maiden warrior, sister of Rinaldo, and the many adventures and vicissitudes that frustrate them. Their marriage concludes the poem. Other notable episodes in the work are: Rinaldo's defence of the Scottish princess Ginevra; Orlando's rescue of Olimpia from the sea monster—two episodes which inspired many operas; the voyage of Astolfo on the hippogriff to the moon, whence he brings back the lost wits of Orlando; and the self-immolation of *Isabella, the widow of the Scottish prince Zerbino, to escape the attentions of the pagan king Rodomont. Orlando's arms and especially his sword Durindana are objects of envy and claimed as his by Mandricardo.

Edmund Spenser, in *The *Faerie Queene*, aimed to 'overgo' Ariosto's epic, and owes much to it for his characters and form of narration. The first complete English version 'in English Heroical Verse' is that of Sir J. *Harington (1591; ed. R. McNulty, 1972). John Hoole's translation (1783) was read and enjoyed by Walter *Scott and Robert *Southey. A version by W. S. Rose (8 vols, 1823–31) in **ottava rima*, though less amusing than Harington's, is more faithful, and was highly praised by Rose's friend Ugo *Foscolo. Recent versions are by G. Waldman (1974) and B. Reynolds (1975). See C. P. Brand, *Ludovico Ariosto: A Preface to Orlando furioso* (1974).

Orlando innamorato A poem by Matteo Maria *Boiardo (Bks I and II, 1484, and with the unfinished third book, 1495), on the subject of the falling in love of *Orlando (the Roland of the *Charlemagne cycle) with Angelica, daughter of Galafron, king of Cathay. She arrives at the court of Charlemagne, with her brother Argalia, under false pretences, to carry off the Christian knights to her father's country. Several knights attempt to win her, the chief among them being Astolfo, Ferrau, Rinaldo, and Orlando. Argalia is slain and Angelica flees, but, drinking from an enchanted fountain, she falls in love with Rinaldo, who, drinking from another enchanted fountain, conceives a violent aversion to her. He runs away, pursued by her, and they reach her father's country, where she is besieged in the capital, Albracca, by Agrican, king of Tartary, to whom her hand had been promised (an incident to which Milton refers in **Paradise Regained*, III. 337 ff.). Orlando comes to Angelica's rescue, slays Agrican, and returns with Angelica to France whither he has been summoned to assist Charlemagne against Agramant, king of the Moors. Drinking once more from the same enchanted fountains, Rinaldo this time falls in love with Angelica, and Angelica into hatred of him. A fierce combat ensues between Orlando and Rinaldo, suppressed by Charlemagne, who entrusts Angelica to Namo, duke of Bavaria. The poem is divided into three books, subdivided into cantos. At the beginning of Book II, Boiardo introduces Ruggiero, as the ancestor of his patrons, the *Este dynasty, and sketches the development of his love for Bradamante.

The poem, which was left unfinished, was refashioned by Francesco *Berni, and translated into English by W. S. Rose (1823). There is some slight evidence that Edmund *Spenser knew Boiardo's poem as well as Ariosto's sequel, **Orlando furioso*, and it was certainly known to John *Milton. There is a modern translation by C. S. Ross (1995). See M. Murrin, *The Allegorical Epic* (1980).

Orley Farm A novel by Anthony *Trollope, published 1862. It was the first of Trollope's novels to be published in shilling numbers (1861–2), and he was especially pleased with the illustrations provided by John Everett *Millais. While Joseph Mason inherits the bulk of his father's property, Orley Farm goes to Lucius Mason, the old man's son by his second marriage. The will is unsuccessfully contested, and matters hang fire until discontented Samuel Dockwrath, formerly a tenant at Orley Farm, discovers irregularities in the evidence brought before the court. The suspicion grows that the codicil was forged by Lucius' mother, Lady Mason, still living at Orley Farm. The case is reopened, and though Lady Mason is not convicted, this is due to the skill of the indefatigable lawyer Chaffanbrass. She confesses her guilt to her aged lover Sir Peregrine Orme, and surrenders the property. Mother and son go into exile abroad.

Ormond A novel by Maria *Edgeworth, published 1817. Largely a tale of life in Ireland, it also describes fashionable Parisian society in the 18th century. The main characters are Harry Ormond, an orphan; his fascinating but unprincipled guardian Sir Ulick O'Shane; the kind-hearted eccentric Cornelius O'shane, the 'king of the Black Islands'; and his daughter Dora, who has been plighted before her birth to one or other of the twin sons of Cornelius' companion Connal, with disastrous results.

Ormulum, The A poem in Middle English, of which about 20,000 short lines survive. Extant in a single manuscript (Oxford, Bodleian Library, MS Junius 1), it was written in the late 12th century in the south Lincolnshire dialect by Orm, an Augustinian canon. The poem is a series of sermons arranged chronologically around the Gospel versions of the life of Christ. The single version that survives comprises just over an eighth (32) of the writer's ambitious original scheme of 242 sermons. The literary merit of the poem is inconsiderable, but it is of great interest and importance as a document in linguistic history, particularly for the semi-phonetic spelling system devised by the writer (largely a matter of doubling consonants after short vowels). It was edited by R. M. White and R. Holt (1878).

Oroonoko, *or The History of the Royal Slave* A novel by Aphra *Behn, published *c.*1688, adapted for the stage by Thomas *Southerne, 1695. Oroonoko, grandson and heir of an African king, loves and wins Imoinda, daughter of the king's general. The king, who also loves her, is enraged and orders her to be sold as a slave. Oroonoko himself is trapped by the captain of an English slave-trading ship and carried off to Surinam, then an English colony, where he is reunited with Imoinda and renamed Caesar by his owners. He rouses his fellow slaves to revolt, is deceived into surrender by deputy governor Byam (a historical figure), and brutally whipped. Oroonoko, determined on revenge but not hoping for victory, kills Imoinda, who dies willingly. He is discovered by her dead body and cruelly executed.

The novel is remarkable as an early protest against the slave trade, and as a description of primitive people in 'the first state of innocence, before men knew how to sin'; the author comments on the superior simplicity and morality of both African slaves and the indigenous Indians, whose Christian oppressors are shown as treacherous and hypocritical. Behn's memories of her own visit to Surinam in 1663 provide a vivid background, and much of the story is narrated as by a personal witness. Southerne's tragedy follows the broad lines of the novel, but the deputy governor's passion for Imoinda is made a chief motive of action, Imoinda herself is presented as the daughter of a white European, and Oroonoko dies by his own hand, changes which make the story less violent, and less provocative.

OROSIUS (*fl.* early 5th century) A priest of Tarragona in Spain, disciple of St *Augustine and friend of St *Jerome, author of the *History against the Pagans*, a universal history and geography which was translated by the circle of King *Alfred in the 890s.

Orphan, The A tragedy in blank verse by Thomas *Otway, produced 1680. Castalio and Polydore are the twin sons of Acasto. Monimia, the orphan daughter of a friend of Acasto's, has been brought up with them. Castalio and Polydore, loyally devoted to one another, have both fallen in love with Monimia, who loves Castalio. But Castalio, out of mistaken consideration for his brother, pretends indifference. Chamont, an honest but rough soldier, brother of Monimia, comes as a guest to Acasto's house; he suspects that Monimia has been wronged by one of the young men, and annoys her with his questions. Castalio and Monimia are secretly married. Polydore, ignorant of this and overhearing them arranging for a meeting in the night, takes Castalio's place in the darkness, and is not detected. Castalio, coming later, is shut out, and curses his wife for what he supposes to be her heartless and rebellious conduct. The truth being discovered through Chamont, the brothers fall into despair. Both kill themselves, and Monimia takes poison. The play was very successful, and was frequently revived. Monimia was one of Elizabeth *Barry's most celebrated parts.

Orpheus A legendary Greek poet, supposedly son of *Apollo by the *Muse Calliope, and renowned as a musician, religious leader, and seer. He was reputed to have made trees and rocks follow his singing, been one of the Argonauts, visited Egypt, and founded mystery cults in several parts of Greece. He was eventually torn to pieces by Maenads (frenzied votaresses of the god Dionysus), and his head and lyre, thrown into the river Hebrus, drifted to Lesbos where the head became an oracle, while *Apollo placed the lyre among the stars. Many writings ascribed to Orpheus and his son *Musaeus are quoted by ancient writers. The best-known story, told by *Virgil in *Georgics*, Book 4, *Ovid in *Metamorphoses*, Book 10, and *Boethius in *De Consolatione Philosophiae*, Book III, is of Orpheus going down into hell, persuading *Hades to let him have back his wife Eurydice, and then losing her because he disregarded the instruction not to look back before they reached the light of day. Orpheus was especially important to John *Milton, who refers to his skill and plight in *'L'Allegro' and *'Il Penseroso', *Lycidas*, and *Paradise Lost*, Book VII. Robert *Burton cites the story of Orpheus as evidence that beasts respond to music, and it inspired one of Nicolas *Poussin's finest paintings. Appropriately opera has been the genre that has made most use of the story in modern times, from *L'Orfeo* (1607) by Claudio Monteverdi (1567–1643), and *Orfeo ed Euridice* (1762; French version, 1774) by Christoph Willibald Gluck (1714–87), to the comic operetta *Orphée aux enfers (Orpheus in the Underworld*, 1858) by Jacques Offenbach (1819–80). Other important modern treatments are Rainer Maria *Rilke's *Die Sonnette an Orpheus* (*Sonnets to Orpheus*, 1923), and Jean *Cocteau's film trilogy *Le Sang d'un poète* (*The Blood of a Poet*, 1930), *Orphée* (1950), and *Le Testament d'Orphée* (*The Testament of Orpheus*, 1960).

Orpheus Caledonius, *or A Collection of the Best Scotch Songs* (1725) The first printed collection of Scots airs for the voice, collected by William Thomson (*c.*1684–*c.*1760), which contains many of the songs first printed by Allan *Ramsay.

ORRERY, earls of *See* Boyle, John; Boyle, Roger.

ORSAY, Alfred Guillaume Gabriel, Count d' (1801–52) A Frenchman who, coming to London in 1821, made himself famous as wit, dandy, and artist. He was adopted by the earl and countess of *Blessington. In 1823, with his benefactors, he travelled to Genoa, where he met Lord *Byron and made a rapid pencil sketch of the poet which has survived. In 1827 he married Lady Harriet Gardiner, Lord Blessington's daughter by a former marriage, but a separation took place almost immediately. He was prominent in the society of Gore House, where Lady Blessington entertained literary, political, and artistic London.

ORTON, Joe (1933–67) Playwright and novelist, born in Leicester. He left school at 16 to train as an actor. His comedies, which include *Entertaining Mr Sloane* (1964), *Loot* (1965), and the posthumously performed *What the Butler Saw* (1969), are black, stylish, satirical, farcical, and violent, and their emphasis on corruption and sexual perversion made them a *succès de scandale*. Orton was battered to death in his Islington home by his friend and companion Kenneth Halliwell, who then committed suicide. At the time of his death he was negotiating terms to provide the script for a new Beatles' film. See *Prick up your Ears* (1978), a biography by John Lahr, which formed the basis of a film scripted (1987) by Alan *Bennett. Lahr also edited *The Orton *Diaries* (1986). Much of Orton's early work has subsequently been published, as his role in the development of 'queer theory' is increasingly recognized.

ORWELL, George (1903–50) Pseudonym of Eric Arthur Blair, novelist and political writer, born in Bengal, India, brought to England when he was 3, and educated at St

Cyprian's prep school (of which his account, 'Such, such were the joys', was considered too libellous to print in this country until 1968) and at Eton College. He went on to serve with the Indian Imperial Police in Burma, 1922–7; his uneasy experiences as a policeman are reflected in his first novel, *Burmese Days* (1934), and in two of his finest essays, 'A Hanging' and 'Shooting an Elephant'. He resigned 'to escape not merely from imperialism but from every form of man's dominion over man', as he later put it, and then worked in Paris and London in a series of ill-paid jobs and lived off and on among tramps (see *Down and Out in Paris and London*, 1933, his first published book), struggling all the while with the repeated rejection of his work by publishers. His second novel, *A Clergyman's Daughter* (1935), describes the adventures of Dorothy Hare, who through loss of memory briefly escapes from the confines of her life to join the vagrants and hop-pickers of Kent. *Keep the Aspidistra Flying* (1936), which he wrote while working in a Hampstead bookshop, recounts the literary aspirations and financial humiliations of Gordon Comstock, a bookseller's assistant. A journey north in 1936, commissioned by Victor *Gollancz, produced his vivid and opinionated account of unemployment, proletarian life, and his fellow socialist intellectuals, *The Road to Wigan Pier* (1937, published by the *Left Book Club). The Spanish Civil War (in which he fought for the Republicans and was wounded) intensified his political preoccupations, honed his style, and resulted in *Homage to Catalonia* (1938). Orwell's simmering disgust with modernity and the threat of imminent war hung over his next novel, *Coming up for Air* (1939), which focuses on the many frustrations of George Bowling, a modern everyman, and his yearning for the lost England of his (and Orwell's) youth. By this stage Orwell saw himself primarily as a political writer, a democratic socialist who avoided party labels, hated totalitarianism, and was to become more and more disillusioned with the methods of communism. V. S. *Pritchett, reviewing Orwell's *The Lion and the Unicorn: Socialism and the English Genius* (1941), compared him to Daniel *Defoe and William *Cobbett both for his 'subversive, non-conforming brand of patriotism' and for his 'lucid conversational style'. His collections of essays include *Inside the Whale* (1940), *Critical Essays* (1946), and *Shooting an Elephant* (1950). But his most popular works were and remain his political satires **Animal Farm* (1945) and **Nineteen Eighty-Four* (1949). His first wife, Eileen, died in 1945, and he married Sonia Mary Brownell in 1949, shortly before his death from tuberculosis, an illness from which he had suffered for many years. His *Complete Works* (20 vols, ed. Peter Davison) appeared in 1998. See Bernard Crick, *George Orwell: A Life* (rev. edn, 1992); Michael Sheldon, *Orwell: The Authorised Biography* (1991).

OSBORNE, Dorothy (1627–95) Letter writer. She met William *Temple on the Isle of Wight in 1648, when she was 21, he 20. After considerable family opposition they married in 1654. Her letters to him during the period 1652–4, mostly written from her family home of Chicksands, came to light when T. P. Courtenay (1782–1841) published some in an appendix to his life of Temple in 1836; Thomas *Macaulay singled them out for praise and Sir Edward Parry (1863–1943) brought out an edition (1888) that was followed by the more scholarly edition of G. C. Moore Smith (1858–1940) in 1928. The letters are lively and witty, though occasionally solemn in their reflections; she believed that letters 'should be as free and easy as one's discourse'. They provide an intimate picture of the life, manners, and reading habits of the times, of the relations between the sexes, and particularly of a woman's attitudes to marriage and filial duty.

OSBORNE, John (1929–94) Playwright, born in Fulham, London, the son of a commercial artist who died in 1940; the first volume of his autobiography, *A Better Class of Person* (1981), describes his childhood in suburbia, his brief spell as a journalist, and his years as an actor in provincial repertory, during which he began to write plays, the first of which was performed in 1950. He made his name with **Look Back in Anger* (1956; pub. 1957), which was followed by *Epitaph for George Dillon* (1957; pub. 1958; written in the mid-1950s in collaboration with Anthony Creighton); *The Entertainer* (1957, which starred Laurence Olivier as Archie Rice, a faded survivor of the great days of music hall); *Luther* (1961, based on the life of Martin *Luther, with much emphasis on his physical as well as his spiritual problems); *Inadmissible Evidence* (1964, the tragedy of a down-at-heel solicitor, Bill Maitland, plunging rhetorically towards self-destruction); and *A Patriot for Me* (1965, a highly theatrical piece set in Vienna, based on the rise and fall of Redl, a homosexual officer in the Austro-Hungarian army, ruined by blackmail). Iconoclastic, energetic, and impassioned, Osborne's works at their most positive praise the qualities of loyalty, tolerance, and friendship, but his later works (which include *West of Suez*, 1971; *A Sense of Detachment*, 1972; *Watch It Come Down*, 1976) became increasingly vituperative in tone, and the objects of his invective apparently more arbitrary; his outbursts of rage against contemporary society are frequently exhilarating, for the anger that made him known as an *'Angry Young Man' remained one of his strongest theatrical weapons, but he also expressed from time to time an ambivalent nostalgia for the past that his own work did so much to alter. His last play, *Déjàvu* (1991), is a sequel to *Look Back in Anger*, presenting the same characters in their regrouped, bad-tempered, but occasionally companionable middle age. *Almost a Gentleman* (1991) was a second volume of autobiography; *Damn You, England* (1994) a miscellany of reviews and letters to the press. See J. Heilpern, *John Osborne: A Patriot for Us* (2006).
See KITCHEN SINK DRAMA.

OSBORNE, Thomas (d. 1767) Bookseller who commissioned Samuel *Johnson to work on the **Harleian Miscellany*. Alexander *Pope ridiculed Osborne's coarseness, and Johnson knocked him down with a folio volume for impertinence.

O'SHAUGHNESSY, Arthur William Edgar (1844–81) Poet, protégé of Edward *Bulwer-Lytton, and friend of D. G. *Rossetti, who worked at the British Museum. He published several volumes of poetry; his best-known piece, 'Ode' ('We are the music-makers'), appeared in *Music and Moonlight* (1874) and was set to music by Edward *Elgar.

OSÓRIO, Jerónimo (Hieronymus Osorius) (1514–80) Portuguese theologian, historian, and political theorist, bishop of Silves from 1564. His impact on the intellectual life of England in the 16th century has never been fully investigated. All his books are in Latin. His treatise on the good ruler, *De Gloria* (1549), was enthusiastically received by Roger *Ascham and his circle. It was much read in the universities. His controversial letter to Queen Elizabeth (1563), inviting her to return to Roman Catholicism, was answered by Walter Haddon (1514/15–1571) and John *Foxe, who also responded to his *De Iustitia* (1572). In later centuries John *Dryden and Alexander *Pope continued to admire Osório's history of the discoveries (1571).

Ossian Variant of *Oisin, a legendary Gaelic warrior and bard.
See MACPHERSON, JAMES; FINGAL.

OSTROVSKY, Aleksandr Nikolaevich (1823–86) Russian playwright and theatre reformer, born into a merchant family in Moscow. He produced about 40 prose plays and eight in blank verse whose characters were drawn from the merchant class and lower officialdom and whose themes were contemporary national preoccupations. He translated William *Shakespeare's *The *Taming of the Shrew* (1865) and was working on a translation of **Antony and Cleopatra* when he died. Among his best plays are *It's a Family Affair—We'll Settle It Ourselves* (1850), *The Poor Bride* (pub. 1852), *The Forest* (1871), and *The Dowerless Girl* (1879). His most powerful drama is *The Storm* (1859), on which the opera *Katia Kabanova*, by the Czech composer Leoš Janáček (1854–1928), is based. Set on the Volga, symbolizing hope and freedom, the play depicts the oppressive household of the Kabanovs, dominated by the matriarch who suppresses the aspirations of her daughter-in-law Katerina, whose quest for happiness and the right to self-expression leads to her suicide. Despite the barrier of Ostrovsky's vivid, idiosyncratic vernacular, often defying translation, his plays have enjoyed successful English adaptations such as Frank *McGuinness's *Storm* (Almeida, 1998) and Alan *Ayckbourn's *Forest* (National, 2000).

OSWALD, St (d. 992) One of the leading figures (along with *Dunstan and *Æthelwold) in the 10th-century Benedictine Revival in England. He became a Benedictine monk at Fleury. On Dunstan's initiative he was appointed bishop of Worcester in 961, founding monasteries at Westbury, Worcester, Winchcombe, and on the Isle of Ramsey. In 971–2 he was made archbishop of York, retaining the see of Worcester, where he is buried. His life was written by Byrhtferth of Ramsey (*fl. c.*986–*c.*1016), and later by Eadmer (*c.*1060–in or after 1126).

OSWALD, Alice (1966–) British poet. Oswald read Classics at Oxford before working as a gardener at Chelsea Physic Garden. Her first collection, *The Thing in the Gap-Stone-Stile* (1996), includes several poems about gardening. *Dart* (2002), which won the T. S. *Eliot Prize, is a book-length evocation of the river, which she has described as 'a songline from source to sea'. The poem mingles the voices of the people who live and work on the banks of the Dart with characters from history and myth to chart the 'mutterings' of the river itself. *Woods etc* (2005) saw her return from the hybrid, dramatized narrative of *Dart* to a more elliptical and mysterious exploration of subjectivity, focused through the natural world. Oswald has continued to probe the boundaries of mainstream poetry, her experiments sometimes linking her, perhaps surprisingly, with innovative language writers, despite the obvious influence of mainstream poets such as Gerard Manley *Hopkins and Ted *Hughes. Although professing not to be a nature poet, Oswald's explicit turn towards the visionary also shows an alliance with earlier writers of the New Apocalypse, particularly Dylan *Thomas.

Othello, the Moor of Venice A tragedy by *Shakespeare, written between 1602 and 1604 when it was performed before James I at Whitehall. It was first printed in quarto in 1622, and again in a different version in the *folio of 1623. The story is taken from *Cinzio, which Shakespeare probably read in Italian, possibly also in French.

The first act (which *Verdi's opera *Otello* omits) is set in Venice. Desdemona, daughter of Brabanzio, a Venetian senator, has secretly married Othello, a Moor in the service of the state. Accused before the duke and senators of having stolen Brabanzio's daughter, Othello explains and justifies his conduct, and is asked by the Senate to lead the Venetian forces against the Turks who are about to attack Cyprus.

In the middle of a storm which disperses the Turkish fleet, Othello lands on Cyprus with Desdemona, Cassio, a young Florentine, who helped him court his wife and whom he has now promoted to be his lieutenant, and Iago, a soldier, bitterly resentful of being passed over for promotion, who now plans his revenge. Iago uses Roderigo, 'a gulled gentleman' in love with Desdemona, to fight with Cassio after he has got him drunk, so that Othello deprives him of his new rank. He then persuades Cassio to ask Desdemona to plead in his favour with Othello, which she warmly does. At the same time he suggests to Othello that Cassio is, and has been, Desdemona's lover, finally arranging through his wife Emilia, who is Desdemona's waiting-woman, that Othello should see Cassio in possession of a handkerchief which he had given to his bride. Othello is taken in by Iago's promptings and in frenzied jealousy smothers Desdemona in her bed. Iago sets Roderigo to murder Cassio, but when Roderigo fails to do this Iago kills him and Emilia as well, after she has proved Desdemona's innocence to Othello. Emilia's evidence and letters found on Roderigo prove Iago's guilt; he is arrested, and Othello, having tried to stab him, kills himself.

According to Thomas *Rymer one of the play's morals was 'a warning to all good wives that they look well to their linen'.

S. T. *Coleridge in a famous phrase described Iago's soliloquy at the end of I. iii as 'the motive-hunting of motiveless malignity'.

ottava rima An Italian stanza of eight eleven-syllable lines, rhyming *abababcc*, possibly invented by *Boccaccio, and later employed by *Ariosto, *Tasso, and others. It was introduced into England by Thomas *Wyatt, and used to great effect by Lord *Byron in **Don Juan*, with a ten-syllable iambic line.

Otter, Captain Thomas, and **Mistress Otter** The ill-matched husband and wife in Ben Jonson's **Epicene*. Charles II, joking about the henpecked state of his brother the duke of York, christened him Tom Otter.

Otterbourne, The Battle of One of the earliest of English ballads, included in Thomas *Percy's **Reliques*. It describes how the Scots, led by James, earl of Douglas, attacked the castle of Otterburn in Northumberland in 1388. They were surprised by Henry Hotspur, Lord Percy. Douglas was killed, and Percy taken prisoner.

Otuel, Sir Pagan knight, miraculously converted, subsequently one of *Charlemagne's *Paladins. See *Otuel* in the Auchinlech manuscript (EETS ES 39, ed. S. J. Herrtage, 1882); *Duke Rowland and Sir Otuell of Spayne* (EETS ES 35, ed. S. J. Herrtage, 1880); *Otuel and Roland* (EETS OS 198, ed. M. O'Sullivan, 1935).

OTWAY, Thomas (1652–85) Playwright, born at Milland near Trotton, Sussex, educated at Winchester College and Christ Church, Oxford. He failed as an actor, being given a part by the kindness of Aphra *Behn. In 1678 he joined the army in the Netherlands and received a commission, but soon returned. He died destitute aged 33. Of his three great tragedies, **Don Carlos*, in rhymed verse, was produced in 1676; *The *Orphan*, in blank verse, in 1680; and **Venice Preserved*, also in blank verse, in 1682. Of his other plays *Alcibiades*, a tragedy, was produced in 1675 (and provided Elizabeth *Barry, for whom Otway cherished an unrequited passion, with her first successful part); *Titus and Berenice*, adapted from a tragedy by *Racine, and *The Cheats of Scapin*, from a comedy by *Molière, in 1676; *The History and Fall of Caius Marius*, an adaptation of **Romeo and Juliet*, in 1679; *Friendship in Fashion*, a comedy, in 1681; and *The Atheist*, also a comedy, in 1683. He also wrote prologues, epilogues, and a few poems. The standard edition by J. C. Ghosh was published in 1932.

OUIDA (1839–1908) Pen-name of Marie Louise de la Ramée, novelist, born in Bury St Edmunds; her mother was English and her father, Louis Ramée, a teacher of French. She was educated at home by her father. Her pseudonym is a childish mispronunciation of 'Louise'. She began her career contributing stories to **Bentley's Miscellany* (1859–60) encouraged by its editor Harrison *Ainsworth. Her first real success was *Held in Bondage* (1863), followed by *Strathmore* (1865). By this time her reputation was established. She spent much time in Italy from 1860 and in 1874 settled in Florence where she pursued her work as a novelist while living in lavish style. Her other popular novels included *Under Two Flags* (1867), perhaps her most famous (a film, starring Ronald Colman, was made in 1936), *Folle-Farine* (1871), which Edward *Bulwer-Lytton considered 'a triumph of modern English fiction', *Two Little Wooden Shoes* (1874), *Moths* (1880), *A Village Commune* (1881), and *In Maremma* (1882). Her 45 novels, often set in a fashionable world far removed from reality, show a spirit of rebellion against the moral ideals reflected in much of the fiction of the time. She suffered frequent ridicule for her extravagantly portrayed heroes, often languid guardsmen, miracles of strength, courage, and beauty, and for her inaccuracies in matters of men's sports and occupations; but her faults were redeemed by her narrative power and emotional energy. She campaigned against vivisection in her later years, and wrote several animal stories, including *A Dog of Flanders* (1872) and *Bimbi, Stories for Children* (1882). After 1890 her popularity waned and she wrote chiefly critical and social articles for magazines. When her literary profits declined, she fell into debt, moved to Lucca in 1894, and from 1904 lived in poverty in Viareggio.

OuLiPo [an acronym for Ouvroir de Littérature Potentielle] was a French movement founded in 1960 by Raymond *Queneau and François Le Lionnais (1901–84). Oulipians were dedicated to exploring connections between mathematics and the formal constraints inherent in literature. Its members have included Georges *Perec, Harry *Mathews, and Italo *Calvino. An example of their practice is the lipogram, which is a text from which one or more letters of the alphabet have been excluded. The best-known lipogram is Perec's *La Disparition* (1969), a 300-page novel in which the letter *e* is not once used (translated into English, without *es*, by Gilbert Adair as *A Void*, 1994). Perec's masterpiece, *La Vie: mode d'emploi* (1978), more fully illustrates the ways in which an arbitrary set of constraints can serve as a catalyst for the imagination. Other Oulipian developments include poems in which the vowels *a e i o u* always occur in that order, and narratives predicated on algorithms, such as Mathews's *Cigarettes* (1987).

Our Mutual Friend Charles *Dickens's last completed novel, published in monthly parts (May 1864–November 1865). The plot is exceptionally complex. John Harmon returns from the exile to which he has been sent by a harsh father, a rich dust-contractor; he expects to receive the inheritance to which his father has attached the condition that he shall marry a certain girl, Bella Wilfer. Bella is unknown to him, and he confides to a mate of the ship which is bringing him home his intention of concealing his identity until he has formed some judgement of his allotted wife. The mate lures him to a riverside haunt, attempts to murder him, throws his body into the river, and is in turn murdered and his body likewise thrown into the river. Harmon recovers and escapes; the mate's body is found after some days, and, owing to Harmon's papers found upon it, it is taken to be that of Harmon.

Harmon's intention of remaining unknown is thus facilitated; he assumes the name of John Rokesmith and becomes the secretary of the kindly, disinterested Mr Boffin, old Harmon's foreman, who, in default of young Harmon, inherits the property. He meets Bella, who is adopted by Boffin and whose wealth has made her a coldly disdainful young woman. Rokesmith nevertheless falls in love with her and is contemptuously rejected. Harmon's identity is now discovered by the amiable Mrs Boffin, and the Boffins, devoted to their old master's son and convinced of Bella's soundness of heart, contrive a plot to prove her. Boffin pretends to be transformed by his wealth into a hard-hearted miser, and heaps indignities on Harmon, who is finally dismissed. Bella, awakened to the evils of wealth and to the merits of Rokesmith, flies from the Boffins and marries her suitor. His identity presently comes to light, and with his assistance the scheme of a one-legged old villain, Silas Wegg, to blackmail Boffin is exposed.

This theme runs alongside the story of the love of Eugene Wrayburn, a careless young barrister, for Lizzie Hexam, daughter of a disreputable boatman. His rival for her affections, Bradley Headstone, a schoolmaster, attempts to murder Wrayburn. Wrayburn is saved by Lizzie and marries her. Among the notable characters in the book are the Veneerings, types of social parvenus; the good Jew Riah; the blackmailing waterside villain Rogue Riderhood; Jenny Wren, the dolls' dressmaker; Bella Wilfer's grotesque father, mother, and sister; and the spirited Betty Higden, an old woman haunted by dread of the workhouse.

Many early reviewers agreed with Henry *James, who found the novel 'forced' and 'wanting in inspiration', but later critics (including Humphry House and Edmund *Wilson) have praised it highly, stressing in particular the complex use of the dirt–money symbolism. Its critical reputation remains strong.

Our Village, *Sketches of Rural Life, Character, and Scenery* By Mary Russell *Mitford, published 1832. The sketches and descriptions which make up the book were written between 1824 and 1832, most of them appearing in the *Lady's Magazine*. The *Sketch Book* of Washington *Irving provided the original idea. The village is based on Three Mile Cross, near Reading, where Mitford and her father lived, but other locations and memories are also used. Before beginning the series, Mitford declared that it would describe 'country scenery and country manners', and that she abhorred sentimentality. Seasons, places, events, and people are described with precision and humour. Her lucid prose was the result of hard work, for she wrote that 'what looks like ease in my style is labour'.

OUSPENSKY, Peter Demianovich (1878–1947) Russian journalist and esoteric philosopher, born in Moscow; he emigrated to England after the October Revolution of 1917. He is best known for his exposition of the ideas of G. I. *Gurdjieff, whom he had met in 1914. In 1947 he published *The Strange Life of Ivan Osokin*, a novel exploring the concept of eternal return, set in Russia and Paris at the turn of the century. See Gary Lachman, *In Search of P. D. Ouspensky* (2004).

Outsider, The (1) A novel by American author Richard *Wright, published 1953. (2) A study by Colin *Wilson, published 1956. (3) The translated title of Albert *Camus's novel *L'Étranger* (1942).

OVERBURY, Sir Thomas (1581–1613) Poet and essayist. Educated at the Queen's College, Oxford, and the Middle Temple, he opposed the marriage of his patron Robert Carr (*c.*1587–1645; afterwards earl of Somerset) with the divorced countess of Essex, and was consigned to the Tower, on a trumped-up charge, where he was poisoned by Lady Essex's agents. Four of these were hanged; Somerset and Lady Essex were convicted and pardoned. *James I was possibly implicated. The prosecution was conducted by Francis *Bacon. Overbury's poem *A Wife* appeared in 1614, and with its second edition his Theophrastian 'Characters'. Later editions added new characters, some by John *Webster and some by Thomas *Dekker (see W. J. Taylor's edition, *The Overburian Characters*, 1936). The types include 'A Roaring Boy', 'A Puny Clerk', 'A Mere Scholar', and the unusually idyllic 'Fair and Happy Milkmaid'; John *Earle responded to their satirical tone with his *Microcosmography*.
See CHARACTER-WRITING.

OVERTON, Richard (*fl.* 1646) One of the leaders of the Leveller movement. His early life is obscure. He may have attended Queens' College, Cambridge, and worked as an actor and playwright. A prolific, forceful, and versatile pamphleteer, he published much of his work anonymously, and some under the pseudonym of Martin Marpriest, in the tradition of *Martin Marprelate. His *Man's Mortality* (1643), arguing that the soul dies with the body, to be raised on the last day, aroused controversy, and he was imprisoned many times for his religious and political views. He adopted John *Lilburne's cause and was imprisoned in 1649 with him, Thomas Prince (*fl.* 1630–57), and William *Walwyn. His stance is rational, tolerant, egalitarian, and antimonarchical, and his style colourful and often caustic (Walwyn praised his 'comic' and 'satiric' pen).

OVID (Publius Ovidius Naso) (43 BC–AD 17) Latin poet. He was born at Sulmo (now Sulmona, in the Abruzzo, Italy), studied oratory at Rome, and visited Athens and other places in the Greek East. Intended for a public career, he broke away and devoted himself to poetry. He became known for his *Amores* (loves) and the mock-didactic *Ars Amatoria* (art of love), poems in *elegiac couplets in which he subverts the serious conventions of the *Propertian elegy. Not suffering but shared pleasure is the key, and Ovid barely pretends to take it seriously. The *Heroides* (heroines) are imaginary verse letters to their lovers from lovelorn women of mythology: Ariadne, abandoned by ungrateful *Theseus; Phaedra, trying to reveal just enough to *Hippolytus; Dido, reproaching Aeneas for desertion. Ovid then took up the challenge of creating a long poem in *hexameters, a rival to the **Aeneid*. He settled on the theme of *Metamorphoses*, transformations of form, by which mythical thought explained natural phenomena. So the cypress tree had been a pretty boy, Cyparissus; the spider had been a girl, Arachne, who challenged Athene to a weaving contest and was hideously transmogrified by the insulted goddess. Most of the stories were of unhappy loves. Ovid carried the theme through fifteen books with enormous panache. An attempt to re-establish himself morally, in the puritanical last years of Augustus, was his *Fasti*, versifying the Roman calendar and its festivals. He had written six books when in AD 8 the angry emperor packed him off into permanent exile in Tomis on the Black Sea. The cause remains unclear: Ovid speaks of a poem (his *Ars*) and an unexplained 'mistake'. The collections of elegies entitled *Tristia* (sorrows) and *Epistulae ex Ponto* (letters from Pontus) express his grief, despair, and occasional hope. Ovid's posthumous influence was enormous. *Chaucer and *Gower both borrowed his stories. The late 16th and early 17th centuries were England's Ovidian Age: Thomas *Lodge, Christopher *Marlowe, Edmund *Spenser, *Shakespeare, George *Chapman, Michael *Drayton were all indebted to him directly or through Arthur *Golding's translation of the *Metamorphoses*. Other notable translators include Marlowe, George *Sandys, John *Dryden, and Ted *Hughes. Ovid has been an unrivalled source of subjects for painters and composers. See L. P. Wilkinson, *Ovid Surveyed* (1960); Charles Martindale (ed.), *Ovid Renewed* (1988).

Ovide moralisé A French work in octosyllabic couplets, written by an anonymous author early in the 14th century. It moralizes fifteen books of Ovid's *Metamorphoses* and is highly significant in the development of late medieval and Renaissance literature by bringing secular literature into the official canon. It was particularly influential on *Chaucer and on the *Ovidius Moralizatus* of Pierre Bersuire (d. 1362), which is Book XV of his huge *Reductorium Morale*, completed in 1340. Compare John Ridewall's *Fulgentius metaforalis* (*c.*1330) for the practice of allegorizing the stories of classical authors.

OWEN, Alun (1925–94) Welsh-Liverpudlian playwright, actor, and television scriptwriter, born in Menai Bridge, north Wales, and educated at Oulton High School, Liverpool. During the war he worked as a Bevin Boy down the coal mines. He is principally remembered for his gritty, realist television dramas, which helped to shape the emerging style of TV drama in the 1960s: these include *No Trams to Lime Street* (1959), and *After the Funeral* (1960); *A Little Winter Love* (1964) was a stage play. He also wrote the screenplay for the *Beatles' film *A Hard Day's Night* (1964).

OWEN, John (?1563–1622) Writer of *epigrams, educated at Winchester College and New College, Oxford, famous throughout Europe for his volumes of Latin epigrams, which were translated into several languages and frequently reprinted down to the 19th century.

OWEN, Robert (1771–1858) Socialist and philanthropist. He was born in Wales, the son of a shopkeeper, and became the wealthy owner of cotton-spinning mills in Manchester. In 1799 he purchased the New Lanark mills in Scotland, where he established his model community and village, organized on principles of mutual cooperation, as well as infant schools and other educational institutions. His example was instrumental in bringing about the Factory Act of 1819, although, disappointed with the slow rate of reform, he left Britain in 1821 for some years to set up another ideal community, New Harmony, in America. Owen was a pioneer of cooperation between workers and consumers, and his ideas strengthened the growing cooperative movement. He published *A New View of Society* in 1813 and *The Revolution in Mind and Practice of the Human Race* in 1849. Owen was notorious in later life for his atheism. The standard life is by G. D. H. Cole (1925). See Owen's *Selected Works*, ed. G. Claeys, 4 vols (1993).

OWEN, Wilfred (1893–1918) Poet, born in Shropshire, and educated at the Birkenhead Institute and Shrewsbury Technical School. After a period as a lay assistant at Dunsden, near Reading, he left in 1913 to teach English in France, where he became friends with the poet Laurent Tailhade. Owen returned to England in 1915, joining the Artists' Rifles and then the Manchester Regiment, as an officer. After concussion and shell-shock he was invalided to Craiglockhart War Hospital in Edinburgh, where he was greatly encouraged in his writing by Siegfried *Sassoon. He returned to France in 1918, won the MC, and was killed on the Sambre Canal a week before the Armistice. He found his own voice as a poet of the trenches, and most of the poems for which he is remembered were written in a creative burst between the summer of 1917 and the autumn of the following year. After the war, his reputation slowly grew, greatly assisted by Edmund *Blunden's edition of his poems, with a memoir, in 1931, and he is now generally regarded as a war poet of the first rank. His bleak realism, his energy and indignation, his compassion, and his high technical skills (he was a master of metrical variety, *assonance, and *pararhyme) are evident in most of his work. His poems were chosen by Benjamin *Britten for his *War Requiem* (1961). *The Complete Poems and Fragments* was published in 1983, and *Collected Letters* in 1967. See Jon *Stallworthy, *Wilfred Owen* (1974); Dominic Hibberd, *Wilfred Owen* (2002).

OWENSON, Sydney *See* MORGAN, LADY.

'O Westren winde' The opening words of an early 16th-century quatrain. As a carol, it inspired masses by Christopher Tye (*c.*1505–*c.*1572), John Sheppard (d. 1559?), and John Taverner (*c.*1490–1545). The lines are used to great effect by Virginia *Woolf (in *The *Waves*) and Ernest *Hemingway (in *A Farewell to Arms*). See *Medieval English Lyrics*, ed. R. T. Davies (1963).

Owl and the Nightingale, The An early Middle English poem of 1,794 lines of *octosyllabic couplets, from the beginning or middle of the 13th century, two of the three known manuscripts of which survive. It is a debate between the birds concerning the benefits each confers on mankind, the symbolic implications of which have been much disputed. A learned work, it touches with light, scholastic legalism on many matters of serious contemporary interest, including foreknowledge, music, confession, and papal missions. It is a virtuoso poem, highly accomplished in its style and in its humorous tone, which reaches no definite conclusion. The debate is to be submitted at the end to the judgement of 'Nicholas of Guildford', who has been thought to be the author, although there is no further evidence to support this. See text and translation by Neil Cartlidge (2001); see also the edition by E. G. Stanley (1960).

Owlglass *See* EULENSPIEGEL.

OXFORD, Edward De Vere, seventeenth earl of (1550–1604) Poet and courtier, educated at Queens' College, Cambridge. Arthur *Golding, the translator of *Ovid, was his uncle. Oxford married Lord *Burghley's daughter Anne, and he raised high hopes as a courtier and patron, but they were dissipated by his capricious and violent temper. His most famous quarrel was with Philip *Sidney, whom, according to Fulke *Greville, he called a 'puppy' in a dispute at the tennis court in 1579; there is also some evidence that Oxford planned to kill Sidney. It is perhaps appropriate that one of the sixteen or so surviving poems attributed to Oxford is entitled 'Love compared to a tennis play'. He had some reputation as a poet during his lifetime, but the idea, initiated by John Thomas Looney (1870–1944) in 1920 and subsequently promoted by 'Oxfordians', that he was the author of William *Shakespeare's plays is without foundation.
See SHAKESPEARE: AUTHORSHIP OF THE WORKS.

Oxford and Cambridge Magazine A periodical of the year 1856, of which twelve monthly numbers appeared, financed mainly by William *Morris. Among its (anonymous) contributors were Morris and Edward *Burne-Jones (of Oxford), Henry Lushington (1812–55) of Cambridge, and by invitation D. G. *Rossetti, whose 'Burden of Nineveh' appeared in its pages. The contents were predominantly literary, and included poems, tales, fairy stories, essays, and reviews.

Oxford English Dictionary, The The scheme of 'a completely new English Dictionary' was conceived in 1858, chiefly as the result of the reading of two papers 'On some Deficiencies in Our English Dictionaries' by Richard *Trench to the Philological Society in 1857. Herbert Coleridge (1830–61), and after him Frederick *Furnivall, were the first editors. Their work, which covered twenty years, consisted mainly in the collection of materials, and it was not until James *Murray took over in 1878 that the preparation of the dictionary took shape. The first part (*A–Ant*) was published in 1884, when Murray estimated that the whole might be completed in another twelve years. It was not in fact finished until 1928, 70 years from its beginning. Murray, who planned the work, did not live to see it completed (at his death, T had been reached); but more than half was produced under his personal editorship. His co-editors were Henry *Bradley (from 1888), William Craigie (from 1901), and Charles Onions (from 1914).

The essential feature of the dictionary is its historical method, by which the meaning and form of the words are traced from their earliest appearance on the basis of an immense number of quotations, collected by more than 800 voluntary workers. The dictionary contains a record of 414,825 words, whose history is illustrated by 1,827,306 quotations. The original title of the main work was 'A New English Dictionary on Historical Principles' (abbreviated as *NED*). The title *The Oxford English Dictionary* first appeared in the reprint of 1933, with a supplement of 867 pages. In 1957 work began, under the editorship of Robert Burchfield (1923–2004), on a new supplement, superseding that of 1933, and treating all the vocabulary which came into use while the main dictionary was being published or after its completion. The outcome of this work, entitled *A Supplement to the Oxford English Dictionary*, contains a record of approximately 120,000 words and is about one-third of the length of the main dictionary. The second edition, by J. Simpson and E. Weiner, was published in 1989, and further new material has appeared in the Oxford English Dictionary Additions Series, two volumes in 1993, and another in 1997. It is also available in electronic form on CD-ROM, and online. A third edition, expected to double the length of the dictionary, is currently in preparation, and will represent a nearly complete overhaul of the work. The online database is updated quarterly with revisions that will be included in the third edition.

Oxford Gazette The first real newspaper, other than a newsletter, to be published in England. It appeared in November 1665, the court being then at Oxford owing to the great plague, and was started by Henry *Muddiman under the direction of his patron Sir Joseph Williamson (1633–1701). It became the *London Gazette* in 1666. It still survives, not now a newspaper, but a record of official appointments, notices of bankruptcy, and other public events, having passed in 1923 into the keeping of the Stationery Office. See P. M. Handover, *A History of the London Gazette 1665–1965* (1965), in which she traces its slow evolution to its present form, and describes its anomalies and eccentricities as 'relics of ancient pride and state'.
See NEWSPAPERS.

Oxford Movement (Tractarian Movement) A movement of thought and doctrine within the Church of England, centred at Oxford, which began with the Assize Sermon on National Apostasy preached by John *Keble in 1833. It criticized the tendencies of the Anglican Church to accept the authority of the state, and to tolerate a range of theological positions. The movement aimed to defend the Church of England as a divine institution with an independent spiritual status, and to revive the High Church traditions of the 17th century. The Reform Act of 1832, and the views of *Broad Church supporters such as Thomas *Arnold, had led many to believe that the church was in danger of increasing subordination to civil control. Keble's sermon inspired John Henry *Newman, Richard Hurrell *Froude, and others to launch their series *Tracts for the Times* in 1833 (which gave the Tractarian movement its name); the series gained the influential support of Edward *Pusey, who gave the movement cohesion and authority. It was Newman's famous Tract XC (1841) on the compatibility of the Thirty-Nine Articles with Roman Catholic theology that brought the Tractarians under official ban, but hostility had already been aroused by the publication of the first volumes of Froude's *Literary Remains* in 1838, with its strictures on the Reformation. *The Ideal of a Christian Church* (1844), by William Ward (1812–82), with its praise of the Roman Catholic Church, intensified suspicions that the Tractarians (and principally Newman) were subversively leading their followers towards Rome. Newman himself became a Roman Catholic in 1845, a decision which dealt a severe blow to the unity of the movement.

The impact of the Tractarians was immense. In literary terms, the revival of interest in the medieval and 17th-century church influenced Alfred *Tennyson, William *Morris and the *Pre-Raphaelites, Christina *Rossetti, and Charlotte *Yonge, among others; it also strengthened the revival of *Gothic architecture associated with Augustus *Pugin. See Richard Church, *The Oxford Movement: Twelve Years, 1833–1845* (1891); Newman's *Apologia pro Vita Sua* (1864); the autobiography of Isaac *Williams, and Mark *Pattison's *Memoirs*; see also P. Nockles, *The Oxford Movement in Context* (1996).

Oxford University Press A publishing and printing business owned by the university and directed by its delegates of the press, of whom the vice-chancellor is *ex officio* chairman. Its aims are to produce books of religious, scholarly, and educational value: since its surplus profits are devoted to financing the editing and production of unremunerative works of this kind, and to supporting the university, it has charitable status.

Printing in Oxford by independent craftsmen began in 1478 (*see* UNIVERSITY PRESSES), and in 1584 one of these was appointed 'Printer to the University'. This title was borne by a succession of printers in the 17th century and was revived in 1925 for the head of the printing department of the press. One press at Oxford was excepted from the prohibition of printing outside London by a decree of the Star Chamber in 1586, and in 1632 a royal charter allowed the university three presses and to print and sell 'all manner of books'. William *Laud in 1634 bound the university to provide itself with a printing house; but a press under its immediate control did not come into being until 1690. In the meantime John *Fell had won an international reputation for scholarly Oxford books by setting up a press (1669) in the Sheldonian Theatre. By his bequest, the unsold books and printing equipment, including the famous 'Fell types', became the university's property in 1690.

Since then, under the delegates' management, the press has produced such famous books as the earl of *Clarendon's *History* (1703–7), William *Blackstone's *Commentaries* (1765–9), Benjamin Kennicott's Hebrew Bible (1776–80), James Clerk Maxwell's *Treatise on Electricity and Magnetism* (1873), the Revised Version of the English Bible (1885), the *Oxford English Dictionary*, completed in 1928, and the *Oxford Dictionary of National Biography* (2004), besides many millions of bibles and prayer books and, in recent times, editions of classical and modern works, monographs, companions, the celebrated World's Classics series, schoolbooks, and dictionaries.

The copyright in Clarendon's works, once very profitable, is secured to the university in perpetuity, and in his honour the Walton Street building to which the press moved in 1829 was named 'the Clarendon Press'. This was formerly the imprint given to learned books published under the supervision of the secretary to the delegates at Oxford. Books of more general appeal, including verse anthologies and reference books, were published between 1880 and 1976 from the press's London offices, subsequently from Oxford.

oxymoron [from two Greek words meaning 'sharp', 'dull'] A rhetorical figure by which two incongruous or contradictory terms are united in an expression so as to give it point, for example 'Faith unfaithful kept him falsely true' (Tennyson, **Idylls of the King*).

OYEYEMI, Helen (1984–) Born in Nigeria; she moved to London when she was 4. She wrote her first novel, *The Icarus Girl* (2006), while she was still at school; her second novel is *The Opposite House* (2007). *Juniper's Whitening* and *Victimese* (2005) are plays written and staged in Cambridge.

OYONO, Ferdinand (1929–) Cameroonian novelist, diplomat, and politician. Of his novels, which offer satirical portraits of the colonial relationship, the best known is *Une vie de boy* (1956; *Houseboy*, 1966). He served as minister of culture in Cameroon from 1997 to 2007.

Oz An underground magazine started in Sydney, Australia (1963–6), by Richard Neville (1941–), and relaunched by him in London in 1966 with Jim Anderson and Felix Dennis. The 'Schoolkids' issue (no. 28) was the occasion of a notorious trial during which the editors were convicted of issuing a publication likely to 'corrupt public morals', but were freed on appeal. *Oz* faded away in the winter of 1973, having reached a peak print-run of 70,000 in 1971.

OZ, Amos (1939–) Israeli novelist and political commentator, born in Jerusalem, of parents who had emigrated to Israel in the 1930s from Russia and Poland. His first novel to be widely translated from the Hebrew was *My Michael* (1968; trans. 1972), which, set in the 1950s, describes a hesitant student marriage, set against the background of the struggles of a newly independent nation: it gives a vivid portrait of unsettling fantasies and of the changing city of Jerusalem. Oz's fictional works (titles include *A Perfect Peace*, 1982, dealing with kibbutz life, *Fima*, 1991, about a failed middle-aged poet, and *Black Box*, which shows the tension of a failed marriage) build up a strong physical and political sense of Israel, and his reportage (see *In the Land of Israel*, 1983) gives a voice to its varied cultures and inhabitants. His memoir *A Tale of Love and Darkness* (2003) recounts his mother's suicide when he was 12.

OZICK, Cynthia (1928–) American novelist, born in New York, whose fiction explores aspects of Jewish American life. Her fiction includes *The Shawl* (1980) and *Heir to the Glimmering World* (2004: UK title *The Bear Boy*). Her essay collections include *Fame & Folly* (1996) and *The Din in the Head* (2006).

P

Pacchiarotto and How He Worked in Distemper: *With Other Poems* A collection of nineteen poems, in various metres, by Robert *Browning, published 1876. The title poem, the three which follow it, and the epilogue were directed at Browning's critics, in satirical or serious vein; the remaining poems are a miscellany on topics of religion, love, and art. 'Numpholeptos', 'St Martin's Summer', and 'A Forgiveness' are all memorable, but the volume's most unusual poem is the ballad 'Hervé Riel', about the heroic exploits of a French sailor in a fight against the British.

PADEL, Ruth (1946–) Poet and scholar, born in London and educated at Oxford University. Her first volume, *Summer Snow* (1990), contained poems evoking Crete; others include *Angel* (1993), *Rembrandt Would Have Loved You* (1998), an intimate exploration of a love affair, and *The Soho Leopard* (2004). Her verse combines classical allusion with a contemporary, often erotic idiom. Her scholarly works display an interest in various kinds of mythologizing, madness, and masculinity, both ancient and modern, and include *In and Out of the Mind: Greek Images of the Tragic Self* (1992) and *I'm a Man: Sex, Gods and Rock 'n' Roll* (2000). She has also published close critical readings of contemporary poems, including *The Poem and the Journey* (2007).

PAGET, Violet *See* LEE, VERNON.

PAINE, Thomas (1737–1809) Revolutionary and author, son of a Quaker staymaker of Thetford. He was dismissed as an exciseman in 1774 after agitating for an increase in pay. At the suggestion of Benjamin *Franklin he sailed for America, where he published in 1776 *Common Sense* and in 1776–83 a series of pamphlets, *The Crisis*, encouraging American resistance to England; he also wrote against slavery and in favour of the emancipation of women. In 1787 he returned to England, and published in 1791 the first part of *The *Rights of Man* in reply to Edmund Burke's **Reflections on the Revolution in France*. The second part appeared in 1792, when, alerted by William *Blake of impending arrest, Paine left for France, where he was elected a member of the Convention. However, he opposed the execution of Louis XVI, and narrowly escaped the guillotine. *The Age of Reason* (1793), an attack on Christianity and the Bible, was answered by Richard *Watson, bishop of Llandaff, and others, and his effigy was repeatedly burned in England. He returned to America in 1802; his last years were saddened by ill health and neglect. Ten years after his death William *Cobbett, once an implacable opponent, exhumed his bones for reburial in England, but they were eventually mislaid. Paine's writings, however, became a textbook for radicals in England, thanks to his clear style and direct connection with the American struggle and the French Revolution. He gave away most of his earnings, in part to the Society of Constitutional Information, founded in 1780.

PAINTER, George Duncan (1914–2005) Biographer, born in Birmingham, and educated at King Edward VI School and at Trinity College, Cambridge. In 1938 he joined the British Museum's Printed Book Department, a career he returned to after the war for a further twenty years. He published a biography of André *Gide (1951) but is most famous for his two-volume biography of *Proust (1959; 1965), which was awarded the Duff Cooper Memorial Prize, and is widely regarded as a milestone in the art of biography. Only the first volume of a planned three-volume biography of the French writer *Chateaubriand was ever published, *Chateaubriand: A Biography,* i: *1768–93: The Longed-for Tempests (1977), winning the James Tait Black Memorial Prize.*

PAINTER, William *See* PALACE OF PLEASURE.

Pair of Blue Eyes, A A novel by Thomas *Hardy, published 1873; Hardy's first popular success. Stephen Smith, a young architect, comes to the Cornish village of Endelstow to restore the church tower and falls in love with Elfride Swancourt, the blue-eyed daughter of the vicar. Her father is incensed that someone of Stephen's humble origin should claim his daughter. Elfride and Stephen elope, but Elfride vacillates over marriage, and Stephen leaves for India. Henry Knight, Stephen's friend and patron, meets Elfride, and after she saves his life on a cliff they become engaged. However, Knight learns of Elfride's affair with Stephen, and rejects her. Eventually he and Stephen meet; Stephen learns that Elfride remains unmarried and Knight learns the innocent facts of her escapade with Stephen. But the train which carries them both to Cornwall also carries Elfride's corpse. They learn when they arrive at Endelstow that she has died, after marrying Lord Luxellian.

Palace of Pleasure, The A collection of translations into English of 'pleasant histories and excellent novels…out of divers good and commendable Authors', made by William Painter (1540?–95), clerk of the ordnance, and published in 1566, 1569, and 1575. Many of the translations are from *Boccaccio, *Bandello, and Marguerite of Navarre (1492–1549; *see* HEPTAMÉRON), but Painter also drew on *Herodotus, *Livy, and *Gellius. The book provided a storehouse of plots for Elizabethan writers, especially dramatists; *Shakespeare used it for *The *Rape of Lucrece* and **All's Well That Ends Well*, and John *Webster drew the plot of *The *Duchess of Malfi* from it. It was edited by Joseph Jacobs (1890).

Paladins In the cycle of *Charlemagne legends, the twelve peers who accompanied the king. The origin of the idea is seen in the *Chanson de Roland* (*see* ROLAND), where the twelve peers or champions are merely an association of particularly brave warriors, under the leadership of Roland and *Oliver, who all perish at Roncesvalles. From the Spanish war the idea was transported by later writers to other parts of the cycle, and Charlemagne is found always surrounded by twelve peers. Their names are differently stated by different authors, most of the original names given by the *Chanson de Roland* having being forgotten; but Roland and Oliver always figure. Among the best known are *Otuel, Fierabras or *Ferumbras, *Ogier the Dane, and the count palatine. In the early 13th century there was a French court, comprising six ecclesiastics and six laymen, known as 'the Twelve Peers of France'; this court in 1202 declared King John deprived of his lands in France. Since the 16th century the word has been applied to any great knightly champion.

Palamon and Arcite The two Theban princes whose love for Emelye is the subject of Chaucer's 'The Knight's Tale' (*see* CANTERBURY TALES, 1), following the *Teseida* of *Boccaccio. The tale was paraphrased in heroic couplets by *Dryden under the title 'Palamon and Arcite'. It is also the subject of *The *Two Noble Kinsmen*.

PALEY, Grace (1922–2007) American short story writer and poet, who grew up in the Bronx, New York city, the daughter of Russian-Jewish parents. She was taught Russian and *Yiddish by her father. She is the author of three acclaimed volumes of short stories: *The Little Disturbances of Man* (1959); *Enormous Changes at the Last Minute* (1974); and *Later the Same Day* (1985). Pungent and laconic, her tragicomic stories resound with the cadences of the city where she was raised and are carried by the spoken word. Paley campaigned on behalf of anti-war movements, nuclear disarmament, and women's rights, and was co-author of *365 Reasons Not to Have Another War* (1989). Her essays and articles on family, community, and politics are collected in *Just as I Thought* (1997). *Begin Again: New and Collected Poems* (1992) features poems written from the 1950s onwards. See Judith Arcana, *Grace Paley's Life Stories* (1993).

PALEY, William (1743–1805) Anglican clergyman and theologian, educated at Christ's College, Cambridge, where for ten years he was a popular tutor. He published three influential works: *Moral and Political Philosophy* (1785), *Evidences of Christianity* (1794), and *Natural Theology* (1802); crisply written with clear examples, they were long used as textbooks at Cambridge. Paley was the major exponent of theological utilitarianism (the doctrine, partly derived from John *Locke, that human happiness lies in obedience to the will of God), and was strongly opposed to contemporary Scottish philosophy, which based ethics on the 'moral sense'. He attempted to rebut David *Hume's scepticism about Christian miracles and a beneficent and omnipotent deity, finding proof of the existence of God in the design apparent in natural phenomena, and particularly in the mechanisms of the human body. Just as a watch must have a watchmaker, so the world must have a designer (*Natural Theology*, ch. 1).

PALGRAVE, Francis Turner (1824–97) Critic and poet, son of barrister, historian, and antiquary Sir Francis Palgrave (1788–1861), who had changed his name from Cohen when he converted to Christianity in 1823. F. T. Palgrave was educated at Balliol College, Oxford; he was an official in the education department, 1855–84, and professor of poetry at Oxford, 1885–95. He is chiefly remembered for his anthology *The Golden Treasury of Best Songs and Lyrical Poems in the English Language* (1861, and much reprinted; 2nd series, 1897). In the selection for the first edition, Palgrave was advised by his close friend Alfred *Tennyson; it contained no work by living poets, and is a reflection of Palgrave's distinctive taste (e.g. no John *Donne and no William *Blake, though work by these poets was added to subsequent editions; Pope only as a lyricist). New and enlarged editions with poems by later writers have since appeared; Christopher Ricks edited the original selection in 1991. Palgrave compiled other anthologies and selections, and published several volumes of his own verse.

PALGRAVE, William Gifford (1826–88) Travel writer and diplomat, son of Sir Francis Palgrave (1788–1861) and brother of Francis Turner *Palgrave, educated at Trinity College, Oxford. He became a Jesuit missionary in Syria and Arabia. After a risky journey through Arabia for Napoleon III, undertaken in the guise of a doctor, he wrote *Narrative of a Year's Journey through Central and Eastern Arabia (1862–63)* (1865), his popular but somewhat unreliable narrative of this expedition. He then left the Jesuits to join the diplomatic service in which he held various posts from 1865. Shortly before his death he became reconciled to the church.

PALIN, Michael (1943–) Actor, television presenter, scriptwriter, and author, born in Sheffield, and educated at Shrewsbury School and Brasenose College, Oxford. He made his name in television with *Monty Python's Flying Circus* (1969–74, with John Cleese and others) and *Ripping Yarns* (1975–9, with Terry Jones). He has written film scripts (including *Time Bandits*, 1981; *The Missionary*, 1982), plays (including *East of Ipswich*, 1987; *The Weekend*, 1994), a novel (*Hemingway's Chair*, 1995), and several books for children. Since the late 1980s he has been best known for his *BBC TV travel documentaries and the books based on them: *Around the World in 80 Days* (1989), *Pole to Pole* (1992), *Full Circle* (1997), *Hemingway Adventure* (1999), *Sahara* (2002), and *Himalaya* (2004). Gently educational, their appeal owes much to Palin's affable curiosity and a wry humour that occasionally sends up the conceit of the lone, intrepid traveller. His *Diaries 1969–1979: The Python Years* appeared in 2006.

palinode [Greek, παλινῳδία, 'song sung over again', 'recantation'] Usually a poem or work in which the author retracts what she or he has formerly said or written. 'Palinode' is the Catholic shepherd in the 'May' eclogue of Edmund *Spenser's *The *Shepheardes Calender.*

Palladianism The 18th-century revival of the architectural style of *Palladio and of his follower Inigo *Jones. The movement, dominant in English architectural theory from *c.*1720 to *c.*1770, marks a turning away from the individual panache of Nicholas Hawksmoor (1661–1736) and Sir John *Vanbrugh towards a purer form of classicism, associated additionally with Vitruvius. Colen Campbell's *Vitruvius Britannicus* (3 vols, 1715–25), a collection of engravings of English buildings inspired by antiquity, and Giacomo Leoni's English version of Palladio's *I quattro libri dell'architettura* (4 vols, 1715–20), established the style. Chiswick House (1725–9), home to the architect-earl Lord Burlington, was built avowedly under the influence of Palladio's Villa Rotonda, and epitomized the movement in England. Alexander *Pope may have advised Burlington on his Palladian transformation of Burlington House in Piccadilly; his *Epistle to Burlington* (1731) both satirizes the excesses of the style (in the grandiose monstrosity of Timon's villa) and defines its aspirations.

PALLADIO, Andrea (1508–80) Influential Italian architect of the late Renaissance, whose style was formed by his passion for antiquity, a knowledge of Vitruvius (*fl.* 40 BC), and his response to High Renaissance and mannerist architects. He was unrivalled in his ability to express the ideas of antiquity in a modern idiom, yet he was a sophisticated mannerist architect, and as his career progressed his treatment of classical themes became increasingly imaginative. Palladio designed the churches of San Giorgio Maggiore (1566–80) and Il Redentore (begun 1577) in Venice, but most of his works are in and around Vicenza; they include many town palaces, like the Teatro Olimpico, which was begun in 1580 and finished by Scamozzi (1558–1615), and many country houses and villas which were to affect English architecture in the early 18th century. The characteristic Palladian villa has a symmetrically planned central block, with a portico deriving from a classical temple front and low wings. The most famous is the untypical Villa Rotonda (1550–51). Palladio's buildings became widely known through his *Quattro libri dell'architettura* (1570).
See also PALLADIANISM.

Palladis Tamia *See* MERES, FRANCIS.

Palliser Novels A term used to describe the political novels (or, as he liked to call them, the 'parliamentary' novels) of Anthony *Trollope, which are **Can You Forgive Her?*, **Phineas Finn, The *Eustace Diamonds, *Phineas Redux, The *Prime Minister,* and *The *Duke's Children.*

Pall Mall Gazette An evening paper founded in 1865 by Frederick Greenwood (1830–1909) and George *Smith to combine the features of a newspaper with political and social articles. Its name was taken from Thackeray's **Pendennis,* where Captain Shandon in the Marshalsea prepares the prospectus of 'The Pall Mall Gazette', 'written by gentlemen for gentlemen'. Early contributors included Sir Henry Maine (1822–88), Anthony *Trollope, James Fitzjames *Stephen, Leslie *Stephen, and Matthew *Arnold (whose *Friendship's Garland* first appeared in it); in 1880 Smith parted with it to his Liberal son-in-law, and John *Morley took over as editor, to be succeeded (1883–9) by W. T. *Stead, whose sensational campaigning journalism altered the character of the paper. Greenwood produced instead the newly founded Conservative *St James's Gazette.* The paper was incorporated into the *Evening Standard* in 1923. See R. Schultz, *Crusader in Babylon: W. T. Stead and the Pall Mall Gazette* (1972).

PALMER, Samuel (1805–81) Romantic painter and etcher, born in Newington, London. His early aspirations were literary, and he greatly admired William *Blake, to whom he was introduced in 1824 by the painter John Linnell (1792–1882). He settled for some years, 1826–32, in Shoreham, Kent, where he painted some of his most celebrated visionary pastoral landscapes. He later travelled in north Wales, Devon, and Italy, all of which provided inspiration. Some of his subjects were drawn from the *Bible and the classics (he produced an English translation of *Virgil's *Eclogues,* published 1881), but he also looked to English literature, such as John *Bunyan and Charles *Dickens (*Pictures from Italy,* 1846). His fine watercolours on the themes of John Milton's *'L'Allegro' and *'Il Penseroso' belong to his later years after 1868. His powerfully poetic imagination has won the admiration of many writers. See Raymond Lister, *Samuel Palmer* (1987).

Palmerin of England (*Palmeirim de Inglaterra*) A chivalric romance attributed to the Portuguese writer Francisco de Moraes (*c.*1500–1572). The Palmerin cycle deals with the exploits and loves of Palmerin d'Oliva, emperor of Constantinople, and his various descendants—one of them, Palmerin of England, is the subject of the sixth tale in the cycle. The daughter of Palmerin d'Oliva, Flerida by name, married Don Duardos, son of Fadrique, king of Great Britain, and became the mother of Palmerin of England and his brother Floriano of the Desert. Duardos having been imprisoned in the castle of the giant Dramusiando by Eutropa, a magician, a savage carries off Palmerin and Floriano intending them as food for his hunting lions, but his wife insists on bringing them up. Palmerin is taken to Constantinople and appointed to become servant to his cousin Polinarda, with whom he falls in love; while Floriano is taken to London and appointed to serve Flerida. Palmerin and Floriano undertake the quest of Don Duardos, and the former is successful. Thereafter the identity of the brothers is revealed and Palmerin marries Polinarda. Then the sultan advances against the Christians and demands the surrender of Polinarda as a condition of peace. Finally the Turks attack Constantinople; all the Turks and most of the Christians perish, but Palmerin survives. Anthony *Munday translated the Palmerin cycle into English (through a French intermediary), 1581–95. It was highly popular with the Elizabethan middle classes, and there are many references to Palmerin in the plays of the time (e.g. *The *Knight of the Burning Pestle*, where the vogue for such chivalric fantasies is mocked). A revised translation by Robert *Southey appeared in 1807, in which Southey suggests debts to *Palmerin* from *Shakespeare, Edmund *Spenser, and Philip *Sidney. See M. Patchell, *The Palmerin Romances in Elizabethan Prose Fiction* (1947). *Palmerin of England* and **Amadis of Gaul* were two romances of chivalry spared from the holocaust of such works in **Don Quixote* (I. 6).

Pamela The heir to the dukedom of Arcadia in Philip *Sidney's romance. Samuel *Richardson took her name for the heroine of his first novel.

***Pamela,** *or Virtue Rewarded* Samuel *Richardson's first novel, published 1740–41. *Pamela* consists entirely of letters and journals, of which Richardson presents himself as the 'editor'. His 'new species of writing' built on the existing form of the *epistolary novel by giving the six correspondents in *Pamela* their own particular style and point of view. Pamela herself provides most of the letters and journals, with the 'hero', Mr B., having only two. Pamela Andrews is a handsome, intelligent girl of 15 when her employer, Lady B., dies. Without protection, Pamela is pursued by Mr B., Lady B.'s son, but she rejects him and remains determined to retain her chastity. Letters reveal Mr B.'s cruel dominance and pride, but also Pamela's half-acknowledged tenderness for him, as well as her vanity and prudence. Mr B. separates her from her friends, Mrs Jervis the housekeeper and Mr Longman the steward, and dispatches her to B—Hall, his remote house in Lincolnshire, where she is imprisoned, guarded, and threatened by the cruel Mrs Jewkes. The chaplain, Mr Williams, is her friend, but he is powerless to help. For 40 days, allowed no visits or correspondence, she keeps a detailed journal, analysing her situation and her feelings. She despairs, and begins to think of suicide. Mr B., supposing her spirit must now be broken, arrives at B—Hall, and, thinking himself generous, offers to make her his mistress and keep her in style. She refuses indignantly, and he later attempts to rape her and then to arrange a mock marriage. Gradually each becomes aware of their faults, and of the genuine nature of their affection. However, Pamela again retreats and refuses his proposal of marriage. She is sent away from B—Hall, but a message gives her a last chance. Overcoming her pride and caution, she decides to trust Mr B., and they are married. Pamela's unimpeachable goodness then wins over Mr B.'s supercilious relations, initially disgusted at his class treachery in marrying a servant. The book was enormously successful and fashionable, generating sermons, poems, stage versions, sequences of paintings, and unauthorized continuations of the story, including Eliza *Haywood's *Anti-Pamela*. Further editions were soon called for, and Richardson's own sequel, usually known as *Pamela in her Exalted Condition*, appeared in 1741, partly to milk the success of the first novel and partly to counter spurious versions. Here Pamela is exhibited as a domestic paragon, patiently leading her profligate husband to reform, breastfeeding her children, and bringing about the penitence of the wicked through her good example. Much space is given over to discussion of moral, domestic, and literary subjects. Though Richardson's novel was a foundational text of a new realism in English fiction, in giving primacy to a working-class woman and her direct self-expression, *Pamela* also generated much controversy and opposition: **Shamela* (1741, anonymous but assumed to be by Henry *Fielding) lampooned what the author regarded as the novel's hypocritical morality; and Fielding's **Joseph Andrews*, which begins as a parody of *Pamela*, appeared in 1742.

pamphleteering, origins of The word 'pamphlet' appears to derive, curiously, from the generalized use of the title of a popular 12th-century French love poem in Latin called *Pamphilus, seu de Amore*, which was adapted to 'Pamphilet'. George *Orwell, in his introduction to *British Pamphleteers* (vol. i, 1948), describes a pamphlet as 'a short piece of polemical writing, printed in the form of a booklet and aimed at a large public', usually of 5,000–10,000 words, and unbound. Although the term can also refer to works in manuscript (it is used in this way by Thomas *Hoccleve), and it could be used of a poem (William *Shakespeare calls *The *Rape of Lucrece* 'this pamphlet'), it is especially associated with printed tracts of an ephemeral and polemical kind.

Pamphleteering may be said to have got fully under way with the Reformation, and during the 16th century became widespread. It was associated as much with low-life *jest book, *coney-catching, and plague literature as with religious and political tracts (*see* NASHE, THOMAS; DEKKER, THOMAS; GREENE, ROBERT; MARTIN MARPRELATE). John *Knox's *First Blast of the Trumpet against the Monstrous Regiment* [i.e. 'government'] *of Women* (1558) was, perhaps, the first British political pamphlet. The religious and political ferment of the 17th century, along with the attendant breakdown of licensing and censorship, produced many thousands of pamphlets, some of high literary quality; John *Milton's are perhaps the best known (but *see also* WINSTANLEY, GERRARD; OVERTON, RICHARD; WALWYN, WILLIAM; CLARKSON, LAURENCE; COPPE, ABIEZER; LILBURNE, JOHN; NEDHAM, MARCHAMONT; BERKENHEAD, SIR JOHN). Many, such as **Tyranipocrit Discovered* and **Light Shining in Buckinghamshire* (1648), were anonymous; George *Thomason made an unusually complete collection of works from this period. The renewal of press control at the Restoration revived the *manuscript circulation of libellous, seditious, and obscene works. In the 18th century, though important works in pamphlet form were produced by writers like Daniel

*Defoe and Jonathan *Swift, and collections of antiquarian tracts such as the *Harleian Miscellany* were produced, the rise of weekly periodicals tended to reduce the demand for this type of publication. The form was effectively and extensively revived during the 19th century by the *Oxford Movement and later by the Fabian Society.

Pan In Greek and Roman mythology a hairy, goat-legged, lecherous god, who inhabited *Arcadia, where he pursued *nymphs unsuccessfully and was sacred to shepherds. As the inventor of the reed pipes, the syrinx, he was associated with both music and poetry. He became a key figure in classical *pastoral, and in Renaissance pastoral, for example in Spenser's **Shepheardes Calender*, he sometimes represented not only the lover and the poet but also Christ, because he is the good shepherd and in Greek Pan signifies all. Late 19th-century and early 20th-century literature saw a revival of interest in Pan, as a figure representing the unruly powers of natural fertility. Those who wrote of him in this guise include *Saki, E. M. *Forster, Arthur *Machen, and D. H. *Lawrence.

Pandarus In Homer's **Iliad*, a son of Lycaon who assisted the Trojans in their war against the Greeks. The role that he plays in *Chaucer's and *Shakespeare's stories of Troilus and Criseyde/Cressida was the invention of *Boccaccio in his **Filostrato* (where he is called Pandaro; see N. R. Havely, *Chaucer's Boccaccio*, 1980). In Boccaccio he is the cousin of Cressida, presumably much the same age as her and Troilus; Chaucer strikingly changes him from her cousin to her uncle and guardian, the effect of which is to increase the sense of irresponsibility towards her in arranging their love affair. His role plays a central part in the atmosphere of sourness in which the events of Shakespeare's play occur. The word 'pander' (as Shakespeare says: III. ii. 197) derives from his role as go-between for Troilus and Criseyde.

Pandemonium A word coined by John *Milton, the abode of all the demons; a place represented by Milton (**Paradise Lost*, I. 756) as the capital of hell, containing the council chamber of the devils.

Pandosto, *or The Triumph of Time* A prose romance by Robert *Greene first published in 1588. It went through eleven editions up to 1636, but is now best known as the source for *The *Winter's Tale*. William *Shakespeare followed Greene closely, except that he preserved the life of Hermione (Bellaria in *Pandosto*), and made Leontes/Pandosto, not Hermione/Bellaria, appeal to the oracle. Pandosto is killed at the end of the romance, 'to close up the comedy with a tragical stratagem'. *Pandosto* is one of Greene's best narratives, and understandably popular in its time.

panegyric A formal public speech in extended and elaborate praise of some person or group; or a written composition of similar laudatory tendency, such as *Dryden's coronation poem for Charles II, *To His Sacred Majesty, a Panegyrick on his Coronation* (1661).

PANIZZI, Antonio (later Sir Anthony) (1797–1879) Born in Italy. He fled to England as a political exile in 1823, where he was befriended by Ugo *Foscolo, William *Roscoe, and Lord *Brougham. He taught Italian before obtaining (1831) a post in the library of the *British Museum, eventually becoming (in 1856) the Museum's principal librarian or director. With his great talent for administration, he was responsible for the preparation of a new catalogue and for the plans of the celebrated circular domed Reading Room which he opened personally in 1857. The inaugural Panizzi Lectures on *book history at the British Library were given by D. F. McKenzie in 1985.

Panopticon Jeremy *Bentham's term (1843) for a proposed type of prison, consisting of cells ranged round a central point from which a warder could observe the prisoners while they could see neither him nor their fellow prisoners in adjacent cells. Michel *Foucault took up the idea in *Surveiller et punir* (1975), his study of the change in the way power was exercised after the 16th century. Before this he claims power was exerted through violence and coercion of the body, whereas the body was subsequently schooled to discipline itself. The Panopticon exemplifies this change; the prisoner, unable to see the guard and know whether observation is taking place at any given time, exercises self-control over behaviour and demeanour.

Pantagruel *See* RABELAIS, FRANÇOIS.

Pantisocracy A utopian scheme invented by S. T. *Coleridge and Robert *Southey in 1794–5, to establish an egalitarian commune of six families in America, based on a joint-stock farm. The scheme ended in acrimony when Southey, to Coleridge's horror, suggested that the Pantisocrats should keep servants.

pantomime (1) Originally a Roman actor, who performed in dumb show, representing by mimicry various characters and scenes. (2) An English dramatic performance, assimilating some of the traditions of the Italian **commedia dell'arte*, originally consisting of action without speech, but in its further development consisting of a dramatized traditional fairy-tale, with singing, dancing, acrobatics, clowning, topical jokes, a transformation scene, and certain stock roles, especially the 'principal boy' (i.e. hero) acted by a woman and the 'dame' acted by a man. *See* MIME.

Paolo and **Francesca** Francesca, daughter of Giovanni da Polenta, count of Ravenna, was given in marriage by him to Giovanni (Sciancato, the Lame) Malatesta, of Rimini, an ill-favoured man, in return for his military services. She fell in love with Paolo, her husband's brother, and, their relations being discovered, the two lovers were put to death in 1289. *Dante, at the end of the fifth canto of the *Inferno*, relates his conversation with Francesca, who told him how her fall was occasioned by the reading of the tale of Launcelot and Guinevere. The 'Galeotto' mentioned by Dante is Galahault, the prince who, in the story of the early loves of Launcelot and Guinevere, not included in *Malory, introduces Launcelot to the queen. The story of Paolo and Francesca was the subject of the poem *The *Story of Rimini* by Leigh *Hunt, and it remained popular throughout the 19th century, most famously in *Tchaikovsky's symphonic fantasy *Francesca da Rimini*.

Paper Money Lyrics Burlesque poems by Thomas Love *Peacock, ridiculing political economists and bankers. They were written in the late 1820s, but not published until 1837, after the death of James *Mill, Peacock's immediate superior at the India Office.

Pap with an Hatchet The title of a tract supporting the bishops contributed in 1589 by John *Lyly to the *Martin Marprelate controversy. The expression appears to be ironical, signifying feeding an infant ('pap' is baby food) with threats, and refers to the 'violent repression of religious dissent' (*OED*). Lyly's *pamphlet is a mixture of abuse and ribaldry.

Paracelsus A dramatic poem in blank verse by Robert *Browning, published 1835. The career of the historical Paracelsus (1493–1541), the maverick physician, provides Browning, despite his claim to the contrary, with an opportunity for his own exploration of the processes of the creative imagination, in particular the conflict between 'Love' (self-forgetting) and 'Knowledge' (self-assertion) in the mind of the artist. The poem's critical success introduced Browning to literary London and launched his career, at first in the (unhappy) direction of the theatre. Browning's works up to the end of **Bells and Pomegranates* were published as by 'Robert Browning, author of Paracelsus'.

paradise The name often given to the biblical garden of *Eden, but also to heaven, the blessed state after death; it can have literal or physical and spiritual or allegorical meanings, and can apply to past, present, or future states, both earthly and heavenly.

See Divina commedia; Earthly Paradise; Paradise Lost; Paradise Regained.

Paradise Lost An epic poem by John *Milton, originally in ten books, subsequently rearranged in twelve, first printed 1667. Milton expressed his intention of writing a great epic poem as early as 1639. An autograph list of possible subjects, some scriptural, some from British history, survives from about 1640–41, with drafts of the scheme of a poem on 'Paradise Lost'. The work was not, however, begun in earnest until 1658, and it was finished, according to John *Aubrey, in 1663. It was licensed for publication by the Revd Thomas Tomkyns, chaplain to the archbishop of Canterbury. Milton sold the copyright to Samuel Simmons for £5 down, and a further £5 when the first impression of 1,300 copies was exhausted. His widow subsequently parted with all further claims for £8. Milton added to later copies of the first edition an 'Argument', summarizing the contents of each book, and also a defence of his choice of blank verse which condemns rhyme as 'the invention of a barbarous age, to set off wretched matter and lame metre'.

Book I. The poet, invoking the 'Heavenly Muse', states his theme, the fall of man through disobedience, and his aim, which is to 'justify the ways of God to men'. He then presents the defeated archangel *Satan, with *Beelzebub, his second in command, and his rebellious angels, lying on the burning lake of hell. Satan awakens his legions, rouses their spirits, and summons a council. The palace of Satan, *Pandemonium (a word coined by Milton), is built.

Book II. The council debates whether another battle for the recovery of Heaven should be hazarded, *Moloch recommending open war, *Belial and *Mammon recommending peace in order to avoid worse torments. Beelzebub announces the creation of 'another world, the happy seat | Of some new race called Man', which may prove a means of revenge. Satan undertakes to visit it alone, passes through hell-gates, guarded by Sin and Death, and flies up through the realm of Chaos.

Book III. Milton invokes celestial light to illumine the 'ever-during dark' of his own blindness, then describes God, who sees Satan's flight towards our world, and foretells his success and the fall and punishment of man, emphasizing that man will fall not through predestination but through free will. The Son of God offers himself as a ransom, is accepted, and exalted as the Saviour. Satan alights on the outer convex of our universe, 'a Limbo large and broad, since called | The Paradise of Fools'. He finds the stairs leading up to heaven, descends to the sun, disguises himself as 'a stripling cherub', and in this shape is directed to earth by Uriel, where he alights on Mount Niphates in Armenia.

Book IV. Satan, at first tormented by doubts, resolves 'evil be thou my good' and journeys on towards the garden of *Eden, where he first sees Adam and Eve 'in naked majesty', and overhears their discourse about the forbidden Tree of Knowledge. He resolves to tempt them to disobey the prohibition but is discovered by the guardian angels Ithuriel and Zephon as he squats like a toad near the ear of Eve, and expelled from the garden by their commander, *Gabriel.

Book V. Eve relates to Adam the disquieting dream of temptation which Satan had inspired. He comforts her, and they set about their daily tasks. Raphael, sent by God, comes to paradise, warns Adam, and enjoins obedience. They discuss reason, free will, and predestination, and Raphael, at Adam's request, relates how Satan, inspired by hatred and envy of the newly anointed Messiah, inspired his legions to revolt, resisted only by Abdiel—'Among the faithless, faithful only he'.

Book VI. Raphael continues his narrative, telling how Michael and Gabriel were sent to fight against Satan. After indecisive battles the Son of God himself, alone, attacked the hosts of Satan, and, driving them to the verge of heaven, forced them to leap down through chaos into the deep.

Book VII. Milton evokes Urania (whom he identifies as the spirit who inspired Moses to write the Book of Genesis), and requests her to aid him to 'fit audience find, though few', in the evil days on which he has fallen; then continues Raphael's narrative, with an account of God's decision to send his Son to create another world from the vast abyss. He describes the six days of creation, ending with the creation of man, and a renewed warning to Adam that death will be the penalty for eating of the fruit of the Tree of Knowledge.

Book VIII. Adam enquires concerning the motions of the heavenly bodies, and is answered 'doubtfully'. The controversy regarding the Ptolemaic and Copernican systems was at its height when *Paradise Lost* was written, and Milton declined to decide between them, as seen in X. 668 ff. Adam relates what he remembers since his own creation, notably his own need for rational fellowship, and his plea to his Maker for a companion, which is answered by the creation of Eve. Adam and Raphael talk of the relations between the sexes, then, with a final warning to 'take heed least passion sway | Thy judgement', Raphael departs.

Book IX. Insisting that his argument is 'not less but more heroic' than the themes of *Homer and *Virgil, Milton describes Satan's entry into the body of the serpent, in which form he finds Eve, she having insisted, despite Adam's warnings, on going gardening alone. He persuades her to eat of the Tree of Knowledge. Eve relates to Adam what has passed and brings him some of the fruit. Adam, recognizing that she is doomed, resolves to perish with her: 'If death | Consort with thee, death is to me as life; | So forcible within my heart I feel | The bond of nature draw me to my own.' He also eats the fruit, and after initial intoxication in their lost innocence, they cover their nakedness and fall to mutual accusation.

Book X. God sends his Son to judge the transgressors. They greet him with guilt and shame, and confess, and he pronounces his sentence. Sin and Death resolve to come to this world, and make a broad highway to it from hell. Satan returns to hell and announces his victory, whereupon, in their moment of triumph, he and his angels are temporarily transformed into serpents chewing ashes. Adam, recognizing that in him 'all posterity stands cursed', at first reproaches Eve and despairs, but she suggests they seek mercy from the Son of God.

Book XI. The Son of God, seeing their penitence, intercedes. God decrees that they must leave paradise, and sends down Michael to carry out his command. Eve laments; Adam pleads not to be banished from the 'bright appearances' of God, but Michael reassures him that God is omnipresent, then unfolds to him the future, revealing to him the consequences of his original sin in the death of Abel and the future miseries of mankind, ending with the Flood and the new Covenant.

Book XII. Michael relates the subsequent history of the Old Testament, then describes the coming of the Messiah, his incarnation, death, resurrection, and ascension, which leads Adam to rejoice over so much good sprung from his own sin. Michael also foretells the corrupt state of the Church until the Second Coming. Eve meanwhile, during these revelations, has been comforted by a dream presaging 'some great good'. Resolved on obedience and submission, and assured that they may possess 'a Paradise within' that will be 'happier far' than the lost one, they are led out of the garden.

Paradise Lost has inspired a mass of critical commentary and interpretation, theological discussion, imitations and adaptations, and illustrations. (For bibliography, *see* MILTON, JOHN.) Illustrators include *Fuseli, 1802; *Blake, 1806; John *Martin, 1827, 1846, 1847, and so on; *Turner, 1835; and *Doré, 1866. See Marcia Pointon, *Milton and English Art* (1970).

Paradise of Dainty Devices, The A collection of works by minor poets of the 1560s and 1570s: they include Lord *Vaux, the earl of *Oxford, Thomas *Churchyard, and William Hunnis (d. 1597). Compiled by Richard *Edwards and containing some of his own poems, the volume was published posthumously in 1576 and frequently reprinted. It was edited by H. E. Rollins (1927).

Paradise Regained An epic poem in four books by John *Milton, published 1671. It is a sequel to **Paradise Lost*, and deals exclusively with the temptation of Jesus in the wilderness. According to the poet's conception, whereas paradise was lost by the yielding of Adam and Eve to *Satan's temptation, it was regained by the resistance of the Son of God to the temptation of the same spirit. Satan is here represented not in the majestic lineaments of *Paradise Lost*, but as a cunning, smooth, and dissembling creature, a 'spirit unfortunate', as he describes himself. The style, by comparison with *Paradise Lost*, is bare, conveying the rigour of Jesus' astringent intelligence.

Book I relates the baptism of Jesus and the proclamation from heaven that he is the Son of God. Satan, alarmed, summons a council of devils, and undertakes his temptation. Jesus is led into the wilderness, not knowing why, but trusting that God will reveal all he needs to know. After 40 days, without food, he is approached by Satan, disguised as 'an aged man in rural weeds', who suggests he should turn the stones around him into bread. Jesus penetrates his disguise and rebukes him for tempting him to distrust God. Night falls on the desert.

Books II and III. Meanwhile Andrew and Simon seek Jesus, and Mary is troubled at his absence. Satan confers again with his council. He once more tries the hunger temptation, conjuring up a sumptuous banquet with the added allure of beautiful female attendants, which Jesus contemptuously rejects. Satan next appeals to the higher appetites for wealth and power, and a disputation follows as to the real value of earthly glory. Satan, confuted, reminds Jesus that the kingdom of David is under the Roman yoke, and suggests that he should free it. He takes Jesus to a high mountain and shows him the kingdoms of the earth. To the east, the powers of Rome and Parthia, displayed in a vision, are pitted against each other, and Satan offers Jesus an alliance with, or conquest of, the Parthians, and the liberation of the Jews then in captivity.

Book IV. Jesus remaining unmoved by Satan's 'politic maxims', the tempter, turning to the western side, draws his attention to Rome and proposes the expulsion of the wicked emperor Tiberius; and finally, pointing out Athens, urges the attractions of its poets, orators, and philosophers. Jesus scornfully rejects these, maintaining that Hebrew poetry far excels Greek. Satan returns Jesus to the wilderness, and assails him during the night with ugly dreams and a terrible storm, but Jesus is undaunted.

On the third morning Satan carries him to the highest pinnacle of the temple and bids him cast himself down, only to receive the enigmatic answer, 'Tempt not the Lord thy God' (a quotation from Deuteronomy 6: 16). Satan falls 'smitten with amazement' and a 'fiery globe' of angels bears Jesus away.
See ELLWOOD, THOMAS.

Paradiso, *of Dante* *See* DIVINA COMMEDIA.

pararhyme *See* RHYME.

Parasitaster, The, *or The Fawn* A comedy by John *Marston, published 1606. Hercules, the widowed duke of Ferrara, wishes his son Tiberio to marry Dulcimel, daughter of a neighbouring prince, and, in order to persuade him, declares that he will marry Dulcimel himself. He sends Tiberio to negotiate the marriage, and under the name of Faunus follows in disguise to see how matters develop. The resourceful Dulcimel falls in love with Tiberio and manages to win him.

parataxis The absence of relative or dependent clauses (subordination), as in 'I came, I saw, I conquered'. The adjectival form is 'paratactic'.
See HYPOTAXIS.

'Pardoner's Tale, The' *See* CANTERBURY TALES, 14.

PARETSKY, Sara (1947–) American novelist, born in Iowa, who has published a series of narratives centring on a female private investigator called V. I. Warshawski, some of which explore the impact of the past on the present: the Nazi concentration camps in *Total Recall* (2001) and the McCarthy era in *Blacklist* (2003).

Paris *See* ILIAD.

PARIS, Matthew (*c.*1200–1259) Benedictine monk and prolific historian, who entered the monastery of St Albans in 1217, succeeding Roger of Wendover (d. 1236) as chronicler, and compiling the *Chronica Majora*, his greatest work, there from 1235 to 1259. The work is outstanding for its expressive liveliness as well as for its historical value. Among Paris's many other works are abbreviated versions of the *Chronica Majora*; the *Historia Anglorum*, a summary of events in England from 1200 to 1253; the *Vitae Duorum Offarum* ('Lives of the two Offas', the king of the Angles and the king of Mercia); saints' lives; and the *Gesta Abbatum Monasterii S. Albani*, the lives of the first 23 abbots up to 1255. He went to Norway on a papal visit in 1248. He may have spent time in Paris, but Paris was a 13th-century English surname.

'Parish Register, The' A poem by George *Crabbe, published 1807. Developing the form of *The *Village*, 'The Parish Register' relates the memories of a country parson as he looks through the entries in his registers of births, marriages, and deaths. The work first revealed Crabbe's gift for narrative, and reaffirmed his determination to present the realities of life, however sordid. The tales include the story of Phoebe Dawson, which pleased Walter *Scott and C. J. *Fox; and the terrible account, written in stanzas (and possibly under the effect of opium) in 'Sir Eustace Grey', of a patient in a madhouse.

PARK, Mungo (1771–1806) Scottish explorer, born near Selkirk. He studied medicine at Edinburgh University, and sailed as assistant surgeon with the East India Company to Sumatra (1793–4) where he collected botanical specimens. In 1794 the African Association appointed him to determine the course of the river Niger, which he reached at Segou where, he confirmed, it flowed eastwards. His best-selling *Travels in the Interior Districts of Africa* (1799) also includes detailed accounts of Mandinka culture. Contemporary readers were impressed by its verisimilitude, but the text also draws on conceptions of the picturesque, the sentimental, and the heroic associated with *Romanticism. He returned to the Niger in 1805 with a much larger party, and travelled 1,500 miles further downstream but died in northern Nigeria. *The Journal of a Mission in the Interior of Africa* (1815) was assembled from Park's surviving notes with additional material from his African guides. His life is the subject of the novel *Water Music* (1981) by T. Coraghessan Boyle. The standard biography is Kenneth Lupton, *Mungo Park, the African Traveller* (1978).

PARKER, Dorothy (1893–1967) Née Rothschild, New York-born American humorist and journalist, legendary for her instant wit and for her satirical verses; she also wrote sketches and short stories, many of them published in the *New Yorker* and various collections. She worked as a screenwriter in Hollywood and was blacklisted in the McCarthy era. See Leslie Frewin, *The Late Mrs Dorothy Parker* (1986).

PARKER, Henry *See* MORLEY, LORD.

PARKER, Matthew (1504–75) Archbishop of Canterbury and patron of scholarship, born in Norwich and educated at Corpus Christi College, Cambridge. In 1544 he was elected master of the college, where he reformed the library, to which he was to bequeath his superb collections of manuscripts, printed books, and plate. Having lost his offices during Queen Mary's reign, he reluctantly accepted the archbishopric of Canterbury on the accession of *Elizabeth I, and was consecrated at Lambeth in 1559. He identified himself with the party (afterwards known as the Anglican party) which sought to establish a *via media* between Roman Catholicism and Puritanism. From 1563 to 1568 he was occupied with the production of the Bishops' Bible (*see* BIBLE, THE ENGLISH), his most distinguished service to the theological studies of the day. In his later years he retired more and more from society, being conscious of the strength of the opposing current, headed by the earl of *Leicester. Buried in his private chapel at Lambeth, in 1648 his remains were disinterred and reburied under a dunghill, but after the Restoration they were restored to their original resting place. Besides being a great benefactor to his college and to the University of Cambridge, he was a patron of scholars and historians, including John *Foxe and John *Stow. Often using his own manuscripts, he instigated editions of *Asser, *Ælfric, *Gildas, the *Flores Historiarum* of Matthew of Westminster, Matthew *Paris, and other early chroniclers (an important manuscript of the **Anglo-Saxon Chronicle*, given by him to Corpus Christi College, is known as the 'Parker Chronicle'). In these editions, along with his own *De Antiquitate Britannicae Ecclesiae et Privilegiis Ecclesiae Cantuariensis, cum Archiepiscopis eiusdem 70* (1572–4), he sought to assert the antiquity and legitimacy of the Church of England. In spite of Elizabeth I's dislike of clerical matrimony, he was married, and left a son.

Parker Society Named after Matthew *Parker, founded in 1840 by Church of England evangelicals to combat the effects of the *Oxford Movement and the spread of *Roman Catholicism. The society published the works of the 16th-century reformers in 54 volumes (1841–55), including William *Tyndale, John *Bale, Thomas *Cranmer, Miles *Coverdale, Hugh *Latimer, Nicholas *Ridley, John Jewel (1522–71), and John Whitgift (1530–1604), and volumes on the Elizabethan *liturgy.

PARKINSON, John (1567–1650) Apothecary to *James I, herbalist, author of *Paradisi in Sole Paradisus Terrestris, or A Garden of All Sorts of Pleasant Flowers which our English Air will Permit to Be Nursed up* (1629), with woodcuts; also of a herbal, *Theatrum Botanicum* (1640).

PARKMAN, Francis (1823–93) American historian, born in Boston. After graduation from Harvard University he travelled in Europe, then journeyed to Wyoming to study Native American life, giving an account of his experiences in *The Oregon Trail* (1849), which was dictated, owing to his own ill health, to his cousin and companion Quincy A. Shaw. His history of the struggle of the English and French for dominion in North America was published in a series of studies, beginning with his *History of the Conspiracy of the Pontiac* (1851) and continuing through several volumes, concluding with *A Half-Century of Conflict* (1892). Donald *Davie pays tribute to Parkman's evocation of historical figures in *A Sequence for Francis Parkman* (1961).

Parleyings with Certain People of Importance in their Day A volume of poems in blank verse by Robert *Browning, published 1887. The phrase 'certain people of importance' derives from a passage in *Dante's *Vita nuova*. Browning refers to a number of obscure historical figures whose works he had studied in his youth. Each of these figures is matched by a contemporary of Browning's. The collection constitutes an oblique autobiography and self-dramatization, and is important to an understanding both of the sources of Browning's art and of the mature processes of that art. Perhaps the most celebrated of the 'Parleyings' are the two concluding ones, with 'Gérard de Lairesse' and 'Charles Avison'.

Parliament of Fowls, The A dream-poem (*c.* late 1370s–early 1380s) by Geoffrey *Chaucer in 699 lines of *rhyme royal. It may (but need not) have been written in connection with the marriage of Richard II to Anne of Bohemia (1382). After a prologue interweaving the themes of love and reading, the narrator reads Cicero's *Dream of Scipio*, in which Africanus, Scipio's grandfather, explains the importance of 'commune profyt'. Having fallen asleep, he dreams that Africanus pushes him into a garden in which the goddess Nature presides over the choosing of mates on St Valentine's Day. Here the theme of common profit is put under severe pressure as three male eagles pay court to a 'formel' (female). There follows a long dispute about the criteria for success in a love suit, the argument centring on the opposition between the eagles' courtly approach and the pragmatism exemplified by the duck. The female is unable to decide which suitor to take, and Nature, while granting the other birds their mates, accedes to her request to wait a year before deciding. The political and philosophical issues that the poem suggests are left undefined and unresolved. Ed. H. Phillips and N. Havely, *Chaucer's Dream Poetry* (1997).

Parnassians A group of 19th-century French poets, headed by *Leconte de Lisle, who sought to free poetry from what they saw as the extravagances of *Romanticism in favour of restraint, discipline, precision, and objectivity. Their name derives from the three collections of their work published under the title *Le Parnasse contemporain* (1866, 1871, 1876: *Contemporary Parnassus*). Also associated with the group were José-Maria de Heredia (1842–1905), whose collection *Les Trophées* (*The Trophies*) appeared in 1893, Catulle Mendès (1841–1909), and René-François-Armand Sully-Prudhomme (1839–1907).

Parnassus Plays, The The name given to a group of three plays produced between 1598 and 1602 by students of St John's College, Cambridge, consisting of *The Pilgrimage to Parnassus* and *The Return from Parnassus*, the latter in two parts. Authorship has not been established, but they seem to be the work of two dramatists, unusually writing academic drama in English rather than Latin (or even Greek), as was more common. They have been attributed to John *Day and, more recently, to John Weever of Queen's and Joseph *Hall. They present the attempts of a group of young men (one apparently modelled on Thomas *Nashe) to resist temptation and to gain preferment or at least a livelihood, and are full of allusions to contemporary literature and drama. In the second play a fool, Gullio, quotes from **Venus and Adonis* and **Romeo and Juliet* and exclaims, 'O sweet Master Shakespeare! I'll have his picture in my study at the court.' The play contains the earliest known parody of Shakespearian verse, written in the *rhyme-royal stanza form of *Lucrece*. In the third, more satirical, section Richard *Burbage and Will *Kemp audition recent students for places in their company, using Richard III's opening soliloquy as a test piece, and the students are shown on their way to London, learning how to catch a patron or cheat a tradesman, and following menial occupations. Eventually, discouraged, they 'return' to Cambridge. The plays were first published together in 1886 and edited by J. B. Leishman (1949).

PARNELL, Charles Stewart (1846–91) Irish politician, born of an Anglo-Irish father and American mother at Avondale, Co. Wicklow, and educated at Magdalene College, Cambridge. He became MP for Meath in 1875 and was elected chairman of the Home Rule party. As president of the Irish National Land League he formulated the tactic of agrarian 'boycotting' in 1880. Parnell's enormous popular influence had gained him the title of 'uncrowned king of Ireland' before his imprisonment under coercion legislation in Kilmainham Jail in 1881. He converted *Gladstone and the Liberal Party to the idea of Home Rule and overthrew the Tory government in 1886. In 1887 a **Times* article, subsequently revealed as a forgery, accused him of condoning the Phoenix Park murders, but he triumphantly vindicated himself two years later. His career was ruined by his citation as co-respondent in a divorce case brought by Captain William O'Shea against his wife; the scandal led to a split amongst Irish nationalists and Parnell's repudiation in a series of by-elections. The fall of Parnell is mythologized in various ways by writers of the *Irish Revival, most notably James *Joyce.

PARNELL, Thomas (1679–1718) Irish poet, educated at Trinity College, Dublin. He was archdeacon of Clogher and a friend of Jonathan *Swift and Alexander *Pope (to whose *Iliad* translation he contributed an introductory essay). He was a member of the *Scriblerus Club. His *Essay on the Different Styles of Poetry* (1713) was dedicated to Viscount *Bolingbroke; his 'Hymn to Contentment' was published in Richard *Steele's *Poetical Miscellanies* (1714) and his mock-heroic *Homer's Battle of the Frogs and Mice with the Remarks of Zoilus* appeared in 1717 (*see* BATRACHOMYOMACHIA), but most of his work was published posthumously by Pope in 1721. His poems include 'The Hermit', in which the mysterious ways of God are revealed to the hermit by the apparently ruthless and amoral actions of a disguised angel, and 'Night-Piece on Death', a *graveyard poem, which in Oliver *Goldsmith's view inspired 'all those night-pieces and churchyard scenes that have since appeared' (Goldsmith's *Life of Parnell*, 1770). Samuel *Johnson praised 'the easy sweetness of his diction'. The first complete edition of his poems, ed. C. Rawson and F. P. Lock, appeared in 1985.

parody A work written in mocking imitation of the style of another work, that style being exaggerated or applied to an incongruous subject, as in *burlesque and *mock-epic verse. It may be distinguished from *pastiche on the basis of its mocking intent, and from *satire on the basis of its focus upon style rather than upon people and their conduct. In some cases, parody incorporates an element of literary criticism: notable English examples of this include Henry Fielding's **Shamela Andrews* (1741), a parodic critique of Samuel Richardson's novel **Pamela*; Jane Austen's **Northanger Abbey* (1818), written in affectionate mockery of the *Gothic novels of Ann *Radcliffe; and Stella Gibbons's **Cold Comfort Farm* (1932), which sends up the oversexed primitivism of Mary *Webb and other rural novelists. The tradition of English parody begins with Chaucer's **Canterbury Tales*, notably in its 'Tale of Sir Thopas'. It flourished in the 18th century in the mock-epic works of Alexander *Pope (who also wrote a bawdy parody of Chaucer) and others, and in the prose of Fielding and of Laurence *Sterne, whose **Tristram Shandy* involves continuous parodic play with the conventions of novelistic narration. The 19th century was a fertile period for verse parody, the distinctive styles of William *Wordsworth, Robert *Browning, and A. C. *Swinburne especially attracting numerous parodic imitations. The celebrated **Rejected Addresses* (1812) of James and Horatio *Smith provide one highlight of that tradition, another being the verses in the *Alice* books of 'Lewis Carroll' (*Dodgson) in absurd imitation of Wordsworth, Isaac *Watts, Robert *Southey, and others. Some poets even engaged in self-parody, for example S. T. *Coleridge ('On a Ruined House in a Romantic Country', 1797) and Swinburne ('Nephelidia', 1880). In the early 20th century, Max *Beerbohm's prose parodies of Henry *James and others in *A Christmas Garland* (1912) were widely admired, but the most versatile and accomplished parodist of the age was James *Joyce in his **Ulysses*: among many other parodic feats here, the fourteenth ('Oxen of the Sun') chapter manages to parody every phase in the development of English prose from the earliest times up to the then contemporary. In the later 20th century, Wendy *Cope established a reputation for verse parody, while parody and pastiche were strong elements in the plays of Tom *Stoppard. See Simon Dentith, *Parody* (2000).

paronomasia A rhetorical term for a pun or play on words, in which the repeated words are similar but not identical; for example, Lady Macbeth: 'I'll gild the faces of the grooms withal, | For it must seem their guilt.'

PARR, Samuel (1747–1825) Teacher and clergyman, educated at Harrow School (where he later taught) and Emmanuel College, Cambridge. He wrote a Latin epitaph on Samuel *Johnson, whom he knew personally, for the monument in St Paul's Cathedral. Because of his support for Charles James *Fox, and his forceful conversational style, he was regarded as 'the Whig Johnson'. Parr's *Works* appeared in eight volumes (1828).

PARRY, Sir Hubert (1848–1918) English composer and writer on music, educated at Eton College and Exeter College, Oxford, where he read widely. The cantata *Scenes from Prometheus Unbound* (based on P. B. *Shelley, 1880) and the choral settings of John *Milton, *Blessed Pair of Sirens* (1887) and *L'Allegro ed Il Penseroso* (1890), established his reputation. In

1895, on the bicentenary of Henry *Purcell's death, he collaborated with Robert *Bridges on the *Invocation to Music*. Later choral works include *The Pied Piper of Hamelin* (after Robert *Browning, 1905), and the six *Songs of Farewell* (1916, with words by Henry *Vaughan, John *Davies, Edmund *Campion, John *Lockhart, and John *Donne). Parry also produced twelve sets of *English Lyrics* for voice and piano. The writers Parry set include William *Shakespeare, Robert *Herrick, John *Keats, Alfred *Tennyson, A. C. *Swinburne, and Rudyard *Kipling. In 1916 Parry made the unison setting of William *Blake's short poem commonly known as 'Jerusalem'. Parry was knighted in 1898 and created baronet in 1902.

PARRY, Sir William Edward (1790–1855) Arctic explorer, whose expeditions are described in his three *Journals* of voyages for the discovery of a North-West Passage, undertaken between 1819 and 1825 (published 1821, 1824, 1826), and in his *Narrative of an Attempt to Reach the North Pole, 1827* (1828).

'Parson's Tale, The' *See* CANTERBURY TALES, 24.

Parthenophil and Parthenophe Published 1591, a collection of sonnets by Barnabe *Barnes, one of the first to appear after Philip *Sidney's **Astrophel and Stella*.

Partisan Review American literary and political periodical, published from 1934 to 2003, founded as a successor to *New Masses*. After the Second World War it moved away from supporting the Communist Party. Its contributors included T. S. *Eliot, George *Orwell, and Saul *Bellow.

PARTRIDGE, Frances (Catherine) (1900–2004) Diarist and translator, educated at Bedales School and Newnham College, Cambridge. She became with her husband Ralph Partridge (1894–1960) assistant editor of *The Greville Memoirs* (ed. Lytton *Strachey and Roger Fulford, 8 vols, 1938; *see* GREVILLE, CHARLES CAVENDISH FULKE). Six volumes of her own diaries (1985–2001), covering her experiences in and beyond the *Bloomsbury Group between the late 1930s and mid-1970s, gained her a wide readership late in life. A remarkably resilient and shrewd survivor, she was still reviewing for the *Spectator* at the age of 99.

Parzifal Middle High German epic poem by *Wolfram von Eschenbach. Composed early in the 13th century, its subject is the legend of *Perceval and the Holy *Grail.
See also TITUREL.

PASCAL, Blaise (1623–62) French mathematician, scientist, and religious thinker. As gifted in science as in letters, he did important work in geometry, hydrodynamics, and atmospheric pressure, and invented a calculating machine, a syringe, and a hydraulic press. He came under the influence of Jansenism, a branch of Catholic thought which emphasized original sin and predestination, from around 1646, and it was in defence of his friends at the convent of Port-Royal that he wrote *Les Provinciales* (1656–7: *The Provincial Letters*; trans. 1657), polemical letters directed against the methods of the Jesuits. His greatest work is the posthumously published *Pensées* (1670: *Thoughts*; trans. 1688), fragments jotted down in preparation for a systematic defence of Christianity which he left unfinished at his death. The *Pensées* paint a dark picture of human beings, their contradictions analysed with an intensity of logic and passion characteristic of all his work. He exercised an influence on a number of later thinkers, notably *Rousseau, Henri *Bergson, and the *existentialists.

PASCOLI, Giovanni (1855–1912) The major precursor of *modernism in Italian poetry. A socialist sympathizer, he was imprisoned for some months after demonstrations in 1879. Nature and simple things often provide his themes, but he draws from *Symbolism the suggestion of enigma and evanescence. His language spans the range from pure sound (animal- and baby-talk) to the literary conventions of lyric tradition. He translated from the classics and English *Romantic poets. The essential Pascoli is in *Myricae* (1891–1903) and *Canti di Castelvecchio* (1903).

PASOLINI, Pier Paolo (1922–75) Italian poet, novelist, critic, and film director. Pasolini's earliest writings were his poems in the Friulan dialect of north-eastern Italy and he continued throughout his life to write often highly innovative poetry in both Italian and Friulan. His best poetry is in *Le ceneri di Gramsci* (1957: *Gramsci's Ashes*). Pasolini's experience of living in the shanty towns around Rome inspired his two novels *Ragazzi di vita* (1955: *The Ragazzi*) and *Una vita violenta* (1958: *A Violent Life*). He is best known for the films he made in the last fifteen years of his life, in particular *Accattone* (1961), *Mamma Roma* (1962), *The Gospel According to Saint Matthew* (1964), *Oedipus Rex* (1967), *Theorem* (1968), *Medea* (1970), *Decameron* (1971), *Canterbury Tales* (1973), *Arabian Nights* (1974), and *Salò* (1975), which frequently used ordinary people instead of trained actors, and variously challenged *neo-realism with its conventions of sentimentalism and linear narrative. His best critical essays are in *Passione e ideologia* (1960: *Passion and Ideology*). A homosexual, Pasolini was murdered by one or more young men in 1975.

Pasquil (Pasquin) 'Pasquino' or 'Pasquillo' was the name popularly given to a mutilated statue disinterred at Rome in 1501, and set up by Cardinal Caraffa at the corner of his palace near the Piazza Navona. It became the custom to salute Pasquin on St Mark's Day in Latin verses. Over time these anonymous *pasquinate* or pasquinades tended to become satirical, and the term began to be applied, not only in Rome but in other countries, to satirical compositions and lampoons, political, ecclesiastical, or personal. According to Mazocchi, the name Pasquino originated in that of a schoolmaster who lived opposite the spot where the statue was found; a later tradition made Pasquino a caustic tailor or shoemaker; another calls him a barber (*OED*). Replies to the pasquinades used to be attached to the *Marforio*, an ancient statue of a river god, thought to be of Mars.

PASQUIN, Anthony *See* WILLIAMS, JOHN.

Passage to India, A Last-written novel by E. M. *Forster, published 1924. It portrays a restive India under the British Raj, the clash between East and West, tensions between Hindus and Muslims, and the disastrous consequences of prejudice and 'muddle'. The story is told in three parts and concerns Aziz, a young Muslim doctor, whose friendliness and enthusiasm for the British turn to bitterness and disillusionment. A sympathy springs up between him and the elderly Mrs Moore, who has come to visit her son Ronny Heaslop, the city magistrate. Accompanying her is Adela Quested, intended for Ronny, who longs to know the 'real' India and tries to disregard the taboos and snobberies of the British. Aziz organizes an expedition to the famous Marabar Caves, where an unforeseen development plunges him into disgrace and rouses deep antagonism between the British and the indigenous population. Adela accuses Aziz of sexually assaulting her in the Caves; he is committed to prison, and stands trial. Adela realizes she has made a terrible mistake and withdraws her charge, but Aziz turns furiously away from the British. In the third part of the book he has moved to a post in a native state, and is bringing up his family in peace, writing poetry and reading Persian. He is visited by his friend Cyril Fielding, the former principal of the Government College, an intelligent, hard-bitten man. They discuss the future of India and Aziz prophesies that only when the British are driven out can he and Fielding really be friends. Among the many characters is Professor Godbole, the detached and saintly Brahman who is the innocent cause of the contretemps. Usually thought of as Forster's finest novel, it won the James Tait Black Memorial Prize for Fiction in 1924.

Passetyme of Pleasure, *or The Historie of Graunde Amoure and La Bel Pucel* An allegorical poem in *rhyme royal and decasyllabic couplets by Stephen *Hawes, written about 1506 and printed by Wynkyn de *Worde in 1509 (edited by *Southey, 1831, and by Thomas *Wright for the Percy Society, 1845). It describes the education of a certain Graunde Amoure in the accomplishments required to make a knight perfect and worthy of the love of La Bel Pucel, and narrates his encounters with giants (representing the vices), his marriage, and his death; the whole constituting an allegory of life in the form of a romance of chivalry. It contains a well-known couplet in perhaps its original form: 'For though the day be never so longe, | At last the belles ryngeth to evensonge.'

'Passing of Arthur, The' *See* 'MORTE D'ARTHUR'.

Passionate Pilgrim, The An unauthorized anthology of twenty poems by various authors, some still unidentified, published by *Jaggard in 1599 in two editions, and attributed on the title page to William *Shakespeare, but containing only two sonnets and three extracts from *Love's Labour's Lost* by him. A third edition with additional poems by Thomas *Heywood appeared in 1612; Heywood protested on his own and on Shakespeare's behalf.

PASTERNAK, Boris Leonidovich (1890–1960) Russian poet and prose writer, born in Moscow, son of the artist Leonid Pasternak and the pianist Rosa Kaufman. He studied philosophy and music before embracing poetry. After an early *symbolist phase, he joined the *Futurist 'Centrifuge' group in 1914. His collection *My Sister Life* (1922) established his poetic reputation. By the mid-1920s Pasternak had moved away from personal themes to reflect on political and moral issues in long poems such as *The Year 1905* and *Lieutenant Shmidt* (both 1927), and *Spektorsky* (1931). His reputation as a prose writer was also made in 1922 with *The Childhood of Luvers*. In 1931 he published his first memoir, *A Safe Conduct*, followed by another major verse collection, *Second Birth* (1932), an attempt to combine public and lyric themes in a plainer style. In the 1930s Pasternak's position became increasingly difficult. After a doomed effort to become a 'Soviet writer', he began what he described as his 'long silent duel' with Stalin. After 1933 no original work by Pasternak could be published for ten years, after which two further poetry collections, *On Early Trains* (1943) and *The Breadth of the Earth* (1945), appeared. Original work gave way to translation. Together with a volume of *Georgian lyrical poetry, he translated the poetry of Walter *Ralegh, Ben *Jonson, P. B. *Shelley, Lord *Byron, John *Keats, and William *Shakespeare. His excellent translations of **Hamlet* (1941), **Romeo and Juliet* (1943), **Antony and Cleopatra* (1944), **Othello* (1945), *1* and *2* **Henry IV* (1948), **King Lear* (1949), and **Macbeth* (1951) became classic versions in Russia. *Goethe's *Faust* (1953) and *Schiller's *Maria Stuart* (1958) were other notable productions. Despite declining health, his literary endeavours were now focused on a work intended to be his testament to the experience of the Russian intelligentsia before, during, and after the revolution, the novel *Doctor Zhivago*. Despairing of publication in the USSR, he gave permission for publication in Italy in 1957. An English version by Max Hayward and Manya Harari followed in 1958. He was awarded the 1958 *Nobel Prize for Literature but was obliged to decline the honour and expelled from the Writers' Union. Olga Ivinskaia, the companion of his last years and on whom Lara, the heroine of *Doctor Zhivago*, was largely based, was arrested and imprisoned. Publication of Pasternak's poetry resumed in the USSR soon after his death, and a volume of his short prose appeared in 1982. But *Doctor Zhivago*, on which his worldwide fame is based, was only published in 1988 in Russia, where his reputation rests on the poetic achievement of *My Sister Life* and *Second Birth*. For translations, see Jon *Stallworthy and Peter France, *Selected Poems* (1984), and for a biography see Peter *Levi, *Boris Pasternak* (1990).

pastiche A literary composition written in imitation of the style of another author or authors, or pieced together from fragments of other writings. T. S. *Eliot's poem *The Waste*

Land (1922) is a celebrated example. Pastiche usually differs from parody in that its imitations involve affectionate or respectful tribute rather than mockery.

Paston Letters A collection of letters preserved by the Pastons, a well-to-do Norfolk family, written between *c.*1420 and 1504. They are of great value for the evidence they give of the language of their time, but even more for the general historical, political, and social interest they provide. They concern three generations of the family, and most were written in the reigns of Henry VI, Edward IV, and Richard III. They are unique as historical material, showing the violence and other complexities of life in 15th-century England, and the domestic conditions in which a family of this class lived. **John Paston I** (1421–66) had a close association with Sir John *Fastolf. The manuscript hands show that although both the men and women used clerks as amanuenses, the men could write, but the women could do so only barely, at best. The letters were published in three volumes, in 1787, 1789, and 1823. The originals were recovered in the second half of the 19th century, and James Gairdner produced a three-volume edition in 1872–5. See *Paston Letters and Papers of the Fifteenth Century*, ed. Norman Davis (1971, 1976), rev. Richard Beadle and Colin Richmond (2004–5); *Selections*, ed. Norman Davis (modernized) (1983); Helen Castor, *Blood and Roses: The Paston Family in the Fifteenth Century* (2004).

pastoral A form of literature that celebrates in conventionally idealized terms the innocent loves and musical pleasures of shepherds and shepherdesses, usually in a mythical Arcadian 'Golden Age' of ease and harmony. Pastoral writing spans the genres of poetry, drama, and prose fiction. Despite its extreme artificiality, it is often capable of oblique or overt social criticism, in which rural harmony is contrasted with the corruptions of court or city. English pastoral writing derives from classical sources (the *Idylls* of *Theocritus and the more influential *Eclogues* of *Virgil, along with the prose romance **Daphnis and Chloe*) mediated through writers of the Italian Renaissance (notably *Petrarch, *Mantuan, and *Tasso). Its earliest appearances are in the **Eclogues* of Alexander *Barclay and in those (styled 'eglogs') of Barnabe *Googe, but the most important early landmark in this tradition is Edmund *Spenser's *The *Shepheardes Calender* (1579), followed by Philip *Sidney's prose romance interspersed with pastoral verses, the *Arcadia* (posthumously published in 1590). Several Elizabethan poets wrote pastoral poems, among them Christopher *Marlowe, Thomas *Lodge, and Michael *Drayton, and some attempted prose romances in this vein, notably Lodge's **Rosalyne* (1590). In drama, the most important pastoral plays are *Shakespeare's **As You Like It* and *The *Winter's Tale*, along with John *Fletcher's *The *Faithful Shepherdess*. Pastoral poetry remained an important category of 17th-century English verse (e.g. in the works of *Milton, Andrew *Marvell, and Robert *Herrick), while the drama and prose romance forms faded. In the 18th century, Alexander *Pope and others wrote pastoral poems, but the classical pastoral conventions increasingly gave way to more realistic forms of bucolic poetry, and eventually to a directly anti-pastoral realism in which the true poverty and hardship of contemporary rural life was stressed, notably by Oliver *Goldsmith, George *Crabbe, John *Clare, and William *Wordsworth. A special sub-genre that proved more enduring was the pastoral *elegy, of which the classic English model is Milton's **Lycidas*, imitated in important 19th-century elegies such as the *Adonais* of P. B. *Shelley and as late as 1867 in Matthew *Arnold's 'Thyrsis'. See Terry Gifford, *Pastoral* (1999).

Pastorella In Edmund *Spenser's **Faerie Queene* (VI. ix-xii), a shepherdess, believed to be the daughter of Meliboe, and loved by the shepherd Coridon and by Sir *Calidore. She is carried off by brigands, rescued by Calidore, and discovered to be the daughter of Sir Bellamour and the Lady Claribell.

pastor fido, Il *See* GUARINI, GIOVANNI BATTISTA.

PATCHEN, Kenneth (1911–72) American writer, born in Ohio, best known for the poetry he began publishing in 1936, which follows the methods of Walt *Whitman and William Carlos *Williams. These had some influence on the *Beat movement. He published a number of plays and experimental novels, the latter including *The Journal of Albion Moonlight* (1941) and *The Memoirs of a Shy Pornographer* (1945). See Larry Smith and Harry Redl, *Kenneth Patchen: Rebel Poet in America* (2000).

Patelin *See* PATHELIN.

PATER, Walter Horatio (1839–94) Writer, born in Stepney, the son of a surgeon who died in 1842; his mother died in 1854. From 1869 he lived with his unmarried sisters Hester and Clara (one of the founders of Somerville College, Oxford). After a childhood in rural Enfield, he was educated at King's School, Canterbury, and the Queen's College, Oxford, where his interests in Hellenism, pre-Socratic and German philosophy, European art, and literature were encouraged by Benjamin *Jowett, the classical scholar W. W. Capes (1834–1914), and Matthew *Arnold. He became a fellow of Brasenose in 1864. His Oxford career was marked by personal and professional controversies. Jowett blocked a university appointment when he suspected Pater's involvement with a student; colleagues attacked the 'Conclusion' to *Studies in the History of the Renaissance* (1873) because it postulated the relativity of existence ('that strange, perpetual, weaving and unweaving of ourselves'), celebrated 'pagan' art, and 'the love of art for its own sake', and advised 'To burn always with this hard gem-like flame, to maintain this ecstasy, is success in life.' Many of his writings on art challenge those of John *Ruskin, then Oxford's Slade professor of art. Gerard Manley *Hopkins was among the students who appreciated his critical and aesthetic independence.

Early essays for the **Westminster Review* and the **Fortnightly Review* articulated a radical critique of absolutism and expressed admiration for Hellenic homoerotic discourse and culture. *Studies in the History of the Renaissance*, later acclaimed by Oscar *Wilde and others as 'the holy writ of beauty', traces the rebirth of Hellenism in medieval France, the art of *Botticelli, *Leonardo da Vinci, and *Michelangelo, and the classicism of *Winckelmann.

Pater's prose fiction examines the possibilities of subjectivity within a specific historical and cultural milieu. The quality of life is always measured against the fact of death; the 'aesthetics of pain' is paramount. **Marius the Epicurean* (1885) is set in the days of Marcus Aurelius; *Gaston de Latour* (published 'unfinished' in 1896 but reissued with new materials in 1995) in the era of *Montaigne and the religious controversies of 16th-century France. 'The Child in the House' (**Macmillan's Magazine*, 1878) is one of many texts blurring the boundaries between autobiography and fiction. Four *Imaginary Portraits* (1887) are experiments in genre-blending. Narratives such as 'Apollo in Picardy' (*Harper's New Monthly*, 1893) exploit the rebirth/twilight of the gods motif. *Appreciations: With an Essay on Style* (1889) and *Essays from the Guardian* (1896) reflect his engagement with Victorian periodical journalism and belles-lettres. *Plato and Platonism* (1893), based on lectures and scholarly essays, represents an eclectic synthesis of ancient and then-contemporary philosophy, and justifies a homoerotic sensibility. 'Demeter and Persephone', an 1876 lecture later published in *Greek Studies* (1895), praises ancient matriarchal religious practices; modernists such as Hilda *Doolittle (H.D.) and Virginia *Woolf were influenced by its revisionary mythmaking and the story of female empowerment.

Pater's works have long been associated with the *'art for art's sake' movement, and the cultivation of decadence in the 1880s and 1890s. W. B. *Yeats insisted that Pater's writings are 'permanent in our literature' because of their 'revolutionary importance'. In the decades immediately following the Wilde trial, many male modernists, including T. E. *Hulme, T. S. *Eliot, and Wyndham *Lewis, felt compelled to denigrate Pater's writings, but his contribution to modernist aesthetics and theories of subjectivity, and his importance to James *Joyce, Woolf, and others, have been affirmed by critics such as F. McGrath (*The Sensible Spirit*, 1986). See *Letters of Walter Pater*, ed. L. Evans (1970); M. Levey, *The Case of Walter Pater* (1978); R. Seiler (ed.), *Walter Pater: A Life Remembered* (1987); L. Brake, *Walter Pater* (1994); L. Brake, L. Higgins, and C. Williams (eds), *Walter Pater: Transparencies of Desire* (2003).

PATERSON, Banjo (Andrew Barton) *See* BULLETIN.

PATERSON, Don (1963–) Poet and jazz musician, born in Dundee. He left school to concentrate on music and moved to London in 1984, where he began to write poetry. Returning to Scotland at the end of the decade, he formed the jazz-folk band Lammas. His first book, *Nil Nil* (1993), introduced a distinctive style which spliced together demotic and recondite vocabulary in tightly wrought, often oblique poems about sex, families, and reading. It won the Forward Prize for best first collection. In *God's Gift to Women* (1997), which won the T. S. *Eliot Prize, a more supple and confident style, influenced by Paul *Muldoon, explores the possibilities of postmodern lyric in a variety of self-conscious forms. Poems about memory, childhood, and failed relationships are connected by the structuring device of a train journey. Its preoccupation with creative adaptations of foreign language poetry led to two major works: *The Eyes: A Version of Antonio Machado* (1999) and *Orpheus: A Version of Rilke's Die Sonneten an Orpheus* (2006). *The White Lie* (2001) was a volume selected for American publication that demonstrated a maturing formal prowess and erudition without compromising the earlier work's playful energy. His keen interest in the cultural uses of poetry, and especially the poem's capacity to internalize and multiply the contexts of its own reception, is examined further in *Landing Light* (2003). In the poem 'A Talking Book', the physical page apparently addresses the reader in the first person, only to conclude 'there is no I to speak of'. Paterson is also a fan of the witty, poignant aphorism, and has published two volumes of aphorisms to date: *The Book of Shadows* (2005) and *The Blind Eye* (2007). He has written two plays and various radio dramas, and has a number of popular editorial publications, including *101 Sonnets: From Shakespeare to Heaney* (1999), *Robert Burns: Poems Selected by Don Paterson* (2001), *Don't Ask Me What I Mean: Poets in their Own Words* (with Clare Brown; 2003), and *New British Poetry* (with Charles *Simic; 2004). He teaches Creative Writing at the University of St Andrews and is poetry editor for Picador.

Pathelin, La Farce de Maistre Pierre The most celebrated of the medieval French *farces, dating from before 1470, of uncertain authorship, and written in *octosyllabic couplets. Its central figure is the duplicitous lawyer Pathelin, who is himself finally fooled by the shepherd Aignelet.

pathetic fallacy A phrase coined by John *Ruskin in 'Of the Pathetic Fallacy' (**Modern Painters*, iii (1856), ch. 12), indicating the tendency of writers and artists to ascribe human emotions and sympathies to nature. Ruskin sees in it morbidity and 'a falseness in all our impressions of external things', preferring the 'very plain and leafy fact' of a primrose to those poets (e.g. Wordsworth in **Peter Bell*) 'to whom the primrose is anything else than a primrose'. The poetic convention by which, for example, clouds 'weep' or flowers 'smile' is found extensively in English verse, and especially in that of the late 18th and early 19th centuries.
See also APOSTROPHE; PERSONIFICATION.

Patience (opera) Opera by *Gilbert and *Sullivan, produced in 1881, a deliberate satire on the pretensions of the *Aesthetic movement; Bunthorne, the central character, is said to be modelled on Oscar *Wilde and Grosvenor on A. C. *Swinburne.

Patience (poem) An alliterative poem in 531 lines from the late 14th century, preserved in Cotton Nero A. X, also the sole manuscript of **Pearl*, **Cleanness*, and *Sir *Gawain and the Green*

Knight. It frames the story of Jonah with exhortations to patience. Modern critics usually treat the four poems in the manuscript as the work of a single author on the basis of stylistic and thematic affinities. Ed. M. Andrew and R. Waldron, *The Poems of the Pearl Manuscript* (2008).

Patient Grissil A comedy by Thomas *Dekker in collaboration with Henry *Chettle and William Haughton (d. 1605), written 1600, printed 1603, which dramatizes Geoffrey *Chaucer's 'Clerk's Tale' (*see* CANTERBURY TALES, 9). It contains the well-known songs 'Art thou poor yet hast thou golden slumbers, | O sweet content' and 'Golden slumbers kiss your eyes'.

PATMORE, Coventry (1823–96) Poet; son of Peter George *Patmore. He published his first volume of *Poems* (including 'The Woodman's Daughter', later the subject of a well-known painting by *Millais) in 1844. In 1846, after his father's financial collapse, he became assistant in the printed book department of the British Museum, on the recommendation of Monckton *Milnes. His work was much admired by the *Pre-Raphaelites, with whom he became acquainted, and he contributed to the *Germ*. In 1847 he married his first wife Emily, who inspired his long and popular sequence of poems in praise of married love, The **Angel in the House* (1854–63); together the Patmores formed a model of perceived ideal domesticity, and as such entertained many eminent literary figures, including Alfred *Tennyson, John *Ruskin, and Robert *Browning, who wrote a poem to Emily. Emily died in 1862, leaving her husband with six children. In 1864 he travelled to Rome, where he met his second wife Marianne, a Roman Catholic, and was himself converted to Catholicism, factors which may have contributed to his decline in popularity as a poet; *The Unknown Eros* (1877) was received with much less enthusiasm than his previous work. It contains odes marked by an erotic mysticism, but also some more autobiographical pieces (now the most anthologized), including 'The Azalea', 'Departure', 'A Farewell', directly inspired by Emily's illness and death, and 'The Toys', inspired by a moment of anger and grief aroused by one of his sons. *Amelia, Tamerton Church-Tower, etc.*, with a preface on English metrical law, appeared in 1878. His second wife died in 1880 and he married Harriet, the governess of his children, who survived him. In his later years he formed new friendships, predominantly with other Catholic writers including Gerard Manley *Hopkins, Francis *Thompson, and Alice *Meynell, who helped to revive interest in his poetry. *The Rod, the Root and the Flower* (1895) is chiefly meditations on religious subjects.

PATMORE, Peter George (1786–1855) Journalist; father of Coventry *Patmore, and a close friend of Charles *Lamb and William *Hazlitt. He edited the **New Monthly Magazine*, 1841–53, and published *My Friends and Acquaintances* (1854), a lively, unreliable account of Lamb, Hazlitt, Thomas *Campbell, Richard Brinsley *Sheridan, and others. He parodied the prose of Hazlitt, Lamb, and John *Wilson in his *Rejected Articles* (1826). Many intimate letters in Hazlitt's **Liber Amoris* are addressed to him.

PATRICK, St (*c.*389–*c.*461) The patron saint of Ireland, probably born in western Roman Britain, son of a deacon. Taken captive to Ireland as an adolescent, he escaped after six years and returned there voluntarily to preach the gospel in 432, after years of study in Gaul. He journeyed first through Ulster and then, it is said, through the whole of Ireland. Many stories, legends, and purported writings of his are current in Ireland. See David Howlett (ed.), *The Book of Letters of Saint Patrick the Bishop* (1994).

patronage Traditionally, financial help, payment in kind, or more indirect assistance or influence, exercised by royalty, the aristocracy, and the wealthy, on behalf of writers, in return for dedications, entertainment, and prestige (as well as sometimes for more altruistic motives). Patronage was of particular importance before writers were able to support themselves through the literary market-place. Thus Geoffrey *Chaucer was assisted by *John of Gaunt, William *Shakespeare by the earl of Southampton, John *Donne by Sir Robert Drury, and William *Wordsworth by Sir George Beaumont. Ben *Jonson's tribute to the *Sidneys in his 'country-house poem' 'To Penshurst' (*see* PENSHURST PLACE) is a product of the system. But the relationship was not always happy, particularly by the 18th century, as commercial sources of income (journalism, and especially the newly popular form of the novel) began to give authors a sense of themselves as more independent figures. Alexander *Pope had begun his career under the protection of several noblemen, but made himself financially secure through the publication by subscription of his *Iliad* translation (dedicated not to an aristocrat but to a fellow writer, William *Congreve); he declared he was 'Above a patron', and ridiculed the art, and pitiful dependency, of dedicators, in the *Epistle to Dr Arbuthnot* and *The *Dunciad*. Many writers were supported by political funding or government sinecures, another source of contempt for Pope. Samuel *Johnson, who had sought, and belatedly received, the patronage of the earl of *Chesterfield for his **Dictionary*, defined a patron as 'a wretch who supports with insolence, and is paid with flattery'. His letter of defiance to Chesterfield has come to be regarded as the end of patronage, though the process was naturally more complex and drawn out (Johnson himself accepted a state pension of £300 in 1762). Patronage passed largely from men of individual wealth to men of professional power or commercial interest, such as literary editors and library owners and suppliers. Johnson himself called the bookseller Robert *Dodsley 'my patron', and Oliver *Goldsmith commented that 'the few poets of England no longer depend on the great for subsistence; they have now no other patrons than the public'. Many authors were also clergymen, and patronage was also sometimes exercised through the gift of clerical livings; George *Crabbe, befriended by the duke of Rutland, wrote of such arrangements in 'The Patron' (1812).

Institutional patronage began formally in 1790 when David Williams (1738–1816) founded the *Royal Literary Fund to support impoverished writers, and in 1837 the Civil List Act permitted the treasury to assist authors by the grant of pensions, provided they could demonstrate 'desert and distress'.

Authors who have benefited include Wordsworth, Alfred Lord *Tennyson, Matthew *Arnold, W. H. *Hudson, W. B. *Yeats, and T. F. *Powys. Joseph *Conrad returned his pension; Dinah *Craik set hers aside for less fortunate authors, and Harriet *Martineau refused several offers. The pension is now worth on average only £600 p.a. It is awarded on the recommendation of the Royal Literary Fund, the *Society of Authors, the *Poetry Society, and other bodies. See D. Griffin, *Literary Patronage in England 1650–1800* (1996).

PATTEN, Brian (1946–) Poet, born and educated (to the age of 15) in Liverpool, where he became one of the *Liverpool poets. He published with Roger *McGough and Adrian *Henri in *The Mersey Sound* (1967), and has many subsequent volumes of his own, including *Little Johnny's Confession* (1967), *Vanishing Trick* (1976), and *Armada* (1996). He is a prolific writer for children in both prose and verse: titles include *Mr Moon's Last Case* (1977), *Gangsters, Ghosts and Dragon Flies* (1981), and *The Story Giant* (2001). Patten's anthologies for children are admired. There is a study by Linda Cookson (1997).

PATTISON, Mark (1813–84) Born in Hornby, Yorkshire, educated at home and at Oriel College, Oxford, a supporter of John Henry *Newman and the *Oxford Movement until Newman's departure for Rome. He was ordained priest in 1843 and became successively fellow and tutor (1843–55) of Lincoln College, Oxford; he would have been elected rector in 1851 but for an intrigue among the reactionary fellows of the college. An influential tutor, he was keenly interested in university reform, and travelled to Germany to study continental systems of education. His ideas on education can be found in *Oxford Studies* (1855) and *Suggestions on Academical Organisation* (1868); his life work—a history of European learning surrounding a biography of Joseph *Scaliger—was never completed. His best-known work was his classic biography *Isaac Casaubon 1559–1614* (1875). Other published works included a contribution to **Essays and Reviews*, 'On the Tendencies of Religious Thought in England, 1688–1750' (1860), a short life of John *Milton (1879), editions of certain of Alexander *Pope's and Milton's poems, and contributions to the **Encyclopaedia Britannica*, articles on *Erasmus, Sir Thomas *More, and *Grotius. In 1861, still embittered from his earlier rejection, he was finally elected rector of Lincoln. In the same year he married Emilia Francis Strong (later Lady *Dilke) who was 27 years his junior; this and the fact that both parties remained apart as far as convention would allow gave rise to the famous theory that Mr and Mrs Pattison were the originals of Casaubon and Dorothea in George Eliot's **Middlemarch*. The question has been often debated and produced many differences of learned opinion. His *Memoirs* (1885) are an important study of 19th-century Oxford. See H. S. Jones, *Intellect and Character in Victorian England: Mark Pattison and the Invention of the Don* (2007).

PAUL, St (d. *c.*65) Early Christian missionary leader and *Bible letter writer. A Jew and a Roman citizen born in Tarsus, Cilicia, Saul (his Hebrew name) was a leading persecutor of the earliest Christians, complicit in the first Christian martyrdom, that of Stephen. On the road to Damascus he had an archetypal conversion experience, a blinding vision of Jesus ('Saul, Saul, why persecutest thou me?', Acts 9: 4), and became, as Paul, the most active apostle of Christianity. His mission was particularly to the Gentiles, rather than the Jews; he travelled, preached, and established and supported churches from Jerusalem to Rome. He was several times imprisoned, once escaping by a miracle, eventually exercising his right as a Roman citizen of appealing to Caesar and being sent to Rome, where he was executed during a persecution of the Christians by Nero. Acts narrates his missionary work.

His principal legacy is fourteen New Testament epistles ascribed to him in the King James Bible (Romans to Hebrews). Romans, 1, 2 Corinthians, Galatians, Philippians, 1 Thessalonians, and Philemon are generally agreed to be authentic, while his authorship of Ephesians, Colossians, and 2 Thessalonians is sometimes questioned; his authorship of the 'pastoral epistles' (1, 2 Timothy, Titus) is more doubtful, and he did not write Hebrews. With his teaching in Acts, these make him the dominant figure in the latter part of the New Testament: his stamp on Christianity has been almost as influential as that of Jesus. His teaching was founded on his belief in Jesus as the risen Messiah rather than on his life and teaching. Inspirational passages such as 1 Corinthians 13 on charity or love, resonant sayings such as 'the wages of sin is death' (Romans 6: 23), and complex theology mix with a dogmatism that is often difficult for modern churches on subjects such as relationships with the Jews or 'the powers that be' (Romans 13: 1) and the status of women.

Paul et Virginie See BERNARDIN DE SAINT-PIERRE, JACQUES-HENRI.

PAULIN, Tom (1949–) Poet and critic, born in Leeds and brought up in Belfast. Paulin was educated at the University of Hull and at Oxford, where he became a lecturer (at Hertford College) in 1994. He is the most overtly 'political' of the leading Northern Irish poets. His poetry and criticism share a fascination with Protestant Dissent, represented positively by the existential urgency he values in mentors such as William *Hazlitt and Emily *Dickinson, and negatively by the degraded Calvinism he discerns in consumerism and Ulster loyalism. The stanzaic and metrical formality of early poetry collections like *The Strange Museum* (1980) gives way to an increasingly spiky and improvisatory colloquial mode in *Walking a Line* (1994) and *The Invasion Handbook* (2002), the latter an ambitious tableau of pre-Second World War Europe. Paulin's prose includes *Writing to the Moment: Selected Critical Essays 1980–1996* (1996) and *Crusoe's Secret: The Aesthetics of Dissent* (2005).

Pauline A poem in blank verse, the first poem to be published by Robert *Browning; it appeared anonymously in 1833.

Subtitled 'A Fragment of a Confession', it is marked by the influence of Browning's Romantic predecessors, notably P. B. *Shelley and Lord *Byron; but its form and theme already declare Browning's independence. The 'confession' is addressed to Pauline by the first in a long series of 'fallen' speakers whose ambivalent rhetoric combines self-reproach and self-justification. The poem was barely noticed, but an important commentary by J. S. *Mill, in the form of an annotated copy, reached Browning through their common friend W. J. *Fox. Mill assumed the speaker of the poem to be the author, and severely criticized his morbidity and self-regard. Partly in response to this misunderstanding of the poem's 'dramatic' form, Browning suppressed it for over 30 years, finally acknowledging it 'with extreme repugnance' in the collected edition of 1867, to avoid the threat of pirate publication.

Paul's, Children of A company of boy actors, recruited from the choristers of St Paul's Cathedral, whose performances enjoyed great popularity from 1575 to 1590, when their tiny theatre within the cathedral was closed, and again from 1599 to 1608. They performed among others the plays of John *Lyly and, later, satirical comedies by John *Marston, George *Chapman, Thomas *Middleton, and others. The Children of the Chapel, recruited from the choristers of the Chapel Royal, was another company enjoying popular favour at the same time. Their rivalry with men actors is alluded to in **Hamlet* (II. ii).

Paul's School, St Founded between 1509 and 1512 by John *Colet. William *Lily was its first high master. The school moved from St Paul's Churchyard to Hammersmith in 1884, and to Barnes in 1968. Among its many distinguished scholars have been William *Camden, John *Milton, Samuel *Pepys, Benjamin *Jowett, R. H. *Barham, E. C. *Bentley, G. K. *Chesterton, Compton *Mackenzie, Edward *Thomas, and John *Fuller.

PAVESE, Cesare (1908–50) Italian novelist and poet, whose powerful last novel, *La luna e i falò* (1950: *The Moon and the Bonfires*), combines realism and myth, lyrical memoir and contemporary reality, with a strongly autobiographical dimension to express the heart-searchings of a solitary man with a restless social conscience. His first novel *Il carcere* (1939: *The Prison*) was followed by *Paesi tuoi* (1941: *The Harvesters*), *Il compagno* (1947: *The Comrade*), *Prima che il gallo canti* (1949: *Before Cock-Crow*), and *La bella estate* (1949: *The Beautiful Summer*); see also *Lavorare stanca* (1936: *Work Wearies*), a volume of poetry. He made many translations from English and American authors (James *Joyce, William *Faulkner, and others) who influenced him; his translation of Melville's **Moby-Dick* is definitive. His suicide was seen as representative of intellectuals broken by the tensions of post-war Europe. See A. O'Healy, *Cesare Pavese* (1988).

PAYN, James (1830–98) Editor and novelist, educated at Eton College and Trinity College, Cambridge. He was a regular contributor to **Household Words*, and became an influential figure in literary London as editor of *Chambers's Journal* (1859–74) and the **Cornhill Magazine* (1882–96). He published a volume of poems in 1853 and several volumes of essays, including *Some Private Views* (1894), *Some Literary Recollections* (1884), *Gleams of Memory* (1894), and *The Backwater of Life* (1899), with an introduction by Leslie *Stephen. He wrote 100 novels of which *Lost Sir Massingberd* (1864) and *By Proxy* (1878) were the most popular.

PAZ, Octavio (1914–98) Acclaimed poet and essayist who was born and died in Mexico City. After an early flirtation with the politics of the radical left, he abandoned Marxism and the idea of committed literature, thereby earning the opprobrium of many Latin American writers and intellectuals. Significant influences on his work include French *Surrealism and Buddhist philosophy; he studied the latter during his years as Mexican ambassador to India (1962–8). He made his name questioning Mexican identity and history in *El laberinto de la soledad* (1950: *The Labyrinth of Solitude: Life and Thought in Mexico*). The collection of prose poetry *¿Águila o sol?* (1951: *Eagle or Sun?*) and the long, cyclical poem 'Piedra de sol' (1957: 'Sunstone') explore Mexican motifs, guided by a fascination with how the mind perceives through language and how poetry and eroticism offer an antidote to the horrors of history. His most admired works are his journey-meditation *El mono gramático* (1974: *The Monkey Grammarian*) and his biography of the Mexican nun and poetess Sor Juana Inés de la Cruz, *Sor Juana o las trampas de la fe* (1986: *Sor Juana, or The Traps of Faith*). Major poetry anthologies include *Poemas (1935–1975)* and the bilingual *The Collected Poems of Octavio Paz, 1957–1987* (1987). His complete works are published by Siglo XXI of Mexico. Paz was a shrewd political commentator, a respected art critic, a translator, and the editor of several distinguished magazines. He was awarded the *Nobel Prize in 1990.

P'BITEK, Okot (1931–82) A poet and anthropologist, who wanted to counter what he saw as the alienation of a new generation of Western-educated Africans. He was born in northern Uganda; his mother was a composer and singer. After touring Britain with the Ugandan football team he stayed to study at Aberystwyth and Oxford. His dramatic monologues, written in an Acholi oral tradition, *Song of Lawino* (1966), *Song of Ocol* (1970), *Song of Prisoner* (1971), and *Song of Malaya* (1971), are scathingly witty indictments of the political corruption of the African middle class, and a celebration of traditional village life.

PEACHAM, Henry (1578–?1643) Early writer on art, and son of Henry Peacham (1546–1634), author of *The Garden of Eloquence* (1577). Educated at Trinity College, Cambridge, he published *The Art of Drawing with the Pen* (1612), later titled *The Gentleman's Exercise*, which went through many editions, as did *The Complete Gentleman* (1622), a guide to the painters, musicians, and poets a young gentleman should know about.

PEACOCK, Thomas Love (1785–1866) Satirist, essayist, and poet, the son of a London glass merchant, though brought up by his mother. He had published two volumes of verse when, in 1812, he met P. B. *Shelley, who became a close friend. Peacock's prose satires, **Headlong Hall* (1816), **Melincourt* (1817), and **Nightmare Abbey* (1818), survey the contemporary political and cultural scene from a radical viewpoint. Formally they owe most to two classical genres: the 'Anatomy', or miscellaneous prose satire, and the Socratic dialogue, especially perhaps *Plato's *Symposium* which, like many of Peacock's convivial arguments, takes place over a dinner table. The debate is diversified by a romantic love-plot, increasingly important in **Crotchet Castle* (1831) and **Gryll Grange* (1860–61), and by songs. Peacock's fictional world is a pleasant one, for he assembles his characters in English country houses, and sends them on excursions into mountain and forest scenery. In **Maid Marian* (1822) and *The *Misfortunes of Elphin* (1829) he employs historical settings, 12th-century England and 6th-century Wales, but the topical satirical reference remains unmistakable. Peacock's early volumes of poetry are of antiquarian interest, but *Rhododaphne* (1818) is a powerful poem, in the mythological manner of John Keats's *'Lamia'. Peacock also wrote touching lyrics, especially 'Long Night Succeeds thy Little Day' (1826) and 'Newark Abbey' (1842). Of his satirical poems, **Paper Money Lyrics* (1837) attack the dogmas of political economists and the malpractices of bankers. Peacock's sceptical attitude to the fashionable cult of the arts is apparent in his two most sustained critical essays, 'Essay on Fashionable Literature' (a fragment, written 1818) and 'The *Four Ages of Poetry' (1820), to which Shelley replied in a **Defence of Poetry*. In 1819 Peacock married Jane Gryffydh, the 'White Snowdonian antelope' of Shelley's 'Letter to Maria Gisborne'; she suffered a breakdown at the death of their third daughter in 1826, though she lived until 1851. His favourite child was his eldest daughter Mary Ellen, who became the first wife of George *Meredith, and features in Meredith's sonnet sequence **Modern Love*. Peacock entered the East India Company's service in 1819 and worked under James *Mill until the latter's death in 1836, when he succeeded to the responsible position of examiner.

There is a biography by C. van Doren (1911); see also M. Butler, *Peacock Displayed* (1979). The standard edition is the *Halliford Edition of the Works of T. L. Peacock*, ed. H. F. B. Brett-Smith and C. E. Jones, 10 vols (1924–34).

PEAKE, Mervyn (1911–68) Novelist, poet, and artist, born at Kuling in China, the son of a medical missionary; he came to England aged 11, was educated at Eltham College, Kent, then attended the Royal Academy Schools. He spent three years from 1934 with a group of artists on the island of Sark, then returned to London, where he taught art, exhibited his own work and illustrated books, and published verse and stories for children. He was invalided out of the army in 1943 after a nervous breakdown, but was later commissioned as a war artist, and also visited Belsen in 1945 on a journalistic expedition for *The Leader*, an experience which profoundly affected him. Meanwhile he was working on a novel, *Titus Groan*, which was published in 1946; it was followed by *Gormenghast* (1950) and *Titus Alone* (1959), which as a trilogy form the work for which Peake is best remembered, a creation of grotesque yet precise *Gothic fantasy, recounting the life of Titus, 77th earl of Groan, in his crumbling castle of Gormenghast, surrounded by a cast of characters which includes the colourful Fuchsia, Dr Prunesquallor, and the melancholy Muzzlehatch. Peake's poetry includes *The Glassblowers* (1950) and *The Rhyme of the Flying Bomb* (1962), a ballad of the Blitz; he illustrated most of his own work, and also produced memorable drawings for *The Rime of the *Ancient Mariner* (1943), **Treasure Island* (1949), and other works. A lighter side of his prolific imagination is seen in his posthumous *A Book of Nonsense* (1972). The last years of his life were overshadowed by Parkinson's disease, as described by his widow Maeve Gilmore in her memoir *A World Away* (1970). For an account of the relationship between his drawings and his prose, see Hilary Spurling's introduction to *The Drawings of Mervyn Peake* (1974).

PEARCE, Philippa (1920–2007) Born in Great Shelford, Cambridgeshire, and educated at Girton College, Cambridge; she became a leading children's writer after writing and producing Schools Radio for the BBC and while working in the Educational Department of Oxford University Press. Her reputation was established with her first novel, *Minnow on the Say* (1955), but it is *Tom's Midnight Garden* (1958), about a boy who travels between the worlds of Victorian and 20th-century England when the clock strikes thirteen, for which she will be remembered. Her best books are sophisticated mixtures of realism and fantasy, past and present.

Pearl An alliterative poem in 1,212 lines of twelve-line *octosyllabic stanzas from the late 14th century, preserved in Cotton Nero A. X, also the sole manuscript of **Patience*, **Cleanness*, and *Sir *Gawain and the Green Knight*. The pearl whose loss is lamented by the poem's narrator is soon identified as a young girl, who died before she was 2 years old. He falls asleep in the garden where she is buried, and has a vision of a river, beyond which lies a paradisal garden. Here he sees a maiden whom he recognizes as the dead girl. She criticizes his excessive grief and describes her blessed state. He questions the justice that makes her queen of heaven when she died so young. Convinced by her, he is granted a vision of the New Jerusalem. He plunges into the river in an attempt to join her, but awakes with renewed commitment to participation in Christian worship, as exemplified by the sacrament of the Eucharist. The poem is distinguished by its verbal precision, its artful word-play, and its use of concatenation, the linking of stanzas and stanza-groups through verbal repetition. Ed. M. Andrew and R. Waldron, *The Poems of the Pearl Manuscript* (2008).

PEARSON, Hesketh (1887–1964) Actor and biographer, born in Hawford, Worcestershire, and educated at Bedford Grammar School; he joined the company of the actor-manager Herbert Beerbohm Tree (1853–1917) as a young man. During the First World War he served in the Middle East and earned the Military Cross. His first book, *Modern Men and Mummers* (1921), contained portraits of many of the theatre personalities of the time. *The Whispering Gallery* (1926), an anonymous work purporting to be 'leaves from the diary of an ex-diplomat', occasioned a scandal, a court case, and an acquittal for Pearson, who went on to write many lively and widely read biographies, of (for example) William *Hazlitt (1934), Sydney *Smith (*The Smith of Smiths*, 1934), George Bernard *Shaw (1942), Oscar *Wilde (1946), Beerbohm Tree (1956), and several others. He also wrote literary travel books in collaboration with Hugh *Kingsmill, and his autobiography, *Hesketh Pearson by Himself*, appeared posthumously in 1965. See Ian Hunter, *Nothing to Repent: The Life of Hesketh Pearson* (1987).

PEARSON, John (1613–86) Theologian, educated at Eton College and Cambridge University, a Royalist chaplain during the Civil War, and after the Restoration master of Jesus College, then of Trinity, Cambridge. He became bishop of Chester in 1673. From 1654 he preached at St Clement's, Eastcheap, the series of lectures which he published in 1659 as his classic *Exposition of the Creed*, the notes of which exhibit deep learning on the writings of the early church *Fathers. He was one of the most learned theologians of his age.

Peasants' Revolt The popular insurrection of Essex and Kent labourers which began in May 1381. Its principal motivation was the wish of tenants to end feudal rights and its immediate cause was the third poll tax. While the Kentish leader Wat Tyler was negotiating with the 14-year-old Richard II, he was pulled from his horse and killed. The rebels dispersed and by the end of June the revolt had been repressed. It has left traces in contemporary literature, most famously in the letters of the preacher John *Ball, who appears to have known about the figure of **Piers Plowman*. *Chaucer refers with mordant wit to *Jack Straw in *The *Canterbury Tales* ('The Nun's Priest's Tale') and John *Gower gives a nightmarish account of the revolt in his Latin poem *Vox Clamantis*. William *Morris's socialist novel *A *Dream of John Ball* is set at the time of the Peasants' Revolt. See R. B. Dobson, *The Peasants' Revolt of 1381* (1983).

PECOCK, Reginald (*c.*1392–*c.*1459) Bishop successively of St Asaph and Chichester. His extant English writings not only confronted the appeal of the *Lollards, but were also intended to provide lay people with systematic orthodox theology in English. He addresses heresy most explicitly in *The Repressor of Over Much Blaming of the Clergy*, which exhibits considerable eloquence and lexical variety. In his *Donet* and the *Folewer to the Donet* he sought to define a body of faith, and the more demanding *Book of Faith* is markedly philosophical in character. He aroused hostility among the clergy, was arraigned before the archbishop of Canterbury, and obliged to resign his bishopric and recant his opinions (1458). He was sent to Thorney Abbey where he probably lived in seclusion. EETS os editions: *The Donet*, ed. E. V. Hitchcock (no. 156, 1918); *The Folewer to the Donet*, ed. E. V. Hitchcock (no. 164, 1923); *The Reule of Christen Religioun*, ed. W. C. Greet (no. 171, 1926). See also *The Repressor*, ed. C. Babington (2 vols, 1860); Wendy Scase, *Reginald Pecock* (1996).

PEELE, George (1556–96) Poet and playwright, educated at *Christ's Hospital, Broadgates Hall (Pembroke College), and Christ Church, Oxford. From about 1581 he lived mainly in London, pursuing a literary career and associating with many other writers of the period. His works fall into three main categories: plays, pageants, and 'gratulatory' and miscellaneous verse. His surviving plays are *The *Arraignment of Paris* (1584); *Edward I* (1593); *The Battle of Alcazar* (1594); *The Old Wife's Tale* (1595); and **David and Fair Bethsabe* (1599). His miscellaneous verse includes **Polyhymnia* (1590) and *The Honour of the Garter* (1593), a gratulatory poem to the earl of Northumberland. Peele extended the range of non-dramatic blank verse: his work is dominated by courtly and patriotic themes. The *jest book *The Merry Conceited Jests of George Peele* (1607) apparently bears little relation to Peele's actual personality. C. T. Prouty edited a three-volume *Life and Works* (1952–70).

Pegasus *See* BELLEROPHON.

PÉGUY, Charles (1873–1914) French poet and essayist. A socialist who gradually became a Catholic, Péguy began by writing for the *Revue socialiste*, but he is best known for his later religious poetry, notably his *Mystère de la charité de Jeanne d'Arc* (1910: *Mystery of the Charity of Joan of Arc*) (*see* JOAN OF ARC), based on his 1897 dramatic trilogy, *Le Porche du mystère de la deuxième vertu* (1911: *The Portico of the Mystery of the Second Virtue*), *Le Mystère des Saints-Innocents* (1912: *The Mystery of the Holy Innocents*), and *Ève* (1913). A reservist, he was killed in the battle of the Marne. He is the subject of a poem by Geoffrey *Hill, *The Mystery of the Charity of Charles Péguy* (1983).

Peg Woffington Charles *Reade's first published novel (1853), based on an episode in the life of the 18th-century actress Peg Woffington, and adapted from his play *Masks and Faces*.

Pelagian Derived from Pelagius, the Latinized form of the name of a British monk (*fl.* *c.*398–418) whose understanding of grace as illumination was fiercely combated by Germanus, bishop of Auxerre, and by St *Augustine, and condemned by Pope Zosimus in 418. The Pelagians denied the doctrine of original sin, asserting that Adam's fall did not involve his posterity, and maintained that the human will is itself capable of good without the assistance of divine grace. In spite of their condemnation, their beliefs died slowly and were only finally defeated by the Augustinian view at the Council of Orange (529) that grace is God-given. Even so, the voluntarist tendency of Pelagianism revived in the Middle Ages; many of the thinkers opposed by *Bradwardine (d. 1349) he called 'modern Pelagians' in their attempts to qualify the immanence of God's grace by their views of free will. See R. E. Evans, *Pelagius: Inquiries and Reappraisals* (1968).

***Pelham**, or The Adventures of a Gentleman* A novel by Edward *Bulwer-Lytton, published 1828. It describes the adventures of Henry Pelham, a young dandy and aspiring politician, who falls in love with Ellen, sister of an old school friend, Reginald Glanville. Reginald is falsely suspected of murder, and tells his story to Pelham, who discovers the real murderer, Thornton (based on the notorious murderer John Thurtell). The novel's success rested on its lively portrayal of fashionable society, and of vivid minor characters such as Lady Frances, Pelham's worldly mother, and Lord Vincent, whose conversation is laced with Latin puns. Bulwer-Lytton mocks the conventions of the *fashionable novel while he exploits them, creating a tone of witty cynicism which pleased contemporary readers, and made the hero's name a catchphrase.

'Pelleas and Ettarre' One of Tennyson's **Idylls of the King*, published 1869. Pelleas woos the heartless Ettarre, is tricked by Gawain, learns of the adultery of Lancelot and Guinevere, and vows to avenge the treasons of the Round Table.

Pelléas et Mélisande *See* MAETERLINCK, MAURICE.

PEMBROKE, Mary Herbert, countess of (1561–1621) The younger sister of Philip *Sidney, whose first version of the **Arcadia* was written for her at Wilton shortly after her marriage to Henry Herbert, second earl of Pembroke (1534–1601), in 1577. After her brother's death in 1586 she became in effect his literary executrix, overseeing the publication of *The Arcadia* and the rest of his works for editions in 1593 and 1598 and undertaking literary projects of which he would have approved. She completed the *Psalms*, of which Sidney had translated only the first 42, rendering them in a very wide variety of English verse forms; they were not published as a whole until 1963, although John *Ruskin had made a selection from them under the title of *Rock Honeycomb* (1877). She translated the *Discourse of Life and Death* by Du Plessis Mornay (1549–1623) and *Antonius*, a Senecan tragedy by Robert Garnier (1544–90). Both were published in 1592; the latter was also published as *Antonie* in 1595. At an unknown date she translated *Petrarch's *Trionfo della morte*. Her reputation as a patroness rivalled her specific achievements (T. S. *Eliot's 1932 essay 'Apology for the Countess of Pembroke' implies her control of a literary clique which probably never existed); but she certainly had links with such writers as Thomas *Nashe, Abraham *Fraunce, Samuel *Daniel, *Nicholas Breton, and John *Harington. A letter from her saying 'we have the man Shakespeare with us', allegedly seen at Wilton by William *Cory, was probably a humorous fabrication. William *Browne's epitaph on her was popular throughout the 17th century:

'Underneath this sable hearse
Lies the subject of all verse:
Sidney's sister, Pembroke's mother.
Death, ere thou hast slain another,
Fair, and learned, and good as she,
Time shall throw a dart at thee.'

There is a two-volume edition of her works by Margaret P. Hannay, Noel J. Kinnamon, and Michael G. Brennan (1998).

PEN An association of Poets, Playwrights, Editors, Essayists, and Novelists founded in 1921 by Amy Dawson Scott (1865–1934) to promote understanding and cooperation between writers in the interests of literature, freedom of expression, and international goodwill. Its first international gathering was in 1923 and it now has branches in more than 100 countries.

Pendennis, The History of A novel by W. M. *Thackeray, serialized in numbers November 1848–December 1850, and illustrated by himself. Publication was interrupted by Thackeray's serious illness in 1849, and the second half of the novel is more sombre in tone. It is a **Bildungsroman* in which the main character, Arthur Pendennis, is the spoiled son of an unworldly widow, Helen. He falls in love with an actress, Emily Costigan ('Miss Fotheringay'), and is only rescued from an unsuitable marriage by the intervention of his uncle, Major Pendennis, who persuades her disreputable old father that Arthur has no money of his own. Pendennis then goes to university, where he runs up bills and is rescued by a loan from Helen's adopted daughter Laura Bell. Helen hopes that Laura and her son will marry, but Pendennis's next entanglement is with Blanche Amory, an affected and hard-hearted girl, daughter of the rich, vulgar Lady Clavering by her first husband. Major Pendennis encourages this match, although he is secretly aware that Blanche's father is an escaped convict who is still alive and is blackmailing Sir Francis Clavering.

Pendennis goes to London, supposedly to read for the bar. He shares chambers with George Warrington (descended from the Warringtons in *The *Virginians*), who starts him on a literary career by introducing him to Captain Shandon, a debt-ridden Irish journalist (based on William *Maginn) who is editing a new magazine, the 'Pall Mall Gazette', from prison. Pendennis has a mild flirtation with a working-class girl, Fanny Bolton, who nurses him through a dangerous illness. Helen Pendennis mistakenly assumes that Fanny is Pendennis's mistress, and treats her very unkindly. Roused to indignation, Pendennis threatens to marry Fanny, but is dissuaded by Warrington, whose life is blighted by his own unfortunate marriage. Fanny finds consolation with a medical student, but Blanche is harder to escape. After the exposure of the existence of her villainous father, Pendennis feels obliged to go through with an engagement to her. Fortunately Blanche decides in favour of Harry Foker, heir to a brewing fortune, and Pendennis and Laura finally marry, after Helen's death. *Pendennis*, which includes many autobiographical details, is among Thackeray's most accomplished novels.

Pendragon A title given to an ancient British or Welsh chief holding or claiming supreme power. In English chiefly known as the title of Uther Pendragon, father of *Arthur. The word means 'chief dragon', the dragon being the war standard.

Penelope *See* ODYSSEY.

Penguin Books The name given to an innovative series of paperbacks launched by Allen *Lane in 1935 and established as an independent publishing company in 1936. The first ten titles—colour-coded orange for fiction, blue for biography, and green for crime—sold for sixpence each, and included works by Agatha *Christie, Ernest *Hemingway, and Dorothy *Sayers. In 1937 both the Penguin Shakespeare and the non-fiction Pelican series were unveiled; Puffin Picture Books for children followed in 1940. Other notable ventures include the inception of Penguin Classics in 1946, edited for many years by E. V. Rieu (1887–1972), whose own translation of the *Odyssey* (1946) was its first and best-selling volume, and the first unexpurgated edition of **Lady Chatterley's Lover* (1960), which led to a celebrated Old Bailey trial and acquittal. Penguin became a public company in 1961 and was acquired by the Pearson Group in 1970. The archives of Penguin Books Ltd are held at the University of Bristol.

PENHALL, Joe (1967–) Playwright, born in London, whose first play, *Some Voices* (1994), about a young schizophrenic unsuccessfully attempting to adjust to life outside the hospital, was produced at the *Royal Court Theatre. Quickly established as an important new writer, with a line in dialogue reminiscent of David *Mamet, his *Blue/Orange* (2000) reopened debates about schizophrenic treatment in the context of a young black man lost in the maze of a collapsing National Health Service. His *Landscape with Weapon*, a play about the invention of a devastating new weapon, was produced at the *National Theatre in 2007.

PENN, William (1644–1718) Quaker and founder of Pennsylvania. He was born in London, educated at Chigwell School, then privately taught in Ireland before attending Christ Church, Oxford. Sent to the Tower in 1668 for publishing *The Sandy Foundation Shaken* (dismissing the doctrine of the Trinity), he wrote *No Cross, No Crown* (1669), a Quaker classic. He went to America to escape persecution, and drew up a democratic constitution for Pennsylvania, a forerunner of the United States Constitution.

PENNANT, Thomas (1726–98) Naturalist, antiquary, and traveller. His works include *A Tour in Scotland* (1771), *A Tour in Wales* (1778–81), *A Tour in Scotland and Voyage to the Hebrides* (1774–6), and *The Journey from Chester to London* (1782). His travel writings were admired by Samuel *Johnson. He was also a distinguished zoologist, author of *British Zoology* (1768–70) and *Arctic Zoology* (1784–7). *Literary Life of the Late Thomas Pennant, Esq., by Himself* appeared in 1793.

penny dreadfuls (*dime novels in the USA) Cheap, sensational texts produced in the 19th century featuring the lurid adventures of Sweeney Todd, Spring-Heeled Jack, and others. They were targeted at boys, but many girls also read them. Robert Louis *Stevenson was among those influenced by their style. Attempts to replace them with 'healthy fiction' included *Chatterbox* and *The Boy's Own Paper*. See E. S. Turner, *Boys will be Boys* (1948).

Penny Magazine *See* KNIGHT, CHARLES.

Penshurst Place, in Kent Owned by the Sidney family since 1552, and the birthplace of Philip and Robert *Sidney. Many writers enjoyed its hospitality, including Ben *Jonson, who paid a graceful tribute in 'To Penshurst' (*The Forest*, 1616), praising the fruitfulness of the landscape and the gardens, the 'high huswifery' of its lady, the generosity of its lord, and the virtues of the whole household, who learned there 'the mysteries of manners, arms and arts'.
See also PATRONAGE.

Pentameron, The A prose work by Walter Savage *Landor, published 1837, an expression of Landor's admiration of *Boccaccio. The book consists of imaginary conversations between *Petrarch and Boccaccio, while the latter lies ill at his village near Certaldo, and Petrarch visits him on five successive days. They speak mainly of Dante's **Divina commedia*; but Petrarch also reproves Boccaccio for the licentious character of some of his tales.

pentameter A verse line with five stressed syllables, almost always iambic in *metre and thus of ten syllables, the stressed normally alternating regularly with the unstressed: 'And never lifted up a single stone' (William *Wordsworth, 'Michael'). This iambic pentameter is the standard line of English verse from *Chaucer onwards, and the basis of several major English verse forms including *blank verse, *heroic couplets, *rhyme royal, and the *sonnet. It is open to flexible variation in syllable count (variant lines may be of eleven or nine syllables), in the use and position of the *caesura, in the number of stressed syllables (variant lines may employ four or six, thus speeding or slowing the movement), and in their placing (stressing the first rather than second syllable of a line is the most common variation).

PEPYS, Samuel [pron. Peeps] (1633–1703) Diarist, son of John Pepys, a London tailor, educated at St *Paul's School, London, and at Magdalene College, Cambridge. In 1655, when 22, he married Elizabeth St Michel, a girl of 15, the daughter of a French father and English mother. He entered the household of Sir Edward Montagu (afterwards first earl of Sandwich), his father's first cousin, in 1656; and his subsequent successful career was largely due to Montagu's patronage. His famous *Diary* opens on 1 January 1660, when Pepys was living in Axe Yard, Westminster, and was very poor. Soon after this he was appointed 'clerk of the King's ships' and clerk of the privy seal, with a salary of £350 (supplemented by fees). In 1665 he became surveyor-general of the victualling office, in which capacity he showed himself an energetic official and a zealous reformer of abuses. Owing to an unfounded fear of failing eyesight he closed his diary on 31 May 1669, and in the same year his wife died. In 1672 he was appointed secretary to the admiralty. He was committed to the Tower on a charge of complicity in the *'Popish Plot' in 1679 and deprived of his office, but was soon set free. In 1683 he was sent to Tangier with Lord Dartmouth and wrote an interesting diary while there. In 1684 he was reappointed secretary to the admiralty, a post which he held until the revolution of 1688, labouring hard to provide the country with an efficient fleet. At the revolution he was deprived of his appointment and afterwards lived in retirement, principally at Clapham. His *Diary* remained in cipher (a system of shorthand) at Magdalene College, Cambridge, until 1825, when it was deciphered by John Smith and edited by Lord Braybrooke. An enlarged edition by Mynors Bright appeared in 1875–9, and an edition in ten volumes (1893–9) by Henry B. Wheatley remained the standard text until the appearance of a new and unbowdlerized transcription by R. Latham and W. Matthews (11 vols, 1970–83). On his death his friend and fellow diarist John *Evelyn remembered him as 'a very worthy, industrious and curious person, none in England exceeding him in knowledge of the navy…universally beloved, hospitable, generous, learned in many things, skilled in music, a very great cherisher of learned men'. Pepys's *Memoirs of the Navy, 1690* were edited by J. R. Tanner (1906). See Claire Tomalin, *Samuel Pepys: The Unequalled Self* (2003). *See also* Restoration.

Perceforest A vast 14th-century French prose romance, in which the author seeks to link the legends of *Alexander the Great and *Arthur. Alexander, after the conquest of India, is driven by a storm on the coast of England, and makes one of his followers, called Perceforest because he has killed a magician in an impenetrable forest, king of the land. Under the latter's grandson the Holy *Grail is brought to England.

Perceval, Sir Probably to be identified with *Peredur of the **Mabinogion*. He first appears in European poetry in the 9,000-line, incomplete *Perceval, ou le conte del Graal* of *Chrétien de Troyes (*c.*1182) and the German *Parzival* (*c.*1205) of *Wolfram von Eschenbach (which was the inspiration for *Wagner's opera). In English he appears in *Sir Perceval of Galles*, a 2,288-line romance, in 16-line stanzas in *tail-rhyme from the 15th century (ed. W. H. French and C. B. Hale, *Middle English Metrical Romances*, 1930), and in Sir Thomas *Malory. The former tells of the childhood of Perceval and his being knighted by Arthur, without any allusion to the Holy *Grail. Malory makes him a son of King Pellinore, describing his success in the quest for the Holy Grail with the knights *Galahad and Bors. In the French prose Vulgate *La Queste del Saint Graal*, the three successful questers are joined on Solomon's ship by Perceval's sister.

PERCY, Thomas (1729–1811) Clergyman and literary scholar, son of a Bridgnorth grocer, educated at Christ Church, Oxford. In 1761 he published a translation (from the Portuguese) of the first Chinese novel to appear in English, *Hau Kiou Choaan*; his *Five Pieces of Runic Poetry Translated from the Islandic Language*, including the 'Incantation of Hervor' and the 'Death-Song of Ragnar Lodbrog' (1763), had a considerable influence on the study of Norse in England. Percy also published poetry (including his ballad *The Hermit of Warkworth*, 1771), translated from the Hebrew and Spanish, and wrote a *Memoir of Goldsmith* (1801). His collection of *ballads, **Reliques of Ancient English Poetry* (3 vols, 1765), tastefully 'improved' (following advice from William *Shenstone and Samuel *Johnson) from materials in the *Percy Folio, was attacked by Joseph *Ritson as unscholarly, but contributed to the revival of interest in older English poetry. Percy was created bishop of Dromore in 1782.

Percy Folio A manuscript in mid-17th-century handwriting, which belonged to Humphrey Pitt of Shifnal, the most important source of our *ballad literature and the basis of Francis Child's (1825–96) collection. It was the source of the ballads included in Thomas *Percy's **Reliques*. It also contains the 14th-century alliterative allegorical poem 'Death and Life' (modelled on **Piers Plowman*) and 'Scottish Field' (mainly on the battle of *Flodden). The Percy Folio was printed in its entirety by J. W. Hales and F. J. *Furnivall in 1867–8. It is now in the British Library.

Percy Society Founded in 1840 by Thomas Crofton *Croker, Alexander *Dyce, James *Halliwell-Phillipps, and John Payne *Collier, for the purpose of publishing old English lyrics and ballads. It was named in honour of Thomas *Percy.

PEREC, Georges (1936–82) French novelist, writer, and member of the *OuLiPo movement, whose work is defined by formal experimentation. *La Disparition* (1969: *A Void*) is a detective novel which avoids using words containing the letter 'e'. *W ou le Souvenir d'enfance* (1975: *W, or The Memory of Childhood*) deals with *Holocaust survival and memory by combining two narratives (one of childhood memories, the other fictional) which converge on an image of a concentration camp. *La Vie, mode d'emploi* (1978: *Life: A User's Manual*) is a vast fresco depicting life in a Parisian apartment block.

Peredur The Arthurian subject of one of the seven tales added by Lady Charlotte Guest (1812–95; an early translator of the **Mabinogion*) to the *Mabinogion* proper and now normally included in it. The Welsh *Peredur* is found most completely in the White Book, rather than the Red Book used by Guest (see *Mabinogion*), and it is found in two additional manuscripts. The story corresponds closely to the *Perceval* of *Chrétien de Troyes, from which however it departs in a number of ways, and also corresponds to a number of other Arthurian texts, such as *Perlesvaus* (ed. F. Nitze *et al.*, 1932).

Peregrine Pickle, The Adventures of A satirical novel by Tobias *Smollett, published 1751. As a boy Peregrine shows 'a certain oddity of disposition' which manifests itself in practical jokes. At Winchester College and at Oxford he plunges into hectic living, and develops further his violent vein of humour. He falls in love with Emilia, who remains through all his wanderings a fixed point to which he always returns. But she is beneath him in fortune and in rank, and pride forbids him to court her. He undertakes a disastrous *Grand Tour, suffering imprisonment in the Bastille and passionately attaching himself to one woman after another. Returning to England, he allies himself in Bath with the misanthrope Crabtree, but when his old friend the comic sailor Commodore Hawser Trunnion falls ill, he nurses the old man lovingly and is filled with grief at his death. Trunnion's legacy to him, however, prompts a new burst of profligacy, and he becomes obsessed with the seduction of Emilia, falling ill when he fails to accomplish this. At this point, the lengthy 'Memoirs of a Lady of Quality' are abruptly inserted as chapter 81, breaking the pell-mell flow of adventure but providing an oblique perspective on Peregrine's life of debauchery. The 'Memoirs' are based on the life story of Frances Anne Hawes, Viscountess Vane (1713–88). When the main story resumes, Peregrine loses money in an attempt to enter politics, and is eventually imprisoned for libel. Another long story, of the generous but unfortunate poet Mackercher, is interpolated at this point. In prison Peregrine becomes morose and withdrawn, quarrels with Trunnion's comrades, the faithful boatswain Pipes and Lieutenant Hatchway, and begins to long for death. But he is rescued by Emilia's brother Godfrey, Emilia returns to him, and he inherits his father's fortune. When he and Emilia marry they reject the fashionable urban world and retire to the country. The novel contained savage caricatures of Henry *Fielding as Mr Spondy (Fielding responded in the *Covent-Garden Journal*), David *Garrick as Marmozet, and Mark *Akenside as the Doctor. It was only moderately successful, and was modified both in form and tone for the second edition of 1758.

PERELMAN, S. J. (Sidney Joseph) (1904–79) American humorist, born in New York, who published comic sketches focused on an innocent abroad, targeting particularly travel and show business. He was a screenwriter in Hollywood for films by the Marx Brothers and others, and helped support Nathanael *West at the beginning of his career. See Dorothy Herrmann, *S. J. Perelman* (1986).

PÉREZ GALDÓS, Benito (1843–1920) Spanish novelist, playwright, and journalist, born in the Canary Islands, who spent most of his life in Madrid, a city of which he became the chronicler. His output was vast: he published a series of 46 historical novels between 1873 and 1912, to which he gave the general title of *Episodios nacionales* (*Scenes from the History of the Nation*). Of his novels of contemporary life, the best known is his masterpiece, *Fortunata y Jacinta* (1887), an extraordinarily rich, realistic, densely populated panoramic work which follows the fortunes of two contrasted women, but also explores Spanish society, history, and politics. Galdós greatly admired both Charles *Dickens and William *Shakespeare, and made many visits to England, where he was elected fellow of the *Royal Society of Literature.

performance poetry A term applied to poetry specifically written to be performed out loud. The work may sometimes transfer successfully to the printed page, but its true power usually lies in the moment of public performance.

Often with an anti-establishment edge, performance poetry covers a wide range of poetic activity, from topical satire and burlesque to ranting and agitprop, including avant-garde sound poetry and mixings of word and music. Usually performed from memory or improvised, rather than read, it can be accompanied by highly choreographed gestures and subtle voice techniques, leading to accusations (not always unjust) of style over substance. A term also in vogue is 'Spoken Word'.

'It is very important to get poetry out of the hands of the professors and out of the hands of the squares,' declared American jazz poet Kenneth *Rexroth (1905–82) in 1958. 'We simply want to make poetry a part of show business.' Rexroth's motivation to broaden the audience remains at the heart of performance poetry today. Performing poets are less likely to appear at literary clubs than in music venues, bars, comedy festivals, and on radio; they may issue a CD before a book.

Jazz (*see* JAZZ POETRY) has been a consistently dominant influence, starting with Langston *Hughes and Vachel Lindsay (1879–1931); to Rexroth's 1950s jazz-poetry collaborations with Lawrence *Ferlinghetti; and continuing since the 1970s, with Amiri *Baraka, Jayne Cortez (1936–), Gil Scott Heron (1949–), and the Last Poets, through to contemporary hip-hop.

In the 1960s, Allen *Ginsberg took oral poetry into coffee houses, pop festivals, and art happenings. In Britain, the spirit was spread by Michael *Horovitz, Adrian *Mitchell, and the *Liverpool poets. Maverick figures with a music-hall tilt followed, including Glaswegian absurdist Ivor Cutler (1923–2006); then, in the mid-1970s, punky quickfire monologuist John Cooper Clarke (1950–), and from the mid-1980s cabaret scene, John Hegley (1953–).

Performance poetry has become most closely identified with black writers such as Benjamin *Zephaniah, Linton Kwesi *Johnson, John *Agard, and James *Berry. The Caribbean tradition from which their work derives is closely associated with the musical forms of calypso, ska, reggae, and dancehall and can be roughly divided into two forms: *'dub poetry', which is performed from memory without accompaniment, and the more improvisational 'toastin', which is accompanied by music.

In 1987, a new wave of performance activity was sparked in the United States when Marc Smith (1950–) started the first Poetry Slam at Chicago's Green Mill Cocktail Bar. These raucous stand-up poetry contests came to worldwide attention after Bob Holman (1948–) introduced them to the Nuyorican Poets Café. The format is now well enough established for Harold *Bloom to have described it in the *Paris Review* (Spring 2000) as 'the death of art', an assessment which supporters have welcomed as an endorsement of its anti-elitist credentials. Leading exponents include Patricia Smith (1955–) and Saul Williams (1972–), who starred in the 1998 film on the subject, *Slam*.

Peri Bathous, *or The Art of Sinking in Poetry* (1727) A mock–critical manual by Alexander *Pope on literary 'bathos', supposedly 'depth' or 'profundity' (by analogy with *Longinus' 'hypsos' or 'sublimity'), but actually a record of the failure of poets to achieve literary sublimity and their tendency to fall flat instead. Pope used as examples quotations from Richard *Blackmore, John *Dennis, Ambrose *Philips, and

Lewis *Theobald, among others. Angry responses were shortly afterwards absorbed into the material for Pope's **Dunciad*.

Pericles and Aspasia A prose work by Walter Savage *Landor, published 1836. The book consists of imaginary letters, most of them between Aspasia and her friend Cleone. Others pass between Pericles and Aspasia, or other prominent figures of the time, including Anaxagoras and Alcibiades. The letters discuss artistic, literary, religious, philosophical, and political subjects, ending with the death of Pericles.

Pericles, Prince of Tyre A romantic drama ascribed to *Shakespeare on its first publication, in a textually corrupt quarto, in 1609 but now generally agreed to have been written in collaboration with George *Wilkins, who seems to have been mainly responsible for the first two acts. It was registered in 1608, when Wilkins's prose narrative *The Painful Adventures of Pericles Prince of Tyre*, based on a performance of the play, was published. Though the quarto was reprinted five times, the play was omitted from the first *folio of 1623, but included in the second issue of the third folio of 1664. The play is based on the story of Apollonius of Tyre (which Shakespeare also used in *The *Comedy of Errors*) in John *Gower's *Confessio Amantis* and a prose version (itself derived from the **Gesta Romanorum*), *The Pattern of Painful Adventures*, registered 1576 and reprinted 1607, by Laurence Twyne.

The play is presented by Gower, who acts as chorus throughout. It tells how Pericles, prince of Tyre, discovers the incestuous relation between King Antiochus and his daughter by solving a riddle, and then finds his life in danger. He leaves his government in the hands of his honest minister Helicanus, and sails from Tyre to Tarsus where he relieves a famine. Off the coast of Pentapolis Pericles alone survives the wreck of his ship, and in a tournament defeats the suitors for the hand of Thaisa, daughter of King Simonides, whom he marries.

Hearing that Antiochus has died, Pericles sets sail for Tyre, and during a storm on the voyage Thaisa gives birth to a daughter, Marina, and collapses. Apparently dead, Thaisa is buried at sea in a chest, which is cast ashore at Ephesus, where Cerimon, a physician, opens it and restores Thaisa to life. She, thinking her husband drowned, becomes a priestess in the temple of Diana. Pericles takes Marina to Tarsus, where he leaves her with its governor Cleon and his wife Dioniza.

When the child grows up Dioniza, jealous of her being more favoured than her own daughter, seeks to kill her; but Marina is carried off by pirates and sold in Mytilene to a brothel, where her purity and piety win the admiration of Lysimachus, the governor of the city, and the respect of the brothel-keeper's servant, Boult, and secure her release. In a vision Pericles sees Marina's tomb, deceivingly erected by Cleon and Dioniza. He puts to sea again and lands at Mytilene, where to his intense joy Pericles discovers his daughter. In a second vision, Diana directs him to go to her temple at Ephesus and there tell the story of his life. In doing this, the priestess Thaisa, his lost wife, recognizes him, and is reunited with her husband and daughter. At the end of the play the chorus tells how Cleon and Dionyza are burnt by the citizens of Tarsus as a penalty for their wickedness.

All editions are necessarily heavily edited; the play is printed in its original form in the Oxford Shakespeare original-spelling edition (1996).

periodical, literary A term which designates a repeating series of literary journal, magazine, or review. The literary periodical began to flourish in the early 18th century. The trade journal **Mercurius Librarius*, begun in 1668, was the first periodical to catalogue books, and the *Universal Historical Bibliotheque* of 1687 the first to invite contributions and include comments on essays and other recent writings. The *Gentleman's Journal* (begun 1692) included much literary material, and the general magazine with some literary content was popularized by the **Tatler* (1709–11) of Joseph *Addison and Richard *Steele and Edmund *Cave's influential **Gentleman's Magazine* (begun 1731); the tradition continued in the 19th century with **Blackwood's Magazine* (1817–1980) and **Bentley's Miscellany* (1837–69). The single-essay periodical, best represented by the **Spectator* (1711–12, 1714) and Samuel *Johnson's **Rambler* (1750–52), had huge contemporary influence and reputation, but the form did not last beyond the end of the 18th century. Periodicals promoted and sustained many other writers of the 18th century, including Daniel *Defoe, Jonathan *Swift, and Henry *Fielding, who was associated with several journals, especially *The *Champion* (1739–41) and the *Covent-Garden Journal* (1752), which held occasional 'trials' of current publications, including those of Tobias *Smollett, another writer heavily involved in literary journalism. Christopher *Smart and Oliver *Goldsmith contributed to a wide range of similar periodicals. Formal book reviews began with the **Monthly Review* (1749–1844) and Smollett's **Critical Review* (1756–90). Several periodicals identified themselves with political positions, such as *The Anti-Jacobin* (1797–8), which opposed the liberal outlook of the *Monthly Review* and of S. T. *Coleridge's *The Watchman* (1796); the **New Monthly Magazine* (1814–84) expressly opposed the radical *Monthly Magazine* (founded 1796).

By the early 19th century the periodicals and their editors (such as Leigh *Hunt in the **Indicator* and John *Scott in the **London Magazine*) were becoming increasingly important for the encouragement and dissemination of literary work. The *Englishman's Magazine* (1831–3) published and defended William *Wordsworth, Alfred *Tennyson, Thomas *Hood, and others. S. T. Coleridge's **Friend* and P. B. Shelley's **Liberal* (1822–4) saw the first publication of much new work. In some cases such writer-driven periodicals were deliberately set against the magisterial opinion-formers of the 19th century such as the **Edinburgh Review* (1802–1929), the **Quarterly Review* (1809–1967), the **Examiner* (1808–81), the **Westminster Review* (1824–1914), the **Athenaeum* (1828–1921), the **Cornhill Magazine* (1860–1975), and the **Fortnightly Review* (1865–1934). Later periodicals established by writers to break away from commercial journalism include the **Yellow Book* (1894–7), the **English Review*, begun in 1908 by writers such as H. G. *Wells and Joseph *Conrad, *Blast* (*see* VORTICISM), T. S. *Eliot's

*Criterion, *Horizon (1940–50), and *Encounter (1953–). Many small-scale literary magazines containing reviews and new writing continue to publish, though some of the functions of the literary periodical have been assumed by the book sections of newspapers such as the *Guardian, The *Times, and the *Observer. In Britain the most eminent periodicals devoted to books are the *Times Literary Supplement (1902–) and the *London Review of Books (1979–).

peripeteia A sudden reversal of the *protagonist's fortunes within a dramatic plot, usually that of a *tragedy.

Perkin Warbeck A historical play by John *Ford, printed 1634: its source is an episode in Francis Bacon's *Henry VII*. The play deals with the arrival of Warbeck at the court of King James IV of Scotland and his marriage, at the king's request and against her father's wish, to Lady Katherine Gordon; the treason of Sir William Stanley and his execution; the expedition of James IV with Warbeck into England; the desertion of Warbeck's cause by James; Warbeck's landing in Cornwall, his defeat, capture, and execution. Ford takes up, in a new key, the much earlier fashion for plays in English history, but departs from his sources in making Perkin convinced that he actually is duke of York, not an impostor. Thus Perkin is a victim, not a villain, and the play is a study of delusion rather than ambition.

PERRAULT, Charles (1628–1703) French writer, lawyer, civil servant, and member of the Académie Française, born in Paris. In his day he was known for his participation in the quarrel between the ancients and moderns (*see* CORNEILLE, PIERRE); however, he is remembered for his collection of *fairy stories published under the name (and possibly with the collaboration) of his son Pierre: *Histoires ou contes du temps passé* (1697), subtitled 'Contes de ma Mère l'Oye' (*see* MOTHER GOOSE). He began by producing ironic verse tales, popular in sophisticated court circles: 'Grisélidis' (the story of Patient Griselda, 1691), 'Les Souhaits ridicules' (in which Jupiter grants three disastrous wishes to a man and his wife, 1693), and 'Peau d'Asne' ('Donkeyskin', in which a princess flees the incestuous advances of her widowed father disguised as a kitchen maid wrapped in a donkey-skin, 1695).

The *Histoires* transformed popular folk tales into moralizing works concluded with ironic verse homilies; they were translated into English as 'Mother Goose Tales' by Robert *Samber in 1729. The original tales consisted of those known in English as 'Hop o' my Thumb'; 'Cinderella'; 'Sleeping Beauty'; 'Blue Beard'; 'The Fairies, or Diamonds and Toads' (about two sisters, one good, one bad, from whose mouths issue the appropriate objects); 'Puss in Boots'; 'Little Red Riding Hood'; and 'Ricky with the Tuft' (in which a hideous but intelligent prince must choose whether to marry a beautiful and stupid woman or her intelligent, ugly sister; he selects the former).

Perseus Mythical Greek hero, son of Zeus (*Jupiter) and Danaë. Aided by divine gifts, including winged sandals, helmet of invisibility, and shield used as a mirror, he cut off the head of the monstrous Gorgon Medusa, whose gaze turned those who looked at her to stone. The winged horse Pegasus sprang up from her blood. *Ovid describes his adventures, including his rescue of Andromeda, in *Metamorphoses* Book 4. Shakespeare and other Renaissance writers assumed that Perseus, not *Bellerophon, was the rider of Pegasus. Keats plays with these narratives in his sonnet 'If by dull rhymes'.

PERSIUS (Aulus Persius Flaccus) (AD 34–62) Roman poet, author of six satires. Persius writes as a Stoic: a serious-minded young man, interested in promoting virtue and rebuking vice. His style is deliberately crabbed and compressed; he assumes that his reader is familiar with *Horace, using Horatian allusions as a kind of shorthand. He produces some fine lines and effective passages; but as a whole, his work is difficult and undeniably bookish. His satires were imitated by John *Donne and translated by John *Dryden. See Kirk Freudenburg (ed.), *The Cambridge Companion to Roman Satire* (2005).

personification (prosopopeia) A figure of speech in which inanimate objects or abstractions are endowed with human qualities or represented as possessing human form, as in 'Let us flee this cruel shore', or 'The leaves laughed in the trees'.

Persuasion A novel by Jane *Austen, written 1815–16, published posthumously 1818. Sir Walter Elliot, a spendthrift baronet and widower, with a swollen sense of his social importance and personal elegance, is obliged to let the family seat, Kellynch Hall. His eldest daughter Elizabeth, haughty and unmarried, is now 29; the second, Anne, who is pretty and intelligent, had previously been engaged to a young naval officer, Frederick Wentworth, but had been persuaded by her trusted friend Lady Russell to break off the engagement, because of his lack of fortune and a misunderstanding of his easy nature. The breach had brought great unhappiness to Anne, and caused angry indignation in Wentworth. When the story opens Anne is 27, and the bloom of her youth is gone. Captain Wentworth, now prosperous, is thrown again into Anne's company by the letting of Kellynch to Admiral and Mrs Croft, his sister and brother-in-law. Sir Walter's youngest daughter Mary is married to Charles Musgrove, the heir of a neighbouring landowner. Wentworth is attracted by Charles's sisters Louisa and Henrietta, and in time becomes involved with Louisa. During a visit of the party to Lyme Regis, Louisa, being 'jumped down' from the Cobb by Wentworth, falls and is badly injured. Wentworth's partial responsibility for the accident increases his obligation to Louisa at the very time that his feelings are being drawn back to Anne. However, during her convalescence Louisa becomes engaged to Captain Benwick, another naval officer, and Wentworth is free to proceed with his courtship. He goes to Bath, where Sir Walter now lives with his two elder daughters and Elizabeth's artful companion Mrs Clay. There Wentworth finds another suitor for Anne's hand, her cousin William Elliot, the heir to the Kellynch estate, who is also flirting with Mrs Clay, in order to detach her from Sir Walter. Anne remains unshaken in her love for Wentworth and learns about the duplicity of William Elliot. Accidentally made aware of Anne's constancy, Wentworth renews his offer of marriage and is accepted.

In this, Jane Austen's last completed work, satire and ridicule take a milder form, and the tone is more grave and tender. There is a tradition—poorly substantiated—that a love story of her own life is reflected in Anne Elliot's, although she wrote to her niece Fanny, 'You may *perhaps* like the heroine, as she is almost too good for me.'

PESSOA, Fernando (1888–1935) Portuguese poet and writer of prose who was educated in South Africa, not returning permanently to Portugal until 1905, when he was 17. Thereafter he lived almost entirely in Lisbon. Pessoa was profoundly influenced by English literature and, in 1918, published, in English, *35 Sonnets and Antinous*. His interest in the occult links him to Aleister *Crowley, whom he knew, and to W. B. *Yeats. The most creative period of his life was probably the years 1913–17, which saw the appearance of the 'heteronyms', fictional alter egos under whose names he composed poetry in many different styles, and whose biographies—and horoscopes—he also compiled. The best known of the many heteronyms are Alberto Caeiro, a pastoral poet of an unusual kind, Álvaro de Campos, who is associated with *Futurism, and the neo-classical Ricardo Reis. Pessoa also wrote poetry under his own name and, as Bernardo Soares, the prose *Livro de desassossego* (*Book of Disquiet*), published posthumously and several times translated. He left a large legacy of poetry and prose, but in his lifetime published relatively little, mostly in magazines. The only book in Portuguese to appear during his life was *Mensagem* (1935: *Message*), a collection of short poems presenting a Messianic vision of Portuguese history. Since the 1980s many different translators have produced versions of his poetry, and he has come to be considered one of the leading European *modernists. The multi-vocal heteronyms, whose poetic identities are constantly shifting, are a compelling expression of the fragmentation of the personality. Nor is it possible to say that the poems signed by the poet in his own name represent in some way the 'real' Pessoa. Since the 1990s the gradual revelation of the extent of his unpublished work has shown how much he is also the poet of the fragmentary and the unfinished.

PETER, St *See* BIBLE.

PETER I, the Great (Emperor Petr Alekseevich) (1672–1725) Russian tsar, born in Moscow, who ruled jointly with his half-brother Ivan V from 1682 to 1696 and then as sole ruler until his death. Ruthless in suppressing opposition, he embarked on a series of wide-reaching reforms, aimed at transforming Russia into a major European power and eradicating practices and customs that he considered impediments to progress (e.g. long coats and longer beards; the old Russian calendar). His modernization programme embraced reform of the administration and subordination of the church, introduction of new taxes and establishment of a meritocratic Table of Ranks, complete reorganization of the army and creation of a navy. His reign was marked by constant wars against the Turks and the Swedes. Soon after the commencement of the Great Northern War, he founded St Petersburg (1703) as a fortress which became his new capital. In 1721 he accepted the title of emperor of 'All the Russias', which were by then considerably larger than those he had inherited. Peter was the first Russian ruler to travel abroad (1697–8), accompanying in transparent incognito, rather than leading, a Grand Embassy that visited European capitals seeking support for Russia's struggle against the Turks. He was more successful in honing his own practical skills in the dockyards of Amsterdam and London and in recruiting naval officers, shipwrights, and all manner of specialists and craftsmen necessary for advancing his technological revolution. After meeting William III in Utrecht, Peter, still incognito, visited England in January 1698. The months he spent in London, working in the shipyards, sailing on the Thames, visiting the Mint and the Arsenal, but also frequenting taverns and theatres and managing to devastate John *Evelyn's house and garden at Sayes Court, provided the colourful anecdotes that ensured Peter's place in British memory and imagination. Despite subsequent deterioration in Anglo-Russian diplomatic relations, Peter became a legendary hero of the *Enlightenment. Painted during his visit by Sir Godfrey *Kneller, he was the subject of vast 19th-century historical canvases by Robert Ker Porter, Daniel Maclise, and Augustus Egg. His engraved portrait has adorned popular and academic biographies, historical novels and adventure tales, and edifying works for children. During the tsar's lifetime Daniel *Defoe published his fake memoir *Impartial History* (1723), and Aaron *Hill's poetic effusion *The Northern Star* went into no fewer than five editions between 1718 and 1739. Peter became the star of dramas, comic operas, and tragedies, beginning with the anonymous *Northern Heroes* (1748), including John *O'Keeffe's *The Czar Peter* (1790), and finishing with Laurence Irving's performed but unpublished five-act tragedy *Peter the Great* (1898). To mark the tercentenary of Peter's visit to London, a statue by the Russian sculptor Mikhail Chemiakin (1943–) was unveiled near the site of the old royal dockyard in Deptford in June 2001. See Lindsey Hughes, *Russia in the Age of Peter the Great* (1998); Anthony Cross, *Peter the Great through British Eyes* (2000).

Peter Bell A poem by William *Wordsworth, written 1798, published with a dedication to Robert *Southey 1819. Bell is a lawless potter, insensible to the beauty of nature. Coming to the edge of the Swale he sees a solitary ass and hopes to steal it. The ass is gazing into the water at some object, which turns out to be the dead body of its owner. After a series of supernatural events Peter mounts the ass, which leads him to the cottage of the drowned man's widow. Peter's spiritual and supernatural experiences on this ride make him a reformed man. The comic nature of part of the poem was seen by some as ludicrous and diverted attention from its merits, and it became the subject of several parodies, including one by P. B. *Shelley, **Peter Bell the Third*.

Peter Bell the Third A satirical poem by P. B. *Shelley written at Florence 1819, published 1839. It parodies William *Wordsworth's poem **Peter Bell*. A second 'Peter Bell' had already been published by John *Keats's friend J. H. *Reynolds. Shelley uses inventive doggerel, outrageous rhymes, and effervescent social satire to mock Wordsworth's 'defection' from the radical cause—'a solemn and unsexual man'. He follows Peter's progress through a black, comic underworld, described in seven sections: 'Death', 'The Devil', 'Hell', 'Sin', 'Grace', 'Damnation', and 'Double Damnation'. Part III begins with the celebrated 'Hell is a city much like London'; while Part V draws a sympathetic cartoon of Peter the poet, who remembered 'Many a ditch and quick-set fence; | Of Lakes he had intelligence'.

Peterborough Chronicle, The The last part of the Laud manuscript of the **Anglo-Saxon Chronicles*, written in Peterborough at various times between 1121 and 1154, the date of its last annal. It is the only part of the chronicles to extend beyond 1080, and is of great linguistic interest in exemplifying the developments between Old and Middle English. The 12th-century entries, in particular, as they describe the disasters and hardships of Stephen's reign, have vigour and circumstantiality far beyond the earlier parts of the chronicles. See C. Clark, *The Peterborough Chronicle 1070–1154* (1958); facsimile edn D. Whitelock (1954); trans. G. N. Garmonsway (1953).

'Peter Grimes' A tale in George *Crabbe's *The *Borough*. Grimes is a fisherman who 'fish'd by water and who filch'd by land'. Forbidden to keep apprentices after several die under his ill treatment, he lives and works alone. Guilt maddens him, and he dies after enduring imagined terrors. He is the principal figure in Benjamin *Britten's opera *Peter Grimes*.

PETER LOMBARD (*c.*1095/1100–*c.*1161) *Magister Sententiarum*, or master of the sentences, born at Novara and educated at Rheims and Paris, where he taught at the cathedral school of Notre Dame. In 1159, he became bishop of Paris. The *Sententiae* were completed by 1157. They are a collection of opinions, derived from the Bible and the church Fathers, on topics such as God, the Creation, the redemption, and the sacraments. They became the standard theological textbook from the 13th century, upon which all those with aspirations to theological authority had to write a commentary (*see* COMESTOR, PETRUS; ALEXANDER OF HALES; DUNS SCOTUS; OCKHAM, WILLIAM OF).

PETER MARTYR (1499–1562) Pietro Martire Vermigli, theologian, born in Florence, an Augustinian monk (who took the name of St Peter Martyr) who accepted the Reformed faith, fled from Italy in 1542 to Switzerland, and subsequently to England, and became Regius professor of divinity at Oxford (1548). He helped Thomas *Cranmer in the preparation of the second *Book of *Common Prayer* (1552) and was responsible for an important collection of *Loci Communes* (theological topics). When the Catholic Mary Tudor came to the throne in 1553, he escaped to Strasbourg and died at Zurich. His first wife is buried in Christ Church Cathedral, Oxford. See Philip McNair, *Peter Martyr in Italy* (1967).

Peter Pan, *or The Boy Who Would Not Grow Up* A play by J. M. *Barrie, first performed in 1904, featuring Peter Pan, who lives in Neverland with fairies, pirates, and the Lost Boys, where he takes the Darling children. It has been adapted as a musical (1954), and filmed by Disney (1953), P. J. Hogan (2003), and, as *Hook*, by Steven Spielberg (1991).
See MCCAUGHREAN, GERALDINE.

Peter Porcupine *See* COBBETT, WILLIAM.

PETERS, Ellis *See* DETECTIVE FICTION.

Peter Wilkins, a Cornishman, The Life and Adventures of (1750) A romance by Robert Paltock (1697–1767), an attorney. Wilkins is shipwrecked in the Antarctic and reaches a land of winged people. One of them, the beautiful Youwarkee, falls outside his hut, and he revives her, and eventually marries her. The work, combining the naturalism of **Robinson Crusoe* with the fantasy of **Gulliver's Travels*, was much admired by S. T. *Coleridge, P. B. *Shelley, Walter *Scott, and others.

'Petra' *See* BURGON, JOHN WILLIAM.

PETRARCH (Francesco Petrarca) (1304–74) Italian poet and humanist, and the most popular Italian poet of the English Renaissance. He was born at Arezzo, the son of a notary who was expelled from Florence (in the same year as *Dante) by the Black Guelfs and migrated to Avignon in 1312. Here in 1327 Petrarch first saw the woman who inspired his love poetry. He calls her Laura; her true identity is unknown. Until 1353 Petrarch's life was centred on Provence (Avignon and his beloved retreat at Vaucluse), but he made extended visits to Italy, on the first of which, in 1341, he was crowned poet laureate in Rome, for him the most memorable episode of his life. From 1353 onwards he resided in Italy, though he travelled widely, both on his own account and at the instance of his patrons. He died in Arquà in the Euganean Hills near Padua. Today Petrarch is best known for the collection of Italian lyrics variously known as the *Canzoniere* or the *Rerum vulgarium fragmenta*, which includes the long series of poems in praise of Laura, now regarded as the fountainhead of the European lyric; but to his contemporaries and the generations that immediately succeeded him he was best known as a devoted student of classical antiquity. This enthusiasm he shared with his friend *Boccaccio. The encouragement which Petrarch gave to Cola di Rienzo in 1347, at the time of the attempted restitution of the Roman republic, may be seen as an expression of the humanist spirit with which he was imbued, and in accordance with which he wrote the majority of his works in Latin. He wrote a large number of treatises, including *De Viris Illustribus* (*On Famous Men*), *De Vita Solitaria* (*On the Solitary Life*), *De Remediis Utriusque Fortunae (Remedies for Fortune Fair and Foul*); a Latin epic, *Africa*, on the struggle between Rome and Carthage; and the *Secretum* (*The Secret*), a self-analysis in the form of a dialogue between himself and St *Augustine. Influenced by Cicero, many of whose letters he rediscovered, Petrarch produced a large number of letters, consciously collecting them for public circulation. See *Rerum Familiarum Libri* (*Letters on Familiar Matters*), *Seniles* (*Letters of Old Age*).

Petrarch is justly regarded as the father of Italian humanism and the initiator of the revived study of Greek and Latin literature, but for English writers his chief inspiration was to the early sonneteers (*see* SONNET); he was imitated and translated by the earl of *Surrey, Thomas *Wyatt, Thomas *Watson, and, later, by *Drummond of Hawthornden. Philip *Sidney, while mocking the poets who slavishly echoed 'poor Petrarch's long deceased woes', yet bears witness to his powerful and pervasive influence. Henry Parker, Lord Morley (1476–1556), translated at some point before 1546 his *Trionfi* as *The Tryumphes of Fraunces Petrarcke* (?1555; ed. D. D. Carnicelli, 1971), and the countess of *Pembroke translated the *Trionfo della morte* into **terza rima*. The Petrarchan vogue declined in the 17th century with the waning popularity of the sonnet sequence, and in 1756 Joseph *Warton in his essay on Alexander *Pope dismissed Petrarch as 'metaphysical and far fetched'. Thomas *Gray, in a note on the last stanza of his *Elegy*, credits Petrarch with his phrase 'trembling hope' (*paventosa speme*), which indicates a renewal of interest in the later 18th century. See George Watson, *The English Petrarchans* (1967); N. Mann, *Petrarch* (1984); K. Foster, *Petrarch, Poet and Humanist* (1984); L. W. Foster, *The Icy Fire: Five Studies in European Petrarchism* (1969).

PETRONIUS ARBITER (probably 1st century AD) Roman satirical novelist, author of the *Satyricon*; traditionally identified with Petronius, the witty favourite of Nero called by Tacitus his *arbiter elegantiae* (arbiter of taste), who was forced to commit suicide in AD 66. The novel's central character is the disreputable Encolpius, a person of some culture but few morals and no money. The story tells of his adventures and those of his glamorous boyfriend, Giton. At times, it is the wrath of Priapus, god of fertility, which pursues them—a burlesque of the angry Poseidon of the **Odyssey* and the angry *Juno of the **Aeneid*. Most celebrated, and longest, of the surviving episodes is the grotesque dinner party given by Trimalchio, a wealthy and ignorant freedman, which burlesques the motif of the philosophical party, a recurrent theme from *Plato's *Symposium* onwards. The story of the Widow of Ephesus is a classic of ribald misogyny. The novel is punctuated by passages of verse, a feature of **Menippean satire*, including a lengthy poem on the Civil Wars covering the same ground as *Lucan. The first English translation was published in 1694 by William Burnaby (1673–1706). Retellings of Petronius include Federico Fellini's film *Satyricon*. See J. P. Sullivan, *Petronius: A Literary Study* (1968).

PETRY, Ann (1908–97) African American writer, born in Connecticut, who published articles and stories about Harlem in the 1940s. She is best known for her first novel *The Street* (1946), describing the efforts of a mother to raise her son in Harlem. She also wrote a number of historical portraits for younger readers.

PETTIE, George (*c*.1548–89) Writer of romances, educated at Christ Church, Oxford. His *A Petite Palace of Pettie his Pleasure*, first published in 1576, with an address to the 'gentle gentlewomen readers', was often reprinted. This collection of twelve 'pretty histories', all but one deriving from classical sources, concerns lovers. They are mainly made up of long speeches with little action, and their style partially anticipates John *Lyly's euphuism. A century after their first publication, Pettie's grand-nephew Anthony *Wood called them 'more fit to be read by a schoolboy, or rustical amoratto, than by a gent. of mode or language'. Pettie's work follows on from William Painter's **Palace of Pleasure* from which he derived his title; his translation of most of *Civil Conversation* (1581) by Stefano Guazzo (1530–93) contributed to the Elizabethan vogue for *courtesy literature.

PETTY, Sir William (1623–76) Political economist, and one of the intellectuals in the Samuel *Hartlib circle. The son of a Hampshire clothier, he became a cabin boy, but was set ashore in Normandy and educated by Jesuits in Caen. A disciple of Francis *Bacon, he championed quantification, and became personal secretary to Thomas *Hobbes. For Oliver *Cromwell he carried out a survey of confiscated lands in Ireland, the first attempt at scientific map-making. He acquiesced in the *Restoration, was knighted, and became a charter member of the *Royal Society in 1662. He published economic treatises, the principal of which were *A Treatise of Taxes* (1662), which examined taxation and public expenditure, *Verbum Sapienti* (1664), which attempted the first serious calculations of national income and wealth, and *Political Arithmetic* (1690), a term denoting what we now call statistics. He was an early proponent of laissez-faire government. See C. Webster, *The Great Instauration* (1975).

Peveril of the Peak A novel by Walter *Scott, published 1823, set in the Restoration England of Titus Oates's *'Popish Plot'. The action is chiefly concerned with corruption at the court of Charles II, with fanaticism turned sour, and with conflicting loyalties. These are worked out most effectively in the characters of Major Bridgenorth and young Julian

Peveril, in both of whom there is profound psychological development.

PEVSNER, Sir Nikolaus Bernhard Leon (1902–83) Architectural historian, born and educated in Germany. He lectured for four years at Göttingen before the rise of Hitler brought him to England, where he became in 1941 associated with *Penguin Books, as editor of King Penguins and of his celebrated county-by-county series *The Buildings of England* (1951–74). His association with Birkbeck College began formally in 1942, where he continued to teach until 1967, and he was professor of fine art at the universities of Cambridge (1949–55) and Oxford (1968–9). His many works on art, design, and architecture include *Pioneers of the Modern Movement* (1936), *High Victorian Design* (1951), and *The Englishness of English Art* (1956).

PEYTON, K. M. (1929–) (Kathleen—'M' is her husband, Michael, a collaborator on some early books.) Children's novelist, born in Birmingham; she attended Manchester Art School. She is known for her stories about horses and hunting, especially the trilogy of books beginning with *Flambards* (1968; televised, 1979). The Pennington books (1970, 1971, 1980) feature a musically talented but difficult working-class boy.

PFEIFFER, Emily (1827–1890) Née Davis, poet and essayist. She published writings diverse in style and form, including *The Wynnes of Wynhavod* (1881); *Flying Leaves from East and West* (1885); *Flowers of the Night* (1889); and various feminist articles which were collected in *Women and Work* (1887).

Phalaris, Epistles of Letters attributed to Phalaris, a tyrant of Acragas in Sicily (6th century BC), with a reputation for extreme cruelty. They were edited by Charles Boyle, fourth earl of Orrery (1674–1731), in 1695, and praised by Sir William *Temple. Richard *Bentley proved that they were spurious and dated from perhaps the 2nd century AD. There is an echo of the controversy in Jonathan Swift's *The *Battle of the Books*.

Phaon (1) In Edmund *Spenser's **Faerie Queene* (II. iv), the unfortunate squire who, deceived by Philemon and under the influence of Furor (mad rage), slays Claribel and poisons Philemon. (2) In classical mythology, the boatman with whom *Sappho is said to have fallen in love. John *Lyly's play *Sapho and Phao* (1584) dramatizes the subject.

Pharsalia *See* LUCAN.

Phèdre *See* RACINE, JEAN; HIPPOLYTUS.

Philaster, *or Love Lies a-Bleeding* A romantic tragicomedy by Francis *Beaumont and John *Fletcher, written 1608–9, printed 1620. One of the most successful of the Beaumont and Fletcher collaborations, the play draws on the conventions of the prose romances, notably on *Montemayor's *Diana* and Sidney's **Arcadia*.

The king of Calabria has usurped the crown of Sicily. The rightful heir, Philaster, loves and is loved by Arethusa, the king's daughter, but the king intends to marry her to Pharamond, prince of Spain. To maintain contact with her, Philaster places his page Bellario in her service. Arethusa reveals to the king that Pharamond (tired of her own frigid reception of him) has embarked on an affair with Megra, a lady of the court; Megra in turn accuses Arethusa of misconduct with the handsome young Bellario. After various pursuits and disasters, during which Bellario shows touching devotion to Philaster, and Philaster himself behaves badly, it emerges that Bellario is in fact Euphrasia, daughter of a Sicilian lord, in love with Philaster. Reassured of Arethusa's virtue, Philaster regains his loved one and his kingdom, whereas Bellario/Euphrasia devotes herself to a life of chastity.

Philip *See* ADVENTURES OF PHILIP.

philippics *See* CICERO, MARCUS TULLIUS; DEMOSTHENES.

Philip Quarll, The Adventures of An adventure story originally published as *The Hermit* (1727) by 'Edward Dorrington', but probably by Peter Longueville. A derivative of **Robinson Crusoe*, it describes Quarll's 50 years of solitude and suffering on a South Sea island. It went through many editions, and was much adapted for children.

PHILIPS, Ambrose (1674–1749) Poet, fellow of St John's College, Cambridge, and MP in the Irish Parliament. He was a member of Joseph *Addison's circle. In 1709 his *Pastorals* were printed in the same miscellany as those of Alexander *Pope; following Thomas *Tickell's praise (in the **Guardian*) of Philips's versions, Pope added an extra paper, no. 40, in which he commended with 'unexampled and unequalled artifice of irony' (Samuel *Johnson) Philips's most risible effects. Philips also wrote *The Distrest Mother* (1712), a successful adaptation of *Racine's *Andromaque*, and a series of infantile trochaics addressed to children which earned him the nickname of 'Namby Pamby'.

PHILIPS, John (1676–1709) Poet, educated at Christ Church, Oxford. In *The Splendid Shilling* (unauthorized 1701, authorized 1705), a burlesque in Miltonic blank verse, Philips contrasts the happy possessor of the shilling, who 'nor hears with pain | New oysters cry'd, nor sighs for chearful ale', with the starving poet in his garret, beset by creditors. In 1705 he published *Blenheim*, written at the suggestion of Robert *Harley and Viscount *Bolingbroke, as a Tory counterpart to Joseph *Addison's *The Campaign*. *Cyder* (1708), a two-book poem in blank verse written in imitation of *Virgil's *Georgics*, celebrates the cultivation, manufacture, and virtues of cider. The poem influenced Alexander Pope's **Windsor-Forest* and

James Thomson's *The *Seasons*, where Philips is praised as 'Pomona's bard' ('Autumn', ll. 640–50).

PHILIPS, Katherine (1631–64) Poet and translator, known as the 'Matchless Orinda', the daughter of Royalist John Fowler, a London merchant. She lived in London until the age of 15, attending Mrs Salmon's School, Hackney. On her father's death her mother married a Welsh baronet, whose castle in Pembrokeshire became Katherine's home. In 1648 she married Parliamentarian James Philips of Cardigan: he was 59, she 17. Her poems were widely circulated in manuscript, inspiring eulogies by Henry *Vaughan ('It was thy light showed me the way' in *Olor Iscanus* and *Thalia Redeviva*); a commendatory poem by 'Orinda' was prefixed to the latter volume. Her translation of *Corneille's *Pompée* was acted in Dublin with great success in 1663, and her version of *Horace*, completed by Sir John *Denham, in 1668. Her collected poems appeared unauthorized in 1664. She died of smallpox, and was mourned in elegies by Abraham *Cowley and Sir William *Temple; her collected poems were published in 1667. They memorialize a coterie, a Platonic Society of Friendship, whose members were known by poetic sobriquets, including Anne Owen (1633–92; Lucasia), Mary Aubrey (1631–1700; Rosania), John *Berkenhead (Cratander), and Sir Charles Cotterell (1615–1701; Poliarchus), her correspondence with whom was published as *Letters from Orinda to Poliarchus* in 1705. These letters show Philips's careful construction of the persona of 'Orinda'. She was pre-eminently a poet of female friendship. Her lyrics, marrying *Cavalier and *metaphysical influences, applied *Petrarchan love conventions to present women's friendship as an ideal. Friendship is 'our passion...the strongest thing I know'. See P. W. Souers, *The Matchless Orinda* (1931); E. Hobby, *The Virtue of Necessity* (1988); Germaine *Greer, *Kissing the Rod* (1988).

Philistine The name of an alien warlike people who in early biblical times constantly harassed the Israelites. The name is applied (1) humorously or otherwise to persons regarded as 'the enemy' into whose hands one may fall, like bailiffs, or literary critics; (2) to persons deficient in liberal culture and enlightenment, from *philister*, the term applied by German students to one who is not a student at the university, but a townsman. In sense (2) the word was introduced into English by Matthew *Arnold ('Heine', *Essays in Criticism*); he describes Heinrich *Heine as a progressive, a lover of ideas and hater of philistinism, and the English as a nation dominated by 'inveterate inaccessibility to ideas'. In other works, notably **Culture and Anarchy*, he develops the concept; the English middle classes are predominantly Philistine, whereas the aristocracy, with its love of field sports, physical prowess, and external graces, is described as 'Barbarian'. The working classes are described as the 'Populace'.

PHILLIPPS, Sir Thomas (1792–1872) Book collector, educated at Rugby School and University College, Oxford. He early developed a passion for collecting books and, particularly, manuscripts (he described himself as 'a perfect vellomaniac'), assembling an extremely valuable library at his home in Broadway, Worcestershire. He also established there a private printing press, the Middle Hill Press, where he printed visitations, extracts from registers, collections of charters, and other works. In 1863 he moved his vast library to Thirlestaine House, Cheltenham, and on his death left some 60,000 manuscripts and 50,000 printed books to his youngest daughter Katharine Fenwick; he was estranged from his eldest daughter Henrietta following her marriage to the Shakespearian scholar J. O. *Halliwell. The collection was gradually dispersed in a series of sales to public libraries and private collectors. Some unique items (such as the manuscript of part of a translation of *Ovid's *Metamorphoses* associated with William *Caxton) came to light as late as 1964: the Caxton manuscript is now reunited with its other half, once owned by Samuel *Pepys, in the Pepys Library at Magdalene College, Cambridge. See A. N. L. *Munby, *Phillipps Studies* (1951–60); N. J. Barker, *Portrait of an Obsession* (1967).

PHILLIPS, Caryl (1958–) Novelist and playwright, born in St Kitts, West Indies. He came to England with his family as a child and was educated in Leeds, Birmingham, and at Oxford University. Early plays such as *Strange Fruit* (1980) and *The Shelter* (1983) broach issues later central to the novels for which he is better known: race, migration, colonial and postcolonial concerns. His first novel, *The Final Passage* (1985), describes the experiences of the post-war immigrant generation from the Caribbean to Britain. In *A State of Independence* (1986), the protagonist experiences dislocation on returning to his West Indian home. Set in the West Indies in the early 19th century, *Cambridge* (1991) juxtaposes the voices of an educated slave and an Englishwoman visiting her father's plantation. *Crossing the River* (1994) counterpoints various travellers in search of emancipation. In *The Nature of Blood* (1997) Phillips suggests analogies between black slavery and oppressed Jewish experience over the centuries. *Dancing in the Dark* (2005) subtly fictionalizes the life of the black American vaudeville performer Bert Williams. Non-fiction works include *The European Tribe* (essays, 1987) and *Foreigners* (2007), a portrait of three black men in England in different eras. *Extravagant Strangers: A Literature of Belonging* (1997), edited by Phillips, is a survey and anthology of non-British-born writers and the invigorating effects of 'mongrelization' on the native tradition.
See POSTCOLONIAL LITERATURE.

PHILLIPS, Edward (1630–?96) Editor, lexicographer, and biographer, brother of John *Phillips and nephew of John *Milton, by whom he was educated. He was tutor to John *Evelyn's son, then to Philip Herbert (1652/3–1683), afterwards seventh earl of Pembroke. His works include an edition of the poems of William *Drummond of Hawthornden (1656); a popular philological dictionary called *The New World of English Words* (1658); and *Theatrum Poetarum* (1675), a collection of literary biographies in the preface to which some have seen the hand of Milton. He also wrote a short life of his uncle, published 1694. *Lives of Edward and John Phillips* by William *Godwin was published in 1815.

PHILLIPS, John (1631–1706) Younger brother of Edward *Phillips, and nephew of John *Milton, by whom he was educated. He wrote a scathing attack on Puritanism in his poem *A Satire against Hypocrites* (1655), supported Charles II and Titus Oates (1649–1705), and worked as translator and hack-writer. He translated *La Calprenède's *Pharamond* and *Scudéry's *Almahide*, and wrote a travesty of **Don Quixote* (1687) in which he mentions **Paradise Lost*, but his biographer William *Godwin (who much prefers his elder brother Edward) was unable to determine whether the reference was 'intended as a compliment or a slur'.

PHILLIPS, Mike (195?–) Innovative crime writer and essayist, born in Guyana; he moved to Britain as a child. Four of his novels feature a black journalist, Sam Dean, whom Phillips describes as 'a moral outlaw'. *A Shadow of Myself* (2000) plays with the doppelgänger theme.

PHILLIPS, Tom (1937–) English painter, illustrator, and composer. Much of his work has explored the material presence of books and the possibility of reordering printed words to reveal latent stories. *A Humument* (1966–) is a 'treated book' based on W. H. *Mallock's 1892 novel *A Human Document*, parts of which are picked out and elaborately illuminated in a process of constant revision. Phillips's portrait of Dame Iris *Murdoch is in the National Portrait Gallery, and he has designed jackets for many of her novels.

Philomela In classical myth raped by Tereus, husband of her sister Procne; he cut out her tongue, but she revealed her fate to Procne in an embroidered tapestry. The sisters took their revenge by serving up Procne's and Tereus' son to his father in a stew. Procne, Tereus, and Philomela were changed into birds, with Philomela in some versions becoming a nightingale. The story is told in *Ovid's *Metamorphoses* Book 6, and echoed in William *Shakespeare's **Titus Andronicus* and **Cymbeline*. The name Philomela or Philomel is often used poetically to designate the nightingale without reference to her story. Elizabeth *Rowe published her poems under the name Philomela.

Philosophes The collective name of a group of 18th-century writers and thinkers who championed the *Enlightenment values of reason, tolerance, and critical scrutiny of political, social, and religious customs and traditions. From the 1750s they came to be seen as an influential party, its members including *Montesquieu, *Voltaire, *Diderot, *Rousseau, *Buffon, *Condillac, *Condorcet, Jean d'Alembert (1717–83), Paul-Henri Batron d'Holbach (1723–89), and Claude Arien Helvétius (1715–71).

Philosophical View of Reform, A A political essay by P. B. *Shelley, written at Pisa 1820, not published until 1920. Intended as an 'instructive and readable' booklet, this was Shelley's most mature political statement about Liberty, Revolution, and Reform: it confirms his position as a radical (rather than a liberal)—but not a violent revolutionary. Chapter 1 is a historical sketch of the continuous overthrow of imperial powers in Europe; it argues that periods of great literary creativity have always coincided with libertarian movements. Chapter 2 describes conditions of political and economic oppression in contemporary Britain and proposes specific measures of radical change, including parliamentary reform and alteration of laws regarding marriage, property inheritance, capital investment, and working hours. Chapter 3 (unfinished) suggests the means of enforcing political change, including non-violent protest, the intervention of 'poets and philosophers', and the 'last resort' of resistance which is 'undoubtedly insurrection'. The essay illuminates the thinking behind Shelley's political poems of 1817–20, and provided much material for the **Defence of Poetry*, such as the concept of 'unacknowledged legislators'.

Philotas A Senecan tragedy in blank verse by Samuel *Daniel, published 1605. The boasts of Philotas, a brave and generous soldier who is much admired among the Macedonians, make Alexander suspicious. He is accused of concealing his knowledge of a conspiracy against the king, is tortured, and, having confessed, is stoned to death. The author had subsequently to defend himself against the charge that the play implied sympathy for the rebellion of Essex. Performance of the play was suppressed in 1604.

Phineas Finn, the Irish Member A novel by Anthony *Trollope, published 1869, the second of the *'Palliser' series. Phineas Finn, a young Irish barrister, is elected to Parliament for the family seat of Loughshane. In London Phineas wins numerous friends, and falls in love with the politically minded Lady Laura Standish. Lady Laura's fortune is diminished after paying the debts of her brother Lord Chiltern, and she feels she must marry the chilly but wealthy Mr Kennedy. Phineas is disappointed, and later deeply grieved by the unhappiness of the Kennedy marriage, but finds consolation elsewhere. He pursues Violet Effingham, Lord Chiltern's childhood sweetheart, but after a quarrel between the two suitors Violet settles for Chiltern, and they are married. Madame Max Goesler, the rich widow of a Viennese banker, is Phineas's next favourite. Phineas loses his government salary by sticking to his principles over the issue of Irish Tenant Right, and cannot cover the cost of re-election. Madame Max wants to help, and when Phineas refuses she offers to marry him, and to finance a fresh political career. But Phineas honours his prior engagement to a pretty Irish girl, Mary Flood-Jones, and returns to Ireland.

Phineas Redux A novel by Anthony *Trollope, published 1874, fourth in the *'Palliser' series. Phineas Finn's young wife Mary dies, and he returns to politics. But his progress is blocked by a series of misfortunes. First Mr Kennedy, enraged by Phineas's visit to his wife Lady Laura in her Dresden exile, tries to shoot him. Then Phineas quarrels with the president of the Board of Trade, Mr Bonteen, and when, later that night, Bonteen is murdered, he becomes a suspect. He is tried, and only the spirited efforts of Madame Max in discovering the true culprit, and a brilliant courtroom performance by Chaffanbrass, succeed in getting him off. Bonteen's murderer turns out to have been Mr Emilius, the converted Jew who married Lizzie Eustace. Emilius is convicted of bigamy and imprisoned, but there is insufficient evidence to hang him. Phineas is shattered by these experiences, but finally rallies, and marries Madame Max.

In this novel the old duke of Omnium dies, and Plantagenet and Lady Glencora become duke and duchess. Madame Max inherits valuable jewels in the old duke's will, but refuses to accept them. Instead they go to Plantagenet's cousin Adelaide Palliser, enabling her to marry the impoverished Gerard Maule.

Phiz *See* BROWNE, HABLOT KNIGHT.

phoenix In classical myth a unique Arabian bird which periodically was consumed by fire and reborn from its own ashes. It became a symbol of resurrection in a Christian sense and also of many kinds of rebirth: in **Annus Mirabilis* John *Dryden portrays a newly deified London rising from the Great Fire. The phoenix motif was of particular importance to D. H. *Lawrence.

Phoenix, The An Old English poem of 677 lines, found in the *Exeter Book. It is a beast allegory of the kind found in the *bestiaries but developed over a greater length than usual. The descriptive part of the poem is closely based on *Carmen de Ave Phoenice*, probably by the early Christian writer Lactantius (*c.*250–*c.*325), but the allegorizing section has not been attributed to a specific source. The poem is admired for the vividness of its imagery and the accomplishment of its syntax. Rev. edn by N. F. Blake (1990).

'Phoenix and the Turtle, The' Regarded by many as William *Shakespeare's greatest non-dramatic poem, an allegorical elegy lamenting the death of the phoenix and the turtle-dove, who are presented as models of ideal, chaste wedded love, and are mourned by other birds. It was first published in 1601 in a collection of poems on the same subject by Ben *Jonson, George *Chapman, John *Marston, and Robert Chester (*fl. c.*1586–1604), whose long poem gave the volume its title *Love's Martyr*. The identity of the dead couple is mysterious. They have been tentatively identified as the Welsh courtier Sir John Salusbury and his wife, to whom the volume is dedicated (but who had ten children, so do not represent 'married chastity'), Elizabeth and Essex, or various Catholic martyrs (a view favoured by those who think Shakespeare a crypto-Catholic).

Phoenix Nest, The A poetical miscellany published in 1593, compiled by the unidentified R.S. It includes poems by the earl of *Oxford, Walter *Ralegh, and Thomas *Lodge, and opens with three elegies on Philip *Sidney, the 'Phoenix' of the title. It was edited by H. E. Rollins (1931).

photography The practice of photography became highly fashionable in Europe and America in the mid-19th century, with writers' portraits among the most popular subjects. In England, Julia Margaret Cameron (1815–79) photographed Alfred *Tennyson, Robert *Browning, Charles *Darwin, and Thomas *Carlyle. In France, Nadar (Gaspard-Félix Tournachon, 1820–1910) recorded all the great composers, artists, and writers of the era, including Honoré de *Balzac, Victor *Hugo, Charles *Baudelaire, and Émile *Zola. Many 20th-century writers became proficient photographers: Leonid *Andreev adopted the Autochrome colour process, while Virginia *Woolf chronicled the Bloomsbury circle. Reportage, combining photographs and text, became an important genre in the 1930s and 1940s, in magazines and books such as Walker Evans and James *Agee's *Let Us Now Praise Famous Men* (1941). W. G. (Max) *Sebald was influential in his integration of photographs with his fictional writing. Important modern essays on photography include Susan *Sontag, *On Photography* (1978), and Roland *Barthes, *Camera Lucida* (1980).

Phyllyp Sparowe A poem by John *Skelton.

'Physician's Tale, The' *See* CANTERBURY TALES, 13.

picaresque [from the Spanish *pícaro*] A wily trickster or picaroon; the form of novel described as 'picaresque' first appeared in 16th-century Spain with the anonymous **Lazarillo de Tormes* (1554 or earlier) and **Guzmán de Alfarache* (Pt I: 1599; Pt II: 1604) by Mateo Alemán (1547–*c.*1614), the fictional autobiographies of ingenious roguish anti-heroes, the servants of several masters. Examples of their descendants in English are **Moll Flanders*, **Roderick Random*, and **Tom Jones*. The term was apparently first used in England in the 19th century; Walter *Scott, for example, writing in 1829, describes the *Memoirs of Vidocq* (1829) as 'a pickaresque tale…a romance of roguery', and *The Bookman* in 1895 defines a picaresque tale as that of a 'trickster'. Nowadays the term is commonly, and loosely, applied to episodic novels, especially those of Henry *Fielding, Tobias *Smollett, and others of the 18th century which describe the adventures of a lively and resourceful hero on a journey. *The Golden Ass* of *Apuleius is regarded as a forerunner of the picaresque novel, while Thomas *Nashe's *The *Unfortunate Traveller* (1594) is commonly accepted as the first picaresque romance in English. See Richard Bjornson, *The Picaresque Hero in European Fiction* (1977).

PICCOLOMINI, Aeneas Silvius (1405–64) Pope Pius II from 1458, patron of letters, humanist, and author of a romance in Latin, *Historia de Duobus Amantibus (The Tale of*

Two Lovers), of a bawdy comedy (*Chrysis*), of treatises on many subjects, and of commentaries on his times, the *Commentarii Rerum Memorabilium* (*Commentaries on Memorable Matters*), 1462–4. His *De Curialium Miseriis* (*On the Misery of the Court*) provided one of the models for the **Eclogues* of Alexander *Barclay. He visited Scotland in 1435, and wrote a hostile report of its poverty-stricken condition. His third-person autobiography was translated as *Memoirs of a Renaissance Pope* by F. A. Gragg (1959).

PICKARD, Tom (1946–) Poet, born and educated in Newcastle-upon-Tyne. In 1963 he instigated a celebrated series of poetry readings at the Mordern Tower in Newcastle, including one by Basil *Bunting, whom he encouraged in the production of his late masterpiece, *Briggflatts*. Pickard's poetry, prominently absorbing such American influences as Robert *Creeley, is often inflected with a Geordie eroticism. His books include *High on the Walls* (1967) and *The Dark Months of May* (2004).

PICKERING, William (1796–1854) Publisher and bookseller, who started business in London in 1820, and raised printing and book-production standards greatly. He published the 'Diamond Classics' 1820–31, adopting the trademark of the Aldine Press (*see* ALDUS MANUTIUS) in 1830. He increased his reputation by his Aldine edition of the English poets in 53 vols.

Pickwick Papers (*The Posthumous Papers of the Pickwick Club*) A novel by Charles *Dickens, first issued in 20 monthly parts April 1836–November 1837, and as a volume in 1837 (when Dickens was only 25 years old). This high-spirited episodic work was very popular, and had an immense influence on the development of Victorian fiction. Samuel Pickwick, chairman of the Pickwick Club, together with Tracy Tupman, Augustus Snodgrass, and Nathaniel Winkle, become the Club's Corresponding Society, reporting their journeys and observations of characters and manners. The Club links a series of incidents, without elaborate plot. The adventures of Mr Pickwick and his friends are interspersed with incidental tales contributed by various characters. The principal elements in the story are: (1) the visit of Pickwick and his associates to Rochester and their falling in with the specious rascal Jingle, who involves Winkle in the prospect of a duel (fortunately averted). (2) The visit to Dingley Dell, the home of the hospitable Mr Wardle; the elopement of Jingle with Wardle's sister Rachael, their pursuit by Wardle and Pickwick, and the recovery of the lady; followed by the engagement of the brisk young Sam Weller as Pickwick's servant. (3) The visit to Eatanswill, where a parliamentary election is in progress, and Mr Pickwick makes the acquaintance of the journalist Pott, and Mrs Leo Hunter. (4) The visit to Bury St Edmunds, where Mr Pickwick and Sam Weller are fooled by Jingle and his servant Job Trotter. (5) The pursuit of Jingle to Ipswich, where Mr Pickwick inadvertently enters the bedroom of a middle-aged lady at night; is in consequence involved in a quarrel with Mr Peter Magnus, her admirer; is brought before Mr Nupkins, the magistrate, on a charge of intending to fight a duel; and is released on exposing the designs of Jingle on Nupkins's daughter. (6) The Christmas festivities at Dingley Dell. (7) The misunderstanding of Mrs Bardell, Mr Pickwick's landlady, regarding her lodger's intentions, which leads to an action for breach of promise of marriage, in which judgement is given for the plaintiff. (8) The visit to Bath, in which Winkle figures prominently, first in the adventure with the blustering Dowler, and secondly in his courtship of Arabella Allen. (9) Mr Pickwick's imprisonment in the Fleet in consequence of his refusal to pay the damages and costs of his action; the discovery of Jingle and Job Trotter in that prison, and their relief by Mr Pickwick. (10) The affairs of Tony Weller (Sam's father) and the second Mrs Weller, ending in the death of the latter and the discomfiture of the hypocritical drunkard Stiggins, deputy shepherd in the Ebenezer Temperance Association. (11) The affairs of Bob Sawyer and Benjamin Allen, medical students and subsequently struggling practitioners. The novel ends with the happy marriage of Emily Wardle and Augustus Snodgrass, and the prosperous retirement of Pickwick and Weller in Dulwich.

PICO DELLA MIRANDOLA, Giovanni (1463–94) Italian humanist and philosopher, born at Mirandola, of which his family were the lords. He spent part of his short life at Florence in the circle of Lorenzo de *Medici. In 1486 he published 900 theses, offering to defend them at Rome, but some of his propositions were pronounced heretical and the public debate did not take place. The famous oration *De Dignitate Hominis*, with which he intended to introduce the debate, is one of the most important philosophical works of the 15th century. Pico was a daring syncretist, who tried to make a synthesis of Christianity, Platonism, Aristotelianism, and the Jewish cabbala. As a pioneer in the study of Hebrew philosophy he influenced *Reuchlin. His life (*The Lyfe of Johan Picus, Erle of Myrandula a Grete Lorde of Italy*) and some of his pious writings were translated by Sir Thomas *More. John *Colet was influenced by Pico.

picturebooks The most distinctive, complex, and underestimated contribution of children's literature to literary and artistic culture. The potential of the form, rooted in the use of wood-blocks in the early history of book production, was demonstrated by the imaginative innovations of figures like William *Blake. It was further developed by the printer Edmund Evans (1826–1905) and his artists Randolph *Caldecott, Kate *Greenaway, and Walter *Crane. Picturebook narratives, as distinct from books with pictures and illustrated texts, are created by the interaction between words and images. They blossomed with the development of offset lithography in the 1920s, with artists such as Edward *Ardizzone and William Nicholson. Contemporary picturebooks commonly push at the boundaries between visual and verbal texts.

picturesque A term which came into fashion in the late 18th century, principally to describe a certain kind of scenery.

Writers on the picturesque include William *Gilpin, William *Mason, William Payne Knight (1750–1824, who published *The Landscape* in 1794), Uvedale Price (1747–1829, who published *Essays on the Picturesque*, 1794), and the landscape gardener Humphry Repton (1752–1818; *see* LANDSCAPE GARDENING). The impact of these writers on the sensibility and vocabulary of writers of the 19th century was considerable. The 'picturesque', as defined by Price, was a new aesthetic category, to be added to Edmund *Burke's recently established categories of the *Sublime and the Beautiful; its attributes were roughness and irregularity, and its most complete exponent in terms of painting was Salvator *Rosa, whose works enjoyed much popularity at this period; John *Constable described him as 'a great favourite with novel writers, particularly the ladies'. Ann *Radcliffe's works dwell frequently on the picturesque, and Jane *Austen and many of her characters were familiar with the works of Gilpin; in **Mansfield Park* she mocks the spirit of 'improvement' in the character of the foolish Mr Rushworth. The entertaining aesthetic disputes of Price and Knight, both of whom owned estates near the Welsh borders, are satirized in Thomas Love Peacock's **Headlong Hall*, and William *Combe's adventures of Dr Syntax are aimed at the movement in general and Gilpin in particular. Although the excesses of picturesque theory became a popular target for satire, these writers made a lasting contribution to our vision, and writers as diverse as Charles *Dickens, George *Eliot, and Henry *James found the term useful. The development of the picturesque movement into *Romanticism is a subject of much complexity and literary interest. See C. Hussey, *The Picturesque* (1927, 1967).

PIEŃKOWSKI, Jan (1936–) Born in Warsaw, educated at King's College, Cambridge; primarily an illustrator/designer of popular series including the *Meg and Mog* books (1972– , text by Helen Nicoll) but also the creator of several innovative *movable books including *The Haunted House* (1979; CD version 1996), *ABC Dinosaurs* (1993), *Botticelli's Bed and Breakfast* (1996), and *The First Noel* (2004).

Pierce Penniless, *his Supplication to the Devil* A fantastic prose satire by Thomas *Nashe, published 1592: the title plays on the rustic name 'Piers'. The author, in the form of a humorous complaint to the devil, comments on modern vices, throwing interesting light on contemporary customs and everyday life. One of the best passages is that relating to the recently developed practice of excessive drinking, 'a sin, that ever since we have mixed ourselves with the Low Countries, is counted honourable', and containing a description of the various types of drunkards, drawn with a coarse Rabelaisian humour and vigour. The work is directed in part against Richard Harvey the astrologer (brother of Gabriel *Harvey) and the Martinists (*see* MARTIN MARPRELATE). It ends with a discussion of hell and devils.

Pierce the Ploughman's Crede An alliterative poem dating from the last decade of the 14th century, mainly concerned with an attack on the four orders of friars. It was heavily influenced by **Piers Plowman*, to which it pays tribute by featuring a poor but charismatic ploughman, also named Piers, who alone has the spiritual authority to teach the poem's narrator not the Apostles' Creed but a markedly polemical alternative. See Helen Barr (ed.), *The Piers Plowman Tradition* (1993).

PIERCY, Marge (1936–) American novelist, born in Detroit, who became active in the civil rights movement of the 1960s. In addition to publishing poetry (most famously *The Moon is Always Female*, 1980), her novels have engaged with feminist subjects. *Woman on the Edge of Time* (1976) combines time travel with investigating the politics of mental care, and *He, She and It* (1991: UK title *Body of Glass*) portrays a woman's relation with a cyborg in a post-apocalyptic America. Her historical novels include *Sex Wars* (2005), set in the post-Civil War USA.

Piers Plowman The greatest poem of the Middle English *Alliterative Revival, thought to be by William *Langland. It survives in about 50 manuscripts, in three principal versions known as the A, B, and C texts. The A-text, totalling 2,567 lines in its longest version, was probably written *c.*1367–70; the B-text, usually considered an extension of the A-text, which both rewrites the parts of the poem that occur in the A-text and adds more than as much again to the end of it, extends to 7,277 lines (or more) and probably dates from *c.*1377–9; and the C-text is a substantial revision of the B-text, about the same length, dating from *c.*1385–6. All these dates remain open to dispute. The existence of a further version, known as Z, has also been argued. Structurally, the poem is divided in a number of ways which are also problematic because of conflicting manuscript evidence. The principal division of the poem has been into two parts, the 'Visio' (vision) and the 'Vita' (life), the 'Visio' comprising the prologue and the first seven *passus* ('step', or section division) in the B-text (prologue and the first eight in A; the first ten *passus* in C, which sometimes does not have a prologue). This 'Visio'–'Vita' distinction has been of much importance to some critics but it is not found in B manuscripts at all (see Schmidt's edition, 1978, p. xx). It is also unclear whether B or C is to be taken as the more authoritative text. The revisions in C have changed the shape of the poem at some points so that it no longer divides into coherent visions, describing falling asleep—vision—awakening. B is complete and coherent in this way, at least according to modern tastes. Moreover, some of the obscurities that C irons out, such as the tearing of the pardon in B.VII, display great imaginative power. Though some claims have been made for its integrity as a poem, the A-text generally receives less critical attention than other versions. The following unified account of the poem follows the B-text (where there is any divergence in the narrative), in its division into eight separate visions.

Vision 1. While wandering on the Malvern Hills, the narrator (who, it transpires later, is called Will) falls asleep and has a vision of a Tower where Truth dwells, a deep Dungeon, and between them 'a fair feeld ful of folk' (prologue, 17) going about their business. The worldly values thus raised are expounded by Lady Holy Church in *Passus* I; the theme is sustained by the analytical trial of Lady Meed in *Passus* II–IV which considers whether Meed (Reward or payment) is to be given to Wrong or according to Conscience and Reason.

Vision 2. The narrator observes the Sermon (preached here by Reason); Confession (by the Seven Deadly Sins, colourfully personified in *Passus* V, the longest in the poem); Pilgrimage (to Truth, led by Piers the Plowman who first appears here); and Pardon (a paper pardon sent by Truth, but torn up by Piers when its validity is questioned by a priest). The conflict with the priest awakens the dreamer; this is the end of the 'Visio' as distinct from 'Vita', if such a distinction is indicated (as in A and C manuscripts).

Vision 3 shows Will turning to the faculties and sources of knowledge and understanding, as the search for Truth (now referred to as 'Dowel') becomes individualized. In *Passus* VIII–XII Will progressively consults Thought, Wit, Study, Clergy, Scripture, Ymagynatyf, and Reason.

Visions 4 and 5. The theme is Charity, and *Passus* XIII–XVII attempt to show in action the ideas concerning doing well which were offered in Vision 3. Piers reappears in a transfigured form in which his action is indistinguishable from that of Christ.

Vision 6. The Passion of Christ is described as the culmination of doing well in *Passus* XVIII, where the death of Christ is evoked with great power (ll. 57–63), and after his death the *Harrowing of Hell.

Visions 7 and 8. These *Passus* (XIX and XX) continue with the liturgical cycle begun in Lent in *Passus* XVI (l. 172) and show the attempts to put into practice the lessons gained from observing the actions of Christ. But these attempts to perfect the church are still frustrated by evildoers, and the poem ends with Conscience setting out to find Piers.

The structure and argument of *Piers Plowman* may initially seem confusing to modern readers, but such effects, which result from the imagination being brought to bear on urgent theological questions, are part of the poem's radicalism. Passages of great imaginative power (such as in *Passus* XVIII) have a sublimity beyond the reach of any other medieval English writer.

The standard editions, based on all the manuscripts, are *Piers Plowman: The A Version*, ed. G. Kane (1960); *Piers Plowman: The B Version*, ed. G. Kane and E. T. Donaldson (1975); *Piers Plowman: The C Version*, ed. G. Russell and G. Kane (1997); A. G. Rigg and Charlotte Brewer, *Piers Plowman: A Working Facsimile of the Z-Text in Oxford, MS Bodley 851* (1994). The most accessible editions are *The Vision of Piers Plowman: A Complete Edition of the B-Text*, ed. A. V. C. Schmidt (1978; rev. 1996); *Piers Plowman: A New Annotated Edition of the C-Text*, ed. D. A. Pearsall (2008). See also the translation by Schmidt (2000).

PILATE, Pontius See Bible.

Pilgrim's Progress, The, *from This World to That Which Is to Come* A prose *allegory by John *Bunyan, written while he was imprisoned in Bedford Jail for conducting services outside the auspices of the Church of England. Part I was published in 1678 (a second edition with additions appeared in the same year, and a third in 1679), Part II in 1684.

The allegory takes the form of a dream by the author. In this he sees Christian, with a burden on his back (sin) and reading in a book (the *Bible), from which he learns that the city in which he and his family dwell will be burned. On the advice of Evangelist, Christian flees from the City of Destruction, having failed to persuade his wife and children to accompany him. He stuffs his fingers in his ears so that he cannot hear their cries. Part I describes his pilgrimage through the Slough of Despond, the Interpreter's House, the House Beautiful, the Valley of Humiliation, the Valley of the Shadow of Death, *Vanity Fair, Doubting Castle, the Delectable Mountains, the country of Beulah, to the Celestial City. On the way he encounters various allegorical personages, among them Mr Worldly Wiseman, Faithful (who accompanies Christian on his way but is put to death in Vanity Fair), Hopeful (who next joins Christian), Giant Despair, the foul fiend Apollyon, and many others.

Part II relates how Christian's wife Christiana, moved by a vision, sets out with her children on the same pilgrimage, accompanied by her neighbour Mercy, despite the objections of Mrs Timorous and others. They are escorted by Greatheart, who overcomes Giant Despair and other monsters and brings them to their destination. The work is a development of the Puritan conversion narrative (*see* Grace Abounding), drawing on popular literature such as *emblem books and *chapbooks, as well as John *Foxe's *Book of Martyrs* and the Bible. Its powerful, resonant, simple and succinct style combines colloquial and biblical English. It circulated at first mainly in uneducated circles, but became an acknowledged religious and literary classic and has been rightly identified as (apart from the Authorized Version of the Bible) the most influential religious work ever published in English. It has been translated into well over 100 languages. It was a seminal text in the development of the realistic novel, and Bunyan's humorously caustic development of the tradition of name symbolism influenced Charles *Dickens, Anthony *Trollope, and W. M. *Thackeray. A version for children by Geraldine *McCaughrean was published in 1999.

PILKINGTON, Laetitia (1708–50) Irish autobiographer and poet, the daughter of the distinguished Dublin physician John Van Lewen and successively a friend of Jonathan *Swift, Colley *Cibber, and Samuel *Richardson. She turned to verse, playwriting, autobiography, and miscellaneous ghostwriting when her husband, the Revd Matthew *Pilkington, publicly disgraced and divorced her. Between 1739 and 1747, when she returned to Ireland for good, she lived in London and supported herself largely through Cibber and his circle of friends at White's coffee house. Appearing between 1748 and 1754, her three-volume *Memoirs* incorporate a fragmentary tragedy and almost all her known poems. The unfinished last volume appeared posthumously, with an appendix by her son John Carteret Pilkington (1730–63). Celebrated for their vignettes of

Swift, the *Memoirs* exhibit a breezy conversational style and a mastery of dialogue uncommon in narrative at so early a date. Ten years after her death John tried to repeat their success with *The Real Story of John Carteret Pilkington*, a *picaresque account of his boyhood travels after he escaped from the scullery of his father's house at the age of 10. See Norma Clarke, *Queen of the Wits: A Life of Laetitia Pilkington* (2008).

PILKINGTON, Matthew (1701–74) Irish poet turned art historian. Educated at Trinity College, Dublin, he was ordained in 1723. Jonathan *Swift helped him to revise his *Poems on Several Occasions* (1730) and procured his appointment as chaplain to the lord mayor of London in 1732. In London Pilkington successfully passed off as Swift's one of his own satires, *An Infallible Scheme to Pay the Public Debt of This Nation in Six Months*, wrote a libellous biography of the mayor, and apparently turned government informer when arrested for his part in publishing Swift's *Epistle to a Lady* (1734). The notoriety surrounding his 1738 divorce from Laetitia *Pilkington seems to have cut short his literary career. By the mid-1750s he had re-emerged as an authority on Old Master paintings. In 1770 he published *The Gentleman's and Connoisseur's Dictionary of Painters* which, periodically revised, expanded, and retitled, remained current for nearly a century.

Pills to Purge Melancholy *See* D'URFEY, THOMAS.

PINDAR (*c.*518–after 446 BC) Greek lyric poet, the majority of whose surviving works are odes celebrating victories in the games at Olympia and elsewhere. Antiquity's most notable exponent of the greater ode, he served as an inspiration to all subsequent poets attempting this difficult genre. His compositions were elevated and formal, distinguished by the boldness of their metaphors and a marked reliance on myth and gnomic utterance. He used a framework of strophe (the opening section), antistrophe (with the same number of lines and metrical arrangement), and epode (of differing length and structure), which his imitators sought to copy, but in Pindar this pattern rested on an elaborate prosodic structure that remained unknown until it was worked out by August Boeckh in his edition of the Odes (1811). The 17th- and 18th-century writers of Pindarics—Abraham *Cowley, John *Dryden, Alexander *Pope, Thomas *Gray—employed a much looser prosodic system, so that their odes, although elevated and rich in metaphor, lack Pindar's architectural quality.
See also ODE.

Pindaric *See* ODE.

PINERO, Sir Arthur Wing (1855–1934) Playwright. Born in London, he left the Spafields Chapel charity school at the age of 10 to work in his father's solicitor's practice, but, stage-struck from youth, became an actor, and was noticed by Henry *Irving who later produced some of his plays. His first one-act play, *Two Hundred a Year*, performed in 1877, heralded a successful and prolific career. The first of his *farces, *The Magistrate* (performed 1885), involves a series of ludicrous confusions between Mr Posket, the magistrate, and his family; it brought Pinero fame and wealth. Later farces, such as *The School-Mistress* (1887), did nearly as well, as did his sentimental comedy *Sweet Lavender* (1888). His first serious play, on what was to be the recurrent theme of double standards for men and women, was *The Profligate* (1889); it was praised by William *Archer, and noted not only for its frankness but also for its absence of the standard devices of soliloquy and aside. *Lady Bountiful* (1891) was the first of the 'social' plays in which Pinero was deemed to display his understanding of women. *The Second Mrs Tanqueray* (1893), returning to the theme of double standards, was a lasting success, and is now the play for which he is best remembered. *The Notorious Mrs Ebbsmith* (1895) again dealt with a woman's dubious past. *Trelawny of the 'Wells'* (1898), a comedy nostalgically recalling his own passion for the theatre he had haunted as a boy, also had great success. He continued to write, but, although knighted in 1909, lived through many years of dwindling reputation and disillusion, eclipsed by the rising popularity of the new theatre of Henrik *Ibsen and George Bernard *Shaw. See J. Dawick, *Pinero: A Theatrical Life* (1993).

PINTER, Harold (1930–2008) Poet and playwright, born in east London, the son of a Jewish tailor, and educated at Hackney Downs Grammar School. He began to publish poetry in periodicals before he was 20, then became a professional actor, working mainly in repertory. His first play, *The Room*, was performed in Bristol in 1957, followed in 1958 by a London production of *The Birthday Party*, in which Stanley, an out-of-work pianist in a seaside boarding house, is mysteriously threatened and taken over by two intruders, an Irishman and a Jew, who present him with a *Kafkaesque indictment of unexplained crimes. Pinter's distinctive voice was soon recognized, and many critical and commercial successes followed, including *The *Caretaker* (1960), *The Lover* (1963), *The *Homecoming* (1965), *Old Times* (1971), and *No Man's Land* (1975). *Betrayal* (1978; film, 1982) is an ironic tragedy which ends in beginning and traces with a reversed chronology the development of a love affair between a man and his best friend's wife. Later plays include *A Kind of Alaska* (1982), based on a work by Oliver *Sacks, *One for the Road* (1984), *Mountain Language* (1988), *Party Time* (1991), and *Ashes to Ashes* (1996, a short drama of the *Holocaust). Pinter's gift for portraying, by means of dialogue which realistically produces the nuances of colloquial speech, the difficulties of communication and the many layers of meaning in language, pause, and silence created a style labelled by the popular imagination as 'Pinteresque', and his themes—nameless menace, erotic fantasy, obsession and jealousy, family hatreds, and mental disturbance—are equally recognizable. Pinter also wrote extensively for radio and television, directed plays, and wrote several screenplays, which include versions of L. P. *Hartley's *The Go-Between* (1969), **À la recherche du temps perdu* (1978), and John *Fowles's *The French Lieutenant's Woman* (1982). *Poems and Prose, 1947–1977* was published in 1978. In 2005 he was awarded the *Nobel Prize for Literature, and used the occasion of his acceptance speech to attack the US invasion of Iraq. See Michael Billington, *The Life and Work of Harold Pinter* (1996).

PINTO, Fernão Mendes (?1509–83) A Portuguese traveller of obscure origins who sailed for India in 1537 and spent the next 21 years travelling, mainly in the Far East. His posthumously published narrative of his voyages and adventures (*Peregrinação*, 1614), written between 1569 and 1578, was translated into English by Henry Cogan (1653), and into several other European languages in many editions. Its veracity and authenticity were doubted from the start. Scholarship now suggests that Pinto drew on his own experiences, others' accounts, and contemporary literary conventions, including *satire and the *picaresque, to produce a complex blend of travel account, fiction, and commentary on Portuguese colonialism.

Pippa Passes By Robert *Browning, published 1841 as no. I of the series **Bells and Pomegranates*. Although subtitled 'A Drama', it was not written for the stage. In its final version it consists of an 'Introduction' in verse, and four parts, entitled 'Morning', 'Noon', 'Evening', and 'Night'. The first two parts have a verse section followed by one in prose; the third part has two verse sections; the fourth part has a prose section followed by one in verse. This combination of verse and prose was perhaps influenced by Browning's study of Elizabethan and Jacobean drama; *see* SOUL'S TRAGEDY.)

The play is set in and around Asolo, a small town in the Veneto which Browning first visited in 1838 (*see* ASOLANDO). The plot is a web of dramatic ironies. The Introduction shows Pippa, a young silk-worker, waking up on the morning of her annual holiday. She contrasts the life of 'Asolo's Four Happiest Ones' with her own, and decides to 'pass' by them all in the course of the day. These four constitute an ascending scale of value, from carnal love (Ottima, wife of a rich silk merchant, and her lover Sebald), through married love (Jules, a sculptor, and his bride), and filial love (the young patriot Luigi and his mother), reaching at last the love of God (the good bishop). Each life turns out to be different from Pippa's imagining of it, though she herself does not realize this. Ottima and Sebald are quarrelling after their murder of Ottima's husband; Jules's bride turns out not to be the cultivated patrician he thought her, but an ignorant peasant girl; Luigi and his mother are disputing over his intention to carry out a political assassination; and the bishop is negotiating with a corrupt official about the destruction of Pippa herself, who turns out to be his own lost niece, heiress to a fortune he might otherwise appropriate. Pippa 'passes' by each of the four main scenes in turn, singing as she goes. Each song, ironically juxtaposed with the action, effects a moral revolution in the characters concerned. The famous concluding lines of Pippa's first song, 'God's in his heaven—All's right with the world!', are often quoted out of context as evidence of Browning's own allegedly naive optimism. At the end of the drama we see Pippa back in her room at nightfall, unaware of the day's events. The ambivalent moral and aesthetic value of Pippa's 'innocence' is developed in the figure of Pompilia in *The *Ring and the Book*.

PIRANDELLO, Luigi (1867–1936) Italian dramatist, short story writer, and novelist, awarded the *Nobel Prize in 1934. His challenge to the conventions of *naturalism was an important influence on European drama. The first part of his literary career, to 1917, was marked by a prolific production of fiction, both novels and short stories. His novels include *L'esclusa* (1893–4: *The Outcast*), which deals with a woman's desire for independence within patriarchal Sicilian society; *Il fu Mattia Pascal* (1904: *The Late Mattia Pascal*), a major example of modernism, in which Pascal goes home to discover it is impossible to alter his status as 'deceased'; and *I vecchi e i giovani* (1909; rev. 1913: *The Old and the Young*), dealing with the effects of the unification of Italy on Sicily at the turn of the century. His first major work for the theatre was *Così è se vi pare* (1917: *Right You Are, If You Think You Are*), which initiated the second half of his career as a playwright of international stature. In the years between 1918 and 1928 he wrote a further 22 plays, of which the most famous are *Sei personaggi in cerca di autore* (1921: *Six Characters in Search of an Author*), and *Enrico IV* (1922: *Henry IV*). Ten of these Pirandello collected and published as *Maschere nude* (1918–22: *Naked Masks*). His plays anticipated the anti-illusionist theatre of Bertolt *Brecht, Thornton *Wilder, and Peter *Weiss; his exploration of the disintegration of personality foreshadowed Samuel *Beckett; his probing of the conflict between reality and appearance has echoes in the work of Eugene *O'Neill; and his examination of the relationship between self and persona, actor and character, face and mask, is a precursor of the work of Jean *Anouilh, Jean *Giraudoux, and Jean *Genet. These years also saw the production of a further novel, *Uno, nessuno e centomila* (1926: *One, No One, and a Hundred Thousand*), on themes connected with his plays. Pirandello is also the author of several important essays on literature and art, including *L'umorismo* (1908: *Humour*). His plays are regularly performed in Britain. See A. H. Caesar, *Characters and Authors in Luigi Pirandello* (1998).

PIRANESI, Giovanni Battista (1720–78) An Italian architect, who published many dramatic etchings of the ruins of classical Rome. In literary circles Piranesi is most famous for the *Carceri d'invenzione* (*c.*1745; rev. edn *c.*1761), dark visions of Roman prisons where chains and instruments of torture swing before massive arches, and isolated figures wander aimlessly along stairs, ladders, and bridges that lead nowhere. Before his death his works were already popular in England, where they were associated with the Burkeian *sublime; Horace *Walpole wrote of 'the sublime dreams of Piranesi…He piles palaces on bridges, and temples on palaces, and scales Heaven with mountains of edifices'; *The *Castle of Otranto* perhaps shows the impact of such images. Piranesi's deepest influence was on the Romantics. In **Confessions of an English Opium Eater* (1821), Thomas *De Quincey compared Piranesi's prisons with the illusions induced by opium: 'With the same power of endless growth and self-reproduction did my architecture proceed in dreams.' Curiously, he had not seen the etchings but had listened to S. T. *Coleridge's description of a print showing Piranesi groping up endless flights of stairs. This passage became famous in France, where *Musset, *Gautier, and *Hugo were fascinated by Piranesi. Later Piranesi appealed to writers who saw the *Carceri* as symbolizing metaphysical despair. See John Wilton-Ely, *The Mind and Art of Giovanni Battista Piranesi* (1988).

Pirate, The A novel by Walter *Scott, published 1821. Set in 17th-century Shetland, it deals with the tension between tradition and new ideas brought into a closed community by outsiders. Mordaunt Mertoun, though the son of a newcomer, has grown up in Shetland, and like many of Scott's heroes occupies a halfway house between tradition and common sense. The heroines, Minna and Brenda Troil, embody an equally familiar contrast between romance and realism. Fantasy is supplied by the half-crazed seer Norna of the Fitful Head, whose schemes control the plot.

PIRSIG, Robert M. (Maynard) (1928–) American writer, born in Minneapolis, best known for his *Zen and the Art of Motorcycle Maintenance* (1974), a best-selling combination of travel narrative and meditation on human values. This was followed in 1991 by *Lila: An Enquiry into Morals.*

Pistyl of Susan (*The Pistil of Swete Susan*) 'The epistle of Susanna', a northern alliterative poem from the late 14th century, in 364 lines of thirteen-line *tail-rhyme stanzas. Similar in genre to **Patience*, it narrates the story of Susanna and the Elders (Daniel 13), celebrating Susan's obedience to God and her husband. Ed. by Russell A. Peck in *Heroic Women of the Old Testament in Middle English Verse* (1991).

PITT-KETHLEY, Fiona (1954–) Poet, travel writer, novelist, and journalist, best known for her outspoken writing about sex. Her satirical poetry collections include *Sky Ray Lolly* (1986), *Private Parts* (1987), *The Perfect Man* (1989), and *Dogs* (1996), her travel books are *Journeys to the Underworld* (1988) and *The Pan Principle* (1994), and she has published two novels, *The Misfortunes of Nigel* (1991) and *Baker's Dozen* (2000). She has also produced an anthology with some of her own translations from Latin, Greek, Italian, and French, *The Literary Companion to Sex* (1992), and essays on red light districts around the world. *The Autobiography of Fiona Pitt-Kethley: My Schooling* appeared in 2000. She is married to the grandmaster and former British chess champion James Plaskett (1960–).

PIX, Mary (*c.*1666–1709) Playwright and novelist. She published a novel, *The Inhumane Cardinal*, in 1696, and between then and her death wrote some dozen plays, of which the comedy *The Spanish Wives* (1696) held the stage longest. She was admired by the critic Charles Gildon (1665–1724) and the dramatist William *Congreve

Plague Year, A Journal of the A historical fiction by Daniel *Defoe, published 1722. It purports to be the narrative of a resident in London during 1664–5, the year of the Great Plague; the initials 'H.F.' which conclude it have been taken to refer to Defoe's uncle Henry Foe. It tells of the gradual spread of the plague, the terror of the inhabitants, and the steps taken by the authorities, such as the shutting up of infected houses and the prohibition of public gatherings. The symptoms of the disease, the circulation of the dead-carts, and the burials in mass graves are described with extraordinary vividness. The *Journal* condensed information from various sources, including official documents; some scenes appear to have been borrowed from Thomas *Dekker's *The Wonderfull Yeare* (1603). Defoe's subject was suggested by fears of another outbreak, following the one in Marseilles in 1721 which occasioned Sir Robert *Walpole's unpopular Quarantine Act.

Plain-Dealer, The A comedy by William *Wycherley, loosely based on *Molière's *Le Misanthrope*, probably performed 1676, published 1677. Though praised by John *Dryden and John *Dennis, it was criticized for obscenity, and performed in the 18th century in a version bowdlerized by Isaac *Bickerstaff. Manly, Wycherley's blunt, principled hero, returns from the Dutch wars to find his love Olivia treacherously wedded to his friend Vernish. Fidelia, who loves Manly, and has followed him to sea in man's clothes, intercedes with Olivia on his behalf, in a scene reminiscent of the Olivia–Viola scene in **Twelfth Night*. Manly forswears Olivia and pledges himself to Fidelia. In the sub-plot widow Blackacre, who has a passion for legal jargon, trains up her son Jerry (a literary ancestor of Tony Lumpkin in **She Stoops to Conquer*) in her footsteps, and thereby overreaches herself.

The *Plain Dealer* is also the name of a periodical established by Aaron *Hill.

Plain Speaker, The A volume of essays by William *Hazlitt, published in 1826, the last such collection to appear before his death. The title reflects his forthright assertion and invective. It includes several of his finest pieces, such as 'On Dreams' ('We are not hypocrites in our sleep') and 'On the Pleasures of Hating', which concludes with Hazlitt's self-description as 'the dupe of friendship, and the fool of love'.

PLANCHÉ, James Robinson (1796–1880) Prolific and popular dramatist of Huguenot descent, born and educated in London. Besides his many original pieces for the stage, mainly burlesques and extravaganzas, he made translations and adaptations from French, Spanish, and Italian authors, including *fairy-tales by the Countess d'*Aulnoy (1855) and by *Perrault (1858). His works include *The Vampire, or The Bride of the Isles* (1820), an adaptation of John *Polidori's 'The Vampyre', which introduced the 'vampire trap' to the English stage (involving two spring leaves that parted under pressure and immediately re-closed, giving the impression a figure was passing through solid matter), and *The Island of Jewels* (1849). He wrote several opera libretti, including *Maid Marian* (1822) adapted from a tale by Thomas Love *Peacock, Carl *Weber's remarkable *Oberon* (1826), and English versions of *William Tell* and *The Magic Flute*. Planché also made a reputation as an antiquary and a scholar of heraldry and costume. His *History of British Costumes* (1834) long remained a standard work, and in 1842 he published an edition of the *Regal and Ecclesiastical Antiquities of England* (1773) by the antiquarian Joseph *Strutt.

PLATER, Alan (1935–) Dramatist and screenwriter, born in Jarrow and educated at Kingston High School, Hull, and King's College, Newcastle-upon-Tyne. After contributing many episodes to BBC TV's *Z Cars* and its sequel *Softly Softly* in the 1960s, several stage plays followed: the moving *Close the Coalhouse Door* (1972, from a story by ex-miner and novelist Sid Chaplin) heralded the effects of pit closures upon regional communities. Life in the north-east, sport, and jazz feature in his considerable television output, the first predominant in *Seventeen Per Cent Said Push Off* (1972) and *The Land of Green Ginger* (1974), while Rugby League features in *Trinity Tales* (1975, a 'Chaucerian' pilgrimage of supporters to a cup final) and the recordings of cornet-player Bix Beiderbecke inspired *The Beiderbecke Affair* (1985). His adaptations for the small screen include Anthony *Trollope's *Barchester Chronicles* (1982) and Olivia *Manning's *The Fortunes of War* (1987) (from her *Balkan Trilogy*). *All Credit to the Lads* (1998) is a stage play about football. Recent work for television includes *The Last of the Blonde Bombshells* (2000), and *Belonging* (2004).

PLATH, Sylvia (1932–63) American poet and novelist, born in Boston, Massachusetts, the daughter of a German immigrant professor, who died when she was 8. She was educated at Smith College, Massachusetts, and Newnham College, Cambridge. She married the poet Ted *Hughes in 1956 and the two often compared drafts of their work. After teaching for a while in America, she and Hughes returned to England in 1959, where they lived in London before moving to Devon in 1961. Her first volume of poetry, *The Colossus*, appeared in 1960, and in 1963 her only novel, *The *Bell Jar*, based on her experience of electroconvulsive therapy, appeared under the pseudonym Victoria Lucas. Less than a month after its publication she committed suicide in London. In 1965 appeared her best-known collection, *Ariel*, which established her reputation with its courageous and controlled treatment of extreme and painful states of mind. Much of her symbolism was deeply rooted in actuality; the poems on bee-keeping ('The Bee Meeting', 'The Arrival of the Bee Box', etc.) are based on her own attempts to keep bees in Devon. Other poems refer directly to her own experiences: 'Lady Lazarus' is based on her two previous suicide attempts, 'Daddy' on the early loss of her father, 'Tulips' on a week spent in hospital undergoing an appendectomy: in 'Lady Lazarus' and 'Daddy' she uses powerful imagery drawn from the *Holocaust, though she was not herself Jewish. Other posthumous volumes include *Crossing the Water* and *Winter Trees* (both 1971); *Johnny Panic and the Bible of Dreams* (1977, collected prose pieces); and *Collected Poems* (1981, with an introduction by Ted Hughes). A volume of letters, *Letters Home*, edited by her mother, Aurelia Plath, with a commentary, appeared in 1975. Hughes's *Birthday Letters* (1998) is a response to the complexities of her marriage and suicide. Her best-known poems deal with illness, suffering, and death; and are expressed through complex shifts of metaphor and tone. Anne *Stevenson's biography *Bitter Fame* (1989) was written with the approval of the Plath estate. Jacqueline Rose's *The Haunting of Sylvia Plath* (1992) examines the processes which transformed Plath into a literary icon.

PLATO (*c*.424/3–*c*.348/7 BC) With *Socrates, who taught him, and *Aristotle, whom he taught, a dominant philosophical figure of classical antiquity, author of numerous dialogues and founder of the Athenian Academy, a school formally closed by Justinian in AD 529 (but without significant effect on the teaching of pagan Platonism). The dialogues—'Socrates' mostly leads; Plato himself is permanently absent—fall stylistically into three chronological groups: (I) *Defence of Socrates* ('*Apology*': actually not a dialogue), *Charmides, Cratylus, Crito, Euthydemus, Euthyphro, Gorgias, Hippias Minor, Ion, Laches, Lysis, Menexenus, Meno, Phaedo, Protagoras, Symposium*; (II) *Parmenides, Phaedrus, Republic, Theaetetus*; (III) *Sophist, Statesman, Philebus, Timaeus, Critias, Laws*. Until the modern period, and the German Romanticists at the beginning of the 19th century, the cosmological *Timaeus* was considered the master-work; for moderns it is the political *Republic*. Central to all periods of Plato's writing is the importance of *dialectic*, that is, philosophy in the form of conversation; in some works, especially those in Group I, the emphasis seems to be on the demolition by Socrates of others' ideas, and their pretence to knowledge, but certain positive ideas are more or less constant. (1) Plato and his Socrates oppose relativism of all kinds, especially value-relativism: things like justice, beauty, and above all the good can be *investigated*, and in principle their natures *discovered* (where what is investigated becomes the 'Form' in each case, in contrast to its instantiations, i.e. the 'particulars' that 'share' in the Form). (2) Plato appears permanently committed to the idea that his fellow human beings radically misunderstand the way things are, which is why they need philosophy (if necessary, the philosophy will be done by others: hence the idea of the 'philosopher–rulers' in the *Republic*); for (3) they will, above all, misunderstand what is truly good—which is what they (we) all, always, desire. 'No one willingly goes wrong', say the dialogues from beginning to end—suggesting a thoroughly optimistic view of human nature, though this appears to sit alongside (4) a more pessimistic view, according to which parts of our souls resemble brute beasts. ('Platonic love' develops the properly Platonic figure of the philosopher–pupil relationship as a passionate but asexual joint search for the truth.) Plato's influence on European philosophy and literature is largely indirect: through *Augustine, through the Florentine Platonists, but above all through the *Neoplatonists, especially *Plotinus, who for many was indistinguishable from Plato. Central, for English literature, was the neo-Platonizing Thomas Taylor, who completed the first English translation of the whole corpus (1804): S. T. *Coleridge and P. B. *Shelley could read Plato for themselves, but Coleridge also read Taylor's translations (complete with his interpretations), as did John *Keats, William *Wordsworth, and W. B. *Yeats; across the Atlantic the 'transcendentalists' around Bronson Alcott (1799–1888) and Ralph Waldo *Emerson were also inspired by Taylor. Modern, direct study of Platonic texts begins seriously with figures like Friedrich von *Schlegel and Schleiermacher (1768–1834) in Germany; but literature is barely touched by *this* Plato—for which, in a recent treatment, see Christopher Rowe, *Plato and the Art of Philosophical Writing* (2007).

Platonists *See* CAMBRIDGE PLATONISTS.

PLATONOV, Andrei Platonovich (1899–1951) The pen-name of Andrei Platonovich Klimentov, Russian prose writer, born in Voronezh in central Russia. He fought for the Bolsheviks during the Revolution, and then qualified as an engineer, before becoming a professional writer in Moscow in 1927, when his first collection of stories, *The Epifan Locks*, appeared. During 1928–30 he wrote his most important works, *Chevengur*, which relates with bitter irony the tale of a group of proletarians who attempt to create a communist utopia, and *The Foundation Pit*, the story of a doomed communal construction project. These works were first published in Russian abroad (1972, 1968), were translated into English (1978, 1973), and appeared in the Soviet Union only in the late 1980s. His story 'For Future Use' (1931) was attacked because of its author's ironic attitude to forced collectivization. Service as a war correspondent did not protect him from expulsion from the Writers' Union in 1946.

PLAUTUS, Titus Maccius (*c.*250–184 BC) Early Roman dramatist who adapted the Greek New Comedy for the Roman stage. The extent of his originality remains uncertain. He does not seem to have translated exactly, but he certainly worked within the Greek convention using the same stock characters—miserly fathers, spendthrift sons, boastful soldiers, resourceful parasites, courtesans, and slaves—and often borrowing the plots of his Greek models. Twenty of his plays have survived, and it was from him and from his successor *Terence that Renaissance Europe learned about ancient comedy. Reading and acting Plautus in Latin was a standard part of humanist education. *Shakespeare drew on his *Menaechmi* in *The *Comedy of Errors*, Ben *Jonson conflated the *Captivi* and the *Aulularia* in *The *Case Is Altered*, and John *Dryden adapted his **Amphitryon*. Stephen Sondheim's long-running musical *A Funny Thing Happened on the Way to the Forum* (1962) borrows exuberantly from Plautine situations.

Playboy of the Western World, The A comedy by J. M. *Synge, performed and published 1907. Christy Mahon, 'a slight young man, very tired and frightened', arrives at a village in Mayo. He gives out that he is a fugitive from justice, who in a quarrel has killed his bullying father, splitting him to the chin with a single blow. He is hospitably entertained, and his character as a dare-devil gives him a great advantage with the women (notably Pegeen Mike and Widow Quin) over the milder-spirited lads of the place. But admiration gives place to angry contempt when the father himself arrives in pursuit of the fugitive, who has merely given him a crack on the head and run away. The implication that Irish peasants would condone a murder and the frankness of some of the language (Christy speaks of 'all the girls in Mayo...standing before me in their shifts') caused outrage and riots when the play was first performed at the *Abbey Theatre. In his preface, Synge compares the 'joyless and pallid' words of the naturalistic theatre of *Ibsen with the 'rich and living' language of 'the country people of Ireland', and this play is his best-known effort to fuse Gaelic idiom and Hiberno-English diction in a dramatic rhetoric of his own making.

Pleasant Satyre of the Thrie Estaitis, Ane, *in Commendatioun of Vertew and Vituperatioun of Vyce* (1552–4) A morality play by Sir David *Lindsay, an early version of which was staged in 1540. In Part I Rex Humanitas is tempted by Sensuality, Wantonness, Solace, and others, while Good Counsel is hustled away, Verity is put in the stocks, and Chastity is warned off. An interlude follows in which are described the adventures of Chastity among humbler folks, a tailor, a soutar (or cobbler), and their wives. Then Chastity is put in the stocks. But Correction's arrival causes change. Verity, Good Counsel, and Chastity are admitted to the king, and Sensuality is banished. After an interlude in which a farmer exposes his sufferings at the hands of the clergy and a pardoner's trade is ridiculed, Part II presents the Three Estates summoned before the king, and their misdeeds denounced by John the Common Weal. The Lords and Commons repent, but the clergy remain impenitent, are exposed, and the malefactors brought to the scaffold. The work is long and exists in three different versions. It is written in a variety of metres and is in advance of all contemporary English plays. It has been editedy by R. J. Lyall (1989).

Pleasures of Hope, The A poem by Thomas *Campbell, published 1799. In Part I Campbell considers the inspiration of Hope and the hard fate of a people deprived of it, described in a passage on Poland's downfall. In Part II he reflects on Love combined with Hope, and on the belief in a future life.

Pleasures of Imagination, The A philosophical poem by Mark *Akenside, published 1744; Akenside began a new version, *The Pleasures of the Imagination*, in 1757 but did not complete it. The poem is influenced by the philosophical and aesthetic doctrines of Joseph *Addison, the third earl of *Shaftesbury, and Francis *Hutcheson; Thomas *Gray found it 'too much infected with the Hutchesonian jargon'. It examines the primary and secondary pleasures of the imagination, the first connected with the *sublime, the wonderful, and the beautiful, the second with passion and sense. The poem was influential through the *Romantic period; Anna *Barbauld edited it, with a sympathetic 'critical essay', in 1794.

Pleasures of Memory, The *See* ROGERS, SAMUEL.

Pléiade A group of seven 16th-century French poets, led by *Ronsard. The name, deriving ultimately from the seven stars of the constellation of the Pleiades, had originally been applied by Alexandrian critics to a group of seven poets from the reign of Ptolemy II. Ronsard's use of the term dates from 1556. The other members of the group were Joachim *Du Bellay, Pontus de Tyard (1521–1605), Jean-Antoine de Baïf (1532–89), Étienne Jodelle (1532–73), Rémy Belleau (*c.*1528–77), and either Jacques Peletier du Mans (1517–82) or, according to some, Jean Dorat (1508–88). The group, inspired by a common interest in the literatures of antiquity and of the Italian Renaissance, sought to promote the claims of the French language to a comparably dignified status as a medium for literary expression, and their aims were set out in Du Bellay's *Défense et illustration de la langue française* of 1549. The Pléiade were largely responsible for the acclimatization of the *sonnet in France, and for the establishment of the *alexandrine as the dominant metrical form for much later French poetry. Indeed, the group did much to create the conditions for the emergence of modern poetry in France.

pleonasm An expression involving the use of superfluous words, for example 'Th'inaudible and noiseless foot of time' (**All's Well That Ends Well*, v. iii. 41), or colloquially 'at this moment in time'.

PLINY THE ELDER (Gaius Plinius Secundus) (AD 23/4–79) Roman compiler of a *Natural History*, which is an encyclopedic rag-bag of popular science. Widely read in the Middle Ages, it provided a cosmology for *Du Bartas's *La Semaine, ou création du monde* (1578), which Josuah *Sylvester's translation established for the 17th century as an English classic. The *Natural History* was translated by Philemon *Holland in 1601.

PLINY THE YOUNGER (Gaius Plinius Caecilius Secundus) (AD *c.*61–*c.*112) Roman letter writer, nephew of *Pliny the elder. Pliny was a more formal writer than *Cicero, and is remembered mainly for his description of the eruption of Vesuvius (6. 16), his official correspondence with Trajan, including an important letter on the early Christians (10. 96), and his accounts of his Tuscan and Laurentine villas (5. 6, 2. 17), of interest to 18th-century landscape gardeners and neoclassical architects such as William *Kent and Sir John *Soane. The vogue for letter writing in the 1690s led to the translation of some of his correspondence, and William Melmoth produced a full but inaccurate version in 1746.

PLOMER, William (1903–73) Poet and novelist, born in Pietersberg, South Africa, and educated at St John's College, Johannesburg, and Rugby School. Several of his works, including his first novel, the savagely satirical *Turbott Wolfe*, published in 1926 by the *Hogarth Press, are portraits of South African life. In 1926, with Roy *Campbell, he founded the magazine *Voorslag* ('Whiplash'). Plomer then spent three years in Japan, an experience reflected in his poems, in *Paper Houses* (1929), and in *Sado* (a novel, 1931). He came to England in 1929 and settled in Bloomsbury, where he was befriended by Leonard and Virginia *Woolf. His first volume of poetry, *Notes for Poems* (1927), was followed by several others, and his *Collected Poems* appeared in 1960 (enl. edn 1973). His poems are largely satirical and urbane, with a sharp eye for character and social setting; many of them, like the title piece of *The Dorking Thigh* (1945), are modern ballads with a macabre touch. His celebrated edition of Francis *Kilvert's *Diary* appeared in three volumes, 1938–40. He wrote four libretti for Benjamin *Britten, including *Gloriana* (1952); his last novel, *Museum Pieces*, appeared in the same year. See P. F. Alexander, *William Plomer* (1989).

PLOTINUS (AD 205–270/71) Greek philosopher/Platonist, the chief figure in the movement described by moderns as *Neoplatonism, and the dominant figure in Western philosophy between *Aristotle and *Augustine. His *Enneads*, like much Platonism before him, downplay what seems sceptical in *Plato; they also create, from authentically Platonic ideas, a new kind of metaphysics, based on a single first principle, the transcendent One, from which everything including matter ultimately derived. Christian thinkers found much to attract them in Plotinus' brilliant but difficult constructions, which also, through Marsilio *Ficino's translation (1492), exercised a wide influence on Renaissance thought, as they did on English Platonism, especially on the *Cambridge Platonists, and on his first English translator, Thomas Taylor (1758–1835). For Taylor—as for the majority of scholars and readers until the beginning of the 19th century—Plotinus' Plato, or a simplified, more rigid, doctrinal version of it, for the most part *was* Plato.

Plough and the Stars, The See O'CASEY, SEAN.

Plowman's Tale, The A late 14th- or early 15th-century poem in 1,380 lines of eight-line stanzas rhyming on alternate lines, sympathetic to John *Wyclif, and indebted to **Pierce the Ploughman's Crede*. A griffin and a pelican debate the merits of endowed and poor clergy. It was mistakenly included in early editions of *Chaucer's works. Ed. James Dean, *Six Ecclesiastical Satires* (1991).

PLUTARCH (before AD 50–after 120) Prolific Greek biographer and moralist. His philosophical position was *Platonist and anti-*Stoic, and for many years he was a priest at Delphi. Fifty lives and 78 miscellaneous works survive. His *Parallel Lives*, which pair illustrious Greeks and Romans such as Alcibiades and *Coriolanus, and *Alexander and Julius *Caesar, illustrate the moral character of his subjects through a series of anecdotes. The influential version by Thomas *North (1579) served as a source-book for Shakespeare's Roman plays. John *Dryden's 'Life of Plutarch' prefaced a very successful five-volume translation of the *Lives* by 42 contributors (1683–6), later revised by Arthur Hugh *Clough. The *Moralia* or *Moral Essays* provide a compendium of ancient wisdom on a variety of topics: moral philosophy, religious belief, education, health,

literary criticism, and social customs. Several Renaissance authors, including Sir Thomas *Wyatt, Sir Thomas *Elyot, and George *Chapman, translated or drew on individual pieces. The first complete version in English, by Philemon *Holland, appeared in 1603, when its popularity was enhanced by the almost simultaneous publication of John *Florio's translation of *Montaigne, for the latter cites Plutarch on nearly every page. There are modern translations of selected essays by Donald Russell and lives by Ian Scott-Kilvert. See D. A. Russell, *Plutarch* (2nd edn, 2001).
See BIOGRAPHY.

Plymley, Letters of Peter By Sydney *Smith, published 1807–8. The letters purport to be written by Peter Plymley to his brother in the country, the Revd Abraham Plymley ('a bit of a goose'), in support of Catholic emancipation. The arguments, both serious and absurd, of the Revd Abraham for maintaining the disabilities of the Catholics are demolished with sense, wit, and humour; while the author makes his own Anglican position plain, and ridicules the 'nonsense' of the Roman Catholic Church.

PN Review A British literary periodical, publishing six times a year. It originated as **Poetry Nation* in 1973, and has been edited by Michael Schmidt for thirty years. It has a reputation for a certain combativeness and has been controversial in both its advocacies and detractions. Catholic in taste, the journal publishes poems, essays, and reviews, and contributors range widely across the spectrum of poetry and culture more generally.

POE, Edgar Allan (1809–49) American writer, born in Boston, the son of itinerant actors. He became an orphan in early childhood, and was taken into the household of John Allan, adopting his foster-father's name as his middle name from 1824 onwards. He came to London with the Allans (1815–20) and attended Manor House school at Stoke Newington (which he describes, imaginatively but with some accurate detail, in his doppelgänger story 'William Wilson', 1839). He published his first volume of verse, *Tamerlane and Other Poems* (1827), anonymously and at his own expense; then enlisted in the US army under the name of Edgar A. Perry. He was sent to Sullivan's Island, South Carolina, which provided settings for 'The Gold Bug' (1843) and 'The Balloon Hoax' (1844). Allan (from whom he had been estranged) procured his discharge from the army, and he entered the military academy West Point in 1830, being dishonourably discharged in 1831. He now turned to journalism, living from 1831 to 1835 with a relative, Mrs Clemm, in Baltimore, whose 13-year-old daughter, his cousin Virginia, he married in 1836. He worked as editor on various papers, including the *Southern Literary Messenger*, publishing numerous reviews and hoax pieces. His first collection of stories, *Tales of the Grotesque and Arabesque* (1839, for 1840), contains one of his most famous works, 'The Fall of the House of Usher', a *Gothic romance in which the narrator visits the crumbling mansion of his childhood companion Roderick Usher to find both Usher and his twin sister Madeline in the last stages of mental and physical weakness. His tales characteristically explore states of obsession and mania. In 1845 his poem 'The Raven', published in a New York paper and then as the title poem of *The Raven and Other Poems* (1845), brought him fame, but not security. He and his ménage continued to suffer poverty and ill health, his wife dying in 1847 and he himself struggling with alcohol addiction and nervous instability. Poe's one attempt at novel writing was the unfinished *Narrative of Arthur Gordon Pym of Nantucket* (1837), which describes a surreal voyage to the Antarctic. *Eureka: A Prose Poem*, an extended meditation on cosmology, appeared in 1848. His posthumous reputation and influence have been great; he was much admired by *Baudelaire, who translated many of his works, and in Britain by Oscar *Wilde, W. B. *Yeats, and others. Freudian critics (and *Freud himself) have been intrigued by the macabre and pathological elements in his work, ranging from hints of necrophilia in his poem *'Annabel Lee' (1849) to the indulgent sadism of 'The Pit and the Pendulum' (1843). Jorge Luis *Borges and many others have been impressed by the cryptograms and mysteries of the stories which feature Poe's detective Auguste Dupin ('The Murders in the Rue Morgue', 1841; 'The Purloined Letter', 1845) and the morbid metaphysical speculation of 'The Facts in the Case of M. Waldemar' (1845). His critical writings include 'The Philosophy of Composition' (on the process of composing 'The Raven') and 'The Poetic Principle' (on unity of effect). See Kenneth Silverman, *Edgar A. Poe* (1991).

Poema Morale ('The Moral Ode') A southern poem in early Middle English of about 400 lines, surviving in seven manuscripts, and dating from *c.*1175. It is a vigorous work on the themes of transience and repentance, and is very early in the Middle English period after the transition from Old English. See R. Morris (ed.), EETS OS 53 (1873).

Poems in Two Volumes A collection of poems by William *Wordsworth, published 1807. In this successor to the **Lyrical Ballads*, Wordsworth continued his avant-garde attempt to set aside *'poetic diction' and to write in what the 'Preface' to the *Lyrical Ballads* describes as the 'real language of men'. Such simple verses as 'We are Seven' were ridiculed in satirical circles and in the **Edinburgh Review*, where *Jeffrey described them as 'an insult on the public taste'. Lord *Byron described Wordworth's manner as 'not simple, but puerile', and further attacked the collection in **English Bards and Scots Reviewers* (1809). Nonetheless, it contains such notable poems as *'Intimations of Immortality from Recollections of Early Childhood', the lines 'Composed upon Westminster Bridge, 3 September 1802' (which begin 'Earth has not any thing to show more fair'), and 'I wandered lonely as a cloud'. In this collection Wordsworth also began to work successfully in the *sonnet form.

Poetaster A comedy by Ben *Jonson, performed by the Children of the Queen's Chapel 1601, printed 1602. The play, a contribution to the so-called War of the Theatres, is Jonson's retaliation to John *Marston's satire of him in *What You Will*.

Set in the court of the emperor Augustus, the main plot concerns the conspiracy of the poetaster (i.e. a poor poet) Crispinus and his friend Demetrius (who represent Marston and Thomas *Dekker) and a swaggering captain, Pantilius Tucca, to belittle Horace, who represents Jonson. The matter is tried before Augustus, with Virgil as judge. Horace is acquitted, the 'dresser of plays' Demetrius is made to wear a fool's coat and cap, and Crispinus is made to vomit up his windy rhetoric. A secondary plot concerns Ovid's love for the daughter of Augustus, and his subsequent banishment. Marston and Dekker replied to the attack in **Satiromastix*, where the main characters of this play reappear.

poetic diction A term used to mean vocabulary and usage peculiar to poetry, which came into prominence with William *Wordsworth's discussion in his preface (1800; supplemented by an appendix in the 1802 edition) to the **Lyrical Ballads*, in which he claims to have taken pains to avoid 'what is usually called poetic diction', and asserts that there is and should be no essential difference between the language of prose and the language of metrical composition. Wordsworth thus implies that there should be no such thing as 'language and usage peculiar to poetry', and illustrates his point by attacking a sonnet of Thomas *Gray, who himself had declared (1742, letter to Richard *West) that 'the language of the age is never the language of poetry'. Wordsworth's attack on poetical archaisms, personifications, hackneyed epithets, circumlocutions, and so on was both forceful and revolutionary, although he did not always consider it necessary to use 'the real language of men' in his own poems, in which we often find such words as 'beauteous', 'elfin', 'haply', 'jocund', 'oftentimes', 'perchance', 'plashy', 'steed', 'verdant', and many others not commonly used in contemporary prose. Wordsworth's faith that the language of low and rustic life is plainer, more emphatic, and more philosophical than the 'gaudiness and inane phraseology' which he condemned was soon repudiated by his collaborator S. T. *Coleridge in **Biographia Literaria* (1817). Although English poetry became less stilted in its language, its vocabulary remained on the whole distinctive throughout the Romantic and Victorian periods and as far as the 1920s in poems by, for example, Thomas *Hardy and Edmund *Blunden. It was not until the 20th century and the advent of the *Georgian and *modernist poets, followed by W. H. *Auden and Philip *Larkin, that a thorough extension of poetic vocabulary towards ordinary speech was achieved. See B. Groom, *The Diction of Poetry from Spenser to Bridges* (1955).

Poetics, The A fragment of a treatise by *Aristotle which greatly influenced the theory of *neo-classicism. It is the source of the principles misinterpreted by later critics as the *unities, and it also introduced many much-discussed concepts related to the theory of tragedy, such as *mimesis* (imitation); *catharsis (purification or purgation of pity and fear); *peripeteia* (reversal); and *hamartia* ('error of judgement', sometimes interpreted as 'tragic flaw'). *Hubris* (overweening pride or confidence) was a form of *hamartia*.

poet laureate The title given to a poet who receives a stipend as an officer of the royal household, with the duty (no longer enforced) of writing court odes and so on. The title was sometimes conferred by certain universities. For a list of poets laureate see Appendix 2. The title of poet laureate in the USA was established in 1985 by the US Senate: the salaried post has been held by, among others, Richard *Wilbur (1987), Joseph *Brodsky (1991), and Rita *Dove (1993).

Poetry: *A Magazine of Verse* (1912–) Founded at Chicago by the American poet and critic Harriet Monroe (1860–1936), who edited it until her death. In its early days it published work by Ezra *Pound, Amy *Lowell, T. S. *Eliot, Robert *Frost, H. D. (Hilda *Doolittle), Ford Madox *Ford, and others, and it has continued to flourish, publishing work by nearly every major American poet of the 20th century.

poetry annuals Published as giftbooks, annuals flourished from the mid-1820s to the 1840s and were the most influential force in poetry publishing in this period. Well-known titles included *The Literary Souvenir*, *The Keepsake*, *Forget-Me-Not*, and *Fisher's Drawing-Room Scrapbook*. Their popularity stemmed from their engravings of famous paintings, fashionable people, and exotic locations: authors produced poems to fit these pictures. The annuals paid well in a disastrous market, and poets such as William *Wordsworth, S. T. *Coleridge, Walter *Scott, and Alfred *Tennyson were tempted into contributing. Annuals also offered employment to women writers, for instance Letitia *Landon and the countess of *Blessington, as contributors and editors.

Poetry London A bi-monthly which became the leading poetry magazine of the 1940s. It was conceived by a group of four, Dylan *Thomas, James Meary Tambimuttu (1915–83), Anthony Dickins, and Keidrych Rhys, and edited by Tambimuttu, who had arrived in 1938 from Ceylon, almost penniless, and entered the literary London of Soho and *Fitzrovia. The first issue appeared in February 1939; Tambimuttu produced fifteen numbers, and it was subsequently edited by Richard Marsh and Nicholas Moore. It published work by George *Barker, Vernon *Watkins, Gavin *Ewart, Harold *Pinter, Charles *Tomlinson, David *Gascoyne, Lawrence *Durrell, and many others.

Poetry Nation A twice-yearly poetry magazine edited by C. B. Cox and Michael Schmidt (6 issues, 1973–6), founded in sympathy with what its first editorial described as 'a renewed popularity and practice of clearly formal writing, a common bridling at vacuous public and private rhetoric'. Contributors included Charles *Tomlinson, Peter *Porter, Elizabeth *Jennings, Geoffrey *Hill, and Douglas *Dunn; Donald *Davie and

C. H. *Sisson became co-editors of its thrice-yearly successor, *PN Review* (1976–).

Poetry Society Founded in 1909 (as the Poetry Recital Society) for the promotion of poetry and the art of speaking verse, and sponsored by many figures in the literary world, including Gilbert *Murray, Thomas Sturge *Moore, Edmund *Gosse, Henry *Newbolt, Arnold *Bennett, and A. C. *Benson. Its many activities now include the organization of poetry competitions, workshops, and slams (open competitions where poets read or recite new work). Its journal, *Poetry Review,* was founded in 1912; its first editor was Harold *Munro, but he had lost control of it by the end of the year.

Poets' Corner Part of the south transept of Westminster Abbey containing the tombs of Geoffrey *Chaucer, Edmund *Spenser, Ben *Jonson, Aphra *Behn, John *Dryden, John *Gay, Samuel *Johnson, Alfred *Tennyson, Robert *Browning, and Charles *Dickens. Writers buried elsewhere but commemorated here include William *Shakespeare, John *Milton, John *Keats, Lord *Byron, Jane *Austen, the *Brontë sisters, and Henry *James. Many of the monuments are by Michael *Rysbrack.

POHL, Frederik (1919–) American *science fiction writer, editor, and literary agent, born in New York. *The Space Merchants* (1953), satirizing the advertising industry, was part of his collaborative partnership with Cyril M. Kornbluth (1923–58). Pohl's stories of the period, such as 'The Midas Plague' (1954), also lampooned American consumerism. During the 1960s he edited the magazines *Galaxy* and *If,* following which he published numerous novels including *Man Plus* (1976) and *Gateway* (1977). Stories are collected in *Platinum Pohl* (2005).

POLIAKOFF, Stephen (1952–) Playwright and film-maker, educated at Westminster School and King's College, Cambridge. He attracted attention as a playwright while still at school, became a writer in residence at the *National Theatre aged 24, and has written prolifically for stage, television, and film, winning many awards, ranging from the Prix Italia to an Emmy. Modern city life and the alienation of young people was an early theme, notably in the play *City Sugar* (1975), and the films *Bloody Kids* (1980) and *Runners* (1983), both given limited cinema release. Multi-part television drama has allowed him to explore the legacy of the past, especially its buried secrets and scandals, in *Caught on a Train* (1980), *Shooting the Past* (1999), and *The Lost Prince* (2003). Since *Hidden City* (1988), he has largely directed his own scripts, and has developed a distinctive televisual form in the overlapping pairs of *Friends and Crocodiles* and *Gideon's Daughter* (2005) and *Joe's Palace* and *Capturing Mary* (2007). He was awarded a CBE in 2007.

POLIDORI, John William (1795–1821) Physician and writer. The son of an Italian translator, he was educated at Ampleforth before taking an Edinburgh medical degree at the age of 19. In 1816 he was hired by Lord *Byron as personal physician and travelling companion for a few months; and kept a journal of this association, much later published as his *Diary* (1911). He participated in the famous ghost story competition in June 1816 that gave rise to Mary *Shelley's **Frankenstein* and eventually to Polidori's only novel, *Ernestus Berchtold* (1819). Byron's incomplete tale 'Augustus Darvell' provided the basis for Polidori's story 'The Vampyre', written in 1816 and misleadingly published as Byron's in 1819 by the **New Monthly Magazine*. Frequently reprinted and adapted for the stage in the 1820s, 'The Vampyre' laid the foundations of modern vampire fiction, notably in the use of an aristocratic villain, Lord Ruthven, evidently modelled upon Byron himself. Polidori established an unsuccessful medical practice in Norwich, and committed suicide in 1821.

POLITIAN *See* POLIZIANO, ANGELO.

Political House that Jack Built, The A satirical pamphlet by William *Hone, with engravings by George *Cruikshank, published 1819. Hone's satirical imitation of the old nursery rhyme was the most successful radical satire of the Regency period, running into over 50 editions. It attacked the Tory government, the church, and the prince regent, who is portrayed as a spendthrift and gluttonous libertine, 'the Dandy of Sixty'.

Political Register (1802–35) A weekly newspaper founded by William *Cobbett. It began as a Tory paper but by 1809 was thoroughly Radical. Cobbett continued to issue it even when imprisoned for an article condemning military flogging. His new version of the paper, produced in 1816 at *2d.*, achieved a remarkable weekly circulation of 40,000–50,000. In 1821 **Rural Rides* began to appear, but Cobbett continued the paper until his death.

POLIZIANO (in English Politian), **Angelo** (1454–94) The name assumed from his birthplace, Montepulciano, by Angelo Ambrogini, Italian humanist and friend of Lorenzo de *Medici, in whose household in Florence he lived as tutor and scholar. In this period he combined philological studies with the composition of poetry in Latin and Italian. In 1479 he moved to Mantua, where he wrote *Orfeo*, the first pastoral drama in Italian. The following year he returned to the chair of Greek and Latin at the University of Florence. The two volumes of editorial and philological studies (*Miscellanea*) that he compiled during this period established him as the greatest textual scholar of his time, and his Greek epigrams showed him to be the first Italian humanist with the fluency in Greek requisite for the composition of poetry of real quality. Thomas *Linacre was one of his students, and George *Chapman translated and imitated his verse.

POLLARD, A. W. (Alfred William) (1859–1944) Honorary secretary of the *Bibliographical Society, instigator of the *Malone Society, keeper of the Department of Printed Books at the *British Museum, 1919–24. An authority on *incunabula, early printing and illustration, Geoffrey *Chaucer, and William *Shakespeare, he published other pioneering works which influenced the study of medieval and Tudor literature. His important contributions to Shakespearian bibliography include *Shakespeare Folios and Quartos, 1594–1685* (1909) and *Shakespeare's Fight with the Pirates* (1917). He was largely responsible for the completion of the *Short-Title Catalogue of Books Printed in England, Scotland, and Ireland, 1475–1640* (1926).

Polly A musical play by John *Gay, published 1729, the sequel to *The *Beggar's Opera*. Its performance was prohibited by the Lord Chamberlain for political reasons, but its publication brought Gay nearly £1,200 in subscriptions. Macheath has been transported to the West Indies, and has escaped from the plantation; he is disguised as the pirate chief Morano. Polly, in search of him, disguises herself as a man, joins the loyal Indians, helps to beat off an attack by the pirates, and takes Morano prisoner, discovering his identity too late to save him from execution. The play concludes with a proposal of marriage from a virtuous Indian prince.

Pollyanna (1913) By Eleanor Porter (1868–1920). Pollyanna is an orphan who changes the lives of everyone around her with her 'glad' game; her name has become synonymous with unquenchable cheerfulness. There were twelve sequels by four authors, a vogue for 'Glad Clubs', and films in 1920 and 1960.

POLO, Marco (1254–1324) A member of a patrician mercantile family of Venice whose father and uncle had reached the court of the great and enlightened Mongol ruler, Kublai Khan, and who accompanied them on their return in 1271 on an embassy from the pope. They travelled overland to China and returned home by sea to the Persian Gulf, reaching Venice after an absence of 24 years. Marco Polo's account of his travels was dictated to Rustichello, a writer of romances, whilst both were imprisoned by the Genoese. The original text was in French, but it subsequently appeared in Latin and in various vernacular versions. The textual complications make it difficult to differentiate what Marco saw himself from his indirect reports; some even doubt he went to China at all. Most scholars, after acknowledging the complexities of the evidence, consider the *Travels* to be a fine travel account and early example of human geography. Since Frampton's edition of 1579, English readers have enjoyed Marco Polo in various anthologies and editions while scholars, notably W. Marsden in 1818 and Henry Yule in 1871, have tried to produce definitive versions. The best modern English edition is the Penguin one by Ronald Latham (1958).

POLYDORE VERGIL *See* VERGIL, POLYDORE.

Polyhymnia A poem by George *Peele written and published in 1590 commemorating the retirement of Sir Henry *Lee from the office of queen's champion, and describing the ceremonies that took place on the occasion at the accession day tilt. At the poem's end is printed the beautiful song 'His golden locks, time hath to silver turned', quoted in part by W. M. *Thackeray in *The Newcomes*, ch. 76.

Poly-Olbion, The (the spelling of the first edition) The most ambitious work of Michael *Drayton. It was written between 1598 and 1622 and consists of 30 'Songs' each of 300–500 lines, in hexameter couplets, in which the author tries to awaken his readers to the beauties and glories of their country. Travelling from the south-west to Chester, down through the Midlands to London, up the eastern counties to Lincoln, and then through Lancashire and Yorkshire to Northumberland and Westmorland, he describes, or at least enumerates, the principal topographical features of the country, but chiefly the rivers and rivulets, interspersing in the appropriate places legends, fragments of history, catalogues of British saints and hermits, of great discoverers, of birds, fishes, and plants with their properties. The first part, published 1612–13, was annotated by John *Selden. The word 'poly-olbion' (from the Greek) means 'having many blessings'.

polyptoton The repetition of the same word or root with varying grammatical inflections, as in 'And singing still dost soar, and soaring ever singest' (P. B. *Shelley), or 'Love is an irresistible desire to be irresistibly desired' (Robert *Frost).

polysyndeton [from Greek, 'using many connectives'] The repetition of conjunctions in close succession for rhetorical effect, as in 'Since brass, nor stone, nor earth, nor boundless sea' (Shakespeare, Sonnet 65).

POMFRET, John (1667–1702) A Bedfordshire vicar whose poem *The Choice* (1700), in the tradition of the sixth satire of *Horace's second book, describes the pleasures of a quiet country estate where the author 'might live genteelly, but not great'. It enjoyed considerable success, and secured its author inclusion in Samuel Johnson's **Lives of the English Poets*, where Pomfret's choice was described as 'such a state as affords plenty and tranquillity, without exclusion of intellectual pleasures'.

Pompey the Great *See* CORNELIA.

POOLE, John (?1786–1872) A successful dramatist, who also produced poems and essays and wrote for many years for the **New Monthly Magazine*. His comedies and farces were produced at Drury Lane, Covent Garden, and the Haymarket, with Charles *Kemble and other well-known actors. There were few years between 1813 and 1829 when no play of his was produced. The most successful were *Paul Pry* (1825), *'Twixt the*

Cup and the Lip (1826), and *Lodgings for a Single Gentleman* (1829). Later in his life Charles *Dickens obtained him a state pension of £100 p.a.

POOLE, Thomas (1765–1837) Farmer and tanner, born at Nether Stowey; he became a close friend of S. T. *Coleridge and William *Wordsworth, and helped them to find homes in his neighbourhood in 1796–7. Coleridge wrote 'This lime tree bower my prison' in Poole's garden, and Sara Coleridge corresponded with him for many years. Another of his friends was Sir Humphry *Davy. He was progressive and generous; Wordsworth said of him, 'he felt for all men as his brothers'.

Poor Tom A name assumed by someone pretending to be mad in the **Fraternity of Vagabonds*, and by Edgar in William *Shakespeare's **King Lear* (II. iii).

POPE, Alexander (1688–1744) Poet, son of a Roman Catholic linen draper of London. His health was damaged and his growth stunted by a severe illness at the age of 12 (probably Pott's disease, a tubercular affliction of the spine). He lived with his parents at Binfield in Windsor Forest and was largely self-educated. His 'Pastorals' were published in Jacob *Tonson's *Miscellany* (vol. vi) in 1709 and demonstrated strong classical knowledge and well-polished metrical skill. His **Essay on Criticism* (1711) made him known to Joseph *Addison's circle, and his *'Messiah' was published in the *Spectator* in 1712. The first version of *The *Rape of the Lock* appeared in Bernard *Lintot's *Miscellanies* in the same year and enlarged and published separately in 1714. In 1713 he published **Windsor-Forest*, grafting support for the Tories' Peace of Utrecht on to a *topographic celebration of the mythic and historical landscape of the Thames valley. Pope now gravitated away from Addison's 'little senate' and became a member of the *Scriblerus Club, a Tory association that included Jonathan *Swift, John *Gay, Thomas *Parnell, John *Arbuthnot, and Robert *Harley. He published in 1715 the first volume of his translation into heroic couplets of Homer's **Iliad*, a version which S. T. *Coleridge thought an 'astonishing product of matchless talent and ingenuity'. It was supplemented in 1725–6 by a translation of the **Odyssey*, with substantial assistance from William Broome (1689–1745) and Elijah Fenton (1683–1730). Published by subscription, the two translations brought him financial independence. Pope moved in 1718 to Twickenham, where he built a villa and spent the rest of his life, devoting much time to *landscape gardening.

In 1717 Pope published a magnificent volume of his *Works*, including new pieces such as 'Verses to the Memory of an Unfortunate Lady', an elegy on a fictitious lady who had killed herself through thwarted love, and *'Eloisa to Abelard', in which Eloisa describes her inner turmoil. These poems may reflect Pope's own emotional conflicts; about this time Pope became strongly attached to Martha Blount (1690–1763), his closest female friend, and to Lady Mary Wortley *Montagu, with whom he later quarrelled. Pope had already become embroiled in several literary controversies: the 'Pastorals' had led to a quarrel with Ambrose *Philips, the *Essay on Criticism* had provoked the lifelong hostility of John *Dennis, he had poisoned the bookseller Edmund *Curll in 1716, and his Homer translations were undermined by Addison and routinely abused as the work of a *Jacobite. In 1723, four years after Addison's death, Pope's portrait of Atticus, a satire on Addison written in 1716, appeared in a newspaper, to be republished by Curll a year later. An extended version appeared as 'A Fragment of a Satire' in a 1727 volume of *Miscellanies* by Pope and his Scriblerian friends, and took its final form in *An Epistle to Dr Arbuthnot* (1735). In the same *Miscellanies* volume Pope published his prose treatise **Peri Bathous*, ridiculing contemporary poets including Lewis *Theobald, who in *Shakespeare Restored* (1726) had pointed out some errors in Pope's edition of Shakespeare (1725). This led to Pope's selection of Theobald as hero of his **Dunciad*, on which he had been working for some time; the first version appeared anonymously in 1728, with a 'variorum' text, complete with mock annotation, coming out in 1729. The poem provoked threats, reprisals, and parodies, which Pope skilfully incorporated into the supplementary material surrounding the poem in its later manifestations.

Influenced in part by the philosophy of his friend Viscount *Bolingbroke, Pope published a series of moral and philosophical poems: *An *Essay on Man* (1733–4), in four Epistles; and **Epistles to Several Persons* (1731–5), again four in number. In 1733 Pope began publishing the series of poems later known as *Imitations of Horace*, beginning with a paraphrase of the first satire of Horace's second book, in the form of a dialogue between the poet and his friend the lawyer William Fortescue (1687–1749). He followed this up with his *Imitations* of Horace's Satires 2. 2 and 1. 2 ('Sober Advice from Horace', published anonymously because of its bawdy content), in 1734; of Epistles 2. 2 and 2. 1 (the latter a substantial 'Epistle to Augustus' on literary and political issues) in 1737; and of Epistles 1. 6 and 1. 1 and the latter part of Satire 2. 6, 'imitated in the manner of Dr Swift', in 1738. In 1735 appeared the *Epistle to Dr Arbuthnot*, later thought of as a prologue to the Horatian Satires, and a brilliant showcase of irony and invective. It contains the famous portraits of Addison (ll. 193–214) and Lord *Hervey, alongside some carefully modulated presentations of intimate domestic life. In 1738 Pope published *One Thousand Seven Hundred and Thirty Eight*, two dialogues ostensibly in Horatian manner but with greater satiric bitterness. Pope was also occupied with the publication of his letters; in 1735 he contrived to have Curll publish a volume of his *Literary Correspondence*, allowing him to promote his own 'authorized' text of the letters in 1737. In 1742 Pope added an additional book, *The New Dunciad*, to his earlier poem; the complete *Dunciad* in four books, with Colley *Cibber replacing Theobald as hero, appeared in 1743. In his later years Pope came under the influence of William *Warburton, who endeavoured to make the poet's oeuvre into a morally consistent and monumental corpus; Warburton's edition of Pope appeared in 1751.

Pope's poetic dominance came under attack from poets and critics such as William *Cowper and Joseph *Warton. He was robustly defended in Samuel Johnson's *Lives of the English Poets* but further onslaughts against his supposed worldliness and artificiality came from William *Wordsworth and William *Blake, with Lord *Byron his major defender in the early 19th century. Matthew *Arnold's famous comment, 'Dryden and Pope are not classics of our poetry, they are classics of our prose' (*Essays in Criticism*, 1880), summed up much 19th-century opinion, and it was not until F. R. *Leavis and William *Empson that serious attempts were made to rediscover Pope's richness, variety, and complexity. The standard edition of Pope's poetry is the Twickenham Edition, general editor John Butt (11 vols, 1938–68). See also Maynard Mack, *Alexander Pope: A Life* (1985).

Popish Plot A plot fabricated in 1678 by Titus Oates (1649–1705). He claimed at the end of September before the Middlesex magistrate Sir Edmond Berry Godfrey (1621–78) that it was intended to murder Charles II, place James on the throne, and suppress Protestantism. Godfrey disappeared on 12 October and was found murdered on 17 October. The existence of the plot was widely believed and great excitement prevailed. Many people, especially Catholics, were falsely accused and executed. These events occasioned John *Caryll's poem *Naboth's Vineyard* (1679) which was an important predecessor of **Absalom and Achitophel* and thus contributed to the flowering of the *mock biblical as a satirical mode.

POPPER, Sir Karl (1902–94) Austrian-born philosopher of science. He studied mathematics, physics, and psychology in Vienna. Originally associated with the Vienna circle, the source of logical positivism, he left for New Zealand on Hitler's rise to power. In 1946 he came to England, joining the London School of Economics, where he was appointed professor of logic and scientific method in 1949. Popper rejected the traditional idea that a scientific hypothesis can be verified by experimental testing. Instead he proposed that a hypothesis is only scientific by virtue of the fact that it can be falsified. On these grounds he dismissed the claims of psychoanalysis to scientific status and challenged the empirical basis and determinist pretensions of some *Marxist historiography. His influential works include *The Logic of Scientific Discovery* (*Logik der Forschung*, 1934); *The Open Society and Its Enemies* (1945), and *The Poverty of Historicism* (1957). See Roberta Corvi, *An Introduction to the Thought of Karl Popper* (1997).

PORTER, Anna Maria (1780–1832) Poet and novelist, younger sister of Jane *Porter. Her martial tale of the French Revolution, *The Hungarian Brothers* (1807), inspired by her sister's successful *Thaddeus of Warsaw*, went into several editions. She published *Don Sebastian* in 1809, together with other novels, ballads, and poems.

PORTER, Endymion (1587–1649) Groom of the bedchamber to Charles I, and the friend and patron of painters and poets. He was painted by Anthony *Van Dyck, and Ben *Jonson, Robert *Herrick, William *D'Avenant, and Thomas *Dekker, among others, celebrated him in verse. He sat in the Long Parliament but was expelled, and lived abroad in poverty.

PORTER, Jane (1776–1850) Novelist and dramatist; elder sister of Anna Maria *Porter. Her historical romance *Thaddeus of Warsaw* (1803) was immensely successful, and led to friendship with one of its heroes, the Polish General Kosciuszko. It describes the adventures of a young Polish nobleman who accompanies his grandfather to join the army of King Stanislas against the invading Russians. *The Scottish Chiefs* (1810) tells the story of William Wallace and Robert the Bruce, ending with the battle of Bannockburn. Also successful, it was translated into German and Russian. It is an interesting precursor of the *historical fiction of Walter *Scott, though Scott was 'disappointed', according to James *Hogg, with Porter's portrayal of Wallace. *The Pastor's Fireside* (1815) is a story of the later Stuarts. Her tragedy *Switzerland*, produced in 1819 with Edmund *Kean and Charles *Kemble, was a disastrous failure, closing after one performance, while her later *Owen, Prince of Powys* (1822) managed only three. Among other volumes she produced *Sir Edward Seaward's Narrative* (1831), on Caribbean exploration, a work which purported to be a genuine diary but which was almost certainly largely fictitious. Porter was much admired by Joanna *Baillie, though George Saintsbury (1845–1933) found 'a general air of silliness' in her work.

PORTER, Katherine Anne (1890–1980) American short story writer and novelist, born in Texas, whose collections of short stories include *Flowering Judas* (1930), *Pale Horse, Pale Rider* (1939), and *The Leaning Tower* (1944). Her novel *Ship of Fools* (1962) is a heavily allegorical treatment of a voyage from Mexico to Germany on the eve of Hitler's rise to power. See Darlene Harbour Unrue, *Katherine Anne Porter* (2005).

PORTER, Peter (1929–) Poet, born and educated in Brisbane, where he worked as a journalist before coming to England in 1951. He was briefly associated with the *Group in the 1960s, and the work in earlier collections such as *Once Bitten, Twice Bitten* (1961) and *The Last of England* (1970) provides a satiric portrait of London in the 'swinging sixties', informed by his early job in advertising. In the 1970s, his poetry, always mentored by the achievement of W. H. *Auden, became more meditative and allusive, although no less colloquial and urbane; its learned references to a vast range of subjects, from Italian baroque to classical mythology, opera, and German Romanticism, bring both richness and obscurity. His technical command of complex stanza forms, sometimes used parodically, is striking. *The Cost of Seriousness* (1978) and *English Subtitles* (1981) introduce a new and sombre exploration of the poet's conflicting responsibilities to his art and to others, the former examining emotions following the death of his first wife in 1974. Later volumes include *Fast Forward* (1984), *The Chair of Babel* (1992), and *Afterburner* (2004). His *Collected Poems 1961–1999* was published in two volumes in 1999. Porter's now very large volume of work, often inflected with an outsider's quizzically sceptical view of English culture and attitudes, maintains a view of poetry as conversation, civility, and decency. See Bruce Bennett, *Spirit in Exile: Peter Porter and his Poetry* (1991).

Portrait of a Lady, The A novel by Henry *James, published 1881, which describes the marriage of an idealistic heiress, Isabel Archer, to an American dilettante expatriate, Gilbert Osmond. He marries her for her fortune and ruins her life, but she remains loyal in spite of her realization of his vileness.

Portrait of the Artist as a Young Man, A An autobiographical novel by James *Joyce, first published in *The *Egoist*, 1914–15. It describes the development of Stephen Dedalus (who reappears in **Ulysses*) from his early boyhood, through bullying at school and an adolescent crisis of faith inspired partly by the famous 'hellfire sermon' preached by the Jesuit Father Arnall (ch. 3) and partly by the guilt of his own precocious sexual adventures, to student days and a gradual sense of his own destiny as dedicated artist who must leave Ireland in order to 'encounter…the reality of experience and to forge in the smithy of my soul the uncreated conscience of my race'. Though not as innovative as the later work (its experimentation lies principally in its prose style changing as the novel progresses to mirror the growth and development of Stephen's mind), the novel foreshadows many of the themes and verbal complexities of *Ulysses*.

Poseidon *See* NEPTUNE.

positivist philosophy *See* COMTE, AUGUSTE.

postcolonial literature Literatures in English emerging from the anglophone world outside Britain, Ireland, and the United States constitute an important and growing body of writing, often referred to as postcolonial or world literature in English. Many of the regions and countries from which this literature emerges—the Caribbean, the Indian subcontinent, West Africa, in particular Nigeria and Ghana, East and southern Africa, and Australasia and the Pacific islands—were once colonies of Britain, and now form part of the Commonwealth, which accounts for the chronological designation of the word 'postcolonial'. However, 'postcolonial' is widely recognized to be a term beset with contradictions. What does it mean to bracket so many diverse traditions of writing under this one heading, and, moreover, to hinge the literary histories of these regions to the single narrative of British colonial history, as the word would seem to imply? Were not the forms of colonial rule and the processes of decolonization too varied to admit of a single definitional category? Does the term contain implied assumptions of a multicultural community in which each country is working towards a sense of shared enterprise and common purpose? And what of the chronological limits of the postcolonial: did empire end with Indian independence in 1947, or in 1956 with Suez, or was it later, when many of the African countries gained their independence?

Such questions and conundrums abound, but the term 'postcolonial literature' is to date still considered to be the most convenient, 'catch-all' way of embracing the powerful and diverse body of literary responses to the challenges presented by decolonization and the transitions to independence and post-independence in a wide variety of political and cultural contexts. Rather than simply being the writing which 'came after' empire, postcolonial literature might be broadly defined as that which critically or subversively scrutinizes the colonial relationship, and offers a reshaping or rewriting of the dominant meanings pertaining to race, authority, space, and identity prevalent under colonial and decolonizing conditions. Furthermore, given that postcolonial writing sets out to resist and challenge colonialist perspectives, it is also important to acknowledge that it can be produced at the time of empire, and within the former imperial metropole (in London or Edinburgh, for example), as well as on the one-time colonial periphery, and in a chronologically post-colonial situation. By this reckoning, Sarojini Naidu (1879–1949), an Indian poet in English at the turn of the 20th century, whose poetry was subtly ironic in its imitation of European forms, is technically postcolonial; as also is the contemporary work of British second-generation migrant writers like Hanif *Kureishi or Monica *Ali.

Many assumptions that are central to postcolonial literary studies, and that inform a number of different approaches to postcolonial writing, emanate from the influential work of the critic Edward *Said, in particular his *Orientalism* (1978), and *Culture and Imperialism* (1993). These include the critical perception that cultural representations (of 'savages' and 'cannibals'; or of primitive Africa or the exotic East) were fundamental first to the process of colonizing other lands, and then again to the process of obtaining independence (imaginative and otherwise) from the colonizer. As Joseph *Conrad was among the first to acknowledge, in his 'Heart of Darkness' (1899), assuming control over a territory or a nation meant not only exerting political or economic power but also having imaginative command. Overturning and replacing imperial systems of control therefore involved contesting these European imaginative and literary versions of the colonial experience, or as Indian-born writer Salman *Rushdie famously put it, it involved the empire 'writing back'.

As writers from places as far apart as Trinidad and Aotearoa/New Zealand, or Kolkata/Calcutta and Kano (Nigeria) have demonstrated, the forms of literary retaliation and writing back are manifold. Postcolonial literature, in seeking to awaken political and cultural nationalism, has dwelt, for example, on popular revolts against colonial rule, exposing the lie of the passive and indolent native. Writers like the Trinidadian C. L. R. *James have brought to the fore neglected black heroes like Toussaint *Louverture, who led the greatest slave revolt in history, defeating French, Spanish, and British military forces to set up Haiti, the first free black republic in the West. History, however, is not an epic narrative of kings and rebels, but a record of the day-to-day existence of the common people; the cane-cutters for instance, whose labour produced the sugar which not only boosted the profits of imperial commerce but, in the 18th century, created a taste among the gentry for taking sweetened tea. By giving voice and character to cane-cutters and the like, postcolonial writers point to the people who truly mattered to history but who, for political and related reasons, were written out. The world-view of such 'lowly' people, expressed in their myths and legends, is given space in postcolonial literature, with writers like the Guyanese Wilson *Harris arguing that Amerindian mythology reveals values and perspectives as complex and mysterious as any originating from the Graeco-Roman or Judaeo-Christian traditions. There is a corresponding reappraisal of oral expression, the riddles and proverbs and songs and stories handed down over generations and shared by the whole community. These forms of orality are often spurned by literary academics as lesser forms of 'literature' and relegated to the dubious category of 'folk tale'. But as the Nigerian writer Chinweizu (1943–) reminds us, the African folk tale is a product of ancient traditions of eloquence and rhetoric, created for courtship or wedding ceremonies, or ceremonies marking birth and death. The folk tale is therefore an 'integral part of the fabric of personal and social life', often with profound religious significance. To ignore it is to ignore the cultural history of a nation.

In a nutshell, as writers as diverse as Caryl *Phillips, Nadine *Gordimer, Peter *Carey, and Arundhati *Roy acknowledge, making a postcolonial world means learning how to live in and represent that world in a profoundly different way. These practices of new and revised representation can be grouped into the following three dominant areas of concern: the search for more authentic and vital forms of self-definition, in order to overcome experiences of alienation under colonialism; the retrieval and excavation of partially lost and buried histories and spaces (for example, sacred sites), for the same purpose; and the adaptation and regeneration of local languages and indigenous myths.

As this third point suggests, repositioning the coordinates of history has importantly involved coming to terms with the language of expression itself. Language is inextricably bound up with culture and identity, and as the colonizers attempted, with varying degrees of success, to impose the English language on subject peoples, the response from the formerly colonized has ranged from the outright rejection of English as a medium through which to exercise their art, to the appropriation of it with subversive intent. After first using English as the medium for his fiction, the Kenyan writer *Ngugi wa Thiong'o finally decided to reject it. For him 'language is at the heart of the two contending forces in the Africa of the 20th century' and is crucial to maintaining control over one's own culture and mental universe. For others, like the Nigerian writer Chinua *Achebe, or Indian novelists Upamanyu *Chatterjee and Amit *Chaudhuri, English has been a means of uniting peoples across continents and of reaching a wider audience than would have been possible in their mother tongues. Whether or not the English language is capable of supplying the rhythms and cadences necessary to dramatize foreign landscapes, this has not prevented writers from doing 'unheard of things with it'. Caribbeanists like Derek *Walcott and V. S. *Naipaul, for instance, have used techniques such as switching in and out of standard English and local Creoles to emphasize that their cultural worlds are irrevocably multicultural and hybridized. The debate as regards 'whose English?' continues to rage, and, although the view is by no means universally shared, there are now many people in all parts of the world who see English as having become detached from Britain or Britishness. They claim the language as their own property, for they have moulded and refashioned it to make it bear the weight of their own experience.

Another important trend within postcolonial writing from the different anglophone regions has been the celebratory and affirmative acknowledgement of women's experiences, following painful legacies of 'double' and in some cases 'triple colonization' (as women, black, lower class, lower caste, 'queer', etc.) under empire. Many of the entrenched and derogatory representations of non-Western women have been powerfully rejected in a host of contemporary writings, which in their different ways refute imaginings deeply rooted in Western traditions of writing and their subsequent over-simplistic depictions. The distinguished and burgeoning list of postcolonial women writers, which includes Jean *Rhys, Anita *Desai, Bessie *Head, Doris *Lessing, Olive *Senior, Nadine *Gordimer, and Tsitsi *Dangarembga, has placed women at the centre of history, as makers and agents of community life, not silent witnesses to it.

Postcolonial literature worldwide has registered the impact of modernist and also postmodernist traditions of Anglo-American writing across the 20th century and into the 21st. The montage effects and mythic adaptations of Anglo-American modernist poetry, for example, were enthusiastically adopted but also extended and enriched from local sources by writers such as Christopher *Okigbo and Wole *Soyinka. The subversive, playful techniques of metropolitan postmodernism have been appropriated by postcolonial writers in order to dramatize the unstable, provisional, and ever-shifting constitution of identities in the aftermath of empire, as in the work of Michael *Ondaatje and Dambudzo *Marechera. However, postcolonial literature has not simply responded to these metropolitan traditions in an imitative way, but, as writers like Rushdie and Derek Walcott recognize, has itself formed and informed modernist and postmodernist techniques.

POSTGATE, Oliver (1925–2008) Born in Hendon, Middlesex, educated at Kingston College of Art and the London Academy of Music and Dramatic Art; he wrote scripts for and book/annual versions of popular children's television programmes such as *Ivor the Engine* (1958–77), *Noggin the Nog* (1959–65), *The Clangers* (1965–74), and *Bagpuss* (1974). See Postgate's *Seeing Things: An Autobiography* (2000).

Post-Impressionism An art movement christened off-the-cuff by Roger *Fry in 1910 to designate the painters Paul Cézanne (1839–1906), Paul Gauguin (1848–1903), Vincent Van Gogh (1853–90), and others. The term (which was assimilated into other European languages) created the appearance of a coordinated group of artists who, according to Fry, gave priority to form over content. The impact in Britain of Fry's first Post-Impressionist exhibition in 1910 was considerable, and reactions ranged from veneration to outrage. Writers influenced by the stress on formalism included Virginia *Woolf. *To The Lighthouse endorses many of Fry's ideas, particularly in the figure of Lily Briscoe, whose 'vision' in the concluding lines coincides with the narrator's own. Wyndham *Lewis admired the *Futurist element in the movement, and D. H. *Lawrence in **Women in Love* expressed an antipathy to what he saw as its cold and inhuman qualities. See J. B. Bullen, *Post-Impressionists in England* (1988).

postmodernism The term applied by some commentators since the early 1980s to the cultural features characteristic of Western societies in the aftermath of artistic *modernism. In this view, 'postmodernity' asserts itself from about 1956 with the exhaustion of the high modernist project, reflected in the work of Samuel *Beckett among others, and the huge cultural impact of television and popular music. The term has been applied as a 'period' label more confidently by architectural historians than by students of literature, and many critics maintain that artistic or literary works described as 'postmodernist' are really continuations of the modernist tradition. Nevertheless, some general literary features of the period have been identified, such as tendencies to *parody, *pastiche, scepticism, irony, fatalism, the mixing of 'high' and 'low' cultural allusions, and an indifference to the redemptive mission of Art as conceived by the modernist pioneers. Postmodernism thus favours random play rather than purposeful action, surface rather than depth, inconclusiveness rather than 'closure'. The kinds of literary work that have been described as postmodernist include the Theatre of the *Absurd and the poetry of, among others, John *Ashbery and Paul *Muldoon. Most commonly, though, it is prose fiction that is held to exemplify the postmodernist mood or style, notably in works by American novelists such as Vladimir *Nabokov, John *Barth, Thomas *Pynchon, Kurt *Vonnegut, and Paul *Auster, and by the British authors John *Fowles, Angela *Carter, Julian *Barnes, Peter *Ackroyd, Salman *Rushdie, and Jeanette *Winterson. Outside the English-speaking world, the fictions of Jorge Luis *Borges and the later work of Italo *Calvino show similar tendencies. Distinctive features of this school include switching between orders of reality and fantasy (*see* MAGIC REALISM), resort to *metafiction, and the playful undermining of supposedly objective kinds of knowledge such as biography and history. See Brian McHale, *Postmodernist Fiction* (1987); Ian Gregson, *Postmodern Literature* (2004).

post-structuralism *See* STRUCTURALISM.

'Pot of Basil, The' *See* 'ISABELLA'.

POTTER, Beatrix (1866–1943) Born in London and never sent to school; she became fascinated with nature on family holidays in Scotland. She taught herself to draw and paint from nature, and as a young woman dissected, drew, and classified fungi. She invented a cipher for writing her private journal; it was eventually decoded by Leslie Linder and published as *The Journal of Beatrix Potter* (1966). *The Tale of Peter Rabbit* started as a letter to the son of her former governess and was published at her own expense in 1901, followed by *The Tailor of Gloucester* (1902). Her books are notable for their interactions between images and text, appealing but pointed use of animals in clothes, elaborate vocabulary, and lack of sentimentality. The publishers F. Warne & Co took over their publication; in 1903, *Squirrel Nutkin* was her first great success. She was briefly engaged to Norman Warne, who died before they married. Her farm at Sawrey in the Lake District, bought in 1905, features in six of her books. In 1913 she married William Heelis, a Lakeland solicitor, and thereafter devoted herself almost entirely to farming and the new National Trust. *Johnny Town-Mouse* (1918) was the last of her books in the old style; later books written for the USA such as *The Fairy Caravan* (1928) are of less interest. There are biographies and studies by Margaret Lane (1946, 1978), Linder (1955, 1966, 1971), and Judy Taylor (1987 and many edited works). The Beatrix Potter Society produces numerous publications and facsimiles and has an extensive website.

POTTER, Dennis (1935–94) Playwright, born in the Forest of Dean, the son of a miner. He was educated at New College, Oxford, where he became involved in left-wing politics, and subsequently worked as journalist and critic. He wrote fiction, stage plays, screenplays, and adapted works for television but is best known for his own television plays, which show an original and inventive use of the medium. These include two plays dealing with the career of an aspiring working-class, Oxford-educated politician, *Vote, Vote, Vote for Nigel Barton* (1965) and *Stand up, Nigel Barton* (1965); *Pennies from Heaven*, a six-part serial (1978); and *Blue Remembered Hills* (1979), a tragic evocation of childhood. Potter's experience of psoriatic arthropathy, a debilitating condition affecting skin and joints, is central to his six-part serial *The Singing Detective* (1986), widely held to be his finest work: this is a multi-layered narrative, moving between a moody 1940s thriller and incorporating songs of that period, and a present-day hospital ward where Philip Marlow, hero of both sequences, is suffering from a skin disease: it dwells on key themes of childhood trauma, disillusion, betrayal, love, and guilt. *Blackeyes* (1989) is a study of sexual exploitation and *Lipstick on your Collar* (1993) is a musical black comedy based on Potter's National Service experiences. His final work was a pair of linked serials completed weeks before his death from cancer: *Karaoke* and *Cold Lazarus* (1996). See H. Carpenter, *Dennis Potter: A Biography* (1998); S. Gilbert, *The Life and Work of Dennis Potter* (1998).

Potter, Harry Orphan hero of J. K. *Rowling's seven-part fantasy series (1997–2007) set in Hogwarts School of Witchcraft and Wizardry. Harry's parents, James and Lily Potter, were killed by Lord Voldemort, the embodiment of evil, when he was an infant, leaving him in the charge of his nasty aunt and uncle who live in the non-magical 'Muggle' world. He was marked with a distinctive lightning-bolt scar in the encounter. On his eleventh birthday Harry is astonished to learn that he is a wizard, and is taken to Hogwarts, where he becomes friends with Ron Weasley and Hermione Granger, and the favourite of headmaster Albus Dumbledore; together they struggle with Voldemort with varying degrees of success. There he discovers that like his father he is a naturally brilliant wizard and skilled player of Quidditch, the school sport. Films, starring Daniel Radcliffe (Warner Brothers, 2001–9 to date), of all seven books are planned.

poulter's measure A *metre consisting of alternate lines of twelve and fourteen syllables, i.e. iambic *hexameters and *fourteeners, used by *Surrey and some other 16th-century poets. The name comes from the customary inconsistency of poulterers in selling eggs as 'dozens' varying from twelve to fourteen.

POUND, Ezra (1885–1972) American poet, born in Idaho. He studied at the University of Pennsylvania, where he met Hilda *Doolittle (H.D.). He taught briefly in Indiana, but was asked to resign, and in 1908 came to Europe and published his first volume of poems, *A Lume Spento* (1908), at his own expense in Italy; he then moved to London, where he lectured for a time in medieval Romance literature at the Regent Street Polytechnic and soon became prominent in literary circles. He published several other volumes of verse, including *Personae* (1909). Together with F. S. Flint (1885–1960), Richard *Aldington, and Hilda Doolittle he founded the *imagist school of poets, advocating the use of free rhythms, concreteness, and concision of language and imagery; in 1914 he edited *Des Imagistes: An Anthology.* Pound also championed the *modernist work of avant-garde writers and artists like James *Joyce, Wyndham *Lewis, Henri *Gaudier-Brzeska, and T. S. *Eliot. Eliot, who described him as 'more responsible for the XXth Century revolution in poetry than any other individual', greatly valued his advice, as may be seen from the history of the composition of *The *Waste Land*. Further volumes of poetry include *Quia Pauper Amavi* (1919, which contains 'Homage to Sextus Propertius') and *Hugh Selwyn Mauberley* (1920). Pound was now increasingly turning away from the constrictions of imagism, and finding freedom partly through translations; his early volumes had contained adaptations from Provençal and early Italian, a version of the Old English *The *Seafarer*, and *Cathay* (1915), translations from the Chinese of Li Po, via a transliteration. Pound was thus moving towards the rich, grandly allusive, multicultural world of the *Cantos*, his most ambitious achievement. The first three Cantos appeared in 1917 in *Poetry.* In 1920 Pound left London for Paris with his English wife Dorothy Shakespear, where he lived until 1924, finding a new literary scene figuring Gertrude *Stein, Ernest *Hemingway, and others. In 1925 he settled permanently in Rapallo, where he continued to work on the Cantos, which appeared intermittently over the next decades until the appearance of the final *Drafts and Fragments of Cantos CX to CXVII* (1970).

In Italy Pound became increasingly preoccupied with economics, embraced Social Credit theories, and was persuaded that 'Usura', or credit capitalism, lay at the root of all social and spiritual evils (see Canto XLV for his violent attack on usury). His own interpretations of these theories led him into anti-Semitism and at least partial support for Mussolini's social programme. During the Second World War he broadcast on Italian radio: in 1945 he was arrested at Genoa, then sent to a US Army Disciplinary Training Centre near Pisa, a period which produced the much-admired *Pisan Cantos* (1948). He was then moved to Washington, found unfit to plead, and confined to a mental institution; he was released in 1958 and returned to Italy, where he died.

Inevitably, Pound's literary reputation was obscured by the tragedy of his last decades, and also by the difficulty of the work itself, which resides principally in its astonishingly wide range of reference and assimilation of cultures; *Hugh Selwyn Mauberley,* despite the advocacy of Eliot and F. R. *Leavis (who described it as 'the summit of Mr Pound's superbly supple and varied art'), never quite reached the 'popular classic' status of *The Waste Land*, and the *Cantos* remain formidable both in style and content. Nevertheless, he is widely accepted both as a great master of traditional verse forms and as the man who regenerated the poetic idiom of his day. See Humphrey Carpenter, *A Serious Character* (1988).

POUSSIN, Nicolas (1593/4–1665) French painter, who worked mainly in Rome. His early works are romantic treatments of subjects from *Ovid and *Tasso; later he developed an austerely classical style. In the early 18th century Poussin was deeply admired by English men of letters, and many of his greatest works found their way to English collections. James *Thomson's descriptions of landscape are indebted to Poussin and, in the second half of the century, poets, travellers, and landscape gardeners frequently contrast the nobility of Poussin's landscapes with the wildness of Salvator *Rosa and the beauty of *Claude Lorrain. In the late 18th century Poussin's most severe works were most admired. William *Hazlitt wrote many passionate descriptions of his painting; John *Keats was inspired by the lyrical Ovidian pictures; but for some artists, such as Benjamin *West and the French neo-classical painter Jacques Louis David (1748–1825), he provided a model for 'history painting'. John *Ruskin described the *Triumph of Flora* (Paris, Louvre) as 'a Keats-like revel of body and soul of most heavenly creatures'. The picture most admired by literary men was Poussin's second treatment of the theme 'Et in Arcadia Ego', *The Shepherds of Arcady* (*c.*1650–55), a picture which fascinated later writers and painters. It has been suggested that Thomas *Gray thought of it when he wrote his **Elegy Written in a Country Church-Yard* (1751); *The Monument in Arcadia: A Dramatic Poem* (1773) by the minor poet George Keate (1729–97) derives from it. English admiration paused with John Ruskin, but revived in the late 19th century when, in a neo-classical revival, he was most admired for his formal brilliance. Paul Cézanne (1839–1906) and the *Post-Impressionists were much influenced by Poussin, and through them Roger *Fry and the *Bloomsbury Group. Anthony *Powell's image of *A Dance to the Music of Time* was inspired by Poussin's picture in the Wallace Collection, London. See Anthony Blunt, *Nicolas Poussin* (1995).

POWELL, Anthony (1905–2000) Novelist, whose initial reputation as a satirist and light comedian rests on five pre-war books, beginning with *Afternoon Men* (1931) which maps a characteristically seedy section of pleasure-loving, party-going London: a territory close to Evelyn *Waugh's, bounded at opposite extremes by Nancy *Mitford and by Powell's Oxford contemporary and friend Henry *Green.

After the war he embarked on a more ambitious sequence of twelve novels, *A Dance to the Music of Time* (named after Nicolas *Poussin's painting, with which the sequence shares a certain classical severity as well as an architectural command of structural rhythm). They are: *A Question of Upbringing* (1951), *A Buyer's Market* (1952), *The Acceptance World* (1955), *At Lady Molly's* (1957), *Casanova's Chinese Restaurant* (1960), *The Kindly Ones* (1962), *The Valley of Bones* (1964), *The Soldier's Art* (1966), *The Military Philosophers* (1968), *Books Do Furnish a Room* (1971), *Temporary Kings* (1973), and *Hearing Secret Harmonies* (1975). The whole cycle is framed and distanced through the eyes of a narrator, Nicholas Jenkins, whose generation grew up in the shadow of the First World War to find their lives dislocated by the Second. Jenkins's canvas, following the perspectives of time rather than space, is hospitable and broad, especially rich in literary and artistic hangers-on, stiffened by a solid contingent from society, politics, and the City, enlivened and sometimes convulsed by eccentrics, derelicts, and drop-outs of all classes and conditions from the socialist peer Erridge to a shifty crew of baleful, semi-fraudulent gurus and seers. Against these looms Kenneth Widmerpool, one of the most memorable characters of 20th-century fiction, whose ruthless pursuit of power, which carries him from innately ludicrous beginnings to a position of increasingly formidable, eventually sinister, authority, is the chief of many threads binding this higgledy-piggledy, jam-packed, panoramic view of England.

The narrative is part humorous, part melancholy, and at times so funny that readers have tended to underrate its sombre, even tragic, sweep and range. Powell's naturalism takes on the almost surrealistic overtones implicit in Jenkins's rule of thumb: 'All human beings, driven as they are at different speeds by the same Furies, are at close range equally extraordinary.' Powell's memoirs, which shed considerable light on the creation of the characters of his fictional world, were published in four volumes, 1976–82, under the general title *To Keep the Ball Rolling*. Later works include the novels *O, How the Wheel Becomes It!* (1983) and *The Fisher King* (1986), two volumes of criticism, *Miscellaneous Verdicts* (1990) and *Under Review* (1992), and *Journals 1982–6* (1995).

POWERS, Tim (1952–) American *science fiction and *fantasy author, born in Buffalo, New York. His fiction often counterpoints historical characters with fantastic plots. Lord *Byron, P. B. *Shelley, and John *Keats, for example, appear in *The Stress of her Regard* (1989) which exploits the Romantics' fascination with vampires. *Declare* (2001) is a similar 'secret history' drawing upon the Cold War.

POWYS, John Cowper (1872–1963) Writer, born at Shirley, Derbyshire, and educated at Sherborne School and Corpus Christi College, Cambridge. Brother of Llewelyn and Theodore *Powys, he was brought up in the Dorset–Somerset countryside which was to become of great importance in his work, even though he spent much of his life between 1909 and 1934 teaching and writing in the USA. His output was prolific, including volumes of poetry and many books and essays on philosophy, religion, literature, and the arts of living, as well as a remarkable *Autobiography* (1934). It is, however, for his highly individual novels that he is chiefly remembered; the first, *Wood and Stone* (1915, NY; 1917, London), contains many hints of the powerful characters and intense relationships, the attachment to place, and the arresting oddity of personal names which were more fully developed in later works. *Rodmoor* (1916) was followed by *Ducdame* (1925) before *Wolf Solent*, his first major novel, and major success, appeared in 1929. It is a crowded work, set again in the West Country, of many interweaving stories, but chiefly concerning Wolf and Gerda, and the destructive pull of opposites. *A Glastonbury Romance* (1932, NY; 1933, London), the best known of his novels, was also conceived on a huge scale; Glastonbury and its legends exert a supernatural influence on the life of the town and on the complex loves, both sacred and sexual, of the town's inhabitants. *Weymouth Sands* (1934, NY) had, because of a libel action, to be recast as *Jobber Skald* (1935), but was restored and republished as *Weymouth Sands* in 1963. *Maiden Castle* (1936, NY; 1937, London) follows the interlocking loves of several couples, no longer young; the lives of the protagonists move towards disillusion and endurance. Most of the later novels, written after Powys had settled in Wales in the late 1930s, share an extravagance of subject and style and strong elements of the supernatural. In *Morwyn* (1937), cast as a letter from the narrator to his son, the theme of man's cruelty, to his fellows and to animals, is carried through various meetings with characters from history. *Owen Glendower* (1940, NY; 1941, London), the most successful of his historical novels, describes the confused events and passions surrounding Owen and his cousin Rhisiart. Set in AD 499, *Porius* (1951) presents a fraught world of giants, Mithraic cults, and Arthurian legend filling the void the Romans have left. This was followed by *The Inmates* (1952), on the theme of madness; *Atlantis* (1954), containing Powys's most extreme flight of imagination, in which Odysseus, returned from Troy, sets out again through a world of giants, heroes, talking animals, and inanimate objects, to discover the continent of America, where he settles; and *The Brazen Head* (1956). Powys's stature as a writer has been much debated. His admirers regard him as an unjustly neglected writer and an arresting major novelist, while others find his talents less convincing and his appeal more obscure. See Morine Krissdottir, *Descents of Memory* (2007).

POWYS, Llewelyn (1884–1939) Writer, born in Dorchester and educated at Sherborne School and Corpus Christi College, Cambridge. Brother of J. C. and T. F. *Powys, his existence was peripatetic, but his output was prolific. The best of his books are generally thought to be *Black Laughter* (1924); *Skin for Skin* (1925), an account of his tuberculosis and the idyllic Dorset interludes when it seemed to be cured;

Impassioned Clay (1931), an intense meditation on the human condition, the Epicurean ethic, and death; and *Love and Death* (1939), an eloquent 'imaginary autobiography', on the theme of lost love and his own approaching end. Apart from these works, a novel, *Apples Be Ripe* (1930), and two volumes of essays, *Earth Memories* (1934) and *Dorset Essays* (1935), are noteworthy. *Damnable Opinions* (1935) offered further evidence of the iconoclastic outlook he shared with J. C. Powys. See R. P. Graves, *The Brothers Powys* (1983).

POWYS, T. F. (Theodore Francis) (1875–1953) Writer, brother of J. C. and L. *Powys, born at Shirley, Derbyshire, and educated at Sherborne preparatory school, Dorset, and Eaton House School, Aldeburgh. He farmed in Suffolk for six years before returning to Dorset in 1901 where the local landscape formed the backdrop to almost all his novels and stories. His first book, *An Interpretation of Genesis* (1907), was followed by *The Soliloquy of a Hermit* (1916) and many other volumes, among the most notable of which are *The Left Leg* (1923), a collection of three long stories; *Black Bryony* (1923), *Mark Only* (1924), and *Mr Tasker's Gods* (1925), three pessimistic novels of village life; and *Mockery Gap* (1923) and *Innocent Birds* (1926), which developed his religious concerns. They were followed in 1927 by the novel for which Powys is best remembered, *Mr Weston's Good Wine*. In this vivid allegory Mr Weston (or God) comes to the worldly village of Folly Down, selling from his old van his vintages of Love and Death; after his departure he leaves no paradise, but the good are happier, and the evil (such as Mrs Vosper, the procuress) are vanquished. *Fables* (1929), the volume of short stories in which Powys's beliefs are most clearly exposed, was followed by another major novel, *Unclay* (1931), in which John Death (or the archangel Michael) arrives in Dodder with instructions from God to 'unclay', or kill, various people; however, he loses his instructions, is unsettled by the mysterious Tinker Jar, and falls in love with a village girl. Other volumes of short stories, including the melancholy *Bottle's Path* (1946) and the sunnier *God's Eyes A-Twinkle* (1947), followed, but Powys's output dwindled significantly around 1940. See R. P. Graves, *The Brothers Powys* (1983).

practical criticism The term used in academic literary studies for an exercise in which students are required to comment upon a poem or short prose passage without knowledge of its authorship, date, or circumstances of composition. This procedure encourages attention to form, diction, and style rather than 'extraneous' associations. It was adopted by I. A. *Richards at the University of Cambridge in the 1920s as an experiment which he records and analyses in his book *Practical Criticism* (1929). Thereafter it became a standard exercise, especially under the influence of the *New Criticism in America. In a more general sense, the term has been used, by S. T. *Coleridge and others, to designate the applied uses of criticism as distinct from the purely theoretical.

Practice of Pietie, The A devotional work by Lewis Bayly (*c.*1575–1631), bishop of Bangor, first published *c.*1612. This extraordinarily popular and influential book, regularly republished and translated into the 19th century, combined a compendium of *Reformation doctrine with guidance on daily life, meditation, prayer, and preparation for death. John *Bunyan had a copy.

PRAED, Winthrop Mackworth (1802–39) Poet, educated at Eton, where he founded the *Etonian*, and at Trinity College, Cambridge. He was called to the bar, went into Parliament, and was appointed secretary to the Board of Control in 1834. He is remembered principally as a humorous poet and composer of elegant **vers de société*; 'The County Ball', 'A Letter of Advice', 'Stanzas on Seeing the Speaker Asleep', and 'The Vicar' are characteristic examples of his light verse. Like Thomas *Hood, with whom he is often compared, he sometimes uses humour to clothe a grim subject, as in 'The Red Fisherman'. He also wrote verse epistles, some to his sister, and historical ballads similar to those of his Cambridge friend Thomas Babington *Macaulay, for example 'Sir Nicholas at Marston Moor'. His verse was published largely in periodicals and annuals, and his early death from consumption prevented him from taking an interest in more formal publication, but his inoffensive satire, gentle wit, and fluent metrical variations assured him a more lasting readership; his *Poems*, with a memoir by his friend Derwent Coleridge, appeared in 1864.

Praeterita ['things past'] Unfinished autobiographical work by John *Ruskin, published in 28 parts and at intervals between 1885 and 1889. Ruskin had no interest in giving a complete account of his life, as he admits. Instead, he writes about 'what it gives me joy to remember, at any length I like' and 'passing in total silence things I have no pleasure in reviewing'. There is therefore no mention of his wife and the annulment of his marriage, and only a fleeting reference to Rose La Touche, the young girl he fell in love with. The work is a lyrical and fragmentary evocation of the past, particularly the lost landscapes of his childhood and the growth of his intense visual imagination. Periods of mental breakdown prevented the completion of this, his last work.

pragmatism In philosophy, the doctrine that the test of the value of any assertion lies in its practical consequences, that is, in its practical bearing upon human interests and purposes. This view is associated chiefly with William *James, but has been revived in literary studies by the American critic Stanley Fish (1938–).

Prague Circle *See* STRUCTURALISM.

PRATCHETT, Sir Terry (1948–) *Fantasy and *science fiction writer, born in Beaconsfield; author of the successful 'Discworld' series. His first story, 'The Hades Business' (1963), was published before he left school for a career in journalism. *The Carpet People* was published in 1971. *The Colour of Magic* (1983) was the first 'Discworld' novel. Since then, Discworld has developed from parodying *fantasy conventions to become a location for thoughtful, witty, and morally acute satire. Abstractions acquire personalities—jokes arise from Death's inability to understand humans—and 'narrative causality' affects events, as characters find themselves having to decide how they *should* behave, rather than behaving according to narrative stereotypes. Granny Weatherwax, in particular, is the conscience of many of the books in which she appears, while the 'Vimes' series beginning with *Guards! Guards!* (1989) increasingly considers the nature of civic society. The collaboration with Neil *Gaiman, *Good Omens* (1990), and books for children such as *Truckers* (1988) address similar themes. In 1998, Pratchett was awarded the OBE for services to literature. *The Amazing Maurice and his Educated Rodents* (2001) won the Carnegie Medal for best children's novel. Pratchett has won a large and enthusiastic following, and was the best-selling British writer of the 1990s. In 2007 he announced his diagnosis with early-onset Alzheimer's disease. See Andrew M. Butler, Edward James, and Farah Mendlesohn (eds), *Terry Pratchett: Guilty of Literature* (2000).

PRATT, Fletcher (1897–1956) American *science fiction author, born in Buffalo, New York; published numerous stories and translations for American science fiction magazines. He co-wrote, with L. Sprague *de Camp, the *fantasy series beginning with *The Incompleat Enchanter* (1941). Among solo novels is *The Well of the Unicorn* (1948).

PRAZ, Mario (1896–1982) Italian critic and scholar, born in Rome, who spent ten years in England, in Liverpool and Manchester (1924–34), as senior lecturer, then professor, of Italian studies, before returning to Rome as professor of English literature. He wrote on many aspects of English literature and the connections between the English and Italian traditions; his best-known work is *La carne, la morte e il diavolo nella letteratura romantica* (1930; published in a translation by Angus Davidson as *The Romantic Agony*, 1933) in which he explores the legacy of the marquis de *Sade, the perverse and pathological elements in *Poe, *Swinburne, Oscar *Wilde, and others, and the cult of the *femme fatale*. His other works include *The Flaming Heart* (1958: essays on Richard *Crashaw, *Machiavelli, T. S. *Eliot, and others) and *La casa della fama* (1952: as *The House of Life*, 1958).

Prelude, The, *Or Growth of a Poet's Mind* An autobiographical poem in blank verse by William *Wordsworth, addressed to S. T. *Coleridge, and begun in 1798–9; a two-book version was composed in 1799 and a complete draft in thirteen books was finished in 1805, but it was several times remodelled, and published posthumously in its final version, in fourteen books in 1850, with its present title, suggested by Mary Wordsworth. The poem was originally intended as an introduction to 'The Recluse', a vast work which Wordsworth planned but never completed (*see* EXCURSION).

In the first book Wordsworth describes his search for a conventional epic theme, moving to an evocation of his own childhood which leads him less by logic than by imaginative association to his central subject, his own development as a poet and the forces that shaped his imagination. Although profoundly autobiographical, the poem does not proceed in terms of strict chronology; it deals with infancy, schooldays, Cambridge, his walking tour through the Alps, his political awakening in France, and consequent horrors, but (for example) the passage describing the 'visionary dreariness' of a highly charged moment in his early boyhood is delayed until Book XI ('Imagination, How Impaired and Restored'). The landscape described there is linked in the immediate past with his sister Dorothy and Coleridge, who are both intermittently addressed throughout the work. The tone is flexible and variable; conversational in some passages, narrative in others, it sometimes rises to an impassioned loftiness. A constant theme is Wordsworth's sense of himself as a chosen being, with an overriding duty to his poetic vocation. Wordsworth was aware that his choice of subject (original in its day, when the confessional mode in poetry was little developed) might be construed as 'self-conceit', but he insisted that he wrote through 'real humility' and 'diffidence'. Apart from its poetic quality, the work is remarkable for its psychological insight into the significance of childhood experience, a theme dear to *Romanticism, but rarely treated with such power and precision. E. de Selincourt published an important edition in 1926, tracing Wordworth's later changes to the poem: increasing the number of books to fourteen, toning down some of its political views, and tidying up structure and syntax. The Norton critical edition of *The Prelude, 1799, 1805, 1850*, ed. J. Wordsworth, M. H. Abrams, and S. Gill (1979), prints the three principal texts of the poem in one volume.

Pre-Raphaelite Brotherhood A group of artists, poets, and critics—John Everett *Millais, Dante Gabriel *Rossetti, William Holman *Hunt, William Michael *Rossetti, Thomas *Woolner, Frederic George Stephens (1828–1907), and James Collinson (1825–81)—who first met as a group, led by the first three, in 1848. Various derivations have been assigned to the term 'Pre-Raphaelite', which indicated the group's admiration for the Italian quattrocento and its defiance of the authority both of *Raphael as a master and of 19th-century academic painting. The initials 'P.R.B.' first appeared on their work in the Royal Academy exhibition of 1849. As its periodical *The *Germ* (1850) suggests, the movement was strongly literary, and some of its most striking paintings were inspired by John *Keats (see Millais's *Isabella*), *Dante, William *Shakespeare, and Alfred *Tennyson. Common aspirations of the group included fidelity to nature (manifested in clarity, brightness, detailed first-hand observation of flora, etc.), and moral seriousness, in some expressed in religious themes or symbolic mystical iconography. Many of the subjects were medieval as well as literary, and the movement (much influenced by John *Ruskin, who became its champion) saw itself in part as a revolt against the ugliness of modern life and dress. Its revolutionary aims thus became in some of its products inextricably mingled with nostalgia. Artists connected with the PRB include Ford Madox Brown (1821–93), William Bell

*Scott, William Dyce (1806–64), Henry Wallis (1830–1916), Arthur Hughes (1831–1915), Simeon Solomon (1840–1905), and William *de Morgan. The first phase of the movement was brief, and the group broke up around 1853; a second phase led by Dante Gabriel Rossetti and involving Edward *Burne-Jones, William *Morris, and A. C. *Swinburne was often labelled 'Pre-Raphaelite' but was more accurately linked to the *Aesthetic movement. Pre-Raphaelite influence amongst British painters was considerable, and the British attachment to material accuracy and startling colour persisted until the end of the century. See Tim Barringer, *Reading the Pre-Raphaelites* (1999).

Presbyterianism A church system overseen by a governing hierarchy of four courts (parochial, local, regional, and national), championed by English Puritans. The term comes from the New Testament Greek word πρεσβύτερος, rendered *presbyter* or *elder* in Protestant English Bibles but *priest* in Roman Catholic translations. The Westminster Assembly of Divines, summoned by the Long Parliament in 1643, issued a set of enduring Presbyterian formularies: directories of *Church-Government* (1644) and *Public Worship* (1645), a *Confession of Faith* (1648), and *Larger and Shorter Catechism* (1648); but a national Presbyterian church was never established in England as it had been in Scotland.

PRESCOTT, William Hickling (1796–1859) American historian, born at Salem, Massachusetts, and educated at Harvard University. His sight was affected by an accident while at college, but he nevertheless devoted himself, with the help of a reader, to the study of ancient and modern literature. His first work, *The History of Ferdinand and Isabella*, appeared in 1838. It was followed by the *History of the Conquest of Mexico* (1843) and the *History of the Conquest of Peru* (1847). The first two volumes of his unfinished *History of Philip II, King of Spain* appeared in 1855, the third in 1858.

PRESTON, Thomas (1537–98) A fellow of King's College, Cambridge, master of Trinity Hall, and vice-chancellor of Cambridge, 1589–90. He is thought to have been the Thomas Preston who wrote *A Lamentable Tragedy Mixed Full of Pleasant Mirth, Containing the Life of Cambyses King of Persia* (?1570) (*see* CAMBYSES).

PRÉVOST, Antoine-François, abbé (1697–1763) French novelist and translator. Successively Jesuit novice, professional soldier, Benedictine priest, Protestant convert, and literary hack, he is best remembered today for *Manon Lescaut* (1731), the story of the mutually destructive passion between the nobleman Des Grieux, who narrates the story, and the pleasure-loving Manon. The novel was very successful, and it formed the basis of operas by Jules Massenet (1842–1912) and *Puccini. Prévost also translated Samuel *Richardson's *Pamela* (1742), *Clarissa* (1751), and *Histoire du Chevalier Grandisson* (1755–8).

Priam *See* ILIAD.

PRICE, Richard (1723–91) Dissenting minister. In *A Review of the Principal Questions in Morals* (1756) he questions Francis *Hutcheson's doctrine of 'moral sense', and argues that the rightness and wrongness of an action belong to it intrinsically. He was from 1758 minister at Newington Green, where he influenced younger writers such as Samuel *Rogers and Mary *Wollstonecraft. He was a friend of Benjamin *Franklin, and supported American independence and the French Revolution; his address to the Revolution Society of 4 November 1789, celebrating the French 'ardour for liberty', provoked Edmund Burke to write **Reflections on the Revolution in France*. In 1791 he became, with Joseph *Priestley, one of the original members of the Unitarian Society.

PRICE, Susan (1955–) Born in Dudley, Staffordshire; she left school at 15 and had her first novel accepted for publication the following year. Her numerous novels combine fantasy, realism, and history. *The Sterkarm Handshake* (1998) and its sequel, *A Sterkarm Kiss* (2003), describe what happens when 21st-century technology allows travel through a Time Tube (not unlike the Channel Tunnel) between centuries, raising ethical questions and creating emotional dilemmas.

PRICE, Uvedale *see* PICTURESQUE.

Pride and Prejudice A novel by Jane *Austen, published 1813. Originally a youthful work entitled 'First Impressions', it was refused by Cadell, a London publisher, in 1797. Austen's most popular novel, and one which has had a series of successful adaptations in film and television, it demonstrates her skill at revealing character through incident and incident through character as she portrays the series of mutual misunderstandings between her clever quick-witted heroine Elizabeth Bennet and the condescending Mr Darcy.

Mr and Mrs Bennet live with their five daughters at Longbourn in Hertfordshire. In the absence of a male heir, the property is due to pass by entail to a cousin, William Collins. Through the patronage of the haughty Lady Catherine de Bourgh, Collins has been presented with a living near Rosings, the Kentish seat of Lady Catherine. Charles Bingley, a rich young bachelor, takes Netherfield, a house near Longbourn, bringing with him his two sisters and his friend Fitzwilliam Darcy, nephew of Lady Catherine. Bingley and Jane, the eldest of the Bennet girls, very soon fall in love. Darcy, though attracted to the next sister, the lively and spirited Elizabeth, offends her by his supercilious behaviour at a ball. This dislike is increased by the account given her by George Wickham, a dashing young militia officer (and son of the late steward of the Darcy property), of the unjust treatment he has met with at Darcy's hands. The aversion is intensified when Darcy and Bingley's two sisters, disgusted with the vulgarity of Mrs Bennet and her two youngest daughters, effectively separate Bingley from Jane.

Meanwhile the fatuous Mr Collins, urged to marry by Lady Catherine (for whom he shows the most grovelling respect), and thinking to remedy the hardship caused to the Bennet girls by the entail, proposes to Elizabeth. When firmly rejected he promptly transfers his affections to Charlotte Lucas, a friend of Elizabeth's, who accepts him. Staying with the newly married couple in their parsonage, Elizabeth again encounters Darcy, who is visiting Lady Catherine. Captivated by her in spite of himself, Darcy proposes to her in terms which reveal the violence the proposal does to his self-esteem. Elizabeth indignantly rejects him, on the grounds of his overweening pride, the part he has played in separating Jane from Bingley, and his alleged treatment of Wickham. Mortified, Darcy writes to justify the separation of his friend and Jane, and makes it clear that Wickham is, in fact, an unprincipled adventurer.

On an expedition to the north of England with her uncle and aunt, Mr and Mrs Gardiner, Elizabeth visits Pemberley, Darcy's seat in Derbyshire, believing Darcy to be absent. However, Darcy appears, welcomes the visitors, and introduces them to his sister. His manner, though still grave, is now gentle and attentive. At this point news reaches Elizabeth that her youngest sister Lydia has eloped with Wickham. With considerable help from Darcy, the fugitives are traced, their marriage is arranged, and (again through Darcy) they are provided for. Bingley and Jane are reunited and become engaged. In spite of the insolent intervention of Lady Catherine, Darcy and Elizabeth also become engaged. The story ends with their marriages, an indication of their subsequent happiness, and an eventual reconciliation with Lady Catherine.

Though a novel of manners, *Pride and Prejudice*, to borrow the words of Ronald *Blythe, extracts more drama out of petty social rivalries and class differences than 'most other writers can get from shipwreck, battle, murder, or mayhem'. Jane Austen regarded Elizabeth Bennet as her favourite among all her heroines.

PRIEST, Christopher (1943–) Novelist and short story writer, born in Cheshire. Like Geoff *Ryman and M. John *Harrison, Priest was first published as a *science fiction writer, with *Indoctrinaire* (1970), *Fugue for a Darkening Island* (1972), and *The Inverted World* (1974), but by the early 1980s he was edging towards the mainstream. In *The Affirmation* (1981), in which a lottery winner is promised eternal life, he patrols the frontier between sanity and insanity, rendering his narrator's fantasy world more real than the 'real' world. *The Glamour* (1984) explored not dissimilar psychological territory in a world where little is what it seems. *The Prestige* (1995) is a compelling tale of doppelgängers and magicians, while *The Extremes* (1998) takes a look at virtual reality, which essentially has been his subject since the beginning. In an interview in *The Third Alternative* in 1998 he remarked that 'perception of memory, and understanding it, is probably the central theme in most of my novels'.

PRIESTLEY, J. B. (John Boynton) (1894–1984) Journalist, novelist, and playwright. He was born in Bradford, the son of a schoolmaster, and worked as junior clerk in a wool office before serving in the infantry in the First World War; he then took a degree at Trinity Hall, Cambridge, and in 1922 settled in London, where he quickly made a name as journalist and critic. His first major popular success as a novelist was with the high-spirited, rambling *The Good Companions* (1929), an account of theatrical adventures on the road, which was followed by the grimmer, somewhat self-consciously *'realist' novel of London life, *Angel Pavement* (1930). His many other novels, which vary greatly in scope, include *Bright Day* (1946), *Festival at Farbridge* (1951), *Lost Empires* (1965), and *The Image Men* (1968). Priestley also wrote some 50 plays and dramatic adaptations; amongst the best known are his 'Time' plays, influenced by the theories of J. W. Dunne (1875–1949) (*Dangerous Corner*, 1932; *I Have Been Here Before*, 1937; *Time and the Conways*, 1937), his psychological mystery drama *An Inspector Calls* (1947), and his West Riding farce *When We Are Married* (1938). He also published dozens of miscellaneous works, including collections of his popular and influential wartime broadcasts (*Britain Speaks*, 1940; *All England Listened*, 1968). He also wrote *Journey down a Rainbow* (1955) with his wife Jacquetta Hawkes (1919–96), describing travels in New Mexico; and several volumes of autobiography, including *Margin Released* (1962) and *Instead of the Trees* (1977). Priestley consciously cultivated various poses—of grumbling patriot, cosmopolitan Yorkshireman, professional amateur, cultured philistine, or reactionary radical. He much admired H. G. *Wells (whose disregard of the 'mandarin conventions' of the literary novel he applauded), and in a sense inherited his role as Man of Letters, who remained nevertheless a spokesman for the common sense of the common man. His plays continue to be successfully revived.

PRIESTLEY, Joseph (1733–1804) Presbyterian minister. He wrote on theology, grammar, education, government, psychology, and history; his *Essay on the First Principles of Government* (1768) influenced Jeremy *Bentham's development of utilitarianism. His scientific research, announced in works such as *Experiments and Observations on Different Kinds of Air* (1774–7), isolated and identified seven gases, oxygen (or 'dephlogisticated air') amongst them. With his friend Richard *Price, Priestley was one of the founders of the Unitarian Society in 1791. In politics he was a radical, labelled 'Gunpowder' Priestley for his remarks about laying gunpowder 'under the old building of error and superstition'; on 14 July 1791 his Birmingham house and laboratory were wrecked by a mob outraged by his public support for the French Revolution. He emigrated to Pennsylvania in 1794. S. T. *Coleridge, in describing him as 'Patriot, and Saint, and Sage' ('Religious Musings', 1796), gave expression to the esteem in which Priestley was held by radical Dissenters.

PRIMAS The nickname ('Primate') given to Hugh, a scholar from Orléans who was at the University of Paris *c.*1142. He was a Goliardic poet (*see* GOLIAS) excelling in Latin lyrics which reveal both scholarship and a pleasure-loving disposition. See

C. J. McDonough, *The Oxford Poems of Hugh Primas and the Arundel Lyrics* (1984).

Prime Minister, The A novel by Anthony *Trollope, published 1876, fifth in the *'Palliser' series. Ferdinand Lopez is disappointed in his marriage to Emily Wharton. He had hoped it would bring him money and social position, but Emily's father ties up her fortune, and Lopez's unscrupulous motives are revealed. The duchess of Omnium promises to help him in the Silverbridge by-election, but the duke, now prime minister, refuses his support. Lopez claims he has been cheated, and presses the duke to pay his election expenses, to the duke's political embarrassment. Facing ruin, Lopez prefers death to exile, and walks in front of a train. The novel also records the duke's political difficulties. He is head of a rickety coalition, which he struggles to hold together for three years, while the duchess makes a determined attempt to support him as a hostess. This austere novel was not among Trollope's popular successes.

primitivism The idea that civilization corrupts the virtues of simplicity and nobility, which can only be rediscovered in remote, undeveloped cultures. A predominantly 18th-century phenomenon, associated with the educational and philosophic theories of Jean-Jacques *Rousseau, it is descended from the classical concept of the Golden Age. Critics such as Richard *Hurd and poets like Thomas *Gray led a mid-century revaluation of medieval, Celtic, and Norse writing; Gray's *The *Progress of Poesy* includes a note on the 'extensive influence of poetic genius over the remotest and most uncivilized nations'. James *Macpherson's 'Ossian' was an attempt to recover the supposed simplicity of ancient Highland life, while Thomas *Percy's researches into early *ballads fed a growing taste for pre-classical simplicity. The phenomenon of the feral child, brought up by animals, also emerged: Lord *Monboddo wrote a preface to a French case history of a 'savage girl' in 1768. (Later versions of the idea appear in Rudyard *Kipling's Mowgli, and Edgar Rice *Burroughs's *Tarzan.) There was also great enthusiasm for travel writings about the 'noble savages' of the South Seas and elsewhere. Omai, brought from the Society Islands by James *Cook, was warmly welcomed in London in 1774 by men of the world like James *Boswell, and Sir Joshua *Reynolds, who painted a magnificent portrait of him; even Samuel *Johnson, who found the primitivist cult puerile and unrealistic, was impressed. The idea of the noble savage had been useful for campaigners against slavery since its ambivalent appearance in Aphra Behn's **Oroonoko*, and it was taken up by writers such as William *Cowper and Thomas *Day. George Colman's **Inkle and Yarico*, George Cumberland's *The *West Indian*, Elizabeth *Inchbald's *The Child of Nature* (1788), and Robert Bage's **Hermsprong* all stress the superiority of 'natural' education and simple living, values which continued into the *Romantic period.

PRIMROSE, Diana (*fl.* 1630) Author of a poem-sequence, *A Chain of Pearl, or A Memorial of...Queen Elizabeth* (1630), based on William *Camden's *Annals of Queen Elizabeth* (1615), which celebrates Elizabeth as a Protestant queen, and obliquely criticizes Charles I's pro-Catholic policies. See Germaine *Greer, *Kissing the Rod* (1988).

Prince, The *See* MACHIAVELLI, NICCOLÒ.

PRINCE, F. T. (Frank Templeton) (1912–2003) Poet, born in South Africa, and educated at Balliol College, Oxford, and Princeton. From 1957 to 1974 he was professor of English at Southampton University. His collections include *Poems* (1938), *Soldiers Bathing and Other Poems* (1954), and *Afterword on Rupert Brooke* (1977). *Collected Poems 1935–1992* was published in 1993. His very varied work ranges from dramatic monologues to lengthy meditations; from technical experiments with little-used verse forms (e.g. the Italian *strambotto*) to the immediacy and pictorial qualities of the title poem of *Soldiers Bathing*, which is a much-anthologized classic of the Second World War. He has been highly celebrated by such diverse modern poets as Geoffrey *Hill and John *Ashbery. His critical work includes *The Italian Element in Milton's Verse* (1951).

PRINCE, Mary (*c.*1788–?1834) Born into slavery in Bermuda. She was brutally treated by different masters in the Caribbean, escaping from one of them in London. She dictated her intimate and idiomatic autobiography, *The History of Mary Prince, a West Indian Slave*, which went into three editions in 1831.

See SLAVERY.

Princess, The: *A Medley* A poem by Alfred *Tennyson, published 1847. Some of the well-known lyrics ('The splendour falls', 'Ask me no more: the moon may draw the sea') were added in the third edition of 1850, but others, including 'Tears, idle tears' (composed in 1834 at Tintern) and 'Now sleeps the crimson petal, now the white', were included in the first. The poem opens with a description of a summer fete based on an event at Park House, near Maidstone, the home of his friend Edmund Lushington (1811–93). It purports to be a tale of fancy composed in turn by some young people, based on an old chronicle.

A prince has been betrothed since childhood to Princess Ida, daughter of neighbouring King Gama. She becomes a devotee of women's rights, rejects marriage, and founds a university. The prince and two companions, Cyril and Florian, gain admission to the university dressed as women, and are detected by the two tutors, Lady Psyche and Lady Blanche, who from different motives conceal their knowledge. The deceit is eventually detected by Ida, but not before the prince has had occasion to rescue her from drowning. Her determination is unshaken, and a combat ensues, between fifty warriors led by the prince and fifty led by Gama's son, during which the three comrades are wounded. The university is turned into a hospital, the prince urges his suit, and he wins Ida (or at least he probably does), envisaging a future in which 'The man [may] be more of woman, she of man'; the epilogue is a plea for gradual social reform: 'Maybe wildest dreams | Are but the needful prelude of the truth.' The work was well received on the whole, an important statement about the public reach of poetry and, in particular, on the topical subject of women's education. It formed the basis of the satirical *Gilbert and Sullivan operetta *Princess Ida* (1884).

Princesse de Clèves, La *See* LAFAYETTE, MARIE-MADELEINE DE LA VERGNE.

PRINGLE, David (1950–) Scottish editor and critic, publisher/editor of **Interzone* magazine 1988–2004.

PRINGLE, Thomas (1789–1834) Poet, who studied at Edinburgh University, became a friend of Walter *Scott, and was briefly editor of the *Edinburgh Monthly Magazine* (later **Blackwood's Magazine*), the first of several editorships. In 1809 he published his first volume of poems, which included 'The Emigrant's Farewell', and emigrated to South Africa. He is chiefly remembered as a poet of that country. His *Ephemerides* (1828) and *African Sketches* (1834) reveal his sympathetic interest in the native peoples and wildlife of Africa, and contain some powerful poems, such as 'The Hottentot' and 'Afar in the Desert', which was highly praised by S. T. *Coleridge.

PRIOR, Matthew (1664–1721) Poet and diplomat, educated at Westminster School and St John's College, Cambridge. He joined with Charles Montagu, later earl of Halifax (1661–1715), in *The Hind and the Panther Transvers'd to the Story of the Country Mouse and the City Mouse* (1687), a satire against John *Dryden. His poem 'The Secretary' (1696) reflects his diplomatic experience as secretary to the ambassador at The Hague during negotiations for the Treaty of Ryswick (1697). His *Carmen Seculare* (1700) celebrates the arrival of William III, but Prior later joined the Tories and in 1711 went to Paris as a secret agent during the negotiations leading to the Treaty of Utrecht (1713). He was recalled on Queen Anne's death and imprisoned for over a year. A magnificent folio edition of his poems, produced with the advice of Alexander *Pope, was published by Jacob *Tonson in 1719 after his release; this gained Prior enough money in subscriptions, with extra assistance from Robert *Harley, to purchase Down Hall in Essex, celebrated in *Down-Hall, a Ballad* (1723). Prior wrote many occasional verses, epigrams, and bawdy pieces, but also large-scale didactic poems such as *Solomon, or The Vanity of the World* (1718). 'Henry and Emma' (1709) (described by William *Cowper as 'enchanting') is a sentimental burlesque of the old ballad 'The Nut-Brown Maid'. See his *Literary Works*, ed. H. B. Wright and M. K. Spears, 2 vols (1959).

'Prioress's Tale, The' *See* CANTERBURY TALES, 16.

Prisoner of Chillon, The A dramatic monologue principally in rhymed octosyllabics by Lord *Byron, written in 1816 after a visit with P. B. *Shelley to the castle of Chillon on Lake Geneva, and published in the same year. It deals with the imprisonment of the Swiss patriot François de Bonnivard (1496–1570), who in the poem describes his years spent chained with his two brothers in the castle's dungeons. He survives their slow deaths, and in time his guards relax their vigilance, and he is able to glimpse the outside world from his barred windows. At first tormented by the vision of the lake, the mountains, and the joy of nature, he is finally reconciled to his fate, consoled by 'long communion' with his fellow inmates, the mice and the spiders: when he is released he leaves his hermitage 'with a sigh'. This simple and powerful work of dignified resignation became one of Byron's most popular poems.

Prisoner of Zenda, The With its sequel **Rupert of Hentzau*, novels by Anthony Hope (*Hawkins), published 1894 and 1898. They deal with the perilous and romantic adventures of Rudolf Rassendyll, an English gentleman, in Ruritania, where, by impersonating the king (to whom he bears a marked physical resemblance), he defeats a plot to usurp him. He falls in love with the king's betrothed, Princess Flavia, and she with him, but gallantly relinquishes her to the restored king. In the sequel he vanquishes the villain Rupert of Hentzau, and has another chance of taking the throne and of marrying Flavia. But he is assassinated before his decision is known. *The Prisoner of Zenda* has repeatedly been adapted for film and television, and the swashbuckling 1937 version (starring Ronald Colman and Douglas Fairbanks, Jr) was especially memorable.

PRITCHETT, Sir V. S. (Victor Sawdon) (1900–97) Novelist, critic, and short story writer. He was born in Ipswich, the son of a travelling salesman who was a Christian Scientist, and spent his childhood in the provinces and various London suburbs before attending Alleyn's School, Dulwich, which he left at 15 to work in the leather trade. He went to Paris at the age of 21, and then became a journalist, writing for the *Christian Science Monitor*, before settling to a literary life in London. His first book, *Marching Spain* (1928), described a journey he had made across that country. Pritchett, an enthusiastic traveller, was to return to the travel-writing genre throughout his long career, most notably in *The Spanish Temper* (1954) and *Foreign Faces* (1964). His first novel, *Clare Drummer* (1929), was followed by several others, including *Dead Man Leading* (1937) and *Mr Beluncle* (1951), but he is principally known for his short stories, which began to appear in magazines in the 1920s. *The Spanish Virgin and Other Stories* (1930) was the first of many collections, including *You Make your Own Life* (1938), *When my Girl Comes Home* (1961), and *The Camberwell Beauty* (1974). Two volumes of *Collected Stories* appeared (1982, 1983). Pritchett was a great admirer of Chekhov and his stories are distinguished by the same shrewd observation of the quirks of human nature and humane irony found in the Russian writer. Pritchett's other works include *The Living Novel* (1946), studies of *Balzac (1973), *Turgenev (1977), and *Chekhov (1988), and two volumes of much-praised autobiography, *The Cab at the Door: Early Years* (1968), an account of a peripatetic childhood spent flitting with his family from lodgings to lodgings as a result of his improvident father's frequent business failures, and *Midnight Oil* (1971), which takes the story of his life to the end of the Second World War. He also edited the *Oxford Book of Short Stories* (1981). As reviewer, he contributed most regularly to the *New Statesman*, of which he was a director from 1946 to 1978. There is a biography (2005) by Jeremy Treglown.

Private Memoirs and Confessions of a Justified Sinner, The A novel by James *Hogg, published 1824, a macabre and original tale, inviting psychological as well as literary interpretation. In the first part of the book Colwan, believing himself to be 'saved' according to the Calvinist doctrine of predestination, and under the influence of a malign stranger who may be interpreted as his evil alter ego, commits a series of horrifying crimes, including the murder of his half-brother. The second section of the book purports to be a memoir written by Colwan, discovered when his grave was opened a century after his suicide. This reveals that he also murdered his mother, a girl, and a preacher, all under the supposed auspices of divine justice, before coming to believe that the stranger who haunts him is in fact the devil. His skull, on exhumation, is found to have two horn-like protuberances. A powerful mixture of *Gothic and psychological fiction, the book has come to be seen as Hogg's masterpiece. The French critic and novelist André *Gide declared that he read 'this astounding book...with a stupefaction and admiration that increased at every page'. The standard edition is by P. Garside (2001).

private presses Presses distinguished by aims that are aesthetic rather than commercial and by printing for the gratification of their owners rather than to order. Many such presses have been set up by enthusiasts for printing and publishing: well-known early examples include Horace *Walpole's 18th-century Strawberry Hill and Sir Thomas *Phillipps's 19th-century Middle Hill presses. At the end of the 19th century private presses were established as a protest against the low artistic standards and degradation of labour in the printing trade. William *Morris set up the Kelmscott Press (1891–8) with this object. He was followed by others, notably C. H. St John Hornby (1867–1946), who founded the Ashendene Press (1895), Charles *Ricketts (the Vale Press, 1896), and T. J. Cobden-Sanderson (1840–1922) and Emery Walker (1851–1933), who established the Doves Press in 1900. The *Cuala Press was established in Ireland in 1902. The 1920s saw the foundation of the *Golden Cockerel, the *Gregynog, and the *Nonesuch presses, and a considerable revival of interest in the art of wood engraving. The term 'private press' is sometimes applied, perhaps unjustifiably, to such publishing companies as Nonesuch, which used commercial printers and called itself 'architects rather than builders' of books. See Roderick Cave, *The Private Press* (2nd edn, 1983).

problem play A term used in two distinct senses, to denote either a play about a social issue such as prison conditions or women's rights, or a *Shakespearian play that some critics have found hard to accept as a *comedy because of its dark or cynical mood (thus a synonym for *tragicomedy). In the latter sense, three plays written at the start of the 17th century were often grouped as 'problem' cases by commentators in the early 20th century: **Measure for Measure*, **All's Well That Ends Well*, and **Troilus and Cressida*, with some critics placing **Hamlet* and **Timon of Athens* in the same category on the psychological basis of Shakespeare's supposed dejection during that phase. The former sense is applied chiefly to dramas written under the influence of *Ibsen in the 1890s and early 20th century, by G. B.*Shaw, *Galsworthy, and others.

PROCTER, Adelaide Anne (1825–64) Poet, daughter of B. W. Procter ('Barry *Cornwall'). She was Charles *Dickens's most published poet in **Household Words*. She lived in London and was a leading member of the Society for Promoting the Employment of Women as well as supporting a hostel for homeless women and children in east London. In addition to her widely admired devotional lyrics Procter wrote witty, ironic poems about women's position ('A Woman's Last Word' is a rewriting of Robert *Browning's poem of the same title) and some lyrical ballads which draw attention to the position of fallen and single women at mid-19th century. She also wrote some humane lyrics about the Crimean War. Her most famous poem, 'A Lost Chord' (*Legends and Lyrics*, 1858–61), was memorably set to music by Arthur *Sullivan. See Gill Gregory, *The Life and Work of Adelaide Procter: Poetry, Feminism and Fathers* (1998).

PROCTER, Brian Waller *See* CORNWALL, BARRY.

Prodigal Son The general subject of a group of plays written about 1540–75, showing the influence of the continental neo-classic writers of the period, particularly Gnaphaeus in his *Acolastus*, on early Tudor dramatists and novelists. The chief of these are *Misogonus*, dating from about 1560 (author unknown), *Jacke Jugeler* (?1562), and George *Gascoigne's *Glasse of Government* (1575). The parable of the Prodigal Son is in Luke 15: 11–32. The theme continued to appeal to dramatists, as in Shakespeare's **Henry IV* plays and the pseudo-Shakespearian *The *London Prodigal*.

Professor, The A novel by Charlotte *Brontë, written in 1846 (before **Jane Eyre*), but not published until 1857. The story is based, like **Villette*, on the author's experiences in Brussels, and uses much of the same material, though the two principal characters are transposed. William Crimsworth, an orphan, after trying his hand at trade in the north of England, goes to seek his fortune in Brussels. At the girls' school where he teaches English he falls in love with Frances Henri, an Anglo-Swiss pupil-teacher and lace mender, whose Protestant honesty and modesty are contrasted with the manipulating duplicity of the Catholic headmistress, Zoraide Reuter. Crimsworth resists Mlle Reuter's overtures; she marries the headmaster of the neighbouring boys' school, M. Pelet. Crimsworth resigns his post, and is able to marry the firm-minded Frances. They establish a school together, and their shared labours, and the fruits of judicious investment, enable them eventually to give up teaching, and to return to England.

Progress of Poesy, The A Pindaric *ode by Thomas *Gray, written 1751–4, published 1757, describing the different kinds of poetry, its primitive origins, and its connections with political liberty. He recounts its progress from Greece, to Italy, to Britain, celebrating particularly William *Shakespeare, John *Milton, and John *Dryden, but finding no 'daring spirit' to continue their line.

PROKOFIEV, Sergei (1891–1953) Russian composer, prolific in many genres, including the film score. His children's tale for narrator and orchestra *Peter and the Wolf* (1936) is well known to English audiences. Towards the end of his self-imposed exile (1918–36) Prokofiev was commissioned to compose music for a theatrical experiment combining excerpts from George Bernard *Shaw's *Caesar and Cleopatra*, Shakespeare's **Antony and Cleopatra*, and Alexander *Pushkin's *Egyptian Nights*, performed in Moscow in 1935. The first version of Prokofiev's ballet *Romeo and Juliet* (1935) was turned down by the Bolshoi Theatre as unsuitable for dancing: the composer revised his score (toying with the idea of a happy ending and supplying extra music at the request of choreographers) and it was finally performed in Leningrad in 1940. In 1939 he composed incidental music for **Hamlet*; he also wrote scores for versions of Pushkin's *Boris Godunov* and *Yevgeny Onegin* (1936). His opera *Betrothal in a Monastery*, based on Richard Brinsley Sheridan's *The *Duenna*, is a brightly lyrical score from which the *Socialist Realism of some of his later work is absent. It was completed by 1941, but not performed until 1946, after the premiere of his greatest opera, the epic adaptation of Lev *Tolstoy's *War and Peace*.

prolepsis An anticipation, either in rhetoric or in narrative: thus the use of a descriptive term prior to the circumstances that would make it truly applicable (Hamlet: 'I am dead, Horatio'); or a 'flashforward' in which a story is interrupted by an account of events that should come much later.

promessi sposi, I Novel by Alessandro *Manzoni first published in 1827 and in the definitive, linguistically revised form in 1840. By far the best-known work of Italian 19th-century fiction, the story is set in 17th-century Lombardy, but Manzoni uses this setting to comment on Italian politics and society, and the Catholic Church of his own day. The novel owes much to the European, especially English, novel of the 18th century, but contains important innovations, such as the choice of protagonists from the working/peasant classes. See *The Betrothed*, trans. B. Penman (1983).

Prometheus (meaning 'Forethought') Appears in Greek myth as one of the *Titans, descended from the original union of Uranus and Gaia. In some stories he is the creator of mankind and he is always their champion. He is supposed to have stolen fire for them from heaven when they were denied it by Zeus, and to have been punished by being fastened to a cliff in the Caucasus where an eagle tore daily at his liver. *Hesiod explains Zeus' enmity to Prometheus and his human dependants by stating that Prometheus had played a trick on him over a sacrifice. In *Aeschylus' *Prometheus Bound* he is the bringer of civilization to mankind and he refuses, despite his sufferings, to submit to the tyrant Zeus. The modern popularity of the myth dates from the 1770s with *Goethe's *Prometheus*. P. B. *Shelley's **Prometheus Unbound* is a highly original sequel to Aeschylus' version; Mary *Shelley's **Frankenstein*, subtitled *The Modern Prometheus*, also reinterprets the myth. Modern retellings include William *Golding's *Pincher Martin* and Ted *Hughes's *Prometheus on his Crag*.

Prometheus Unbound A lyrical drama in four acts by P. B. *Shelley, written in Italy 1818–19, published 1820. It is partly mythical drama and partly political allegory. Shelley began with the idea of completing the Aeschylean story of *Prometheus the fire-bringer and champion of mankind, who is bound to his rock for all eternity by a jealous Jupiter. He combined this with his view of Satan as the hero of **Paradise Lost*, and of God as the Oppressor. Rewriting or updating these two myths, he presents a Prometheus-Lucifer figure of moral perfection and 'truest motives', who is liberated by 'alternative' and benign forces in the universe and triumphs over Tyranny in the name of all mankind. The work is executed in a bewildering variety of verse forms: rhetorical soliloquies, dramatic dialogues, love songs, dream visions, lyric choruses, and prophecies.

Act I shows Prometheus chained in agony, 'in a ravine of Icy rocks in the Indian Caucasus', comforted by his mother Earth, but tempted to yield to Jupiter's tyranny by Mercury and the Furies. Act II introduces Asia and Panthea, the lovely daughters of Ocean, who decide to release Prometheus by confronting the ultimate source of power, *Demogorgon, a volcanic force dwelling in a shadowy underworld. Act III abruptly presents Jupiter vanquished by the eruption of Demogorgon, and Prometheus released and united with his beloved Asia. Their child, the Spirit of the Hour, prophesies the liberation of mankind. Act IV is a cosmic coda, or *epithalamium, sung by a chorus of Hours, Spirits, Earth, and Moon.

The sexual, scientific, and political symbolism of the drama have been variously interpreted, but the concept of liberation is central. The work has an important preface on the role of poetry in reforming society, which links with the **Defence of Poetry*.

PROPERTIUS, Sextus (55/47–15/2 BC) Roman poet, whose four books of elegies celebrate his passion for 'Cynthia'. His poetry ranges from poems of rare elegance and refinement to allusively mythological pieces in the

*Hellenistic tradition to which he was deeply indebted, presenting himself as the Roman *Callimachus. A. E. *Housman prepared an unpublished edition. He is the subject of Ezra *Pound's 'Homage to Sextus Propertius' (1919). See John Patrick Sullivan, *Ezra Pound and Sextus Propertius* (1965).

Prophetic books The name sometimes given to the symbolic and prophetic poems of William *Blake, including *The Book of *Urizen, The Book of Los, *Milton,* and **Jerusalem*.

prose poetry A term usually applied to short, self-contained passages of lyrical prose. It is closely connected with Charles *Baudelaire, and with Arthur *Rimbaud. Baudelaire's *Petits Poèmes en prose* (1869) were translated by Arthur *Symons and appeared as *Poems in Prose* in 1905. In the same year, *Poems in Prose* by Oscar *Wilde was privately printed. Wilde's six prose poems had previously appeared in the **Fortnightly Review* in 1894. In 1906, Edward *Thomas observed that the prose poem 'has never had a real vogue' (Jon *Stallworthy calls it 'the no man's land between prose and poetry'), but it has had some prominent 20th-century exponents, including Geoffrey *Hill. Like *free verse, to which it is akin, prose poetry is associated with literature of the 19th century and later, but not exclusively. In literary criticism, it had long been widely held that poetry need not be in verse. Philip *Sidney says that 'there have been many most excellent poets that never versified'. *Wordsworth notes that 'much confusion has been introduced into criticism by this contradistinction of Poetry and Prose, instead of the more philosophical one of Poetry and Matter of Fact, or Science'. Prose poetry is sometimes distinguished from poetic prose, the latter term applying to passages within longer prose works, but novels or non-fiction are frequently described as containing prose poetry. Extracts from George *Borrow, Sir Thomas *Browne, Thomas *De Quincey, Walter *Pater, and others could stand alone as prose poems. W. B. *Yeats took from Pater's *Studies in the History of the Renaissance* (1873) the famous description of the *Mona Lisa* and, without changing a word, set it out as poetry at the start of *The Oxford Book of Modern Verse* (1936). According to Edward Thomas, 'Borrow really wrote about six prose-poems; yet he now wearies us with six bad books'. Quoting from Baudelaire, Symons speaks of 'the miracle of a poetic prose, musical without rhythm and without rhyme'. See Margueritte S. Murphy, *A Tradition of Subversion* (1992); Mary Ann Caws and Hermine B. Riffaterre (eds), *The Prose Poem in France* (1983).

prosody *See* METRE.

prosopopeia *See* PERSONIFICATION.

'Prosopopoia' The main title of Edmund *Spenser's *'Mother Hubberds Tale'.

protagonist The central or leading character in a story or drama, usually although not necessarily the hero or heroine of the piece. In popular usage, the term has come to mean advocate or champion, regardless of the original dramatic sense; and the commonly found phrase 'main protagonist' is a *pleonasm.

Protestantism Summary term for the convictions and practices shared, to a greater or lesser extent, by the religious traditions deriving from the movements that constitute the *Reformation. The term originated in the *Protestatio* issued by those princes and cities of the Holy Roman Empire who dissented from the prohibition of the teachings of Martin *Luther agreed at the Diet of Speyer in 1529.

Protestantism encompasses the beliefs and practices of the various churches established in northern and western Europe in the 16th and 17th centuries in both the Lutheran and the subsequent Reformed tradition deriving from John *Calvin. Its characteristics are: repudiation of the overarching authority of the pope and the development of separate church polities and ministerial orders; a homiletic and pastoral, rather than sacerdotal, conception of ministry; an emphasis on the importance of faith, rather than works, in the scheme of salvation; a stress on the individual commitment of believers rather than upon obedience to ecclesiastical authority, with a consequent fostering of individualism and introspection; a prioritizing of biblical authority (in the vernacular) over ecclesiastical tradition; a hostility to images; and a tendency towards democratic habits of thought. To disseminate these ideas Protestantism made active use of the printing press and it played a very significant part in encouraging literacy, the habit of reading, and the development of a general reading public in England in the early modern period. The English literary tradition was to remain overwhelmingly Protestant in sensibility until the late 19th century.

Prothalamion A 'Spousall Verse' written by Edmund *Spenser, published 1596, to celebrate the double marriage of Lady Elizabeth and Lady Katherine Somerset, the earl of Worcester's daughters. Each verse ends with 'Sweete *Themmes* runne softly, till I end my Song'. Spenser formed the title on the model of his **Epithalamion*.

PROUDHON, Pierre-Joseph (1809–65) French social philosopher and political activist. His writings laid the basis for the organized anarchist movement in France, and exercised considerable influence on the thought and practice of anarchist and socialist movements throughout Europe. His works include *Qu'est-ce que la propriété?* (1840: *What is Property?*), which begins with the celebrated paradox: 'La propriété, c'est le vol!' ('property is theft'); *L'Idée générale de la révolution* (1851: *The General Idea of Revolution*); *De la justice dans la révolution et dans l'église* (1858: *Of Justice in the Revolution and the Church*); and *De la capacité politique de la classe ouvrière* (1865: *Of the Political Capacity of the Working Class*). His prose style was admired by Charles *Baudelaire and Gustave *Flaubert, and his influence extended to such figures as the painter Gustave Courbet (1819–77) and Leo *Tolstoy, as well as to large numbers of political activists in Italy, Spain, Russia, and elsewhere.

PROULX, E. A. (Annie) (1935–) American novelist, born in Connecticut of French Canadian parents, who has achieved critical and commercial success since her first novel, *Postcards* (1991), made her the first woman to win the PEN/Faulkner prize. Her second, *The Shipping News* (1993), won her other awards and a large British readership. In both of these, in *Accordion Crimes* (1996), and in her collected short stories (*Heart Songs and Other Stories*, USA 1988; *Heart Songs*, UK 1995) she combines two powerful strands of American writing: a regionalist emphasis on particular places and an encyclopedic attempt to grasp the diversity of America. For her short story 'Brokeback Mountain' (1997; a successful film version was released in 2005), she dropped the 'E' and published as Annie Proulx. *That Old Ace in the Hole* (2002) takes place in the Texas panhandle, continuing her preference for rural settings.

PROUST, Marcel (1871–1922) French novelist, essayist, and critic, author of **À la recherche du temps perdu* (1913–27). In the 1890s Proust moved in the most fashionable Parisian circles, but in later years became a virtual recluse, dedicating himself to the completion of *À la recherche*, which occupied him until the end of his life. In 1896 he published a collection of essays, poems, and short stories, *Les Plaisirs et les jours* (*Pleasures and Regrets*), and in the period *c.*1896–1900 worked on an early version of *À la recherche* which was published posthumously, as *Jean Santeuil*, in 1952. He was actively involved, on the side of Alfred *Dreyfus, in the Dreyfus case of 1897–9. Around 1899 he discovered John *Ruskin's art criticism, and subsequently translated Ruskin's *The Bible of Amiens* and *Sesame and Lilies* into French. In 1919 he published a collection of literary parodies, *Pastiches et mélanges*. He explored his own literary aesthetic in *Contre Sainte-Beuve* (1954: *By Way of Sainte-Beuve*), where he defines the artist's task as the releasing of the creative energies of past experience from the hidden store of the unconscious, an aesthetic which found its most developed literary expression in *À la recherche*. See Jean-Yves Tadié, *Marcel Proust*, trans. E. Cameron (2000).

PROUT, Father Pseudonym of Francis *Mahony.

Provençal, *or langue d'oc* (as distinct from the **langue d'oïl*) The language of the southern part of France, and the literary medium of the *troubadours. Their language was a *koiné*, a class language avoiding marked regional features; it was known as *lemosi* (Limousin), probably because some of the most famous troubadours came from the area around Limoges. Provençal declined as a literary language after the defeat of the south in the Albigensian War. The language is now generally called *occitan*, though the terms Provençal and *langue d'oc* are still in use (but *see also* Félibrige). Provençal literature in the medieval period consisted chiefly of the lyric poetry composed by the troubadours for the feudal courts of the Midi, northern Italy, and Spain. The *canso*, the love song in the courtly style which was the troubadours' special achievement, was known all over Western Europe, and inspired the courtly poetry of northern France, the Minnesang of Germany (*see* Minnesänger), and the Petrarchan poetry of Italy. The *sirventes*, the satirical poem mostly on political or moral themes, was also much cultivated by the troubadours. There is little literature of an epic kind, or literature in prose, extant in Old Provençal, and Provençal was considered the language *par excellence* of lyric poetry, courtly in content and very elaborate in style. This poetic flowering came to an end with the decline, after the Albigensian crusade, of the aristocratic society which had produced it. See *Anthology of Troubadour Lyric Poetry*, ed. A. R. Press (1971).

Proverbs, Book of *See* Bible.

Proverbs of Alfred, The An early Middle English poem, surviving in four manuscripts from the 13th century. The poem's 600 lines comprise a section of proverbial instructions concerning the government of society (written *c.*1150–65) and one of parental instruction (written *c.*1200). The attribution of the proverbs to Alfred is no more than traditional, as in *The *Owl and the Nightingale*. See *The Proverbs of Alfred: An Emended Text*, ed. and trans. Olaf Arngart (1978).

'Proverbs of Hell' *See* Marriage of Heaven and Hell.

Provok'd Husband, The, *or A Journey to London* A comedy by Sir John *Vanbrugh, finished by Colley *Cibber from Vanbrugh's incomplete manuscript, produced 1728. Lord Townly, 'provok'd' by the extravagance of his wife, decides to separate from her and to make his reasons public. In Cibber's ending, this brings Lady Townly to her senses, and a reconciliation is promoted by Manly, Lord Townly's sensible friend. The 'journey to London' is performed by Sir Francis Wronghead, a country gentleman, with his family. Count Basset, an unprincipled gambler, plans to entice Wronghead's daughter into a secret marriage, and to effect a match between Wronghead's son and his own cast-off mistress. The plot is frustrated by Manly.

Provoked Wife, The A comedy by Sir John *Vanbrugh, produced 1697, but possibly written before *The *Relapse*. Its serious main plot centres on the unhappy marriage of Sir John and Lady Brute (played by Thomas *Betterton and Elizabeth *Barry in the first production) and incorporates quotation from John *Milton's divorce pamphlets. Flirtation and intrigue are supplied by the gallants Constant and Heartfree, Lady Brute's niece Belinda, and the jealous, affected Lady Fanciful. In a famous scene Sir John, disguised as a parson (or, in Vanbrugh's rewriting, as a woman), is arrested by the watch for brawling and returns home to find the two gallants hidden in a closet.

Provost, The A novel by John *Galt, published 1822, a book in which Galt's analytic skills are at their best. The provost, Mr Pawkie, reflects on the arts of authority and rule, and his own successful manipulation of them throughout his life. The ironic revelation of his self-righteous, contriving character is of more importance in this work than the Scottish social scene he describes.

PRUDENTIUS (Aurelius Prudentius Clemens) (348–after 405) A Christian Latin poet born in Spain, the composer of many hymns and of the *Psychomachia*, an allegorical account of the battle for the soul of man which was a very important influence on the development of medieval and Renaissance allegorical works. It is given extended attention in *The Allegory of Love* by C. S. *Lewis, who had little admiration for the work. It is translated (along with some of the hymns) in Harold Isbell's *The Last Poets of Imperial Rome* (1971).

'Prufrock, The Love Song of J. Alfred' A poem which became a keystone of *modernism, by T. S. *Eliot, written 1910–11, published 1915, and collected in *Prufrock* (1917).

Pryderi *See* MABINOGION.

PRYNNE, J. H. (Jeremy Halvard) (1936–) Poet, born in Kent and educated at Cambridge University. Following a year at Harvard he returned to Cambridge and secured a fellowship at Gonville and Caius College, where he taught until 2003, only retiring as college librarian in 2006. His first collection, *Force of Circumstance and Other Poems* (1962), bore similarities to Donald *Davie's gently modernist *Movement poetry, but his subsequent involvement in the British Poetry Revival exposed his work to the legacy of American Objectivism, particularly Charles *Olson, and shifted it in a more experimental direction. He has since suppressed his first volume. His work usually appears as pamphlets published by small local presses aligned with the so-called "Cambridge School'. Volumes of the late 1960s and 1970s—including *Kitchen Poems* (1968), *Aristeas* (1968), *Brass* (1971), *Wound Response* (1974), *High Pink on Chrome* (1975), and *Down Where Changed* (1979)—were collected as *Poems* in 1982, gaining a slightly broader audience for a poet whose desire for personal obscurity is often confounded with a perceived desire for poetic obscurity. The notorious difficulty of this work—its daunting erudition and syntactic innovation—has grown over time, say proponents, not to fulfil some esoteric or elitist urge but as a means of encouraging new forms of linguistic engagement with an increasingly heterodox human experience. During the 1980s, volumes like *The Oval Window* (1983), *Bands around the Throat* (1987), and *Word Order* (1989) developed concerns with physical human agency and the body as a site of interaction. *Not-You* (1993), *Her Weasels Wild Returning* (1994), and *For the Monogram* (1997) moved away from the smooth stylistics associated with the 'Cambridge School', casting even the smallest parts of speech in newly energized roles. He published in Chinese for the first time during this decade (as Pu Ling-en), and contemporary Chinese poetry has become a dominant influence on recent work, including *Pearls That Were* (1999), *Triodes* (2000), *Acrylic Tips* (2002), *Biting the Air* (2003), and *To Pollen* (2006). The comprehensive collection *Poems* (2nd edn, 2005) has cemented his reputation as the pre-eminent English experimentalist. His prose publications are numerous but uncollected.

PRYNNE, William (1600–69) Puritan pamphleteer. He was educated at Bath Grammar School and Oriel College, Oxford, and was a barrister of Lincoln's Inn. He wrote against *Arminianism from 1627, and endeavoured to reform the manners of his age. He published *Histriomastix*, an enormous work attacking stage plays, in 1633. For a supposed aspersion on Charles I and his queen in it he was sentenced by the Star Chamber, in 1634, to be imprisoned during life, to be fined £5,000, and to lose both his ears in the pillory. He continued to write in the Tower of London, and in 1637 was again fined £5,000, deprived of the remainder of his ears, and branded on the cheeks with the letters S. L. ('seditious libeller'), which Prynne humorously asserted to mean 'Stigmata Laudis' (i.e. of Archbishop *Laud). He was released by the Long Parliament, and his sentences declared illegal in November 1640. He continued an active paper warfare, attacking Laud, then the independents, then the army (1647), then, after being arrested by Colonel Thomas Pride, the government. In 1660 he asserted the rights of Charles II, and was thanked by him. He was MP for Bath in the Convention Parliament and was appointed keeper of the records in the Tower of London. He published his most valuable work, *Brevia Parliamentaria Rediviva*, in 1662. He published altogether about 200 books and pamphlets.

Psalms One of the books of the Old Testament, a collection of 150 poems traditionally ascribed to *David, king of Israel, though it is now assumed that they were written by several authors at different times, probably as a part of early Jewish *liturgy. The word 'psalm' originally meant a song sung to the harp. They cover a variety of subjects, for example praise of God and his creation (95, 100), thanks for the salvation of Israel (46, 115), and laments on behalf of the individual (42) or of Israel in exile (137). There are significant allusions to psalms in the New Testament (e.g. Matthew 21: 9; Acts 2: 25); *Jesus quotes Psalm 22 on the cross. Christian interpreters read the psalms as prefiguring the coming of Jesus and his relationship with the church, and for centuries they have been used for both public worship and private devotion. Miles *Coverdale's version in the *Book of *Common Prayer* has been far more influential than that in the Authorized Version (*see* BIBLE, THE ENGLISH). The popular metrical version by *Sternhold, Hopkins, and others, known as the Old Version (1562), was longer lasting than the New Version (1692) by *Tate and Brady designed to replace it. The Psalms have been translated and imitated by many English poets, including Thomas *Wyatt, Philip *Sidney and the countess of *Pembroke, George *Herbert, John *Milton, Joseph *Addison, Isaac

*Watts, and Christopher *Smart (whose *A Song to David* celebrates their supposed author, and whose *Jubilate Agno* displays many characteristics of antiphonal psalms).

Pseudodoxia Epidemica: *or Enquiries into Very Many Received Tenets, and Commonly Presumed Truths* Often referred to as *Vulgar Errors*; by Sir Thomas *Browne, first published 1646, revised and augmented 1650, 1658, and 1672. Whereas **Religio Medici* made him famous for wit, this, his longest work, established him as a man of learning. Fulfilling Francis *Bacon's desire in *The *Advancement of Learning* for a 'Calendar of Dubitations, or Problems' and a 'Calendar of False-hoods, and of popular Errors', it comprises one general book, treating of the sources and propagation of error (original sin, popular gullibility, logical fallacy, learned credulity and laziness, reverence for antiquity and authority, influential authors, and Satan), and six particular books, three on natural history (mineralogy, botany, zoology, physiology) and three on civil, ecclesiastical, and literary history (iconography, magic and folklore, chronology, historical geography, and biblical, classical, and medieval history). Browne examines more than 100 problems in the light of his extensive learning, the verdicts of reasoned argument, and the results of his own experiments and observations. The standard edition, comprising a critical text with introduction and full commentary, is by R. Robbins (1981).

psychoanalytic criticism A form of literary interpretation that employs the terms of psychoanalysis (like the unconscious, repression, the Oedipus complex) to illuminate aspects of literature in its connection with conflicting psychological states. The beginnings of this modern tradition are found in Sigmund *Freud's *The Interpretation of Dreams* (1900), which provides a method of interpreting apparently unimportant details of narratives as 'displacements' of repressed wishes or anxieties. Freud often acknowledged his debts to the poets, and his theory of the Oedipus complex is itself a sort of commentary upon *Sophocles' drama. He also attempted posthumous analyses of *Michelangelo, *Shakespeare, Ernst *Hoffmann, and other artists. Ambitious interpretations of literary works as symptoms betraying the authors' neuroses are found in 'psychobiographies' of writers, such as Marie Bonaparte's *Edgar Poe* (1935), which diagnoses sadistic necrophilia as the problem underlying Poe's tales. A more sophisticated study in this vein is Edmund *Wilson's *The Wound and the Bow* (1941). As Lionel *Trilling and others have objected, this approach risks reducing art to pathology. More profitable are analyses of fictional characters, beginning with Freud's own suggestions about Prince Hamlet, later developed by his British disciple Ernest Jones (1879–1958): Hamlet feels unable to kill his uncle because Claudius' crimes embody his own repressed incestuous and patricidal wishes, in a perfect illustration of the Oedipus complex. A comparable exercise is Wilson's essay 'The Ambiguity of Henry James' (1934), which interprets the ghosts in *The *Turn of the Screw* as imaginary projections of the governess's repressed sexual desires. A third possible object of analysis, after the author and the fictional protagonist, is the readership. Here the question is why certain kinds of story have such a powerful appeal to us, and numerous answers have been given in Freudian terms, usually focusing on the overcoming of fears (as in *Gothic fiction) or the resolution of conflicting desires (as in comedy and romance). Although Freud's writings are the most influential, some interpretations employ the concepts of heretical psychoanalysts, notably Alfred Adler (1870–1937), Carl *Jung, and Melanie Klein (1882–1960); or evolve their own partly Freudian schemes, as with Harold *Bloom. Since the 1970s, the theories of Jacques *Lacan have inspired a new school of psychoanalytic critics who illustrate the laws of 'desire' through a focus upon the language of literary texts. The advent of post-*structuralism has tended to cast doubt upon the authority of the psychoanalytic critic who claims to unveil a true 'latent' meaning behind the disguises of a text's 'manifest' contents. The subtler forms of psychoanalytic criticism make allowance for ambiguous and contradictory significances, rather than merely discover hidden sexual symbolism in literary works. See Elizabeth Wright, *Psychoanalytic Criticism* (2nd edn 1998).

PTOLEMY (Claudius Ptolemaeus) Lived at Alexandria in the 2nd century AD; a celebrated mathematician, astronomer, astrologer, and geographer. He devised a system of astronomy according to which the sun, planets, and stars revolved round the earth, generally accepted until displaced by that of *Copernicus. Combined with *Aristotle's natural philosophy, which saw Nature as orderly, hierarchical, and teleological, Ptolemaic astronomy when suitably Christianized formed the core of the medieval world picture. Ptolemy's work on this subject is generally known by its Arabic name of *Almagest*. His great geographical treatise remained a textbook until superseded by the discoveries of the 15th century. *Chaucer's Wife of Bath appeals to the authority of the *Almagest*, and the lustful astrologer Nicholas in 'The Miller's Tale' owns a copy.

Public Lending Right A right achieved by Act of Parliament in 1979. The idea that the author of a book (in copyright) should be paid for its use by a public, commercial, or other kind of lending library was first advanced by the novelist John Brophy (1899–1965) in 1951. It was then formally adopted by the *Society of Authors which conducted a prolonged campaign—for what became known as 'Public Lending Right' (PLR). The campaign was reinforced and brought ultimately to a successful conclusion by the Writers' Action Group—which was set up in 1972 by Brigid *Brophy (daughter of the campaign's originator) and Maureen *Duffy. Initially the campaign was opposed by many librarians, who feared that the payments to authors would have to come from library budgets. There was also disagreement among authors themselves over the nature of the proposed right and how the payments should be calculated. PLR was finally secured, not by amendment to the Copyright Act, but by a separate statute, followed three years later by the PLR scheme which set out detailed arrangements for the operation of the new right. The scheme is administered by the Registrar of PLR from an office in Stockton-on-Tees and is financed by a central government grant. Qualifying authors received their first payments in 1984.

publishing, subscription A system by which the author collected a pre-publication list of buyers prepared to pay for a book in advance; it was sometimes used to support deserving but impoverished authors such as Stephen *Duck and Robert *Burns, but more often to facilitate large-scale or multi-volume publications with high production costs or high prestige. Subscription lists were normally printed at the front of the ensuing publication. William *Caxton, in the late 15th century, secured promises of sales before producing major works, but the first book published by a fully developed form of the system was John Minsheu's *Guide into Tongues* of 1617. The system flourished most widely in the 18th century. Alexander *Pope's subscription list for his **Iliad* translation is the best example of assiduous lobbying rewarded with financial success, though in the *Epistle to Dr Arbuthnot* Pope mocked the importunity of authors: 'Others roar aloud, "Subscribe, Subscribe"'. Samuel *Johnson, who had great trouble with the list for his edition of Shakespeare, remarked, 'he that asks subscriptions soon finds that he has enemies'.

PUCCINI, Giacomo (1858–1924) Italian opera composer. Few of his completed operas have a strong connection with English literature: both *Madame Butterfly* (1904) and *La Fanciulla del West* (1910, from *The Girl of the Golden West*) are based on plays by the American actor-manager and playwright David Belasco, the former taken in its turn from a magazine story by John Luther Long. *La Bohème* (1896) perhaps derives something from Du Maurier's **Trilby*. At various stages of his career, he considered works based on **Enoch Arden*, **Oliver Twist*, Edward *Bulwer-Lytton's *Last Days of Pompeii*, and **Lorna Doone*.

Puck Originally an evil or malicious spirit or demon of popular superstition; from the 16th century the name of a mischievous, tricksy goblin or sprite, also called Robin Goodfellow and Hobgoblin. In this character he figures in William *Shakespeare's *A *Midsummer Night's Dream* (II. i. 40) and Michael *Drayton's **Nimphidia* (xxxvi).

PUDNEY, John Sleigh (1909–77) Poet, novelist, and journalist, born at Langley, Buckinghamshire, and educated at Gresham's School, in Norfolk, where he was a contemporary and friend of W. H. *Auden and Benjamin *Britten. His first volume of verse, *Spring Encounter* (1933), was followed by ten works of fiction, but he is principally remembered for his poem lamenting pilots who died in the war, 'For Johnny' ('Do not despair | For Johnny-head-in-air'), written while he was an intelligence officer with the RAF in 1941, and first published in the *News Chronicle*. It became one of the most quoted poems of the Second World War.

PUGH, Sheenagh (1950–) Poet, novelist, and translator, born in Birmingham and educated at the University of Bristol; she lives in Cardiff and identifies strongly with Wales. Her volumes include *Crowded by Shadows* (1977); *Earth Studies and Other Voyages* (1982); *Beware Falling Tortoises* (1987); *Sing for the Taxman* (1993), the title poem of which makes the country singer Willie Nelson's touring to clear his revenue debts a witty paradigm of artistic endeavour; *Stonelight* (1999); and *The Movement of Bodies* (2005). Pugh's poetry is marked by an ecological sensitivity and a defiantly populist directness of address. Her other writings include *Folk Music* (1999), a novel, and *The Democratic Genre* (2005), a study of fan fiction.

PUGIN, Augustus Welby Northmore (1812–52) Architect, son of the French artist Auguste-Charles Pugin (1762–1832). He was a protagonist and theorist of the *Gothic Revival, and developed his thesis that Gothic was the only proper Christian architecture in *Contrasts, or A Parallel between the Noble Edifices of the Fourteenth and Fifteenth Centuries and Similar Buildings of the Present Day, Shewing the Present Decay of Taste* (1836), an important work that foreshadowed John *Ruskin and Thomas *Carlyle's *Past and Present*. He wrote various other works on architectural and ecclesiastical matters, including *An Apology for the Revival of Christian Architecture in England* (1843), and was also responsible for designing the decorations and furniture for Charles Barry's Houses of Parliament. See Rosemary Hill, *God's Architect* (2007).

PULCI, Luigi (1432–84) Florentine poet of the circle of Lorenzo de' *Medici. His poem **Morgante maggiore* was the first romance epic to be written by an Italian, and his influence on *Ariosto and *Boiardo is clear. His poem was a major source for *Rabelais. He was much admired by Lord *Byron. See M. Davie, *Half Serious Rhymes: The Narrative Poetry of Luigi Pulci* (1998).

Pulitzer Prizes Annual prizes established since 1917 under the will of Joseph Pulitzer (1847–1911), an American newspaper proprietor of Hungarian birth, who used sensational journalism for the correction of social abuses. The prizes, which are confined to American citizens, are offered in the interest of letters (American history and biography, poetry, drama, and novel writing), music, and good newspaper work. A fund of $500,000 was set aside for the prizes, which are controlled by the School of Journalism at Columbia University.

PULLEIN-THOMPSON, Josephine (1924–), **Christine** (1925–2005), and **Diana** (1925–) Born in Wimbledon, Surrey; they attended Wychwood School, Oxford. The sisters began long and prolific careers as writers of pony stories by co-authoring *It Began with Picotee* (1946). See their autobiography, *Fair Girls and Grey Horses* (1996).

PULLMAN, Philip (1946–) Born in Norwich, educated at Ysgol Ardudwy, Harlech, and Exeter College, Oxford, children's writer whose reputation was established with the trilogy

His Dark Materials (1995–2000). Other works include an inventive quartet of novels (*The Ruby in the Smoke*, 1985; *The Shadow in the North*, first published as *The Shadow in the Plate*, 1986; *The Tiger in the Well*, 1990; *The Tin Princess*, 1994) set in the 19th century and featuring the female detective Sally Lockhart (played by Billie Piper in the 2006 television adaptation). Like all Pullman's fiction, they display an interest in storytelling, referencing the contents and conventions of Victorian melodrama while also deliberately including anachronistic elements: Sally conducts herself like a 20th-century feminist rather than a suffragette.

Pullman has written several innovative shorter books for younger readers that demonstrate his admiration for the *comic strips of his youth. *Spring-Heeled Jack* (1989) is a comic version of the story about the legendary character—in this case cast as a superhero—told through a combination of prose and graphics. The *metafictional and much darker *Clockwork* (1996, made into an opera in 2004) is about a wind-up prince whose mechanical heart is rusting away, Gretel, whose love saves him, the Faust-like Dr Kalmenius whose murderous wind-up model is on the loose, and the relationship between characters, stories, and their tellers. *I was a Rat!* (1999, televised 2001) follows one of the rats in the Cinderella story who is accidentally left as a page-boy when the clock strikes midnight. Although this story ends happily, many of Pullman's novels and tales for younger readers reject happy endings in favour of more realistic, emotionally challenging endings. *Lyra's Oxford* (2003) is what Pullman describes as a stepping-stone between the trilogy and a forthcoming sequel (*The Book of Dust*) that provides information about the Oxford in which Lyra, the central female character in *His Dark Materials*, lives. He has also written plays, including an adaptation of *Frankenstein* (1990) and *Sherlock Holmes and the Limehouse Horror* (1992).

Pullman is a notable reteller and creator of *fairy stories including short *picture books such as *Aladdin* (1995) and the novel-length *The Scarecrow and his Servant* (2004). Nicholas Tucker's *Darkness Visible* (2003) combines biography and analysis for a popular audience.

Punch The principal character in the most famous of English puppet plays, distinguished by humped back, hooked nose, and a tendency to beat his wife Judy and other victims: he is accompanied by his faithful dog Toby. The name of Punch came into the language after the Restoration through Pulcinella, a similar character in the **commedia dell'arte*.
See GUIGNOL.

Punch, *or The London Charivari* An illustrated weekly comic periodical, founded in 1841; at first a strongly radical paper, gradually becoming blander and less political. It suspended publication in 1992, was revived in 1996, and closed in 2002.

Various accounts have been given of this famous paper's birth. One or two illustrated comic papers had already appeared in London, notably Gilbert Abbott *À Beckett's *Figaro in London* (1831) and *Punchinello* (1832), illustrated by George *Cruikshank. It appears that the idea of starting in London a comic paper along the lines of Philippon's Paris *Charivari* first occurred to Ebenezer Landells, draughtsman and wood-engraver, who submitted it to Henry *Mayhew. Mayhew took up the proposal and enlisted the support of Mark *Lemon and Joseph Stirling Coyne (1803–68), who became the first joint editors. The first number appeared on 17 July 1841. Joseph Last was the first printer, and Landells the first engraver. Gilbert Abbott À Beckett and Douglas *Jerrold were among the original staff, soon joined by W. M. *Thackeray, Thomas *Hood, John *Leech, and John *Tenniel, among others. Shirley Brooks (1816–74) became editor in 1870, Tom *Taylor in 1874, and Francis *Burnand in 1880. Sir Owen Seaman was editor from 1906 to 1932; he was succeeded by E. V. Knox, 1932–49; Kenneth Bird (better known as the cartoonist 'Fougasse'), 1949–52; Malcolm *Muggeridge, 1953–7; Bernard Hollowood, 1958–68; William Davis, 1969–78; and Alan Coren (who introduced full-colour cartoon covers) from 1978. Contributors included Melvyn *Bragg, Hunter Davies, Benny Green, and Alan Brien.

The magazine's draughtsmen include Charles Keene (1823–91), who first contributed in 1851 and joined the staff in 1860, and George *du Maurier, who drew for the magazine from 1860 and joined the staff in 1864. Richard *Doyle's famous cover drawing was used from 1849 to 1956, to be replaced by a full-colour design, different each week. Punch and the dog Toby usually appeared on the cover until 1969, and the last vestige of Doyle's image disappeared from the inside pages in 1978. Ronald Searle, Bill Tidy, Michael Heath, Norman Thelwell, and Gerald Scarfe are among the cartoonists who contributed to the magazine in its later years. For an account of *Punch's* early history, see R. Altick, *Punch: The Lively Youth of a British Institution, 1841–1851* (1997); S. and A. Briggs, *Cap and Bell: Punch's Chronicle of English History in the Making, 1841–61* (1972).

puppet play *See* MOTION.

PURCELL, Henry (1659–95) English composer, who began his musical career as a chorister and later organist of the Chapel Royal, and at the age of 20 succeeded John *Blow, who had taught him, as organist at Westminster Abbey. Much of his output consists of anthems and other sacred works, with words by Abraham *Cowley, Nahum *Tate, Francis *Quarles, Thomas *Flatman, and others. He also set various secular odes and 'Welcome' songs for royal occasions. Throughout his career, Purcell wrote songs and catches (a type of musical round in which two or more voices sing the same tune, or variations on the same tune, beginning at different times), eventually amounting to some 250 in number; these range from simple tunes, almost like *folk song in manner, which could be sung by amateurs, to elaborate sequences of recitative and aria that developed the declamatory style introduced from Italy by Henry *Lawes and Matthew *Locke. Many of the songs were written for the 50 or so stage works (by Nathaniel *Lee, John *Dryden, Thomas *Shadwell, Thomas *D'Urfey, Thomas *Southerne, William *Congreve, and others) for which Purcell is known to have provided music; a theme from Purcell's music for Aphra *Behn's play *Abdelazer* was chosen by Benjamin *Britten for his set of variations, *The Young Person's Guide to the Orchestra* (1945). After the accession of William and Mary the court became less central to musical life than it had been under the Stuarts, though Purcell continued in his official posts and wrote birthday odes, and funeral music, for Queen Mary. Purcell's *opera *Dido and Aeneas* (modelled in part on Blow's *Venus and Adonis*) was written to a *libretto by Nahum Tate and performed by the young gentlewomen of Josias Priest's boarding school at Chelsea in 1689. Though short, *Dido* achieves a wide range of dramatic expression, from the ribald vitality of the sailors to the fiery exchanges between Dido and Aeneas and the dignified resignation of Dido's lament 'When I am laid in earth'. Purcell provided music for five 'semi-operas' in the last five years of his life, though only *King Arthur* (by Dryden, 1691) was written with Purcell's music in mind; the song 'Fairest Isle' comes in the fifth act. The music for *The Prophetess, or The History of Dioclesian* (1690), adapted from Francis *Beaumont and John *Fletcher by Thomas *Betterton, includes a well-known *masque, and *The Fairy Queen* (1692), an elaboration of *A *Midsummer Night's Dream*, consists almost entirely of masques: the longest of Purcell's dramatic works, it contains no setting of *Shakespeare's words. *The Indian Queen*, to a text by Dryden and Robert Howard (1626–98), and a final Shakespearian adaptation, Shadwell's arrangement of Dryden and Sir William *D'Avenant's version of *The *Tempest*, which includes settings of 'Come unto these yellow sands' and 'Full fathom five', were both performed in the last year of Purcell's life. 'The Author's extraordinary Talent in all sorts of Musick is sufficiently known', wrote John Playford in 1698, 'but he was especially admir'd for the *Vocal*, having a peculiar Genius to express the Energy of *English* Words, whereby he mov'd the Passions of all his Auditors.' Purcell's death was lamented to an unusual degree by his fellow musicians, and he was the subject of a famous sonnet by Gerard Manley *Hopkins.

PURCHAS, Samuel (1577–1626) Editor and publisher of travel literature, born at Thaxted, Essex, educated at St John's College, Cambridge, who held various church benefices, latterly in London. *Purchas his Pilgrimage*...(1613), essentially a religious geography, was followed in 1619 by *Purchas his Pilgrim...the Historie of Man*. In 1624–5 came his major work incorporating materials left by *Hakluyt, *Hakluytus Posthumus, or Purchas his Pilgrimes, Contayning a History of the World in Sea Voyages and Land Travell*. At 4,000 folio pages in four volumes this was the largest work ever printed in England. From the travels of the biblical patriarchs to the latest reports of English voyages, *Pilgrimes* covered the whole world in space and time. The first section, after an introductory book, contains accounts of voyages to India, China, Japan, Africa, and the Mediterranean. The second part deals with attempts to discover the North-West Passage, the Muscovy expeditions, and explorations of the West Indies and Florida. Among the best narratives are William Adams's description of his voyage to Japan and residence there and William Hawkins's account of the court of the great mogul at Agra. The collection became a source for later writers, notably *Dryden, *Milton in **Paradise Lost* and S. T. *Coleridge for **Kubla Khan*. Purchas used travel accounts for polemical religious purposes and was often a careless and irresponsible editor, so his reputation has been mixed, but his work remains an indispensable mine for historians.

PURDY, James (1923–2009) American novelist, born in Ohio, whose work explores homosexuality, family breakdown, and sexual experimentation. His first novels, *Malcolm* (1959) and *The Nephew* (1961), sold well, but his work has generally been undervalued in the USA, despite numerous awards. In addition to novels, he has also published a number of plays, short story collections, and volumes of poetry.

Purgatorio, *of Dante* *see* DIVINA COMMEDIA.

Puritan, The, *or The Widow of Watling-Street* A comedy published in 1607 as 'written by W.S.' and included in the third and fourth Shakespeare folios, but by some other hand, almost certainly Thomas *Middleton's. The play is a farcical comedy of London manners, concerned with the tricks played on the widow and her daughter by Captain Idle and George Pye-boord to win their hands, with scenes in the Marshalsea prison.

Puritanism The term 'Puritan' became current during the 1560s as a pejorative nickname for Protestants who wished to continue the process of *reformation beyond the compromise of the established Elizabethan Protestant church, which retained government by bishops and a liturgy modelled on that of Rome. Puritan dissent from this *via media* (middle way) ranged from declining to observe particular ceremonies to refusal to attend the parish church, rejection of the validity of episcopal orders, and separatism. Puritans came to propose a variety of alternative models of church government and, as they came into conflict with state authorities, a variety of alternative constitutional political models.

Puritanism desired to recover the purity of doctrine, simplicity of worship, commitment of ministry, and integrity of faith that was thought to characterize the first three Christian centuries, after which the ascendancy of the church of Rome had supposedly corrupted the Christian gospel. Its revolutionary politics, leading in the mid-17th century to Civil War, regicide, and the ensuing Republic and Protectorate of Oliver *Cromwell, hoped to create a constitutional order that would return to the godly practice of the early (or 'primitive' in the sense of 'pristine') church. The prospect of 'paradise regained' haunts the Puritan imagination of John *Milton and John *Bunyan, as of George *Fox and Richard *Baxter. Such aspirations, however, were readily lampooned as hypocrisy in the comedies of Ben *Jonson and *Shakespeare and in the poetry of Samuel *Butler.

See BAPTISTS; CONGREGATIONALISM; PRESBYTERIANISM; PROTESTANTISM; QUAKERS.

Purple Island, The See FLETCHER, PHINEAS.

PUSEY, Edward Bouverie (1800–82) Churchman, educated at Christ Church, Oxford, elected a fellow of Oriel College in 1823. In 1828 he was ordained deacon and priest, and appointed Regius professor of Hebrew. He became attached to the *Oxford Movement in 1833 and joined John *Keble and John Henry *Newman in contributing to the *Tracts for the Times*. Pusey's deep learning lent authority to the movement (which was often termed Puseyism by contemporaries), and when Newman withdrew in 1841 he became its leader. He was an influential preacher, and his sermon on 'The Holy Eucharist, a Comfort to the Penitent' (1843) was condemned for heresy by the university authorities. He was a stalwart defender of the doctrines of the High Church movement, and his passionate belief in the union of the English and Roman churches led him to try to discourage defections to the Roman Catholic Church.

PUSHKIN, Aleksandr Sergeevich (1799–1837) Russia's greatest poet, born in Moscow. From 1811 he attended the recently established Imperial Lyceum at Tsarskoe Selo, outside St Petersburg, where he began to write poetry. He entered government service, but was expelled from the capital in 1820 for writing revolutionary epigrams and permitted to return only in 1826. In the interim he had served in southern Russia until his dismissal in 1824 for 'atheism' and subsequently lived on his mother's estate at Mikhailovskoe, near Pskov. In 1831 he married Natalia Goncharova and it was the attentions paid to her by Baron Georges D'Anthès, a French royalist in Russian service, that led to the duel in which Pushkin was fatally wounded. Pushkin was prolific in a wide variety of genres, poetry and prose. It was his early narrative poems, beginning with *Ruslan and Ludmilla* (1820), that brought him initial popularity, particularly the so-called southern or *Byronic poems, *The Prisoner of the Caucasus* (1820–21), *The Fountain of Bakhchisarai* (1822), and *The Gypsies* (1824); but his mature masterpiece is *The Bronze Horseman* (1833), set during the great flood of 1824, when the statue of Peter the Great chases the distraught and fleetingly rebellious clerk Evgeny through the streets of Petersburg. It is another Evgeny who is better known to English audiences as the hero of Pushkin's finest work, his novel in verse *Eugene Onegin* (1823–31), available in no fewer than twelve English-language versions, beginning with Colonel Henry Spalding's in 1881, embracing *Nabokov's idiosyncratic unrhymed iambics and extraordinary commentary (1964; rev. edn 1977), and finishing with Roger Clarke's prose (2000), to stress 'novel' rather than 'verse'. It was however Charles Johnston's influential stanzaic version (1977) that inspired the first genuine attempt to emulate in English the poetry and form of Pushkin's great work, Vikram *Seth's *The Golden Gate* (1986). Pushkin's dramatic work includes the *blank verse historical drama *Boris Godunov* (1825) and the four 'Little Tragedies' (1830), while in prose, which increasingly attracted him in the 1830s, he wrote *The Tales of Belkin* (1830), *The Queen of Spades* (1834), *The Captain's Daughter* (1836), and historical works. Pushkin became widely read in English literature and was influenced at different times and to different degrees by the works of William *Shakespeare, Lord *Byron, Samuel *Richardson, Laurence *Sterne, Walter *Scott, and William *Wordsworth. First mentioned in the English press in 1821, Pushkin found his first translator in George *Borrow (*The Talisman: From the Russian of Alexander Pushkin, With Other Pieces*, St Petersburg, 1835) and an early champion and translator in Thomas Budge Shaw (*Blackwood's*, 1845). Every line that Pushkin wrote is now available in English in *The Complete Works of Alexander Pushkin* (15 vols, 1999–2003). See also T. J. Binyon, *Pushkin* (2002).

PUTTENHAM, George (1529–1590/91) Writer and critic; born in Hampshire, he was educated at Christ's College, Cambridge, and the Middle Temple. A nephew of Sir Thomas *Elyot, Puttenham was a quarrelsome man who was imprisoned on several occasions. He was almost certainly the author of *The Art of English Poesie*, although it has sometimes been ascribed to his brother Richard or to John, Lord Lumley. It was published anonymously in 1589, but a version may have been composed perhaps twenty years earlier. Both a critical treatise and a rhetorical manual, it is divided into three books, *Of Poets and Poesie*, *Of Proportion*, and *Of Ornament*, and is important as a record of early Elizabethan taste and theory. The author's tone is lively and personal; he mingles anecdotes with serious appraisal, illustrating the view that epitaphs should be brief by recounting that he was locked up in a cathedral by the sexton while reading a long one. He condemns John *Gower for 'false orthography', finds John *Skelton 'a rude railing rhymer and all his doings ridiculous', and praises Sir Thomas *Wyatt and the earl of *Surrey as the stars of a 'new company of courtly makers'. In the second book he discusses 'courtly trifles' such as anagrams, *emblems, and posies, showing a fondness for 'ocular representations'—in particular for poems shaped like eggs and pillars. The third book defines and illustrates various figures of speech, suggesting new common terms for Greek and Latin originals, like 'single supply, ringleader and middlemarcher' (zeugma, prozeugma, and mezozeugma), 'the dry mock' (irony), 'the bitter taunt' (sarcasm), and 'the over reacher' (hyperbole). He attacks excessive use of foreign words, but was aware of the rapidly changing vernacular. Among the illustrative quotations in the *Art* are extracts from poems in manuscript by *Elizabeth I, Edward *Dyer, and Philip *Sidney and from printed works including Richard *Tottel's *Miscellany* and volumes by George *Turbervile and George *Gascoigne. There are also extracts from Puttenham's own royal panegyric, *Partheniades*, which survives in a single manuscript, unlike the many copies of his defence of the execution of Mary Queen of Scots (written 1586–8). The *Art* was edited by G. D. Willcock and Alice Walker (1936).

PUZO, Mario (1920–99) American novelist of Sicilian origins, born in New York, best known for his novels dealing with the Mafia in the USA. His first novel was *The Dark Arena* (1955) but he achieved fame with *The Godfather* (1969), which was filmed with two sequels by Francis Ford Coppola. A follow-up volume of essays on the novel, *The Godfather Papers*, appeared in 1972. His last novel, *The Family* (2001), was completed by Carol Gino.

Pwyll In Welsh mythology, prince of Dyfed and 'head of Hades', the subject of the first story in *The* **Mabinogion*. The stories of Sir Pelleas and King Pelles in *Malory are perhaps connected with his myth. See J. Rhys, *Studies in the Arthurian Legend* (1891).

PYE, Henry James (1745–1813) He became *poet laureate in 1790, largely for political reasons, and was the constant butt of contemporary ridicule.

Pygmalion Legendary king who because of his disgust for real women made himself a beautiful statue with which he fell in love. *Venus, in answer to his prayer, then transformed her into a woman. *Ovid tells the story in *Metamorphoses*, Book 10, William *Shakespeare draws on it in *The* **Winter's Tale*; George Bernard *Shaw clothes it in modern dress in *Pygmalion*.

Pylon School A nickname for the group of younger left-wing poets of the 1930s, chiefly the 'MacSpaunday' group, W. H. *Auden, Cecil *Day-Lewis, Louis *MacNeice, and Stephen *Spender. Cyril *Connolly referred to them as the 'Pylon Boys', alluding to their rather self-conscious use of modern technology. Spender's poem 'The Pylons' was published in 1933, and pylons and skyscrapers appear in Day-Lewis's poem to Auden ('Look west, Wystan, lone flyer') in *The Magnetic Mountain* (1933). Auden's verse, such as 'Out on the lawn I lie in bed' (1933), features power stations, and landscapes of arterial roads and filling stations are evoked in, for instance, Auden and Christopher *Isherwood's *The Dog beneath the Skin* (1935). MacNeice's earlier poetry features many trains and trams (see, for instance, 'Birmingham', 1933).

PYM, Barbara (1913–80) Novelist, born in Oswestry, Shropshire, educated at Huyton College, Liverpool, and St Hilda's College, Oxford, where she read English. After serving in the Women's Royal Naval Service during the Second World War, she worked as an editor at the International African Institute in London from 1946 until 1974. The anthropological perspective this familiarized her with is apparent in the six novels, starting with *Some Tame Gazelle*, that she published between 1950 and 1961: wry comedies of manners that record the habits and habitats of predominantly celibate women and men, usually of literary tastes, in a High Anglican milieu. After the rejection of her seventh novel, *An Unsuitable Attachment*, in 1963 (it eventually appeared in 1982), she remained unpublished until David *Cecil and Philip *Larkin revived interest in her work by nominating her among 'the most underrated novelists of the century' in a **Times Literary Supplement* survey in 1977. The novels she subsequently published—*Quartet in Autumn* (1977), *The Sweet Dove Died* (1978), and *A Few Green Leaves* (1980)—are her finest, adding elegiac resonances to the ironic wit with which she scrutinizes the comedy and pathos of people who lead lives of decorous stoicism. A selection of her diaries, letters, and notebooks was posthumously published in 1984, edited by Hazel Holt, who also published a biography of her, *A Lot to Ask* (1990).

PYNCHON, Thomas (1937–) American novelist, born on Long Island, New York, and educated at Cornell University. His novels are less concerned with character than with the effects of historical and political processes on individual behaviour. Their fragmented *picaresque narratives are often based on outlandish quests, and blend paranoia, literary game-playing, bawdy humour, social satire, and fantasy. Science provides an important source of metaphor and subject matter. He began his first novel while working as a technical writer for the Boeing Aircraft Corporation. This was *V.* (1963), a long and complex allegorical fable interweaving the picaresque adventures of a group of contemporary Americans with the secret history of a shape-changing spy, 'V', who represents a series of female archetypes. *The Crying of Lot 49* (1966) is a paranoid mystery story mixing philosophical speculation with satirical observation of American culture in the 1960s. *Gravity's Rainbow* (1973) is a multi-layered black comedy set at the close of the Second World War: its convoluted plots and conspiracies reflect the socio-political processes threatening personal freedom. In *Vineland* (1990), a darkly humorous conspiracy thriller, participants in the 'counter-culture' of the 1960s face up to the conservative political scene of the 1980s. *Mason & Dixon* (1997) is a pastiche *historical novel, based on the adventures of the two 18th-century British surveyors who established the Mason–Dixon line, drawing parallels between the political and scientific upheavals of the Age of Reason and those of the late 20th century. *Against the Day* (2006) describes the uncertainties of the period from the Chicago World's Fair (1893) up to the impending outbreak of the First World War.

Pyrochles In Edmund *Spenser's **Faerie Queene*, symbolizes rage. He is the brother of Cymochles, the son of 'old *Acrates* and *Despight*' (II. iv. 41). On his shield is a flaming fire, with the words '*Burnt I do burne*'. Overcome by Sir *Guyon (II. v), he tries to drown himself in a lake to quench his flames. He is rescued and healed by *Archimago (II. vi. 42–51), and finally killed by Prince Arthur (II. viii).

pyrrhic *See* METRE.

PYTHAGORAS (*fl.* mid-6th century BC) A native of Samos who emigrated to Croton (Crotone) in the south of Italy, and there founded a movement that spread through southern Italy and Sicily; the movement continued after his death, but before long broke up, to be replaced in later centuries by scattered manifestations of 'Pythagoreanism', often distinguished by modern scholars as 'neo-Pythagoreanism'. While Pythagoras' name is associated especially with developments in mathematics (including 'Pythagoras' theorem') and musical theory, and with the idea of the 'transmigration' of souls ('metempsychosis',—their repeated incarnation in different bodies, whether human, animal, or plant), how much actually went back to Pythagoras is unclear. 'Pythagoreanism' itself varied between respectable scientific thinking, with later figures like Archelaus (5th century BC) and Philolaus (*c*.470–*c*.385 BC), and something more akin to folk wisdom. *Plato because of his Pythagorean borrowings is sometimes himself represented—mistakenly—as a neo-Pythagorean, not least by Marsilio *Ficino and others in the Renaissance.

Pythias *See* DAMON AND PYTHIAS.

Q

'Q' *See* JERROLD, DOUGLAS WILLIAM; QUILLER-COUCH, SIR ARTHUR.

Quakers Members of the Society of *Friends.

QUARITCH, Bernard (1819–99) Antiquarian bookseller. Born in Saxony, in London he was initially employed by Henry *Bohn, starting his own firm in 1847. He was the first to publish Edward *FitzGerald's *The Rubáiyát of *Omar Khayyám* (1859). His interests were wide and above all he was known as a dealer in *incunabula, fine manuscripts, bibles, Shakespeariana, early English literature, and cartography. The catalogues issued by the firm remain valuable bibliographical reference works.

QUARLES, Francis (1592–1644) Poet, born near Romford in Essex, educated at Christ's College, Cambridge, and at Lincoln's Inn. He made his reputation in the 1620s by a series of biblical paraphrases (e.g. *A Feast for Worms*, 1620), and in 1629 published a 'vain amatory poem', *Argalus and Parthenia*, based on an episode in Philip *Sidney's **Arcadia*. He is chiefly remembered for his extremely successful and popular **Emblems* (1635) and *Hieroglyphics of the Life of Man* (1638). In 1639 he was appointed chronologer to the City of London. From 1640 he turned to prose, publishing pamphlets, some anonymous, holding a constitutionalist–Royalist position. A petition circulated against him in 1644 accused him of popery, but Anthony *Wood declared that he was a Puritan. *Eclogues* (1646) and a comedy, *The Virgin Widow* (1649), were published posthumously. A nearly complete collection of his works was edited by Alexander *Grosart (3 vols, 1880–81), and additional poems by J. Hordern (1960).

Quarterly Review (1809–1967) Founded by John *Murray as a Tory rival to the Whig **Edinburgh Review*. Walter *Scott, who had been harshly reviewed in the *Edinburgh*, became an ardent supporter of the venture but refused the editorship. The journal stood for the defence of the established order, church, and Crown; its unwavering adherence to the bishops and the Church was satirized by Thomas Love *Peacock in **Melincourt*. Its tone was magisterial from the beginning, and its influence, both literary and political, was for the best part of the century matched only by that of the *Edinburgh*. The first editor, William *Gifford, brought with him several clever writers from the **Anti-Jacobin*, including George *Canning and John *Frere, but the quality of his chief writers (largely Scott and Robert *Southey) could not match that of the *Edinburgh*, who had William *Hazlitt, Thomas *Macaulay, Thomas *Carlyle, and Francis *Jeffrey, among many others. The *Quarterly's* enemies argued that its political bias strongly affected its literary criticism. However, unlike the *Edinburgh*, it supported the *'Lake School' and *Byron, although it fiercely condemned John *Keats, Leigh *Hunt, Hazlitt, Charles *Lamb, P. B. *Shelley, and later Alfred *Tennyson, Macaulay, Charles *Dickens, and Charlotte *Brontë. Two of its more famous early articles were those of Scott in praise of Jane Austen's **Emma*, and John *Croker's hostile review of Keats's *'Endymion'. Gifford was succeeded as editor in 1825 by John *Lockhart, who was followed by a distinguished line, including members of the Murray family. The journal ceased publication in 1967.

QUASIMODO, Salvatore (1901–68) Italian poet associated with *hermeticism, and translator of *Shakespeare, *Ruskin, and *Homer, awarded the *Nobel Prize (1959). His main collections are *Acque e terre* (1930: *Water and Land*), *Oboe sommerso* (1932: *Sunken Oboe*), and *Ed è subito sera* (1942: *And it's Suddenly Evening*). After the Second World War his hermeticism yielded to a more extrovert poetry of social conscience, as in *Con il piede straniero sopra il cuore* (1946: *With the Alien Foot on our Heart*), *La vita non è sogno* (1949: *Life Is Not Dream*), and *Dare e avere* (1966: *Giving and Having*). He has been translated by Richard *Wilbur.

quatrain A *stanza of four lines, or a group of four rhyming lines within a *sonnet. Varieties of quatrain stanza are distinguished by *metre and *rhyme scheme. The quatrain of rhymed *pentameters is known as the 'heroic quatrain'. More often found are those employing four-stress lines only (known as 'long measure') or in combination with three-stress lines arranged 4343 ('common measure', as in many *ballads) or 3343 ('short measure', as in some *hymns). The principal rhyme schemes are *abcb* (especially in ballads), *abab*, *aabb*, and *abba*; the quatrain of *octosyllabic lines rhyming *abba* is sometimes called the **In Memoriam* stanza.

QUEEN, Ellery Pseudonym created in 1928 by two American cousins, Daniel Nathan (Frederic Dannay) (1905–82) and Manford Lepofsky (Manfred Bennington Lee) (1905–71), who co-wrote numerous detective novels and stories under that name. In 1941 they founded *Ellery Queen's*

Mystery Magazine, which became a key outlet for *detective fiction.

Queen Mab A visionary and ideological poem by P. B. *Shelley, written in England and Wales during his early period of political activism, published privately 1813, when he was 21. The poem is in nine cantos, using 'didactic and descriptive' blank verse greatly indebted to *Milton and to Robert *Southey's *Thalaba*. Despite its lyrical opening, invoking 'Death and his brother Sleep' and Mab the Fairy Queen in her time-chariot, the poem largely consists of attacks on monarchy, war, commerce, and religion. In place of these Shelley celebrates a future of Republicanism, Free Love, Atheism, and Vegetarianism. The verse is furiously polemical in style, with occasional passages of grandiloquent beauty, such as Canto VIII, presaging Asia's speeches in **Prometheus Unbound*. Seventeen prose Notes are attached as appendices, many of them substantial essays, 'against Jesus Christ, & God the Father, & the King, & the Bishops, & Marriage, & the Devil knows what', as Shelley himself later put it. Note 9 on Free Love is especially striking, showing the influence of David *Hume, William *Godwin, Mary *Wollstonecraft, and Jean-Jacques *Rousseau. The work was extremely popular among working-class radicals, and ran to over a dozen cheap editions by 1840.

Queen's Maries (Marys), the The four ladies named Mary attendant on *Mary Queen of Scots. The list is variously given, including: Mary Seton, Mary Beaton, Mary Livingstone, Mary Fleming, Mary Hamilton, and Mary Carmichael. They are frequently mentioned in Scottish ballads.

Queen's Wake, The A poem by James *Hogg, published 1813. Seventeen bards hold a competition to welcome Mary Queen of Scots to Holyrood in 1561. Their 'songs' are verse tales in various styles. The supernatural tale *'Kilmeny', originally committed to an artificially archaic Scots but Anglicized for subsequent, extended editions of the poem, has been much admired and anthologized, as has the grotesque ballad 'The Witch of Fife'.

QUENEAU, Raymond (1903–76) French poet, novelist, and essayist. His works, deftly translated by Barbara Wright, experiment with literary form and explore the often problematic divergence between spoken and written language; the best known is *Zazie dans le métro* (1959: *Zazie in the Underground*; successfully filmed in 1960, dir. Louis Malle). He co-founded the *OuLiPo movement in 1960.

QUENNELL, Sir Peter (1905–93) Poet, biographer, and editor, born in Bromley, Kent, son of social historians Marjorie and C. H. B. Quennell, educated at Berkhamsted Grammar School and Balliol College, Oxford. He was editor of the **Cornhill Magazine* (1944–51) and founder and editor of *History Today* (1951–79). His first volume, *Masques and Poems* (1922), was followed by many other works, including *Four Portraits* (1945; studies of James *Boswell, Edward *Gibbon, Laurence *Sterne, and John *Wilkes) and works on Alexander *Pope, Lord *Byron, John *Ruskin, and Samuel *Johnson. He published two volumes of autobiography, *The Marble Foot* (1976) and *Wanton Chase* (1980). He received a knighthood in 1992 at the age of 87.

Quentin Durward A novel by Walter *Scott, published 1823. One of the most vigorous of Scott's novels, it is set in 15th-century France. It was Scott's first imaginative venture to the mainland of Europe, and his story of a young Scots soldier of fortune serving in the guard of Louis XI was enthusiastically received in Paris. Like many of Scott's novels, it deals with the breakdown of traditional chivalric values and the opposition (and here, the reconciliation) of romance and reality.

Quest for Corvo, The: *An Experiment in Biography* A life of Frederick *Rolfe by A. J. A. *Symons, published in 1934. This account dwells as much on the author's pursuit of his eccentric subject as on his findings, and established a new genre of biography, in which the biographer's difficulties are part of the story: see Ian *Hamilton's life of J. D. *Salinger, and Richard *Holmes, *Footsteps* (1985).

QUEVEDO Y VILLEGAS, Francisco de (1580–1645) Spanish satirist, courtier, and wit. He was educated in Madrid by the Jesuits and at the universities of Alcalá de Henares and Valladolid. He wrote the *picaresque novel *La vida del buscón* (1626: *The Life of the Scoundrel*), translated into English (through a French intermediary) by John Davies of Kidwelly (1657). His *Sueños* (1627: *Dreams*), which are biting satirical portraits of all classes of society, were translated by Richard Croshawe of the Inner Temple (from the French) as *Visions, or Hels Kingdome* (1640), and later by Roger *L'Estrange (1667). Quevedo also wrote political works, moral and theological treatises, and a wide variety of poetry.

quietism In its religious sense, a passive form of Christian *mysticism, in which the believer focuses entirely on the inner life and neglects social action and the outer life of the church. In its political sense it means accepting political or social conditions unquestioningly.
See GUYON, MADAME; FRIENDS, SOCIETY OF.

QUILLER-COUCH, Sir Arthur (1863–1944) Son of a Cornish doctor, educated at Clifton College, Bristol, and Trinity College, Oxford, where he began writing parodies under his lifelong pseudonym 'Q'. His writing career opened with a novel of adventure, *Dead Man's Rock* (1887), after which followed a vast output of fiction, verse, anthologies, and literary journalism. In 1900 he edited the first *Oxford Book of English Verse*, which had considerable influence and large sales. A knighthood in 1910 was followed in 1912 by the chair of English at Cambridge, where in 1917 he established the final honours school in that subject. Two influential volumes of lectures, *On the Art of Writing* and *On the Art of Reading*, appeared in 1916 and 1920, and his edition of the *New Cambridge Shakespeare* began to appear in 1921. In 1928 his collected novels and stories appeared in 30 volumes. The first volume of his unfinished autobiography, *Memories and Opinions* (1944), covers his early years. See a life by F. Brittain (1947).

QUILTER, Roger (1877–1953) English composer, chiefly remembered for his songs, which were sensitively written and very popular as recital pieces. They are mostly settings of English poems from the Elizabethan, Romantic, and Victorian periods, and include four sets of *Shakespeare Songs*, P. B. *Shelley's 'Love's Philosophy', Alfred *Tennyson's 'Now sleeps the crimson petal', *Seven Elizabethan Lyrics* (1908), and *Three Songs of William *Blake* (1917).

QUINTILIAN (Marcus Fabius Quintilianus) (AD *c.*35–*c.*100) Roman rhetorician, educationist, and literary critic. His monumental *De Institutione Oratoria* ('On the Education of an Orator') is not only a treatise on rhetoric, but also discusses the training of an ideal orator for whom Quintilian like *Cicero advocates a wide general education; Book 10 contains a critical history of Greek and Roman literature. *Petrarch lamented in his *Epistle to Quintilian* that 'he came torn and mangled into my hands'; the complete text of the *Institutio* became known only after Poggio Bracciolini unearthed a complete text in Saint-Gall in 1416, after which it served the humanists as a guide on all literary and educational matters. Ben *Jonson excerpted it in **Timber*, *Milton referred to it in the *Tetrachordon* sonnet, and John *Dryden cited it on a number of points.

Quinze Joyes de mariage, Les A French misogynistic satire, of unknown authorship, dating from the late 14th/early 15th century. Several English versions of the work appeared in the 17th and 18th centuries, including one by Thomas *Dekker, entitled *The Batchelars Banquet* (1603), and a 1682 version called *The Fifteen Comforts of Rash and Inconsiderate Marriage*.

Quixote *See* DON QUIXOTE DE LA MANCHA.

Quo Vadis? A popular novel set in 1st-century AD Rome, published in 1896 and widely translated, helping its Polish author Henryk Sienkiewicz (1846–1916) to win the *Nobel Prize in 1905. Taking its title from Peter's question to Jesus, 'Where are you going?', the story of love between a Christian woman, Lygia, and a Roman patrician, Marcus Vinicius, is set against the turbulent background of Nero's dissolute rule and the Great Fire of AD 64, with historical figures including St Peter and St Paul. It bears some similarities to Edward *Bulwer-Lytton's **Last Days of Pompeii* (1834) and the two were frequently filmed from 1911 onwards.

Qur'ān (Koran) The 'Recitation', the sacred Scripture of Islam. For Muslims it is the word of God, revealed in Arabic by the archangel Gabriel to Muhammad and thence to mankind. The revelations were oral and in prose, most of them apparently consisting of a relatively short number of verses (*āyāt* 'signs'). These basic revelations were then drawn into *sūras* (chapters), the working units of the Qur'ān. The processes of revelation and compilation started about 610 and ended with Muhammad's death in 632. There are 114 *sūras*, of widely disparate length. The canonical *sūra* order avoids chronological questions by placing them in rough order of length. There is evidence that parts of the Qur'ān were committed to writing in Muhammad's lifetime, but written versions became important only after his death.

The central theme of the Qur'ān is belief in one God, whose omnipotence is to be seen everywhere. Disobedience will lead to an apocalypse, which will be the prelude to the Day of Judgement, when each individual will be judged and the righteous conveyed to heaven and the unrighteous to hell. The message is strengthened by stories of prophets and of peoples who have been destroyed for not heeding them. Some are Arabian, but many more echo the Old Testament (and sometimes later Midrashic stories). Moses, Abraham, and Noah are all prominent. A smaller amount of material recalls the New Testament and Christian apocryphal sources, mostly telling of Jesus and Mary. The Qur'ān rejects the doctrine of the Trinity and also denies the Crucifixion. After Muhammad's move to Medina in 622 there are numerous passages offering more specific guidance on religious and legal matters and others arguing against Judaism and Christianity.

Stylistically the Qur'ān calls on the four main high-level registers of Arabic current in 7th-century Arabia: the clipped, gnomic style of soothsayers, the admonitory, exhortative, and argumentative style of orators, the narrative techniques of storytellers, and the dramatic style of some poetry—though the Qur'ān itself denies any link with poets or poetry. The verses containing social legislation appear to approximate to the style used in formal written agreements. Assonance is so prominent a feature that later generations used it to divide *sūras* into verses. It preponderates in early pieces and decreases in use in later revelations.

In Britain the first translation direct from Arabic was that of George Sale (1734), which was extremely influential in the 18th and 19th centuries, but is now very dated. He has been followed by John Rodwell (1861), Edward Palmer (1880), Richard Bell (1937–9), Arthur Arberry (1955), and Alan Jones (2007). There have been nearly 40 translations into English from the Indian sub-continent, by far the best of which is that of Muhammed Marmaduke Pickthall (1930), an English convert to Islam who lived in Hyderabad. There are also several translations by Arabs. The best of these is that by Majid Fakhry (1997), who, unlike N. J. Dawood (1956) and Abdel Haleem (2004), does not fall back on the extensive use of paraphrase.

R

RABAN, Jonathan (1942–) Travel writer, novelist, and essayist, born in Norfolk and educated at the University of Hull, where he read English literature. Raban taught at the universities of Aberystwyth and East Anglia before turning to writing full-time and moving to London in 1969. He is best known as a travel writer but, like several practitioners of the genre, including Jan *Morris and Bruce *Chatwin, dislikes the term. His travel books skilfully blend novelistic plots and character sketches with autobiography, historical information, acute observations on individual and national character, and political commentary. An example is *Coasting: A Private Voyage* (1986), a work that combines an account of Raban's journey by boat round the British Isles with reflections on his childhood in post-war Britain, on his relationship with his parents (his father was an Anglican clergyman), and on the national march to war over the Falklands. In *Old Glory* (1981) Raban travels on the Mississippi in the wake of *Huckleberry Finn, his journey providing a vehicle for an examination both of himself and of the United States through the places and people he encounters. His other books include *Soft City* (1974), a study of London life; *Arabia through the Looking Glass* (1979), written as an antidote to romantic and nostalgic views of the desert; *Hunting Mister Heartbreak* (1990), a journey exploring US emigration and identity; and *Passage to Juneau: A Sea and its Meanings* (1999). *For Love and Money* (1987) collects essays and short travel pieces. In 1990 Raban settled in Seattle, from where he has written many sharp portraits of his adopted country.

RABE, David (1940–) American playwright and screenwriter, born in Iowa, who served in the Vietnam War 1965–7. This experience was used in his trilogy of plays about Vietnam draftees: *Sticks and Stones* (1971), *The Basic Training of Pavlo Hummel* (1972), and *In the Boom Boom Room* (1973). His screenplays include *The Firm* (1993).

RABELAIS, François (d. 1553) French humanist, physician, and author of comic fictions. The son of a Touraine lawyer, he became successively a Franciscan monk, the secretary of the bishop of Maillezais (*c.*1524), and a bachelor of medicine from Montpellier (1530). He travelled in France and Italy, and acquired a widespread reputation for his erudition and medical skill. For much of his life he enjoyed the patronage of Cardinal Jean du Bellay (1492–1560) and the protection of Francis I, but he was subject to frequent proscriptions and condemnations. He published various works on archaeology and medicine in Latin, though he is best remembered for his comic fictions in French, *Pantagruel* (1532), *Gargantua* (1534–5), *Le Tiers Livre* (1546: *Third Book*), *Le Quart Livre* (1548–52: *Fourth Book*) and *Le Cinquième Livre* (1562–4: *Fifth Book*), though the authenticity of the latter is disputed. These fictions are characterized both by unparalleled linguistic inventiveness, embracing obscenity, wit, and elaborate word-play, and by an encyclopedic frame of reference, encompassing virtually all the fields of knowledge of his day—theology, law, medicine, natural science, politics, military art, navigation, botany, ancient and modern languages—and many aspects of everyday life and society. They therefore read as dazzlingly complex and wonderfully disorienting images of the Renaissance world, distorted through Rabelais's inimitable comic lens. Although he was known to Gabriel *Harvey and Francis *Bacon, he was not translated into English until Sir Thomas *Urquhart's version of 1653 (*Pantagruel* and *Gargantua*) and 1693–4 (*Le Tiers Livre*, together with Peter *Motteux's translation of *Le Quart Livre* and *Le Cinquième Livre*), which was revised and elaborated upon by John Ozell in 1737; amongst more recent translations, that of Donald M. Frame (1991) stands out as particularly successful. His influence on English literature has been widespread, and is particularly marked on Samuel *Butler, Jonathan *Swift, Laurence *Sterne, Thomas Love *Peacock, and James *Joyce.

RACINE, Jean (1639–99) French dramatist, author of eleven tragedies and one comedy. He was educated by the Jansenists of Port-Royal, but was estranged from them between 1666 and 1677, during which time he wrote the majority of his plays. His tragedies derive from various sources, including Greek and Roman literature (*Andromaque*, 1667; *Iphigénie*, 1674; *Phèdre*, 1677), Roman history (*Britannicus*, 1669; *Bérénice*, 1670; *Mithridate*, 1673), recent Turkish history (*Bajazet*, 1672), and the Bible (*Esther*, 1689; *Athalie*, 1691). His comedy *Les Plaideurs* (1668: *The Litigants*) is drawn from *Aristophanes. Central to most of his tragedies is a sense of the blind folly of human passion, continually enslaved to the pursuit of its object and destined always to be unsatisfied. The plays were extensively translated into English from the 1660s by, amongst others, Thomas *Otway, though Racine's distinctive musicality and unique blend of formal restraint and passionate excess have often been considered untranslatable. The most famous of the early English versions was *The Distrest Mother*, an adaptation of *Andromaque* by Ambrose *Philips, which was still being published in the 1820s. There are important modern versions of *Phèdre* by Robert *Lowell (1961), Tony *Harrison (1975), Derek *Mahon (1996), and Ted *Hughes (1998).

RACKHAM, Arthur (1867–1939) Children's book illustrator, born in London and educated at the Lambeth School of Art. Amongst his most successful works are *Fairy Tales of the Brothers Grimm* (1900), *Rip Van Winkle* (1905), which established him as the fashionable illustrator of his time, and *Peter Pan in Kensington Gardens* (1906). Rackham's vein of fantasy is Nordic—he created a sinister world, full of the twisting roots and tendrils of gnarled trees with gnome-like faces, and peopled by goblins, birds, mice, and monsters. Rackham believed passionately in 'the stimulating and educative power of fantastic and playful pictures and writings for children in their impressionable years'.
See FAIRY STORIES.

RADCLIFFE, Ann (1764–1823) *Gothic novelist. She was daughter of a London tradesman, William Ward; she married in 1786 William Radcliffe, manager of the *English Chronicle*. In the next twelve years she published five novels, *The Castles of Athlin and Dunbayne* (1789), *A Sicilian Romance* (1790), *The Romance of the Forest* (1791), *The *Mysteries of Udolpho* (1794), and *The Italian* (1797), and a description of journeys to the Netherlands, Germany, and the Lake District. A further romance, *Gaston de Blondeville*, and her journals of travels in southern England were published after her death. She and her husband led such a retired life that unfounded rumours that she was already dead or insane circulated towards the end of her life. She was asthmatic, and died of pneumonia.

Radcliffe was the leading exponent of the early Gothic novel. Her portrayals of the raptures and terrors of her characters' imagination in solitude are compelling, and she was one of the first novelists to include vivid descriptions of landscape, weather, and effects of light. Her plots were wild and improbable, but she was expert at maintaining suspense and devising striking incidents. Radcliffe's stories, unlike those of her contemporary Matthew *Lewis, contain no supernatural elements; supposedly ghostly events turn out to have rational explanations. Her novels were immensely popular throughout Europe and were much imitated. She had an unlikely admirer in the shape of the marquis de *Sade. A best-seller in her day, the £500 advance which Radcliffe received for *Udolpho* was then unprecedented for a novel. See a memoir by T. N. *Talfourd, in *Posthumous Works of Ann Radcliffe* (1833); R. Miles, *Ann Radcliffe: The Great Enchantress* (1995); R. Norton, *Mistress of Udolpho: The Life of Ann Radcliffe* (1999).

radio Originally developed by Nikola Tesla (1856–1943), Guglielmo Marconi (1874–1937), and others as 'wireless telegraphy', and first demonstrated publicly in Oxford in 1894. Early uses included marine communication and military signalling during the First World War, before broadcast programmes began in many countries in the early 1920s. In Britain, the *BBC became an important commissioner of talks, by such writers as E. M. *Forster and J. B. *Priestley, and of original radio drama. Ezra *Pound's pioneering radio opera *The Testament of François Villon* was transmitted by the BBC in 1931, and W. H. *Auden and Christopher *Isherwood included radio bulletins and songs in their experimental verse play *The Ascent of F6* (1937). Working with Louis *MacNeice and other writers, Dallas Bower (1907–99) would create a new form of epic radio drama in the 1940s, attuned to propaganda needs, which would lead to a post-war golden age of radio drama on the BBC's Third Programme, which broadcast Dylan *Thomas's *Under Milk Wood* (1954), and the inventive 'radio ballads' that began with *Singing the Fishing* in 1960, produced by the American jazz musician Charles Parker (1920–55) with music by Ewan MacColl (1915–89) and Peggy Seeger (1935–). Many leading contemporary playwrights have continued to contribute to BBC radio drama, including Harold *Pinter and Tom *Stoppard.

Raffles *See* HORNUNG, E. W.

Ragged Trousered Philanthropists, The *See* TRESSELL, ROBERT.

Rainbow, The A novel by D. H. *Lawrence, published 1915. Beginning as a family saga, it focuses first on the farmer Tom Brangwen and his marriage to a Polish widow; then on Anna, her daughter from her first marriage, who marries Tom's nephew Will. It gradually becomes a **Bildungsroman* concerned with Anna and Will's daughter Ursula. It traces Ursula's relationships—with Anton Skrebensky, son of a Polish émigré, and with Winifred Inger, a schoolmistress—and her trials as a teacher and a student. The book is remarkable for the rhythms and stylistic range of Lawrence's prose, for its study of the 'recurrence of love and conflict' within each generation's relationships, and for its attempt to capture the flux of human personality. The novel evolved from a draft called 'The Sisters'; the story of Ursula and of her sister Gudrun is continued in Lawrence's **Women in Love* (1920).

RAINE, Craig (1944–) Poet and critic, born in Bishop Auckland, County Durham, and educated at Exeter College, Oxford. For a time he edited the *little magazine *Quarto* and is the founding editor of *Areté*. In 1981 he became poetry editor at Faber & Faber, returning to Oxford in 1991 as a fellow of New College. His first collection of poetry, *The Onion, Memory*, was published in 1978 and his second, *A Martian Sends a Postcard Home*, in 1979. In both books he displays great metaphoric vitality and individuality, and as a result of his inventive transformations of the everyday was credited with having initiated a 'Martian' school of poetry: the term was coined by James *Fenton. The manner persists, with variations, in *A Free Translation* (1981) and *Rich* (1984), in which Raine's father appears in a central prose account of his childhood, 'A Silver Plate'. *History: The Home Movie* (1994) is a lengthy, ambitious 'novel' in verse, a chronicle of the Raine and Pasternak families set against the background of 20th-century European history. *Clay: Whereabouts Unknown*, written in a much sparer, less accommodated and accommodating style, appeared in 1996, and *À la recherche du temps perdu*, an elegy for a former lover written with unconsoled frankness, in 2000. Raine's *Collected Poems 1978–1999* appeared in 1999. He has also published an opera libretto based on a text by Boris *Pasternak, and a version of *Racine's *Andromaque*. His criticism includes *Haydn and the Valve Trumpet* (1990) and *T. S. Eliot* (2007).

RAINE, Kathleen (1908–2003) Poet, born in London and educated at Girton College, Cambridge, where she read Natural Sciences. She published many collections of poetry, from her first, *Stone and Flower* (1943), illustrated by Barbara Hepworth, to her *Collected Poems* of 2002, and also three volumes of autobiography, collected as *Autobiographies* in 1991: the final volume includes an account of her important relationship with Gavin *Maxwell. Later collections include *The Oracle in the Heart* (1980) and *Living with Mystery* (1992). Much of her poetry is inspired by the landscapes of Scotland, particularly of Wester Ross, and has what she described as 'a sense of the sacred', an intense and mystic vision of the vitality of the natural world which also informs her critical work on William *Blake and the *Neoplatonic tradition. In 1981 she founded the review *Temenos*, a journal exploring 'the intimate link between the arts and the sacred'.

RAINOLDS, John (1549–1607) An Oxford academic among whose pupils was Richard *Hooker. As well as composing Latin lectures on Aristotle which contributed to the development of euphuism (*see* EUPHUES), he produced controversial works and Protestant apologetics. Having acted as an undergraduate in Richard *Edwards's *Palaemon and Arcite* (1566), he later took part in a controversy over the lawfulness of acting plays, publishing his contributions in *The Overthrow of Stage Plays* (1599).

Rake's Progress, The A series of engravings by William *Hogarth which inspired an opera by Igor *Stravinsky of the same title with a libretto by W. H. *Auden in collaboration with Chester Kallman (1921–75).

RALEGH, Sir Walter (1554–1618) Explorer and author, born at Hayes in south Devon; the sailor Sir Humfrey Gilbert (1537–83) was his half-brother. Before entering Oriel College, Oxford, in 1572 he had spent some time as a volunteer with the Huguenot forces in France, being present at the battle of Montcontour in 1569. After Oxford and a period in London attached to the Middle Temple and at court, Ralegh began his long career as an explorer and colonizer. In Ireland in 1580 he became acquainted with Edmund *Spenser, who approved of Ralegh's commanding role in the massacre of Smerwick, in which 600 Spanish mercenaries were killed. Throughout the 1580s he seems to have enjoyed royal favour, though Thomas *Fuller's story of his throwing a plush cloak over a puddle for *Elizabeth I to tread on is most unlikely to be true. His marriage to Elizabeth Throckmorton, one of the queen's maids of honour, led to a period of imprisonment in the summer of 1592. The journey to Guiana (now Venezuela) in 1595 in search of gold was in part a bid for royal favour; his leadership of the expedition to sack Cadiz harbour in June 1596 was a more successful one, and by adroitly dissociating himself from the earl of *Essex he maintained a strong position until the queen's death. Ralegh's trial, on largely trumped-up charges of high treason, was one of the first events of James I's reign, and from 1603 to 1616 he was imprisoned in the Tower with his wife and family, a dead man in the eyes of the law. He was released to search out the gold mine he claimed to have discovered in Guiana twenty years before. On returning from this disastrous expedition, in which his eldest son was killed and his chief lieutenant, Keymis, committed suicide, a commission of inquiry set up under Spanish pressure determined that the gold mine was a fabrication, the old charge of treason was renewed, and on 29 October 1618 Ralegh was executed.

His poems are beset by uncertainties as to date and authenticity, though a few of them, including the fragmentary '21th: and last booke of the Ocean to Scinthia', survive in his own handwriting. Two well-known poems formerly attributed to him, 'Walsingham' ('As you came from the holy land') and 'The Passionate Man's Pilgrimage' ('Give me my scallop shell of quiet'), are not now thought to be his work. Among the authentic poems are his 'An Epitaph upon Sir Philip Sidney' and the prefatory sonnet to *The *Faerie Queene* which begins, 'Methought I saw the grave, where *Laura* lay'. There are numerous prose works. His *Report of the Truth of the Fight about the Isles of Açores* (1591) was a source of Alfred *Tennyson's 'The Revenge' (1878). His *Discovery of Guiana* (1596) includes a description of 'El Dorado', and describes the plain-lands as a natural Eden: 'still as we rowed, the deer came down feeding by the water's side, as if they had been used to a keeper's call.'

The History of the World (1614), written during Ralegh's long imprisonment, was originally intended for Henry, prince of Wales (d. 1612). This ambitious book, which Ralegh worked on with the help of several assistants, deals with Greek, Egyptian, and biblical history up to 168 BC. The preface, at the beginning of which he affirms his 'fidelity towards her, whom I must still honour in the dust', summarizes modern European history, demonstrating the unchangeableness of God's judgement. The *History* contains many reflective passages, most characteristically elegiac in tone: 'For this tide of man's life, after it once turneth and declineth, ever runneth, with a perpetual ebb and falling stream, but never floweth again: our leaf once fallen, springeth no more, neither doth the sun or the summer adorn us again, with the garments of new leaves and flowers.' The best-known such passage comes on the final page: 'O eloquent, just and mighty Death! whom none could advise, thou hast persuaded; what none hath dared, thou hast done; and whom all the world hath flattered, thou only hast cast out of the world and despised: thou hast drawn together all the far-stretched greatness, all the pride, cruelty, and ambition of man, and covered it all over with these two narrow words, *Hic iacet* ['Here lies'].'

The poems were edited by M. Rudick (1999); the letters by A. Latham and J. Youings (1999); C. A. Patrides edited selections from *The History of the World* (1971). There are studies by P. Lefranc (1968) and S. May (1989).

Ralph Roister Doister The earliest-known English comedy, by Nicholas *Udall, probably performed about 1552 and printed about 1566, and perhaps played by Westminster boys while Udall was headmaster there. The play, in short rhymed doggerel, represents the courting of the widow Christian Custance, who is betrothed to Gawin Goodlucke, an absent merchant, by Roister, a swaggering simpleton, prompted by the mischievous Mathewe Merygreeke. Roister is sent packing by Custance and her maids; and Goodlucke, after being deceived by false rumours, is reconciled to her. The play is similar to the comedies of *Plautus and *Terence.

RALSTON, William (1828–89) Scholar and translator of Russian literature, born in London and educated at Cambridge. It was during his employment in the Department of Printed Books at the *British Museum from 1853 until his resignation in 1875 that, having taught himself Russian, he became Britain's foremost interpreter and translator of Russian literature and folk culture. He enjoyed easy relations with many leading British writers including Thomas *Carlyle, George *Eliot, and Alfred *Tennyson. It was Tennyson who heralded Ralston's *Krylov and his Fables* (1869), finding his versions 'good and pithy beyond the wont of fables'. Despite the rendition of *Krylov's sprightly verse and racy idiom in somewhat pedestrian prose, his translations proved extremely popular with his Victorian audience and went through four, ever expanded, editions by 1883. The third edition brought an enthusiastic review in the **Academy* in 1871 from Ivan *Turgenev, with whom Ralston had corresponded since 1866 and who thought very highly of Ralston's *Lisa* (1869), the translation of his novel *Dvorianskoe gnezdo* (*A Nest of the Gentry*). Ralston paid visits to Russia in 1868 and 1870 and developed friendships with Russian philologists, folklorists, and writers. His endeavours on behalf of Russian culture, which included three significant books, *The Songs of the Russian People* (1872), *Russian Folk-Tales* (1873), and *Early Russian History* (1874), brought him corresponding membership of several Russian institutions, including the Academy of Sciences. Ralston was a founder member of the Folklore Society and among his many publications was *Tibetan Tales* (1882).

Rambler A twice-weekly *periodical by Samuel *Johnson in 208 numbers, published 20 March 1750 to 14 March 1752. Edward *Cave was the publisher. The essays treat a great variety of subjects: ethics; crime; marriage and family life; economics; education; prostitution; history; self-knowledge; and many others. They include character studies, allegories, Eastern fables, and literary criticism (including a series on John *Milton). The moral seriousness of his enterprise is indicated by Johnson's prayer on beginning the work; a fine account of the inception and writing of the papers is given in James Boswell's *Life of Johnson*. Minor contributions came from Samuel *Richardson, Elizabeth *Carter, Hester *Chapone, and Catherine Talbot (1720–70). Despite initial protests against its 'solemn' tone, the *Rambler* was pirated and imitated, and went through ten numbered reprintings in Johnson's lifetime.

RAMSAY, Allan (1684–1758) Scottish poet, born in Leadhills, Lanarkshire, who came to Edinburgh where he spent most of his life. He was a wig-maker, then a bookseller, and an important figure in Edinburgh literary society; he opened the first *circulating library in Edinburgh in 1726. In 1718 he brought out anonymously several editions of **Christis Kirk on the Green*, with supplementary verses of his own in fake antique *Scots, and also various vernacular mock elegies. A collection of his elegies and satires appeared in 1721. In 1724–37 he issued *The Tea-Table Miscellany*, one of the more famous 18th-century collections of songs and ballads, and in 1724 *The Ever Green*, which contained work by the great poets of late medieval Scotland, notably William *Dunbar and Robert *Henryson, though with revisions and additions of his own. These contributed much to the revival of vernacular Scottish poetry, and in his preface to the latter Ramsay makes clear his patriotic intentions: 'When these good old Bards wrote, we had not yet made Use of imported Trimming.' Ramsay's pastoral comedy *The Gentle Shepherd* (1725), with its Scots songs, was very successful and much admired by James *Boswell among others for its 'beautiful rural imagery' and its 'real picture of manners'.

RAMUS, Peter (Pierre de la Ramée) (1515–72) French philosopher and grammarian. A convert to Protestantism from *c.*1560, he perished in the massacre of St *Bartholomew, an event portrayed by Christopher *Marlowe in *The *Massacre at Paris*. His *Dialectique* (1555), which can lay claim to being the first major philosophical work in French, systematically challenged Aristotelian and *scholastic logic. It was introduced into England in the late 16th century and obtained wide academic currency, especially at Cambridge. His followers were known as Ramists and his anti-scholastic system of logic as Ramism. See Walter J. Ong, *Ramus* (1958).

RAND, Ayn (1905–82) Russian-born American novelist (born Alisa Zinov'yevna Rosenbaum), who devised the philosophy of 'Objectivism', which she promoted through her fiction, especially *The Fountainhead* (1943) and *Atlas Shrugged* (1957). She expressed controversial right-wing views on many social issues in essays collected in *For the New Intellectual* (1961) and other volumes. The Ayn Rand Institute was founded in 1985 to promote her ideas and works.

RANDOLPH, Thomas (1605–35) Poet, playwright, and wit, follower of Ben *Jonson, educated at Westminster School and Trinity College, Cambridge, where he became known as a writer in English and Latin verse. He returned to London in 1632. His principal plays are **Hey for Honesty*, based on Aristophanes' *Plutus*, perhaps his first play but not printed till 1651, *The *Muses Lookinge-Glasse* (?1630), printed 1638, and *Amyntas*, a pastoral comedy acted at court (?1631). He wrote an eclogue included in *Annalia Dubrensia*, verses in celebration of the Cotswold Games (an annual celebration of sports held in the Cotswolds). His plays and poems were edited by W. C. *Hazlitt (1875).

RANKIN, Ian (1960–) Scottish crime novelist, born in Cardenden, Fife, and educated at the University of Edinburgh. His Rebus series of novels, set in a vividly evoked Edinburgh and featuring the working-class police inspector John Rebus, includes *Knots and Crosses* (1987), *Let It Bleed* (1995), *Black and Blue* (1997), *The Falls* (2001), *Fleshmarket Close* (2004), and *Exit Music* (2007).

RANSOM, John Crowe (1888–1974) American poet and critic, born in Tennessee. From 1937 to 1958 he was a professor at Kenyon College, Ohio, where he founded and edited the important *Kenyon Review*, a scholarly publication committed to the close textual analysis associated with the *New Criticism. He co-founded the Fugitives group, which included Allen *Tate and Robert Penn *Warren. His critical works include *God without Thunder* (1930) and *The New Criticism* (1941), the latter an independent survey of the works of I. A. *Richards, Yvor *Winters, and others. His period of activity as a poet was relatively brief, but his output, notably in *Chills and Fever* (1924) and *Two Gentlemen in Bonds* (1927), is impressive, and he is particularly remembered for his formal, subtle, taut ballad-portraits and elegies. See Thomas Daniel Young, *Gentleman in a Dustcoat* (1977).

RANSOME, Arthur Michell (1884–1967) Journalist and author, born in Leeds and educated at Rugby. He started work in London as office boy for Grant Richards, graduated to ghostwriting, reviewing, and short story writing, finally becoming a reporter, first for the **Daily News*, then (in 1919) for the **Manchester Guardian*. He went to Russia in 1913 to learn the language, and covered the revolution at first hand; his Russian legends and fairy stories, *Old Peter's Russian Tales* (1916), had considerable success. Ransome is best remembered for his sequence of novels for children, beginning with *Swallows and Amazons* (1930) and ending with *Great Northern?* (1947). The books describe the adventures of the Walker (Swallow) and Blackett (Amazon) families, and various of their friends, in the Lake District, the Norfolk Broads, and other vividly drawn locations. He was the first winner of the Carnegie Medal for *children's literature, awarded for *Pigeon Post* in 1936. There is an autobiography, edited by Rupert Hart-Davis (1976), and a biography by Hugh Brogan (1984).

Ranters A miscellaneous sect of Puritan extremists whose 'heresies', which mushroomed in the late 1640s and early 1650s, were founded on belief in the inner light shining in each believer, and included freedom from the moral law (*see* ANTINOMIAN), community of goods and women, abolition of tithes, the futility of the Bible, the non-existence of hell, the excellence of tobacco and alcohol, and mystical Pantheism (Jacob Bauthumley's 'God in an ivy-leaf'). Notorious Ranters included Laurence *Clarkson, Abiezer *Coppe, Richard Coppin (*fl.* *c.*1645–1659), and Joseph Salmon (*fl.*1647–56). Hack-writers exploited their reputation for orgiastic sex by inventing sensational reports, leading some modern historians to claim that 'there was no Ranter movement' (J. C. Davis, *Fear, Myth and History* (1986)). However, Christopher *Hill has written persuasively about their revolutionary anarchism in *The World Turned Upside Down* (1972). See also Nigel Smith (ed.), *A Collection of Ranter Writings* (1983); and. (ed.), *Perfection Proclaimed* (1989).

RAO, Raja (1909–2006) Indian writer, born at Hassan, Karnataka, and educated at Nizam College, Hyderabad, and the universities of Montpellier and the Sorbonne. His first novel, *Kanthapura* (1938), an account of the Independence movement seen from the perspective of a small south Indian village grandmother, attempts to forge an Indian idiom and tempo through the medium of the English language, as the famous preface declares. This was followed by *The Serpent and the Rope* (1960), the story of a young Indian Brahman intellectual, Rama, and his French wife Madeleine in their search for spiritual truth in India, France, and England. Rao's stories have been collected in *The Cow of the Barricades* (1947), *The Policeman and the Rose* (1978), and *On the Ganga Ghat* (1989). Later works include *The Chessmaker and his Moves* (1988). His work is characterized throughout by the spiritual searching of the characters, a preoccupation which was increasingly important to Rao himself. Between 1966 and 1980 he taught as professor of philosophy at the University of Texas.
See ANGLO-INDIAN LITERATURE.

rap The performance of a rhythmic monologue over a pre-recorded instrumental backing. Rap was developed in the dance halls and clubs of North America in the 1980s as a way of exciting the crowds and allowing the rappers to show off their ability to rhyme. Rap studio recordings are now recognized as a legitimate branch of popular music. Many of the poets now referred to as rap poets are concerned not only with their rhyming skills but also with lyrical content.

Rape of Lucrece, The (*Lucrece*) A poem in the seven-line *rhyme royal by *Shakespeare, published 1594 and dedicated to Henry Wriothesley, earl of Southampton. It is presumably the 'graver labour' which he promised to the earl in the dedication of **Venus and Adonis* the previous year. It is a highly rhetorical expansion of the story as told by *Ovid (in the *Fasti*) and *Livy.
See LUCRETIA.

Rape of the Lock, The A poem by Alexander *Pope. A two-canto version was published in Bernard *Lintot's *Miscellany* (1712) as 'The Rape of the Locke'; a much-enlarged version in five cantos appeared as a separate publication in 1714. The poem was prompted by an incident in which Robert, seventh Baron Petre (1690–1713), cut a lock of hair from Arabella Fermor (*c.*1689–1738), giving rise to a quarrel between the families. In an attempt to mollify the parties, Pope treated the subject in a playful *mock-heroic poem, in which the great set pieces of epic are miniaturized into the coffee-drinking, card-playing rituals of fashionable metropolitan living. Belinda's use of cosmetics is modelled on the arming of Achilles; the cutting of the lock is likened to the fall of Troy; Belinda's depression recalls the underworld voyages of epic; in the final battle the belles and beaus use fans and snuff-boxes as if they were heroic weapons. The Olympian gods are scaled down into the 'machinery' of sylphs and gnomes, drawn from *Le Comte de Gabalis*, a series of playful discourses by the abbé de Montfaucon de Villars, which appeared in English in 1680. The overall effect is more benign than *The *Dunciad*, and the poem has been enduringly popular; Samuel *Johnson called it 'the most attractive of all ludicrous compositions', in which 'New things are made familiar and familiar things are made new'. More recently the underlying sexual politics of the poem has been the focus of much *feminist criticism. The 1714 version appeared with six illustrations; Aubrey *Beardsley produced eleven designs for the poem (1896–7).

RAPHAEL (Raffaello Sanzio) (1483–1520) Italian painter, born in Urbino. He worked in Perugino's studio and then in Florence, and succeeded Bramante as architect of St Peter's. Throughout the 17th, 18th, and 19th centuries Raphael was generally revered as the greatest of all painters; his supremacy was challenged by the romantic admirers of *Michelangelo in the 18th century but endorsed by the first president of the Royal Academy, Sir Joshua *Reynolds. In the 19th century he continued to be revered by members of the Academy, but the High Renaissance tradition was powerfully attacked first by the young John *Ruskin in *Modern Painters* then by the *Pre-Raphaelites who idealistically romanticized the purity, simplicity, and naturalism of Gothic art.

RAPHAEL, Frederic (?1931–) Novelist and screenwriter, born in Chicago, educated at St John's College, Cambridge, and long resident in England. His novels, many dealing with the dilemmas of educated middle-class life, include *Obbligato* (1956), *The Limits of Love* (1960, set partly in Jewish north London), and *The Graduate Wife* (1962). *Lindmann* (1963), based on the break-up of the illegal Jewish immigrant ship SS *Broda* off the Turkish coast in 1942, uses the device of a screenplay written by a London-based writer. Other novels include *Orchestra and Beginners* (1967), *Heaven and Earth* (1985), and *Coast to Coast* (1998). Raphael's screenplays include a mid-term report on the Swinging Sixties, *Darling* (1965, John Schlesinger), a six-part TV series, *The Glittering Prizes* (1976), following a group of artistic Cambridge undergraduates from 1952 to the 1970s, and *Eyes Wide Shut* (1999), based on *Dream Story* (1926), a novella by the Austrian writer Arthur Schnitzler (1862–1931), for Stanley Kubrick. Raphael also translated *Catullus (1978, with K. McLeish) and *Aeschylus (1991). A memoir series based on unpublished notebooks, *Personal Terms*, reached its fourth volume in 2008.

Rasselas A philosophical romance by Samuel *Johnson, written during the evenings of a week to pay for his mother's funeral, and published as *The Prince of Abissinia: A Tale* (1759). It is an essay on the 'choice of life', a phrase repeated throughout the work. Rasselas, a son of the emperor of Abyssinia, weary of the joys of the 'happy valley' where the inhabitants know only 'the soft vicissitudes of pleasure and repose', escapes to Egypt, accompanied by his sister Nekayah, her attendant Pekuah, and the much-travelled philosopher Imlac. Here they study the various conditions of men's lives, discovering in the main dissatisfaction and self-delusion. The story illustrates the themes of *The *Vanity of Human Wishes*, stressing that no single system produces happiness, and demonstrating that philosophers, scientists, hermits, and the wealthy all fail to achieve it. The characters are stripped of their illusions, but retain a humane awareness that while imagination may be delusive and that desire brings disappointment, they are also necessary to keep life 'in motion'. In a 'conclusion, in which nothing is concluded' the characters resolve to return to Abyssinia. Though milder in tone, *Rasselas* bears some resemblance in plan to *Voltaire's *Candide*, published in the same year; Johnson himself later commented on the similarity. In the course of the narrative Imlac voices Johnson's celebrated definition of the 'business of a poet', which is to 'examine not the individual, but the species'; and to write 'as the legislator of mankind...presiding over the thoughts and manners of future generations', an unexpected anticipation of P. B. *Shelley's phrasing in his **Defence of Poetry*.

RASTELL, John (*c.*1475–1536) Innovative printer, barrister, playwright, and brother-in-law of Sir Thomas *More. He wrote and published an *interlude called *Four Elements* (*c.*1520), and two comedies of *c.*1525, *Calisto and Melebea* and *Gentleness and Nobility*. The latter has been attributed to Rastell's son-in-law John *Heywood.

Rat, the Cat, and Lovel the dog, the In the political rhyme

The Rat, the Cat, and Lovel the dog
Rule all England under the Hog,

refer to three adherents of Richard III: Sir Richard Ratcliffe (killed at Bosworth, 1485), Sir John Catesby (d. 1487), and Francis, first Viscount Lovell (1457–*c.*1488). The Hog is the boar that is featured as one of the supporters of the royal arms.

RATTIGAN, Sir Terence Mervyn (1911–77) The son of a diplomat. Educated at Harrow School and Trinity College, Oxford, he immediately embarked on a career as a playwright. His first West End success was a comedy, *French without Tears* (1936). This was followed by many other works, including *The Winslow Boy* (1946), a drama in which a father fights to clear his naval-cadet son of the accusation of petty theft; it was filmed in 1948, and again, directed and with a screenplay by David *Mamet, in 1999. *The Browning Version* (1948) depicts a repressed and unpopular schoolmaster with a faithless wife. The heroine of *The Deep Blue Sea* (1952) is a judge's wife suffering from passion for a test pilot. *Separate*

Tables (1954) comprises two one-act plays set in a hotel, both studies of emotional failure and inadequacy, and *Ross* (1960) is based on the life of T. E. *Lawrence. He created the character of 'Aunt Edna', the average middle-brow matinée attender whom playwrights must take into account, and critics were later to use this light-hearted invention as a focus for their complaints about the middle-class, middle-brow nature of his own plays; the so-called *kitchen sink dramatists of the 1950s and 1960s reacted against Rattigan (expressly, in the case of Shelagh *Delaney), but his works are still much performed and admired, and David *Rudkin in a BBC Radio 3 programme in 1976 stressed not his celebrated 'craftsmanship' but his sense of 'existential bleakness and irresolvable carnal solitude'. A biography by M. Darlow and G. Hodson (1979) gives an account of his troubled personal life and successful career; see also G. Wansell, *Terence Rattigan* (1995).

Rauf Coilyear A rhymed poem of the *Charlemagne cycle, in alliterative thirteen-line stanzas, printed in Scotland in 1572 (written probably *c.*1475). Charlemagne, disguised, takes refuge in the hut of Rauf, a plain-spoken charcoal-burner, who then comes to court, discovers who his guest was, and becomes a knight. Ed. S. J. Herrtage (EETS ES 39, 1882).

RAVEN, Simon (1927–2001) Novelist, educated at Charterhouse and King's College, Cambridge. In 1957 he resigned his infantry commission to become a professional writer and reviewer. His first novel, *The Feathers of Death* (1959), brought him instant recognition. His major work is a ten-volume series of novels, *Alms for Oblivion*, consisting of *The Rich Pay Late* (1964), *Friends in Low Places* (1965), *The Sabre Squadron* (1966), *Fielding Gray* (1967, chronologically the first in the series), *The Judas Boy* (1968), *Places Where They Sing* (1970), *Sound the Retreat* (1971), *Come Like Shadows* (1972), *Bring Forth the Body* (1974), and *The Survivors* (1976). The sequence presents an uncompromising panorama of post-war life from 1945 to 1973 through the lives and vicissitudes of the same group of characters. Some of these also appear in the seven-volume series *The First-Born of Egypt*, which began with *Morning Star* (1984) and concluded with *The Troubadour* (1992). *The Old School* (1986), a work of non-fiction, reflects Raven's ambivalent attitude to the British public-school system, which he found at once detestable and fascinating. He also published plays and essays.

RAVENHILL, Mark (1966–) Playwright, born in Haywards Heath, Sussex, and educated at Bristol University. He shot to prominence with the *Royal Court production of *Shopping and Fucking* (1996), the title of which summed up the play's deliberately confrontational analysis of the interconnectedness of sex and consumerism in a surreally realized 'queer' world. *Some Explicit Polaroids* (1999) extended the analysis of the modern world with a clash of generations, and *Mother Clap's Molly House* (2002) was a sexual romp that moved between the 18th century and the present. Audiences at the *National Theatre behaved almost as at a revival of *The Rocky Horror Show*, making it appropriate that he should be invited to write the first ever pantomime, *Dick Whittington and his Cat*, for the National in 2006.

Ravenshoe A novel by Henry *Kingsley, published 1862, containing among its many dramatic episodes an animated description of the Charge of the Light Brigade.

RAVERAT, Gwen (Gwendolen Mary) (1885–1957) Née Darwin, wood-engraver and granddaughter of Charles *Darwin. Born in Cambridge, and educated at the Slade School of Art, her childhood is described in her autobiographical *Period Piece: A Cambridge Childhood* (1952). She was a close friend of Rupert *Brooke and associate of the *Bloomsbury Group. Works illustrated by her include *Spring Morning* (1915) by her cousin Frances *Cornford, and various anthologies in association with Kenneth *Grahame. Her husband, the French painter Jacques Raverat (1885–1925), suffered from multiple sclerosis. The correspondence between herself, Jacques, and Virginia *Woolf was edited by her grandson William Pryor (2004). See Francis Spalding, *Gwen Raverat: Family and Affections* (2001).

RAY, John (1627–1705) The son of a blacksmith, who became one of England's greatest naturalists. He was pre-eminently a botanist (he originated the division of plants into monocotyledons and dicotyledons), but also took up the unfinished zoological work of his friend Francis Willughby (1635–72). His *Historia Plantarum* was published 1686–1704, and his *Wisdom of God Manifested in the Works of Creation* (1691) went through many editions. He also published *A Collection of English Proverbs* (1670) and was keenly interested in philology.

READ, Sir Herbert (1893–1968) Poet, novelist, and critic, born in Yorkshire, and educated at Leeds University; he served in France throughout the First World War. In the 1920s and 1930s he worked in the Victoria and Albert Museum, then as professor of fine art in Edinburgh, and as editor of the *Burlington Magazine*. His poetry, influenced initially by *imagism, includes philosophical poetry, dialogues, and modernist lyrics; a *Collected Poems* appeared in 1966. His only novel, *The Green Child* (1935), admired by Graham *Greene, is a philosophical fantasy about forms of utopia. He was prolific as a critic of art, society, and literature, explicating modernist work in literature, painting, and sculpture: important works include *Education through Art* (1943), *Collected Essays in Literary Criticism* (1951), *The Philosophy of Modern Art* (1952), and *Anarchy and Order* (1954). See James King, *The Last Modern: A Life of Herbert Read* (1990).

READ, Piers Paul (1941–) Novelist, son of Sir Herbert *Read, educated at Ampleforth and St John's College, Cambridge. His novels often combine the psychological study and moral analysis of character (Read is himself a Catholic) with elements of the political thriller and the historical novel. They include *Game in Heaven with Tussy Marx* (1966), *A Married Man* (1979), *The Villa Golitsyn* (1981), *A Patriot in Berlin*, 1995) and

Alice in Exile (2001). Read has also written books of reportage, including *Alive: The Story of the Andes Survivors* (1974) and *The Train Robbers* (1978), about the Great Train Robbery.

READE, Charles (1814–84) Playwright and novelist, born at Ipsden, in Oxfordshire, the son of a respectable country squire. In 1831 he won a scholarship to Magdalen College, Oxford, beginning a long association which brought him a fellowship and various college offices over the years. He travelled abroad, then in 1842 began to study for the bar; in 1846 he tried studying medicine in Edinburgh; and in 1847, he began to deal in violins. After publishing a stage version of Smollett's **Peregrine Pickle* in 1851, he entered on his long career as theatre manager and dramatist. *Masks and Faces*, successfully produced in that year, became his first novel, **Peg Woffington*, in 1853. In that year he also published *Christie Johnstone*, urging the reform of prisons and the treatment of criminals, which was followed in 1856 by *It Is Never Too Late to Mend*, a highly successful work in the same reforming genre, which was later dramatized. *Gold!*, a play converted in 1869 into the novel *Foul Play*, also appeared in this prolific year. At the same time Reade was writing short stories, working as a journalist, and writing plays. In 1854 he met the actress Laura Seymour, with whom he lived until her death in 1879. *The Autobiography of a Thief* and *Jack of All Trades* (both greatly admired by George *Orwell) appeared in 1858; *Love Me Little, Love Me Long* in 1859; and in 1861 the work for which he is chiefly remembered, *The *Cloister and the Hearth*. **Hard Cash*, a *sensation novel exposing the scandal of lunatic asylums (which Reade considered 'my best production'), appeared in 1863, and in 1866 **Griffith Gaunt*. Its sexual frankness provoked litigation, in which Reade pugnaciously defended himself against 'the Prurient Prudes'. For much of the rest of his life he was engaged in various personal and legal controversies. A long collaboration with *Boucicault, a highly successful adapter of plays and novels, began in 1867, and the last of Reade's major novels, *Put Yourself in his Place*, attacking the trade union practice of 'rattening' or enforcing membership, appeared in 1870. In 1871 he published another novel, *A Terrible Temptation*, and in 1872 quarrelled with Anthony *Trollope over *Shilly-Shally*, his unauthorized dramatic version of Trollope's *Ralph the Heir* (1871), following this with a libel action in 1873 over his own new novel, *The Simpleton*. *The Wandering Heir* (1873), suggested by the Tichborne trial, was again both novel and play; Reade persuaded Ellen *Terry to emerge from retirement to perform in the stage version. He continued to produce short stories, journalistic work, and plays for his touring company, and to be embroiled in disputes and legal actions. By the time he published *A Woman Hater* (1877) he had lost his determination to present honestly the problems of sex in society, and meekly agreed to all *Blackwood's objections. After the death of Laura Seymour in 1879 he wrote little, turned to religion, and in 1882 gave up theatrical management. *A Perilous Secret* appeared posthumously in 1884.

Reade was very successful, and often seen as the natural successor of *Dickens (whose novels had considerably influenced him). Among critics, both the young Henry *James and *Swinburne were admirers, placing his work above that of George *Eliot (a view which at the time did not seem eccentric). But his reputation has dimmed, and he is largely remembered only for *The Cloister and the Hearth* and *Griffith Gaunt*. The 'realism' of his novels was based on immense research, recorded in intricate detail in his mass of notebooks; for *The Cloister and the Hearth*, he read *Erasmus, *Froissart, *Luther, *chronicles, *jest books, and all the records he could find. He wanted to impart an authentic reality to his work, and also to discipline the 'inner consciousness', which he distrusted; but the accumulation of detail often threatens to overwhelm his narratives. His interest in sexual frustration and fantasy (celibacy, he wrote, is 'an invention wholly devilish'), and its place in religious feeling, was much stifled by the proprieties of the time. See M. Elwin, *Charles Reade* (1931); W. Burns, *Charles Reade: A Study in Victorian Authorship* (1961).

READE, William Winwood (1838–75) Explorer, novelist, and nephew of Charles *Reade. His explorations in West and south-west Africa are described in *Savage Africa* (1863), *The African Sketch-Book* (1873), and *The Story of the Ashanti Campaign* (1874). His other works, which aroused some controversy for their criticism of religion, include the notable *The Martyrdom of Man* (1872), which reflects the author's freethinking views and influenced H. G. *Wells.

reading, cultures of *See introductory essay.*

READING, Peter (1946–) Poet, born in Liverpool, where he studied and taught at Liverpool College of Art. A prolific, hugely original poet, his first volume was *Water and Waste* (1970); numerous further books, which are usually organized around particular themes or motifs, include *Nothing for Anyone* (1977), *C* (1984, a grim meditation on cancer), *Ukulele Music* (1985), a fantasia on Thatcherite Britain which many regard as his outstanding single volume, *Perduta Gente* (1989), *Last Poems* (1994), and *Faunal* (2002). His *Collected Poems 1997–2003* was published in 2003. Reading's work displays a fertile inventiveness and aggression in typography, verse form, and subject matter. Characteristically, he contrasts a reporter's unsparing evocation of the underside and underclass of contemporary Britain—pub life, domestic brutality, street violence—with a mocking command of classical metrics. '"Unemployed/Hopeless" doesn't sufficiently | Serve to explain Cro Magnon atrocities' (*Stet*, 1986) might stand as a motto for most of his output, in which evolutionary time and mankind's place within it supplies various, sometimes lacerating, ironies of perspective. A driven, even obsessive, gallows-humour assault on decay and self-destruction is a prominent note in the later work which also includes, however, sometimes poignant poetic rehearsals of his long-standing interest in birds.

Real Charlotte, The *See* Somerville and Ross.

realism A broad tendency in literature that emphasizes fidelity to the observable and complex facts of life, in contradistinction to the idealized or simplified representations of *romance or *melodrama. It is associated particularly with prose fiction and drama since the mid-19th century, although realism has also been identified as a feature of some works in earlier periods, from Chaucer's General Prologue to the **Canterbury Tales* to Defoe's **Moll Flanders*, and can be found in some deliberately anti-romantic modern poetry, as in works by Rupert *Brooke, Wilfred *Owen, W. H. *Auden, and Philip *Larkin. Literary realism of the 19th century was a major international tendency (although not quite a 'movement', except in the French realism that evolved into the *naturalism of *Zola) in fiction under the influences of Honoré de *Balzac, *Stendhal, and Gustave *Flaubert; and later in drama under the influence of *Ibsen. It turned away from the visionary or heroic ideals of *Romanticism in order to depict unheroic lives, usually of the middle or working class, commonly in unglamorous provincial settings, and to offer accurate and credible descriptions of imperfect characters (i.e. neither perfectly virtuous nor purely villainous) within specific material and social circumstances, stressing the inescapable pressures of economic necessity. In English fiction, the most celebrated exemplars are the novels of George *Eliot, notably **Middlemarch*, and of Arnold *Bennett, especially *The Old Wives' Tale*. The novels of Jane *Austen too, although pre-dating that major phase of realism, exemplify many of its features, while those of Henry *James, while not dealing with provincial penury, extend realist methods with new technical sophistication towards a 'psychological realism' that was further developed by *modernism. The tradition survived into the 20th century, for example in the novels of E. M. *Forster and Winifred *Holtby, the early novels of D. H. *Lawrence and of George *Orwell, and the novels and stories of Somerset *Maugham. The tradition of realism in English drama is less distinguished, and appears mostly in socially concerned plays by e.g. John *Galsworthy and the *kitchen sink dramatists of the 1950s. Realism has been condemned on various grounds: commonly in the late 19th century as too pessimistic and distressing; later by Virginia *Woolf in her attacks on Bennett as materialistic; and generally in the climate of post-*structuralism as ideologically regressive. See Pam Morris, *Realism* (2003).

Rebecca Novel by Daphne *du Maurier, published in 1938. The unnamed narrator becomes the second wife of Maxim de Winter and mistress of Manderley, his Cornish estate. Insecure in the role created by Maxim's glamorous first wife Rebecca, she is tormented by her failure to match her predecessor's social confidence, especially by the servant Mrs Danvers, who remains obsessively loyal to Rebecca's memory. Having assumed that Maxim also adored his first wife, the narrator discovers that in fact he hated and murdered her, disguising her death as a boating accident. The discovery of Rebecca's boat threatens to expose Maxim's guilt, but the coroner is led to record a verdict of suicide. The de Winters go into exile after Mrs Danvers sets fire to Manderley. The novel has echoes of **Jane Eyre* and of the wider *Gothic tradition. An award-winning film adaptation, directed by Alfred *Hitchcock, was released in 1940.

Rebecca and Rowena A humorous sequel by W. M. *Thackeray to Scott's **Ivanhoe*, published as a Christmas book in 1850, with illustrations by Richard *Doyle. Ivanhoe tires of domestic life with Rowena, and after various comic vicissitudes is reunited with Rebecca.

RECHY, John (1934–) American novelist, born in El Paso, Texas, whose writings explore the world of gay sexual hustlers. He achieved fame with his first book *City of Night* (1963), drawing on his experience of New Orleans. Among his subsequent works, *The Sexual Outlaw* (non-fiction, 1977) addresses homophobia and *Rushes* (1979) collects the stories of patrons to an inner-city gay bar. See Charles Casillo, *Outlaw* (2002).

'Recluse, The' *See* EXCURSION, THE.

Records of Woman A volume of nineteen poems by Felicia *Hemans. Published in 1828 at the height of her poetic reputation, the volume records the legacies of famous women from history and legend, and Hemans capitalizes on her own fame, displaying her poetic mastery and authority through the use of a range of stanzaic forms and genres. The volume is dedicated to the Scottish female poet and playwright Joanna *Baillie, whom Hemans never met but who shared her interest in historic figures and strong passions. The opening poem in the set, 'Arabella Stuart', is written in the form of a dramatic monologue and tells of the narrator's longing for her absent husband, a recurring theme of Hemans's verse. Hemans also draws upon literary figures, as in 'The Switzer's Wife', taken from *Schiller's anti-Napoleonic play *Wilhelm Tell* (1804), which features an intensely patriotic Swiss wife. Throughout she often deploys the type of third-person sympathetic voice, familiar from Lord *Byron, fusing the personal and the political. Other poems address the female artist, notably the elegy 'The Grave of a Poetess', referring to the Irish poet Mary *Tighe, which has a poignant epigraph, taken from Madame de *Staël's *Corinne*, and may be translated as: 'Don't pity me; if only you knew how much suffering this tomb has spared me.'

Recruiting Officer, The A comedy by George *Farquhar, produced 1706 and performed more than 500 times during the 18th century; it is said to be the first play performed in Australia (1789). It draws on Farquhar's own experience of military recruiting in country towns. Captain Plume flirts with women to secure their followers as recruits; Kite, his resourceful sergeant, assumes the character of an astrologer, for the same purpose. Sylvia is in love with Plume but cannot marry him without the consent of her father, Justice Balance; she disguises herself as a man, gets herself arrested, is brought before her father, and is handed over by him to Plume, as a recruit. Meanwhile Captain Brazen, a boastful rival recruiting officer, endeavours to marry the rich Melinda, but is fobbed off with her maid.

recusant A term applied to Roman Catholics who refused to attend Church of England services as required by an Elizabethan law of 1559. In the reigns of *Elizabeth I and *James I recusants were subject to fines and imprisonment, and many priests were executed, including Edmund *Campion and Robert *Southwell. Catholics were still subject to fines in the 18th century, as described by Alexander *Pope in *Imitations of Horace*.
See ROMAN CATHOLICISM.

Red Badge of Courage, The A novel by Stephen *Crane, published 1895, describing the experiences of a raw young recruit in the American Civil War, famous for its *impressionistic technique.

Red Book of Hergest *See* MABINOGION.

Red Cotton Night-Cap Country, *or Turf and Towers* A poem in blank verse by Robert *Browning, published 1873. The title refers ironically to the description by Browning's friend Anne Thackeray *Ritchie of a district in Normandy as 'white cotton night-cap country'; Browning undertakes to show that the 'red' of passion and violence should replace the 'white'.

The story is based on a contemporary scandal, involving the wealthy heir to a Paris jewellery business, Antoine Mellerio (in the poem, Léonce Miranda). As Browning tells it, Miranda's life was dominated by the opposed principles of sensual indulgence and religious fanaticism, symbolized by the 'turf' and 'towers' of the sub-title. He lived with his mistress Anna (in the poem, Clara) at a luxurious estate in Normandy. His mother's death in Paris occasioned a fit of violent remorse, in which he renounced Clara and mutilated himself by burning off both his hands. However, he soon resumed his relationship with Clara and, in the period before his death, made extravagant donations to a convent near his estate, which housed a famous statue of the Virgin. He died by falling from the top of his belvedere, leaving his fortune to the convent, with a life interest for Clara. The will was challenged by his family, but their suit was comprehensively rejected by the courts, which upheld the will and declared Miranda's death to be due to an accident. Browning, however, maintains that Miranda leapt from the tower in a deliberate test of the power of the Virgin to save him, to resolve the struggle in his spirit between idealism and materialism. This struggle is the real topic of the poem: Miranda, weak-headed victim of a self-imposed dualism, is a nightmare parody of the figure of the artist in Browning. The poem has never been popular, because of its sordid plot and harsh, sardonic style; but contains, in Miranda's long interior monologue before he jumps, one of the most powerful single passages of Browning's late work.

Redcrosse Knight In Book I of Edmund *Spenser's *The *Faerie Queene*, St George, the patron saint of England. The 'patron' or champion of Holiness, he represents the Anglican Church. Separated from *Una (the true religion) by the wiles of *Archimago (hypocrisy), he is led away by *Duessa (the Roman Catholic religion) to the House of Pride. There he drinks from an enchanted stream, loses his strength, and is made captive by the giant Orgoglio (pride). Orgoglio is killed by Prince *Arthur, and Una leads her knight to the House of Holiness, to learn repentance and be healed. The Knight and Una are finally betrothed, after he has killed the dragon besieging her parents' castle.

Redgauntlet A novel by Walter *Scott, published 1824. In this novel, Scott returns after several years and with great success to the period and setting in which he was always most at home. The plot concerns an apocryphal attempt by Prince Charles Edward to regain the throne, twenty years after 1745. Under the name of Herries of Birrenswork, Hugh Redgauntlet, a fanatical Jacobite, leads the attempt and kidnaps his nephew Darsie Latimer (unknown to himself, Sir Arthur Darsie Redgauntlet and head of the family) in order to strengthen the cause. The plot collapses when the conspirators realize that the Hanoverian government does not take them seriously enough even to arrest them; that, in the words of Redgauntlet, the cause is lost forever. Apart from Darsie, the novel contains some memorable characters, notably Redgauntlet himself, the Quaker Joshua Geddes, the crazy litigant Peter Peebles (a parody of the situation of the Young Pretender) and particularly Saunders Fairford, an affectionate and probably accurate portrait of Scott's own father. It also contains, embedded in the novel and thematically linked to it, Scott's fine short story 'Wandering Willie's Tale'.

REDGROVE, Peter (1932–2003) Poet and novelist, educated at Queens' College, Cambridge, where he read Natural Sciences. A long-time resident in Cornwall, he figures its landscapes and seascapes in many poems. A founder member of the *Group, his first volume of poetry, *The Collector and Other Poems* (1960), was followed by many others, including *The Force and Other Poems* (1966), *The Weddings at Nether Powers* (1979), *Assembling a Ghost* (1996), and *From the Virgil Caverns* (2002). A *Selected Poems* appeared in 1999. His poetry is marked by a richness of visual imagery, a sense of physical immediacy, and a deep preoccupation with religious and sexual mysteries; it offers a world transformed by an intense pressure of imaginative focus. His novels, which include *In the Country of the Skin* (1973) and *The Beekeepers* (1980), are also rich in imagery, written in a highly poetic prose. He wrote several works in collaboration with Penelope *Shuttle, including *The Terrors of Dr Treviles* (1974), a novel of the occult and the psychic based on the relationship of psychologist Gregory Treviles and his witch-wife Robyn; and *The Wise Wound* (1978), a study of the mythology and reality of menstruation. Although Redgrove's work has some affinity with that of the *magic realists, it appears to spring from a different, possibly less cerebral source; with him, the artist as magician is less of a conjurer, more of a mystic. See Neil Roberts, *The Lover, the Dreamer and the World: The Poetry of Peter Redgrove* (1994).

Red Lion Playhouse London's first playhouse, built in the garden of a farm in Stepney by John Brayne (*c.*1541–1586), brother-in-law of James *Burbage, in 1567. Its stage measured 40 feet by 30 feet and was 5 feet high, and it had a single gallery and a 30-foot turret whose purpose is unclear. It was built without foundations, which may explain why it seems not to have lasted longer than a few months.

REED, Henry (1914–86) Poet, translator, and radio dramatist, educated at the University of Birmingham. He is best known for his book of verse *A Map of Verona* (1946), which contained his much-anthologized poem, inspired by his wartime experiences, 'Naming of Parts'. His plays made a notable contribution to *BBC radio drama in the 1950s, and two collections have been published: *The Streets of Pompeii* (1971), which contains five verse plays, and *Hilda Tablet and Others* (1971), which contains his four prose comedies of contemporary cultural life, based on the central character of the fictional composer Hilda Tablet. Reed's *Collected Poems*, edited by Jon *Stallworthy, appeared in a new edition in 2007.

REED, Isaac (1742–1807) Biographer, editor, and bibliophile. He practised, reluctantly, as a conveyancer, but devoted his life to literature: he produced a new edition of Robert *Dodsley's *Select Collection of Old Plays* (1780); *Biographica Dramatica* (2 vols 1782); contributions to Samuel *Johnson's **Lives of the English Poets*; and the 'first variorum' edition of *Shakespeare (21 vols, 1803), based on a long association with George *Steevens. He was unusually generous with his large library and was much consulted by contemporary scholars and antiquaries such as John *Nichols. See *The Reed Diaries 1762–1804*, ed. C. E. Jones (1946); Arthur Sherbo, *Isaac Reed: Editorial Factotum* (1989).

REED, Ishmael (Scott) (1938–) African American novelist, born in Chattanooga, Tennessee, who moved to New York in 1962, where he was active within the *Black Arts Movement, co-founding the *East Village Other*. His fiction tends to involve parodies of accepted genres: of the detective novel in *Mumbo Jumbo* (1972) and slave narratives in *Flight to Canada* (1976). His *Neo-HooDoo Manifesto* (1969) set out his subversive credo as a new 'religion'. He has courted controversy over feminism in his *Reckless Eyeballing* (1986) and his essays have been collected in *Shrovetide in Old New Orleans* (1978). In addition, Reed has published volumes of poetry, and edited *From Totems to Hip-Hop* (2003) among other anthologies. See Jay Boyer, *Ishmael Reed* (1993).

REED, John (Jack) (1887–1920) American journalist, born in Oregon, famous for his account of the Russian Revolution in *Ten Days that Shook the World* (1919). His other best-known publication was *Insurgent Mexico* (1914). John Reed Clubs, affiliated to the Communist Party, were widespread in the USA during the 1930s. See Eric Homberger, *John Reed* (1990).

REED, Talbot Baines (1852–93) Writer, born in Hackney, London; educated at the City of London School, he helped establish the conventions of the boys' *school story. His novels were often serialized in the *Boy's Own Paper*: 'My First Football Match, by an Old Boy' appeared on the front page of its first number, and he effectively donated his copyrights to its publishers, the *Religious Tract Society. His books' ethos mingles athleticism, duty, religion, and nationalism. Reed also worked in the family type-foundry and his *The History of Old English Letter Foundries* (1887) became a standard work.

REEVE, Clara (1729–1807) Novelist, who was born and died in Ipswich. *The Champion of Virtue: A Gothic Story*, published 1777, was reprinted in 1778 as *The Old English Baron*, and enjoyed great success. It was often published with Horace *Walpole's *The *Castle of Otranto*, of which it was confessedly a descendant. Reeve found Walpole's supernatural machinery absurd and had therefore reduced it to 'reason and probability'; Walpole, in turn, declared that Reeve's story was 'so probable, that any trial for murder at the Old Bailey would make a more interesting story'. The virtuous and noble Edmund moves resolutely through many adventures of romantic horror in order to obtain his rightful heritage, but the ghost of the murdered baron provides the only element of the supernatural. The story concludes with a dramatic day of trial and retribution. Clara Reeve wrote poems and several other novels, and an important critical dialogue on *The Progress of Romance* (1785).

'Reeve's Tale, The' *See* CANTERBURY TALES, 3.

Reflections on the Revolution in France By Edmund *Burke, published 1790. The treatise was provoked by Richard *Price's *Discourse of the Love of our Country*, delivered November 1789, in which Price exulted in the French Revolution and asserted that the king of England owed his throne to the choice of the people, who are at liberty to remove him for misconduct. Burke repudiated this constitutional doctrine, and contrasted inherited rights, which the English hold dear, with the 'rights of man' of the French revolutionaries, based on 'extravagant and presumptuous speculations', inconsistent with an ordered society and leading to poverty and chaos. Burke examined the character of the men who instigated the French Revolution, and the proceedings of their National Assembly, a 'profane burlesque of that sacred institute'. The well-known eloquent passage on the downfall of Marie Antoinette leads to the lament that 'the age of chivalry is gone… All the decent drapery of life is to be rudely torn off' in deference to 'the new conquering empire of light and reason'. Burke's general conclusion is that the defective institutions of the old regime should have been reformed, not destroyed.

***Reflector*, The** (1810–11) Founded and edited by Leigh *Hunt, a literary and political quarterly consisting of 'a collection of essays'. Hunt and Charles *Lamb were the principal contributors, and in its pages Lamb's essays on William *Hogarth and on the plays of *Shakespeare first appeared.

Reformation Referring primarily to the religious history of Europe in the early 16th century, though it can include both John *Wyclif and the 15th-century *Lollards and the later period to 1700. In its primary sense, the initiating event was the challenge to the selling of indulgences issued by Martin *Luther in 1517. This attack on corrupt practices quickly developed into a repudiation of the primacy of the pope and the ecclesiastical authority of Rome, and, led by Jean *Calvin in Geneva, Ulrich Zwingli (1484–1581) in Zurich, and John *Knox in Scotland, to the development of a distinctively Protestant conception of the Christian life, and the establishment of separate national, regional, and local congregational churches in northern and western Europe.

Under *Henry VIII England separated from Rome in the 1530s for political, rather than religious, reasons. Nevertheless, through the liturgy of Thomas *Cranmer, the sermons of Hugh *Latimer, and the biblical translations of William *Tyndale, the national Church of England became increasingly Protestant, adopting under *Elizabeth I a *via media* (middle way) between Rome and continental Reformed churches. The integrity of this course, and the distinctive piety associated with it (afterwards known as Anglicanism), was first enunciated and defended in the *Apologia Ecclesiae Anglicanae* (1562) of John Jewel (1522–71), and subsequently in the work of Richard *Hooker, Lancelot *Andrewes, John *Donne, Henry Hammond (1605–60), and Jeremy *Taylor. It was attacked by *Puritan writers (such as *Martin Marprelate and John *Milton) and Roman Catholics (such as Robert Parsons (1546–1610)).

Reformation, History of the *See* KNOX, JOHN.

Reform Bills The Reform Bill of 1832, introduced by Lord John Russell (1792–1878) in 1831, extended the parliamentary vote to include the prosperous middle classes, and redistributed members of Parliament to correspond with industrial centres of population. The Reform Bill of 1867 more than doubled the electorate, giving the vote to many male members of the working class, and the Bill of 1884 took in (with the exception of certain categories, i.e. lunatics, convicted criminals, and peers) all males over 21. In 1872 voting by secret ballot was introduced. Women over 30 were enfranchised in 1918; and women over 21 received the vote in 1928. In 1969, the franchise was extended to those over the age of 18. Electoral reform is a theme in many Victorian novels, notably in George Eliot's **Middlemarch* and **Felix Holt*.

regional novel A novel describing people and landscapes outside the metropolis. Early examples are set in Ireland (Maria *Edgeworth, **Castle Rackrent*) and Scotland (John *Galt, *The *Provost*) and are primarily studies of individual characters. The regional novels of Walter *Scott begin to combine a historically informed feeling for local customs with an appreciation of natural scenery. By the mid-19th century the localities described are often smaller and more exact, the focus being partly sociological, as in Charlotte *Brontë's **Shirley* (Yorkshire) and in the fiction of Elizabeth *Gaskell (Cheshire) and George *Eliot (the Midlands). In the works of Thomas *Hardy, set in a fictional Wessex, sensitivity to landscape complements a concern with agricultural and economic issues. These two approaches subsequently tend to diverge. In the mid-19th century, industrial or urban novels set in a specific town or city include Gaskell's **Mary Barton*, *Dickens's **Hard Times*, and Eliot's **Middlemarch*, and the tradition continued in the 20th century in the work of James *Joyce. Following Emily *Brontë's **Wuthering Heights* and R. D. *Blackmore's portrayal of Exmoor in **Lorna Doone*, other novelists adopted remote locations as settings for romantic dramas (Samuel Rutherford *Crockett's Galloway, Eden Phillpotts's (1862–1960) Dartmoor, Hugh *Walpole's Cumberland). The popularity of regional novels is reflected in the invention of fictional counties (Anthony *Trollope's Barsetshire, Winifred *Holtby's South Riding) or towns (Margaret *Oliphant's Carlingford). The genuinely regional work of Richard *Jefferies (Wiltshire), Constance Holme (1880–1955; Westmorland), and Francis Brett *Young (Worcestershire) combines social analysis with a celebration of local loyalties, as do the domestic novels set in Radstowe (Bristol) of Emily Hilda Young (1880–1949). More didactically slanted accounts of particular regions are found in the Shropshire romances of Mary *Webb and the early work of Henry *Williamson (Devon), in which country life is contrasted favourably with that of towns. Continued divergence between romantic and realistic handling of regionalism in the 20th century was reflected in the enormous popularity enjoyed by the Cornish novels of Daphne *du Maurier and the Tyneside ones of Catherine *Cookson; Winston Graham (1909–2003) gained a considerable following for his *historical Cornish novels, the Poldark series, of which the first (*Ross Poldark*) appeared in 1945. Examples of regionalism of a naturalistic kind are Arnold *Bennett's tales of the Staffordshire 'Five Towns' and the accounts of farming life of Sheila *Kaye-Smith (Kent and Sussex) and Adrian Bell (1901–80; Suffolk). Emphasis on social realism becomes more pronounced in the 1920s in the work of Phyllis Bentley (1894–1977), born in Halifax, who wrote of the textile industry in the West Riding of Yorkshire in many works including *Inheritance* (1932), a family saga; and H. E. *Bates (Northamptonshire). In D. H. *Lawrence's *The *Rainbow* (Nottinghamshire) and *A Glastonbury Romance* by John Cowper *Powys the potential limitations of the genre are surmounted through the integration of particular landscapes and places with individual psychological, religious, and emotional experience. In the second half of the 20th century regional writers continued to favour a realist approach, as in the work of Leo Walmsley (1892–1966), Yorkshire novelist born at Robin Hood's Bay, whose works include the saga *Three Fevers* (1932), *Phantom Lobster* (1933), and *Sally Lunn* (1937), a trilogy set on the north Yorkshire coast dealing with the lives of fishermen and their families; or John Moore (1907–67) with works based in Gloucestershire, Tewkesbury, and the surrounding villages (see the 'Brensham trilogy', 1946–8). The regional novel has often become a sociologically attuned vehicle for working-class concerns, *A Scots Quair* by Lewis Grassic *Gibbon anticipating the novels of Durham-born ex-miner Sid Chaplin (1916–86: see his *The Day of the Sardine*, 1961), Alan *Sillitoe, and Stan *Barstow in replacing nostalgia with radical questioning and social realism. See K. D. M. Snell (ed.), *The Regional Novel in Britain and Ireland: 1800–1990* (1998).

Register, Stationers' *See* STATIONERS' COMPANY.

Rehearsal, The A farcical comedy attributed to George Villiers, second duke of *Buckingham, but probably written by him in collaboration with others, among whom are mentioned Samuel *Butler and Martin Clifford (*c.*1624–1677), master of the Charterhouse; printed 1672. The play satirizes the heroic tragedies of the day, and consists of a series of parodies of passages from these, strung together in an absurd heroic plot. The author of the mock play is evidently a laureate (hence his name 'Bays'), and Sir William *D'Avenant was probably intended; but there are also hits at John *Dryden (particularly his *Conquest of Granada*) and his brothers-in-law, Edward (bap. 1624, d. 1712) and Robert Howard (1626–98). Bays takes two friends, Smith and Johnson, to see the rehearsal of his play, and the absurdity of this work (which includes the two kings of Brentford, entering hand in hand), coupled with the comments of Bays, his instructions to the actors, and the remarks of Smith and Johnson, remains highly entertaining. Prince Pretty-man, Prince Volscius, and Drawcansir are among the characters. It was one of the earliest of English dramatic *burlesques, and was much performed during the 18th century, during which period the genre developed to one of its highest points in Richard Brinsley Sheridan's *The *Critic*. The work helped to inspire Andrew *Marvell's *The Rehearsal Transprosed* (1672; Pt II, 1673).

REID, Christopher (1949–) Poet, born in Hong Kong and educated at Oxford. He was poetry editor at Faber & Faber between 1991 and 1999. His first book, *Arcadia* (1979), was widely regarded as a contribution to the 'Martian' kind of poetry which James *Fenton identified in relation to Craig *Raine's volume *A Martian Sends a Postcard Home*; and Reid is adept with the *defamiliarizing metaphors characteristic of the style. However, after his second book, *Pea Soup* (1982), the exuberant playfulness of that manner was turned decisively towards melancholy in *Katerina Brac* (1985). Here Reid writes in the persona of a woman poet, translated into English, from an unspecified Eastern European country under a communist regime. Acutely imitating the syntactical hesitations and inflections of some translations, Reid now employs defamiliarizations edged with new political point or menace: the 'tin lily' of a loudspeaker issuing threats, for instance, is 'not surrealism, | but an image of the new reality, | a counterblast to Copernicus'. At the same time, the volume is a sophisticated exploration of the potentials, paradoxes, pitfalls, and peculiarities of the acts of translation, ventriloquism, self-concealment, and self-revelation that constitute the making of all poems, not only translations. It has been followed by *In the Echoey Tunnel* (1991), *Expanded Universes* (1996), and *For and After* (2002), which includes many translations from actual, not fictional, poets, among them *Leopardi, *Pushkin, *Verlaine, and Antonio *Machado; it also includes the outstanding 'Bollockshire', a disabused, alliterating English anti-pastoral, more bilious than bucolic. *Mr Mouth* (2005) is a further sequence of poems concerning a single 'character', whom it traces from birth to death. Charting an extraordinary ordinary life, the volume is a compendium of emotions and kinds: whimsy, melancholy, fantasy, humour, wit, and grief all attach themselves to its prematurely voluble, preternaturally gluttonous human exhibit. A selection of Reid's work, *Mermaids Explained*, edited by Charles *Simic, was published in the USA in 2001. Reid has also published children's books, including *All Sorts* (1999), with his own press, Ondt and Gracehoper.

REID, Forrest (1875–1947) Novelist, journalist, and literary scholar, born in Belfast and educated at the Royal Belfast Academical Institution and, after some years in the tea trade, Christ's College, Cambridge. His largely uneventful life was spent in and around his native city. His sixteen novels include *The Kingdom of Twilight* (1904), *The Garden God* (1905), *Following Darkness* (1912), and a later trilogy, *Uncle Stephen* (1931), *The Retreat* (1936), and *Young Tom* (1944), published in one volume in 1955 as *Tom Barber*, with an introduction by his friend E. M. *Forster. Reid's dominant subject is boyhood and adolescence; he evokes a lyrical world of 'lonely garden and sombre grove', in which hints of the supernatural are contrasted with the realities of everyday. His autobiographies, *Apostate* (1926) and *Private Road* (1940), vividly describe his sense of the numinous in nature. See *The Green Avenue* (1980), a critical biography by B. Taylor.

REID, 'Captain' Thomas Mayne (1818–83) A celebrated writer of boys' adventure stories, born in Ballyroney, County Down; he travelled extensively in the USA, participating in the Mexican War (1846–8). His first book, *The Rifle Rangers* (1850), was based on his experiences; his first 'juvenile' was *The Desert Home* (1852). His admirers included Theodore Roosevelt. See Elizabeth Reid, *Captain Mayne Reid* (1900).

Rejected Addresses By James and Horatio *Smith, published 1812. A competition was held to find a suitable address to celebrate the opening of the new *Drury Lane Theatre in 1812. James and Horatio Smith produced a large batch of bogus entries, purporting to be by William *Wordsworth, Lord *Byron, Thomas *Moore, Robert *Southey, S. T. *Coleridge, George *Crabbe, Walter *Scott, William *Cobbett, and others. The parodies are mixed in quality, but the brilliance of some made the Smiths famous, and caused Thomas *Campbell to feel annoyed that he had been left out.

Relapse, The, *or Virtue in Danger* Sir John *Vanbrugh's highly successful first play, produced 1696. A continuation of *Love's Last Shift* by Colley *Cibber, it has two plots. In the first, Loveless, a reformed libertine, living happily in the country with his wife Amanda, suffers a relapse, on a visit to London, under the temptation of Berinthia, an unscrupulous young widow. In the comic sub-plot the absurd Sir Novelty Fashion, who has recently become (by purchase) Lord Foppington, plans to marry Miss Hoyden, daughter of Sir Tunbelly Clumsey, a country squire, but is foiled by his younger brother, Young Fashion, who marries her himself. The play was adapted by Richard Brinsley *Sheridan as *A Trip to Scarborough*.

Religio Laici A poem by John *Dryden, published 1682. Written in defence of Anglicanism against Deist, Catholic, and Dissenting arguments, *Religio Laici* combines an exalted recognition of religious sublimity with a defence of a 'layman's' reasonable and straightforward religious attitudes. The poem's opening lines, beginning 'Dim as the borrowed beams of moon and stars', are among the finest Dryden wrote.

Religio Medici *('The Religion of a Doctor')* A personal account of his religious faith by Sir Thomas *Browne, composed about 1635, first published in an unauthorized edition 1642, reprinted 1643 with authorial corrections and additions. It is written in magnificently sonorous yet intimate prose, and in its humanity, lack of prejudice, tolerance of other religious persuasions, self-revelation, and frank self-doubt, it resembles *Montaigne's *Essays* (which, however, Browne said he had not read when he wrote it). Its wit and learning made it a European best-seller, and it has been often reprinted, and translated into many languages. Its unorthodox views were deplored by Sir Kenelm *Digby in his *Observations* (1643) and it was placed on the papal index of prohibited books in 1645.

Religious Tract Society Founded in 1799 to distribute cheap religious literature by the same interdenominational group of evangelicals who had earlier set up the London Missionary Society and were later to found the British and Foreign Bible Society. Its methods were influenced by Hannah *More's *Cheap Repository Tracts*, and its productions were much more readable than those put out by the *SPCK. A famous example from the early 19th century was Legh *Richmond's *The Dairyman's Daughter*, the account of the religious reformation and early death of a working-class woman from the Isle of Wight. In the course of the century it published a great deal of children's literature, by authors such as Favell Bevan (1802–78) and Talbot Baines *Reed, a popular contributor to the Society's widely read *Boy's Own Paper*. See Gordon Hewitt, *Let the People Read* (1949).

Reliques of Ancient English Poetry A collection of ballads, historical songs, and metrical romances published in 3 volumes (1765) by Thomas *Percy. With its introductory 'Essay on the Ancient English Minstrels', the collection was an important landmark in the recovery of folk poetry (*see* PRIMITIVISM). Most of the texts were extracted from the *Percy Folio and 'restored' by Percy with advice from William *Shenstone and Samuel *Johnson. Some were from medieval times, others were as recent as the reign of Charles I. Ancient poems from other sources and a few relatively modern pieces (by e.g. George *Wither, John *Dryden, and Richard *Lovelace), were added by the editor. Joseph *Ritson was sharply critical of Percy's editorial method. The editions of 1767, 1775, and 1794 each contained new matter.

REMARQUE, Erich Maria (1898–1970) German novelist, known best as the author of *Im Westen nichts Neues* (1929: *All Quiet on the Western Front*), a fictionalized account of his experiences in the First World War which was translated into many languages and made into an acclaimed film by Lewis Milestone for Universal Studios (1930). The novel's anti-war stance, for which it was denounced and publicly burnt in Nazi Germany, helped shape the attitudes of an inter-war generation that included William *Golding. Remarque left Germany for Switzerland in 1938, and in 1939 settled permanently in the United States. A stage adaptation of the novel by Robin Kingsland was performed in 2006.

Remorse A tragedy by S. T. *Coleridge, written in 1797 as *Osorio* and produced at Drury Lane 1813. The story, set in Granada at the time of the Spanish Inquisition, tells of the slow corruption of the character of Osorio, a man who supposed himself strong but who is gradually led by temptations and events into guilt and evil.

Renaissance The great flowering of art, architecture, politics, and the study of literature, usually seen as the end of the Middle Ages and the beginning of the modern world, which came about under the influence of Greek and Roman models. The Renaissance (some scholars prefer to use the term 'early modern period') is generally said to have begun in Italy in the late 14th century and to have culminated in the High Renaissance in the early 16th century (the period of *Michelangelo and *Machiavelli), and spread to the rest of Europe in the 15th century and afterwards. Its emphasis was humanist: that is, regarding the human figure and reason without necessarily relating them to the superhuman; but much of its energy also came from the *Neoplatonic tradition in writers such as *Pico della Mirandola. The term 'Renaissance' has been applied in the 20th century to earlier periods which manifested a new interest in and study of the classics, such as the 12th century and the age of Charlemagne. But the Italian Renaissance is still seen as a watershed in the development of civilization, both because of its extent and because of its emphasis on the human, whether independent of or in association with the divine. The pioneering account is Jacob *Burckhardt, *The Civilization of the Renaissance in Italy* (1860; English trans., S. G. C. Middlemore, 1878); see also Walter *Pater, *Studies in the History of the Renaissance* (1873) and John Addington *Symonds, *History of the Renaissance in Italy* (1875–86).

RENAN, Ernest (1823–92) French Hebraist, historian, and archaeologist. After a childhood spent in his native Brittany he studied for the priesthood in Paris, but withdrew because of doubts about the divinity of Jesus and the divine inspiration of the Bible. His eccentric sexuality, which was aroused by the veiled and the inaccessible, seems eventually to have focused on his sister Henriette, about whom he was to write rhapsodically years after her death in *Ma Sœur Henriette* (1895: *My Sister Henriette*), not least for her role in the preparation of his controversial masterpiece *La Vie de Jésus* (1863: *The Life of Jesus*), the first of a seven-volume account of the historical origins of Christianity (*Histoire des origines du Christianisme* (*History of the Origins of Christianity*)). *La Vie de Jésus* is a fusion of Renan's romantic Christianity, which centred on its aesthetic and emotional significance, and his solid historical scholarship, which led him to subject the biblical accounts of the life of Jesus to sceptical scrutiny. Translated into English twice in 1864 alone, it earned him both fame and persecution. His thinking had a significant impact on religious thought in Victorian Britain, and was particularly important to the cultural criticism of Matthew Arnold. Besides his historical and philological works, Renan published a number of critical, reflective, and prophetic essays, including *Essais de morale et de critique* (1859: *Moral and Critical Essays*), *La Réforme intellectuelle et morale* (1871: *Intellectual and Moral Reform*), *Examen de conscience philosophique* (1888: *Examination of Philosophical Conscience*), and *L'Avenir de la science* (1890: *The Future of Science*). His early years are recalled in *Souvenirs d'enfance et de jeunesse* (1883: *Memories of Childhood and Youth*).

RENAULT, Mary (1905–83) Pseudonym of Mary Challans, novelist, known principally for her *historical novels, most of which are lively first-person narratives set in ancient Greece or Asia Minor, incorporating the new anthropological and historical insights of the 20th century. They include *The King Must Die* (1958) and *The Bull from the Sea* (1962), both retelling the legend of Theseus, and *The Persian Boy* (1972), set in the time of Alexander the Great.

RENDELL, Ruth Barbara, Baroness Rendell of Babergh (1930–) Writer of detective fiction and psychological thrillers, educated at Loughton High School, Essex; she worked as a journalist before becoming a full-time writer. Starting with her first book, *From Doon with Death* (1964), her novels featuring Detective Chief Inspector Reginald Wexford and his colleague Mike Burden in the fictional Sussex town of Kingsmarkham increasingly use the 'police procedural' genre to explore contemporary social issues. Tense crime novels (among which *A Judgement in Stone*, 1977, and *The Keys to the Street*, 1996, are outstanding) portray and probe aberrant psychologies and personalities warped by phobias. Under the pseudonym Barbara Vine, she has also written fictional studies of crime and violence (from *A Dark-Adapted Eye*, 1986, to *The Birthday Present*, 2008), often set in the past and more spacious in their evocation of place and period. There are two volumes of *Collected Short Stories* (1987 and 2008). Her many awards include four Gold Daggers from the Crime Writers Association and three Edgar Allen *Poe awards from the Mystery Writers of America. She was made a life peer in 1996.

RENÉ D'ANJOU, count of Provence (1409–80) Known as 'le bon Roi René', son of Louis II, duke of Anjou, and titular king of Naples, the two Sicilies, and Jerusalem, 'whose large style agrees not with the leanness of his purse' (Shakespeare, 2 **Henry VI*, I. i). His daughter *Margaret of Anjou was wife of Henry VI. As count of Provence, he was a great patron of the arts, and showed indifference to political affairs. There is a picture of his court in Walter Scott's **Anne of Geierstein*. He figures in *Henry VI* as 'Reignier'. He wrote a handbook of tournament ritual and two allegories.

RENI, Guido (1575–1642) Bolognese painter much admired in England in the 18th and early 19th centuries, when he was ranked second only to *Raphael. P. B. *Shelley, in Bologna in 1818, wrote rapturously to Thomas Love *Peacock of the Renis in the Pinacoteca, and from Rome (1819) exclaimed that only Raphael, Reni, and Salvator *Rosa could sustain comparison with antiquity. A painting traditionally described as a portrait of Beatrice Cenci, almost certainly not by Reni himself but loosely derived from his *St Andrew Led to Martyrdom* (1608), cast a spell over the Romantics: Shelley describes it in his preface to *The *Cenci*, and later it fascinated Thomas *De Quincey, Charles *Dickens, A. C. *Swinburne, Herman *Melville, and many others: Nathaniel *Hawthorne uses it and Reni's *Archangel Michael* in *The *Marble Faun* to symbolize various aspects of his central characters. But John *Keats disliked his 'melodramatic mawkishness' and his reputation plunged with John *Ruskin: only recently has the true stature of his work again been recognized. See Richard Spear, *The 'Divine' Guido* (1997).

REPTON, Humphry *See* PICTURESQUE.

'Resolution and Independence' A poem by William *Wordsworth, written 1802, published 1807, sometimes known as 'The Leech Gatherer'. The poet describes his elation as he walks over the moors on a fine spring morning after a storm, and his sudden descent into apprehension and dejection, as he ponders the fate of earlier poets, such as Thomas *Chatterton: 'We Poets in our youth begin in gladness, | But thereof come in the end despondency and Madness.' At this point he meets the aged leech gatherer, and cross-questions him in characteristically Wordsworthian manner about his way of life; the old man responds with cheerful dignity, and the poet resolves to remember him as an admonishment. The poem was based on a meeting recorded in Dorothy *Wordsworth's *Journal*, 3 October 1800, with an 'old man almost double', whose trade was to gather leeches. Its mixture of elevated language and sentiment with prosaic detail is peculiarly Wordsworthian, and led S. T. *Coleridge to comment on its 'inconstancy of style'. Wordsworth's own comments on his use of imagery in the poem and 'the conferring, the abstracting, and the modifying powers of the Imagination' in his 1815 preface are of great interest.

RESTIF DE LA BRETONNE, Nicolas-Edme (1734–1806) French novelist and thinker. His fictions, rich in the material reality of daily life in late 18th-century France, often reflect the dissipations of his own life as a well-to-do peasant in Paris (*Le Paysan perverti*, 1775: *The Perverted Peasant*; *La Paysanne pervertie*, 1784: *The Perverted Peasant Girl*), a life chronicled in his sixteen-volume autobiography *Monsieur Nicolas* (1794–97). His *Nuits de Paris* (1788–94: *Paris Nights*) offers a fascinating insight into life in Paris during the revolution.

Restoration The re-establishment of monarchy in England, with the return of Charles II (1660); also the period marked by this event of which the chief literary figures are John *Dryden, John Wilmot, earl of *Rochester, John *Bunyan, Samuel *Pepys, John *Locke, and the Restoration dramatists. One of the characteristic genres of the period is Restoration comedy, or the comedy of manners, which developed upon the reopening of the theatres. Its principal writers were William *Congreve, Sir George *Etherege, George *Farquhar, Sir John *Vanbrugh, and William *Wycherley, and its predominant tone was witty, bawdy, cynical, and amoral. The plays were mainly in prose, with passages of verse for the more romantic moments; the plots were complex and usually double, sometimes triple, though repartee and discussions of marital behaviour provide much of the interest, reflecting the fashionable manners of the day. Standard characters include fops, bawds, scheming valets, country squires, and sexually voracious young widows and older women; the principal theme is sexual intrigue, either for its own sake or for money. Playwrights came under heavy attack for frivolity, blasphemy, and immorality (*see* Collier, Jeremy): they and their subsequent admirers defended their works as serious social criticism, and mirrors to the age. During the 18th century the plays were presented in more 'genteel' versions, and in the 19th century hardly at all: the 20th century saw a considerable revival of interest, with such notable productions as Congreve's *The *Way of the World*, one of the masterpieces of the period, in 1924 with Edith Evans as Millamant.

Resurrection *See* Bible.

Retaliation An unfinished poem by Oliver *Goldsmith, published 1774, consisting of a string of humorous epitaphs on David *Garrick, Sir Joshua *Reynolds, Edmund *Burke, and other friends, in reply to Garrick's mock epitaph on him: 'Here lies Nolly Goldsmith, for shortness called Noll, | Who wrote like an angel, but talked like poor Poll.'

Retrospective Review (1820–8) Founded by Henry Southern (1799–1853), its first editor, as a 'Review of past literature', the object of which was 'to exhibit a bird's-eye view of the rise and progress of our literature' and to rouse interest 'in the old and venerable literature of the country'. Extracts from poetry, essays, drama, and other prose, chiefly drawn from the 16th and 17th centuries, included the work of Francis *Bacon, Sir Thomas *Browne, George *Chapman, George *Herbert, Ben *Jonson, Henry *Vaughan, and many others. Some three-quarters of the work was English; the rest consisted of translations from past European literature. Southern also questioned the authority of contemporary critics, such as those of the **Quarterly* and the **Edinburgh* reviews, claiming that they substituted prejudice for true critical principles. The method of the *Review* was to consider each piece or extract as if it were just from the press, sometimes comparing the quality of the old with work of the 'moderns'. The *Review* was briefly revived in 1853–4.

Return of the Native, The A novel by Thomas *Hardy, published 1878. The scene is the sombre Egdon Heath, powerfully and symbolically present throughout the novel. Damon Wildeve, once an engineer but now a publican, dallies between the gentle Thomasin Yeobright and passionate Eustacia Vye. Thomasin rejects the humble reddleman Diggory Venn (he sells the 'reddle' ochre used by farmers to mark their sheep), and is eventually married to Wildeve, whose strongest motive in the union is a wish to hurt Eustacia. Thomasin's cousin Clym Yeobright, a diamond merchant in Paris, disgusted with his trivial occupation, returns to Egdon to become a schoolmaster in his native heath. He falls in love with Eustacia, and she marries him, hoping to escape the Heath by moving to Paris. But to her despair he will not return; his sight fails and he becomes a humble furze-cutter on the heath. She divides Clym from his beloved mother, and unintentionally causes the mother's death. This, together with the discovery that Eustacia's relationship with Wildeve has continued, leads to a violent scene between Clym and his wife. Eustacia flees, and she and Wildeve are drowned. Clym, blaming himself for the deaths of his wife and mother, becomes an itinerant preacher, and the widowed Thomasin marries Diggory Venn.

REUCHLIN, Johann (1455–1522) Celebrated German humanist scholar. Born at Pforzheim, he studied at Freiburg, Paris, and Basle and became the leading Hebraist of his day, producing the first Hebrew grammar. Through his extensive knowledge of Jewish writings, in particular the Cabbala, he became embroiled in the controversy over the suppression of Jewish books advocated by Johannes Pfefferkorn and the Dominicans. This controversy was the occasion of the **Epistolae Obscurorum Virorum*. Already an old man at the time of Martin *Luther's challenge, he vainly sought to keep *Melanchthon, his grand-nephew, loyal to Rome.

Revelation, Book of *See* Apocalypse; Bible.

revels, master of the An officer appointed to superintend *masques and other entertainments at court. He is first mentioned in the reign of Henry VII. The first permanent master of the revels was Sir Thomas Cawarden (*c.*1514–1559), appointed in 1545. Holders of the office in William *Shakespeare's day were Edmund Tilney, 1579–1610, and Sir George Buc, 1610–22 (he had been deputy master since 1603).

Revenge of Bussy D'Ambois, The A tragedy by George *Chapman, written 1610/11, printed 1613, a sequel to **Bussy D'Ambois*. Clermont D'Ambois, brother of Bussy, described by his close friend the duc de Guise as the ideal 'Senecal [i.e. Stoical] man', noble and 'fixed in himself', is urged by his brother's ghost to avenge his murder, but will only do so by the honourable method of a duel. He sends a challenge to Montsurry, who evades it; urged again by the ghost, he enters Montsurry's house, forces him to fight, and kills him. Learning of the assassination of the duc de Guise, and refusing to live amid 'all the horrors of the vicious time' as 'the slave of power', he kills himself. The hero's reluctance to exact revenge recalls certain aspects of **Hamlet*.
See also REVENGE TRAGEDY.

Revenger's Tragedy, The A tragedy published anonymously in 1607, and from 1656 ascribed to Cyril *Tourneur; its authorship has been much disputed but since the later part of the 20th century Thomas *Middleton's claims have prevailed.

The central character is Vendice (or Vindice), intent on revenging the death of his mistress, poisoned by the lecherous old duke. The court is deeply corrupt; the duchess's youngest son is convicted of rape, she herself seduces Spurio, the duke's illegitimate son, and her two older sons, the duke's stepsons, plot against each other and against Lussurioso, the duke's heir. Vendice, disguised as Piato, pretends to try to prostitute his own sister Castiza to Lussurioso; she resists, but their mother Gratiana temporarily succumbs to his bribes and agrees to help him. Vendice murders the duke by tricking him into kissing the poisoned skull of his mistress, and most of the remaining characters die in a final masque of revengers and murderers; Vendice, who survives the bloodbath, owns up to the murder of the duke, and is condemned to death with his brother and accomplice Hippolite by the duke's successor, old Antonio. He is content to 'die after a nest of dukes'. The play is marked by a tragic intensity of feeling, a powerfully satiric wit, and passages of great poetic richness, all combined, for example, in Vendice's address to 'the bony lady', his dead mistress: 'Does the silkworm expend her yellow labours | For thee?' (III. iv).
See also REVENGE TRAGEDY.

revenge tragedy A dramatic genre that flourished in the late Elizabethan and Jacobean period, sometimes known as 'the tragedy of blood'. Kyd's *The *Spanish Tragedy* (*c.*1587), a much-quoted prototype, helped to establish the popularity of the form; later examples are Christopher Marlowe's *The *Jew of Malta*, Shakespeare's **Titus Andronicus*, Thomas *Middleton's *The *Revenger's Tragedy*, and, most notably, **Hamlet*; there are also strong revenge elements in John *Webster. Common ingredients include: the hero's quest for vengeance, often at the prompting of the ghost of a murdered kinsman or loved one; scenes of real or feigned insanity; a play-within-a-play; scenes in graveyards, severed limbs, and scenes of carnage and mutilation. Many of these features were inherited from *Seneca, with the difference that in revenge tragedy violence was not reported but took place on stage: as Vindice in *The Revenger's Tragedy* rather baldly puts it, while in the process of slowly murdering the Duke, 'When the bad bleeds, then is the tragedy good.' The revenge code also produced counter-attacks, as in *The *Atheist's Tragedy*, in Chapman's *The *Revenge of Bussy D'Ambois*, and again in *Hamlet*, in which the heroes refuse or hesitate to follow the convention.

Review (1) a *periodical started by Daniel *Defoe in 1704, originally under the title of *A Weekly Review of the Affairs of France*, signalling one of its key areas of interest. It became *A Review of the State of the British Nation* in 1707 and continued until 1713, when the war with France ended. It appeared three times a week and was written almost entirely by Defoe himself, voicing opinions on current political, economic, and military topics. Supposedly non-partisan but essentially Protestant and Whig in perspective, it promoted mercantile interests and European trade as the key to national prosperity, but also contained articles on love, marriage, crime, gambling, and other social issues, and 'Advice from the Scandal Club', a section of lighter stories. (2) A quarterly magazine of poetry and criticism, founded in 1962 and edited by Ian *Hamilton. It ran for 30 issues, and was succeeded by the *New Review*, also edited by Hamilton, which ran from 1974 to 1979.

Revolt of Islam, The An epic political poem by P. B. *Shelley, written at Great Marlow in 1817 (under the title 'Laon and Cythna: or The Revolution in the Golden City, A Vision of the Nineteenth Century'), published 1818. The poem is Shelley's idealized and orientalized version of the French Revolution, and the prose preface considers reactions to the revolution. It is composed in Spenserian stanzas, forming twelve cantos. The revolt is organized by a brother and sister, Laon and Cythna, whose temporary success is celebrated in incestuous love-making. But the tyrants recover power, and Islam is subject to plague and famine, vividly described. Brother and sister are burnt at the stake, but sail together with an illegitimate child to a visionary Hesperides. Though cumbersome, diffuse, and obsessive (there is much-disguised autobiography), the poem contains powerful images of struggle and renewal which Shelley returns to in his poems of 1819. The figure of Cythna, the revolutionary feminist, is of historical interest.

Revue des deux mondes, La A celebrated French monthly review which first appeared in 1829 and which continues to be published today. Under the editorship (1831–77) of François Buloz it became one of the leading periodicals of its kind in Europe, dealing with foreign and domestic politics as well as literature, philosophy, and the fine arts, and attracting contributions from such writers as *Balzac, *Sainte-Beuve, *Dumas *père*, *Hugo, *Vigny, and *Sand.

reward books There is a long tradition of giving books to children as rewards and prizes; in the 19th century the creation of suitable books for this purpose became a distinct part of the publishing industry. Reward books combined attractive presentation with warnings against such social evils as intemperance and discontent and the promotion of virtuous behaviour.

REXROTH, Kenneth (1905–82) American writer, born in Indiana, who had a multifaceted career in literature and painting. His poetry from *In What Hour* (1940) onwards continues the line of *modernism, although Rexroth wrote many polemical essays, in *With Eye and Ear* (1970) among other volumes, stressing the value of an indigenous tradition of American writing. He also edited a number of anthologies and produced translations from Japanese and other languages. See Linda Hamalian, *A Life of Kenneth Rexroth* (1991).

Reynard the Fox The central character in the *Roman de Renart*, a series of popular satirical fables, related to the *bestiaries and in the tradition of *Aesop's Fables, written in France at various times *c*.1175–1250. The first known cycle is a Latin one by Nivard of Ghent, *Ysengrimus* (*c*.1148), and this was followed by the Middle High German *Reinhard Fuchs* (*c*.1180). There is a Flemish version from *c*.1250; another Flemish version (now lost) was translated into English and printed by William *Caxton in 1481. In these anthropomorphic stories, the fox is the man who preys on society, is brought to justice, but escapes by his cunning. The popularity of the series was most marked in French (which took from it the German word *Regin-hart*, 'strong in counsel', to become 'renard', for 'fox'), but there are some derived and related English works. The most important of these is the Middle English 'The Fox and the Wolf' (in *Early Middle English Verse and Prose*, ed. J. A. W. Bennett and G. V. Smithers (2nd edn 1968)), written in rhyming couplets and dating from the late 13th century. The encounter between the fox and cockerel in this poem anticipates that in Chaucer's 'The Nun's Priest's Tale' (*see* CANTERBURY TALES, 20), while its satire on ecclesiastical practices (in this case confession) make it an early example of a tradition to which Robert *Henryson's 'Morall Fabillis of Esope' (where the fox is called Lowrence) also belong. Later examples of the Reynard tradition are J. C. *Harris's Uncle Remus stories (where the role of the fox is taken by Brer Rabbit). The principal characters in Caxton's version include Reynard, King Noble the Lion, Isengrym the Wolf, Bruin the Bear, Bellyn the Ram, Chanticleer the Cock, and Partlet the Hen. Ermeline is Reynard's wife and Malperdy his castle. *The History of Reynard the Fox Translated from the Dutch Original by William Caxton*, ed. N. F. Blake (EETS os 263, 1970).

REYNOLDS, Alastair (1966–) *Science fiction author, born in Barry, south Wales. *Revelation Space* (2000) began a series of darkly *Gothic far-future novels, somewhat in the neo-space opera vein of Peter F. *Hamilton or Iain M. *Banks, but with a significant vein of baroque moral ambiguity.

REYNOLDS, John Hamilton (1796–1852) Poet, and a close friend and correspondent of John *Keats (Keats's letter to Reynolds of May 1818 on *The *Fall of Hyperion* is particularly important). In 1814 Reynolds published *Safie*, an *oriental novel reminiscent of Lord *Byron, and *The Eden of the Imagination*, which echoes late 18th-century verse. *The Garden of Florence* (1821) contains his most effective serious work, and includes two verse tales from *Boccaccio, as part of a Boccaccio volume he and Keats intended to write together, and for which Keats originally produced *'Isabella'. He had great skill in parody and comic verse; his anticipatory parody of William *Wordsworth's **Peter Bell* appeared in 1819 even before the original was published, *The Fancy*, a mock heroic poem on pugilism, in 1820, and *Odes and Addresses to Great People* (with Thomas *Hood) in 1825. See Leonidas M. Jones, *The Life of John Hamilton Reynolds* (1984).

REYNOLDS, Sir Joshua (1723–92) Painter, born in Devon. He was apprenticed in London (1740–44) and studied in Italy (1750–52); on his return to London (1753) he swiftly became the most successful portrait painter of his age. Reynolds sought to give new dignity to British portraiture by relating it to the Grand Style of European art. His portraits are immensely varied and enriched by allusions to the antique and to Renaissance and 17th-century Italian art. He was a distinguished man of letters; it was he who suggested the idea of the *Club to his friend Samuel *Johnson. He painted Johnson at least five times and wrote a memoir of him and two Johnsonian dialogues; James *Boswell dedicated his *Life of Johnson* to the painter, and Oliver *Goldsmith dedicated *The *Deserted Village* to him. Reynolds's first literary works were three essays published in *The *Idler* (1759). In 1768 he was made first president of the Royal Academy and his *Discourses*, delivered to the students (1769–90), are his most significant achievement as a writer. He supported the values of academic art, and stressed the importance of study of the great masters of the past. Yet the *Discourses* reveal that he was sensitive to the new ideals of Romantic art; the last is a tribute to *Michelangelo, whose sublimity Reynolds had come to value above the perfection of *Raphael. William *Hazlitt pointed out the contradictions in the *Discourses* and William *Blake, in a series of annotations to his copy of the *Works*, attacked Reynolds for his lack of faith in the inspiration of genius—on the title page he wrote, 'This man was hired to depress art.' Yet he was admired by John *Constable, J. M. W. *Turner, and John *Ruskin, and William *Wordsworth paid tribute to him in lines on Sir George *Beaumont's cenotaph to his memory at Coleorton. See *Discourses on Art*, ed. Robert R. Wark (1975; repr. 1997); Nicholas Penny, *Reynolds* (1986); Richard Wendorf, *Sir Joshua Reynolds: The Painter in Society* (1996).

REZNIKOFF, Charles (1894–1976) American poet, born in New York; a leading member of the Objectivists group. His major work was *Testimony* (1978–9), an assembly (or 'recitative') of American stories 1855–1915, taken initially from court records. Reznikoff used a similar method for his volume on the Nazi concentration camps, *Holocaust* (1975). See Stephen Fredman, *A Menorah for Athena* (2001).
See also HOLOCAUST.

rhetoric The ancient art of speaking (or by extension, writing) persuasively, much cultivated in antiquity, and revived as a major element of the medieval and Renaissance school syllabus up to the 17th century. This tradition of learning ultimately laid the foundations for English literature as an academic discipline, notably in the lectures of Hugh *Blair at Edinburgh. Literary rhetoric is concerned chiefly with the conscious exploitation of the various figures of speech, which were extensively named and categorized in antiquity and are still mostly known under their Greek names (although George *Puttenham attempted to provide colourful English translations for them). These are commonly divided into three kinds: (i) major 'figures of thought', also called 'tropes', which transform the meanings of words and expressions, as with *metaphor, *metonymy, *personification, *irony, and *hyperbole; (ii) lesser 'figures of speech' which arrange words in attractive or memorable ways, as with *anaphora, *asyndeton, *chiasmus, *epanalepsis, *syllepsis, and dozens of others; and (iii) 'figures of sound', such as *alliteration and *onomatopoeia. A growing number of English schoolboys in the 15th, 16th, and 17th centuries, including Shakespeare and Milton, were required to identify, memorize, and illustrate examples of more than a hundred such figures, thus encouraging a vibrant culture of linguistic exuberance in these periods. See Edward P. J. Corbett and Robert J. Connors, *Classical Rhetoric for the Modern Student* (1998); Jennifer Richards, *Rhetoric* (2007); Brian Vickers, *In Defence of Rhetoric* (1988).

RHODES, William Barnes (1772–1826) A banker, who translated the *Satires* of *Juvenal in 1801 and the *Epigrams* in 1803. He did not acknowledge his authorship of his highly successful farce *Bombastes furioso* (1810) until 1822. Rhodes collected volumes of plays, old and new, and bought heavily at the *Roxburghe sale in 1812.

rhyme Correspondence of vowel and consonantal sounds in pairs of stressed syllables or of syllable-groups beginning with a stressed syllable, most commonly found at the ends of verse lines. There are various kinds of rhyme, the most common distinction being between 'masculine' rhymes on single stressed syllables only (born/forlorn) and 'feminine' rhymes with a further unstressed syllable included in the rhymed element (together/weather). Triple rhymes are also sometimes found, with two unstressed syllables following the main stress (beautiful/dutiful). Where more than one word makes up one of the rhymed pair of sounds in a feminine or triple rhyme (dreamy/see me), this is called 'mosaic rhyme'. All the rhyming pairs illustrated here are examples of 'full' or 'true' rhyme, a norm from which various other forms deviate. These include *rime riche*, in which the consonants preceding the stressed syllable also match (veil/vale); 'eye rhyme', in which spellings match but pronunciation does not (bough/through); half-rhyme, in which the stressed vowel sounds do not match but the consonants (and sometimes unstressed syllables) coming after them do (love/have, lover/never); and pararhyme, a 'rich' version of half-rhyme in which stressed vowel sounds again fail to correspond while the preceding consonants as well as those following do (grieve/grave).

The ordered pattern in which rhyming sounds recur at the line-endings of a *stanza or poem is called the rhyme scheme, this being conventionally represented by alphabetical notation whereby each line-ending is allotted a letter in order, the same letter being allotted to all the lines that rhyme with it: thus a quatrain with two alternate rhymes has the rhyme scheme *abab*, while the rhyme scheme of Shakespeare's *sonnets is *ababcdcdefefgg*.

Rhyme is not essential to English poetry, and in the Old English and much of the Middle English periods was either an incidental device in *alliterative verse or a minor tradition subordinate to it. Rhyming poems appear with greater frequency after the Norman Conquest, as with *The *Owl and the Nightingale*, but they become the standard only in *Chaucer's work and thereafter. Chaucer made rhyming easier for himself by concluding many lines with French-derived words ending in '-esse', '-age', '-aunce', etc. Rhyming is generally harder in English than in French, but nonetheless rhymes have been found for most English words apart from 'month', 'orange', and a handful of others. Non-standard forms of rhyming such as pararhyme and half-rhyme were unusual until the early 20th century, when W. B. *Yeats, Wilfred *Owen, W. H. *Auden, Dylan *Thomas, and many others adopted them regularly. See John Hollander, *Rhyme's Reason* (1989).

rhyme (rime) royal A seven-line *stanza form of iambic *pentameter, rhyming *ababbcc*, used for narrative poetry from Chaucer (*Troilus and Criseyde*) to William *Morris.

Rhymers Club A group of poets that met at the Cheshire Cheese in Fleet Street for several years, from 1890, to read and discuss each other's poetry. The group was augmented in 1891 through association with Herbert Horne's artists' community at Fitzroy Street. Members and associates included W. B. *Yeats, Ernest *Rhys, Richard *Le Gallienne, Ernest *Dowson, Lionel *Johnson, and Arthur *Symons. It published two collections of verse, 1892 and 1894.

Rhyming Poem, The An Old English poem from the *Exeter Book, therefore no later than the 10th century. The two halves of its alliterating lines rhyme (an occasional feature in later Old English poetry). It contrasts the misfortunes of a fallen king with his past glory, a common Boethian, elegiac theme in Old English. It may be a paraphrase of Job 29 and 30. Ed. Bernard Muir, *The Exeter Anthology of Old English Poetry* (2000).

Rhyming Weavers A loose generic term for the Ulster *Scots poets of the late 18th and early 19th centuries, some of whom worked in the linen industry. Many were radical Presbyterians and a few, notably James Orr (1770–1816), were involved in the United Irishmen and the Rebellion of 1798. They often thought of themselves as simultaneously Irish and Scottish, referring to Ireland as 'Eirlan'. Verse in Scots reflecting the impact of Allan *Ramsay's anthologies was published in broadsheets, newspapers, and other media in Ulster from as early as the 1750s but greatly increased in quantity towards the end of the century in response to the popularity of Robert *Burns. Many of the Ulster poets produced sentimental imitations of Scottish originals but the work of some, particularly Samuel Thomson (1766–1816) and Orr, is individual and sophisticated. See John Hewitt, *Rhyming Weavers and Other Country Poets from Antrim and Down* (1974).

RHYS, Ernest (1859–1946) Editor, journalist, and poet, born in Islington, London, and brought up in Carmarthen and Newcastle-upon-Tyne. After qualifying as a mining engineer, Rhys embarked on a career as a professional writer in London in 1886. He helped found the *Rhymers Club and supplied an important Welsh dimension to the early Celtic enthusiasms of W. B. *Yeats. Though *A London Rose* (1896) was praised by Robert Louis *Stevenson and others, and poems from his subsequent collections widely anthologized, Rhys is chiefly remembered for his role in setting up and sustaining the *Everyman's Library. *Everyman Remembers* (1931) provides a lively portrait of literary London over five decades.

RHYS, Jean (Ella Gwendolen Rees Williams) (1890–1979) Novelist, born in Dominica, the daughter of a Welsh doctor. She came to England in 1907, attended the Academy of Dramatic Art, then worked as chorus girl and film extra, an experience she drew upon in her third novel, *Voyage in the Dark* (1934). In 1919 she left England for Holland to marry the first of three husbands, and remained abroad for many years, living mainly in Paris, where she began to write and where much of her early work is set. *The Left Bank: Sketches and Studies of Present-Day Bohemian Paris* appeared in 1927 with an introduction by Ford Madox *Ford, who became her lover and whom she portrayed as the predatory H. J. Heidler in *Postures* (1928; repr. 1969 under its American title, *Quartet*). The figure who came to be known as 'the Jean Rhys Woman'—lonely, impoverished, drinking too much, a prey to untrustworthy men—was already established and would recur in Rhys's fiction under different names and guises in such novels as *After Leaving Mr Mackenzie* (1930) and *Good Morning, Midnight* (1939). A long silence followed this last novel, during which Rhys returned to England, living quietly in the West Country, until a radio adaptation of *Good Morning, Midnight* in 1958 brought her back to public attention. She began publishing short stories in magazines and in 1966 produced a new novel, *Wide Sargasso Sea*. A poetic, dreamlike narrative set in Dominica and Jamaica during the 1830s, it describes the early life and marriage of Antoinette Cosway, a Creole heiress who becomes the mad Mrs Rochester in **Jane Eyre*. The book won several awards, and Rhys's earlier novels were reprinted to considerable acclaim. She subsequently published two collections of short stories, *Tigers Are Better Looking* (1968) and *Sleep It Off, Lady* (1976), set largely among the desperate and dispossessed. *Smile Please* (1979) is an unfinished autobiography, and her *Letters 1931–66*, ed. F. Wyndham and D. Melly, were published in 1984. See Carole Angier, *Jean Rhys* (1990).

RHYS, John Llewellyn (Llewelyn) (1910–40) Author, killed in action with the RAF during the Second World War. His three books all reflect his passion for flying and his life as a pilot: E. E. Mavrogordato said of his first book, *The Flying Shadow* (1936), that 'the protagonist of this novel is Flying—Flying as enlightenment and Flying as routine'. This was followed by *The World Owes Me a Living* (1939), and *England Is my Village* (1941), a volume of short stories for which he was posthumously awarded the Hawthornden Prize in 1942. His widow, Jane Oliver, established in 1942 the prize that bears his name. Originally awarded to writers under 30 years old, it is now available to British and Commonwealth writers (of fiction, drama, poetry, or non-fiction) aged 35 or under. The prize is administered by a charity called Booktrust. Shortlisted authors are also awarded a prize. The first winner was Michael Richey, for an article called 'Sunk by a Mine' (1941). Other winners include Alun *Lewis (1944), for *The Last Inspection*; Elizabeth Jane *Howard (1951), for *The Beautiful Visit*; V. S. *Naipaul (1958), for *The Mystic Masseur*; Dan *Jacobson (1959), for *A Long Way from London*; David *Storey (1961), for *Flight into Camden*; Margaret *Drabble (1966), for *The Millstone*; Angela *Carter (1968), for *The Magic Toyshop*; Melvyn *Bragg (1969), for *Without a City Wall*; Susan *Hill (1972), for *The Albatross*; A. N. *Wilson (1978 and 1981), for *The Sweets of Pimlico* and *The Laird of Abbotsford*; William *Boyd (1982), for *An Ice-Cream War*; Andrew *Motion (1984), for *Dangerous Play*; Jeannette *Winterson (1987), for *The Passion*; Jonathan *Coe (1994), for *What a Carve Up!*; Peter Ho Davies (1998), for *The Ugliest House in the World*; Uzodinma Iweala (2005), for *Beasts of No Nation*; and Sarah Hall (2007) for *The Carhullan Army*.

Rhythm (1911–13) Superseded in 1913 by the *Blue Review*, a periodical edited by J. M. *Murry, with Michael *Sadleir and Katherine *Mansfield. Murry conceived it as '*The *Yellow Book* of the modern movement', and it published work by D. H. *Lawrence, Mansfield, Ford Madox *Ford, Pablo Picasso, Henri *Gaudier-Brzeska, and others.

RICE, Anne (1941–) American novelist, born in New Orleans. Her 'Vampire Chronicles', beginning with *Interview with the Vampire* (1976), highlighted the sexual undercurrents of the vampire mythos. Following her return to the Roman Catholic faith of her youth, she began a fictionalized biography of Jesus with *Christ the Lord: Out of Egypt* (2005).

RICE, Elmer (1892–1967) American dramatist, born Elmer Reizenstein in New York. His first major play was the expressionist drama *The Adding Machine* (1923), which satirized increasing regimentation and mechanization through the posthumous adventures of Mr Zero, a book-keeper. His plays of the 1930s (*We, the People*, 1933; *Judgment Day*, 1934; *Between Two Worlds*, 1934) are a response to the Depression and international ideological conflict. Rice was a campaigner for social justice and an outspoken critic of censorship. He wrote many other plays, some of them farces and melodramas, four novels, and a memoir, *Minority Report* (1963). See Robert Hogan, *The Independence of Elmer Rice* (1965).

RICE, James (1843–82) Novelist and journalist, educated at Queens' College, Cambridge. While editing the failing periodical *Once a Week* he made the acquaintance of Walter *Besant, and suggested that they should collaborate: the result was *Ready-Money Mortiboy* (1872), the tale of a Prodigal Son who returns home 'ten times worse than when he went away' and ruins his father. Their successful association produced several novels and volumes of short stories. Rice also published a history of English racing in 1879.

RICH, Adrienne (1929–) American poet, essayist, and critic, born in Baltimore. She has held a variety of academic posts, most recently professor in Stanford University, California. Rich has published steadily since *A Change of World* (1951), though it was only with her third collection, *Snapshots of a Daughter in Law* (1956), that her characteristic, fractured, free verse, frequently in lengthy sequences, began to emerge. Rich's volumes through the 1960s, 1970s, and 1980s keep pace with her own increasing politicization and involvement with first the anti-war movement, and then lesbian/feminist politics. Her poetry allies the personal ever more closely with the political, typically juxtaposing scenes of domestic life with reminders of horrifying instances of history. *Diving into the Wreck* (1971) and *The Dream of a Common Language* (1978) are outstanding collections, while *The Fact of a Doorframe: Poems Selected and New, 1950–1984* presents much of her most achieved work. Rich's essays, particularly *Compulsory Heterosexuality and Lesbian Existence* (1981), have been seminal for her generation of feminists. Some of her prose work is published in *Lies, Secrets and Silence* (1978) and in *Bread, Blood, and Poetry* (1984). *Poetry and Commitment* (2007) examines the cultural status of poetry.

RICH, Barnaby (1542–1617) Writer. He fought at Le Havre, in Ireland, and in the Netherlands, rising to the rank of captain; from 1574 he turned to literature, writing romances in the style of John *Lyly's **Euphues*, *pamphlets, and reminiscences. From 1587 he received a pension. His best-known romance is *Rich, his Farewell to Military Profession* (1581), which includes 'Apolonius and Silla', the source of *Shakespeare's **Twelfth Night*. It was edited by T. M. Cranfill (1959).

RICH, Penelope (1563–1607) The sister of Robert Devereux, earl of *Essex. Her father's dying wish, when she was only 13 or 14, that she should marry Philip *Sidney, came to nothing; in 1581 she was unhappily married to Robert, Lord Rich, providing the model for Sidney's 'Stella' in *Astrophil and Stella*. Having had five children with Rich, she became the mistress of Charles Blount, Lord Mountjoy (later earl of Devonshire), and had six children with him: they were married in 1605, after she had been legally separated from Lord Rich, by William *Laud, but the legality of the match was not accepted: both died soon after. A famous beauty and a good linguist, especially in Spanish, she took part in masques by Ben *Jonson and Samuel *Daniel, and was addressed by other poets besides Sidney, e.g. Henry *Constable and John *Ford. According to the Jesuit John Gerard (1564–1637), she died a Roman Catholic.

RICHARD I (1157–99) 'Cœur de Lion', king of England 1189–99, was one of the leaders of the Third Crusade and became a romantic figure in England (in the *Robin Hood legends, for instance, and in Walter Scott's *The *Talisman* and **Ivanhoe*), in spite of the fact that only six months of his ten-year reign were spent in England. For the Middle English verse romance see **Richard Cœur de Lion*.

Richard II, King A historical tragedy by *Shakespeare, probably written and acted 1595. It was an immediate success and the first quarto of 1597 was followed by two more in 1598. After the death of *Elizabeth I a fourth quarto was issued in 1608, which contained the first appearance in print of the deposition scene (IV. i. 154–318), probably previously suppressed because of the politically contentious subject of the queen's succession, upon which it could be taken to reflect. The scene was included in the text printed in the first *folio of 1623. Shakespeare's main source was the *Chronicles* of *Holinshed, but he appears possibly to have known the anonymous play about Richard II called *Woodstock*, and to have drawn on Samuel *Daniel's narrative poem *The *Civil Wars*.

The play begins with the quarrel between Henry Bolingbroke, son of John of Gaunt, and Thomas Mowbray, duke of Norfolk, which King Richard resolves arbitrarily by exiling Mowbray for life and Bolingbroke for ten years. When 'time-honoured' John of Gaunt dies Richard confiscates his property to pay for his Irish wars, for which he leaves the country. Bolingbroke returns to claim his inheritance and takes Berkeley Castle, which the duke of York has as regent to yield him. The king returns to Wales, hears that his Welsh supporters have deserted him and that Bolingbroke has executed the king's favourites Bushy and Green. Accompanied by York's son Aumerle, he withdraws to Flint Castle, where Bolingbroke accepts his surrender. The first half of the play ends with a discussion between a gardener and Richard's queen about the government of the garden-state and the possibility of the king's deposition (III. iv).

In London Richard relinquishes his crown to Bolingbroke, who sends him to the Tower. The earls of Carlisle and Aumerle plot to kill Bolingbroke, who has now proclaimed himself Henry IV, but are foiled by York. Richard is transferred to Pomfret Castle, where he hears of Henry's coronation and is murdered by Sir Piers Exton.

Richard II, like *1 *Henry VI* and **King John*, is written entirely in verse and it contains some of Shakespeare's most famous speeches, including John of Gaunt's evocation of England as 'This royal throne of kings, this sceptred isle'. Its telling 'sad stories of the death of kings' contributed to its potent appeal. On the day before the earl of *Essex's planned revolt in 1601 his supporters paid for a performance of a play about Richard II, which was almost certainly Shakespeare's.

Richard III, King A historical tragedy by *Shakespeare, probably written and performed 1592–3. It was first published in a quarto in 1597, which was reprinted five times before it appeared again, in a fuller and variant text in the first *folio of 1623. The play's chief sources are the chronicles of Raphael *Holinshed and Edward *Hall which contained material from Polydore *Vergil's *Anglicae Historiae* and Sir Thomas More's *The History of King *Richard the Third*. A favourite with actors, it was played for many years in Colley *Cibber's adaptation (1700), which gives the king even more prominence than the original.

The play completes the tetralogy whose first three parts are the **Henry VI* plays. It centres on the character of Richard of Gloucester, afterwards King Richard III, ambitious and bloody, bold and subtle, treacherous, yet brave in battle, a murderer, and usurper of the crown. The play begins with the deformed Richard's announcement: 'Now is the winter of our discontent | Made glorious summer by this son of York', that is the king, Edward IV, who is dying. Richard, determined to succeed to the throne, sets out to eliminate any opposition and secure his position. He has his brother the duke of Clarence, who has been imprisoned in the Tower, murdered. As she accompanies the corpse of her dead father-in-law Henry VI, Anne, the widow of Edward, prince of Wales, is wooed by Richard, and they are later married.

When the king dies Richard begins his attack on the queen's family and supporters, helped by the duke of Buckingham. Hastings, Rivers, and Gray are all executed, and Buckingham persuades the citizens of London to proclaim Richard king. After his coronation he murders his nephews, the princes in the Tower, and following the death of his wife Anne, which he hastens, tries to marry his niece, Elizabeth of York. However, Buckingham rebels and goes to join Henry Tudor, earl of Richmond, who has landed in Wales at Milford Haven to claim the crown. Buckingham is captured and Richard has him executed, but he must now face Richmond's army at Bosworth. On the night before the battle the ghosts of those murdered by Richard appear to him and foretell his defeat. In the battle the next day he loses his horse and is killed by Richmond, who is then proclaimed Henry VII, the first of the Tudor monarchs.

Richard Cœur de Lion A romance in 7,136 lines of short couplets dating from the early 14th century, which some scholars suggest may be by the same writer as two other long romances of the same period, *Of *Arthour and of Merlin* and **King Alisaunder* (see introduction to the latter by G. V. Smithers for discussion of authorship). The writer says he is taking his poem from a French source, but it is marked by spirited English patriotism and contempt for the French King Philip. It is assumed that the source is Anglo-Norman, dating from about 1230–50. The poem describes the defeat of the Saracens in the course of the Third Crusade and breaks off, unfinished, when a three-year truce is arranged. There are several manuscripts and fragments. Quotations from it are found in the notes to Walter Scott's *The *Talisman*, referring to the cooking and eating of the Saracen's head, and of the heads served to the Paynim (or pagan) ambassadors. The edition by K. Brunner (Vienna, 1913) is a critical edition of the seven manuscripts then known.

Richard the Third, The History of King A history of the King's life by Sir Thomas *More, written in English and Latin and included in his *Works* (1557) and his *Omnia Opera* (1565). It is distinguished from earlier English chronicles by its unity of form and dramatic effectiveness. William *Shakespeare probably used More's work only as filtered through Edward *Hall and Raphael *Holinshed; it was More, however, who was ultimately responsible for the image of Richard as a *Machiavellian tyrant which Shakespeare transmits in **Richard III*.
See also BIOGRAPHY.

RICHARDS, Alun (1929–2004) Welsh short story writer, novelist, and playwright, born in Pontypridd, Glamorgan. Drawing on his experiences as a probation officer and teacher, his work portrays an urban, post-industrial, emphatically unromantic Wales. His critical reputation rests mainly on two collections of stories, *Dai Country* (1973) and *The Former Miss Merthyr Tydfil* (1976); the novel *Home to an Empty House* (1973); and the autobiography *Days of Absence* (1986), though he published much else besides. *Ennal's Point* (1977) and *Barque Whisper* (1979) belong to an unfinished marine trilogy. Richards scripted many episodes of the 1970s television series *The Onedin Line*, and edited the *Penguin Book of Welsh Short Stories* (1976). *A Touch of Glory* (1980) celebrates Welsh rugby.

RICHARDS, Frank Pseudonym of Charles *Hamilton.

RICHARDS, I. A. (Ivor Armstrong) (1893–1979) Rhetorician, born in Cheshire, the son of a factory manager, and educated at Clifton College, Bristol, before studying moral sciences at Magdalene College, Cambridge. He became one of the first lecturers in English at Cambridge (1919–29), where he wrote his best-known works. With his friend C. K. Ogden (1889–1957) he published two early books, *The Foundations of Aesthetics* (1922, with J. Wood) and *The Meaning of Meaning* (1923), but he is best known for the next three, *Principles of Literary Criticism* (1924), *Science and Poetry* (1926), and above all *Practical Criticism: A Study of Literary Judgement* (1929). The last of these helped to establish *practical criticism as a central feature of literary education, at Cambridge and then more widely; while the first two proposed that poetry promotes vital kinds of psychological flexibility, in part because it offers 'pseudo-statements' rather than true or false propositions. This decoupling of literature from 'belief' proved controversial, and was resisted by his friend T. S. *Eliot, among others. Richards's attacks on vagueness, sentimentality, and laziness in poets and readers, and his praise of irony ('a characteristic of poetry of the highest order'), ambiguity, complexity, and allusiveness, did much to create the climate which accepted *modernism, and greatly influenced William *Empson (his student from 1928 to 1929), F. R. *Leavis, and the American *New Critics. In 1929–30 and again in 1936–8 he visited China, partly to promote his and Ogden's language-learning system known as Basic English (a much-simplified version of English, with a vocabulary of only 850 words). His last specifically literary book was *Coleridge on Imagination* (1934): after moving to Harvard (1939–63), he wrote on more general questions of rhetoric, communication, and education, while also publishing some volumes of verse. There is a life by J. P. Russo (1989), and a *Selected Letters* (ed. John Constable) appeared in 1990.

RICHARDSON, Dorothy Miller (1873–1957) Novelist, the third of four daughters of an impoverished gentleman. Born in Abingdon, Oxfordshire, and educated in Worthing, Sussex, and Southborough House, Putney, she was obliged to earn her living from an early age, first as governess, then as secretary, translator, and journalist. She became an intimate friend of H. G. *Wells and other avant-garde thinkers of the day, who encouraged her to write. In 1915 appeared *Pointed Roofs*, the first of a sequence of thirteen highly autobiographical novels entitled *Pilgrimage*. She pioneered the *stream-of-consciousness technique—May *Sinclair imported the term from psychology to describe Richardson's work—narrating the action through the mind of her heroine Miriam. She argued for an unpunctuated 'feminine prose', and Virginia *Woolf, reviewing *Revolving Lights* in 1923, credited her with inventing 'the psychological sentence of the feminine gender'. *Pilgrimage* was also innovative in the open-endedness of its narrative; the final volume, *March Moonlight*, did not appear in Richardson's lifetime, being published only in 1967. Though *Pilgrimage* was her primary achievement, she also wrote on cinema for *Close-Up*, and wrote short fiction; for the latter, see Trudi Tate (ed.), *Journey to Paradise* (1989).

The formidable length of her great work deterred many readers, but interest revived in the 1960s and 1970s with the growth of *feminist criticism. Angus *Wilson ('Sexual Revolution', *Listener*, Oct. 1968) acclaimed her as a defiant writer who 'enters more fully than any novelist I know into the material and spiritual struggles of a young, very gifted, but at the same time utterly underprivileged woman in a world made by men for men'. *Pilgrimage* was reissued in 1979 in four volumes by the *Virago Press; there is as yet no scholarly edition, but see George H. Thomson, *Notes on Pilgrimage* (1999). See also Gloria Fromm, *Dorothy Richardson* (1977), a biography, and Fromm (ed.), *Windows on Modernism* (1995), selected letters.

RICHARDSON, Henry Handel (1870–1946) Penname of Ethel Florence Lindesay Richardson, Australian novelist who lived her adult life in Germany then England. In 1888 Richardson went to Leipzig to study music, meeting John George Robertson, whom she married in 1895; they moved to London in 1903. Her first novel, *Maurice Guest* (1908), is an unconventional tale of *grande passion* set in Leipzig, while her second and most economical, *The Getting of Wisdom* (1910) reflects her school experience at the Presbyterian Ladies' College in Melbourne. Richardson's most ambitious work is *The Fortunes of Richard Mahony* (1930), initially published in three volumes: *Australia Felix* (1917), *The Way Home* (1925), and *Ultima Thule* (1929). The novel is a magnificent chronicle of individuals, notably the volatile Mahony, his stoic wife Mary, and their daughter Cuffy, and of a place, the colony of Victoria. Clearly based on the biography of her own parents, the epic story traces the attempts of its protagonist to find a psychological home between Britain and Australia. Later works include *The End of a Childhood and Other Stories* (1934), *Young Cosima* (based on the life of Cosima Wagner), and the autobiography, *Myself When Young* (1948), unfinished at her death.

RICHARDSON, Jonathan, the elder (1665–1745) British portrait painter, highly successful in his day. He also wrote about art, and the science of connoisseurship. His *Theory of Painting* (1715) was the first significant work on aesthetic theory by an English author; in the second edition, 1725, he added an influential essay on the *sublime. He was a connoisseur with a superlative collection of drawings; he had a wide circle of literary friends, amongst them Alexander *Pope, John *Gay, and Matthew *Prior, and with his son wrote a book *Explanatory Notes on Paradise Lost* (1734). He drew and painted Pope and his family many times. His son researched a guidebook to Italy which was a popular companion on the *Grand Tour.

RICHARDSON, Samuel (1689–1761) Printer and novelist, the son of a joiner. Richardson appears to have received (in his own words) 'only common School-learning', though it is possible that he attended Merchant Taylors' School, Middlesex. He read widely, told stories to his friends, and wrote letters on behalf of young lovers. In 1706 he was apprenticed to a printer, and in 1715 he was admitted a freeman of the *Stationers' Company, later rising to the office of renter warden (1727) and master (1754). He set up in business on his own in 1721, combining printing and publishing, and producing books, journals, advertisement posters, and other miscellaneous work. In 1723 he took over the printing of an influential Tory journal. In 1733 he published his *The Apprentice's Vade Mecum*, a conduct manual. In 1738 he began renting in Fulham a weekend 'country' house, which he always referred to as 'North End', which later became the setting for literary gatherings. He published in 1739 his own version, heavily moralized, of *Aesop's Fables*. The inspiration for his first novel, **Pamela*, came from a series of 'familiar letters' which fellow printers had encouraged him to write on the concerns of everyday life; these were published separately as *Letters…to and for Particular Friends* (1741). *Pamela* was written between November 1739 and January 1740, and was published later in that year. The morality and realism of the work were much praised, but complaints about its impropriety persuaded him to revise his second edition considerably. In 1741 there appeared a riotously irreverent but astute parody called *An Apology for the Life of Mrs *Shamela Andrews*, which Richardson believed, probably correctly, to be by Henry *Fielding and which he never forgave. Fielding's **Joseph Andrews*, also begun as a parody of *Pamela*, appeared in 1742.

Richardson's business continued to prosper, despite poor health and occasional accusations of *Jacobite involvement. In 1733 he had begun printing for the House of Commons and in 1742 he secured the lucrative post of printer of its journals. His circle of friends now included many admiring young women known as his 'songbirds' or 'honorary daughters', as well many members of the *Blue Stocking circle. During the writing of **Clarissa*, which was probably begun in 1744, Richardson tirelessly canvassed friends for comments and advice, reading passages aloud to them in his 'grotto' (or summer house) at North End. The first two volumes of *Clarissa* appeared in 1747 and were very favourably received. A further five volumes appeared in 1748. *Clarissa* was an undoubted success (even Fielding admired it) but there were complaints about both its length and its sexual content, and it was not reprinted as often as *Pamela*.

In the 1750s Richardson published, supported, or became friendly with several notable authors, among them Charlotte *Lennox, Sarah *Fielding, Edward *Young, and George *Lyttelton. In 1750 he contributed to Samuel *Johnson's **Rambler*. In 1752 Johnson (with many of Richardson's other friends) read the draft of *Sir Charles *Grandison*, his final novel, published in seven volumes 1753–4. The book sold well and rapidly became fashionable, but was assailed in various critical pamphlets for its prolixity, tedium, improbability, and dubious morality. He published in 1755 *A Collection of the Moral and Instructive Sentiments…in the Histories of Pamela, Clarissa, and Sir Charles Grandison*, which he considered contained the essence of all his work. **Johnson's Dictionary*, published the same year, contained 97 citations from *Clarissa*. In 1756, when Johnson was arrested for debt, it was Richardson who came to his aid financially. In that year Richardson was asked by Sir William *Blackstone for advice on the reform of *Oxford University Press. He continued to revise his novels heavily, and remained active in his business until his death.

All Richardson's novels were *epistolary, a form which he appreciated for its immediacy ('writing to the moment' as he called it), and which he developed to an unprecedented level of intensity. Richardson was acutely aware of the problems of prolixity and worked hard but somewhat ineffectually to prune his drafts. In Johnson's view, 'if you were to read Richardson for the story, your impatience would be so much fretted that you would hang yourself. But you must read him for the sentiment, and consider the story as only giving occasion to the sentiment'. Johnson always maintained the superiority of Richardson's psychological insight over Fielding's comic characterization. A selection of Richardson's letters (6 vols, 1804) was edited by Anna Barbauld; see also *Selected Letters of Samuel Richardson*, ed. J. Carroll (1964); T. C. D. Eaves and B. D. Kimpel, *Samuel Richardson: A Biography* (1971).

RICHELIEU, Armand du Plessis, cardinal de (1585–1642) French politician and statesman. He first came into prominence as bishop of Luçon in 1607, before becoming first minister of Louis XIII in 1628. He disciplined the nobles by a series of executions, destroyed the political importance of the Protestants by the siege and capture of La Rochelle (1628), and intervened successfully in the Thirty Years War (1618–48). He founded the *Académie Française. He figures in *Les Trois Mousquetaires* of *Alexandre *Dumas père*, and is the anti-hero of a blank verse drama by Edward *Bulwer-Lytton and a novel by Alfred de *Vigny.

RICHLER, Mordecai (1931–2001) Canadian novelist and screenwriter, born in Montreal, who spent the 1960s in England, returning to Canada in 1972. His first novel, *The Acrobats* (1954), was followed by *The Apprenticeship of Duddy Kravitz* (1959), describing a Jewish boyhood in Montreal, which he adapted as an Oscar-nominated screenplay, *The Incomparable Atuk* (1963), a satire on popular culture, and *Cocksure* (1968), a ribald extravaganza set in theatrical London. *St Urbain's Horseman* (1971), also set in 1960s London, has a Jewish-Canadian film director acquitted of a rape charge. *Joshua Then and Now*, a semi-autobiographical novel set in Montreal, was filmed by Ted Kotcheff in 1985. His other witty and irreverent novels include *Solomon Gursky Was Here* (1989), considered by some his masterpiece: an ambitious epic which interweaves Jewish themes and Inuit folklore in a gripping exploration of Canada's multicultural roots through the Gursky family saga. *Barney's Version* (1997) recounts the unreliable and outrageous memories of Barney Panofsky in Montreal, London, and Paris.

RICHMOND, Legh (1772–1827) An evangelical clergyman who lived in the Isle of Wight, and wrote highly successful pious tales, published between 1809 and 1814, including *The Dairyman's Daughter*, *The Young Cottager*, and *The Negro Slave*.

RICHTER, Conrad (1890–1968) American novelist, born in Pennsylvania, who is best known for his Ohio (Awakening Land) Trilogy: *The Trees* (1940), *The Fields* (1946), and *The Town* (1950). These works were informed by historical research and a desire to recreate the vernacular of the region. See David R. Johnson, *Conrad Richter* (2001).

RICHTER, Johann Paul Friedrich (1763–1825) German novelist, who wrote under the name 'Jean Paul'. From humble beginnings, he became a successful writer and a significant figure in German *Romanticism. His eccentric combination of irony, pathos, humour, and visionary idealism was appreciated by Thomas *De Quincey, for whom he was a significant influence, and Thomas *Carlyle. Both helped bring him to wider notice in England through essays and translations, but he was already of great importance to S. T. *Coleridge who incorporated and adapted his ideas in his *Notebooks*. His best-known works include: *Quintus Fixlein* (1796), *Siebenkäs* (1796–7), and the unfinished *Flegeljahre* (1804–5).

RICKETTS, Charles (1866–1931) English aesthete, illustrator, designer, and painter. His brilliant conversation and rarefied tastes attracted many writers to his house in the Vale, Chelsea, and later to Townshend House; among his friends were Oscar *Wilde, John *Gray, W. B. *Yeats, G. B. *Shaw, 'Michael *Field' (Edith Cooper and Katherine Bradley), and Laurence *Binyon. Ricketts illustrated and designed many of Wilde's books; most beautiful are *A House of Pomegranates* (1891) and *The Sphinx* (1894). After Wilde's death he wrote a memoir of him, *Recollections of Oscar Wilde* (1932). With Charles Shannon (1865–1937), Ricketts edited *The *Dial* (1889–97), a lavishly illustrated literary magazine deeply influenced by the then little-known works of French and Belgian symbolists. His Vale Press, founded in 1896, was one of the most important of the *private presses. Later Ricketts worked as a stage designer; G. B. Shaw's *Saint Joan* (1924) was his most successful production. Ricketts was a distinguished collector, connoisseur, and writer on art, and in his last years designed and illustrated two of his own prose works, *Beyond the Threshold* (1929) and *Unrecorded Histories* (1933). See J. G. Paul Delaney, *Charles Ricketts: A Biography* (1990); M. Watry, *The Vale Press: Charles Ricketts, a Publisher in Earnest* (2004).

RICKS, Sir Christopher (1933–) Literary critic and scholar, born in London, and educated at King Alfred's School, Wantage, and Balliol College, Oxford. He held academic appointments from 1958 at Oxford, Bristol, and Cambridge universities until he moved in 1986 to Boston University. His major scholarly achievement is the annotated *Poems of Tennyson* (1969). His critical writings, clearly influenced by William *Empson, have been notable for their close attention to the sounds, semantic nuances, and verbal echoes of poetry, often re-echoed in his own punning style of commentary. His principal critical works include *Milton's Grand Style* (1963), *Keats and Embarrassment* (1974), *The Force of Poetry* (1984), *T. S. Eliot and Prejudice* (1988), and *Beckett's Dying Words* (1993). He has also edited the *Oxford Book of English Verse* (1999) and the *New Oxford Book of Victorian Verse* (1987), and has frequently championed the merits of Bob *Dylan as a poet, notably in his book *Dylan's Visions of Sin* (2004). In 2004 he was elected professor of poetry at Oxford.

RICKWORD, Edgell (1898–1982) Poet, critic, and radical; born in Colchester, Essex, and educated at Colchester Royal Grammar School and Pembroke College, Oxford. The literary periodical he edited from 1925 to 1927, the **Calendar of Modern Letters*, influenced the critical attitudes of F. R. *Leavis, as did the two volumes of criticism he edited under the title *Scrutinies* (1928, 1932). Rickword also edited the *Left Review* (1936–8), and *Our Time* (1944–7). *Essays and Opinions* (1921–51), edited by A. Young, appeared in 1974, and *Collected Poems* in 1976.

Riddle of the Sands, The See CHILDERS, ERSKINE.

RIDING, Laura (1901–91) American poet and critic, born Laura Reichenthal in New York, who lived and worked with Robert *Graves from 1927 until 1939. Her elliptical verses were brought together in *Collected Poems* (1938), but around 1941 she renounced poetry. Critical works include (with Graves) *A Survey of Modernist Poetry* (1927) and *Contemporaries and Snobs* (1928). A novel, *A Trojan Ending*, appeared in 1937, and *Lives of Wives*, on various marriages in history, in 1939. See Elizabeth Friedman, *A Mannered Grace* (2005).

RIDLEY, Nicholas (*c*.1502–1555) Fellow and master of Pembroke College, Cambridge, one of Thomas *Cranmer's chaplains, and bishop successively of Rochester and London in the reign of Edward VI. He gradually rejected many Roman Catholic doctrines and ceremonies and became one of the leaders of the *Reformation in England, ordering the destruction of altars in London churches. Following Edward's death in July 1553 and the accession of the Roman Catholic Mary he was arrested and imprisoned with Cranmer and Hugh *Latimer. He and Latimer were condemned on the charge of heresy and burnt alive at Oxford on 16 October 1555, an occasion made famous in John *Foxe's *Book of Martyrs*. His theological treatises and letters, including his 'Last Farewell', appeared after his death. See *The Works of Nicholas Ridley*, ed. Henry Christmas (Parker Society, 1843).

RIDLEY, Philip (1967–) Playwright, novelist, artist, photographer, songwriter, poet, screenplay writer, and film director; he has been described as a 'one man cultural revolution'. Born in the East End of London, he studied fine art at St Martin's School of Art. He has written twelve novels, of which nine are for children, including *Krindlekrax* (1991), and has also written stage work for young people. *The Pitchfork Disney* (1991), a new brutalist work with scenes of vomiting and cockroach-eating, *The Fastest Clock in the Universe* (1992), and *Ghost from a Perfect Place* (1994) mix magic realism with the depiction of raw emotion. Amongst his work for the cinema, he is perhaps best known for the screenplay for *The Krays* (1990).

Rights of Man, The A political treatise by Thomas *Paine in two parts, published 1791 and 1792. Part I is a reply to Edmund *Burke's **Reflections on the Revolution in France*; Paine accuses Burke of 'rancour, prejudice and ignorance', and of seeking theatrical effects at the expense of truth. He denies that one generation can bind another as regards the form of government, and argues that the constitution of a country is an act of the people constituting the government. He traces the incidents of the French Revolution up to the adoption of the Declaration of the Rights of Man by the National Assembly, and criticizes Burke's account of these incidents as over-emotional and inaccurate. Part II compares the new French and American constitutions with those of British institutions, to the disadvantage of the latter. The work also contains Paine's far-sighted proposals for family allowances, maternity grants, and tax reform.

RIIS, Jacob (1849–1914) Danish-born American journalist remembered for his descriptions and photographs of the poor of New York, in *How the Other Half Lives* (1890) and other volumes.

RILEY, Denise (1948–) Poet, born in Carlisle and educated at Cambridge. Her first volume of poetry, *Marxism for Infants*, was published in 1977 and has been followed by *Dry Air* (1985), *Stair Spirit* (1982), and *Mop Mop Georgette* (1993): all are small press publications. A *Selected Poems* was published in 2000. Riley's prose, ranging from *War in the Nursery: Theories of the Child and Mother* (1983) to *Impersonal Passion: Language as Affect* (2005), includes work in feminist, psychoanalytical, and linguistic theory; and these preoccupations are reflected in her challenging poetry too. It characteristically slips between matters of philosophical and linguistic moment, reworkings of mythology, sudden plangencies associated with desire and death, political inspection and reproach, and a warily feminist delight in popular culture, particularly the pop music of the early 1960s. Its primarily impersonal modes are sometimes fractured by a difficult early autobiography readable between the lines.

RILEY, Joan (1958–) Born in Jamaica, moving to Britain as an adolescent. Her novels *The Unbelonging* (1985), *Waiting in the Twilight* (1987), and *Romance* (1988) focus on girls' and women's experience of migration and exile. *A Kindness to the Children* (1992) is a collection of short stories.

RILKE, Rainer Maria (1875–1926) German poet, born in Prague where he briefly studied philosophy. Of decisive importance were visits to Russia in 1899 and 1900 which deepened his religious experience and led to *Das Stunden-Buch* (1905: *The Book of Hours*), in which death is a central preoccupation. The intense subjectivity of the early work began to give way to poetry of a more objective kind. The transition is seen in *Das Buch der Bilder* (1902: *The Book of Pictures*) and finds mature expression in the *Neue Gedichte* (1907–8: *New Poems*). The aesthetic of objectivity was developed under the influence of the French sculptor Rodin (1840–1917) for whom Rilke worked briefly as secretary. His poetic novel *Die Aufzeichnungen des Malte Laurids Brigge* (1910: *Sketches of Malte Laurids Brigge*) is the portrait of a poet living in poverty in Paris. The *Duineser Elegien* (1923: *Duino Elegies*), begun shortly before the First World War and completed not long afterwards, arose from Rilke's attempt to find or create for himself in art a spiritual basis for existence in the face of the prevailing scientific materialism. In their wake came the 55 poems of *Die Sonette an Orpheus* (1923: *Sonnets to Orpheus*), written in a brief and extraordinary burst of creativity, which represent the jubilant culmination of that attempt. As one of the most admired and influential lyric poets of the 20th century, his work has been translated into many languages. Various collections have appeared in English translated by J. B. Leishman (1902–63), sometimes in collaboration with Stephen *Spender, by Michael *Hamburger, Sean *O'Brien, Michael *Hofmann, Stephen Cohn, Stephen Mitchell, and others. His extensive correspondence is also of great literary interest. See D. A. Prater, *A Ringing Glass: The Life of Rainer Maria Rilke* (1986).

RIMBAUD, Arthur (1854–91) French poet. One of the most revolutionary figures in 19th-century literature, he was by the age of 16 in full revolt against every form of authority. Expressing the exhilaration of his regular escapes from maternal discipline and his fascination with cabbalistic and alchemical imagery, his verse was already fiercely independent of religious, political, and literary orthodoxy. By the age of 17 he had written his most famous poem, 'Le Bateau ivre' ('The Drunken Boat), a hymn to the quest for unknown realities, which became a sacred text for the next two generations of writers, and which Samuel *Beckett famously translated in 1932. Between 1871 and 1873—the period of his association with Paul *Verlaine and his sojourns in England—he undertook a programme of 'disorientation of the senses' in order to try to turn himself into a *voyant*, or seer. This resulted in his most original work, two collections of prose poems, *Les Illuminations*, which explored the visionary possibilities of this experiment, and *Une saison en enfer* (*A Season in Hell*), recording its moral and psychological failure; these have been translated particularly effectively by Enid Rhodes Peschel (1973) and by Martin Sorrell (2001). By the time he was 19, his poetic career was over, and he spent the rest of his life travelling, first in Europe, and later in Aden and north-east Africa. See Graham Robb, *Rimbaud* (2000).

Rime of the Ancient Mariner, The See ANCIENT MARINER, THE RIME OF THE.

Rimini, The Story of See STORY OF RIMINI, THE.

RINEHART, Mary Roberts (1876–1958) American author of mystery fiction, born in Pennsylvania, who published her first novel, *The Circular Staircase*, in 1908. Her use of a country-house setting here and elsewhere in her numerous works spanning the period 1908–53 earned her the sobriquet of the 'American Agatha *Christie'.

Ring and the Book, The A poem in blank verse, in twelve books, totalling over 21,000 lines, by Robert *Browning, published in four monthly instalments November 1868–February 1869. The poem was a critical and popular success, and established Browning's contemporary reputation. The

'Ring' of the title is a figure for the process by which the artist transmutes the 'pure crude fact' of historical events into living forms; the 'Book' is a collection of documents relating to the Italian murder trial of the late 17th century on which the poem is based. Browning found the volume on a market stall in Florence, and offered it to several of his acquaintances (including Alfred *Tennyson and Anthony *Trollope) before finally deciding to use it himself.

The story in bare outline is as follows. Pietro and Violante Comparini were a middle-aged childless couple living in Rome. Their income could only be secured after Pietro's death if they had a child; so Violante bought the child of a prostitute and passed it off as her own. This child, Pompilia, was eventually married to Count Guido Franceschini, an impoverished nobleman from Arezzo. The marriage was unhappy, and the Comparini, disappointed by life in Arezzo, returned to Rome, where they sued Guido for the restoration of Pompilia's dowry on the grounds of her illegitimacy, which Violante now revealed. Pompilia herself eventually fled from Arezzo in the company of a young priest, Giuseppe Caponsacchi. Guido pursued them and had them arrested on the outskirts of Rome; as a result, Caponsacchi was exiled to Civita Vecchia for three years, and Pompilia was sent to a convent while the lawsuits were decided. But then, because she was pregnant, she was released into the custody of the Comparini. A fortnight after the birth of her child, Guido and four accomplices murdered her and her putative parents. They were arrested and tried for the murder, Guido claiming justification on the grounds of his wife's adultery with Caponsacchi; nevertheless he and his accomplices were convicted and sentenced to death. Guido then pleaded exemption for himself, but his appeal was rejected and the five were executed.

In Browning's poem, the story is told by a succession of speakers—citizens of Rome, the participants themselves, the lawyers, and the pope—each of whose single, insufficient perceptions combines with the others to form, it may be, the 'ring' of the truth. This design represents Browning's response to a number of pressing concerns in his own creative life and in contemporary philosophies of art and religion, and to John Stuart *Mill's liberal conviction that truth will be established by debate. Browning offered 'truth' as both absolute (in its divine essence) and relative (in its human manifestation); the artist partakes of either quality, all means of expression (such as language) being an inadequate 'witness' to the true life of the imagination, just as historical witnesses give a partial and inadequate account of 'real' events.

In its immense but ordered size and scope; in the vitality of its characters and the rich evocation of time and place; and in its magnificently troubled exposition of the relation between human testimony and objective verity, and its zesty prefigurement of the modern detective novel, the poem stands at the centre of Browning's work.

RIORDAN, Maurice (1953–) London-based Irish poet, born in Lisgoold, Co. Cork, educated at University College, Cork. His poems reflect an interest in science and anthropology and bring a detached tone and fastidious eye for detail to their presentations of domestic situations. He has published *A Word from the Loki* (1995) and *Floods* (2000), which opens with the bravura archaeological meditation 'The Sloe'. His third collection, *The Holy Land* (2007), a wry memorial to Riordan's farmer father, includes a sequence of eighteen pastoral prose poems.

'Rip Van Winkle' A story by Washington *Irving published in *The Sketch Book* (1820). Rip Van Winkle, taking refuge from a nagging wife in a solitary ramble in the Catskill mountains, falls asleep, and wakes after twenty years, to find his wife dead, his house in ruins, and the world completely changed.

RITCHIE, Anne Isabella Thackeray, Lady (1837–1919) Novelist, memoir writer, and biographer of her father W. M. *Thackeray. She grew up in France; her mother suffered post-natal depression which became prolonged mental illness. Her younger sister Minny, who died in 1875, was the first wife of Leslie *Stephen, and she was thus aunt to Virginia *Woolf, as well as a good friend of Woolf's mother, Julia Stephen. Woolf drew a portrait of her in **Night and Day* as 'Mrs Hilbery'. Her impressionistic *Old Kensington* (1873) and *From an Island* (1877) are probably the best remembered of her novels today. She also wrote two collections of modern fairy stories, *Five Old Friends and a Young Prince* (1868) and *Bluebeard's Keys* (1874). She wrote biographical introductions to her father's complete works (1898–9) as well as reminiscences of the literary figures she had known in her youth: *Records of Tennyson, Ruskin and Robert and Elizabeth Browning* (1892) and *Chapters from Some Memoirs* (1894), among others. See Henrietta Garnett, *Anny: A Life of Anne Thackeray Ritchie* (2004).

RITSON, Joseph (1752–1803) Antiquary. An implacable advocate of textual fidelity in the editing of early texts, he challenged Thomas *Warton's *History of English Poetry* (1782) and also Samuel *Johnson's and George *Steevens's edition of Shakespeare. In 1783 he published *A Select Collection of English Songs*, in which he accused Thomas *Percy of falsifying the texts in his **Reliques*. In 1795 appeared his *Robin Hood: A Collection of All the Ancient Poems, Songs and Ballads Now Extant Relative to That Outlaw*, with illustrations by Thomas *Bewick: Walter *Scott, one of his few friends, attributed a 'superstitious scrupulosity' to this work, which he thought excessively comprehensive. Ritson's *Ancient English Metrical Romances* appeared in 1802. He also published collections of songs, children's verses, and *fairy stories, and advised Scott on his **Minstrelsy of the Scottish Border*. In later life he became a fanatical vegetarian (his diet was originally inspired by reading Bernard *Mandeville), and finally insane. See B. H. Bronson, *Joseph Ritson: Scholar-at-Arms*, 2 vols (1938).

Rival Queens, The, *or The Death of Alexander the Great* A tragedy by Nathaniel *Lee, founded on the *Cassandre* of *La Calprenède, produced 1677. Colley *Cibber attributed its success to the performance of Thomas *Betterton, but it held the stage for 100 years. Statira, daughter of Darius and wife of Alexander, learning that Alexander has again fallen a victim to the charms of his first wife Roxana, whom he had promised to discard, vows never to see him again. Alexander, returning from his campaign and passionately loving Statira, is deeply distressed. Roxana goads Statira to fury, Statira revokes her vow, and Alexander banishes Roxana, who later stabs her rival to death. Alexander is poisoned by the conspirator Cassander.

Rivals, The A comedy by R. B. *Sheridan, produced 1775. This was Sheridan's first play, written rapidly when he was only 23; its first performance (17 January) was poorly received, but a rapidly revised version (28 January) met with the better success, and the play has held the stage into modern times. Captain Absolute, son of Sir Anthony Absolute, a warm-hearted but demanding old gentleman, is in love with Lydia Languish, the niece of Mrs Malaprop (whose comic verbal mistakes have given rise to the term 'malapropism'). As he knows the romantic Lydia prefers a poor half-pay lieutenant to the heir of a baronet, he has assumed the character of Ensign Beverley, and is favourably received. But Lydia will lose half her fortune if she marries without her aunt's consent, and Mrs Malaprop will not approve of a low-ranking soldier, especially after Sir Anthony arrives in Bath to propose a match between his son and Lydia, a proposal Mrs Malaprop welcomes. Captain Absolute is now afraid of revealing his deception to Lydia in case he loses her; while Bob Acres, who is also Lydia's suitor and has heard of Beverley's courtship, is provoked by the fiery Irishman Sir Lucius O'Trigger to ask Captain Absolute to carry a challenge to Beverley. Sir Lucius himself, who has been deluded into thinking that some love letters received by him from Mrs Malaprop are really from Lydia, likewise finds Captain Absolute in his path, and challenges him. But when Acres finds that Beverley is in fact his friend Absolute, he declines the duel and resigns all claim to Lydia. Sir Lucius' misapprehension is removed by the arrival of Mrs Malaprop, and Lydia, after a pretty quarrel with her lover for shattering her hopes of a romantic elopement, forgives him.

Road to Oxiana, The *See* BYRON, ROBERT.

Roaring Girl, The, *or Moll Cut-Purse* A comedy by Thomas *Middleton and Thomas *Dekker, written and acted about 1611. In this play Moll Cutpurse, a notorious thief in real life, is portrayed as an honest girl, who helps lovers and defends herself with her sword. Sebastian Wentgrave loves and is betrothed to Mary Fitzallard, but his grasping father forbids the match. Sebastian pretends he has fallen desperately in love with Moll Cutpurse and is about to marry her; Moll good-naturedly cooperates. Old Wentgrave, appalled, is only too glad to give his blessing when the real bride turns out to be Mary Fitzallard. There are bustling scenes in which the life of the London streets is vividly presented, shopkeepers selling tobacco and feathers, their wives flirting, and Moll talking thieves' slang and putting overbold admirers in their place. There is a Revels edition (1987) by Paul Mulholland.

ROBB, Graham (1958–) Cultural historian and biographer, born in Manchester and educated at the Royal Grammar School, Worcester, and Exeter College, Oxford. He has a particular interest in the cultural history of France. Robb has published *Balzac: A Biography* (1994), *Victor Hugo* (1997), *Rimbaud* (2000), and *Strangers: Homosexual Love in the 19th Century* (2003). His *The Discovery of France* (2007) won the 2008 Ondaatje Prize.

ROBBE-GRILLET, Alain (1922–2008) French novelist, screenwriter, and film-maker. A leading proponent of the **nouveau roman*, his essays *Pour un nouveau roman* (1963: *Towards a New Novel*) helped define the movement, with their interrogation of traditional narrative techniques, and stress on the instability and unreliability of representation. They crystallized questions he had already begun to explore in his novels. In *Les Gommes* (1953: *The Rubbers*), the erasers of the title represent the erasure of one version of events and its replacement by another. The title of *Le Voyeur* (1955) refers equally to author, narrator, and reader. In *La Jalousie* (1957; *Jealousy*, trans. Richard Howard, 1959), the very precision of description betrays the anxious presence of a narrator convinced of his wife's infidelity and intent on finding evidence to prove it. Novels of the 1970s and 1980s, such as *Djinn* (1981), confirmed Robbe-Grillet's preoccupation with *metafiction, as did his trilogy of novelistic memoirs published in the 1980s and 1990s. Cinema was also an ongoing concern, from *L'Année dernière à Marienbad* (1961: *Last Year at Marienbad*), the screenplay for Alain Resnais's landmark film, to *Gradiva (C'est Gradiva qui vous appelle*, 2006).

ROBBINS, Tom (1936–) American novelist, born in North Carolina, whose works combine an eccentric inventiveness with satirical elements. He devised his writing style while reporting on a Doors concert in 1967 and his fiction has been linked to the *Beats. His novels include *Even Cowgirls Get the Blues* (1976) and *Skinny Legs and All* (1990).

Robene and Makyne A pastoral by Robert *Henryson, on the model of the French *pastourelle*, included in Thomas Percy's **Reliques*. Robene, a shepherd, is loved by Makyne (a form of Malkin, diminutive of Matilda, which seems to have been a stereotypical name for an unattractive woman: see **Piers Plowman* B I. 184). He rejects her advances, then changes his mind and appeals to her. She rebuffs him. See *The Poems of Robert Henryson*, ed. Denton Fox (1981).

ROBERT OF GLOUCESTER (*fl. c.*1260–1300) The author of part of a metrical Chronicle of England from Brutus to

Henry III, much of which draws on *Laȝamon, and which was probably composed in the abbey of Gloucester. It is written in long lines, running to fourteen syllables and more, and is not the work of a single hand. A famous passage narrates the death of Simon de Montfort (1208–65) at the battle of Evesham. Ed. W. A. Wright, Rolls Series 86 (1887).

ROBERT THE DEVIL Sixth duke of Normandy and father of William the Conqueror, legendary for his violence and cruelty. In *The Life of Robert the Devil*, Robert is represented as having been devoted to Satan by his mother, but as repenting and marrying the emperor's daughter (he in fact died on a pilgrimage to Palestine). This verse tale, printed *c.*1500 by Wynkyn de *Worde, is a translation from French. Thomas *Lodge wrote a prose version.

Robert Elsmere A novel by Mary Augusta *Ward (Mrs Humphry Ward), published in 1888; the best-selling novel of ideas of the 19th century. It tells the story of an idealistic young clergyman, Robert Elsmere, who loses his Anglican faith as a result of his encounters with the cynical squire Roger Wendover, and the rationalist works he recommends. Despite the distress of his devout wife Catherine, Robert abandons the supernatural elements of religion, resigns his orders, and adopts an ethical approach to his calling, emphasizing practical work among the poor and ignorant. He establishes a settlement, the 'New Brotherhood of Christ', among the working people of east London. His arduous labours bring his life to a premature end, after a reconciliation with his wife. The novel was spectacularly successful, early interest having been generated by W. E. *Gladstone's searching but largely favourable review in the **Nineteenth Century*. It sold more than a million copies, and its ideas were widely debated. Sales figures were also very high in America, where at one point pirated copies were given away free with bars of Balsam Fir Soap.

ROBERTS, Adam (1965–) Academic, critic, and *science fiction writer, born in London; *Salt* (2000) began a sequence of richly thoughtful science fiction. *Splinter* (2007) is inspired by Jules *Verne. Under various transparent pseudonyms, Roberts also parodies best-selling *fantasy and science fiction such as **Star Wars*.

ROBERTS, Keith (1935–2000) *Science fiction author, illustrator, and editor, born in Kettering. His *Pavane* (1968), a collection of linked short stories, is a much-admired *alternate history. Roberts's dark, *fantasy-tinged science fiction may otherwise be seen to best effect in *The Chalk Giants* (1974) and *Kaeti & Company* (1986).

ROBERTS, Lynette (1909–95) Poet, born in Buenos Aires to Australian parents of Welsh extraction, who wrote much of her work in the 1940s in the remote village of Llanybri, Carmarthenshire, during her nine-year marriage to the editor and nationalist activist Keidrych Rhys (1915–87). *Poems* (1944) and the book-length sequence *Gods with Stainless Ears* (1951), a wartime meditation remarkable for its use of arcane, *defamiliarizing diction, were published with the encouragement of T. S. *Eliot. Roberts contributed copious, if less than wholly reliable Welsh materials to Robert *Graves for *The White Goddess* (1948), the first edition of which bore a dedication to her. See *Collected Poems*, ed. P. McGuinness (2005); *Diaries, Letters and Recollections* (2007).

ROBERTS, Michael (1902–48) Poet, critic, and editor; born in Bournemouth, Dorset, educated at Bournemouth School, King's College London, and Trinity College, Cambridge. His anthologies *New Signatures* (1932), *New Country* (1933), and *The *Faber Book of Modern Verse* (1936) helped shape the *modernist canon. His own poetry, influenced by T. S. *Eliot, Herbert *Read, and Hart *Crane, drew on his love of mountaineering and his knowledge of science. His criticism broadened in scope from the primarily literary concerns of *Critique of Poetry* (1934) to the larger social and cultural questions of *The Recovery of the West* (1941) and *The Estate of Man* (1951). The latter, written 1947–8, issued a then unfashionable warning about the devastation of the earth's resources. See *Selected Poems and Prose*, ed. Frederick Grubb (1980).

ROBERTS, Michèle (1949–) Novelist and poet, born in Hertfordshire and educated at Oxford. A leading feminist writer since the 1970s, she was poetry editor of the magazine *Spare Rib* from 1975 to 1977 and her first novel, *A Piece of the Night* (1978), was the first original fiction published by the Women's Press. Other novels include *The Wild Girl* (1984), *The Book of Mrs Noah* (1987), *Daughters of the House* (1992), *Impossible Saints* (1997), which was partly inspired by the life of St *Teresa of Avila, *Fair Exchange* (1999), which reworks episodes from the lives of William *Wordsworth and Mary *Wollstonecraft, *The Mistressclass* (2003), and *Reader, I Married Him* (2005). *During Mother's Absence* (1993) and *Playing Sardines* (2001) are volumes of short stories. Her poetry includes *The Mirror of the Mother* (1986), and *All the Selves I Was* (1995); *Paper Houses* (2007) is a memoir of the 1970s.

ROBERTSON, Thomas William (1829–71) Began life as an actor, but retired from the stage and became a dramatist. His plays *Society* (1865), *Ours* (1866), *Caste* (1867), *Play* (1868), *School* (1869), and *M.P.* (1870) introduced a new and more natural type of comedy to the English stage than had been seen during the first half of the century. His earlier drama *David Garrick* (1864) was also well received. Marie Wilton (Lady Bancroft) was the great exponent of Robertson's best female characters.

Robin Hood A legendary outlaw. 'Robertus Hood fugitivus' is mentioned in the portion of the Pipe Roll of 1230 relating to Yorkshire. He is mentioned in **Piers Plowman*. As a historical character he appears in *The Orygynale Cronykil* (*c.*1420) by the historian Andrew Wyntoun (*c.*1350–*c.*1422), and is referred to as a ballad hero by Abbot Bower (d. 1449),

John *Mair and John *Stow. The first detailed history, *Lytell Geste of Robyn Hode* (printed *c.*1500), locates him in south-west Yorkshire; later writers place him in Sherwood and Plumpton Park (Cumberland), and finally make him earl of Huntingdon. Joseph *Ritson, who collected the ancient songs and ballads about him, says that he was born at Locksley, Nottinghamshire, *c.*1160, that his name was Robert Fitz-Ooth, and that he was reputed to have been earl of Huntingdon. There is an account of the activities of his band in Michael *Drayton's **Poly-Olbion*, song 26. According to Stow, there were *c.*1190 many robbers and outlaws, among whom were Robin Hood and Little John, who lived in the woods, robbed the rich, killed only in self-defence, allowed no woman to be molested, and spared poor men's goods. Martin Parker (*True Tale*, *c.*1632) and the antiquary Ralph Thoresby (1658–1725) dated his death as 18 November 1247 and William *Stukeley supplied his pedigree. Legend claims that he was bled to death by a treacherous nun at Kirklees, Yorkshire. According to Joseph Hunter (antiquary, 1783–1861), with support from the court rolls of the manor of Wakefield, Yorkshire, he was a contemporary of Edward II (1307–27) and adherent of Thomas of Lancaster. He is the centre of a cycle of ballads, one of the best of which is *Robin Hood and Guy of Gisborne*, printed in Thomas *Percy's **Reliques*. Popular plays embodying the legend appear to have developed out of the village May Day Game, Robin and *Maid Marian replacing the king and queen of May. Works on this theme were written by Anthony *Munday, Henry *Chettle, Alfred *Tennyson, and others. The *True Tale of Robbin Hood* was published *c.*1632, *Robin Hood's Garland* in 1670, and a prose narrative in 1678. He figures in Thomas Love *Peacock's **Maid Marian*, and Walter *Scott's **Ivanhoe* as Locksley.

ROBINSON, E. A. (Edwin Arlington) (1869–1935) American poet, born in Maine, who recorded that at the age of 17 he became 'violently excited over the structure and music of English blank verse'. His admiration for Thomas *Hardy, George *Crabbe, and Robert *Browning is manifest in his many volumes of poetry about New England life, beginning with *The Torrent and the Night Before* (1896) and *The Children of the Night* (1897), which introduce, often through dramatic monologues, the population of his fictitious and representative Tilbury Town. As well as New England character sketches, he also wrote several long blank verse narratives, including an Arthurian trilogy (*Merlin*, 1917; *Lancelot*, 1920; *Tristram*, 1927) and *The Man Who Died Twice* (1924), a tale of genius destroyed. See Scott Donaldson, *Edwin Arlington Robinson* (2007).

ROBINSON, Henry Crabb (1775–1867) Diarist and journalist, born in Bury St Edmunds; he attended the Nonconformist Devizes academy and was articled to a solicitor in Colchester. He became a barrister, but is chiefly remembered for his diaries (over 30 volumes), reading-lists, and letters, first collected in 1869, which provide valuable information about the writers and events of his time. He was the friend of William *Wordsworth, S. T. *Coleridge, Charles *Lamb, William *Hazlitt, and later Thomas *Carlyle, and because of his indefatigable attendance at public lectures was able to provide useful descriptions of the lecturing of Coleridge (with his 'immethodical rhapsody'), Hazlitt, and others. He was an admirer of the German writers, of *Goethe in particular, travelled in Germany, and did much to popularize German culture in England. For many years he wrote for *The *Times*, at home and abroad, and he was one of the founders of both University College London, and the Athenaeum Club. See Edith J. Morley, *The Life and Times of Henry Crabb Robinson* (1935).

ROBINSON, Kim Stanley (1952–) American *science fiction writer, born Waukegan, Illinois, resident in California. *The Wild Shore* (1984) began a trio of novels experimenting with utopian and *dystopian versions of southern California. *Red Mars* (1992) and its sequels considered our own planet's ecological and political uncertainties through the problems of colonizing and 'terraforming' (i.e. modifying to resemble earth) Mars. *Antarctica* (1997) replayed these themes in an apparently less science fictional near future, a technique repeated when we confront the politics of global warming in *Forty Signs of Rain* (2004).

ROBINSON, Mary (1757/8–1800) Née Darby, poet, novelist, and actress, educated in Bristol, Chelsea, and lastly Marylebone. In 1774 she married Thomas Robinson, who incurred debts and was committed to debtors' prison. There, still not yet 20, she published a volume of *Poems* (1775). After her husband's release from jail she became a principal at Drury Lane, notably in a famous 1779 production of *The *Winter's Tale*. In the same year she became mistress of the prince of Wales (later George IV) who styled himself Florizel to her Perdita. Cast off by the prince and abandoning her feckless husband, she became the mistress of the army officer Banastre Tarleton, who had distinguished himself in the American War of Independence. In 1783 she became semi-paralysed, possibly as the result of a miscarriage. She turned once again to writing, and was prolific. She was a key member of the *Della Cruscan poetic coterie and produced a large number of publications in the 1790s, including *Modern Manners* (1793), **Sappho and Phaon* (1796), and several novels, such as the popular **Vancenza* (1792) and *The Natural Daughter* (1799). Her poetry was admired by S. T. *Coleridge and her **Lyrical Tales* (1800) were influenced by the **Lyrical Ballads*. Her daughter edited her *Memoirs, with Some Posthumous Pieces* (1801) and her *Poetical Works* (1806). See J. Pascoe, *Mary Robinson: Selected Poems* (2000); P. Byrne, *Perdita: The Life of Mary Robinson* (2005).

ROBINSON, Mary (later Darmesteter, later Duclaux) (1857–1944) Poet, born at Leamington Spa and educated at University College London. She was scholarly and knew many significant literary figures, Vernon *Lee, John Addington *Symonds, and Dante Gabriel *Rossetti among them. She gathered her many volumes of verse into *Collected Poems* in 1901, but continued to write. Her last volume, *Images* *and Meditations* (1923), was a meditation on the First World War.

ROBINSON, William Heath (1872–1944) Illustrator and artist, born in Islington, London, whose 'Heath Robinson contraptions' remain distinctive and instantly recognizable: he delighted in creating elaborate and unlikely devices, often for absurd purposes. He parodied the machine age with wit and style, and his drawings appeared in many magazines.

Robinson Crusoe, *The Life and Strange and Surprizing Adventures of* A novel by Daniel *Defoe, published 1719. The story was in part inspired by the adventures of Alexander *Selkirk, who had joined a privateering expedition under William *Dampier, and in 1704 was put ashore after a quarrel on one of the uninhabited islands of the Juan Fernández archipelago. He was rescued in 1709 by Woodes Rogers (1679–1732). The story was told by Richard *Steele in *The Englishman* (1713), and elsewhere. Defoe's novel (told, like all his novels, in the first person, and presented as a true story) is vastly more vivid, detailed, and psychologically powerful, giving an extraordinarily convincing account of the shipwrecked Crusoe's efforts to survive in isolation. With the help of a few stores and utensils saved from the wreck and the dedicated exercise of labour and ingenuity, Crusoe builds himself a refuge, maps the island, domesticates goats, sows crops, and constructs a boat. Suffering from dreams and illness, he struggles to accept the workings of Providence, and has disturbing encounters with cannibals from other islands, from whom he rescues the man he later names 'Friday'. After 28 years, an English ship with a mutinous crew arrives; by some delicate management Crusoe subdues the mutineers, and returns, finally prosperous, to Britain. In *The Farther Adventures of Robinson Crusoe* (1719), Crusoe revisits his island, is attacked by a fleet of canoes on his departure, and loses Friday in the encounter. *Serious Reflections...of Robinson Crusoe...with his Vision of the Angelick World*, offering a pious and allegorical interpretation of the adventures, appeared in 1720. The influence of the *Robinson Crusoe* story has been enormous. The book had immediate and permanent success; it was pirated, adapted, and abridged in *chapbooks, translated into many languages, and inspired many imitations, known generically as 'Robinsonnades', including **Philip Quarll*, **Peter Wilkins*, and *The *Swiss Family Robinson*. Jean-Jacques *Rousseau (in *Émile*) recommended it as the first book that should be studied by a growing boy, S. T. *Coleridge praised its evocation of 'the universal man', and Karl *Marx in *Das Kapital* used it to illustrate economic theory in action. It was extremely popular with male readers of the 19th century, being affectionately remembered by William *Wordsworth, Lord *Macaulay, John Stuart *Mill, George *Borrow, Robert Louis *Stevenson, and John *Ruskin. The novel has also inspired many artists and film-makers. More recently it has been seen as an apologia for, or an ironic critique of, economic individualism, capitalism, and imperialism; a study in alienation; and an allegorical spiritual autobiography. See Ian Watt, *The Rise of the Novel* (1957); Pat Rogers, *Robinson Crusoe* (1979); Michael Seidel, *Robinson Crusoe: Island Myths and the Novel* (1991); David Blewett, *The Illustrations of Robinson Crusoe* (1995).

Robinsonnades A group of primarily children's island adventure stories originating in Daniel Defoe's **Robinson Crusoe*. Best known are *The *Swiss Family Robinson* (1812–13), Frederick *Marryat's *Masterman Ready* (1841–2), Ballantyne's *The *Coral Island* (1857), Robert Louis *Stevenson's *Treasure Island* (1881), J. M. Barrie's **Peter Pan* (1904), and William *Golding's *The Lord of the Flies* (1954).

Rob Roy A novel by Walter *Scott, published 1817. The novel, set in the period preceding the first Jacobite rebellion (1715), portrays the rise of a prosperous Whig mercantile class, personified by Francis Osbaldistone and Bailie Nicol Jarvie, over the fox-hunting, Tory world of Osbaldistone Hall, ruled by Francis's elder brother Sir Hildebrand. Francis's son Frank, on refusing to enter his father's business, is exiled to Osbaldistone Hall; in exchange, his father decides to give his youngest nephew Rashleigh the place designed for his son. The plot is complicated by Frank's and Rashleigh's rival interest in their cousin Diana Vernon, one of Scott's most vivid heroines. Rashleigh is entangled in plans for the forthcoming rebellion and uses his place in the firm to rob and ruin Francis. Frank, attempting to save his father's credit, goes to Scotland to seek the help of the firm's Scottish correspondent, Bailie Nicol Jarvie, the real hero of the novel. They search for Rob Roy in the Highlands. Jarvie's defence of the practical benefits to Scotland of the Union is set against a portrayal of the ignorance, brutality, and squalor of the Highlands which Scott is sometimes thought to romanticize. Rob Roy Macgregor does not appear until late in the novel. A historical figure and member of a proscribed clan, he has been driven by injustice to outlawry but is still capable of generosity. He is involved in Rashleigh's plans for the rebellion, but Frank needs his help to frustrate his cousin's designs. The rebellion fails, Rashleigh is killed by Rob Roy, and Frank inherits Osbaldistone Hall and marries Diana. His incorrigible manservant Andrew Fairservice is one of Scott's great characters.

ROBSART, Amy (1532–60) Daughter of Sir John Robsart, married to Sir Robert Dudley, afterwards earl of *Leicester, in 1550; she figures in Walter Scott's **Kenilworth*.

ROBSON, Justina (1968–) *Science fiction author, born in Leeds; her novels, including *Silver Screen* (1999), *Mappa Mundi* (2001), and *Natural History* (2003) involve many of the preoccupations of the 21st century: artificial intelligence, identity, and nanotechnologies that destroy the boundaries between them.

ROCHESTER, John Wilmot second earl of (1647–80) Lyric poet, satirist, and a leading member of the group of 'court wits' surrounding Charles II. He was born at Ditchley in Oxfordshire, his father a Cavalier hero and his mother a deeply religious woman related to many prominent Puritans. In his early teens he was sent to Wadham College, Oxford, the home of the *Royal Society, and then went on a European tour, returning to the court late in 1664. At the age of 18 he romantically abducted the sought-after heiress Elizabeth Malet in a coach-and-six. Despite the resistance of her family, and after a delay of eighteen months (during which Rochester fought with conspicuous gallantry in the naval wars against the Dutch), she married him. Subsequently his time was divided between periods of domesticity with Elizabeth at his mother's home in the country (the couple had four children), and fashionable life in London with, among several mistresses, the brilliant actress Elizabeth *Barry, and his riotous male friends, who included the earl of Dorset (Charles *Sackville) and George Villiers, the second duke of *Buckingham. Wherever he was staying he tried to keep up the other side of his life through letters, many of which survive. Although Samuel *Johnson dismissed Rochester's lyrics, their wit and emotional complexity give him some claim to be considered one of the last important *metaphysical poets of the 17th century, and he was one of the first of the *Augustans, with his social and literary verse satires. He wrote scurrilous lampoons—some of them impromptu—dramatic prologues and epilogues, 'imitations' and translations of classical authors, and several other brilliant poems which are hard to categorize, such as his tough self-dramatization 'The Disabled Debauchee' and the grimly funny 'Upon Nothing'. He wrote more frankly about sex than anyone in English before the 20th century, and is one of the wittiest poets in the language. Although his output was small (he died young), it was very varied. Andrew *Marvell admired him, John *Dryden, Jonathan *Swift, and Alexander *Pope were all influenced by him (he was Dryden's patron for a time), and he has made an impression on many subsequent poets—*Goethe and Alfred *Tennyson, for example, and in modern Britain, William *Empson and Peter *Porter.

Rochester is famous for having, in Samuel Johnson's words, 'blazed out his youth and health in lavish voluptuousness'. He became very ill in his early thirties and engaged in discussions and correspondence with a number of theologians, particularly the Deist Charles Blount (1654–93) and the rising Anglican churchman Gilbert *Burnet, an outspoken royal chaplain who superintended and subsequently wrote up the poet's deathbed conversion. It was the final contradiction in a personality whose many oppositions—often elegantly or comically half-concealed—produced an important body of poems. See *Works*, ed. Harold Love (1999); *Letters*, ed. J. Treglown (1980). *A Profane Wit* is a life by J. W. Johnson (2004); see also Graham *Greene, *Lord Rochester's Monkey* (1974).

Roderick Hudson The first novel of Henry *James, published in 1876. It is the story of a young man transplanted from a lawyer's office in a Massachusetts town to a sculptor's studio in Rome. Incapable of adjustment to his environment, he fails in both art and love, and meets a tragic end in Switzerland.

Roderick Random, The Adventures of A novel by Tobias *Smollett, published 1748. Smollett's first novel, narrated with youthful vigour in the first person, is strongly influenced by *Lesage's *Gil Blas*, which Smollett translated the following year. In his preface the author declares his wish to arouse 'generous indignation...against the vicious disposition of the world'. Roderick, a Scot, is combative, often violent, but essentially innocent and genuine, capable of great affection and generosity. His father, on being disinherited, has left Scotland, leaving his young son penniless. Roderick is befriended by his uncle, Lieutenant Tom Bowling of the navy. After a brief apprenticeship to a surgeon, Roderick travels with Strap, an old schoolmate, to London, where he encounters assault, deception, and other tribulations. Despite his qualifications as a surgeon's mate, he is pressed as a common sailor aboard a man-of-war, where he eventually becomes mate to the ebullient Welsh surgeon Morgan. After much suffering and ill treatment Roderick returns to England. Here he lives under a false name as a footman, falls in love with Narcissa, and is once again kidnapped, this time by smugglers, who bear him off to France. He finds and helps his uncle Tom Bowling, joins the French army, and fights at Dettingen. He again encounters the generous Strap, who arranges his release from the army and serves as Roderick's valet. Once more in London, Roderick becomes embroiled in riotous living and a series of amatory adventures, but his attempts to court rich women all come to grief. Again he meets Narcissa, but is imprisoned for debt, and, unable to find her on his release, he sinks into despair. He is once more rescued by Tom Bowling, and embarks as surgeon on a ship under Bowling's command; in the course of the voyage he meets Don Roderigo, who turns out to be his long-lost father, now a wealthy merchant. When they return to England Roderick marries Narcissa, and Strap marries her maid, Miss Williams. In a digression, Smollett inserts the story of Melopoyn, partly based on his own experience in trying to get his *The Regicide* accepted for the stage, and containing a character widely assumed to be a caricature of David *Garrick.

RODKER, John (1894–1955) Poet and publisher, born in Manchester to Jewish parents; he moved to the East End of London at the age of 6. His earliest works were published in the *New Age* (in 1912) and the **Egoist* (in 1914). A conscientious objector, he was arrested and imprisoned during the First World War: he described his experiences in *Memoirs of Other Fronts* (published anonymously in 1932), and in the poem 'A CO's Biography'. He married Mary *Butts in 1918, but by 1920 the marriage had broken down; they divorced in 1926. Rodker had privately published his first collection of poems in 1914. He established the brief-lived Ovid Press, publishers of T. S. *Eliot's *Ara Vus Prec* (1920), Ezra *Pound's *Hugh Selwyn Mauberley* (1920), volumes of drawing by Edward Wadsworth and Wyndham *Lewis, and of his second volume of poems, *Hymns* (1920). He was later, under other imprints, to publish Pound's *Draft of the Cantos 17–27* (1928), Paul *Valéry's *Introduction to the Method of Leonardo da Vinci* (1929), and, through the Imago Press, psychoanalytic texts in English and German.

His poetry, long neglected, draws on *imagism, but interweaves impersonal images with a more subjective and personal vocabulary. His poems are powerful in their presentation of bodily experience and in their use of somatic metaphor; marked by neither D. H. *Lawrence's sexualized vitalism nor James *Joyce's fastidious detachment, they speak from the indistinct territory between emotion, thought, and bodily sensation. The dominant emotion is fear. His oeuvre also includes prose poems and an experimental dumb-show drama, *Theatre Muet* (1915). Several of his longer prose works proved unpublishable, and two appeared in French translations: *Montagnes russes* (1923) (known in English as 'The Switchback'); and *Dartmoor* (1926), an extract from *Memoirs of Other Fronts. The Future of Futurism* (1927), a brief and lively critical book, is atypical, but its speculations on the evolution of man in a world of machines give an indication of Rodker's world-view. *Adolphe 1920* (1929), a phantasmagoric prose narrative, conveys a vivid sense of embodied mental life. See *Poems & Adolphe 1920*, ed. Andrew Crozier (1996).

Rodomont In **Orlando innamorato* and **Orlando furioso*, the king of Sarza, arrogant, ferocious and valiant, the doughtiest of the followers of the king Agramant and his chief general in the attack on Paris. His boastfulness gave rise to the word 'rodomontade'. In the *Innamorato*, he leads the first Saracen invasion into France. Doralice, princess of Granada, is betrothed to him, but in the *Furioso* is not unwillingly seduced by Mandricardo. After a duel between the two Saracen heroes, the conflict is referred to the princess herself, who, to Rodomont's surprise, expresses her preference for Mandricardo. Rodomont retires in disgust to the south of France. Here *Isabella falls into his power and, preferring death, tricks him into slaying her. In remorse, he builds a bridge in her memory and takes toll of all who pass that way. Orlando, coming in his madness to the bridge, throws Rodomont into the river. Rodomont is also defeated by Bradamante. Humiliated, he temporarily retires from arms, emerges once more, and is finally killed by Ruggero.

ROETHKE, Theodore (1908–63) American poet, born in Michigan, who taught from 1947 at the University of Washington. His first book of poems, *Open House* (1941), already displays characteristic imagery of vegetable growth and decay, rooted in childhood memories of the greenhouses of his father, who was a keen horticulturalist. It was followed by various volumes including *The Lost Son* (1948), *Praise to the End* (1951), a book of light verse (divided into 'Nonsense' and 'Greenhouse' poems) called *I Am! Says the Lamb* (1961), and a posthumous collection, *The Far Field* (1964). See Allan Seager, *The Glass House* (1968).

ROGERS, Samuel (1763–1855) The son of a banker and himself a banker for some years, in his lifetime a highly successful poet, and well known as an art collector and for the celebrated 'breakfasts' which he held for over 40 years. In 1792 he published *The Pleasures of Memory*, in which the author wanders reflectively round the villages of his childhood. The work went into four editions in its first year, and by 1816 over 23,000 copies had been sold. In 1810 he published a fragmentary epic, *Columbus*; in 1814 *Jacqueline*; in 1822–8 *Italy*, a collection of verse tales; and in 1832 *Poems*. His work was praised by Francis *Jeffrey and admired by Lord *Byron, who came to believe that only Rogers and George *Crabbe were free from 'a wrong revolutionary system'. But William *Hazlitt spoke for many younger writers when he declared in a lecture in 1818 that in Rogers's work 'the decomposition of prose is substituted for the composition of poetry'.

Roget's Thesaurus, of English Words and Phrases By Dr Peter Mark Roget (1779–1879), English physician and scholar, is a compilation of words classified in groups according to the ideas they express, the purpose of which is to supply a word, or words, which most aptly express a given idea; conversely, a dictionary explains the meaning of words by supplying the ideas they are meant to convey. The volume, first published in 1852, has been followed by many successive revised editions: by Roget's son John Lewis Roget (from 1879), and his grandson Samuel Romilly Roget (from 1933). The family connection came to an end with the death of Samuel Roget in 1953.

rogue literature A very popular type of writing about the underworld in the 16th and 17th centuries. Its practitioners include the Kentish landowner Thomas Harman (*fl.* 1547–67), whose *Caveat for Common Cursitors* first appeared in 1566; Robert Copland (*see* High Way to the Spital House); Robert *Greene, whose *pamphlets describe 'coney-catching', that is, the deception of innocents; and Thomas *Dekker. Rogue literature is generally vividly descriptive and often allegedly confessional, providing an important source for our knowledge of everyday common life and its language, as well as for the language of thieves and beggars. It can be related to stories about *Robin Hood, *jest book literature, and early attempts at writing fiction and autobiography. A large collection of such tracts was edited by A. V. Judges in 1930 and a smaller selection by G. Salgãdo in 1972.

ROJAS, Fernando de (*c.*1473/6–1541) Spanish author born at Puebla de Montalbán, near Toledo, his family being *conversos*, or Jews converted to Christianity. He studied law at the University of Salamanca and, in spite of continued family difficulties owing to his racial origin, rose to the position of mayor of Talavera de la Reina, where he practised as a civil lawyer. He is famous for the masterpiece **Celestina*, of which he claimed to have found the anonymous opening act while a student at Salamanca and to have completed it there. There is no record of any other work by his hand.

Rokeby A poem in six cantos by Walter *Scott, published 1813. The scene is laid chiefly at Rokeby in Yorkshire, immediately after the battle of Marston Moor (1644). The complicated plot involves conspiracy, attempted murder, and disguise: young Redmond O'Neale, who has helped to frustrate an attack on Rokeby Castle, is revealed as the lost son of Philip of Mortham, and marries Matilda, daughter of Lord Rokeby.

Roland The most famous of the *Paladins of Charlemagne. According to the chronicler Einhard, his legend has a factual basis. In August 778 the rearguard of the French army of Charlemagne was surprised in the valley of Roncevaux by the Basque inhabitants of the mountains; the baggage was looted and all the rearguard killed. In later poetic versions, the Saracens were substituted for the Basques, and Roland becomes the commander of the rearguard, appointed to the post at the instance of the traitor Ganelon, who is in league with the Saracen king Marsile. Roland's companion Oliver is introduced, the brother of Aude, Roland's betrothed. Oliver thrice urges Roland to summon aid by sounding his horn, but pride prevents him from doing so until too late. Charlemagne returns and destroys the pagan army. Ganelon is tried and executed. The legend has been handed down in three principal forms: in the fabricated Latin chronicle of the 12th century mistakenly attributed to Archbishop Turpin (d. *c.*800); in the *Carmen de Proditione Guenonis* of the same epoch; and in the *Chanson de Roland*, in medieval French, also of the early 12th century. Roland, as Orlando, is the hero of Boiardo's **Orlando innamorato* and Ariosto's **Orlando furioso*. Roland's sword was called 'Durandal' or 'Durindana', and his horn 'Olivant'.
See OLIVER.

ROLFE, Frederick William (1860–1913) Writer who styled himself 'Baron Corvo', or, equally misleadingly, Fr Rolfe, by turns schoolmaster, painter, and writer. From a Dissenting background, he was a convert to Roman Catholicism and an unsuccessful candidate for the priesthood. His most outstanding novel, *Hadrian the Seventh* (1904), combines autobiographical elements with wish-fulfilment, in which Rolfe's protagonist, George Arthur Rose, is rescued from a life of literary poverty and elected pope. His other writings include *Stories Toto Told Me* (published in 1898, after first appearing in the **Yellow Book*), *Chronicles of the House of Borgia* (1901, an eccentric historical study), and *Don Tarquinio: A Kataleptic Phantasmatic Romance* (1905, a novel relating 24 hours in the life of a young nobleman in the company of the Borgias in 1495). Rolfe moved to Venice in 1908, and in his last work, *The Desire and Pursuit of the Whole: A Romance of Modern Venice*, written largely in 1909 but not published until 1934, he describes his poverty, his homoerotic fantasies, and the beauties of Venice, as well as abusing in characteristic vein many of those who had previously befriended him, including R. H. Benson (1871–1914). W. H. *Auden in a 1961 foreword describes him as 'one of the great masters of vituperation'. Two other novels (*Nicholas Crabbe, or The One and the Many*, 1958; *Don Renato: An Ideal Content*, 1963) and several fragments were also published posthumously. Rolfe's style is highly ornate and idiosyncratic; his vocabulary is arcane, his allusions erudite, and although he had admirers during his lifetime, he alienated most of them by his persistent paranoia and requests for financial support. The story of his unhappy life is told by A. J. *Symons in *The Quest for Corvo: An Experiment in Biography* (1934). See also D. Weeks, *Corvo* (1971).

ROLLAND, Romain *See* ROMAN-FLEUVE.

ROLLE, Richard of Hampole (*c.*1305/10–1349) One of the principal 14th-century English writers of religious prose and poetry. He was born in north Yorkshire and is said to have left Oxford in his nineteenth year to become a hermit. He lived at various places in Yorkshire, finally at Hampole where he died, near a Cistercian nunnery to which he was religious adviser. Among his disciples was Margaret Kirkby (d. 1391/4), who became an anchoress (i.e. a woman who withdraws from the world for religious reasons) and to whom a number of his major English works (notably the vernacular anchoritic manual *The Form of Living*) are addressed. He wrote in the Yorkshire dialect, in a highly rhetorical language which makes much use of alliteration. The essential element in his mysticism is personal enthusiasm; the echoing words he returns to are *fervor, dulcor, canor*: warmth, sweetness, melodiousness. Among his best-known vernacular works are *Ego Dormio, The Commandment of Love*, and his translation of *The English Psalter*. The canon of his works, in Latin as well as English, is very large. See H. E. Allen, *Writings Ascribed to Richard Rolle* (1927); *The English Writings of Richard Rolle*, ed. H. E. Allen (1931); C. T. Horstman, *Yorkshire Writers: Rolle and his Followers* (2 vols, 1895–6).

Rollo, Duke of Normandy *See* BLOODY BROTHER, THE.

Rolls Series Otherwise *Chronicles and Memorials of Great Britain and Ireland from the Invasion of the Romans to the Reign of Henry VIII*. Their publication was authorized in 1847 at the suggestion of Joseph Stevenson, the archivist, and the recommendation of Sir John Romilly, master of the rolls, and it produced texts of many of the most important literary and historical writings of the Middle Ages and Renaissance. Among its most celebrated editors were James Gairdner (1828–1912) and J. H. Round (1854–1928).

ROMAINS, Jules *See* ROMAN-FLEUVE.

roman à clef i.e. a 'novel with a key', in which the reader (or some readers) is intended to identify real people disguised more or less obviously as fictional characters. The key is sometimes literal, sometimes figurative, and sometimes provided by the author, as in the case of Delarivier *Manley's *The New Atalantis*, sometimes published separately by others, as in the case of Benjamin Disraeli's **Coningsby*. A modern example is *The Ghost* by Robert *Harris (2007), a thinly veiled novel about Tony Blair.

Roman Actor, The A tragedy by Philip *Massinger, acted 1626, printed 1629. The play is based on the life of the emperor Domitian as told by *Suetonius and Dio Cassius. The cruel and lustful Domitian forcibly steals Domitia from her husband Aelius Lamia, a Roman senator. He executes Lamia and makes Domitia his empress. He dotes on her, but she falls in love with the actor Paris. So well does he act before her a scene in which, as Iphis scorned by Anaxarete, he threatens to take his life, that she betrays her feelings to her enemies, who warn Domitian. The emperor finds her wooing Paris, and kills the actor with his own hand in the course of a play in which he takes the part of an injured husband and Paris the part of a false servant. Domitia escapes punishment but, angered by the death of Paris and confident of her power over the emperor, she taunts him. Finally he includes her name in a list of those marked for death. Domitia finds the list while he sleeps, and joins others whose names appear on the list in a conspiracy. Domitian is lured from the protection of his guards and assassinated.

Roman Catholicism The beliefs and practices of the Roman Catholic Church. The spread of Islam in the 7th century overran all but two of the five patriarchates of the early Christian church (Alexandria, Antioch, Constantinople, Jerusalem, and Rome). Political and doctrinal tensions between the surviving claimants to Christian primacy, Constantinople and Rome, led to an enduring schism between the (Eastern or Greek) Orthodox Church and the (Western or Latin) Roman Catholic Church in 1054. The Church of Rome, however, has always maintained that, with papal authority deriving in direct succession from St Peter (Matthew 16: 18), it alone is the true apostolic and catholic church.

The Synod of Whitby in 664 determined that Celtic Christianity, originating in conversions during the Roman occupation of Britain, would henceforth adopt the Roman Catholic practices introduced by the mission of St *Augustine in 597. From *Bede onward, Medieval English literature was Roman Catholic in its context, apparatus, and emphases, not only in devotional and homiletic texts but in its romances, in the *mystery cycles and *morality plays, and in its poetry. Within a generation of *Henry VIII's *Reformation, however, a virulent strain of anti-popery marked texts such as *The *Faerie Queene*. This was fuelled by the excommunication of *Elizabeth I by Pope Pius V in 1570 which, by releasing English Catholics from their allegiance, appeared to foster sedition, and by the Armada and the Gunpowder Plot. Hailing England as an elect Protestant nation, writers such as John *Bale, John *Foxe, and John *Milton took the pope to be Antichrist. In *Jacobean drama, Roman Catholics are commonly scheming Machiavellians. With the exception of Robert *Southwell, Richard *Crashaw, John *Dryden, and Alexander *Pope, not until after the emancipation of Roman Catholics from civil disadvantage in 1829 was a Roman Catholic allegiance and sensibility once more confidently to be articulated in English (by, for example, John Henry *Newman and Gerard Manley *Hopkins).
See PROTESTANTISM.

romance [from the medieval Latin *romanice*, 'in a Romance language'] The Old French *roman*, derived from the phrase 'mettre en romanz', 'to translate into French', became synonymous with the popular courtly stories in verse on three traditional subjects: legends about Arthur; Charlemagne and his knights; and classical heroes (*see* MATTER). English equivalents, almost always translations, are found from the 13th century onwards. The best known include **King Horn*, **Havelok*, *Sir *Gawain and the Green Knight*, **Sir Orfeo* (*see* BRETON LAYS). From the 15th century, English romances are mostly in prose, and some 16th-century examples were the inspiration for Edmund *Spenser and *Shakespeare. A new interest in medieval romance (in writers such as Walter *Scott and John *Keats) contributed to the naming of 19th-century *Romanticism, though the term was also applied to some sentimental novels from the 18th century onwards, as in the *Mills and Boon romances of the modern era.

Roman de la Rose, Le The first 4,058 lines of this allegorical romance were written in *c*.1225–40 by Guillaume de Lorris to expound 'the whole art of love'; the remaining 17,622 lines were composed in *c*.1270–78 by Jean de Meun (d. 1305) as a more wide-ranging anatomy of love within a social and philosophical framework. The story in Guillaume's part of the poem is an allegorical presentation of *courtly love; the allegorical figures mostly embody various aspects of the lady whom the lover-narrator meets in his endeavours to reach the rose which symbolizes the lady's love. The story is set in the walled garden of the god of love, the unpleasant realities of life being depicted on the walls outside. In the second part Jean de Meun shows love in a wider context of scholarship, philosophy, and morals, shifting the work from the courtly to the encyclopedic literary tradition, in line with the rationalist and compendious spirit of the 13th century. The poem, in its allegorical dream form and in its presentation of both the courtly and the philosophical discussions of love, remained an immense literary influence all through the later Middle Ages, both inside and outside France. About one-third of the whole (ll. 1–5,154 and 10,679–12,360) is translated in the Middle English **Romaunt of the Rose*, the first part of which may be by *Chaucer. See F. Lecoy (ed.) (Paris, 1965–70); trans. F. Horgan (1999); also S. Huot, *The Romance of the Rose and its Medieval Readers* (2007).

roman-fleuve [French, 'river novel'] The term for a series of novels which follow the fortunes of a character or family and which thus give an account of a social period. Inspired by *Balzac and *Zola, the form reached its high point in the first half of the 20th century. Its major exemplars were: Romain Rolland (1866–1944), whose *Jean Christophe* (10 vols, 1904–12) describes the career of a musical genius; Roger Martin du Gard (1881–1958), whose *Les Thibault* (10 vols, 1922–40) explores the reaction of two brothers against their bourgeois inheritance; Georges Duhamel (1884–1966), whose *Chronique des Pasquiers* (10 vols, 1933–41: *The Pasquier Chronicles*) traces the moral and cultural development of a Parisian family; and Jules Romains (1885–1972), whose *Les Hommes de bonne volonté* (27 vols, 1932–47: *Men of Good Will*) offers a panorama of French society between 1910 and 1940. Translations of these works have been popular in England, but the English version of the phenomenon, descending from Anthony *Trollope and including such novelists as John *Galsworthy and C. P. *Snow, did not have the same impact.

romantic comedy *See* COMEDY.

romantic fiction A broad category of story, in which the trials and eventual triumphs of heterosexual love constitute the focus of narrative interest. *'Romance' is often used to designate medieval tales of courtly love written in the 'popular' languages derived from Latin, as opposed to *epic, which denotes narratives of heroism in the classical languages. Seventeenth-century prose fiction contains many stories of illicit love generally now thought of as romances, though there was often no clear distinction between romance and the emergent form of the *novel; Samuel *Richardson's novels, especially **Pamela* and **Clarissa*, may be said to fuse high aristocratic romance with the realistic world of the novel, presenting respectively comic and tragic versions of love and marriage. In *The Progress of Romance* (1785), Clara *Reeve differentiated the novel, which deals in the realistic details of everyday life, from the romance, which she conceived of as a more elevated form concerned with high emotion, aristocratic life, and the past. By this time romantic fiction had already become a scapegoated genre, irretrievably gendered female; an early straw in the wind was Charlotte Lennox's *The *Female Quixote*, with its deluded heroine comically adrift in the real world thanks to an excess of romance reading. As the size of the reading public (especially amongst women) was perceived to increase and create its own market demands, much anxiety, amongst both early feminists such as Mary *Wollstonecraft and reactionary commentators of both sexes, focused on the likelihood of female readers being led astray by unrealistic fantasy fiction. Reeve, having attempted to domesticate the emergent *Gothic form in her own novel, *The Champion of Virtue* (1777), attempted in her essay to endow romance with a literary value equivalent to that of epic, but the situation became still more acute with the arrival in the 1790s of popular Gothic romances, such as those of Ann *Radcliffe or Charlotte *Dacre, which were widely denounced for their pernicious effects on female minds.

Much of what remains as canonical in the history of the novel was written in conscious reaction against the romance. In the early 19th century, Jane *Austen, having mocked the potential errors of female reading of romances in **Northanger Abbey* and elsewhere, strengthened the major model of romantic fiction, the 'Cinderella' narrative in which the worthy but disadvantaged heroine wins the noblest hero, with wit, irony, psychological depth, and a hard-nosed interest in property. Walter *Scott fused history with romance in an attempt to masculinize the genre. Literary novels have, however, by drawing on romance conventions, spawned further romantic fictions. The *Brontë sisters inherited a set of Gothic fixtures, including wild landscapes, tormented heroes, and haunted houses, but Emily Brontë may be said to have established a standard for the romance of doomed love in **Wuthering Heights*, while Charlotte Brontë's **Jane Eyre* is a template for the romance of a young woman's climb towards moral independence and a love validated by intellectual equality. The much-read and much-castigated *sensation novelists of the end of the century, such as Wilkie *Collins and Mary *Braddon, draw on these models, and not only for the secrets found in the attic or the family tree. Daphne du Maurier's **Rebecca* (1938), with its pure young heroine, sinister housekeeper, and fatal hero, is a later debtor to the Gothic romance. Best-selling 20th-century writers of romantic fiction include Ethel M. Dell (1881–1939), whose *The Way of an Eagle* (1912) began a series of melodramatic adventures centred on strong, virtuous heroines; Edith M. Hull (1880–1947), whose exotic sexual fantasy *The Sheik* (1919) shocked an avid public; Georgette Heyer (1902–74) in her guise as a historical novelist; Catherine *Cookson, who reinvented the rags-to-riches tale of the resourceful northern heroine; and Joanna Trollope (1943–), whose *Aga sagas have a more middle-class appeal. The 1980s and 1990s saw the rise of blockbuster romances by Jackie Collins (1937–), Judith Krantz (1928–), Barbara Taylor Bradford (1933–), Jilly Cooper (1937–), and Danielle Steele (1947–), who explored a more sexually liberated version of female power. The novels of Anita *Brookner, Mary *Wesley, and Margaret *Drabble might be said to contain elements of romantic fiction, and in the hands of playful postmodernists, such as David *Lodge in *Small World: An Academic Romance* (1984) or A. S. *Byatt in *Possession* (1990), romance has once again been turned into literary fiction. In serene defiance of all such trends, the simplest brand of romance, the formulaic fictions of the *Mills and Boon series, continue to sell millions of books a year in the UK alone. See Barbara Fuchs, *Romance* (2004).

Romanticism A profound transformation in artistic styles, in cultural attitudes, and in the relations between artist and society evident in Western literature and other arts in the first half of the 19th century. In Britain, a stark contrast appears between representative works of the preceding *Augustan age and those of leading figures in what became known as the Romantic movement or 'Romantic Revival' in the period from about 1780 to about 1848 (the 'Romantic period'): William *Blake, Robert *Burns, Charlotte *Smith, William *Wordsworth, S. T. *Coleridge, Mary *Robinson (1757/8–1800), Robert *Southey, Walter *Scott, Lord *Byron, P. B. *Shelley, John *Keats, William *Hazlitt, Thomas *De Quincey, Thomas *Carlyle, Emily *Brontë, and Charlotte *Brontë. To define the general character or basic principle of this momentous shift, which later historians have called Romanticism, is notoriously difficult, partly because the Romantic temperament itself resisted the very impulse of definition, favouring the indefinite and the boundless.

In the most abstract terms, Romanticism may be regarded as the triumph of the values of imaginative spontaneity, visionary originality, wonder, and emotional self-expression over the classical standards of balance, order, restraint, proportion, and objectivity. Its name derives from *romance, the literary form in which desires and dreams prevail over everyday realities.

Romanticism arose from a period of turbulence, euphoria, and uncertainty. Political and intellectual movements of the late 18th century encouraged the assertion of individual and national rights, denying legitimacy (forcibly in the American and French revolutions) to kings and courtiers. In Britain, the expansions of commerce, journalism, and literacy had loosened the dependency of artists and writers upon noble patrons, releasing them to discover their own audiences in an open cultural market-place—as Scott and Byron did most successfully—or to toil in unrewarded obscurity, like Blake. Nourished by Protestant conceptions of intellectual liberty, the Romantic writers tended to cast themselves as prophetic voices crying in the wilderness, dislocated from the social hierarchy. The Romantic author, unlike the more socially integrated Augustan writers, was often seen a sort of modern hermit or exile, who usually granted a special moral value to similar outcast figures in his or her own writing: the pedlars and vagrants in Wordsworth's poems, Coleridge's *Ancient Mariner, Mary *Shelley's man-made monster, and the many tormented pariahs in the works of Byron and P. B. Shelley—who were themselves wandering outcasts from respectable English society. From this marginal position, the Romantic author wrote no longer to or on behalf of a special caste but, in Wordsworth's phrase, as 'a man speaking to men', his utterance grounded in the sincerity of his personal vision and experience. To most of the Romantics, the polished wit of the Augustans seemed shallow, heartless, and mechanically bound by artificial 'rules' of *neo-classical taste. Although some (notably Keats and Shelley) continued to employ elements of Greek mythology and to adapt the classical form of the *ode, they scorned the imitation of classical models as an affront to the autonomy of the all-important creative imagination. Well above *Horace or *Juvenal they revered *Shakespeare and *Milton as their principal models of the *sublime embodied in the poet's boundless imaginative genius. In this, they took the partly nationalistic direction followed by Romantic poets and composers in other countries, who likewise rediscovered and revalued their local vernacular traditions.

Although inheriting much of the humane and politically liberal spirit of the *Enlightenment, the Romantics largely rejected its analytic rationalism, associating it with the coldly calculating mentality of contemporary commerce, politics, and moral philosophy (as for example in the work of Jeremy *Bentham). Wordsworth warned against the destructive tendency of the 'meddling intellect' to intrude upon the sanctities of the human heart, and he argued that the opposite of poetry was not prose but science. The Romantic revolt against scientific empiricism is compatible with the prevailing trend of German philosophy, notably Immanuel *Kant's 'transcendental' idealism, of which Coleridge and Carlyle were dedicated students. This new philosophical idealism endorsed the Romantics' view of the human mind as organically creative, and encouraged most of them to regard the natural world as a living mirror to the soul, not as dead matter for scientific dissection.

In reaction against the spiritual emptiness of the modern calculating age, Romanticism cultivated various forms of nostalgia and of *primitivism, following *Rousseau in contrasting the 'natural' man (or child) with the hypocrisies and corruptions of modern society. The imaginative sovereignty of the child, in the works of Blake and Wordsworth, implicitly shames the inauthenticity of adulthood, while the dignified simplicity of rural life is more generally invoked in condemnation of urban civilization. The superior nobility of the past tends also to be, as we now say, 'romanticized', although less for its actual social forms than for its imaginative conceptions of the ideal and the heroic, as reflected in Shakespeare, in chivalric romance, and in balladry. Antiquaries of the 18th century, notably Thomas *Percy in his **Reliques* and James *Macpherson in his Ossianic poems, had won a new respect for the older forms of popular or 'folk' poetry and legend, upon which Southey, Scott, and several other Romantic writers drew for materials and forms, notably in the **Lyrical Ballads* (1798, 1800) of Wordsworth and Coleridge.

These kinds of change manifest themselves in the literary productions of the Romantic writers in widely varied ways, as may be expected in a movement that unleashed individualism and that privileged the particular experience over the general rule. In general, though, Romantic writing exhibits a new emotional intensity taken to unprecedented extremes of joy or dejection, rapture or horror, and an extravagance of apparently egotistic self-projection. As a whole, it is usually taken to represent a second renaissance of literature in Britain, especially in lyric and narrative poetry, which displaced the Augustan cultivation of satiric and didactic modes. The prose styles of Hazlitt, De Quincey, Charles *Lamb, and Leigh *Hunt also show a marked renewal of vitality, flexibility, subjective tone, and what Hazlitt called 'gusto'. The arts of prose fiction were extended by Scott's historical novels, by the sensational effects of *Gothic fiction, and by the emergence of the short story form in the Edinburgh and London magazines. Although Byron, Shelley, and others wrote important dramatic poems, drama written for the theatres is not seen as the strongest aspect of Romantic literature. On the other hand, alongside the often vituperative and partisan conduct of reviewing in **Blackwood's Magazine* and other periodicals, this was a great age of literary criticism and theory, most notably in the writings of Coleridge and Hazlitt, and in major essays by Wordsworth and Shelley.

Simplified accounts of Romanticism in Britain date its arrival from the appearance in 1798 of the *Lyrical Ballads* or in 1800 of Wordsworth's preface (effectively a manifesto) to that collection. Several important tendencies in the latter part of the 18th century, however, have been recognized as 'pre-Romantic' currents, suggesting a more gradual evolution. Important developments here include *'graveyard poetry', the novel of *sentiment, the cult of the sublime, and the **Sturm und Drang* phase of German literature in the 1770s led by *Schiller and the young *Goethe; all of these influences encouraged a deeper emotional emphasis than Augustan or neo-classical convention allowed.

Romanticism flourished in the United States in the somewhat later period, between 1820 and 1860, with James Fenimore *Cooper's historical romances, Ralph Waldo *Emerson's essays, Herman *Melville's novels, Edgar Allan *Poe's tales and poetry, Henry Wadsworth *Longfellow, Walt *Whitman, and the nature writings of Henry *Thoreau.

The convenient and conventional divisions of literary history into distinct 'periods' are particularly misleading if they obscure the extent to which the Romantic tradition remains unbroken in the later 19th century and beyond. The associated work of John *Ruskin, the *Pre-Raphaelite Brotherhood, and the Victorian advocates of the *Gothic Revival, indeed displays a hardening of Romantic attitudes in its nostalgia and its opposition to an unpoetical modern civilization; and the same might be said of W. B. *Yeats and D. H. *Lawrence in the early 20th century. Culture continues to display latter-day Romantic features, ranging from the rebelliousness of rock lyrics and other forms of songwriting, to the anti-Enlightenment themes of post-*structuralist literary theory.

Critical opposition to the Romantic inheritance, in the name of *'classical' ideals, was advanced by Matthew *Arnold in the 1850s, and by some later critics under his influence, including the American scholar Irving *Babbitt, whose book *Rousseau and Romanticism* (1919) condemned the Romantic movement as an irresponsible 'pilgrimage in the void' that had licensed self-indulgent escapism and nationalist aggression. His student T. S. *Eliot continued the anti-Romantic campaign, although Eliot's own poetry, like Arnold's, was nonetheless inescapably 'romantic' in its nostalgia and sense of alienation. Some damage was done by Eliot's disciples to the reputations of Shelley and other Romantic writers, from which they have since recovered. See M. H. Abrams, *Natural Supernaturalism* (1971); M. Butler, *Romantics, Rebels, and Reactionaries* (1981); D. Wu, *Romanticism: An Anthology* (1995).

Romany Rye, The A novel by George *Borrow, published 1857. 'Romany Rye' in Romany language means 'Gypsy Gentleman', a name applied to Borrow by Ambrose Smith, the Norfolk gypsy. This book is a sequel to **Lavengro*, and continues, in episodic fashion, the story of the author's wanderings and adventures.

Romaunt of the Rose, The A translation into Middle English octosyllabics of about one-third of the **Roman de la Rose*, lines 1–5,154 and 10,679–12,360, made in the time of Geoffrey *Chaucer and previously attributed to him. W. W. *Skeat argued that only Part A, a closer translation than the other sections, is by Chaucer, and that B and C are not his. Almost all modern authorities agree.

In the Garden of Mirth, the dreamer-narrator falls in love with a rosebud. Parts A and B describe the dreamer's instructions by the god of love. He is befriended by the imprisoned Bialacoil, opposed by Daunger and other adverse figures, and (in the section by Jean de Meun (d. 1305)) challenged by the discourse of Resoun; Part C satirizes the various hypocrisies of religion, women, and society. See *The Romaunt of the Rose and Le Roman de la Rose: A Parallel-Text Edition*, ed. R. A. Sutherland (1967).

Romeo and Juliet *Shakespeare's first romantic tragedy, based on the poem *The Tragical History of Romeus and Juliet* (1562) by Arthur Brooke (d. 1563), a translation from the French of Boaistuau of one of Matteo *Bandello's *Novelle*. Shakespeare's play was probably written about 1595 and first printed in a 'bad' quarto in 1597; a good quarto published in 1599 and reprinted in 1609 served as the copy for the play's text in the first *folio of 1623.

The Montagues and Capulets, the two chief families of Verona, are bitter enemies; Escalus, the prince, threatens anyone who disturbs the peace with death. Romeo, son of old Lord Montague, is in love with Lord Capulet's niece Rosaline. But at a feast given by Capulet, which Romeo attends disguised by a mask, he sees and falls in love with Juliet, Capulet's daughter, and she with him. After the feast he overhears, under her window, Juliet's confession of her love for him, and wins her consent to a secret marriage. With the help of Friar Laurence, they are wedded next day. Mercutio, a friend of Romeo, meets Tybalt, of the Capulet family, who is infuriated by his discovery of Romeo's presence at the feast, and they quarrel. Romeo arrives, and tries to reason with Tybalt, but Tybalt and Mercutio fight, and Mercutio falls dead. Then Romeo draws his sword and Tybalt is killed. The prince, Montague, and Capulet appear, and Romeo is sentenced to banishment. After spending the night with Juliet, he leaves Verona for Mantua, counselled by the friar, who intends to reveal Romeo's marriage at the right moment. Capulet proposes to marry Juliet to Count Paris, despite her attempts to avoid the match. Juliet consults the friar, who advises her to consent, but on the night before the wedding to drink a potion which will render her apparently lifeless for 42 hours. He will warn Romeo, who will rescue her from the vault when she wakes and carry her to Mantua. The friar's message to Romeo goes astray, and Romeo hears that Juliet is dead. Buying poison, he comes to the vault to have a last sight of Juliet. He chances upon Count Paris outside the vault; they fight and Paris is killed. Then Romeo, after a last kiss on Juliet's lips, drinks the poison and dies. Juliet wakes to find Romeo dead by her side, the cup still in his hand. Guessing what has happened, she stabs herself and dies. The friar and Count Paris's page reveal the story, and Montague and Capulet, faced by the tragic results of their quarrel, are reconciled.

The play begins with a sonnet spoken by the chorus and in its poetry, language, and plot reflects the sonnet vogue of the 1590s, from which period Shakespeare's own sonnet sequence probably dates.

ROMNEY, George (1734–1802) Portrait painter, born in Dalton-in-Furness, the son of a builder. He spent two years in Italy (1773–5) and the poise and graceful rhythms of his most distinguished works suggest his love of *Raphael and the antique. Yet Romney (who was a friend of William *Hayley, who later wrote Romney's life, and that of David *Flaxman) felt trapped by the demands of portraiture. His many drawings of literary and historical subjects develop from a neoclassical treatment towards a wilder, more violent style; and his increasing obsession with *sublime and horrific subject matter from *Aeschylus, John *Milton, and William *Shakespeare links him to Henry *Fuseli and J. H. Mortimer (*c.*1741–1779). Romney, after 1781, became obsessed with Emma Hart, later Lady Hamilton, whom he painted many times. See Alex Kidson, *George Romney* (2002).

Romola A novel by George *Eliot, published 1863. The background of the novel (meticulously researched by Eliot) is Florence at the end of the 15th century, the troubled period, following the expulsion of the Medici, of the expedition of Charles VIII, distracted counsels in the city, the excitement caused by the preaching of *Savonarola, and acute division between the popular party and the supporters of the Medici. Various historical figures, including Charles VIII, *Machiavelli, and Savonarola himself, are drawn with great care. The story describes the trials of the noble Romola, devoted daughter of a blind scholar. Into their lives comes a clever, adaptable young Greek, Tito Melema, whose self-indulgence develops into utter perfidy. He robs and abandons in prison the benefactor of his childhood, Baldassare. He cruelly goes through a mock marriage ceremony with the innocent little contadina Tessa. After marrying Romola he wounds her deepest feelings by betraying her father's solemn trust. He plays a double game in the political intrigues of the day. He is eventually destroyed by Baldassare, who escapes from imprisonment crazed with sorrow and suffering. Romola, her love for her husband turned to contempt, and her trust in Savonarola destroyed by his falling away from his high prophetic mission, is left alone, until she discovers her duty in self-sacrifice. She devotes her life to the care of Tessa and her children. The novel was illustrated by Frederic *Leighton, much to George Eliot's satisfaction. It is her most austerely uncompromising investigation of the moral nature of the self as it is shaped by individual and historical circumstances.

rondeau A medieval French verse form revived in English by A. C. *Swinburne, Austin *Dobson, and others in the later 19th century. It normally consists of thirteen octosyllabic lines (in three stanzas, of five, three, and five lines), having only two rhymes throughout, and with the opening words used twice as a refrain. A related form, the rondel, also uses only two rhymes, but with repetition of the opening two lines as lines 7 and 8, and of the first line as line 13. The term 'roundel' may refer to either of these forms or to an eleven-line variant upon them invented by Swinburne in *A Century of Roundels* (1883).

rondel *See* RONDEAU.

RONSARD, Pierre de (1524–85) French poet, leader of the *Pléiade. He published his first four books of *Odes* in 1550, followed by a fifth in 1552, with which he also published *Les amours* (*Loves*), a cycle of 183 decasyllabic love sonnets. A second cycle of love poetry followed in two collections: the *Continuation des amours* (1555: *Continuation of Loves*) and the *Nouvelle Continuation des amours* (1556: *New Continuation of Loves*). His last important love sequence, the *Sonnets pour Hélène* (1578: *Sonnets for Hélène*), was dedicated to Hélène de Surgères, lady-in-waiting to Catherine de *Médicis. Ronsard also wrote on a wide variety of political, philosophical, pastoral, and religious themes, including *Les Hymnes* (1555–6: *Hymns*), poems conceived as miniature epics on classical models; the *Discours* and the *Continuation du Discours des misères de ce temps* (1562: *Discourse* and *Continuation of the Discourse on the Present Troubles*), written at the beginning of the Wars of Religion; and the unfinished national epic *La Franciade* (1572: *Legend of France*), intended to trace the origins of France's royal dynasty to the legendary Trojan hero Francus, son of Hector. Imitated by Alexander *Montgomerie and plagiarized by Thomas *Lodge, Ronsard exerted a considerable influence on 16th- and 17th-century English poets, notably *Shakespeare, Robert *Herrick, and Andrew *Marvell. John *Keats and Andrew *Lang both translated him in the 19th century.

Room at the Top *See* BRAINE, JOHN.

Room of one's Own, A By Virginia *Woolf, a key work of the feminist movement, published 1929 and based on two lectures on 'Women and Fiction' that Woolf delivered in Cambridge in 1928. It begins with the visit of the imaginary Mary Beton to an imaginary Oxbridge college where she feels a complete outsider. Woolf goes on to describe the educational, social, and financial disadvantages against which women have struggled throughout history, arguing that women will not be able to write well and freely until they have privacy and financial independence. She pays tribute to women writers of the past; to women's achievements in the form of the novel; and projects a future in which increasing equality would enable women to become not only novelists but poets. In the last chapter she discusses 'androgyny': 'Perhaps a mind that is purely masculine cannot create, any more than a mind that is purely feminine.'

Room with A View, A Novel by E. M. *Forster, published 1908. It opens in a Florence *pensione*, where Lucy Honeychurch and her chaperone Charlotte Bartlett reluctantly accept the room with a view that the socially inferior Mr Emerson and his son George offer to vacate for them. Other guests at the Pensione Bertolini include a clergyman, Mr Beebe, and a lady novelist, Miss Lavish. Lucy is disturbed by witnessing a murder, and by an embrace from George Emerson, and a scandalized Miss Bartlett returns her to Summer Street, Surrey, where Lucy becomes engaged to Cecil Vyse. Mr Beebe reappears as the local vicar and the Emersons take a cottage nearby. Lucy comes to realize that she loves George, not Cecil, and the remainder of the novel is played out against a background of tennis and tea parties, piano recitals and muddle. It ends in the Pensione Bertolini, with George and Lucy on their honeymoon. An award-winning film adaptation was released in 1985.

ROPER, Margaret (1505–44) Daughter of Sir Thomas *More. According to Thomas Stapleton (1535–98), she purchased the head of her dead father nearly a month after it had been exposed on London Bridge and preserved it in spices until her death. It is believed that it was buried with her. Alfred *Tennyson alludes to this: 'her, who clasped in her last trance | Her murdered father's head' ('A Dream of Fair Women').

ROPER, William (1495/8–1578) Of Lincoln's Inn. He married Sir Thomas *More's daughter Margaret *Roper and wrote an early life of his father-in-law first published at Saint-Omer (1626).

RORTY, Richard (1931–2007) American philosopher, and the best-known contemporary advocate of pragmatism in the tradition of John *Dewey. Influenced also by *Heidegger, *Derrida, and the later *Wittgenstein, his critique of the traditional philosophical project leads many to identify him as an exponent of *postmodernism. His major work *Philosophy and the Mirror of Nature* (1979) rejects conceptions of language and thought as representations mirroring an independent reality, while *Contingency, Irony and Solidarity* (1989) applies this anti-foundationalist perspective to ethics and politics, presenting an 'ironic' defence of liberalism.

ROS, Amanda McKittrick (1860–1939) Née Anna Margaret McKittrick, Irish writer, known as 'the World's Worst Novelist'. Her fiction was remarkable for its extraordinary and unselfconsciously colourful prose, to which Aldous *Huxley devoted an essay, 'Euphues Redivivus' (1923). *Irene Iddesleigh* (1897), her first novel, provides many choice examples: 'Every sentence the able and beautiful girl uttered caused Sir John to shift his apparently uncomfortable person nearer and nearer, watching at the same time minutely the divine picture of innocence, until at last, when her reply was ended, he found himself, altogether unconsciously, clasping her to his bosom, whilst the ruby rims which so recently proclaimed accusations and innocence met with unearthly sweetness, chasing every fault over the hills of doubt, until hidden in the hollow of immediate hate.' She was also a ludicrous poet, publishing *Poems of Puncture* (1912) and *Fumes of Formation* (1933). See J. Loudan, *O Rare Amanda* (1954).

ROSA, Salvator (1615–73) Neapolitan painter, etcher, satirical poet, and actor. He painted genre scenes, battles, marines, and ambitious figure compositions, but has remained most famous for his macabre subjects (witches, monsters, meditations on death) and for his wild, craggy landscapes. In England his reputation rose steadily throughout the 18th century. Horace *Walpole, crossing the Alps in 1739, exclaimed 'Precipices, mountains, torrents, wolves, rumblings—Salvator Rosa', and writers on the *picturesque frequently invoked his name. His stormy personality also fascinated artists, and with the publication of a biography by Lady *Morgan in 1824 the legends associated with him—that he had lived with bandits and fought in a popular uprising in Naples—became more important than his pictures. He came to represent the archetypal Romantic artist, outlawed by a corrupt society, whose genius bore comparison with William *Shakespeare. See Jonathan Scott, *Salvator Rosa: His Life and Times* (1995).

Rosalind (1) in Edmund *Spenser's *Shepheardes Calender* and *Colin Clouts Come Home Againe*, an unknown lady celebrated by the figure of the poet as his love; (2) the heroine of William *Shakespeare's *As You Like It*, whose chief source was Thomas *Lodge's *Rosalynde*.

Rosalynde, *Euphues' Golden Legacy* A pastoral romance in the style of John *Lyly's *Euphues*, interspersed with sonnets and eclogues, written by Thomas *Lodge during his voyage to the Canaries ('every line was wet with a surge'), published 1590.

The story is borrowed in part from *The Tale of *Gamelyn* and was dramatized by William *Shakespeare in *As You Like It*. Lodge's Rosader is Shakespeare's Orlando; Saladyne is Oliver; Alinda, Celia; and Rosalind is common to both. Jaques and Touchstone have no equivalents. The ill treatment of Rosader (Orlando) is more fully developed by Lodge, and the rightful duke has his dukedom returned through force of arms instead of persuasion. Lodge's romance, which includes such lyrics as 'Love in my bosom like a bee | Doth suck his sweet', is also diversified by a variety of rhetorical speeches and descriptions.

ROSAMOND, Fair (Rosamond Clifford) (d. ?1176) Probably mistress of Henry II in 1174. She was buried in the choir of Godstow Abbey near Oxford, and her remains were removed to the chapter house there *c.*1191. A legend transmitted by John *Stow, following *Higden*, declares that Henry kept her in a maze-like house in Woodstock where only he could find her, but the queen, *Eleanor of Aquitaine, traced her whereabouts by following a thread and 'so dealt with her that she lived not long after'. The story is told in a ballad by *Deloney included in Percy's *Reliques*; Samuel *Daniel published in 1592 'The *Complaint of Rosamund', a poem in *rhyme royal; and *Addison wrote an opera, *Rosamond*, in 1707.

Rosciad, The (1761) A *mock-heroic verse satire by Charles *Churchill, originally 730 lines, but greatly expanded in later editions. It describes the attempt to find a worthy successor to Roscius, the Roman actor who died *c.*62 BC, and provides satiric sketches of many famous theatrical personalities of the day, including James Quin (1693–1766), Samuel *Foote, and George *Colman. David *Garrick, the chosen successor, is praised highly, but the poem was very controversial and a bad review in the *Critical Review* prompted Churchill's *Apology* (1761), attacking the editor, Tobias *Smollett.

ROSCOE, William (1753–1831) Lawyer and banker, book-collector, writer, scholar, and botanist, born in Liverpool. Largely self-educated, he published his early verses in 1777, and from then until the end of his life, a considerable number of works of poetry, biography, jurisprudence, botany, and arguments against the slave trade (see *Wrongs of Africa*, 1788). His principal work was his *Life of Lorenzo de' Medici* (1795). In 1805 (having learned Greek) he published the *Life of Leo the Tenth* (the 16th-century pope), and in 1806 *The Butterfly's Ball and the Grasshopper's Feast*, which became a children's classic. His edition of Alexander *Pope appeared in 1824. He did much to stimulate an interest in Italy and Italian literature in England. His son Henry Roscoe published a *Life* (2 vols) of his father in 1833.

Rose and the Ring, The A *fairy story written and illustrated by W. M. *Thackeray, first published 1855. The magic rose and ring have the property of making those who have possession of them seem irresistibly attractive, which introduces comic complications into the story of Prince Giglio and Princess Rosalba, who have been ousted from their positions as a result of the Fairy Blackstick's benevolent wish that they shall suffer 'a little misfortune'. Thackeray makes gentle fun both of fairy-story conventions, and of 'improving' children's books in this 'Fireside Pantomime for Great and Small Children'.

ROSEN, Michael (1946–) Born in Pinner, Middlesex, son of Harold and Connie Rosen, educationalists. Rosen is a broadcaster, poet, and polemicist specializing in childhood culture. Since his first book of verse, *Mind your Own Business* (1974), he has written around 100 books, including anthologies, retellings, and *picturebooks. After the sudden death of his son Eddie he wrote *Michael Rosen's Sad Book* (2004) and, for adults, *Carrying the Elephant* (2002). Rosen received the Eleanor Farjeon Award in 1997. See also his introductory essay on 'Children's Literature'.

ROSENBERG, Isaac (1890–1918) Poet, born in Bristol. He moved with his family to Whitechapel, London, in 1897. His parents were émigrés of Lithuanian origin, and his father, a scholarly Jew, worked as a pedlar and market dealer. During his irregular East End schooling Isaac learned to paint, and began to experiment with poetry. He became an apprentice engraver at 14, but in 1911 three Jewish women paid for him to attend the Slade School of Art. In 1912 he published at his own expense a collection of poems, *Night and Day*, and was encouraged by Gordon Bottomley, Ezra *Pound, and others. He went to South Africa in 1914, but returned in 1915 and published another volume of verse, *Youth*, which passed largely unregarded. In the same year he defied his family's pacifist views and joined the army, arriving as a private in the trenches in 1916. He was killed in action. His poetry is forceful, rich in its vocabulary, and starkly realistic in its attitudes to war (Rosenberg greatly disliked Rupert *Brooke's 'begloried sonnets'). His poor Jewish urban background gives the poems a note not found in the work of his fellow war poets. Bottomley edited a selection of his poems, introduced by Laurence *Binyon, in 1922, but it was only after the publication in 1937 of his *Collected Works*, with a foreword by Siegfried *Sassoon, that his importance became generally accepted. Vivien Noakes edited *The Poems and Plays of Isaac Rosenberg* (2004). See Jean Liddiard, *Isaac Rosenberg* (1975). Liddiard also edited *Selected Poems and Letters* (2003).

Rosencrantz and Guildenstern Are Dead A comedy by Tom *Stoppard, performed and published 1966, which places the peripheral 'attendant lords' from **Hamlet* at the centre of a drama in which they appear as bewildered witnesses and predestined victims. This device is used to serious as well as to comic effect, for underlying the verbal wit and Shakespearian parody there is a pervasive sense of man's solitude and lack of mastery over his own life reminiscent of Samuel *Beckett, whom Stoppard greatly admires. Stoppard's two protagonists consciously echo Vladimir and Estragon, from Beckett's **Waiting for Godot*, in their existentialist *angst* and their attempts to pass the time while they wait for something to happen.

ROSENTHAL, Jack (1931–2004) Dramatist, born in Manchester, educated at Sheffield University. He is best known for an unusually wide-ranging television output. He wrote 150 early episodes of Granada Television's *Coronation Street*, and introduced a more demotic speech into the sitcom genre in *The Dustbin Men*. *The Evacuees* (1975) and *Bar Mitzvah Boy* (1976) were single plays drawing on his Jewish background; their wry and compassionate humour appealed to a wide audience. *The Knowledge* (1979) portrayed London cabdrivers facing a malevolent invigilator. *London's Burning* (1986) dramatized the perils of the fire service, and *And a Nightingale Sang* (1989) evoked wartime nostalgia. *Eskimo Day* (1996) and its successor *Cold Enough for Snow* (1997) depicted the tragicomic effects of social class upon parents as their children entered university. Rosenthal was one of the few television writers at the time still commissioned to produce single dramas. His autobiography, *By Jack Rosenthal* (2006), was published posthumously and, soon after, a four-part radio version, *Jack Rosenthal's Last Act*, was broadcast, adapted by his daughter Amy and with his wife, the actress Maureen Lipman, played by herself.

Rose Theatre, the On Bankside, Southwark, built in 1587, and altered and enlarged in 1592, closing in 1602. Philip *Henslowe was its owner and Edward *Alleyn its leading actor. Shakespeare is thought to have acted there. Its foundations, close to the reconstructed Globe, were discovered and partially excavated in 1989; they await fuller investigation. In the meantime they are cared for by the Rose Theatre Trust.

Rosicrucian A member of a supposed society or order, 'the brethren of the Rosy Cross', reputedly founded by one Christian Rosenkreuz in 1484, but first mentioned in 1614. Its manifestos were the *Fama Fraternitatis* (1614) and the *Confessio Fraternitatis* (1615), which aroused intense interest on the Continent and in Britain. Its members were said to claim various forms of secret and magic knowledge, such as the transmutation of metals, the prolongation of life, and power over the elements and elemental spirits, and to derive much of their alchemy and mystical preoccupations from *Paracelsus. No Rosicrucian society appears to have actually existed, and the Rosicrucian movement seems to have been rooted in some kind of anti-Jesuit Protestant alliance, with deep religious interests, as well as interests in alchemy, medicine, and the Cabbala (a school of thought based on mystical interpretations of Judaism). Frances *Yates, in her study *The Rosicrucian Enlightenment* (1972), describes the term as representing 'in the purely historical sense...a phase...intermediate between the Renaissance and the so-called scientific revolution of the 17th century', 'a historical label for a style of thinking', and names as major figures in the English Rosicrucian movement John *Dee, Robert *Fludd, and Elias *Ashmole; she also discusses the Rosicrucian connections of Francis *Bacon, *Comenius, Isaac *Newton, *Leibniz, and many others.

ROSS, Alan (1922–2001) Poet, travel writer, and editor, born in Calcutta and educated at St John's College, Oxford. He published several volumes of poetry and prose, many evocatively describing travels and stays abroad. *Open Sea* (1975) collects poems about the Second World War from earlier works, and includes his compressed epic 'J.W.51B', a haunting, first-hand description of naval endurance on the Arctic convoy route. A posthumous collection of his work, *Poems*, appeared in 2005. He edited the **London Magazine* from 1961 until his death.

ROSS, Alexander (1699–1784) Scottish poet and schoolmaster, born on Deeside and educated at Marischal College, Aberdeen, author of *The Fortunate Shepherdess* (1768), later called *Helenore*, a lengthy pastoral poem in north-eastern *Scots. His songs 'Woo'd and Married and a'' and 'The Rock and the Wee Pickle Tow' were lastingly popular.

ROSS, Martin *See* SOMERVILLE AND ROSS.

ROSSETTI, Christina Georgina (1830–94) Poet, sister of Dante Gabriel and William Michael *Rossetti. Born in London, she was educated at home, sharing her family's strong intellectual interests. Ill health (possibly strategic when young, but later severe) ended her attempts to work as a governess, and confined her to a quiet life. Her engagement to the painter James Collinson (1825–81), an original member of the *Pre-Raphaelites, was broken off in 1850 when he rejoined the Roman Catholic Church; Christina, like her mother and sister Maria, was a devout High Anglican, much influenced by the Tractarians (*see* OXFORD MOVEMENT). She contributed to *The *Germ* (1850), where five of her poems appeared under a pseudonym. In 1861 **Macmillan's Magazine* published 'Up-hill' and 'A Birthday', two of her best-known poems. **Goblin Market and Other Poems* appeared in 1862, *The Prince's Progress and Other Poems* in 1866, *Sing-Song, a Nursery Rhyme Book* (with illustrations by Arthur Hughes) in 1872, and *A Pageant and Other Poems* in 1881. She also published poems elsewhere and wrote numerous prose works, including *Speaking Likenesses* (1874), a collection of fairy-tales; *Time Flies: A Reading Diary* (1885), which consists of short passages linked to each day of the year, and several devotional works. Rossetti's technical virtuosity was considerable and her poems are distinctive for their beautifully constructed forms. Her work ranges from poems of fantasy and children's verse to ballads, love lyrics, sonnets, and religious poetry. Much of her poetry reflects her strong religious beliefs: it is also fascinated by loss, melancholy, and death, secrets, and unhappy or frustrated love. Many of her finest poems are teasingly subtle in their veiled eroticism and their continual play on revelation versus concealment, and they often lend themselves to feminist interpretations. Rossetti's reputation as a relatively minor poet underwent a seismic shift with the advent of feminist criticism, and since the late 20th century she has been regarded as a leading Victorian woman poet, a peer of Emily *Brontë, E. B. *Browning, and Emily *Dickinson, and as a major Victorian poet irrespective of gender. Her collected poems, ed. R. W. Crump (2001), are available from Penguin; see also *Christina Rossetti: Poems and Prose*, ed. Simon Humphries (2008).

ROSSETTI, Dante Gabriel (1828–82) Poet and painter, whose full first names were Gabriel Charles Dante (but his form of these has become customary); born in London, the son of Gabriele Rossetti (1783–1854), an Italian patriot who came to England in 1824, and brother to Christina *Rossetti, and William Michael *Rossetti. He was brought up in an atmosphere of keen cultural and political activity which contributed more to his artistic development than his formal education at King's College School, London. He studied painting with John Everett *Millais and Holman *Hunt, and in 1848, with them and four others, founded the *Pre-Raphaelite Brotherhood. For many years he was known only as a painter, though he began to write poetry early. Several of his poems, including 'The *Blessed Damozel' and 'My Sister's Sleep', and a prose piece, 'Hand and Soul', were published in *The *Germ* (1850). In the same year he first met Elizabeth *Siddal (or Siddall), who modelled for him and many of his circle. In 1854 he met John *Ruskin, who did much to establish the reputation of the Pre-Raphaelite painters, and in 1856 William *Morris, whom he greatly influenced; Morris's wife Jane was to become Rossetti's muse and lover. In 1860 Rossetti and Lizzie married: she died of an overdose, probably self-administered, in 1862, and Rossetti buried with her a manuscript containing many of his poems. Later that year he moved to 16 Cheyne Walk, Chelsea, where A. C. *Swinburne and George *Meredith were briefly joint tenants; he filled the house with antiques, bric-à-brac, and a curious selection of animals, including a wombat. In 1868 he showed a renewed interest in poetry, possibly inspired by renewed contact with Jane Morris; sixteen sonnets, including the 'Willowwood' sequence, were published in March 1869 in the **Fortnightly Review*. That summer he wrote many more and also arranged the exhumation of the poems buried with his wife. *Poems* (1870) contained 'Sister Helen', 'Troy Town', 'Eden Bower', *'Jenny', and the first part of his sonnet sequence *The *House of Life*; it was well received, partly because Rossetti took care that his friends should review it. In 1871 Morris and Rossetti took a joint lease of Kelmscott Manor, where Rossetti continued his intimacy with Jane, with Morris's apparent consent, and continued to paint her; there also he wrote the ballad 'Rose Mary' and further sonnets for *The House of Life* sequence. In October 1871 Robert *Buchanan's notorious attack 'The Fleshly School of Poetry' appeared (under the pseudonym Thomas Maitland) in the **Contemporary Review*. This accused Rossetti and his associates of impurity and obscenity. The sonnet 'Nuptial Sleep' was singled out for particular criticism and was not reprinted in the 1881 edition, though the prolonged and bitter controversy which Buchanan aroused ended with the Pre-Raphaelites largely victorious. Rossetti's reply, 'The Stealthy School of Criticism', appeared in the **Athenaeum*, December 1872. Rossetti's later years were overshadowed by ill health and the abuse of the drug chloral, though he continued to paint and write and was recognized by a new generation of aesthetes, including Walter *Pater and Oscar *Wilde, as a source of inspiration; the admiration was not wholly mutual. *Poems* and *Ballads and Sonnets* both appeared in 1881; the first was largely rearrangements of earlier works, and the second completed *The House of Life* with 47 new sonnets, and also contained other new work, including 'The King's Tragedy' and 'The White Ship', both historical *'ballads'.

Many of Rossetti's poems were written as commentaries on his own and other paintings, and his finest poems have a Pre-Raphaelite sharpness of detail and undeniable emotional and erotic power, although his equal fondness for vast and cloudy generalities about Life, Love, and Death can be offputting to readers. His letters reveal another side of his colourful and extravagant personality; they are witty, irreverent, at times coarse, and demonstrate the wide range of his artistic interests. Rossetti was also a gifted translator from the Italian (*The Early Italian Poets Together with Dante's Vita Nuova*, 1861, known later as *Dante and his Circle*, 1874), and of *Villon. A new edition of his *Collected Poetry and Prose*, ed. Jerome McGann, appeared in 2003 and a new edition of his letters, ed. William Fredeman and others (2002–), is ongoing. See also Jan Marsh, *Dante Gabriel Rossetti: Painter and Poet* (1999).

ROSSETTI, William Michael (1829–1919) Man of letters, art critic, and editor, brother of Dante Gabriel *Rossetti and Christina *Rossetti, educated at King's College School, London; he worked as an official of the Inland Revenue. He was a member of the *Pre-Raphaelite Brotherhood, edited *The *Germ*, and wrote the sonnet that was printed on its cover. His reviews of art exhibitions for the **Spectator* were published as *Fine Art: Chiefly Contemporary* (1867). He edited fifteen volumes of *Moxon's Popular Poets, and was responsible for important editions of William *Blake and P. B. *Shelley. He edited Walt *Whitman in 1868, introducing him to a British public, and the two corresponded frequently. He translated *Dante, and was responsible for encouraging James *Thomson (1834–82). He also edited many of his family's papers, letters, and diaries, and wrote memoirs of his brother and his sister. See *Ruskin: Rossetti: Preraphaelitism* (1899); *Preraphaelite Diaries and Letters* (1900); *Rossetti Papers, 1862–70* (1903); *D. G. Rossetti: His Family Letters, with a Memoir* (1895); *Family Letters of Christina Rossetti* (1908). His *Some Reminiscences* (1906) is a valuable biographical source. His diary for 1870–3 was edited with notes by O. Bornand (1977).

ROSSINI, Gioachino (1792–1868) Italian opera composer. After early success with comic opera, Rossini devoted himself to serious drama, beginning with *Otello* (1816). The text, adapted by a wealthy dilettante, Francesco di Salsa, was berated by Lord *Byron: 'the music is good, but lugubrious; but as for the words, all the real scenes with Iago cut out, and the greatest nonsense inserted; the handkerchief turned into a *billet-doux*, and the singer would not black his face, for some exquisite reasons.' Rossini's *La donna del lago* (1819) was based on Walter *Scott's *The *Lady of the Lake*; *Ivanhoe* (1826) and *Robert Bruce* (1846) were compiled by others from Rossini's works. When news of Byron's death reached London, Rossini produced, from music already written, *Pianto delle muse in morte di Lord Byron*, performed at the second of his London concerts in 1824. In that year *Stendhal published a biography of Rossini.

ROSTAND, Edmond (1868–1918) French playwright, author of *Les Romanesques* (1894: *The Romancers*), *La Princesse lointaine* (1895: *The Faraway Princess*), *La Samaritaine* (1897: *The Samaritan Woman*), *L'Aiglon* (1900: *The Eaglet*; based on the life of Napoleon's son), and *Chantecler* (1910). The poetic drama *Cyrano de Bergerac* (1897), his most popular and successful work, is about the 17th-century soldier and duellist *Cyrano de Bergerac. It has been translated into Glaswegian demotic by Edwin *Morgan (1992), and was successfully filmed (1990) with Gérard Depardieu in the title role, with English subtitles rendered into rhyming verse by Anthony *Burgess.

ROSTEN, Leo (1908–1997) Jewish American novelist and screenwriter, born in Łódź, Poland, who grew up in Chicago. He published a series of humorous sketches of beginners learning English, *The Education of H*Y*M*A*N K*A*P*L*A*N* (1937) and *The Return of Hyman Kaplan* (1938). In addition to novels, Rosten published a portrait of the movie capital, *Hollywood* (1941), and an exploration of Jewish humour in *The Joys of Yiddish* (1968).

ROSZAK, Theodore (1933–) American social commentator and novelist, who produced a study of the underground in *The Making of a Counter Culture* (1969) and of computing in *The Cult of Information* (1994). His novels include *Bugs* (1981), a cybernetic fantasy, and *Flicker* (1991), a postmodern investigation of an experimental film-maker.

ROTA, Bertram (1903–66) Bookseller, who entered the book trade in 1918 in the bookshop conducted by his uncles Percy and Arthur Dobell. In 1923, at the age of 19, he began his own business with £100 borrowed from his mother's savings. The firm has continued its tradition of specializing in the sale of first editions of literature of the last 100 years or so and, especially to US libraries, of literary archives.

ROTH, Henry (1906–1995) Jewish American novelist, born in Galicia, who grew up in New York. His 1934 novel *Call It Sleep* describes a boy's coming of age. Roth then did not write any further pieces until he published his four-part novel sequence *Mercy of a Rude Stream* (1994–8). See Stephen G. Kellman, *Redemption* (2005).

ROTH, Joseph (1894–1939) Austrian novelist and essayist. Born of Jewish parents in Galicia, he studied at Lemberg and Vienna. A highly regarded and successful journalist, he published numerous novels both before and during his self-exile in France: acutely aware of the threat of Nazism, he moved to Paris in 1933. In his works, he is a sardonic and clear-sighted chronicler of his times as well as a nostalgic apologist for the pre-1914 empire of Hapsburg Austria. His family epic *Radetskymarsch* (1932: *The Radetzky March*) has remained his best-known work in England, but recent translations of earlier writing including *The Spider's Web* (2004), as well as translations of essays and journalistic pieces by Michael *Hofmann—*The Wandering Jews* (2001: *Juden auf Wanderschaft*, 1927), *What I Saw: Reports from Berlin 1920–33* (2003), and *In the White Cities: Reports from France 1925–1939* (2004)—have enabled a fuller reception of his work.

ROTH, Philip (1933–) Jewish American novelist, born in Newark, New Jersey. His writing career has been combined with various teaching posts in America. His complex relationship with his Jewish background is reflected in most of his works, and his portrayal of contemporary Jewish life has aroused much controversy. His works include *Goodbye, Columbus* (1959, a novella with five short stories), *Letting Go* (1962), and a sequence of novels featuring Nathan Zuckerman, a Jewish novelist who has to learn to contend with success: *My Life as a Man* (1974), *The Ghost Writer* (1979), *Zuckerman Unbound* (1981), *The Anatomy Lesson* (1983), *The Prague Orgy* (1985). *Portnoy's Complaint* (1969) was a *succès de scandale* which records the intimate confessions of Alexander Portnoy to his psychiatrist. *The Breast* (1972) is a Kafkaesque fantasy. Later novels include *Patrimony: A True Story* (1991), about his father Herman Roth; and *Operation Shylock: A Confession* (1993), in which the author meets his double, whose self-appointed task is to lead the Jews out of Israel and back to Europe. *American Pastoral* was published in 1997. *The Plot against America* (2004) is an example of *alternate history where Charles Lindbergh the aviator has become president. *Everyman* (2006) is a bleak study of mortality, while *Exit Ghost* (2007) records Zuckerman's final fictional appearance. *Indignation* (2008) is set on the campus of a conservative college in Ohio at the time of the Korean War. Roth published an autobiography, *The Facts*, in 1988.

ROUBILIAC, Louis-François (d. 1762) French rococo sculptor, who settled in London *c.*1732. His first success was the statue of *Handel (1738) commissioned for Vauxhall Gardens, which introduced a new informality into English sculpture. Roubiliac was successful as a tomb sculptor; the monuments to General Hargrave (1757) and to Lady Elizabeth Nightingale (1761), both in Westminster Abbey, are his most famous works. As a portrait sculptor Roubiliac attracted a very wide circle of patrons; his image of Alexander *Pope (there are four marble busts dating from 1738, 1740, and 1741, all inscribed *ad vivum*; and one terracotta model) is unflinchingly realistic yet deeply poignant. Roubiliac also executed a series of vivid historical busts of famous scientists, writers, and men of letters for the library of Trinity College, Cambridge.

Round Table In the Arthurian legend, the symbol of the common purpose of Arthur's court and knights. According to *Malory (in Vinaver's Tale 1) it was made for *Uther Pendragon who gave it to King Lodegrean of Camelerde (Cornwall). The latter gave it as a wedding gift, with 100 knights, to Arthur when he married Guinevere, his daughter. It would seat 150 knights, and all places round it were equal. The 'Siege Perilous' was reserved for the knight who should achieve the quest of the *Grail. In *Laȝamon's *Brut*, however, the table was made for Arthur by a crafty workman. It is first mentioned by the poet *Wace.

ROUSSEAU, Jean-Jacques (1712–78) Swiss writer and philosopher. Born into a Protestant artisan family at Geneva, he was brought up by various family members, his mother having died soon after his birth. At the age of 15, he embarked upon the first of the travels which would take him to many parts of Switzerland, France, and Italy, and (in 1766–7) to England, where he famously quarrelled with David *Hume. Rousseau's fiery personality, extreme sensitivity, and penchant for controversy fill his career with dramatic episodes such as this; nevertheless, his contributions to social and political philosophy, the novel, autobiography, moral theology, and educational theory mark him out as one of the dominant writers and thinkers of the age.

Rousseau made his name with the publication in 1751 of his *Discours sur les sciences et les arts* (*Discourse on the Sciences and Arts*), which had won first prize in an essay competition organized by the Academy of Dijon; within a year, it had twice been translated into English. In the *Discours*, Rousseau argues that the development and spread of knowledge and culture, far from improving human behaviour, has corrupted it by promoting inequality, idleness, and luxury. The *Discours sur l'origine et les fondements de l'inégalité* (1755: *Discours on the Origin and Foundations of Inequality*), reviewed by Adam *Smith in the first **Edinburgh Review*, contrasts the innocence and contentment of primitive man in a 'state of nature'—his mode of existence determined by none but genuine needs—with the dissatisfaction and perpetual agitation of modern social man, most of whom are condemned to the legally sanctioned servitude necessary to preserve the institution of private property. The suggestion by d'Alembert in his *Encyclopédie* article on Geneva that a theatre should be established in Rousseau's native city prompted the *Lettre sur les spectacles* (1758: *Letter on Theatre*), in which the passive nature of playgoing, the preoccupation of modern plays with love, and the consequent unnatural bringing forward of women are seen as dangerous symptoms of the ills of society.

A return to primitive innocence being impossible, these ills were only to be remedied, Rousseau held, by reducing the gap separating modern man from his natural archetype and by modifying existing institutions in the interest of equality and happiness. Such is the theme of his two novels: in *Julie, ou la Nouvelle Héloïse* (1761: *Julie, or the New Heloise*), a critical account of contemporary manners and ideas is interwoven with the story of the passionate love of the tutor Saint Preux and his pupil Julie, their separation, Julie's marriage to the Baron Wolmar, and the dutiful, virtuous life shared by all three on the baron's country estate; and *Émile* (1762) lays down the principles for a new scheme of education in which the child is to be allowed full scope for individual development in natural surroundings, shielded from the harmful influences of civilization, in order to form an independent judgement and a stable character. Also in 1762 Rousseau published *Du contrat social* (*The Social Contract*), his theory of politics, in which he advocated universal justice through equality before the law, a more equitable distribution of wealth, and defined government as fundamentally a matter of contract providing for the exercise of power in accordance with the 'general will' and for the common good, by consent of the citizens as a whole, in whom sovereignty ultimately resides.

As examples of unparalleled self-insight and subtle self-analysis, Rousseau's last works, his posthumously published autobiographical *Confessions* (1782–9) and *Rêveries du promeneur solitaire* (1782: *Reveries of the Solitary Walker*) are landmarks of the literature of personal revelation (*see* AUTOBIOGRAPHY).

ROUTH, Martin Joseph (1755–1854) President of Magdalen College, Oxford, for 63 years; he edited the *Gorgias* and *Eutheydemus* of *Plato, and *Reliquiae Sacrae* (1814–43), a collection of writings of ecclesiastical authors of the 2nd and 3rd centuries. Immensely learned, Routh was a strong, old-fashioned 'High Churchman'. He is said to be the last man in England who always wore a wig. His longevity lends weight to his famous advice: 'I think, Sir, you will find it a very good practice *always to verify your references*.' See R. D. Middleton, *Dr Routh* (1938).

ROWE, Elizabeth Singer (1674–1737) Poet, born in Ilchester, Somerset, and largely home educated, whose verses appeared under the pseudonym 'Philomela' and who is chiefly known for the fervently devotional pieces in *Divine Hymns and Poems on Several Occasions* (1704) and *A Collection of Divine Hymns and Poems* (1709). Her elegy on the death of her husband (the poet Thomas Rowe, 1687–1715) was much admired by Alexander *Pope; her much-reprinted *Friendship in Death: or, Twenty Letters from the Dead to the Living* (1728), a volume of prose stories celebrating the afterlife, was dedicated to Edward *Young. Isaac *Watts edited her posthumous collection, *Devout Exercises of the Heart in Meditation and Soliloquy, Prayer and Praise* (1737).

ROWE, Nicholas (1674–1718) Playwright, born in Little Barford, Bedfordshire, educated at Westminster School. He became a barrister of the Middle Temple, but abandoned the legal profession for literature. As a dramatist Rowe declared himself the descendant of Thomas *Otway, whose work highlighted tenderness and pathos. Apart from one unsuccessful comedy (*The Biter*, 1704), Rowe concentrated on verse tragedy: *The Ambitious Stepmother* (1700), **Tamerlane* (1701), *The *Fair Penitent* (1703), *Ulysses* (1705), *The Royal Convert* (1707), *Jane Shore* (1714), and *Lady Jane Grey* (1715). His greatest successes were the 'She-Tragedies' (his own phrase), which stressed the suffering and penitence of victimized women, and attempted to arouse 'pity; a sort of regret proceeding from good-nature'. Later in the century Sarah *Siddons played Rowe's heroines to great applause. Rowe was editor of the first modern edition of *Shakespeare (1709), using his theatrical experience to supply stage directions and act and scene divisions, making the text more intelligible, and giving the earliest substantial biography of the author. Rowe's poems include a painstaking translation of *Lucan's *Pharsalia* (1719), 'one of the greatest productions of English poetry', according to Samuel *Johnson. A loyal Whig, Rowe was made *poet laureate in 1715. His grave is in *Poets' Corner. See *Three Plays by Nicholas Rowe*, ed. J. R. Sutherland (1929).

ROWLANDS, Samuel (?1565–1630) A writer of satirical tracts, epigrams, and jests, mainly in verse. His works include a satire on the manners of Londoners, *The Letting of Humour's Blood in the Head-Vein* (1600); *'Tis Merry When Gossips Meet* (1602), a vivid and dramatic character sketch of a widow, a wife, and a maid who meet in a tavern and converse; *Greene's Ghost* (1602), on the subject of 'coney-catchers' (*see* GREENE, ROBERT); *Democritus, or Doctor Merryman his Medicines against Melancholy Humours* (1607); and *The Melancholy Knight* (1615). His *Complete Works*, including *Martin Mark-All* (1610), now considered spurious, were edited with an essay by Edmund *Gosse and S. J. H. Herrtage in 1880.

ROWLANDSON, Thomas (1756–1827) Painter, book illustrator, and caricaturist, born in London, studied at the Royal Academy; famous for his comic depiction of scenes from social life. Among his most important productions were *The Loyal Volunteers of London and Environs* (1799); *The Microcosm of London* (1808–10), with A. C. Pugin (*c.*1768/9–1832); *The Three Tours of Doctor Syntax*, for William *Combe; *The English Dance of Death* (1815–16); and *The Dance of Life* (181617), also with Combe, all of which issued from Rudolph *Ackermann. Rowlandson was equally adept at rendering the *picturesque landscape and the caricatured human figure. He is best remembered for his comic invention, for the spontaneity and fluid quality of his draughtsmanship, and for the often ribald jocularity of his social commentary. See Bernard Falk, *Thomas Rowlandson: His Life and Art* (1949); John T. Hayes, *The Art of Thomas Rowlandson* (1990).

ROWLEY, Samuel (*fl.* 1597–1624) An actor in the Admiral's Company and a playwright employed by Philip *Henslowe; he is believed to be responsible for the comic additions to Christopher Marlowe's **Dr Faustus*. His only extant play is a chronicle drama about Henry VIII, *When You See Me, You Know Me*, acted 1603.

ROWLEY, William (?1585–1626) Dramatist and actor. That he was Samuel *Rowley's brother is no more than a guess. His first compositions were episodic adventure-plays for Queen Anne's Men, *The Travels of the Three English Brothers* (1607), written with John *Day and George *Wilkins, *Fortune by Land and Sea* (1607–9; printed 1655), with Thomas *Heywood, and, unassisted, *A Shoemaker, a Gentleman* (1607–9; printed 1638). Collaborations, in which he usually contributed a comic subplot, account for nearly all of his surviving dramatic work. His most notable partnership was with Thomas *Middleton with whom he wrote *Wit at Several Weapons* (1613; printed 1647), *A *Fair Quarrel* (1616; printed 1617), *The Old Law* (1618–29, printed 1656), *The World Tossed at Tennis* (acted and printed 1620), and *The *Changeling* (1622; printed 1653). He also assisted in *The *Witch of Edmonton* (1621; printed 1658), with Thomas *Dekker and John *Ford; *The Maid in the Mill* (1623; printed 1647), with John *Fletcher; *A *Cure for a Cuckold* (1624–5; printed 1661), with John *Webster; and *A New Wonder, a Woman Never Vexed* (1624–6; printed 1632), with an unknown collaborator. His non-dramatic work includes a satirical pamphlet, *A Search for Money* (1609), and elegies on Prince Henry and a fellow actor, Hugh Attwell. From 1609 he was a member of the Duke of York's (later Prince Charles's) Men, and by 1616 had become leader of the company. His speciality as an actor was the role of a fat clown, and he took the part of Jacques in his own **All's Lost by Lust* (c.1619). By 1623 he had joined the King's Men. In 1625 he was cited in a legal action over *Keep the Widow Waking*, a sensational dramatization, now lost, of two contemporary scandals which he had written with Dekker, Ford, and Webster. He died before he could testify, and was buried at St James's, Clerkenwell.

ROWLING, J. K. (Joanne Kathleen) (1965–) OBE, born in Yate, near Bristol, educated at Exeter University. Her seven-part series of books about Harry *Potter, beginning with *Harry Potter and the Philosopher's Stone* (1997), has been phenomenally successful worldwide, as have the accompanying films, computer games, and merchandise. From the publication of book four, *The Goblet of Fire* (2000), sales of Rowling's *crossover books have broken all records, with unprecedented levels of media coverage and security surrounding the manuscripts. Before becoming a publishing phenomenon, Rowling taught English in Portugal and French in Edinburgh.

In many ways the books, which largely take place at Hogwarts School of Witchcraft and Wizardry, are *school stories with a *fantasy twist; however, when Bloomsbury bought the series in 1996, Rowling had already decided that her characters would age by a year from book to book, so adjusting the convention which sees characters staying perpetually schoolchildren or being replaced by a new generation of pupils as series evolve. As a consequence, her original audience of child readers matured with her characters and gradually the books became *young adult novels and arguably, in the case of book six, *Harry Potter and the Half-Blood Prince* (2005), and book seven, *Harry Potter and the Deathly Hallows* (2007), largely for adults, though they continue to have crossover appeal.

The series begins with the orphan Harry living miserably with his abusive guardians, the Dursleys. On learning that he is a wizard and being inducted into the world of wizards, Harry discovers that his world comprises 'Muggles' (non-magical people presumably living in the world we know) and wizards. Much of the books' comedy stems from interactions between the two. Rowling mixes genres and modes in her reworking of the battle between 'good', represented by Harry and his friends including Albus Dumbledore, headmaster of Hogwarts, and 'evil' in the form of Lord Voldemort and his followers. As an orphan, Harry is seeking knowledge about his parents, murdered by Voldemort when Harry was a baby. Voldemort's attack not only left Harry with his signature scar in the shape of a lighting bolt running down his forehead but also inextricably linked the two in various ways, interestingly complicating the battle between them. The ambiguities around this relationship characterize the books: with the exception of Harry's close friends Ron Weasley (and his family including his sister Ginny who becomes Harry's girlfriend in book six) and Hermione Granger, it is impossible to tell who is trustworthy. The mysteries around character become darker over time, possibly reflecting increasing uncertainties in global politics though also in line with Harry's adolescent perception of the world.

In 2001 Rowling produced two light-hearted works ostensibly from the Hogwarts library in aid of Comic Relief.

Roxana, *or The Fortunate Mistress* A novel by Daniel *Defoe, published 1724. It is presented as the autobiography of Mademoiselle de Beleau, the daughter of French Protestant refugees, brought up in England and married to a London brewer, who, having squandered his property, deserts her and her five children. Like the heroine of **Moll Flanders*, Roxana supports herself as a kept mistress, passing from one protector to another, but her behaviour is presented as more flamboyant and ruthless than Moll's. Her adventures take place in England, at the court of Charles II, where she receives the name 'Roxana' after performing a 'Turkish' dance, and on the Continent, where she is later known as the countess de Wintselsheim. She amasses great wealth, about which she consults a banker, the historical figure Sir Robert Clayton (1629–1707). She marries a respectable Dutch merchant and lives as a woman of rank. When one of her daughters appears, Roxana dares not acknowledge her, for fear that her past life will be revealed; Amy, Roxana's faithful maid and alter ego, says she will murder the girl to silence her, and Roxana is both horrified and relieved. The disturbing conclusion of the novel does not resolve the exact sequence of events, but Roxana experiences a catastrophic descent into poverty and remorse.

ROXBURGHE, John Ker, third duke of (1740–1804) An ardent bibliophile, who formed an unrivalled collection of books from William *Caxton's press. His splendid library, housed in St James's Square, was sold in 1812. Valdarfer's edition of *Boccaccio (1471), for which the second duke had paid 100 guineas, was bought by the marquess of Blandford for £2,260. To celebrate this event the chief bibliophiles of the day dined together on 17 June 1812 under the presidency of Lord Spencer, and inaugurated the Roxburghe Club, the first of the 'book-clubs', consisting of 25 members, with T. F. *Dibdin as its first secretary. The Club's first publication from an original manuscript was the metrical romance of *Havelok the Dane* (1828). Each member is expected once in his or her career to present (and pay for a limited edition of) a volume of some rarity. See N. Barker, *The Publications of the Roxburghe Club 1814–1962* (1964).

ROY, Arundhati (1961–) Novelist, scriptwriter, and anti-globalization essayist and campaigner, born in Bengal and brought up in southern India. Her semi-autobiographical novel set in Kerala and much influenced by Salman *Rushdie, *The God of Small Things*, won the 1997 *Booker Prize.

Royal Court Theatre Built in 1888; it has a historic association with new writing. Under the management of J. E. Vedrenne and Harley *Granville-Barker from 1904 to 1907, it staged premieres by George Bernard *Shaw, John *Galsworthy, W. B. *Yeats, and John *Masefield. But it was with the foundation of the *English Stage Company in 1956, under the direction of George Devine (1910–66), that it became a national centre of new writing. The initial intention was to encourage novelists to write for the stage but, although work by Angus *Wilson and Nigel *Dennis was presented, it was the production of *Look Back in Anger* by John *Osborne (8 May 1956) that liberated other writers through its scalding rhetoric and social candour. The Court has subsequently championed many living dramatists including Arnold *Wesker, John *Arden, Edward *Bond, David *Storey, Brian *Friel, Athol *Fugard, Caryl *Churchill, Mustapha Matura (1939–), and Timberlake *Wertenbaker as well as reviving, through the advocacy of Peter Gill, neglected masters such as D. H. *Lawrence. From 1979 until the late 1990s, Max Stafford-Clark and Stephen Daldry successively encouraged a new generation of socially angry, anti-materialist young writers, including Sarah *Kane and Mark *Ravenhill, and the Royal Court acquired fresh impetus through its encouragement and its promotion of eloquent new Irish dramatists, notably Martin *McDonagh and Conor *McPherson. In 1998 Ian Rickson took over as artistic director and, in the year celebrating the fiftieth anniversary of the formation of the English Stage Company (2006), he was succeeded by Dominic Cooke.

Royal Geographical Society Founded in London in 1830; it became the most significant non-governmental promoter of travel and exploration and its resulting literature. The immediate forebear was the Raleigh Travellers' Club, while the African Association was soon absorbed. Thus an element in the original make-up of the RGS was the tradition of the *Grand Tour and polite learning with travel as a spur to literary production. Lord *Byron's friend John Cam *Hobhouse was a founder. Literary and historical concerns were evident in early years with articles on the battle of Marathon or the 'Regio Cinnamomifera of the Ancients'. However, the concerns of the practical servicemen and administrators building up Britain's interests around the world soon became dominant: blank spaces on the map must be filled in and practical information made available. Under its presidents Roderick Murchison in the 1850s and 1860s and, later, Clements Markham, the Society had a quasi-official status, since explorers like David *Livingstone raised questions of public policy. Arguably, too, taking other parts of the world into intellectual possession by mapping and describing them could be a prelude to actual imperialism. More noticeable at the time was the role of the Society in making heroes of explorers in inhospitable tropical or frozen environments, so creating a demand for their published work. The impact on boys' adventure stories by writers such as R. M. *Ballantyne is important. In the middle years of the 19th century, the search for the remains of Sir John *Franklin's expedition in the Arctic and the quest for the sources of the Nile in the middle of Africa raised enormous public interest and sometimes controversy, as when Henry *Stanley 'found' Livingstone in 1871. The Society's own numerous publications made a substantial contribution to travel literature.

Oddly, little work on Britain appeared. Geography remained ill defined until Halford Mackinder united physical and human geography in the 1880s and 1890s and made the subject a university study. Thereafter the RGS became more of a forum for academic geographers. However, the tradition of fostering expeditions persisted in the 20th century, not least in support of attempts to conquer Everest.

Royal Historical Society Founded in 1868; granted the title 'Royal' in 1887. It promotes the study of history by publishing historical material, supporting conferences and lectures, and offering grants and prizes. Its papers appear annually as *Transactions*. It amalgamated with the *Camden Society in 1897, and now publishes the Camden Series.

Royal Literary Fund A benevolent society for authors and their dependants in distress, founded in 1790 as the Literary Fund Society at the instigation of the Revd David Williams (1738–1813), a Dissenting minister. In 1818 it was granted a royal charter, and was permitted to add 'Royal' to its title in 1845. Beneficiaries have included S. T. *Coleridge, Thomas Love *Peacock, James *Hogg, John *Clare, D. H. *Lawrence, Edith *Nesbit, James *Joyce, and Dylan *Thomas. It has also made grants to literary refugees, including *Chateaubriand. The Fund receives no government subsidy and depends on gifts, subscriptions, and legacies—including authors' royalties.

Royal Society More correctly the Royal Society of London for the Improving of Natural Knowledge; obtained its royal charters in 1662 and 1663. The prehistory of the Society extends back to scientific meetings held in London and Oxford from 1645 onwards. Traditionally, the originator of these is identified as Theodore Haak (1605–90), known also as the first to translate John *Milton into German. Francis *Bacon provided the major philosophical inspiration for the Society; Solomon's House in **New Atlantis* has been taken as its model. No scientific society has made a more conspicuous debut—its founders and early members included Robert *Boyle, Robert Hooke (1635–1703), Sir William *Petty, John *Ray, John Wilkins (1614–72), and Christopher *Wren. Among more literary figures, Elias *Ashmole, John *Aubrey, Abraham *Cowley, John *Dryden, John *Evelyn, and Edmund *Waller were members. The Society features prominently in Dryden's **Annus Mirabilis*. Its *Philosophical Transactions* (1665–), first edited by Henry Oldenburg (*c.*1619–1677), is the first permanent scientific journal. Individual members of the Royal Society made an outstanding scientific contribution, but the Society itself was not entirely successful. It was attacked and ridiculed by a bizarre coalition of interests, including Henry Stubbe (1632–76), Samuel *Butler, and Thomas *Shadwell, whose *The Virtuoso* satirized its experiments, including some actually carried out by Boyle and Hooke. The Society was also drawn into the ancients versus moderns controversy (*see* BATTLE OF THE BOOKS). In replies to attacks by the ancients, the modernism of the Society was defended by Joseph *Glanvill and Thomas *Sprat. The latter's *History of the Royal Society* (1667) is known for its defence of the 'close, naked, natural way' of style. The Society risked degenerating into a squabbling London club, but its decline was temporarily arrested under Isaac *Newton, and its fortunes revived in the later 19th century. Its present location is in Carlton House Terrace and its chief function is funding scientific research.

Royal Society of Edinburgh Established in 1783 for 'the cultivation of every branch of science, erudition, and taste'. The membership was originally divided into the Physical Class and a larger Literary Class, the latter including Archibald *Alison, James *Beattie, Hugh *Blair, Edmund *Burke, Alexander *Carlyle, Adam *Ferguson, Alexander *Gerard, John *Home, John *Jamieson, Henry *Mackenzie, Thomas Reid (1710–96), and William Robertson (1721–93). Dugald *Stewart was a member of the Physical Class. Walter *Scott was president 1820–32, and Alfred *Tennyson and Thomas *Carlyle had honorary membership. Science and mathematics came to dominate the Society's work in the 19th century, but the Literary Class was revived in 1976, its fellows including Norman *MacCaig, Sorley *Maclean, and Muriel *Spark. Since the reopening of the Scottish Parliament in 1999 the Society has grown in importance as a governmental advisory agency. It also provides grants for research and enterprise. The RSE library holds most of David *Hume's correspondence and surviving manuscripts.

Royal Society of Literature Founded in 1820 at the suggestion of Thomas Burgess (1756–1837), bishop of St David's, and under the patronage of George IV, who assigned the sum of 1,100 guineas to be applied in pensions of 100 guineas to each of ten Royal Associates, and in a premium of 100 guineas for a prize dissertation. Associates were elected by the council of the Society (Thomas *Malthus and S. T. *Coleridge were among the first ten). The Society published papers under the title *Transactions*; publication was suspended during the First World War and a new series was resumed in 1921 as *Essays by Divers Hands*. The Society has members, fellows, and, since 1961, companions; recipients of the title of companion have included John *Betjeman, Arthur *Koestler, E. M. *Forster, Angus *Wilson, and many others. It sponsors readings and lectures, awards prizes, and campaigns on matters of interest to writers. See I. Quigly, *The Royal Society of Literature* (2000).

RÓŻEWICZ, Tadeusz (1921–) Polish poet and playwright. With his compatriots Zbigniew *Herbert and Czesław *Miłosz he is one of the most influential writers of post-war Eastern Europe. His stark, powerful poems provide an often disturbingly realistic account of his country's recent history. *They Came to See a Poet: Selected Poems* (trans. Adam Czerniawski) appeared in 1991. Much of his controversial political drama, including *The Trap* (1982; trans. 1997), has also been published in English.

Rubáiyát of Omar Khayyám, The See OMAR KHAYYÁM, THE RUBÁIYÁT OF.

RUBENS, Bernice Ruth (1923–2004) Prolific novelist, born into an immigrant Jewish family of musical prodigies in Cardiff, a background that frequently informs her fiction. She was educated at the University of Wales, Cardiff. *Madame Sousatzka* (1962) describes the struggle of a piano teacher to keep possession of a preternaturally gifted pupil, while *Spring Sonata* (1979) depicts the development of a violinist quite literally *in utero*. Other novels include *The Elected Member* (1969, *Booker Prize 1970), about a former child prodigy who takes to drugs and becomes the scapegoat in his orthodox Jewish family; *Brothers* (1983), a historical account of the persecution of four generations of a Russian Jewish family; and *Kingdom Come* (1990), based on the life of a 17th-century Messiah in Turkey. A strain of fantasy and quirky comedy is a characteristic feature of such novels as *Mr Wakefield's Crusade* (1985), about a man inadvertently caught up in an elaborate plot involving transvestism and possible murder.

RUBENS, Peter Paul (1577–1640) Flemish painter, the chief northern exponent of the baroque. Studying first under Flemish masters, he went to Italy in 1600 and became court painter to the duke of Mantua. He returned to Antwerp in 1608, became court painter to the Spanish ruler of Flanders, and set up a large and productive workshop with numerous assistants. In addition he served on various diplomatic missions, visiting Spain in 1628 and England in 1629, where he was knighted and commissioned to paint the ceiling of the Banqueting House. During his visit Rubens stayed with his friend the Zeeland-born painter and architect Sir Balthazar Gerbier (?1591–1667) whose children appear in his magnificent *Allegory of Peace and War* (1629). Rubens was a prolific and vital painter. His style was based on the great Italian masters, but in later life he painted for his own pleasure landscapes with a new feeling for the country. One of the few English writers to appreciate his full stature was George *Eliot, who wrote from Munich (1858, in a letter), 'His are such real, breathing men and women.... What a grand, glowing, forceful thing life looks in his pictures.' See Fiona Donovan, *Rubens and England* (2004).

RUDY, Rucker (1946–) American computer scientist and *science fiction author, born in Louisville, Kentucky. *White Light* (1990) fuses a *cyberpunk sensibility with his background as a mathematician, resulting in what he calls 'transrealism'. *Postsingular* (2007) explores the 'singularity'—the point where computing processing power allows humanity to transcend everyday existence.

RUDKIN, David (1936–) Playwright, born in London, the son of a Nonconformist minister, and educated at King Edward's School, Birmingham, and Oxford University; he then became a schoolteacher. He made his name with a powerful drama set in a rural district of the Black Country, *Afore Night Come* (1962); subsequent works, informed by a dark and passionate surreal mysticism, include *Ashes* (1974), *Penda's Fen* (TV 1974), *Sons of Light* (1976), *The Triumph of Death* (1981), *Space Invaders* (1983), and *The Saxon Shore* (1986). In 2004, he returned to the theatre with *Red Sun*, which characteristically borrowed from an eclectic mixture of mythological material.

RUGGLE, George *See* IGNORAMUS.

'Ruin, The' A 45-line poem in Old English in the *Exeter Book. The poem describes the result of the devastation of a city, which the references to hot springs may identify as Bath, which was a ruin in Anglo-Saxon times. Some of the poem's lines are illegible through damage. Ed. Bernard Muir, *The Exeter Anthology of Old English Poetry* (2000).

'Ruined Cottage, The' ('The Story of Margaret') A poem by William *Wordsworth, written in 1797, and subsequently embodied in Book I of *The *Excursion*. A story of suffering, it tells of a cottager who leaves his home to join a troop of soldiers going to a distant land. His wife Margaret pines for his return in increasing wretchedness, until she dies and the cottage falls into ruin.

'Ruines of Time, The' A poem by Edmund *Spenser, included in the *Complaints* published in 1591. It is an allegorical elegy on the death of Sir Philip *Sidney, which had also been the occasion of his earlier elegy *'Astrophel'. The poet passes to a lament on the decline of patronage and the neglect of literature, referring to his own case. The poem is dedicated to Mary Herbert, countess of *Pembroke, Sidney's sister.

RUKEYSER, Muriel (1913–1980) American poet, born in New York, whose first volume, *Theory of Flight* (1935), set a keynote for her combination of the personal and the political. She used her poetry as a medium for social protest, experimenting with documentary techniques in *U.S. 1* (1938) and other volumes. In addition to poetry, she wrote a number of biographies and plays, and a fictionalized memoir, *The Orgy* (1965). In the 1960s and 1970s she opposed the Vietnam War and also translated a number of works by Octavio *Paz. See Anne F. Herzog and Janet E. Kaufman, *How Shall We Tell Each Other of the Poet?* (2001).

Rule a Wife and Have a Wife A comedy by John *Fletcher, performed 1624. Margarita, a rich heiress of Seville, plans to marry, but only to provide a cover for her pleasures; she must therefore choose a husband 'of easy faith', who will allow her to dominate him, and serve as 'a shadow, an umbrella, | To keep the scorching world's opinion' from her good name. Altea, her companion, plots to win her for her brother Leon; he pretends to be a fool, but, once married, abandons meekness, asserts his authority, and finally wins her affection.

'Rule, Britannia' Patriotic British song with words by James *Thomson and music by Thomas *Arne, composed for *Alfred* (1740), a masque by Thomson and David *Mallet. It became popular during the Jacobite rebellion of 1745.

RUMENS, Carol (1944–) British poet, born in south London. Rumens studied philosophy at Bedford College, University of London, but did not complete her degree. Her first full-length volume, *A Strange Girl in Bright Colours* (1973), combined an interest in gender with wider political commitments. Her later collections saw her developing an interest in Eastern Europe and Russia, and she has translated the work of several Russian poets. Her books include *Direct Dialling* (1985); *The Greening of Snow Beach* (1988); *Best China Sky* (1995), written during her residency in Belfast; and *Hex* (2002). Her substantial *Poems 1964–2004* (2004) defines her as one of the most versatile and outward-looking poets of her generation. She is also the editor of *Making for the Open* (1984) and *New Women Poets* (1992) and a series of lectures on poetry, *Self into Song*. She holds a chair in creative writing at the University of Wales, Bangor.

RŪMĪ, Jalāl ad-Dīn Muhammad (1207–73) Born in Balkh (Afghanistan), a Persian *Sufi famous as the author of the *Masnavī-i ma`nawī* ('Spiritual Couplets'), a vast poem that muses in myriad ways on how to escape from material preoccupations. Rūmī was also the inspirer, and probably the founder, of the Mevlevi Sufi order, better known as the 'Whirling Dervishes'.

rune A letter or character of the earliest surviving Germanic script, most extensively used in inscriptions on wood or stone by the Scandinavians and Anglo-Saxons. The earliest runic alphabet seems to date from about the 3rd century AD, and is formed by modifying the letters of the Greek and

Roman alphabets. Magical and mysterious powers were associated with runes from the Anglo-Saxon period, perhaps because of their employment in riddles, as in the *Rune Poem*, a 94-line piece illustrating the runes of the Anglo-Saxon runic alphabet, the *futhorc* (see ASPR 6, 28–30 for edition). The other important occurrence of runes in Old English literature is the runic signature to the poems of *Cynewulf. See R. W. V. Elliott, *Runes: An Introduction* (1959).

RUNYON, Damon (1884–1946) American writer, born in Kansas, who became famous for his sketches of New York life, particularly the world of Broadway, from the Prohibition era and onwards, including *Guys and Dolls* (1932) and *My Old Man* (1939), and numerous subsequent collections. Runyon also worked as a baseball columnist and sports correspondent. See John Mosedale, *The Men Who Invented Broadway* (1981).

Rupert Bear *Comic-strip character created by Mary Tortel (1920–35), Alfred Bestall (1935–73), and John Harrold (1973–). The young bear, with his distinctive white fur, check trousers, yellow jumper, and scarf, features in the *Daily Express* and many annuals. The limited comic-strip text is supplemented by verse narratives.

Rupert of Hentzau A novel published in 1898 by Anthony Hope (*Hawkins), a sequel to *The *Prisoner of Zenda* (1894).

Rural Rides Essays by William *Cobbett, published 1830, after appearing in the **Political Register*. Sceptical of proposed remedies for the agricultural distress that followed the war, Cobbett 'made up his mind to see for himself, and to enforce, by actual observation of rural conditions, the statements he had made in answer to the arguments of the landlords before the Agricultural Committee'. The result was this series of lively, opinionated accounts of his travels on horseback between September 1822 and October 1826, largely in the south and east of England. Later journeys, in the Midlands and the north, were described in subsequent editions. He rails against tax collectors, 'tax-eaters', landlords, gamekeepers, stockjobbers, and excisemen, and against the monstrous swelling of the 'Great Wen' of London; but the work is animated by his knowledge and love of the land, and breaks occasionally into rapturous praise for a landscape, a hedgerow, a hanging wood. See *The Social and Political Writings of William Cobbett*, ed. N. Thompson and D. Eastwood, 16 vols (1998).

Ruritania An imaginary kingdom in central Europe, the scene of *The *Prisoner of Zenda* by Anthony Hope (*Hawkins). The name connotes more generally a world of make-believe romance, chivalry, and intrigue.

RUSHDIE, Salman (1947–) Novelist and short story writer, born in Bombay (Mumbai) to a Muslim family, educated at Rugby School and King's College, Cambridge; he worked as an actor and as an advertising copywriter before becoming a novelist. His first book, *Grimus* (1975), an abstruse fantasy based on a medieval Sūfī poem, was followed by *Midnight's Children* (1981, *Booker Prize), a swarming comic saga which won him literary prominence. In it Saleem Sinai, born as midnight strikes the dawn of India's Independence, symbolizes his nation's changing fortunes and its intractable divisions. *Shame* (1983), a savage satirical fable interspersed with chapters of authorial comment, depicts lethal splits in Pakistan, especially between military and civilian rule (represented by thinly disguised versions of General Zia and the Bhutto family). Migration and displacement (from countries, cultures, and ideologies) are the central themes in his phantasmagoric novel *The Satanic Verses* (1988), which was denounced as blasphemous by some Muslims and led to his being sentenced to death in a *fatwa* issued by the Ayatollah Khomeini in 1989. Forced to live in hiding, under police protection, for many years, he continued to write, and published works such as *Haroun and the Sea of Stories*, an engaging novel for children about the pleasures and perils of storytelling (1990, adapted for the stage at the *National Theatre, 1998), *Imaginary Homelands*, a collection of essays and reviews (1991), and a volume of short stories about cultural tensions, *East, West* (1994). *The Moor's Last Sigh* (1995), Rushdie's first novel after the *fatwa*, is narrated by a hunted man who ages at twice the normal rate. Subsequent novels—*The Ground beneath her Feet* (1999) in which the myth of Orpheus and Eurydice is recast as the story of two rock musicians; *Fury* (2001), set in New York; *Shalimar the Clown* (2005), about the ruination of Kashmir and the making of a terrorist; and *The Enchantress of Florence* (2008), which travels between the Mughal court of the emperor Akbar and Renaissance Italy—have shown an increasing willingness to incorporate sensational and floridly fantastic material. Like all Rushdie's fiction, they proclaim, often in allegorical or surreal ways, the evils of ideological single-mindedness and the moral, social, and artistic benefits of pluralism and tolerance.

RUSKIN, John (1819–1900) Critic. The only child of John James and Margaret Ruskin, he was born in London, and grew up in Herne Hill, in south London. His father built up the wine business of which he was a founding partner, and was able to pass on to his son a large fortune, of which Ruskin gave much away. To his parents Ruskin also owed a close knowledge of the Bible, a strong affection for romantic literature, stern political views, and an early attraction to contemporary landscape painting. Much of his schooling was given at home, and from 1836 to 1842 he was at Christ Church, Oxford, where he won the Newdigate Prize but found the curriculum unprofitable. Travel was more important to his education. The family took regular tours in Britain, and, from 1833, on the Continent. These fixed Ruskin's lifelong preference for French cathedral towns, the Alps, and certain cities of northern Italy, and focused his main passion, the study of the facts of nature. His early publications included essays in Loudon's *Magazine of Natural History* (1834 and 1836), 'The Poetry of Architecture' (*Architectural Magazine*, 1837–8) and numerous Byronesque poems and stories written for Christmas annuals. He contributed regularly from 1835 to 1846, mainly to *Friendship's Offering*, whose editor, W. H. Harrison, acted as his personal literary adviser. He admired the art of Copley Fielding, J. D. Harding, Clarkson Stanfield, James Holland, David Roberts, Samuel Prout, and, above all, J. M. W. *Turner. He took lessons from two of these artists (Fielding and Harding), made friends of several, and bought the work of all. With the first of the five volumes of **Modern Painters* (1843), an immediate success, he became their public champion.

Seven months' work in Italy in preparation for *Modern Painters II* (1846) confirmed Ruskin's 'function as interpreter'. They also compelled him to write of the medieval buildings of Europe before they should be destroyed by neglect, restoration, industrialization, and revolutions. He postponed further enquiry into natural beauty and its representation, and *Modern Painters III* and *IV* did not appear until 1856. The interval produced *The Seven Lamps of Architecture* (1849) and *The *Stones of Venice* (1851–3), both written during the period of his marriage to Euphemia Chalmers Gray, for whom the lastingly popular fable, *The King of the Golden River* had been a gift (written 1841; pub. 1851). In 1854, after six unhappy years, the marriage was annulled, and soon afterwards she married John Everett *Millais. Ruskin had defended Millais and the *Pre-Raphaelites in letters to *The *Times* and the pamphlet *Pre-Raphaelitism* (1851). He continued to notice their work in *Notes on the Royal Academy* (1855–9 and 1875), guides intended to influence public taste and to intervene in the production and distribution of a national art.

Ruskin's middle years were extraordinarily active, and he became a prominent public figure. He wrote for the Arundel Society (*Giotto and his Works in Padua*, 1853–4, 1860), taught at the Working Men's College, produced drawing manuals, helped with plans for the Oxford Museum of Natural History building, arranged for the National Gallery the drawings of the Turner bequest, and tried to guide the work of individual artists, including Dante Gabriel *Rossetti, John Inchbold (1830–88), and John Brett (1831–1902). He gave evidence before parliamentary committees, and lectured extensively throughout the country. Some of these addresses appeared in *Lectures on Architecture and Painting* (1854) and *The Two Paths* (1859). But Ruskin's was a critical, not a collaborative intervention, and his judgements often offended. Speaking in Manchester on *The Political Economy of Art* (1857), Ruskin challenged economic laws affecting matters in which he had a standing. In the final volume of *Modern Painters* (1860) he denounced greed as the deadly principle guiding English life. In attacking the 'pseudo-science' of John Stuart *Mill and David Ricardo (1772–1823) in *Unto this Last* (1860) and *Essays on Political Economy* (1862–3; later *Munera Pulveris*, 1872), Ruskin entered new territory and declared open warfare against the spirit and science of his times.

This fight, against competition and self-interest, for the recovery of heroic, feudal, and Christian social ideals was to occupy Ruskin for the rest of his life. It is expressed in considerations of engraving or Greek myth (*The Cestus of Aglaia*, 1865–6; *The Queen of the Air*, 1869), geological lectures for children (*The Ethics of the Dust*, 1866), essays on literature and the respective duties of men and women (*Sesame and Lilies*, 1865, 1871), lectures on war, work, and trade (*The Crown of Wild Olives*, 1866, 1873), or letters to a workman (*Time and Tide, by Weare and Tyne*, 1867). In the serial letters of **Fors Clavigera* (1871–8) he found a form well suited to his public teaching and to the diversity of his interests, which also expressed themselves during the 1870s and 1880s in a multitude of writings on natural history, travel, painting, etc., and in practical projects, many associated with the Guild of St George, a utopian society (still thriving) founded by Ruskin under his own mastership in 1871.

In 1870 Ruskin became the first Slade professor of art at Oxford. He started a drawing school, arranged art collections of his own gift, and drew crowds to his eleven courses of lectures. Seven volumes of them were published shortly after delivery: *Lectures on Art* (1870), *Aratra Pentelici*, *The Relation between Michael Angelo and Tintoret*, *The Eagle's Nest* (all 1872), *Love's Meinie* (1873, 1881), and *Ariadne Fiorentina* (1873–6). But, despite caution, Ruskin did not keep his 'own peculiar opinions' out of his lectures. Senior members of the university were alarmed, Ruskin offended: he resigned in 1878. Although Ruskin returned to Oxford in 1883 and gave two more courses of lectures, some of his statements were even more startling than before, and he resigned again in 1885.

The isolation of his later years was mitigated by the loyalty of his disciples, including J. W. Bunney and George Allen, both students of the Working Men's College, and W. G. Collingwood, who acted as Ruskin's secretary at Brantwood, the house in the Lake District which was his home after 1870. Older friends, such as Sir Henry Acland and Thomas *Carlyle, remained doubtful about the schemes, the vehemence, and the frequent obscurity of his later pronouncements. They were also disturbed by Ruskin's passion for Rose La Touche. In middle and old age he made many young girls the objects of his affection. Rose, an Anglo-Irish girl, was 11 when Ruskin came across her in 1858, 18 when he proposed in 1866. But he could not share her evangelical religious views, her parents were also opposed, and she died, mad, in 1875. Three years later Ruskin himself went through the first of a series of delirious illnesses. He often wrote for her and, indirectly, of her, in later life, and in *Praeterita*, the autobiography on which he worked sporadically between 1885 and 1889, he would have spoken of her directly; but he did not complete it. After 1889 Ruskin wrote nothing and spoke rarely, but was cared for by his cousin Joan Severn at Brantwood. The influence of his thought on art and politics was profound, and enduring. See T. Hilton, *John Ruskin: The Early Years* (1985); *John Ruskin: The Later Years* (2000).

RUSS, Joanna (1937–) American *science fiction author, born in New York. *The Female Man* (1975) described both the utopian and the dystopic preoccupations of the American women's movement. The novel, with its dark and uncompromising humour, attracted much controversy within the science fiction field, inspiring and encouraging other feminist writers such as Ursula K. *Le Guin and James *Tiptree Jr to continue exploring their own ideas, and was widely read outside it by a new generation of feminists. *Alyx* (1976) incorporated earlier work about a female mercenary hero. *How to Suppress Women's Writing* (1983) is a collection of essays.

RUSSELL, Bertrand, third Earl Russell (1872–1970) Philosopher and social critic, educated privately and at Trinity College, Cambridge. He wrote voluminously on philosophy, logic, education, economics, and politics, and throughout his life was the champion of advanced political and social causes. While much of his writing was aimed at a wide audience, he also contributed work of lasting importance in some of the most technical fields of philosophy and logic. He was the inventor of the Theory of Descriptions. *The Principles of Mathematics* (1903) and *Principia Mathematica* (the latter in collaboration with A. N. Whitehead (1861–1947), 1910) quickly became classics of mathematical logic. Other important philosophical works include *The Analysis of Mind* (1921), *An Inquiry into Meaning and Truth* (1940), and *Human Knowledge, Its Scope and Limits* (1948). Russell was awarded the *Nobel Prize for Literature in 1950. He published a three-volume *Autobiography* (1967–9); see also the two-volume biography by Ray Monk (1997, 2001).

RUSSELL, Eric Frank (1905–78) Born in Sandhurst, the first British *science fiction writer to receive a *Hugo award, for 'Allamagoosa' (1955), his cheerful lampoon of military bureaucracy. *Sinister Barrier* (1943) suggests we are property, harvested by aliens. His wisecracking style and iconoclastic speculations made him a popular writer.

RUSSELL, George William (Æ) (1867–1935) Poet, dramatist, novelist, mystic, painter, and social reformer, born in Lurgan, Co. Armagh, and educated at the Dublin Metropolitan School of Art, where he met W. B. *Yeats. The ethereal lyrics of *Homeward* (1894) set the *Celtic Twilight signature of the poetry of the early years of the *Irish Revival. His poetic drama *Deirdre* was performed in 1902 at the Irish National Theatre (later the *Abbey). From 1905 to 1923 he edited the widely influential *Irish Homestead*, which encouraged interest in agriculture, home economics, and arts and crafts; meanwhile he continued to publish poetry, including *The Divine Vision* (1904), *The Interpreters* (1922), and *Midsummer Eve* (1928), and did much to support young writers, from Padraic *Colum to Patrick *Kavanagh. From 1923 until 1930 he edited the *Irish Statesman*. His prophetic novel *The Avatars* aroused much interest in 1933, the year he left Ireland in disgust at the emerging character of the new state.

RUSSELL, Lord John *See* Reform Bills.

RUSSELL, Mary Doria (1950–) American novelist, born in Chicago. Her Arthur C. Clarke Award-winning *The Sparrow* (1996) and its sequel *Children of God* (1998) explore the effect on a Jesuit priest of first contact with an alien race. *A Thread of Grace* (2005) is set in Italy during the Second World War.

RUSSELL, Willy (1947–) Playwright, born near Liverpool, the son of a factory worker; he left school at 15 and became a hairdresser. He subsequently trained as a teacher at St Katharine's College of Education. *John Paul George Ringo... and Bert* (1974), a play about the Beatles, first brought him to public notice. *Breezeblock Park* (1975) deals with life on a Liverpool housing estate; *Stags and Hens* (1978) describes the parties held by a couple on the eve of their wedding; *Educating Rita* (1980; filmed 1983), is about the transformative relations between an Open University tutor and Rita, his working-class student. *Blood Brothers* (1983) treats the lives of twins separated at birth and brought up in very differently; *Shirley Valentine* (1986; filmed 1989), describes a Liverpool housewife's escape from her dull life after a holiday in Greece.

Russian Fever Also known as 'the Russian Disease', was a term describing the Western European vogue for Russian culture in the years leading up to the First World War. It was particularly associated with the performances of Russian ballet and opera organized by Sergei Diaghilev (1872–1929), but also with exhibitions of Russian folk arts and crafts. 'Russianness' became a commodity that was marketed on the basis of its primitive and exotic image, a contrast to the products of Western European bourgeois culture.

The Ballets Russes performed annually in London from 1912, and at the gala performance to mark the coronation of King George V in 1911; at the same time, Russian ballerinas featured regularly on the programmes of the city's music halls. Among the admirers of the Russian ballet were Lady Ottoline *Morrell, Lytton *Strachey, Osbert *Sitwell, and Rupert *Brooke. Critics appreciated the way in which the productions by the Ballets Russes were shaped by an overriding artistic idea, using music, scenery, and costume to create an artistic whole. Although some ballets, such as *Petrushka*, performed in London in 1913, and *The Firebird*, were based on Russian themes, most of them tended towards *oriental settings, and lavish displays of sex and violence, confirming the association between Russianness, the exotic, and the primitive.

Similar associations contributed to the appeal of peasant-produced artefacts, which found ready purchasers in London, Paris, Leipzig, and in the USA. Traditional peasant handicrafts had been revived in Russia in the late 19th century by wealthy patrons influenced by the ideas of John *Ruskin and William *Morris. Hand-made peasant goods were displayed at the 1900 Paris Exhibition in a mock-up of a traditional Russian village; a Russian village also featured at the 1913 Ideal Home Exhibition in London. A considerable part of the appeal was these items' direct connection with what was perceived as one of Europe's few remaining primitive cultures. The export value of folk art was also recognized by the Soviet state, which continued to exhibit peasant handicrafts at international trade fairs through the 1920s.

Other art forms also contributed to Russian Fever: the music of composers such as Igor *Stravinsky, who incorporated motifs from folk music, the singing of operatic bass superstar Fedor Shaliapin (1873–1938), who performed the title role in *Boris*

Godunov in London in 1913, and the paintings of Post-Impressionist artists such as Nikolai Roerikh (1874–1947) and Kuzma Petrov-Vodkin (1878–1938).

The orientalism evident in the stage design and costume of the Ballets Russes was echoed in the use of bright, unconventional colour combinations in fashion and interior decoration; Parisian couturier Paul Poiret (1879–1944) used Russian peasant clothing as an inspiration. Theatrical design and book production were also influenced by the Russian style. See Wendy R. Salmond, *Arts and Crafts in Late Imperial Russia: Reviving the Kustar Art Industries 1870–1917* (1996); Charles Spencer, *The World of Serge Diaghilev* (1974).

Russian film or more accurately Soviet film, made a dramatic cultural and political impact outside Soviet Russia in the late 1920s, when rumours of its bold new style began to circulate. *Battleship Potemkin* by Sergei Eisenstein (1898–1948) opened in Germany in 1926, causing a sensation and provoking censorship and bans in many countries. The home secretary assured Parliament that it would be kept out, and it was not seen in Britain until a private screening in 1929, organized by the *Film Society and attended by Eisenstein. Although the Film Society had been formed four years earlier to circumvent draconian censorship mainly of German films, the new Soviet films of Eisenstein, Vsevelod Pudovkin (1893–1953), and Dziga Vertov (1896–1954) quickly became fashionable, and were eagerly analysed in the magazine *Close Up*, funded by *Bryher, and including criticism by H.D. (Hilda *Doolittle) and Dorothy *Richardson.

Also inspired by the techniques and themes of Soviet 'montage' cinema, with its emphasis on industrial transformation, the British *documentary film movement emerged under the leadership of John Grierson (1898–1972). Many of its future members attended classes given by Eisenstein in London in 1929, and Grierson would briefly engage W. H. *Auden and Benjamin *Britten in film work, and launch the career of Humphrey *Jennings as Britain's leading film poet. When Soviet cinema turned towards more nationalistic themes, with Eisenstein's operatic *Alexander Nevsky* (1938), this inspired the first of the verse plays for *radio produced by Dallas Bower (1907–99), written by Louis *MacNeice and broadcast immediately after the Japanese attack on the American naval base at Pearl Harbor, Hawaii, in 1941.

Soviet film made a fresh impact abroad in the 1960s, when **Hamlet* (1964), by the film-maker Grigori Kozintsev (1905–73), appeared, based on Boris *Pasternak's translation. It was widely shown and admired, and was followed by his **King Lear* in 1971. The films of Andrei Tarkovsky (1932–86) also had a wide cultural impact, especially *Andrei Rublev* (1966), *Solaris* (1972), and *Stalker* (1979), during the final decades of the Soviet regime, evoking a more traditional Russian spirituality in modern form.

Russian formalism A school of literary criticism which originated in pre-revolutionary Russia and was suppressed in the early 1930s. Most of its founders were young men under the age of 20 who held that literature should be studied not as a reflection of an author's life, nor as a mirror of the society in which it had been produced, but as an autonomous phenomenon governed by its own laws. Major figures associated with formalism include Roman *Jakobson, who led the Moscow Linguistic Circle, founded in 1915, and Viktor Shklovsky (1893–1984), Iurii Tynianov (1894–1943), and Boris Eikhenbaum (1886–1959), members of the St Petersburg-based Society for the Study of Poetic Language, founded in 1916. The formalists aimed to transform the discipline of literary studies by adopting scientific and objective methodology. Their often belligerent rejection of established authorities was in tune with the turbulent times; after the 1917 Revolution several formalists occupied prominent academic positions, but their insistence on the autonomy of literature contradicted the Bolshevik view of literature as a servant of the state. They were attacked by orthodox *Marxist critics for their refusal to treat literature as a reflection of social structures, and for their 'irrelevant' and 'escapist' concern with the specifics of poetic language.

Early formalist studies concentrated on examining the specific formal properties of poetic language, and identifying the ways in which certain 'devices' worked in a text to produce the quality of 'literariness'. One such 'device' was identified as the process of 'making strange' or defamiliarization, deliberately slowing down readers' perceptions of the world so as to bypass habitual responses and enable them to perceive the world anew. A good deal of work was done in the study of poetry, examining the systems of metre, rhyme, sound repetition, and the way in which sound and meaning in poetry were connected. More accessible to non-Russian readers are studies of narrative devices in prose fiction. In the 1920s the scope of formalist investigations broadened to take in literary history, viewing it as a dynamic process of evolution, of constant change and struggle. Many of their studies focused on 19th-century Russian literature, although contemporary literature did receive some attention.

In the later 1920s the formalists, now on the defensive, attempted to develop their work in directions which might be less controversial, recognizing, to some extent, the influence of society on literature, and, in some cases, reverting to something resembling a more traditional 'life and works' approach to authors. Their opponents' attacks became increasingly savage, and, by 1930, practitioners either moved into other areas, including fiction, or steered clear of methodological questions. Yet even after formalism as a school of literary criticism faded from view, its theories and methods helped to shape literary studies in the Soviet Union, and its 'rediscovery' in the 1960s proved influential both there and in the West. See Stephen Bann and John E. Bowlt (eds), *Russian Formalism: A Collection of Articles and Texts in Translation* (1973); Victor Erlich, *Russian Formalist: History—Doctrine* (1980).

Russian novel The first Russian novels were adaptations of Western European 18th-century works such as the epistolary novel *The Letters of Ernest and Doravra* (1766) by Fedor Emin (*c.*1735–1770), based on *Rousseau's *La Nouvelle Heloïse*, and *The Comely Cook* (1770) by Mikhail Chulkov (1734–92), drawn from Fougeret de Montbron's *Margot la ravadeuse*. In the early 19th century Russian novelists continued to look to the West for inspiration and Russia's first historical novel, *Iurii Miloslavskii* (1829) by Mikhail Zagoskin (1789–1852), owed its conception to Walter *Scott's example which continued to influence numerous emulators in the 1830s, culminating in Alexander *Pushkin's *The Captain's Daughter* (1836), which nonetheless projects an authentic Russian voice. Pushkin's novel in verse *Eugene Onegin* (1823–31), inspired by Lord *Byron's *Don Juan*, is the first truly Russian novel, initiating the period from 1830 to 1880 when the major Russian classics by Pushkin, *Lermontov, *Gogol, *Goncharov, *Turgenev, *Tolstoy, and *Dostoevsky were published. In its Russian context the novel, while portraying typical Russian heroes and heroines, invariably reflected social and political issues, and engaged with moral questions. In this the Russians were prompted by their English counterparts, particularly Charles *Dickens and George *Eliot, who were greatly admired. When the Russian novel was discovered by English readers in the 1880s, it was indeed its moral timbre that appealed to them, making Russian realism, 'the higher realism of mental and spiritual truth' as the **Saturday Review* put it in 1887, superior to what was perceived as the coldly objective, amoral naturalism of the contemporary French novel. Russian realism was based more on sympathetic portraiture and ideas than ingenious plotting and adventures. Dostoevsky's legacy of the ideological novel was the crowning achievement of an unparalleled half-century of novel writing that ended with Tolstoy's renunciation of literature in 1880 and the deaths of Dostoevsky in 1881 and Turgenev in 1883. The *symbolist movement (1890–1910) reacted against their predecessors' commitment to civic and moral issues, celebrating instead the values of beauty, mysticism, and untrammelled individualism in stylistically experimental works. Outstanding examples of symbolist novels are Fedor Sologub's *Petty Demon* (1907), Valerii Briusov's *Fiery Angel* (1908), and *Bely's *Silver Dove* (1909) and *Petersburg* (1916). The inheritance of social engagement was, however, evident in *Gorky's early novels. His *Mother* (1907) was later adopted as a pattern for the *Socialist Realist novels that dominated the Stalinist period 1932–53. A less regimented depiction of Soviet reality was permitted after Stalin's death. Previously unpublishable novels now passed the censorship; most notably *Bulgakov's *The Master and Margarita* (1966–7), written in 1928–40. Official interference, however, prevented the publication in their homeland of *Pasternak's *Doctor Zhivago* (1957) and *Solzhenitsyn's novels until 1989. These were in the mainstream of the classic Russian novels, and their traditional social and moral commitment contributed to the demise of the Soviet Union in 1991. See Gilbert Phelps, *The Russian Novel in English Fiction* (1956); John Garrard (ed.), *The Russian Novel from Pushkin to Pasternak* (1983); Richard Freeborn, *The Russian Revolutionary Novel* (1985); Malcolm V. Jones and Robin Feuer Miller (eds), *Cambridge Companion to the Russian Novel* (1998).

Ruth *See* BIBLE.

Ruth A novel by Elizabeth *Gaskell, published 1853. Ruth Hilton, a 15-year-old orphan apprenticed to a dressmaker, is seduced and then deserted by wealthy Henry Bellingham. She is rescued from suicide by Thurston Benson, a Dissenting minister, who with the help of his sister and his outspoken servant Sally takes her into his house under an assumed name as a widow. She bears Bellingham's son, and is redeemed by love for her child and by Benson's guidance. Later she becomes a governess in the home of tyrannical Mr Bradshaw, where she is discovered by Bellingham, whose offer of marriage she rejects. Bradshaw, learning of her past, brutally dismisses her. Ruth regains respect by becoming a heroic nurse during a cholera epidemic, and dies after nursing Bellingham to recovery. In arousing sympathy for 'fallen women' who had been victims of seduction, Gaskell shocked many contemporary readers.

RUTHERFORD, Mark *See* WHITE, WILLIAM HALE.

Ruthwell Cross A stone monument over five metres high, in the parish church at Ruthwell, Dumfriesshire, dating perhaps from the 8th century, on which are inscribed in *runes some alliterating phrases closely corresponding to parts of the Old English poem **Dream of the Rood*. It was thrown down by Presbyterians and the inscriptions partly effaced. The monument has further significance as a preaching cross: on it may still be seen carvings including the Evangelists and representations of incidents from the life of Christ. Some of the latter, such as the Resurrection, strongly cohere with the themes of the runic inscription and the later poem in the *Vercelli Book. There are also Latin inscriptions and decorations with vine tracery. See Éamonn Ó Carragáin, *Ritual and the Rood: Liturgical Images and the Old English Poems in the Dream of the Rood Tradition* (2005); *The Dream of the Rood*, ed. Michael Swanton (1996).

RYMAN, Geoff (1951–) Canadian-born author resident in the UK. His first novel, *The Warrior Who Carried Life* (1985) was an acclaimed *fantasy; much of his subsequent work, including *Air* (2005), which won multiple awards including the Arthur C. Clarke Award, is *science fiction. His work also includes the web-based 'hypertext novel' *253* (published as a book 1998), and *The King's Last Song* (2006), set in modern and 12th-century Cambodia; and as writer and editor Ryman constantly questions genre boundaries. *Was* (1992) uses the device of a 'real' Dorothy who is the model for the protagonist of L. Frank *Baum's *The Wonderful Wizard of Oz* to explore America's dreams and dark fantasies.

RYMER, Thomas (1642/3–1713) Historian and critic, probably born in Yafforth, Yorkshire, educated at Sidney Sussex College, Cambridge. He wrote a verse 'Heroick Tragedy', *Edgar, or The English Monarch* (1678), but is better known as the critic whose *The Tragedies of the Last Age Considered* (1678) and *A Short View of Tragedy* (1692) brutally lambasted British dramatists (including William Shakespeare, whose **Othello* is particularly condemned) for failing to observe the practice of the ancients (*see* BATTLE OF THE BOOKS) and French *neo-classical principles. These works were treated with respect by

John *Dryden, Alexander *Pope, and Samuel *Johnson. Rymer also produced, with Robert Sanderson (1660–1741), *Foedera* (20 vols, 1704–35), a massive collection of documents covering British history down to 1654.

RYSBRACK, Michael (1694–1770) Flemish sculptor, trained in Antwerp, who settled in England; the classicism of his style made him popular with the virtuosi in the circle of Lord Burlington (1694–1753). Rysbrack's Roman reliefs in the chimney pieces at Houghton Hall (Norfolk) and Clandon Park (Surrey) satisfied the taste of an era formed by the writings of *Shaftesbury, and his bust of Daniel Finch, earl of Nottingham (1723), introduced the fashion for the portrait bust into English sculpture. Alexander *Pope (of whom he made an idealized bust, 1730) collaborated with him on some of his monuments in Westminster Abbey, where his most famous work is the monument to Sir Isaac *Newton; his contributions to *Poets' Corner include memorials to Ben *Jonson (*c*.1737), John *Gay (1736), Matthew *Prior, and Nicholas *Rowe. The national pride that inspired Poets' Corner found striking expression in the cult of British Worthies; William *Kent's Temple of British Worthies (1733) at Stowe is decorated with many busts by Rysbrack.

S

SAADI, Suhayl (1961–) Doctor, dramatist, librettist, novelist, and poet, born in Yorkshire to Afghan-Pakistani parents and brought up in Glasgow. Recent work includes the novel *Psychorag* (2004). He writes that 'the pen in some metaphysical way holds out the possibility of re-writing the world'.

SABA, Umberto (1883–1957) Italian poet. Born Umberto Poli in Trieste of a Jewish mother, he adopted the name Saba from his nurse, his father having deserted him before his birth. He draws on different strands of Italian literary tradition, *Petrarch, Giovanni *Pascoli, Gabriele *d'Annunzio, and from Freudian ideas; but on the surface he remains a simple poet of nature and domestic affections. His main poems are in his *Canzoniere*, issued in various states from 1919; the definitive edition is 1961. He has been translated by Robert *Lowell.

Sabine farm *See* HORACE.

SACHS, Hans (1494–1576) German poet, born in Nuremberg. A shoemaker by trade, he was author of a large body of verse, including *Meisterlieder* and some 200 plays. The subject of a poem by *Goethe, he is known outside Germany chiefly as the hero of *Wagner's opera *Die Meistersinger von Nürnberg* (1868). *See* MEISTERSINGER.

SACKS, Oliver (1933–) London-born neurologist and writer, educated at St Paul's School, the Queen's College, Oxford, and Middlesex Hospital; he has worked for many years as clinician and instructor in New York. *Awakenings* (1973, the source of *A Kind of Alaska* by Harold *Pinter) is a description, with vividly written case histories, of the reactions of post-encephalitic 'sleeping-sickness' patients of the 1916–17 epidemic to the new drug L-Dopa. Other works include *Seeing Voices* (1989), *An Anthropologist on Mars* (1995), and *The Island of the Colour-Blind and Cycad Island* (1996). *The Man Who Mistook his Wife for a Hat* was adapted by Peter *Brook as *L'Homme qui* (Paris, 1993: UK, *The Man Who*, 1994). His autobiographical *Uncle Tungsten: Memories of a Chemical Boyhood* appeared in 2001; *Oaxaca Journal* (2002) is an account of an expedition is search of ferns; *Musicophilia: Tales of Music and the Brain* (2007) describes the healing power of music.

SACKVILLE, Charles, Lord Buckhurst and later sixth earl of Dorset (1638–1706) A favourite of Charles II and noted for dissipation, who later became a loyal supporter of William III. He was a friend and patron of poets, was praised as a poet by Matthew *Prior and John *Dryden, and has been identified with the Eugenius of the latter's *Of Dramatick Poesy*. His poems, which appeared with those of Sir Charles *Sedley in 1701, include some biting satires and the ballad 'To all you ladies now at land'.

SACKVILLE, Thomas, first earl of Dorset and Baron Buckhurst (*c.*1536–1608) Writer and administrator, son of Sir Richard Sackville (d. 1566). Probably educated at Oxford, he became a barrister of the Inner Temple, entered Parliament in 1558, was raised to the peerage in 1567, and held a number of high official positions, including those of lord treasurer and chancellor of Oxford University. He wrote the Induction and *The *Complaint of Buckingham* for *A *Mirror for Magistrates*, and collaborated (probably writing only the last two acts) with Thomas Norton (1532–84) in the tragedy of **Gorboduc*. He was an ancestor of Vita *Sackville-West and is discussed in her *Knole and the Sackvilles* (1922).

SACKVILLE-WEST, 'Vita' (Victoria Mary) (1892–1962) Writer, born at Knole, Kent, and educated by governesses and at Miss Woolff's day school, London. She wrote eight novels as a child before publishing *Poems of East and West* (1917). Her first novel, *Heritage* (1919), *Knole and the Sackvilles* (1922), *The Heir* (1922, a novel), and her acclaimed novel *The Edwardians* (1930) all centre on her childhood home. In 1913 she married Harold *Nicolson, with whom she travelled widely before they settled at Sissinghurst, Kent, in 1930. In 1922 she met Virginia *Woolf; Sackville-West wrote *Seducers in Ecuador* (1924) for her and received *Orlando* (1928) in return. Her other works include a pastoral poem, *The Land* (1926, Hawthornden Prize, 1927), *All Passion Spent* (1931, novel), and many works on travel, gardening, and biography. Her unorthodox but harmonious marriage was described by her son Nigel Nicolson in *Portrait of a Marriage* (1973). See Victoria *Glendinning, *Vita* (1983).

SADE, Donatien-Alphonse-François, marquis de (1740–1814) French novelist, dramatist, and philosopher. A controversial figure from an early age, he spent prolonged periods in prison, during which time he wrote his pornographic novels *Les 120 Journées de Sodome* (1784–5: *The 120 Days of Sodom*), *Justine ou les malheurs de la vertu* (1791: *Justine,* or *The Misfortunes of Virtue*), *La Philosophie dans le boudoir* (1795: *Philosophy in the Boudoir*), and *La Nouvelle Justine* (1797: *The New Justine*). With their fascination with the minutiae of sexual pathology and their hedonistic nihilism, these texts have been seen to anticipate *Nietzsche, *Freud, and *Foucault. Long censored in Britain, but now readily available, they have also had a considerable influence on English literature, inspiring imitation and parody from writers as diverse as A. C. *Swinburne, Angus *Wilson, and Angela *Carter. Sade's period of imprisonment at the mental hospital of Charenton (where he died) was the basis of Peter *Weiss's play, commonly known as the 'Marat/Sade' (1964), which, through Peter *Brook's production, had a powerful impact on British theatre. Sade's name is the origin of the term 'sadism'. See M. Lever, *Marquis de Sade*, trans. A. Goldhammer (1993).

SA'DĪ of Shiraz (d. *c.*1290) Famous Persian literary figure, whose adventurous life included a spell as a prisoner of the Crusaders in Syria. He was already well known as a poet when, back in Shiraz, he wrote his two principal works, the *Bustān* or 'Orchard' (1257), comprising ten sections of verse on moralistic topics, and the *Gulistān* or 'Rose Garden' (1258), a lighter, more humorous prose work interspersed with passages of verse. Their freshness and sharp wit brought them a popularity that they still retain. They are often used as early reading for those studying Persian, and Sir William *Jones and, later, Edward *FitzGerald knew them well. Ralph Waldo *Emerson's acquaintance with Sa'dī, about whom he wrote, came through a 19th-century German translation.

SADLEIR (formerly Sadler), **Michael** (1888–1957) Bibliographer and novelist, born in Oxford, and educated at Rugby School and Balliol College, Oxford. He became director of the publishing house of Constable in 1920. He amassed an unrivalled collection of 19th-century books, often of less-known authors, and wrote important bibliographical works, including *Excursions in Victorian Bibliography* (1922) and *Nineteenth Century Fiction* (2 vols, 1951). He wrote several novels portraying the seamy side of Victorian London; his best-known, *Fanny by Gaslight* (1940), was made into a film.

Sad Shepherd, The, *A Tale of Robin Hood* The last and unfinished play of Ben *Jonson, a pastoral tragicomedy written *c.*1635, printed 1641. Robin Hood invites shepherds and shepherdesses to a feast in Sherwood Forest, but it is marred by the arts of the witch Maudlin, aided by her familiar, Puck-Hairy. Aeglamour, the Sad Shepherd, relates the loss of his beloved Earine, believed drowned in the Trent. In reality Maudlin has stolen her clothes to adorn her daughter and shut her up in an oak as a prey for her son, the rough swineherd Lorel. Assuming the form of Maid Marian, Maudlin sends away the festive venison, abuses Robin, and throws his guests into confusion. But Lorel fails to win Earine, Maudlin's wiles are detected, and Robin's huntsmen pursue her. Only three acts exist; there are continuations by Francis Waldron (1783) and Alan Porter (1935).

saga An Old Norse word meaning 'spoken narrative', applied to narrative compositions produced in Iceland and Norway in the 13th, 14th, and 15th centuries, but typically set much earlier. There are three main types of saga: family sagas, dealing with the first settlers of Iceland and their descendants; kings' sagas, historical works about the kings of Norway; and legendary or heroic sagas, fantastic adventure stories about legendary heroes. The family sagas and the kings' sagas share an elegant, laconic style, notable for its air of detached objectivity. Where early scholars supposed that the family sagas were reliably historical, being based almost wholly on oral traditions from an earlier period, modern critics see these works as literary fictions with some historical basis. The most celebrated of the family sagas is **Njáls saga*. The main concerns of this outstanding saga (the growth of social stability, legal and political, among the settlers of a new community, and the part played by human emotions, especially rivalry, loyalty, and sexual jealousy, in the course of this development) are characteristic of the other family sagas too, though *Njáls saga* stands out because of its scope and breadth of characterization. *Eyrbyggja saga* is especially concerned with the emergence of a politically stable community, though it also recounts some supernatural incidents. *Laxdaela saga* deals with the theme of a tragic love-triangle and the fortunes of one of Iceland's most powerful families at that time. *Grettis saga* tells, with remarkable psychological depth and subtlety, the story of a famous Icelandic outlaw. Grettir's fights with the monstrous walking corpse Glámr and with a troll woman are analogous to Beowulf's fight with Grendel and Grendel's mother (*see* BEOWULF). Snorri Sturluson's **Heimskringla* comprises a history of the kings of Norway; **Völsunga saga* recounts the legends of the Goths and Burgundians which underlie Richard *Wagner's *Ring des Nibelungen* cycle. *Sturlunga saga*, with its five feuding families, is unique in being a compilation of sagas about figures almost contemporary with their 13th-century authors. William *Morris did much to popularize Icelandic literature in England (*see* SIGURD THE VOLSUNG). See also *Njáls saga*, trans. M. Magnusson and H. Pálsson (1960); *Eyrbyggja saga*, trans. H. Pálsson and P. Edwards (1973); *Laxdaela saga*, trans. M. Magnusson and H. Pálsson (1969); *The Saga of Grettir the Strong*, trans. G. A. Hight (1965); *The Sagas of Icelanders: A Selection*, with a preface by Jane Smiley and an introduction by Robert Kellogg (1997).

SAGAN, Carl (1934–96) American astronomer and writer, born in New York; author of numerous books of popular science. His novel *Contact* (1985; filmed 1997) concerns the search for extra-terrestrial life.

SAID, Edward (1935–2003) American critic, born in Jerusalem to Christian Palestinian parents, and educated at Victoria College, Cairo, then at Princeton and Harvard. He taught from 1963 at Columbia University, New York. His works of general literary theory, *Beginnings* (1975) and *The World, the Text and the Critic* (1983), show the influence of Michel *Foucault. His most influential book, *Orientalism* (1978), argues that

Western writers and 'experts' have constructed a myth of the 'Orient'; it is a founding text of modern *postcolonial theory, complemented by the essays collected in *Culture and Imperialism* (1993). He was also a music critic and a noted public defender of the Palestinian cause. *Out of Place* (1999) is his memoir.

ST AUBYN, Edward (1960–) Novelist, author of a trilogy of short novels *Never Mind* (1992), *Bad News* (1992), and *Some Hope* (1994): the first describes with horrific conviction the indulged but appalling childhood of Patrick Melrose, sexually abused by his father on holiday in the south of France in the 1960s, and the two later volumes follow Patrick to New York (where his father lies dead in a funeral parlour) and back to London, as he struggles to cope with his drug addiction and his terrible paternal legacy. *On the Edge* (1998) is a journey through the New Age cults of the 1990s, from Findhorn to California, and follows with some unease the spiritual and sexual quests of several pilgrims, including a drop-out English banker. *A Clue to the Exit* (2000) and *Mother's Milk* (2006) continues his complex and often painful portrayal of family allegiances and betrayals.

SAINTE-BEUVE, Charles-Augustin (1804–69) French critic, poet, and novelist. His famous articles in periodicals such as *La Revue de Paris* and *La *Revue des deux mondes* were collected as *Critiques et portraits littéraires* (1832, 1836–9: *Critiques and Literary Portraits*). Between 1849 and 1869 he contributed weekly critical essays to Paris newspapers; these were the celebrated 'Causeries du lundi', appearing on Mondays and collected in book form as *Causeries du lundi* (15 vols, 1851–62: *Monday Chats*) and *Nouveaux Lundis* (13 vols, 1863–70: *New Mondays*). His two long studies, each of which began life as a course of lectures, *Port-Royal* (6 books, 1840–59), are classics of literary and biographical criticism. To the care and method of the professional critic Sainte-Beuve joined a subtle and enquiring curiosity about books and authors, wide-ranging interests, and a tolerant spirit. He is generally regarded as one of the founders of modern criticism. Some of his early essays, and notably his *Tableau historique et critique de la poésie française et du théâtre français au XVIe siècle* (1828: *Historical and Critical Survey of Sixteenth-Century French Poetry and Theatre*), helped to promote the poetry of the Romantic movement in France by tracing its affinities with 16th-century poetry.

SAINT-ÉVREMOND, Charles de Marguetel de Saint-Denis, sieur de (1613–1703) French essayist and dramatist. He spent the latter part of his life in exile in England, where he acted as arbiter of taste from the reign of Charles II to that of William III. In his sceptical Epicureanism (*see* EPICURUS) he was a representative freethinker who wrote with witty sobriety on a variety of subjects, including English comedy. His works were translated in 1714, some of his essays having previously appeared in English in 1693, with a preface by John *Dryden.

SAINT-EXUPÉRY, Antoine de (1900–44) French novelist. He was actively involved in the early years of commercial aviation, and his novels, all quickly translated into English, are intimately linked with his flying experiences: *Courrier-Sud* (1928: *Southern Mail*), *Vol de nuit* (1931: *Night Flight*), *Terre des hommes* (1939: *Wind, Sand and Stars*), and *Pilote de guerre* (1942: *Flight to Arras*). He also wrote a deceptively simple book for children, *Le Petit Prince* (1943: *The Little Prince*). He failed to return from a reconnaissance mission in North Africa: his presumed death in the desert contributed to the success of a posthumously published unfinished collection of desert meditations, *Citadelle* (1948: *Wisdom of the Sands*).

SAINT-JOHN PERSE (1887–1975) Pseudonym of Alexis Saint-Léger Léger, French poet and diplomat. His early poems, *Éloges* (1911: *Eulogies*), evoked his childhood in the French West Indies. He travelled widely for most of his life, his career in the French foreign service taking him as far afield as Beijing. He first became known to the English-speaking world through T. S. *Eliot's translation of his epic poem *Anabase* (1924: *Anabasis*), a chronicle of Asiatic tribal migrations. Exiled to the United States after 1940, he produced a succession of highly wrought prose poems of great rhythmic subtlety: *Exil* (1942: *Exile*), *Pluies* (1943: *Rain*), *Neiges* (1944: *Snow*), and *Vents* (1946: *Wind*). He was awarded the *Nobel Prize in 1960.

St Leon A novel by William *Godwin, published 1799. Godwin tells the story of Reginald St Leon who has discovered the philosopher's stone and the alchemical grails of immortality and the secret of turning base metal into gold. The story mixes *Gothic elements with the socio-political concerns of his earlier **Caleb Williams*. The story influenced his daughter Mary *Shelley's **Frankenstein*.

St Ronan's Well A novel by *Walter Scott, published 1823. One of only two set within Scott's lifetime, it is the only one in which he attempts contemporary social *satire. St Ronan's Well is a tawdry, third-rate spa, inhabited by meretricious, pretentious characters. Against this background, he sets the melodrama of two half-brothers, sons of the late earl of Etherington, both of whom are involved with Clara Mowbray, daughter of the local laird. The younger son impersonates the elder, Francis, at a midnight marriage with Clara, who is thus married to a man she detests, and the novel ends in unrelieved misery.

Saint's Everlasting Rest, The *See* BAXTER, RICHARD.

SAINT-SIMON, Claude-Henri de Rouvroy, comte de (1760–1825) French social philosopher and political economist, whose father was a cousin of the duc de *Saint-Simon. In his various writings Saint-Simon laid down a set of principles for the reorganization of European society after the French Revolution in conformity with current scientific and economic notions. Conceiving of a nation as a vast productive enterprise, he proposed that industrialists should hold political power and that spiritual authority should be vested in scientists and artists in order to secure the physical and moral improvement of all classes. After his death his followers formed a religious association and elaborated his ideas along broadly socialist lines into the doctrine known as *Saint-Simonisme*, for which Thomas *Carlyle and John Stuart *Mill showed some enthusiasm in the 1830s. The Saint-Simonians advocated the abolition of the right of private inheritance and its transfer to the state, the institution of a hierarchy of merit, and the enfranchisement of women. The association was declared illegal in 1832.

SAINT-SIMON, Louis de Rouvroy, duc de (1675–1755) Writer of memoirs. After a period of reluctant army service, he sought advancement at court until 1723, when the death of his patron, the duc d'Orléans, put an end to his participation in public affairs. His great work, the *Mémoires*, composed during the twenty years of his retirement but only published in its entirety at the turn of the 20th century, offers an incomparable record of life at court in the latter part of Louis XIV's reign. The dynamism of his writing, the liveliness of his observation, and the penetration of his portraits have made this work a classic of the genre. It was among *Proust's favourite reading.

SAKI (1870–1916) Pseudonym of Hector Hugh Munro, short story writer, born in Burma and educated, briefly, at Bedford Grammar School (later Bedford School). In 1900 he published *The Rise of the Russian Empire*, and in the same year began to write political satire which he signed 'Saki', the name of the 'cypress-slender Minister of Wine' in *The Rubáiyát of *Omar Khayyám*. His short stories from this period were collected as *Reginald* (1904), followed by *Reginald in Russia* (1910), *The Chronicles of Clovis* (1911), *Beasts and Super-Beasts* (1914), *The Toys of Peace* (1919), and *The Square Egg* (1924). *The Unbearable Bassington* (1912) and *When William Came* (1913), about a successful invasion of England by the Kaiser, are both novels. In 1914 he enlisted as a trooper and was killed in France two years later. His stories mix the satiric, the comic, the macabre, and the supernatural, and show a marked interest in the use of animals as agents of revenge upon mankind. See Sandie Byrne, *The Unbearable Saki* (2007).

SALA, George Augustus (1828–96) Journalist and illustrator. Born in London, he was educated partly in France. He began his bohemian literary career as editor of *Chat* in 1848, and became a regular contributor to **Household Words* (1851–6). He was sent by Charles *Dickens to Russia as correspondent at the end of the Crimean War and subsequently wrote copiously for the **Daily Telegraph*. His first-hand reporting from overseas conflicts, including the American Civil War and the Franco-Prussian War, made him a journalistic pioneer. He published books of travel, and much racy fiction, including *The Seven Sons of Mammon* (1862), a satirical account of ruthless capitalist practices, and edited the popular 18th-century romance *The Strange Adventures of Captain Dangerous* (1863).

SALADIN (Salah ad-Din Yusuf ibn Ayyub) (*c.*1138–1193) A Sunni Kurd and the founder of the Ayyubid dynasty. He became sultan of Egypt in 1171, and took over southern Syria and Damascus in 1174. For the next dozen years he concentrated on subduing his Muslim adversaries to the north and east. Action against the Crusaders was rare and largely unsuccessful. When a truce ended in April 1187, he launched a *jihad* against them, winning a decisive victory at Hattin on 4 July. Acre surrendered 10 July; and he then besieged and captured Jerusalem (2 October), precipitating the Third Crusade. After several defeats by forces led by *Richard I, Cœur de Lion, he concluded a truce in 1192 which allowed Henry of Champagne, titular king of Jerusalem, a strip of coastal land around Acre and access to Jerusalem itself. But his conquests remained considerable at his death in 1193. The Arab chroniclers had mixed opinions about him, his supporters depicting him as chivalrous, just, and magnanimous. This view was widely taken up by Christian authors in the west (probably originally as a justification for the termination of the Third Crusade): by *Boccaccio who represents him thus in two stories in the **Decameron* (Day 1, Tale 3; Day 10, Tale 9); by *Dante who places him in the limbo of heroes (*Inferno*, IV. 129; *see* DIVINA COMMEDIA); and by English writers such as Walter *Scott in *The *Talisman*.

SALINGER, J. D. (Jerome David) (1919–) American novelist and short story writer, born in New York. He served with the 4th Infantry Division in the Second World War and was stationed in Devon for a time. He is best known for his novel *The Catcher in the Rye* (1951), the story of adolescent Holden Caulfield who runs away from boarding school in Pennsylvania to New York, where he preserves his innocence despite various attempts to lose it. The colloquial, lively, first-person narration, with its attacks on the 'phoniness' of the adult world and its clinging to family sentiment in the form of Holden's affection for his sister Phoebe, made the novel accessible to and popular with a wide readership, particularly with the young. A sequence of works about the eccentric Glass family began with *Nine Stories* (1953, published in Britain as *For Esmé—With Love and Squalor*) and was followed by *Franny and Zooey* (1961), *Raise High the Roof Beam, Carpenters*, and *Seymour: An Introduction* (published together, 1963), containing stories reprinted from the **New Yorker*. A notably reclusive character, he was the subject of Ian Hamilton's *In Search of J. D. Salinger* (1988). See also P. Alexander, *Salinger* (1999).

SALKEY, Andrew (1928–95) Caribbean poet, short story writer, editor, and broadcaster; born in Colón, Panama, of Jamaican parents, and educated in Jamaica and at London University. He was active in the promotion of Caribbean culture in Britain and abroad: his later years were spent teaching at Amherst, Massachusetts. His novels include *Escape* *to an Autumn Pavement* (1960) and *A Quality of Violence* (1978). His many publications include stories and fables for younger readers, such as *Anancy's Score* (1973), which takes its name from the Jamaican trickster spider of creation myths, Ananse. *Havana Journal* is a portrait of Cuba, and *Georgetown Journal* (1972) describes a visit to Guyana on the occasion of its independence celebrations in 1970.

SALLUST (Gaius Sallustius Crispus) (probably 86–35 BC) Roman historian whose surviving works are two monographs, *Bellum Catilinae (The Conspiracy of Catiline)*, a major source for Ben *Jonson's **Catiline*, and *Belum Iugurthinum* (*The War against Jugurtha*). His practice of including speeches, gnomic sayings, and character sketches in his narrative was copied by the 12th-century *William of Malmesbury. The *Jugurtha* was translated by Alexander *Barclay early in the 16th century, and Thomas *Heywood translated both monographs from the French (1608); there were several translations in the 18th century, for example by the radical Whig Thomas Gordon (1744). Sallust's condemnations of corruption were much savoured by the architects of the American Revolution.

SALMASIUS (1588–1653) Professional name of Claude de Saumaise, an eminent French scholar, professor at Leiden University in 1649 when Charles II was living at The Hague. At the age of 19 he discovered the Palatine library at Heidelberg and unearthed the 10th-century Palatine Anthology (*The Greek *Anthology*). He was commissioned by Charles to draw up a defence of his father and an indictment of the regicide government. This took the form of the Latin *Defensio Regia* which reached England by the end of 1649. John *Milton was ordered by the Council in 1650 to prepare a reply to it, and in 1651 issued his *Pro Populo Anglicano Defensio*, also in Latin, a work which brought him an international reputation and attracted great attention, much of it hostile. It is a repetitious work, a mixture of scholarship and personal abuse, but Milton himself was well satisfied with it. Salmasius rejoined in his *Responsio*, published posthumously in 1660. Thomas *Hobbes in his *Behemoth* said he found the two *Defensiones* 'very good Latin both...and both very ill reasoning'.

SAMBER, Robert (bap. 1682, d. *c.*1745) Translator who is chiefly remembered for his 1729 version of Charles *Perrault's fairy-tales as *Mother Goose's Tales: Histories, or Tales of Passed Times. With Morals*. Samber often produced dual-language editions for the purposes of teaching French to English children.

Samson *See* BIBLE.

Samson Agonistes A tragedy by John *Milton, published 1671, in the same volume as **Paradise Regained*. Probably written after the *Restoration, though W. R. Parker and others have dated it much earlier, possibly as early as 1647. It is modelled on Greek tragedy, and has been frequently compared to *Prometheus Bound* by *Aeschylus or *Oedipus at Colonus* by *Sophocles. Other critics have claimed that its spirit is more Hebraic (or Christian) than Hellenic. Predominantly in blank verse, it also contains passages of metrical freedom and originality, and some rhyme. In a preface, Milton says it was never intended for the stage. 'Agonistes' means in Greek a contestant in the games or a champion. Based loosely on the biblical Book of Judges, the tragedy deals with the last phase of Samson's life when he is blinded and captive, a phase many have likened to Milton's situation after the collapse of the Commonwealth. In the course of the drama Samson is visited successively by friends from his tribe (the chorus), his father Manoa, his wife Dalila, Harapha, a strong man of Gath, and a Philistine officer who summons him to perform feats of strength to entertain his masters in the temple of *Dagon. After his exit, a messenger brings news of his final feat—pulling down the supporting pillars and destroying himself and the audience. No work of Milton's has undergone more reinterpretation in modern times. It used to be regarded as celebrating Samson's spiritual regeneration, but some commentators now see it as condemning Samson's violence or 'genocide', and he has been compared to a suicide bomber. See J. Wittreich, *Interpreting 'Samson Agonistes'* (1986), and for a summary of the debate *Milton: Complete Shorter Poems*, ed. J. Carey (2nd edn 1997).

SANCHO, Ignatius (?1729–80) Afro-British letter writer, born on a slave ship during the Middle Passage from Africa to the Americas. Brought to England as a child, he eventually became valet to the duke of Montague, who helped him to establish a Westminster grocery shop in 1774. Sancho published letters in newspapers on public affairs and was known as a correspondent and admirer of Laurence *Sterne. Sancho also composed music, wrote (lost) plays, and was the first Afro-British patron of white writers and artists. He called Phillis *Wheatley a 'genius in bondage'. A former correspondent published *Letters of the Late Ignatius Sancho, an African* (1782), now available in modern editions, increasing Sancho's fame as writer, devoted husband and father, wit, man of feeling, critic, opponent of slavery and racial discrimination in England, Africa, and India, and friend of Sterne, David *Garrick, and John Hamilton Mortimer (1740–79). His portrait was painted by Thomas *Gainsborough in 1768. Sancho's letters have attracted many literary and social commentators, including Thomas *Jefferson.
See also SLAVERY.

SAND, George (1804–76) Pseudonym of Aurore Dupin, baronne Dudevant, French novelist. After separating from her husband, she went to Paris in 1831 to begin an independent life as a writer. Her fame now largely derives from two groups of novels: the first includes *Indiana* (1832), *Lélia* (1833), and *Jacques* (1834), which portray the struggles of the individual woman against social constraints, especially those of marriage; and the second includes *La Mare au diable* (1846: *The Devil's Pool*), *La Petite Fadette* (1848: *Little Fadette*), and *François le Champi* (1850: *François the Waif*), which are set in the region of Berry in central France, where she had a country property at Nohant, and depict the idylls of rustic life. *Elle et lui* (1859: *Her and Him*) fictionalizes her liaison with Alfred de *Musset; *Un hiver à Majorque* (1841: *Winter in Majorca*) describes an episode in her relationship with Frédéric Chopin; *Histoire de ma vie* (4 vols, 1854: *Story of my Life*) is an autobiography. Sand aroused much interest in Victorian England: in 1844 Elizabeth Barrett *Browning addressed to her two sonnets, 'A Desire' and 'A Recognition'; and in 1847 there appeared an incomplete edition of *The Works of George Sand*, edited by the radical Matilda M. Hays (*c.*1820–1897). See B. Jack, *George Sand* (1999).

SANDBURG, Carl August (1878–1967) American poet, born in Chicago, with Swedish Lutheran ancestry. He challenged contemporary taste by his use of colloquialism and free verse, and became the principal among the authors writing in Chicago during and after the First World War. He published *Chicago Poems* (1916), *Cornhuskers* (1918), *Smoke and Steel* (1920), *Slabs of the Sunburnt West* (1922), *Good Morning America* (1928), and *Complete Poems* (1950). His film reviews are collected in *Carl Sandburg at the Movies* (1988). He also compiled a collection of folk songs, *The American Songbag* (1927), and wrote stories and poems for children. His major prose work is his six-volume life of Abraham Lincoln (1926–39); his novel *Remembrance Rock* (1948) is on an epic scale and traces the growth of an American family from its English origins and its crossing on the *Mayflower* to the present day. *Always the Young Strangers* (1953) is an autobiography. See N. Callahan, *Carl Sandburg: His Life and Times* (1987).

SANDFORD, Jeremy (1930–) Television playwright, born in London, remembered for his powerful BBC television drama *Cathy Come Home* (1966), directed by Ken Loach, which focused attention on the plight of a young family trapped in a downward spiral of poverty and homelessness. One of the landmarks of the socially committed drama documentary of the 1960s, it was followed by *Edna the Inebriate Woman* (1971, BBC), directed by Ted Kotcheff, a sympathetic portrayal of an elderly 'bag lady'.

Sanditon An unfinished novel by Jane *Austen, written 1817. Mr Parker is obsessed with the ambition to transform the small village of Sanditon, on the south coast, into a fashionable resort. His unquenchable enthusiasm sees crescents and terraces, a hotel and a library, and bathing machines. Charlotte Heywood, an attractive, alert young woman, is invited to stay with the Parkers, where she catches the fancy of Lady Denham, the local great lady. Denham's nephew and niece, Sir Edward and Miss Denham, live nearby, and the second heroine of the novel, Clara Brereton, is staying with her. Edward plans (with a frankness of expression new to the author) to seduce Clara; but his aunt intends him to marry a West Indian heiress, under the care of a Mrs Griffiths and her entourage, whose visit to Sanditon is anticipated shortly. After a ludicrous series of complications, involving both Mrs Griffiths's party and a ladies' seminary from Camberwell, the excited inhabitants of Sanditon find the expected invasion of visitors consists merely of Mrs Griffiths and three young ladies.

This entertaining fragment was written in the first three months of 1817, when Jane Austen was already suffering from Addison's disease (of which she died on 18 July); one of its remarkable features is the spirit with which the author satirizes the hypochondria of the sisters and brother of Mr Parker (Diana, Susan, and Arthur) and the scorn she pours on their dependence on patent medicines and tonics for their imaginary illnesses.

SANDYS, George (1578–1644) English traveller, poet, and colonist, educated at St Mary Hall, Oxford. He travelled, starting in 1610, to France, Italy, Constantinople, Egypt, Mount Sinai. Palestine, Cyprus, Sicily, Naples, and Rome, and published his fascinating *Relation of a Journey* in 1615. In 1621 he went to America as treasurer of the Virginia Company, becoming a member of the Council in 1624, and advocating a lenient policy towards the Indians. He returned to England about 1631. He published a widely read verse translation of *Ovid's *Metamorphoses* (1621–6), a verse *Paraphrase upon the Psalms* (1636), and *Christ's Passion: A Tragedy*, translated from the Latin of Hugo *Grotius (1640). He was a member of the circle of Lucius Cary, second Viscount *Falkland, at Great Tew and became an increasingly outspoken critic of absolutist government and the confrontational policies of Archbishop *Laud. See J. Ellison, *George Sandys: Travel, Colonialism and Tolerance in the 17th Century* (2002).

Sanglier, Sir In Edmund *Spenser's **Faerie Queene* (V. i), the wicked knight who has cut off his lady's head, and is forced by Sir *Artegall to bear it before him, as a mark of his shame. He is thought to represent the Irish leader Shane O'Neill, second earl of Tyrone (*c.*1530–1567), who invaded the Pale in 1566 and was killed by the Scots, his head being sent to Sir Henry Sidney (1529–86). Sanglier in French means 'wild boar'.

SANNAZAR (Sannazzaro), **Jacopo** (1458–1530) Neapolitan author whose writings celebrate the charms of nature and the rustic life. He was the author of an influential pastoral, in prose and verse, the **Arcadia*, and of Latin *eclogues and other poems including five piscatorial (or angling) eclogues, a genre of his own invention which was later adopted by Izaak *Walton. See C. Kidwell, *Sannazaro and Arcadia* (1993).

Sansfoy, Sansjoy, and **Sansloy** Three brothers in Edmund *Spenser's **Faerie Queene* (I. ii. 25 ff.). Sansfoy ('faithless') is slain by the *Redcrosse Knight, who also defeats Sansjoy ('joyless'), but the latter is saved from death by *Duessa. Sansloy ('lawless') carries off *Una and kills her lion (I. iii). This incident is supposed to refer to the suppression of the Protestant religion in the reign of Queen Mary.

SANSOM, William (1912–76) Short story writer, travel writer, and novelist, born in London and educated at Uppingham. He travelled widely as a young man, and worked at various jobs, including that of copywriter for an advertising agency. His first stories were published in literary periodicals (*_Horizon_, _New Writing_, the *_Cornhill Magazine_, and others) and his first volume, _Fireman Flower and Other Stories_ (1944), reflects his experiences with the National Fire Service in wartime London. This was followed by many other collections of stories, some set in London, others making full use of backdrops from Germany, Scandinavia, and the Mediterranean. His most successful novel, _The Body_ (1949), is set in London. A collection of stories, with an introduction by Elizabeth *Bowen, appeared in 1963.

SANTAYANA, George (1863–1952) Spanish-born writer and philosopher, brought up in Boston and educated at Harvard University, where he taught. From 1912 until his death he was resident in Europe. He was a speculative philosopher, of a naturalist tendency and opposed to German idealism, whose views are embodied in his _The Life of Reason_ (1905–6). He later modified and supplemented his philosophy in a series of four books, _Realms of Being_ (1927–40). Santayana also published poetry, criticism (see _Essays in Literary Criticism_, 1956), reviews, and memoirs; other works include _Soliloquies in England_ (1922), essays on the English character; _Character and Opinion in the United States_ (1920), one of several studies of American life; and his three-volume _Persons and Places_ (1944–53). His only novel, _The Last Puritan_ (1935), describes at length the antecedents and brief life of Boston-born Oliver Alden, whose European wanderings end in death by motor accident just after Armistice Day. He strongly influenced Wallace *Stevens, whose poem 'To an Old Philosopher in Rome' is a tribute to him. Santayana's letters have been published in eight volumes (2001–6). See Irving Singer, _George Santayana_ (2000).

SAPPER (1888–1937) The pseudonym of Herman Cyril McNeile, born in Bodmin, taken from the nickname of the Royal Engineers with whom he served during the First World War; he created the character of Hugh 'Bulldog' Drummond, the hearty, charming, xenophobic British ex-army officer who foils the activities of Carl Peterson, the international crook. He appears in _Bull-dog Drummond_ (1920), _The Female of the Species_ (1928), and many other popular thrillers; after McNeile's death the series was continued under the same pseudonym by his friend and collaborator G. T. Fairlie. See R. Usborne, _Clubland Heroes_ (1953, 1974).

Sapphics Verses written in imitation of a predominantly trochaic *metre used in Greek by *Sappho and in Latin by *Horace in stanzas of four lines in which the first three lines have eleven syllables, the last line five. Philip *Sidney, A. C. *Swinburne, Ezra *Pound and Peter *Reading are among those who attempted English Sapphics.

SAPPHO (b. _c._ late 7th century BC) The most famous woman poet of antiquity, a native of Lesbos. Evidence for her life and career is scanty and controversial. She had a husband and a daughter, Cleis, whose name occurs among her literary remains. She writes of female erotic feelings. Some poems are homosexual in colouring, but there are also *epithalamia, celebrating marriages. She figured posthumously in Attic comedies, and romantic fantasies and scandal grew up about her name: she was a priestess of Aphrodite; she was a Lesbian, in the modern sense; she threw herself into the sea, for love of a man, Phaon. *Ovid includes this last doomed affair among the _Heroides_, and Alexander *Pope translated it as _Sapho_ [sic] _to Phaon_. *Catullus closely imitated her one complete surviving ode. Her poems were collected and arranged into nine books (_c._300 BC). Sappho was praised for the directness, simplicity, and power of her poetry. The surviving fragments bear out that praise, and the loss of most of her work is a grievous one. See Margaret Reynolds, _The Sappho Companion_ (2000).

Sappho and Phaon A collection of sonnets by Mary *Robinson (1757/8–1800), published 1796. The sonnet sequence relates the story of *Sappho's doomed love for the boatman Phaon. Robinson declares that the versions of the story found in *Ovid and Alexander *Pope serve rather to 'depreciate than to adorn the Grecian Poetess' and she offers a more 'liberal account of that illustrious woman'. Rather than the more common Shakespearian sonnet, the sequence uses a Petrarchan form in imitation of 'that sublime Bard' John *Milton.

SARAMAGO, José (1922–) Portuguese novelist who was first brought to the attention of English readers with the translation (1988) of his novel _Memorial do convento_ (1982; trans. as _Baltasar and Blimunda_). This subversive historical novel treats the 18th century in Portugal from a left-wing perspective. In his next novel, _O ano da morte de Ricardo Reis_ (1984: _The Year of the Death of Ricardo Reis_), Dr Ricardo Reis returns to Lisbon after a sixteen-year absence, and roams the city with, among others, the recently dead poet Fernando *Pessoa. Set in 1936, this novel (generally considered Saramago's masterpiece) evokes a world where war is imminent, and where conventional boundaries between reality and illusion have lost their meaning. In _Ensaio sobre a cegueira_ (1995: _Blindness_), in which the spread of an epidemic of white blindness brings about the collapse of a civilized society, Saramago uses allegory to illustrate the threat of latent human savagery. It was followed by _Ensaio sobre a lucidez_ (2004: _Seeing_). He was awarded the *Nobel Prize in 1998.

SARBAN (1910–89) Pseudonym of John W. Wall, diplomat and author, born in Mexborough, Yorkshire. _The Sound of his Horn_ (1952) is a nightmarish *alternate history, in which the Nazis have won the Second World War and political prisoners are hunted down for sport by the ruling classes.

Sardanapalus A poetic drama by Lord *Byron, published 1821. The subject was taken from the *Bibliotheca Historica* of *Diodorus Siculus. Sardanapalus is represented as a self-indulgent but courageous monarch. When Beleses, a Chaldean soothsayer, and Arabaces, governor of Media, lead a revolt against him, he shakes off his sloth and, encouraged by Myrrha, his favourite Greek slave, fights bravely. Defeated, he arranges for the safety of his queen, Zarina, and of his supporters, then prepares a funeral pyre round his throne and dies in it with Myrrha.

SARGENT, Pamela (1948–) American *science fiction author, born in Ithaca, New York. She edited the influential 'Women of Wonder' series of anthologies of stories by women (1975–8: an updated 1995 volume featured later decades). *Cloned Lives* (1976) describes the lives of a group of cloned children.

SAROYAN, William (1908–81) Armenian American writer, born in Fresno, California, who achieved fame with his portraits of Armenian American life in collections like *My Name is Aram* (1940). In addition to numerous short stories he wrote a number of plays and briefly worked in Hollywood as a screenwriter. *The Bicycle Rider of Beverly Hills* (1952) is the first of his memoirs. See John Leggett, *A Daring Young Man* (2002). His son Aram (1943–) is also a writer.

SARRAUTE, Nathalie (1900–99) Russian-born French writer. Alongside Michel *Butor and Alain *Robbe-Grillet, she became known in the 1950s as a leading proponent of the **nouveau roman*. Central to her work is the exploration of 'tropism', a term adapted from biology to describe the pre-linguistic movements of attraction and repulsion she sees being played out in human relationships. In consultation with Sarraute, Maria Jolas translated many of Sarraute's novels, including *Le Planétarium* (1959; *The Planetarium*, 1963) and *Les Fruits d'or* (1963; *The Golden Fruits*, 1965), as well as *L'Ère du soupçon* (1956; *The Age of Suspicion*, 1964), a collection of essays in which she sets out her theory of the novel. Later, the translator Barbara Wright also produced lucid versions of Sarraute's work, also in consultation with the author.

SARTORIS, Adelaide (?1814–79) Née Kemble, singer and author, sister of Fanny *Kemble. After a distinguished operatic career she settled with her husband in Rome. She had many friends in the literary and artistic world, some of whom (notably Frederic *Leighton as Kioski) appear in *A Week in a French Country House* (1867), her **roman à clef*.

Sartor Resartus: *The Life and Opinions of Herr Teufelsdröckh* By Thomas *Carlyle, originally published in **Fraser's Magazine* (1833–4), and as a separate volume at Boston, Massachusetts, in 1836 (partly through the intervention of Ralph Waldo *Emerson, who had visited Carlyle in Craigenputtock in 1833); the first English edition followed in 1838.

The work was written under the influence of German *Romanticism, particularly *Richter. It consists of two parts: a discourse on the philosophy of clothes (*sartor resartus* means 'the tailor repatched') based on the speculations of an imaginary Professor Teufelsdröckh, and leading to the conclusion that all symbols, forms, and human institutions are properly clothes, and as such temporary; and a biography of Teufelsdröckh himself, which is in part Carlyle's autobiography, particularly in the description of the village of Entepfuhl and of the German university (suggested by Ecclefechan and Edinburgh), and still more in the notable chapters on 'The Everlasting No', 'The Centre of Indifference', and 'The Everlasting Yea', which depict a spiritual crisis such as Carlyle himself had experienced during his early Edinburgh days. The prose, dotted with capital letters, exclamation marks, phrases in German, compound words of the author's own invention, wild appeals to the reader, and outbursts of bitter satire, is a memorable early example of what came to be known as 'Carlylese'. Contemporary readers were generally bewildered, but the book is now acknowledged as a major landmark in Carlyle's development.

SARTRE, Jean-Paul (1905–80) French philosopher, novelist, playwright, literary critic, and political activist. He was the principal exponent of *existentialism in France, and, together with his friend and companion from her university days, Simone de *Beauvoir, had a considerable influence on French intellectual life in the decades following the Second World War. He studied philosophy and psychology at the École Normale Supérieure, and subsequently spent a period studying phenomenology at the French Institute in Berlin. He held various teaching posts in France until the outbreak of war. Mobilized in 1939, taken prisoner in 1940, he was released the following year and played a part in the Resistance movement. After the war he devoted himself exclusively to writing and to the pursuit of socialist political objectives. Through the great range of his creative and critical energies, his personal involvement in many of the important issues of his time, and his unceasing concern with problems of freedom, commitment, and moral responsibility, he won a wide audience for his ideas. He made important contributions in many areas: existentialist and Marxist philosophy (*L'Être et le néant*, 1943: *Being and Nothingness*; *Critique de la raison dialectique*, 1960: *Critique of Dialectical Reason*); the novel (*La Nausée*, 1938: *Nausea*; *Les Chemins de la liberté*, 1945–9: *The Roads to Freedom*: an unfinished trilogy, comprising *L'Âge de raison*: *The Age of Reason*, *Le Sursis*: *The Reprieve*, and *La Mort dans l'âme*: *Iron in the Soul*); drama (*Les Mouches*, 1943: *The Flies*; *Huis clos*, 1945: *In Camera*; *Les Mains sales*, 1948: *Dirty Hands*; *Les Séquestrés d'Altona*, 1960: *Loser Wins*); literary criticism (*Qu'est-ce que la littérature?*, 1948: *What is Literature?*); and biography, with studies of Charles *Baudelaire (1947), Jean *Genet (1952), and Gustave *Flaubert (1971–2). He was one of the founders of the influential literary and political review *Les Temps modernes* (1945). His autobiography, *Les Mots* (*Words*) appeared in 1964, in which year he was awarded the *Nobel Prize for Literature. His works have been widely translated into English, helping to ensure his significant influence on thought and writing outside France. See B.-H. Lévy, *Sartre* (2003).

SASSOON, Siegfried (1886–1967) Poet, educated at Marlborough College, Wiltshire, and Clare College, Cambridge. After university, he lived in Kent and Sussex, following country pursuits and publishing verse in private pamphlets. In the trenches in the First World War he began to write the poetry for which he is remembered: his bleak realism, his contempt for war leaders and patriotic cant, and his compassion for his comrades found expression in verse that was unlikely to be admired by the wartime public. During his first spell in the front line he was awarded the MC. Dispatched as 'shell-shocked' to Craiglockhart War Hospital in Edinburgh, he encountered and encouraged Wilfred *Owen, and organized a public protest against the war. In 1917 he published his war poems in *The Old Huntsman* and in 1918 further poems in *Counter-Attack*, both with scant success. From the late 1920s Sassoon began to think of himself as a religious poet, and converted to Roman Catholicism in 1957. After a series of homosexual relationships, he had married in 1933.

He also achieved success as a prose writer. His semi-autobiographical trilogy (*Memoirs of a Fox-Hunting Man*, 1928; *Memoirs of an Infantry Officer*, 1930; and *Sherston's Progress*, 1936) relates the life of George Sherston, a lonely boy whose loves are cricket and hunting, who grows into a thoughtless young gentleman and eventually finds himself a junior officer in the trenches, where he is brutally thrust into adulthood. The three books were published together as *The Complete Memoirs of George Sherston* in 1937. In 1938 Sassoon published *The Old Century and Seven More Years*, an autobiography of his childhood and youth, and his own favourite among his books. *The Weald of Youth* (1942) and *Siegfried's Journey* (1945) brought his story up to 1920. His attachment to the countryside emerges as a major theme in his post-1918 poetry and in most of his prose work. Three volumes of diaries (1915–18, 1920–2, and 1923–5), edited by Rupert Hart-Davis, were published between 1981 and 1985. See Jean Moorcroft Wilson's two-volume biography (1998 and 2003); and Max Egremont, *Siegfried Sassoon* (2005).

Satan The devil, God's primary antagonist, the figure who tempts Job in the Old Testament and Jesus in the New (Luke, ch. 4), and who is identified with the serpent who tempts Eve (Genesis, ch. 2) and the dragon who fights St *Michael in the war in heaven and is cast down into the lake of fire (Revelation, chs 12 and 20). Satan before his fall is known as Lucifer, the morning star; he is also associated with Apollyon, the angel of the bottomless pit (Revelation 9: 11), with whom Christian fights in **Pilgrim's Progress*, and Beelzebub, the prince of devils. He was popularly portrayed with horns and cloven feet: *Othello looks down at Iago's feet for evidence of his diabolic nature. In **Paradise Lost* by contrast Satan has the characteristics of an implacable hero of classical epic. He was a popular subject for 19th-century apocalyptic painters like John *Martin.

'Satanic school' The name under which Robert *Southey attacks Lord *Byron and the younger Romantics in the preface to his *A *Vision of Judgement*.

satire A poem or prose composition in which prevailing vices or follies are held up to ridicule or scorn; or a vein of such mockery found incidentally in many kinds of literary work, especially comic drama and fiction. In English literature, satire may be held to have begun with *Chaucer in his General Prologue to the **Canterbury Tales*. He was followed by many 15th- and 16th-century writers, including William *Dunbar, John *Skelton, George *Gascoigne, Thomas *Lodge, and John *Marston. The first important dramatic satires are the major plays of Ben *Jonson, notably **Volpone*. The great age of English satire began in the 1660s with the enormous popularity of Butler's **Hudibras*, and was further stimulated by John *Dryden, who perfected the epigrammatic and antithetical use of the *heroic couplet for satirical purposes in **Mac Flecknoe* and other works. He was followed by the major satirists Alexander *Pope and Jonathan *Swift, along with John *Gay, Matthew *Prior, and others in the Augustan period (*see* MOCK EPIC). The same tradition was followed by Charles *Churchill, and brilliantly revived by Lord *Byron in **English Bards and Scotch Reviewers*. With the exception of some of A. H. *Clough's poems, the Victorian age was not noted for verse satire, although the novel proved an excellent vehicle for social satire with Charles *Dickens, W. M. *Thackeray, and others. In the early 20th century, Thomas *Hardy, T. S. *Eliot, Siegfried *Sassoon, and Louis *MacNeice variously contributed to a revival of verse satire, while prose satire flourished in the novels of E. M. *Forster, Evelyn *Waugh, Wyndham *Lewis, Aldous *Huxley, Christopher *Isherwood, and George *Orwell. British culture of the 1960s was enlivened by a 'satire boom' launched in the stage revue *Beyond the Fringe* (1960) by Alan *Bennett, Jonathan Miller (1934–), Peter Cook (1937–95), and Dudley Moore (1935–2002), and continued in the lampoons of the fortnightly magazine *Private Eye* (1962–). Since then, satire has been strongly evident in fiction, for example in works by Malcolm *Bradbury, Jonathan *Coe, Alasdair *Gray, and Salman *Rushdie. See Ruben Quintero (ed.), *A Companion to Satire* (2006).

***Satiromastix**, or The Untrussing of the Humorous Poet* A comedy by Thomas *Dekker, written 1601 as part of the 'war of the theatres' (with John *Marston?), printed 1602.

Ben *Jonson in his **Poetaster* had satirized Dekker and Marston, under the names of Demetrius and Crispinus, while he himself figures as Horace. Dekker here replies, bringing the same Horace, Crispinus, and Demetrius on the stage once more. Horace is seen sitting in a study laboriously writing an *epithalamium, and stuck for a rhyme. Crispinus and Demetrius enter and reproach him for his bad temper.

Presently Captain Tucca (of the *Poetaster*) enters, mocking and abusing Horace. Horace's peculiarities of dress and appearance, his vanity and bitterness, are ridiculed; he is finally crowned with nettles.

The satirical part of the play uses a somewhat inappropriate romantic setting—the wedding of Sir Walter Terill at the court of William Rufus, and the drinking of poison (as she thinks) by his wife Caelestine, but really of a sleeping potion, to escape the king's attentions.

Saturday Review An influential weekly review founded in 1855, pungently conservative in its early days, which ran until 1938. In the mid-Victorian period, its anonymous fiction reviews were sometimes savage—Charles *Dickens, W. M. *Thackeray, and Anthony *Trollope were among those who suffered. Contributors included Henry Maine (1822–88), James Fitzjames *Stephen, J. R. *Green, and E. A. *Freeman. It later became more literary in its interests (notably under the editorship of Frank *Harris, 1894–8), publishing work by Thomas *Hardy, H. G. *Wells, Max *Beerbohm, Arthur *Symons, and others. George Bernard *Shaw was dramatic critic from 1895 to 1898, and James Agate (1877–1947) from 1921 to 1923.

Saturn (Greek 'Cronos') God whose throne was usurped by his son *Jupiter (Greek 'Zeus'). Saturn's reign was identified with the Golden Age in classical mythology: *Virgil's fourth eclogue prophesies its restoration. Later literary depictions usually follow Virgil, but John *Keats's **Hyperion* portrays Saturn and his brethren the *Titans helplessly recognizing the beauty and power of the young gods who replace them.
See Four Ages.

Satyrane, Sir In Edmund *Spenser's **Faerie Queene* (I. vi), a knight 'Plaine, faithfull, true, and enimy of shame', son of a satyr and the nymph Thyamis. He rescues *Una from the satyrs, perhaps symbolizing the liberation of the true Protestant religion by Martin *Luther.

satyr drama A humorous performance with a chorus of satyrs that ancient Athenian dramatists were expected to append to tragic trilogies offered for competition. This practice, which had the incidental virtue of providing light relief, may have been due to the belief mentioned by *Aristotle (*Poetics*, ch. 4) that tragedy had its origin in performances by actors dressed as satyrs. The surviving fragments of *Aeschylus' *Diktyoulkoi* (The Net-Drawers) and *Sophocles' *Ichneutai* (The Trackers) reveal sympathy for the promptings of animal impulse and a lyrical feeling for nature. Only one satyric drama has survived intact, the *Cyclops* of *Euripides. Tony *Harrison's *The Trackers of Oxyrhynchus* (1988) is an English satyr play adapted from the fragmentary *Ichneutai*.

Satyricon *See* Petronius, Arbiter.

Saul *See* Bible.

SAUSSURE, Ferdinand de (1857–1913) Swiss linguistician, born in Geneva. Having studied Indo-European languages at the University of Leipzig for four years, he went to Paris in 1881 where he taught for ten years. In 1891 he became professor at Geneva where, between 1907 and 1911, he delivered the three courses of lectures which were reconstructed from students' notes into the *Cours de linguistique générale* (1915: *Course in General Linguistics*), a book which is the basis of modern *linguistics and of much modern literary criticism. His most important and influential idea was the conception of language as a system of signs, arbitrarily assigned and only intelligible in terms of the particular system as a whole. This idea was applied outside language in the new science called semiotics. Language is a structure whose parts can only be understood in relation to each other; this *'Structuralism' has been very influential in literary criticism and in other fields, such as sociology. Furthermore, he established crucial distinctions between *langage* (the human capacity of using language), *langue* (the particular language as a whole: e.g. English), and *parole* (a particular utterance or occurrence of language), though successive translators (Wade Baskin, 1966; Roy Harris, 1983) have struggled to render these terms adequately in English; and he divided language study into *synchronic* (the examination of a particular language as a system at one stage of its existence) and *diachronic* (the historical study of the development of a language). Saussure's emphasis was on the value of synchronic study (with which the term 'linguistics' is sometimes used synonymously, as distinct from 'philology' for historical study), rather than the diachronic philology with which he had previously been concerned. One of the compilers of the *Cours* was Charles Bally (1865–1947), who developed the ideas of Saussure and, with other followers, is sometimes assigned to the 'Geneva School'. See J. Culler, *Saussure* (1976).

SAVAGE, Richard (*c.*1698–1743) Poet, who claimed to be the illegitimate son of the fourth Earl Rivers (*c.*1674–1712) and the countess of Macclesfield (1667/8–1753); but the account given by Samuel *Johnson, in his psychologically intense biography (1744), contains much unverifiable detail. After some success as a playwright, Savage was convicted of murder in 1727, and subsequently pardoned; he then wrote verse tributes to Queen Caroline (1683–1737) in a self-appointed capacity as 'volunteer laureate', and produced longer poems such as 'The Bastard' (1728), and *The *Wanderer* (1729). Savage acted as Alexander *Pope's spy in *Grub Street, and Pope helped him financially, but he died penniless in a Bristol jail. See Richard *Holmes, *Dr Johnson and Mr Savage* (1993).

Savage Club A club with strong literary and artistic connections founded in 1857, with George *Sala as one of the founder members; it was named after the poet Richard *Savage. Members have included Edgar *Wallace, George and Weedon *Grossmith, and Dylan *Thomas.

Saved A play by Edward *Bond, which caused much controversy when it was first seen (members only) at the *Royal Court in 1965, having been refused a licence for public performance. In short, minimalist-realist scenes, with dialogue of stark and stylized crudity, Bond evokes a bleak south London landscape of domestic and street violence and the somewhat caricatured impoverished pastimes of the working class—fishing, football pools, TV, pop music. In the central episode Pam's baby, which has been neglected by her and which cries loudly through much of the preceding action, is tormented and stoned to death in its pram by a gang of youths and its putative father, Fred. The subsequent lack of response to the child's death adds to the sense of dramatic shock.

SAVILE, George *See* HALIFAX, GEORGE.

SAVILE, Sir Henry (1549–1622) Scholar educated at Brasenose College, Oxford, and a fellow and subsequently warden of Merton College and provost of Eton College. He was secretary of the Latin tongue to *Elizabeth I, perhaps also teaching her Greek, and one of the scholars commissioned to prepare the authorized translation of the *Bible. He translated the *Histories* of *Tacitus (1591) and published a magnificent edition of St John *Chrysostom (1610–13) and of *Xenophon's *Cyropaedia* (1613) at Eton. He assisted Sir Thomas *Bodley in founding his library and established the Savilian professorships of geometry and astronomy at Oxford. He left a collection of manuscripts and printed books, now in the Bodleian Library.

Savile Club Founded in 1868 as the Eclectic Club, renamed in 1869 the New Club, and from 1871, when it moved to independent premises in Savile Row, known as the Savile Club. It moved to its present home, 69 Brook Street, in 1927. The club has always had a strong literary tradition; members have included Edmund *Gosse, Robert Louis *Stevenson, Thomas *Hardy, W. B. *Yeats, Lytton *Strachey, Henry *James. It was in the Savile billiards room that Stevenson is alleged to have said to Herbert *Spencer 'that to play billiards well was the sign of an ill-spent youth', though other clubs also claim this honour.

SAVONAROLA, Fra Girolamo (1452–98) Dominican friar from Ferrara, who was invited to Florence by Lorenzo de' Medici and became prior of San Marco. An eloquent and powerful preacher, he castigated the artistic licence, interest in paganism, and moral corruption of late 15th-century Italy. After the expulsion of the *Medici (1494) he became the de facto ruler of Florence. His political and moral invectives antagonized the pope, Alexander VI *Borgia, but only the threat of interdict deprived Savonarola of his widespread support among elite and populace alike. He was burnt at the stake in 1498. There is a sympathetic portrayal of him in George Eliot's **Romola*. The many editions of his sermons testify to his influence and appeal.

Savoy A short-lived but important 'art and literature' magazine, edited by Arthur *Symons, of which eight issues appeared in 1896, with contributions by Aubrey *Beardsley, Joseph *Conrad, Ernest *Dowson, W. B. *Yeats, and others.

Sawles Warde A work of alliterative prose, found in three manuscripts with the saints' lives called 'The *Katherine Group', dating from the end of the 12th century and from the west Midlands (probably Herefordshire). It is a loose translation of part of *De Anima* by Hugh of St Victor, and it presents a morality in which the body is the dwelling place of the soul and is attacked by the vices. It has connections with the morality castle, an allegorical representation of body and soul, found from *Grosseteste's *Chasteau d'Amour* to *The *Castle of Perseverance*. Its prose has the same elegance and colloquialism as **Ancrene Wisse* and the Katherine Group. Ed. R. Morris, *Old English Homilies and Homiletic Treatises*, EETS os 29 (1867, repr. 1998).

SAWYER, Robert (1960–) Canadian *science fiction writer, born in Ottawa. *Hominids* (2002), about the discovery of an *alternate world where Neanderthals became the dominant human species, won a *Hugo award. Like its sequels, it explores the differences between the two versions of humanity.

SAXO GRAMMATICUS A 13th-century Danish historian, author of the *Gesta Danorum*, a partly mythical Latin history of the Danes (which contains the **Hamlet* story). See *A History of the Danes*, vol. i, trans. P. Fisher (1970); vol. ii: *Commentary*, by H. Ellis-Davidson (1980).

SAXTON, Josephine (1935–) *Science fiction writer, born in Yorkshire. Her work is often closer to fabulation than science fiction, but has often, as in *The Travails of Jane Saint* (1980) and *Queen of the States* (1986), used its forms to engage with feminist concerns for liberation.

SAYERS, Dorothy L. (1893–1957) Crime writer and playwright, born in Oxford and educated by governesses, at the Godolphin School, Salisbury, and at Somerville College, Oxford. She worked as an advertising copywriter (1922–31) before the success of her novels brought her financial independence. They are outstanding for their literariness, well-researched backgrounds, observant characterization, and ingenious plotting, as well as for their detective Lord Peter Wimsey (*see* DETECTIVE FICTION). Her first novel was *Whose Body?* (1923) and she reached her peak the following decade with *Murder Must Advertise* (1933), *The Nine Tailors* (1934), and *Gaudy Night* (1935). From the mid-1930s she also wrote plays, including *Busman's Holiday* (1936), which were mainly for radio broadcast, while her learning, wit, and pugnacity made her a formidable theological polemicist. From the early 1940s she threw herself into translating Dante's **Divina commedia*. See Barbara Reynolds, *Dorothy L. Sayers: Her Life and her Soul* (rev. edn 1998).

SCALIGER, Joseph Justus (1540–1609) The son of Julius Caesar *Scaliger, one of the greatest scholars of the *Renaissance. His edition of the 1st-century AD Roman author Manilius (1579) and his *De Emendatione Temporum* (1583) revolutionized ancient chronology by insisting on the recognition of the historical material relating to the Jews, the Persians, the Babylonians, and the Egyptians. He also issued critical editions of many classical authors. He angered the Jesuits and retired from France to Lausanne in 1572, and subsequently to Leiden. He was attacked in his old age by Gaspar Scioppius (1576–1649) on behalf of the Jesuits, who contested the claim of the Scaligers to belong to the Della Scala family. See Anthony Grafton, *Joseph Scaliger: A Study in the History of Classical Scholarship* (2 vols, 1983, 1993).

SCALIGER, Julius Caesar (1484–1558) Classical scholar, born at Riva on Lake Garda. He settled at Agen in France as a physician. In the Renaissance debate about the purity of Latin, he was an advocate of *Cicero and so found himself in dispute with *Erasmus, against whom he wrote two tracts (1531, 1536). He wrote an important treatise on poetics (1561) which contained the earliest expression of the conventions of classical tragedy.

SCANNELL, Vernon (1922–2007) Poet, born in Spilsby, Lincolnshire. His first volume of verse, *Graves and Resurrections* (1948), was followed by several others including *The Masks of Love* (1960), *A Sense of Danger* (1962), and *The Loving Game* (1975). Later collections include *Funeral Games* (1987), *Dangerous Ones* (1991), *A Time for Fire* (1991), and *Views and Distances* (2000). *Collected Poems 1950–1993* appeared in 1998. Many of the poems combine informal colloquial language and domestic subjects with a sense of underlying violence: poetry and human love 'build small barriers against confusion' in an essentially hostile world. His several volumes of autobiography include *An Argument of Kings* (1987), an account of his wartime experiences in the British army, which included both the Normandy landings and the crime of desertion. The war figures in the poems too, including the well-known 'Walking Wounded'. He also published several novels, including *Ring of Truth* (1983).

Scarlet Letter, The A novel by Nathaniel *Hawthorne, published 1850. Set in the Puritan New England of the 17th century, the novel describes how Hester Prynne is punished for adultery by having to wear a scarlet letter A, whose significance shifts positively as the novel develops. Hester's defiance of the authorities and her protection of her love-child Pearl make a study in independence. Her husband, in disguise, torments her lover, a respected clergyman who is concealing his guilt until a final public confession.

SCARRON, Paul (1610–60) French poet, novelist, and comic dramatist. He is best remembered as the author of a collection of short fiction, *Nouvelles tragi-comiques* (1655–60: *Tragicomic Stories*), an English translation of which, by John Davies (1625–93), ran to six editions by 1700, and a burlesque novel, *Le Roman comique* (1651–7: *The Comic Novel*), recounting the adventures of a touring company of actors in the town of Le Mans, which was translated by John Bulteel (*c*.1627–1692) in 1665. Scarron's burlesque verse includes *Virgile travesti* (1648–51: *Virgil Travestied*), a *mock-heroic parody of the **Aeneid* in which the ancient gods and heroes speak like ordinary mortals, and which inspired Charles *Cotton's popular *Scarronides* (1664–5).

SCARRY, Richard (1919–94) Popular American author-illustrator, born in Boston, Massachusetts, educated at Boston's School of the Museum of Fine Arts; best known for *The Best Word Book Ever* (1963) which depicts and labels huge numbers of everyday objects, and his many books about Busytown featuring Lowly Worm and his friends.

Scenes of Clerical Life Three stories by George *Eliot, her first published fiction; they appeared in **Blackwood's Magazine* (1857), and were published in two volumes, 1858. Her purpose was to create fiction grounded in the moral realities of everyday experience.

'The Sad Fortunes of the Rev. Amos Barton' is the sketch of a commonplace clergyman, curate of Shepperton, who earns the affection of his parishioners by his misfortune—the death from overwork and general wretchedness of his gentle wife Milly.

'Mr Gilfil's Love-Story' tells of a man whose nature has been warped by tragedy. Maynard Gilfil was parson at Shepperton before the days of Amos Barton. The ward of Sir Christopher Cheverel and his domestic chaplain, he had fallen deeply in love with Caterina Sarti (Tina), the daughter of an Italian singer, adopted by the Cheverels. But Captain Wybrow, the selfish heir of Sir Christopher, had flirted with Tina and won her heart. At his uncle's bidding he had abandoned her for a wealthier rival. This brings Tina to the verge of lunacy, as Gilfil watches with helpless sorrow and unabated love. Tina rallies for a time under his devoted care and finally marries him, but soon dies, leaving Gilfil like a tree lopped of its best branches.

'Janet's Repentance' describes the influence of a sympathetic human soul. The Revd Edgar Tryan, earnest and evangelical, comes to Milby, an industrial town sunk in religious apathy, unmoved by the scanty ministration of the old curate, Mr Crewe. Tryan's efforts are vigorously opposed by a group of inhabitants led by Dempster, a drunken lawyer, who bullies his long-suffering wife Janet and drives her to drink. She shares her husband's prejudices against Tryan, until she discovers in him a sympathetic fellow sufferer. Her husband's brutality causes her to appeal to Tryan, and with his help she turns away from drink. Eliot's account of her struggle amounts to the first sympathetic treatment of alcoholism in English fiction. Dempster dies, and Janet gradually achieves self-conquest. Tryan's death from consumption leaves her bereaved, but strengthened for a life of service.

scepticism A philosophical stance which questions the possibility of attaining lasting knowledge about the reality, as distinct from the appearance, of things, and which rejects all dogmatism, fanaticism, and intolerance. As a historical movement, scepticism had its origin in the teaching of some of the Sophists in the 5th century BC. 'Pyrrhonian' scepticism, associated with Pyrrho in the following century, held that any argument supporting one side of a case could be balanced by a contrary argument of equal weight, so that the wise person suspends judgement and cultivates tranquillity and indifference to outward things. 'Academic' scepticism, associated with the Academy of Carneades, held that although the same evidence is always compatible with two contrary conclusions, some beliefs are more reasonable than others and we can act upon the balance of probabilities. *Montaigne and Pierre *Bayle in France and Joseph *Glanvill in England could combine scepticism with a devout theism, and sceptical techniques have frequently been practised by both supporters and opponents of religion to show that it rests on faith rather than reason. David *Hume carried the study to new lengths in his **Treatise of Human Nature* in a detailed analysis of the rational factors which generate scepticism and the psychological factors which allay or moderate it. Since the time of *Descartes critics of scepticism, particularly in religion and morals, have tended to depict it as a form of negative dogmatism, i.e. as seeking actually to deny the existence of anything whose nature is in doubt.

SCÈVE, Maurice (*c.*1500–1560) French poet and humanist, best known for his *Délie, objet de plus haute vertu* (1544), a sequence of 449 decasyllabic *dizains*, accompanied by 50 emblematic woodcuts, which is primarily concerned with the problems and conflicts of love. He also wrote a pastoral *eclogue, *La Saulsaye* (1547), and *Le Microcosme* (1562), an *epic poem dealing with the history of mankind since the fall of Adam. Writing in the **London Magazine*, Henry *Cary compared Scève to John *Donne.

SCHELLING, Friedrich Wilhelm Joseph von (1775–1854) German philosopher. Born in Leonberg, he studied at Tübingen, and on *Goethe's advice was appointed professor of philosophy at Jena in 1798 where he associated with such important figures in German *Romanticism as *Novalis, Ludwig Tieck (1773–1853), and the *Schlegel brothers. Initially a disciple of *Fichte's idealism, his ideas soon developed independently. His *Naturphilosophie* conceives nature as a single organism and as visible spirit, just as spirit is invisible nature. Schelling's early works include *Ideen zu einer Philosophie der Natur* (1797: *Ideas towards a Philosophy of Nature*), *System des transcendentalen Idealismus* (1800: *System of Transcendental Idealism*) and *Philosophische Untersuchungen* (1809: *Philosophical Investigations*). The relative clarity of these writings was sacrificed as his work moved increasingly in a mystical and quasi-religious direction, and his reputation as a philosopher suffered due to *Hegel's disparagement. Schelling's ideas on the relation of mind and nature were incorporated by S. T. *Coleridge, without acknowledgement, in his **Biographia Literaria* (1817).

SCHILLER, Johann Christoph Friedrich von (1759–1805) German dramatist and poet. Born in Marbach as the son of an army surgeon, he was educated in medicine at a military academy, but eventually rebelled against military discipline and fled the Stuttgart regiment to make his way in theatre. His first play *Die Räuber* (1781: *The Robbers*), the story of a nobleman who turns robber, caused a sensation at its first performance. It was quickly followed by three others—*Die Verschwörung des Fiesko zu Genua* (1783: *The Conspiracy of Fiesco at Genoa*), *Kabale und Liebe* (1784: *Cabal and Love*), and *Don Carlos* (1787)—which are regarded as his **Sturm und Drang* works, although the blank verse form of the last clearly marks a new phase in his development. In 1787 he settled in Weimar, then Germany's literary capital, where he embarked on studies in philosophy, especially aesthetics and *Kant's idealism, and history. Books on the revolt of the Netherlands against Spanish rule in the 16th century and the Thirty Years War led to his appointment, thanks to *Goethe's recommendation, as professor of history at Jena. The 1790s saw a series of important essays on various literary topics ranging from tragedy to the sublime. The most important of these, *Über naïve und sentimentalische Dichtung* (1795–6: *On Naive and Sentimental Poetry*), contributed a distinction between types of poetry still referred to in modern critical discourse. After a gap of ten years he returned to works for the stage with the *Wallenstein* trilogy (1797–1800), *Maria Stuart* (1801), *Die Jungfrau von Orleans* (1801: *The Maid of Orleans*), *Die Braut von Messina* (1803: *The Bride of Messina*), and *Wilhelm Tell* (1804), all verse plays frequently termed his 'classical' works. Schiller's reception in Britain dates from a lecture on German theatre by Henry *Mackenzie in 1788. During the 1790s German drama enjoyed a vogue in England, and both Matthew *Lewis and Walter *Scott produced translations of plays by Schiller. Almost from the first his work was admired as a critique of tyranny and political oppression, and it attracted none of the moral opprobrium which affected Goethe's reputation. Schiller had translated **Macbeth* and his admiration of *Shakespeare was a further reason for approval. His work was appreciated by William *Hazlitt and S. T. *Coleridge, who translated the two final parts of *Wallenstein*, and in 1825 Thomas *Carlyle's previously serialized *Life of Schiller* appeared in book form. Later in the century George *Eliot was an admirer, and Matthew *Arnold valued highly Schiller's correspondence with Goethe (the *Briefwechsel zwischen Schiller und Goethe*, 1828–9) for its many critical insights. Schiller's theatrical work also achieved notice through celebrated operatic adaptations by *Rossini (*Guillaume Tell*, 1829) and *Verdi (*Luisa Miller*, 1849, after *Kabale und Liebe*, and *Don Carlo*, 1869). Despite Edward *Bulwer-Lytton's translation of the poetry (*Poems and Ballads of Schiller*, 1844) Schiller's verse has been less widely known and appreciated here; the 'Ode to Joy' (*An die Freude*, 1782), familiar chiefly through its setting by *Beethoven in the Ninth Symphony, is the exception. In the 20th century *Maria Stuart* was translated and adapted by

Stephen *Spender (1959), and the second centenary of his death was marked in England by notable and successful London productions of this play (trans. Peter Oswald) and of *Don Carlos* (adapted by Mike Poulton) with Derek Jacobi as King Philip. See T. J. Reed, *Schiller* (1991); Lesley Sharpe, *Friedrich Schiller: Drama, Thought, and Politics* (1991).

SCHLEGEL, August Wilhelm von (1767–1845) German scholar, critic, and translator. He studied at Göttingen, and with his brother Friedrich *Schlegel co-edited *Das Athenäum* (1798–1800), the most important journal for early German Romantic writers such as *Novalis. His fame, however, was established chiefly by his verse translations—with Ludwig Tieck (1773–1853) and others—of *Shakespeare's plays and his series of lectures *Über dramatische Kunst und Literatur* (1809–11). These were translated by John Black (1783–1855) as *Lectures on Dramatic Art and Literature* (1815), and those dealing with Shakespeare were greatly admired by William *Wordsworth and William *Hazlitt. In his own lecture series of 1811 S. T. *Coleridge borrowed ideas and passages from Schlegel without acknowledgement.

SCHLEGEL, Friedrich von (1772–1829) German critic, essayist, and scholar. The younger brother of A. W. *Schlegel, he studied law and classics at Göttingen and Leipzig. He is notable for his studies in the history of literature, particularly *Geschichte der alten und neuen Literatur* (1815), trans. John *Lockhart as *Lectures on the History of Literature, Ancient and Modern* (1818) and his work on Sanskrit language and poetry, *Sprache und Weisheit der Inder* (1808: *Language and Wisdom of the Indians*) which was an important early contribution to oriental studies in the West. His critical fragments and essays, many of them published in the periodical he wrote with his brother, *Das Athenäum* (1798–1800), were particularly fertile and made him a leading figure in the German *Romantic movement. His early creative efforts, the novel *Lucinde* (1799) and the tragedy *Alarcos* (1802), though the sexual frankness of the former caused a sensation, are of less significance.

SCHOENBAUM, Samuel (1927–96) American scholar. His *Shakespeare's Lives* (1970; rev. 1991) is a scintillating history of accounts of Shakespeare's life; his *William Shakespeare: A Documentary Life* (1975) reproduces and comments authoritatively on most of the relevant documents; it was revised as *William Shakespeare: A Compact Documentary Life* (1977). A supplementary volume is *William Shakespeare: Records and Images* (1981).
See also SHAKESPEARE: AUTHORSHIP OF THE WORKS.

'Scholar-Gipsy, The' A poem by Matthew *Arnold, published 1853. The poem, pastoral in setting, is loosely based on a tale narrated by Joseph *Glanvill in *The Vanity of Dogmatizing*. Arnold's version concerns an 'Oxford scholar poor', who, tired of seeking preferment, joined the gypsies to learn their lore, roamed with them, and still haunts the Oxford countryside. With this is woven a vivid evocation of the places Arnold visited with his Oxford friends (Bagley Wood, Hinksey, the Cumnor moors, etc.) and reflections on the contrast between the single-minded faith of the scholar-gypsy and the modern world, 'the strange disease of modern life, | With its sick hurry, its divided aims'. The tone, as in many of Arnold's best works, is elegiac though it hails nonetheless a figure who has avoided modern contamination. 'The Gipsy Scholar at best awakens a pleasing melancholy', said Arnold later. 'But this is not what we want.'

scholasticism The doctrines of medieval schoolmen, and the theological and philosophical teachings of the period 1100–1500, mainly an attempt to reconcile *Aristotle with the Scriptures, and Reason with Faith. It is characterized by its dialectical method of argument, often associated with *Abelard. Its best-known monument is the *Summa Theologica* of *Aquinas. Between the 14th and the 16th centuries, scholasticism gradually exhausted itself as an intellectual movement. See M. Colish, *Medieval Foundations of the Western Intellectual Tradition, 400–1400* (1997).

School for Scandal, The A comedy by R. B. *Sheridan, produced with great success at Drury Lane in May 1777; the prologue was by David *Garrick and the epilogue by George *Colman. The play contrasts two brothers: Joseph Surface, a sanctimonious hypocrite, and Charles, a good-natured, reckless spendthrift. Charles is in love with Maria, the ward of Sir Peter Teazle; Joseph is courting the same girl for her fortune, while at the same time dallying with Lady Teazle, a young woman whom Sir Peter has recently married and whose flirting and frivolity torments him. Her social group is the 'school for scandal', the gossips Sir Benjamin Backbite, Crabtree, Lady Sneerwell, and Mrs Candour. Sir Oliver Surface, the rich uncle of Joseph and Charles, returns unexpectedly from India, and decides to test the characters of his nephews. He visits Charles disguised as a moneylender, Mr Premium, and Charles, always short of money, cheerfully sells him the family portraits, with the exception of the portrait of 'the ill-looking little fellow over the settee', who is Sir Oliver himself; by this he unwittingly wins the old man's heart. Meanwhile Joseph receives a visit from Lady Teazle and attempts to seduce her. The arrival of Sir Peter obliges Lady Teazle to hide behind a screen, where she is filled with remorse as she listens to proof of Sir Peter's generosity to her, even though he suspects her of infidelity with Charles. At the arrival of Charles, Sir Peter hides in a cupboard, and hears enough conversation to show that his suspicions of Charles were unfounded. On Joseph's leaving the room, Sir Peter emerges and he and Charles agree to reveal the 'little French milliner' who, according to Joseph, is hiding behind the screen. Lady Teazle is revealed instead, and begs Sir Peter's forgiveness. Joseph returns, to be upbraided by both. Sir Oliver then enters in the character of a needy relative. Joseph refuses assistance, giving as his reason the avarice of his uncle, Sir Oliver, thus finally revealing his character. Charles is united to Maria, and Sir Peter and Lady Teazle are happily reconciled.

Schoolmaster, The See Ascham, Roger.

School of Abuse, The See Gosson, Stephen.

School of Night A name drawn from a line in William *Shakespeare's *Love's Labour's Lost* (IV. iii), and first ascribed by Arthur Acheson in *Shakespeare and the Rival Poet* (1903) to a supposed circle of speculative thinkers, led by Thomas *Harriot and Walter *Ralegh, and including Christopher *Marlowe, George *Chapman, the explorer Lawrence Keymis (1564/5–1618), and the 'Wizard Earl', Henry Percy, ninth earl of Northumberland (1564–1632). J. Dover *Wilson, G. B. Harrison in his edition of *Willobie his Avisa* (1926), and M. C. Bradbrook in *The School of Night* (1936) supported the theory that Shakespeare's play was an attack upon this coterie, which engaged in free-thinking philosophical debate (not necessarily atheistic) and dabbled in hermeticism, alchemy, and the occult. The existence of such a secret society is now widely disbelieved.

school stories A genre associated with writing for children. The earliest examples—beginning with Sarah *Fielding's *The Governess, or Little Female Academy* (1749)—were essentially didactic. The basic elements of the modern school story (the new child, the bully, codes of behaviour) were established in Harriet *Martineau's 'The Crofton Boys' (1841) and Thomas Hughes's **Tom Brown's School Days* (1857). Despite being debunked by Rudyard *Kipling's neo-realistic *Stalky & Co.* (1899), school stories were hugely popular in the early 20th century with writers like Charles *Hamilton and Angela *Brazil. They survive in J. K. *Rowling's 'Harry Potter' books. *See also* Blyton, Enid (Malory Towers); Brent-Dyer, Elinor (Chalet School).

SCHOPENHAUER, Arthur (1788–1860) German philosopher, born in Danzig. After a schooling which included a brief period in England, he studied science and philosophy at Göttingen, Berlin, and Jena. His principal work *Die Welt als Wille und Vorstellung* (1819: *The World as Will and Idea*), without attempting to construct a philosophical system, articulates a profoundly pessimistic view of existence, denying free will and the existence of god as illusions. As a young lecturer in Berlin he attempted, unsuccessfully, to challenge *Hegel's preeminence there, but achieved recognition in later life. His work, which influenced Richard *Wagner, Friedrich *Nietzsche, Thomas *Mann, and Ludwig *Wittgenstein, is sometimes seen as anticipating Sigmund *Freud's psychology of the unconscious. Various claims for his influence on English literature have been made, from George *Eliot, to Joseph *Conrad, and Samuel *Beckett. See B. Magee, *The Philosophy of Schopenhauer* (1997).

SCHREINER, Olive (1855–1920) Writer, born in Cape Colony, South Africa, the daughter of a missionary. She began to write while working as a governess, and when she came to England in 1881 had completed her best-known novel, *The *Story of an African Farm*, published to much acclaim in 1883 under the pseudonym 'Ralph Iron'. Set in the vividly evoked landscape of her childhood, it recounts the lives of two orphaned cousins, stay-at-home Em and unconventional Lyndall, greeted by feminists as one of the first *'New Women', who breaks away from her Bible-belt origins, becomes pregnant by a lover whom she refuses to marry, and dies after the death of her baby; also of Waldo, son of the farm's German overseer, whose rebellious spirit is aroused (as was Schreiner's) by reading Herbert *Spencer's *First Principles*. This novel won her the friendship of Havelock *Ellis, and while in England she moved in progressive literary and political circles, returning in 1889 to South Africa, where she married the farmer and politician Samuel Cron Cronwright. In 1914 she came back to England, returning to the Cape to die. Her other novels, both with feminist themes, *From Man to Man* (1927) and *Undine* (1929), appeared posthumously. Works published during her lifetime include collections of allegories and stories, articles on South African politics, *Trooper Peter Halkett of Mashonaland* (1897; an attack on Cecil Rhodes's activities), and *Woman and Labour* (1911). Courageous and unconventional as a woman and public figure, Schreiner has been acknowledged as a pioneer both in her treatment of women and in her fictional use of the African landscape. See Ruth First and Ann Scott, *Olive Schreiner* (1980); Joyce Avrech Berkman, *The Healing Imagination of Olive Schreiner* (1989); Cherry Clayton, *Olive Schreiner* (1997).

SCHUBERT, Franz (1797–1828) Austrian composer, successor to *Haydn, *Mozart, and *Beethoven in the Viennese classical school of symphonic, chamber, and piano composition. Schubert also wrote more than 600 songs for voice and piano, mostly settings of popular German poets such as *Schiller, *Goethe, and *Heine. About 24 songs have a British origin, though all were set in German translation; these include versions of Abraham *Cowley, Alexander *Pope, and Colley *Cibber's 'The Blind Boy'. Ten settings of passages from *Ossian, and the Scottish ballad *Edward*, indicate an interest in romantic Scotland, also typified in the songs Schubert drew from Walter *Scott, especially Ellen's three songs from *The *Lady of the Lake* (1825) which include the 'Ave Maria'. From the same source came the part-song 'Coronach'. Three more Scott songs, 'Lied der Anne Lyle', 'Gesang der Norna', and 'Romanze des Richard Löwenherz' (from **Ivanhoe*), were written at the same time, though not published until 1828. Most famous of all, however, are the Shakespeare settings of 1826, including 'Hark, hark, the lark' and 'Who is Sylvia?'

SCHULBERG, Budd (1914–2009) American novelist and screenwriter, born in New York, who is best known for his novel about a cynical opportunist achieving success in Hollywood, *What Makes Sammy Run?* (1941). Schulberg was a leading screenwriter and fictionalized his collaboration with F. Scott *Fitzgerald in *The Disenchanted* (1950). See Nicholas Beck, *Budd Schulberg* (2001).

SCHUMANN, Robert (1810–56) German composer and writer on music, with strong literary interests. Schumann's first major choral work, *Das Paradies und die Peri* (1843), was a setting of Thomas *Moore's **Lalla Rookh*, treated as a kind of secular oratorio. After failing to finish an opera based on Lord *Byron's **Corsair*, begun in 1844, Schumann produced incidental music for Byron's **Manfred* (1849), apparently envisaging (unlike Byron) a stage presentation. Schumann also wrote an overture to **Julius Caesar* (1852). One Shakespeare song, 'When that I was', from **Twelfth Night*, in the new translation by Ludwig Tieck and *Schlegel, appeared in 1840. Schumann made many part-song and solo settings of Robert *Burns: eight were included in the *Myrthen* cycle (1840), with a Byron song, 'Mein Herz ist schwer'. Schumann made three settings from Byron's *Hebrew Melodies* in 1849. His five *Gedichte der Königin Maria Stuart* (1852) set texts attributed to *Mary Queen of Scots.

SCHUYLER, James (1923–1991) American poet, born in Chicago, who later became a leading figure in the *New York School. He served as a curator in the New York Museum of Modern Art (1955–1961) and began publishing his collections with *Alfred and Guinevere* (1958). His early poetry uses Dadaist techniques and his later work evokes day-to-day situations in concrete detail. Schuyler was a close friend of Frank *O'Hara and John *Ashbery, collaborating with the latter on a novel, *A Nest of Ninnies* (1969).

SCHWARTZ, Delmore (1913–68) American poet and short story writer, born into a Jewish family in New York. He achieved early recognition with his family-dream story 'In Dreams Begin Responsibilities', published in 1937 in the **Partisan Review* (which he was later to edit, 1943–55). *The World is a Wedding* (1948) is a collection of stories; *Shenandoah* (1941) is a verse drama. Volumes of verse include *Summer Knowledge* (1959) and *Last and Lost Poems* (1979). Schwartz's decline into drinking and loneliness and his death in a cheap hotel room created a 'doomed poet' legend, and inspired elegies from John *Berryman. Saul *Bellow depicted him in *Humboldt's Gift* (1975). See James Atlas, *Delmore Schwartz* (1977).

SCIASCIA, Leonardo (1921–89) Italian novelist, essayist, and journalist, city councillor for Palermo (1975–7), and Radical MP (1979). Almost all his writings are concerned with his native Sicily and aim through historical enquiry, *detective fiction, and political and personal observation to expose the endemic corruption and criminal collusion of the island's society past and present, and more widely of Italian politics. His best-known works are *Il giorno della civetta* (1961: *The Day of the Owl*) whose title is derived from Shakespeare's *3 Henry VI; Candido*, a homage to *Voltaire as well as a critique of Sicily in the later 20th century, and *L'Affaire Moro*, Sciascia's *Zolaesque denunciation of the terrorism and the political shenanigans which led to the death of the Italian prime minister Aldo Moro.

science, the literature of Science writing is built on the Victorian belief that important scientific ideas should be communicated to a wide audience. Charles Lyell (1797–1875) with his *Principles of Geology* (1830–3) and Charles *Darwin, with a stream of successful books, were 19th-century pioneers, but John *Tyndall was also an important popularizer. His American tours rivalled the success of those of Charles *Dickens. The periodical *Nature*, edited by Norman Lockyer, was founded in 1869 to bring scientific information to the public, with the support of Darwin, T. H. *Huxley, and Tyndall. The archetypal 20th-century scientist, Albert Einstein (1879–1955), wrote about his scientific work (notably in *The Theory of Relativity*, 1905) and also about wider issues (*Why War?*, 1933; *The World as I See It*, 1935). But the widest publicity for the theory of relativity came from astronomer Arthur Eddington (1882–1944), an early contributor to the great tradition of astronomers who have written accessibly. Eddington's contemporary James Jeans (1877–1946), also an active astronomer, had no university post after 1912 but devoted himself to popular books and broadcasting.

In the biological sciences, Julian Huxley (1887–1975) summed up the theory of evolution for both scientists and lay persons with *Evolution: The Modern Synthesis* (1942), while a quantum physicist turned biologist, Erwin Schrödinger (1887–1961), pointed the way to an understanding of the genetic code with his enormously influential *What is Life?* (1944). Among those who were impressed was Francis Crick (1916–2004), who, with James Watson (1928–), determined the structure of DNA. Watson went on to write the best-seller *The Double Helix* (1968), and other genetic researchers, notably Jacques Monod (1910–76) with *Chance and Necessity* (1970), presented their ideas to a wide public. Sir Peter Medawar (1915–87), zoologist and immunologist, addressed a large readership with works such as *The Future of Man* (1960) and *The Limits of Science* (1984). George Gamow (1904–68) also became an important scientific interpreter, particularly with his 'Mr Tompkins' series. In the late 20th century, the stars have been the vociferously atheist biologist Richard Dawkins (1941–), Stephen Jay Gould (1941–2002), and the Pulitzer Prize-winning Edward O. Wilson (1929–), author of *On Human Nature* (1978) and *The Diversity of Life* (1992). Other scientists who became successful writers include Fred Hoyle (1915–2001) and Nobel Prize-winning physicist Richard Feynman (1918–88). The phenomenal sales of *A Brief History of Time* (1988) by Stephen Hawking (1942–) have created a flood of books by scientists, and the genre continues to flourish.

Scientific progress led to the rise of *science fiction: although much of what is called science fiction today is actually *fantasy, there is a sub-genre, known as *'hard science fiction', which presents science and scientists realistically. The great exponents of hard science fiction in its heyday of the 1950s were Isaac *Asimov and Arthur C. *Clarke: practitioners also include Gregory *Benford (*Against Infinity*, 1983; *Across the Sea of Suns*, 1984), John Cramer (*Twistor*, 1989), and Hal Clement (*Heavy Planet*, 2002).

science fiction There are many definitions of science fiction (SF), all incomplete. Differences between E. E. *Smith's

'Lensman' series, begun in 1937, and Margaret *Atwood's *Oryx and Crake* (2003) might be more numerous than similarities, yet experienced readers recognize them as, in some way, belonging to the same category. A useful description (rather than definition) is that of critic Paul Kincaid (1952–), suggesting a series of generic or sub-generic strands braided together, any one of which may be removed (still leaving 'science fiction') but none of which *is* the genre. 'Science fiction' suggests a hybrid, not quite ordinary fiction, not quite science, yet partaking of both. Beneath the label, we might find utopianism / dystopianism, *fantasy, *horror, or books on UFOs. One of the pleasures of reading this fiction is that it challenges readers to decide whether what they are reading is within the bounds of the possible. The machine of H. G. *Wells's *The Time Machine* (1895) is an impossibility as far as we know; but the book has been taken seriously as both sociological and cosmological speculation ever since its publication.

Another broad definition of science fiction is that it considers the mythologies of power: to travel through time or space, to enter the thoughts of another, to overcome death, or the process of evolutionary forces. The long-running TV series **Star Trek* utilizes all these elements. In this way it is able, within a predictable format, to produce those surprises which are a vital part of the genre.

Such features, touching on basic human fears, have a long ancestry. There are science fiction-like speculations in many periods. Mary *Shelley's **Frankenstein* (1818) reflects on the levers of power and human control. Shelley was well versed in the science of her time, rejecting any kind of supernatural agency in Victor Frankenstein's creation of life. Only when Frankenstein has engaged in scientific research does he achieve the seemingly impossible, giving us an iconic thought-experiment whereby we may examine the workings of the mind and the consequences of 'ardent curiosity'. As if she wished to be understood as the mother of science fiction, Shelley published *The Last Man* in 1826: a plague wipes out all humanity except for one man. It was less successful than *Frankenstein*, but was followed by Jane Louden Webb's *The Mummy!* (1827), which drew on both of Shelley's great texts. Science fiction became a genre, without yet having a name.

Jules *Verne's vigorous adventure writings, such as *Journey to the Centre of the Earth* (1864), proved to be the next great worldwide success. Yet Wells was the great innovator, perfecting many themes, such as invasion, invention, and time travel, which have since been extensively cultivated. His influence touched Olaf *Stapledon, who in *Star Maker* presents a vision of the cosmos, past, present, and to come. C. S. *Lewis's *Out of the Silent Planet* (1938) is written against Wells's secular, scientific progressivism. Through reprints in Hugo *Gernsback's magazines, Wells was introduced to a new generation of American readers.

The invention in the 1880s of linotype machines, cheaper and faster than their predecessors, led to a proliferation of magazines, all avid for short stories. **Amazing Stories*, beginning publication in 1926, fostered a vigorous fandom. The 1950s 'Paperback Revolution' increased the number of novels available as readers looked towards the coming Space Age. With television, another channel opened. Science fiction's ability to generate strange and striking images had made it an ideal medium for visual effects. Both the movies (with Georges Mélies (1861–1938)) and British television (with Nigel Kneale's Quatermass series and George Orwell's **Nineteen Eighty-Four*) first acquired their mass audiences with science-fictional themes. The computer has again diversified and diluted the original strain of ideas.

British science fiction was perhaps less cut off from the main vein of literary culture than its American cousin. Edward *Bulwer-Lytton, Rudyard *Kipling, E. M. *Forster, Aldous *Huxley, George *Orwell, Kingsley *Amis, Anthony *Burgess, and, most considerably, Doris *Lessing have all written in this mode. In the 1960s, the British magazine *New Worlds* was taken over and transformed by Michael *Moorcock. Among Moorcock's revolutionaries, the names of J. G. *Ballard and Brian *Aldiss stand out. These three followed the English pattern, writing in other modes without entirely forsaking science fiction. Events, however, made the USA the centre of a science-fictional industry which encroaches not only on movies and television, but also on such institutions as NASA; it is no coincidence that the revival of science fiction in China coincides with its space programme. Inevitably, the wider popularity of science fiction has sometimes led to a dilution of challenging ideas. Yet there are those who still succeed in making readers think while being entertained. Among these are authors of long standing, such as Arthur C. *Clarke, who commanded a worldwide audience with *Childhood's End* (1953), and his collaboration with Stanley Kubrick (1928–99); Stephen *Baxter; and the idiosyncratic Iain M. *Banks, who rose to prominence with his first novel, *The Wasp Factory* (1984). The creator of Discworld, Terry *Pratchett, has been an immensely popular and productive contributor to the field. Some of the best-known names in the international language of science fiction have been American. A. E. *Van Vogt, Robert *Heinlein, Philip K. *Dick, Frank *Herbert, Harry *Harrison, Ursula K. *Le Guin, William *Burroughs, William *Gibson and the *cyberpunks, Gregory *Benford, and Greg *Bear. Bear's *Blood Music* (1985) is all that science fiction should be: its narrative makes us see the world anew.

A significant development in recent years has been the growth of science fiction scholarship. Institutions like the SFRA (Science Fiction Research Association) and the lively IAFA (International Association for the Fantastic in the Arts) publish learned papers and hold annual conferences. The *Science Fiction Foundation, with its research library in Liverpool, is the British equivalent. See Brian W. Aldiss, with David Wingrove, *Trillion Year Spree: The History of Science Fiction* (1986); John Clute and Peter Nicholls (eds), *The Encyclopaedia of Science Fiction* (1993).

science fiction drama One of the first major works of 20th-century *science fiction was a play: Karel *Čapek's *R.U.R. (Rossum's Universal Robots)*. George Bernard *Shaw's *Back to Methusaleh* (1931) and J. B. *Priestley's *Time and the Conways* (1937) treat classic science fiction themes like time and the future of humanity, but little subsequent science fiction, with the exception of Ray *Bradbury's adaptation of his own work, has found its way into the theatre. Ken *Campbell's 'Science fiction theatre of Liverpool' in the late 1970s was humorous and imaginative. The concerns if not the form of some kinds of science fiction feature in Tom *Stoppard's explorations of science and knowledge, while Alan *Ayckbourn (*Henceforward*, 1987) has used straightforward science fiction tropes, including robots. However, science fiction's sense of spectacle often sits uneasily in the theatre unless the audience's imagination can make amends for lack of special effects. In contrast, radio and television drama are fruitful areas.

Science Fiction Foundation Established by authors and researchers in 1971 at the North East London Polytechnic, the Foundation aids research into *science fiction through the critical journal *Foundation* and its important research library and archive (now administered by the University of Liverpool).

science fiction poetry Science fiction's experiments with image and language make it fertile territory for poetry. Practitioners include Thomas M. *Disch, Ursula K. *Le Guin, and Brian *Aldiss. D. M. *Thomas's poems in **New Worlds*, and the anthology *Holding your Eight Hands* (1970) stimulated interest in Britain, where science fiction is a significant part of the work of the Scottish poet Edwin *Morgan. Longer examples include *Aniara* (1956) by the Swedish Harry Martinson (1904–78). The Science Fiction Poetry Association (founded by Suzette Haden *Elgin) offers an annual 'Rhysling' Award.

scientific romance A term taken from C. H. Hinton's collection *Scientific Romances* (1886) to describe the fiction and non-fiction which would draw upon scientific speculations to become what was later called *science fiction. It was particularly applied to the work of H. G. *Wells. In Britain particularly, the term may be said to describe the Wellsian legacy: a more reflective and literary tradition than the stories of inventor-heroes or action-adventure tales featured in the American 'pulp' magazines.

Scilla's Metamorphosis A poem by Thomas *Lodge, first published 1589, and later (1610) as *Glaucus and Scilla*. The earliest of many Ovidian epyllia, or minor epics, in the Elizabethan period, it describes the sea god Glaucus' courtship of the nymph Scilla, who is punished for her cruelty to him by being metamorphosed into a lonely rock in the sea. It bears a generic and a specific relationship to William *Shakespeare's **Venus and Adonis*, including a brief account of Adonis' death beginning: 'He that hath seen the sweet *Arcadian* boy | Wiping the purple from his forced wound.'

SCOGAN, Henry (?1361–1407) The dedicatee of *Chaucer's 'Lenvoy a Scogan'. His only surviving literary work is the 'Moral Balade' (*c.*1406/7), probably dedicated to the four sons of Henry IV to whom he was tutor. The 'Balade' appears in vol. vii of W. W. *Skeat's edition of Chaucer's *Works* (1897).

SCOGGIN (Scogan), John (*fl.* 1480) Allegedly Edward IV's celebrated jester, whose exploits, real or imagined, are recorded in *The Jests of Skogyn* (*c.*1570). He was associated with Henry *Scogan.

SCOT, Reginald *See* SCOTT, REGINALD.

Scots A historical offshoot of the Northumbrian dialect of Anglo-Saxon. The precise measure to which the Anglian of Lothian and the Anglo-Danish of Yorkshire were intermediaries in its development has been disputed. Gaelic, French (Parisian as well as Norman), and Dutch elements combined to enhance the distinctiveness of Lowland speech, to which the political independence of Scotland gave national significance. Scots became the vehicle of a considerable poetic literature in John *Barbour, Robert *Henryson, William *Dunbar, Gawin *Douglas, and Sir David *Lindsay. The Union of Crowns in 1603 and of Parliaments in 1707 served, along with the general acceptance of the Authorized Version (*see* BIBLE, THE ENGLISH), to extend the influence of English and prevent the evolution of an all-purpose Scots prose. The 18th-century literary revival of Scots by Allan *Ramsay, Robert *Fergusson, and Robert *Burns was confined to poetry. In fiction from Walter *Scott, through Robert Louis *Stevenson and the *'Kailyard school' to Nan *Shepherd, Scots has been used mainly to represent rural speech. While some 20th-century poets (e.g. Hugh *MacDiarmid and Sydney Goodsir *Smith) attempted to develop the range of Scots to include modern themes, others, like William *Soutar and Robert *Garioch, wrote in a more colloquial idiom, a practice in which they have been followed by contemporary poets like Kathleen *Jamie and Don *Paterson (who write mainly in English). In Northern Ireland since the 1990s there have been attempts to revive for literary purposes the Ulster Scots that flourished briefly in the work of the *Rhyming Weavers. See the online *Dictionary of the Scots Language* (www.dsl.ac.uk).

Scots Musical Museum, The (1787–1803) Song collection edited by James Johnson (*c.*1750–1811) in six volumes. Each volume contained 100 songs, presented in each case by melody and bass. The songs, one-third of them by Robert *Burns, who acted as editorial adviser to the project, were variously antique, refurbished, and new.

'Scots wha hae' A battle song by Robert *Burns composed in 1793. It is the anthem of the Scottish National Party.

SCOTT, C. P. *See* MANCHESTER GUARDIAN.

SCOTT, Geoffrey (1884–1929) Poet and biographer, son of a Unitarian manufacturer and nephew of C. P. Scott, editor of the **Manchester Guardian*. He was educated at Rugby School and New College, Oxford, where he won the

*Newdigate Prize in 1906. His interest in architectural theory was confirmed by his friendship with Bernard *Berenson, and culminated in his study *The Architecture of Humanism* (1914). Scott had great conversational talents, which, combined with what the artist William Rothenstein (1872–1945) described as his 'Botticellian' beauty, made him disastrously attractive to women, not least, it would appear, to Berenson's wife Mary. Scott's best-known book is *The Portrait of Zélide* (1925), an elegant and evocative life of Isabelle de *Charrière which his friend Edith *Wharton described as a 'wellnigh perfect' book. In the same year appeared *Four Tales* by de Charrière, translated by Scott's wife Lady Sybil (née Cuffe; d. 1943). Scott was working on a biography of James *Boswell when he died.

SCOTT, John (1783–1821) Educated at the same Aberdeen school as Lord *Byron; the first editor, 1820–1, of the remarkable *London Magazine*; he had previously edited *The Champion*, and published *A Visit to Paris* (1814) and *Paris Revisited* (1816), books whose admirers included William *Wordsworth. He was impressed by *Blackwood's Magazine*'s 'spirit of life', and based the *London* on roughly the same plan, but with a greater emphasis on original writing. He attracted a brilliant set of contributors; Thomas De Quincey's *Confessions of an English Opium Eater*, Charles *Lamb's earlier 'Elia' essays, and much of William *Hazlitt's *Table-Talk* first appeared in the *London Magazine*, as well as work by John *Keats, John *Clare, Thomas *Hood, George *Darley, Thomas *Carlyle, Allan *Cunningham, and others. His reviewers aimed to praise rather than to condemn, and were permitted no political bias. Scott's own writing on Wordsworth, Walter *Scott, P. B. *Shelley, Keats, Byron, and other young writers is of high quality. Conflict with *Blackwood's* was inevitable; he came to detest what he saw as its 'duplicity and treachery', and he felt obliged to defend his *'Cockney School'. His attacks on *Blackwood's*, in particular on John *Lockhart, led to a series of confusions which culminated in a duel with J. H. Christie, a close friend of Lockhart, in which Scott was killed. See P. O'Leary, *Regency Editor* (1983).

SCOTT, Melissa (1960–) American *science fiction writer, born in Little Rock, Arkansas. Her vividly imagined novels like *Trouble and her Friends* (1994) and *The Jazz* (2000) often engage with the themes of *cyberpunk—computer-hacking, virtual reality, an all-pervasive internet—from a feminist perspective, subtly undermining assumptions about, for instance, sexuality.

SCOTT (SCOT), **Michael** (d. *c.*1235) A Scottish scholar, possibly born at Balwearie, who studied at Oxford, Bologna, and Paris, and was attached to the court of Frederick II at Palermo, probably in the capacity of official astrologer. He translated works of *Aristotle from Arabic to Latin (including *De Anima*, pre-1220), and perhaps *Averroës' great Aristotelian Commentary. Because the science he studied was astronomy, legends of his magical power grew up and served as a theme for many writers from the disapproving *Dante (*Inferno*, XX. 116) to Walter Scott in *The *Lay of the Last Minstrel*. Works of his on astronomy and alchemy, and various translations, still remain in manuscript. See Lynn Thorndike, *Michael Scot* (1965).

SCOTT, Paul (1920–78) Novelist, born in north London, educated at Winchmore Hill Collegiate School (a private establishment which he was forced to leave at the age of 14 when his family ran into financial difficulties); he began a career in accountancy before conscription into the army in 1940. After being posted to India in 1943, he returned to Britain in 1946 and worked in publishing and for a literary agency. His first novel, *Johnnie Sahib* (1952), was followed by six others, often drawing on his experiences with the armed forces and in India. But it is the four novels known as the *Raj Quartet*—*The Jewel in the Crown* (1966), *The Day of the Scorpion* (1968), *The Towers of Silence* (1971), and *A Division of the Spoils* (1975)—which constitute his major achievement. Set in India during and immediately after the Second World War, these interlinked narratives, which brilliantly deploy a wide diversity of viewpoints and settings, give a panoramic picture, teeming with vividly realized characters, of political, personal, racial, and religious conflicts in the period leading up to Independence and Partition. A coda to this epic undertaking, Scott's last novel, *Staying On* (1977, *Booker Prize), looks at the new India through the eyes of two minor characters from the Quartet, the emblematically named Smalleys, who have remained after Independence and attempted to adjust to changed conditions. After the success of a fine television adaptation of *Staying On* in 1980, the *Raj Quartet* was televised to wide acclaim in fourteen parts in 1984 as *The Jewel in the Crown*.

SCOTT (SCOT), **Reginald** (d. 1599) Educated at Hart Hall (now Hertford College), Oxford, and MP for New Romney, 1589, author of *A Perfect Platform of a Hop Garden* (1574) and *The Discovery of Witchcraft* (1584). Written with the aim of preventing the persecution of poor, aged, and simple people who were popularly believed to be witches, *The Discovery* exposed the impostures and credulity that supported the common belief in sorcery. Scott's learned scepticism about witches was attacked by the future *James I.

SCOTT, Robert Falcon (1868–1912) Antarctic explorer, born near Devonport; he joined the navy as a boy. He described his first Antarctic expedition (1901–4), which sledged further south than anyone previously, in *The Voyage of the 'Discovery'* (1905). His second expedition (1910–12) became an epic tragedy when his party, beaten by Amundsen in a race to the Pole, perished on the harrowing trek back. His final diaries, published as *Scott's Last Expedition* (1913), and other accounts, including Apsley *Cherry-Garrard's, told a heroic story of nobility and bravery sacrificed for empire, though some questioned his leadership. Literary versions of the tragedy include Douglas Stewart's verse drama *The Fire on the*

Snow (1941), Ted Tally's play *Terra Nova* (1977), and Beryl Bainbridge's novel *The Birthday Boys* (1991).

SCOTT, Sarah (1723–95) Née Robinson, novelist, sister of Elizabeth *Montagu. After a brief marriage (1751–2), ending in legal separation, she lived in Bath with Lady Barbara Montagu (*c.*1722–1765), engaging in small-scale philanthropy on an income supplemented by the proceeds of writing. Between 1750 and 1772 she published, anonymously, five novels, a translation of a French novel, and three historical works, including *The History of Gustavus Ericson, King of Sweden* (1761). The hero of *Sir George Ellison* (1766), perhaps conceived in the wake of Samuel Richardson's *Sir Charles *Grandison*, first appeared in her best-known novel, the utopian **Millenium Hall* (1762).

SCOTT, Thomas (1747–1821) Clergyman, autobiographer, and biblical scholar, born in Lincolnshire, the son of a farmer. As a curate in Buckinghamshire he was strongly influenced by John *Newton, whose *evangelical views he originally resisted. In his much-reprinted spiritual autobiography *The Force of Truth* (1779), which William *Cowper polished stylistically, he described his intellectual journey from fashionable Socinian or *unitarian views back to *Calvinist ones. He wrote an influential commentary on the *Bible (4 vols, 1788–92), originally published in weekly numbers.

SCOTT, Sir Walter (1771–1832) Author, son of Walter Scott, a lawyer. Scott was born in College Wynd, Edinburgh, educated at Edinburgh High School and University, and apprenticed to his father. He was called to the bar in 1792. His interest in the old Border tales and ballads was stimulated by Thomas Percy's **Reliques* and by the study of the old romantic poetry of France and Italy and of the modern German poets. After exploring the Border country, in 1797 he published anonymously *The Chase and William and Helen*, a translation of Bürger's 'Der wilde Jäger' ('The *Wild Huntsman') and *'Lenore', and in 1799 a translation of *Goethe's *Götz von Berlichingen*. In 1797 he married Margaret Charlotte Charpentier, or Carpenter (1770–1826), daughter of Jean Charpentier of Lyons in France, and was appointed sheriff-depute of Selkirkshire in 1799. In 1802–3 appeared the three volumes of Scott's **Minstrelsy of the Scottish Border*; and in 1805 his first considerable original work, the romantic poem *The *Lay of the Last Minstrel*. He then became a partner in James *Ballantyne's printing business and published **Marmion* in 1808. This was followed by *The *Lady of the Lake* (1810), **Rokeby* and *The Bridal of Triermain* (1813), *The Lord of the Isles* (1815), and *Harold the Dauntless* (1817), his last long poem. In 1809 he had entered into partnership with James's brother John Ballantyne in the bookselling business known as 'John Ballantyne & Co.', and in 1811 he had purchased the estate he renamed Abbotsford on the Tweed, where he built himself a substantial house. Scott supported the foundation in 1809 of the Tory **Quarterly Review*, after ceasing his contributions to the **Edinburgh Review*, alienated by its Whig attitude. In 1813 he refused the offer of the *poet laureateship and recommended Robert *Southey for the honour. Eclipsed by Lord *Byron's fame as a poet, in spite of the popularity of his verse romances, he now turned his attention to the novel as a means of expressing his erudition, humour, and sympathies. His novels appeared anonymously in the following order: **Waverley* (1814); **Guy Mannering* (1815); *The *Antiquary* (1816); *The *Black Dwarf* and **Old Mortality* (1816), as the first series of **Tales of my Landlord*; **Rob Roy* (1817); *The *Heart of Midlothian* (1818), the second series of *Tales of my Landlord*; *The *Bride of Lammermoor* and *A *Legend of Montrose* (1819), the third series of *Tales of my Landlord*; **Ivanhoe* (1819); *The *Monastery* (1820); *The *Abbot* (1820); **Kenilworth* (1821); *The *Pirate* (1821); *The *Fortunes of Nigel* (1822); **Peveril of the Peak* (1823); **Quentin Durward* (1823); **St Ronan's Well* (1823); **Redgauntlet* (1824); *The *Betrothed* and *The *Talisman* (1825), together as *Tales of the Crusaders*; **Woodstock* (1826); **Chronicles of the Canongate* (1827, containing 'The Highland Widow', 'The *Two Drovers', and 'The *Surgeon's Daughter'); *Chronicles of the Canongate* (2nd series): *Saint Valentine's Day, or The *Fair Maid of Perth* (1828); **Anne of Geierstein* (1829); *Tales of my Landlord* (4th series): **Count Robert of Paris* and **Castle Dangerous* (1831). Scott was created a baronet in 1820, and claimed authorship of the novels in 1827. In 1826 James Ballantyne & Co. became involved in the bankruptcy of Constable & Co., and Scott, as partner of the former, found himself liable for a debt of about £114,000. He shouldered the whole burden, and henceforth worked heroically, shortening his life by strenuous efforts to pay off the creditors, who received full payment after his death.

Scott's dramatic work, in which he did not excel, includes *Halidon Hill* (1822), *Macduff's Cross* (1823), *The Doom of Devorgoil: A Melodrama* and *Auchindrane, or The Ayrshire Tragedy* (both 1830). Of these *Auchindrane* is the best. It is founded on the case of Mure of Auchindrane in Pitcairn's *Ancient Criminal Trials*. He also wrote or edited historical, literary, and antiquarian works: *The Works of Dryden* with a life (1808); *The Works of Swift* with a life (1814); *Provincial Antiquities of Scotland* (1819–26); an abstract of the 'Eyrbyggja Saga' in *Northern Antiquities* (1814); *Description of the Regalia of Scotland* (1819); *Lives of the Novelists* prefixed to Ballantyne's Novelist's Library (1821–4); essays on Chivalry (1818), the Drama (1819), and Romance (1824) contributed to the **Encyclopaedia Britannica*; *The Life of Napoleon Buonaparte* (1827); *The *Tales of a Grandfather* (1827–30); *History of Scotland* (1829–30); *Letters on Demonology and Witchcraft* (1830); *Original Memoirs Written during the Great Civil War of Sir H. Slingsby and Captain Hodgson* (1806); the **Military Memoirs of Captain Carleton* (1808); the *State Papers of Sir Ralph Sadler* (1809); the *Secret History of James I* (1811); and *Memorie of the Somervilles* (1815). *Paul's Letters to his Kinsfolk* appeared in 1816. Scott founded the *Bannatyne Club in 1823. In 1826 he addressed to the *Edinburgh Weekly Journal* three letters 'from Malachi Malagrowther', 'Thoughts on the proposed Change of Currency', defending the rights of Scotland.

The Life of Scott by John *Lockhart, published in 1837–8, is one of the great biographies of the 19th century. Scott's *Journal* was published in 1890 and again in 1939–46, in three volumes, edited by J. G. Tait; there is a modern edition by W. E. K. Anderson (1972). An edition of his letters in twelve volumes was published by H. J. C. Grierson (1932–7) with an index and notes by J. C. Corson (1979). *Sir Walter Scott: The Great Unknown*, a biography by Edgar Johnson, two volumes, was published in 1970; see also J. Sutherland, *The Life of Sir Walter Scott* (1995). The magisterial Edinburgh Edition of the Waverley Novels in 30 volumes (1993–2006) is the standard edition of Scott's fiction.

Scott's influence as a novelist was incalculable; he established the form of the *historical novel, and, according to V. S. *Pritchett, the form of the short story (with 'The Two Drovers' and 'The Highland Widow'). He was read and imitated throughout the 19th century, not only by historical novelists such as Harrison *Ainsworth and Edward *Bulwer-Lytton, but also by writers like Elizabeth *Gaskell, George *Eliot, the *Brontës, and many others, who treated rural themes, contemporary peasant life, or regional speech in a manner that owed much to Scott. His reputation gradually declined (though his medieval and Tudor romances retained a popular readership) until there was a revival of interest from European *Marxist critics in the 1930s, who interpreted his works in terms of historicism. In 1951 three seminal essays were published, David Daiches's 'Scott's Achievement as a Novelist' (*Nineteenth-Century Fiction*), Arnold Kettle's chapter in his *Introduction to the English Novel* (vol. i), and S. Stewart Gordon's '*Waverley* and the "Unified Design"' (*English Literary History*, 18); these heralded an upsurge of scholarly activity and reappraisal, most of which singles out the Scottish 'Waverley' novels (including *The Antiquary*, *Old Mortality*, and *The Heart of Midlothian*) as his masterpieces. For a survey of critical attitudes, see *Walter Scott: Modern Judgements*, ed. D. D. Devlin (1968); T. Crawford, *Walter Scott* (1982).

SCOTT, William Bell (1811–90) Poet, artist, and art critic; born in Edinburgh and trained at the Trustees' Academy there, he taught for many years in Newcastle-upon-Tyne. His mural *Iron and Coal* (1862) at Wallington Hall, Northumberland, is one of the earliest representations in art of heavy industry. Scott was a friend of Dante Gabriel *Rossetti (who made his acquaintance through an admiring letter) and later of A. C. *Swinburne; he was associated with the birth of the *Pre-Raphaelite Movement, and contributed to *The *Germ*. His poems and verses (of which he published several volumes, some illustrated by himself) range from rambling Pindaric *odes to *sonnets and medieval-style *ballads. His *Autobiographical Notes* (1892), edited by W. Minto, gave much offence to the Rossetti family.

Scottish Enlightenment Retrospective term for the flowering of intellectual enquiry, centred on the city and University of Edinburgh but also involving the universities of Glasgow and Aberdeen, in 18th-century Scotland. Though the scientists, philosophers, and *literati associated with the movement differed widely in attitude and opinion, they shared a faith in the primacy of reason, a commitment to social and economic 'improvement' through the application of their findings, an insistence on the interconnectedness of human activities, and a quest for underlying philosophical principles. They contributed significantly to the development of the disciplines of medicine, law, economics, and history, and to most branches of philosophy. The main philosophers were Francis *Hutcheson, David *Hume, Adam *Smith, Adam *Ferguson; and Hume's 'common-sense' antagonists Thomas *Reid and Dugald *Stewart. The political, economic, and social thought of Hume, Smith, and Ferguson was powerfully influential in France and America, and the ideas of Reid, Stewart, and Hugh *Blair helped shape American higher education. The scientists included William Cullen (1710–90), who established chemistry as a separate discipline; his student Joseph Black (1728–99), who propounded the theories of latent and specific heat; the latter's friend James Hutton (1726–97), founder of modern geology, and the father and son team of Alexander and Alexander Monro (1697–1767; 1733–1817), pioneering anatomists. The engineers James Watt (1736–1819) and John McAdam (1756–1836) emerged from the same milieu. Some literary figures, like John *Home and James *Macpherson, identified with the values of the Enlightenment, while others, such as James *Boswell, Robert *Fergusson, and Robert *Burns, were to varying degrees ambivalent, and at times antagonistic towards them. Numerous learned societies and journals flourished during the period, and the **Encyclopaedia Britannica* was founded. See A. Broadie (ed.), *The Cambridge Companion to the Scottish Enlightenment* (2003).

Scottish Renaissance A movement in literature and politics, and to a lesser extent in music and the visual arts. It had its origins in Montrose, Angus, in the 1920s, where Edwin and Willa *Muir, the composer Francis George Scott (1880–1958), and the future novelist Fionn McColla (1906–75) all either lived or holidayed in proximity to Hugh *MacDiarmid, then at the most energetic phase of his career as poet and propagandist. All shared a sense of the degraded condition of post-war Scotland and a desire to internationalize the country's intellectual life and reanimate aspects of national tradition diminished by Protestantism and unionism. Other north-eastern writers like Lewis Grassic *Gibbon and Nan *Shepherd shared MacDiarmid's conviction that language and idiom were central to Scottish literary authenticity. Scotland was also being reimagined in the 1920s and 1930s in the fiction of Neil M. *Gunn, the poetry of William *Soutar, and the iconoclastic biography of Robert *Burns by Catherine *Carswell.

Scottish Text Society Founded in 1882 for the purpose of furnishing scholarly but popularly accessible editions of historically significant Scottish texts. It has published more than 150 volumes of poetry, drama, and prose, including John *Barbour's *Bruce*, *The Original Chronicle of Andrew of Wyntoun*, *The *Kingis Quair*, and the poems of Robert *Henryson, William *Dunbar, Sir David *Lindsay, and William *Drummond of Hawthornden. Although the Society's primary concern has been with medieval and Renaissance works, it has also produced important editions of later writers, including Allan *Ramsay and Robert *Fergusson, along with the 19th-century ballad collection *The Song Repertoire of Amelia and Jane Harris*.

SCOTUS ERIUGENA, John (John the Scot) (*fl.* *c.*845–70) Distinguished philosopher of Irish origin, employed as a teacher at the court of Charles the Bald *c.*847. *De Divisione Naturae* expounds his philosophy of the unity of nature; this proceeds from (1) God, the first and only real being (Nature which creates and is not created); through (2) the Creative Ideas (Nature which creates and is created); to (3) the sensible Universe (Nature which is created and does not create); everything is ultimately resolved into (4) its First Cause (immanent, unmoving God: Nature which is not created and does not create). He was one of the originators of medieval mysticism, as well as a precursor of *scholasticism. The originality of his theology lies in elements drawn from Pseudo-Dionysius and others in the *Neoplatonic tradition. The Neoplatonic element in medieval philosophy owes much to his influence. See *Works* in Jacques-Paul *Migne's *Patrologia Latina*, 122.

Scriblerus Club An informal group which included the writers Jonathan *Swift, John *Arbuthnot, Thomas *Parnell, Alexander *Pope, John *Gay, and the politician Robert *Harley. The group appears to have met regularly only from January to July 1714, with the object of burlesquing false science and scholarship through the figure of an educated fool, 'Martinus Scriblerus'. A number of short satires under this name were printed or reprinted in miscellanies by Pope and Swift from 1727, and works such as **Gulliver's Travels*, **Peri Bathous*, and *The *Dunciad* were in part inspired by the original idea. *Memoirs of *Martinus Scriblerus* appeared in 1741. See Patricia C. Brückmann, *A Manner of Correspondence* (1997).

Scrutiny A quarterly periodical of literary criticism which ran for 19 volumes, 1932–53, edited for most of this period by L. C. Knights, D. W. Harding, and F. R. *Leavis, the latter being the dominant critical voice and the most regular reviewer. The editorial business was carried out from his and his wife Q. D. *Leavis's home in Cambridge. Its other regular contributors included H. A. Mason, Denys Thompson, W. H. Mellers (on music), John Spiers (on medieval literature), D. A. Traversi, and Martin Turnell (on French literature); and there were occasional contributions from W. H. *Auden, I. A. *Richards, Edgell *Rickword, D. J. *Enright, and M. C. Bradbrook. Inspired in part by the example of the **Calendar of Modern Letters*, it became an important vehicle for the views of the new Cambridge school of criticism, and published many seminal essays, particularly in the pre-war years, on *Shakespeare, *Marvell, and the traditions of the English novel. The major works of F. R. Leavis himself in this period—*Revaluation* (1936), *The Great Tradition* (1948), and *The Common Pursuit* (1952)—were based upon articles that had appeared in *Scrutiny*. Its critical strictures proved notoriously destructive when applied to contemporary writing: it mauled Graham *Greene and Dylan *Thomas, dismissed Ernest *Hemingway as second-rate, derided much of Virginia *Woolf's writing (describing **Between the Acts* as a work of 'extraordinary vacancy and pointlessness'), and repeatedly lamented the aridity of T. S. *Eliot's later work and the 'immaturity' of Auden's. The journal's stance was one of embattled rearguard defence of standards against a general cultural debasement abetted by the 'London literary establishment' comprising the BBC, the *Times Literary Supplement*, the British Council, and reviewers influenced by the *Bloomsbury Group. It had a powerful influence on two generations of literary academics and schoolteachers, consolidated after the journal's closure by Boris Ford's *Pelican Guide to English Literature* (7 vols, 1954–61), in which many of the contributors were former 'Scrutineers'. The Cambridge University Press reprinted the full run in 1963 with a twentieth volume containing an index and an important 'Retrospect' by F. R. Leavis. This was followed by *A Selection from Scrutiny* (2 vols, 1968). See Francis Mulhern, *The Moment of 'Scrutiny'* (1979).

SCUDÉRY, Madeleine de (1608–1701) Author of French heroic romances. Her *Artamène, ou le Grand Cyrus* (10 vols, 1649–53), trans. Frances Gifford (1653–5), and *Clélie, histoire romaine* (10 vols, 1654–60; trans. 1656–61) consist of an interweaving of elaborate tales of love and war in an antique setting with ingenious systems of contemporary allusions. They had an immense vogue throughout Europe, even influencing heroic plays of the court of Charles II.

SEACOLE, Mary (1805–81) Born in Jamaica, the daughter of a Scottish officer and a free black businesswoman, 'an admirable doctress'. Seacole's autobiography *The Wonderful Adventures of Mrs Seacole in Many Lands* (1857) tells how she travelled as a humane entrepreneur and healer, most notably during the Crimean War.

Seafarer, The An Old English poem of *c.*124 lines in the *Exeter Book. The opening section is a powerful evocation of the miseries and attractions of life at sea, the speaker contrasting a compulsion to be at sea with the comforts of life on land. This section gives way to moral reflections on the transience of life and an explicitly Christian part (the text of which is uncertain), concluding with a prayer. Ezra *Pound made a loose but highly evocative translation of the first half of the poem. The structure of the poem and the coherence of the relationship between its two halves have been much debated. Some critics regard the didactic second part as an appendage to an earlier secular poem; others see the whole as an allegorical representation of human exile from God on the sea of life. Ed. Bernard Muir, *The Exeter Anthology of Old English Poetry* (2000).

Seasons, The A poem in blank verse, in four books, by James *Thomson, published 1726–30. The first version of 'Winter', of 405 lines, appeared in 1726; it was gradually expanded to 1,069 lines by 1746. It describes the power of the elements and the sufferings of men and animals; the best-known episode narrates the death of a shepherd in a snowdrift. 'Summer' (1727) sets forth the progress of a summer's day, with scenes of hay-making and sheep-shearing, followed by a panegyric to Great Britain. The episode in which Damon beholds Musidora bathing was highly popular, according to

William *Wordsworth, because of its sexual content. 'Spring' (1728) describes the influence of the season on all the natural world, and ends with a panegyric on nuptial love; its opening lines were particularly admired by John *Clare. 'Autumn' (1730) gives a vivid picture of hunting, harvesting, and wine-making, and ends with a hymn to the 'pure pleasures of the rural life'. It includes the episode of Palemon who falls in love with Lavinia, a gleaner, based on the biblical story of Ruth and Boaz. The whole was completed by a Hymn (1730) and illustrations by William *Kent. The work contains many elegant compliments to Thomson's patrons, such as George *Lyttelton and George Bubb *Dodington. It went through many editions in the 18th and 19th centuries, and was at the centre of the crucial *copyright cases of the 1770s. The text of *Haydn's oratorio *Die Jahreszeiten* (1801) was adapted from Thomson's poem. See the edition by J. Sambrook (1981).

SEBALD, W. G. (Winfried Georg Maximilian (Max)) (1944–2001) German novelist, poet, and critic. Born in Bavaria, he studied at Freiburg, Fribourg (Switzerland), and Manchester, and spent almost all his adult life working in the UK, chiefly at the University of East Anglia, where he was appointed professor of German in 1987 and founding director of the British Centre for Literary Translation in 1989. Unusual in the use they make of photographs, his novels owe much of their strange and haunting quality to their unique narrative voice, through which—typically in winding intricate sentences—'characters' are remembered in the act of remembering. These include *The Emigrants* (1996), *The Rings of Saturn* (1999), *Vertigo* (1999), and *Austerlitz* (2001). Lectures delivered in Zurich challenging German literature for its failure to record the trauma of Allied fire-bombing of German cities also instance his concern with the ethics of memory; on publication in 1999 they aroused great controversy (*On the Natural History of Destruction*, 2003). In 2001 two volumes of poetry appeared, *After Nature* (trans. Michael *Hamburger) and *For Years Now* (with images by Tess Jaray). The fact that his works were written in England and often translated under the auspices of his own institute lends the translations a particular authority, and gives them a special place in English as well as German literature.

'Second Nun's Tale' *See* CANTERBURY TALES, 21.

Secret Agent, The Novel by Joseph *Conrad, published 1907. A seedy Soho shop provides cover for Verloc, the lazy secret agent in question; he moonlights lackadaisically as a spy for a foreign embassy and an informer for the police. Winnie has married him chiefly to provide security for her simple-minded younger brother, Stevie. Verloc's shop is a meeting place for a bunch of anarchist misfits, comprising the Russian *agent provocateur* Vladimir; 'The Professor', a terrorist; and Ossipon, Yundt, and Michaelis, who are happy to fit their principles to their material needs. The embassy is planning a series of outrages aimed at discrediting the revolutionary groups to which London has been so accommodating, with the first target being the Greenwich Observatory. Verloc exploits Stevie as an accomplice, but the boy, rather than the Observatory, is blown to pieces. An outraged Winnie kills Verloc, flees, and, in terror of being hanged, throws herself overboard from a ferry.

Secreta Secretorum A compendium of pronouncements on political and ethical matters, written in Syriac in the 8th century AD and claiming to be advice from *Aristotle to *Alexander the Great. It reached Europe through Arabic and 12th-century Hispano-Arabic. The main version in Latin was translated in Spain *c.*1230 and was influential on poets from then until the 16th century. It influenced in particular the tradition of writing works of advice to kings; it was translated in part by John *Lydgate, and Egidio Colonna's *De Regimine Principum* (an important source for *Hoccleve's *Regiment of Princes*) drew on it.

Secret Commonwealth of Elves, Fauns and Fairies, The A tract on the fairy world, second sight, and related subjects by Robert Kirk (?1641–92), minister of Aberfoyle. The earliest surviving text (1815) is from a 1691 manuscript. It was printed with a commentary by Andrew *Lang in 1893 and edited by Robert Bontine *Cunninghame Graham in 1933.

Secret Garden, The (1911) By Frances Hodgson *Burnett, tells the romantic story of the regeneration of two sickly, spoiled children, Mary Lennox and her cousin Colin, through contact with nature. One of the most intricately symbolic books in the children's literature canon, it was filmed in 1919, 1949, and 1993.

SEDLEY (Sidley), **Sir Charles** (?1639–1701) Dramatist and poet, friend of *Rochester and John *Dryden, famous for his wit and urbanity and notorious for his profligate escapades. His tragedy *Antony and Cleopatra* (1677) was followed by two comedies, **Bellamira* (1687) and *The Mulberry Garden* (1668), which was based partly on *Molière's *L'École des maris*. His poems and songs ('Phillis is my only joy', 'Love still has something of the sea', etc.) were published in 1702, with his *Miscellaneous Works*. Edmond *Malone identified him as the Lisideius of Dryden's **Of Dramatick Poesy*, who defends the imitation of French drama in English. He also had a hand in a translation of *Corneille's *Pompée* (performed 1643) with Edmund *Waller, Sidney *Godolphin, Charles *Sackville, and Sir Robert *Filmer.

SEFERIS, George (1900–71) Greek poet and diplomat, born in Smyrna and educated in Athens. He spent several periods in Britain, including some years as ambassador (1957–62), and in 1963 was awarded the *Nobel Prize. He published several volumes of poetry, from 1931 onwards, much of it strongly imbued with classical mythology: translations include *Poems* (1960), by Rex *Warner, and *Collected Poems* (1981), by

E. Keeley and P. Sherrard. *The Complete Poems*, translated by Keeley and Sherrard, appeared in a new edition in 1993.

SEGALEN, Victor (1878–1919) French explorer, archaeologist, ethnographer, and writer, born in Brest. Segalen studied medicine in Bordeaux and then travelled and lived in Polynesia, where he worked as a naval doctor, 1903–5, and in China 1909–14 and in 1917. During his lifetime he published a novel, *Les Immémoriaux* (1907), based on his experiences in Tahiti, and two collections of poetry, *Stèles* (1912) and *Peintures* (1916), influenced by his time in China. His posthumous publications include the novel *René Leys* (1922); *Équipée* (1929), an account of an imaginary expedition based on his various journeys in China; *Lettres de Chine* (1967); and *Essai sur l'exotisme* (1978). After his mysterious death in a Breton forest, Segalen enjoyed only a minor reputation until the publication of Henry Bouillier's 1961 study *Victor Segalen*. Subsequently there has been increasing scholarly interest in Segalen's reflections on cultural difference and exoticism. His *œuvres complètes* appeared in 1995. See Charles Forsdick, *Victor Segalen and the Aesthetics of Diversity* (2000).

Sei personaggi in cerca di autore *See* PIRANDELLO, LUIGI.

Sejanus his Fall A Roman tragedy by Ben *Jonson, performed by the King's Men 1603, with *Shakespeare and Richard *Burbage in the cast, printed 1605. At its first performance it was hissed from the stage.

Based mainly on *Tacitus, the play deals with the rise of Sejanus during the reign of Tiberius, his destruction of the family of Germanicus, and his poisoning of Tiberius' son Drusus. Suspicious of Sejanus, Tiberius leaves Rome, setting his agent Macro to spy on him. Tiberius denounces Sejanus in a letter to the Senate, which condemns him to death. The mob, stirred up by Macro, tears him to pieces. The play was successfully revived by the Royal Shakespeare Company in 2005.

SELBY, Hubert, Jr (1928–2004) American novelist, born in New York, who achieved fame with his first novel *Last Exit to Brooklyn* (1964), which was prosecuted in Britain for obscenity. Selby was helped in his career by Gilbert *Sorrentino and Amiri *Baraka, and shared many of the concerns of the *Beats. His later novels include *Requiem for a Dream* (1978).

SELDEN, John (1584–1654) English jurist, orientalist, and legal historian, born near Worthing, Sussex, and educated at Hart Hall, Oxford. He became an eminent lawyer and bencher of the Inner Temple. Among his early works was *The Duello* (1610), a history of trial by single combat, and notes to the first eighteen cantos of Michael *Drayton's **Poly-Olbion* (1613). His *De Diis Syriis* (1617), a work of comparative religion far ahead of its time, won him European fame as an orientalist. John *Milton, an admirer of Selden's learning, consulted it when writing of the pagan gods in his *Nativity Ode*. Selden's valuable collection of oriental manuscripts mostly passed at his death to the Bodleian Library. His *History of Tithes* (1618) offended the bishops, and he was called before the Privy Council and forced to retract his opinions. In Parliament he took an active part against the Crown, insisting on the rights and privileges of the House of Commons, and was twice imprisoned. He seems later to have inclined to the Royalist cause and in 1635 he dedicated his *Mare Clausum* to Charles I. This was an answer to the *Mare Liberum* of Hugo *Grotius, which had justified the activities of Dutch fishermen poaching in the waters off the English coast by denying that the seas were susceptible to sovereignty. In the Long Parliament he opposed the exclusion of the bishops from the House of Lords, but in 1647 he was voted £5,000 by Parliament in compensation for his sufferings during the evil days of the monarchy. He withdrew from public affairs in 1649 on the principle that 'The wisest way for men in these times is to say nothing.' His *Table Talk*, drawn from the last twenty years of his life, and composed by his secretary Richard Milward (bap. 1609, d. 1680), appeared in 1689. With Patrick Young (1584–1652) and Richard James (bap. 1581, d. 1638) he compiled a catalogue of the Arundel Marbles in 1628. He was buried in the Temple Church and his tomb can be seen through glass plates in the floor. His works were collected by Dr David Wilkins (1685–1745) in 1726.

Select Society An association of educated Scotsmen formed in 1754, whose members met in Edinburgh to discuss philosophical questions. David *Hume and William Robertson (1721–93) were among its prominent members.

SELF, Will (1961–) Novelist and journalist, educated at University College School, London, and Exeter College, Oxford. A former cartoonist, he has published short stories, novellas, and novels—such as *The Book of Dave* (2006)—much indebted to Martin *Amis in their fascination with the scabrous and penchant for surreal satire, lurid caricature, and arcane vocabulary. He has also published two collections of his journalism, *Junk Mail* (1995), which includes pieces about his drug addiction, and *Feeding Frenzy* (2001).

SELKIRK, Alexander (1676–1721) Scottish seaman and castaway, born in Fife. He ran away to sea and joined the privateering expedition of William *Dampier in 1703. Having quarrelled with his captain, Thomas Stradling, he was put ashore on one of the uninhabited Pacific islands of Juan Fernández in 1704, and remained there until 1709 when he was rescued by Woodes Rogers (*c.*1679–1732). He returned to Britain in 1711 after further voyages. Rogers gave an account of him in *A Cruising Voyage round the World* (1712). An essay by Sir Richard *Steele in the *Englishman* (3 Dec. 1713) repeats some of its details with a more explicit moral. Selkirk is often advanced as a likely model for **Robinson Crusoe* (1719) by Daniel *Defoe. He also inspired a poem by William *Cowper published in 1782.

SELLAR, W. C. (Walter Carruthers) (1898–1951) and **YEATMAN, R. J.** (Robert Julian) (1897–1968) Remembered for *1066 and All That: 'A memorable history of England, comprising All the Parts You Can Remember, including 103 Good Things, 5 Bad Kings and 2 genuine Dates'* (1930), a gentle satire on education and history: its jokes require an extensive grounding in English history. Sellar taught at Charterhouse; Yeatman was an advertising manager; both wrote for **Punch* and together also produced *And Now All This* (1932), *Horse Nonsense* (1933), and *Garden Rubbish and Other Country Bumps* (1936).

SELVON, Sam (Samuel Dickson) (1923–94) Born and educated in San Fernando in Trinidad; he wrote novels, plays, and short stories. He began to write while serving as a wireless operator in the Royal Navy during the Second World War, and came to England in 1950, travelling on the same boat as George *Lamming. His first novel, *A Brighter Sun* (1952), set in Trinidad during the war, was written in London: it describes the life and brightening prospects of Tiger, a young Indian peasant. Selvon became well known for his novels about London: these include *The Lonely Londoners* (1956), *Moses Ascending* (1975), and *Moses Migrating* (1983), which chart with comedy, sympathy, and a pioneering use of Caribbean idiom the experiences of black immigrants trying to find fame and fortune, or at least a bed, in the unknown terrain of Earls Court, Notting Hill, and Bayswater. Selvon also wrote many plays for *BBC radio before leaving to settle in Canada in 1978.
See also BLACK BRITISH LITERATURE.

SEMBÈNE, Ousmane (1923–2007) Senegalese novelist and film-maker. Unlike contemporaries such as Léopold *Senghor, Sembène was not a product of the French colonial education system. His involvement with working-class movements in France and Africa led to a critical engagement with both the idea of *Négritude articulated by Senghor, and postcolonial Senegalese society. His most famous novel, *Les Bouts de bois de Dieu* (1960; *God's Bits of Wood*), is about the Dakar–Nigeria railway strike of 1947–8. Films such as *Mandabi* (1968) and *Xala* (1975) offer a satirical portrait of the Senegalese political elite.

SENANCOUR, Étienne Pivert de (1770–1846) French author, now chiefly remembered for his *Obermann* (1804), a novel made up of letters from Obermann to a friend, supposedly written over a period of years and mostly from a remote Alpine valley. Disappointed in love, the hero reflects on the society he has fled and on man, describing his own frustrated inactivity, melancholy, and ennui, his solitude and mystical attachment to Nature. The mental and emotional condition given voice in *Obermann* appealed to many first-generation Romantic writers in France. Senancour was much admired by Charles-Augustin *Sainte-Beuve and by Matthew *Arnold, who saw in his sentimentalism a distinctive 'gravity and severity'. Two well-known poems by Arnold, 'Stanzas in Memory of the Author of Obermann' (1852) and 'Obermann Once More' (1867), take the form of reflections on Senancour's book in its Alpine setting. Arnold also wrote an essay 'Obermann' (**Academy*, 9 Oct. 1869).

SENDAK, Maurice (1928–) American author-illustrator, born in Brooklyn; he studied at the Art Students League in New York. In 2003 he shared the Astrid Lindgren Award. **Where the Wild Things Are* (1963; Caldecott medal, 1964), *In the Night Kitchen* (1970), and *Outside Over There* (1981) established his reputation. More recent work includes *We Are All in the Dumps with Jack and Guy* (1993) depicting street children, and the Holocaust-inspired *Brundibar* (2003), an illustrated book based in the opera of the same name, with a text by Tony Kushner (1956–). Sendak also works as a designer for theatre, opera, and ballet.

SENECA, Lucius Annaeus (4 BC/AD 1–65) Roman Stoic philosopher, tragic poet, and, like his father the elder Seneca, a noted rhetorician; born in Córdoba, Spain. He was appointed tutor to the young Nero and, when the latter became emperor, acted as one of his chief advisers, checking his crimes for a period; but, finding this position untenable, he withdrew from the court in 62. Three years later he was accused of being implicated in a conspiracy and was forced to commit suicide. His writings consist of tragedies in verse, dialogues, treatises, and letters in prose, which in their different ways all aim to teach *Stoicism. Most of his nine plays are on subjects drawn from Greek mythology and treated in extant Greek dramas, but his manner is very different from that of Greek tragedy. He uses an exaggerated rhetoric, dwells habitually on bloodthirsty details, and introduces ghosts and magic; the plays were almost certainly not intended for performance but for reading aloud, probably by the author himself, to a select audience.

Senecan drama was familiar in the 16th century at a time when Greek tragedies were scarcely known; all the nine plays were translated and imitated by dramatists from the time of **Gorboduc* onwards. Shakespeare's **Titus Andronicus* is the best-known example. Seneca's prose writings consist of moral treatises, some in the form of dialogues, on such topics as anger, clemency, providence, consolation for loss, and tranquillity of mind, and letters suppposedly addressed to Lucilius after the author's retirement, constituting a practical course in Stoicism. These moral writings were widely read and taken to heart in the 17th and 18th centuries, and Seneca's antithetical style, often contrasted with *Cicero's, was much imitated, for example by Ben *Jonson. *L'Estrange's digest, *Seneca's Morals* (1678), was reprinted many times, and there is an undercurrent of Stoicism in much early 18th-century thinking. See T. S. *Eliot, 'Seneca in Elizabethan Translation' and 'Shakespeare and the Stoicism of Seneca' (1927); George Williamson, *The Senecan Amble* (1966).

SENGHOR, Léopold Sédar (1906–2001) Senegalese poet, intellectual, and politician. He left Senegal in 1928 to pursue his education in Paris, where he met fellow colonial subjects Aimé *Césaire and Léon Damas (1912–78). Together, they founded the *Négritude movement. In keeping with the notion of Négritude, Senghor's poetry, first translated in the 1960s, celebrates a black identity which has its roots in traditional African spirituality, while at the same time seeking out universal values which can cut across racial difference. Following Senegal's independence from France in 1960, Senghor served as its first president until 1980.

SENIOR, Olive (1941–) Poet and short story writer who was born and brought up in Jamaica, and educated at Carleton University, Ottawa; she divides her time between Jamaica and Canada. Her collections of poetry, *Talking of Trees* (1985), *Gardening in the Tropics* (1994), and *Over the Roofs of the World* (2005), employ a wide range of voices, from the colloquial and the conversational to the prophetic, to explore the struggles and history of her land and its people. Her volumes of short stories are *Summer Lightning* (1986) which won the Commonwealth Writers' Prize, *Arrival of the Snake Woman* (1989), and *Discerner of Hearts* (1995). Her stories often give a child's view of the world, and are alert to the range of Jamaican ethnicities. She writes that travelling to Canada forced her to look at Jamaica: 'my search for personal identity and the search for national identity came together.'

sensation, novel of An enormously popular genre of fiction that flourished from *c.*1860 onwards. It relocated the terrors of the *Newgate and *Gothic novel to a recognizably modern, middle-class England. Its high-impact narrative style employed cliffhanging conclusions to chapters, which gave the genre a reputation for 'preaching to the nerves'. Its plots commonly involved guilty family secrets, bigamy, arson, adultery, insanity, forgery, and murder (especially poisoning), often taking inspiration from real criminal cases. This accounts for an intense interest in legal papers, telegrams, diary entries, and written testimony. Indeed, many of Wilkie *Collins's sensation novels represent themselves as bundles of documents authored by witnesses in the case. The genre was also noted for its energetic—and frequently criminal—heroines, and for its enervated, hypersensitive heroes. The 'sensation' label, however, was a negative one, and its practitioners rarely declared themselves as such. The most influential works in the genre are Wilkie Collins's *The *Woman in White* (1860) and *The *Moonstone* (1868); Ellen Wood's **East Lynne* (1861); Mary Braddon's **Lady Audley's Secret* (1862); Charles Reade's **Hard Cash* (1863); and Sheridan Le Fanu's **Uncle Silas* (1864). The novels of Rhoda *Broughton and *Ouida are usually considered to be on the margins of the genre. Most mid-Victorian novelists show some traces of its influence, including Thomas *Hardy, Charles *Dickens, George *Eliot, and Anthony *Trollope. *Detective fiction can trace its roots back to sensation fiction. See L. Pykett, *The Sensation Novel from The Woman in White to The Moonstone* (1994); A. Mangham, *Violent Women and Sensation Fiction* (2007).

Sense and Sensibility A novel by Jane *Austen, which grew from a sketch entitled 'Elinor and Marianne'; revised 1797–8 and again 1809; published 1811. The title of this tale about two sisters reflects its subject. Elinor, the eldest, is the embodiment of good sense while her younger sister Marianne suffers from a potentially fatal excess of romantic sensibility. However, far from being a simplistic moral tale advocating the importance of reason over passion, *Sense and Sensibility* subtly explores the psychology of romantic love and the restrictions placed upon individual desire by social probity and family duty.

Mrs Henry Dashwood and her daughters Elinor and Marianne, together with the younger Margaret, are left with little money, because the estate of which Mrs Dashwood's husband had the life interest has passed to her stepson John Dashwood. Henry Dashwood, before his death, had appealed to John to look after his stepmother and sisters, but John and his grasping wife (the daughter of the arrogant Mrs Ferrers) are too selfish to help them. Mrs Henry Dashwood and her daughters retire to a cottage in Devon, but not before Elinor and Edward Ferrers, brother of Mrs John Dashwood, have become attracted to each other. However, Edward shows a strange uneasiness in his relations with Elinor. In Devon Marianne is thrown into the company of John Willoughby, an attractive but poor and unprincipled young man, with whom she falls desperately—and very obviously—in love. Willoughby seems to respond, and their engagement is expected daily. Willoughby suddenly departs for London, leaving Marianne in acute distress. Eventually Elinor and Marianne also go to London, on the invitation of their tactless and garrulous old friend Mrs Jennings. Here Willoughby shows complete indifference to Marianne, and finally, in a cruel and insolent letter, informs her of his approaching marriage to a rich heiress. Marianne makes no effort to hide her grief. Meanwhile Elinor has learned, under pledge of secrecy, from Lucy Steele (a sly, self-seeking young woman) that she and Edward Ferrers have been secretly engaged for four years. Elinor, whose self-control contrasts with Marianne's demonstrative emotions, silently conceals her distress. Edward's engagement, which had been kept secret from his mother, now becomes known to her. Infuriated by Edward's refusal to break his promise to Lucy, she dismisses him from her sight, and settles on his younger brother Robert the property that would otherwise have gone to Edward. At this juncture a small living is offered to Edward, and the way seems open for his marriage with Lucy. But the shallow Robert falls in love with Lucy, who, seeing her best interest in a marriage with the wealthier brother, throws over Edward and marries Robert. Edward, immensely relieved to be released from an engagement he has painfully regretted, proposes to Elinor and is accepted. Marianne, slowly recovering from the despair that followed her abandonment by Willoughby, accepts the proposal of Colonel Brandon, an old family friend, whose quiet attractions had been eclipsed by his brilliant rival.

sentiment, novel of A form of fiction, popular in the 18th century, illustrating and promoting 'sensibility', a combination of virtue, ready sympathy, and charitable impulse, based on the ethics of philosophers such as *Shaftesbury and on medical theories of the nervous system. The novels of

Samuel *Richardson and Sarah *Fielding stressed the importance of sentiment in the 1740s, and Henry Brooke's *The *Fool of Quality* (1765–70), Laurence Sterne's *A *Sentimental Journey* (1768), and Henry Mackenzie's *The *Man of Feeling* (1771) concentrated almost exclusively, though sometimes with comic irony, on feeling. The *Gothic novel later incorporated many of the conventions of sentimental fiction, and its decline was hastened by Jane Austen's mockery of its weeping heroines, and her suggestion, in **Northanger Abbey* and **Sense and Sensibility*, of the self-indulgence and delusion underlying its moral claims.

Sentimental Journey, A, *through France and Italy* By Laurence *Sterne, published 1768. Sterne travelled abroad in 1762–5 and wrote when the vogue for the *Grand Tour was at its height, parodying the travel journal and the novel as well as travel itself when he commented 'I seldom go to the place I set out for.' The narrative only gets as far as Lyons. The narrator is the amiable Parson Yorick (from **Tristram Shandy*), a 'sentimental' traveller who 'interests his heart in everything', is frequently moved to tears, and fights his susceptibility to women of all ranks met along the way. He contrasts his own pleasure in France with the condemnation of Smelfungus, a caricature of Tobias *Smollett. After Sterne's death in 1768, the narrative was continued by a 'Eugenius', Yorick's friend and correspondent, assumed wrongly to be Sterne's old friend John *Hall-Stevenson.

series books Are the staple of popular and children's literature, their *lack* of variation being their primary attraction. Famous examples include Enid *Blyton's 'Famous Five' and R. L. *Stine's 'Point Horror'. Series can develop their own internal dynamics and subtleties of character and narrative, as in Arthur Ransome's *Swallows and Amazons.

Series of Plays, A Collection of dramas by the Scottish poet and dramatist Joanna *Baillie, first published anonymously in 1798, and thought initially to be written by a man. The full title is illuminating: *A Series of Plays on the Passions: in which it is Attempted to Delineate the Stronger Passions of the Mind, Each Passion Being the Subject of a Tragedy and a Comedy.* Each play examines the effects of a key passion on the psychology and actions of the leading character: *Count Basil* (a tragedy) on love, *The Tryal* (a comedy) also on love, and *De Montfort* (a tragedy) on hate. The whole is prefaced by a justificatory 72-page 'Introductory Discourse', where Baillie explains that the 'design' of her drama to investigate psychological character development is based upon our curiosity about human nature and psychological motivation. She argues that it is characters in extraordinary situations that fascinate us most, although she also shares William *Wordsworth's and S. T. *Coleridge's preoccupation in **Lyrical Ballads* with socially marginal figures and altered states of being. Many of the age's leading writers admired Baillie, among them Wordsworth, Samuel *Rogers, Walter *Scott, Robert *Southey, Anna Laetitia *Barbauld, Maria *Edgeworth, and, most particularly Felicia *Hemans, who shared her fascination with the drama of the human passions and dedicated *Records of Woman* (1828) to her.

Serious Money By Caryl *Churchill (1987). Inspired by the 1986 deregulation of the City, known as the Big Bang, the play, written largely in spirited rhyming verse, evokes the ruthless greed, buoyant materialism, changing culture, and cynicism of the financial world in the monetarist 1980s. The play opens with a short satirical extract on speculation from Thomas *Shadwell's comedy *The Volunteers, or The Stockjobbers* (pub. 1693), and then introduces a noisy gallery of contemporary traders, dealers, jobbers, bankers, and stockbrokers. The plot involves a possible murder and insider dealing in the context of an attempted takeover bid of the symbolically named company Albion: Churchill's ear for the new jargon of the media, PR, and the City itself is acute and the play, launched at the *Royal Court, was also a West End success, much enjoyed by those it mocked. The play ends with a chorus singing in praise and hope of 'Five more Glorious Years' —'pissed and promiscuous, the money's ridiculous—five more glorious years', a reference to the possibility of the then prime minister Margaret Thatcher being re-elected.

Sermon on the Mount *See* BIBLE.

SERRAILLIER, Ian (1912–94) Children's writer, born in London, educated at Brighton College and St Edmund Hall, Oxford; he wrote poetry and adventure stories and retold classic texts, and is remembered for *The Silver Sword* (1956), set in Poland about the journey of four refugee children to Switzerland to find their parents.

SERVICE, Robert (1874–1958) Poet, born in Preston, Lancashire, and brought up in Glasgow. He emigrated to Canada in 1895 where he observed the gold rush in the Yukon; this inspired his best-known ballads, which include 'The Shooting of Dan McGrew' and 'The Cremation of Sam McGee', published in *Songs of a Sourdough* (1907, Toronto; as *The Spell of the Yukon*, New York). Its sequel, *Ballads of a Cheechako*, followed in 1909. Other volumes include *Rhymes of a Rolling Stone* (1912) and *Rhymes of a Red Cross Man* (1916). *Ploughman of the Moon* (1945) and *Harper of Heaven* (1948) are both autobiographical. He also wrote six novels varying in subject matter and genre. Collected volumes appeared in 1933, 1955, and 1960.

SERVISS, Garrett Putnam (1851–1929) American journalist, astronomer and *science fiction writer, born in Sharon Springs, New York. *Edison's Conquest of Mars* (1898) was published as an unauthorized sequel to H. G. *Wells's *The War of the Worlds*. Later novels, such as *The Second Deluge* (1912), were published in the popular magazines.

sestina An unrhymed poem of six six-line stanzas with a final three-line 'envoy', composed according to a fixed formula of repeated line-endings: in place of rhymed endings it employs full repetition of six words which reappear as line-endings in a different order in each successive stanza, in the sequence *abcdef, faebdc, cfdabe, ecbfad, deacfb, bdfeca*. Stanzas are thus linked by recurrence of the same line-ending in the final line of one stanza and the first line of the next. In the envoy, all six words reappear, three of them as line-endings. There is no required metre. The form originated among French *troubadour poets and was brought into English by Philip *Sidney in the **Arcadia*. Later poets who wrote English sestinas include *Swinburne, W. H. *Auden ('Paysage moralisé', 1933), and John *Ashbery ('The Painter', 1970).

SETH, Vikram (1952–) Poet, novelist, librettist, and travel writer, born in India, educated at Corpus Christi, Oxford, Stanford University, and Nanjing University, China, acclaimed for the versatility of his style and the brilliance of his generic ventriloquism. Early works included the collections of poems, *Mappings* (1981) and *The Humble Administrator's Garden* (1985), and a travel book, *From Heaven Lake: Travels through Sinkiang and Tibet* (1983). Poetry has continued throughout to be his *métier* of choice. The internationally praised *The Golden Gate* (1986) is a verse-novel set in San Francisco written in rhyming *tetrameter sonnet-stanzas, an insightful performance of Byronic verve dealing with modern professional protagonists in a traditional medium drawn in part from *Pushkin's *Eugene Onegin*. *A Suitable Boy* (1993) is an intricately structured novel in the realist tradition of the British Victorian multi-decker about the Mehra family's search for a suitable husband for their younger daughter, the entirely ordinary Lata. Noticeably tracing a trajectory away from magical-exotic evocations of South Asia, the novel is set in India some years after Independence and Partition, and the domestic and the political are entwined in the interlocking lives of four families, the Mehras, Kapoors, and Chatterjis (all Hindu), and the Khans (Muslim). Other works by this multilingual author include *Beastly Tales* (1992), *Three Chinese Poets* (1992, translation), *Arion and the Dolphin* (1994), *Two Lives* (2005, a memoir), and his second novel, *An Equal Music* (1999), concerning a violinist haunted by the memory of a former love.
See ANGLO-INDIAN LITERATURE.

SETTLE, Elkanah (1648–1724) Poet and playwright, educated at Trinity College, Oxford, the author of a series of bombastic oriental melodramas which threatened John *Dryden's popularity and aroused his hostility. He appears to have written *Cambyses* (1667) while still at Oxford, and his *The Empress of Morocco* (1673) had such a vogue that Dryden, with John *Crowne and Thomas *Shadwell, wrote a pamphlet of criticism of it. Settle retorted with an attack on Dryden's *Almanzor and Almahide*, and Dryden vented his resentment by satirizing Settle as Doeg in the second part of **Absalom and Achitophel*. Settle published *Absalom Senior, or Achitophel Transprosed* in 1682, and *Reflections on Several of Mr Dryden's Plays* in 1687. He was appointed city poet in 1691, took to writing *drolls for Bartholomew Fair (as he may have done before his success), and died in the Charterhouse, a charitable foundation. He also wrote two interesting rogue biographies (*see* ROGUE LITERATURE).

SEUSS, Dr (Theodor Seuss Geisel) (1904–1991) American writer of hugely successful books for children, born in Springfield, Massachusetts; he began work in advertising and as a cartoonist. *And to Think That I Saw it on Mulberry Street* (1937) introduced Seuss's anarchic visual and verbal style, used in the 'Beginner Book' series which commenced with *The Cat in the Hat* (1957). These books used a limited vocabulary, although he later 'came to despise' the idea. Legend has it that he wrote the best-selling *Green Eggs and Ham* (1960) on a bet from Bennett Cerf that he could not write a children's book using only 50 different words. Perhaps paradoxically, his wild, fluid *'nonsense' rhymes and surreal cartoon-drawings are designed to help children learn the discipline of reading. A political cartoonist for the New York newspaper *PM* (1941–3), his liberal views are expressed in some of his children's books: *The Lorax* (1971) can be read as an environmentalist tract, while *The Butter Battle Book* (1984) is a satire on the arms race. Many films have been made from his books including feature films of *How the Grinch Stole Christmas* (2000) and *The Cat in the Hat* (2003).

Seven Champions of Christendom, The Famous History of the *See* JOHNSON, RICHARD.

seven deadly sins Usually pride, envy, anger, sloth, covetousness, gluttony, and lust; frequently personified (e.g. **Piers Plowman*, B, *Passus V*; William *Dunbar's 'The Dance of the Sevin Deidly Synnis'; Edmund *Spenser's **Faerie Queene*) and used in *Chaucer's 'Parson's Tale' (*see* CANTERBURY TALES, 24). See M. W. Bloomfield, *The Seven Deadly Sins* (1952).

Seven Sages of Rome, The A metrical romance of the early 14th century, varying in length in different versions from 2,500 to 4,300 lines. In form it is a framed collection of tales, derived through Latin and French from Eastern collections, the original of which is the Indian *Book of Sindibad*, and is of interest as one of the earliest English instances of the form of verse story used by Chaucer in *The *Canterbury Tales*.

The Emperor Diocletian's son is educated by seven sages. Jealous of the boy, his stepmother accuses him to the emperor of attempting to seduce her; the boy is silent for seven days, under the influence of the stepmother's magic, and he is ordered to execution. On each of the seven nights a tale is told by the queen to illustrate the dangers of supplantation of the emperor by his son, and on each of the following mornings a tale is told by one of the sages on the theme of the danger of trusting women. When the seven days are passed, the boy speaks and exposes the stepmother, who is burnt. The most widely attested manuscript version ('A') in 3,974 lines of short couplets has been edited by K. Brunner (EETS os 191,

1933; repr. 1971). See also the edition of the Midlands version by J. Whitelock (EETS os 324, 2005).

SEVERN, Joseph (1793–1879) Painter, and devoted friend and correspondent of John *Keats, of whom he made several drawings and portraits, and of whom he took a death-mask. He won the Royal Academy Gold Medal in 1818 but had little public success. He accompanied Keats to Italy in 1820 and attended him at his death. His care of Keats brought him to general notice and for a time he prospered as a painter, especially in English circles in Rome. He attempted fiction, without success, but published *The Vicissitudes of Keats's Fame* in 1863. He was eventually given the British consulship in Rome. See *Joseph Severn: Letters and Memoirs*, ed. Grant F. Scott (2005).

SÉVIGNÉ, Marie de Rabutin-Chantal, marquise de (1626–96) French letter writer. Orphaned early, she was brought up by an uncle and became widely cultured. She frequented the Hôtel de Rambouillet, made a fashionable marriage in 1644, and was widowed seven years later, when her husband was killed in a duel over another woman. Her reputation rests on her voluminous correspondence with her daughter, published posthumously in the 18th century and translated into English anonymously in 1727 and 1757–65, which gives a lively insight into both public life in Paris under Louis XIV and the private life of an aristocratic woman and loving mother.
See LETTERS AND CORRESPONDENCE.

SEWARD, Anna (1742–1809) Poet and letter writer, from Eyam, Derbyshire; known as the 'Swan of Lichfield', where she lived from the age of 10, and where her father, who edited the works of *Beaumont and Fletcher (10 vols, 1750) was canon. Her grandfather John Hunter (*c.*1674–1741) had taught Samuel *Johnson, and she furnished James *Boswell with many details of Johnson's early life. Her poems included *Elegy on Captain Cook* (1780), which Johnson commended, and *Llangollen Vale, with Other Poems* (1796), the title poem recalling a visit to the Ladies of Llangollen, Lady Eleanor Butler (?1739–1829) and Miss Sarah Ponsonby (?1735–1831). Her friends included Erasmus *Darwin (of whom she wrote a memoir, 1804), Thomas *Day, and William *Hayley. In 1802 she wrote an admiring letter to Walter *Scott, who edited her works in three volumes, with a memoir, in 1810, at her suggestion. Her letters were published in 1811 (6 vols), and there is a selection in Hesketh *Pearson's *The Swan of Lichfield* (1936).

SEWELL, Anna *See* BLACK BEAUTY.

SEWELL, Elizabeth Missing (1815–1906) Novelist and educationalist, born in Newport, on the Isle of Wight, and educated (though 'not well', according to her own later recollection), at the Misses Aldridge's school in Bath. Elizabeth was one of twelve siblings, and several of her brothers were to achieve successful public careers, including Richard (bap. 1803, d. 1864; lawyer), William (1804–74; fellow of Exeter College, Oxford, and founder of Radley College), Henry (1807–79; the first prime minister of New Zealand), and James Edwards Sewell (1810–1903; warden of New College, Oxford). Nevertheless, the family was not wealthy, and Sewell's literary earnings were important to their continuing prosperity after her father died in 1842, leaving only debts. Sewell was especially close to her brother William, and as a young woman she shared his allegiance to the *Oxford Movement. Her earliest novels, including the popular *Amy Herbert* (1844), were published as having been edited by William Sewell. But relations with the volatile William became troublesome as Sewell's success grew, and her later works, like the powerful *Ursula* (1858), warned young female readers of the dangers of idolizing brothers. Sewell combined her writing with work as a teacher, and she founded and ran two schools on the Isle of Wight. Her strongest novels, including *The Experience of Life* (1853) and *Katharine Ashton* (1854), address the need for young women to have the means to achieve independence and self-respect, whether or not they marry; a serious and disciplined education is therefore necessary for their well-being. She published a down-to-earth account of the values she had developed in her years as a teacher in *Principles of Education Drawn from Nature and Revelation* (1865). See *The Autobiography of Elizabeth M. Sewell*, edited by Eleanor Sewell (Elizabeth Sewell's niece) in 1907.

SEXTON, Anne (1928–74) American poet, born in Massachusetts. Following an early elopement, children, and a breakdown, she started to write poetry as therapy. She attended Robert *Lowell's classes with Sylvia *Plath, with whom she shares the use of a dramatic, *confessional 'I', and the thematic territory of family life, jealous passion, and mental illness. Her early work makes dynamic use of strict poetic form, but, from the *Pulitzer Prize-winning *Live or Die* (1966), this is replaced by free verse which relies on dense, sometimes surreal, metaphors, wit, and rhythmic lists for impact. Her later work is increasingly haunted by a troubled relationship with God. Despite much success, especially with her adaptation of the *Grimm brothers' fairy-tales, *Transformations* (1971), Sexton took her own life in 1974. See Diane Wood Middlebrook, *Anne Sexton* (1992).

SFORZA family Dukes of Milan from 1450 until the end of the independent duchy of Milan in the mid-16th century. The family came to prominence with **Francesco** (1401–66), who served as condottiere to the last *Visconti duke and seized power shortly after the latter's death. Francesco's political acumen is celebrated by *Machiavelli in *The Prince*. The Sforza were notable patrons of the arts; *Leonardo da Vinci spent almost twenty years (1481–99) in Milan working for **Ludovico Sforza**, il Moro ('The Moor') (1452–1508).

SHACKLETON, Sir Ernest (1874–1922) Antarctic explorer, born Kildare, Ireland, and raised in Sydenham, Kent. Shackleton left Dulwich College at 16 to join the mercantile marine. In 1901 he joined Robert *Scott's first Antarctic expedition, maintaining his literary interests by editing the first *South Polar Times*. He was invalided home after a long-distance sledge journey into the interior. He led his own expedition on the *Nimrod* from 1907–9. He sledged to within 100 miles of the South Pole, recounting the harrowing journey in *The Heart of the Antarctic* (1909). In 1914, during his attempt to cross the continent, his ship *Endurance* was crushed by pack ice. To seek help, Shackleton led an epic voyage in an open boat to South Georgia, and climbed the uncharted Allardyce Range. He published his account, *South*, in 1919. Shackleton died on board the *Quest* in 1922, during his fourth expedition to the Antarctic.

Shadow of a Gunman, The See O'CASEY, SEAN.

SHADWELL, Thomas (?1642–92) Dramatist, born in Norfolk and educated at Gonville and Caius College, Cambridge, whose first play *The Sullen Lovers* (1668) was based on *Molière's *Les Fâcheux*; in its preface he proclaimed himself a follower of Ben *Jonson's comedy of humours. He wrote some fourteen comedies, including *The Squire of Alsatia* (1688), *The Virtuoso* (1676, a satire on the *Royal Society), *Epsom Wells* (1672), and *Bury Fair* (1689); the last two give an interesting if scurrilous picture of contemporary manners, watering places, and amusements. He also wrote operas, adapting William *Shakespeare's *The* **Tempest* as *The Enchanted Island* (1674). A successful dramatist in his day, he has been perhaps unfairly remembered for his 1682 quarrel with John *Dryden. He was probably the author of *The Medal of John Bays* (1682) and other anonymous attacks on Dryden; Dryden's counter-attacks include **Mac Flecknoe* and the second part of **Absalom and Achitophel*, where Shadwell appears as Og. Shadwell somewhat plaintively defends himself from the charge of dullness in his dedication to Sir Charles *Sedley of his translation of the *Tenth Satire of Juvenal* (1687). As a 'true-blue' Whig, he succeeded Dryden as poet laureate and historiographer at the revolution in 1689; their quarrel had been partly political, for Shadwell had been virtually unable to get his plays performed during the last years of Charles II's reign, or in James II's.

SHAFFER, Peter (1926–) Playwright, born in Liverpool, and educated at Trinity College, Cambridge. His first play, *Five Finger Exercise* (1958), a drama of middle-class family life, was followed by many other successes, including *The Royal Hunt of the Sun* (1964), an epic about the conquest of Peru; *Black Comedy* (1965), a cleverly constructed *farce set in a London apartment which reverses dark and light, so that the cast, in full glare of the lights and view of the audience, stumbles around during the pitch darkness of a dramatic electricity failure; *Equus* (1973), a drama about an analyst's relationship with his horse-obsessed patient; *Amadeus* (1979), which deals with the nature of creativity through a portrayal of the composers *Mozart and Salieri; *Lettice and Lovage* (1987); and *The Gift of the Gorgon* (1992). His twin brother Anthony Shaffer (d. 2001), author of *Sleuth* (1970), was also a successful playwright.

SHAFTESBURY, Anthony Ashley Cooper, first Baron Ashley and first earl of (1621–83) A statesman prominent on the king's side in the Civil War, as leader of the parliamentary opposition to Oliver *Cromwell, after the *Restoration as a member of the cabal and chancellor. After his dismissal he was leader of the opposition, a promoter of the Exclusion Bill, and a supporter of the duke of Monmouth (1649–85). He is closely associated with the foundation of the Whig party and was for a time its most prominent politician. He died in the Netherlands. He was satirized as Achitophel in John *Dryden's **Absalom and Achitophel*, by Thomas *Otway in **Venice Preserv'd*, and by many others.

SHAFTESBURY, Anthony Ashley Cooper, third earl of (1671–1713) Moral philosopher. His principal writings, which employ irony, indirection, ambiguity, and juxtaposition to achieve a broad range of witty effects, were collected in *Characteristics of Men, Manners, Opinions, and Times*, published 1711 (rev. edn 1714). Shaftesbury was influenced by *Deism and opposed the self-interest theory of conduct advocated by Thomas *Hobbes. Man has 'affections', Shaftesbury held, not only for himself but for the creatures about him. 'To have one's affections right and entire, not only in respect of oneself, but of society and the public: this is rectitude, integrity, or virtue.' Moreover, man has a capacity for distinguishing right and wrong, the beauty or ugliness of actions and affections, and this he calls the 'moral sense'. To be truly virtuous, a man must have a disinterested affection for what he perceives to be right. Such views are echoed in Alexander *Pope's **Essay on Man*, in the novels of Henry *Fielding, and in the philosophy of Francis *Hutcheson. Shaftesbury's aesthetic thought, which asserts a close connection between art and morality, influenced later writers such as James *Arbuckle and Mark *Akenside. See the edition of *Characteristicks* by L. E. Klein (1999).

SHAH, Idries (1924–96) Writer and teacher, born in the north of India, whose many works have done much to introduce Sūfī thought to the West. They include *The Sufis* (1964), *The Tales of the Dervishes* (1967), *Caravan of Dreams* (1968), *The Way of the Sufi* (1968), and *Learning How to Live* (1978, with an introduction by Doris *Lessing, 1981: Lessing has been much influenced by his work). He collected stories from the *Nasrudin corpus and published other selections of oriental tales. His works are unconventional mixtures of jokes, anecdotes, questions, precepts, and illuminations, inspired by Sūfī wisdom and psychology.

SHAH, Tahir (1966–) Travel writer and documentary film-maker educated at Bryanston School, Dorset, and at the United States International University; Shah's several books, mostly accounts of journeys in Africa, Asia, and the Americas, include *Trail of Feathers* (2001), *In Search of King Solomon's Mines* (2002), and *House of the Tiger King* (2004).

SHAKESPEARE, Nicholas (1957–) Novelist and biographer, born in Worcester and educated at Cambridge. Shakespeare worked as a literary journalist and published his first novel, *The Vision of Elena Silves*, a story of religious visions and revolutionary dreams in South America, in 1989. On the strength of this book and his second novel, *The High Flyer* (1993), he was chosen as one of **Granta*'s 'Best of Young British Novelists' in 1993. Subsequent novels include *The Dancer Upstairs* (1995), another tale of love and politics set in South America, *Snowleg* (2004), about a failed love affair in Cold War East Germany and its long-term consequences, and *Secrets of the Sea* (2007). His biography of the novelist and travel writer Bruce *Chatwin was published in 1999.

SHAKESPEARE, William (1564–1616) Dramatist, actor, man of the theatre, and poet, baptized in Holy Trinity Church, Stratford-upon-Avon, on 26 April 1564. His birth is traditionally celebrated on 23 April, which is also known to have been the date of his death. He was the eldest son of John Shakespeare, a glover and dealer in other commodities who played a prominent part in local affairs, becoming bailiff and justice of the peace in 1568, but whose fortunes later declined. John had married *c.*1557 Mary Arden, who came from a family of higher social standing. Of their eight children, four sons and one daughter survived childhood.

The standard and kind of education indicated by William's writings are such as he might have received at the local grammar school, whose records for the period are lost. On 28 November 1582 a bond was issued permitting him to marry Anne Hathaway of Shottery, a village close to Stratford. She was eight years his senior. A daughter, Susanna, was baptized on 26 May 1583, and twins, Hamnet and Judith, on 2 February 1585. We do not know how Shakespeare was employed in early manhood; the best-authenticated tradition is John *Aubrey's: 'he had been in his younger years a schoolmaster in the country.' This has fed speculation that he is the 'William Shakeshafte' named in the will of the Alexander Houghton, of Lea Hall, Lancashire, in 1581, who refused to attend Anglican church services, and in turn that he had Catholic sympathies.

Nothing is known of his beginnings as a writer, nor when or in what capacity he entered the theatre. In 1587 an actor of the Queen's Men was killed shortly before the company visited Stratford. That Shakespeare may have filled the vacancy is an intriguing speculation. The first printed allusion to him is from 1592, in the pamphlet **Greene's Groat's-Worth of Wit*, ostensibly by Robert *Greene but possibly by Henry *Chettle. Mention of 'an upstart Crow' who 'supposes he is as well able to bombast out a blank verse as the best of you' and who 'is in his own conceit the only Shake-scene in a country' suggests rivalry, and parody of a line from *3 *Henry VI* shows that Shakespeare was established on the London literary scene. He was a leading member of the Lord Chamberlain's Men soon after their refoundation in 1594. With them he worked and grew prosperous for the rest of his career as they developed into London's leading company, occupying the *Globe Theatre from 1599, becoming the King's Men on James I's accession in 1603, and taking over the Blackfriars as a winter house in 1608. He is the only prominent playwright of his time to have had so stable a relationship with a single company.

Theatrical life centred on London, which necessarily became Shakespeare's professional base, as various records testify. But his family remained in Stratford. In 1596 his father applied, successfully, for a grant of arms, and so became a gentleman; in August William's son Hamnet died, and was buried in Holy Trinity churchyard. In October Shakespeare was lodging in Bishopsgate, London, and in May of the next year he bought a substantial Stratford house, New Place. His father died in 1601, and in the following year William paid £320 for 127 acres of land in Old Stratford. In 1604 he lodged in London with a Huguenot family called Mountjoy. In the next year he paid £440 for an interest in the Stratford tithes, and there in June 1607 his daughter Susanna married a physician, John Hall. His only granddaughter, Elizabeth Hall, was christened the following February; in 1608 his mother died and was buried in Holy Trinity.

Evidence of Shakespeare's increasing involvement with Stratford at this time suggests that he was withdrawing to New Place, but his name continues to appear in London records; in March 1613, for instance, he paid £140 for a gatehouse close to the Blackfriars Theatre, probably as an investment. In the same month he and the actor/artist Richard *Burbage received 44 shillings each for providing an *impresa*, a tilting shield for the earl of Rutland at a court tournament. This is Shakespeare's last known literary enterprise. In February 1616 his second daughter Judith married Thomas Quiney, causing her father to make alterations to the draft of his will, which he signed on 25 March. He died, according to the inscription on his monument, on 23 April, and was buried in Holy Trinity. His widow died in 1623 and his last surviving descendant, Elizabeth Hall, in 1670.

Shakespeare's only writings for the press are the narrative poems **Venus and Adonis* and *The *Rape of Lucrece*, published 1593 and 1594 respectively, each with the author's dedication to Henry Wriothesley, earl of Southampton, and the short poem 'The *Phoenix and the Turtle', published in 1601 in Robert Chester's *Love's Martyr*, a collection of poems by various hands. His *sonnets, mostly dating probably from the mid-1590s, appeared in 1609. Whether he authorized the publication is disputed. They bear a dedication to the mysterious 'Mr W.H.' over the initials of the publisher, Thomas Thorpe. The volume also includes the poem 'A *Lover's Complaint', whose authorship also is disputed.

Shakespeare's plays were published by being performed. Scripts of only half of them appeared in print in his lifetime, some in short, sometimes manifestly corrupt, texts, often known as 'bad quartos'. Records of performance are scanty and haphazard: as a result dates and order of composition, especially of the earlier plays, are often difficult to establish. The list that follows gives dates of first printing of all the plays other than those that first appeared in the 1623 *folio.

Probably Shakespeare began to write for the stage in the late 1580s. The ambitious trilogy on the reign of Henry VI, now known as *Henry VI* Parts 1, 2, and 3, and its sequel *Richard III*, are among his early works. Parts 2 and 3 were printed in variant texts as *The First Part of the Contention betwixt the Two Famous Houses of York and Lancaster* (1594) and *The True Tragedy of Richard, Duke of York* (1595). *Henry VI Part 1* may have been written after these, perhaps with a collaborator. A variant quarto of *Richard III* appeared in 1597. Shakespeare's first Roman tragedy is *Titus Andronicus*, printed in 1594, probably written with George *Peele; his earliest comedies are *The *Two Gentlemen of Verona*, *The *Taming of the Shrew* (a derivative play, *The Taming of a Shrew*, was printed 1594), *The *Comedy of Errors* (acted 1594), and *Love's Labour's Lost* (printed 1598). All these plays are thought to have been written by 1595.

Particularly difficult to date is *King John*: scholars still dispute whether a two-part play, *The Troublesome Reign of John, King of England*, printed 1591, is its source or (as seems more probable) a derivative. *Richard II*, printed 1597, is usually dated 1595. For some years after this, Shakespeare concentrated on comedy, in *A *Midsummer Night's Dream* and *The *Merchant of Venice* (both printed 1600), *The *Merry Wives of Windsor* (related to the later history plays, and printed in a variant text 1602), *Much Ado About Nothing* (printed 1600), *As You Like It* (mentioned in 1600), and *Twelfth Night*, probably written in 1600 or soon afterwards. *Romeo and Juliet* (ascribed to the mid-1590s) is a tragedy with strongly comic elements, and the tetralogy begun by *Richard II* is completed by three comical histories: *Henry IV* Parts 1 and 2, each printed a year or two after composition (Part 1 1598, Part 2 1600), and *Henry V*, almost certainly written 1599, printed, in a shortened, possibly corrupt, text, 1600.

In 1598 Francis *Meres, a minor writer, published praise of Shakespeare in *Palladis Tamia: Wit's Treasury*, mentioning twelve of the plays so far listed (assuming that by *Henry the 4* he means both Parts) along with another, *Love's Labour's Won*, apparently either a lost play or an alternative title for an extant one.

Late in the century Shakespeare turned again to tragedy. A Swiss traveller, Thomas Platter, saw *Julius Caesar* in London in September 1599. *Hamlet* apparently dates from the following year, but was only entered for publication in the register of the *Stationers' Company in July 1602; a short text probably reconstructed from memory by an actor appeared in 1603, and a good text printed from Shakespeare's manuscript in late 1604 (some copies bear the date 1605). A play that defies easy classification is *Troilus and Cressida*, probably written 1602, printed 1609. The comedy *All's Well That Ends Well*, too, is probably of this period, as is *Measure for Measure*, played at court in December 1604. The surviving text may have been lightly adapted by Thomas *Middleton. The tragedy *Othello*, played at court the previous month, did not reach print until 1622. *King Lear* probably dates, in its first version, from 1605; the quarto printed in 1608, once regarded as a corrupt text, is now thought to have been badly printed from Shakespeare's original manuscript. The text printed in the folio appears to represent a revision dating from a few years later. Much uncertainty surrounds *Timon of Athens*, printed in the folio from uncompleted papers, and probably written in collaboration with Middleton. *Macbeth*, probably adapted by Middleton, is generally dated 1606, *Antony and Cleopatra* 1606–7, and *Coriolanus* 1607–9.

Towards the end of his career, though while still in his early forties, Shakespeare turned to romantic tragicomedy. *Pericles*, probably written with George *Wilkins and printed in a debased text in 1609, certainly existed in the previous year; it and *The *Two Noble Kinsmen* are the only surviving plays generally believed to be largely by Shakespeare that were not included in the 1623 folio. Simon *Forman, the astrologer, records seeing both *Cymbeline* and *The *Winter's Tale* in 1611. *The *Tempest* was given at court in November 1611.

The last three plays associated with Shakespeare appear to have been written in collaboration with John *Fletcher. They are *All Is True*, retitled *Henry VIII* in the folio, which 'had been acted not passing 2 or 3 times' before the performance at the Globe during which the theatre burnt down on 29 June 1613; a lost play, *Cardenio*, acted by the King's Men in 1613 and attributed to the two dramatists in a Stationers' Register entry of 1653; and *The *Two Noble Kinsmen*, which appears to incorporate elements from a 1613 masque by Francis *Beaumont, and which was first printed in 1634. No Shakespeare play survives in authorial manuscript, though three pages of revisions to a manuscript play, *Sir Thomas *More*, variously dated about 1593 or 1601, are often thought to be by Shakespeare and in his hand.

It may have been soon after Shakespeare died, in 1616, that his colleagues John *Heminges and Henry Condell (d. 1627) began to prepare *Mr William Shakespeare's Comedies, Histories, and Tragedies*, better known as the first folio, which appeared in 1623. Only once before, in the 1616 Ben *Jonson folio, had an English dramatist's plays appeared in collected form. Heminges and Condell, or their agents, worked with care, assembling manuscripts, providing reliable printed copy when it was available, but also causing quartos to be brought wholly or partially into line with prompt-books. Their volume includes a dedicatory epistle to William and Philip Herbert, earls of Pembroke and Montgomery, an address 'To the great Variety of Readers' by themselves, and verse tributes, most notably the substantial poem by Jonson in which he declares that Shakespeare 'was not of an age, but for all time'. Above all, the folio is important because it includes sixteen plays which in all probability would not otherwise have survived. Its title-page engraving, by *Droeshout, is, along with the half-length figure bust by Gheerart Janssen erected in Holy Trinity, Stratford, by 1623, the only image of Shakespeare with strong claims to authenticity. The folio was reprinted three times in the 17th century; the second issue (1664) of the third edition adds *Pericles* and six more plays. Other plays, too, have been ascribed to Shakespeare, but few scholars would add anything to the accepted canon except part (or even all) of *Edward III*, printed anonymously 1596.

Over 200 years after Shakespeare died, doubts were raised about the authenticity of his works (*see* SHAKESPEARE: AUTHORSHIP OF THE WORKS). The documents committed to print between 1593 and 1634 have generated an enormous amount of varied kinds of human activity. The first editor to try to bring them into order, reconcile their discrepancies, correct their errors, and present them for readers of his time was the dramatist Nicholas *Rowe, in 1709. His 18th-century successors include Alexander *Pope (1723–5), Lewis *Theobald (1733), Samuel *Johnson (1765), Edward *Capell (1767–8), and Edmond *Malone (1790; third variorum 1821 by James Boswell the younger, out of Malone's edition). The most important 19th-century edition is the Cambridge Shakespeare (1863–6; rev. 1891–3), on which the Globe text (1864) was based. The American New Variorum edition, still in progress, began to appear in 1871. Early in the 20th century advances in textual studies transformed attitudes to the text. Subsequent editions include *Quiller-Couch's and J. Dover *Wilson's New Shakespeare (Cambridge, 1921–66), G. L. Kittredge's (1936), Peter Alexander's (1951), and the Riverside (1974). The Arden edition appeared originally 1899–1924; it was revised and largely replaced 1951–81. A new series, Arden 3, started to appear in 1995. The Oxford multi-volume edition (paperbacked as World's Classics) started to appear in 1982, and the New Cambridge in 1983. The Oxford single-volume edition, edited by S. Wells and G. Taylor, was published in 1986 with a second edition, including full texts of *Sir Thomas More* and *Edward III*, in 2005. A Royal Shakespeare Company edition, general editors Jonathan Bate and Eric Rasmussen, privileging the folio, appeared in 2007.

Great critics who have written on Shakespeare include John *Dryden, Samuel *Johnson, S. T. *Coleridge, William *Hazlitt, A. C. *Bradley, and (less reverently) George Bernard *Shaw. The German *Shakespeare Jahrbuch* has been appearing since 1865; other major periodicals are *Shakespeare Survey* (annual from 1948), *Shakespeare Quarterly* (from 1950), and *Shakespeare Studies* (annual from 1965). The standard biographical studies are E. K. *Chambers, *William Shakespeare: A Study of Facts and Problems* (2 vols, 1930) and S. *Schoenbaum, *William Shakespeare: A Documentary Life* (1975). The play scripts have been translated into over 90 languages and have inspired poets, novelists, dramatists, painters, composers, choreographers, film-makers, and other artists at all levels of creative activity. They have formed the basis for the English theatrical tradition, and they continue to find realization in readers' imaginations and, in richly varied transmutations, on the world's stages.

Shakespeare: authorship of the works Shakespeare's authorship of the works commonly attributed to him is amply demonstrated by documentary evidence from his own time and beyond. His name first appears in print on the title pages of **Venus and Adonis* (1593) and *The *Rape of Lucrece* (1594). As was customary, his earliest plays were published without ascription to their author, but his name appears on title pages of many plays from 1598 onwards and of the sonnets in 1609. Many writers refer to him by name as the author of plays and poems during his lifetime and later, most significantly in the private conversations of around Christmas 1618 between Ben *Jonson and William *Drummond of Hawthornden. There are numerous manuscript allusions. The first *folio of 1623 prints tributes including Jonson's 'To the Memory of my Beloved the Author Mr William Shakespeare and What He Hath Left Us', in which Shakespeare is described as the 'sweet swan of Avon'. The inscriptions on the memorial in Holy Trinity Church Stratford-upon-Avon compare him to great figures of antiquity and praise 'what he hath writ'.

No questions were raised until the late 18th century, when James Wilmot, a literary scholar and clergyman, came up with the idea that the true author of the works was Francis *Bacon. The idea resurfaced in *The Romance of Yachting* (1848) a book by an American lawyer, Colonel Joseph C. Hart, and gathered force with the work of Delia Bacon, a mad American who in 1856 sought to open the Stratford grave in the hope of finding evidence to support her case that the plays were the work of a committee including Francis Bacon, Edmund *Spenser, and Sir Walter *Ralegh. This resulted in the forming of both an American and an English Bacon Society, which still exist. It grew in force in the following years, since when at least 60 candidates, from *Elizabeth I downwards, have been proposed. In recent times the most popular have been Bacon, Christopher *Marlowe, and the earl of *Oxford. The list grows year by year.

The commonest anti-Stratfordian arguments are that Shakespeare was of relatively humble origins, is not known to have travelled overseas, and came from a small provincial town where he could not have received a good enough education to have written the plays. The facts are that it is not necessary to be an aristocrat to be a great writer—Jonson, who like Shakespeare did not attend a university, was the son of a bricklayer, Marlowe's father was a cobbler—that the plays show no knowledge of foreign countries that could not have been obtained from books or from conversation, and that Stratford had a good grammar school whose pupils received a rigorous education in the classics which would more than account for the learning displayed in the works. Anti-Stratfordians too easily ignore the logical necessity to disprove the evidence that Shakespeare wrote the works before trying to argue that someone else did. See S. *Schoenbaum, *Shakespeare's Lives* (1970; rev. 1991).

'Shalott, The Lady of' *See* 'LADY OF SHALOTT, THE'; LAUNCELOT OF THE LAKE, SIR.

Shamela Andrews, An Apology for the Life of Mrs A lively travesty of Samuel Richardson's **Pamela*, published anonymously in 1741, almost certainly by Henry *Fielding. The gullible Parson Tickletext writes to his friend, Parson Oliver, commending the beauty and virtue of 'sweet, dear, pretty Pamela'; Oliver, however, has in his possession letters which reveal the true history of the heroine. The main events of Richardson's story are preserved, but Parson Williams now appears as a scheming hypocrite, Mr B. as the foolish Mr Booby, and Pamela as a calculating and promiscuous slut, already the mother of an illegitimate child, and determined to use her reputation for 'vartue' to capture her master. Richardson's prized device of 'writing to the moment' is also ridiculed. Richardson was convinced the work was Fielding's and never forgave him. The novel's title alludes ironically to *An Apology for the Life of Colley *Cibber* (1740).

SHANGE, Ntozake (1948–) Born Paulette Williams, African American playwright and novelist, born in New Jersey, who changed her name in 1971. Her first play, or rather 'choreopoem', was *For Coloured Girls Who Have Considered Suicide When the Rainbow is Enuf* (1975). She has also published a number of volumes of poetry and her novels include *Sassafrass, Cypress & Indigo* (1982) and *I Live in Music* (1994), a mixed-media portrait of a trumpet player.

SHAPCOTT, Jo (1953–) Poet, born in London and educated at Trinity College, Dublin, Oxford, and Harvard. Her first collection was *Electroplating the Baby* (1988), whose title poem explored a characteristic vein of scientific and medical fantasia. *Phrase Book* (1992) followed, with its invigoratingly feminist sequence of 'Mad Cow' poems and its widely celebrated title poem, written during the Gulf War. *My Life Asleep* appeared in 1998. A selection from these volumes, *Her Book: Poems 1988–1998*, was published in 2000; and *Tender Taxes*, versions of *Rilke's poems in French, appeared in 2002. Her poetry combines contemporary references (to film, cartoon, and news stories) with literary and historical allusions, and is distinguished by sharp word-play and a disturbing surreal animism.

SHAPIRO, Karl (1913–2000) American poet, born in Baltimore, who began publishing poetry while serving in the Pacific during the Second World War. His 1945 collection *V-Letter* won the Pulitzer Prize. *The Younger Son* (1988) and *Reports of my Death* (1990) are volumes of autobiography; *Edsel* (1971) is his only novel.

SHARP, Cecil (1859–1924) English musician and folk-music collector. Sharp began collecting English rural *folk songs in 1903, and soon became the most important of all the workers in this field, transcribing during the course of his life a total of 4,977 tunes of which he published 1,118. He was active in the Folk-Song Society, and founded the Folk Dance Society in 1911; his efforts profoundly influenced a whole school of English composers, including Ralph *Vaughan Williams and Gustav *Holst.

SHARP, William ('Fiona Macleod') (1855–1905) Novelist, mystic and biographer born in Paisley, Scotland, and educated at Glasgow University. He wrote under his own name essays, verse, minor novels, and lives of D. G. *Rossetti (1882), P. B. *Shelley (1887), Heinrich *Heine (1888), and Robert *Browning (1890). He is chiefly remembered for his mystic Celtic tales and romances of peasant life written by his feminized persona 'Fiona Macleod', in the spirit of *The *Celtic Twilight*. The first work by 'Fiona Macleod' was *Pharais* (1894), followed by *The Mountain Lovers* (1895), *The Sin Eater* (1895), and plays, including *The House of Usna* (1903) and *The Immortal Hour* (1900). Sharp successfully concealed the identity of 'Fiona Macleod' (including writing a bogus entry in **Who's Who*) until his death.

SHARPE, Tom (1928–) Novelist, born in London and educated at Lancing School and Pembroke College, Cambridge. He spent some years in South Africa (1951–61) and his first two novels, *Riotous Assembly* (1971) and *Indecent Exposure* (1973), are political satires set in that country. On his return to England he taught for a decade in Cambridge, and *Porterhouse Blue* (1974) is a farcical *campus novel set in a fictitious college. Other works, all in a vein of fierce and sometimes grotesque satiric comedy, include *Blott on the Landscape* (1975), *Wilt* (1976), and *Ancestral Vices* (1980).

SHAW, Bob (1931–96) Irish *science fiction writer, born in Belfast. His story 'Light of Other Days' (1966) is a classic example of extrapolating the possibilities of an imaginary technology, seen also in novels like *Orbitsville* (1975) and *The Ragged Astronauts* (1986). His humorous lectures are fondly remembered.

SHAW, George Bernard (1856–1950) Dramatist and critic, born in Dublin, the youngest child of unhappily married and inattentive parents. In 1876 he moved to London, joining his mother and sister, and began his literary career by ghosting music criticism and writing five unsuccessful novels (including *Cashel Byron's Profession*, 1886). From 1885 he contributed music, art, and literary criticism to the *Dramatic Review*, *Our Corner*, the **Pall Mall Gazette*, *The World*, and *The Star* (as 'Corno di Bassetto'). He was a drama critic for the **Saturday Review* (1895–8) and produced a series of controversial articles voicing his impatience with the artificiality of the London theatrical scene and pleading for the performance of plays dealing with contemporary social and moral problems. He campaigned for a theatre of ideas in Britain comparable to that of Henrik *Ibsen and August *Strindberg in Scandinavia. He took up various causes and joined several literary and political organizations, notably the Fabian Society, serving on the executive committee from 1885 to 1911. He wrote tracts setting down his socialist and collectivist principles. He was a freethinker, a supporter of women's rights, and an advocate of income equality, the abolition of private property, and a change in the voting system. He also agitated for the simplification of spelling and punctuation and the reform of the English alphabet. He was already well known as a journalist and public speaker when his first play, *Widowers' Houses*, was produced, with little success, in 1892. There followed, among others, *Arms and the Man* (1894), *The Devil's Disciple* (1897), *You Never Can Tell* (1899), *Mrs Warren's Profession* (1902, though published earlier), and **John Bull's Other Island* (1904), a play originally intended for the *Abbey Theatre and one which, thanks to its characteristic 'Shavian' wit, brought his first popular success in London.

The huge dramatic output of Shaw's maturity included *Man and Superman* (1905), *Major Barbara* (1905), *The Doctor's Dilemma* (1906), *Androcles and the Lion* (1913), **Pygmalion* (1913), *Heartbreak House* (1920), *Back to Methuselah* (1921), *Saint Joan*

(1923), *Too True to be Good* (1932), *Village Wooing* (1934), *In Good King Charles's Golden Days* (1939), and *Buoyant Billions* (1948). These plays were published (some in collections: *Plays Pleasant and Unpleasant*, 1898; *Three Plays for Puritans*, 1901) with lengthy prefaces in which Shaw expressed his rationalist, anti-romantic, ameliorist views. The conflict in the plays involves a clash of thought and belief rather than of will or temperament. The witty, paradoxical dialogue won audiences over to the idea that mental and moral passion could produce absorbing drama. Shaw believed that war, disease, and the unnecessary brevity of our lifespan frustrate the 'Life Force' and that functional adaptation, a current of creative evolution activated by human will power, was essential to progress and the survival of the species. His major non-dramatic works include *The Quintessence of Ibsenism* (1891; expanded 1913), *The Perfect Wagnerite* (1898); *Common Sense about the War* (1914); and *The Intelligent Woman's Guide to Socialism and Capitalism* (1928). He was a prolific letter writer. His correspondence with the actresses Ellen *Terry and Mrs Patrick Campbell (aka Margot Schneider, 1865–1940), and with colleagues such as H. G. *Wells and the film producer Gabriel Pascal (1894–1954), as well as several volumes of collected letters, have been published.

In 1898 Shaw married Charlotte Payne-Townshend, with whom he appears to have lived in celibate companionship until her death in 1943. He was a strict vegetarian and never drank spirits, coffee, or tea, and remained active as a playwright and controversialist until his death at 94. He was awarded the *Nobel Prize in 1925. See *The Bodley Head Collected Plays with their Prefaces* (7 vols, 1970–4).

SHEBBEARE, John (1709–88) A surgeon who gave up medicine for writing in about 1754, when he published a satirical novel, *The Marriage Act*, for which he was arrested. Another novel, *Lydia* (1755), uses the figure of a noble savage, the Iroquois Cannassatego, to attack, in the spirit of *primitivism, the corruptions of British society. Shebbeare's inflammatory writings were condemned by Tobias *Smollett, who satirized him as Ferret in *Sir Launcelot *Greaves*. Later Shebbeare wrote much against John *Wilkes.

SHECKLEY, Robert (1928–2005) American *science fiction writer, born in Poughkeepsie, New York. His sardonic stories have been issued in several collections. Novels such as *Immortality, Inc.* (1959), *The Status Civilisation* (1960), and *The Alchemical Marriage of Alistair Crompton* (1978) often featured confused, even paranoid protagonists in bizarre situations.

SHEFFIELD, Charles (1935–2002) Physicist and author of *hard science fiction, born in Hull, resident in America for much of his life. *The Web between the Worlds* (1979) described a fictional 'space elevator' linking earth and an orbiting satellite.

SHEFFIELD, John, third earl of Mulgrave, first duke of Buckinghamshire, and marquess of Normanby (1647–1721) Courtier and poet. He was a patron of John *Dryden, and erected the Dryden monument in *Poets' Corner. Sheffield was an early friend of Alexander *Pope, who drew on his *Essay upon Poetry* (1682) in the **Essay on Criticism* and later edited his works (1723).

SHELLEY, Mary Wollstonecraft (1797–1851) Novelist, editor, biographer and travel writer, only daughter of William *Godwin and Mary *Wollstonecraft, born in London. Her mother died a few days after her birth. Educated in London, in 1814 she eloped to Italy with P. B. *Shelley, and married him in 1816 on the death of his wife Harriet. Only one of their children, Percy, survived infancy. She returned to England in 1823, after Shelley's death the previous year, and pursued a professional writing career. She is famous for **Frankenstein, or The Modern Prometheus* (1818), but she is the author also of six further novels. *Valperga* (1823) is a romance set in 14th-century Italy; *The *Last Man* (1826), a novel set in the future. *Perkin Warbeck* (1830), a historical romance bearing the influence of Walter *Scott, addresses the historically contentious theory that the duke of York (the younger of the two princes imprisoned in the tower and allegedly put to death by Richard III) was the same person as the rebel leader Perkin Warbeck. There followed *Lodore* (1835) which returns to the theme of primitivism evident in *Frankenstein* and *The Last Man*; the heroine, Ethel, is taken as a child by her father, Lord Lodore, to the wilds of Illinois and reared amidst the grandest objects of nature, whence she returns to a life of romance and penury in a London reminiscent of Mary Shelley's early years. Her sixth and last novel *Falkner* (1837) was composed during the year of her father's death, an event that clearly influenced the novel's primary plot line, which concerns the father–daughter relationship between Falkner and his adopted charge, Elizabeth. She also published several biographies and short stories, most of which were published in the *Keepsake*; some have *science fiction elements, others are Gothic (*see* GOTHIC FICTION) or historical (*see* HISTORICAL FICTION), and many are continental in setting. Her *Rambles in Germany and Italy, in 1840, 1842 and 1843* (1844) was well received. She also edited her husband's *Poems* (1839) and his *Essays, Letters from Abroad, Translations and Fragments* (1840). Her children's story *Maurice*, written in 1820, about a kidnapped boy's chance meeting with his father, was rediscovered in 1997 and published in 1998 with an introduction by Claire *Tomalin. See *The Journals of Mary Shelley*, ed. P. R. Feldman and D. Scott-Kilvert, 2 vols (1987); *The Letters of Mary Wollstonecraft Shelley*, ed. B. T. Bennett, 3 vols (1980–8); *The Novels and Selected Works of Mary Shelley*, ed. N. Crook and P. Clemit, 8 vols (1996).

SHELLEY, Percy Bysshe (1792–1822) English poet and radical. The eldest son of the MP for Horsham (and later baronet), he was born at Field Place, Sussex, and destined for a parliamentary career. Mischievous and imaginative as a child, he was conventionally educated at Syon House Academy, Eton College, and University College, Oxford; an upbringing that made him unhappy and rebellious. At school he was bullied as 'Mad Shelley' and the 'Eton Atheist'; at home he was worshipped by a tribe of younger sisters; a pattern that recurs throughout his life.

Encouraged in his 'printing freaks', he privately published a series of *Gothic novels and verses in his teens: *Zastrozzi* (1810); *Original Poetry by Victor and Cazire* (1810, with his beloved sister Elizabeth); and *St Irvyne, or The Rosicrucian* (1811). At Oxford he read radical authors—William *Godwin, Thomas *Paine, *Condorcet—dressed and behaved eccentrically, and in March 1811 was expelled for circulating a pamphlet, 'The Necessity of *Atheism', written with his friend T. J. *Hogg. He quarrelled with his father, and eloped to Scotland with 16-year-old Harriet Westbrook, the daughter of a coffee-house proprietor. They married in Edinburgh in August 1811, though Shelley disapproved of matrimony, as well as royalty, meat-eating, and religion. Three years of nomadic existence followed. At York he tried sharing Harriet with Hogg; in the Lakes he argued with Robert *Southey; in Dublin he spoke on public platforms, and published *An Address to the Irish People* (1812) and *Proposals* for reform associations. He corresponded with Godwin; circulated pamphlets on vegetarianism and on the free press (*A Letter to Lord Ellenborough*, 1812); and fly-posted a democratic broadsheet, *A Declaration of Rights* (for which his servant was democratically arrested). He tried setting up a radical commune of 'like spirits' first at Lynmouth, Devon, and later at Tremadoc, north Wales. Much of his early philosophy, both in poetry and politics, is expressed in **Queen Mab* (1813), with its remarkable *Notes*: they show Shelley as the direct heir to the French and British revolutionary intellectuals of the 1790s.

In 1814 his marriage with Harriet collapsed, despite the birth of two children and the kindly intervention of Thomas Love *Peacock. Shelley eloped abroad with Mary Godwin (Mary *Shelley), together with her 15-year-old stepsister Jane Clairmont (she subsequently called herself 'Claire'). Their triangular relationship endured for the next eight years. His unfinished novella *The Assassins* (1814) reflects their dreamy travels through post-war France, Switzerland, and Germany, as does their combined journal, *History of a Six Weeks Tour* (1817). He returned to London, an annuity of £1,000, and, after many upheavals, a house with Mary on the edge of Windsor Great Park. Here he wrote **Alastor* (1816), a non-political poem of haunting beauty, which first brought him general notice and reviews. His favourite son William was born. The summer of 1816 was spent on Lake Geneva with Lord *Byron. Mary began **Frankenstein*, and Shelley composed two philosophic poems much influenced by William *Wordsworth, the 'Hymn to Intellectual Beauty' (partly about his childhood) and 'Mont Blanc', a meditation on the nature of power in a Godless universe.

In the autumn of 1816 Harriet drowned herself in the Serpentine. Shelley immediately married Mary and began a Chancery case for the custody of his first two children, which he lost. The experience shook him deeply, and is recalled in many verse fragments, such as the 'Invocation to Misery', 'Lines: The cold earth slept below…', and the cursing 'To the Lord Chancellor' (1817—a so-called *'flyting'). However, friendships developed with Leigh *Hunt, John *Keats, William *Hazlitt, and others of the liberal **Examiner* circle; while Peacock, now a close friend, drew a portrait of Shelley as Scythrop Glowry in **Nightmare Abbey*. In 1817 the family settled at Great Marlow, on the Thames, where Shelley wrote his polemical 'Hermit of Marlow' pamphlets, drafted a self-searching 'Essay on Christianity', and slowly composed 'Laon and Cythna', which was published, with alterations to avoid prosecution, as *The *Revolt of Islam* in 1818.

Harried by creditors, ill health, and 'social hatred', Shelley took his household permanently abroad, to Italy in the spring of 1818, leaving behind his sonnet 'Ozymandias' and a mass of unpaid bills. He stayed at Lucca, where he translated *Plato's *Symposium* and wrote a daring essay 'On the Manners of the Ancient Greeks'; and then at Venice and Este, where he composed *'Julian and Maddalo', based on his friendship with Byron. He wintered in Naples, where he wrote the passionately unhappy 'Stanzas Written in Dejection'; he also registered a mysterious baby, Elena Adelaide Shelley, as his adopted—or probably illegitimate—child. In the spring of 1819 he was working on **Prometheus Unbound*.

His domestic situation was increasingly strained. His little daughter Clara had died at Venice; now his favourite 'Willmouse' died at Rome and Mary suffered a nervous breakdown. The shaken family settled in Tuscany: first outside Livorno, then at Florence, and finally at Pisa, which became their more or less permanent home until 1822.

Yet the twelve months from the summer of 1819 saw Shelley's most extraordinary and varied burst of major poetry. He completed the fourth act of *Prometheus* (pub. 1820); wrote *The *Mask of Anarchy* (September 1819); *'Ode to the West Wind' (October 1819); the satirical **Peter Bell the Third* (December 1819); his long political odes, 'To Liberty' and 'To Naples' (both spring 1820); the lively, intimate 'Letter to Maria Gisborne' (July 1820); and the *'Witch of Atlas' (August 1820). Much of this work was inspired by news of political events, which also produced a number of short, angry, propaganda poems: 'Young Parson Richards', 'Song to the Men of England', and 'Sonnet: England 1819'. At the same time he dashed off several pure lyric pieces, including 'To a Skylark' and 'The Cloud' (both spring 1820), of dazzling metrical virtuosity; and completed a verse melodrama, *The *Cenci* (1819). Yet despite this period of creativity, he could get little accepted for publication in England, and he felt increasingly isolated and despondent. The birth of his youngest son, Percy Florence, cheered his domestic life.

The quieter period at Pisa which followed (1820–1) saw him at work on a number of prose pieces: *A *Philosophical View of Reform* (1820); the impish 'Essay on the Devil'; and his famous **Defence of Poetry* (1821). He also wrote some of his most delicate, low-keyed, and visually suggestive short poems: 'The Two Spirits', 'To the Moon', 'The Aziola', and 'Evening: Ponte Al Mare, Pisa'.

In the spring of 1821 news of the death of Keats in Rome produced **Adonais*. The absence of Claire and growing restlessness precipitated a platonic love affair with Emilia Viviani, a beautiful 17-year-old heiress 'tyrannized' in a convent at Pisa. Instead of a third elopement this resulted in **Epipsychidion* (1821).

In the winter of 1821 Byron also moved to Pisa, and a raffish circle formed round the two poets, including Edward *Trelawny, Edward and Jane Williams, and eventually Leigh Hunt, who came from England to edit a monthly journal, *The *Liberal* (1822–4). Shelley was roused again to public utterance: his last completed verse drama, **Hellas* (1822), though 'a mere improvise', was inspired by the Greek War of Independence. He also began 'Charles I', a political drama of the English Civil War, with its touching song by Archy, the jester, 'A widow-bird sat mourning for her love'.

In April 1822 he moved his household to an isolated beach house on the bay of Lerici. Here Mary suffered a dangerous miscarriage; Claire reacted violently to news of the sudden death of Allegra, her daughter by Byron; and Shelley saw the ghost of a child in the sea. Here he began his last major poem, *The *Triumph of Life*. At the same time he composed a number of short lyrics, some to Jane Williams, of striking melodic grace: 'When the lamp is shattered', 'With a Guitar, to Jane', and the melancholy 'Lines Written in the Bay of Lerici'. His letters, still full of political hope and magically descriptive of the Italian seascape, are nonetheless shadowed with personal premonitions. Shelley was drowned in August 1822, in his small schooner the *Ariel*, together with Edward Williams and an English boatboy, on a return trip from visiting Byron and Hunt at Livorno. Overtaken by a violent summer squall, the boat went down without lowering its sails.

His lyric powers and romantic biography have until recently obscured Shelley's most enduring qualities as a writer: his intellectual courage and originality; his hatred of oppression and injustice; and his mischievous, sometimes macabre, sense of humour (especially evident in his light verse and letters). He was widely read in the classics, philosophy, and contemporary science; he translated from Greek (Plato and Homer), Latin (Spinoza), Spanish (Calderón), German (Goethe), Italian (Dante), and some Arabic fragments. His essays—very few published in his lifetime—are highly intelligent, his political pamphlets both angry and idealistic.

Writers antipathetic to the poet, notably F. R. *Leavis, have seen in his work imprecision and rhetorical abstraction, intellectual arrogance, and moments of intense self-pity. But in great poems like the 'West Wind', or in magnificent prose like passages from the *Defence*, it is precisely these limitations that he transcends, and indeed explodes. His critical fortunes fell in the middle of the 20th century, but he has recovered his position as an undoubted major figure amongst the English Romantics: the poet of volcanic hope for a better world, of fiery aspirations shot upwards through bitter gloom.

Shelley's *Letters* have been edited by F. L. Jones, 2 vols (1964); the standard life remains that by N. I. White, 2 vols (1947); see also Richard *Holmes, *The Pursuit* (1974). Two major scholarly editions are in progress, the three-volume Longman *The Poems of Shelley* and the seven-volume *The Complete Poetry of Percy Bysshe Shelley* published by the Johns Hopkins University Press. The major political reinterpretations of his career are by K. N. Cameron, *Young Shelley: Genesis of a Radical* (1951) and P. M. S. Dawson's *The Unacknowledged Legislator: Shelley and Politics* (1980). Excellent modern criticism has been produced by Harold Bloom (1959), Neville Rogers (1967), Judith Chernaik (1972), Timothy Webb (1976), Timothy Clark (1989), Benjamin Colbert (2005), and Cian Duffy (2005); while biographical memoirs by Trelawny, *Peacock, and Hogg remain vivid and amusing.

Shelley, Memoirs of By Thomas Love *Peacock, published 1858. Not a full-dress biography, it originated as a review of reminiscences by Edward *Trelawny and T. J. *Hogg, which Peacock thought inaccurate, particularly in relation to P. B. *Shelley's first wife Harriet Westbrook (1795–1816). Peacock's book is polished and reliable, but its reticence and its willingness to question Shelley's truthfulness have not endeared it to the poet's admirers.

SHENSTONE, William (1714–63) Poet, educated at Solihull School and Pembroke College, Oxford, where he published *Poems upon Various Occasions* (1737), which included an early version of *The Schoolmistress*, the mock-Spenserian poem for which he is best known and which he later revised substantially (1742, 1748). From 1743 he transformed the Leasowes, his estate near Halesowen, in the west Midlands of England, into a *ferme ornée* or 'natural' landscape garden, beautified with cascades, vistas, and a grove to *Virgil, encircled by a winding walk. His friends included Lord *Lyttelton at nearby Hagley, to whom he addressed *The Judgement of Hercules* (1741), William *Somervile, Lady Luxborough (1699–1756), Richard *Graves, and Richard *Jago. He helped to edit Robert *Dodsley's *Collection of Poems*, advised the Birmingham printer John *Baskerville, and worked with Thomas *Percy on the **Reliques of Ancient English Poetry*. He wrote many elegies, odes, songs, 'levities', and a 'Pastoral Ballad' which Thomas *Arne set to music. The poetry won moderate praise from Samuel *Johnson in his **Lives of the English Poets*, though Johnson gently mocked Shenstone's improvident gardening obsessions. *Essays on Men, Manners, and Things*, the second volume of Dodsley's edition of Shenstone's works (3 vols, 1764–9), contains his influential essay on 'landskip gardening'. Shenstone's extensive correspondence was edited by M. Williams (1939).
See also LANDSCAPE GARDENING.

SHEPARD, E. H. (Ernest Howard) (1879–1976) Author-illustrator, born in London, educated at St Paul's School and Heatherley's School of Fine Art. He worked for **Punch* from 1907 but is remembered for his illustrations for A. A. *Milne's children's books and Kenneth Grahame's *The *Wind in the Willows* (1931). His own children's books include *Ben and Brock* (1965). There are autobiographical works and a life by Arthur Chandler (2000).

SHEPARD, Lucius (1947–) American *science fiction writer of sometimes *Conradian intensity, born in Lynchburg, Virginia. *Life during Wartime* (1987) has a near-future USA at war in Central America, a location used in other fictions. Stories are collected in *Barnacle Bill the Spacer and Other Stories* (1997).

SHEPARD, Sam (1943–) American playwright and actor, born in Illinois. Having staged his first plays in New York, Shepard spent four years (from 1971) living in London, where a number of his plays were produced at the *National Theatre and the *Royal Court. His work deals with American mythologies, the death of the American dream, and Americans' relationship to their land and history. In his most famous work, *True West* (1980), two brothers in southern California argue over the nature of the 'true' American West—where each character fights to maintain his own identity and destroy his brother's. Shepard's 40 other plays include *Buried Child* (1978), which won the 1979 *Pulitzer Prize for drama, and which links *True West* in a trilogy with *Curse of the Starving Class* (1976); and *Fool for Love* (1983), which Shepard directed off-Broadway and acted in on screen. He is also the author of a number of screenplays, including *Zabriskie Point* (1970, Michelangelo Antonioni) and *Paris, Texas* (1984, Wim Wenders), and has appeared in some 40 films, notably as the test pilot Chuck Yeager in *The Right Stuff* (1983) and in a number of *westerns.

Shepheardes Calender, The The earliest important work of Edmund *Spenser, published anonymously in 1579, and dedicated to Philip *Sidney. It was illustrated by original woodcuts and had accompanying glosses by one 'E.K.' (*see* KIRKE, EDWARD).

It consists of twelve *eclogues, one for each month of the calendar year, beginning with January, modelled on the eclogues of *Theocritus, *Virgil, and more modern writers, such as *Mantuan and *Marot. The pastorals are written in deliberately archaic language and, except for the first and last, take the form of dialogues among shepherds. 'January' and 'December' are complaints by 'Colin Clout', the poet's persona: the first introduces his unhappy love for Rosalind which also features in June. Each eclogue is supplied with an argument and a woodcut and ends with one or more emblems or mottoes, followed by E.K.'s glosses, the whole work being framed by a poem 'To his Booke', a dedicatory epistle, a general argument, an envoi, and a final motto. The eclogues deal with moral, religious, and political, matters, as well as with the nature, practice, and patronage of poetry itself; they show off the new poet's virtuosity in using new genres, such as pastoral elegy or a singing-match, new verse forms, such as the *sestina, and new metres.

Spenser follows contemporary practice by using pastoral and complaint to talk about 'secrete and particular' people and matters. The extent to which the work shadows a specific allegorical meaning has been disputed: some individuals, such as Algrind (Grindal), Roffy (John Young, bishop of Rochester), Dido and Elisa (*Elizabeth I), Tityrus (Geoffrey *Chaucer), Hobbinol (Gabriel *Harvey), or Wrenock (Richard *Mulcaster), seem clearly meant to be recognizable. Yet the works' engagement with contemporary politics, and in particular with the queen's courtship by the French king's brother, the duc d'Alençon (*see also* STUBBE, JOHN), is problematic. Although hugely influential in Spenser's time and up to Alexander *Pope (and beyond), Samuel *Johnson mocked the poems' quaint language and use of dialogue.

SHEPHERD, Nan (1893–1981) Scottish novelist and nature writer brought up in Deeside and educated at the University of Aberdeen. *The Quarry Wood* (1928), a wryly realistic **Bildungsroman*, and *The Weatherhouse* (1930), a complex, polyphonic variation on the novel of rural community, are distinguished by Shepherd's superb ear for Scottish speech and by an anti-romantic acknowledgement of the constriction of women's lives. Published belatedly in 1977, *The Living Mountain* combines lyricism and science in its meditation on the Grampians and how they have been perceived.

Shepherd's Calendar, The A volume of verse by John *Clare, published 1827. It describes rural and agricultural life in and around Clare's home village of Helpstone in Northamptonshire. Like *Spenser's **Shepheardes Calender*, it consists of twelve poems, one for each month of the year. Though not a commercial success on first publication, it has come to be seen as one of the poet's finest achievements.

Shepherd's Week, The A series of six pastorals by John *Gay, published 1714 and dedicated to Viscount *Bolingbroke. They are in mock-classical style, based somewhat loosely on *Virgil, but presenting shepherds and milkmaids of naive bucolic modernity rather than of Golden Age innocence, and so producing ironic contrast. They were in part designed to parody the pastorals of Ambrose *Philips, which had been praised for their 'modern' simplicity at the expense of Alexander *Pope's classical exercises in the genre. Gay portrays his comic rustics (Blouzelinda, Bowzybeus, Cloddipole, Grubbinol) at work as well as at play, paints (in his own words) a 'lively landscape', and includes many references to folklore, games, and superstitions. See William *Empson, *Some Versions of Pastoral* (1935).

SHERIDAN, Frances (1724–66) Novelist, wife of Thomas *Sheridan and mother of R. B. *Sheridan. She was encouraged in her writing by Samuel *Richardson, to whom she dedicated her novel of *sentiment *The Memoirs of Miss Sydney Biddulph* ('after the manner of **Pamela*') in 1761. The novel, which ends in despair, describes the terrible misfortunes and distress of conscience of Sydney, who feels she has not the first claim to her beloved Faulkland. The novel was warmly received and was translated into French by the abbé *Prévost, though Samuel *Johnson declared, 'I know not, Madam, that you have a right, upon moral principles, to make your readers suffer so much.' An expanded version appeared in 1767. *The Discovery*, a comedy starring David *Garrick, was very successful in 1763; it was adapted by Aldous *Huxley in 1924. *The History of Nourjahad*, an *oriental tale, appeared posthumously in 1767: in this, an apparently indulgent sultan permits his friend to indulge all desires; but it is a trick, and retribution follows.

SHERIDAN, Richard Brinsley (1751–1816) The son of Thomas *Sheridan (1719–88), an Irish actor-manager, and Frances *Sheridan. He was educated, unhappily, at Harrow

School. In Bath, where he began writing, he met a singer, Eliza Linley (1754–92), and eloped with her to France; they were not lawfully married until 1773. Being short of money, he wrote *The *Rivals*, which was produced with great success at Covent Garden in 1775. It was followed in a few months by a farce, *St Patrick's Day*, and in the autumn by an opera, *The *Duenna*, both also successful. In 1776 Sheridan, with partners, bought David *Garrick's half-share in the *Drury Lane Theatre and became its manager. Early in 1777 appeared a musical play, *A Trip to Scarborough*, loosely based on Sir John Vanbrugh's *The *Relapse*. In March of that year Sheridan was elected a member of the *Club, on the proposal of Samuel *Johnson. *The *School for Scandal* was produced, with Garrick's help and with a brilliant cast, in May. The play was universally acclaimed; it had 73 performances between 1777 and 1789 and made a profit of £15,000. *The Critic* (1779) was likewise a hit. But Sheridan, whose literary success brought him into expensive social circles, was nonetheless dogged by financial anxieties. In 1779 he became the sole proprietor of Drury Lane, and began to live far beyond his means. He turned to politics, became the friend and ally of Charles James *Fox, and in 1780 won the seat at Stafford. After only two years as an MP he became the under-secretary for foreign affairs, but he neglected his work both as a politician and as theatrical manager, though his father had secured the services of both Sarah *Siddons and J. P. *Kemble, who brought audiences to the theatre. In 1783 he became secretary to the treasury and established a reputation as a brilliant orator in the House of Commons. In 1787 Edmund *Burke persuaded him into supporting the impeachment of Warren Hastings (1732–1818), and he was made manager of the trial. He was by now confirmed as an intimate friend of the prince regent and other royal figures. But in 1792 the Drury Lane Theatre was declared unsafe and had to be demolished. Sheridan raised £150,000 for a new theatre with apparent ease, but he was plunging himself yet deeper into debt, and payments to his actors became more uncertain than ever. **Pizarro*, adapted by Sheridan from *Kotzebue, was performed in 1799 and was successful enough to bring a brief reprieve, but in 1802 the theatre funds were impounded. Enormous sums were owing to the landlord, the architect, the actors, and stage staff. Although he was still speaking daily at the Commons, Sheridan's friendship with Fox was fading, and when Lord Grenville formed the 'ministry of all the talents' in 1806 Sheridan was offered only the treasurership to the navy, without cabinet rank. In 1809 the new Drury Lane was destroyed by fire, the debts became crushing, and Sheridan was excluded from all aspects of management. In 1811 he lost his seat at Stafford, and in 1813 he was arrested for debt. He died in July 1816 and was given a fine funeral, with four lords as pall-bearers. He wished to be remembered as a man of politics and to be buried next to Fox, but he was, perhaps more appropriately, laid near Garrick instead. The standard edition of the plays is by C. Price (2 vols, 1973). See also Price's edition of the *Letters* (3 vols, 1966). Recent biographies of Sheridan include those by L. Kelly and F. O'Toole (both 1997).

SHERIDAN, Thomas (1719–88) Irish actor, educationalist, and elocutionist, educated at Westminster School and Trinity College, Dublin, author of the farce *The Brave Irishman, or Captain O'Blunder* (1743). *British Education, or The Source of the Disorders of Great Britain* (1756) was the first of his influential works on elocution. His lecturing career took him to Edinburgh to enlighten the *literati on pronunciation. He was the husband of Frances *Sheridan and the father of Richard Brinsley *Sheridan.

SHERRIFF, R. C. (Robert Cedric) (1896–1975) Playwright, born in Hampton Wick, Middlesex, educated at Kingston Grammar School, who worked in a local insurance office and began to write plays to raise money for his rowing club. His best-known play was *Journey's End* (1928; pub. 1929), based on his experiences in the trenches as a captain during the First World War. Realistic and low-key, it was praised by George Bernard *Shaw as a 'useful corrective to the romantic conception of war', and has also proved lastingly popular on the stage. It portrays the relationships under stress of Captain Stanhope, new lieutenant Raleigh (with whose sister Stanhope is in love), the reliable second-in-command Osborne, and Hibbert, who has lost his nerve, and ends in mid-battle after the deaths of Osborne and Raleigh. Other plays include *Badger's Green* (1930), a comedy of village politics and cricket; *St Helena* (1934), about Napoleon's last years; *Home at Seven* (1950), in which a banker suffering from amnesia fears he may have committed a crime; and *The White Carnation* (1953), a ghost story about a conscience-stricken stockbroker. Sherriff also wrote screenplays, most memorably *Good-bye Mr Chips* (1939; from the 1934 book by James *Hilton), and *The Four Feathers* (1939; from A. E. W. *Mason's 1902 novel), and several novels, including *The Fortnight in September* (1931).

SHERWOOD, Mary Martha (1775–1851) Writer and educationalist, born in Stanford-on-Teme, Worcestershire, educated at the Abbey School in Reading, Berkshire, Sherwood wrote numerous books, stories, and tracts, many for children, teaching the rewards of virtue. *Susan Gray*, written for her Sunday School scholars, appeared in 1802; *Little Henry and his Bearer* (1814), drawing on time spent in India, was translated into French, German, Hindustani, Chinese, and Sinhalese. The best known of all her works is *The History of the Fairchild Family* (1818), its tremendous success leading to sequels 1842 and 1847. M. Nancy Cutt has written a study (1974).

She Stoops to Conquer, (*The Mistakes of a Night*) A comedy by Oliver *Goldsmith, produced 1773. The principal characters are Mr and Mrs Hardcastle, and Miss Hardcastle their daughter; Mrs Hardcastle's son by a former marriage, the idle but cunning Tony Lumpkin, doted on by his mother; and young Marlow, 'one of the most bashful and reserved young fellows in the world', except with barmaids and servant-girls. His father, Sir Charles Marlow, proposes a match between young Marlow and Miss Hardcastle, and he and his friend Hastings accordingly travel down to visit the Hardcastles. They arrive in the dark at an inn, the Three Jolly Pigeons, where Tony Lumpkin mischievously directs them to a neighbouring inn, which is in reality the Hardcastles' house. In the resulting misunderstanding, Marlow treats Hardcastle as a pub landlord, and attempts to seduce Miss Hardcastle, whom he takes for one of the servants. This contrasts with his bashful behaviour when presented to her in her real character. The arrival of Sir Charles Marlow clears up the misconception and all ends well. The mistaking of a private residence for an inn was said by Goldsmith's sister to have been founded on an actual incident in his own youth. The play was an immense success, and was seen as a victory in the battle against more sentimental forms of comedy, as outlined in Goldsmith's essay 'A Comparison between Laughing and Sentimental Comedy' of the same year. It is still regularly performed.

She Would if She Could Sir George *Etherege's second comedy produced in 1668. Sir Oliver and Lady Cockwood and Sir Joslin Jolley, with his young kinswomen Ariana and Gatty, come up from the country to London for pleasure. Lady Cockwood pursues Mr Courtal, a gentleman of the town, while he and his friend Mr Freeman strike up acquaintance with the young ladies. Various farcical scenes follow, one set in the Bear in Drury Lane. In the happy ending the young couples are united and Lady Cockwood resolves to confine herself in future to family matters.

SHIEL, Matthew Phipps (1865–1947) Montserrat-born British writer known for his baroque style. *The Yellow Danger* (1898) expresses the invasion fears of contemporary Britain. *The Purple Cloud* (1901), his most famous novel, is a 'last man' story reminiscent of Mary *Shelley's, but with almost hallucinatory impact. His fiction, which includes much that would now be called supernatural or *science fiction, is marked by melodramatic, even paranoid, energy and an attention to Nietzschean religious and social philosophies.

SHIELDS, Carol (1935–2003) Novelist and poet, born in Oak Park, Illinois; she lived mainly in Canada after her marriage to a Canadian civil engineer in 1957. She studied at Hanover College and the University of Ottawa. Her first published books were volumes of poetry, *Others* (1972) and *Intersect* (1974), and were followed in 1975 by a study of the 19th-century writer, Susanna Moodie. The title of her first novel, *Small Ceremonies* (1975), suggested the often domestic territory of the everyday that she would explore in her fiction and would illuminate and transform both by her use of language and by subverting traditional narrative forms. Several more novels and two volumes of short stories followed, but none of her work was published in the UK until 1990, when *Mary Swann* (originally published in Canada as *Swann*, 1987) established her as a major 'new' writer. Her international reputation was made by *The Stone Diaries* (1993), a novel which uses the conventions of biography (including photographs purporting to depict the book's characters) to tell the story of one woman's life in the 20th century. It was shortlisted for the *Booker Prize, won the Governor General's Award, and both a Pulitzer and the National Critics' Circle Prize. *Larry's Party* won the Orange Prize in 1998, the same year Shields was diagnosed with cancer. Defying the prognoses of her doctors, Shields survived to produce a new volume of stories, *Dressing Up for the Carnival* (2000), a brief life of Jane Austen (2001), and a final novel, *Unless* (2002), which was shortlisted for the *Man Booker Prize.

SHINER, Lewis (1950–) American *science fiction writer, born Eugene, Oregon. Associated at one time with *cyberpunk, he has explored broader regions of science fiction such as time travel in *Deserted Cities of the Heart* (1988). *Glimpses* (1993) won the World Fantasy Award.

'Shipman's Tale, The' *See* CANTERBURY TALES, 15.

Ship of Fools, The A translation of Sebastian Brant's famous *Narrenschiff* by Alexander *Barclay. The original *Narrenschiff*, written in Swabian dialect and first published in 1494, became extremely popular and was translated into several languages. Published in England in 1509, Barclay's translation is an adaptation which gives an interesting picture of contemporary English life. Its theme is the shipping off of fools of all kinds from their home to the Land of Fools, and its popularity was enhanced by the humorous woodcut illustrations. The work is notable as an early collection of satirical types, and its influence is seen in **Cock Lorell's Boat*.

Shirley A novel by Charlotte *Brontë, published 1849. The story is set in Yorkshire, during the latter part of the Napoleonic Wars, the time of the Luddite riots, when the wool industry was suffering from the collapse of exports. In spite of these conditions, the forceful mill-owner Robert Gérard Moore, half English and half Belgian, persists in introducing the latest labour-saving machinery, undeterred by the opposition of the workers, which culminates in an attempt to destroy his mill and take his life. To overcome his financial difficulties he proposes to Shirley Keeldar, an heiress of independent spirit, while under the mistaken impression that she is in love with him; he himself loves his gentle cousin Caroline Helstone, who is pining away for love of him and through enforced idleness in the oppressive atmosphere of her uncle's rectory. Robert is indignantly rejected by Shirley, who is in fact in love with his brother Louis, a tutor in her family, also of proud and independent spirit. The misunderstandings are resolved, and the two couples united.

Despite touches of melodrama (such as the sub-plot, which reveals that Shirley's companion and one-time governess Mrs Pryor is in fact Caroline's long-lost mother) this is Charlotte Brontë's most social novel, intended in her own words to be 'unromantic as Monday morning'. One of its recurrent themes is its plea for useful occupations for women, condemned either to matrimony or, as old maids, to a life of self-denial and acts of private charity. Caroline is forbidden even the career of governess by her uncle, and this career is itself painted by Mrs Pryor as 'sedentary, solitary, constrained, joyless, toilsome'. Shirley herself is an attempt to portray a woman with the freedom and power to act. Charlotte told Elizabeth *Gaskell that she was intended to be what Emily *Brontë might have been 'had she been placed in health and prosperity', but despite certain recognizable characteristics (her relationship with her dog Tartar, her physical courage, her nickname of 'Captain'), Shirley seems to shed little light on her enigmatic original.

SHIRLEY, James (1596–1666) Born in London and educated at Merchant Taylors' School, St John's College, Oxford, and St Catharine's Hall, Cambridge. His first work, a poem on Echo and Narcissus, was published in 1618. An Anglican clergyman and, till 1624, master at St Albans Grammar School, he apparently converted to Roman Catholicism and moved to London, where he lived in Gray's Inn. His first recorded play, *Love Tricks* (1625), was followed by some forty tragedies, comedies, and tragicomedies. Among the best known are *The *Traitor* (1631), **Hyde Park* (1632), *The *Gamester* (1633), *The *Lady of Pleasure* (1635), and *The *Cardinal* (1641). During the plague closure of 1636–7 he went to Ireland, where he wrote a number of plays, including *St Patrick for Ireland* (*c.*1639), for the theatre in Werburgh Street, Dublin, the first theatre built in Ireland, which was only a year old when Shirley arrived. In London, most of his plays were performed by Queen Henrietta's Men, and he attracted royal favour by a sarcastic reference to William *Prynne (then awaiting trial for writing *Histriomastix*) in the dedication to *The Bird in a Cage* (1632–3). As a further sign of royal allegiance he wrote the masque *The *Triumph of Peace* (1634), presented at Whitehall by the gentlemen of the Inns of Court. On his return from Ireland in 1640 he succeeded Philip *Massinger as principal dramatist for the King's Men, but the outbreak of the Civil War put an end to this career. He served in the Royalist army under the duke of *Newcastle, returned to London after the Royalist defeat, was patronized by Thomas *Stanley, and assisted John *Ogilby in his translations of Homer. He took up schoolmastering again and wrote some pieces for school performance, among them *The Contention of Ajax and Ulysses* (pub. 1659), a dramatic debate interspersed with songs, which contains his most famous work, the lyric 'The glories of our blood and state', which was a favourite with Charles II. Shirley and his wife are said to have died as a result of terror and exposure when they were driven from their home by the Great Fire of London. See S. A. Burner, *James Shirley: A Study of Literary Coteries and Patronage* (1988).

SHIRLEY, John (*c.*1366–1456) The scribe of many works of *Chaucer, *Lydgate, and others, whose attributions have been particularly important for the ascriptions to Chaucer of some of the shorter poems, including the Complaints 'To Pity', 'To his Lady', and 'Of Mars'; 'Adam Scriveyn'; 'Truth'; 'Lak of Stedfastnesse'; and 'The Complaint of Venus'. A central figure in the literary culture of 15th-century London, he also translated a number of works from French and Latin, among the latter being 'A Full Lamentable Cronycle of the Dethe and False Murdure of James Stewarde, Late Kynge of Scotys' (*see* JAMES I OF SCOTLAND).

SHIRLEY, John (1954–) American *science fiction writer and musician, born Houston, Texas. Linked to *cyberpunk, he collaborated with William *Gibson: the 1989 collection *Heatseeker* brings together his influential stories. He has also written *horror fiction and screenplays. *Crawlers* (2003) combines science fiction nanotechnology with apocalyptic horror.

Shoemakers' Holiday, The, *or The Gentle Craft* A comedy by Thomas *Dekker, written 1599, published 1600. Rowland Lacy, a kinsman of the earl of Lincoln, loves Rose, the daughter of the lord mayor of London. To prevent the match the earl sends him to France in command of a company of men. Lacy gives his place to a friend and, disguised as a Dutch shoemaker, takes service with Simon Eyre, who supplies the family of the lord mayor with shoes. Here he successfully pursues his suit, is married in spite of the efforts of the earl and the lord mayor to prevent it, and is pardoned by the king. The most entertaining characters in the play are Eyre, the cheery, eccentric master shoemaker, who becomes lord mayor of London, and his wife Madgy.
See also DELONEY, THOMAS.

SHOLOKHOV, Mikhail Aleksandrovich (1905–84) Russian novelist, born in Veshenskaya of mixed peasant and lower-middle-class background. He became well known in the West for his lengthy regional epic novel about Cossack life in the early 20th century, *And Quiet Flows the Don* (4 vols, 1928–40; trans. Robert Daglish, ed. and rev. Brian Murphy, 1997), which has been much admired despite allegations, since refuted, that he made use of the manuscript of a dead White Army officer. His other works include a novel described as a classic of *Socialist Realism, *Virgin Soil Upturned* (vol. i 1932, vol ii 1960; trans. Robert Daglish, 1979), which chronicles life during the early period of agricultural collectivization in southern Russia. Sholokhov was awarded the *Nobel Prize in 1965.

SHORE, Jane (d. 1526/7?) Mistress of Edward IV. Born Elizabeth Lambert, the daughter of a Cheapside textile merchant, her marriage to William Shore was annulled in 1476. With her beauty and wit, she greatly influenced Edward IV, and after his death became mistress of Thomas Grey, first marquess of Dorset (1455–1501). She was made to do public penance in 1483, and tradition holds that she died in poverty.

Sir Thomas *More's *History of Richard the Third*, provides a remarkable account of her. She is the subject of a ballad included in Thomas *Percy's **Reliques*, appears in Thomas *Churchyard's *Shore's Wife* in *A *Mirror for Magistrates*, and is the subject of a descriptive note by Michael *Drayton in *England's Heroical Epistles*. She was first called Jane Shore in Thomas *Heywood's plays on Edward IV (1599) and is the *eponymous heroine of Nicholas *Rowe's tragedy (1714).

SHORTHOUSE, Joseph Henry (1834–1903) Novelist, born into a Birmingham Quaker family. His severe stammer led to a home education, and he joined his father's manufacturing business at the age of 16. He converted to Anglicanism, and the historical novel by which he is remembered, *John Inglesant* (1881, privately printed 1880), is an evocation of 17th-century religious intrigue and faith. Inglesant becomes a tool of the Jesuit faction, joins the court of Charles I, and after the king's death visits Italy to seek vengeance for his brother's murder; the book includes a vivid account of Nicholas *Ferrar's religious community at *Little Gidding. Inglesant falls in love with Mary Collet in a wholly fictitious episode, but the background is on the whole drawn in accurate detail. The novel was immensely successful, and something of a cult formed around it. It bears witness to the religious and historical interests revived by the *Oxford Movement and the *Pre-Raphaelites. His subsequent novels, largely introspective stories of guilt and doubt, were less successful.

Short View See COLLIER, JEREMY.

SHOSTAKOVICH, Dmitry Dimitryevich (1906–75) Prolific Russian composer whose work was produced under the shadow of Soviet aesthetics. His opera, *Lady Macbeth of the Mtsensk District* (1932), from a story by Nikolai *Leskov, occasioned the official displeasure of Stalin, to which he responded with the ostensibly patriotic Fifth Symphony (1937). After writing incidental music for performances of *Hamlet* (1931–2) and *King Lear* (1941), Shostakovich produced scores for film versions (*Hamlet*, 1964; *King Lear*, 1970). His group of *Six Romances* (1942) sets texts by Walter *Ralegh, Robert *Burns, and *Shakespeare, and he also set words by Alexander *Pushkin and Mikhail *Lermontov. His unfinished opera *The Gamblers* (1941–2) was based on a text by Nikolai *Gogol.

Shropshire Lad, A See HOUSMAN, A. E.

SHUTE, Nevil (1899–1960) The pen-name of Nevil Shute Norway, popular novelist, born in London and educated at Shrewsbury School and Balliol College, Oxford, who later (1950) settled in Australia. His many readable, fast-moving novels, several based on his involvement with the aircraft industry and his own wartime experiences, include *Pied Piper* (1942); *No Highway* (1948); *A Town Like Alice* (1950), in which an English girl is captured by the Japanese and survives the war to settle in Australia; and *On the Beach* (1957), which describes events after a nuclear holocaust.

SHUTTLE, Penelope (1947–) Poet and novelist, born in Staines, Middlesex. Her first volume of poetry was *The Orchard Upstairs* (1980), which was followed by several others, including *Adventures with my Horse* (1988), *A Leaf out of his Book* (1999), and *Selected Poems 1980–1996* (1998). Her poetry is distinguished by a rich, sensuous awareness of sexuality and the natural and animal worlds: her use of female imagery is arresting and celebratory. Her novels include *Wailing Monkey Embracing a Tree* (1973). She was married to Peter *Redgrove, with whom she collaborated on several works, including *The Wise Wound* (1978), a study of the reality and mythology of menstruation. Her volume *Redgrove's Wife* (2006) movingly celebrates and elegizes their life together.

Shylock The Jewish moneylender in *Shakespeare's *The *Merchant of Venice*.

Sibylline Leaves A volume of poems by S. T. *Coleridge, published 1817. It is most notable for the publication of the revised and expanded version of the *The Rime of the *Ancient Mariner* with marginal notes, here acknowledged for the first time as Coleridge's poem.

SIDDAL (Siddall), **Elizabeth** ('Lizzie') (1829–62) Painter, poet, and model to the *Pre-Raphaelites. Siddal met D. G. *Rossetti in 1850, and in 1852 modelled for John Everett *Millais as the drowning Ophelia. She attended art school at Sheffield, drawing subjects from medieval lore and works by John *Keats, Alfred *Tennyson, and Robert *Browning; John *Ruskin praised her later watercolours. Her poems reflect the unhappiness of her relationship with Rossetti. The two married in 1860, and, having long suffered ill health, Siddal gave birth in 1861 to a stillborn child. In 1862 she died, after taking an overdose of laudanum, and was buried in Highgate Cemetery. In 1869 Rossetti exhumed the manuscript notebook of his poems with which Siddal had been buried.

SIDDONS, Sarah (1755–1831) The eldest child of the actor-manager Roger Kemble (1721–1802), and sister of Charles *Kemble and J. P. *Kemble. From 1782 she was without dispute the greatest tragic actress of her generation, in such roles as Jane *Shore (as conceived by Nicholas *Rowe), Belvidera in Thomas Otway's *Venice Preserved*, and Lady *Macbeth. Her friends included Samuel *Johnson, Horace *Walpole, and Joshua *Reynolds, who painted her as *The Tragic Muse*. Thomas *Gainsborough also painted a portrait of her. William *Hazlitt wrote that 'She was Tragedy personified'; she rarely attempted comedy. She retired in 1812, making a brief, undistinguished comeback in 1819.

SIDGWICK, Henry (1838–1900) Philosopher, educated at Rugby and Trinity College, Cambridge, where he became a fellow in 1859. He was from 1883 professor of moral philosophy, and an influential figure in the university. A follower of John Stuart *Mill, his reputation rests on *The Methods of Ethics* (1874), where he considered ways of determining the right courses of action, and the practical obstacles which hinder our following them. In 1876 Sidgwick married Eleanor Balfour (1845–1936), who was from 1892 to 1910 principal of Newnham College, Cambridge; it was partly through their efforts on behalf of women's higher education that the college was founded. She and Sidgwick's brother Arthur wrote a memoir of Henry (1906).

SIDNEY, Algernon (1622–83) Grand-nephew of Sir Philip *Sidney. He took up arms against Charles I and was wounded at Marston Moor. Employed on government service until the *Restoration, he aroused Oliver *Cromwell's hostility by his implacable republicanism (which he emphasized by staging a performance of *Julius Caesar* with himself as Brutus). At the Restoration he refused to give pledges to Charles II, and lived abroad in poverty and exile until 1677. On his return he joined the opposition to Stuart absolutism, was imprisoned in the Tower after the discovery of the Rye House Plot, tried before the notorious judge George Jeffreys (1645–89), condemned without adequate evidence, and executed. His *Discourses Concerning Government* (1698) were widely read in the American colonies. Thomas *Jefferson regarded them as a philosophical basis for liberty and human rights. The Latin motto of Massachusetts (usually translated 'By the sword we seek peace but only under liberty') is ascribed to Sidney.

SIDNEY, Sir Philip (1554–86) Writer and courtier, born at *Penshurst Place, eldest son of Sir Henry Sidney (who was thrice lord deputy governor of Ireland), nephew of Robert Dudley, earl of *Leicester. Educated at Shrewsbury School (with his close friend Fulke *Greville), and Christ Church, Oxford, where his contemporaries included William *Camden, Richard *Hakluyt, and Walter *Ralegh, he may have spent some time also at Cambridge. Between 1572 and 1575 he travelled in France, witnessing the massacre of St *Bartholomew's Day in Paris, and in Germany, Austria, and Italy. During his year in Italy, most of it spent in Venice, he was painted by Veronese, but devoted himself to serious study of history and ethics, and to correspondence with the elderly Protestant statesman Hubert Languet (1518–81). After his return to England, in spite of a successful embassy to Vienna in 1577, Sidney did not achieve any official post which matched his ambitions until his appointment as governor of Flushing (Vlissingen, in the Netherlands) in 1585. His knighthood was awarded for reasons of court protocol in 1583, the year in which he married Frances, daughter of Sir Francis Walsingham.

Years of comparative idleness enabled him to write and revise the **Arcadia*, and to complete *A *Defence of Poetry, The *Lady of May,* and **Astrophel and Stella*. The first *Arcadia*, and probably other works, were composed while he was staying with his younger sister Mary, countess of *Pembroke, at Wilton. The exact nature of his relations with Penelope Devereux (later *Rich) are not known; however, verbal and heraldic references leave no room for doubt that she was the 'Stella' of Sidney's sonnet sequence. During these years Sidney also became a notable literary patron, receiving dedications from a variety of authors, the best known being that of Edmund *Spenser's *The *Shepheardes Calender* (1579). Sidney was interested in experimenting with English verse in classical metres along the lines prescribed by Thomas Drant (*c.*1540–1578), but it is unlikely that his discussion of this and other matters with Greville, Edward *Dyer, and Spenser (the 'Areopagus') amounted to anything so formal as an academy or learned society. His last year was spent in the Netherlands, where his greatest military success was a surprise assault on the town of Axel. On 22 September 1586 he led an attack on a Spanish convoy bringing supplies to the fortified city of Zutphen; he received a musket shot in his thigh and died of infection three weeks later. Greville, who was not present, subsequently told the story of the death with two famous embellishments, claiming that Sidney left off his thigh-armour deliberately, so as not to be better armed than a fellow soldier, and that as he was being carried wounded from the field he saw a dying soldier gazing at his water bottle, and gave it to him with the words 'Thy necessity is yet greater than mine.'

Sidney was buried in St Paul's Cathedral, and the almost immediate appearance of volumes of Latin elegies from Oxford, Cambridge, and the Continent testified to the great political and literary promise he had shown. Among many English elegies on him the best known, Spenser's *'Astrophel', was not printed until 1595, among his *Complaints*. This included elegies by Lodowick Bryskett (1546–1609/12), Matthew Roydon (*fl.* 1583–1622), Ralegh, and Dyer. Roydon's is unusual in evoking the hero's presence, his 'sweet attractive kind of grace'. Sidney's posthumous reputation, as the perfect Renaissance patron, soldier, lover, and courtier, far outstripped his documented achievements, and can be seen as having a life independent of them which has become proverbial, as when W. B. *Yeats paid tribute to Major Robert *Gregory as 'our Sidney and our perfect man'.

None of Sidney's works was published during his lifetime. The revised *Arcadia* was published under Greville's editorship in 1590; in 1593 the countess of Pembroke printed that version with the last three books of the earlier one appended; *Astrophel and Stella* was published in 1591, first in a pirated and then in an authorized text; and *A Defence of Poetry,* also in two slightly varying texts, in 1595. Editions of the *Arcadia* from 1598 onwards included all the literary works except his version of the Psalms. These were completed posthumously by his sister, and not printed until 1823. Sidney's complete *Poems* were edited by W. A. Ringler in 1962, the *Old Arcadia* (1973) by Jean Robertson, *The New Arcadia* by Victor Skretkowicz (1987), and the *Miscellaneous Prose* by K. Duncan-Jones and J. van Dorsten (1973); the standard life is by M. W. Wallace (1915). See also K. Duncan-Jones, *Sir Philip Sidney: Courtier and Poet* (1991).

SIDNEY, Sir Robert (1563–1626) Poet and courtier, the younger brother of Sir Philip *Sidney. His early career closely followed that of his brother, whom he succeeded as governor of Flushing (Vlissingen, in the Netherlands) in 1589, a post he continued to hold for over 25 years. He was created Baron Sidney by James I in 1603, Viscount Lisle in 1605, and earl of Leicester in 1618; he held the post of lord chamberlain to Anne of Denmark. Robert Dowland (1591–1641), who was his godson, dedicated *A Musical Banquet* (1610) to him. Sidney's estate and generous hospitality at *Penshurst Place were warmly praised by Ben *Jonson. An autograph manuscript of Sidney's poems, consisting of sonnets, pastorals, songs, and epigrams, apparently written in the later 1590s, was identified by P. J. Croft in 1973; he edited them in 1984.

Siege of Corinth, The A poem by Lord *Byron, published 1816. The poem is founded on the story of the Turkish siege of Corinth, then held by the Venetians, and it was the last of Byron's Eastern tales. The Turks, guided by the fierce and daring traitor Alp, who loves the daughter of the Venetian governor Minotti, enter the fortress. Minotti, discovering the betrayal, destroys both victors and defenders, including himself.

Siege of Rhodes, The One of the earliest attempts at English opera, by Sir William *D'Avenant, performed 1656. Dramatic performances having been suppressed by the Commonwealth government, D'Avenant obtained permission in 1656 to produce at Rutland House an 'Entertainment after the manner of the ancients', in which Diogenes and *Aristophanes argue against and for public amusements, and a Londoner and Parisian compare the merits of their two cities; this was accompanied by vocal and instrumental music, composed by Henry *Lawes. Immediately after this prologue was given *The Siege of Rhodes* (at first in one, but in 1662 in two parts), a heroic play, the 'story sung in recitative music', which was composed by Dr Charles Coleman (d. 1664) and George Hudson (d. 1672/3). The play deals with the siege of Rhodes by Solyman the Magnificent, and the devotion by which Ianthe, wife of the Sicilian Duke Alphonso, saves her husband and the defenders of the island.

SIGAL, Clancy (1926–) American novelist and screenwriter, born in Chicago and educated at the University of California. He worked in Hollywood in the 1950s and came to England in 1957, where he wrote *Weekend in Dinlock* (1960), a fictionalized exploration of life in a mining community in Yorkshire. *Going Away* (1963) is a first-person 'road' novel. *Zone of the Interior* (USA 1976) is set in England. Sigal lived for some 30 years in England, and contributed regularly to the *New Statesman* and other periodicals. He now lives and writes in California.

Sigismonda *See* GHISMONDA.

Sigurd the Volsung and the Fall of the Niblungs, The Story of An epic in *anapaestic couplets by William *Morris, founded on the **Völsunga Saga*, and published 1876. Although a loose rendering, and at times free in its versification, it did much to awaken popular interest in Icelandic literature. Morris described its subject as 'the Great Story of the North which should be to all our race what the Tale of Troy was to the Greeks'. It is in four books; the first, 'Sigmund', is the story of Volsung's son Sigmund and of the fatal marriage of his sister Signy to the king of the Goths; the second and third, 'Regin' and 'Brynhild', deal with Sigmund's son Sigurd, his betrothal to Brynhild, his subsequent marriage (under the influence of a magic potion) to Gudrun, the Niblung king's daughter, and the deaths of Sigurd and Brynhild; the last, 'Gudrun', tells of Gudrun's own death and the fall of the Niblungs.
See SAGA.

Silas Marner A pastoral novel by George *Eliot, published 1861. Silas Marner, a linen-weaver, is driven out of his religious community by a false charge of theft, and takes refuge in the agricultural village of Raveloe. He consoles himself with a growing pile of gold, which is stolen by the squire's reprobate son Dunstan Cass, who disappears. Dunstan's elder brother Godfrey loves Nancy Lammeter, but is secretly married to a working-class woman in a neighbouring town. Enraged by Godfrey's refusal to acknowledge her, this woman carries her child one New Year's Eve to Raveloe, intending to force her way into his house; but dies in the snow. Her golden-haired child, Eppie, toddles into Silas's cottage and is adopted by him, giving his life new meaning. After many years, a drained pond near Silas's door reveals the body of Dunstan with the gold. Moved by this revelation, Godfrey, now married to Nancy, acknowledges Eppie as his daughter, but she refuses to leave Silas. The serious tone of the story is varied by the humour of the rustic Rainbow Inn, and the genial motherliness of Silas's friend Dolly Winthrop.

Silent Woman, The *See* EPICENE.

SILKIN, Jon (1930–97) Poet, born in London, the son of a solicitor, and educated at Wycliffe and Dulwich colleges. He established himself as a poet while working as a manual labourer, then as a teacher, and subsequently lectured extensively. His first volume, *The Peaceable Kingdom* (1954), was followed by many others, including *Nature with Man* (1965, which contains many of his piercingly observed 'flower poems'), *Amana Grass* (1971, with work inspired by visits to Israel and America), and *The Principle of Water* (1974); his *Selected Poems* was published in 1980. Other volumes include *The Psalms with their Spoils* (1980), *Autobiographical Stanzas* (1984), and *The Lens-Breakers* (1992). His anthologies include *Out of Battle: Poetry of the Great War* (1972). He founded the literary quarterly **Stand* in 1952; his wife Lorna Tracy, short story writer, was his co-editor.

SILLITOE, Alan (1928–) Writer, brought up in Nottingham, son of an illiterate and often unemployed labourer; he married the American poet Ruth *Fainlight. He started work aged 14 in a bicycle factory, served in the RAF in Malaya, and began to write while in hospital recovering from tuberculosis. During a subsequent stay in Majorca, Robert *Graves encouraged him to write a novel set in Nottingham. His first volume of verse, *Without Beer or Bread* (1957), was followed by his much-praised first novel, *Saturday Night and Sunday Morning* (1958), which describes the life of Arthur Seaton, a dissatisfied young Nottingham factory worker. It differed from other provincial novels of the 1950s (see COOPER, WILLIAM; AMIS, KINGSLEY; LARKIN, PHILIP; BRAINE, JOHN; WAIN, JOHN) in that its hero is a working man, not a rising member of the lower middle class. The title story of *The Loneliness of the Long Distance Runner* (1959) is a first-person portrait of a rebellious and anarchic Borstal boy. Many other books followed, including the novels *The Death of William Posters* (1965) and *A Start in Life* (1970); the semi-autobiographical *Raw Material* (1972); a collection of short stories, *Men, Women and Children* (1973); and a collection of autobiographical and critical essays, *Mountains and Caverns* (1975). His *Collected Poems* appeared in 1993. *A Man of his Time* (2004) is a sequel to *Saturday Night and Sunday Morning*.

SILONE, Ignazio (1900–78) Pseudonym of Secondino Tranquilli, Italian novelist, critic, and founder member of the Italian Communist Party in 1921, from which he was later expelled (1931) over his refusal to condemn Trotsky. To escape *Fascist persecution he went into exile in Switzerland in 1930, where he remained until 1945 and where his early novels were first published, in German. The peasant south, its deprivation, and the impact on it of Fascism are the themes of his best-known novels, *Fontamara* (Italian edn 1934; rev. 1949) and *Pane e vino* (Italian edn 1937; rev. 1955 as *Vino e pane*: *Wine and Bread*). His autobiographical memoir *Uscita di sicurezza* (1949; rev. 1965: *The God That Failed*) indicates his importance for Anglo-American culture as the type of the European ex-communist. Silone is also the author of a play on the figure of Pope Celestine V ('he who made, through cowardice, the great refusal' in *Dante's words), *L'avventura di un povero cristiano* (1968: *The Story of a Humble Christian*, 1970). See M. Nicolai Paynter, *Ignazio Silone: Beyond the Tragic Vision* (2000).

Silurist, the *See* VAUGHAN, HENRY.

SILVA, Feliciano de (*c.*1491–1554) A Spanish romance writer, who composed sequels to **Amadis of Gaul* and **Celestina*, and was ridiculed in **Don Quixote* (I. 6).

SILVERBERG, Robert (1935–) American *science fiction writer, born in New York; known for his prolific output in the 1950s and the astonishing range of the next decade, including *A Time of Changes* (1971), where a society forbids the use of the first person, and *Dying Inside* (1972) a bitter novel of a telepath losing his gift. Many of these novels were influenced by, and influenced in return, the greater thematic openness of the *New Wave. *Lord Valentine's Castle* (1980) began a series of *fantasy-influenced novels.

silver-fork school *See* FASHIONABLE NOVEL.

SIMAK, Clifford Donald (1904–88) American newspaperman and *science fiction author, born in Millville, Wisconsin. His pastoral includes *City* (1952); stories about humanity abandoning earth, told by the dogs who remain, and the *Hugo-winning *Way Station* (1963), a fine example of how science fiction looks obliquely on violence and war.

SIMENON, Georges (1903–89) Franco-Belgian novelist. Born in Liège, he moved to Paris in 1922 and began a prolific career as a writer. His most famous creation, Inspector Maigret, made his first appearance in *Pietr-le-Letton* (1931), and established Simenon as a leading exponent of *detective fiction. Maigret featured in 75 novels and numerous short stories, having his last outing in *Maigret et Monsieur Charles* (1972). Simenon's sustained international success can be traced both to his evocation of ordinary life, and to his dogged attempts to articulate the complexities of human motivations.

SIMIC, Charles (1938–) Serbian-born poet, who moved to America at the age of 15. His portrayal of the familiar in startling, often unsettling ways runs through his later collections, most notably *Charon's Cosmology* (1977), *Classic Ballroom Dances* (1980), and *Austerities* (1982), and betrays the influence of the *Surrealists, as well as of Serbian poetry, which he has done much to promote. Much of his work deals with this dual identity, as a Serbian writer who returns to his 'psychic roots', but 'with foreign words in my mouth'.

simile An explicit likening of one object, scene, or action with another, e.g. 'as weak as a kitten', inviting imaginative comparison between the two terms rather than the more forceful identification suggested by *metaphor. A more elaborately extended variety is the *epic simile.

SIMMONDS, Dan (1948–) American *science fiction author, born in Peoria, Illinois. His epic *Hyperion* (1989) employs literary echoes—including the life of John *Keats—to begin a metaphysical space opera. *Ilium* (2003) likewise draws upon *Homer, with post-humans observing events from the **Iliad*.

SIMMS, William Gilmore (1806–70) American novelist, born in South Carolina, who produced a series of romances like *The Yemassee* (1835), depicting early phases of Southern history. He published several volumes of poetry and a number of historical studies. He supported slavery and attacked **Uncle Tom's Cabin* through a rejoinder novel, *The Sword and the Distaff* (1852).

SIMON, Neil (1927–) Prolific Jewish American playwright and screenwriter, born in New York, whose plays include *Come Blow your Horn* (1961) and *The Odd Couple* (1965).

Simple Story, A A novel by Elizabeth *Inchbald, published 1791, with the avowed purpose of showing the value of 'a proper education'. Miss Milner, a clever but headstrong heiress, falls in love with her attractive and sensitive guardian Dorriforth, a Roman Catholic priest: when he inherits the title of Lord Elmwood he renounces his vows and marries her, but later becomes violently autocratic. During his prolonged absence overseas she is unfaithful to him, and dies. Their daughter Matilda, forbidden her father's presence, and brought up under many restrictions, is finally reconciled with him, and marries her father's favourite, Rushbrook. The novel's blend of *melodrama, *Gothic sexual intensity, and psychological observation has provoked much commentary. The expiation of jealousy and guilt over two generations has been compared to *The *Winter's*

Tale, in which Inchbald may have acted, and Dorriforth is taken to be modelled in part on her friend J. P. *Kemble.

SIMPSON, Habbie (1550–1620) Subject of 'The Life and Death of the Piper of Kilbarchan', a comic elegy by Robert Sempill of Beltrees (*c*.1595–1659) which circulated in broadsheet before its inclusion in *A Choice Collection of Comic and Serious Scots Poems both Ancient and Modern* (1706–11), published by the printer and bookseller James Watson (?1664–1722). Sempill's six-line stanza was adopted by Allan *Ramsay, who called it 'Standart Habbie', and further developed by Robert *Fergusson and Robert *Burns. Sometimes called 'the Burns stanza', it has been used by Douglas *Dunn, Seamus *Heaney (in his uncollected 'Open Letter', 1983), and Iain Crichton *Smith.

SIMPSON, Helen (1959–) Short story writer, born in Bristol, brought up in London, and educated at Oxford, where she undertook postgraduate work in *Restoration comedy. After winning the *Vogue* talent contest, she worked for the magazine for several years. Her first collection of stories, *Four Bare Legs in a Bed* (1990), established her reputation as a wry and elegant chronicler of modern life, winning the *Sunday Times* Young Writer of the Year Award and a Somerset *Maugham Award. A novella, 'Flesh and Grass', appeared with one by Ruth *Rendell in *Unguarded Hours* (1990), and although she has otherwise published only short stories, in 1993 she was chosen as one of *Granta*'s 'Best of Young British Novelists'. Subsequent volumes include *Dear George* (1995), *Hey Yeah Right Get a Life* (2000), which drew upon her experiences of motherhood and won the Hawthornden Prize, *Constitutional* (2005), and *In the Driver's Seat* (2007).

SIMPSON, Matt (1936–2009) Poet, born in Bootle, Liverpool. Although of the same generation as his better-known contemporaries, the *Liverpool poets, Simpson's haunted, uneasy lyricism and his exploration of the vernacular mark an altogether more literary aesthetic. His main subject matters—his working-class upbringing, his relationship with his seafaring father, and his negotiations with Liverpool's imperial past—connect him to poets such as Tony *Harrison, Seamus *Heaney, and Douglas *Dunn. Collections include *Making Arrangements* (1982), *An Elegy for the Galosherman: New and Selected Poems* (1990), *Catching up with History* (1995), *Cutting the Clouds Towards* (1998), *Getting There* (2001), and *In Deep* (2006).

SIMPSON, N. F. (Norman Frederick) (1919–) Playwright, whose surreal comedies *A Resounding Tinkle* (1957) and *One-Way Pendulum* (1959) established him as a writer of the Theatre of the *Absurd. His work shows an affinity with that of Eugène Ionesco (1909–94), which enjoyed a considerable vogue in Britain in the late 1950s. Other works include *The Cresta Run* (1965) and a novel, *Harry Bleachbaker* (1976).

SINCLAIR, Catherine (1800–64) Philanthropist and prolific Scottish writer of travel, biography, children's books, novels, essays, and reflections. In *Holiday House* (1839) she produced a classic children's book that consciously resisted the prevailing fashion for moralizing tales for the young; her popular *Picture Letters* (1861–4) sold up to 100,000 copies each.

SINCLAIR, Clive (1948–) Novelist and short story writer, born in London and educated at the universities of East Anglia and California, Santa Cruz. The title of his first novel, *Bibliosexuality* (1973), indicates an idiosyncratic strain of verbal play and erotic bravura that characterizes much of his work. It was followed by two volumes of short stories, *Hearts of Gold* (1979) and *Bedbugs* (1982). Sinclair was chosen as one of *Granta*'s original 'Best of Young British Novelists' in 1983. His other novels include *Cosmetic Effects* (1989), set in England and Israel and featuring a film studies lecturer unwittingly involved in a terrorist plot, *Augustus Rex* (1992), and *Meet the Wife* (2002). *The Lady with the Laptop* (1996) is a further collection of short stories. *A Soap Opera from Hell* (1998) consists of non-fiction pieces. Sinclair has also written a study of the brothers *Singer (1983).

SINCLAIR, Iain (1943–) British poet, novelist, London chronicler, and film-maker, born in Cardiff, educated in Dublin, based in London. Early poetry collections *Lud Heat* (1975) and *Suicide Bridge* (1979) were followed by his first novel, *White Chapell* (1987), which established his recurrent themes: the mythology of *Jack the Ripper and the 'psychogeography' of east London, based on the belief of Guy Debord (1931–94) in 'the effects of the geographical environment on the emotions and behaviour of individuals'. *Downriver* (1991) views the changing face of London from its rail and waterways. *Slow Chocolate Autopsy* (1997) is a collection of short stories and graphic tales (with artist Dave McKean) and *Lights out for the Territory* (1997), based on a series of London walks, explores such enthusiasms as the churches of Nicholas Hawksmoor, the secret state, and the films of Patrick Keiller (1950–). He has since collaborated on a film about the M25, *London Orbital* (screened in 2002), with Chris Pettit.

SINCLAIR, May (Mary Amelia St Clair) (1863–1946) Novelist. Born near Birkenhead, Cheshire, Sinclair was almost entirely educated at home; she never married, and supported herself by reviewing, translating, and writing fiction. She was a supporter of women's suffrage, and deeply interested in psychoanalysis; her reviews and novels show considerable knowledge of both *Jung and *Freud. Among the most notable of her 24 novels are *The Divine Fire* (1904); *The Three Sisters* (1914), a study in female frustration with echoes of the lives of the *Brontë sisters; *The Tree of Heaven* (1917); *Mary Olivier: A Life* (1919); and *Life and Death of Harriett Frean* (1922). The last two are *stream-of-consciousness novels, taking a woman from girlhood to unmarried middle age. The plots of both are informed by ideas of degeneration, and both are keenly aware of the tendency towards self-denial in women's lives. See Suzanne Raitt, *May Sinclair: A Modern Victorian* (2000).

SINCLAIR, Upton (1878–1968) American novelist and journalist, born in Baltimore, who is best known for his novel *The Jungle* (1906), an exposé of the Chicago meat-packing industry, which resulted in a government investigation of the yards; it also marks a conversion to socialism on the part of its author and of its protagonist. Other novels include *The Metropolis* (1908), *King Coal* (1917), *Oil!* (1927), and *Boston* (1928). His Lanny Budd series, focusing on the illegitimate son of a munitions manufacturer, was designed as a panorama of modern history, including *World's End* (1940), *Dragon's Teeth* (1942), *The Return of Lanny Budd* (1953), and other works. Sinclair ran unsuccessfully for the governorship of California in 1934 and wrote studies of economics, extra-sensory perception, the Soviet Union and other subjects. See Anthony Arthur, *Radical Innocent* (2006).

SINGER, Isaac Bashevis (1904–91) Polish-born American writer, the son and grandson of rabbis. In 1935 he emigrated to New York, in the footsteps of his brother, the novelist Israel Joshua Singer (1893–1944), and became a journalist, writing in *Yiddish for the *Jewish Daily Forward*, which published most of his short stories. The first of his works to be translated into English was *The Family Moskat* (1950), which was followed by many other works, including *Satan in Goray* (Yiddish, 1935; English, 1955); *The Magician of Lublin* (1960); *The Slave* (1962); *The Manor* (1967) and its sequel *The Estate* (1969). His collections of stories include *Gimpel the Fool* (1957); *The Spinoza of Market Street* (1961); *Zlateh the Goat* (1966); and *A Friend of Kafka* (1970). Singer's work portrays the lives of Polish Jews in many periods of Polish history, coloured by hints of the mystical and supernatural. Many of his novels and stories describe the conflicts between traditional religion and rising scepticism, between varying forms of nationalism, and between the primitive, the exotic, and the intellectually progressive. Singer was awarded the *Nobel Prize for Literature in 1978. See Paul Kresh, *Isaac Bashevis Singer* (1979); Clive Sinclair, *The Brothers Singer* (1983); the latter includes an account of the life of the Singers' sister, novelist Esther Kreitman (1891–1954).

Singleton, The Life, Adventures and Piracies of the Famous Captain A novel by Daniel *Defoe, published 1720. Singleton tells how he was kidnapped in infancy and sent to sea. After a mutiny he is put ashore in Madagascar with his comrades; he crosses the continent of Africa from east to west, encountering many adventures and obtaining much gold, which he dissipates in England. He then becomes a pirate, acquiring great wealth from depredations in the West Indies, Indian Ocean, and China Seas; he returns home, unpunished but vaguely repentant, and marries the sister of his shipmate, William, a colourful Quaker pirate.

Sir Courtly Nice, *or It Cannot Be* A comedy by John *Crowne, produced 1685, based on *No puede ser el guardar una mujer*, by the Spanish dramatist Moreto (1618–69). Leonora loves Farewel, a young man of quality, but her brother Lord Bellguard opposes the match owing to a family feud. He keeps her under watch by her aunt, 'an old amorous envious maid', and a pair of spies, Hothead and Fanatic, comical religious bigots of contrary convictions. Thanks to the resourcefulness of Crack, who introduces himself in an assumed character into Bellguard's house, Farewel carries off and marries Leonora. His rival, the fop Sir Courtly Nice, whose 'linen is all made in Holland by neat women that dip their fingers in rosewater', is fobbed off with the aunt; and Surly, an ill-mannered cynic, gets no wife at all. There is a critical edition by C. B. Hughes (1966).

Sir Launfal By Thomas Chestre (*fl.* late 14th–early 15th century), a late 14th-century *Breton lay, in 1,044 lines in twelve-line, *tail-rhyme stanzas. It is one of the two English versions of *Marie de France's *Lanval*. Launfal is a knight of the *Round Table who leaves the court, affronted by tales of *Guinevere's misconduct. He falls in love with a fairy lady, Tryamour. When he returns to Arthur's court Guinevere declares her love for him, but he rejects her, declaring that his beloved's maids are more beautiful. The queen accuses him of trying to seduce her and at his trial he is asked to produce the beautiful lady he has boasted of. Tryamour appears, breathes on Guinevere's eyes, blinding her, and the lovers depart. The poem has been much edited in romance anthologies. See Anne Laskaya and Eve Salisbury (eds), *The Middle English Breton Lays* (1995).

Sir Patrick Spens An early Scottish ballad, included in Thomas *Percy's **Reliques*. Sir Patrick goes to sea on a mission, has a premonition of disaster, and is lost with his ship's company. In Walter *Scott's version, the mission was to bring to Scotland the Maid of Norway (1283–90), who died on her voyage to marry Edward, prince of Wales.

Sir Thomas More *See* MORE, SIR THOMAS.

SISMONDI, Léonard Simonde de (1773–1842) Swiss historian whose most famous work was the sixteen-volume *Histoire des républiques italiennes* (1807–18: *History of the Italian Republics*). He also published a massive *Histoire des Français* (1821–44: *History of the French*), and the influential *De la littérature du midi de l'Europe* (1813: *Historical View of the Literature of the South of Europe*, trans. Thomas Roscoe, 1823). He was an important influence on John *Ruskin's understanding of Italian history.

SISSAY, Lemn (?1967–) Dramatist, scriptwriter, and poet, born in Ethiopia but fostered by a British couple; he lost touch with his birth family. His work focuses on his search for them: poetry collections include *Tender Fingers in a Clenched Fist* (1988) and *The Emperor's Watchmaker* (2000).

SISSON, C. H. (Charles Hubert) (1914–2003) Poet, translator, and essayist, born in Bristol, and educated at Bristol

University. Exposure to the febrile political rhetoric of 1930s Germany was a formative experience, as was his conversion from *Methodism to High Anglicanism. He joined the Civil Service in 1936 to begin a career which, unusually amongst his contemporaries, combined writing and public office. Inviting comparisons with Andrew *Marvell, Jonathan *Swift, and Barnabe *Barnes, he sought to integrate poetry and politics: not simply in his 'political poetry' (Tory reaction to the *Pylon School) but also his 'poetic politics'. His constitutional study *The Spirit of British Administration* (1959) appeals to an ancient and mystical bond between God, Crown, and nation. His literary work, however, explores the persuasive rhythms and imaginative insights of poetry as the best means to expound this obscure tradition. Volumes published include *The London Zoo* (1961), *Numbers* (1965), *Metamorphoses* (1968), *Anchises* (1976), *In the Trojan Ditch* (1974), *God Bless Karl Marx!* (1988), and *Antidotes* (1991). Both *free verse and metrical forms are employed to trace tensions between an idealist, traditionalist vision and the discourses conspiring to oust it. Biblical and classical themes are mingled with *Arthurian references and juxtaposed with portrayals of contemporary society. The result is often caustic satire, combining a Christian preoccupation with man's fallen nature and a classical view of his limitations. Sisson is sometimes seen as the antithesis to the *Movement in conservative post-war English poetry, but his association with Donald *Davie suggests the poets formed the two feet of a bridge between the Movement and the legacy of T. S. *Eliot and Ezra *Pound. His prolific translations—of Heinrich *Heine, Jean *Racine, *Catullus, *Horace, *Lucretius, *Virgil, Dante's **Divina commedia* (1980), and others—sometimes appear to domesticate the works as a compromise to the Movement's insular audience. He published two novels: *An Asiatic Romance* (1953), which calls upon wartime experiences in India, and *Christopher Homm* (1965), which pre-empts Martin *Amis's *Time's Arrow* in recounting a life backwards from death to birth. A partial autobiography, *On the Look Out*, appeared in 1989. The major collections are *The Avoidance of Literature: Collected Essays* (1978), *Collected Translations* (1996), and *Collected Poems* (1998).

SITWELL, Dame Edith (1887–1964) Poet and writer, born in Scarborough and educated at home. She began to write poetry when young, and her first published poem, 'Drowned Suns', appeared in the *Daily Mirror* in 1913. She despised much of the work published in **Georgian Poetry*, and from 1916 to 1921 edited *Wheels*, an anti-Georgian magazine. Her first volume of verse, *The Mother and Other Poems* (1915), was followed by many others, including *Gold Coast Customs* (1929), and she quickly acquired a reputation as an eccentric and controversial figure, confirmed by the first public performance, in 1923, of *Façade* (1922), with verses in syncopated rhythms and music by William *Walton. Her prose works include a biography of Alexander *Pope (1930), *English Eccentrics* (1933), and *Victoria of England* (1936). Her only novel, *I Live under a Black Sun* (1937), was poorly received, but it was followed by a period of great acclaim, aroused by her poems of the Blitz and the atom bomb (*Street Songs*, 1942; *Green Song*, 1944; *The Song of the Cold*, 1945; *The Shadow of Cain*, 1947); as John *Lehmann said, 'The hour and the poet were matched.' Triumphal lecture tours in America followed the war, but in the 1950s her reputation began to slowly fade. She remained, however, a considerable public figure, well known outside literary circles for her theatrical dress and manner (recorded by many artists and photographers) and by her indignant response to real or suspected criticism. F. R. *Leavis had claimed in 1932 that 'the Sitwells belong to the history of publicity, rather than that of poetry', but Edith's status as a poet survived this dismissal, although it remains less than secure. She was made a DBE in 1954. An autobiography, *Taken Care Of* (1965) appeared posthumously. See Victoria *Glendinning, *Edith Sitwell* (1981).

SITWELL, Sir Osbert (1892–1969) Poet and writer, born in London and educated at Eton College; brother of Edith and Sacheverell *Sitwell. He joined the army (the Sherwood Rangers, transferring to the Grenadier Guards) and served reluctantly in the First World War; his early poetry (e.g. *The Winstonburg Line*, 1919) is sharply satirical and pacifist in tone. He went on to produce further volumes of poetry (including *Argonaut and Juggernaut*, 1919, and *At the House of Mrs Kinfoot*, 1921), fiction, and autobiography, and was, with his brother and sister, an outspoken enemy of the *Georgian poets (whom he regarded as philistine) and an ardent supporter of their *modernist counterparts. His prose works include *Triple Fugue* (1924), a collection of six satirical stories; *Before the Bombardment* (1926), a novel describing the shock German naval shelling of Scarborough in 1914 and its effects on the town; *Winters of Content* (1932), describing travels in Italy; and *Escape with Me!* (1939), describing travels in China and the Far East. His most sustained achievement remains his autobiography, in five volumes (*Left Hand! Right Hand!*, 1945; *The Scarlet Tree*, 1946; *Great Morning!*, 1948; *Laughter in the Next Room*, 1949; *Noble Essences*, 1950: with a later addition, *Tales my Father Taught Me*, 1962). These are remarkable for the portrait of the eccentric, exasperating figure of his father Sir George, and their tone is romantic, acidic, nostalgic, and affectionate in turn. He was appointed CBE in 1956 and CH in 1958. See P. Ziegler, *Osbert Sitwell* (1998).

SITWELL, Sir Sacheverell (1897–1988) Poet and writer, born in Scarborough and educated at Eton College and at Balliol College, Oxford; brother of Osbert and Edith *Sitwell. His first volume of verse, *The People's Palace*, was published in 1918, his last, *An Indian Summer*, in 1982. His prose works include *Southern Baroque Art* (1924) and *German Baroque Art* (1927); the monumental *British Architects and Craftsmen* (1945); and *Bridge of the Brocade Sash* (1959), on the arts of Japan. He also wrote biographies of *Mozart* (1932), *Liszt* (1934), and *Scarlatti* (1935). His imaginative prose includes *The Dance of the Quick and the Dead* (1936), a series of interlocked reflections on literature, art, travel, etc.; *Valse des fleurs* (1941), a recreation of a day in St Petersburg in 1868; and *Journey to the Ends of Time* (1959). He was made a Companion of Honour in 1984. See S. Bradford, *Sacheverell Sitwell* (1993).

Six Characters in Search of an Author See PIRANDELLO, LUIGI.

skaldic (scaldic) **verse** A form of Old Norse poetry distinguished by elaborate *metre, *alliteration, *consonance, and resourceful diction that includes the *kenning. The most usual metre is 'dróttkvaett', eight six-syllable lines, all ending in trochees. Usually each odd line contains two alliterating syllables in stressed positions; alliteration is continued on one stressed syllable in each following even line. Odd lines contain two internal half-rhymes, even lines two full rhymes. Skaldic verse flourished in the 10th and 11th centuries and much was composed to commemorate the deeds of chieftains then ruling in Norway. Such verses are preserved mainly in the kings' sagas; occasional verses, and some love poetry are included in the family sagas (*see* SAGA). E. O. G. Turville-Petre, *Scaldic Poetry* (1976), gives parallel translation and discussion. A nine-volume collection, *Skaldic Poetry of the Scandinavian Middle Ages*, has begun to appear.

SKEAT, W. W. (1835–1912) 19th-century editor of Old and Middle English literature. He became a mathematics lecturer at Christ's College, Cambridge (1864), but spent much time in the study of Early English and was appointed to the chair of Anglo-Saxon (1878). His edition of *Lancelot of the Laik* (1865) was among the first publications of the *Early English Text Society. He edited *Ælfric, John *Barbour's *Bruce*, Thomas *Chatterton, and the Anglo-Saxon Gospels. He also edited **Piers Plowman* (1886), setting out in parallel the three manuscript versions, the existence of which he discovered, and *Chaucer (7 vols, 1894–7, largely establishing the canon, with non-canonical works in vol. vii). He founded the English Dialect Society (1873). His *Etymological Dictionary* (1879–82; rev. and enl. 1910) was begun in order to collect material for the *New English Dictionary* (*see* MURRAY, SIR JAMES).

SKEFFINGTON, Sir Lumley St George (1771–1850) Dandy, playwright, and lover of the theatre. His most successful works, *The Word of Honour, The High Road to Marriage*, and *The Sleeping Beauty*, were produced in the years 1802–5. He was caricatured by James *Gillray, and his dramatic works were described by Lord *Byron in **English Bards and Scotch Reviewers* (1809) as 'skeletons of plays'.

SKELTON, John (?1460–1529) Poet, created 'laureate' by the universities of Oxford, Louvain, and Cambridge, an academical distinction. He became tutor to Prince Henry (later Henry VIII). He was admitted to holy orders in 1498 and became rector of Diss in Norfolk, although certainly from 1518 he lived in Westminster. Skelton's extraordinary poetry is marked by its unrivalled linguistic and metrical inventiveness. He pioneered the verse form now known as 'Skeltonic verse', consisting of short lines grouped by end-rhymes. His principal works include: *The *Bowge of Courte* (the title refers to free board at the king's table), a satire on the court of Henry VII, printed by Wynkyn de *Worde; *A Garlande of Laurell* (a self-laudatory allegory, describing the crowning of the author among the great poets of the world); *Phyllyp Sparowe* (a lamentation put into the mouth of Jane Scrope, a young lady whose sparrow has been killed by a cat, followed by a eulogy of her by Skelton, and a defence of himself and the poem); and **Collyn Clout* (a complaint by a vagabond of the misdeeds of ecclesiastics), which influenced Edmund *Spenser. Not only this last poem, but also his satires *Speke Parrot* and *Why come ye nat to Courte*, contained attacks on Cardinal Wolsey. However, *A Garlande of Laurell* and his poem on the duke of Albany, both of 1523, are dedicated to Wolsey, and the cardinal commissioned *A Replycacion agaynst Certayne Yong Scolers Abjured of Late* (printed *c.*1528), in which Skelton condemns the folly of Thomas Bilney and Thomas Arthur, two Cambridge scholars who had abjured heresies. *The Tunnyng of Elynour Rummyng* is a vigorous satire. His play **Magnificence* is an example of the *morality, although it may have been intended to satirize the expulsion from the privy chamber of some of Henry VIII's associates. Skelton's *Ballade of the Scottysshe Kynge* is a spirited celebration of the defeat of the Scots at the battle of *Flodden Field (1513). A number of Skelton's poems were printed and reprinted in the 16th century, most of the extant copies being, though undated, evidently later than the poet's death; in 1568 appeared a fairly full collected edition in one volume. See *The Complete English Poems*, ed. John Scattergood (1983).

Sketches by Boz A collection of vivid sketches of life and manners, by Charles *Dickens, first published in various periodicals, and in book form 1836–7 (in one volume, 1839). They represent some of Dickens's earliest literary work.
See BOZ.

SKINNER, B. F. (Burrhus Frederic) (1904–90) American behavioural psychologist, born in Pennsylvania, who invented the operant conditioning chamber, an item of laboratory equipment used in the study of animal behaviour. His only novel, *Walden Two* (1948), describes a visit to a utopian community and *Beyond Freedom and Dignity* (1971) explores a technology of behaviour.

SKINNER, John (1721–1807) Episcopal minister and controversialist, born in Birse, Aberdeenshire, and educated at Mariscal College, who is chiefly remembered as the author of 'Tullachgorum' (1776), pronounced by Robert *Burns 'the best Scotch song Scotland ever saw'. His poems and songs were published in vol. iii of his *Theological Works* (1809).

ŠKVORECKY, Josef (1924–) Czech novelist, born in Náchod in north-east Bohemia, and educated at Charles University, Prague. He worked for a while in publishing, and emigrated to Canada in 1969 with his novelist wife Zdena Salivarová (1933–), where they founded a Czech-language publishing house. He is known internationally for his comic and frequently subversive novels of wartime and post-war life, many of them featuring his hero Danny, passionate about women and jazz, who graduates from small-town adolescence in Bohemia to become a professor in Canada. Titles include *Zbabělci* (*The Cowards*, 1958) and *The Engineer of Human Souls* (1977). Recent works include *When Eve Was Naked: Stories of a Life's Journey* (2002), a collection of translated shorter fiction, and *Ordinary Lives* (2008).

SLADEK, John T. (1937–2000) American *science fiction writer, born in Minnesota. During a lengthy stay in Britain, he became involved with the *New Wave of science fiction. With Thomas M. *Disch, he also wrote pseudonymous *Gothics like *The House that Fear Built* (1966). Much of his work draws on the absurdity of the human-robot contrast. *Roderick* (1980) described the **Candide*-like moral education of a young robot. *Maps* (2002) is a posthumous collection showing his surreal gifts as a short story writer.

slavery, literature of Literature written during or about the period between the 16th and 19th centuries when Europeans colonized the Americas and the Caribbean using slave labour from Africa. Slavery is treated ambivalently in Aphra Behn's **Oroonoko* (1688) and Thomas *Southerne's play of the same name (1696), and in Daniel Defoe's **Robinson Crusoe* and **Colonel Jack*. Later in the 18th century the anti-slavery movement began to attract writers; Thomas *Day's narrative poem about a runaway slave, *The Dying Negro* (1773), became one of the best-known abolitionist poems of the period, but other poets such as William *Cowper, William *Blake, Robert *Southey, and William *Wordsworth contributed notably to the cause. George *Colman the younger's popular play **Inkle and Yarico* (1787) was only the most sentimental of dozens of versions of the tale (from Richard Steele's **Spectator*, 13 Mar. 1711) of the betrayal and abandonment of a 'noble savage' by a supposedly cultivated European. Such critiques of civilization and commerce link anti-slavery with *primitivism. *Sentimental novels such as Henry *Mackenzie's *Julia de Roubigné* (1777) and Sarah *Scott's *The History of Sir George Ellison* (1766) also used slavery as a focus for pathos, though the depiction of the slave's predicament is often designed to stimulate the sensibility and benevolence of the reader rather than to challenge the institution of slavery. Even sympathetic observers such as John *Stedman, whose *Narrative* (1796), illustrated by Blake, catalogued the horrors of slavery in Surinam, argued for amelioration of the slaves' conditions rather than their freedom. Anti-slavery politics did not usually transcend the belief in the superiority of European culture and rarely provided insights into the experiences of slaves as individuals. However, literature produced by ex-slaves, such as the *Interesting Narrative of the Life... of Olaudah *Equiano* (1789) and the *Letters* (1782) of Ignatius *Sancho, played an important role in the abolition movement because writing and art were valued as expressions of humanity and civilization. The 19th century produced many more slave narratives, especially in America; the most famous of them are by Frederick *Douglass and Harriet *Jacobs. Such writings have formed the basis of newly constructed *African American canons (*see also* BLACK BRITISH LITERATURE). Literature has continued to be produced which rewrites the experience of slavery; the most famous of these to come out of America was Toni Morrison's **Beloved* (1987): she stated that her aim in writing was 'to fill in the blanks that the slave narratives left, to part the veil that was so frequently drawn'. In Britain, Fred *D'Aguiar, David *Dabydeen, Caryl *Phillips, and Beryl Gilroy (1924–2001) have written literature that reimagines the history of slavery, and novels by Phillipa Gregory (1954–), Barry *Unsworth, and Marina *Warner have explored the role slavery played in British society. In the Caribbean, the need to develop a postcolonial identity has encouraged writers such as George *Lamming, Derek *Walcott, and Earl Lovelace (1935–) to reinterpret the slave past. See Peter Hulme, *Colonial Encounters* (1986); A. Rampersad, *Slavery and the Literary Imagination* (1989); V. Carretta, *Unchained Voices* (1996); M. Wood, *Slavery, Empathy, and Pornography* (2000).

'Sleepy Hollow, The Legend of' A popular story by Washington *Irving, included in *The Sketch Book* (1820). Ichabod Crane is a schoolmaster and suitor for the hand of Katrina van Tassel. He meets his death, or, according to another report, leaves the neighbourhood, in consequence of being pursued at night by a headless horseman, an incident for which his rival Brom Bones is suspected of having been responsible. The story forms the basis of a film starring Johnny Depp (1999).

SLESSOR, Kenneth (1901–71) Australian poet and journalist, born Kenneth Adolphe Schloesser, in Orange (New South Wales). He worked mainly in Sydney and was Australia's official war correspondent 1940–4. Slessor's reputation as a *bon vivant* and writer of light verse belies the technical virtuosity of the small number of poems on which his critical reputation largely rests. Among these are 'Five Bells' (written 1935–7), an elegy on a drowned friend set in Sydney Harbour, and 'Beach Burial'.

Slough of Despond In John *Bunyan's **Pilgrim's Progress*, a bog into which Christian and Pliable fall shortly after quitting the City of Destruction. Calvinist horror of sin accompanying conversion is symbolized as a rank fen which the king's surveyors have been attempting to drain 'for this sixteen hundred years' (i.e. since Christ's crucifixion). As fen drainage was a preoccupation of the age, the image had immediacy, and has since become proverbial.

Small House at Allington, The A novel by Anthony *Trollope, published 1864, fifth in the *'Barsetshire' series, and one of the most enduringly popular. Lily Dale is engaged to the ambitious Adolphus Crosbie, but Crosbie is invited to a house party at Courcy Castle where he proposes to Lady Alexandrina de Courcy. Learning that Crosbie has jilted her, Lily accepts his perfidy stoically, but Johnny Eames, who loves her, assaults Crosbie at Paddington station. Crosbie's marriage fails; Lady Alexandrina returns to her family and Crosbie takes refuge in bachelordom. Meanwhile Eames grows out of his juvenile dissipations, clears up an unfortunate entanglement with the daughter of his London boarding-house keeper, and begins to spend much time at Allington. He becomes the protégé of Lord de Guest, and renews his suit to Lily. Lily, however, is stubbornly loyal to Crosbie. Meanwhile, Lily's sister Bell is expected to marry the heir of Squire Dale of the Great House at Allington, but instead chooses the worthy Dr Crofts.

SMART, Christopher (1722–71) Poet, born near Maidstone, Kent, and educated at Pembroke Hall, Cambridge, where he distinguished himself as a classical scholar and as a poet, winning the Seatonian Prize for sacred poetry five times. In 1749 he came to London and began to write poems and reviews under various pseudonyms, including 'Mrs Midnight', for John *Newbery, whose stepdaughter he married in 1752. Newbery published his first collection of verse, *Poems on Several Occasions* (1752), which included a blank verse georgic in two books, 'The Hop-Garden'. *The Hilliad*, a *mock-heroic satire on the quack doctor John Hill (1714–75), written with Arthur *Murphy and modelled on *The *Dunciad*, appeared in 1753. In 1756 Smart was dangerously ill, and a year later he was admitted to a hospital for the insane; he spent the years 1759–63 in a private home for the mentally ill in Bethnal Green. His derangement took the form of a compulsion to public prayer, which occasioned the famous comment of Samuel *Johnson: 'I'd as lief pray with Kit Smart as anyone else.' After being rescued from the asylum he published *A Song to David* (1763), a hymn of praise to David as author of the Psalms; the poem is built on a mathematical and mystical ordering of stanzas grouped in threes, fives, and sevens, and was likened by Robert *Browning to a great cathedral. Smart also published translations of the Psalms, of the fables of Phaedrus, and of *Horace, two oratorios, and *Hymns for the Amusement of Children* (1770; ed. Edmund *Blunden, 1947). William *Mason, who on reading the *Song to David* declared Smart 'as mad as ever', was, with Charles *Burney, a supportive friend. Smart died within the 'Rules' of the King's Bench Prison, confined for debt. His work was little known until the publication of his extraordinary work *Jubilate Agno* in 1939 (ed. W. F. Stead as *Rejoice in the Lamb: A Song from Bedlam*). This unfinished work had been composed between 1758/9 and 1763, largely at Bethnal Green; Smart described it as 'my Magnificat', and it celebrates the Creation in a verse form based on the antiphonal principles of Hebrew poetry. It was to consist of parallel sets of verses, one beginning 'Let…', with a response beginning 'For…'. The arrangement of the lines intended by Smart himself was demonstrated in W. H. Bond's 1954 edition, based on the autograph manuscript in the Houghton Library at Harvard. It contains an extremely wide range of references, biblical, botanical, scientific (in opposition to Isaac *Newton's view of the universe), cabbalistic, and personal; the most celebrated passage is the one beginning 'For I will consider my cat Jeoffry…'. Benjamin *Britten set parts of the poem to music in 1943. There is a scholarly edition of the complete works, by K. Williamson and M. Walsh (5 vols, 1980–96); Smart's letters were edited by B. Rizzo and R. Mahoney (1991). See A. Sherbo, *Christopher Smart: Scholar of the University* (1967); C. Mounsey, *Christopher Smart: Clown of God* (2001).

SMART, Elizabeth (1913–86) Canadian-born writer, born in Ottawa, who went to England in 1930 to study music and settled there after the Second World War. She is remembered for her prose poem *By Grand Central Station I Sat Down and Wept* (1945), an account of her love for George *Barker, whom she met in California in 1940, and by whom she was to have four children. It is passionate and lyrical, with biblical echoes from the Song of Songs, and was described by Brigid *Brophy as 'shelled, skinned, nerve-exposed'. She also published poetry (*A Bonus*, 1977; *In the Meantime*, 1984) and her journals have been edited (1986, 1994) by Alice Van Wart.

Smectymnuus The name under which five Presbyterian clergymen, Stephen Marshall (?1594/5–1655), Edmund Calamy (1600–66), Thomas Young (*c.*1587–1655), Matthew Newcomen (d. 1669), and William Spurstowe (d. 1666), published a pamphlet in 1641 attacking episcopacy and Bishop Joseph *Hall. It was answered by Hall, and defended by John *Milton (who had been a pupil of Young, the eldest of the five) in his *Animadversions upon the Remonstrant's Defence against Smectymnuus* (1641) and his *An Apology against a Pamphlet Call'd A Modest Confutation of the Animadversions upon the Remonstrant against Smectymnuus* (1642). In the latter Milton also defends himself against the allegations of the anonymous *A Modest Confutation* (possibly by Hall's son or by the Revd Robert Duncan (?1599–?1622), which include the charge that Milton had 'spent his youth in loitering, bezelling and harlotting', and that he had been 'vomited out' of the university: it contains an interesting account of his early studies. From 'Smectymnuus' is derived the 'Legion Smec' in Samuel *Butler's **Hudibras* (II. ii) (where the Presbyterians: 'New modell'd the army and cashier'd | All that to Legion Smec adher'd').

SMEDLEY, Agnes (1892–1950) Political activist and writer born in Missouri to a family of labourers; she did not complete her formal education but worked as a domestic servant and teacher.

In 1916 she joined the Socialist Party of America. She was a campaigner against British rule in India and for birth control. Smedley is best known for her articles and books on China, where she went in 1928 and spent much of the 1930s, becoming closely involved with the Communist cause and marching with its armies. After her return to the United States in 1941 she was monitored by the FBI, partly as a result of which she moved to England in late 1949. Her books include the autobiographical novel *Daughter of Earth* (1929) and the extraordinary works of reportage *China Fights Back* (1938) and *Battle Hymn of China* (1943). A 2005 biography by Ruth Price presents evidence that Smedley was a Soviet spy.

SMEDLEY, Francis Edward (1818–64) Editor and novelist, disabled from childhood, born at Great Marlow, Buckinghamshire, and privately educated. He was for three years editor of *Cruikshank's Magazine* and author of high-spirited novels of sport, romance, and adventure, including the popular *Frank Fairleigh* (1850), illustrated by George *Cruikshank, *Lewis Arundel* (1852), and *Harry Coverdale's Courtship* (1855).

SMETANA, Bedřich (1824–84) Czech composer, best known for his symphonic poem cycle *Má Vlast* ('My Fatherland', 1879–80). Smetana was devoted to Czech language and culture and set no English texts, but admired *Shakespeare: one of his earliest orchestral works was the symphonic poem based on **Richard III* (1857–8) written when the composer was seeking recognition in Sweden: it includes a musical portrait of the hunchbacked king with his uneven, halting walk. In 1867 Smetana returned to the theme of Richard with fanfares for brass and timpani. Smetana also wrote a substantial piano piece, *Sketch to the Scene Macbeth and the Witches* (1859). In 1874–5 and 1883–4 Smetana, having successfully produced a number of Czech-themed operas, worked on *Viola*, an opera based on **Twelfth Night*: a fragmentary act survives.

SMILES, Samuel (1812–1904) Writer and reformer. Son of a shopkeeper in Haddington, near Edinburgh, he was educated at Edinburgh University and had a varied career as surgeon, newspaper editor, and secretary for a railway company. He devoted his leisure to the advocacy of political and social reform, on the lines of the *Manchester school, and to the biography of industrial leaders and humble self-taught students. He published a *Life of George Stephenson* (1875), *Lives of the Engineers* (1861–2), *Josiah Wedgwood* (1894), and many similar works, but is now principally remembered for his immensely successful *Self-Help* (1859), which was translated into many languages. Advocating industry, thrift, and self-improvement, and attacking 'over-government'; it has been seen as a work symbolizing the ethics and aspirations of mid-19th-century bourgeois individualism. The titles of other works on similar themes (*Character*, 1871; *Thrift*, 1875; *Duty*, 1880) are self-explanatory. His *Autobiography* was published posthumously (1905).

SMILEY, Jane (1951–) American novelist, born in Los Angeles, best known for her novel *A Thousand Acres* (1991), for which she was awarded the *Pulitzer Prize for fiction. In this grim retelling of the **King Lear* story, set like much of Smiley's work in the American Midwest, Smiley describes the tragic consequences of a farm-owner's decision to retire and pass his farm down to his three daughters. Other novels include the thriller *Duplicate Keys* (1984) and *Moo* (1995), a wryly satirical look at university campus life in Midwestern America. *Ten Days in the Hills* (2007) describes a Hollywood house party. She has also published a collection of short stories, *The Age of Grief* (1988). *Thirteen Ways of Looking at the Novel* (2005) gives her reflections on her chosen medium.

SMITH, Adam (1723–90) Scottish moral philosopher and political economist, born in Kirkcaldy and educated at Glasgow University (where he was taught by Francis *Hutcheson) and Balliol College, Oxford. His public lectures on rhetoric and belles-lettres in Edinburgh from 1748 to 1751 won him the friendship of Hugh *Blair, Adam *Ferguson, and David *Hume. He was appointed professor of logic at Glasgow in 1751, moving to the chair of moral philosophy the following year. His contributions to the original **Edinburgh Review* (1755–6) included a respectful but critical assessment of Samuel *Johnson's *Dictionary*. In 1759 he published *The *Theory of Moral Sentiments*, and five years later resigned his professorship to accompany the young duke of Buccleuch as tutor to France, Switzerland, and Germany. While in Europe he met *Voltaire and other **Philosophes*, and renewed an existing acquaintance with Benjamin *Franklin. In 1766 he returned to Kirkcaldy to devote himself to the preparation of *An Inquiry into the Nature and Causes of the *Wealth of Nations*, published in 1776 at the end of a three-year sojourn in London (during the course of which he had been admitted to the *Royal Society and the *Club). The argument of *The Wealth of Nations* that conventional 'mercantilist' policies restricted growth and perpetuated poverty revolutionized economic theory and (in due course) governmental practice. Most of Smith's voluminous and various manuscript writings were destroyed, in accordance with his instructions, on his death. *Essays on Philosophical Subjects* (1795) collected what was left. See Iain MacLean, *Adam Smith, Radical and Egalitarian: An Interpretation for the Twenty-First Century* (2006).

SMITH, Alexander (1829–67) Scottish poet, born in Kilmarnock, who left school at the age of 11 to work as a muslin pattern designer in Glasgow. *Poems* (1853), which included the already well-known 'A Life Drama', was greeted with enthusiasm. *Sonnets on the War* (1855), a patriotic sequence written in collaboration with Sydney *Dobell, was less successful, and was satirized, along with other works of the vehemently intense *Spasmodic school, in William *Aytoun's *Firmilian*. 'Glasgow', from *City Poems* (1857), continues to be anthologized. *A Summer in Skye* (1865) is a vividly individual evocation of the island where Smith spent his annual vacation from 1858.

SMITH, Ali (1962–) Novelist and short story writer, born in Inverness and educated at Aberdeen and Cambridge. Her first volume of stories, *Free Love* (1995) won the Saltire First Book of the Year Award, and was followed by her acclaimed first novel, *Like* (1997). A distinctly literary and genuinely original writer, she uses language and structure inventively and often experimentally, while always remaining highly readable and often very funny. *Hotel World* (2001), which won both the Encore Prize and the Scottish Arts Council Book Award, devotes five interlinking sections to five different women (including a ghost). Similarly, *The Accidental* (2004), which won the Whitbread Novel Award, gives a distinctive voice to each of the four very different members of a family whose holiday is invaded by a disruptive young woman. *Girl Meets Boy* (2007) retells the gender-swapping story of Iphis from *Ovid's *Metamorphoses*.

SMITH, Charlotte (1749–1806) Née Turner, poet and novelist, who also wrote many stories and sketches, and enjoyed considerable success. Born into prosperity in London, and educated at Chichester, Kensington, and at home, she was married at 15 to Benjamin Smith, the son of a London merchant (a circumstance she likened to being sold to 'slavery'). Abandoned by her spendthrift husband, she turned to writing to support her large family, beginning her literary career with **Elegiac Sonnets* in 1784, followed by a second volume of sonnets (a form for which she was particularly admired) in 1797. Her poetry was valued by William *Wordsworth, who called on Smith on his way to France in 1790, and S. T. *Coleridge. Like the Lake Poets, Smith's poetry is concerned with the notion of the solitary poet meditating on the beauty and sublimity of the landscape. However, her poetry does not share the Wordsworthian confidence in the restorative potential of nature. She initially welcomed the French Revolution but renounced it as it progressed into the Terror. Her political position is articulated in *The *Emigrants*. The melancholy of much of her poetry was not merely fashionable, as some supposed, but sprang in part from intense marital, family, and financial difficulties. *Beachy Head: With Other Poems* was published posthumously in 1807. Her eleven novels appeared between 1788 and 1802, and include *Emmeline* (1788), which impressed Walter *Scott, who included her in his *Lives of the Novelists*, and *The *Old Manor House* (1793), which many consider to be her best. Her novels mix aspects of the *Gothic, sentimental, and domestic literary modes and are also socio-politically engaged.

Wordsworth labelled Charlotte Smith a poet 'to whom English verse is under greater obligations than are likely to be either acknowledged or remembered', and until the late 20th century, when there was an upsurge of interest in Smith, his prophecy was accurate. See L. Fletcher, *Charlotte Smith: A Critical Biography* (1998); *The Works of Charlotte Smith*, ed. S. Curran, 14 vols (2005–7).

SMITH, Clark Ashton (1893–1961) American *fantasy author, painter, poet, and sculptor, born in Long Valley, California. His stories of far futures (Zothique) or distant pasts (Hyperborea) were frequently, like those of his correspondents H. P. *Lovecraft and Robert E. *Howard, published in **Weird Tales* and reprinted in numerous collections.

SMITH, Cordwainer (1913–66) Pseudonym of Paul Myron Anthony Linebarger, American *science fiction writer and psychological war expert. Born in Milwaukee, Wisconsin, but brought up in China, he was influenced by Chinese narrative techniques for the 'Instrumentality' series which, apart from three pre-1950 non-science fiction novels, were his major work. The sequence exists as an extensive, baroque future history, including the liberation of the animal-derived 'underpeople'.

SMITH, Dodie (Dorothy Gladys) (1896–1990) Playwright and novelist, born in Manchester, educated at the Royal Academy of Dramatic Art. Her output comprises ten plays, among them *Dear Octopus* (1938), and six adult novels, including the romantic minor classic *I Capture the Castle* (1949; filmed 2003). She is best known for her children's book *One Hundred and One Dalmatians* (1956), adapted by Disney in 1961 and 1996, with a sequel in 2000. See Valerie Grove, *Dear Dodie* (2006).

SMITH, Edward Elmer (1890–1965) American *science fiction author, born in Sheboygan, Wisconsin. Known as 'Doc' Smith because of his Ph.D., his serials in **Amazing Stories* and **Astounding Science-Fiction* magazines, such as the 'Lensman' series (begun in 1937), shaped science fiction through their epic conflict and sense of wonder.

SMITH, George (1824–1901) Publisher, born in London, educated at Merchant Taylors' School and the City of London School. He joined in 1838 the firm of Smith & Elder, publishers and East India agents, which his father had founded in partnership with Alexander Elder in 1816, soon after coming to London as a young man from his native town of Elgin. In 1843 Smith took charge of some of the firm's publishing operations, and on his father's death in 1846 became head of the firm. Under his control the business grew in both the India agency and publishing directions. The chief authors whose works he published in his early career were John *Ruskin, Charlotte *Brontë, whose **Jane Eyre* he issued in 1847, and W. M. *Thackeray, whose *The *History of Henry Esmond* he brought out in 1852. Charlotte Brontë visited Smith and his mother in London on friendly terms, and Smith later acknowledged that 'In **Villette* my mother was the original of "Mrs Bretton", several of her expressions are given verbatim. I myself, I discovered, stood for "Dr John"' ('Recollections of Charlotte Brontë', *Cornhill Magazine*, Dec. 1900).

In 1853 he took a business partner, H. S. King, and after weathering the storm of the Indian Mutiny, founded in 1859 the **Cornhill Magazine*, with Thackeray as editor and numerous leading authors and artists as contributors. In 1865 Smith (with Frederick Greenwood) founded the **Pall Mall Gazette*, a London evening newspaper of independent character and literary quality, which he owned until 1880. In 1868 he dissolved partnership with King, leaving him to carry on the India agency branch of the old firm's business, and himself taking over the publishing branch. His chief authors now included Robert *Browning, Matthew *Arnold, Leslie *Stephen, and Anne Thackeray *Ritchie, all of whom were personal friends. He was founder (1882) and proprietor of the **Dictionary of National Biography*. Shrewd and discriminating, Smith was one of the most successful and influential literary publishers of his day.

SMITH, Horatio (Horace) (1779–1849) Brother of James *Smith. He became famous overnight as the author, with his brother, of **Rejected Addresses* in 1812, and of *Horace in London* (1813), imitations of odes of *Horace, chiefly written by his brother. He then turned to the writing of historical romance. In 1826 his *Brambletye House*, the story of a young Cavalier and a pale shadow of *Scott's *Woodstock* (published in the same year), went through many editions. *The Tor Hill* followed in the same year, and between then and 1846 he wrote nearly twenty further novels, as well as plays, poems, and work for the **New Monthly Magazine*.

SMITH, Iain Crichton (Iain Mac a'Ghobhainn) (1928–98) Scottish poet, novelist, and short story writer, born in Glasgow and brought up in Lewis. He was educated at the University of Aberdeen and taught English in secondary schools for many years, first in Dumbarton and then (1955–77) in Oban. Smith was a prolific writer who used both English and (to a diminishing degree) his native Gaelic. In volumes such as *Thistles and Roses* (1961), *The Law and the Grace* (1965), and *The Leaf and the Marble* (1998), Smith's poetry juxtaposes the spontaneous and creative with the authoritarian and dogmatic, associating the latter categories with the Roman Empire, the abstractions of ideology, and (persistently) the Scottish Free Church in which the poet was brought up. *Consider the Lilies* (1962) is an austere psychological novel of the Clearances, and *Murdo* (1981) a series of surreal, darkly hilarious sketches of Highland life.

SMITH, James (1775–1839) Elder brother of Horatio *Smith. He was solicitor to the Board of Ordnance, and produced with his brother **Rejected Addresses* (1812), the famous collection of parodies of contemporary writers including William *Wordsworth, S. T. *Coleridge, and Walter *Scott, and *Horace in London* (1813), imitations of odes of *Horace, largely written by James. He also wrote entertainments for the comic actor Charles Mathews (1776–1835).

SMITH, John (1618–52) *See* CAMBRIDGE PLATONISTS.

SMITH, Captain John (1580–1631) Soldier and colonial governor; he set out with the Virginia colonists in 1606 and is said to have been rescued by Pocahontas, a Native American woman, when taken prisoner by the Native Americans. He became head of the colony and explored the coasts of the Chesapeake. He was author of *The General History of Virginia, New England, and the Summer Isles* (1624). See *Complete Works*, ed. P. L. Barbour (1986); D. and T. Hoobler, *Captain John Smith, Jamestown, and the Birth of the American Dream* (2006).

SMITH, John Thomas (1776–1833) Engraver and artist, and eventually keeper of prints and drawings at the British Museum. He was particularly interested in the history and character of London. Among other writings he published *Antiquities of London* (1800) and *Vagabondiana* (1817), a description of London's beggars, illustrated by himself. He wrote a remarkably candid life of the sculptor Joseph *Nollekens, published in 1828, and in 1839 *Cries of London: A Book for a Rainy Day, or Recollections of the Events of the Years 1766–1833* (1845), which provides a lively account of the literary and artistic life of the time.

SMITH, Ken (1938–2003) Poet, born in Rudston, east Yorkshire, educated at Leeds University. *The Pity* (1967) introduced a nature poet with a strong human focus too. His work then appeared fugitively until *Bloodaxe Books published *Burned Books* (1981) and *The Poet Reclining: Selected Poems 1962–1980* (1982), which showed Smith's kinship with American speech-based poetry (rather than the image-driven practice of English contemporaries) when he dealt, in fragmentary form, with themes of loss and exile. *Fox Running* (1980), his most celebrated work, applies these methods to a period of breakdown in London. *Terra* (1986) is Smith's reading of the Thatcher–Reagan years 'from below', while *Wormwood* (1987) draws on experience as writer in residence at HM Prison Wormwood Scrubs. After 1989 Smith travelled extensively in Eastern Europe. His acclaimed volume *Shed* appeared in 2002. From 1963 to 1972 he co-edited **Stand*. See Ken Smith, *You Again: Last Poems and Tributes* (2004).

SMITH, Logan Pearsall (Lloyd Pearsall Smith) (1865–1946) Essayist and scholar, born in Philadelphia of Quaker stock. He spent most of his life in England, devoting himself to the study of literature and the English language; he was (with Robert *Bridges and others) a founder of the Society for Pure English. One of his sisters became the first wife of Bertrand *Russell, another married Bernard *Berenson, and his own circle of literary friends included Roger *Fry, Henry *James, and Cyril *Connolly. His works include *Trivia* (1902), *More Trivia* (1921), and *Afterthoughts* (1931), collections of much-polished observations and aphorisms; one of his more memorable, 'People say that life is the thing, but I prefer reading', indicates the nature of his success and limitations as an author. See *Recollections of Pearsall Smith* (1949), an unsparing account by R. Gathorne-Hardy.

SMITH, Stevie (1902–71) Poet and novelist, born in Hull but brought up in Palmers Green, north London, where she spent most of her adult life with an aunt. Educated at Palmers Green High School and North London Collegiate for Girls, she wrote three novels, *Novel on Yellow Paper* (1936), *Over the Frontier* (1938), and *The Holiday* (1949), but has been more widely recognized for her caustic and enigmatic verse, much of it illustrated by her own drawings. Her first volume, *A Good Time Was Had by All* (1937), was followed by seven others, including *Not Waving but Drowning* (1957), of which the title poem is probably her best known. Her *Collected Poems*, edited by James MacGibbon, appeared in 1975. She was an extraordinary reader of her own verse: Seamus *Heaney brilliantly characterizes her performances as 'pitching between querulousness and keening', both cajoling and forbidding. During her lifetime she was frequently condescended to as eccentric, fey, and whimsical; but she has been read since as one of the most notable poets of her time. Largely this is the consequence of both her absorption by feminist criticism and her impact on a range of women poets (including Sylvia *Plath). Her slyly subversive narratives and rewritings of legend and myth have been particularly influential, and so too have her treatments of solitude, death, loneliness, and conventionality. In many respects what was once seen as levity has been newly appreciated as an oblique, stoical manner of exploring some of the darkest, most disintegrative emotions and experiences. The poems rehearse a sceptical mistrust of marriage, painful feeling connected with relationships between mothers and daughters, and frustrated libidinous desire; and they are frequently drawn to molestation and murder. A newly appreciative attentiveness has also been given to the rationale for her use of experimental forms, and particularly for her interest in oral modes such as *ballad, *folksong, *hymn and *carol, which are sometimes read as undermining certain masculinist assumptions about the literary, and about the authority or primacy of the textual. If still enigmatic, her work has come to seem very richly and provocatively so. See Romana Huk, *Stevie Smith: Between the Lines* (2005).

SMITH, Sydney (1771–1845) Author, clergyman, and wit, educated at Winchester College and New College, Oxford. He lived for a time as a tutor in Edinburgh, where he became a friend of Francis *Jeffrey and Henry *Brougham with whom he founded the **Edinburgh Review* in 1802. He was himself the original 'projector' of the *Review*, the object of which was to provide a voice for liberal and Whig opinion to balance the Tory **Quarterly Review*. Smith was a humane man, who campaigned vigorously, in the *Review* and elsewhere, against the Game Laws, transportation, prisons, slavery, and for Catholic emancipation, church reform, and many other matters. He tried for a time to restrain what he saw as Jeffrey's tendency, as editor of the *Review*, to 'analyse and destroy'; but his own contributions became less frequent, then ceased altogether, as he came to feel that Jeffrey was making it 'perilous' for a cleric to be connected with the *Review*. He came to London in 1803, lectured with great success on moral philosophy at the Royal Institution, and became the wittiest and one of the most beloved of the Whig circle at *Holland House. In 1807 he published *The Letters of Peter *Plymley* in defence of Catholic emancipation, and he published many sermons, speeches, essays, and letters. He held the livings, first of Foston in Yorkshire, then of Combe Florey in Somerset, and in 1831 was made a canon of St Paul's, London. His remarkable wit was chiefly evident in his conversation, but may also be found in his letters, reviews, and essays. See biography by H. Pearson, *The Smith of Smiths* (1934).

SMITH, Sydney Goodsir (1915–75) Poet, born in Wellington, New Zealand, who moved to Edinburgh in 1928 when his father, the scientist Sydney (later Sir Sydney) Alfred Smith, took up the chair of forensic medicine there. Smith was educated at Edinburgh University and Oriel College, Oxford, and later worked for many years as art critic for the *Scotsman*. His first collection, *Skail Wind* (1941), included 'Epistle to John Guthrie', a wittily defiant apologia for his decision to write in *Scots. His most ambitious work is *Under the Eildon Tree* (1948), a sequence of 24 elegiac meditations on love, with a cast of characters ranging from *Dido and *Cuchulain to the poet's friend and mentor Hugh *MacDiarmid. The 'novel' *Carotid Cornucopius* (1947; rev. and extended, 1964) deploys flamboyantly erudite cross-linguistic puns to celebrate pub life and debauchery in Edinburgh. Smith's play *The Wallace* (1960) was revived at the 1985 Edinburgh Festival.

Smith, W. H., and Son, Ltd A firm of stationers, newsagents, and booksellers, which originated in a small newsvendor's shop opened in London in Little Grosvenor Street in 1792 by Henry Walton Smith and his wife Anna. He died within a few months, leaving the shop to his widow, who on her death in 1816 left it to her sons; the younger, William Henry Smith (1792–1865), gave the firm its name of W. H. Smith in 1828. When his son, also William Henry (1825–91), became a partner in 1846, the words 'and Son' were added, and have remained ever since. The business prospered, profiting from the railway boom by opening station bookstalls throughout the country (of which the first was at Euston, 1848), and establishing a circulating library in competition with *Mudie's which lasted until 1961; it was a joint owner (from 1966) of Book Club Associates. In the 20th century the wholesale and retail activities of the business expanded greatly, and the name of W. H. Smith is now associated with a wide range of products. The W. H. Smith Literary Award (1959–2006) was awarded for a work of any genre that constitutes 'the most outstanding contribution to English literature' in the year under review.

SMITH, Sir William (1813–93) Lexicographer, classical scholar, and editor of the **Quarterly Review* (1867–93). He is associated with the revival of classical teaching in England, and among his numerous and much-used educational works were the *Dictionary of Greek and Roman Antiquities* (1842), a *Dictionary of Greek and Roman Biography and Mythology* (1844–9), and a *Dictionary of the Bible* (1860–3).

SMITH, Zadie (1975–) Novelist, born in London to an English father and a Jamaican mother, and educated at Cambridge. Her first novel, *White Teeth* (2000), tells its story through three ethnically varied families. It won the *Guardian*'s and Whitbread's First Book Awards and was the overall winner of the Commonwealth Writers' Prize Best First Book Award. Though the novel is not autobiographical, Smith notes that when 'you come from a mixed-race family, it makes you think a bit harder about inheritance'. Her second novel, *The Autograph Man* (2002), is concerned with celebrity; the third, *On Beauty* (2005), which won the Orange Prize and the Europe and South Asia section of the Commonwealth Writers' Prize, pays homage to E. M. Forster's **Howards End*. Set mainly in Boston, it wittily domesticates the fashionable academic posturing that humiliates student enthusiasm with the use of arcane jargon.

SMOLLETT, Tobias (1721–71) Novelist and critic, the son of a Scots laird, born at Dalquhurn, Dunbartonshire. After attendance at Glasgow University he was apprenticed to a surgeon. He wrote a play, *The Regicide*, which he brought to London in 1739, but he could not get it accepted. He joined the navy, became surgeon's mate, and sailed in 1741 for the West Indies on an expedition against the Spaniards. In 1744 he set himself up as a surgeon in Downing Street. Although never a *Jacobite, Smollett's first publication, in 1746, was a poem, 'The Tears of Scotland', elicited by the duke of Cumberland's treatment of the Scots after 1745. Further poems followed, notably two satires on London life, *Advice* (1746) and *Reproof* (1747). *The Adventures of *Roderick Random*, drawing in part on Smollett's own naval experience, was published in 1748. In 1750 he moved to Chelsea, where he entertained freely in his fine large house. In the same year he received the degree of MD from Aberdeen, and travelled to Paris, a journey of which he made use in *The Adventures of *Peregrine Pickle* (1751). He may have been the author, in 1752, of the scurrilous pamphlet *The Faithful Narrative of Habbakkuk Hilding*, attacking Henry *Fielding for plagiarism. In 1753 he published *The Adventures of *Ferdinand Count Fathom*, a story of cruelty and treachery which did not sell well. His translation of *Cervantes, *The History and Adventures of the Renowned Don Quixote*, appeared in 1755, also to a disappointing reception. In 1756 he became co-founder and editor of the **Critical Review*; his editorship lasted till 1763. In 1757–8 he published his *Complete History of England*, which engendered much controversy, but sold well enough for Smollett to feel financially secure at last. Also in 1757 his naval farce *The Reprisal* was staged successfully at Drury Lane by David *Garrick. In 1760 *The Life and Adventures of Sir Launcelot *Greaves* began to appear in instalments in the *British Magazine*, Smollett's new venture, which ran until 1767. Also in 1760, Smollett was fined £100 and sentenced to three months' imprisonment for a libel on Admiral Knowles in the *Critical Review*. His edition of a new translation of *The Works of...Voltaire* began to appear in 1761. In 1762–3 Smollett wrote and edited the Tory journal the *Briton*, which was successfully opposed by Wilkes's **North Briton*. Smollett's health had long been deteriorating, and in 1763 he left England with his wife for France and Italy; they returned in 1765 and in 1766 he published his *Travels through France and Italy*, a caustic work which earned him from Laurence *Sterne the nickname of Smelfungus. In 1768 he and his wife left again for Italy, and in 1769 appeared *The Adventures of an Atom*, a rancorous satire on public men and affairs. *The Expedition of *Humphry Clinker*, an *epistolary novel generally agreed to be Smollett's crowning achievement, was published in 1771, some months before Smollett died at his home near Livorno. See J. C. Beasley, *Tobias Smollett, Novelist* (1988).

SMYTH, Dame Ethel Mary (1858–1944) Composer and autobiographer, born in Sidcup, London, and brought up near Aldershot; her father was a general and both he and her French mother disapproved of the intensity of her passion for music; she eventually escaped to Leipzig to study composition, where she met the German composers Johannes Brahms (1833–97) and Clara Schumann (1819–96). Her most famous compositions are her *Mass in D* (1891) and her opera *The Wreckers* (1902–4). She became a supporter of the women's suffrage movement in 1910 and was briefly imprisoned for militant activities; her *March of Women* became the anthem of the movement. She was made a dame in 1922. In later life her deafness meant she was unable to compose. Smyth is also renowned for her passionate attachments to women. Having met Virginia *Woolf when she was 72 and Virginia 48, she developed an immediate passion for her. Woolf read her autobiographical writing which she found richly evocative of a previous age, and admired her struggles and resistance, her 'great rush at life'. Smyth became the model for Rose Pargiter in Woolf's novel *The Years* (1937) and Miss La Trobe in *Between the Acts* (1941). Smyth's numerous volumes of memoirs, which she began to write in her fifties, include *Impressions that Remained* (1919), *Streaks of Life* (1924), and *Female Pipings in Eden* (1934). She dedicated *As Time Went On* (1936) to Virginia Woolf. See Louise Collis, *Impetuous Heart: The Story of Ethel Smyth* (1985).

Snobs of England, The A very successful series of comic papers by W. M. *Thackeray which originally appeared in **Punch* (1846–7); published in one volume in 1848. A satirical investigation of 'thinking meanly of mean things', the work introduced the word 'snob' in its modern meaning to the English language.

SNORRI STURLUSON (1178/9–1241) Icelandic historian and literary antiquary, distinguished author of **Heimskringla*, the Prose *Edda, and perhaps *Egils saga*, the biography of a Viking poet. Snorri is the most important figure in Old Icelandic literature; our knowledge of Norse myth and understanding of Old Norse poetry is due largely to him. He was ambitious, involved in the chief political intrigues of his time, and was ignominiously assassinated on the order of King Håkon of Norway.

SNOW, C. P. (Charles Percy) Baron Snow of Leicester (1905–80) Novelist, born in Leicester, and educated there and at Cambridge where he became a fellow of Christ's College in 1930. *Death under Sail* (1932), his first novel, was a detective story, but his major work is the **roman-fleuve Strangers and Brothers*. Published between 1940 and 1970, this traces the life of its narrator, Lewis Eliot, a barrister who, like Snow himself, rises from lower-middle-class provincial origins to enjoy worldly success and influence in academic and public life. *The Masters* (1951), a study of the internal politics of a Cambridge college, is the best known of the sequence but another, *The Corridors of Power* (1964), added a phrase to the language of the day. So too did his Rede Lecture on *The *Two Cultures and the Scientific Revolution* (1959). Snow was married to the novelist Pamela Hansford *Johnson.

Snowman, The (1978) Raymond *Briggs's wordless *picturebook uses *comic-strip techniques to depict the relationship between a boy and a snowman who comes alive in the night but melts the next day. It has been made into an animated film (1982), a musical (1998), and is frequently reformatted.

SNYDER, Gary (1930–) American poet, born in San Francisco, whose interest in mountaineering fed into his early poetry. Snyder was associated with the *Beats, and the poet Philip Whalen (1923–2002) was a close friend. He became a serious student of Zen Buddhism, living in Japan from 1956 to 1968. His environmental concerns are reflected in the sequence *Mountains and Rivers without End* (1996) and his essays began appearing with *Earth House Hold* (1969), continuing with *Back on the Fire* (2007).

SOANE, Sir John (1753–1837) Architect. He was architect to the Bank of England from 1788 to 1833 and founder of the museum in Lincoln's Inn Fields which bears his name and contains his library, antiquities, and works of art—perhaps most notably his collection of William *Hogarth paintings. The library is famous for its hoard of architectural drawings by Christopher *Wren, John (1721–92), James (1732–94), and Robert (1728–92) Adam, George Dance (1741–1825), and Soane. He published several volumes of his own designs and an extensive description of the museum. His Royal Academy lectures, his only major literary enterprise, were published in 1929. See Ptolemy Dean, *Sir John Soane and London* (2006).

soap opera Named after the detergent manufacturers who first sponsored popular serial drama on American radio in the 1930s. It began with *Clara, Lu and Em*, about the lives of three women in the small-town Midwest, initially on WGN Chicago then networked. The first British *radio soap (as such series are conventionally known) was *Mrs Dale's Diary*, which ran from 1948 to 1969, but *The Archers* has run continuously since 1951, and remains a mainstay of BBC Radio 4. The play *The Killing of Sister George* by Frank Marcus (1928–96), staged in 1964, explored the gulf between a soap's benign fictional world and the emotional turmoil among its cast. It was filmed by Robert Aldrich (1918–83) in 1968. The film *The Truman Show* (1998) portrayed its hero's life as an elaborate fake, broadcast as a soap. British *television's major soaps, ITV's *Coronation Street* (1960–) and BBC's *EastEnders* (1985–), regularly promote behind the scenes stories about their stars and guest appearances.

Socialist Realism A style of realistic art adopted as the official artistic and literary doctrine of the Soviet Union in 1934 at the First Congress of Soviet Writers, and subsequently adopted by its satellite Communist Parties. Party official Andrei Zhdanov's statements about the nature of Socialist Realism as a 'method' at the 1934 Congress emphasized the truthful depiction of everyday reality 'in its revolutionary development', and the writer's task of educating readers 'in the spirit of socialism'. The conventions governing matters of style and content were provided by a retrospectively constructed canon of model texts, including an early novel by Maxim *Gorky, *The Mother* (1906–7). *Modernist works such as those of James *Joyce or Franz *Kafka were condemned as symptoms of decadent bourgeois pessimism. Soviet writers were required instead to affirm the struggle for socialism by portraying positive heroic actions in texts that were accessible to a mass readership. These principles were condemned by major *Marxist critics and writers like Bertolt *Brecht, Georg Lukács (1885–1971), or Leon Trotsky (1879–1940) for propagandist optimism and aesthetic conservatism, and many writers sympathetic to communism found them an embarrassment. Socialist Realism entailed a significant shift in the relationship between the state and writers; now cast as 'engineers of the soul' who were expected to educate their readers through works which addressed themes considered by the state to be of contemporary political importance. Failure to address such themes or to conform to stylistic norms could have severe consequences. Under Stalin's tyranny, the doctrine was employed as a pretext for the persecution and silencing of nonconformist writers (see Anna *Akhmatova, Osip *Mandelshtam, Boris *Pasternak), as well as a means of controlling published writers through censorship and critical attacks in the press. Both plot and characters in Socialist Realist texts are formulaic; novels frequently feature an exemplary 'positive hero' who encounters and overcomes difficulties in his progress towards mature socialist enlightenment. Canonical texts include Nikolai *Ostrovsky's *How the Steel was Tempered* (1934), a Socialist Realist classic, and Mikhail *Sholokhov's *Virgin Soil Upturned* (1932). Katerina Clark's analysis of Socialist Realist conventions (*The Soviet Novel*, 1981) provides an illuminating decoding of works often ignored as propaganda. In *On Socialist Realism* (1960), Abram Tertz (pseudonym of Andrei Siniavsky) explores the contradictions inherent in Socialist Realist literature as a neo-classical formulaic genre which nevertheless aspires to the realism of *Tolstoy. The most accessible legacy of Socialist Realism is in painting and statuary of the Soviet period, typified by the omnipresent image of the muscular and smiling tractor-driver.

social problem novel A phrase used (alongside terms such as 'the industrial novel', or the *'condition of England' novel) to describe mid-19th-century fiction which examines abuses and hardships affecting the working classes. These included many of the topics which were simultaneously being exposed by non-fictional writers, such as poor housing and sanitation; conditions in factories; child labour; the exploitation of seamstresses; and the exhausting nature of agricultural work. Largely written from a middle-class perspective, it sometimes sought to stimulate legislation, or (as in Elizabeth Gaskell's *North and South*, 1854–5) to promote understanding between masters and men on the basis of shared humanity, and shared material interests, as a way forward. Other notable examples include Harriet *Martineau's 'A Manchester Strike', in her *Illustrations of Political Economy* (1835; an early example of the genre); Charles Kingsley's **Yeast* (1848) and **Alton Locke* (1850), Benjamin Disraeli's **Sybil* (1845), Frances *Trollope's

Michael Armstrong, the Factory Boy (1840) and *Jessie Phillips* (1842–3), and Charlotte Elizabeth Tonna's *Helen Fleetwood* (1841). Whilst Charles *Dickens's fiction is usually regarded as more complex in its focus than many of these novels, much of his writing, especially **Oliver Twist* (1838), *The *Chimes* (1845), **Bleak House* (1852), and **Hard Times* (1854), deals very directly with poverty, inequality, and their consequences. The term can be extended to include writing about 'fallen women' and prostitution (as in Gaskell's **Ruth*, 1853; Felicia Skene's *Hidden Depths*, 1866). In its search for resolution, whether practical or emotional, the social problem novel differs from later realist fiction by writers like George *Gissing and Arthur *Morrison. See J. M. Guy, *The Victorian Social-Problem Novel* (1996).
See also CONDITION OF ENGLAND.

Society for Psychical Research A body founded in 1882 by Frederic *Myers, Henry *Sidgwick, and others 'to examine without prejudice...those faculties of man, real or supposed, which appear to be inexplicable in terms of any recognised hypothesis'. The Society, in a period of intense interest in spiritualism and the supernatural, investigated with high standards of scientific detachment such matters as telepathy, apparitions, etc., and was instrumental in exposing the fraudulent claims of, for example, Madame *Blavatsky. Its presidents included Arthur *Balfour, William *James, and Sir Oliver Lodge (1851–1940, a physicist less sceptical than many of the SPR); members and associates have included John *Ruskin, Alfred *Tennyson, William *Gladstone, and Alfred Russel *Wallace. See R. Haynes, *The Society for Psychical Research 1882–1982* (1982).

Society of Authors An organization founded in 1884 by Walter *Besant to promote the business interests of authors and fight for their rights, especially in *copyright. Progress was slow, but by 1914 much had been achieved; Britain had joined the International Copyright Convention (Berne Union), the USA had offered limited protection to foreign authors, while domestic copyright had undergone a major reform under the Copyright Act of 1911. By then too the Society had succeeded in radically improving publishing contracts and in dealing with recalcitrant publishers in and out of the courts.

Besant's example was followed by George Bernard *Shaw, who fought arduously for playwrights *vis-à-vis* theatre managers, and to liberalize stage censorship; the League of Dramatists was founded in 1931 as an autonomous section of the Society. Since then the Society has formed other specialized groups, and has also improved the author's lot with regard to taxation, libel, and social security. It conducted a successful 28-year campaign for *Public Lending Right, and has helped to set up the Authors' Lending and Copyright Society, in order to secure income in respect of rights (e.g. photocopying) only possible on a collective basis. The work of the Society continues. Its quarterly publication is the *Author*. See Victor Bonham-Carter, *Authors by Profession*, 2 vols (1978, 1984).

Society of Friends, the *See* FRIENDS, SOCIETY OF.

Socinianism *See* UNITARIANISM.

SOCRATES (469–399 BC) Athenian who dominated classical Greek philosophy in company with *Plato and *Aristotle. He wrote nothing, but his ideas and methods provided the foundations not only for Platonic philosophy but for many of what we call the 'Hellenistic' philosophical 'schools', notably Cynicism and *Stoicism. Plato uses a 'Socrates' as main speaker in most of his dialogues; other, rather different portraits are offered by *Aristophanes and *Xenophon. We may say with some probability that while claiming to know nothing, he was a master of argument, and that he thought argument (philosophy) essential to life—because (he claimed) our desires are, universally, for what is really good, and we go wrong only because of our mistaken *beliefs* about what our good really is. His execution by his fellow citizens (for impiety), despite an exemplary courage and incorruptibility, later evoked comparisons with Christ; admirers included *Erasmus and the third earl of *Shaftesbury.

'Sohrab and Rustum' A poem by Matthew *Arnold, published 1853. The story is taken from *Firdausī's Persian *epic, via a French translation by Jules Mohl in *Le Livre des rois* (1838–76). It recounts, in blank verse adorned by *epic similes, the fatal outcome of Sohrab's search for his father Rustum, the leader of the Persian forces. Rustum (who believes his own child to be a girl) accepts the challenge of Sohrab, now leader of the Tartars: the two meet in single combat, at first unaware of one another's identity, which is confirmed only when Sohrab has been mortally wounded.

soldan [from the Arabic 'sultan'] The soldan or souldan, in Edmund *Spenser's **Faerie Queene* (V. viii) represents Philip II of Spain. He is encountered by Prince *Arthur and Sir *Artegall with a bold defiance from Queen Mercilla (*Elizabeth I), and the combat is undecided until the prince unveils his shield and terrifies the soldan's horses, so that they overturn his chariot and the soldan is torn 'all to rags'. The unveiling of the shield signifies divine interposition.

Solomon, Song of (Song of Songs) *See* BIBLE.

Solyman and Perseda *See* KYD, THOMAS.

SOLZHENITSYN, Aleksandr Isaievich (1918–2008) Russian prose writer born in Kislovodsk in the Caucasus, the son of an army officer. He studied mathematics and physics at the University of Rostov-on-Don before joining the Red Army in 1941. Arrested in 1945 for criticism of Stalin in a letter, he was sent first to labour camps, then in 1953 into exile in Kazakhstan. He received treatment for cancer in Tashkent 1954–5. 'Rehabilitated' in 1956, he returned to Riazan to work as a teacher. His first published story, *One Day in the Life of Ivan Denisovich* (1962), based on his labour camp experiences, brought immediate recognition. It was followed by *Matrena's House* (1963) and other stories. He was expelled from the Soviet Writers' Union in 1969 following the publication abroad of his major novels *Cancer Ward* (1968) and *The First Circle* (1969) which had been confiscated by the KGB in 1965. He was awarded the 1970 *Nobel Prize for Literature. Publication in the West of *August 1914* (1971) and *The Gulag Archipelago* (1974), an epic 'history and geography' of the labour camps, led to his deportation to West Germany in 1971. He lived in Zurich 1974–6, then in Vermont, USA, 1976–94, where he continued a series of novels begun with *August 1914*, offering an alternative picture of Soviet history: an English version, *The Red Wheel: A Narrative in Discrete Periods of Time*, appeared in 1989. Meanwhile, with perestroika, his works were published in Russia and he was readmitted to the Writers' Union in 1989. His memoirs were translated by H. T. Willets as *The Oak and the Calf* (1980). See also D. M. *Thomas, *Alexander Solzhenitsyn* (1998).

Some Experiences of an Irish R.M. Published 1899, first and most famous of a series of three collections of stories by Edith *Somerville and Martin Ross. The others are *Further Experiences of an Irish R.M.*, 1908, and *In Mr Knox's Country*, 1915. The stories are narrated by Major Yeates, the resident magistrate, whose misfortune is to attract calamity. With his gallant wife Philippa, he lives at the centre of a vigorous and wily community as the tenant of a dilapidated County Cork demesne, Shreelane, which he rents from a well-to-do rogue, Flurry Knox, whose grandmother lives in squalid splendour at neighbouring Aussolas. Frequent rain, flowing drink, unruly hounds, and the eccentricities of the populace contribute to innumerable confusions involving collapsing carts, missed meals, sinking boats, shying horses, and outraged visitors. Few of the stories are merely farcical, however, and some are shadowed by the agrarian tensions of the day.

SOMERVILE, William (1675–1742) Gentleman of Edstone, Warwickshire, whose *The Chace* (1735), a four-book poem in Miltonic *blank verse on hunting, had considerable success. *Hobbinol* (1740) a *mock-heroic account of rural games in Gloucestershire, was dedicated to William *Hogarth. *Field Sports*, a short poem on hawking, appeared in 1742. Somervile was a friend of Allan *Ramsay and William *Shenstone. Samuel *Johnson commented that 'he set a good example to men of his own class'.

SOMERVILLE (Edith) and **ROSS** (Martin) The pen-names of second cousins Edith Œnone Somerville (1858–1949, born in Corfu) and Violet Florence Martin (1862–1915, born in Co. Galway), who first met in 1886. Separately and together they wrote many books, mainly set in Ireland, as well as many articles, letters, diaries, and jottings. Their first collaboration, *An Irish Cousin* (1889), was well received. In their most sustained novel, *The Real Charlotte* (1894), Francie Fitzpatrick, a beautiful girl from Dublin, finds herself, on the estate of the wealthy Dysarts, becoming enmeshed with the malign Charlotte Mullen, who is jealous of the attention devoted to Francie by the flash estate manager Lambert. Francie, finding herself in love with a handsome English officer, discovers he is already engaged and marries Lambert, only to be killed riding her horse. In 1897 came *The Silver Fox*, their first book with hunting as a major theme, then **Some Experiences of an Irish R.M.* (1899). The international success of this book led in 1908 to *Further Experiences of an Irish R.M.* and in 1915 to the third of the series, *In Mr Knox's Country.* After Martin Ross's death Edith Somerville wrote another thirteen books, including *The Big House at Inver* (1925), a historical romance, but continued to name Ross as co-author.

'Somnium Scipionis' (Dream of Scipio) The fable with which *Cicero ends his *De Republica*, based on the myth of Er at the end of *Plato's *Republic*. The only extant manuscript of Cicero's treatise breaks off early in the last book, and the 'Somnium' has survived because in the 4th century it was reproduced by Macrobius, who furnished it with a Neoplatonist commentary that was of great importance for medieval thinkers. The fable relates how the younger Scipio saw his grandfather, the elder Scipio, in a dream and was shown the dwelling set aside in the Milky Way for those who follow virtue and especially for those who distinguish themselves in the service of their country. The 'Somnium' may have inspired *Petrarch's choice of Scipio Africanus as the hero of his epic *Africa*. Since the fable expressed to perfection the humanist ideal of combining a quest for personal distinction with tranquillity of mind and patriotic effort, it attracted numerous editors during the Renaissance. *Chaucer gives a poetical summary of it in *The *Parliament of Fowls*.

'Song of the Shirt, The' A poem by Thomas *Hood, originally published anonymously in **Punch* in 1843. One of Hood's best-known serious poems, it takes the form of a powerful protest by an overworked and underpaid seamstress—

It is not linen you're wearing out
But human creatures' lives.

The poem was a popular theme for illustration, and was treated by John *Leech in *Punch* and by the painters Richard Redgrave (1844) and G. F. Watts (1850).

Songs of Experience *See* Songs of Innocence.

Songs of Innocence A collection of poems written and etched by William *Blake, published 1789. Most of the poems are about childhood, some of them written, with apparent simplicity, as if by children (e.g. 'Little lamb, who made thee?' and 'The Chimney Sweeper'); others commenting on the state of infancy ('The Ecchoing Green'); and yet others introducing the prophetic tone and personal imagery of Blake's later work ('The Little Girl Lost', 'The Little Girl Found').

In 1795 Blake issued a further volume, entitled *Songs of Innocence and of Experience: Shewing the Two Contrary States of the Human Soul*, to which he added the 'Songs of Experience', some of them (e.g. 'The Chimney Sweeper' and 'Nurse's Song') bearing identical titles to poems in the first collection, but replying to them in a tone that questions and offsets their simplicities, and manifests with great poetic economy Blake's original vision of the interdependence of good and evil, of energy and restraint, of desire and frustration. They range from straightforward, if highly provocative, attacks on unnatural restraint ('The Garden of Love', 'London') to the extraordinary lyric intensity of 'Infant Sorrow', 'Ah! Sun-Flower', and 'Tyger! Tyger!'

sonnet A short rhyming lyric poem, usually of fourteen lines of iambic *pentameter. The term may be applied to poems of different lengths ranging from ten-and-a-half lines in some sonnets of Gerard Manley *Hopkins to sixteen in those of George *Meredith and Tony *Harrison, and some sonnets by Philip *Sidney and others have been composed in *alexandrines, but the widely accepted standard is fourteen pentameters. The *rhyme schemes of the sonnet have also varied, but fall into two basic patterns. (1) The Italian or Petrarchan sonnet begins with an octave using two rhymes (*abbaabba*), followed by a sestet with two or three further rhymes (either *cdcdcd* or *cdecde*), with a pause or redirection in the thought (called the 'turn' or *volta*) after the octave. English practitioners of this form, notably John *Milton and William *Wordsworth, have sometimes adapted it to allow a third rhyme in the octave (*abbaacca*) and a 'turn' in a later position around the tenth line. (2) The English sonnet comprising four *quatrains and a couplet has two major versions, the Spenserian form in which the quatrains are linked by rhyme, thus preserving the Italian restriction to five rhymes (*ababbabccdcdee*), and the Shakespearian scheme of seven rhymes in which the quatrains remain unlinked (*ababcdcdefefgg*).

Italian in origin, and brought to prominence in the love poems of *Petrarch, the sonnet was introduced to England by *Wyatt, developed by *Surrey, and thereafter widely used, notably in the sonnet sequences of *Shakespeare (*see* SONNETS OF SHAKESPEARE), Sidney, Samuel *Daniel, Edmund *Spenser, and others, most of which are amatory in nature. In the early 17th century, the major sonneteers were John *Donne and Milton, who both extended the subject-matter to religious, political, and philosophical themes. The sonnet was largely neglected by poets of the Restoration and early 18th-century periods, but underwent a significant revival from the late 18th, in the verse of Charlotte *Smith and S. T. *Coleridge, then in the early 19th in the work of Wordsworth and John *Keats. Wordsworth's 'Nuns fret not at their Convent's narrow room' (1807) and Keats's 'If by dull rhymes our English must be chain'd' (posthumously published 1848) both comment self-consciously on the sonnet's formal restraints, Keats's poem exhibiting the unorthodox rhyme scheme *abcabdcabdede*. Important Victorian sonneteers include Meredith, Hopkins, D. G. *Rossetti, and E. B. *Browning. Major early 20th-century practitioners include W. B. *Yeats and W. H. *Auden; and the form continues to flourish. See Michael Spiller, *The Development of the Sonnet* (1992).

Sonnets from the Portuguese A sonnet sequence by Elizabeth Barrett *Browning first published 1850; the so-called 'Reading Edition' of 1847 was a forgery by T. J. *Wise. The sequence reimagines the growth and development of her love for Robert *Browning, at first hesitating to involve him in her sorrowful invalid life, then yielding to gradual conviction of his love for her, and finally rapturous in late-born happiness. The title was chosen in part to disguise the personal nature of the poems by suggesting that they were a translation. The force of the sequence derives in part from its imaginative challenge to the conventional female role as beloved (*Petrarch's Laura and Philip *Sidney's Stella are the obvious examples) by placing the woman as author, and lover of the (silent) man.

sonnets of Shakespeare Printed in 1609 and probably dating from the 1590s. In 1598 Francis *Meres referred to William *Shakespeare's 'sugred Sonnets among his private friends', but these are not necessarily identical with the ones we now have. Most of them trace the course of the writer's affection for a young man of rank and beauty: the first seventeen urge him to marry to reproduce his beauty, numbers 18 to 126 form a sequence of 108 sonnets, the same number as in Sidney's sequence **Astrophel and Stella*. The complete sequence of 154 sonnets (of which two, numbers 138 and 144, had been published in a 1599 miscellany, *The Passionate Pilgrim*) was issued by the publisher Thomas Thorpe (1571/2–1625), whether authorized by Shakespeare or not is not known, in 1609, with a dedication 'To the onlie begetter of these insuing sonnets Mr W.H.' Mr W.H. has been identified as (among others) William, Lord Herbert (1580–1630), afterwards third earl of Pembroke, or Henry Wriothesley, earl of Southampton (1573–1624), and further as the young man addressed in the sonnets. Other views are that Mr W.H. was an unknown friend of Thorpe who may have procured the manuscript for him, or that W.H. is a printer's error for W.S., Shakespeare's initials. Other characters alluded to in the sequence include a mistress stolen by a friend (40–2), a rival poet (78–80 and 80–6), and a dark lady loved by the author (127–52). The dark lady has been variously identified as Mary Fitton (bap. 1578, d. 1641) or the poet Emilia *Lanier, and the rival poet as Christopher *Marlowe or George *Chapman. But all such identifications are purely speculative. For the form of these poems *see* SONNET. Notable editions are by John Kerrigan (1986), Katherine Duncan-Jones (1997), and Colin Burrow (2002).

Sons and Lovers By D. H. *Lawrence, published 1913, an autobiographical **Bildungsroman* set in the Nottinghamshire coal-mining village of Bestwood. Walter Morel has married Gertrude, 'delicate' but 'resolute', a high-minded woman better educated than himself. She shrinks from his lack of fine feeling; embittered, she turns their marriage into a battle. Walter, baffled and thwarted, is sometimes violent; Gertrude turns her love towards her four children, particularly her two eldest sons, William and Paul. Dissatisfied with her social station, she is determined that her boys will not become miners. William and Paul find clerical work in London and Nottingham respectively; William develops pneumonia and dies. Gertrude, numbed by despair, is roused only when Paul also falls ill. She nurses him back to health, and subsequently their attachment deepens. Paul is friendly with the Leivers family of Willey Farm, and a tenderness grows between him and the daughter Miriam, a soulful, shy girl. They read poetry together; Paul instructs her in French and algebra, and shows her his sketches. Gertrude fears that Miriam will exclude her and tries to break up their relationship, while Paul, himself sickened at heart by Miriam's romantic love and fear of physical warmth, turns away. He becomes involved with Clara Dawes, a married woman and supporter of women's rights, separated from her husband Baxter. Paul is promoted at work, and begins to be noticed as a painter and designer. His affair with Clara peters out and she returns to her husband. Meanwhile, Paul's mother falls ill with cancer and he is dejected at the thought of losing her. At last, unable to bear her suffering, he and his sister Annie give her an overdose of morphia. Paul resists the urge to follow her 'into the darkness' and, with a great effort, turns towards life. *Sons and Lovers* was perhaps the first English novel with a truly working-class background, and certainly Lawrence's first major novel. The original text was heavily edited by Edward *Garnett. The Cambridge Edition (1992) restores several passages. An early draft, *Paul Morel*, was published in 2003.

SONTAG, Susan (1933–2004) American cultural critic, essayist, and novelist. Born in New York, she studied at the universities of California, Chicago, Harvard, Oxford, and the Sorbonne. Settling in New York as a teacher and an essayist for **Partisan Review* and other journals, she wrote two experimental novels, *The Benefactor* (1963) and *Death Kit* (1967), and collected her essays in two volumes, *Against Interpretation* (1966) and *Styles of Radical Will* (1969), in which she surveys a range of topics, from the 'camp' sensibility and pornographic writing to avant-garde music and painting. These early essays foreshadow many of the emphases of *postmodernism. While undergoing treatment for cancer in the 1970s, she wrote two provocative essays, *On Photography* (1977) and *Illness as Metaphor* (1978), and collected her short stories as *I, Etcetera* (1978). Later works include *AIDS and its Metaphors* (1989) and a historical romance about Horatio Nelson and the Hamiltons, *The Volcano Lover* (1992; *see* HAMILTON, SIR WILLIAM). She also worked as a theatrical and cinematic director, and in her later years became embroiled in feminist controversy. See Sohnya Sayres, *Susan Sontag* (1990).

SOPHOCLES (496/5–406 BC) Greek tragedian who wrote *c.*120 plays, of which seven survive, including *Ajax, The Women of Trachis, Electra*, and *Philoctetes*. The group known as the Theban plays, *Oedipus the King, Oedipus at Colonus*, and *Antigone*, have long been influential in English literature, either directly or in versions by *Seneca. Thomas *Watson's 16th-century translation of the *Antigone* into Latin was widely read, and both John Milton's **Samson Agonistes* and John *Dryden and Nathaniel *Lee's *Oedipus* draw on Sophocles. Many translations and adaptations into verse and prose have been made from the 18th to the 21st century. In the 19th century Edward *Bulwer-Lytton adapted *Oedipus the King*; Matthew *Arnold produced his Sophoclean play *Merope* and two Sophoclean fragments, *Antigone* and *Dejaneira*; A. C. *Swinburne introduced Sophoclean touches into his *Erechtheus*. In the early 20th century Sigmund *Freud coined the phrase 'Oedipus complex', but it has little to do with the play. W. B. *Yeats produced a version of *Oedipus*, and Ezra *Pound adapted *Women of Trachis*. Recent adaptations include Seamus *Heaney's *Cure at Troy*, Steven *Berkoff's *Greek*, and Derek *Mahon's *Oedipus*. See Edith Hall and Fiona Macintosh, *Greek Tragedy and the British Theatre 1660–1914* (2005); *Archive of Performances of Greek and Roman Drama*, http://www.apgrd.ox.ac.uk. *See* AESCHYLUS; EURIPIDES; POETICS.

Sordello A narrative poem in iambic pentameter couplets by Robert *Browning, published 1840. The poem took seven years to complete, and was interrupted by the composition of **Paracelsus* and *Stafford*; Browning intended it to be more 'popular' than the former, but the poem was received with incomprehension and derision by the critics and the public, and its notorious 'obscurity' caused severe and prolonged damage to Browning's reputation. The *Pre-Raphaelites, intrigued, were *Sordello*'s first defenders, followed later by Ezra *Pound; some still regard it as an important poem, and even of central importance in the interpretation of Browning's work, particularly in the light of his negotiation with a *Romantic inheritance. Its genuine difficulty springs partly from the swiftness and compression of the language, the convoluted time-scheme of the narrative, and the fusion of intense specificity (of historical detail, landscape, etc.) with the abstract ideas which form the core of the argument.

The narrative, which defies summary, is set in Italy during the period of the Guelf–Ghibelline wars of the late 12th and 13th centuries, and traces the 'development of a soul', that of the troubadour Sordello, along a path of self-realization where political, aesthetic, and metaphysical ideas reflect each other; all this in the framework of a plot strongly influenced by the elements of fairy-tale, including the lost heir, wicked stepmother, and unattainable princess.

SORLEY, Charles Hamilton (1895–1915) Poet, born in Aberdeen and educated at Marlborough College, Wiltshire. He spent a year in Germany before returning on the outbreak of war in 1914. He was commissioned in the Suffolk Regiment, and served in the trenches in France, where he was killed by a sniper. He left only 37 complete poems: his posthumous collection, *Marlborough and Other Poems* (1916), was a popular and critical success in the 1920s, but his verse was then long neglected, despite the efforts of Edmund *Blunden and Robert *Graves (who considered him, with Wilfred *Owen and Isaac *Rosenberg, 'one of the three poets of importance killed during the War'). Poems such as 'The Song of the Ungirt Runners', 'Barbury Camp', and the last, bitter, 'When you see millions of the mouthless dead' have become well known. His parents selected *The Letters of Charles Sorley* (1919). See Jean Moorcroft Wilson, *Charles Hamilton Sorley* (1985).

SORRENTINO, Gilbert (1929–2006) American novelist, born in New York. His novels include the *postmodern meta-narrative *Mulligan Stew* (1979) and he also published a number of volumes of poetry. His essays are collected in *Something Said* (1984).

Soul's Tragedy, A A play by Robert *Browning, published 1846, together with **Luria*, as no. VIII of **Bells and Pomegranates*. Its subtitle—'Act First, being what was called the Poetry of Chiappino's life: and Act Second, its Prose'—indicates both the play's genre, tragicomedy, and also its unusual form: the division (as opposed to mixture) of verse and prose represents Browning's idiosyncratic adaptation of Elizabethan and Jacobean models (*see also* PIPPA PASSES). Chiappino, the 'hero', is a discontented liberal in 16th-century Faenza, who, at the climax of Act I, nobly (or perhaps egotistically) takes on himself the punishment for the supposed assassination of the tyrannical provost by his friend Luitolfo. He expects to be lynched by the provost's guards, but is instead acclaimed by the people as their liberator, and is unable to resist the temptation of his new-found role. The provost turns out not to have been killed after all and, just as Chiappino is about to become the new provost himself, he is unmasked by the papal legate Ogniben, who has sardonically played up to his self-deceiving justification for seizing power. Ogniben, who had arrived in Faenza remarking that he had seen 'three-and-twenty leaders of revolts', utters the famous line 'I have seen *four*-and-twenty leaders of revolts!' as he watches Chiappino fleeing the town after his humiliation.

SOUTAR, William (1898–1943) Scottish poet, born in Perth, the son of a master joiner, and educated at Perth Academy. He served in the navy during the First World War, and contracted the ankylosing spondylitis which, after his subsequent studies at Edinburgh University, left him paralysed for the fourteen years leading up to his death of tuberculosis. Soutar wrote lyrics in *Scots and (less successfully) English. Though rarely adventurous in its rhythms, the Scots work is remarkable for its idiomatic purity and its dialogue with the *ballad and other elements of folk tradition. It includes the haunting 'The Tryst' and the wryly anti-Calvinist 'The Philosophic Taed', along with epigrams, riddles, pieces for children ('bairn-rhymes'), and the extravagant miniatures the poet called 'whigmaleeries'. See Soutar, *The Diary of a Dying Man* (1991); C. MacDougall and D. Gifford, *Into a Room: Selected Poems of William Soutar* (2000).

SOUTHERN, Terry (1924–95) American novelist and screenwriter, born in Texas, who is known for the grotesque dimension to his satires. His first novel (co-written with Mason Hoffenberg) was *Candy* (1957) followed in 1959 by *The Magic Christian*, a satire on national greed. His most famous screenplays were *Dr Strangelove* (1962, also published as a novel) and *The Loved One* (1965), which have become classics of black humour.

SOUTHERNE (Southern), **Thomas** (1659–1746) Irish dramatist, educated at Trinity College, Dublin; he came to London 1678 and entered the Middle Temple. He wrote prologues and epilogues for several of his friend John *Dryden's plays, whose *Cleomenes* he revised and completed. His first tragedy, *The Persian Prince, or The Loyal Brother* (1682), was, like Thomas *Otway's **Venice Preserv'd*, its immediate contemporary, an attack on *Shaftesbury and the Whigs. He wrote several comedies, but is chiefly remembered for his two highly successful tragedies, *The *Fatal Marriage* (1694) and **Oroonoko* (1695), both based on novels by Aphra *Behn. Jonathan *Swift, John *Dennis, Colley *Cibber, and other friends testified to his good nature, but little is known of his life. He is regarded as a successor to Otway in the art of pathos, and as a link between *Restoration tragedy and the sentimental tragedies of the 18th century. See J. W. Dodds, *Thomas Southerne, Dramatist* (1933).

SOUTHEY, Robert (1774–1843) Poet, the son of a Bristol linen draper. Much of his lonely childhood was spent in the home of an eccentric aunt, Miss Tyler, where he acquired a precocious love of reading; he gives a vivid account of these years in letters written when he was 46 to his friend John May. He was expelled from Westminster School for founding a magazine, the *Flagellant*, and proceeded to Oxford with 'a heart full of poetry and feeling, a head full of Rousseau and Werther, and my religious principles shaken by Gibbon'. He became friendly with S. T. *Coleridge and together they planned their Pantisocratic society (*see* PANTISOCRACY). At Oxford he wrote a play, *Wat Tyler*, and another with Coleridge, *The *Fall of Robespierre*. From this time on his literary output was prodigious. In 1795 he travelled to Portugal, married Edith Fricker (Coleridge married her sister Sara), and wrote *Joan of Arc* (1796). Between 1796 and 1798 he wrote many ballads, including 'The *Inchcape Rock' and 'The Battle of Blenheim', which had an influence in loosening the constrictions of 18th-century verse. In 1800 he went to Spain, and on his return settled in the Lake District, where he remained for the rest of his life as one of the *'Lake Poets'. A narrative *oriental verse romance, *Thalaba*, appeared in 1801, but sold poorly. In 1803 he published a translation of **Amadis of Gaul* (revised from an older version); in 1805, **Madoc*; and in 1807, the year in which he received a government pension, appeared a version of **Palmerin of England* and *Letters from England by Don Manuel Alvarez Espriella*, purporting to be from a young Spaniard and giving a lively account of life and manners in England. In 1808 he translated the *Chronicle of the Cid* and in 1809 began his long association with the **Quarterly Review*, which provided almost his only regular income for most of the rest of his life. A long oriental poem, *The Curse of Kehama*, featuring much complex Hindu mythology, appeared in 1810 and *Omniana*, an original commonplace book, with contributions by Coleridge, in 1812. He was appointed *poet laureate in 1813, a post which he came greatly to dislike, and in the same year published his short but admirable *Life of Nelson*. A narrative poem *Roderick: The Last of the Goths* appeared in 1814. In 1817 he produced an edition of *Malory and had to endure the publication, by his enemies, of his youthful and revolutionary *Wat Tyler.* The final volume of his *History of Brazil*, 3 vols (1810–19) appeared a year before his *Life of Wesley.* In 1821, to commemorate the death of George III, he wrote *A *Vision of Judgement*, in the preface to which he vigorously attacked Lord *Byron as the leader of the *'satanic School of poetry'. Byron's parody in riposte, *The *Vision of Judgment*, appeared in 1822, and Southey is frequently mocked in **Don Juan*. From 1823 to 1832 Southey was working on his *History of the Peninsular War.* In 1824 appeared *The Book of the Church* and in 1825 *A Tale of Paraguay.* His *Sir Thomas More*, in which he converses with the ghost of More, came out in 1829. In the same year appeared *All for Love; and The Pilgrim to Compostella*, and in 1832 *Essays Moral and Political* and the last volume of *History of the Peninsular War* (1823–32), which was overshadowed by the work on the same subject by William Napier (1785–1860). Between 1832 and 1837 he worked on a life and an edition of William *Cowper, and on his *Lives of the British Admirals* (1833). In 1835 he was granted a pension of £300 by Peel. His wife died in 1837, and in 1839 he married Caroline *Bowles. *The *Doctor* was begun in 1834, 7 vols (1834–47). Southey's last years were marked by an increasing mental decline.

His longer poems, now little read, were admired by men as diverse as William *Fox, Walter *Scott, and Thomas Babington *Macaulay. Although an honest, generous man (who was particularly kind to Coleridge's abandoned family), he alienated many of his contemporaries, in particular William *Hazlitt and Byron, who felt that in accepting pensions and the laureateship, and in denying his youthful Jacobinism, he was betraying principles. In **Melincourt* Thomas Love Peacock caricatures him as Mr Feathernest. See J. Simmons, *Robert Southey* (1945); *New Letters of Robert Southey*, ed. K. Curry (1965); *Robert Southey: The Critical Heritage*, ed. L. Madden (1972); W. A. Speck, *Robert Southey: Entire Man of Letters* (2006). Southey's *Poetical Works* in eight volumes is edited by T. Fulford and L. Pratt (2004–11).

SOUTHWELL, St Robert (1561–95) Poet and martyr, educated by the Jesuits at Douai and Rome, he became a Roman Catholic priest, coming to England in 1586 with Henry Garnet. In 1589 he became domestic chaplain to the countess of Arundel, was captured in 1592, imprisoned, repeatedly tortured, and executed. In his poems, mainly written in prison, he sought to make spiritual love, instead of 'unworthy affections', the subject. His chief work was *St Peter's Complaint*, published 1595, a long narrative of the closing events of Christ's life in the mouth of the repentant Peter, in which the spiritual is contrasted with the material by numerous comparisons and antitheses. He also wrote many fine shorter devotional poems (some of them collected under the title *Moeoniae*, 1595), notably 'The Burning Babe', praised by Ben *Jonson. Beatified in 1929, he was canonized in 1970. His poems were edited by J. H. McDonald and N. P. Brown (1967).

SOYINKA, Wole (1934–) Nigerian novelist, poet, and playwright, educated at the universities of Ibadan and Leeds. He was play reader at the *Royal Court Theatre, London, where his *The Swamp Dwellers* (1958), *The Lion and the Jewel*, and *The Invention* (both 1959) were produced. These already demonstrated his development from simple village comedies to a more complex and individual drama incorporating mime and dance. After his return to Nigeria in 1960, university posts and the opportunity of producing and acting in his own plays gave him the self-confidence to undertake even more daring innovations, for instance in *A Dance of the Forests* (1960), a half-satirical, half-fantastic celebration of Nigerian independence. Soyinka's first novel, *The Interpreters* (1965), captures the idealism of young Nigerians regarding the development of a new Africa, possibly anticipating a new Biafra. In prison for pro-Biafran activity during 1967–9, he produced increasingly bleak verse and prose, *Madmen and Specialists* (1970), his second novel, *Season of Anomy* (1973), and *The Man Died* (1972), a prison memoir. His translation of the *Bacchae* of *Euripides was commissioned by and performed at the *National Theatre in 1973. *Death and the King's Horseman* (1975) embodied his post-Biafran cultural philosophy, enunciated in *Myth, Literature and the African World* (1976), of the need for the aesthetics of Africa and Europe to cross-fertilize each other. Another bleak period, coloured by the deteriorating political situation in Nigeria, followed this patch of optimism: later works include the drama *A Play of Giants* (1984), savagely portraying a group of African ex-dictators taking refuge in New York, and *The Open Sore of a Continent* (1996), denouncing the military regime in Nigeria, and the brutal execution in November 1995 of Nigerian writer and political activist Ken Saro-Wiwa. Soyinka himself had his Nigerian passport confiscated in 1994, and has since lived abroad, largely in the USA, while continuing actively to campaign for human rights. His account of his childhood, *Aké* (1981), is witty and celebratory; he continues the story in *Isara* (1989) and published a long memoir in 2006, *You Must Set Forth at Dawn*. He was awarded the *Nobel Prize in 1986.

Spanish Bawd, The *See* CELESTINA.

Spanish Curate, The A comedy by John *Fletcher, probably in collaboration with Philip *Massinger, written and performed 1622, and based on *Gerardo, the Unfortunate Spaniard* (1622), translated from the Spanish of Céspedes by Leonard Digges (1588–1635). It was very popular after the *Restoration.

The main plot deals with the schemes of Don Henrique's mistress Violante, the failure of which leads to the reconciliation of Don Henrique with his divorced wife Jacinta and his brother Don Jamie; Violante is sent to a nunnery. In the subplot, from which the play takes its name, Leandro, a rich young gentleman, plays on the greed of a priest and his sexton, and, with their help, on that of the lawyer Bartolus, the jealous husband of a beautiful wife, Amaranta, to facilitate his affair with her.

Spanish Friar, The A tragicomedy by John *Dryden, produced and published 1681. The serious plot is characteristically about a usurpation. Torrismond, though he does not know it, is legitimate heir to the throne, and secretly marries the reigning but unlawful queen, who has allowed Torrismond's father, the true king, to be murdered in prison. The sub-plot is dominated by Father Dominic, a monstrous corrupt friar, who uses the jargon of Dissenters and who pimps for the dissolute and politically liberal Lorenzo. The latter is a highly dubious character, yet ironically it is through his agency that the lawful Torrismond is rescued. The woman Lorenzo is pursuing, however, turns out to be his sister. The play is like **Mr Limberham* in challenging comic as well as tragic convention, and in its deeply sceptical treatment of religious and political orthodoxies.

Spanish Gipsy, The (1) A romantic comedy by Thomas *Middleton and others (1623); (2) A dramatic poem by George *Eliot (1868).

Spanish Tragedy, The A tragedy, mostly in blank verse, by Thomas *Kyd, written *c.*1587, printed eleven times between 1592 and 1633. The political background of the play is loosely related to the victory of Spain over Portugal in 1580. Lorenzo and Bel-imperia are the children of Don Cyprian, duke of Castile (brother of the king of Spain); Hieronimo is marshal of Spain and Horatio his son. Balthazar, son of the viceroy of Portugal, has been captured in the war. He courts Bel-imperia, and Lorenzo and the king of Spain favour his suit for political reasons. Lorenzo and Balthazar discover that Bel-imperia loves Horatio; they surprise the couple by night in Hieronimo's garden and hang Horatio on a tree. Hieronimo discovers his son's body and runs mad with grief. He succeeds nevertheless in identifying the murderers, and revenges himself by means of a play, *Solyman and Perseda*, in which Lorenzo and Balthazar are killed, and Bel-imperia stabs herself. Hieronimo bites out his tongue before killing himself. The whole action is watched over by Revenge and the ghost of Andrea, previously killed in battle by Balthazar.

The play was the prototype of the English *revenge tragedy genre. It returned to the stage for decades and was seen by Samuel *Pepys as late as 1668. There have been successful modern revivals.

Ben *Jonson is known to have been paid for additions to the play, but the additional passages in the 1602 edition are probably not his. The play was one of *Shakespeare's minor sources for **Hamlet* and the alternative title given to it in 1615, *Hieronimo Is Mad Again*, provided T. S. *Eliot with the penultimate line of *The *Waste Land*.

SPARK, Dame Muriel (1918–2006) Née Camberg, novelist and poet, born and educated in Edinburgh, where she attended James Gillespie's High School for Girls, immortalized in her novel about the charismatic teacher of a group of schoolgirls in the 1930s, *The Prime of Miss Jean Brodie* (1961); the novel later became a play (1968), a film (1969), and a television series (1978). After six years in Rhodesia (recalled in stories in *The Go-Away Bird*, 1958, and *Voices At Play*, 1961), where her marriage to a man thirteen years her senior, Sydney Oswald Spark, broke down, she returned to Britain in 1944. Editing *Poetry Review* from 1947 to 1949, she wrote studies of Mary *Shelley, Emily *Brontë, and John *Masefield, and published a book of poems, *The Fanfarlo and Other Verse*, in 1952. But it was fiction, to which she turned after winning an *Observer* short story competition in 1951, that established her as one of the most distinctive and distinguished writers of her age. Her first novel, *The Comforters* (1957), begun after she converted to Roman Catholicism (a crucial factor in the view of life her fiction transmits), was followed by a rapid succession of highly original and highly accomplished novels hallmarked by economy of style and structure, authorial omniscience, telling disruptions of normal chronology, ironic wit, and concentration on small worlds which are simultaneously satirized and given allegorical significance. Among them her sardonic survey of old age, *Memento Mori* (1959), and *The Girls of Slender Means* (1963), set in a Kensington hostel between VE and VJ days, particularly stand out. In 1963 she left Britain, eventually settling in Italy. While never quite matching the brilliance of her earlier work, the fiction of her expatriate years still beguilingly retained her sharp wit, poetic flair, and characteristic mix of insouciant tone and moral rigour. Her *Collected Poems* and *Collected Plays* (written for both stage and radio) were published in 1967; a collected edition of her stories, in 1986. A volume of autobiography, *Curriculum Vitae* (1992), gives an account of her early years, which two novels of reminiscence, *Loitering with Intent* (1981) and *A Far Cry from Kensington* (1988), imaginatively complement. A further volume of poetry, *Going up to Sotheby's*, was published in 1982. The last of her 22 novels, *The Finishing School*, appeared in 2004.

Spasmodic school A term applied by W. E. *Aytoun to a loosely affiliated group of poets which included P. J. *Bailey, J. W. *Marston, Sydney *Dobell, and Alexander *Smith. Most of the so-called 'spasmodic' poets came from lower-class backgrounds and were encouraged in their poetic ambitions by the well-known Scottish critic George *Gilfillan. Their works briefly enjoyed great popularity, particularly in the case of Smith's *A Life-Drama* (1853) and Dobell's **Balder* (1854): the former was favourably reviewed by A. H. *Clough in comparison to Matthew *Arnold's early poems. Spasmodic poems tended to describe intense interior psychological drama, were violent and verbose, and were characterized by obscurity, *pathetic fallacy, and extravagant imagery. Their language and imagery is often highly derivative and much of it was drawn wholesale from poets they admired, including William *Shakespeare, John *Keats, and Alfred *Tennyson. Spasmodics combined an uneasy blend of political and sexual radicalism with fantastic settings and events, and generally focused on heroes (owing much to Lord *Byron and *Goethe) who were lonely, aspiring, disillusioned, and frequently poets themselves. Although spasmodism was rapidly discredited and became a laughing-stock after the publication of Aytoun's parody of the genre, *Firmilian* (1854), it had a significant influence on Victorian poetry. Poems such as Tennyson's **Maud* (1855) and Elizabeth Barrett *Browning's **Aurora Leigh* (1856), plus works by Arnold, Clough, and A. C. *Swinburne, have been linked to spasmodic principles. See M. A. Weinstein, *W. E. Aytoun and the Spasmodic Controversy* (1968).

SPCK (Society for Promoting Christian Knowledge) Founded in 1698 by Dr Thomas Bray (1658–1730), it was a *Church of England society with an ambitious programme at home and in the American colonies for improving the education of the clergy through the establishment of libraries, teaching poor children to read and write and to understand the principles of the Christian religion, and distributing bibles and devotional and didactic works to poor families, servants, prisoners, soldiers, and sailors. In 1701 its overseas activities and missionary work were brought under a separate society, the Society for the Propagation of the Gospel in Foreign Parts (SPG). From the point of view of *Methodists and evangelicals it was objectionable because the devotional works it distributed—such as *The *Whole Duty of Man* and Robert *Nelson's *Companion for the Festivals and Fasts of the Church of England*—ignored what they regarded as the essential doctrines of the gospel. But its methods were a significant influence in the formation of other tract societies: it perfected the process whereby a list of suitable books was chosen by committee, kept in print, and given to members to distribute to the poor. In the mid-18th century it began to employ its own official publishers, Rivingtons, and the Society has remained a major publisher of popular religious books ever since.

Specimens of English Dramatic Poets Who Lived about the Time of Shakespeare By Charles *Lamb, published 1808; an anthology, with brief but cogent and illuminating critical comments, of extracts of scenes and speeches from Elizabethan and Jacobean dramatists, many of them little known or regarded in Lamb's day. His selections include extracts from Francis *Beaumont and John *Fletcher, Ben *Jonson, Christopher *Marlowe, John *Webster, and some dozen others. The book did much to draw the attention of Lamb's contemporaries to this period of drama, which Lamb himself enjoyed 'beyond the diocese of strict conscience'.

Spectator (1) A periodical conducted by Richard *Steele and Joseph *Addison, from 1 March 1711 to 6 December 1712, succeeding the **Tatler*. It was revived by Addison in 1714, when 80 further numbers (556–635) were issued. It appeared daily, except Sundays, and was immensely popular with a middle-class and professional readership; it was strongly associated with London and its new meeting places, especially coffee houses. Addison and Steele were the principal contributors, in about equal proportions; other contributors included Alexander *Pope, Thomas *Tickell, Eustace Budgell (1686–1737), Ambrose *Philips, Laurence *Eusden, and Lady Mary Wortley *Montagu. It centres on a small club of characters, including Sir Roger de Coverley, who represents the Tory-inclined country gentry, the Whig merchant Sir Andrew Freeport, Captain Sentry of the army, and Will Honeycomb, a man about town. Mr Spectator himself, who writes the papers, is a man of travel and learning, who frequents London as an observer, but (for the most part) keeps clear of political faction. The papers are mainly concerned with contemporary manners, morals, and literature; the most important literary papers are Addison's nineteen papers on **Paradise Lost* and his eleven essays on the 'pleasures of the imagination'. The tone is lightly satirical and the papers seek 'to enliven morality with wit, and to temper wit with morality'. Edward *Young declared that the periodical provided 'a wholesome and pleasant regimen'; both its style and its ethos were considered exemplary by Samuel *Johnson and Hugh *Blair, among other commentators. The papers were collected and regularly reprinted in book form during the centuries that followed; an annotated five-volume edition by Donald F. Bond was published in 1965. (2) A weekly periodical started in 1828 by Robert Stephen Rintoul, with funds provided by Joseph Hume and others, as an organ of 'educated radicalism'. It supported Lord John Russell's *Reform Bill of 1831 with a demand for 'the Bill, the whole Bill, and nothing but the Bill'. R. H. *Hutton was joint editor, 1861–97; John St Loe Strachey (1860–1927) was editor and proprietor from 1898 to 1925, and his cousin Lytton *Strachey was a frequent contributor. Other notable contributors in later years include Peter *Fleming, Graham *Greene, Evelyn *Waugh, Peter *Quennell, Kingsley *Amis, Clive James (1939–), Bernard Levin (1928–2004), Peregrine Worsthorne (1923–), Katharine Whitehorn (1928–), and Auberon *Waugh. From 1999 to 2005 it was edited by the Conservative MP Boris Johnson, continuing a long association with that party.

speculative fiction A term used by Robert A. *Heinlein in 1947 to describe what *science fiction *did*, extrapolating from known facts; now used to suggest a broader range of exploratory genres (including *fantasy) or to establish a class distinction between so-called 'literary' fiction and science fiction.

SPEDDING, James (1808–81) Literary editor and biographer, educated at Trinity College, Cambridge. He was a friend of Alfred *Tennyson, Edward *FitzGerald, and Thomas *Carlyle (who said of him that 'There is a grim strength in Spedding, quietly, very quietly, invincible'). He is now chiefly remembered for his pioneering edition of *The Works of Francis Bacon* (7 vols, 1857–9). His *Evenings with a Reviewer* (1848) was a refutation of T. B. *Macaulay's 'Essay' on *Bacon which he subsequently developed in his *The Letters and Life of Francis Bacon* (1861–72).

SPEGHT, Rachel (b. 1597, *fl.*1621) Daughter of a London Puritan minister, James Speght; she published at the age of 19 a spirited rebuttal of the misogynist *Arraignment of Lewd, Idle, Froward and Inconstant Women* by Joseph Swetnam (d. 1621). Her *A Mouzell for Melastomus* (1617: *A Muzzle for a Black Mouth*) objected to the 'excrement of your raving cogitations' as a slander on woman, who, as Eve's daughter, was fashioned from Adam's side, not his head or foot, 'near his heart, to be his equal'. In 1621 she published *Mortalities Memorandum, with* *a Dreame Prefixed*, the latter being an allegorical narrative poem urging the education of women, under guidance of tutelary female personifications (Thought, Experience, Industry, Desire, Truth). *A Mouzell* is reprinted in S. Shepherd (ed.), *The Women's Sharp Revenge* (1984).

SPEKE, John Hanning (1827–64) Explorer in Africa, born near Bideford, Devon, and unhappily educated at Barnstaple Grammar School and Blackheath proprietary school before entering the Indian army; he joined Sir Richard *Burton on expeditions to Somalia and then Lake Tanganyika in 1858. While Burton was ill, Speke diverted to Lake Victoria, claiming it was the Nile source. The relationship with Burton deteriorated badly. Speke was chosen to vindicate his claim and did so at the Ripon Falls in July 1862. Burton and other geographers questioned whether Speke had seen the real source. The matter remained in doubt for a dozen years. Speke was then dead, having accidentally shot himself the day before a planned debate with Burton. Although Speke solved the greatest of all geographical problems, his fame has not lasted while his *Journal of the Discovery of the Source of the Nile* (1863), having needed to be 'improved' by a publisher's reader, has not become a travel classic. Nevertheless, it contains fascinating material, particularly on Buganda.

SPENCE, Alan (1947–) Glasgow-born novelist and poet whose works include *The Magic Flute* (1990), *Way to Go* (1998), and *The Pure Land* (2006), a historical novel connecting 19th-century Aberdeenshire to Nagasaki at the time of its atomic bombing in 1945.

SPENCE, Joseph (1699–1768) Clergyman, anecdotist, scholar, born in Kingsclere, Hampshire, educated at Winchester College and Oxford University. He succeeded Thomas *Warton as professor of poetry at Oxford in 1728. A man of much generosity, he befriended Robert *Dodsley in his early days, later helping him to edit his celebrated *Collection of Poems*, and also Stephen *Duck, whose life he wrote (1731, reprinted with Duck's poems, 1736). He also wrote a life of the blind poet Thomas *Blacklock (1754). He was a close friend of Alexander *Pope, whose version of the **Odyssey* he defended, and from 1726 collected anecdotes and recorded conversations with Pope and other literary figures. These, although not published until 1820, were well known and widely quoted during the 18th century, and were made available to and used by William *Warburton and Samuel *Johnson. They are usually referred to under the title *Spence's Anecdotes*: an edition by J. M. Osborn appeared in 1966 under the title *Observations, Anecdotes, and Characters of Books and Men, Collected from Conversation*.

SPENCE, Thomas (1750–1814) English radical, bookseller, and satirist. Originally from Newcastle, Spence became a central figure in English radicalism in the 1790s. He wrote and printed radical tracts and spent several spells in prison for his pains. Spence also wrote widely circulated radical squibs against William Pitt and the Tory government. His 'Spencean philanthropy' was espoused by the Society of Spencean Philanthropists.

SPENCER, Herbert (1820–1903) Philosopher and social theorist. Born in Derby, the son of a schoolmaster, Spencer was largely self-taught and showed few intellectual interests until he was over 16. He worked as a civil engineer, then turned his attention to philosophy and published *Social Statics* (1850) and *Principles of Psychology* (1855). In 1860, after reading Charles *Darwin, he announced a systematic series of treatises, to the elaboration of which he devoted the remainder of his life: *First Principles* (1862), *Principles of Biology* (1864–7), *Principles of Sociology* (1876–96), and *Principles of Ethics* (1879–93). Among his other works were *Essays on Education* (1861), *The Classification of the Sciences* (1864), *The Study of Sociology* (1873), *Man versus the State* (1884), and *Factors of Organic Evolution* (1887).

Spencer was the founder of evolutionary philosophy, proposing the unification of all knowledge on the basis of the principle of evolution, whose laws hold good of the visible universe as well as of smaller aggregates, suggesting the conception of past and future evolutions such as that which is now proceeding. He is the origin of the phrase 'survival of the fittest'. His philosophical writing was widely popular and achieved mass sales, though its reputation declined rapidly in the 1880s and 1890s.

Spencer's attempts to define an ethical system, based on the right to liberty of every individual, so long as others are not harmed, were less successful. He wanted to reconcile utilitarian with evolutionary ethics, but had to confess that for the purpose of deducing ethical principles 'the Doctrine of Evolution has not furnished guidance to the extent that I had hoped'.

In a literary context Spencer is remembered for his friendship with George *Eliot, whom he met in 1851. Though he found her 'the most admirable woman, mentally, I have ever met', after her death he was at pains to quell any rumour that they had ever been more than friends. She appears to have been more strongly attached to him, but transferred her affections to G. H. Lewes (*c*.1852–3). Spencer died a bachelor. See Mark Francis, *Herbert Spencer and the Invention of Modern Life* (2007).

SPENCER, Sir Stanley (1891–1959) A biblically inspired artist famous for his religious images of the village of Cookham-on-Thames in Berkshire, where he was born, and spent his life. He was one of the models for Gully Jimson, the painter in Joyce *Cary's novel *The Horse's Mouth*. See T. Hyman and P. Wright (eds), *Stanley Spencer* (exhibition catalogue, Tate Gallery, London, 2001).

SPENDER, Sir Stephen (1909–95) Poet and critic, born in Kensington, London, and educated at University College School, London, and University College, Oxford, where he became friendly with W. H. *Auden and Isaiah Berlin (1909–

97). After leaving Oxford he lived in Germany for a period, in Hamburg and near Christopher *Isherwood in Berlin, an experience which sharpened his political consciousness. In 1930 a small collection of his verse, *Twenty Poems*, was published; his *Poems* (1933) were received with great acclaim and contained both personal and political pieces, including 'I Think Continually of Those who were Truly Great', 'The Landscape near an Aerodrome', and 'The Pylons', which gave the nickname of the *Pylon poets to himself and his friends. He also published a critical work, *The Destructive Element* (1935), mainly on Henry *James, which ends with a section called 'In Defence of a Political Subject', in which he discusses the work of Auden and Edward *Upward, and argues the importance of treating 'politico-moral' subjects in literature. During the Spanish Civil War he briefly belonged to the Communist Party and did propaganda work in Spain for the Republicans, a period reflected in his volume of poems *The Still Centre* (1939). During the Second World War he was a member of the Auxiliary Fire Service. He retracts a number of his earlier positions in *The Creative Element* (1953), while he gives an account of his relationship with the Communist Party in his frank and very successful autobiography *World within World* (1951). His interest in the public and social role and duty of the writer (a duty which he maintained from 1971 in his work for the magazine *Index on Censorship*) has tended to obscure the essentially personal and private nature of much of his own poetry, including his elegies for his sister-in-law, in *Poems of Dedication* (1947), and many of the poems in such later volumes as *Collected Poems 1928–1953* (1955). His other works include *Trial of a Judge* (1938), *The Thirties and after* (1978, a volume of memoirs), *Collected Poems 1982–85* (1985), and his lively and often comically self-deprecating *Journals 1939–83* (1985). *The Temple* (1989) is a novel inspired by an abandoned manuscript written in 1929 about a young Englishman in Germany, and rewritten as 'a complex of memory, fiction and hindsight'. He was knighted in 1983. See John Sutherland, *Stephen Spender: The Authorized Biography* (2004).

SPENSER, Edmund (?1552–1599) Poet, probably the elder son of John Spenser from Lancashire, who may have been a journeyman in the art of cloth-making. The poet claimed to be related to the Spencers of Althorp.

Edmund Spenser was probably born in Smithfield, London, and was educated at Merchant Taylors' School, London under Richard *Mulcaster, and Pembroke Hall, Cambridge. In 1569, while still at Cambridge, he contributed a number of 'Visions' and sonnets, translations from *Petrarch and *Du Bellay, to Jan van der Noodt's *Theatre for Voluptuous Worldlings*. To the 'greener times' of his youth belong also the 'Hymne in Honour of Love' and that of 'Beautie' (first published 1596), which reflect his study of *Neoplatonism. After possibly spending some time in the north, he became secretary to John Young, bishop of Rochester (*c.*1532–1605), in 1578, and in 1579, through his college friend and tutor Gabriel *Harvey, obtained a place in Robert Dudley, earl of *Leicester's household. There he became acquainted with Philip *Sidney, to whom he dedicated his **Shepheardes Calender* (1579). He married Maccabaeus Childe in the same year, and also began to write *The *Faerie Queene*. In 1580 he was appointed secretary to Lord Grey of Wilton (1536–93), then going to Ireland as lord deputy. During the later 1580s he became one of the 'undertakers' for the settlement of Munster, having acquired Kilcolman Castle in Co. Cork. Here he settled and occupied himself with literary work, writing his elegy *'Astrophel', on Sidney, and preparing *The Faerie Queene* for the press. The first three books of it were entrusted to the publisher during his visit to London with Walter *Ralegh in 1589. He returned reluctantly to Kilcolman, which he liked to regard as a place of exile, in 1591, recording his visit to London and return to Ireland in **Colin Clouts Come Home Againe* (printed 1595). The success of *The Faerie Queene* led the publisher, Ponsonby, to issue his minor verse and juvenilia, in part rewritten, as *Complaints, Containing Sundrie Small Poemes of the Worlds Vanitie* (1591). This volume included 'The *Ruines of Time', which was a further elegy on Sidney, dedicated to Sidney's sister, the countess of *Pembroke, *'Mother Hubberds Tale', *'Muiopotmos', 'The *Teares of the Muses', and *'Virgils Gnat'. *Daphnaïda*, an elegy on Douglas Howard, the daughter of Lord Byndon and wife of Sir Arthur *Gorges, was also published in 1591.

Spenser married Elizabeth Boyle, whom he had wooed in his *Amoretti*, in 1594 and celebrated the marriage in his superb **Epithalamion*: the works were printed together in 1595. He was probably in London for the publication of Books IV–VI of *The Faerie Queene* and his *Fowre Hymnes* in 1596, staying at the house of his friend the earl of Essex, where he may have written his **Prothalamion* and completed his well-informed though propagandist *View of the Present State of Ireland*. He returned to Ireland, depressed both in mind and health, in 1596 or 1597. His castle of Kilcolman was burnt in October 1598, in a sudden insurrection of native rebels, chiefly O'Neills, under the earl of Desmond; Spenser was compelled to flee to Cork with his wife and three children. It is not known what works, if any, were lost at Kilcolman, but Ponsonby in 1591 had mentioned various other pieces by Spenser which are not now extant, and in *The Shepheardes Calender* reference is made to his discourse of the 'English Poet'. He died in London at a lodging in King Street, Westminster. His funeral expenses were borne by the earl of Essex, and he was buried near his favourite Geoffrey *Chaucer in Westminster Abbey. His monument, set up some twenty years later by Lady Anne *Clifford, describes him as 'the prince of poets in his tyme': there have been few later periods in which he has not been admired, and the poetry of both John *Milton and John *Keats had its origins in the reading of Spenser. There is a biography by A. C. Judson (1945), a chronology by W. Maley (1994), and an encyclopedia ed. A. C. Hamilton (1990).

Spenserian stanza The stanza invented by Edmund *Spenser, in which he wrote *The *Faerie Queene*. It consists of eight five-foot iambic lines, followed by an iambic line of six feet (an alexandrine); it rhymes *ababbcbcc* (*see* METRE).

SPILLANE, Mickey (Frank Morrison Spillane) (1918–2006) American novelist, born in New York, who achieved fame from a series of novels centring on the detective Mike Hammer and commencing with *I, the Jury* (1947). A number of these novels were adapted into films.

SPINOZA, Benedict de (Baruch de Spinoza) (1632–77) Amsterdam-born Jewish philosopher of Portuguese origin, expelled from the Jewish community for religious unorthodoxy. Spinoza's philosophy is pantheistic. He rejects René *Descartes's dualism of spirit and matter, acknowledging only 'one infinite substance, of which finite existences are modes or limitations'. God is synonymous with this infinite substance. Denial of free will and of personal immortality are consequences of Spinoza's system. In his *Ethics* (finished about 1665, pub. 1677) he takes a relativist position (nothing is intrinsically good or bad). Reality is perfect: failure to see this comes from deficient perception. Emotion comes from inadequate understanding. Blessedness consists in being conscious of ourselves and Nature. Spinoza lived simply, working as a lens-grinder. The *Ethics* and the *Tractatus Theologico-politicus* (published 1670) have influenced modern philosophers including Gilles *Deleuze, and Ludwig *Wittgenstein. See S. Hampshire, *Spinoza and Spinozism* (1951, 2005).

SPINRAD, Norman (1940–) American *science fiction writer, born in New York; associated with the *New Wave when his controversial *Bug Jack Barron* (1969) was serialized in **New Worlds* (1967–8). *The Iron Dream* (1972) satirized both science fiction and fascism by describing an alternate Hitler who renounces politics for science fiction.

Spirit of the Age, The Essays by William *Hazlitt, published 1825, presented as a portrait gallery of the eminent writers of his time: Jeremy *Bentham, William *Godwin, S. T. *Coleridge, William *Wordsworth, Walter *Scott, Lord *Byron, Robert *Southey, Thomas *Malthus, Charles *Lamb, and several others. The essays combine character sketches with lively critical assessments of the subjects' works and summaries of their reputations, placed in the context of the political and intellectual ferment of their times. They are strongly animated by Hazlitt's political loyalties, especially in the sustained assault upon the Tory critic William *Gifford for his 'ridiculous pedantry and vanity'.

spondee *See* METRE.

SPRAT, Thomas (1635–1713) Educated at Wadham College, Oxford, bishop of Rochester and dean of Westminster. Politically he was inclined to be a *'Vicar of Bray'; he sat on James II's objectionable ecclesiastical commission in 1686 and allowed the Declaration of Indulgence to be read (amid deep murmurs of disapproval) in the abbey. As a writer he is chiefly remembered for his *History of the *Royal Society* (1667), of which he was one of the first members, but he was also known as a poet (*The Plague of Athens*, 1659, was his most popular poem) and for a biography of his friend Abraham *Cowley, which was attached to Cowley's works from 1668 onwards.

sprung (or 'abrupt') **rhythm** A term invented by G. M. *Hopkins to describe his own idiosyncratic poetic metre, as opposed to normal 'running' rhythm, the regular alternation of stressed and unstressed syllables. It was based partly on Greek and Latin quantitative metre and influenced by the rhythms of Welsh poetry and Old and Middle English *alliterative verse. Hopkins maintained that sprung rhythm existed, unrecognized, in Old English poetry and in *Shakespeare, *Dryden, and *Milton (notably in **Samson Agonistes*). It is distinguished by a metrical foot consisting of a varying number of syllables. The extra, 'slack' syllables added to the established patterns are called 'outrides' or 'hangers'. Hopkins demonstrated the natural occurrence of this rhythm in English by pointing out that many nursery rhymes employed it, for instance 'Díng, Dóng, Béll, | Pússy's in the wéll'. Conventional metres may be varied by the use of 'counterpoint', by which Hopkins meant the reversal of two successive feet in an otherwise regular line of poetry; but sprung rhythm itself cannot be counterpointed because it is not regular enough for the pattern to be recognized under the variations. Hopkins, an amateur composer, often described his theory in terms of musical notation, speaking of rests, crotchets, and quavers. He felt strongly that his poetry should be read aloud, but seems to have felt that the words themselves were not enough to suggest the intended rhythms, and frequently added various diacritical markings to indicate where a sound was to be drawn out, and where syllables were to be spoken quickly. Some critics have suggested that sprung rhythm is not a poetic metre at all, properly speaking, merely Hopkins's attempt to force his own personal rhythm into an existing pattern, or recognizable variation of one, and that his sprung rhythm is in fact closer to some kinds of free verse or polyphonic prose. Variants of it are widely used in modern and contemporary verse.

SPURLING, Hilary Susan (1940–) CBE, biographer, born in Stockport and educated at Somerville College, Oxford. She worked as a reviewer and then literary editor for the *Spectator* during the 1960s before her two-volume biography of Ivy *Compton-Burnett was published (1974, 1984). This was followed by a biography of Paul *Scott (1990) and a two-volume biography of the French painter Henri Matisse (1869–1954), *The Unknown Matisse* (1998) and *Matisse the Master* (2005). Her biography of George *Orwell's wife Sonia (1918–80), *The Girl from the Fiction Department*, was published in 2002.

spy fiction One of the most popular forms of fiction over the last hundred years, the British spy novel emerged during the international tensions of the years preceding the First World War. In the following century, two world wars, revolutions, the Cold War, and the war on terror continued to provide writers with material and subject matter for spy fiction.

Erskine *Childers's *The Riddle of the Sands* (1903), a suspenseful tale of two amateur British agents foiling a German invasion plot, is often described as the first spy novel. But the first spy writer to spring to public fame was William Le Queux (1864–1927), whose highly successful invasion novel *The Great War in England in 1897* (1894), featuring an enemy spy, heralded a cascade of best-sellers over the next three decades. Le Queux's great Edwardian rival was E. Phillips Oppenheim (1866–1946), who wrote a succession of novels, including *The Kingdom of the Blind* (1916) and *The Great Impersonation* (1920), which featured glamorous seductresses and society high life. The year 1920 saw the creation by *Sapper (Herman Cyril McNeile) of the unabashed xenophobe and anti-Semite Bulldog Drummond, a muscular agent who robustly thwarted the plots of the communist arch-villain Carl Peterson in such titles as *The Black Gang* (1922), *The Final Count* (1926), and *The Return of Bulldog Drummond* (1932).

From this early period the writer who has best endured is John *Buchan, whose secret agent hero Richard Hannay first appeared in *The Thirty-Nine Steps* (1915), a novel its author described as 'a romance where the incidents defy the probabilities, and march just inside the borders of the possible', which defines much other spy fiction. There followed such classics as *Greenmantle* (1916), *Mr Standfast* (1919), and *The Three Hostages* (1924).

The First World War, the Great Depression, and the rise of *Fascism created a sombre inter-war climate that saw the emergence of a new generation of spy writers who broke sharply with the patriotic orthodoxies of their predecessors. Some, like Somerset *Maugham, had worked for British wartime intelligence and painted a far less glamorized picture of the secret agent's life. Maugham's *Ashenden* (1928) was an influential collection of short stories based closely on his personal experience.

In the 1930s, Eric *Ambler crafted plots of considerable technical skill and authenticity, combined with a leftist outlook, that featured innocent protagonists caught up in the machinations of 'merchants of death' and other capitalist villains. His best-known and most successful novel was *The Mask of Dimitrios* (1939). Ambler's ideological outlook was shared by Graham *Greene, whose *Stamboul Train* (1932), *The Confidential Agent* (1939), and *The Ministry of Fear* (1943) foreshadowed his even better-known spy novels that appeared after the Second World War when he worked as a British intelligence officer for the Secret Intelligence Service (MI6): *The Quiet American* (1955), *Our Man in Havana* (1958), and *The Human Factor* (1978).

The dominating figure of the immediate post-war years was Ian *Fleming, whose *Casino Royale* (1953) introduced the iconic figure of James *Bond, undoubtedly the most famous fictional secret agent of all time. By 1964, the year of Fleming's death, his eleven Bond spy novels, including such classics as *From Russia with Love* (1957) and *Goldfinger* (1959), had sold over 40 million copies and his hero was beginning to appear in the blockbuster movies that continue to this day.

The 1961 building of the Berlin Wall brought a serious chill to the Cold War climate, and in *The Spy Who Came in from the Cold* (1963) John *le Carré marked out the territory that was to dominate spy fiction until the end of the Cold War. Making an explicit and conscious break with Bond, he created the anti-heroic figure of George Smiley, the protagonist of several of his novels that culminate in *Smiley's People* (1980), an eternally middle-aged and all too human intelligence officer who grapples with the moral ambiguities of real-life Cold War espionage. *The Looking-Glass War* (1965) is a particularly bleak dissection of a Cold War operation, while *Tinker, Tailor, Soldier, Spy* (1974), inspired by the infamous case of Kim Philby, explores the theme of the Soviet 'mole' within the service.

Exploring similar terrain were novelists like Len Deighton (1929–) who made his name with *The Ipcress File* (1962) and *Funeral in Berlin* (1964), and went on to write three trilogies in the 1980s and 1990s featuring the Secret Service agent Bernard Samson; the former intelligence officer Ted Allbeury (1917–2005), whose first novel, *A Choice of Enemies*, appeared in 1973; and Anthony Price (1928–), creator of the historian and spy Dr David Audley. Yet even as le Carré and others explored the moral ambiguities of Cold War espionage, Frederick Forsyth (1938–) was marking yet another shift in mood. In thrill-packed best-sellers such as *The Day of the Jackal* (1971) and *The Odessa File* (1972), he returned to adventure stories on a global scale in which tough male heroes save the world from a variety of disasters, a trend also reflected in the novels of Ken Follett (1949–) such as *The Eye of the Needle* (1978) and *The Man from St Petersburg* (1982).

One of the many consequences of the ending of the Cold War could have been the death of the spy novel but writers of espionage fiction have found ways of dealing with the disappearance of their richest source of plots. Le Carré has continued to publish best-selling fiction but has turned his attention to the iniquities of global capitalism in novels such as *The Constant Gardener* (2001). Forsyth has embraced the fictional opportunities offered by recent history and his 2006 novel *The Afghan* features an undercover agent working to thwart an al-Qaeda terror plot. Younger writers such as Henry Porter (1953–), author of *A Spy's Life* (2001) and *Brandenburg* (2005) amongst others, and Charles Cumming (1971–), who made an acclaimed debut as a novelist with *A Spy by Nature* (2001), have shown that there is life in the genre yet.

SQUIRE, Sir J. C. (John Collings) (1884–1958) Born in Plymouth and educated at Plymouth Grammar School, Blundell's School, Tiverton, and St John's College, Cambridge; he became a *Georgian poet, an influential literary journalist and editor, and a skilful parodist. He published a number of volumes of prose and poetry, established the **London Mercury* in 1919, and exercised considerable power through his editorship, so much so that he and his friends formed a literary establishment—irreverently known as 'the Squirearchy'—which was vigorously opposed by the *Sitwells, the *Bloomsbury Group, and the *modernist avant-garde. Squire edited a large number of successful anthologies and between 1921 and 1934 edited three widely popular volumes of *Selections* *from Modern Poets*. His *Collected Parodies* appeared in 1921, he was knighted in 1933, and an autobiography, *The Honeysuckle and the Bee*, appeared in 1937. His *Collected Poems*, edited by John *Betjeman, were published in 1959.

Squire of Dames A comic character in Edmund *Spenser's **Faerie Queene* (III. vii). He had been ordered by his lady to 'do service unto gentle Dames' and at the end of twelve months to report his progress. A year later he was able to bring 'pledges' or evidence of 300 conquests. Thereupon his lady ordered him not to return to her till he had found an equal number of dames who rejected his advances. After three years he had only found three: he had been rejected by a courtesan because he would not pay her enough, a nun because she could not trust his discretion, and a 'Damzell' of low degree 'in countrey cottage found by chaunce'.

Squire of Low Degree, The A metrical romance, probably mid-15th century, opening with the much-quoted distich: 'It was a squier of lowe degree | That loved the Kings doughter of Hungré.' The squire declares his love to the princess, who consents to marry him when he has proved himself a distinguished knight. But he is seen in his tryst by a steward, whom he kills after the steward reports to the king. He is imprisoned but finally released because the princess is inconsolable, whereupon he sets out on his quest, proves his worth, and marries her. There is no manuscript of the full-length, 1,131-line version; the romance is known from a printing *c.*1560 by W. Copland and fragments of a 1520 printing by Wynkyn de *Worde; de Worde's edition is dramatically entitled 'Undo youre Dore' from one of its episodes. Ed. D. B. Sands, *Middle English Verse Romances* (1966).

'Squire's Tale, The' *See* CANTERBURY TALES, 11.

STABLEFORD, Brian (1948–) *Science fiction author and critic, born in Shipley, West Yorkshire, whose work ranges from routine space operas to erudite explorations of *Gothic/decadence. In the 'Hooded Swan' series from *The Halcyon Drift* (1972), he developed a sardonic voice which moved towards subverting the expectations of the form. With the stories collected in *Sexual Chemistry* (1991), and the 'Emortality' series, beginning with *Inherit the Earth* (1998), Stableford refuses to abandon science fiction's desire to examine the future. He is also one of the field's finest scholars.

STABLES, Gordon (*c.*1840–1910) Retired naval surgeon and children's writer, born in Aberchirder, Marnoch, Scotland, educated at Aberdeen University; he produced numerous books and articles, usually for boys, though he contributed health advice to the *Girl's Own Paper*. Stables wrote adventure and animal stories and about health.

STACPOOLE, H. (Henry) **de Vere** (1863–1951) Novelist and sea captain, born near Dublin, and educated at Portarlington School in Ireland and Malvern College, Worcestershire. He achieved popularity with *The Crimson Azaleas* (1907), a sea adventure, but is chiefly remembered for his best-selling romance *The Blue Lagoon* (1908), the story of two cousins, Dick and Emmeline, marooned at the age of 8 on a tropical island where they grow up and produce a baby. It has been several times successfully filmed.

STAËL, Anne-Louise-Germaine Necker, Madame de (1766–1817) French writer of Swiss parentage and a major precursor of French Romanticism. Daughter of the finance minister Necker and mistress of Benjamin *Constant, she occupied a central place in French intellectual life for over three decades. Her critical study *De la littérature considérée dans ses rapports avec les institutions sociales* (1800: *On Literature Considered in Relation to Social Institutions*) was the first piece of criticism to treat literature as a product of social history and environment. Another study, *De l'Allemagne* (1810: *On Germany*), banned in France by Napoleon, was published in London in 1813 and had a huge impact, in both France and England, on views of contemporary German thought and literature. Her two novels, *Delphine* (1802) and *Corinne* (1807), offer a distinctive image of woman as independent artist in a male-dominated society.

STAFFORD, Jean (1915–1979) American writer, born in California, who began publishing with her novel *Boston Adventure* (1944). Her first marriage was to Robert *Lowell and her *Collected Stories* (1969) won the *Pulitzer Prize. See Anne Hulbert, *The Interior Castle* (1992).

STAFFORD-CLARK, Max (1941–) Theatre director, born in Cambridge, educated at Felsted School and Trinity College, Dublin. He is the single most important force in the introduction of new playwrights and plays into the modern British theatre. He ran the Traverse Theatre, Edinburgh, from 1968 and was director of its Theatre Workshop Company until 1974, the year that he co-founded the Joint Stock Theatre Company, an innovative workshop-based organization that nurtured the careers of many new writers. From 1979 to 1993 he was the longest-serving artistic director of the *Royal Court. There he actively supported new writing, including Caryl *Churchill's **Top Girls*. In 1993 he founded Out of Joint, with which he continues to promote the work of new writers. He is the author of *Letters to George* (1997), an account of his rehearsals for George *Etherege's *The Man of Mode*, and in 2007 he and Philip Roberts published *Taking Stock: The Theatre of Max Stafford-Clark*.

STAINER, Pauline (1941–) Poet, born in Stoke-on-Trent and educated at St Anne's College, Oxford. Her first collection, *The Honeycomb* (1989), quite out of key with its time, introduced a characteristic mingling of sacred, archaeological, and scientific imagery, and a spare lyric line. This was followed by *Sighting the Slave Ship* (1992), containing poems in homage to various artists, including Rembrandt, Satie, Henry Moore, and illustrator and war artist Eric Ravilious. Other volumes include *The Wound-Dresser's Dream* (1996) and *A Litany of High Waters* (2002). *The Lady and the Hare: New and Selected Poems* was published in 2003.

STALLWORTHY, Jon (1935–) Poet and biographer, born in London and educated at Rugby School and Magdalen College, Oxford. He subsequently worked for Oxford University Press and taught in Oxford, where in 1992 he became a professor of English literature. His first volume, *The Astronomy of Love* (1961), was followed by several others, including *A Familiar Tree* (1978), a sequence which mixes family and local history with a story of migration, *The Guest from the Future* (1995), which celebrates female survival in the person of Anna *Akhmatova and others, and *Body Language* (2004). The title of *Rounding the Horn: Collected Poems* (1998) pays homage, as do many of his individual poems, to his New Zealand ancestry. His translations of Boris *Pasternak (with Peter France) appeared in a revised edition in 1984. He has published notable biographies of Wilfred *Owen (1974), whose work he has also edited, and Louis *MacNeice (1995).

Stand A literary quarterly founded in 1952 by Jon *Silkin, who would sell it in pubs and student halls, and published from 1965 in Newcastle-upon-Tyne; subsequently edited by John Whale and Elaine Glover. Political considerations have characterized its sense of the place of poetry, and a representative anthology in 1973 was entitled *Poetry of the Committed Individual*; it has also been warmly accommodating to work in translation. It publishes poetry, fiction, and criticism, and contributors have included Geoffrey *Hill, Seamus *Heaney, Simon *Armitage, Ken *Smith, a one-time editor, and, in translation, work by Miroslav *Holub, Joseph *Brodsky, and Evgenii *Evtushenko.

STANFORD, Sir Charles Villiers (1852–1924) British composer and teacher, born in Dublin and educated at Queens' College Cambridge, where he wrote incidental music for Henry Wadsworth *Longfellow's *The Spanish Student*. With Hubert *Parry, Stanford was a leading figure of the English musical renaissance of the late 19th century. His pupils at the Royal College of Music included Frank Bridge, John Ireland, George *Butterworth, Ivor *Gurney, Gustav *Holst, Ralph *Vaughan Williams, and Arthur *Bliss. Stanford made a large number of settings for voice and chorus, almost exclusively from Victorian writers onwards: Alfred *Tennyson (*The Revenge*, 1886), Robert *Bridges (the oratorio *Eden*, 1891), and Henry *Newbolt (the cantatas *Songs of the Sea*, 1904, and *Songs of the Fleet*, 1910). Stanford's nine operas include *Shamus O'Brien* (1896, with a text after Sheridan *Le Fanu), *Much Ado About Nothing* (1901), *The *Critic* (based on Richard Brinsley *Sheridan's play, 1916), and *The Travelling Companion* (1926), with a libretto by Henry *Newbolt after Hans Christian *Anderson.

STANHOPE, Lady Hester (1776–1839) Traveller, born Chevening, Kent, her father later the third Earl Stanhope, her mother the sister of William *Pitt the younger, in whose house Hester gained a reputation as a formidable political hostess. In 1810 she left Europe for good with her wealthy young lover Michael Bruce (1787–1861), and travelled in style and without inhibition in Egypt and the Middle East, the first European woman to reach Palmyra. Bruce returned home and she stayed on in Lebanon, living in great magnificence among a semi-oriental retinue and wielding some political power. In later years her debts accumulated and her eccentricity increased. She claimed to be a prophetess and mistress of occult sciences. She was visited by distinguished European travellers, including Alphonse de *Lamartine and Alexander *Kinglake. Her letters were edited posthumously by her physician and companion, Charles Meryon (1783–1877), and confirmed her as a legendary figure of female independence and unconventionality.

Stanhope press An iron printing press invented by Charles, third Earl Stanhope (1753–1816), the father of Lady Hester *Stanhope. He also devised a stereotyping process, and a microscopic lens which bears his name.

STANIHURST, Richard (1547–1618) Irish chronicler, literary theorist, translator, poet, and alchemist, born in Dublin and educated at University College, Oxford. He wrote most of the Irish materials in *Holinshed's *Chronicles*, drawing on researches he had conducted with Edmund *Campion. *The First Four Books of Virgil's 'Aeneis' Translated into English Heroicall Verse* (1582) includes a dissertation on *prosody and the principles of spelling, and an appendix of poems embodying his somewhat eccentric views on these subjects. After the death of his second wife in 1602 Stanihurst became a Jesuit in Flanders.

STANLEY, Arthur Penrhyn (1815–81) Clergyman and historian, educated at Rugby School under Thomas *Arnold and at Balliol College, Oxford. He was commissioned to write Arnold's biography by his widow: *The Life and Correspondence of Thomas Arnold* (1844). He became dean of Westminster (1863). Stanley was a leader of the *Broad Church movement, and a champion of religious toleration.

STANLEY, Sir Henry Morton (1841–1904) Explorer and journalist, born John Rowlands in Denbigh, Wales, where he spent his early years in a workhouse. In 1859 he went as a cabin boy to New Orleans, where, he claims, he was adopted by a merchant named Stanley. In 1869, as a reporter for the *New York Herald*, he was instructed by James Gordon Bennett Jr, a proponent of the 'new journalism', to find Dr David *Livingstone, whom he eventually encountered at Ujiji in 1871. The resulting book, *How I Found Livingstone* (1872), includes the famous, much-ridiculed greeting 'Dr Livingstone, I presume'. Stanley's further explorations and discoveries in

Africa are described in *Through the Dark Continent* (1878), which traced his journey across Africa from east to west, and in *In Darkest Africa* (1890), his narrative of the disastrous and highly controversial Emin Pasha Relief Expedition. In 1890 he married the painter Dorothy Tennant (1855–1926), who edited his autobiography in 1909. From 1895 to 1900 he served as a Unionist MP. He was knighted in 1899. Stanley introduced a new journalistic and sensationalist style into writings of African exploration. He was adept at narrating his experiences for a popular readership. Associated with the new imperialism and responsible for assisting the creation of King Leopold of Belgium's Congo Free State, Stanley was a brutal but complex man through whom many of the contradictions of Victorian Britain may be seen.

STANLEY, Thomas (1625–78) Educated at Pembroke Hall, Cambridge, author of *The History of Philosophy* (1655–62), an edition of *Aeschylus (1663), and translations from *Theocritus, *Bion, the Latin poet and rhetorician Ausonius (*c*.310–395), *Moschus, and Giambattista *Marino, besides original poems. See *Poems and Translations*, ed. G. M. Crump (1962).

stanza A group of verse lines, popularly called a 'verse', of which the length, metrical scheme, and rhyming pattern correspond with those of at least one other such group of verse lines in a poem, often with those of all. Poems are described as stanzaic if they are composed of such matching groups, spatially separated when written or printed. In length, stanzas of English verse are most commonly of four lines (i.e. *quatrains), but various forms of five-line (quintain), six-line (sestet), seven-line (septet), eight-line (octave), and longer stanzas are also found. Possible permutations of *metre and *rhyme are numerous: metrically, stanzas divide between those in which lines are of uniform length and those combining longer with shorter lines. Stanzaic rhyme schemes are summarized by a customary alphabetic notation in which each rhymed or unrhymed line-ending is allotted a letter in sequence, recurrence of the same letter indicating rhymed lines: thus *abcb* for the standard quatrain 'ballad stanza' in which only the second and fourth lines rhyme, but *abab* for the quatrain of alternate rhymes often found in hymns. Most stanza forms are nameless, but exceptions among those longer than the quatrain include the six-line 'Burns stanza' of which the fourth and sixth are of two stresses while the remainder are four-stress lines, with the rhyme scheme *aaabab*; the *'rhyme-royal' stanza of seven iambic *pentameters rhyming *abbabbcc*; the Italianate octave known as **ottava rima*; and the nine-line *Spenserian stanza.

Stanzaic Life of Christ, The A 14th-century compilation surviving in three 15th-century manuscripts in 10,840 lines of English quatrains, drawn from the *Polychronicon* of Ranulf *Higden and the *Legenda Aurea* of Jacobus de Voragine (*see* GOLDEN LEGEND). It was written by a monk of St Werburgh's, Chester, and it was an influence on the Chester *mystery plays. Ed. F. A. Foster (EETS OS 166, 1926).

Staple of News, The A comedy by Ben *Jonson, performed 1626, printed 1631. Pennyboy Junior learns from a beggar, whom he takes on as a servant, that his father has died. He begins to squander his inheritance, buying gaudy clothes, pursuing the rich Lady Pecunia, his miserly uncle's ward, and purchasing a clerkship for his barber at the Staple of News, an office for the collection, sorting, and dissemination of news and gossip, 'authentical and apocryphal'. The beggar reveals that he is Pennyboy's father, and, appalled by his extravagance, disinherits him, but Pennyboy redeems himself, and wins the hand of Lady Pecunia, when he thwarts a plot to ruin his father hatched by the scheming lawyer Picklock. The play is watched throughout by four gossips, Mirth, Tattle, Expectation, and Censure, who sit on the stage and offer an undiscerning commentary at the end of each act.

STAPLEDON, Olaf (1886–1950) *Science fiction writer, philosopher, and activist, born in Wallasey, near Liverpool. His novels *Last and First Men* (1930) and *Star Maker* (1937) have been seen as among the greatest works of science fiction (which Stapledon knew little about at the time of writing them), having been widely cited as influences by Arthur C. *Clarke, Brian W. *Aldiss, Gregory *Benford, Doris *Lessing, and Stephen *Baxter, among others, influencing several generations of authors. *Last and First Men* is a future history of epic proportions, covering the history of humanity from the 20th century, ending two billion years hence when the eighteenth species of humanity, now on Neptune, is facing destruction as the sun explodes. Throughout, the ethical conflict between two essential forces, the intellectual and the spiritual, and an astonishing range of biological and sociological speculation, powers a narrative of mythic proportions. This entire account is a tiny proportion of *Star Maker*, a Dantesque vision of the universe evolving towards a cosmic mind. *Odd John* (1935), with its tragic mutant superman, and *Sirius* (1944), about a dog with superhuman intelligence, are lesser only by comparison. See Robert Crossley, *Olaf Stapledon: Speaking for the Future* (1994).

Star Trek American *science fiction television series, devised and produced by Gene Roddenberry (1921–99), which originally ran 1966–9 and was brought back after a campaign by fans. Its basic scenario, the voyages of the starship *Enterprise* headed by Captain Kirk and his half-alien first officer Spock, allowed for numerous adventures, often exploring moral dilemmas. Several well-known writers, such as Robert *Bloch, Harlan *Ellison, and Theodore *Sturgeon, contributed scripts. Since the first series, numerous motion pictures and spin-offs—*The Next Generation, Deep Space Nine, Voyager, Generations*—have been produced, together with an industrial quantity of books, comics, and games.

Star Wars Originally a single American *science fiction film (1977, dir. George Lucas), *Star Wars* has become a popular-culture franchise rivalled only by **Star Trek*. Celebrated for astonishing special effects, it drew heavily on the American magazines of the 1930s; the first draft of the sequel *The Empire Strikes Back* (1980) was written by Leigh *Brackett. *The Return of the Jedi* followed in 1983. The series was completed by the prequels *The Phantom Menace* (1999), *Attack of the Clones* (2002), and *Revenge of the Sith* (2005).

STARK, Dame Freya (1893–1993) Travel writer and explorer, born in Paris, and educated at Bedford College and the School of Oriental Studies, London. In 1927, having mastered Arabic, she began travelling in the Middle East, and in the next decade made adventurous solitary journeys in that region. During the Second World War she worked for the Ministry of Information in Aden, Cairo, Baghdad, the USA, and India. In 1947 she married the writer Stewart Perowne (1901–87); the couple separated in 1952. Throughout her wanderings her home base was Italy, and she settled in Asolo. She was appointed a fellow of the *Royal Geographical Society in 1936, and made a DBE in 1972. Among her many books on her travels in Iran, Iraq, southern Arabia, and Turkey, the most notable are *The Valleys of the Assassins* (1934), *The Southern Gates of Arabia* (1936), *A Winter in Arabia* (1940), *Iona: A Quest* (1954), and *The Lycian Shore* (1956). Their focus is principally archaeological and antiquarian, yet they also offer a rich account of the remote communities through which she passed. Stark was also an accomplished photographer, illustrating her books with striking portraits of the people and places she encountered. Four volumes of autobiography, including *Traveller's Prelude* (1950), appeared 1950–61, and eight volumes of letters 1974–82; a selection of the latter is available in *Over the Rim of the World*, ed. Caroline Moorehead (1988). Several biographies are also available, among them Molly Izzard's rather hostile *Freya Stark: A Biography* (1993) and Jane Fletcher Geniesse's more sympathetic *Passionate Nomad: The Life of Freya Stark* (1999).

STARKE, Mariana *See* MURRAY, JOHN.

Stationers' Company A London livery company concerned with the book trade and its related crafts. The Company existed from at least 1403 and was incorporated by royal charter in 1557. Under its provisions, only members of the Company might print anything for sale in the kingdom unless authorized by special privilege or patent. Since every member of the Company was required to enter in the register of the Company (the Stationers' Register) the name of any book that he desired to print, these registers furnish valuable information regarding printed matter during the latter part of the 16th century and well into the 17th century. The Company was not responsible for licensing or censorship: by payment of a small fee, the Register established the holder's right to the copy entered in the Register, but by no means all legitimately published works were entered in the Registers. Although the Company's regulatory control of the printing trade waned during the 17th century, it retained its right to print such works as psalters, almanacs, school- and lawbooks. The Stationers' Company merged with the Newspaper Makers' Company in 1937 and their extensive archives, including the original Registers, are kept at Stationers' Hall.

STATIUS, Publius Papinius (AD *c.*45–96) Roman poet, born at Naples. His *Silvae* ('trees' or 'materials'), in five books, is a collection of poems in various metres, some of considerable length, on various occasional topics such as thanks to patrons and descriptions of country houses. His epic *Thebais*, in twelve books, tells the story of the Theban War, from blinded *Oedipus' curse on his sons Eteocles and Polynices, to the expedition of the Seven against Thebes. The precedent of the **Aeneid*, in language and conception, is everywhere visible. He died before completing his second epic, *Achilleis*. Statius appears as a Christian convert in *Dante's *Purgatory*. Ben *Jonson's *Forest* owes a debt to *Silvae*; Alexander *Pope and Thomas *Gray tried their hands at translating the *Thebais*. See Philip Hardie, *The Epic Successors of Virgil* (1993).

STEAD, Christina Ellen (1902–83) Australian novelist, born in Sydney and educated at Sydney University Teachers' College. She came to London in 1928 and subsequently worked and travelled in Europe and America with her companion, then husband, William J. Blake. In 1953 they settled near London; she returned to Australia on his death in 1968. Her wandering life and her left-wing views (which also raised difficulties for her when she worked as a Hollywood scriptwriter) may have contributed to the neglect of her work, particularly in her native country, but towards the end of her life she received renewed attention and admiration. Her first collection of stories, *The Salzburg Tales*, and her first novel, *Seven Poor Men of Sydney*, were both published in 1934. Her best-known work, *The Man Who Loved Children* (1940), is a bitterly ironic view of family life and family conflict, focused on a monstrously egotistical and self-serving patriarch, Sam Pollit, and his dominance over his wife and children. Stead's other novels include *For Love Alone* (1945), in which the central character, Teresa, escapes to Australia to seek her own freedom, *Letty Fox: Her Luck* (1946), a first-person narration describing the adventurous, unconventional, and ambitious life of a New York office girl, and *Cotter's England* (1967; USA as *Dark Places of the Heart*, 1966), which presents a vivid portrait of post-war working-class Britain, centred on the extraordinary personality of chain-smoking, emotional, destructive Nellie Cook, née Cotter, an insatiably curious journalist, working on a left-wing London paper.

STEAD, C. K. (Christian Karlson) (1932–) New Zealand poet, critic, and novelist, born and brought up in Auckland; he went to university there and taught in the English department 1959–86. In 1964 he published his first volume of poems, *Whether the Will Is Free*, and a well-received critical book, *The New Poetic: Yeats to Eliot*. He covered something of the same ground with renewed incisiveness and persuasiveness in *Pound, Yeats, Eliot and the Modernist Movement* (1986). He has published several novels, including *All Visitors Ashore*

(1984), *The Death of the Body* (1986), and *The Singing Whakapapa* (1994), which characteristically mix New Zealand personal material with experimental techniques. *Mansfield* (2004) is a fictional portrait of the New Zealand short story writer Katherine *Mansfield. *My Name is Judas* (2006) fictionally recreates the life of Judas Iscariot (*see* BIBLE). As editor (for example of *The Faber Book of Contemporary South Pacific Stories*, 1994) and as reviewer, Stead has a reputation for provocation. *The Black River*, a selection of poems, appeared in 2007.

STEAD, W. T. (William Thomas) (1849–1912) Journalist. Born at Embleton, Northumberland, he was educated at Silcoates School, Wakefield, and in 1880 moved to London to become assistant editor of the *Pall Mall Gazette*. On becoming editor (1883–8) of the paper, he transformed it into a vigorous, modern, and campaigning journal. He achieved wide notoriety for his 'Maiden Tribute of Modern Babylon' (1885) exposing sexual vice, which prompted Parliament to raise the age of consent to 16 years. His role in the campaign led to a brief term of imprisonment. He founded the *Review of Reviews* in 1890 and continued his work for peace, friendship with Russia, and spiritualism (for which he was much ridiculed). He was drowned in the *Titanic* disaster.

STEDMAN, John Gabriel (1744–97) Army officer and author, born in Dendermonde, the Netherlands, of a Scots father and Dutch mother. After serving for eleven years as a mercenary in the Low Countries, he volunteered to help put down a slave rebellion in the Dutch Caribbean, departing in 1772 and returning in 1777, later resettling in England. His *Narrative of a Five Years' Expedition against the Revolted Negroes of Surinam* (1796) provides a detailed and multi-layered portrait of plantation society as well as telling the story of the author's love affair with a young slave—fictionalized in Beryl Gilroy's *Stedman and Joanna* (1991). Stedman was not an abolitionist, but his blunt descriptions of the cruel treatment of slaves were seized on by anti-slavery campaigners. The book included engravings by William *Blake from Stedman's own drawings. A critical edition by Richard and Sally Price based on the original (1790) manuscript appeared in 1988.

STEELE, Anne (1717–78) Baptist poet and *hymn-writer, born at Broughton, Hampshire, where she died unmarried. In her lifetime she published *Poems on Subjects Chiefly Devotional* (1760) in two volumes under the name Theodosia; after her death the Baptist minister Caleb Evans (1737–91) republished these and added *Miscellaneous Pieces in Prose and Verse* (1780), again by Theodosia, but identifying her in the advertisement. Many of her hymns were included in *A Collection of Hymns Adapted to Public Worship* (1769), edited by Evans and John Ash, which went through seven editions, and her work was well known and loved in the late 18th-century evangelical world.

STEELE, Sir Richard (1672–1729) Whig essayist, born in Dublin and educated at Charterhouse, where he met Joseph *Addison, and subsequently at Merton College, Oxford. Steele joined the Life Guards, eventually attaining the rank of captain. His distaste for military life informs his tract *The Christian Hero* (1701). *The Funeral* (also 1701) was the first and most successful of three early comedies. In 1707 he was appointed gazetteer and married Mary Scurlock ('dear Prue'), his second wife. In 1709 he launched the *Tatler*, which he ran with the help of Addison until 1711 when it foundered in the new Tory hegemony, which also cost him the gazetteership. In April 1711 he and Addison set up the less political *Spectator*. This was followed by the *Guardian*, to which Addison, George *Berkeley, and Alexander *Pope contributed, and which was attacked by the Tory *Examiner* and the *Englishman* (1713–14). In 1713 Steele was elected MP for Stockbridge. The publication of *The Crisis*, a pamphlet in favour of the Hanoverian succession, led to his expulsion from the House in 1714. In the same year he issued *Apology for Himself and his Writings* and edited the *Lover*, a paper in the manner of the *Spectator*. On the accession of George I he was appointed supervisor of Drury Lane Theatre, and was knighted in 1715. His 1718 denunciation in *The Plebeian* of Lord Sunderland's Peerage Bill led to the revocation of his Drury Lane patent, and to an estrangement from Addison. He established the *Theatre*, a bi-weekly paper, which continued until 1720. His last and most popular comedy, *The *Conscious Lovers*, was produced in 1722. Money difficulties forced him to leave London in 1724, and he died at Carmarthen. His letters to Mary Scurlock were printed in 1787. Though Steele's light, rapid essays were less highly regarded than Addison's, his influence was great; his attacks on *Restoration drama; his approval of the 'sober and polite Mirth' of *Terence; his praise of tender affections and family life; and his own reformed and sentimental dramas did much to create an image of polite behaviour for the new century.

Steel Glass, The A satire in verse by George *Gascoigne, published 1576. The poet's 'steel glass' reveals abuses and how things should be, whereas the common looking-glass offers 'a seemly show', i.e. shows things much better than they really are. Looking into his 'steel glass', the author sees himself with his faults and then successively the faults of kings; covetous lords and knights; greedy, braggart, and drunken soldiers; false judges; merchants; and priests. Finally, the ploughman is held up as a model:

> Behold him (priests) and though he stink of sweat
> Disdain him not: for shall I tell you what?
> Such climb to heaven, before the shaven crowns.

STEEVENS, George (1736–1800) Shakespearian commentator, educated at Eton College and King's College, Cambridge. In 1766 he issued in four volumes *Twenty of the Plays of Shakespeare* from the earliest quarto texts (*see* FOLIOS AND QUARTOS), and in 1773 a ten-volume annotated edition, a revision of Samuel *Johnson's edition, further revised in 1778. He helped Edmond *Malone produce two supplementary volumes in 1780, but their increasing rivalry led Steevens to produce a further edition (1793), with materials for still another left in the hands of Isaac *Reed. Steevens supplied to his editions a vast range of illustrative quotations from Elizabethan writings, but is also thought to have planted various hoax documents to mislead other scholars. He assisted Thomas *Tyrwhitt in his work on Thomas *Chatterton's Rowley poems, and attacked W. H. *Ireland's Shakespeare forgeries. He was elected to the *Club in 1774, at Johnson's nomination, but constantly quarrelled with his associates and was called by William *Gifford 'the Puck of commentators'.

STEGNER, Wallace (1909–93) American writer and naturalist, born in Iowa. His novels include *The Big Rock Candy Mountain* (1943), and *The Preacher and the Slave* (1950) about the American labour activist Joe Hill. He also published a number of studies of the American landscape. See Jackson J. Benson, *Wallace Stegner* (1984).

STEIN, Gertrude (1874–1946) American author, born in Pennsylvania into a progressive and intellectual family of German-Jewish origin. She studied psychology under William *James, who introduced her to automatic writing. In 1902 she went with her brother Leo to Paris, where her home became a literary salon and art gallery. Visitors included *Picasso, Ford Madox *Ford, and Ernest *Hemingway. Her friend, secretary, and companion from 1907 was San Francisco-born Alice B. Toklas (1877–1967), whom she made the ostensible author of her own memoir, *The Autobiography of Alice B. Toklas* (1933). Her fiction includes *Three Lives* (1909), of which the second portrait, 'Melanctha', was described by Richard *Wright as 'the first long serious literary treatment of Negro life in the United States'; *The Making of Americans* (written 1906–8; pub. 1925), an enormously long work intended as a history of her family; and *A Long Gay Book* (1932). *Tender Buttons* (1914) presents lexical experiments and an attempt at Cubist prose. Her characteristic repetitions and reprises, her flowing, unpunctuated prose, and her attempts to capture the 'living moment' owe much to William James and to Henri *Bergson's concept of time, and represent a highly personal but nevertheless influential version of the *stream-of-consciousness technique. She produced a series of prose portraits like *Picasso* (1938) and in the 1930s she became particularly interested in film, in which she found analogies for her own prose methods. Her many varied published works include essays, sketches of life in France, works of literary theory, short stories, portraits of her friends, a lyric drama called *Four Saints in Three Acts*, and *Wars I Have Seen* (1945), a personal account of occupied Paris. See James R. Mellow, *Charmed Circle* (1974); Janet Hobhouse, *Everybody Who Was Anybody* (1975); Janet Malcolm, *Two Lives: Gertrude and Alice* (2007).

STEINBECK, John (1902–68) American novelist, born in California. He took his native state as the background for his early short stories and novels and described the lives of those working on the land. *Tortilla Flat* (1935) was his first success, and he confirmed his growing reputation with two novels about landless rural workers, *In Dubious Battle* (1936) and *Of Mice and Men* (1937), the story of two itinerant farm labourers, one of huge strength and weak mind, exploited and protected by the other. His best-known work, *The Grapes of Wrath* (1939), is an epic account of the efforts of an emigrant farming family from the dust bowl of Oklahoma to reach the 'promised land' of California. Among his later novels are *East of Eden* (1952), a family saga, and *The Winter of our Discontent* (1961). His screenplays include *The Forgotten Village* (1941), a documentary, and *Viva Zapata!* (1952). *America and Americans* (2003) collects important non-fiction. He was awarded the *Nobel Prize in 1962. See Jackson J. Benson, *The True Adventures of John Steinbeck, Writer* (1984).

STEINER, George (Francis George Steiner) (1929–) American critic and author, born in Paris of émigré Austrian parents who took him to the USA in 1940, and educated at the Sorbonne, the University of Chicago, Harvard, and Oxford. He has held many academic positions including founding fellow of Churchill College, Cambridge (1961) and professor of English and comparative literature at the University of Geneva (1974–94). His critical works include *Tolstoy or Dostoevsky* (1959); *The Death of Tragedy* (1961); *Language and Silence* (1967); *In Bluebeard's Castle* (1971); and *After Babel: Aspects of Language and Translation* (1975). Steiner's criticism is wide-ranging and multilingual in its references and controversial in its content: one of his recurrent themes is the way in which the 20th-century experiences of the Holocaust, world wars, and totalitarianism have destroyed the assumption that literature is a humanizing influence. The Holocaust is also the subject of his novella *The Portage to San Cristobal of A.H.* (1979), which puts into the mouth of Hitler (who is supposed to have survived the war) the argument that the Jews (through monotheism, Christianity, and Marxism) had provoked their own destruction by offering 'the blackmail of transcendence…the virus of Utopia'. Other works include *Real Presences* (1989), a response to *deconstruction, and *Proofs and Three Parables* (fiction, 1992). *Errata: An Examined Life* (1997) is a memoir, *Lessons of the Masters* (2003) a study of mentors and protégés.

Stella (1) The chaste lady, based on Penelope *Rich, loved by Astrophel in Philip *Sidney's sonnet sequence **Astrophel and Stella*; (2) Jonathan *Swift's name for Esther Johnson, employed particularly in his *Journal to Stella*.

STENDHAL (1783–1842) Pseudonym of Henri Beyle, French novelist, who spent his early years in his native Grenoble and later lived for long periods in Italy. He is best known for two masterpieces: *Le Rouge et le noir* (1830: *The Red and the Black*), which follows the rise and fall of the young provincial Julien Sorel in the France of the Restoration (1814–30); and *La Chartreuse de Parme* (1839: *The Charterhouse of Parma*), which chronicles the fortunes of Fabrice del Dongo at a small Italian court during the same period. First translated into English at the turn of the 20th century, these novels are remarkable for their political dimension, for the detail and variety of the experience portrayed, for the dynamism of the principal characters, and for their penetrating psychological analysis. Stendhal also wrote studies of music, art history (*Histoire de la* *peinture en Italie*, 1817: *History of Italian Painting*), travel books (*Rome, Naples et Florence en 1817*, 1817), and much occasional journalism. *De l'amour* (1822: *On Love*) considers love both psychologically and in relation to historical and social conditions. He championed his own version of Romanticism in *Racine et Shakespeare* (1823–5). Of his other fictional works, *Armance* (1827) and *L'Abbesse de Castro* (1839) appeared during his lifetime; the unfinished *Lucien Leuwen* (1834–6) and the fragmentary *Lamiel* (*c*.1839) were published posthumously, as were his autobiographical *Vie de Henri Brulard* (*The Life of Henri Brulard*), covering the years 1801–15, and *Souvenirs d'égotisme* (*Memoirs of an Egotist*), covering the years 1822–30. See J. Keates, *Stendhal* (1994).

STEPHEN, Sir James Fitzjames (1829–94) Lawyer and journalist, son of Sir James Stephen (1789–1859) and brother of Leslie *Stephen, a barrister, legal member of council in India (1869–72), and high court judge (1879–91). In 1861 he was counsel for Rowland Williams in the **Essays and Reviews* case. He was a member of the *Apostles and the *Metaphysical Society and contributed vigorous articles on social and literary subjects to periodicals including the **Saturday Review*, where he was particularly influential, **Fraser's Magazine* and the **Cornhill Magazine*; he was chief writer for the **Pall Mall Gazette* for five years. Among his works were *A History of the Criminal Law in England* (1883), *Horae Sabbaticae* (1892, collected articles from the *Saturday Review*), and *Liberty, Equality, Fraternity* (1873; repub. 1967) in which he criticized John Stuart *Mill's utilitarian position in his essay *On Liberty*. There is a life by Leslie Stephen; see also K. J. M. Smith, *James Fitzjames Stephen: Portrait of a Victorian Rationalist* (1988).

STEPHEN, James Kenneth (1859–92) Barrister, journalist, and poet, younger son of Sir James Fitzjames *Stephen and cousin of Virginia *Woolf, educated at Eton College and King's College, Cambridge. He was called to the bar but devoted most of his time to journalism and in 1888 began a weekly paper called *The Reflector*, chiefly written by himself. He was author (as 'J.K.S.') of highly successful parodies and light verse, collected as *Lapsus Calami* and *Quo Musa Tendis* (both 1891). His promising career ended as a result of an accident in 1886 which slowly drove him insane, and he has been implausibly suggested as a candidate for the role of *Jack the Ripper. See M. Harrison, *Clarence* (1972).

STEPHEN, Sir Leslie (1832–1904) Biographer and critic. Son of Sir James Stephen (1789–1859) and brother of Sir James Fitzjames *Stephen, he was born in Kensington Gore, London, and educated at Eton College and Trinity Hall, Cambridge, where he became tutor, having taken orders. From his family he inherited a strong tradition of evangelicalism and muscular Christianity, and he became a noted mountaineer: he edited the *Alpine Journal*, 1868–72, and the best of his Alpine essays were collected in 1871 as *The Playground of Europe*. Stephen's reading of John Stuart *Mill, *Comte, and *Kant inclined him to scepticism, and he was increasingly influenced by Darwinism; by 1864, having abandoned his religious vocation, he had embarked on a literary career of prodigious industry and output, contributing articles to many periodicals. In 1871 he became editor of the **Cornhill Magazine*, a post he held until 1882 when he undertook the editorship of the **Dictionary of National Biography* (*DNB*). During these years he published several volumes, some defining his position as an agnostic; his great work, *History of English Thought in the 18th Century* (1876), reviews the Deist controversy of that age, and the intuitional and utilitarian schools of philosophy. He also contributed several biographies to the English Men of Letters series, including lives of Samuel *Johnson (1878), Alexander *Pope (1880), and Jonathan *Swift (1882), despite the amount of time consumed by the vast undertaking of the *DNB*, to which he himself contributed almost 400 entries, and from which strain and ill health forced him to resign in 1891. His last important volume was *English Literature and Society in the Eighteenth Century* (1904). Stephen's first wife was W. M. *Thackeray's daughter 'Minny', who died in 1875. He then married Julia Duckworth, with whom he had four children, including Virginia *Woolf; after Julia's death in 1895, he wrote *The Mausoleum Book*, ostensibly as a record of their mother for his children and stepchildren, but it is also a form of autobiography. Woolf portrays some aspects of her conflictual relationship with her father in her portrait of Mr Ramsay in **To the Lighthouse* (1927). See also Noël Annan, *Leslie Stephen: His Thought and Character in Relation to his Time* (1951; rev. 1984).

STEPHENS, James (1880/82–1950) Irish poet and story writer, born in Dublin and raised in a Protestant orphanage. The prose fantasy *The Crock of Gold* (1912) and many of his best-known poems share a whimsical quality that is less than entirely characteristic. The sharp proletarian portraiture of *Insurrections* (1909), Stephens's first collection of poems, and the angry, grotesque variations on *Ó Bruadair and other Gaelic poets in *Reincarnations* (1918) have their counterparts in the psychological realism and concern for social privation that offset the fairy-tale extravagance of his novels *The Charwoman's Daughter* (1912) and *The Demi-Gods* (1914). *The Insurrection in Dublin* (1916) offers a vivid first-hand account of the Easter Rising. Stephens lived in later life in England, where he became a widely known broadcaster.

STEPHENSON, Neal (1959–) American *science fiction writer, born in Fort Meade, Maryland. Novels such as *Snow Crash* (1992) and *The Diamond Age* (1995) developed *cyberpunk preoccupations with the social effects of computers and nanotechnology. *Cryptonomicon* (1999) explored the history of computing; much of it is set during the Second World War, with Alan Turing (1912–54) at the Bletchley Park code-breaking centre a major character. *Quicksilver* (2003) speculates about 17th-century systems of knowledge, and is as much *historical novel as science fiction.

STERLING, Bruce (1954–) American author and journalist, born in Brownsville, Texas; instrumental in defining and promoting *cyberpunk. With William *Gibson, he co-wrote *The Difference Engine* (1990); elsewhere he explores our futures. Climate change and longevity are the themes of *Heavy Weather* (1994) and *Holy Fire* (1996).

STERLING, John (1806–44) Writer, born on the Isle of Bute and educated at Trinity College and Trinity Hall, Cambridge, a leading member of the *Apostles and a disciple of S. T. *Coleridge. With F. D. *Maurice he was briefly proprietor of the **Athenaeum* (1828). Sterling owes his fame to his friend Thomas *Carlyle, whose vivid *Life of Sterling* (1851) reveals the tragic history of Sterling's life, dogged by persistent ill health. His monthly meetings of literary friends, from 1838, became known as the Sterling Club; among its members were Carlyle, Julius *Hare, John Stuart *Mill, and Alfred *Tennyson. He contributed to various periodicals, and among his published works were a novel, *Arthur Coningsby* (1833), *Poems* (1839), and *Essays and Tales* (1848). They were collected and edited with a memoir by Hare, to whom with Carlyle his papers were entrusted.

STERNE, Laurence (1713–68) Novelist, the son of an impoverished infantry officer. He spent his early childhood in various barracks in Ireland and England, where he developed the affection for military men evident in his writings. He was sent, on a scholarship founded by his great-grandfather Richard Sterne (1596/7–1683), archbishop of York, to Jesus College, Cambridge, where he met John *Hall-Stevenson. He took holy orders and in 1738 obtained the living of the Yorkshire parish of Sutton-on-the-Forest. In 1741 he became a prebendary of York Cathedral, and married Elizabeth Lumley, a cousin of Elizabeth *Montagu, who described her as possessed of many virtues which however 'stand like quills upon the fretful porcupine'. They had one surviving daughter, Lydia, who edited Sterne's letters and sermons after his death. Sterne earned a good reputation as a country pastor and preached many sermons at York Minster, and in 1744 he added the living of Stillington to that of Sutton. He played the violin, read widely, painted, and led a very sociable life. In 1759, in the course of an ecclesiastical quarrel, he wrote *A Political Romance* (later entitled *The History of a Good Warm Watch Coat*), a satire offensive enough to be suppressed by the authorities. In the same year he began **Tristram Shandy*. The first version of vols i and ii was rejected by the London publisher Robert *Dodsley. The next version of vols i and ii, 'written under the greatest heaviness of heart', caused by deaths and illness in the family, was published in York in 1759, with Dodsley agreeing to take half the printing for sale in London. Early in 1760 Sterne found himself famous. He went to London and (although his book was not liked by Samuel *Johnson, Oliver *Goldsmith, and Samuel *Richardson, who disapproved of its 'odd' manner and tolerant moral stance) he was fêted by society, had his portrait painted by Sir Joshua *Reynolds, and was invited to court. In the same year he was presented with a third Yorkshire living, that of Coxwold, where he settled himself into 'Shandy Hall'. He published *The Sermons of Mr Yorick*, a volume whose title was taken by some as an insult to his profession, and continued with *Tristram Shandy*, four further volumes of which appeared in 1761. Sterne had contracted tuberculosis at college and his health now deteriorated steadily. In 1762 his voice was badly affected, and in the hope of improvement he and his wife and daughter left for France, where they lived at Toulouse and Montpellier until 1764, when Sterne returned alone to England to publish vols vii and viii of *Tristram Shandy* (1765). He returned to France, visited his wife and daughter, and undertook an eight-month tour of France and Italy, which provided him with material for *A *Sentimental Journey through France and Italy*. In 1766 appeared two further volumes of sermons. The ninth and last volume of *Tristram Shandy* appeared, under pressure of fading health, in 1767. In the same year Sterne met Elizabeth Draper (1744–78), the young wife of an official of the East India Company, and after her enforced departure for India began his *Journal to *Eliza*. He finished and published *A Sentimental Journey* in the same year, but his health collapsed and he died in London in March 1768. His epitaph was written by David *Garrick. His body was stolen by grave-robbers, and is said to have been recognized at an anatomy lecture in Cambridge, and secretly reburied; a skull believed to be that of Sterne was recovered in 1969 and buried in Coxwold.

Sterne's work has some links with the *Renaissance tradition of 'learned fooling' and the unflinching self-examination of essayists such as *Montaigne. His attention to the nuances and misunderstandings of mental processes makes him a progenitor of the *stream-of-consciousness novel, albeit in comic guise. He acknowledges in *Tristram Shandy* his own debt in this respect to John *Locke, whose **Essay Concerning Human Understanding* seemed to Sterne 'a history-book…of what passes in man's own mind'. Throughout his work he plays with the developing conventions of the still-new 'novel', and its problems in presenting in language the realities of consciousness, space, and time. His lively conversations with imaginary readers and bizarre experiments with typographic conventions have made him a popular object of study among theorists of narrative. The standard life is by A. H. Cash, *Laurence Sterne: The Early and Middle Years* (1975) and *Laurence Sterne: The Later Years* (1986). See also *The Florida Edition of the Works of Laurence Sterne*, ed. M. New and others (6 vols to date, 1978–).

STERNHOLD, Thomas (d. 1549) and **HOPKINS, John** (1520/1–1570) Joint versifiers of the *Psalms. A collection of 44 metrical Psalms appeared in 1549; music was first supplied in the Geneva edition of 1556, and by 1640 about 300 editions had been published. In 1562 *The Whole Book of Psalms*, by Sternhold, Hopkins, Thomas Norton (1530/32–1584), and others, was added to the Prayer Book. John *Dryden ridiculed this version in **Absalom and Achitophel* (II. 403), and it provoked *Rochester's epigram 'Spoken Extempore to a Country Clerk after Having Heard Him Sing Psalms':

Sternhold and Hopkins had great qualms
When they translated David's psalms
To make the heart full glad;
But had it been poor David's fate
To hear thee sing, and them translate,
By God! 'twould have made him mad.

STEVENS, Wallace (1879–1955) Major American poet, born in Pennsylvania and educated at Harvard, where he met George *Santayana. He became a lawyer, and from 1916 worked at Hartford, Connecticut, on the legal staff of the Hartford Accident and Indemnity Company, where he remained until his death, becoming vice-president in 1934. Meanwhile, he had begun to publish poems in **Poetry* and elsewhere, and his first volume, *Harmonium*, which contains 'Thirteen Ways of Looking at a Blackbird', was published in 1923. This was followed by other collections, including *Ideas of Order* (1935) and *Notes towards a Supreme Fiction* (1942). The 'supreme fiction' in the latter denotes a satisfactory conceptualization of reality, more often an aim in his poetry rather than an achieved end. His enigmatic, elegant, intellectual, and occasionally startling meditations on order and the imagination and on the function of poetry can also be seen in his volume of essays *The Necessary Angel* (1951). Stevens also wrote several plays and explored the relation between poetry and painting in his writing; he was himself an art collector. See Joan Richardson, *Wallace Stevens*, 2 vols (1986, 1988).

STEVENSON, Anne (1933–) Poet, critic, and biographer, born in Cambridge of American parents and educated in America; she settled in Britain in the 1960s and has lived partly in Wales. Her collections include *Living in America* (1965), *Correspondences* (1973), which is a historical and contemporary saga of a New England family written in letters, prose, and verse, and perhaps her most admired work, *The Fiction Makers* (1985), *The Other House* (1990), and *A Report from the Border* (2003). *Poems 1955–2005* was published in 2005. Many of Stevenson's poems celebrate the landscapes and cultures of her two nations, and their interconnections: her tone is at times conversational, at times lyrical, at times wry. Her controversial biography of Sylvia *Plath, *Bitter Fame*, appeared in 1989, and her critical writing includes *Five Looks at Elizabeth Bishop* (1998), who is an important influence (*see* BISHOP, ELIZABETH), and *Between the Iceberg and the Ship: Selected Essays* (1998).

STEVENSON, Robert Louis (originally Lewis) (1850–94) Scottish novelist, essayist, and poet, born in Edinburgh and educated at Edinburgh University. Poor health and a distaste for office work led Stevenson to spurn the profession of lighthouse engineer in which his father and grandfather had won distinction. He qualified as a lawyer, but had already begun publishing essays in the **Cornhill Magazine* and elsewhere when admitted advocate in 1875. In the same year he became friends with W. E. *Henley, with whom he collaborated on four plays, performed with little success 1880–5. Stevenson suffered from a chronic bronchial condition (possibly bronchiectasis), and much of life was spent going from country to country in search of health; travelling in due course emerged as a defining trope of his writing. In France in 1876 he met Mrs Fanny Osbourne, ten years his senior, recording his feelings for her in the essay 'On Falling in Love' (1877). *An Inland Voyage*, an account of a canoe expedition in Belgium and France, appeared in 1878. The following year, after the publication of *Travels with a Donkey in the Cevennes*, he set off for California by emigrant ship and train in response to a telegram from Fanny, whom he married in March 1880, four months after her divorce. The couple stayed at an abandoned mine in Calistoga, as described in *The Silverado Squatters* (1883), before returning to Europe and settling for three years in Bournemouth, where Stevenson consolidated a friendship with Henry *James. By this time many of his miscellaneously published stories, essays, and travel pieces had been collected in volume form (*Virginibus Puerisque*, 1881; *Familiar Studies of Men and Books*, 1882; *New Arabian Nights*, 1882). His first full-length work of fiction, **Treasure Island*, begun on holiday in Braemar in Scotland and issued in book form in 1883, brought him fame, which increased with the publication of *The Strange Case of *Dr Jekyll and Mr Hyde* (1886). This was followed by two novels with Scottish settings, **Kidnapped* (1886), a bravura recasting of the historical novel as coming-of-age romance, and *The *Master of Ballantrae* (1889), at once a tale of high adventure and an acute analysis of sibling rivalry.

In 1888 Stevenson set out from San Francisco with his family entourage for the South Seas, where he was greeted as a celebrity. His visit to the leper colony at Molokai inspired *Father Damien: An Open Letter* (1890), his indignant defence of the Catholic 'Apostle of the Lepers' against the criticisms of C. M. Hyde, a Presbyterian clergyman based in Honolulu. He settled in Samoa at Vailima, where he temporarily regained his health, and became known as 'Tusitala' or 'The Story Teller'. He died there from a brain haemorrhage while working on **Weir of Hermiston* (1896), even in its fragmentary, unfinished state the most richly orchestrated of his four Scottish novels. (*Catriona*, a sequel to *Kidnapped*, had appeared in 1893.)

Other books by Stevenson include *The Merry Men* (1887, which collected the supernatural *Scots tale 'Thrawn Janet', the *Gothic pastiche 'Olalla', and four other stories); *The Black Arrow* (1888), a historical romance; *Island Nights' Entertainments* (1893); and *St Ives* (1897, unfinished, completed by Sir Arthur *Quiller-Couch), an episodic novel of the Napoleonic Wars. With his stepson Lloyd Osbourne he wrote the mischievous comedy *The Wrong Box* (1889) and *The Wrecker* (1892). *The Ebb-Tide* (1894), first drafted with Osbourne but comprehensively rewritten by Stevenson, vividly exposes European imperial corruption in the South Pacific, a concern also of 'The Beach of Falesá' (1893). He published three volumes of poetry, *A Child's Garden of Verses* (1885), a classic of children's literature; *Underwoods* (1887), a collection of *lyrics in English and Scots and of *ballads in English; and *Songs of Travel* (1896), which celebrates the Pacific and pines for Scotland with equal plangency. The poetry shares the combination of surface delicacy with subterranean disturbance that characterizes Stevenson's fiction. The theme of dualism recurs in his work, as does a fascination with morally ambiguous heroes or anti-heroes. The concern with patrimony implicit in *Treasure Island* and *Kidnapped* emerges with full thematic force in the fierce father–son conflict of *Weir of Hermiston*. Stevenson's wide popularity has occluded the slow but inexorable growth of his critical reputation; his heavyweight admirers have included not only his friend James, but G. M. *Hopkins, *Nabokov,

*Borges, and Graham *Greene (a distant relative). There are lives by Jenni Calder (1980) and Ian Bell (1993). See *The Letters of Robert Louis Stevenson*, ed. B. A. Booth and E. Mehew, 8 vols (1994–5).

STEWART, Dugald (1753–1828) Scottish philosopher, born in Edinburgh and educated at Edinburgh and Glasgow universities, where he was taught by Hugh *Blair and Thomas Reid (1710–96) respectively. Appointed professor of mathematics at Edinburgh in 1775, he moved to the chair of moral philosophy in 1785. Much of his impact on Scottish intellectual life came through his innovative and inspirational teaching. His lectures on political economy, eagerly attended by the young Whigs who founded the **Edinburgh Review*, owed much to Adam *Smith. A debt to Reid is evident in Stewart's most significant work, *Elements of the Philosophy of the Human Mind* (1792, 1814, 1827). His lives of Smith, the historian and Edinburgh University principal William Robertson (1721–93), and Reid in *Biographical Memoirs* (1810) ponder the origins and nature of what we now know as the *Scottish Enlightenment. Stewart befriended Robert *Burns in 1786–9 but later came to disapprove of his lifestyle.

STEWART, George Rippey (1895–1980) American *science fiction author and academic, born in Sewickley, Pennsylvania. *Earth Abides* (1949), an elegiac chronicle of the attempts of a few survivors of a worldwide plague to rebuild civilization, set mostly in California, is an exceptionally influential novel.

STEWART, J. I. M. (John Innes Mackintosh) (1906–94) Novelist and critic, born in Edinburgh and educated at the Edinburgh Academy and Oriel College, Oxford. After lecturing in English literature at the universities of Leeds and Adelaide and the Queen's University of Belfast, he became a student (i.e. a fellow) of Christ Church, Oxford, in 1949 and remained there for over twenty years. Under the pseudonym Michael Innes he wrote donnish *detective fiction, rich in literary allusions and quotations, featuring Inspector John Appleby. Published over a 50-year period, the Appleby books include *Death at the President's Lodging* (1936), *Hamlet, Revenge!* (1937), *Appleby on Ararat* (1941), *The Long Farewell* (1958), *Appleby at Allington* (1968), *Appleby's Answer* (1973), and *Appleby and the Ospreys* (1986). Under his own name he wrote literary criticism and a quintet of novels (1974–8) about life in Oxford with the collective title *A Staircase in Surrey*.

stichomythia In classical Greek drama, dialogue in alternate lines of verse, employed in sharp disputation. The form is sometimes imitated in English drama, e.g. in the dialogue between Richard III and Elizabeth in *Shakespeare's **Richard III* (IV. iv).

STINE, R. L. (Robert Lawrence) (1943–) American writer born in Columbus, Ohio, educated at Ohio State University, known for his Point Horror, Goosebumps, and Fear Street series popular with young people during the 1990s. His *young adult novels are occasionally frightening, but his work often borders on pastiche.

Stoicism A system of thought which originated in Athens during the 3rd century BC, flourished in Rome *c.*100 BC–*c.* AD 200, and enjoyed a vigorous revival at the time of the Renaissance. The Stoics' prime concern was ethics, but they held that right behaviour must be grounded on a general understanding of the universe, and their theories extended to cover the nature of the physical world, logic, rhetoric, epistemology, and politics. The founders, notably Zeno of Citium (*c.*334–*c.*262 BC) and Chrysippus of Soli (*c.*280–*c.*207 BC), held that 'virtue' or excellence was the only good, and that 'virtue' consisted in following reason, unaffected by the passions, passions being caused by false judgements. Echoing *Socrates, they said that ordinary 'goods' such as health or money were merely 'preferred', not good. Only fragments of these founders remain; the Stoics whose writings survive whole are those who lived under the Roman Empire, especially *Seneca, *Epictetus, and *Marcus Aurelius. The development of Christian thinking is often closely involved with Stoic ideas. *Petrarch in the 14th century expounded a Christian Stoicism in his *De Remediis Fortunae*, and in the 16th century a manufactured version of Marcus Aurelius' ideas, *Libro Aureo del Emperador Marco Aurelio* (translated into French and English in the 1530s, well before the *Meditations* became widely available, by Antonio de Guevara (*c.*1480–1545)) may have served to promote the Stoic revival ('neo-Stoicism') which came at the end of the century with *Montaigne's *Essais* (1580) and *Lipsius' *De Constantia* (1585). In England the years 1595–1615 saw translations of Lipsius, Montaigne, his disciple Charron (1541–1603), Epictetus, and Seneca, and the influence of Stoicism can be traced in a great number of writers from George *Chapman and Ben *Jonson to the third earl of *Shaftesbury and Francis *Hutcheson. See Brad Inwood (ed.), *The Cambridge Companion to the Stoics* (2003).

STOKER, Bram (Abraham) (1847–1912) Writer, born in Dublin and educated at Trinity College, Dublin. He gave up his career as a civil servant in 1878 to become Sir Henry *Irving's secretary and business manager for the next 27 years, an experience that produced his two-volume tribute, *Personal Reminiscences of Henry Irving* (1906). Stoker wrote a number of adventure novels and short stories, as well as some dramatic criticism, but is chiefly remembered for his vampire novel **Dracula* (1897), influenced by 'Carmilla', one of the tales in Sheridan Le Fanu's **In a Glass Darkly* (1872).

STONE, Robert (1937–) American novelist, born in New York, whose second novel, *Dog Soldiers* (1974), dealt with drug-smuggling in Vietnam. *A Flag for Sunrise* (1981) describes the politics of a small Central American republic. *Prime Green* (2007) is a memoir of the 1960s counter-culture.

Stones of Venice, The By John *Ruskin, published in three volumes, the first in 1851, the second and third in 1853. A study of the architecture of Venice, it combines extensive and painstaking scholarship with an eloquent account of the moral, political, and religious significance of the city's rise and fall. Its impact on contemporary readers was profound and lasting, and the work confirmed Ruskin's reputation as one of the leading cultural critics of his generation. Ruskin's celebration of *Byzantine and *Gothic architecture had a widespread influence on Victorian architects, and Venetian designs, combined with new uses of colour derived from the architecture of Venice and Verona, became prominent features of mid-19th-century building.

The first volume sets out first principles for discrimination between good and bad architecture, followed, in the second and third volumes, with a cultural and architectural history of the city. Ruskin describes the rise of medieval Venice, whose power he attributes to creativity, discipline, and religious faith, and its subsequent decline into what Ruskin saw as the pride, infidelity, and hedonism of the Renaissance. Ruskin's *Protestant and conservative sympathies shape this analysis, for the book was written when his suspicion of Roman *Catholicism was at its height, and one of the things he admired about the early history of Venice was the city's long-standing resistance to the authority of Rome. The famous chapter 'The Nature of Gothic' contrasts the imaginative freedom possible for the workmen who constructed the great Gothic buildings of Venice with the rigid confinement resulting from the division of labour and mechanical mass production in English manufacturing industries of the 19th century. William *Morris described it as 'one of the very few necessary and inevitable utterances of the century' in his preface to the Kelmscott edition (1892), and its passionate plea for the liberty of the workman still carries weight.

STOPPARD, Sir Tom (1937–) OM, CBE, dramatist, born in Czechoslovakia; he eventually settled in England after the war. He worked as a journalist before his play **Rosencrantz and Guildenstern Are Dead* (1966) created an overnight sensation. It was followed by many witty and inventive plays, including *The Real Inspector Hound* (1968, a play-within-a-play that parodies the conventions of the stage thriller); **Jumpers* (1972); **Travesties* (1974); *Dirty Linen* (1976, a satire of political life and parliamentary misdemeanours); *Every Good Boy Deserves Favour* (1977, about a political dissident in a Soviet psychiatric hospital); *Night and Day* (1978, about the dangers of the 'closed shop' in journalism); *The Real Thing* (1982, a marital tragicomedy); *Arcadia* (1993, with a parallel setting in the present day and in 1809); and *Indian Ink* (1995, an exploration of cultural identity). *The Invention of Love* (1997) presents, through the contrasted fates of A. E. *Housman and Oscar *Wilde, the sexual complexities of the *Aesthetic movement, and the conflicts between art and scholarship. Stoppard has also written many works for film, radio, and television, including *Professional Foul* (TV, 1977), set in Prague, which portrays the concurrent visits of an English philosopher and an English football team, and dramatizes the inner conflicts of the philosopher, caught between the abstractions of his own discipline and the realities of a regime which stifles free intellectual exchange. Stoppard's work displays a metaphysical wit, a strong theatrical sense, and a talent for pastiche which enables him to move from mode to mode within the same scene with great flexibility and rapidity; yet the plays appear far from frivolous in intention, posing (though not always choosing to solve) ethical challenges. *The Coast of Utopia* (2002), a trilogy about political radicalism in Russia, was received better in the USA than in Britain. His sympathy for, and work on behalf of, dissident voices stifled in the Soviet Empire is evident in much of his work, and his *Rock 'n' Roll* (2006) looked at the dual history of his homeland, Czechoslovakia, from the Prague Spring of 1968 to the Velvet Revolution, and that of the British left seen from a right-wing perspective.

STOREY, David Malcolm (1933–) Novelist and playwright, born in Wakefield, the third son of a miner; he was educated at the Queen Elizabeth Grammar School, Wakefield, and at the Slade School of Fine Art. He worked as professional footballer, teacher, farm worker, and erector of show tents, acquiring a variety of experience which is evident in his works. His first novel, *This Sporting Life* (1960), describes the ambitions and passions of a young working man, Arthur Machin, a Rugby League player who becomes emotionally involved with his landlady. This was followed by *Flight into Camden* (1960), about the unhappy affair of a miner's daughter with a married teacher, and the highly ambitious *Radcliffe* (1963), a sombre, violent, Lawrentian novel about class conflict, the Puritan legacy, and destructive homosexual passion. Later novels include *Pasmore* (1972, an account of a young lecturer in a state of mental breakdown) and *Saville* (1976, *Booker Prize), an epic set in a south Yorkshire mining village. Meanwhile Storey had also established himself as a playwright, with such works as *In Celebration* (1969), a play in which three educated sons return north to visit their miner father; *The Contractor* (1970), which presents the audience with the construction, then the dismantling, of a wedding marquee, a spectacle which forms the background for the presentation of the relationship of the contractor Ewbank (who had appeared in *Radcliffe*) with his university-educated son; *Home* (1970), set in a mental home; *The Changing Room* (1971), again using Rugby League as a setting; *Life Class* (1974), set in an art college; and *Mother's Day* (1976), a violent black comedy set on a housing estate. Action, in Storey's plays, tends to be offstage, obliquely presented through low-key, episodic encounters in a realistic setting; both plays and novels show a preoccupation with social mobility and the disturbance it frequently appears to cause, and combine documentary naturalism with the symbolic and unspoken. Later works include the plays *Sister* (1978), *Early Days* (1980), and *The March on Russia* (1989) and the novels *A Prodigal Child* (1982) and *Present Times* (1984). A collection of poems, *Storey's Lives: Poems 1951–1991*, appeared in 1992.

STORR, Catherine (1913–2001) Children's writer and psychiatrist, born in Kensington, London, educated at St Paul's Girls' School and Newnham College, Cambridge. Her stories display her understanding of the juvenile psyche as in *Marianne Dreams* (1958, filmed as *Paper House*, 1988; Storr also wrote it as an opera libretto) in which two ill, prepubescent children meet in a dreamscape where, by overcoming various threats and anxieties, they heal each other. Her stories strike a balance between fear and reassurance, reality and fantasy; the popular tales about Clever Polly, beginning with *Clever Polly and the Stupid Wolf* (1955), have an everyday setting into which the wolf from fairy-tales regularly intrudes and tries to capture and eat Polly. Time and again Polly outwits him, making her a strong girl character at a time when these were rare in children's books; such girls appear regularly in Storr's writing.

Story of An African Farm, The A novel by the South African writer Olive *Schreiner, published in two volumes in 1883, at first under the pseudonym 'Ralph Iron'. It was largely completed before Schreiner left Africa for England in 1881, and it is set in the landscape of the Karoo, where she had spent her childhood. It tells the stories of two orphaned cousins, stay-at-home Em and unconventional Lyndall, who was greeted by feminists as one of the first *'New Women'. Lyndall rejects her early religious training, becomes pregnant by a lover whom she refuses to marry, and dies, exhausted, after the death of her baby. She is devotedly tended in her final illness by the English farmer Gregory Rose, who disguises himself as a woman in order to act as a nurse. Gregory later proposes marriage to Em, and is accepted. The novel also describes the intellectual and spiritual development of the sceptic Waldo, son of the farm's German overseer, whose rebellious spirit is aroused (as was Schreiner's) by reading Herbert *Spencer's *First Principles*. Passionate, uncompromising, and enterprising, the book was much admired in progressive circles, and gave Schreiner access to the leading literary and intellectual society of London.

Story of Rimini, The A poem by Leigh *Hunt, published 1816 and in a heavily revised version in 1844. The work is based on *Dante's story of Paolo and Francesca. On a fine May morning Francesca leaves Ravenna as a bride, and journeys in moonlight to Rimini. The events which overtake her, and the feelings which arise, lead to her adulterous love for Paolo. The lovers are discovered, and their deaths conclude the poem. The work, with its flexible couplets, its use of both common speech and new words, and its luxuriant southern imagery, suggested new possibilities to the younger Romantic poets. **Blackwood's Magazine*, in attacking 'the Cockney School', derided Hunt's 'glittering and rancid obscenities'.

STOW, John (1524/5–1605) Chronicler and antiquary. Born in London, in 1547 he was admitted a freeman of the Merchant Taylors' Company. At first Stow's interest was English poetry; then from about 1564 he began to collect and transcribe manuscripts and to compose historical works, the first to be based on systematic study of public records. He was suspected of recusancy (i.e. evading the legal obligation to attend the *Church of England), and in 1569 and 1570 was accused of possessing popish and dangerous writings; the charge was dropped. He is said to have spent as much as £200 a year on books and manuscripts; he was patronized by the earl of *Leicester and from 1579 received a pension from the Merchant Taylors. A fine effigy of Stow, based on one erected by his wife, survives in the church of St Andrew Undershaft, Leadenhall Street, London.

As well as assisting Matthew *Parker with editing historical texts, his chief publications were: editions of the works of *Chaucer (1561; further notes were subsequently printed by T. Speght (d. 1631) in 1598) and of John *Skelton (1568); *Summary of English Chronicles* (1565), an original historical work; *The Chronicles of England* (1580), later entitled *The Annals of England* (1592); the second edition of Raphael *Holinshed's *Chronicles* (1585–7); and lastly *A Survey of London* (1598 and 1603), invaluable for the detailed information it gives about the ancient city and its customs. It was brought down to his day by John *Strype in 1720, and modernized and annotated editions have since been published. The fullest edition of the original work was C. L. Kingsford's of 1908.

STOW, Randolph (1935–) Australian novelist and poet, born in Geraldton, Western Australia, resident in England since 1966. Stow's first book, *Act One: Poems* (1957), received the Gold Medal of the Australian Literature Society, while his best known is the semi-autobiographical *The Merry-Go-Round in the Sea* (1965). *To the Islands* (1958), *Tourmaline* (1963), and *Visitants* (1979) are complex, innovative novels which respond to dilemmas of spirituality and colonial relations, particularly in Australia and its near north.

STOWE, Harriet Beecher (1811–96) Née Beecher, born in Connecticut, sister of Henry Ward Beecher (1813–87, divine, religious author, and journalist). She was a schoolteacher in Cincinnati before marrying in 1836 Calvin Stowe, a professor at her father's theological seminary. Her anti-slavery novel **Uncle Tom's Cabin*, was her first book; it was serialized in the *National Era* in 1851–2 and published as a volume in 1852, had a sensational success, and stirred up great public feeling. A powerful tale, it describes the sufferings of pious Uncle Tom, who is sold by his well-intentioned Kentucky owner, Mr Shelby, to meet his debts. He is taken first to a New Orleans household and eventually beaten to death by a brutal cotton plantation owner. This action is counterpointed against a parallel plot describing the escape to freedom in Canada of Shelby's slave Eliza, her child, and her husband George. Stowe's stress on the anguish of parted families formed part of the novel's overt polemic, although this was offset by generalizations applying the period's race theory. The phrase 'Uncle Tom' came to indicate a supine collaboration with the oppressor. *A Key to Uncle Tom's Cabin* (1853) documents many of Stowe's sources for the novel. The latter's success brought Stowe to England in 1853, 1856, and 1859, where she was rapturously received, and honoured by Queen *Victoria, although she later alienated

British opinion by her *Lady Byron Vindicated* (1870), in which she charged Lord *Byron with incestuous relations with his half-sister. Her other works include *Dred: A Tale of the Dismal Swamp* (1856), which also deals with slavery; *The Minister's Wooing* (1859), a protest against the doctrines of Calvinism; *Old Town Folks* (1869), set in New England; and *Poganuc People* (1878), another tale of New England family life. See Joan D. Hedrick, *Harriet Beecher Stowe* (1994).

STRACHEY, Lytton (1880–1932) Biographer and essayist, born in London; he was the eleventh child of an eminent soldier and public administrator who had served for more than 30 years in India, and he was named after his godfather, the first earl of *Lytton, viceroy of India. He attended Abbotsholme and Leamington college as a boarder but was mostly educated at home; he studied Latin, Greek, and English literature at Liverpool University and then went on to Trinity College, Cambridge, where he became a member of the *Apostles and a friend of the philosopher George Edward Moore (1873–1958), the economist John Maynard Keynes (1883–1946), and Leonard *Woolf. He was thereafter a prominent member of the *Bloomsbury Group, advocating both in words and life its faith in tolerance in personal relationships: he spent the last sixteen years of his life in a *ménage à trois* with Dora *Carrington and her husband Ralph Partridge. He was also, in the First World War, a conspicuous conscientious objector. After an abortive attempt at an academic career, Strachey began to write extensively for periodicals (including the **Spectator*, the **Edinburgh Review*, the **Nation*, the **Athenaeum*, and, later, *Life and Letters*). His flamboyant *Landmarks in French Literature* appeared in 1912, but he did not achieve fame until 1918, with the publication of **Eminent Victorians*, itself a landmark in the history of *biography. This was a collection of four biographical essays, on Cardinal Manning, Florence *Nightingale, Thomas *Arnold, and General Gordon; Strachey's wit and narrative powers captured a large (though at times hostile) readership; the standard criticism of the work was that Strachey used secondary sources and provided no references. However this important debunking of the moral pretensions of the Victorian age meant, as Edmund *Wilson wrote in 1932, that no one was 'able to feel quite the same about the legends that had dominated their pasts'; he equally brought a new literary inventiveness to the genre of biography. His irreverent but affectionate life of Queen *Victoria (1921), which combined careful construction and telling anecdote, was also highly successful. His last full-length work, *Elizabeth and Essex: A Tragic History* (1928), with its emphasis on *Elizabeth I's relationship with her father and its effect on her treatment of Essex, shows a clear (and early) debt to Sigmund *Freud. Various collections of Strachey's essays, on subjects ranging from *Voltaire to the *Muggletonians, appeared during his life and posthumously. Michael *Holroyd's biography, first published in 1967–8, was revised as *Lytton Strachey: The New Biography* in 1995.

Strafford A tragedy in blank verse by Robert *Browning, published 1837. It was written at the instigation of William *Macready, who produced it at Covent Garden on the day of publication, with himself in the title role. The play received mixed notices and had only a brief run; it has never been professionally revived. Browning's prose life of Strafford (Sir Thomas Wentworth, 1593–1641) was originally written for John *Forster and published in his 'Lives of Eminent British Statesmen' series: the Browning Society reissued it in 1892.

The action deals with the events surrounding the impeachment of Strafford; Browning's interest lies in the interplay of love and loyalty between Strafford and the three other main characters: King Charles I, whose weakness causes Strafford's downfall; John Pym, his closest friend until Strafford joined the Royalist party and 'betrayed' the people; and Lady Carlisle, whose love for him Strafford, blinded by his devotion to the king, does not perceive. As with his other historical works, Browning's speculations about the characters' motives are searching and inventive. The action of the play is not closely related to the actual course of events.

STRAHAN, William (1715–85) Printer, born in Edinburgh, where he served his apprenticeship. He opened his first business in London in 1738, and soon became established in the forefront of his trade, receiving the patent as king's printer in 1770. He was on terms of some intimacy with David *Hume, Benjamin *Franklin, and Samuel *Johnson, whose *Dictionary* he printed, and had friendly business relations with many of the leading writers of the age, including Edward *Gibbon, Adam *Smith, Tobias *Smollett, and Oliver *Goldsmith. He was an MP from 1774 to 1784. Strahan's scrupulously maintained business records are kept in the British Library.

STRANGFORD, Percy Clinton, sixth Viscount (1780–1855) Born and educated in Dublin. He became a successful diplomat and public man. Profiting by his first posting to Lisbon, he published in 1803 *Poems from the Portuguese of Camoens*, which went into many editions. Mocked as 'Hibernian' Strangford by Lord *Byron in **English Bards and Scotch Reviewers* (1809), he was the friend of Thomas *Moore, John Wilson *Croker, Samuel *Rogers, and other literary men, and a contributor to the **Gentleman's Magazine*.

STRAPAROLA, Gianfrancesco (d. 1557) Italian author of *novelle* entitled *Piacevoli Notti* (*Pleasant Nights*), published in two parts, 1550 and 1553. It enjoyed much popularity and introduced various folk tales to European literature, including the stories of 'Puss in Boots' and 'Beauty and the Beast'. William Painter, in his **Palace of Pleasure*, drew on Straparola among others.

STRAUB, Peter (1943–) American author of *horror and dark *fantasy, born in Milwaukee. *Ghost Story* (1979) shows his careful handling of the complexities of the form, which he adapts and updates. *Floating Dragon* (1983) is a supernatural thriller. He collaborated with Stephen *King in *The Talisman* (1984) and *Black House* (2001). *Koko* (1988) won a World Fantasy Award, although the fantasy elements in the novel—about the hunt for the killer of Vietnam War veterans—are muted and subtle.

STRAUSS, David Friedrich (1808–74) German biblical scholar, who studied and taught theology at Tübingen. He resigned his teaching post in 1833. His most famous work, *Das Leben Jesu, kritisch bearbeitet* (1835–6: *The Life of Jesus, Critically Examined*), was a notorious example of German 'Higher Criticism' which scandalized Europe. In it Strauss subjected the Gospel accounts to close historical scrutiny, judging them based on myth rather than fact, and denied the divinity of Jesus. George *Eliot translated the work into English in 1846, and her study of it helped confirm her break with Christianity.

STRAUSS, Richard (1864–1949) German composer, who rose to fame through his symphonic 'tone poems', such as *Also Sprach Zarathustra*, after Friedrich *Nietzsche (1896). Strauss had written incidental music for **Romeo and Juliet* in 1887; a year later he composed the tone poem *Macbeth* (rev. 1891); it was not performed until after the success of *Don Juan*, in 1890. Strauss returned to William *Shakespeare with three Ophelia songs in the *Sechs Lieder* (1918). Most of Strauss's song texts are German, though there are settings of Robert *Burns and Lord *Byron. The success of Strauss's operatic version of Oscar *Wilde's *Salome* (1905) was partly due to an element of scandal, but within two years this *fin-de-siècle* decadent piece had been performed at 50 opera houses; it has remained a staple of the repertoire. None of the operas Strauss wrote in collaboration with Hugo von *Hofmannsthal had an English source, but after Hofmannsthal's death he accepted from Stefan *Zweig a libretto based on Ben *Jonson's **Epicene*, which became *Die schweigsame Frau*, one of the most brilliant of his operas: it received four performances in 1935, but was then banned because of the Jewish origins of the librettist.

STRAVINSKY, Igor Fyodorovich (1882–1971) Russian composer. Stravinsky's early work includes a number of ballets on Russian themes as well as the controversial *Rite of Spring* (1913). In 1914 he left for Switzerland, moving to France in 1920 and taking French citizenship in 1934. His opera-oratorio *Oedipus Rex* (1926) was based on a text by Jean *Cocteau, after *Sophocles. In 1939 Stravinsky went to America, taking citizenship in 1945. His most important composition to English words is the opera *The Rake's Progress* (1951). The *libretto, by W. H. *Auden, assisted by Chester Kallman, was based on the famous series of *Hogarth engravings, with a vivid 18th-century environment which Stravinsky matched with strongly marked operatic conventions. Stravinsky's neoclassical style then underwent a profound change, absorbing aspects of the serial practice developed by the Austrian composer Arnold Schoenberg (1874–1951): the little *Cantata* (1952), made up of four late medieval English lyrics, and the *Three Songs from William Shakespeare* (1953), are in the new style. Auden offered Stravinsky another libretto (a masque entitled *Delia*) but Stravinsky turned to Dylan *Thomas, who proposed as a subject 'the rediscovery of our planet following an atomic misadventure'. The composer left a touching account of their one meeting in 1953, but the only music that resulted from it was *In Memoriam Dylan Thomas* (1954), a setting of 'Do not go gentle' for tenor, string quartet, and four trombones. Another 'in memoriam' piece is the miniature *Elegy for J.F.K.* (1964), for baritone and three clarinets, to Auden's 'very quiet little lyric'. The death of his friend T. S. *Eliot produced the short *Introitus*, first heard in April 1965 together with the orchestral *Variations* dedicated to the memory of another close friend, Aldous *Huxley. His only setting of an Eliot text was the short polyphonic *Anthem* for unaccompanied chorus, 'The Dove descending breaks the air' (1962, 'Little Gidding', *Four Quartets*). Stravinsky's last work for the stage was the 'musical play' *The Flood*, a version of part of the York miracle play. His last composition was a setting for soprano and piano of Edward *Lear's 'The Owl and the Pussycat', dedicated to his wife. Stravinsky produced many books on music in collaboration with the American conductor Robert Craft (1923–).

stream of consciousness A term used variously to describe either the continuity of impressions and thoughts in the human mind, or a special literary method for representing this psychological principle in unpunctuated or fragmentary forms of *interior monologue. The term was coined in William *James's *Principles of Psychology* (1890), in the first sense. The literary sense of the term was introduced in 1918 by May *Sinclair in a review of early volumes in Dorothy *Richardson's novel sequence *Pilgrimage* (1915–38), which include the first notable English uses of the technique. As used by Richardson, and more famously by James *Joyce in his novel **Ulysses* (1922), the stream-of-consciousness style represents the 'flow' of impressions, memories, and sense-impressions through the mind by abandoning accepted forms of syntax, punctuation, and logical connection. Joyce himself attributed the origin of the technique to the little-known French novel *Les Lauriers sont coupés* (1888) by Édouard Dujardin (1861–1949). After Joyce's virtuoso demonstration of its possibilities in the unpunctuated final chapter of *Ulysses*, the stream-of-consciousness method of rendering characters' thought processes became an accepted part of the modern novelist's repertoire, used by Virginia *Woolf, William *Faulkner, and others.

STREATFEILD, Noel (1895–1983) OBE, born in Frant, Sussex, educated at the Academy of Dramatic Art in London; she wrote children's books featuring creative, hard-working, middle-class children. *Ballet Shoes* (1936) was her first success; *The Circus is Coming* won the Carnegie Medal (1939). *The Painted Garden* (1949) is based on filming *The *Secret Garden*. *A Vicarage Family* (1963) commences a semi-autobiographical sequence.

Strephon The shepherd whose lament for his lost love Urania forms the opening of Philip *Sidney's revised **Arcadia*. 'Strephon' has been adopted as a conventional name for a rustic lover.

STRETTON, Hesba (1832–1911) The pen-name of Sarah Smith, novelist and short story writer. Born in Wellington, Shropshire, the daughter of a printer and bookseller, she was educated at Old Hall, a school in Wellington, but also read widely among her father's wares. She qualified as a governess, but began a career as a writer in 1858, publishing stories in periodicals including Charles *Dickens's *All the Year Round*. She wrote prolifically for children, and had a long publishing career with the *Religious Tract Society. **Jessica's First Prayer* (1867), a powerful account of a neglected child, was extraordinarily successful, and sold two million copies in her lifetime. It was in part an attack on the hypocrisy of prosperous church and chapel congregations who ignored the plight of the poor. But it was also motivated by Stretton's concern for the welfare of children, a cause for which she campaigned throughout her life. It was widely translated, and was for a while (by order of Tsar Alexander II) compulsory reading in all Russian schools. She also wrote well-received novels for adults, including *The Doctor's Dilemma* (1872) and *Through a Needle's Eye* (1879). She never married, and lived with her sister Elizabeth throughout most of her adult life.

STRINDBERG, (Johan) **August** (1849–1912) Swedish author and playwright, born in Stockholm, the son of a steamship agent who married his housekeeper after she had already borne him three sons: hence the title of his autobiography, *The Son of a Servant* (1886). He achieved literary success only after much difficulty and attempts at other careers, and his works, dramatic and non-dramatic, are marked by a deeply neurotic response to religion, social class, and sexuality; he married three times, gained a reputation for anti-feminism and misogyny, and was tried for blasphemy, though acquitted. His first important play, *Master Olof* (written 1872–7; performed 1881), was followed by others, including *The Father* (1887), *Miss Julie* (1888), and *Creditors* (1889), works which combine a highly aggressive and original version of *naturalism with a sense of the extreme and pathological. His later works are tense, symbolic, psychic dramas, marked by a sense of suffering and a longing for salvation and absolution; they include *To Damascus* (1898–1901; 3 parts), *The Dance of Death* (1901), *A Dream Play* (1902), and *The Ghost Sonata* (1907), all distinctive, experimental plays which anticipate *Expressionism and which influenced the psychological and symbolic dramas of Eugene *O'Neill and the writers of the Theatre of the *Absurd. G. B. *Shaw, who met Strindberg in Stockholm in 1908 and saw a specially arranged performance of *Miss Julie*, was a generous advocate of his work, but it took until the 1920s before many of his plays were adequately performed in England.

Strindberg's non-dramatic works include a novel, *The Red Room* (1879), *Getting Married* (1884, 1885; 2 vols of short stories), which he wrote in response to *Ibsen's *A Doll's House*, and *Inferno* (written and published in French, 1898), an extraordinary account of his life in Paris after the collapse of his second marriage, when, driven to the verge of insanity by guilt and a sense of failure, he studied *Swedenborg, dabbled in alchemy, and suffered severe hallucinations. Many of Strindberg's plays have been translated into English by Michael Meyer, who also published a biography in 1985, and several of his works have been translated by Mary Sandbach.

STRODE, Ralph (d. 1387) Scholastic philosopher and logician of repute, fellow of Merton College, Oxford, where he was the colleague of John *Wyclif, with whom he entered into controversy. As 'philosophical Strode' (V. 1857) he was a dedicatee of Chaucer's **Troilus and Criseyde*, along with John *Gower.

STRODE, William (1600–45) Poet and dramatist, educated at Oxford University, where his tragicomedy *The Floating Island* (pub. 1655) was performed before Charles I by the students of Christ Church in 1636, with songs set to music by Henry *Lawes. His poems were collected by the literary scholar Bertram Dobell (1842–1914) from manuscript and published with the play as *The Poetical Works of William Strode* (1907), with a memoir of the author. The poems include some fine love lyrics and epitaphs.

STRONG, L. A. G. (Leonard Alfred George) (1896–1958) Poet and novelist, born at Compton Gifford, Devon, and educated at Brighton College and Wadham College, Oxford. He later taught at an Oxford preparatory school, before becoming a full-time writer in 1930. His first two volumes of poetry were *Dublin Days* (1921) and *The Lowery Road* (1923), and his many novels (which show a strain of the macabre and violent) include his first, *Dewer Rides* (1929, set on Dartmoor), *Sea Wall* (1933), and *The Director* (1944). He also wrote many works of non-fiction and an autobiography of his early years, *Green Memory* (1961).

STROSS, Charles (1964–) Born in Leeds. He has been publishing *science fiction stories since 1987 although his first published novel was *Singularity Sky* (2003). Like *Accelerando* (2005) and *Glasshouse* (2006), it focuses on the evolutionary implications of technological developments leading to post-human artificial intelligences.

structuralism and **post-structuralism** Broad schools of thought that arose in Paris from the 1950s to the 1970s, asserting a powerful influence across a range of different kinds of cultural analysis, from anthropology to literary criticism. Structuralism aimed to create a single general 'science of signs' called semiotics or semiology and so to uncover the basic codes or systems of meaning underlying all human cultural activity. Post-structuralism abandons such grand scientific ambitions, while still roving freely among different cultural forms. Both currents share the same founding principle, which is the primacy of 'Language', conceived as an abstract system of differences, over the human mind, hitherto assumed to be the autonomous maker of all meanings, which is demoted to a subordinate position as 'the subject' generated by Language. This agreed, structuralism and post-structuralism disagree on whether Language is knowably fixed as an object of science, or unstably indeterminate and slippery. Opposed conclusions about the relations between literature and science follow: for structuralism, fictional texts are to be seen as instances of scientific laws, while post-structuralism often regards scientific laws as instances of textual fictions.

The origins of these movements lie in the foundation of modern linguistics by the Swiss scholar Ferdinand de *Saussure, who redirected the study of languages away from 'diachronic' questions of their historical development and towards 'synchronic' study of their workings at a given time. Structuralism and post-structuralism avoid historical enquiry into the origins of phenomena, usually dismissing notions of evolution and progress as 19th-century superstitions. Saussure's second condition for the reconstruction of linguistics as a science was that its object of study should be, not individual utterances and their meanings (*parole*), but the system of rules and distinctions (the *langue*) that underlies them in a given language. So structuralism shows less interest in what a cultural product (a poem, an advertisement, a culinary ritual) may mean than in the implicit rules that allow it to mean something. The key principle of Saussure's linguistic theory is that a word is an 'arbitrary sign': that is, its form and meaning derive not from any natural quality of its referent in the world outside language, but solely from its differences from other words. Saussure's general conclusion here is that 'in a language, there are only differences, without positive terms'. Meanings are, then, not to be found 'in' words but only through the differential relations between them, as conventionally established within a given language. Structuralism and post-structuralism alike are founded upon this principle of the 'relational' nature of signification. Abstracting from Saussure's work, which applies to the analysis of a given language such as English, they often invoke 'Language' as such, as a self-contained realm or general principle of differentiation. This permits the discovery of 'Language' in realms not usually regarded as properly linguistic: cuisine, costume, dance, and structures of kinship, for example, may all be read as 'sign-systems'. Indeed, for the influential structuralist psychoanalyst Jacques *Lacan, it is Language that turns infants into human 'subjects', splitting their minds into conscious and unconscious levels as they enter its system of interchangeable pronouns.

After Saussure, the second founding father was the Russian linguist Roman Jakobson (1896–1982), whose early work in the Russian *formalist school grows into full-blown structuralism in his later writings. Jakobson helped to shape the ideas of the leading French structuralists of the 1960s—Claude *Lévi-Strauss, Roland *Barthes, Lacan, and the Marxist philosopher Louis Althusser (1918–90)—with his claim that the basic principles by which all sign-systems combine their elements into meaningful compounds are those of *metaphor and *metonymy.

As applied to the analysis of particular literary works, the structuralist method is not concerned with critical evaluation, but with uncovering the basic 'binary oppositions' (nature/culture, male/female, active/passive, etc.) that govern the text. It rejects traditional conceptions in which literature is held to express an author's meaning or to reflect the real world; instead, it regards the 'text' as a self-contained structure in which conventional codes of meaning are activated. In the English-speaking world, some critics such as Frank *Kermode, David *Lodge in his *Modes of Modern Writing* (1977), and Jonathan Culler in his *Structuralist Poetics* (1975) adopted elements of structuralist analysis, albeit cautiously.

Post-structuralism cannot be disentangled fully from structuralism: some of its leading figures, notably Barthes, move from one to the other. In general, post-structuralism pursues structuralist arguments about the autonomy of Language from the world, to the point at which structuralism's own authority is undermined. The philosophical pioneer in this new phase was Jacques *Derrida, who began to unpick the logic of structuralism in 1966, questioning the founding concepts of 'structure' and 'binary opposition'. Under his corrosive re-examination, fixed structures appear to dissolve, binary opposites appear to contaminate one another, and determinate meanings become indeterminate. Post-structuralism challenges the 'scientific' pretensions, not only of structuralism but of other explanatory systems, by appealing to the inherent uncertainty of Language. In particular, it discredits all 'metalanguages' (that is, uses of language that purport to explain other uses: linguistics, philosophy, criticism, etc.) by pointing out that they are just as unreliable as the kinds of language they claim to comprehend. Post-structuralism usually allows no appeal to a reality outside Language that could act as a foundation for linguistic meanings; instead, it sees every kind of 'discourse' as circularly self-confirming. This is not the same as denying the existence of a real world outside Language, although Derrida's notorious declaration that 'il n'y a pas d'hors-texte' (unhelpfully Englished as 'there is nothing outside the text') gave that impression. The radical scepticism of this movement reflected in part the libertarian politics of the 1960s and in part the influence of Friedrich *Nietzsche, in its rejection of 'hierarchical' and 'totalitarian' systems of thought, its denial of objectivity, and its hostility to the 'grand narratives' of historical explanation associated with the *Enlightenment.

In terms of linguistic theory, the distinctive view of post-structuralism is that the 'signifier' (a written word, for example) is not fixed to a particular 'signified' (a concept), and so all meanings are provisional. Derrida's philosophical account of this idea found support in the psychoanalytic teachings of Lacan, which stress the instability of individual identity within Language. Lacan's writings created an intersection of psychological, linguistic, and political concerns in which much post-structuralist theory operates, notably the work of Julia *Kristeva, Gilles *Deleuze, and Jean-François *Lyotard. A similar conjunction characterizes the work of Michel *Foucault, which examines the power of Language as revealed in institutionalized 'discourses' and intellectual systems. In the social sciences and beyond, this body of post-structuralist theory encouraged cultural relativism and the associated view that our models of reality are 'constructed' in Language or discourse. It also shaped the concept of *postmodernism.

In academic literary criticism, post-structuralism has won a greater influence than the more narrowly scientific propositions of structuralism, partly because it respects such literary values as verbal complexity and paradox. In some versions, indeed, it threatens to treat history, philosophy, anthropology, and even natural science merely as branches of literature or 'text'. Post-structuralist literary theory and criticism have assumed varied forms, from the kind of linguistic and rhetorical analysis inspired by Derrida and known as *deconstruction, to the *New Historicism inspired by Foucault. They include a version of *feminist criticism derived in part from Lacan and associated with the work of Kristeva. Another important figure is Barthes, whose writings of the 1970s present the process of reading less as a decoding of structures than as a kind of erotic sport. Both Barthes and Kristeva championed *modernist literary experiment, in which they detected a politically liberating value opposed to the conservative implications of literary *realism. Post-structuralist criticism is in general more sympathetic to 'open', unstable, or self-referential writing than to what it regards as 'closed' literary forms; and it disparages realism in particular because it disguises the active power of Language in 'constructing' reality. See J. Sturrock (ed.), *Structuralism and since* (1979); M. Sarup, *An Introductory Guide to Post-structuralism and Postmodernism* (1988).

STRUGATSKY, Arkady (1925–91) and **BORIS** (1933–) Russian brothers who collaborated as *science fiction writers. Translations of their works, widely admired for their imaginative power and satirical force, include *Hard to be a God* (1973), *Roadside Picnic* (1977: filmed as *Stalker*, 1979), and *Definitely Maybe* (1978).

STRUTT, Joseph (1749–1802) Author, artist, engraver, and antiquary, author of many works valuable for their research and engravings, including a *Chronicle of England* (1777–8), *Dresses and Habits of the English People* (1796–9), and *Sports and Pastimes of the People of England* (1801). An unfinished novel by Strutt was completed by Walter *Scott (*Queenhoo Hall*, 1808), and suggested to him the publication of his own **Waverley*.

STUART, Daniel (1766–1846) Journalist, and an early press baron, who in 1795 bought the **Morning Post* and increased its circulation fourfold, later amalgamating with it the *Gazetteer* and the *Telegraph*. In 1796 he bought the **Courier* and when he sold the *Morning Post* in 1803 he proceeded to do for the *Courier* what he had done for his earlier paper. He employed excellent journalists and writers, including Robert *Southey, Charles *Lamb, William *Wordsworth, and S. T. *Coleridge. Between 1799 and 1802 Coleridge wrote many articles, both political and literary, for the *Post*.

STUBBE (Stubbs), **John** (*c.*1541–1590) Religious writer, educated at Trinity College, Cambridge, and Lincoln's Inn. In August 1579 he published *The Discovery of a Gaping Gulf Whereinto England is Like to be Swallowed* against the queen's marriage to the French king's brother François, duc d'Alençon. For this Stubbe was imprisoned and had his right hand cut off, whereupon (according to William *Camden) he 'put off his hat with his left and said with a loud voice "God save the Queen" '. The *pamphlet was edited by L. E. Berry (1968).

STUBBES (Stubbs), **Philip** (*c.*1555–*c.*1610) A *Puritan pamphleteer, author of *The Anatomy of Abuses* (1583), a denunciation of contemporary evil customs which, in the author's opinion, needed abolition. It contains a section on stage plays and is one of the principal sources of information on the social and economic conditions of the period. His account of his wife Katherine, who died aged 19, *A Chrystal Glass for Christian Women* (1591), was very popular.

STUBBS, George (1724–1806) The greatest of the English 18th-century animal painters. Stubbs was also a brilliant anatomist. His paintings of sporting and country pursuits, in which grooms feature as prominently as their noble employers, are realistic and honest. His pictures of horses attacked by lions, a theme which recurred in his work from 1763 when his *Startled Horse* moved Horace *Walpole to verse (*Public Advertiser*, 4 Nov. 1763), anticipated *Romanticism. *Reapers* and *Haymakers* (1783, 1785), possibly painted to appeal to the taste for pastoral scenes inspired by James *Thomson's *The *Seasons*, proved too unsentimental to be widely popular.

STUBBS, William (1825–1901) Historian and bishop of Oxford. Educated at Ripon Grammar School and Christ Church, Oxford, he was elected a fellow of Trinity College, Oxford, in 1848 but resigned in 1850 to take the living of Navestock, Essex; in 1866 he was appointed Regius professor of modern history at Oxford. He may be said to have created the discipline of English medieval history single-handed. His great *Constitutional History of [Medieval] England*, 3 vols (1874–8), has been described as 'one of the most astonishing achievements of the Victorian mind', fit to rank with Charles Darwin's **Origin of Species*. See J. W. Burrow, *A Liberal Descent* (1981).

Stukeley A character in George Peele's **Battle of Alcazar*. The real Thomas Stucley (*c.*1520–1578) was said to be a natural son of *Henry VIII. An adventurer, spy, soldier, and pirate, he was killed at the battle of Alacazar.

STUKELEY, William (1687–1765) He qualified as a doctor, and later as a clergyman, but in 1718 became a founder member of the Society of Antiquaries, of which he was secretary. He wrote on many topics, from flute music to earthquakes, but he was famous for claiming, in elaborate, illustrated discussions of Stonehenge (*Stonehenge: A Temple Restor'd to the British Druids*, 1740) and Avebury (*Abury*, 1743) that they were druid monuments, an idea earlier promoted by John *Aubrey. Stukeley believed that the druid beliefs were 'near akin to the Christian doctrine', and that their alleged human sacrifices prefigured the Crucifixion. His views may have influenced William *Blake's vision of *Albion; William

*Wordsworth was also familiar with them. See D. B. Haycock, *William Stukeley* (2002).

STURGEON, Theodore (1918–1985) American *science fiction writer, born in New York; his work explores aspects of human love. Novels include *More Than Human* (1953), about the coalescing of a hive-mind, and *Some of your Blood* (1962).

STURGIS, Howard Overing (1855–1920) American-born novelist who lived for many years in England. He is remembered for *Belchamber* (1904), a novel describing the marriage of the heir to the country house in the title. Sturgis numbered Henry *James among his close friends.

Sturm und Drang [Storm and Stress] The term applied to a period of cultural ferment prevailing in Germany during the latter part of the 18th century and to the associated movements in literature and music. The name itself derives from the title of a play by F. M. Klinger (1752–1831) of 1776 about the American Revolution. The literary movement, which was greatly influenced by Jean-Jacques *Rousseau, was characterized by a revolt against highly sophisticated literary conventions and a preference for folk poetry, the cult of genius and veneration of *Shakespeare, a 'return to nature', and the expression of extreme emotion. It is generally represented as a challenge to *Enlightenment values and a precursor of *Romanticism. The principal figures of the movement were J. G. Hamann (1730–88), the young Johann Wolfgang von *Goethe, Johann Gottfried *Herder, J. M. R. Lenz (1751–92), and Friedrich von *Schiller. The name is also commonly applied to a group of symphonies by Joseph *Haydn.

STURT, Charles (1795–1869) Australian explorer and public servant, born in Chunar-Ghur, Bengal, son of an East India Company judge. Educated in England, including two years at Harrow School, he joined the army and arrived in Sydney in 1827. The most honoured of Australian land explorers, Sturt gained fame for his expeditions in 1828–30 mapping and naming the Darling and Murray rivers. His favourable reports helped determine the site for South Australia. Sturt later moved there, precariously occupying senior administrative posts. In the drought of 1844–6 he led a harrowing journey from Adelaide into the centre of Australia, which conclusively disproved his dream of an inland sea, and confirmed the reputation of the 'dead heart' as pitiless desert. Better read than many Australian explorers, Sturt published *Two Expeditions into the Interior of Southern Australia* (1833) and *Narrative of an Expedition into Central Australia* (1849).

STURT, George (1863–1927) Diarist and writer on rural crafts, born in Farnham, Surrey, where in 1884 he inherited the long-established family business described in *The Wheelwright's Shop* (1923), which records the traditions of and changes in local craftsmanship and relationships. Earlier works, published as 'George Bourne', include *The Bettesworth Book* (1901) and *Change in the Village* (1912). Selections from his journal were edited by Geoffrey *Grigson (1941) and E. D. Mackerness (1967).

STYRON, William, Jr (1925–2006) American novelist, born in Virginia, who created controversy with *The Confessions of Nat Turner* (1967), about the 1831 slave revolt. *Sophie's Choice* (1979) describes a survivor of the Holocaust. *This Quiet Dust* (1982) collects Styron's non-fiction and *Darkness Visible* (1990) is a memoir of depression. See James L. W. West III, *William Styron* (1998).

sublime A concept associated with awe, vastness, natural magnificence, and strong emotion, which fascinated 18th-century literary critics and aestheticians. Its development marks a movement away from *neo-classicism towards *Romanticism; it was connected with the idea of original genius which soars powerfully above rules and constraints. Sublimity was first analysed in an anonymous Greek work, *On the Sublime*, attributed to *Longinus, which was widely admired in England after Nicholas *Boileau's French translation of 1674. The concept was elaborated by many writers, including Alexander *Pope, Joseph *Addison, John *Dennis, David *Hume, and Hugh *Blair. The most widely read work on the subject was Burke's **Philosophical Enquiry into the Origin of our Ideas of the *Sublime and Beautiful** (1757), which put a new emphasis on terror as 'productive of the strongest emotion which the mind is capable of feeling'. The discussion was not confined to literature. Longinus had described the immensity of objects in the natural world, such as stars, mountains, volcanoes, and the ocean, as a source of the sublime, and this idea was of profound importance to a growing appreciation of the grandeur and violence of nature. Enthusiasm for wild scenery and cosmic grandeur was already apparent in the writings of Edward *Young and James *Thomson; the poems of Thomas *Gray, the Ossianic writings of James *Macpherson, and the *Gothic novels of Ann *Radcliffe also promoted sublime landscapes. Many 18th-century writers making the *Grand Tour dwelt on the sublimity of the Alps, comparing them with the pictures of Salvator *Rosa, whose stormy landscapes provided a pattern for 18th-century depictions of savage nature. From the 1760s travellers began to seek out the exhilarating perils of the remote mountain peak and the gloomy forest; sublimity became a fashion, pandered to by the dramatic storms shown by Philippe de Loutherbourg's 'Eidophusikon' (1781), a small theatre with lantern slides, and later by John *Martin's vast panoramas of cosmic disaster. The macabre paintings, crowded with monsters and ghosts, of Henry *Fuseli, and the landscapes of the paintings of J. M. W. *Turner, may in their different ways also be considered as belonging to the sublime tradition. The *Romantic poets rejected the categories of the 18th-century theorists, but the works of William *Blake, P. B. *Shelley, and William *Wordsworth in particular reflect the development of sublime aesthetics. See S. H. Monk, *The Sublime: A Study of Critical Theories in XVIII Century England* (1935); P. de Bolla, *The Discourse of the Sublime* (1989).

Sublime and Beautiful, *A Philosophical Enquiry into the Origin of our Ideas of the* A treatise by Edmund *Burke, published anonymously in 1757, with an 'Introduction on Taste' added in 1759. Burke distinguishes between the *sublime, which suggests infinity, vastness, darkness, solitude, and terror, and inspires a drive to self-preservation, and the beautiful, which consists in relative smallness, smoothness, and brightness of colour, and promotes an instinct for sociability. The treatise coincided with a renewed interest in wild landscapes, pre-civilized writing (*see* PRIMITIVISM), and the imagination. Burke's new emphasis on the power of the emotions, and of terror in particular, gave the *Gothic novel some legitimacy, but the treatise also had a strong influence on continental aestheticians such as G. E. *Lessing and Immanuel *Kant. See the edition by David Womersley (1998) and vol. i: *Early Writings* (1997) of *The Writings and Speeches of Edmund Burke*, ed. P. Langford.

SUCKLING, Sir John (1609–42) Poet and dramatist, of an old Norfolk family, educated at Trinity College, Cambridge. He inherited large estates, travelled on the Continent, and was knighted on his return in 1630. In 1631 he was in Germany, as a member of Sir Henry Vane's embassy to Gustavus Adolphus. He returned to London in 1632 and lived at court in great splendour. He became a leader of the Royalist party in the early troubles, then fled to France and is said by John *Aubrey to have committed suicide in Paris. His chief works are included in *Fragmenta Aurea* (1646) and consist of poems, plays, letters, and tracts, among them the famous 'Ballad upon a Wedding'. His 'Sessions of the Poets', in which various writers of the day, including Ben *Jonson, Thomas *Carew, and Sir William *D'Avenant, contend for the laurel, was written in 1637, and is interesting as an expression of contemporary opinion on these writers. Suckling's play *Aglaura* (with two fifth acts, one tragic, the other not) was lavishly staged and printed in 1638 at his own expense. *The Goblins* (1646), a romantic drama in which outlaws disguise themselves as devils, was said by John *Dryden to illustrate Suckling's professed admiration for William *Shakespeare, 'his Reginella being an open imitation of Shakespeare's Miranda; his spirits, though counterfeit, yet are copied from Ariel.' *Brennoralt* (1646), an expansion of the *Discontented Colonel* (1640), a tragedy, is interesting for the light which the melancholy colonel throws on the author himself. The plays are, however, chiefly valuable for their lyrics, and Suckling has enjoyed a steady reputation as one of the most elegant and brilliant of the *Cavalier poets. D'Avenant speaks of his sparkling wit, describing him further as the greatest gallant and gamester of his day. According to Aubrey, he invented the game of cribbage. A two-volume edition of his works, ed. T. Clayton and L. A. Beaurline, appeared in 1971.
See FALKLAND, LUCIUS.

SUE, Eugène (1804–57) Prolific French novelist, author of serialized thrillers, most notably *Les Mystères de Paris* (1842–3: *The Mysteries of Paris*), which was hugely popular in England and inspired *The Mysteries of London* (1845–55) by G. W. M. Reynolds (1814–79). Sue also wrote *Le Juif errant* (1844–5: *The Wandering Jew*).

SUETONIUS (Gaius Suetonius Tranquillus) (*c.* AD 70–*c.*130) Roman biographer whose major surviving work, the *Lives of the Caesars*, was composed in part while he was in charge of the imperial archives. Suetonius, writing about the Julio-Claudian and Flavian emperors under a new dynasty, saw no reason to treat them as heroes. His aim was to bring out the moral (or immoral) character of his subjects, and he paid attention to their private habits as well as to their imperial policy. His method was adopted by later Roman biographers. Philemon *Holland translated *Twelve Caesars* (1605), and Thomas *De Quincey imitated and expanded Suetonius in *The Caesars* (1853). The flavour of his writing has been best caught by Robert *Graves in *I, Claudius* and *Claudius the God*.

Sūfī A follower of Sūfism, Islamic mysticism, which originated in the 8th century. Sūfism has always attracted many devotees, including important authors in all the major Islamic languages. Its influence was particularly pervasive in Persian poetry, and it was translations from Persian by Sir William *Jones and Edward *FitzGerald that first brought it to the notice of English readers. Another channel was the German translations of Persian poetry taken up by Ralph Waldo *Emerson.

SUKENICK, Ronald (1932–2004) American novelist, born in New York, who studied the poetry of Wallace *Stevens at Cornell University, publishing books on his work in 1962 and 1967. His novels are usually meta-narratives exploiting different aspects of language and narrative construction, as in *Out* (1973) and *Blown Away* (1986). He founded the *Fiction Collective and his essays on fiction are collected in *In Form* (1985). *Down and In* (1987) is a memoir of the counter-culture.

SULLIVAN, Sir Arthur (1842–1900) English composer, conductor, and teacher, educated at the Royal Academy of Music. Best known for his collaborations on the *Gilbert and Sullivan operas, Sullivan had a distinguished career as a composer in his own right, and was considered the leading musician in the period preceding Hubert *Parry and Charles Villiers *Stanford. His Opus 1, written when he was a 19-year-old student at Leipzig, was a group of twelve pieces of incidental music for *The *Tempest*: their first performance in London (1862) made Sullivan famous, winning the approval of Charles *Dickens. Later, in Paris, Sullivan played them in a piano duet version with Gioachino *Rossini. He wrote incidental music for other *Shakespeare plays—*The *Merchant of Venice* (1871), *The *Merry Wives of Windsor* (1874), **Henry VIII* (1877), **Macbeth* (1888)—and there are *Shakespeare settings in the cantata *Kenilworth* (1865). His *Five Shakespeare Songs* (1866) include a famous setting of 'Orpheus with his lute', and were among the earliest of an enormous number of songs and ballads for the Victorian drawing room, of which 'The Lost Chord', to a poem by Adelaide *Procter, is the most famous. Sullivan collaborated with Alfred *Tennyson on a song cycle,

The Window, or The Songs of the Wrens (1871). He also composed hymn tunes, including the melody for 'Onward, Christian soldiers'. His large-scale choral works were mostly on sacred subjects, though *The Golden Legend*, Sullivan's own favourite, is based on Henry Wadsworth *Longfellow. His one attempt at serious opera, *Ivanhoe* (after Walter *Scott, 1891), opened with much publicity, but could not compare with the brilliance of the comic operas. Sullivan was knighted in 1883.

SULLIVAN, Tricia (1968–) American *science fiction writer, born in New Jersey, resident in Britain. *Dreaming in Smoke* (1999) won the Arthur C. Clarke Award. *Maul* (2004) imagines a world where the male population has almost been eliminated. As Valery Leith, she also writes *fantasy.

'Sumer is icumen in' One of the earliest known English lyrics, found in British Library MS Harley 978, a miscellany of Reading Abbey from the first half of the 13th century. The music, and Latin instructions for singing it, are also in the manuscript.

Summer's Last Will and Testament A play by Thomas *Nashe, published 1600, but written in the autumn of 1592 or 1593. It is framed by the playful comments of Will Summers, **Henry VIII's* jester (who died *c.*1560), and is an allegorical pageant in which Summer, seen as a dying old man, decides who should inherit his riches. The play reflects fear of the plague, of which there was a prolonged outbreak in 1592–3, in the famous lyric

Adieu, farewell earth's bliss,
This world uncertain is,
Fond are life's lustful joys,
Death proves them all but toys,
None from his darts can fly;
I am sick, I must die:
Lord, have mercy on us.

There is an edition in Nashe's *Selected Writings*, ed. S. Wells (1964).

'Summoner's Tale, The' *See* CANTERBURY TALES, 8.

Supposes A comedy in prose, one of the earliest in English, by George *Gascoigne, translated from *Ariosto's *I suppositi*, and performed at Gray's Inn in 1566. It concerns a series of disguises and confused identities; the scenes with servants are effectively comic, especially those with the old nurse Balia. It influenced *Shakespeare's *The *Taming of the Shrew.*

'Surgeon's Daughter, The' A tale by Walter *Scott, published 1827 as one of the stories in the *Chronicles of the Canongate*. This melodramatic tale is set in India (a country Scott never visited). The orphaned Richard Middlemas is reared with Dr Gideon Grey's daughter Menie, whom he later lures to India to be sold as a concubine to Tippoo Sahib. Menie is rescued but dies single; Richard is killed on the order of Hyder Ali, a local potentate and Tippoo's father, by being trampled to death by an elephant.

'Surprised by joy—impatient as the wind' A sonnet by William *Wordsworth, first published in 1815, suggested by the death of his daughter Catherine in 1812, but written, by his own account, 'long after'.

Surrealism An artistic and literary movement founded in Paris as a breakaway from the Dada group by André *Breton with his first *Manifeste du Surréalisme* (1924). It was conceived as a revolutionary mode of thought and action in politics, philosophy, and psychology as well as literature and art. The *Manifeste* attacked rationalism and 'bourgeois' logic: drawing on Sigmund *Freud's theories of the unconscious and its relation to dreams, it called for the exploration of hidden and neglected areas of the human psyche, and the resolution 'of the apparently contradictory states of dream and reality'. Breton's group of writers, painters, and film-makers, mostly French and Spanish, experimented with automatic processes, which were considered the best means of producing the surreal poetic image: the spontaneous coupling of unrelated objects. The principal literary works of the group were Louis *Aragon's *Le Paysan de Paris* (1926), Breton's *Nadja* (1928), and the poems of Paul *Éluard. In the 1930s several Surrealists joined the Communist Party. Surrealism was a significant intellectual current between the wars, although as it spread internationally in the 1930s interest tended to concentrate on its visual rather than literary art. In England the movement attracted some attention among literary circles, but it was only after the appearance of the youthful David *Gascoyne's *Short Survey of Surrealism* (1935) and the International Surrealist Exhibition of June 1936 in London that a Surrealist group was formed, its members including Gascoyne, Herbert *Read, Roland Penrose (1900–84), Humphrey *Jennings, Roger Roughton (1916–41), and Hugh Sykes Davies (1909–84). The impact of Surrealism can be felt in the early stories of Dylan *Thomas, in Lawrence *Durrell's *The Black Book* (1938), and in the poems of Gascoyne, Charles *Madge, and Sykes Davies, among others. The English group was broken up by wartime conditions, but the legacy of Surrealism was repeatedly drawn upon by post-war writers in English, notably by the American poets Frank *O'Hara, John *Ashbery, and Robert *Bly. See Michel Remy, *Surrealism in Britain* (1999); Edward B. Germain's anthology, *Surrealist Poetry in English* (1978).

SURREY, Henry Howard, earl of (by courtesy) (1516/17–1547) Poet, the son of Thomas Howard (1473–1554; afterwards third duke of Norfolk). He married Lady Frances de Vere in 1532. He was with the army during the war with France (1544–6), being wounded before Montreuil, and was commander of Boulogne, 1545–6. Accused of various minor offences, he was, however, tried and executed on the charge of treasonably quartering the royal arms. His works consist of sonnets, poems, and translations in various metres notable for their elegance of construction. Like Sir Thomas *Wyatt he studied Italian models, especially *Petrarch, but his sonnets were predominantly in the 'English' form (*ababcdcdefefgg*), later to be used by *Shakespeare, which appears to have been his invention (*see* SONNET). A still more durable innovation was his use of blank verse in his translation of the **Aeneid*, Books 2 and 4. Forty of his poems were printed by Richard *Tottel in his *Miscellany* (1557). Thomas *Nashe and Michael *Drayton built up a picture of Surrey as the languishing lover of 'Geraldine' (Elizabeth, daughter of the ninth earl of Kildare); but he seems to have done no more than address a single sonnet to this lady, possibly when she was as young as 9.

Surrey's poems were edited together with those of Wyatt by G. F. Nott (1815–16); and, in selection, by Emrys Jones in 1964.

SURTEES, Robert (1779–1834) Educated at Christ Church, Oxford, an antiquary and topographer. He spent his life in collecting materials for his *History of Durham* (1816–40), and is commemorated in the Surtees Society, which publishes original materials relating to the history of the region constituting the old kingdom of Northumbria. His fake ballad 'The Death of Featherstonhaugh' is included in Scott's **Minstrelsy of the Scottish Border.*

SURTEES, Robert Smith (1805–64) Journalist and novelist, born in Durham, the son of a country squire. After attending Durham Grammar School he became articled to a solicitor and practised as a lawyer. From 1830 he built up a reputation as a sporting journalist, contributing to the *Sporting Magazine*, and in 1831 founded (with Rudolph *Ackermann) and edited the *New Sporting Magazine* to which he contributed his comic sketches of Mr Jorrocks, the sporting cockney grocer, later collected as *Jorrocks's Jaunts and Jollities* (1838, illustrated by 'Phiz', the pseudonym of Hablot Knight *Browne, and later by Henry Thomas Alken (1785–1851)). Jorrocks, whose adventures to some extent suggested the original idea of **Pickwick Papers*, reappears in *Handley Cross* (1843; expanded and illustrated by John *Leech, 1854), one of Surtees's most successful novels, and in *Hillingdon Hall* (1845). His second great character, Mr Soapey Sponge, appears in the popular *Mr Sponge's Sporting Tour* (1853, illustrated by Leech); another celebrated character was Mr Facey Romford, who appears in his last novel, *Mr Facey Romford's Hounds* (1865). Surtees inherited his father's Hamsterley estate in 1838, and thereafter devoted his time to his favourite pursuits of hunting and shooting (he became high sheriff of Durham in 1856) while continuing his literary work. His eight long novels deal mainly with characteristic aspects of English fox-hunting society, but his vivid caricatures and the absurd scenes he describes, together with his convincing dialect, frequent catchphrases, and perceptive social observation distinguish him from other writers of this genre and won praise from W. M. *Thackeray and others; the illustration of his novels by Leech, Alken, and Phiz also contributed to their success. *Young Tom Hall*, originally serialized in the **New Monthly Magazine* in 1853, remained unfinished and was first published in book form in 1926.

Survey of London, A *See* STOW, JOHN.

'Suspiria de Profundis' Visionary prose by Thomas *De Quincey, published 1846 in **Blackwood's Magazine*, and a companion piece to the same author's **Confessions of an English Opium Eater.* Another meditation on De Quincey's 'prostration before the dark idol' of opium and fascination with dreaming, it contains the remarkable 'Levana and our Ladies of Sorrow', a description of the author's dreams, while at Oxford, of the goddess Levana and the three mysterious sisters: 'Mater Lachrymarum, Our Lady of Tears', 'Mater Suspiriorum, Our Lady of Sighs' and 'Mater Tenebrarum, Our Lady of Darkness'.

SUTCLIFF, Rosemary (1920–92) CBE, novelist, born in West Clanden, Surrey; she suffered from Still's disease and was confined to a wheelchair for much of her life; disability features in many of her books. She was largely educated by her mother, though she spent three years (from the age of 14) in Bideford Art School. Sutcliff remains the foremost writer of historical novels for children (although her books are essentially *crossover books); her major theme is reconciliation. She wrote about many historical periods, from the prehistoric (*Warrior Scarlet*, 1958) through the Roman (*The Eagle of the Ninth*, 1954) and Arthurian (*Sword at Sunset*, 1963) to the Saxon invasions of England (*Dawn Wind*, 1961). She is noted for her sense of historical continuity (symbolized by a signet ring that passes from generation to generation of her characters), and of developing appropriate argots for each period. She won the Carnegie Medal for *The Lantern Bearers* (1959), illustrated by Charles Keeping. Her final published book was *Sword Song* (1997). *Blue Remembered Hills* (1983) is autobiographical.

SVEVO, Italo (1861–1928) Pseudonym of Ettore Schmitz, Italian novelist, who also wrote plays, short stories, and criticism, born in Trieste from a Jewish Italo-German background (indicated by his pen-name). His novels are: *Una vita* (1892: *A Life*), *Senilità* (1898: a title translated by James *Joyce as *As a Man Grows Older*), *La coscienza del Zeno* (1923: *Confessions of Zeno*), *La novella del buon vecchio e della bella fanciulla* (1926: *The Tale of the Good Old Man and of the Lovely Young Girl*). He was working on a fifth novel, *Il vecchione* (1967: *The Grand Old Man*), when he died in a car crash. Svevo's work was unknown until Joyce met him in Trieste and helped him to publish his masterpiece, *Confessions of Zeno*. Svevo's style stood out against prevailing trends based on Gabriele *d'Annunzio and Antonio *Fogazzaro. *Zeno* is a complex and delicately balanced novel in which time and point of view are relative. Arguing with his psychoanalyst, Zeno struggles with chance, time, marriage, and tobacco, disclosing the source of his malady as the Oedipus complex.

Swallows and Amazons (1930) Arthur *Ransome's novel about children sailing and camping in the Lake District, noted for its egalitarian tone, slow pace, circular construction, and adherence to family codes. The first in a sequence of twelve, it was adapted for television in 1963 and filmed in 1985.

Swan Theatre Built by Frances Langley on the Bankside in London in 1595, and closed down temporarily in 1597, following a performance by Lord Pembroke's Company of Ben *Jonson and Thomas *Nashe's controversial play *The Isle of Dogs*. The Lady Elizabeth's Company is believed to have performed *A *Chaste Maid in Cheapside* there around 1613. Johannes de Witt's sketch (*c*.1596) of the theatre is believed to be the only surviving representation of the interior of an Elizabethan playhouse. The name was adopted by the Royal Shakespeare Company for its galleried playhouse, which opened in Stratford in 1986.

SWANWICK, Michael (1950–) American *science fiction writer, born in Philadelphia. *The Iron Dragon's Daughter* (1993) combines the archetypes of *fantasy with the technological transformations of science fiction. *Stations of the Tide* (1991) and *Jack Faust* (1997) are convincing multi-layered revoicings of *The *Tempest* and **Faust*.

SWEDENBORG, Emanuel (1688–1772) Swedish philosopher, scientist, and mystic. Towards the end of his long career as a scientist he became concerned with uncovering the spiritual structure of the universe, and he began to experience visions and to converse with angels, not only in his dreams, but, he claimed, in his waking life. His prolific writings, mostly in Latin, were designed to promote his peculiar interpretation of the Bible. Swedenborg died in London, and his followers there organized themselves into the New Jerusalem Church, of which William *Blake was for a while an active member. Blake was initially deeply influenced by Swedenborg's writings, which began to appear in English from the 1760s, but he then parodied them mercilessly. Ralph *Emerson, Henry James, Sr, and W. B. *Yeats were also devotees of Swedenborg. See Kathleen *Raine, *Blake and Tradition* (2 vols, 1969).

SWEENEY, Matthew (1952–) Irish poet and children's writer, born in Co. Donegal. He has lived mainly in London since 1973. His collections include *A Round House* (1983), *Blue Shoes* (1989), *A Smell of Fish* (2000), and *Black Moon* (2007). Influences from Franz *Kafka and Charles *Simic as well as from oral tradition are detectable in Sweeney's strange, often sinister, verse narratives. His work for children includes fiction (*The Snow Vulture*, 1992; *Fox*, 2003) and poetry (*Up on the Roof: New and Selected Poems*, 2001). He edited *The New Faber Book of Children's Verse* (2001).

Sweeney, the Frenzy of (*Buile Shuibhne*) 12th-century Irish text surviving in one 17th- and one 18th-century manuscript. Mixing prose and verse, it tells of the madness that overtook Sweeney, an Ulster king, at the 7th-century battle of Mag Rath (Moira, Co. Down) as a result of the curse of St Ronan, whose psalter he had cast into a lake. Sweeney flies from perch to perch in Ireland and Scotland, living off berries and alternately cursing his condition and praising the landscape in a series of impassioned lyrics. In *The White Goddess* Robert *Graves describes *Buile Shuibhne* as 'the most ruthless and bitter description in all European literature of an obsessed poet's predicament'. Sweeney features as an alter ego of Seamus *Heaney in 'Sweeney Redivivus' (1984) and as a character in Flann *O'Brien's *At Swim-Two-Birds* and Neil *Gaiman's *American Gods*. Heaney has translated the 18th-century manuscript version as *Sweeney Astray* (1983).

SWEET, Henry (1845–1912) A great phonetician and, after A. J. Ellis (1814–90) one of the founders of that study in England, educated at Heidelberg University and Balliol College, Oxford, where he was awarded a fourth class in Lit. Hum. (1873). He lived in Oxford from 1895 until his death, but he never fully received the recognition there that his eminence warranted; the readership in phonetics he was given in 1901 was a poor compensation for his failure to gain a number of chairs. He is said to have been the inspiration for George Bernard *Shaw's Henry Higgins in **Pygmalion*. His works are still a staple of the study of Old English and the philology of English; the most celebrated are *History of English Sounds* (1874, 1888); *Anglo-Saxon Reader* (1876); *Anglo-Saxon Primer* (1882); *A New English Grammar* (1892, 1898); *The History of Language* (1900); and *The Sounds of English: An Introduction to Phonetics* (1908).

SWIFT, Graham (1949–) Novelist and short story writer, born in London, educated at Dulwich College and Queens' College, Cambridge, who worked as a teacher before publishing his first novel, *The Sweet Shop Owner* (1980), a portrait of an unfulfilled shopkeeper. *Shuttlecock* (1981) features an archivist who unearths wartime secrets which question his father's integrity. *Learning to Swim* (1982) was a collection of short stories. Focusing on a history teacher, *Waterland* (1984), one of Swift's finest novels, intertwines a story of family disorder with a retrospective panorama of the English fen country. *Out of This World* (1988) about a troubled photo-journalist, and *Ever After* (1992), in which a professor who has attempted suicide turns to ancestral research, likewise delve into the past. Secrets further surface in Swift's masterly *Last Orders* (1996, *Booker Prize-winner), a poignant and funny novel in which four south Londoners journey to the coast to scatter a friend's ashes. *The Light of Day* (2003) and *Tomorrow* (2007) continue his patient, precise surveying of characters caught in domestic predicaments entangled with the past.

SWIFT, Jonathan (1667–1745) Clergyman and writer, born in Dublin, but predominantly of English ancestry. He was educated, with William *Congreve, at Kilkenny Grammar School, then at Trinity College, Dublin, where he obtained his degree only by 'special grace' (he was awarded the degree of doctor of divinity by Trinity in 1702). In 1689 he became secretary to Sir William *Temple. He wrote Pindaric *odes, one of which provoked, according to Samuel *Johnson, John *Dryden's remark, 'Cousin Swift, you will never be a poet.' In 1695 Swift was ordained in the Church of Ireland.

He returned to Temple at Moor Park in 1696, where he edited Temple's correspondence, and in 1697 wrote *The *Battle of the Books*, which was published in 1704 with *A *Tale of a Tub*. On the death of Temple in 1699, Swift went again to Ireland, where he was given the living of Laracor. In the course of frequent visits to London he became acquainted with Joseph *Addison, Richard *Steele, and Congreve. He was entrusted in 1707 with a mission to obtain the grant of Queen Anne's Bounty for Ireland, and in 1708 began a series of pamphlets on church questions with his ironical *Argument against Abolishing Christianity*, followed in the same year by his *Letter Concerning the Sacramental Test*, an attack on the Irish Presbyterians, and *The Sentiments of a Church of England Man with Respect to Religion and Government*. He also diverted himself with the series of squibs upon the astrologer John Partridge (1644–1715) known as the 'Bickerstaff Papers'. His poems of London life, 'Description of a City Shower' and 'Description of the Morning', appeared in the **Tatler* (1709).

From 1710 Swift aligned himself with the Tory ministry of Robert *Harley and Viscount *Bolingbroke; he attacked the Whig ministers in *The Virtues of Sid Hamet the Magician's Rod* (1710), and in the **Examiner*, and in 1711 promoted the peace under negotiation in *The Conduct of the Allies* and *Some Remarks on the Barrier Treaty*. Swift's *Proposal for Correcting, Improving and Ascertaining the English Tongue* (1712), one of the few works to bear his name, dates from this moment of political power. *The Importance of the Guardian Considered* (1713) and *The Public Spirit of the Whigs* (1714), in reply to Steele's *Crisis*, were his last major statements of this kind. He was appointed dean of St Patrick's in 1713, Queen Anne having apparently vetoed any high preferment in England. In 1714 he became friendly with like-minded wits such as Alexander *Pope, John *Arbuthnot, John *Gay, meeting at the short-lived *Scriblerus Club, but in August that year he returned to Ireland. Swift's *History of the Four Last Years of the Queen*, his 'official' account of this period, was not published until 1758, but during his time in London Swift had written the so-called *Journal to Stella*, a series of intimate, teasing letters (1710–13) to Esther Johnson, whom he had first encountered at Moor Park, and her companion Rebecca Dingley, who had moved to Ireland in 1700/1, giving a vivid account of Swift's daily life in London in the company of the Tory ministers. This was first published in 1766. Stella was Swift's closest female companion; the *Journal* mentions his meeting with another woman, Esther Vanhomrigh (pron. 'Vanummery'; d. 1723), who appears to have pursued him; his relationship with her is playfully portrayed in the poem **Cadenus and Vanessa*.

Swift now occupied himself with Irish affairs in such pamphlets as *A Proposal for the Universal Use of Irish Manufacture* (1720). His **Drapier's Letters* (1724) prevented the introduction of 'Wood's half-pence' into Ireland. He came to England in 1726, visited Pope and Gay, and dined with Sir Robert Walpole (1676–1745), to whom he addressed a letter of remonstrance on Irish affairs. He published **Gulliver's Travels*, with its bitter allegory of Irish dependence, in the same year, and paid a last visit to England in 1727, returning to Ireland in time to witness the death of Stella (28 January 1728). Swift continued to publicize the problems faced by Ireland in *A Short View of the State of Ireland* (1728) and *A *Modest Proposal* (1729); he also wrote several ballads on topical subjects for popular distribution. His more important poems include *Verses on the Death of Dr Swift* (1731; pub. 1739), in which he reviews his life and work with ironic detachment, and the satirical *On Poetry, a Rhapsody* (1733). Poems such as *The Lady's Dressing-Room*, *A Beautiful Young Nymph Going to Bed*, and *Strephon and Chloe*, once considered obscene or misogynistic, are now much studied for their refusal to adopt patronizingly 'polite' attitudes towards women. His last prose works were the ironic *Directions to Servants* (written about 1731 and published after his death) and his *Complete Collection of Polite and Ingenious Conversation* (1738). Swift kept up his correspondence with Bolingbroke, Pope, Gay, and Arbuthnot, and attracted to himself a small circle of friends; the *Memoirs* of Laetitia *Pilkington contain much material relating to Swift's personality and behaviour at this time. In 1735 the Dublin printer George Faulkner (1699–1755) published the first major collected edition of his work. The symptoms of the illness from which he suffered for most of his life (now thought to have been Menière's disease) became very marked in his last years, and in 1742 he was suspended from his duties. He was buried by the side of Stella, in St Patrick's, Dublin, his own famous epitaph 'ubi saeva indignatio ulterius cor lacerare nequit' (where fierce indignation cannot further tear apart the heart) being inscribed on his tomb. John *Boyle, Samuel Johnson, Lord *Macaulay, and William *Thackeray, among many other writers, were alienated by his ferocity and coarseness, but the 20th century has seen a revival of biographical and critical interest, stressing Swift's verbal inventiveness, restless and sometimes anarchic energy, and satirical courage rather than his alleged misanthropy.

See Irvin Ehrenpreis, *Swift: The Man, his Works and the Age* (3 vols, 1962–83). The edition of the *Prose Works* by Herbert Davis (16 vols, 1939–74) will be replaced by the *Cambridge Edition of the Works of Jonathan Swift*, ed. C. Rawson and others (15 vols, 2008–). See also Swift's *Complete Poems*, ed. P. Rogers (1983); *The Correspondence of Jonathan Swift*, ed. D. Woolley, 4 vols (1999–2007).

Swift, Tom The juvenile hero of a long-running series of American adventure stories started in 1910, written by ghost-writers, and credited to the house name of 'Victor *Appleton'.

SWINBURNE, Algernon Charles (1837–1909) Poet and critic, born into an old Northumbrian family. He spent much of his childhood in the Isle of Wight, where he acquired a lasting love of the sea, reflected in much of his work. He was educated at Eton College and at Balliol College, Oxford, where he was associated with Dante Gabriel *Rossetti, and the *Pre-Raphaelite circle. His first published volume, *The Queen-Mother and Rosamond* (1860), echoes Elizabethan dramatists, notably George *Chapman, and attracted only modest attention, but **Atalanta in Calydon* (1865), a drama in classical Greek form, with choruses (e.g. 'When the hounds of spring are on winter's traces') that revealed his exceptional metrical skills, brought him celebrity; Alfred *Tennyson wrote praising his 'wonderful rhythmic invention'. *Chastelard*, the first of three dramas on the subject of *Mary Queen of Scots, which appeared the same year, raised some doubts about the morality of Swinburne's verse, doubts reinforced by the first series of *Poems and Ballads* (1866), which received some criticism, notably from Robert *Buchanan and John *Morley. The volume contains many of his best poems (*'Dolores', 'Itylus', 'Hymn to Proserpine', 'The Triumph of Time', 'Faustine', 'Laus Veneris', etc.) which clearly demonstrate preoccupations with non-Christian belief structures, moral conundrums, distracting beauties, the links between sex and pain. Swinburne had a complicated regard for Christianity (he was critical but continually drawn to the subject). Thomas *Hardy makes his heroine Sue Bridehead (in **Jude the Obscure*) an admirer of his rejection of Christian belief. *A Song of Italy* (1867) and *Songs before Sunrise* (1871) express his support for Mazzini in the struggle for Italian independence, and an impatience with authority which connects him to William *Blake, of whom Swinburne was an early and important admirer. *Bothwell* (1874) and a second Greek drama, *Erechtheus* (1876), were followed by the more subdued *Poems and Ballads: Second Series* (1878), which contains 'A Forsaken Garden', richly imbued with resistance to Christianity. By this time Swinburne's health, always delicate and subject to fits of intense nervous excitement, was seriously undermined by heavy drinking. In 1879 he moved to Putney with his friend Theodore *Watts-Dunton, who gradually weaned him from alcoholism and restored his health. He published many more volumes, including *Mary Stuart* (1881), **Tristram of Lyonesse and Other Poems* (1882), **Marino Faliero* (1885, a tragedy on the same subject as Lord *Byron's), and *Poems and Ballads: Third Series* (1889), a volume concerned with elegy and less controversial than its predecessor.

Swinburne wrote extensively in classical metres, and commanded an exceptional variety of verse forms, including burlesques, modern and mock-antique ballads, and roundels; he also translated the ballads of François *Villon. His published prose works include two novels, *A Year's Letters* (serialized pseudonymously 1877; republished 1905 as *Love's Cross Currents*) and the sado-masochistic 'flogging novel' *Lesbia Brandon* (ed. R. Hughes, 1952). His presence in the work of aesthetes including Walter *Pater was considerable, and he was an important channel through which elements from contemporary French verse, including Charles *Baudelaire's, entered British culture. Neither T. S. *Eliot nor F. R. *Leavis admired him. Swinburne was a critic of originality and brilliance; his studies of Chapman (1875), Christopher *Marlowe (1883, **Encyclopaedia Britannica*), Thomas *Middleton (1887), Cyril *Tourneur (1889, *EB*), and others were the first important successors to Charles *Lamb in the revival of interest in Elizabethan and Jacobean drama, and those of Blake (1868) and the *Brontës (1877, 1883, etc.) in many ways laid the foundation of modern readings. His letters were edited in six volumes, 1959–62, by C. Y. Lang. There is a biography by Rikky Rooksby (1997).

SWINDELLS, Robert (1939–) Writer, born in Bradford, Yorkshire; he had little formal education before becoming a teacher. His *young adult novels move between social critique and the supernatural: *Brother in the Land* (1984) is about a nuclear holocaust; *Stone Cold* (1993), murdered homeless teenagers; *Abomination* (1998), abusive Christian parents.

SWINNERTON, Frank (1884–1982) Critic and prolific novelist. He left school at 14 and worked as office boy, proofreader, then editor at Chatto and Windus. His novels, often set in contemporary London, include *Nocturne* (1917, his greatest success) and *Harvest Comedy* (1937). He was literary critic of *Truth and Nation*, the *Evening News*, and the **Observer* and a familiar figure in the literary life of the first half of the 20th century, Arnold *Bennett and John *Galsworthy being among his friends. His knowledge of the period provided material for his literary reminiscences, notably *The Georgian Literary Scene* (1935), and two autobiographical works, *Swinnerton: An Autobiography* (1937) and *Reflections from a Village* (1969). *Arnold Bennett: A Last Word* (1978) appeared in his 94th year. He was president of the *Royal Literary Fund (1962–6).

Swiss Family Robinson, The The story of a family wrecked on a desert island, written in German by Johann David Wyss (1743–1818), a Swiss pastor. Firmly Christian and moral in tone, it was published in two parts in Zurich in 1812–13. The first English translation came a year later. 'Robinson' refers to Daniel *Defoe's **Robinson Crusoe*; it is not the name of the family. The tale survives, usually expanded and changed, in many different forms, including numerous film and television adaptations.

sword and sorcery Term used to describe the heroic *fantasy exemplified (though not originated) by Robert E. *Howard's 'Conan the Barbarian' stories, published in **Weird Tales* in the 1930s. Conan gained a new lease of life in the 1970s with reprints and 'new' stories composed by L. Sprague *de Camp, Lin *Carter, and others. The term was coined by Fritz Leiber whose 'Newhon' series added irony and character interplay to the simple 'barbarian fights supernatural monster' format. The surprising flexibility of the form was further exploited by writers including C. L. *Moore, Samuel R. *Delany, and Michael *Moorcock.

sword-dance A medieval folk custom, one of the origins of the *mummers' play and so of English drama. It probably symbolized the year's death and resurrection. Stock characters were the fool, dressed in an animal skin, and the 'Bessy', a man in woman's clothes. In many surviving dances one character is surrounded with the swords of the others, or slain.

SYAL, Meera (1963–) British-born writer, actor, and comedian. She wrote the script for Gurinder Chadha's film *Bhaji on the Beach* (1994) and is well known as a writer and actor in the television series *Goodness Gracious Me* and *The Kumars at No. 42*. Her novels *Anita and Me* (1996) and *Life Isn't All Ha Ha*

Hee Hee (1999) explore satirically and sympathetically the position of British Asian girls and women.

Sybil, *or The Two Nations* A novel by Benjamin *Disraeli, published 1845; the second book of the trilogy **Coningsby*—*Sybil*—**Tancred*. Like *Coningsby*, it celebrates the ideas of the 'Young England' Tories and was designed to describe 'the Condition of the People' and of the 'Two Nations of England, the Rich and the Poor' (*see* SOCIAL PROBLEM NOVEL). In this ambitious book, Disraeli suggests reforms a generation before his government was able to introduce them. Poverty and oppression are described with feeling, and the radical *Chartist spirit is sympathetically shown in Gerard, Morley, and others; aspects of the wealthy social and political world, particularly as seen in Mowbray Castle, are described with ironic contempt.

The background is set in the prime ministership of *Wellington. Charles Egremont, younger brother of the pitiless landowner Lord Marney, master of splendid Marney Abbey, falls in love with the beautiful Sybil. She is the daughter of the Chartist Walter Gerard (who becomes Egremont's friend) and is loved by Stephen Morley, a radical and atheist; all three live in the oppressed industrial town of Mowbray some miles away. When Sybil refuses Egremont because of his rank, he begins to live a life painfully divided between the poverty-stricken town of Mowbray, his brother's glittering social circle, and his parliamentary life in London. He sets out to discover the true condition of the poor in Mowbray and to understand the feelings of the Chartists and incendiaries. The plight of the poor, whose land has been taken by the rich, is compared with that of the Saxons despoiled by the Normans, and Sybil's ancestry turns out to entitle her to the lands of Marney. Much of the narrative is concerned with the development of the Chartist rising, Gerard's imprisonment, the activities of Morley, the radical parson St Lys, and with Egremont's struggle in the House of Commons to secure reforms. Five years of increasing poverty culminate in violent riots. Gerard is killed, Lord Marney stoned to death, Morley shot, and the castle burned down. Egremont rescues Sybil, and the pair are later married.

Sydney *Bulletin* *See* BULLETIN, THE.

syllabics Lines of verse composed according to a regular counting of the number of syllables to a line, regardless of stress patterns (*see* METRE). Syllabic verse is the standard metrical principle of modern Romance languages such as French, as it is in Chinese and Japanese; but in English poetry it is a minor tradition of modern experiment inaugurated by Robert *Bridges in 'Poor Poll' (1921), and adapted later in some poems by W. H. *Auden, Dylan *Thomas, Marianne *Moore, Thom *Gunn, and Sylvia *Plath, among others. Uniform length of lines is favoured by some practitioners, as for instance in the twelve-syllable line of Bridges's long poem *The Testament of Beauty* (1929); but Moore and others favoured *stanza forms combining lines of different lengths. The *haiku, imported from the Japanese, is the most widely practised syllabic form.

syllepsis A figure of speech by which a word, or a particular form or inflection of a word, is made to refer to two or more words in the same sentence, while properly applying to them in different senses: e.g. 'Miss Bolo...went home in a flood of tears and a sedan chair' (Dickens, **Pickwick Papers*, ch. 35).
See also ZEUGMA.

SYLVESTER, Josuah (*c.*1563–1618) A London merchant, whose translation into rhyming couplets of *The Divine Weeks and Works* of *Du Bartas was, according to John *Davies of Hereford, 'admir'd of all'. The first instalment appeared in 1592, more in 1598, further parts in 1605–7, and a complete translation in 1608, which was reprinted for the fifth time in 1641. The edition of 1621 contained many of Sylvester's other works, including his poems in the important collection *Lachrymae Lachrymarum* (1613). This contained elegies by Joseph *Hall and John *Donne, among others, on Prince Henry, to whom Sylvester had attached himself. His translation of Du Bartas has been edited by Susan Snyder (2 vols, 1973).

Sylvia's Lovers A novel by Elizabeth *Gaskell, published 1863; her only historical novel. The scene is the whaling port of Monkshaven (based on Whitby in Yorkshire) during the Napoleonic Wars, and the plot hinges on the activities of the press-gangs, whose seizure of Monkshaven men to man naval warships provokes bitter resentment. Sylvia's father, the farmer Daniel Robson, leads a mob attack on the press-gang's headquarters, and is hanged. Her lover, the 'specksioneer' (harpooner) Charley Kinraid, is carried off by the press-gang, but sends a message promising constancy and return through Sylvia's cousin, the pedantic shopkeeper Philip Hepburn, who has long loved Sylvia. Philip conceals the message, and Sylvia, believing Charley dead, and left in poverty after her father's execution, agrees to marry him. Years later, Charley returns and Philip's treachery is revealed. Sylvia swears never to forgive him. Philip flees from Monkshaven and enlists, but, having saved Charley's life on the battlefield, eventually returns as a disfigured beggar. Recognized on his deathbed, he is forgiven, and dies in the arms of the repentant Sylvia. Sylvia herself does not live long. The book is particularly notable for its early chapters, with their vivid reconstruction of life in the little town dominated by the whaling industry (which Gaskell carefully researched) and at the farm where noisy, unreasonable Daniel Robson, his quiet, devoted wife, and their sturdy old servant Kester combine to cherish the lovely but hapless Sylvia. Gaskell felt that this tale of betrayal and irremediable loss was 'the saddest story I ever wrote'.

Symbolism, symbolists A group of French writers of the 19th century. The term is widely applied, but in its most useful and restricted sense refers to the period *c.*1880–95. The movement may be seen as a reaction against dominant *realist and *naturalist tendencies in literature generally and, in the case of poetry, against the descriptive precision and 'objectivity' of the *Parnassians. The symbolists stressed the priority of suggestion and evocation over direct description and explicit analogy (compare Stéphane *Mallarmé's dictum, 'Peindre, non la chose, mais l'effet qu'elle produit'; 'To paint, not the thing, but the effect it produces'), and the symbol was identified as an important means of distilling a private mood, or evoking subtle affinities between the material and spiritual worlds. Symbolist writers were particularly concerned to explore the musical properties of language, through the interplay of suggestive sound relationships, but were deeply interested in all the arts and much influenced by Richard *Wagner's music dramas. Other influences on the movement were the mystical writings of *Swedenborg, and the poetry of Gérard de *Nerval, Charles *Baudelaire, and Edgar Allan *Poe. Generally associated with the symbolist movement are: the poets Mallarmé, Paul *Verlaine, Arthur *Rimbaud, and Jules *Laforgue; the dramatists Auguste *Villiers de l'Isle-Adam and Maurice *Maeterlinck, whose *Pelléas et Mélisande* (1892) was the source of Claude *Debussy's opera of that name; and the novelists Joris-Karl *Huysmans and Édouard Dujardin (1861–1949), whose *Les Lauriers sont coupés* (1888: *The Laurels Are Cut*) influenced James *Joyce. The movement exercised an influence on painters, including Odilon Redon (1840–1916) and Gustave Moreau (1826–98) and on a wide range of 20th-century writers, including Ezra *Pound, T. S. *Eliot, Wallace *Stevens, W. B. *Yeats, Joyce, Virginia *Woolf, Paul *Claudel, Paul *Valéry, Stefan George (1868–1933), and Rainer Maria *Rilke. It was the subject of A. W. *Symons's *The Symbolist Movement in Literature* (1899) and played a part in the development of the Russian symbolist movement and of the *modernista* movement in Latin America.

SYMONDS, John Addington (1840–93) Poet and critic, born in Bristol, the son of an eminent physician, educated at Harrow School and Balliol College, Oxford, where he won the *Newdigate Prize, and became a fellow of Magdalen College. He suffered from tuberculosis, and spent much of his life in Italy and Switzerland. He was attracted by the Hellenism of the Renaissance, and both his prose and poetry reveal his interest in *Platonic love and his admiration for male beauty. His largest work, *Renaissance in Italy* (1875–86), is more picturesque than scholarly, and at times overburdened with detail and anecdote. His works include volumes on Ben *Jonson, Philip *Sidney, P. B. *Shelley, Walt *Whitman, and *Michelangelo; collections of travel sketches and impressions; several volumes of verse; a translation of the autobiography of *Cellini (1888); and translations of Greek and Italian poetry. He had a wide circle of literary friends (among them Edward *Lear, A. C. *Swinburne, Leslie *Stephen, and Robert Louis *Stevenson). He married in 1864, but increasingly acknowledged his own homosexuality, and discreetly campaigned for legal reform. His privately printed pamphlets *A Problem in Greek Ethics* (1883) and *A Problem in Modern Ethics* (1891) were reproduced in part by Havelock *Ellis in *Sexual Inversion* (1897). See Phyllis Grosskurth, *John Addington Symonds* (1964).

SYMONS, A. J. A. (Alphonse James Albert) (1900–41) Writer and bibliographer, born in London, the son of a Jewish immigrant; he became an authority on the literature of the 1890s and published *An Anthology of 'Nineties' Verse* (1928). He wrote several biographies, but is best remembered for *The *Quest for Corvo: An Experiment in Biography* (1934), a life of F. W. *Rolfe. *A. J. A. Symons: His Life and Speculations* (1950), by his brother Julian *Symons, is a vivid evocation of his paradoxical personality and diverse interests as book-collector, dandy, and epicure.

SYMONS, Arthur William (1865–1945) Literary scholar and author. A prolific writer, by 21 he had published many articles, reviews, and poems, as well as his first book, an *Introduction to the Study of Robert Browning* (1886). Symons was fascinated by French decadent poetry, which influenced the poems of his *Days and Nights* (1889) and *London Nights* (1895). Travelling in France, he met Stéphane *Mallarmé, Paul *Verlaine, and Joris-Karl *Huysmans, and in 1890 joined the *Rhymers Club where he befriended W. B. *Yeats. Throughout the 1890s he was a proponent of *'art for art's sake', publishing an influential article, 'The Decadent Movement in Literature' (1892) and *The Symbolist Movement in England* (1899). He was editor of the *Savoy* (1896), which published, among others, Aubrey *Beardsley, Joseph *Conrad, and Ernest *Dowson; and wrote critical studies of writers including William *Blake, Charles *Baudelaire, Walter *Pater, and Oscar *Wilde. In 1908 he suffered a mental breakdown and, though he largely recovered, published little thereafter.

SYMONS, Julian Gustave (1921–94) Crime writer, critic, biographer, and scholar of crime fiction, born in London, brother of A. J. A. *Symons. His many novels, which include *Bland Beginning* (1949) and *The Belting Inheritance* (1965), showed interests in anarchy, forgery, and bibliography. His survey of the genre, *Bloody Murder: From the Detective Story to the Crime Novel*, appeared in 1972.
See also DETECTIVE FICTION.

synecdoche [pron. 'sinekdoki'] A figure of speech which substitutes a whole for a part or a part for a whole, e.g. 'the police are coming' to refer to one police officer, or 'Australia' in reference to its cricket team; conversely 'the Press' in reference to the world of newspapers, or 'per head' meaning per person. A special form of *metonymy, it is found especially in politics ('Westminster' for the British government, etc.) and sport. In literary uses it commonly takes the form of reference to a bodily part in place of a whole person (Blake: 'And did those feet in ancient time…').

SYNGE, John Millington (1871–1909) Irish playwright and poet, born in Rathfarnham, Co. Dublin and educated at Trinity College, Dublin, where he was taught Irish as part of his divinity degree by a native speaker, Revd James Goodman. Abandoning plans to become a professional musician, he spent some years in Paris, where he met W. B. *Yeats in 1896. Following a suggestion from Yeats, he went to the Aran Islands, and stayed there annually from 1898 to 1902, perfecting his Irish and collecting material that would form the basis not only of his prose study *The Aran Islands* (1907) but of much of his drama. His six mature plays fuse Gaelic syntax and idioms with the rhythms of Hiberno-English to create a dramatic language simultaneously brutal and lyrical, realist and ironic. *In the Shadow of the Glen* (1903) is a grim one-act 'peasant' comedy in which an elderly husband feigns death to test his wife's fidelity. In *Riders to the Sea* (1904), a compressed tragedy, the elderly mother, Maurya, stoically anticipates 'a great rest' after the drowning of the last of her six sons. *The Well of the Saints* (1905) dramatizes a beggar couple's choice to return to blindness after having their sight miraculously restored. Synge's best-known play, the extravagant comedy *The *Playboy of the Western World*, caused riots when first performed in 1907 because it was seen by a section of nationalist opinion as a slur on Irish womanhood. All of the above were produced at the *Abbey Theatre, of which Synge became a director in 1906. *The Tinker's Wedding* (written 1902) was first performed in London in 1908, as Yeats judged that its disrespectful portrayal of a priest would further inflame sentiment if staged in Dublin. Synge's sinewy, compact lyrics, many of them shadowed by his impending death, were published in *Poems and Translations* (1909). From 1897 Synge had suffered from Hodgkin's disease, and he brought his last play, *Deirdre of the Sorrows*, close to completion as he was dying. It was finished by Yeats and Synge's fiancée Molly Allgood and performed and published in 1910. The authorized biography is *J. M. Synge 1871–1909* (1959) by D. H. Greene and E. M. Stephens, and the *Collected Works* (4 vols, 1962–8) were edited by Robin Skelton; his *Collected Letters*, edited by Ann Saddlemyer, appeared 1983–4.

Syntax, Dr *See* Combe, William.

SZIRTES, George (1948–) Poet and translator, born in Budapest into a family of Jewish origin, who entered Britain as refugees in 1956 after fleeing a perceived upsurge in fascism stirred up in the wake of the Hungarian Revolution. Having studied at art colleges in London and Leeds, he took to writing poetry. His first collection, *The Slant Door* (1979), won the Faber Memorial Prize and his second, *November and May* (1982), saw him elected to the *Royal Society of Literature. His return to Budapest in 1984 energized his writing and precipitated a string of acclaimed translations. His poetry, formally precise and subtly shaded with emotional and cultural complexities, explores themes of exile, identity, and the interdependent structures of personal and political experience. It has appeared in numerous volumes, including *Reel* (2004), which won the T. S. *Eliot Prize. He maintains a strong public profile and runs his own website and blog: www.georgeszirtes.co.uk.

SZYMBORSKA, Wisława (1923–) Polish poet. After completing her studies at the University of Cracow, in 1953 she joined the staff of the literary journal *Życie Literackie*, where she was to work as poetry editor for almost 30 years. During this time she published six collections of poetry; *People on a Bridge* (1986, trans. Adam Czerniawski, 1990) is among the most widely admired. She was awarded the *Nobel Prize in 1996, and has continued to add to her body of work: recent volumes include *Moment* (2002); *Rhymes for Big Kids* (2003); and *Colon* (2005).

T

TABART, Benjamin (?1767–1833). Little is known of his early life but he began selling books—notably a well-developed Juvenile Library comprising both instructional and entertaining works—in London in 1801. He is best known for his influential collections of fairy-tales, beginning in 1804 with *Collection of Popular Stories*.

TABUCCHI, Antonio (1943–) Italian novelist, translator (from Portuguese), and critic, born in Pisa. His works include *Notturno indiano* (1984, trans. 1988 by Tim Parks as *Indian Nocturne*), *Requiem* (published first in Portuguese, 1991, then Italian 1992; English trans. 1994), a haunted evocation of Lisbon in July, and *Sostiene Pereira* (1994: *Declares Pereira*, 1995), a concentrated, deceptively simple, and resonant novel set in 1938 in Portugal, in which a middle-aged cultural journalist finds himself obliged to confront political repression and violence. This was subsequently turned into a film (1996). *Piccoli equivoci senza importanza* (1985: *Little Misunderstandings of No Importance*, 1988) is a volume of short stories. His most recent fiction is *Si sta facendo sempre più tardi* (2001: *It's Getting Later All the Time*), an *epistolary novel. His writings show the influence of Joseph *Conrad, and Henry *James among others.

TACITUS, Cornelius (*c.* AD 56–after 117) The greatest historian of imperial Rome. His first work was a biography of his father-in-law Julius Agricola (98), followed by an ethnographical account of the German tribes. The former provides a useful description of Roman Britain, the latter contains one of the earliest representations of the Noble Savage (*see* PRIMITIVISM). He also wrote a dialogue on the shortcomings of contemporary oratory. His fame rests on his *Annals* and his *Histories*, which related events from the death of Augustus to the Flavian period. About a third of the *Histories* and over half of the *Annals* survive. Tacitus' aim was to keep alive the memory of virtuous and vicious actions so that posterity could judge them, and his great achievement was to have drawn a picture of how men must live under tyranny. Little known in the Middle Ages, Tacitus was rediscovered by *Boccaccio in the 14th century. The *Agricola* and the *Histories* were translated into English by Sir Henry *Savile (1591), the *Germania* and *Annals* by Richard Grenewey (1598); after this Tacitus became in John *Donne's phrase the 'Oracle of Statesmen' or at least the model for historians such as Sir John *Hayward and Francis *Bacon. He was also influential as a stylist in the 17th century, when attempts were made to imitate his concision and trenchancy.

TAGORE, Rabindranath (1861–1941) Most eminent modern Bengali poet. He was also critic, essayist, composer, and author of short fiction of a kind that was new to Bengali literature. He is known outside India principally in English translation. *Gitanjali: Song Offering* (1912), his free verse recreations of his Bengali poems modelled on medieval Indian devotional lyrics, won him the *Nobel Prize for Literature in 1913, its first award to an Asian. Representative translations followed, of philosophical plays such as *Chitra* (1913) and *The King of the Dark Chamber* (1914), and of his novels *The Home and the World* (1919) and *Gora* (1924). His short fiction often comments powerfully and courageously on Indian national and social concerns, in the collections *Hungry Stones* (1916), *Broken Ties* (1925), and *The Housewarming* (1965), and in the novella *The Broken Nest* (1971). Tagore had an excellent command of English, but he wrote primarily in Bengali and tirelessly encouraged writers of the Indian vernaculars.

Taillefer (Incisor Ferri) A minstrel in the army of William the Conqueror who (according to the *Carmen de Hastingae Proelio* and to *Henry of Huntingdon and Geffrei *Gaimar) marched in front of the army at Hastings, singing of the deeds of *Roland to encourage the Normans.

tail-rhyme [translated from the Latin *rhythmus caudatus*] The measure associated in particular with a group of Middle English *romances in which a pair of rhyming lines is followed by a single line of different length and the three-line pattern is repeated to make up a six-line stanza. *Chaucer's 'Sir Thopas' (*see* CANTERBURY TALES, 17) is an example; six are edited by M. Mills in *Six Middle English Romances* (1973).

Táin-Bó-Cuailnge The chief epic of the Ulster cycle of Irish mythology, an account in prose and verse of the raid by Queen *Maeve of Connaught to secure the Brown Bull of Cooley, and her defeat by *Cuchulain. There are modern translations by Thomas *Kinsella (1969) and Ciaran *Carson (2007).

TAINE, Hippolyte-Adolphe (1828–93) French philosopher, historian, and critic, the leading exponent in his age of the view that historical and artistic phenomena can be explained by the methods of natural science. Taine's determinist and mechanistic theory of mental activity is fully set out in *De l'intelligence* (1870: *On Intelligence*, 1871). Its moral corollary was given a provocative formulation in the introduction to his *Histoire de la littérature anglaise* (3 vols, 1863: *History of English Literature*, 1871): 'vice and virtue are products like vitriol and sugar.' In the same introduction he laid down the principle that hereditary, environmental, and historical factors ('la race, le milieu, le moment') could sufficiently account for the entire range and character of a national literature. Taine wrote widely on art and aesthetics, e.g. *Philosophie de l'art* (1865: *The Philosophy of Art*, 1865), *De l'idéal dans l'art* (1867: *The Ideal in Art*, 1870), as well as books on the art of Italy, Greece, and the Low Countries. *Les Origines de la France contemporaine* (6 vols, 1875–93: *The Origins of Contemporary France*, 1876–94) is a history of France in the late 18th and early 19th centuries, focusing on the revolutionary period and deploring the centralizing tendency of which, to his mind, the revolution was an expression. Taine's numerous travel books include *Notes sur l'Angleterre* (1872: *Notes on England*, 1872), impressions of the country and of life and manners gathered during his stays in England, together with reflections on the English mind and system of government.

Tale of a Tub, A A comedy by Ben *Jonson, performed 1633, printed 1640. Various suitors, including John Clay the tilemaker, Squire Tub, and Justice Preamble, try to marry Audrey, the daughter of Toby Turf, high constable of Kentish Town. She finally marries Pol Martin, 'a groom was never dreamt of'. This was Jonson's last completed play.

Tale of a Tub, A A satire in prose by Jonathan *Swift, written, according to his own statement, about 1696, but not published until 1704, when it appeared anonymously. The main story tells of a father who leaves as a legacy to his three sons a coat apiece, with directions that on no account are the coats (which represent religion) to be altered. The sons are named Peter, to symbolize the *Roman Catholic Church, Martin (from Martin *Luther) to represent the *Church of England, and Jack (from John *Calvin), as the *Protestant Dissenter. The sons gradually disobey the terms of the will (that is, the *Bible), finding excuses for adding shoulder-knots or gold lace according to the prevailing fashion. Martin and Jack quarrel with Peter (the Reformation), then with each other, and separate. The satire ridicules especially Peter's papal bulls and dispensations, and the doctrine of transubstantiation, but Jack's fanatical delusions are also ridiculed. Martin, representing Swift's own church, is the least reprehensible. The narrative is interspersed with digressions, by the supposed hack author of the *Tale*, on critics, on learning, 'in praise of digressions', and on madness. The *Tale* was one of Swift's own favourite works, though its cavalier treatment of religion is said to have been the cause of Queen Anne's hostility to him. Its dizzying paradoxes, brilliant scientific parodies, and unsparing, audacious ironies have inspired much controversy since its publication. In the 5th edition (1710) Swift added plates, notes, and an unsigned and not entirely straightforward 'Apology', in response to critical failures to understand his satiric purpose. See the edition by M. Walsh (2010).

Tale of Two Cities, A A novel by Charles *Dickens, published 1859. The 'two cities' are Paris, at the time of the French Revolution, and London. Dr Manette, a French doctor, has been imprisoned in the Bastille for eighteen years, to secure his silence about the vicious crimes of the marquis de St Évremonde and his brother. He maintains a precarious sanity by cobbling shoes. When the story opens he is brought to England, where he gradually recovers his balance of mind. Charles Darnay, who conceals the fact that he is a nephew of the marquis, has left France and renounced his heritage from detestation of the cruelty of the old French nobility; he falls in love with Lucie, Dr Manette's daughter, and they are happily married. During the Terror he goes to Paris to try to save a faithful servant, who is accused of having served the nobility. He is arrested, condemned to death, and saved only at the last moment by Sydney Carton, a reckless wastrel of an English barrister, whose character is redeemed by his generous devotion to Lucie. Carton, who strikingly resembles Darnay in appearance, smuggles the latter out of prison, and takes his place on the scaffold. The book's vivid picture of Paris at this period was modelled on Thomas *Carlyle's *The *French Revolution*, which Dickens greatly admired. Critics complained of its lack of humour, but it later achieved wide popularity, partly through successful dramatizations and film adaptations. Carton's dramatic words as he goes to his death—'It is a far, far better thing that I do, than I have ever done'—became a celebrated moment in Dickens's fiction.

Tales in Verse A collection of poems by George *Crabbe, published 1812. There is humour and tenderness, as well as horror, in these 21 tales, intended to reveal the destruction of happiness by uncontrolled passions.

Tales of my Landlord Four series of novels by Walter *Scott: *The *Black Dwarf*, *Old Mortality* (1st series); *The *Heart of Midlothian* (2nd series); *The *Bride of Lammermoor, A *Legend of Montrose* (3rd series); *Count Robert of Paris, *Castle Dangerous* (4th series). Jedediah Cleishbotham, schoolmaster and parish clerk of Gandercleugh, by a fiction of Scott, sold these tales to a publisher. They were supposed to be compiled by his assistant Peter Pattieson. As Scott admitted, the title is misleading, for the tales were not told by any fictional landlord.

Tales of the Hall A collection of poems by George *Crabbe, published 1819. The work shows some decline in formal skill, but is otherwise similar in character to *Tales in Verse*.

TALFOURD, Sir Thomas Noon (1795–1854) Son of a Reading brewer, a judge and member of Parliament but also a literary critic and author of *Ion* (1836), *The Athenian Captive* (1838), and other ambitious tragedies in blank verse, for which William *Macready's acting helped to secure celebrity. His reputation as a playwright, once high, did not last, but Talfourd is still remembered for his editing of the letters of his friend Charles *Lamb, and for having introduced an Act securing real legal protection for authors' copyright. The friendships of this generous and eccentric man spanned the literary generation from Lamb and S. T. *Coleridge to Mary Russell *Mitford and Charles *Dickens, who dedicated *Pickwick Papers* to him. He was a model for Dickens's character Tommy Traddles in **David Copperfield*. See J. A. Brain, *An Evening with Thomas Noon Talfourd* (1889).

TALIESIN (*fl.*550) A British bard first mentioned in the *Saxon Genealogies* appended to the *Historia Britonum* (*c.*690). A mass of poetry, probably of later date, has been ascribed to him, and the *Book of Taliesin* (14th century) is a collection of poems by different authors and of different dates. The village of Tre-Taliesin in Cardiganshire sprang up near the supposed site of his grave. Taliesin, still a mysterious figure, features prominently in Peacock's *The *Misfortunes of Elphin*, and he is mentioned in Tennyson's **Idylls of the King* as one of the Round Table.

Talisman, The A novel by Walter *Scott, published 1825. The novel describes the adventures of a poor but brave Scottish knight, Sir Kenneth, who is caught up in the intrigues between Richard I of England, the king of France, the duke of Austria, and the Knights Templars. He is eventually discovered to be Prince David of Scotland. The most striking portrait in the novel is that of *Saladin, whose wisdom and chivalry is contrasted throughout with the scheming and corruption of the Christian leaders.

TALLIS, Thomas (*c.*1505–1585) English composer and chorister of the Chapel Royal. For this choir Tallis wrote liturgical music, mostly on Latin texts, some of it suggesting Roman Catholic leanings even after the accession of *Elizabeth I. In 1575 he and William *Byrd were granted in 1575 a 21-year patent for the printing of music; in that year they published their *Cantiones Quae ab Argumento Sacrae Vocantur*. The melody known as the 'Tallis Canon' was composed for Matthew *Parker's *Whole Psalter* (1567), which also contained the tune that underlies *Vaughan Williams's *Fantasia on a Theme by Thomas Tallis* (1910).

Talus A character in Edmund *Spenser's *The *Faerie Queene*. When Astraea left the world and returned to heaven, 'she left her groome | An yron man, which did on her attend | Alwayes, to execute her stedfast doome' (V. i. 12). Wielding an iron flail, with which he dispatches criminals, he attends on *Artegall, and represents the executive power of government.

TAMBIMUTTU, James Meary *See* POETRY LONDON.

Tamburlaine the Great A drama in blank verse by Christopher *Marlowe, written not later than 1587, published 1590. Its blank verse was livelier and more sophisticated that that of **Gorboduc*, and it was immediately popular. The material for it was taken by the author from Pedro Mexia's *Spanish Life of Timur*, translated into English in 1571.

Part I of the drama deals with the rise to power of the Scythian shepherd-robber Tamburlaine; he supports Cosroe's rebellion against his brother, the king of Persia, then challenges him for the crown and defeats him. Tamburlaine's ambition and cruelty carry all before him. He conquers the Turkish emperor *Bajazet and leads him about, a prisoner in a cage, taunting him and his empress Zabina until they dash out their brains against the bars of the cage. His ferocity is softened only by his love for his captive Zenocrate, daughter of the sultan of Egypt, and when he takes Damascus she persuades him to spare the sultan's life.

Part II deals with his further conquests, which extend to Babylon, where he is drawn in a chariot dragged by the kings of Trebizond, Soria, Anatolia, and Jerusalem, 'pampered Jades of Asia' (a phrase quoted by Pistol in Shakespeare, *2 *Henry IV*, II. iv), The play ends with Tamburlaine's death.

Tamerlane A tragedy by Nicholas *Rowe, produced 1701, with the professed intention of celebrating William III as the high-minded conqueror of the title, and of vilifying Louis XIV under the character of the defeated Bajazet. The play was, until about 1815, revived annually on 5 November, the date of William's landing in England.

Taming of the Shrew, The A comedy by *Shakespeare, first printed in the *folio of 1623, probably written *c.*1592 or earlier and based in part on the **Supposes* adapted by George *Gascoigne from *Ariosto. In 1594 a quarto text called *The Taming of a Shrew* was published; this was once thought to be Shakespeare's source, but is more likely to be a derivative version.

The play begins with an induction in which Christopher Sly, a drunken Warwickshire tinker, picked up by a lord and his huntsmen on a heath, is brought to a castle, sumptuously treated, and in spite of his protestations is assured that he is a lord who has been out of his mind. He is set down to watch the play that follows, performed solely for his benefit by strolling players. Sly appears again at the end of I. ii, but disappears after that in the folio text; in *A Shrew* he is given five more short scenes throughout the play, some or all of which are often imported into Shakespeare's text in performance.

Baptista Minola of Padua has two daughters, Katherina the Shrew, who is the elder of the two, and Bianca, who has many suitors, but who may not marry until a husband has been found for Katherina. Petruccio, a gentleman from Verona, undertakes to woo the shrew to gain her dowry and to help his friend Hortensio win Bianca. To tame her he pretends to find her rude behaviour courteous and gentle and humiliates her by being late for their wedding and appearing badly dressed. He takes her off to his country house and, under the pretext that nothing there is good enough for her, prevents her from eating or sleeping. By the time they return to Baptista's house, Katherina has been successfully tamed, and Lucentio, a Pisan, has won Bianca by disguising himself as her schoolmaster, while the disappointed Hortensio has to console himself with marriage to a rich widow. At the feast which follows the three bridegrooms wager on whose wife is the most docile and submissive. Katherina argues that 'Thy husband is thy lord, thy life, thy keeper, | Thy head, thy sovereign' and Petruccio wins the bet.

A play by John *Fletcher, *The *Woman's Prize*, shows Petruccio tamed in a second marriage after Kate's death. Petruccio's three times repeated request 'kiss me, Kate' supplied the title for Cole Porter's popular musical of 1948.

'Tam o' Shanter' A narrative poem by Robert *Burns, which had its origins in the poet's request that an illustration of Kirk Alloway be included in Francis Grose's *Antiquities of Scotland*. Burns in return was to supply a witch story to accompany the illustration. He came up with three, and in the autumn of 1790, in a state of high excitement, combined aspects of all of them in a poem he immediately recognized as his masterpiece. 'Tam o' Shanter' was published in the *Edinburgh Herald* and the *Edinburgh Magazine* in March 1791 before appearing a month later as a double column footnote in the second volume of Grose's *Antiquities*. A mock moral tale, the poem is characterized by swift changes of perspective as it recounts the homeward progress of Tam from a snug Ayr alehouse, past 'Alloway's auld haunted kirk', to the brig o' Doon. Though terrifying witches pursue him after his drunken, licentious shout interrupts their Sabbath in the mysteriously lit kirk, he escapes with his life but without the tail of his faithful mare, Meg. The poem brilliantly reconciles the vernacular tradition with the neo-classical aesthetics Burns had been vainly trying to serve in his English verses since 1787.

TAN, Amy (1952–) Chinese American novelist, born in California, whose first publication, *The Joy Luck Club* (1989), describes the experiences of Chinese American immigrants. Tan collaborated over its 1993 movie adaptation. Her 2001 novel *The Bonesetter's Daughter* is typical of Tan's work in exploring the relation between daughters and mothers. *The Opposite of Fate* (2003) is a non-fiction volume of reflections.

Tanaquil In Roman legend, the wife of Tarquinius Priscus, the first of the Tarquin (Etruscan) kings of Rome. Edmund *Spenser uses the name to signify *Elizabeth I in the introduction to Book I of *The *Faerie Queene*.

Tancred, *or The New Crusade* A novel by Benjamin *Disraeli, published 1847; the last of the trilogy **Coningsby*—**Sybil*—*Tancred*. More mystical than its predecessors, and less directly concerned with social and political reform, the novel attempts to resolve the antagonism between Judaism and Christianity and to establish a role for a reforming faith and revitalized church in a progressive society. Tancred, brilliant and beautiful, declares to his bewildered parents, Lord and Lady Montacute, that he intends to learn the secrets of the 'Asian mystery' in the Holy Land. He abandons fashionable London and travels to Jerusalem, and thence to Sinai, where he receives a revelation from the Angel of Arabia of 'a common Father'. But he becomes embroiled in intrigue between the Druses and the Maronites, and is used as a pawn to increase the power of the fiery Fakredeen, a brilliant emir, who manoeuvres Tancred into battle. Tancred, wounded and captured, is saved by by the beautiful Jewish woman Eva, with whom he falls in love. This, and his conviction that Christianity owes everything to the Jews, leads him to propose marriage. But in the final scenes of the novel his parents, the duke and duchess, arrive in Jerusalem to claim him.

Tancred and Gismund, The Tragedy of, *or Gismond of Salerne* A rhetorical love tragedy by Robert Wilmot (*c.*1550–*c.*1608) and others, published 1591 but dating from 1566 or 1568. Act II is possibly by Henry Noel (d. 1597), Act IV by Sir Christopher *Hatton. The play is the first of many to use an Italian tale as source material—in this case a story by *Boccaccio (*see* GHISMONDA).

TANIZAKI, Junichiro (1886–1965) Japanese novelist, born in Tokyo, whose early work is marked by a conscious air of *fin-de-siècle* French decadence. After moving to Osaka in 1923, in the wake of the Tokyo earthquake, he explored the tensions between modern, Westernized life and classical Japanese culture. His most famous novels in the West are *Makioka Sisters* (1943–8), *The Key* (1956), and his masterpiece of erotic obsession, *Diary of a Mad Old Man* (1961–2).

TANNAHILL, Robert (1774–1810) Scottish poet, born in Paisley. At 12 he was apprenticed to his weaver father and showed signs of poetic talent. At 17 he walked to Alloway to see the setting of *'Tam o' Shanter' and began writing songs. From 1805 his work began to appear in newspapers and journals and in 1807 he published *Poems and Songs*, which included a harshly criticized dramatic 'interlude', 'The Soldier's Return'. Embittered by having a revised edition declined by two publishers, he burnt his manuscripts and drowned himself in a culvert near Paisley.

TANNHÄUSER, Der (*c.*1200–*c.*1270) Important Middle High German lyric poet. Little is known of his life, but he took part in a crusade and was later a court poet in Austria. His work represents a significant development in the tradition of courtly love poetry (*see* MINNESÄNGER) as it introduces elements of humour and even parody. Perhaps in consequence of the frank eroticism of his work he became the subject of a folk legend narrated in the 16th-century ballad the *Tannhäuserlied* where he is depicted as the lover of a beautiful woman who keeps him ensnared in the grotto of Venus in the 'Venusberg'. Emerging repentant, he goes to Rome to seek absolution which is denied. After his departure in despair, however, the miraculous flowering of the pope's pilgrim staff indicates the possibility of forgiveness. Tannhäuser is sent for but has returned to Venusberg and is never found. Interest in the legend revived in the 19th century, and Thomas *Carlyle translated a version by Ludwig Tieck (1773–1853) in *German Romance* (1827). The ballad was one of Richard *Wagner's sources for the opera *Tannhäuser* (1845) although new elements are introduced and the hero achieves redemption. Wagner's version is the basis of a poem by Edward Robert *Lytton, and the legend recurs as the subject of A. C. *Swinburne's poem 'Laus Veneris' (1866). Aubrey *Beardsley's unfinished *Under the Hill* (commenced 1894) offers a further retelling of the legend.

TARKINGTON, Booth (1869–1946) American novelist, born in Indianapolis, whose works include *The Gentleman from Indiana* (1899), *Monsieur Beaucaire* (1900, the historical romance which first won him popularity), *The Magnificent Ambersons* (1918, a chronicle of the Midwest), and *Alice Adams* (1921). Works like *Penrod* (1914) were addressed to younger readers.

TARLTON, Richard (d. 1588) Actor, a man of humble origin and imperfect education, who is said to have attracted attention as a young man by his 'happy unhappy answers' and was introduced to *Elizabeth I through the earl of *Leicester. He became one of the queen's players in 1583, winning immense popularity with his jests, comic acting, and improvisations of doggerel verse. He is sometimes identified with *Spenser's 'Pleasant Willy' (*see* 'Teares of the Muses, The') and Shakespeare's *Yorick. Many fictitious anecdotes connected with him were published, notably *Tarlton's Jests*, in three parts (1613), and *Tarlton's News out of Purgatory* (1590).
See also fool.

Tarzan *See* Burroughs, Edgar Rice.

Task, The A poem in six books by William *Cowper, published 1785. When Cowper's friend Lady Austen (whom he met in 1781) suggested to him the sofa in his room as the subject of a poem, the poet set about 'the task'. Its six books are entitled 'The Sofa', 'The Time-Piece', 'The Garden', 'The Winter Evening', 'The Winter Morning Walk', and 'The Winter Walk at Noon'. Cowper opens with a mock-heroic account of the evolution of the sofa ('I sing the sofa') but thereafter addresses a wide range of topics, from cucumbers to salvation, in an accessible, emotionally fluent style of blank verse. The poem stresses the delights of a retired life ('God made the country, and man made the town', Bk I, 749); describes the poet's own search for peace ('I was a stricken deer, that left the herd', Bk III, 108); and evokes the consolations of religious faith, the pleasures of gardening, and the comforts of evenings by the fireside. It condemns aristocratic diversions, French fashions, *slavery, and cruelty to animals; the poet shows tenderness not only for his pet hare, but even for worms and snails. The poem was an immediate success; Robert *Burns found it 'a glorious poem' that expressed 'the Religion of God and Nature', and William Wordsworth's *The *Prelude* contains many echoes of Cowper's passages of natural description and reflective autobiography.

TASSO, Torquato (1544–95) Italian poet and playwright, son of Bernardo Tasso (author of an epic on *Amadis of Gaul). He was born at Sorrento and spent many years at the court of Ferrara. He was from early life in constant terror of persecution and adverse criticism, and his conduct at Ferrara was such as to make it necessary for the duke, Alphonso II of *Este, to lock him up as mad from 1579 to 1586. The legend of his passion for Leonora d'Este, the duke's discovery of it, and his consequent imprisonment was for long widely believed; John *Milton refers to it (in a Latin poem), Lord *Byron's *The Lament of Tasso* is based on it, and *Goethe's play *Torquato Tasso* (1790) supports it, as does *Donizetti's opera (1833) of the same title. Tasso was released on condition that he would leave Ferrara, and he spent the rest of his life wandering from court to court, unhappy, poverty-stricken, and paranoid, though widely admired. He died in Rome.

His chief works were *Rinaldo*, a romance epic (1562); a pastoral play, *Aminta* (1573; English translation 1591), which had a great success; **Jerusalem Delivered* (1580–1); and a less successful tragedy, *Torrismondo* (1586–7). He was also a prolific and brilliant lyric poet in a variety of metres including *Pindaric odes, and Edmund *Spenser used his sonnets in many of his **Amoretti*. Tasso's epics and his critical works (*Discorsi dell'arte poetica, Discorsi del poema eroico*) had a great influence on English literature, displayed in the works of Samuel *Daniel, Milton, Giles and Phineas *Fletcher, Abraham *Cowley, John *Dryden, and others; Milton refers to his theory of the epic in *The Reason of Church Government* and *Of Education*. Edward *Fairfax's translation of *Jerusalem Delivered* (1600) also had an influence in its own right; according to Dryden, Edmund *Waller said that he 'derived the harmony of his numbers' from it. In the following century, Thomas *Gray translated a passage (XIV. 32–9), and William *Collins recorded ('Ode on the Popular Superstitions of the Highlands') his great admiration for both Tasso and Fairfax:

> How have I trembled, when at Tancred's stroke
> Its gushing blood, the gaping Cypress pour'd.

See C. P. Brand, *Torquato Tasso* (1965).

TASSONI, Alessandro (1565–1635) Italian poet, philosopher, historian, politician, and member of several learned Academies. He joined the entourage of Cardinal Ascanio *Sforza in Rome (1597) and later became a court official first in Turin and then in his native Modena. His most famous work is the mock-heroic, pseudo-historical epic *La secchia rapita* (1622; rev. 1630: *The Stolen Bucket/The Rape of the Bucket*) which may have inspired Alexander *Pope.

TATE, Allen (1899–1979) American poet and critic, born in Kentucky. He began his literary career as editor of the *little magazine the Tennessee *Fugitive* (1922–5), which published work by John Crowe *Ransom and others, and supported a sense of Southern regionalism. He is best known for his poetry; his collections include *Mr Pope and Other Poems* (1928) and *Poems 1928–1931* (1932). His essays are collected in *On the Limits of Poetry* (1948) and other volumes. *The Fathers* (1938) was his only novel. See Thomas A. Underwood, *Allen Tate: Orphan of the South* (2000).

TATE, Nahum (1652–1715) Playwright, most of whose dramatic works were adaptations from earlier writers; his 1681 version of **King Lear* omits the Fool, makes Edgar and Cordelia fall in love, and ends happily. It was highly popular; Samuel *Johnson defended it on the grounds that the original is too painful, and the full text was not restored until the 19th century: Edmund *Kean was the first actor to conclude with Lear's death. Tate also wrote, with John *Dryden, the second part of **Absalom and Achitophel*; also the libretto of Henry *Purcell's *Dido and Aeneas*. In 1696 he published with Nicholas Brady (1659–1726) the well-known metrical version of the Psalms that bears their name. He was appointed *poet laureate in 1692, and was mocked by Alexander *Pope in *The *Dunciad*.

TATE and **BRADY** *See* TATE, NAHUM.

Tatler A *periodical founded by Richard *Steele, of which the first issue appeared on 12 April 1709; it appeared three times a week until 2 January 1711, numbering 271 issues in all. The author assumes the character of Isaac Bickerstaff, a name borrowed from Jonathan *Swift (some of whose poems first appeared in the *Tatler*), from his hoaxes against the astrologer John Partridge (1644–1715). According to no. 1, the *Tatler* was to include 'Accounts of Gallantry, Pleasure and Entertainment... under the Article of White's Chocolate House'; poetry under that of Will's Coffee House; foreign and domestic news from St James's Coffee house; learning from the Grecian; and so on. Several 'lucubrations' are issued 'from my own apartment' and the paper also regularly included letters, stories, reviews of recent plays and publications, and spoof advertisements alongside genuine ones. Gradually it adopted a loftier moral tone, attacking the evils of duelling and gambling, and discussing all questions of good manners from the standpoint of humane civilization and gentlemanly taste. The *Tatler* was republished in book form and was very widely read. Its vein of light satire was much imitated: Alexander Pope's **Rape of the Lock*, for example, borrows freely from the periodical's account of contemporary fashions. From an early stage in the history of the *Tatler* Steele had the collaboration of Joseph *Addison, who contributed notes, suggestions, and a number of complete papers. It was succeeded by the **Spectator*, which they edited jointly. See the edition by Donald F. Bond (3 vols, 1987).

TAUCHNITZ, Christian Bernhard von (1816–95) Founder of a publishing house at Leipzig which in 1841 began to issue piratically, and from 1843 to 1943 by sanction or copyright, a series of 5,370 volumes eventually called 'Collection of British and American Authors'. Although specified for sale only on the Continent, the series prefigured and then exemplified the commercial and cultural success of the paperback market. The books were distributed worldwide and sold in tens of millions of copies.

TAVENER, John (1944–) English composer, educated at the Royal Academy of Music. Tavener's prolific output draws inspiration from liturgy, mysticism, and poetry, and includes operas on biblical themes and choral or solo settings of *Sappho, *Shakespeare, John *Donne, George *Herbert, William *Blake, W. B. *Yeats, and T. S. *Eliot. Tavener was knighted in 2000.

TAYLOR, A. J. P. (Alan John Percivale) (1906–90) Historian, born in Birkdale, Lancashire, educated at Bootham School, York, and Oriel College, Oxford. His many publications include *The Habsburg Monarchy* (1941), *The Troublemakers* (1957, from his Ford lectures), *The Origins of the Second World War* (1961), and a life of Lord *Beaverbrook (1972). He also became widely known as a journalist and television personality, and his autobiography, *A Personal History* (1983), gives a lively and frequently iconoclastic account of his colleagues and acquaintances (including a hostile portrait of Dylan *Thomas), and traces the evolution of his political sympathies from his support of the workers in the General Strike to his support of the Campaign for Nuclear Disarmament. See Kathleen Burk, *Troublemaker: The Life and History of A. J. P. Taylor* (2000).

TAYLOR, Edward (*c.*1642–1729) American poet and pastor, born in England. He emigrated to Boston in 1668, and was educated at Harvard University. His devotional poems remained in manuscript, at his own request, and were not published until 1937. *God's Determinations* and the *Preparatory Meditations* are particularly important devotional sequences. His poetry belongs in the metaphysical tradition of George *Herbert and Francis *Quarles. A full edition of his works, ed. D. E. Stanford, was published in 1960.

TAYLOR, Elizabeth (1912–75) Novelist and short story writer, educated at the Abbey School, Reading; she then worked as tutor and librarian until she married in 1936 and settled in Buckinghamshire. Many of her books are set in provincial towns and villages amongst the middle classes, a circumstance which has sometimes led to this shrewd, witty, but compassionate observer of snobbery and the deceits and disappointments of everyday life being underrated. Taylor was in fact an atheist who joined the Communist Party in her early twenties and remained an active supporter of the Labour Party throughout her life, and there is nothing in the least bit cosy about her books. Angus *Wilson perceptively summed up her qualities by referring to her 'warm heart and sharp claws'. Her first novel, *At Mrs Lippincote's* (1945), was followed by eleven more, which are written with an elegant and often deadly precision. *Angel* (1957), for example, describes the appalling and destructive self-deception of a popular novelist who genuinely believes in the ludicrous fantasy world she purveys in her books. Taylor was often compared with Jane *Austen, and *Palladian* (1946), in which a governess is employed by a widower, knowingly brings the conventions of the Romantic novel up against the stark realities of the present day. Her equally fine short stories, first published in such periodicals as the *New Yorker*, were collected in several volumes, including *The Blush* (1958), *A Dedicated Man* (1965), and *The Devastating Boys* (1972). The title novella of the collection *Hester Lily* (1954) is a minor masterpiece, describing the havoc wreaked on a marriage by the husband's much younger but apparently unremarkable cousin, while the childhood bond between two cousins in another of Taylor's best books, *A Game of Hide and Seek* (1951), persists catastrophically into adulthood. As in the work of her admirer Ivy *Compton-Burnett, children and domestic staff often provide some of the most comic and disturbing characters in Taylor's books. Her later novels include *Mrs Palfrey at the Claremont* (1971), a funny but unsparing portrait of impoverished but genteel old age, and the posthumously published *Blaming* (1976).

TAYLOR, Sir Henry (1800–86) Dramatist and man of letters. He held an appointment in the Colonial Office from 1824 to 1872, during which time he published a number of popular verse dramas: the most admired was *Philip van Artevelde* (1834), a long work set in Flanders in the 14th century; he describes its hero, a retiring citizen raised to prominence during the power struggles between Ghent and Bruges, as 'a statesman and a man of business', two particularly important roles for Taylor. His *The Statesman* (1836) was an ironical exposition of the arts of succeeding as a civil servant: its apparent cynicism dismayed some readers, but it was a significant text in the sustained 19th-century reassessment of *Machiavelli (see also, for instance, John *Galt's *The Provost*, 1822). Twentieth-century editors (H. J. Laski, 1927; L. Silberman, 1957) found it also a culturally valuable commentary on the changing and expanding role of the Civil Service. Taylor was a friend of Robert *Southey and his literary executor. His *Autobiography 1800–75* was published in 1885 (privately printed 1877) and his complete works in five volumes appeared in 1877–8.

TAYLOR, Jane (1783–1824) and **Ann** (1782–1866). They came from a literary family ('The Taylors of Ongar') and were probably the most imitated poets for children of the 19th century. *Original Poems for Infant Minds* (1804–5), which also contained poems by Adelaide O'Keefe (1776–1855), ran to 50 editions. It contains one of the most popular poems of the century, 'My Mother', and was part of the 'awful warning' school of poetry. *Rhymes from the Nursery* (1806) contained the classic 'The Star' ('Twinkle, twinkle, little star'), famously parodied by Lewis *Carroll, and rhymes with a republican flavour. Walter *Scott and Robert *Browning admired their work.

TAYLOR, Jeremy (1613–67) Clergyman and religious writer, born at Cambridge, the son of a barber. He was educated at Gonville and Caius College, Cambridge. Having attracted William *Laud's attention as a preacher, he was sent by him to Oxford and became a fellow of All Souls College. He was chaplain to Laud and Charles I, and was appointed rector of Uppingham in 1638. He was taken prisoner in the Royalist defeat before Cardigan Castle in 1645, and retired to Golden Grove, Carmarthenshire, where he wrote most of his greater works. After the *Restoration he was made bishop of Down and Connor, Ireland, and subsequently of Dromore. He died at Lisburn and was buried in his cathedral of Dromore. His fame rests on the combined simplicity and splendour of his style, of which *The Rule and Exercises of Holy Living* (1650) and *The Rule and Exercises of Holy Dying* (1651) are perhaps the best examples. Among his other works, *The Liberty of Prophesying*, an argument for toleration, appeared in 1647; his *Eniautos*, or series of sermons for the Christian year, in 1653; *The Golden Grove*, a manual of daily prayers, in 1655; his *Ductor Dubitantium*, 'a general instrument of moral theology' for determining cases of conscience, in 1660; and *The Worthy Communicant* in the same year.

TAYLOR, John (1580–1653) The 'water poet', born of humble parentage in Gloucester. He was sent to Gloucester Grammar School, but becoming 'mired' in his Latin grammar was apprenticed to a waterman, pressed for the navy, and was present at the siege of Cadiz. He then became a Thames waterman, and increased his earnings by writing rollicking verse and prose; he obtained the patronage of Ben *Jonson and others, and diverted both court and City. He went on foot from London to Braemar, visited the Continent, started from London to Queenborough in a brown-paper boat and narrowly escaped drowning, and accomplished other journeys, each one resulting in a booklet with an odd title. He published in 1630 a collected edition of his works, *All the Works of John Taylor, the Water-Poet* (reprinted, with other pieces, by the Spenser Society, 1868–78), but continued to write a good deal after this, notably Royalist ballads and news-sheets.

TAYLOR, John (1781–1864) Publisher, who first distinguished himself, amid much controversy, by identifying *'Junius' as Sir Philip Francis (1740–1818) in 1813. After the death of John *Scott, he became the editor of the *London Magazine*, 1821–4, and he became a very perceptive partner in the publishing firm of Taylor and Hessey. He published the work of Thomas *De Quincey, Charles *Lamb, William *Hazlitt, John *Keats, John *Clare, and others, many of whom had already appeared in the *London Magazine*. He greatly encouraged and assisted Clare, published his first volume of *Poems* in 1820, and raised a subscription, to which he contributed generously himself, for the joint benefit of Clare and Keats. But Clare felt that the comparative failure of *The *Shepherd's Calendar* in 1827 was Taylor's fault, and although Taylor offered Clare all the remaining copies to sell for his own benefit, he advanced no more money to the poet and was not the publisher of *The Rural Muse* (1835). He offended Keats, and other writers, by his occasional 'revisions' of their works. He held regular dinners for writers, lent money to Keats to travel to Italy, and seems to have combined the qualities of businessman and friend.

TAYLOR, Philip Meadows (1808–76) Anglo-Indian novelist and historian, born in Liverpool. He joined the Indian army and became a correspondent for *The *Times* from 1840 to 1853. He was author of the successful *Confessions of a Thug*

(1839), a result of his investigation into Thuggism, the secret terrorist movement in India. His reputation rests mainly on stories written after his retirement to England in 1860, notably the trilogy *Tara: A Mahratta Tale* (1843), *Ralph Darnell* (1865), and *Seeta* (1872), which delineate epochs of Indian history from the 17th century to his own time. His autobiography, ed. A. M. Taylor (his daughter), appeared in 1877.

TAYLOR, Tom (1817–80) Educated at Trinity College, Cambridge, of which he became a fellow, editor of **Punch*, 1874–80. He produced many successful plays (some in collaboration with Charles *Reade), most of them adaptations. His comedy *Our American Cousin* (1858) contained the character of the brainless peer Lord Dundreary, played with great panache by E. A. (Edward Askew) Sothern (1826–81). He edited Benjamin Robert *Haydon's autobiography in 1853.

TAYLOR, William (1765–1836) Critic and translator, born in Norwich. He was significant for his role as an early advocate of German literature in England although his translations, which included Bürger's ballads (*see* 'LENORE'), Gotthold Ephraim *Lessing's *Nathan der Weise* in 1791, and Johann Wolfgang von *Goethe's *Iphigenia auf Tauris* in 1793, never became widely known. By the time the three volumes of his *Historic Survey of German Poetry* appeared (1828–30), in which he brought together his many magazine contributions on the subject, it was badly out of date—August von *Kotzebue was ludicrously overrated—and was savaged by Thomas *Carlyle in the **Edinburgh Review*. Like Henry Crabb *Robinson, Taylor's influence as a popularizer of German writers was chiefly personal. He encouraged Walter *Scott's interest in German and was a friend of Robert *Southey, his correspondence with whom is included in a *Memoir* by J. W. Robberds (1843).

TCHAIKOVSKY, Peter Ilich (1840–93) Russian composer of symphony and opera. His fantasy overture *Romeo and Juliet* (1869), initially proposed to him by *Balakirev, is perhaps the most widely heard of any *Shakespeare-inspired musical work. It was his first masterpiece (revised in 1870, and again in 1880), integrating the dramatic and passionate elements of the play into a compact musical structure. In the last months of his life Tchaikovsky used the famous love motif as the basis for a duet version of the opening of Act III scene v of Shakespeare's play, but it does not appear that he planned to make an opera on the subject. There are two other important Shakespearian orchestral works: the symphonic fantasia *The Tempest* (1873) and the fantasy overture *Hamlet* (1888); the symphonic poem *Francesca da Rimini* (1877) is based on *Dante. The *Manfred Symphony* (1885), after Lord *Byron, was urged upon Tchaikovsky by Balakirev, and caused him much pain, in part because he was tiring of music with a narrative 'programme': 'the symphony has turned out to be huge, serious and difficult,' he wrote, 'absorbing all my time, sometimes to my utter exhaustion.'

'Teares of the Muses, The' A poem by Edmund *Spenser, included in the *Complaints*, published 1591. In this the poet deplores, through the mouth of several *Muses, the decay of literature and learning.

TEATE, Faithfull (*fl.* 1650s) Poet and clergyman, father of Nahum *Tate, born in Co. Cavan and educated at Trinity College, Dublin. Teate went to England after the rebellion of 1641, in which three of his children were killed. His *Ter Tria* (1658) is a long, 'metaphysical' Trinitarian poem remarkable for its figurative vigour.

TEILHARD DE CHARDIN, Pierre (1881–1955) French palaeontologist and Jesuit priest, author of a series of posthumously published works in which he sought to reconcile evidence about the origin of mankind with his Christian faith. Among these, the best known is *Le Phénomène humain* (written 1938–40; pub. 1955: *The Human Phenomenon*), in which he elaborated a system of cosmic evolution, explaining the emergence of mind from matter by the increase in complexity and consciousness, and suggesting the development of a specifically human sphere of activity, known as the noosphere, or domain of thought, which is to reach its ultimate stage of development, the point of maximum differentiated unity, known as Omega Point.

Telemachus *See* ODYSSEY.

television Grew out of *radio broadcasting and initially followed a similar programming pattern, with the BBC transmitting a limited service of music, news, and drama from 1936 until the outbreak of war in 1939. Programmes resumed in 1946 and interest was boosted by Elizabeth II's coronation in 1953, watched by an estimated 20 million viewers. After the single BBC channel was joined by a commercial channel in 1956 and BBC2 in 1964, British television drama became a highly competitive arena, with writers such as Harold *Pinter and Alun *Owen contributing to ABC's Armchair Theatre in the late 1950s, before BBC's Wednesday Play and Play for Today series took the lead in the mid-1960s with challenging naturalistic work by two early specialists in television drama, David *Mercer and John Hopkins (1931–98), as well as original scripts by Dennis *Potter and Jim Allen (1926–99), and improvised drama by Mike *Leigh. Channel 4 supported films rather than television drama from 1982, and the 'single play' has largely disappeared from British television, replaced by drama series.

Tempest, The A romantic drama by *Shakespeare probably written in 1611, when it was performed before *James I at Whitehall; in 1613 it was included in the wedding celebrations for the Princess Elizabeth and the elector palatine. It was not printed until 1623 when it appeared as the first play in the first *folio. It is usually taken to be his last play written without a collaborator. Although there are several analogues for the story of *The Tempest*, and contemporary accounts of the shipwreck of the *Sea-Venture* in 1609 on the Bermudas and passages from Arthur *Golding's Ovid and John *Florio's Montaigne contribute details to the play, no single source for it is known. As Samuel *Johnson observed, *The Tempest*'s 'plan is regular', that is, it conforms to the *unities.

Prospero, duke of Milan, ousted by his brother Antonio and turned adrift on the sea with his child Miranda, is a castaway on a lonely island, once the place of banishment of the witch Sycorax. Prospero uses his knowledge of magic to release various spirits (including *Ariel) imprisoned by the witch, and these now obey his orders. He also keeps in service the witch's son Caliban, a misshapen monster, formerly the sole inhabitant of the island. Prospero and Miranda have lived in this way for twelve years. When the play begins a ship carrying the usurper, his confederate Alonso, king of Naples, Alonso's brother Sebastian and son Ferdinand, is by Prospero's art wrecked on the island. The passengers are saved, but Ferdinand is thought by the rest to be drowned, and he thinks this is their fate. According to Prospero's plan Ferdinand and Miranda are thrown together, and fall in love. Prospero appears to distrust Ferdinand and sets him to carrying logs. On another part of the island Sebastian and Antonio plot to kill Alonso and Gonzalo, an old councillor who had helped Prospero in his banishment. Caliban offers his services to Stefano, a drunken butler, and Trinculo, a jester, and persuades them to try to murder Prospero. As the conspirators approach, Prospero breaks off the masque of Iris, Juno, and Ceres, which Ariel has presented to Ferdinand and Miranda. Caliban, Stefano, and Trinculo are driven off and Ariel brings the king and his courtiers to Prospero's cell. There he greets 'My true preserver' Gonzalo, forgives his brother Antonio, on the condition that he restores his dukedom to him, and reunites Alonso with his son Ferdinand, who is discovered playing chess with Miranda. While Alonso repents for what he has done, Antonio and Sebastian do not speak directly to Prospero, but exchange ironic and cynical comments with each other. The boatswain and master of the ship appear to say that it has been magically repaired and that the crew is safe. Before all embark for Italy Prospero frees Ariel from his service, renounces his magic, and leaves Caliban once more alone on the island.

The Tempest has inspired numerous works of art, including Milton's **Comus*, P. B. *Shelley's 'Ariel to Miranda' (*see* ARIEL), Robert *Browning's 'Caliban upon Setebos', music by *Berlioz and *Tchaikovsky, W. H. *Auden's series of poetic meditations *The Sea and the Mirror*, a science fiction film, *Forbidden Planet* (1954), Marina *Warner's novel *Indigo* (1992), and an opera (2004) by Thomas Adès.

Templars, Knights An order founded after the First Crusade and endorsed by the church in 1129. It consisted originally of nine knights whose profession was to safeguard pilgrims to Jerusalem. They were granted by Baldwin II, king of Jerusalem, a dwelling place in his palace near the temple. They became a source of weakness to the Christian king of Jerusalem because of their dependence on the pope and violation of treaties with Muslim powers. After the battle of the Horns of Hattin (1187) *Saladin beheaded them all, about 200 in number. The order lost support and was suppressed by the kings of Europe under circumstances, especially in France, of great cruelty. It was suppressed by the pope and the Council of Vienne (1312). Robert *Browning's poem 'The Heretic's Tragedy' alludes to the burning of Jacques de Bourg-Molay, the grand master, in 1314.

TEMPLE, Sir William (1628–99) Diplomat and writer, educated at Emmanuel College, Cambridge. He was envoy at Brussels in 1666, and visited The Hague, where he negotiated the triple alliance between England, the Netherlands, and Sweden, to protect Spain from French ambition. He went again to The Hague in 1674, where he brought about the marriage between William of Orange and Mary. In 1654 he married Dorothy *Osborne, whose letters to him give a vivid picture of the times. He settled first at Sheen, then at Moor Park, near Farnham, Surrey, where he was much occupied with gardening, and where Jonathan *Swift was a member of his household. His principal works include *Observations upon... the Netherlands* (1672), an essay upon *The Advancement of Trade in Ireland* (1673), and three volumes of *Miscellanea* (1680, 1692, 1701). The second of these contains 'Of Ancient and Modern Learning', an essay which, by its uncritical praise of the spurious epistles of *Phalaris, exposed Temple to the censure of Richard *Bentley and led to a vigorous controversy. The *Miscellanea* also include 'Upon the Gardens of Epicurus', 'Of Health and Long Life', 'Of Heroic Virtue', and 'Of Poetry'. Temple's letters were published by Jonathan Swift, 1700–3, after Temple's death. His *Memoirs*, relating to the period 1672–9, published in 1692, are an interesting blend of public and private affairs.

Temptation of Christ *See* BIBLE.

Tenant of Wildfell Hall, The The second and last of Anne *Brontë's novels, published 1848. Written in the first person with a male narrator, Gilbert Markham, it has a complex epistolary and diary structure. Markham, a young farmer, falls in love with Helen Graham, a young widow and talented painter newly arrived in the neighbourhood with her son Arthur. She is the tenant of the title. Her youth, beauty, and seclusion, and her mysterious relationship with her landlord Lawrence, give rise to local gossip, which Markham refuses to credit until he himself overhears Helen and Lawrence in intimate conversation. He violently assaults Lawrence, and Helen, distressed at the threatened rupture of their friendship, reveals the truth of her past to him through a lengthy document. Despite her family's warnings, she had married Arthur Huntingdon, who had lapsed into a dissolute life. She had fled, to protect her child, to Wildfell Hall, provided for her by Lawrence, who is her brother. Shortly after the revelation of this secret, Helen returns to nurse her husband through a fatal illness, his death hastened by alcohol, and the way is left clear for Markham successfully to renew his suit. In her 'Biographical Notice' (1850) Charlotte *Brontë suggested that the portrait of Huntingdon was based on their brother Branwell, in whom Anne Brontë had had ample opportunity to observe 'the terrible effects of talents misused and faculties abused', and the novel was generally considered 'coarse', 'brutal', and excessively morbid. The author defended it in a preface to the second edition: 'I am at a loss to conceive how a man should permit himself to write anything that would be really disgraceful to a woman, or why a woman should be censured for writing anything that would be proper and becoming for a man.' Its forthright treatment of Arthur's alcoholic decline, and of Helen's resolute defiance of his attempts to control her, has since attracted much critical interest and admiration.

Ten Commandments *See* MOSES.

TENN, William (1920–) Pseudonym of American *science fiction writer Philip Klass, born in London; noted for the darkly comic anti-war story 'The Liberation of Earth' (1953). *Of Men and Monsters* (1968), his only novel, imagines humanity as vermin scavenging among conquering aliens.

TENNANT, Emma (1937–) Novelist, born in London but brought up largely in Scotland. She founded and edited the literary review *Bananas*. Her novels include early neo-*Gothic and *magic realist works such as *Hotel de Dream* (1976) and *The Bad Sister* (1978), and later revisionist versions of classic texts, among them *Pemberley* (1993), a sequel to **Pride and Prejudice*, and *The French Dancer's Bastard* (2006), which attempts to complement and continue **Jane Eyre*.

TENNANT, William (1784–1848) Educated at St Andrews University, a parish schoolmaster, at Anstruther in Fife, who became professor of oriental languages at St Andrews. He is remembered for his poem *Anster Fair* (1812), a mock-heroic description of the fair in James V's reign, and of the courting, with fairy intervention, of Maggie Lauder by Rob the Ranter.

TENNIEL, Sir John (1820–1914) Illustrator. He worked for **Punch* from 1850, and from 1864 succeeded John *Leech as its chief cartoonist; 'Dropping the Pilot' (1890), referring to Bismarck's resignation, is one of his best-known cartoons. His illustrations for *Alice's Adventures in Wonderland* (1865) and *Through the Looking-Glass* (1871) by Lewis Carroll (Charles *Dodgson) are perfect examples of the integration of illustration with text. See Roger Simpson, *Sir John Tenniel* (1994).

TENNYSON, Alfred, first Baron Tennyson (1809–92) Poet, born at Somersby, Lincolnshire, the third surviving son of the rector, George Tennyson. He went to Trinity College, Cambridge, where he joined the *Apostles and became friends with Arthur Henry *Hallam. In 1829 he won the Chancellor's Medal for English verse with 'Timbuctoo', the first poem in blank verse to win. *Poems by Two Brothers* (1827) contains some early work that he chose not to reprint even in his juvenilia, as well as poems by his brothers Charles and Frederick. *Poems Chiefly Lyrical* (1830, including *'Mariana') was unfavourably reviewed by John *Lockhart and John *Wilson (1785–1854). In 1832 he travelled with Hallam on the Continent, visiting among other places Cauteret, which provided him with lasting inspiration. Hallam, who had done much to encourage and promote Tennyson's work, died in Vienna in 1833. That year Tennyson began **In Memoriam*, a long elegy that he published seventeen years later; it is written in what has become known as the Tennysonian stanza.

In December 1832 he published a further volume of *Poems* (dated 1833), which included 'The *Lady of Shalott', 'The Two Voices', 'Oenone', 'The Lotos-Eaters', and 'A Dream of Fair Women'; 'Tithonus', published 1860, was composed 1833–4. In 1842 a selection from the previous two volumes appeared, many of the poems much revised, with new poems, including *'Morte d'Arthur' (the germ of **Idylls of the King*), *'Locksley Hall', *'Ulysses', and 'St Simeon Stylites'. From 1845 until his death he received a Civil List pension of £200 per annum. In 1847 he published *The *Princess* and in 1850 *In Memoriam*; that year he was also appointed *poet laureate in succession to William *Wordsworth; and he married Emily Sellwood (1813–96), after a long engagement. He wrote his 'Ode' on the death of *Wellington in 1852 and 'The *Charge of the Light Brigade' in 1854, having at this time settled in Farringford on the Isle of Wight.

Tennyson's fame was now firmly established, and **Maud, and Other Poems* (1855) and the first four *Idylls of the King* (1859) sold extremely well. Among many friends and admirers who visited Farringford were Edward *FitzGerald (who had helped him financially in early years), Edward *Lear, Coventry *Patmore, Arthur Hugh *Clough, Francis Turner *Palgrave, and William *Allingham. Prince Albert called in 1856, but despite the high esteem in which she held him, Queen *Victoria never visited, preferring to summon him to Osborne or Windsor. Although suspicious of unknown admirers, Tennyson was a sociable man, with a fondness for declaiming his work to a respectful audience; his wife and his son Hallam protected him from hostile criticism, to which he was sensitive. In London he frequented the literary and artistic salon of Sarah Prinsep (1816–87) at Little Holland House; her sister, the photographer Julia Margaret *Cameron, moved to the Isle of Wight in 1860, where she used Tennyson and his family as subjects and was later commissioned by him to produce photographic illustrations for some of his poems. **Enoch Arden Etc.* appeared in 1864; *The Holy Grail and Other Poems* (including 'Lucretius') in 1869 (dated 1870); 'The Last Tournament' in the **Contemporary Review* in 1871; and **Gareth and Lynette, etc.* in 1872. Tennyson began building his second residence, Aldworth, near Haslemere in Surrey, in 1868. His dramas *Queen Mary* and *Harold* were published in 1875 and 1876, and *The Falcon*, *The Cup*, and *Becket* in 1884, in which year he was made a peer. He published **Tiresias, and Other Poems* in 1885, and *The Foresters* appeared in 1892. He was buried in Westminster Abbey, and a life by his son Hallam appeared in 1897 (*Tennyson: A Memoir by his Son*, 2 vols).

In his later years there were signs that widespread admiration of Tennyson's work was beginning to wane; but after mixed responses from early 20th-century authors and critics, his place as one of the most important poets in English literary tradition was confirmed. Thomas *Carlyle felt that the *Idylls* were 'finely elaborated' but that they expressed 'the inward perfectn. of *vacancy*'. This characteristic of Tennyson's work, which Walt *Whitman termed his 'finest verbalism', continues to divide readers' views, some considering it to betray at times a hollowness of conviction, while others appreciate the richness, poise, and precision it creates in Tennyson's responses to diverse emotional and political subject matter. In 1870, Alfred *Austin described Tennyson's work as 'poetry of the drawing room', and for a time critical opinion tended to endorse W. H. *Auden's view that 'his genius was lyrical', rather than narrative, epic, or dramatic. T. S. *Eliot, however, called him 'the great master of metric as well as of melancholia', who has 'the finest ear of any English poet since Milton'. Revival of serious interest in his work began with some of the longer poems, ('Locksley Hall', *The Princess*, 'Enoch Arden'), and his work continues to suggest excellent new readings in its emotional, political, formal, and linguistic aspects. The standard annotated edition is by Christopher *Ricks (1989, 3 vols); see also his *Tennyson* (1972; 1989). There is a life by Robert Martin (1980).

TENNYSON, Frederick (1807–98) Poet, eldest brother of Alfred *Tennyson. He contributed (with Charles *Tennyson Turner) to *Poems by Two Brothers* (1827), and published *Days and Hours* (1854), *The Isles of Greece* (1890), and other volumes of verse.

TENNYSON TURNER, Charles (1808–79) Poet, elder brother of Alfred *Tennyson. He contributed (with Frederick *Tennyson) to *Poems by Two Brothers* (1827) and published from time to time volumes of sonnets (1830–80), simple and spare in manner, some of them depicting life in the Lincolnshire wolds.

TEPPER, Sheri Stewart (1929–) American *science fiction writer born in Littleton, Colorado; her work explores feminist and ecological ideas to memorable effect in novels like *The Gate to Woman's Country* (1988), *Grass* (1989), and *Gibbon's Decline and Fall* (1996). She has also written mysteries under various pseudonyms.

TERENCE (Publius Terentius Afer) (d. *c.*159 BC) Roman comic poet, allegedly born in Carthage and a slave at Rome. Four of his plays, *Andria*, *Adelphi*, *Eunuchus*, and *Heautontimorumenos*, are adaptations of *Menander; his other two plays, *Hecyra* and *Phormio*, are also imitations of Greek originals. Although he employs the same limited range of characters that is found in *Plautus, he gives them greater depth and presents a world of genuine relationships. He was famed in antiquity for the elegance and colloquial character of his Latin. It was as a stylist that he was studied in the Middle Ages and figured in the curriculum of most Tudor schools: there is an early translation of the *Andria* (*c.*1520), a later one specifically for schools by Maurice Kyffin (1588), and a much-reprinted English version of all the six comedies by Richard Bernard (1598). Ben *Jonson partly derived his view of comedy from commentators on Terence. But Terence was known more through imitations than through translations. Along with Plautus, he contributed plots, characters, and tone to the mainstream of Renaissance comedy in 16th-century Italy, then (with original features) in the France of *Corneille and *Molière, from where it spread to Restoration London.

TERESA (or Theresa), **St** (Teresa of Ávila) (1515–82) A Spanish saint, famous for her mystical writings. Her *Libro de la vida*: *Life* (written ?1561–6, pub. 1588) and *Libro de las fundaciones* (*The Book of the Foundations*, written 1573–82, pub. 1610) narrate her spiritual growth, evolving commitment to reforming the Carmelite order, and ceaseless journeys founding new convents. *Camino de perfección* (*The Way of Perfection*, written ?1562–79, pub. 1583), and *Moradas del castillo interior* (*The Interior Castle*, written 1577, pub. 1588) are further penetrating accounts of the inner life. She is the subject of Richard *Crashaw's 'Hymne to Sainte Teresa', which relates her childish attempt to court martyrdom by preaching to the Moors (an incident taken from her own spiritual autobiography) and her progress towards a state of mystic ecstasy or spiritual 'marriage'. She is also the subject of Bernini's masterpiece *The Ecstasy of Saint Teresa* (1645) in S. Maria della Vittoria, Rome. George *Eliot refers to her inspiring example in the 'Prelude' to her great novel **Middlemarch*. Rowan Williams, archbishop of Canterbury (2003–), has written on her work; see his *Teresa of Avila* (2003).

TERKEL, Studs (1912–2008) American writer and radio broadcaster, born in New York, who was active during the 1930s in the Federal Writers' Project, a government scheme to support writers during the Depression. He is particularly known for his oral histories like *Division Street: America* (1967), *Hard Times* (1970), which collects accounts of the Depression, and *Working* (1974). *Touch and Go* (2007) is an autobiographical memoir.

TERRY, Dame Ellen (1847–1928) Celebrated actress, and member of a distinguished theatrical family. Born in Coventry, she received little formal education, and married the painter George Frederick Watts (1817–1904) in 1864, when only 16. The union soon ended, and she later had two children by Edward William Godwin (1833–86), the architect and theatrical designer, one of whom was Gordon *Craig. She was Henry *Irving's leading lady during his brilliant management of the Lyceum Theatre. She became a Dame Grand Cross of the Order of the British Empire in 1925.

TERSON, Peter (1932–) The pseudonym of Peter Patterson, playwright, born in Newcastle-upon-Tyne; he was associated with the Victoria Theatre, Stoke-on-Trent, with its tradition of social documentary and theatre-in-the-round, then with the National Youth Theatre, where he excelled in writing for large casts. His works include *Mooney and his Caravans* (TV 1966), a poignant play about a young and inadequate couple victimized by the owner of a caravan site; *Zigger Zagger* (1967), about a football fan, which skilfully incorporates the drama of the football terraces; and *Good Lads at Heart* (1971), set in a Borstal. Later works include *Geordie's March* (1979) and *Strippers* (1984), about a group of working-class women forced to take up stripping to support themselves.

terza rima The measure adopted by *Dante in the **Divina commedia*, consisting of eleven-syllable lines in sets of three, the middle line of each rhyming with the first and third lines of the next set (*aba, bcb, cdc*, etc.). It was also used by *Petrarch for his *Trionfi* and by *Boccaccio in the *Caccia di Diana* (*Diana's Hunt*).

Tess of the D'Urbervilles: *A Pure Woman* A novel by Thomas *Hardy, published 1891. The sub-title was important to Hardy's purpose. Tess Durbeyfield is the daughter of a poor villager of Blackmoor Vale, whose father is told that they are descended from the ancient family of D'Urberville. Tess is cunningly seduced (perhaps raped) by Alec, a wealthy young man, whose family has bought the name of D'Urberville. Tess gives birth to a child, which dies after an improvised midnight baptism by its mother. Later, while working as a dairymaid on a prosperous farm, she becomes blissfully engaged to Angel Clare, a clergyman's son. On their wedding night she confesses to him the seduction by Alec; and Angel, although himself no innocent, hypocritically abandons her. Misfortunes and bitter hardships come upon her and her family, and accident throws her once more in the path of Alec D'Urberville. He has become an itinerant preacher, but his temporary religious conversion does not prevent him from persistently pursuing her. When her appeals to her husband, now in Brazil, remain unanswered, she is driven for the sake of her family to become the mistress of Alec. Clare, returning from Brazil and repenting of his harshness, finds her living with Alec in Sandbourne. Maddened by this second wrong that has been done her by Alec, Tess stabs and kills him. After a brief and happy period of concealment with Clare in the New Forest, Tess is arrested at Stonehenge, tried, and hanged. Hardy's closing summary reads: ' "Justice" was done, and the President of the Immortals (in Aeschylean phrase) had ended his sport with Tess.'

The publication of the novel, like that of **Jude the Obscure*, created a violent sensation. Some reviewers were deeply impressed, but most considered the work immoral, pessimistic, disagreeable, and, as Henry *James wrote, 'chockful of faults and falsity'. It has since become one of the most widely read of Hardy's works.

TESSIMOND, A. S. J. (Arthur Seymour John) (1902–62) Poet, born in Birkenhead and educated at Charterhouse School and Liverpool University. He published three volumes of verse in his lifetime (*The Walls of Glass*, 1934; *Voices in a Giant City*, 1947; *Selection*, 1958), and his *Collected Poems* (ed. Hubert Nicholson) appeared in 1985. He is remembered for his wry, low-key, urban pieces, some of them much anthologized, which include 'Cats', 'The Man in the Bowler Hat', and 'Not Love Perhaps'.

Testament, Old and New *See* BIBLE.

Testament of Cresseid, The A poem in 616 lines of *rhyme royal by Robert *Henryson. Henryson circumvents the authority of Chaucer's **Troilus and Criseyde* by having his narrator take up another (fictional) source that enables him to tell a different version. Diomede leaves Cresseid, for which she reproaches Venus and Cupid. A council of the gods discusses the punishment for her blasphemy; Saturn deprives her of joy and beauty, and she is struck with leprosy. As she sits by the roadside, Troilus passes and, though the leper brings Cresseid to his mind, he does not recognize her, nor she him. She receives alms from him and then learns who he is. She dies after sending him a ring he had once given her. See Denton Fox, *The Poems of Robert Henryson* (1981).

Testament of Love, The *See* USK, THOMAS.

tetrameter A verse line with four stressed syllables, the most common kind in English.
See METRE.

TEVIS, Walter Stone (1928–84) American novelist and short story writer, born in San Francisco. *The Hustler* (1959) was filmed in 1961. *The Man Who Fell to Earth* (1963), a *science fiction novel of the gradual corruption of an alien by human society, was filmed in 1976 by Nicholas Roeg.

THACKERAY, Anne Isabella *See* RITCHIE, ANNE THACKERAY.

THACKERAY, William Makepeace (1811–63) Novelist, born in Calcutta (Kolkata), the son of Richmond Thackeray, a collector in the East India Company's service. His father died when he was 3, and Thackeray was sent home to England in 1817, to be rejoined by his mother, who had married again, in 1820. Thackeray was educated at Charterhouse, where he was not happy, and at Trinity College, Cambridge, where he became a close friend of Edward *FitzGerald. He left Cambridge in June 1830 without taking a degree, having lost some of his inheritance through gambling. He visited Paris, and spent the winter of 1830–1 in Weimar, where he met *Goethe. He entered the Middle Temple, but had little enthusiasm for the law, and never practised as a barrister. Thackeray began his career in journalism by becoming the proprietor of a struggling weekly paper, the *National Standard*, in 1833. It ceased publication a year later, but it had given Thackeray an entrée to the London literary world. He also studied in a London art school and a Paris atelier. By the end of 1833 virtually all his inherited money had been lost, and from 1834 until 1837 he lived in Paris, making a meagre living from journalism. He briefly had a regular income as Paris correspondent of the *Constitutional*, a newspaper bought by his stepfather, and he married Isabella Shawe in 1836, the year in which his first publication in volume form, *Flore et Zephyr*, a series of ballet caricatures, appeared. The *Constitutional* failed, and the Thackerays returned to London, where their first child Anne (Anne Thackeray *Ritchie) was born in 1837. Thackeray began to contribute regularly to **Fraser's Magazine*, and also wrote for many other periodicals, including the **Morning Chronicle*, the **New Monthly Magazine*, and *The *Times*. A second daughter born in 1839 did not live long, and after the birth of their third child, Harriet Marian (later the first wife of Leslie *Stephen), in 1840 Isabella Thackeray suffered a mental breakdown which proved permanent. Thackeray placed her first in the care of a French doctor, later in a private home in England, and sent his children to live with his mother in Paris.

During the 1840s Thackeray began to make a name for himself as a writer. He came to the attention of the public with *The Yellowplush Papers*, a critique of what Thomas *Carlyle called 'flunkeyism' which appeared in *Fraser's Magazine* in 1837–8, delivered through the device of a footman-narrator. These were followed by **Catherine*, narrated by 'Ikey Solomon' (1839), and 'A Shabby Genteel Story' (1840). His first full-length volume, *The Paris Sketch Book*, containing miscellaneous early journalism, appeared in the same year, followed in 1841 by *The Great Hoggarty Diamond*, a mock-heroic tale about a diamond which brings bad luck to Samuel Titmarsh, an amiable young clerk who inherits the gem. It is narrated by Sam's cousin, Michael Angelo Titmarsh, who provided Thackeray with his most familiar pseudonym. Other pseudonyms included 'George Savage FitzBoodle', a bachelor clubman, 'author' of *The FitzBoodle Papers* (1842–3), narrator of **Men's Wives* (1843) and 'editor' of *The *Luck of Barry Lyndon* (1844), 'Jeames de la Pluche', and 'Our Fat Correspondent'. *The Irish Sketch Book* of 1843 (a personal, impressionistic, and prejudiced account of an 1842 tour of Ireland) has a preface signed, for the first time, with Thackeray's own name.

Thackeray began his association with **Punch* in 1842, and *contributed caricatures, articles, and humorous sketches. *The Snobs of England, by One of Themselves* (later published as *The Book of Snobs*, 1848), narrated by 'Mr Snob', appeared there 1846–7: this constitutes his great anatomy of the English vice of snobbery, a term he invented. *Mr Punch's Prize Novelists* (1847) parodies the leading writers of the day. His children returned to live with him in 1846. In 1847 his first major novel, **Vanity Fair*, began to appear in monthly numbers, with illustrations by the author. **Pendennis* followed in 1848–50. In 1841 Thackeray's increasing love for Jane Brookfield, the wife of an old Cambridge friend, led to a rupture in their friendship, and his next novel, *The *History of Henry Esmond*, shows signs, as Thackeray confessed, of his melancholy at this time. It was published in three volumes in 1852, and was followed by *The *Newcomes*, published in numbers in 1853–5.

As well as the major novels, Thackeray continued to produce lighter work. He wrote for *Punch* until 1854, and produced a series of 'Christmas Books' which he illustrated himself: *The *Rose and the Ring* (by 'Mr M. A. Titmarsh'), a high-spirited children's story, was published in 1855. In 1851 he gave a series of lectures on *The English Humourists of the Eighteenth Century*, and in 1855–7 he lectured on *The Four Georges*. He twice lectured in the United States, in 1852–3 and 1855–6. *The *Virginians*, set partly in America, appeared in numbers in 1857–9. In 1860 he became the first editor of the **Cornhill Magazine*, for which he wrote his engagingly casual improvisations, the *Roundabout Papers*. **Lovel the Widower*, *The Adventures of Philip*, and the unfinished **Denis Duval* all first appeared in the *Cornhill*. Thackeray died suddenly on Christmas Eve 1863.

There is an authoritative biography of Thackeray by Gordon Ray in two volumes: *Thackeray: The Uses of Adversity* (1955) and *Thackeray: The Age of Wisdom* (1958). Ray also edited Thackeray's *Letters and Private Papers* (1945–6), and his study of the relation between Thackeray's fiction and his life, *The Buried Life*, was published in 1952. Anne Thackeray Ritchie published *Chapters from Some Memoirs* in 1894, and her introductions to the *Biographical Edition* (1899) of her father's works contain many anecdotes about his life. See also D. J. Taylor, *Thackeray* (1999).

theatre criticism In the journalistic sense, began in Britain in the early 18th century. Despite earlier attempts by John *Dryden in his prefaces and Thomas *Rymer in *A Short View of Tragedy* to uphold French neo-classical principles, it was not governed by a continental adherence to aesthetic rules. Its emergence was determined by pragmatic factors: the rise of the opinionated essayist, the strength of Restoration acting, and the need to protect the stage from moral censure. All three converge in Richard *Steele who, writing on the death of Thomas *Betterton in 1710, claims, 'There is no human invention so aptly calculated for the forming a free-born people as that of the theatre.' While Steele and Joseph *Addison were occasional commentators, Aaron *Hill and William Popple (1701–64) in *The Prompter* (1734–6) became the first professional theatre critics, pursuing a campaign for realistic acting that paved the way for David *Garrick. But it was Leigh *Hunt and William *Hazlitt who transformed dramatic criticism from a transient record into a durable art. Both were writing, between 1805 and 1830, in the period William *Archer called 'the winter solstice of English drama': both, however, were witness to legendary performances. Hunt was often at his best writing about comic actors, whilst Hazlitt was inspired by the demonic genius of Edmund *Kean. His reviews of Kean's Shakespearian performances combine astute technical analysis with vivid impressionistic images.

Hazlitt argued that Shakespeare's best commentators were his actors; and actor-led criticism continued in the later 19th century with G. H. *Lewes and Joseph Knight. But, with the emergence of Henrik *Ibsen and the new drama, the rules changed. George Bernard *Shaw used his coruscating columns in the **Saturday Review* in the 1890s to attack the reigning actor-manager Henry *Irving, and to endorse a drama that addressed social and moral issues. Shaw's successor, Max

*Beerbohm, was more a whimsical essayist than an embattled campaigner and James Agate (1877–1947), who wrote for the *Sunday Times* from 1923 to 1947, was a distinguished connoisseur of acting rather than a reliable analyst of plays. But the separate traditions of graphic reporter and militant enthusiast converged in Kenneth *Tynan, who both enshrined legendary performances, particularly those of Olivier, and used his *Observer* columns to champion Bertolt *Brecht and John *Osborne. Harold Hobson, his opposite number on the *Sunday Times*, was equally persuasive about the work of Samuel *Beckett, Harold *Pinter, and Marguerite *Duras. American theatre criticism, with a shorter historical tradition, in the 20th century produced a pugnacious essayist in George Jean *Nathan, a gracious stylist in Stark Young, and a distinguished blend of academic, practitioner, and journalist in Eric Bentley, Robert Brustein, and Harold Clurman. In Britain, the development of an alternative theatre movement from the mid-1960s and, in particular, the publication of the London magazine *Time Out* (together with its regional counterparts) has led to a lesser credence for a small group of dominant critics, although the work of Michael Billington for the *Guardian* has the occasional capacity to revive, in a less flamboyant manner, the campaigning edge of Tynan in his heyday.

Théâtre de Complicité Influential physical theatre group founded in 1983 by Annabel Arden, Simon McBurney, Marcello Magni, and Fiona Gordon. Their early work fed on European mime traditions and surreal British humour and later embraced a fascination with a wide range of textual sources. A production of Friedrich *Dürrenmatt's *The Visit* in 1988 was a powerful spectacle of post-war nightmare, revenge, and materialism. *The Street of Crocodiles* (1992) and *Out of a House Walked a Man* (1994), both co-produced with the *National Theatre, gave stunning new articulation to the forgotten absurdists Bruno Schulz and Daniel Kharms. Complicité helped to redraw the map of British theatre in the 1980s, raising the ensemble performance stakes alongside the continuing wealth of new playwriting. Their version of John *Berger's *The Three Lives of Lucie Cabrol* (1994) combined the best of both worlds in a work of intellectual passion and physical distinction. Their use of extant texts has yielded wonderfully diverse theatrical experiences, demonstrated in their productions of Eugène Ionesco's *The Chairs* (1997) and their take on Haruki Murakam's short stories, *The Elephant Vanishes* (2003).

Theatre of the Absurd *See* ABSURD, THEATRE OF THE.

Thel, The Book of *See* BLAKE, WILLIAMS.

THELWALL, John (1764–1834) English radical and poet who in 1794 was arrested with John Horne *Tooke for his revolutionary views, and subsequently tried and acquitted. He published several volumes of verse, most notably *Poems on Various Subjects* (1787), political essays, and tracts on elocution. He was an acquaintance of William *Wordsworth and S. T. *Coleridge, whom he visited in Somerset in 1797, having walked on foot from London, a journey described in part (although anonymously) in the **Monthly Magazine*, 1799. His most significant book, *The Peripatetic, or Sketches of the Heart, of Nature and Society; in a Series of Politico-Sentimental Journals* (1793), is part fictional travelogue in the manner of Laurence *Sterne, part radical call to arms. Wordsworth described him as a 'a man of extraordinary talent'.

THEOBALD, Lewis (1688–1744) Poet, critic, and Shakespearian scholar. His *Shakespeare Restored* (1726) exposed *Pope's faults as an editor of *Shakespeare; Pope retaliated with a devastating portrait of Theobald (or 'Tibbald') as hero of his *The *Dunciad*, making gleefully expert use of Theobald's earlier poems (such as *The Cave of Poverty*, 1715) and his pantomimes (*Harlequin Sorcerer* and *The Rape of Proserpine*, both 1725). Pope did incorporate some of Theobald's corrections in the second edition of his Shakespeare, but Theobald's own edition of 1733–4 superseded Pope's, and some 300 emendations made to the texts by Theobald are still given credence by modern editors. Theobald was a pioneer in the study of Shakespeare's sources and the writings of his contemporaries. *Double Falsehood* (1727) was announced by Theobald as his adaptation of **Cardenio*, which he ascribed to Shakespeare; but his manuscript sources were not made public and satirists including Pope (in **Peri Bathous*) and Henry *Fielding (in *A *Journey from this World to the Next*) regarded the play as spurious. See P. Seary, *Lewis Theobald and the Editing of Shakespeare* (1990).

THEOCRITUS (early 3rd century BC) Author of the *Idylls*, a collection of poems in the Doric dialect of Greek; he was probably a native of Sicily and may have lived in Cos and Alexandria. His most famous poems evoke the life and rustic arts of Sicilian shepherds, maintaining a successful balance between idealization and realism; they were imitated by *Virgil in the **Eclogues*, and established the formal characteristics and setting that *pastoral poetry was to retain for centuries. Six of the *Idylls* were translated anonymously in 1588, and in 1684 Thomas Creech translated them into English, a year before John *Dryden contributed some translations to Jacob *Tonson's *Sylvae*. Many English elegies, notably John Milton's **Lycidas*, ultimately derive from Theocritus' lament for Daphnis. Victorian imitators, such as Alfred **Tennyson* in 'The Lotos-Eaters' (1833), delighted in the sensuality of Theocritus' world. There is a recent translation by Robert Wells (1988). *See* ECLOGUE.

THEODORE (602–90) Archbishop of Canterbury, a native of Tarsus in Cilicia. He studied at Athens and was consecrated archbishop in 668. He imposed the Roman order and was the first archbishop of Canterbury to whom (according to *Bede) the whole English church agreed in submitting after the divisions leading up to the Synod of Whitby (663/4). He was a distinguished ecclesiastical administrator and scholar, under whose aegis the important *Poenitentiale* was produced. See Michael Lapidge (ed.), *Archbishop Theodore* (1995).

THEOPHRASTUS (*c.*371–287 BC) Greek philosopher, head of the Peripatetic school after *Aristotle. He is said to have written on style, and two of his works on plants survive. But his influence on English literature stems from his *Characters*, thirty brief sketches of human types embodying particular faults: the flatterer, the overproud, the bad-mannered. The popularity of Theophrastus in modern times dates from the edition of the 23 *Characters* then known with Latin translations by Isaac *Casaubon (1592). An English version by John Healey (*c.*1585–*c.*1616) appeared in 1616, but before then Joseph *Hall enlarged Theophrastus' scope, adding good qualities to bad in his *Characters of Vertues and Vices* (1608). The genre remained popular throughout the century, and left its mark on 18th-century periodicals such as the **Spectator*.
See CHARACTER-WRITING; OVERBURY, SIR THOMAS.

Theory of Moral Sentiments, The A philosophical work by Adam *Smith, published 1759, and originally delivered in the form of lectures at Glasgow. The author advances the view that all moral sentiments arise from sympathy, the principle which gives rise to our notions of the merit or demerit of the agent. The basis of morality is pleasure in mutual sympathy, which moderates our natural egocentricity. The desire for such pleasure requires us to see ourselves 'in the light in which others see us', a thought quoted admiringly by Robert *Burns in 'To a Louse':

> O wad some Pow'r the giftie gie us
> *To see oursels as others see us!*

Smith's account of the role of the imagination in the operation of sympathy influenced Laurence *Sterne, in *A Sentimental Journey*, and other contemporary writers.

Theosophical Society *See* BLAVATSKY, MADAME ELENA.

THERESA, St *see* TERESA, ST.

THEROUX, Paul Edward (1941–) Prolific travel writer, novelist, short story writer, and journalist, born in Medford, Massachusetts, and educated at Medford High School and the University of Massachusetts, from which he graduated in 1963. After a short spell in Italy, Theroux taught in Malawi (then called Nyasaland) as a member of the Peace Corps 1963–5, and afterwards in Uganda. In 1968 he began teaching English at the University of Singapore. His time there inspired a collection of stories, *Sinning with Annie* (1972), and a novel, *Saint Jack* (1973). His first novel *Waldo* had been published in 1967. There followed *Fong and the Indians* (1968), *Girls at Play* (1969), and *Jungle Lovers* (1971), all set in Africa. Theroux made his reputation with a series of vivid travel books about epic railway journeys: *The Great Railway Bazaar* (1975), describing a journey across Europe and Russia to Japan; *The Old Patagonian Express* (1979), depicting travels in South America; and *Riding the Iron Rooster* (1988), an account of a journey through China. The first two of these have been credited with reviving the popularity of travel writing as a genre. In *The Kingdom by the Sea* (1983) Theroux turned his attention to the coastline of Britain, his adopted home for many years. *The Happy Isles of Oceania* (1992) describes a voyage in the South Pacific and *The Pillars of Hercules* (1995) a tour of the Mediterranean. He continued to publish novels, of which *The Mosquito Coast* (1982) is probably the best known. *My Other Life* (1996) is an 'imaginary memoir' which disconcertingly mixes fact and fiction. *Sir Vidia's Shadow: A Friendship across Five Continents* (1998) charts the decline of Theroux's long-standing friendship with V. S. *Naipaul. Shorter travel essays are collected in *Sunrise with Sea Monsters* (1985) and *Fresh-Air Fiend* (2000). *Dark Star Safari* (2002) recounts an overland trip from Cairo to Cape Town. In *Ghost Train to the Eastern Star: On the Tracks of The Great Railway Bazaar* (2008), Theroux revisits Eastern Europe and Asia thirty years after the journey recounted in *The Great Railway Bazaar.*

Thersites The most irritable and repellent member of the Greek army in the Trojan War. He laughs at Achilles' grief over the death of Penthesilea, the queen of the Amazons, and Achilles kills him for it. He appears in Shakespeare's **Troilus and Cressida* as a harsh cynic. See Alexander *Pope's translation of the **Iliad* (2. 255–74).

Theseus A son of the Greek god Poseidon, or, according to later legend, of Aegeus, king of Athens. His exploits (in association with Medea, the Minotaur, Ariadne, and Phaedra) figure in many literary works, including *Sophocles' *Oedipus at Colonus* and *Euripides' *Hippolytus*. He appears as the duke of Athens in *Shakespeare's *A *Midsummer Night's Dream*, with his newly won bride *Hippolyta, and also in Shakespeare and John Fletcher's *The *Two Noble Kinsmen*.

THESIGER, Sir Wilfred (1910–2003) Travel writer, explorer, and photographer, born in Addis Ababa, Abyssinia (now Ethiopia), where his father was a British diplomat. He was educated at Eton College and Oxford. In 1933–4 he explored the little-known territories of the Danakil people in eastern Ethiopia (see his *Danakil Diary*, pub. 1998) and became increasingly taken with a desire to escape modern civilization. After war service in the Sudan, he spent several years living in the Empty Quarter of Arabia with the Bedu, and then a further period living in the marshes of southern Iraq. His experiences are recorded in *Arabian Sands* (1959) and *The Marsh Arabs* (1964), which offer an elegiac account of traditional tribal culture in these regions. He lived in Kenya from 1960 to the mid-1990s, when failing health forced his return to Britain. His other works include *Desert, Marsh and Mountain* (1979, an account of travels in Persia and Iraqi Kurdistan); *The Life of my Choice* (1987); *My Kenya Days* (1994); *Among the Mountains: Travels in Asia* (1998); *A Vanished World* (2001); and an extensive collection of photographs, left to the Pitt-Rivers Museum in Oxford. See Alexander Maitland, *Wilfred Thesiger: The Life of the Great Explorer* (2006).

Thierry King of France, and his Brother Theodoret, The Tragedy of A play by John *Fletcher, with the collaboration probably of Philip *Massinger and possibly of Francis *Beaumont, written *c.*1613, published 1621.

Theodoret, king of Austrasia, reproaches his mother Brunhalt for her loose behaviour, and to revenge herself she tries unsuccessfully to alienate him from his younger brother Thierry. Aided by her lover Protaldy and a physician specializing in poisons, she destroys the happiness of Thierry and his young bride Ordella, then has Theodoret assassinated, then attempts to bring about the death of Ordella, and finally poisons Thierry. Vengeance then falls upon Brunhalt and her accomplices. There are incidents in the play which may be allusions to the queen regent of France, Marie de Médicis, and her favourite Concini (murdered in 1617).

Thiong'o *See* NGUGI WA THIONG'O.

THIRKELL, Angela (1890–1961) Novelist and journalist, born in Kensington, London, and educated at St Paul's Girls' School, London, and a Paris finishing school. She was a granddaughter of Edward *Burne-Jones, a cousin of Rudyard *Kipling, and the god-daughter of J. M. *Barrie; her son (by her first husband) was Colin *McInnes. Her second husband, George Thirkell, was an engineer, but the marriage failed, and having spent some ten years in Australia, she returned to England to earn her living (very successfully in the 1930s but less so after the war) as a writer of idealized English country life. Many of her novels are set in a Barsetshire borrowed from Anthony *Trollope, such as *Ankle Deep* (1933), *August Folly* (1936), and *The Brandons* (1939). See Margot Strickland, *Angela Thirkell* (1977).

THIRLWALL, Connop (1797–1875) Historian and liberal bishop, educated at Charterhouse and Trinity College, Cambridge, where he became a fellow in 1818; ordained in 1828. He translated the *Essay on the Gospel of St Luke* (1825) by Schleirmacher (1768–1834), demonstrating exceptional knowledge of German theology, and *Niebuhr's *History of Rome* (1828–42; with Julius *Hare). Also with Hare he edited the *Philological Museum* (1832–3) which contained Thirlwall's important essay on 'The Irony of Sophocles'. His liberal views on the admission of Dissenters to the universities forced his resignation from Trinity College in 1834; he subsequently wrote his chief work, the *History of Greece* (1835–44, for *Lardner's Cyclopaedia*, rev. 1847–52). As bishop of St David's (from 1840), he supported the admission of Jews to Parliament and the disestablishment of the Irish Church, and allowed John Colenso, bishop of Natal, to preach in his diocese.

THOMAS À KEMPIS (Thomas Hämmerlein or Thomas Hämmerken) (*c.*1380–1471) Born of humble parents at Kempen near Cologne. He became an Augustinian monk and wrote Christian mystical works, including the famous *De Imitatione Christi* (*The Imitation of Christ*), which has been translated from the Latin into many languages (into English in the middle of the 15th century). This work was at one time attributed to Jean Charlier de Gerson, a French theologian. It traces in four books the gradual progress of the soul to Christian perfection, its detachment from the world, and union with God; and obtained wide popularity by its simplicity and sincerity and the universal quality of its religious teaching. Its influence was persistent: Maggie Tulliver, for instance, finds comfort and support in its 'lasting record of human needs and human consolations' in George *Eliot's *The *Mill on the Floss*.

THOMAS, D. M. (Donald Michael) (1935–) Poet, novelist, and translator, born in Cornwall and educated there, in Australia, and at New College, Oxford. His work is much influenced by his familiarity with Russian literature. He has published translations of the poetry of Alexander *Pushkin, Anna *Akhmatova, and Evgenii *Evtushenko, and volumes of his own poetry such as *Two Voices* (1968) and *Love and Other Deaths* (1975). His first novel, *The Flute-Player* (1979), a fantasy set in a totalitarian state, pays tribute to the persecuted creative spirit of 20th-century Russian poets. *The White Hotel* (1981), which combines an invented case history of one of *Freud's patients, and the steps that lead her and her stepson to death in the 1941 massacre at Babi Yar, won him international success. *Ararat* (1983) shows a similar brooding on the theme of *holocaust (this time of the Armenians) and on the relationship between sex and death. It was followed by novels such as *Sphinx* (1986), *Lying Together* (1990), and *Eating Pavlova* (1994). A volume of autobiography, *Memories and Hallucinations*, was published in 1988. *Alexander Solzhenitsyn: A Century in his Life* (1997) is a biography.

THOMAS, Dylan (1914–53) Poet, born in Swansea, the son of the English master at Swansea Grammar School, where he himself was educated. He knew very little Welsh. He began to write poetry while still at school, and worked in Swansea as a journalist before moving to London in 1934. His first volume of verse, *18 Poems*, appeared in the same year. He then embarked on a *Grub Street career of journalism, broadcasting, and film-making, spending much time in the flourishing afternoon drinking clubs of the era, and rapidly acquiring a reputation for exuberance and flamboyance, as both poet and personality. In 1937 he married Caitlin Macnamara. They settled for a while at Laugharne in Wales, returning there permanently, after many wanderings, in 1949. Despite some allegations of deliberate obscurity, Thomas's romantic, affirmative, rhetorical style gradually won a large following. It was both new and influential (and much imitated by his contemporaries of the New Apocalypse Movement), and the publication of *Deaths and Entrances* (1946), which contains some of his best-known work (including 'Fern Hill' and 'A Refusal to Mourn the Death by Fire of a Child in London'), established him with a wide public: his *Collected Poems 1934–1952* (1952) sold extremely well. His worksheets, minutely and continually laboured over, reveal him as an impassioned, even obsessional, craftsman—a great part of his mature work consists of the reworking of the early poetic outbursts of his youth, controlled by a strict discipline.

Thomas also wrote a substantial quantity of prose. *The Map of Love* (1939) is a collection of prose and verse; *Portrait of the Artist as a Young Dog* (1940) is a collection of largely autobiographical short stories; *Adventures in the Skin Trade* (1955) is a collection of stories, including the unfinished title story (also edited separately by his friend Vernon *Watkins, 1955); *A Prospect of the Sea* (1955) is a collection of stories and essays. He was a popular entertainer on radio and with students. In 1950, he undertook the first of his lecture tours to the United States, and he died there on his fourth visit, as legend grew about his wild living and hard drinking. Shortly before his death he took part in a reading in New York of what was to be his most famous single work, **Under Milk Wood*. In 1971, *The Poems* was published with authoritative critical notes and personal comments by his friend and early collaborator, the composer Daniel Jones. Thomas's *Notebooks* were published in 1968, edited by Ralph Maud. With Walford Davies, Maud edited *Collected Poems* (1988). See Constantine Fitzgibbon, *The Life of Dylan Thomas* (1965); Paul Ferris, *Dylan Thomas* (1977). Ferris also edited *The Collected Letters* (1985).

THOMAS, Edward (1878–1917) Poet, born in Lambeth and educated at St Paul's School and Lincoln College, Oxford. He married young and supported his family by producing many volumes of prose, much of it topographical and biographical, including a biography of Richard *Jefferies (1909), who profoundly influenced him. He was also a prolific but perceptive book reviewer. With the encouragement of Robert *Frost, he turned to poetry soon after the start of the war. In 1915, Thomas joined the army, and he was killed at Arras. Most of his poetry was published posthumously, though a few pieces appeared under the pseudonym 'Edward Eastaway' between 1915 and 1917. Both he and Frost advocated the use of natural diction, and of colloquial speech rhythms in metrical verse. F. R.*Leavis singled him out as 'an original poet of rare quality, who has been associated with the Georgians by mischance', and his work, including his prose, is now highly regarded. There are memoirs by his widow, Helen (*As It Was*, 1926; and *World without End*, 1931), and by Eleanor *Farjeon. See R. George Thomas, *Edward Thomas: A Portrait* (1985). R. George Thomas also edited *The Collected Poems* (1978) and *Selected Letters* (1995).

THOMAS, R. S. (Ronald Stuart) (1913–2000) Welsh poet and clergyman, born in Cardiff and brought up in Holyhead; he was educated at St Michael's College, Llandaff, and University College, Bangor, where he studied classics. Ordained in 1936, Thomas was appointed rector of Manafon, Montgomeryshire, six years later. He became vicar of Eglwysfach, Ceredigion, in 1954, and of Aberdaron, on the Llŷn peninsula, in 1967. He retired in 1978. Though reviewers of *Song at the Year's Turning* (1955), *Tares* (1961), and other collections up to *Not that He Brought Flowers* (1968) dwelt mainly on Thomas's anti-pastoral portraits of Welsh rural life, recent criticism has seen the early work as scarcely less characterized by irony and allusiveness, and no less haunted by a sense of the absence of God, than the speculative, discursive poems of *H'm* (1972), *Laboratories of the Spirit* (1975), and *Frequencies* (1978). Thomas's poetry progressively abandons stanzaic and metrical formality in favour of a low-key, disenchanted idiom which displays immense technical cunning in its repudiation of the customary charms of lyricism. Disconsolate meditations on the denationalized condition of Wales give way to more abstract protests in which ecological and metaphysical deprivations mirror each other, and the Machine looms as a despoiler alike of the present and the future. *Ingrowing Thoughts* (1985) contains poetic responses to famous paintings; *The Echoes Return Slow* (1988) plays off quizzical verse commentaries against autobiographical prose fragments; *No Truce with the Furies* (1995) and the posthumously published *Residues* (2002) restate established themes while bringing renewed figurative stamina to their treatment of old age and memory (and its loss). *Neb* ('No one', 1985), a laconic third-person prose autobiography in Welsh, has been translated by Jason Walford Davies along with three shorter texts as *Autobiographies* (1997). 'There is a kind of narrowness in my work which a good critic would condemn,' observed Thomas in 1999: if thinness is one undeniable attribute of his poetry, however, profundity and precision are others. See *Collected Poems* (1993); *Collected Later Poems* (2004); Byron Rogers, *The Man Who Went into the West: The Life of R. S. Thomas* (2006).

THOMASON, George (*c*.1602–1666) A London bookseller and publisher and friend of William *Prynne and of John *Milton, whose sonnet 'When Faith and Love which parted from thee never' was written in 1646 on the death of Thomason's wife Catharine. Thomason's comprehensive collection of more than 22,000 political tracts and broadsides published between the outbreak of the Civil War and the Restoration is preserved in the British Library; it includes four items donated by Milton personally. The tracts were catalogued in 1908 by G. K. Fortescue.

THOMPSON, E. P. (Edward Palmer) (1924–93) Historian, born in Oxford and educated at Corpus Christi College, Cambridge; for many years (1948–65) an extramural lecturer at Leeds University. His works include an influential study of William *Morris (1955) and *The Making of the English Working Class* (1963), in which he sought 'to rescue the poor stockinger, the Luddite cropper, the "obsolete" hand-loom weaver, the "utopian" artisan, and even the deluded follower of Joanna Southcott, from the enormous condescension of posterity'. He also worked to support the Campaign for Nuclear Disarmament. *Witness against the Beast*, a study of William *Blake, was published posthumously (1993). See H. J. Kaye and K. McClelland (eds), *E. P. Thompson: Critical Perspectives* (1990).

THOMPSON, Flora (1876–1947) Author, daughter of a builder's labourer, born at Juniper Hill, near Brackley, Oxfordshire. She left school at 14, and worked as a post office clerk before marrying another post office worker, John Thompson. They moved to Bournemouth, Hampshire, and lived from 1916 at Liphook, Hampshire, moving in 1928 to

Dartmouth, Devon; she supplemented their meagre income with journalism, writing nature essays for national magazines and newspapers. She published her first book, a volume of verse called *Bog-Myrtle and Peat*, in 1921, but she is chiefly remembered for her semi-autobiographical trilogy *Lark Rise to Candleford* (1945), published originally as *Lark Rise* (1939), *Over to Candleford* (1941), and *Candleford Green* (1943), works which evoke through the childhood memories and youth of 'Laura' a vanished world of agricultural customs, rustic culture, and rural decline. The trilogy was adapted for television in 2008. Her final book, *Still Glides the Stream*, appeared posthumously in 1948. See Gillian Lindsay, *Flora Thompson* (1990).

THOMPSON, Francis (1859–1907) Poet, son of a Roman Catholic doctor, born in Preston, Lancashire, and educated at Ushaw College. He was intended for the priesthood, but was judged not to have a vocation. He also failed to qualify as a doctor, and in 1885 left home to spend three years of homeless and opium-addicted destitution in London, till he was rescued by Wilfrid and Alice *Meynell, who secured him literary recognition and organized his life in London lodgings and monasteries in Sussex and Wales. He never married, and never for long freed himself from opium which, together with tuberculosis, caused his early death. His best-known poems are 'The Hound of Heaven' and 'The Kingdom of God'; he published three volumes of verse, in 1893, 1895, and 1897, and much literary criticism in Meynell's *Merry England*, the **Academy*, and the **Athenaeum*. His finest work conveys intense religious experience in imagery of power, he admired especially P. B. *Shelley, Thomas *De Quincey, and Richard *Crashaw. He has retained a following particularly among Catholic readers.

The standard life is by Everard Meynell (1913): see also J. C. Reid, *Francis Thompson, Man and Poet* (1959), which gives a full and scholarly account of the poet's opium addiction, and John Walsh, *Strange Harp, Strange Symphony* (1968), which has the fullest account of his personal life.

THOMPSON, Hunter S. (1937–2005) American journalist and writer, born in Louisville, Kentucky. He spent many years writing for *Rolling Stone* magazine, in which the two works for which he is best known first appeared. *Fear and Loathing in Las Vegas* (1972), subtitled 'a savage journey to the heart of the American Dream', is an account of a heavily drugged visit to Las Vegas, offering a dissection of American culture. No less provocative was *Fear and Loathing on the Campaign Trail '72* (1973), his coverage of the 1972 American presidential campaign. He spent a year riding with the Hell's Angels (his book about them appeared in 1966), ran for sheriff of Aspen, Colorado, in 1970, and subsequently awarded himself a doctorate. With Tom *Wolfe and Joan *Didion, he was a pioneer of *New (or *gonzo) Journalism, a mode blurring the border between reportage and fiction.- His own irreverent political and cultural writing has been collected in four volumes as *The Gonzo Papers* (1979–94). *Proud Highway*, the first volume of his *Letters*, was published in 1997, and a novel *The Rum Diary* (written in 1959) in 1998.
See GONZO JOURNALISM.

THOMS, William John (1803–85) Antiquary; successively clerk and deputy librarian to the House of Lords. He wrote *The Book of the Court* (1838), and edited a number of volumes including *Early Prose Romances* (1827–8) and *The History of Reynard the Fox* (1844) for the *Percy Society. He was secretary of the *Camden Society (1838–73). In 1846, in an article in the **Athenaeum* headed 'Folk Lore', he introduced this term into the English language. Encouraged by Charles *Dilke he founded **Notes and Queries* in 1849.

THOMSON, James (1700–48) Poet, born at Ednam, Roxburghshire, and educated at Edinburgh University. Encouraged by his friend David *Mallet, he came to London in 1725, and wrote 'Winter', the first of *The *Seasons*. *Britannia*, a poem promoting British interests against Spain, appeared in 1729. Thomson made the acquaintance of Alexander *Pope, Richard *Savage, and Aaron *Hill, and found patrons, including George Bubb *Dodington and Lord *Lyttelton. He travelled in France and Italy as tutor to Charles Talbot, son of the solicitor-general, and in 1735–6 published a long patriotic poem *Liberty*, celebrating the progress of Liberty from ancient Greece and Rome to Britain. Thomson wrote a series of declamatory and high-minded tragedies, beginning with *Sophonisba* (1730), for which Pope and Mallet wrote a prologue. Pope made a rare personal appearance at the theatre to support *Agamemnon* (1738) and commended the pathos of Thomson's *Edward and Eleanora* (1739), which was banned by the Lord Chamberlain on the eve of performance. *Tancred and Sigismunda* was acted in 1745 with David *Garrick as Tancred; it held the stage longer than any of Thomson's other plays. *Coriolanus* (1749) was performed posthumously. Despite their ancient settings, the plays were conspicuously aligned with political opposition to Sir Robert Walpole (1676–1745), to whom Thomson had earlier dedicated an elegy on Sir Isaac *Newton (1727). In 1740 the masque of *Alfred*, by Thomson and Mallet, was performed; it contains Thomson's *'Rule, Britannia'. In 1748, a few weeks before his death, appeared *The *Castle of Indolence*, including a portrait of himself, perhaps written by Lyttelton, which affectionately mocks the poet's notorious love of idleness. He was buried in Richmond church; his friend William *Collins wrote an elegy, 'In yonder Grave a Druid lies' (1749). *The Seasons*, one of the most frequently reprinted and illustrated of English poems, developed in a highly distinctive manner the range of *topographical poetry; William *Wordsworth recognized Thomson as the first poet since John *Milton to offer new images of 'external nature'. Thomson's landscapes were influenced by those of *Claude, *Poussin, and *Rosa, and were in turn greatly admired by J. M. W. *Turner. See the biography by J. Sambrook (1991).

THOMSON, James (1834–82) Born in Scotland, the son of a poor merchant seaman. He attended the Royal

Caledonian Asylum school when the family moved to London. He was trained as an army schoolmaster, in which capacity he was sent in 1851–2 to Ireland, where he met Charles *Bradlaugh, who became his staunch friend, and also a young girl, Matilda Weller, who died in 1853 but who became an important symbolic figure in Thomson's later poetry. Between 1852 and 1862 he worked at army stations in England and Ireland and wrote much poetry, some of which was accepted by various journals, including Bradlaugh's *National Reformer.* For his early work he used the pseudonym 'B.V.', representing his admiration for P. B. *Shelley with 'Bysshe' and for the German poet *Hardenberg ('Novalis') with 'Vanolis'. Signs of growing alcoholism appeared in the late 1850s and in 1862 Thomson was discharged from the army, probably for drunkenness. He came to London, and until 1868 lodged with the Bradlaughs. He took various jobs and wrote poems, essays, and translations for several magazines, publishing among other work 'Vane's Story', 'Sunday up the River', and 'Sunday at Hampstead'. 'Weddah', a long poem relating a tragic Arabian love story, appeared in 1871, and led to friendship with W. M. *Rossetti. For part of 1872 Thomson was with a gold company in Colorado, and in 1873 in Spain as a war reporter; on his return he completed his best-known poem, 'The City of Dreadful Night', which appeared in the *National Reformer* in 1874, and received some favourable notice, including encouragement from George *Eliot and later from George *Meredith. This long poem, which much influenced the mood of *fin-de-siècle* poetic pessimism, is a powerful evocation of a half-ruined city, a 'Venice of the Black Sea', through which flows the River of the Suicides; the narrator, in vain search of 'dead Faith, dead Love, dead Hope', encounters tormented shades wandering in a Dantesque vision of a living hell, over which presides the sombre and sublime figure of Melancolia (based on Albrecht *Dürer's engraving of 1514). In 1880 his first volume of verse, *The City of Dreadful Night and Other Poems,* and a second volume later in the same year, were well received. *Essays and Phantasies* appeared in 1881. But his alcoholism was by now out of control; *Satires and Profanities* was published posthumously in 1884. There is a life by H. S. Salt, 1889; see also *Poems and Some Letters of James Thomson,* edited with a biographical introduction by Anne Ridler (1963). See also Tom *Leonard, *Places of the Mind: The Life and Work of James Thomson* (1993).

THOMSON, Sir William, first Baron Kelvin (1824–1907) Physicist and mathematician, born in Belfast and educated at Glasgow, where he later became professor of natural philosophy, and at Peterhouse, Cambridge. His formulation of the second law of thermodynamics, predicting that the world would sooner or later suffer a heat death as a result of entropy, contributed significantly to late 19th-century pessimism. The ignorance of this law displayed by most 20th-century literary intellectuals was used as an illustration of the gap between the *'two cultures' by C. P. *Snow. See C. Smith and W. N. Wise, *Energy and Empire: A Biographical Study of Lord Kelvin* (1989).

'Thopas, The Tale of Sir' *See* CANTERBURY TALES, 17.

THOREAU, Henry David (1817–62) American author, born in Concord, Massachusetts, and educated at Harvard University. He became a follower and friend of Ralph Waldo *Emerson, and was, in his own words, 'a mystic, a transcendentalist, and a natural philosopher to boot'. He supported himself by a variety of occupations, as lead pencil-maker (his father's trade), schoolteacher, tutor, and surveyor; a few of his poems were published in *The *Dial,* but he made no money from literature, and published only two books in his lifetime. The first, *A Week on the Concord and Merrimack River* (1849), described a journey undertaken in 1839 with his brother; the second, *Walden, or Life in the Woods* (1854), attracted little attention, but has since been recognized as a literary masterpiece and as one of the seminal books of the century. It describes his two-year experiment in self-sufficiency (1845–7) when he built himself a wooden hut on the edge of Walden Pond, near Concord; he describes his domestic economy, his agricultural experiments, his visitors and neighbours, the plants and wildlife, and his sense of the Indian past, with a challenging directness that questions the materialism and the prevailing work ethic of the age. Equally influential in future years was his essay on 'Civil Disobedience' (1849; originally entitled 'Resistance to Civil Government'), in which he argues the right of the individual to refuse to pay taxes when conscience dictates, as he and Bronson Alcott (1799–1888) had done in 1843, in protest against the Mexican War and slavery, for which he had in 1845 been briefly imprisoned. Thoreau's reputation as philosopher and political thinker, as well as naturalist, was strengthened by a biography (1890) by the British socialist Henry S. Salt (1851–1939), and by the admiration of Edward *Carpenter and Havelock *Ellis in Britain; his technique of passive resistance, as described in 'Civil Disobedience', was adopted by Gandhi. He has also been hailed as a pioneer ecologist. His *Journal* (14 vols) was published in 1906, his collected *Writings* (20 vols) also in 1906, and a new scholarly edition of works, *The Writings of Henry D. Thoreau* (the Princeton edition) began publication in 1971.

THORNBURY, George Walter (1828–76) Prolific writer, born in London and informally educated, who contributed to Charles *Dickens's periodicals on topics including travel and crime. His art criticism included a biography of J. M. W. *Turner (1861), partly overseen by John *Ruskin, and he published novels, poetry, and translations.

Thornton Manuscript One of two manuscript anthologies produced by Robert Thornton (in or before 1397–in or before ?1465), from north Yorkshire. Containing both secular literature, including the alliterative **Morte Arthure*, and religious meditations and prayers, it assembles what Brewer and Owen call a 'private library'. See facsimile edn with an introduction by D. S. Brewer and A. E. B. Owen (1977).

THORPE, Adam (1956–) Poet and novelist, born in Paris, brought up in India, Cameroon, and England, and educated at Marlborough College and Magdalen College, Oxford. He left England in 1990 to live in France. His first volume of poetry was *Mornings in the Baltic* (1988); others include *Meeting Montaigne* (1990) and *Nine Lessons from the Dark* (2003). His first novel was *Ulverton* (1992), a tour de force which places a fictional Wessex village at the centre of three centuries of social, linguistic, and historical flux, with each chapter narrated in an appropriate style. Others include *Still* (1995), *Pieces of Light* (1998), and *The Rules of Perspective* (2005), set in a German museum at the end of the Second World War. His poems, like his novels, are much preoccupied with people in particular landscapes, pitted against historical forces. His work meditates on the continuum of history and explores ideas of Englishness.

Thousand and One Nights, The See ARABIAN NIGHTS ENTERTAINMENTS.

THRALE, Hester Lynch (1741–1821) Née Salusbury, born near Pwllheli; she showed an early inclination to literature and learned several languages. In 1763 she married Henry Thrale, a wealthy brewer. In 1765 they met, through Arthur *Murphy, Samuel *Johnson, who wrote election addresses for Thrale, and at one period became almost domesticated at their house in Streatham Place. The Thrales also took Johnson to north Wales (1774) and Paris (1775). Mrs Thrale bore twelve children; four daughters survived to maturity. Henry Thrale died in 1781, and three years later, against opposition from her daughters and friends (including Fanny *Burney), she married Gabriel Piozzi (1740–1809), an Italian musician. Johnson sent her a letter of violent, anguished protest; their friendship, already under strain, was ruined. She published *Anecdotes of the Late Samuel Johnson*, an intimate portrait, in 1786, and a selection of her correspondence with Johnson in 1788. Later works include a book of travels (1789), *British Synonymy* (1794), and *Retrospection* (1801). *Thraliana*, a mixture of diary, anecdotes, poems, and jests, covering the period 1776–1809, begun at the suggestion of Johnson, was edited in 1942 (rev. 1951), 2 vols, by K. C. Balderston. See J. L. Clifford, *Hester Lynch Piozzi (Mrs Thrale)* (rev. edn 1987).

Three Clerks, The A novel by Anthony *Trollope, published 1858. The three clerks are Harry Norman, Alaric Tudor, and Alaric's gauche cousin Charley. In the course of the novel each marries one of the daughters of Mrs Woodward, a widow living near Hampton Court. Alaric sucessfully competes with Harry for the affection of the eldest daughter Gertrude. He is also successful in the new system of promotion by examination in the Civil Service. But he is tempted to abuse a trust fund, and, despite the efforts of the lawyer Chaffanbrass, tried and imprisoned. His wife Gertrude, and dependable Harry Norman, help him through the ordeal and into Australian exile. Meanwhile Charley builds a literary reputation, wins promotion, and settles down to married life. Charley's experiences reflect Trollope's own early days as a clerk at the Post Office.

THUBRON, Colin (1939–) Novelist and travel writer, born in London, educated at Eton College. His travel writings began in the eastern Mediterranean and include *Mirror to Damascus* (1967), *The Hills of Adonis* (1968), and *Journey into Cyprus* (1975), which provided the setting for his first novel, *The God in the Mountain* (1977). Later travel books took on increasingly difficult terrain and reflect Thubron's curiosity about societies that his generation found threatening. They include *Among the Russians* (1983), *Behind the Wall* (1987), *The Lost Heart of Asia* (1994), *In Siberia* (1999), and *Shadows of the Silk Road* (2006). Thubron's travel writing is characterized by historical detail, careful prose, conscientious character observation, and a self-effacing narrator. Many of Thubron's novels, which include *Emperor* (1978), *A Cruel Madness* (1984), *Distance* (1996), and *To the Last City* (2002), feature enclosed spaces and interior worlds; Thubron himself has remarked on the contrast with his travel books.

THUCYDIDES (*c*.460/455–*c*.400 BC) Athenian historian who left a brilliant account in eight books of the Peloponnesian War, waged disastrously by Athens against Sparta. Giving the story the inexorable dignity of a tragedy, he traced effects to natural human causes and emphasized the scientific value of eyewitness accounts, while creating powerful speeches for the leading figures in his narrative, of which Pericles' funeral oration (Bk 2) is the most famous. The first English translation from the Greek was by Thomas *Hobbes (1629) (that by Thomas Nicholls (1550) was from a French version). In 1830–5 Thomas *Arnold published a commentary in which he tried to derive lessons for his own time from Thucydides' text, and Benjamin *Jowett's elegant translation followed in 1881. Rex *Warner's translation (1954) with notes by Moses Finley has been frequently reissued.

Thunderer, The A nickname given to *The *Times* in the middle of the 19th century, in allusion to the style of writing of Edward Sterling (1773–1847), a member of its staff, and father of John *Sterling.

THURBER, James (1894–1961) American humorist, many of whose essays, stories, and sketches appeared in the **New Yorker*, including one of his best-known short stories, 'The Secret Life of Walter Mitty' (1932), which describes the colourful escapist fantasies of a docile husband. Many of his sketches ridicule contemporary fads like *Let your Mind Alone!* (1937). See Thomas Fensch, *The Man Who Was Walter Mitty* (2001).

THURLOW, Edward, second Baron Thurlow (1781–1829) Public servant and writer, who contributed frequently to the **Gentleman's Magazine*. His books include an edition of Philip Sidney's *A *Defence of Poetry* (1810), his own *Poems* (1813), *Angelica* (1822), and a continuation of Shakespeare's *The *Tempest*.

THWAITE, Anthony (1930–) Poet, born in Chester, and educated at Christ Church, Oxford. His career has included some years as producer for the BBC, and he was co-editor of **Encounter* from 1973 to 1985. His volumes of poetry include *Home Truths* (1957), *The Stones of Emptiness* (1967), *New Confessions* (1974), a meditation on St Augustine, and one of his most highly regarded volumes, and *A Move in the Weather* (2003). An early allegiance to Philip *Larkin has expanded into a wide variety of theme and subject matter, ranging from the domestic to the exotic, and prominently figuring historical material. *Victorian Voices* (1980) is a collection of fourteen *dramatic monologues which takes as subjects Victorian figures such as Philip Henry Gosse, John Churton Collins (1848–1908), and Lawrence Alma-Tadema. *Selected Poems 1956–1996* appeared in 1997. Thwaite is editor of two collected editions of Larkin's poems, and of his *Selected Letters* (1992).

'Thyrsis, A Monody *to commemorate the author's friend, Arthur Hugh Clough, who died at Florence, 1861'* A poem by Matthew *Arnold, first published in **Macmillan's Magazine*, 1866. The poem is a pastoral elegy lamenting *Clough as Thyrsis, recalling his 'golden prime' in the days when he and Arnold wandered through the Oxfordshire countryside, their youthful rivalry as poets, and Clough's departure for a more troubled world

> where his poetry took on 'a stormy note
> Of men contention-tossed'.

It invokes the *Scholar-Gipsy as a fragile image of hope and perpetual quest: 'Roam on! The light we sought is shining still.'

Tibert The cat in the *Roman de Renart* (*see* REYNARD THE FOX). The name is the same as Tybalt (see the exchange between Mercutio and Tybalt in **Romeo and Juliet*, III. i. 74–7: 'Tybalt, you rat-catcher...Good King of Cats, nothing but one of your nine lives').

TIBULLUS, Albius (55/48–19 BC) Roman elegiac poet, noted for his refined and simple style and his idealization of the countryside. Of the three books bearing his name, the first celebrates his love for a mistress (Delia) and a boy (Marathus), the second describes his love for a woman whom he calls Nemesis, and the third is a collection of poems by members of his literary circle. John *Dryden called Charles *Sedley 'a more elegant Tibullus'. Dante Gabriel *Rossetti painted 'The Return of Tibullus to Delia'.

TICKELL, Thomas (1685–1740) Poet, educated at the Queen's College, Oxford. He contributed to the **Guardian* the essays praising Ambrose *Philips that irritated Alexander *Pope. His poem *On the Prospect of Peace* (1712) drew Pope's admiration, though he considered it a potential rival to his own **Windsor-Forest*. Tickell was a friend of Joseph *Addison, whose posthumous *Works* he later edited (1721); in 1715 he published, with Addison's approval, a translation of the first book of the **Iliad*, which Pope took as a direct challenge to his own translation. From 1724 Tickell lived in Dublin, where he became friendly with Jonathan *Swift. His sentimental *ballad *Lucy and Colin* (1725) was much admired by Thomas *Gray and Oliver *Goldsmith.

TIGHE, Mary (1772–1810) Poet, born in County Wicklow, she later moved to London, which she experienced as displacement. She is best known for *Psyche, or The Legend of Love* (1805). Written in *Spenserian stanzas, it recounts in richly erotic language Cupid's forbidden love for Psyche. Some critics argue that Tighe is writing from an Irish standpoint of loss and dislocation, whilst others suggest that she is reworking the tradition of the Spenserian epic from a feminine perspective.

Till Eulenspiegel *See* EULENSPIEGEL, TILL.

TILLOTSON, John (1630–94) Clergyman and preacher, educated at Clare Hall, Cambridge; a latitudinarian (i.e. conforming to the government and ritual of the *Church of England, but denying its divine origin and authority) who became archbishop of Canterbury. His sermons, which were very popular, show a marked difference from the earlier *metaphysical style of John *Donne and Lancelot *Andrewes. They were both plainer and shorter, and were praised as models of lucidity and good sense through most of the 18th century.

Time and Tide: *An Independent Non-Party Weekly Review* A periodical founded in 1920 by Viscountess Rhondda (Margaret Haig Thomas, 1883–1958), with the support of Rebecca *West, Cicely Hamilton (1872–1952), and others. Originally a strongly left-wing and feminist publication, under the editorship of Helen Archdale, it went through many shades of political opinion before its disappearance in 1977. Its contributors included D. H. *Lawrence, Virginia *Woolf, Aldous *Huxley, Storm *Jameson, George Bernard *Shaw, and Robert *Graves; in 1929 it serialized E. M. *Delafield's *Diary of a Provincial Lady*; John *Betjeman's poem 'Caprice' describes how he was sacked from his post as its literary adviser in 1953. For its feminist aspect, see Dale Spender, *Time and Tide Wait for No Man* (1984).

Times, The Founded under the name of *The Daily Universal Register* on 1 January 1785 by John Walter; it became *The Times* in 1788. The founder and his son introduced great improvements both in newspaper printing and in the collection of news. *The Times* was one of the first papers to employ special foreign correspondents: H. C. *Robinson was sent to north Germany in this capacity in 1807, and W. H. Russell (1821–1907) was an important war correspondent, reporting from the Crimea. Notable writers who contributed to *The Times* in the 19th century include George *Borrow (from Spain), Leigh *Hunt, and Benjamin *Disraeli. The 'Times New Roman' font was designed for the newspaper by Stanley Morrison (1889–1967) in 1932. *The Times* has been edited in modern times by George Geoffrey Dawson (1912–19 and 1923–41); Henry Wickham Steed (1919–22); Robert Barrington

Ward (1941–8); William Francis Casey (1948–52); William Haley (1952–66); William Rees-Mogg (1966–81); Harold Evans (1981–2); Charles Douglas-Home (1982–5); Charles Wilson (1985–90); Simon Jenkins (1990–2); Peter Stothard (1992–2002); Robert Thomson (2002–7), and James Harding (2007–). There are three weekly supplements: the *Times *Literary Supplement* (founded 1901), the *Times Educational Supplement* (founded 1910), and the *Times Higher Educational Supplement* (founded 1971). In 1967 both *The Times* and the *Sunday Times* came under the umbrella of Times Newspapers Limited, a company set up by Lord Thomson of Fleet (1894–1976); in 1981 all the titles were acquired by News Corporation.

Times Literary Supplement (1902–) A weekly literary periodical of high international standing which first appeared with *The *Times* in 1902, then in 1914 became a separate publication. The first editor, Bruce Richmond, supported and encouraged many writers of his time, including Virginia *Woolf, T. S. *Eliot, J. M. *Murry, and Edmund *Blunden, both by commissioning reviews from them and by covering their own works. Contributions were anonymous until 1974 when under the editorship of John Gross they began to be signed. The journal tries to cover most of the important works of literature and scholarship, and remains influential. There is an official history by Derwent May, *Critical Times* (2001).

Timias In Edmund *Spenser's *The *Faerie Queene*, Prince *Arthur's squire; he may represent Walter *Ralegh. When wounded (III. v), he is healed by *Belphoebe. The episode in IV. vii. 35–6, where Belphoebe is angered by *Amoret's kissing Timias, may allude to Ralegh's relationship with Elizabeth Throckmorton.

Timon Athenian misanthrope described by *Plutarch, the subject of one of *Lucian's Dialogues and *Shakespeare's **Timon of Athens*. Alexander *Pope's Timon, in *An Epistle to Burlington*, ll. 98–168, is an example of ostentatious wealth without sense or taste.

Timon of Athens A drama by *Shakespeare, now generally acknowledged to be a collaboration with Thomas *Middleton, written probably about 1607 and apparently left unfinished; it was not printed until the first *folio of 1623. The material for the play is in *Plutarch's *Life of Antony*, William Painter's **Palace of Pleasure*, *Lucian's *Timon, or The Misanthrope*, and possibly an anonymous play *Timon* among the *Dyce MSS in the Victoria and Albert Museum.

Timon, a noble and good-natured Athenian, ruins himself by his generosity to flatterers and parasites. He turns to the richest of his friends for help, and finds himself abandoned by those who had previously kept company with him. He surprises them by inviting them to another banquet; but when the covers are removed from the dishes (Timon crying, 'Uncover, dogs, and lap', III. vii. 84), they contain only warm water, which he throws in his guests' faces. Cursing the city, he retires to a cave, where he lives in disillusioned solitude. While digging for roots he finds a hoard of gold, which has now no value for him. His embittered spirit is revealed in his talk with the exiled Alcibiades, the churlish philosopher Apemantus, the thieves and flatterers attracted by the gold, and his faithful steward Flavius. When the senators of Athens, pressed by Alcibiades' attack, come to ask him to return to the city and help them, he offers them his fig tree, on which to hang themselves as a refuge from trouble. Soon his tomb is found by the seashore, with an epitaph expressing his hatred of mankind.

The edition by John Jowett (2004) makes the strongest case for Middleton's part-authorship.

TINDAL, Matthew *See* DEISM.

TINDAL, William *See* TYNDALE, WILLIAM.

TINDALL, Gillian (1938–) Novelist, critic, and historian, born in London, and educated at Oxford. Her novels, which show a sensitive interest in contemporary social and moral issues, and frequently feature the dilemmas of the liberal conscience, include *The Youngest* (1967), *Fly Away Home* (1971), *The Traveller and his Child* (1975), *Give Them All my Love* (1989), and *Spirit Weddings* (1992). Her fiction also reflects her appreciation of the importance of place; in her non-fiction, this appreciation is even clearer. Indeed one of her books, *Countries of the Mind* (1991), is subtitled 'The Meaning of Place to Writers'. *The Fields Beneath* (1977) is a study of Kentish Town in north London, *Célestine* (1995) recreates the vanished world of a 19th-century French village, and *The House by the Thames* (2006) is an exploration of one old house and its role in London history.

Tintagel A castle on the north coast of Cornwall, of which ruins remain. It figures in *Malory as the castle where *Uther Pendragon was wedded to Igraine, and subsequently as the home of King *Mark of Cornwall.

'Tintern Abbey, Lines Composed a Few Miles above, *On Revisiting the Banks of the Wye during a Tour* A poem by William *Wordsworth published in the first edition of the **Lyrical Ballads* (1798). Wordsworth had visited Tintern in 1793; the second visit recorded in this work was with his sister Dorothy, who is addressed in its closing passage, and the poem was composed as they walked towards Bristol. Written in *blank verse, its style is very different from the deliberately 'low' manner of the ballads, and Wordsworth himself referred to 'the impassioned music of the versification', which resembled the elevation of an ode. It is a central statement of Wordsworth's faith in the restorative and associative power of nature; he describes the development of his own love of nature from the 'coarser pleasures' of boyhood, through the 'aching joys' and 'dizzy raptures' of young manhood, to the more reflective, moral, philosophic pleasures of maturity, informed by 'the still, sad music of humanity'.

TIPPER, Elizabeth (*fl.* 1693–8) Poet, author of *The Pilgrim's Viaticum, or The Destitute but not Forlorn* (1698), a book of pious reflections on personal struggles, as in 'Some Experimental Passages of my Life'; Tipper also draws humour from her alternate situations as governess, teacher, servant, and book-keeper. John *Dunton published some of her verse.

TIPPETT, Sir Michael (1905–98) English composer, one of the leading figures of 20th-century British music. He made a substantial impression with the oratorio *A Child of our Time* (1944). At an early stage he had interested T. S. *Eliot in writing the *libretto; Eliot eventually declined, suggesting Tippett would do better to write the words himself. Tippett followed this advice and adopted the same procedure in the five operas of his maturity, *The Midsummer Marriage* (1955), *King Priam* (1962), *The Knot Garden* (1970), *The Ice Break* (1977), and *New Year* (1989). His most important song settings are both for solo voice and piano: the cantata *Boyhood's End* (1943), to words by W. H. *Hudson, and the song cycle *The Heart's Assurance* (1951), to poems by Alun *Lewis and Sidney *Keyes. Tippett's choral works include settings of Edith *Sitwell (the motet *The Weeping Babe*, 1944), Christopher *Fry (the cantata *Crown of the Year*, 1958), P. B. *Shelley and W. B. *Yeats (*Music for Words Perhaps*, 1960). *The Vision of St Augustine* (1965) is a dense and complex setting of words from St *Augustine and the Bible, arranged by the composer as a personal spiritual testament. Tippett published a book of essays, *Moving into Aquarius* (1958), and an autobiography, *Those Twentieth-Century Blues* (1991). He was knighted in 1996.

TIPTREE, James, Jr (1915–87) Pseudonym of Alice Bradley Sheldon, American *science fiction writer, born in Chicago. As a child, she travelled with her parents. During the Second World War, she joined the army, then worked for the CIA before taking a doctorate in psychology. She began publishing in 1968 as 'Tiptree', including 'The Women Men Don't See' (1973). Its rejection of the masculine world observed by a male 'unreliable narrator' invented by a woman writing as a pseudonymous man is fascinatingly recursive. She also published as Racoona Sheldon. Her uncompromisingly feminist work, touched by a sense of death and sexuality, was much praised; after her female identity was revealed in 1977 she continued publishing. *Her Smoke Rose up Forever* (1990) collects the best of her short fiction. See Julie Phillips, *James Tiptree Jr.* (2006).

Tiresias Seer of Thebes, whose divinely inflicted blindness was compensated with the gift of prophecy. In the underworld in *Homer's **Odyssey* Book 11 he foretells Odysseus' final voyage, and he is a key figure in *Sophocles' *Oedipus* and *Antigone*. The blind John *Milton associates himself with Tiresias and other blind seers in **Paradise Lost* Book III. In one tradition, drawn on by *Ovid in *Metamorphoses* Book 3, he changed sex. T. S. *Eliot described his explicitly bisexual Tiresias as 'the most important personage' in *The *Waste Land*.

'Tiresias' A dramatic monologue in blank verse by Alfred *Tennyson, published 1885, but mostly composed in 1833. The prophet Tiresias, blinded and doomed to 'speak the truth that no man may believe' as a consequence of glimpsing Athene naked, urges Menoeceus, son of Creon, to sacrifice himself for Thebes.

TIRSO DE MOLINA (1583–1648) The pseudonym of Gabriel Téllez, a Spanish friar and dramatist, famous outside Spain principally as the creator of the prototype of *Don Juan in his play *El burlador de Sevilla* (1630: *The Seville Deceiver* or *Jester*).

'Tis Pity She's a Whore A tragedy by John *Ford, printed 1633. The play deals with the guilty passion between Giovanni and his sister Annabella. Pregnant, Annabella marries Soranzo, who discovers her condition. She refuses to name her lover, though threatened with death by Soranzo. On the advice of Vasques, his faithful servant, Soranzo pretends forgiveness, while Vasques succeeds in discovering the truth. Soranzo invites Annabella's father and the dignitaries of the city, with Giovanni, to a grand feast, intending to exact vengeance. Although warned of Soranzo's plans, Giovanni boldly comes. He has a last meeting with Annabella just before the feast and, to forestall Soranzo's vengeance, stabs her himself. He enters the banqueting room with her heart on his dagger, defiantly tells what he has done, kills Soranzo, and is killed by Vasques.

'Tis Pity is an obsessive play, focusing on the incest taboo, but treating it seriously and with penetrating honesty (see Act I sc. ii). The love between Giovanni and Annabella is portrayed, with rich symbolic imagery, as doomed but intensely beautiful, making this Ford's most famous play, in the study and on the stage.

Titans According to *Hesiod's *Theogony*, the twelve children of Uranus and Gaia, the original gods of heaven and earth, including Oceanus, Hyperion, Cronos (Roman *Saturn), and their descendants, including *Prometheus, grandson of Oceanus. Intergenerational warfare is an essential part of the myth: Cronos defeated Uranus; the Olympian gods Zeus (Roman *Jupiter), son of Cronos, and his siblings waged war against the first generation of Titans, who were cast down to Tartarus (*see* HADES).

TITIAN (Tiziano Vecellio) (*c.*1487–1576) Venetian painter, famous for his use of colour. He painted religious and history paintings, allegorical and mythological scenes, and many portraits. He was a close friend of Pietro *Aretino. His early work was influenced by Giovanni Bellini (*c.*1430–1516) and *Giorgione with whom the authorship of such works as *Fête Champêtre* (*c.*1508) is closely linked. His pagan subjects, such as the *Bacchus and Ariadne* (1523), are profoundly sensuous. *The Death of St Peter Martyr* (completed 1530), once his most famous picture, was destroyed by fire in 1867. His late style is characterized by its extraordinarily free and expressive handling. It has been suggested that William *Shakespeare's Adonis may have been inspired by Titian's *Adonis*. Travellers on the *Grand Tour invariably commented on the *Venus of Urbino* (1538, Uffizi, Florence). The Romantics, Benjamin *Haydon, William *Hazlitt, Sir Thomas *Lawrence, and John *Keats admired the *Bacchus and Ariadne*. His eroticism appealed to A. C. *Swinburne and Dante Gabriel *Rossetti. See Charles Hope, *Titian* (2003).

Titmarsh, Michael Angelo A pseudonym used by W. M. *Thackeray for much of his early journalism. 'Michael Angelo' is a comic reference to his broken nose and to his aspirations to be an artist. Samuel Titmarsh appears as a character in Thackeray's *The Great Hoggarty Diamond*.

Titurel A German *Grail legend of the 13th century, left incomplete by *Wolfram von Eschenbach. Titurel (the great-grandfather of Parsifal) is entrusted by heaven with the guardianship of the Grail. He builds a chapel at Mount Selvagge (Montsalvatsch) for its safe keeping, and organizes a band of defenders for it.

Titus Andronicus A tragedy by *Shakespeare with, probably, George *Peele. It is probably his earliest tragedy and may date from 1590; in 1594 it was published in a quarto which was reprinted twice before its appearance in the first *folio of 1623, with an added scene (III. ii). Various sources have been put forward, including the *Hecuba* of *Euripides. *Seneca's *Thyestes* and *Troades* contributed to the plot, as did *Ovid's version of 'the tragic tale of Philomel', in *Metamorphoses* Book 13, and *Plutarch.

The first half of the play deals with the return of Titus Andronicus to Rome after his sixth victory over the Goths. He brings with him their Queen Tamora and her three sons, the eldest of whom, Alarbus, is sacrificed to avenge his own sons' deaths. Titus is offered the imperial throne, but gives it instead to the late emperor's eldest son Saturninus, offering his daughter Lavinia as Saturninus' bride. But Lavinia is already promised to Saturninus' brother Bassianus, who steals her away, with the help of her brothers. Titus kills his son Mutius, who had tried to prevent his pursuit of the lovers. Saturninus renounces Lavinia, and marries Tamora, who engineers a false reconciliation between the emperor and Titus, whom she plans to destroy. With the encouragement of her lover Aaron, the Moor, Tamora's sons Chiron and Demetrius murder Bassianus, whose body is thrown into a pit, rape Lavinia, and cut off her tongue and hands. Titus' sons Quintus and Martius are then lured by Aaron to fall into the pit, where they are found and accused of Bassianus' murder. Aaron tells Titus that his sons will not be executed if he sacrifices his hand and sends it to the emperor. Titus does so, but gets it back again with the heads of his two sons.

In the second half of the play Titus discovers who raped and mutilated his daughter, and with his brother Marcus, and last remaining son Lucius, vows revenge. Lucius leaves Rome, but returns with an army of Goths, which captures Aaron and his child by Tamora. Tamora and her sons Demetrius and Chiron visit Titus disguised as Revenge, Rapine, and Murder and ask him to have Lucius' banquet at his house, where the emperor and the empress and her sons will be brought. Titus recognizes his enemies and with the help of Lavinia slits the throats of Chiron and Demetrius and uses their flesh in a pie, some of which Tamora eats at the banquet before Titus kills her. He also stabs Lavinia, but is killed by Saturninus, who is in turn killed by Lucius. Lucius is elected emperor and sentences Aaron to be buried breast-deep in the ground and starved to death.

Critical judgement of the play has been generally unfavourable. It was dismissed by its *Restoration adapter Edward Ravenscroft (*fl.* 1659–97): 'It seems rather a heap of Rubbish than a Structure.' More recent critics have related the play to *revenge tragedy, and praised it for its anticipation of Shakespeare's great tragedies, in particular **Othello* and **King Lear*. A drawing ascribed to Henry *Peacham depicting 'Tamora pleading for her sons going to execution' perhaps dated 1595 is at Longleat and is the first known surviving illustration of one of Shakespeare's plays.

Andr*o*nicus in the play is accentuated thus, on the second syllable; in Latin it is Andronicus. For authorship, see Brian Vickers, *Shakespeare, Co-Author* (2004).

'To Autumn' A poem by John *Keats, written September 1819, published 1820. It was his last major poem, and although usually included in a discussion of the Odes (*see* ODE), Keats himself did not call it an ode. The poem, in three stanzas, is at once a celebration of the fruitfulness of autumn (lightly personified as a figure in various autumnal landscapes) and an elegy for the passing of summer and the transience of life, and its mood has been generally taken to be one of acceptance. Keats's association of autumn and early death is poignantly revealed in a letter to J. H. *Reynolds (21 September 1819), written immediately after the composition of the poem, in which he says, 'I always somehow associate Chatterton with the autumn.'

TOCQUEVILLE, Alexis de (1805–59) French historian and political thinker. Until the *coup d'état* of 1851 he was active in the legal profession and in politics, serving for a time as foreign minister. An official visit to the United States in 1851 produced the first of his two classic works, *De la démocratie en Amérique* (1835–40: *Democracy in America*), a subtle analysis of the strengths and weaknesses of a democratic society in evolution. The second, *L'Ancien Régime et la Révolution* (1856: *The Ancien Régime and the Revolution*), is a social and political study of pre-revolutionary France, regarded as the source rather than the contradiction of the revolution that destroyed it. No 19th-century historian discerned with greater exactness the tensions hidden in large-scale contemporary communities. He corresponded extensively with J. S. *Mill and became a friend of Henry Reeve (1813–95), who translated him. See H. Brogan, *Alexis de Tocqueville* (2007).

TODHUNTER, John (1839–1916) Poet, playwright, and pioneer of the Irish literary movement, educated at Trinity College, Dublin, where he three times won the vice-chancellor's prize for English verse. He took his MD in Dublin, but did not practise medicine for long before turning to literature. *The Banshee* (1888) and *Three Irish Bardic Tales* (1896) were considered among his best poetic works. Prose works include his published lecture on *The Theory of the Beautiful* (1872) and *A Study of Shelley* (1879).

TÓIBÍN, Colm (1955–) Irish novelist, journalist, and travel writer, born in Enniscorthy, Co. Wexford, educated at the Christian Brothers School there, and at St Peter's College, Wexford, and University College, Dublin. Three years spent in Barcelona led to *Homage to Barcelona* (1990) and his first novel, *The South* (1990), about an Irish woman artist living in Spain in the 1950s. Toíbín's lyrical style and political concerns are displayed in *The Heather Blazing* (1992) which won the Encore Prize. Travels in South America resulted in *The Story of the Night* (1996), about a gay man in Argentina during the Falklands War. *The Blackwater Lighthouse* (1999) describes a family reunion at the sickbed of a man with Aids and is complemented by the collection of essays *Love in a Dark Time* (2002). *The Master* (2004), a novel about Henry *James, won the International Impac Dublin Literary Award. Toíbín's stories were collected in *Mothers and Sons* (2006), the title of which announces a recurrent theme of his fiction.

TOKLAS, Alice B. *See* STEIN, GERTRUDE.

TOLAND, John (1670–1722) Freethinker and controversialist, born, probably into an Irish-speaking family, on Inishowen in Donegal. 'Educated from the cradle in the grossest superstition', as he says in his *Apology* (1697), he repudiated *Roman Catholicism at the age of 15. After studying at universities in Scotland and the Netherlands, he settled in Oxford, where he completed *Christianity not Mysterious* (1696), which made him notorious. It also began the *Deist controversy and initiated the greatest epoch of Irish philosophy. In 1702 he travelled to Berlin, where he addressed *Letters of Serena* (1704) to the queen of Prussia. Toland's materialistic pantheism—he coined the word 'pantheist' in 1705—is flamboyantly expressed in *Pantheisticon* (1720). In 1698 he wrote a life of John *Milton and edited his prose works. *Tetradymus* (1720) contains perhaps the first essay on the esoteric/exoteric distinction, or the difference between specialized or obscure knowledge and knowledge that is publicly available to all. Alexander *Pope ridiculed Toland; Jonathan *Swift called him 'the great Oracle of the Anti-Christians'.

TOLKIEN, J. R. R. (John Ronald Reuel) (1892–1973) Scholar and novelist. A member of the *'Inklings' group, he was Merton professor of English language and literature at Oxford University, 1945–59, and published a number of philological and critical studies, including 'Beowulf: The Monsters and the Critics' (in *Proceedings of the British Academy*, 1936). Alongside his scholarly career, he became internationally known for two books based on a complex mythology of his own devising: *The Hobbit* (1937) and its sequel *The *Lord of the Rings* (3 vols, 1954–5). *The Silmarillion* (1977), which occupies an earlier place in this sequence of stories, was published posthumously. When *The Lord of the Rings* became a best-seller in the United States during the 1960s, Tolkien was unimpressed, referring ruefully to his 'deplorable cultus'. Enthusiasts nonetheless multiplied and developed a vast network of societies, publications, and, from the 1990s onwards, mailing lists and websites, all devoted to exploring Tolkien's Middle Earth and its denizens. After Tolkien's death, his son Christopher supervised publication of a series of posthumous works and the negotiation of adaptation rights. Film versions (2001–3) of the three volumes of *The Lord of the Rings* have created many new admirers for Tolkien's fiction. A life by Humphrey Carpenter was published in 1977, while Tom Shippey has published two studies of the man, his mythology, and his vast influence on late 20th-century culture: *The Road to Middle-Earth* (1982) and *J. R. R. Tolkien: Author of the Century* (2000).
See also FANTASY FICTION.

TOLLER, Ernst (1893–1939) German poet and dramatist, born near Bromberg. Of Jewish family, he studied in Grenoble but enlisted in 1914 on the German side. The experience of war made him a radical pacifist. Associated with the short-lived Bavarian communist government of 1918, he was imprisoned for five years after the war, during which period he wrote *Expressionist plays such as *Die Maschinenstürmer* (1922: *The Machine Wreckers*). After the rise of Hitler he moved to New York, where he committed suicide, an act commemorated in an elegy by W. H. *Auden ('In Memory of Ernst Toller'), who had met Toller in 1936 in Portugal and translated the lyrics for his satirical musical play *Nie wieder Friede!* (1937: *No More Peace!*).

TOLLET, Elizabeth (1694–1754) Poet, daughter of the commissioner of the navy George Tollet (d. 1719), who gave her a comparatively full education. Her anonymous *Poems on Several Occasions: With Anne Boleyn to King Henry VIII. An Epistle* (1724) was reissued posthumously (1755), bearing her name and including much additional work. Tollet wrote several poems on contemporary figures such as Isaac *Newton, William *Congreve, Lady Mary Wortley *Montagu, Anne Finch, countess of *Winchilsea, and Alexander *Pope. Her poem 'To my Brother at St John's College in Cambridge' deftly explores male and female patterns of reading; her most substantial poem, 'Hypatia', has a strongly *feminist argument.

TOLSTOY, Count Lev Nikolaevich (1828–1910) Russian prose writer, dramatist, and publicist, born near Tula at Iasnaia Poliana, his home until his death. He attended Kazan University 1844–7 and St Petersburg University as a law student 1849. He served in the army 1852–6, seeing action in the Caucasus and at Sevastopol during the Crimean War. Reading Laurence *Sterne's *A Sentimental Journey* in 1850 prompted him to devote his life to writing. He read widely, admiring, apart from Sterne, *Plato, *Rousseau, W. M. *Thackeray, George *Eliot, and Charles *Dickens. The influence of **David Copperfield* was apparent in his first published work, *Childhood* (1852), the opening part of a trilogy completed by *Boyhood* (1854) and *Youth* (1857). His experience of warfare informed his Caucasian tale *The Raid* (1853), and *Sevastopol Sketches* (1855–6). His first visit to the West in 1857 led to 'Lucerne', a lyrical short story attacking English behaviour. On his return he founded a school at Iasnaia Poliana and began to develop his ideas on child-centred education. He then published *Family Happiness* (1859) and *The Cossacks* (1863), but the following years (1863–9) were engaged in the creation of *War and Peace*, an epic historical novel of the Napoleonic campaigns and the lives of two aristocratic families. This was followed by *Anna Karenina*, begun in 1873 and published 1875–8, the story of a married woman's passion for a young officer and her tragic fate. From about 1880 Tolstoy's constant concern with moral questions developed into a spiritual crisis leading to his renunciation of literature as art. Henceforth his writing was to display a purely moral purpose, apparent in such works as *A Confession* (1879–82), *What Men Live By* (1882), *What I Believe* (1883), and *What is Art?* (1898). The major fictional works of this late period, bearing the imprint of changes in his thinking, are *The Death of Ivan Ilyich* (1886), *The Kreutzer Sonata* (pub. 1891), *Master and Man* (1895), *Resurrection* (1899–1900), and *Hadji Murad* (1904, published posthumously in 1912). Tolstoy's moral positions, involving non-resistance to evil, the renunciation of property, and the abolition of governments and churches, led to the banning of many of his works and to his excommunication by the Orthodox Church in 1901. But his teachings led to the formation of Tolstoyan communities throughout Europe and America, motivated the kibbutz movement in Palestine, and were an inspiration to penal reformers in Britain and to Gandhi in South Africa. His few plays, including *The Fruits of Enlightenment* and *The Power of Darkness*, are mainly didactic in intent. George Bernard *Shaw reworked the latter as *The Shewing-up of Blanco Posnet* (1910) and the former was reflected in his *Heartbreak House* (1919). Others who played a part in establishing his English reputation were Matthew *Arnold, John *Galsworthy, E. M. *Forster, and D. H. *Lawrence. His works were translated by Louise and Aylmer Maude, *The Centenary Edition of Tolstoy* (21 vols, 1928–37). A. N. *Wilson, *Tolstoy* (1988) is a life. For affinities with Britain see W. Gareth Jones (ed.), *Tolstoi and Britain* (1995).

TOMALIN, Claire (1933–) Biographer, born in London, educated at Newnham College, Cambridge. Her biographies, which have been notable for their scholarly and sensitive reclamation of women's lives from historical neglect or misunderstanding, include *The Life and Death of Mary Wollstonecraft* (1974), *Katherine Mansfield: A Secret Life* (1987), *The Invisible Woman: The Story of Nelly Ternan and Charles Dickens* (1990), *Mrs Jordan's Profession* (1994, a study of the actress Dorothy *Jordan, inspired by her research into the theatrical profession during her work on Ellen Ternan), and *Jane Austen: A Life* (1997). More recently she has published an award-winning biography of Samuel *Pepys (2002) and *Thomas Hardy: The Time-Torn Man* (2006).

Tom and **Jerry** The two chief characters in Pierce *Egan's *Life in London*; hence used in various allusive ways, for instance to suggest riotous behaviour: they gave their names to the well-known cartoon characters.

Tom Brown's Schooldays (1857) Seminal *school story by Thomas *Hughes, set in Rugby School in the 1830s. It helped establish staples of the genre with a God-like headmaster (Thomas *Arnold) and the ultimate bully, *Flashman. There is a film (1951, Gordon Parry); Stephen Fry featured in the 2005 television adaptation.

Tom Jones, The History of A novel by Henry *Fielding, published 1749. Although very long, the novel is highly organized, and was thought by S. T. *Coleridge to have one of the three great plots of all literature. The kindly, prosperous widower Mr Allworthy (based on Ralph *Allen and the dedicatee, Lord *Lyttelton) lives at 'Paradise Hall' in Somerset with his ill-humoured sister Bridget. Late one evening Allworthy finds a baby boy on his bed. He is charmed, names the baby Tom, and adopts him, adding the surname Jones on the assumption that the mother is Jenny Jones, a maidservant to the wife of the schoolmaster Partridge, who is accused of being the father and dismissed his post. Bridget marries the obnoxious Captain Blifil and they have a son, Master Blifil, who is taught, with Tom, by the sadistic chaplain Thwackum and the philosopher Square. When Tom is 19, his childhood affection for the beautiful and sweet-natured Sophia (supposedly a portrait of Fielding's first wife), daughter of the neighbouring fox-hunting Squire Western, matures into love. However, Sophia is destined by her father for Master Blifil, and Tom allows himself to be distracted by the more accessible charms of Molly Seagrim, daughter of the gamekeeper (and poacher) Black George. By clever misrepresentation the scheming young Blifil gradually poisons Allworthy's affection for the good-natured but unruly Tom, and with the help of Thwackum and Square he succeeds in having Tom expelled from the house. Filled with despair at alienating his beloved foster-father, Tom sets off for Bristol intending to go to sea. Meanwhile Sophia, disgusted by Blifil's courtship, runs away with her maid Honour. Amid numerous adventures on the road, Tom encounters Partridge, once supposed to be his father, who is now travelling the country as a barber-surgeon. Tom and Sophia both arrive at an inn at Upton, but because of Partridge's malicious stupidity Sophia believes that Tom, then in bed with a woman known as Mrs Waters, no longer loves her, and flees on towards London. Tom follows, and in London is ensnared by the rich and amorous Lady Bellaston, Sophia's kinswoman. Lady Bellaston and her friend Lord Fellamar contrive together to keep Tom away from Sophia, on whom Lord Fellamar has designs, but the abrupt eruption of Squire Western into the picture is sufficient to save Sophia from the artistocrat's schemes of seduction. Partridge now reveals that Mrs Waters is Jenny Jones, supposedly Tom's mother, and Tom briefly believes he has committed incest. But Jenny reveals that Tom's mother was really Bridget Allworthy, who has confessed to her brother on her deathbed. Tom's enemies arrange for him to be press-ganged, but instead a fight develops in which it at first appears that Tom has killed his assailant; he is in consequence arrested. Blifil arranges for the gang to give evidence against Tom, who despairs of obtaining Sophia's forgiveness; but with the help of a letter of confession and repentance from Square to Allworthy, Blifil's long-running envious machinations are finally revealed, and Tom is reinstated in his uncle's affection. He meets Sophia again, learns that she loves him, and receives the hearty blessing of her father. In the generosity of his heart, Tom forgives all who have wronged him.

In chapter 1, 'Bill of Fare', Fielding informs the reader that 'The provision...we have here made is no other than Human Nature' and in his Dedication to Lord Lyttelton declares, 'that to recommend goodness and innocence hath been my sincere endeavour in this history'. The book's robust characterization, occasional exercises in *mock-heroic diction, and magisterial narrative voice defined a widely influential compromise between the new world of the 'realistic' novel and the more timeless genres of comedy and epic, and the book was an immediate success, selling some 10,000 copies in its first year. Fielding's highly individual moral sense (which permits his high-spirited hero various sexual escapades before his final blissful marriage) was however a severe irritant to many, including Samuel *Johnson, who thought the book too 'vicious' to be read by women. To James *Boswell, who openly admired Fielding, Johnson sternly maintained the superiority of Samuel *Richardson's psychological analysis, declaring 'there is more knowledge of the heart in one letter of Richardson's, than in all *Tom Jones*'.

TOMKINS, Thomas (1572–1656) Welsh composer, taught by William *Byrd. A book of his *madrigals was published in 1622; his sacred works appeared as *Musica Deo Sacra* (1668). He also annotated some important music manuscripts.

TOMKIS, Thomas (?1580–?1634) Fellow of Trinity College, Cambridge, and author of two university comedies, *Lingua, or The Combat of the Tongue and the Five Senses for Superiority* (1607) and *Albumazar* (1615). The latter was acted before *James I at Cambridge. Albumazar (historically an Arabian astronomer, 805–85) is a rascally wizard who transforms the rustic Trincalo into the person of his master, with absurd consequences. It was revived (1668) with a prologue by John *Dryden, wrongly charging Ben *Jonson with adopting it as a model for *The *Alchemist*. It was again revived by David *Garrick in 1747.

TOMLINSON, Charles (1927–) Poet and artist, born in Stoke-on-Trent and educated at Queens' College, Cambridge, where he was taught by Donald *Davie. He was for many years professor of English at the University of Bristol. His qualities as a graphic artist (*Eden: Graphics and Poems* was published in 1989) are reflected in the visual qualities of his verse, which frequently figures paintings among its subjects. It also shows strong American influences, including Wallace *Stevens, William Carlos *Williams, and Marianne *Moore. Tomlinson has spent a great deal of time in the USA and has been an enthusiastic exponent of modernist American poetry: *Some Americans* (1981) commemorates his relationships with such poets and painters as George *Oppen and Georgia O'Keeffe (1887–1986). American landscapes, notably those of New Mexico, also figure prominently in the poems, as do those of Italy, Mexico, and Japan, along with those of rural Gloucestershire where he has lived for many years. Tomlinson is both a poet of place and a poet between places, and his poems maintain a dialogue between rootedness and instability, celebration and wry rumination. The natural world is characteristically scrutinized into a human significance while also remaining instructively, even caustically, other. The celebrated 'Swimming Chenango Lake' is exemplary in this regard: a swimming human body 'reads the water...making a where' for itself only by recognizing that this is

> a possession to be relinquished
> Willingly at each stroke

Tomlinson's first volume, *Relations and Contraries* (1951), has been followed by numerous others including *Seeing is Believing* (USA 1958; London 1960), *The Way of the World* (1969), *Written on Water* (1972), *The Way in and Other Poems* (1974), which uncharacteristically explores his working-class childhood in Stoke, *Notes from New York* (1984), *Jubilation* (1995), and *Cracks in the Universe* (2006). A volume of *Collected Poems* was published in 1985. Tomlinson has also been prominent as a translator, producing versions of such poets as Fyodor Tyutchev (1803–73), Antonio *Machado, Cesar Vallejo (1892–1938), Octavio *Paz, and Attilio Bertolucci (1911–2000). He edited *The Oxford Book of Verse in Translation* in 1980, and his critical work includes *Poetry and Metamorphosis* (1983).

TOMLINSON, H. M. (Henry Major) (1873–1958) Journalist and novelist, born in Poplar, London, the son of a dockyard foreman. His early love of ships and the sea is reflected in his life and works, including his first book, *The Sea and the Jungle* (1912, an account of a voyage to Brazil and some 2,000 miles up the Amazon and the Madeira, its longest tributary), *London River* (1921, essays and reflections), and his first novel, *Gallions Reach* (1927). *All our Yesterdays* (1930) is an anti-war novel born of his experiences as an official war correspondent (1914–17). As a journalist he contributed to the radical *Morning Leader* and the **Daily News* and was literary editor of *The Nation* from 1917 to 1923.

Tommy Thumb's Song Book A collection of *nursery rhymes presumably printed and distributed by Mary *Cooper. Although no copy of this work has been located, Cooper advertised it in 1744 and copies of *Tommy Thumb's Pretty Song Book* (vol. ii, 1744), containing many well-known verses, survive.

Tom o' Bedlam A wandering beggar. After the dissolution of the religious houses, where before the Reformation the poor used to be relieved, there was for a long time no settled provision for them. They wandered over the country, many assuming disguises designed to promote charitable giving. Some pretended to be mad and were called Bedlam beggars (like 'Diccon the Bedlam' in **Gammer Gurton's Needle*). Edgar, in **King Lear*, II. iii, adopts this disguise:

> Of Bedlam beggars, who, with roaring voices,
> Strike in their numb'd and mortified bare arms
> Pins, wooden pricks, nails, sprigs of rosemary.

In Thomas *Dekker's *Bellman of London* (1608) 'Tom of Bedlam's band of madcaps' are listed among types of beggars. Some of these Bedlam beggars sang mad songs, examples of which are given in Thomas *Percy's **Reliques*. They were also called 'Abraham-men', possibly from the parable of the beggar Lazarus in Luke 18.

Tom Sawyer, The Adventures of A novel by Mark *Twain, published 1876, which describes a series of escapades centring on Tom, a lively and adventurous lad, and his companion Huckleberry Finn. At the close of the novel, they divide the treasure they discover between them, which marks the starting point for the classic sequel *The Adventures of *Huckleberry Finn*. Tom also features in *Tom Sawyer Abroad* (1894) and *Tom Sawyer, Detective* (1896).

Tom Thumb, a Tragedy A *mock-heroic farce by Henry *Fielding, performed and published in 1730, and republished in 1731 in an extended version as *The Tragedy of Tragedies, or The Life and Death of Tom Thumb the Great*, with an apparatus of mock-scholarly notes in the manner of Alexander *Pope's **Dunciad Variorum*. William *Hogarth supplied the frontispiece. The play burlesqued the 'Bombastic Greatness' of heroic tragedies by James *Thomson and others. In the denouement, Thumb is eaten by a cow and the entire cast, including Thumb's ghost, is murdered. Jonathan *Swift claimed that he had laughed only twice in his life, once at a Merry-Andrew, or clown, and once at *Tom Thumb*.

TONE, Theobald Wolfe (1763–98) Irish barrister, revolutionary, and adjutant general in the French army, born in Dublin and educated at Trinity College there, who founded the United Irishmen and died, by his own hand, while awaiting execution for his part in organizing French incursions to Ireland. For his famously stylish writings—pamphlets, speeches, correspondence, and diaries—see *The Writings of Theobold Wolfe Tone*, ed. T. W. Moody, R. B. McDowell, and C. J. Woods (3 vols, 1998–2007).

TONKS, Rosemary (1932–?) British novelist and poet, born in London, educated at Wentworth School, London. Tonks moved to Karachi after her marriage in the early 1950s, but was forced to return to Britain due to serious illness. There she worked for the BBC, writing and reviewing for the European Service. Since the 1990s there has been an increasing interest in her work, particularly among poets, and poems have appeared in a wide range of 20th-century poetry anthologies. Her surreally inflected poetics of modern urban life—what she has described as its 'enraged excitement, its great lonely joys'—harness huge lyrical and colloquial energies. Tonks stopped publishing in the 1970s due to strong religious convictions, and her whereabouts is not currently publicly known. Poems include *Notes on Cafés and Bedrooms* (1963) and *Iliad of Broken Sentences* (1967) and novels include *Opium Fogs* (1963), *The Bloater* (1968), and *The Halt during the Chase* (1972).

TONSON, Jacob (1655–1736) Publisher and bookseller, the son of a barber-surgeon; he established himself in 1678 with his brother Richard (1653–90) and eventually took his nephew Jacob (1682–1735) into the business, resigning it to him *c.*1718; the firm was continued by a great-nephew of the same name. Tonson was the major literary publisher of his age and secretary of the *Kit-Cat Club. His long association with John *Dryden began in 1679, with Dryden's version of *Troilus and Cressida*; he also published Aphra *Behn, the earl of *Rochester, Thomas *Otway, Abraham *Cowley, Nicholas *Rowe, Matthew *Prior, William *Congreve, Joseph *Addison, and Richard *Steele, among many others. He bought up several lucrative copyrights, and published major editions of **Paradise Lost*, of the plays of William *Shakespeare (1709) and of the works of Edmund *Spenser (1715). His series of *Miscellanies*, in six parts, of which the earliest were compiled by Dryden, appeared 1684–1709, and contained translations from *Horace, *Ovid, *Virgil, among other Latin poets, as well as work by Alexander *Pope, Ambrose *Philips, and Jonathan *Swift. Tonson was the butt of occasional satire from Dryden, who mocked his 'two left legs, and Judas-coloured hair' (Judas was traditionally supposed to have had red hair), and from Pope, who nonetheless respected the publisher's knowledge, taste, and literary intelligence.

TOOKE, John Horne (1736–1812) Radical politician, the son of a poulterer named Horne; he added the name of his friend William Tooke of Purley to his own in 1782. He vigorously supported John *Wilkes in connection with the Middlesex election, but later quarrelled with him. He was more than once in conflict with the authorities, and was tried for high treason and acquitted in 1794. His varied acquaintance included James *Boswell, Jeremy *Bentham, William *Godwin, Thomas *Paine, and S. T. *Coleridge. His principal work, *Epea Pteroenta, or The Diversions of Purley* (1786–1805, two volumes of a planned three) established his reputation as a philologist and was extremely popular.

TOOLE, John Kennedy (1937–69) American novelist, born in New Orleans, whose works were published after his suicide at the age of 32. His comic novel *A Confederacy of Dunces* was published in 1980 with the help of the novelist Walker Percy (1916–90). His other novel was *The Neon Bible* (1989).

TOOMER, Jean (1894–1967) African American writer, born Nathan Pinchback in Washington, DC, who is primarily remembered for his mixed-media volume *Cane* (1923), which uses *modernist techniques to explore the gathering of sugar in Georgia. Toomer was an important figure in the *Harlem Renaissance but from the 1930s he withdrew from society. See Cynthia Earl Kerman and Richard Elridge, *The Lives of Jean Toomer* (1989).

Top Girls A play by Caryl *Churchill, first performed at the *Royal Court Theatre in 1982, is a feminist questioning of Thatcherite individualist assumptions. The first act is set in a London restaurant as Marlene celebrates her promotion as managing director of the 'Top Girls' employment agency: her guests are five historical and quasi-historical characters, including Isabella *Bird and *Patient Griselda, who have different stories of female experience to relate. The second and third acts, which move between the agency office and the poor East Anglian home of Marlene's sister, reveal the hard choices Marlene has made to achieve her success, and how her 'sister' has been denied the same possibilities. Each member of the all-female cast (apart from Marlene) plays several parts. The play explores the changing social, sexual, and above all financial expectations of British women in the 1980s, and contrasts them both with historical attitudes and with contemporary aspirations.

TOPLADY, Augustus Montague (1740–78) Clergyman and writer of *hymns, educated at Westminster School and Trinity College, Dublin. His best-known hymn is 'Rock of Ages', published in the *Gospel Magazine* in 1776. Initially influenced by John *Wesley, he soon became his bitter opponent, and an extreme *Calvinist.

topographical poetry Described by Samuel *Johnson as 'local poetry, of which the fundamental object is some particular landscape...with the addition of...historical retrospection or incidental meditation', normally distinguished from poems praising country estates, such as Ben *Jonson's 'To Penshurst' or Andrew *Marvell's 'Upon Appleton House'. *Cooper's Hill* (1642), by Sir John *Denham, is regarded as the model for the genre, which includes poems by John *Dyer, Sir Samuel *Garth, Alexander *Pope, James *Thomson (1700–48), Richard *Jago, and Oliver *Goldsmith. 'Prospect poems' survey a large landscape from a high point; William *Wordsworth's 'Lines Composed a Few Miles above *Tintern Abbey' is a late example. *Remains of Elmet* (1979) and the less precisely located *River* (1983), poetic sequences by Ted *Hughes, lie partially within the topographical tradition, as does Alice *Oswald's *Dart* (2002).

To the Lighthouse Fifth novel by Virginia *Woolf, published 1927. It draws powerfully on her memories of family holidays at St Ives, Cornwall, when she was a girl, although the setting is ostensibly the Isle of Skye. Woolf's parents were the inspiration for the maternal, gracious, managing, but manipulative Mrs Ramsay (the novel was published on the thirty-second anniversary of Woolf's mother's death), and the self-centred, self-pitying, absurd, yet tragic Mr Ramsay, who together provide the focus for Woolf's most profound exploration of the conflicts between men and women and the dynamics of marriage. The novel is in three sections, of which the first and longest, 'The Window', describes the late afternoon and evening of an Edwardian September day, with the Ramsays on holiday with their eight children (Andrew, Cam, James, Jasper, Nancy, Prue, Roger, and Rose) and assorted guests (the lethargic elderly poet Augustus Carmichael; the painter Lily Briscoe; the awkward young academic Charles Tansley; William Bankes, a gentleman botanist; Paul Rayley; and Minta Doyle). Family tension centres on the desire of the youngest child, James, to visit the lighthouse, and his father's apparent desire to thwart him; the frictions of the day are momentarily resolved around the dinner table and a triumphant *bœuf en daube*. The second section, 'Time Passes', is a comparatively brief, lyrical treatment of the 1914–18 period and records, parenthetically, the deaths of Mrs Ramsay, Andrew Ramsay (killed in the war), and Prue, who dies in childbirth. It dwells with a desolate lyricism on the abandonment of the family summer home and its gradually being brought back to life by Mrs McNab and Mrs Bast, and ends with the arrival of the Ramsays, Lily Briscoe, Carmichael, and others in September 1919. The last section, 'The Lighthouse', describes the finally successful efforts of Lily to complete the painting which she had abandoned ten years earlier and the parallel but equally successful efforts of Mr Ramsay, Cam, and James to reach the lighthouse, despite the undercurrents of rivalry, loss, and rebellion that torment them. The novel is a triumphant fusion of rapture and grief, tragedy and comedy, devotion and tyranny, and is widely acknowledged one of the greatest novels in the English literary canon.

TOTTEL, Richard (*c*.1528–1593) A publisher who carried on business at 'The Hand and Star' within Temple Bar from 1553 to 1593. He is chiefly known as the compiler (with Nicholas *Grimald) of *Songs and Sonnets*, known as *Tottel's Miscellany* (1557), in which many of Sir Thomas *Wyatt's and the earl of *Surrey's poems were printed for the first time. Besides law-books, he also published Sir Thomas *More's *Dialogue of Comfort* (1553) and Surrey's *Aeneid* (1557).

Slender, in William *Shakespeare's *The *Merry Wives of Windsor*, had 'rather than forty shillings' he had Tottel's 'book of Songs and Sonnets' with him when courting Anne Page; and the grave-digger in **Hamlet* sings a version of Lord Vaux's poem from the same collection.

TOURNEUR, Cyril (?1575–1626) Dramatist. Practically nothing is known of his life. He appears to have worked for a time in the Netherlands, and died at Kinsale in Ireland after accompanying Sir Edward Cecil to Cadiz in 1625 on an unsuccessful raid of Spanish treasure ships. His small known output includes an allegorical poem, *The Transformed Metamorphosis* (1600), a lost play, *The Nobleman* (1612), *The *Atheist's Tragedy* (1611), an elegy on the death of Prince Henry (1613), and

several minor and disputed works. *The *Revenger's Tragedy*, printed anonymously in 1607, was first ascribed to him in 1656 by Edward Archer in a play list, and was generally accepted as his until the end of the 19th century, when Thomas *Middleton was proposed as the author. Since then there has been prolonged debate over attribution, with Middleton gradually emerging as the most likely candidate, a view confirmed by recent statistical and linguistic analysis. The *Complete Works* were edited by Allardyce Nicoll (1930); see S. Schuman, *Cyril Tourneur* (1977).
See also REVENGE TRAGEDY.

TOURNIER, Michel (1924–) French novelist and short story writer. Tournier is known in particular for his reworkings of stories, myths, and legends from Western literature and the Judaeo-Christian tradition. His first novel, *Vendredi, ou Les Limbes du Pacifique* (1967; trans. as *Friday*, 1969), restaged Daniel Defoe's **Robinson Crusoe* by having Man Friday rather than Crusoe himself leave the island for civilization. *Le Coq de Bruyère* (1978; trans. as *The Fetishist*, 1984) includes retellings of the Adam and Eve story and Charles *Perrault's 'Le Petit Poucet' (Tom Thumb).

TOUSSAINT LOUVERTURE, François *See* LOUVERTURE, TOUSSAINT.

TOWNSEND, John Rowe (1922–) Children's writer, historian, and critic, born in Leeds, England, and educated at Leeds Grammar School and Emmanuel College, Cambridge. While Children's Books Editor for the *Guardian* in the 1970s he became concerned with the way children's books helped shape attitudes to social issues including class, gender, and the environment. *Gumble's Yard* (1961) and its sequels include working-class characters; *The Intruder* (1969) is about identity theft. Later works explore fantasy and future worlds and teenage romance. *Written for Children* (1965, frequently revised), a historical overview of children's literature, is a standard work in the field.

TOWNSEND, Sue (1946–) Born in Leicester; she left school at 15; known for *The Secret Diary of Adrian Mole Aged 13¾* (1982) and its four sequels (televised 1985). Adrian reports on his own and others' behaviour, revealing concerns about his adolescent desires and body in an inadvertently comic way. The books comment on the politics, attitudes, and events of Britain in the 1980s and 1990s; later books for adults similarly combine political observation and humour.

TOWNSHEND, Aurelian (?1583–?1643) Poet. He travelled in France and Italy, then appears in 1632 as a writer of court *masques. He seems to have collaborated with Inigo *Jones in *Albion's Triumph* and to have contributed verses for the queen's masque of *Tempe Restored*. He enjoyed favour at the court of Charles I, as his lyric 'On his Hearing Her Majesty Sing' records. His poems were not collected, but scattered through various miscellanies, until E. K. *Chambers's edition, *Poems and Masks* (1912).

Toxophilus *See* ASCHAM, ROGER.

toy books Books designed to stimulate play and so which function as toys have existed since the 18th century, but the term is usually applied to the large (usually 10.5 × 9 inches) colourful picture books, usually based on traditional tales and nursery rhymes, published in the 19th century in tandem with—and possibly stimulating—developments in colour printing. They are particularly associated with the printer-engraver Edmund Evans (1826–1905) and his stable of artists including Walter *Crane, Randolph *Caldecott, and Kate *Greenaway. Together they set the standard for the modern *picturebook, with its sophisticated interplay of word and image. They were sold inexpensively in vast print runs; a first printing usually started at 10,000 copies. See Tomoko Masaki, *A History of Victorian Popular Picture Books* (2006).

TOYNBEE, Arnold Joseph (1889–1975) Historian, educated at Winchester College and Balliol College, Oxford. He was professor of Byzantine and modern Greek language, literature, and history at King's College, London, 1919–24, the director of studies at the Royal Institute of International Affairs, and research professor of international history until he retired in 1955. His great work *A Study of History*, published in ten volumes between 1934 and 1954, is a survey of the chief civilizations of the world, and an enquiry into cycles of creativity and decay. His view that the fragmentation and waning of Western civilization could already be detected, and that hope lay in a new universal religion which would recapture 'spiritual initiative', aroused much controversy. His other works include *Civilization on Trial* (1948) and *The World and the West* (1953). *Comparing Notes: A Dialogue across a Generation* (1963) was written with his son, novelist, critic, and journalist Philip Toynbee (1916–81). Polly Toynbee (1946–), daughter of Philip, is a distinguished journalist and writer on social policy.

Tractarian Movement, *Tracts for the Times* *See* OXFORD MOVEMENT.

TRADESCANT, John (d. 1638) Traveller and collector, gardener successively to the earls of Salisbury, George Villiers, first duke of Buckingham (1592–1628), and Charles I. He travelled with Sir Dudley Digges (1582/3–1639) to Archangel in 1619 (his account contains the earliest known description of Russian plants) and to the Levant and Algiers in an expedition against the Barbary pirates (1620), from which he brought back the 'Algier apricot'. From his botanical garden in Lambeth he and his son John (1608–62), also a traveller and collector, introduced many foreign plants to English gardens. The genus *Tradescantia* is named after them. The younger Tradescant published *Musaeum Tradescantianum* in 1656, and his collection, given by Elias *Ashmole to the University of Oxford, became the world's first University Museum, the Ashmolean. Both Tradescants are buried in the churchyard of St-Mary-at-Lambeth, now the Museum of Garden History. See Mea Allan, *The Tradescants* (1964); Jennifer Potter, *Strange Blooms* (2006).

tragedy A dramatic (or, by extension, narrative) work in which events move to a fatal or disastrous conclusion for the *protagonist, whose potential greatness is cruelly wasted through error or the mysterious workings of fate. Aristotle's **Poetics* was the first attempt to define the characteristics of tragedy as practised by *Sophocles and others, presenting its effect upon spectators in terms of pity, terror, and purification ('catharsis'). Roman tragedies, especially those of *Seneca, exerted a stronger influence upon the emergence of English tragic drama than did Greek practice or precept. A distinct contributory tradition was that of late medieval verse narratives recounting the fall of great men: after the example of *Boccaccio, *Chaucer's 'Monk's Tale' (*see* CANTERBURY TALES, 19), John *Lydgate's *Fall of Princes*, and eventually the collaborative **Mirror for Magistrates* exemplify this monitory genre. Following the precedent of Norton and Sackville's **Gorboduc* (1561), tragic stage plays flourished in the late Elizabethan and Jacobean periods (*c.*1590–1625), notably in the form of *revenge tragedy. The leading Elizabethan practitioners, Thomas *Kyd, Christopher *Marlowe, and *Shakespeare, developed new tragic conventions including the presentation of deaths onstage and an often rapid succession of scenes, in Kyd's *The *Spanish Tragedy*, Marlowe's **Tamburlaine the Great* and **Dr Faustus*, and Shakespeare's **Romeo and Juliet*, **Julius Caesar*, and **Hamlet*. The Jacobean period is even richer in English stage tragedies, including the mature work of Shakespeare in **Macbeth*, **King Lear*, **Othello*, and **Antony and Cleopatra*, along with Thomas Middleton and William Rowley's *The *Changeling* and John Webster's *The *Duchess of Malfi*. The rediscovery and codification of Aristotle's theory of tragedy in the rules of *neo-classicism gave rise to a purer form of tragic drama in France, of which *Racine's work is the great exemplar, but in England after the closure of the theatres in the mid-17th century the tragic tradition withered: some imitative neo-classical tragedies were attempted, notably John Dryden's **All for Love* (1678), while John *Milton's **Samson Agonistes* (1671) was a dramatic poem not intended for the stage (a *'closet drama', like some later tragic poems, e.g. Lord *Byron's **Manfred*). Serious English drama thereafter adopted various forms of *tragicomedy such as the 'heroic drama' of Dryden, or lapsed into *melodrama, although there were recurrent unsuccessful attempts at tragedy in the Shakespearian manner, notably P. B. *Shelley's *The *Cenci*. Novels aiming at traditional tragic effects appeared in the 19th century, notably Thomas *Hardy's *The *Mayor of Casterbridge*, but the dramatic tradition, although revived in modern conditions by Henrik *Ibsen, has survived only fitfully in English, most clearly in the plays of Arthur *Miller. In his book *The Death of Tragedy* (1961), George *Steiner attributed the decline of tragedy since the 17th century to the optimistic world-view of the *Enlightenment and its heirs. See Adrian Poole, *Tragedy* (2005).

tragicomedy A play that combines elements of *tragedy and *comedy in varying darker and lighter moods, or that cannot be placed clearly in either category. This mixed form was first practised and justified in the 16th century by the Italian dramatists *Cinzio and *Guarini, especially in *pastoral plays combining 'high' and 'low' styles and characters. English dramatists of the early 17th century, notably Francis *Beaumont and John *Fletcher in *Philaster* and other works, developed both this mixture and the associated plot structure of surprising reversals that pluck happy endings from seemingly tragic stories. *Shakespeare had independently exploited similar reversals in such 'dark' comedies as *The *Merchant of Venice* and **Measure for Measure* (*see* PROBLEM PLAY) and continued with the device in his late 'romance' plays, notably *The *Winter's Tale*. These developments all show the strict separation of comic from tragic modes breaking down in the late 16th century and early 17th, so that many kinds of drama thereafter may, unless they clearly adhere to classical principles, be regarded as tragicomedy: the sentimental comedy of the 18th century, the *melodrama of the 19th, and many plays by *Ibsen, *Chekhov, G. B. *Shaw, and *Brecht, for example, have been seen in this light. In particular, *Beckett's designation of his **Waiting for Godot* as a tragicomedy revived interest in the term in the 1950s and 1960s, in part as a clue to the enigmas of *Pinter's plays and of the Theatre of the *Absurd more generally. See D. L. Hirst, *Tragicomedy* (1984).

TRAHERNE, Thomas (1637–74) Poet and visionary, the son of a shoemaker in Hereford. He and his brother Philip were seemingly orphaned as infants, and brought up by a wealthy innkeeper, Philip Traherne, twice mayor of Hereford. Thomas went up to Brasenose College, Oxford, in March 1653 and took his BA in October 1656. In 1657 the Parliamentary commissioners appointed him rector of Credenhill, Herefordshire, but he seems not to have resided there until 1661. At Credenhill he may have joined a religious circle centring on the religious polemicist Susanna Hopton (1627–1709) at Kington, for whom he perhaps wrote the *Centuries*, a series of short meditations. During this period he evidently travelled to Oxford to work in the Bodleian Library on *Roman Forgeries* (published 1673), which exposes the falsifying of ecclesiastical documents by the Church of Rome. Probably in recognition of this work he gained his BD in 1669, and also his appointment the same year as chaplain to Sir Orlando Bridgeman, lord keeper of the great seal, which necessitated his moving to London. He was buried at Teddington. He led a 'single and devout life', according to Anthony *Wood, and he left five houses in Hereford in trust for the poor people of All Saints parish. He told John *Aubrey that he had visions, seeing, on one occasion, the phantom of an apprentice who was asleep in the same house, and on another a basket of fruit sailing in the air over his bed. Traherne's *Centuries* and many of his poems were discovered in a notebook (now in the Bodleian) which was picked up for a few pence on a London bookstall in the winter of 1896–7 by W. T. Brooke. The scholar Bertram Dobell (1842–1914) identified Traherne as the author, and edited the *Poetical Works* (1903) and the *Centuries of Med-*

itations (1908). More poems, prepared for publication by Traherne's brother Philip as 'Poems of Felicity', were discovered in a British Museum manuscript and published by H. I. Bell in 1910. A further manuscript of *Select Meditations* is in the collection of the late J. M. Osborn. His *Christian Ethics* (1675) was prepared for the press before he died. The *Thanksgivings*, written in exuberant, unconventional verse, and at times foreshadowing Walt *Whitman, appeared in 1699. His memories, in the *Centuries*, of his own early intuitions are the first convincing depiction of childhood experience in English literature. He is also among the first English writers to respond imaginatively to new ideas about infinite space, which he at times virtually equates with God, and he develops a theory, seemingly unique to him, that God needs man and can enjoy the universe only through man's enjoyment of it. The boundless potential of man's mind and spirit is his recurrent theme, as is the need for adult man to regain the wonder and simplicity of the child. In this he was influenced by *Neoplatonism, especially by the Hermetic books. See *Centuries, Poems and Thanksgivings*, ed. H. M. Margoliouth (2 vols, 1958); *Christian Ethicks*, ed. C. L. Marks and G. R. Guffey (1968); *Select Meditations*, ed. Julia Smith (1997); K. W. Salter, *Thomas Traherne, Mystic and Poet* (1964); L. S. Marcus, *Childhood and Cultural Despair* (1978). For accounts of recently discovered Traherne manuscripts in Lambeth and Washington see Julia Smith and Laetitia Yeandle, *TLS*, 7 Nov. 1997; Denise Inge and Cal Macfarlane, *TLS*, 2 June 2000.

Traitor, The A tragedy by James *Shirley, acted 1631, printed 1635. This play was highly successful both before and after the Civil War; Samuel *Pepys saw it several times and praised it highly. It is based on the assassination of the Florentine Duke Alessandro de' Medici by his kinsman Lorenzo. Unlike the hero of the best-known play on this subject, Alfred de *Musset's *Lorenzaccio*, Shirley's Lorenzo is a scheming villain who talks of republicanism and liberty only to gain the support of others. The plot combines a number of devices used by earlier dramatists. Lorenzo encourages the duke's lust for Amidea, sister of Sciarrha, while simultaneously urging Sciarrha to take revenge on the duke. The duke, unmoved by a moral masque presented him by Sciarrha, is nearly converted by Amidea's courageous virtue. Later, Lorenzo persuades him to blackmail her into yielding to save her brother's life. Sciarrha, to test Amidea's virtue, threatens to kill her unless she accepts this proposal; she, to save him from the guilt of murder, pretends to accept, whereupon he stabs her for dishonouring him. Her final act of virtue is to pretend that her death was suicide. The duke comes to her bed, finding only a corpse. Lorenzo kills him, and he and Sciarrha then kill each other.

Transcendental Club A group of American intellectuals who met informally for philosophical discussion at Ralph Waldo *Emerson's house and elsewhere. They represent a movement of thought, philosophical, religious, social, and economic, produced in New England between 1830 and 1850 by the spirit of revolutionary Europe, German philosophy, and William *Wordsworth, S. T. *Coleridge, and Thomas *Carlyle. The philosophical views of this Transcendentalism may be gathered from Emerson's short treatise *Nature* (1836). Its literary organ was *The *Dial*. Its utopian aspect was reflected in the Brook Farm community (1841–7) of George Ripley (1802–80), unflatteringly portrayed in Nathaniel *Hawthorne's *The *Blithedale Romance*.

transition: *an international quarterly for creative experiment* A periodical founded in 1927 in Paris by Eugène and Maria Jolas, and edited for some ten years by Eugène Jolas and Elliot Paul. Central to the experimental work it published, and exemplary of its 'revolution of the word', was James *Joyce's 'Work in Progress' (**Finnegans Wake*); other authors included Gertrude *Stein, Hart *Crane, Dylan *Thomas, and Samuel *Beckett; its distinguished art coverage included work by Max Ernst, Marcel Duchamp, Joan Miró, and Man Ray.

translation A vital dimension of English literary culture since the time of King *Alfred, who himself translated several works from the Latin. From *Ælfric in the 10th century until 1611 the most important translations into English were biblical (*see* BIBLE, THE ENGLISH). Otherwise medieval translation was dominated by devotional texts from Latin sources, interspersed by secular romances from the French, as with the **Romaunt of the Rose* attributed in part to *Chaucer. The most prolific translator of the 15th century was John *Lydgate in his lengthy *Troy Book* (from the Latin of *Guido delle Colonne) and *Fall of Princes* (from a French version of *Boccaccio), among other works. England's first printing press was devoted in part to the publication of William *Caxton's own translations of French works.

The great humanistic programme of rendering the classics of antiquity into the vernaculars arrived with Gawin *Douglas's Scots version of *Virgil's *Aeneid* (1553) and with *Surrey's version of the same poem's fourth book (1554). The wealth of classical translation in the later 16th and early 17th centuries includes Arthur *Golding's version of *Ovid's *Metamorphoses* (1565–7); George *Gascoigne's *Jocasta* (1575, from an Italian version of Euripides); the tragedies of *Seneca, Englished by Jasper Heywood and others from 1559; Sir Thomas *North's translation of Plutarch's *Lives* (1579, from a French version), drawn upon by *Shakespeare for his Roman plays; Christopher *Marlowe's translation of Ovid's *Amores* (*c.*1599); Philemon *Holland's versions of Livy (1600), Pliny (1601), and Suetonius (1606); and George *Chapman's *Works of Homer* (1616).

Meanwhile other works had come into English from Italian and French, notably in Thomas *Wyatt's versions of *Petrarch's lyrics, Geoffrey Fenton's tales from *Bandello (1567), Sir John *Harington's translation of *Ariosto (1591), Edward *Fairfax's rendering of *Tasso's *Gerusalemme liberata* (as *Godfrey of Bulloigne*, 1600), Florio's translation of *Montaigne's *Essays* (1603), and the unattributed English **Decameron* of 1620 (possibly also by John *Florio). Particularly fruitful was William Painter's **Palace of Pleasure* (1566–7), a two-volume anthology of tales translated from Boccaccio, Bandello,

*Cinzio, and others, later raided by Shakespeare and John *Webster for the plots of their plays.

In the later 17th and 18th centuries, the principal landmarks in prose are Sir Thomas *Urquhart's first two books of *Rabelais (1653), Peter *Motteux's *Don Quixote* (1700–03), and Tobias *Smollett's *Gil Blas* (1749, from the French of *Lesage), while the great verse translations are John *Dryden's of Virgil's works (1697) and Alexander *Pope's of Homer's **Iliad* (1715–20) and **Odyssey* (1725–6).

The early 19th century witnessed a significant discovery of modern German literature, in S. T. *Coleridge's translation of the last two parts of *Schiller's *Wallenstein* (1800), and in Thomas *Carlyle's version of *Goethe's novel *Wilhelm Meister's Apprenticeship* (1824, 1827). Henry *Cary's blank verse translation of Dante's **Divina commedia* (1805, 1814) meanwhile established itself as the standard for successive generations. The Victorian age is notable for disagreements over principles of translation from the ancient Greek, as in Matthew *Arnold's *On Translating Homer* (1861) and in Robert *Browning's defiantly literal **Agamemnon of Aeschylus* (1877). Victorian writers also achieved significant importations from remoter languages: Edward *FitzGerald's free interpretation of the Persian poet *The Rubáiyát of *Omar Khayyám* (1859) became widely popular. The theatre critic William *Archer introduced the major works of Henrik *Ibsen to English audiences, translating and producing *A Doll's House* (1889) and *Ghosts* (1891) among many others, thereby provoking a transformation of serious English drama. The modern Russian prose writers were brought into English almost single-handedly by the efforts of Constance *Garnett, who from 1894 until her death translated as many as 70 volumes of Turgenev, Tolstoy, Dostoevsky, Gogol, Chekhov, and others. Also significant in this period were Arthur *Waley's versions of Japanese and Chinese classics, in his *A Hundred and Seventy Chinese Poems* (1918), his *Tale of Genji* (1925–33), and his *Monkey* (1942). Ezra *Pound had already drawn upon the work of the American scholar Ernest Fenollosa to produce verse translations from the Chinese in his *Cathay* (1915).

Among the more notable 20th-century translations from modern European writers are the legendary translation of Marcel *Proust's *À la recherche du temps perdu* by C. K. Scott-Moncrieff (1889–1930) under the fanciful title *Remembrance of Things Past* (1922–30), Edwin and Willa *Muir's versions of Franz *Kafka's works (1930–49), and Stephen *Spender's translation with J. B. Leishman of Rainer Maria *Rilke's *Duino Elegies* (1939). In the realm of the classics, Louis *MacNeice's *Agamemnon* (1936) and Cecil *Day-Lewis's Virgil (*Georgics*, 1940; *Aeneid*, 1952) ushered in a period in which leading modern poets engaged regularly with the ancients, notably in Christopher *Logue's *War Music* (1981), Tony *Harrison's *Oresteia* (1981), Ted *Hughes's *Tales from Ovid* (1997), and Seamus *Heaney's *Beowulf* (1999).

translation for children Although translated books for children have been very influential historically, currently translations into English comprise less than 2 per cent of material published for the young. The earliest translated children's book is generally agreed to be John Amos *Comenius' (Czech) *Orbis Sensualiam Pictus* (1658; *A World of Things Obvious to the Senses*, 1659). In the 18th century, translations specifically for children tended to lag behind their adult counterparts. The **Arabian Nights Entertainments* were first translated in 1706–21, but not adapted for children until *c.*1791 (*The Oriental Moralist*, published by Elizabeth Newbery). Similarly, Madame d'Aulnoy's *Contes des fées* were first translated into English in 1699, but not for children until Frances Newbery's *Mother Bunch's Fairy Tales* in 1773. The translation of Charles *Perrault's *Histoires ou contes du temps passé* in 1729, however, suggests that the children's market was at least partially considered, while Edgar Taylor's 1823 translation of the *Grimm brothers' *Kinder- und Hausmärchen* (1812–14) as *German Popular Stories* 'had the amusement of some young friends principally in view'. The popularity of folk and fairy tales associated with other cultures in the 19th century is demonstrated by a group of retellings rather than translations, for example, Annie and Eliza Keary's *The Heroes of Asgard* (1857) and Charles *Kingsley's version of the Greek myths, *The Heroes* (1856), which has the curious distinction of having been translated *into* Greek. Equally influential was the work of Hans Christian *Andersen, translated in five different versions in 1846. The translation of folk-tale materials continued into the 20th century with Arthur *Ransome's *Old Peter's Russian Tales* (1916).

Outside the folk- and fairy-tale traditions, several 19th-century translated works have now been virtually naturalized into English culture, including *Der schweizerische Robinson* (1812–13), a version of which appeared in English in 1814 (*The Family Robinson Crusoe*, possibly translated by William *Godwin); Johanna Spyri's *Heidi's Lehr- und Wanderjahre* (1881) (*Heidi's Early Experiences* and *Heidi's Further Experiences*, 1884), Carlo Collodi's *Pinocchio* (1883), and Heinrich Hoffmann's satire on the moral tale that became a worldwide phenomenon, *Lustiges Geschichten und drollige Bilder* (1845; *The English Struwwelpeter*, 1848).

Perhaps the most influential 20th-century children's book in translation was Erich Kästner's *Emile und die Detektive* (1929; *Emile and the Detectives*, 1930), a precursor of child-detective *series such as Enid *Blyton's 'Famous Five'. Scandinavia has contributed three long-lasting series: Tove Jansson's eco-fable about the Moomins, beginning with *Kometjakten* (1946; *Comet in Moominland*, 1951), Astrid Lindgren's books about Pippi Longstocking (*Pippi Långstrump*, 1945; *Pippi Longstocking*, 1954), and Alf Proysen's *Kjerringa som ble så lita some ei teskje* (1957; *Little Old Mrs Pepperpot*, 1959). The French have contributed Babar the elephant by Jean de Brunhoff (1932–93) and the graphic/comic books of René Goscinny and Albert Uderzo ('Astérix'); Belgium has contributed the graphic/comic 'Tintin' series by Georges Remi (Hergé). In recent years, despite the efforts of publishers such as Klaus Flugge (Andersen Press) and Aidan *Chambers, and the establishment of the biennial Marsh Award for Children's Literature in Translation (1996), the traffic of translation has remained almost entirely one-way.

TRAPIDO, Barbara (1941–) South African-born novelist, resident in England since 1963. Her first novel *Brother of the More Famous Jack* (1982), the story of a timid student's involvement with a bohemian family, has been followed by five more, including *The Travelling Hornplayer* (1998) and *Frankie and Stankie* (2003).

TRAPNEL, Anna (*fl.* 1642–60) Prophetess, born in Poplar, Middlesex, the daughter of a shipwright. She joined the radical dissenting Fifth Monarchist movement in 1652, and was associated with the revolutionary church of John Simpson (1614/5–1662) at All Hallows the Great in London. Her spiritual and political extemporizations flowed forth in trances and were transcribed in shorthand. She achieved notoriety by a twelve-day ecstasy at Whitehall attacking Oliver *Cromwell's Protectorate, after which she travelled to Cornwall, was arrested on suspicion of sedition, and committed to Bridewell, a journey she vividly recorded in *Anna Trapnel's Report and Plea*. Other accounts of her activities appeared in *Strange and Wonderful News from Whitehall*, *The Cry of a Stone*, and *A Legacy for Saints*, all published in 1654. See E. Hobby, *Virtue of Necessity* (1989); S. H. Wright, *Women's Writings of the Early Modern Period* (2002); E. Longfellow, *Women and Religious Writing in Early Modern England* (2004).

Traveller, The, *or A Prospect of Society* A *topographical poem by Oliver *Goldsmith, published 1764. It is dedicated and addressed to Goldsmith's brother, a clergyman, whose stable country existence is presented as a contrast to the melancholy, wandering poet. From a vantage point in the Alps, the poet compares the national characteristics and social conditions of the surrounding countries, showing that the best aspects of each nation are balanced by some opposite demerit: even in Britain, the love of 'Liberty' leads to a loss of social interaction. Many of the landscapes (Italy, the Loire valley, the Netherlands) are vividly recalled from Goldsmith's own continental tour of 1755–6. Samuel *Johnson, who reviewed the poem warmly in the *Critical Review*, contributed at least nine lines to the conclusion (420, 429–34, and 437–8).

travel writing Many critics and practitioners have commented on the difficulty of defining travel writing, pointing to its employment of different literary forms, or its position between genres, and to its mixture of fact and fiction. A straightforward definition would identify travel texts as first-person accounts by authors who have experienced the events they describe. However, questions about the authenticity and truthfulness of many works that are broadly accepted as travel writing, including some of its foundational texts, such as the 14th-century travel book ascribed to Sir John *Mandeville, and the versions of Marco *Polo's journey to China, illustrate the difficulties involved. To add to the problem of authorial identity and veracity, travels may be related in letters, journals, diaries, memoir, essays, reportage, verse, or other literary forms, each of which has been utilized by travel writers, sometimes, as in W. H. *Auden and Louis *MacNeice's *Letters from Iceland* (1937), within a single volume. Furthermore, travel writing often draws on characteristics of the novel (e.g. plotting, characterization, the construction of a narrator); and certain types of novel, such as the *picaresque and the **Bildungsroman*, are structured around journey motifs. Celebrated novels such as Jonathan *Swift's **Gulliver's Travels* (1726) and Laurence *Sterne's *A *Sentimental Journey* (1768), were presented as travel writing. Others, including John *Bunyan's *The *Pilgrim's Progress* (1678) and Mark *Twain's *The Adventures of *Huckleberry Finn* (1884), depend upon journeys for their plot and themes. *Gothic novels turned to European travel accounts for their scene-setting. Poems of the *Romantic period, too, particularly those of S. T. *Coleridge and Lord *Byron, were informed, even inspired, by travel books, while the narratives of explorers James *Bruce and Mungo *Park exhibit qualities associated with *Romanticism, including in the character of their protagonists.

Since the last quarter of the 20th century, under the influence of Edward *Said's *Orientalism* (1978), travel writing has been examined for its associations with imperialism and colonialism. Certainly, the major periods of global British expansion produced some of the most notable narratives of travel and exploration. Richard *Hakluyt's monumental anthology *The Principall Navigations* (1589, 1598–1600) collected voyage and travel reports to promote *Protestantism and the English nation. Later, tourist accounts, especially those of the *Grand Tour and of the Middle East, recorded and contributed to the acquisition of knowledge that helped Britons exercise cultural and political authority. Not all travel writing has been concerned with outward movement: a long tradition of travel and social exploration within Britain takes in books by Samuel *Johnson, William *Cobbett, and George *Orwell, while post-Freudian travel writing, such as Graham *Greene's *Journey without Maps* (1936), has explicitly drawn parallels between physical and psychological journeys. The 1920s and 1930s were rich decades for the production of literary travels as modernist aesthetics combined with scrutiny of the politics of representation. E. E. *Cummings, D. H. *Lawrence, and Wyndham *Lewis are among those who wrote important travel books in these years. The 1970s saw the beginning of a resurgence in travel writing, to which Paul *Theroux, Bruce *Chatwin, Jonathan *Raban, and the best-selling Bill *Bryson prominently contributed, though Chatwin's and Raban's detestation of the term (for its insufficient recognition of imagination and inventiveness) is testament to the low esteem in which travel writing has been held. The work of women travellers, such as Mary *Kingsley, has enjoyed popular reprints and scholarly enquiry into its differences from that of men. In *Tracks* (1980), Australian Robyn *Davidson scorned the sexism and racism of her white compatriots, and reflected on her experience of being marketed as a woman celebrity. For all its conservatism, there has been much innovative and radical travel writing, including left-wing, *postmodern, *postcolonial, feminist, gay, and 'green' texts. Meanwhile, non-anglophone travel narratives from cultures outside Western Europe and the United States have attracted increased scholarly attention. Travel writing has proven to be one of the most adaptable and dynamic of literary forms.

TRAVERS, Ben *See* FARCE.

TRAVERS, P. L. (Pamela Lyndon) (1906–96) Novelist and journalist, born in Queensland, Australia; she came to

England in 1924. Her accounts of her life involved some myth-making: she was allegedly influenced by W. B. *Yeats and Æ (George *Russell), and later by the Russian mystic G. I. *Gurdijeff. She disapproved of the Disney version of her *Mary Poppins series. Her other notable works include a refugee story, *I Go by Sea, I Go by Land* (1941), *Friend Monkey* (1971), and an address to the Library of Congress, 'Only Connect' (1967). Ellen Dooling Draper and Jenny Koralek have edited a volume of essays on her work: *A Lively Oracle* (1999).

Travesties A comedy by Tom *Stoppard, performed 1974, published 1975. The play is largely set, with various time shifts, in Zurich during the First World War, where Lenin, James *Joyce, and the Romanian Dadaist poet Tristan Tzara (1896–1963) happened to be residing; they appear as characters, as does the marginally historical figure of Henry Carr (1894–1962), through whose memories much of the action is portrayed. Stoppard takes a minor incident from Richard *Ellmann's life of Joyce, describing a semi-amateur performance in Zurich in 1918 of *The *Importance of Being Earnest*, in which Joyce and Carr were involved, and builds from it an extravaganza which plays on Oscar *Wilde's original (in terms of stylistic parody and of the plot of assumed and mistaken identities) to produce a theatrical, informative, and witty commentary on the birth of Dada, the writing of **Ulysses*, and the genesis of the doctrine of *Socialist Realism, and the nature of the artist as revolutionary or conformist. Stoppard uses a dazzling range of literary and theatrical effects, from Wildean epigram to a scene written entirely in limericks, from a suggestion of striptease to a lecture on Marxist theory.

TREASE, Geoffrey (1909–98) Children's writer, born in Nottingham. He received a scholarship to the Queen's College, Oxford, but left after a year; the experience may have stimulated his political radicalism. He became a teacher and, inspired by a Soviet project to develop young readers, began to write children's fiction which challenged dated ideas about empire, class, and gender characteristic of writing for the young. *Bows against the Barons* (1934) features a Robin Hood who supports peasants against an oppressive ruling class, told without the mock-historical language then typical of historical fiction. *Cue for Treason* (1940) features a theatre troupe who work with *Shakespeare, and two children who foil a plot against *Elizabeth I. It is notable for including a bold and intelligent girl at the centre of the action. *Shadow under the Sea* (1990) takes place during the Gorbachev years. There is a three-part autobiography (1971, 1974, 1998).

Treasure Island A novel by Robert Louis *Stevenson, published 1883, having first appeared in *Young Folks*, July 1881–June 1882, under the title 'The Sea Cook, or Treasure Island'. The flamboyant anti-hero Long John Silver was suggested by Stevenson's friend W. E. *Henley. The book's impact on the popular image of pirates (one-legged rogues, with parrots on their shoulders, in search of buried treasure) has been huge.

The narrator is Jim Hawkins, whose mother keeps the Admiral Benbow inn on the west coast of England in the 18th century. An old seaman comes to stay, with a map marking the whereabouts of Captain Flint's treasure hidden in his chest. His former confederates, led by the sinister blind pirate Pew, descend on the inn in a bid to steal it. But Jim Hawkins secures the map, and gives it to Squire Trelawney. The squire and his friend Dr Livesey set off for Treasure Island in the schooner *Hispaniola* taking Jim with them. Some of the crew are the squire's faithful dependants, but most are old buccaneers recruited by Long John Silver. Their design to seize the ship and kill the squire's party is discovered by Jim, and after a series of thrilling fights and adventures is defeated. The squire, with the help of the marooned pirate Ben Gunn, secures the treasure.

Treatise of Human Nature, A A philosophical work by David *Hume, written in France 1734–7, published in three volumes in London 1739–40. After being largely ignored, the work was rewritten as three separate works published between 1748 and 1757: *An Enquiry* (originally *Philosophical Essays*) *Concerning Human Understanding*, *An Enquiry Concerning the Principles of Morals*, and *A Dissertation on the Passions*. Hume's work is sometimes treated as the culmination of the empiricist understanding of mind attributed to John *Locke; equally influential is the view that Hume sought to extend and redirect the philosophy of Francis *Hutcheson. Other influences include Bernard *Mandeville, *Cicero, *Descartes, and *Bayle.

In the first part, 'Of the Understanding', Hume agreed with Locke that there are no innate ideas, and that all the data of reason stem from experience. But he argued that reason has insufficient data in experience to form adequate ideas of the external world, bodily identity, causality, the self, and other minds, and that any beliefs we form about these must fall short of the full rational knowledge represented by abstract mathematics. We use the experience of acquired associations to identify causes and effects, past events and future contingencies; but this process cannot be independently justified. It ceases to be rational altogether when it involves inferences beyond the bounds of familiar experience (as with religion). Compensating for such inadequacies are certain 'natural instincts' by which the imagination forges its own links between distinct ideas according to principles of association and habituation. Through these associations, which Hume called 'fictions' (that is, they are not given directly by experience), and which he assumed were explicable in terms of the brain science of the day, we project onto the world a sense of the continuity of bodies, and the predictable sequencing of cause and effect. Hume's account of the self as a somewhat confused 'bundle or collection of different perceptions', a striking departure from Locke, was not altogether satisfactory to Hume himself, though it was influential in other spheres. Hume characterized his general standpoint as 'mitigated scepticism', arguing that 'philosophical decisions are nothing but the reflections of common life, methodized and corrected' by the balanced interplay of reason, sense, and natural instinct. The second part of the *Treatise* dealt with 'passions' (emotions), and Part III with morals. Hume accepted Hutcheson's belief in a moral sense, but not his theological framework or psychological model. Insofar as there is a common structure of human nature, which approves whatever gives happiness to the parties affected without giving unhappiness to others, and enables us by the mechanisms of association to share the sentiments of others, there can be general consensus as to the motives and acts that are judged virtuous or vicious. Hume's distinction between natural virtues (such as benevolence) and artificial virtues (such as justice, which involves the application of appropriate conventions in circumstances of need) was widely misconstrued in his lifetime; the book was attacked by James *Beattie and Thomas Reid (1710–96), but was acknowledged as a prime stimulus by philosophers as various as Immanuel *Kant and Jeremy *Bentham.

TREECE, Henry (1911–66) Writer and teacher, born in Wednesbury, Staffordshire, educated at Birmingham University. He began his writing career as a poet, producing seven volumes of verse. He was associated with the *New Apocalypse movement, and co-edited, with James Findlay Henry (1912–86), *The White Horseman: Prose and Verse of the New Apocalypse* (1941). He is best known for his *historical novels for young people, such as *Viking's Dawn* (1955), the first in a trilogy about Harald Sigurdson, who grows from youth to manhood, moving from oarsman to leader and undertaking lengthy voyages including to North America. *The Horned Helmet* (1963), one of his best-known books, begins a trilogy for younger readers tracing the development of Beorn, an Icelandic boy who is adopted by a Viking warrior and participates in raids on the Scottish coast. His last book, *The Dreamtime* (1967), about a Stone Age boy's desire not to become a warrior, was published posthumously. Treece is recognized as one of the 20th century's leading writers of historical fiction for the young.

TRELAWNY, Edward John (1792–1881) Novelist and memoirist. Of Cornish descent, though born in London, he is remembered principally for his connection with and records of P. B. *Shelley and Lord *Byron. When he met Shelley in Pisa in January 1822 Trelawny had survived unhappy years as a midshipman in the navy, followed by marriage and divorce: from this time he attached himself first to Shelley (he was present at Livorno when Shelley was drowned) and later to Byron, whom he accompanied to Greece in July 1823. Byron had remarked on first meeting that Trelawny was 'the personification of my Corsair', and he did his best to live up to that image. He was the author of the notable *Adventures of a Younger Son* (1831), an autobiographical novel published with the encouragement of Mary *Shelley (who provided its title); it tells the story of a handsome, romantic, buccaneering youth, a lawless daredevil, warped in youth by the harshness of his father, who deserts from the navy and takes to a life of wandering during which he becomes involved in many wild escapades and desperate ventures. It is highly unreliable as autobiography, but written with much verve. His other publication was *Recollections of the Last Days of Shelley and Byron* (1858), again unreliable, but again written with great poetry and panache; it was later expanded to *Records of Shelley, Byron, and the Author* (1878). See William St Clair, *Trelawny: The Incurable Romancer* (1977) David Crane, *Lord Byron's Jackal* (1998).

TREMAIN, Rose (1943–) Novelist, short story writer, and playwright, born in London, educated at the Sorbonne and at the University of East Anglia. Her first novel, *Sadler's Birthday* (1976), was followed by *Letter to Sister Benedicta* (1978), *The Cupboard* (1981), and *The Swimming Pool Season* (1985). Her best-known work of fiction, *Restoration* (1989), is a first-person historical novel in which the central character is taken up by Charles II but suffers the king's disfavour after he marries Charles's former mistress. *Sacred Country* (1992) moves from Suffolk to Tennessee in its exploration of gender and identity. *The Way I Found Her* (1997) describes a summer in Paris, seen through the eyes of a 13-year-old boy. *Music & Silence* (1999) returns to the 17th century and tells the story of a lutenist at the court of the melancholy Christian IV of Denmark. *The Colour* (2003) takes place in New Zealand in the mid-19th century; *The Road Home* (2007) examines Britain from the perspective of an economic migrant from Eastern Europe. *The Colonel's Daughter* (1984), *The Garden of the Villa Mollini* (1987), *Evangelista's Fan* (1994), and *The Darkness of Wallis Simpson* (2005) are collections of Tremain's short stories. She has also written plays for radio and TV.

TRENCH, Richard Chenevix (1807–86) Philologist and poet, educated at Trinity College, Cambridge, and afterwards dean of Westminster and archbishop of Dublin. He was the author of works dealing with history and literature, poetry, divinity, and philology. As a philologist, and notably by his *On the Study of Words* (1851) and *English Past and Present* (1855), he popularized the scientific study of language. The scheme of what became the **Oxford English Dictionary* originated partly in a resolution passed at his suggestion in 1858 by the Philological Society. He also published several volumes of poetry, and his anthology *Sacred Latin Poetry, Chiefly Lyrical* (1849) drew attention to the masterpieces of Latin hymnody.

TRESSELL, Robert (1870–1911) The pen-name of Robert Noonan, born in Dublin; he earned his living as a sign-writer and house painter. He is remembered for his posthumously published novel *The Ragged Trousered Philanthropists* (1914), edited from a manuscript left in the care of his daughter. It draws on his experiences while working for a builder in Hastings, where he settled in 1901 after various wanderings. He died of tuberculosis in Liverpool en route to Canada, where he intended to make a new life. An abridged edition of his novel appeared in 1918, but on the discovery of the original handwritten manuscript in 1946 it became clear that the author's intentions had been widely altered, and it reappeared, edited by F. C. Ball, in 1955.

The action centres on the lives of a group of working men in the town of Mugsborough, and the novel is a bitter exposure of the greed, dishonesty, and gullibility of employers and workers alike. Debates on socialism, competition, employment, and capitalism are skilfully interwoven with a realistic and knowledgeable portrayal of the decorating and undertaking business, and with the human stories of the families of the workers. Principal characters include Frank Owen, socialist craftsman and atheist; Barrington, socialist son of a wealthy father, who wants first-hand experience of labour; the inadequate but well-intentioned Eastons with their unfortunate baby whom they feed on fried bacon; and Slyme, a canting and unprincipled teetotaller. Noonan's coining of names for local worthies—Sweater, Didlum, Grinder, Botchit, etc.—indicates his attitude towards the widespread corruption and hypocrisy, and the book has become a classic text of the Labour movement. The ironically named 'philanthropists' of the title are the workers who for pitiful wages 'toil and sweat at their noble and unselfish task of making money' for their employers, while doing nothing to improve their lot. See F. C. Ball's account of Tressell's life and times (1973).

TREVELYAN, Sir George Otto (1838–1928) Statesman and author, nephew of T. B. *Macaulay. He was educated at Harrow School and Trinity College, Cambridge. He entered Parliament as a Liberal in 1865 and held several important offices. Some of his early humorous writings were collected in *The Ladies in Parliament* (1869), others mainly about India included *The Dawk Bungalow* (1863, a comedy), *The Competition Wallah* (1864), and *Cawnpore* (1865). The first of his great works, *The Life and Letters of Lord Macaulay*, appeared in 1876, and was followed by a *History of the American Revolution*, 6 vols (1899–1914) and *The Early History of George the Third and Charles Fox* (1912–14). His son, the historian G. M. *Trevelyan, published a memoir of him (1932).

TREVELYAN, G. M. (George Macaulay) (1876–1962) Historian, son of Sir George Otto *Trevelyan, educated at Harrow School and Trinity College, Cambridge, where he became a member of the *Apostles. He was appointed Regius professor of modern history at Cambridge in 1927, and master of Trinity in 1940. He was author of three remarkable works on the Italian leader Giuseppe Garibaldi (1807–82), *Garibaldi's Defence of the Roman Republic* (1907), *Garibaldi and the Thousand* (1909), and *Garibaldi and the Making of Italy* (1911), which owe some of their vividness of narrative and description to the fact that Trevelyan himself, a tireless walker, retraced on foot every mile of the scenes of campaign. His many other works include lives of John Bright (1913), Lord Grey (1920), and Grey of Falloden (1937); a three-volume work on *England under Queen Anne* (1930–4); and his popular and nostalgic *English Social History* (1944). In *Layman's Love of Letters* (1954), delivered in 1953 as the Clark Lectures, he speaks warmly of Robert *Browning, Walter *Scott, George *Meredith, A. E. *Housman, the poetry of mountaineering, etc., and mildly deplores the professional view of literature as 'a set of intellectual conundrums, to be solved by certain rules. It is joy, joy in our inmost heart.' He published *An Autobiography and Other Essays* in 1949. See David Cannadine, *G. M. Trevelyan: A Life in History* (1992).

TREVISA, John of (*c.*1342–*c.*1402) Born in Cornwall, a fellow of Exeter (1362–9) and the Queen's (1369–79) colleges, Oxford. He was expelled from Oxford and, having become vicar of Berkeley (1374), he subsequently became chaplain to the Berkeley family (1379). He translated the *Polychronicon* of Ranulf *Higden (1397), one of his most famous additions to which is the prefatory *Dialogue between a Lord and a Clerk* which contains important reflections on the cultural politics of translation into the vernacular at this time. The *Polychronicon* translation is written in a vigorous and colloquial style, though he also has claims to a more elaborate manner. A translation of Giles of Rome's *De Regimine Principum* is attributed to him and by 1399 he had translated the *De Proprietatibus Rerum* of *Bartholomaeus Anglicus. He also translated Richard Fitzralph's *Defensio Curatorum* and William of *Ockham's *Dialogus Inter Militem et Clericum*. See D. C. Fowler, *John Trevisa* (1993).

TREVOR, William (1928–) Novelist, short story writer, and sculptor, born in Mitchelstown, Co. Cork, and educated at Trinity College, Dublin; he has divided his life between Ireland and England, both countries providing the settings for his works. His novels include *The Old Boys* (1964), *Mrs Eckdorf in O'Neill's Hotel* (1969), *Elizabeth Alone* (1973), *The Children of Dynmouth* (1976), *Fools of Fortune* (1983), *Felicia's Journey* (1994), and *The Story of Lucy Gault* (2002); collections of short stories include *The Day We Got Drunk on Cake* (1969), *The Ballroom of Romance* (1972), *Beyond the Pale* (1981), *Family Sins* (1989), *The Hill Bachelors* (2000), and *Cheating at Canasta* (2007). *Two Lives*, made up of the novellas 'Reading Turgenev' and 'My House in Umbria', appeared in 1991. Trevor's low-key, evocative prose covers a remarkably wide social range, from Catholic Irish small farmers to representatives of the declining Anglo-Irish ascendancy, from Dublin and London professionals to lower-middle-class characters in the Irish provinces and English Midlands. A long-standing concern with the elderly, the lonely, and the unsuccessful has been complemented from the 1980s by an increasing preoccupation with history and politics and with the complexities of communication across the Catholic–Protestant divide in Ireland and between Irish and English perspectives. Collected editions of Trevor's short stories were published in 1983, 1992, and 2003. *Excursions in the Real World* (1994) gathers personal essays on childhood, people, and places.

Trilby A novel written and illustrated by George *du Maurier, published 1894. The story's setting reflects the writer's years studying art in Paris, and the student friends of Trilby O'Ferrall (the Laird, *Little Billee, and Taffy) are portraits of friends. Trilby, an artist's model, slowly falls under the mesmeric spell of Svengali, a German-Polish musician, who trains her voice and establishes her fame as a singer. His power over her is so complete that when he dies her voice collapses, and she languishes and dies herself. The novel was immensely popular for many years, and in 1895 was dramatized with Herbert Beerbohm Tree (1853–1917) as Svengali. Trilby's hat, a soft felt with an indented crown, is the origin of the 'trilby'.

TRILLING, Lionel (1905–75) American critic who taught at Columbia University (1932–75), and whose many works include *Matthew Arnold* (1939), *The Opposing Self* (1955), *Beyond Culture* (1965), *Sincerity and Authenticity* (1972), and his most widely admired book of essays, *The Liberal Imagination* (1950). He was a leading figure in the predominantly left-wing Jewish circle around **Partisan Review*, sometimes called the New York Intellectuals; this included his wife Diana Trilling (1905–96), a noted essayist. His varied essays, written from the standpoint of liberal humanism and under the influence of Edmund *Wilson, show admiration for a wide range of writers from Jane *Austen and Henry *James to Sigmund *Freud, and a recurrent preoccupation with the conjunctions of literature, politics, and psychology. His works appeared in a twelve-volume edition, 1978–80. He also wrote one novel, *The Middle of the Journey* (1947).

trilogy In Greek antiquity, a series of three tragedies (originally connected in subject) performed at Athens at the festival of Dionysus. Hence any series of three related dramatic or other literary works.

trimeter A verse line of three stresses.
See METRE.

TRIMMER, Sarah (1741–1810) Née Kirby, born in Ipswich. One of the foremost educationalists of the late 18th century, she ran her own Sunday Schools from 1772. Trimmer wrote educational texts for charity schools and edited *The Family Magazine* (1778–89) 'to counteract the pernicious tendency of immoral books', and *The Guardian of Education* (1802–6). Her first book was *Easy Introduction to the Knowledge of Nature* (1780); her most famous book, *Fabulous Histories* (1786; known from *c.*1820 as *The History of the Robins*), was an antidote to fairy stories.

Trimmer, Character of a *See* HALIFAX, GEORGE.

triolet A poem of eight lines, with two rhymes, in which the first line is repeated as the fourth and seventh, and the second as the eighth.

triplet A set of three successive verse lines rhyming together, occasionally introduced among *heroic couplets, e.g. by John *Dryden. The term is sometimes applied to a three-line stanza, more commonly called a tercet.

'Tristram and Iseult' A poem in three parts by Matthew *Arnold, published 1852. This is the first modern version of the story that was made familiar by Richard *Wagner, Alfred *Tennyson, and A. C. *Swinburne. It deals with the death of Tristram (Tristan, in earlier editions of the same work), who lies dying, watched over by Iseult of Brittany, and dreaming in his fever of his love for Iseult of Ireland, the wife of Marc. She arrives, and after a brief passionate dialogue he dies. In Part III Iseult of Brittany tells her children the story of *Merlin, entranced by Vivian.

Tristram and Isoud (*Tristan and Isolde*) The story of Tristram de Lyones is the fifth of Vinaver's eight *Works* of Sir Thomas *Malory. The love of Tristram and Isoud is much older than the corresponding Arthurian story of Launcelot and Guinevere, and it was incorporated into the Arthurian legends only at a late stage. There are three versions of Tristram romances surviving from the 12th century: Béroul's fragment of 4,485 lines in the Norman dialect; Thomas of Britain's French fragment; and the version in literary Rhenish German by Eilhart von Oberge. Gottfried von Strassburg's German version is based to some extent on Thomas. The first English version is *Sir Tristrem*, a northern 3,344-line romance in eleven-line stanzas, dating from *c.*1300. In Malory's version, which draws on the 13th-century French prose *Tristan*, Tristram is the child of Meliodas, king of Lyonesse, and Elizabeth, the sister of King Mark of Cornwall, whose attitude to him varies in different versions from great affection to jealousy. Tristram defeats and kills Sir Marhalt, the brother of the queen of Ireland. Sent to Ireland to be cured of his wounds, Tristram falls in love with the queen's daughter, Isoud; when the queen discovers that he killed her brother, Tristram returns to Cornwall. King Mark sends Tristram to seek for him the hand of Isoud. The princess and her maid Brangwayn travel by ship to Cornwall; Brangwayn has been given a love potion to be given on their wedding night to Isoud and King Mark, which will bind them in unending love. By mistake Tristram and Isoud drink the potion and are bound in endless passion, although Isoud has to marry Mark. The rest of the story concerns the fated love of Tristram and Isoud and their subterfuges: as in the Lancelot romances, love is represented as a value that transcends morality. While fighting for Howell of Brittany, Tristram agrees to marry his daughter, Isoud of the White Hands, although the marriage is unconsummated. On the invitation of Isoud of Ireland, he returns to Cornwall, where he is killed by Mark while playing his harp before Isoud. In some versions his death is not mentioned at all; in the most celebrated (adopted by Richard *Wagner) Tristram sends for Isoud while he lies dying in Brittany. If she is on the ship when it returns, a white flag is to be flown; if not, a black one. The flag is white, but Isoud of the White Hands tells Tristram it is black, whereupon he dies. When Isoud comes to his bedside, she dies too. The story is celebrated for its strong mythical overtones and elements such as Tristram's temporary madness, his harping, and his importance as an exponent of chivalric values.

Tristram of Lyonesse A poem in heroic couplets by A. C. *Swinburne, published 1882, which tells the story of Tristram's love for Queen Iseult, his marriage to Iseult of Brittany, and his death. The poem challenged Alfred *Tennyson's handling of the same story in *Idylls of the King*.

Tristram Shandy, Gentleman, The Life and Opinions of A novel by Laurence *Sterne, published 1759–67. 'Shandy', a Yorkshire dialect word, means 'crack-brained, half-crazy'; Tristram declares his story a 'civil, nonsensical, good humoured *Shandean* book'. The slim story is constantly interrupted by digressions on a huge variety of scientific and philosophical matters, deliberately disordering the sequence of events; Tristram mocks the conventional linear development of narrative, highlighting the disparity between the comically unpredictable processes of mental life and the novelistic attempt to order experience rationally. He can never write fast enough to catch up with the life that he is living. The normal illusions of novelistic prose are further disrupted by wayward typography, including asterisks, dashes, diagrams, blank pages, multiple typefaces, and other devices. Volume i opens with Tristram's risibly inefficient conception, after which the other main characters, all comically idiosyncratic and burdened with variously obsessional 'hobby-horses', are introduced: Tristram's excitable father Walter, a sort of benign *Scriblerus, whose reading comprehends all arts and sciences without practical result; the bewildered Mrs Shandy; Uncle Toby, Walter's innocent soldier brother, interested only in the problems of military fortifications; Corporal Trim, Toby's devoted, talkative servant; and the impulsive parson Yorick. Volume ii concentrates on the past military experiences of Toby and Corporal Trim and introduces the irrepressible servant Obadiah. Tristram's birth is described in volume iii, after many diversions, including the comically overdue Preface. Volume iv contains Walter's exposition to his bemused brother Toby of Slawkenbergius' Latin treatise on noses, and an account of the misnaming of the infant 'Tristram' instead of 'Trismegistus'. Volume v covers the death of Tristram's brother Bobby, and the devising of the ill-fated *Tristapaedia* for Tristram's education. Volume vi includes the *sentimental tale of Lieutenant Le Fever and his son, a ludicrous discussion on the putting of Tristram into breeches, a description of the tremendous model of military earthworks constructed by Toby and Trim in the garden, and Toby's tentative courtship of the amorous widow Wadman. In volume vii the family narrative is broken by a description of Tristram's travels in France, with Death in pursuit. Volume viii follows Toby's amour and Trim's attempt to tell his story of the king of Bohemia. Volume ix includes the pathetic tale of mad Maria (who reappears in *A *Sentimental Journey*). At the end, a conversation about Walter's bull gives rise to the famous inconclusive conclusion: 'L—d! said my mother, what is all this story about?—A COCK and a BULL, said Yorick—And one of the best of its kind, I ever heard.' The work made Sterne famous, although Samuel *Richardson, Oliver *Goldsmith, and others disliked its literary manner ('Nothing odd will do long', declared Samuel *Johnson; '*Tristram Shandy* did not last'), and its insistent innuendo and tolerant bawdiness. In the 20th century the novel was celebrated as a humane comedy in the tradition of *Rabelais, *Cervantes, and Richard *Burton, and as a brilliantly ironic meditation on the new science of psychology, as found in John *Locke's **Essay Concerning Human Understanding*. Its radical, experimental narrative mode has also endeared it to literary theorists. See the edition by Melvin New (3 vols, 1978–84).

Triumph of Life, The An unfinished visionary poem by P. B. *Shelley, written in the bay of Lerici in summer 1822, published from rough drafts 1824. Composed in **terza rima*, the poem is strongly influenced by *Dante's *Inferno*, *Petrarch's *Trionfi*, and the carvings of Roman triumphal processions Shelley had seen in the Forum. The 'triumph' or masquerade (as in *The *Mask of Anarchy*) belongs to the cruel Chariot of Life, here shown as one of Shelley's tyrant figures. Life appears to vanquish all hope, dragging in its train even the greatest, like *Plato, *Alexander, or Napoleon. Only the 'sacred few', like Jesus and *Socrates, who early 'Fled back like eagles to their native noon', escape compromise and captivity. The poetry has a bitter, lucid directness that is new to Shelley, with a grim passage about growing old and sexually disillusioned (ll. 137–69).

Triumph of Peace, The A *masque by John *Shirley, acted and printed 1634. This was the best known of all 17th-century masques, mainly because of the spectacular torchlight procession (or 'triumph') of the masquers, from Holborn to Whitehall, which preceded the masque proper. It was an expression of loyalty to the Crown on the part of the four Inns of Court, after William *Prynne—a member of Lincoln's Inn—had published his *Histriomastix* (1633) with a dedication to his fellow benchers at the Inn. Shirley's plot is simple: the chief anti-masquer, Fancy, presents a series of interludes showing the benefit and abuses of Peace; these are finally driven away by the entry of Peace, Law, and Justice—qualities which, the lawyers were eager to point out, cannot flourish separately. The masque was designed by Inigo *Jones, and its score (by William *Lawes and Simon Ives (bap. 1600, d. 1662) is among the few examples of masque music to have survived. There is an edition in *A Book of Masques* (1967).

TRIVET, Nicholas (1257/65–?1334) Of a family with connections in Norfolk and Somerset, a Dominican who studied at Oxford and Paris. He made early commentaries on classical texts, including *Boethius, but is most celebrated as the writer of three histories in the 1320s: his Anglo-Norman Chronicle, extending from the Creation to 1285, surviving in eight manuscripts and containing the tale of Constance, told by John *Gower in *Confessio Amantis* and by *Chaucer's Man of Law (*see* CANTERBURY TALES, 5); secondly, *Annals of Six Kings of England 1136–1307*, pro-Angevin and particularly useful for the reign of Edward I; and the *Historia ab Orbe Condito* (1327–9), an encyclopedic history influenced by *Vincent of Beauvais.

Trivia, *or The Art of Walking the Streets of London* A poem in three books by John *Gay, published 1716. Drawing on the 'town eclogue' as exemplified by Jonathan *Swift's 'Description of a City Shower' (1710), Gay adds mock-didactic elements akin to the *Georgics* of *Virgil. The poem is an imaginary perambulation of the streets of London, by day and by night, with much jovially satirical comment on the hazards of pavements, gutters, and rubbish, and on the characters of the streets: boot-boys, ballad-singers, footmen, thieves, bullies, fishwives. 'Trivia' is one of the titles of Hecate as goddess of the crossroads, and the humour is often dark: Gay refers to the murder of Laius by Oedipus at the crossroads (III. 217). In its mock-heroic coupling of ancient myth with insalubrious modern reality (as in the comic passage on Cloacina, goddess of the sewers) the poem is an important source for Alexander Pope's *The *Dunciad*.

trochee, trochaic *See* METRE.

Troilus and Cressida A drama by *Shakespeare probably written 1602, conjecturally with a performance at one of the Inns of Court in mind. It was first printed in 1609, in a quarto of which there are two issues, with different title pages, one of which has a prefatory epistle, 'A never writer, to an ever reader. News.' This was not included in the first *folio, where a variant text is the first play in the section of tragedies. As well as *Homer's and *Chaucer's handling of material concerning the lovers and the siege of Troy, Shakespeare knew of Robert Henryson's **Testament of Cresseid*, William *Caxton's *Recuyell of the Historyes of Troye*, and John *Lydgate's *Troy Book*, and drew on *Ovid's *Metamorphoses* Books 11 and 12, Robert *Greene's *Euphues his Censure to Philautus* (1587), and George *Chapman's *Seven Books of the Iliads* (1598).

Shakespeare's treatment of the love of Troilus and Cressida and its betrayal, against the setting of the siege of Troy by the Greeks, is conventional. The play contains much formal debate, and takes the story up to the death of Hector at the hands of Achilles: Troilus fails to kill his rival Diomedes, and the cynically railing Thersites escapes death. Modern critics have tended to agree with S. T. *Coleridge's view that 'there is none of Shakespeare's plays harder to characterize'. It was performed only in adaptation until the 20th century, but its concern with love, sex, and war have increased its appeal since the 1950s.

Troilus and Criseyde Geoffrey *Chaucer's longest complete poem, in 8,239 lines of *rhyme royal, probably written during the first half of the 1380s. Chaucer takes the narrative from *Boccaccio's *Il filostrato*, adapting its eight books to five and changing the characters of Criseyde and *Pandarus. In Boccaccio Troilo falls in love with Criseida whose cousin, Troilo's friend Pandaro, persuades her, not unwillingly, to become Troilo's lover. In the end Criseida has to leave the Trojan camp to join her father who had defected to the Greeks; in the Greek camp she betrays Troilo by falling in love with Diomede. While following the same story in outline, Chaucer layers the narrative in several ways: by making Pandaro Criseida's voyeuristic uncle; by showing her deliberating at more length, and by having his narrator explicitly call into question the conventionally harsh judgement passed on her throughout the course of literary history; by introducing philosophical material, principally from *Boethius, calling into question the lovers' freedom of action and foregrounding their respective insights into their situation; and by complicating the texture of the narrative through the interpolation of *Ovidian and other classical references. The poem ends with an exhortation to the young to turn away from worldly vanity and to place their trust, not in unstable fortune as Troilus did, but in God. Discussion of the poem has centred largely on the appropriateness of the epilogue to the preceding action, on the attitudes to love (*courtly love in particular) in the poem, and on the voice of the narrator and his effect on the narrative. The love story has no basis in classical antiquity but is the invention of *Benoît de Sainte-Maure in his *Roman de Troie*, which was based on the pretended histories of Troy by *Dares Phrygius and *Dictys Cretensis. Boccaccio's intermediate source was *Guido delle Colonne. After Chaucer, the story was treated by Robert *Henryson in *The *Testament of Cresseid* and by William *Shakespeare in **Troilus and Cressida*. Ed. B. A. Windeatt (1984). N. R. Havely, *Chaucer's Boccaccio* (1980); B. A. Windeatt, *Troilus and Criseyde* (1992); S. A. Barney (ed.), *Chaucer's Troilus: Essays in Criticism* (1980).

Trojan War *See* AENEID; ILIAD.

TROLLOPE, Anthony (1815–82) Novelist, born in London. His father, a fellow of New College, Oxford, before his marriage, failed both as a lawyer and as a farmer. The family's poverty made Trollope miserable at school (he went to both Harrow School and Winchester College), and when financial difficulties became acute, the family moved to Belgium, where Trollope's father died. Frances *Trollope, Trollope's mother, had already begun to support the family with her pen; she was in her fifties when her successful *Domestic Manners of the Americans* was published in 1832. Trollope became a junior clerk in the General Post Office in London in 1834, but only began to succeed when transferred to Ireland in 1841. He married Rose Heseltine of Rotherham in 1844. They had two sons, the younger of whom was to settle in Australia. Trollope did not return permanently to England until 1859, although he travelled extensively on Post Office business, and became an important if also highly individual civil servant (he introduced the pillar-box for letters to Great Britain). He resigned from the Post Office in 1867, and stood unsuccessfully for Parliament as a Liberal in 1868, a painful experience often recalled in his fiction. He edited the *St Paul's Magazine*, 1867–70.

His literary career began with the appearance of *The Macdermots of Ballycloran* in 1847, but not until his fourth novel, *The *Warden* (1855), did he establish the manner and material by which he is best known. This, the first of the 'Barsetshire' series, was followed by **Barchester Towers* (1857), **Doctor Thorne* (1858), **Framley Parsonage* (1861), *The *Small House at*

Allington (1864), and *The *Last Chronicle of Barset* (1867). The action of these novels is for the most part set in the imaginary West Country county of Barset and its chief town, Barchester, of which Trollope says in the *Autobiography*, 'I had it all in my mind—its roads and railroads, its towns and parishes, its members of Parliament, and the different hunts which rode over it. I knew all the great lords and their castles, the squires and their parks, the rectors and their churches...' The Barset novels are connected by characters who appear repeatedly, and Trollope developed this technique in his second series, known as the 'political', 'parliamentary', or 'Palliser' novels. This series began with **Can You Forgive Her?* (1864) and continued with **Phineas Finn* (1869), *The *Eustace Diamonds* (1873), **Phineas Redux* (1876), *The *Prime Minister* (1876), and *The *Duke's Children* (1880). The two series taken together thus span over twenty years of Trollope's writing life. Trollope established the novel sequence in English fiction. His use of reappearing characters had been anticipated by *Balzac, though there is no evidence that Trollope was in any way indebted to him.

Modest in claiming literary excellence, Trollope prided himself on his workmanlike attitude towards his art. He attributed his remarkable output, which included 47 novels, several travel books, biographies, as well as collections of short stories and sketches, to a disciplined regularity of composition. He produced a given number of words in the early morning before leaving for his post office duties (which he combined with an almost fanatical devotion to hunting). More concerned with character than with plot, he made the degree to which an author really knows his characters a fundamental test of his or her merit. In the *Autobiography* Trollope writes of the novelist's need to live with his creatures 'in the full reality of established intimacy. They must be with him as he lies down to sleep, and as he wakes from dreams.' He also stresses the importance of recording the effects of time: 'On the last day of each month recorded, every person in his novel should be a month older than on the first.' His popularity, which has proved enduring, was at its peak during the 1860s; readers admired his treatment of family and professional life, the variety and delicacy of his heroines, and the photographic accuracy of his pictures of social life.

Trollope's other principal novels include: *The *Three Clerks* (1857), *The Bertrams* (1859), **Orley Farm* (1862), *The *Belton Estate* (1866), *The *Claverings* (1867), **He Knew He Was Right* (1869), *The *Vicar of Bullhampton* (1870), *The *Way We Live Now* (1875), *The *American Senator* (1877), *Doctor Wortle's School* (1881), **Ayala's Angel* (1881), **Mr Scarborough's Family* (1883). The *Autobiography* records that, down to 1879, his publications had brought him some £70,000, which he thought 'comfortable, but not splendid'. He was a popular figure in London and literary society in his later years. He greatly admired W. M. *Thackeray, of whom he wrote a clear-sighted study (1879), and was a friend of George *Eliot and G. H. *Lewes. Writing in 1883, Henry *James summed up his achievement by saying that 'His great, his inestimable merit was a complete appreciation of the usual...Trollope's great apprehension of the real, which was what made him so interesting, came to him through his desire to satisfy us on this point—to tell us what certain people were and what they did in consequence of being so.' His *Autobiography*, written 1875–6, published posthumously 1883, describes his life with a characteristic blend of candour and reticence; see also V. Glendinning, *Trollope* (1992); *Letters*, ed. N. John Hall (2 vols, 1983).

TROLLOPE, Frances (1780–1863) Travel writer and novelist, born in Bristol. A woman of tireless energy, who made an unfortunate marriage, conducted several ventures into, for instance, farming, and when she was past 50 wrote the first of over 40 books, by which she proceeded to support her large family, and eventually achieved wealth and fame. After the failure of their farm at Harrow (later to appear in her son Anthony *Trollope's *Orley Farm*) she sailed to New Orleans in 1827 with utopian aspirations and three of her children, and opened an exotic bazaar in Cincinnati. This venture failing, she travelled for fifteen months in America, then in 1832, back in England, published her caustic *Domestic Manners of the Americans*. Its resounding success brought contracts to write on the Belgians, the French, the Austrians, and others, and she lived for the next few years on the Continent. *Paris and the Parisians* appeared with great success in 1835, *Vienna and the Austrians* in 1838, and in 1842 *A Visit to Italy* (where she became the friend of the *Brownings, Charles *Dickens, and W. S. *Landor). Meanwhile, by working both early and late every day, she was writing a long sequence of vivid popular novels, some of which, like *Michael Armstrong, the Factory Boy* (1840), dealt with social issues, and by the early 1840s was earning a considerable income. Her writing, long neglected, has attracted increasing attention and admiration in recent years. See P. Neville-Sington, *Fanny Trollope: The Life and Adventures of a Clever Woman* (1997).
See also SOCIAL PROBLEM NOVEL.

troubadours Poets composing in Occitan (a Romance language spoken in southern France and parts of Italy and Spain) during the 12th and early 13th centuries (and perhaps earlier). They were famous for the complexity of their verse forms, and for the conception of *courtly love which their poems to a great extent founded. Guilhem IX (1071–1126), count of Poitou and duke of Aquitaine, is the first known troubadour; Jaufre Rudel (*fl.*1125–48) developed the theme of 'amor de lonh', love from afar. The most celebrated troubadour love poets are Bernart de Ventadorn (*fl.* 1147–70), Raimbaut d'Aurenga (*c.*1143–1173), Guiraut de Bornelh (*c.*1165–1212), and Arnaut Daniel (*fl.* 1180–1200), later admired by *Dante and *Petrarch, and Ezra *Pound. The troubadours flourished in the courts of Spain, Italy, and northern France, as well as in the south of France, and courtly poetry was being written and cultivated in Italy in the later 13th century (see Robert *Browning's **Sordello*) when it was disappearing in the Midi. Through their influence on the northern French poets (such as *Chrétien de Troyes, and the writers of the **Roman de la Rose*) and on the German poets (notably the **Minnesänger*) they had a major effect on the development of European lyric poetry. Love was their major but not their only subject; they also composed moralizing, satirical, and political poems called sirventes (of which Guiraut de Bornelh was the recognized master), and military poems in which Bertran de Born (*c.*1140–*c.*1215) excelled. See A. R. Press (ed. and trans.), *Anthology of Troubadour Lyric Poetry* (1971: parallel text); L. T. Topsfield, *Troubadours and Love* (1975).

Troubles, literature of the The term 'the Troubles' is used to refer both to the years of the war for Irish independence (1919–21) and subsequent civil war (1922–3), and to the later (not unconnected) post-1968 period of Northern Irish violence which culminated in the ceasefires of 1994. In the first sense, the Troubles inspired work by W. B. *Yeats, Sean *O'Casey, Liam *O'Flaherty, Frank *O'Connor, and other writers, many of whom had participated in the turbulent politics of the time, and gave a title to J. G. *Farrell's *historical novel *Troubles* (1970). The discord in Northern Ireland, the second Troubles, also produced an important body of writing. It informs to a more or less direct degree much of the poetry of Seamus *Heaney, Michael *Longley, Ciaran *Carson, Paul *Muldoon, and other poets who came to prominence just before or in the early years of the conflict, and has given rise to a sub-genre, 'the Troubles novel', which includes Glenn Patterson's *Burning your Own* (1988), Robert McLiam Wilson's *Eureka Street* (1996), and Eoin McNamee's *Resurrection Man* (1994) and *The Ultras* (2004). The first of these works by McNamee fictionalizes the activities of the Shankhill Butchers, a notorious Loyalist gang who tortured and murdered Catholics in the 1970s, while the second is based on the events surrounding the unsolved disappearance of the undercover British officer Captain Robert Nairac in 1977. Other historically focused novels include Naomi May's *Troubles* (1976), which has as one of its themes the defeat of liberalism among unionists during the 1960s; Maurice Leitch's *Silver's City* (1981), a depiction of terrorism, corruption, and brutality in a ravaged Protestant quarter of Belfast; John Morrow's blackly comic *The Essex Factor* (1982), in which an unfortunate opposition backbencher on a fact-finding trip to Northern Ireland tries and fails to make sense of the confusion; and Eugene McEldowney's thriller *A Kind of Homecoming* (1994). Many of the most celebrated Irish works of fiction from the later decades of the 20th century, from Jennifer *Johnston's *Shadows on our Skin* (1977) and Benedict Kiely's *Proxopera* (1977), through William *Trevor's 'Beyond the Pale' (1981) and Bernard *MacLaverty's *Cal* (1983), to Brian *Moore's *Lies of Silence* (1990) and Seamus *Deane's bleakly enigmatic family romance *Reading in the Dark* (1996), take a more indirect approach to the Troubles, exploring the moral ambiguities thrown up by sectarian conflict and by the struggle between paramilitary organizations and a state which fails to command the loyalty of considerable numbers of its citizens.

trouvères Poets composing narrative, dramatic, satiric, comic, and especially lyric verse in the north of France during the late 12th and 13th centuries. They were either professional entertainers, overlapping with *jongleurs* (or public entertainers), *clercs* (or scholars), or feudal lords composing fashionable verse. *Chrétien de Troyes was a *clerc*; other prominent trouvères were Conon de Béthune (d. *c.*1224), a Picard nobleman who composed crusading songs, Gâce Brulé (d. *c.*1220), *Blondel de Nesle, and Thibaut de Champagne (1201–53), count of Champagne and king of Navarre. Their poetry was much influenced by that of the Provençal *troubadours, one of whom, Bernart de Ventadorn (*fl.* 1150–80), came north to the court of *Eleanor of Aquitaine, who was herself the granddaughter of Guilhem IX of Aquitaine (1071–1126), the first known troubadour.

True Tragedy of Richard, Duke of York and the Good King Henry the Sixth, The *See* HENRY VI.

Trumpet Major, The A novel by Thomas *Hardy, published 1880; his only historical fiction. The story is set during the Napoleonic Wars, against a backdrop of preparations for invasion. It describes the courtship of Anne Garland, whose mother is tenant of a part of Overcombe Mill, where the dragoons come down from the nearby camp to water their horses. Among them is John Loveday, the trumpet major, the gentle, unassuming son of the miller. He loves Anne, but has a rival in his brother Bob, a cheerful, light-hearted sailor. Her third suitor is the boorish yeoman Festus Derriman. In the course of events Anne meets King George III, on a military inspection, and later watches the departure of the *Victory* for Trafalgar. The story ends with the defeat of Festus and the success of Bob's courtship, while John marches away, to die on a battlefield in Spain.

TRUSS, Lynne (1955–) Novelist, journalist, and playwright, born in Kingston upon Thames, educated at the University of London, literary editor of the **Listener* 1986–90. She has worked as a columnist and reviewer and has written many plays, dramatic monologues, short stories, and talks for BBC Radio, some of them collected in *A Certain Age* (2007). She has published three novels: *With One Lousy Free Packet of Seed* (1994), *Tennyson's Gift* (1996), a comic re-creation of the poet laureate's circle of friends and fellow artists on the Isle of Wight in the 1860s, and *Going Loco* (1999). *Eats, Shoots and Leaves* (2003), an idiosyncratic plea for attention to the importance of punctuation, became a surprise best-seller on both sides of the Atlantic. *Talk to the Hand* (2005) is a complementary attack on contemporary forms of rudeness.

TRUTH, Sojourner (Isabella Baumfree) (1797–1883) Preacher and autobiographer, born in Ulster County, New York. She lived as a slave until 1827; thereafter she became a travelling preacher, speaking on behalf of abolition and women's rights. *The Narrative of Sojourner Truth* was published in 1850. Her legendary phrase 'Ain't I a Woman?' was part of a speech in Ohio in 1854.
See SLAVERY.

TSVETAEVA, Marina Ivanovna (1892–1941) Russian poet and prose writer. Born in Moscow, the daughter of a professor of art and a gifted pianist, she spent much of her childhood in Western Europe. She published her early poetry privately as *Evening Album* (1910) with great success. In 1912 she married Sergei Iakovlevich Efron, who became an officer in the tsarist army, and published a second book of poetry. She totally rejected the October Revolution of 1917 and wrote a cycle of poems *Demesne of the Swans* (Munich 1957; trans. Robin Kemball, 1980), glorifying the White Army. At the end of the fighting she got permission to join her husband (whom she had thought dead in action against the Bolsheviks) in Prague, and in 1922 much of her poetry appeared in Moscow and Berlin, consolidating her reputation. In exile she engaged in an exalted correspondence with Rainer Maria *Rilke and Boris *Pasternak, two poets whom she greatly admired. In 1925 she moved to Paris, and in March 1926 spent two weeks in London. She became increasingly estranged from her fellow emigrants, who thought her too sympathetic to Soviet Russia. Consequently she found it difficult to publish her work, and lived in great poverty, while continuing to write poetry and critical prose of lasting importance, including her autobiographical prose works of 1934–7. Her husband became increasingly pro-Soviet, and on the orders of the Soviet secret police took part in arranging a political assassination in 1937, then fled to the USSR. Ostracized by Russian emigrants, Tsvetaeva decided, despite her better judgement, to return to Russia. She arrived in Moscow in June 1939 to be shunned by most of her former friends; later that year her daughter Ariadna was arrested and her husband arrested and shot. During the war she was evacuated to the Tatar town of Elabuga, near Kazan, where in despair she hanged herself. Much of her poetry was republished in the Soviet Union after 1961, and her passionate yet articulate and precise work, with its daring linguistic experimentation, brought her increasing recognition as a major poet. She has been much translated into English, notably in *Selected Poems* (trans. Elaine *Feinstein, 1999), *Selected Poems* (trans. David McDuff, 1987), and in *A Captive Spirit: Selected Prose* (trans. J. Marin King, 1980). See Elaine Feinstein, *A Captive Lion: The Life of Marina Tsvetayeva* (1987).

Tuatha Dé Danann (Tuath Dé) In Gaelic mythology, the gods, the 'Folk of the goddess Danu', enemies of the *Fomorians. They are represented as invaders of Ireland, subsequent to the Fomorians and the *Fir Bolgs. They rout the Fomorians at the battle of Moytura, and are ousted in their turn by the *Milesians. Conspicuous among the Tuatha Dé Danann are Lugh, the Gaelic sun god, their leader; and *Lêr, the god of the sea.

TUBMAN, Harriet (*c.*1820–1913) Née Araminta Ross, famous abolitionist. Born a slave in Maryland, she escaped in 1849, and began escorting many other slaves to freedom, using the network known as the Underground Railroad. Herself illiterate, she was the subject of an influential biography by an admirer, Sarah H. Bradford, *Scenes in the Life of Harriet Tubman* (1869). See Catherine Clinton, *Harriet Tubman: The Road to Freedom* (2004).
See SLAVERY.

Tuirenn, The Fate of the Sons of One of the 'three sorrowful tales of Erin', a mythological tale in which the three sons of Tuirenn are punished for killing Cian, the father of the hero god Lugh, by being required, by way of a fine, to achieve a number of quests, in the last of which they perish.

TULLY *See* CICERO.

TUOHY, Frank (John Francis) (1925–99) Novelist, born in Uckfield, Sussex, educated at Stowe School and King's College, Cambridge. His experiences as a lecturer for the British Council are reflected in three novels—*The Animal Game* (1957), *The Warm Nights of January* (1960), and *The Ice Saints* (1964), which won the James Tait Black Memorial Prize and the Geoffrey Faber Memorial Prize. The ironic wit, stylistic elegance, powers of cultural evocation and analysis, and ability to portray a wide range of characters which they display are also exhibited in his three volumes of short stories, a collected edition of which appeared in 1984. He published a notable biography of W. B. *Yeats in 1976.

TUPPER, Martin Farquhar (1810–89) Prolific writer of verse and prose, educated at Christ Church, Oxford. His *Proverbial Philosophy* (1838–76, four series), presenting maxims and reflections couched in vaguely rhythmical form, became the favourite of millions of readers, and remained a best-seller in Britain and America for more than a generation. Among his numerous other published works were two novels, *The Crock of Gold* (1844) and *Stephan Langton* (1858).

TURBERVILE, George (1543/4–*c.*1597) Poet and translator, educated at Winchester College, New College, Oxford, and the Inns of Court. He published *Epitaphs, Epigrams, Songs and Sonnets* (1567), various translations from *Ovid and *Mantuan, including Mantuan's eclogues (1567); and a verse account of the state of 'Moscovia', later reprinted by Richard *Hakluyt. Turbervile's *The Book of Falconry* (1575) is usually found bound with *The Noble Art of Venery or Hunting* (1575; repr. 1908): adapted from an unidentified French manual, the latter may be the work of George *Gascoigne. Turbervile's poems reflect the use of Italian models and show the influence of Sir Thomas *Wyatt and the earl of *Surrey.

TURGENEV, Ivan Sergeevich (1818–83) Russian novelist and playwright, born in Orel. Brought up on his family's gentry estate, he studied at Moscow and St Petersburg universities 1833–7, and the University of Berlin 1838–41. After a brief period in the Ministry of the Interior 1843–5, he devoted himself to country pursuits, writing, and travel. He formed a relationship with the singer Pauline Garcia Viardot (1821–1910), and travelled with her and her husband to France 1845–50. He was confined to his country estate 1852–3 for political writings and left Russia in 1856 to live first in Baden-Baden and then in Paris with the Viardots from 1871 until his death in Bougival. His first important prose work was *A Sportsman's Sketches* (1847–51), translated by J. D. Meiklejohn in 1855 as

Russian Life in the Interior. This was followed by a series of novels in which individual lives are examined to illuminate the social, political, and philosophical issues of the day: *Rudin* (1856), *A Nest of Gentlefolk* (1859), *On the Eve* (1860), *Fathers and Sons* (1862), in which, in Bazarov, he created a nihilist hero, *Smoke* (1867), and *Virgin Soil* (1877). His greatest short stories are 'Asia' (1858), 'First Love' (1860), and 'Torrents of Spring' (1870). The best of his ten plays is *A Month in the Country* (first version 1850; perf. 1872), a psychological comedy of frustrated love and inertia which anticipated the drama of *Chekhov. Turgenev was the first major Russian writer to find success in the rest of Europe. He was closer than his contemporaries *Tolstoy and *Dostoevsky in both sensibility and literary practice to Western Europe where he was personally acquainted with *Flaubert, *George Sand, *Merimée, and others. Turgenev first visited England in 1847 and returned many times up to 1881: *Fathers and Sons* was conceived on the Isle of Wight. He received an honorary doctorate in civil laws at Oxford in 1879 for 'advancing the liberation of the Russian serfs'. He was extremely widely read in English literature; of his English contemporaries, he most valued Charles *Dickens and George *Eliot, both of whom he knew. He was acquainted with W. M. *Thackeray, Anthony *Trollope, Thomas *Carlyle, Robert *Browning, Alfred *Tennyson, the *Rossettis, and A. C. *Swinburne, and in correspondence with George *Gissing. He was one of the earliest admirers of Henry *James, who first met him in Paris in 1875 and on whom he had a substantial influence. For James Turgenev was 'the novelist's novelist'. Perhaps the greatest English debt to him is owed by G. A. *Moore whose mature career was given shape by the discovery of Turgenev's artistry. By 1890 most of Turgenev's major work had appeared in English and exerted its influence on such writers as John *Galsworthy, Joseph *Conrad, and Virginia *Woolf. The most complete early translation is Constance *Garnett's *The Novels of Turgenev* (1894–9). For a biography see Leonard Shapiro, *Turgenev: His Life and Times* (1978); for a critical study Richard Freeborn, *Turgenev: The Novelist's Novelist* (1978); and, for his relationship with Britain, Patrick Waddington (ed.), *Turgenev and Britain* (1995).

TURNER, Frederick Jackson (1861–1932) American historian, who formulated his 'Frontier Thesis' in 1893, arguing that American prosperity was directly related to the westward movement of its frontier.

TURNER, George (1916–97) Australian novelist, born in Melbourne, who turned to *science fiction criticism, and then to writing science fiction. *The Sea and Summer* (1987), his best-known novel, won the Arthur C. Clarke Award for its description of an Australia suffering from the ravages of global warming.

TURNER, J. M. W. (Joseph Mallord William) (1775–1851) English landscape painter, whose mature works convey a Romantic vision of the violence of the elements. He travelled in England and in France, Switzerland, and Italy, and his subjects and styles are astonishingly varied. He moved from conventional topographical watercolours of *picturesque subjects to historical landscapes which vie with the grandeur of Nicolas *Poussin and *Claude Lorrain; in his late, increasingly violent, and almost abstract works (*Snowstorm at Sea*, 1842; *Rain, Steam and Speed*, 1844) forms are dissolved in the sweep of light and brilliant colour patterning the surface of the canvas. Turner was devoted to the 18th-century doctrine of *ut pictura poesis* ('as is painting, so is poetry': *Horace, *Ars Poetica*, 361) and was often inspired by contemporary poetry. He was committed to the values of the Royal Academy, where he was appointed professor of perspective in 1807 and lectured in 1811, and sought to ennoble the genre of landscape painting by suggesting that it could attain the imaginative power and complexity of poetry. From 1798 many of his pictures exhibited at the Royal Academy were accompanied by verses printed in the catalogue; from 1800 he added lines composed by himself. His quotations are frequently from James *Thomson (1700–48), who influenced his literary style, and in 1811 his picture *Thomson's Aeolian Harp* was accompanied by 32 lines honouring the poet. *Snowstorm; Hannibal and His Army Crossing the Alps* (1812) was exhibited with the first quotation taken from his gloomy 'M. S. P. Fallacies of Hope'. There is no trace of this projected epic poem beyond excerpts in Royal Academy catalogues; it was influenced by Mark *Akenside's **Pleasures of Imagination* and Thomas *Campbell's **Pleasures of Hope*. Between 1806 and 1815 Turner frequently wrote poems beside the drawings in his sketchbooks; they have been transcribed by Jack Lindsay in *The Sunset Ship* (1968). In the 1830s Turner did many designs for book illustrations, amongst them charming vignettes for Samuel *Rogers's *Italy* (1830) and *Poems* (1834). He also illustrated works by John *Milton, Lord *Byron, Walter *Scott, and Thomas *Campbell. Turner endured much ridicule, including William *Hazlitt's famous description of his work as 'pictures of nothing and very like', but John *Ruskin became his passionate admirer and the first volume of **Modern Painters* (1843) was written in his defence. See Luke Herrmann, *J. M. W. Turner* (2007).

TURNER, Sharon (1768–1847) A lawyer who became an enthusiastic student of Icelandic and Anglo-Saxon literature, and found much new material, especially among the unexplored Cottonian manuscripts (*see* Cotton, Sir Robert). His interest was, however, more historical than literary. Between 1799 and 1805 he published his *History of the Anglo-Saxons from the Earliest Period to the Norman Conquests*, which was greatly admired, by Henry *Hallam, Robert *Southey, and Walter *Scott, amongst others. He continued his histories up to the death of *Elizabeth I. His insistence on the use of original first sources was important to future historiography. As John *Murray's legal adviser, he was involved in the controversies surrounding the publication of Lord *Byron's **Don Juan*. He was also legal adviser to the **Quarterly Review*.

TURNER, W. J. R. (Walter James Redfern) (1889–1946) Poet, novelist, and critic, born in Melbourne, Australia, and educated at Carlton state school and Scotch College, Melbourne. He arrived in London in 1907, where in time he became music critic of the **New Statesman* (until 1940), drama critic of the **London Mercury* (1919–23), literary editor of the

Daily Herald (1920–3) and literary editor of the **Spectator* (1942–6). He wrote novels, including *The Aesthetes* (1927), *Blow for Balloons* (1935), *Henry Airbubble* (1936) and *The Duchess of Popocatapetl* (1939); a satirical comedy, *The Man Who Ate the Popomack* (1922); and several volumes of verse. His poetry was generously represented by W. B. *Yeats in his *Oxford Book of Modern Verse* (1936). Turner's poem 'Romance', with the lines

> Chimborazo, Cotopaxi,
> They have stolen my heart away!

was published in his first collection, *The Hunter and Other Poems* (1916). See Wayne McKenna, *W. J. Turner: Poet and Music Critic* (1990).

Turn of the Screw, The A novella by Henry *James, published 1898. The narrator is a young governess, sent off to a country house, Bly, to take charge of two orphaned children, Miles and Flora. She gradually becomes convinced that the children are communicating with the spirits of an ex-valet and former governess, both dead. The narrative is a classic example of James's ambiguity and incorporates his interest in psychical research. Benjamin *Britten wrote a chamber opera (1954) based on this tale.

TURTLEDOVE, Harry (1949–) *Science fiction and *fantasy writer, born in Los Angeles; his work usually explores *alternate history. *The Misplaced Legion* (1987) and sequels draws upon his studies of Byzantine history. *How Few Remain* (1997) begins a cycle where the South has won the American Civil War.

TUSSER, Thomas (*c.*1524–1580) Agricultural writer and poet, educated at St Paul's Cathedral school, Eton College, King's College, and Trinity Hall, Cambridge. He farmed at Cattiwade, Suffolk, and introduced the culture of barley to the area. In 1557, he published his *Hundreth Good Points of Husbandry* (amplified to *Five Hundreth Points* in 1573) in quaint and pointed verse. The immensely popular work comprises a collection of instructions on farming, gardening, and housekeeping, together with humorous and wise maxims on conduct in general: many proverbs can be traced to it.

TUTTLE, Lisa (1952–) Novelist, born in Houston, Texas, resident in Scotland. Her work ranges through *science fiction, dark *fantasy, and *horror without solidifying into generic forms. In *Gabriel* (1987) a woman believes a young boy is her dead husband. *The Mysteries* (2005) echoes Celtic folkore.

TUTUOLA, Amos (1920–97) Novelist, born in Abeokuta, Nigeria, trained as a blacksmith. His inventive novel *The Palm-Wine Drinkard* (1952) polarized opinion; Dylan *Thomas's review praised it as bewitching but African critics disapproved of its mythological idiosyncrasy as it traces a drunk's excursion into the ghost world. Other works include *My Life in the Bush of Ghosts* (1952), *Simbi and the Satyr of the Dark Jungle* (1955), *The Brave African Huntress* (1958), *Feather Woman of the Jungle* (1962), *Ajaiyi and his Inherited Poverty* (1968), and *The Witch Herbalist of the Remote Town* (1981); they often draw on elements of myth and folklore.

TWAIN, Mark (1835–1910) Pseudonym of Samuel Langhorne Clemens, American writer, born in Florida, Missouri, where he was brought up. After his father's death in 1847 he was apprenticed to a printer, and wrote for his brother's newspaper. From 1857 to 1861 he was a river pilot on the Mississippi, and from 1862 worked as a newspaper correspondent for various Nevada and Californian magazines, coming under the influence of the humorist Artemus *Ward. He adopted the pseudonym 'Mark Twain', familiar to him from the call of crewmen testing the depth of the water on the Mississippi riverboats. Under this name he published his first successful story, 'Jim Smiley and his Jumping Frog', in 1865 in the New York *Saturday Press*. This comic version of an old folk tale became the title story of *The Celebrated Jumping Frog of Calaveras County, and Other Sketches* (1867), which established him as a leading humorist, a reputation consolidated by *The *Innocents Abroad* (1869), an account of a voyage through the Mediterranean. *Roughing It* (1872), an account of his adventures as miner and journalist in Nevada, appeared in the year of his first English lecture tour; England provided the background for his democratic historical fantasy *The Prince and the Pauper* (1882), in which Edward VI as a boy changes places with Tom Canty, a beggar, and for *A Connecticut Yankee in King Arthur's Court* (1889), a disturbing fantasy that satirizes both past and present. Meanwhile appeared his most famous works, both deeply rooted in his own childhood, *The Adventures of *Tom Sawyer* (1876) and its sequel *The Adventures of *Huckleberry Finn* (1884), the latter combining satire with vernacular narration. *Life on the Mississippi* (1883), an autobiographical account of his life as a river pilot, contains a notable attack on the influence of Walter *Scott, whose romanticism did 'measureless harm' to progressive ideas and progressive works, creating, Twain alleges, the myth of the southern gentleman that did much to precipitate the Civil War. In the last two decades of his life Clemens was beset with financial anxieties and dissipated time and money on chimerical business enterprises, trying to recoup by lecture tours (in 1895–6 he toured New Zealand, Australia, India, and South Africa) and by writing potboilers; his pessimism and bitterness were increased by the death of his wife in 1904, of two of his three daughters, and by other family troubles. In these last years, however, he wrote some memorable if sombre works, including *The Man that Corrupted Hadleyburg* (1900), a fable about the venality of a smug small town, and *The Mysterious Stranger* (published posthumously in 1916, in a much-edited version), an extraordinary tale set in 16th-century Austria, in which Satan appears as a morally indifferent but life-enhancing visitor, to reveal the hypocrisies and stupidities of the village of Eseldorf. He dictated his autobiography during his last years to his secretary A. B. Paine, and various versions of it have appeared. See Ron Powers, *Mark Twain* (2005).

Twelfth Night, *or What You Will* A comedy by *Shakespeare probably written 1601. The diarist John Manningham (*c.*1575–1622) saw a performance of it in the Middle Temple in February 1602; it was first printed in the *folio of 1623. Shakespeare's immediate source for the main plot was 'The History of Apolonius and Silla' in Barnaby *Rich's *Riche his Farewell to Military Profession* (1581). This is derived from Belleforest's version, which by way of Matteo *Bandello can be traced back to a Sienese comedy *Gl'ingannati* (*The Deceived*), written and performed 1531.

Sebastian and Viola, twin brother and sister who look very much alike, are separated in a shipwreck off the coast of Illyria. Viola, brought to shore in a boat, disguises herself as a youth, Cesario, and takes service as page with Duke Orsino, who is in love with the lady Olivia. Olivia rejects the duke's suit and will not meet him. Orsino makes a confidant of Cesario and sends her to press his suit on Olivia, much to Cesario's distress, for she has fallen in love with Orsino. Olivia in turn falls in love with Cesario. Sebastian and Antonio, captain of the ship that had rescued Sebastian, now arrive in Illyria. Cesario, challenged to a duel by Sir Andrew Aguecheek, a rejected suitor of Olivia, is rescued from her predicament by Antonio, who takes her for Sebastian. Antonio, being arrested at that moment for an old offence, claims from Cesario a purse that he had entrusted to Sebastian, is denied it, and hauled off to prison. Olivia, coming upon the true Sebastian, takes him for Cesario, invites him to her house, and promptly marries him. Orsino comes to visit Olivia. Antonio, brought before him, claims Cesario as the youth he has rescued from the sea; while Olivia claims Cesario as her husband. The duke, deeply wounded, is bidding farewell to Olivia and the 'dissembling cub' Cesario, when the arrival of the true Sebastian clears up the confusion. The duke, having lost Olivia, and becoming conscious of the love that Viola has revealed, turns his affection to her, and they are married.

Much of the play's comedy comes from the sub-plot dealing with the members of Olivia's household: Sir Toby Belch, her uncle, Sir Andrew Aguecheek, his friend, Malvolio, her pompous steward, Maria, her waiting-gentlewoman, and her clown Feste. Exasperated by Malvolio's officiousness, the other members of the household make him believe that Olivia is in love with him and that he must return her affection. In courting her he behaves so outrageously that he is imprisoned as a madman. Olivia has him released and the joke against him is explained, but he is not amused, threatening, 'I'll be revenged on the whole pack of you.'

The play's gentle melancholy and lyrical atmosphere is captured in two of Feste's beautiful songs 'Come away, come away, death' and

> When that I was and a little tiny boy,
> With hey, ho, the wind and the rain.

Twentieth Century *See* Nineteenth Century.

Two Cultures and the Scientific Revolution, The 'The Two Cultures' is a phrase coined by C. P. *Snow in the Rede Lecture delivered at Cambridge in 1959 and published the same year. In it, he contrasts the culture of 'literary intellectuals' and that of 'scientists, and as the most representative, physical scientists'. He describes the increasing gulf between them, claiming that 30 years earlier the two sides could at least manage 'a frozen smile' but are now incapable of communication. His analysis of the educational attitudes that produced this situation and his recommendations for change were strongly attacked by F. R. *Leavis in his Richmond Lecture *Two Cultures? The Significance of C. P. Snow* (1962).
See Thomson, Sir William.

'Two Drovers, The' A short story by Walter *Scott, one of the **Chronicles of the Canongate*, published 1827. One of the strongest of Scott's shorter tales, the tragedy turns on the conflict between Highland and Lowland views of life. Robin Oig M'Combich and Harry Wakefield, long-standing companions on the drove-roads, quarrel. Wakefield wants to settle the matter with his fists, English fashion; Robin Oig rejects this idea as beneath the dignity of a Highland gentleman. Knocked down by his friend, he kills him with his dirk in revenge. 'I give a life for the life I took,' he says, when he is arrested, 'and what can I do more?'

Two Foscari, The A poetic melodrama by Lord *Byron, published 1821. The son of Francesco Foscari, the doge of Venice, Jacopo, twice banished, once for corruption and once for complicity in murder, has been brought back from exile on a charge of treason, and the play opens with his interrogation on the rack. His broken-hearted father signs the sentence for his third, perpetual exile. But Jacopo's love for Venice is so intense that he dies in horror at the prospect. The Council of Ten decides to require the abdication of the old doge. He immediately leaves the palace, and as he descends the steps he falls and dies.

Two Gentlemen of Verona, The A comedy by *Shakespeare, probably written about 1590, often regarded as Shakespeare's first play. There is no record of a performance before the *Restoration. It was first printed in the *folio of 1623, where it is the second play in the section of comedies. Its main source is the story of Felix and Felismena in the *Diana* of Jorge de *Montemayor.

The two gentlemen of Verona are the friends Valentine and Proteus. Proteus loves Julia, who returns his affection. Valentine leaves Verona for Milan 'to see the wonders of the world abroad', and there falls in love with Silvia, the duke of Milan's daughter. Presently Proteus also sets off on his travels, exchanging vows of constancy with Julia before starting. But arriving at Milan, Proteus is at once captivated by Silvia, and, betraying both his friend and his former love, reveals to the duke Valentine's plan to carry off Silvia. Valentine is banished and becomes a captain of outlaws, while Proteus continues to court Silvia. Meanwhile Julia, pining for Proteus, comes to Milan dressed as a boy and takes service as Proteus' page, unrecognized by him. Silvia, to escape marriage with Thurio, her father's choice, leaves Milan to rejoin Valentine, is captured by outlaws and rescued from them by Proteus. Proteus is violently pressing his suit on Silvia when Valentine comes on the scene. Proteus is struck with such remorse that Valentine surrenders Silvia to him, to the dismay of Proteus' page, the disguised Julia. She faints, and is recognized by Proteus. Her faithfulness wins back his love. The duke and Thurio arrive. Thurio shows cowardice in face of Valentine's determination, and the duke approves the match with Silvia, and pardons the outlaws. Lance, the clownish servant of Proteus, and his dog Crab, 'the sourest-natured dog that lives', provide much humour.

Two Nations, The Subtitle of the novel **Sybil*, by Benjamin *Disraeli.

Two Noble Kinsmen, The A tragicomedy attributed to John *Fletcher and *Shakespeare on its publication in 1634. In spite of its absence from the first *folio (1623), recent studies suggest that it is probably a genuine work of collaboration between Fletcher and Shakespeare, taking more or less equal shares and with Shakespeare responsible especially for the first and last acts, written for the King's Men in about 1613.

The play is closely based on *Chaucer's 'Knight's Tale' (*see* CANTERBURY TALES, 1), which Shakespeare had previously drawn on in *A *Midsummer Night's Dream*. The main addition to the plot is the unnamed Jailer's Daughter who is crazed by unrequited love for Palamon, and is cured by a lower-class wooer pretending to be Palamon. The overall tone is lighter than in Chaucer's poem, the play being diversified with songs and lyrical passages such as Emilia's reminiscence of her friendship with Flavina (I. iii. 55–82); there is also a country festival with morris dancing, presided over by a pedantic schoolmaster (III. v). Theseus is a much less ominous figure than in Chaucer, and Arcite's death is rapid and dignified. The play is rarely performed.

Two on a Tower A novel by Thomas *Hardy, published 1882. Lady Constantine, whose disagreeable husband is away, falls in love with Swithin St Cleeve, a young astronomer who works at the top of a tower, where many of the scenes of the novel occur. Believing her husband dead, Lady Constantine secretly marries Swithin, but learns that marriage would deprive him of a legacy; and that her husband, though now dead, was alive when she married Swithin. The union is therefore void, and she insists on his leaving, to find employment abroad. She discovers that she is pregnant, and accepts an offer of marriage from Bishop Helmsdale. A son is born. Swithin returns after the bishop's death, and is appalled that she is no longer young. He proposes marriage, but she falls dead in his arms, overcome with joy. Hardy's ambition was 'to set the history of two infinitesimal lives against the tremendous background of the stellar universe'

2001: A Space Odyssey Film (1968) directed by Stanley Kubrick and scripted by Arthur C. *Clarke.

Two Years Ago The last of Charles *Kingsley's reforming novels, published 1857. Kingsley describes the arrival of cholera in the fishing village of Aberalva, attacks the sanitary conditions and public apathy that allowed it to take hold, and praises the heroism of various inhabitants. These include the doctor, Tom Thurnall, rescued from shipwreck by the schoolmistress Grace Harvey, who converts him to Christianity and whose love he finally wins, and Frank Headley, the High Church curate. A secondary plot involves a denunciation of slavery in America, influenced by Harriet Beecher *Stowe's **Uncle Tom's Cabin*, and there are also references to the Crimean War, which brings about a crisis in Thurnall's spiritual life. Contrasted with the practical Thurnall is Elsley Vavasour (once an apothecary's assistant under his real name, John Briggs), an opium-taking poet evidently of the *Spasmodic school, who prefers Art to Action and demonstrates the dangers of unleashed emotion by running wild on Snowdon, before a deathbed scene in which he desires that his poetry be burned and his children dissuaded from writing verse. This caused a quarrel with Alfred *Tennyson, who wrongly supposed Vavasour to be modelled on him.

TYLER, Anne (1941–) American novelist, born in Minneapolis, who began publishing with *If Morning Ever Comes* (1964). *Breathing Lessons* (1988) won the *Pulitzer Prize. Most of her fiction has been set in Baltimore and she has been praised as a chronicler of the day-to-day.

TYLER, Wat (d. 1381) The leader of the Peasants' Revolt of 1381, who led the peasants of Kent and Essex to London. He was killed by William Walworth, the lord mayor of London, in the course of a discussion with Richard II at Smithfield. He is the subject of a drama by Robert *Southey.
See JACK STRAW.

TYNAN, Katharine (1861–1931) Poet and novelist, born in Dublin, early confidante of W. B. *Yeats. Her first volume of verse, *Louise de La Vallière and Other Poems* (1885), was followed by seventeen others, which fuse feminism, Catholicism, and an ethic of service increasingly at odds with the separatist enthusiasm of her compatriots. In addition to scores of novels and twelve collections of short stories, she published four volumes of memoirs.

TYNAN, Kenneth Peacock (1927–80) Dramatic critic, educated at Magdalen College, Oxford. He wrote for various papers, most influentially for the **Observer* (1954–63), and championed the plays of John *Osborne, Arnold *Wesker, Shelagh *Delaney, N. F. *Simpson, Samuel *Beckett, and others, playing a leading role in the shift of taste from drawing-room comedy and the poetic drama of T. S. *Eliot and Christopher *Fry (which he disliked) to naturalism and 'working-class drama' (*see* KITCHEN SINK DRAMA). He also vigorously attacked theatre censorship. His various collections of reviews and essays include *Curtains* (1967), *The Sound of Two Hands Clapping* (1975), and *A View of the English Stage* (1976), which pay tribute to the role of the *English Stage Company in the development of British theatre. Tynan was also a moving force in the creation of the *National Theatre, and its literary

manager from 1963 to 1969. There is a life by his widow Kathleen Tynan (1987) who also edited his *Letters* (1994). The *Diaries* were published in 2001.
See also THEATRE CRITICISM.

TYNDALE, William (*c.*1494–1536) Translator of the *Bible, born in Gloucestershire and educated at Magdalen Hall, Oxford. About 1522 he formed the project of translating the Scriptures into the vernacular, but finding difficulties in England emigrated to Germany. An incomplete edition of Tyndale's translation of the New Testament was printed at Cologne in 1525; an edition of the whole translation was produced at Worms in 1526; when copies of this and the Cologne fragment were introduced into England, they were denounced by the bishops and destroyed. Tyndale eventually settled at Antwerp, becoming an active pamphleteer, and writing *An Answer* to Sir Thomas *More's *Dialogue* (1531). He was betrayed to imperial officers, arrested for heresy, imprisoned at Vilvorde in 1535, and strangled and burnt at the stake there, in spite of the intercession of Thomas Cromwell (*c.*1485–1540). Tyndale was one of the most remarkable leaders of the *Reformation; his original writings show sound scholarship, but his translation of the Bible—the New Testament (1525), Pentateuch (1530), and Jonah (1531?)—whose accuracy, straightforward style, and vivid language were endorsed by the translators of the Authorized Version, is his surest title to fame. There is a life by David Daniell (1994).

TYNDALL, John (1820–93) Professor of natural history at the Royal Institution in 1853, and later superintendent there, who did much in his vigorous writings and lectures to popularize science. He had many friends in literary and scientific circles, including Alfred *Tennyson, Charles *Darwin, Herbert *Spencer, and Leslie *Stephen. His famous address to the British Association in Belfast in 1874, on the relation between science and theology, gave rise to acute controversy.
See SCIENCE.

Typee, *or A Peep at Polynesian Life* A novel by Herman *Melville, published 1846, first in Britain under the title *Narrative of a Four Months Residence among the Natives of a Valley of the Marquesas Islands*. It was Melville's first book, and his most popular during his lifetime. Like Melville himself, *Typee's* hero Tommo and his friend Toby jump ship in the Marquesas, but their perception of the island paradise is darkened by fears of cannibalism. *Omoo* (1847) continues the narrative.

Tyranipocrit Discovered An anonymous radical pamphlet, published in Rotterdam in 1649. A plea for social equality, it attacks the 'White Devil' of tyrannical power, idleness, and greed disguised as Christian piety. There is an edition by A. Hopton (1990), and extracts in George *Orwell and Reginald Reynolds, *British Pamphleteers* (1948).

Tyrannic Love, *The Royal Martyr* A heroic play by John *Dryden, produced and published 1669. Based on the legend of the martyrdom of St Catherine by the Roman emperor Maximin, it contains some of Dryden's most extravagant heroic verse. Possibly deliberately comic at times, it is also seriously concerned with contrasting Lucretian and Christian conceptions of God. It was ridiculed in *The *Rehearsal*, and by Thomas *Shadwell. Dryden himself satirizes its excesses in **Mac Flecknoe*.

TYRWHITT, Thomas (1730–86) Scholar, educated at Eton College and the Queen's College, Oxford. He was clerk of the House of Commons, 1762–8. His *Observations and Conjectures upon Some Passages of Shakespeare* (1766) insisted on the importance of careful collation of early texts, criticizing Samuel *Johnson's edition for its neglect in this respect. Tyrwhitt was much consulted by later editors. His edition of *Chaucer's **Canterbury Tales* (4 vols, 1775, with glossary, 1778) was the first on recognizably modern editorial principles. In 1777 he published an edition of Thomas *Chatterton's 'Rowley' poems, adding to the third edition an appendix (1778) proving that they were modern, not ancient, a view elaborated in his *Vindication of the Appendix* (1782). Tyrwhitt was appointed curator of the British Museum, 1784.

U

ubi sunt Derived from the opening words of a type of Medieval Latin poem ('Where are they?'), taken up in Old English poems such as *The* **Wanderer* (ll. 92–3) and in many Middle English lyrics (especially the one beginning 'Where beth they, beforen us weren', *c.*1300). Many later medieval French poems use the theme, famously François *Villon's 'Ballade des dames du temps jadis' with its refrain, 'Mais où sont les neiges d'antan?'—'Where are the snows of yesteryear?'

UDALL (Uvedale), **Nicholas** (1504–56) Dramatist and scholarly translator, educated at Winchester College and Corpus Christi College, Oxford, successively headmaster of Eton College and Westminster School. He was author of **Ralph Roister Doister*, the earliest known English comedy, translated selections from *Terence and other works, and wrote Latin plays on sacred subjects. Thomas *Tusser (*Five Hundreth Points*, 1573) complains of having been severely flogged by Udall 'For fault but small, or none at all'. Udall was prosecuted for, and admitted, buggery of a pupil in 1541, while at Eton, and was sent to the Marshalsea prison by the Privy Council, but went on to become canon of St George's Chapel, Windsor, ten years later. He figures in Ford Madox *Ford's novel *The Fifth Queen* (1906).

Udolpho, The Mysteries of *See* MYSTERIES OF UDOLPHO.

UGLOW, Jenny (1947–) Biographer and critic. Brought up in Cumbria, then Dorset, she was educated at Cheltenham Ladies' College and St Anne's College, Oxford. She compiled a *Dictionary of Women's Biography* (1982), followed by full-length biographies of two women writers, George *Eliot (1987) and Elizabeth *Gaskell (1993). Subsequent work has included a biography of Henry *Fielding (1995); *Hogarth: A Life and a World* (1997), and *Thomas Bewick* (2006). *Words & Pictures* (2008) explores relationships between writers and artists. Her study of the Lunar Society which included Erasmus *Darwin, Matthew Boulton, James Watt, Joseph *Priestley, and Josiah Wedgwood, *The Lunar Men* (2003), won the James Tait Black Memorial Prize.

UGOLINO DELLA GHERARDESCA (d. 1289) An Italian leader, from a noble Ghibelline family, who allied himself to the Guelf party, for which he was deemed a traitor. He twice made himself master of Pisa in 1284 and 1288, by forming an underhand intrigue with the Ghibelline leader Ruggieri degli Ubaldini. But Ruggieri betrayed him in turn, and he was locked with his two sons and two of his grandsons in a tower and starved to death. The story is told by Ugolino himself in *Dante's *Inferno*, XXXIII, and it is among the tragedies of Fortune told in Chaucer's 'The Monk's Tale' (*see* CANTERBURY TALES, 19; VII. 2407–62); though he knew the source was Dante, Chaucer tells of three sons and says the youngest was 5 years old, although three of the four in Dante were grown men. The story was used again as the basis for a poem in Seamus *Heaney's *Field Work* (1981).

Ulysses Novel by James *Joyce, begun in 1914 and partly serialized in the **Little Review* (Chicago), 1918–20, and the **Egoist*. The editors of the *Little Review* were found guilty of publishing an obscenity, which is why the entire novel was first published in Paris in 1922. Copies of the first English edition were burned by the New York post office authorities and Folkestone customs officials seized the second edition in 1923. Various later editions appeared abroad, but after the United States District Court found the book not obscene in 1933, it was freely published in the USA in 1934 and the UK in 1936. The novel deals with the events of one day in Dublin, 16 June 1904 (the anniversary of Joyce's first walk with Nora Barnacle, who became his wife), now known as 'Bloomsday'. The principal characters are Stephen Dedalus (the hero of Joyce's earlier, largely autobiographical, *A *Portrait of the Artist as a Young Man*); Leopold Bloom, a part-Jewish advertisement canvasser; and his wife Molly. The plot follows the wanderings of Stephen and Bloom through Dublin, and their eventual meeting; the last chapter is an extended monologue by Molly Bloom. The eighteen chapters roughly correspond to the episodes of Homer's **Odyssey* (Stephen representing Telemachus, Bloom Odysseus, and Molly Penelope), and are, in order: 'Telemachus', 'Nestor', 'Proteus', 'Calypso', 'Lotus Eaters', 'Hades', 'Aeolus', 'Lestrygonians', 'Scylla and Charybdis', 'Wandering Rocks', 'Sirens', 'Cyclops', 'Nausicaa', 'Oxen of the Sun', 'Circe', 'Eumaeus', 'Ithaca' and 'Penelope'. The style is highly allusive and employs a variety of techniques, especially those of *interior monologue and of *parody, and ranges from extreme realism to fantasy. Joyce described the theme of the *Odyssey* to one of his students in 1917 as the 'most beautiful, all-embracing theme…greater, more human, than that of *Hamlet*, Don Quixote, Dante, *Faust*', and refers to Ulysses himself as a pacifist, father, wanderer, musician, and artist: 'I am almost afraid to treat such a theme; it's overwhelming.'

But he pulled it off and produced one of the most consummate, controversial, and famous novels in the history of the genre.

'Ulysses' A poem by Alfred *Tennyson, composed 1833, published 1842. In a dramatic monologue Ulysses describes how he plans to set forth again from Ithaca after his safe return from his wanderings after the Trojan War, 'to sail beyond the sunset'. The episode is based not on *Homer but on *Dante (*Inferno*, XXVI), which Tennyson probably read in the translation of Henry *Cary. The poem is exceptionally divided about the nature of its hero, but took some of its energy from 'the need of going forward and braving the struggle of life' after the death of A. H. *Hallam.

Una In Book I of Edmund *Spenser's *The *Faerie Queene*, typifies singleness of the true religion. She is separated from the *Redcrosse Knight of Holiness (the Anglican Church) by the wiles of *Archimago, but meets and is protected by a lion, until it is killed by Sansloy (*see* SANSFOY, SANSJOY, AND SANSLOY), who carries Una off to a forest. She is rescued by fauns and satyrs, and is finally united with and betrothed to the Redcrosse Knight.

Uncle Remus *See* HARRIS, JOEL.

Uncle Silas A *sensation novel by Sheridan *Le Fanu, published 1864. Maud Ruthyn, aged 17, is the only child of Austin Ruthyn, a rich elderly recluse. Her mother, whom he married late in life, is dead. Austin has a younger brother Silas, suspected by many of the murder of a wealthy gambler at Bartram-Haugh, Silas's Derbyshire home. Believing in Silas's innocence, Austin at his death makes Silas Maud's guardian. He will inherit her fortune if she dies under age. Silas summons Maud to Bartram-Haugh, where he attempts to marry her to his boorish son Dudley, who is in fact already secretly married. When she refuses, he imprisons her at Bartram-Haugh, where Silas and Dudley, aided by a grotesque and sinister French governess, Madame de la Rougierre, try to kill her. The plot miscarries and the governess is horribly murdered by Dudley in mistake for Maud, who escapes. The tale has no supernatural element; but Maud's mounting terror is powerfully conveyed. Uncle Silas is a fearful figure, tall, marble-faced, with black eyebrows and long silver hair, a laudanum-taker, prone to strange trances.

Uncle Tom's Cabin, *or Life among the Lowly* Novel by Harriet Beecher *Stowe, published in 1852, which was triggered by the passage of the Fugitive Slave Act in 1850. It mounted a powerful attack on slavery, which led President Lincoln to attribute the American Civil War partly to its effectiveness. It became a best-seller and was followed in 1853 by *A Key to Uncle Tom's Cabin*, where Stowe assembled much of her source material.

UNDERDOWNE, Thomas (*fl.* 1566–77) He translated the **Aethiopica* of Heliodorus under the title *An Aethiopian History* (?1569; rev. 1577).

Under Milk Wood A radio drama by Dylan *Thomas, first broadcast by the *BBC on 25 January 1954 and subsequently adapted for the stage; the published version was completed shortly before his death, although he was still at work on the text. Set in the small Welsh seaside town of Llareggub (Thomas had a backwards reading in mind: censoring editors changed the name to Llaregyb on the play's initial publication) it evokes the lives of the inhabitants—Myfanwy Price the dressmaker, and her lover Mog Edwards the draper; twice-widowed Mrs Ogmore-Pritchard; Butcher Beynon and his daughter Gossamer; the Reverend Eli Jenkins; the romantic and prolific Polly Garter; nostalgic Captain Cat, dreaming of lost loves; and many others. The poetic, alliterative prose is interspersed with songs and ballads. An earlier version of the first part of this play appeared in **Botteghe oscure* in 1952 under the title 'Llaregyb'.

Under the Greenwood Tree A novel by Thomas *Hardy, published 1872. Gentle and humorous, this short novel skilfully interweaves the love story of Dick Dewy and Fancy Day with the fortunes and misfortunes of a group of villagers, many of whom are musicians and singers in Mellstock church. Dick Dewy, the son of the local 'tranter', or carrier, falls in love with the new schoolmistress, the capricious Fancy Day. Dick finally triumphs over Shiner, a rich local farmer, and Maybold, the vicar in charge of the school, who also court Fancy. Dick and his father are among the musicians who have always sung and played in the gallery of Mellstock church, and who find themselves ousted by the new-fangled organ. This story of the displaced musicians reflects Hardy's own experience at the church at Stinsford, and Hardy originally wished to call his book 'The Mellstock Choir'. The novel marks the first appearance of Hardy's village rustics, who drew much critical comment, both favourable and unfavourable, and who were to reappear frequently in later novels.

Unfortunate Traveller, The, *or The Life of Jack Wilton* A prose tale by Thomas *Nashe, published 1594, the earliest *picaresque romance in English, and the most remarkable work of the kind before Daniel *Defoe. It is dedicated to the third earl of Southampton (1573–1624).

Jack Wilton is 'a certain kind of an appendix or page' at the court of Henry VIII during the siege of Tournai. He lives by his wits, playing tricks on a mean old supplier of provisions and other naive occupants of the camp, and gets whipped for his pains. He goes to Münster, which the Anabaptists are holding against the emperor, and sees John of Leyden hanged. The earl of *Surrey, the supposed lover of the Fair Geraldine, takes him to Italy as his page. During their travels they meet *Erasmus, Sir Thomas *More, H. C. *Agrippa, and *Aretino. They hear Martin *Luther disputing at Wittenberg. Wilton passes himself off as Surrey and runs away with an

Italian courtesan. After a tourney at Florence, where the earl defeats all-comers in honour of the Fair Geraldine, Wilton leaves him, and is at Rome during an outbreak of the plague. Here, turning from lighter themes, he recounts scenes of violence and tragedy, rapes, murders, tortures, and executions. Depressed by his experiences, he is converted to a better way of life, marries his courtesan, and is last seen at the Field of the Cloth of Gold, in the English king's camp. The book includes much literary parody and pastiche, including of Philip *Sidney's **Arcadia*.

UNGARETTI, Giuseppe (1888–1970) Italian poet. He founded hermeticism with his first two collections of poems *L'allegria di naufragi* (written 1914–19: *Gaiety of Shipwrecks*) and *Il porto sepolto* (1916: *The Buried Port*), in which he used neither rhyme nor punctuation. His later poems, of which the best are in *Il dolore* (1947: *Sorrow*) and *Sentimento del tempo* (1933: *The Feeling of Time*, 1950), depart from hermeticism by reviving the tradition of *Leopardi and *Petrarch. He translated William *Blake's visionary poems (*Visioni di William Blake*, 1965) and from *Shakespeare, and was himself translated by Robert *Lowell.

Unitarianism A system of Christian belief which rejects the Trinity and the divinity of Christ in favour of the single personality of the Godhead. Unitarianism is more radical in its anti-Trinitarianism than *Arianism. Though the term was not used in English until the 1680s, and Unitarianism was not legally tolerated as a religious denomination until the early 19th century, it had its origins in 16th- and 17th-century Polish Socinianism, from Fausto Sozzini (1539–1604), known as Socinus. Socinianism was sometimes used as an equivalent label. John Biddle (1615/16–62), regarded as the father of English Unitarianism, published Socinian tracts in the 1650s. In the 18th century Dissenting congregations, particularly the English Presbyterians, turned first to Arian and then to Unitarian views. Joseph *Priestley in his *Appeal to the Serious and Candid Professors of Christianity* (1770) defended Unitarian principles, and in 1774 Theophilus Lindsey (1723–1808) formed the first Unitarian denomination, opening the Essex Street Chapel in London. Both Priestley and his friend Richard *Price became original members of the Unitarian Society in 1791. S. T. *Coleridge briefly contemplated becoming a Unitarian minister. In the 19th century James *Martineau influenced the organization of the Unitarian body in England and Ireland and led the development of rational Unitarianism. Elizabeth *Gaskell's fiction is imbued with Unitarian values.

unities Principles of dramatic composition derived questionably from Aristotle's **Poetics*. Recording the practice of the tragedians whose works he knew, Aristotle states that a play should have the unity of a living organism, the action it represents lasting, if possible, no longer than a single revolution of the sun. From these hints, Ludovico *Castelvetro and other 16th-century critics developed the rule of the three unities: action, time, and place, in the belief that audiences would be confused by the time of the action lasting longer than the time of its performance and that they would not accept changes of scene. These principles were adopted in French drama, but with some latitude: the exclusion of subplots became the rule in France only after the controversy over *Corneille's *Le Cid* (1637). The time allowed for the action of a tragedy was extended by common consent to 24 hours; and the place the stage represented was allowed to shift from one point to another within a palace or even a city. Some dramatists circumvented the limitations of the unities by avoiding the mention of specific times and places. The later impact of this *neo-classicism on English tragedy was weakened by the taste for exciting action that was a legacy from the Jacobean stage, and especially by the example of *Shakespeare's irregular dramatic structures (only two of his plays, *The *Two Gentlemen of Verona* and *The *Tempest*, conform to the unities). John Dryden's essay **Of Dramatick Poesy* (1668) offers the unities only half-hearted support, and in spite of the efforts of the French-inspired critics Thomas *Rymer and John *Dennis, neo-classical drama never took firm root in England. After the decline of neo-classicism, some later plays nonetheless abided by the unities inadvertently or, as with Samuel *Beckett's *Endgame* (*Fin de partie*, 1957), with self-conscious irony.

university presses By the end of the 16th century the appointment of printers by European academies to produce learned books under their control and protection was common. As early as 1470 Johann Heynlin (*c.*1425–1496), rector of the Sorbonne, brought printers from Germany to work in the college; but his press had no sanction from the University of Paris and lasted only two years. A printer worked at Oxford from 1478 until 1486, but his relationship with the university is unknown.

With the advent of the 'new learning' universities needed new texts and printers needed help and protection in issuing them. The University of Leipzig, devoted to humane studies since 1502, took the lead in attracting printers, directing them to Greek and elegant Latin, and defending their books from attack by conservative authorities. The advantages of printing in a university were exemplified in the polyglot *Bible produced in 1514–22 at Alcalá de Henares, Spain.

The modern conception of a university press owes much to Leiden. The academy founded there in 1575 appointed an official printer from the first, and was served in that capacity by Christopher Plantin (in 1584–5), by the erudite Franciscus Raphelengius (1539–97), and three generations of Elzeviers. Their books, edited or approved by the resident professors and well corrected at the press, established the advantages that a university can bestow in publishing.

In England, from 1534 a royal charter gave Cambridge University power to appoint printers to work in its precinct and sell books anywhere, mainly, no doubt, with a view to combating heresy (*see* Cambridge University Press). It exercised the power from 1583, and Oxford followed the year after (*see* Oxford University Press), apparently with only oral warrant from the queen. Costly conflicts with vested interests contesting the universities' right to override monopolies in such lucrative works as the *Bible in English, *The Book of *Common Prayer*, and the metrical Psalms induced both universities to forgo this privilege in return for money during most of two centuries and to sponsor only scholarly works.

The press owned, financed, and conducted by a university, as distinct from one censored and protected by it but privately financed and managed, had its origin in England and is still generally confined to English-speaking countries. Oxford acquired such a press in 1690, with John *Fell's bequest of printing equipment and rights in copy. Cambridge took immediate control of its printing in 1698 and exercises it through a board of syndics.

The style of 'university press' is used by many publishing firms, particularly in Great Britain, the USA, and Canada. They are variously related to the academies from which they take their names. In the USA Cornell opened a small press in 1869, which lasted until 1894, and Johns Hopkins established an agency for publishing in 1875. The University of Chicago has owned its printing and publishing office since 1894. Among the leading North American and Canadian university presses are or have been Harvard, Yale, Princeton, Columbia, California, and Toronto.

University Wits Name given by the critic George Saintsbury (1845–1933) to a group of Elizabethan playwrights and pamphleteers. The chief Wits were Christopher *Marlowe, Thomas *Nashe, George *Peele, Thomas *Kyd, Robert *Greene, John *Lyly, and Thomas *Lodge.

unreason, abbot of *See* MISRULE, KING, LORD, OR ABBOT OF.

UNSWORTH, Barry (1930–) Novelist, son of a mining family, born and brought up in Durham, and educated at the University of Manchester. His subsequent travels in Greece and Turkey as a language teacher and his fascination with history (especially imperial concerns) are vividly reflected in his work. After his first novel, *The Partnership* (1966), set in 1960s Cornwall, he has largely written novels located in the past and overseas. Outstanding among them are *Pascali's Island* (1980), which takes place on the fringe of the decaying Ottoman Empire, *Stone Virgin* (1985), which recreates different periods of Venice's history, and *Morality Play* (1995), a chillingly atmospheric tale of travelling players in 14th-century Northumbria. His longest novel, *Sacred Hunger* (*Booker Prize, 1992), unrolls a grim panorama of the 18th-century slave trade. In his autobiographical black comedy *After Hannibal* (1996), the themes of greed, exploitation, and clashes between cultures that suffuse his historical fiction are transposed to the contemporary Umbria of expatriate homes, where he now lives. Typifying the virtuoso restlessness of his imagination, his most recent novels, *The Songs of the Kings* (2002) and *The Ruby in her Navel* (2006), are respectively set in ancient Greece and medieval Sicily.

UPDIKE, John (1932–2009) American novelist, short story writer, and poet, born in Pennsylvania, where his early works are set. His novels include the tetralogy *Rabbit, Run* (1960), *Rabbit Redux* (1971), *Rabbit is Rich* (1981), and *Rabbit at Rest* (1990), a small-town domestic tragicomedy which traces the career of ex-basketball champion Harry Angstrom from the early days of his precarious (but, as it turns out, lasting) marriage to alcoholic Janice, through the social and sexual upheavals of the 1960s, to the compromises of middle age. *The Centaur* (1963) uses a mythological framework to explore the relationship of a schoolmaster father and his teenage son and *Couples* (1968) is a portrait of sexual passion and realignment amongst a group of young married couples in a small Massachusetts town. Updike's characteristic preoccupations with the erotic, with the pain and striving implicit in human relationships, and with the sacred in daily life are conveyed in an ornate, highly charged prose which reaches its most flamboyant in an atypical work, *The Coup* (1979), an exotic first-person narration by the ex-dictator of a fictitious African state. Other novels include *The Witches of Eastwick* (1984, subsequently filmed) and *Toward the End of Time* (1997), an excursion into science fiction. *A Month of Sundays* (1975), *Roger's Version* (1986), and *S* (1988) form a linked sequence based on reworkings of Nathaniel *Hawthorne's *The *Scarlet Letter*. His volumes of short stories include *Pigeon Feathers and Other Stories* (1962), *Museums and Women* (1972), *Problems and Other Stories* (1979), *Trust Me* (1987), and *The Afterlife and Other Stories* (1995). His reviews and essays have been collected in *Assorted Prose* (1965), *Picked-up Pieces* (1978), *Hugging the Shore* (1983), *Just Looking: Essays on Art* (1990), and *Odd Jobs: Essays and Criticism* (1991). *Self-Consciousness* (1989) is an autobiographical memoir. His *Collected Poems 1953–1992* were published in 1993. *Due Considerations*, a volume of essays and criticism, appeared in 2007.

UPTON, Florence (1873–1922) Artist and illustrator, born in Flushing, New York, of English parents, educated at the National Academy of Design. She is famous for illustrating a series of thirteen texts written by her mother, Bertha Upton (1849–1912), from *The Adventures of Two Dutch Dolls and a 'Golliwogg'* (1895) to *Golliwogg in the African Jungle* (1909). There is some dispute as to which of them invented the name, but the Golliwogg, a gentlemanly and heroic figure in the books, became a highly popular toy, especially in Europe, where it was second only to the teddy bear. It was adopted as a brand image by the English makers of preserves James Robertson, 1910–2001, and used, negatively, as a character by Enid *Blyton. From the 1960s the golliwog has been regarded as a racist creation and widely censored. See N. S. Davis's *A Lark Ascends: Florence K. Upton, Artist and Illustrator* (1992).

UPWARD, Edward (1903–2009) Novelist, born in Essex, and educated at Repton School and Corpus Christi College, Cambridge, with Christopher *Isherwood, whose lifelong friend he became; at Cambridge they both wrote *Barbellion-inspired diaries, and invented the surreal imaginary world of 'Mortmere'. A long Mortmere fragment appeared in Upward's *The Railway Accident and Other Stories* (1969) and its fantasies are described in Isherwood's *Lions and Shadows* (1938), in which Upward appears as Allen Chalmers. Upward's *Journey to the Border* (1938) describes the progress of a neurotic tutor in an upper-middle-class household towards commitment to the workers' movement (Upward was for some years a member of the Communist Party); his trilogy *In the Thirties* (1962), *The Rotten Elements* (1969), and *No Home but the Struggle* (1977), published together in 1977 as *The Spiral Ascent*, describes the alternating political and artistic conflicts, over some decades, in the life of Marxist poet and schoolmaster Alan Sebrill. The last, and most introspective, volume affirms the narrator's need for a union of personal and political commitment in his work.

URFÉ, Honoré d' (1567–1625) French novelist, author of *L'Astrée* (1607–27), a pastoral novel set in 5th-century Gaul celebrating the virtues of a refined life which enjoyed great popularity, influencing English playwrights under Charles I. It was praised by Jean de *La Fontaine and Jean-Jacques *Rousseau for the sensitivity of its descriptions of nature.

Urizen A principal character in the symbolic books of William *Blake, represented as god of reason and law-maker, to some extent to be identified with the Hebrew Jehovah. His name might derive from 'your reason' or from the Greek term *οὐριζειν*, to limit. *The Book of Urizen* (1794) is Blake's version of the myth of Genesis, describing the creation of the material world by Urizen from the 'abominable void', from which is engendered Urizen's opponent, Los, and Pity, the first female form, who is named Enitharmon. The spirit of the book is of anguish, revolt, and suffering. Urizen, after long struggles with Los, surveys his creation with a sorrow that creates a web, 'The Net of Religion'. In the first plate of **Europe*, Urizen is portrayed majestically as an aged, Newtonian figure leaning down from the sun with a great pair of compasses to create the world.

Urn Burial See HYDRIOTAPHIA.

URQUHART, Sir Thomas (1611–60) Writer and translator of Cromarty, Scotland, educated at King's College, Aberdeen. He fought at Turriff against the Covenanters, withdrew to London, and was knighted in 1641. At the Royalist defeat at Worcester he lost many of his manuscripts, was imprisoned 1651–2, and died abroad. His best-known work is a translation of the first three books of *Rabelais, the first two 1653, the third 1693 (completed by Peter *Motteux). He wrote a plan for a universal language, and curious treatises on mathematics and other subjects, with strange Greek titles, collected in 1774 and 1834, among them *Ekskubalauron* (1651, known as 'The Jewel'), which contains in his 'Vindication of the Honour of Scotland' the story of the 'Admirable' *Crichton. He is said to have died laughing at news of the *Restoration. See *The Jewel*, ed. R. D. S. Jack and R. J. Lyall (1984); R. Boston, *The Admirable Urquhart* (1975).

USK, Thomas (*c*.1354–1388) The author of *The Testament of Love*. He was a professional scribe who became under-sheriff of London in 1387, by the mandate of Richard II. He became embroiled in the complex London politics of the 1380s and experienced only intermittent success in public life. Eventually accused of involvement in a plot against the duke of Gloucester, he was proceeded against and executed by the 'Merciless Parliament' in 1388. *The Testament of Love* is an allegorical and philosophical prose work with some autobiographical elements, written as a dialogue between a prisoner and a Lady in the tradition of *Boethius' *Consolation of Philosophy.* It was written after 1384, as is clear from its borrowings from **Troilus and Criseyde* and **Piers Plowman*. The first letters of the sections form an acrostic reading 'Margaret of virtu have merci on THINUSK', i.e. 'thine Usk'. See *The Testament of Love*, ed. R. A. Shoaf (1998).

Usnach, the Sons of *See* DEIRDRE.

USSHER, James (1581–1656) Theologian, historian, and key figure in the development of the Church of Ireland. Born in Dublin and educated at the newly founded Trinity College there, Ussher was the nephew of Richard *Stanihurst, with whom he maintained correspondence across the Reformation divide. He was appointed archbishop of Armagh in 1625. His *Annales Veteris et Novi Testamenti* (1650, 1654), a chronology of world history from the Creation to the dispersal of the Jews, was the source of the dates later inserted in the margins of the Authorized Version of the Bible. Ussher fixes the time of Creation as 23 October 4004 BC.

Uther Pendragon In the Arthurian legend, king of the Britons and father of *Arthur. Pendragon means 'chief dragon'. The narrative outline of Uther's life was established in *Geoffrey of Monmouth's *History of the Kings of Britain*. He was the brother of Aurelius Ambrosius and Constans. After he became king of the Britons, he lusted after *Igraine, wife of Gorlois, duke of Cornwall. He picked a quarrel with Gorlois and was transformed by Merlin's magic into his shape, whereupon he slept with Igraine three hours after Gorlois's death. In Sir Thomas *Malory's version, Arthur was conceived that night and Uther subsequently married Igraine.

'Utilitarianism' An influential essay by John Stuart *Mill, first published in a series of articles in **Fraser's Magazine* in 1861, in book form 1863. The term 'utilitarian' was first adopted by Mill in 1823, from John Galt's **Annals of the Parish*. In this work, Mill, while accepting the Benthamite principle (*see* BENTHAM, JEREMY) that Utility, or the greatest happiness of the greatest number, is the foundation of morals, departs from it by maintaining that pleasures differ in kind or quality as well as in quantity, 'that some *kinds* of pleasure are more desirable and more valuable than others'; also by recognizing in 'the conscientious feelings of mankind' an 'internal sanction' to be added to Bentham's 'external sanctions'. 'The social feelings of mankind, the desire to be in unity with our fellow creatures' constitute 'the ultimate sanction of the greatest happiness, morality'.

Utopia The principal literary work of Sir Thomas *More, is an essay in two books, originally written in Latin and published in 1516 at Louvain: *Erasmus supervised its printing. The form was influenced by such contemporary narratives of voyages as the accounts of the explorer Amerigo Vespucci (1454–1512), printed 1507. The first book describes the current condition of England, implicitly contrasting it in Book II with the account of 'Utopia', 'Nowhere land', described by Raphael Hythloday, whom More says he met at Antwerp. The Utopians practise a form of communism, extending a national system of education to men and women alike, and allowing the freest toleration of religion: they have only recently been introduced to Christianity and to printing. The work at once became popular, and was translated by Ralph Robinson (1520–77) into English in 1551, and into French, German, Italian, and Spanish.

The name 'Utopia', coined by More, passed into general usage, and has been adopted to describe, retrospectively, *Plato's *Republic*, and many subsequent fictions, fantasies, and blueprints for the future, including Francis *Bacon's **New Atlantis*, James *Harrington's *The *Commonwealth of Oceana*, William *Morris's *News from Nowhere*, and Edward *Bellamy's *Looking Backward*. Satirical utopias include Jonathan *Swift's **Gulliver's Travels* and Samuel *Butler's **Erewhon*. The word *'dystopia' ('bad place') has been coined to describe nightmare visions of the future, such as Aldous *Huxley's **Brave New World*, Evgenii Ivanovich Zamiatin's *We*, and George *Orwell's **Nineteen Eighty-Four*, in which present-day social, political, and technological tendencies are projected in an extreme and unpleasant form. Many works of *science fiction use the utopian and dystopian forms.

UTTLEY, Alison (1884–1976) Writer, born in Cromford, Derbyshire, the second female honours graduate from the University of Manchester (physics). Author of series about 'Little Grey Rabbit' and 'Sam Pig', she wrote over 100 books, including the distinguished historical fantasy *A Traveller in Time* (1940) and many country books, notably the largely autobiographical *The Country Child* (1931). Her papers are at the John Rylands Library, Manchester; Denis Judd's biography was revised in 2001.

Vala *See* FOUR ZOAS, THE.

Valentine and Orson The subject of an early French romance. Bellisant, King Pepin's sister, is married to Alexander, emperor of Constantinople. Accused of adultery, she is banished. Orson, one of her children, is carried away by a bear and reared as a wild man. The other (Valentine) is found by Pepin and brought up as a knight. Valentine meets Orson, conquers him, brings him to court, and tames him. The principal subsequent adventure is the imprisonment of Bellisant, Valentine, and Orson in the castle of Clerimond, sister of the giant Ferragus, and their rescue by Pacolet, Ferragus' dwarf messenger, who has a wooden magic horse which conveys him instantly wherever he wishes.

The story appeared in English *c.*1510 translated by Henry Watson, and again *c.*1555 as *The History of the Two Valiant Brethren, Valentine and Orson*. A ballad in Thomas *Percy's **Reliques* deals with it.

Valentinian, The Tragedy of A play by John *Fletcher, performed between 1610 and 1612, published 1647. A sensational drama with elements of *revenge tragedy, it deals with the vengeance of Maximus, a general under Valentinian III, for the dishonour of his wife by the emperor, and her suicide. A dense web of intrigue and treachery results in the slow death of Valentinian by poisoning (to the accompaniment of the well-known lyric 'Care-charming sleep'), and the subsequent death of Maximus, poisoned, again to musical accompaniment, by the widowed empress Eudoxa, as he is inaugurated as Valentinian's successor.

VALÉRY, Paul (1871–1945) French poet, essayist, and critic. As a young man he was deeply influenced by the *symbolists and, in particular, by the work of Stéphane *Mallarmé. He became widely known for the poetry of *La Jeune Parque* (1917: *The Young Fate*) and the collection *Charmes* (1922: *Charms*), the latter containing 'Le Cimetière marin' ('The Graveyard by the Sea'), memorably translated by Cecil *Day-Lewis (1946), by Graham D. Martin (1971), and (into Scots) by Douglas Young (1989). He wrote little poetry after 1922, but published essays on a variety of literary, philosophical, and aesthetic subjects (*Variété* [*Variety*] 1924–44) and two Socratic dialogues, *Eupalinos ou l'architecte* and *L'Âme et la danse* (1923: *Eupalinos, or The Architect* and *Soul and Dance*). His notebooks (*Cahiers*), covering the years 1894 to 1945, were published posthumously.

Valperga, *or The Life and Adventures of Castruccio, Prince of Lucca* A novel by Mary *Shelley, published 1823. The successor to **Frankenstein*, it is a *historical fiction about the 14th-century Italian warrior Castruccio, tyrannical but fascinating, as he seeks to reclaim the land from which his family had been exiled by the Guelfs. It also recounts his ill-fated liaisons with two women: Beatrice, a beautiful heretic, and Euthenasia, the countess of Valperga, who is torn between Castruccio and her Guelf family.

VANBRUGH, Sir John (1664–1726) Dramatist and architect, son of a London tradesman, whose father, a merchant of Ghent, had fled to England from Alva's persecutions. He was imprisoned in France between 1688 and 1692 for spying. In 1696 he produced *The *Relapse, or Virtue in Danger*, with immense success, and *The *Provoked Wife* in 1697. His other principal comedies are *The Confederacy* (1705) and *The *Provok'd Husband*, which he left unfinished and Colley *Cibber completed and brought out in 1728. His collected dramatic works appeared in 1730. He, together with William *Congreve, was specially attacked by Jeremy *Collier in his **Short View*.

Vanbrugh's first building was Castle Howard, 1699–1726. This already shows the grandeur and dramatic quality of his style, which reaches its climax in Blenheim Palace. Nicholas Hawksmoor (1661–1736) assisted him in many of his projects. Vanbrugh was Clarenceux king-of-arms and in 1714 was the first man knighted by George I.
See RESTORATION.

VANCE, Jack (1916–) Born San Francisco; writer generally of *science fiction and *fantasy, but also of mysteries under his real name, John Holbrook Vance. He is noted for the engagingly baroque invention of the stories collected as *The Dying Earth* (1970) and the novels in the 'Alastor' series, beginning with *Trullion: Alastor 2262* (1973), with their imagined societies sparkling with a sense of ironized decadence.

Vancenza By Mary *Robinson (1757/8–1800), published 1792. Subtitled 'the Dangers of Credulity: A Moral Tale', *Vancenza* embeds a moral message within a historical narrative. Set in 15th-century Spain, it portrays a virtuous but doomed heroine, Elvira. Uneducated in the ways of the world, she dies of a fever on learning that the man she loves is her half-brother. A plea for the improvement of female education, the novel sold out on publication, due, in part, to Robinson's personal celebrity.

VANDERMEER, Jeff (1968–) American writer, born in Belfonte, Pennsylvania; his work is influenced by *science fiction and *fantasy. *City of Saints and Madmen* (2001) is a collection of short stories set in Ambergris, an imaginary city which is also the location of *Shriek: An Afterword* (2006).

van der POST, Sir Laurens Jan (1906–96) Writer, soldier, farmer, and explorer, born in South Africa, whose many works of travel, anthropology, and adventure (much influenced by Carl *Jung) include *The Lost World of the Kalahari* (1958), *The Heart of the Hunter* (1961), *A Story Like the Wind* (1972), *A Far-Off Place* (1974), *A Mantis Carol* (1975), *Jung and the Story of our Time* (1976), *Yet Being Someone Other* (1982), and *A Walk with a White Bushman* (1986). He was knighted in 1981.

Van DYCK, Sir Anthony (1599–1641) Flemish painter, born in Antwerp, who worked in *Rubens's studio in his youth. In 1623 he came to England as court painter to Charles I. He was knighted and enjoyed great success, painting many portraits of the royal family and the court. He married a lady of the Scottish house of Ruthven in 1640. He died in England and was buried in Old St Paul's. Van Dyck's success lay in his ability to portray the poetic ideals that sustained the Caroline court. He painted the king both as warrior monarch and as perfect gentleman; his mythological portraits, like Venetia, Lady Digby (1600–33), as Prudence, and those which convey an Arcadian mood suggest the atmosphere of the *masque. Van Dyck was the friend of men of letters and of the most cultivated patrons of his day; among others, he painted the second earl of Arundel (1585–1646), William *Laud, Endymion *Porter, and Thomas *Killigrew the elder. Edmund *Waller praised his portraits for showing

> Not the form alone, and grace
> But art and power of a face.

See Susan J. Barnes, *Anton van Dyck* (2004).

Vanity Fair A novel by W. M. *Thackeray, published in numbers 1847–8, illustrated by the author. The story is set at the time of the Napoleonic Wars, and gives a satirical picture of a worldly society, which Thackeray intended to illuminate his own times. Its title is derived from John Bunyan's *The *Pilgrim's Progress*. The novel follows the fortunes of Rebecca (Becky) Sharp, the penniless orphaned daughter of an artist and a French opera dancer, and Amelia Sedley, the sheltered child of a rich City merchant. The two girls, as unlike in character as they are in fortune, have been educated at Miss Pinkerton's Academy for young ladies. Becky fails to force a proposal of marriage from Amelia's elephantine brother Jos, and becomes governess to the children of Sir Pitt Crawley, a brutal old man. She manages to charm the Crawley family, becoming a favourite of Miss Crawley, Sir Pitt's rich and capricious sister. When his wife dies Sir Pitt proposes to Becky, but she has to confess that she is already married, to his younger son Rawdon. The young couple abruptly fall from favour with Miss Crawley, and have to live on Becky's wits.

Meanwhile Amelia's apparently secure life has disintegrated. Her father has lost his money, and her engagement to George Osborne, the handsome but shallow son of another City magnate, has been broken off in consequence. William Dobbin, George's awkward, loyal friend, who secretly loves Amelia, persuades George to defy his father and marry Amelia, and Mr Osborne disinherits his son.

George, Rawdon, and Dobbin are all in the army, and Amelia and Becky accompany their husbands to Belgium, where Becky carries on an intrigue with George Osborne. George is killed at Waterloo, and Amelia, with her baby son Georgy, goes to live in poverty with her parents, while Becky and Rawdon manage to make a brilliant display in London society on 'nothing a year'. Amelia's devotion to her son is contrasted with Becky's neglect of hers, but she is finally forced by poverty to part with Georgy, who is growing up to be much like his father, to his grandfather. Dobbin, despairing of winning Amelia's love, has spent ten years in India. Becky and Rawdon part, after Rawdon has discovered his wife in a compromising situation with Lord Steyne, who has, it turns out, been paying for Becky's extravagances. Becky leads an increasingly disreputable life on the Continent, and it is hinted that she may be responsible for the death of Jos Sedley, who has insured his life in her favour. Rawdon becomes governor of Coventry Island, and dies of fever. Amelia steadfastly refuses to marry Dobbin, until a chance meeting with Becky, who tells her of George Osborne's infidelity. Disillusioned, she marries Dobbin, but by then his love for her has cooled. *Vanity Fair* has never lost its standing as Thackeray's most popular and widely admired novel.

Vanity of Human Wishes, The A poem in heroic couplets by Samuel *Johnson, published 1749, in imitation of the Tenth Satire of *Juvenal. It was the first complete work to which Johnson put his name. Less topical and more sombre than his other long poem, **London*, it prefigures the serious ethical concerns of **Rasselas*. Johnson illustrates the doomed futility of various ambitions—for power, learning, and military glory—citing the examples of Cardinal Wolsey (1470/1–1530), the earl of *Clarendon, Archbishop *Laud, Jonathan *Swift, and others: the passage on Charles XII of Sweden (d. 1718), whose glorious military career ended in bathetic failure, is the most celebrated in the poem, 'quite perfect in form', according to T. S. *Eliot. The bleak *Stoicism of Juvenal's conclusion is modulated by Johnson's hard-won Christian perspective.

van VOGT, Alfred Elton (1912–2000) Canadian-born *science fiction writer, born in Manitoba, later resident in California. His first story, 'Black Destroyer' (1939) became part of *The Voyage of the Space Beagle* (1950). The popular *Slan* (1946), and *The World of Null-A* (1948) are examples of the dreamlike plot reversals that influenced Philip K. *Dick.

VARGAS LLOSA, Mario (1936–) Novelist, playwright, essayist, journalist, and critic, born in Arequipa (Peru) and educated in Lima at the Leoncio Prado Military Academy and San Marcos University. Fleetingly a communist, and a supporter of the Cuban Revolution, he became disillusioned with the left and narrowly failed to be elected president of Peru as a liberal in 1990. *La ciudad y los perros* (1963: *The Time of the Hero*) is a scandalous exposé of the Leoncio Prado Military Academy and a key novel of the *Boom. This and later works show the influence of William *Faulkner's manipulation of time, narrative viewpoint, and structure. His *La casa verde* (1966: *The Green House*) and *Conversación en la catedral* (1969: *Conversation in the Cathedral*) are experimentally realist novels which depict social evils in Peru. While *La tía Julia y el escribidor* (1977: *Aunt Julia and the Script Writer*) is a comic, semi-autobiographical novel, *La guerra del fin del mundo* (1981: *The War of the End of the World*) portrays fanaticism in 19th-century Brazil, and *La fiesta del chivo* (2000: *The Feast of the Goat*) the horrors of dictatorship in the Dominican Republic. His memoir, *El pez en el agua* (*A Fish in the Water*), was published in 1993; two collections of essays have appeared in English as *Making Waves* (1996) and *Touchstones* (2007). See Efraín Kristal, *Temptation of the Word: The Novels of Mario Vargas Llosa* (1998).

VARLEY, John (1947–) American author of libertarian *science fiction, born in Austin, Texas. His work is likened to that of Robert A. *Heinlein, who is explicitly referred to in *The Golden Globe* (2004). Varley's futures, as in *The Ophiuchi Hotline* (1977) assume cloning and sex change as routine possibilities.

VASARI, Giorgio (1511–74) Italian painter, architect, and author of *The Lives of the Most Excellent Italian Architects, Painters and Sculptors* (1550 and 1568), for generations the main source for the history of Italian art. Selections translated by G. Bull appeared in 1965 and 1987. See Patricia Rubin, *Giorgio Vasari* (1995).

VASSILTCHIKOV, Princess Marie Illarionovna (1917–78) Diarist, born in St Petersburg, Russia, to aristocratic parents who left Russia after the 1917 Revolution, and lived in Germany, France, and Lithuania. She worked in Germany during the Second World War and kept a diary which described the plot to kill Hitler and the bombing of Berlin, later published as *Berlin Diaries 1940–45* (1988).

***Vathek,** an Arabian Tale* By William *Beckford, published in English 1786. The book was written in French and translated into English, with the author's assistance, by Samuel Henley, who published his translation with copious scholarly notes on matters Eastern, without the author's consent. It was one of the most successful of the *oriental tales then in fashion.

The cruel and sensual Caliph Vathek, whose eye can kill with a glance, is compelled, by the influence of his sorceress mother and the unbridled pride of his own nature, to serve Eblis, the Devil. He makes a sacrifice of 50 children, and sets off from his capital, Samarah, to the ruined city of Istakar, where he is to be shown the treasure of the pre-Adamite sultans. On the way he falls in love with Nouronihar, the exquisite daughter of one of his emirs, who accompanies him on his journey. After various exotic and terrifying incidents, he obtains admission to the great subterranean halls of Eblis, only to discover the sickening worthlessness of the riches that he sees there, and to receive the penalty of his sin, when his own heart and the hearts of all the damned burst into flame in their living bodies. The febrile excitement of the story is sustained by the use of rapid action, exotic locales, and exaggerated passions, often cruel or prurient. William *Hazlitt objected to 'the diabolical levity of its contempt for mankind', but critics disagree as to whether the tale is related with a sly irony, with some seeing black humour throughout in the manner of Voltaire's **Candide*. Because of its supernatural elements, the novel has sometimes, perhaps mistakenly, been associated with the *Gothic novel. Beckford wrote three further 'Episodes' (the last unfinished) for insertion in the story, and included them in his French version of 1815.

vaudeville Term deriving from a combination of the irreverent 'vau de Vire' from Normandy and the courtly 'voix de ville' of Paris, originally denoting a satirical song. Because of the incorporation of such songs in French musical theatre, the term came to refer to music-hall entertainments and variety shows.

'Vaudracour and Julia' *See* WORDSWORTH, WILLIAM.

VAUGHAN, Henry (1621–95) Poet, born at Newton-upon-Usk, Breconshire, the eldest son of a Welsh gentleman, Thomas Vaughan of Tretower. Henry's twin brother Thomas *Vaughan became a 'natural magician'. Probably in 1628 a third brother William was born. Henry and Thomas were brought up bilingual in Welsh and English, tutored by Matthew Herbert, a noted schoolmaster at Llangattock. By May 1638 Thomas was at Jesus College, Oxford, and Henry almost certainly accompanied him. Around 1640 Henry probably went to London to study law. He returned to Breconshire, probably at the outbreak of the Civil War, and saw military service on the Royalist side. About 1646 he married Catherine Wise. They had a son, Thomas, and three daughters. His wooing of Catherine is apparently recalled in the poem 'Upon the Priory Grove' printed in *Poems with the Tenth Satire of Juvenal Englished* (1646), his first collection. His second, *Olor Iscanus* (The Swan of Usk), has a dedication bearing the date 1647, but was not published till 1651. The poems in these two volumes are almost wholly secular, including fashionable love verses and translations from *Ovid, the Latin poet and rhetorician Ausonius (*c.*310–395), *Boethius, and the Polish Jesuit Latin poet Casimir Sarbiewski (1595–1640). The great religious poetry of Vaughan's next volume, *Silex Scintillans* (1650: *Flashing Flint*), suggests a profound spiritual experience, perhaps connected with the death of his brother William (1648) and the defeat of the Royalist cause. Further devotional works followed: *The Mount of Olives, or Solitary Devotions* (1652) and *Flores Solitudinis* (1654), which includes a life of St Paulinus of

Nola. In 1655 the second edition of *Silex Scintillans* had an added second part with a translation of the *Hermetical Physic* of Heinrich Nolle (*fl.*1612–19). A translation of Nolle's *The Chemist's Key* followed in 1657. After his first wife's death, Vaughan married her younger sister Elizabeth, probably in 1655. They had a son, Henry, and three daughters. By that date he had been a medical practitioner 'for many years with good success'. *Thalia Rediviva* (1678) contained poems by both brothers. Vaughan acknowledged his great debt to George *Herbert, but his own religious poetry is unique and his beliefs are unusual. He thought that plants and animals would be resurrected at the last judgement, and that even stones had feeling. He was seized with the idea of the child's recollections of prenatal glory. He was fascinated by Hermeticism (*see* Hermes Trismegistus), and the idea of sympathetic bonds uniting microcosm and macrocosm. Many of his poems share ideas and even phrases with his brother Thomas's alchemical treatises. On the title pages of *Olor Iscanus* and *Silex Scintillans* Vaughan calls himself a 'Silurist', presumably because his native Brecon was anciently inhabited by the British tribe of Silures. See *Works*, ed. L. C. Martin (2nd edn 1957); *Complete Poems*, ed. Alan Rudrum (1976); F. E. Hutchinson, *Henry Vaughan: A Life and Interpretation* (1947; corrected repr. 1971); S. Davies, *Henry Vaughan* (1995). The Vaughan Society was founded in 1995.

VAUGHAN, Thomas (1621–66) Philosopher and alchemist, twin brother of Henry *Vaughan, whose entry gives details of his background. Thomas, an Anglican minister, was evicted from his living in 1650 for alleged misconduct. He published treatises on alchemy and magic, including *Anima Magia Abscondita* (1650), *Magia Adamica* (1650), *Aula Lucis* (1652), and a preface to a *Rosicrucian work, *The Fame and Confession of the Fraternity…of the Rosy Cross* (1652). He published under the pseudonym 'Eugenius Philalethes' ('Good Truth-Loving Man'), and engaged in furious controversy with Henry More (*see* Cambridge Platonists) who had attacked his *Anthroposophia* (1650) as nonsense. After the *Restoration he was patronized by Sir Robert Moray (1608/9–73), first president of the *Royal Society. Together they accompanied the court to Oxford to flee the plague in 1665, and Vaughan died at Albury. Jonathan *Swift described him as a writer of the greatest gibberish 'ever published in any language'. *Works*, ed. A. Rudrum with J. Drake-Brockman (1984).

VAUGHAN WILLIAMS, Ralph (1872–1958) Composer, educated at Charterhouse and the Royal College of Music, where he was taught by Hubert *Parry and Charles Villiers *Stanford and formed a friendship with Gustav *Holst. He also studied at Trinity College, Cambridge, where he met Bertrand *Russell. His interest in *folk song and early English composers (signalled in the orchestral *Fantasia on a Theme of Thomas *Tallis*, 1910) enabled him to break the dominance of *Romanticism. He profoundly reshaped English hymnody with his *English Hymnal* (1906). His first published work was the song 'Linden Lea' (1902, words by William *Barnes); other English settings include poems from D. G. Rossetti's 'The *House of Life' (1903), *Songs of Travel* (Robert Louis *Stevenson, 1904), the A. E. *Housman cycle *On Wenlock Edge* (1909), and *Five Mystical Songs* (George *Herbert, 1911). Later came settings of *Chaucer, John *Skelton, *Ten *Blake Songs* (1957), and many choral settings of Walt *Whitman. *Serenade to Music* (1938) set words from the last act of *The *Merchant of Venice*. *An Oxford Elegy* (1949) embeds Matthew Arnold's 'The *Scholar-Gipsy' and *'Thyrsis' in a work for speaker, chorus, and orchestra. The opera *Hugh the Drover* (1924) leaned heavily on folk song, and *Sir John in Love* (1929) counterposed an English *Falstaff to *Verdi's. *Riders to the Sea* (1937) is an intense setting of John Millington *Synge's tragedy. His opera *The Pilgrim's Progress* (1951) was based on John *Bunyan; another opera, *Thomas the Rymer*, was nearly complete when he died. Vaughan Williams declined a knighthood, but accepted the Order of Merit in 1935.

VAUVENARGUES, Luc de Clapiers, marquis de (1715–47) French moralist. After serving as an army officer in the War of the Austrian Succession, he was forced by ill health into premature retirement. His *Introduction à la connaissance de l'esprit humain, suivie de réflexions et de maximes* (1746: *Introduction to the Understanding of the Human Mind, Followed by Reflections and Maxims*) put him in the literary tradition of Blaise *Pascal and *La Rochefoucauld. Less sceptical than the first and less cynical than the second, he sought in people's natural feelings the source of their best thought and the springs of their moral energy.

VAUX, Thomas, second Baron Vaux (1509–56) Poet, said to have been educated at Cambridge. He was employed by Thomas Wolsey (1470/1–1530) and *Henry VIII until 1536, when he fell from favour until Mary's accession. A contributor to Richard *Tottel's *Miscellany* and *The *Paradise of Dainty Devices*, he is chiefly remembered now as the author of 'The Aged Lover Renounceth Love', the poem sung by the grave-digger in *Hamlet*. George *Puttenham praised 'the facility of his metre, and the aptness of his descriptions'.

VEGA, Garcilaso *See* Garcilaso de la Vega.

VEGA CARPIO, Lope Félix de (1562–1635) Spanish poet and playwright, born and educated in Madrid. He took part in the expedition to the Azores in 1582, and sailed with the Armada in 1588, an experience which inspired one of his less-regarded works, an epic in ten cantos, *La Dragontea* (1598), which violently attacks England and Francis *Drake. His personal life was passionate and turbulent; his many love poems are addressed to several mistresses. Immensely prolific and versatile in many genres, he is regarded as the founder of Spanish Golden Age drama; he claimed to have written 1,500 plays, of which several hundred survive. These include dramas of intrigue and chivalry, historical dramas, sacred dramas, plays of peasant life, and plays on biblical subjects. Other works include pastoral romances, imitations of Torquato *Tasso, and a novel in dialogue called *La Dorotea* (1632). The energy and fecundity of his imagination made a profound impact not only in Spain, but on European literature in general, particularly on that of France. See Melveena McKendrick, *Theatre in Spain 1490–1700* (1989).

Venice Preserv'd, *or A Plot Discovered* A tragedy in blank verse by Thomas *Otway, produced 1682. Jaffeir, a noble Venetian youth, secretly married to Belvidera, is persuaded by Pierre to join a conspiracy against the republic. Finding her father is one of the intended victims, Belvidera persuades Jaffeir to reveal the plot to the Senate, on condition the conspirators' lives will be spared. They are arrested, and the senators, despite their promise, condemn them to death. Jaffeir threatens to kill Belvidera unless she secures their pardon. She succeeds, but too late, and she goes mad. Jaffeir stabs Pierre on the scaffold and then himself. Belvidera dies broken-hearted. With Thomas *Betterton as Jaffeir and Elizabeth *Barry as Belvidera, the play was well received and remained popular throughout the 18th and early 19th centuries. The bawdy comic scenes featuring the masochistic senator Antonio (a caricature of the first earl of *Shaftesbury) were often cut.

Venus In Roman mythology the goddess of love (Greek 'Aphrodite'), daughter of *Jupiter, wife of Vulcan, mother of *Cupid, and lover of Mars. In the **Aeneid* she is the hero's mother by the mortal Anchises and tries to protect her son from *Juno. *Lucretius' *De Rerum Natura* 1 opens with an invocation to her, as does Chaucer's **Troilus and Criseyde*, III. She is also a major force in *The *Faerie Queene*, IV. x, and Edmund *Spenser' telling of the story of Venus and Adonis in III. vi (derived from *Ovid's *Metamorphoses*, 10) is very different from *Shakespeare's.

Venus and Adonis A narrative poem by *Shakespeare, published in 1593, the same year in which Christopher Marlowe's **Hero and Leander* was registered, and dedicated, like *The *Rape of Lucrece* (1594), to Henry Wriothesley, earl of Southampton, who has been connected with the *sonnets. Based on a short episode in *Ovid's *Metamorphoses*, the poem is written in the six-line stanza form known as *sesta rima*, a quatrain followed by a couplet, which Edmund *Spenser used in **Astrophel* (1595) and Thomas *Lodge in **Scilla's Metamorphosis* (1589). Shakespeare's poem was probably his first publication, and was first printed by Richard Field, another Stratford man, in 1593: it was extremely popular, being reprinted at least fifteen times before 1640.

Venus, in love with the youth Adonis, keeps him from hunting but cannot win his love. She begs him to meet her the next day, but he is then to hunt the boar. She tries in vain to dissuade him. When the morning comes she hears his hounds at bay; terrified, she searches for him and finds him killed by the boar.

VERA, Yvonne (1964–2005) Zimbabwean novelist, short story writer, and editor of remarkable originality and imaginative vigour. Her work, alongside that of Bessie *Head, broke the mould of African women's writing, incorporating in a distinctive narrative voice violent revelations, lyrical evocations of place, and the vitality of orality. Vera was born in Bulawayo and graduated and obtained her doctorate in Canada. Returning to Zimbabwe in 1995, she was regional director of the Zimbabwe National Gallery at Bulawayo 1997–2003. Despite her love for her country, she left Zimbabwe for Canada reluctantly in 2004 because of the oppressive political climate. All her books appeared first in Zimbabwe except the last which was published in the USA. Her first book was a collection of short stories, *Why Don't You Carve Other Animals?* (1992), in which she opens up twin themes that will be pursued in her later books, the oppressed position of peasant women and the power of the imagination to liberate. *Nehanda* (1993) is set in the 1890s during the African rebellion against colonialism in Rhodesia but told in the present tense; Nehanda's spirit possession inspires her people, through dreams and traditional lore, to resist: 'We danced the future into our midst.' In *Without a Name* (1994), which can be read allegorically, Mazvita is raped during the war of liberation and kills her son, betrayed as she is by African patriarchal domination. Another taboo is exposed in *Under the Tongue* (1996); Zhizha knows 'a stone is buried in my mouth, carried under my tongue'. The silent stone is the fact that her father raped her, symbolizing the systematic abuse of African women within black as well as colonial rule. *Butterfly Burning* (1998) takes place in 1940s Rhodesia; *The Stone Virgins* (2002) is set in post-independence Zimbabwe.

Vercelli Book An Old English manuscript, made in England before the year 1000, now in the possession of the chapter of Vercelli in north Italy. It contains prose sermons and about 3,500 lines of Old English poetry; its most distinguished contents are the poems **Dream of the Rood* and **Andreas*, and two of the four signed poems of **Cynewulf*: *Elene* and *The Fates of the Apostles*. See ASPR 2, *The Vercelli Book Poems*, ed. F. P. Magoun (1960).

Verdant Green, The Adventures of Mr *see* BRADLEY, EDWARD.

VERDI, Giuseppe (1813–1901) Italian composer of operas, of which two, *I due foscari* (1844) and *Il corsaro* (*The Corsair*, 1848), are based on texts by Lord *Byron. Three more are based on William *Shakespeare, beginning with *Macbeth* (1847): here Verdi gave his librettist (Francesco Piave) an unusually rough passage in his determination to bring the text under his imaginative control. He took immense pains over the first production, and subjected the opera to a thorough revision for Paris in 1865. The Paris version, in which the opera is now heard, betrayed its dual origin, but Verdi was stung by Parisian criticism that he did not know his Shakespeare: 'Maybe I haven't done **Macbeth* justice', he wrote, 'but that I don't know, don't feel, don't understand Shakespeare—no, for God's sake no. I have had him in my hands from earliest youth, and I read and re-read him continually.' This preoccupation continued throughout his life, although his next project, for a **King Lear*, proved abortive: the problem of the libretto always made Verdi hesitate to set Shakespeare. But at the end of his life, after he had apparently concluded his career with the *Requiem Mass*, he found in Arrigo *Boito a librettist of inspiring skill and imagination. Their collaboration produced the two greatest of all Shakespeare operas: *Otello* (1887), which explored a fluid and emotionally responsive style, and the fleeting, boisterously tender wisdom of *Falstaff* (1893), Verdi's most personal expression of love for the English writer.

VERGA, Giovanni (1840–1922) Italian novelist, dramatist, and writer of short stories, born at Catania. His finest works portray life at the lower levels of society in his native Sicily. The novels *I malavoglia* (1881) and *Mastro-don Gesualdo* (1889) deal respectively with a family of poor Sicilian fisherfolk and an ambitious master stonemason in economic competition with the local gentry. The story 'Cavalleria rusticana' (1880: 'Rustic Chivalry'), after being dramatized by the author, was adapted as a libretto for Mascagni's opera. True to the principles of **verismo*, Verga sought to eliminate from his works all trace of his own personality and outlook, and perfected a unique narrative style, which combined the literary language with idioms and constructions from popular and dialect speech. His English translators include D. H. *Lawrence, whose *Little Novels of Sicily* (1925) and *Cavalleria rusticana and Other Stories* (1928) contain the best of Verga's tales. See also *Cavalleria rusticana*, trans. G. H. McWilliam (1999). Lawrence also translated the second of the great Sicilian novels under the title *Master don Gesualdo* (1923).

VERGIL, Polydore (*c.*1470–1555) Historian; he came from near Urbino, and arrived in England in 1502 as sub-collector of Peter's pence (an annual donation to the pope). He held various ecclesiastical preferments and was a friend of Sir Thomas *More and other English humanists. His *Anglica Historia* was published in 1534 and in revised and extended editions in 1546 and 1555; the chronicle is of special value for the reign of Henry VII. He was also author of a *Proverbiorum Libellus* (Venice, 1498) which anticipated *Erasmus' *Adagia*.

verismo A movement in 19th-century Italian literature akin to *naturalism, whose greatest exponent was the Sicilian Giovanni *Verga. The principle of making language and style harmonize with the social class and origins of the characters portrayed contrasted both with national policies for linguistic unification after the Unification of Italy (1870), and with Alessandro *Manzoni's programme for a standard literary language. The literature of *verismo* sought to document social conditions—particularly of the lower classes, but unlike the work of Émile *Zola, tends to focus more on the rural than the urban poor. *Verismo* influenced the early works of Gabriele *d'Annunzio and Luigi *Pirandello, and subsequently post-war *neo-realism.

VERLAINE, Paul (1844–96) French poet. Some of his poems appeared in *Le Parnasse contemporain* of 1866; his *Poèmes saturniens* (*Saturnian Poems*) were published in the same year, and his *Fêtes galantes* in 1869. From the end of 1871 he came under the influence of Arthur *Rimbaud, with their intense relationship culminating in Verlaine's arrest and imprisonment, in 1873, for wounding Rimbaud with a revolver. Perhaps his most significant work, characterized by an intense musicality and metrical inventiveness, appeared in *Romances sans paroles* (1874: *Songs without Words*). His influential 'Art poétique' ('De la musique avant toute chose', 'Music before Everything') dates from the same time, but remained unpublished for ten years. *Sagesse* (*Wisdom*), a religious work, written after his conversion to Catholicism, appeared in 1881, *Jadis et naguère* (*Once Upon a Time*) in 1884, and in the same year he published a number of short studies of contemporary poets (including *Mallarmé and Rimbaud) under the title *Les Poètes maudits* (*The Outcast Poets*). Verlaine's relationship with Rimbaud is the subject of a play by Christopher *Hampton, *Total Eclipse* (1968).

VERNE, Jules (1828–1905) French novelist, who achieved great popularity with a series of books combining adventure and popular science. Among his most successful novels are *Voyage au centre de la terre* (1864: *Voyage to the Centre of the Earth*), *Vingt mille lieues sous les mers* (1870: *Twenty Thousand Leagues under the Sea*), and *Le Tour du monde en quatre-vingts jours* (1873: *Round the World in Eighty Days*), recounting the travels of the Englishman Phileas Fogg. These were quickly translated into English for one of three popular series of Verne's works in the 1860s and 1870s by, amongst others, W. H. G. *Kingston.

Vernon Manuscript The most substantial surviving collection of important Middle English writings. It was compiled in the Midlands in the later 1380s and its large number of vernacular religious texts may indicate both clerical and lay use. The Simeon Manuscript, kept in the British Library (BL MS Add. 22283), provides a close parallel. See the facsimile ed. A. I. Doyle (1987).

vers de société A term applied to a form of light verse dealing with events in polite society, usually in a satiric or playful tone, sometimes conversational, sometimes employing intricate forms such as the *villanelle or the *rondeau. English writers noted for their *vers de société* include Matthew *Prior, Oliver *Goldsmith, W. M. *Praed, C. S. *Calverley, Austin *Dobson, and Frederick *Locker-Lampson.

verse for children Isaac *Watts, in the Introduction to *Divine Songs* (1715), argued that verse was particularly suitable for the religious education of children; his advice was followed into the 19th century by versifiers such as Ann and Jane *Taylor, many of whom were parodied by Lewis *Carroll. A new pattern for childhood sentimental and realistic verse was set by Robert Louis *Stevenson with *A Child's Garden of Verses* (1885), imitated by writers such as A. A. *Milne and Rose Fyleman (1877–1957). Major poets, notably Rudyard *Kipling and Ted *Hughes, have contributed to the form. In the late 20th century there has been a revival, with a great deal of light, humorous, 'urchin verse', a form used to serious effect by, for example, Michael *Rosen and Roger *McGough, and *performance poetry, particularly by West Indian poets including Grace *Nichols and Benjamin *Zephaniah. See M. Styles, *From the Garden to the Street* (1998).

vers libre The French term often used in the early 20th century to denote many forms of metrically irregular verse, now more commonly referred to as *free verse.

VERTUE, George (1684–1756) Engraver and antiquary, whose notes for a history of the arts in Britain are a major source of information. His notebooks were sold to Horace *Walpole, who used them as a basis for his *Anecdotes of Painting in England*, 4 vols (1762–71); they were published separately by the Walpole Society, 6 vols (1930–55).

VERY, Jones (1813–80) American poet, essayist, and clergyman, born in Massachusetts. He became a friend of Ralph Waldo *Emerson and published a volume of poems characterized by Christian mysticism and reflecting a sense of mission. See Edwin Gittleman, *Jones Very: The Effective Years* (1965).

Very Hungry Caterpillar, The *See* CARLE, ERIC.

Very Woman, A *See* MASSINGER, PHILIP.

VESEY, Elizabeth (*c*.1715–1791) An Irishwoman, the first, and perhaps the most loved and successful, of the *Blue Stocking hostesses. In the early 1750s she decided, with the support of her husband, who was an Irish MP, to open her doors to literary and fashionable society for an entirely new kind of evening party. Vivacious, intelligent, but always modest, she liked to break her parties into small, ever-changing groups; Horace *Walpole, a devoted attender at all Blue Stocking functions, described her gatherings as 'Babels'. She set the pattern of Blue Stocking evenings for the next 50 years and, according to Hannah *More in her poem *Bas Bleu*, shared with Elizabeth *Montagu and Frances Boscawen (1719–1805) 'the triple crown' among Blue Stocking hostesses.

Vestiges of Creation *See* CHAMBERS, ROBERT.

VIAN, Boris *See* ABSURD, THEATRE OF THE.

VIAZEMSKY, Prince Petr Andreevich (1792–1878) Russian poet, critic, and memoirist, born in Moscow to a Russian aristocrat and an Irish mother (née O'Reilly). An intimate friend of Aleksandr *Pushkin, he himself wrote elegant, witty, and often bitingly satirical poems. He was a leading theorist of Romanticism, among the first to use the term in Russia (1817). He was a great admirer of Lord *Byron and Walter *Scott and did much to advance their reputation in Russia, but visiting England for the first and last time in 1838, he found much to criticize in English life and mores. Viazemsky's own work is little known in England, although he was one of the poets John Bowring (1792–1872) chose for his *Russian Anthology* (1821–3) to introduce Russian poetry to the English public. A sympathetic obituary by William *Ralston appeared in the *Athenaeum* in 1879.

'Vicar of Bray, The' A satirical song, dating from the early 18th century, in which a clergyman boasts of keeping his position by adapting to the various religious policies in force from Charles II to George I. The idea is much older. Thomas *Fuller, annotating the proverb 'the Vicar of Bray, will be Vicar of Bray still', cited an unnamed priest (sometimes identified as Simon Aleyn or Allen, vicar 1540–88) of the Berkshire village of Bray who had switched from Catholic to Protestant and back several times from the reign of Henry VIII to that of Elizabeth I, declaring 'I alwaies kept my Principle, which is this, to live and die the Vicar of Bray'.

Vicar of Bullhampton, The A novel by Anthony *Trollope, published 1870. Carry Brattle is a 'fallen woman', and her brother Sam is accused of the murder of a local farmer. There follows a battle between the arbitrary old marquis of Trowbridge and the vicar, Frank Fenwick, a worldly and energetic clergymen, who takes the side of the unfortunate Brattles. Sam's name is finally cleared and Carry is restored to her family at the mill. A sub-plot concerns the love of Fenwick's friend Harry Gilmore for Mary Lowther. She allows herself to be persuaded by the Fenwicks to accept him, but breaks her engagement when her previous suitor Walter Marrable unexpectedly comes into the family estate. The novel is concerned with the ideal of English manliness in action.

Vicar of Wakefield, The A novel by Oliver *Goldsmith, published 1766. The manuscript was sold to John *Newbery for £60 by Samuel *Johnson on Goldsmith's behalf, to prevent the author's arrest for debt. The story contains many of the plot devices of *sentimental fiction. Dr Primrose and his wife Deborah live an idyllic life in a country parish with their children, George and Moses, Olivia and Sophia. On the eve of George's wedding to Arabella Wilmot, the vicar loses all his money through the bankruptcy of a merchant, preventing the marriage. George leaves to find work, and the family move to a meagre living on the land of Squire Thornhill. An eccentric friend, Burchell, rescues Sophia from drowning, but her attraction to him is discouraged by her ambitious mother. The dashing squire captivates Olivia and encourages the social pretensions of Mrs Primrose. Olivia then disappears, causing the vicar to fall ill with anguish and fever. Thornhill reappears, now seriously courting Arabella; he obtains a commission in the army for his rival, George, who has been found in a troupe of travelling players. Primrose discovers his daughter Olivia being ejected from an inn; she has been seduced by Thornhill under pretence of marriage and cast off. The vicar receives her with joy, and they proceed home, only to find a terrible fire destroying their house. Thornhill is unrepentant, and offers to find a husband for the ailing Olivia. When he is rejected he demands his rent, which Primrose cannot pay, so Thornhill has him removed to the debtors' prison where he encounters every mortification: he hears of Olivia's death, is told that Sophia has been abducted, and finds that George has been brought half-dead into the prison, having been set upon by Thornhill's servants. At this point Sophia appears with Burchell. She explains how he rescued her from abduction by Thornhill, and in his gratitude the vicar sanctions her marriage to Burchell. Meanwhile George recognizes Burchell as Sir William Thornhill, Squire Thornhill's noble uncle. The nephew is denounced, and Arabella is united with George. It transpires that Olivia is not, after all, dead, and was in fact actually married to Thornhill. All proceed home, where Sophia and Sir William, with Arabella and George, are married at a double ceremony. The well-known poems 'The Hermit', the 'Elegy on the Death of a Mad Dog', and 'When lovely woman stoops to folly' are placed at three turning points of the story.

Vice A *fool or buffoon introduced into some of the *interludes and later moralities as a figure of evil. The descent of the figure from characters in *mystery cycles and *morality plays (such as 'The Vices', the *Seven Deadly Sins) is likely, though they are related too to the mischievous devil figure. See L. W. Cushman, *The Devil and the Vice in the English Dramatic Literature before Shakespeare* (1900; 1970); B. Spivack, *Shakespeare and the Allegory of Evil* (1958).

VICO, Giambattista (1668–1744) Italian philosopher and classical scholar. The son of a poor Neapolitan bookseller, he taught rhetoric at the University of Naples, and was appointed royal historiographer in 1735. His most important work is *Principii di una scienza nuova intorno alla natura delle nazioni* (1725; rev. 1729–30, 1744: *Principles of a New Science of Nations*), in which he developed his theory of historical change as a redemptive design based on 'corsi' and 'ricorsi'—recurring cycles of barbarism, heroism, and reason. To each of these phases correspond cultural, linguistic, and political modes, and at the end of each cycle of phases there is a fall into disorder from which the next cycle is born. The language of poetry, being metaphoric and sensuous, flourishes in the heroic age. It is typified by the Homeric *epics, for which Vico was first to postulate collective authorship. Prose enters with the age of reason. This scheme of cycles was put to artistic use by James *Joyce.

VICTORIA (1819–1901) Queen of England from 1837. She wrote innumerable letters and accumulated over 100 volumes of diaries and journals, kept from the age of 13 until shortly before her death. Much was excised by her family, at her wish, but many selections have been published. They are factual and practical, but observant and often vivid in detail. Her only writings published in her lifetime were *Leaves from a Journal of our Life in the Highlands 1848–61*, which appeared in 1868. The queen's love of Scotland enlivens her observations on the views, the weather, and the domestic events of her holidays. Expeditions, such as that up Lochnagar, are undertaken in all weathers, by pony and on foot, with lengthy pauses for spartan picnics and to watch Prince Albert shoot. *More Leaves* covered the years 1862–3 and appeared in 1883. Apart from her huge official correspondence, the queen's lively letters to her eldest daughter Vicky have been published, together with a selection of her daughter's replies.

In her diaries the queen notes her reading, which included sermons, *Shakespeare, Thomas *Macaulay, Frances *Burney, and Jane *Austen. Though she took an interest in the novelists of her own reign, including Walter *Scott, Charles *Dickens, the *Brontës, Elizabeth *Gaskell, George *Eliot, and Benjamin *Disraeli, she preferred poetry ('in all shapes'), an enthusiasm which led to her friendship with Alfred *Tennyson, whom she regarded as the perfect poet of 'love and loss'. Their correspondence has been published. Her role in the political and social culture of her nation and empire has recently attracted much scholarly and critical attention. E. Longford published the authorized version of her life (1964); see also M. Homans and A. Munich (eds), *Remaking Queen Victoria* (1997); J. Plunkett, *Queen Victoria: First Media Monarch* (2003).

VIDAL, Gore (1925–) American novelist and essayist, born at West Point, New York, where his father was an instructor at the US Military Academy. He saw army service during the Second World War, the experience of which was drawn on for his first novel, *Williwaw* (1946). In *A Search for the King* (1950), concerning the affection of a troubadour for Richard the Lionheart, he signalled his interest in using history, often as a means of analysing the present. Novels in this vein include *Julian* (1964), about the Roman emperor; *Two Sisters* (1970), based partly on the Roman world of the 4th century; and *Creation* (1981), set in the 5th century BC, the period of Darius, Xerxes, and Confucius. A sequence of 'Narratives of a Golden Age', chronicling the history of America from the mid-19th century, includes *Washington, D.C.* (1967), *1876* (1976), *Lincoln* (1984), *Empire* (1987), *Burr* (1973), and *Hollywood* (1990). His most celebrated novel, *Myra Breckenridge* (1968), wittily chronicled the adventures of a transsexual; its sequel, *Myron*, was published in 1974. Other works include *The Judgement of Paris* (1952), a contemporary version of the classic tale, and *Kalki* (1978), a satire on feminism. *Live from Golgotha* (1992) was a satirical fantasy on television culture. His elegant and pungent essays on history, literature, culture, and politics have been collected in *Matters of Fact and of Fiction* (1977), *The Second American Revolution* (1982), *Armageddon?* (1987), and *Sexually Speaking* (1999), among other volumes. He has also written plays for television and the stage, including *Visit to a Small Planet* (1956), and detective stories under the pseudonym Edgar Box. *Palimpsest* (1995) is a candid memoir, followed by *Point to Point Navigation* (2006).

VIGNY, Alfred de (1797–1863) French Romantic poet, dramatist, and novelist. After an undistinguished ten-year military career, he established himself as a poet and a novelist in 1826, publishing his *Poèmes antiques et modernes* (*Poems Ancient and Modern*) and his historical novel *Cinq-Mars*, based on a conspiracy against *Richelieu. This novel, together with his three tales *Servitude et grandeur militaires* (1835: *Military Servitude and Grandeur*), illustrating the self-sacrifice of Napoleon's armies, and his Romantic drama *Chatterton* (1835), which uses Thomas *Chatterton as a symbol of the solitary poet in the world, forms part of what he called his 'epic of disillusionment', which argued in favour of a reasoned pessimism as a condition for survival. A number of powerful individual poems, such as 'La Mort du loup' ('The Death of the Wolf'), 'Le Mont des oliviers' ('The Mount of Olives'), and 'La Bouteille à la mer' ('The Bottle in the Sea'), collected posthumously in 1863, proclaim a more positive, though equally Romantic, faith in 'man's unconquerable mind'.

Village, The A poem in two books by George *Crabbe, published 1783, based in part on his experiences as a country doctor and curate. The poem contrasts the dispiriting realities of country life with the idealized pastoral favoured by poets such as Oliver *Goldsmith. The poem was shown before publication to Samuel *Johnson, who contributed some six lines; Crabbe's patron Edmund *Burke also assisted. Johnson correctly predicted that the poem would establish Crabbe's reputation as a writer.

villanelle A poem consisting of an uneven number (normally five) of three-lined stanzas (tercets) rhyming *aba* and a final *quatrain rhyming *abaa*, with only two rhymes throughout. The first and third lines of the first tercet are repeated alternately as final lines in the succeeding tercets, and form a final couplet in the quatrain. The form originated in 16th-century France, and was employed for *pastoral song. In English it appeared in light verse of the 19th century, but in the 20th century was used to more serious purpose by W. H. *Auden, William *Empson, Derek *Mahon, and in the best-known such poem, Dylan *Thomas's 'Do not go gentle into that good night' (1951).

VILLEHARDOUIN, Geoffroi de (*c.*1150–*c.*1216) Member of a powerful French crusading family which ruled over a great court at Achaea; marshal of Champagne. He was an eyewitness of the events described in his *Conquête de Constantinople*, an account of the so-called Fourth Crusade, the first great literary work in French prose. Villehardouin relates with picturesque vigour the negotiations with the doge of Venice, the departure of the crusading host, its diversion from its proper purpose to various more secular undertakings, including the capture of Constantinople, the subsequent dissensions and intrigues, culminating in the crowning of Baldwin of Flanders as emperor of the East, and the grant of the kingdom of Macedonia to Boniface of Montferrat. See J. Beer, *Villehardouin* (1986).

Villette Charlotte *Brontë's last completed novel, published 1853. Like its predecessor *The *Professor* (then unpublished), it is based on Brontë's experiences in Brussels, here renamed Villette, and centres on a pupil-teacher relationship. The narrator, Lucy Snowe, poor and plain, finds herself a post as teacher in a girls' school in Villette, where she wins the respect of the capable, if unscrupulous, headmistress, Madame Beck, and gains authority over the boisterous girls. She becomes deeply attached to the handsome John Bretton, the school's English doctor, in whom she recognizes an acquaintance from her childhood, the son of her own godmother. She watches his infatuation with the shallow and flirtatious Ginevra Fanshawe, followed by a happier love for his childhood friend Paulina Home, and represses her own strong feelings for him. These feelings gradually attach themselves to the waspish, despotic, but good-hearted little professor Monsieur Paul Emanuel, Madame Beck's cousin, whose own response to her changes from asperity to esteem and affection, despite Madame Beck's attempts to discourage the friendship. His generosity leaves her mistress of her own school when he is called away on business to the West Indies. The ending is ambiguous, implying but not confirming that Paul Emanuel is drowned on his way home. The novel's vivid portrayal of Belgian daily life highlights the religious tensions generated by the Protestant Lucy's responses to a Catholic culture. Brontë makes use of elements of *Gothic fiction, with hints of the supernatural (the story of a ghostly nun, a visit to the mysterious and deformed Madame Walravens) heightening the impression of her heroine's nervous isolation and heroic fortitude; but all the apparitions are found to have realistic explanations, and in Paul Emanuel she successfully creates an unromantic hero very far removed from the *Byronic Rochester of **Jane Eyre*.

VILLIERS DE L'ISLE-ADAM, Auguste (Jean-Marie-Mathias-Philippe-Auguste), comte de (1838–89) French novelist and dramatist. His best-known work, the visionary drama *Axël* (1890; trans. 1925), which first appeared in symbolist reviews and which John *Keats read in French, is a Wagnerian narrative of love and death set in an isolated German castle, which enshrines *Rosicrucian mysteries. Its symbolic subtleties have exerted an influence on English writing which has only recently begun to be recognized; it provided a title for Edmund *Wilson's study of symbolist writers, *Axel's Castle* (1931).

VILLON, François (*c.*1431–after 1463) French poet. The little that is known of his life suggests nearly constant turmoil: he was imprisoned several times for rioting and theft, and narrowly escaped death by hanging in 1463. His two major poems are the *Lais* (or *Petit Testament*), which he wrote in 1456, and the *Testament* (or *Grand Testament*), which he wrote in 1461–2 and which was first published posthumously in 1489. Both take the form of a mock will; the latter contains the famous 'Ballade des dames du temps jadis' ('Ballad of the ladies of bygone times'), with its refrain, 'Mais où sont les neiges d'antan?' ('Where are the snows of yesteryear?') (*see* UBI SUNT). In addition, a number of short poems survive, including Villon's own epitaph, 'Frères humains qui après nous vivez'

('Human brothers who survive us'), written under sentence of death. His poetry was popular in England in the late 19th century, with translations of individual poems by D. G. *Rossetti, A. C. *Swinburne, and W. E. *Henley, and prose adaptations by John *Synge; of more recent versions, those by Basil *Bunting and Robert *Lowell stand out.

VINCENT OF BEAUVAIS (*c.*1190–*c.*1264) The Dominican author of the *Speculum Maius*, the general title of a Latin encyclopedic work of which three parts were completed: *Speculum Naturale, Historiale, Doctrinale* (mid-13th century). A compilation of all received knowledge at the time, it was widely circulated, translated into some vernaculars, and was cited as an authority. Vincent is mentioned by *Chaucer in the G version of the prologue to *The *Legend of Good Women* (G 307).

Vindication of the Rights of Woman, A By Mary *Wollstonecraft, published 1792. Wollstonecraft attacks the educational restrictions and 'mistaken notions of female excellence' that keep women in a state of 'ignorance and slavish dependence'. She argues that girls are forced into passivity, vanity, and credulity by a lack of physical and mental stimulus, and by a constant insistence on the need to please; she attacks the educational theories of the 'unmanly, immoral' *Chesterfield, of Jean-Jacques *Rousseau (who in her view made false and discriminatory distinctions in his approach to the sexes in *Émile*), and others, concluding that 'From the tyranny of man...the greater number of female follies proceed.' The work was much acclaimed and is now seen as a founding document in modern feminism, but it also inevitably attracted contemporary hostility; Horace *Walpole referred to Wollstonecraft as 'a hyena in petticoats'.

VINE, Barbara Pseudonym of Ruth *Rendell.

VINGE, Joan D. (1948–) American *science fiction writer, born in Baltimore; author of the *Hugo award-winning *The Snow Queen* (1980), which echoes Robert *Graves and Hans Christian *Andersen to show the relationship between a world, the galactic civilization, and the ambitions of the titular 'Queen'.

Virago Press British publishing house founded by Carmen Callil in 1972. Its first book (*Fenwomen* by Mary Chamberlain) appeared the following year. For more than three decades, Virago was one of the leading publishers of feminist writing in the English-speaking world, and the works of major feminist thinkers such as Kate Millett, Sheila Rowbotham, and Elaine Showalter have appeared under its imprint. In its Virago Modern Classics series, which was launched in 1978, it has republished and championed neglected classics by Antonia *White, Willa *Cather, Christina *Stead, Elizabeth *Taylor, and other women writers. It has also contributed to the ever-increasing popular and academic interest in women's history and women's studies that began in the 1970s. Although owned by several different companies over the years (since 2006 it has been part of the Hachette Publishing empire), Virago has largely succeeded in maintaining its reputation as an independent and innovative publisher.

Virgidemiarum, Sex Libri By Joseph *Hall, two volumes of English satires, 1597 and 1598. The first volume, called 'Toothless', satirizes literary conventions in the spirit of *Martial and *Horace; the second, imitating *Juvenal, 'bites' such evils as sexual promiscuity, ostentatious piety, economic injustice, and impostures in astrology and genealogy. The title means 'sheaves of rods' (for corporal punishment). In a crackdown on satire in 1599 Hall's books were condemned to be burnt, along with satires by John *Marston, Thomas *Nashe, and others, but then reprieved.

VIRGIL (Publius Vergilius Maro) (70–19 BC) The greatest of Roman poets, born near Mantua. His first publication was the *pastoral *Eclogues* (*c.*39–38), indebted to the *Idylls* of *Theocritus. The family land was confiscated to settle civil war veterans (41–40): that experience is echoed in *Eclogues* 1 and 9, but they are not otherwise autobiographical. *Eclogue* 4 (later famous as the 'Messianic Eclogue') gave Virgil quasi-prophetic status in Christian Europe: it prophesies the birth of a child with whom a glorious new era will begin: as he matures, the Golden Age will return. The poem offers an apocalyptic vision of hope in a time of despair. Virgil's **Georgics* (published 29), a didactic and celebratory poem in four books about the life of the farmer which partly imitates the *Works and Days* of *Hesiod, is dedicated to his patron *Maecenas, the trusted counsellor of Octavian (later the emperor Augustus), who is said to have suggested the project. The **Aeneid*, Virgil's *epic in twelve books about the remote legendary origins of what eventually became the Roman Empire, was composed during the last ten years of his life and was not quite finished at his death. It seems to have grown out of his response to pressure placed on the poets of the day to produce a poem in praise of Augustus' martial exploits. Augustus as soldier and statesman is reflected in Virgil's account of his mythical ancestor Aeneas, the Trojan martial hero who escaped from his ruined city to become the nation-building founder of a new colony on the Italian mainland from which mighty Rome would eventually develop. Virgil's narrative of adventure and conquest, and keenly felt human suffering and loss, builds on the achievement of earlier Latin epic poets such as *Ennius. It deliberately invites comparison with *Homer, announcing its theme as both arms, as in the **Iliad*, and a man, an individual hero, as in the **Odyssey*. The treatment of Dido, queen of Carthage, loved and abandoned by Aeneas on his way to fulfilling his destiny and the destiny of Rome, shows the influence of Greek tragedy and probably also alludes to Cleopatra, another foreign queen who had recently, and disastrously, become involved in the history of Rome. The poem contrives to bring together the legendary past and the moral, political, and religious concerns of Virgil's own times, most notably at the centre of the poem, in the sixth book, where Aeneas descends into the underworld, the place of the dead, and the future imperial destiny of Rome is revealed to him. This episode influenced John *Milton's hell in *_Paradise Lost_ and *Dante's _Inferno_. Virgil is Dante's guide through both hell and purgatory. The melancholy as well as the heroism of the _Aeneid_ commended itself to Alfred *Tennyson and the poem has been much translated by other poets from Gawin *Douglas and John *Dryden to Cecil *Day-Lewis. Edmund *Spenser and to some extent Alexander *Pope modelled their careers on the Virgilian ladder (from pastoral to georgic to epic). See Charles Martindale (ed.), _Virgil and his Influence_ (1984); Theodore Ziolkowski, _Virgil and the Moderns_ (1993); Sarah Spence (ed.), _Poets and Critics Read Vergil_ (2001). _See also_ MARCELLUS.

'Virgils Gnat' A poem by Edmund *Spenser, published in the _Complaints_ of 1591, and adapted from the _Culex_ (or 'Gnat') attributed to *Virgil. A shepherd sleeping in the shade is about to be attacked by a serpent, when a gnat, to warn him, stings him on the eyelid. The shepherd crushes the gnat, and sees and kills the serpent. The next night the ghost of the gnat reproaches him for his cruelty. The shepherd, filled with remorse, raises a monument to the gnat. In what way, if any, the poem reflects Spenser's relations with the 'late deceased' earl of *Leicester, to whom it was dedicated 'Long since', will probably never be known.

Virginians, The A *historical novel of the American Revolution by W. M. *Thackeray, published in numbers, November 1857–October 1859, and illustrated by the author. The prominent part played by George Washington offended some American readers. The novel takes up the story of the Esmond family after the events of _The *History of Henry Esmond_, and traces the fortunes of Esmond's grandsons George and Harry Warrington. Their mother, Esmond's daughter Rachel, favours the cheerful Harry, and is capricious in her treatment of the more bookish George. George is thought to be killed in action against the French. Harry, now the heir, visits England, is corrupted by his dissipated Castlewood relations, and is trapped into an engagement to his much older cousin Maria. Imprisoned for debt, he is rescued by the reappearance of George, who has escaped from the French and come to England. Maria releases Harry from his engagement, since he is no longer the heir. George marries Theo, the daughter of a poor soldier, and is only saved from penury by becoming the heir of Sir Miles Warrington, of the English branch of the family. Harry joins the army, and is with Wolfe at the capture of Quebec. When the War of Independence breaks out, Harry joins Washington, and George, who is in the British army, resigns his commission rather than run the risk of fighting against his brother. He settles in England, and gives up the Virginian property to Harry. George Warrington in *_Pendennis_ is a descendant of the Warrington family of this novel.

Virgin Martyr, The A tragedy by Philip *Massinger and Thomas *Dekker, printed 1622. The emperor Diocletian asks his daughter Artemia to select a husband. She chooses Antoninus, a brave soldier, son of Sapritius, governor of Caesarea. He declines the dangerous honour, being moreover devoted to Dorothea, a maid of the oppressed Christian sect. Theophilus, a zealous persecutor, and his secretary Harpax, 'an evil spirit', betray Antoninus and Dorothea to Artemia, who orders them to execution, but presently allows Theophilus to send his daughters to Dorothea to convert her to paganism. The daughters are instead converted by Dorothea to Christianity, and on their boldly professing it are killed by their own father. Dorothea, attended by her 'good spirit' Angelo, is tortured and executed, Antoninus dying by her side. In the last act, Angelo and Harpax, the good and evil spirits, contend for Theophilus' soul. Theophilus, summoned before Diocletian, proclaims his conversion to Christianity, courageously suffers torture, and dies. The same story has been treated in poems by A. C. *Swinburne and Gerard Manley *Hopkins.

VISCONTI family Ancient feudal family who ruled as imperial vicars and then as hereditary lords of Milan from the 14th century until 1447. By the early 15th century their territories covered much of northern Italy. They founded the University of Pavia (1361) and collected a magnificent library (988 volumes in the inventory of 1426). Among those who enjoyed Visconti patronage was *Petrarch. The film director **Luchino Visconti** (1906–76) was a descendant of the younger branch of the family.

Vision of Judgement, A A poem in hexameters by Robert *Southey, published 1821, when he was *poet laureate. The preface, written in defence of the poem's metrical innovation, also contains a violent attack on the works of Lord *Byron, 'those monstrous combinations of horrors and mockery, lewdness and impiety'. Byron responded with his parody _The *Vision of Judgment_. The poet in a trance sees George III (who died in 1820) rise from the tomb and, after receiving from the shade of the former prime minister Spencer Perceval (1762–1812) news of affairs in England, proceed to the gates of heaven. The devil, accompanied by the radical John *Wilkes, comes forward to accuse him, but retires defeated, and the king, after receiving a eulogy from George Washington, is admitted to paradise.

Vision of Judgment, The A satirical poem in *_ottava rima_ by Lord *Byron, published in the *_Liberal_, 1822. In 1821 Robert *Southey published _A *Vision of Judgement_, which described Byron as the leader of the *'Satanic school' of poetry. Byron's reply is an exuberant parody of Southey's poem. George III, at the celestial gate, is claimed by Satan, who lists his crimes against freedom and the national and individual woes that he condoned: Satan then calls a crowd of witnesses, including the 'merry, cock-eyed', and forgiving spirit of John *Wilkes and the unforgiving *Junius, to testify to the king's disastrous reign. Southey is swept up from the Lake District by a devil, and is mocked by Byron for his 'spavin'd dactyls' and derided as a political traitor, and literary hack. Southey demonstrates his corruption by offering to add Satan's biography to his life of John *Wesley. The poem ends as Southey attempts to read from his own manuscript; this causes such distress to the assembled spirits that he is knocked back down to his own lake by St Peter, and in the confusion King George slips into heaven. The work is a triumph of mock-heroic wit, savage in its attack, yet buoyant with its own inventiveness. The condemnation of the king himself is lightened by references to his dull domestic virtues—

> A better farmer ne'er brushed dew from lawn,
> A worse king never left a realm undone!

Vita nuova *See* DANTE, ALIGHIERI.

VITTORINI, Elio (1908–66) Italian novelist, critic, translator, and literary editor; he was responsible for introducing into Italian literature many of the techniques of modern American fiction. He translated works by Edgar Allan *Poe, Erskine *Caldwell, William *Faulkner, John *Steinbeck, D. H. *Lawrence, and Daniel *Defoe. His best-known novel *Conversazione in Sicilia* (1941: *In Sicily*) reveals the American influence in particular in its use of allusion. In the post-war period he was influential, through working as commissioning editor for the publisher Giulio Einaudi (1912–99), in promoting the work of Italo *Calvino.

Vivian Grey The first of Benjamin *Disraeli's novels, anonymously published 1826, with a continuation in 1827; written, as he later observed, 'with imagination acting upon knowledge not acquired by experience'. It began a group of three novels (the others were *Alroy* and **Contarini Fleming*). Vivian, brilliant and difficult, is expelled from school, and discovers that charm can secure political advancement. By playing on the follies of discontented peers and MPs, he builds a faction round the powerful but disappointed marquis of Carabas. His secret efforts to create a new party are exposed by the tempestuous Mrs Lorraine (a reminiscence of Lady Caroline *Lamb). Challenged to a duel by the outraged Cleveland, leader-designate of the party, Vivian kills him. Ruined, he leaves England and begins a desultory life of intrigue and adventure among German princelings. The last four books were added by popular demand in 1827.

Disraeli came to dislike the novel, and the character of the unprincipled Vivian dogged him for years. He tried to suppress the book, but pirated editions abroad forced him to reprint, and in 1853 he drastically revised the work. Among various identifications, the kindly, scholarly Mr Grey represents Disraeli's father Isaac *D'Israeli, the dashing Lord Alhambra has something of Lord *Byron, the marquis of Carabas of John *Murray (who was extremely angry), and Cleveland of John Gibson *Lockhart.

VIZENOR, Gerald (1934–) Native American writer and ethnologist, born in Minneapolis, who served during the 1960s as director of the American Indian Employment and Guidance Centre in that city. His first novel was *Darkness in Saint Louis Bearheart* (1978). Subsequent works drew on traditional trickster tales, and on the writings of the Native American writer Navarre Scott *Momaday. In addition to his fiction and poetry, Vizenor has published studies of Native American culture like *Narrative Chance* (1989) and *Manifest Manners: Postindian Warriors of Survivance* (1994). Vizenor uses *postmodern strategies to question the cultural construction of 'Indian'. *Interior Landscapes* (1990) is an autobiography.

VIZETELLY, Henry (1820–94) Son of a printer and engraver, of a family Italian in origin, but long settled in England; he became an engraver, printer, publisher, journalist, and editor, whose defiance of censorship and policy of issuing cheap reprints had a considerable impact on the literary scene. In 1885 he joined forces with George *Moore to publish a cheap one-volume edition of *A Mummer's Wife*, an act which did much to break the power of the *circulating libraries and the three-decker novel. The following year, 1886, with Havelock *Ellis he founded the Mermaid Series of unexpurgated reprints of 'The Best Plays of the Old Dramatists'. He also published translations of *Flaubert, *Gogol, *Tolstoy, the *Goncourts, etc., and seventeen novels by *Zola; it was his publication of Zola's *La Terre* that led to his three-month imprisonment in 1888 on an obscenity charge, despite the protests of Charles *Bradlaugh, Edmund *Gosse, Ellis, and others. This bankrupted his publishing company. Vizetelly had many friends in the artistic and literary world, including W. M. *Thackeray, Gustave *Doré, and George *Sala, and his memoirs, *Glances Back through Seventy Years* (1893), give a lively portrait of bohemian society.

VOLNEY, Constantin-François de Chasseboeuf, comte de (1757–1820) French historian, travel writer, and **philosophe*, author of *Les Ruines, ou méditation sur les révolutions des empires* (1791: *Ruins, or Meditations on the Revolutions of Empires*), in which contemplation of the ruins of Palmyra becomes the occasion for reflections on the rise, progress, and decline of ancient civilizations and the prospect for modern ones. The soul of the narrator, enlightened by a spirit, the Genius of Tombs and Ruins, comprehends through a conspectus of human history that man's miseries have at all times been the result of his ignorance, greed, and neglect of natural law; but that, guided by Nature and Reason, he will at last come to know his own best interest. Putting aside the dual tyranny of religious superstition and political despotism, he will perfect his nature and establish freedom, equality, and justice. *Les Ruines* was translated into English as early as 1792 and remained popular in England in the early 19th century, especially among rationalists and freethinkers. It was a favourite book of P. B. *Shelley's, providing the plan for his **Queen Mab*; in Mary Shelley's **Frankenstein* it is one of four books by means of which the monster receives his education.

Volpone, *or The Fox* A comedy by Ben *Jonson, performed by the King's Men in 1605–6, printed 1607. Volpone, a rich and childless Venetian, pretends to be dying in order to draw gifts from his would-be heirs. Mosca, his accomplice, persuades each of these in turn that he is to be the heir, extracting costly presents from them. One of them, Corvino, even attempts to offer his wife to Volpone in hope of the inheritance. Finally Volpone overreaches himself. To enjoy the mortification of the vultures awaiting his death, he bequeaths his property to Mosca and pretends to be dead. Mosca then blackmails Volpone, but rather than be defeated Volpone chooses to reveal all to the authorities. They direct that Volpone shall be cast in irons until he is as infirm as he pretended to be, Mosca whipped and confined to the galleys, Corvino made to parade in ass's ears, and his wife be returned to her family with a trebled dowry. A secondary plot involves Sir Politic Would-be, an English traveller with absurd schemes for improving trade and curing diseases, and his Lady, a hectoring pedant. Sir Politic is chastened when Peregrine, a wiser English traveller, pretends to have him arrested for treason. The names of the principal characters, Volpone (the fox), Mosca (the fly), Voltore (the vulture), Corbaccio (the crow), Corvino (the raven), indicate their roles and natures.

Völsunga saga A prose version of a lost cycle of heroic songs of which fragments survive in the poetic *Edda, dealing with the families of the Volsungs and the Niblungs. It has been translated by William *Morris and Eirikr Magnusson (1888). For the treatment in it of the story of Sigurd and Brunhild, *see* SIGURD THE VOLSUNG.

VOLTAIRE (1694–1778) Pseudonym of François-Marie Arouet, prolific French poet, dramatist, historian, satirist, fiction writer, polemicist, thinker, critic, and correspondent. He was the universal genius of the *Enlightenment. He made his name as a tragic dramatist, writing some 30 tragedies, from *Œdipe* (1718: *Oedipus*) to *Irène* (1778), and as a poet, publishing *La Ligue* (1723: *The League*; later retitled *La Henriade*, 1728), his epic poem about Henri de Navarre. Following early imprisonment in the Bastille for his satirical verse (1717–18), he spent a period in exile in England (1726–8), which inspired his first great prose work, the controversial *Lettres philosophiques* (1734: *Philosophical Letters*), the first edition of which was in English (1733), and which creates a satirical contrast between the liberty and tolerance of England and the abuses of the French *ancien régime*. Thereafter Voltaire spent most of his life away from Paris, staying first in Champagne with Madame Du Châtelet, subsequently in Berlin with Frederick II, and finally at Ferney, near Geneva. His other prose works include his histories, which won the admiration of Hugh *Blair, notably *Le Siècle de Louis XIV* (1751: *The Century of Louis XIV*), which disregards providence as an explanatory principle, seeking instead evidence of social and moral progress, and his philosophical tales, most famously **Candide* (1759), in which his wit, the concision of his style, and the precision of his mind are put to the service of satirizing philosophical systems which take no account of the reality of evil and suffering in the world. His championing of justice and tolerance and his mockery of the cruelty and obscurantism of the civil and ecclesiastical establishments were relentless from the late 1750s onwards, symbolized by his campaign to 'écraser l'Infâme' ('crush Infamy'). This was the source of both his persecution and his immense international prestige. Most of his works were translated into English as they appeared (*Candide*, for instance, was translated twice in 1759 alone); there were also English collected works, in particular the 35-volume edition masterminded by Tobias *Smollett and Thomas Francklin (1721–84), which began to appear in 1761. See R. Pearson, *Voltaire Almighty* (2005).

VON ARNIM, Elizabeth (1866–1941) Novelist and cousin of Katherine *Mansfield, born in Sydney, Australia, and educated at Blythwood House School, Southgate, and Queen's College School, Acton, London. In 1890 she married Count Henning August von Arnim-Schlagenthin, the 'Man of Wrath' in her best-known work, *Elizabeth and her German Garden*, published anonymously in 1898; part satire, part idyll, it describes her life at Nassenheide in Pomerania. E. M. *Forster and Hugh *Walpole were tutors to her children there. After von Arnim's death she married in 1916 the second Earl Russell, brother of Bertrand Russell, the philosopher and writer. She published many novels, including *The Pastor's Wife* (1914), *Vera* (1921), *The Enchanted April* (1922; adapted for film in 1992), *Love* (1925), and a quirky autobiography, *All the Dogs of my Life* (1936). Noted for its descriptive power and irreverent wit, her work reveals a keen sense of women's struggle for autonomy within marriage.

VON HARBOU, Thea (1888–1954) German scriptwriter and novelist, born in Tauperlitz; wife of (until 1932) and co-scriptwriter with the director Fritz Lang. Her novel of the script for **Metropolis* (1927) illuminates the film. Other *science fiction includes *Frau im Mond* (*The Girl in the Moon*) (1928).

VONNEGUT, Kurt (1922–2007) American novelist and short story writer, born in Indianapolis, who attended Cornell University before serving in the air force in the Second World War. Captured by the Germans, he survived the bombing of Dresden in 1945, an experience that he would later use in his most famous novel, *Slaughterhouse-Five, or The Children's Crusade* (1969). His earlier works drew on *science fiction and *fantasy to satirize the increasing mechanization and dehumanization of the post-war world. His first novel, *Player Piano* (1952), envisages a New York factory town whose automated structure turns its workers and scientists into virtual robots. *Cat's Cradle* (1963) imagines how a scientific discovery threatens to destroy the planet. He has also written plays, of which *Happy Birthday Wanda June* (1970) is the best known, and collections of stories, chief among which is *Welcome to the Monkey House* (1968). Other novels include *Breakfast of Champions* (1973), *Slapstick* (1976), *Jailbird* (1979), and *Deadeye Dick* (1983). Vonnegut often masked his sardonic views of contemporary America with a faux-naïf voice. He shared *black humour techniques with Joseph *Heller, who was a close friend. He illustrated some of his own works.

Vorticism A literary and artistic movement that flourished 1912–15, dominated by Wyndham *Lewis and Ezra *Pound, and including Henri *Gaudier-Brzeska, the painters C. R. Nevinson (1889–1946) and Edward Wadsworth (1889–1949), and the photographer Alvin Langdon Coburn (1882–1966). It adopted some of the strategies and styles of the continental avant-garde, but defined itself in opposition to *Futurism, an Italian-dominated movement. At its heart was a concern to reconcile the dynamism of modernity with form in art. The vortex, being both energetic and well shaped, served as a model of good aesthetic form. The movement also emphasized the rational shaping power of the artist: it criticized other modern tendencies for passively recording sense-impressions. The vorticists rejected the dynamism of the futurists, describing their work as 'accelerated impressionism', and mocked their obsession with speed. In the visual arts its revolutionary fervour was expressed in abstract compositions of bold lines, sharp angles, and planes. **Blast*, the vorticist periodical, attempted to draw together artists and writers of the English avant-garde. Several artists adapted the vorticist style to First World War subjects, but the real impetus petered out after the vorticist Exhibition held at the Doré Gallery in 1915.

Vortigern A legendary 5th-century British king reputed to have enlisted *Hengist and Horsa against the Picts, thus causing the transfer of Britain to the Anglo-Saxons. After a lifetime of feuds and alliances with the Germanic invaders, in the course of which he meets Merlin and is astonished by his prophecies, he is burnt alive in the Welsh tower to which he had retired. His story is told by *Nennius, *Bede, *Geoffrey of Monmouth, and *Laȝamon.

Vortigern and Rowena *See* IRELAND, WILLIAM.

VOYNICH, Ethel Lillian (1864–1960) Née Boole, novelist, born in Cork, the daughter of the mathematician George Boole (1815–64). She was introduced to radical political circles through her marriage to the Polish Count Wilfrid Voynich (1865–1930), and is now remembered for her revolutionary novel *The Gadfly* (1897), set in pre-1848 Italy, which sold in vast quantities in translation in the Soviet Union. She later published two sequels, *An Interrupted Friendship* (1910) and *Put off thy Shoes* (1945). Much of her later life was spent in the United States.

Vulgar Errors *See* PSEUDODOXIA EPIDEMICA.

Vulgate [from the Latin *versio vulgata*, 'common translation'] The name given to the Latin version of the Bible collected together in the 6th century. St *Jerome's translation of the Old Testament from the Hebrew, completed 405, forms the greater part. The Clementine edition (1592) was for centuries the authorized Latin text of the *Roman Catholic Church. In 1979 it was replaced by the *Nova Vulgata*.
See BIBLE.

Vulgate cycle An important group of Arthurian romances in French prose, dating from *c.*1215–35. It comprises the *Estoire del Saint Graal* (*The History of the Holy Grail*), a version of Robert de *Boron's partially surviving *Estoire de Merlin* (*The History of Merlin*), and the three romances which make up the Prose *Lancelot*, namely the *Lancelot propre* (*Lancelot Proper*), the *Queste del Saint Graal* (*The Quest for the Holy Grail*), and *Mort Artu* (*The Death of Arthur*). The group is the most influential version of the Arthurian legends between *Geoffrey of Monmouth and *Malory. Ed. Norris J. Lacy (1992–6).

WACE (*fl.* 12th century) Author, in French verse of 15,000 short couplets, of the *Roman de Brut*, completed in 1155 and dedicated to *Eleanor of Aquitaine, a highly popular adaptation of *Geoffrey of Monmouth's *Historia Regum Britanniae* (*The History of the Kings of Britain*). Characterized in particular by its beautifully written descriptive passages, the *Roman de Brut* survives in 22 manuscripts, including the four manuscripts of *Gaimar in which Wace's poem has been substituted for Gaimar's account of the *Historia*. It was the principal source of *Laȝamon's *Brut* in the early 13th century, and it retained considerable influence up to the 14th century. Wace also wrote the *Roman de Rou*, a history of the dukes of Normandy in the course of which he provides some apparently autobiographical information. He was made a canon of Bayeux by Henry II. Ed. I. Arnold (2 vols, 1938–40); trans. in E. Mason, *Arthurian Chronicles* (1912).

WADDELL, Helen Jane (1889–1965) Medievalist and translator, born in Tokyo, and educated at Queen's University, Belfast. She is best remembered for her popular study of the 'vagantes' of the Middle Ages, *The Wandering Scholars* (1927), for her anthology of imaginative but sometimes misleading translations from their works in her *Medieval Latin Lyrics* (1929), and for her novel *Peter Abelard* (1933), based on the life of *Abelard.

Wade's boat In Geoffrey *Chaucer's 'The Merchant's Tale' (*see* Canterbury Tales, 10): widows 'konne so muchel craft on Wades boot' (IV. 1424). Wade was also mentioned in Sir Thomas *Malory (Caxton vii. ix: possibly Caxton's addition; not in Vinaver's *Sir Gareth: Works*, 188). The 'tale of Wade' is also mentioned in **Troilus and Criseyde*, III. 614. In the 13th-century German *epic *Kudrun*, Hettel, king of the Hegelings, wishes to marry Hilde, daughter of Hagen, king of Ireland. Hettel's servant Wade sails to Ireland, his fleet including a boat with a removable deck, beneath which he conceals an army. He and his men distract King Hagen while his daughter is lured onto the boat. The army emerges, kills her protectors, and abducts her so that she may marry Hettel.

'Waggoner, The' A poem by William *Wordsworth, composed 1805, published 1819 with a dedication to Charles *Lamb. Wordsworth's comic narrative tells how Benjamin the Waggoner, driving his team of eight horses through the night among the Lakeland hills, escapes the temptation of the Swan Inn, but falls victim to that of the Cherry-Tree, and loses his place in consequence. But no one else can drive the team, and Lakeland loses both waggoner and wain.

WAGNER, Karl Edward (1945–94) American editor, publisher, *science fiction and *horror writer; born in Knoxville, Tennessee. He edited collections of Robert E. *Howard's 'Conan' stories and also wrote fiction featuring Howard's characters. His own 'Kane', a cursed anti-hero who may be immortal, appears in several novels and collections including *Darkness Weaves* (1970) and *Bloodstone* (1975).

WAGNER, Richard (1813–83) German composer, dramatist, and writer. His theoretical writings reached beyond the musical field: a revolutionary in 1848–9, he later came under the influence of Arthur *Schopenhauer, and his works contain much that has social, political, and cultural implications. As a composer, Wagner attempted to create a new synthesis of music and drama, writing both words and music. His ideas were on the grandest scale: *Der Ring des Nibelungen* (based on the **Nibelungenlied*), planned as a single drama, developed backwards (each episode requiring previous explanation for its proper understanding) until the finished work required four separate evenings and eventually the construction of a new type of theatre. A. C. *Swinburne wrote poems on the preludes to *Lohengrin* and *Tristan* and an elegy, 'The Death of Richard Wagner' (*A Century of Roundels*, 1883), but Wagner's first critical champion in this country was G. B. *Shaw; later Ernest Newman (1868–1959) became 'the perfect Wagnerite'. Wagner's prose works were translated into English by W. Ashton Ellis (8 vols, 1892–9). D. H. *Lawrence's *The Trespasser* (originally entitled *The Saga of Siegmund*) contains much Wagnerian symbolism, and three deeply influential works of the 20th century, *The *Waste Land*, **Ulysses*, and **Finnegans Wake*, all quote directly from Wagner's operas. Wagner's mature operas use exclusively German texts: of his early works, however, *Das Liebesverbot* (1836) is an adaptation of **Measure for Measure*: its successor, *Rienzi* (1842), is partly based on Edward *Bulwer-Lytton's novel of that title.

waif stories Socially conscious novels with great melodramatic potential, especially when concerned with deprived and abused children, popular in the 19th century. Best-sellers included Maria Louisa Charlesworth (1819–80) with *Ministering Children* (1854) and Hesba *Stretton's (Sarah Smith) *Jessica's*

First Prayer (1867)—a critique of the religious system that produced it—which sold over 1.5 million copies. The genre was susceptible to bathos, a charge some make against Brenda (Georgina Castle Smith, née Meyrick, 1845–1933), whose tear-jerker *Froggy's Little Brother* (1875) was hugely popular and influential. Notable episodes in the same tradition include the opening of *The *Water-Babies* and the scenes about *Dickens's crossing-sweeper, Jo, in **Bleak House* (1852–3). In the USA, waif stories overlapped the genre of self-help books such as Horatio *Alger Jr's *Ragged Dick* (1868), stressing social mobility and individual effort rather than religion or philanthropy. Vestiges of the genre survived into the 20th century in Frances Hodgson *Burnett's *A Little Princess* (1905).

WAIN, John Barrington (1925–94) Poet, critic, and novelist, born in Stoke-on-Trent and educated at Newcastle-under-Lyme and St John's College, Oxford. He lectured at Reading University, 1947–55, and was professor of poetry at Oxford 1973–8. His first novel, *Hurry on Down* (1953), a *picaresque account of a university graduate rebelling against the middle-class career that beckons him, has been linked with the work of the so-called *'Angry Young Men' of the 1950s, although Wain himself disliked the term. Other novels include *The Contenders* (1958), *Strike the Father Dead* (1962), *Young Shoulders* (1982), and a trilogy set in Oxford (*Where the Rivers Meet*, 1988; *Comedies*, 1990; and *Hungry Generations*, 1994). As a poet Wain was associated with the *Movement and contributed to **New Lines*. He published several volumes of verse, collected in *Poems 1949–79* (1981), an autobiography, *Sprightly Running* (1962), and a biography of Samuel *Johnson (1974).

WAINEWRIGHT, Thomas Griffiths (1794–1852) Apprentice painter, soldier, then art journalist. He wrote as an art critic for the **London Magazine*, 1820–3, and became the friend of William *Hazlitt, Charles *Lamb, Thomas *De Quincey, and others. He exhibited at the Royal Academy, 1821–5, began to live far beyond his means, and forged an order on the bank. In 1827 he published *The Life of Egomet Bonmot Esq.*, largely consisting of sneers at writers. After insurance frauds, a poisoning, and prison in Paris, he was tried and transported to Tasmania, where he died. He is the original of Varney in Edward *Bulwer-Lytton's *Lucretia* and the victim in Charles *Dickens's story 'Hunted Down'. See Andrew Motion, *Wainewright the Poisoner* (2000).

Waiting for Godot The first stage play of Samuel *Beckett, published in French as *En attendant Godot*, 1952, staged in French in Paris, 1953, first staged in English at the Arts Theatre, London, 1955. One of the most influential plays of the post-war period, it portrays two tramps, Estragon and Vladimir, trapped in an endless waiting for the arrival of the mysterious Godot, while disputing the appointed place and hour of his coming. They amuse themselves meanwhile with bouts of repartee and word-play, and are for a while diverted by the arrival of whip-cracking Pozzo, driving the oppressed and burdened Lucky on the end of a rope. Towards the end of each of the two acts, a boy arrives, heralding Godot's appearance, but he does not come; each act ends with the interchange between the two tramps, 'Well, shall we go?' 'Yes, let's go', and the stage direction, 'They do not move.' There are strong biblical references throughout, but Beckett's powerfully symbolic portrayal of the human condition as one of ignorance, delusion, paralysis, and intermittent flashes of human sympathy, hope, and wit has been subjected to varying interpretations. The vitality and versatility of the play have been demonstrated by performances throughout the world. *See* ABSURD, THEATRE OF THE.

WAKOSKI, Diane (1934–) American poet, born in California, whose work originally used 'deep image' techniques (generally stylized and heroic in manner), and which has been influenced by William Carlos *Williams and Allen *Ginsberg. *Towards a New Poetry* (1980) is a volume of essays.

WALCOTT, Derek (1930–) Poet and playwright, born in St Lucia, in the West Indies, and educated at the University College of the West Indies. He founded the Trinidad Theatre Workshop in 1959, and many of his own plays had their first performances there. These include *Dream on Monkey Mountain* (1967; pub. 1970), *The Joker of Seville* (1974; pub. 1978; based on *Tirso de Molina's *El burlador de Sevilla*), *O Babylon!* (1976; pub. 1978; set amongst a Rastafarian community in Kingston, Jamaica), and *The Haitian Trilogy* (2002). His collections of poetry include *In a Green Night: Poems 1948–60* (1962), *The Castaway and Other Poems* (1965), *Sea Grapes* (1976), *The Fortunate Traveller* (1982), *Midsummer* (1984), *The Arkansas Testament* (1987), *Tiepolo's Hound* (2001), *The Prodigal* (2004) and his epic Caribbean Odyssey *Omeros* (1990). Both plays and poetry show a preoccupation with the national identity of the West Indies and their literature, and with the conflict between the heritage of European and West Indian culture ('the choice of home or exile, self-realization or spiritual betrayal of one's country', in his own words). Though he asserts that the English language is the property of the imagination, he is haunted by history:

> but we live like our names and you would have
> to be colonial to know the difference,
> to know the pain of history words contain.

Walcott's plays mingle verse and prose, *Creole vocabulary and the rhythms of calypso, and his poems, many of which are confessional and self-questioning, are rich in classical allusion and evoke with equal vividness both Caribbean and European landscapes. A wry wit enlivens his essays as well as plays and poems. He was awarded the *Nobel Prize for Literature in 1992. See Bruce King, *Derek Walcott: A Caribbean Life* (2000). *See also* POSTCOLONIAL LITERATURE.

Walden, or Life in the Woods *See* THOREAU, HENRY.

Waldensians [in French, *Vaudois*] The adherents of a religious sect which originated in the south of France about 1170 through the preaching of Peter Waldo, a rich merchant of

Lyons. They rejected the authority of the pope and various rites, and were excommunicated in 1184 and subjected to persecution. But they survived and eventually became a separately organized church, which associated itself with the Protestant Reformation of the 16th century and still exists, chiefly in northern Italy and the adjacent regions. Their persecution by the duke of Savoy in 1655 led to John *Milton's sonnet, 'Avenge, O Lord, thy slaughtered saints', and caused Oliver *Cromwell to insist on his new ally, France, putting an immediate end to the massacre.

'Waldhere' The name given to two fragments of an Old English poem in a manuscript from the Royal Library, Copenhagen, of the late 10th century, totalling 63 lines. Waldhere was the son of a king of Aquitaine, who became one of Attila the Hun's generals. He escaped with Hiltgund, a Burgundian princess. They were attacked, and Waldhere, after slaying his assailants in a fist fight, was ambushed and wounded the next day. But they were finally married. There is a 10th-century Latin poem *Waltharius*. See the edition by F. Norman (1933; rev. 1949).

WALDROP, Howard (1946–) American *science fiction writer, born in Houston, Mississippi; his short stories such as 'Night of the Cooters' (1987) are characterized by humour, energy, and a deep feeling for popular culture. *Them Bones* (1984) is a time-travel novel exploring several alternate cultures.

WALEY, Arthur (1889–1966) Poet and authority on Chinese and Japanese literature, which he introduced to a wide public through his well-known translations. He taught himself the languages while working in the Print Room at the *British Museum, and in 1918 published *A Hundred and Seventy Chinese Poems*. His translations are unrhymed, elegant, and lucid; his rhythms had, he believed, something in common with G. M. Hopkins's *sprung rhythm. His other translations in prose and verse include *The Tale of Genji* (1925–33), *The Pillow-Book of Sei Shonagon* (1928), and *Monkey* (1942). He also published many works on oriental art, history, and culture, but, despite frequent invitations, never visited the Far East. He spent most of his life in Bloomsbury, where he was on friendly terms with many of the *Bloomsbury Group and the *vorticists. See Alison Waley, *A Half of Two Lives: A Personal Memoir* (1982).

WALKER, Alice (1944–) African American novelist, poet, and short story writer, born in Georgia, best known as the writer of *The Color Purple* (1982), which won the *Pulitzer Prize for fiction in 1983, but which also provoked controversy for its hostile depiction of African American men. This novel tells the story of Celie, a young black woman in the South, raped by the man she believes to be her father and then forced to marry an older man she despises. It is narrated through letters from Celie to God, and to and from her missionary sister Nettie. Walker has published collections of poetry, including *Once: Poems* (1968) and *Revolutionary Petunias and Other Poems* (1973). Her other work includes short stories and a collection of essays, *In Search of my Mother's Garden: Womanist Prose* (1983). Her novel *Possessing the Secret of Joy* (1992) examines female circumcision, and *The Same River Twice* (1996) is a memoir. See Evelyn C. Scott, *Alice Walker* (2004).

WALKER, Thomas (1784–1836) Author and magistrate, educated at Trinity College, Cambridge, and called to the bar 1812. He was the author of a weekly periodical, *The Original*, of which 29 numbers appeared (20 May to 2 December 1835). Its purpose was to raise 'the national tone in whatever concerns us socially or individually', and it is especially remembered for Walker's admirable papers on health and gastronomy.

WALLACE, Alfred Russel (1823–1913) Naturalist and traveller, born at Usk, Monmouthshire; he left school at 14 and found work surveying and teaching. A self-taught botany enthusiast, he joined a collecting expedition to the Amazon in 1848. While his huge collection was destroyed by fire on the return voyage, his 1853 account of the expedition was a best-seller. During an eight-year journey described in *The Malay Archipelago* (1869) he, independently of *Darwin, developed the theory of natural selection. Darwin presented their joint findings to the Linnean Society (*see* LINNAEUS, CARL VON) in 1858. Wallace coined the term 'survival of the fittest' and mapped 'Wallace's line' demarcating the Asian and Australasian faunal regions. He was doomed to be remembered (as Margaret *Drabble has put it) as 'forgotten', overshadowed by the more established Darwin and marginalized by his interests in spiritualism, socialism, and women's suffrage. His voluminous writing embraced travel, science, and social criticism. He published an autobiography in 1905. See Martin Fichman, *An Elusive Victorian* (2004).

WALLACE, Edgar (1875–1932) Writer and playwright, born in Greenwich, London. He left school at 12 and published his first book, a collection of ballads, in 1898. He became an extremely successful and remarkably prolific writer of thrillers, including *The Four Just Men* (1905), *The Crimson Circle* (1922), and *The Green Archer* (1923). He also wrote successful plays, and died in Hollywood, where he had been working on the screenplay of *King Kong* (1933).

WALLACE, Sir William (d. 1305) A Scottish patriot of the time of Edward I, who devoted his life to resistance to the English and was finally captured by treachery and executed in London. He is the subject of a long poem (*see* HARY'S WALLACE). *Braveheart* (1995), Mel Gibson's stirring film about his life, greatly enhanced his status as national hero.

WALLER, Edmund (1606–87) Poet and politician, educated at Eton College and King's College, Cambridge. He is said to have entered Parliament at 16. In 1643 he plotted to seize London for Charles I, and was banished. He travelled with John *Evelyn in Switzerland and Italy, but made his peace with Oliver *Cromwell in 1651, and returned to England. After the death of his first wife, an heiress whom he had married surreptitiously, he unsuccessfully courted

Lady Dorothy Sidney, the 'Sacharissa' of his poems. His use of the heroic couplet led John *Dryden to praise him as 'the father of our English numbers'. 'Go, lovely rose' (from *Poems*, 1645) is his best-known lyric, and 'Of the Last Verses in the Book' contains the famous lines

> The Soul's dark cottage, battered and decayed,
> Lets in new light through chinks that time hath made.

See *Poems*, ed. G. Thorn-Drury (2 vols, 1893).

WALMSLEY, Leo *See* REGIONAL NOVEL.

WALPOLE, Horace, fourth earl of Orford (1717–97) Author and politician, fourth son of Sir Robert Walpole (1676–1745), educated at Eton College, where he formed a 'Quadruple Alliance' with Thomas *Gray, Richard West (1716–42), and Thomas Ashton (1715–75); then at King's College, Cambridge. In 1737 his mother, to whom he was deeply attached, died, and six months later his father married his mistress Maria Skerrett (1702–38), who died shortly afterwards. In 1739–41 Walpole travelled in France and Italy with Gray, and met in Florence the diplomat Horace Mann (1701–86), who became one of his most valued correspondents. At Reggio he and Gray quarrelled and parted company. Walpole was MP successively for Callington, Castle Rising, and Lynn, 1741–67. From 1741 he catalogued the collection of paintings at his father's house at Houghton, Norfolk, producing *Aedes Walpolianae* in 1747. His father died in 1745, and in 1747 Walpole settled in Twickenham in the house he made known as Strawberry Hill, rebuilding it as 'a little Gothic castle' which later became a tourist attraction for which Walpole printed his own *Description*. In 1757 he established his own printing press here; his first publication was Gray's Pindaric *Odes, he and Gray having been lastingly reconciled in 1745. In 1758 he printed his own *A Catalogue of the Royal and Noble Authors of England* and *Fugitive Pieces in Verse and Prose*, and in 1762 his *Anecdotes of Painting in England*. His *Gothic novel *The *Castle of Otranto* appeared late in 1764. In 1765 Walpole made the first of several visits to Paris, where he met Madame *du Deffand, with whom he formed a lasting friendship. In 1768 he published *Historic Doubts on the Life and Reign of King Richard the Third*, in which he attempted to acquit Richard of the crimes imputed to him by historians, and in the same year printed but did not publish his tragedy *The *Mysterious Mother*. He became embroiled in the controversy surrounding Thomas *Chatterton when the young poet sent him a fake manuscript about early English painting which, after consultation with Gray and William *Mason, he rejected; accused of hastening Chatterton's apparent suicide by his neglect, he defended himself in a pamphlet of 1782. In 1787/8 he met the sisters Agnes and Mary Berry, who became the intimate friends of his last years; in 1791 they settled at Little Strawberry Hill, where the actress Katherine (Kitty) Clive (1711–85) had been Walpole's neighbour until her death six years earlier. In the same year he succeeded his nephew to the earldom. Walpole left his Memoirs ready for publication in a sealed chest, which was opened in 1818. *Memoirs of the Last Ten Years of the Reign of George II* was first edited in 1822 (modern edition by J. Brooke, 3 vols, 1985); *Memoirs of the Reign of King George the Third* first appeared in 1845 (modern edition by D. Jarrett, 4 vols, 2000). Some of Walpole's letters appeared with his *Works* in 1798, edited by Mary Berry: the monumental Yale edition of the *Correspondence*, ed. W. S. Lewis *et al.* (48 vols, 1937–83) has established Walpole's reputation as an assiduous, stylish, and witty observer of his age. This edition, together with modern biographies (such as R. W. Ketton-Cremer's *Horace Walpole*, 1946), extensive critical study of *The Castle of Otranto*, and the unflagging efforts of W. S. Lewis (1897–1979) to collect anything and everything related to Walpole (culminating in the establishment of the Lewis Walpole Library in Connecticut) have done much to dispel the 19th-century image of Walpole, inspired by Lord *Macaulay's attack in the **Edinburgh Review*, 1833, as merely a malicious and affected gossip.

WALPOLE, Sir Hugh (1884–1941) Novelist, born in Auckland, New Zealand, and educated (briefly) at King's School, Canterbury, and at Emmanuel College, Cambridge. The first of his 36 novels was *The Wooden Horse* (1909); his third novel, *Mr Perrin and Mr Traill* (1911), reflected his short experience of teaching. *The Dark Forest* (1915) is based on his wartime service with the Russian Red Cross. Other works include *Jeremy* (1919) and the *Herries Chronicle*, a historical sequence set in Cumberland (where Walpole lived from 1924), consisting of *Rogue Herries* (1930), *Judith Paris* (1931), *The Fortress* (1932), *Vanessa* (1933), and two further novels. Although proud of his popularity, he worried that his work was old-fashioned and he was deeply offended by Somerset *Maugham's portrait of him as Alroy Kear, a hypocritical literary opportunist, in *Cakes and Ale* (1930). He was knighted in 1937.

WALSH, Jill (Gillian) **Paton** (1937–) CBE London-born novelist and children's writer, educated at St Anne's College, Oxford. Her novels include *Lapsing* (1986), set in Oxford of the 1950s; *A School for Lovers* (1989), a country-house romance, and *Knowledge of Angels* (1994), a medieval romance which discusses the nature and grounds of belief, and the question of whether or not we have innate knowledge of the existence of God. Her reputation as a children's writer was established with *Goldengrove* (1972) and its sequel *Unleaving* (1976) about the end of childhood; *The Emperor's Winding-Sheet* (1974), set during the fall of Constantinople, the time-slip fantasy *A Chance Child* (1978), and the plague story *A Parcel of Patterns* (1984). Her novelization of Grace Darling's life, *Grace* (1992), was widely praised. Walsh also writes detective stories featuring Imogen Quy. *Thrones, Dominations* (1998) is a continuation of an unfinished work by Dorothy *Sayers.

WALSH, William (1663–1708) Poet, author of *eclogues, elegies, songs, and light satires, educated at Wadham College, Oxford. John *Dryden commended him as 'the best Critick of our Nation' in 1697. Walsh advised Alexander *Pope on matters of stylistic correctness in his 'Pastorals', and Pope praised him in his **Essay on Criticism* as 'the Muse's judge and friend'.

WALTON, Izaak (1593–1683) Born at Stafford. He was apprenticed in London to a kinsman who was a draper and a member of the Ironmongers' Company, and later carried on trade there on his own account. He was a friend of John *Donne and Sir Henry *Wotton and of Bishops Morley (?1598–1684), Sanderson (1587–1663), and Henry *King. He was twice married, and spent the latter part of his life at Winchester, where his son-in-law was a clergyman. His biographies of Donne (1640), Wotton (1651), Richard *Hooker (1665), George *Herbert (1670), and Sanderson (1678) are gentle and admiring in tone. He is chiefly known for *The *Compleat Angler*, first published 1653, and largely rewritten for the second edition (1655), which is half as long again. Often reprinted, this work combines practical information about angling with folklore, quotations from writers as diverse as *Pliny, Guillaume de Saluste *Du Bartas, and Herbert, pastoral interludes of songs and ballads, and glimpses of an idyllic rural life of well-kept inns and tuneful milkmaids. *See* COTTON, CHARLES.

WALTON, Sir William (1902–83) English composer, educated at Christ Church, Oxford, where he was befriended by the Sitwell family. Walton's innovative *Façade* (1922), for voice and six instruments, was based on 21 poems by Edith *Sitwell (recited at early performances by the poet herself). Walton also set three of her poems as independent songs. The text of his dramatic cantata *Belshazzar's Feast* (1931) was arranged by Osbert *Sitwell from biblical sources. A later choral work, *In Honour of the City of London* (1937), was a setting of William *Dunbar. Walton also set poems by A. C. *Swinburne and Louis *MacNeice. His opera *Troilus and Cressida* (1954) follows *Chaucer's version; his *The Bear* (1967) is distantly based on Anton *Chekhov. Walton produced incidental music for a stage production of **Macbeth* (1942), and scores for Laurence Olivier's Shakespeare films **Henry V* (1944), **Hamlet* (1947), and **Richard III* (1955). Walton was knighted in 1951.

WALWYN, William (*c.*1600–1681) Pamphleteer and a leader of the Leveller movement, born in Newland, Worcestershire. Apprenticed to a London silk merchant, he became a master weaver. He married Anne Gundell in 1627 and they had twenty children. Private theological and philosophical study led him to champion complete religious freedom and voluntary community of property, which he advocated in a series of tracts. He quoted *Montaigne in support of his own humane rationalism. In the 1640s he led the protest against the imprisonment of John *Lilburne and other Levellers. He was imprisoned himself in 1649 with Lilburne, Richard *Overton, and Thomas Prince (*fl.*1630–67) as one of the authors of *England's New Chains Discovered*, a criticism of the new Parliamentary regime. In later life he practised as a physician. See H. N. Brailsford, *The Levellers and the English Revolution* (1961, 1976); J. R. MacMichael and B. Taft (eds). *The Writings of William Walwyn* (1989).

Wanderer, The An Old English poem of 115 lines in the *Exeter Book, one of the group known as 'elegies'. Beginning with the hardships of a man who has lost his lord, it becomes a plangent lament for the transience of life, culminating towards its end in a powerful **ubi sunt* passage. It begins and ends with a brief and bald statement of Christian consolation, but that is not the prevailing sentiment of the poem. It is paralleled in spirit and structure by *The *Seafarer*, particularly in the latter's first half, and similar arguments have been advanced for and against the coherence of organization in both poems. The poem was admired by W. H. *Auden, among other modern poets, and he translated it loosely. Ed. R. F. Leslie (1966), A. J. Bliss and T. P. Dunning (1969).

Wanderer, The A poem in five cantos by Richard *Savage, published 1729. The suffering wanderer is taught to interpret the landscapes and figures of a 'strange visionary land' by an angelic hermit. The poem has several narrative episodes, advice on the life of the poet, passages of vivid natural description and dark reflections on murder, death, and suicide. Samuel *Johnson called it 'a heap of shining materials thrown together by accident, which strikes...with the solemn magnificence of a stupendous ruin'.

Wanderer, The, *or Female Difficulties* The last novel of Fanny *Burney, published in 1814. Less successful than her earlier works, it was criticized for its improbabilities (William *Hazlitt in the **Edinburgh Review* commented that the female difficulties were 'created out of nothing') and its convoluted style—according to Thomas Babington *Macaulay 'a sort of broken Johnsonese, a barbarous *patois*'. It describes the adventures of its mysterious and, for much of the novel, nameless heroine, Juliet, escaped from revolutionary France and hard pressed by poverty, unwanted male attention, and the social conventions which prevent her from earning her own living. Her friend and foil, the passionate Elinor Joddrel, who loves Juliet's admirer Harleigh, provides an interesting portrait of the emancipated woman of the period, possibly based in part on Madame de *Staël, whom Burney had met in 1793, as one of a circle of French émigrés which included her own future husband. The novel's vigorous social satire has drawn critical attention in recent years.

WANDOR, Michelene (1940–) Playwright, poet, and critic, born in London, educated at Newnham College, Cambridge. An important figure in the history of British feminism, she was involved in the Women's Liberation movement from 1969, and edited *The Body Politic*, a collection of feminist essays, in 1972. She has had more than twenty plays produced, including *The Wandering Jew* (1987), the first play by a woman put on at the *National Theatre. These interests combined in her editorship of the first four volumes of the ground-breaking *Plays by Women*, and she is the author of *Carry On, Understudies: Theatre and Sexual Politics* (1986, an expanded version of *Understudies* 1981) and *Post-war British Drama: Looking Back in Gender* (2001, a reworking of *Look Back in Gender* 1987). She worked with the founding women's theatre groups Women's Theatre Group and Monstrous Regiment, and was the poetry editor of *Time Out* from 1971 to 1982. Her *Music of the Prophets*

(2007) commemorates the 350th anniversary of the Jews' return to England in 1657.

WANLEY, Humfrey (1672–1726) Scholar. He was apprenticed to a Coventry draper, but studied Anglo-Saxon and palaeography and became an assistant in the Bodleian Library, Oxford, in 1695, contributing to Edward Bernard's *Catalogi Librorum Manuscriptorum Angliae et Hiberniae* (1697). His catalogue of Anglo-Saxon manuscripts was published in 1705. His diary (ed. C. E. and R. C. Wright, 1966) records his work as librarian to Robert *Harley and his son Edward, from 1708, when he began a catalogue of the *Harleian manuscripts. Through Harley, Wanley became friendly with Alexander *Pope, John *Gay, and Matthew *Prior.

WANLEY, Nathaniel (1632/3–80) Clergyman and poet, and father of Humfrey *Wanley. He published *The Wonders of the Little World* (1678), a collection of tales and superstitions in which Robert *Browning found the story of the 'Pied Piper of Hamelin' and other oddities. His poems, some in the vein of Henry *Vaughan, were edited by L. C. Martin (1928).

WARBURTON, Eliot (Bartholomew Elliott George) (1810–52) An Irish barrister, educated at Trinity College, Cambridge, and called to the Irish bar in 1837; he abandoned his profession for travel and the literary life. His account of an Eastern tour, *The Crescent and the Cross, or Romance and Realities of Eastern Travel* (1845), was a highly successful work which covered much the same ground as his friend Alexander *Kinglake's *Eothen*. Among Warburton's other works were *Memoirs of Prince Rupert and the Cavaliers* (1849) and two historical novels, *Reginald Hastings* (1850) and *Darien* (1852).

WARBURTON, John (1682–1759) Antiquary and manuscript collector. His manuscripts of Elizabethan and Jacobean plays, some of them unique, were mostly destroyed by Betsy Baker, his cook, who burned them or put them 'under pye bottoms'. Warburton's list of 55 destroyed plays (three more, with one fragment, were saved) is in the British Library, with other surviving mansucripts.

WARBURTON, William (1698–1779) Clergyman and writer, vigorously engaged in theological debate. His most famous work was *The Divine Legation of Moses* (1738–41), a controversial attack on *Deism. He defended the orthodoxy of Alexander *Pope's **Essay on Man*, and became a close associate, and literary executor, of the poet; he produced a supposedly authoritative edition of his works (1751), source of many subsequent editions. His combative edition of *Shakespeare (1747) attacked Lewis *Theobald, a former friend. Warburton denounced the 'natural religion' of Pope's friend Viscount *Bolingbroke in *A View of Lord Bolingbroke's Philosophy* (1754). In 1760 he became bishop of Gloucester, and in other works he opposed the 'enthusiasm' of John *Wesley and David *Hume's views on miracles. Despite Warburton's capacity for making enemies, Samuel *Johnson remained grateful for his early commendation of Johnson's essay on **Macbeth* (1747): 'He praised me at a time when praise was of value to me.'

WARD, Artemus (1834–67) The pen-name of Charles Farrar Browne, American humorist, born in Maine, who purported to describe the experiences of a travelling showman, using, like 'Josh Billings' (Henry Wheeler Shaw, 1818–85), his own comic phonetic spelling. He met Mark *Twain in Nevada in the 1860s and helped shape his career. See John J. Pullen, *Comic Relief* (1983).

WARD, Edward ('Ned') (1667–1731) Tavern-keeper and writer (under various pseudonyms) of *Hudibrastic verse, travel stories, and satires. *The London Spy*, issued in 18 monthly parts (1698–1700) recounts the sights, sounds, smells, and characters encountered in a series of walks through the capital. Ward was fined and pilloried for *Hudibras Redivivus*, a burlesque poem, published in 24 monthly parts (1705–7). Alexander *Pope satirized him in *Peri Bathous* and *The Dunciad* and Ward wrote at least two responses.

WARD, John (*c.*1590–1638) English composer of *madrigals; his *First Set of English Madrigals* (1613) contains settings of Philip *Sidney and Michael *Drayton, and the famous 'Come, sable night'.

WARD, Mary Augusta Novelist and philanthropist, commonly known as Mrs Humphry Ward (1851–1920), granddaughter of Thomas *Arnold of Rugby, and daughter of the literary scholar and teacher Thomas Arnold (1823–1900), whose religious vacillations caused his family much distress. Born in Hobart, Tasmania, she was partly educated at a boarding school in Ambleside run by Anne Jemima Clough (1820–92), who later became the first principal of Newnham College, Cambridge. But her childhood, largely spent in separation from her family in a series of boarding schools, was unhappy, and her education patchy. Her father's reconversion to Anglicanism allowed him to teach in Oxford, where she joined the family, read widely, and met Thomas Humphry Ward, then an Oxford don and later on the staff of *The *Times* in London, whom she married in 1872. Her most famous novel, *Robert Elsmere* (1888), is in part a vivid evocation of the Oxford of Walter *Pater, Mark *Pattison, and T. H. *Green, and of the many varieties of religious faith and doubt which succeeded the ferment of the *Oxford Movement. Its protagonist, an earnest but questioning clergyman, resigns his orders for a life of social service in the East End, to the distress of his devout wife Catherine. It became one of the most popular novels of the 19th century, its success initially stimulated by a long and thoughtful review it received from W. E. *Gladstone; the author herself compared it to J. A. *Froude's *The Nemesis of Faith* and J. H. *Newman's *Loss and*

Gain, novels which also dealt with the crisis of mid-Victorian faith. Most of her other novels deal with social, political, and religious themes, frequently contrasting traditional belief with the values of progress and intellectual freedom. They include *The History of David Grieve* (1892), *Marcella* (1894), *Helbeck of Bannisdale* (1898), *Lady Rose's Daughter* (1903), and *The Marriage of William Ashe* (1905). She inherited the Arnold sense of high moral purpose, was an active philanthropist and a leading figure in the intellectual life of her day; she supported the movement for higher education for women, but opposed women's suffrage, on the grounds that women's influence was stronger in the home than in public life. She was a tireless propagandist in the First World War, and did much to mobilize support in America, where she had always been popular. Her *A Writer's Recollections* (1918) draws a striking picture of Oxford life and of the domestic influence of William *Morris, Edward *Burne-Jones, and Liberty prints; it also contains portraits of Benjamin *Jowett, Pater, Henry *James, and other friends. In the year she died (1920), she became one of England's first women magistrates. See J. Sutherland, *Mrs Humphry Ward* (1990).

WARD, Plumer Robert (1765–1846) A lawyer and MP who held minor government posts and wrote on legal and political matters. When he was 60 he unexpectedly published his first fiction, *Tremaine, or A Man of Refinement* (1825), a *fashionable novel. His motives were didactic, and he hoped that his works of fiction (which he did not care to call 'novels') would display 'Philosophy teaching by examples', and demonstrate how the standards of public and private morality could be upheld amid the dissipation of the times. In 1827 appeared *De Vere, or The Man of Independence* and in 1841 *De Clifford, or The Constant Man*.

Warden, The A short novel by Anthony *Trollope, published 1855, the first in the *'Barsetshire' series. It represents a turning point in Trollope's career. The income of Hiram's Hospital, a charitable institution, has grown down the centuries, but the twelve bedesmen have not benefited. The surplus has created a pleasant sinecure for the gentle warden, Septimus Harding, a fact which John Bold, a local surgeon with a passion for reform, makes known to the national press. Harding is subjected to unpleasant publicity, and his son-in-law, the conservative Archdeacon Grantly, bullies him to dispute the case along party lines. But Harding sees the anomaly in his position, and with considerable personal courage resigns. The novel ends in an atmosphere of quiet goodwill, with Bold withdrawing his accusations and marrying the warden's daughter Eleanor, and Harding receiving a new preferment in the cathedral close. Meanwhile, the Hospital falls into neglect, and the bedesmen find no profit in their new situation.

WARLOCK, Peter (1894–1930) Pseudonym of Philip Heseltine, English song composer, educated at Eton College. Under his official name he was much involved in the recovery of early English music; he wrote a study of Thomas *Whythorne, among much editorial work. Many of his songs were based on poems of this period, such as 'Sleep' (1922, to a poem by John *Fletcher, for voice and string quartet). But his choice of texts was extremely varied, and includes poems by Arthur *Symons, Hilaire *Belloc, and Bruce Blunt (1899–1957). He had a troubled friendship with D. H. *Lawrence, who at one stage intended to portray him in **Women in Love*. Warlock's friendship with Frederick *Delius (about whom he also wrote) greatly influenced the harmonic idiom of his later songs. The intense, haunting cycle *The Curlew* (1922), to words by W. B. *Yeats, for tenor and six instruments, is considered his masterpiece.

WARNER, Alan (1964–) Scottish novelist and short story writer, born in Oban, Argyll, and resident in Co. Wicklow. His acclaimed first novel, *Morvern Callar* (1995), is written in the voice of a semi-literate young woman living in the West Highlands of Scotland in the early 1990s. Her mysterious older boyfriend kills himself, leaving money and an unpublished manuscript: she appropriates both and runs away to a life of dissolution in Spain. The novel's style combines banal colloquialism with sophisticated lyricism. Warner's second and rather more experimental novel, *These Demented Lands* (1997), continues the story of Morvern to evoke a New Age nightmare of shipwreck on an offshore island, with echoes of William *Golding and Joseph *Conrad. *The Sopranos* (1998), a traditionally structured story about a group of drunken Highland schoolgirls on a day trip to Edinburgh, enjoyed greater popular than critical success. *The Man Who Walks* (2002) presents a darkly comic, partly fantastical narrative of the interactions of a group of Scottish misfits, while the widely admired *The Worms Can Carry Me to Heaven* (2006) recounts the colourful, self-deluding life of Manolo, a Spanish playboy who learns that he is HIV-positive. Warner has sometimes been seen as a leader of the so-called 'Chemical Generation', along with Irvine *Welsh. The term refers loosely to a group of younger writers, predominantly Scottish, whose work displays a comfortable familiarity with 1990s youth culture: music, fashion, nightclubs, and drugs.

WARNER, Marina (1946–) CBE, novelist, critic, and cultural historian, born in London and educated at Lady Margaret Hall, Oxford. Her novels include *The Skating Party* (1983), *The Lost Father* (1988), *Indigo, or Mapping the Waters* (1992), an exploration of colonialism and displacement, set on an imaginary Caribbean island, and *The Leto Bundle* (2001). She has also published volumes of short stories and several books for children. Her scholarly works include *Alone of All her Sex* (1976), a study of the myth and cult of the Virgin Mary, *Joan of Arc: The Image of Female Heroism* (1981) and *From the Beast to the Blonde* (1994), a study of *fairy-tales. *No Go the Bogeyman* (1998) investigates what scares us and how we master our fears by translating them into art and narrative; *Signs and Wonders* (2003) is a collection of essays on literature and culture.

WARNER, Rex (1905–86) Poet, novelist, and translator, born in Amberley, Gloucestershire, and educated at St George's School, Harpenden, and Wadham College, Oxford, where he was a close friend of Cecil *Day-Lewis; W. H. *Auden and Stephen *Spender were also Oxford friends. His *Poems* appeared in 1937, as did his striking and well-received first novel, *The Wild Goose Chase* (1937). *The Professor* (1938), and his best work of fiction, *The Aerodrome* (1941; ironically subtitled 'A Love Story'), followed in quick succession and are more sombre political parables which reflect the gathering gloom of the 1930s; in *The Aerodrome* in particular, the matter-of-fact and the uncanny mingle with disturbing effect. His later fiction is based largely on Greek or Roman historical subjects, and he also translated the *Medea* (1944), *Hippolytus* (1950), and *Helen* (1951) of *Euripides, and the *Prometheus Bound* (1947) of *Aeschylus.

WARNER, Sylvia Townsend (1893–1978) Novelist and poet, born in Harrow, the daughter of a housemaster at Harrow School, educated privately and haphazardly. She worked as an editor of *Tudor Church Music* (10 vols, 1922–9) and her love of early music is reflected in her later fiction. Her first volume of poems, *The Espalier* (1925), was followed by several others, including *Opus 7* (1931), a novel in verse. Her *Collected Poems* appeared in 1982, but her original voice is heard more strongly in her novels, which often draw on folklore and include *Lolly Willowes* (1926), the story of a maiden aunt who realizes her vocation as a witch; *Mr Fortune's Maggot* (1927), which describes the eponymous missionary's sojourn on a remote South Sea island, where he makes only one doubtful convert and in the process loses his own faith; and *The True Heart* (1929), set in the Essex marshes, which retells the story of *Cupid and Psyche through the medium of a Victorian orphan. Another old story is retold in a contemporary setting in *After the Death of Don Juan* (1938), an allegorical novel of the Spanish Civil War. *The Corner That Held Them* (1948) is set in a closed community of nuns in fourteenth-century East Anglia. Later works include a translation of *Proust's *Contre Sainte-Beuve* (1958), a biography of T. H. *White (1967), and several collections of short stories, many previously first published in the *New Yorker*. Her *Letters* (1982, ed. W. Maxwell) and *Diaries* (1994, ed. C. Harman) describe her many friendships, notably with T. F. *Powys, and her love for the poet Valentine Ackland, with whom she lived in Dorset until the latter's death in 1969. See Claire Harman, *Sylvia Townsend Warner* (1989).

WARNER, William (1558/9–1609) Poet and author; also an attorney in London. He published *Pan his Syrinx*, seven prose tales (1584), and a translation of the *Menaechmi* of *Plautus (1595) may be his. His chief work was *Albion's England*, a metrical British history, written in *fourteeners, with mythical and fictitious episodes, extending in the first edition (1586) from Noah to the Norman Conquest. It was brought up to *Elizabeth I's reign in 1592; and a continuation, reaching *James I, was published in 1606. Francis *Meres, in his *Palladis Tamia* (1598), claimed to have heard Warner called 'our English Homer', and Michael *Drayton praised him in his elegy *To Henery Reynolds*; the assessment of C. S. *Lewis was that 'The good things in *Albion's England* are as far divided as the suns in space.'

War of the Worlds, The ;A *scientific romance by H. G. *Wells, published 1898, written while he was living in Woking. It describes the arrival of the Martians in Woking, driven from their own planet by its progressive cooling to take refuge in a warmer world. In a letter Wells described his plan for the work, in which: 'I completely wreck and sack Woking—killing my neighbours in painful and eccentric ways—then proceed via Kingston and Richmond to London, selecting South Kensington for feats of peculiar atrocity'; much of the novel's power depends on the contrast between the familiar complacent reactions of the humans and the terrifying destructive intelligence of the Martians, who consist of round bodies, each about four feet in diameter, each body containing a huge brain. They live by the injection into themselves of the fresh living blood of other creatures, mostly of human beings, and they devastate the country before eventually falling victims to terrestrial bacteria. A radio broadcast by Orson *Welles of a dramatization of the novel in the USA on 30 October 1938 caused a furore, many of its millions of listeners taking it for a factual report of the invasion of New Jersey by Martians.

war poetry, 20th-century It is generally agreed that the First World War (1914–18) inspired poetry of the highest order, some of it ground-breaking in both treatment of subject and technique: combatants included Wilfred *Owen, Siegfried *Sassoon, Isaac *Rosenberg, Robert *Graves, Charles Hamilton *Sorley, Edward *Thomas, and Rupert *Brooke (the last of whom died before seeing active service). Memorable poems and elegies on the theme were contributed by Thomas *Hardy, Laurence *Binyon, A. E *Housman, and others. Rudyard *Kipling's poetry struck a different and more patriotic note from that of most of his contemporaries, but the anguish of losing his son to the conflict left a deep mark on him and his work. The Spanish Civil War (1936–9), very much a writers' war, attracted some important British poets, including John *Cornford, Stephen *Spender, W. H *Auden, and Louis *MacNeice, as well as less well-remembered names like those of Clive Branson (1907–44), Bernard Gutteridge (1916–85), and H. B. Mallalieu (1914–88). (See Valentine Cunningham, *The Penguin Book of Spanish Civil War Verse*, 1980.) The Second World War produced a more disparate response: the poets most commonly associated with it are Keith *Douglas, Alun *Owen, and Sidney *Keyes, all of whom died in the conflict. However, F. T. *Prince, John *Pudney, and Henry *Reed are widely remembered for single, much-anthologized war poems, as well as other work, and later anthologies have revealed a considerable wealth and diversity of responses, some by writers like Alan *Ross and Charles *Causley who moved on to other subjects, some by writers who moved on to other careers. See Brian Gardner (ed.), *The Terrible Rain: The War Poets 1939–1945* (1966; rev. 1987); Desmond Graham

(ed.), *Poetry of the Second World War: An International Anthology* (1995); Catherine W. Reilly (ed.), *Scars upon my Heart: Women's Poetry and Verse of the First World War* (1981).
See also HOLOCAUST; HARSENT, DAVID.

WARREN, John Byrne Leicester, Baron de Tabley (1835–95) Poet, educated at Christ Church, Oxford. He published verse under the pseudonyms 'George F. Preston' (1859–62) and 'William Lancaster' (1863–8), and two tragedies, also under pseudonyms, *Philoctetes* (1866) and *Orestes* (1867). In 1893–5 he published under his own name two series of *Poems, Dramatic and Lyrical*; also *A Guide to the Study of Book Plates* (1880). He was a botanist, and some of his poems reveal a close observation of nature.

WARREN, Robert Penn (1905–89) American poet, novelist, and critic, born in Kentucky and educated at the universities of California, Yale, and Harvard. In the 1930s he was a member of the Southern Agrarians (a group of twelve traditionalist and conservative populist writers, including John Crowe *Ransom and Allen *Tate). His novels include *All the King's Men* (1946), a study of a power-crazed Southern politician modelled on Huey Long (1893–1935), *Band of Angels* (1955), *The Cave* (1959), and *Meet Me in the Green Glen* (1971); his volumes of poetry include *Promises* (1957), *Now and Then* (1978), and *Portrait of a Father* (1988). His critical works are associated with the *New Criticism, and include two anthologies-with-commentaries, compiled in collaboration with Cleanth *Brooks, *Understanding Poetry* (1938) and *Understanding Fiction* (1943). See Joseph Blotner, *Robert Penn Warren* (1997).

WARREN, Samuel (1807–77) Lawyer and novelist. Born near Wrexham, Wales, he studied medicine at Edinburgh, then became successively barrister, recorder of Hull, MP for Midhurst, and master in lunacy, with jurisdiction over the estates of those declared insane. Despite these multiple careers, from early youth he aimed for literary fame. His first publication, the morbidly melodramatic *Passages from the Diary of a Late Physician* (1830–7), first published in **Blackwood's*, provoked criticism from the *Lancet* for revealing professional secrets. Warren is best remembered for the sensationally popular comic novel *Ten Thousand a-Year* (1840–1), a story of greed and imposture concerning Mr Tittlebat Titmouse, a draper's assistant who inherits a vast fortune by way of documents forged by the lawyers Quirk, Gammon, and Snap, and whose unexpected elevation to wealth leads to absurd consequences.

Wars of the Roses, The The collective title given to John Barton and Peter *Hall's three-part adaptation of Shakespeare's history cycle of **Henry VI*, Parts 1, 2, and 3, and **Richard III*, first performed at Stratford in 1963, directed by Peter Hall. Barton composed about 1,400 lines of it.

war stories for children *Children's literature has included stories about war almost since its inception. Some books have depicted the hardships, injustices, and tragedies of war, not least for children—this is particularly true of more recent events such as the First World War, the Holocaust, and other genocidal conflicts. Many writers, however, treat war as romantic and dramatic; a time when children can be valiant and have adventures as in the stories of G. A. *Henty and Robert *Westall. There are sub-genres about Second World War evacuees, typified by Nina *Bawden's *Carrie's War* (1975), and refugees: Alem in Benjamin *Zephaniah's *Refugee Boy* (2001) has fled civil war in Africa. *Series books, magazines, and *comics have all included war stories. Futuristic wars often raise ethical questions as in Orson Scott *Card's *Ender's Game* (1994), in which adults use children, who think they are playing computer games, to exterminate an alien race. See Kate Agnew and Geoff Fox, *Children at War* (2004).

WARTON, Joseph (1722–1800) Clergyman, poet, and critic, educated at Winchester College (of which he was headmaster, 1766–93) and Oriel College, Oxford. He was the son of Thomas *Warton (1688–1745), whose poems he edited, with unacknowledged additions, with his brother Thomas *Warton (1728–90). His own early poems, such as *The Enthusiast, or The Lover of Nature* (1744), *Odes on Various Subjects* (1746), and *An Ode to Evening* (1749), reacted against the poetic dominance of Alexander *Pope. Warton's *An Essay on the Writings and Genius of Pope* (1756, 1782) ranks poets of the *sublime, such as William *Shakespeare, Edmund *Spenser, and John *Milton, above poets of ethical reasoning, such as Pope, a critique to which Samuel *Johnson responded in his account of Pope in **Lives of the English Poets*. Warton had contributed to the *Adventurer* at Johnson's request, and was elected a member of the *Club in 1777. His last completed work was an edition of Pope (1797).

WARTON, Thomas (1688–1745) Clergyman and poet, educated at Magdalen College, Oxford, and from 1718 to 1728 professor of poetry at Oxford. A collection of his odes, light satires, and 'runic' verse, with an imitation of Edmund *Spenser, was published (and in part written) by his sons Joseph and Thomas *Warton as *Poems on Several Occasions* (1748).

WARTON, Thomas (1728–90) Scholar and literary historian, educated at Trinity College, Oxford. He was the son of Thomas *Warton (1688–1745) whose poems he edited and partly fabricated with his brother Joseph *Warton. He made his mark with *Observations on the Faery Queen of Spenser* (1754) and was professor of poetry at Oxford 1757–67. He wrote much satiric verse and edited *The Oxford Sausage* (1764), an anthology of university poems; his serious verse includes many *sonnets, a form he helped to revive. He was a friend of Samuel *Johnson, contributed three numbers to the **Idler*, and was elected to the *Club in 1782. His *History of English Poetry* (3 vols, 1774–81) was the first substantial literary history of England, and showed unusual admiration for Geoffrey *Chaucer and other medieval authors. In 1782 Warton demonstrated that the poems produced by Thomas *Chatterton could not be medieval. His edition of the shorter poems of John *Milton appeared in 1785, the year he became poet laureate.

WASHINGTON, Booker T. (Taliaferro) (1856–1915) African American writer, born into slavery on a Virginia plantation. Freed, he taught himself to read, studied at the Hampton Institute in Virginia, and became the founder and head of the Tuskegee Institute, Alabama, a school for African Americans. He was an eloquent speaker and a voluminous writer, and became a spokesman for his people, though criticized by some for his accommodationist attitude to racism. His works include an autobiography, *Up from Slavery* (1901), and *Working with the Hands* (1904). See Louis R. Harlan, *Booker T. Washington*, 2 vols. (1972, 1983).
See also SLAVERY.

Washington Square A novel by Henry *James, published 1881. Catherine Sloper lives in Washington Square, New York, with her widowed father, a rich physician. She is plain and shy, and is approached by a handsome fortune-hunter, who drops his suit when her father threatens disinheritance. After the latter's death, he tries again, but is turned down by Catherine.

Waste Land, The A poem by T. S. *Eliot, first published 1922 in **Criterion* and a few days later in *The *Dial*. It consists of five sections, 'The Burial of the Dead', 'A Game of Chess', 'The Fire Sermon', 'Death by Water', and 'What the Thunder Said'. Boni and Liveright's edition of 1922 was the first to include Eliot's own 'Notes', which source his many allusions, quotations, and half-quotations (from John *Webster, *Dante, Paul *Verlaine, Thomas *Kyd, etc.), and indicate his general indebtedness to the *Grail legend and to the vegetation ceremonies in *Frazer's *The Golden Bough*. (Eliot himself was later to describe these 'Notes' as 'a remarkable exposition of bogus scholarship', written to pad out the text of the poem for book publication: 'The Frontiers of Criticism', 1956.) The poem was rapidly acclaimed as a statement of the post-war sense of futility; it was seriously praised by I. A. *Richards as 'a perfect emotive description of a state of mind which is probably inevitable for a while to all meditative people' (*Science and Poetry*, 1926), and less seriously but significantly hailed as a kind of protest against the older generation by the undergraduates of the day. Complex, erudite, cryptic, satiric, spiritually earnest, and occasionally lyrical, it became one of the most recognizable landmarks of *modernism, an original voice speaking through many echoes and parodies of echoes. Eliot himself found the poem's reputation a burden, and later remarked that it could be seen not so much as 'an important bit of social criticism', but as 'the relief of a personal and wholly insignificant grouse against life; it is just a piece of rhythmical grumbling.' Valerie Eliot's edition, *The Waste Land: A Facsimile and Transcript of the Original Drafts* (1971), shed much light on the circumstances of the poem's composition, and particularly on the well-heeded and detailed textual advice offered by Ezra *Pound (through which the poem's length was very considerably reduced); Lawrence Rainey's work has clarified the dates of composition. See L. Rainey (ed.), *The Annotated Waste Land* (2005).

Watchman, The (1796) A political and literary journal, of ten issues only, produced by S. T. *Coleridge. The journal was pacifist and opposed the Tory government of William Pitt, and included literary contributions from, among others, Thomas Lovell *Beddoes and Thomas *Poole.

Water-Babies, The: *A Fairy Tale for a Land-Baby* By Charles *Kingsley; serialized in **Macmillan's Magazine* 1862–3, published in book form in 1863 with illustrations by Sir (Joseph) Noël Paton (1821–1901). Supposedly written for Kingsley's son Grenville, the book is a Rabelaisian collection of fantasy episodes punctuated by authorial digressions on a wide range of the author's religious, philosophical, sexual, and social preoccupations. Consequently, although it is often celebrated as the first book in the 'first golden age' of children's literature, its address to children is highly ambiguous. It begins with a realistic picture of chimney-sweep Tom's Godless life in London with his drunken master Mr Grimes. While sweeping the chimneys of a large house, Tom gets lost, emerging into the symbolically white bedroom of the little girl Ellie, and is hounded by the household to his death (by drowning). He is then transformed into a water-baby, and the story effectively becomes a redemption allegory with the figures of Mrs Doasyouwouldbedoneby and Mrs Bedonebyasyoudid helping to develop Tom from a mindless slave to a moral being who appreciates the living world. This redemption extends to Grimes, after which Tom is reunited with Ellie. The book has survived into the 21st century largely in abridgements and adaptations. It was filmed by Lionel Jefferies in 1988. The standard text is edited by Brian Alderson (1995).

WATERHOUSE, Keith Spencer (1929–) Journalist, novelist, and dramatist, born and educated in Leeds. He had a considerable success with his second novel, *Billy Liar* (1959) a regional comedy about a youth who attempts to escape his dull family life through fantasy, which he adapted for the stage in 1960, with his long-standing friend and collaborator Willis Hall (1925–2005). Other novels include *Billy Liar on the Moon* (1976), *Office Life* (1978), *Maggie Muggins* (1981), and *Unsweet Charity* (1992). Waterhouse and Hall worked together on many stage, screen, and television plays, adaptations, and musicals, including the film *Whistle down the Wind* (1961). Waterhouse also wrote the screenplay of Stan *Barstow's *A Kind of Loving* (1960). *Jeffrey Bernard Is Unwell* (1989) was his successful adaptation for the stage of Bernard's **Spectator* columns. *City Lights* (1994) is the first part of his autobiography; it was followed by *Streets Ahead: Life After 'City Lights'* (1995).

water poet, the *See* TAYLOR, JOHN (1580–1653).

WATERS, Sarah (1966–) Novelist, born in Pembrokeshire; she studied English at the universities of Kent,

Lancaster, and London (where she wrote a thesis on lesbian and gay fiction from 1870 to the present), and was a tutor for the Open University before becoming a full-time writer. Her first three books each look back at a different decade of the Victorian age. *Tipping the Velvet* (1998) brings a music-hall swagger to its accounts of a young lesbian's escapades in the 1880s. *Affinity* (1999) gives resonances reminiscent of Emily *Dickinson or Henry *James to a haunting tale of spinsters and spiritualists in the 1870s. *Fingersmith* (2002) plunges into the lurid world of the 1860s *sensation novel. Uncovering lesbian existences scarcely glimpsed in 19th-century fiction motivated the writing of these books. With *The Night Watch* (2006), Waters moved into the 20th century, spotlighting covert, mainly homosexual, lives in the 1940s and portraying the impact on them of the Second World War and its aftermath. Like all her work, this powerful and atmospheric novel is much concerned with constraint and liberation, evokes the look and sound of an era with intense imaginative skill, and draws on extensive historical research (including immersion in the literature of the period being recreated). *The Little Stranger* (2009) is a *ghost story.

WATKINS, Vernon (1906–67) Poet, born in Wales of Welsh-speaking parents, and educated at Magdalene College, Cambridge. Spending most of his life near Swansea, he was a long-standing friend of Dylan *Thomas. Although sometimes associated with the *New Apocalypse, his poetry was, as Philip *Larkin—a perhaps unlikely admirer—was to record, 'much more controlled than theirs and reached further back to the symbolist poets of Europe'. The long, outstanding title poem of his first volume *Ballad of the Mari Lwyd* (1941) is rooted in Welsh folklore and mythology, whereas 'The Collier' and other poems in the collection are marked by a relative simplicity. Watkins's lyric gift was developed in many subsequent volumes, including *The Lamp and the Veil* (1945) and *Fidelities* (1968). His work shows an awareness of, and was influenced by, German and French poetry, and he translated Heinrich *Heine. *New Selected Poems* was published in 2006.

WATSON, Ian (1943–) *Science fiction writer, born in North Shields: his first novel *The Embedding* (1973), an exploration of linguistics, won the French Prix Apollo for its 1975 translation. He has since published a stream of fiercely intelligent novels and stories. *Miracle Visitors* (1978) is one of the comparatively few science fiction novels to take the issue of UFOs seriously. *Lucky's Harvest* (1993) begins a series based upon the Finnish epic the *Kalevala*; *Mockymen* (2003) combines Nazi occultists and alien visitors bringing gifts.

WATSON, John *See* KAILYARD SCHOOL.

WATSON, Richard (1737–1816) Clergyman, educated at Trinity College, Cambridge. In 1776 Watson published *An Apology for Christianity*, in opposition to Edward *Gibbon's sceptical account of the early history of Christianity. In 1782 he became bishop of Llandaff. Originally an orthodox Whig, Watson was later seen as a reactionary; William *Wordsworth's *Letter to the Bishop of Llandaff* (written 1793; pub. 1876) was a reply to Watson's attack on the French Revolution in his sermon on the 'Wisdom and Goodness of God' in creating both rich and poor. Watson's *Apology for the Bible* (1796) was a response to Thomas *Paine's *Age of Reason*. His autobiographical *Anecdotes* appeared in 1817.

WATSON, Thomas (1556/7–92) Poet and translator, educated at Winchester College and Oxford, he spent seven years in France and Italy, returning to study law in London. He published a Latin version of *Sophocles' *Antigone*, with an appendix of Latin allegorical poems and experiments in classical metres (1581). His major work was *The Ἑκατομπαθια or Passionate Century of Love* (1582), eighteen-line poems, called sonnets, often based on classical, French, and Italian sources, and accompanied by learned explanatory notes. His Latin-verse lamentations, *Amyntas* (1585), were translated without authority by Abraham *Fraunce (1587); they were followed by a translation of *Helenae Raptus* from the Greek of Colluthus (1586). Watson published *The First Set of Italian Madrigals Englished* (1590) with music by Luca Marenzio and William *Byrd and in the same year an *Eglogue*, in Latin and English versions, on the death of Sir Francis Walsingham (*c.*1532–1590). His Latin *pastoral *Amintae Gaudia* appeared posthumously (1592), and he may have written the *sonnet sequence *The Tears of Fancy* (1593). He was a close friend of Christopher *Marlowe, and was mentioned as 'Amyntas' in Edmund *Spenser's **Colin Clouts Come Home Againe*. There is an edition of his works by D. Sutton (1996).

WATSON, Sir William (1858–1935) Poet, born in Yorkshire and brought up in Liverpool, educated privately. He gained distinction with *Wordsworth's Grave and Other Poems* (1890) and *Lachrymae Musarum* (1892, verses on the death of Alfred *Tennyson). He was not sympathetic to *modernist forms of writing though he continued to write well into the 20th century.

Watsons, The An unfinished novel by Jane *Austen, written some time between 1804 and 1807. This story is sometimes seen, almost certainly mistakenly, as an early version of **Emma*. Although it is only a fragment, probably never revised, the characters are fully realized. The story is set at a social level below that of the other novels, and largely concerns the efforts of Emma Watson's three sisters to get themselves married. Emma, who has been brought up by a well-to-do aunt, returns to her family, who live unfashionably in genteel poverty in a Surrey village. A pretty, sensible girl, Emma is here surrounded by people in every way inferior to herself. Even her good-natured sister Elizabeth is as intent on a favourable match as her unpleasant sisters Margaret and Penelope. The other principal characters are Lady Osborne, handsome and dignified; her son, Lord Osborne, a fine but cold young man; Mr Howard, a gentlemanly clergyman; and Tom Musgrave, a cruel and hardened flirt. The intention appears to have been that the heroine should marry Mr

Howard, but Austen left no hint as to the future course of events, or why she abandoned the novel.

WATT, Robert (1774–1819) Scottish bibliographer, who began life as a farm and road labourer, and in his boyhood met Robert *Burns—'an extraordinary character'. He learned Greek and Latin, and proceeded to Glasgow and then Edinburgh University, where he studied classics, anatomy, and divinity, becoming a very successful doctor. His remarkable bibliographical compilation, which occupied him for some twenty years, *Bibliotheca Britannica, or A General Index to British and Foreign Literature*, provides lists of both authors and subjects, arranged alphabetically and then chronologically; it was published 1819–24.

WATTEAU, Jean-Antoine (1684–1721) French rococo painter who invented the 'fête-galante'—small pictures where elegant men and women, among them players from the **commedia dell'arte*, play music, and make love in a soft and dreamy parkland; the most famous of them is *The Embarkation for* [or *from*] *Cythera* (1717). Watteau died young, of consumption, and was notorious for his discontent and restlessness; his popularity declined in the late 18th century, but Romantic writers, among them Théophile *Gautier and Gérard de *Nerval, created around him an aura of mystery; they saw him as the tragic artist whose work is touched with melancholy and the transience of human pleasure. A vision of the enchanted, aristocratic 18th century in contrast to the bourgeois 19th century (expressed, notably, in an evocative essay by the *Goncourt brothers in *L'Art du dix-huitième siècle*), inspired many *fin-de-siècle* poets and artists, including Austin *Dobson, Aubrey *Beardsley, Charles *Ricketts, and Michael *Field; Walter *Pater's story 'A Prince of Court Painters' (in *Imaginary Portraits*, 1877), a study of ill-fated genius, is based on Watteau's life. See Julie-Ann Plax, *Watteau and the Cultural Politics of Eighteenth-Century France* (2000).

WATTS, Isaac (1674–1748) *Congregational minister, hymn-writer, educator, philosopher, and theologian, born in Southampton, and educated at a Dissenting academy in London. He was the leading Dissenting writer in the first half of the 18th century. Because of ill health he relied on an assistant in his ministry and amanuenses for his writing, and spent much of his life in the homes of his benefactors the Abneys. He published four collections of verse, *Horae Lyricae* (1706; enl. 1709), *Hymns and Spiritual Songs* (1707; enl. 1709), *Divine Songs for the Use of Children* (1715), and *The Psalms of David Imitated* (1719), regarding poetry as a divine gift which should be dedicated to God but which had been profaned. He was included in *The *Lives of the English Poets* at Samuel *Johnson's own suggestion. His *hymns had phenomenal sales and influence right through the 19th century, and his *Divine Songs* were imitated and parodied by William *Blake and Lewis Carroll (C. L. *Dodgson). His educational and philosophical works include *Logic: or the Right Use of Reason* (1725), *The Doctrine of the Passions* (1729), and *The Improvement of the Mind* (1741). With his *Humble Attempt towards the Revival of Practical Religion* (1731) he was an early instigator of the *Evangelical Revival, and he published the first edition of Jonathan *Edwards's *Faithful Narrative* (1737). See A. P. Davis, *Isaac Watts: His Life and Works* (1948).

WATTS-DUNTON, Theodore (1832–1914) Novelist and poet, born Watts at St Ives, Huntingdonshire; he gave up his profession as solicitor to devote himself to literature. He reviewed for *the *Examiner*, and then from 1876 to 1902 was one of the most influential writers for the **Athenaeum*; as its chief poetry reviewer, he supported the work of his friends in the *Pre-Raphaelite movement. Like George *Borrow, whom he met in 1872, he was interested in the Gypsies; his collection of poetry *The Coming of Love* (1898), reprinted from the *Athenaeum*, features the gypsy girls Rhona Boswell and Sinfi Lovell. These characters reappear in his novel *Aylwin* (1898), which recounts the love of Henry Aylwin for a Welsh girl, Winifred, his separation from her through a Gnostic curse, and his pursuit of her until their final reunion (with Sinfi Lovell's aid) on Snowdon. Its romantic mysticism and sensational plot brought it much success. His other works include introductions to Borrow's **Lavengro* (1893) and *The *Romany Rye* (1900), reminiscent sketches of D. G. *Rossetti, Alfred *Tennyson, etc., collected as *Old Familiar Faces* (1916), an article on 'Poetry' in the **Encyclopaedia Britannica* (9th edn 1885) and an essay, 'The Renascence of Wonder in English Poetry' (in Chambers's *Cyclopaedia of English Literature*, vol. iii, 1901), in which he strongly defends the Romantic movement. He is probably best remembered, however, for his loyal support of A. C. *Swinburne, whom he rescued from declining health in 1879, and who lived with him until his death in 1909, at the Pines, Putney, in an intimacy little interrupted by Watts-Dunton's late marriage, in 1905, to a woman much younger than himself.

WAUGH, Alec (1898–1981) Novelist and travel writer, born in Hampstead, London, and educated at Sherborne School and the Royal Military College, Sandhurst. His first novel, *The Loom of Youth* (1917), became a notorious success through its frank treatment of public-school homosexuality. It was followed by many others, including the late success *Island in the Sun* (1956), and several autobiographical volumes, such as *The Early Years of Alec Waugh* (1962) and *My Brother Evelyn and Other Profiles* (1967).

WAUGH, Auberon (1939–2001) Novelist, journalist, diarist, and editor of the *Literary Review* from 1986 until his death. Son of Evelyn *Waugh, he was educated at Downside School and Oxford University. His first novel, *The Foxglove Saga* (1960), written after sustaining serious injuries during National Service, is based on his experiences of illness, school, and military life. Other novels, including *The Path of Dalliance* (1963) and *A Bed of Flowers* (1972), followed, but Waugh abandoned fiction because, he claimed, it was impossible to make a living from it. He went on to publish several works of non-fiction, including collected articles from his columns in the *Spectator and the *Daily Telegraph, and an autobiography (*Will This Do?*, 1991). Two volumes of diaries, originally published in the satirical magazine *Private Eye*, full of tongue-in-cheek prejudice, fantasy, and vituperative attacks on those of whom he disapproved, appeared in 1976 and 1985.

WAUGH, Evelyn (1903–66) Writer, born in West Hampstead, London, and educated at Lancing College, Sussex, and Hertford College, Oxford, where he devoted himself more to social than to academic life. He took a third-class degree, then worked for some years as a schoolmaster, a largely unhappy experience which provided material for *Decline and Fall* (1928), his immensely successful first novel, which followed the publication of his study of Dante Gabriel *Rossetti earlier that year. In 1928 he married Evelyn Gardner; in 1930 he was divorced, and received into the Roman Catholic Church. His career as a novelist prospered, with *Vile Bodies* (1930), *Black Mischief* (1932, set in Africa), *A Handful of Dust* (1934), and *Scoop* (1938), works of high comedy and social satire which capture the brittle, cynical, determined frivolity of the inter-war generation, all being well received. He also established himself as journalist and travel writer with accounts of a journey through Africa (*Remote People*, 1931), a journey through South America (*Ninety-Two Days*, 1934), and Mussolini's invasion of Abyssinia (*Waugh in Abyssinia*, 1936). In 1937 he married Laura Herbert, a cousin of his first wife, and from this time onwards made his home in the West Country, first at Piers Court in Gloucestershire, then at Combe Florey in Somerset, where he cultivated the image of the country squire, with, eventually, a family of six children. The war, however, intervened; *Put out More Flags* (1942) was written while he was serving in the army, and his wartime experiences in Crete and Yugoslavia provided the material for his trilogy *Sword of Honour* (1965), originally published as *Men at Arms* (1952), *Officers and Gentlemen* (1955), and *Unconditional Surrender* (1961). In the interim appeared one of his most popular works, *Brideshead Revisited* (1945), and a macabre comedy about Californian funeral practices, *The Loved One* (1948). *Helena* was published to indifferent reviews in 1950 and *The Ordeal of Gilbert Pinfold*, a bizarre novel about a famous 50-year-old Roman Catholic novelist, corpulent, heavy-drinking, insomniac, out of tune with modern life, plagued by disgust and boredom, appeared in 1957. Waugh's other works include a biography of *Edmund *Campion* (1935) and a volume of autobiography, *A Little Learning* (1964). His *Diaries* appeared in 1972; his *Letters* in 1980, and his *Essays, Articles and Reviews* in 1983. There is a two-volume life by Martin Stannard (1986, 1992).

Waverley The first of the novels of Walter *Scott, published 1814. Much of it had been written, and thrown aside, some years before. Edward Waverley, a romantic young man, has been brought up partly by a Hanoverian father, partly by his uncle Sir Everard Waverley, a rich landowner of *Jacobite leanings. Ambivalent in politics, he is commissioned in the army in 1745 and joins his regiment in Scotland. He visits his uncle's friend the Baron Bradwardine, a kind-hearted but pedantic old Jacobite, and attracts the interest of his daughter Rose. Curious, he visits Donald Bean Lean, a Highland freebooter, and Fergus MacIvor (Vich Ian Vohr) of Glennaquoich, a young Highland Jacobite chieftain. At Glennaquoich, he falls in love with Fergus's sister Flora, whose beauty and ardent loyalty to the Stuarts appeal to his romantic disposition. These visits, unwise in a British officer at a time of political tension, compromise Edward with his colonel. Through the intrigues of Donald Bean Lean, he is accused of encouraging mutiny in his regiment and is arrested. He is rescued by the action of Rose Bradwardine and, influenced by a sense of unjust treatment, by Flora's enthusiasm, and by a kind reception by Prince Charles Edward, he joins the Jacobite forces. At the battle of Prestonpans he saves from death Colonel Talbot, a distinguished English officer and friend of his family, and Talbot's influence, after the eventual defeat of the Pretender's army, secures his pardon and the rehabilitation of Baron Bradwardine. Decisively rejected by the spirited Flora, Edward turns his affections to Rose, whom he marries. Fergus, convicted of treason, meets his end bravely; Flora retires to a convent.

Scott claimed to have written *Waverley* in haste and 'without much skill'; in fact, it is one of the best plotted of his novels. Equally skilful is the progress of Waverley ('a sneaking piece of imbecility' in Scott's own words) from woolly-minded ignorance at the opening to the knowledge of the world gained from experience. In his first novel, Scott explored the opposition of romance and realism which was to reappear in many of his later works.

Waves, The A novel by Virginia *Woolf, published in 1931 and commonly regarded as the most experimental of her works. It traces the lives of a group of friends (Bernard, Susan, Louis, Rhoda, Neville, and Jinny) from infancy to late middle age, evoking their personalities through their reflections on themselves, on one another, and on their friend Percival, a largely absent colonial administrator. The characters are presented through successive brief monologues: though the friends gather together on several occasions, they rarely respond directly to each other's words; Louis and Rhoda are the exceptions. And though their speech patterns are undifferentiated, their individuality as characters emerges through their divergent lives and through recurring concerns, phrases, and images. The narrator exists only in the formula 'said Bernard', 'said Susan', etc., and in the lyrical prose 'interludes' between episodes which describe the rise and fall of the sun over a seascape. Bernard, however, assumes a quasi-narratorial role in the final episode. Though the characters' lives are uneventful, the death of Percival, and the rhythms of separation and reunion throughout provide the occasion for reflections on the mortality both of individuals and of the group as a unit, and on the forms taken by friendship and love. While it was long seen as Woolf's most poetic novel and the least political of her works, recent critics have focused increasingly on questions of authority, in particular Percival's power to unite the group and the narrative authority of Bernard's final summing-up.

Way of All Flesh, The A novel by Samuel *Butler (1835–1902), published posthumously 1903. This celebrated dissection of the stultifying effects of family life reflects many of Butler's own experiences. It was completed some seventeen years before his death, but the second half was not revised. The story (narrated by a family friend, Overton) was originally called *Ernest Pontifex*; Ernest is the awkward and unhappy great-grandson of John Pontifex, a village carpenter, whose instinctive character he comes to revere. His own father, Theo, is tyrannical, repeating the attitudes of Ernest's grandfather George. After his ordination the inept Ernest mistakes a respectable woman for a prostitute and is sentenced to prison, where he tries to return to the simplicity of Old Pontifex. On his release he plunges into a disastrous union with Ellen, a drunken maidservant. Fortunately she turns out to be already married, and Ernest's beloved aunt Alethea leaves him sufficient money to devote himself to literature, rejoicing in his freedom from the oppressive institution of the family. Aunt Alethea was based on Butler's friend Eliza Savage, who helped with the first half of the book before her death. The book attracted much praise, notably from George Bernard *Shaw, and reached the height of its success in the 1920s.

Way of the World, The A comedy by William *Congreve, produced 1700, in which Mirabell eventually wins the hand of Millamant, niece of the wealthy Lady Wishfort, who had wanted Millamant to marry her boisterous and good-natured country nephew Sir Wilful Witwoud. The plot is extremely complicated. In pursuit of his schemes Mirabell pretends to woo Lady Wishfort, and he also plans to get his servant Waitwell to marry her, disguised as Mirabell's uncle, Sir Rowland. Waitwell is in fact already married to Lady Wishfort's maid Foible. Mirabell's plans are opposed by the passionate and scheming Mrs Marwood, who hates him because he has rejected her advances, and by her lover Fainall, Mirabell's false friend, who attempts to blackmail Lady Wishfort. The dialogue is brilliant, and Mirabell's undisguised materialism together with Millamant's insistence on retaining her freedom after marriage give the play exceptional sophistication.

Way We Live Now, The A novel by Anthony *Trollope, published 1875. Augustus Melmotte is supposedly a great financier, who entertains the emperor of China, and is offered a seat in Parliament. No one thinks to examine the nature of his fortune until he is caught forging the deeds to an estate. His prize speculation, a Central American railway, is revealed as a gigantic confidence trick, and when it becomes clear that he has tampered with his daughter's trust fund, his disgrace is complete. After a drunken appearance in the House of Commons he commits suicide. Melmotte's worthless career is matched by his daughter Marie's experiences in the marriage market. She is treated as a commodity by the cautious Lord Nidderdale, and as a diversion by the dissipated Sir Felix Carbury. Carbury entices her to elope, but lets her down. She finally marries the devious Hamilton K. Fisker. Meanwhile, Lady Carbury's shifts as a glib authoress expose the shabbiness of literary life. Trollope conceived this bleak and powerful novel as an attack on 'the commercial profligacy of the age', dishonest at all levels. His perspective is shared by the upright Roger Carbury, head of the dissolute Carbury family.

weak ending The occurrence of an unstressed monosyllable (such as a preposition, conjunction, or auxiliary verb) in the normally stressed position at the end of an iambic verse line.

Wealth of Nations, An Inquiry into the Nature and Causes of the A treatise on political economy by Adam *Smith, published 1776, originally delivered in the form of lectures at Glasgow. A third edition (1784) contained substantial additions. Smith did not share the view of some economists that land is the sole source of wealth; instead he regarded the labour of a nation as the source of its economic strength. In the first book, Smith argues that Labour is the standard of value, and was originally the sole determinant of price; but in a more advanced society three elements enter into price: wages, profit, and rent. The second book deals with the 'nature, accumulation and employment' of capital, arguing that with the increase of capital there is an increase of productive labour and a decrease in the rate of interest. The third book consists of historical observations on the 'different progress of opulence in different nations', and the fourth mounts a forceful attack on the restrictions of the mercantile system. Smith forcefully advocates freedom of commerce and industry, and views self-interest as the proper criterion of economic action; but the universal pursuit of personal advantage contributes, in his theory, to the general public interest.

WEAVER, Harriet Shaw (1876–1961) Editor, publisher, and benefactor, born in Frodsham, Cheshire. Business manager and later (1914) editor of the **Egoist*, she saw James *Joyce's *A *Portrait of the Artist as a Young Man* through serial publication (1914–15), changing the journal's printers to do so. When Joyce could find no British publisher for the book, Weaver brought it out under the imprint of the Egoist Press; the Press also published work by T. S. *Eliot, Hilda *Dolittle, Marianne *Moore, and others. In 1917 she anonymously provided the first of many benefactions to Joyce. the *Egoist* published work by Ezra *Pound, T. S. Eliot, Wyndham *Lewis, William Carlos *Williams, and others, as well as early instalments of **Ulysses*. It ceased publication in December 1919 and the press closed in 1923. Weaver continued her financial support of Joyce and became literary executor of his estate. See Jane Lidderdale and Mary Nicholson, *Dear Miss Weaver* (1970).

WEBB, Beatrice (1858–1943) Writer, diarist, and social reformer, born near Gloucester into a wealthy and well-connected family and educated by governesses. She was from an early age deeply interested in both the theoretical and practical aspects of social reform, political economy, and sociology, concerns that were shared by her husband Sidney Webb (1859–1947), whom she married in 1892. From 1891, both were leading spirits in the Fabian Society, and they produced jointly numerous works on social history, served on many royal commissions, and helped to found the London School of Economics. Beatrice Webb also wrote two autobiographical works (*My Apprenticeship*, 1926; *Our Partnership*, 1948), and kept a remarkable diary, of which selections were published in 1952 and 1956 and a fuller, four-volume edition, edited by N. and J. Mackenzie, appeared between 1982 and 1985. It reveals the width of her human and intellectual interests and considerable literary skill, and is a valuable record of the period's social life and progressive thought. Sidney and Beatrice Webb are lampooned in H. G. *Wells's novel *The New Machiavelli* (1911) as the Baileys, 'two active, self-centred people, excessively devoted to the public service...the most formidable and distinguished couple conceivable'.

WEBB, Jane Loudon (1807–58) Born in Birmingham; she became a leading writer on horticulture after marrying John Loudon. Before her marriage, she published the pre-*science fiction *The Mummy!* (1827), borrowing the image of a future England with balloon transportation from Mary *Shelley's *The *Last Man* (1826), together with ideas from **Frankenstein*.

WEBB, Mary (1881–1927) Novelist, born at Leighton, Shropshire, and educated by governesses and at Mrs Walmsley's Finishing School, Southport, Lancashire. In 1912 she married Henry Webb; they lived for some years in Shropshire before moving to London in 1921. She had contracted Graves' disease in 1901, an affliction which found its fictional counterpart in the harelip of Prudence Sarn, the narrator of her fifth and most famous novel, *Precious Bane* (1924). Her five other novels are *The Golden Arrow* (1916), *Gone to Earth* (1917), *The House in Dormer Forest* (1920), *Seven for a Secret* (1922), and *Armour Wherein he Trusted*, which appeared posthumously in 1929. They are tales of rustic life, romantic, passionate, morbid, and frequently naive, written in a fervid prose easily ridiculed by Stella *Gibbons in **Cold Comfort Farm*. They had relatively little success on first publication but were immensely popular in the 1930s and 1940s; her posthumous reputation was due largely to the championship of Stanley Baldwin, who wrote an introduction to a reprint of *Precious Bane* in 1928 in which he praised her lyrical intensity, her evocation of the Shropshire landscape, and her 'blending of human passion with the fields and skies'. See G. M. Coles, *Mary Webb* (1990).

WEBER, Carl Maria von (1786–1826) German composer. After the European success of his opera *Der Freischütz* (1821), Weber was asked in 1824 by Charles *Kemble to write and conduct an opera for Covent Garden, on the subject of either *Faust or Oberon. Weber began an intensive programme of English lessons, which helped with another commission, to provide ten Scottish songs (including poems by Walter *Scott and Robert *Burns) with instrumental accompaniment, early in 1825. James *Planché provided, after much delay, a *libretto for *Oberon, or The Elf King's Oath*: based on the German poet Wieland's *Oberon* (itself a reworking of the story of *Huon of Bordeaux), the libretto's main Shakespearian element is the quarrel between Oberon and Titania (already incorporated by Wieland from *A *Midsummer Night's Dream*). The premiere of Weber's *Oberon* (1826) was a triumphant success, but Weber's insecure health was broken by the strain of rapid composition and he died shortly afterwards.

WEBSTER, Augusta (1837–94) Née Davies, poet and feminist writer, born in Poole, Dorset, the daughter of a vice-admiral. She was a fluent linguist and trained at the Cambridge School of Art: she was expelled from South Kensington Art School for whistling. In 1867, she married Thomas Webster, a lawyer. Her earliest works were published under the pseudonym 'Cecil Home': under her own name appeared *Dramatic Studies* (1866), *A Woman Sold and Other Poems* (1867), and *Portraits* (1870). Her inventive use of the *dramatic monologue, partly derived from her admiration and imitation of Robert *Browning, is particularly evident in the forceful presentation of female character and predicament. 'The Castaway' (1870) is a lively challenge to conventional notions of prostitution. Her last volume, an incomplete sonnet sequence called *Mother and Daughter*, appeared in 1895 with a preface by W. M. *Rossetti.

WEBSTER, Daniel (1782–1852) American statesman and orator, born in New Hampshire. He rose to great eminence in the law courts, the American House of Representatives and Senate, and in public speeches, when he urged the union of the American states. He was twice secretary of state. His speeches, even in ordinary criminal trials, show a literary quality comparable to that of speeches by Edmund *Burke. Among the best known are the discourse on the 200th anniversary of the landing of the Pilgrims (1825), the Bunker Hill oration (1825), and the Adams and Jefferson speech (1826).

WEBSTER, Jason (1970–) Writer, born in California, raised in England and Germany, educated at Oxford University. After spells in Italy and Egypt he settled in Spain, the subject of his books: *Duende: A Journey in Search of Flamenco* (2002), *Andalus: Unlocking the Secrets of Moorish Spain* (2004), and *¡Guerra! Living in the Shadows of the Spanish Civil War* (2006).

WEBSTER, John (*c.*1578–*c.*1638) Playwright, the son of a prosperous London coachmaker of Smithfield. He attended the Merchant Taylors' Company, and combined the careers of coachmaker and playwright. He wrote several plays in collaboration with other dramatists; these include **Westward Ho* and **Northward Ho*, with Thomas *Dekker, written 1604 and 1605, both printed 1607; *A *Cure for a Cuckold* (printed 1661, written ? 1624), probably with William *Rowley (and possibly Thomas *Heywood); and a lost play with John *Ford, Dekker, and Rowley, *Keep the Widow Waking* (1624). It has also been suggested that he had a hand in Thomas *Middleton's *Anything for a Quiet Life* (1661, written ?1621) and John *Fletcher's *The Fair Maid of the Inn* (1623). He expanded John *Marston's *The*

Malcontent for the King's Men in 1604, and published elegies on Prince Henry in 1613 with Heywood and Cyril *Tourneur. In 1615 he contributed 32 sketches to the sixth impression of Thomas *Overbury's *Characters*, which he may have edited, perhaps acting as Overbury's literary executor. *The Devil's Law Case*, a tragicomedy, published 1623, written 1617–21, mentions in its dedication a lost play, *Guise*, which would have brought Webster's total of single-handed plays up to four; as it is, his great reputation rests on his two major works, *The *White Devil* (which dates from between 1609 and 1612, when it was published) and *The *Duchess of Malfi* (published 1623, written 1612/13). With these two tragedies Webster has achieved a reputation second only to Shakespeare's; in the 20th century, they were revived more frequently than those of any other of *Shakespeare's contemporaries. However, critics have by no means agreed on his virtues. Attempts by Nathan *Tate and Lewis *Theobald to accommodate the plays to 18th-century taste were followed in 1808 by Charles *Lamb's influential *Specimens*, which singled out the 'beauties', in terms of poetic passages, and many 19th-century critics continued to complain about Webster's poor sense of structure, his inconsistencies, his excessive use of horror. George Saintsbury (1845–1933), writing on *The Duchess* in 1887, claimed that 'the fifth act is a kind of gratuitous appendix of horrors stuck on without art or reason'. The 20th century however saw a strong revival of interest in the plays as drama, and in Webster as satirist and moralist. Increasing critical sophistication brought deeper understanding of the structural principles underlying his plays. The works were edited by F. L. Lucas (1894–1967) (4 vols, 1927), and by David Gunby and others (1995–). Editions of individual plays are published in the major series. There is a critical biography by M. C. Bradbrook (1980); see also C. R. Forker, *Skull beneath the Skin: The Achievement of John Webster* (1986).

WEBSTER, Noah (1758–1843) American lexicographer, born in Connecticut. He was educated at Yale University, and worked subsequently as teacher, lawyer, and journalist. The work for which he is chiefly remembered is his great and scholarly *An American Dictionary of the English Language*, 2 vols (1828), in which he challenged the parochialism of British dictionaries and, with a strong national pride and spirit, established Americanisms and American usages. He also published a speller in 1783, which ran through numerous editions.
See DICTIONARY.

WEDDERBURN, James (*c.*1495–1553) Scottish reformer and poet, born in Dundee and educated at St Andrew's University, who with his brothers John (*c.*1505–1556) and Robert (*c.*1510–1555/60) produced a collection of verse *Ane Compendeous Buke, of Godlye Psalmes and Spirituall Sangis* (1565). Possibly dating from *c.*1540, it contains psalm translations as well as versions of popular songs designed to promote *Protestant doctrine.

WEDEKIND, Frank (1864–1918) German poet, playwright, actor, and cabaret performer. Born in Hanover and brought up in Switzerland, he studied briefly at Lausanne and Munich. His first important play *Frühlings Erwachen* (1891: *Spring Awakening*) is also the work for which he is best known in Britain; Edward *Bond's translation was performed at the *National Theatre in 1972, and in 1995 the Royal Shakespeare Company staged a translation commissioned from Ted *Hughes. In its day, the work's frank representation of sexuality and satirical attack on bourgeois hypocrisy led to its being censored. *Erdgeist* (1895) and *Die Büchse der Pandora* (1904), in which Wedekind acted the part of *Jack the Ripper, formed the basis of the silent film *Pandora's Box* (1929) of Georg Wilhelm Pabst (1885–1967) and the unfinished opera *Lulu* (1937) of Alban Berg (1885–1935). These plays were translated by Stephen *Spender in *The Lulu Plays and Other Sex Tragedies* (1972). Although *Frühlings Erwachen* contains naturalistic elements, his work generally was hostile to *naturalism and as such greatly valued by Bertolt *Brecht. See Alan Best, *Frank Wedekind* (1975).

WEDGWOOD, Dame (Cicely) **Veronica** (1910–97) OM, historian, educated privately and at Lady Margaret Hall, Oxford. Her publications include *Strafford* (1935), *The Thirty Years' War* (1938), *Oliver Cromwell* (1939; rev. 1973), *The King's Peace* (1955), which she worked on for twelve years, *The King's War* (1958), and *The Great Rebellion* (1966). She was awarded the Order of Merit in 1969.

WEELKES, Thomas (?1576–1623) English composer. With John *Wilbye, he was the most important of the English *madrigal composers after Thomas *Morley's introduction of the form. Weelkes's *Madrigals to 3. 4. 5. & 6. Voyces* appeared in 1597; a year later he became organist at Winchester College, afterwards holding the same post at Chichester Cathedral. *Balletts and Madrigals to Five Voyces* came out in 1598, and the best of his works, the *Madrigals of 5. and 6. Parts, Apt for the Viols and Voices*, in 1600. He contributed one madrigal to *The Triumphes of Oriana* in 1601 (*see* MORLEY, THOMAS); his last collection was *Ayeres or Phantasticke Spirites for Three Voices* (1608). Weelkes developed the Italianate manner of Morley into a more characteristically English style, often more serious in content and laid out for larger forces, with great contrapuntal brilliance and richness of harmony. The authors of the texts are generally not known.

WEEVER, John (1575/6–1632) Poet and antiquary, born in Lancashire and educated at Queens' College, Cambridge. His first publication, *Epigrams in the Oldest Cut, and Newest Fashion* (1599), is a collection of verse reflecting his Cambridge friendships and his knowledge of the London literary scene: a Shakespearian sonnet is addressed 'Ad Gulielmum Shakespear'. The Ovidian epyllion, or minor *epic, *Faunus and Melliflora* (1600) shows a knowledge of *Shakespeare's works, especially of **Venus and Adonis*. Weever probably wrote the anonymous *pamphlet *The Whipping of the Satyre* (1601), which led to his being mocked by some of the leading dramatists. In the same year he published *The Mirror of Martyrs*, a verse account of Sir John *Oldcastle. He subsequently devoted himself to collecting funeral epitaphs and inscriptions for *Ancient Funeral Monuments* (1631). There is a study (1987) by E. Honigmann which seeks to establish the nature of his links with Shakespeare.

WEIL, Simone (1909–43) French philosopher. Equally independent in her life and her work, she devoted herself to resisting the oppression inherent in organized institutions and to achieving identification with the sufferings of its victims. Although qualified to teach philosophy, she worked for a year on the shop floor of the Renault factory, joined the International Brigade, formed to fight for the Republic in the Spanish Civil War, in 1936, and after the outbreak of war found employment as a farm servant. Broken by her voluntary privations, and suffering from tuberculosis, she died in England where she had been engaged by the provisional French government. Her moral and intellectual authority became generally apparent only posthumously. *La Pesanteur et la grâce* (1947: *Gravity and Grace*), *L'Attente de Dieu* (1950: *Waiting for God*), and *Cahiers* (1951–6: *Notebooks*) have earned her a unique respect for their intensity of thought, their moral commitment, and their religious inwardness. See D. McLellan, *Simone Weil* (1989).

WEILL, Kurt (1900–50) German composer, born in Dessau of a Jewish family. He first achieved fame with the music he wrote for Bertolt *Brecht's *Threepenny Opera* (1928) and *Mahagonny* (1930). In keeping with Brecht's rejection of dramatic and bourgeois operatic tradition, the music mingled popular song ('Mack the Knife') and jazz rhythms with ironic echoes of high opera. He fled Germany and settled finally in New York in 1935. In America he enjoyed great success as a composer of popular songs and writer of music for the stage.

WEINBAUM, Stanley (1902–35) American *science fiction writer born in Louisville, Kentucky. With the publication of 'A Martian Odyssey' (1934) in *Wonder Stories* he transformed the way alien beings were depicted in science fiction. *The New Adam* (1939) is a tragic story of a mutant 'superman'.

Weird Tales One of the most influential magazines in supernatural and *science fiction during its original incarnation (1923–54). The magazine, with its striking, sometimes lurid covers, published many of the writers central to the field: H. P. *Lovecraft, Robert E. *Howard, C. L. *Moore, Ray *Bradbury; together with early stories from a wider range of writers such as Tennessee *Williams. Several attempts to revive it were made from the 1970s onward, most recently the current version (from 1988).

Weir of Hermiston An unfinished novel by Robert Louis *Stevenson, published 1896, containing some of his most powerful work. Archie Weir is the only child of Adam Weir, Lord Hermiston, the lord justice clerk, a formidable 'hanging judge', based on the character of Robert Macqueen, Lord Braxfield (1722–99), known as 'the Jeffrey of Scotland'. His mother is an ineffectually religious woman who dies young, leaving Archie to the care of a father he dreads. The conflict comes to a head when Archie witnesses his father hounding a wretched criminal to death at a trial; he confronts him, speaking out against capital punishment, and is banished to Hermiston, a remote Lowland village. There he lives with Kirstie, his devoted housekeeper and distant relative, who is aunt to the four 'Black Elliotts', brothers famed for hunting down their father's murderer. Archie falls in love with their sister Christina. The novel ends as Archie, warned by Kirstie, tells Christina that their secret meetings must end. We know from Stevenson's notes that the story was to conclude with another confrontation between father and son, in which Archie is on trial for his life for the murder of Christina's seducer Frank Innes. Archie and Christina are rescued by the Black Elliotts and escape to America, but the old man dies of shock. In this novel, Stevenson returns to the Edinburgh and Lowland landscapes of his youth, which he evokes with grim intensity. Archie's rebellion might be seen as Stevenson's rejection of his Calvinist ancestry, though he was able to achieve a reconciliation and understanding with his own parents, who came to approve of his career as a writer. Many feel that the novel promised to be the most ambitious and profound of his works.

WEISS, Peter (1916–82) Swedish-German playwright and novelist. Born in Berlin to a German mother and Hungarian Jewish father, he trained as a visual artist in Berlin, London, and Prague. He settled in Sweden before the Second World War and took Swedish nationality in 1946. Best known in England for his *Marat/Sade* (*The Persecution and Assassination of Marat as Performed by the Inmates of the Asylum of Charenton under the Direction of the Marquis de Sade*), the work was first performed in London in 1964 in an adaptation by Geoffrey Skelton and Adrian *Mitchell, directed by Peter *Brook. A landmark in the theatre of the 1960s, the work explores the clash of antithetical philosophies, revolutionary *Marxism (voiced by Marat), and a nihilistic individualism (voiced by de Sade). His vast drama/oratorio *Die Ermittlung* (1965: *The Investigation*), in which harrowing testimony about Auschwitz given at the Frankfurt war crimes trial is rendered in serene verse, is a monumental and challenging example of literature of the *Holocaust. It was performed as a stage reading under Peter Brook's direction by the Royal Shakespeare Company, and on *BBC radio and Granada Television. His best-known novel is *The Aesthetics of Resistance* (1975–81).

WELCH, Denton (1915–48) Writer, born in Shanghai and educated at Repton School, Derbyshire (from which, aged 16, he ran away), and Goldsmiths' College School of Art, London. He intended to be a painter, but in 1935 he was involved in a serious bicycle accident. His injuries included a fractured spine and he was an invalid for the rest of his life. He continued to paint, but his focus switched to writing. A semi-autobiographical novel, *Maiden Voyage* (1943), was followed by a novel about adolescence, *In Youth is Pleasure* (1945), and a volume of short stories, *Brave and Cruel, and Other Stories* (1949). His most distinctive work is *A Voice through a Cloud* (1950), his not-quite-finished, autobiographical, vivid, and at times painfully sensitive account of accident and illness. See James Methuen-Campbell, *Denton Welch, Writer and Artist* (2002).

WELDON, Fay (1933–) Novelist, dramatist, and screenwriter, born in Worcester, educated at South Hampstead High School for Girls and the University of St Andrews, employed in advertising before becoming a full-time writer. From *The Fat Woman's Joke* (1967) onwards, she has kept up a copious fictional output in which feminist polemic and hostility to such concerns as psychotherapy and genetic research have found didactic and whimsical expression. *The Life and Loves of a She-Devil* (1983), is prominent among the works by which she gained attention. *Big Women* (1998) is a fictionalized account of the founding of the feminist publishing company the *Virago Press. There is a memoir, *Auto Da Fay* (2002), which is partially continued in her hybrid novel *Mantrapped* (2004).

Well-Beloved, The A novel by Thomas *Hardy, published serially 1892, revised and reissued 1897. The story is set on the Isle of Slingers (i.e. Portland), and the central figure is Jocelyn Pierston, a sculptor, who falls in love successively with three generations of island women: Avice Caro, her daughter, and her granddaughter, all of the same name. He seeks the perfect form in woman, the 'well-beloved', as he seeks it in stone. Misfortune, and the varying natures of the women, prevent him from capturing any of them. In despair, he marries an early love, Marcia, when both he and she have been, like the rock of Portland, subjected to the raspings and chisellings of time.

WELLES, Orson (1915–84) American actor and director, best remembered for his work in the cinema, notably *Citizen Kane* (1941), widely regarded as the greatest of all films; and *The Magnificent Ambersons* (1942), both of which he directed, and for his role in *The Third Man* (1949), directed by Carol Reed from a script by Graham *Greene. His radio version of H. G. *Wells's *The *War of the Worlds* (1938) created an early sensation. He also directed himself in three *Shakespeare films: as *Macbeth* (1948), *Othello* (1952), and as *Falstaff in his own adaptation, *Chimes at Midnight* (1966).

WELLESLEY, Dorothy (1889–1956) Poet, born at White Waltham, Berkshire, and educated privately. She published *Early Poems* in 1913, followed by *Poems* (1920), *Genesis* (1926), *Deserted House* (1931), *Poems of Ten Years* (1934), and six further volumes of verse. She is now chiefly remembered through the admiration of W. B. *Yeats, who included her in his *Oxford Book of Modern Verse* (1936) and introduced *Selections from the Poems of Dorothy Wellesley* (1936); his *Letters on Poetry*, originally written to Wellesley, were published in 1940. She was a friend of Vita *Sackville-West and edited the 'Living Poets' series for the *Hogarth Press. Her autobiography, *Far Have I Travelled*, appeared in 1952.

WELLINGTON, Arthur Wellesley, first duke of (1769–1852) Soldier and statesman, who fought in the Indian Campaign (1799–1803), the Peninsular Campaign (1808–14), and was the hero of the battle of Waterloo (18 June 1815) at which Napoleon was decisively defeated. He first became a national figure with the victory of Talavera in 1809, and was created marquess of Douro and duke of Wellington in 1814. He was prime minister 1828–30, and secretary of state for foreign affairs 1834–5. Known as the 'Iron Duke' (or 'Old Nosey'), he was much portrayed by caricaturists, notably John Doyle (father of Richard *Doyle) and William Heath ('Paul Pry', 1795–1840). A less romantic figure than Napoleon, his exploits and his phlegmatic utterances (e.g. 'Publish and be damned', attributed to him) nevertheless caught the imagination of writers: the battle of Waterloo is depicted in Lord Byron's **Childe Harold's Pilgrimage* (III. xxi, 'There was a sound of revelry by night') and in **Vanity Fair*; he inspired much of the juvenilia of Charlotte *Brontë; and he appears in historical novels by Arthur Conan *Doyle, G. A. *Henty, and others. He was given the most magnificent state funeral ever accorded to a subject, commemorated in Alfred *Tennyson's 'Ode on the Death of the Duke of Wellington' (1852). Wellington's literary presence persists in Bernard Cornwell's (1944–) long-running and immensely popular series of historical novels featuring the fictional soldier Richard Sharpe, who shadows Wellington's campaigns. There is a biography (2 vols, 1969, 1973) by Elizabeth Longford; see also Richard *Holmes, *Wellington: The Iron Duke* (2002).

Well of Loneliness, The See HALL, RADCLYFFE.

WELLS, Charles Jeremiah (1800–79) Lawyer and poet; he was a member of John *Keats's circle, and author of *Joseph and his Brethren: A Scriptural Drama* (1824), a verse play with a Keatsian richness of language and imagery that was admired by Dante Gabriel *Rossetti. It became a cult text for the *Pre-Raphaelites, and was republished in 1876 with an essay by A. C. *Swinburne.

WELLS, H. G. (Herbert George) (1866–1946) Writer, born in Bromley, Kent, the son of an unsuccessful small tradesman and professional cricketer, educated at Thomas Morley's Commercial Academy. He was apprenticed to a draper in early life, a period reflected in several of his novels. He then became assistant teacher at Midhurst Grammar School, studying by night and winning a scholarship in 1884 to the Normal School of Science in South Kensington, where he came under the lasting influence of T. H. *Huxley. For some years, in poor health, he struggled as a teacher, studying and writing articles in his spare time; his marriage in 1891 to his cousin Isabel proved unhappy, and he eloped with his student Amy Catherine ('Jane') Robbins, whom he married in 1895 (though this did not prevent him from embarking on further liaisons, and continuing to criticize conventional marriage). In 1903 he joined the Fabian Society, but was soon at odds with it, his sponsor George Bernard *Shaw, and Sidney and Beatrice *Webb. Impatient and turbulent, his career as writer and thinker was marked by a provocative independence.

His literary output was vast and extremely varied. As a novelist he is perhaps best remembered for his scientific romances, among the earliest products of the new genre of *science fiction. The first, *The Time Machine* (1895), is a social allegory set in the year 802701, describing a society divided into two classes, the subterranean workers, called Morlocks, and the decadent Eloi. This was followed by *The Wonderful Visit* (1895), *The *Island of Doctor Moreau* (1896), *The *Invisible Man* (1897), *The *War of the Worlds* (1898, a powerful and apocalyptic vision of the world invaded by Martians), *When the Sleeper Wakes* (1899), *The First Men in the Moon* (1901), *Men Like Gods* (1923), and others. These combine, in varying degrees, political satire, warnings about the dangerous new powers of science, and a desire to foresee a possible future (see also *A Modern Utopia*, 1905); Wells's preoccupation with social as well as scientific progress distinguishes them from the fantasies of Jules *Verne.

Another group of novels evokes in comic and realistic style the lower-middle-class world of his youth. *Love and Mr Lewisham* (1900) tells the story of a struggling teacher; *Kipps* (1905) that of an aspiring draper's assistant, undone by an unexpected inheritance and its consequences; *The History of Mr Polly* (1910) recounts the adventures of Alfred Polly, an inefficient shopkeeper who liberates himself by burning down his own shop and bolting for freedom, which he discovers as man-of-all-work at the Potwell Inn.

Among his other novels, *Ann Veronica* (1909) is a feminist tract about a girl who, fortified by the concept of the *'New Woman', defies her father and conventional morality by running off with the man she loves. *Tono-Bungay* (1909), one of his most successful works (described by himself as 'a social panorama in the vein of Balzac'), is a picture of English society in dissolution, and of the advent of a new class of rich, embodied in Uncle Ponderevo, an entrepreneur intent on peddling a worthless patent medicine. *The Country of the Blind, and Other Stories* (1911), his fifth collection of short stories, contains, as well as the well-known title story, originally published in 1904, the memorable 'The Door in the Wall' (originally published 1906). *The New Machiavelli* (1911), about a politician involved in sexual scandal, was seen to mark a decline in his creative power, evident in later novels, which include *Mr Britling Sees it Through* (1916) and *The World of William Clissold* (1926). He continued to reach a huge audience, however, notably with his massive *The Outline of History* (1920) and its shorter offspring *A Short History of the World* (1922), and with many works of scientific and political speculation (including *The Shape of Things to Come*, 1933) which confirmed his position as one of the great popularizers and one of the most influential voices of his age; the dark pessimism of his last prediction, *Mind at the End of its Tether* (1945), may be seen in the context of his own ill health and the course of the Second World War. One of his last statements (made after Hiroshima) was an exhortation to man to confront his 'grave and tragic' destiny with dignity and without hysteria.

His *Experiment in Autobiography* (1934) is a striking portrait of himself, his contemporaries (including Arnold *Bennett, George *Gissing, and the Fabians) and their times. See also a life by N. and J. MacKenzie, *The Time Traveller* (1973), and *Aspects of a Life* (1984), a memoir by Anthony West (1914–87), his son by Rebecca *West.

WELSH, Irvine (1957–) Scottish writer, born in Edinburgh, generally seen as the first and most important member of the so-called 'Chemical Generation' of younger British writers, politically disaffected, culturally sophisticated, and centrally engaged with the music, drugs, and mores of 1990s club culture. Welsh grew up in Muirhouse, one of Edinburgh's peripheral housing estates. After leaving school at 16, he did many jobs in Edinburgh and London, among them TV repair work, property development, and working for local government for the City of Edinburgh District Council. He took an MBA at Heriot-Watt University, Edinburgh, in 1990. His first novel, *Trainspotting* (1993), about a group of young heroin addicts in 1980s Edinburgh, was sexually and scatologically explicit, written in a pungent Edinburgh vernacular, and distinguished by great comic verve. It quickly became a best-seller and cultural byword; a stage version was followed by a film adaptation (1996), which was a great success. Welsh's subsequent works of fiction include two short story collections, *The Acid House* (1994) and *Ecstasy: Three Tales of Chemical Romance* (1996), and two novels, *Marabou Stork Nightmares* (1995) and *Filth* (1998). The language is progressively explicit, and often extreme in its use of obscenity and violence: *Filth*, the story of a corrupt Edinburgh policeman, includes the narrative 'voice' of the protagonist's own excrement. *Glue* (2001) tells of the bonds uniting four characters over several decades. *Porno* (2002) considers the consequences of pornography for those who produce or consume it. *The Bedroom Secrets of the Master Chefs* (2006) describes a civil servant who unwittingly curses a fellow worker. *If You Liked School You'll Love Work* (2007) is a collection of short stories. He has written several plays, and is also interested in music, having worked as a DJ in London and Amsterdam in the mid-1990s.

WELSH, Jane *See* CARLYLE, JANE.

WELTY, Eudora (1909–2001) American short story writer, novelist, and photographer, born in Jackson, Mississippi, her lifelong home. The stories of *A Curtain of Green* (1941) derive from her experiences with the New Deal's Works Progress Administration in the 1930s, for which she travelled through her native state photographing inhabitants. Her first novel, *The Robber Bridegroom* (1942), is an elaborately worked fairy-tale set in the Natchez Trace country *c.*1798. *The Golden Apples* (1949) is a series of linked stories and *Losing Battles* (1970) returns to the Depression for its subject. *The Optimist's Daughter* (1972) centres on the antagonism after a judge's death between his middle-aged daughter and insensitive young widow. *The Eye of the Story* (1978) collects essays and in *One Writer's Beginnings* (1984) she traces her imaginative development. See Suzanne Marrs, *Eudora Welty* (2005).

WERTENBAKER, Timberlake (1951–) Dramatist who grew up in the Basque country near Saint-Jean-de-Luz, France, educated in America and Europe but long resident in Britain. She is best known for *Our Country's Good* (1987), based on Thomas *Keneally's novel *The Playmaker*, which dealt with the first play (George *Farquhar's *The *Recruiting Officer*) performed by penal settlers in Australia: it has been much revived around the world. Other plays include *The Grace of Mary Travers* (1985), which dealt with a woman coming to personal and political awareness during the Gordon riots of the 1780s, and *Three Birds Alighting on a Field* (1992), which dealt with the commercial art market at the height of the Thatcher economic boom. *After Darwin* (1998) uses the historical figure of Charles *Darwin and mixes past and present in an examination of evolution and extinction. She has also written frequent stage, radio, and TV adaptations, including Edith *Wharton's *The Children*; Pierre *Marivaux's *False Admissions* and *Successful Strategies* (both for Shared Experience touring players) and his *La Dispute*; Jean *Anouilh's *Leocadia*; Maurice *Maeterlinck's *Pelléas et Mélisande*; Mnouchkine's *Mephisto*; *Sophocles' *Theban Plays* (for the RSC); and *Euripides' *Hecuba*. Her work, frequently directed by Max *Stafford-Clark, has always made much use of workshop development. Recent productions include a modern reworking of the Cinderella story, *The Ash Girl* (2000), *A Credible Witness* (2001), about the struggle for identity in the contemporary world, *Galileo's Daughter* (2004), and *Divine Intervention* (2006).

Wertherism A cultural phenomenon resulting from the fame throughout Europe of Johann Wolfgang von *Goethe's early work *Die Leiden des jungen Werthers* (1774: *The Sorrows of Young Werther*) an *epistolary novel which concerns the unfulfilled love of the sensitive hero for a married woman, Lotte. A notable example of the novel of *sensibility, it owed its notoriety chiefly to its supposed defence of the hero's suicide. In the immediate wake of the novel's success, there was a vogue for things to do with Werther, imitations, illustrations, supposed discoveries of 'new' letters, etc. Though it was still admired by Romantic writers such as P. B. *Shelley, Thomas *Carlyle disapproved of Werther, and by the mid-19th century the term had come to stand for a self-indulgent melancholy or lachrymose sensitivity. Charles *Kingsley accused his brother-in-law J. A. *Froude of catching the disease of Wertherism in his youthful novel *The Nemesis of Faith* (1849) and W. M. *Thackeray wrote well-known verses in mocking parody of the lovers.

WESKER, Sir Arnold (1932–) Playwright, born in Stepney of Jewish immigrant parents, and educated in Hackney. He left school at 16 and worked at various jobs (including furniture-maker's apprentice and pastrycook) before making his name as a playwright. His early work was closely associated with the *English Stage Company, although his first play to be performed, *Chicken Soup with Barley* (1958), transferred there from the Belgrade Theatre, Coventry, which also put on the first productions of *Roots* (1959) and *I'm Talking about Jerusalem* (1960), three plays now grouped together as the Wesker Trilogy. *The Kitchen* (1959), which first appeared at the *Royal Court, shows the stresses and conflicts of life behind the scenes in a restaurant, which culminate in tragedy; its use of the rhythms of working life was highly innovative and did much to stimulate the growth of what was to be known (though in a slightly different sense) as *kitchen sink drama. Wesker's political commitments were also manifested in 1960–1 in his efforts to establish Centre 42, a movement which aimed to popularize the arts through trade union support. His subsequent plays include *Chips with Everything* (1962), a study of class attitudes in the RAF during National Service; *The Four Seasons* (1965), about a love affair; *Their Very Own and Golden City* (1966) and *The Friends* (1970), both of which deal in different ways with the disappointment of political and social hope; *The Merchant* (1977; subsequently retitled *Shylock*), which attacks anti-Semitism through the story of *Shylock; *Caritas* (1981), which shows the spiritual anguish of a 14th-century anchoress who realizes she has mistaken her vocation; and *Annie Wobbler* (1984), one of several one-woman plays. He has also published essays, screenplays, and volumes of short stories; the title story of *Love Letters on Blue Paper* (1974), about the relationship of a dying trade unionist and his wife, was televised and adapted (1978) for the stage. *As Much as I Dare*, a volume of autobiography, was published in 1994. *The Birth of Shylock and the Death of Zero Mostel* (1997) is a gripping account of the disastrous events attending the New York production of *Shylock*. He has continued to produce stage work, including, in 2000, *Badenheim* and *Denial*, about false memory syndrome. *Honey* (2005) is his first novel. He was knighted in 2006.

WESLEY, Charles (1707–88) Church of England clergyman and hymn-writer, one of the founders of *Methodism, educated at Christ Church, Oxford. He was a lifelong associate of his brother John *Wesley, though they had significant disagreements. He was an active member of the Oxford Methodists, was ordained in 1735, briefly accompanied John to Georgia, experienced conversion before him, and like him began field-preaching. However he had doubts about the employment of lay preachers, fearing that they would instigate the separation of the Methodist societies from the Church, and he was appalled when John ordained ministers for America in 1784. His hymns, which resonate with allusions to the *Bible, *The Book of *Common Prayer*, and John *Milton, are his great contribution to Methodism and to poetry. They began appearing in *Hymns and Sacred Poems* (1739), and dominate John's standard edition, *A Collection of Hymns for the Use of the People called Methodists* (1780). A full edition of his *Journal* (first published 1849) is in preparation. See Kenneth G. C. Newport and Ted A. Campbell (eds), *Charles Wesley: Life, Literature, Legacy* (2007).

WESLEY, John (1703–91) Church of England clergyman, one of the founders of *Methodism, born in Epworth, Lincolnshire, the son of Samuel and Susanna Wesley. His mother profoundly influenced his religious upbringing. He was educated at Christ Church, Oxford, became a fellow of

Lincoln College in 1726, and was ordained in 1728. In Oxford from 1729 to 1735 he was one of a loose association (including his brother Charles *Wesley, and George *Whitefield) nicknamed the 'Holy Club' or 'Methodists' for their religious practices. In 1735 he was sent by the Society for the Propagation of the Gospel (*see* SPCK) on an unsuccessful mission to Georgia, where he was much influenced by German *Moravians. On his return in 1738, he had an evangelical conversion, visited the Moravians in Germany, and in 1739, following Whitefield's example, began field-preaching in Bristol. He quarrelled with Whitefield over predestination, always emphasizing Christian perfection and social holiness as the key teachings of Methodism. For over 50 years he conducted his ministry with extraordinary energy, travelling thousands of miles through the British Isles, mainly on horseback, and by carriage in old age, in order to preach to all who would listen and to encourage and regulate his followers. Wesley's importance for popular publishing cannot be overestimated: he was editor and author of more publications than any other single figure in 18th-century Britain, with his own distribution system for his societies and from 1778 his own printing press in London. Of the over 400 titles he published (several representing multiple works), the majority are books he edited and abridged, chosen from a wide range of authors of different denominations, such as *Thomas à Kempis, Jonathan *Edwards, and William *Law. His main collections are *A Christian Library*, 50 vols (1749–55); *The Works of the Rev. John Wesley*, 32 vols (1771–4); *The Arminian Magazine* (1778–91, continued after his death). Of his original works the most important is his *Journal*, published in parts from 1740 to 1791. See *The Works of John Wesley* (Abingdon Press, 1975–); Henry Rack, *Reasonable Enthusiast: John Wesley and the Rise of Methodism* (3rd edn 2002).

WESLEY, Mary (1912–2002) Novelist and children's writer, born into an army family and brought up largely by governesses. Her first book for adults, *Jumping the Queue* (1983), published when she was 71, established her reputation for dark comedy. This was enhanced by her enormously popular second novel, *The Camomile Lawn* (1984), a family saga in which five cousins shuttle between a blacked-out London and a large house on the Cornish coast during the Second World War, discovering the delights and complications of sex. Drawing on her own aristocratic-bohemian (and often unhappy) background, she published eight further novels in which characters sometimes recurred and in which she explored such favourite themes as 'the ideal house', death, unorthodox sexual relationships, illegitimacy, and other uncertainties about identity. Wesley's books are skilfully written, creating a coherent and attractive fictional world, and they command a devoted readership. See Patrick Marnham, *Wild Mary* (2006).

WESLEY, Mehitabel (Hetty) (1697–1750) Poet, daughter of the Reverend Samuel Wesley (1662–1735) and sister of John and Charles *Wesley. She was educated at home, apparently to the extent of learning New Testament Greek. In 1725, after eloping and becoming pregnant, she was forcibly married to William Wright, a plumber and glazier. She bitterly attacked marriage in 'Wedlock: A Satire' (written *c*.1730; pub. 1862) and other poems. Only a few of her poems were published during her life: the **Gentleman's Magazine* printed 'To an Infant Expiring the Second Day of its Birth' in 1733 and an elegy on one of her sisters in 1736.

Wessex The name used by Thomas *Hardy to designate the south-west counties, principally Dorset, which form the setting of many of his works.

WEST, Benjamin (1738–1820) An American painter who studied in Rome and settled in London in 1763. He was a founder member of the Royal Academy in 1768 and succeeded Joshua *Reynolds as president in 1792. A mediocre painter, his importance derives from his invention of the modern history painting with *The Death of Wolfe* (1770), with characters wearing contemporary dress, contrary to the dictates of the grand manner. His innovation was an important turning point in taste. Later, with *Death on a Pale Horse* (1802), he anticipated *Romanticism, and with his paintings of the life of Edward III (1787–9) pioneered a medieval subject. See Effra von Helmut, *The Paintings of Benjamin West* (1986).

WEST, Jane (1758–1852) Novelist, poet, and moralist. She wrote poetry from an early age, publishing in the **Gentleman's Magazine*, and began writing fiction and conduct literature in the 1790s in the wake of the French Revolution, of which she disapproved. Her anti-Jacobin politics are evident in such works such as *A Tale of the Times* (1799) and *The Infidel Father* (1802). She supported women's education, but disliked the feminism of Wollstonecraft's **Vindication of the Rights of Woman* (1792). She wrote two works of conduct literature, *Letters to a Young Man* (1801) and *Letters to a Young Lady* (1806), and was the author of *Alicia de Lacy: An Historical Romance* (1814) and *Ringrove, or, Old Fashioned Notions* (1827).

WEST, Nathanael (1903–40) The pseudonym of Nathan Wallenstein Weinstein, American novelist, born in New York. He is known principally for two novels, *Miss Lonelyhearts* (1933), the story of a heavy-drinking agony columnist who becomes involved in the life of one of his correspondents, and *The Day of the Locust* (1939), a satire of Hollywood life based on West's own experiences as a scriptwriter. He was killed in a car crash. See Jay Martin, *Nathanael West* (1970).

WEST, Dame Rebecca The adopted name of Cecily Isabel Fairfield (1892–1983), daughter of Charles Fairfield, of Anglo-Irish descent, who became known in London for his witty defence of extreme individualism in debates with Herbert *Spencer and G. B. *Shaw. He moved his family to Edinburgh, where he died, leaving his widow and four daughters with little money. Rebecca (who adopted this name, after

Henrik *Ibsen's heroine in *Rosmersholm*, at 19) was educated in Edinburgh, trained briefly for the stage in London, then became a feminist and journalist, much influenced at this stage by the Pankhursts and the movement to gain votes for women; from 1911 she wrote for *The Freewoman*, the *New Freewoman*, and *The Clarion*. Many of her shrewd, witty, and combative pieces have been collected and reprinted as *The Young Rebecca* (1982, ed. Jane Marcus); this includes her outspoken review of H. G. *Wells's *Marriage* (1912), which led to a ten-year love affair and the birth of a son, Anthony West (1914–87). Her first novel, *The Return of the Soldier* (1918), which describes the return home of a shell-shocked soldier, was followed by *The Judge* (1922), *The Strange Necessity* (1928), *Harriet Hume* (1929), and *The Thinking Reed* (1936); then, after a long gap, *The Fountain Overflows* (1956) and *The Birds Fall down* (1966). Meanwhile, in 1930, she had married a banker, Henry Maxwell Andrews, who accompanied her on the journey which produced her two-volume study of the Yugoslav nation, *Black Lamb and Grey Falcon* (1941). She was present at the Nuremberg trials, and *The Meaning of Treason* (1949) grew out of articles originally commissioned by the **New Yorker*; an updated version in 1965 added accounts of more recent spy scandals to her study of the Nazi propaganda broadcaster 'Lord Haw Haw' (William Joyce, 1906–46) and others. She continued to write and to review with exceptional vigour almost until her death, at 90. The reputation of her novels tends to have been eclipsed by the aggressive panache of her reportage and journalism, but feminist reassessments have admired her strong and unconventional heroines, and her fine craftsmanship.

WEST, Richard (1716–42) Poet, son of a lawyer. He became at Eton College a close friend of Thomas *Gray and Horace *Walpole. Gray wrote a moving sonnet on his early death, 'In vain to me the smileing Mornings shine', first printed in 1775, which William *Wordsworth used to illustrate his views on poetic diction in the Preface of 1800 to the **Lyrical Ballads*.

WESTALL, Robert (1929–93) Born in Newcastle-upon-Tyne, educated at Durham University and the Slade School, prolific author of *war stories, realistic *young adult fiction, and supernatural tales. *The Machine-Gunners* (1975) established him as a writer prepared to use language and explore topics previously considered unsuitable for young readers.

western The name given to American novels and stories set in the Old West, usually in the period 1850–1900. The earliest examples were *dime novels, but the first western novel is usually taken to be Owen *Wister's *The Virginian* (1902). The genre was consolidated by the fiction of Zane *Grey and Max Brand (1892–1944); and has continued to evolve, as in the novels of Cormac *McCarthy and Larry *McMurtry. In film and fiction alike traditional western subjects have included the conflict between settlers and Native Americans, and between law officers and 'gunslingers'.

West Indian, The A comedy by Richard *Cumberland, successfully produced by David *Garrick in 1771. Stockwell, having secretly married in Jamaica the daughter of his employer, old Belcour, has had a son by her, who has been brought up by old Belcour as a foundling. The young Belcour comes home, but Stockwell decides to postpone recognizing him as his son until he has tested his character. Young Belcour falls in love with Louisa, but is misled into thinking her the mistress of Charles, who is actually her brother. Belcour generously assists Louisa's father, but his impetuous gift to Louisa of some jewels entrusted to him leads to further complications. Eventually Belcour discovers his mistakes, marries Louisa, and is acknowledged by Stockwell. The play's central character is a *Rousseauesque child of nature and the action explores the comic potential of *primitivism; it was much performed in America into the 19th century.

Westminster Review (1824–1914) Established by James Mill, an ardent supporter of Jeremy *Bentham, as the journal of the 'philosophical radicals', in opposition to the **Edinburgh Review* and the **Quarterly Review*. The conservatism of the *Quarterly* and the quality of the *Edinburgh* reviewers both came under attack. Lord *Byron, S. T. *Coleridge, Alfred *Tennyson, and Thomas *Carlyle were among the literary figures it supported, but political and philosophical attitudes were always put first. The journal's influence survived several changes of name and ownership, and under the editorship of John *Chapman from 1851 (when George *Eliot played a defining role in running the magazine) published Herbert *Spencer, J. A. *Froude, Mark *Pattison, Walter *Pater, George Eliot herself, and other important writers. It became a monthly in 1887, and in the 20th century dropped its literary interests.

Westward Ho A comedy by John *Webster and Thomas *Dekker, printed 1607. The main plot deals with the escapades of three merry wives, whose innocence is eventually established. In the sub-plot Justiniano, an Italian merchant, convinced of his wife's infidelity, abandons her and lives disguised, enjoying the comedy of London life. Mistress Justiniano is involved in an affair with a spendthrift earl, but conscience intervenes and repentance and reconciliation follow.

Westward Ho! *See* Kingsley, Charles.

WEYMAN, Stanley John (1855–1928) Historical novelist. Born in Ludlow, and educated at Shrewsbury School and Christ Church, Oxford, he established his reputation with *A Gentleman of France* (1893, dealing with the period of Henry of Navarre), followed by other comparably vigorous romances, including *The Red Cockade* (1895), *Under the Red Robe* (1896), *Count Hannibal* (1901, based on the massacre of St *Bartholomew), and *Chippinge* (1906, in an English setting, at the time of the *Reform Bill).

WHARTON, Edith (1862–1937) Née Newbold Jones, American novelist and short story writer, born in New York of a distinguished and wealthy New York family. She was educated privately at home and in Europe, where she travelled widely; she married Edward Robbins Wharton in 1885 and they settled in France in 1907. The marriage was not happy; she suffered from nervous illnesses, and her husband's mental health declined in later years. They were divorced in 1913. She devoted her considerable energy to a cosmopolitan social life, which included a close friendship with Henry *James, and to a literary career, which began with the publication of poems and stories in *Scribner's Magazine*. Her first volume of short stories, *The Greater Inclination* (1899), was followed by a novella, *The Touchstone* (1900), but it was *The House of Mirth* (1905), the tragedy of failed social climber Lily Bart, which established her as a leading novelist. Many other works followed, including the less characteristic but much-admired *Ethan Frome* (1911), a grim and ironic tale of passion and vengeance on a poor New England farm; *Madame de Treymes* (1907), which describes the American-born marquise de Malrive's adjustments to aristocratic Parisian society; *The Reef* (1912), also set in France, at the chateau of Givré, where widowed Anna Leath's expectations of a happy second marriage are frustrated when she learns of her fiancé's fleeting past dalliance with her daughter's governess; and *The *Custom of the Country* (1913). *The Age of Innocence* (1920) describes the frustrated love of a New York lawyer, Newland Archer, for Ellen Olenska, the separated wife of a dissolute Polish count; her unconventional and artistic nature is contrasted with the timid but determined calculations of Archer's fiancée May, who, backed by all the authority of society, keeps him within her grasp and marries him. *The Mother's Recompense* (1925) concerns the struggle between runaway mother Kate Clephane and her daughter Anne for the hand of the same young man, and *Hudson River Bracketed* (1929) contrasts Midwest with New York society. She also published many volumes of short stories, various travel books, and an autobiography, *A Backward Glance* (1934). Edith Wharton's chief preoccupation is with the conflict between social and individual fulfilment which frequently leads to tragedy. Her observant, satiric, witty portrayal of social nuance, both in America and Europe, shows her keen interest in anthropology and in what she called the 'tribal behaviour' of various groups. See Hermione *Lee, *Edith Wharton* (2007).

What Maisie Knew A novel by Henry *James, published 1897. Maisie, the child of divorced parents, is used as a pawn in the power games of the adults who surround her; her perception of their corrupt lives leads her to a disconcerting maturity, yet she retains a fundamental honesty and innocence.

What You Will The subtitle of Shakespeare's **Twelfth Night*; it is his only play (with the possible exception of **Henry VIII*) with an alternative title—its meaning is 'whatever you want to call it'. It is clearly connected, in some way, with John *Marston's *What You Will* which probably appeared in 1601.

WHEATLEY, Dennis (1897–1977) Born in London; British writer of thrillers covering historicals (*The Launching of Roger Brook*, 1947), espionage (*V for Vengeance*, 1942), and occasional *science fiction (*Star of Ill-Omen*, 1952). He is chiefly remembered for his novels of black magic, including *The Devil Rides Out* (1935).

WHEATLEY, Phillis (?1753–84) African American poet, born in Gambia, Africa, and shipped as a child to the slave market of Boston, where she was purchased by John Wheatley, who encouraged her literary talent. Her *Poems on Various Subjects, Religious and Moral* were first published in London in 1773. *See* SLAVERY.

WHEELER, Sara (1961–) Travel writer, biographer, and journalist, educated at Oxford University, whose publications include *Chile: Travels in a Thin Country* (1994), *Cherry: A Life of Apsley Cherry-Garrard* (2001), and *Too Close to the Sun: The Life and Times of Denys Finch-Hatton* (2006). The work that established her reputation, *Terra Incognita: Travels in Antarctica* (1996), an often lyrical and spiritual account of the Antarctic, provides a woman's perspective on a region more often associated with tales of masculine adventure. Wheeler mocks the public-school humour and attitudes of the male scientists whose base she shares for several weeks, but she comes to respect the endurance and fortitude shown by Robert Falcon *Scott and his companions. Her book offers a complicated and ambivalent view on the gendered associations of the Antarctic.

Where the Wild Things Are (1963) A ground-breaking and much-analysed *picturebook by Maurice *Sendak. Max is sent to bed and fantasizes about sailing to an island inhabited by Wild Things. Sendak experiments with frames, pace, and viewpoint, arguably raising the picturebook to a new artistic level. There is an opera (Oliver Knussen, 1980; libretto by Sendak); Spike Jonze has directed a film version.

WHETSTONE, George (1550–87) Poet and playwright, born in London where he studied at the Inns of Court. He wrote miscellaneous verse, especially elegies, and prose tales, but is principally remembered for *Promos and Cassandra* (1578), a two-part play in rhymed verse (based on a tale in *Cinzio's *Hecatommithi*), which provided the plot for William *Shakespeare's **Measure for Measure* and is an early example of English romantic comedy. There is a life by T. C. Izard (1942).

WHICHCOTE, Benjamin *See* CAMBRIDGE PLATONISTS.

WHISTLER, James Abbott McNeill (1834–1903) An American painter, who moved between Paris and London. He was first influenced by the realism of Gustave Courbet (1819–77), but later emphasized that a painting is 'an arrangement of line, form and colour first'. His most famous works are the *Nocturnes*, paintings of the Thames at dusk. George du

*Maurier's *Trilby* describes his bohemian life as a student in Paris (1855–9). Whistler moved to London in 1859; as a neighbour of Dante Gabriel *Rossetti, he mixed in *Pre-Raphaelite circles, and discussed his ideas on art with A. C. *Swinburne; Swinburne dedicated a poem to the *Little White Girl* (1864). Whistler, notorious as a dandy and wit, was at the centre of the *Aesthetic movement. In 1877 John *Ruskin attacked him for 'flinging a pot of paint into the public's face'; Whistler sued him, won, and was awarded a farthing damages. The trial stimulated Whistler's gifts as a polemicist; he wrote a series of pamphlets and vituperative letters to the press, later published together in *The Gentle Art of Making Enemies* (1890). His most serious and elegant attack on Ruskin's belief in the moral purpose of art was his *Ten O'Clock Lecture*. He had discussed many of his ideas with Oscar *Wilde, whom he later accused of plagiarism; Whistler's influence is evident in Wilde's lectures in America (1882) and in 'The Decay of Lying' and 'The Critic as Artist'. After 1891 Whistler again lived in Paris, where both his writing and the shadowy beauty of his pictures were deeply admired by symbolist writers. Stéphane *Mallarmé, a close friend, translated his *Ten O'Clock Lecture* (1888). Marcel *Proust's Elstir is generally considered to be drawn from the characters of Whistler and Claude Monet (1840–1926). See Richard Dorment, *James McNeil Whistler* (1994).

WHITAKER, Joseph (1820–95) Publisher and editor, son of a silversmith, who was apprenticed to a bookseller in Oxford and then moved to London. He was editor of the **Gentleman's Magazine* (1856–9), where he became interested in readers' questions. He founded the *Educational Register* (1850), Whitaker's *Clergyman's Diary* (1850), the *Artist* (1855), the *Bookseller* (1858), and *Whitaker's Almanack* (1868), a compendium of general information regarding the government, finances, population, and commerce of the world, with special reference to the British Commonwealth and the United States.
See ALMANACS.

WHITE, Antonia (1899–1979) Novelist and translator, born in London, the daughter of a classics scholar and schoolmaster. She was educated at a convent in Roehampton, and at St Paul's School for Girls. In 1930 she married H. T. Hopkinson, later editor of *Picture Post*. Her convent childhood is described in her first autobiographical novel, *Frost in May* (1933). The heroine of this work, Nanda Grey, becomes Clara Batchelor in three subsequent novels, *The Lost Traveller* (1950), *The Sugar House* (1952), and *Beyond the Glass* (1954), which provide a fictionalized account of her own experiences as a struggling writer, her complex relationships with her father and with other men, and the mental illness which led to her confinement in an asylum. *The Hound and the Falcon* (1966) describes her reconversion to Catholicism. Antonia White also translated many of the novels of *Colette. There is a life by Jane Dunn (1998).

WHITE, E. B. (Elwyn Brooks) (1899–1985) Born in Mount Vernon, New York, author and critic who wrote for the **New Yorker* for eleven years. His most widely read book, apart from his best-selling revision of William Strunk Jr's *Elements of Style* (popularly known as Strunk and White, 1959), is *Charlotte's Web* (1952). This highly regarded book mixes realism and fantasy: farmer's daughter Fern Zuckerman saves Wilbur, a runt piglet, from slaughter, helped by a literate spider, Charlotte, who weaves words starting with 'Some Pig' in her web over Wilbur's head, and Templeton the rat. *Charlotte's Web* was made into an animated film in 1973 and a feature film in 2006. *Stuart Little* (1945) has an uneasy premiss—a mouse born to humans; it was filmed in 1999 with a 2002 sequel. White received a Pulitzer Prize by special citation in 1978.
See ANIMAL STORIES.

WHITE, Edmund (1940–) American novelist and essayist, born in Cincinnati. *Nocturnes for the King of Naples* (1978) is a non-realistic novel dealing with homosexual themes which were pursued more realistically in *A Boy's Own Story* (1982), a semi-autobiographical description of the gay adolescence of a child of divorced parents. This work brought him much acclaim, and was followed by the sequels *The Beautiful Room Is Empty* (1988) and *The Farewell Symphony* (1997), the last of which moves into the AIDS era. Other works include *States of Desire: Travels in Gay America* (1980) and the autobiographical *My Lives* (2006). He has also published biographies of Jean *Genet (1993) and Marcel *Proust (1998).

WHITE, Gilbert (1720–93) Clergyman and naturalist, born at Selborne in Hampshire, educated at Oriel College, Oxford. White chose to spend most of his life as curate of Selborne. He began in 1751 a 'Garden Kalendar' and later a 'Naturalist's Journal'. He sent detailed local observations on birds, bats, plants, weather conditions, and other natural phenomena to Thomas *Pennant and Daines Barrington (1727–1800), the correspondence forming the basis of his *Natural History and Antiquities of Selborne* (published 1788, dated 1789), a work read with appreciation by figures as various as S. T. *Coleridge, William *Cobbett, Charles *Darwin, and Richard *Jefferies. The work has proved enduringly popular, and has been continuously in print since its first publication. Selections from White's journals appeared as *A Naturalist's Calendar*, ed. Dr John Aikin (1795), and *Gilbert White's Journals*, ed. W. Johnson (1931).

WHITE, Henry Kirke (1785–1806) Poet, son of a butcher, articled to a lawyer in Nottingham. His volume of verses in 1803 attracted the attention of Robert *Southey, who encouraged and helped him. His overwork as a student at Cambridge helped to bring about his early death. Southey collected his works, with a memoir, and published them in 1807.

WHITE, James (1928–99) Northern Irish *science fiction writer, born in Belfast; whose 'Sector General' series of novels and stories about a vast space-hospital combine ingenious alien biologies with a light but sincere message about cooperation. Examples are *Hospital Surgeon* (1962) and *Final Diagnosis* (1997).

WHITE, Joseph Blanco (1775–1841) Theologian and poet, born in Seville. He became a Catholic priest, but soon abandoned the priesthood, and came to England in 1810. With the help of Lord Holland he started a journal, *El español*, which ran from 1810 to 1814. He wrote for the **New Monthly Magazine* and later for John Stuart *Mill's *London Review*. He went to study at Oxford and became an Anglican cleric, and the friend of Richard Whately (1787–1863), John Henry *Newman, Edward *Pusey, and Richard Hurrell *Froude. His *Evidences against Catholicism* appeared in 1825. His other publications include *Observations on Heresy and Orthodoxy* (1835), translations into Spanish of William *Paley's *Evidences*, and other widely read ecclesiastical works. In 1828 *The Bijou* published his sonnet 'Night and Death', which S. T. *Coleridge extravagantly described as 'the finest…sonnet in our language'. Towards the end of his life White became a Unitarian, and lived among the *Unitarian community of Liverpool. See M. Murphy, *Blanco White: Self-Banished Spaniard* (1989).

WHITE, Patrick (1912–90) Australian novelist and playwright, born in England, the first Australian to win the *Nobel Prize for Literature, in 1973. After attending Cheltenham College, White returned to Australia (where he had spent his childhood), working on farms and writing three unpublished novels. *Thirteen Poems* (1929 or 1930) and *The Ploughman* (1935), also poetry, were published by his mother. After studying modern languages at Cambridge (1932–5), White travelled in Europe and the United States, publishing the novels *Happy Valley* (1939) and *The Living and the Dead* (1941). He joined the RAF in 1941, serving as an intelligence officer in the Mediterranean. While on leave he met Manoly Lascaris, who became his lifelong partner and returned with him to Sydney in 1948. White's first major novel, *The Aunt's Story* (1948), sold well in the USA, receiving a positive review by James Stern in the *New York Times*. From the mid-1950s he wrote plays, short stories, and a series of *epic novels which collectively attempt to reconfigure the values of Australian society, rejecting equally the tenets of realist writing, and suburban cant: *The Tree of Man* (1955), *Voss* (1957), *Riders in the Chariot* (1961), *The Solid Mandala* (1966), and *The Vivisector* (1970). His biographer, David Marr, notes that 'White's explorers, spinsters, dames, Jews, painters, Aborigines, farmers, washerwomen and tramps…shake off their past to pursue a calling and reach, in the end, some vision of the holiness, the wonder of life' (see *Patrick White: A Life*, 1991). His most studied novel, *Voss*, tells the story of the doomed attempt of Johann Voss to cross the Australian continent, describing the mystic communion that binds him to Laura Trevelyan, who, at home in Sydney, suffers with him and is released from fever at the moment of his death. *The Eye of the Storm* (1973) and *A Fringe of Leaves* (1976) create powerful female characters, a White signature, while *The Twyborn Affair* (1979) in some respects echoes Virginia *Woolf's *Orlando* with its gender-switching protagonist. *Flaws in the Glass* (1981), an autobiography, offers frank insights into White's writing and thought. In 2006 the National Library of Australia announced the purchase of White's manuscripts, thought to have been destroyed.

WHITE, T. H. (Terence Hanbury) (1906–64) Born in Bombay (Mumbai), India, educated at Cheltenham College and Queen's College, Cambridge; he is remembered for the *crossover novels comprising *The Once and Future King* (1958) based on Arthurian legends. This begins with *The Sword in the Stone* (1938), made into a Disney film in 1963. *Mistress Masham's Repose* (1947), featuring a girl who becomes involved with some Lilliputians, is a children's classic. Other books include *The Goshawk* (1951), about training a falcon, and *The Book of Beasts* (1954), translated from a Latin *bestiary. See S. T. Warner, *T. H. White: A Biography* (1967).

WHITE, William Hale (1831–1913) Known as a writer under the pseudonym of 'Mark Rutherford', author and civil servant, born in Bedford, the son of William White, Dissenter, bookseller, and later a well-known doorkeeper in the House of Commons and author of *The Inner Life of the House of Commons* (1897). Hale White was educated to become an independent minister, but became disillusioned with his training. In 1854 he entered the Civil Service, rising to a responsible post as assistant director of contracts at the admiralty. He supplemented his income as a journalist, and in 1881 published *The Autobiography of Mark Rutherford, Dissenting Minister*, the book for which he is best remembered. It describes the spiritual development of a young Dissenter, supposedly edited after his death by his friend Reuben Shapcott. Rutherford attends a Dissenting college and becomes a minister, but is beset by theological doubts and distressed by the narrow views of his colleagues and congregations. He loses his faith, becoming as disillusioned by the Unitarians as he was by his own church. It is a powerful account of the progress of 19th-century doubt. Rutherford cannot believe in personal immortality (though he is attracted to Wordsworthian pantheism), and finally sees himself as one born 100 years too late, for whom it would be 'a mockery to think about love for the only God whom I knew, the forces that maintained the universe'. The book was well received, and was followed by other imaginative works under the same pseudonym: these were *Mark Rutherford's Deliverance* (1885), *The Revolution in Tanner's Lane* (1887, a sympathetic portrait of Dissent, radical politics, and working men's lives earlier in the century), *Miriam's Schooling and Other Papers* (1893), *Catherine Furze* (1893), and *Clara Hopgood* (1896). Works published under his own name include a life of John *Bunyan (1905), a writer who profoundly influenced him. His life was overshadowed by the illness of his wife, who died in 1891; he saw her patient suffering as 'salvation through Crucifixion'. See a biography by C. D. Maclean (1955); also C. R. Harland, *Mark Rutherford: Mind and Art of William Hale White* (1988).

White Devil, The A tragedy by John *Webster, written between 1609 and 1612, when it was published. The duke of Brachiano, husband of Isabella, the sister of Francisco, duke of

Florence, is weary of her and in love with Vittoria, wife of Camillo. The *Machiavellian Flamineo, Vittoria's brother, helps Brachiano to seduce her, and contrives (at her suggestion, delivered indirectly in a dream) the death of Camillo. Brachiano causes Isabella to be poisoned. Vittoria is tried for adultery and murder in the celebrated central arraignment scene (III. ii), and defends herself with great spirit; Charles *Lamb's phrase for her manner was 'innocence-resembling boldness', and William *Hazlitt found in her 'that forced and practised presence of mind' of the hardened offender, pointing out that she arouses sympathy partly through the hypocrisy of her accusers. She is sentenced to confinement in 'a house of penitent whores', whence she is carried off by Brachiano, who marries her. Flamineo quarrels with his younger brother, the virtuous Marcello, and kills him; he dies in the arms of their mother Cornelia, who later, driven out of her wits by grief, sings the dirge 'Call for the robin redbreast, and the wren', a scene which elicits from Flamineo a speech of remorse.

('I have a strange thing in me to the which
I cannot give a name, without it be
Compassion.')

Meanwhile Francisco, at the prompting of Isabella's ghost (*see* REVENGE TRAGEDY), avenges her death by poisoning Brachiano. Vittoria and Flamineo, both of whom die Stoic deaths, are murdered by Brachiano's dependants. The play has been one of the most frequently revived of *Jacobean tragedies.

WHITEFIELD, George (1714–70) Popular evangelical preacher, journal writer, and leader of the Calvinistic *Methodists. He came under the influence of Charles *Wesley while an undergraduate at Pembroke College, Oxford, and after his ordination as deacon and first successes as a preacher, in 1738 followed the Wesley brothers to Georgia, where he founded an orphanage. On his return he was ordained priest and attracted much attention at large open-air meetings by his fervent and emotional sermons. Whitefield encouraged John *Wesley to imitate him by preaching out of doors, but his own increasingly Calvinistic views resulted in a rift between them. A genius at public speaking and fund-raising, Whitefield published his naively enthusiastic journals relating his experiences in England and America (1738–41) and accounts of his early life (1740, 1747) to raise money for his orphanage (in 1756 he published an abridged and expurgated version). He became the focus of the transatlantic *Evangelical Revival, his activities generating as much hostility as adulation, and also made several preaching journeys to Scotland and Wales. In 1748 he became domestic chaplain to the countess of *Huntingdon and began to recruit more aristocratic hearers. He died near Boston on the last of his seven visits to America. He was widely ridiculed in novels, plays, prints, and poems, for example by Samuel *Foote in *The Minor*, Richard *Graves in *The Spiritual Quixote*, and William *Hogarth.

WHITEHEAD, Charles (1804–62) Poet, novelist, and dramatist. In 1831 he published *The Solitary*, a poem which met with warm approval. His quasi-historical romances *The Autobiography of Jack Ketch* (1834) and *Richard Savage* (1842), and his play *The Cavalier* (1836), were also successful. His career was ruined by his drinking, and he died miserably in Australia.

WHITEHEAD, William (1715–85) Poet and playwright, educated at Winchester College, and Clare Hall, Cambridge. In 1741 he published *The Danger of Writing Verse*, a verse epistle, and in 1743 *An Essay on Ridicule* and *Ann Boleyn to Henry VIII* (1743). His tragedy *The Roman Father*, based on *Corneille's *Horace*, was successfully staged in 1750 with David *Garrick in the leading role. In 1757 he was appointed *poet laureate after Thomas *Gray declined the office. His *Charge to the Poets* (1762) prompted a derogatory response from Charles *Churchill. His *Poems and Plays* (2 vols, 1774) was supplemented by a third volume, containing a 'Memoir' by William *Mason, in 1788.

WHITING, John (1917–63) Playwright, whose plays, at first ill received, marked a historic break from the prevailing vogue for drawing-room comedy. *A Penny for a Song* (1956), *Saint's Day* (1951), *Marching Song* (1954), and *The Gates of Summer* (1956) show a powerful and individual talent, but he did not achieve popular success until *The Devils*, adapted from *The Devils of Loudun* by Aldous *Huxley, was performed by the Royal Shakespeare Company in 1961. A highly theatrical piece, influenced by Bertolt *Brecht, it deals with a case of hysterical demonic possession in a French nunnery. His *Collected Plays* (1969, ed. R. Hayman) includes several performed posthumously.

WHITMAN, Walt (1819–92) American poet, born on Long Island, New York. He had little formal education, and started work as an office boy; he subsequently worked as printer, wandering schoolteacher, and contributor to and editor of various magazines and newspapers, entering politics as a Democrat, and travelling in 1848 to New Orleans, where he wrote for the *Crescent*. He returned to New York and the *Brooklyn Times* via St Louis and Chicago, and the experience of the frontier merged with his admiration for Ralph Waldo *Emerson to produce the first, self-published edition of *Leaves of Grass* in 1855, a sequence celebrating America through free verse, avoiding European models. When Emerson was sent a copy he replied hailing the work as 'the most extraordinary piece of wit and wisdom that America has yet contributed'. The second edition (1856) added 21 poems, and the third edition (1860) 122, including the group entitled 'Calamus', which has been taken as a reflection of the poet's homosexuality, although in his own words they celebrate the 'beautiful and sane affection of man for man'. The six further editions that appeared in Whitman's lifetime were revised or expanded, the work enlarging as the poet developed. During the Civil War Whitman worked as a clerk in Washington, but his real business was as a volunteer hospital visitor among the wounded, an experience which affected him deeply, as can be seen in his prose *Memoranda during the War* (1875) and in the poems published under the title of *Drum-Taps* in 1865. In the *Sequel* to these poems (1865–6) appeared the great elegy on Abraham

Lincoln, 'When Lilacs Last in the Dooryard Bloom'd'. Whitman continued to revise *Leaves of Grass* up to his death. In spite of his achievement, and his efforts at self-publicity, he was disregarded by the public at large, some of whom were offended by his outspokenness on sexual matters, some by his pose as rough working man; his reputation began to rise after recognition in England by D. G. *Rossetti, A. C. *Swinburne, and others. After a paralytic stroke in 1873 he left Washington and lived quietly in Camden, New Jersey, still writing, though without the originality of his early years. The free, vigorous sweep of his verse conveys subjects at once national ('Pioneers! O Pioneers!', 1865), mystically sexual ('I sing the body electric', 1855), and deeply personal ('Out of the Cradle Endlessly Rocking', 1860), and his work proved a liberating force for many of his successors, including Henry *Miller and the poets of the *Beat Generation. See *The Collected Writings of Walt Whitman*, ed. Sculley Bradley *et al.*, 17 vols (1961–84); Justin Kaplan, *Walt Whitman* (1980); Gary Schmidgall, *Walt Whitman* (1997).

WHITNEY, Geoffrey *See* EMBLEM BOOK.

WHITNEY, Isabella (*fl.*1566–73) The first English female poet to acknowledge her authorship of a volume of secular verse. She was brought up in London and may have been the sister of the *emblem book writer Geoffrey Whitney. Her two collections of poems are *The Copy of a Letter* (1566–7) and *A Sweet Nosegay* (1573): both survive only in single copies. The first consists of four complaints voiced by two female and two male speakers about their unhappiness in love; in the second the poet (or her persona) describes her social and domestic circumstances and the reasons for her deciding to leave London. The final piece in the volume is a poetical last 'Will and Testament' which provides a striking picture of contemporary London, especially of its low life.

WHITTIER, John Greenleaf (1807–92) American poet, born of Quaker parents in Massachusetts. He began life as a farmer's boy, and supported himself while at Haverhill Academy by shoemaking and teaching. He became an ardent Abolitionist, and wrote tracts and edited various periodicals for the cause as well as writing poems on the subject of slavery, collected as *Voices of Freedom* (1846). He was a regular contributor to the **Atlantic Monthly*, which he helped to found. A prolific and popular poet and hymn-writer (his hymns include 'Dear Lord and Father of mankind'), he wrote in many genres; his first book, *Legends of New-England in Prose and Verse* (1831) demonstrates his lifelong interest in local history. See Edward Wagenknecht, *John Greenleaf Whittier* (1967).

Whole Duty of Man, The A devotional work published 1658, in which man's duties to God and his fellow men are analysed and discussed in detail. The book was at one time attributed to Lady Dorothy Pakington (d. 1679). She was, however, probably only the copyist. The book, by internal evidence, is the work of a practised scholar, acquainted with Hebrew, Syriac, and Arabic, probably Richard Allestree (1619–81), chaplain in ordinary to the king, Regius professor of divinity, and provost of Eton College. It had enormous popularity, lasting for over a century; it is comparable in this respect to *Thomas à Kempis's *De Imitatio Christi* and William *Law's *Serious Call*.

Who's Who An annual biographical dictionary of contemporary men and women published by A. & C. Black. It was first issued in 1849 but took its present form in 1897, when it incorporated material from another biographical work, *Men and Women of the Time*; earlier editions of *Who's Who* had consisted merely of professional lists, etc. Inclusion is regarded as a mark of prominence in public life, though definitions of what constitutes prominence have not entirely kept step with fashion. Members of the peerage are automatically included, while sports people or pop stars may not be. The entries are compiled with the assistance of the subjects themselves and updated annually. This allows information which may not be a matter of public record elsewhere to be included and for the style to reflect particular personalities, though information may sometimes be partial or unreliable. Once included in *Who's Who*, no subject is removed until death. The first *Who Was Who 1897–1916* appeared in 1920, and the eighth (1981–90) in 1991. These volumes contain entries for subjects who have died, with final details and date of death added. They are now added every five years. An online edition of *Who's Who* was launched in 2005 and a history of *Who's Who* was published in 1998 in its 150th year.

WHYTE-MELVILLE, George John (1821–78) Novelist, born in Fife, educated at Eton; he is celebrated (with Anthony *Trollope and Robert *Surtees) as a hunting novelist. He joined the 93rd Highlanders, then the Coldstream Guards, and served in the Crimean War. Returning to England, he devoted his time to field sports. His first novel, *Digby Grand*, was published in 1853; John *Galsworthy, at Oxford, fell under the spell of the 'Bright Things' in Whyte-Melville's novels, and Digby Grand was Jolyon's (in *The *Forsyte Saga*) first idol. He won fame with *Holmby House* (1859), a historical romance describing the Civil War. *Market Harborough* (1861) and *The Gladiators* (1863), also very popular, were followed by a number of similar novels. *Riding Recollections* (1879) was a notable book on horsemanship. He was killed in a hunting accident.

WHYTHORNE, Thomas (1528–96) Poet and musician, educated at Magdalen College, Oxford. After three years as 'servant and scholar' in the household of John *Heywood he became a music tutor. His *Songes for Three, Fower and Five Voyces* (1571) was one of the first English *madrigal books; *Duos, or Songs for Two Voices* appeared in 1590. Whythorne's pioneering autobiography, *A Book of Songs and Sonetts*, written *c.*1576, was discovered in 1955 and edited by James M. Osborn (1961). A revealing document of Tudor social life, it is written in phonetic spelling and thus offers a key to contemporary pronunciation.

WICKHAM, Anna (1883–1947) Pseudonym of Edith Harper, poet, born in Wimbledon, and educated in Queensland and New South Wales, Australia. She returned to London in 1905 to study singing, went to Paris to be coached for opera by de Reszke, but married in 1906 Patrick Hepburn, solicitor and astronomer, by whom she had four sons. More popular in the USA and France than at home, she was an original and copious poet, in imagery and subject matter in advance of her time. She charted the struggle of a woman artist to achieve freedom to work as well as to fulfil herself as wife and mother. Her friends included D. H. *Lawrence, Malcolm *Lowry, Kate *O'Brien, and Dylan *Thomas. Her publications include *The Contemplative Quarry* (1915), *The Little Old House* (1921), and *Thirty-Six New Poems* (1936). A collection, *The Writings of Anna Wickham* (1984), was edited by R. D. Smith.

WICKS, Susan (1947–) British poet and novelist. Wicks read French at the universities of Hull and Sussex, writing a dissertation on the work of André *Gide. Her poetry collections include *Singing Underwater* (1992); *Open Diagnosis* (1994), which saw her coming to terms with multiple sclerosis; *The Clever Daughter* (1996), which details the after effects of her mother's death and her relationship with her father; *The Night Toad: New and Selected Poems*; and *De-Iced* (2007). Wicks has also written a short memoir, *Driving my Father*, and two novels, *The Key* (1997) and *Little Thing* (1998). The American poet Sharon *Olds has been important to her work, but although a strong element of emotional risk is central to her autobiographical explorations of family relationships, Wicks also combines a strong interest in narrative with a restrained and acutely judged bareness of language.

Widsith A poem of 143 lines in Old English in the *Exeter Book. 'Widsith', its opening word, is the poet who unlocks the 'word-hoard' that constitutes the poem. It contains three 'thulas' (i.e. mnemonic name-lists), connected by his ostensible experience: the first names great rulers; the second lists the tribes among whom he claims to have travelled; the third names people whom he sought out. Ed. K. Malone (1962); *The Exeter Anthology of Old English Poetry*, ed. Bernard Muir (2000).

WIENERS, John (1934–2002) American poet, born in Massachusetts, who studied at Black Mountain College with Charles *Olson. Wieners spent much of his life in Boston and focused his poetry on the subjects of drugs and gay sexuality. His best-known collection is *Nerves* (1970). *The Journal of John Wieners* was published in 1996.

'Wife of Bath's Tale, The' *See* CANTERBURY TALES, 6.

Wife of Usher's Well, The A ballad of the Scottish border. The wife sends her three sons to sea, and soon gets tidings of their death. Their ghosts come back on one of the long nights of Martinmas, and the mother, deceived by the apparitions, orders a feast; but at cock-crow they disappear.

Wife's Lament, The An Old English poem of 53 lines in the *Exeter Book, one of the group usually called 'elegies'. That the speaker is female is established by feminine grammatical endings in the first two lines, making it (like *'Wulf and Eadwacer') a rare early English example of a *Frauenlied*. It is a poem about the pain of separation, apparently visited on the speaker by the absent husband/lover and his family. The precise situation is impossible to determine; the speaker has been made to live in an earth-barrow so the poem can plausibly be interpreted as a revenant voice from the grave. As in the other elegies, the situation seems to be an image of the separation of the soul from God; but, as in *The *Seafarer* (the opening of which this poem echoes closely), the obscure literal location is hauntingly evoked. By the 20th century it had become one of the most admired Old English short poems. See R. Hamer (ed. and trans.), *A Choice of Anglo-Saxon Verse* (1970); B. J. Muir (ed.), *The Exeter Anthology of Old English Poetry* (1994).

WIGGIN, Kate Douglas (1856–1923) American children's writer and educationalist, born in Philadelphia, Pennsylvania, trained to be a teacher at Abbott Academy, Massachusetts, the author of sentimental but popular books; notably *The Birds' Christmas Carol* (1887), *Rebecca of Sunnybrook Farm* (1903), and *Mother Carey* (1911). See her autobiography (1923).

WIGGLESWORTH, Michael (1631–1705) Puritan American poet and minister, born in Lincolnshire, who emigrated in 1638. He is known chiefly for his long Calvinistic poem in ballad metre, *The Day of Doom: A Poetical Description of the Great and Last Judgement* (1662). See Richard Crowder, *No Feather Bed to Heaven* (1961).

WILBERFORCE, William (1759–1833) Politician, leading evangelical, and philanthropist, educated at St John's College, Cambridge, and MP for the county of Yorkshire. He devoted himself to the abolition of the slave trade and to other philanthropic projects. He published *A Practical View of the Prevailing Religious System of Professed Christians* (1797), an influential and widely read work. A close friend of Hannah *More, he was the leading layman of the evangelical *'Clapham Sect', and lived just long enough to see carried the second reading of the Bill abolishing slavery.

WILBUR, Richard (1921–) American poet, born in New York, and educated at Amherst College and Harvard University. His elegant, urbane, and witty poetry appears in several collections, starting with *Ceremony* (1950), and he has also translated plays by *Molière and *Racine. In 1987 he was appointed US poet laureate.

WILBYE, John (1574–1638) English composer, born in Norfolk. Wilbye was one of the most important of the English *madrigal composers following the lead of Thomas *Morley. Wilbye spent most of his life in the service of the Kytson family at Hengrave Hall, in Suffolk. He published *The First Set of English Madrigals* (1598), and *The Second Set of Madrigals* (1609), and contributed one madrigal to *The Triumphes of Oriana* (1601). Wilbye stayed closer than his rival Thomas *Weelkes to Morley's Italianate manner: 'Adew, sweet Amarillis', for four voices, is a famous example of the delicate balance and harmonic ingenuity he achieved in this style. The second set is often regarded as the finest English madrigal collection of all, for its subtle poetic understanding, musical expressiveness, purity of style, and variety of texture; the melancholy six-part 'Draw on sweet night' is perhaps the outstanding example.

WILCOX, Ella Wheeler (1850–1919) American writer, born in Wisconsin, whose many volumes of romantic, sentimental, and mildly erotic verse, especially *Poems of Passion* (1883), brought her a vast readership. She also wrote short stories and novels; *The Worlds and I* (1918) is her autobiography. In her writings she pursued long-standing interests in *Rosicrucianism, the New Thought Movement and Theosophy (*see* BLAVATSKY, MADAME ELENA).

WILDE, Jane Francesca ('Speranza') (1821–96) Poet, Irish nationalist, translator, and mother of Oscar *Wilde. 'Speranza' was a pseudonym used to avoid identification with her nationalistic writing. An advocate of women's rights, she campaigned for better education for women and fought against differing legal and moral codes for the sexes. Her first collection of *Poems* appeared in 1864.

WILDE, Oscar (1854–1900) Irish dramatist and wit, born in Dublin, son of the ophthalmologist and antiquarian Sir William Wilde, and the literary hostess Jane Francesca Elgee (the nationalist poet 'Speranza'; *see* WILDE, JANE). A brilliant classical scholar, Wilde studied at Trinity College, Dublin, then at Magdalen College, Oxford, where in 1878 he won the Newdigate Prize for his poem 'Ravenna'. On his move to London in 1879 he attracted attention, much of it hostile, for his flamboyant aestheticism; he affected green velvet knee-breeches and silk stockings, and proclaimed himself a disciple of Walter *Pater and the cult of *'Art for art's sake' mocked in *Gilbert and Sullivan's **Patience* (1881). Wilde successfully lived up to the image of the satire, and its impetus took him on a lecture tour of the United States in 1882, after the publication of *Poems* (1881). In 1883 he attended the first performance of his four-act nihilist drama *Vera* in New York but the play received poor reviews and closed after a week. In 1884 he married Constance Lloyd, daughter of a well-connected Dublin family, and in 1888 published a volume of fairy stories, *The Happy Prince and Other Tales*. In 1891 followed *Lord Arthur Savile's Crime, and Other Stories* and his only novel, *The Picture of Dorian Gray*, a *Gothic melodrama which had aroused scandalized protest when it appeared in *Lippincott's Magazine* (1890), and which first brought his glittering epigrammatic style before a wide public. Wilde claimed in his preface, 'There is no such thing as a moral or an immoral book. Books are well written or badly written. That is all.' In 1891 he also published a further volume of fairy stories, *A House of Pomegranates*. His second play, the verse tragedy *The Duchess of Padua*, was almost a decade old when it was produced with some success in New York in 1891, under the title *Guido Ferranti*. Theatrical celebrity came the following year with the London production of *Lady Windermere's Fan*. *A Woman of No Importance* (1893) and *An Ideal Husband* (1895) swiftly followed. All three are moralizing social comedies which combine teasing wit with shrewd observation of upper-middle-class English manners. *The *Importance of Being Earnest* (1895), almost universally acclaimed as Wilde's masterpiece, eschews the didacticism of these plays in favour of a more sustained display of paradox and a more enigmatic commentary on social and sexual identity. *Salomé* (now known chiefly by way of Richard *Strauss's opera), written in French, was refused a licence, but was performed in Paris in 1896 and published in 1894 in an English translation by Lord Alfred *Douglas with illustrations by Aubrey *Beardsley. Lord Alfred's father, the marquess of Queensberry, disapproved of his son's association with Wilde and publicly insulted the playwright. After the failure of a libel action against Queensberry, Wilde was prosecuted for homosexual offences and sentenced to two years' hard labour in May 1895. He was declared bankrupt while in prison and wrote a letter of bitter reproach to Lord Alfred, published in part in 1905 as *De Profundis*: in it he provided a sometimes self-pitying apologia for his conduct, claiming to have stood 'in symbolic relation to the art and culture' of his age. He was released in 1897 and went to France where he wrote the best-selling poem *The Ballad of Reading Gaol* (1898), inspired by his prison experience. In exile he adopted the name Sebastian Melmoth, after the romance by Charles *Maturin (his great-uncle). He died in Paris. A century after his death, the critical penchant for identity issues has put Wilde's Irishness and his homosexuality—sometimes in conjunction with one another, as in Terry *Eagleton's play *St Oscar* (1989)—at the centre of assessments of his achievement. His aesthetic dialogues ('The Decay of Lying' and 'The Critic as Artist', in *Intentions*, 1891), his anarchistic political meditation *The Soul of Man under Socialism* (written after hearing G. B. *Shaw speak, and first published in the **Fortnightly Review* in 1891), and his fictionalized homoerotic meditation on *Shakespeare's sonnets, *The Portrait of Mr W.H.* (published as an article in **Blackwood's Magazine* in 1899 and subsequently greatly extended in a version issued in book form in 1920), have attracted increasing attention. The publication of his *Collected Works* (1908) was organized by his loyal friend Robert Ross. See *The Complete Letters of Oscar Wilde*, ed. Merlin Holland (2000); Richard Ellman, *Oscar Wilde* (1987), one of many biographies.

WILDER, Cherry (1930–2002) Pseudonym of New Zealand-born author Cherry Barbara Grimm who began writing *science fiction and *fantasy with *The Luck of Brin's Five* (1977), published for teenagers, and other series including 'Rulers of Hylor', beginning with *A Princess of the Chameln* (1984).

WILDER, Laura Ingalls (1867–1957) American author; born in Pepin, Wisconsin; her 'Little House' books, from *Little House in the Big Woods* (USA, 1932/UK, 1956) to *These Happy Golden Years* (1943/64), are edited versions of the Ingalls family's travels from Wisconsin to Kansas, Minnesota, and South Dakota between 1871 and 1889. These widely popular books, written in collaboration with Wilder's journalist daughter, Rose, idealize Pa Ingalls and incorporate an anti-New Deal political agenda. Supplementary volumes including *The First Four Years* (1971/3) were written without Rose's help. There are further books about Rose's life by Roger Lea MacBride, who inherited the copyrights, together with spin-off volumes and a long-running television series.

WILDER, Thornton (1897–1975) American novelist and dramatist, born in Wisconsin. *The Bridge of San Luis Rey* (1927) is the best known of his novels, describing the convergence of fortunes of those involved in the collapse of a bridge, and *The Ides of March* (1948) deals with the assassination of Julius *Caesar. He scored considerable success in the theatre with *Our Town* (1938), *The Skin of our Teeth* (1942), and *The Merchant of Yonkers* (1938), a comedy which was revised as *The Matchmaker* (1954) and adapted as the musical comedy *Hello, Dolly!* (1963). See Gilbert A. Harrison, *The Enthusiast* (1983).

Wild-Goose Chase, The A comedy by John *Fletcher, acted with great success in 1621, printed 1652; it was very popular on the *Restoration stage. Mirabell, the 'wild goose', a boastful Don Juan with an aversion to marriage, is 'chased' by Oriana, who tries various wiles to bring him to the altar. She pretends to be driven mad by love, but he sees through the pretence, and she finally traps him in the disguise of a rich Italian lady. His two companions, Pinac and Belleur, less assured and more at the mercy of their high-spirited mistresses, alternately pursue and are pursued by Rosalura and Lillia-Bianca. George *Farquhar's comedy *The Inconstant* is based on this play.

Wild Huntsman A ghostly hunter of German folklore and the title of a ballad by Walter *Scott, written in imitation of 'Der wilde Jäger' by Gottfried August Bürger (1747–94). The ballad, a specimen of '*Gothic terror', was included in *The Chase and William and Helen: Two Ballads from the German* and published anonymously in 1797. It concerns a 'Wildgrave', the keeper of a royal forest, who not only hunted on the Sabbath but also oppressed the peasantry. Damned for his sins, he is himself hunted perpetually through the forest after his death. *See* 'Lenore'.

Wild Swans *See* Chang, Jung.

WILKES, John (1727–97) Politician and libertine, educated at Leiden University. He was elected MP for Aylesbury in 1757 and in 1762 founded the **North Briton* in which, aided by Charles *Churchill, he attacked Lord Bute's government. He was arrested for libel, but released; he was then expelled from Parliament for his part in the *Essay on Woman* (an obscene parody of Alexander Pope's **Essay on Man*), and went to Paris. He returned in 1768, but was kept out of Parliament until 1774. On 15 May 1776 he had a surprisingly friendly meeting over dinner with Samuel *Johnson, who had written vehemently against Wilkes's claims as a champion of fundamental civil liberties. The occasion was contrived by James *Boswell, who records it in elaborate detail in the *Life of Johnson*. Johnson later sent Wilkes a set of the **Lives of the English Poets*.

WILKIE, William (1721–72) Scottish poet, academic, and Presbyterian clergyman, born in Dalmeny and educated at Edinburgh University. He was author of *The Epigoniad*, an epic poem in heroic couplets, in nine books, on the theme of the siege of Thebes: it was modelled on *Homer and inspired by the 'heroic Tragedy' of *Sophocles, and went into two editions (1757, 1759). It was highly regarded by David *Hume and by Adam *Smith. Wilkie was raised on a farm, and claimed to have 'shaken hands with poverty up to the very elbow'; he became a skilled classicist and mathematician and was appointed professor of natural philosophy at St Andrews. He was a member of the *Select Society.

WILKINS, George (d. 1618) Pamphleteer, playwright, and innkeeper. Little is known of his early life; although he describes himself as a scholar he is not known to have attended university. Amongst his writings are a pamphlet on which he collaborated with Thomas *Dekker, published in 1607, and a play, *The Miseries of Enforced Marriage*, acted by the King's Men, published and probably acted in 1607; based on the events that lie behind another King's Men play, *A *Yorkshire Tragedy*. It was popular, with new editions in 1611, 1629, and 1637. He was almost certainly joint author, with *Shakespeare, of **Pericles*, and the novel of the play, *The Painful Adventures of Pericles Prince of Tyre*, in 1608. A disreputable and violent character, from no later than 1610 he had opened an inn that doubled as brothel. In 1611 he allegedly kicked a pregnant woman in the belly, and after that was frequently prosecuted for violence and other offences. See Roger Prior, 'The Life of George Wilkins', *Shakespeare Survey*, 25 (1972); McDonald P. Jackson, *Defining Shakespeare: Pericles as Test Case* (2003).

WILKINS, John (1614–72) Scientist, religious writer, and language theorist, successively warden of Wadham College, Oxford, and master of Trinity College, Cambridge, during the Interregnum, and first secretary of the *Royal Society and bishop of Chester after the Restoration. His handbook *Ecclesiastes* (1646) went through many editions and revisions and greatly influenced the development of a plainer preaching style. He attempted to classify knowledge in his *Essay towards a Real Character and a Philosophical Language* (1668). *Of the*

Principles and Duties of Natural Religion (1675), edited by John *Tillotson, was an important expression of the reasonableness of religion in the face of contemporary scepticism.

WILLARD, Barbara (1909–94) Prolific, reclusive children's writer born in Brighton, educated at the Convent of La Sainte Union, Southampton. She began writing for adults but her reputation was established with the eight-book Mantlemass series (1970–80); set in the Sussex house where Willard lived, it tells the interconnecting stories of the Mallory and Medley families over 250 years, beginning with *The Lark and the Laurel* about the end of the Wars of the Roses. Willard's approach to history reflects the changing attitudes to women at the time she was writing: her female characters are usually strong women typified by Lilias Forstal (*The Iron Lily*, 1974), who, despite a crooked shoulder and unknown parentage, becomes respected by the workmen (who call her master) at the iron workings she manages.

William The character created by Richmal *Crompton as an ironic response to the early 20th-century 'beautiful child' cult. With his companions, 'the Outlaws', Ginger, Henry, and Douglas, long-suffering elder siblings Robert and Ethel, confederate Violet Elizabeth Bott, and rival gang led by Hubert Lane, William Brown became part of English culture through 37 collections of short stories and one novel (*Just William's Luck*, 1948) between 1919 and 1970. A detailed guide is Mary Cadogan's *The William Companion* (1990).

'William and Helen' *See* 'Lenore'.

WILLIAM OF MALMESBURY (*c.*1090–*c.*1142) The first full-scale writer of history in England after *Bede. He was educated at Malmesbury Abbey in Wiltshire, of which he became librarian. His major works were the *Gesta Regum Anglorum*, a history of England from 449 to 1120; the *Gesta Pontificum Anglorum*, an ecclesiastical history of England from 597 to 1125; the *Historia Novella*, the sequel to the *Gesta Regum*, dealing with 1128 to 1142 and left unfinished at his death; *De Antiquitate Glastoniensis Ecclesiae*; a treatise on miracles associated with the Virgin Mary; and *hagiographical works including lives of St Patrick, St Dunstan, and St Wulfstan. As well as being an authoritative and serious historian, William was a picturesque, circumstantial writer who enlivened his narrative with topographical observation, anecdote, reminiscence, and comment. The *Gesta Regum* includes two stories about *Arthur whom William regards as a great warrior while discrediting many of the stories about him. See A. Gransden, *Historical Writing in England, c.550–c.1307* (1974); R. M. Thomson, *William of Malmesbury* (1987).

William of Palerne One of the earliest of the 14th-century English romances of the *Alliterative Revival, of 5,540 lines in a west Midland dialect. It was written for Humphrey de Bohun, based on the late 12th-century French *Roman de Guillaume de Palerne*. William is a prince of Apulia who is saved from his uncle's attempts to poison him by a werewolf who is really a prince of Spain turned into that shape by his wicked stepmother. William falls in love with and wins the daughter of the Roman emperor and finally defeats the king of Spain, forcing the queen to undo her dastardly magic and restore the prince to his rightful form. While William and his love, Melior, are fleeing, they disguise themselves as bears and deer. Within this improbable framework, the poet has incorporated a discussion of courtliness and love which is not without sophistication. See EETS ES 1, ed. W. W. Skeat (1867; repr. Kraus, 1973).

WILLIAM OF WYKEHAM (*c.*1324–1404) Bishop of Winchester and chancellor of England, founder of New College, Oxford (1379), and Winchester College (1382). He was first employed as clerk of the king's works at Windsor, and he administered the rebuilding of Windsor Castle for Edward III. He became chancellor in 1367 but was dismissed, as a symbol of the clerical establishment, in 1371. He was one of the leaders of the bishops who opposed *John of Gaunt, and he was a lifelong opponent of Wycliffism. His political power waned with the ascendance of Gaunt, who seized Wykeham's lands, after the death of Edward III in 1377.

WILLIAMS, Anna (1706–83) Poet, daughter of Zachariah Williams (*c.*1672–1755), an unsuccessful inventor; Samuel *Johnson wrote a pamphlet promoting his scheme for determining the longitude at sea in 1755. She published a *Life of the Emperor Julian*, translated from a French source, in 1746. She became completely blind in 1752, living in Johnson's household for much of the rest of her life. At Johnson's prompting David *Garrick put on a benefit performance of Aaron *Hill's *Merope* for her in 1756. Her *Miscellanies in Prose and Verse* (1766) included a story by Johnson, and was supported by other friends such as Thomas *Percy, Hester *Thrale, and Elizabeth *Carter. Among the contents are verses in praise of Samuel Richardson's *Sir Charles *Grandison*, light satires ('The Nunnery'), elegies, odes, 'Rasselas to Imlac', and a sonnet in imitation of Edmund *Spenser. Williams also received assistance from Elizabeth *Montagu. She features prominently in James Boswell's *Life of *Johnson*.

WILLIAMS, Charles (1886–1945) Poet, novelist, and theological writer, born in Holloway, London, and educated at St Albans School and London University. The first of over 40 books was *The Silver Stair* (1912), but he is best known for his novels, which have been described as supernatural thrillers, and include *War in Heaven* (1930), *Descent into Hell* (1937), and *All Hallows Eve* (1944). Of his theological works the most important is *The Descent of the Dove* (1939). In verse he wrote a number of plays on religious themes, including *Thomas Cranmer* (1936) and *Seed of Adam* (1948), but his most original poetic achievement is his cycle on the Arthurian legend, *Taliessin through Logres* (1938) and *The Region of the Summer Stars* (1944), afterwards reissued in one volume (1974) together with *Arthurian Torso*, a study of Williams's poetry by his friend C. S. *Lewis. He was a member of the literary group known as the *Inklings.

WILLIAMS, Edward ('Iolo Marganwg') (1747–1826) Welsh stonemason, antiquarian, and poet, born in Llancarfan, Glamorgan, who collected a vast store of manuscripts and, under his 'bardic' pseudonym, made extravagant claims about the antiquity and continuity of Welsh tradition. See Geraint Jenkins (ed.), *A Rattleskull Genius: The Many Faces of Iolo Morganwg* (2005).

WILLIAMS, Emlyn (1905–87) Welsh actor and dramatist, born at Mostyn in Flintshire and educated at Christ Church, Oxford, whose plays include *Night Must Fall* (1935), *The Corn Is Green* (1938), and *The Wind of Heaven* (1945).

WILLIAMS, Helen Maria (?1761–1827) Poet and translator. She published her first poem, a ballad, *Edwin and Eltruda*, in 1782, which provided an entrée into London literary society where she was admired by Elizabeth *Montagu and Samuel *Johnson. In 1788, she travelled to Paris, where she was chiefly to live. She became friendly with the leading Girondists, and made the acquaintance of Mary *Wollstonecraft; her *Letters from France* (1790–5) contain interesting information on the state of Paris and France just before and during the revolution. She was a friend of *Bernardin de Saint-Pierre, whose *Paul et Virginie* she translated (1796); she also translated Alexander von *Humboldt's travels (1814–29). William *Wordsworth's first printed poem was 'Sonnet on Seeing Miss Helen Maria Williams Weep at a Tale of Distress' (1787, under the pseudonym 'Axiologus'), but despite its title he appears not to have met her until 1820 in Paris.

WILLIAMS, Hugo (1942–) Poet and travel writer, born in Windsor, the son of actor Hugh Williams, who is vividly remembered in *Writing Home* (1985). Educated at Eton College, he worked for the *London Magazine* from 1961 to 1970. His first volume, *Symptoms of Loss*, was published in 1965; others include *Sugar Daddy* (1970), *Dock Leaves* (1994), *Billy's Rain* (1999), and *Dear Room* (2006). His *Collected Poems* was published in 2002. Williams's poems are extremely distinctive, characteristically offering the potent combination of an insouciant flaneur's self-deprecation with sudden chasms of loss, grief, and yearning; they also have elements of the risqué, and they are prominently taken up with matters of style—of clothes and of music, as well as living. His travel books include *No Particular Place to Go* (1981); a collection of his much-admired columns in the *Times Literary Supplement*, *Freelancing: Adventures of a Poet*, appeared in 1995. He was awarded the Queen's Medal for Poetry in 2004.

WILLIAMS, Isaac (1802–65) Poet and theologian, educated at Trinity College, Oxford, where he was influenced by John *Keble and participated in the *Oxford Movement. He was the author of poems in *Lyra Apostolica* and other poetical works including *The Cathedral* (1838) and *The Baptistery* (1842). His contribution to *Tracts for the Times* on 'Reserve in communicating Religious Knowledge' lost him the election to the chair of poetry (1842). His autobiography (edited by Sir G. Prevost, 1892) is a significant record of the history of the Oxford Movement.

WILLIAMS, John (known as 'Anthony Pasquin') (1761–1818) A voluminous satirist and miscellaneous writer, often threatened with prosecution for libel. *The Children of Thespis* (1786–8) was his most successful poem, but he produced various volumes of poetry, biography, politics, satire, and plays. William *Gifford in *The Baviad* (1791) condemned the 'rank fume of Tony Pasquin's brains'. Williams sued Gifford's publisher for libel, and lost.

WILLIAMS, John A. (John Alfred) (1925–) African American novelist, born in Mississippi, whose best-known novel is *The Man Who Cried I Am* (1967). His non-fiction includes *This Is my Country Too* (1965) and *The Most Native of Sons* (1970), a biography of Richard *Wright. His career has included contributions to journals, TV scripts, and editing several anthologies.

WILLIAMS, Raymond (1921–88) Critic and novelist. The son of a railway signalman, he was born in Pandy, near Abergavenny, where he attended the grammar school. His studies at Trinity College, Cambridge, were interrupted by wartime service in an anti-tank regiment. He taught first as an adult education tutor in Sussex from 1946 to 1961, then at Cambridge as fellow of Jesus College and later as professor of drama. His best-known book, *Culture and Society, 1780–1950* (1958), surveys the history of the idea of 'culture' in British thought; and his later works, beginning with *The Long Revolution* (1961) and *Modern Tragedy* (1966), attempt to extend this concept in more democratic directions than those envisaged by T. S. *Eliot and others. These include short studies in historical semantics, in *Keywords* (1976). His critical investigations included television as well as the history and sociology of drama and fiction. More traditional literary studies include *The English Novel from Dickens to Lawrence* (1970) and *The Country and the City* (1974), both challenging the view of English literature and society presented by F. R. *Leavis. A leading figure of the British 'New Left', he tried to move beyond the limits of orthodox *Marxist literary criticism into a more dynamic materialist view of cultural changes, explored in *Marxism and Literature* (1977) and other books. His early novels, including *Border Country* (1960) and *Second Generation* (1964), are semi-autobiographical works in the realist tradition which, as a critic, he defended against the new orthodoxy of *modernism. There is a life by Fred Inglis (1995).

WILLIAMS, Roy (1968–) Winner of the 2001 Evening Standard Theatre Award for most promising playwright 2001. *Fallout* (2003), loosely based on the murders of Damilola

Taylor and Stephen Lawrence, and *Clubland* (2001) were staged at the *Royal Court Theatre, and *Sing yer Heart out for the Lads* (2002) at the *National Theatre.

WILLIAMS, Tad (1957–) American author of *science fiction and *fantasy novels, born in San Jose, California. *The Dragonbone Chair* (1988) begins the 'Memory, Sorrow and Thorn' series, which subtly engages with *Tolkien's moral framework. The 'Otherland' sequence (1996–2001) shows virtual realities copying literary 'worlds'.

WILLIAMS, Tennessee (Thomas Lanier Williams III) (1911–83) American dramatist, born in Mississippi. He studied at Washington, St Louis, and Iowa, and in New York, while embarking on a career as a playwright with *American Blues* (1939; pub. 1945) and *Battle of Angels* (1940; pub. 1945; rev. 1957 as *Orpheus Descending*). He achieved success with the semi-autobiographical *The Glass Menagerie* (1944; pub. 1945), a poignant and painful family drama set in St Louis, in which a frustrated mother persuades her rebellious son to provide a 'gentleman caller' for her crippled daughter Laura. His next big success was *A Streetcar Named Desire* (1947), a study of sexual repression, violence, and aberration, set in New Orleans, in which Blanche Dubois's fantasies of refinement and grandeur are brutally destroyed by her brother-in-law Stanley Kowalski. Williams continued to write prolifically, largely in a *Gothic and macabre vein, but with insight into human passion and its perversions, and a considerable warmth and compassion; his other works include *The Rose Tattoo* (1950), a comedy about a Sicilian woman and her quest for love; the symbolic and anti-naturalistic *Camino Real* (1953); *Cat on a Hot Tin Roof* (1955), a Freudian family drama which takes place at wealthy cotton planter Big Daddy's 65th birthday celebration; *Suddenly Last Summer* (1958); *Sweet Bird of Youth* (1959); *The Night of the Iguana* (1962); and a novella, *The Roman Spring of Mrs Stone* (1950), about an ageing actress's affair with a gigolo. He also published collections of poems, and his *Memoirs* appeared in 1975. *The Theatre of Williams* collects his plays, 7 vols (1972–81). See Lyle Leverich, *Tom: The Unknown Tennessee Williams* (1995).

WILLIAMS, Ursula Moray (1911–2006) Author-illustrator, born in Petersfield, Hampshire, educated at home and briefly at Winchester College of Art, remembered for *Adventures of the Little Wooden Horse* (1938), about a courageous toy, and *Gobbolino the Witch's Cat* (1942), describing the exploits of a witch's kitten who wants an ordinary home.

WILLIAMS, William ('Pantycelin') (1718–91) Hymn-writer, poet, theologian, and Methodist organizer, born in Llanfair-ar-y-bryn, Carmarthenshire, whose hymns, combining classical with dialect Welsh, and biblical allusion with force of individual personality, have been seen as the earliest and perhaps greatest achievement of Welsh romanticism.

WILLIAMS, William Carlos (1883–1963) American poet, novelist, short story writer, and, for many years, a paediatrician in his home town of Rutherford, New Jersey. His profession as doctor deeply affected his literary life, giving him, in his own words, an entry into 'the secret gardens of the self.' In his student days he was a friend of Ezra *Pound and Hilda *Doolittle (known as H.D.), and some early poems are *imagist, although he soon moved on to what he called Objectivism (a literary approach which presented the poem as an object, comprising a clear, intelligent reflection of the world). *Kora in Hell* (1920) is a volume of improvisations from this period. His poems range from the minimal, eight-line, sixteen-word 'The Red Wheelbarrow' (1923) to his most ambitious production, *Paterson* (1946–58), a long, five-part, free verse, collage evocation of the New Jersey industrial city, with the mystic motif, 'man is himself a city'. The title of his last collection, *Pictures from Brueghel* (1963), suggests the plain, poverty-stricken subjects of some of his verse and prose; and his skill at painting the ordinary with freshness and compassion is manifested in his short stories, collected as *The Farmers' Daughters* (1961). Other prose works include *In the American Grain* (1925), an important series of essays exploring the nature of American literature and the influence of *Puritanism in American culture. Williams produced an important sequence of novels: *White Mule* (1937), *In the Money* (1940), and *The Build-Up* (1952); and his *Autobiography* in 1951. See Paul L. Mariani, *Williams*, 2 vols (1975, 1981).

WILLIAMSON, David (1942–) Popular Australian playwright, born in Melbourne. Initially associated with the counter-cultural 'New Wave' drama of the late 1960s and 1970s in Melbourne, with award-winning works such as *Don's Party* (1971), *The Removalists* (1972), and *The Club* (1976), Williamson has over the course of writing nearly 40 plays increasingly become the leading chronicler and critic, in theatre, of the experiences and attitudes of his own generation of well-educated middle-class Australians. *After the Ball* (1997) employs autobiography to reflect on Australia's social changes in the previous 30 years. The satire and social criticism often seem blunted by Williamson's many brilliant one-liners and sheer comic verve, which have earned critical censure but delighted audiences.

WILLIAMSON, Henry (1895–1977) Writer, born in south London, the son of a bank clerk, and educated at Colfe's Grammar School, Lewisham. Service in the First World War affected him profoundly and its influence can be felt in much of his fiction, although his best-known work, *Tarka the Otter* (1927), is the vivid, unsentimental account of the life of a wild animal. It was followed by other such tales, including *Salar the Salmon* (1935). Williamson's flirtation with *Fascism (he was an admirer of Sir Oswald Mosley in the 1930s) has led, his admirers maintain, to the neglect of his most ambitious work, a series of fifteen novels known under the collective title *A Chronicle of Ancient Sunlight*. These trace the life, from childhood in the 1890s to the 1950s, of a writer whose experiences in the First World War, and with the Mosley-like character Sir Hereward Birkin, echo Williamson's own.

WILLIAMSON, Jack (1908–2006) Born in Bisbee, Arizona Territory; Williamson grew up with *science fiction and shaped it. His first story was in **Amazing Stories* in 1928; his last novel published 2005. Stories collected as *The Legion of Time* (1952) influenced later time-travel fictions; *With Folded Hands* (1947) questions the wisdom of trusting superior machines.

WILLIS, Connie (1945–) *Science fiction writer, born in Denver; her work has remarkable range. Both the *Hugo-winning *Domesday Book* (1992) and *To Say Nothing of the Dog* (1998) involve time travel; the former approaches tragedy, the latter comedy, as befits a title borrowed from Jerome K. *Jerome.

WILLIS, Lord Ted (1918–92) Playwright, born and educated in Tottenham. He is now best remembered for his work on the *BBC TV series *Dixon of Dock Green* (1955–63), with his central character the amiable copper George Dixon brought back from the dead from Willis's earlier screenplay for *The Blue Lamp* (1950). However, his early life had been spent in political activity to the left of the Labour Party, and his early plays were produced for the left-wing Unity Theatre, with which he was involved throughout most of the 1940s. After the end of the Second World War, he became increasingly involved in popular drama, particularly for the developing medium of television, but, however far subsequent work may have moved from his original ideological base, his drama never lost its sense of social engagement in a real world. He is the author of a biographical work, the title of which derives from his most famous character's opening words each Saturday evening episode, *Evening All: Fifty Years of Slaving over a Hot Typewriter* (1991).

Willobie his Avisa One of the books which, with Gabriel *Harvey's and Thomas *Nashe's satirical works, was censored in 1599. The poem, first published in 1594, consists of 74 serviceable but uninspired songs and a few other poems by Henry Willoughby (1574/5–1597/1605). They narrate the unsuccessful courting of Avisa, a country innkeeper's wife, by a nobleman before her marriage, and by four foreign suitors after it. The last of these has a 'familiar friend W.S.' as a companion; he has been identified with Shakespeare, who is also mentioned as author of *The Rape of Lucrece* in prefatory verses. The enigmatic and apparently allusive nature of the work has never been satisfactorily explained.

WILLS, W. G. (William Gorman) (1828–91) Irish dramatist, novelist and portrait painter, born in Kilkenny and educated at Trinity College, Dublin, whose plays revived the popularity of verse drama in Victorian London. The success of such early works as *A Man and his Shadow* (1865) and *Man o' Airlie* (1867) led to his appointment as 'Dramatist to the Lyceum' and the composition of many historical dramas, including *Charles I* (1872), which, like a number of its successors, starred Henry *Irving. He produced a version of **Faust* in 1885, and a long poem, *Melchior*, dedicated to Robert *Browning, in the same year.

WILMOT, John *See* Rochester, John.

WILMOT, Robert *See* Tancred and Gismund.

WILSON, A. N. (Andrew Norman) (1950–) Novelist, biographer, and reviewer, born in Stone, Staffordshire, educated at Rugby School and New College, Oxford, literary editor of the **Spectator*, 1981–3. His first novels, *The Sweets of Pimlico* (1977) and *Unguarded Hours* (1978), are acid social comedies much influenced by Evelyn *Waugh. Satire blended with more complex exploration of character in two of his best fictional works: *The Healing Art* (1980), about a mistaken diagnosis of cancer, and *Wise Virgin* (1982), a study of a father–daughter relationship. Among his many other novels, *Incline our Hearts* (1989), *A Bottle in the Smoke* (1990), *Daughters of Albion* (1991), *Hearing Voices* (1995), and *A Watch in the Night* (1996) comprise the Lampitt Papers quintet, about a rogue biographer. Wilson has published biographies of Walter *Scott (1980), *Milton (1983), Hilaire *Belloc (1994), *Tolstoy (1988), C. S. *Lewis (1990), and John *Betjeman (2006), and a controversial memoir, *Iris Murdoch as I Knew Her*, in 2003. *Winnie and Wolf* (2007) fictionalizes the relationship between Winifred Wagner and Adolf Hitler.

WILSON, Sir Angus (Frank Johnstone) (1913–91) Novelist, born in Bexhill, educated at Westminster School and Merton College, Oxford. During the war he worked on decoding at Bletchley Park, returning in 1946 to the *British Museum where he became deputy superintendent of the Reading Room, a post he resigned in 1955 to become a freelance writer. His first two volumes, *The Wrong Set* (1949) and *Such Darling Dodos* (1950), were of short stories, and revealed an outstanding talent for satiric mimicry and sharp social observation. Along with a Dickensian relish for the macabre and farcical, these skills were also on display in his first novel, *Hemlock and After* (1952), about an attempt to establish a writers' centre in a country house, and *Anglo-Saxon Attitudes* (1956), whose plot revolves around an archaeological forgery reminiscent of the Piltdown case. A further volume of sardonic stories, *A Bit off the Map* (1957), was followed by *The Middle Age of Mrs Eliot* (1958), a novel with deeper emotional dimensions, about the wife of an apparently wealthy barrister, who finds herself suddenly widowed in reduced circumstances. With *The Old Men at the Zoo* (1961), Wilson gave allegorical expression to his fascination with conflicts between the wild and the tame, the disciplined and the free. *Late Call* (1964) focuses with careful social and psychological naturalism on a retired woman obliged to live in a New Town with her widowed son. *No Laughing Matter* (1967), Wilson's most ambitious and masterly novel, chronicles the fortunes of a large middle-class family, and, making brilliant use of parody and pastiche, opens up a vivid panorama of more than half a century of English cultural, political, social, and sexual life. His *picaresque novel *As if by Magic* (1973) juxtaposes the often bizarre experiences of a plant geneticist and his hippie god-daughter as they journey around Asia. More tightly constructed, *Setting the World on Fire* (1980) contrasts the characters and destinies of two brothers, one a theatre director in love with artistic daring, the other a lawyer dismayed by disorder and encroaching chaos. Wilson also wrote on *Zola (1952), *Dickens (1970), and *Kipling (1977), and explored his own creative processes in *The Wild Garden* (1963). A biography by Margaret *Drabble was published in 1995.

WILSON, Colin Henry (1931–) Writer, born and brought up in Leicester; he left school at 16 and gained instant fame when he published *The Outsider*, a study of alienated genius, in 1956. Wilson has since written many works on mysticism, crime, and the occult and has published novels in various genres including *Ritual in the Dark* (1960), *The Mind Parasites* (1967), and *The Space Vampires* (1976). *Dreaming to Some Purpose* (2004) is an autobiography.

WILSON, Edmund (1895–1972) American author, born in Red Bank, New Jersey, and educated at Princeton University. He served with the US army in France during the First World War, an experience which inspired verse and short stories published in a lively and eccentric little anthology about death, *The Undertaker's Garland* (1922, with his friend J. P. *Bishop). He then worked for various magazines, including *Vanity Fair* (1920–5), the *New Republic* (1925–31), and the **New Yorker* (1943–8). His novel *I Thought of Daisy* (1929; rev. 1967) is set in bohemian literary New York, and his short stories, *Memoirs of Hecate Country* (1946), are also set largely in New York. He is principally known for his influential and wide-ranging works of literary and social criticism, which include *Axel's Castle* (1931), a study of *modernist writing as a continuation of *Symbolism (discussing W. B. *Yeats, *Valéry, James *Joyce, *Stein, and others); *The Triple Thinkers* (1938); *To the Finland Station* (1940), which traces socialist and revolutionary theory from Jules *Michelet and Robert *Owen through *Marx to Lenin; *The Wound and the Bow* (1941), a series of essays employing *psychoanalytic approaches to Charles *Dickens and others; and *Patriotic Gore: Studies in the Literature of the American Civil War* (1962), a comprehensive survey of major and minor writers of the period, and the war's roots in the national psyche. His other works include experimental plays, collections of articles and reviews (*The Shores of Light*, 1952, and others), and memoirs of early and later life (*A Prelude*, 1967; *Upstate*, 1971). He was an inspiring example and mentor to Lionel *Trilling and a larger circle of critics associated from 1937 with the **Partisan Review* and known as the New York Intellectuals: among these was his third wife, the novelist Mary *McCarthy. He was a friend from college days of Scott *Fitzgerald, whose posthumously published works he edited. Wilson's own posthumous works include diaries (*The Twenties*, 1975; *The Thirties*, 1980; *The Forties*, 1983) and *Letters on Literature and Politics* (ed. Elena Wilson, 1977). The standard life is by Lewis Dabney (2005).

WILSON, Frank Percy (1889–1963) Merton professor of English literature at Oxford University (1947–57). Apart from his general editorship from 1935 of the *Oxford History of English Literature* and revision of *The Oxford Dictionary of English Proverbs* (1970), he was chiefly concerned with Elizabethan and Jacobean literature. His works include *The Plague in Shakespeare's London* (1927; rev. 1963), *Shakespeare and the New Bibliography* (1945; rev. 1970), and his revision of Ronald *McKerrow's edition of Thomas *Nashe's works (1958).

WILSON, Harriette (1786–1846) Née Dubochet, courtesan, one of fifteen children of a Swiss-born London shopkeeper. She wrote a spirited account of her adventures and amours in the fashionable Regency world in *Memoirs of Harriette Wilson, Written by Herself* (1825), which went through many editions. It opens with panache, with the sentence 'I shall not say why and how I became at the age of fifteen, the mistress of the earl of Craven', and proceeds to describe with much frankness and some art her impressions of, and friendships with, Beau Brummell (1778–1840), Prince Esterhazy, the dukes of *Wellington, Argyle, Beaufort, Leinster, and others. She also wrote two slight novels, *Paris Lions and London Tigers* (1825) and *Clara Gazul* (1830), both **romans à clef*. See Frances Wilson, *The Courtesan's Revenge: Harriette Wilson, the Woman who Blackmailed the King* (2003).

WILSON, Dame Jacqueline (1945–) Popular children's writer, born in Bath, educated at Coombe Girls' School, Surrey. From *Ricky's Birthday* (1973) she has appealed to young readers as a writer who acknowledges their problems and resourcefulness. A champion of literacy initiatives and reading aloud, Wilson is known for her books for pre-teenagers which deal with the challenges of growing up in contemporary Britain. *The Story of Tracy Beaker* (1991; four television series 2001–8) purports to be written by a 10-year-old girl living in a children's home; *The Suitcase Kid* (1992) is the first of several to explore the impact of divorce on families; the 'Girls' books, from *Girls in Love* (1997) to *Girls in Tears* (2002), deal with issues such as anorexia and boyfriends. Wilson has campaigned to revive classic texts including stories by Noel *Streatfeild and Eve *Garnett. She was children's laureate 2005–7. See the autobiography, *Jacky Daydream* (2007).

WILSON, John (?1627–96) Playwright, educated at Oxford. He became recorder of Londonderry. His two principal plays, of which the first was popular, are *The Cheats* (1663) and *The Projectors* (printed 1665, no recorded performance); they are Jonsonian satires in which sharks, gulls, usurers, and astrologers are vigorously and effectively displayed.

WILSON, John (1785–1854) Tory satirist, journalist, and poet. He enjoyed a brilliant university career at Glasgow and

Oxford, and as a young man was a friend of William *Wordsworth and S. T. *Coleridge (to whose *Friend* he contributed). He joined the editorial staff of *Blackwood's Magazine* shortly after its foundation and became its most copious single contributor. For the 'Maga' he provided more than half of the series *Noctes Ambrosianae*, in which he appears as 'Christopher North'; he was part-author of the notorious *'Chaldee MS'; he wrote a ferocious attack on Coleridge's *Biographia Literaria*; and joined in John *Lockhart's prolonged onslaught on the *Cockney School. He admired P. B *Shelley's poetry though not his politics, and dubbed Wordsworth, Walter *Scott, and Lord *Byron, as poets, 'the three great master-spirits of our day'. Wilson's praise alternated bewilderingly with derision and he declared, 'I like to abuse my friends.' He wrote several volumes of verse, notably *The Isle of Palms* (1812), and three sentimental novels of Scottish life, *Lights and Shadows of Scottish Life* (1822); *The Trials of Margaret Lyndsay* (1823); and *The Foresters* (1825), which Wordsworth described as 'mawkish stuff'. In 1820 Wilson was appointed, for political reasons, to the chair of moral philosophy at Edinburgh, a post he held for three decades.

WILSON, John Dover (1881–1969) Shakespearian scholar and editor. Using the methods of the 'new bibliography', scientifically rigorous in examining every aspect of a text's transmission, he was responsible for editing most of the plays in the New Cambridge Shakespeare series which was begun in 1921. He also produced several popular and influential books about Shakespeare, notably the 'biographical adventure' *The Essential Shakespeare* (1932), *What Happens in Hamlet* (1935), and *The Fortunes of Falstaff* (1943).

WILSON, Thomas (1523/4–81) Humanist, educated at Eton College and King's College, Cambridge; he was made a privy counsellor and a secretary of state in 1577. He published *The Rule of Reason*, a work on logic (1551), and the *Art of Rhetoric* (1553; rev. and improved, 1560). The *Art* is a notable landmark in the history of English prose. Wilson provides interesting and useful models for letters and speeches in a variety of English styles. Some of the more amusing examples, such as the famous *'inkhorn' letter from a Lincolnshire clergyman seeking preferment, exhibit the worst excesses of Latinism and affectation: 'There is a sacerdotal dignity in my native country contiguate to me, where I now contemplate: which your worshipful benignity could soon impetrate for me, if it would like you to extend your schedules, and collaud me in them to the right honourable Lord Chancellor, or rather Archigrammatian of England.'

Wilton, Jack *See* UNFORTUNATE TRAVELLER, THE.

Wilton House In Wiltshire, the seat of the earls of Pembroke, is associated with Mary, countess of *Pembroke, whose brother Philip *Sidney is said to have written much of the first version of the *Arcadia* while staying there. According to John *Aubrey, 'In her time Wilton house was like a college, there were so many learned and ingenious persons.' She was undoubtedly an important literary patroness of authors, including Samuel *Daniel and Abraham *Fraunce, but W. J. *Cory's report in 1865 of a letter mentioning that William *Shakespeare was at Wilton and that *As You Like It* was performed there before *James I may have been meant as a joke.

WINCHILSEA, Anne Finch, countess of (1661–1720) Née Kingsmill, poet, born near Newbury. In 1684 she married Colonel Heneage Finch, who inherited the Winchilsea earldom in 1712. Writing as 'Ardelia', Anne Finch addressed many lyrics to 'Daphnis', her husband, and she wrote freely in many other forms. Her influential 'The Spleen: A Pindaric Poem' was published with three other poems of hers and some verses by Nicholas *Rowe in her praise in 1701 in *A New Collection of Poems on Several Occasions*, ed. Charles Gildon (1665–1724). Jonathan *Swift addressed a poem to her in 1709. Her *Miscellany Poems, on Several Occasions* 'Written by a Lady', appeared in 1713; this included her two best-known poems, 'The Petition for an Absolute Retreat' and 'A Nocturnal Reverie', each celebrating the virtues of retirement, privacy, and contentment. She exchanged verses with Alexander *Pope and contributed a commendatory poem to his *Works* of 1717; Pope included eight of her poems in a miscellany, *Poems on Several Occasions* (1717). Though her reputation faded, William *Wordsworth praised her nature imagery and chose seventeen of her poems for a gift album in 1819. Virginia *Woolf wrote of Finch's melancholy in *A *Room of one's Own* (1928), and John Middleton *Murry edited a selection of her verse in 1928. The major edition by M. Reynolds (1903) has been supplemented by *The Anne Finch Wellesley Manuscript Poems*, ed. B. McGovern and C. H. Hinnant (1998), but a complete edition is still awaited. See B. McGovern, *Anne Finch and her Poetry: A Critical Biography* (1992).

WINCKELMANN, Johann Joachim (1717–68) The son of a German shoemaker, who became the founder of the modern study of Greek sculptures and antiquities. By his understanding of the ideal of Greek art, its spiritual quality, its sense of proportion, and its 'noble simplicity and quiet grandeur', he exerted an immense influence on subsequent thought and literature (e.g. on Johann Wolfgang von *Goethe and Friedrich *Schiller). Friedrich *Nietzsche later rebelled against Winckelmann's 'Apollonian' view of Greek culture in his first work, *The Birth of Tragedy.* Winckelmann was the subject of an essay by Walter *Pater and of *The Conversion of Winckelmann* by Alfred *Austin. See Alex Potts, *Flesh and the Ideal: Winckelmann and the Origins of Art History* (1994).

Wind in the Willows, The (1908) Kenneth *Grahame's account of riverbank society. The Toad sections are based on stories and letters for Grahame's son Alistair. Alan *Bennett adapted it for the National Theatre (1990). There are sequels by Jan Needle (1981) and William Horwood (1993).

Windsor-Forest A *topographical poem by Alexander *Pope, begun in 1704, and published in 1713 to celebrate the Treaty of Utrecht. Partly modelled on Sir John *Denham's *Cooper's Hill*, it also draws on the *Georgics* of *Virgil, Jacobean court *masques and William *Camden's **Britannia*. Under the unifying symbols of castle, forest, and river Thames, the poem combines natural description and seasonal observation with reflections on history, politics, and poetry, closing with an epic prophecy of Britain's future as a world power.

Wings of the Dove, The A novel by Henry *James, published 1902, which explores the triangular relationship between the impoverished Kate Croy, the journalist Merton Densher, and the rich heiress Milly Theale, who sickens and dies prematurely.

'Winkle, Rip Van' *See* 'Rip Van Winkle'.

Winnie-the-Pooh The bear of very little brain in A. A. *Milne's children's stories. The archetypal amiable teddy bear, greedy and loyal, he has become something of a new-age shaman in books such as Benjamin Hoff's *The Tao of Pooh* (1982). Since 1961 his film rights have been owned by Disney.

WINSTANLEY, Gerrard (*c.*1609–1676) Pamphleteer and leader of the Diggers, or True Levellers. Born in Wigan, the son of a textile merchant, he went to London as a clothing apprentice, set up in business, failed, and worked as a hired labourer. In 1649 with a group of comrades he started cultivating the common land on St George's Hill, Surrey, in a short-lived attempt to claim it for 'the common people of England'. His first Digger manifesto, *The True Levellers' Standard Advanced*, dated 20 April 1649, was followed by *A Watchword to the City of London, and the Army* (1649), *Fire in the Bush* (1650), and *The Law of Freedom, in a Platform* (1652). His work expresses compassion for the poor and ardour for social justice. See *The Works of Gerrard Winstanley*, ed. G. H. Sabine (1941); *The Law of Freedom and Other Writings*, ed. Christopher *Hill (1973).

WINTERS, Yvor (1900–68) American poet and critic, whose own poems exemplify his critical doctrine of classicism, restraint, moral judgement, and 'cold certitude' (*see* New Criticism). His *In Defense of Reason* (1947) contains three earlier works, *Primitivism and Decadence* (1937), *Maule's Curse* (1938), and *The Anatomy of Nonsense* (1943), all of which attack obscurantism and *Romanticism, and an essay on his friend, the highly dissimilar Hart *Crane, for whom he also wrote an elegy, 'Orpheus'.

WINTERSON, Jeanette (1959–) OBE, novelist, born in Manchester and adopted by Pentecostal evangelists, educated at Accrington Girls' Grammar School and St Catherine's College, Oxford. Her training for evangelical service and her recognition that she was lesbian inspired *Oranges Are Not the Only Fruit* (1985), which won the Whitbread Award for a first novel. Winterson subsequently adapted it for television (1990). Other early books include *The Passion* (1987), in which Napoleon's hero-worshipping chef falls in love with a bisexual, web-footed Venetian girl, and *Sexing the Cherry* (1989). Winterson's novels are noted for formal experimentation: *Written on the Body* (1992) explores gender within a triangular relationship; *Art & Lies* (1994), set in an authoritarian future, deploys three narrative voices from different historical periods; and *Gut Symmetries* (1997) draws on quantum physics and the nature of time. *The Powerbook* (2000) is also concerned with time and was adapted by the author for the *National Theatre in 2002. Later novels include *Lighthousekeeping* (2004) and *The Stone Gods* (2007).

Winter's Tale, The A play by *Shakespeare written 1610 or 1611, in which year it was performed at the *Globe (recorded by Simon *Forman). It was one of the plays put on to celebrate the marriage of Princess Elizabeth and the elector palatine in 1612–13 and was first printed in the *folio of 1623 where it is the last play in the section of comedies. Its main source is Robert *Greene's **Pandosto*, and it also draws on his coney-catching pamphlets (*see* rogue literature).

Leontes, king of Sicily, and Hermione, his virtuous wife, are visited by Leontes' childhood friend Polixenes, king of Bohemia. Leontes convinces himself that Hermione and Polixenes are lovers, tries to poison Polixenes, and on his escape imprisons Hermione, who in prison gives birth to a daughter. Paulina, wife of Antigonus, a Sicilian lord, tries to move the king's compassion by bringing the baby to him, but in vain. He orders Antigonus to abandon the child on a desert shore to die. He ignores a Delphian oracle declaring Hermione innocent. He soon learns that his son Mamillius has died of sorrow for Hermione's treatment, and then he is told that Hermione herself is dead, and is filled with remorse. Meanwhile Antigonus leaves the baby girl, Perdita, on the shore of Bohemia (in fact Bohemia is landlocked), and is himself pursued and eaten by a bear. Perdita is found and brought up by a shepherd. Sixteen years pass. When she grows up, Florizel, son of King Polixenes, falls in love with her, and his love is returned. This is discovered by Polixenes, to avoid whose anger Florizel, Perdita, and the old shepherd flee from Bohemia to the court of Leontes, where the identity of Perdita is discovered, to Leontes' great joy, and the revival of his grief for the loss of Hermione. Paulina offers to show him a statue that perfectly resembles Hermione, and when the king's grief is intensified at the sight, the statue comes to life and reveals itself as the living Hermione, whose death Paulina had falsely reported in order to save her life. Polixenes is reconciled to the marriage of his son with Perdita, on finding that the shepherd-girl is really the daughter of his former friend Leontes. The tricks and songs (including the famous 'When daffodils begin to peer' and 'Jog on, jog on, the footpath way') of Autolycus, pedlar and 'snapper-up of unconsidered trifles', enliven the later scenes of the play.

WINTON, Tim (1960–) Novelist and short story writer, born in Perth, Western Australia, educated at Curtin

University, Perth. Damage is the central preoccupation in the novels and stories—usually set in his native Western Australia—that Winton has published since his first book, *An Open Swimmer*, in 1982. His breakthrough novel, *Cloudstreet* (1991), about two working-class families, begins with one character losing four fingers and another suffering brain injury. In all his books, the repercussions of physical and emotional injuries are explored with a tough sensitivity reminiscent of Raymond *Carver. Ecological damage (Winton is a dedicated environmental campaigner) is another continuing preoccupation. *Shallows* (1984) depicts clashes between conservationists and whalers in an Australian harbour town. *The Turning* (2005), a subtly interlinked collection of stories which returns to this setting two decades later, and *Breath* (2008), set in the world of surfing, are particularly impressive displays of his keenly sensuous response to his environment, psychological and social acuteness, skill at conveying intense physical experience, narrative power, vivid prose, lively dialogue, and deadpan humour. He has also written children's books, such as the Lockie Leonard series, and co-authored books about the Australian landscape.

WIREKER, Nigel (1135–1198) Benedictine monk of Christ Church, Canterbury, and author of *Burnellus* or *Speculum Stultorum*, a satire on monks featuring *Burnell the ass.

Wisdom (also ***Mind, Will and Understanding*** or ***Wisdom, Who Is Christ***) A *morality play from *c.*1460, one of the group called *Macro plays, describing the seduction by Lucifer of Mind, Will, and Understanding in a series of dances. Ed. Mark Eccles in *The Macro Plays* (EETS 262, 1969).

WISE, Thomas James (1859–1937) Bibliographer, collector, and editor, who formed the Ashley Library, which was acquired by the British Museum in 1937. In 1934 his reputation was gravely damaged by the publication of John Carter and Graham Pollard's *An Enquiry into the Nature of Certain 19th-Century Pamphlets*, which proved that a large number of rare *pamphlets whose authenticity depended upon Wise's statements were his forgeries. The most notorious of these was an edition of E. B. *Browning's **Sonnets from the Portuguese* said to have been published in Reading in 1847. Wise also stole leaves from plays in the British Museum.

WISTER, Owen (1860–1938) American novelist, born in Pennsylvania, who published a series of *westerns. *The Virginian* (1902), describing a cowboy caught up in the Wyoming range war, is a prototype of the genre.

Witch, The A play by Thomas *Middleton, written before 1616, not printed until 1778. The principal part of the plot is based on the story of the revenge exacted by Rosamond in 572 on her husband Alboin, ruler of Lombardy. In Middleton's play the duchess is obliged by her husband to drink a health at a banquet out of a cup made from her father's skull and, to avenge herself, purchases by her pretended favours the help of a courtier, Almachides, to kill her husband. (The same subject is treated in William *D'Avenant's *Albovine*, and in A. C. *Swinburne's *Rosamund, Queen of the Lombards*.) In this and the subordinate intrigue, the assistance of the witch Hecate is called in, and part of the interest of the play lies in the comparison between Middleton's Hecate and the witches in Shakespeare's **Macbeth*. Charles *Lamb in his *Specimens* indicated the difference between them.

'Witch of Atlas, The' A poem by P. B. *Shelley, written in the summer of 1820, on his return from a solitary pilgrimage to Monte San Peligrino, Lucca, in Italy, published 1824. Shelley composed this playful fantasy of 78 stanzas in **ottava rima* within the space of three days. The beautiful Witch is the daughter of *Apollo, and the spirit of mischief and poetry. She enjoys herself amid exuberant imagery of magic boats, airships, storms, and fireballs, with her mysterious companion, the Hermaphrodite. Together they circle the globe, weaving spells over stubborn kings, priests, soldiers, and young lovers (whose inhibitions are blissfully dissolved). Mary *Shelley disliked the poem; Shelley replied in verse, asking if she were 'critic-bitten'.

Witch of Edmonton, The A tragicomedy by Thomas *Dekker, John *Ford, William *Rowley, 'etc.' (possibly John *Webster), first performed probably 1621, not published until 1658. It is partly based on the story of Elizabeth Sawyer, who was hanged as a witch in April 1621.

Frank Thorney marries his fellow servant Winifred, without his father's knowledge and against his will. To save himself from being disinherited, at his father's bidding he also marries Susan Carter, and presently, to extract himself, murders her and attempts to blame her two rejected suitors, but is discovered and executed.

In a second distinct plot, the old woman of Edmonton is persecuted by her neighbours because she is, in her own words, 'poor, deformed and ignorant', and to revenge herself she sells her soul to the devil, who appears to her in the form of a dog.

> Some call me witch;
> And being ignorant of myself, they go
> About to teach me how to be one.

Her character is notable for the characteristic sympathy shown by Dekker for the poor outcast, and the tone of the play is markedly humane. Both plots are engaged with the theme of revenge, but are otherwise little connected.

WITHER, George (1588–1667) Poet and pamphleteer, born at Bentworth, Hampshire, educated at Magdalen College, Oxford. His satires *Abuses Stripped and Whipped* (1613) earned him imprisonment in the Marshalsea, where he wrote the pastorals *The Shepherd's Hunting*, a continuation of his friend William *Browne's *The Shepherd's Pipe*. *Fidelia*, a poetic epistle by a lovelorn nymph (1615), was reprinted in 1619 with the famous song 'Shall I, wasting in despair', included by Thomas *Percy in his **Reliques*. Wither was again briefly imprisoned for his satire *Wither's Motto* (1621). *Fair-Virtue, the*

Mistress of Phil'Arete (1622) was followed by *Hymns and Songs of the Church* (1623), a book of *emblems (1634–5), and *Halleluiah* (1641), which contains his best religious poetry. He was satirized (as 'Chronomastix') in Ben *Jonson's masque *Time Vindicated* (1623). During the Civil War he raised a troop of horse and wrote pamphlets for Parliament. His *Poetry* was edited by F. Sidgwick (1902).

Wits, The A comedy by Sir William *D'Avenant, published 1636, revised by him after the *Restoration, and generally considered his best comedy. Young Pallatine, a wit, who lives in London on an allowance, but finds it unequal to his wants, is in love with Lucy, who sells her jewels to provide him with money and is in consequence turned out by her cruel aunt, who suspects her of misconduct. She takes refuge with Lady Ample, the rich ward of Sir Tyrant Thrift, who proposes to force an unwelcome marriage on his ward before he loses control over her. Meanwhile Pallatine's wealthy elder brother comes to town, with old Sir Morglay Thwack, for a spell of dissipation. He tells young Pallatine that he will give him no more money, but that he must live by his wits, as he himself and Thwack propose to do. In pursuit of this purpose they become involved in a series of adventures, are thoroughly fooled, and the elder Pallatine is released from his troubles only on making liberal provision for his brother and Lucy. Thrift is likewise fooled and held to ransom.

WITTGENSTEIN, Ludwig Josef Johann (1889–1951) Anglo-Austrian philosopher, born in Vienna to a family of Jewish descent which had converted to Christianity. Educated at Linz and Berlin, he came to England in 1908 to pursue a doctorate in aeronautics at Manchester. Through the study of the logical foundations of mathematics with Bertrand Russell he became interested in philosophy. After serving in the Austrian army during the First World War he published the *Tractatus Logico-Philosophicus* (1921) in which he claimed to have solved the problems of philosophy by defining those areas in which the meaningful use of language was possible and in which it was not. Having begun to doubt his conclusions, he returned to England in 1929 to teach philosophy at Cambridge, where he held the chair from 1939 to 1947, acquiring British citizenship in 1939. His new approach stressed that language had a multiplicity of uses and that the traditional problems of philosophy arose from a misunderstanding of the use of those concepts in terms of which the problems arose; thus, by carefully bringing out the true character of the language in which they were framed, the problems of philosophy were to be 'dissolved' rather than solved. Among other posthumously published writings, the *Philosophical Investigations* (1953) contain a full account of this later position. He is generally accounted a philosopher of genius, widely studied and variously interpreted. Outside philosophy, his writings have been of influence in literary theory and are much alluded to in criticism: recently, his later ideas on language have been variously seen as representing a serious challenge to, or as support for, those espoused by *deconstructionist thinkers. See R. Monk, *Ludwig Wittgenstein: The Duty of Genius* (1990).

Wives and Daughters The last and unfinished novel of Elizabeth *Gaskell, published in the *Cornhill Magazine* 1864–6 (illustrated by George *du Maurier), and in volume form 1866. Complex and assured, the novel centres on two families, the Gibsons and the Hamleys. Mr Gibson is a widower with one daughter, Molly, a child when the story starts. As she grows up her father proposes to a widow, Mrs Kirkpatrick, formerly governess in the family of Lord Cumnor, the local magnate. Molly resents her father's marriage, and is made unhappy by her graceful stepmother's selfishness, but she loyally tries to accept the new situation. Her lot is improved when her stepmother's daughter by her previous marriage, Cynthia, who has been brought up in France, joins the household. Cynthia is beautiful, and more sincere than her mother, but has few moral principles.

The Hamleys are a county family—the proud and hot-tempered squire, his invalid wife, their elder son Osborne who is handsome and clever and his parents' favourite, and a younger son, Roger, sturdy, honest, and a late developer. Staying with the Hamleys, Molly accidentally discovers that Osborne is secretly married to a French nursery-maid. Molly begins to love and admire Roger, but he becomes engaged to Cynthia, and, now a successful scientist, leaves on an expedition to Africa. Cynthia is in fact already secretly engaged to Preston, Lord Cumnor's clever but ill-bred agent, and she enlists Molly's help in extricating herself from this entanglement, by a series of secret meetings which compromise Molly's reputation. Osborne Hamley is bitterly estranged from his father, but when Osborne dies and the secret of his marriage is revealed, Squire Hamley, repenting his harshness, adopts Osborne's baby son. Cynthia throws over Roger Hamley and marries a man more suited to her, and when Roger returns he has realized that it is Molly whom he really loves. The novel, almost complete when Gaskell died in November 1865, was clearly intended to conclude with their marriage.

Wizard of Oz, The Wonderful (1900) L. Frank *Baum's fantasy (named after the O–Z drawer in his filing cabinet). It recounts how Dorothy and her dog Toto are transported from dry, miserable Kansas to bright, colourful Oz. Dorothy accidentally defeats the Wicked Witch of the West, and with her companions, a Tin Man, a Scarecrow, and a Cowardly Lion, is tricked by the 'Wizard' (a 'Great Humbug') into finding their missing desires (heart, brain, courage, and Dorothy's Kansas home). W. W. Denslow's illustrations contributed to the book's success, and it has become a seminal American text. Baum wrote fourteen sequels; his son Frank Jr and others continued the series. The 1939 MGM film, with Judy Garland, remains popular. There is a musical companion, *Wicked*, told from the Witch's perspective (music, Stephen Schwartz; book, Winnie Holzman). The book can be read as a satirical or utopian metaphor for the USA.

WODEHOUSE, Sir P. G. (Pelham Grenville) (1881–1975) Novelist and short story writer, born in Guildford, the son of a civil servant who became a judge in Hong Kong. He spent much of his childhood in England in the care of various aunts, and was educated at Dulwich College, which he always remembered with affection; sporting schoolboys and formidable aunts would feature frequently in his fiction. He soon abandoned a career with the Hong Kong Bank for literature, writing short stories for boys' magazines, and later published extensively in the *Strand Magazine*, *Punch, etc., establishing himself as one of the most widely read humorists of his day. Several of his early novels, including his first, *The Pothunters* (1902), were school stories, and his fictional world retained an attractively child-like innocence. His prolific output of over 120 volumes included *The Man with Two Left Feet* (1917), the collection of stories which first introduced the amiably dim-witted Bertie Wooster and his wily manservant, Jeeves, whose joint antics continued in *My Man Jeeves* (1919), *The Inimitable Jeeves* (1923), *Carry On, Jeeves* (1925), etc. Other characters, including Psmith, Lord Emsworth (and his prize sow, the Empress of Blandings), and Mr Mulliner, had series of novels written about them. While Wodehouse himself remained quintessentially English, he spent much of his life in America, which provided new settings for his novels. He wrote plays, worked in Hollywood, and had a notable career in musical theatre, working with Jerome Kern, George Gershwin, and others. In 1934 he left America to live in France, where he was captured at Le Touquet by the invading Germans in 1940. Taken to Berlin, he was persuaded to make some radio broadcasts which were in themselves innocuous but which caused a furore back in England, where he was accused of collaboration and even treason. He consequently settled in America after the war, taking American citizenship in 1955. He continued to write prolifically until the end of his life. His last novel, *Sunset at Blandings* (1977), was left unfinished at his death but completed by the Wodehouse scholar Richard Usborne. See Frances Donaldson, *P. G. Wodehouse* (1982).

WOFFINGTON, Peg (Margaret) (*c.*1714–1760) Celebrated actress, daughter of a Dublin bricklayer. She was engaged by the theatre manager John *Rich (1692–1761) for Covent Garden in 1740, and was immediately successful, acting in a great number of leading comic roles. She had many lovers, and lived for some time with David *Garrick. She is the subject of *Masks and Faces* (1852), a play by Charles *Reade and Tom Taylor (1817–80), on which Reade based his novel *Peg Woffington* (1853).

WOLCOT, John (1738–1819) Satirist, who wrote under the pseudonym 'Peter Pindar'. He began his career as a physician, was ordained, then returned to the practice of medicine until 1778, when he came to London and began the writing of vigorous and witty satirical verses. Among these were *Lyric Odes to the Royal Academicians* (1782–5), mocking their painting; a *mock-heroic poem, *The *Lousiad*, published in five cantos between 1785 and 1795, and various other satires on George III. *Bozzy and Piozzi*, in which James *Boswell and Hester *Thrale set forth their reminiscences of Samuel *Johnson, appeared in 1786, as did his *Poetical and Congratulatory Epistle to James Boswell*. In 1787 appeared *Instructions to a Celebrated Laureate*, which professes to teach Thomas *Warton (1728–90) how he should celebrate the visit of George III to Whitbread's brewery. He brawled with William *Gifford in a London bookshop in 1800, the year of the latter's 'An Epistle to Peter Pindar', which describes Wolcot as an 'unhappy dotard' and a 'wrinkled profligate'.

WOLF, Christa (1929–) Née Ihlenfeld, German novelist and essayist, born in Landsberg an der Warthe (then in Germany; now Gorzów Wielkopolski in Poland) where her parents, Herta and Itto Ihlenfeld, owned a grocery. Her family fled in 1945 to Mecklenberg, which would become part of East Germany. Wolf attended school in Bad Frankenhausen and then university in Jena and Leiden. She achieved recognition with her first novel, *The Divided Heaven* (1963), which was followed by *The Quest for Christa T* (1968); her emphasis on subjective meaning brought her into conflict with the state. Her more directly autobiographical work *Patterns of Childhood* (1976) was followed by two books, *No Place on Earth* (1977) and *Cassandra* (1983), which developed her questioning of the present through the medium of the past. Her more recent work, *What Remains* (1990), describes her surveillance by the Stasi, while her biographical work *One Day a Year* was published in 2003.

WOLFE, Bernard (1915–85) American writer, born in Connecticut, who served as secretary to Leon Trotsky in 1937 and in his later years worked as a screenwriter in Hollywood. His main novels are the dystopian *Limbo* (1952), a grotesque depiction of attempts to remove Cold War aggression by amputation, and *The Great Prince Died* (1959), an account of Trotsky's assassination.

WOLFE, Charles (1791–1823) Irish poet, educated at Trinity College, Dublin, curate of Donoughmore, Co. Down, from 1818 to 1821. He was the author of the well-known lines on 'The Burial of Sir John Moore', his only poem of note, apparently based on Robert *Southey's narrative in the **Annual Register*, and first published in the *Newry Telegraph* in 1817. His *Poems*, with a memoir by C. L. Falkiner, were published in 1903.

WOLFE, Gene (1931–) American author of *fantasy and *science fiction, who dissolves the boundaries between the two by means of his command of language, storytelling, and subtle manipulation of viewpoint. *The Book of the New Sun* (1980–3), set in the far future as the sun cools, has been published both as fantasy and science fiction. Wolfe has been described as a North American *Borges: he shares Borges's sense of literary playfulness. *The Fifth Head of Cerberus* (1972) contains three related stories which require a close concentration upon the questions of identity to be fully understood as a whole. Wolfe's technique frequently involves narrators who remember (but do not necessarily *tell us*) everything (Severian in *The Book of the New Sun*), or who forget everything (Latro in *Soldier of the Mist*, 1986) or who emphatically point out that they are summarizing or paraphrasing (*Pirate Freedom*, 2007).

WOLFE, Humbert (1886–1940) Prolific writer and full-time civil servant, born in Milan and educated at Bradford Grammar School and Wadham College, Oxford. *London Sonnets* (1920) was followed by many other volumes of serious light verse, more urbane than *Georgian in tone, including *The Unknown Goddess* (1925), *Requiem* (1927), and *Kensington Gardens in Wartime* (1940). He was appointed CB in 1925. His autobiographical works include *Now a Stranger* (1933) and *The Upward Anguish* (1938).

WOLFE, Reyner (Reginald Wolfe) (*c.*1530–1573) Bookseller and printer. From Strasbourg, he came to London, established himself in St Paul's Churchyard, and enjoyed the patronage of Archbishop *Cranmer. He was the earliest printer in England to possess a stock of Greek type of good quality, and he printed in 1543, with Greek and Latin text, the *Homilies* of *Chrysostom, edited by Sir John *Cheke, the first Greek book printed in England. In 1547 he was appointed king's printer in Latin, Greek, and Hebrew.

WOLFE, Thomas Clayton (1900–38) American novelist, born in North Carolina, the son of a stonecutter, and educated at the university there and at Harvard, where he studied playwriting. He made his name with his autobiographical novel *Look Homeward, Angel* (1929), which describes at length and with much intensity the adolescence of Eugene Gant. The original version was reconstructed and published as *O Lost* (2000). *Of Time and the River* (1935) was a sequel, and various posthumous works have been published, including *The Web and the Rock* (1939) and its sequel *You Can't Go Home Again* (1940). Passionate, prolix, and rhetorical, Wolfe's novels often lacked discipline and his work owed much in its published form to editorial assistance. He died of an infection following pneumonia. See David Herbert Donald, *Look Homeward* (1989).

WOLFE, Tom (1931–) American novelist and journalist; born in Richmond, Virginia, he began his career as a journalist reporting for the *Washington Post* (1959–62). With his contemporaries Joan *Didion and Hunter S. *Thompson, he was a pioneer of *New Journalism (he co-edited the anthology *The New Journalism* in 1973), bringing to journalism techniques of writing usually employed by fiction writers. He published a number of volumes of non-fiction in the 1960s and 1970s (much of which had first appeared in periodicals such as *Rolling Stone* magazine), including *The Electric Kool-Aid Acid Test* (1968) and *The Right Stuff* (1979), about the early stages of the American space programme. His other works of non-fiction include *From Bauhaus to our House* (1981), a succinct overview of 20th-century architecture.

He is now best known for his satirical first novel *The Bonfire of the Vanities* (1987), a sharply critical look at Ronald Reagan's America, which traces the downfall of an ambitious Wall Street dealer. His 2004 novel *I Am Charlotte Simmons* deals with sexual promiscuity in a small American university.

WOLFF, Tobias (1945–) American writer, born in Alabama, whose first collection of stories, *Hunters in the Snow* (1982) established his characteristic subject of alienation in small-town America. This was followed in 1984 by *The Barracks Thief*, a short novel set during the Vietnam War, and by further story collections. He is also known for two volumes of autobiography: *This Boy's Life* (1989) describing his early adolescence; followed by an account of his experiences of service in Vietnam, *In Pharaoh's Army* (1994). His 2003 novel *Old School* describes the experience of boarding school.

WOLFRAM VON ESCHENBACH (*c.*1170–*c.*1220) Important Middle High German poet. Little is known of his life, but his principal works were the epics *Parzival* (*see* PERCEVAL, SIR), the unfinished *Willehalm*, and fragments of *Titurel*. He also composed a small number of lyrical *Tagelieder* (dawn songs or *aubades). Wolfram features as a character in Richard *Wagner's *Tannhäuser*.
See MINNESÄNGER.

WOLLSTONECRAFT, Mary (1759–97) Writer and feminist, born in Spitalfields, London; she briefly attended a day school in Beverley, Yorkshire, but was largely self-taught. After an unhappy childhood, she opened a school at Newington Green in 1784 with her sister Eliza and a friend; there she made the acquaintance of Richard *Price and other eminent Dissenters. In 1786, after writing *Thoughts on the Education of Daughters* (1787) (*see* EDUCATION, LITERATURE OF), she went to Ireland as governess to Lord Kingsborough's children; she returned in 1788 and spent some years writing reviews and translations for the radical publisher Joseph *Johnson, who published her fiction *Mary* (1788), her *A Vindication of the Rights of Men* (1790, an early reply to Edmund *Burke), and her most famous work, **Vindication of the Rights of Woman* (1792). During these years she encountered leading members of Johnson's circle, including William *Godwin, Thomas *Holcroft, and Henry *Fuseli. In 1792 she went to Paris, where she met Gilbert *Imlay, an American writer, by whom she had a daughter, Fanny, in 1794; in the same year she published her 'View' of the French Revolution. In 1795 she travelled through Scandinavia, accompanied by her maid and her daughter, a journey which produced her remarkable and observant travel book *Letters Written during a Short Residence in Sweden, Norway and Denmark*, published by Johnson in January 1796 She returned to London later in 1795, where Imlay's neglect drove her to two suicide attempts; she reintroduced herself in 1796 to Godwin, and in 1797 she married him. She died from septicaemia shortly after the birth of her daughter, the future Mary *Shelley. Godwin published a memoir in 1798, edited her *Posthumous Works* (which included her unfinished novel *The *Wrongs of Woman*) in the same year, and portrayed her in his novel **St Leon* (1799). See Claire *Tomalin, *The Life and Death of Mary Wollstonecraft* (1974); *A Short Residence*, published with Godwin's *Memoirs*, ed. Richard *Holmes (1987); Barbara Taylor, *Mary Wollstonecraft and the Feminist Imagination* (2003); Janet Todd has edited with Marilyn Butler *The Works*, 7 vols (1989) and is the author of *Mary Wollstonecraft* (2000).

Wolsey, The Life and Death of Cardinal See CAVENDISH, GEORGE.

WOMACK, Jack (1956–) Born in Lexington, Kentucky; the post-*cyberpunk flavour of his *science fiction is strengthened by his command of language in depicting the grotesque near future of America in *Ambient* (1987) or the former Soviet Union in *Let's Put the Future Behind Us* (1996).

Woman in the Moon, The A prose play by John *Lyly, published 1597. The shepherds of Utopia ask Nature to provide a woman to comfort their 'sole estate'. Nature creates Pandora, endowing her with the qualities of the Seven Planets (Saturn, for instance, is melancholy and grave; Jupiter is generous and jovial). Pandora's moods and actions vary as the planets in turn become dominant, with consequent complications among the shepherds.

Woman in White, The A novel by Wilkie *Collins, published 1860. It was an early and influential example of the novel of *sensation, and its popularity has proved enduring. The novel's complex narrative strategy was among its innovations, combining diaries, documentary testimony, and legal evidence to give the dramatic twists of the story an air of solid reality. Walter Hartright encounters a mysterious woman dressed in white on a lonely road at midnight, and helps her to escape from pursuers. Working as a drawing master in the family of Mr Fairlie, a selfish hypochondriac, he falls in love with his niece Laura, who strikingly resembles the woman in white. She returns his love, but is engaged to the vicious Sir Percival Glyde, whom she marries. It comes to light that Sir Percival has married Laura to gain possession of her wealth, and that he was responsible for the confinement of the woman in white, Anne Catherick, in an asylum. Anne Catherick and her mother know a secret concerning Sir Percival, the revelation of which he is determined to prevent. Unable to obtain Laura's signature to the surrender of her money, Sir Percival and his friend Count Fosco (fat, smooth, and villainous) contrive to get Laura confined in an asylum as Anne Catherick, while Anne Catherick, who dies, is buried as Laura Glyde. The scheme is uncovered through the courage and resource of Marian Halcombe, Laura's half-sister, and Laura is rescued. Hartright, who has been abroad, returns and takes Laura and Marian under his care, and discovers Sir Percival's secret (that he was born out of wedlock and has no right to the title). Sir Percival is burnt to death while tampering with a parish register in a last effort to save his position. Fosco is forced to supply the information which restores Laura to her identity, and is killed by a member of an Italian secret society which he has betrayed. Laura, now an heiress, marries Walter, and the pair live happily with Marian as a close companion.

Woman Killed with Kindness, A A domestic *tragedy by Thomas *Heywood, acted about 1603, printed 1607. Frankford, a country gentleman, is the husband of Anne, a 'perfect' wife. But his happiness is ruined by the treachery of Wendoll, a guest to whom Frankford has shown every kindness and hospitality. Frankford discovers the adultery of Anne and Wendoll, but instead of taking immediate vengeance on her, he determines to 'kill her even with kindness'. He sends her to live in comfort in a lonely manor house, only prohibiting her from seeing him or her children again. She dies from remorse, after having sent for Frankford to ask forgiveness on her deathbed and received it. The sub-plot, in which Susan Mountford is used as a pawn to redeem her bankrupt brother from prison, but finds herself loved by her new husband, offers interesting perspectives on the main plot. The play is one of the most successful examples of English domestic tragedy.

Woman's Prize, The, *or The Tamer Tamed* A *comedy by John *Fletcher, written 1609–11, printed 1647. It was expurgated for performance before Charles I and his queen in 1633, when it was given back to back with *Shakespeare's play, as also by the Royal Shakespeare Company in 2003. It shows the second marriage of Petruccio, from Shakespeare's *The *Taming of the Shrew*; Katharine is dead, and he marries Maria, who locks him out of his house on his wedding night, and further humiliates him until he is thoroughly subdued. There is an edition by G. Taylor and C. Daileader (2007).

Woman Who Did, The See ALLEN, GRANT.

Women Beware Women A *tragedy by Thomas *Middleton, written *c*.1621, published 1657. Set in Florence, the action involves two interwoven plots. The sub-plot is concerned with the guilty love of Hippolito for his niece Isabella. Hippolito's sister Livia acts as go-between, persuading Isabella she is no blood relation of her uncle: Isabella then consents to marry a foolish young heir as a screen for her own passion for Hippolito. The main plot is loosely based on the life of the historical Bianca Cappello, who became the mistress, and then the consort, of Francesco de' Medici (1541–87), second grand duke of Tuscany. In Middleton's version, she is at the opening of the play innocently but secretly married to the poor but honest young Leantio, a merchant's clerk. The duke sees her at a window and falls in love with her. While Livia outwits Leantio's mother at chess (a scene invoked by T. S. *Eliot in *The *Waste Land*), the duke gains access to Bianca and seduces her. Both she and Leantio are consumed by the corruption of the court. Bianca becomes the duke's mistress: the duke, reproved by the cardinal, his brother, for his sin, contrives the death of Leantio. These crimes finally meet with retribution in a wholesale massacre of the characters, through the theatrical medium of a masque accompanied by poisoned incense. Bianca destroys herself by drinking deliberately from a poisoned cup.

Women in Love Novel by D. H. *Lawrence, published in New York, 1920, and London, 1921. The sisters Ursula and Gudrun Brangwen (who first appear in *The *Rainbow*, 1915) live in Beldover, a small Midlands colliery town. Ursula has been teaching for some years at the local school and Gudrun has just returned from art school in London. Ursula is in love with Rupert Birkin (a self-portrait of Lawrence), a school inspector involved in an unsatisfactory affair with Hermione Roddice, an eccentric and dominating literary hostess based on Lady Ottoline *Morrell. Gudrun meets Gerald Crich, son of the local colliery owner, and the two are drawn together as if by a powerful electrical force. His father is dying and he takes over management of the mine, his ruthless efficiency being both feared and respected by the miners; but with Gudrun he becomes increasingly helpless. Birkin breaks free from Hermione and hopes to find with Ursula the complete union between man and woman in which he believes. Gerald suffers in his relationship with Gudrun, his mixture of violence and weakness arousing a destructive demon in her. Birkin recognizes an emptiness in Gerald, and offers him love and friendship to be based on a new intimacy between men, but Gerald is unable to accept. Ursula and Birkin are married and together with Gudrun and Gerald they take a trip to the Alps where they meet the sculptor Loerke, with whom Gudrun flirts. The relationship between Gudrun and Gerald becomes increasingly destructive until finally, in blankness and despair, Gerald wanders off into the snow and dies, leaving only Birkin to grieve for him. Lawrence completed *Women in Love* in 1916 but was unable to find a publisher until 1920 in the USA and the following year in London. *Women in Love* and *The Rainbow* are Lawrence's most experimental novels; he thought the former his best work.

WOOD, Anthony (1632–95) or, as he later called himself, Anthony à Wood. Historian and antiquary, educated at New College School, Oxford, Thame School, and Merton College, Oxford. He prepared a treatise on the history of the University of Oxford, which was translated into Latin and edited (with alterations) by Dr John *Fell and published as *Historia et Antiquitates Univ. Oxon.* (1674). Of this an English version by Wood, issued by John Gutch (1746–1831), is the standard edition. He received much ill-acknowledged help from John *Aubrey. Wood published *Athenae Oxonienses* (1691–2), a biographical dictionary of Oxford writers and bishops, containing severe judgements on some of these, and was expelled from the university in 1693 at the instance of Henry Hyde (1638–1709), for a libel which the work contained on his father Edward Hyde, the first earl of *Clarendon (1609–74). Several antiquarian manuscripts left by Wood were published posthumously. His *Life and Times*, ed. A. Clark, occupy five volumes of the Oxford Historical Society's publications (1891–1900), in which series, also edited by Clark, appeared his *History of the City of Oxford* (3 vols, 1889–99).

WOOD, Ellen (Mrs Henry Wood) (1814–87) Née Price, novelist and journalist. The daughter of a glove manufacturer, she was educated at home. She lived till her marriage at Worcester, whose neighbourhood she used as the background for her *Johnny Ludlow* short story series (1868–89). Largely brought up by her grandmother, she was disabled as a girl by a spinal disorder that left her in poor health for the rest of her life. In 1836 she married Henry Wood, a banker, and lived in the Dauphiné till she returned in 1856 to spend the rest of her life in London. Her husband was financially unsuccessful, and Wood began to write fiction to help support her family. She had an immense success with **East Lynne* (1861), her second novel, which combines the excitement of the novel of *sensation with the emotional appeal of domestic fiction. Wood subsequently owned and edited the magazine the **Argosy*, and wrote nearly 40 novels, among the best of which are *Mrs Halliburton's Troubles* (1862), *The Channings* (1862), and *The Shadow of Ashlydyat* (1863). Her ingenious plots about murders, thefts, and forgeries, her numerous court scenes and well-planted clues, make her in such novels as *Lord Oakburn's Daughters* (1864), *Elster's Folly* (1866), and *Roland Yorke* (1869) one of the forerunners of the modern *detective story. The sensational, and occasionally supernatural, events in her novels are presented in solidly detailed settings of middle-class country-town communities of doctors and lawyers, bankers and manufacturers. Conservative and Christian, Wood grounds her thrilling narratives in a firmly moral view of the world, in which vice is punished and character strengthened by adversities courageously endured. She is consistently sympathetic to the situation of women trapped in unsatisfactory marriages, without financial resources of their own. She often used industrial and trade union problems—slumps, unemployment, strikes—in her novels; her hostile description of a strike in *A Life's Secret* (1867) caused her publisher's office to be besieged by an angry mob. Many of her books were world best-sellers, widely read in America, and outstripping even Charles *Dickens in Australian sales. *East Lynne* was repeatedly dramatized and filmed, and translated into many languages, from Welsh to Hindustani. See C. W. Wood, *Memorials of Mrs Henry Wood* (1894).

WOODFORDE, Revd James (1740–1803) Diarist, educated at Winchester College and New College, Oxford. He was rector of Weston Longeville, Norfolk, from 1774 until his death. He kept a daily diary, plain but vivid in style, for 43 years, from which large selections were eventually published as *The Diary of a Country Parson* (ed. J. Beresford, 5 vols, 1924–31). It covers the period of the American War of Independence and the French Revolution, but the life Woodforde describes is more concerned with local tradesmen, squires, friends, sporting events, travels, prices, gossip, and crime. He writes of agricultural matters but not of landscape or the natural world. His love of food and drink is recorded in frequent descriptions of meals (such as 'Fowls boiled, Rabbitts smothered in onions'). The manuscript of Woodforde's diary, together with that of his niece Anna Woodforde (1757–1830), is in the Bodleian Library, Oxford.

Woodlanders, The A novel by Thomas *Hardy, published 1887. In Little Hintock, a village in the forest country of Dorset, live the native woodlanders, whose living depends upon trees, and a group of outsiders with whom their lives become entwined. Giles Winterbourne, who tends trees and travels in the autumn with his cider-press, loves and is betrothed to Grace Melbury, daughter of a well-to-do Hintock timber merchant. But she is educated outside Wessex, and seems too much of a lady to marry Giles. He suffers financial misfortune, and these facts together induce Grace's father to bring the engagement to an end, and to persuade his daughter to marry Edred Fitzpiers, an attractive young doctor who has settled nearby. Meanwhile Marty South, a village girl who had always loved Giles, has to sell her splendid hair to provide for herself and her sick father. Fitzpiers is lured away from Grace by a wealthy widow, Felice Charmond, who has come to live in the great house. The hope of divorce brings Grace and the faithful Giles together again. But the hope is illusory, and when Fitzpiers returns from his travels with Mrs Charmond Grace flies to Giles's cottage in the woods. To protect her honour Giles, although ill, leaves his cottage and sleeps outside. Grace discovers his condition, drags him back into his hut, and fetches Fitzpiers to help, but despite their efforts Giles dies. The loving, faithful Marty meets Grace by Giles's deathbed, and together they regularly visit his burial-place. With Mrs Charmond's death Grace and Fitzpiers are reconciled, and Marty is left alone to tend Giles's grave. Writing to a friend in 1912, Hardy said of *The Woodlanders*, 'I think I like it, *as a story*, the best of all.'

Woodstock, *or The Cavalier* A novel by Walter *Scott, published 1826. The work was written when Scott was oppressed by financial difficulty, his wife's death, and the serious illness of his beloved grandson. There are clear parallels between the situation of Sir Henry Lee and himself. Set in the Civil War, it describes the escape from England of Charles II after the battle of Worcester. The scene is laid in the royal lodge and park of Woodstock, where the old Cavalier, Sir Henry Lee, is ranger. His nephew Everard Markham, who, to his uncle's displeasure, has taken the Parliamentarian side, is in love with Lee's daughter Alice. Charles arrives, disguised as the page of Lee's son Colonel Albert Lee. The climax, when Oliver *Cromwell arrives to capture the king, and discovers that he has escaped, results first in Cromwell's ordering the execution of all his prisoners, down to Sir Henry's wolfhound, and then in his pardoning them. The novel was highly successful.

WOOLER, T. J. (*c.*1796–1853) Publisher, editor, and radical reformer. A Yorkshireman apprenticed to a printer, he moved to London where he became the publisher of a number of radical and freethinking periodicals: *The Reasoner*, *The Republican*, and, most notably, the *Black Dwarf* (1817–24), a mixture of incendiary polemic and sharp satire. He was twice prosecuted for seditious libel and spent fifteen months in prison. Wooler also published works by liberal and radical authors such as Jeremy *Bentham and Thomas *Paine.

WOOLF, Leonard (1880–1969) Writer, political commentator, and publisher, born in Kensington, London, and educated at St Paul's School, London, and at Trinity College, Cambridge, where he became a member of the *Apostles, a friend of Lytton *Strachey and E. M. *Forster, and was much influenced by the philosopher G. E. Moore (1873–1958). He entered the colonial Civil Service and in 1904 went to Ceylon (Sri Lanka). His experiences there would form the substance of his first novel, *The Village in the Jungle* (1913), including the profound anti-imperialist disquiet which built up within him during his time in the East. Woolf returned to England on leave in 1911, and in 1912 resigned from his post to marry Virginia Stephen (*see* Woolf, Virginia); the marriage was largely a happy one and survived until her death in 1941. After the publication of his second and last novel, *The Wise Virgins* (1914), Woolf devoted himself to journalism and political writing, although he and his wife continued to share a close intellectual comradeship and, from 1917, a commitment to fiction in the form of the *Hogarth Press. He wrote on the Cooperative movement, socialism, imperialism, the League of Nations, and international affairs, was literary editor of the *Nation* (1923–30), and co-founder and joint editor of the *Political Quarterly* (1931–59). *After the Deluge* (2 vols, 1931 and 1939) and *Principia Politica* (1953) were his most sustained attempts to formulate a political philosophy, but the five volumes of his autobiography reached a wider audience: *Sowing* (1960), *Growing* (1961), *Beginning Again* (1964), *Downhill All the Way* (1967), and *The Journey Not the Arrival Matters* (1969) together constitute a clear-sighted view of a life devoted to social progress and international understanding, and rich in intellectual and literary friendships. His late relationship with the artist Trekkie Ritchie Parsons is revealed in their *Love Letters* (2001), ed. Judith Adamson. See Victoria *Glendinning, *Leonard Woolf* (2006).

WOOLF, Virginia (1882–1941) Writer and publisher, daughter of Sir Leslie *Stephen and his second wife Julia Duckworth (1846–95), born at Hyde Park Gate, Kensington, London, where she lived with her sister Vanessa (later the artist Vanessa *Bell) and her brothers until her father's death in 1904, and educated at home: see *Hyde Park Gate News: The Stephen Family Newspaper*, by Virginia Woolf and Vanessa Bell with Thoby Stephen, ed. Gill Lowe (2005). Summer vacations at Talland House, St Ives, Cornwall, provided the inspiration for much of her writing and one of the mainstays of her life. The four Stephen children moved to Bloomsbury in 1904, where, in time, they formed the nucleus of the *Bloomsbury Group. In 1905 Woolf began to write for the **Times Literary Supplement*, a connection which lasted almost until her death, and in due course began to review regularly for other journals and newspapers. In 1912 she married Leonard *Woolf; she had been working on her first novel, *The Voyage Out*, since 1908 and it was published in 1915. Conventional in form and approach, but foreshadowing the lyric intensity of her subsequent work, it describes the voyage to South America of a young Englishwoman, Rachel Vinrace; her engagement there to Terence Hewet; and her subsequent fever and rapid death. Woolf herself had meanwhile experienced several bouts of acute mental disturbance, brought on in part by her mother's death in 1895 and her half-sister Stella's even more untimely death in 1897. Woolf's first serious breakdown was in 1904, when she threw herself out of a window; her mental health collapsed again in 1910, and in 1913 she took a near-fatal overdose. She suffered another major collapse in 1915, and it was partly as therapy for her that she and Leonard founded, in 1917, the *Hogarth Press; its first production was *Two Stories*, one by each of them. Her second novel, *Night and Day* (1919), set in London, centres on Katharine Hilbery, granddaughter of a famous Victorian poet, whose humdrum existence and restricted pursuits are contrasted with her friend Mary Datchet's involvement with the women's suffrage movement. *Jacob's Room* (1922), a novel which spasmodically evokes the life and death (in the First World War) of Jacob Flanders (clearly related to the death from typhoid of Woolf's elder brother Thoby in 1906), was recognized, in its stunningly mischievous ellipses and its often absent protagonist, as a new development in the art of fiction; it was hailed by friends such as T. S. *Eliot ('you have freed yourself from any compromise between the traditional novel and your original gift') and attacked by, for example, John Middleton *Murry for its lack of plot. Shortly afterwards she published one of her important statements on modern fiction, 'Mr Bennett and Mrs Brown' (afterwards revised and reprinted in various forms), which attacked the realism of Arnold *Bennett and advocated a more fluid and impressionistic approach to the problem of characterization and the representation of reality. From this time onwards Woolf was regarded as one of the principal exponents of *modernism, and her subsequent major novels, **Mrs Dalloway* (1925), **To the Lighthouse* (1927), and *The *Waves* (1931), established, and have been instrumental in preserving, her reputation. She also wrote *Orlando* (1928), a fantastic biography inspired by her friend Vita *Sackville-West, which traces the history of the youthful, beautiful, and aristocratic Orlando through four centuries and both male and female manifestations (it was made into a highly successful film in 1993); *Flush* (1933), a biography of Elizabeth Barrett *Browning's spaniel; *The Years* (1937), a chronicle of the Pargiter family from 1880 to the present day, and her last work, *Between the Acts* (1941). It was shortly after finishing it, and before its publication, that Woolf drowned herself in the river Ouse, near her home at Rodmell, Sussex, in March 1941. Virginia Woolf is now acclaimed as one of the greatest novelists in the literary canon; many of her experimental techniques (such as the use of *free indirect discourse and *interior monologue) have been absorbed into mainstream fiction. She was also a literary critic, essayist, and journalist of distinction. *A *Room of one's Own* (1929) is a classic of the feminist movement; a sequel, *Three Guineas* (1938), articulates Woolf's view that patriarchal tyranny at home is intimately connected with tyranny abroad. Her critical essays were published in several collections, including *The Common Reader* (1925; 2nd series, 1932), and the posthumous *The Death of the Moth* (1942), *The Captain's Death Bed* (1950), and *Granite and Rainbow* (1958). Four volumes of her collected *Essays* (1986–) have appeared under the editorship of Andrew McNeillie and two more volumes are to appear, edited by Stuart N. Clarke. Woolf was also a tireless letter writer and diarist. Her *Letters* (ed. Nigel Nicolson and J. Trautmann, 6 vols, 1975–80) are a dazzling evocation of a world of literary and social friendships and intrigues, with a cast list that includes Lytton *Strachey, the *Sitwells, Ottoline *Morrell, Roger *Fry, and many others; her *Diary* (5 vols, ed. Anne Olivier Bell assisted by A. McNeillie, 1977–84) is a unique record of the joys and pains of the creative process. *A Passionate Apprentice: The Early Journals* (rev. edn 2004) and *Moments of Being* (rev. edn 2002), which collects some of Woolf's most fascinating autobiographical writings, including 'A Sketch of the Past', are also significant. See Hermione *Lee, *Virginia Woolf* (1996); Julia Briggs, *Virginia Woolf: An Inner Life* (2005).

WOOLMAN, John (1720–72) American Quaker, itinerant preacher, and anti-slavery campaigner. His *Journal* (1774) records his spiritual life and humanitarian and social concerns in a style which, according to J. G. *Whittier, 'has a sweetness as of violets'. Charles *Lamb declared, 'Get the writings of John Woolman by heart, and love the early Quakers.'

WOOLNER, Thomas (1825–92) Poet and sculptor, one of the original *Pre-Raphaelite Brotherhood, who contributed to *The *Germ* two cantos of what was to become *My Beautiful Lady* (1863). At first he met with small success as a sculptor, and in 1852 sailed for the Australian gold fields (his departure inspiring Ford Madox Brown's picture *The Last of England*), but returned in 1854 and became a prosperous portrait sculptor in the neo-classical mode, particularly with busts and statues of (among many others) Alfred *Tennyson, John Henry *Newman, Charles *Kingsley, and John Stuart *Mill. His other poems include the blank verse *Pygmalion* (1881). 'The Piping Shepherd', which appears as a frontispiece to Francis Turner *Palgrave's *Golden Treasury*, is by him.

WORDE, Wynkyn de (*fl.*1479–1535) Printer at Westminster and in London. His place of birth is not certainly known, but his name suggests he came from Woerden, near Gouda and Leiden. By 1479 he was a tenant of Westminster Abbey and was probably William *Caxton's principal assistant until his death in 1492, whereupon de Worde succeeded to the printing business, moving it to Fleet Street in 1500. He printed large numbers of important vernacular works, including poems by *Chaucer, religious books, and grammars, which were highly in demand. Many of his books are illustrated with woodcuts. See J. Moran, *Wynkyn de Worde, Father of Fleet Street* (3rd edn 2003).

WORDSWORTH, Dorothy (1771–1855) Poet and diarist, the sister of William *Wordsworth and his treasured companion throughout their adult lives. After an unsettled and partly orphaned childhood, away from her three brothers, Dorothy settled with William in 1795, and from that time they lived together, through William's marriage until his death. After a short time in Dorset they moved to Alfoxden in Somerset, to be near S. T. *Coleridge at Nether Stowey. Here in 1798, when she, William, and Coleridge walked and talked, as Coleridge wrote, 'as three persons with one soul', she began her first journal. This was the *Alfoxden Journal*, but the manuscript has disappeared and only the months January–April 1798 remain. It is, however, valuable, not only for its close description of the Quantocks and the sea, but for the revelation of the companionship of the three friends in the heady year of the *Lyrical Ballads. In 1799 William and Dorothy moved to Dove Cottage at Grasmere in the Lake District. The *Grasmere Journal* covers the years 1800–3 and was begun 'because I shall give William pleasure by it'. The entries are again filled with her love of landscape, season, walking, and weather; her skill with words is evident in the precise descriptions both of the world about them and of the daily events of life in Dove Cottage.

Dorothy kept several other journals of travels and expeditions, which also were unpublished until after her death. She wrote a brief journal of a 'Visit to Hamburgh and a Journey…to Goslar' (1798–9). In 1805 she finished *Recollections of a Tour Made in Scotland*, which exists in five manuscripts; the earlier, less formal, versions vividly describe the wild countryside and weather, the tremulous horse, the uneatable oatcake, and the wet sheets. (Coleridge, overwhelmed, abandoned the expedition at Loch Long.) Her spirited accounts of an 'Excursion on the Banks of Ullswater' (1805) and 'An Excursion up Scawfell Pike' (1818) were both used by Wordsworth in his *Guide to the Lakes* (1823). A long *Journal of a Tour on the Continent 1820* conveys her intoxication with, especially, Switzerland, and the rubs of life on the road with William. A sprightly *Journal of a Second Tour in Scotland* followed in 1822, and a *Journal of a Tour in the Isle of Man* in 1828.

It is clear from passages in his notes and from certain of his poems (most notably, 'I wandered lonely as a cloud') that Wordsworth made use of his sister's journals. Coleridge seems also to have used the Alfoxden journal for certain passages in *'Christabel'. Several of Wordsworth's poems, as well as the famous closing lines of *'Tintern Abbey', are addressed to Dorothy, including 'The Glow Worm', 'Ode to Lycoris', and 'To the Same'. Dorothy died, after many years of illness and senility, from arteriosclerosis. In his 1933 biography, her editor Ernest de Selincourt calls her 'probably…the most distinguished of English writers who never wrote a line for the general public'.

WORDSWORTH, William (1770–1850) English poet, born at Cockermouth, Cumbria, the son of an attorney; he attended (with Mary Hutchinson, his future wife) the infants' school in Penrith and, from 1779 to 1787, Hawkshead Grammar School. His mother died in 1778, his father in 1783, losses recorded in *The *Prelude*, which describes the mixed joys and terrors of his boyhood with a peculiar intensity. He attended St John's College, Cambridge, but disliked the academic course. In 1790 he went on a walking tour of France, the Alps, and Italy, and returned to France late in 1791, to spend a year there. During this period he was fired by a passionate belief in the French Revolution and republican ideals, and also fell in love with the daughter of a surgeon at Blois, Annette Vallon, who bore him a daughter (see E. Legouis, *William Wordsworth and Annette Vallon*, 1922). This love affair is reflected in 'Vaudracour and Julia', composed ?1804, published 1820, and incorporated somewhat anomalously in Book IX of *The Prelude*. After his return to England he published in 1793 two poems in heroic couplets, *An Evening Walk* and *Descriptive Sketches*, both conventional attempts at the *picturesque and the *sublime, the latter describing the Alps. In this year he also wrote (but did not publish) a *Letter to the Bishop of Llandaff* (*see* WATSON, RICHARD) in support of the French Republic. England's declaration of war against France shocked him deeply, but the institution of the Terror marked the beginning of his disillusion with the French Revolution, a period of depression reflected in his verse drama *The Borderers* (composed 1796–7; pub. 1842) and in 'Guilt and Sorrow' (composed 1791–4; pub. in part in 1798 as 'The Female Vagrant'). In 1795 he received a legacy of £900 from his friend Raisley Calvert, intended to enable him to pursue his vocation as a poet, which also allowed him to be reunited with his sister Dorothy (*see* WORDSWORTH, DOROTHY); they settled first at Racedown in Dorset, then at Alfoxden in Somerset, where they had charge of the son of their friend Basil *Montagu. The latter move (aided by Thomas *Poole) was influenced by a desire to be near S. T. *Coleridge, then living at Nether Stowey, whom Wordsworth had met in 1795. This was a period of intense creativity for both poets, which produced the **Lyrical Ballads* (1798), a landmark in the history of English *Romanticism (*see* ANCIENT MARINER; 'IDIOT BOY'; 'TINTERN ABBEY').

The winter of 1798–9 was spent in Goslar in Germany, where Wordsworth wrote sections of what was to be *The Prelude* and the enigmatic *'Lucy' poems. In 1799 he and Dorothy settled in Dove Cottage, Grasmere; to the next year belong 'The Recluse', Book I (later *The *Excursion*), 'The Brothers', *'Michael', and many of the poems included in the 1800 edition of the *Lyrical Ballads* (which, with its provocative preface on *poetic diction, aroused much criticism). In 1802 Wordsworth and Dorothy visited Annette Vallon in France, and later that year William married Mary Hutchinson, his financial position having been improved by the repayment of a debt on the death of Lord Lonsdale. In the same year he composed *'Resolution and Independence', and began his ode on *'Intimations of Immortality from Recollections of Early Childhood', both of which appeared in **Poems in Two Volumes* (1807), along with many of his most celebrated lyrics, including the famous 'I wandered lonely as a cloud'. To the same period belong the birth of five children (of whom the eldest, John, was born in 1803), travels with Dorothy and Coleridge, and new friendships, notably with Walter *Scott, George *Beaumont, and Thomas *De Quincey. Wordsworth's domestic happiness was overcast by the shipwreck and death of his sailor brother John in 1805 (which inspired several poems, including 'Elegiac Stanzas Suggested by a Picture of Peele Castle', 1807), the early deaths of two of his children (one of which inspired his sonnet *'Surprised by joy', 1815), and the physical deterioration of Coleridge, from whom he was for some time estranged, and with whom he was never entirely reconciled. But his productivity continued, and his popularity gradually increased. *The Excursion* was published in 1814, *The White Doe of Rylstone* and two volumes of *Miscellaneous Poems* in 1815, and **Peter Bell* and *The *Waggoner* in 1819. In 1813 he had been appointed stamp distributor for Westmorland, a post which brought him some £400 a year, and in the same year moved from Allan Bank (where he had lived from

1808) to Rydal Mount, Ambleside, where he lived the rest of his life. The great work of his early and middle years was now over, and Wordsworth slowly settled into the role of patriotic, conservative public man, abandoning the radical politics and idealism of his youth. Much of the best of his later work was topographical, inspired by his love of travel; it records journeys to Scotland, along the river Duddon, to the Continent, etc. He was left a legacy by Sir George Beaumont in 1827, and in 1842 received a Civil List pension of £300 a year; in 1843 he succeeded Robert *Southey as *poet laureate. He died at Rydal Mount, after the publication of a finally revised text of his works, 6 vols (1849–50), and *The Prelude* was published posthumously in 1850. His prose works include an essay, *Concerning the Relations of Great Britain, Spain and Portugal… as Affected by the Convention of Cintra* (1809), castigating the supine English policy on the Iberian peninsular, and *A Description of the Scenery of the Lakes in the North of England*, written in 1810 as an introduction to Wilkinson's *Select Views of Cumberland*.

De Quincey wrote of Wordsworth in 1835, 'Up to 1820 the name of Wordsworth was trampled underfoot; from 1820 to 1830 it was militant; from 1830 to 1835 it has been triumphant.' Early attacks in the **Edinburgh Review* and by the anonymous author of a parody, *The Simpliciad* (1808), were followed by criticism and satire by the second generation of Romantics; Lord *Byron and P. B. *Shelley mocked him as 'simple' and 'dull', John *Keats distrusted what he called the *'egotistical sublime', and William *Hazlitt, and later Robert *Browning, deplored him as 'The Lost Leader', who had abandoned his early radical faith. But these doubts were counterbalanced by the enormous and lasting popularity of much of his work, which was regarded by writers such as Matthew *Arnold and John Stuart *Mill with almost religious veneration, as an expression in an age of doubt of the transcendent in nature and the good in man. A great innovator, he permanently enlarged the range of English poetry, both in subject matter and in treatment. His notions of the creative imagination and of the centrality of poetic selfhood were essential to the development of English *Romanticism.

Wordsworth's *Poetical and Prose Works*, together with Dorothy Wordsworth's *Journals*, ed. W. Knight, appeared in 1896, and his *Poetical Works* (ed. E. de Selincourt and H. Darbishire, 5 vols) in 1940–9 and 1952–4. Whereas these volumes privilege Wordsworth's final published versions of his poems (the poet was a persistent reviser of his work), the Cornell Wordsworth series (1975–) aims to 'bring the early Wordsworth into view', focusing on the earliest versions of the individual poems. *The Letters of William and Dorothy Wordsworth* (ed. E. de Selincourt, 6 vols) were published in 1935–9 and were revised by A. G. Hill (1967–93). Wordsworth's *Prose Works* were edited in 1974 by W. J. B. Owen and J. W. Smyser (3 vols). Important modern scholarship on Wordsworth has been produced by J. Jones (1954), G. Hartman (1964), J. Wordsworth (1982), J. Chandler (1984), A. Liu (1988), N. Roe (1988), and J. Bate (1991). His biography by M. Moorman was published in 1968 (2 vols), and a long-lost collection of letters between Mary and William appeared as *The Love Letters of William and Mary Wordsworth*, ed. B. Darlington (1982). See also Stephen Gill, *William Wordsworth* (1989).

World's Classics A series of affordable reprints of standard works of classic English literature and foreign literature in translation, launched in 1901 in small hardback format by Grant Richards (1872–1948); its first titles included **Jane Eyre* and *The *Vicar of Wakefield*, and the spine decoration of the series was designed by Laurence *Housman. In 1906 the series was bought by Henry Frowde (1841–1927) for *Oxford University Press; he introduced pocket editions on thin, Oxford India paper. The series grew rapidly and modern writers, such as Virginia *Woolf and T. S. *Eliot, were commissioned to write introductions. The series was relaunched in paperback in 1980 and rebranded as Oxford World's Classics in 1998.

WOTTON, Sir Henry (1568–1639) Educated at Winchester College and New and the Queen's colleges, Oxford, where he became a friend of John *Donne. He travelled widely on the Continent collecting intelligence for the earl of *Essex, and prudently left England within hours of Essex's arrest. *James I appointed him ambassador to Venice (1604–21, with intervals at The Hague and in Vienna). He defined an ambassador as 'an honest man, sent to lie abroad for the good of his country'. He was provost of Eton College, 1624–39, and published *Elements of Architecture* (1624). *Reliquiae Wottonianae* (1651; enlarged edns 1672, 1685) collects his poetical and other writings including the 'Character of a Happy Life' and 'You meaner beauties of the night' (honouring James I's daughter Elizabeth). His life was written by his friend Izaak *Walton (1651). See Logan Pearsall *Smith, *Life and Letters* (1907); G. Curzon, *Wotton and his Worlds* (2004).

'Wreck of the Deutschland, The' A poem by Gerard Manley *Hopkins, occasioned by the shipwreck in December 1875 of a German transatlantic steamer off the Kentish coast. Among the dead were five Franciscan sisters from Westphalia; the poem identifies them as victims of Bismarck's anti-Catholic 'Falk' laws, which forced many into exile. The two-part poem wonders about the role of violence in God's scheme, turning to the shipwreck as an instance of God's ability to make himself known through calamity. It concludes with a hope for England's re-conversion to Catholicism. The text experiments with a new metric Hopkins 'long had haunting [his] ear', *sprung rhythm. *The Month*, a Jesuit journal, declined to publish the poem in 1876; Robert *Bridges included it in the 1918 edition of Hopkins's poetry, and it is now recognized as central in Hopkins's work.

WREN, Sir Christopher (1632–1723) Architect, mathematician, and astronomer, son of Christopher Wren, dean of Windsor (1635–58), educated at Westminster School and Wadham College, Oxford. He was a prominent member of the circle of scholars who later were founder members of the *Royal Society. With them he studied anatomy, mathematics, and astronomy, being appointed professor of anatomy at Gresham College, London, in 1657 and Savilian professor of astronomy at Oxford in 1661. His first architectural works were the chapel of Pembroke College, Cambridge (1663–5), and the Sheldonian Theatre, Oxford (1664–9). A few days after the fire of London in 1666, he presented a plan for rebuilding the City, but it was not adopted. He was, however, made surveyor in charge of the City churches, and designed 52 of them. He had prepared a scheme for repairing St Paul's before the fire, and when it became clear in 1668 that it must be rebuilt he prepared designs: work began on the new building in 1675 and it was finished in 1710. Wren also designed many other buildings, including the library of Trinity College, Cambridge, and Tom Tower, Christ Church, Oxford. *Parentalia, or Memories of the Family of the Wrens* (1750) is a collection of family documents made by Wren's son Christopher (1675–1747). Lisa Jardine's biography, *On a Grander Scale: The Outstanding Career of Sir Christopher Wren*, was published in 2002.

WREN, P. C. (Percival Christopher) (1875–1941) Novelist, born in Deptford, London, educated at West Kent School and as a non-collegiate student at Oxford. Between 1903 and 1917 he worked for the Indian Educational Service. His first book of stories, *Dew and Mildew* (1912), was set in India; he went on to publish over 30 more novels, but did not achieve popular success until the publication of *Beau Geste* (1924), one of his many Foreign Legion novels, a romantic adventure story which became a best-seller and which was filmed three times (1926, 1939, and 1966). *Beau Sabreur* (1926), *Beau Ideal* (1928), and others followed.

WRIGHT, Austin Tappan (1883–1931) American lawyer whose single novel *Islandia* (1942), written as a hobby, charts the reaction of an American visitor to an imaginary southern continent. Its pastoral exploration of love and politics influenced Ursula K. *Le Guin.

WRIGHT, David (1920–94) Poet, born in Johannesburg, who lost his hearing at the age of 7. He was educated at Oriel College, Oxford, and subsequently lived in London, Cornwall, and the Lake District. His volumes of poetry include *Poems* (1949), which appeared in James Meary Tambimuttu's **Poetry London* imprint: he himself was a founder editor of the quarterly review *X*, 1959–62. He also published translations of **Beowulf* (1957) and *The *Canterbury Tales* (1964). *Deafness: A Personal Account* was published in 1969.

WRIGHT, Joseph, of Derby (1734–97) English painter, who worked mainly in Derby. Wright's subjects are novel—scientific experiments, industrial activity—and he was celebrated for effects of light—candlelight, moonlight, the flames of a forge, the windows of a mill at night. Wright was patronized by Josiah Wedgwood (1730–95) and Richard Arkwright (1732–92), and his works reflect the scientific curiosity that dominated intellectual life in the industrial Midlands. He was a friend of Erasmus *Darwin, whose poem *The Botanic Garden* is close in subject and feeling to Wright's pictures; painter and poet move easily from modern engineering to classical allegory. In the 1770s and 1780s Wright, a friend of William *Hayley, began to choose his subjects from literature; he was attracted by the macabre and by the Romantic melancholy of contemporary literature. He painted scenes from William *Shakespeare, John *Milton, and from contemporary writers, including James *Beattie, Laurence *Sterne, and John *Langhorne. *The Dead Soldier*, from Langhorne, became a highly popular engraving. See Elizabeth Barker *et al.*, *Joseph Wright of Derby in Liverpool* (exhibition catalogue, 2007).

WRIGHT, Judith (1915–2000) Australian poet, born in Armidale, New South Wales, to a wealthy pastoral family. Her first book, *The Moving Image* (1946), made her reputation, subsequently enhanced through more than a dozen volumes (see *Collected Poems*, 1994). Wright's poems are intensely imagined and beautifully crafted, concerned with human relationships (as in 'Woman to Man'), rural and wild landscapes ('South of my Days'), and the violence of colonial history ('Nigger's Leap'). She is the author of a fine work of criticism, *Preoccupations in Australian Poetry* (1965), and an important work of colonial history, *The Generations of Men* (1965). An original and impassioned thinker, from the 1960s Wright immersed herself in struggles for conservation and for a treaty with Indigenous Australians, chronicled in Veronica Brady's biography, *South of my Days* (1998).

WRIGHT, Kit (1944–) Poet and children's writer, born in Kent, educated at Oxford. Wright has been praised as a master of light verse, for his comic observations of human behaviour, and his offbeat wit. His poems reveal a fascination with English eccentricity, and include compassionate portraits of characters who are often lost, failed, or doubting their sanity. *The Bear Looked over the Mountain* (1977) was followed by *Bump-Starting the Hearse* (1983), which includes 'The Day Room', a moving sequence on life in a psychiatric ward, and *Short Afternoons* (1989). *Hoping It Might Be So: Poems 1974–2000* was published in 2000. Wright's children's books include *Hot Dogs and Other Poems* (1982) and *Cat among the Pigeons* (1987).

WRIGHT, Richard (1908–60) African American writer, born in Mississippi and brought up in Memphis, largely self-educated. He joined the Communist Party in the 1930s, but left in the 1940s, as he records in *American Hunger* (1977). *Uncle Tom's Children* (1938) brought him recognition with stories of Southern racism. His first novel *Native Son* (1940), based on an actual case, describes the killing of a white girl in Chicago by her African American driver and the subsequent trial. Estranged from American society by its racism and by being dogged by the FBI, Wright moved to Paris in 1947, where he met James *Baldwin. He continued writing with his *existential novel *The Outsider* (1953). *The Colour Curtain* (1956) and *White Man, Listen!* (1957) both reported on third-world politics and racism in the post-war world. See John A. *Williams, *The Most Native of Sons* (1970).

WRIGHT, Sydney Fowler (1874–1965) British writer and poet whose early novels and stories were *scientific romances comparable with, and often written in antagonism to, those of H. G. *Wells. *Deluge* (1928) describes a flooded England. *The New Gods Lead* (1932) collected some of his dystopian stories.

WRIGHT, Thomas (1810–77) Historian and antiquary, educated at Trinity College, Cambridge. He played an important part in founding the *Camden, *Percy, and *Shakespeare societies, and his work helped to show the importance of vernacular writings in understanding the lives and beliefs of people in the Middle Ages.

Wrongs of Woman, The, *or Maria* A fiction by Mary *Wollstonecraft, published posthumously in 1798. The (semi-autobiographical) narrative tells of Maria, who flees to France with her infant daughter to escape her dissolute husband, but is intercepted en route and confined on his instruction in a madhouse. Here she falls in love with fellow prisoner Darnford, and bonds with her female janitor, also a victim of patriarchy. The fiction is a revolutionary defence of a woman's right to assert her sexuality.

'Wulf and Eadwacer' An Old English poem in nineteen lines of varying length, from the *Exeter Book. Its theme is thought to be the separation of lovers, but it is very cryptic, despite its powerfully suggestive atmosphere. Modern translations include a version by Craig *Raine in *Rich* (1984). See also M. Green (ed.), *The Old English Elegies* (1983).

WULFSTAN (d. 1023) Archbishop of York, author of homilies in English including the famous 'Address of the Wolf to the English', *Sermo Lupi ad Anglos*, in which he describes the desolation brought about by the Danish raids and castigates the demoralization of the people. Like his predecessor *Oswald he held the sees of Worcester and York simultaneously from 1002 to his death, whereupon he was buried at Ely. He was bishop of London in 996 and is said to have reformed St Peter's, Gloucester. He had contacts with *Ælfric, with whom he shares a distinction as a writer of rhythmical, *alliterative prose. He drafted codes of laws for Ethelred from 1008 to 1015, and for Cnut (*Canute), despite his earlier deploring of the Danish raids, from his accession in 1016 to Wulfstan's death in 1023. *Sermo Lupi ad Anglos*, ed. D. Whitelock (1939; rev. 1963); *Homilies*, ed. D. Bethurum (1957).

WURLITZER, Rudolph (1937–) American novelist and screenwriter, whose first novels, *Nog* (1969, UK title *The Octopus*) and *Flats* (1970), show a debt to Samuel *Beckett in austerely problematizing their own narrative procedures. *Slow Fade* (1984) describes the last stages of a movie director's career and *Walker* (1987) presents Wurlitzer's script for the film of that name. *Drop Edge of Yonder* (2008) describes the experiences of a mountain man, travelling at the beginning of the Mexican revolution.

Wuthering Heights Emily *Brontë's only novel, published 1847. The story begins with the journal of Lockwood, temporary tenant of Thrushcross Grange, who stumbles unsuspecting into the violent world of Wuthering Heights, home of his landlord Heathcliff. The narration is taken up by the housekeeper, Nelly Dean, who had witnessed the interlocked destinies of the original owners of the Heights, the Earnshaw family, and of the Grange, the Linton family. In a series of brilliantly handled flashbacks and time shifts, Emily Brontë unfolds a tale of exceptional emotional and imaginative force. Events are set in motion by the arrival at the Heights of Heathcliff, picked up as a waif in the streets of Liverpool by the elder Earnshaw, who brings him home to rear as one of his own children. Bullied and humiliated after Earnshaw's death by his son Hindley, Heathcliff's passionate nature finds its complement in Earnshaw's daughter Catherine. Their childhood collusions develop into an increasingly intense though vexed attachment, but Heathcliff, overhearing Catherine tell Nelly that she cannot marry him because it would degrade her, and failing to stay to hear her declare her passion for him, leaves the house. He returns three years later, mysteriously enriched, to find Catherine married to the gentlemanly Edgar Linton. Heathcliff is welcomed by Hindley, now widowed with a son, Hareton, and a hardened drinker and gambler. Heathcliff's destructive force is unleashed; he marries Edgar's sister Isabella and cruelly ill-treats her, hastens Catherine's death by his passion as she is about to give birth to a daughter, Cathy, and brings Hindley and his son Hareton under his power, brutalizing Hareton in revenge for Hindley's treatment of himself as a child. Edgar Linton dies, after trying to prevent a friendship between Cathy and Heathcliff's feeble son Linton; Heathcliff has lured Cathy to his house, and forces a marriage between her and young Linton in order to secure the Linton property. Linton also dies, and an affection springs up between her, an unwilling prisoner at the Heights, and the ignorant Hareton, whom she attempts to educate. Heathcliff's lust for revenge has now worn itself out, and he longs for the death that will reunite him with Catherine; at his death, it is implied that the contrasting worlds represented by the Heights and the Grange will be united in the marriage of Cathy and Hareton.

Early reviewers often deplored the novel's painful aspects, but their criticism has been overtaken by a general recognition of the mastery of an extremely complex structure, acute evocation of place, poetic grandeur of vision, and a highly original handling of *Gothic and Romantic elements. It has become one of the most popular and widely admired of all Victorian novels.

WYATT, Sir Thomas (*c.*1503–1542) Poet, from a Yorkshire family, educated at St John's College, Cambridge. He held various diplomatic posts in the service of *Henry VIII in France, Italy, and Spain. His first visit to Italy in 1527 probably stimulated him to translate and imitate the poems of *Petrarch. In the same year he made a version of a *Plutarch essay, based on the Latin translation of Guillaume Budé (1467–1540), *The Quiet of Mind*, which he dedicated to the queen (Catherine of Aragon) whom the king was in process of divorcing. Wyatt's relationship with Henry VIII's next bride, Anne Boleyn, was more problematic. He was certainly closely acquainted with her before her marriage and, according to three 16th-century accounts, confessed to the king that she had been his mistress and was not fit to be a royal consort. If true, this frankness may explain why Wyatt was not executed, along with Anne's alleged lovers, in 1536, suffering only a period of imprisonment in the Tower. After his release his career soon recovered; he became a sheriff of Kent, and in 1537–9 held the important post of ambassador to Charles V's court in Spain. He celebrated his departure from Spain, June 1539, in the epigram 'Tagus, farewell'. In 1540 the tide of Wyatt's fortunes turned, with the execution of his friend and patron Thomas Cromwell (*c.*1485–1540), which is probably referred to in the sonnet (based on Petrarch) 'The pillar perished is whereto I lent'. Wyatt himself was arrested, on charges of treason, in January 1541; though released two months later he never fully regained favour. He died in October 1542, of a fever contracted on a last diplomatic errand for the king.

Wyatt's poetry is beset by problems in three main areas; authorship, biographical relevance, and artistic aims. Though the canon of his poems is generally taken to include all the poems in the Egerton Manuscript (which contains autograph material), even this cannot be proved with certainty, and there are many other poems whose attribution to him depends mainly upon association. The authenticated poems and translations include *sonnets, *rondeaux, *epigrams, epistolary satires, lute songs, and a version in **terza rima* of the seven Penitential *Psalms, whose framing poems depict *David repenting of his adulterous love for Bathsheba. Much controversy surrounds Wyatt's artistic purpose in making translations from Italian poems. His metre must have been perceived as irregular even fifteen years after his death, since Richard *Tottel in his *Songs and Sonnets* (1557) adapted many of Wyatt's poems to conventional iambic stress, including 'They flee from me that sometime did me seek'. Modern critical estimates of Wyatt's poetry have varied widely. C. S. *Lewis called him 'the father of the Drab Age', but others have viewed him as a complex and original writer whose love poems anticipate those of *Donne. The poems have been frequently edited, for instance by Kenneth *Muir and P. Thomson (1969), by Joost Daalder (1975), and by R. A. Rebholz (1978). Muir and Thomson's *Life and Letters* (1963) assembles most of the biographical material; Thomson's *Critical Heritage* collection (1974) assembles critical views.

WYCHERLEY, William (1641–1715) Playwright, of a Shropshire family. He was educated first in France, then at the Queen's College, Oxford, but he never matriculated, afterwards enrolling as a student in the Inner Temple. His first play, *Love in a Wood, or St James's Park*, a comedy of intrigue set in St James's Park, was probably acted in 1671, and published in 1672, and brought him the favour of the countess of Castlemaine (bap. 1640, d. 1709), the king's mistress. In 1679 he secretly married the widowed countess of Drogheda (d. 1685), daughter of the first earl of Radnor, and incurred thereby the displeasure of Charles II, who had offered him the tutorship of his son, the duke of Richmond. His second play, *The *Gentleman Dancing-Master*, was probably acted 1671, published 1673; *The *Country Wife* was published and probably first acted 1675; his last play, *The *Plain-Dealer*, was probably acted 1676, published 1677. His *Miscellany Poems* (1704) led to a friendship with Alexander *Pope, who revised many of his writings. His *Posthumous Works* appeared in 1728.

Wycherley's plays, admired by Charles *Lamb but condemned by T. B. *Macaulay as licentious and indecent, are highly regarded for their acute social criticism, particularly of sexual morality and the marriage conventions; his characterization and thematic organization are also strong, and his last two plays have been successfully revived many times. The standard edition is by A. Friedman (1979).
See RESTORATION.

WYCLIF, John (d. 1384) Theologian and controversialist, probably born to a north Yorkshire family. He attended Oxford from *c.*1350, was master of Balliol College (1360–1), and became warden of Canterbury College in 1365. He was studying theology by *c.*1362–3 and became rector of Lutterworth, Leicestershire, in 1374. Wyclif's views regarding the authority of the pope and the temporal possessions of the church aroused suspicion in 1377, when Gregory XI issued five bulls condemning his views. While his attacks on ecclesiastical abuses marked him out as reformist, in 1381 he came under renewed suspicion at Oxford principally on account of the view that, in the sacrament of the Eucharist, material bread remained after the words of consecration had been spoken. At the Blackfriars Council of 1382, ten arguments were condemned as heretical, and fourteen as erroneous, the issues concerned ranging from the church's temporalities and the powers of the pope to the sacraments of confession and the Eucharist. Wyclif was not named in these proceedings, but the growing controversy surrounding his views on a range of matters had already led to his retirement to Lutterworth in 1381, where he remained until his death. In 1428, according to a decree passed at the Council of Constance in 1415, Wyclif's bones were exhumed and burnt, and the ashes were thrown into the river Swift. Nevertheless, his ideas continued to trouble the ecclesiastical authorities long after his death: he had written prolifically in a number of genres from sermons to polemical treatises, and had received a significant degree of support from contemporaries at Oxford. In 1401 a statute was passed whereby those condemned for heresy could be executed by burning, and heresy trials occurred throughout the 15th century. Although modern scholars are reluctant to attribute any extant English writings to Wyclif himself, his influence on English religious thought of this period is partly reflected in a significant body of writings in English directly influenced or at least inspired by his ideas. This includes two versions of the *Bible in English, a substantial sermon cycle, many polemical works and the *Testimony of William Thorpe*, which depicts the interrogation of a suspected Wycliffite by Thomas Arundel, archbishop of Canterbury. See K. B. Macfarlane, *John Wycliffe and the Beginnings of English Nonconformity* (1952); M. Aston, *Lollards and Reformers* (1984); A. Hudson (ed.), *Selections from English Wycliffite Writings* (1978); A. Hudson (ed.), *The Premature Reformation: Wycliffite Texts and Lollard History* (1988).

WYLIE, Elinor (1885–1928) Née Hoyt, American writer and painter, born in New Jersey, whose third husband was the poet William Rose Benet (1886–1950), brother of Stephen Vincent *Benet. Her works include *Nets to Catch the Wind* (1921, poems); *The Venetian Glass Nephew* (1925, novel); and *The Orphan Angel* (1926, UK title *Mortal Image*), a fantasy-continuation of the life of P. B. *Shelley, for whom she had a lifelong admiration. Her *Collected Poems* appeared in 1932, many focusing on delicate and fugitive impressions. See Stanley Olson, *Elinor Wylie: A Life Apart* (1979).

WYNDHAM, Francis (1924–) Writer, born in London and educated at Eton College and Christ Church, Oxford, before joining the army in 1943. He is the author of two volumes of interlinked short stories, *Out of the War* (1974) and *Mrs Henderson and Other Stories* (1985), and *The Other Garden* (1987), a novella set during the Second World War. *The Theatre of Embarrassment* (1991) collects his essays and journalism, and he co-edited (with Diana Melly) the *Letters* of Jean *Rhys (1984). His *Collected Fiction* (1992) is introduced by Alan *Hollinghurst.

WYNDHAM, John (1903–69) The best-known pseudonym of John Wyndham Parkes Lucas Beynon Harris, *science fiction writer, born in Knowle, Warwickshire, who tried several different careers before settling to a successful life as a writer. He was attracted to science fiction partly through his early admiration of H. G. *Wells. He published numerous stories in the American science fiction magazines and elsewhere, adopting 'John Wyndham' for *The Day of the Triffids* (1951), which introduced science fiction to a mass British audience to whom it was largely unknown but whose anxieties it reflected. He preferred the description 'logical fantasy' for his own works, which also included *The Kraken Wakes* (1953), *The Chrysalids* (1955), *The Midwich Cuckoos* (1957), and *Chocky* (1968). Several of his works were filmed; most are distinguished by the contrast between a comfortable English background and the sudden invasion of catastrophe which reveals the precariousness of the initial situation. The blindness which strikes in *Triffids*, for instance, lays humanity open to predatory mobile carnivorous plants until then safely domesticated for their oil. The proto-feminist novella 'Consider her Ways' (1956) postulates a plague which wipes out men, leaving women to develop a social structure based upon antlike 'castes'.

Wynnere and Wastour An alliterative dream-poem of *c.*500 lines in a north-west Midland dialect, certainly written after 1352, discussing contemporary economic problems. The narrator sees in a dream two armies drawn up on the plain, with Edward III encamped above them. The king sends his son, the Black Prince (1330–76), to intervene and prevent the battle. The poem becomes more of a traditional debate as the leaders of the two armies explain their causes: with Winner (the gainer of wealth in society) are the pope and the traditionally avaricious friars; with Waster (the prodigal spender) are the nobility and the soldiery. In the king's judgement speech (which is unfinished), he sends Waster to the markets of London to stimulate the economy and Winner to the rich courts of the pope and the cardinals. In its concerns and methods, the poem has often been compared to **Piers Plowman*. Ed. Stephanie Trigg (1990).

Xanadu In S. T. *Coleridge's *'Kubla Khan', the place where the khan decreed 'a stately pleasure-dome'.

XAVIER, St Francis (1506–52) A Spaniard, one of the founders of the Society of Jesus, and a famous missionary in the Far East. He died on his way to China and is buried in Goa. John *Dryden's life of St Francis Xavier (1688), a translation of a French work, *La Vie de Saint François Xavier* (1682), by Dominique Bouhours, is dedicated to Mary of Modena, the queen of James II.

XENOPHON (*c.*428–354 BC) Athenian writer and associate of *Socrates. He joined the Greek mercenaries recruited by the Persian Cyrus the younger in a failed rebellion, then enlisted as a Spartan mercenary, fought against the Athenians, and was formally exiled. His banishment was later annulled and he returned to Athens. His many works include *Anabasis* (the march up country), the first-hand story of the Greeks' expedition and their epic retreat to the Black Sea; *Hellenica*, a continuation of *Thucydides' history; *Cyropaedia* (the education of Cyrus), a work of edifying fiction, describing the formation of a perfect ruler, the Persian King Cyrus the Great; and a group of Socratic memoirs: *Apology*, supposed to have been spoken by Socrates at his trial, *Memorabilia*, which relates anecdotes of Socrates' conversation, and *Symposium*, which unlike *Plato's text of that name shows Socrates giving practical advice. As a soldier-writer Xenophon was much admired by humanists. An English translation of *Cyropaedia* was published in 1554 by William Barker (*fl.* 1540–76), and *Memoirs of Socrates* by Sarah *Fielding (1762).

XIMÉNEZ DE CISNEROS, Cardinal Francisco (1436–1517) Spanish Franciscan, religious reformer, archbishop of Toledo, statesman, and grand inquisitor. He founded the University of Alcalá de Henares in 1508 and recruited the team of scholars who produced the Complutensian Polyglot Bible.

Y

YARBRO, Chelsea Quin (1942–) American writer, born in Berkeley, California; author of *Hotel Transylvania* (1978), first of a series featuring Saint-Germain, an immortal vampire, ranging from ancient Rome to modern America. *Time of the Fourth Horseman* (1976) is a *science fiction novel about a macabre experiment in population control.

YATES, Dornford (1885–1960) Pseudonym of Cecil William Mercer, novelist and short story writer, born at Upper Walmer, Kent, and educated at Harrow School and University College, Oxford. His sequence of ten books featuring Berry Pleydell and his family includes *The Brother of Daphne* (1914), *Berry and Co.* (1920), and *The House that Berry Built* (1945). Both this group and Yates's nine Chandos thrillers (including *Blind Corner*, 1927) reflect a world of wealth and idleness and were immensely popular between the wars. See A. J. Smithers, *Dornford Yates* (1982).

YATES, Dame Frances Amelia (1899–1981) Renaissance scholar, who taught at the Warburg Institute. Some of her most important work was on *Neoplatonism, hermeticism, and the *Rosicrucian tradition in *Renaissance thought, and their connections with politics, religion, and literature. Her publications include studies of John *Florio (1934), *The French Academies of the Sixteenth Century* (1947; rev. 1988), *The Valois Tapestries* (1959; rev. 1975), Giordano *Bruno (1964), *The Art of Memory* (1966), and *Astraea: The Imperial Theme in the Sixteenth Century* (1975).

year books Reports of English common law cases for the period 1268–1535, of great interest from a historical as well as a legal standpoint. They were succeeded by the law 'Reports'. F. W. Maitland (1850–1906) began editing them, and the work is still continuing.

YEARSLEY, Ann (1752–1806) Née Cromartie, poet, born at Clifton, Bristol. She received no regular education but read widely and began writing while working as a dairywoman. In 1784 Hannah *More learned of her local reputation and, with Elizabeth *Montagu, arranged the publication of Yearsley's *Poems, on Several Occasions* (1785). Fanny *Burney, Horace *Walpole, Anna *Seward, and Sir Joshua *Reynolds were among the subscribers. As a supposed curiosity of literary *primitivism, 'Lactilla' provoked much interest, and the book's profits were invested by More on Yearsley's behalf. Yearsley, who had higher aspirations, furiously rejected this arrangement, denouncing More in an 'Autobiographical Narrative' attached to the fourth edition of the *Poems*. Under different *patronage Yearsley produced *Poems on Various Subjects* (1787); a *Poem on the Inhumanity of the Slave Trade* (1788); a tragedy, *Earl Goodwin* (1791), a novel, *The Royal Captives* (1795), and some final poems, *The Rural Lyre* (1796). From 1793 she ran a *circulating library. See Mary Waldron, *Lactilla: Milkwoman of Clifton* (1996).

Yeast: A Problem A novel by Charles *Kingsley, published in **Fraser's Magazine* 1848, in volume form in 1851. The first of Kingsley's novels, *Yeast* is unformed as a literary work. It deals with social and religious problems of the day (the miserable conditions of the rustic labourer, the Game Laws, and Tractarianism: *see* OXFORD MOVEMENT), largely by means of dialogues between the hero and other characters. The story is that of the reactions of the generous but undisciplined nature of Lancelot Smith to the influences exercised on him by the philosophical Cornish gamekeeper Tregarva, the worldly Colonel Bracebridge, the Romanizing curate Luke, Lancelot's orthodox love Argemone Lavington, and the philanthropic banker Barnakill; he is seen suffering the loss, first of his fortune, and then of Argemone. The story ends in a vague and semi-mystical indication that Lancelot is to seek his salvation in working towards the regeneration of England.

YEATS, Jack Butler (1871–1957) Painter, illustrator, novelist, and dramatist, brother of W. B. *Yeats; he contributed for many years to **Punch* (1910–41) under the pseudonym 'W. Bird', and also did many illustrations for the *Cuala Press. His writings convey an anarchic spirit and a democratic sympathy strikingly at odds with the values associated with his famous brother. Three of his plays were produced at the *Abbey Theatre's Peacock subsidiary in 1939, 1942, and 1949. He remains best known for his oil paintings of Irish life and landscape, which became increasingly Expressionist in his later career. See Hilary Pyle, *The Different Worlds of Jack B. Yeats* (1994).

YEATS, John Butler (1839–1922) Irish portrait painter and rationalist, father of W. B. and J. B. *Yeats; his *Letters to his Son W. B. Yeats and Others, 1869–1922* (ed. J. Hone, 1946) give a vivid portrait of cultural life in Ireland, London (where he lived for some years from 1887 in Bedford Park), and New York (where he spent his last fourteen years, renowned, in Hone's words, less as a painter than as 'a critic, philosopher and conversationalist').

YEATS, William Butler (1865–1939) Poet, dramatist, essayist, autobiographer, and dominating figure of the *Irish Revival. The eldest son of J. B. *Yeats and brother of Jack *Yeats, he was born in Dublin and grew up there and in London, spending his summers at his maternal grandparents' home in Sligo: all three locations were significant for a career that would explore Irish mythological and political subject matter in terms of the English Romantic tradition and celebrate the landscapes and the folklore of the west of Ireland. For three years he studied at the Dublin Metropolitan School of Art, where with his fellow student G. W. *Russell (Æ) he developed an interest in mystical religion and the supernatural. At 21 he abandoned art as a profession in favour of literature, writing the novels *John Sherman and Dhoya* (published pseudonymously in 1891) and editing *The Poems of William Blake* (1893), *The Works of William Blake* (with F. J. Ellis, 3 vols, 1893), and *Poems of Spenser* (1906). The transfer of political power from his own Anglo-Irish ascendancy caste to the majority *Roman Catholic community and the associated movement towards Irish independence provide the context for Yeats's long struggle to assert spiritual and heroic values in the face of egalitarian modernity, a struggle which gave central prominence to the theatre. Founding an Irish Literary Society in London in 1891 and another in Dublin in 1892, he applied himself to the creation of an Irish national theatre, an objective which, with the help of Lady *Gregory and others, was partly realized in 1899 when his play *The Countess Cathleen* (1892) was acted in Dublin. The English actors engaged by the *Irish Literary Theatre gave way to an Irish amateur company, which produced his and Gregory's incendiary nationalist prose play *Cathleen ni Houlihan* in 1902. This Irish National Theatre Company then acquired, with the help of Annie *Horniman, the building in Dublin's Lower Abbey Street which became the *Abbey Theatre in 1904. Yeats's early interest in the lore of the countryside resulted in the anthology *Fairy and Folk Tales of the Irish Peasantry* (1888) and a compilation of his own essays and case studies, *The Celtic Twilight* (1893). Associated mystical concerns are explored in the short fictions of *The Secret Rose* (1897), which introduce Michael Robartes and Owen Aherne, characters who would feature importantly in the mature poetry. The Indian and Arcadian settings of Yeats's first poems yielded around 1886 to what he called 'Irish scenery'. Mythological and faery themes, along with delicate evocations of the weather, topography, and place-names of the west of Ireland, characterize *The Wanderings of Oisin and Other Poems* (1889), *The Countess Kathleen and Various Legends and Lyrics* (1892), and *The Wind among the Reeds* (1899), an intricately organized volume which combines *symbolist techniques with an antique courtliness. Yeats's 19th-century poems at once dramatize and ironize the appeal of escape from the burdens of modern living, many of them exploring his hopeless love for the beautiful nationalist activist Maud Gonne. Subsequent collections show the poet moving from the elaborate style of the 1890s to an increasingly colloquial and socialized idiom. *In the Seven Woods* (1903) was followed by *The Green Helmet and Other Poems* (1910) and the laconic and disenchanted *Responsibilities* (1914). Yeats's mounting disillusionment with Irish politics came to a head in 1912 and 1913 with the controversy over the Hugh Lane bequest of French Impressionist paintings to the city of Dublin. The Easter Rising of 1916, however, restored his faith in the heroic character of his country and produced the self-rebuking if ultimately ambiguous political encomium 'Easter 1916', his first fully modern lyric masterpiece. The following year he married George Hyde-Lees (1892–1968), a young Englishwoman who on their honeymoon attempted automatic writing, an event that exercised a profound effect on his life and work. His wife's 'communicators' ultimately provided him with the philosophical 'system' set out in *A Vision* (1925) and exploited in some of the poems in *Michael Robartes and the Dancer* (1921), and in the two richly orchestrated volumes that stand at the apex of his achievement, *The Tower* (1928) and *The Winding Stair and Other Poems* (1933). *The Wild Swans at Coole* (1917), a transitional collection, marks the beginning of a shift towards the compacted, symbolically freighted meditative style perfected in the latter works. *Parnell's Funeral and Other Poems* (1935), *New Poems* (1938), and the posthumously published *Last Poems* (1939) explore a variety of modes, from the esoteric to the raucous, and contain both the most obscurely allusive and the most direct verse of his career. Yeats served as a senator of the Irish Free State from 1922 to 1928, was chairman of the commission on coinage, and in 1923 received the *Nobel Prize for Literature. He developed an increasingly adversarial relationship with Ireland as the country grew more theocratic in the 1930s. He died in the south of France, and in 1948 his body was brought back to Ireland and interred at Drumcliff in his beloved Sligo. Yeats's dramatic output, which includes five plays in which he develops the character of *Cuchulain as a tragic alter ego, has slowly grown in critical stature. One of the Cuchulain cycle, *At the Hawk's Well* (performed 1916; pub. 1917), is the first example of *Nōh drama in English. Some of Yeats's major critical writings are collected in *Essays and Introductions* (1961), while the memoirs he published in his lifetime were brought together as *Autobiographies* in 1955. A fifteen-volume edition of his correspondence is in preparation under the general editorship of John Kelly. There is an exhaustive *Life* by the historian R. F. Foster (i: *The Apprentice Mage*, 1997; ii: *The Arch-Poet*, 2003).

yellowbacks Cheap (usually costing 2*s*., or 2*s*. 6*d*.) editions of novels, so called from being bound in yellow boards. First produced in the 1850s, they were the ordinary 'railway novels' of the 1870s and 1880s.

Yellow Book (1894–7) A journal devoted to literature and art, startling in its time for being bound as a book with bright yellow covers. Published and promoted by John *Lane and edited by Henry *Harland, with Aubrey *Beardsley initially as art editor, its first issue (which included Max *Beerbohm's essay 'A Defence of Cosmetics') provoked a public storm which did not subside during the three years of the *Book*'s life. Writers published included Henry *James, Robert *Gissing, John *Davidson, Ernest *Dowson, Ella *Dixon, and Arnold *Bennett; among artists represented were Aubrey *Beardsley, Walter Sickert (1860–1942), and Wilson Steer (1860–1942).

YEVTUSHENKO, Yevgenii Aleksandrovich *See* EVTUSHENKO, EVGENII ALEKSANDROVICH.

Yiddish Language of the Jews of Central and Eastern Europe. Incorporating elements of Germanic, Balto-Slavic, Hebrew, and some Romance languages, its written and printed form uses the Hebrew alphabet. Millions of its speakers were victims of the Holocaust, but the language survives and has moved with its speakers to various parts of the world. In America numerous words of Yiddish origin have been Anglicized, and Howard *Jacobson's *Kalooki Nights* (2006) illustrates the continued use of Yiddish vocabulary and phrases in Jewish communities in England. The works of the great Yiddish novelist Isaac Bashevis *Singer have been translated into many languages.

YOLEN, Jane (1939–) American author and editor of numerous books of *fantasy and *science fiction for children and adults, born in New York. She often draws on folklore and fairy-tales. *Briar Rose* (1992) uses the traditional tale to reflect the narrator's experiences during the Second World War.

YONGE, Bartholomew (1560–1612) Translator. He travelled in Spain in 1578–80, and produced translations of Guazzo (1586), *Boccaccio (1587), and the Spanish romance *Diana* by *Montemayor. His version was published in 1598, with a dedication to Lady *Rich (Penelope Rich). It has been edited by J. M. Kennedy (1968).

YONGE, Charlotte M. (Mary) (1823–1901) Novelist, born in Otterbourne, in the parish of Hursley, Hampshire; she lived all her life there. She was educated at home by her parents. In 1836, the Revd John *Keble, one of the founders of the *Oxford Movement, was appointed to the parish and became her mentor; his influence pervades her writing. Yonge published over 150 works, including novels, historical, educational, and religious textbooks, short stories of village life, a life of the prince consort (1890), and many children's books. Her most famous novel is the *Tractarian *The *Heir of Redclyffe* (1853); others include *Countess Kate* (1852) and *Hopes and Fears* (1860). Yonge's novels were often interlinked family sagas advocating a life of submission and duty, primarily designed for young female readers. Some, notably *The Daisy Chain, or Aspirations* (1856), which she described as 'of a nondescript class', are *crossover books, appealing to both adult and young readers. Her historical novel for children *The Little Duke* (1854) inspired Mark *Twain's *The Prince and the Pauper* (1881). She edited the magazines the *Monthly Packet* (1851–99), *The Monthly Paper of Sunday Teaching* (1860–75), and the journal of the Mother's Union, *Mothers in Council* (1890–1900). Her pamphlet *What Books to Lend and What to Give* (1887) is one of the earliest critical works on children's literature. The Charlotte Mary Yonge Fellowship has an exhaustive website including an annotated bibliography. See www.cmyf.org.uk.

Yorick (1) in Shakespeare's *Hamlet* (V. i), the king's jester, whose skull the grave-diggers throw up when digging Ophelia's grave; (2) in Laurence Sterne's *Tristram Shandy*, 'the lively, witty, sensible, and heedless parson', of Danish extraction, and probably a descendant of Hamlet's Yorick. Sterne adopted 'Yorick' as a pseudonym in his *Sentimental Journey* and entitled his own homilies *The Sermons of Mr Yorick*, first published in 1760.

Yorkshire Tragedy, A A brief but powerful play published in 1608, stated in the title to be by *Shakespeare and to have been acted by the King's Men as part of an otherwise unknown *Four Plays in One*. It was reprinted by Thomas Pavier (d. 1625) along with other Shakespearian and pseudo-Shakespearian plays in 1619. It was published along with other plays of dubious authorship in the third *folio, but internal evidence makes it extremely improbable that Shakespeare had any part in its authorship. It is probably by Thomas *Middleton. The play is based on a pamphlet, *Two Most Unnatural and Bloody Murders* (1605) describing actual murders committed in that year. George *Wilkins's play *The Miseries of Enforced Marriage* (1607) is also based on the case. In the play the unnamed husband, a brutal and depraved gamester, suddenly filled with remorse when he realizes his shame, murders his two children, and stabs his docile and devoted wife.

YOUNG, Andrew (1885–1971) Poet, born in Scotland, educated at school and university in Edinburgh, ordained a minister of the Free Church in 1912. In 1910 his father paid for the publication of his *Songs of Night*, the first of many slim volumes of poetry which were greatly admired by an ever-widening circle. The first *Collected Poems* appeared in 1936 and the verse play *Nicodemus* in 1937. In 1939 Young was ordained in the Church of England. *The Green Man* (1947) is sometimes considered his best collection. In 1952 he published a long, disturbing poem, 'Into Hades', which was later combined with the visionary 'A Traveller in Time' to create *Out of the World and Back* (1958), his most ambitious work. His lifelong interest in botany was reflected in a prose account of his travels and searches, *A Prospect of Flowers* (1945), but in many lyrics, too, whose subjects also included many aspects of the natural world. His spare line, sharp specific imagery, quiet concision, and skill with conceit brought him much admiration. The influence of literary fashions barely touched him, but he acknowledged a particular debt to Thomas *Hardy, and to George *Crabbe and George *Herbert. *The Complete Poems* was revised in 1974.

YOUNG, Arthur (1741–1820) Agricultural theorist, author of several county-based surveys of agriculture. His *Tour in Ireland* (1780) was praised for its accuracy by Maria *Edgeworth. His *Travels in France* (1793) was based on three tours to France, with excursions to Catalonia and Italy, undertaken 1787–9 'with a view of ascertaining the cultivation, wealth, resources and national prosperity' of France. Young was editor of *Annals of Agriculture* (1784–1809). He knew Fanny *Burney, who described his house, Bradfield Hall, Suffolk, in **Camilla*. A selection from his autobiographical papers and correspondence was published in 1898 by M. Betham Edwards; see also the biography by J. G. Gazley (1973).

YOUNG, Edward (1683–1765) Poet and clergyman, educated at Winchester College and Oxford University. His early literary contacts included Joseph *Addison, Thomas *Tickell, Aaron *Hill, Jonathan *Swift, and Alexander *Pope. His tragedy *Busiris* was produced at Drury Lane in 1719, and another, *The Revenge*, was performed there in 1721. In 1725–8 he published a series of verse satires on the 'Love of Fame' under the title *The Universal Passion*, and in 1730, two *Epistles to Mr. Pope Concerning the Authors of the Age*. In that year Young became rector of Welwyn, where he spent the rest of his life. His most celebrated poem was *The Complaint, or *Night Thoughts on Life, Death and Immortality* (1742–5). *The Brothers*, a tragedy written decades earlier, was performed in 1753. Young's prose satire *The Centaur Not Fabulous* appeared in 1755; his essay *Conjectures on Original Composition* (1759), addressed to his close friend Samuel *Richardson, marked an important cultural shift towards an emphasis on originality and genius. Samuel *Johnson, another friend, cited Young extensively in **Johnson's Dictionary* and added commentary on the poems to the biography of Young by Sir Herbert Croft (1751–1816) included in **Lives of the English Poets*. See H. Forster, *Edward Young: Poet of the Night Thoughts* (1986).

YOUNG, Francis Brett (1884–1954) Novelist, short story writer, and poet, born in Halesowen, Worcestershire. He was educated at Epsom College and the University of Birmingham, was a doctor for some years in Devon, and served during the First World War in East Africa. He is remembered largely for his best-selling, solid, traditional novels of the West Midlands, which include *Portrait of Clare* (1927) and *My Brother Jonathan* (1928), but he also wrote novels based on his African experiences, including *Jim Redlake* (1930) and *They Seek a Country* (1937). *Poems 1916–1918* (1919) was written in Africa while he was convalescing from what proved permanent damage to his health, and *The Island* (1944) is a verse history of England, employing the verse forms of succeeding periods in strict chronological sequence.

YOUNG, Gavin (1928–2001) Travel writer, he spent his early years in Wales, where he was born, and in Cornwall. He was educated at Rugby School and, after National Service 1946–8, during which he was stationed in Palestine and Jordan, at Oxford University. At the age of 22, he joined a shipping company in Basra. In Iraq he met Wilfred *Thesiger, who took him to visit the Marsh Arabs, with whom he stayed for two years. He then spent two years in south-western Arabia, before moving in 1956 to North Africa, where he worked for Radio Maroc. Young became foreign correspondent of the *Observer* in 1960, covering many conflicts, including those in Algeria, the Congo, and Vietnam. His books include *Slow Boats to China* (1981), and *In Search of Conrad* (1991; *see* CONRAD, JOSEPH). *A Wavering Grace* (1997) follows the fortunes of a Vietnamese family whom he befriended during the war.

young adult literature An area of 'children's' literature addressed to the adolescent/teenage market. Originating in the USA, they were originally greeted sceptically in the UK; however, since the 1970s, books for the 13–18 age-range have dominated the juvenile market. Initially restricted by a supposed need for balance and resolution, and caution about content, over the past 30 years young adult (YA) novels have pushed back the boundaries of what is acceptable in technique (Aidan *Chambers) and content (Judy *Blume, Robert *Cormier, and Melvin *Burgess). *Salinger's *The Catcher in the Rye* (1951) was a powerful influence, inspiring thousands of 'problem' novels: notable exponents have been Paul Zindel (*The Pigman*, 1968), Cynthia Voight (*Homecoming*, 1981), and Jacqueline *Wilson. While many commercial *series such as 'Point Horror' are designed for the YA market, many strong *crossover novels, including those by Philip *Pullman, have also originated there. See Roberta Seelinger Trites, *Disturbing the Universe* (2000).

YOURCENAR, Marguerite (1903–87) Pseudonym of Marguerite de Crayencour, French historical novelist, poet, dramatist, and critic. The novel which brought her international acclaim was the meticulously researched *Mémoires d'Hadrien* (1951: *Memoirs of Hadrian*), translated in 1954 by her partner Grace Frick. She was elected to the Académie Française in 1980, the institution's first woman member.

Ywain and Gawain A northern *romance from the first half of the 14th century of 4,032 lines in short couplets, surviving in a single manuscript. The poem is a translation (with variations) from the 6,818 lines of *Yvain* by *Chrétien de Troyes. The translation has elements in common with other versions of the story (such as the Welsh *Owein*) and is admired for its narrative life and clarity of diction. Ywain kills the knight of a castle and, aided by her serving-lady Lunet, marries his widow Alundyne. Gawain persuades him to abandon his lady and go in search of adventure, assisted by a lion. The two knights have many adventures, eventually fighting each other incognito; but they recognize each other and are reconciled. Ywain is reconciled to Alundyne, again by the skills of Lunet. Ed. A. B. Friedman and N. T. Harrington, EETS os 254 (1964) and Mary Flowers Braswell (1995).

Z

ZAMIATIN, Evgenii Ivanovich (1884–1937) Russian writer, born in Tambov province. Joining the Bolshevik Party in 1905 and almost immediately arrested and exiled, he nevertheless graduated from the St Petersburg Polytechnic Institute in 1908 and joined the faculty, teaching naval architecture. He spent eighteen months in 1916–17 in Newcastle-upon-Tyne, supervising the construction of Russian ice-breakers, and the two stories that sprang from this experience, 'Islanders' (1917) and 'The Fisher of Men' (1918), reveal his opposition to the restrictions and bourgeois values of English life as he saw it. After the October Revolution of 1917 Zamiatin produced a steady flow of stories, among the best of which are 'The North' (1918), 'The Cave' (1920), 'Mamai' (1920), 'The Yawl' (1928), and 'The Flood' (1929), in which his major themes, the cult of the primitive and condemnation of the city, appear. He also edited collections by H. G. *Wells, George Bernard *Shaw, Jack *London, and O. *Henry. He greatly admired Wells and his 'social-fantastic novels', especially *The Time Machine*, which influenced him in the writing of his best-known work, the dystopian satire *We* (1920). Suppressed in Russia (until 1988), it appeared first in English translation in 1924. Its influence on *Nineteen Eighty-Four* was acknowledged by George *Orwell, though its widely suggested influence on *Brave New World* was denied by Aldous *Huxley. Vilified for the novel in his homeland, Zamiatin was allowed to leave in November 1931, settling and dying in Paris.

ZANGWILL, Israel (1864–1926) Born in London of Russian and Polish immigrant parents; he obtained a degree part-time at London University and became a teacher before turning to writing. The popular novel *Children of the Ghetto* (1892) established his reputation through its realistic and sympathetically critical portrayal of London's poor Jews. *Ghetto Tragedies* (1893), *Ghetto Comedies* (1907), and *The King of Schnorrers* (1894), a *jeu d'esprit*, contain vignettes of Jewish life. The historical *Dreamers of the Ghetto* (1898) testifies both to Judaism's inner strength and to its role in civilization. *The War for the World* (1916) and *The Voice of Jerusalem* (1920) combine apologia with polemic. His plays are vehicles for ideas, notably *The Melting Pot* (1909), which coined the phrase. See J. Udelson's biography (1990).

Zanzis (or possibly **'Zeuzis'**) Described by *Chaucer in **Troilus and Criseyde* (IV. 414) as a wise writer. This may be Zeuxis, a sage in the Alexander story, or the Athenian painter mentioned in 'The Physician's Tale' (*see* CANTERBURY TALES, 13; VI. 16), and by John *Gower.

Zarathustra, Thus Spake *See* NIETZSCHE, FRIEDRICH.

Zastrozzi *See* SHELLEY, PERCY.

Zeitgeist [German, 'time-spirit'] The word signifies the prevailing or defining intellectual or cultural climate of an era. It entered English in the 19th century, its first recorded use being by Matthew *Arnold.

ZELAZNY, Roger (1937–1995) American *science fiction writer, born in Euclid, Ohio; best known for the 'Amber' series beginning with *Nine Princes in Amber* (1976). He won two *Hugo awards for best novel, including *Lord of Light* (1967) in which technology has allowed humans literally to become gods.

ZÉLIDE *See* CHARRIÈRE, ISABELLE DE.

Zeluco A novel by John *Moore, published 1786, which 'traces the windings of vice' through the life of a wholly wicked man. Zeluco, a Sicilian noble, exhibits from childhood a character of cruelty, treachery, lust, and violence. He tyrannizes, maims, and murders, even killing his own child and driving his mother mad. In the end he is himself killed in a duel. The savagery is interspersed with humorous episodes, several of which involve a comic pair of Scotsmen, Buchanan and Targe.

ZEPHANIAH, Benjamin (1958–) Poet and playwright who left school aged 13, and spent most of his teenage years in youth institutions and the criminal underworld of Birmingham. He came to public attention as a *performance poet with the anti-racist demonstrations of the late 1970s and early 1980s. *Job Rocking* (pub. 1989) is recognized as Britain's first rap play. In 1991 he co-wrote *Dread Poets Society*, a BBC-TV play, in which he played himself in a fictional encounter with P. B. *Shelley, Mary *Shelley, and Lord *Byron. After *Streetwise* (1990), he stopped writing for the stage on the grounds that most theatre did not reach ethnic minorities or the most disadvantaged communities. Collections of poetry include *City Psalms* (1992) and *Propa Propaganda* (1996). Novels for teenagers include *Teacher's Dead* (2007); he also writes poetry for children.

zeugma A figure of speech by which a single word is made to refer to two or more words in a sentence, when properly

applying literally to only one of them; e.g. 'See Pan with flocks, with fruits Pomona crowned'.
See also SYLLEPSIS.

Zeus *See* JUPITER.

ZHUKOVSKY, Vasilii Andreevich (1783–1852) Russian poet, translator, and critic, born at Mishenskoe, near Tula, and educated at home and in Moscow. His first publication (1802), a translation of Thomas *Gray's 'Elegy', was seen as ushering in a new age of lyricism and feeling. He popularized the ballad form and gained fame for his adaptations of Bürger's *'Lenore', 'Liudmila' (1808), and 'Svetlana' (1813), perhaps his most famous work and, together with other of his poems, translated into English by John Bowring (1792–1872) in 1821–3. Zhukovsky, who believed that 'a translator in prose is a slave; a translator in verse is a rival', played a major role in introducing to Russia the works of European Romantic poets, particularly English and German. Among the poets he adapted and 'rivalled' were *Schiller and Uhland, and, among the English, James *Thomson, Oliver *Goldsmith, Thomas *Campbell, Robert *Southey, Walter *Scott, Thomas *Moore, and Lord *Byron. His version of 'The Prisoner of Chillon', written after a visit to the Swiss castle in 1821, was particularly admired. In 1839, Zhukovsky, visiting England in the suite of the future Alexander II, went to Stoke Poges, where he sketched the church and was inspired to compose his second, fundamentally different, version of Gray's poem.

Zofloya A novel by Charlotte *Dacre, published 1806. A *Gothic tale of criminality and sexual misconduct depicting the liaison between the callous *femme fatale* Victoria, set a bad example by her flighty mother, and the sexually magnetic and diabolical Moor, Zofloya, to whom she willingly surrenders her soul. Reviewers were shocked by the novel's frenzied sublimity and sexual charge, despite the declared moral purpose to warn vulnerable young readers against the dangers of seduction and the corrupting influence of parental immorality.

ZOLA, Émile (1840–1902) French novelist and leading figure of the *naturalist movement. Zola was influenced by *realist writers such as *Balzac, and by the scientific doctrines of positivism and determinism formulated by Hippolyte *Taine. He saw the novel as a laboratory in which the ingredients dictating human behaviour—Taine's famous trilogy of race, milieu, and moment—could be combined and tested. The essays of *Le Roman expérimental* (1880: *The Experimental Novel*) are his most sustained theoretical discussion of naturalism, though by the time of their publication, he had been putting his theories into practice for several years. His first naturalist novel, *Thérèse Raquin*, was published in 1867; and the appearance of *La Fortune des Rougon* (*The Fortune of the Rougons*) in 1871 marked the start of his most ambitious project. *Les Rougon-Macquart* is a twenty-novel cycle chronicling the activities of the Rougons and the Macquarts, two branches of a family whose conduct is conditioned through several generations by environment and inherited characteristics, chiefly drunkenness and mental instability. It offers a carefully documented panorama of life in Second Empire France exploring the powerful claims of human appetites and instincts. *Germinal* (1885) depicts the life of a mining community, and *La Terre* (1887: *The Earth*) that of the agricultural peasant; *La Bête humaine* (1890: *The Human Beast*) portrays the railway age, and *La Débâcle* (1892: *The Debacle*) the catastrophe of the Franco-Prussian War; the cycle concludes with *Le Docteur Pascal* (1893: *Doctor Pascal*). Throughout his texts, Zola's scientific ambitions exist in tension with a lyrical and impressionistic descriptive style. The later trilogy *Les Trois Villes* (*The Three Cities*)—*Lourdes* (1894), *Rome* (1896), *Paris* (1898)—examines the claims of the religious and social organizations of the day to minister to human needs. The novels of his final work, *Les Quatre Évangiles* (*The Four Gospels*)—*Fécondité* (1899: *Fertility*), *Travail* (1901: *Work*), *Vérité* (1903: *Truth*), and the unfinished *Justice*—are optimistic presentations of social ideals. *Vérité* refers to the *Dreyfus case in which Zola intervened with trenchant vigour, notably in 'J'accuse' ('I Accuse'), his letter to the newspaper *L'Aurore*. To avoid the sentence of imprisonment for libel that followed its publication, he spent eleven months in exile in England (1898–9), where, a decade earlier, Henry *Vizetelly had been found guilty of charges of obscenity for publishing his large-scale translation of Zola, totalling eighteen volumes between 1884 and 1888. See F. Brown, *Zola* (1996).

ZOLINE, Pamela (1941–) American writer and artist, born in Chicago. The much-anthologized 'The Heat Death of the Universe' (1967), published in **New Worlds*, applies the concept of entropy to the life of a Californian housewife. It and others appear in *Busy about the Tree of Life* (1988).

ZUKOFSKY, Louis (1904–78) American poet, born in New York. In 1931 with Ezra *Pound's sponsorship he edited the 'Objectivists' issue of **Poetry*, Chicago, followed in 1932 by *An 'Objectivists' Anthology*, featuring among others Carl Rakosi (1903–2004), George *Oppen, and Basil *Bunting. Zukofsky's lyrics, collected in the *Complete Short Poetry* (1991), are vividly textual, often witty, always stylish. The interpretative drive within Objectivism, a movement which presented poems as objects, differentiated it from *imagism's lyric base. It is fully explored in Zukofsky's *modernist long poem *A*, written over 45 years in 24 categorical parts. *A* shows itself as a compendium of forms and forces, in which translation, music, drama, and reiteration hustle and contend. *Bottom: On Shakespeare* (1963) combines Zukofsky's tribute to *Shakespeare with a running meditation on Western culture. *Propositions* (1967 and 1981) collects his critical essays and his *Autobiography* appeared in 1970. See Mark Scroggins, *The Poem of a Life* (2007).
See also WILLIAMS, W. C.

Zuleika Dobson Max *Beerbohm's only novel, published in 1911. Zuleika is a mesmerizing *femme fatale* who pays a fatal visit to her grandfather, the warden of Judas College, Oxford, during the Eights Week regatta. All the young men fall madly in love with her and, when rejected, they rush 'like lemmings' into the Thames and drown themselves. At the end, Zuleika determines to leave for Cambridge by special train.

ZWEIG, Stefan (1881–1942) Austrian novelist and biographer. Born in Vienna to secular Jewish parents, he studied philosophy and literature there and at Berlin. The first of his many biographies, of Paul *Verlaine, appeared in 1902. A committed pacifist, he took no part in the First World War. During the 1920s and 1930s he published many novellas and short stories, collected in two volumes in 1936. Though mainly remembered for his fiction and historical biographies, including those on Marie Antoinette (1932), *Erasmus (1934), and *Mary Queen of Scots (1935), he also published two early volumes of verse, three plays, and wrote the libretto for Richard *Strauss's *Die schweigsame Frau* (1935: *The Silent Woman*) based on Ben *Jonson's *Epicene*; his earlier translation of **Volpone* had enjoyed some success on the stage. Zweig's only full-length novel, *Ungeduld des Herzens* (1938: *Beware of Pity*), concerns the psychological destructiveness of pity. His autobiography, *The World of Yesterday* (1942), records his meetings and friendship with, among many others, W. B. *Yeats, James *Joyce, Rainer Maria *Rilke, and Sigmund *Freud. Following the rise of Hitler he fled Austria in 1934, moving to England, America, and eventually Brazil where, in despair at Europe's descent into barbarism, he committed suicide. See D. A. Prater, *European of Yesterday: A Biography of Stefan Zweig* (rev. edn 2004).

Appendix 1 · Chronology

The Chronology has two related lines of information, allowing readers to review key works of English literature in relation to their time. In the left-hand column are listed some of the significant literary works published in a given year. In the right-hand column a parallel range of information is provided on ruling monarchs; historical and literary events; birth and death dates of important authors, thinkers, musicians, and painters; and a selection of significant works of European literature, musical works, etc.

Date	*Principal literary works*	*Other events*
*c.*1000	Four surviving MSS of Anglo-Saxon poetry: Vercelli, Exeter, Cædmon, and *Beowulf*	
1042		**Edward the Confessor** (–1066)
1066		Battle of Hastings; **William I** (–1087)
1086		Doomsday survey
1087		**William II** (–1100)
1100		**Henry I** (–1135)
1135		**Stephen** (–1154)
*c.*1136	Geoffrey of Monmouth, *Historia Regum Britanniae*	
1139–53		Civil war between Stephen and Matilda
1154		**Henry II** (–1189)
1155		Geoffrey of Monmouth d.
*c.*1155	Wace, *Roman de Brut*	
1170		Thomas Becket murdered
1175	*Poema Morale*	
1187		Jerusalem captured by Saladin
1189		**Richard I** (–1199)
*c.*1190–1225	Katherine Group of devotional prose works	
1199		**John** (–1216)
*c.*1200	*The Owl and the Nightingale*	
*c.*1205?	Laȝamon, *Brut*	
1215		Magna Carta signed
1216		**Henry III** (–1272)
1221		Dominicans arrive in England
1224		Franciscans arrive in England
*c.*1225	*King Horn*	
*c.*1230	*Ancrene Wisse* (*Ancrene Riwle*)	Guillaume de Lorris, *Roman de la Rose*
*c.*1235–59	Matthew Paris, *Chronica Majora*	
1237		Guillaume de Lorris d.
1249		University College, Oxford, founded
1259		Matthew Paris d.

Date	*Principal literary works*	*Other events*
1265		Simon de Montfort's Parliament
1272		**Edward I** (–1307)
1282–4		**Edward I**'s conquest of Wales
1284		Peterhouse, Cambridge, founded
1290		Jews expelled from England
*c.*1290–4		Dante, *Vita nuova*
1295		**Edward I**'s Model Parliament
1296		**Edward I** invades Scotland
*c.*1300	*Cursor Mundi*	Richard Rolle b.
1305		Execution of William Wallace
1306		Robert Bruce crowned
*c.*1307–21		Dante, *Divina commedia*
1307		**Edward II** (–1327)
1314	*King Alisaunder; Sir Orfeo*	Battle of Bannockburn
1321		Dante d.
1327		**Edward III** (–1377)
*c.*1330		John Gower b.; John Wyclif b.; William Langland b.
1337		Hundred Years War begins
*c.*1340	*Harley Lyrics*	Geoffrey Chaucer b.
1342		Julian of Norwich b.
1346		Battle of Crécy
1348		First outbreak of plague in Britain
1349		Richard Rolle d.
*c.*1350	Thomas Chestre, *Sir Launfal*	
*c.*1350–2		Boccaccio, *Decameron*
*c.*1350–1400	*The Cloud of Unknowing*	
1356		English victory at Poitiers
*c.*1367–70	Langland, *Piers Plowman* (A-text)	
*c.*1369	Chaucer, *Book of the Duchess*	Thomas Hoccleve b.
*c.*1370		John Lydgate b.
1372–86	Chaucer, *The Legend of Good Women*	
*c.*1373		Margery Kempe b.
*c.*1374–85	Chaucer, *The House of Fame*	
1377		**Richard II** (–1399); First Poll Tax
*c.*1377–9	Langland, *Piers Plowman* (B-text)	
1378		The Great Schism (–1417)
*c.*1380	Bible tr. into vernacular by Wyclif and others	
*c.*1380–6	Chaucer, *The Parliament of Fowls*	
1381		Peasants' Revolt
1384		John Wyclif d.
*c.*1385	Chaucer, *Troilus and Criseyde*	
*c.*1385–6	Langland, *Piers Plowman* (C-text)	
1386		Treaty of Windsor
*c.*1387–1400	Chaucer, *The Canterbury Tales*	

Date	Principal literary works	Other events
c.1390	Gower, *Confessio Amantis*	William Langland d.
1396		Walter Hilton d.
1397		R. Whittington lord mayor of London
1399		**Henry IV** (–1413)
1400		Chaucer d.
c.1400	Sole surviving MS (Cotton Nero A x) of *Sir Gawain and the Green Knight*, Pearl, Cleanness, *and* Patience	Fra Angelico b.
1408		John Gower d.
1411	Hoccleve, *The Regiment of Princes*	
1412–20	Lydgate, *Troy Book*	
1413		**Henry V**
1415		Battle of Agincourt
c.1420 (–1504)	The Paston Letters	
1420–2	Lydgate, *The Siege of Thebes*	
1421	Hoccleve; The 'Series' Poems (–1422)	
1422		**Henry VI** (–1461)
c.1422		William Caxton b.
c.1424		Robert Henryson b.
1426		Thomas Hoccleve d.
1429		Siege of Orleans
1431		Joan of Arc burned
1431–8	Lydgate, *The Fall of Princes*	
c.1432–8	Margery Kempe, *The Book of Margery Kempe*	
c.1438		Margery Kempe d.
1441		King's College, Cambridge, founded; Jan van Eyck d.
1444		Sandro Botticelli b.
1449		John Lydgate d.
c.1450	*The Floure and the Leaf*	Hieronymus Bosch b.
1452		Leonardo da Vinci b.
1455		Battle of St Albans; Wars of the Roses begin; Fra Angelico d.
c.1460		John Skelton b.; William Dunbar b.
1461		**Henry VI** deposed; **Edward IV** (–1470)
1466		Donatello d.
c.1467		Desiderius Erasmus b.
1469		Niccolò Machiavelli b.
1470		**Henry VI** restored (–1471)
1471		**Henry VI** deposed and murdered; **Edward IV** restored (–1483); Sir Thomas Malory d.; Albrecht Dürer b.
1473–4	Caxton, *Recuyell of the Historyes of Troye*	

Date	*Principal literary works*	*Other events*
1474		Ludovico Ariosto b.
1475		Michelangelo b.
*c.*1475	Caxton, *The Game and Playe of the Chesse*	Alexander Barclay b.
*c.*1476	Caxton, *The Canterbury Tales*	Gavin Douglas b.;
*c.*1476–8		Giorgione b.
*c.*1478		Thomas More b.
1483	Caxton, *The Golden Legend*; Caxton, *Confessio Amantis*	**Edward V** (reigns two months); **Richard III** (–1485); Raphael b.
1484	Caxton, *Troilus and Criseyde*	
1485	Caxton, *Le Morte Darthur*	Battle of Bosworth; **Henry VII** (–1509)
*c.*1487		Titian b.
*c.*1490		Thomas Elyot b.; Robert Henryson d.
1492		Columbus lands in W. Indies; Piero della Francesca d.; William Caxton d.
*c.*1494		François Rabelais b.
*c.*1497–8		Hans Holbein b.
*c.*1498	Skelton, *The Bowge of Courte*	
1500		Wynkyn de Worde establishes new press
*c.*1500–6		Leonardo, *Mona Lisa*
1503	Atkinson, [Aquinas] *Imitation of Christ* (first English tr.); Erasmus, *Enchiridion Militis Christiani*	Thomas Wyatt b.
1504		Nicholas Udall b.; Colet made Dean of St Paul's
*c.*1505		Thomas Tallis b.
1506		Columbus d.
1509	Barclay, *The Ship of Fools*	**Henry VIII** (–1547); Jean Calvin b.
*c.*1509–19	(Anon.), *Everyman*	
1510		Giorgione d.; Botticelli d.
1511	Erasmus, *Encomium Moriae* (The Praise of Folly)	Erasmus at Cambridge
1513	Skelton, *Ballade of the Scottysshe Kynge*	Battle of Flodden Field; Machiavelli, *Il principe* (The Prince) written
*c.*1513		William Dunbar d.
*c.*1515		Roger Ascham b.
1516	More, *Utopia*; Skelton, *Magnificence*	John Foxe b.; Ariosto, *Orlando furioso* (see 1532); Hieronymus Bosch d.
1517		Henry Howard, earl of Surrey, b.; Magellan's first voyage; Luther's Wittenberg theses
1518		Tintoretto b.
1519		Leonardo da Vinci d.
1520	Murdoch Nisbet (tr.), Scots New Testament	Field of the Cloth of Gold; Raphael d.

Date	*Principal literary works*	*Other events*
1521		Luther condemned at Diet of Worms; Magellan killed in Philippines
1522		Gavin Douglas d.
1523	Skelton, *The Garlande of Laurell*	
1525	Tyndale (tr.), New Testament (printed at Worms)	
1527		Machiavelli d.; Sack of Rome
1528		Dürer d.; Castiglione, *Il cortegiano*
1529		John Skelton d.; fall of Cardinal Wolsey
1530	Tyndale (tr.), the Pentateuch (pub. Antwerp)	Wolsey d.; Andrea del Sarto d.
1531	Elyot, *The Boke named the Governour*	**Henry VIII** separates from Catherine of Aragon
1532	Chaucer (d. 1400), *Works*, ed. W. Thynne	Ariosto, *Orlando furioso* (final form); Rabelais, *Pantagruel*, i
1533	J. Heywood, *The Play of the Weather*; More, *The Apology of Syr Thomas More*	Michel de Montaigne b.; **Henry VIII** marries Anne Boleyn
*c.*1533	Elyot, *The Doctrinall of Princis*	
1534	J. Heywood, *A Play of Love*	Rabelais, *Pantagruel* (*Gargantua*), ii.; Act of Supremacy
1535	Coverdale's Bible (first pub. probably Zürich)	Sir Thomas More executed; St John Fisher executed; Ariosto d.
1536		William Tyndale burned; Anne Boleyn executed; Erasmus d.; dissolution of the monasteries (–1539); Calvin, *Institution de la religion chrétienne* (Latin edn)
*c.*1536	Elyot, *The Castell of Helthe*	
1537	Coverdale's Bible (modified version): first Bible printed in England; Cranmer, *Institution of a Christian Man*	
1538	Elyot, *Dictionary* (Latin–English)	
1539	The Great Bible	Act of Six Articles
1540	Elyot, *The Image of Governance*	Thomas Cromwell executed
1541	Udall (tr.), *Apophthegms of Erasmus*	Paracelsus d.; Calvin, *Institution de la religion chrétienne* (French edn)
1542		Sir Thomas Wyatt d.
1543	More, *History of Richard III* (in Grafton's *Chronicle*)	Copernicus (d. 1543), *De Revolutionibus*; Holbein d.
*c.*1543		William Byrd b.
1544		Torquato Tasso b.
1545	Ascham, *Toxophilus*	*Mary Rose* sinks in Solent; Council of Trent (–1563)
1546		Martin Luther d.; Sir Thomas Elyot d.

Date	Principal literary works	Other events
1547		**Edward VI** (–1553); Henry Howard executed; Miguel de Cervantes (Saavedra) b.; Nicholas Hilliard b.
1548	Bale, *King John* perf. 1538	
1549	Cranmer, *Book of Common Prayer*	
1550		Vasari, *Lives of the Artists* (completed 1568)
1551		William Camden b.
1552		Alexander Barclay d.; Christ's Hospital founded
*c.*1552		Edmund Spenser b.
1553		**Lady Jane Grey** (reigns nine days); **Mary I** (–1558); Rabelais d.
1554		Philip Sidney b.; Walter Ralegh b.
1555		**Mary I** marries Philip of Spain; Hugh Latimer and Nicholas Ridley burned
1556	Foxe, *Christus Triumphans*; the Geneva Psalter; J. Heywood, *The Spider and the Fly*	Thomas Cranmer burned; Nicholas Udall d.; Agricola, *De Re Metallica*
1557	North, *The Dial of Princes*; Surrey (tr.), *Aeneid* (Bks II, IV); Tottel and Grimald, *Songs and Sonnets* (*Tottel's Miscellany*)	Stationers obtain Charter of Incorporation
1558	Knox, *First Blast of the Trumpet against the Monstrous Regiment of Women*	English lose Calais; **Elizabeth I** (–1603); Robert Greene b.; Thomas Kyd b.; Thomas Lodge b.
1559	*A Mirror for Magistrates*	Act of Uniformity
1560	The Geneva ('Breeches') Bible	Westminster School founded
1561	Hoby, *The Courtier* (tr. of Castiglione's *Il libro del cortegiano*, 1528); Norton (tr.), [Calvin] *The Institution of Christian Religion*	Francis Bacon b.; Merchant Taylors' School founded
1562		Samuel Daniel b.; Lope de Vega b.
1563	Foxe, *Acts and Monuments* ('Book of Martyrs'); the Thirty-Nine Articles	Michael Drayton b.; John Dowland b.
1564		William Shakespeare b.; Christopher Marlowe b.; Galileo b.; Michelangelo d.; Calvin d.; Hawkins's first voyage opens slave trade
1565	Norton and Sackville, *Gorboduc* (perf. 1561)	
*c.*1566	Udall (d. 1556), *Ralph Roister Doister* pub. (perf. *c.*1552)	
1566	Gascoigne, *Supposes*	
1567		Thomas Nashe b.; Thomas Campion b.
1568	The Bishops' Bible	
1569		Pieter Bruegel (the elder) d.
1570	Ascham (d. 1568), *The Schoolmaster*	**Elizabeth I** excommunicated by Pius V

Date	Principal literary works	Other events
c.1570		Thomas Dekker b.; Thomas Middleton b.
1571		Kepler b.; battle of Lepanto; Caravaggio b.
1572		St Bartholomew's Day massacre; John Donne b.; John Knox d.
1572–4	Matthew Parker, *De Antiquitate Britannicae*	
1573	Gascoigne, *A Hundred Sundry Flowers*	
c.1573		Ben Jonson b.
1575	*Gammer Gurton's Needle*	Titian d.
c.1575		John Marston b.; Cyril Tourneur b.
1576		Burbage's Theatre built in London
1577	Holinshed, *Chronicles*	Robert Burton b.; Drake's circumnavigation of the globe (–1580); Rubens b.
1578	Lyly, *Euphues. The Anatomy of Wit*	Master of the revels becomes censor of plays
1579	North (tr.), Plutarch's *Lives*; Spenser, *The Shepheardes Calender*; P. Sidney, *A Defence of Poetry* (–1580)	John Fletcher b.
1580	Stow, *Chronicles of England*	Camoëns d.
c.1580		John Webster b.
1581	Sidney, *Old Arcadia* (completed by)	
1582	Hakluyt, *Divers Voyages Touching the Discoverie of America*	Shakespeare marries Anne Hathaway
1583	Stubbes, *Anatomy of Abuses*	
1583–4	Sidney, *New Arcadia* (completed by)	
1584	Peele, *Arraignment of Paris*; Scot, *Discovery of Witchcraft*	
1585		Thomas Tallis d.; Virginia colonized by W. Ralegh
1586	Camden, *Britannia*	Sir Philip Sidney d.
1587	Hakluyt, *Voyages Made into Florida*; Knox, *History of the Reformation in Scotland*	Mary Queen of Scots executed; Foxe d.
c.1587	Kyd, *The Spanish Tragedy*	
1588		Defeat of Spanish Armada; Thomas Hobbes b.; Martin Marprelate controversy (–1590); Byrd, *Psalmes, Sonets and Songs*
1589	Greene, *Menaphon*; Hakluyt, *Principal Navigations, Voiages, and Discoveries...*; Lodge, *Scillaes Metamorphosis*; Nashe, *The Anatomy of Absurdity*; Puttenham, *The Art of English Poesie*	Byrd, *Songs of Sundrie Natures*
1590	Greene, *Greene's Mourning Garment*; Lodge, *Rosalynde*; Marlowe, *Tamburlaine*; Sidney	

Date	Principal literary works	Other events
	(d. 1586), *Arcadia* (revised version); Spenser, *Faerie Queene*, i–iii	
*c.*1590	Shakespeare, *The Comedy of Errors* written (pub. 1623); *Titus Andronicus* written (pub. 1594)	
1590–2	Shakespeare, *1 Henry VI* written (pub. 1623); *2 Henry VI* written (pub. 1594, anon. and retitled); *3 Henry VI* written (pub. 1595, anon. and retitled)	
1591	Harrington (tr.), *Orlando furioso*; Lyly, *Endymion*; Sidney, *Astrophel and Stella*	Robert Herrick b.
*c.*1591	Shakespeare, *Richard III* written (pub. 1597)	
1592	*Arden of Faversham*; Daniel, *Delia*; Greene, *Greene's Groat's-Worth of Wit*; Lyly, *Midas*; Nashe, *Pierce Penniless, his Supplication to the Devil*	Montaigne d.; plague closes theatres for two years; Greene d.
*c.*1592	Shakespeare, *The Taming of the Shrew* written (pub. 1623)	
1593	Drayton, *Idea*; Hooker, *Of the Laws of Ecclesiastical Politie*, i–iv; Nashe, *Christ's Tears over Jerusalem*; Shakespeare, *Venus and Adonis*; Sidney, *Arcadia* (revised version plus three books of early version)	Izaak Walton b.; George Herbert b.; Christopher Marlowe d.
1594	Drayton, *Idea's Mirror*; Greene, *Orlando furioso*; Marlowe (d. 1593), *Edward II*; Nashe, *The Terrors of the Night*; *The Unfortunate Traveller*; Shakespeare, *The Rape of Lucrece*	Lord Chamberlain's Men established; Tintoretto d.; T. Kyd d.
1595	Sidney, *A Defence of Poetry*	Robert Southwell executed; Tasso d.
*c.*1595	Shakespeare, *Love's Labour's Lost* written (pub. 1598); *Romeo and Juliet* written (pub. 1597, 1599); *Richard II* written (pub. 1597)	
1595–6	Shakespeare, *A Midsummer Night's Dream* written (pub. 1600)	
1596	Davies, *Orchestra*; Nashe, *Have with You to Saffron-Walden*; Spenser, *Faerie Queene*, iv–vi	René Descartes b.; Essex storms Cadiz
*c.*1596–8	Shakespeare, *The Merchant of Venice* written (pub. 1600)	
1597	Bacon, *Essays* (other edns 1612, 1625); Gerard, *Herbal*; Hooker, *Laws of Ecclesiastical Politie*, v	Dowland, *The First Booke of Songes*
*c.*1597	Shakespeare, *1 Henry IV* written (pub. 1598); *2 Henry IV* written (pub. 1600); *The Merry Wives of Windsor* written (pub. 1602, 1623)	
1598	Marlowe (d. 1593), *Hero and Leander*; Stow, *A Survey of London* (and 1603)	Edict of Nantes
*c.*1598–9	Shakespeare, *Much Ado About Nothing* written (pub. 1600)	
1599	Nashe, *Nashe's Lenten Stuff*; Shakespeare, *Henry V* written (pub. 1600)	Edmund Spenser d.; first Globe Theatre opened; Anthony Van Dyck b.

Date	Principal literary works	Other events
c.1599	Shakespeare, *Julius Caesar* written (pub. 1623); *As You Like It* registered (pub. 1623)	
1599–1601	Shakespeare, *Hamlet* written (pub. 1603; short text)	
1600	Dekker, *The Shoemakers' Holiday*; Jonson, *Every Man out of His Humour* (perf. 1599); Nashe, *Summer's Last Will and Testament* (perf. 1599)	East India Company founded; Dowland, *Second Booke of Songes*; Pedro Calderón de la Barca b.; Claude Lorraine (Gellée) b.
1601	Holland (tr.), Pliny's *Natural History*; Jonson, *Every Man in His Humour* (perf. 1598); Shakespeare, *Twelfth Night* written (pub. 1623); 'The Phoenix and the Turtle' (in Chester's *Loves Martyr*)	Earl of Essex executed; Thomas Nashe d.; Poor Law Act
1602	Campion, *Art of English Poesie*; Dekker, *Satiromastix*; Marston, *Antonio and Mellida*; *Antonio's Revenge*	Bodleian Library opened
c.1602	Shakespeare, *Troilus and Cressida* written (pub. 1609)	
c.1602–4	Shakespeare, *Othello* written (pub. 1622)	
1603	Daniel, *Defence of Rhyme*; Dekker, *The Wonderful Year*; Florio (tr.), Montaigne's *Essays*	**James I** (–1625); Dowland, *Third and Last Booke of Songes*
1603–4	Shakespeare, *All's Well that Ends Well* written (pub. 1623)	
1604	Dekker, *The Honest Whore* (Parts I and II) (1604–5), *Westward Ho*; Marlowe (d. 1593), *Dr Faustus*; Marston, *The Malcontent*	Hampton Court Conference; *Book of Common Prayer* authorized
c.1604	Shakespeare, *Measure for Measure* written (pub. 1623)	
1604–5	Shakespeare, *King Lear* written (pub. 1608)	
1605	Bacon, *Advancement of Learning*; Jonson, *Sejanus his Fall* (perf. 1603)	Gunpowder Plot; Sir Thomas Browne b.; Byrd, *Ave Verum Corpus*; Cervantes, *Don Quixote*, i
1606	Dekker, *News from Hell*	Edmund Waller b.; John Lyly d.; Pierre Corneille b.; Rembrandt b.
c.1606	Shakespeare, *Macbeth* written (pub. 1623)	
c.1606–7	Shakespeare, *Antony and Cleopatra* written (pub. 1623)	
1607	Chapman, *Bussy D'Ambois*; T. Heywood, *A Woman Killed with Kindness*; Jonson, *Volpone* (perf. 1605–6); Marston, *What You Will*; *The Revenger's Tragedy* (Tourneur? Middleton?)	Monteverdi, *Orfeo*; settlement of Virginia
c.1607	Beaumont, *The Knight of the Burning Pestle* perf.; Shakespeare (with Middleton?), *Timon of Athens* written (pub. 1623)	
1608	Middleton, *A Mad World, my Masters*	John Milton b.

Date	Principal literary works	Other events
c.1608	Shakespeare, *Coriolanus* written (pub. 1623)	
1609	Dekker, *The Gull's Horn-Book*; Shakespeare, *Sonnets*	Edward Hyde, earl of Clarendon, b.
1609–10	Shakespeare, *Cymbeline* written (pub. 1623)	
1610	Donne, *Pseudo-Martyr*	Monteverdi, *Vespers*; Caravaggio d.
1610–11	Shakespeare, *The Winter's Tale* written (pub. 1623)	
1611	Authorized Version of the Bible; Jonson, *Catiline* perf.; Tourneur, *The Atheist's Tragedy*	Bermuda settled
c.1611	Shakespeare, *The Tempest* written (pub. 1623)	
1612	Bacon, *Essays* (2nd edn.); Drayton, *Poly-Olbion*, i (completed 1622); Jonson, *The Alchemist* (perf. 1610); Webster, *The White Devil*	Henry, prince of Wales d.
1613	Samuel Purchas, *Purchas his Pilgrimage*	Samuel Butler b.; Jeremy Taylor b.; Sir Thomas Bodley d.; Globe Theatre burns down
1614	Ralegh, *History of the World*	Addled Parliament
1615	Beaumont and Fletcher, *Cupid's Revenge*	Cervantes, *Don Quixote*, ii
1616	Chapman, *The Whole Works of Homer*; Jonson, *Mercury Vindicated*; *Epicene* (perf. 1609–10)	William Shakespeare d.; Francis Beaumont d.; Cervantes d.; Harvey expounds circulation of the blood
1618		Sir Walter Ralegh executed; Thirty Years War; Ben Jonson poet laureate
1619	Beaumont (d. 1616) and Fletcher, *The Maid's Tragedy*	Samuel Daniel d.; Nicholas Hilliard d.
1619–22		Inigo Jones designs the Banqueting House, Whitehall
1620	Bacon, *Novum Organum*	Pilgrim Fathers emigrate to New World; John Evelyn b.; Thomas Campion d.
1621	Burton, *The Anatomy of Melancholy*; Dekker *et al.*, *The Witch of Edmonton*	Andrew Marvell b.; Henry Vaughan b.; Thomas Vaughan b.; Jean de La Fontaine b.
1622	Drayton, *Poly-Olbion*, ii	Virginia settlers massacred
c.1622	Middleton and Rowley, *The Changeling*	
1623	Webster, *The Duchess of Malfi*; Shakespeare (d. 1616), 'First Folio', ed. Heminge and Condell	William Byrd d.; Blaise Pascal b.; Camden d.
1624	Donne, *Devotions upon Emergent Occasions*	War against Spain
1625	Bacon, *Essays* (3rd edn)	**Charles I** (–1649); John Fletcher d.
1626		Francis Bacon d.; Cyril Tourneur d.; John Dowland d.
1627		Robert Boyle b.; war against France; Thomas Middleton d.
1628	Earle, *Microcosmography*; W. Harvey, *De Motu Cordis*	John Bunyan b.; Buckingham assassinated; Fulke Greville d.

Date	Principal literary works	Other events
1629	Lancelot Andrewes, *XCVI Sermons*	
1630	Middleton (d. 1627), *A Chaste Maid in Cheapside*	
1631	Jonson, *Bartholomew Fair* (perf. 1614); Stow, *Annals of England* (final form)	John Dryden b.; John Donne d.; Michael Drayton d.; peace with Spain
1632	Donne (d. 1631), *Death's Duel*	John Locke b.; Benedict de Spinoza b.; Thomas Dekker d.; Jan Vermeer b.; Jean-Baptiste Lully b. John Webster d.
1633	Donne (d. 1631), *Poems*; Ford, *The Broken Heart*; *'Tis Pity She's a Whore*; Herbert (d. 1633), *The Temple*; Marlowe (d. 1593), *The Jew of Malta*; Massinger, *A New Way to Pay Old Debts*	Samuel Pepys b.; George Herbert d.; Laud appointed archbishop of Canterbury
1634		John Marston d.
1635	Francis Quarles, *Emblems*	
1636		Nicholas Boileau b.
1637	Milton, *Comus* (perf. 1634)	Ben Jonson d.
c.1637		Thomas Traherne b.
1638	Milton, *Lycidas*	Monteverdi, *Madrigals of Love and War*; Sir William D'Avenant poet laureate
1639		First Bishops' War
1640	Donne (d. 1631), *LXXX Sermons* (with life by I. Walton); Carew, *Poems*	The Long Parliament; Aphra Behn b.; Philip Massinger d.; Rubens d.
c.1640		John Ford d.
1641		Strafford executed; Irish rebellion; Thomas Heywood d.
1642	Denham, *Cooper's Hill* (final version 1655); Milton, *Reason of Church Government*; *Apology for Smectymnuus*	Civil War begins (–1649); public theatres closed (–1660); Galileo d.
1643	Browne, *Religio Medici*; D'Avenant, *The Unfortunate Lovers*	Solemn League and Covenant
1644	Milton, *Areopagitica*	Battle of Marston Moor
1645	Milton, *Tetrachordon*; *Poems*; Waller, *Poems*	William Laud executed; battle of Naseby
1646	Browne, *Pseudodoxia Epidemica*; Crashaw, *Steps to the Temple*; H. Vaughan, *Poems*	
1647		John Wilmot, earl of Rochester, b.
1648	Beaumont, *Psyche*; Herrick, *Hesperides*	
1649	Lovelace, *Lucasta*; Milton, *Tenure of Kings and Magistrates*; *Eikonoklastes*	Execution of **Charles I**; **The Commonwealth** (–1660); William Drummond d.
1650	Baxter, *The Saints' Everlasting Rest*; Taylor, *Rule and Exercise of Holy Living*; H. Vaughan, *Silex Scintillans*; T. Vaughan, *Anthroposophia Theomagica*	Descartes d.; massacres of Drogheda and Wexford

Date	*Principal literary works*	*Other events*
1651	D'Avenant, *Gondibert*; Donne (d. 1631), *Essays in Divinity*; Hobbes, *Leviathan* (definitive Latin text 1668); Taylor, *Rules and Exercises of Holy Dying*	Battle of Worcester
1652	Ashmole, *Theatrum Chemicum*; H. Vaughan, *Mount of Olives*	Act of Settlement (Ireland)
1652–4		First Dutch War
1653	Walton, *The Compleat Angler* (2nd edn 1655)	Oliver Cromwell becomes Protector
1656	Bunyan, *Some Gospel Truths Opened*; Cowley, *Poems*	War against Spain (–1659)
1657		Richard Lovelace d.
1658	Browne, *Hydriotaphia, or Urn Burial*; Massinger (d. 1640), *The City Madam* (perf. 1632)	Oliver Cromwell dies; succeeded by his son Richard
1659	Lovelace (d. 1657), *Posthume Poems*	
1660		The Restoration; **Charles II** (–1685); Samuel Pepys begins his diary (–1669); Bunyan imprisoned; Velázquez d.; Anne Marshall first woman on English stage
1661		Anne Finch, countess of Winchilsea, b.
*c.*1661		Daniel Defoe b.
1662	Prayer Book (final version); Butler, *Hudibras*; Fuller (d. 1661), *Worthies of England*	Act of Uniformity; Dunkirk sold to France; Royal Society's first charter
1663	Butler, *Hudibras*, ii	
1664	Dryden, *The Rival Ladies*	Sir John Vanbrugh b.; Matthew Prior b.
1665	Bunyan, *The Holy City*; Lord Herbert of Cherbury, *Poems*; Marvell, *The Character of Holland*	The Great Plague; Second Dutch War (–1667)
1666	Bunyan, *Grace Abounding*; Glanvill, *Philosophical Considerations Concerning Witches and Witchcraft*	James Shirley d.; Thomas Vaughan d.; Great Fire of London; Molière, *Le Misanthrope*; *Le Médecin malgré lui*
1667	Dryden, *Annus Mirabilis*; Milton, *Paradise Lost* (10 books); Sprat, *History of the Royal Society*	Jonathan Swift b.; Jeremy Taylor d.; Abraham Cowley d.; Racine, *Andromaque*; Molière, *Tartuffe*
1668	Dryden, *Essay of Dramatick Poesy*; Etherege, *She Would if She Could*	William D'Avenant d.; Dryden poet laureate; Racine, *Les Plaideurs*; La Fontaine, *Fables*, i; François Couperin b.
1669	Dryden, *The Wild Gallant*	Rembrandt d.
1670		William Congreve b.; Pascal (d. 1662), *Pensées*; Molière, *Le Bourgeois Gentilhomme*
1671	Milton, *Paradise Regained*; *Samson Agonistes*	
1672	Buckingham *et al.*, *The Rehearsal*	Joseph Addison b.; Richard Steele b.; Molière, *Les Femmes savantes*
1672–4		Third Dutch War

Date	Principal literary works	Other events
1673	Aphra Behn, *The Dutch Lover*; D'Avenant (d. 1668), *Collected Works*; Dryden, *Marriage-à-la-Mode*	Test Act passed
1674	Milton (d. 1674), *Paradise Lost* (2nd edn, 12 books)	Robert Herrick d.; John Milton d.; Thomas Traherne d.; Edward Hyde d.
1675	Traherne (d. 1674), *Christian Ethics*; Wycherley, *The Country Wife*	Jan Vermeer d.
1676	Etherege, *The Man of Mode*	
1677	Aphra Behn, *The Rover*, i; Wycherley, *The Plain Dealer*	Spinoza (d. 1677), *Ethics*; Racine, *Phèdre*
1678	Bunyan, *Pilgrim's Progress*, i (ii pub. 1684); Butler, *Hudibras*, iii	Popish Plot; Andrew Marvell d.; La Fontaine, *Fables*, ii; Mme de Lafayette, *La Princesse de Clèves*
1679		Thomas Hobbes d.
1680	Bunyan, *The Life and Times of Mr Badman*	Samuel Butler d.; Joseph Glanvill d.; John Wilmot, earl of Rochester, d.; La Rochefoucauld d.
1681	Aphra Behn, *The Rover*, ii; Dryden, *Absalom and Achitophel*, i; Hobbes (d. 1679), *Behemoth*; Marvell (d. 1678), *Miscellaneous Poems*	
1682	Bunyan, *The Holy War*; Dryden, *Religio Laici*; *Mac Flecknoe*, i; *Absalom and Achitophel*, ii; Otway, *Venice Preserv'd*	Sir Thomas Browne d.; Claude Lorraine d.
1683		Rye House Plot; Izaak Walton d.; Turks besiege Vienna
1684	Bunyan, *Pilgrim's Progress*, ii	Corneille d.; Jean-Antoine Watteau b.
1685		**James II** (–1688); John Gay b.; Thomas Otway d.; Monmouth's rebellion; J. S. Bach b.; G. F. Handel b.
1687	Dryden, *Song for St Cecilia's Day*; *The Hind and the Panther*	Jean-Baptiste Lully d.
1688	Dryden, *Britannia Rediviva*	**James II** abdicates; Glorious Revolution; Alexander Pope b.; John Bunyan d.
*c.*1688	A. Behn, *Oroonoko*	
1689	Marvell (d. 1678), *Poems on Affairs of State* (–1697)	**Mary II** (–1694) and **William III** (–1702); siege of Londonderry; Samuel Richardson b.; Aphra Behn d.; Thomas Shadwell poet laureate
1690	Locke, *Essay Concerning Human Understanding*	Battle of the Boyne
1691	Wood, *Athenae Oxonienses*	Sir George Etherege d.; Richard Baxter d.; Robert Boyle d.; George Fox d.; Purcell, *Dido and Aeneas*
1692		Purcell, *The Fairy Queen*; Nahum Tate poet laureate

Date	Principal literary works	Other events
1693	Congreve, *The Old Bachelor*; Cotton Mather, *Wonders of the Invisible World*	La Fontaine, *Fables*, iii; Mme de Lafayette d.
1694	Congreve, *The Double Dealer*; Dryden, *Love Triumphant*	**Mary II** d.; **William III** reigns alone; Bank of England founded; Voltaire (François-Marie Arouet) b.
1695	Congreve, *Love for Love*	Henry Vaughan d.; Jean de La Fontaine d.; Purcell, *The Indian Queen*; Purcell d.
1696	Aubrey, *Miscellanies*	
1697	Dryden, *Alexander's Feast*; Vanbrugh, *The Relapse*; *The Provok'd Wife*	William Hogarth b.
1698		J. Collier attacks stage profanity
1699		Jean Racine d.; Fénelon, *Télémaque*
1700	Congreve, *The Way of the World*	James Thomson b.; John Dryden d.
1701	Dryden (d. 1700), *Collected Plays*	Act of Settlement; War of Spanish Succession begins
1702	Clarendon, *History of the Rebellion* (completed 1704); Defoe, *Shortest Way with Dissenters*	**Anne** (–1714)
1703		Defoe pilloried and imprisoned; Samuel Pepys d.; Perrault d.
1704	Swift, *A Tale of a Tub*; *The Battle of the Books*	Battle of Blenheim; John Locke d.; Bossuet d.
1705	Addison, *The Campaign*	
1706	Defoe, *Apparition of Mrs Veal*; Farquhar, *The Recruiting Officer*	Act of Succession; Benjamin Franklin b.; John Evelyn d.
1707	Farquhar, *The Beaux' Stratagem*; Watts, *Hymns*	Henry Fielding b.; George Farquhar d.; Union of England and Scotland
1709	Berkeley, *New Theory of Vision*; Defoe, *History of the Union of Great Britain*; Swift, *Baucis and Philemon*	Steele starts the *Tatler* (–1711); first Copyright Act; Samuel Johnson b.
1710	Berkeley, *Principles of Human Knowledge*; Swift, *Meditations upon a Broomstick*	
1711	Pope, *Essay on Criticism*; Shaftesbury, *Characteristics of Men and Manners*	The *Spectator* started (–1712); David Hume b.; Boileau d.
1712	Pope, *The Rape of the Lock* (in Lintot's *Miscellanies*); Swift, *Proposal for Correcting the English Language*	Jean-Jacques Rousseau b.; Stamp Act
1713	Addison, *Cato*; Pope, *Windsor-Forest*	Laurence Sterne b.; Swift becomes Dean of St Paul's; Denis Diderot b.
1714		**George I** (–1727); Leibniz, *Monadologie*
1715	Pope (tr.), *Iliad*, i (ii: 1716; iii: 1717; iv: 1718; v–vi: 1720); Watts, *Divine Songs for Children*	First Jacobite Rebellion; Nicholas Rowe poet laureate; Louis XIV d.
1716		Thomas Gray b.; William Wycherley d.; Leibniz d.

Date	*Principal literary works*	*Other events*
1717	Pope, *Collected Works* (inc. 'Verses to the Memory of an Unfortunate Lady' and 'Eloisa to Abelard')	Horace Walpole b.; David Garrick b.; Handel, *Water Music*
1718		Laurence Eusden poet laureate; Handel, *Acis and Galatea*
1719	Defoe, *Robinson Crusoe*; Watts, *Psalms of David*	Joseph Addison d.
1720	Defoe, *Memoirs of a Cavalier*; *Captain Singleton*; Gay, *Collected Poems*	South Sea Bubble; Giovanni Battista Piranesi b.
1721	Swift, *Letter to a Young Gentleman*; *Letter of Advice to a Young Poet*	William Collins b.; Tobias Smollett b.; Mark Akenside b.; Matthew Prior d.; Bach, Brandenburg Concertos 1–6; Watteau d.
1722	Defoe, *Journal of the Plague Year*; *Moll Flanders*; *Colonel Jack*	Christopher Smart b.; Joseph Wharton b.
1723		Adam Smith b.; Sir Joshua Reynolds b.
1724	Defoe, *Roxana*; *Tour through…Great Britain* (completed 1726); Oldmixon, *Critical History of England* (completed 1726); Swift, *Drapier's Letters*	Immanuel Kant b.; Bach, *St John Passion*
1725	Pope (ed.), Shakespeare's Works (2nd edn, 1728); (tr., with William Broome and Elijah Fenton) *Odyssey*, i–iii (iv–v: 1726); Swift, *Jonathan Wild*	
1726	Swift, *Gulliver's Travels*; Theobald, *Shakespeare Restored* (criticism of Pope's edn of Shakespeare); Thomson, *Winter*	Charles Burney b.; Sir John Vanbrugh d.; Voltaire in England (three years)
1727	Defoe, *History and Reality of Apparitions*; Dyer, *Grongar Hill*; Gay, *Fables*, i (ii: 1738; completed 1750); Thomson, *Summer*	**George II** (–1760); John Wilkes b.; Sir Isaac Newton d.; Bach, *St Matthew Passion*; Thomas Gainsborough b.
1728	Gay, *The Beggar's Opera*; Law, *A Serious Call to a Devout and Holy Life*; Pope, *The Dunciad*, i–iii; iv (the *New Dunciad*): 1742; complete 1743; Swift, *Short View of the State of Ireland*; Thomson, *Spring*	Robert Bage b.; Gay's *Polly* banned by Lord Chamberlain
1729	Swift, *A Modest Proposal*	Edmund Burke b.; Richard Steele d.; William Congreve d.; G. E. Lessing b.
1730	Fielding, *Tom Jones*; Thomson, *The Seasons* (inc. *Autumn*)	Oliver Goldsmith b.; Colley Cibber poet laureate
1731	Pope, *Of Taste*	William Cowper b.; Daniel Defoe d.; Prévost, *L'Histoire du chevalier des Grieux et de Manon Lescaut*
1732	Gay, libretto for *Acis and Galatea* (Handel); Pope, *Of the Use of Riches*; Swift, *The Lady's Dressing-Room*; *The Beast's Confession to the Priest*	John Gay d.; Voltaire, *Zaïre*; Franz Joseph Haydn b.
1733	Pope, *An Essay on Man* (1733–4); *Imitations of Horace*, i; Swift, *A Serious and Useful Scheme…*	Joseph Priestley b.; François Couperin d.

Date	*Principal literary works*	*Other events*
1734	Fielding, *Don Quixote in England*; Gay, *The Distressed Wife*; Pope, *Imitations of Horace*, ii; George Sale (tr.), the Qur'ān; Swift, *A Beautiful Young Nymph Going to Bed*	Bach, *Christmas Oratorio*; Joseph Wright (of Derby) b.
1735	Pope, *Epistle to Dr Arbuthnot*; Thomson, 'Italy'; 'Greece'; 'Rome' (Pts i–iii of *Liberty*)	
1736	Thomson, 'Britain'; 'The Prospect' (Pts iv and v of *Liberty*)	
1737	Shenstone, *Poems upon Various Occasions*	Edward Gibbon b.; Thomas Paine b.; Robert Walpole's Licensing Act
1738	Gay, *Fables*, ii; Johnson, *London*; Swift, *A Complete Collection of Polite and Ingenious Conversation*	
1739	Hume, *Treatise of Human Nature* (completed 1740); Swift, *Verses on the Death of Dr Swift*	John and Charles Wesley, *Hymns and Sacred Poems*; War of Jenkins's Ear
1740	Cibber, *An Apology for the Life of Mr Colley Cibber*; Dyer, *The Ruins of Rome*; Thomson, *Alfred* (containing 'Ode in Honour of Great Britain', i.e. 'Rule Britannia'); Richardson, *Pamela*	James Boswell b.; War of the Austrian Succession
1741	Fielding, *Shamela*; Hume, *Essays Moral and Political* (completed 1742); Shenstone, *The Judgement of Hercules*; Watts, *Improvement of the Mind*	Edmond Malone b.; Choderlos de Laclos b.; Vivaldi d.
1742	Collins, *Persian Eclogues*; Fielding, *Joseph Andrews*; Pope, *New Dunciad*; Shenstone, *The Schoolmistress*; Young, *The Complaint, or Night Thoughts...* (–1745)	Richard Bentley d.; Voltaire, *Mahomet*; Handel, *Messiah*
1743	Blair, *The Grave*	
1744	Akenside, *Pleasures of Imagination*; Thomson, *The Seasons* (revised version); J. Warton, *The Enthusiast*	Alexander Pope d.; John and Charles Wesley, *A Collection of Psalms and Hymns*
1745	Akenside, *Odes on Several Subjects*	Second Jacobite Rebellion; Jonathan Swift d.
1746	Collins, *Odes on Several Descriptive and Allegorical Subjects*; J. Warton, *Odes on Various Subjects*	Robert Blair d.; battle of Culloden; Francisco de Goya b.
1747	Gray, *Ode on a Distant Prospect of Eton College*; Johnson, *Plan of a Dictionary of the English Language*; Richardson, *Clarissa* (8 vols, 1747–9); J. Warton, *The Pleasures of Melancholy*; Warburton's edition of Shakespeare; Wortley Montagu, *Town Eclogues*	Voltaire, *Zadig*
1748	Hume, *Enquiry Concerning Human Understanding*; Smollett, *The Adventures of Roderick Random*; Thomson (d. 1748), *The Castle of Indolence*	Jeremy Bentham b.; James Thomson d.; Isaac Watts d.

Date	Principal literary works	Other events
1749	Cleland, *Memoirs of a Woman of Pleasure* (*Fanny Hill*; see 1750); Fielding, *The History of Tom Jones*; Johnson, *The Vanity of Human Wishes*; *Irene*; Smollett (tr.), *Gil Blas*; J. Warton, *The Triumph of Isis*	Bach, Mass in B minor
1750	Cleland, *Memoirs of Fanny Hill* (abridged version of Cleland, 1749); Thomson (d. 1748), *Poems on Several Occasions*	J. S. Bach d.
1751	Fielding, *Amelia*; Gray, *Elegy Written in a Country Church-Yard*; Hume, *Enquiry Concerning Principles of Morals*; Smollett, *The Adventures of Peregrine Pickle*	Richard Brinsley Sheridan b.
1752	Law, *The Way to Divine Knowledge*; Lennox, *The Female Quixote*; Smart, *Poems on Several Occasions*	Thomas Chatterton b.; Fanny Burney b.; Gregorian Calendar adopted: eleven days 'lost'
1753	Richardson, *The History of Sir Charles Grandison* (7 vols, 1753–4); Smollett, *The Adventures of Ferdinand Count Fathom*	John and Charles Wesley, *Hymns and Spiritual Songs*; charter of the British Museum
1754	Hume, *History of England*, i (ii: 1757; final version 1762)	George Crabbe b.; Henry Fielding d.
1755	Fielding (d. 1754), *Journal of a Voyage to Lisbon*; Johnson, *A Dictionary of the English Language*	Lisbon earthquake
1756	J. Warton, *Essay on the Writings and Genius of Pope*	William Godwin b.; Thomas Rowlandson b.; Mozart b.; Seven Years War
1757	Burke, *Philosophical Enquiry into…the Sublime and the Beautiful*; Dyer (d. 1757), *The Fleece*; Gray, *Odes by Mr Gray* (inc. 'The Progress of Poesy', 'The Bard'); Smollett, *A Complete History of England* (completed 1758)	William Blake b.; Colley Cibber d.; John Dyer d.; William Whitehead poet laureate
1758	Akenside, *Ode to the Country Gentlemen of England*; Johnson, the *Idler* (in the *Universal Chronicle*, collected 1758)	
1759	Goldsmith, *An Enquiry into the Present State of Polite Learning*; Johnson, *Rasselas, Prince of Abyssinia*; Sterne, *A Political Romance*	Robert Burns b.; Mary Wollstonecraft b.; William Beckford b.; William Collins d.; Handel d.; Schiller b.; Voltaire, *Candide*; British Museum opens; capture of Quebec
1760	Macpherson, *Fragments of Ancient Poetry, Collected in the Highlands*; Sterne, *The Life and Opinions of Tristram Shandy*, i–ii (iii–vi: 1761–2; vii and viii: 1765; ix: 1767); *Sermons of Yorick* (completed 1769)	**George III** (–1811)

Date	*Principal literary works*	*Other events*
1761	Churchill, *The Rosciad*; *The Apology*	Samuel Richardson d.; William Law d.; Kotzebue d.; Rousseau, *Julie, ou la nouvelle Héloïse*
1762	Churchill, *The Ghost*, i–iii (iv: 1763); Goldsmith, *The Citizen of the World*; Macpherson, *Fingal, an Ancient Epic Poem*; Smollett, *The Adventures of Sir Launcelot Greaves*; Walpole, *Anecdotes of Painting* (completed 1780); E. Young, *Resignation*	William Cobbett b.; Lady Mary Wortley Montagu d.; Rousseau, *Du contrat social*; *Émile*; Wilkes starts *North Briton*
1763	Hugh Blair, *A Critical Dissertation on the Poems of Ossian*; Macpherson, *Temora*; C. Smart, *A Song to David*	Samuel Rogers b.; William Shenstone d.; John Wilkes prosecuted; Johnson meets Boswell; Jean-Paul Richter b.; Peace of Paris
1764	Goldsmith, *The History of England in a Series of Letters*; *The Traveller*; T. Warton the younger (ed.), *The Oxford Sausage*	Ann Radcliffe b.; Charles Churchill d.; William Hogarth d.; Voltaire, *Dictionnaire philosophique portatif*; Jean-Philippe Rameau d.
1765	Blackstone, *Commentaries on the Laws of England* (completed 1769); Johnson (ed.), *The Works of Shakespeare*; Macpherson, *Works of Ossian*; Percy, *Reliques of Ancient English Poetry*; Smart (tr.), *The Psalms of David*; Walpole, *The Castle of Otranto*	Edward Young d.
1766	Anstey, *The New Bath Guide*; Goldsmith, *The Vicar of Wakefield*; Smollett, *Travels through France and Italy*	Thomas Malthus b.; Robert Bloomfield b.; Mme de Staël b.; Lessing, *Laokoon*
1767		Maria Edgeworth b.; John and Charles Wesley, *Hymns for the Use of Families*
1768	Boswell, *An Account of Corsica*; Gray, *Poems by Mr Gray* (inc. 'The Fatal Sisters', 'The Descent of Odin'); Sterne (d. 1768), *A Sentimental Journey through France and Italy*; Walpole, *The Mysterious Mother*	Laurence Sterne d.; Royal Academy of Arts founded; Chateaubriand b.; Canaletto d.
1769	Smollett, *The Adventures of an Atom*	Amelia Opie b.; Garrick's Shakespeare Jubilee; Napoleon b.; James Watt's steam engine patented
1770	Goldsmith, *The Deserted Village*; Percy, *Northern Antiquities*	William Wordsworth b.; James Hogg b.; Mark Akenside d.; Thomas Chatterton d.; Holbach, *Le Système de la nature*; Hölderlin b.; Beethoven b.
1771	Beattie, *The Minstrel*, i (ii: 1774); Smollett, *The Expedition of Humphrey Clinker*	Sir Walter Scott b.; Thomas Gray d.; Tobias Smollett d.
1772	'Junius', *Letters*	S. T. Coleridge b.; Emanuel Swedenborg d.

Date	Principal literary works	Other events
1773	Barbauld, *Poems*; Goldsmith, *She Stoops to Conquer*; Richard Graves, *The Spiritual Quixote*; Sterne (d. 1768), *Letters from Yorick to Eliza*	James Mill b.; Boston Tea Party
1774	Burke, *Speech on American Taxation*; Chesterfield, *Letters to his Natural Son*; T. Warton the younger, *History of English Poetry* (3 vols, 1774–81)	Robert Southey b.; Oliver Goldsmith d.; Goethe, *Die Leiden des jungen Werthers* (The Sorrows of Young Werther); Bürger, *Lenore*
1775	Johnson, *A Journey to the Western Islands of Scotland*; Sheridan, *The Rivals*	Jane Austen b; Charles Lamb b.; Walter Savage Landor b.; M. G. Lewis b.; War of American Independence; J. M. W. Turner b.; John Constable b.; Beaumarchais, *Le Barbier de Seville*
1776	Gibbon, *Decline and Fall of the Roman Empire*, i (ii and iii: 1781; iv–vi: 1788); Smith, *The Wealth of Nations*	David Hume d.; American Declaration of Independence
1777	Chatterton (d. 1770), *Poems, Supposed to Have Been Written by Thomas Rowley*; Sheridan, *The School for Scandal* perf.	
1778	Burney, *Evelina* (pub. anonymously)	Rousseau d.; Piranesi d.
1779	Richard Graves, *Columella*; Johnson, *The Works of the English Poets*; Sheridan, *The Critic* perf.	
1780	Crabbe, *The Candidate*	Gordon Riots; Wieland, *Oberon*
1781	Bage, *Mount Henneth*; Crabbe, *The Library*; Gibbon, *Decline and Fall of the Roman Empire*, ii and iii	Rousseau (d. 1778), *Les Confessions*, i–vi (vii–xii: 1788); G. E. Lessing d.; British surrender at Yorktown
1782	Burney, *Cecilia*; Cowper, *Poems*; 'The Diverting History of John Gilpin' (in *Public Advertiser*; repr. 1785); I. Sancho, *Letters*	C. R. Maturin b.; Laclos, *Les Liaisons dangereuses*
1783	Beckford, *Dreams, Waking Thoughts and Incidents*; Blake, *Poetical Sketches*; Crabbe, *The Village*; Thomas Day, *The History of Sandford and Merton*	Peace of Versailles; Washington Irving b.; Stendhal b.
1784	Bage, *Barham Downs*	Leigh Hunt b.; Samuel Johnson d.; Diderot d.; Beaumarchais, *Le Mariage de Figaro*
1785	Boswell, *Journal of Tour of the Hebrides with Johnson*; Cowper, *The Task* (also inc. 'John Gilpin'); Richard Graves, *Eugenius*; Paley, *The Principles of Moral and Political Philosophy*; Rudolf Raspe, *Baron Munchausen's Travels*	Thomas De Quincey b.; Thomas Love Peacock b.; Thomas Warton poet laureate
1786	Beckford, *Vathek* (first English tr.); Burns, *Poems Chiefly in the Scottish Dialect*; Hester Lynch Piozzi, *Anecdotes of Samuel Johnson*	Frederick the Great d.; Mozart, *Le nozze di Figaro* (The Marriage of Figaro)
1787	Bage, *The Fair Syrian*; Wollstonecraft, *Thoughts on the Education of Daughters*	Mary Russell Mitford b.; American Constitution signed; Mozart, *Don Giovanni*

Date	Principal literary works	Other events
1788	Bage, *James Wallace*; Gibbon, *Decline and Fall of the Roman Empire*, iv–vi; 'Peter Pindar', *The Poetical Works of Peter Pindar*	Byron b.; Charles Wesley d.; Thomas Gainsborough d.; trial of Warren Hastings; *The Times* started
1789	Blake, *Songs of Innocence*; *The Book of Thel*; E. Darwin, *Loves of the Plants*; Equiano, *Interesting Narrative*; G. White, *The Natural History of Selborne*	French Revolution
1790	Blake, *The Marriage of Heaven and Hell*; Burke, *Reflections on the Revolution in France*; Radcliffe, *A Sicilian Romance*	Adam Smith d.; Henry James Pye poet laureate; Benjamin Franklin d.; Lamartine b.; Mozart, *Così fan tutte*
1791	Blake, *The French Revolution*; Boswell, *The Life of Samuel Johnson*; Burns, 'Tam o' Shanter'; Isaac D'Israeli, *Curiosities of Literature*, i (ii: 1793; iii: 1817; iv and v: 1823; vi: 1834); Benjamin Franklin (d. 1790), *Autobiography*; Paine, *The Rights of Man*, i (ii: 1792); Radcliffe, *Romance of the Forest*	Michael Faraday b.; the *Observer* started; Mozart, *Die Zauberflöte* (The Magic Flute); Mozart d.; Louis XVI's flight to Varennes (June)
1792	Aiken and Barbauld, *Evenings at Home*; Bage, *Man as He Is*; Blake, *Song of Liberty*; Holcroft, *Anna St Ives*; Rogers, *The Pleasures of Memory*; Mary Wollstonecraft, *A Vindication of the Rights of Woman*	Percy Bysshe Shelley b.; John Keble b.; Frederick Marryat b.; Sir Joshua Reynolds d.; Paine flees to France; monarchy abolished in France
1793	Blake, *Visions of the Daughters of Albion*; *America*; Burns, *Poems*; Godwin, *An Enquiry Concerning Political Justice*; Wordsworth, *An Evening Walk*; *Descriptive Sketches*	John Clare b.; Gilbert White d.; execution of Louis XVI (Jan.); war with France
1794	Blake, *Songs of Experience*; *Europe*; *The Book of Urizen*; Godwin, *Caleb Williams*; Paine, *The Age of Reason*, i (ii: 1795; iii: 1811); Paley, *View of the Evidences of Christianity*; Radcliffe, *The Mysteries of Udolpho*	Edward Gibbon d.; execution of Robespierre
1795	Blake, *The Book of Los*; *The Book of Ahania*; *The Song of Los*; *Songs of Innocence and Experience*; Chatterton (d. 1770), *Poetical Works*; Landor, *Poems*	John Keats b.; Thomas Carlyle b.; Thomas Arnold b.; James Boswell d.; Goethe, *Wilhelm Meisters Lehrjahre* (Wilhelm Meister's Apprenticeship, 1795–6)
1796	Bage, *Hermsprong*; Burney, *Camilla*; Lewis, *The Monk*	Robert Burns d.
1797	Bewick, *A History of British Birds*; Radcliffe, *The Italian*; Southey, *Poems*; *Letters Written in Spain and Portugal*	Mary Wollstonecraft Godwin d.; Edmund Burke d.; Horace Walpole d.; Franz Schubert b.; Alfred de Vigny b.; Joseph Wright (of Derby) d.; Haydn, *Die Schöpfung* (The Creation, 1797–8)
1798	Coleridge, 'Fears in Solitude', 'France: An Ode', 'Frost at Midnight'; Landor, *Gebir*; Malthus, *An Essay on the Principles of Population*; Wordsworth and Coleridge, *Lyrical Ballads* (1st edn; see 1800, 1802)	

Date	Principal literary works	Other events
1799	T. Campbell, *The Pleasures of Hope*; Godwin, *St Leon*; M. G. Lewis, *Tales of Terror*; Mungo Park, *Travels in the Interior of Africa*	Thomas Hood b.; Religious Tract Society founded; Napoleon First Consul; Balzac b.
1800	Bloomfield, *The Farmer's Boy*; Burns (d. 1796), *Works* (with life); Coleridge, tr. of Schiller's *Wallenstein*; Dibdin, *History of the English Stage*; Edgeworth, *Castle Rackrent*; Wordsworth and Coleridge, *Lyrical Ballads* (2 vols: preface, 1798 poems, and new poems)	Thomas Babington Macaulay b.; Edward Pusey b.; William Cowper d.; Beethoven, Symphony No. 1
1801	Edgeworth, *Moral Tales for Young People*; *Belinda*; M. G. Lewis, *Tales of Wonder*; T. Moore, *Poems by Thomas Little*; Southey, *Thalaba the Destroyer*	J. H. Newman b.; Robert Bage d.; Union with Ireland; Chateaubriand, *Atala*; Haydn, *Die Jahreszeiten* (The Seasons)
1802	Lamb, *John Woodvil*; Landor, *Poetry by the Author of Gebir*; Paley, *Natural Theology*; W. Scott, *Minstrelsy of the Scottish Border*; Wordsworth and Coleridge, *Lyrical Ballads* (3rd edn, with new preface)	Harriet Martineau b.; Erasmus Darwin d.; Peace of Amiens; Alexandre Dumas (Dumas *père*) b.; Victor Hugo b.; Mme de Staël, *Delphine*
1803	E. Darwin (d. 1802), *The Temple of Nature*; Repton, *Theory and Practice of Landscape Gardening*; Southey (tr.), *Amadis of Gaul*	T. L. Beddoes b.; George Borrow b.; Ralph Waldo Emerson b.; Edward Bulwer (Lytton) b.; Prosper Merimée b.; Hector Berlioz b.; Beethoven, Symphony No. 3 ('Eroica')
1804	Blake, *Jerusalem* (1804–20); *Milton* (1804–8); Edgeworth, *Popular Tales*; *A Modern Griselda*	Benjamin Disraeli b.; Nathaniel Hawthorne b.; John Wilkes d.; Napoleon crowned emperor; Kant d.; George Sand (Lucile-Aurore Dupin) b.
1805	Cary (tr.), Dante's *Inferno*; W. Scott, *The Lay of the Last Minstrel*; Southey, *Madoc*	W. H. Ainsworth b.; Robert Surtees b.; battle of Trafalgar; battle of Austerlitz; Schiller d.; Samuel Palmer b.; Beethoven, *Fidelio*
1806	Byron, *Fugitive Pieces*; Landor, *Simonidea*; Lingard, *Antiquities of the Anglo-Saxon Church*; W. Scott, *Ballads and Lyrical Pieces*	Elizabeth Barrett b.; J. S. Mill b.; Charles James Fox d.
1807	Byron, *Hours of Idleness*; *Poems on Various Occasions*; Crabbe, *Poems* (inc. 'The Parish Register'); Charles and Mary Lamb, *Tales from Shakespeare*; T. Moore, *Irish Melodies*; Southey, *Letters from England*; Wordsworth, *Poems in Two Volumes*	Henry Wadsworth Longfellow b.; Mme de Staël, *Corinne*
1808	M. G. Lewis, *Romantic Tales*; W. Scott, *Marmion*; S. Smith, *The Letters of Peter Plymley*	Peninsular War begins; Convention of Cintra; Goethe, *Faust*, i; Beethoven, Symphony No. 6 ('Pastoral')

Date	Principal literary works	Other events
1809	Byron, *English Bards and Scotch Reviewers*; Coleridge, the *Friend* (–1810); Wordsworth, *Concerning the Relations of Great Britain, Spain and Portugal as Affected by the Convention of Cintra*	Charles Darwin b.; Alfred Tennyson b.; W. E. Gladstone b.; Thomas Paine d.; Edgar Allan Poe b.; Haydn d.
1810	Crabbe, *The Borough*; W. Scott, *The Lady of the Lake*; P. B. Shelley, *Original Poetry by Victor and Cazire*; *Zastrozzi*; Southey, *The Curse of Kehama*	Elizabeth Gaskell b.; Robert Schumann b.; Frédéric Chopin b.
1811	Austen, *Sense and Sensibility* (pub. anonymously); W. Scott, *The Vision of Don Roderick*; P. B. Shelley, *The Necessity of Atheism*	W. M. Thackeray b.; **Regency declared**; Shelley expelled from Oxford; Gautier b.; Liszt b.
1812	Byron, *Childe Harold*, i and ii; *The Curse of Minerva*; Cary (tr.), Dante's *Purgatorio* and *Paradiso*; Combe, *Tour of Dr Syntax in Search of the Picturesque*; Edgeworth, *Tales of Fashionable Life*, 2nd ser.; Southey and Coleridge, *Omniana*	Robert Browning b.; Charles Dickens b.; Edward Lear b.; Edmond Malone d.; French retreat from Moscow
1813	Austen, *Pride and Prejudice* (pub. anonymously); Byron, *The Bride of Abydos*; *The Giaour*; Coleridge, *Remorse*; W. Scott, *Rokeby*; P. B. Shelley, *Queen Mab*; Southey, *Life of Nelson*	Southey poet laureate; Richard Wagner b.; Giuseppe Verdi b.
1814	Austen, *Mansfield Park* (pub. anonymously); Byron, *The Corsair*; *Lara*; *Ode to Napoleon*; Hunt, *Feast of the Poets* (book form); W. Scott, *Waverley* (pub. anonymously); Southey, *Roderick, the Last of the Goths*; Wordsworth, *The Excursion*	Charles Reade b.; abdication of Napoleon
1815	Byron, *Hebrew Melodies*; Hunt, *The Descent of Liberty*; W. Scott, *Guy Mannering*; *The Lord of the Isles*; *The Field of Waterloo*	Anthony Trollope b.; Byron married; Wellington and Blücher defeat Napoleon at Waterloo, 18 June
1816	Austen, *Emma* (pub. anonymously); Byron, *The Prisoner of Chillon and Other Poems*; *Childe Harold*, iii; *The Siege of Corinth*; Coleridge, *Christabel and Other Poems* (inc. 'Kubla Khan', 'The Pains of Sleep'); Hunt, *The Story of Rimini*; Lady Caroline Lamb, *Glenarvon*; Peacock, *Headlong Hall*; W. Scott, *The Antiquary* (*Tales of my Landlord*, 1st ser.); P. B. Shelley, *Alastor and Other Poems*	Charlotte Brontë b.; Richard Brinsley Sheridan d.; Shelley's marriage to Mary Godwin; Leigh Hunt's essay on Shelley and Keats in the *Examiner*; Rossini, *Il barbiere di Siviglia*; Benjamin Constant, *Adolphe*
1817	Byron, *Manfred*; *The Lament of Tasso*; Coleridge, *Sybilline Leaves*; Hazlitt, *Characters of Shakespeare's Plays*; Keats, *Poems* (inc. 'Sleep and Poetry'); T. Moore, *Lalla Rookh*; Peacock, *Melincourt*; W. Scott, *Rob Roy*; P. B. Shelley, *Laon and Cythna* (see 1818); Southey, *Wat Tyler*	G. H. Lewes b.; Jane Austen d.; Henry David Thoreau b.; *Blackwood's Magazine* started; Mme de Staël d.
1818	Austen (d. 1817), *Northanger Abbey* and *Persuasion* (with Memoir); Bowdler, *The Family*	Emily Brontë b.; M. G. Lewis d.; Shelley's final departure from

Date	Principal literary works	Other events
	Shakespeare; Byron, *Childe Harold*, iv; *Beppo*; Hazlitt, *Lectures on the English Poets*; Keats, *Endymion*; T. Moore, *The Fudge Family in Paris*; Peacock, *Nightmare Abbey*; *Rhododaphne*; W. Scott, *The Heart of Midlothian* (*Tales of my Landlord*, 2nd ser.); M. Shelley, *Frankenstein*; P. B. Shelley, *The Revolt of Islam* (orig. *Laon and Cythna*, 1817)	England; attack on Keats in *Quarterly Review*; Karl Marx b.
1819	Byron, *Mazeppa*; *Don Juan*, i and ii; Hazlitt, *Lectures on the English Comic Writers*; Lockhart, *Peter's Letters to his Kinfolk*; Macaulay, *Pompeii*; Mitford, *Our Village* (in *Lady's Magazine*; pub. in book form 1824–32); J. H. Reynolds, *Peter Bell*; W. Scott, *The Bride of Lammermoor* (in *Tales of my Landlord*, 3rd ser.); *Ivanhoe*; P. B. Shelley, *The Cenci*; *Rosalind and Helen*; Wordsworth, *Peter Bell*; *The Waggoner*	Charles Kingsley b.; John Ruskin b.; A. H. Clough b.; George Eliot (Mary Ann Evans) b.; Walt Whitman b.; Peterloo Massacre
1820	Elizabeth Barrett, *The Battle of Marathon*; Clare, *Poems, Descriptive of Rural Life*; Galt, *The Ayrshire Legatees*; Irving, *The Sketch Book of Geoffrey Crayon*; Keats, *Lamia, The Eve of St Agnes, Hyperion, and Other Poems*; C. Lamb, *Essays of Elia* (in *London Magazine* 1820–3, collected 1823); Maturin, *Melmoth the Wanderer*; Peacock, *The Four Ages of Poetry*; W. Scott, *The Abbot*; *The Monastery*; P. B. Shelley, *Prometheus Unbound and Other Poems*; Southey, *Life of John Wesley*; Wordsworth, *The River Duddon*; *Vaudracour and Julia*	**George IV** (–1830); Anne Brontë b.; Herbert Spencer b.; Jean Ingelow b.; trial of Queen Caroline
1821	Beddoes, *The Improvisatore*; Byron, *Cain*; *Don Juan*, iii–v; *Marino Faliero*; Clare, *The Village Minstrel and Other Poems*; J. F. Cooper, *The Spy*; De Quincey, *Confessions of an English Opium Eater* (in *London Magazine*; pub. separately 1822); Egan, *Life in London* (vol. pub.); Galt, *Annals of the Parish*; Hazlitt, *Table Talk* (completed 1822); W. Scott, *Kenilworth*; Shelley, *Epipsychidion*; *Adonais*; Southey, *A Vision of Judgement*	Keats d.; Greek War of Liberation; famine in Ireland (1821–3); Baudelaire b.; Flaubert b.; Dostoevsky b.; Napoleon d.
1822	Beddoes, *The Bride's Tragedy*; Byron, *Werner*; *The Vision of Judgment* (in the *Liberal*: see 1821, Southey); Galt, *The Provost*; Irving, *Bracebridge Hall*; Peacock, *Maid Marian*; S. Rogers, *Italy*, i (ii: 1828; completed 1830); W. Scott, *The Fortunes of Nigel*; *The Pirate*; *Peveril of the Peak*; Shelley, *Hellas*; Wordsworth, *Ecclesiastical Sketches*	Matthew Arnold b.; Shelley d.; *Sunday Times* started

Date	*Principal literary works*	*Other events*
1823	Byron, *Don Juan*, vi–viii (July); ix–xi (Aug.); xii–xiv (Dec.); Carlyle, *Life of Schiller* (in *London Magazine*, pub. separately 1825); J. F. Cooper, *The Pioneers*; Galt, *The Entail*; Hazlitt, *Liber Amoris*; C. Lamb, *Essays of Elia* (see 1820); T. Moore, *The Loves of the Angels*; W. Scott, *Quentin Durward*; Southey, *History of the Peninsular War* (completed 1832)	Charlotte Yonge b.; Coventry Patmore b.; Ann Radcliffe d.; Beethoven, *Missa Solemnis* (completed)
1824	Byron, *Don Juan*, xv and xvi; *The Deformed Transformed*; Hogg, *Confessions of a Justified Sinner*; Landor, *Imaginary Conversations of Literary Men and Statesmen*, i; M. R. Mitford, *Our Village* (completed 1832); W. Scott, *Redgauntlet*; *St Ronan's Well*	Wilkie Collins b.; Byron d.; National Gallery, London, founded; Beethoven, Symphony No. 9 ('Choral')
1825	Coleridge, *Aids to Reflection*; Hazlitt, *The Spirit of the Age*; W. Scott, *The Talisman*; *The Betrothed*; Southey, *A Tale of Paraguay*	T. H. Huxley b.; R. D. Blackmore b.; Stockton and Darlington railway opened
1826	J. F. Cooper, *The Last of the Mohicans*; Landor, *Imaginary Conversations*, ii; M. Shelley, *The Last Man*	
1827	Clare, *The Shepherd's Calendar*; De Quincey, 'Murder as One of the Fine Arts' (in *Blackwood's Magazine*); Keble, *The Christian Year*; W. Scott, *Chronicles of the Canongate*, 1st ser.	William Blake d.; Thomas Rowlandson d.; Thomas Arnold becomes headmaster of Rugby School; Beethoven d.
1828	Landor, *Imaginary Conversations*, iii; Lockhart, *Life of Robert Burns*; Napier, *History of the Peninsular War* (completed 1840); W. Scott, *Tales of a Grandfather*, 1st ser.; *Chronicles of the Canongate*, 2nd ser.	D. G. Rossetti b.; George Meredith b.; Taine b.; Tolstoy b.; Ibsen b.; Schubert d.; Goya d.
1829	Hood, *The Dream of Eugene Aram* (in *The Gem*, pub. separately 1831); Landor, *Imaginary Conversations*, iv and v; Lytton, *Devereux*; Peacock, *The Misfortunes of Elfin*; W. Scott, *Anne of Geierstein*; *Tales of a Grandfather*, 2nd ser.	J. E. Millais b.; Catholic Emancipation; Rossini, *Guillaume Tell*
1830	Cobbett, *Rural Rides*; Lytton, *Paul Clifford*; W. Scott, *Tales of a Grandfather*, 3rd and 4th ser.; Tennyson, *Poems, Chiefly Lyrical* (inc. 'Mariana')	**William IV** (–1837); Christina Rossetti b.; William Hazlitt d.; Camille Pisarro b.; Mendelssohn, Hebrides Overture (rev. 1832); Berlioz, *Symphonie fantastique*
1831	Peacock, *Crotchet Castle*; Poe, *Poems*; Trelawny, *Adventures of a Younger Son*	Hegel d.; Stendhal, *Le Rouge et le noir*
1832	Disraeli, *Contarini Fleming*; Lytton, *Eugene Aram*; W. Scott, *Tales of my Landlord*, 4th ser.; Tennyson, *Poems* (dated 1833, inc. 'The Lady of Shalott'); F. Trollope, *Domestic Manners of the Americans*	Lewis Carroll (Charles Lutwidge Dodgson) b.; Leslie Stephen b.; Sir Walter Scott d.; Jeremy Bentham d.; George Crabbe d.; First Reform Bill;

Date	Principal literary works	Other events
		Goethe, *Faust*, ii; Balzac, *Le Peau de chagrin*; *Le Curé de Tours*; Goethe d.
1833	R. Browning, *Pauline*; Carlyle, *Sartor Resartus* (in *Fraser's Magazine* 1833–4; first English edn 1838); Lamb, *Last Essays of Elia*; Lytton, *Godolphin*; *England and the English*; Newman, Pusey *et al.*, *Tracts for the Times* (90 numbers, 1833–41)	William Wilberforce d.; A. H. Hallam d.; Keble's sermon on 'national apostasy'; Balzac, *Eugénie Grandet*; Johannes Brahms b.
1834	Ainsworth, *Rookwood*; Lady Blessington, *Conversations with Lord Byron*; Lytton, *The Last Days of Pompeii*; Southey, *The Doctor*	William Morris b.; George du Maurier b.; S. T. Coleridge d.; Thomas Malthus d.; slavery abolished in British Empire; Edgar Degas b.; James Abbott McNeill Whistler b.
1835	R. Browning, *Paracelsus*; Dickens, *Sketches by Boz*, 1st ser.; Lytton, *Rienzi*; T. Moore, *The Fudges in England*; Mary Shelley, *Lodore*; Wordsworth, *Yarrow Revisited and Other Poems*	Samuel Butler b.; William Cobbett d.; Mark Twain (Samuel Langhorne Clemens) b.; Balzac, *Le Père Goriot*
1836	Dickens, *Sketches by Boz*, 2nd ser.; *The Posthumous Papers of the Pickwick Club* (monthly Apr. 1836–Nov. 1837); Marryat, *Mr Midshipman Easy*; Newman, Keble, *et al.*, *Lyra Apostolica*	W. S. Gilbert b.; William Godwin d.; Francis Bret Harte b.
1837	Carlyle, *The French Revolution*; Dickens, *The Pickwick Papers* (vol. pub.); *Oliver Twist* (monthly, Feb. 1837–Apr. 1839); Disraeli, *Henrietta Temple*; *Venetia*; Hawthorne, *Twice-told Tales* (2nd ser., 1842); Lockhart, *Life of Scott* (completed 1838); Lytton, *Ernest Maltravers*; Thackeray, *The Yellowplush Papers* (in *Fraser's Magazine*, 1837–8)	**Victoria** (–1901); Algernon Charles Swinburne b.; John Constable d.; Berlioz, *Grande Messe des morts*
1838	Elizabeth Barrett, *The Seraphim*; Dickens, *Nicholas Nickleby* (monthly, Apr. 1838–Oct. 1839); Lady Charlotte Guest (tr.), *The Mabinogion*; Surtees, *Jorrocks's Jaunts and Jollities* (orig. serialized 1831–4); Wordsworth, *Sonnets*	English Historical Society founded; Anti-Corn Law League established; Sir Charles Lyell, *Elements of Geology*
1839	Ainsworth, *Jack Sheppard*; C. Darwin, *Journal of Researches into the Geology and Natural History of the Various Countries Visited by H.M.S. Beagle*; Dickens, *Nicholas Nickleby* (vol. pub.); Thackeray, *Catherine* (serialized pseudonymously 1839–40; vol. pub. 1869)	Walter Pater b.; John Galt d.; Chartist Riots; Paul Cézanne b.
1840	Ainsworth, *The Tower of London*; Barham, *The Ingoldsby Legends*, 1st ser.; R. Browning, *Sordello*; J. F. Cooper, *The Pathfinder*; Dickens, *The Old Curiosity Shop* (weekly, 25 Apr. 1840–6 Feb. 1841)	Thomas Hardy b.; **Queen Victoria** marries Prince Albert; penny post introduced; Zola b.; Claude Monet b.; Auguste Rodin b.; Peter Ilich Tchaikovsky b.

Date	*Principal literary works*	*Other events*
1841	Ainsworth, *Old Saint Paul's*; Boucicault, *London Assurance*; R. Browning, *Pippa Passes*; Carlyle, *On Heroes, Hero-Worship and the Heroic in History*; Dickens, *The Old Curiosity Shop* (vol. pub.); *Barnaby Rudge* (weekly, 13 Feb.–27 Nov. 1841); Lever, *Charles O'Malley*; Marryat, *Masterman Ready*	*Punch* started; Pierre-Auguste Renoir b.; Antonin Dvořák b.
1842	Dickens, *American Notes*; Lytton, *Zanoni*; Macaulay, *Lays of Ancient Rome*; Tennyson, *Poems* (inc. 'Locksley Hall', 'Morte d'Arthur'); Wordsworth, *Poems Chiefly of Early and Late Years*	Thomas Arnold d.; Mallarmé b.; Stendhal d.
1843	Ainsworth, *Windsor Castle*; Borrow, *The Bible in Spain*; Carlyle, *Past and Present*; Dickens, *A Christmas Carol*; *Martin Chuzzlewit* (monthly, Jan. 1843–July 1844); Horne, *Orion*; Lytton, *The Last of the Barons*; Macaulay, *Critical and Historical Essays*; J. S. Mill, *System of Logic*; Ruskin, *Modern Painters*, i (ii: 1846; iii and iv 1856; v: 1860); Surtees, *Handley Cross* (expanded 1854)	Henry James b.; Robert Southey d.; Wordsworth poet laureate
1844	Barnes, *Poems of Rural Life in the Dorset Dialect*; Elizabeth Barrett, *Poems*; Dickens, *Martin Chuzzlewit* (vol. pub.); Disraeli, *Coningsby*; Horne, *The New Spirit of the Age*; Kinglake, *Eothen*; Thackeray, *The Luck of Barry Lyndon* (serialized Jan.–Dec. 1846, rev. and repr. 1856)	Robert Bridges b.; Gerard Manley Hopkins b.; William Beckford d.; railway mania (–1845); Verlaine b.; Nietzsche b.; Dumas, *Les Trois Mousquetaires*
1845	Dickens, *The Cricket on the Hearth*; Poe, *Tales of Mystery and Imagination*	Thomas Hood d.; Sydney Smith d.; Mérimée, *Carmen*
1846	C. Brontë, E. Brontë, and A. Brontë, *Poems by Currer, Ellis and Acton Bell*; Dickens, *Pictures from Italy*; *Dombey and Son* (monthly, Oct. 1846–Apr. 1848); G. Eliot, tr. Strauss's *The Life of Jesus Critically Examined*; Hawthorne, *Mosses from an Old Manse*; Lear, *A Book of Nonsense* (enlarged edns 1861, 1863); Melville, *Typee*; Ruskin, *Modern Painters*, ii	Marriage of Robert Browning and Elizabeth Barrett; Corn Laws abolished; Balzac, *La Cousine Bette*; Berlioz, *La Damnation de Faust*
1847	A. Brontë, *Agnes Grey* (by 'Acton Bell'); C. Brontë, *Jane Eyre* (by 'Currer Bell'); E. Brontë, *Wuthering Heights* (by 'Ellis Bell'); Disraeli, *Tancred*; Marryat, *Children of the New Forest*; Tennyson, *The Princess*; Thackeray, *Vanity Fair* (monthly, Jan. 1847–July 1848); Trollope, *The Macdermots of Ballycloran*	Balzac, *Le Cousin Pons*

Date	Principal literary works	Other events
1848	Ainsworth, *The Lancashire Witches*; A. Brontë, *The Tenant of Wildfell Hall*; Catherine Crowe, *The Night-side of Nature*; Dickens, *Dombey and Son* (vol. pub.); Gaskell, *Mary Barton*; Lytton, *Harold*; J. S. Mill, *Principles of Political Economy*; Thackeray, *Vanity Fair* (vol. pub.); *The History of Pendennis* (monthly, Nov. 1848–Dec. 1850)	Emily Brontë d.; Branwell Brontë d.; Frederick Marryat d.; Pre-Raphaelite Brotherhood formed; revolution in France; Chateaubriand d.; Marx and Engels, *Communist Manifesto*
1849	M. Arnold, *The Strayed Reveller and Other Poems*; C. Brontë, *Shirley*; Dickens, *David Copperfield* (monthly, May 1849–Nov. 1850); Macaulay, *History of England*, i and ii (iii and iv: 1855); Ruskin, *The Seven Lamps of Architecture*	Edmund Gosse b.; Anne Brontë d.; Maria Edgeworth d.; T. L. Beddoes d.; Edgar Allan Poe d.; *Notes and Queries* started; Sir Austin Layard, *Nineveh and its Remains*; Frédéric Chopin d.
1850	Beddoes (d. 1849), *Death's Jest Book*; E. B. Browning, *Poems* (inc. 'Sonnets from the Portuguese'); R. Browning, *Christmas Eve and Easter Day*; W. Collins, *After Dark*; Dickens, *David Copperfield* (vol. pub.); Hawthorne, *The Scarlet Letter*; Hunt, *Autobiography*; Kingsley, *Alton Locke*; Lytton, *The Caxtons*; Tennyson, *In Memoriam*; Wordsworth (d. 1850), *The Prelude*	R. L. Stevenson b.; Wordsworth d.; Tennyson poet laureate; Guy de Maupassant b.; Balzac d.; Wagner, *Lohengrin*; Public Libraries Act initiates modern public library system
1851	Borrow, *Lavengro*; Hawthorne, *The House of the Seven Gables*; Kingsley, *Yeast*; Melville, *Moby-Dick*; Meredith, *Poems*; Ruskin, *The King of the Golden River*; *The Stones of Venice*, i (ii and iii: 1853)	The Great Exhibition; Turner d.; Verdi, *Rigoletto*
1852	M. Arnold, *Empedocles on Etna and Other Poems*; Dickens, *Bleak House* (monthly, Mar. 1852–Sept. 1853); Stowe, *Uncle Tom's Cabin*; Thackeray, *The History of Henry Esmond*	George Moore b.; Thomas Moore d.
1853	M. Arnold, *Poems* (inc. 'Sohrab and Rustum', 'The Scholar-Gipsy'); C. Brontë, *Villette*; Dickens, *Bleak House* (vol. pub.); Gaskell, *Ruth*; *Cranford* (vol. pub.); Hawthorne, *Tanglewood Tales*; Kingsley, *Hypatia*; Surtees, *Mr Sponge's Sporting Tour*; Thackeray, *The Newcomes* (monthly, Oct. 1853–Aug. 1855)	Vincent van Gogh b.; Verdi, *Il trovatore*; *La traviata*
1854	W. Collins, *Hide and Seek*; Dickens, *Hard Times* (weekly, 1 Apr.–12 Aug. 1854, and vol. pub.); Patmore, *The Betrothal* (*The Angel in the House*, i); Tennyson, 'The Charge of the Light Brigade' (*Examiner*, 9 Dec.); Thoreau, *Walden*; Yonge, *The Little Duke*	Oscar Wilde b.; Crimean War (–1856); Rimbaud b.
1855	R. Browning, *Men and Women*; Dickens, *Little Dorrit* (monthly, Dec. 1855–June 1859); Gaskell, *Lizzie Leigh and Other Tales*; *North and South*	Charlotte Brontë d.; Mary Russell Mitford d.; *Daily Telegraph* started; Stamp Duty abolished

Date	*Principal literary works*	*Other events*
	(vol. pub.; serialized Sept. 1854–Jan. 1855); Kingsley, *Westward Ho!*; G. H. Lewes, *Life of Goethe*; Longfellow, *Hiawatha*; Tennyson, *Maud and Other Poems*; Trollope, *The Warden*; Whitman, *Leaves of Grass*	
1856	Kingsley, *The Heroes*; Melville, *The Piazza Tales*; Patmore, *The Espousals* (*The Angel in the House*, ii); Ruskin, *Modern Painters*, iii and iv	George Bernard Shaw b.; National Portrait Gallery founded; Freud b.; Heine d.; Flaubert, *Madame Bovary*; Robert Schumann d.
1857	Borrow, *The Romany Rye*; C. Brontë (d. 1855), *The Professor*; E. B. Browning, *Aurora Leigh*; Gaskell, *Life of Charlotte Brontë*; T. Hughes, *Tom Brown's Schooldays*; Trollope, *Barchester Towers*	Joseph Conrad b.; George Gissing b.; Museum of Ornamental Art (Victoria and Albert Museum) founded; Edward Elgar b.; Baudelaire, *Les Fleurs du mal*
1858	Clough, *Amours de voyage*; G. Eliot, *Scenes of Clerical Life*; Farrar, *Eric, or Little by Little*; Holmes, *The Autocrat of the Breakfast Table*; MacDonald, *Phantastes*; Trelawny, *Recollections of the Last Days of Shelley and Byron*; Trollope, *Doctor Thorne*; *The Three Clerks*	Indian Mutiny; Giacomo Puccini b.
1859	C. Darwin, *On the Origin of Species by Means of Natural Selection*; Dickens, *A Tale of Two Cities* (monthly, Apr.–Nov., and vol. pub.); G. Eliot, *Adam Bede*; E. Fitzgerald, *The Rubáiyát of Omar Khayyám*; Meredith, *The Ordeal of Richard Feverel*; J. S. Mill, *On Liberty*; Tennyson, *Idylls of the King* ('Enid', 'Vivien', 'Elaine', 'Guinevere'); Trollope, *The Bertrams*	Arthur Conan Doyle b.; Kenneth Grahame b.; A. E. Housman b.; Thomas de Quincey d.; Leigh Hunt d.; Lord Macaulay d.; War of Italian Liberation; Georges Seurat b.
1860	E. B. Browning, *Poems before Congress*; Collins, *The Woman in White* (vol. pub.; serialized 26 Nov. 1859–25 Aug. 1860); Dickens, *Great Expectations* (weekly, 1 Dec. 1860–3 Aug. 1861); G. Eliot, *The Mill on the Floss*; Patmore, *Faithful for Ever* (*The Angel in the House*, iii); Ruskin, *Modern Painters*, v	J. M. Barrie b.; Chekhov b.; Gustav Mahler b.; Walter Sickert b.; Schopenhauer d.
1861	Beeton, *Book of Household Management* (serialized 1859–61); Dickens, *Great Expectations* (vol. pub.); G. Eliot, *Silas Marner*; T. Hughes, *Tom Brown at Oxford*; Palgrave, *The Golden Treasury* (2nd ser. 1897); Peacock, *Gryll Grange* (serialized 1860); Reade, *The Cloister and the Hearth*; Thackeray, *Lovel the Widower* (serialized Jan.–June 1860); Trollope, *Framley Parsonage* (serialized Jan. 1860–Apr. 1861)	Elizabeth Barrett Browning d.; A. H. Clough d.; Prince Albert d.; American Civil War (–1865)
1862	Borrow, *Wild Wales*; Braddon, *Lady Audley's Secret*; E. B. Browning (d. 1861), *Last Poems* (ed.	M. R. James b.; Edith Wharton b.; Hugo, *Les Misérables*; Claude Debussy b.

Date	Principal literary works	Other events
	R. Browning); W. Collins, *No Name* (serialized Mar. 1862–Jan. 1863); Lytton, *A Strange Story*; Meredith, *Modern Love*; Patmore, *Victories of Love (The Angel in the House*, iv); C. Rossetti, *Goblin Market and Other Poems*; Trollope, *Orley Farm* (serialized Mar. 1861–Oct. 1862)	
1863	G. Eliot, *Romola*; Gaskell, *Sylvia's Lovers*; Kingsley, *The Water Babies*; Kinglake, *The Invasion of the Crimea*, i and ii (iii–iv: 1868; v: 1875; vi: 1880; vii and viii: 1887); Le Fanu, *The House by the Churchyard*; M. Oliphant, *Salem Chapel* (first of the Chronicles of Carlingford series); Reade, *Hard Cash* (serialized Mar.–Dec. 1863); Thackeray (d. 1863), *Roundabout Papers* (serialized Jan. 1860–Feb. 1863)	Arthur Quiller-Couch b.; W. M. Thackeray d.; Tolstoy, *War and Peace* (1863–9); Edvard Munch b.
1864	Dickens, *Our Mutual Friend* (monthly, May 1864–Nov. 1865); Gaskell, *Cousin Phillis*; Le Fanu, *Uncle Silas*; *Wylder's Hand*; Newman, *Apologia pro Vita Sua*; Trollope, *The Small House at Allington* (serialized Sept. 1862–Apr. 1864); *Can You Forgive Her?* (serialized Jan. 1864–Aug. 1865)	W. S. Landor d.; John Clare d.; R. S. Surtees d.; Nathaniel Hawthorne d.; Henri de Toulouse-Lautrec b.; Richard Strauss b.
1865	M. Arnold, *Essays in Criticism*, 1st ser.; Carroll, *Alice in Wonderland*; Dickens, *Our Mutual Friend* (vol. pub.); Meredith, *Rhoda Fleming*; Swinburne, *Atalanta in Calydon*; Trollope, *The Belton Estate* (serialized May 1865–Jan. 1866)	Rudyard Kipling b.; W. B. Yeats b.; A. E. W. Mason b.; Elizabeth Gaskell d.; Palmerston d.; Abraham Lincoln assassinated; Jean Sibelius b.; Wagner, *Tristan und Isolde*
1866	W. Collins, *Armadale* (serialized Nov. 1864–June 1866); Gaskell (d. 1865), *Wives and Daughters*; Kingsley, *Hereward the Wake*; Reade, *Griffith Gaunt*; Ruskin, *The Ethics of the Dust*; *The Crown of Wild Olives*; Swinburne, *Poems and Ballads*, 1st ser.	H. G. Wells b.; Thomas Love Peacock d.; John Keble d.; Jane Welsh Carlyle d.; Dostoevsky, *Crime and Punishment*
1867	M. Arnold, *New Poems* (inc. 'Thyrsis'); Bagehot, *The English Constitution*; Swinburne, *Song of Italy*; Trollope, *The Last Chronicle of Barset* (serialized Dec. 1866–July 1867); *The Claverings* (serialized Feb. 1866–May 1867)	Arnold Bennett b.; John Galsworthy b.; Arthur Rackham b.; Baudelaire d.; Second Reform Bill
1868	Alcott, *Little Women*; R. Browning, *The Ring and the Book*; W. Collins, *The Moonstone* (serialized Jan.–Aug. 1868); Morris, *The Earthly Paradise*, i (completed 1870); Queen Victoria, *Leaves from a Journal of our Life in the Highlands*	Gioachino Rossini d.; Dostoevsky, *The Idiot*
1869	M. Arnold, *Culture and Anarchy*; Blackmore, *Lorna Doone*; Gilbert, *Bab Ballads*; J. S. Mill, *On the Subjection of Women*; Tennyson, *The Holy Grail and Other Poems*; Trollope, *Phineas Finn:*	Suez Canal opened; André Gide b.; Gandhi b.; Berlioz d.; Henri Matisse b.

Date	*Principal literary works*	*Other events*
	The Irish Member (serialized Oct. 1867–May 1869); *He Knew He Was Right* (serialized Oct. 1868–May 1869)	
1870	Dickens, *The Mystery of Edwin Drood* (6 of 12 monthly parts completed, Apr.–Sept.); Disraeli, *Lothair*; Trollope, *The Vicar of Bullhampton* (serialized July 1869–May 1870)	Hilaire Belloc b.; Charles Dickens d.; Franco-Prussian War (–1871); Dumas d.; Mérimée d.; Lenin b.; first Married Women's Property Act
1871	Carroll, *Through the Looking-Glass*; G. Eliot, *Middlemarch* (8 parts, Dec. 1871–Dec. 1872); Hardy, *Desperate Remedies*; Lear, *Nonsense Songs, Stories, Botany and Alphabets*; Lytton, *The Coming Race*; MacDonald, *At the Back of the North Wind*; Meredith, *The Adventures of Harry Richmond*; Ruskin, *Fors Clavigera* (8 vols, 1871–84); Swinburne, *Songs before Sunrise*	Marcel Proust b.; Paul Valéry b.; Verdi, *Aida*
1872	S. Butler, *Erewhon*; G. Eliot, *Middlemarch* (vol. pub.); Forster, *Life of Dickens*, i (ii: 1873; iii: 1874); Hardy, *Under the Greenwood Tree*; Lear, *More Nonsense, Pictures, Rhymes, Botany etc.*; MacDonald, *The Princess and the Goblin*; Tennyson, *Gareth and Lynette*	Max Beerbohm b.; Bertrand Russell b.; Aubrey Beardsley b.; Ralph Vaughan Williams b.; Gautier d.; voting by ballot introduced
1873	M. Arnold, *Literature and Dogma*; Hardy, *A Pair of Blue Eyes*; J. S. Mill (d. 1873), *Autobiography*; Pater, *Studies in the Renaissance*; Trollope, *The Eustace Diamonds* (serialized July 1871–Feb. 1873)	Walter de la Mare b.; J. S. Mill d.; Edward Bulwer-Lytton d.; Tolstoy, *Anna Karenina* (–1877); Sergei Rachmaninov b.
1874	Hardy, *Far from the Madding Crowd*; J. Thomson, *City of Dreadful Night* (in *National Reformer*, pub. separately 1880); Trollope, *Phineas Redux* (serialized July 1873–Jan. 1874)	G. K. Chesterton b.; Winston Churchill b.; Somerset Maugham b.; Gertrude Stein b.; Arnold Schoenberg b.; Verdi, *Requiem*; Wagner, *Ring* cycle completed
1875	Keble, *Sermons for the Christian Year* (1875–80); Trollope, *The Way We Live Now* (serialized Feb. 1874–Sept. 1875)	Charles Kingsley d.; Maurice Ravel b.
1876	Carroll, *The Hunting of the Snark*; G. Eliot, *Daniel Deronda*; Hardy, *The Hand of Ethelberta*; H. James, *Roderick Hudson*; Meredith, *Beauchamp's Career*; Morris, *The Story of Sigurd the Volsung, and the Fall of the Niblungs*; Trollope, *The Prime Minister* (serialized May 1876–July 1877); Twain, *Adventures of Tom Sawyer*	George Sand d.; Brahms, First Symphony (completed)
1877	H. James, *The American*; Lear, *Laughable Lyrics*; Trollope, *The American Senator*	Ibsen, *Pillars of Society*; Tchaikovsky, *Swan Lake*
1878	Hardy, *The Return of the Native*; H. James, *The Europeans*; Swinburne, *Poems and Ballads*, 2nd ser.; Trollope, *Is He Popinjoy?* (serialized Oct. 1877–July 1878)	John Masefield b.; G. H. Lewes d.; Augustus John b.
1879	H. James, *Daisy Miller*; Meredith, *The Egoist*	E. M. Forster b.; Ibsen, *A Doll's House*; Tchaikovsky, *Eugene Onegin*; Stalin b.

Date	Principal literary works	Other events
1880	Disraeli, *Endymion*; Hardy, *The Trumpet-Major*; Joel Chandler Harris, *Uncle Remus*; Shorthouse, *John Inglesant*; Trollope, *The Duke's Children* (serialized Oct. 1879–July 1880)	Lytton Strachey b.; George Eliot d.; First Anglo-Boer War (–1881); Flaubert d.; Dostoevsky, *The Brothers Karamazov*
1881	Revised Version of the New Testament; Hardy, *A Laodicean*; H. James, *Portrait of a Lady*; *Washington Square*; D. G. Rossetti, *Ballads and Sonnets*; Stevenson, *Virginibus Puerisque*; Wilde, *Poems*	P. G. Wodehouse b.; Thomas Carlyle d.; Benjamin Disraeli d.; George Borrow d.; Samuel Palmer d.; Ibsen, *Ghosts*; Dostoevsky d.; Pablo Picasso b.; Béla Bartók b.
1882	Anstey, *Vice Versa*; Hardy, *Two on a Tower*; Jefferies, *Bevis*; Stevenson, *The New Arabian Nights*	James Joyce b.; Virginia Woolf b.; W. H. Ainsworth d.; Charles Darwin d.; Ralph Waldo Emerson d.; D. G. Rossetti d.; Anthony Trollope d.; second Married Women's Property Act; Wagner, *Parsifal*
1883	MacDonald, *The Princess and Curdie*; Schreiner, *The Story of an African Farm*; Stevenson, *Treasure Island* (serialized Oct. 1881–Jan. 1882); Trollope (d. 1882), *Mr Scarborough's Family* (serialized May 1882–June 1883); *An Autobiography*	William Carlos Williams b.; Nietzsche, *Also sprach Zarathustra*; Wagner d.; Marx d.; Mussolini b.
1884	Gissing, *The Unclassed*; Twain, *The Adventures of Huckleberry Finn*	Sean O'Casey b.; Hugh Walpole b.; Ivy Compton Burnett b.; Charles Reade d.; first *OED* begins to appear (–1928); Society of Authors founded; Huysmans, *À rebours*.
1885	Revised Version of the Old Testament; H. Rider Haggard, *King Solomon's Mines*; Meredith, *Diana of the Crossways*; Pater, *Marius the Epicurean*; Ruskin, *Praeterita* (completed 1889); Stevenson, *A Child's Garden of Verses*; *More New Arabian Nights*; Swinburne, *Marino Faliero*; Tennyson, *Tiresias and Other Poems*	D. H. Lawrence b.; Ezra Pound b.; fall of Khartoum; Victor Hugo d.; Zola, *Germinal*; Brahms, Fourth Symphony
1886	Alcott, *Jo's Boys*; Burnett, *Little Lord Fauntleroy*; Hardy, *The Mayor of Casterbridge*; H. James, *The Bostonians*; *The Princess Casamassima*; Kipling, *Departmental Ditties*; Stevenson, *The Strange Case of Dr Jekyll and Mr Hyde*; *Kidnapped*; Tennyson, *Locksley Hall Sixty Years after*	Charles Williams b.; Ronald Firbank b.; Franz Liszt d.
1887	Conan Doyle, *A Study in Scarlet*; Haggard, *She*; *Allan Quartermain*; Hardy, *The Woodlanders*; Pater, *Imaginary Portraits*	Rupert Brooke b.; Edith Sitwell b.; Richard Jefferies d.; Verdi, *Otello*
1888	M. Arnold (d. 1888), *Essays in Criticism*, 2nd ser.; Barrie, *Auld Licht Idylls*; Hardy, *Wessex Tales*; H. James, *The Aspern Papers*; Kipling, *Plain Tales from the Hills*; Stevenson, *The Black Arrow*	T. S. Eliot b.; T. E. Lawrence b.; Raymond Chandler b.; Eugene O'Neill b.; Matthew Arnold d.; Edward Lear d.

Date	*Principal literary works*	*Other events*
1889	Carroll, *Sylvie and Bruno*; Conan Doyle, *The Sign of Four*; Jerome, *Three Men in a Boat*; Stevenson, *The Master of Ballantrae*; *The Wrong Box* (with Lloyd Osbourne); Swinburne, *Poems and Ballads*, 3rd ser.; Tennyson, *Demeter and Other Poems*; Twain, *A Connecticut Yankee in King Arthur's Court*	Robert Browning d.; Gerard Manley Hopkins d.; Wilkie Collins d.; Tolstoy, *The Kreutzer Sonata*; Adolf Hitler b.; Ibsen's *A Doll's House* perf. in England
1890	Kipling, *The Light that Failed*	Agatha Christie b.; J. H. Newman d.; Ibsen, *Hedda Gabler*; Tchaikovsky, *The Sleeping Beauty*; Vincent van Gogh d.
1891	Bierce, *Tales of Soldiers and Civilians*; Conan Doyle, *The Adventures of Sherlock Holmes*; Gissing, *New Grub Street*; Hardy, *Tess of the d'Urbervilles*; *A Group of Noble Dames*; Kipling, *Life's Handicap*; Wilde, *Lord Arthur Savile's Crime and Other Stories*; *The Picture of Dorian Gray*	Herman Melville d.; Rimbaud d.; Huysmans, *Là-bas*; Sergei Prokofiev b.; Stanley Spencer b.
1892	Gissing, *Born in Exile*; Kipling, *Barrack-Room Ballads*; Shaw, *Widowers' Houses*	J. R. R. Tolkien b.; H. MacDiarmid b.; Rebecca West (Cecily Fairfield) b.; Lord Tennyson d.; Ibsen, *The Master Builder*; Tchaikovsky, *Nutcracker*
1893	Conan Doyle, *The Memoirs of Sherlock Holmes*; Stevenson, *Catriona*; Weyman, *A Gentleman of France*; Wilde, *Lady Windermere's Fan* (perf. 1892); Yeats, *The Celtic Twilight*	Guy de Maupassant d.; Taine d.; Joan Miró b.; Tchaikovsky, Sixth Symphony ('Pathétique'); Tchaikovsky d.; Dvořák, Symphony No. 9 ('From the New World')
1894	du Maurier, *Trilby*; G. and W. Grossmith, *The Diary of a Nobody*; Hardy, *Life's Little Ironies*; Hope, *The Prisoner of Zenda*; Kipling, *The Jungle Book*; Moore, *Esther Waters*; Swinburne, *Astrophel and Other Poems*; Wilde, *A Woman of No Importance* (perf. 1893); *Salomé* (English tr. Lord Alfred Douglas, illus. Aubrey Beardsley; perf. Paris 1896); Yeats, *The Land of Heart's Desire*	Aldous Huxley b.; J. B. Priestley b.; Robert Louis Stevenson d.; Walter Pater d.; Christina Rossetti d.; Beardsley *et al.*, *The Yellow Book* (–1897); Debussy, *Prélude à 'L'Après-midi d'un faune'*
1895	Grant Allen, *The Woman Who Did*; Conrad, *Almayer's Folly*; Crane, *The Red Badge of Courage*; Hardy, *Jude the Obscure*; Kipling, *The Second Jungle Book*; Wells, *The Time Machine*	Robert Graves b.; L. P. Hartley b.; F. R. Leavis b.; Chekhov, *The Seagull*; Jameson's raid into the Transvaal
1896	Belloc, *A Bad Child's Book of Beasts*; Conrad, *An Outcast of the Islands*; Housman, *A Shropshire Lad*; Stevenson (d. 1894), *Weir of Hermiston*; Wells, *The Island of Dr Moreau*	F. Scott Fitzgerald b.; William Morris d.; Coventry Patmore d.; George du Maurier d.; Alfred Austin poet laureate; J. E. Millais d.; Verlaine d.; Strauss, *Also sprach Zarathustra*; Puccini, *La Bohème*
1897	Conrad, *The Nigger of the 'Narcissus'*; Hardy, *The Well-Beloved*; H. James, *What Maisie Knew*; *The Spoils of Poynton*; Maugham, *Liza of Lambeth*; Meredith, *Essay on Comedy*; Wells, *The Invisible Man*; Yeats, *Adoration of the Magi*	Tate Gallery opened; Rostand, *Cyrano de Bergerac*; Brahms d.

Date	Principal literary works	Other events
1898	Hardy, *Wessex Poems*; H. James, *The Two Magics* (inc. 'The Turn of the Screw'); Wells, *The War of the Worlds*; Wilde, *The Ballad of Reading Gaol*	C. S. Lewis b.; Ernest Hemingway b.; Lewis Carroll d.; Mallarmé d.; Aubrey Beardsley d.; Zola, 'J'accuse'
1899	Hornung, *The Amateur Cracksman*; H. James, *The Awkward Age*; Kipling, *Stalky & Co.*; Somerville and Ross, *Some Experiences of an Irish R. M.*; Wilde, *The Importance of Being Earnest* (perf. 1895); *An Ideal Husband* (perf. 1895)	Noël Coward b.; Second Anglo-Boer War (–1902); Vladimir Nabokov b.; Tolstoy, *Resurrection*; Elgar, *Enigma Variations*; Sibelius, *Finlandia*
1900	Conrad, *Lord Jim*; Dreiser, *Sister Carrie*; Wells, *Love and Mr Lewisham*	John Ruskin d.; Oscar Wilde d.; Nietzsche d.; Boxer Rising (–1901); S. Freud, *The Interpretation of Dreams*; Elgar, *The Dream of Gerontius*; Mahler, Fourth Symphony; Puccini, *Tosca*; Kurt Weill b.
1901	Bennett, *Anna of the Five Towns*; Butler, *Erewhon Revisited*; Hardy, *Poems of the Past and Present*; Jacobs, *Light Freights*; Kipling, *Kim*; Wells, *The First Men in the Moon*	**Edward VII** (–1910); Roy Campbell b.; C. M. Yonge d.; Chekhov, *Three Sisters*; Walt Disney b.; Giuseppe Verdi d.; Toulouse-Lautrec d.
1902	Barrie, *The Admirable Crichton* (perf.; pub. 1914); *Quality Street* (perf.; pub. 1913); Conrad, *Youth*; *Typhoon*; de la Mare, *Songs of Childhood* (as 'Walter Ramal'); Conan Doyle, *The Hound of the Baskervilles*; H. James, *The Wings of the Dove*; W. James, *The Varieties of Religious Experience*; Kipling, *Just So Stories*; Mason, *The Four Feathers*; Potter, *Peter Rabbit*; Yeats, *Cathleen Ni Houlihan*	Samuel Butler d.; *Times Literary Supplement* started; Zola d.; C. Rhodes d.; William Walton b.; Debussy, *Pelléas et Mélisande*; Anglo-Japanese Treaty
1903	Butler (d. 1902), *The Way of All Flesh*; Childers, *The Riddle of the Sands*; Gissing (d. 1903), *The Private Papers of Henry Ryecroft*; H. James, *The Ambassadors*; London, *The Call of the Wild*; Yeats, *Ideas of Good and Evil*	George Orwell (Eric Blair) b.; Evelyn Waugh b.; George Gissing d.; Herbert Spencer d.; *Daily Mirror* started; J. A. M. Whistler d.; Paul Gauguin d.
1904	Barrie, *Peter Pan* (stage version); Chesterton, *The Napoleon of Notting Hill*; Conrad, *Nostromo*; Hardy, *The Dynasts*, i; Hudson, *Green Mansions*; H. James, *The Golden Bowl*; M. R. James, *Ghost Stories of an Antiquary*; Rolfe, *Hadrian the Seventh*	Graham Greene b.; Christopher Isherwood b.; C. Day-Lewis b.; Sir Leslie Stephen d.; Abbey Theatre, Dublin, founded; Chekhov, *The Cherry Orchard*; Chekhov d.; Salvador Dali b.; Dvořák d.; Puccini, *Madame Butterfly*
1905	Forster, *Where Angels Fear to Tread*; Orczy, *The Scarlet Pimpernel*; Shaw, *Major Barbara* (perf., pub. 1907); Wells, *A Modern Utopia*; *Kipps*; Wharton, *The House of Mirth*; Wilde (d. 1900), *De Profundis*	C. P. Snow b.; Arthur Koestler b.; Jean-Paul Sartre b.; Debussy, *La Mer*; mutiny on *Battleship Potemkin*; Sinn Fein founded in Dublin
1906	Barrie, *Peter Pan in Kensington Gardens*; Conrad, *The Mirror of the Sea*; Galsworthy, *A Man of Property*; Hardy, *The Dynasts*, ii; Kipling, *Puck of Pook's Hill*; London, *White Fang*; Nesbit, *The Railway Children*	Samuel Beckett b.; Ibsen d.; Cézanne d.; Elgar, *The Kingdom*

Date	*Principal literary works*	*Other events*
1907	Belloc, *Cautionary Tales for Children*; Conrad, *The Secret Agent*; Forster, *The Longest Journey*; Gosse, *Father and Son*; Joyce, *Chamber Music*; Synge, *The Playboy of the Western World*; Yeats, *Deirdre*	W. H. Auden b.; Louis MacNeice b.; Daphne du Maurier b.; J. K. Huysmans d.; H. Bergson, *L'Evolution créatrice*
1908	Barrie, *What Every Woman Knows*; Bennett, *The Old Wives' Tale*; Chesterton, *The Man Who Was Thursday*; W. H. Davies, *The Autobiography of a Super-Tramp*; Forster, *A Room with a View*; Grahame, *The Wind in the Willows*; Hardy, *The Dynasts*, iii; Pound, *A Lume Spento*; Wells, *The War in the Air*	Ian Fleming b.; Simone de Beauvoir b.
1909	Hardy, *Time's Laughingstocks*; Pound, *Personae*; Wells, *Tono-Bungay*	George Meredith d.; A. C. Swinburne d.; J. M. Synge d.; S. Spender b.
1910	Bennett, *Clayhanger*; Buchan, *Prester John*; Forster, *Howards End*; Kipling, *Rewards and Fairies*; Wells, *The History of Mr Polly*	**George V** (–1936); William James d.; Mark Twain d.; Tolstoy d.; Elgar, Violin Concerto; Vaughan Williams, *Fantasia on a Theme by Tallis*; Stravinsky, *The Firebird*; Henri ('Douanier') Rousseau d.
1911	Beerbohm, *Zuleika Dobson*; Bennett, *Hilda Lessways*; R. Brooke, *Poems 1911*; Burnett, *The Secret Garden*; Chesterton, *The Innocence of Father Brown*; Conrad, *Under Western Eyes*; Munro ('Saki'), *Chronicles of Clovis*; Pound, *Canzoni*; Hugh Walpole, *Mr Perrin and Mr Traill*; Wells, *The Country of the Blind*; Wharton, *Ethan Frome*	William Golding b.; Mervyn Peake b.; Terence Rattigan b.; Tennessee Williams b.; W. S. Gilbert d.; Gustave Mahler d.; Strauss, *Der Rosenkavalier*; Agadir crisis; Copyright Act extends posthumous copyright
1912	E. C. Bentley, *Trent's Last Case*; de la Mare, *The Listeners and Other Poems*; Munro ('Saki'), *The Unbearable Bassington*; Pound, *Ripostes*; Shaw, *Pygmalion*	Lawrence Durrell b.; Roy Fuller b.; Patrick White b.; Thomas Mann, *Der Tod in Venedig* (Death in Venice); Jackson Pollock b.; John Cage b.; Ravel, *Daphnis et Chloé*
1913	Conrad, *Chance*; de la Mare, *Peacock Pie*; Flecker, *The Golden Journey to Samarkand*; D. H. Lawrence, *Sons and Lovers*; Mackenzie, *Sinister Street*, i	Angus Wilson b.; S. Freud, *Totem and Taboo*; Proust, *Du côté de chez Swann* (*Swann's Way*, vol. i of *À la recherche du temps perdu*, completed 1927); Alain-Fournier, *Le Grand Meaulnes*; Benjamin Britten b.; Stravinsky, *The Rite of Spring*; Robert Bridges poet laureate;
1914	Hardy, *Satires of Circumstance*; Joyce, *Dubliners*; Mackenzie, *Sinister Street*, ii; Yeats, *Responsibilities*	Dylan Thomas b.; Britain declares war on Germany (4 Aug.); Alain-Fournier d.; Vaughan Williams, *The Lark Ascending*
1915	R. Brooke, *1914 and Other Poems*; Buchan, *The Thirty-Nine Steps*; Conrad, *Victory*; F. M. Ford, *The Good Soldier*; D. H. Lawrence, *The Rainbow*;	Rupert Brooke d.; Mary Elizabeth Braddon d.; James Elroy Flecker d.; first Zeppelin attack on London

Date	Principal literary works	Other events
	Maugham, *Of Human Bondage*; Pound, *Cathay*; D. Richardson, *Pointed Roofs* (*Pilgrimage*, I); V. Woolf, *The Voyage Out*; Yeats, *Reveries over Childhood and Youth*	
1916	Bennett, *These Twain*; Buchan, *Greenmantle*; Graves, Over *the Brazier*; Joyce, *A Portrait of the Artist as a Young Man*; G. Moore, *The Brook Kerith*; Pound, *Lustra*	Henry James d.; H. H. Munro ('Saki') d.; battle of Verdun 21 Feb.–16 Dec.; battle of the Somme 1 July–8 Nov.; Easter Rising, Dublin; execution of Roger Casement, 3 Aug.
1917	Conrad, *The Shadow-Line*; T. S. Eliot, *Prufrock and Other Observations*; A. Waugh, *The Loom of Youth*; Mary Webb, *Gone to Earth*; Yeats, *The Wild Swans at Coole*	Anthony Burgess b.; Edward Thomas d.; battle of Paschendaele 31 July–6 Nov.; Russian Revolution; Auguste Rodin d.; Edgar Degas d.
1918	R. Brooke (d. 1915), *Collected Poems* (memoir by E. Marsh); Hopkins (d. 1889), *Poems* (ed. R. Bridges); Joyce, *Exiles*; W. Lewis, *Tarr*; Strachey, *Eminent Victorians*; R. West, *The Return of the Soldier*	Wilfred Owen d.; 'Spanish flu' pandemic; Armistice (11 Nov.); women over 30 gain vote; Guillaume Apollinaire d.; Claude Debussy d.
1919	Ashford, *The Young Visiters*; Beerbohm, *Seven Men*; Buchan, *Mr Standfast*; T. S. Eliot, *Poems*; Hardy, *Collected Poems*; M. Keynes, *The Economic Consequences of the Peace*; Pound, *Quia Pauper Amavi*; Sassoon, *War Poems*; Shaw, *Heartbreak House*; May Sinclair, *Mary Olivier: A Life*; V. Woolf, *Night and Day*	Elgar, Cello Concerto; Renoir d.; Treaty of Versailles; Lady Astor first woman MP
1920	T. S. Eliot, *The Sacred Wood*; F. Scott Fitzgerald, *This Side of Paradise*; Galsworthy, *In Chancery*; D. H. Lawrence, *Women in Love*; O'Neill, *Beyond the Horizon*; Pound, *Hugh Selwyn Mauberley*; Wells, *The Outline of History*; Wharton, *The Age of Innocence*; Yeats, *Michael Robartes and the Dancer*	Paul Scott b.; Amedeo Modigliani d.; League of Nations established
1921	de la Mare, *Memoirs of a Midget*; Galsworthy, *To Let*; A. Huxley, *Crome Yellow*; Shaw, *Back to Methuselah*; Svevo, *Confessions of Zeno*; Yeats, *Four Plays for Dancers*	Irish Free State established; Vaughan Williams, Pastoral Symphony; Prokofiev, *The Love of Three Oranges*
1922	Crompton, *Just William*; T. S. Eliot, *The Waste Land*; F. Scott Fitzgerald, *Tales of the Jazz Age*; *The Beautiful and the Damned*; Galsworthy, *The Forsyte Saga* (in one vol.); D. Garnett, *Lady into Fox*; Hardy, *Late Lyrics and Earlier*; Joyce, *Ulysses*; D. H. Lawrence, *Aaron's Rod*; May Sinclair, *The Life and Death of Harriet Frean*; V. Woolf, *Jacob's Room*; Yeats, *Later Poems*	Philip Larkin b.; Wilfrid Scawen Blunt d.; T. S. Eliot founds the *Criterion*; Marcel Proust d.; Michael Collins assassinated; Gandhi imprisoned for civil disobedience; Mussolini's march on Rome; Wittgenstein, *Tractatus Logico-Philosophicus*
1923	Bennett, *Riceyman Steps*; Conrad, *The Rover*; A. Huxley, *Antic Hay*; D. H. Lawrence, *Kangaroo*;	Katherine Mansfield d.

Date	*Principal literary works*	*Other events*
	Masefield, *Collected Poems*; E. Sitwell, *Façade*; W. Stevens, *Harmonium*	
1924	Arlen, *The Green Hat*; R. Firbank, *Prancing Nigger*; Forster, *A Passage to India*; Milne, *When We Were Very Young*; I. A. Richards, *Principles of Literary Criticism*; Shaw, *Saint Joan*; Webb, *Precious Bane*; Wodehouse, *The Inimitable Jeeves*	James Baldwin b.; Joseph Conrad d.; Franz Kafka d.; first Labour government; Lenin d.; Puccini d.
1925	Compton-Burnett, *Pastors and Masters*; Coward, *Hay Fever*; Dreiser, *An American Tragedy*; T. S. Eliot, *Poems 1905–25*; F. Scott Fitzgerald, *The Great Gatsby*; A. Huxley, *Those Barren Leaves*; Loos, *Gentlemen Prefer Blondes*; O'Casey, *Juno and the Paycock*; Pound, *A Draft of XVI Cantos*; Wodehouse, *Carry on, Jeeves*; V. Woolf, *Mrs Dalloway*; *The Common Reader*, 1st ser.; Yeats, *A Vision*	Sir Henry Rider Haggard d.; A. C. Benson d.; *New Yorker* started; Hitler, *Mein Kampf*, vol. i; S. Eisenstein, *Battleship Potemkin*
1926	Christie, *The Murder of Roger Ackroyd*; Hemingway, *Fiesta* (*The Sun Also Rises*); D. H. Lawrence, *The Plumed Serpent*; T. E. Lawrence, *The Seven Pillars of Wisdom*; Milne, *Winnie-the-Pooh*; O'Casey, *The Plough and the Stars*; Warner, *Lolly Willowes*	Ronald Firbank d.; General Strike 3–12 May; Rainer Maria Rilke d.; Claude Monet d.; Alban Berg, *Wozzeck*; Hitler, *Mein Kampf*, vol. ii; Fritz Lang, *Metropolis*; Rudolf Valentino d.
1927	Forster, *Aspects of the Novel*; Hemingway, *Men without Women*; R. Lehmann, *Dusty Answer*; S. Lewis, *Elmer Gantry*; Milne, *Now We Are Six*; T. F. Powys, *Mr Weston's Good Wine*; Wilder, *The Bridge of San Luis Rey*; V. Woolf, *To the Lighthouse*	Jerome K. Jerome d.; *The Jazz Singer*, with Al Jolson; Rex Whistler's frescos for Tate Gallery
1928	T. S. Eliot, *For Lancelot Andrewes*; R. Hall, *The Well of Loneliness*; A. Huxley, *Point Counter Point*; Joyce, *Anna Livia Plurabelle*; D. H. Lawrence, *Lady Chatterley's Lover* (privately printed, Florence); Milne, *The House at Pooh Corner*; J. Rhys, *Quartet*; Sassoon, *Memoirs of a Fox-Hunting Man*; E. Waugh, *Decline and Fall*; V. Woolf, *Orlando*; Yeats, *The Tower*	Thomas Hardy d.; Edmund Gosse d.; Ravel, *Boléro*; Women's Suffrage extended to women over 21
1929	Bridges, *The Testament of Beauty*; Compton-Burnett, *Brothers and Sisters*; Faulkner, *The Sound and the Fury*; Graves, *Goodbye to All That*; H. Green, *Living*; Hemingway, *A Farewell to Arms*; R. Hughes, *A High Wind in Jamaica*; Priestley, *The Good Companions*; Wolfe, *Look Homeward, Angel*; V. Woolf, *A Room of one's Own*; Yeats, *The Winding Stair*	John Osborne b.
1930	Auden, *Poems*; Coward, *Private Lives*; Delafield, *The Diary of a Provincial Lady*; Empson, *Seven*	D. H. Lawrence d.; Sir Arthur Conan Doyle d.; Robert Bridges d.; John

Date	Principal literary works	Other events
	Types of Ambiguity; Faulkner, *As I Lay Dying*; Hammett, *The Maltese Falcon*; A. W. Lewis, *The Apes of God*; Maugham, *Cakes and Ale*; Priestley, *Angel Pavement*; H. Walpole, *The Herries Chronicle* (completed 1933); E. Waugh, *Vile Bodies*	Masefield poet laureate; Ted Hughes b.; *The Blue Angel*, with Marlene Dietrich; France begins building Maginot line
1931	Coward, *Cavalcade*; Hanley, *Boy*; O'Neill, *Mourning Becomes Electra*; Powell, *Afternoon Men*; E. Wilson, *Axel's Castle*; V. Woolf, *The Waves*	Arnold Bennett d.; Oswald Mosley forms new party; Britain abandons gold standard; *Frankenstein*, with Boris Karloff
1932	Auden, *The Orators*; T. S. Eliot, *Sweeney Agonistes*; *Selected Essays*; Gibbons, *Cold Comfort Farm*; Hardy (d. 1928), *Collected Poems*; Hemingway, *Death in the Afternoon*; A. Huxley, *Brave New World*; Isherwood, *The Memorial*; D. H. Lawrence, *Lady Chatterley's Lover* (expurgated); F. R. Leavis, *New Bearings in English Poetry*; Powell, *Venusberg*; E. Waugh, *Black Mischief*; Yeats, *Words for Music Perhaps*	Lytton Strachey d.; Kenneth Grahame d.; *Scrutiny* started
1933	Auden, *The Dance of Death*; Day-Lewis, *The Magnetic Mountain*; T. S. Eliot, *The Use of Poetry and the Use of Criticism*; Orwell, *Down and Out in Paris and London*; J. C. Powys, *A Glastonbury Romance*; Sayers, *Murder Must Advertise*; Spender, *Poems*; Stein, *The Autobiography of Alice B. Toklas*; Wells, *The Shape of Things to Come*; A. White, *Frost in May*; Yeats, *Collected Poems*	Joe Orton b.; John Galsworthy d.; George Moore d.; Mario Praz, *The Romantic Agony*; Hitler becomes German chancellor
1934	Christie, *Murder on the Orient Express*; F. Scott Fitzgerald, *Tender is the Night*; Graves, *I, Claudius*; *Claudius the God*; J. Hilton, *Goodbye Mr Chips*; H. Miller, *Tropic of Cancer*; Sayers, *The Nine Tailors*; E. Waugh, *A Handful of Dust*; W. Carlos Williams, *Collected Poems*	Sir Edward Elgar d.; Gustav Holst d.; Frederick Delius d.
1935	Bagnold, *National Velvet*; E. F. Benson, *Mapp and Lucia*; Day-Lewis, *A Time to Dance*; T. S. Eliot, *Murder in the Cathedral*; Empson, *Some Versions of Pastoral*; *Poems*; Isherwood, *Mr Norris Changes Trains*; MacNeice, *Poems*; Wodehouse, *Blandings Castle*; Yeats, *A Full Moon in March*	T. E. Lawrence d.; A. Hitchcock, *The Thirty-Nine Steps*
1936	Auden, *Look, Stranger!*; Auden and Isherwood, *The Ascent of F6* (perf. 1937); T. S. Eliot, *Collected Poems 1909–35* (inc. 'Burnt Norton'); Faulkner, *Absalom, Absalom!*; Forster, *Abinger Harvest*; A. Huxley, *Eyeless in Gaza*; C. S. Lewis, *The Allegory of Love*; Mitchell, *Gone with the Wind*; Orwell,	**Edward VIII** (Jan.–Dec.); **Edward VIII** abdicates (11 Dec.); **George VI** (–1952); G. K. Chesterton d.; Rudyard Kipling d.; A. E. Housman d.; M. R. James d.; Penguin Books founded by Allen Lane; BBC Television Service

Date	Principal literary works	Other events
	Keep the Aspidistra Flying; Sassoon, *Sherston's Progress*; Dylan Thomas, *Twenty-Five Poems*	begins (Nov.); Spanish Civil War; Maxim Gorky d.; Luigi Pirandello d.
1937	Auden and MacNeice, *Letters from Iceland*; Hemingway, *To Have and Have Not*; D. Jones, *In Parenthesis*; Kipling (d. 1936), *Something of Myself*; Orwell, *The Road to Wigan Pier*; Priestley, *Time and the Conways*; Steinbeck, *Of Mice and Men*; Tolkien, *The Hobbit*; V. Woolf, *The Years*	J. M. Barrie d.; Edith Wharton d.; Ravel d.; Picasso, *Guernica*; W. Disney, *Snow White and the Seven Dwarfs*
1938	Beckett, *Murphy*; E. Bowen, *The Death of the Heart*; Connolly, *Enemies of Promise*; Dos Passos, *U.S.A.*; du Maurier, *Rebecca*; Orwell, *Homage to Catalonia*; E. Waugh, *Scoop*; Wodehouse, *The Code of the Woosters*; Yeats, *New Poems*	Munich agreement (30 September); Prokofiev, *Romeo and Juliet*; A. Hitchcock, *The Lady Vanishes*; S. Eisenstein, *Alexander Nevsky*
1939	Ambler, *The Mask of Dimitrios*; Compton-Burnett, *A Family and a Fortune*; T. S. Eliot, *The Family Reunion*; *Old Possum's Book of Practical Cats*; Forester, *Captain Hornblower, RN*; Greene, *The Confidential Agent*; Household, *Rogue Male*; A. Huxley, *After Many a Summer*; Isherwood, *Goodbye to Berlin*; Joyce, *Finnegans Wake*; MacNeice, *Autumn Journal*; H. Miller, *Tropic of Capricorn*; F. O'Brien, *At Swim Two-Birds*; Orwell, *Coming up for Air*; Steinbeck, *The Grapes of Wrath*; Flora Thompson, *Lark Rise*; T. H. White, *The Sword in the Stone*; Yeats (d. 1939), *Last Poems and Two Plays*	W. B. Yeats d.; Ford Madox Ford d.; Second World War begins (3 Sept.); film of *Gone with the Wind*; Arthur Rackham d.; Sigmund Freud d.; *The Wizard of Oz*, with Judy Garland
1940	Auden, *Another Time*; Betjeman, *Old Lights for New Chancels*; Chandler, *Farewell, my Lovely*; Day-Lewis, *Poems in Wartime*; T. S. Eliot, 'East Coker' (in *New English Weekly*); Greene, *The Power and the Glory*; Hemingway, *For Whom the Bell Tolls*; Koestler, *Darkness at Noon*; Dylan Thomas, *Portrait of the Artist as a Young Dog*	F. Scott Fitzgerald d.; W. H. Davies d.; fall of France; Battle of Britain; Leon Trotsky d.; C. Chaplin, *The Great Dictator*
1941	Auden, *New Year Letters* (*The Double Man*); Compton-Burnett, *Parents and Children*; Coward, *Blithe Spirit*; T. S. Eliot, 'The Dry Salvages' (in *New English Weekly*); F. Scott Fitzgerald (d. 1940), *The Last Tycoon*; P. Hamilton, *Hangover Square*; E. Wilson, *The Wound and the Bow*; V. Woolf (d. 1941), *Between the Acts*	James Joyce d.; Virginia Woolf d.; J. G. Frazer d.; Rabindranath Tagore d.; Sherwood Anderson d.; Japanese attack Pearl Harbor; USA, and Soviet Union enter war; Brecht, *Mutter Courage*; Orson Welles, *Citizen Kane*
1942	de la Mare, *Collected Poems*; T. S. Eliot, 'Little Gidding' (in *New English Weekly*); C. S. Lewis, *The Screwtape Letters*; E. Waugh, *Put out More Flags*; V. Woolf (d. 1941), *The Death of the Moth*	Walter Sickert d.; Anouilh, *Antigone*; fall of Singapore; *Casablanca*, with Humphrey Bogart

Date	Principal literary works	Other events
1943	Graves, *Wife to Mr Milton*	Allied invasion of Italy; Rachmaninov d.; M. Powell and E. Pressburger, *Life and Death of Colonel Blimp*
1944	Auden, *For the Time Being*; Betjeman, *New Bats in Old Belfries*; J. Cary, *The Horse's Mouth*; Compton-Burnett, *Elders and Betters*; T. S. Eliot, *Four Quartets*; L. P. Hartley, *The Shrimp and the Anemone*	Normandy landings (6 June); Education Act introduces system of grammar schools, secondary technical schools, and secondary modern schools; Laurence Olivier's film of *Henry V*; Saint-Exupéry d.; Sartre, *Huis Clos* (In Camera); Edvard Munch d.
1945	Connolly, *The Unquiet Grave*; T. S. Eliot, *What is a Classic?*; H. Green, *Loving*; N. Mitford, *The Pursuit of Love*; Orwell, *Animal Farm*; E. Waugh, *Brideshead Revisited*; Wells, *Mind at the End of its Tether*	Charles Williams d.; Theodor Dreiser d.; Second World War ends (VE Day 8 May; VJ Day 15 Aug. / 2 Sept. (USA)); Hitler d.; F. D. Roosevelt d.; Mussolini d.; Paul Valéry d.; Britten, *Peter Grimes*; Béla Bartók d.; David Lean, *Brief Encounter*
1946	R. Campbell, *Talking Bronco*; de la Mare, *The Traveller*; L. P. Hartley, *The Sixth Heaven*; O'Neill, *The Iceman Cometh*; Peake, *Titus Groan*; Priestley, *An Inspector Calls*; Rattigan, *The Winslow Boy*	M. Sinclair d.; H. G. Wells d.; Damon Runyon d.; Nuremberg trials; nationalization of major industries begins; Bertrand Russell, *History of Western Philosophy*; Prokofiev, *Betrothal in a Monastery* (*The Duenna*)
1947	Graves, *The White Goddess*; L. P. Hartley, *Eustace and Hilda*; Larkin, *A Girl in Winter*; Lowry, *Under the Volcano*; MacNeice, *The Dark Tower*; Snow, *The Light and the Dark*; T. Williams, *A Streetcar Named Desire*	Flora Thompson d.; Partition of India, Pakistan established; Camus, *La Peste* (The Plague)
1948	Auden, *The Age of Anxiety*; Betjeman, *Selected Poems*; T. S. Eliot, *Notes towards the Definition of Culture*; Greene, *The Heart of the Matter*; F. R. Leavis, *The Great Tradition*; Mailer, *The Naked and the Dead*; Paton, *Cry, the Beloved Country*; Pound, *Pisan Cantos*; Rattigan, *The Browning Version*; E. Waugh, *The Loved One*	Gandhi assassinated; Strauss, *Four Last Songs*; *Hamlet*, with L. Olivier; the *Empire Windrush* brings first large group of West Indian immigrants to Britain
1949	C. Fry, *The Lady's Not for Burning*; Orwell, *Nineteen Eighty-Four*; A. Miller, *Death of a Salesman*; N. Mitford, *Love in a Cold Climate*; Snow, *Time of Hope*	NATO founded; Richard Strauss d.; film of *The Third Man* (see Greene 1950)
1950	Auden, *Collected Shorter Poems 1930–1944*; T. S. Eliot, *The Cocktail Party*; Greene, *The Third Man*; C. S. Lewis, *The Lion, the Witch, and the Wardrobe*; D. Lessing, *The Grass is Singing*; Peake, *Gormenghast*; Pound, *Seventy Cantos*; A. Wilson, *Such Darling Dodos*	Bernard Shaw d.; George Orwell d.; Kurt Weill d.; Korean War begins

Date	Principal literary works	Other events
1951	Auden, *Nones*; W. Robertson Davies, *Tempest-Tost* (*The Salterton Trilogy*, i); Forster, *Two Cheers for Democracy*; Greene, *The End of the Affair*; Powell, *A Question of Upbringing* (first vol. in *A Dance to the Music of Time*); Salinger, *The Catcher in the Rye*; Snow, *The Masters*; Wyndham, *The Day of the Triffids*	André Gide d.; Schoenberg d.; Britten, *Billy Budd*; defection of Burgess and Maclean; *The Archers* begins on BBC Light Programme
1952	Christie, *The Mousetrap*; R. Ellison, *Invisible Man*; Hemingway, *The Old Man and the Sea*; F. R. Leavis, *The Common Pursuit*; D. Lessing, *Martha Quest*; Powell, *A Buyer's Market*; Dylan Thomas, *Collected Poems 1934–52*; E. Waugh, *Men at Arms*; A. Wilson, *Hemlock and After*	**Elizabeth II**; Britain produces atomic bomb; Mau Mau active in Kenya
1953	Baldwin, *Go Tell It on the Mountain*; Beckett, *Watt* (written 1944); R. Bradbury, *Fahrenheit 451*; Brophy, *Hackenfeller's Ape*; I. Fleming, *Casino Royale*; L. P. Hartley, *The Go-Between*; R. Lehmann, *The Echoing Grove*; A. Miller, *The Crucible*; Wain, *Hurry on Down*	Dylan Thomas d.; Hilaire Belloc d.; Eugene O'Neill d.; Stalin d.; Prokofiev d.; conquest of Everest; coronation of Elizabeth II (2 June); execution of Rosenbergs in USA
1954	K. Amis, *Lucky Jim*; Betjeman, *A Few Late Chrysanthemums*; W. Robertson Davies, *Leaven of Malice* (*The Salterton Trilogy*, ii); T. S. Eliot, *The Confidential Clerk*; Golding, *Lord of the Flies*; T. Gunn, *Fighting Terms*; A. Huxley, *The Doors of Perception*; D. Lessing, *A Proper Marriage*; MacNeice, *Autumn Sequel*; Murdoch, *Under the Net*; Rattigan, *Separate Tables*; W. Stevens, *Collected Poems*; Dylan Thomas (d. 1953), *Under Milk Wood* (broadcast); Tolkien, *The Fellowship of the Ring*; *The Two Towers* (Pts i and ii of *The Lord of the Rings*)	Henri Matisse d.; Nasser seizes power in Egypt; E. Kazan, *On the Waterfront*
1955	K. Amis, *That Uncertain Feeling*; Auden, *The Shield of Achilles*; Beckett, *Waiting for Godot* (pub. in French 1952); Donleavy, *The Ginger Man*; Greene, *The Quiet American*; Larkin, *The Less Deceived*; C. S. Lewis, *Surprised by Joy*; Nabokov, *Lolita*; Powell, *The Acceptance World*; Tolkien, *The Return of the King* (Pt iii of *The Lord of the Rings*); E. Waugh, *Officers and Gentlemen*; T. Williams, *Cat on a Hot Tin Roof*	Thomas Mann d.; Albert Einstein d.; *Rebel without a Cause*, with James Dean; L. Olivier's film of *Richard III*
1956	Baldwin, *Giovanni's Room*; Beckett, *Malone Dies* (French, 1951); Bedford, *A Legacy*; Highsmith, *The Talented Mr Ripley*; R. Macaulay, *The Towers of Trebizond*; O'Neill (d. 1953), *Long Day's Journey into Night* (written 1940–1); J. Osborne, *Look*	Walter de la Mare d.; Sir Max Beerbohm d.; Jackson Pollock d.; Suez crisis; Copyright Act; first Aldermaston march; Hungarian uprising; *My Fair Lady*

Date	Principal literary works	Other events
	Back in Anger; A. Wilson, *Anglo-Saxon Attitudes*; C. Wilson, *The Outsider*	
1957	Braine, *Room at the Top*; L. Durrell, *Justine* (*Alexandria Quartet*, i); T. S. Eliot, *On Poetry and Poets*; Ted Hughes, *The Hawk in the Rain*; Kerouac, *On the Road*; J. Osborne, *The Entertainer*; Powell, *At Lady Molly's*; E. Waugh, *The Ordeal of Gilbert Pinfold*; P. White, *Voss*	Malcolm Lowry d.; D. Richardson d.; Dorothy L. Sayers d.; Sibelius d.; Bernstein, *West Side Story*; I. Bergman, *The Seventh Seal*
1958	Achebe, *Things Fall Apart*; Bates, *The Darling Buds of May*; Beckett, *Krapp's Last Tape*; W. Robertson Davies, *A Mixture of Frailties* (*The Salterton Trilogy*, iii); Delaney, *A Taste of Honey*; L. Durrell, *Balthazar*; *Mountolive* (*Alexandria Quartet*, ii and iii); Galbraith, *The Affluent Society*; Greene, *Our Man in Havana*; Murdoch, *The Bell*; Pinter, *The Birthday Party*; Sillitoe, *Saturday Night and Sunday Morning*; A. Wilson, *The Middle Age of Mrs Eliot*	Roy Campbell d.; Ralph Vaughan Williams d.; European Common Market
1959	M. Bradbury, *Eating People is Wrong*; Burroughs, *The Naked Lunch*; R. Ellmann, *James Joyce*; L. Lee, *Cider with Rosie*; R. Lowell, *Life Studies*; G. Painter, *Proust* (vol. i); Peake, *Titus Alone*; Sillitoe, *The Loneliness of the Long Distance Runner*; Spark, *Memento Mori*; Waterhouse, *Billy Liar*	Raymond Chandler d.; Stanley Spencer d.; Jacob Epstein d.; Leavis and Snow 'Two Cultures' debate
1960	K. Amis, *Take a Girl Like You*; Auden, *Homage to Clio*; L. Banks, *The L-Shaped Room*; Barstow, *A Kind of Loving*; Betjeman, *Summoned by Bells*; Bolt, *A Man for all Seasons*; L. Durrell, *Clea* (*Alexandria Quartet*, iv); Ted Hughes, *Lupercal*; D. H. Lawrence (d. 1930), *Lady Chatterley's Lover* (full text); O. Manning, *The Great Fortune* (*The Balkan Trilogy*, i); Harper Lee, *To Kill a Mockingbird*; E. O'Brien, *The Country Girls*; Pinter, *The Caretaker*; Powell, *Casanova's Chinese Restaurant*; Storey, *This Sporting Life*; Updike, *Rabbit, Run*	Boris Pasternak d.; A. Eichmann captured; J. F. Kennedy wins US presidential election
1961	New English Bible (New Testament); Heller, *Catch-22*; Murdoch, *A Severed Head*; Naipaul, *A House for Mr Biswas*; Spark, *The Prime of Miss Jean Brodie*; E. Waugh, *Unconditional Surrender*; A. Wilson, *The Old Men at the Zoo*	Ernest Hemingway d.; Augustus John d.; C. G. Jung d.; Berlin Wall built
1962	Albee, *Who's Afraid of Virginia Woolf?*; Baldwin, *Another Country*; Burgess, *A Clockwork Orange*; M. Duffy, *That's How It Was*; Gunn, *My Sad*	Britten, *War Requiem*; Faulkner d.

Date	Principal literary works	Other events
	Captains; D. Lessing, *The Golden Notebook*; O. Manning, *The Spoilt City* (*The Balkan Trilogy*, ii); P. Mortimer, *The Pumpkin Eater*; Powell, *The Kindly Ones*; A. Wesker, *Chips with Everything*	
1963	Burgess, *Inside Mr Enderby*; Le Carré, *The Spy Who Came in from the Cold*; M. McCarthy, *The Group*; Plath, *The Bell Jar*; Pynchon, *V*; S. Selvon, *Lonely Londoners*; Spark, *The Girls of Slender Means*	C. S. Lewis d.; Aldous Huxley d.; William Carlos Williams d.; Robert Frost d.; Plath d.; Beatles' first LP; J. F. Kennedy assassinated
1964	Bellow, *Herzog*; Brophy, *The Snow Ball*; Golding, *The Spire*; B. S. Johnson, *Albert Angelo*; Orton, *Entertaining Mr Sloane*; J. Osborne, *Inadmissible Evidence*; Powell, *The Valley of Bones*; Snow, *Corridors of Power*; Trevor, *The Old Boys*; A. Wilson, *Late Call*	Sean O'Casey d.; Edith Sitwell d.; Ian Fleming d.; Brendan Behan d.; Vietnam War (–1975); Nelson Mandela imprisoned
1965	Larkin, *The Whitsun Weddings*; O. Manning, *Friends and Heroes* (*The Balkan Trilogy*, iii); G. Painter, *Proust* (vol. ii); Pinter, *The Homecoming*; Plath, *Ariel*	T. S. Eliot d.; Somerset Maugham d.; Sir Winston Churchill d.; Albert Schweitzer d.; Malcolm X assassinated
1966	Bunting, *Briggflatts*; Drabble, *The Millstone*; Fowles, *The Magus*; Greene, *The Comedians*; Heaney, *Death of a Naturalist*; Orton, *Loot*; Powell, *The Soldier's Art*; J. Rhys, *Wide Sargasso Sea*; P. Scott, *The Jewel in the Crown* (*The Raj Quartet*, i)	Evelyn Waugh d.; F. O'Brien d.
1967	Ayckbourn, *Relatively Speaking*; A. Carter, *The Magic Toyshop*; Holroyd, *Lytton Strachey* (vol. i); F. O'Brien (d. 1966), *The Third Policeman*; Stoppard, *Rosencrantz and Guildenstern Are Dead*; A. Wilson, *No Laughing Matter*	P. Kavanagh d.; John Masefield d.; Joe Orton d.; S. Sassoon d.; Sexual Offences Act partially decriminalizes homosexual acts in private between two men; Six-Day War (Israel); Nigerian Civil War
1968	Ackerley, *My Father and Myself*; G. Hill, *King Log*; Mailer, *The Armies of the Night*; Powell, *The Military Philosophers*; P. Scott, *The Day of the Scorpion* (*The Raj Quartet*, ii); Stoppard, *The Real Inspector Hound*; Vidal, *Myra Breckenridge*	Mervyn Peake d.; John Steinbeck d.; Martin Luther King assassinated; Theatres Act abolishes power of lord chamberlain; civil rights march in Derry; C. Day-Lewis poet laureate
1969	K. Amis, *The Green Man*; Atwood, *The Edible Woman*; Blythe, *Akenfield*; D. Dunn, *Terry Street*; Fowles, *The French Lieutenant's Woman*; Greene, *Travels with my Aunt*; B. S. Johnson, *The Unfortunates*; D. Lessing, *The Four-Gated City*; Roth, *Portnoy's Complaint*	Dame Ivy Compton-Burnett d.; John Wyndham d.; Jack Kerouac d.; manned landing on the moon; first Booker-McConnell Prize for Fiction (P. H. Newby, *Something to Answer For*)
1970	W. Robertson Davies, *Fifth Business* (*The Deptford Trilogy*, i); Hampton, *The Philanthropist*; Hare, *Slag*; Ted Hughes, *Crow*; J. Mortimer,	E. M. Forster d.; John Dos Passos d.; Bertrand Russell d.

Date	Principal literary works	Other events
	A Voyage round my Father; Pound, *Drafts and Fragments of Cantos CX to CXVII*	
1971	Forster (d. 1970), *Maurice* (written 1913–14); G. Hill, *Mercian Hymns*; Murdoch, *An Accidental Man*; Naipaul, *In a Free State*; Powell, *Books Do Furnish a Room*; P. Scott, *The Towers of Silence* (*The Raj Quartet*, iii); Storey, *The Changing Room*; Updike, *Rabbit Redux*	Igor Stravinsky d.
1972	Ayckbourn, *Absurd Person Singular*; Berger, *G*; W. Robertson Davies, *The Manticore* (*The Deptford Trilogy*, ii); Heaney, *Wintering Out*; Stoppard, *Jumpers*	Ezra Pound d.; C. Day-Lewis d.; Sir John Betjeman poet laureate; L. P. Hartley d.; Sir Compton Mackenzie d.; Berryman d.; 'Bloody Sunday' (Belfast) 30 October
1973	M. Amis, *The Rachel Papers*; Ayckbourn, *The Norman Conquests*; J. G. Farrell, *The Siege of Krishnapur*; Greene, *The Honorary Consul*; B. S. Johnson, *Christy Malry's Own Double-Entry*; Murdoch, *The Black Prince*; Powell, *Temporary Kings*; Pynchon, *Gravity's Rainbow*; Shaffer, *Equus*	W. H. Auden d.; J. R. R. Tolkien d.; Noël Coward d.; B. S. Johnson d.; Britain enters Common Market; Watergate hearings; Picasso d.; American troops withdraw from Vietnam
1974	K. Amis, *Ending up*; Bainbridge, *The Bottle Factory Outing*; S. Hill, *In the Springtime of the Year*; Larkin, *High Windows*; Le Carré, *Tinker, Tailor, Soldier, Spy*; D. Lessing, *The Memoirs of a Survivor*	H. E. Bates d.; David Jones d.
1975	M. Amis, *Dead Babies*; Bellow, *Humboldt's Gift*; M. Bradbury, *The History Man*; W. Robertson Davies, *World of Wonders* (*The Deptford Trilogy*, iii); Drabble, *The Realms of Gold*; S. Heaney, *North*; Jhabvala, *Heat and Dust*; D. Lodge, *Changing Places*; Pinter, *No Man's Land*; Powell, *Hearing Secret Harmonies* (last vol. in *Dance to the Music of Time*); P. Scott, *A Division of the Spoils* (*The Raj Quartet*, iv); Theroux, *The Great Railway Bazaar*	P. G. Wodehouse d.
1976	Bawden, *Afternoon of a Good Woman*; Banville, *Doctor Copernicus*; Gunn, *Jack Straw's Castle*	Agatha Christie d.; Benjamin Britten d.
1977	Chatwin, *In Patagonia*; Fowles, *Daniel Martin*; P. Scott, *Staying On*; Ted Hughes, *Gaudete*	Sir Terence Rattigan d.; Robert Lowell d.; Vladimir Nabokov d.; *Gay News* trial
1978	K. Amis, *Jake's Thing*; M. Amis, *Success*; Bainbridge, *Young Adolf*; Byatt, *The Virgin in the Garden*; Greene, *The Human Factor*; Hare, *Plenty*; Irving, *The World According to Garp*; McEwan, *The Cement Garden*; Murdoch, *The Sea, the Sea*; Pinter, *Betrayal*; Potter, *Brimstone and Treacle*	Paul Scott d.; F. R. Leavis d.

Date	*Principal literary works*	*Other events*
1979	A. Carter, *The Bloody Chamber and Other Stories*; P. Fitzgerald, *Offshore*; Golding, *Darkness Visible*; Gordimer, *Burger's Daughter*; Heaney, *Field Work*; Mailer, *The Executioner's Song*; Naipaul, *A Bend in the River*; Raine, *A Martian Sends a Postcard Home*	Jean Rhys d.; J. G. Farrell d.; Public Lending Right established; Conservative government elected in Britain
1980	Burgess, *Earthly Powers*; Friel, *Translations*; Golding, *Rites of Passage*; Hoban, *Riddley Walker*; Le Carré, *Smiley's People*; Muldoon, *Why Brownlee Left*; A. N. Wilson, *The Healing Art*	C. P. Snow d.; Olivia Manning d.; Jean-Paul Sartre d.
1981	Banville, *Kepler*; Boyd, *A Good Man in Africa*; Brookner, *A Start in Life*; Coetzee, *Waiting for the Barbarians*; W. Robertson Davies, *The Rebel Angels* (*The Cornish Trilogy*, i); M. Duffy, *Gor Saga*; A. Gray, *Lanark*; Rushdie, *Midnight's Children*; Spark, *Loitering with Intent*; D. M. Thomas, *The White Hotel*	Pamela Hansford Johnson d.; Samuel Barber d.
1982	P. Barker, *Union Street*; Boyd, *An Ice-Cream War*; Keneally, *Schindler's Ark*; Theroux, *The Mosquito Coast*	Falklands campaign
1983	Ackroyd, *The Last Testament of Oscar Wilde*; Coetzee, *The Life and Times of Michael K.*; Edgar, *Maydays*; S. Hill, *The Woman in Black*; Kelman, *Not Not While the Giro*; G. Swift, *Waterland*; Trevor, *Fools of Fortune*; Weldon, *The Life and Loves of a She-Devil*	Rebecca West d.; Tennessee Williams d.; Arthur Koestler d.; Sir William Walton d.; Joan Miró d.
1984	M. Amis, *Money*; Ballard, *Empire of the Sun*; Bainbridge, *Watson's Apology*; I. Banks, *The Wasp Factory*; J. Barnes, *Flaubert's Parrot*; Brookner, *Hotel du Lac*; A. Carter, *Nights at the Circus*; A. Gray, *Janine*; R. Holmes, *Footsteps*; Lodge, *Small World*; Raine, *Rich*	Sir John Betjeman d.; Ted Hughes poet laureate; J. B. Priestley d.
1985	Ackroyd, *Hawksmoor*; Atwood, *The Handmaid's Tale*; Carey, *Illywhacker*; W. Robertson Davies, *What's Bred in the Bone* (*The Cornish Trilogy*, ii); Dunn, *Elegies*; Ishiguro, *An Artist of the Floating World*; Winterson, *Oranges Are Not the Only Fruit*	Philip Larkin d.; Robert Graves d.; Marc Chagall d.
1986	K. Amis, *The Old Devils*; Banville, *Mefisto*; Cope, *Making Cocoa for Kingsley Amis*; Seth, *The Golden Gate*	Christopher Isherwood d.; Simone de Beauvoir d.; Henry Moore d.; Chernobyl nuclear accident
1987	Ackroyd, *Chatterton*; Alan Bennett, *Talking Heads* (televised; pub. 1988); Boyd, *The New Confessions*; C. Churchill, *Serious Money*; Drabble, *The Radiant Way*; Golding, *Close Quarters*; Lively, *Moon Tiger*; McEwan, *The Child*	James Baldwin d.; Jean Anouilh d.

Date	Principal literary works	Other events
	in Time; T. Morrison, *Beloved*; Naipaul, *The Enigma of Arrival*	
1988	Atwood, *Cat's Eye*; Carey, *Oscar and Lucinda*; W. Robertson Davies, *The Lyre of Orpheus* (*The Cornish Trilogy*, iii); Larkin (d. 1985), *Collected Poems*; Hollinghurst, *The Swimming Pool Library*; D. Lessing, *The Fifth Child*; Lodge, *Nice Work*; Rushdie, *The Satanic Verses*; T. Wolfe, *The Bonfire of the Vanities*	Alan Paton d.
1989	M. Amis, *London Fields*; Bainbridge, *An Awfully Big Adventure*; Banville, *The Book of Evidence*; J. Barnes, *A History of the World in 10½ Chapters*; Bedford, *Jigsaw*; Fenton, *Manila Envelope*; Golding, *Fire Down Below*; Ishiguro, *The Remains of the Day*; Tremain, *Restoration*	Samuel Beckett d.; Bruce Chatwin d.; Daphne du Maurier d.; Robert Penn Warren d.; *fatwa* issued against Salman Rushdie; Salvador Dali d.
1990	Boyd, *Brazzaville Beach*; Byatt, *Possession*; Coetzee, *Age of Iron*; Mosley, *Hopeful Monsters*; Walcott, *Omeros*	Patrick White d.; Lawrence Durrell d.; Sir Tim Berners-Lee initiates the World Wide Web; reunification of Germany; Iraq invades Kuwait; resignation of Margaret Thatcher; R. Lehmann d.; Nelson Mandela released
1991	M. Amis, *Time's Arrow*; P. Barker, *Regeneration*; A. Carter, *Wise Children*; Longley, *Gorse Fires*; J. Osborne, *Déjavu*; C. Phillips, *Cambridge*	Graham Greene d.; Angus Wilson d.; Roy Fuller d.; John Cage d.
1992	McEwan, *Black Dogs*; Ondaatje, *The English Patient*	Angela Carter d.
1993	P. Barker, *The Eye in the Door*; R. Doyle, *Paddy Clarke Ha Ha Ha*; Fenton, *Out of Danger*; Malouf, *Remembering Babylon*; Seth, *A Suitable Boy*; Stoppard, *Arcadia*; Welsh, *Trainspotting*	Anthony Burgess d.; William Golding d.; Dame Freya Stark d.; Mandela and de Klerk share Nobel Peace Prize
1994	Atwood, *The Robber Bride*; Edgar, *Pentecost*; Kelman, *How Late It Was, How Late*; A. Miller, *Broken Glass*; Muldoon, *The Annals of Chile*; Raine, *History: The Home Movie*	Opening of Channel Tunnel; John Osborne d.; Dennis Potter d.; J. I. M. Stewart d.; John Wain d.; Mandela becomes president of South Africa
1995	M. Amis, *The Information*; Barker, *The Ghost Road*; Boyd, *The Destiny of Nathalie 'X'*; P. Fitzgerald, *The Blue Flower*; Hornby, *High Fidelity*; Rushdie, *The Moor's Last Sigh*; Pullman, *His Dark Materials* (–2000)	Kingsley Amis d.; Robert Bolt d.; Gerald Durrell d.; Julian Symons d.; Ken Saro-Wiwa hanged in Nigeria
1996	Byatt, *Babel Tower*; Deane, *Reading in the Dark*; Heaney, *The Spirit Level*; G. Swift, *Last Orders*	George Mackay Brown d.; Norman MacCaig d.; Charles Madge d.
1997	Crace, *Quarantine*; D'Aguiar, *Feeding the Ghosts*; Kennedy, *Original Bliss*; McEwan, *Enduring Love*; Michéle Roberts, *Impossible Saints*; Self, *Great Apes*	Laurie Lee d.; S. MacLean d.; A. L. Rowse d.; Jon Silkin d.; Labour government elected in Britain; Diana,

Date	Principal literary works	Other events
		princess of Wales d.; Mother Teresa of Calcutta d.
1998	Ted Hughes, *Birthday Letters*; Michael Cunningham, *The Hours*; W. Boyd, *Armadillo*; A. Hollinghurst, *The Spell*; N. Hornby, *About a Boy*; T. Hughes, *Birthday Letters*; I. McEwan, *Amsterdam*	Ted Hughes d.; Dame Iris Murdoch d.; British Library opens at St Pancras
1999	J. Crace, *Being Dead*; J. M. Coetzee, *Disgrace*; M. Holroyd, *Basil Street Blues*; D. Lessing, *Mara and Dann*; V. Seth, *An Equal Music*; R. Tremain, *Music and Silence*	J. Heller d.; Sarah Kane d.; Andrew Motion poet laureate; war in Kosovo; introduction of the euro
2000	M. Bradbury, *To the Hermitage*; Zadie Smith, *White Teeth*; M. Atwood, *The Blind Assassin*; Lorna Sage, *Bad Blood*	M. Bradbury d.; A. Powell d.; R. S. Thomas d.; Tate Modern opens
2001	B. Bainbridge, *According to Queeney*; J. Coe, *The Rotters' Club*; Ali Smith, *Hotel World*	Lorna Sage d.; R. K. Narayan d.; 9/11 terrorist attack in New York; USA invades Afghanistan
2002	A. S. Byatt, *A Whistling Woman*; C. Hampton, *The Talking Cure*; T. Stoppard, *The Coast of Utopia*	W. Cooper d.; D. J. Enright d.; M. Wesley d.; terrorists bomb Bali
2003	Monica Ali, *Brick Lane*; M. Frayn, *Democracy*; C. Phillips, *A Distant Shore*	C. Causley d.; K. Raine d.; P. Redgrove d.; E. Said d.; second Gulf War in Iraq
2004	Maggie Gee, *The Flood*; Alan Hollinghurst, *The Line of Beauty*; Andrea Levy, *Small Island*; V. Brittain and G. Slovo, *Guantanamo*	J. Derrida d.; T. Gunn d.; S. Sontag d.; George W. Bush re-elected US president; Boxing Day tsunami in Indian Ocean
2005	J. Barnes, *Arthur and George*; K. Ishiguro, *Never Let Me Go*; I. McEwan, *Saturday*; S. Rushdie, *Shalimar the Clown*; D. Hare, *Stuff Happens*	S. Bellow d.; C. Fry d.; A. Miller d.; British detainees released from Guantanamo; hurricane floods New Orleans
2006	Martin Amis, *The House of Meetings*; David Mitchell, *Black Swan Green*; Sarah Waters, *The Night Watch*; Seamus Heaney, *District and Circle*	Muriel Spark d.; Naguib Mahfouz d.; William Styron d.; Israeli troops invade Lebanon; Ban-ki Moon appointed Secretary-General of United Nations
2007	Jim Crace, *The Pesthouse*; Ian McEwan, *On Chesil Beach*; Doris Lessing, *The Cleft*; J. K. Rowling, *Harry Potter and the Deathly Hallows*; Hermione Lee, *Edith Wharton*	Elizabeth Jolley d.; Norman Mailer d.; Grace Paley d.; Gordon Brown succeeds Tony Blair as British prime minister; Benazir Bhutto assassinated in Pakistan
2008	Sebastian Barry, *The Secret Scripture*; Toni Morrison, *A Mercy*; Ciaran Carson, *For All We Know*; Philip Roth, *Indignation*; Michael Holroyd, *A Strange Eventful History*	Arthur C. Clarke d.; Alexander Solzhenitsyn d.; Harold Pinter d.; financial crisis threatens global economy; Barack Obama elected president of the United States of America

Appendix 2 · Poets Laureate

1616–37	Ben *Jonson
1638–?	Sir William *D'Avenant

OFFICIAL HOLDERS

1668–89	John *Dryden
1689–92	Thomas *Shadwell
1692–1715	Nahum *Tate
1715–18	Nicholas *Rowe
1718–30	Laurence *Eusden
1730–57	Colley *Cibber
1757–85	William *Whitehead
1785–90	Thomas *Warton
1790–1813	Henry James *Pye
1813–43	Robert *Southey
1843–50	William *Wordsworth
1850–92	Alfred *Tennyson
1896–1913	Alfred *Austin
1913–30	Robert *Bridges
1930–67	John *Masefield
1968–72	Cecil *Day-Lewis
1972–84	Sir John *Betjeman
1984–98	Ted *Hughes
1999–2009	Andrew *Motion
2009–	Carol Ann *Duffy

Appendix 3 · Children's Laureates

1999–2001	Quentin *Blake
2001–03	Anne *Fine
2003–05	Michael *Morpurgo
2005–07	Jacqueline *Wilson
2007–09	Michael *Rosen
2009–	Anthony Browne

Appendix 4 · Literary Awards

(A) NOBEL PRIZE FOR LITERATURE

1901	René-François-Armand-Sully Prudhomme
1902	Theodor Mommsen
1903	Björnstjerne Björnson
1904	José Echegaray / Frédéric Mistral
1905	Henryk Sienkiewicz
1906	Giosuè *Carducci
1907	Rudyard *Kipling
1908	Rudolf Eucken
1909	Selma Lagerlöf
1910	Paul Heyse
1911	Maurice *Maeterlinck
1912	Gerhart *Hauptmann
1913	Rabindranath *Tagore
1914	No award
1915	Romain Rolland
1916	Verner von Heidenstam
1917	Karl Gjellerup / Henrik Pontoppidan
1918	No award
1919	Carl Spitteler
1920	Knut *Hamsun
1921	Anatole *France
1922	Jacinto Benavente y Martínez
1923	W. B. *Yeats
1924	Władysław Reymont
1925	G. B. *Shaw
1926	Grazia *Deledda
1927	Henri *Bergson
1928	Sigrid Undset
1929	Thomas *Mann
1930	Sinclair *Lewis
1931	Erik Axel Karlfeldt
1932	John *Galsworthy
1933	Ivan *Bunin
1934	Luigi *Pirandello
1935	No award
1936	Eugene *O'Neill
1937	Roger Martin du Gard
1938	Pearl S. *Buck
1939	F. E. Sillanpää
1940–3	No awards
1944	Johannes V. Jensen
1945	Gabriela Mistral
1946	Hermann *Hesse
1947	André *Gide
1948	T. S. *Eliot
1949	William *Faulkner
1950	Bertrand *Russell
1951	Pär Lagerkvist
1952	François *Mauriac
1953	Winston S. *Churchill
1954	Ernest *Hemingway
1955	Halldór Laxness
1956	Juan Ramón Jiménez
1957	Albert *Camus
1958	Boris *Pasternak
1959	Salvatore *Quasimodo
1960	*Saint-John Perse
1961	Ivo Andrić
1962	John *Steinbeck
1963	George *Seferis
1964	Jean-Paul *Sartre
1965	Mikhail *Sholokhov
1966	S. Y. Agnon / Nelly Sachs
1967	Miguel Angel Asturias
1968	Yasunari *Kawabata
1969	Samuel *Beckett
1970	Alexander *Solzhenitsyn
1971	Pablo *Neruda
1972	Heinrich *Böll
1973	Patrick *White
1974	Eyvind Johnson / Harry Martinson
1975	Eugenio *Montale
1976	Saul *Bellow
1977	Vicente Aleixandre
1978	Isaac Bashevis *Singer
1979	Odysseus *Elytis
1980	Czesław *Miłosz
1981	Elias *Canetti
1982	Gabriel *García Márquez
1983	William *Golding

1984 Jaroslav Seifert
1985 Claude Simon
1986 Wole *Soyinka
1987 Joseph *Brodsky
1988 Naguib *Mahfouz
1989 Camilo José Cela
1990 Octavio *Paz
1991 Nadine *Gordimer
1992 Derek *Walcott
1993 Toni *Morrison
1994 Kenzaburo *Oë
1995 Seamus *Heaney
1996 Wisława *Szymborska
1997 Dario *Fo
1998 José *Saramago
1999 Günter *Grass
2000 Gao Xingjian
2001 V. S. *Naipaul
2002 Imre Kertesz
2003 J. M. *Coetzee
2004 Elfriede Jelinek
2005 Harold *Pinter
2006 Orhan Pamuk
2007 Doris *Lessing
2008 Jean-Marie *Le Clézio

(B) PULITZER PRIZE FOR FICTION

1918 Ernest Poole, *His Family*
1919 Booth *Tarkington, *The Magnificent Ambersons*
1920 No award
1921 Edith *Wharton, *The Age of Innocence*
1922 Booth *Tarkington, *Alice Adams*
1923 Willa *Cather, *One of Ours*
1924 Margaret Wilson, *The Able McLaughlins*
1925 Edna *Ferber, *So Big*
1926 Sinclair *Lewis, *Arrowsmith*
1927 Louis Bromfield, *Early Autumn*
1928 Thornton *Wilder, *The Bridge of San Luis Rey*
1929 Julia Peterkin, *Scarlet Sister Mary*
1930 Oliver *La Farge, *Laughing Boy*
1931 Margaret Ayer Barnes, *Years of Grace*
1932 Pearl S. *Buck, *The Good Earth*
1933 T. S. Stribling, *The Store*
1934 Caroline Miller, *Lamb in his Bosom*
1935 Josephine Winslow Johnson, *Now in November*
1936 Harold L. Davis, *Honey in the Horn*
1937 Margaret *Mitchell, *Gone with the Wind*
1938 John Phillips Marquand, *The Late George Apley*
1939 Marjorie Kinnan Rawlings, *The Yearling*
1940 John *Steinbeck, *The Grapes of Wrath*
1941 No award
1942 Ellen *Glasgow, *In This our Life*
1943 Upton *Sinclair, *Dragon's Teeth*
1944 Martin Flavin, *Journey in the Dark*
1945 John *Hersey, *A Bell for Adano*
1946 No award
1947 Robert Penn *Warren, *All the King's Men*
1948 James A. *Michener, *Tales of the South Pacific*
1949 James Gould Cozzens, *Guard of Honour*
1950 A. B. Guthrie Jr, *The Way West*
1951 Conrad *Richter, *The Town*
1952 Herman Wouk, *The Caine Mutiny*
1953 Ernest *Hemingway, *The Old Man and the Sea*
1954 No award
1955 William *Faulkner, *A Fable*
1956 Mackinley Kanter, *Andersonville*
1957 No award
1958 James *Agee, *A Death in the Family*
1959 Robert Lewis Taylor, *The Travels of Jamie McPheeters*
1960 Allen *Drury, *Advise and Consent*
1961 Harper *Lee, *To Kill a Mockingbird*
1962 Edwin O'Connor, *The Edge of Sadness*
1963 William *Faulkner, *The Reivers*
1964 No award
1965 Shirley Ann Grau, *The Keepers of the House*
1966 Katherine Anne *Porter, *The Collected Stories of Katherine Anne Porter*
1967 Bernard *Malamud, *The Fixer*
1968 William *Styron, *The Confessions of Nat Turner*
1969 N. Scott *Momaday, *House Made of Dawn*
1970 Jean *Stafford, *Collected Stories*
1971 No award
1972 Wallace *Stegner, *Angle of Repose*
1973 Eudora *Welty, *The Optimist's Daughter*
1974 No award
1975 Michael Shaara, *The Killer Angels*
1976 Saul *Bellow, *Humboldt's Gift*
1977 No award
1978 James Alan McPherson, *Elbow Room*
1979 John *Cheever, *The Stories of John Cheever*
1980 Norman *Mailer, *The Executioner's Song*
1981 John Kennedy *Toole, *A Confederacy of Dunces*

1982 John *Updike, *Rabbit is Rich*
1983 Alice *Walker, *The Color Purple*
1984 William Kennedy, *Ironweed*
1985 Alison *Lurie, *Foreign Affairs*
1986 Larry *McMurtry, *Lonesome Dove*
1987 Peter Taylor, *A Summons to Memphis*
1988 Toni *Morrison, *Beloved*
1989 Anne *Tyler, *Breathing Lessons*
1990 Oscar Hijuelos, *The Mambo Kings Play Songs of Love*
1991 John *Updike, *Rabbit at Rest*
1992 Jane *Smiley, *A Thousand Acres*
1993 Robert Olen Butler, *A Good Scent from a Strange Mountain*
1994 E. A. *Proulx, *The Shipping News*
1995 Carol *Shields, *The Stone Diaries*
1996 Richard *Ford, *Independence Day*
1997 Steven Millhauser, *Martin Dressler: The Tale of an American Dreamer*
1998 Philip *Roth, *American Pastoral*
1999 Michael Cunningham, *The Hours*
2000 Jhumpa Lahiri, *Interpreter of Maladies*
2001 Michael Chabon, *The Amazing Adventures of Kavalier & Clay*
2002 Richard Russo, *Empire Falls*
2003 Jeffrey Eugenides, *Middlesex*
2004 Edward P. Jones, *The Known World*
2005 Marilynne Robinson, *Gilead*
2006 Geraldine Brooks, *March*
2007 Cormac *McCarthy, *The Road*
2008 Junot Diaz, *The Brief Wondrous Life of Oscar Wao*
2009 Elizabeth Strout, *Olive Kitteridge*

(C) CILIP (LIBRARY ASSOCIATION) CARNEGIE MEDALLISTS

Instituted in 1936 to mark the centenary of the birth of Andrew Carnegie, philanthropist and benefactor of libraries, the CILIP (Library Association) Carnegie Medal is awarded annually for an outstanding book for children written in English and receiving its first publication in the United Kingdom during the preceding year. Before 2007 the year refers to when the book was published rather than when the medal was awarded i.e. the 2005 winner was announced and the medal presented in July 2006.

1936 Arthur *Ransome, *Pigeon Post*
1937 Eve *Garnett, *The Family from One End Street*
1938 Noel *Streatfeild, *The Circus is Coming*
1939 Eleanor Doorly, *The Radium Woman* (children's biography of Marie Curie)
1940 Kitty Barne, *Visitors from London*
1941 Mary Treadgold, *We Couldn't Leave Dinah*
1942 'B. B.' (D. J. Watkins-Pitchford), *The Little Grey Men*
1943 No award
1944 Eric *Linklater, *The Wind on the Moon*
1945 No award
1946 Elizabeth *Goudge, *The Little White Horse*
1947 Walter *de la Mare, *Collected Stories for Children*
1948 Richard Armstrong, *Sea Change*
1949 Agnes Allen, *The Story of your Home* (non-fiction)
1950 Elfrida Vipont, *The Lark on the Wing*
1951 Cynthia *Harnett, *The Wool-Pack*
1952 Mary *Norton, *The Borrowers*
1953 Edward Osmond, *A Valley Grows Up* (non-fiction)
1954 Ronald Welch, *Knight Crusaders*
1955 Eleanor *Farjeon, *The Little Bookroom*
1956 C. S. *Lewis, *The Last Battle*
1957 William *Mayne, *A Grass Rope*
1958 Philippa *Pearce, *Tom's Midnight Garden*
1959 Rosemary *Sutcliff, *The Lantern Bearers*
1960 Ian W. Cornwall and Howard M. Maitland, *The Making of Man* (non-fiction)
1961 Lucy M. *Boston, *A Stranger at Green Knowe*
1962 Pauline Clarke, *The Twelve and the Genii*
1963 Hester Burton, *Time of Trial*
1964 Sheena Porter, *Nordy Bank*
1965 Philip Turner, *The Grange at High Force*
1966 No award
1967 Alan *Garner, *The Owl Service*
1968 Rosemary Harris, *The Moon in the Cloud*
1969 K. M. *Peyton, *The Edge of the Cloud*
1970 Edward Blishen and Leon *Garfield, *The God Beneath the Sea*
1971 Ivan Southall, *Josh*
1972 Richard *Adams, *Watership Down*
1973 Penelope *Lively, *The Ghost of Thomas Kempe*
1974 Mollie Hunter, *The Stronghold*
1975 Robert *Westall, *The Machine-Gunners*
1976 Jan *Mark, *Thunder and Lightnings*
1977 Gene Kemp, *The Turbulent Term of Tyke Tyler*
1978 David Rees, *The Exeter Blitz*

1979 Peter *Dickinson, *Tulku*
1980 Peter *Dickinson, *City of Gold*
1981 Robert *Westall, *The Scarecrows*
1982 Margaret *Mahy, *The Haunting*
1983 Jan *Mark, *Handles*
1984 Margaret *Mahy, *The Changeover*
1985 Kevin *Crossley-Holland, *Storm*
1986 Berlie Doherty, *Granny Was a Buffer Girl*
1987 Susan *Price, *The Ghost Drum*
1988 Geraldine *McCaughrean, *A Pack of Lies*
1989 Anne *Fine, *Goggle-Eyes*
1990 Gillian *Cross, *Wolf*
1991 Berlie Doherty, *Dear Nobody*
1992 Anne *Fine, *Flour Babies*
1993 Robert *Swindells, *Stone Cold*
1994 Theresa Breslin, *Whispers in the Graveyard*
1995 Philip *Pullman, *Northern Lights*
1996 Melvin *Burgess, *Junk*
1997 Tim Bowler, *River Boy*
1998 David *Almond, *Skellig*
1999 Aidan *Chambers, *Postcards from No Man's Land*
2000 Beverley Naidoo, *The Other Side of Truth*
2001 Terry *Pratchett, *The Amazing Maurice and his Educated Rodents*
2002 Sharon Creech, *Ruby Holler*
2003 Jennifer Donnelly, *A Gathering Light*
2004 Frank Cottrell Boyce, *Millions*
2005 Mal Peet, *Tamar*
2007 Meg Rosoff, *Just in Case*
2008 Philip Reeve, *Here Lies Arthur*
2009 Siobhan Dowd, *Bog Child*

(D) MAN BOOKER PRIZE FOR FICTION (Booker Prize until 2002)

1969 P. H. *Newby, *Something to Answer for*
1970 Bernice *Rubens, *The Elected Member*
1971 V. S. *Naipaul, *In a Free State*
1972 John *Berger, *G*
1973 J. G. *Farrell, *The Siege of Krishnapur*
1974 Nadine *Gordimer, *The Conservationist*; Stanley *Middleton, *Holiday*
1975 Ruth Prawer *Jhabvala, *Heat and Dust*
1976 David *Storey, *Saville*
1977 Paul *Scott, *Staying On*
1978 Iris *Murdoch, *The Sea, the Sea*
1979 Penelope *Fitzgerald, *Offshore*
1980 William *Golding, *Rites of Passage*
1981 Salman *Rushdie, *Midnight's Children*
1982 Thomas *Keneally, *Schindler's Ark*
1983 J. M. *Coetzee, *Life and Times of Michael K*
1984 Anita *Brookner, *Hotel du Lac*
1985 Keri Hulme, *The Bone People*
1986 Kingsley *Amis, *The Old Devils*
1987 Penelope *Lively, *Moon Tiger*
1988 Peter *Carey, *Oscar and Lucinda*
1989 Kazuo *Ishiguro, *The Remains of the Day*
1990 A. S. *Byatt, *Possession*
1991 Ben *Okri, *The Famished Road*
1992 Michael *Ondaatje, *The English Patient*; Barry *Unsworth, *Sacred Hunger*
1993 Roddy *Doyle, *Paddy Clarke Ha Ha Ha*
1994 James *Kelman, *How Late It Was, How Late*
1995 Pat *Barker, *The Ghost Road*
1996 Graham *Swift, *Last Orders*
1997 Arundhati *Roy, *The God of Small Things*
1998 Ian *McEwan, *Amsterdam*
1999 J. M. *Coetzee, *Disgrace*
2000 Margaret *Atwood, *The Blind Assassin*
2001 Peter *Carey, *True History of the Kelly Gang*
2002 Yann *Martel, *Life of Pi*
2003 DBC Pierre, *Vernon God Little*
2004 Alan *Hollinghurst, *The Line of Beauty*
2005 John *Banville, *The Sea*
2006 Kiran *Desai, *The Inheritance of Loss*
2007 Anne *Enright, *The Gathering*
2008 Aravind Adiga, *The White Tiger*

(E) KING'S AND QUEEN'S GOLD MEDAL FOR POETRY

The Gold Medal for Poetry was instituted by George V in 1933 at the suggestion of the poet laureate, John Masefield. The medal is awarded for an outstanding book of verse published by an author from the United Kingdom or (from 1985) the Commonwealth. The nominating committee is chaired by the poet laureate and announcement of the award is made on the birthday of William Shakespeare.

1934 Laurence Whistler
1937 W. H. *Auden
1940 Michael Thwaites
1952 Andrew *Young
1953 Arthur *Waley
1954 Ralph *Hodgson
1955 Ruth Pitter

1956 Edmund *Blunden
1957 Siegfried *Sassoon
1959 Frances *Cornford
1960 John *Betjeman
1962 Christopher *Fry
1963 William *Plomer
1964 R. S. *Thomas
1965 Philip *Larkin
1967 Charles *Causley
1968 Robert *Graves
1969 Stevie *Smith
1970 Roy *Fuller
1971 Stephen *Spender
1973 John *Heath-Stubbs
1974 Ted *Hughes
1977 Norman *Nicholson
1981 D. J. *Enright
1986 Norman *MacCaig
1988 Derek *Walcott
1989 Allen *Curnow
1990 Sorley *Maclean
1991 Judith *Wright
1992 Kathleen *Raine
1996 Peter *Redgrove
1998 Les *Murray
2000 Edwin *Morgan
2001 Michael *Longley
2002 Peter *Porter
2003 U. A. *Fanthorpe
2004 Hugo *Williams
2006 Fleur *Adcock
2007 James *Fenton

(F) T. S. ELIOT PRIZE FOR POETRY

The T. S. Eliot Poetry Prize is awarded by the Poetry Book Society annually to the best collection of new poetry in English published in the UK or the Republic of Ireland. It was inaugurated in 1993, to celebrate the Poetry Book Society's 40th birthday and honour its founding poet, T. S. Eliot. The prize money is donated by his widow, Valerie Eliot.

1993 Ciaran *Carson, *First Language: Poems*
1994 Paul *Muldoon, *The Annals of Chile*
1995 Mark Doty, *My Alexandria*
1996 Les *Murray, *Subhuman Redneck Poems*
1997 Don *Paterson, *God's Gift to Women*
1998 Ted *Hughes, *Birthday Letters*
1999 Hugo *Williams, *Billy's Rain*
2000 Michael *Longley, *The Weather in Japan*
2001 Anne Carson, *The Beauty of the Husband*
2002 Alice *Oswald, *Dart*
2003 Don *Paterson, *Landing Light*
2004 George *Szirtes, *Reel*
2005 Carol Ann *Duffy, *Rapture*
2006 Seamus *Heaney, *District and Circle*
2007 Sean *O'Brien, *The Drowned Book*
2008 Jen *Hadfield, *Nigh-No-Place*

Index of New and Heavily Revised Entries by Contributor

The following list identifies by initials (see *Editors and Contributors*, p.xi) those who have added new entries, replaced previously existing entries, or significantly revised existing material in this edition of the *Companion*. Revised entries are indicated by an asterisk; others are new.